D0645953

Collins
gem

Collins
French
Dictionary

HarperCollins Publishers
Westerhill Road
Bishopbriggs
Glasgow
G64 2QT
Great Britain

Ninth edition/Neuvième édition
2006

Reprint 10 9 8 7 6

© William Collins Sons & Co. Ltd
1979, 1988
© HarperCollins Publishers 1993,
1997, 2000, 2001, 2003, 2005, 2006

ISBN 978-0-00-722397-8

Collins Gem® is a registered
trademark of HarperCollins
Publishers Limited

www.collinslanguage.com

A catalogue record for this book is
available from the British Library

HarperCollins Publishers,
10 East 53rd Street,
New York, NY 10022

COLLINS GEM FRENCH DICTIONARY.
Eighth US Edition 2005

ISBN 978-0-00-712622-4

www.harpercollins.com

HarperCollins books may be
purchased for educational,
business or sales promotional use.
For information, please write to:
Special Markets Department,
HarperCollins Publishers, 10 East
53rd Street, New York, NY 10022

Typeset by/Photocomposition
Thomas Callan

Printed in Italy by/Imprimé en
Italie par LEGO Spa, Lavis (Trento),
ITALY.

TABLE DES MATIÈRES   CONTENTS

Acknowledgements

We would like to thank those authors and publishers who kindly gave permission for copyright material to be used in the Collins Word Web. We would also like to thank Times Newspapers Ltd for providing valuable data.

MANAGING EDITOR/CHEF DE PROJET
Michela Clari

CONTRIBUTORS/RÉDACTION
Jean-François Allain
Gaëlle Amiot-Cadey
Cécile Aubinière-Robb
Sabine Citron
Wendy Lee
Catherine Love
Rose Rociola

COORDINATION/COORDINATION
Joyce Littlejohn

SERIES EDITOR/
COLLECTION DIRIGÉE PAR
Lorna Knight

Based on the first edition of the Collins Gem French Dictionary under the direction of Pierre-Henri Cousin

Nous sommes très heureux que vous ayez choisi ce dictionnaire et espérons que vous aimerez l'utiliser et que vous en tirerez profit au lycée, à la maison, en vacances ou au travail.

Cette introduction a pour but de vous donner quelques conseils sur la façon d'utiliser au mieux votre dictionnaire, en vous référant non seulement à son importante nomenclature mais aussi aux informations contenues dans chaque entrée. Ceci vous aidera à lire et à comprendre, mais aussi à communiquer et à vous exprimer en anglais contemporain.

Au début du dictionnaire, vous trouverez la liste des abréviations utilisées dans le texte et celle de la transcription des sons par des symboles phonétiques. Vous y trouverez également la liste des verbes irréguliers en anglais, suivis d'une section finale sur les nombres et sur les expressions de temps.

COMMENT UTILISER VOTRE DICTIONNAIRE
Ce dictionnaire offre une richesse d'informations et utilise diverses formes et tailles de caractères, symboles, abréviations, parenthèses et crochets. Les conventions et symboles utilisés sont expliqués dans les sections qui suivent.

ENTRÉES
Les mots que vous cherchez dans le dictionnaire - les entrées - sont classés par ordre alphabétique. Ils sont imprimés en couleur pour pouvoir être repérés rapidement. Les entrées figurant en haut de page indiquent le premier (sur la page

de gauche) et le dernier mot (sur la page de droite) des deux pages en question.

Des informations sur l'usage ou sur la forme de certaines entrées sont données entre parenthèses, après la transcription phonétique. Ces indications apparaissent sous forme abrégée et en italiques (par ex. (*fam*), (*Comm*)).

Pour plus de facilité, les mots de la même famille sont regroupés sous la même entrée (ronger, rongeur; accept, acceptance) et apparaissent également en couleur.

Les expressions courantes dans lesquelles apparaît l'entrée sont indiquées par des caractères romains gras différents (par exemple retard : [...] **avoir du ~**).

TRANSCRIPTION PHONÉTIQUE
La transcription phonétique de chaque entrée (indiquant sa prononciation) est indiquée entre crochets immédiatement après l'entrée (par ex. fumer [fyme]; knee [ni:]). La liste des symboles phonétiques figure page xiii.

TRADUCTIONS
Les traductions des entrées apparaissent en caractères ordinaires ; lorsque plusieurs sens ou usages coexistent, ces traductions sont séparées par un point-virgule. Vous trouverez des synonymes de l'entrée en italiques entre parenthèses avant les traductions (par ex. poser (*installer : moquette, carrelage*)) ou des mots qui fournissent le contexte dans lequel l'entrée est susceptible d'être utilisée (par ex. poser (*question*)).

Une importance particulière est accordée à certains mots français et anglais qui sont considérés comme des « mots-clés » dans chacune des langues. Cela peut être dû à leur utilisation très fréquente ou au fait qu'ils ont divers types d'usage (par ex. vouloir, plus; get, that). L'utilisation de triangles et de chiffres aide à distinguer différentes catégories grammaticales et différents sens. D'autres renseignements utiles apparaissent en italiques et entre parenthèses dans la langue de l'utilisateur.

Les catégories grammaticales sont données sous forme abrégée et en italiques après la transcription phonétique (par ex. *vt, adv, conj*). Les genres des noms français sont indiqués de la manière suivante : *nm* pour un nom masculin et *nf* pour un nom féminin. Le féminin et le pluriel irrégulier de certains noms sont également indiqués (par ex. directeur, -trice ; cheval, -aux).

Le masculin et le féminin des adjectifs sont indiqués lorsque ces deux formes sont différentes (par ex. noir, e). Lorsque l'adjectif a un féminin ou un pluriel irrégulier, ces formes sont clairement indiquées (par ex. net, nette). Les pluriels irréguliers des noms, et les formes irrégulières des verbes anglais sont indiqués entre parenthèses, avant la catégorie grammaticale (par ex. man [...] (*pl* **men**) *n* ; give (*pt* **gave**; *pp* **~n**) *vt*).

INTRODUCTION

We are delighted that you have decided to buy this dictionary and hope you will enjoy and benefit from using it at school, at home, on holiday or at work.

This introduction gives you a few tips on how to get the most out of your dictionary – not simply from its comprehensive wordlist but also from the information provided in each entry. This will help you to read and understand modern French, as well as communicate and express yourself in the language. This dictionary begins by listing the abbreviations used in the text and illustrating the sounds shown by the phonetic symbols. You will also find French verb tables, followed by a final section on numbers and time expressions.

USING YOUR DICTIONARY

A wealth of information is presented in the dictionary, using various typefaces, sizes of type, symbols, abbreviations and brackets. The various conventions and symbols used are explained in the following sections.

HEADWORDS

The words you look up in a dictionary – 'headwords' – are listed alphabetically. They are printed in colour for rapid identification. The headwords appearing at the top of each page indicate the first (if it appears on a left-hand page) and last word (if it appears on a right-hand page) dealt with on the page in question.

Information about the usage or form of certain headwords is given in brackets after the phonetic spelling. This usually appears in abbreviated form and in italics (e.g. (fam), (Comm)).

Where appropriate, words related to headwords are grouped in the same entry (ronger, rongeur; accept, acceptance) and are also in colour. Common expressions in which the headword appears are shown in a bold roman type (e.g. retard: [...] **avoir du ~**).

PHONETIC SPELLINGS

The phonetic spelling of each headword (indicating its pronunciation) is given in square brackets immediately after the headword (e.g. fumer [fyme]; knee [niː]). A list of these symbols is given on page xiii.

TRANSLATIONS

Headword translations are given in ordinary type and, where more than one meaning or usage exists, these are separated by a semi-colon. You will often find other words in italics in brackets before the translations. These offer suggested contexts in which the headword might appear (e.g. rough (*voice*), [...] (*weather*)) or provide synonyms (e.g. rough (*violent*)). The gender of the translation also appears in italics immediately following the key element of the translation.

KEY WORDS

Special status is given to certain French and English words which are considered as 'key' words in each language. They may, for example, occur very frequently or have several types of usage (e.g. vouloir, plus; get, that). A combination of triangles and numbers helps you to distinguish different parts of speech and different meanings. Further helpful information is provided in brackets and italics.

Parts of speech are given in abbreviated form in italics after the phonetic spellings of headwords (e.g. *vt, adv, conj*). Genders of French nouns are indicated as follows: *nm* for a masculine and *nf* for a feminine noun. Feminine and irregular plural forms of nouns are also shown (**directeur, -trice; cheval, -aux**).

Adjectives are given in both masculine and feminine forms where these forms are different (e.g. **noir, e**). Clear information is provided where adjectives have an irregular feminine or plural form (e.g. **net, nette**).

ABRÉVIATIONS

ABBREVIATIONS

abréviation	*ab(b)r*	abbreviation
adjectif, locution adjectivale	*adj*	adjective, adjectival phrase
administration	*Admin*	administration
adverbe, locution adverbiale	*adv*	adverb, adverbial phrase
agriculture	*Agr*	agriculture
anatomie	*Anat*	anatomy
architecture	*Archit*	architecture
article défini	*art déf*	definite article
article indéfini	*art indéf*	indefinite article
automobile	*Aut(o)*	the motor car and motoring
aviation, voyages aériens	*Aviat*	flying, air travel
biologie	*Bio(l)*	biology
botanique	*Bot*	botany
anglais britannique	*BRIT*	British English
chimie	*Chem*	chemistry
commerce, finance, banque	*Comm*	commerce, finance, banking
informatique	*Comput*	computing
conjonction	*conj*	conjunction
construction	*Constr*	building
nom utilisé comme adjectif	*cpd*	compound element
cuisine	*Culin*	cookery
article défini	*def art*	definite article
déterminant: article; adjectif démonstratif ou indéfini *etc*	*dét*	determiner: article, demonstrative *etc*
économie	*Écon, Econ*	economics
électricité, électronique	*Élec, Elec*	electricity, electronics
en particulier	*esp*	especially
exclamation, interjection	*excl*	exclamation, interjection
féminin	*f*	feminine
langue familière (! emploi vulgaire)	*fam(!)*	colloquial usage (! particularly offensive)
emploi figuré	*fig*	figurative use
(verbe anglais) dont la particule est inséparable	*fus*	(phrasal verb) where the particle is inseparable
généralement	*gén, gen*	generally
géographie, géologie	*Géo, Geo*	geography, geology
géométrie	*Géom, Geom*	geometry
langue familière (! emploi vulgaire)	*inf(!)*	colloquial usage (! particularly offensive)
infinitif	*infin*	infinitive
informatique	*Inform*	computing
invariable	*inv*	invariable
irrégulier	*irreg*	irregular
domaine juridique	*Jur*	law

grammaire, linguistique	Ling	grammar, linguistics
masculin	m	masculine
mathématiques, algèbre	Math	mathematics, calculus
médecine	Méd, Med	medical term, medicine
masculin ou féminin	m/f	masculine or feminine
domaine militaire, armée	Mil	military matters
musique	Mus	music
nom	n	noun
navigation, nautisme	Navig, Naut	sailing, navigation
nom ou adjectif numéral	num	numeral noun or adjective
	o.s.	oneself
péjoratif	péj, pej	derogatory, pejorative
photographie	Phot(o)	photography
physiologie	Physiol	physiology
pluriel	pl	plural
politique	Pol	politics
participe passé	pp	past participle
préposition	prép, prep	preposition
pronom	pron	pronoun
psychologie, psychiatrie	Psych	psychology, psychiatry
temps du passé	pt	past tense
quelque chose	qch	
quelqu'un	qn	
religion, domaine ecclésiastique	Rel	religion
	sb	somebody
enseignement, système	Scol	schooling, schools
scolaire et universitaire		and universities
singulier	sg	singular
	sth	something
subjonctif	sub	subjunctive
sujet (grammatical)	su(b)j	(grammatical) subject
superlatif	superl	superlative
techniques, technologie	Tech	technical term, technology
télécommunications	Tél, Tel	telecommunications
télévision	TV	television
typographie	Typ(o)	typography, printing
anglais des USA	US	American English
verbe (auxiliaire)	vb (aux)	(auxiliary) verb
verbe intransitif	vi	intransitive verb
verbe transitif	vt	transitive verb
zoologie	Zool	zoology
marque déposée	®	registered trademark
indique une équivalence culturelle	≈	introduces a cultural equivalent

TRANCRIPTION PHONÉTIQUE

CONSONNES

CONSONANTS

NB. p, b, t, d, k, g sont suivis
d'une aspiration en anglais.

NB. p, b, t, d, k, g are
not aspirated in French.

poupée	p	puppy
bombe	b	baby
tente thermal	t	tent
dinde	d	daddy
coq qui képi	k	cork kiss chord
gage bague	g	gag guess
sale ce nation	s	so rice kiss
zéro rose	z	cousin buzz
tache chat	ʃ	sheep sugar
gilet juge	ʒ	pleasure beige
	tʃ	church
fer phare	dʒ	judge general
verveine	f	farm raffle
	v	very revel
	θ	thin maths
	ð	that other
lent salle	l	little ball
rare rentrer	R	
	r	rat rare
maman femme	m	mummy comb
non bonne	n	no ran
agneau vigne	ɲ	
	ŋ	singing bank
	ɲ	hat rehearse
yeux paille pied	j	yet
nouer oui	w	wall wail
huile lui	ɥ	
	x	loch

DIVERS

MISCELLANEOUS

pour l'anglais: le r final se
prononce en liaison devant
une voyelle

in English transcription:
final r can be pronounced
before a vowel

pour l'anglais: précède la ' syllabe accentuée

in French wordlist:
no liaison before
aspirate h

En règle générale, la prononciation est donnée entre crochets après
chaque entrée. Toutefois, du côté anglais-français et dans le cas des
expressions composées de deux ou plusieurs mots non réunis par un trait
d'union et faisant l'objet d'une entrée séparée, la prononciation doit être
cherchée sous chacun des mots constitutifs de l'expression en question.

PHONETIC TRANSCRIPTION

VOYELLES		VOWELS
NB. La mise en équivalence de certains sons n'indique qu'une ressemblance approximative.		NB. The pairing of some vowel sounds only indicates approximate equivalence.
ici vie lyrique	i i:	heel bead
	ɪ	hit pity
jouer été	e	
lait jouet merci	ɛ	set tent
plat amour	a æ	bat apple
bas pâte	ɑ ɑ:	after car calm
	ʌ	fun cousin
le premier	ə	over above
beurre peur	œ	
peu deux	ø ə:	urgent fern work
or homme	ɔ	wash pot
mot eau gauche	o ɔ:	born cork
genou roue	u	full hook
	u:	boom shoe
rue urne	y	

DIPHTONGUES		DIPHTHONGS
	ɪə	beer tier
	ɛə	tear fair there
	eɪ	date plaice day
	aɪ	life buy cry
	aʊ	owl foul now
	əʊ	low no
	ɔɪ	boil boy oily
	ʊə	poor tour

NASALES		NASAL VOWELS
matin plein	ɛ̃	
brun	œ̃	
sang an dans	ɑ̃	
non pont	ɔ̃	

In general, we give the pronunciation of each entry in square brackets after the word in question. However, on the English-French side, where the entry is composed of two or more unhyphenated words, each of which is given elsewhere in this dictionary, you will find the pronunciation of each word in its alphabetical position.

FRENCH VERB TABLES

1 Present participle 2 Past participle 3 Present 4 Imperfect 5 Future
6 Conditional 7 Present subjunctive

acquérir 1 acquérant 2 acquis
3 acquiers, acquérons,
acquièrent 4 acquérais
5 acquerrai 7 acquière

ALLER 1 allant 2 allé 3 vais, vas, va,
allons, allez, vont 4 allais 5 irai
6 irais 7 aille

asseoir 1 asseyant 2 assis 3 assieds,
asseyons, asseyez, asseyent
4 asseyais 5 assiérai 7 asseye

atteindre 1 atteignant 2 atteint
3 atteins, atteignons
4 atteignais 7 atteigne

AVOIR 1 ayant 2 eu 3 ai, as, a,
avons, avez, ont 4 avais 5 aurai
6 aurais 7 aie, aies, ait, ayons,
ayez, aient

battre 1 battant 2 battu 3 bats, bat,
battons 4 battais 7 batte

boire 1 buvant 2 bu 3 bois, buvons,
boivent 4 buvais 7 boive

bouillir 1 bouillant 2 bouilli 3 bous,
bouillons 4 bouillais 7 bouille

conclure 1 concluant 2 conclu
3 conclus, concluons
4 concluais 7 conclue

conduire 1 conduisant 2 conduit
3 conduis, conduisons
4 conduisais 7 conduise

connaître 1 connaissant 2 connu
3 connais, connaît, connaissons
4 connaissais 7 connaisse

coudre 1 cousant 2 cousu 3 couds,
cousons, cousez, cousent
4 cousais 7 couse

courir 1 courant 2 couru 3 cours,
courons 4 courais 5 courrai
7 coure

couvrir 1 couvrant 2 couvert
3 couvre, couvrons 4 couvrais
7 couvre

craindre 1 craignant 2 craint
3 crains, craignons 4 craignais
7 craigne

croire 1 croyant 2 cru 3 crois,
croyons, croient 4 croyais
7 croie

croître 1 croissant 2 crû, crue, crus,
crues 3 croîs, croissons
4 croissais 7 croisse

cueillir 1 cueillant 2 cueilli
3 cueille, cueillons 4 cueillais
5 cueillerai 7 cueille

devoir 1 devant 2 dû, due, dus,
dues 3 dois, devons, doivent
4 devais 5 devrai 7 doive

dire 1 disant 2 dit 3 dis, disons,
dites, disent 4 disais 7 dise

dormir 1 dormant 2 dormi 3 dors,
dormons 4 dormais 7 dorme

écrire 1 écrivant 2 écrit 3 écris,
écrivons, écrivais 7 écrive

ÊTRE 1 étant 2 été 3 suis, es, est,
sommes, êtes, sont 4 étais
5 serai 6 serais 7 sois, sois, soit,
soyons, soyez, soient

FAIRE 1 faisant 2 fait 3 fais, fais,
fait, faisons, faites, font
4 faisais 5 ferai 6 ferais 7 fasse

falloir 2 fallu 3 faut 4 fallait
5 faudra 7 faille

FINIR 1 finissant 2 fini 3 finis,
finis, finit, finissons, finissez,
finissent 4 finissais 5 finirai
6 finirais 7 finisse

fuir 1 fuyant 2 fui 3 fuis, fuyons,
fuient 4 fuyais 7 fuie

joindre 1 joignant 2 joint 3 joins,
joignons 4 joignais 7 joigne

lire 1 lisant 2 lu 3 lis, lisons 4 lisais
7 lise

luire 1 luisant 2 lui 3 luis, luisons

4 luisais 7 luise

maudire 1 maudissant 2 maudit
3 maudis, maudissons
4 maudissait 7 maudisse

mentir 1 mentant 2 menti 3 mens,
mentons 4 mentais 7 mente

mettre 1 mettant 2 mis 3 mets,
mettons 4 mettais 7 mette

mourir 1 mourant 2 mort 3 meurs,
mourons, meurent 4 mourais
5 mourrai 7 meure

naître 1 naissant 2 né 3 nais, naît,
naissons 4 naissais 7 naisse

offrir 1 offrant 2 offert 3 offre,
offrons 4 offrais 7 offre

PARLER 1 parlant 2 parlé 3 parle,
parles, parle, parlons, parlez,
parlent 4 parlais, parlais,
parlait, parlaient, parliez,
parlaient 5 parlerai, parleras,
parlera, parlerons, parlerez,
parleront 6 parlerais, parlerais,
parlerait, parlerions, parleriez,
parleraient 7 parle, parles,
parle, parlions, parliez, parlent
impératif parle! parlons! parlez!

partir 1 partant 2 parti 3 pars,
partons 4 partais 7 parte

plaire 1 plaisant 2 plu 3 plais, plaît,
plaisons 4 plaisais 7 plaise

pleuvoir 1 pleuvant 2 plu 3 pleut,
pleuvent 4 pleuvait 5 pleuvra
7 pleuve

pourvoir 1 pourvoyant 2 pourvu
3 pourvois, pourvoyons,
pourvoient 4 pourvoyais
7 pourvoie

pouvoir 1 pouvant 2 pu 3 peux,
peut, pouvons, peuvent 4
pouvais 5 pourrai 7 puisse

prendre 1 prenant 2 pris 3 prends,
prenons, prennent 4 prenais
7 prenne

prévoir like voir 5 prévoirai

RECEVOIR 1 recevant 2 reçu
3 reçois, reçois, reçoit, recevons,
recevez, reçoivent 4 recevais

5 recevrai 6 recevrais 7 reçoive

RENDRE 1 rendant 2 rendu
3 rends, rends, rend, rendons,
rendez, rendent 4 rendais
5 rendrai 6 rendrais 7 rende

résoudre 1 résolvant 2 résolu
3 résous, résout, résolvons
4 résolvais 7 résolve

rire 1 riant 2 ri 3 ris, rions 4 riais
7 rie

savoir 1 sachant 2 su 3 sais,
savons, savent 4 savais 5 saurai
7 sache impératif sache! sachons!
sachez!

servir 1 servant 2 servi 3 sers,
servons 4 servais 7 serve

sortir 1 sortant 2 sorti 3 sors,
sortons 4 sortais 7 sorte

souffrir 1 souffrant 2 souffert
3 souffre, souffrons 4 souffrais
7 souffre

suffire 1 suffisant 2 suffi 3 suffis,
suffisons 4 suffisais 7 suffise

suivre 1 suivant 2 suivi 3 suis,
suivons 4 suivais 7 suive

taire 1 taisant 2 tu 3 tais, taisons
4 taisais 7 taise

tenir 1 tenant 2 tenu 3 tiens,
tenons, tiennent 4 tenais
5 tiendrai 7 tienne

vaincre 1 vainquant 2 vaincu
3 vaincs, vainc, vainquons
4 vainquais 7 vainque

valoir 1 valant 2 valu 3 vaux, vaut,
valons 4 valais 5 vaudrai 7 vaille

venir 1 venant 2 venu 3 viens,
venons, viennent 4 venais
5 viendrai 7 vienne

vivre 1 vivant 2 vécu 3 vis, vivons
4 vivais 7 vive

voir 1 voyant 2 vu 3 vois, voyons,
voient 4 voyais 5 verrai 7 voie

vouloir 1 voulant 2 voulu 3 veux,
veut, voulons, veulent 4 voulais
5 voudrai 7 veuille; impératif
veuillez!

VERBES IRRÉGULIERS ANGLAIS

PRÉSENT	PASSÉ	PARTICIPE	PRÉSENT	PASSÉ	PARTICIPE
arise	arose	arisen	fight	fought	fought
awake	awoke	awoken	find	found	found
be	was, were	been	flee	fled	fled
(am, is,			fling	flung	flung
are; being)			fly	flew	flown
bear	bore	born(e)	forbid	forbad(e)	forbidden
beat	beat	beaten	forecast	forecast	forecast
become	became	become	forget	forgot	forgotten
begin	began	begun	forgive	forgave	forgiven
bend	bent	bent	forsake	forsook	forsaken
bet	bet,	bet,	freeze	froze	frozen
	betted	betted	get	got	got,
bid (at auction,	bid	bid			(us) gotten
cards)			give	gave	given
bid (say)	bade	bidden	go (goes)	went	gone
bind	bound	bound	grind	ground	ground
bite	bit	bitten	grow	grew	grown
bleed	bled	bled	hang	hung	hung
blow	blew	blown	hang (execute)	hanged	hanged
break	broke	broken	have	had	had
breed	bred	bred	hear	heard	heard
bring	brought	brought	hide	hid	hidden
build	built	built	hit	hit	hit
burn	burnt,	burnt,	hold	held	held
	burned	burned	hurt	hurt	hurt
burst	burst	burst	keep	kept	kept
buy	bought	bought	kneel	knelt,	knelt,
can	could	(been able)		kneeled	kneeled
cast	cast	cast	know	knew	known
catch	caught	caught	lay	laid	laid
choose	chose	chosen	lead	led	led
cling	clung	clung	lean	leant,	leant,
come	came	come		leaned	leaned
cost	cost	cost	leap	leapt,	leapt,
cost (work	costed	costed		leaped	leaped
out price of)			learn	learnt,	learnt,
creep	crept	crept		learned	learned
cut	cut	cut	leave	left	left
deal	dealt	dealt	lend	lent	lent
dig	dug	dug	let	let	let
do (does)	did	done	lie (lying)	lay	lain
draw	drew	drawn	light	lit,	lit,
dream	dreamed,	dreamed,		lighted	lighted
	dreamt	dreamt	lose	lost	lost
drink	drank	drunk	make	made	made
drive	drove	driven	may	might	—
dwell	dwelt	dwelt	mean	meant	meant
eat	ate	eaten	meet	met	met
fall	fell	fallen	mistake	mistook	mistaken
feed	fed	fed	mow	mowed	mown,
feel	felt	felt			mowed

PRÉSENT	PASSÉ	PARTICIPE	PRÉSENT	PASSÉ	PARTICIPE
must	(had to)	(had to)	spend	spent	spent
pay	paid	paid	spill	spilt,	spilt,
put	put	put		spilled	spilled
quit	quit,	quit,	spin	spun	spun
	quitted	quitted	spit	spat	spat
read	read	read	spoil	spoiled,	spoiled,
rid	rid	rid		spoilt	spoilt
ride	rode	ridden	spread	spread	spread
ring	rang	rung	spring	sprang	sprung
rise	rose	risen	stand	stood	stood
run	ran	run	steal	stole	stolen
saw	sawed	sawed,	stick	stuck	stuck
		sawn	sting	stung	stung
say	said	said	stink	stank	stunk
see	saw	seen	stride	strode	stridden
seek	sought	sought	strike	struck	struck
sell	sold	sold	strive	strove	striven
send	sent	sent	swear	swore	sworn
set	set	set	sweep	swept	swept
sew	sewed	sewn	swell	swelled	swollen,
shake	shook	shaken			swelled
shear	sheared	shorn,	swim	swam	swum
		sheared	swing	swung	swung
shed	shed	shed	take	took	taken
shine	shone	shone	teach	taught	taught
shoot	shot	shot	tear	tore	torn
show	showed	shown	tell	told	told
shrink	shrank	shrunk	think	thought	thought
shut	shut	shut	throw	threw	thrown
sing	sang	sung	thrust	thrust	thrust
sink	sank	sunk	tread	trod	trodden
sit	sat	sat	wake	woke,	woken,
slay	slew	slain		waked	waked
sleep	slept	slept	wear	wore	worn
slide	slid	slid	weave	wove	woven
sling	slung	slung	weave (wind)	weaved	weaved
slit	slit	slit	wed	wedded,	wedded,
smell	smelt,	smelt,		wed	wed
	smelled	smelled	weep	wept	wept
sow	sowed	sown,	win	won	won
		sowed	wind	wound	wound
speak	spoke	spoken	wring	wrung	wrung
speed	sped,	sped,	write	wrote	written
	speeded	speeded			
spell	spelt,	spelt,			
	spelled	spelled			

LES NOMBRES

		NUMBERS
un (une)	1	one
deux	2	two
trois	3	three
quatre	4	four
cinq	5	five
six	6	six
sept	7	seven
huit	8	eight
neuf	9	nine
dix	10	ten
onze	11	eleven
douze	12	twelve
treize	13	thirteen
quatorze	14	fourteen
quinze	15	fifteen
seize	16	sixteen
dix-sept	17	seventeen
dix-huit	18	eighteen
dix-neuf	19	nineteen
vingt	20	twenty
vingt et un (une)	21	twenty-one
vingt-deux	22	twenty-two
trente	30	thirty
quarante	40	forty
cinquante	50	fifty
soixante	60	sixty
soixante-dix	70	seventy
soixante-et-onze	71	seventy-one
soixante-douze	72	seventy
quatre-vingts	80	eighty
quatre-vingt-un (-une)	81	eighty-one
quatre-vingt-dix	90	ninety
cent	100	a hundred, one hundred
cent un (une)	101	a hundred and one
deux cents	200	two hundred
deux cent un (une)	201	two hundred and one
quatre cents	400	four hundred
mille	1000	a thousand
cinq mille	5000	five thousand
un million	1000000	a million

LES NOMBRES

premier (première), 1ᵉʳ (1ᵉʳᵉ)
deuxième, 2ᵉ or 2ᵉᵐᵉ
troisième, 3ᵉ or 3ᵉᵐᵉ
quatrième, 4ᵉ or 4ᵉᵐᵉ
cinquième, 5ᵉ or 5ᵉᵐᵉ
sixième, 6ᵉ or 6ᵉᵐᵉ
septième
huitième
neuvième
dixième
onzième
douzième
treizième
quatorzième
quinzième
seizième
dix-septième
dix-huitième
dix-neuvième
vingtième
vingt-et-unième
vingt-deuxième
trentième
centième
cent-unième
millième

LES FRACTIONS ETC

un demi
un tiers
un quart
un cinquième
zéro virgule cinq, 0,5
trois virgule quatre, 3,4
dix pour cent
cent pour cent

EXEMPLES

elle habite au septième (étage)
il habite au sept
au chapitre/à la page sept
il est arrivé (le) septième

NUMBERS

first, 1st
second, 2nd
third, 3rd
fourth, 4th
fifth, 5th
sixth, 6th
seventh
eighth
ninth
tenth
eleventh
twelfth
thirteenth
fourteenth
fifteenth
sixteenth
seventeenth
eighteenth
nineteenth
twentieth
twenty-first
twenty-second
thirtieth
hundredth
hundred-and-first
thousandth

FRACTIONS ETC

a half
a third
a quarter
a fifth
(nought) point five, 0.5
three point four, 3.4
ten per cent
a hundred per cent

EXAMPLES

she lives on the 7th floor
he lives at number 7
chapter/page 7
he came in 7th

L'HEURE	THE TIME
quelle heure est-il?	*what time is it?*
il est …	*it's ou it is …*
minuit	midnight, twelve p.m.
une heure (du matin)	one o'clock (in the morning), one (a.m.)
une heure cinq	five past one
une heure dix	ten past one
une heure et quart	a quarter past one, one fifteen
une heure vingt-cinq	twenty-five past one, one twenty-five
une heure et demie, une heure trente	half-past one, one thirty
deux heures moins vingt-cinq, une heure trente-cinq	twenty-five to two, one thirty-five
deux heures moins vingt, une heure quarante	twenty to two, one forty
deux heures moins le quart, une heure quarante-cinq	a quarter to two, one forty-five
deux heures moins dix, une heure cinquante	ten to two, one fifty
midi	twelve o'clock, midday, noon
deux heures (de l'après-midi), quatorze heures	two o'clock (in the afternoon), two (p.m.)
sept heures (du soir), dix-sept heures	seven o'clock (in the evening), seven (p.m.)
à quelle heure?	*(at) what time?*
à minuit	at midnight
à sept heures	at seven o'clock
dans vingt minutes	in twenty minutes
il y a un quart d'heure	fifteen minutes ago

a [a] *vb voir* **avoir**

◯ **MOT-CLÉ**

à [a] (*à + le* = **au**, *à + les* = **aux**) *prép*
1 (*endroit, situation*) at, in; **être à Paris/
au Portugal** to be in Paris/Portugal;
être à la maison/à l'école to be at
home/at school; **à la campagne** in the
country; **c'est à 10 km/à 20 minutes
(d'ici)** it's 10 km/20 minutes away
2 (*direction*): **aller à Paris/au
Portugal** to go to Paris/Portugal; **aller
à la maison/à l'école** to go home/to
school; **à la campagne** to the country
3 (*temps*): **à 3 heures/minuit** at 3
o'clock/midnight; **au printemps/
mois de juin** in the spring/the month
of June; **à Noël/Pâques** at Christmas/
Easter; **à demain/lundi!** see you
tomorrow/on Monday!
4 (*attribution, appartenance*) to); **le livre
est à Paul/à lui/à nous** this book is
Paul's/his/ours; **un ami à moi** a

friend of mine; **donner qch à qn** to
give sth to sb
5 (*moyen*) with; **se chauffer au gaz** to
have gas heating; **à bicyclette** on a *ou*
by bicycle; **à pied** on foot; **à la main/
machine** by hand/machine
6 (*provenance*) from; **boire à la
bouteille** to drink from the bottle
7 (*caractérisation, manière*): **l'homme
aux yeux bleus** the man with the blue
eyes; **à leur grande surprise** much
to their surprise; **à ce qu'il prétend**
according to him, from what he says;
à la russe the Russian way; **à nous
deux nous n'avons pas su le faire**
we couldn't do it, even between the
two of us
8 (*but, destination*): **tasse à café** coffee
cup; **maison à vendre** house for sale;
je n'ai rien à lire I don't have anything
to read; **à bien réfléchir** ... thinking
about it ..., on reflection ...
9 (*rapport, évaluation, distribution*): **100
km/unités à l'heure** 100 km/units per
ou an hour; **payé au mois/à l'heure**
paid monthly/by the hour; **cinq à six**
five to six; **ils sont arrivés à quatre**
four of them arrived

abaisser [abese] *vt* to lower, bring
down; (*manette*) to pull down;
s'abaisser *vi* to go down; (*fig*) to
demean o.s.

abandon [abɑ̃dɔ̃] *nm* abandoning;
giving up; withdrawal; **être à l'~** to
be in a state of neglect; **laisser à l'~**
to abandon

abandonner [abɑ̃dɔne] *vt* (*personne*)
to abandon; (*projet, activité*) to
abandon, give up; (*Sport*) to retire *ou*
withdraw from; (*céder*) to surrender; **s'~
à** (*paresse, plaisirs*) to give o.s. up to

abat-jour [abaʒuʀ] *nm inv* lampshade

abats [aba] *nmpl* (*de bœuf, porc*) offal *sg*;
(*de volaille*) giblets

abattement [abatmɑ̃] *nm*:
abattement fiscal ≈ tax allowance

abattoir [abatwaʀ]

slaughterhouse

abattre [abatʀ] vt (*arbre*) to cut down, fell; (*mur, maison*) to pull down; (*avion, personne*) to shoot down; (*animal*) to shoot, kill; (*fig*) to wear out, tire out; to demoralize; **s'abattre** vi to crash down; **ne pas se laisser ~** to keep one's spirits up, not to let things get one down; **s'~ sur** to beat down on; (*fig*) to rain down on; **~ du travail ou de la besogne** to get through a lot of work

abbaye [abei] nf abbey

abbé [abe] nm priest; (*d'une abbaye*) abbot

abcès [apsɛ] nm abscess

abdiquer [abdike] vi to abdicate

abdominaux [abdɔmino] nmpl: **faire des ~** to do sit-ups

abeille [abɛj] nf bee

aberrant, e [abɛʀɑ̃, ɑ̃t] adj absurd

aberration [abɛʀasjɔ̃] nf aberration

abîme [abim] nm abyss, gulf

abîmer [abime] vt to spoil, damage; **s'abîmer** vi to get spoilt ou damaged

aboiement [abwamɑ̃] nm bark, barking

abolir [abɔliʀ] vt to abolish

abominable [abɔminabl] adj abominable

abondance [abɔ̃dɑ̃s] nf abundance

abondant, e [abɔ̃dɑ̃, ɑ̃t] adj plentiful, abundant, copious; **abonder** vi to abound, be plentiful; **abonder dans le sens de qn** to concur with sb

abonné, e [abɔne] nm/f subscriber; season ticket holder

abonnement [abɔnmɑ̃] nm subscription; (*transports, concerts*) season ticket

abonner [abɔne] vt: **s'~ à** to subscribe to, take out a subscription to

abord [abɔʀ] nm: **au premier ~** at first sight, initially; **abords** nmpl (*environs*) surroundings; **d'~** adv first

abordable [abɔʀdabl] adj (*prix*) reasonable; (*personne*) approachable

aborder [abɔʀde] vi to land ▷ vt (*sujet, difficulté*) to tackle; (*personne*) to

aboutir [abutiʀ] vi (*négociations etc*) to succeed; **~ à** to end up at; **n'~ à rien** to come to nothing

aboyer [abwaje] vi to bark

abréger [abʀeʒe] vt to shorten

abreuver [abʀœve]: **s'abreuver** vi to drink; **abreuvoir** nm watering place

abréviation [abʀevjasjɔ̃] nf abbreviation

abri [abʀi] nm shelter; **être à l'~** to be under cover; **se mettre à l'~** to take cover; **à l'~ de** (*vent, soleil*) sheltered from; (*danger*) safe from

abricot [abʀiko] nm apricot

abriter [abʀite] vt to shelter; **s'abriter** vt to shelter, take cover

abrupt, e [abʀypt] adj sheer, steep; (*ton*) abrupt

abruti, e [abʀyti] adj stunned, dazed ▷ nm/f (*fam*) idiot, moron; **~ de travail** overworked

absence [apsɑ̃s] nf absence; (*Méd*) blackout; **avoir des ~s** to have mental blanks

absent, e [apsɑ̃, ɑ̃t] adj absent ▷ nm/f absentee; **absenter: s'absenter** vi to take time off work; (*sortir*) to leave, go out

absolu, e [apsɔly] adj absolute; **absolument** adv absolutely

absorbant, e [apsɔʀbɑ̃, ɑ̃t] adj absorbent

absorber [apsɔʀbe] vt to absorb; (*gén Méd: manger, boire*) to take

abstenir [apstəniʀ] vb: **s'~ de qch/de faire** to refrain from sth/from doing

abstrait, e [apstʀɛ, ɛt] adj abstract

absurde [apsyʀd] adj absurd

abus [aby] nm abuse; **~ de confiance** breach of trust; **il y a de l'~!** (*fam*) that a bit much!; **abuser** vi to go too far, overstep the mark; **abuser de** (*duper*) to take advantage of; **s'abuser** (*se méprendre*) to be mistaken; **abusif, -ive** adj exorbitant; (*punition*) excessive

académie [akademi] nf academy; (*Scol: circonscription*) ≈ regional education authority

▸ **ACADÉMIE FRANÇAISE**

The **Académie française** was founded by Cardinal Richelieu in 1635, during the reign of Louis XIII. It is made up of forty elected scholars and writers who are known as 'les Quarante' or 'les Immortels'. One of the **Académie**'s functions is to keep an eye on the development of the French language, and its recommendations are frequently the subject of lively public debate. It has produced several editions of its famous dictionary and also awards various literary prizes.

acajou [akaʒu] nm mahogany

acariâtre [akarjɑtr] adj cantankerous

accablant, e [akablɑ̃, ɑ̃t] adj (chaleur) oppressive; (témoignage, preuve) overwhelming

accabler [akable] vt to overwhelm, overcome; ~ **qn d'injures** to heap ou shower abuse on sb; ~ **qn de travail** to overwork sb

accalmie [akalmi] nf lull

accaparer [akapare] vt to monopolize; (suj: travail etc) to take up (all) the time ou attention of

accéder [aksede]: ~ **à** vt (lieu) to reach; (accorder: requête) to grant, accede to

accélérateur [akseleratœr] nm accelerator

accélérer [akselere] vt to speed up ▸ vi to accelerate

accent [aksɑ̃] nm accent; (Phonétique, fig) stress; **mettre l'~ sur** (fig) to stress; ~ **aigu/grave/circonflexe** acute/grave/circumflex accent; **accentuer** vt (Ling) to accentuate; (fig) to accentuate, emphasize; **s'accentuer** vi to become more marked ou pronounced

acceptation [akseptasjɔ̃] nf acceptance

accepter [aksepte] vt to accept; ~ **de**

faire to agree to do; **acceptez-vous les cartes de crédit?** do you take credit cards?

accès [aksɛ] nm (à un lieu) access; (Méd: de toux) fit; (: de fièvre) bout; **d'~ facile** easily accessible; **facile d'~** easy to get to; **accès de colère** fit of anger; **accessible** adj accessible; (livre, sujet) **accessible à qn** within the reach of sb

accessoire [akseswar] adj secondary; incidental ▸ nm accessory; (Théâtre) prop

accident [aksidɑ̃] nm accident; **par ~** by chance; **j'ai eu un ~** I've had an accident; **accident de la route** road accident; **accidenté, e** adj damaged; injured; (relief, terrain) uneven; hilly; **accidentel, le** adj accidental

acclamer [aklame] vt to cheer, acclaim

acclimater [aklimate]: **s'acclimater** vi (personne) to adapt (o.s.)

accolade [akɔlad] nf (amicale) embrace; (signe) brace

accommoder [akɔmɔde] vt (Culin) to prepare; **s'accommoder de** vt to put up with; (se contenter de) to make do with

accompagnateur, -trice [akɔ̃paɲatœr, tris] nm/f (Mus) accompanist; (de voyage: guide) guide; (de voyage organisé) courier

accompagner [akɔ̃paɲe] vt to accompany, be ou go ou come with; (Mus) to accompany

accompli, e [akɔ̃pli] adj accomplished; voir aussi **fait**

accomplir [akɔ̃plir] vt (tâche, projet) to carry out; (souhait) to fulfil; **s'accomplir** vi to be fulfilled

accord [akɔr] nm agreement; (entre des styles, tons etc) harmony; (Mus) chord; **d'~!** OK!; **se mettre d'~** to come to an agreement; **être d'~ (pour faire qch)** to agree (to do sth)

accordéon [akɔrdeɔ̃] nm (Mus) accordion

accorder [akɔrde] vt (faveur, délai) to

grant; (*harmoniser*) to match; (*Mus*) to tune; (*valeur, importance*) attach

accoster [akɔste] vt (*Navig*) to draw alongside ▸ vi to berth

accouchement [akuʃmã] nm delivery, (child)birth; labour

accoucher [akuʃe] vi to give birth, have a baby; ~ **d'un garçon** to give birth to a boy

accouder [akude] vi: **s'~ à/contre/sur** to rest one's elbows on/against/on; **accoudoir** nm armrest

accoupler [akuple] vt to couple; (*pour la reproduction*) to mate; **s'accoupler** vt to mate

accourir [akuriʁ] vi to rush ou run up

accoutumance [akutymãs] nf (*gén*) adaptation; (*Méd*) addiction

accoutumé, e [akutyme] adj (*habituel*) customary, usual

accoutumer [akutyme] vt: **s'~ à** to get accustomed ou used to

accroc [akʁo] nm (*déchirure*) tear; (*fig*) hitch, snag

accrochage [akʁɔʃaʒ] nm (*Auto*) collision; (*dispute*) clash, brush

accrocher [akʁɔʃe] vt (*fig*) to catch, attract; **s'accrocher** (*se disputer*) to have a clash ou brush; **~ qch à** (*suspendre*) to hang sth (up) on; (*attacher: remorque*) to hitch sth (up) on; **~ qch (à)** (*déchirer*) to catch sth (on); **il a accroché ma voiture** he bumped into my car; **s'~ à** (*rester pris à*) to catch on; (*agripper, fig*) to hang on ou cling to

accroissement [akʁwasmã] nm increase

accroître [akʁwatʁ]: **s'accroître** vi to increase

accroupir [akʁupiʁ]: **s'accroupir** vi to squat, crouch (down)

accru, e [akʁy] pp de **accroître**

accueil [akœj] nm welcome; **comité d'~** reception committee; **accueillir** vt to welcome; (*aller chercher*) to meet, collect

accumuler [akymyle] vt to accumulate, amass; **s'accumuler** vi to accumulate; to pile up

accusation [akyzasjɔ̃] nf (*gén*) accusation; (*Jur*) charge; (*partie*): **l'~** the prosecution

accusé, e [akyze] nm/f accused; defendant; **accusé de réception** acknowledgement of receipt

accuser [akyze] vt to accuse; (*fig*) to emphasize, bring out; to show; **~ qn de** to accuse sb of; (*Jur*) to charge sb with; **~ réception de** to acknowledge receipt of

acéré, e [asere] adj sharp

acharné, e [aʃaʁne] adj (*efforts*) relentless; (*lutte, adversaire*) fierce, bitter

acharner [aʃaʁne] vb: **s'~ contre** to set o.s. against; (*suj: malchance*) to dog; **s'~ à faire** to try doggedly to do; (*persister*) to persist in doing; **s'~ sur qn** to hound sb

achat [aʃa] nm purchase; **faire des ~s** to do some shopping; **faire l'~ de qch** to purchase sth

acheter [aʃ(ə)te] vt to buy, purchase; (*soudoyer*) to buy; **~ qch (à** (*marchand*) to buy ou purchase sth from; (*ami etc: offrir*) to buy sth for; **où est-ce que je peux ~ des cartes postales?** where can I buy (some) postcards?; **acheteur, -euse** nm/f buyer; shopper; (*Comm*) buyer

achever [aʃ(ə)ve] vt to complete, finish; (*blessé*) to finish off; **s'achever** vi to end

acide [asid] adj sour, sharp; (*Chimie*) acid(ic) ▸ nm (*Chimie*) acid; **acidulé, e** adj slightly acid; **bonbons acidulés** acid drops

acier [asje] nm steel; **aciérie** nf steelworks sg

acné [akne] nf acne

acompte [akɔ̃t] nm deposit

à-côté [akote] nm side-issue; (*argent*) extra

à-coup [aku] nm: **par ~s** by fits and starts

acoustique [akustik] nf (*d'une salle*) acoustics pl

acquéreur [akerœr] nm buyer, purchaser

acquérir [akerir] vt to acquire

acquis, e [aki, iz] pp de **acquérir** ▷ nm (accumulated) experience; **son aide nous est ~e** we can count on her help

acquitter [akite] vt (Jur) to acquit; (facture) to pay, settle; **s'acquitter de** (devoir) to discharge; (promesse) to fulfil

âcre [akr] adj acrid, pungent

acrobate [akrɔbat] nm/f acrobat; **acrobatie** nf acrobatics sg

acte [akt] nm act, action; (Théâtre) act; **prendre ~ de** to note, take note of; **faire ~ de candidature** to apply; **faire ~ de présence** to put in an appearance; **acte de naissance** birth certificate

acteur [aktœr] nm actor

actif, -ive [aktif, iv] adj active ▷ nm (Comm) assets pl; (fig): **avoir à son ~** to have to one's credit; **population active** working population

action [aksjɔ̃] nf (gén) action; (Comm) share; **une bonne ~** a good deed; **actionnaire** nm/f shareholder; **actionner** vt (mécanisme) to activate; (machine) to operate

activer [aktive] vt to speed up; **s'activer** vi to bustle about; to hurry up

activité [aktivite] nf activity; **en ~** (volcan) active; (fonctionnaire) in active life

actrice [aktris] nf actress

actualité [aktɥalite] nf (d'un problème) topicality; (événements): **l'~** current events; **actualités** nfpl (Cinéma, TV) the news; **d'~** topical

actuel, le [aktɥɛl] adj (présent) present; (d'actualité) topical; **à l'heure ~le** at the present time; **actuellement** adv at present, at the present time

⚠ Attention à ne pas traduire **actuellement** par **actually**.

acupuncture [akypɔ̃ktyr] nf acupuncture

adaptateur [adaptatœr] nm (Élec) adapter

adapter [adapte] vt to adapt; **s'adapter (à)** (suj: personne) to adapt (to); **~ qch à** (approprier) to adapt sth to (fit); **~ qch sur/dans/à** (fixer) to fit sth on/into/to

addition [adisjɔ̃] nf addition; (au café) bill; **l'~, s'il vous plaît** could I have the bill, please?; **additionner** vt to add (up)

adepte [adɛpt] nm/f follower

adéquat, e [adekwa(t), at] adj appropriate, suitable

adhérent, e [adera, ɑ̃t] nm/f member

adhérer [adere]: **~ à** vt (coller) to adhere ou stick to; (se rallier à) to join; **adhésif, -ive** adj adhesive, sticky; **ruban adhésif** sticky ou adhesive tape

adieu, x [adjø] excl goodbye ▷ nm farewell

adjectif [adʒɛktif] nm adjective

adjoint, e [adʒwɛ̃, wɛ̃t] nm/f assistant; **adjoint au maire** deputy mayor; **directeur adjoint** assistant manager

admettre [admɛtr] vt (laisser entrer) to admit; (candidat: Scol) to pass; (tolérer) to allow, accept; (reconnaître) to admit, acknowledge

administrateur, -trice [administratœr, tris] nm/f (Comm) director; (Admin) administrator

administration [administrasjɔ̃] nf administration; **l'A~** = the Civil Service

administrer [administre] vt (firme) to manage, run; (biens, remède, sacrement etc) to administer

admirable [admirabl] adj admirable, wonderful

admirateur, -trice [admiratœr, tris] nm/f admirer

admiration [admirasjɔ̃] nf admiration

admirer [admire] vt to admire

admis, e [admi, iz] pp de **admettre**

admissible [admisibl] adj (candidat) eligible; (comportement) admissible, acceptable

ADN sigle m (= acide désoxyribonucléique) DNA

adolescence [adɔlesɑ̃s] *nf* adolescence

adolescent, e [adɔlesɑ̃, ɑ̃t] *nm/f* adolescent, teenager

adopter [adɔpte] *vt* to adopt; **adoptif, -ive** *adj* (parents) adoptive; (fils, patrie) adopted

adorable [adɔrabl] *adj* delightful, adorable

adorer [adɔre] *vt* to adore; (Rel) to worship

adosser [adose] *vt*: **~ qch à** ou **contre** to stand sth against; **s'adosser à/contre** to lean with one's back against

adoucir [adusiʀ] *vt* (goût, température) to make milder; (avec du sucre) to sweeten; (peau, voix) to soften; (caractère) to mellow

adresse [adrɛs] *nf* (domicile) address; (dextérité) skill, dexterity; **~ électronique** email address

adresser [adrese] *vt* (lettre: expédier) to send; (: écrire l'adresse sur) to address; (injure, compliments) to address; **s'adresser à** (parler à) to speak to, address; (s'informer auprès de) to go and see; (: bureau) to inquire at; (suj: livre, conseil) to be aimed at; **~ la parole à** to speak to, address

adroit, e [adʀwa, wat] *adj* skilful, skilled

ADSL *sigle m* (= asymmetrical digital subscriber line) ADSL, broadband

adulte [adylt] *nm/f* adult, grown-up ▷ *adj* (chien, arbre) fully-grown, mature; (attitude) adult, grown-up

adverbe [adverb] *nm* adverb

adversaire [adverser] *nm/f* (Sport, gén) opponent, adversary

aération [aerasjɔ̃] *nf* airing; (circulation de l'air) ventilation

aérer [aere] *vt* to air; (fig) to lighten

aérien, ne [aerjɛ̃, jɛn] *adj* (Aviat) air *cpd*, aerial; (câble, métro) overhead; (fig) light; **compagnie ~ne** airline

aéro... [aero] *préfixe*: **aérobic** *nm* aerobics *sg*; **aérogare** *nf* airport (buildings); (en ville) air terminal;

aéroglisseur *nm* hovercraft; **aérophagie** *nf* (Méd) wind, aerophagia (Méd); **aéroport** *nm* airport; **aérosol** *nm* aerosol

affaiblir [afeblir]: **s'affaiblir** *vi* to weaken

affaire [afɛr] *nf* (problème, question) matter; (criminelle, judiciaire) case; (scandaleuse etc) affair; (entreprise) business; (marché, transaction) deal; business *no pl*; (occasion intéressante) bargain; **affaires** *nfpl* (intérêts publics et privés) affairs; (activité commerciale) business *sg*; (effets personnels) things, belongings; **ce sont mes ~s** (cela me concerne) that's my business; **occupe-toi de tes ~s!** mind your own business!; **ça fera l'~** that will do (nicely); **se tirer d'~** to sort it out to things out for o.s.; **avoir ~ à** (être en contact) to be dealing with; **les A~s étrangères** Foreign Affairs;

affairer [afere]: **s'affairer** *vi* to busy o.s., bustle about

affamé, e [afame] *adj* starving

affecter [afɛkte] *vt* to affect; **~ qch à** to allocate ou allot sth to; **~ qn à** to appoint sb to; (diplomate) to post sb to

affectif, -ive [afɛktif, iv] *adj* emotional

affection [afɛksjɔ̃] *nf* affection; (mal) ailment; **affectionner** *vt* to be fond of; **affectueux, -euse** *adj* affectionate

affichage [afiʃaʒ] *nm* billposting; (électronique) display; **"~ interdit"** "stick no bills"; **affichage à cristaux liquides** liquid crystal display, LCD

affiche [afiʃ] *nf* poster; (officielle) notice; (Théâtre) notice; **être à l'~** to be on

afficher [afiʃe] *vt* (affiche) to put up; (réunion) to put up a notice about; (électroniquement) to display; (fig) to exhibit, display; **"défense d'~"** "no bill posters"; **s'afficher** *vr* (péj) to flaunt o.s.; (électroniquement) to be displayed

affilée [afile]: **d'~** *adv* at a stretch

affirmatif, -ive [afirmatif, iv] *adj* affirmative

affirmer [afirme] *vt* to assert

affligé, e [afliʒe] adj distressed, grieved; **~ de** (maladie, tare) afflicted with

affliger [afliʒe] vt (peiner) to distress, grieve

affluence [aflyɑ̃s] nf crowds pl; **heures d'~** rush hours; **jours d'~** busiest days

affluent [aflyɑ̃] nm tributary

affolement [afɔlmɑ̃] nm panic

affoler [afɔle] vt to throw into a panic; **s'affoler** vi to panic

affranchir [afrɑ̃ʃiʀ] vt to put a stamp ou stamps on; (à la machine) to frank (BRIT), meter (us); (fig) to free, liberate; **affranchissement** nm postage

affreux, -euse [afʀø, øz] adj dreadful, awful

affront [afʀɔ̃] nm affront; **affrontement** nm clash, confrontation

affronter [afʀɔ̃te] vt to confront, face

affût [afy] nm: **à l'~ (de)** (gibier) lying in wait (for); (fig) on the look-out for

Afghanistan [afganistɑ̃] nm: **l'~** Afghanistan

afin [afɛ̃]: **~ que** conj so that, in order that; **~ de faire** in order to do, so as to do

africain, e [afʀikɛ̃, ɛn] adj African ▷ nm/f: **A~, e** African

Afrique [afʀik] nf: **l'~** Africa; **l'Afrique du Nord/Sud** North/South Africa

agacer [agase] vt to irritate

âge [ɑʒ] nm age; **quel ~ as-tu?** how old are you?; **prendre de l'~** to be getting on (in years); **le troisième ~** (période) retirement; (personnes âgées) senior citizens; **âgé, e** adj old, elderly; **âgé de 10 ans** 10 years old

agence [aʒɑ̃s] nf agency, office; (succursale) branch; **agence de voyages** travel agency; **agence immobilière** estate (BRIT) ou real estate (us) agent's (office)

agenda [aʒɛ̃da] nm diary; **~ électronique** PDA

Attention à ne pas traduire **agenda** par le mot anglais **agenda**.

agenouiller [aʒ(ə)nuje]: **s'agenouiller** vi to kneel (down)

agent, e [aʒɑ̃, ɑ̃t] nm/f (aussi: **~(e) de police**) policeman(policewoman); (Admin) official, officer; **agent immobilier** estate agent (BRIT), realtor (us)

agglomération [aglɔmeʀasjɔ̃] nf town; built-up area; **l'~ parisienne** the urban area of Paris

aggraver [agʀave]: **s'aggraver** vi to worsen

agile [aʒil] adj agile, nimble

agir [aʒiʀ] vi to act; **il s'agit de** (ça traite de) it is about; (il est important de) it's a matter ou question of; **il s'agit de faire** we (ou you etc) must do; **de quoi s'agit-il?** what is it about?

agitation [aʒitasjɔ̃] nf (hustle and) bustle; (trouble) agitation, excitement; (politique) unrest, agitation

agité, e [aʒite] adj fidgety, restless; (troublé) agitated, perturbed; (mer) rough

agiter [aʒite] vt (bouteille, chiffon) to shake; (bras, mains) to wave; (préoccuper, exciter) to perturb

agneau, x [aɲo] nm lamb

agonie [agɔni] nf (mortal agony, death pangs pl; (fig) death throes pl

agrafe [agʀaf] nf (de vêtement) hook, fastener; (de bureau) staple; **agrafer** vt to fasten; to staple; **agrafeuse** nf stapler

agrandir [agʀɑ̃diʀ] vt to enlarge; **s'agrandir** vi (ville, famille) to grow, expand; (trou, écart) to get bigger; **agrandissement** nm (Photo) enlargement

agréable [agʀeabl] adj pleasant, nice

agréé, e [agʀee] adj: **concessionnaire ~** registered dealer

agréer [agʀee] vt (requête) to accept; **~ à** to please, suit; **veuillez ~, Monsieur/Madame, mes salutations distinguées** (personne nommée) yours sincerely; (personne non nommée) yours faithfully

agrégation

agrégation [agregasjɔ̃] nf highest teaching diploma in France; **agrégé, e** nm/f holder of the agrégation

agrément [agremɑ̃] nm (accord) consent, approval; (attraits) charm, attractiveness; (plaisir) pleasure

agresser [agrese] vt to attack; **agresseur** nm aggressor, attacker; (Pol, Mil) aggressor; **agressif, -ive** adj aggressive

agricole [agrikɔl] adj agricultural; **agriculteur** nm farmer; **agriculture** nf agriculture, farming

agripper [agripe] vt to grab, clutch; **s'agripper à** to cling (on) to, clutch, grip

agro-alimentaire [agroalimɑ̃tɛr] nm farm-produce industry

agrumes [agrym] nmpl citrus fruit(s)

aguets [age] nmpl: **être aux ~** to be on the lookout

ai [e] vb voir **avoir**

aide [ed] nm/f assistant; carer ▷ nf assistance, help; (secours financier) aid; **à l'~ de** (avec) with the help ou aid of; **appeler (qn) à l'~** to call for help (from sb); **à l'~!** help!; **aide judiciaire** legal aid; **aide ménagère** = home help (BRIT) ou helper (US); **aide-mémoire** inv memoranda pages pl; (key facts) handbook; **aide-soignant, e** nm/f auxiliary nurse

aider [ede] vt to help; **~ à qch** to help (towards) sth; **~ qn à faire qch** to help sb to do sth; **pouvez-vous m'~?** can you help me?; **s'aider de** (se servir de) to use, make use of

aïe [aj] excl ouch!

aie etc [e] vb voir **avoir**

aigle [egl] nm eagle

aigre [egr] adj sour, sharp; (fig) sharp, cutting; **aigre-doux, -ce** adj (sauce) sweet and sour; **aigreur** nf sourness; sharpness; **aigreurs d'estomac** heartburn sg

aigu, ë [egy] adj (objet, douleur) sharp; (son, voix) high-pitched, shrill; (note) high(-pitched)

aiguille [egɥij] nf needle; (de montre) hand; **aiguille à tricoter** knitting needle

aiguiser [egize] vt to sharpen; (fig) to stimulate; (: sens) to excite

ail [aj] nm garlic

aile [ɛl] nf wing; **aileron** nm (de requin) fin; **ailier** nm winger

aille etc [aj] vb voir **aller**

ailleurs [ajœr] adv elsewhere, somewhere else; **partout/nulle part ~** everywhere/nowhere else; **d'~** (du reste) moreover, besides; **par ~** (d'autre part) moreover, furthermore

aimable [ɛmabl] adj kind, nice

aimant [ɛmɑ̃] nm magnet

aimer [eme] vt to love; (d'amitié, affection, par goût) to like; (souhait): **j'aimerais ...** I would like ...; **j'aime faire du ski** I like skiing; **je t'aime** I love you; **bien ~ qn/qch** to like sb/sth; **j'aime mieux Paul** I prefer Paul (to Pierre); **j'aimerais mieux faire** I'd much rather do

aine [ɛn] nf groin

aîné, e [ene] adj elder, older; (le plus âgé) eldest, oldest ▷ nm/f oldest child ou one, oldest boy ou son/girl ou daughter

ainsi [ɛ̃si] adv (de cette façon) like this, in this way, thus; (ce faisant) thus ▷ conj thus; so; **~ que** (comme) (just) as; (et aussi) as well as; **pour ~ dire** so to speak; **et ~ de suite** and so on

air [ɛr] nm air; (mélodie) tune; (expression) look, air; **prendre l'~** to get some (fresh) air; **avoir l'~** (sembler) to look, appear; **il a l'~ triste/malade** he looks sad/ill; **avoir l'~ de** to look like; **il a l'~ de dormir** he looks as if he's sleeping; **en l'~** (promesses) empty

airbag [ɛrbag] nm airbag

aisance [ɛzɑ̃s] nf ease; (richesse) affluence

aise [ɛz] nf comfort; **être à l'~** ou **à son ~** to be comfortable; (pas embarrassé) to be at ease; (financièrement) to be comfortably off; **se mettre à l'~** to make o.s. comfortable; **être mal à l'~**

to be uncomfortable; **(gêne)** to be ill at ease; **en faire à son ~** to do as one likes; **aisé, e** adj easy; **(assez riche)** well-to-do, well-off

aisselle [ɛsɛl] nf armpit

ait [ɛ] vb voir **avoir**

ajonc [aʒɔ̃] nm gorse no pl

ajourner [aʒuʀne] vt **(réunion)** to adjourn; **(décision)** to defer, postpone

ajouter [aʒute] vt to add

alarme [alaʀm] nf alarm; **donner l'~** to give ou raise the alarm; **alarmer** vt to alarm; **s'alarmer** vi to become alarmed

Albanie [albani] nf: **l'~** Albania

album [albɔm] nm album

alcool [alkɔl] nm: **l'~** alcohol; **un ~** a spirit, a brandy; **bière sans ~** non-alcoholic ou alcohol-free beer; **alcool à brûler** methylated spirits **(BRIT)**, wood alcohol **(US)**; **alcool à go=** surgical spirit; **alcoolique** adj, nm/f alcoholic; **alcoolisé e** adj alcoholic; **une boisson non alcoolisée** a soft drink; **alcoolisme** nm alcoholism; **alco(o)test®** nm Breathalyser® **(test)** breath-test

aléatoire [aleatwaʀ] adj uncertain; **(Inform)** random

alentour [alɑ̃tuʀ] adv around, round about; **alentours** nmpl **(environs)** surroundings; **aux ~s de** in the vicinity ou neighbourhood of the area; **(temps)** round about

alerte [alɛʀt] adj agile, nimble; brisk, lively ▷ nf alert; warning; **alerte à la bombe** bomb scare; **alerter** vt to alert

algèbre [alʒɛbʀ] nf algebra

Alger [alʒe] n Algiers

Algérie [alʒeʀi] nf: **l'~** Algeria; **algérien, ne** adj Algerian ▷ nm/f: **Algérien, ne** Algerian

algue [alg] nf **(gén)** seaweed no pl **(Bot)** alga

alibi [alibi] nm alibi

aligner [aliɲe] vt to align, line up; **(idées, chiffres)** to string together; **(adapter)**: **~ qch sur** to bring sth into

alignment with; **s'aligner (sur)** **(Pol)** to line up behind; **s'~ sur (Pol)** to bring o.s. into line with

aliment [alimɑ̃] nm food; **alimentation** nf **(commerce)** food trade; **(magasin)** grocery store; **(régime)** diet; **(en eau etc, de moteur)** supplying; **(Inform)** feed; **alimenter** vt to feed; **(Tech)**: **alimenter (en)** to supply **(with)**; to feed (with); **(fig)** to sustain, keep going

allaiter [alete] vt to (breast-)feed, nurse; **(suj: animal)** to suckle

allécher [aleʃe] vt: **~ qn** to make sb's mouth water; to tempt ou entice sb

allée [ale] nf **(de jardin)** path; **(en ville)** avenue, drive; **~s et venues** comings and goings

allégé, e [aleʒe] adj **(yaourt etc)** low-fat

alléger [aleʒe] vt **(voiture)** to make lighter; **(chargement)** to lighten; **(souffrance)** to alleviate, soothe

Allemagne [almaɲ] nf: **l'~** Germany; **allemand, e** adj German ▷ nm/f: **Allemand, e** German ▷ nm **(Ling)** German

aller [ale] nm **(trajet)** outward journey; **(billet: aussi: ~ simple)** single ou one-way(= ticket); **~ (et) retour** return **(ticket)** journey; round-trip ticket **(us)** ▷ vi **(gén)** to go; **~ à (convenir)** to suit; **(suj: forme, pointure etc)** to fit; **~ (bien) avec (couleurs, style etc)** to go (well) with; **je vais y /me fâcher** I'm going to go/to get angry; **~ chercher qn** to go and get ou fetch **(BRIT)** sb; **~ voir** to go and see, to go to see; **allez!** come on!; **allons!** come now!; **comment allez-vous?** how are you?; **comment ça va?** how are you?; **(affaires etc)** how are things?; **il va bien/mal** he's well/not well, he's fine/ill; **ça va bien/mal (affaires etc)** things are going well/not going well; **~ mieux** to be better; **s'en ~ (partir)** to be off, go, leave; **(disparaître)** to disappear

allergie [alɛʀʒi] nf allergy

allergique [alɛʀʒik] adj: **~ à** allergic to; **je suis ~ à la pénicilline** I'm allergic to penicillin

alliance [aljɑ̃s] *nf* (Mil, Pol) alliance; (*bague*) wedding ring

allier [alje] *vt* (Pol, gén) to ally; (*fig*) to combine; **s'allier** to become allies; to combine

allô [alo] *excl* hullo, hallo

allocation [alɔkasjɔ̃] *nf* allowance; **allocation (de) chômage** unemployment benefit; **allocations familiales** ≈ child benefit

allonger [alɔ̃ʒe] *vt* to lengthen, make longer; (*étendre: bras, jambe*) to stretch (out); **s'allonger** *vi* to get longer; (*se coucher*) to lie down, stretch out; **~ le pas** to hasten one's step(s)

allumage [alymaʒ] *nm* (Auto) ignition

allume-cigare [alymsigar] *nm inv* cigar lighter

allumer [alyme] *vt* (lampe, phare, radio) to put on *ou* switch on; (*pièce*) to put on switch the light(s) on in; (*feu*) to light; **s'allumer** *vi* (*lumière, lampe*) to come *ou* go on; **je n'arrive pas à ~ le chauffage** I can't turn the heating on

allumette [alymɛt] *nf* match

allure [alyr] *nf* (*vitesse*) speed, pace; (*démarche*) walk; (*aspect, air*) look; **avoir de l'~** to have style; **à toute ~** at top speed

allusion [a(l)lyzjɔ̃] *nf* allusion; (*sous-entendu*) hint; **faire ~ à** to allude *ou* refer to; to hint at

---

⊙ **MOT-CLÉ**

alors [alɔr] *adv* 1 (*à ce moment-là*) then, at that time; **il habitait alors à Paris** he lived in Paris at that time
2 (*par conséquent*) then; **tu as fini? alors je m'en vais** have you finished? I'm going then; **et alors?** so what?
▷ *conj*: **alors que** 1 (*au moment où*) when, as; **il est arrivé alors que je partais** he arrived as I was leaving
2 (*pendant que*) whereas, while; **alors que son frère travaillait dur, lui se reposait** while his brother was

working hard, HE would rest
3 (*bien que*) even though; **il a été puni alors qu'il n'a rien fait** he was punished, even though he had done nothing

alourdir [alurdir] *vt* to weigh down, make heavy

Alpes [alp] *nfpl*: **les ~** the Alps

alphabet [alfabɛ] *nm* alphabet; (*livre*) ABC (book)

alpinisme [alpinism] *nm* mountaineering, climbing

alsace [alzas] *nf* Alsace; **alsacien, ne** *adj* Alsatian ▷ *nm/f*: **Alsacien, ne** Alsatian

altermondialisme [altɛrmɔ̃djalism] *nm* anti-globalism; **altermondialiste** *adj, nm/f* anti-globalist

alternatif, -ive [altɛrnatif, iv] *adj* alternating; **alternative** *nf* (*choix*) alternative; **alterner** *vi* to alternate

altitude [altityd] *nf* altitude, height

alto [alto] *nm* (*instrument*) viola

aluminium [alyminjɔm] *nm* aluminium (BRIT), aluminum (US)

amabilité [amabilite] *nf* kindness

amaigrissant, e [amegrisɑ̃, ɑ̃t] *adj* (*régime*) slimming

amande [amɑ̃d] *nf* (*de l'amandier*) almond; **amandier** *nm* almond (tree)

amant [amɑ̃] *nm* lover

amas [amɑ] *nm* heap, pile; **amasser** *vt* to amass

amateur [amatœr] *nm* amateur; **en ~** (*péj*) amateurishly; **amateur de musique/sport** music/sport lover

ambassade [ɑ̃basad] *nf* embassy; **l'~ de France** the French Embassy; **ambassadeur, -drice** *nm/f* ambassador(-dress)

ambiance [ɑ̃bjɑ̃s] *nf* atmosphere; **il y a de l'~** there's a great atmosphere

ambigu, ë [ɑ̃bigy] *adj* ambiguous

ambitieux, -euse [ɑ̃bisjø, jøz] *adj* ambitious

ambition [ɑ̃bisjɔ̃] *nf* ambition

ambulance [ɑ̃bylɑ̃s] *nf* ambulance;

appelez une ~! call an ambulance!;
ambulancier, -ière nm/f ambulance
man(-woman); paramedic (us)
âme [am] nf soul; **âme sœur** kindred
spirit
amélioration [ameljɔrasjɔ̃] nf
improvement
améliorer [ameljɔre] vt to improve;
s'améliorer vi to improve, get better
aménager [amenaʒe] vt (agencer,
transformer) to fit out; to lay out;
(: quartier, territoire) to develop;
(installer) to fix up, put in; **ferme
aménagée** converted farmhouse
amende [amɑ̃d] nf fine; **faire ~
honorable** to make amends
amener [am(ə)ne] vt to bring; (causer)
to bring about; **s'amener** vi to show
up (fam), turn up; **~ qn à faire qch** to
lead sb to do something
amer, amère [amɛʀ] adj bitter
américain, e [amerikɛ̃, ɛn] adj
American ▷ nm/f: **A~, e** American
Amérique [amerik] nf: l'~ America;
Amérique centrale/latine Central/
Latin America; **l'Amérique du Nord/
Sud** North/South America
amertume [amɛʀtym] nf bitterness
ameublement [amœblamɑ̃] nm
furnishing; (meubles) furniture
ami, e [ami] nm/f friend; (amant/
maîtresse) boyfriend/girlfriend ▷ adj:
pays/groupe ~ friendly country/
group; **petit ~/petite ~e** boyfriend/
girlfriend
amiable [amjabl]: **à l'~** adv (Jur) out of
court; (gén) amicably
amiante [amjɑ̃t] nm asbestos
amical, e, -aux [amikal, o] adj
friendly; **amicalement** adv in a
friendly way; (dans une lettre) with
best wishes
amincir [amɛ̃siʀ] vt: **~ qn** to make sb
thinner ou slimmer; (suj: vêtement) to
make sb look slimmer
amincissant, e [amɛ̃sisɑ̃, ɑ̃t] adj:
régime ~ (slimming) diet; **crème ~e**
slimming cream

amiral, -aux [amiral, o] nm admiral
amitié [amitje] nf friendship; **prendre
en ~** to befriend; **faire ou présenter
ses ~s à qn** to send sb one's best
wishes; **"~s"** (dans une lettre) "(with)
best wishes"
amonceler [amɔ̃s(ə)le] vt to pile ou
heap up; **s'amonceler** vi to pile ou
heap up; (fig) to accumulate
amont [amɔ̃]: **en ~** adv upstream
amorce [amɔʀs] nf (sur un hameçon)
bait; (explosif) cap; primer; priming; (fig:
début) beginning; start
amortir [amɔʀtiʀ] vt (atténuer: choc)
to absorb, cushion; (bruit, douleur) to
deaden; (Comm: dette) to pay off; **~ un
achat** to make a purchase pay for itself;
amortisseur nm shock absorber
amour [amuʀ] nm love; **faire l'~** to
make love; **amoureux, -euse** adj
(regard, tempérament) amorous; (vie,
problèmes) love cpd; (personne): **être
amoureux (de qn)** to be in love (with
sb); **tomber amoureux (de qn)** to
fall in love (with sb) ▷ nmpl courting
couple(s); **amour-propre** nm self-
esteem, pride
ampère [ɑ̃pɛʀ] nm amp(ere)
amphithéâtre [ɑ̃fiteatʀ] nm
amphitheatre; (d'université) lecture hall
ou theatre
ample [ɑ̃pl] adj (vêtement) roomy,
ample; (gestes, mouvement) broad;
(ressources) ample; **amplement** adv:
c'est amplement suffisant that's
more than enough; **ampleur** nf (de
dégâts, problème) extent
amplificateur [ɑ̃plifikatœʀ] nm
amplifier
amplifier [ɑ̃plifje] vt (fig) to expand,
increase
ampoule [ɑ̃pul] nf (électrique) bulb;
(de médicament) phial; (aux mains, pieds)
blister
amusant, e [amyzɑ̃, ɑ̃t] adj
(divertissant, spirituel) entertaining,
amusing; (comique) funny, amusing
amuse-gueule [amyzɡœl] nm inv

appetizer, snack

amusement [amyzmã] nm
(divertissement) amusement; (jeu etc)
pastime, diversion

amuser [amyze] vt (divertir) to
entertain, amuse; (égayer, faire rire) to
amuse; **s'amuser** vi (jouer) to play; (se
divertir) to enjoy o.s., have fun; (fig) to
mess around

amygdale [amidal] nf tonsil

an [ã] nm year; **avoir quinze ans** to be
fifteen (years old); **le jour de l'an, le
premier de l'an, le nouvel an** New
Year's Day

analphabète [analfabet] nm/f
illiterate

analyse [analiz] nf analysis; (Méd) test;
analyser vt to analyse; to test

ananas [anana(s)] nm pineapple

anatomie [anatɔmi] nf anatomy

ancêtre [ãsetr] nm/f ancestor

anchois [ãʃwa] nm anchovy

ancien, ne [ãsjɛ̃, jɛn] adj old; (de
jadis, de l'antiquité) ancient; (précédent,
ex-) former, old; (par l'expérience)
senior ▷ nm/f (dans une tribu) elder;
ancienneté [ãsjɛnte] nf (Admin) (length of)
service; (privilèges obtenus) seniority

ancre [ãkr] nf anchor; **jeter/lever l'~** to
cast/weigh anchor; **ancrer** vt (Constr:
câble etc) to anchor; (fig) to fix firmly

Andorre [ãdɔr] nf Andorra

andouille [ãduj] nf (Culin) sausage made
of chitterlings; (fam) clot, nit

âne [an] nm donkey, ass; (péj) dunce

anéantir [aneãtir] vt to annihilate,
wipe out; (fig) to obliterate, destroy

anémie [anemi] nf anaemia;
anémique adj anaemic

anesthésie [anɛstezi] nf anaesthesia;
faire une ~ locale/générale à qn to
give sb a local/general anaesthetic

ange [ãʒ] nm angel; **être aux ~s** to be
over the moon

angine [ãʒin] nf throat infection;
angine de poitrine angina

anglais, e [ãglɛ, ɛz] adj English ▷ nm/f:
A~, e Englishman(-woman) ▷ nm

(Ling) English; **les A~** the English; **filer à
l'~e** to take French leave

angle [ãgl] nm angle; (coin) corner;
angle droit right angle

Angleterre [ãglətɛr] nf: **l'~** England

anglo- [ãglɔ] préfixe Anglo-, anglo(-);
anglophone adj English-speaking

angoisse [ãgwas] nf anguish, distress;
angoissé, e adj (personne) distressed

anguille [ãgij] nf eel

animal, e, -aux [animal, o] adj, nm
animal

animateur, -trice [animatœr, tris]
nm/f (de télévision) host; (de groupe)
leader, organizer

animation [animasjõ] nf (voir animé)
busyness; liveliness; (Cinéma: technique)
animation

animé, e [anime] adj (lieu) busy, lively;
(conversation, réunion) lively, animated

animer [anime] vt (ville, soirée) to liven
up; (mener) to lead

anis [ani(s)] nm (Culin) aniseed; (Bot)
anise

ankyloser [ãkiloze]: **s'ankyloser** vi
to get stiff

anneau, x [ano] nm (de rideau, bague)
ring; (de chaîne) link

année [ane] nf year

annexe [anɛks] adj (problème) related;
(document) appended; (salle) adjoining
▷ nf (bâtiment) annex(e); (jointe à une
lettre) enclosure

anniversaire [aniversɛr] nm
birthday; (d'un événement, bâtiment)
anniversary

annonce [anɔ̃s] nf announcement;
(signe, indice) sign; (aussi: ~ publicitaire)
advertisement; **les petites ~s** the small
classified advertisements, the small
ads

annoncer [anɔ̃se] vt to announce; (être
le signe de) to herald; **s'~ bien/difficile**
to look promising/difficult

annuaire [anɥɛr] nm yearbook,
annual; **annuaire téléphonique**
(telephone) directory, phone book

annuel, le [anɥɛl] adj annual, yearly

annulation [anylɑsjɔ̃] nf cancellation

annuler [anyle] vt (rendez-vous, voyage) to cancel, call off; (jugement) to quash (BRIT), repeal (US); (Math, Physique) to cancel out; **je voudrais ~ ma réservation** I'd like to cancel my reservation

anonymat [anɔnima] nm anonymity; **garder l'~** to remain anonymous

anonyme [anɔnim] adj anonymous; (fig) impersonal

anorak [anɔrak] nm anorak

anorexie [anɔrɛksi] nf anorexia

anormal, e, -aux [anɔrmal, o] adj abnormal

ANPE sigle f (= Agence nationale pour l'emploi) national employment agency

antarctique [ɑ̃taʀktik] adj Antarctic ▷ nm: **l'A~** the Antarctic

antenne [ɑ̃tɛn] nf (de radio) aerial; (d'insecte) antenna, feeler; (poste avancé) outpost; (petite succursale) sub-branch; **passer à l'~** to go on the air; **antenne parabolique** satellite dish

antérieur, e [ɑ̃teʀjœʀ] adj (d'avant) previous, earlier; (de devant) front

anti... [ɑ̃ti] préfixe anti...:

antialcoolique adj anti-alcohol;
antibiotique nm antibiotic;
antibrouillard adj: **phare antibrouillard** fog lamp (BRIT) ou light (US)

anticipation [ɑ̃tisipasjɔ̃] nf: **livre/ film d'~** science fiction book/film

anticipé, e [ɑ̃tisipe] adj: **avec mes remerciements ~s** thanking you in advance anticipation

anticiper [ɑ̃tisipe] vt (événement, coup) to anticipate, foresee

anti... : **anticorps** nm antibody;
antidote nm antidote; **antigel** nm antifreeze; **antihistaminique** nm antihistamine

antillais, e [ɑ̃tijɛ, ɛz] adj West Indian, Caribbean ▷ nm/f: **A~, e** West Indian, Caribbean

Antilles [ɑ̃tij] nfpl: **les ~** the West Indies; **les Grandes/Petites ~** the Greater/Lesser Antilles

antilope [ɑ̃tilɔp] nf antelope

anti... : **antimite(s)** adj, nm: **(produit) antimite(s)** mothproofer; moth repellent; **antimondialisation** nf anti-globalization; **antipathique** adj unpleasant, disagreeable;
antipelliculaire adj anti-dandruff

antiquaire [ɑ̃tikɛʀ] nm/f antique dealer

antique [ɑ̃tik] adj antique; (très vieux) ancient, antiquated; **antiquité** nf (objet) antique; **l'Antiquité** Antiquity; **magasin d'antiquités** antique shop

anti... : **antirabique** adj rabies cpd;
antirouille adj inv anti-rust cpd;
antisémite adj anti-Semitic;
antiseptique adj, nm antiseptic

antivirus [ɑ̃tiviʀys] nm (Inform) antivirus; **antivol** adj, nm: **(dispositif) antivol** anti-theft device

anxieux, -euse [ɑ̃ksjø, jøz] adj anxious, worried

AOC sigle f (= appellation d'origine contrôlée) label guaranteeing the quality of wine

août [u(t)] nm August

apaiser [apeze] vt (colère, douleur) to soothe; (personne) to calm (down), pacify; **s'apaiser** vi (tempête, bruit) to die down, subside; (personne) to calm down

apercevoir [apɛʀsəvwaʀ] vt to see; **s'apercevoir de** vt to notice; **s'~ que** to notice that

aperçu [apɛʀsy] nm (vue d'ensemble) general survey

apéritif [apeʀitif] nm (boisson) aperitif; (réunion) drinks pl

à-peu-près [apøpʀɛ] (péj) nm inv vague approximation

apeuré, e [apœʀe] adj frightened, scared

aphte [aft] nm mouth ulcer

apitoyer [apitwaje] vt to move to pity; **s'apitoyer (sur)** to feel pity (for)

aplatir [aplatiʀ] vt to flatten; **s'aplatir** vi to become flatter; (écrasé) to be flattened

aplomb [aplɔ̃] nm (équilibre) balance, equilibrium; (fig) self-assurance; nerve; **d'~** steady

apostrophe [apɔstrɔf] nf (signe) apostrophe

apparaître [apaʀɛtʀ] vi to appear

appareil [apaʀɛj] nm (outil, machine) piece of apparatus; device; (électrique, ménager) appliance; (avion) (aero)plane, aircraft inv; (téléphonique) phone; (dentier) brace (BRIT), braces (US); **"qui est à l'~?"** "who's speaking?"; **dans le plus simple ~** in one's birthday suit; **appareil(-photo)** camera; **appareiller** vi (Navig) to cast off, get under way ▷ vt (assortir) to match up

apparemment [apaʀamɑ̃] adv apparently

apparence [apaʀɑ̃s] nf appearance; **en ~** apparently

apparent, e [apaʀɑ̃, ɑ̃t] adj visible; (évident) obvious; (superficiel) apparent

apparenté, e [apaʀɑ̃te] adj: **~ à** related to; (fig) similar to

apparition [apaʀisjɔ̃] nf appearance; (surnaturelle) apparition

appartement [apaʀtəmɑ̃] nm flat (BRIT), apartment (US)

appartenir [apaʀtəniʀ]: **~ à** vt to belong to; **il lui appartient de** it is his duty to

apparu, e [apaʀy] pp de **apparaître**

appât [apɑ] nm (Pêche) bait; (fig) lure, bait

appel [apɛl] nm call; (nominal) roll call; (: Scol) register; (Mil: recrutement) call-up; **faire ~ à** (invoquer) to appeal to; (avoir recours à) to call on; (nécessiter) to call for, require; **faire ou interjeter ~** (Jur) to appeal; **faire l'~** to call the roll; (Scol) to call the register; **sans ~** (fig) final, irrevocable; **faire un ~ de phares** to flash one's headlights; **appel d'offres** (Comm) invitation to tender; **appel (téléphonique)** (tele)phone call

appelé [ap(ə)le] nm (Mil) conscript

appeler [ap(ə)le] vt to call; (faire venir: médecin etc) to call, send for; **s'appeler** vi: **elle s'appelle Gabrielle** her name is Gabrielle, she's called Gabrielle; **comment vous appelez-vous?** what's your name?; **comment ça s'appelle?** what is it called?; **être appelé à** (fig) to be destined to

appendicite [apɑ̃disit] nf appendicitis

appesantir [apəzɑ̃tiʀ]: **s'appesantir** vi to grow heavier; **s'~ sur** (fig) to dwell on

appétissant, e [apetisɑ̃, ɑ̃t] adj appetizing, mouth-watering

appétit [apeti] nm appetite; **bon ~!** enjoy your meal!

applaudir [aplodiʀ] vt to applaud ▷ vi to applaud, clap; **applaudissements** nmpl applause sg, clapping sg

application [aplikasjɔ̃] nf application

appliquer [aplike] vt to apply; (loi) to enforce; **s'appliquer** vi (élève etc) to apply o.s.; **s'~ à** to apply to

appoint [apwɛ̃] nm (extra) contribution ou help; **avoir/faire l'~** to have/give the right change ou money; **chauffage d'~** extra heating

apporter [apɔʀte] vt to bring

appréciable [apʀesjabl] adj appreciable

apprécier [apʀesje] vt to appreciate; (évaluer) to estimate, assess

appréhender [apʀeɑ̃de] vt (craindre) to dread; (arrêter) to apprehend

apprendre [apʀɑ̃dʀ] vt to learn; (événement, résultats) to learn of, hear of; **~ qch à qn** (informer) to tell sb sth; (enseigner) to teach sb sth; **~ à faire qch** to learn to do sth; **~ à qn à faire qch** to teach sb to do sth; **apprenti, e** nm/f apprentice; **apprentissage** nm learning; (Comm, Scol: période) apprenticeship

apprêter [apʀɛte] vt: **s'~ à faire qch** to get ready to do sth

appris, e [apʀi, iz] pp de **apprendre**

apprivoiser [apʀivwaze] vt to tame

approbation [apʀɔbasjɔ̃] nf approval

approcher [apʀɔʃe] vi to approach, come near ▷ vt to approach; *(rapprocher):* ~ **qch (de qch)** to bring or put sth near (to sth); **s'approcher de** to approach, go up, come near to; ~ **de** *(lieu, but)* to draw near to; *(quantité, moment)* to approach

approfondir [apʀɔfɔ̃diʀ] vt to deepen; *(question)* to go further into

approprié, e [apʀɔpʀije] adj: ~ **(à)** appropriate (to), suited to

approprier [apʀɔpʀije]: **s'approprier** vt to appropriate, take over; **s'~ en** to stock up with

approuver [apʀuve] vt to agree with; *(trouver louable)* to approve of

approvisionner [apʀɔvizjɔne] vt to supply; *(compte bancaire)* to pay funds into; **s'approvisionner en** to stock up with

approximatif, -ive [apʀɔksimatif, iv] adj approximate, rough; *(termes)* vague

appt abr = **appartement**

appui [apɥi] nm support; **prendre ~ sur** to lean on; *(objet)* to rest on; **l'~ de la fenêtre** the windowsill, the window ledge

appuyer [apɥije] vt *(poser):* ~ **qch sur/ contre** to lean or rest sth on/against; *(soutenir: personne, demande)* to support, back (up) ▷ vi: ~ **sur** *(bouton)* to press, push; *(mot, détail)* to stress, emphasize; ~ **sur le frein** to brake, to apply the brakes; **s'appuyer sur** to lean on; *(fig: compter sur)* to rely on

après [apʀɛ] prép after ▷ adv afterwards; **2 heures ~** 2 hours later; ~ **qu'il est** ou **soit parti** after he left; ~ **avoir fait** after having done; **d'~** *(selon)* according to; ~ **coup** after the event, afterwards; ~ **tout** *(au fond)* after all; **et (puis) ~?** so what?; **après-demain** adv the day after tomorrow; **après-midi** nm ou nf inv afternoon; **après-rasage** nm inv aftershave; **après-shampooing** nm inv conditioner; **après-ski** nm inv snow boot

après-soleil [apʀɛsɔlɛj] adj inv after-sun cpd ▷ nm after-sun cream ou lotion

apte [apt] adj capable; ~ **à qch/faire qch** capable of sth/doing sth; ~ **(au service)** *(Mil)* fit (for service)

aquarelle [akwaʀɛl] nf watercolour

aquarium [akwaʀjɔm] nm aquarium

arabe [aʀab] adj Arabic; *(désert, cheval)* Arabian; *(nation, peuple)* Arab ▷ nm/f: **A~** Arab ▷ nm *(Ling)* Arabic

Arabie [aʀabi] nf: **l'~ (Saoudite)** Saudi Arabia

arachide [aʀaʃid] nf *(plante)* groundnut (plant); *(graine)* peanut, groundnut

araignée [aʀeɲe] nf spider

arbitraire [aʀbitʀɛʀ] adj arbitrary

arbitre [aʀbitʀ] nm *(Sport)* referee; *(: Tennis, Cricket)* umpire; *(fig)* arbiter, judge; *(Jur)* arbitrator; **arbitrer** vt to referee; to umpire; to arbitrate

arbre [aʀbʀ] nm tree; *(Tech)* shaft

arbuste [aʀbyst] nm small shrub

arc [aʀk] nm *(arme)* bow; *(Géom)* arc; *(Archit)* arch; **en ~ de cercle** semi-circular

arcade [aʀkad] nf arch(way); **arcades** nfpl *(série)* arcade sg, arches

arc-en-ciel [aʀkɑ̃sjɛl] nm rainbow

arche [aʀʃ] nf arch; **arche de Noé** Noah's Ark

archéologie [aʀkeɔlɔʒi] nf arch(a)eology; **archéologue** nm/f arch(a)eologist

archet [aʀʃɛ] nm bow

archipel [aʀʃipɛl] nm archipelago

architecte [aʀʃitɛkt] nm architect

architecture [aʀʃitɛktyʀ] nf architecture

archives [aʀʃiv] nfpl *(collection)* archives

arctique [aʀktik] adj Arctic ▷ nm: **l'A~** the Arctic

ardent, e [aʀdɑ̃, ɑ̃t] adj *(soleil)* blazing; *(amour)* ardent, passionate; *(prière)* fervent

ardoise [aʀdwaz] nf slate

ardu, e [aʀdy] adj *(travail)* arduous; *(problème)* difficult

arène [aʀɛn] nf arena; **arènes** nfpl (amphithéâtre) bull-ring sg

arête [aʀɛt] nf (de poisson) bone; (d'une montagne) ridge

argent [aʀʒɑ̃] nm (métal) silver; (monnaie) money; **argent de poche** pocket money; **argent liquide** ready money, (ready) cash; **argenterie** nf silverware

argentin, e [aʀʒɑ̃tɛ̃, in] adj Argentinian ▷ nm/f: **A-, e** Argentinian

Argentine [aʀʒɑ̃tin] nf: **l'~** Argentina

argentique [aʀʒɑ̃tik] adj (appareil-photo) film cpd

argile [aʀʒil] nf clay

argot [aʀgo] nm slang; **argotique** adj slang cpd; (très familier) slangy

argument [aʀgymɑ̃] nm argument

argumenter [aʀgymɑ̃te] vi to argue

aride [aʀid] adj arid

aristocratie [aʀistɔkʀasi] nf aristocracy; **aristocratique** adj aristocratic

arithmétique [aʀitmetik] adj arithmetic(al) ▷ nf arithmetic

arme [aʀm] nf weapon; **armes** nfpl (armement) weapons, arms; (blason) (coat of) arms; **~s de destruction massive** weapons of mass destruction; **arme à feu** firearm

armée [aʀme] nf army; **armée de l'air** Air Force; **armée de terre** Army

armer [aʀme] vt to arm; (arme à feu) to cock; (appareil-photo) to wind on; **~ qch de** to reinforce sth with; **s'armer de** to arm o.s. with

armistice [aʀmistis] nm armistice; **l'A-** = Remembrance (BRIT) ou Veterans (US) Day

armoire [aʀmwaʀ] nf (tall) cupboard; (penderie) wardrobe (BRIT), closet (US)

armure [aʀmyʀ] nf armour no pl, suit of armour; **armurier** nm gunsmith

arnaque [aʀnak] (fam) nf swindling; **c'est de l'~** it's a rip-off; **arnaquer** (fam) vt to swindle

arobase [aʀobaz] nf (symbole) at symbol; **"paul – société point fr"** "paul

at société dot fr"

aromates [aʀɔmat] nmpl seasoning sg, herbs (and spices)

aromathérapie [aʀɔmateʀapi] nf aromatherapy

aromatisé, e [aʀɔmatize] adj flavoured

arôme [aʀom] nm aroma

arracher [aʀaʃe] vt to pull out; (page etc) to tear off, tear out; (légumes, herbe) to pull up; (bras etc) to tear off; **s'arracher** vt (article recherché) to fight over; **~ qch à qn** to snatch sth from sb; (fig) to wring sth out of sb

arrangement [aʀɑ̃ʒmɑ̃] nm agreement, arrangement

arranger [aʀɑ̃ʒe] vt (gén) to arrange; (réparer) to fix, put right; (régler) to settle, sort out; (convenir à) to suit, be convenient for; **cela m'arrange** that suits me (fine); **s'arranger** vi (se mettre d'accord) to come to an agreement; **je vais m'~** I'll manage; **ça va s'~** it'll sort itself out

arrestation [aʀɛstasjɔ̃] nf arrest

arrêt [aʀɛ] nm stopping; (de bus etc) stop; (Jur) judgment, decision; **à l'~** stationary; **tomber en ~ devant** to stop short in front of; **sans ~** (sans interruption) non-stop; (très fréquemment) continually; **arrêt de travail** stoppage (of work)

arrêter [aʀete] vt to stop; (chauffage etc) to turn off, switch off; (fixer: date etc) to appoint, decide on; (criminel, suspect) to arrest; **s'arrêter** vi to stop; **~ de faire** to stop doing; **arrêtez-vous ici/au coin, s'il vous plaît** could you stop here/at the corner, please?

arrhes [aʀ] nfpl deposit sg

arrière [aʀjɛʀ] nm back; (Sport) fullback ▷ adj inv: **siège/roue ~** back ou rear seat/wheel; **à l'~** behind, at the back; **en ~** behind; (regarder) back, behind; (tomber, aller) backward(s); **arrière-goût** nm aftertaste; **arrière-grand-mère** nf great-grandmother; **arrière-grand-père** nm great-grandfather;

arrière-pays nm inv hinterland;
arrière-pensée nf ulterior motive;
mental reservation; **arrière-plan** nm
background; **à l'arrière-plan** in the
background; **arrière-saison** nf late
autumn

arrimer [aʀime] vt to secure;
(cargaison) to stow

arrivage [aʀivaʒ] nm consignment

arrivée [aʀive] nf arrival; (ligne d'arrivée)
finish

arriver [aʀive] vi to arrive; (survenir)
to happen, occur; **il arrive à Paris à
8h** he gets to ou arrives in Paris at 8; **à
quelle heure arrive le train de Lyon?**
what time does the train from Lyons
get in?; **~ à** (atteindre) to reach; **~ à
faire qch** to succeed in doing sth; **en ~ à**
(finir par) to come to; **il arrive que** it
happens that; **il lui arrive de faire** he
sometimes does

arrobase [aʀɔbaz] nf (Inform) @,
'at' sign

arrogance [aʀɔgɑ̃s] nf arrogance

arrogant, e [aʀɔgɑ̃, ɑ̃t] adj arrogant

arrondissement [aʀɔ̃dismɑ̃] nm
(Admin) ≈ district

arroser [aʀoze] vt to water; (victoire) to
celebrate (over a drink); (Culin) to baste;
arrosoir nm watering can

arsenal, -aux [aʀsənal, o] nm (Navig)
naval dockyard; (Mil) arsenal; (fig) gear,
paraphernalia

art [aʀ] nm art

artère [aʀtɛʀ] nf (Anat) artery; (rue)
main road

arthrite [aʀtʀit] nf arthritis

artichaut [aʀtiʃo] nm artichoke

article [aʀtikl] nm article; (Comm)
item, article; **à l'~ de la mort** at the
point of death

articulation [aʀtikylasjɔ̃] nf
articulation; (Anat) joint

articuler [aʀtikyle] vt to articulate

artificiel, le [aʀtifisjɛl] adj artificial

artisan [aʀtizɑ̃] nm artisan, (self-
employed) craftsman; **artisanat** nm

cottage industry cpd; **de fabrication
artisanale** home-made; **artisanat** nm
arts and crafts pl

artiste [aʀtist] nm/f artist; (de variétés)
entertainer; (musicien etc) performer;
artistique adj artistic

as¹ [a] vb voir **avoir**

as² [ɑs] nm ace

ascenseur [asɑ̃sœʀ] nm lift (BRIT),
elevator (US)

ascension [asɑ̃sjɔ̃] nf ascent;
(de montagne) climb; **l'A~** (Rel) the
Ascension

  ● ASCENSION
  ●
  ● The **fête de l'Ascension** is a public
  ● holiday in France. It always falls on
  ● a Thursday, usually in May. Many
  ● French people take the following
  ● Friday off work too and enjoy a long
  ● weekend.

asiatique [azjatik] adj Asiatic, Asian
▷ nm/f: **A~** Asian

Asie [azi] nf: **l'~** Asia

asile [azil] nm (refuge) refuge,
sanctuary; (Pol): **droit d'~** (political)
asylum

aspect [aspɛ] nm appearance, look;
(fig) aspect, side; **à l'~ de** at the sight of

asperge [aspɛʀʒ] nf asparagus no pl

asperger [aspɛʀʒe] vt to spray, sprinkle

asphalte [asfalt] nm asphalt

asphyxier [asfiksje] vt to suffocate,
asphyxiate; (fig) to stifle

aspirateur [aspiʀatœʀ] nm vacuum
cleaner; **passer l'~** to vacuum

aspirer [aspiʀe] vt (air) to inhale;
(liquide) to suck (up); (suj: appareil) to
suck up; **~ à** to aspire to

aspirine [aspiʀin] nf aspirin

assagir [asaʒiʀ]: **s'assagir** vi to
quieten down, settle down

assaisonnement [asɛzɔnmɑ̃] nm
seasoning

assaisonner [asɛzɔne] vt to season

assassin [asasɛ̃] nm murderer;

assassin; assassiner vt to murder; (esp Pol) to assassinate

assaut [aso] nm assault, attack; prendre d'~ to storm, assault; donner l'~ à to attack

assécher [asefe] vt to drain

assemblage [asãblaʒ] nm (action) assembling; (de couleurs, choses) collection

assemblée [asãble] nf (réunion) meeting; (assistance) gathering; (Pol) assembly; l'A~ nationale the National Assembly (the lower house of the French Parliament)

assembler [asãble] vt (joindre, monter) to assemble, put together; (amasser) to gather (together), collect (together); s'assembler vi to gather

asseoir [aswaʀ] vt (malade, bébé) to sit up; (personne debout) to sit down; (autorité, réputation) to establish; s'asseoir vi to sit (o.s.) down

assez [ase] adv (suffisamment) enough, sufficiently; (passablement) rather, quite, fairly; ~ de pain/livres enough ou sufficient bread/books; vous en avez ~? have you got enough?; j'en ai ~! I've had enough!

assidu, e [asidy] adj (appliqué) assiduous, painstaking; (ponctuel) regular

assied etc [asje] vb voir asseoir

assiérai etc [asjeʀe] vb voir asseoir

assiette [asjet] nf plate; (contenu) plate(ful); il n'est pas dans son ~ he's not feeling quite himself; assiette à dessert dessert plate; assiette anglaise assorted cold meats; assiette creuse (soup) dish, soup plate; assiette plate (dinner) plate

assimiler [asimile] vt to assimilate, absorb; (comparer): ~ qch/qn à to liken ou compare sth/sb to; s'assimiler vr (s'intégrer) to be assimilated, assimilate

assis, e [asi, iz] pp de asseoir ▷ adj sitting (down), seated

assistance [asistãs] nf (public) audience; (aide) assistance; enfant de

l'A~ publique child in care

assistant, e [asistã, ãt] nm/f assistant; (d'université) probationary lecturer; assistant(e) social(e) social worker

assisté, e [asiste] adj (Auto) power assisted; ~ par ordinateur computer-assisted; ~ direction ~e power steering

assister [asiste] vt (aider) to assist; ~ à (scène, événement) to witness; (conférence, séminaire) to attend, be at; (spectacle, match) to be at, see

association [asɔsjasjɔ̃] nf association

associé, e [asɔsje] nm/f associate; (Comm) partner

associer [asɔsje] vt to associate; s'associer vi to join together; s'~ à qn pour faire to join (forces) with sb to do; s'~ à (couleurs, qualités) to be combined with; (opinions, joie de qn) to share in; ~ qn à (profits) to give sb a share of; (affaire) to make sb a partner in; (joie, triomphe) to include sb in; ~ qch à (allier à) to combine sth with

assoiffé, e [aswafe] adj thirsty

assommer [asɔme] vt (étourdir, abrutir) to knock out, stun

Assomption [asɔ̃psjɔ̃] nf: l'~ the Assumption

assorti, e [asɔʀti] adj matched, matching; (varié) assorted; ~ à matching; assortiment nm assortment, selection

assortir [asɔʀtiʀ] vt to match; ~ qch à to match sth with; ~ qch de to accompany sth with

assouplir [asupliʀ] vt to make supple

(fig) to relax; **assouplissant** nm *(fabric)* softener

assumer [asyme] vt *(fonction, emploi)* to assume, take on

assurance [asyʀɑ̃s] nf *(certitude)* assurance; *(confiance en soi)* (self-)confidence; *(contrat)* insurance *(policy)*; *(secteur commercial)* insurance; **assurance au tiers** third-party insurance; **assurance maladie** health insurance; **assurance tous risques** *(Auto)* comprehensive insurance; **assurances sociales** ≈ National Insurance *(BRIT)*, ≈ Social Security *(US)*; **assurance-vie** nf life assurance ou insurance

assuré, e [asyʀe] adj *(certain: réussite, échec)* certain, sure; *(air)* assured; *(pas)* steady ▷ nm/f insured *(person)*; **assurément** adv assuredly, most certainly

assurer [asyʀe] vt *(Finance)* to insure; *(victoire etc)* to ensure; *(frontières, pouvoir)* to make secure; *(service)* to provide, operate; **s'assurer (contre)** *(Comm)* to insure o.s. (against); **s'~ de/ que** *(vérifier)* to make sure of/that; **s'~ (de)** *(aide de qn)* to secure; **~ à qn que** to assure sb that; **~ qn de** to assure sb of

asthmatique [asmatik] adj, nm/f asthmatic

asthme [asm] nm asthma

asticot [astiko] nm maggot

astre [astʀ] nm star

astrologie [astʀɔlɔʒi] nf astrology

astronaute [astʀonot] nm/f astronaut

astronomie [astʀɔnɔmi] nf astronomy

astuce [astys] nf shrewdness, astuteness; *(truc)* trick, clever way; **astucieux, -euse** adj clever

atelier [atəlje] nm workshop; *(de peintre)* studio

athée [ate] adj atheistic ▷ nm/f atheist

Athènes [atɛn] n Athens

athlète [atlɛt] nm/f *(Sport)* athlete; **athlétisme** nm athletics sg

atlantique [atlɑ̃tik] adj Atlantic ▷ nm: **l'(océan) A~** the Atlantic (Ocean)

atlas [atlas] nm atlas

atmosphère [atmɔsfɛʀ] nf atmosphere

atome [atom] nm atom; **atomique** adj atomic, nuclear

atomiseur [atɔmizœʀ] nm atomizer

atout [atu] nm trump; *(fig)* asset

atroce [atʀɔs] adj atrocious

attachant, e [ataʃɑ̃, ɑ̃t] adj engaging, lovable, likeable

attache [ataʃ] nf clip, fastener; *(fig)* tie

attacher [ataʃe] vt to tie up; *(étiquette)* to attach, tie on; *(ceinture)* to fasten ▷ vi *(poêle, riz)* to stick; **s'attacher à** *(par affection)* to become attached to; **~ qch à** to tie ou attach sth to

attaque [atak] nf attack; *(cérébrale)* stroke; *(d'épilepsie)* fit

attaquer [atake] vt to attack ▷ vi to attack; **s'attaquer à** vt to attack; *(problème)* to tackle; **~ qn en justice** to bring an action against sb, sue sb

attarder [ataʀde]: **s'attarder** vi to linger

atteindre [atɛ̃dʀ] vt to reach; *(blesser)* to hit; *(émouvoir)* to affect; **atteint, e** adj *(Méd)*: **être atteint de** to be suffering from; **atteinte** nf: **hors d'atteinte** out of reach; **porter atteinte à** to strike a blow at

attendant [atɑ̃dɑ̃] adv: **en ~** meanwhile, in the meantime

attendre [atɑ̃dʀ] vt *(gén)* to wait for; *(être destiné ou réservé à)* to await, be in store for ▷ vi to wait; **s'attendre à (ce que)** to expect (that); **attendez-moi, s'il vous plaît** wait for me, please; **~ un enfant** to be expecting a baby; **~ de faire/d'être** to wait until one does/is; **attendez qu'il vienne** wait until he comes; **~ qch de** to expect sth of

⚠ Attention à ne pas traduire **attendre** par to attend.

attendrir [atɑ̃dʀiʀ] vt to move (to pity); *(viande)* to tenderize

attendu, e [atɑ̃dy] *adj* (*visiteur*) expected; (*événement*) long-awaited; **~ que** considering that, since

attentat [atɑ̃ta] *nm* assassination attempt; **attentat à la pudeur** indecent assault *no pl*; **attentat suicide** suicide bombing

attente [atɑ̃t] *nf* wait; (*espérance*) expectation

attenter [atɑ̃te] : **~ à** *vt* (*liberté*) to violate; **~ à la vie de qn** to make an attempt on sb's life

attentif, -ive [atɑ̃tif, iv] *adj* (*auditeur*) attentive; (*examen*) careful; **~ à** careful to

attention [atɑ̃sjɔ̃] *nf* attention; (*prévenance*) thoughtfulness *no pl*; **à l'~ de** for the attention of; **faire ~ (à)** to be careful (of); **faire ~ (à ce) que** to be ou make sure that; **~!** carefull, watch out!; **~ à la voiture!** watch out for that car!; **attentionné, e** *adj* thoughtful, considerate

atténuer [atenɥe] *vt* (*douleur*) to alleviate, ease; (*couleurs*) to soften; **s'atténuer** *vi* to ease; (*violence etc*) to abate

atterrir [aterir] *vi* to land; **atterrissage** *nm* landing

attestation [atɛstasjɔ̃] *nf* certificate

attirant, e [atirɑ̃, ɑ̃t] *adj* attractive, appealing

attirer [atire] *vt* to attract; (*appâter*) to lure, entice; **~ qn dans un coin/vers soi** to draw sb into a corner/towards one; **~ l'attention de qn** to attract sb's attention; **~ l'attention de qn sur** to draw sb's attention to; **s'~ des ennuis** to bring trouble upon o.s., get into trouble

attitude [atityd] *nf* attitude; (*position du corps*) bearing

attraction [atraksjɔ̃] *nf* (*gén*) attraction; (*de cabaret, cirque*) number

attrait [atrɛ] *nm* appeal, attraction

attraper [atrape] *vt* (*gén*) to catch; (*habitude, amende*) to get, pick up; (*fam: duper*) to con; **se faire ~** (*fam*) to

be told off

attrayant, e [atrejɑ̃, ɑ̃t] *adj* attractive

attribuer [atribɥe] *vt* (*prix*) to award; (*rôle, tâche*) to allocate, assign; (*imputer*): **~ qch à** to attribute sth to; **s'attribuer** *vt* (*s'approprier*) to claim for o.s.

attrister [atriste] *vt* to sadden

attroupement [atrupmɑ̃] *nm* crowd

attrouper [atrupe]: **s'attrouper** *vi* to gather

au [o] *prép* +*dét* = **à** +**le**

aubaine [obɛn] *nf* godsend

aube [ob] *nf* dawn, daybreak; **à l'~** at dawn ou daybreak

aubépine [obepin] *nf* hawthorn

auberge [obɛrʒ] *nf* inn; **auberge de jeunesse** youth hostel

aubergine [obɛrʒin] *nf* aubergine

aucun, e [okœ̃ yn] *dét* no, *tournure négative* +any; (*positif*) any ▷ *pron* none, *tournure négative* +any; any(one); **sans ~ doute** without any doubt; **plus qu'~ autre** more than any other; **il le fera mieux qu'~ de nous** he'll do it better than any of us; **~ des deux** neither of the two; **~ d'entre eux** none of them

audace [odas] *nf* daring, boldness; (*péj*) audacity; **audacieux, -euse** *adj* daring, bold

au-delà [od(a)la] *adv* beyond ▷ *nm*: **l'~** the hereafter; **~ de** beyond

au-dessous [odsu] *adv* underneath; below; **~ de** under(neath); below; (*limite, somme etc*) below, under; (*dignité, condition*) below

au-dessus [odsy] *adv* above; **~ de** above

au-devant [od(a)vɑ̃]: **~ de** *prép*: **aller ~ de** (*personne, danger*) to go (out) and meet; (*souhaits de qn*) to anticipate

audience [odjɑ̃s] *nf* audience; (*Jur: séance*) hearing

audiovisuel, le [odjovizɥɛl] *adj* audiovisual

audition [odisjɔ̃] *nf* (*ouïe, écoute*)

hearing; (Jur: de témoins) examination; (Mus, Théâtre: épreuve) audition

auditoire [oditwar] nm audience

augmentation [ɔgmɑ̃tasjɔ̃] nf increase; **augmentation (de salaire)** rise (in salary) (BRIT), (pay) raise (US)

augmenter [ɔgmɑ̃te] vt (gén) to increase; (salaire, prix) to increase, raise, put up; (employé) to increase the salary of ▷ vi to increase

augure [ogyr] nm: **de bon/mauvais ~** of good/ill omen

aujourd'hui [oʒurdɥi] adv today

aumône [omon] nf inv alms sg;

aumônier nm chaplain

auparavant [oparavɑ̃] adv before(hand)

auprès [oprɛ]: **~ de** prép next to, close to; (recourir, s'adresser) to; (en comparaison de) compared with

auquel [okɛl] prép +pron = **à +lequel**

aurai etc [ɔre] vb voir **avoir**

aurons etc [ɔrɔ̃] vb voir **avoir**

aurore [`ɔr] nf dawn, daybreak

ausculter [oskylte] vt to sound (the chest of)

aussi [osi] adv (également) also, too; (de comparaison) as ▷ conj therefore, consequently; **~ fort que** as strong as; **moi ~** me too

aussitôt [osito] adv straight away, immediately; **~ que** as soon as

austère [ostɛr] adj austere

austral, e [ostral] adj southern

Australie [ostrali] nf: **l'~** Australia; **australien, ne** adj Australian ▷ nm/f: **Australien, ne** Australian

autant [otɑ̃] adv (intensité) so much; **je ne savais pas que tu la détestais ~** I didn't know you hated her so much; (comparatif): **~ (que)** as much (as); (nombre) as many (as); **~ (de)** so much (ou many); as much (ou many); **~ partir** (ou you etc) may as well leave; **~ dire que ...** one might as well say that ...; **pour ~** for all that; **d'~ plus/mieux (que)** all the more/the

better (since)

autel [otɛl] nm altar

auteur [otœr] nm author

authentique [otɑ̃tik] adj authentic, genuine

auto [oto] nf car

auto...: **autobiographie** nf autobiography; **autobronzant** nm self-tanning cream (or lotion etc);
autobus nm bus; **autocar** nm coach

autochtone [otɔktɔn] nm/f native

auto...: **autocollant, e** adj self-adhesive; (enveloppe) self-seal ▷ nm sticker; **autocuiseur** nm pressure cooker; **autodéfense** nf self-defence; **autodidacte** nm/f self-taught person; **auto-école** nf driving school; **autographe** nm autograph

automate [otɔmat] nm (machine) (automatic) machine

automatique [otɔmatik] adj automatic ▷ nm: **l'~** direct dialling

automne [otɔn] nm autumn (BRIT), fall (US)

automobile [otɔmɔbil] adj motor cpd, car cpd ▷ nf (motor) car; **automobiliste** nm/f motorist

autonome [otɔnɔm] adj autonomous; **autonomie** nf autonomy; (Pol) self-government, autonomy

autopsie [otɔpsi] nf post-mortem (examination), autopsy

autoradio [otoradjo] nm car radio

autorisation [otɔrizasjɔ̃] nf permission, authorization; (papiers) permit

autorisé, e [otɔrize] adj (opinion, sources) authoritative

autoriser [otɔrize] vt to give permission for, authorize; (fig) to allow (for)

autoritaire [otɔritɛr] adj authoritarian

autorité [otɔrite] nf authority; **faire ~** to be authoritative; **les ~s** the authorities

autoroute [otorut] nf motorway (BRIT), highway (US); **~ de**

l'information (*Inform*) information superhighway

AUTOROUTE

Motorways in France, indicated by blue road signs with the letter **A** followed by a number, are toll roads. The speed limit is 130 km/h (110 km/h when it is raining). At the tollgate, the lanes marked 'réservé' and with an orange 't' are reserved for people who subscribe to 'télépéage', an electronic payment system.

auto-stop [otostɔp] *nm*: **faire de l'~** to hitch-hike; **prendre qn en ~** to give sb a lift; **auto-stoppeur, -euse** *nm/f* hitch-hiker

autour [otuʀ] *adv* around; **~ de** around; **tout ~** all around

 MOT-CLÉ

autre [otʀ] *adj* **1** (*différent*) other, different; **je préférerais un autre verre** I'd prefer another *ou* a different glass
2 (*supplémentaire*) other; **je voudrais un autre verre d'eau** I'd like another glass of water
3: **autre chose** something else; **autre part** somewhere else; **d'autre part** on the other hand
▷ *pron*: **un autre** another (one); **nous/vous autres** us/you; **d'autres** others; **l'autre** the other (one); **les autres** the others; (*autrui*) others; **l'un et l'autre** both of them; **se détester l'un l'autre/les uns les autres** to hate each other *ou* one another; **d'une semaine à l'autre** from one week to the next; (*incessamment*) any week now; **entre autres** (*personnes*) among others; (*choses*) among other things

autrefois [otʀəfwa] *adv* in the past
autrement [otʀəmɑ̃] *adv* differently;

(*d'une manière différente*) in another way; (*sinon*) otherwise; **~ dit** in other words
Autriche [otʀiʃ] *nf*: **l'~** Austria; **autrichien, ne** *adj* Austrian ▷ *nm/f*: **Autrichien, ne** Austrian
autruche [otʀyʃ] *nf* ostrich
aux [o] *prép +dét* = **à +les**
auxiliaire [ɔksiljɛʀ] *adj, nm/f* auxiliary
auxquelles [okɛl] *prép +pron* = **à +lesquelles**
auxquels [okɛl] *prép +pron* = **à +lesquels**
avalanche [avalɑ̃ʃ] *nf* avalanche
avaler [avale] *vt* to swallow
avance [avɑ̃s] *nf* (*de troupes etc*) advance; progress; (*d'argent*) advance; (*sur un concurrent*) lead; **avances** *nfpl* (*amoureuses*) advances; (**être**) **en ~** (to be) early; (*sur un programme*) (to be) ahead of schedule; **à l'~, d'~** in advance
avancé, e [avɑ̃se] *adj* advanced; (*travail*) well on, well under way
avancement [avɑ̃smɑ̃] *nm* (*professionnel*) promotion
avancer [avɑ̃se] *vi* to move forward, advance; (*projet, travail*) to make progress; (*montre, réveil*) to be fast; ▷ *vt* to move forward, advance; (*argent*) to advance; (*montre, pendule*) to put forward; **s'avancer** *vi* to move forward, advance; (*fig*) to commit o.s.
avant [avɑ̃] *prép, adv* before ▷ *adj inv*: **siège/roue** ~ front seat/wheel ▷ *nm* (*d'un véhicule, bâtiment*) front; (*Sport: joueur*) forward; ~ **qu'il (ne) parte** before he goes *ou* leaves; ~ **de partir** before leaving; ~ **tout** (*surtout*) above all; **à l'~** (*dans un véhicule*) in (the) front; ~ (*se pencher, tomber*) forward(s); **partir en** ~ to go on ahead; **en** ~ **de** in front of
avantage [avɑ̃taʒ] *nm* advantage; **avantages sociaux** fringe benefits; **avantager** *vt* (*favoriser*) to favour; (*embellir*) to flatter; **avantageux, -euse** *adj* (*prix*) attractive
avant...: **avant-bras** *nm inv* forearm; **avant-coureur** *adj inv*: **signe avant-**

coureur advance indication ou sign; **avant-dernier, -ière** adj, nm/f next to last, last but one; **avant-goût** nm foretaste; **avant-hier** adv the day before yesterday; **avant-première** nf (de film) preview; **avant-veille** nf: **l'avant-veille** two days before

avare [avaʀ] adj miserly, avaricious ▷ nm/f miser; **~ de** (compliments etc) sparing of

avec [avɛk] prép with; (à l'égard de) to(wards); with; **et ~ ça?** (dans magasin) anything else?

avenir [avniʀ] nm future; **à l'~** in future; **politicien/métier d'~** politician/job with prospects ou a future

aventure [avɑ̃tyʀ] nf adventure; (amoureuse) affair; **aventureux, -euse** adj adventurous, venturesome; (projet) risky, chancy

avenue [avny] nf avenue

avérer [aveʀe]: **s'avérer** vb +attrib to prove (to be)

averse [avɛʀs] nf shower

averti, e [avɛʀti] adj (well-)informed

avertir [avɛʀtiʀ] vt: **~ qn (de qch/que)** to warn sb (of sth/that); (renseigner) to inform sb (of sth/that); **avertissement** nm warning; **avertisseur** nm horn, siren

aveu, x [avø] nm confession

aveugle [avœgl] adj blind ▷ nm/f blind man/woman

aviation [avjasjɔ̃] nf aviation; (sport) flying; (Mil) air force

avide [avid] adj eager; (péj) greedy, grasping

avion [avjɔ̃] nm (aero)plane (BRIT), (air)plane (US); **aller (quelque part) en ~** to go (somewhere) by plane, fly (somewhere); **par ~** by airmail; **avion à réaction** jet (plane)

aviron [aviʀɔ̃] nm oar; (sport): **l'~** rowing

avis [avi] nm opinion; (notification) notice; **à mon ~** in my opinion; **changer d'~** to change one's mind;

jusqu'à nouvel ~ until further notice

aviser [avize] vt (informer): **~ qn de/que** to advise ou inform sb of/that ▷ vi to think about things, assess the situation; **nous ~ons sur place** we'll work something out once we're there; **s'~ de qch/que** to become suddenly aware of sth/that; **s'~ de faire** to take it into one's head to do

avocat, e [avɔka, at] nm/f (Jur) barrister (BRIT), lawyer ▷ nm (Culin) avocado (pear); **~ de la défense** counsel for the defence; **avocat général** assistant public prosecutor

avoine [avwan] nf oats pl

MOT-CLÉ

avoir [avwaʀ] nm assets pl, resources pl; (Comm) credit
▷ vt 1 (posséder) to have; **elle a 2 enfants/une belle maison** she has (got) 2 children/a lovely house; **il a les yeux bleus** he has (got) blue eyes; **vous avez du sel?** do you have any salt?; **avoir du courage/de la patience** to be brave/patient

2 (âge, dimensions) to be; **il a 3 ans** he is 3 (years old); **le mur a 3 mètres de haut** the wall is 3 metres high; voir aussi **faim; peur** etc

3 (fam: duper) to do, have; **on vous a eu!** (dupé) you've been done ou had!; (fait une plaisanterie) we ou they had you there

4: **en avoir après** ou **contre qn** to have a grudge against sb; **en avoir assez** to be fed up; **j'en ai pour une demi-heure** it'll take me half an hour

5 (obtenir, attraper) to get; **j'ai réussi à avoir mon train** I managed to get ou catch my train; **j'ai réussi à avoir le renseignement qu'il me fallait** I managed to get (hold of) the information I needed

6 (éprouver): **avoir de la peine** to be ou feel sad
▷ vb aux 1 to have; **avoir mangé/dormi**

to have eaten/slept

2 (*avoir +à +infinitif*): **avoir à faire qch**
to have to do sth; **vous n'avez qu'à lui
demander** you only have to ask him
▷ *vb impers* **1: il y a** (+ *singulier*) there is; (+
pluriel) there are; **il y avait du café/des
gâteaux** there was coffee/there were
cakes; **qu'y-a-t-il?, qu'est-ce qu'il y a?**
what's the matter?, what is it?; **il doit
y avoir une explication** there must be
an explanation; **il n'y a qu'à ...** we (*ou*
you *etc*) will just have to ...; **il ne peut y
en avoir qu'un** there can only be one
2 (*temporel*): **il y a 10 ans** 10 years ago;
il y a 10 ans/longtemps que je le sais
I've known it for 10 years/a long time; **il
y a 10 ans qu'il est arrivé** it's 10 years
since he arrived

avortement [avɔʀtəmɑ̃] *nm* abortion
avouer [avwe] *vt* (*crime, défaut*) to
confess (to); **~ avoir fait/que** to admit
ou confess to having done/that
avril [avʀil] *nm* April
axe [aks] *nm* axis; (*de roue etc*) axle;
(*fig*) main line; **axe routier** main road,
trunk road, highway (BRIT), highway (US)
ayons *etc* [ɛjɔ̃] *vb voir* **avoir**

bâbord [babɔʀ] *nm:* **à ~** to port, on the
port side
baby-foot [babifut] *nm* table football
bac [bak] *abr m* = **baccalauréat** ▷ *nm*
(*récipient*) tub
baccalauréat [bakalɔʀea] *nm* high
school diploma
bâcler [bakle] *vt* to botch (up)
baffe [baf] (*fam*) *nf* slap, clout
bafouiller [bafuje] *vi, vt* to stammer
bagage [bagaʒ] *nm* piece of luggage;
(*connaissances*) background,
knowledge; **nos ~s ne sont pas arrivés**
our luggage hasn't arrived; **bagage à
main** piece of hand-luggage
bagarre [bagaʀ] *nf* fight, brawl;
bagarrer: se bagarrer *vi* to have a
fight *ou* scuffle, fight
bagnole [baɲɔl] (*fam*) *nf* car
bague [bag] *nf* ring; **bague de
fiançailles** engagement ring
baguette [bagɛt] *nf* stick; (*cuisine
chinoise*) chopstick; (*de chef d'orchestre*)
baton; (*pain*) stick of (French) bread;

baguette magique magic wand
baie [bɛ] nf (Géo) bay; (fruit) berry; **baie (vitrée)** picture window
baignade [bɛɲad] nf bathing; "**~ interdite**" "no bathing"
baigner [bɛɲe] vt (bébé) to bath; **se baigner** vi to have a swim, go swimming ou bathing; **baignoire** nf bath(tub)
bail [baj, bo] (pl baux) nm lease
bâiller [baje] vi to yawn; (être ouvert) to gape
bain [bɛ̃] nm bath; **prendre un ~** to have a bath; **se mettre dans le ~** (fig) to get into it ou things; **bain de bouche** mouthwash; **bain moussant** bubble bath; **bain de soleil: prendre un bain de soleil** to sunbathe; **bain-marie** nm: **faire chauffer au bain-marie** (boîte etc) to immerse in boiling water
baiser [beze] nm kiss ▷ vt (main, front) to kiss; (fam!) to screw (!)
baisse [bɛs] nf fall, drop; **être en ~** to be falling, be declining
baisser [bese] vt to lower; (radio, chauffage) to turn down ▷ vi to fall, drop, go down; (vue, santé) to fail, dwindle; **se baisser** vi to bend down
bal [bal] nm dance; (grande soirée) ball; **bal costumé** fancy-dress ball
balade [balad] (fam) nf (à pied) walk, stroll; (en voiture) drive; **balader** (fam): **se balader** vi to go for a walk ou stroll; to go for a drive; **baladeur** nm personal stereo, Walkman®
balai [balɛ] nm broom, brush
balance [balɑ̃s] nf scales pl; (signe): **la B~** Libra; **balance commerciale** balance of trade
balancer [balɑ̃se] vt to swing; (fam: lancer) to fling, chuck; (: jeter) to chuck out; **se balancer** vi to swing, rock; **se ~ de** (fam) not to care about; **balançoire** nf swing; (sur pivot) seesaw
balayer [baleje] vt (feuilles etc) to sweep up, brush up; (pièce) to sweep; (objections) to sweep aside; (suj: radar) to scan; **balayeur, -euse** nm/f

roadsweeper
balbutier [balbysje] vi, vt to stammer
balcon [balkɔ̃] nm balcony; (Théâtre) dress circle; **avez-vous une chambre avec ~?** do you have a room with a balcony?
Bâle [bal] n Basle, Basel
Baléares [balɛaʀ] nfpl: **les ~** the Balearic Islands, the Balearics
baleine [balɛn] nf whale
balise [baliz] nf (Navig) beacon; (marker) buoy; (Aviat) runway light, beacon; (Auto, Ski) sign, marker; **baliser** vt to mark out (with lights etc)
balle [bal] nf (de fusil) bullet; (de sport) ball; (fam) franc
ballerine [bal(ə)ʀin] nf (danseuse) ballet dancer; (chaussure) ballet shoe
ballet [balɛ] nm ballet
ballon [balɔ̃] nm (de sport) ball; (jouet, Aviat) balloon; **ballon de football** football
balnéaire [balneɛʀ] adj seaside cpd; **station ~** seaside resort
balustrade [balystʀad] nf railings pl, handrail
bambin [bɑ̃bɛ̃] nm little child
bambou [bɑ̃bu] nm bamboo
banal, e [banal] adj banal, commonplace; (péj) trite; **banalité** nf banality
banane [banan] nf banana; (sac) waist-bag, bum-bag
banc [bɑ̃] nm seat, bench; (de poissons) shoal; **banc d'essai** (fig) testing ground
bancaire [bɑ̃kɛʀ] adj banking; (chèque, carte) bank cpd
bancal, e [bɑ̃kal] adj wobbly
bandage [bɑ̃daʒ] nm bandage
bande [bɑ̃d] nf (de tissu etc) strip; (Méd) bandage; (motif) stripe; (magnétique etc) tape; (groupe) band; (péj) bunch; **faire ~ à part** to keep to o.s.; **bande dessinée** comic strip; **bande sonore** sound track
bande-annonce [bɑ̃danɔ̃s] nf trailer
bandeau, x [bɑ̃do] nm headband; (sur les yeux) blindfold
bander [bɑ̃de] vt (blessure) to bandage;

~ **les yeux à qn** to blindfold sb
bandit [bɑ̃di] nm bandit
bandoulière [bɑ̃duljɛʁ] nf: **en ~** (slung ou worn) across the shoulder
Bangladesh [bɑ̃ɡladɛʃ] nm: **le ~** Bangladesh
banlieue [bɑ̃ljø] nf suburbs pl; **lignes/quartiers de ~** suburban lines/areas; **trains de ~** commuter trains
bannir [baniʁ] vt to banish
banque [bɑ̃k] nf bank; (activités) banking; **banque de données** data bank
banquet [bɑ̃kɛ] nm dinner; (d'apparat) banquet
banquette [bɑ̃kɛt] nf seat
banquier [bɑ̃kje] nm banker
banquise [bɑ̃kiz] nf ice field
baptême [batɛm] nm christening; baptism; **baptême de l'air** first flight
baptiser [batize] vt to baptize, christen
bar [baʁ] nm bar
baraque [baʁak] nf shed; (fam) house; (dans une fête foraine) stall, booth; **baraqué, e** (fam) adj well-built, hefty
barbare [baʁbaʁ] adj barbaric
barbe [baʁb] nf beard; **la ~!** (fam) damn it!; **quelle ~!** (fam) what a drag ou bore!; **à la ~ de qn** under sb's nose; **barbe à papa** candy-floss (BRIT), cotton candy (US)
barbelé [baʁbəle] adj, nm: **(fil de fer) ~** barbed wire no pl
barbiturique [baʁbityʁik] nm barbiturate
barbouiller [baʁbuje] vt to daub; **avoir l'estomac barbouillé** to feel queasy
barbu, e [baʁby] adj bearded
barder [baʁde] (fam) vi: **ça va ~** sparks will fly, things are going to get hot
barème [baʁɛm] nm (Scol) scale; (table de référence) table
baril [baʁi(l)] nm barrel; (poudre) keg
bariolé, e [baʁjɔle] adj gaudily-coloured
baromètre [baʁɔmɛtʁ] nm barometer

baron, ne [baʁɔ̃] nm/f baron(ess)
baroque [baʁɔk] adj (Art) baroque; (fig) weird
barque [baʁk] nf small boat
barquette [baʁkɛt] nf (pour repas) tray; (pour fruits) punnet
barrage [baʁaʒ] nm dam; (sur route) roadblock, barricade
barre [baʁ] nf (Navig) helm; (écrite) line, stroke
barreau, x [baʁo] nm bar; (Jur): **le ~** the Bar
barrer [baʁe] vt (route etc) to block; (mot) to cross out; (chèque) to cross (BRIT); (Navig) to steer; **se barrer** (fam) ▷ vi to clear off
barrette [baʁɛt] nf (pour cheveux) (hair) slide (BRIT) ou clip (US)
barricader [baʁikade]: **se barricader** vi to barricade o.s.
barrière [baʁjɛʁ] nf fence; (obstacle) barrier; (porte) gate
barrique [baʁik] nf barrel, cask
bar-tabac [baʁtaba] nm bar (which sells tobacco and stamps)
bas, basse [bɑ, bɑs] adj low ▷ nm bottom, lower part; (vêtement) stocking ▷ adv low; (parler) softly; **au ~ mot** at the lowest estimate; **en ~** down below; (d'une liste, d'un mur etc) at/to the bottom; (dans une maison) downstairs; **en ~ de** at the bottom of; **un enfant en ~ âge** a young child; **à ~ ...!** down with ...!
bas-côté [bakote] nm (de route) verge (BRIT), shoulder (US)
basculer [baskyle] vi to fall over, topple (over); (benne) to tip up ▷ vt (contenu) to tip out; (benne) to tip up
base [baz] nf base; (Pol) rank and file; (fondement, principe) basis; **de ~** basic; **à ~ de café** coffee etc -based; **base de données** database; **baser** vt to base; **se baser sur** (preuves) to base one's argument on
bas-fond [bafɔ̃] nm (Navig) shallow; **bas-fonds** nmpl (fig) dregs
basilic [bazilik] nm (Culin) basil

basket [basket] *nm* trainer (BRIT), sneaker (US); (aussi: **~-ball**) basketball

basque [bask] *adj* Basque ▷ *nm/f* B-Basque; **le Pays Basque** the Basque Country

basse [bɑs] *adj voir* **bas** ▷ *nf* (*Mus*) bass; **basse-cour** *nf* farmyard

bassin [basɛ̃] *nm* (*pièce d'eau*) pond, pool; (*de fontaine*,: *Géo*) basin; (*Anat*) pelvis; (*portuaire*) dock

bassine [basin] *nf* (*ustensile*) basin; (*contenu*) bowl(ful)

basson [bɑsɔ̃] *nm* bassoon

bat [ba] *vb voir* **battre**

bataille [bataj] *nf* (*Mil*) battle; (*rixe*) fight; **elle avait les cheveux en ~** her hair was a mess

bateau, x [bato] *nm* boat, ship; **bateau-mouche** *nm* passenger pleasure boat (*on the Seine*)

bâti, e [bati] *adj*: **bien ~** well-built; **terrain ~** piece of land that has been built on

bâtiment [batimɑ̃] *nm* building; (*Navig*) ship, vessel; (*industrie*) building trade

bâtir [batir] *vt* to build

bâtisse [batis] *nf* building

bâton [batɔ̃] *nm* stick; **parler à ~s rompus** to chat about this and that

bats [ba] *vb voir* **battre**

battement [batmɑ̃] *nm* (*de cœur*) beat; (*intervalle*) interval; **10 minutes de ~** 10 minutes to spare

batterie [batri] *nf* (*Mil, Élec*) battery; (*Mus*) drums *pl*, drum kit; **batterie de cuisine** pots and pans *pl*, kitchen utensils *pl*

batteur [batœr] *nm* (*Mus*) drummer; (*appareil*) whisk

battre [batr] *vt* to beat; (*blé*) to thresh; (*passer au peigne fin*) to scour; (*cartes*) to shuffle ▷ *vi* (*cœur*) to beat; (*volets etc*) to bang, rattle; **se battre** *vi* to fight; **~ la mesure** to beat time; **~ son plein** to be at its height, be going full swing; **~ des mains** to clap one's hands

baume [bom] *nm* balm

bavard, e [bavar, ard] *adj* (very) talkative; gossipy; **bavarder** *vi* to chatter; (*commérer*) to gossip; (*divulguer un secret*) to blab

baver [bave] *vi* to dribble; (*chien*) to slobber; **en ~** (*fam*) to have a hard time (of it)

bavoir [bavwar] *nm* bib

bavure [bavyr] *nf* smudge; (*fig*) hitch; (*policière*) blunder

bazar [bazar] *nm* general store; (*fam*) jumble; **bazarder** (*fam*) *vt* to chuck out

BCBG *sigle adj* (= *bon chic bon genre*) preppy, smart and trendy

BD *sigle f* = **bande dessinée**

bd *abr* = **boulevard**

béant, e [beɑ̃, ɑ̃t] *adj* gaping

beau, bel, belle [bo, bɛl] (*mpl* **~x**) *adj* beautiful, lovely; (*homme*) handsome; (*femme*) beautiful ▷ *adv*: **il fait ~** the weather's fine ▷ *nm*: **faire le ~** (*chien*) to sit up and beg; **un ~ jour** one (fine) day; **de plus belle** more than ever, even more; **on a ~ essayer** however hard we try; **bel et bien** well and truly; **le plus ~ c'est que ...** the best of it is that ...

⭕ **MOT-CLÉ**

beaucoup [boku] *adv* **1** a lot; **il boit beaucoup** he drinks a lot; **il ne boit pas beaucoup** he doesn't drink much ou a lot

2 (*suivi de plus, trop etc*) much, a lot; **il est beaucoup plus grand** he is much ou a lot taller; **c'est beaucoup plus cher** it's a lot ou much more expensive; **il a beaucoup plus de temps que moi** he has much ou a lot more time than me; **il y a beaucoup plus de touristes ici** there are a lot ou many more tourists here; **beaucoup trop vite** much too fast; **il fume beaucoup trop** he smokes far too much

3: **beaucoup de** (*nombre*) many, a lot of; (*quantité*) a lot of; **beaucoup d'étudiants/de touristes** a lot of ou many students/tourists; **beaucoup**

de courage a lot of courage; **il n'a pas beaucoup d'argent** he hasn't got much *ou* a lot of money
4: **de beaucoup** by far

beau...: beau-fils nm son-in-law; *(remariage)* stepson; **beau-frère** nm brother-in-law; **beau-père** nm father-in-law; *(remariage)* stepfather

beauté [bote] nf beauty; **de toute ~** beautiful; **finir qch en ~** to complete sth brilliantly

beaux-arts [bozar] nmpl fine arts

beaux-parents [boparɑ̃] nmpl wife's/husband's family, in-laws

bébé [bebe] nm baby

bec [bɛk] nm beak, bill; *(de théière)* spout; *(de casserole)* lip; *(fam)* mouth; **bec de gaz** (street) gaslamp

bêche [bɛʃ] nf spade; **bêcher** vt to dig

bedaine [bədɛn] nf paunch

bedonnant, e [bədɔnɑ̃, ɑ̃t] adj potbellied

bée [be] adj: **bouche ~** gaping

bégayer [begeje] vt, vi to stammer

beige [bɛʒ] adj beige

beignet [bɛɲɛ] nm fritter

bel [bɛl] adj voir **beau**

bêler [bele] vi to bleat

belette [bəlɛt] nf weasel

belge [bɛlʒ] adj Belgian ⊳ nm/f: **B-** Belgian

Belgique [bɛlʒik] nf: **la ~** Belgium

bélier [belje] nm ram; *(signe)*: **le B-** Aries

belle [bɛl] adj voir **beau** ⊳ nf *(Sport)*: **la ~** the decider; **belle-fille** nf daughter-in-law; *(remariage)* stepdaughter; **belle-mère** nf mother-in-law; stepmother; **belle-sœur** nf sister-in-law

belvédère [belvedɛr] nm panoramic viewpoint (or small building more)

bémol [bemɔl] nm *(Mus)* flat

bénédiction [benediksjɔ̃] nf blessing

bénéfice [benefis] nm *(Comm)* profit; *(avantage)* benefit; **bénéficier de** vt to enjoy; *(situation)* to benefit by *ou* from; **bénéfique** adj beneficial

Benelux [benelyks] nm: **le ~** Benelux, the Benelux countries

bénévole [benevɔl] adj voluntary, unpaid

bénin, -igne [benɛ̃, iɲ] adj minor, mild; *(tumeur)* benign

bénir [benir] vt to bless; **bénit, e** adj consecrated; **eau bénite** holy water

benne [bɛn] nf skip; *(de téléphérique)* (cable) car; **benne à ordures** *(amovible)* skip

béquille [bekij] nf crutch; *(de bicyclette)* stand

berceau, x [bɛrso] nm cradle, crib

bercer [bɛrse] vt to rock, cradle; *(suj: musique etc)* to lull; **~ qn de** *(promesses etc)* to delude sb with; **berceuse** nf lullaby

béret [berɛ] nm *(aussi: ~ basque)* beret

berge [bɛrʒ] nf bank

berger, -ère [bɛrʒe, ɛr] nm/f shepherd(-ess); **berger allemand** alsatian (BRIT), German shepherd

Berlin [bɛrlɛ̃] n Berlin

Bermudes [bɛrmyd] nfpl: **les (îles) ~** Bermuda

Berne [bɛrn(ə)] n Bern

berner [bɛrne] vt to fool

besogne [bəzɔɲ] nf work no pl, job

besoin [bəzwɛ̃] nm need; **avoir ~ de qch/faire qch** to need sth/to do sth; **au ~** if need be; **le ~** *(pauvreté)* need, want; **être dans le ~** to be in need *ou* want; **faire ses ~** to relieve o.s.

bestiole [bɛstjɔl] nf *(tiny)* creature

bétail [betaj] nm livestock, cattle pl

bête [bɛt] nf animal; *(bestiole)* insect, creature ⊳ adj stupid, silly; **il cherche la petite ~** he's being pernickety *ou* overfussy; **bête noire** pet hate; **bête sauvage** wild beast *ou* animal

bêtise [betiz] nf stupidity; *(action)* stupid thing (to say *ou* do)

béton [betɔ̃] nm concrete; **(en) ~** *(alibi, argument)* cast iron; **béton armé** reinforced concrete

betterave [bɛtrav] nf beetroot (BRIT), beet (US); **betterave sucrière**

sugar beet

Beur [bœʀ] nm/f person of North African origin living in France

beurre [bœʀ] nm butter; **beurrer** vt to butter; **beurrier** nm butter dish

biais [bjɛ] nm (moyen) device, expedient; (aspect) angle; **en ~**, **de ~** (obliquement) at an angle; **par le ~ de** by means of

bibelot [biblo] nm trinket, curio

biberon [bibʀɔ̃] nm (feeding) bottle; **nourrir au ~** to bottle-feed

bible [bibl] nf bible

biblio... [biblo] préfixe: **bibliobus** nm mobile library van; **bibliothécaire** nm/f librarian; **bibliothèque** nf library; (meuble) bookcase

bic® [bik] nm Biro®

bicarbonate [bikaʀbɔnat] nm: **~ (de soude)** bicarbonate of soda

biceps [bisɛps] nm biceps

biche [biʃ] nf doe

bicolore [bikɔlɔʀ] adj two-coloured

bicoque [bikɔk] (péj) nf shack

bicyclette [bisiklɛt] nf bicycle

bidet [bidɛ] nm bidet

bidon [bidɔ̃] nm can ▷ adj inv (fam) phoney

bidonville [bidɔ̃vil] nm shanty town

bidule [bidyl] (fam) nm thingumajig

MOT-CLÉ

bien [bjɛ̃] nm **1** (avantage, profit): **faire du bien à qn** to do sb good; **dire du bien de** to speak well of; **c'est pour son bien** it's for his own good
2 (possession, patrimoine) possession, property; **son bien le plus précieux** his most treasured possession; **avoir du bien** to have property; **biens de consommation** etc (consumer etc) goods
3 (moral): **le bien** good; **distinguer le bien du mal** to tell good from evil
▷ adv **1** (de façon satisfaisante) well; **elle travaille/mange bien** she works/eats well; **croyant bien faire, je/il ...** thinking I/he was doing the

right thing, I/he ...; **tiens-toi bien!** (assieds-toi correctement) sit up straight!; (debout) stand up straight!; (sois sage) behave yourself!; (prépare-toi) wait for it!; **c'est bien fait!** it serves him (ou her etc) right!
2 (valeur intensive) quite; **bien jeune** quite young; **bien assez** quite enough; **bien mieux** (very) much better; **j'espère bien y aller** I do hope to go; **je veux bien le faire** (concession) I'm quite willing to do it; **il faut bien le faire** it has to be done; **Paul est bien venu, n'est-ce pas?** Paul did come, didn't he?; **où peut-il bien être passé?** where can he have got to?
3 (beaucoup): **bien du temps/des gens** quite a time/a number of people
4 (au moins) at least; **cela fait bien deux ans que je ne l'ai pas vu** I haven't seen him for at least ou a good two years
▷ adj inv **1** (en bonne forme, à l'aise): **je me sens bien** I feel fine; **je ne me sens pas bien** I don't feel well; **on est bien dans ce fauteuil** this chair is very comfortable
2 (joli, beau) good-looking; **tu es bien dans cette robe** you look good in that dress
3 (satisfaisant) good; **elle est bien, cette maison/secrétaire** it's a good house/she's a good secretary; **c'est bien?** is that ou it O.K.?; **c'est très bien (comme ça)** that's fine (like that)
4 (moralement) right; (: personne) good, nice; (: respectable) respectable; **ce n'est pas bien de ...** it's not right to ...; **elle est bien, cette femme** she's a nice woman, she's a good sort; **des gens bien** respectable people
5 (en bons termes): **être bien avec qn** to be on good terms with sb
▷ préfixe: **bien-aimé, e** adj, nm/f beloved; **bien-être** nm well-being; **bienfaisance** nf charity; **bienfait** nm act of generosity, benefaction; (de la science etc) benefit; **bienfaiteur, -trice**

nm/f benefactor/benefactress; **bien-
fondé** *nm* soundness; **bien que** *conj*
(al)though; **bien sûr** *adv* certainly

bientôt [bjɛ̃to] *adv* soon; **à ~** see
you soon
bienveillant, e [bjɛ̃vɛjɑ̃, ɑ̃t] *adj* kindly
bienvenu, e [bjɛ̃vny] *adj* welcome;
bienvenue *nf*: **souhaiter la
bienvenue à** to welcome; **bienvenue
à** welcome to
bière [bjɛʀ] *nf* (*boisson*) beer; (*cercueil*)
bier; **bière blonde** lager; **bière brune**
brown ale (BRIT), dark beer (US); **bière
(à la) pression** draught beer
bifteck [biftɛk] *nm* steak
bigorneau, x [bigɔʀno] *nm* winkle
bigoudi [bigudi] *nm* curler
bijou, x [biʒu] *nm* jewel; **bijouterie**
nf jeweller's (shop); **bijoutier, -ière**
nm/f jeweller
bikini [bikini] *nm* bikini
bilan [bilɑ̃] *nm* (*fig*) (net) outcome; (: *de
victimes*) toll; (*Comm*) balance sheet(s);
un ~ de santé (a) medical checkup;
faire le ~ de to assess, review; **déposer
son ~** to file a bankruptcy statement
bile [bil] *nf* bile; **se faire de la ~** (*fam*) to
worry o.s. sick
bilieux, -euse [biljø, øz] *adj* bilious;
(*fig*: *colérique*) testy
bilingue [bilɛ̃g] *adj* bilingual
billard [bijaʀ] *nm* (*jeu*) billiards *sg*;
(*table*) billiard table
bille [bij] *nf* (*gén*) ball; (*du jeu de billes*)
marble
billet [bijɛ] *nm* (*aussi*: **~ de banque**)
(bank)note; (*de cinéma, de bus etc*)
ticket; (*courte lettre*) note; **billet
électronique** e-ticket; **billetterie**
nf ticket office; (*distributeur*) ticket
machine; (*Banque*) cash dispenser
billion [biljɔ̃] *nm* billion (BRIT), trillion
(US)
bimensuel, le [bimɑ̃sɥɛl] *adj*
bimonthly
bio [bjo] *adj inv* organic
bio... [bjo] *préfixe* bio...; **biochimie**

nf biochemistry; **biographie** *nf*
biography; **biologie** *nf* biology;
biologique *adj* biological; (*produits,
aliments*) organic; **biométrie** *nf*
biometrics; **biotechnologie** *nf*
biotechnology; **bioterrorisme** *nm*
bioterrorism
Birmanie [biʀmani] *nf* Burma
bis [bis] *adv*: **12 ~ 12a** ou A ▷ *excl, nm*
encore
biscotte [biskɔt] *nf* toasted bread (*sold
in packets*)
biscuit [biskɥi] *nm* biscuit (BRIT),
cookie(US)
bise [biz] *nf* (*fam*: *baiser*) kiss; (*vent*)
North wind; **grosses ~s (de)** (*sur lettre*)
love and kisses (from)
bisexuel, le [bisɛksɥɛl] *adj* bisexual
bisou [bizu] (*fam*) *nm* kiss
bissextile [bisɛkstil] *adj*: **année ~**
leap year
bistro(t) [bistʀo] *nm* bistro, café
bitume [bitym] *nm* asphalt
bizarre [bizaʀ] *adj* strange, odd
blague [blag] *nf* (*propos*) joke; (*farce*)
trick; **sans ~!** no kidding!; **blaguer**
vi to joke
blaireau, x [blɛʀo] *nm* (*Zool*) badger;
(*brosse*) shaving brush
blâme [blɑm] *nm* blame; (*sanction*)
reprimand; **blâmer** *vt* to blame
blanc, blanche [blɑ̃, blɑ̃ʃ] *adj* white;
(*non imprimé*) blank ▷ *nm/f* white,
white(-)man/(-)woman ▷ *nm* (*couleur*)
white; (*espace non écrit*) blank; (*aussi*: **~
d'œuf**) (egg-)white; (*aussi*: **~ de poulet**)
breast, white meat; (*aussi*: **vin ~**) white
wine; **cassé** off-white; **chèque en ~**
blank cheque; **à ~** (*chauffer*) white-hot;
(*tirer, charger*) with blanks; **blanche**
nf (*Mus*) minim (BRIT), half-note (US);
blancheur *nf* whiteness
blanchir [blɑ̃ʃiʀ] *vt* (*gén*) to whiten;
(*linge*) to launder; (*Culin*) to blanch; (*fig*:
disculper) to clear ▷ *vi* (*cheveux*) to go
white; **blanchisserie** *nf* laundry
blason [blazɔ̃] *nm* coat of arms
blasphème [blasfɛm] *nm* blasphemy

blazer [blɛzɛʀ] nm blazer
blé [ble] nm wheat; **blé noir** buckwheat
bled [blɛd] (péj) nm hole
blême [blɛm] adj pale
blessé, e [blese] adj injured ▷ nm/f injured person, casualty
blesser [blese] vt to injure; (délibérément) to wound; (offenser) to hurt; **se blesser** to injure o.s.; **se ~ au pied** to injure one's foot; **blessure** nf (accidentelle) injury; (intentionnelle) wound
bleu, e [blø] adj blue; (bifteck) very rare ▷ nm (couleur) blue; (contusion) bruise; (vêtement: aussi: **~s**) overalls pl; (fromage) blue cheese; **bleu marine** navy blue
bleuet [bløɛ] nm cornflower
bloc [blɔk] nm (de pierre etc) block; (de papier à lettres) pad; (ensemble) group, block; **serré à ~** tightened right down; **en ~** as a whole; **bloc opératoire** operating ou theatre block; **blocage** nm (des prix) freezing; (Psych) hang-up; **bloc-notes** nm note pad
blog, blogue [blɔg] nm blog; **bloguer** vi to blog
blond, e [blɔ̃, blɔ̃d] adj fair, blond; (sable, blés) golden
bloquer [blɔke] vt (passage) to block; (pièce mobile) to jam; (crédits, compte) to freeze
blottir [blɔtiʀ]: **se blottir** vi to huddle up
blouse [bluz] nf overall
blouson [bluzɔ̃] nm blouson jacket; **blouson noir** (fig) ≈ rocker
bluff [blœf] nm bluff
bobine [bɔbin] nf (fil) reel; (Élec) coil
bobo [bɔbo] abr m/f = bourgeois bohème (fam) boho
bocal, -aux [bɔkal, o] nm jar
bock [bɔk] nm glass of beer
bœuf [bœf] nm ox; (Culin) beef
bof [bɔf] (fam) excl don't care!; (pas terrible) nothing special
bohémien, ne [bɔemjɛ̃, -ɛn] nm/f gipsy
boire [bwaʀ] vt to drink; (s'imprégner

de) to soak up; **~ un coup** (fam) to have a drink
bois [bwa] nm wood; **de ~, en ~** wooden; **boisé, e** adj woody, wooded
boisson [bwasɔ̃] nf drink
boîte [bwat] nf box; (fam: entreprise) firm; **aliments en ~** ou tinned (BRIT) foods; **boîte à gants** glove compartment; **boîte à ordures** dustbin (BRIT), trashcan (US); **boîte aux lettres** letter box; **boîte d'allumettes** box of matches; (vide) matchbox; **boîte de conserves** can ou tin (BRIT) of food; **boîte de nuit** night club; **boîte de vitesses** gear box; **boîte postale** PO Box; **boîte vocale** (Tél) voice mail
boiter [bwate] vi to limp; (fig: raisonnement) to be shaky
boîtier [bwatje] nm case
boive etc [bwav] vb voir **boire**
bol [bɔl] nm bowl; **un ~ d'air** a breath of fresh air; **j'en ai ras le ~** (fam) I'm fed up with this; **avoir du ~** (fam) to be lucky
bombarder [bɔ̃baʀde] vt to bomb; **~ qn de** (cailloux, lettres) to bombard sb with
bombe [bɔ̃b] nf bomb; (atomiseur) (aerosol) spray

○ **MOT-CLÉ**

bon, bonne [bɔ̃, bɔn] adj 1 (agréable, satisfaisant) good; **un bon repas/restaurant** a good meal/restaurant; **être bon en maths** to be good at maths (BRIT) ou math (US)

2 (charitable): **être bon (envers)** to be good (to)

3 (correct) right; **le bon numéro/moment** the right number/moment

4 (souhaits): **bon anniversaire!** happy birthday!; **bon voyage!** have a good trip!; **bonne chance!** good luck!; **bonne année!** happy New Year!; **bonne nuit!** good night!

5 (approprié, apte): **bon à/pour** fit to/for; **à quoi bon?** what's the use?

6: **bon enfant** adj inv accommodating,

easy-going; **bonne femme** (*péj*) woman; **de bonne heure** early; **bon marché** *adj inv* cheap; **bon mot** witticism; **bon sens** common sense; **bon vivant** jovial chap; **bonnes œuvres** charitable works, charities ▷ *nm* **1** (*billet*) voucher; (*aussi:* **bon cadeau**) gift voucher; **bon d'essence** petrol coupon; **bon du Trésor** Treasury bond

2: **avoir du bon** to have its good points; **pour de bon** for good ▷ *adv*: **il fait bon** it's *ou* the weather is fine; **sentir bon** to smell good; **tenir bon** to stand firm ▷ *excl* good!; **ah bon?** really?; **bon, je reste** then, I'll stay; *voir aussi* **bonne**

bonbon [bɔ̃bɔ̃] *nm* (boiled) sweet
bond [bɔ̃] *nm* leap; **faire un ~** to leap in the air
bondé, e [bɔ̃de] *adj* packed (full)
bondir [bɔ̃diʀ] *vi* to leap
bonheur [bɔnœʀ] *nm* happiness; **porter ~ (à qn)** to bring (sb) luck; **au petit ~** haphazardly; **par ~** fortunately
bonhomme [bɔnɔm] (*pl* **bonshommes** [bɔ̃zɔm]) *nm* fellow; **bonhomme de neige** snowman
bonjour [bɔ̃ʒuʀ] *excl, nm* hello; (*selon l'heure*) good morning/afternoon; **c'est simple comme ~** it's as easy as pie!
bonne [bɔn] *adj voir* **bon** ▷ *nf* (*domestique*) maid
bonnet [bɔnɛ] *nm* hat; (*de soutien-gorge*) cup; **bonnet de bain** bathing cap
bonsoir [bɔ̃swaʀ] *excl* good evening
bonté [bɔ̃te] *nf* kindness *no pl*
bonus [bɔnys] *nm* no-claims bonus; (*de DVD*) extras *pl*
bord [bɔʀ] *nm* (*de table, verre, falaise*) edge; (*de rivière, lac*) bank; (*de route*) side; (*monter*) **à ~** (*to go*) on board; **jeter par-dessus ~** to throw overboard; **le commandant de/les hommes du ~** the ship's master/crew; **au ~ de la mer** at the seaside; **au ~ de la route** at the

roadside; **être au ~ des larmes** to be on the verge of tears
bordeaux [bɔʀdo] *nm* Bordeaux (wine) ▷ *adj inv* maroon
bordel [bɔʀdɛl] *nm* brothel; (*fam!*) bloody mess (!)
border [bɔʀde] *vt* (*être le long de*) to line; (*qn dans son lit*) to tuck up; (*garnir*): **~ qch de** to edge sth with
bordure [bɔʀdyʀ] *nf* border; **en ~ de** on the edge of
borne [bɔʀn] *nf* boundary stone; (*aussi:* **~ kilométrique**) kilometre-marker; = milestone; **bornes** *nfpl* (*fig*) limits; **dépasser les ~s** to go too far
borné, e [bɔʀne] *adj* (*personne*) narrow-minded
borner [bɔʀne] *vt*: **se ~ à faire** (*se contenter de*) to content o.s. with doing; (*se limiter à*) to limit o.s. to
bosniaque [bɔsnjak] *adj* Bosnian ▷ *nm/f* **B** ≈ Bosnian
Bosnie-Herzégovine [bɔsniɛʀzegɔvin] *nf* Bosnia-Herzegovina
bosquet [bɔskɛ] *nm* grove
bosse [bɔs] *nf* (*de terrain etc*) bump; (*enflure*) lump; (*du bossu, du chameau*) hump; **avoir la ~ des maths** *etc* (*fam*) to have a gift for maths *etc*; **il a roulé sa ~** (*fam*) he's been around
bosser [bɔse] *vi* (*travailler*) to work; (*travailler dur*) to slave (away)
bossu, e [bɔsy] *nm/f* hunchback
botanique [bɔtanik] *nf* botany ▷ *adj* botanic(al)
botte [bɔt] *nf* (*soulier*) (high) boot; (*gerbe*): **~ de paille** bundle of straw; **botte de radis/d'asperges** bunch of radishes/asparagus; **bottes de caoutchouc** wellington boots
bottin [bɔtɛ̃] *nm* directory
bottine [bɔtin] *nf* ankle boot
bouc [buk] *nm* goat; (*barbe*) goatee; **bouc émissaire** scapegoat
boucan [bukã] (*fam*) *nm* din, racket
bouche [buʃ] *nf* mouth; **faire du ~ à ~ à qn** to give sb the kiss of life *ou* mouth-

to-mouth resuscitation (BRIT); **rester ~ bée** to stand open-mouthed; **bouche d'égout** manhole; **bouche d'incendie** fire hydrant; **bouche de métro** métro entrance

bouché, e [buʃe] adj (flacon etc) stoppered; (temps, ciel) overcast; (péj fam: personne) thick (pej); **c'est un secteur ~** there's no future in that area; **avoir le nez ~** to have a blocked(-up) nose; **l'évier est ~** the sink's blocked

bouchée [buʃe] nf mouthful; **bouchées à la reine** chicken vol-au-vents

boucher, -ère [buʃe, ɛʀ] nm/f butcher ▷ vt (trou) to fill up; (obstruer) to block (up); **se boucher** vi (tuyau etc) to block up, get blocked up; **j'ai le nez bouché** my nose is blocked; **se ~ le nez** to hold one's nose; **boucherie** nf butcher's (shop); (fig) slaughter

bouchon [buʃɔ̃] nm stopper; (de tube) top; (en liège) cork; (fig: embouteillage) holdup; (Pêche) float

boucle [bukl] nf (forme, figure) loop; (objet) buckle; **boucle (de cheveux)** curl; **boucle d'oreille** earring

bouclé, e [bukle] adj (cheveux) curly

boucler [bukle] vt (fermer: ceinture etc) to fasten; (terminer) to finish off; (fam: enfermer) to shut away; (quartier) to seal off ▷ vi to curl

bouder [bude] vi to sulk ▷ vt to stay away from

boudin [budɛ̃] nm: **~ (noir)** black pudding; **boudin blanc** white pudding

boue [bu] nf mud

bouée [bwe] nf buoy; **bouée (de sauvetage)** lifebuoy

boueux, -euse [bwø, øz] adj muddy

bouffe [buf] (fam) nf grub (fam), food

bouffée [bufe] nf (de cigarette) puff; **une ~ d'air pur** a breath of fresh air; **bouffée de chaleur** hot flush (BRIT) ou flash (US)

bouffer [bufe] (fam) vi to eat

bouffi, e [bufi] adj swollen

bouger [buʒe] vi to move; (dent etc) to be loose; (s'activer) to get moving ▷ vt

to move; **les prix/les couleurs n'ont pas bougé** prices/colours haven't changed

bougie [buʒi] nf candle; (Auto) spark(ing) plug

bouillabaisse [bujabɛs] nf type of fish soup

bouillant, e [bujā, āt] adj (qui bout) boiling; (très chaud) boiling (hot)

bouillie [buji] nf (de bébé) cereal; **en ~** (fig) crushed

bouillir [bujiʀ] vi to boil; **~ d'impatience** to seethe with impatience

bouilloire [bujwaʀ] nf kettle

bouillon [bujɔ̃] nm (Culin) stock no pl; **bouillonner** vi to bubble; (fig: idées) to bubble up

bouillotte [bujɔt] nf hot-water bottle

boulanger, -ère [bulāʒe, ɛʀ] nm/f baker; **boulangerie** nf bakery

boule [bul] nf (gén) ball; (de pétanque) bowl; **boule de neige** snowball

boulette [bulɛt] nf (de viande) meatball

boulevard [bulvaʀ] nm boulevard

bouleversement [bulvɛʀsəmā] nm upheaval

bouleverser [bulvɛʀse] vt (émouvoir) to overwhelm; (causer du chagrin) to distress; (pays, vie) to disrupt; (papiers, objets) to turn upside down

boulimie [bulimi] nf bulimia

boulimique [bulimik] adj bulimic

boulon [bulɔ̃] nm bolt

boulot, te [bulo, ɔt] adj plump, tubby ▷ nm (fam: travail) work

boum [bum] nm bang ▷ nf (fam) party

bouquet [bukɛ] nm (de fleurs) bunch (of flowers), bouquet; (de persil etc) bunch; **c'est le ~!** (fam) that takes the biscuit!

bouquin [bukɛ̃] (fam) nm book; **bouquiner** (fam) vi to read

bourdon [buʀdɔ̃] nm bumblebee

bourg [buʀ] nm small market town

bourgeois, e [buʀʒwa, waz] (péj) adj ≈ (upper) middle class; **bourgeoisie** nf ≈ upper middle classes pl

bourgeon [buʀʒɔ̃] nm bud

Bourgogne [buʀgɔɲ] nf: **la ~** Burgundy
▷ nm: **bourgogne** burgundy (wine)

bourguignon, ne [buʀgiɲɔ̃, ɔn] adj of
ou from Burgundy, Burgundian

bourrasque [buʀask] nf squall

bourratif, -ive [buʀatif, iv] (fam) adj
filling, stodgy (pej)

bourré, e [buʀe] adj (fam: ivre)
plastered, tanked up (BRIT); (rempli): **~
de** crammed full of

bourrer [buʀe] vt (pipe) to fill; (poêle) to
pack; (valise) to cram (full)

bourru, e [buʀy] adj surly, gruff

bourse [buʀs] nf (subvention) grant;
(porte-monnaie) purse; **la B~** the Stock
Exchange

bous [bu] vb voir **bouillir**

bousculade [buskylad] nf (hâte) rush;
(cohue) crush; **bousculer** vt (heurter) to
knock into; (fig) to push, rush

boussole [busɔl] nf compass

bout [bu] vb voir **bouillir** ▷ nm bit; (d'un
bâton etc) tip; (d'une ficelle, table, rue,
période) end; **au ~ de** at the end of, after;
pousser qn à ~ to push sb to the limit;
venir à ~ de to manage to finish; **à ~
portant** (at) point-blank (range)

bouteille [butɛj] nf bottle; (de gaz
butane) cylinder

boutique [butik] nf shop

bouton [butɔ̃] nm button; (sur la
peau) spot; (Bot) bud; **boutonner**
vt to button up; **boutonnière** nf
buttonhole; **bouton-pression** nm
press stud

bovin, e [bɔvɛ̃, in] adj bovine; **bovins**
nmpl cattle pl

bowling [buliŋ] nm (tenpin) bowling;
(salle) bowling alley

boxe [bɔks] nf boxing

BP abr = **boîte postale**

bracelet [bʀaslɛ] nm bracelet

braconnier [bʀakɔnje] nm poacher

brader [bʀade] vt to sell off; **braderie**
nf cut-price shop/stall

braguette [bʀagɛt] nf fly ou flies pl
(BRIT), zipper (us)

braise [bʀɛz] nf embers pl

brancard [bʀɑ̃kaʀ] nm (civière)
stretcher; **brancardier** nm stretcher-
bearer

branche [bʀɑ̃ʃ] nf branch

branché, e [bʀɑ̃ʃe] (fam) adj trendy

brancher [bʀɑ̃ʃe] vt to connect (up); (en
mettant la prise) to plug in

brandir [bʀɑ̃diʀ] vt to brandish

braquer [bʀake] vi (Auto) to turn (the
wheel) ▷ vt (revolver etc): **~ qch sur**
to aim sth at, point sth at; (mettre en
colère): **~ qn** to put sb's back up

bras [bʀɑ] nm arm; **~ dessus, ~ dessous**
arm in arm; **se retrouver avec qch sur
les ~** (fam) to be landed with sth; **bras
droit** (fig) right hand man

brassard [bʀasaʀ] nm armband

brasse [bʀas] nf (nage) breast-stroke;
brasse papillon butterfly (stroke)

brassée [bʀase] nf armful

brasser [bʀase] vt to mix; **~ l'argent/
les affaires** to handle a lot of money/
business

brasserie [bʀasʀi] nf (restaurant) café-
restaurant; (usine) brewery

brave [bʀav] adj (courageux) brave; (bon,
gentil) good, kind

braver [bʀave] vt to defy

bravo [bʀavo] excl bravo ▷ nm cheer

bravoure [bʀavuʀ] nf bravery

break [bʀɛk] nm (Auto) estate car

brebis [bʀəbi] nf ewe; **brebis galeuse**
black sheep

bredouiller [bʀəduje] vi, vt to
mumble, stammer

bref, brève [bʀɛf, ɛv] adj short, brief
▷ adv in short; **d'un ton ~** sharply,
curtly; **en ~** in short, in brief

Brésil [bʀezil] nm Brazil

Bretagne [bʀətaɲ] nf Brittany

bretelle [bʀətɛl] nf (de vêtement, de
sac) strap; (d'autoroute) slip road (BRIT),
entrance/exit ramp (us); **bretelles**
nfpl (pour pantalon) braces (BRIT),
suspenders (us)

breton, ne [bʀətɔ̃, ɔn] adj Breton
▷ nm/f: **B~, ne** Breton

brève [bʀɛv] adj voir **bref**

brevet [bʀəvɛ] nm diploma, certificate; **brevet des collèges** exam taken at the age of 15; **brevet (d'invention)** patent; **breveté, e** adj patented

bricolage [bʀikɔlaʒ] nm: **le ~** do-it-yourself

bricoler [bʀikɔle] vi (petits travaux) to do DIY jobs; (passe-temps) to potter about ▷ vt (réparer) to fix up; **bricoleur, -euse** nm/f handyman(-woman), DIY enthusiast

bridge [bʀidʒ] nm (Cartes) bridge

brièvement [bʀijɛvmã] adv briefly

brigade [bʀigad] nf (Police) squad; (Mil) brigade; **brigadier** nm sergeant

brillamment [bʀijamã] adv brilliantly

brillant, e [bʀijã, ãt] adj (remarquable) bright; (luisant) shiny, shining

briller [bʀije] vi to shine

brin [bʀɛ̃] nm (de laine, ficelle etc) strand; (fig): **un ~ de** a bit of

brindille [bʀɛ̃dij] nf twig

brioche [bʀijɔʃ] nf brioche (bun); (fam: ventre) paunch

brique [bʀik] nf brick; (de lait) carton

briquet [bʀikɛ] nm (cigarette) lighter

brise [bʀiz] nf breeze

briser [bʀize] vt to break; **se briser** vi to break

britannique [bʀitanik] adj British ▷ nm/f: **B~** British person, Briton; **les B~s** the British

brocante [bʀɔkãt] nf junk, second-hand goods pl; **brocanteur, -euse** nm/f junkshop owner; junk dealer

broche [bʀɔʃ] nf brooch; (Culin) spit; (Méd) pin; **à la ~** spit-roasted

broché, e [bʀɔʃe] adj (livre) paper-backed

brochet [bʀɔʃe] nm pike inv

brochette [bʀɔʃɛt] nf (ustensile) skewer; (plat) kebab

brochure [bʀɔʃyʀ] nf pamphlet, brochure, booklet

broder [bʀɔde] vt to embroider ▷ vi: **~ (sur les faits ou une histoire)** to embroider the facts; **broderie** nf embroidery

bronches [bʀɔ̃ʃ] nfpl bronchial tubes; **bronchite** nf bronchitis

bronze [bʀɔ̃z] nm bronze

bronzer [bʀɔ̃ze] vi to get a tan; **se bronzer** to sunbathe

brosse [bʀɔs] nf brush; **coiffé en ~** with a crewcut; **brosse à cheveux** hairbrush; **brosse à dents** toothbrush; **brosse à habits** clothesbrush; **brosser** vt (nettoyer) to brush; (fig: tableau etc) to paint; **se brosser les dents** to brush one's teeth

brouette [bʀuɛt] nf wheelbarrow

brouillard [bʀujaʀ] nm fog

brouiller [bʀuje] vt (œufs, message) to scramble; (idées) to mix up; (rendre trouble) to cloud; (désunir: amis) to set at odds; (gens): **se ~ (avec)** to fall out (with)

brouillon, ne [bʀujɔ̃, ɔn] adj (sans soin) untidy; (qui manque d'organisation) disorganized ▷ nm draft; **(papier) ~** rough paper

broussailles [bʀusaj] nfpl undergrowth sg; **broussailleux, -euse** adj bushy

brousse [bʀus] nf: **la ~** the bush

brouter [bʀute] vi to graze

brugnon [bʀynɔ̃] nm (Bot) nectarine

bruiner [bʀɥine] vb impers: **il bruine** it's drizzling, there's a drizzle

bruit [bʀɥi] nm: **un ~** a noise, a sound; (fig: rumeur) a rumour; **le ~** noise; **sans ~** without a sound, noiselessly; **bruit de fond** background noise

brûlant, e [bʀylã, ãt] adj burning; (liquide) boiling (hot)

brûlé, e [bʀyle] adj (fig: démasqué) blown ▷ nm: **odeur de ~** smell of burning

brûler [bʀyle] vt to burn; (suj: eau bouillante) to scald; (consommer: électricité, essence) to use; (feu rouge, signal) to go through ▷ vi to burn; (jeu): **tu brûles!** you're getting hot!; **se brûler** to burn o.s.; (s'ébouillanter) to scald o.s.

brûlure [bʀylyʀ] nf (lésion) burn; **brûlures d'estomac** heartburn sg

brume | 36

brume [bʀym] nf mist

brun, e [bʀœ̃ bʀyn] adj (gén, bière) brown; (cheveux, tabac) dark; **elle est ~e** she's got dark hair

brunch [bʀœntʃ] nm brunch

brushing [bʀœʃiŋ] nm blow-dry

brusque [bʀysk] adj abrupt

brut, e [bʀyt] adj (minerai, soie) raw; (diamant) rough; (Comm) gross; **(pétrole)** ~ **crude** (oil)

brutal, e, -aux [bʀytal, o] adj brutal

Bruxelles [bʀysɛl] n Brussels

bruyamment [bʀɥijamɑ̃] adv noisily

bruyant, e [bʀɥijɑ̃, ɑ̃t] adj noisy

bruyère [bʀɥijɛʀ] nf heather

BTS sigle m (= brevet de technicien supérieur) vocational training certificate taken at the end of a higher education course

bu, e [by] pp de **boire**

buccal, e, -aux [bykal, o] adj: **par voie ~e** orally

bûche [byʃ] nf log; **prendre une ~** (fig) to come a cropper; **bûche de Noël** Yule log

bûcher [byʃe] nm (funéraire) pyre; (supplice) stake ▷ vi (fam) to swot (BRIT), slave (away) ▷ vt (fam) to swot up (BRIT), slave away at

budget [bydʒɛ] nm budget

buée [bɥe] nf (sur une vitre) mist

buffet [byfɛ] nm (meuble) sideboard; (de réception) buffet; **buffet (de gare)** (station) buffet, snack bar

buis [bɥi] nm box tree; (bois) box(wood)

buisson [bɥisɔ̃] nm bush

bulbe [bylb] nm (Bot, Anat) bulb

Bulgarie [bylgaʀi] nf Bulgaria

bulle [byl] nf bubble

bulletin [byltɛ̃] nm (communiqué, journal) bulletin; (Scol) report; **bulletin d'informations** news bulletin; **bulletin (de vote)** ballot paper; **bulletin météorologique** weather report

bureau, x [byʀo] nm (meuble) desk; (pièce, service) office; **bureau de change** (foreign) exchange office ou bureau; **bureau de poste** post office; **bureau de tabac** tobacconist's (shop); **bureaucratie** [byʀokʀasi] nf bureaucracy

bus[1] [by] vb voir **boire**

bus[2] [bys] nm bus; **à quelle heure part le ~?** what time does the bus leave?

buste [byst] nm (torse) chest; (seins) bust

but[1] [by] vb voir **boire**

but[2] [by(t)] nm (cible) target; (fig) goal, aim; (Football etc) goal; **de ~ en blanc** point-blank; **avoir pour ~ de faire** to aim to do; **dans le ~ de** with the intention of

butane [bytan] nm (camping) butane; (usage domestique) Calor gas®

butiner [bytine] vi (abeilles) to gather nectar

buvais etc [byvɛ] vb voir **boire**

buvard [byvaʀ] nm blotter

buvette [byvɛt] nf bar

C

c' [s] dét voir **ce**

ça [sa] pron (pour désigner) this; (: plus loin) that; (comme sujet indéfini) it; **ça m'étonne que ...** it surprises me that ...; **comment ça va?** how are you?; **ça va?** (d'accord?) O.K?, all right?; **où ça?** where's that?; **pourquoi ça?** why's that?; **qui ça?** who's that?; **ça alors!** well really!; **ça fait 10 ans (que)** it's 10 years (since); **c'est ça** that's right; **ça y est** that's it

cabane [kaban] nf hut, cabin

cabaret [kabaʀɛ] nm night club

cabillaud [kabijo] nm cod inv

cabine [kabin] nf (de bateau) cabin; (de piscine etc) cubicle; (de camion, train) cab; (d'avion) cockpit; **cabine d'essayage** fitting room; **cabine (téléphonique)** call ou (tele)phone box

cabinet [kabinɛ] nm (petite pièce) closet; (de médecin) surgery (BRIT), office (US); (de notaire etc) office; (: clientèle) practice; (Pol) Cabinet; **cabinets** nmpl (w.-c.) toilet sg; **cabinet de toilette**

toilet

câble [kabl] nm cable; **le ~** (TV) cable television, cablevision (US)

cacahuète [kakaɥɛt] nf peanut

cacao [kakao] nm cocoa

cache [kaʃ] nm mask, card (for masking)

cache-cache [kaʃkaʃ] nm: **jouer à ~** to play hide-and-seek

cachemire [kaʃmir] nm cashmere

cacher [kaʃe] vt to hide, conceal; **se cacher** vi (volontairement) to hide; (être caché) to be hidden ou concealed; **~ qch à qn** to hide ou conceal sth from sb

cachet [kaʃɛ] nm (comprimé) tablet; (de la poste) postmark; (rétribution) fee; (fig) style, character

cachette [kaʃɛt] nf hiding place; **en ~** on the sly, secretly

cactus [kaktys] nm cactus

cadavre [kadavʀ] nm corpse, (dead) body

caddie® [kadi] nm (supermarket) trolley (BRIT), (grocery) cart (US)

cadeau, x [kado] nm present, gift; **faire un ~ à qn** to give sb a present ou gift; **faire ~ de qch à qn** to make a present of sth to sb, give sb sth as a present

cadenas [kadnɑ] nm padlock

cadet, te [kadɛ, ɛt] adj younger; (le plus jeune) youngest ▷ nm/f youngest child ou one

cadran [kadʀɑ̃] nm dial; **cadran solaire** sundial

cadre [kadʀ] nm frame; (environnement) surroundings pl ▷ nm/f (Admin) managerial employee, executive; **dans le ~ de** (fig) within the framework ou context of

cafard [kafaʀ] nm cockroach; **avoir le ~** (fam) to be down in the dumps

café [kafe] nm coffee; (bistro) café ▷ adj inv coffee(-coloured); **café au lait** white coffee; **café noir** black coffee; **café tabac** tobacconist's or newsagent's serving coffee and spirits; **cafetière** nf (pot) coffee-pot

cage [kaʒ] nf cage; **cage (d'escalier)** stairwell; **cage thoracique** rib cage

cageot [kaʒo] nm crate

cagoule [kagul] nf (passe-montagne) balaclava

cahier [kaje] nm notebook; **cahier de brouillon** jotter (BRIT), rough notebook; **cahier d'exercices** exercise book

caille [kaj] nf quail

caillou, x [kaju] nm (little) stone; **caillouteux, -euse** adj (route) stony

Caire [KER] nm: **le ~** Cairo

caisse [kes] nf box; (tiroir où l'on met la recette) till; (où l'on paye) cash desk (BRIT), check-out; (de banque) cashier's desk; **caisse d'épargne** savings bank; **caisse de retraite** pension fund; **caisse enregistreuse** cash register; **caissier, -ière** nm/f cashier

cake [kek] nm fruit cake

calandre [kalɑ̃dR] nf radiator grill

calcaire [kalkER] nm limestone ▷ adj (eau) hard; (Géo) limestone cpd

calcul [kalkyl] nm calculation; **le ~** (Scol) arithmetic; **calcul (biliaire)** (gall)stone; **calculatrice** nf calculator; **calculer** vt to calculate, work out; **calculette** nf pocket calculator

cale [kal] nf (de bateau) hold; (en bois) wedge

calé, e [kale] (fam) adj clever, bright

caleçon [kalsɔ̃] nm (d'homme) boxer shorts; (de femme) leggings

calendrier [kalɑ̃dRije] nm calendar; (fig) timetable

calepin [kalpɛ̃] nm notebook

caler [kale] vt to wedge ▷ vi (moteur, véhicule) to stall

calibre [kalibR] nm calibre

câlin, e [kɑlɛ̃, in] adj cuddly, cuddlesome; (regard, voix) tender

calmant [kalmɑ̃] nm tranquillizer, sedative; (pour la douleur) painkiller

calme [kalm] adj calm, quiet ▷ nm calm(ness), quietness; **sans perdre son ~** without losing one's cool (inf) ou composure; **calmer** vt to calm (down);

(douleur, inquiétude) to ease, soothe; **se calmer** vi to calm down

calorie [kalɔRi] nf calorie

camarade [kamaRad] nm/f friend, pal; (Pol) comrade

Cambodge [kɑ̃bɔdʒ] nm: **le ~** Cambodia

cambriolage [kɑ̃bRijolaʒ] nm burglary; **cambrioler** vt to burgle (BRIT), burglarize (US); **cambrioleur, -euse** nm/f burglar

camelote [kamlɔt] (fam) nf rubbish, trash, junk

caméra [kameRa] nf (Cinéma, TV) camera; (d'amateur) cine-camera

Cameroun [kamRun] nm: **le ~** Cameroon

caméscope® [kameskɔp] nm camcorder®

camion [kamjɔ̃] nm lorry (BRIT), truck; **camion de dépannage** breakdown (BRIT) ou tow (US) truck; **camionnette** nf (small) van; **camionneur** nm (chauffeur) lorry (BRIT) ou truck driver; (entrepreneur) haulage contractor (BRIT), trucker (US)

camomille [kamɔmij] nf camomile; (boisson) camomile tea

camp [kɑ̃] nm camp; (fig) side

campagnard, e [kɑ̃paɲaR, aRd] adj country cpd

campagne [kɑ̃paɲ] nf country, countryside; (Mil, Pol, Comm) campaign; **à la ~** in the country

camper [kɑ̃pe] vi to camp ▷ vt to sketch; **se ~ devant** to plant o.s. in front of; **campeur, -euse** nm/f camper

camping [kɑ̃piŋ] nm camping; **faire du ~** to go camping; (terrain de) **camping** campsite, camping site; **camping-car** nm camper, motorhome (US); **camping-gaz®** nm inv camp(ing) stove

Canada [kanada] nm: **le ~** Canada; **canadien, ne** adj Canadian ▷ nm/f: **Canadien, ne** Canadian; **canadienne** nf (veste) fur-lined jacket

canal, -aux [kanal, o] nm canal;

(naturel, TV) channel; **canalisation** nf (tuyau) pipe

canapé [kanape] nm settee, sofa

canard [kanaʀ] nm duck; (fam: journal) rag

cancer [kɑ̃sɛʀ] nm cancer; (signe): **le C~** Cancer

cancre [kɑ̃kʀ] nm dunce

candidat, e [kɑ̃dida, at] nm/f candidate; (à un poste) applicant, candidate; **candidature** nf (Pol) candidature; (à poste) application; **poser sa candidature à un poste** to apply for a job

cane [kan] nf (female) duck

canette [kanɛt] nf (de bière) (flip-top) bottle

canevas [kanva] nm (Couture) canvas

caniche [kaniʃ] nm poodle

canicule [kanikyl] nf scorching heat

canif [kanif] nm penknife, pocket knife

canne [kan] nf (walking) stick; **canne à pêche** fishing rod; **canne à sucre** sugar cane

cannelle [kanɛl] nf cinnamon

canoë [kanɔe] nm canoe; (sport) canoeing; **canoë (kayak)** kayak

canot [kano] nm ding(h)y; **canot de sauvetage** lifeboat; **canot pneumatique** inflatable dinghy

cantatrice [kɑ̃tatʀis] nf (opera) singer

cantine [kɑ̃tin] nf canteen

canton [kɑ̃tɔ̃] nm district consisting of several communes; (en Suisse) canton

caoutchouc [kautʃu] nm rubber; **caoutchouc mousse** foam rubber

cap [kap] nm (Géo) cape; (promontoire) headland; (fig: tournant) watershed; (Navig): **changer de ~** to change course; **mettre le ~ sur** to head ou steer for

CAP sigle m (= Certificat d'aptitude professionnelle) vocational training certificate taken at secondary school

capable [kapabl] adj able, capable; **~ de qch/faire** capable of sth/doing

capacité [kapasite] nf (compétence) ability; (Jur, contenance) capacity

cape [kap] nf cape, cloak; **rire sous ~** to laugh up one's sleeve

CAPES [kapɛs] sigle m (= Certificat d'aptitude pédagogique à l'enseignement secondaire) teaching diploma

capitaine [kapiten] nm captain

capital, e, -aux [kapital, o] adj (œuvre) major; (question, rôle) fundamental ▷ nm (aussi: fig) stock; **d'une importance ~e** of capital importance; **capitaux** nmpl (fonds) capital sg; **capital (social)** authorized capital; **capitale** nf (ville) capital; (lettre) capital (letter); **capitalisme** nm capitalism; **capitaliste** adj, nm/f capitalist

caporal, -aux [kapɔʀal, o] nm lance corporal

capot [kapo] nm (Auto) bonnet (BRIT), hood (US)

câpre [kɑpʀ] nf caper

caprice [kapʀis] nm whim, caprice; **faire des ~s** to make a fuss; **capricieux, -euse** adj (fantasque) capricious, whimsical; (enfant) awkward

Capricorne [kapʀikɔʀn] nm: **le ~** Capricorn

capsule [kapsyl] nf (de bouteille) cap; (Bot etc, spatiale) capsule

capter [kapte] vt (ondes radio) to pick up; (fig) to win, capture

captivant, e [kaptivɑ̃, ɑ̃t] adj captivating

capturer [kaptyʀe] vt to capture

capuche [kapyʃ] nf hood

capuchon [kapyʃɔ̃] nm hood; (de stylo) cap, top

car [kaʀ] nm coach ▷ conj because, for

carabine [kaʀabin] nf rifle

caractère [kaʀaktɛʀ] nm (gén) character; **avoir bon/mauvais ~** to be good-/ill-natured; **en ~s gras** in bold type; **en petits ~s** in small print; **~s d'imprimerie** (block) capitals

caractériser [kaʀakteʀize] vt to be characteristic of; **se ~ par** to be characterized ou distinguished by

caractéristique [kaʀakteʀistik] adj,

nf characteristic

carafe [karaf] nf (pour eau, vin ordinaire) carafe

caraïbe [karaib] adj Caribbean ▷ n: **les C~s** the Caribbean (Islands)

carambolage [karɑ̃bɔlaʒ] nm multiple crash, pileup

caramel [karamel] nm (bonbon) caramel, toffee; (substance) caramel

caravane [karavan] nf (caravan); **caravaning** nm caravanning

carbone [karbɔn] nm carbon; (double) carbon (copy)

carbonique [karbɔnik] adj: **gaz ~** carbon dioxide; **neige ~** dry ice

carbonisé, e [karbɔnize] adj charred

carburant [karbyrɑ̃] nm (motor) fuel

carburateur [karbyratœr] nm carburettor

cardiaque [kardjak] adj cardiac, heart cpd ▷ nm/f heart patient; **être ~** to have heart trouble

cardigan [kardigɑ̃] nm cardigan

cardiologue [kardjɔlɔg] nm/f cardiologist, heart specialist

carême [karɛm] nm: **le C~** Lent

carence [karɑ̃s] nf (manque) deficiency

caresse [kares] nf caress

caresser [karese] vt to caress; (animal) to stroke

cargaison [kargɛzɔ̃] nf cargo, freight

cargo [kargo] nm cargo boat, freighter

caricature [karikatyr] nf caricature

carie [kari] nf: **la ~ (dentaire)** tooth decay; **une ~** a bad tooth

carnaval [karnaval] nm carnival

carnet [karnɛ] nm (calepin) notebook; (de tickets, timbres etc) book; **carnet de chèques** cheque book

carotte [karɔt] nf carrot

carré, e [kare] adj square; (fig: franc) straightforward ▷ nm (Math) square; **mètre/kilomètre ~** square metre/ kilometre

carreau, x [karo] nm (par terre) (floor) tile; (au mur) (wall) tile; (de fenêtre) (window) pane; (motif) check, square; (Cartes: couleur) diamonds pl; **tissu à ~x**

checked fabric

carrefour [karfur] nm crossroads sg

carrelage [karlaʒ] nm (sol) (tiled) floor

carrelet [karlɛ] nm (poisson) plaice

carrément [karemɑ̃] adv (franchement) straight out, bluntly; (sans hésiter) straight; (intensif) completely; **c'est ~ impossible** it's completely impossible

carrière [karjɛr] nf (métier) career; (de roches) quarry; **militaire de ~** professional soldier

carrosserie [karɔsri] nf body, coachwork no pl

carrure [karyr] nf build; (fig) stature, calibre

cartable [kartabl] nm satchel, (school)bag

carte [kart] nf (de géographie) map; (marine, du ciel) chart; (d'abonnement, à jouer) card; (au restaurant) menu; (aussi: **~ de visite**) (visiting) card; **pouvez-vous me l'indiquer sur la ~?** can you show me (it) on the map?; **à la ~** (au restaurant) à la carte; **est-ce qu'on peut voir la ~?** can we see the menu?; **donner ~ blanche à qn** to give sb a free rein; **carte bancaire** cash card; **Carte Bleue®** debit card; **carte à puce** smart card; **carte de crédit** credit card; **carte de fidélité** loyalty card; **carte d'identité** identity card; **carte de séjour** residence permit; **carte grise** (Auto) ≈ (car) registration book, logbook; **carte memoire** (d'appareil-photo numérique) memory card; **carte postale** postcard; **carte routière** road map

carter [kartɛr] nm sump

carton [kartɔ̃] nm (matériau) cardboard; (boîte) (cardboard) box; **faire un ~** (fam) to score a hit; **carton (à dessin)** portfolio

cartouche [kartuʃ] nf cartridge; (de cigarettes) carton

cas [kɑ] nm case; **ne faire aucun ~ de** to take no notice of; **en aucun ~** on no account; **au ~ où** in case; **en ~ de** in case of, in the event of; **en ~ de besoin**

if need be; **en tout ~** in any case, at any rate

cascade [kaskad] *nf* waterfall, cascade

case [kɑz] *nf* (hutte) hut; (compartiment) compartment; (sur un formulaire, de mots croisés etc) box

caser [kɑze] (fam) *vt* (placer) to put (away); (loger) to put up; **se caser** *vi* (se marier) to settle down; (trouver un emploi) to find a (steady) job

caserne [kazɛʀn] *nf* barracks pl

casier [kɑzje] *nm* (pour courrier) pigeonhole; (compartiment) compartment; (à clef) locker; **casier judiciaire** police record

casino [kazino] *nm* casino

casque [kask] *nm* helmet; (chez le coiffeur) (hair-)drier; (pour audition) (head-)phones *pl*, headset

casquette [kaskɛt] *nf* cap

casse...: casse-croûte *nm inv* snack; **casse-noix** *nm inv* nutcrackers *pl*; **casse-pieds** (fam) *adj inv* **il est casse-pieds** he's a pain in the neck

casser [kɑse] *vt* to break; (Jur) to quash; **se casser** *vi* to break; **~ les pieds à qn** (fam: irriter) to get on sb's nerves; **se ~ la tête** (fam) to go to a lot of trouble

casserole [kasʀɔl] *nf* saucepan

casse-tête [kɑstɛt] *nm inv* (difficultés) headache (fig)

cassette [kasɛt] *nf* (bande magnétique) cassette; (coffret) casket

cassis [kasis] *nm* blackcurrant

cassoulet [kasulɛ] *nm* bean and sausage hot-pot

catalogue [katalog] *nm* catalogue

catalytique [katalitik] *adj*: **pot ~** catalytic convertor

catastrophe [katastʀɔf] *nf* catastrophe, disaster

catéchisme [kateʃism] *nm* catechism

catégorie [kategɔʀi] *nf* category; **catégorique** *adj* categorical

cathédrale [katedʀal] *nf* cathedral

catholique [katɔlik] *adj, nm/f* (Roman) Catholic; **pas très ~** a bit shady ou fishy

cauchemar [koʃmaʀ] *nm* nightmare

cause [koz] *nf* cause; (Jur) lawsuit, case; **à ~ de** because of, owing to; **pour ~ de** on account of, owing to; **(et) pour ~** and for a (very) good reason; **être en ~** (intérêts) to be at stake; **remettre en ~** to challenge; **causer** *vt* to cause ▷ *vi* to chat, talk

caution [kosjɔ̃] *nf* guarantee, security; (Jur) bail (bond); (fig) backing, support; **libéré sous ~** released on bail

cavalier, -ière [kavalje, jɛʀ] *adj* (désinvolte) offhand ▷ *nm/f* rider; (au bal) partner ▷ *nm* (Échecs) knight

cave [kav] *nf* cellar

CD *sigle m* (= compact disc) CD

CD-ROM [sederɔm] *sigle m* CD-ROM

MOT-CLÉ

ce, cette [sə, sɛt] (devant nm **cet** + voyelle ou h aspiré; pl **ces**) dét (proximité) this; these *pl*; (non-proximité) that; those *pl*; **cette maison(-ci/là)** this/that house; **cette nuit** (qui vient) tonight; (passée) last night

▷ *pron* 1: **c'est** it's ou it is; **c'est un peintre** it's ou he's a painter; **ce sont des peintres** they're ou they are painters; **c'est le facteur** etc (à la porte) it's the postman; **c'est toi qui lui a parlé** it's you who spoke to him; **qui est-ce?** who is it?; (en désignant) who is he/she?; **qu'est-ce?** what is it?

2: **ce qui, ce que** ce qui me plaît, **c'est sa franchise** what I like about him ou her is his ou her frankness; **il est bête, ce qui me chagrine** he's stupid, which saddens me; **tout ce qui bouge** everything that ou which moves; **tout ce que je sais** all I know; **ce dont j'ai parlé** what I talked about; **ce que c'est grand!** it's so big!; voir aussi **-ci**; **est-ce que**; **n'est-ce pas**; **c'est-à-dire**

ceci [səsi] *pron* this

céder [sede] *vt* (donner) to give up ▷ *vi* (chaise, barrage) to give way; (personne) to give in; **~ à** to yield to, give in to

CEDEX [sedɛks] *sigle m (= courrier d'entreprise à distribution exceptionnelle) postal service for bulk users*

cédille [sedij] *nf* cedilla

ceinture [sɛtyʀ] *nf* belt; *(taille)* waist; **ceinture de sécurité** safety ou seat belt

cela [s(ə)la] *pron* that; *(comme sujet indéfini)* it; **~ m'étonne que ...** it surprises me that ...; **quand/où ~?** when/where (was that)?

célèbre [selɛbʀ] *adj* famous; **célébrer** *vt* to celebrate

céleri [selʀi] *nm* **~ (-rave)** celeriac; **céleri en branche** celery

célibataire [selibatɛʀ] *adj* single, unmarried ▷ *nm* bachelor ▷ *nf* unmarried woman

celle, celles [sɛl] *pron voir* **celui**

cellule [selyl] *nf (gén)* cell; **~ souche** stem cell

🅞 MOT-CLÉ

celui, celle [səlɥi, sɛl] *(mpl* **ceux**, *fpl* **celles)** *pron* **1**: **celui-ci/là, celle-ci/là** this one/that one; **ceux-ci, celles-ci** these (ones); **ceux-là, celles-là** those (ones)
2: **celui qui bouge** the one which ou that moves; *(personne)* the one who moves; **celui que je vois** the one (which ou that) I see; *(personne)* the one (whom) I see; **celui dont je parle** the one I'm talking about; **celui de mon frère** my brother's; **celui du salon/du dessous** the one in (ou from) the lounge/below
3 *(valeur indéfinie)*: **celui qui veut** whoever wants

cendre [sɑ̃dʀ] *nf* ash; **cendres** *nfpl (d'un défunt)* ashes; **sous la ~** *(Culin)* in (the) embers; **sous la ~** ashtray

censé, e [sɑ̃se] *adj*: **être ~ faire** to be supposed to do

censeur [sɑ̃sœʀ] *nm (Scol)* deputy-head

(BRIT), vice-principal *(US)*

censure [sɑ̃syʀ] *nf* censorship; **censurer** *vt (Cinéma, Presse)* to censor; *(Pol)* to censure

cent [sɑ̃] *num* a hundred, one hundred ▷ *nm (US, Canada etc)* cent; *(partie de l'euro)* cent; **centaine** *nf*: **une centaine (de)** about a hundred, a hundred or so; **des centaines (de)** hundreds (of); **centenaire** *adj* hundred-year-old ▷ *nm (anniversaire)* centenary; *(monnaie)* cent; **centième** *num* hundredth; **centigrade** *nm* centigrade; **centilitre** *nm* centilitre; **centime** *nm* centime; **centime d'euro** euro cent; **centimètre** *nm* centimetre; *(ruban)* tape measure, measuring tape

central, e, -aux [sɑ̃tʀal, o] *adj* central ▷ *nm*: **~ (téléphonique)** (telephone) exchange; **centrale** *nf* power station; **centrale électrique/nucléaire** power/nuclear power station

centre [sɑ̃tʀ] *nm* centre; **centre commercial/sportif/culturel** shopping/sports/arts centre; **centre d'appels** call centre; **centre-ville** *nm* town centre, downtown (area) *(us)*

cèpe [sɛp] *nm (edible)* boletus

cependant [s(ə)pɑ̃dɑ̃] *adv* however

céramique [seʀamik] *nf* ceramics *sg*

cercle [sɛʀkl] *nm* circle; **cercle vicieux** vicious circle

cercueil [sɛʀkœj] *nm* coffin

céréale [seʀeal] *nf* cereal

cérémonie [seʀemɔni] *nf* ceremony; **sans ~** *(inviter, manger)* informally

cerf [sɛʀ] *nm* stag

cerf-volant [sɛʀvɔlɑ̃] *nm* kite

cerise [s(ə)ʀiz] *nf* cherry; **cerisier** *nm* cherry (tree)

cerner [sɛʀne] *vt (Mil etc)* to surround; *(fig: problème)* to delimit, define

certain, e [sɛʀtɛ̃, ɛn] *adj* certain ▷ *dét* certain; **d'un ~ âge** past one's prime, not so young; **un ~ temps** (quite) some time; **un ~ Georges** someone called Georges; **~s** *pron* some; **certainement** *adv (probablement)* most probably ou

likely; **(bien sûr)** certainly, of course
certes [sɛʁt] adv **(sans doute)** admittedly; **(bien sûr)** of course
certificat [sɛʁtifika] nm certificate
certifier [sɛʁtifje] vt: **~ qch à qn** to assure sb of sth; **copie certifiée conforme** certified copy of the original
certitude [sɛʁtityd] nf certainty
cerveau, x [sɛʁvo] nm brain
cervelas [sɛʁvəla] nm saveloy
cervelle [sɛʁvɛl] nf (Anat) brain; (Culin) brains
ces [se] dét voir **ce**
CES sigle m (= collège d'enseignement secondaire) ≈ (junior) secondary school (BRIT)
cesse [sɛs]: **sans ~** adv **(tout le temps)** continually, constantly; **(sans interruption)** continuously; **il n'a eu de ~ que** he did not rest until; **cesser** vt to stop ▷ vi to stop, cease; **cesser de faire** to stop doing; **cessez-le-feu** nm inv ceasefire
c'est-à-dire [sɛtadiʁ] adv that is (to say)
cet, cette [sɛt] dét voir **ce**
ceux [sø] pron voir **celui**
chacun, e [ʃakœ̃, yn] pron each; **(indéfini)** everyone, everybody
chagrin [ʃagʁɛ̃] nm grief, sorrow; **avoir du ~** to be grieved
chahut [ʃay] nm uproar; **chahuter** vt to rag, bait ▷ vi to make an uproar
chaîne [ʃɛn] nf chain; (Radio, TV: stations) channel; **travail à la ~** production line work; **réactions en ~** chain reaction sg; **chaîne de montagnes** mountain range; **chaîne (hi-fi)** hi-fi system
chair [ʃɛʁ] nf flesh; **avoir la ~ de poule** to have goosepimples ou gooseflesh; **bien en ~** plump, well-padded; **en ~ et en os** in the flesh; **à saucisse** sausage meat
chaise [ʃɛz] nf chair; **chaise longue** deckchair
châle [ʃɑl] nm shawl
chaleur [ʃalœʁ] nf heat; (fig: accueil) warmth; **chaleureux, -euse** adj warm

chamailler [ʃamaje]: **se chamailler** vi to squabble, bicker
chambre [ʃɑ̃bʁ] nf bedroom; (Pol, Comm) chamber; **faire ~ à part** to sleep in separate rooms; **je voudrais une ~ pour deux personnes** I'd like a double room; **chambre à air** (de pneu) (inner) tube; **chambre à coucher** bedroom; **chambre à un lit/à deux lits** (à l'hôtel) single-/twin-bedded room; **chambre d'amis** spare ou guest room; **chambre d'hôte** ≈ bed and breakfast; **chambre meublée** bedsit(ter) (BRIT), furnished room; **chambre noire** (Photo) darkroom
chameau, x [ʃamo] nm camel
chamois [ʃamwa] nm chamois
champ [ʃɑ̃] nm field; **champ de bataille** battlefield; **champ de courses** racecourse
champagne [ʃɑ̃paɲ] nm champagne
champignon [ʃɑ̃piɲɔ̃] nm mushroom; (terme générique) fungus; **champignon de Paris** ou **de couche** button mushroom
champion, ne [ʃɑ̃pjɔ̃, jɔn] adj, nm/f champion; **championnat** nm championship
chance [ʃɑ̃s] nf: **la ~** luck; **chances** nfpl (probabilités) chances; **avoir de la ~** to be lucky; **il a des ~ de réussir** he's got a good chance of passing; **bonne ~!** good luck!
change [ʃɑ̃ʒ] nm (devises) exchange
changement [ʃɑ̃ʒmɑ̃] nm change; **changement de vitesses** gears pl
changer [ʃɑ̃ʒe] vt (modifier) to change, alter; (remplacer, Comm) to change ▷ vi to change, alter; **se changer** vi to change (o.s.); **~ de** (remplacer: adresse, nom, voiture etc) to change one's; (échanger: place, train etc) to change; **~ d'avis** to change one's mind; **~ de vitesse** to change gear; **il faut ~ à Lyon** you ou we etc have to change in Lyons; **où est-ce que je peux ~ de l'argent?** where can I change some money?
chanson [ʃɑ̃sɔ̃] nf song

chant [ʃɑ̃] nm song; (art vocal) singing; (d'église) hymn

chantage [ʃɑ̃taʒ] nm blackmail; **faire du ~** to use blackmail

chanter [ʃɑ̃te] vt, vi singing; **si cela lui chante** (fam) if he feels like it; **chanteur, -euse** nm/f singer

chantier [ʃɑ̃tje] nm (building) site; (sur une route) roadworks pl; **mettre en ~** to put in hand; **chantier naval** shipyard

chantilly [ʃɑ̃tiji] nf voir **crème**

chantonner [ʃɑ̃tɔne] vi, vt to sing to oneself, hum

chapeau, x [ʃapo] nm hat; **~!** well done!

chapelle [ʃapɛl] nf chapel

chapitre [ʃapitʀ] nm chapter

chaque [ʃak] dét each, every; (indéfini) every

char [ʃaʀ] nm (Mil): **~ (d'assaut)** tank; **~ à voile** sand yacht

charbon [ʃaʀbɔ̃] nm coal; **charbon de bois** charcoal

charcuterie [ʃaʀkytʀi] nf (magasin) pork butcher's shop and delicatessen; (produits) cooked pork meats pl; **charcutier, -ière** nm/f pork butcher

chardon [ʃaʀdɔ̃] nm thistle

charge [ʃaʀʒ] nf (fardeau) load, burden; (Élec, Mil, Jur) charge; (rôle, mission) responsibility; **charges** nfpl (du loyer) service charges; **à la ~ de** (dépendant de) dependent upon; (aux frais de) chargeable to; **prendre en ~** to take charge of; (suj: véhicule) to take on; (dépenses) to take care of; **charges sociales** social security contributions

chargement [ʃaʀʒəmɑ̃] nm (objets) load

charger [ʃaʀʒe] vt (voiture, fusil, caméra) to load; (batterie) to charge ▷ vi (Mil etc) to charge; **se ~ de** to see to, take care of

chariot [ʃaʀjo] nm trolley; (charrette) waggon

charité [ʃaʀite] nf charity; **faire la ~ à** to give (something) to

charmant, e [ʃaʀmɑ̃, ɑ̃t] adj charming

charme [ʃaʀm] nm charm; **charmer**

vt to charm

charpente [ʃaʀpɑ̃t] nf frame(work); **charpentier** nm carpenter

charrette [ʃaʀɛt] nf cart

charter [ʃaʀtɛʀ] nm (vol) charter flight

chasse [ʃas] nf hunting; (au fusil) shooting; (poursuite) chase; (aussi: **~ d'eau**) flush; **prendre en ~** to give chase to; **tirer la ~ (d'eau)** to flush the toilet, pull the chain; **~ à courre** hunting; **chasse-neige** nm inv snowplough (BRIT), snowplow (US); **chasser** vt to hunt; (expulser) to chase away ou out, drive away ou out; **chasseur, -euse** nm/f hunter ▷ nm (avion) fighter

chat¹ [ʃa] nm cat

chat² [tʃat] nm (Internet) chat room

châtaigne [ʃatɛɲ] nf chestnut

châtain [ʃatɛ̃] adj inv (cheveux) chestnut (brown); (personne) chestnut-haired

château, x [ʃato] nm (forteresse) castle; (résidence royale) palace; (manoir) mansion; **château d'eau** water tower; **château fort** stronghold, fortified castle

châtiment [ʃatimɑ̃] nm punishment

chaton [ʃatɔ̃] nm (Zool) kitten

chatouiller [ʃatuje] vt to tickle; **chatouilleux, -euse** adj ticklish

chatte [ʃat] nf (she-)cat

chatter [tʃate] vi (Internet) to chat

chaud, e [ʃo, ʃod] adj (gén) warm; (très chaud) hot; **il fait ~** it's warm; it's hot; **avoir ~** to be warm; to be hot; **ça me tient ~** it keeps me warm; **rester au ~** to stay in the warm

chaudière [ʃodjɛʀ] nf boiler

chauffage [ʃofaʒ] nm heating; **chauffage central** central heating

chauffe-eau [ʃofo] nm inv water-heater

chauffer [ʃofe] vt to heat ▷ vi to heat up, warm up; (trop chauffer: moteur) to overheat; **se chauffer** vi (au soleil) to warm o.s.

chauffeur [ʃofœʀ] nm driver; (privé) chauffeur

chaumière [ʃomjɛr] nf (thatched) cottage

chaussée [ʃose] nf road(way)

chausser [ʃose] vt (bottes, skis) to put on; (enfant) to put shoes on; **~ du 38/42** to take size 38/42

chaussette [ʃosɛt] nf sock

chausson [ʃosɔ̃] nm slipper; (de bébé) bootee; **chausson (aux pommes)** (apple) turnover

chaussure [ʃosyr] nf shoe; **chaussures basses** flat shoes; **chaussures montantes** ankle boots; **chaussures de ski** ski boots

chauve [ʃov] adj bald; **chauve-souris** nf bat

chauvin, e [ʃovɛ̃, in] adj chauvinistic

chaux [ʃo] nf lime; **blanchi à la ~** whitewashed

chef [ʃɛf] nm head, leader; (de cuisine) chef; **commandant en ~** commander-in-chief; **chef d'accusation** charge; **chef d'entreprise** company head; **chef d'État** head of state; **chef de famille** head of the family; **chef de file** (de parti etc) leader; **chef de gare** station master; **chef d'orchestre** conductor; **chef-d'œuvre** nm masterpiece; **chef-lieu** nm county town

chemin [ʃ(ə)mɛ̃] nm path; (itinéraire, direction, trajet) way; **en ~** on the way; **chemin de fer** railway (BRIT), railroad (US)

cheminée [ʃ(ə)mine] nf chimney; (à l'intérieur) chimney piece, fireplace; (de bateau) funnel

chemise [ʃ(ə)miz] nf shirt; (dossier) folder; **chemise de nuit** nightdress

chemisier [ʃ(ə)mizje] nm blouse

chêne [ʃɛn] nm oak (tree); (bois) oak

chenil [ʃ(ə)nil] nm kennels pl

chenille [ʃ(ə)nij] nf (Zool) caterpillar

chèque [ʃɛk] nm cheque (BRIT), check (US); **est-ce que je peux payer par ~?** can I pay by cheque?; **chèque sans provision** bad cheque; **chèque de voyage** traveller's cheque; **chéquier** [ʃekje] nm cheque book

chic [ʃik] adj inv chic, smart; (fam:

cher, -ère [ʃɛr] adj (aimé) dear; (coûteux) expensive, dear ▷ adv: **ça coûte ~** it's expensive

chercher [ʃɛrʃe] vt to look for; (gloire etc) to seek; **aller ~** to go for, go and fetch; **~ à faire** to try to do; **chercheur, -euse** nm/f researcher, research worker

chéri, e [ʃeri] adj beloved, dear; **(mon) ~** darling

cheval, -aux [ʃ(ə)val, o] nm horse; (Auto): **~ (vapeur)** horsepower no pl; **faire du ~** to ride; **à ~** on horseback; **à ~ sur** astride; (fig) overlapping; **cheval de course** racehorse

chevalier [ʃ(ə)valje] nm knight

chevalière [ʃ(ə)valjɛr] nf signet ring

chevaux [ʃavo] nmpl de **cheval**

chevet [ʃ(ə)vɛ] nm: **au ~ de qn** at sb's bedside; **lampe de chevet** bedside lamp

cheveu, x [ʃ(ə)vø] nm hair; **cheveux** nmpl (chevelure) hair sg; **avoir les ~x courts** to have short hair

cheville [ʃ(ə)vij] nf (Anat) ankle; (de bois) peg; (pour une vis) plug

chèvre [ʃɛvr] nf (she-)goat

chèvrefeuille [ʃɛvrəfœj] nm honeysuckle

chevreuil [ʃavrœj] nm roe deer inv; (Culin) venison

🔵 **MOT-CLÉ**

chez [ʃe] prép **1** (à la demeure de) at; (: direction) to; **chez qn** at/to sb's house ou place; **je suis chez moi** I'm at home; **je rentre chez moi** I'm going home; **allons chez Nathalie** let's go to Nathalie's

2 (: profession) at; (: direction) to; **chez le boulanger/dentiste** at ou to the baker's/dentist's

3 (dans le caractère, l'œuvre de) in; **chez ce poète** in this poet's work; **c'est ce que je préfère chez lui** that's what I like best about him

généreux) nice, decent ▷ nm stylishness; **~ (alors)!** (fam) great!; **avoir le ~ de** to have the knack of

chicorée [ʃikɔre] nf (café) chicory; (salade) endive

chien [ʃjɛ̃] nm dog; **chien d'aveugle** guide dog; **chien de garde** guard dog

chienne [ʃjɛn] nf dog, bitch

chiffon [ʃifɔ̃] nm (piece of) rag; **chiffonner** vt to crumple; (fam: tracasser) to concern

chiffre [ʃifʀ] nm (représentant un nombre) figure, numeral; (montant, total) total, sum; **en ~s ronds** in round figures; **chiffre d'affaires** turnover; **chiffrer** vt (dépense) to put a figure to, assess; (message) to (en)code, cipher; **se chiffrer à** to add up to, amount to

chignon [ʃiɲɔ̃] nm chignon, bun

Chili [ʃili] nm: **le ~** Chile; **chilien, ne** adj Chilean ▷ nm/f: **Chilien, ne** Chilean

chimie [ʃimi] nf chemistry; **chimiothérapie** [ʃimjoterapi] nf chemotherapy; **chimique** adj chemical; **produits chimiques** chemicals

chimpanzé [ʃɛ̃pãze] nm chimpanzee

Chine [ʃin] nf: **la ~** China; **chinois, e** adj Chinese ▷ nm/f: **Chinois, e** Chinese ▷ nm (Ling) Chinese

chiot [ʃjo] nm pup(py)

chips [ʃips] nfpl crisps (BRIT), (potato) chips (US)

chirurgie [ʃiʀyʀʒi] nf surgery; **chirurgie esthétique** plastic surgery; **chirurgien, ne** nm/f surgeon

chlore [klɔʀ] nm chlorine

choc [ʃɔk] nm (heurt) impact, shock; (collision) crash; (moral) shock; (affrontement) clash

chocolat [ʃɔkɔla] nm chocolate; **chocolat au lait** milk chocolate

chœur [kœʀ] nm (chorale) choir; (Opéra, Théâtre) chorus; **en ~** in chorus

choisir [ʃwaziʀ] vt to choose, select

choix [ʃwa] nm choice, selection; **avoir le ~** to have the choice; **premier ~** (Comm) class one; **de ~** choice, selected;

au ~ as you wish

chômage [ʃomaʒ] nm unemployment; **mettre au ~** to make redundant, put out of work; **être au ~** to be unemployed ou out of work; **chômeur, -euse** nm/f unemployed person

choquer [ʃɔke] vt (offenser) to shock; (deuil) to shake

chorale [kɔʀal] nf choir

chose [ʃoz] nf thing; **c'est peu de ~** it's nothing (really)

chou, x [ʃu] nm cabbage; **mon petit ~** (my) sweetheart; **chou à la crème** choux bun; **chou de Bruxelles** Brussels sprout; **choucroute** nf sauerkraut

chouette [ʃwɛt] nf owl ▷ adj (fam) great, smashing

chou-fleur [ʃuflœʀ] nm cauliflower

chrétien, ne [kʀetjɛ̃, jɛn] adj, nm/f Christian

Christ [kʀist] nm: **le ~** Christ; **christianisme** nm Christianity

chronique [kʀɔnik] adj chronic ▷ nf (de journal) column, page; (historique) chronicle; (Radio, TV): **la ~ sportive** the sports review

chronologique [kʀɔnɔlɔʒik] adj chronological

chronomètre [kʀɔnɔmɛtʀ] nm stopwatch; **chronométrer** vt to time

chrysanthème [kʀizɑ̃tɛm] nm chrysanthemum

- **CHRYSANTHÈME**
-
- Chrysanthemums are strongly
- associated with funerals in France,
- and therefore should not be given
- as gifts.

chuchotement [ʃyʃɔtmã] nm whisper

chuchoter [ʃyʃɔte] vt, vi to whisper

chut [ʃyt] excl sh!

chute [ʃyt] nf (fait) (déchet) scrap; **faire une ~ (de 10 m)** to fall (10 m); **chute (d'eau)** waterfall; **chute libre** free fall; **chutes de pluie/neige** rainfall/ snowfall

Chypre [ʃipʀ] nm/f Cyprus

-ci [si] adv voir **par** ▷ dét: **ce garçon~** this boy; **ces femmes~** these women

cible [sibl] nf target

ciboulette [sibulɛt] nf (small) chive

cicatrice [sikatʀis] nf scar; **cicatriser** vt to heal

ci-contre [sikɔ̃tʀ] adv opposite

ci-dessous [sidəsu] adv below

ci-dessus [sidəsy] adv above

cidre [sidʀ] nm cider

Cie abr (= compagnie) Co.

ciel [sjɛl] nm sky; (Rel) heaven

cieux [sjø] nmpl de **ciel**

cigale [sigal] nf cicada

cigare [sigaʀ] nm cigar

cigarette [sigaʀɛt] nf cigarette

ci-inclus, e [siɛ̃kly, yz] adj, adv enclosed

ci-joint, e [siʒwɛ̃, ɛ̃t] adj, adv enclosed

cil [sil] nm (eye)lash

cime [sim] nf top; (montagne) peak

ciment [simɑ̃] nm cement

cimetière [simtjɛʀ] nm/f cemetery; (d'église) churchyard

cinéaste [sineast] nm/f film-maker

cinéma [sinema] nm cinema

cinq [sɛ̃k] num five; **cinquantaine** nf: **une cinquantaine (de)** about fifty; **avoir la cinquantaine** (âge) to be around fifty; **cinquante** num fifty; **cinquantenaire** adj, nm/f fifty-year-old; **cinquième** num fifth ▷ nf (Scol) year 8 (BRIT), seventh grade (US)

cintre [sɛ̃tʀ] nm coat-hanger

cintré, e [sɛ̃tʀe] adj (chemise) fitted

cirage [siʀaʒ] nm (shoe) polish

circonflexe [siʀkɔ̃flɛks] adj: **accent ~** circumflex accent

circonstance [siʀkɔ̃stɑ̃s] nf circumstance; (occasion) occasion; **circonstances atténuantes** mitigating circumstances

circuit [siʀkɥi] nm (Élec, Tech) circuit; (trajet) tour, (round) trip

circulaire [siʀkylɛʀ] adj, nf circular

circulation [siʀkylasjɔ̃] nf circulation; (Auto): **la ~** (the) traffic

circuler [siʀkyle] vi (sang, devises) to circulate; (véhicules) to drive (along); (passants) to walk along; (train, bus) to run; **faire ~** (nouvelle) to spread (about); circulate; (badauds) to move on

cire [siʀ] nf wax; **ciré** nm oilskin; **cirer** vt to wax, polish

cirque [siʀk] nm circus; (fig) chaos, bedlam; **quel ~!** what a carry-on!

ciseau, x [sizo] nm: **~ (à bois)** chisel; **ciseaux** nmpl (paire de ciseaux) (pair of) scissors

citadin, e [sitadɛ̃, in] nm/f city dweller

citation [sitasjɔ̃] nf (d'auteur) quotation; (Jur) summons sg

cité [site] nf town; (plus grande) city; **cité universitaire** students' residences pl

citer [site] vt (un auteur) to quote (from); (nommer) to name; (Jur) to summon

citoyen, ne [sitwajɛ̃, jɛn] nm/f citizen

citron [sitʀɔ̃] nm lemon; **citron pressé** (fresh) lemon juice; **citron vert** lime; **citronnade** nf still lemonade

citrouille [sitʀuj] nf pumpkin

civet [sivɛ] nm: **~ de lapin** rabbit stew

civière [sivjɛʀ] nf stretcher

civil, e [sivil] adj (mariage, poli) civil; (non militaire) civilian; **en ~** in civilian clothes; **dans le ~** in civilian life

civilisation [sivilizasjɔ̃] nf civilization

clair, e [klɛʀ] adj light; (pièce) light, bright; (eau, son, fig) clear ▷ adv: **voir ~** to see clearly; **tirer qch au ~** to clear sth up, clarify sth; **mettre au ~** (notes etc) to tidy up ▷ nm: **~ de lune** moonlight; **clairement** adv clearly

clairière [klɛʀjɛʀ] nf clearing

clandestin, e [klɑ̃dɛstɛ̃, in] adj clandestine, secret; (mouvement) underground; (travailleur, immigration) illegal; **passager ~** stowaway

claque [klak] nf (gifle) slap; **claquer** vi (porte) to bang, slam; (fam: mourir) to snuff it ▷ vt (porte) to slam, bang; (doigts) to snap; (fam: dépenser) to blow; **il claquait des dents** his teeth were chattering; **être claqué** (fam) to be dead tired; **se claquer un muscle** to pull *ou* strain a muscle; **claquettes** *nfpl* tap-dancing *sg*; (*chaussures*) flip-flops

clarinette [klaʀinɛt] *nf* clarinet

classe [klɑs] *nf* class; (Scol: *local*) class(room); (: *leçon, élèves*) class; **aller en ~** to go to school; **classement** *nm* (*rang*: Scol) place; (: *Sport*) placing; (*liste*: Scol) class list (in order of merit); (: *Sport*) placings *pl*

classer [klɑse] *vt* (*idées, livres*) to classify; (*papiers*) to file; (*candidat, concurrent*) to grade; (*Jur: affaire*) to close; **se ~ premier/dernier** to come first/last; (Sport) to finish first/last; **classeur** *nm* (*cahier*) file

classique [klasik] *adj* classical; (*sobre: coupe etc*) classic(al); (*habituel*) standard, classic

clavecin [klav(ə)sɛ̃] *nm* harpsichord

clavicule [klavikyl] *nf* collarbone

clavier [klavje] *nm* keyboard

clé [kle] *nf* key; (*Mus*) clef; (*de mécanicien*) spanner (BRIT), wrench (US); **prix ~s en main** (*d'une voiture*) on-the-road price; **clé de contact** ignition key; **clé USB** USB key

clef [kle] *nf* = **clé**

clergé [klɛʀʒe] *nm* clergy

cliché [kliʃe] *nm* (*fig*) cliché; (*négatif*) negative; (*photo*) print

client, e [klijɑ̃, klijɑ̃t] *nm/f* (*acheteur*) customer, client; (*d'hôtel*) guest, patron; (*du docteur*) patient; (*de l'avocat*) client; **clientèle** *nf* (*du magasin*) customers *pl*, clientèle; (*du docteur, de l'avocat*) practice

cligner [kliɲe] *vi*: **~ des yeux** to blink (one's eyes); **~ de l'œil** to wink; **clignotant** *nm* (*Auto*) indicator; **clignoter** *vi* (*étoiles etc*) to twinkle; (*lumière*) to flicker

climat [klima] *nm* climate

climatisation [klimatizasjɔ̃] *nf* air conditioning; **climatisé, e** *adj* air-conditioned

clin d'œil [klɛ̃dœj] *nm* wink; **en un clin d'œil** in a flash

clinique [klinik] *nf* private hospital

clip [klip] *nm* (*boucle d'oreille*) clip-on; **(vidéo) ~** (pop) video

cliquer [klike] *vt* to click; **~ sur** to click on

clochard, e [klɔʃaʀ, aʀd] *nm/f* tramp

cloche [klɔʃ] *nf* (*d'église*) bell; (*fam*) clot; **clocher** *nm* church tower; (*en pointe*) steeple ▷ *vi* (*fam*) to go *ou* go wrong; **de clocher** (*péj*) parochial

cloison [klwazɔ̃] *nf* partition (wall)

clonage [klɔnaʒ] *nm* cloning

cloner [klɔne] *vt* to clone

cloque [klɔk] *nf* blister

clore [klɔʀ] *vt* to close

clôture [klotyʀ] *nf* closure; (*barrière*) enclosure

clou [klu] *nm* nail; **clous** *nmpl* (*passage clouté*) pedestrian crossing; **pneus à ~s** studded tyres; **le ~ du spectacle** the highlight of the show; **clou de girofle** clove

clown [klun] *nm* clown

club [klœb] *nm* club

CNRS *sigle m* (= Centre nationale de la recherche scientifique) ≈ SERC (BRIT), ≈ NSF (US)

coaguler [kɔagyle] *vt, vi* (*aussi: se ~*: *sang*) to coagulate

cobaye [kɔbaj] *nm* guinea-pig

coca [kɔka] *nm* Coke®

cocaïne [kɔkain] *nf* cocaine

coccinelle [kɔksinɛl] *nf* ladybird (BRIT), ladybug (US)

cocher [kɔʃe] *vt* to tick off

cochon, ne [kɔʃɔ̃, ɔn] *nm* pig ▷ *adj* (*fam*) dirty, smutty; **cochon d'Inde** guinea pig; **cochonnerie** (*fam*) *nf* (*saleté*) filth; (*marchandise*) rubbish, trash

cocktail [kɔktɛl] *nm* cocktail; (*réception*) cocktail party

cocorico [kɔkɔriko] *excl, nm* cock-a-doodle-do

cocotte [kɔkɔt] *nf* (*en fonte*) casserole; **ma ~** (*fam*) sweetie (*pie*); **cocotte (minute)®** pressure cooker

code [kɔd] *nm* code ▷ *adj*: **phares ~s** dipped lights; **se mettre en ~(s)**

one's (head)lights; **code à barres** bar code; **code de la route** highway code; **code pénal** penal code; **code postal** (numéro) post ou zip (US) code

cœur [kœr] nm heart; (Cartes: couleur) hearts pl; (: carte) heart; **avoir bon ~** to be kind-hearted; **avoir mal au ~** to feel sick; **par ~** by heart; **de bon ~** willingly; **cela lui tient à ~** that's (very) close to his heart

coffre [kɔfr] nm (meuble) chest; (d'auto) boot (BRIT), trunk (US); **coffre-fort** nm safe; **coffret** nm casket

cognac [kɔɲak] nm brandy, cognac

cogner [kɔɲe] vi to knock; **se ~ contre** to knock ou bump into; **se ~ la tête** to bang one's head

cohérent, e [kɔerã, ãt] adj coherent, consistent

coiffé, e [kwafe] adj: **bien/mal ~** with tidy/untidy hair; **~ d'un chapeau** wearing a hat

coiffer [kwafe] vt (fig: surmonter) to cover, top; **se coiffer** vi to do one's hair; **~ qn** to do sb's hair; **coiffeur, -euse** nm/f hairdresser; **coiffeuse** nf (table) dressing table; **coiffure** nf (cheveux) hairstyle, hairdo; (art): **la coiffure** hairdressing

coin [kwɛ̃] nm corner; (pour coincer) wedge; **l'épicerie du ~** the local grocer; **dans le ~** (aux alentours) in the area, around about; (habiter) locally; **je ne suis pas du ~** I'm not from here; **au ~ du feu** by the fireside; **regard en ~** sideways glance

coincé, e [kwɛ̃se] adj stuck, jammed; (fig: inhibé) inhibited, hung up (fam)

coïncidence [kɔɛ̃sidãs] nf coincidence

coing [kwɛ̃] nm quince

col [kɔl] nm (de chemise) collar; (encolure, cou) neck; (de montagne) pass; **col de l'utérus** cervix; **col roulé** polo-neck

colère [kɔlɛr] nf anger; **une ~** a fit of anger; **(se mettre) en ~** (contre qn) (to get) angry (with sb); **coléreux, -euse, colérique** adj quick-tempered,

irascible

colin [kɔlɛ̃] nm hake

colique [kɔlik] nf diarrhoea

colis [kɔli] nm parcel

collaborer [kɔ(l)labɔre] vi to collaborate; **~ à** to collaborate on; (revue) to contribute to

collant, e [kɔlã, ãt] adj sticky; (robe etc) clinging, skintight; (péj) clinging ▷ nm (bas) tights pl; (de danseur) leotard

colle [kɔl] nf glue; (à papiers peints) (wallpaper) paste; (fam: devinette) teaser, riddle; (Scol: fam) detention

collecte [kɔlɛkt] nf collection; **collectif, -ive** adj collective; (visite, billet) group cp

collection [kɔlɛksjɔ̃] nf collection; (Édition) series; **collectionner** vt to collect; **collectionneur, -euse** nm/f collector

collectivité [kɔlɛktivite] nf group; **collectivités locales** (Admin) local authorities

collège [kɔlɛʒ] nm (école) (secondary) school; (assemblée) body; **collégien** nm schoolboy

collègue [kɔ(l)lɛg] nm/f colleague

coller [kɔle] vt (papier, timbre) to stick (on); (affiche) to stick up; (enveloppe) to stick down; (morceaux) to stick ou glue together; (Comput) to paste; (fam: mettre, fourrer) to stick, shove; (Scol: fam) to keep in ▷ vi (être collant) to be sticky; (adhérer) to stick; **~ à** to stick to; **être collé à un examen** (fam) to fail an exam

collier [kɔlje] nm (bijou) necklace; (de chien, Tech) collar

colline [kɔlin] nf hill

collision [kɔlizjɔ̃] nf collision, crash; **entrer en ~ (avec)** to collide (with)

collyre [kɔlir] nm eye drops

colombe [kɔlɔ̃b] nf dove

Colombie [kɔlɔ̃bi] nf: **la ~** Colombia

colonie [kɔlɔni] nf colony; **colonie (de vacances)** holiday camp (for children)

colonne [kɔlɔn] nf column; **se mettre en ~ par deux** to get into twos;

colonne (vertébrale) spine, spinal column

colorant [kɔlɔʀɑ̃] nm colouring

colorer [kɔlɔʀe] vt to colour (in)

colorier [kɔlɔʀje] vt to colour (in)

coloris [kɔlɔʀi] nm colour, shade

colza [kɔlza] nm rape(seed)

coma [kɔma] nm coma; être dans le ~ to be in a coma

combat [kɔ̃ba] nm fight, fighting no pl; combat de boxe boxing match; combattant nm: ancien combattant war veteran; combattre vt to fight; (épidémie, ignorance) to combat, fight against

combien [kɔ̃bjɛ̃] adv (quantité) how much; (nombre) how many; ~ de (quantité) how much; (nombre) how many; ~ de temps how long; ~ ça coûte/pèse? how much does it cost/ weigh?; on est le ~ aujourd'hui? (fam) what's the date today?

combinaison [kɔ̃binɛzɔ̃] nf combination; (astuce) scheme; (de femme) slip; (de plongée) wetsuit; (bleu de travail) boiler suit (BRIT), coveralls pl (US)

combiné [kɔ̃bine] nm (aussi: ~ téléphonique) receiver

comble [kɔ̃bl] adj (salle) packed (full) ▷ nm (du bonheur, plaisir) height; combles nmpl (Constr) attic rooms sg, loft sg; c'est le ~! that beats everything!

combler [kɔ̃ble] vt (trou) to fill in; (besoin, lacune) to fill; (déficit) to make good; (satisfaire) to fulfil

comédie [kɔmedi] nf comedy; (fig) playacting no pl; faire la ~ (fam) to make a fuss; comédie musicale musical; comédien, ne nm/f actor(-tress)

comestible [kɔmɛstibl] adj edible

comique [kɔmik] adj (drôle) comical; (Théâtre) comic ▷ nm (artiste) comic, comedian

commandant [kɔmɑ̃dɑ̃] nm (gén) commander, commandant; (Navig, Aviat) captain

commande [kɔmɑ̃d] nf (Comm)

order; commandes nfpl (Aviat etc) controls; sur ~ to order; commander vt (Comm) to order; (diriger, ordonner) to command; commander à qn de faire to command ou order sb to do; je peux commander, s'il vous plaît? can I order, please?

🔵 MOT-CLÉ

comme [kɔm] prép 1 (comparaison) like; tout comme son père just like his father; fort comme un bœuf as strong as an ox; joli comme tout ever so pretty

2 (manière) like; faites-le comme ça do it like this, do it this way; comme ci, comme ça so-so, middling; comme il faut (correctement) properly

3 (en tant que) as; donner comme prix to give as a prize; travailler comme secrétaire to work as a secretary

▷ conj 1 (ainsi que) as; elle écrit comme elle parle she writes as she talks; comme si as if

2 (au moment où, alors que) as; il est parti comme j'arrivais he left as I arrived

3 (parce que, puisque) as; comme il était en retard, il ... as he was late, he ...

▷ adv: comme il est fort/c'est bon! he's so strong/it's so good!

commencement [kɔmɑ̃smɑ̃] nm beginning, start

commencer [kɔmɑ̃se] vt, vi to begin, start; ~ à ou de faire to begin ou start doing

comment [kɔmɑ̃] adv how; ~? (que dites-vous) pardon?; et ~! and how!

commentaire [kɔmɑ̃tɛʀ] nm (remarque) comment, remark; (exposé) commentary

commerçant, e [kɔmɛʀsɑ̃, ɑ̃t] nm/f shopkeeper, trader

commerce [kɔmɛʀs] nm (activité) trade, commerce; (boutique) business; ~ électronique e-commerce; ~

équitable fair trade; **commercial, e, -aux** adj commercial, trading; (péj) commercial; **les commerciaux** the sales people; **commercialiser** vt to market

commissaire [kɔmisɛʀ] nm (de police) ≈ (police) superintendent; **commissaire aux comptes** (Admin) auditor; **commissariat** nm police station

commission [kɔmisjɔ̃] nf (comité, pourcentage) commission; (message) message; (course) errand; **commissions** nfpl (achats) shopping sg

commode [kɔmɔd] adj (pratique) convenient, handy; (facile) easy; (personne) **pas ~** awkward (to deal with) ▷ nf chest of drawers

commun, e [kɔmœ̃, yn] adj common; (pièce) communal, shared; (effort) joint; **ça sort du ~** it's out of the ordinary; **le ~ des mortels** the common run of people; **en ~** (faire) jointly; **mettre en ~** to pool, share; **communs** nmpl (bâtiments) outbuildings; **d'un ~ accord** by mutual agreement

communauté [kɔmynote] nf community

commune [kɔmyn] nf (Admin) commune, ≈ district; (: urbaine) ≈ borough

communication [kɔmynikasjɔ̃] nf communication

communier [kɔmynje] vi (Rel) to receive communion

communion [kɔmynjɔ̃] nf communion

communiquer [kɔmynike] vt (nouvelle, dossier) to pass on, convey; (peur etc) to communicate ▷ vi to communicate; **se communiquer à** (se propager) to spread to

communisme [kɔmynism] nm communism; **communiste** adj, nm/f communist

commutateur [kɔmytatœʀ] nm (Élec) (change-over) switch, commutator

compact, e [kɔ̃pakt] adj (dense) dense;

(appareil) compact

compagne [kɔ̃paɲ] nf companion

compagnie [kɔ̃paɲi] nf (firme, Mil) company; **tenir ~ à qn** to keep sb company; **fausser ~ à qn** to give sb the slip, slip ou sneak away from sb; **compagnie aérienne** airline (company)

compagnon [kɔ̃paɲɔ̃] nm companion

comparable [kɔ̃paʀabl] adj: **~ (à)** comparable (to)

comparaison [kɔ̃paʀɛzɔ̃] nf comparison

comparer [kɔ̃paʀe] vt to compare; **~ qch/qn à** ou **et** (pour choisir) to compare sth/sb with ou and; (pour établir une similitude) to compare sth/sb to

compartiment [kɔ̃paʀtimɑ̃] nm compartment; **un ~ non-fumeurs** a non-smoking compartment (BRIT) ou car (US)

compas [kɔ̃pa] nm (Géom) (pair of) compasses pl; (Navig) compass

compatible [kɔ̃patibl] adj compatible

compatriote [kɔ̃patʀijɔt] nm/f compatriot

compensation [kɔ̃pɑ̃sasjɔ̃] nf compensation

compenser [kɔ̃pɑ̃se] vt to compensate for, make up for

compétence [kɔ̃petɑ̃s] nf competence

compétent, e [kɔ̃petɑ̃, ɑ̃t] adj (apte) competent, capable

compétition [kɔ̃petisjɔ̃] nf (gén) competition; (Sport: épreuve) event; **la ~ automobile** motor racing

complément [kɔ̃plemɑ̃] nm complement; (reste) remainder; **complément d'information** (Admin) supplementary ou further information; **complémentaire** adj complementary; (additionnel) supplementary

complet, -ète [kɔ̃plɛ, ɛt] adj complete; (plein: hôtel etc) full ▷ nm (aussi: **~-veston**) suit; **pain complet** wholemeal bread; **complètement** adv completely; **compléter** vt (porter à la quantité voulue) to complete;

(*augmenter: connaissances, études*) to complement, supplement; (: *garde-robe*) to add to

complexe [kɔ̃plɛks] *adj, nm* complex; **complexe hospitalier/industriel** hospital/industrial complex; **complexé, e** *adj* mixed-up, hung-up

complication [kɔ̃plikasjɔ̃] *nf* complexity, intricacy; (*difficulté, ennui*) complication; **complications** *nfpl* (*Méd*) complications

complice [kɔ̃plis] *nm* accomplice

compliment [kɔ̃plimɑ̃] *nm* (*louange*) compliment; **compliments** *nmpl* (*félicitations*) congratulations

compliqué, e [kɔ̃plike] *adj* complicated, complex; (*personne*) complicated

comportement [kɔ̃pɔrtəmɑ̃] *nm* behaviour

comporter [kɔ̃pɔrte] *vt* (*consister en*) to consist of, comprise; (*inclure*) to have; **se comporter** *vi* to behave

composer [kɔ̃poze] *vt* (*musique, texte*) to compose; (*mélange, équipe*) to make up; (*numéro*) to dial; (*constituer*) to make up, form ▷ *vi* (*transiger*) to come to terms; **se composer de** to be composed of, be made up of; **compositeur, -trice** *nm/f* (*Mus*) composer; **composition** *nf* composition; (*Scol*) test

composter [kɔ̃pɔste] *vt* (*billet*) to punch

● **COMPOSTER**
●
● In France you have to punch your
● ticket on the platform to validate it
● before getting onto the train.

compote [kɔ̃pɔt] *nf* stewed fruit *no pl*; **compote de pommes** stewed apples

compréhensible [kɔ̃preɑ̃sibl] *adj* comprehensible; (*attitude*) understandable

compréhensif, -ive [kɔ̃preɑ̃sif, iv] *adj* understanding

▌ Attention à ne pas traduire *compréhensif* par *comprehensive*.

comprendre [kɔ̃prɑ̃dr] *vt* to understand; (*se composer de*) to comprise, consist of

compresse [kɔ̃prɛs] *nf* compress

comprimé [kɔ̃prime] *nm* tablet

compris, e [kɔ̃pri, iz] *pp de* **comprendre** ▷ *adj* (*inclus*) included; **~ entre** (*situé*) contained between; **l'électricité -e/non ~e, y/non ~ l'électricité** electricity included/excluding electricity; **100 euros tout ~** = 100 euros all inclusive ou all-in

comptabilité [kɔ̃tabilite] *nf* (*activité*) accounting, accountancy; (*comptes*) accounts *pl*, books *pl*; (*service*) accounts office

comptable [kɔ̃tabl] *nm/f* accountant

comptant [kɔ̃tɑ̃] *adv*: **payer ~** to pay cash; **acheter ~** to buy for cash

compte [kɔ̃t] *nm* count; (*total, montant*) count, (right) number; (*bancaire, facture*) account; **comptes** *nmpl* (Finance) accounts, books; (*fig*) explanation *sg*; **en fin de ~** all things considered; **s'en tirer à bon ~** to get off lightly; **pour le ~ de** on behalf of; **pour son propre ~** for one's own benefit; **régler un ~** (*s'acquitter de qch*) to settle an account; (*se venger*) to get one's own back; **rendre ~s à qn** (*fig*) to be answerable to sb; **tenir ~ de** to take account of; **travailler à son ~** to work for oneself; **rendre ~ (à qn) de qch** to give (sb) an account of sth; *voir aussi* **rendre**; **compte à rebours** countdown; **compte courant** current account; **compte rendu** account, report; (*de film, livre*) review; **compte-gouttes** *nm inv* dropper

compter [kɔ̃te] *vt* to count; (*facturer*) to charge for; (*avoir à son actif, comporter*) to have; (*prévoir*) to allow, reckon; (*penser, espérer*): **~ réussir** to expect to succeed ▷ *vi* to count; (*être économe*) to economize; (*figurer*): **~ parmi** to be ou rank among; **~ sur** to count (up)on;

~ avec qch/qn to reckon with *ou* take account of sth/sb; **sans ~ que** besides which

compteur [kɔ̃tœʀ] *nm* meter; **compteur de vitesse** speedometer

comptine [kɔ̃tin] *nf* nursery rhyme

comptoir [kɔ̃twaʀ] *nm* (*de magasin*) counter; (*bar*) bar

con, ne [kɔ̃, kɔn] (*fam!*) *adj* damned *ou* bloody (BRIT) stupid (!)

concentrer [kɔ̃sɑ̃tʀe] *vt* to concentrate; **se concentrer** *vi* to concentrate

concerner [kɔ̃sɛʀne] *vt* to concern; **en ce qui me concerne** as far as I am concerned

concert [kɔ̃sɛʀ] *nm* concert; **de ~** (*décider*) unanimously

concessionnaire [kɔ̃sesjɔnɛʀ] *nm/f* agent, dealer

concevoir [kɔ̃s(ə)vwaʀ] *vt* (*idée, projet*) to conceive of; (*comprendre*) to understand; (*enfant*) to conceive; **bien/mal conçu** well-/badly-designed

concierge [kɔ̃sjɛʀʒ] *nm/f* caretaker

concis, e [kɔ̃si, iz] *adj* concise

conclure [kɔ̃klyʀ] *vt* to conclude; **conclusion** *nf* conclusion

conçois *etc* [kɔ̃swa] *vb voir* **concevoir**

concombre [kɔ̃kɔ̃bʀ] *nm* cucumber

concours [kɔ̃kuʀ] *nm* competition; (*Scol*) competitive examination; (*assistance*) aid, help; **concours de circonstances** combination of circumstances; **concours hippique** horse show

concret, -ète [kɔ̃kʀɛ, ɛt] *adj* concrete

conçu, e [kɔ̃sy] *pp de* **concevoir**

concubinage [kɔ̃kybinaʒ] *nm* (*Jur*) cohabitation

concurrence [kɔ̃kyʀɑ̃s] *nf* competition; **faire ~ à** to be in competition with; **jusqu'à ~ de** up to

concurrent, e [kɔ̃kyʀɑ̃, ɑ̃t] *nm/f* (*Sport, Écon etc*) competitor; (*Scol*) candidate

condamner [kɔ̃dane] *vt* (*blâmer*) to condemn; (*Jur*) to sentence; (*porte,*

ouverture) to fill in, block up; **~ qn à 2 ans de prison** to sentence sb to 2 years' imprisonment

condensation [kɔ̃dɑ̃sasjɔ̃] *nf* condensation

condition [kɔ̃disjɔ̃] *nf* condition; **conditions** *nfpl* (*tarif, prix*) terms; (*circonstances*) conditions; **sans ~s** unconditionally; **à ~ de ou que** provided that; **conditionnel, le** *nm* conditional (tense)

conditionnement [kɔ̃disjɔnmɑ̃] *nm* (*emballage*) packaging

condoléances [kɔ̃dɔleɑ̃s] *nfpl* condolences

conducteur, -trice [kɔ̃dyktœʀ, tʀis] *nm/f* driver ▷ *nm* (*Élec etc*) conductor

conduire [kɔ̃dɥiʀ] *vt* to drive; (*délégation, troupeau*) to lead; **se conduire** *vi* to behave; **~ vers/à** to lead to; **~ qn quelque part** to take sb somewhere; to drive sb somewhere

conduite [kɔ̃dɥit] *nf* (*comportement*) behaviour; (*d'eau, de gaz*) pipe; **sous la ~ de** led by

confection [kɔ̃fɛksjɔ̃] *nf* (*fabrication*) making; (*Couture*): **la ~** the clothing industry

confesser [kɔ̃fese] *vt* to confess; **confession** *nf* confession; (*culte: catholique etc*) denomination

confetti [kɔ̃feti] *nm* confetti *no pl*

confiance [kɔ̃fjɑ̃s] *nf* (*en l'honnêteté de qn*) confidence, trust; (*en la valeur de qch*) faith; **avoir ~ en** to have confidence *ou* faith in, trust; **faire ~ à qn** to trust sb; **mettre qn en ~** to win sb's trust; **confiance en soi** self-confidence

confiant, e [kɔ̃fjɑ̃, jɑ̃t] *adj* confident; trusting

confidence [kɔ̃fidɑ̃s] *nf* confidence; **confidentiel, le** *adj* confidential

confier [kɔ̃fje] *vt*: **~ à qn** (*objet, travail*) to entrust to sb; (*secret, pensée*) to

confide to sb; **se ~ à qn** to confide in sb
confirmation[kɔ̃firmasjɔ̃] nf
confirmation
confirmer[kɔ̃firme] vt to confirm
confiserie[kɔ̃fizri] nf (magasin)
confectioner's ou sweet shop;
confiseries nfpl (bonbons)
confectionery sg
confisquer[kɔ̃fiske] vt to confiscate
confit, e[kɔ̃fi, it] adj: **fruits ~s**
crystallized fruits; **confit d'oie** nm
conserve of goose
confiture[kɔ̃fityr] nf jam
conflit[kɔ̃fli] nm conflict
confondre[kɔ̃fɔ̃dr] vt (jumeaux, faits)
to confuse, mix up; (témoin, menteur) to
confound; **se confondre** vi to merge;
se ~ en excuses to apologize profusely
conforme[kɔ̃form] adj: **~ à** (loi, règle)
in accordance with; **conformément**
adv: **conformément à** in accordance
with; **conformer** vt: **se conformer à**
to conform to
confort[kɔ̃fɔr] nm comfort; **tout ~**
(Comm) with all modern conveniences;
confortable adj comfortable
confronter[kɔ̃frɔ̃te] vt to confront
confus, e[kɔ̃fy, yz] adj (vague)
confused; (embarrassé) embarrassed;
confusion nf (voir confus) confusion;
embarrassment; (voir confondre)
confusion, mixing up
congé[kɔ̃ʒe] nm (vacances) holiday; **en
~** on holiday; **semaine/jour de ~** week/
day off; **prendre ~ de qn** to take one's
leave of sb; **donner son ~ à** to give in
one's notice to; **congé de maladie** sick
leave; **congé de maternité** maternity
leave; **congés payés** paid holiday
congédier[kɔ̃ʒedje] vt to dismiss
congélateur[kɔ̃ʒelatœr] nm freezer
congeler[kɔ̃ʒ(ə)le] vt to freeze; **les
produits congelés** frozen foods
congestion[kɔ̃ʒɛstjɔ̃] nf congestion
Congo[kɔ̃go] nm: **le ~** Congo, the
Democratic Republic of the Congo
congrès[kɔ̃grɛ] nm congress
conifère[kɔnifɛr] nm conifer

conjoint, e[kɔ̃ʒwɛ̃, wɛ̃t] adj joint
▷ nm/f spouse
conjonctivite[kɔ̃ʒɔ̃ktivit] nf
conjunctivitis
conjoncture[kɔ̃ʒɔ̃ktyr] nf
circumstances pl; **la ~ actuelle** the
present (economic) situation
conjugaison[kɔ̃ʒygɛzɔ̃] nf (Ling)
conjugation
connaissance[kɔnɛsɑ̃s] nf (savoir)
knowledge no pl; (personne connue)
acquaintance; **être sans ~** to be
unconscious; **perdre/reprendre ~** to
lose/regain consciousness; **à ma/sa
~** to (the best of) my/his knowledge;
faire la ~ de qn to meet sb
connaisseur, -euse[kɔnɛsœr, øz]
nm/f connoisseur
connaître[kɔnɛtr] vt to know;
(éprouver) to experience; (avoir: succès)
to have, enjoy; **~ de nom/vue** to know
by name/sight; **ils se sont connus à
Genève** they (first) met in Geneva; **s'y
~ en qch** to know a lot about sth
connecter[kɔnɛkte] vt to connect; **se
~ à Internet** to log onto the Internet
connerie[kɔnri] (fam!) nf stupid thing
(to do/say)
connexion[kɔnɛksjɔ̃] nf connection
connu, e[kɔny] adj (célèbre) well-
known
conquérir[kɔ̃kerir] vt to conquer;
conquête nf conquest
consacrer[kɔ̃sakre] vt (employer) to
devote, dedicate; (Rel) to consecrate; **se
~ à qch** to dedicate ou devote o.s. to sth
conscience[kɔ̃sjɑ̃s] nf conscience;
(perception) consciousness;
avoir/prendre ~ de to be/become
aware of; **perdre ~** to lose
consciousness; **avoir bonne/
mauvaise ~** to have a clear/guilty
conscience; **consciencieux, -euse**
adj conscientious; **conscient, e** adj
conscious
consécutif, -ive[kɔ̃sekytif, iv] adj
consecutive; **~ à** following upon
conseil[kɔ̃sej] nm (avis) piece of
advice; (assemblée) council; **des ~s**

advice; **prendre ~ (auprès de qn)** to take advice (from sb); **conseil d'administration** board (of directors); **conseil des ministres** = the Cabinet; **conseil municipal** town council

conseiller, -ère [kɔ̃seje, ɛʀ] nm/f adviser ▷ vt (personne) to advise; (méthode, action) to recommend, advise; **~ à qn de** to advise sb to; **pouvez-vous me ~ un bon restaurant?** can you suggest a good restaurant?

consentement [kɔ̃sɑ̃tmɑ̃] nm consent

consentir [kɔ̃sɑ̃tiʀ] vt to agree, consent

conséquence [kɔ̃sekɑ̃s] nf consequence; **en ~** (donc) consequently; (de façon appropriée) accordingly; **conséquent, e** adj logical, rational; (fam: important) substantial; **par conséquent** consequently

conservateur, -trice [kɔ̃sɛʀvatœʀ, tʀis] nm/f (Pol) conservative; (de musée) curator ▷ nm (pour aliments) preservative

conservatoire [kɔ̃sɛʀvatwaʀ] nm academy

conserve [kɔ̃sɛʀv] nf (gén pl) canned ou tinned (BRIT) food; **~** canned, tinned (BRIT)

conserver [kɔ̃sɛʀve] vt (faculté) to retain, keep; (amis, livres) to keep; (préserver, Culin) to preserve

considérable [kɔ̃sideʀabl] adj considerable, significant, extensive

considération [kɔ̃sideʀasjɔ̃] nf consideration; (estime) esteem

considérer [kɔ̃sideʀe] vt to consider; **~ qch comme** to regard sth as

consigne [kɔ̃siɲ] nf (de gare) left luggage (office) (BRIT), checkroom (US); (ordre, instruction) instructions pl; **consigne automatique** left-luggage locker

consister [kɔ̃siste] vi: **~ en/à faire** to consist of/in doing

consoler [kɔ̃sɔle] vt to console

consommateur, -trice [kɔ̃sɔmatœʀ, tʀis] nm/f (Écon) consumer; (dans un café) customer

consommation [kɔ̃sɔmasjɔ̃] nf (boisson) drink; (Écon) consumption; **de ~** (biens, sociétés) consumer cpd

consommer [kɔ̃sɔme] vt (suj: personne) to eat ou drink, consume; (: voiture, machine) to use, consume; (mariage) to consummate ▷ vi (dans un café) to (have a) drink

consonne [kɔ̃sɔn] nf consonant

constamment [kɔ̃stamɑ̃] adv constantly

constant, e [kɔ̃stɑ̃, ɑ̃t] adj constant; (personne) steadfast

constat [kɔ̃sta] nm (de police, d'accident) report; **~ (à l')amiable** jointly-agreed statement for insurance purposes; **~ d'échec** acknowledgement of failure

constatation [kɔ̃statasjɔ̃] nf (observation) (observed) fact, observation

constater [kɔ̃state] vt (remarquer) to note; (Admin, Jur: attester) to certify

consterner [kɔ̃stɛʀne] vt to dismay

constipé, e [kɔ̃stipe] adj constipated

constitué, e [kɔ̃stitɥe] adj: **~ de** made up ou composed of

constituer [kɔ̃stitɥe] vt (équipe) to set up; (dossier, collection) to put together; (suj: éléments: composer) to make up, constitute; (représenter, être) to constitute; **se ~ prisonnier** to give o.s. up

constructeur, -trice [kɔ̃stʀyktœʀ, tʀis] nm/f manufacturer, builder

constructif, -ive [kɔ̃stʀyktif, iv] adj constructive

construction [kɔ̃stʀyksjɔ̃] nf construction, building

construire [kɔ̃stʀɥiʀ] vt to build, construct

consul [kɔ̃syl] nm consul; **consulat** nm consulate

consultant [kɔ̃syltɑ̃] adj, nm consultant

consultation [kɔ̃syltasjɔ̃] nf consultation; **heures de ~** (Méd)

consulter | 56

surgery (BRIT) ou office (US) hours
consulter [kɔ̃sylte] vt to consult ▷ vi
(médecin) to hold surgery (BRIT), be in
(the office) (US)

contact [kɔ̃takt] nm contact; **au ~
de** (air, peau) on contact with; (gens)
through contact with; **mettre/
couper le ~** (Auto) to switch on/off
the ignition; **entrer en ou prendre
~ avec** to get in touch ou into contact
with; **contacter** vt to contact, get in
touch with

contagieux, -euse [kɔ̃taʒjø, jøz] adj
infectious; (par le contact) contagious

contaminer [kɔ̃tamine] vt to
contaminate

conte [kɔ̃t] nm tale; **conte de fées**
fairy tale

contempler [kɔ̃tɑ̃ple] vt to
contemplate, gaze at

contemporain, e [kɔ̃tɑ̃pɔʀɛ̃, ɛn] adj,
nm/f contemporary

contenir [kɔ̃t(ə)niʀ] vt to contain;
(avoir une capacité de) to hold

content, e [kɔ̃tɑ̃, ɑ̃t] adj pleased, glad;
~ de pleased with; **contenter** vt to
satisfy, please; **se contenter de** to
content o.s. with

contenu [kɔ̃t(ə)ny] nm (d'un récipient)
contents pl; (d'un texte) content

conter [kɔ̃te] vt to recount, relate

conteste [kɔ̃tɛst]: **sans ~** adv
unquestionably, indisputably;
contester vt to question ▷ vi (Pol, gén)
rebel (against established authority)

contexte [kɔ̃tɛkst] nm context

continent [kɔ̃tinɑ̃] nm continent

continu, e [kɔ̃tiny] adj continuous;
faire la journée ~e to work without
taking a full lunch break; **(courant)
continu** direct current, DC

continuel, le [kɔ̃tinɥɛl] adj (qui se
répète) constant, continual; (continu)
continuous

continuer [kɔ̃tinɥe] vt (travail, voyage
etc) to continue (with), carry on (with),
go on (with); (prolonger: alignement, rue)
to continue ▷ vi (vie, bruit) to continue,

go on; **~ à ou de faire** to go on ou
continue doing

contourner [kɔ̃tuʀne] vt to go round;
(difficulté) to get round

contraceptif, -ive [kɔ̃tʀaseptif, iv]
adj, nm contraceptive; **contraception**
nf contraception

contracté, e [kɔ̃tʀakte] adj tense

contracter [kɔ̃tʀakte] vt (muscle etc)
to tense, contract; (maladie, dette) to
contract; (assurance) to take out; **se
contracter** vi (muscles) to contract

contractuel, le [kɔ̃tʀaktɥɛl] nm/f
(agent) traffic warden

contradiction [kɔ̃tʀadiksjɔ̃] nf
contradiction; **contradictoire** adj
contradictory, conflicting

contraignant, e [kɔ̃tʀɛɲɑ̃, ɑ̃t] adj
restricting

contraindre [kɔ̃tʀɛ̃dʀ] vt: **~ qn à
faire** to compel sb to do; **contrainte**
nf constraint

contraire [kɔ̃tʀɛʀ] adj, nm opposite; **~
à** contrary to; **au ~** on the contrary

contrarier [kɔ̃tʀaʀje] vt (personne:
irriter) to annoy; (fig: projets) to thwart,
frustrate; **contrariété** nf annoyance

contraste [kɔ̃tʀast] nm contrast

contrat [kɔ̃tʀa] nm contract

contravention [kɔ̃tʀavɑ̃sjɔ̃] nf
parking ticket

contre [kɔ̃tʀ] prép against; (en échange)
(in exchange) for; **par ~** on the other
hand

contrebande [kɔ̃tʀəbɑ̃d] nf (trafic)
contraband, smuggling; (marchandise)
contraband, smuggled goods pl; **faire
la ~ de** to smuggle

contrebas [kɔ̃tʀəba]: **en ~** adv (down)
below

contrebasse [kɔ̃tʀəbas] nf (double)
bass

contre...: **contrecoup** nm
repercussions pl; **contredire** vt
(personne) to contradict; (faits) to refute
contrefaçon [kɔ̃tʀəfasɔ̃] nf forgery
contre-...: **contre-indication** (pl
contre-indications) nf (Méd) contra-

indication; **"contre-indication en cas d'eczéma"** "should not be used by people with eczema"; **contre-indiqué, e** adj (Méd) contraindicated; (déconseillé) unadvisable, ill-advised
contremaître [kɔ̃trəmɛtr] nm foreman
contre-plaqué [kɔ̃trəplake] nm plywood
contresens [kɔ̃trəsɑ̃s] nm (erreur) misinterpretation; (de traduction) mistranslation; **à ~** the wrong way
contretemps [kɔ̃trətɑ̃] nm hitch; **à ~** (fig) at an inopportune moment
contribuer [kɔ̃tribɥe]: **~ à** vt to contribute towards; **contribution** nf contribution; **mettre à contribution** to call upon; **contributions directes/ indirectes** direct/indirect taxation
contrôle [kɔ̃trol] nm checking no pl, check; (des prix) monitoring, control; (test) test, examination; **perdre le ~ de** (véhicule) to lose control of; **contrôle continu** (Scol) continuous assessment; **contrôle d'identité** identity check
contrôler [kɔ̃trole] vt (vérifier) to check; (surveiller: opérations) to supervise; (: prix) to monitor, control; (maîtriser, Comm: firme) to control; **contrôleur, -euse** nm/f (de train) (ticket) inspector; (de bus) (bus) conductor(-tress)
controversé, e [kɔ̃trɔvɛrse] adj (personnage, question) controversial
contusion [kɔ̃tyzjɔ̃] nf bruise, contusion
convaincre [kɔ̃vɛ̃kr] vt: **~ qn (de qch)** to convince sb (of sth); **~ qn (de faire)** to persuade sb (to do)
convalescence [kɔ̃valesɑ̃s] nf convalescence
convenable [kɔ̃vnabl] adj suitable; (assez bon, respectable) decent
convenir [kɔ̃vnir] vi to be suitable; **~ à** to suit; **~ de** (bien-fondé de qch) to acknowledge; (date, somme etc) to agree upon; **~ que** (admettre) to admit that; **~ de faire** to agree to do

convention [kɔ̃vɑ̃sjɔ̃] nf convention; **conventions** nfpl (convenances) conventions sg; **convention collective** (Écon) collective agreement; **conventionné, e** adj (Admin) applying charges laid down by the state
convenu, e [kɔ̃vny] pp de **convenir** ▷ adj agreed
conversation [kɔ̃vɛrsasjɔ̃] nf conversation
convertir [kɔ̃vɛrtir] vt: **~ qn (à)** to convert sb (to); **se convertir (à)** to be converted (to); **~ qch en** to convert sth into
conviction [kɔ̃viksjɔ̃] nf conviction
convienne etc [kɔ̃vjɛn] vb voir **convenir**
convivial, e, -aux [kɔ̃vivjal, jo] adj (Inform) user-friendly
convocation [kɔ̃vɔkasjɔ̃] nf (document) notification to attend; (: Jur) summons sg
convoquer [kɔ̃vɔke] vt (assemblée) to convene; (subordonné) to summon; (candidat) to ask to attend
coopération [kɔɔperasjɔ̃] nf co-operation; (Admin): **la C~** = Voluntary Service Overseas (BRIT), = Peace Corps (US)
coopérer [kɔɔpere] vi: **~ (à)** to co-operate (in)
coordonné, e [kɔɔrdɔne] adj coordinated; **coordonnées** nfpl (adresse etc) address and telephone number
coordonner [kɔɔrdɔne] vt to coordinate
copain [kɔpɛ̃] (fam) nm mate, pal; (petit ami) boyfriend
copie [kɔpi] nf copy; (Scol) script, paper; **copier** vt, vi to copy; **copier coller** (Comput) copy and paste; **copier sur** to copy from; **copieur** nm (photo)copier
copieux, -euse [kɔpjø, jøz] adj copious
copine [kɔpin] (fam) nf mate, pal; (petite amie) girlfriend
coq [kɔk] nm cock, rooster

coque [kɔk] nf (de noix, mollusque) shell; (de bateau) hull; **à la ~** (Culin) (soft-)boiled

coquelicot [kɔkliko] nm poppy

coqueluche [kɔklyʃ] nf whooping-cough

coquet, te [kɔkε, εt] adj appearance-conscious; (logement) smart, charming

coquetier [kɔk(ə)tje] nm egg-cup

coquillage [kɔkijaʒ] nm (mollusque) shellfish inv; (coquille) shell

coquille [kɔkij] nf shell; (Typo) misprint; **coquille St Jacques** scallop

coquin, e [kɔkε̃, in] adj mischievous, roguish; (polisson) naughty

cor [kɔr] nm (Mus) horn; (Méd): **~ (au pied)** corn

corail, -aux [kɔraj, o] nm coral no pl

Coran [kɔrɑ̃] nm: **le ~** the Koran

corbeau, x [kɔrbo] nm crow

corbeille [kɔrbεj] nf basket; **corbeille à papier** waste paper basket ou bin

corde [kɔrd] nf rope; (de violon, raquette) string; **usé jusqu'à la ~** threadbare; **corde à linge** washing ou clothes line; **corde à sauter** skipping rope; **cordes vocales** vocal cords; **cordée** nf (d'alpinistes) rope, roped party

cordialement [kɔrdjalmɑ̃] adv (formule épistolaire) (kind) regards

cordon [kɔrdɔ̃] nm cord, string; **cordon de police** police cordon; **cordon ombilical** umbilical cord

cordonnerie [kɔrdɔnri] nf shoe repairer's (shop); **cordonnier** nm shoe repairer

Corée [kɔre] nf: **la ~ du Sud/du Nord** South/North Korea

coriace [kɔrjas] adj tough

corne [kɔrn] nf horn; (de cerf) antler

cornée [kɔrne] nf cornea

corneille [kɔrnεj] nf crow

cornemuse [kɔrnəmyz] nf bagpipes pl

cornet [kɔrnε] nm (paper) cone; (de glace) cornet, cone

corniche [kɔrniʃ] nf (route) coast road

cornichon [kɔrniʃɔ̃] nm gherkin

Cornouailles [kɔrnwaj] nf Cornwall

corporel, le [kɔrpɔrεl] adj bodily; (punition) corporal

corps [kɔr] nm body; **à ~ perdu** headlong; **prendre ~** to take shape; **corps électoral** the electorate; **corps enseignant** the teaching profession

correct, e [kɔrεkt] adj correct; (fam: acceptable: salaire, hôtel) reasonable, decent; **correcteur, -trice** nm/f (Scol) examiner; **correction** nf (voir corriger) correction; (voir correct) correctness; (coups) thrashing

correspondance [kɔrεspɔ̃dɑ̃s] nf correspondence; (de train, d'avion) connection; **cours par ~** correspondence course; **vente par ~** mail-order business

correspondant, e [kɔrεspɔ̃dɑ̃, ɑ̃t] nm/f correspondent; (Tél) person phoning (ou being phoned)

correspondre [kɔrεspɔ̃dr] vi to correspond, tally; **~ à** to correspond to; **~ avec qn** to correspond with sb

corrida [kɔrida] nf bullfight

corridor [kɔridɔr] nm corridor

corrigé [kɔriʒe] nm (Scol: d'exercice) correct version

corriger [kɔriʒe] vt (devoir) to correct; (punir) to thrash; **~ qn de** (défaut) to cure sb of

corrompre [kɔrɔ̃pr] vt to corrupt; (acheter: témoin etc) to bribe

corruption [kɔrypsjɔ̃] nf corruption; (de témoins) bribery

corse [kɔrs] adj, nm/f Corsican ▷ nf: **la C~** Corsica

corsé, e [kɔrse] adj (café) full-flavoured; (sauce) spicy; (problème) tough

cortège [kɔrtεʒ] nm procession

cortisone [kɔrtizɔn] nf cortisone

corvée [kɔrve] nf chore, drudgery no pl

cosmétique [kɔsmetik] nm beauty care product

cosmopolite [kɔsmɔpɔlit] adj cosmopolitan

costaud, e [kɔsto, od] (fam) adj strong, sturdy

costume [kɔstym] nm (d'homme) suit; (de théâtre) costume; **costumé, e** adj dressed up; **bal costumé** fancy dress ball

cote [kɔt] nf (en Bourse) quotation; **cote d'alerte** danger ou flood level; **cote de popularité** (popularity) rating

côte [kot] nf (rivage) coast(line); (pente) hill; (Anat) rib; (d'un tricot, tissu) rib, ribbing no pl; **à ~ side by side;** **la Côte (d'Azur)** the (French) Riviera

côté [kote] nm (gén) side; (direction) way, direction; **de chaque ~ (de)** on each side (of); **de tous les ~s** from all directions; **de quel ~ est-il parti?** which way did he go?; **de ce/de l'autre ~** this/the other way; **du ~ de** (provenance) from; (direction) towards; (proximité) near; **de** (regarder) sideways; **mettre qch de ~** to put sth aside; **mettre de l'argent de ~** to save some money; **à ~** (right) nearby; (voisins) next door; **à ~ de** beside, next to; (en comparaison) compared to; **être aux ~s de** to be by the side of

Côte d'Ivoire [kotdivwaʀ] nf: **la Côte d'Ivoire** Côte d'Ivoire, the Ivory Coast

côtelette [kotlɛt] nf chop

côtier, -ière [kotje, jɛʀ] adj coastal

cotisation [kɔtizasjɔ̃] nf subscription, dues pl; (pour une pension) contributions pl

cotiser [kɔtize] vi: **~ (à)** to pay contributions (to); **se cotiser** vi to club together

coton [kɔtɔ̃] nm cotton; **coton hydrophile** cotton wool (BRIT), absorbent cotton (US); **Coton-tige®** nm cotton bud

cou [ku] nm neck

couchant [kuʃɑ̃] adj: **soleil ~** setting sun

couche [kuʃ] nf layer; (de peinture, vernis) coat; (de bébé) nappy (BRIT), diaper (US); **couches sociales** social levels ou strata

couché, e [kuʃe] adj lying down; (au lit) in bed

coucher [kuʃe] vt (enfant) to put to bed; (: loger) to put up; (objet) to lay on its side ▷ vi to sleep; **~ avec qn** to sleep with sb; **se coucher** vi (pour dormir) to go to bed; (pour se reposer) to lie down; (soleil) to set; **coucher de soleil** sunset

couchette [kuʃɛt] nf couchette; (pour voyageur, sur bateau) berth

coucou [kuku] nm cuckoo

coude [kud] nm (Anat) elbow; (de tuyau, de la route) bend; **~ à ~** shoulder to shoulder, side by side

coudre [kudʀ] vt (bouton) to sew on ▷ vi to sew

couette [kwɛt] nf duvet, quilt; **couettes** nfpl (cheveux) bunches

couffin [kufɛ̃] nm Moses basket

couler [kule] vi to flow, run; (fuir: stylo, récipient) to leak; (nez) to run; (sombrer: bateau) to sink ▷ vt (cloche, sculpture) to cast; (bateau) to sink; (faire échouer: personne) to bring down

couleur [kulœʀ] nf colour (BRIT), color (US); (Cartes) suit; **film/télévision en ~** colo(u)r film/television; **de ~** (homme, femme: vieilli) colo(u)red

couleuvre [kulœvʀ] nf grass snake

coulisses [kulis] nfpl (Théâtre) wings; (fig): **dans les ~** behind the scenes

couloir [kulwaʀ] nm corridor, passage; (d'avion) aisle; (de bus) gangway; **~ aérien/de navigation** air/shipping lane

coup [ku] nm (heurt, choc) knock; (affectif) blow, shock; (agressif) blow; (avec arme à feu) shot; (de l'horloge) stroke; (tennis, golf) stroke; (boxe) blow; (fam: fois) time; **donner un ~ de balai** to give the floor a quick sweep; **boire un ~** (fam) to have a drink; **être dans le ~** (impliqué) to be in on it; (à la page) to be hip ou trendy; **du ~ ...** as a result; **d'un seul ~** (subitement) suddenly; (à la fois) at one go; **du premier ~** first time; **du même ~** at the same time; **à tous les ~s** (fam) every time; **tenir le ~** to hold out; **après ~** afterwards; **à ~ sûr** definitely, without fail; **~ sur** in

quick succession; **sur le ~** outright;
sous le ~ de (surprise etc) under the
influence of; **coup de chance** stroke
of luck; **coup de coude** nudge (with
the elbow); **coup de couteau** stab (of
a knife); **coup d'envoi** kick-off; **coup
d'essai** first attempt; **coup d'État**
coup; **coup de feu** shot; **coup de filet**
(Police) haul; **coup de foudre** (fig) love
at first sight; **coup de frein** (sharp)
braking no pl; **coup de grâce** coup
de grâce, death blow; **coup de main**:
donner un coup de main à qn to give
sb a (helping) hand; **coup d'œil** glance;
coup de pied kick; **coup de poing**
punch; **coup de soleil** sunburn no pl;
coup de sonnette ring of the bell;
coup de téléphone phone call; **coup
de tête** (fig) (sudden) impulse; **coup de
théâtre** (fig) dramatic turn of events;
coup de tonnerre clap of thunder;
coup de vent gust of wind; **en coup
de vent** (rapidement) in a tearing hurry;
coup franc free kick

coupable [kupabl] adj guilty ▷ nm/f
(gén) culprit; (Jur) guilty party

coupe [kup] nf (verre) goblet; (à
fruits) dish; (Sport) cup; (de cheveux, de
vêtement) cut; (graphique, plan) (cross)
section

couper [kupe] vt to cut; (retrancher)
to cut (out); (route, courant) to cut off;
(appétit) to take away; (vin à table) to
dilute ▷ vi to cut; (prendre un raccourci)
to take a short-cut; **se couper** vi (se
blesser) to cut o.s.; **~ la parole à qn** to
cut sb short; **nous avons été coupés**
we've been cut off

couple [kupl] nm couple

couplet [kuplɛ] nm verse

coupole [kupɔl] nf dome

coupon [kupɔ̃] nm (ticket) coupon;
(reste de tissu) remnant

coupure [kupyʀ] nf cut; (billet de
banque) note; (de journal) cutting;
coupure de courant power cut

cour [kuʀ] nf (de ferme, jardin)
(court)yard; (d'immeuble) back yard; (Jur,

royale) court; **faire la ~ à qn** to court sb;
cour d'assises court of assizes; **cour
de récréation** playground

courage [kuʀaʒ] nm courage,
bravery; **courageux, -euse** adj brave,
courageous

couramment [kuʀamɑ̃] adv
commonly; (parler) fluently

courant, e [kuʀɑ̃, ɑ̃t] adj (fréquent)
common; (Comm, gén: normal) standard;
(en cours) current ▷ nm current; (fig)
(opinion) trend; **être
au ~ (de)** (fait, nouvelle) to know
(about); **mettre qn au ~ (de)** to tell sb
(about); (nouveau travail etc) to teach
sb the basics (of); **se tenir au ~ (de)**
(techniques etc) to keep o.s. up-to-date
(on); **dans le ~ (de)** (pendant) in the
course of; **le 10 ~** (Comm) the 10th
inst.; **courant d'air** draught; **courant
électrique** (electric) current, power

courbature [kuʀbatyʀ] nf ache

courbe [kuʀb] adj curved ▷ nf curve

coureur, -euse [kuʀœʀ, øz]
nm/f (Sport) runner (ou driver); (péj)
womanizer/manhunter

courge [kuʀʒ] nf (Culin) marrow;
courgette nf courgette (BRIT),
zucchini (US)

courir [kuʀiʀ] vi to run ▷ vt (Sport:
épreuve) to compete in; (risque) to run;
(danger) to face; **~ les magasins** to go
round the shops; **le bruit court que** the
rumour is going round that

couronne [kuʀɔn] nf crown; (de fleurs)
wreath, circlet

courons etc [kuʀɔ̃] vb voir **courir**

courriel [kuʀjɛl] nm e-mail

courrier [kuʀje] nm mail, post; (lettres
à écrire) letters pl; **est-ce que j'ai du ~?**
are there any letters for me?; **courrier
électronique** e-mail

> ⚠ Attention à ne pas traduire **courrier**
> par le mot anglais **courier**.

courroie [kuʀwa] nf strap; (Tech) belt

courrons etc [kuʀɔ̃] vb voir **courir**

cours [kuʀ] nm (leçon) class;
(: particulier) lesson; (série de leçons,

cheminement) course; *(écoulement)* flow; *(Comm: de devises)* rate; *(: de denrées)* price; **donner libre ~ à** to give free expression to; **avoir ~** *(Scol)* to have a class ou lecture; **en ~** *(année)* current; *(travaux)* in progress; **en ~ de route** on the way; **au ~ de** in the course of, during; **le ~ de change** the exchange rate; **cours d'eau** waterway; **cours du soir** night school

course [kuʀs] *nf* running; *(Sport: épreuve)* race; *(d'un taxi)* journey, trip; *(commission)* errand; **courses** *nfpl (achats)* shopping *sg;* **faire des ~s** to do some shopping

court, e [kuʀ, kuʀt(ə)] *adj* short ▷ *adv* short ▷ *nm:* **~ (de tennis)** (tennis) court; **à ~ de** short of; **prendre qn de ~** to catch sb unawares; **court-circuit** *nm* short-circuit

courtoisie [kuʀtwazi] *nf* courtesy

couru, e [kuʀy] *pp de* **courir**

cousais *etc* [kuze] *vb voir* **coudre**

couscous [kuskus] *nm* couscous

cousin, e [kuzɛ̃, in] *nm/f* cousin

coussin [kusɛ̃] *nm* cushion

cousu, e [kuzy] *pp de* **coudre**

coût [ku] *nm* cost; **le ~ de la vie** the cost of living

couteau, x [kuto] *nm* knife

coûter [kute] *vt, vi* to cost; **combien ça coûte?** how much is it?, what does it cost? **ça coûte trop cher** it's too expensive; **coûte que coûte** at all costs; **coûteux, -euse** *adj* costly, expensive

coutume [kutym] *nf* custom

couture [kutyʀ] *nf* sewing; *(profession)* dressmaking; *(points)* seam; **couturier** *nm* fashion designer; **couturière** *nf* dressmaker

couvent [kuvɑ̃] *nm (de sœurs)* convent; *(de frères)* monastery

couver [kuve] *vt* to hatch; *(maladie)* to be coming down with ▷ *vi (feu)* to smoulder; *(révolte)* to be brewing

couvercle [kuvɛʀkl] *nm* lid; *(de bombe aérosol etc, qui se visse)* cap, top

couvert, e [kuvɛʀ, ɛʀt] *pp de* **couvrir** ▷ *adj (ciel)* overcast ▷ *nm* place setting; *(place à table)* place; **couverts** *nmpl (ustensiles)* cutlery *sg;* **~ de** covered with ou in; **mettre le ~** to lay the table

couverture [kuvɛʀtyʀ] *nf* blanket; *(de livre, assurance, fig)* cover; *(presse)* coverage

couvre-lit [kuvʀəli] *nm* bedspread

couvrir [kuvʀiʀ] *vt* to cover; **se couvrir** *vi (s'habiller)* to cover up; *(se coiffer)* to put on one's hat; *(ciel)* to cloud over

cow-boy [koboj] *nm* cowboy

crabe [kʀab] *nm* crab

cracher [kʀaʃe] *vi, vt* to spit

crachin [kʀaʃɛ̃] *nm* drizzle

craie [kʀɛ] *nf* chalk

craindre [kʀɛ̃dʀ] *vt* to fear, be afraid of; *(être sensible à: chaleur, froid)* to be easily damaged by

crainte [kʀɛ̃t] *nf* fear; **de ~ de/que** for fear of/that; **craintif, -ive** *adj* timid

crampe [kʀɑ̃p] *nf* cramp; **j'ai une ~ à la jambe** I've got cramp in my leg

cramponner [kʀɑ̃pɔne] *vt:* **se ~ (à)** to hang ou cling on (to)

cran [kʀɑ̃] *nm (entaille)* notch; *(de courroie)* hole; *(fam: courage)* guts *pl*

crâne [kʀɑn] *nm* skull

crapaud [kʀapo] *nm* toad

craquement [kʀakmɑ̃] *nm* crack, snap; *(du plancher)* creak, creaking *no pl*

craquer [kʀake] *vi (bois, plancher)* to creak; *(fil, branche)* to snap; *(couture)* to come apart; *(fig: accusé)* to break down; *(: fam)* to crack up ▷ *vt (allumette)* to strike; **j'ai craqué** *(fam)* I couldn't resist it

crasse [kʀas] *nf* grime, filth; **crasseux, -euse** *adj* grimy, filthy

cravache [kʀavaʃ] *nf (riding)* crop

cravate [kʀavat] *nf* tie

crawl [kʀol] *nm* crawl; **dos ~é** backstroke

crayon [kʀɛjɔ̃] *nm* pencil; **crayon à bille** ball-point pen; **crayon de couleur** crayon, colouring pencil; **crayon-feutre** *(pl* **crayons-feutres)**

création [kreasjɔ̃] nf creation

crèche [krɛʃ] nf (de Noël) crib; (garderie) crèche, day nursery

crédit [kredi] nm (gén) credit; **crédits** nmpl (fonds) funds; **payer/acheter à ~** to pay/buy on credit ou on easy terms; **faire ~ à qn** to give sb credit; **créditer** vt: **créditer un compte (de)** to credit an account (with)

créer [kree] vt to create

crémaillère [kremajɛʀ] nf: **pendre la ~** to have a house-warming party

crème [kʀɛm] nf cream; (entremets) cream dessert ▷ adj inv cream(-coloured); **un (café) ~** = a white coffee; **crème anglaise** (egg) custard; **crème Chantilly** whipped cream; **crème à raser** shaving cream; **crème solaire** suntan lotion

créneau, x [kʀeno] nm (de fortification) crenel(le); (dans marché) gap, niche; (Auto): **faire un ~** to reverse into a parking space (between two cars alongside the kerb)

crêpe [kʀɛp] nf (galette) pancake ▷ nm (tissu) crêpe; **crêperie** nf pancake shop ou restaurant

crépuscule [kʀepyskyl] nm twilight, dusk

cresson [kʀesɔ̃] nm watercress

creuser [kʀøze] vt (trou, tunnel) to dig; (sol) to dig a hole in; (fig) to go (deeply) into; **ça creuse** that gives you a real appetite; **se ~ la cervelle** (fam) to rack one's brains

creux, -euse [kʀø, kʀøz] adj hollow ▷ nm hollow; **heures creuses** slack periods; (électricité, téléphone) off-peak periods; **avoir un ~** (fam) to be hungry

crevaison [kʀəvɛzɔ̃] nf puncture

crevé, e [kʀəve] (fam) adj (fatigué) shattered (BRIT), exhausted

crever [kʀəve] vt (ballon) to burst ▷ vi (pneu) to burst; (automobiliste) to have a puncture (BRIT) ou a flat (tire) (US); (fam) to die

crevette [kʀəvɛt] nf: **~ (rose)** prawn;

~ grise shrimp

cri [kʀi] nm cry, shout; (d'animal: spécifique) cry, call; **c'est le dernier ~** (fig) it's the latest fashion

criard, e [kʀijaʀ, kʀijaʀd] adj (couleur) garish, loud; (voix) yelling

cric [kʀik] nm (Auto) jack

crier [kʀije] vi (pour appeler) to shout, cry (out); (de douleur etc) to scream, yell ▷ vt (injure) to shout (out), yell (out)

crime [kʀim] nm crime; (meurtre) murder; **criminel, le** nm/f criminal; (assassin) murderer

crin [kʀɛ̃] nm (de cheval) hair no pl

crinière [kʀinjɛʀ] nf mane

crique [kʀik] nf creek, inlet

criquet [kʀikɛ] nm grasshopper

crise [kʀiz] nf (Méd) attack; (: d'épilepsie) fit; **piquer une ~ de nerfs** to go hysterical; **crise cardiaque** heart attack; **crise de foie**: **avoir une crise de foie** to have really bad indigestion

cristal, -aux [kristal, o] nm crystal

critère [kʀitɛʀ] nm criterion

critiquable [kʀitikabl] adj open to criticism

critique [kʀitik] adj critical ▷ nm/f (de théâtre, musique) critic ▷ nf criticism; (Théâtre etc: article) review

critiquer [kʀitike] vt (dénigrer) to criticize; (évaluer) to assess, examine (critically)

croate [kʀɔat] adj Croatian ▷ nm/f: **C~** Croat, Croatian

Croatie [kʀɔasi] nf: **la ~** Croatia

crochet [kʀɔʃɛ] nm hook; (détour) detour; (Tricot: aiguille) crochet hook; (: technique) crochet; **vivre aux ~s de qn** to live ou sponge off sb

crocodile [kʀɔkɔdil] nm crocodile

croire [kʀwaʀ] vt to believe; **se ~ fort** to think one is strong; **~ que** to believe ou think that; **~ à, ~ en** to believe in

croisade [kʀwazad] nf crusade

croisement [kʀwazmã] nm (carrefour) crossroads sg; (Bio) crossing; (: résultat) crossbreed

croiser [kʀwaze] vt (personne, voiture)

to pass; (route) to cross, cut across; (Bio) to cross; **se croiser** vi (personnes, véhicules) to pass each other; (routes, lettres) to cross; (regards) to meet; **~ les jambes/bras** to cross one's legs/fold one's arms

croisière [kʀwazjɛʀ] nf cruise

croissance [kʀwasɑ̃s] nf growth

croissant [kʀwasɑ̃] nm (à manger) croissant; (motif) crescent

croître [kʀwatʀ] vi to grow

croix [kʀwa] nf cross; **la Croix Rouge** the Red Cross

croque-monsieur [kʀɔkməsjø] nm inv toasted ham and cheese sandwich

croquer [kʀɔke] vt (manger) to crunch; (: fruit) to munch; (dessiner) to sketch; **chocolat à croquer** plain dessert chocolate

croquis [kʀɔki] nm sketch

crotte [kʀɔt] nf droppings pl; **crottin** nm dung, manure; (fromage) (small round) cheese (made of goat's milk)

croustillant, e [kʀustijɑ̃, ɑ̃t] adj crisp

croûte [kʀut] nf crust; (du fromage) rind; (Méd) scab; **en ~** (Culin) in pastry

croûton [kʀutɔ̃] nm (Culin) crouton; (bout du pain) crust, heel

croyant, e [kʀwajɑ̃, ɑ̃t] nm/f believer

CRS sigle fpl (= Compagnies républicaines de sécurité) state security police force ▷ sigle m member of the CRS

cru, e [kʀy] pp de **croire** ▷ adj (non cuit) raw; (lumière, couleur) harsh; (paroles) crude ▷ nm (vignoble) vineyard; (vin) wine; **un grand ~** a great vintage; **jambon ~** Parma ham

crû [kʀy] pp de **croître**

cruauté [kʀyote] nf cruelty

cruche [kʀyʃ] nf pitcher, jug

crucifix [kʀysifi] nm crucifix

crudités [kʀydite] nfpl (Culin) selection of raw vegetables

crue [kʀy] nf (inondation) flood

cruel, le [kʀyɛl] adj cruel

crus etc [kʀy] vb voir **croire; croître**

crûs etc [kʀy] vb voir **croître**

crustacés [kʀystase] nmpl shellfish

Cuba [kyba] nf Cuba; **cubain, e** adj Cuban ▷ nm/f: **Cubain, e** Cuban

cube [kyb] nm cube; (jouet) brick; **mètre ~** cubic metre; **2 au ~** 2 cubed

cueillette [kœjɛt] nf picking; (quantité) crop, harvest

cueillir [kœjiʀ] vt (fruits, fleurs) to pick, gather; (fig) to catch

cuiller [kɥijɛʀ], **cuillère** [kɥijɛʀ] nf spoon; **cuiller à café** coffee spoon; (Culin) ≈ teaspoonful; **cuiller à soupe** soup-spoon; (Culin) ≈ tablespoonful; **cuillerée** nf spoonful

cuir [kɥiʀ] nm leather; **cuir chevelu** scalp

cuire [kɥiʀ] vt (aliments) to cook; (au four) to bake ▷ vi to cook; **bien cuit** (viande) well done; **trop cuit** overdone

cuisine [kɥizin] nf (pièce) kitchen; (art culinaire) cookery, cooking; (nourriture) cooking, food; **faire la ~** to cook; **cuisiné, e** adj: **plat cuisiné** ready-made meal ou dish; **cuisiner** vt to cook; (fam) to grill ▷ vi to cook; **cuisinier, -ière** nm/f cook; **cuisinière** nf (poêle) cooker

cuisse [kɥis] nf thigh; (Culin) leg

cuisson [kɥisɔ̃] nf cooking

cuit, e [kɥi, kɥit] pp de **cuire**

cuivre [kɥivʀ] nm copper; **les cuivres** (Mus) the brass

cul [ky] nm (fam!) arse ø!

culminant, e [kylminɑ̃, ɑ̃t] adj: **point ~** highest point

culot [kylo] nm (fam) nm (effronterie) cheek

culotte [kylɔt] nf (de femme) knickers pl (BRIT), panties pl

culte [kylt] nm (religion) religion; (hommage, vénération) worship; (protestant) service

cultivateur, -trice [kyltivatœʀ, tʀis] nm/f farmer

cultivé, e [kyltive] adj (personne) cultured, cultivated

cultiver [kyltive] vt to cultivate; (légumes) to grow, cultivate

culture [kyltyʀ] nf cultivation; (connaissances etc) culture; **les ~s**

intensives intensive farming; **culture physique** physical training; **culturel, le** *adj* cultural

cumin [kymɛ̃] *nm* cumin

cure [kyʀ] *nf* (*Méd*) course of treatment; **cure d'amaigrissement** slimming (*BRIT*) *ou* weight-loss (*US*) course; **cure de repos** rest cure

curé [kyʀe] *nm* parish priest

cure-dent [kyʀdɑ̃] *nm* toothpick

curieux, -euse [kyʀjø, jøz] *adj* (*indiscret*) curious, inquisitive; (*étrange*) strange, curious ▷ *nmpl* (*badauds*) onlookers; **curiosité** *nf* curiosity; (*site*) unusual feature

curriculum vitae [kyʀikylɔmvite] *nm inv* curriculum vitae

cutané, e [kytane] *adj* skin

cuve [kyv] *nf* vat; (*à mazout etc*) tank

cuvée [kyve] *nf* vintage

cuvette [kyvɛt] *nf* (*récipient*) bowl, basin; (*Géo*) basin

CV *sigle m* (*Auto*) = **cheval vapeur**; (*Comm*) = **curriculum vitae**

cybercafé [sibɛʀkafe] *nm* Internet café

cyberespace [sibɛʀɛspas] *nm* cyberspace

cybernaute [sibɛʀnot] *nm/f* Internet user

cyclable [siklabl] *adj*: **piste ~** cycle track

cycle [sikl] *nm* cycle; **cyclisme** *nm* cycling; **cycliste** *nm/f* cyclist ▷ *adj* cycle *cpd*; **coureur cycliste** racing cyclist

cyclomoteur [siklomotœʀ] *nm* moped

cyclone [siklon] *nm* hurricane

cygne [siɲ] *nm* swan

cylindre [silɛ̃dʀ] *nm* cylinder; **cylindrée** *nf* (*Auto*) (cubic) capacity; **une (voiture de) grosse cylindrée** a big-engined car

cymbale [sɛ̃bal] *nf* cymbal

cynique [sinik] *adj* cynical

cystite [sistit] *nf* cystitis

d

d' [d] *prép voir* **de**

dactylo [daktilo] *nf* (*aussi*: **~graphe**) typist; (*aussi*: **~graphie**) typing

dada [dada] *nm* hobby-horse

daim [dɛ̃] *nm* (*fallow*) deer *inv*; (*cuir suédé*) suede

daltonien, ne [daltɔnjɛ̃, jɛn] *adj* colour-blind

dame [dam] *nf* lady; (*Cartes, Échecs*) queen; **dames** *nfpl* (*jeu*) draughts *sg* (*BRIT*), checkers *sg* (*US*)

Danemark [danmaʀk] *nm* Denmark

danger [dɑ̃ʒe] *nm* danger; **être en ~** (*personne*) to be in danger; **mettre en ~** (*personne*) to put in danger; (*projet, carrière*) to jeopardize; **dangereux, -euse** *adj* dangerous

danois, e [danwa, waz] *adj* Danish ▷ *nm/f*: **D~, e** Dane ▷ *nm* (*Ling*) Danish

 MOT-CLÉ

dans [dɑ̃] *prép* 1 (*position*) in; (*à l'intérieur de*) inside; **c'est dans le tiroir/le salon**

it's in the drawer/lounge; **dans la boîte** in *ou* inside the box; **je l'ai lu dans le journal** I read it in the newspaper; **marcher dans la ville** to walk about the town

2 (*direction*) into; **elle a couru dans le salon** she ran into the lounge; **monter dans une voiture/le bus** to get into a car/on to the bus

3 (*provenance*) out of, from; **je l'ai pris dans le tiroir/salon** I took it out of *ou* from the drawer/lounge; **boire dans un verre** to drink out of *ou* from a glass

4 (*temps*) in; **dans 2 mois** in 2 months, in 2 months' time

5 (*approximation*) about; **dans les 20 euros** about 20 euros

danse [dɑ̃s] *nf*: **la ~** dancing; **une ~** a dance; **la ~ classique** ballet; **danser** *vi, vt* to dance; **danseur, -euse** *nm/f* ballet dancer; (*au bal etc*) dancer; (: *cavalier*) partner

date [dat] *nf* date; **de longue ~** longstanding; **date de naissance** date of birth; **date limite** deadline; **dater** *vt, vi* to date; **dater de** to date from; **à dater de** (as) from

datte [dat] *nf* date

dauphin [dofɛ̃] *nm* (*Zool*) dolphin

davantage [davɑ̃taʒ] *adv* more; (*plus longtemps*) longer; **~ de** more

⬤ MOT-CLÉ

de, d' [də] (*de +le* = **du**, *de +les* = **des**) *prép*

1 (*appartenance*) of; **le toit de la maison** the roof of the house; **la voiture d'Ann/de mes parents** Ann's/my parents' car

2 (*provenance*) from; **il vient de Londres** he comes from London; **elle est sortie du cinéma** she came out of the cinema

3 (*caractérisation, mesure*): **un mur de brique/bureau/acajou** a brick wall/ mahogany desk; **un billet de 50 euros** a 50 euro note; **une pièce de 2 m de long** *ou* **large de 2 m** a room 2m wide,

a 2m-wide room; **un bébé de 10 mois** a 10-month-old baby; **12 mois de crédit/ travail** 12 months' credit/work; **être payé 20 euros de l'heure** to be paid 20 euros an *ou* per hour; **augmenter de 10 euros** to increase by 10 euros; **de 14 à 18** from 14 to 18

4 (*moyen*) with; **je l'ai fait de mes propres mains** I did it with my own two hands

5 (*cause*): **mourir de faim** to die of hunger; **rouge de colère** red with fury

6 (*devant infinitif*) to; **il m'a dit de rester** he told me to stay

▷ *dét* **1** (*phrases affirmatives*) some (*souvent omis*): **du vin, de l'eau, des pommes** (some) wine, (some) water, (some) apples; **des enfants sont venus** some children came; **pendant des mois** for months

2 (*phrases interrogatives et négatives*) any; **a-t-il du vin?** has he got any wine?; **il n'a pas de pommes/d'enfants** he hasn't (got) any apples/children, he has no apples/children

dé [de] *nm* (*à jouer*) die *ou* dice; (*aussi*: **dé à coudre**) thimble

déballer [debale] *vt* to unpack

débarcadère [debaʁkadɛʁ] *nm* wharf

débardeur [debaʁdœʁ] *nm* (*maillot*) tank top

débarquer [debaʁke] *vt* to unload, land ▷ *vi* to disembark; (*fig: fam*) to turn up

débarras [debaʁɑ] *nm* (*pièce*) lumber room; (*placard*) junk cupboard; **bon ~!** good riddance!; **débarrasser** *vt* to clear; **se débarrasser de** *vt* to get rid of; **débarrasser qn de** (*vêtements, paquets*) to relieve sb of; **débarrasser (la table)** to clear the table

débat [deba] *nm* discussion, debate; **débattre** *vt* to discuss, debate; **se débattre** *vi* to struggle

débit [debi] *nm* (*d'un liquide, fleuve*) flow; (*d'un magasin*) turnover (of goods); (*élocution*) delivery; (*bancaire*) debit; **débit de boissons** drinking establishment; **débit de tabac** tobacconist's

déblayer [debleje] vt to clear

débloquer [debloke] vt (prix, crédits) to free

déboîter [debwate] vt (Auto) to pull out; **se ~ le genou** etc to dislocate one's knee etc

débordé, e [deborde] adj: **être ~ (de)** (travail, demandes) to be snowed under (with)

déborder [deborde] vi to overflow; (lait etc) to boil over: **~ (de) qch** (dépasser) to extend beyond sth; **~ de** (joie, zèle) to be brimming over with ou bursting with

débouché [debuʃe] nm (pour vendre) outlet; (perspective d'emploi) opening

déboucher [debuʃe] vt (évier, tuyau etc) to unblock; (bouteille) to uncork ▷ vi: **~ de** to emerge from; **~ sur** (études) to lead on to

debout [d(ə)bu] adv: **être ~** (personne) to be standing, stand; (: levé, éveillé) to be up; **se mettre ~** to stand up; **se tenir ~** to stand; **~! I** stand up!; (du lit) get up!; **cette histoire ne tient pas ~** this story doesn't hold water

déboutonner [debutone] vt to undo, unbutton

débraillé, e [debraje] adj slovenly, untidy

débrancher [debrãʃe] vt to disconnect; (appareil électrique) to unplug

débrayage [debrɛjaʒ] nm (Auto) clutch; **débrayer** vi (Auto) to declutch; (cesser le travail) to stop work

débris [debri] nmpl fragments; **des ~ de verre** bits of glass

débrouillard, e [debrujar, ard] (fam) adj smart, resourceful

débrouiller [debruje] vt to disentangle, untangle; **se débrouiller** vi to manage; **débrouillez-vous** you'll have to sort things out yourself

début [deby] nm beginning, start; **débuts** nmpl (de carrière) début sg; **~**

juin in early June; **débutant, e** nm/f beginner, novice; **débuter** vi to begin, start; (faire ses débuts) to start out

décaféiné, e [dekafeine] adj decaffeinated

décalage [dekalaʒ] nm gap; **décalage horaire** time difference

décaler [dekale] vt to shift

décapotable [dekapɔtabl] adj convertible

décapsuleur [dekapsylœr] nm bottle-opener

décédé, e [desede] adj deceased

décéder [desede] vi to die

décembre [desãbr] nm December

décennie [deseni] nf decade

décent, e [desã, ãt] adj decent

déception [desɛpsjɔ̃] nf disappointment

décès [desɛ] nm death

décevoir [des(ə)vwar] vt to disappoint

décharge [deʃarʒ] nf (dépôt d'ordures) rubbish tip ou dump; (électrique) electrical discharge; **décharger** vt (marchandise, véhicule) to unload; (tirer) to discharge; **décharger qn de** (responsabilité) to relieve sb of, release sb from

déchausser [deʃose] vt (skis) to take off; **se déchausser** vi to take off one's shoes; (dent) to come ou work loose

déchet [deʃɛ] nm (reste) scrap; **déchets** nmpl (ordures) refuse sg, rubbish sg; **~s nucléaires** nuclear waste

déchiffrer [deʃifre] vt to decipher

déchirant, e [deʃirã, ãt] adj heart-rending

déchirement [deʃirmã] nm (chagrin) wrench, heartbreak; (gén pl: conflit) rift, split

déchirer [deʃire] vt to tear; (en morceaux) to tear up; (arracher) to tear out; (fig: conflit) to tear (apart); **se déchirer** vi to tear, rip; **se ~ un muscle** to tear a muscle

déchirure [deʃiryr] nf (accroc) tear, rip; **déchirure musculaire** torn muscle

décidé, e [deside] adj (personne, air) determined; **c'est ~** it's decided; **décidément** adv really

décider [deside] vt: **~ qch** to decide on sth; **~ de faire/que** to decide to do/that; **~ qn (à faire qch)** to persuade sb to do sth); **se décider (à faire)** to decide (to do), make up one's mind (to do); **se ~ pour** to decide on ou in favour of

décimal, e, -aux [desimal, o] adj decimal

décimètre [desimɛtʀ] nm decimetre

décisif, -ive [desizif, iv] adj decisive

décision [desizjɔ̃] nf decision

déclaration [deklaʀasjɔ̃] nf declaration; (discours: Pol etc) statement; **déclaration d'impôts ou de revenus** = tax return; **déclaration de vol: faire une déclaration de vol** to report a theft

déclarer [deklaʀe] vt to declare; (décès, naissance) to register; **se déclarer** vi (feu) to break out

déclencher [deklɑ̃ʃe] vt (mécanisme etc) to release; (sonnerie) to set off; (attaque, grève) to launch; (provoquer) to trigger off; **se déclencher** vi (sonnerie) to go off

décliner [dekline] vi to decline ▷ vt (invitation) to decline; (nom, adresse) to state

décoiffer [dekwafe] vt: **~ qn** to mess up sb's hair; **je suis toute décoiffée** my hair is in a real mess

déçois etc [deswa] vb voir **décevoir**

décollage [dekɔlaʒ] nm (Aviat) takeoff

décoller [dekɔle] vt to unstick ▷ vi (avion) to take off; **se décoller** vi to come unstuck

décolleté, e [dekɔlte] adj low-cut ▷ nm low neck(line); (plongeant) cleavage

décolorer [dekɔlɔʀe] vt: **se décolorer** vi to fade; **se faire ~ les cheveux** to have one's hair bleached

décommander [dekɔmɑ̃de] vt to cancel; **se décommander** vi to cry off

déconcerter [dekɔ̃sɛʀte] vt to disconcert, confound

décongeler [dekɔ̃ʒ(ə)le] vt to thaw

déconner [dekɔne] (fam) vi to talk rubbish

déconseiller [dekɔ̃seje] vt: **~ qch (à qn)** to advise (sb) against sth; **c'est déconseillé** it's not recommended

décontracté, e [dekɔ̃tʀakte] adj relaxed, laid-back (fam)

décontracter [dekɔ̃tʀakte] vi to relax

décor [dekɔʀ] nm décor; (paysage) scenery; **décorateur** nm (interior) decorator; **décoration** nf decoration; **décorer** vt to decorate

décortiquer [dekɔʀtike] vt to shell; (fig: texte) to dissect

découdre [dekudʀ]: **se découdre** vi to come unstitched

découper [dekupe] vt (papier, tissu etc) to cut up; (viande) to carve; (article) to cut out

décourager [dekuʀaʒe] vt to discourage; **se décourager** vi to lose heart, become discouraged

décousu, e [dekuzy] adj unstitched; (fig) disjointed, disconnected

découvert, e [dekuvɛʀ, ɛʀt] adj (tête) bare, uncovered; (lieu) open, exposed ▷ nm (bancaire) overdraft; **découverte** nf discovery; **faire la découverte de** to discover

découvrir [dekuvʀiʀ] vt to discover; (enlever ce qui couvre) to uncover; (dévoiler) to reveal; **se découvrir** vi (chapeau) to take off one's hat; (vêtement) to take something off; (ciel) to clear

décrire [dekʀiʀ] vt to describe

décrocher [dekʀɔʃe] vt (détacher) to take down; (téléphone) to take off the hook; (: pour répondre) to lift the receiver; (: fam: contrat etc) to get, land ▷ vi (fam: abandonner) to drop out; (: cesser d'écouter) to switch off

déçu, e [desy] pp de **décevoir**

dédaigner [dedeɲe] vt to despise, scorn; (négliger) to disregard, spurn;

dédaigneux, -euse adj scornful, disdainful; **dédain** nm scorn, disdain

dedans [dədɑ̃] adv inside; (pas en plein air) indoors, inside ▷ nm inside; **au ~** inside

dédicacer [dedikase] vt: **~ (à qn)** to sign (for sb), autograph (for sb)

dédier [dedje] vt: **~ à** to dedicate to

dédommagement [dedɔmaʒmɑ̃] nm compensation

dédommager [dedɔmaʒe] vt: **~ qn (de)** to compensate sb (for)

dédouaner [dedwane] vt to clear through customs

déduire [deduir] vt: **~ qch (de)** (ôter) to deduct sth (from); (conclure) to deduce ou infer sth (from)

défaillance [defajɑ̃s] nf (syncope) blackout; (fatigue) (sudden) weakness no pl; (technique) fault, failure; **défaillance cardiaque** heart failure

défaire [defɛr] vt to undo; (installation) to take down, dismantle; **se défaire** vi to come undone; **se ~ de** to get rid of

défait, e [defɛ, ɛt] adj (visage) haggard, ravaged; **défaite** nf defeat

défaut [defo] nm (moral) fault, failing, defect; (tissus) fault, flaw; (manque, carence): **~ de** shortage of; (Inform): **prendre qn en ~** to catch sb out; **faire ~** (manquer) to be lacking; **à ~ de** for lack ou want of

défavorable [defavɔrabl] adj unfavourable (BRIT), unfavorable (US)

défavoriser [defavɔrize] vt to put at a disadvantage

défectueux, -euse [defɛktɥø, øz] adj faulty, defective

défendre [defɑ̃dr] vt to defend; (interdire) to forbid; **se défendre** vi to defend o.s.; **~ à qn qch/de faire** to forbid sb sth/to do; **il se défend** (fam: se débrouille) he can hold his own; **se ~ de/contre** (se protéger) to protect o.s. from/against; **se ~ de** (se garder de) to refrain from

défense [defɑ̃s] nf defence; (d'éléphant etc) tusk; **ministre de la ~** Minister of Defence (BRIT), Defence Secretary (US);

"~ de fumer" "no smoking"

défi [defi] nm challenge; **lancer un ~ à qn** to challenge sb; **sur un ton de ~** defiantly

déficit [defisit] nm (Comm) deficit

défier [defje] vt (provoquer) to challenge; (mort, autorité) to defy; **qn de faire qch** to challenge sb to do sth

défigurer [defigyre] vt to disfigure

défilé [defile] nm (Géo) (narrow) gorge ou pass; (soldats) parade; (manifestants) procession, march

défiler [defile] vi (troupes) to march past; (sportifs) to parade; (manifestants) to march; (visiteurs) to pour, stream; **faire ~ un document** (Comput) to scroll a document; **se défiler** vi: **il s'est défilé** (fam) he wriggled out of it

définir [definir] vt to define

définitif, -ive [definitif, iv] adj (final) final, definitive; (pour longtemps) permanent, definitive; (refus) definite; **définitive** nf: **en définitive** eventually; (somme toute) in fact; **définitivement** adv (partir, s'installer) for good

déformer [defɔrme] vt to put out of shape; (pensée, fait) to distort; **se déformer** vi to lose its shape

défouler [defule]: **se défouler** vi to unwind, let off steam

défunt, e [defœ̃, œ̃t] adj (mort) late before n ▷ nm/f deceased

dégagé, e [degaʒe] adj (route, ciel) clear; **sur un ton ~** casually

dégager [degaʒe] vt (exhaler) to give off; (délivrer) to free, extricate; (désencombrer) to clear; (isoler: idée, aspect) to bring out; **~ qn de** (engagement, parole etc) to release ou free sb from; **se dégager** vi (passage, ciel) to clear

dégâts [dega] nmpl damage sg; **faire des ~** to cause damage

dégel [deʒɛl] nm thaw; **dégeler** vt to thaw (out)

dégivrer [deʒivre] vt (frigo) to defrost; (vitres) to de-ice

dégonflé, e [degɔ̃fle] adj (pneu) flat

dégonfler [degɔ̃fle] vt (pneu, ballon) to let down, deflate; **se dégonfler** vi (fam) to chicken out

dégouliner [deguline] vi to trickle, drip

dégourdi, e [degurdi] adj smart, resourceful

dégourdir [degurdiʀ] vt: **se dégourdir les jambes** to stretch one's legs (fig)

dégoût [degu] nm disgust, distaste; **dégoûtant, e** adj disgusting; **dégoûté, e** adj disgusted; **dégoûté de** sick of; **dégoûter** vt to disgust; **dégoûter qn de qch** to put sb off sth

dégrader [degrade] vt (Mil: officier) to degrade; (abîmer) to damage, deface; **se dégrader** vi (relations, situation) to deteriorate

degré [dəgʀe] nm degree

dégressif, -ive [degʀesif, iv] adj on a decreasing scale

dégringoler [degʀɛ̃gɔle] vi to tumble (down)

déguisement [degizmɑ̃] nm (pour s'amuser) fancy dress

déguiser [degize]: **se déguiser (en)** vi (se costumer) to dress up (as); (pour tromper) to disguise o.s. (as)

dégustation [degystasjɔ̃] nf (de fromages etc) sampling; **~ de vins** wine-tasting session

déguster [degyste] vt (vins) to taste; (fromages etc) to sample; (savourer) to enjoy, savour

dehors [dəɔʀ] adv outside; (en plein air) outdoors ▷ nm outside ▷ nmpl (apparences) appearances; **mettre ou jeter ~** (expulser) to throw out; **au ~** outside; **au ~ de** outside; **en ~ de** (hormis) apart from

déjà [deʒa] adv already; (auparavant) before, already

déjeuner [deʒœne] vi to (have) lunch; (le matin) to have breakfast ▷ nm lunch

delà [dəla] adv: **en ~ (de), au ~ (de)** beyond

délacer [delase] vt (chaussures) to undo

délai [delɛ] nm (attente) waiting period; (sursis) extension (of time); (temps accordé) time limit; **sans ~** without delay; **dans les ~s** within the time limit

délaisser [delese] vt to abandon, desert

délasser [delase] vt to relax; **se délasser** vi to relax

délavé, e [delave] adj faded

délayer [deleje] vt (Culin) to mix (with water etc); (peinture) to thin down

delco(r) [delko] nm (Auto) distributor

délégué, e [delege] nm/f representative

déléguer [delege] vt to delegate

délibéré, e [delibeʀe] adj (conscient) deliberate

délicat, e [delika, at] adj delicate; (plein de tact) tactful; (attention) thoughtful; **délicatement** adv delicately; (avec douceur) gently

délice [delis] nm delight

délicieux, -euse [delisjø, jøz] adj (au goût) delicious; (sensation) delightful

délimiter [delimite] vt (terrain) to delimit, demarcate

délinquant, e [delɛ̃kɑ̃, -ɑ̃t] adj, nm/f delinquent

délirer [deliʀe] vi to be delirious; **tu délires!** (fam) you're crazy!

délit [deli] nm (criminal) offence

délivrer [delivʀe] vt (prisonnier) to (set) free, release; (passeport) to issue

deltaplane(r) [dɛltaplan] nm hang-glider

déluge [delyʒ] nm (pluie) downpour; (biblique) Flood

demain [d(ə)mɛ̃] adv tomorrow; **~ matin/soir** tomorrow morning/evening

demande [d(ə)mɑ̃d] nf (requête) request; (revendication) demand; (d'emploi) application; (Écon): **la ~** demand; **"~s d'emploi"** (annonces) "situations wanted"

demandé, e [d(ə)mɑ̃de] adj (article etc): **très ~** (very) much in demand

demander [d(ə)mɑ̃de] vt to ask for;

(chemin, heure etc) to ask; (nécessiter) to require, demand; **~ qch à qn** to ask sb for sth; **~ un service à qn** to ask sb a favour; **~ à qn de faire qch** to ask sb to do sth; **je ne demande pas mieux que de ...** I'll be only too pleased to ...; **se ~ si/pourquoi** etc to wonder whether/ why etc; **demandeur, -euse** nm/f: **demandeur d'emploi** job-seeker; **demandeur d'asile** asylum-seeker

démangeaison [demãʒezɔ̃] nf itching; **avoir des ~s** to be itching

démanger [demãʒe] vi to itch

démaquillant [demakijã] nm make-up remover

démaquiller [demakije] vt: **se démaquiller** to remove one's make-up

démarcation [demarkasjɔ̃] nf

démarche [demarʃ] nf (allure) gait, walk; (intervention) step; (fig: intellectuelle) thought processes pl; **faire les ~s nécessaires (pour obtenir qch)** to take the necessary steps (to obtain sth)

démarrage [demaraʒ] nm start

démarrer [demare] vi (conducteur) to start (up); (véhicule) to move off; (travaux) to get moving; **démarreur** nm (Auto) starter

démêlant [demelã] nm conditioner

démêler [demele] vt to untangle; **démêlés** nmpl problems

déménagement [demenaʒmã] nm move; **camion de déménagement** removal van

déménager [demenaʒe] vt (meubles) to (re)move ▷ vi to move (house); **déménageur** nm removal man

démerder [demɛʀde] vt: **se démerder** (fam!) vi to sort things out for o.s.

démettre [demɛtʀ] vt: **~ qn de** (fonction, poste) to dismiss sb from; **se ~ l'épaule** etc to dislocate one's shoulder etc

demeurer [d(ə)mœʀe] vi (habiter) to live; (rester) to remain

demi, e [dəmi] adj half ▷ nm (bière) = half-pint (0,25 litres) ▷ préfixe: **~... half-**, semi..., demi-; **trois heures/bouteilles**

et **~es** three and a half hours/bottles, three hours/bottles and a half; **il est 2 heures et ~e/midi et ~** it's half past 2/half past 12; **à ~** half-; **à la ~** (heure) on the half-hour; **demi-douzaine** nf half-dozen, half a dozen; **demi-finale** nf semifinal; **demi-frère** nm half-brother; **demi-heure** nf half-hour, half an hour; **demi-journée** nf half-day, half a day; **demi-litre** nm half-litre, half a litre; **demi-livre** nf half-pound, half a pound; **demi-pension** nf (à l'hôtel) half-board; **demi-pensionnaire** nm/f: **être demi-pensionnaire** to take school lunches

démis, e [demi, iz] adj (épaule etc) dislocated

demi-sœur [dəmisœʀ] nf half-sister

démission [demisjɔ̃] nf resignation; **donner sa ~** to give ou hand in one's notice; **démissionner** vi to resign

demi-tarif [dəmitaʀif] nm half-price; **voyager à ~** to travel half-fare

demi-tour [dəmituʀ] nm about-turn; **faire ~** to turn (and go) back

démocratie [demɔkʀasi] nf democracy; **démocratique** adj democratic

démodé, e [demɔde] adj old-fashioned

demoiselle [d(ə)mwazɛl] nf (jeune fille) young lady; (célibataire) single lady, maiden lady; **demoiselle d'honneur** bridesmaid

démolir [demɔliʀ] vt to demolish

démon [demɔ̃] nm (enfant turbulent) devil, demon; **le D~** the Devil

démonstration [demɔ̃stʀasjɔ̃] nf demonstration

démonter [demɔ̃te] vt (machine etc) to take down, dismantle; **se démonter** (meuble) to be dismantled, be taken to pieces; (personne) to lose countenance

démontrer [demɔ̃tʀe] vt to demonstrate

démouler [demule] vt to turn out

démuni, e [demyni] adj (sans argent) impoverished; **~ de** without

dénicher [deniʃe] (fam) vt (objet)

unearth; (restaurant etc) to discover
dénier [denje] vt to deny
dénivellation [denivelasjɔ̃] nf (pente) slope
dénombrer [denɔ̃bʀe] vt to count
dénomination [denɔminasjɔ̃] nf designation, appellation
dénoncer [denɔ̃se] vt to denounce; **se dénoncer** to give o.s. up, come forward
dénouement [denumã] nm outcome
dénouer [denwe] vt to unknot, undo
denrée [dãʀe] nf: **denrées alimentaires** foodstuffs
dense [dãs] adj dense; **densité** nf density
dent [dã] nf tooth; **dent de lait/de sagesse** milk/wisdom tooth; **dentaire** adj dental; **cabinet dentaire** dental surgery (BRIT), dentist's office (US)
dentelle [dãtɛl] nf lace no pl
dentier [dãtje] nm denture
dentifrice [dãtifʀis] nm toothpaste
dentiste [dãtist] nm/f dentist
dentition [dãtisjɔ̃] nf teeth
dénué, e [denɥe] adj: **~ de** devoid of
déodorant [deodoʀã] nm deodorant
déontologie [deɔ̃tolɔʒi] nf code of practice
dépannage [depanaʒ] nm: **service de ~** (Auto) breakdown service
dépanner [depane] vt (voiture, télévision) to fix, repair; (fig) to bail out, help out; **dépanneuse** nf breakdown lorry (BRIT), tow truck (US)
dépareillé, e [depaʀeje] adj (collection, service) incomplete; (objet) odd
départ [depaʀ] nm departure; (Sport) start; **au ~** at the start; **la veille de son ~** the day before he leaves/left
département [depaʀtəmã] nm department

○ **DÉPARTEMENT**

● France is divided into 96
● administrative units called
● **départements**. These local
● government divisions are headed

● by a state-appointed 'préfet',
● and administered by an elected
● 'Conseil général'. **Départements**
● are usually named after prominent
● geographical features such as rivers
● or mountain ranges.

dépassé, e [depase] adj superseded, outmoded; **il est complètement ~** he's completely out of his depth, he can't cope
dépasser [depase] vt (véhicule, concurrent) to overtake; (endroit) to pass, go past; (somme, limite) to exceed; (fig: en beauté etc) to surpass, outshine ▷ vi (jupon etc) to show; **se dépasser** to excel o.s.
dépaysé, e [depeize] adj disoriented
dépaysement [depeizmã] nm (changement) change of scenery
dépêcher [depeʃe]: **se dépêcher** vi to hurry
dépendance [depãdãs] nf dependence; (bâtiment) outbuilding
dépendre [depãdʀ]: **~ de** vt to depend on; (financièrement etc) to be dependent on; **ça dépend** it depends
dépens [depã] nmpl: **aux ~ de** at the expense of
dépense [depãs] nf spending no pl, expense, expenditure no pl; **dépenser** vt to spend; (énergie) to expend, use up; **se dépenser** vi to exert o.s.
dépeupler [depœple]: **se dépeupler** vi to become depopulated
dépilatoire [depilatwaʀ] adj: **crème ~** hair-removing ou depilatory cream
dépister [depiste] vt to detect; (voleur) to track down
dépit [depi] nm vexation, frustration; **en ~ de** in spite of; **en ~ du bon sens** contrary to all good sense; **dépité, e** adj vexed, frustrated
déplacé, e [deplase] adj (propos) out of place, uncalled-for
déplacement [deplasmã] nm (voyage) trip, travelling no pl; **en ~** away
déplacer [deplase] vt (table, voiture) to

move, shift; **se déplacer** vi to move; (voyager) to travel; **je me suis déplacé une vertèbre** to slip a disc

déplaire [deplεʀ] vt: **ça me déplaît** I don't like this, I dislike this; **se déplaire** vi to be unhappy; **déplaisant, e** adj disagreeable

dépliant [deplijɑ̃] nm leaflet

déplier [deplije] vt to unfold

déposer [depoze] vt (gén: mettre, poser) to lay on down; (à la banque, à la consigne) to deposit; (passager) to drop (off), set down; (roi) to depose; (plainte) to lodge; (marque) to register; **se déposer** vi to settle; **dépositaire** nm/f (Comm) agent; **déposition** nf statement

dépôt [depo] nm (à la banque, sédiment) deposit; (entrepôt) warehouse, store

dépourvu, e [depuʀvy] adj: **~ de** lacking in, without; **prendre qn au ~** to catch sb unprepared

dépression [depʀesjɔ̃] nf depression; **dépression (nerveuse)** (nervous) breakdown

déprimant, e [depʀimɑ̃, ɑ̃t] adj depressing

déprimer [depʀime] vi to be/get depressed

 MOT-CLÉ

depuis [dəpɥi] prép 1 (point de départ dans le temps) since; **il habite Paris depuis 1983/l'an dernier** he has been living in Paris since 1983/last year; **depuis quand?** since when?; **depuis quand le connaissez-vous?** how long have you known him?

2 (temps écoulé) for; **il habite Paris depuis 5 ans** he has been living in Paris for 5 years; **je le connais depuis 3 ans** I've known him for 3 years

3 (lieu): **il a plu depuis Metz** it's been raining since Metz; **elle a téléphoné depuis Valence** she rang from Valence

4 (quantité, rang) from; **depuis les plus petits jusqu'aux plus grands** from the

youngest to the oldest

▷ adv (temps) since (then); **je ne lui ai pas parlé depuis** I haven't spoken to him since (then); **depuis que** conj (ever) since; **depuis qu'il m'a dit ça** (ever) since he said that to me

député, e [depyte] nm/f (Pol) ≈ Member of Parliament (BRIT), ≈ Member of Congress (US)

dérangement [deʀɑ̃ʒmɑ̃] nm (gêne) trouble; (gastrique etc) disorder; **en ~** (téléphone, machine) out of order

déranger [deʀɑ̃ʒe] vt (personne) to trouble, bother; (projets) to disrupt, upset; (objets, vêtements) to disarrange; **se déranger** vi: **surtout ne vous dérangez pas pour moi** please don't put yourself out on my account; **est-ce que cela vous dérange si ...?** do you mind if ...?

déraper [deʀape] vi (voiture) to skid; (personne, semelles) to slip

dérégler [deʀegle] vt (mécanisme) to put out of order; (estomac) to upset

dérisoire [deʀizwaʀ] adj derisory

dérive [deʀiv] nf: **aller à la ~** (Navig, fig) to drift

dérivé, e [deʀive] nm (Tech) by-product

dermatologue [dɛʀmatɔlɔg] nm/f dermatologist

dernier, -ière [dɛʀnje, jɛʀ] adj last; (le plus récent) latest, last; **lundi/le mois ~** last Monday/month; **c'est le ~ cri** it's the very latest thing; **en ~** last; **ce ~, cette ~** the latter; **dernièrement** adv recently

dérogation [deʀɔgasjɔ̃] nf (special) dispensation

dérouiller [deʀuje] vt: **se ~ les jambes** to stretch one's legs (fig)

déroulement [deʀulmɑ̃] nm (d'une opération etc) progress

dérouler [deʀule] vt (ficelle) to unwind; **se dérouler** vi (avoir lieu) to take place; (se passer) to go (off); **tout s'est déroulé comme prévu** everything went as planned

dérouter [deʀute] vt (avion, train) to

reroute, divert; (*étonner*) to disconcert, throw (out)

derrière [dɛRjɛR] *adv, prép* behind ▷ *nm* (*d'une maison*) back; (*postérieur*) behind, bottom; **les pattes de ~** the back *ou* hind legs; **par ~** from behind; (*fig*) behind one's back

des [de] *dét voir de* ▷ *prép* +*dét* = **de +les**

dès [dɛ] *prép* from; **~ que** as soon as; **~ son retour** as soon as he was (*ou* is) back

désaccord [dezakɔR] *nm* disagreement

désagréable [dezagreabl] *adj* unpleasant

désagrément [dezagremã] *nm* annoyance, trouble *no pl*

désaltérer [dezaltere] *vt*: **se désaltérer** to quench one's thirst

désapprobateur, -trice [dezapRɔbatœR, tRis] *adj* disapproving

désapprouver [dezapRuve] *vt* to disapprove of

désarmant, e [dezaRmã, ãt] *adj* disarming

désastre [dezastR] *nm* disaster; **désastreux, -euse** *adj* disastrous

désavantage [dezavãtaʒ] *nm* disadvantage; **désavantager** *vt* to put at a disadvantage

descendre [desãdR] *vt* (*escalier, montagne*) to go (*ou* come) down; (*valise, paquet*) to take *ou* get down; (*étagère etc*) to lower; (*fam: abattre*) to shoot down ▷ *vi* to go (*ou* come) down; (*passager: s'arrêter*) to get out, alight; **~ à pied/en voiture** to walk/drive down; **~ de** (*famille*) to be descended from; **~ du train** to get out of *ou* get off the train; **~ de cheval** to dismount; **~ d'un arbre** to climb down from a tree; **~ à l'hôtel** to stay at a hotel

descente [desãt] *nf* descent, going down; (*chemin*) way down; (*Ski*) downhill (race); **au milieu de la ~** halfway down; **descente de lit** bedside rug; **descente (de police)** (police) raid

description [dɛskRipsjɔ̃] *nf*

description

déséquilibre [dezekilibR] *nm* (*position*): **en ~** unsteady; (*fig: des forces, du budget*) imbalance

désert, e [dezɛR, ɛRt] *adj* deserted ▷ *nm* desert; **désertique** *adj* desert *cpd*

désespéré, e [dezɛspere] *adj* desperate

désespérer [dezɛspere] *vi*: **~ (de)** to despair (of); **désespoir** *nm* despair; **en désespoir de cause** in desperation

déshabiller [dezabije] *vt* to undress; **se déshabiller** *vi* to undress (o.s.)

déshydraté, e [dezidRate] *adj* dehydrated

désigner [dezine] *vt* (*montrer*) to point out, indicate; (*dénommer*) to denote; (*candidat etc*) to name

désinfectant, e [dezɛ̃fɛktã, ãt] *adj, nm* disinfectant

désinfecter [dezɛ̃fɛkte] *vt* to disinfect

désintéressé, e [dezɛ̃terese] *adj* disinterested, unselfish

désintéresser [dezɛ̃terese] *vt*: **se ~ (de)** to lose interest in

désintoxication [dezɛ̃tɔksikasjɔ̃] *nf*: **faire une cure de ~** to undergo treatment for alcoholism (*ou* drug addiction)

désinvolte [dezɛ̃vɔlt] *adj* casual, off-hand

désir [dezir] *nm* wish; (*sensuel*) desire; **désirer** *vt* to want, wish for; (*sexuellement*) to desire; **je désire ...** (*formule de politesse*) I would like

désister [deziste]: **se désister** *vi* to stand down, withdraw

désobéir [dezɔbeiR] *vi*: **~ (à qn/qch)** to disobey (sb/sth); **désobéissant, e** *adj* disobedient

désodorisant [dezɔdɔRizã] *nm* air freshener, deodorizer

désolé, e [dezɔle] *adj* (*paysage*) desolate; **je suis ~** I'm sorry

désordonné, e [dezɔRdɔne] *adj* untidy

désordre [dezɔRdR] *nm* disorder(liness), untidiness; (*anarchie*)

disorder; **en ~** in a mess, untidy
désormais [dezɔʀmɛ] *adv* from
now on

desquelles [dekɛl] *prép +pron* = **de
+lesquelles**

desquels [dekɛl] *prép +pron* = **de
+lesquels**

dessécher [deseʃe] : **se dessécher** *vi*
to dry out

desserrer [desere] *vt* (*loosen*); (*frein*)
to release

dessert [desɛʀ] *nm* dessert, pudding

desservir [desɛʀviʀ] *vt* (*ville, quartier*)
to serve; (*débarrasser*): **~ (la table)**
to clear the table

dessin [desɛ̃] *nm* (*œuvre, art*) drawing;
(*motif*) pattern, design; dessin animé
cartoon (film); **dessin humoristique**
cartoon; **dessinateur, -trice** *nm/f*
(*industriel*) draughtsman(-woman)
(BRIT), draftsman(-woman) (US);
(*de bandes dessinées*) cartoonist;
(*industriel*) draughtsman(-woman)
(BRIT), draftsman(-woman) (US);
dessiner *vt* to draw; (*concevoir*) to
design; **se dessiner** *vi* (*forme*) to be
outlined; (*fig: solution*) to emerge

dessous [d(ə)su] *adv* underneath,
beneath ▷ *nm* underside ▷ *nmpl*
(*sous-vêtements*) underwear *sg*; **en ~,
par ~** underneath; **au-~ (de)** below;
(*peu digne de*) beneath; **avoir le ~** to get
the worst of it; **les voisins du ~** the
downstairs neighbours; **dessous-de-
plat** *nm inv* tablemat

dessus [d(ə)sy] *adv* on top; (*collé, écrit*)
on it ▷ *nm* top; **en ~** above; **par ~** *adv*
over it ▷ *prép* over; **au-~ (de)** above; **les
voisins de ~** the upstairs neighbours;
avoir le ~ to get the upper hand; **sens
~ dessous** upside down; **dessus-de-lit**
nm inv bedspread

destin [dɛstɛ̃] *nm* fate; (*avenir*) destiny

destinataire [dɛstinatɛʀ]
nm/f (*Postes*) addressee; (*d'un colis*)
consignee

destination [dɛstinasjɔ̃] *nf* (*lieu*)
destination; (*usage*) purpose; **à ~ de**
bound for, travelling to

destiner [dɛstine] *vt*: **~ qch à qn**

(*envisager de donner*) to intend sb to have
sth; (*adresser*) to intend sth for sb; **être
destiné à** (*usage*) to be meant for; **se ~
à l'enseignement** to intend to become
a teacher

détachant [detaʃɑ̃] *nm* stain remover

détacher [detaʃe] *vt* (*enlever*) to detach,
remove; (*délier*) to untie; (*Admin*): **~
qn (auprès de ou à)** to post sb (to); **se
détacher** *vi* (*se séparer*) to come off;
(: *page*) to come out; (*se défaire*) to come
undone; **se ~ sur** to stand out against;
se ~ de (*se désintéresser*) to grow away
from

détail [detaj] *nm* detail; (*Comm*): **le ~**
retail; **en ~** in detail; **au ~** (*Comm*) retail;
détaillant *nm* retailer; **détaillé, e** *adj*
(*plan, explications*) detailed; (*facture*)
itemized; **détailler** *vt* (*expliquer*) to
explain in detail

détecter [detɛkte] *vt* to detect

détective [detɛktiv] *nm*: **détective
(privé)** private detective

déteindre [detɛ̃dʀ] *vi* (*au lavage*) to
run, lose its colour; **~ sur** (*vêtement*) to
run into; (*fig*) to rub off on

détendre [detɑ̃dʀ] *vt* (*corps, esprit*) to
relax; **se détendre** *vi* (*ressort*) to lose its
tension; (*personne*) to relax

détenir [det(ə)niʀ] *vt* (*record, pouvoir,
secret*) to hold; (*prisonnier*) to detain,
hold

détente [detɑ̃t] *nf* relaxation

détention [detɑ̃sjɔ̃] *nf* (*d'armes*)
possession; (*captivité*) detention;
détention préventive custody

détenu, e [det(ə)ny] *nm/f* prisoner

détergent [detɛʀʒɑ̃] *nm* detergent

détériorer [deteʀjɔʀe] *vt* to damage;
se détériorer *vi* to deteriorate

déterminé, e [detɛʀmine] *adj* (*résolu*)
determined; (*précis*) specific, definite

déterminer [detɛʀmine] *vt* (*fixer*) to
determine; **~ qn à faire qch** to decide
sb to do sth; **se ~ à faire qch** to make
up one's mind to do sth

détester [detɛste] *vt* to hate, detest

détour [detuʀ] *nm* detour; (*tournant*)

bend, curve: **ça vaut le ~** it's worth the trip; **sans ~** (fig) plainly

détourné, e [deturne] adj (moyen) roundabout

détourner [deturne] vt (détourner) to divert; (par la force) to hijack; (yeux, tête) to turn away; (de l'argent) to embezzle; **se détourner** vi to turn away

détraquer [detrake] vt to put out of order; (estomac) to upset; **se détraquer** vi (machine) to go wrong

détriment [detrimā] nm: **au ~ de** to the detriment of

détroit [detrwa] nm strait

détruire [detrɥir] vt to destroy

dette [dɛt] nf debt

DEUG sigle m (= diplôme d'études universitaires générales) diploma taken after 2 years at university

deuil [dœj] nm (perte) bereavement; (période) mourning; **être en ~** to be in mourning

deux [dø] num two; **tous les ~** both; **ses ~ mains** both his hands, his two hands; **~ fois** twice; **deuxième** num second; **deuxièmement** adv secondly; **deux-pièces** nm inv (tailleur) two-piece suit; (de bain) two-piece (swimsuit); (appartement) two-roomed flat (BRIT) ou apartment (US); **deux-points** nm inv colon sg; **deux-roues** nm inv two-wheeled vehicle

devais [dəvɛ] vb voir **devoir**

dévaluation [devaluasjɔ̃] nf devaluation

devancer [d(ə)vāse] vt (coureur, rival) to get ahead of; (arriver) to arrive before; (prévenir: questions, désirs) to anticipate

devant [d(ə)vā] adv in front; (à distance: en avant) ahead ▷ prép in front of; (en avant) ahead of; (avec mouvement: passer) past; (en présence de) before, in front of; (étant donné) in view of ▷ nm front; **prendre les ~s** to make the first move; **les pattes de ~** the front legs, the forelegs; **par ~** (boutonner) at the front; (entrer) the front way; **aller au-~ de**

qn to go out to meet sb; **aller au-~ de** (désirs de qn) to anticipate

devanture [d(ə)vātyr] nf (étalage) display; (vitrine) shop window

développement [dev(ə)lɔpmā] nm development; **pays en voie de ~** developing countries

développer [dev(ə)lɔpe] vt to develop; **se développer** vi to develop

devenir [dəv(ə)nir] vb +attrib to become; **que sont-ils devenus?** what has become of them?

devez [dəve] vb voir **devoir**

déviation [devjasjɔ̃] nf (Auto) diversion (BRIT), detour (US)

devienne etc [dəvjɛn] vb voir **devenir**

deviner [d(ə)vine] vt to guess; (apercevoir) to distinguish; **devinette** nf riddle

devis [d(ə)vi] nm estimate, quotation

devise [dəviz] nf (formule) motto, watchword; **devises** nfpl (argent) currency sg

dévisser [devise] vt to unscrew, undo; **se dévisser** vi to come unscrewed

devoir [d(ə)vwar] nm duty; (Scol) homework no pl; (: en classe) exercise ▷ vt (argent, respect) to owe (à qn) sb; (+infin: obligation): **il doit le faire** he has to do it, he must do it; (: intention): **le nouveau centre commercial doit ouvrir en mai** the new shopping centre is due to open in May; (: probabilité): **il doit être tard** it must be late; (: fatalité): **cela devait arriver** it was bound to happen; **combien est-ce que je vous dois?** how much do I owe you?

dévorer [devɔre] vt to devour

dévoué, e [devwe] adj devoted

dévouer [devwe]: **se dévouer** vi (se sacrifier): **se ~ (pour)** to sacrifice o.s. (for); (se consacrer): **se ~ à** to devote ou dedicate o.s. to

devrai [dəvre] vb voir **devoir**

dézipper [dezipe] vt to unzip

diabète [djabɛt] nm diabetes sg; **diabétique** nm/f diabetic

diable [djɑbl] nm devil
diabolo [djabolo] nm (boisson) lemonade with fruit cordial
diagnostic [djagnɔstik] nm diagnosis sg; **diagnostiquer** vt to diagnose
diagonal, e, -aux [djagɔnal, o] adj diagonal; **diagonale** nf diagonal; **en diagonale** diagonally
diagramme [djagʀam] nm chart, graph
dialecte [djalɛkt] nm dialect
dialogue [djalɔg] nm dialogue
diamant [djamɑ̃] nm diamond
diamètre [djamɛtʀ] nm diameter
diapositive [djapozitiv] nf transparency, slide
diarrhée [djaʀe] nf diarrhoea
dictateur [diktatœʀ] nm dictator; **dictature** nf dictatorship
dictée [dikte] nf dictation
dicter [dikte] vt to dictate
dictionnaire [diksjɔnɛʀ] nm dictionary
dièse [djɛz] nm sharp
diesel [djezɛl] nm diesel ▷ adj inv diesel
diète [djɛt] nf (jeûne) starvation diet; (régime) diet; **diététique** adj: **magasin diététique** health food shop (BRIT) or store (US)
dieu, x [djø] nm god; **D~** God; **mon D~!** good heavens!
différemment [difeʀamɑ̃] adv differently
différence [difeʀɑ̃s] nf difference; **à la ~ de** unlike; **différencier** vt to differentiate
différent, e [difeʀɑ̃, ɑ̃t] adj (dissemblable) different; **~ de** different from; (divers) different, various
différer [difeʀe] vt to postpone, put off ▷ vi: **~ (de)** to differ (from)
difficile [difisil] adj difficult; (exigeant) hard to please; **difficilement** adv with difficulty
difficulté [difikylte] nf difficulty; **en ~** (bateau, alpiniste) in difficulties
diffuser [difyze] vt (chaleur) to diffuse;

(émission, musique) to broadcast; (nouvelle) to circulate; (Comm) to distribute
digérer [diʒeʀe] vt to digest; (fam: accepter) to stomach, put up with; **digestif** nm (after-dinner) liqueur; **digestion** nf digestion
digne [diɲ] adj dignified; **~ worthy of**; **~ de foi** trustworthy; **dignité** nf dignity
digue [dig] nf dike, dyke
dilemme [dilɛm] nm dilemma
diligence [diliʒɑ̃s] nf stagecoach
diluer [dilɥe] vt to dilute
dimanche [dimɑ̃ʃ] nm Sunday
dimension [dimɑ̃sjɔ̃] nf (grandeur) size; (dimensions) dimensions
diminuer [diminɥe] vt to reduce, decrease; (ardeur etc) to lessen; (dénigrer) to belittle ▷ vi to lessen, diminish; **diminutif** nm (surnom) pet name
dinde [dɛ̃d] nf turkey
dindon [dɛ̃dɔ̃] nm turkey
dîner [dine] nm dinner ▷ vi to have dinner
dingue [dɛ̃g] (fam) adj crazy
dinosaure [dinɔzɔʀ] nm dinosaur
diplomate [diplɔmat] adj diplomatic ▷ nm diplomat; (fig) diplomatist; **diplomatie** nf diplomacy
diplôme [diplom] nm diploma; **avoir des ~s** to have qualifications; **diplômé, e** adj qualified
dire [diʀ] nm: **au ~ de** according to ▷ vt to say; (secret, mensonge, heure) to tell; **~ qch à qn** to tell sb sth; **~ à qn qu'il fasse** ou **de faire** to tell sb to do; **on dit que** they say that; **ceci** ou **cela dit** that being said; **si cela lui dit** (plaire) if he fancies it; **que dites-vous** de (penser) what do you think of; **on dirait que** it looks (ou sounds etc) as if; **dis/dites (donc)!** I say!; **se ~ (à soi-même)** to say to o.s.; **se ~ malade** (se prétendre) to claim one is ill; **ça ne se dit pas** (impoli) you shouldn't say that; (pas en usage) you don't say that
direct, e [diʀɛkt] adj direct ▷ nm (TV):

en ~ live; **directement** adv directly
directeur, -trice [dirɛktœr, tris] nm/f (d'entreprise) director; (de service) manager(-eress); (d'école) head(teacher) (BRIT), principal (US)
direction [dirɛksjɔ̃] nf (sens) direction; (d'entreprise) management; (Auto) steering; **"toutes ~s"** "all routes"
dirent [dir] vb voir **dire**
dirigeant, e [diriʒɑ̃, ɑ̃t] adj (classe) ruling ▷ nm/f (d'un parti etc) leader
diriger [diriʒe] vt (entreprise) to manage, run; (véhicule) to steer; (orchestre) to conduct; (recherches, travaux) to supervise; ~ **sur** (arme) to point ou level ou aim at; ~ **son regard sur** to look in the direction of; **se diriger** vi (s'orienter) to find one's way; **se ~ vers** ou **sur** to make ou head for
dis [di] vb voir **dire**
discerner [disɛrne] vt to discern, make out
discipline [disiplin] nf discipline; **discipliner** vt to discipline
discontinu, e [diskɔ̃tiny] adj intermittent
discontinuer [diskɔ̃tinɥe] vi: **sans ~** without stopping, without a break
discothèque [diskɔtɛk] nf (boîte de nuit) disco(thèque)
discours [diskur] nm speech
discret, -ète [diskrɛ, ɛt] adj discreet; (parfum, maquillage) unobtrusive; **discrétion** nf discretion; **à discrétion** as much as one wants
discrimination [diskriminasjɔ̃] nf discrimination; **sans ~** indiscriminately
discussion [diskysjɔ̃] nf discussion
discutable [diskytabl] adj debatable
discuter [diskyte] vt (débattre) to discuss; (contester) to question, dispute ▷ vi to talk; (protester) to argue; ~ **de** to discuss
dise [diz] vb voir **dire**
disjoncteur [disʒɔ̃ktœr] nm (Élec) circuit breaker
disloquer [dislɔke]: **se disloquer** vi

(parti, empire) to break up; (meuble) to come apart; (épaule) to be dislocated
disons [dizɔ̃] vb voir **dire**
disparaître [disparɛtr] vi to disappear; (se perdre: traditions etc) to die out; **faire ~** (tache) to remove; (douleur) to get rid of
disparition [disparisjɔ̃] nf disappearance; **espèce en voie de ~** endangered species
disparu, e [dispary] nm/f missing person ▷ adj: **être porté ~** to be reported missing
dispensaire [dispɑ̃sɛr] nm community clinic
dispenser [dispɑ̃se] vt: ~ **qn de** to exempt sb from
disperser [dispɛrse] vt to scatter; **se disperser** vi to break up
disponible [dispɔnibl(ə)] adj available
disposé, e [dispoze] adj: **bien/mal ~** (humeur) in a good/bad mood; ~ **à** (prêt à) willing ou prepared to
disposer [dispoze] vt to arrange ▷ vi: **vous pouvez ~** you may leave; ~ **de** to have (at one's disposal); **se ~ à faire** to prepare to do, be about to do
dispositif [dispozitif] nm device; (fig) system, plan of action
disposition [dispozisjɔ̃] nf (arrangement) arrangement, layout; (humeur) mood; **prendre ses ~s** to make arrangements; **avoir des ~s pour la musique** etc to have a special aptitude for music etc; **à la ~ de qn** at sb's disposal; **je suis à votre ~** I am at your service
disproportionné, e [disprɔpɔrsjɔne] adj disproportionate, out of all proportion
dispute [dispyt] nf quarrel, argument; **disputer** (match) to play; (combat) to fight; **se disputer** vi to quarrel
disqualifier [diskalifje] vt to disqualify
disque [disk] nm (Mus) record; (forme, pièce) disc; (Sport) discus; **disque compact** compact disc; **disque dur**

hard disk; **disquette** nf floppy disk, diskette

dissertation [disɛʀtasjɔ̃] nf (Scol) essay

dissimuler [disimyle] vt to conceal

dissipé, e [disipe] adj (élève) undisciplined, unruly

dissolvant [disɔlvɑ̃] nm nail polish remover

dissuader [disɥade] vt: ~ qn de faire to dissuade sb from doing

distance [distɑ̃s] nf distance; (fig: écart) gap; **à ~** at ou from a distance; **distancer** vt to outdistance

distant, e [distɑ̃, ɑ̃t] adj (réservé) distant; **~ de** (lieu) far away from

distillerie [distilʀi] nf distillery

distinct, e [distɛ̃(kt), ɛ̃kt] adj distinct; **distinctement** adv distinctly, clearly; **distinctif, -ive** adj distinctive

distingué, e [distɛ̃ge] adj distinguished

distinguer [distɛ̃ge] vt to distinguish; **se ~ de** to be distinguished by

distraction [distʀaksjɔ̃] nf (inattention) absent-mindedness; (passe-temps) distraction, entertainment

distraire [distʀɛʀ] vt (divertir) to entertain, divert; (déranger) to distract; **se distraire** vi to amuse ou enjoy o.s.; **distrait, e** adj absent-minded

distrayant, e [distʀɛjɑ̃, ɑ̃t] adj entertaining

distribuer [distʀibɥe] vt to distribute, hand out; (Cartes) to deal (out); (courrier) to deliver; **distributeur** nm (Comm) distributor; **distributeur (automatique)** (vending) machine; **distributeur de billets** (cash) dispenser

dit, e [di, dit] pp de **dire** adj (fixé): le jour ~ the arranged day; (surnommé): X, ~ Pierrot X, known as Pierrot

dites [dit] vb voir **dire**

divan [divɑ̃] nm divan

divers, e [divɛʀ, ɛʀs] adj (varié) diverse, varied; (différent) different, various; **~es**

personnes various ou several people

diversité [divɛʀsite] nf (variété) diversity

divertir [divɛʀtiʀ]: **se divertir** vi to amuse ou enjoy o.s.; **divertissement** nm distraction, entertainment

diviser [divize] vt to divide; **division** nf division

divorce [divɔʀs] nm divorce; **divorcé, e** nm/f divorcee; **divorcer** vi to get a divorce, get divorced; **divorcer de** ou **d'avec qn** to divorce sb

divulguer [divylge] vt to disclose

dix [dis] num ten; **dix-huit** num eighteen; **dix-huitième** num eighteenth; **dixième** num tenth; **dix-neuf** num nineteen; **dix-neuvième** num nineteenth; **dix-sept** num seventeen; **dix-septième** num seventeenth

dizaine [dizɛn] nf: **une ~ (de)** about ten, ten or so

do [do] nm (note) C; (en chantant la gamme) do(h)

docile [dɔsil] adj docile

dock [dɔk] nm dock; **docker** nm docker

docteur [dɔktœʀ] nm doctor; **doctorat** nm doctorate

doctrine [dɔktʀin] nf doctrine

document [dɔkymɑ̃] nm document; **documentaire** adj, nm documentary; **documentation** nf documentation, literature; **documenter** vt: **se documenter (sur)** to gather information (on)

dodo [dodo] nm (langage enfantin): **aller faire ~** to go to beddy-byes

dogue [dɔg] nm mastiff

doigt [dwa] nm finger; **à deux ~s de** within an inch of; **un ~ de lait/whiskey** a drop of milk/whisky; **doigt de pied** toe

doit etc [dwa] vb voir **devoir**

dollar [dɔlaʀ] nm dollar

domaine [dɔmɛn] nm estate, property; (fig) domain, field

domestique [dɔmɛstik] adj domestic ▷ nm/f servant, domestic

domicile [dɔmisil] nm home, place
of residence; **à ~** at home; **livrer à ~** to
deliver; **domicilié, e** adj: **"domicilié
à …"** "address …"

dominant, e [dɔminɑ̃, ɑ̃t] adj (opinion)
predominant

dominer [dɔmine] vt to dominate;
(sujet) to master; (surpasser) to outclass,
surpass; (surplomber) to tower above,
dominate ▷ vi to be in the dominant
position; **se dominer** vi to control o.s.

domino [dɔmino] nm domino;
dominos nmpl (jeu) dominoes sg

dommage [dɔmaʒ] nm: **~s** (dégâts)
damage no pl; **c'est ~!** what a shame!;
c'est ~ que it's a shame ou pity that

dompter [dɔ̃(p)te] vt to tame;
dompteur, -euse nm/f trainer

DOM-ROM [dɔmrɔm] sigle m
(= départements et régions d'outre-mer)
French overseas departments and regions

don [dɔ̃] nm gift; (charité) donation;
avoir des ~s pour to have a gift ou
talent for; **elle a le ~ de m'énerver**
she's got a knack of getting on my
nerves

donc [dɔ̃k] conj therefore, so; (après une
digression) so, then

donné, e [dɔne] adj (convenu: lieu, heure)
given; (pas cher: fam): **c'est ~** it's a gift;
étant ~ que … given that …; **données**
nfpl data

donner [dɔne] vt to give; (vieux habits
etc) to give away; (spectacle) to put on;
~ qch à qn to give sb sth, give sth to sb;
~ sur (suj: fenêtre, chambre) to look (out)
onto; **ça donne soif/faim** it makes
you (feel) thirsty/hungry; **se ~ à fond**
to give one's all; **se ~ du mal** to take
(great) trouble; **s'en ~ à cœur joie** (fam)
to have a great time

MOT-CLÉ

dont [dɔ̃] pron relatif 1 (appartenance:
objets) whose, of which; (appartenance:
êtres animés) whose; **la maison dont
le toit est rouge** the house whose roof is

which is red, the house whose roof is
red; **l'homme dont je connais la sœur**
the man whose sister I know
2 (parmi lesquel(le)s): **2 livres, dont
l'un est …** 2 books, one of which is …;
**il y avait plusieurs personnes, dont
Gabrielle** there were several people,
among them Gabrielle; **10 blessés,
dont 2 grièvement** 10 injured, 2 of
them seriously
3 (complément d'adjectif, de verbe): **le fils
dont il est si fier** the son he's so proud
of; **le pays dont il est originaire** the
country he's from; **la façon dont il l'a
fait** the way he did it; **ce dont je parle**
what I'm talking about

dopage [dɔpaʒ] nm (Sport) drug use; (de
cheval) doping

doré, e [dɔʀe] adj golden; (avec dorure)
gilt, gilded

dorénavant [dɔʀenavɑ̃] adv
henceforth

dorer [dɔʀe] vt to gild; **(faire) ~** (Culin)
to brown

dorloter [dɔʀlɔte] vt to pamper

dormir [dɔʀmiʀ] vi to sleep; (être
endormi) to be asleep

dortoir [dɔʀtwaʀ] nm dormitory

dos [do] nm back; (de livre) spine; **"voir
au ~"** "see over"; **de ~** from the back

dosage [dozaʒ] nm mixture

dose [doz] nf dose; **doser** vt to measure
out; **il faut savoir doser ses efforts**
you have to be able to pace yourself

dossier [dosje] nm (documents) file; (de
chaise) back; (de Presse) feature; (Comput)
folder; **un ~ scolaire** a school report

douane [dwan] nf customs pl;
douanier, -ière adj customs cpd ▷ nm
customs officer

double [dubl] adj, adv double ▷ nm (2
fois plus): **le ~ (de)** twice as much (ou
many) as; (autre exemplaire) duplicate,
copy; (sosie) double; (Tennis) doubles sg;
en ~ (exemplaire) in duplicate; **faire
~ emploi** to be redundant; **double-
cliquer** vi (Inform) to double-click

doubler [duble] vt (multiplier par 2) to double; (vêtement) to line; (dépasser) to overtake, pass; (film) to dub; (acteur) to stand in for ▷ vi to double

doublure [dublyr] nf lining; (Cinéma) stand-in

douce [dus] adj voir **doux**; **douceâtre** adj sickly sweet; **doucement** adv gently; (lentement) slowly; **douceur** nf softness; (de quelqu'un) gentleness; (de climat) mildness

douche [duʃ] nf shower; **prendre une ~** to have ou take a shower; (Douche): **se doucher** vi to have ou take a shower

doué, e [dwe] adj gifted, talented; **être ~ pour** to have a gift for

douille [duj] nf (Élec) socket

douillet, te [dujɛ, ɛt] adj cosy; (péj: à la douleur) soft

douleur [dulœr] nf pain; (chagrin) grief, distress; **douloureux, -euse** adj painful

doute [dut] nm doubt; **sans ~** no doubt; (probablement) probably; **sans aucun ~** without a doubt; **douter** vt to doubt; **douter de** (sincérité de qn) to have (one's) doubts about; (réussite) to be doubtful of; **douter que** to doubt if ou whether; **se douter de qch/que** to suspect sth/that; **je m'en doutais** I suspected as much; **douteux, -euse** adj (incertain) doubtful; (péj) dubious-looking

Douvres [duvr] n Dover

doux, douce [du, dus] adj soft; (sucré) sweet; (peu fort: moutarde, climat) mild; (pas brusque) gentle

douzaine [duzɛn] nf (12) dozen; (environ 12): **une ~ (de)** a dozen or so

douze [duz] num twelve; **douzième** num twelfth

dragée [draʒe] nf sugared almond

draguer [drage] vt (rivière) to dredge; ~ (fam) to try to pick up

dramatique [dramatik] adj dramatic; (tragique) tragic ▷ nf (TV) (television) drama

drame [dram] nm drama

drap [dra] nm (de lit) sheet; (tissu) woollen fabric

drapeau, x [drapo] nm flag

drap-housse [draus] nm fitted sheet

dresser [drese] vt (mettre vertical, monter) to put up, erect; (liste) to draw up; (animal) to train; **se dresser** vi (obstacle) to stand; (personne) to draw o.s. up; ~ **qn contre qn** to set sb against sb; ~ **l'oreille** to prick up one's ears

drogue [drɔg] nf drug; **la ~** drugs pl; **drogué, e** nm/f drug addict; **droguer** vt (victime) to drug; **se droguer** vi (aux stupéfiants) to take drugs; (péj: de médicaments) to dose o.s. up; **droguerie** nf hardware shop; **droguiste** nm keeper/owner of a hardware shop

droit, e [drwa, drwat] adj (non courbe) straight; (vertical) upright, straight; (fig: loyal) upright, straight(forward); (opposé à gauche) right, right-hand ▷ adv straight ▷ nm (prérogative) right; (taxe) duty, tax; (: d'inscription) fee; (Jur): **le ~** law; **avoir le ~ de** to be allowed to; **avoir ~ à** to be entitled to; **être dans son ~** to be within one's rights; **à -e** on the right; (direction) (to the) right; **droits d'auteur** royalties pl; **droits d'inscription** enrolment fee; **droite** nf (Pol): **la droite** the right (wing); **droitier, -ière** adj right-handed

drôle [drol] adj funny; **une ~ d'idée** a funny idea

dromadaire [drɔmadɛr] nm dromedary

du [dy] dét voir **de** ▷ prép +dét = **de + le**

dû, due [dy] vb voir **devoir** ▷ adj (somme) owing, owed; (causé par): **dû à** due to ▷ nm due

dune [dyn] nf dune

duplex [dyplɛks] nm (appartement) split-level apartment, duplex

duquel [dykɛl] prép +pron = **de +lequel**

dur, e [dyr] adj (pierre, siège, travail, problème) hard; (voix, climat) harsh; (sévère) hard, harsh; (cruel) hard(-hearted); (porte, col) stiff; (viande) tough ▷ adv hard ▷ nm (fam:

meneur) tough nut; **~ d'oreille** hard of hearing

durant [dyʀɑ̃] *prép (au cours de)* during; *(pendant)* for; **des mois ~** for months

durcir [dyʀsiʀ] *vt, vi* to harden; **se durcir** *vi* to harden

durée [dyʀe] *nf* length; *(d'une pile etc)* life; **de courte ~** *(séjour)* short

durement [dyʀmɑ̃] *adv* harshly

durer [dyʀe] *vi* to last

dureté [dyʀte] *nf* hardness; harshness; stiffness; toughness

durit(r) [dyʀit] *nf (car radiator)* hose

duvet [dyve] *nm* down; *(sac de couchage)* down-filled sleeping bag

DVD *sigle m* (= digital versatile disc) DVD

dynamique [dinamik] *adj* dynamic; **dynamisme** *nm* dynamism

dynamo [dinamo] *nf* dynamo

dyslexie [disleksi] *nf* dyslexia, word-blindness

eau, x [o] *nf* water; **eaux** *nfpl (Méd)* waters; **prendre l'~** to leak, let in water; **tomber à l'~** *(fig)* to fall through; **eau de Cologne** eau de Cologne; **eau courante** running water; **eau de javel** bleach; **eau de toilette** toilet water; **eau douce** fresh water; **eau gazeuse** sparkling (mineral) water; **eau minérale** mineral water; **eau plate** still water; **eau salée** salt water; **eau-de-vie** *nf* brandy

ébène [ebɛn] *nf* ebony; **ébéniste** *nm* cabinetmaker

éblouir [ebluiʀ] *vt* to dazzle

éboueur [ebwœʀ] *nm* dustman (*BRIT*), garbageman (*US*)

ébouillanter [ebujɑ̃te] *vt* to scald; *(Culin)* to blanch

éboulement [ebulmɑ̃] *nm* rock fall

ébranler [ebʀɑ̃le] *vt* to shake; *(affaiblir)* to weaken; **s'ébranler** *vi (partir)* to move off

ébullition [ebylisjɔ̃] *nf* boiling point; **en ~** boiling

écaille [ekaj] nf (de poisson) scale; (matière) tortoiseshell; **écailler** vt (poisson) to scale; **s'écailler** vi to flake ou peel (off)

écart [ekar] nm gap; **à l'~** out of the way; **à l'~ de** away from; **faire un ~** (voiture) to swerve

écarté, e [ekarte] adj (lieu) out-of-the-way, remote; (ouvert): **les jambes ~es** legs apart; **les bras ~s** arms outstretched

écarter [ekarte] vt (séparer) to move apart, separate; (éloigner) to push back, move away; (ouvrir: bras, jambes) to spread, open; (: rideau) to draw (back); (éliminer: candidat, possibilité) to dismiss; **s'écarter** vi to part; (s'éloigner) to move away; **s'~ de** to wander from

échafaudage [eʃafodaʒ] nm scaffolding

échalote [eʃalɔt] nf shallot

échange [eʃɑ̃ʒ] nm exchange; **en ~ de** in exchange ou return for; **échanger** vt: **échanger qch (contre)** to exchange sth (for)

échantillon [eʃɑ̃tijɔ̃] nm sample

échapper [eʃape] vt: **~ à** (gardien) to escape (from); (punition, péril) to escape; **s'échapper** vi to escape; **~ à qn** (détail, sens) to escape sb; (objet qu'on tient) to slip out of sb's hands; **laisser ~** (cri etc) to let out; **l'~ belle** to have a narrow escape

écharde [eʃard] nf splinter (of wood)

écharpe [eʃarp] nf scarf; **avoir le bras en ~** to have one's arm in a sling

échauffer [eʃofe] vt (moteur) to overheat; **s'échauffer** vi (Sport) to warm up; (dans la discussion) to become heated

échéance [eʃeɑ̃s] nf (d'un paiement: date) settlement date; (fig) deadline; **à brève ~** in the short term; **à longue ~** in the long run

échéant [eʃeɑ̃]: **le cas ~** adv if the case arises

échec [eʃɛk] nm failure; (Échecs): **~ et mat/au roi** checkmate/check; **échecs**

nmpl (jeu) chess sg; **tenir en ~** to hold in check

échelle [eʃɛl] nf ladder; (fig, d'une carte) scale

échelon [eʃ(ə)lɔ̃] nm (d'échelle) rung; (Admin) grade; **échelonner** vt to space out

échiquier [eʃikje] nm chessboard

écho [eko] nm echo; **échographie** nf: **passer une échographie** to have a scan

échouer [eʃwe] vi to fail; **s'échouer** vi to run aground

éclabousser [eklabuse] vt to splash

éclair [eklɛr] nm (d'orage) flash of lightning, lightning no pl; (gâteau) éclair

éclairage [eklɛraʒ] nm lighting

éclaircie [eklɛrsi] nf bright interval

éclaircir [eklɛrsir] vt to lighten; (fig: mystère) to clear up; (: point) to clarify; **s'éclaircir** vi (ciel) to clear; **s'~ la voix** to clear one's throat; **éclaircissement** nm (sur un point) clarification

éclairer [eklere] vt (lieu) to light (up); (personne: avec une lampe etc) to light the way for; (fig: problème) to shed light on ▷ vi: **~ mal/bien** to give a poor/good light; **s'~ à la bougie** to use candlelight

éclat [ekla] nm (de bombe, de verre) fragment; (du soleil, d'une couleur etc) brightness, brilliance; (d'une cérémonie) splendour; (scandale): **faire un ~** to cause a commotion; **éclats de voix** shouts; **éclat de rire** roar of laughter

éclatant, e [eklatɑ̃, ɑ̃t] adj brilliant

éclater [eklate] vi (pneu) to burst; (bombe) to explode; (guerre) to break out; (groupe, parti) to break up; **~ en sanglots/de rire** to burst out sobbing/laughing

écluse [eklyz] nf lock

écœurant, e [ekœrɑ̃, ɑ̃t] adj (gâteau etc) sickly; (fig) sickening

écœurer [ekœre] vt: **~ qn** (nourriture) to make sb feel sick; (conduite, personne) to disgust sb

école [ekɔl] nf school; **aller à l'~** to go

to school; **école maternelle** nursery school; **école primaire** primary (BRIT) ou grade (US) school; **école secondaire** secondary (BRIT) ou high (US) school; **écolier, -ière** nm/f schoolboy(-girl)

écologie [ekɔlɔʒi] nf ecology; **écologique** adj environment-friendly; **écologiste** nm/f ecologist

économe [ekɔnɔm] adj thrifty ▷ nm/f (de lycée etc) bursar (BRIT), treasurer (US)

économie [ekɔnɔmi] nf economy; (gain: d'argent, de temps etc) saving; (science) economics sg; **économies** nfpl (pécule) savings; **économique** adj (avantageux) economical; (Écon) economic; **économiser** vt, vi to save

écorce [ekɔrs] nf bark; (de fruit) peel

écorcher [ekɔrʃe] vt: **s'- le genou/la main** to graze one's knee/one's hand; **écorchure** nf graze

écossais, e [ekɔsɛ, ɛz] adj Scottish ▷ nm/f: **É-, e** Scot

Écosse [ekɔs] nf: **l'-** Scotland

écouter [ekute] vt to listen to; **s'écouter** (malade) to be a bit of a hypochondriac; **si je m'écoutais** if I followed my instincts; **écouteur** nm (Tél) receiver; **écouteurs** nmpl (casque) headphones pl, headset

écran [ekrɑ̃] nm screen; **petit ~** television; **~ total** sunblock

écrasant, e [ekrazɑ̃, ɑ̃t] adj overwhelming

écraser [ekraze] vt to crush; (piéton) to run over; **s'écraser** vi to crash; **s'~ contre** to crash into

écrémé, e [ekreme] adj (lait) skimmed

écrevisse [ekrəvis] nf crayfish inv

écrire [ekrir] vt to write; **s'écrire** to write to each other; (se) dit; **ça s'écrit comment?** how is it spelt?; **écrit** nm (examen) written paper; **par écrit** in writing

écriteau, X [ekrito] nm notice, sign

écriture [ekrityr] nf writing; **écritures** nfpl (Comm) accounts, books; **l'É- (sainte), les É-s** the Scriptures

écrivain [ekrivɛ̃] nm writer

écrou [ekru] nm nut

écrouler [ekrule]: **s'écrouler** vi to collapse

écru, e [ekry] adj (couleur) off-white, écru

écume [ekym] nf foam

écureuil [ekyrœj] nm squirrel

écurie [ekyri] nf stable

eczéma [ɛgzema] nm eczema

EDF sigle f (= Électricité de France) national electricity company

Édimbourg [edɛ̃bur] n Edinburgh

éditer [edite] vt (publier) to publish; (annoter) to edit; **éditeur, -trice** nm/f publisher; **édition** nf edition; (industrie du livre) publishing

édredon [edrədɔ̃] nm eiderdown

éducateur, -trice [edykatœr, tris] nm/f teacher; (en classe spécialisée) instructor

éducatif, -ive [edykatif, iv] adj educational

éducation [edykasjɔ̃] nf education; (familiale) upbringing; (manières) (good) manners pl; **éducation physique** physical education

éduquer [edyke] vt to educate; (élever) to bring up

effacer [efase] vt to erase, rub out; **s'effacer** vi (inscription etc) to wear off; (pour laisser passer) to step aside

effarant, e [efarɑ̃, ɑ̃t] adj alarming

effectif, -ive [efɛktif, iv] adj real ▷ nm (Scol) (pupil) numbers pl; (entreprise) staff, workforce; **effectivement** adv (réellement) actually, really; (en effet) indeed

effectuer [efɛktɥe] vt (opération) to carry out; (trajet) to make

effervescent, e [efɛrvesɑ̃, ɑ̃t] adj effervescent

effet [efɛ] nm effect; (impression) impression; **effets** nmpl (vêtements etc) things; **faire ~** (médicament) to take effect; **faire de l'~** (impressionner) to make an impression; **faire bon/mauvais ~ sur qn** to make a good/bad impression on sb; **en ~** indeed; **effet de**

serre greenhouse effect
efficace [efikas] *adj (personne)* efficient; *(action, médicament)* effective; **efficacité** *nf* efficiency; effectiveness
effondrer [efɔ̃dʀe]: **s'effondrer** *vi* to collapse
efforcer [efɔʀse]: **s'efforcer de** *vt:* **s'~ de faire** to try hard to do
effort [efɔʀ] *nm* effort
effrayant, e [efʀɛjɑ̃, ɑ̃t] *adj* frightening
effrayer [efʀeje] *vt* to frighten, scare; **s'~ (de)** to be frightened *ou* scared (by)
effréné, e [efʀene] *adj* wild
effronté, e [efʀɔ̃te] *adj* cheeky
effroyable [efʀwajabl] *adj* horrifying, appalling
égal, e, -aux [egal, o] *adj* equal; *(constant: vitesse)* steady ▷ *nm/f* equal; **être ~ à** *(prix, nombre)* to be equal to; **ça lui est ~** it's all the same to him, he doesn't mind; **sans ~** matchless, unequalled; **d'~ à ~** as equals; **également** *adv* equally; *(aussi)* too, as well; **égaler** *vt* to equal; **égaliser** *vt (sol, salaires)* to level (out); *(chances)* to equalize ▷ *vi (Sport)* to equalize; **égalité** *nf* equality; **être à égalité** to be level
égard [egaʀ] *nm:* **~s** *mpl* consideration *sg;* **à cet ~** in this respect; **par ~ pour** out of consideration for; **à l'~ de** towards
égarer [egaʀe] *vt* to mislay; **s'égarer** *vi* to get lost, lose one's way; *(objet)* to go astray
églefin [egləfɛ̃] *nm* haddock
église [egliz] *nf* church; **aller à l'~** to go to church
égoïsme [egoism] *nm* selfishness; **égoïste** *adj* selfish
égout [egu] *nm* sewer
égoutter [egute] *vt* to drip; **s'égoutter** *vi* to drip; **égouttoir** *nm* draining board; *(mobile)* draining rack
égratigner [egʀatiɲe] *vt* to scratch; **égratignure** *nf* scratch
Égypte [eʒipt] *nf:* **l'~** Egypt; **égyptien, ne** *adj* Egyptian ▷ *nm/f:*

Égyptien, ne Egyptian
eh [e] *excl* hey!; **eh bien!** well!
élaborer [elabɔʀe] *vt* to elaborate; *(projet, stratégie)* to work out; *(rapport)* to draft
élan [elɑ̃] *nm (Zool)* elk, moose; *(Sport)* run up; *(fig: de tendresse etc)* surge; **prendre son ~** to gather speed
élancer [elɑ̃se]: **s'élancer** *vi* to dash, hurl o.s.
élargir [elaʀʒiʀ] *vt* to widen; **s'élargir** *vi* to widen; *(vêtement)* to stretch
élastique [elastik] *adj* elastic ▷ *nm (de bureau)* rubber band; *(pour la couture)* elastic *no pl*
élection [elɛksjɔ̃] *nf* election
électricien, ne [elɛktʀisjɛ̃, jɛn] *nm/f* electrician
électricité [elɛktʀisite] *nf* electricity; **allumer/éteindre l'~** to put on/off the light
électrique [elɛktʀik] *adj* electric(al)
électrocuter [elɛktʀɔkyte] *vt* to electrocute
électroménager [elɛktʀomenaʒe] *adj, nm:* **appareils ~s, l'~** domestic (electrical) appliances
électronique [elɛktʀɔnik] *adj* electronic ▷ *nf* electronics *sg*
élégance [elegɑ̃s] *nf* elegance
élégant, e [elegɑ̃, ɑ̃t] *adj* elegant
élément [elemɑ̃] *nm* element; *(pièce)* component, part; **élémentaire** *adj* elementary
éléphant [elefɑ̃] *nm* elephant
élevage [el(ə)vaʒ] *nm* breeding; *(de bovins)* cattle rearing; **truite d'~** farmed trout
élevé, e [el(ə)ve] *adj* high; **bien/mal ~** well-/ill-mannered
élève [elɛv] *nm/f* pupil
élever [el(ə)ve] *vt (enfant)* to bring up, raise; *(animaux)* to breed; *(hausser: taux, niveau)* to raise; *(édifier: monument)* to put up, erect; **s'élever** *vi (avion)* to go up; *(niveau, température)* to rise; **s'~ à** *(suj: frais, dégâts)* to amount to, add up to; **s'~ contre qch** to rise up against

sth; **~ la voix** to raise one's voice; **éleveur, -euse** *nm/f* breeder

éliminatoire [eliminatwaʀ] *nf* (Sport) heat

éliminer [elimine] *vt* to eliminate

élire [eliʀ] *vt* to elect

elle [ɛl] *pron* (sujet) she; (: chose) it; (complément) her; it; **~s** (sujet) they; (complément) them; **~-même** herself; itself; **~-s-mêmes** themselves; *voir aussi* **il**

éloigné, e [elwaɲe] *adj* distant, far-off; (parent) distant

éloigner [elwaɲe] *vt* (échéance) to put off, postpone; (soupçons, danger) to ward off; (objet): **~ qch (de)** to move *ou* take sth away (from); (personne): **~ qn (de)** to take sb away *ou* remove sb (from); **s'éloigner (de)** (personne) to go away (from); (véhicule) to move away (from); (affectivement) to grow away (from)

élu, e [ely] *pp de* **élire** ⊳ *nm/f* (Pol) elected representative

Élysée [elize] *nm*: **(le palais de) l'~** the Élysée Palace (the French president's residence)

émail, -aux [emaj, o] *nm* enamel

e-mail [imɛl] *nm* e-mail; **envoyer qch par ~** to e-mail sth

émanciper [emɑ̃sipe]: **s'émanciper** *vi* (fig) to become emancipated *ou* liberated

emballage [ɑ̃balaʒ] *nm* (papier) wrapping; (boîte) packaging

emballer [ɑ̃bale] *vt* to wrap (up); (dans un carton) to pack (up); (fig: fam) to thrill (to bits); **s'emballer** *vi* (moteur) to race; (cheval) to bolt; (fig: personne) to get carried away

embarcadère [ɑ̃baʀkadɛʀ] *nm* wharf, pier

embarquement [ɑ̃baʀkəmɑ̃] *nm* (de passagers) boarding; (de marchandises) loading

embarquer [ɑ̃baʀke] *vt* (personne) to embark; (marchandise) to load; (fam) to cart off ⊳ *vi* (passager) to board;

s'embarquer *vi* to board; **s'~ dans** (affaire, aventure) to embark upon

embarras [ɑ̃baʀa] *nm* (gêne) embarrassment; **mettre qn dans l'~** to put sb in an awkward position; **vous n'avez que l'~ du choix** the only problem is choosing

embarrassant, e [ɑ̃baʀasɑ̃, ɑ̃t] *adj* embarrassing

embarrasser [ɑ̃baʀase] *vt* (encombrer) to clutter (up); (gêner) to hinder, hamper; **~ qn** to put sb in an awkward position; **s'~ de** to burden o.s. with

embaucher [ɑ̃boʃe] *vt* to take on, hire

embêter [ɑ̃bete] *vt* to bother; **s'embêter** (s'ennuyer) to be bored

emblée [ɑ̃ble]: **d'~** *adv* straightaway

embouchure [ɑ̃buʃyʀ] *nf* (Géo) mouth

embourber [ɑ̃buʀbe]: **s'embourber** *vi* to get stuck in the mud

embouteillage [ɑ̃butejaʒ] *nm* traffic jam

embranchement [ɑ̃brɑ̃ʃmɑ̃] *nm* (routier) junction

embrasser [ɑ̃brase] *vt* to kiss; (sujet: période) to embrace, encompass

embrayage [ɑ̃brɛjaʒ] *nm* clutch

embrouiller [ɑ̃bruje] *vt* to muddle up; (fils) to tangle (up); **s'embrouiller** *vi* (personne) to get in a muddle

embruns [ɑ̃brœ̃] *nmpl* sea spray *sg*

embué, e [ɑ̃bɥe] *adj* misted up

émeraude [emʀod] *nf* emerald

émerger [emɛrʒe] *vi* to emerge; (faire saillie, aussi fig) to stand out

émeri [em(ə)ri] *nm*: **toile** *ou* **papier ~** emery paper

émerveiller [emɛrveje] *vt* to fill with wonder; **s'émerveiller de** to marvel at

émettre [emɛtr] *vt* (son, lumière) to give out, emit; (message etc: Radio) to transmit; (billet, timbre, emprunt) to issue; (hypothèse, avis) to voice, put forward ⊳ *vi* to broadcast

émeus *etc* [emø] *vb voir* **émouvoir**

émeute [emøt] *nf* riot

émigrer [emigre] *vi* to emigrate

émincer [emɛ̃se] *vt* to cut into thin

slices

émission [emisjɔ̃] nf (Radio, TV)
programme, broadcast; (d'un message)
transmission; (de timbre) issue

emmêler [ãmele] vt to tangle (up);
(fig) to muddle up; **s'emmêler** vi to get
in a tangle

emménager [ãmenaʒe] vi to move in;
~ **dans** to move into

emmener [ãmne] vt to take (with
one); (comme otage, capture) to take
away; ~ **qn au cinéma** to take sb to
the cinema

emmerder [ãmɛʀde] (fam!) vt to bug,
bother; **s'emmerder** vi to be bored stiff

émoticone [emotikon] nm smiley

émotif, -ive [emotif, iv] adj emotional

émotion [emosjɔ̃] nf emotion

émouvoir [emuvwaʀ] vt to move;
s'émouvoir vi to be moved; (s'indigner)
to be roused

empaqueter [ãpakte] vt to parcel up

emparer [ãpaʀe]: **s'emparer de** vt
(objet) to seize, grab; (comme otage, MIL)
to seize; (suj: peur etc) to take hold of

empêchement [ãpɛʃmã] nm
(unexpected) obstacle, hitch

empêcher [ãpeʃe] vt to prevent; ~ **qn
de faire** to prevent ou stop sb from
doing; **il n'empêche que** nevertheless;
il n'a pas pu s'~ de rire he couldn't
help laughing

empereur [ãpʀœʀ] nm emperor

empiffrer [ãpifʀe]: **s'~** (fam) vi to
stuff o.s.

empiler [ãpile] vt to pile (up)

empire [ãpiʀ] nm empire; (fig)
influence

empirer [ãpiʀe] vi to worsen,
deteriorate

emplacement [ãplasmã] nm site

emploi [ãplwa] nm (utilisation) use;
(Comm, Écon) employment; (poste) job,
situation; **mode d'~** directions for use;
emploi du temps timetable, schedule

employé, e [ãplwaje] nm/f employee;
employé de bureau office employee
ou clerk

employer [ãplwaje] vt to use; (ouvrier,
main-d'œuvre) to employ; **s'~ à faire**
to apply ou devote o.s. to doing;
employeur, -euse nm/f employer

empoigner [ãpwaɲe] vt to grab

empoisonner [ãpwazɔne] vt to
poison; (empester: air, pièce) to stink out;
(fam): ~ **qn** to drive sb mad

emporter [ãpɔʀte] vt to take (with
one); (en dérobant ou enlevant, emmener:
blessés, voyageurs) to take away;
(entraîner) to carry away; **s'emporter** vi
(de colère) to lose one's temper; **l'~ (sur)**
to get the upper hand (of); **plats à ~**
take-away meals

empreinte [ãpʀɛ̃t] nf: ~ **(de pas)**
footprint; **empreintes (digitales)**
fingerprints

empressé, e [ãpʀese] adj attentive

empresser [ãpʀese]: **s'empresser** vi:
s'~ auprès de qn to surround sb with
attentions; **s'~ de faire** (se hâter) to
hasten to do

emprisonner [ãpʀizɔne] vt to
imprison

emprunt [ãpʀœ̃] nm loan

emprunter [ãpʀœ̃te] vt to borrow;
(itinéraire) to take, follow

ému, e [emy] pp de **émouvoir** ▷ adj
(gratitude) touched; (compassion) moved

○ **MOT-CLÉ**

en [ã] prép **1** (endroit, pays) in; (direction)
to; **habiter en France/ville** to live in
France/town; **aller en France/ville** to
go to France/town
2 (moment, temps) in; **en été/juin** in
summer/June; **en 3 jours** in 3 days
3 (moyen) by; **en avion/taxi** by
plane/taxi
4 (composition) made of; **c'est en verre**
it's (made of) glass; **un collier en
argent** a silver necklace
5 (description, état): **une femme
(habillée) en rouge** a woman (dressed)
in red; **peindre qch en rouge** to paint
sth red; **en T/étoile** T/star-shaped; **en**

chemise/chaussettes in one's shirt-sleeves/socks; **en soldat** as a soldier; **cassé en plusieurs morceaux** broken into several pieces; **en réparation** being repaired, under repair; **en vacances** on holiday; **en deuil** in mourning; **le même en plus grand** the same but ou only bigger

6 (avec gérondif) while, on, by; **en dormant** while sleeping, as one sleeps; **en sortant** on going out, as he etc went out; **sortir en courant** to run out

7 (comme) as; **je te parle en ami** I'm talking to you as a friend

▶ **pron 1** (indéfini): **j'en ai/veux** I have/want some; **en as-tu?** have you got any; **je n'en veux pas** I don't want any; **j'en ai 2** I've got 2; **combien y en a-t-il?** how many (of them) are there?; **j'en ai assez** I've got enough (of it ou them); (j'en ai marre) I've had enough

2 (provenance): **j'en viens** I've come from there

3 (cause): **il en est malade/perd le sommeil** he is ill/can't sleep because of it

4 (complément de nom, d'adjectif, de verbe): **j'en connais les dangers** I know its ou the dangers; **j'en suis fier** I am proud of it ou him ou the ou them; **j'en ai besoin** I need it ou them

encadrer [ɑ̃kɑdʀe] vt (tableau, image) to frame; (fig: entourer) to surround; (personnel, soldats etc) to train

encaisser [ɑ̃kese] vt (chèque) to cash; (argent) to collect; (fam: coup, défaite) to take

en-cas [ɑ̃kɑ] nm inv snack

enceinte [ɑ̃sɛ̃t] adj f: **~ (de 6 mois)** (6 months) pregnant ▶ nf (mur) wall; (espace) enclosure; **enceinte (acoustique)** (loud)speaker

encens [ɑ̃sɑ̃] nm incense

enchaîner [ɑ̃ʃene] vt to chain up; (mouvements, séquences) to link (together) ▶ vi to carry on

enchanté, e [ɑ̃ʃɑ̃te] adj (ravi)

delighted; (magique) enchanted; **~ (de faire votre connaissance)** pleased to meet you

enchère [ɑ̃ʃɛʀ] nf bid; **mettre/vendre aux ~s** to put up for (sale by)/sell by auction

enclencher [ɑ̃klɑ̃ʃe] vt (mécanisme) to engage; **s'enclencher** vi to engage

encombrant, e [ɑ̃kɔ̃bʀɑ̃, ɑ̃t] adj cumbersome, bulky

encombrement [ɑ̃kɔ̃bʀəmɑ̃] nm: **être pris dans un ~** to be stuck in a traffic jam

encombrer [ɑ̃kɔ̃bʀe] vt to clutter (up); (gêner) to hamper; **s'~ de** (bagages etc) to load ou burden o.s. with

○ **MOT-CLÉ**

encore [ɑ̃kɔʀ] adv **1** (continuation) still; **il y travaille encore** he's still working on it; **pas encore** not yet

2 (de nouveau) again; **j'irai encore demain** I'll go again tomorrow; **encore une fois** (once) again; **(et puis) quoi encore?** what next?

3 (en plus) more; **encore un peu de viande?** a little more meat?; **encore deux jours** two more days

4 (intensif) even, still; **encore plus fort/mieux** even louder/better, louder/better still

5 (restriction) even so ou then, only; **encore pourrais-je le faire si ...** even so, I might be able to do it if ...; **si encore** if only

encourager [ɑ̃kuʀaʒe] vt to encourage; **~ qn à faire qch** to encourage sb to do sth

encourir [ɑ̃kuʀiʀ] vt to incur

encre [ɑ̃kʀ] nf ink; **encre de Chine** Indian ink

encyclopédie [ɑ̃siklopedi] nf encyclopaedia

endetter [ɑ̃dete]: **s'endetter** vi to get into debt

endive [ɑ̃div] nf chicory no pl

endormi, e [ãdɔʀmi] adj asleep
endormir [ãdɔʀmiʀ] vt to put to sleep; (suj: chaleur etc) to send to sleep; (Méd: dent, nerf) to anaesthetise; (fig: soupçons) to allay; **s'endormir** vi to fall asleep, go to sleep
endroit [ãdʀwa] nm place; (opposé à l'envers) right side; **à l'~** (vêtement) the right way out; (objet posé) the right way round
endurance [ãdyʀãs] nf endurance
endurant, e [ãdyʀã, ãt] adj tough, hardy
endurcir [ãdyʀsiʀ] **s'endurcir** vi (physiquement) to become tougher; (moralement) to become hardened
endurer [ãdyʀe] vt to endure, bear
énergétique [enɛʀʒetik] adj (aliment) energy-giving
énergie [enɛʀʒi] nf (Physique) energy; (Tech) power; (morale) vigour, spirit; **énergique** adj energetic, vigorous; (mesures) drastic, stringent
énervant, e [enɛʀvã, ãt] adj irritating, annoying
énerver [enɛʀve] vt to irritate, annoy; **s'énerver** vi to become, get worked up
enfance [ãfãs] nf childhood
enfant [ãfã] nm/f child; **enfantin, e** adj (puéril) childlike; (langage, jeu etc) children's cpd
enfer [ãfɛʀ] nm hell
enfermer [ãfɛʀme] vt to shut up; (à clef, interner) to lock up; **s'enfermer** vi to shut o.s. away
enfiler [ãfile] vt (vêtement) to slip on, slip into; (perles) to string; (aiguille) to thread
enfin [ãfɛ̃] adv at last; (en énumérant) lastly; (toutefois) still; (pour conclure) in a word; (somme toute) after all
enflammer [ãflame] **s'enflammer** vi to catch fire; (Méd) to become inflamed
enflé, e [ãfle] adj swollen
enfler [ãfle] vi to swell (up)
enfoncer [ãfɔ̃se] vt (clou) to drive in; (faire pénétrer): **~ qch dans** to push (ou

drive) sth into; (forcer: porte) to break open; **s'enfoncer** vi to sink; **s'~ dans** to sink into; (forêt, ville) to disappear into
enfouir [ãfwiʀ] vt (dans le sol) to bury; (dans un tiroir etc) to tuck away
enfuir [ãfɥiʀ]: **s'enfuir** vi to run away ou off
engagement [ãɡaʒmã] nm commitment; **sans ~** without obligation
engager [ãɡaʒe] vt (embaucher) to take on; (: artiste) to engage; (commencer) to start; (lier) to bind, commit; (impliquer) to involve; (investir) to invest, lay out; (inciter) to urge; (introduire: clé) to insert; **s'engager** (promettre) to commit o.s.; (Mil) to enlist; (débuter: conversation etc) to start (up); **s'~ à faire** to undertake to do; **s'~ dans** (rue, passage) to turn into; (fig: affaire, discussion) to enter into, embark on
engelures [ãʒlyʀ] nfpl chilblains
engin [ãʒɛ̃] nm machine; (outil) instrument; (Auto) vehicle; (Aviat) aircraft inv

> Attention à ne pas traduire **engin** par le mot anglais **engine**.

engloutir [ãɡlutiʀ] vt to swallow up
engouement [ãɡumã] nm (sudden) passion
engouffrer [ãɡufʀe] vt to swallow up, devour; **s'engouffrer dans** to rush into
engourdir [ãɡuʀdiʀ] vt to numb; (fig) to dull, blunt; **s'engourdir** vi to go numb
engrais [ãɡʀɛ] nm manure; **engrais chimique** chemical fertilizer
engraisser [ãɡʀese] vt to fatten (up)
engrenage [ãɡʀənaʒ] nm gears pl, gearing; (fig) chain
engueuler [ãɡœle] (fam) vt to bawl at
enhardir [ãaʀdiʀ]: **s'enhardir** vi to grow bolder
énigme [eniɡm] nf riddle
enivrer [ãnivʀe] vt: **s'~** to get drunk
enjamber [ãʒãbe] vt to stride over
enjeu, x [ãʒø] nm stakes pl
enjoué, e [ãʒwe] adj playful

enlaidir [ɑ̃ledir] vt to make ugly ▷ vi to become ugly

enlèvement [ɑ̃lɛvmɑ̃] nm (rapt) abduction, kidnapping

enlever [ɑ̃l(ə)ve] vt (ôter: gén) to remove; (: vêtement, lunettes) to take off; (emporter: ordures etc) to take away; (kidnapper: to abduct, kidnap; (obtenir: prix, contrat) to win; (prendre): ~ **qch à qn** to take sth (away) from sb

enliser [ɑ̃lize]: **s'enliser** vi to sink, get stuck

enneigé, e [ɑ̃neʒe] adj (route, maison) snowed-up; (paysage) snowy

ennemi, e [ɛnmi] adj hostile; (Mil) enemy cpd ▷ nm/f enemy

ennui [ɑ̃nɥi] nm (lassitude) boredom; (difficulté) trouble no pl; **avoir des ~s** to have problems; **ennuyer** [ɑ̃nɥije] vt to bother; (lasser) to bore; **s'ennuyer** vi to be bored; **si cela ne vous ennuie pas** if it's no trouble (to you); **ennuyeux, -euse** adj boring, tedious; (embêtant) annoying

énorme [enɔrm] adj enormous, huge; **énormément** adv enormously; **énormément de neige/gens** an enormous amount of snow/number of people

enquête [ɑ̃kɛt] nf (de journaliste, de police) investigation; (judiciaire, administrative) inquiry; (sondage d'opinion) survey; **enquêter** vi: **enquêter (sur)** to investigate

enragé, e [ɑ̃raʒe] adj (Méd) rabid, with rabies; (fig) fanatical

enrageant, e [ɑ̃raʒɑ̃, ɑ̃t] adj infuriating

enrager [ɑ̃raʒe] vi to be in a rage

enregistrement [ɑ̃r(ə)ʒistrəmɑ̃] nm recording; **enregistrement des bagages** baggage check-in

enregistrer [ɑ̃r(ə)ʒistre] vt (Mus etc) to record; (fig: mémoriser) to make a mental note of; (bagages: à l'aéroport) to check in

enrhumer [ɑ̃ryme] vt: **s'~, être enrhumé** to catch a cold

enrichir [ɑ̃riʃir] vt to make rich(er); (fig) to enrich; **s'enrichir** vi to get rich(er)

enrouer [ɑ̃rwe]: **s'enrouer** vi to go hoarse

enrouler [ɑ̃rule] vt (fil, corde) to wind (up); **s'~ (autour de qch)** to wind (around) sth

enseignant, e [ɑ̃sɛɲɑ̃, ɑ̃t] nm/f teacher

enseignement [ɑ̃sɛɲ(ə)mɑ̃] nm teaching; (Admin) education

enseigner [ɑ̃seɲe] vt, vi to teach; **~ qch à qn** to teach sb sth

ensemble [ɑ̃sɑ̃bl] adv together ▷ nm (groupement) set; (vêtements) outfit; (totalité): **l'~ du/de la** the whole ou entire; (unité, harmonie) unity; **impression/idée d'~** overall ou general impression/idea; **dans l'~** (en gros) on the whole

ensoleillé, e [ɑ̃soleje] adj sunny

ensuite [ɑ̃sɥit] adv then, next; (plus tard) afterwards, later

entamer [ɑ̃tame] vt (pain, bouteille) to start; (hostilités, pourparlers) to open

entasser [ɑ̃tase] vt (empiler) to pile up, heap up; **s'entasser** vi (s'amonceler) to pile up; **s'~ dans** (personnes) to cram into

entendre [ɑ̃tɑ̃dr] vt to hear; (comprendre) to understand; (vouloir dire) to mean; **s'entendre** vi (sympathiser) to get on; (se mettre d'accord) to agree; **j'ai entendu dire que** I've heard (it said) that; **~ parler de** to hear of

entendu, e [ɑ̃tɑ̃dy] adj (réglé) agreed; (au courant: air) knowing; **(c'est) ~** all right, agreed; **bien ~** of course

entente [ɑ̃tɑ̃t] nf understanding; (accord, traité) agreement; **à double ~** (sens) with a double meaning

enterrement [ɑ̃tɛrmɑ̃] nm (cérémonie) funeral, burial

enterrer [ɑ̃tere] vt to bury

entêtant, e [ɑ̃tɛtɑ̃, ɑ̃t] adj heady

en-tête [ɑ̃tɛt] nm heading; **papier à ~** headed notepaper

entêté, e [ɑ̃tete] adj stubborn

entêter [ɑ̃tete]: **s'entêter** vi: **s'~ (à faire)** to persist (in doing)

enthousiasme [ɑ̃tuzjasm] nm enthusiasm; **enthousiasmer** vt to fill with enthusiasm; **s'enthousiasmer (pour qch)** to get enthusiastic (about sth); **enthousiaste** adj enthusiastic

entier, -ère [ɑ̃tje, jɛʀ] adj whole; (total: satisfaction etc) complete; (fig: caractère) unbending ▷ nm (Math) whole; **en ~** totally; **lait ~** full-cream milk; **entièrement** adv entirely, wholly

entonnoir [ɑ̃tɔnwaʀ] nm funnel

entorse [ɑ̃tɔʀs] nf (Méd) sprain; (fig): **~ au règlement** infringement of the rule

entourage [ɑ̃tuʀaʒ] nm circle; (famille) circle of family/friends; (ce qui enclôt) surround

entourer [ɑ̃tuʀe] vt to surround; (apporter son soutien à) to rally round; **~ de** to surround with; **s'~ de** to surround o.s. with

entracte [ɑ̃tʀakt] nm interval

entraide [ɑ̃tʀɛd] nf mutual aid

entrain [ɑ̃tʀɛ̃] nm spirit; **avec/sans ~** spiritedly/half-heartedly

entraînement [ɑ̃tʀɛnmɑ̃] nm training

entraîner [ɑ̃tʀene] vt (charrier) to carry ou drag along; (Tech) to drive; (emmener: personne) to take (off); (influencer) to lead; (Sport) to train; (impliquer) to entail; **s'entraîner** vi (Sport) to train; **s'~ à qch/à faire** to train o.s. to ou to do; **~ qn à faire** (inciter) to lead sb to do; **entraîneur, -euse** nm/f (Sport) coach, trainer ▷ nm (Hippisme) trainer

entre [ɑ̃tʀ] prép between; (parmi) among(st); **l'un d'~ eux/nous** one of them/us; **ils se battent ~ eux** they are fighting among(st) themselves; **~ autres (choses)** among other things; **entrecôte** nf entrecôte ou rib steak

entrée [ɑ̃tʀe] nf entrance; (accès: au cinéma etc) admission; (billet) (admission) ticket; (Culin) first course

entre…: entrefilet nm paragraph (short article); **entremets** nm (cream) dessert

entrepôt [ɑ̃tʀəpo] nm warehouse

entreprendre [ɑ̃tʀəpʀɑ̃dʀ] vt (se lancer dans) to undertake; (commencer à) to begin ou start (upon)

entrepreneur, -euse [ɑ̃tʀəpʀənœʀ, øz] nm/f: **entrepreneur (en bâtiment)** (building) contractor

entreprise [ɑ̃tʀəpʀiz] nf (société) firm, concern; (action) undertaking, venture

entrer [ɑ̃tʀe] vi to go (ou come) in, enter ▷ vt (Inform) to enter, input; **(faire) ~ qch dans** to get sth into; **~ dans** (gén) to enter; (pièce) to go (ou come) into, enter; (club) to join; (heurter) to run into; **~ à l'hôpital** to go into hospital; **faire ~** (visiteur) to show in

entre-temps [ɑ̃tʀətɑ̃] adv meanwhile

entretenir [ɑ̃tʀət(ə)niʀ] vt to maintain; (famille, maîtresse) to support, keep; **~ qn (de)** to speak to sb (about)

entretien [ɑ̃tʀətjɛ̃] nm maintenance; (discussion) discussion, talk; (pour un emploi) interview

entrevoir [ɑ̃tʀəvwaʀ] vt (à peine) to make out; (brièvement) to catch a glimpse of

entrevue [ɑ̃tʀəvy] nf (audience) interview

entrouvert, e [ɑ̃tʀuvɛʀ, ɛʀt] adj half-open

énumérer [enymeʀe] vt to list

envahir [ɑ̃vaiʀ] vt to invade; (suj: inquiétude, peur) to come over; **envahissant, e** (péj) adj (personne) intrusive

enveloppe [ɑ̃v(ə)lɔp] nf (de lettre) envelope; (crédits) budget; **envelopper** vt to wrap; (fig) to envelop, shroud

enverra etc [ɑ̃veʀa] vb voir **envoyer**

envers [ɑ̃vɛʀ] prép towards, to ▷ nm other side; (d'une étoffe) wrong side; **à l'~** (verticalement) upside down; (pull) back to front; (chaussettes) inside out

envie [ɑ̃vi] nf (sentiment) envy; (souhait) desire, wish; **avoir ~ de (faire)** to feel like (doing); (plus fort) to want (to do); **avoir ~ que** to wish that; **cette glace me fait ~** I fancy some of that ice cream; **envier** vt to envy; **envieux, -euse** adj envious

environ [ãvirɔ̃] adv: **~ 3 h/2 km** (around) about 3 o'clock/2 km; voir aussi **environs**

environnant, e [ãvirɔnã, ãt] adj surrounding

environnement [ãvirɔnmã] nm environment

environs [ãvirɔ̃] nmpl surroundings; **aux ~ de** (round) about

envisager [ãvizaʒe] vt to contemplate, envisage; **~ de faire** to consider doing

envoler [ãvɔle]: **s'envoler** vi (oiseau) to fly away ou off; (avion) to take off; (papier, feuille) to blow away; (fig) to vanish (into thin air)

envoyé, e [ãvwaje] nm/f (Pol) envoy; (Presse) correspondent; **envoyé spécial** special correspondent

envoyer [ãvwaje] vt to send; (lancer) to hurl, throw; **~ chercher** to send for; **~ promener qn** (fam) to send sb packing

épagneul, e [epaɲœl] nm/f spaniel

épais, se [epɛ, ɛs] adj thick; **épaisseur** nf thickness

épanouir [epanwir]: **s'épanouir** vi (fleur) to bloom, open out; (visage) to light up; (personne) to blossom

épargne [eparɲ] nf saving

épargner [eparɲe] vt to save; (ne pas tuer ou endommager) to spare ▷ vi to save; **~ qch à qn** to spare sb sth

éparpiller [eparpije] vt to scatter; **s'éparpiller** vi to scatter; (fig) to dissipate one's efforts

épatant, e [epatã, ãt] (fam) adj super

épater [epate] (fam) vt (étonner) to amaze; (impressionner) to impress

épaule [epol] nf shoulder

épave [epav] nf wreck

épée [epe] nf sword

épeler [ep(ə)le] vt to spell

éperon [ep(ə)rɔ̃] nm spur

épervier [epɛrvje] nm sparrowhawk

épi [epi] nm (de blé, d'orge) ear; (de

maïs) cob

épice [epis] nf spice

épicé, e [epise] adj spicy

épicer [epise] vt to spice

épicerie [episri] nf grocer's shop; (denrées) groceries pl; **épicerie fine** delicatessen; **épicier, -ière** nm/f grocer

épidémie [epidemi] nf epidemic

épiderme [epidɛrm] nm skin

épier [epje] vt to spy on, watch closely

épilepsie [epilɛpsi] nf epilepsy

épiler [epile] vt (jambes) to remove the hair from; (sourcils) to pluck

épinards [epinar] nmpl spinach sg

épine [epin] nf thorn, prickle; (d'oursin etc) spine

épingle [epɛ̃gl] nf pin; **épingle de nourrice** ou **de sûreté** safety pin

épisode [epizɔd] nm episode; **film/roman à ~s** serial; **épisodique** adj occasional

épluche-légumes [eplyʃlegym] nm inv (potato) peeler

éplucher [eplyʃe] vt (fruit, légumes) to peel; (fig) to go over with a fine-tooth comb; **épluchures** nfpl peelings

éponge [epɔ̃ʒ] nf sponge; **éponger** vt (liquide) to mop up; (surface) to sponge; (fig: déficit) to soak up

époque [epɔk] nf (de l'histoire) age, era; (de l'année, la vie) time; **d'~** (meuble) period cpd

épouse [epuz] nf wife; **épouser** vt to marry

épousseter [epuste] vt to dust

épouvantable [epuvãtabl] adj appalling, dreadful

épouvantail [epuvãtaj] nm scarecrow

épouvante [epuvãt] nf terror; **film d'~** horror film; **épouvanter** vt to terrify

époux [epu] nm husband ▷ nmpl (married) couple

épreuve [eprœv] nf (d'examen) test; (malheur, difficulté) trial, ordeal; (Photo) print; (Typo) proof; (Sport) event; **à toute ~** unfailing; **mettre à l'~** to put to the test

éprouver [epruve] vt (tester) to

test; (marquer, faire souffrir) to afflict, distress; (ressentir) to experience

épuisé, e[epчize] adj exhausted; (livre) out of print; **épuisement** nm exhaustion

épuiser[epчize] vt (fatiguer) to exhaust, wear ou tire out; (stock, sujet) to exhaust; **s'épuiser** vi to wear ou tire o.s. out, exhaust o.s.

épuisette[epчizɛt] nf shrimping net

équateur[ekwatœʀ] nm equator; **(la république de) l'É~** Ecuador

équation[ekwasjɔ̃] nf equation

équerre[ekɛʀ] nf (à dessin) (set) square

équilibre[ekilibʀ] nm balance; **garder/perdre l'~** to keep/lose one's balance; **être en ~** to be balanced; **équilibré, e** adj well-balanced; **équilibrer** vt to balance

équipage[ekipaʒ] nm crew

équipe[ekip] nf team; **travailler en ~** to work as a team

équipé, e[ekipe] adj: **bien/mal ~** well-/poorly-equipped

équipement[ekipmɑ̃] nm equipment

équiper[ekipe] vt to equip; **~ qn/qch de** to equip sb/sth with

équipier, -ière[ekipje, jɛʀ] nm/f team member

équitation[ekitasjɔ̃] nf (horse-)riding; **faire de l'~** to go riding

équivalent, e[ekivalɑ̃, ɑ̃t] adj, nm equivalent

équivaloir[ekivalwaʀ]: **~ à** vt to be equivalent to

érable[eʀabl] nm maple

érafler[eʀafle] vt to scratch; **éraflure** nf scratch

ère[ɛʀ] nf era; **en l'an 1050 de notre ~** in the year 1050 A.D.

érection[eʀɛksjɔ̃] nf erection

éroder[eʀɔde] vt to erode

érotique[eʀɔtik] adj erotic

errer[eʀe] vi to wander

erreur[eʀœʀ] nf mistake, error; **faire ~** to be mistaken; **par ~** by mistake

éruption[eʀypsjɔ̃] nf eruption; (Méd) rash

es[ɛ] vb voir **être**

ès[ɛs] prép: **licencié ès lettres/sciences** ≈ Bachelor of Arts/Science

ESB sigle f (= encéphalopathie spongiforme bovine) BSE

escabeau, x[ɛskabo] nm (tabouret) stool; (échelle) stepladder

escalade[ɛskalad] nf climbing no pl; (Pol etc) escalation; **escalader** vt to climb

escale[ɛskal] nf (Navig: durée) call; (endroit) port of call; (Aviat) stop(over); **faire ~** (Navig) to put in at; (Aviat) to stop over at; **vol sans ~** nonstop flight

escalier[ɛskalje] nm stairs pl; **dans l'~** ou **les ~s** on the stairs; **escalier mécanique** ou **roulant** escalator

escapade[ɛskapad] nf: **faire une ~** to go on a jaunt; (s'enfuir) to run away ou off

escargot[ɛskaʀgo] nm snail

escarpé, e[ɛskaʀpe] adj steep

esclavage[ɛsklavaʒ] nm slavery

esclave[ɛsklav] nm/f slave

escompte[ɛskɔ̃t] nm discount

escrime[ɛskʀim] nf fencing

escroc[ɛskʀo] nm swindler, conman; **escroquer** vt: **escroquer qch (à qn)** to swindle sth (out of sb); **escroquerie** nf swindle

espace[ɛspas] nm space; **espacer** vt to space out; **s'espacer** vi (visites etc) to become less frequent

espadon[ɛspadɔ̃] nm swordfish inv

espadrille[ɛspadʀij] nf rope-soled sandal

Espagne[ɛspaɲ] nf: **l'~** Spain; **espagnol, e** adj Spanish ▷ nm/f: **Espagnol, e** Spaniard ▷ nm (Ling) Spanish

espèce[ɛspɛs] nf (Bio, Bot, Zool) species inv; (gén: sorte) sort, kind, type; (péj): **~ de maladroit/de brute!** you clumsy oaf/you brute!; **espèces** nfpl (Comm) cash sg; **payer en ~s** to pay (in) cash

espérance[ɛspeʀɑ̃s] nf hope; **espérance de vie** life expectancy

espérer[ɛspeʀe] vt to hope for;

j'espère (bien) I hope so; **~ que/faire** to hope that/to do

espiègle[ɛspjɛgl] adj mischievous

espion, ne[ɛspjɔ̃, jɔn] nm/f spy; **espionnage** nm espionage, spying; **espionner** vt to spy (up)on

espoir[ɛspwar] nm hope; **dans l'~ de/que** in the hope of/that; **reprendre ~** not to lose hope

esprit[ɛspri] nm (intellect) mind; (humour) wit; (mentalité, d'une loi etc, fantôme etc) spirit; **faire de l'~** to try to be witty; **reprendre ses ~s** to come to; **perdre l'~** to lose one's mind

esquimau, de, -x[ɛskimo, od] adj Eskimo ⊳ nm/f: **E~, de** Eskimo ⊳ nm: **E~®** ice lolly (BRIT), popsicle (US)

essai[esɛ] nm (tentative) attempt, try; (de produit) testing; (Rugby) try; (Littérature) essay; **à l'~** on a trial basis; **mettre à l'~** to put to the test

essaim[esɛ̃] nm swarm

essayer[eseje] vt to try (on); (vêtement, chaussures) to try (on); (méthode, voiture) to try (out) ⊳ vi to try; **~ de faire** to try ou attempt to do

essence[esɑ̃s] nf (de voiture) petrol (BRIT), gas(oline) (US); (extrait de plante) essence; (espèce d'arbre) species inv

essentiel, le[esɑ̃sjɛl] adj essential; **c'est l'~** (ce qui importe) that's the main thing; **l'~ de** the main part of

essieu, x[esjø] nm axle

essor[esɔr] nm (de l'économie etc) rapid expansion

essorer[esɔre] vt (en tordant) to wring (out); (par la force centrifuge) to spin-dry; **essoreuse** nf spin-dryer

essouffler[esufle]: **s'essouffler** vi to get out of breath

essuie-glace[esɥiglas] nm inv windscreen (BRIT) ou windshield (US) wiper

essuyer[esɥije] vt to wipe; (fig: échec) to suffer; **s'essuyer** vi (après le bain) to dry o.s.; **~ la vaisselle** to dry up

est[e] vb voir **être**

est²[ɛst] nm east ⊳ adj inv east; (région)

east(ern); **à l'~** in the east; (direction) to the east, east(wards); **à l'~ de** to (the) east of

est-ce que[ɛskə] adv: **~ c'est cher/ c'était bon?** is it expensive/was it good?; **quand est-ce qu'il part?** when does he leave?, when is he leaving?; voir aussi **que**

esthéticienne[ɛstetisjɛn] nf beautician

esthétique[ɛstetik] adj attractive

estimation[ɛstimasjɔ̃] nf valuation; (chiffre) estimate

estime[ɛstim] nf esteem, regard; **estimer** vt (respecter) to esteem; (expertiser: bijou etc) to value; (évaluer: coût etc) to assess, estimate; (penser): **estimer que/être** to consider that/o.s. to be

estival, e, -aux[ɛstival, o] adj summer cpd

estivant, e[ɛstivɑ̃, ɑ̃t] nm/f (summer) holiday-maker

estomac[ɛstɔma] nm stomach

estragon[ɛstragɔ̃] nm tarragon

estuaire[ɛstɥɛr] nm estuary

et[e] conj and; **et lui?** what about him?; **et alors!** so what!

étable[etabl] nf cowshed

établi[etabli] nm (work)bench

établir[etablir] vt (papiers d'identité, facture) to make out; (liste, programme) to draw up; (entreprise) to set up; (réputation, usage, fait, culpabilité) to establish; **s'établir** vi to be established; **s'~ (à son compte)** to set up in business; **s'~ à/près de** to settle in/near

établissement[etablismɑ̃] nm (entreprise, institution) establishment; **établissement scolaire** school, educational establishment

étage[etaʒ] nm (d'immeuble) storey, floor; **à l'~** upstairs; **au 2ème ~** on the 2nd (BRIT) ou 3rd (US) floor; **c'est à quel ~?** what floor is it on?

étagère[etaʒɛr] nf (rayon) shelf; (meuble) shelves pl

étai [ete] nm stay, prop

étain [etɛ̃] nm pewter no pl

étais etc [etɛ] vb voir **être**

étaler [etale] vt (carte, nappe) to spread (out); (peinture) to spread; (échelonner: paiements, vacances) to spread, stagger; (marchandises) to display; (connaissances) to parade; **s'étaler** vi (liquide) to spread out; (fam) to fall flat on one's face; **s'~ sur** (suj: paiements etc) to be spread out over

étalon [etalɔ̃] nm (cheval) stallion

étanche [etɑ̃ʃ] adj (récipient) watertight; (montre, vêtement) waterproof

étang [etɑ̃] nm pond

étant [etɑ̃] vb voir **être; donné**

étape [etap] nf stage; (lieu d'arrivée) stopping place; (Cyclisme) staging point

état [eta] nm (Pol, condition) state; **en mauvais ~** in poor condition; **en ~ (de marche)** in (working) order; **remettre en ~** to repair; **hors d'~** out of order; **être en ~/hors d'~ de faire** to be in a/in no fit state to do; **être dans tous ses ~s** to be in a state; **faire ~ de** (alléguer) to put forward; **l'É~** the State; **état civil** civil status; **état des lieux** inventory of fixtures; **États-Unis** nmpl: **les États-Unis** the United States

etc. [ɛtsetera] adv etc

et c(a)etera [ɛtsetera] adv et cetera, and so on

été [ete] pp de **être** ▷ nm summer

éteindre [etɛ̃dʀ] vt (lampe, lumière, radio) to turn ou switch off; (cigarette, feu) to put out, extinguish; **s'éteindre** vi (feu, lumière) to go out; (mourir) to pass away; **éteint, e** adj (fig) lacklustre, dull; (volcan) extinct

étendre [etɑ̃dʀ] vt (pâte, liquide) to spread; (carte etc) to spread out; (linge) to hang up; (bras, jambes) to stretch out; (fig: agrandir) to extend; **s'étendre** vi (augmenter, se propager) to spread; (terrain, forêt etc) to stretch; (s'allonger) to stretch out; (se coucher) to lie down;

(fig: expliquer) to elaborate

étendu, e [etɑ̃dy] adj extensive

éternel, le [etɛʀnɛl] adj eternal

éternité [etɛʀnite] nf eternity; **ça a duré une ~** it lasted for ages

éternuement [etɛʀnymɑ̃] nm sneeze

éternuer [etɛʀnɥe] vi to sneeze

êtes [ɛt(z)] vb voir **être**

Éthiopie [etjɔpi] nf: **l'~** Ethiopia

étiez [etje] vb voir **être**

étinceler [etɛ̃s(ə)le] vi to sparkle

étincelle [etɛ̃sɛl] nf spark

étiquette [etiket] nf label; (protocole): **l'~** etiquette

étirer [etire]: **s'étirer** vi (personne) to stretch; (convoi, route): **s'~ sur** to stretch out over

étoile [etwal] nf star; **à la belle ~** in the open; **étoile de mer** starfish; **étoile filante** shooting star; **étoilé, e** adj starry

étonnant, e [etɔnɑ̃, ɑ̃t] adj amazing

étonnement [etɔnmɑ̃] nm surprise, amazement

étonner [etɔne] vt to surprise, amaze; **s'étonner que/de** to be amazed that/at; **cela m'~ait (que)** (j'en doute) I'd be very surprised (if)

étouffer [etufe] vt to suffocate; (bruit) to muffle; (scandale) to hush up ▷ vi to suffocate; (avoir trop chaud): **on étouffe** it's stifling

étourderie [eturdəri] nf (caractère) absent-mindedness no pl; (faute) thoughtless blunder

étourdi, e [eturdi] adj (distrait) scatterbrained, heedless

étourdir [eturdir] vt (assommer) to stun, daze; (griser) to make dizzy ou giddy; **étourdissement** nm dizzy spell

étrange [etrɑ̃ʒ] adj strange

étranger, -ère [etrɑ̃ʒe, ɛr] adj foreign; (pas de la famille, non familier) strange ▷ nm/f foreigner; stranger ▷ nm: **à l'~** abroad

étrangler [etrɑ̃gle] vt to strangle; **s'étrangler** vi (en mangeant etc) to choke

○ **MOT-CLÉ**

être [ɛtʀ] nm being; **être humain** human being
▷ vb +attrib **1** (état, description) to be; **il est instituteur** he is ou he's a teacher; **vous êtes grand/clever/tired** you are ou you're tall/clever/tired
2 (+à: appartenir) to be; **le livre est à Paul** the book is Paul's ou belongs to Paul; **c'est à moi/eux** it is ou it's mine/theirs
3 (+de: provenance): **il est de Paris** he is from Paris; (: appartenance): **il est des nôtres** he is one of us
4 (date): **nous sommes le 10 janvier** it's the 10th of January (today)
▷ vi to be; **je ne serai pas ici demain** I won't be here tomorrow
▷ vb aux **1** +adjectif: **être arrivé/ allé** to have arrived/gone; **il est parti** he has left, he has gone
2 (forme passive): **être fait par** to be made by; **il a été promu** he has been promoted
3 (+à: obligation): **c'est à réparer** it needs repairing; **c'est à essayer** it should be tried; **il est à espérer que ...** it is ou it's to be hoped that ...
▷ vb impers **1**: **il est +adjectif** it is +adjective: **il est impossible de le faire** it's impossible to do it
2 (heure, date): **il est 10 heures** it is ou it's 10 o'clock
3 (emphatique): **c'est moi** it's me; **c'est à lui de le faire** it's up to him to do it

étrennes [etʀɛn] nfpl Christmas box sg
étrier [etʀije] nm stirrup
étroit, e [etʀwa, wat] adj narrow; (vêtement) tight; (fig: liens, collaboration) close; **à l'~** cramped; **~ d'esprit** narrow-minded
étude [etyd] nf studying; (ouvrage, rapport) study; (Scol: salle de travail) study room; **études** nfpl (Scol) studies; **être à l'~** (projet etc) to be under consideration; **faire des ~s (de droit/**

médecine) to study (law/medicine)
étudiant, e [etydjã, jãt] nm/f student
étudier [etydje] vt, vi to study
étui [etɥi] nm case
eu, eue [y] pp de **avoir**
euh [ø] excl er
euro [øʀo] nm euro
Europe [øʀɔp] nf: **l'~** Europe; **européen, ne** adj European ▷ nm/f: **Européen, ne** European
eus etc [y] vb voir **avoir**
eux [ø] pron (sujet) they; (objet) them
évacuer [evakɥe] vt to evacuate
évader [evade]: **s'évader** vi to escape
évaluer [evalɥe] vt (expertiser) to appraise, evaluate; (juger approximativement) to estimate
évangile [evãʒil] nm gospel; **É~** Gospel
évanouir [evanwiʀ]: **s'évanouir** vi to faint; (disparaître) to vanish, disappear; **évanouissement** nm (syncope) fainting fit
évaporer [evapɔʀe]: **s'évaporer** vi to evaporate
évasion [evazjɔ̃] nf escape
éveillé, e [eveje] adj awake; (vif) alert, sharp; **éveiller** vt to (a)waken; (soupçons etc) to arouse; **s'éveiller** vi to (a)waken; (fig) to be aroused
événement [evɛnmã] nm event
éventail [evãtaj] nm fan; (choix) range
éventualité [evãtɥalite] nf eventuality; possibility; **dans l'~ de** in the event of
éventuel, le [evãtɥɛl] adj possible
Attention à ne pas traduire **éventuel** par eventual.
éventuellement adv possibly
Attention à ne pas traduire **éventuellement** par eventually.
évêque [evɛk] nm bishop
évidemment [evidamã] adv (bien sûr) of course; (certainement) obviously
évidence [evidãs] nf obviousness; (fait) obvious fact; **de toute ~** quite obviously ou evidently; **être en ~** to be clearly visible; **mettre en ~** (fait) to highlight; **évident, e** adj obvious,

évident; ce n'est pas évident! (fam) it's not that easy!

évier [evje] nm (kitchen) sink

éviter [evite] vt to avoid; **~ de faire** to avoid doing; **~ qch à qn** to spare sb sth

évoluer [evɔlɥe] vi (enfant, maladie) to develop; (situation, moralement) to evolve, develop; (aller et venir) to move about; **évolution** nf development, evolution

évoquer [evɔke] vt to call to mind, evoke; (mentionner) to mention

ex- [ɛks] préfixe ex-; **son ~ mari** her ex-husband; **son ~ femme** his ex-wife

exact, e [ɛgza(kt), ɛgzakt] adj exact; (correct) correct; (ponctuel) punctual; **l'heure ~e** the right ou exact time; **exactement** adv exactly

ex aequo [ɛgzeko] adj equally placed; **arriver ~** to finish neck and neck

exagéré, e [ɛgzaʒere] adj (prix etc) excessive

exagérer [ɛgzaʒere] vt to exaggerate ▷ vi to exaggerate; (abuser) to go too far

examen [ɛgzamɛ̃] nm examination; (Scol) exam, examination; **à l'~** under consideration; **examen médical** (medical) examination; (analyse) test

examinateur, -trice [ɛgzaminatœr, tris] nm/f examiner

examiner [ɛgzamine] vt to examine

exaspérant, e [ɛgzasperɑ̃, ɑ̃t] adj exasperating

exaspérer [ɛgzaspere] vt to exasperate

exaucer [ɛgzose] vt (vœu) to grant

excéder [ɛksede] vt (dépasser) to exceed; (agacer) to exasperate

excellent, e [ɛksɛlɑ̃, ɑ̃t] adj excellent

excentrique [ɛksɑ̃trik] adj eccentric

excepté, e [ɛksɛpte] adj, prép: **les élèves ~ s, ~ les élèves** except for the pupils

exception [ɛksɛpsjɔ̃] nf exception; **à l'~ de** except for, with the exception of; **d'~** (mesure, loi) special, exceptional; **exceptionnel, le** adj exceptional; **exceptionnellement** adv

exceptionally

excès [ɛksɛ] nm surplus ▷ nmpl excesses; **faire des ~** to overindulge; **excès de vitesse** speeding no pl; **excessif, -ive** adj excessive

excitant, e [ɛksitɑ̃, ɑ̃t] adj exciting ▷ nm stimulant; **excitation** nf (état) excitement

exciter [ɛksite] vt to excite; (suj: café etc) to stimulate; **s'exciter** vi to get excited

exclamer [ɛksklame]: **s'exclamer** vi to exclaim

exclure [ɛksklyʀ] vt (faire sortir) to expel; (ne pas compter) to exclude, leave out; (rendre impossible) to exclude, rule out; **il est exclu que** it's out of the question that ...; **il n'est pas exclu que** ... it's not impossible that ...; **exclusif, -ive** adj exclusive; **à l'exclusion de** with the exclusion ou exception of; **exclusion** nf exclusion; **exclusivité** nf (Comm) exclusive rights pl; **film passant en exclusivité à** film showing only at

excursion [ɛkskyʀsjɔ̃] nf (en autocar) excursion, trip; (à pied) walk, hike

excuse [ɛkskyz] nf excuse; **excuses** nfpl (regret) apology sg, apologies; **excuser** vt to excuse; **s'excuser (de)** to apologize (for); **excusez-moi** I'm sorry; (pour attirer l'attention) excuse me

exécuter [ɛgzekyte] vt (tuer) to execute; (tâche etc) to execute, carry out; (Mus: jouer) to perform, execute; **s'exécuter** vi to comply

exemplaire [ɛgzɑ̃plɛʀ] nm copy

exemple [ɛgzɑ̃pl] nm example; **par ~** for instance, for example; **donner l'~** to set an example

exercer [ɛgzɛʀse] vt (pratiquer) to exercise, practise; (influence, contrôle) to exert; (former) to exercise, train; **s'exercer** vi (sportif, musicien) to practise

exercice [ɛgzɛʀsis] nm exercise

exhiber [ɛgzibe] vt (montrer: papiers, certificat) to present, produce; (péj) to

display, flaunt; **s'exhiber** vi to parade; (suj: exhibitionniste) to expose o.s.
exhibitionniste nm/f flasher
exigeant, e [ɛgziʒɑ̃, ɑ̃t] adj demanding; (péj) hard to please
exiger [ɛgziʒe] vt to demand, require
exil [ɛgzil] nm exile; **en ~** in exile; **s'exiler** vi to go into exile
existence [ɛgzistɑ̃s] nf existence
exister [ɛgziste] vi to exist; **il existe un/des** there is a/are (some)
exorbitant, e [ɛgzɔrbitɑ̃, ɑ̃t] adj exorbitant
exotique [ɛgzɔtik] adj exotic; **yaourt aux fruits ~s** tropical fruit yoghurt
expédier [ɛkspedje] vt (lettre, paquet) to send; (troupes) to dispatch; (fam: travail etc) to dispose of, dispatch; **expéditeur, -trice** nm/f sender; **expédition** [ɛkspedisjɔ̃] nf sending; (scientifique, sportive, Mil) expedition
expérience [ɛksperjɑ̃s] nf (de la vie) experience; (scientifique) experiment
expérimenté, e [ɛksperimɑ̃te] adj experienced
expérimenter [ɛksperimɑ̃te] vt to test out, experiment with
expert, e [ɛkspɛr, ɛrt] adj, nm expert; **~ en objets d'art** appraiser; **expert-comptable** ≈ chartered accountant (BRIT), ≈ certified public accountant (US)
expirer [ɛkspire] vi (prendre fin, mourir) to expire; (respirer) to breathe out
explication [ɛksplikasjɔ̃] nf explanation; (discussion) discussion; (dispute) argument
explicite [ɛksplisit] adj explicit
expliquer [ɛksplike] vt to explain; **s'expliquer** to explain (o.s.); **s'~ avec qn** (discuter) to explain o.s. to sb; **son erreur s'explique** one can understand his mistake
exploit [ɛksplwa] nm exploit, feat; **exploitant, e** nm/f: **exploitant (agricole)** farmer; **exploitation** nf exploitation; (d'une entreprise) running; **exploitation agricole** farming

concern; **exploiter** vt (personne, don) to exploit; (entreprise, ferme) to run, operate; (mine) to exploit, work
explorer [ɛksplɔre] vt to explore
exploser [ɛksploze] vi to explode, blow up; (engin explosif) to go off; (personne: de colère) to flare up; **explosif, -ive** adj, nm explosive; **explosion** nf explosion; (de joie, colère) outburst
exportateur, -trice [ɛkspɔrtatœr, tris] adj export cpd, exporting ▷ nm exporter
exportation [ɛkspɔrtasjɔ̃] nf (action) exportation; (produit) export
exporter [ɛkspɔrte] vt to export
exposant [ɛkspozɑ̃] nm exhibitor
exposé, e [ɛkspoze] nm talk ▷ adj: **~ au sud** facing south
exposer [ɛkspoze] vt (marchandise) to display; (peinture) to exhibit, show; (parler de) to explain, set out; (mettre en danger, orienter, Photo) to expose; **s'~ à** (soleil, danger) to expose o.s. to; **exposition** [ɛkspozisjɔ̃] nf (manifestation) exhibition; (Photo) exposure
exprès¹ [ɛksprɛ] adv (délibérément) on purpose; (spécialement) specially; **faire ~ de faire qch** to do sth on purpose
exprès², -esse [ɛksprɛs] adj inv (lettre, colis) express
express [ɛksprɛs] adj, nm: **(café) ~** espresso (coffee); **(train) ~** fast train
expressif, -ive [ɛkspresif, iv] adj expressive
expression [ɛkspresjɔ̃] nf expression
exprimer [ɛksprime] vt (sentiment, idée) to express; (jus, liquide) to press out; **s'exprimer** vi (personne) to express o.s
expulser [ɛkspylse] vt to expel; (locataire) to evict; (Sport) to send off
exquis, e [ɛkski, iz] adj exquisite
extasier: s'extasier sur vt to go into raptures over
exténuer [ɛkstenɥe] vt to exhaust
extérieur, e [ɛksterjœr] adj (porte, mur etc) outer, outside; (au dehors: escalier, w.-c.) outside; (commerce)

foreign; (*influences*) external; (*apparent: calme, gaieté etc*) surface cpd ▷ nm (*d'une maison, d'un récipient etc*) outside, exterior; (*apparence*) exterior; **à l'~** outside; (*à l'étranger*) abroad

externat [ɛkstɛrna] nm day school

externe [ɛkstɛrn] adj external, outer ▷ nm/f (*Méd*) non-resident medical student (BRIT), extern (US); (*Scol*) day pupil

extincteur [ɛkstɛ̃ktœr] nm (fire) extinguisher

extinction [ɛkstɛ̃ksjɔ̃] nf: **extinction de voix** loss of voice

extra [ɛkstra] adj inv first-rate; (*fam*) fantastic ▷ nm inv extra help

extraire [ɛkstrɛr] vt to extract; **~ qch de** to extract sth from; **extrait** nm extract; **extrait de naissance** birth certificate

extraordinaire [ɛkstraɔrdinɛr] adj extraordinary; (*Pol: mesures etc*) special

extravagant, e [ɛkstravagɑ̃, ɑ̃t] adj extravagant

extraverti, e [ɛkstravɛrti] adj extrovert

extrême [ɛkstrɛm] adj, nm extreme; **d'un ~ à l'autre** from one extreme to another; **extrêmement** adv extremely; **Extrême-Orient** nm Far East

extrémité [ɛkstremite] nf end; (*situation*) straits pl, plight; (*geste désespéré*) extreme action; **extrémités** nfpl (*pieds et mains*) extremities

exubérant, e [ɛgzybɛrɑ̃, ɑ̃t] adj exuberant

f

F abr = **franc**; (*appartement*): **un F2/F3** a one-/two-bedroom flat (BRIT) ou apartment (US)

fa [fa] nm inv (*Mus*) F; (*en chantant la gamme*) fa

fabricant, e [fabrikɑ̃, ɑ̃t] nm/f manufacturer

fabrication [fabrikasjɔ̃] nf manufacture

fabrique [fabrik] nf factory; **fabriquer** vt to make; (*industriellement*) to manufacture; (*fig*): **qu'est-ce qu'il fabrique?** (*fam*) what is he doing?

fac [fak] (*fam*) abr f (*Scol*) = **faculté**

façade [fasad] nf front, façade

face [fas] nf face; (*fig: aspect*) side ▷ adj: **le côté ~** heads; **en ~ de** opposite; (*fig*) in front of; **de ~** (*voir*) face on; **~ à** facing; (*fig*) faced with, in the face of; **faire ~ à** to face; **~ à ~** adv facing each other ▷ nm inv encounter

fâché, e [faʃe] adj angry; (*désolé*) sorry

fâcher [faʃe] vt to anger; **se fâcher (contre qn)** vi to get angry (with sb);

se ~ avec (se brouiller) to fall out with
facile [fasil] adj easy; (caractère) easy-going; **facilement** adv easily; **facilité** nf easiness; (disposition, don) aptitude; **facilités** nfpl (possibilités) facilities; (Comm) terms; **faciliter** vt to make easier
façon [fasɔ̃] nf (manière) way; (d'une robe etc) making-up; cut; **façons** nfpl (péj) fuss sg; **de ~ à/à ce que** so as to/that; **de toute ~** anyway, in any case; **sans ~** (accepter) without fuss; **non merci, sans ~** no thanks, honestly
facteur, -trice [faktœr] nm/f postman(-woman) (BRIT), mailman(-woman) (US) ▷ nm (Math, fig: élément) factor
facture [faktyʀ] nf (à payer: gén) bill; (Comm) invoice
facultatif, -ive [fakyltatif, iv] adj optional
faculté [fakylte] nf (intellectuelle, d'université) faculty; (pouvoir, possibilité) power
fade [fad] adj insipid
faible [fɛbl] adj weak; (voix, lumière, vent) faint; (rendement, revenu) low ▷ nm (pour quelqu'un) weakness, soft spot; **faiblesse** nf weakness; **faiblir** vi to weaken; (lumière) to dim; (vent) to drop
faïence [fajɑ̃s] nf earthenware no pl
faillir [fajiʀ] vi: **j'ai failli tomber** I almost ou very nearly fell
faillite [fajit] nf bankruptcy; **faire ~** to go bankrupt
faim [fɛ̃] nf hunger; **avoir ~** to be hungry; **rester sur sa ~** (aussi fig) to be left wanting more
fainéant, e [fɛneɑ̃, ɑ̃t] nm/f idler, loafer

○ **MOT-CLÉ**

faire [fɛʀ] vt 1 (fabriquer, être l'auteur de) to make; **faire du vin/une offre/un film** to make wine/an offer/a film; **faire du bruit** to make a noise
2 (effectuer: travail, opération) to do; **que faites-vous?** (quel métier etc) what do you do?; (quelle activité: au moment de la question) what are you doing?; **faire la lessive** to do the washing
3 (études) to do; (sport, musique) to play; **faire du droit/du français** to do law/French; **faire du rugby/du piano** to play rugby/the piano
4 (simuler): **faire le malade/l'innocent** to act the invalid/the innocent
5 (transformer, avoir un effet sur): **faire de qn un frustré/avocat** to make sb frustrated/a lawyer; **ça ne me fait rien** (m'est égal) I don't care ou mind; (me laisse froid) it has no effect on me; **ça ne fait rien** it doesn't matter; **faire que** (impliquer) to mean that
6 (calculs, prix, mesures): **2 et 2 font 4** 2 and 2 are ou make 4; **ça fait 10 m/15 euros** it's 10 m/15 euros; **je vous le fais 10 euros** I'll let you have it for 10 euros; **je fais du 40** I take a size 40
7 (distance): **faire du 50 (à l'heure)** to do 50 (km an hour); **nous avons fait 1000 km en 2 jours** we did ou covered 1000 km in 2 days; **faire l'Europe** to tour ou do Europe; **faire les magasins** to go shopping
8: **qu'a-t-il fait de sa valise?** what has he done with his case?
9: **ne faire que: il ne fait que critiquer** (sans cesse) all he (ever) does is criticize; (seulement) he's only criticizing
10 (dire): **"vraiment", fit-il** "really" he said
11 (maladie) to have; **faire du diabète** to have diabetes sg
▷ vi 1 (agir, s'y prendre) to act, do; **il faut faire vite** we (ou you etc) must act quickly; **comment a-t-il fait pour?** how did he manage to?; **faites comme chez vous** make yourself at home
2 (paraître) to look; **faire vieux/démodé** to look old/old-fashioned; **ça fait bien** it looks good
▷ vb substitut to do; **ne le casse pas comme je l'ai fait** don't break it as I did; **je peux le voir? — faites!** can I see

it? — please do!

▷ *vb impers* **1: il fait beau** *etc* the weather is fine *etc; voir aussi* **jour; froid** *etc*

2 *(temps écoulé, durée)*: **ça fait 2 ans qu'il est parti** it's 2 years since he left; **ça fait 2 ans qu'il y est** he's been there for 2 years

▷ *vb semi-aux* **1: faire** *(+infinitif: action directe)* to make; **faire tomber/bouger qch** to make sth fall/move; **faire démarrer un moteur/chauffer de l'eau** to start up an engine/heat some water; **cela fait dormir** it makes you sleep; **faire travailler les enfants** to make the children work ou get the children to work; **il m'a fait traverser la rue** he helped me to cross the street

2 *(indirectement, par un intermédiaire)*: **faire réparer qch** to get ou have sth repaired; **faire punir les enfants** to have the children punished

se faire *vi* **1** *(être convenable)*: **cela se fait beaucoup/ne se fait pas** it's done a lot/not done

2: se faire *+nom ou pron*: **se faire une jupe** to make o.s. a skirt; **se faire des amis** to make friends; **se faire du souci** to worry; **il ne s'en fait pas** he doesn't worry

3: se faire *+adj (devenir)*: **se faire vieux** to be getting old; **se faire beau** to do o.s. up

4: se faire à *(s'habituer)* to get used to; **je n'arrive pas à me faire à la nourriture/au climat** I can't get used to the food/climate

5: se faire *+infinitif*: **se faire examiner la vue/opérer** to have one's eyes tested/have an operation; **se faire couper les cheveux** to get one's hair cut; **il va se faire tuer/punir** he's going to get himself killed/get punished; **il s'est fait aider** he got somebody to help him; **il s'est fait aider par Simon** he got Simon to help him; **se faire faire un vêtement** to get a garment made for o.s.

6 *(impersonnel)*: **comment se fait-il/faisait-il que?** how is it/was it that?

faire-part [fɛʀpaʀ] *nm inv* announcement *(of birth, marriage etc)*

faisan, e [fəzɑ̃, an] *nm/f* pheasant

faisons [fəzɔ̃] *vb voir* **faire**

fait, e [fɛ, fɛt] *adj (mûr: fromage, melon)* ripe ▷ *nm (événement)* event, occurrence; *(réalité, donnée)* fact; **être au ~ (de)** to be informed (of); **au ~ (à propos)** by the way; **en venir au ~** to get to the point; **du ~ de ceci/qu'il a menti** because of *ou* on account of this/his having lied; **de ce ~** for this reason; **en ~** in fact; **prendre qn sur le ~** to catch sb in the act; **c'est bien ~ pour lui** *(ou eux etc)* it serves him *(ou them etc)* right; **fait divers** news item

faites [fɛt] *vb voir* **faire**

falaise [falɛz] *nf* cliff

falloir [falwaʀ] *vb impers*: **il faut qu'il parte/a fallu qu'il parte** *(obligation)* he has to *ou* must leave/had to leave; **il a fallu le faire** it had to be done; **il faudrait qu'elle rentre** she should come *ou* go back, she ought to come *ou* go back; **il faut faire attention** you have to be careful; **il me faudrait 100 euros** I would need 100 euros; **il vous faut tourner à gauche après l'église** you have to turn left past the church; **nous avons ce qu'il (nous) faut** we have what we need; **il ne fallait pas** you shouldn't have (done); **comme il faut** *(personne)* proper; *(agir)* properly; **s'en falloir** *vr*: **il s'en est fallu de 100 euros/5 minutes** we/they *etc* were 100 euros short/5 minutes late *ou* too late; **il s'en faut de beaucoup qu'il soit** he is far from being; **il s'en est fallu de peu que cela n'arrive** it very nearly happened

famé, e [fame] *adj*: **mal ~** disreputable, of ill repute

fameux, -euse [famø, øz] *adj (illustre)* famous; *(bon: repas, plat etc)* first-rate, first-class; *(valeur intensive)* real, downright

familial, e, -aux[familjal, jo] adj family cpd

familiarité[familjarite] nf familiarity

familier, -ère [familje, jɛʀ] adj (connu) familiar; (atmosphère) informal, friendly; (Ling) informal, colloquial ▷ nm regular (visitor)

famille[famij] nf family; **il a de la ~ à Paris** he has relatives in Paris

famine[famin] nf famine

fanatique[fanatik] adj fanatical ▷ nm/f fanatic

faner[fane]: **se faner** vi to fade

fanfare[fɑ̃faʀ] nf (orchestre) brass band; (musique) fanfare

fantaisie[fɑ̃tezi] nf (spontanéité) fancy, imagination; (caprice) whim ▷ adj: **bijou ~** costume jewellery

fantasme[fɑ̃tasm] nm fantasy

fantastique[fɑ̃tastik] adj fantastic

fantôme[fɑ̃tom] nm ghost, phantom

faon[fɑ̃] nm fawn

FAQ sigle f (= foire aux questions) FAQ

farce[faʀs] nf (viande) stuffing; (blague) (practical) joke; (Théâtre) farce; **farcir** vt (viande) to stuff

farder[faʀde]: **se farder** vi to make (o.s.) up

farine[faʀin] nf flour

farouche[faʀuʃ] adj (timide) shy, timid

fart[faʀt] nm (ski) wax

fascination[fasinasjɔ̃] nf fascination

fasciner[fasine] vt to fascinate

fascisme[faʃism] nm fascism

fasse etc [fas] vb voir **faire**

fastidieux, -euse [fastidjø, jøz] adj tedious, tiresome

fatal, e[fatal] adj fatal; (inévitable) inevitable; **fatalité** nf (destin) fate; (coïncidence) fateful coincidence

fatidique[fatidik] adj fateful

fatigant, e[fatigɑ̃, ɑ̃t] adj tiring; (agaçant) tiresome

fatigue[fatig] nf tiredness, fatigue; **fatigué, e** adj tired; **fatiguer** vt to tire, make tired; (fig: agacer) to annoy ▷ vi (moteur) to labour, strain; **se fatiguer**

to get tired

fauché, e[foʃe] (fam) adj broke

faucher[foʃe] vt (herbe) to cut; (champs, blés) to reap; (fig: véhicule) to mow down; (fam: voler) to pinch

faucon[fokɔ̃] nm falcon, hawk

faudra[fodʀa] vb voir **falloir**

faufiler[fofile]: **se faufiler** vi: **se ~ dans** to edge one's way into; **se ~ parmi/entre** to thread one's way among/between

faune[fon] nf (Zool) wildlife, fauna

fausse[fos] adj voir **faux; faussement** adv (accuser) wrongly, wrongfully; (croire) falsely

fausser[fose] vt (objet) to bend, buckle; (fig) to distort; **~ compagnie à qn** to give sb the slip

faut[fo] vb voir **falloir**

faute[fot] nf (erreur) mistake, error; (mauvaise action) misdemeanour; (Football etc) offence; (Tennis) fault; **c'est de sa/ma ~** it's his or her/my fault; **être en ~** to be in the wrong; **~ de** (temps, argent) for ou through lack of; **sans ~** without fail; **faute de frappe** typing error; **faute professionnelle** professional misconduct no pl

fauteuil[fotœj] nm armchair; (au théâtre) seat; **fauteuil roulant** wheelchair

fautif, -ive [fotif, iv] adj (responsable) at fault, in the wrong; (incorrect) incorrect, inaccurate; **il se sentait ~** he felt guilty

fauve[fov] nm wildcat ▷ adj (couleur) fawn

faux[1][fo] nf scythe

faux[2], fausse [fo, fos] adj (inexact) wrong; (voix) out of tune; (billet) fake, forged; (sournois, postiche) false ▷ adv (Mus) out of tune ▷ nm (copie) fake, forgery; **faire ~ bond à qn** to let sb down; **faire un ~ pas** to trip; (fig) to make a faux pas; **fausse alerte** false alarm; **fausse couche** miscarriage; **faux frais** nmpl extras, incidental expenses; **faux mouvement** awkward movement; **fausse note** wrong note; **faux témoignage** (délit) perjury; **faux-filet** nm sirloin

faveur [favœʀ] nf favour; **traitement de ~** preferential treatment; **en ~ de** in favour of

favorable [favɔʀabl] adj favourable

favori, te [favɔʀi, it] adj, nm/f favourite

favoriser [favɔʀize] vt to favour

fax [faks] nm fax

fécond, e [fekɔ̃, ɔ̃d] adj fertile; **féconder** vt to fertilize

féculent [fekylɑ̃] nm starchy food

fédéral, e, -aux [federal, o] adj federal

fée [fe] nf fairy

feignant, e [fɛɲɑ̃, ɑ̃t] nm/f =**fainéant, e**

feindre [fɛ̃dʀ] vt to feign; **~ de faire** to pretend to do

fêler [fele] vt to crack; **se fêler** to crack

félicitations [felisitasjɔ̃] nfpl congratulations

féliciter [felisite] vt: **~ qn (de)** to congratulate sb (on)

félin, e [felɛ̃, in] nm (big) cat

femelle [fəmɛl] adj, nf female

féminin, e [feminɛ̃, in] adj feminine; (sexe) female; (équipe, vêtements etc) women's ▷ nm (Ling) feminine; **féministe** adj feminist

femme [fam] nf woman; (épouse) wife; **femme au foyer** housewife; **femme de chambre** chambermaid; **femme de ménage** cleaning lady

fémur [femyʀ] nm femur, thighbone

fendre [fɑ̃dʀ] vt (couper en deux) to split; (fissurer) to crack; (traverser: foule, air) to cleave through); **se fendre** vi to crack

fenêtre [f(ə)nɛtʀ] nf window

fenouil [fənuj] nm fennel

fente [fɑ̃t] nf (fissure) crack; (de boîte à lettres etc) slit

ferai etc [fəʀe] vb voir **faire**

fer-blanc [fɛʀblɑ̃] nm tin(plate)

férié, e [feʀje] adj: **jour ~** public holiday

ferions etc [fəʀjɔ̃] vb voir **faire**

ferme [fɛʀm] adj firm ▷ adv (travailler etc) hard ▷ nf (exploitation) farm; (maison) farmhouse

fermé, e [fɛʀme] adj closed, shut; (gaz, eau etc) off; (fig: milieu) exclusive

fermenter [fɛʀmɑ̃te] vi to ferment

fermer [fɛʀme] vt to close; shut; (cesser l'exploitation de) to close down, shut down; (eau, électricité, robinet) to turn off; (aéroport, route) to close ▷ vi to close, shut; (magasin: définitivement) to close down, shut down; **~ à clef** to lock; **se fermer** vi to close, shut

fermeté [fɛʀməte] nf firmness

fermeture [fɛʀmətyʀ] nf closing; (dispositif) catch; **heures de ~** closing times; **fermeture éclair®** ou **à glissière** zip (fastener) (BRIT), zipper (US)

fermier [fɛʀmje] nm farmer

féroce [feʀɔs] adj ferocious, fierce

ferons [fəʀɔ̃] vb voir **faire**

ferrer [feʀe] vt (cheval) to shoe

ferroviaire [feʀɔvjɛʀ] adj rail(way) cpd (BRIT), rail(road) cpd (US)

ferry-(boat) [feʀe(-bot)] nm ferry

fertile [fɛʀtil] adj fertile; **~ en incidents** eventful, packed with incidents

fervent, e [fɛʀvɑ̃, ɑ̃t] adj fervent

fesse [fɛs] nf buttock; **fessée** nf spanking

festin [fɛstɛ̃] nm feast

festival [fɛstival] nm festival

festivités [fɛstivite] nfpl festivities

fêtard, e [fɛtaʀ, aʀd] (fam) nm/f high liver, merry-maker

fête [fɛt] nf (religieuse) feast; (publique) holiday; (réception) party; (kermesse) fête, fair; (du nom) feast day, name day; **faire la ~** to live it up; **faire ~ à qn** to give sb a warm welcome; **les ~s (de fin d'année)** the festive season; **la salle des ~s** the village hall; **la ~ des Mères/**

Pères Mother's/Father's Day; **fête foraine** (fun) fair; **fêter** vt to celebrate; (personne) to have a celebration for

feu, x [fø] nm (gén) fire; (signal lumineux) light; (de cuisinière) ring; **feux** nmpl (Auto) (traffic) lights; **au ~!** (incendie) fire!; **à ~ doux/vif** (Culin) over a slow/brisk heat; **à petit ~** (Culin) over a gentle heat; **à ~ doux** slowly; **faire ~** to fire; **ne pas faire long ~** not to last long; **prendre ~** to catch fire; **mettre le ~ à** to set fire to; **faire du ~** to make a fire; **avez-vous du ~?** (pour cigarette) have you (got) a light?; **feu arrière** rear light; **feu d'artifice** (spectacle) fireworks pl; **feu de joie** bonfire; **feu orange/rouge/vert** amber (BRIT) ou yellow (US)/red/green light; **feu de brouillard** fog lights ou lamps; **feux de croisement** dipped (BRIT) ou dimmed (US) headlights; **feux de position** sidelights; **feux de route** headlights

feuillage [fœja3] nm foliage, leaves pl

feuille [fœj] nf (d'arbre) leaf; (de papier) sheet; **feuille de calcul** spreadsheet; **feuille d'impôts** tax form; **feuille de maladie** medical expenses claim form; **feuille de paie** pay slip

feuillet [fœjɛ] nm leaf

feuilleté, e [fœjte] adj: **pâte ~** flaky pastry

feuilleter [fœjte] vt (livre) to leaf through

feuilleton [fœjtɔ̃] nm serial

feutre [føtR] nm felt; (chapeau) felt hat; (aussi: **stylo-~**) felt-tip pen; **feutré, e** adj (atmosphère) muffled

fève [fɛv] nf broad bean

février [fevrije] nm February

fiable [fjabl] adj reliable

fiançailles [fjɑ̃saj] nfpl engagement sg

fiancé, e [fjɑ̃se] nm/f fiancé(e) ▷ adj: **être ~ (à)** to be engaged (to)

fiancer [fjɑ̃se]: **se fiancer (avec)** vi to become engaged (to)

fibre [fibR] nf fibre; **fibre de verre** fibreglass, glass fibre

ficeler [fis(ə)le] vt to tie up

ficelle [fisɛl] nf string no pl; (morceau) piece ou length of string

fiche [fiʃ] nf (pour fichier) (index) card; (formulaire) form; (Élec) plug; **fiche de paye** pay slip

ficher [fiʃe] vt (dans un fichier) to file; (Police) to put on file; (fam: faire) to do; (: donner) to give; (: mettre) to stick ou shove; **fiche(-moi) le camp!** (fam) clear off!; **fiche-moi la paix!** (fam) leave me alone!; **se ficher de** (fam: rire de) to make fun of; (être indifférent à) not to care about

fichier [fiʃje] nm file; **~ joint** (Comput) attachment

fichu, e [fiʃy] pp de **ficher** (fam) ▷ adj (fam: fini, inutilisable) bust, done for; (: intensif) wretched, darned ▷ nm (foulard) (head)scarf; **mal ~** (fam) feeling lousy

fictif, -ive [fiktif, iv] adj fictitious

fiction [fiksjɔ̃] nf fiction; (fait imaginé) invention

fidèle [fidɛl] adj faithful ▷ nm/f (Rel): **les ~s** (à l'église) the congregation sg; **fidélité** nf (d'un conjoint) fidelity, faithfulness; (d'un ami, client) loyalty

fier¹ [fje]: **se fier à** vt to trust

fier², fière [fjɛR] adj proud; **être ~ de** to be proud of; **fierté** nf pride

fièvre [fjɛvR] nf fever; **avoir de la ~/39 de ~** to have a high temperature/a temperature of 39 °C; **fiévreux, -euse** adj feverish

figer [fiʒe]: **se figer** vi (huile) to congeal; (personne) to freeze

fignoler [fiɲɔle] (fam) vt to polish up

figue [fig] nf fig; **figuier** nm fig tree

figurant, e [figyrɑ̃, ɑ̃t] nm/f (Théâtre) walk-on; (Cinéma) extra

figure [figyR] nf (visage) face; (forme, personnage) figure; (illustration) picture, diagram

figuré, e [figyre] adj (sens) figurative

figurer [figyre] vi to appear ▷ vt to represent; **se figurer que** to imagine that

fil [fil] nm (brin, fig: d'une histoire) thread;

(*électrique*) wire; (*d'un couteau*) edge; **au ~ des années** with the passing of the years; **au ~ de l'eau** with the stream *ou* current; **coup de ~** (*fam*) phone call; **donner/recevoir un coup de ~** to make/get *ou* receive a phone call; **fil de fer** wire; **fil de fer barbelé** barbed wire

file [fil] *nf* line; (*Auto*) lane; **en indienne** in single file; **à la ~** (*d'affilée*) in succession; (*d'attente*) queue (BRIT), line (US)

filer [file] *vt* (*tissu, toile*) to spin; (*prendre en filature*) to shadow, tail; (*fam: donner*): **~ qch à qn** to slip sb sth ▷ *vi* (*bas*) to run; (*aller vite*) to fly past; (*fam: partir*) to make *ou* be off; **~ doux** to toe the line

filet [filɛ] *nm* net; (*Culin*) fillet; (*d'eau, de sang*) trickle; **filet (à provisions)** string bag

filiale [filjal] *nf* (*Comm*) subsidiary

filière [filjɛʀ] *nf* (*carrière*) path; **suivre la ~** (*dans sa carrière*) to work one's way up (through the hierarchy)

fille [fij] *nf* girl; (*opposé à fils*) daughter; **vieille ~** old maid; **fillette** *nf* (little) girl

filleul, e [fijœl] *nm/f* godchild, godson/daughter

film [film] *nm* (*pour photo*) (roll of) film; (*œuvre*) film, picture, movie

fils [fis] *nm* son; **fils à papa** daddy's boy

filtre [filtʀ] *nm* filter; **filtrer** *vt* to filter; (*fig: candidats, visiteurs*) to screen

fin¹ [fɛ̃] *nf* end; **fins** *nfpl* (*but*) ends; **prendre ~** to come to an end; **mettre ~ à** to put an end to; **à la ~** in the end, eventually; **en ~ de compte** in the end; **sans ~** endless; **~ juin** at the end of June; **fin prêt** quite ready

fin², e [fɛ̃, fin] *adj* (*papier, couche, fil*) thin; (*cheveux, visage*) fine; (*taille*) neat, slim; (*esprit, remarque*) subtle ▷ *adv* (*couper*) finely; **fines herbes** mixed herbs; **avoir la vue/l'ouïe fine** to have keen eyesight/hearing; **repas/vin fine** gourmet meal/fine wine

final, e [final, o] *adj* final ▷ *nm* (*Mus*) finale; **finale** *nf* final; **quarts de finale** quarter finals; **finalement** *adv* finally,

in the end; (*après tout*) after all

finance [finɑ̃s]: **finances** *nfpl* (*situation*) finances; (*activités*) finance *sg*; **moyennant ~** for a fee; **financer** *vt* to finance; **financier, -ière** *adj* financial

finesse [finɛs] *nf* thinness; (*raffinement*) fineness; (*subtilité*) subtlety

fini, e [fini] *adj* finished; (*Math*) finite ▷ *nm* (*d'un objet manufacturé*) finish

finir [finiʀ] *vt* to finish ▷ *vi* to finish, end; **~ par faire** to end up *ou* finish up doing; **~ de faire** to finish doing; (*cesser*) to stop doing; **il finit par m'agacer** he's beginning to get on my nerves; **en ~ avec** to be have done with; **il va mal ~** he will come to a bad end

finition [finisjɔ̃] *nf* (*résultat*) finish

finlandais, e [fɛ̃lɑ̃dɛ, ɛz] *adj* Finnish ▷ *nm/f*: **F~, e** Finn

Finlande [fɛ̃lɑ̃d] *nf*: **la ~** Finland

finnois, e [finwa, waz] *adj* Finnish ▷ *nm* (*Ling*) Finnish

fioul [fjul] *nm* fuel oil

firme [fiʀm] *nf* firm

fis [fi] *vb voir* **faire**

fisc [fisk] *nm* tax authorities *pl*; **fiscal, e, -aux** *adj* tax *cpd*, fiscal; **fiscalité** *nf* tax system

fissure [fisyʀ] *nf* crack; **fissurer** *vt* to crack; **se fissurer** *vi* to crack

fit [fi] *vb voir* **faire**

fixation [fiksasjɔ̃] *nf* (*attache*) fastening; (*Psych*) fixation

fixe [fiks] *adj* fixed; (*emploi*) steady, regular ▷ *nm* (*salaire*) basic salary; (*téléphone*) landline; **à heure ~** at set time; **menu à prix ~** set menu

fixé, e [fikse] *adj*: **être ~ (sur)** (*savoir à quoi s'en tenir*) to have made up one's mind (about)

fixer [fikse] *vt* (*attacher*): **~ qch (à/sur)** to fix *ou* fasten sth (to/onto); (*déterminer*) to fix, set; (*regarder*) to stare at; **se fixer** (*s'établir*) to settle down; **se ~ sur** (*suj: attention*) to focus on

flacon [flakɔ̃] *nm* bottle

flageolet [flaʒɔlɛ] nm (Culin) dwarf kidney bean

flagrant, e [flagʀɑ̃, ɑ̃t] adj flagrant, blatant; **en ~ délit** in the act

flair [flɛʀ] nm sense of smell; (fig) intuition; **flairer** vt (humer) to sniff (at); (détecter) to scent

flamand, e [flamɑ̃, ɑ̃d] adj Flemish ▷ nm (Ling) Flemish ▷ nm/f: **F~, e** Fleming

flamant [flamɑ̃] nm flamingo

flambant, e [flɑ̃bɑ̃, ɑ̃t] adv: **~ neuf** brand new

flambé, e [flɑ̃be] adj (Culin) flambé

flambée [flɑ̃be] nf blaze; (fig: des prix) explosion

flamber [flɑ̃be] vi to blaze (up)

flamboyer [flɑ̃bwaje] vi to blaze (up)

flamme [flɑm] nf flame; (fig) fire, fervour; **en ~s** on fire, ablaze

flan [flɑ̃] nm (Culin) custard tart ou pie

flanc [flɑ̃] nm side; (Mil) flank

flancher [flɑ̃ʃe] (fam) vi to fail, pack up

flanelle [flanɛl] nf flannel

flâner [flɑne] vi to stroll

flanquer [flɑ̃ke] vt to flank; (fam: mettre) to chuck, shove; (: jeter): **~ par terre/à la porte** to fling to the ground/chuck out

flaque [flak] nf (d'eau) puddle; (d'huile, de sang etc) pool

flash [flaʃ] (pl **~es**) nm (Photo) flash; **flash d'information** newsflash

flatter [flate] vt to flatter; **se ~ de qch** to pride o.s. on sth; **flatteur, -euse** adj flattering

flèche [flɛʃ] nf arrow; (de clocher) spire; **monter en ~** (fig) to soar, rocket; **partir en ~** to be off like a shot; **fléchette** nf dart

flétrir [fletʀiʀ]: **se flétrir** vi to wither

fleur [flœʀ] nf flower; (d'un arbre) blossom; **en ~** (arbre) in blossom; **à ~s** flowery

fleuri, e [flœʀi] adj (jardin) in flower ou bloom; (tissu, papier) flowery

fleurir [flœʀiʀ] vi (rose) to flower; (arbre) to blossom; (fig) to flourish ▷ vt (tombe) to put flowers on; (chambre) to decorate with flowers

fleuriste [flœʀist] nm/f florist

fleuve [flœv] nm river

flexible [flɛksibl] adj flexible

flic [flik] (fam: péj) nm cop

flipper [flipœʀ] nm pinball (machine)

flirter [flœʀte] vi to flirt

flocon [flɔkɔ̃] nm flake

flore [flɔʀ] nf flora

florissant, e [flɔʀisɑ̃, ɑ̃t] adj (économie) flourishing

flot [flo] nm flood, stream; **flots** nmpl (de la mer) waves; **être à ~** (Navig) to be afloat; **entrer à ~s** to stream ou pour in

flottant, e [flɔtɑ̃, ɑ̃t] adj (vêtement) loose

flotte [flɔt] nf (Navig) fleet; (fam: eau) water; (: pluie) rain

flotter [flɔte] vi to float; (nuage, odeur) to drift; (drapeau) to fly; (vêtements) to hang loose; (fam: pleuvoir) to rain; **faire ~** to float; **flotteur** nm float

flou, e [flu] adj (flou) fuzzy, blurred; (fig) woolly, vague

fluide [flɥid] adj fluid; (circulation etc) flowing freely ▷ nm fluid

fluor [flyɔʀ] nm: **dentifrice au ~** fluoride toothpaste

fluorescent, e [flyɔʀesɑ̃, ɑ̃t] adj fluorescent

flûte [flyt] nf flute; (verre) flute (glass); (pain) (thin) French stick; **~! drat it!**; **flûte traversière/à bec** flute/recorder

flux [fly] nm incoming tide; (écoulement) flow; **le ~ et le reflux** the ebb and flow

foc [fɔk] nm jib

foi [fwa] nf faith; **digne de ~** reliable; **être de bonne/mauvaise ~** to be sincere/insincere; **ma ~ ...** well ...

foie [fwa] nm liver; **crise de ~** stomach upset

foin [fwɛ̃] nm hay; **faire du ~** (fig: fam) to kick up a row

foire [fwaʀ] nf fair; (fête foraine) (fun) fair; **faire la ~** (fig: fam) to whoop it up; **~ aux questions** (Internet) FAQs; **foire (exposition)** trade fair

fois [fwa] *nf* time; **une/deux ~** once/twice; **2 ~ 2** 2 times 2; **une ~ (passé)** once; **(futur)** sometime; **une ~ pour toutes** once and for all; **une ~ que** once; **des ~ (parfois)** sometimes; **à la ~ (ensemble)** at once

fol [fɔl] *adj voir* **fou**

folie [fɔli] *nf (d'une décision, d'un acte)* madness, folly; *(état)* madness, insanity; **la ~ des grandeurs** delusions of grandeur; **faire des ~s** *(en dépenses)* to be extravagant

folklorique [fɔlklɔʀik] *adj* folk *cpd*; *(fam)* weird

folle [fɔl] *adj, nf voir* **fou**; **follement** *adv* *(très)* madly, wildly

foncé, e [fɔse] *adj* dark

foncer [fɔse] *vi* to go darker; *(fam: aller vite)* to tear ou belt along; **~ sur** to charge at

fonction [fɔksjɔ̃] *nf* function; *(emploi, poste)* post, position; **fonctions** *nfpl (professionnelles)* duties; **voiture de ~** company car; **en ~ de** *(par rapport à)* according to; **faire ~ de** to serve as; **la ~ publique** the state ou civil *(BRIT)* service; **fonctionnaire** *nm/f* state employee, local authority employee; *(dans l'administration)* ≈ civil servant; **fonctionner** *vi* to work, function

fond [fɔ̃] *nm (d'un récipient, trou)* bottom; *(d'une salle, scène)* back; *(d'un tableau, décor)* background; *(opposé à la forme)* content; *(Sport)*: **le ~** long distance (running); **au ~ de** at the bottom of; at the back of; **à ~ (connaître, soutenir)** thoroughly; *(appuyer, visser)* right down ou home; **à ~ (de train)** full tilt; **dans le ~, au ~ (en somme)** basically, really; **de ~ en comble** from top to bottom; **fond de teint** foundation (cream); *voir aussi* **fonds**

fondamental, e, -aux [fɔ̃damɑtal, o] *adj* fundamental

fondant, e [fɔ̃dɑ̃, ɑ̃t] *adj (neige)* melting; *(poire)* that melts in the mouth

fondation [fɔ̃dasjɔ̃] *nf* founding; *(établissement)* foundation; **fondations**

nfpl (d'une maison) foundations

fondé, e [fɔ̃de] *adj (accusation etc)* well-founded; **être ~ à** to have grounds for ou good reason to

fondement [fɔ̃dmɑ̃] *nm*: **sans ~ (rumeur etc)** groundless, unfounded

fonder [fɔ̃de] *vt* to found; *(fig)* to base; **se fonder sur** *(suj: personne)* to base o.s. on

fonderie [fɔ̃dʀi] *nf* smelting works *sg*

fondre [fɔ̃dʀ] *vt (aussi:* **faire ~)** to melt; *(dans l'eau)* to dissolve; *(fig: mélanger)* to merge, blend ▷ *vi (à la chaleur)* to melt; *(dans l'eau)* to dissolve; *(fig)* to melt away; *(se précipiter)*: **~ sur** to swoop down on; **~ en larmes** to burst into tears

fonds [fɔ̃] *nm (Comm)*: **~ (de commerce)** business ▷ *nmpl (argent)* funds

fondu, e [fɔ̃dy] *adj (beurre, neige)* melted; *(métal)* molten; **fondue** *nf (Culin)* fondue

font [fɔ̃] *vb voir* **faire**

fontaine [fɔ̃tɛn] *nf* fountain; *(source)* spring

fonte [fɔ̃t] *nf* melting; *(métal)* cast iron; **la ~ des neiges** the (spring) thaw

foot [fut] *(fam) nm* football

football [futbol] *nm* football, soccer; **footballeur** *nm* footballer

footing [futiŋ] *nm* jogging; **faire du ~** to go jogging

forain, e [fɔʀɛ̃, ɛn] *adj* fairground *cpd* ▷ *nm (marchand)* stallholder; *(acteur)* fairground entertainer

forçat [fɔʀsa] *nm* convict

force [fɔʀs] *nf* strength; *(Physique, Mécanique)* force; **forces** *nfpl (physiques)* strength *sg*; *(Mil)* forces; **à ~ de** by dint of insisting; as he *(ou* I *etc)* kept on insisting; **de ~** forcibly, by force; **dans la ~ de l'âge** in the prime of life; **les forces de l'ordre** the police *no f*

forcé, e [fɔʀse] *adj* forced; **c'est ~ (fam)** it's inevitable; **forcément** *adv* inevitably; **pas forcément** not necessarily

forcer [fɔʀse] vt to force; (voix) to strain ▷ vi (Sport) to overtax o.s.; **~ la dose** (fam) to overdo it; **se ~ (à faire)** to force o.s. (to do)

forestier, -ère [fɔʀɛstje, jɛʀ] adj forest cpd

forêt [fɔʀɛ] nf forest

forfait [fɔʀfɛ] nm (Comm) all-in deal ou price; **déclarer ~** to withdraw; **forfaitaire** adj inclusive

forge [fɔʀʒ] nf forge, smithy; **forgeron** nm (black)smith

formaliser [fɔʀmalize]: **se formaliser** vi: **se ~ (de)** to take offence (at)

formalité [fɔʀmalite] nf formality; **simple ~** mere formality

format [fɔʀma] nm size; **formater** vt (disque) to format

formation [fɔʀmasjɔ̃] nf (développement) forming; (apprentissage) training; **formation permanente** ou **continue** continuing education

forme [fɔʀm] nf (gén) form; (d'un objet) shape, form; **formes** nfpl (bonnes manières) proprieties; (d'une femme) figure sg; **en ~ de poire** pear-shaped, in the shape of a pear; **être en ~** (Sport etc) to be on form; **en bonne et due ~** in due form

formel, le [fɔʀmɛl] adj (catégorique) definite, positive; **formellement** adv (absolument) positively; **formellement interdit** strictly forbidden

former [fɔʀme] vt to form; (éduquer) to train; **se former** vi to form

formidable [fɔʀmidabl] adj tremendous

formulaire [fɔʀmylɛʀ] nm form

formule [fɔʀmyl] nf (gén) formula; (expression) phrase; **formule de politesse** polite phrase; (en fin de lettre) letter ending

fort, e [fɔʀ, fɔʀt] adj (gros, solide); (intensité, rendement) high, great; (corpulent) stout; (doué) good, able ▷ adv (serrer, frapper) hard; (parler) loud(ly); (beaucoup) greatly, very much; (très) very ▷ nm (édifice) fort; (point fort) strong point,

forte; **forte tête** rebel; **forteresse** nf stronghold

fortifiant [fɔʀtifjɑ̃] nm tonic

fortune [fɔʀtyn] nf fortune; **faire ~** to make one's fortune; **de ~** makeshift; **fortuné, e** adj wealthy

forum [fɔʀɔm] nm forum; **~ de discussion** (Internet) message board

fosse [fos] nf (grand trou) pit; (tombe) grave

fossé [fose] nm ditch; (fig) gulf, gap

fossette [fosɛt] nf dimple

fossile [fosil] nm fossil

fou (fol), folle [fu, fɔl] adj mad; (déréglé etc) wild, erratic; (fam: extrême, très grand) terrific, tremendous ▷ nm/f madman(-woman) ▷ nm (du roi) jester; **être fou de** to be mad ou crazy about; **avoir le fou rire** to have the giggles

foudre [fudʀ] nf: **la ~** lightning

foudroyant, e [fudʀwajɑ̃, ɑ̃t] adj (progrès) lightning cpd; (succès) stunning; (maladie, poison) violent

fouet [fwɛ] nm whip; (Culin) whisk; **de plein ~** (se heurter) head on; **fouetter** vt to whip; (crème) to whisk

fougère [fuʒɛʀ] nf fern

fougue [fug] nf ardour, spirit; **fougueux, -euse** adj fiery

fouille [fuj] nf search; **fouilles** nfpl (archéologiques) excavations; **fouiller** vt to search; (creuser) to dig ▷ vi to rummage; **fouillis** nm jumble, muddle

foulard [fular] nm scarf

foule [ful] nf crowd; **la ~** crowds pl; **une ~ de** masses of

foulée [fule] nf stride

fouler [fule] vt to press; (sol) to tread upon; **se ~ la cheville** to sprain one's ankle; **ne pas se ~** not to overexert o.s.; **il ne se foule pas** he doesn't put himself out; **foulure** nf sprain

four [fuʀ] nm oven; (de potier) kiln; (Théâtre: échec) flop

fourche [fuʀʃ] nf pitchfork

fourchette [fuʀʃɛt] nf fork; (Statistique) bracket, margin

fourgon [fuʀgɔ̃] nm van; (Rail)

wag(g)on; **fourgonnette** nf (small) van

fourmi [fuʀmi] nf ant; **avoir des ~s dans les jambes/mains** to have pins and needles in one's legs/hands; **fourmilière** nf ant-hill; **fourmiller** vi to swarm

fourneau, x [fuʀno] nm stove

fourni, e [fuʀni] adj (barbe, cheveux) thick; (magasin): **bien ~ (en)** well stocked (with)

fournir [fuʀniʀ] vt to supply; (preuve, exemple) to provide, supply; (effort) to put in; **~ qch à qn** to supply sth to sb, supply ou provide sb with sth; **fournisseur, -euse** nm/f supplier; **fournisseur d'accès à Internet** (Internet) service provider, ISP; **fourniture** nf supply(ing); **fournitures scolaires** school stationery

fourrage [fuʀaʒ] nm fodder

fourré, e [fuʀe] adj (bonbon etc) filled; (manteau etc) fur-lined ▷ nm thicket

fourrer [fuʀe] (fam) vt to stick, shove; **se fourrer dans/sous** to get into/under

fourrière [fuʀjɛʀ] nf pound

fourrure [fuʀyʀ] nf fur; (sur l'animal) coat

foutre [futʀ] (fam!) vt = **ficher; foutu, e** (fam!) adj = **fichu, e**

foyer [fwaje] nm (maison) home; (famille) family; (de cheminée) hearth; (de jeunes etc) (social) club; (résidence) hostel; (salon) foyer; **lunettes à double ~** bi-focals

fracassant, e [fʀakasã, ãt] adj (succès) thundering

fraction [fʀaksjɔ̃] nf fraction

fracture [fʀaktyʀ] nf fracture; **fracture du crâne** fractured skull; **fracturer** vt (coffre, serrure) to break open; (os, membre) to fracture; **se fracturer le crâne** to fracture one's skull

fragile [fʀaʒil] adj fragile, delicate; (fig) frail; **fragilité** nf fragility

fragment [fʀagmã] nm (d'un objet)

fragment, piece

fraîche [fʀɛʃ] adj voir **frais; fraîcheur** nf coolness; (d'un aliment) freshness; **fraîchir** vi to get cooler; (vent) to freshen

frais, fraîche [fʀɛ, fʀɛʃ] adj fresh; (froid) cool ▷ adv (récemment) newly, fresh(ly) ▷ nm: **mettre au ~** to put in a cool place ▷ nmpl (gén) expenses; (Comm) costs; **il fait ~** it's cool; **servir ~** serve chilled; **prendre le ~** to take a breath of cool air; **faire des ~** to go to a lot of expense; **frais de scolarité** school fees (pl); tuition (us); **frais généraux** overheads

fraise [fʀɛz] nf strawberry; **fraise des bois** wild strawberry

framboise [fʀɑ̃bwaz] nf raspberry

franc, franche [fʀɑ̃, fʀɑ̃ʃ] adj (personne) frank, straightforward; (visage) open; (net: refus) clear; (: coupure) clean; (intensif) downright ▷ nm franc

français, e [fʀɑ̃sɛ, ɛz] adj French ▷ nm/f: **F~, e** Frenchman(-woman) ▷ nm (Ling) French

France [fʀɑ̃s] nf: **la ~** France; **~ 2, ~3** public-sector television channels

● **FRANCE TÉLÉVISION**

● **France 2** and **France 3** are public-
● sector television channels. France
● 2 is a national general interest and
● entertainment channel; France
● 3 provides regional news and
● information as well as programmes
● for the national network.

franche [fʀɑ̃ʃ] adj voir **franc; franchement** adv frankly; (nettement) definitely; (tout à fait: mauvais etc) downright

franchir [fʀɑ̃ʃiʀ] vt (obstacle) to clear, get over; (seuil, ligne, rivière) to cross; (distance) to cover

franchise [fʀɑ̃ʃiz] nf frankness; (douanière) exemption; (Assurances) excess

franc-maçon[fʀɑ̃masɔ̃] nm freemason

franco[fʀɑ̃ko] adv (Comm): **~ (de port)** postage paid

francophone[fʀɑ̃kɔfɔn] adj French-speaking

franc-parler[fʀɑ̃paʀle] nm inv outspokenness; **avoir son ~** to speak one's mind

frange[fʀɑ̃ʒ] nf fringe

frangipane[fʀɑ̃ʒipan] nf almond paste

frappant, e[fʀapɑ̃, ɑ̃t] adj striking

frappé, e[fʀape] adj iced

frapper[fʀape] vt to hit, strike; (étonner) to strike; **~ dans ses mains** to clap one's hands; **frappé de stupeur** dumbfounded

fraternel, le[fʀatɛʀnɛl] adj brotherly, fraternal; **fraternité** nf brotherhood

fraude[fʀod] nf fraud; (Scol) cheating; **passer qch en ~** to smuggle sth in (ou out); **fraude fiscale** tax evasion

frayeur[fʀejœʀ] nf fright

fredonner[fʀədɔne] vt to hum

freezer[fʀizœʀ] nm freezing compartment

frein[fʀɛ̃] nm brake; **mettre un ~ à** (fig) to curb, check; **frein à main** handbrake; **freiner** vi to brake ▷ vt (progrès etc) to check

frêle[fʀɛl] adj frail, fragile

frelon[fʀəlɔ̃] nm hornet

frémir[fʀemiʀ] vi (de peur, d'horreur) to shudder; (de colère) to shake; (feuillage) to quiver

frêne[fʀɛn] nm ash

fréquemment[fʀekamɑ̃] adv frequently

fréquent, e[fʀekɑ̃, ɑ̃t] adj frequent

fréquentation[fʀekɑ̃tasjɔ̃] nf frequenting; **fréquentations** nfpl (relations) company sg; **avoir de mauvaises ~s** to be in with the wrong crowd, keep bad company

fréquenté, e[fʀekɑ̃te] adj: **très ~** (very) busy; **mal ~** patronized by disreputable elements

fréquenter[fʀekɑ̃te] vt (lieu) to frequent; (personne) to see; **se fréquenter** to see each other

frère[fʀɛʀ] nm brother

fresque[fʀɛsk] nf (Art) fresco

fret[fʀɛ(t)] nm freight

friand, e[fʀijɑ̃, fʀijɑ̃d] adj: **~ de** very fond of ▷ nm: **~ au fromage** cheese puff

friandise[fʀijɑ̃diz] nf sweet

fric[fʀik] (fam) nm cash, bread

friche[fʀiʃ]: **en ~** adj, adv (lying) fallow

friction[fʀiksjɔ̃] nf (massage) rub, rub-down; (Tech, fig) friction

frigidaire®[fʀiʒidɛʀ] nm refrigerator

frigo[fʀigo] (fam) nm fridge

frigorifique[fʀigɔʀifik] adj refrigerating

frileux, -euse[fʀilø, øz] adj sensitive to (the) cold

frimer[fʀime] (fam) vi to show off

fringale[fʀɛ̃gal] (fam) nf: **avoir la ~** to be ravenous

fringues[fʀɛ̃g] (fam) nfpl clothes

fripé, e[fʀipe] adj crumpled

frire[fʀiʀ] vt, vi: **faire ~** to fry

frisé, e[fʀize] adj (cheveux) curly; (personne) curly-haired

frisson[fʀisɔ̃] nm (de froid) shiver; (de peur) shudder; **frissonner** vi (de fièvre, froid) to shiver; (d'horreur) to shudder

frit, e[fʀi, fʀit] pp de **frire** ▷ adj nf: **(pommes) frites** chips (BRIT), French fries; **friteuse** nf chip pan; **friteuse électrique** deep fat fryer; **friture** nf (huile) (deep) fat; (plat): **friture (de poissons)** fried fish

froid, e[fʀwa, fʀwad] adj, nm cold; **il fait ~** it's cold; **avoir/prendre ~** to be/catch cold; **être en ~ avec** to be on bad terms with; **froidement** adv (accueillir) coldly; (décider) coldly

froisser[fʀwase] vt to crumple (up), crease; (fig) to hurt, offend; **se froisser** vi to crumple, crease; (personne) to take offence; **se ~ un muscle** to strain a muscle

frôler[fʀole] vt to brush against; (suj: projectile) to skim past; (fig) to come very close to

fromage [fʀɔmaʒ] nm cheese; **fromage blanc** soft white cheese

froment [fʀɔmɑ̃] nm wheat

froncer [fʀɔ̃se] vt to gather; **~ les sourcils** to frown

front [fʀɔ̃] nm forehead, brow; (Mil) front; **de ~** (se heurter) head-on; (rouler) together (i.e. 2 or 3 abreast); (simultanément) at once; **faire ~ à** to face up to

frontalier, -ère [fʀɔ̃talje, jɛʀ] adj border cpd, frontier cpd; **(travailleurs) ~s** people who commute across the border

frontière [fʀɔ̃tjɛʀ] nf frontier, border

frotter [fʀɔte] vi to rub, scrape ▷ vt to rub; (pommes de terre, plancher) to scrub; **~ une allumette** to strike a match

fruit [fʀɥi] nm fruit gen no pl; **fruits de mer** seafood(s); **fruits secs** dried fruit sg; **fruité, e** adj fruity; **fruitier, -ère** adj: **arbre fruitier** fruit tree

frustrer [fʀystʀe] vt to frustrate

fuel(-oil) [fjul(ɔjl)] nm fuel oil; (domestique) heating oil

fugace [fygas] adj fleeting

fugitif, -ive [fyʒitif, iv] adj (fugace) fleeting ▷ nm/f fugitive

fugue [fyg] nf: **faire une ~** to run away, abscond

fuir [fɥiʀ] vt to flee from; (éviter) to shun ▷ vi to run away; (gaz, robinet) to leak

fuite [fɥit] nf flight; (écoulement, divulgation) leak; **être en ~** to be on the run; **mettre en ~** to put to flight

fulgurant, e [fylgyʀɑ̃, ɑ̃t] adj lightning cpd, dazzling

fumé, e [fyme] adj (Culin) smoked; (verre) tinted; **fumée** nf smoke

fumer [fyme] vi to smoke; (soupe) to steam ▷ vt to smoke

fûmes [fym] vb voir **être**

fumeur, -euse [fymœʀ, øz] nm/f smoker

fumier [fymje] nm manure

funérailles [fyneʀɑj] nfpl funeral sg

fur [fyʀ]: **au ~ et à mesure** adv as one goes along; **au ~ et à mesure que** as

furet [fyʀɛ] nm ferret

fureter [fyʀ(ə)te] (péj) vi to nose about

fureur [fyʀœʀ] nf fury; **être en ~** to be infuriated; **faire ~** to be all the rage

furie [fyʀi] nf fury; (femme) shrew, vixen; **en ~** (mer) raging; **furieux, -euse** adj furious

furoncle [fyʀɔ̃kl] nm boil

furtif, -ive [fyʀtif, iv] adj furtive

fus [fy] vb voir **être**

fusain [fyzɛ̃] nm (Art) charcoal

fuseau, x [fyzo] nm (pour filer) spindle; (pantalon) (ski) pants; **fuseau horaire** time zone

fusée [fyze] nf rocket

fusible [fyzibl] nm (Élec: fil) fuse wire; (: fiche) fuse

fusil [fyzi] nm (de guerre, à canon rayé) rifle, gun; (de chasse, à canon lisse) shotgun, gun; **fusillade** nf gunfire no pl, shooting no pl; **fusiller** vt to shoot; **fusiller qn du regard** to look daggers at sb

fusionner [fyzjɔne] vi to merge

fût [fy] vb voir **être** ▷ nm (tonneau) barrel, cask

futé, e [fyte] adj crafty; **Bison ~®** TV and radio traffic monitoring service

futile [fytil] adj frivolous

futur, e [fytyʀ] adj, nm future

fuyard, e [fɥijaʀ, aʀd] nm/f runaway

g

Gabon [gabɔ̃] nm: **le ~** Gabon
gâcher [gɑʃe] vt (gâter) to spoil; (gaspiller) to waste; **gâchis** nm waste no pl
gaffe [gaf] nf blunder; **faire ~** (fam) to be careful
gage [gaʒ] nm (dans un jeu) forfeit; (fig: de fidélité, d'amour) token; **gages** nmpl (salaire) wages; **mettre en ~** to pawn
gagnant, e [gaɲɑ̃, ɑ̃t] adj: **billet/ numéro ~** winning ticket/number ▷ nm/f winner
gagne-pain [gaɲpɛ̃] nm inv job
gagner [gaɲe] vt to win; (somme d'argent, revenu) to earn; (aller vers, atteindre) to reach; (envahir: sommeil, peur) to overcome; (: mal) to spread to ▷ vi to win; (fig) to gain: **~ du temps/de la place** to gain time/save space; **~ sa vie** to earn one's living
gai, e [ge] adj cheerful; (un peu ivre) merry; **gaiement** adv cheerfully; **gaieté** nf cheerfulness; **de gaieté de cœur** with a light heart

gain [gɛ̃] nm (revenu) earnings pl; (bénéfice: gén pl) profits pl
gala [gala] nm official reception; **de ~** (soirée etc) gala
galant, e [galɑ̃, ɑ̃t] adj (courtois) courteous, gentlemanly; (entreprenant) flirtatious, gallant; (scène, rendez-vous) romantic
galerie [galʀi] nf gallery; (Théâtre) circle; (de voiture) roof rack; (fig: spectateurs) audience; **galerie de peinture** (private) art gallery; **galerie marchande** shopping arcade
galet [galɛ] nm pebble
galette [galɛt] nf flat cake; **galette des Rois** cake eaten on Twelfth Night

---

GALETTE DES ROIS

A **galette des Rois** is a cake eaten on Twelfth Night containing a figurine. The person who finds it is the king (or queen) and gets a paper crown. They then choose someone else to be their queen (or king).

---

galipette [galipɛt] nf somersault
Galles [gal] nfpl: **le pays de ~** Wales; **gallois, e** adj Welsh ▷ nm/f: **Gallois, e** Welshman(-woman) ▷ nm (Ling) Welsh
galon [galɔ̃] nm (Mil) stripe; (décoratif) piece of braid
galop [galo] nm gallop; **galoper** vi to gallop
gambader [gɑ̃bade] vi (animal, enfant) to leap about
gamin, e [gamɛ̃, in] nm/f kid ▷ adj childish
gamme [gam] nf (Mus) scale; (fig) range
gang [gɑ̃g] nm (de criminels) gang
gant [gɑ̃] nm glove; **gant de toilette** face flannel (BRIT), face cloth
garage [gaʀaʒ] nm garage; **garagiste** nm/f garage owner; (employé) garage mechanic
garantie [gaʀɑ̃ti] nf guarantee; **(bon de) ~** guarantee ou warranty slip
garantir [gaʀɑ̃tiʀ] vt to guarantee; **~ à**

qn que to assure sb that

garçon [gaʀsɔ̃] nm boy; (célibataire): **vieux ~** bachelor; **garçon (de café)** (serveur) waiter; **garçon de courses** messenger

garde [gaʀd(ə)] nm (de prisonnier) guard; (de domaine etc) warden; (soldat, sentinelle) guardsman ▶ nf (soldats) guard; **de ~** on duty; **monter la ~** to stand guard; **mettre en ~** to warn; **prendre ~ (à)** to be careful (of); **garde champêtre** nm rural policeman; **garde du corps** nm bodyguard; **garde à vue** nf (Jur) ≈ police custody; **garde-boue** nm inv mudguard; **garde-chasse** nm gamekeeper

garder [gaʀde] vt (conserver) to keep; (surveiller: enfants) to look after; (: immeuble, lieu, prisonnier) to guard; **se garder** vi (aliment: se conserver) to keep; **se ~ de faire** to be careful not to do; **~ le lit/la chambre** to stay in bed/indoors; **pêche/chasse gardée** private fishing/hunting (ground)

garderie [gaʀdəʀi] nf day nursery, crèche

garde-robe [gaʀdəʀɔb] nf wardrobe

gardien, ne [gaʀdjɛ̃, jɛn] nm/f (garde) guard; (de prison) warder; (de domaine, réserve) warden; (de musée etc) attendant; (de phare, cimetière) keeper; (d'immeuble) caretaker; (fig) guardian; **gardien de but** goalkeeper; **gardien de la paix** policeman; **gardien de nuit** night watchman

gare[1] [gaʀ] nf station; **gare routière** bus station

gare[2] [gaʀ] excl: **à ...!** mind ...!; **à toi!** watch out!

garer [gaʀe] vt to park; **se garer** vi to park

garni, e [gaʀni] adj (plat) served with vegetables (and chips or rice etc)

garniture [gaʀnityʀ] nf (Culin) vegetables pl; **garniture de frein** brake lining

gars [gɑ] (fam) nm guy

Gascogne [gaskɔɲ] nf Gascony; **le**

golfe de ~ the Bay of Biscay

gas-oil [gazɔjl] nm diesel (oil)

gaspiller [gaspije] vt to waste

gastronome [gastʀɔnɔm] nm/f gourmet; **gastronomique** adj gastronomic

gâteau, x [gɑto] nm cake; **gâteau sec** biscuit

gâter [gɑte] vt to spoil; **se gâter** vi (dent, fruit) to go bad; (temps, situation) to change for the worse

gâteux, -euse [gɑtø, øz] adj senile

gauche [goʃ] adj left, left-hand; (maladroit) awkward, clumsy ▶ nf (Pol) left (wing); **le bras ~** the left arm; **le côté ~** the left-hand side; **à ~** on the left; (direction) (to) the left; **gaucher, -ère** adj left-handed; **gauchiste** nm/f leftist

gaufre [gofʀ] nf waffle

gaufrette [gofʀɛt] nf wafer

gaulois, e [golwa, waz] adj Gallic ▶ nm/f: **G~, e** Gaul

gaz [gaz] nm inv gas; **ça sent le ~** I can smell gas, there's a smell of gas

gaze [gaz] nf gauze

gazette [gazɛt] nf news sheet

gazeux, -euse [gazø, øz] adj (boisson) fizzy; (eau) sparkling

gazoduc [gazɔdyk] nm gas pipeline

gazon [gazɔ̃] nm (herbe) grass; (pelouse) lawn

geai [ʒɛ] nm jay

géant, e [ʒeɑ̃, ɑ̃t] adj gigantic; (Comm) giant-size ▶ nm/f giant

geindre [ʒɛ̃dʀ] vi to groan, moan

gel [ʒɛl] nm frost

gélatine [ʒelatin] nf gelatine

gelée [ʒ(ə)le] nf jelly; (gel) frost

geler [ʒ(ə)le] vt, vi to freeze; **il gèle** it's freezing

gélule [ʒelyl] nf (Méd) capsule

Gémeaux [ʒemo] nmpl: **les ~** Gemini

gémir [ʒemiʀ] vi to groan, moan

gênant, e [ʒɛnɑ̃, ɑ̃t] adj (irritant) annoying; (embarrassant) embarrassing

gencive [ʒɑ̃siv] nf gum

gendarme [ʒɑ̃daʀm] nm gendarme;

gendarmerie nf military police force in countryside and small towns; their police station or barracks

gendre [ʒɑ̃dʀ] nm son-in-law

gêné, e [ʒene] adj embarrassed

gêner [ʒene] vt (incommoder) to bother; (encombrer) to be in the way; (embarrasser): **~ qn** to make sb feel ill-at-ease; **se gêner** to put o.s. out; **ne vous gênez pas!** don't mind me!

général, e, -aux [ʒeneʀal, o] adj, nm general; **en ~** usually, in general; **généralement** adv generally; **généraliser** vt, vi to generalize; **se généraliser** vi to become widespread; **généraliste** nm/f general practitioner, G.P.

génération [ʒeneʀasjɔ̃] nf generation

généreux, -euse [ʒeneʀø, øz] adj generous

générique [ʒeneʀik] nm (Cinéma) credits pl

générosité [ʒeneʀozite] nf generosity

genêt [ʒ(ə)nɛ] nm broom no pl (shrub)

génétique [ʒenetik] adj genetic

Genève [ʒ(ə)nɛv] n Geneva

génial, e, -aux [ʒenjal, jo] adj of genius; (fam: formidable) fantastic, brilliant

génie [ʒeni] nm genius; (Mil): **le ~** the Engineers pl; **génie civil** civil engineering

genièvre [ʒənjevʀ] nm juniper

génisse [ʒenis] nf heifer

génital, e, -aux [ʒenital, o] adj genital; **les parties ~es** the genitals

génoise [ʒenwaz] nf sponge cake

genou, x [ʒ(ə)nu] nm knee; **à ~x** on one's knees; **se mettre à ~x** to kneel down

genre [ʒɑ̃ʀ] nm kind, type, sort; (Ling) gender; **avoir bon ~** to look a nice sort; **avoir mauvais ~** to be coarse-looking; **ce n'est pas son ~** it's not like him

gens [ʒɑ̃] nmpl (f in some phrases) people pl

gentil, le [ʒɑ̃ti, ij] adj kind; (enfant: sage) good; (endroit etc) nice;

gentillesse nf kindness; **gentiment** adv kindly

géographie [ʒeɔgʀafi] nf geography

géologie [ʒeɔlɔʒi] nf geology

géomètre [ʒeɔmɛtʀ] nm/f (arpenteur) (land) surveyor

géométrie [ʒeɔmetʀi] nf geometry; **géométrique** adj geometric

géranium [ʒeʀanjɔm] nm geranium

gérant, e [ʒeʀɑ̃, ɑ̃t] nm/f manager(-eress); **gérant d'immeuble** (managing) agent

gerbe [ʒɛʀb] nf (de fleurs) spray; (de blé) sheaf

gercé, e [ʒɛʀse] adj chapped

gerçure [ʒɛʀsyʀ] nf crack

gérer [ʒeʀe] vt to manage

germain, e [ʒɛʀmɛ̃, ɛn] adj: **cousin ~** first cousin

germe [ʒɛʀm] nm germ; **germer** vi to sprout; (semence) to germinate

geste [ʒɛst] nm gesture

gestion [ʒɛstjɔ̃] nf management

Ghana [gana] nm: **le ~** Ghana

gibier [ʒibje] nm (animaux) game

gicler [ʒikle] vi to spurt, squirt

gifle [ʒifl] nf slap (in the face); **gifler** vt to slap (in the face)

gigantesque [ʒigɑ̃tɛsk] adj gigantic

gigot [ʒigo] nm leg (of mutton ou lamb)

gigoter [ʒigɔte] vi to wriggle (about)

gilet [ʒile] nm waistcoat; (pull) cardigan; **gilet de sauvetage** life jacket

gin [dʒin] nm gin; **~-tonic** gin and tonic

gingembre [ʒɛ̃ʒɑ̃bʀ] nm ginger

girafe [ʒiʀaf] nf giraffe

giratoire [ʒiʀatwaʀ] adj: **sens ~** roundabout

girofle [ʒiʀɔfl] nf: **clou de ~** clove

girouette [ʒiʀwɛt] nf weather vane ou cock

gitan, e [ʒitɑ̃, an] nm/f gipsy

gîte [ʒit] nm (maison) home; (abri) shelter; **gîte (rural)** (country) holiday cottage (BRIT), gîte (self-catering accommodation in the country)

givre [ʒivʀ] nm (hoar) frost; **givré, e** adj

covered in frost; (fam: fou) nuts; **orange givrée** orange sorbet (served in peel)

glace [glas] nf ice; (crème glacée) ice cream; (miroir) mirror; (de voiture) window

glacé, e [glase] adj (mains, vent, pluie) freezing; (lac) frozen; (boisson) iced

glacer [glase] vt to freeze; (gâteau) to ice; (fig): ~ **qn** (intimider) to chill sb; (paralyser) to make sb's blood run cold

glacial, e [glasjal, jo] adj icy

glacier [glasje] nm (Géo) glacier; (marchand) ice-cream maker

glacière [glasjɛʀ] nf icebox

glaçon [glasɔ̃] nm icicle; (pour boisson) ice cube

glaïeul [glajœl] nm gladiolus

glaise [glɛz] nf clay

gland [glɑ̃] nm acorn; (décoration) tassel

glande [glɑ̃d] nf gland

glissade [glisad] nf (par jeu) slide; (chute) slip; **faire des ~s sur la glace** to slide on the ice

glissant, e [glisɑ̃, ɑ̃t] adj slippery

glissement [glismɑ̃] nm: **glissement de terrain** landslide

glisser [glise] vi (avancer) to glide ou slide along; (coulisser, tomber) to slide; (déraper) to slip; (être glissant) to be slippery ▷ vt to slip; **se glisser dans/entre** to slip into/between

global, e, -aux [glɔbal, o] adj overall

globe [glɔb] nm globe

globule [glɔbyl] nm (du sang): ~ **blanc/rouge** white/red corpuscle

gloire [glwaʀ] nf glory

glousser [gluse] vi to cluck; (rire) to chuckle

glouton, ne [glutɔ̃, ɔn] adj gluttonous

gluant, e [glyɑ̃, ɑ̃t] adj sticky, gummy

glucose [glykoz] nm glucose

glycine [glisin] nf wisteria

GO sigle f (= grandes ondes) LW

goal [gol] nm goalkeeper

gobelet [gɔblɛ] nm (en étain, verre, argent) tumbler; (d'enfant, de pique-nique) beaker; (à dés) cup

goéland [gɔelɑ̃] nm (sea)gull

goélette [gɔelɛt] nf schooner

goinfre [gwɛ̃fʀ] nm glutton

golf [gɔlf] nm golf; (terrain) golf course; **golf miniature** crazy (BRIT) ou miniature golf

golfe [gɔlf] nm gulf; (petit) bay

gomme [gɔm] nf (à effacer) rubber (BRIT), eraser; **gommer** [gɔme] vt to rub out (BRIT), erase

gonflé, e [gɔ̃fle] adj swollen; **il est** ~ (fam: courageux) he's got some nerve; (impertinent) he's got a nerve

gonfler [gɔ̃fle] vt (pneu, ballon: en soufflant) to blow up; (: avec une pompe) to pump up; (nombre, importance) to inflate ▷ vi to swell (up); (Culin: pâte) to rise

gonzesse [gɔ̃zɛs] (fam) nf chick, bird (BRIT)

gorge [gɔʀʒ] nf (Anat) throat; (vallée) gorge; **gorgée** nf (petite) sip; (grande) gulp

gorille [gɔʀij] nm gorilla; (fam) bodyguard

gosse [gɔs] (fam) nm/f kid

goudron [gudʀɔ̃] nm tar; **goudronner** vt to tar(mac) (BRIT), asphalt (US)

gouffre [gufʀ] nm abyss, gulf

goulot [gulo] nm neck; **boire au** ~ to drink from the bottle

goulu, e [guly] adj greedy

gourde [guʀd] nf (récipient) flask; (fam) (clumsy) clot ou oaf ▷ adj oafish

gourdin [guʀdɛ̃] nm club, bludgeon

gourmand, e [guʀmɑ̃, ɑ̃d] adj greedy; **gourmandise** nf greed; (bonbon) sweet

gousse [gus] nf: **gousse d'ail** clove of garlic

goût [gu] nm taste; **avoir bon** ~ to taste good; **de bon** ~ tasteful; **de mauvais** ~ tasteless; **prendre** ~ **à** to develop a taste ou a liking for

goûter [gute] vt (essayer) to taste; (apprécier) to enjoy ▷ vi to have (afternoon) tea ▷ nm (afternoon) tea; **je peux** ~? can I have a taste?

goutte [gut] nf drop; (Méd) gout; (alcool) brandy; **tomber** ~ **à** ~ to drip;

une ~ de whisky a drop of whisky; **goutte-à-goutte** nm (*Méd*) drip
gouttière [gutjɛʀ] nf gutter
gouvernail [guvɛʀnaj] nm rudder; (*barre*) helm, tiller
gouvernement [guvɛʀnəmɑ̃] nm government
gouverner [guvɛʀne] vt to govern
grâce [gʀɑs] nf (*charme, Rel*) grace; (*faveur*) favour; (*Jur*) pardon; **faire ~ à qn de qch** to spare sb sth; **demander ~** to beg for mercy; **~ à** thanks to; **gracieux, -euse** adj graceful
grade [gʀad] nm rank; **monter en ~** to be promoted
gradin [gʀadɛ̃] nm tier; step; **gradins** nmpl (*de stade*) terracing sg
gradué, e [gʀadɥe] adj: **verre ~** measuring jug
graduel, le [gʀadɥel] adj gradual
graduer [gʀadɥe] vt (*effort etc*) to increase gradually; (*règle, verre*) to graduate
graffiti [gʀafiti] nmpl graffiti
grain [gʀɛ̃] nm (*gén*) grain; (*Navig*) squall; **grain de beauté** beauty spot; **grain de café** coffee bean; **grain de poivre** peppercorn
graine [gʀɛn] nf seed
graissage [gʀesaʒ] nm lubrication, greasing
graisse [gʀes] nf fat; (*lubrifiant*) grease; **graisser** vt to lubricate, grease; (*tacher*) to make greasy; **graisseux, -euse** adj greasy
grammaire [gʀa(m)mɛʀ] nf grammar
gramme [gʀam] nm gramme
grand, e [gʀɑ̃, gʀɑ̃d] adj (*haut*) tall; (*gros, vaste, large*) big, large; (*long*) long; (*plus âgé*) big; (*adulte*) grown-up; (*important, brillant*) great ▷ adv: **~ ouvert** wide open; **au ~ air** in the open (air); **les grands blessés** the severely injured; **grand ensemble** housing scheme; **grand magasin** department store; **grande personne** grown-up; **grande surface** hypermarket; **grandes écoles** prestigious schools at university

level; **grandes lignes** (*Rail*) main lines; **grandes vacances** summer holidays (*BRIT*) ou vacation (*US*); **grand-chose** nm/f inv: **pas grand-chose** not much; **Grande-Bretagne** nf (Great) Britain; **grandeur** nf (*dimension*) size; **grandeur nature** life-size; **grandiose** adj imposing; **grandir** vi to grow ▷ vt: **grandir qn** (*suj: vêtement, chaussure*) to make sb look taller; **grand-mère** nf grandmother; **grand-peine**: **à grand-peine** adv with difficulty; **grand-père** nm grandfather; **grands-parents** nmpl grandparents
grange [gʀɑ̃ʒ] nf barn
granit [gʀanit] nm granite
graphique [gʀafik] adj graphic ▷ nm graph
grappe [gʀap] nf cluster; **grappe de raisin** bunch of grapes
gras, se [gʀɑ, gʀɑs] adj (*viande, soupe*) fatty; (*personne*) fat; (*surface, main*) greasy; (*plaisanterie*) coarse; (*Typo*) bold ▷ nm (*Culin*) fat; **faire la ~e matinée** to have a lie-in (*BRIT*), sleep late (*US*); **grassement** adv: **grassement payé** handsomely paid
gratifiant, e [gʀatifjɑ̃, jɑ̃t] adj gratifying, rewarding
gratin [gʀatɛ̃] nm (*plat*) cheese-topped dish; (*croûte*) cheese topping; (*fam: élite*) upper crust; **gratiné, e** (*Culin*) au gratin
gratis [gʀatis] adv free
gratitude [gʀatityd] nf gratitude
gratte-ciel [gʀatsjɛl] nm inv skyscraper
gratter [gʀate] vt (*avec un outil*) to scrape; (*enlever: avec un outil*) to scrape off; (: *avec un ongle*) to scratch; (*enlever avec un ongle*) to scratch off ▷ vi (*irriter*) to be scratchy; (*démanger*) to itch; **se gratter** to scratch (o.s.)
gratuit, e [gʀatɥi, ɥit] adj (*entrée, billet*) free; (*fig*) gratuitous
grave [gʀav] adj (*maladie, accident*) serious, bad; (*sujet, problème*) serious, grave; (*air*) grave, solemn; (*voix, son*)

deep, low-pitched; **gravement** adv seriously; (parler, regarder) gravely

graver [gʀave] vt (plaque, nom) to engrave; (CD, DVD) to burn

graveur [gʀavœʀ] nm engraver; **graveur de CD/DVD** CD/DVD writer

gravier [gʀavje] nm gravel no pl; **gravillons** nmpl loose chippings ou gravel sg

gravir [gʀaviʀ] vt to climb (up)

gravité [gʀavite] nf (de maladie, d'accident) seriousness; (de sujet, problème) gravity

graviter [gʀavite] vi to revolve

gravure [gʀavyʀ] nf engraving; (reproduction) print

gré [gʀe] nm: **à son ~** to one's liking; **de bon ~** willingly; **contre le ~ de qn** against sb's will; **de son (plein) ~** of one's own free will; **bon ~ mal ~** like it or not; **de ~ ou de force** whether one likes it or not; **savoir ~ à qn de qch** to be grateful to sb for sth

grec, grecque [gʀɛk] adj Greek; (classique: vase etc) Grecian ▷ nm/f: **G~, Grecque** Greek ▷ nm (Ling) Greek

Grèce [gʀɛs] nf: **la ~** Greece

greffe [gʀɛf] nf (Bot, Méd: de tissu) graft; (Méd: d'organe) transplant; **greffer** vt (Bot, Méd: tissu) to graft; (Méd: organe) to transplant

grêle [gʀɛl] adj (very) thin ▷ nf hail; **grêler** vb impers: **il grêle** it's hailing; **grêlon** nm hailstone

grelot [gʀəlo] nm little bell

grelotter [gʀəlɔte] vi to shiver

grenade [gʀənad] nf (explosive) grenade; (Bot) pomegranate; **grenadine** nf grenadine

grenier [gʀənje] nm attic; (de ferme) loft

grenouille [gʀənuj] nf frog

grès [gʀɛ] nm sandstone; (poterie) stoneware

grève [gʀɛv] nf (d'ouvriers) strike; (plage) shore; **se mettre en/faire ~** to go on/be on strike; **grève de la faim** hunger strike; **grève sauvage** wildcat strike

gréviste [gʀevist] nm/f striker

grièvement [gʀijevmɑ̃] adv seriously

griffe [gʀif] nf claw; (de couturier) label; **griffer** vt to scratch

grignoter [gʀiɲɔte] vt (personne) to nibble at; (souris) to gnaw at ▷ vi to nibble

gril [gʀil] nm steak ou grill pan; **faire cuire au ~** to grill; **grillade** nf (viande etc) grill

grillage [gʀijaʒ] nm (treillis) wire netting; (clôture) wire fencing

grille [gʀij] nf (clôture) wire fence; (portail) (metal) gate; (d'égout) (metal) grate; (fig) grid

grille-pain [gʀijpɛ̃] nm inv toaster

griller [gʀije] vt (pain) to toast; (viande) to grill; (fig: ampoule etc) to blow; **faire ~** to toast; to grill; (châtaignes) to roast; **~ un feu rouge** to jump the lights

grillon [gʀijɔ̃] nm cricket

grimace [gʀimas] nf grimace; (pour faire rire): **faire des ~s** to pull ou make faces

grimper [gʀɛ̃pe] vi, vt to climb

grincer [gʀɛ̃se] vi (objet métallique) to grate; (plancher, porte) to creak; **~ des dents** to grind one's teeth

grincheux, -euse [gʀɛ̃ʃø, øz] adj grumpy

grippe [gʀip] nf flu, influenza; **grippe aviaire** bird flu; **grippé, e** adj **être grippé** to have flu

gris, e [gʀi, gʀiz] adj grey; (ivre) tipsy

grisaille [gʀizaj] nf greyness, dullness

griser [gʀize] vt to intoxicate

grive [gʀiv] nf thrush

Groenland [gʀɔenlɑ̃d] nm Greenland

grogner [gʀɔɲe] vi to growl; (fig) to grumble; **grognon, ne** adj grumpy

grommeler [gʀɔm(ə)le] vi to mutter to o.s.

gronder [gʀɔ̃de] vi to rumble; (fig: révolte) to be brewing ▷ vt to scold; **se faire ~** to get a telling-off

gros, se [gʀo, gʀos] adj big, large; (obèse) fat; (travaux, dégâts) extensive; (épais) thick; (rhume, averse) heavy ▷ adv: **risquer/gagner ~** to risk/win a lot ▷ nm/f fat man/woman ▷ nm (Comm): **le ~** the wholesale business; **le ~ de** the bulk of; **prix de gros** wholesale price; **par ~ temps/grosse mer** in rough weather/heavy seas; **en ~** roughly; (Comm) wholesale; **gros lot** jackpot; **gros mot** swearword; **gros plan** (Photo) close-up; **gros sel** cooking salt; **gros titre** headline; **grosse caisse** big drum

groseille [gʀozɛj] nf: **~ (rouge/blanche)** red/white currant; **groseille à maquereau** gooseberry

grosse [gʀos] adj voir **gros; grossesse** nf pregnancy; **grosseur** nf size; (tumeur) lump

grossier, -ière [gʀosje, jɛʀ] adj coarse; (insolent) rude; (dessin) rough; (travail) roughly done; (imitation, instrument) crude; (erreur) erreur) gross; **grossièrement** adv (sommairement) roughly; (vulgairement) coarsely; **grossièreté** nf rudeness; (mot): **dire des grossièretés** to use coarse language

grossir [gʀosiʀ] vi (personne) to put on weight ▷ vt (exagérer) to exaggerate; (au microscope) to magnify; (suj: vêtement): **~ qn** to make sb look fatter

grossiste [gʀosist] nm/f wholesaler

grotesque [gʀɔtɛsk] adj (extravagant) grotesque; (ridicule) ludicrous

grotte [gʀɔt] nf cave

groupe [gʀup] nm group; **groupe de parole** support group; **groupe sanguin** blood group; **groupe scolaire** school complex; **grouper** vt to group; **se grouper** vi to unite

grue [gʀy] nf crane

GSM [ʒeɛsɛm] nm, adj GSM

guenon [gənɔ̃] nf female monkey

guépard [gepaʀ] nm cheetah

guêpe [gɛp] nf wasp

guère [gɛʀ] adv (avec adjectif, adverbe): **ne ... ~** hardly; (avec verbe: pas beaucoup): **ne ... ~** + tournure négative +much; (pas souvent) hardly ever; (pas longtemps) tournure négative +(very) long; **il n'y a**

~ que/de there's hardly anybody (ou anything) but/hardly any; **ce n'est ~ difficile** it's hardly difficult; **nous n'avons ~ de temps** we have hardly any time

guérilla [geʀija] nf guerrilla warfare

guérillero [geʀijeʀo] nm guerrilla

guérir [geʀiʀ] vt (personne, maladie) to cure; (membre, plaie) to heal ▷ vi (malade, maladie) to be cured; (blessure) to heal; **guérison** nf (de maladie) curing; (de membre, plaie) healing; (de malade) recovery; **guérisseur, -euse** nm/f healer

guerre [gɛʀ] nf war; **en ~** at war; **faire la ~ à** to wage war against; **guerre civile/mondiale** civil/world war; **guerrier, -ière** adj warlike ▷ nm/f warrior

guet [gɛ] nm: **faire le ~** to be on the watch ou look-out; **guet-apens** [gɛtapɑ̃] nm ambush; **guetter** vt (épier) to watch (intently); (attendre) to watch (out) for; (hostilement) to be lying in wait for

gueule [gœl] nf (d'animal) mouth; (fam: figure) face; (: bouche) mouth; **ta ~!** (fam) shut up!; **avoir la ~ de bois** (fam) to have a hangover, be hung over; **gueuler** (fam) vi to bawl

gui [gi] nm mistletoe

guichet [giʃɛ] nm (de bureau, banque) counter; **les ~s** (à la gare, au théâtre) the ticket office sg

guide [gid] nm (personne) guide; (livre) guide (book) ▷ nf (éclaireuse) guide; **guider** vt to guide

guidon [gidɔ̃] nm handlebars pl

guignol [giɲɔl] nm ≈ Punch and Judy show; (fig) clown

guillemets [gijmɛ] nmpl: **entre ~** in inverted commas

guindé, e [gɛde] adj (personne, air) stiff, starchy; (style) stilted

Guinée [gine] nf Guinea

guirlande [giʀlɑd] nf (fleurs) garland; **guirlande de Noël** tinsel garland

guise [giz] nf: **à votre ~** as you wish ou

please; **en ~ de** by way of
guitare [gitar] *nf* guitar
Guyane [gɥijan] *nf*: **la ~ (française)**
French Guiana
gym [ʒim] *nf* (*exercices*) gym; **gymnase**
nm gym(nasium); **gymnaste** *nm/f*
gymnast; **gymnastique** *nf* gymnastics
sg; (*au réveil etc*) keep-fit exercises *pl*
gynécologie [ʒinekɔlɔʒi] *nf*
gynaecology; **gynécologique** *adj*
gynaecological; **gynécologue** *nm/f*
gynaecologist

habile [abil] *adj* skilful; (*malin*) clever;
habileté [abilte] *nf* skill, skilfulness;
cleverness
habillé, e [abije] *adj* dressed; (*chic*)
dressy
habiller [abije] *vt* to dress; (*fournir en
vêtements*) to clothe; (*couvrir*) to cover;
s'habiller *vi* to dress (o.s.); (*se déguiser,
mettre des vêtements chic*) to dress up
habit [abi] *nm* outfit; **habits** *nmpl*
(*vêtements*) clothes; **habit (de soirée)**
evening dress; (*pour homme*) tails *pl*
habitant, e [abitɑ̃, ɑ̃t] *nm/f*
inhabitant; (*d'une maison*) occupant;
loger chez l'~ to stay with the locals
habitation [abitasjɔ̃] *nf* house;
habitations à loyer modéré (block of)
council flats
habiter [abite] *vt* to live in ▷ *vi*: **~
à/dans** to live in; **où habitez-vous?**
where do you live?
habitude [abityd] *nf* habit; **avoir l'~ de
qch** to be used to sth; **avoir l'~ de faire**
to be in the habit of doing; (*expérience*)

to be used to doing; **d'** usually; **comme d'** as usual

habitué, e [abitye] nm/f (de maison) regular visitor; (de café) regular (customer)

habituel, le [abituɛl] adj usual

habituer [abitye] vt: **~ qn à** to get sb used to; **s'habituer à** to get used to

hache ['aʃ] nf axe

hacher ['aʃe] vt (viande) to mince; (persil) to chop; **hachis** nm mince no pl; **hachis Parmentier** ≈ shepherd's pie

haie ['ɛ] nf hedge; (Sport) hurdle

haillons ['ajɔ̃] nmpl rags

haine ['ɛn] nf hatred

haïr ['aiʀ] vt to detest, hate

hâlé, e ['ale] adj (sun)tanned, sunburnt

haleine [alɛn] nf breath; **hors d'~** out of breath; **tenir en ~** (attention) to hold spellbound; (incertitude) to keep in suspense; **de longue ~** long-term

haleter ['alte] vi to pant

hall ['ol] nm hall

halle ['al] nf (covered) market; **halles** nfpl (d'une grande ville) central food market sg

hallucination [alysinasjɔ̃] nf hallucination

halte ['alt] nf stop, break; (endroit) stopping place ▷ excl stop!; **faire halte** to stop

haltère [altɛʀ] nm dumbbell, barbell; **haltères** nmpl: **(poids et) ~s** (activité) weightlifting sg; **haltérophilie** nf weightlifting

hamac ['amak] nm hammock

hameau, x ['amo] nm hamlet

hameçon [amsɔ̃] nm (fish) hook

hanche ['ãʃ] nf hip

handball ['ãdbal] nm handball

handicapé, e ['ãdikape] adj disabled, handicapped ▷ nm/f handicapped person; **handicapé mental/physique** mentally/physically handicapped person; **handicapé moteur** person with a movement disorder

hangar ['ãgaʀ] nm shed; (Aviat) hangar

hanneton ['antɔ̃] nm cockchafer

hanter ['ãte] vt to haunt

hantise ['ãtiz] nf obsessive fear

harceler ['aʀsəle] vt to harass; **harceler qn de questions** to plague sb with questions

hardi, e ['aʀdi] adj bold, daring

hareng ['aʀɑ̃] nm herring; **hareng saur** kipper, smoked herring

hargne ['aʀɲ] nf aggressiveness; **hargneux, -euse** adj aggressive

haricot ['aʀiko] nm bean; **haricot blanc** haricot bean; **haricot vert** green bean; **haricot rouge** kidney bean

harmonica [aʀmɔnika] nm mouth organ

harmonie [aʀmɔni] nf harmony; **harmonieux, -euse** adj harmonious; (couleurs, couple) well-matched

harpe ['aʀp] nf harp

hasard ['azaʀ] nm: **le hasard** chance, fate; **un hasard** a coincidence; **au hasard** (aller) aimlessly; (choisir) at random; **par hasard** by chance; **à tout hasard** (en cas de besoin) just in case; (en espérant trouver ce qu'on cherche) on the off chance (BRIT)

hâte ['at] nf haste; **à la hâte** hurriedly, hastily; **en hâte** posthaste, with all possible speed; **avoir hâte de** to be eager ou anxious to; **hâter** vt to hasten; **se hâter** vi to hurry; **hâtif, -ive** adj (travail) hurried; (décision, jugement) hasty

hausse ['os] nf rise, increase; **être en hausse** to be going up; **hausser** vt to raise; **hausser les épaules** to shrug (one's shoulders)

haut, e ['o, 'ot] adj high; (grand) tall ▷ adv high ▷ nm top (part); **de 3 m de haut** 3 m high, 3 m in height; **des hauts et des bas** ups and downs; **en haut lieu** in high places; **à haute voix, (tout) haut** aloud, out loud; **du haut de** from the top of; **de haut en bas** from top to bottom; **plus haut** higher up, further up; (dans un texte) above;

(parler) louder; **en haut** (être/aller) at/to the top; (dans une maison) upstairs; **en haut de** at the top of; **'haut débit** nm broadband

'hautain, e [otɛ̃, ɛn] adj haughty

'hautbois ['obwa] nm oboe

'hauteur ['otœʀ] nf height; **à la hauteur de** (accident) near; (fig: tâche, situation) equal to; **à la hauteur** (fig) up to it

'haut-parleur nm (loud)speaker

Hawaï [awai] n: **les îles ~** Hawaii

'Haye ['ɛ] n: **la Haye** the Hague

hebdomadaire [ɛbdɔmadɛʀ] adj, nm weekly

hébergement [ebɛʀʒəmɑ̃] nm accommodation

héberger [ebɛʀʒe] vt (touristes) to accommodate, lodge; (amis) to put up; (réfugiés) to take in

hébergeur [ebɛʀʒœʀ] nm (Internet) host

hébreu, x [ebʀø] adj m, nm Hebrew

Hébrides [ebʀid] nf: **les ~** the Hebrides

hectare [ɛktaʀ] nm hectare

hein ['ɛ̃] excl eh?

'hélas ['elɑs] excl alas! ▷ adv unfortunately

'héler ['ele] vt to hail

hélice [elis] nf propeller

hélicoptère [elikɔptɛʀ] nm helicopter

helvétique [ɛlvetik] adj Swiss

hématome [ematɔm] nm nasty bruise

hémisphère [emisfɛʀ] nm: **l'~ nord/sud** the northern/southern hemisphere

hémorragie [emɔʀaʒi] nf bleeding no pl, haemorrhage

hémorroïdes [emɔʀɔid] nfpl piles, haemorrhoids

'hennir ['eniʀ] vi to neigh, whinny

hépatite [epatit] nf hepatitis

herbe [ɛʀb] nf grass; (Culin, Méd) herb; **~s de Provence** mixed herbs; **en ~** unripe; (fig) budding; **herbicide** nm weed-killer; **herboriste** nm/f herbalist

héréditaire [eʀeditɛʀ] adj hereditary

'hérisson ['eʀisɔ̃] nm hedgehog

héritage [eʀitaʒ] nm inheritance; (coutumes, système) heritage, legacy

hériter [eʀite] vi: **~ de qch (de qn)** to inherit sth (from sb); **héritier, -ière** nm/f heir(-ess)

hermétique [ɛʀmetik] adj airtight; watertight; (fig: obscur) abstruse; (: impénétrable) impenetrable

hermine [ɛʀmin] nf ermine

hernie ['ɛʀni] nf hernia

héroïne [eʀɔin] nf heroine; (drogue) heroin

héroïque [eʀɔik] adj heroic

héron ['eʀɔ̃] nm heron

héros ['eʀo] nm hero

hésitant, e [ezitɑ̃, ɑ̃t] adj hesitant

hésitation [ezitasjɔ̃] nf hesitation

hésiter [ezite] vi: **~ (à faire)** to hesitate (to do)

hétérosexuel, le [eteʀɔsɛksɥɛl] adj heterosexual

'hêtre ['ɛtʀ] nm beech

heure [œʀ] nf hour; (Scol) period; (moment) time; **c'est l'~** it's time; **quelle ~ est-il?** what time is it?; **2 ~s (du matin)** 2 o'clock (in the morning); **être à l'~** to be on time; (montre) to be right; **mettre à l'~** to set right; **à une ~ avancée (de la nuit)** at a late hour (of the night); **de bonne ~** early; **à toute ~** at any time; **24 ~s sur 24** round the clock, 24 hours a day; **à l'~ qu'il est** at this time (of day); by now; **sur l'~** at once; **à quelle ~ ouvre le musée/magasin?** what time does the museum/shop open?; **heures de bureau** office hours; **heure de pointe** rush hour; (téléphone) peak period; **heures supplémentaires** overtime sg

heureusement [œʀøzmɑ̃] adv (par bonheur) fortunately, luckily

heureux, -euse [œʀø, øz] adj happy; (chanceux) lucky, fortunate

heurt ['œʀ] nm (choc) collision; (conflit) clash

'heurter ['œʀte] vt (mur) to strike, hit; (personne) to collide with

hexagone [ɛgzagɔn] *nm* hexagon; **l'H~** (la France) France (because of its shape)

hibérner [ibɛRne] *vi* to hibernate

hibou, x ['ibu] *nm* owl

hideux, -euse [idø, øz] *adj* hideous

hier [jɛR] *adv* yesterday; **~ matin/midi** yesterday morning/lunchtime; **~ soir** last night, yesterday evening; **toute la journée d'~** all day yesterday; **toute la matinée d'~** all yesterday morning

hiérarchie ['jeRaRʃi] *nf* hierarchy

hindou, e [ɛ̃du] *adj* Hindu ▷ *nm/f*: **H~, e** Hindu

hippique [ipik] *adj* equestrian, horse *cpd*; **un club ~** a riding centre; **un concours ~** a horse show; **hippisme** *nm* (horse)riding

hippodrome [ipodRom] *nm* racecourse

hippopotame [ipopotam] *nm* hippopotamus

hirondelle [iRɔ̃dɛl] *nf* swallow

hisser ['ise] *vt* to hoist, haul up

histoire [istwaR] *nf* (science, événements, récit) history; (anecdote, récit, mensonge) story; (affaire) business no *pl*; **histoires** *nfpl* (chichis) fuss no *pl*; (ennuis) trouble *sg*; **historique** *adj* historical; (important) historic ▷ *nm*: **faire l'historique de** to give the background to

'hit-parade ['itpaRad] *nm*: **le hit-parade** the charts

hiver [ivɛR] *nm* winter; **hivernal, e, -aux** *adj* (glacial) wintry; **hiverner** *vi* to winter

HLM *nm ou f* (= habitation à loyer modéré) council flat; **des ~** council housing

hobby ['ɔbi] *nm* hobby

hocher ['ɔʃe] *vt*: **hocher la tête** to nod; (signe négatif ou dubitatif) to shake one's head

hockey ['ɔkɛ] *nm*: **hockey (sur glace/gazon)** (ice/field) hockey

hold-up ['ɔldœp] *nm inv* hold-up

hollandais, e ['ɔlɑ̃dɛ, ɛz] *adj* Dutch ▷ *nm* (Ling) Dutch ▷ *nm/f*: **Hollandais, e** Dutchman(-woman)

'Hollande ['ɔlɑ̃d] *nf*: **la Hollande** Holland

homard ['ɔmaR] *nm* lobster

homéopathique [ɔmeopatik] *adj* homoeopathic

homicide [ɔmisid] *nm* murder; **homicide involontaire** manslaughter

hommage [ɔmaʒ] *nm* tribute; **rendre ~ à** to pay tribute to

homme [ɔm] *nm* man; **homme d'affaires** businessman; **homme d'État** statesman; **homme de main** hired man; **homme de paille** stooge; **l'homme de la rue** the man in the street

homo...: **homogène** *adj* homogeneous; **homologue** *nm/f* counterpart; **homologué, e** *adj* (Sport) ratified; (tarif) authorized; **homonyme** *nm* (Ling) homonym; (d'une personne) namesake; **homosexuel, le** *adj* homosexual

'Hong Kong ['ɔ̃gkɔ̃g] *n* Hong Kong

'Hongrie ['ɔ̃gRi] *nf*: **la Hongrie** Hungary; **hongrois, e** *adj* Hungarian ▷ *nm/f*: **Hongrois, e** Hungarian ▷ *nm* (Ling) Hungarian

honnête [ɔnɛt] *adj* (intègre) honest; (juste, satisfaisant) fair; **honnêtement** *adv* honestly; **honnêteté** *nf* honesty

honneur [ɔnœR] *nm* honour; (mérite) credit; **en l'~ de** in honour of; (événement) on the occasion of; **faire ~ à** (engagements) to honour; (famille) to be a credit to; (fig: repas etc) to do justice to

honorable [ɔnɔRabl] *adj* worthy, honourable; (suffisant) decent

honoraire [ɔnɔRɛR] *adj* honorary; **professeur ~** professor emeritus; **honoraires** *nmpl* fees

honorer [ɔnɔRe] *vt* to honour; (estimer) to hold in high regard; (faire honneur à) to do credit to

'honte ['ɔ̃t] *nf* shame; **avoir honte de** to be ashamed of; **faire honte à qn** to make sb (feel) ashamed; **'honteux, -euse** *adj* ashamed; (conduite, acte) shameful, disgraceful

hôpital, -aux [ɔpital, o] nm hospital; **où est l'~ le plus proche?** where is the nearest hospital?

'hoquet [ɔkɛ] nm: **avoir le hoquet** to have (the) hiccoughs

horaire [ɔRɛR] adj hourly ⊳ nm timetable, schedule; **horaires** nmpl (d'employé) hours; **horaire souple** flexitime

horizon [ɔRizɔ̃] nm horizon

horizontal, e, -aux [ɔRizɔ̃tal, o] adj horizontal

horloge [ɔRlɔʒ] nf clock; **l'~ parlante** the speaking clock; **horloger, -ère** nm/f watchmaker; clockmaker

'hormis [ɔRmi] prép save

horoscope [`skɔp] nm horoscope

horreur [ɔRœR] nf horror; **quelle ~!** how awful; **avoir ~ de** to loathe ou detest; **horrible** adj horrible; **horrifier** vt to horrify

'hors [ˈɔR] prép: **hors de** out of; **hors pair** outstanding; **hors de propos** inopportune; **être hors de soi** to be beside o.s.; **'hors d'usage** out of service; **'hors-bord** nm inv speedboat (with outboard motor); **'hors-d'œuvre** nm inv hors d'œuvre; **'hors-la-loi** nm inv outlaw; **'hors-service** adj inv out of order; **'hors-taxe** adj (boutique, articles) duty-free

hortensia [ɔRtɑ̃sja] nm hydrangea

hospice [ɔspis] nm (de vieillards) home

hospitalier, -ière [ɔspitalje, jɛR] adj (accueillant) hospitable; (Méd: service, centre) hospital cpd

hospitaliser [ɔspitalize] vt to take/ send to hospital, hospitalize

hospitalité [ɔspitalite] nf hospitality

hostie [ɔsti] nf host (Rel)

hostile [ɔstil] adj hostile; **hostilité** nf hostility

hôte [ot] nm (maître de maison) host; (invité) guest

hôtel [otɛl] nm hotel; **aller à l'~** to stay in a hotel; **hôtel de ville** town hall; **hôtel (particulier)** (private) mansion; **hôtellerie** nf hotel business

HÔTELS

There are six categories of hotel in France, from zero ('non classé') to four stars and luxury four stars ('quatre étoiles luxe'). Prices include VAT but not breakfast. In some towns, guests pay a small additional tourist tax, the 'taxe de séjour'.

hôtesse [otɛs] nf hostess; **hôtesse (de l'air)** stewardess, air hostess (BRIT)

'houblon [ˈublɔ̃] nm (Bot) hop; (pour la bière) hops pl

'houille [ˈuj] nf coal; **'houille blanche** hydroelectric power

'houle [ˈul] nf swell; **'houleux, -euse** adj stormy

'hourra [ˈuRa] excl hurrah!

'housse [ˈus] nf cover

'houx [ˈu] nm holly

hublot [yblo] nm porthole

'huche [yʃ] nf: **huche à pain** bread bin

'huer [ˈɥe] vt to boo

huile [ɥil] nf oil

huissier [ɥisje] nm usher; (Jur) = bailiff

'huit [ˈɥi(t)] num eight; **samedi en huit** a week on Saturday; **dans huit jours** in a week; **'huitaine** nf: **une huitaine (de jours)** a week or so; **'huitième** num eighth

huître [ɥitR] nf oyster

humain, e [ymɛ̃, ɛn] adj human; (compatissant) humane ⊳ nm human (being); **humanitaire** adj humanitarian; **humanité** nf humanity

humble [œ̃bl] adj humble

humer [ˈyme] vt (plat) to smell; (parfum) to inhale

humeur [ymœR] nf mood; **de bonne/ mauvaise ~** in a good/bad mood

humide [ymid] adj damp; (main, yeux) moist; (climat, chaleur) humid; (saison, route) wet

humilier [ymilje] vt to humiliate

humilité [ymilite] nf humility, humbleness

humoristique [ymɔRistik] adj

humorous

humour [ymur] nm humour; **avoir de l'~** to have a sense of humour; **humour noir** black humour

'huppé, e [ype] (fam) adj posh

'hurlement ['yrləmã] nm howling no pl, howl, yelling no pl, yell

'hurler ['yrle] vi to howl, yell

'hutte ['yt] nf hut

hydratant, e [idratã, ãt] adj (crème) moisturizing

hydraulique [idrolik] adj hydraulic

hydravion [idravjɔ̃] nm seaplane

hydrogène [idrɔʒɛn] nm hydrogen

hydroglisseur [idrɔglisœr] nm hydroplane

hyène [jɛn] nf hyena

hygiène [iʒjɛn] nf hygiene

hygiénique [iʒenik] adj hygienic

hymne [imn] nm hymn

hyperlien [iperljɛ̃] nm hyperlink

hypermarché [ipermarʃe] nm hypermarket

hypermétrope [ipermetrɔp] adj long-sighted

hypertension [ipertãsjɔ̃] nf high blood pressure

hypnose [ipnoz] nf hypnosis; **hypnotiser** vt to hypnotize

hypocrisie [ipɔkrizi] nf hypocrisy; **hypocrite** adj hypocritical

hypothèque [ipɔtɛk] nf mortgage

hypothèse [ipɔtɛz] nf hypothesis

hystérique [isterik] adj hysterical

iceberg [ajsberg] nm iceberg

ici [isi] adv here; **jusqu'~** as far as this; (temps) so far; **d'~ demain** by tomorrow; **d'~ là** by then, in the meantime; **d'~ peu** before long

icône [ikon] nf icon

idéal, e, -aux [ideal, o] adj ideal ▷ nm ideal; **idéaliste** adj idealistic ▷ nm/f idealist

idée [ide] nf idea; **avoir dans l'~ que** to have an idea that; **se faire des ~s** to imagine things, get ideas into one's head; **avoir des ~s noires** to have black ou dark thoughts; **idées reçues** received wisdom sg

identifier [idãtifje] vt to identify; **s'identifier** vi: **s'~ avec** ou **à qn/qch** (héros etc) to identify with sb/sth

identique [idãtik] adj: **~ (à)** identical (to)

identité [idãtite] nf identity

idiot, e [idjo, idjɔt] adj idiotic ▷ nm/f idiot

idole [idɔl] nf idol

if [if] nm yew

ignoble [iɲɔbl] adj vile

ignorant, e [iɲɔrɑ̃, ɑ̃t] adj ignorant; **~ de** ignorant of, not aware of

ignorer [iɲɔre] vt not to know; (personne) to ignore

il [il] pron he; (animal, chose, en tournure impersonnelle) it; **il fait froid** it's cold; **Pierre est-il arrivé?** has Pierre arrived?; **il a gagné** he won; voir aussi **avoir**

île [il] nf island; **l'île Maurice** Mauritius; **les îles anglo-normandes** the Channel Islands; **les îles britanniques** the British Isles

illégal, e, -aux [i(l)legal, o] adj illegal

illimité, e [i(l)limite] adj unlimited

illisible [i(l)lizibl] adj illegible; (roman) unreadable

illogique [i(l)lɔʒik] adj illogical

illuminer [i(l)lymine] vt to light up; (monument, rue: pour une fête) to illuminate; (: au moyen de projecteurs) to floodlight

illusion [i(l)lyzjɔ̃] nf illusion; **se faire des ~s** to delude o.s.; **faire ~** to delude ou fool people

illustration [i(l)lystrɑsjɔ̃] nf illustration

illustré, e [i(l)lystre] adj illustrated ▷ nm comic

illustrer [i(l)lystre] vt to illustrate; **s'illustrer** to become famous, win fame

ils [il] pron they

image [imaʒ] nf (gén) picture; (métaphore) image; **image de marque** brand image; (fig) public image; **imagé, e** adj (texte) full of imagery; (langage) colourful

imaginaire [imaʒinɛr] adj imaginary

imagination [imaʒinɑsjɔ̃] nf imagination; **avoir de l'~** to be imaginative

imaginer [imaʒine] vt to imagine; (inventer: expédient) to devise, think up; **s'imaginer** vt (se figurer: scène etc) to imagine, picture; **s'~ que** to imagine that

imbécile [ɛ̃besil] adj idiotic ▷ nm/f idiot

imbu, e [ɛ̃by] adj: **~ de** full of

imitateur, -trice [imitatœr, tris] nm/f (gén) imitator; (Music-Hall) impersonator

imitation [imitɑsjɔ̃] nf imitation; (de personnalité) impersonation

imiter [imite] vt to imitate; (contrefaire) to forge; (ressembler à) to look like

immangeable [ɛ̃mɑ̃ʒabl] adj inedible

immatriculation [imatrikylasjɔ̃] nf registration

● **IMMATRICULATION**
●
● The last two numbers on vehicle
● licence plates show which
● 'département' of France the vehicle
● is registered in. For example, a car
● registered in Paris has the number 75
● on its licence plates.

immatriculer [imatrikyle] vt to register; **faire/se faire ~** to register

immédiat, e [imedja, jat] adj immediate ▷ nm: **dans l'~** for the time being; **immédiatement** adv immediately

immense [i(m)mɑ̃s] adj immense

immerger [imɛrʒe] vt to immerse, submerge

immeuble [imœbl] nm building; (à usage d'habitation) block of flats

immigration [imigrɑsjɔ̃] nf immigration

immigré, e [imigre] nm/f immigrant

imminent, e [iminɑ̃, ɑ̃t] adj imminent

immobile [i(m)mɔbil] adj still, motionless

immobilier, -ière [imɔbilje, jɛr] adj property cpd ▷ nm: **l'~** the property business

immobiliser [imɔbilize] vt (gén) to immobilize; (circulation, véhicule, affaires) to bring to a standstill; **s'immobiliser** (personne) to stand still; (machine, véhicule) to come to a halt

immoral, e, -aux [i(m)mɔraL, o] *adj* immoral

immortel, le [imɔrtɛl] *adj* immortal

immunisé, e [im(m)ynize] *adj*: **~ contre** immune to

immunité [imynite] *nf* immunity

impact [ɛ̃pakt] *nm* impact

impair, e [ɛ̃pɛr] *adj* odd ▷ *nm* faux pas, blunder

impardonnable [ɛ̃pardɔnabl] *adj* unpardonable, unforgivable

imparfait, e [ɛ̃parfɛ, ɛt] *adj* imperfect

impartial, e, -aux [ɛ̃parsjal, jo] *adj* impartial, unbiased

impasse [ɛ̃pas] *nf* dead end, cul-de-sac; (*fig*) deadlock

impassible [ɛ̃pasibl] *adj* impassive

impatience [ɛ̃pasjɑ̃s] *nf* impatience

impatient, e [ɛ̃pasjɑ̃, jɑ̃t] *adj* impatient; **impatienter**: **s'impatienter** *vi* to get impatient

impeccable [ɛ̃pekabl] *adj* (*parfait*) perfect; (*propre*) impeccable; (*fam*) smashing

impensable [ɛ̃pɑ̃sabl] *adj* (*événement hypothétique*) unthinkable; (*événement qui a eu lieu*) unbelievable

impératif, -ive [ɛ̃peratif, iv] *adj* imperative ▷ *nm* (*Ling*) imperative; **impératifs** *nmpl* (*exigences: d'une fonction, d'une charge*) requirements; (: *de la mode*) demands

impératrice [ɛ̃peratris] *nf* empress

imperceptible [ɛ̃persɛptibl] *adj* imperceptible

impérial, e, -aux [ɛ̃perjal, jo] *adj* imperial

impérieux, -euse [ɛ̃perjø, jøz] *adj* (*caractère, ton*) imperious; (*obligation, besoin*) pressing, urgent

impérissable [ɛ̃perisabl] *adj* undying

imperméable [ɛ̃permeabl] *adj* waterproof; (*fig*): **~ à** impervious to ▷ *nm* raincoat

impertinent, e [ɛ̃pertinɑ̃, ɑ̃t] *adj* impertinent

impitoyable [ɛ̃pitwajabl] *adj* pitiless, merciless

implanter [ɛ̃plɑ̃te]: **s'implanter** *vi* to be set up

impliquer [ɛ̃plike] *vt* to imply; **~ qn (dans)** to implicate sb (in)

impoli, e [ɛ̃pɔli] *adj* impolite, rude

impopulaire [ɛ̃pɔpylɛr] *adj* unpopular

importance [ɛ̃pɔrtɑ̃s] *nf* importance; (*de somme*) size; (*de retard, dégâts*) extent; **sans ~** unimportant

important, e [ɛ̃pɔrtɑ̃, ɑ̃t] *adj* important; (*en quantité: somme, retard*) considerable, sizeable; (: *dégâts*) extensive; (*péj: airs, ton*) self-important ▷ *nm*: **l'~** the important thing

importateur, -trice [ɛ̃pɔrtatœr, tris] *nm/f* importer

importation [ɛ̃pɔrtasjɔ̃] *nf* importation; (*produit*) import

importer [ɛ̃pɔrte] *vt* (*Comm*) to import; (*maladies, plantes*) to introduce ▷ *vi* (*être important*) to matter; **il importe qu'il fasse** it is important that he should do; **peu m'importe** (*je n'ai pas de préférence*) I don't mind; (*je m'en moque*) I don't care; **peu importe (que)** it doesn't matter (if); *voir aussi* **n'importe**

importun, e [ɛ̃pɔrtœ̃, yn] *adj* irksome, importunate; (*arrivée, visite*) inopportune, ill-timed ▷ *nm* intruder; **importuner** *vt* to bother

imposant, e [ɛ̃pozɑ̃, ɑ̃t] *adj* imposing

imposer [ɛ̃poze] *vt* (*taxer*) to tax; **s'imposer** (*être nécessaire*) to be imperative; **~ qch à qn** to impose sth on sb; **en ~ à** to impress; **s'~ comme** to emerge as; **s'~ par** to win recognition through

impossible [ɛ̃posibl] *adj* impossible; **il m'est ~ de le faire** it is impossible for me to do it, I can't possibly do it; **faire l'~** to do one's utmost

imposteur [ɛ̃postœr] *nm* impostor

impôt [ɛ̃po] *nm* tax; **impôt foncier** land tax; **impôt sur le chiffre d'affaires** corporation (BRIT) ou corporate (US) tax; **impôt sur le revenu** income tax; **impôts locaux** rates, local taxes (US), ...

≈ council tax (BRIT)

impotent, e [ɛ̃pɔtɑ̃, ɑ̃t] adj disabled

impraticable [ɛ̃pratikabl] adj (projet) impracticable, unworkable; (piste) impassable

imprécis, e [ɛ̃presi, iz] adj imprecise

imprégner [ɛ̃preɲe] vt (tissu) to impregnate; (lieu, air) to fill; **s'imprégner de** (fig) to absorb

imprenable [ɛ̃prənabl] adj (forteresse) impregnable; **vue ~** unimpeded outlook

impression [ɛ̃presjɔ̃] nf impression; (d'un ouvrage, tissu) printing; **faire bonne/mauvaise ~** to make a good/bad impression; **impressionnant, e** adj (imposant) impressive; (bouleversant) upsetting; **impressionner** vt (frapper) to impress; (bouleverser) to upset

imprévisible [ɛ̃previzibl] adj unforeseeable

imprévu, e [ɛ̃prevy] adj unforeseen, unexpected ▷ nm (incident) unexpected incident; **des vacances pleines d'~** holidays full of surprises; **en cas d'~** if anything unexpected happens; **sauf ~** unless anything unexpected crops up

imprimante [ɛ̃primɑ̃t] nf printer; **imprimante (à) laser** laser printer

imprimé [ɛ̃prime] nm (formulaire) printed form; (Postes) printed matter no pl; (tissu) printed fabric; **~ à fleur** floral print

imprimer [ɛ̃prime] vt to print; (publier) to publish; **imprimerie** nf printing; (établissement) printing works sg; **imprimeur** nm printer

impropre [ɛ̃prɔpr] adj inappropriate; **~ à** unfit for

improviser [ɛ̃prɔvize] vt, vi to improvise

improviste [ɛ̃prɔvist]: **à l'~** adv unexpectedly, without warning

imprudence [ɛ̃prydɑ̃s] nf (d'une personne, d'une action) carelessness no pl; (d'une remarque) imprudence no pl; **commettre une ~** to do something foolish

imprudent, e [ɛ̃prydɑ̃, ɑ̃t] adj (conducteur, geste, action) careless; (remarque) unwise, imprudent; (projet) foolhardy

impuissant, e [ɛ̃pɥisɑ̃, ɑ̃t] adj helpless; (sans effet) ineffectual; (sexuellement) impotent

impulsif, -ive [ɛ̃pylsif, iv] adj impulsive

impulsion [ɛ̃pylsjɔ̃] nf (Élec, instinct) impulse; (élan, influence) impetus

inabordable [inabɔrdabl] adj (cher) prohibitive

inacceptable [inaksɛptabl] adj unacceptable

inaccessible [inaksesibl] adj inaccessible; **~ à** impervious to

inachevé, e [inaʃ(ə)ve] adj unfinished

inactif, -ive [inaktif, iv] adj inactive; (remède) ineffective; (Bourse: marché) slack

inadapté, e [inadapte] adj (gén): **~ à** not adapted to, unsuited to; (Psych) maladjusted

inadéquat, e [inadekwa(t), kwat] adj inadequate

inadmissible [inadmisibl] adj inadmissible

inadvertance [inadvɛrtɑ̃s]: **par ~** adv inadvertently

inanimé, e [inanime] adj (matière) inanimate; (évanoui) unconscious; (sans vie) lifeless

inanition [inanisjɔ̃] nf: **tomber d'~** to faint with hunger (and exhaustion)

inaperçu, e [inapɛrsy] adj: **passer ~** to go unnoticed

inapte [inapt] adj: **~ à** incapable of; (Mil) unfit for

inattendu, e [inatɑ̃dy] adj unexpected

inattentif, -ive [inatɑ̃tif, iv] adj inattentive; **~ à** (dangers, détails) heedless of; **inattention** nf lack of attention; **une faute ou une erreur d'inattention** a careless mistake

inaugurer [inogyre] vt (monument) to unveil; (exposition, usine) to open; (fig) to inaugurate

inavouable [inavwabl] *adj* shameful; *(bénéfices)* undisclosable

incalculable [ɛ̃kalkylabl] *adj* incalculable

incapable [ɛ̃kapabl] *adj* incapable; **~ de faire** incapable of doing; *(empêché)* unable to do

incapacité [ɛ̃kapasite] *nf (incompétence)* incapability; *(impossibilité)* incapacity; **dans l'~ de faire** unable to do

incarcérer [ɛ̃karsere] *vt* to incarcerate, imprison

incassable [ɛ̃kasabl] *adj* unbreakable

incendie [ɛ̃sɑ̃di] *nm* fire; **incendie criminel** arson *no pl*; **incendie de forêt** forest fire; **incendier** *vt (mettre le feu à)* to set fire to, set alight; *(brûler complètement)* to burn down

incertain, e [ɛ̃sɛrtɛ̃, ɛn] *adj* uncertain; *(temps)* unsettled; *(imprécis: contours)* indistinct, blurred; **incertitude** *nf* uncertainty

incessamment [ɛ̃sesamɑ̃] *adv* very shortly

incident [ɛ̃sidɑ̃] *nm* incident; **incident de parcours** minor hitch *ou* setback; **incident technique** technical difficulties *pl*

incinérer [ɛ̃sinere] *vt (ordures)* to incinerate; *(mort)* to cremate

incisive [ɛ̃siziv] *nf* incisor

inciter [ɛ̃site] *vt*: **~ qn à (faire) qch** to encourage sb to do sth; *(à la révolte etc)* to incite sb to do sth

incivilité [ɛ̃sivilite] *nf (grossièreté)* incivility; **incivilités** *nfpl* antisocial behaviour *sg*

inclinable [ɛ̃klinabl] *adj*: **siège à dossier ~** reclining seat

inclination [ɛ̃klinasjɔ̃] *nf (penchant)* inclination

incliner [ɛ̃kline] *vt (pencher)* to tilt ▷ *vi*: **~ à qch/à faire** to incline towards sth/doing; **s'incliner** *vr (se pencher)* to bow; **s'~ devant** *(par respect)* to pay one's respects

inclure [ɛ̃klyr] *vt* to include; *(joindre à un envoi)* to enclose

inclus, e [ɛ̃kly, -yz] *pp de* **inclure** ▷ *adj* included; *(joint à un envoi)* enclosed ▷ *adv*: **est-ce que le service est ~?** is service included?; **jusqu'au 10 mars ~** until 10th March inclusive

incognito [ɛ̃kɔɲito] *adv* incognito ▷ *nm*: **garder l'~** to remain incognito

incohérent, e [ɛ̃kɔerɑ̃, ɑ̃t] *adj (comportement)* inconsistent; *(geste, langage, texte)* incoherent

incollable [ɛ̃kɔlabl] *adj (riz)* non-stick; **il est ~** *(fam)* he's got all the answers

incolore [ɛ̃kɔlɔr] *adj* colourless

incommoder [ɛ̃kɔmɔde] *vt (chaleur, odeur)*: **~ qn** to bother sb

incomparable [ɛ̃kɔ̃parabl] *adj* incomparable

incompatible [ɛ̃kɔ̃patibl] *adj* incompatible

incompétent, e [ɛ̃kɔ̃petɑ̃, ɑ̃t] *adj* incompetent

incomplet, -ète [ɛ̃kɔ̃plɛ, ɛt] *adj* incomplete

incompréhensible [ɛ̃kɔ̃preɑ̃sibl] *adj* incomprehensible

incompris, e [ɛ̃kɔ̃pri, iz] *adj* misunderstood

inconcevable [ɛ̃kɔ̃s(ə)vabl] *adj* inconceivable

inconfortable [ɛ̃kɔ̃fɔrtabl(ə)] *adj* uncomfortable

incongru, e [ɛ̃kɔ̃gry] *adj* unseemly

inconnu, e [ɛ̃kɔny] *adj* unknown ▷ *nm/f* stranger ▷ *nm*: **l'~** the unknown; **inconnue** *nf* unknown factor

inconsciemment [ɛ̃kɔ̃sjamɑ̃] *adv* unconsciously

inconscient, e [ɛ̃kɔ̃sjɑ̃, jɑ̃t] *adj* unconscious; *(irréfléchi)* thoughtless, reckless; *(sentiment)* subconscious ▷ *nm (Psych)*: **l'~** the unconscious; **~ de** unaware of

inconsidéré, e [ɛ̃kɔ̃sidere] *adj* ill-considered

inconsistant, e [ɛ̃kɔ̃sistɑ̃, ɑ̃t] *adj (fig)* flimsy, weak

inconsolable [ɛ̃kɔ̃sɔlabl] *adj*
inconsolable

incontestable [ɛ̃kɔ̃tɛstabl] *adj*
indisputable

incontinent, e [ɛ̃kɔ̃tinɑ̃, ɑ̃t] *adj*
incontinent

incontournable [ɛ̃kɔ̃turnabl] *adj*
unavoidable

incontrôlable [ɛ̃kɔ̃trolabl]
adj unverifiable; (*irrépressible*)
uncontrollable

inconvénient [ɛ̃kɔ̃venjɑ̃] *nm*
disadvantage, drawback; **si vous n'y
voyez pas d'~** if you have no objections

incorporer [ɛ̃kɔrpɔre] *vt*: **~ (à)** to
mix in (with); **~ (dans)** (*paragraphe
etc*) to incorporate (in); (*Mil: appeler*)
to recruit (into); **il a très bien su s'~
à notre groupe** he was very easily
incorporated into our group

incorrect, e [ɛ̃kɔrɛkt] *adj* (*impropre,
inconvenant*) improper; (*défectueux*)
faulty; (*inexact*) incorrect; (*impoli*)
impolite; (*déloyal*) underhand

incorrigible [ɛ̃kɔriʒibl] *adj*
incorrigible

incrédule [ɛ̃kredyl] *adj* incredulous;
(*Rel*) unbelieving

incroyable [ɛ̃krwajabl] *adj* incredible

incruster [ɛ̃kryste] *vt* (*Art*) to inlay;
s'incruster *vi* (*invité*) to take root

inculpé, e [ɛ̃kylpe] *nm/f* accused

inculper [ɛ̃kylpe] *vt*: **~ (de)** to charge
(with)

inculquer [ɛ̃kylke] *vt*: **~ qch à** to
inculcate sth in *ou* instil sth into

Inde [ɛ̃d] *nf*: **l'~** India

indécent, e [ɛ̃desɑ̃, ɑ̃t] *adj* indecent

indécis, e [ɛ̃desi, iz] *adj* (*par nature*)
indecisive; (*temporairement*) undecided

indéfendable [ɛ̃defɑ̃dabl] *adj*
indefensible

indéfini, e [ɛ̃defini] *adj* (*imprécis,
incertain*) undefined; (*illimité, Ling*)
indefinite; **indéfiniment** *adv*
indefinitely; **indéfinissable** *adj*
indefinable

indélébile [ɛ̃delebil] *adj* indelible

indélicat, e [ɛ̃delika, at] *adj* tactless

indemne [ɛ̃dɛmn] *adj* unharmed;
indemniser *vt*: **indemniser qn (de)** to
compensate sb (for)

indemnité [ɛ̃dɛmnite] *nf*
(*dédommagement*) compensation *no pl*;
(*allocation*) allowance; **indemnité de
licenciement** redundancy payment

indépendamment [ɛ̃depɑ̃damɑ̃]
adv independently; **~ de** (*abstraction
faite de*) irrespective of; (*en plus de*) over
and above

indépendance [ɛ̃depɑ̃dɑ̃s] *nf*
independence

indépendant, e [ɛ̃depɑ̃dɑ̃, ɑ̃t] *adj*
independent; **~ de** independent of;
travailleur ~ self-employed worker

indescriptible [ɛ̃dɛskriptibl] *adj*
indescribable

indésirable [ɛ̃dezirabl] *adj*
undesirable

indestructible [ɛ̃dɛstryktibl] *adj*
indestructible

indéterminé, e [ɛ̃detɛrmine] *adj*
(*date, cause, nature*) unspecified; (*forme,
longueur, quantité*) indeterminate

index [ɛ̃dɛks] *nm* (*doigt*) index finger;
(*d'un livre etc*) index; **mettre à l'~** to
blacklist

indicateur [ɛ̃dikatœr] *nm* (*Police*)
informer; (*Tech*) gauge, indicator ▷ *adj*:
panneau ~ signpost; **indicateur des
chemins de fer** railway timetable;
indicateur de rues street directory

indicatif, ive [ɛ̃dikatif, iv] *adj*: **à titre
~** for (your) information ▷ *nm* (*Ling*)
indicative; (*Radio*) theme *ou* signature
tune; (*Tél*) dialling code (BRIT), area
code (US); **quel est l'~ de ...** what's the
code for ...?

indication [ɛ̃dikasjɔ̃] *nf* indication;
(*renseignement*) information *no
pl*; **indications** *nfpl* (*directives*)
instructions

indice [ɛ̃dis] *nm* (*marque, signe*)
indication, sign; (*Police: lors d'une
enquête*) clue; (*Jur: présomption*) piece
of evidence; (*Science, Écon, Tech*) index;

~ de protection (sun protection) factor

indicible [ɛ̃disibl] *adj* inexpressible

indien, ne [ɛ̃djɛ̃, jɛn] *adj* Indian
▷ *nm/f:* **I~, ne** Indian

indifféremment [ɛ̃diferamɑ̃] *adv*
(*sans distinction*) equally (well)

indifférence [ɛ̃diferɑ̃s] *nf* indifference

indifférent, e [ɛ̃diferɑ̃, ɑ̃t] *adj* (*peu
intéressé*) indifferent; **ça m'est ~** it
doesn't matter to me; **elle m'est ~e**
I am indifferent to her

indigène [ɛ̃diʒɛn] *adj* native,
indigenous; (*des gens du pays*) local
▷ *nm/f* native

indigeste [ɛ̃diʒɛst] *adj* indigestible

indigestion [ɛ̃diʒɛstjɔ̃] *nf* indigestion
no pl; **avoir une ~** to have indigestion

indigne [ɛ̃diɲ] *adj* unworthy

indigner [ɛ̃diɲe] *vt:* **s'~ de qch** to get
annoyed about sth; **s'~ contre qn** to
get annoyed with sb

indiqué, e [ɛ̃dike] *adj* (*date, lieu*)
agreed; (*traitement*) appropriate;
(*conseillé*) advisable

indiquer [ɛ̃dike] *vt* (*suj: pendule, aiguille*)
to show; (: *étiquette, panneau*) to show,
indicate; (*renseigner sur*) to point out,
tell; (*déterminer: date, lieu*) to give, state;
(*signaler, dénoter*) to indicate, point
to: **~ qch/qn à qn** (*montrer du doigt*) to
point sth/sb out to sb; (*faire connaître:
médecin, restaurant*) to tell sb of sth/sb;
**pourriez-vous m'~ les toilettes/
l'heure?** could you direct me to the
toilets/tell me the time?

indiscipliné, e [ɛ̃disipline] *adj*
undisciplined

indiscret, -ète [ɛ̃diskrɛ, ɛt] *adj*
indiscreet

indiscutable [ɛ̃diskytabl] *adj*
indisputable

indispensable [ɛ̃dispɑ̃sabl] *adj*
indispensable, essential

indisposé, e [ɛ̃dispoze] *adj* indisposed

indistinct, e [ɛ̃distɛ̃(kt), ɛ̃kt] *adj*
indistinct; **indistinctement** *adv* (*voir,
prononcer*) indistinctly; (*sans distinction*)
indiscriminately

individu [ɛ̃dividy] *nm* individual

individuel, le *adj* (*gén*) individual;
(*responsabilité, propriété, liberté*)
personal; **chambre individuelle** single
room; **maison individuelle** detached
house

indolore [ɛ̃dɔlɔr] *adj* painless

Indonésie [ɛ̃dɔnezi] *nf* Indonesia

indu, e [ɛ̃dy] *adj:* **à une heure ~e** at
some ungodly hour

indulgent, e [ɛ̃dylʒɑ̃, ɑ̃t] *adj* (*parent,
regard*) indulgent; (*juge, examinateur*)
lenient

industrialisé, e [ɛ̃dystrijalize] *adj*
industrialized

industrie [ɛ̃dystri] *nf* industry;
industriel, le *adj* industrial ▷ *nm*
industrialist

inébranlable [inebrɑ̃labl] *adj* (*masse,
colonne*) solid; (*personne, certitude, foi*)
unshakeable

inédit, e [inedi, it] *adj* (*correspondance,
livre*) hitherto unpublished; (*spectacle,
moyen*) novel, original; (*film*) unreleased

inefficace [inefikas] *adj* (*remède,
moyen*) ineffective; (*machine, employé*)
inefficient

inégal, e, -aux [inegal, o] *adj*
unequal; (*irrégulier*) uneven; **inégalable**
adj matchless; **inégalé, e** *adj* (*record*)
unequalled; (*beauté*) unrivalled;
inégalité *nf* inequality

inépuisable [inepɥizabl] *adj*
inexhaustible

inerte [inɛrt] *adj* (*immobile*) lifeless;
(*sans réaction*) passive

inespéré, e [inɛspere] *adj*
unexpected, unhoped-for

inestimable [inɛstimabl] *adj*
priceless; (*fig: bienfait*) invaluable

inévitable [inevitabl] *adj*
unavoidable; (*fatal, habituel*) inevitable

inexact, e [inɛgza(kt), akt] *adj*
inaccurate

inexcusable [inɛkskyzabl] *adj*
unforgivable

inexplicable [inɛksplikabl] *adj*
inexplicable

in extremis [inɛkstremis] *adv* at the last minute *ou* moment

infaillible [ɛ̃fajibl] *adj* infallible

infarctus [ɛ̃farktys] *nm*: **~ (du myocarde)** coronary (thrombosis)

infatigable [ɛ̃fatigabl] *adj* tireless

infect, e [ɛ̃fɛkt] *adj* revolting; *(personne)* obnoxious; *(temps)* foul

infecter [ɛ̃fɛkte] *vt (atmosphère, eau)* to contaminate; *(Méd)* to infect; **s'infecter** to become infected *ou* septic; **infection** *nf* infection; *(puanteur)* stench

inférieur, e [ɛ̃ferjœr] *adj* lower; *(en qualité, intelligence)* inferior; **~ à** *(somme, quantité)* less *ou* smaller than; *(moins bon que)* inferior to

infernal, e, -aux [ɛ̃fɛrnal, o] *adj* *(insupportable: chaleur, rythme)* infernal; *(: enfant)* horrid; *(satanique, effrayant)* diabolical

infidèle [ɛ̃fidɛl] *adj* unfaithful

infiltrer [ɛ̃filtre]: **s'infiltrer** *vr*: **s'~ dans** to get into; *(liquide)* to seep through; *(fig: groupe, ennemi)* to infiltrate

infime [ɛ̃fim] *adj* minute, tiny

infini, e [ɛ̃fini] *adj* infinite ▷ *nm* infinity; **à l'~** endlessly; *(Photo)* infinitely; **infiniment** *adv* infinitely; **infinité** *nf*: **une infinité de** an infinite number of

infinitif [ɛ̃finitif] *nm* infinitive

infirme [ɛ̃firm] *adj* disabled ▷ *nm/f* disabled person

infirmerie [ɛ̃firməri] *nf* medical room

infirmier, -ière [ɛ̃firmje] *nm/f* nurse; **infirmière chef** sister

infirmité [ɛ̃firmite] *nf* disability

inflammable [ɛ̃flamabl] *adj* (in)flammable

inflation [ɛ̃flasjɔ̃] *nf* inflation

influençable [ɛ̃flyɑ̃sabl] *adj* easily influenced

influencer [ɛ̃flyɑ̃se] *nf* influence; **influencer** *vt* to influence; **influent, e** *adj* influential

informaticien, ne [ɛ̃fɔrmatisjɛ̃, jɛn] *nm/f* computer scientist

information [ɛ̃fɔrmasjɔ̃] *nf* *(renseignement)* piece of information; *(Presse, TV: nouvelle)* item of news; *(diffusion de renseignements, Inform)* information; *(Jur)* inquiry, investigation; **informations** *nfpl* (TV) news *sg*

informatique [ɛ̃fɔrmatik] *nf* *(technique)* data processing; *(science)* computer science ▷ *adj* computer *cpd*; **informatiser** *vt* to computerize

informer [ɛ̃fɔrme] *vt*: **~ qn (de)** to inform sb (of); **s'informer** *vr*: **s'~ (de/si)** to inquire ou find out (about/whether); **s'~ sur** to inform o.s. about

infos [ɛ̃fo] *nfpl*: **les ~** the news *sg*

infraction [ɛ̃fraksjɔ̃] *nf* offence; **~ à** violation *ou* breach of; **être en ~** to be in breach of the law

infranchissable [ɛ̃frɑ̃ʃisabl] *adj* impassable; *(fig)* insuperable

infrarouge [ɛ̃fraruʒ] *adj* infrared

infrastructure [ɛ̃frastryktyr] *nf* *(Aviat, Mil)* ground installations *pl*; *(Écon: touristique etc)* infrastructure

infuser [ɛ̃fyze] *vt, vi (thé)* to brew; *(tisane)* to infuse; **infusion** *nf (tisane)* herb tea

ingénier [ɛ̃ʒenje]: **s'ingénier** *vi*: **s'~ à faire** to strive to do

ingénierie [ɛ̃ʒeniri] *nf* engineering

ingénieur [ɛ̃ʒenjœr] *nm* engineer; **ingénieur du son** sound engineer

ingénieux, -euse [ɛ̃ʒenjø, jøz] *adj* ingenious, clever

ingrat, e [ɛ̃gra, at] *adj* *(personne)* ungrateful; *(travail, sujet)* thankless; *(visage)* unprepossessing

ingrédient [ɛ̃gredjɑ̃] *nm* ingredient

inhabité, e [inabite] *adj* uninhabited

inhabituel, le [inabituɛl] *adj* unusual

inhibition [inibisjɔ̃] *nf* inhibition

inhumain, e [inymɛ̃, ɛn] *adj* inhuman

inimaginable [inimaʒinabl] *adj* unimaginable

ininterrompu, e [inɛ̃terɔ̃py] *adj* *(file, série)* unbroken; *(flot, vacarme)* uninterrupted, non-stop; *(effort)* unremitting, continuous; (suite, ligne) unbroken

initial, e, -aux [inisjal, jo] *adj* initial; **initiales** *nfpl* (d'un nom, sigle etc) initials

initiation [inisjasjɔ̃] *nf*: **~ à** introduction to

initiative [inisjativ] *nf* initiative

initier [inisje] *vt*: **~ qn à** to initiate sb into; (faire découvrir: art, jeu) to introduce sb to

injecter [ɛ̃ʒɛkte] *vt* to inject; **injection** *nf* injection; **à injection** (Auto) fuel injection *cpd*

injure [ɛ̃ʒyr] *nf* insult, abuse *no pl*; **injurier** *vt* to insult, abuse; **injurieux, -euse** *adj* abusive, insulting

injuste [ɛ̃ʒyst] *adj* unjust, unfair; **injustice** *nf* injustice

inlassable [ɛ̃lasabl] *adj* tireless

inné, e [i(n)ne] *adj* innate, inborn

innocent, e [inɔsɑ̃, ɑ̃t] *adj* innocent; **innocenter** *vt* to clear, prove innocent

innombrable [i(n)nɔ̃brabl] *adj* innumerable

innover [inɔve] *vi* to break new ground

inoccupé, e [inɔkype] *adj* unoccupied

inodore [inɔdɔr] *adj* (gaz) odourless; (fleur) scentless

inoffensif, -ive [inɔfɑ̃sif, iv] *adj* harmless, innocuous

inondation [inɔ̃dasjɔ̃] *nf* flood

inonder [inɔ̃de] *vt* to flood; **~ de** to flood with

inopportun, e [inɔpɔrtœ̃ yn] *adj* ill-timed, untimely

inoubliable [inublijabl] *adj* unforgettable

inouï, e [inwi] *adj* unheard-of, extraordinary

inox [inɔks] *nm* stainless steel

inquiet, -ète [ɛ̃kjɛ, ɛkjɛt] *adj* anxious; **inquiétant, e** *adj* worrying, disturbing; **s'inquiéter** to worry; **s'inquiéter de** to worry about; (s'enquérir de) to inquire about; **inquiétude** *nf* anxiety

insaisissable [ɛ̃sezisabl] *adj* (fugitif, ennemi) elusive; (différence, nuance)

imperceptible

insalubre [ɛ̃salybr] *adj* insalubrious

insatisfait, e [ɛ̃satisfɛ, ɛt] *adj* (non comblé) unsatisfied; (mécontent) dissatisfied

inscription [ɛ̃skripsjɔ̃] *nf* inscription; (immatriculation) enrolment

inscrire [ɛ̃skrir] *vt* (marquer: sur son calepin etc) to note ou write down; (: sur un mur, une affiche etc) to write; (: dans la pierre, le métal) to inscribe; (mettre: sur une liste, un budget etc) to put down; **s'inscrire** (pour une excursion etc) to put one's name down; **s'~ (à)** (club, parti) to join; (université) to register ou enrol at; (examen, concours) to register (for); **~ qn à** (club, parti) to enrol sb at

insecte [ɛ̃sɛkt] *nm* insect; **insecticide** *nm* insecticide

insensé, e [ɛ̃sɑ̃se] *adj* mad

insensible [ɛ̃sɑ̃sibl] *adj* (nerf, membre) numb; (dur, indifférent) insensitive

inséparable [ɛ̃separabl] *adj* inseparable ▷ *nm*: **~s** (oiseaux) lovebirds

insigne [ɛ̃siɲ] *nm* (d'un parti, club) badge; (d'une fonction) insignia ▷ *adj* distinguished

insignifiant, e [ɛ̃siɲifjɑ̃, jɑ̃t] *adj* insignificant; trivial

insinuer [ɛ̃sinɥe] *vt* to insinuate; **s'insinuer dans** (fig) to worm one's way into

insipide [ɛ̃sipid] *adj* insipid

insister [ɛ̃siste] *vi* to insist; (continuer à sonner) to keep on trying; **~ sur** (détail, sujet) to lay stress on

insolation [ɛ̃sɔlasjɔ̃] *nf* (Méd) sunstroke *no pl*

insolent, e [ɛ̃sɔlɑ̃, ɑ̃t] *adj* insolent

insolite [ɛ̃sɔlit] *adj* strange, unusual

insomnie [ɛ̃sɔmni] *nf* insomnia *no pl*; **avoir des ~s** to sleep badly, not be able to sleep

insouciant, e [ɛ̃susjɑ̃, jɑ̃t] *adj* carefree; **~ du danger** heedless of (the) danger

insoupçonnable [ɛ̃supsɔnabl] *adj* unsuspected; (personne) above suspicion

insoupçonné, e [ɛ̃supsɔne] adj
unsuspected

insoutenable [ɛ̃sut(ə)nabl] adj
(argument) untenable; (chaleur)
unbearable

inspecter [ɛ̃spɛkte] vt to inspect;
inspecteur, -trice nm/f inspector;
inspecteur d'Académie (regional)
director of education; **inspecteur
des finances** ≈ tax inspector (BRIT),
≈ Internal Revenue Service agent
(US); **inspecteur (de police)** (police)
inspector; **inspection** nf inspection

inspirer [ɛ̃spire] vt (gén) to inspire ▷ vi
(aspirer) to breathe in; **s'inspirer vr: s'~
de** to be inspired by

instable [ɛ̃stabl] adj unstable; (meuble,
équilibre) unsteady; (temps) unsettled

installation [ɛ̃stalasjɔ̃] nf (mise en
place) installation; **installations** nfpl
(de sport, dans un camping) facilities;
l'installation électrique wiring

installer [ɛ̃stale] vt (loger, placer) to put;
(meuble, gaz, électricité) to put in; (rideau,
étagère, tente) to put up; (appartement)
to fit out; **s'installer** (s'établir: artisan,
dentiste etc) to set o.s. up; (se loger) to
settle; (emménager) to settle in; (sur
un siège, à un emplacement) to settle
(down); (fig: maladie, grève) to take a
firm hold

instance [ɛ̃stɑ̃s] nf (Admin: autorité)
authority; **affaire en** ~ matter pending;
être en ~ **de divorce** to be awaiting
a divorce

instant [ɛ̃stɑ̃] nm moment, instant;
dans un ~ in a moment; **à l'** ~ this
instant; **je l'ai vu à l'** ~ I've just this
minute seen him, I saw him a moment
ago; **pour l'** ~ for the moment, for the
time being

instantané, e [ɛ̃stɑ̃tane] adj (lait, café)
instant; (explosion, mort) instantaneous
▷ nm snapshot

instar [ɛ̃star]: **à l'** ~ **de** prép following
the example of, like

instaurer [ɛ̃stɔre] vt to institute;

(couvre-feu) to impose; **s'instaurer** vr
(paix) to be established; (doute) to set in

instinct [ɛ̃stɛ̃] nm instinct;
instinctivement adv instinctively

instituer [ɛ̃stitɥe] vt to establish

institut [ɛ̃stity] nm institute; **institut
de beauté** beauty salon; **Institut
universitaire de technologie**
≈ polytechnic

instituteur, -trice [ɛ̃stitytœr, tris]
nm/f (primary school) teacher

institution [ɛ̃stitysjɔ̃] nf institution;
(collège) private school; **institutions**
nfpl (structures politiques et sociales)
institutions

instructif, -ive [ɛ̃stryktif, iv] adj
instructive

instruction [ɛ̃stryksjɔ̃] nf
(enseignement, savoir) education;
(Jur) (preliminary) investigation and
hearing; **instructions** nfpl (ordres, mode
d'emploi) instructions; **instruction
civique** civics sg

instruire [ɛ̃strɥir] vt (élèves) to teach;
(recrues) to train; (Jur: affaire) to conduct
the investigation for; **s'instruire** vr to
educate o.s.; **instruit, e** adj educated

instrument [ɛ̃strymɑ̃] nm
instrument; **instrument à cordes/à
vent** stringed/wind instrument;
instrument de mesure measuring
instrument; **instrument de musique**
musical instrument; **instrument de
travail** (working) tool

insu [ɛ̃sy] nm: **à l'** ~ **de qn** without sb
knowing (it)

insuffisant, e [ɛ̃syfizɑ̃, ɑ̃t] adj (en
quantité) insufficient; (en qualité)
inadequate; (sur une copie) poor

insulaire [ɛ̃syler] adj island cpd;
(attitude) insular

insuline [ɛ̃sylin] nf insulin

insulte [ɛ̃sylt] nf insult; **insulter** vt
to insult

insupportable [ɛ̃sypɔrtabl] adj
unbearable

insurmontable [ɛ̃syrmɔ̃tabl] adj
(difficulté) insuperable; (aversion)

unconquerable

intact, e [ɛ̃takt] *adj* intact

intarissable [ɛ̃tarisabl] *adj* inexhaustible

intégral, e, -aux [ɛ̃tegral, o] *adj* complete; **texte ~** unabridged version; **bronzage ~** all-over suntan; **intégralement** *adv* in full; **intégralité** *nf* whole; **dans son intégralité** in full; **intégrant, e** *adj*: **faire partie intégrante de** to be an integral part of

intègre [ɛ̃tegr] *adj* upright

intégrer [ɛ̃tegre]: **s'intégrer** *vr*: **s'~ à** *ou* **dans qch** to become integrated into sth; **bien s'~** to fit in

intégrisme [ɛ̃tegrism] *nm* fundamentalism

intellectuel, le [ɛ̃telɛktɥɛl] *adj* intellectual ▷ *nm/f* intellectual; (*péj*) highbrow

intelligence [ɛ̃teliʒɑ̃s] *nf* intelligence; (*compréhension*): **l'~ de** the understanding of; (*complicité*): **regard d'~** glance of complicity; (*accord*): **vivre en bonne ~ avec qn** to be on good terms with sb

intelligent, e [ɛ̃teliʒɑ̃, ɑ̃t] *adj* intelligent

intelligible [ɛ̃teliʒibl] *adj* intelligible

intempéries [ɛ̃tɑ̃peri] *nfpl* bad weather *sg*

intenable [ɛ̃t(ə)nabl] *adj* (*chaleur*) unbearable

intendant, e [ɛ̃tɑ̃dɑ̃] *nm/f* (*Mil*) quartermaster; (*Scol*) bursar

intense [ɛ̃tɑ̃s] *adj* intense; **intensif, -ive** *adj* intensive; **un cours intensif** a crash course

intenter [ɛ̃tɑ̃te] *vt*: **~ un procès contre** *ou* **à** to start proceedings against

intention [ɛ̃tɑ̃sjɔ̃] *nf* intention; (*Jur*) intent; **avoir l'~ de faire** to intend to do; **à l'~ de** for; (*renseignement*) for the benefit of; (*film, ouvrage*) aimed at; **à cette ~** with this aim in view; **intentionné, e** *adj*: **bien intentionné** well-meaning *ou* -intentioned; **mal intentionné** ill-intentioned

interactif, -ive [ɛ̃teraktif, iv] *adj* (*Comput*) interactive

intercepter [ɛ̃tersɛpte] *vt* to intercept; (*lumière, chaleur*) to cut off

interchangeable [ɛ̃terʃɑ̃ʒabl] *adj* interchangeable

interdiction [ɛ̃terdiksjɔ̃] *nf* ban; **interdiction de fumer** no smoking

interdire [ɛ̃terdir] *vt* to forbid; (*Admin*) to ban, prohibit; (: *journal, livre*) to ban; **~ à qn de faire** to forbid sb to do; (*suj: empêchement*) to prevent sb from doing

interdit, e [ɛ̃terdi, it] *pp de* **interdire** ▷ *adj* (*stupéfait*) taken aback; **film – aux moins de 18/12 ans =** 18-/12A-rated film; **"stationnement –"** "no parking"

intéressant, e [ɛ̃teresɑ̃, ɑ̃t] *adj* interesting; (*avantageux*) attractive

intéressé, e [ɛ̃terese] *adj* (*parties*) involved, concerned; (*amitié, motifs*) self-interested

intéresser [ɛ̃terese] *vt* (*captiver*) to interest; (*toucher*) to be of interest to; (*Admin: concerner*) to affect, concern; **s'intéresser** *vr*: **s'~ à** to be interested in

intérêt [ɛ̃tere] *nm* interest; (*égoïsme*) self-interest; **tu as ~ à accepter** it's in your interest to accept; **tu as ~ à te dépêcher** you'd better hurry

intérieur, e [ɛ̃terjœr] *adj* (*mur, escalier, poche*) inside; (*commerce, politique*) domestic; (*cour, calme, vie*) inner; (*navigation*) inland ▷ *nm*: **l'~** (*d'une maison, d'un récipient etc*) the inside; (*d'un pays, aussi: décor, mobilier*) the interior; **à l'~ (de)** inside; **ministère de l'I~e =** Home Office (*BRIT*), ≈ Department of the Interior (*US*); **intérieurement** *adv* inwardly

intérim [ɛ̃terim] *nm* interim period; **faire de l'~** to temp; **assurer l'~ (de)** to deputize (for); **par ~** interim

intérimaire [ɛ̃terimer] *adj* (*directeur, ministre*) acting; (*secrétaire, personnel*) temporary ▷ *nm/f* (*secrétaire*) temporary secretary, temp (*BRIT*)

interlocuteur, -trice [ɛ̃terlɔkytœr, tris] *nm/f* speaker; **son ~** the person he

was speaking to
intermédiaire [ɛ̃tɛʁmedjɛʁ] adj
intermediate; (solution) temporary
▷ nm/f intermediary; (Comm)
middleman; **sans ~** directly; **par l'~
de** through
interminable [ɛ̃tɛʁminabl] adj
endless
intermittence [ɛ̃tɛʁmitɑ̃s] nf: **par ~**
sporadically, intermittently
internat [ɛ̃tɛʁna] nm boarding school
international, e, -aux
[ɛ̃tɛʁnasjɔnal, o] adj, nm/f
international
internaute [ɛ̃tɛʁnot] nm/f Internet
user
interne [ɛ̃tɛʁn] adj internal ▷ nm/f
(Scol) boarder; (Méd) houseman
Internet [ɛ̃tɛʁnɛt] nm: **l'~** the Internet
interpeller [ɛ̃tɛʁpəle] vt (appeler) to
call out to; (apostropher) to shout at;
(Police, Pol) to (concerner) to
concern
interphone [ɛ̃tɛʁfɔn] nm intercom;
(d'immeuble) entry phone
interposer [ɛ̃tɛʁpoze] vt: **s'interposer**
to intervene; **par personnes
interposées** through a third party
interprète [ɛ̃tɛʁpʁɛt] nm/f
interpreter; (porte-parole)
spokesperson; **pourriez-vous nous
servir d'~?** could you act as our
interpreter?
interpréter [ɛ̃tɛʁpʁete] vt to
interpret; (jouer) to play; (chanter)
to sing
interrogatif, -ive [ɛ̃teʁɔgatif, iv] adj
(Ling) interrogative
interrogation [ɛ̃teʁɔgasjɔ̃] nf
question; (action) questioning; **~
écrite/orale** (Scol) written/oral test
interrogatoire [ɛ̃teʁɔgatwaʁ] nm
(Police) questioning no pl; (Jur, aussi fig)
cross-examination
interroger [ɛ̃teʁɔʒe] vt to question;
(Inform) to consult; (Scol) to test
interrompre [ɛ̃teʁɔ̃pʁ] vt (gén) to
interrupt; (négociations) to break off;

(match) to stop; **s'interrompre** to
break off; **interrupteur** nm switch;
interruption nf interruption; (pause)
break; **sans interruption** without
stopping; **interruption (volontaire)
de grossesse** termination of
pregnancy)
intersection [ɛ̃tɛʁsɛksjɔ̃] nf
intersection
intervalle [ɛ̃tɛʁval] nm (espace)
space; (de temps) interval; **dans l'~** in
the meantime; **à deux jours d'~** two
days apart
intervenir [ɛ̃tɛʁvəniʁ] vi (gén) to
intervene; **~ auprès de qn** to intervene
with sb; **intervention** nf intervention;
(discours) speech; **intervention
chirurgicale** (Méd) (surgical) operation
interview [ɛ̃tɛʁvju] nf interview
intestin [ɛ̃tɛstɛ̃] nm intestine
intime [ɛ̃tim] adj intimate; (vie)
private; (conviction) inmost; (dîner,
cérémonie) quiet ▷ nm/f close friend; **un
journal ~** a diary
intimider [ɛ̃timide] vt to intimidate
intimité [ɛ̃timite] nf: **dans l'~** in
private; (sans formalités) with only a few
friends, quietly
intolérable [ɛ̃tɔleʁabl] adj intolerable
intox [ɛ̃tɔks] (fam) nf brainwashing
intoxication [ɛ̃tɔksikasjɔ̃] nf:
intoxication alimentaire food
poisoning
intoxiquer [ɛ̃tɔksike] vt to poison;
(fig) to brainwash
intraitable [ɛ̃tʁɛtabl] adj inflexible,
uncompromising
intransigeant, e [ɛ̃tʁɑ̃ziʒɑ̃, ɑ̃t] adj
intransigent
intrépide [ɛ̃tʁepid] adj dauntless
intrigue [ɛ̃tʁig] nf (scénario) plot;
intriguer vt to puzzle, intrigue
introduction [ɛ̃tʁɔdyksjɔ̃] nf
introduction
introduire [ɛ̃tʁɔdɥiʁ] vt to introduce;
(visiteur) to show in; (aiguille, clef): **~ qch
dans** to insert ou introduce sth into;
s'introduire vr (techniques, usages) to

be introduced; **s'~ (dans)** to get in(to); (dans un groupe) to get o.s. accepted (into)

introuvable [ɛ̃truvabl] adj which cannot be found; (Comm) unobtainable

intrus, e [ɛ̃try, yz] nm/f intruder

intuition [ɛ̃tɥisjɔ̃] nf intuition

inusable [inyzabl] adj hard-wearing

inutile [inytil] adj useless; (superflu) unnecessary; **inutilement** adv unnecessarily; **inutilisable** adj unusable

invalide [ɛ̃valid] adj disabled ▷ nm: **~ de guerre** disabled ex-serviceman

invariable [ɛ̃varjabl] adj invariable

invasion [ɛ̃vazjɔ̃] nf invasion

inventaire [ɛ̃vɑ̃tɛr] nm inventory; (Comm: liste) stocklist; (: opération) stocktaking no pl

inventer [ɛ̃vɑ̃te] vt to invent; (subterfuge) to devise, invent; (histoire, excuse) to make up, invent; **inventeur** nm inventor; **inventif, -ive** adj inventive; **invention** nf invention

inverse [ɛ̃vɛrs] adj opposite ▷ nm: **l'~** the opposite; **dans l'ordre ~** in the reverse order; **en sens ~** in (ou from) the opposite direction; **dans le sens ~ des aiguilles d'une montre** anticlockwise; **tu t'es trompé, c'est l'~** you've got it wrong, it's the other way round; **inversement** adv conversely; **inverser** vt to invert, reverse; (Élec) to reverse

investir [ɛ̃vɛstir] vt to invest; **~ qn de** (d'une fonction, d'un pouvoir) to vest ou invest sb with; **s'investir** vr: **s'~ dans** (Psych) to put a lot into; **investissement** nm investment

invisible [ɛ̃vizibl] adj invisible

invitation [ɛ̃vitasjɔ̃] nf invitation

invité, e [ɛ̃vite] nm/f guest

inviter [ɛ̃vite] vt to invite; **~ qn à faire qch** to invite sb to do sth

invivable [ɛ̃vivabl] adj unbearable

involontaire [ɛ̃vɔlɔ̃tɛr] adj (mouvement) involuntary; (insulte) unintentional; (complice) unwitting

invoquer [ɛ̃vɔke] vt (Dieu, muse) to call

upon, invoke; (prétexte) to put forward (as an excuse); (loi, texte) to refer to

invraisemblable [ɛ̃vrɛsɑ̃blabl] adj (fait, nouvelle) unlikely, improbable; (insolence, habit) incredible

iode [jɔd] nm iodine

irai etc [ire] vb voir **aller**

Irak [irak] nm Iraq; **irakien, ne** adj Iraqi ▷ nm/f: **Irakien, ne** Iraqi

Iran [irɑ̃] nm Iran; **iranien, ne** adj Iranian ▷ nm/f: **Iranien, ne** Iranian

irions etc [irjɔ̃] vb voir **aller**

iris [iris] nm iris

irlandais, e [irlɑ̃dɛ, ɛz] adj Irish ▷ nm/f: **I~, e** Irishman(-woman)

Irlande [irlɑ̃d] nf Ireland; **la République d'~** the Irish Republic; **la mer d'~** the Irish Sea; **Irlande du Nord** Northern Ireland

ironie [irɔni] nf irony; **ironique** adj ironical; **ironiser** vi to be ironical

irons etc [irɔ̃] vb voir **aller**

irradier [iradje] vi to irradiate

irraisonné, e [irɛzɔne] adj irrational

irrationnel, le [irasjɔnɛl] adj irrational

irréalisable [irealizabl] adj unrealizable; (projet) impracticable

irrécupérable [irekyperabl] adj beyond repair; (personne) beyond redemption

irréel, le [ireɛl] adj unreal

irréfléchi, e [irefleʃi] adj thoughtless

irrégularité [iregylarite] nf irregularity; (de travail, d'effort, de qualité) unevenness no pl

irrégulier, -ière [iregylje, jɛr] adj irregular; (travail, effort, qualité) uneven; (élève, athlète) erratic

irrémédiable [iremedjabl] adj irreparable

irremplaçable [irɑ̃plasabl] adj irreplaceable

irréparable [ireparabl] adj (objet) beyond repair; (dommage etc) irreparable

irréprochable [ireprɔʃabl] adj irreproachable, beyond reproach

irrésistible | 136

(tenue) impeccable

irrésistible [iʀezistibl] *adj* irresistible; (besoin, désir, preuve, logique) compelling; (amusant) hilarious

irrésolu, e [iʀezɔly] *adj* (personne) irresolute; (problème) unresolved

irrespectueux, -euse [iʀespɛktɥø, øz] *adj* disrespectful

irresponsable [iʀɛspɔ̃sabl] *adj* irresponsible

irriguer [iʀige] *vt* to irrigate

irritable [iʀitabl] *adj* irritable

irriter [iʀite] *vt* to irritate

irruption [iʀypsjɔ̃] *nf*: **faire ~ (chez qn)** to burst in (on sb)

Islam [islam] *nm*: **l'~** Islam; **islamique** *adj* Islamic; **islamophobie** *nf* Islamophobia

Islande [islɑ̃d] *nf* Iceland

isolant, e [izɔlɑ̃, ɑ̃t] *adj* insulating; (insonorisant) soundproofing

isolation [izɔlasjɔ̃] *nf* insulation: **~ acoustique** soundproofing

isolé, e [izɔle] *adj* isolated; (contre le froid) insulated

isoler [izɔle] *vt* to isolate; (prisonnier) to put in solitary confinement; (ville) to cut off, isolate; (contre le froid) to insulate; **s'isoler** *vi* to isolate o.s.

Israël [israɛl] *nm* Israel; **israélien, ne** *adj* Israeli ▷ *nm/f*: **Israélien, ne** Israeli; **israélite** *adj* Jewish ▷ *nm/f*: **Israélite** Jew (Jewess)

issu, e [isy] *adj*: **~ de** (né de) descended from; (résultant de) stemming from; **issue** *nf* (ouverture, sortie) exit; (solution) way out, solution; (dénouement) outcome; **à l'issue de** at the conclusion ou close of; **voie sans issue** dead end; **issue de secours** emergency exit

Italie [itali] *nf* Italy; **italien, ne** *adj* Italian ▷ *nm/f*: **Italien, ne** Italian ▷ *nm* (Ling) Italian

italique [italik] *nm*: **en ~** in italics

itinéraire [itineʀɛʀ] *nm* itinerary, route; **itinéraire bis** alternative route

IUT *sigle m* = **Institut universitaire de technologie**

IVG *sigle f* (= interruption volontaire de grossesse) abortion

ivoire [ivwaʀ] *nm* ivory

ivre [ivʀ] *adj* drunk; **~ de** (colère, bonheur) wild with; **ivrogne** *nm/f* drunkard

J

j' [ʒ] *pron voir* **je**

jacinthe [ʒasɛ̃t] *nf* hyacinth

jadis [ʒadis] *adv* long ago

jaillir [ʒajir] *vi* (liquide) to spurt out; (cris, réponses) to burst forth

jais [ʒɛ] *nm* jet; **(d'un noir) de ~** jet-black

jalousie [ʒaluzi] *nf* jealousy; (store) slatted blind

jaloux, -ouse [ʒalu, uz] *adj* jealous; **être ~ de** to be jealous of

jamaïquain, e [ʒamaikɛ̃, -ɛn] *adj* Jamaican ▷ *nm/f*: **J~, e** Jamaican

Jamaïque [ʒamaik] *nf*: **la ~** Jamaica

jamais [ʒamɛ] *adv* never; (sans négation) ever; **ne ... ~** never; **je ne suis ~ allé en Espagne** I've never been to Spain; **si vous passez dans la région, venez nous voir** if you happen to be/if you're ever in this area, come and see us; **à ~ for ever**

jambe [ʒɑ̃b] *nf* leg

jambon [ʒɑ̃bɔ̃] *nm* ham

jante [ʒɑ̃t] *nf* (wheel) rim

janvier [ʒɑ̃vje] *nm* January

Japon [ʒapɔ̃] *nm* Japan; **japonais, e** *adj* Japanese ▷ *nm/f*: **Japonais, e** Japanese ▷ *nm* (Ling) Japanese

jardin [ʒardɛ̃] *nm* garden; **jardin d'enfants** nursery school; **jardinage** *nm* gardening; **jardiner** *vi* to do some gardening; **jardinier, -ière** *nm/f* gardener; **jardinière** *nf* planter; (de fenêtre) window box; **jardinière de légumes** (Culin) mixed vegetables

jargon [ʒargɔ̃] *nm* (baragouin) gibberish; (langue professionnelle) jargon

jarret [ʒarɛ] *nm* back of knee; (Culin) knuckle, shin

jauge [ʒoʒ] *nf* (instrument) gauge; **jauge (de niveau) d'huile** (Auto) dipstick

jaune [ʒon] *adj, nm* yellow ▷ *adv* (fam): **rire ~** to laugh on the other side of one's face; **jaune d'œuf** (egg) yolk; **jaunir** *vi, vt* to turn yellow; **jaunisse** *nf* jaundice

Javel [ʒavɛl] *nf voir* **eau**

javelot [ʒavlo] *nm* javelin

je, j' [ʒə] *pron* I

jean [dʒin] *nm* jeans *pl*

Jésus-Christ [ʒezykri(st)] *n* Jesus Christ; **600 avant/après** *ou* **J.-C.** 600 B.C./A.D.

jet [ʒɛ] *nm* (lancer: action) throwing *no pl*; (: résultat) throw; (jaillissement: d'eaux) jet; (: de sang) spurt; **jet d'eau** spray

jetable [ʒ(ə)tabl] *adj* disposable

jetée [ʒəte] *nf* jetty; (grande) pier

jeter [ʒ(ə)te] *vt* (gén) to throw; (se défaire de) to throw away *ou* out; **~ qch à qn** to throw sth to sb; (de façon agressive) to throw sth at sb; **~ un coup d'œil (à)** to take a look (at); **~ un sort à qn** to cast a spell on sb; **se ~ sur qn** to rush at sb; **se ~ dans** (suj: fleuve) to flow into

jeton [ʒ(ə)tɔ̃] *nm* (au jeu) counter

jette *etc* [ʒɛt] *vb voir* **jeter**

jeu, x [ʒø] *nm* (divertissement, Tech: d'une pièce) play; (Tennis: partie, Football etc: façon de jouer) game; (Théâtre etc) acting; (série d'objets, jouet) set; (Cartes) hand; (au casino): **le ~** gambling; **remettre en ~** (Football) to throw in; **être en ~** (fig) to be at stake; **entrer/mettre en ~** (fig) to come/bring into play; **jeu de cartes** pack of cards; **jeu d'échecs** chess set; **jeu de hasard** game of chance; **jeu de mots** pun; **jeu de société** board game; **jeu télévisé** television quiz; **jeu vidéo** video game

jeudi [ʒødi] nm Thursday

jeun [ʒœ̃]: **à ~** adv on an empty stomach; **être à ~** to have eaten nothing; **rester à ~** not to eat anything

jeune [ʒœn] adj young; **jeunes** nmpl: **les ~s** young people; **jeune fille** girl; **jeune homme** young man; **jeunes gens** young people

jeûne [ʒøn] nm fast

jeunesse [ʒœnɛs] nf youth; (aspect) youthfulness

joaillier, -ière [ʒɔaje, -jɛʀ] nm/f jeweller

jogging [dʒɔgiŋ] nm jogging; (survêtement) tracksuit; **faire du ~** to go jogging

joie [ʒwa] nf joy

joindre [ʒwɛ̃dʀ] vt to join; (à une lettre): **~ qch à** to enclose sth with; (contacter) to contact, get in touch with; **se ~ à qn** to join sb; **se ~ à qch** to join in sth

joint, e [ʒwɛ̃, ɛ̃t] adj: **pièce ~e** (de lettre) enclosure; (de mail) attachment ▷ nm joint; (ligne) join; **joint de culasse** cylinder head gasket

joli, e [ʒɔli] adj pretty, attractive; **une ~e somme/situation** a tidy sum/a nice little job; **c'est du ~!** (ironique) that's very nice!; **c'est bien ~, mais ...** that's all very well but ...

jonc [ʒɔ̃] nm (bul)rush

jonction [ʒɔ̃ksjɔ̃] nf junction

jongleur, -euse [ʒɔ̃glœʀ, øz] nm/f juggler

jonquille [ʒɔ̃kij] nf daffodil

Jordanie [ʒɔʀdani] nf: **la ~** Jordan

joue [ʒu] nf cheek

jouer [ʒwe] vt to play; (somme d'argent, réputation) to stake, wager; (simuler: sentiment) to affect, feign ▷ vi to play; (Théâtre, Cinéma) to act; (au casino) to

gamble; (bois, porte: se voiler) to warp; (clef, pièce: avoir du jeu) to be loose; **~ sur** (miser) to gamble on; **~ de** (Mus) to play; **~ à** (jeu, sport, roulette) to play; **~ un tour à qn** to play a trick on sb; **~ serré** to play a close game; **~ la comédie** (fig) to put on an act; **à toi/nous de ~** it's your/our go ou turn; **bien joué!** well done!; **on joue Hamlet au théâtre X** Hamlet is on at the X theatre

jouet [ʒwe] nm toy; **être le ~ de** (illusion etc) to be the victim of

joueur, -euse [ʒwœʀ, øz] nm/f player; **être beau/mauvais ~** to be a good/bad loser

jouir [ʒwiʀ] vi (sexe: fam) to come ▷ vt: **~ de** to enjoy

jour [ʒuʀ] nm day; (opposé à la nuit) day, daytime; (clarté) daylight; (fig: aspect) light; (ouverture) gap; **de ~** (crème, service) day cpd; **travailler de ~** to work during the day; **voyager de ~** to travel by day; **au ~ le ~** from day to day; **de nos ~s** these days; **du ~ au lendemain** overnight; **il fait ~** it's daylight; **au grand ~** (fig) in the open; **mettre au ~** to disclose; **mettre à ~** to update; **donner le ~ à** to give birth to; **voir le ~** to be born; **le J** D-Day; **jour férié** public holiday; **jour ouvrable** working day

journal, -aux [ʒuʀnal, o] nm (news)paper; (spécialisé) journal; (intime) diary; **journal de bord** log; **journal parlé/télévisé** radio/ television news sg

journalier, -ière [ʒuʀnalje, jɛʀ] adj daily; (banal) everyday

journalisme [ʒuʀnalism] nm journalism; **journaliste** nm/f journalist

journée [ʒuʀne] nf day; **faire la ~ continue** to work over lunch

joyau, x [ʒwajo] nm gem, jewel

joyeux, -euse [ʒwajø, øz] adj joyful, merry; **~ Noël!** merry Christmas!; **~ anniversaire!** happy birthday!

jubiler [ʒybile] vi to be jubilant, exult

judas [ʒyda] nm (trou) spy-hole

judiciaire [ʒydisjɛʀ] adj judicial
judicieux, -euse [ʒydisjø, jøz] adj judicious
judo [ʒydo] nm judo
juge [ʒyʒ] nm judge: **juge d'instruction** examining (BRIT) ou committing (US) magistrate: **juge de paix** justice of the peace
jugé [ʒyʒe]: **au** ~ adv by guesswork
jugement [ʒyʒmɑ̃] nm judgment; (Jur: au pénal) sentence; (: au civil) decision
juger [ʒyʒe] vt to judge; (estimer) to consider; ~ **qn/qch satisfaisant** to consider sb/sth (to be) satisfactory; ~ **bon de faire** to see fit to do
juif, -ive [ʒɥif, ʒɥiv] adj Jewish ▷ nm/f: **J~, ive** Jew (Jewess)
juillet [ʒɥijɛ] nm July

14 JUILLET

  Le 14 juillet is a national holiday in France and commemorates the storming of the Bastille during the French Revolution. Throughout the country there are celebrations, which feature parades, music, dancing and firework displays. In Paris a military parade along the Champs-Élysées is attended by the President.

juin [ʒɥɛ̃] nm June
jumeau, -elle, x [ʒymo, ɛl] adj, nm/f twin
jumeler [ʒymle] vt to twin
jumelle [ʒymɛl] adj, vt voir **jumeau**; **jumelles** nfpl (appareil) binoculars
jument [ʒymɑ̃] nf mare
jungle [ʒɔ̃ɡl] nf jungle
jupe [ʒyp] nf skirt
jupon [ʒypɔ̃] nm waist slip
juré, e [ʒyʀe] nm/f juror ▷ adj: **ennemi ~** sworn enemy
jurer [ʒyʀe] vt (obéissance etc) to swear, vow ▷ vi (dire des jurons) to swear, curse; (dissoner) ~ **(avec)** to clash (with); ~ **de qch** (s'en porter garant) to swear to sth

juridique [ʒyʀidik] adj legal
juron [ʒyʀɔ̃] nm curse, swearword
jury [ʒyʀi] nm jury; (Art, Sport) panel of judges; (Scol) board of examiners
jus [ʒy] nm juice; (de viande) gravy. (meat) juice; **jus de fruit** fruit juice
jusque [ʒysk]: **jusqu'à** prép (endroit) as far as, (up) to; (moment) until, till; (limite) up to; ~ **sur/dans** up to; (y compris) even on/in; **jusqu'à ce que** until; **jusqu'à présent** ou **maintenant** so far; **jusqu'où?** how far?

justaucorps [ʒystokɔʀ] nm leotard
juste [ʒyst] adj (équitable) just, fair; (légitime) just; (exact) right; (pertinent) apt; (étroit) tight; (insuffisant) on the short side ▷ adv rightly, correctly; (chanter) in tune; (exactement, seulement) just; ~ **assez/au-dessus** just enough/ above; **au** ~ exactly; **le** ~ **milieu** the happy medium; **c'était** ~ it was a close thing; **pouvoir tout** ~ **faire** to be only just able to do; (précisément) just; **justement** adv justly; (précisément) just, precisely; **justesse** nf (précision) accuracy; (d'une remarque) aptness; (d'une opinion) soundness; **de justesse** only just
justice [ʒystis] nf (équité) fairness, justice; (Admin) justice; **rendre** – **à qn** to do sb justice
justificatif, -ive [ʒystifikatif, iv] adj (document) supporting; **pièce justificative** written proof
justifier [ʒystifje] vt to justify; ~ **de** to prove

juteux, -euse [ʒytø, øz] adj juicy
juvénile [ʒyvenil] adj youthful

kiwi [kiwi] *nm* kiwi
klaxon [klaksɔn] *nm* horn; **klaxonner**
  vi, vt to hoot (BRIT), honk (US)
km *abr* = **kilomètre**
km/h *abr* (= *kilomètres/heure*) ≈ mph
K.-O. (*fam*) *adj inv* shattered, knackered
Kosovo [kɔsɔvo] *nm* Kosovo
Koweit, Kuweit [kɔwɛt] *nm*: **le ~**
  Kuwait
k-way® [kawɛ] *nm* (lightweight nylon)
  cagoule
kyste [kist] *nm* cyst

K [kɑ] *nm* (*Inform*) K
kaki [kaki] *adj inv* khaki
kangourou [kɑ̃guʀu] *nm* kangaroo
karaté [kaʀate] *nm* karate
kascher [kaʃɛʀ] *adj* kosher
kayak [kajak] *nm* canoe, kayak; **faire**
  du ~ to go canoeing
képi [kepi] *nm* kepi
kermesse [kɛʀmɛs] *nf* fair; (*fête de*
  charité) bazaar, (charity) fête
kidnapper [kidnape] *vt* to kidnap
kilo [kilo] *nm* = **kilogramme**
kilo...: kilogramme *nm* kilogramme;
  kilométrage *nm* number of kilometres
  travelled, ≈ mileage; **kilomètre** *nm*
  kilometre; **kilométrique** *adj* (*distance*)
  in kilometres
kinésithérapeute [kineziteʀapøt]
  nm/f physiotherapist
kiosque [kjɔsk] *nm* kiosk, stall
kir [kiʀ] *nm* kir (*white wine with*
  blackcurrant liqueur)
kit [kit] *nm* kit; **~ piéton** *ou* **mains libres**
  hands-free kit; **en ~** in kit form

l' [l] *art déf voir* **le**

la [la] *art déf voir* **le** ▷ *nm* (Mus) A; (*en chantant la gamme*) la

là [la] *adv* there; (*ici*) here; (*dans le temps*) then; **elle n'est pas là** she isn't here; **c'est là que** this is where; **là où** where; **de là** (*fig*) hence; **par là** (*fig*) by that; *voir aussi* **-ci; ce; celui; là-bas** *adv* there

laboratoire [labɔʀatwaʀ] *nm* laboratory; **laboratoire de langues** language laboratory

laborieux, -euse [labɔʀjø, jøz] *adj* (*tâche*) laborious

labourer *vt* to plough

labyrinthe [labiʀɛ̃t] *nm* labyrinth, maze

lac [lak] *nm* lake

lacet [lase] *nm* (*de chaussure*) lace; (*de route*) sharp bend; (*piège*) snare

lâche [lɑʃ] *adj* (*poltron*) cowardly; (*desserré*) loose, slack ▷ *nm/f* coward

lâcher [lɑʃe] *vt* to let go of; (*ce qui tombe, abandonner*) to drop; (*oiseau, animal: libérer*) to release, set free; (*fig: mot, remarque*) to let slip, come out with ▷ *vi* (*freins*) to fail; **~ les amarres** (Navig) to cast off (the moorings); **~ prise** to let go

lacrymogène [lakʀimɔʒɛn] *adj*: **gaz ~** teargas

lacune [lakyn] *nf* gap

là-dedans [ladədɑ̃] *adv* inside (there), in it; (*fig*) in that

là-dessous [ladsu] *adv* underneath, under there; (*fig*) behind that

là-dessus [ladsy] *adv* on there; (*fig: sur ces mots*) at that point; (: *à ce sujet*) about this

lagune [lagyn] *nf* lagoon

là-haut [lao] *adv* up there

laid, e [lɛ, lɛd] *adj* ugly; **laideur** *nf* ugliness *no pl*

lainage [lɛnaʒ] *nm* (*vêtement*) woollen garment; (*étoffe*) woollen material

laine [lɛn] *nf* wool

laïque [laik] *adj* lay, civil; (Scol) state *cpd* ▷ *nm/f* layman(-woman)

laisse [lɛs] *nf* (*de chien*) lead, leash; **tenir en ~** to keep on a lead ou leash

laisser [lese] *vt* to leave ▷ *vb aux*: **~ qn faire** to let sb do; **se ~ aller** to let o.s. go; **laisse-toi faire** let me (*ou him etc*) do it; **laisser-aller** *nm* carelessness, slovenliness; **laissez-passer** *nm inv* pass

lait [lɛ] *nm* milk; **frère/sœur de ~** foster brother/sister; **lait concentré/condensé**/evaporated milk; **lait écrémé/entier** skimmed/full-cream (BRIT) *ou* whole milk; **laitage** *nm* dairy product; **laiterie** *nf* dairy; **laitier, -ière** *adj* dairy *cpd* ▷ *nm/f* milkman (dairywoman)

laiton [lɛtɔ̃] *nm* brass

laitue [lety] *nf* lettuce

lambeau, x [lɑ̃bo] *nm* scrap; **en ~x** in tatters, tattered

lame [lam] *nf* blade; (*vague*) wave; (*lamelle*) strip; **lame de fond** ground swell *no pl*; **lame de rasoir** razor blade; **lamelle** *nf* thin strip *ou* blade

lamentable [lamɑ̃tabl] *adj* appalling

lamenter [lamɑ̃te] *vb*: **se ~ (sur)** to

moan (over)

lampadaire [lɑ̃padɛʀ] nm (de salon) standard lamp; (dans la rue) street lamp

lampe [lɑ̃p] nf lamp; (Tech) valve; **lampe à bronzer** sun lamp; **lampe à pétrole** oil lamp; **lampe de poche** torch (BRIT), flashlight (US); **lampe halogène** halogen lamp

lance [lɑ̃s] nf spear; **lance d'incendie** fire hose

lancée [lɑ̃se] nf: **être/continuer sur sa ~** to be under way/keep going

lancement [lɑ̃smɑ̃] nm launching

lance-pierres [lɑ̃spjɛʀ] nm inv catapult

lancer [lɑ̃se] nm (Sport) throwing no pl, throw ▷ vt to throw; (émettre, projeter) to throw out, send out; (produit, fusée, bateau, artiste) to launch; (injure) to hurl, fling; **se lancer** vi (prendre de l'élan) to build up speed; (se précipiter): **se ~ sur ou contre** to rush at; **se ~ dans** (discussion) to launch into; (aventure) to embark on; **~ qch à qn** to throw sth to sb; (de façon agressive) to throw sth at sb; **un cri ou un appel** to shout ou call out; **lancer du poids** putting the shot

landau [lɑ̃do] nm pram (BRIT), baby carriage (US)

lande [lɑ̃d] nf moor

langage [lɑ̃gaʒ] nm language

langouste [lɑ̃gust] nf crayfish inv; **langoustine** nf Dublin Bay prawn

langue [lɑ̃g] nf (Anat, Culin) tongue; (Ling) language; **tirer la ~ (à)** to stick out one's tongue (at); **de ~ française** French-speaking; **quelles ~s parlez-vous?** what languages do you speak?; **langue maternelle** native language, mother tongue; **langues vivantes** modern languages

langueur [lɑ̃gœʀ] nf languidness

languir [lɑ̃giʀ] vi to languish; (conversation) to flag; **faire ~ qn** to keep sb waiting

lanière [lanjɛʀ] nf (de fouet) lash; (de sac, bretelle) strap

lanterne [lɑ̃tɛʀn] nf (portable) lantern;

(électrique) light, lamp; (de voiture) (side)light

laper [lape] vt to lap up

lapidaire [lapidɛʀ] adj (fig) terse

lapin [lapɛ̃] nm rabbit; (peau) rabbitskin; (fourrure) cony; **poser un ~ à qn** (fam) to stand sb up

Laponie [laponi] nf Lapland

laps [laps] nm: **- de temps** space of time, time no pl

laque [lak] nf (vernis) lacquer; (pour cheveux) hair spray

laquelle [lakɛl] pron voir **lequel**

larcin [laʀsɛ̃] nm theft

lard [laʀ] nm (bacon) (streaky) bacon; (graisse) fat

lardon [laʀdɔ̃] nm: **-s** chopped bacon

large [laʀʒ] adj wide, broad; (fig) generous ▷ adv: **calculer/voir ~** to allow extra/think big ▷ nm (largeur): **5 m de ~** 5 m wide ou in width; (mer): **le ~** the open sea; **au ~ de** off; **large d'esprit** broad-minded; **largement** adv widely; (de loin) greatly; (au moins) easily; (généreusement) generously; **c'est largement suffisant** that's ample; **largesse** nf generosity; **largesses** nfpl (dons) liberalities; **largeur** nf (qu'on mesure) width; (impression visuelle) wideness, width; (d'esprit) broadness

larguer [laʀge] vt to drop; **~ les amarres** to cast off (the moorings)

larme [laʀm] nf tear; (fam: goutte) drop; **en ~s** in tears; **larmoyer** vi (yeux) to water; (se plaindre) to whimper

larvé, e [laʀve] adj (fig) latent

laryngite [laʀɛ̃ʒit] nf laryngitis

las, lasse [lɑ, lɑs] adj weary

laser [lazɛʀ] nm: **(rayon) ~** laser (beam); **chaîne ou platine ~** laser disc (player); **disque ~** laser disc

lasse [lɑs] adj voir **las**

lasser [lɑse] vt to weary, tire; **se lasser de** vt to grow weary ou tired of

latéral, e, -aux [lateʀal, o] adj side cpd, lateral

latin, e [latɛ̃, in] adj Latin ▷ nm/f: **L-, e** Latin ▷ nm (Ling) Latin

latitude [latityd] nf latitude
lauréat, e [lɔʁea, at] nm/f winner
laurier [lɔʁje] nm (Bot) laurel; **feuille de ~** (Culin) bay leaf
lavable [lavabl] adj washable
lavabo [lavabo] nm washbasin; **lavabos** nmpl (toilettes) toilet sg
lavage [lavaʒ] nm washing no pl, wash; **lavage de cerveau** brainwashing no pl
lavande [lavɑ̃d] nf lavender
lave [lav] nf lava no pl
lave-linge [lavlɛ̃ʒ] nm inv washing machine
laver [lave] vt to wash; (tache) to wash off; **se laver** vi to have a wash, wash; **se ~ les mains/dents** to wash one's hands/clean one's teeth; **~ la vaisselle/le linge** to wash the dishes/clothes; **~ qn de** (accusation) to clear sb of; **laverie** nf: **laverie (automatique)** launderette; **lavette** nf dish cloth; (fam) drip; **laveur, -euse** nm/f cleaner; **lave-vaisselle** nm inv dishwasher; **lavoir** nm wash house; (évier) sink
laxatif, -ive [laksatif, iv] adj, nm laxative
layette [lejɛt] nf baby clothes

○ **MOT-CLÉ**

le [lə], **la, l'** (pl **les**) art déf **1** : **le livre/la pomme/l'arbre** the book/the apple/the tree; **les étudiants** the students
2 (noms abstraits): **le courage/l'amour/la jeunesse** courage/love/youth
3 (indiquant la possession): **se casser la jambe** etc to break one's leg etc; **levez la main** put your hand up; **avoir les yeux gris/le nez rouge** to have grey eyes/a red nose
4 (temps): **le matin/soir** in the morning/evening; **mornings/evenings**; **le jeudi** etc (d'habitude) on Thursdays etc; (ce jeudi-là etc) on (the) Thursday
5 (distribution, évaluation) a, an; **10**

euros le mètre/kilo 10 euros a ou per metre/kilo; **le tiers/quart de** a third/quarter of
▷ pron **1** (personne: mâle) him; (: femelle) her; (: pluriel) them; **je le/la/les vois** I can see him/her/them
2 (animal, chose: singulier) it; (: pluriel) them; **je le (ou la) vois** I can see it; **je les vois** I can see them
3 (remplaçant une phrase): **je ne le savais pas** I didn't know (about it); **il était riche et ne l'est plus** he was once rich but no longer is

lécher [leʃe] vt to lick; (laper: lait, eau) to lick ou lap up; **se ~ les doigts/lèvres** to lick one's fingers/lips; **lèche-vitrines** nm: **faire du lèche-vitrines** to go window-shopping
leçon [l(ə)sɔ̃] nf lesson; **faire la ~ à** (fig) to give a lecture to; **leçons de conduite** driving lessons; **leçons particulières** private lessons ou tuition sg (BRIT)
lecteur, -trice [lɛktœʀ, tʀis] nm/f reader; (d'université) foreign language assistant ▷ nm (Tech.): **~ de cassettes/CD/DVD** cassette/CD/DVD player; **lecteur de disquette(s)** disk drive; **lecteur MP3** MP3 player
lecture [lɛktyʀ] nf reading
┃ Attention à ne pas traduire lecture
┃ par le mot anglais lecture.
ledit [lədi], **ladite** (mpl **lesdits**, fpl **lesdites**) dét the aforesaid
légal, e, -aux [legal, o] adj legal; **légaliser** vt to legalize; **légalité** nf law
légendaire [leʒɑ̃dɛʀ] adj legendary
légende [leʒɑ̃d] nf (mythe) legend; (de carte, plan) key; (de dessin) caption
léger, -ère [leʒe, ɛʀ] adj light; (bruit, retard) slight; (personne: superficiel) thoughtless; (: volage) free and easy; **à la légère** (parler, agir) rashly, thoughtlessly; **légèrement** adv (s'habiller, bouger) lightly; (un peu) slightly; **manger légèrement** to eat a light meal; **légèreté** nf lightness; (d'une remarque) flippancy

législatif, -ive [leʒislatif, iv] adj
legislative; **législatives** nfpl general
election sg

légitime [leʒitim] adj (Jur) lawful,
legitimate; (fig) rightful, legitimate; **en
état de ~ défense** in self-defence

legs [leg] nm legacy

léguer [lege] vt: **~ qch à qn** (Jur) to
bequeath sth to sb

légume [legym] nm vegetable;
légumes secs pulses; **légumes verts**
green vegetables, greens

lendemain [lɑ̃dmɛ̃] nm: **le ~** the next
ou following day; **le ~ matin/soir** the
next ou following morning/evening; **le
~ de** the day after

lent, e [lɑ̃, lɑ̃t] adj slow; **lentement** adv
slowly; **lenteur** nf slowness no pl

lentille [lɑ̃tij] nf (Optique) lens sg;
(Culin) lentil; **lentilles de contact**
contact lenses

léopard [leɔpar] nm leopard

lèpre [lɛpr] nf leprosy

lequel, laquelle [ləkɛl, lakɛl] (mpl
lesquels, fpl **lesquelles**) (à + lequel =
auquel, de + lequel = **duquel** etc) pron
1 (interrogatif) which, which one; **lequel
des deux?** which one?
2 (relatif: personne: sujet) who; (: objet,
après préposition) whom; (: chose) which
▷ adj: **auquel cas** in which case

les [le] dét voir **le**

lesbienne [lɛsbjɛn] nf lesbian

léser [leze] vt to wrong

lésiner [lezine] vi: **ne pas ~ sur les
moyens** (pour mariage etc) to push the
boat out

lésion [lezjɔ̃] nf lesion, damage no pl

lessive [lesiv] nf (poudre) washing
powder; (linge) washing no pl, wash;
lessiver vt to wash; (fam: fatiguer) to
tire out, exhaust

lest [lɛst] nm ballast

leste [lɛst] adj sprightly, nimble

lettre [lɛtr] nf letter; **lettres** nfpl
(littérature) literature sg; (Scol) arts
(subjects); **à la ~** literally; **en toutes ~s**
in full; **lettre piégée** letter bomb

leucémie [løsemi] nf leukaemia

leur [lœr] adj possessif their; **leur
maison** their house; **leurs amis** their
friends
▷ pron **1** (objet indirect) (to) them; **je leur
ai dit la vérité** I told them the truth;
je le leur ai donné I gave it to them, I
gave them it
2 (possessif): **le(la) leur, les leurs** theirs

levain [ləvɛ̃] nm leaven

levé, e [ləve] adj: **être ~** to be up; **levée**
nf (Postes) collection

lever [l(ə)ve] vt (vitre, bras etc) to raise;
(soulever de terre, supprimer: interdiction,
siège) to lift; (impôts, armée) to levy ▷ vi
to rise ▷ nm: **au ~** on getting up; **se
lever** vi to get up; (soleil) to rise; (jour)
to break; (brouillard) to lift; **ça va se
lever** (temps) it's going to clear up; **lever de
soleil** sunrise; **lever du jour** daybreak

levier [ləvje] nm lever

lèvre [lɛvr] nf lip

lévrier [levrije] nm greyhound

levure [l(ə)vyr] nf yeast; **levure
chimique** baking powder

lexique [lɛksik] nm vocabulary;
(glossaire) lexicon

lézard [lezar] nm lizard

lézarde [lezard] nf crack

liaison [ljɛzɔ̃] nf (rapport) connection;
(transport) link; (amoureuse) affair;
(Phonétique) liaison; **entrer/être en ~
avec** to get/be in contact with

liane [ljan] nf creeper

liasse [ljas] nf wad, bundle

Liban [libɑ̃] nm: **le ~** (the) Lebanon

libeller [libele] vt (chèque, mandat): **~
(au nom de)** to make out (to); (lettre)
to word

libellule [libelyl] nf dragonfly

libéral, e, -aux [liberal, o] *adj,
nm/f* liberal; **profession ~e** (liberal)
profession

libérer [libere] *vt* (*délivrer*) to free,
liberate; (*relâcher: prisonnier*) to
discharge, release; (: *d'inhibitions*) to
liberate; (*gaz*) to release; **se libérer** *vi*
(*de rendez-vous*) to get out of previous
engagements

liberté [liberte] *nf* freedom; (*loisir*) free
time; **libertés** *nfpl* (*privautés*) liberties;
mettre/être en ~ to set/be free; **en ~
provisoire/surveillée/conditionnelle**
on bail/probation/parole

libraire [librer] *nm/f* bookseller

librairie [libreri] *nf* bookshop

> Attention à ne pas traduire *librairie*
> par *library*.

libre [libr] *adj* free; (*route, voie*) clear;
(*place, salle*) free; (*ligne*) not engaged; (*Scol*) non-state; **~ de qch/de faire**
free from sth/to do; **la place est ~?** is this
seat free?; **libre arbitre** free will; **libre-
échange** *nm* free trade; **libre-service**
nm self-service store

Libye [libi] *nf*: **la ~** Libya

licence [lisɑ̃s] *nf* (*permis*) permit;
(*diplôme*) degree; (*liberté*) liberty;
licencié, e *nm/f* (*Scol*): **licencié
ès lettres/en droit** = Bachelor of
Arts/Law

licenciement [lisɑ̃simɑ̃] *nm*
redundancy

licencier [lisɑ̃sje] *vt* (*débaucher*) to
make redundant, lay off; (*renvoyer*)
to dismiss

licite [lisit] *adj* lawful

lie [li] *nf* dregs *pl*, sediment

lié, e [lje] *adj*: **très ~ avec** very friendly
with ou close to

Liechtenstein [liʃtɛnʃtajn] *nm*: **le ~**
Liechtenstein

liège [ljɛʒ] *nm* cork

lien [ljɛ̃] *nm* (*corde, fig: affectif*) bond;
(*rapport*) link, connection; **lien de
parenté** family tie; **lien hypertexte**
hyperlink

lier [lje] *vt* (*attacher*) to tie up; (*joindre*)

to link up; (*fig: unir, engager*) to bind;
~ conversation (avec) to strike up a
conversation (with); **~ connaissance
avec** to get to know

lierre [ljɛr] *nm* ivy

lieu, x [ljø] *nm* place; **lieux** *nmpl*
(*locaux*) premises; (*endroit: d'un accident
etc*) scene *sg*; **en ~ sûr** in a safe place; **en
premier ~** in the first place; **en dernier
~** lastly; **avoir ~** to take place; **tenir ~
de** to serve as; **donner ~ à** to give rise
to; **au ~ de** instead of; **arriver/être sur
les ~x** to arrive at/be on the scene; **lieu
commun** cliché; **lieu-dit** (*pl* **lieux-dits**)
nm locality

lieutenant [ljøt(ə)nɑ̃] *nm* lieutenant

lièvre [ljɛvr] *nm* hare

ligament [ligamɑ̃] *nm* ligament

ligne [liɲ] *nf* (*gén*) line; (*Transports:
liaison*) service; (: *trajet*) route;
(*silhouette*) figure; **garder la ~** to keep
one's figure; **entrer en ~ de compte** to
come into it; **en ~** (*Inform*) online; **~ fixe**
(*Tél*) land line (phone)

lignée [liɲe] *nf* line, lineage

ligoter [ligote] *vt* to tie up

ligue [lig] *nf* league

lilas [lila] *nm* lilac

limace [limas] *nf* slug

limande [limɑ̃d] *nf* dab

lime [lim] *nf* file; **lime à ongles** nail file;
limer *vt* to file

limitation [limitasjɔ̃] *nf*: **limitation
de vitesse** speed limit

limite [limit] *nf* (*de terrain*) boundary;
(*partie ou point extrême*) limit; **à la ~** (*au
pire*) if the worst comes (*ou* came) to the
worst; **vitesse/charge ~** maximum
speed/load; **cas ~** borderline
case; **date ~** deadline; **date ~ de
vente/consommation** sell-by/best-
before date; **limiter** *vt* (*restreindre*) to
limit, restrict; (*délimiter*) to border;
limitrophe *adj* border *cpd*

limoger [limoʒe] *vt* to dismiss

limon [limɔ̃] *nm* silt

limonade [limonad] *nf* lemonade

lin [lɛ̃] *nm* (*tissu*) linen

linceul [lɛ̃sœl] *nm* shroud

linge [lɛ̃ʒ] *nm* (serviettes etc) linen; (lessive) washing; (aussi: ~ de corps) underwear; **lingerie** *nf* lingerie, underwear

lingot [lɛ̃go] *nm* ingot

linguistique [lɛ̃gɥistik] *adj* linguistic ▷ *nf* linguistics *sg*

lion, ne [ljɔ̃, ljɔn] *nm/f* lion (lioness); (signe): **le L-** Leo; **lionceau, x** *nm* lion cub

liqueur [likœʀ] *nf* liqueur

liquidation [likidasjɔ̃] *nf* (vente) sale

liquide [likid] *adj* liquid ▷ *nm* liquid; (Comm): **en ~** in ready money *ou* cash; **je n'ai pas de ~** I haven't got any cash; **liquider** *vt* to liquidate; (Comm: articles) to clear, sell off

lire [liʀ] *nf* (monnaie) lira ▷ *vt*, *vi* to read

lis [lis] *nm* = **lys**

Lisbonne [lizbɔn] *n* Lisbon

lisible [lizibl] *adj* legible

lisière [lizjɛʀ] *nf* (de forêt) edge

lisons [lizɔ̃] *vb voir* **lire**

lisse [lis] *adj* smooth

liste [list] *nf* list; **faire la ~ de** to list; **liste de mariage** wedding (present) list; **liste électorale** electoral roll; **listing** *nm* (Inform) printout

lit [li] *nm* bed; **petit ~, ~ à une place** single bed; **grand ~, ~ à deux places** double bed; **faire son ~** to make one's bed; **aller/se mettre au ~** to go/to get into bed; **lit de camp** campbed; **lit d'enfant** cot (BRIT), crib (US)

literie [litʀi] *nf* bedding, bedclothes *pl*

litige [litiʒ] *nm* dispute

litre [litʀ] *nm* litre

littéraire [liteʀɛʀ] *adj* literary ▷ *nm/f* arts student; **elle est très ~** she's very literary

littéral, e, -aux [literal, o] *adj* literal

littérature [liteʀatyʀ] *nf* literature

littoral, -aux [litɔʀal, o] *nm* coast

livide [livid] *adj* livid, pallid

livraison [livʀɛzɔ̃] *nf* delivery

livre [livʀ] *nm* book ▷ *nf* (monnaie) pound; (poids) half a kilo, ≈ pound; **livre**

de poche paperback

livré, e [livʀe] *adj*: **~ à soi-même** left to o.s. *ou* one's own devices

livrer [livʀe] *vt* (Comm) to deliver; (otage, coupable) to hand over; (secret, information) to give away; **se livrer à** (se confier) to confide in; (se rendre, s'abandonner) to give o.s. up to; (faire: pratiques, actes) to indulge in; (enquête) to carry out

livret [livʀɛ] *nm* booklet; (d'opéra) libretto; **livret de caisse d'épargne** (savings) bank-book; **livret de famille** (official) family record book; **livret scolaire** (school) report book

livreur, -euse [livʀœʀ, øz] *nm/f* delivery boy *ou* man/girl *ou* woman

local, e, -aux [lɔkal, o] *adj* local ▷ *nm* (salle) premises *pl*; *voir aussi* **locaux**; **localité** *nf* locality

locataire [lɔkatɛʀ] *nm/f* tenant; (de chambre) lodger

location [lɔkasjɔ̃] *nf* (par le locataire, le loueur) renting; (par le propriétaire) renting out, letting; (Théâtre) booking office; "**~ de voitures**" "car rental"; **habiter en ~** to live in rented accommodation; **prendre une ~ (pour les vacances)** to rent a house *etc* (for the holidays)

> Attention à ne pas traduire **location** par le mot anglais **location**.

locomotive [lɔkɔmɔtiv] *nf* locomotive, engine

locution [lɔkysjɔ̃] *nf* phrase

loge [lɔʒ] *nf* (Théâtre: d'artiste) dressing room; (: de spectateurs) box; (de concierge, franc-maçon) lodge

logement [lɔʒmɑ̃] *nm* accommodation *no pl* (BRIT), accommodations *pl* (US); (appartement) flat (BRIT), apartment (US); (Pol, Admin): **le ~** housing *no pl*

loger [lɔʒe] *vt* to accommodate ▷ *vi* to live; **être logé, nourri** to have board and lodging; **se loger** *vr*: **trouver à se ~** to find somewhere to live; **se ~ dans** (suj: balle, flèche) to lodge itself in;

logeur, -euse nm/f landlord(-lady)

logiciel [lɔʒisjɛl] nm software

logique [lɔʒik] adj logical ▷ nf logic

logo [lɔgo] nm logo

loi [lwa] nf law; **faire la ~** to lay down the law

loin [lwɛ̃] adv far; (dans le temps: futur) a long way off; (: passé) a long time ago; **plus ~** further; **~ de** far from; **c'est ~ d'ici** is it far from here?; **au ~** far off; **de ~** from a distance; (fig: de beaucoup) by far

lointain, e [lwɛ̃tɛ̃, ɛn] adj faraway, distant; (dans le futur, passé) distant; (cause, parent) remote, distant ▷ nm: **dans le ~** in the distance

loir [lwaʀ] nm dormouse

Loire [lwaʀ] nf: **la ~** the (River) Loire

loisir [lwaziʀ] nm: **heures de ~** spare time; **loisirs** nmpl (temps libre) leisure sg; (activités) leisure activities; **avoir le ~ de faire** to have the time ou opportunity to do; **à ~** at leisure

londonien, ne [lɔ̃dɔnjɛ̃, jɛn] adj London cpd, of London ▷ nm/f: **L~, ne** Londoner

Londres [lɔ̃dʀ] n London

long, longue [lɔ̃, lɔ̃g] adj long ▷ adv: **en savoir ~** to know a great deal ▷ nm: **de 3 m de ~** 3 m long, 3 m in length; **ne pas faire ~ feu** not to last long; **(tout) le ~ de** (all) along; **tout au ~ de** (année, vie) throughout; **de ~ en large** (marcher) to and fro, up and down; voir aussi **longue**

longer [lɔ̃ʒe] vt to go (ou walk ou drive) along(side); (suj: mur, route) to border

longiligne [lɔ̃ʒiliɲ] adj long-limbed

longitude [lɔ̃ʒityd] nf longitude

longtemps [lɔ̃tɑ̃] adv (for) a long time, (for) long; **avant ~** before long; **pour ou pendant ~** for a long time; **mettre ~ à faire** to take a long time to do; **il en a pour ~?** will he be long?

longue [lɔ̃g] adj voir **long** ▷ nf: **à la ~** in the end; **longuement** adv (longtemps) for a long time; (en détail) at length

longueur [lɔ̃gœʀ] nf length;

longueurs nfpl (fig: d'un film etc) tedious parts; **en ~** lengthwise; **tirer en ~** to drag on; **à la journée** all day long

longуeurs

lorgner [lɔʀɲe] vt to eye; (fig) to have one's eye on

lors [lɔʀ]: **~ de** prép at the time of; during

lorsque [lɔʀsk] conj when, as

losange [lɔzɑ̃ʒ] nm diamond

lot [lo] nm (part) share; (de loterie) prize; (fig: destin) fate, lot; (Comm, Inform) batch; **le gros ~** the jackpot

loterie [lɔtʀi] nf lottery

lotion [losjɔ̃] nf lotion; **lotion après rasage** aftershave lotion

lotissement [lɔtismɑ̃] nm housing development; (parcelle) plot, lot

loto [lɔto] nm lotto

lotte [lɔt] nf monkfish

louanges [lwɑ̃ʒ] nfpl praise sg

loubard [lubaʀ] (fam) nm lout

louche [luʃ] adj shady, fishy, dubious ▷ nf ladle; **loucher** vi to squint

louer [lwe] vt (maison: suj: propriétaire) to let, rent (out); (: locataire) to rent; (voiture etc: entreprise) to hire out (BRIT), rent (out); (: locataire) to hire, rent; (réserver) to book; (faire l'éloge de) to praise; **"à ~"** "to let" (BRIT), "for rent" (US); **je voudrais ~ une voiture** I'd like to hire (BRIT) ou rent (US) a car

loup [lu] nm wolf; **jeune ~** young go-getter

loupe [lup] nf magnifying glass; **à la ~** in minute detail

louper [lupe] (fam) vt (manquer) to miss; (examen) to flunk

lourd, e [luʀ, luʀd] adj, adv heavy; **c'est trop ~** it's too heavy; **~ de** (conséquences, menaces) charged with; **il fait ~** the weather is close, it's sultry; **lourdaud, e** (péj) adj clumsy; **lourdement** adv heavily

loutre [lutʀ] nf otter

louveteau, x [luv(ə)to] nm wolf-cub; (scout) cub (scout)

louvoyer [luvwaje] vi (fig) to hedge,

evade the issue

loyal, e, -aux [lwajal, o] *adj (fidèle)* loyal, faithful; *(fair-play)* fair; **loyauté** *nf* loyalty, faithfulness; fairness

loyer [lwaje] *nm* rent

lu, e [ly] *pp de* **lire**

lubie [lybi] *nf* whim, craze

lubrifiant [lybʀifjɑ̃] *nm* lubricant

lubrifier [lybʀifje] *vt* to lubricate

lubrique [lybʀik] *adj* lecherous

lucarne [lykaʀn] *nf* skylight

lucide [lysid] *adj* lucid; *(accidenté)* conscious

lucratif, -ive [lykʀatif, iv] *adj* lucrative, profitable; **à but non ~** non profit-making

lueur [lɥœʀ] *nf (pâle)* (faint) light; *(chatoyante)* gleam **no** *pl; (fig)* glimmer; gleam

luge [lyʒ] *nf* sledge (BRIT), sled (US)

lugubre [lygybʀ] *adj* gloomy, dismal

 MOT-CLÉ

lui [lɥi] *pron* **1** *(objet indirect: mâle)* (to) him; *(: femelle)* (to) her; *(: chose, animal)* (to) it; **je lui ai parlé** I have spoken to him (ou to her); **il lui a offert un cadeau** he gave him (ou her) a present **2** *(après préposition, comparatif: personne)* him; *(: chose, animal)* it; **elle est contente de lui** she is pleased with him; **je la connais mieux que lui** I know her better than he does; I know her better than him; **ce livre est à lui** this book is his, this is his book; **c'est à lui de jouer** it's his turn ou go **3** *(sujet, forme emphatique)* he; **lui, il est à Paris** HE is in Paris; **c'est lui qui l'a fait** HE did it **4** *(objet, forme emphatique)* him; **c'est lui que j'attends** I'm waiting for HIM **5: lui-même** himself; itself

luire [lɥiʀ] *vi* to shine; *(en rougeoyant)* to glow

lumière [lymjɛʀ] *nf* light; **mettre en ~** *(fig)* to highlight; **lumière du jour** daylight

luminaire [lyminɛʀ] *nm* lamp, light

lumineux, -euse [lyminø, øz] *adj* luminous; *(éclairé)* illuminated; *(ciel, couleur)* bright; *(rayon)* of light, light *cpd; (fig: regard)* radiant

lunatique [lynatik] *adj* whimsical, temperamental

lundi [lœ̃di] *nm* Monday; **on est ~** it's Monday; **le(s) ~(s)** on Mondays; **"à ~"** "see you on Monday"; **lundi de Pâques** Easter Monday

lune [lyn] *nf* moon; **lune de miel** honeymoon

lunette [lynɛt] *nf:* **~s** *nfpl* glasses, spectacles; *(protectrices)* goggles; **lunette arrière** *(Auto)* rear window; **lunettes de soleil** sunglasses; **lunettes noires** dark glasses

lustre [lystʀ] *nm (de plafond)* chandelier; *(fig: éclat)* lustre; **lustrer** *vt* to shine

luth [lyt] *nm* lute

lutin [lytɛ̃] *nm* imp, goblin

lutte [lyt] *nf (conflit)* struggle; *(sport)* wrestling; **lutter** *vi* to fight, struggle

luxe [lyks] *nm* luxury; **de ~** luxury *cpd*

Luxembourg [lyksɑ̃buʀ] *nm:* **le ~** Luxembourg

luxer [lykse] *vt:* **se ~ l'épaule** to dislocate one's shoulder

luxueux, -euse [lyksɥø, øz] *adj* luxurious

lycée [lise] *nm* = secondary school; **lycéen, ne** *nm/f* secondary school pupil

Lyon [ljɔ̃] *n* Lyons

lyophilisé, e [ljɔfilize] *adj (café)* freeze-dried

lyrique [liʀik] *adj* lyrical; *(Opéra)* lyric; **artiste ~** opera singer

lys [lis] *nm* lily

m

M abr = **Monsieur**

m' [m] pron voir **me**

ma [ma] adj voir **mon**

macaron [makaʀɔ̃] nm (gâteau) macaroon; (insigne) (round) badge

macaronis [makaʀɔni] nmpl macaroni sg; **~ au fromage** ou **en gratin** macaroni cheese (BRIT), macaroni and cheese (US)

macédoine [masedwan] nf: **~ de fruits** fruit salad; **~ de légumes** mixed vegetables; **la M~** Macedonia

macérer [maseʀe] vi, vt to macerate; (dans du vinaigre) to pickle

mâcher [maʃe] vt to chew; **ne pas ~ ses mots** not to mince one's words

machin [maʃɛ̃] (fam) nm thing (umajig); (personne): **M~(e)** nm(f) what's-his(ou her)-name

machinal, e, -aux [maʃinal, o] adj mechanical, automatic

machination [maʃinasjɔ̃] nf frame-up

machine [maʃin] nf machine; (locomotive) engine; **machine à laver/coudre** washing/sewing machine; **machine à sous** fruit machine

mâchoire [maʃwaʀ] nf jaw

mâchonner [maʃɔne] vt to chew (at)

maçon [masɔ̃] nm builder; (poseur de briques) bricklayer; **maçonnerie** nf (murs) brickwork; (pierres) masonry, stonework

Madagascar [madagaskaʀ] nf Madagascar

Madame [madam] (pl **Mesdames**) nf: **~ Dupont** Mrs Dupont; **occupez-vous de ~/Monsieur/Mademoiselle** please serve this lady/gentleman/(young) lady; **bonjour ~/Monsieur/Mademoiselle** good morning; (ton déférent) good morning Madam/Sir/Madam; (le nom est connu) good morning Mrs/Mr/Miss X; **~/Monsieur/Mademoiselle!** (pour appeler) Madam/Sir/Miss!; **~/Monsieur/Mademoiselle** (sur lettre) Dear Madam/Sir/Madam; **chère ~/ cher Monsieur/chère Mademoiselle** Dear Mrs/Mr/Miss X; **Mesdames** Ladies; **mesdames, mesdemoiselles, messieurs** ladies and gentlemen

madeleine [madlɛn] nf madeleine, small sponge cake

Mademoiselle [madmwazɛl] (pl **Mesdemoiselles**) nf Miss; voir aussi **Madame**

madère [madɛʀ] nm Madeira (wine)

Madrid [madʀid] n Madrid

magasin [magazɛ̃] nm (boutique) shop; (entrepôt) warehouse; **en ~** (Comm) in stock

magazine [magazin] nm magazine

Maghreb [magʀɛb] *nm:* **le ~** North Africa; *Maghreb,* e *adj* North African ▷ *nm/f:* **Maghrébin,** e North African

magicien, ne [maʒisjɛ̃, jɛn] *nm/f* magician

magie [maʒi] *nf* magic; **magique** *adj* magic; *(enchanteur)* magical

magistral, e, -aux [maʒistʀal, o] *adj (œuvre, adresse)* masterly; *(ton)* authoritative; **cours ~** lecture

magistrat [maʒistʀa] *nm* magistrate

magnétique [maɲetik] *adj* magnetic

magnétophone [maɲetɔfɔn] *nm* tape recorder; **magnétophone à cassettes** cassette recorder

magnétoscope [maɲetɔskɔp] *nm* video-tape recorder

magnifique [maɲifik] *adj* magnificent

magret [magʀɛ] *nm:* **~ de canard** duck steaklet

mai [mɛ] *nm* May

○ MAI
○
○ **Le premier mai** is a public holiday
○ in France and commemorates the
○ trades union demonstrations in the
○ United States in 1886 when workers
○ demanded the right to an eight-hour
○ working day. Sprigs of lily of the
○ valley are traditionally exchanged.
○ **Le 8 mai** is also a public holiday and
○ commemorates the surrender of
○ the German army to Eisenhower
○ on 7 May, 1945. It is marked by
○ parades of ex-servicemen and ex-
○ servicewomen in most towns.

maigre [mɛgʀ] *adj* (very) thin, skinny; *(viande)* lean; *(fromage)* low-fat; *(végétation)* thin, sparse; *(fig)* poor, meagre, skimpy; **jours ~s** days of abstinence, fish days; **maigreur** *nf* thinness; **maigrir** *vi* to get thinner, lose weight; **maigrir de 2 kilos** to lose 2 kilos

mail [mɛl] *nm* e-mail

maille [maj] *nf* stitch; **maille à l'endroit/l'envers** plain/purl stitch

maillet [majɛ] *nm* mallet

maillon [majɔ̃] *nm* link

maillot [majo] *nm (aussi:* **~ de corps)** vest; *(de sportif)* jersey; **maillot de bain** swimming ou bathing (BRIT) costume, swimsuit; *(d'homme)* swimming ou bathing (BRIT)) trunks *pl*

main [mɛ̃, mɛt] *nf* hand; **à la ~** *(tenir, avoir)* in one's hand; *(faire, tricoter etc)* by hand; **se donner la ~** to hold hands; **donner** ou **tendre la ~ à qn** to hold out one's hand to sb; **se serrer la ~** to shake hands; **serrer la ~ à qn** to shake hands with sb; **sous la ~** to ou at hand; **haut les ~s!** hands up!; **attaque à ~ armée** armed attack; **à remettre en ~s propres** to be delivered personally; **mettre la dernière ~ à** to put the finishing touches to; **se faire/perdre la ~** to get one's hand in/lose one's touch; **avoir qch bien en ~** to have (got) the hang of sth; **main-d'œuvre** *nf* manpower, labour; **mainmise** *nf (fig)* **mainmise sur** complete hold on; **mains libres** *adj inv (téléphone, kit)* hands-free

maint, e [mɛ̃, mɛt] *adj* many a; **~s** many; **à ~es reprises** time and (time) again

maintenant [mɛ̃t(ə)nɑ̃] *adv* now; *(actuellement)* nowadays

maintenir [mɛ̃t(ə)niʀ] *vt (retenir, soutenir)* to support; *(contenir: foule etc)* to hold back; *(conserver, affirmer)* to maintain; **se maintenir** *vi (prix)* to keep steady; *(amélioration)* to persist

maintien [mɛ̃tjɛ̃] *nm (sauvegarde)* maintenance; *(attitude)* bearing

maire [mɛʀ] *nm* mayor; **mairie** *nf (bâtiment)* town hall; *(administration)* town council

mais [mɛ] *conj* but; **~ non!** of course not!; **~ enfin** but after all; *(indignation)* look here!

maïs [mais] *nm* maize (BRIT), corn (US)

maison [mɛzɔ̃] *nf* house; *(chez-soi)*

home; (Comm) firm ▷ adj inv (Culin) home-made; (fig) in-house, own; **à la ~** at home; (direction) home; **maison de repos** convalescent home; **maison de retraite** old people's home; **maison close** ou **de passe** brothel; **maison de santé** mental home; **maison des jeunes** = youth club; **maison mère** parent company

maître, -esse [mɛtʀ, mɛtʀɛs] nm/f master (mistress); (Scol) teacher, schoolmaster(-mistress) ▷ nm (peintre etc) master; (titre): **M~** Maître, term of address open for a barrister ▷ adj (principal, essentiel) main; **être ~ de** (soi, situation) to be in control of; **une ~sse femme** a managing woman; **maître chanteur** blackmailer; **maître d'école** schoolmaster; **maître d'hôtel** (domestique) butler; (d'hôtel) head waiter; **maître nageur** lifeguard; **maîtresse** nf (amante) mistress; **maîtresse (d'école)** (school)mistress; **maîtresse de maison** hostess; (ménagère) housewife

maîtrise [mɛtʀiz] nf (aussi: **~ de soi**) self-control, self-possession; (habileté) skill, mastery; (suprématie) mastery, command; (diplôme) ≈ master's degree; **maîtriser** vt (cheval, incendie, inflation) to (bring under) control; (sujet) to master; (émotion) to control, master; **se maîtriser** to control o.s.

majestueux, -euse [maʒɛstɥø, øz] adj majestic

majeur, e [maʒœʀ] adj (important) major; (Jur) of age ▷ nm (doigt) middle finger; **en ~e partie** for the most part; **la ~e partie** de most of

majorer [maʒɔʀe] vt to increase

majoritaire [maʒɔʀitɛʀ] adj majority cpd

majorité [maʒɔʀite] nf (gén) majority; (parti) party in power; **en ~** mainly; **avoir la ~** to have the majority

majuscule [maʒyskyl] adj, nf: **(lettre) ~** capital (letter)

mal [mal, mo] (pl **maux**) nm (opposé

au bien) evil; (tort, dommage) harm; (douleur physique) pain, ache; (maladie) illness, sickness no pl ▷ adv badly; (pas bien) wrong; **être ~ à l'aise** to be uncomfortable; **être ~ avec qn** to be on bad terms with sb; **il a ~ compris** he misunderstood; **se sentir** ou **se trouver ~** to feel ill ou unwell; **dire/penser du ~** to speak/think ill of; **ne voir aucun ~ à** to see no harm in, see nothing wrong in; **faire ~ à qn** to hurt sb; **se faire ~** to hurt o.s.; **avoir du ~ à faire qch** to have trouble doing sth; **se donner du ~ pour faire qch** to go to a lot of trouble to do sth; **ça fait ~** it hurts; **j'ai ~ au dos** my back hurts; **avoir ~ à la tête/à la gorge/aux dents** to have a headache/a sore throat/toothache; **avoir le ~ du pays** to be homesick; voir aussi **cœur; maux**; **mal de mer** seasickness; **mal en point** in a bad state

malade [malad] adj ill, sick; (poitrine, jambe) bad; (plante) diseased ▷ nm/f invalid, sick person; (à l'hôpital) patient; **tomber ~** to fall ill; **être ~ du cœur** to have heart trouble ou a bad heart; **malade mental** mentally ill person; **maladie** nf (spécifique) disease, illness; (mauvaise santé) illness, sickness; **maladif, -ive** adj sickly; (curiosité, besoin) pathological

maladresse [maladʀɛs] nf clumsiness no pl; (gaffe) blunder

maladroit, e [maladʀwa, wat] adj clumsy

malaise [malɛz] nm (Méd) feeling of faintness; (fig) uneasiness, malaise; **avoir un ~** to feel faint

Malaisie [malɛzi] nf: **la ~** Malaysia

malaria [malaʀja] nf malaria

malaxer [malakse] vt (pétrir) to knead; (mélanger) to mix

malbouffe [malbuf] (fam) nf: **la ~** junk food

malchance [malʃɑ̃s] nf misfortune, ill luck no pl; **par ~** unfortunately; **malchanceux, -euse** adj unlucky

mâle [mɑl] *adj (aussi Élec, Tech)* male; *(viril: voix, traits)* manly ▷ *nm* male

malédiction [malediksjɔ̃] *nf* curse

mal...: malentendant, e *nm/f*: **les malentendants** the hard of hearing; **malentendu** *nm* misunderstanding; **il y a eu un malentendu** there's been a misunderstanding; **malfaçon** *nf* fault; **malfaisant, e** *adj* evil, harmful; **malfaiteur** *nm* lawbreaker, criminal; *(voleur)* burglar, thief; **malfamé, e** *adj* disreputable

malgache [malgaʃ] *adj* Madagascan, Malagasy ▷ *nm/f*: **M~** Madagascan, Malagasy ▷ *nm (Ling)* Malagasy

malgré [malgre] *prép* in spite of, despite; **~ tout** all the same

malheur [malœʀ] *nm (situation)* adversity, misfortune; *(événement)* misfortune; *(: très grave)* disaster, tragedy; **faire un ~** to be a smash hit; **malheureusement** *adv* unfortunately; **malheureux, -euse** *adj (triste)* unhappy, miserable; *(infortuné, regrettable)* unfortunate; *(malchanceux)* unlucky; *(insignifiant)* wretched ▷ *nm/f* poor soul

malhonnête [malɔnɛt] *adj* dishonest; **malhonnêteté** *nf* dishonesty

malice [malis] *nf* mischievousness; *(méchanceté)*: **par ~** out of malice ou spite; **sans ~** guileless; **malicieux, -euse** *adj* mischievous

> Attention à ne pas traduire *malicieux* par *malicious*.

malin, -igne [malɛ̃, maliɲ] *adj (futé: f gén: aussi:* **maline**) smart, shrewd; *(Méd)* malignant

malingre [malɛ̃gʀ] *adj* puny

malle [mal] *nf* trunk; **mallette** *nf* (small) suitcase; *(porte-documents)* attaché case

malmener [malməne] *vt* to manhandle; *(fig)* to give a rough handling to

malodorant, e [malɔdɔʀɑ̃, ɑ̃t] *adj* foul-*ou* ill-smelling

malpoli, e [malpɔli] *adj* impolite

malsain, e [malsɛ̃, ɛn] *adj* unhealthy

malt [malt] *nm* malt

Malte [malt] *nf* Malta

maltraiter [maltʀete] *vt* to manhandle, ill-treat

malveillance [malvejɑ̃s] *nf (animosité)* ill will; *(intention de nuire)* malevolence

malversation [malvɛʀsasjɔ̃] *nf* embezzlement

maman [mamɑ̃] *nf* mum(my), mother

mamelle [mamɛl] *nf* teat

mamelon [mam(ə)lɔ̃] *nm (Anat)* nipple

mamie [mami] *(fam) nf* granny

mammifère [mamifɛʀ] *nm* mammal

mammouth [mamut] *nm* mammoth

manche [mɑ̃ʃ] *nf (de vêtement)* sleeve; *(d'un jeu, tournoi)* round; *(Géo)*: **la M~** the Channel ▷ *nm (de pelle, pioche etc)* handle; *(de pelle, pioche etc)* shaft; **à ~s courtes/longues** short-/long-sleeved; **manche à balai** broomstick; *(Inform, Aviat)* joystick m inv

manchette [mɑ̃ʃɛt] *nf (de chemise)* cuff; *(coup)* forearm blow; *(titre)* headline

manchot [mɑ̃ʃo] *nm* one-armed man; armless man; *(Zool)* penguin

mandarine [mɑ̃daʀin] *nf* mandarin (orange), tangerine

mandat [mɑ̃da] *nm (postal)* postal ou money order; *(d'un député etc)* mandate; *(procuration)* power of attorney, proxy; *(Police)* warrant; **mandat d'arrêt** warrant for arrest; **mandat de perquisition** search warrant; **mandataire** *nm/f (représentant)* representative; *(Jur)* proxy

manège [manɛʒ] *nm* riding school; *(à la foire)* roundabout, merry-go-round; *(fig)* game, ploy

manette [manɛt] *nf* lever, tap; **manette de jeu** joystick

mangeable [mɑ̃ʒabl] *adj* edible, eatable

mangeoire [mɑ̃ʒwaʀ] *nf* trough, manger

manger [mɑ̃ʒe] *vt* to eat; *(ronger: suj: rouille etc)* to eat into ou away ▷ *vi* to eat; **donner à ~ à** *(enfant)* to feed; **est-**

ce qu'on peut ~ quelque chose? can we have something to eat?

mangue [mɑ̃g] nf mango

maniable [manjabl] adj (outil) handy; (voiture, voilier) easy to handle

maniaque [manjak] adj finicky, fussy ▷ nm/f (méticuleux) fusspot; (fou) maniac

manie [mani] nf (tic) odd habit; (obsession) mania; **avoir la ~ de** to be obsessive about

manier [manje] vt to handle

manière [manjɛʀ] nf (façon) way, manner; **manières** nfpl (attitude) manners; (chichis) fuss sg; **de ~ à so as to; de cette ~** in this way ou manner; **d'une certaine ~** in a way; **de toute ~** in any case; **d'une ~ générale** generally speaking, as a general rule

maniéré, e [manjeʀe] adj affected

manifestant, e [manifɛstɑ̃, ɑ̃t] nm/f demonstrator

manifestation [manifɛstasjɔ̃] nf (de joie, mécontentement) expression, demonstration; (symptôme) outward sign; (culturelle etc) event; (Pol) demonstration

manifeste [manifɛst] adj obvious, evident ▷ nm manifesto; **manifester** vt (volonté, intentions) to show, indicate; (joie, peur) to express, show ▷ vi to demonstrate; **se manifester** (émotion) to show ou express itself; (difficultés) to arise; (symptômes) to appear

manigancer [manigɑ̃se] vt to plot

manipulation [manipylasjɔ̃] nf handling; (Pol, génétique) manipulation

manipuler [manipyle] vt to handle; (fig) to manipulate

manivelle [manivɛl] nf crank

mannequin [mankɛ̃] nm (Couture) dummy; (Mode) model

manœuvre [manœvʀ] nf (gén) manoeuvre (BRIT), maneuver (US) ▷ nm labourer; **manœuvrer** vt to manoeuvre (BRIT), maneuver (US); (levier, machine) to operate ▷ vi to

manoeuvre

manoir [manwaʀ] nm manor ou country house

manque [mɑ̃k] nm (insuffisance): **~ de** lack of; (vide) emptiness, gap; (Méd) withdrawal; **être en état de ~** to suffer withdrawal symptoms

manqué, e [mɑ̃ke] adj failed; **garçon ~** tomboy

manquer [mɑ̃ke] vi (faire défaut) to be lacking; (être absent) to be missing; (échouer) to fail ▷ vt to miss ▷ vb impers: **il (nous) manque encore 10 euros** we are still 10 euros short; **il manque des pages (au livre)** there are some pages missing (from the book); **il/cela me manque** I miss him/this; **~ à** (règles etc) to be in breach of, fail to observe; **~ de** to lack; **je ne ~ai pas de le lui dire** I'll be sure to tell him; **il a manqué (de) se tuer** he very nearly got killed

mansarde [mɑ̃saʀd] nf attic; **mansardé, e** adj: **chambre mansardée** attic room

manteau, x [mɑ̃to] nm coat

manucure [manykyʀ] nf manicurist

manuel, le [manɥɛl] adj manual ▷ nm (ouvrage) manual, handbook

manufacture [manyfaktyʀ] nf factory; **manufacturé, e** adj manufactured

manuscrit, e [manyskʀi, it] adj handwritten ▷ nm manuscript

manutention [manytɑ̃sjɔ̃] nf (Comm) handling

mappemonde [mapmɔ̃d] nf (plane) map of the world; (sphère) globe

maquereau, x [makʀo] nm (Zool) mackerel; (fam) pimp

maquette [makɛt] nf (à échelle réduite) (scale) model; (d'une page illustrée) paste-up

maquillage [makijaʒ] nm making up; (crème etc) make-up

maquiller [makije] vt (personne, visage) to make up; (truquer: passeport, statistique) to fake; (: voiture volée) to do over (respray etc); **se maquiller** vi to make up (one's face)

maquis [maki] nm (Géo) scrub; (Mil) maquis, underground fighting no pl

maraîcher, -ère [maʀeʃe, ɛʀ] adj: **cultures maraîchères** market gardening sg ▷ nm/f market gardener

marais [maʀɛ] nm marsh, swamp

marasme [maʀasm] nm stagnation, slump

marathon [maʀatɔ̃] nm marathon

marbre [maʀbʀ] nm marble

marc [maʀ] nm (de raisin, pommes) marc

marchand, e [maʀʃɑ̃, ɑ̃d] nm/f shopkeeper, tradesman(-woman); (au marché) stallholder; (de vins, charbon) merchant ▷ adj: **prix/valeur ~(e)** market price/value; **marchand de fruits** fruiterer (BRIT), fruit seller (US); **marchand de journaux** newsagent; **marchand de légumes** greengrocer (BRIT), produce dealer (US); **marchand de poissons** fishmonger (BRIT), fish seller (US); **marchander** vi to bargain, haggle; **marchandise** nf goods pl, merchandise no pl

marche [maʀʃ] nf (d'escalier) step; (activité) walking; (promenade, trajet, allure) walk; (démarche) walk, gait; (Mil etc, Mus) march; (fonctionnement) running; (des événements) course; **dans le sens de la ~** (Rail) facing the engine; **en ~** (monter etc) while the vehicle is moving ou in motion; **mettre en ~** to start; **se mettre en ~** (personne) to get moving; (machine) to start; **être en état de ~** to be in working order; **marche à suivre** (correct) procedure; **marche arrière** reverse (gear); **faire marche arrière** to reverse; (fig) to backtrack, back-pedal

marché [maʀʃe] nm market; (transaction) bargain, deal; **faire du ~ noir** to buy and sell on the black market; **marché aux puces** flea market

marcher [maʀʃe] vi to walk; (Mil) to march; (aller: voiture, train, affaires) to go; (prospérer) to go well; (fonctionner) to work, run; (fam: consentir) to go along, agree; (: croire naïvement) to be taken in; **faire ~ qn** (taquiner) to pull sb's leg; (tromper) to lead sb up the garden path; **comment est-ce que ça marche?** how does this work?; **marcheur, -euse** nm/f walker

mardi [maʀdi] nm Tuesday; **Mardi gras** Shrove Tuesday

mare [maʀ] nf pond; (flaque) pool

marécage [maʀekaʒ] nm marsh, swamp; **marécageux, -euse** adj marshy

maréchal, -aux [maʀeʃal, o] nm marshal

marée [maʀe] nf tide; (poissons) fresh (sea) fish; **marée haute/basse** high/low tide; **marée noire** oil slick

marelle [maʀɛl] nf: **(jouer à) la ~** (to play) hopscotch

margarine [maʀgaʀin] nf margarine

marge [maʀʒ] nf margin; **en ~ de** (fig) on the fringe of; **marge bénéficiaire** profit margin

marginal, e, -aux [maʀʒinal, o] nm/f (original) eccentric; (déshérité) dropout

marguerite [maʀgəʀit] nf marguerite, (oxeye) daisy; (d'imprimante) daisy-wheel

mari [maʀi] nm husband

mariage [maʀjaʒ] nm marriage; (noce) wedding; **mariage civil/religieux** registry office (BRIT) ou civil wedding/ church wedding

marié, e [maʀje] adj married ▷ nm (bride)groom; **les ~s** the bride and groom; **les (jeunes) ~s** the newly-weds

marier [maʀje] vt to marry; (fig) to blend; **se ~ (avec)** to marry, get married to

marin, e [maʀɛ̃, in] adj sea cpd, marine ▷ nm sailor

marine [maʀin] adj voir **marin** ▷ adj inv navy (blue) ▷ nm (Mil) marine ▷ nf navy; **marine marchande** merchant navy

mariner [maʀine] vt: **faire ~ to** marinade

marionnette [maʀjɔnɛt] nf puppet

maritalement [maʀitalmã] adv:
vivre ~ to live as husband and wife

maritime [maʀitim] adj sea cpd;
maritime

mark [maʀk] nm mark

marmelade [maʀməlad] nf stewed
fruit, compote; **marmelade d'oranges**
marmalade

marmite [maʀmit] nf (cooking-)pot

marmonner [maʀmɔne] vt, vi to
mumble, mutter

marmotter [maʀmɔte] vt to mumble

Maroc [maʀɔk] nm: **le ~** Morocco;
marocain, e [maʀɔkɛ̃, ɛn] adj
Moroccan ▷ nm/f: **Marocain, e**
Moroccan

maroquinerie [maʀɔkinʀi] nf
(articles) fine leather goods pl; (boutique)
shop selling fine leather goods

marquant, e [maʀkɑ̃, ɑ̃t] adj
outstanding

marque [maʀk] nf mark; (Comm: de
nourriture) brand; (: de voiture, produits
manufacturés) make; (de disques) label;
de ~ (produits) high-class; (visiteur
etc) distinguished, well-known; **une
grande ~ de vin** a well-known brand of
wine; **marque de fabrique** trademark;
marque déposée registered
trademark

marquer [maʀke] vt to mark; (inscrire)
to write down; (bétail) to brand; (Sport:
but etc) to score; (: joueur) to mark;
(accentuer: taille etc) to emphasize;
(manifester: refus, intérêt) to show
▷ vi (événement) to stand out, be
outstanding; (Sport) to score; **~ les
points** to keep the score

marqueterie [maʀkətʀi] nf inlaid
work, marquetry

marquis [maʀki] nm marquis,
marquess

marraine [maʀɛn] nf godmother

marrant, e [maʀɑ̃, ɑ̃t] (fam) adj funny

marre [maʀ] (fam) adv: **en avoir ~ de** to
be fed up with

marrer [maʀe]: **se ~** (fam) vi to have a

(good) laugh

marron [maʀɔ̃] nm (fruit) chestnut
▷ adj inv brown; **marrons glacés**
candied chestnuts; **marronnier** nm
chestnut (tree)

mars [maʀs] nm March

Marseille [maʀsɛj] n Marseilles

marteau, x [maʀto] nm hammer; **être
~** (fam) to be nuts; **marteau-piqueur**
nm pneumatic drill

marteler [maʀtəle] vt to hammer

martien, ne [maʀsjɛ̃, jɛn] adj
Martian, of/from Mars

martyr, e [maʀtiʀ] nm/f martyr ▷ adj:
enfants ~s battered children; **martyre**
nm martyrdom; (fig: sens affaibli) agony,
torture; **martyriser** vt (Rel) to martyr;
(fig) to bully; (enfant) to batter, beat

marxiste [maʀksist] adj, nm/f Marxist

mascara [maskaʀa] nm mascara

masculin, e [maskylɛ̃, in] adj
masculine; (sexe, population) male;
(équipe, vêtements) men's; (viril) manly
▷ nm masculine

masochiste [mazɔʃist] adj
masochistic

masque [mask] nm mask; **masque de
beauté** face pack ou mask; **masque
de plongée** diving mask; **masquer** vt
(cacher: paysage, porte) to hide, conceal;
(dissimuler: vérité, projet) to mask,
obscure

massacre [masakʀ] nm massacre,
slaughter; **massacrer** vt to massacre,
slaughter; (fam: texte etc) to murder

massage [masaʒ] nm massage

masse [mas] nf (gén, Élec) earth;
(maillet) sledgehammer; (péj): **la ~** the
masses pl; **une ~ de** (fam) masses ou
loads of; **en ~** adv (acheter) in bulk;
(en foule) en masse ▷ adj (exécutions,
production) mass cpd

masser [mase] vt (assembler: gens) to
gather; (pétrir) to massage; **se masser**
vi (foule) to gather; **masseur, -euse**
nm/f masseur(-euse)

massif, -ive [masif, iv] adj (porte)
solid, massive; (visage) heavy, large;

(bois, or) solid; *(dose)* massive; *(déportations etc)* mass cpd ▷ nm *(montagneux)* massif; *(de fleurs)* clump, bank; **le M~ Central** the Massif Central

massue [masy] nf club, bludgeon

mastic [mastik] nm *(pour vitres)* putty; *(pour fentes)* filler

mastiquer [mastike] vt *(aliment)* to chew, masticate

mat, e [mat] adj *(couleur, métal)* mat(t); *(bruit, son)* dull ▷ adj inv *(Échecs)*: **être ~** to be checkmate

mât [mɑ] nm *(Navig)* mast; *(poteau)* pole, post

match [matʃ] nm match; **faire ~ nul** to draw; **match aller** first leg; **match retour** second leg, return match

matelas [mat(ə)lɑ] nm mattress; **matelas pneumatique** air bed ou mattress

matelot [mat(ə)lo] nm sailor, seaman

mater [mate] vt *(personne)* to heel, subdue; *(révolte)* to put down

matérialiser [materjalize]: **se matérialiser** vi to materialize

matérialiste [materjalist] adj materialistic

matériau [materjo] nm material; **matériaux** nmpl material(s)

matériel, le [materjɛl] adj material ▷ nm equipment no pl; *(de camping etc)* gear no pl; *(Inform)* hardware

maternel, le [matɛrnɛl] adj *(amour, geste)* motherly, maternal; *(grand-père, oncle)* maternal; **maternelle** nf *(aussi:* **école maternelle)** (state) nursery school

maternité [maternite] nf *(établissement)* maternity hospital; *(état de mère)* motherhood, maternity; *(grossesse)* pregnancy; **congé de ~** maternity leave

mathématique [matematik] adj mathematical; **mathématiques** nfpl *(science)* mathematics sg

maths [mat] *(fam)* nfpl maths

matière [matjɛr] nf matter; *(Comm, Tech)* material, matter no pl; *(fig: d'un*

livre etc) subject matter, material; *(Scol)* subject; **en ~ de** as regards; **matières grasses** fat content sg; **matières premières** raw materials

Matignon [matiɲɔ̃] nm: **(l'hôtel) ~** the French Prime Minister's residence

matin [matɛ̃] nm, adv morning; **le ~** *(pendant le matin)* in the morning; **demain/hier/dimanche ~** tomorrow/yesterday/Sunday morning; **tous les ~s** every morning; **une heure du ~** one o'clock in the morning; **du ~ au soir** from morning till night; **de bon ou grand ~** early in the morning; **matinal, e, -aux** adj *(toilette, gymnastique)* morning cpd; **être matinal** *(personne)* to be up early; to be an early riser; **matinée** nf morning; *(spectacle)* matinée

matou [matu] nm tom(cat)

matraque [matrak] nf *(de policier)* truncheon *(BRIT)*, billy club *(US)*

matricule [matrikyl] nm *(Mil)* regimental number; *(Admin)* reference number

matrimonial, e, -aux [matrimɔnjal, jo] adj marital, marriage cpd

maudit, e [modi, -it] *(fam)* adj *(satané)* blasted, confounded

maugréer [mogree] vi to grumble

maussade [mosad] adj sullen; *(temps)* gloomy

mauvais, e [mɔvɛ, ɛz] adj bad; *(faux)*: **le ~ numéro/moment** the wrong number/moment; *(méchant, malveillant)* malicious, spiteful ▷ adv: **il fait ~** the weather is bad; **sentir ~** to have a nasty smell, smell nasty; **la mer est ~e** the sea is rough; **mauvais joueur** bad loser; **mauvaise herbe** weed; **mauvaise langue** gossip, scandalmonger *(BRIT)*; **mauvaise plaisanterie** nasty trick

mauve [mov] adj mauve

maux [mo] nmpl de **mal**

maximum [maksimɔm] adj, nm maximum; **au ~** *(le plus possible)* as much as one can; (tout au plus) at the (very) most ou maximum; **faire le ~** to do one's level best

mayonnaise [majɔnɛz] nf mayonnaise

mazout [mazut] nm (fuel) oil

me, m' [m(ə)] pron (direct: téléphoner, attendre etc) me; (indirect: parler, donner etc) (to) me; (réfléchi) myself

mec [mɛk] (fam) nm bloke, guy

mécanicien, ne [mekanisjɛ̃, jɛn] nm/f mechanic; (Rail) (train ou engine) driver; **pouvez-vous nous envoyer un ~?** can you send a mechanic?

mécanique [mekanik] adj mechanical ▷ nf (science) mechanics sg; (mécanisme) mechanism; **ennui ~** engine trouble no pl

mécanisme [mekanism] nm mechanism

méchamment [meʃamɑ̃] adv nastily, maliciously, spitefully

méchanceté [meʃɑ̃ste] nf nastiness, maliciousness; **dire des ~s à qn** to say spiteful things to sb

méchant, e [meʃɑ̃, ɑ̃t] adj nasty, malicious, spiteful; (enfant: pas sage) naughty; (animal) vicious

mèche [mɛʃ] nf (de cheveux) lock; (de lampe, bougie) wick; (d'un explosif) fuse; **se faire faire des ~s** to have highlights put in one's hair; **de ~ avec** in league with

méchoui [meʃwi] nm barbecue of a whole roast sheep

méconnaissable [mekɔnɛsabl] adj unrecognizable

méconnaître [mekɔnɛtʀ] vt (ignorer) to be unaware of; (mésestimer) to misjudge

mécontent, e [mekɔ̃tɑ̃, ɑ̃t] adj: **~ (de)** discontented ou dissatisfied ou displeased (with); (contrarié) annoyed (at); **mécontentement** nm dissatisfaction, discontent, displeasure; (irritation) annoyance

Mecque [mɛk] nf: **la ~** Mecca

médaille [medaj] nf medal

médaillon [medajɔ̃] nm (bijou) locket

médecin [med(ə)sɛ̃] nm doctor

médecine [med(ə)sin] nf medicine

média [medja] nmpl: **les ~** the media; **médiatique** adj media cpd

médical, e, -aux [medikal, o] adj medical; **passer une visite ~e** to have a medical

médicament [medikamɑ̃] nm medicine, drug

médiéval, e, -aux [medjeval, o] adj medieval

médiocre [medjɔkʀ] adj mediocre, poor

méditer [medite] vi to meditate

Méditerranée [mediteʀane] nf: **la (mer) ~** the Mediterranean (Sea); **méditerranéen, ne** adj Mediterranean ▷ nm/f: **Méditerranéen, ne** native ou inhabitant of a Mediterranean country

méduse [medyz] nf jellyfish

méfait [mefɛ] nm (faute) misdemeanour, wrongdoing; **méfaits** nmpl (ravages) ravages, damage sg

méfiance [mefjɑ̃s] nf mistrust, distrust

méfiant, e [mefjɑ̃, jɑ̃t] adj mistrustful, distrustful

méfier [mefje]: **se méfier** vi to be wary; to be careful; **se ~ de** to mistrust, distrust, be wary of

mégaoctet [megaɔktɛ] nm megabyte

mégarde [megaʀd] nf: **par ~** (accidentellement) accidentally; (par erreur) by mistake

mégère [meʒɛʀ] nf shrew

mégot [mego] (fam) nm cigarette end

meilleur, e [mɛjœʀ] adj, adv better ▷ nm: **le ~** the best; **le ~ des deux** the better of the two; **il fait ~ qu'hier** it's better weather than yesterday; **meilleur marché** (inv) cheaper

mél [mɛl] nm e-mail

mélancolie [melɑ̃kɔli] nf melancholy, gloom; **mélancolique** adj melancholic, melancholy

mélange [melɑ̃ʒ] nm mixture;

mélanger vt to mix; (vins, couleurs) to blend; (mettre en désordre) to mix up, muddle (up)

mêlée [mele] nf mêlée, scramble; (Rugby) scrum(mage)

mêler [mele] vt to mix; (embrouiller) to muddle (up), mix up; **se ~ à** (personne: se joindre) to join; (: s'associer à) to mix with; **se ~ de** (suj: personne) to meddle with, interfere in; **mêle-toi de ce qui te regarde** ou **de tes affaires!** mind your own business!

mélodie [melɔdi] nf melody; **mélodieux, -euse** adj melodious

melon [m(ə)lɔ̃] nm (Bot) (honeydew) melon; (aussi: **chapeau ~**) bowler (hat)

membre [mɑ̃bʀ] nm (Anat) limb; (personne, pays, élément) member ▷ adj member cpd

mémé [meme] (fam) nf granny

🅞 MOT-CLÉ

même [mɛm] adj 1 (avant le nom) same; **en même temps** at the same time; **ils ont les mêmes goûts** they have the same ou similar tastes
2 (après le nom: renforcement): **il est la loyauté même** he is loyalty itself; **ce sont ses paroles mêmes** they are his very words
▷ pron: **le(la) même** the same one
▷ adv 1 (renforcement): **il n'a même pas pleuré** he didn't even cry; **même lui l'a dit** even HE said it; **ici même** at this very place; **de même** si even if
2: **à même: à même la bouteille** straight from the bottle; **à même la peau** next to the skin; **être à même de faire** to be in a position to do, be able to do
3: **de même: faire de même** to do likewise; **lui de même** he (ou did ou is) he; **de même que** just as; **il en va de même pour** the same goes for

mémoire [memwaʀ] nf memory ▷ nm

(Scol) dissertation, paper; **mémoires** nmpl (souvenirs) memoirs; **à la ~ de** to the ou in memory of; **de ~** from memory; **mémoire morte** read-only memory, ROM; **mémoire vive** random access memory, RAM

mémorable [memɔʀabl] adj memorable, unforgettable

menace [mənas] nf threat; **menacer** vt to threaten

ménage [menaʒ] nm (travail) housework; (couple) (married) couple; (famille, Admin) household; **faire le ~** to do the housework; **ménagement** nm care and attention; **ménager, -ère** adj household cpd, domestic ▷ vt (traiter: personne) to handle with tact; (utiliser) to use sparingly; (prendre soin de) to take (great) care of, look after; (organiser) to arrange; **ménagère** nf housewife

mendiant, e [mɑ̃djɑ̃, jɑ̃t] nm/f beggar
mendier [mɑ̃dje] vi to beg ▷ vt to beg (for)

mener [m(ə)ne] vt to lead; (enquête) to conduct; (affaires) to manage ▷ vi: **~ à/dans** (emmener) to take to/into; **~ qch à bien** to see sth through to a successful conclusion), complete sth successfully

meneur, -euse [mənœʀ, øz] nm/f leader; (péj) agitator

méningite [menɛ̃ʒit] nf meningitis no pl

ménopause [menopoz] nf menopause

menottes [mənɔt] nfpl handcuffs

mensonge [mɑ̃sɔ̃ʒ] nm lie; (action) lying no pl; **mensonger, -ère** adj false

mensualité [mɑ̃sɥalite] nf (traite) monthly payment

mensuel, le [mɑ̃sɥɛl] adj monthly

mensurations [mɑ̃syʀasjɔ̃] nfpl measurements

mental, e, -aux [mɑ̃tal, o] adj mental; **mentalité** nf mentality

menteur, -euse [mɑ̃tœʀ, øz] nm/f liar

menthe [mɑ̃t] nf mint

mention [mɑ̃sjɔ̃] nf (annotation) note,

comment; (Scol) grade; **~ bien** = grade B, = good pass; (Université) = upper 2nd class pass (BRIT); = pass with (high) honors (US); (Admin): **"rayer les ~s inutiles"** "delete as appropriate"; **mentionner** vt to mention

mentir [mɑ̃tiʀ] vi to lie

menton [mɑ̃tɔ̃] nm chin

menu, e [məny] adj (personne) slim, slight; (frais, difficulté) minor ▷ adv (couper, hacher) very fine ▷ nm menu; **~ touristique/gastronomique** economy/gourmet's menu

menuiserie [mənɥizʀi] nf (métier) joinery, carpentry; (passe-temps) woodwork; **menuisier** nm joiner, carpenter

méprendre [mepʀɑ̃dʀ]: **se méprendre** vi: **se ~ sur** to be mistaken (about)

mépris [mepʀi] nm (dédain) contempt, scorn; **au ~ de** regardless of, in defiance of; **méprisable** adj contemptible, despicable; **méprisant, e** adj scornful; **méprise** nf mistake, error; **mépriser** vt to scorn, despise; (gloire, danger) to scorn, spurn

mer [mɛʀ] nf sea; (marée) tide; **en ~** at sea; **en haute** ou **pleine ~** off shore, on the open sea; **la ~ du Nord/Rouge/Noire/Morte** the North/Red/Black/Dead Sea

mercenaire [mɛʀsənɛʀ] nm mercenary, hired soldier

mercerie [mɛʀsəʀi] nf (boutique) haberdasher's shop (BRIT), notions store (US)

merci [mɛʀsi] excl thank you ▷ nf: **à la ~ de qn/qch** at sb's mercy/the mercy of sth; **~ beaucoup** thank you very much; **~ de** thank you for; **sans ~** merciless(ly)

mercredi [mɛʀkʀədi] nm Wednesday; **~ des Cendres** Ash Wednesday; voir aussi **lundi**

mercure [mɛʀkyʀ] nm mercury

merde [mɛʀd] (fam!) nf shit ▷ excl (bloody) hell (!)

mère [mɛʀ] nf mother; **mère célibataire** single parent, unmarried mother; **mère de famille** housewife, mother

merguez [mɛʀgɛz] nf merguez sausage (type of spicy sausage from N Africa)

méridional, e, -aux [meʀidjɔnal, o] adj southern ▷ nm/f Southerner

meringue [məʀɛ̃g] nf meringue

mérite [meʀit] nm merit; **avoir du ~ (à faire qch)** to deserve credit (for doing sth); **mériter** vt to deserve

merle [mɛʀl] nm blackbird

merveille [mɛʀvɛj] nf marvel, wonder; **faire ~** to work wonders; **à ~** perfectly, wonderfully; **merveilleux, -euse** adj marvellous, wonderful

mes [me] adj voir **mon**

mésange [mezɑ̃ʒ] nf tit (mouse)

mésaventure [mezavɑ̃tyʀ] nf misadventure, misfortune

Mesdames [medam] nfpl de **Madame**

Mesdemoiselles [medmwazɛl] nfpl de **Mademoiselle**

mesquin, e [mɛskɛ̃, in] adj mean, petty; **mesquinerie** nf meanness; (procédé) mean trick

message [mesaʒ] nm message; **est-ce que je peux laisser un ~?** can I leave a message?; **~ SMS** text message; **messager, -ère** nm/f messenger; **messagerie** nf (Internet): **messagerie électronique** e-mail; **messagerie vocale** (service) voice mail; **messagerie instantanée** instant messenger

messe [mɛs] nf mass; **aller à la ~** to go to mass

Messieurs [mesjø] nmpl de **Monsieur**

mesure [m(ə)zyʀ] nf (évaluation, dimension) measurement; (récipient) measure; (Mus: cadence) time, tempo; (: division) bar; (retenue) moderation; (disposition) measure, step; **sur ~** (costume) made-to-measure; **dans la ~ où** insofar as, inasmuch as; **à ~ que** as; **être en ~ de** to be in a position to; **dans une certaine ~** to a certain extent

mesurer [mazyʀe] vt to measure; (juger) to weigh up, assess; (modérer: ses

paroles etc) to moderate

métal, -aux [metal, o] *nm* metal;
métallique *adj* metallic

météo [meteo] *nf* (*bulletin*) weather report

météorologie [meteɔʀɔlɔʒi] *nf* meteorology

méthode [metɔd] *nf* method; (*livre, ouvrage*) manual, tutor

méticuleux, -euse [metikylø, øz] *adj* meticulous

métier [metje] *nm* (*profession: gén*) job; (: *manuel*) trade; (*artisanal*) craft; (*technique, expérience*) (acquired) skill ou technique; (*aussi*: **~ à tisser**) (weaving) loom

métis, se [metis] *adj, nm/f* half-caste, half-breed

métrage [metʀaʒ] *nm*: **long/moyen/court ~** full-length/medium-length/short film

mètre [mɛtʀ] *nm* metre; (*règle*) rule; (*ruban*) tape measure; **métrique** *adj* metric

métro [metʀo] *nm* underground (BRIT), subway

métropole [metʀɔpɔl] *nf* (*capitale*) metropolis; (*pays*) home country

mets [mɛ] *nm* dish

metteur [metœʀ] *nm*: **~ en scène** (*Théâtre*) producer; (*Cinéma*) director

 MOT-CLÉ

mettre [mɛtʀ] *vt* **1** (*placer*) to put;
mettre en bouteille/en sac to bottle/put in bags ou sacks

2 (*vêtements: revêtir*) to put on; (: *porter*) to wear; **mets ton gilet** put your cardigan on; **je ne mets plus mon manteau** I no longer wear my coat

3 (*faire fonctionner: chauffage, électricité*) to put on; (: *réveil, minuteur*) to set; (*installer: gaz, eau*) to put in, lay on;
mettre en marche to start up

4 (*consacrer*): **mettre du temps à faire qch** to take time to do sth ou over sth

5 (*noter, écrire*) to say, put (down);

qu'est-ce qu'il a mis sur la carte?
what did he say ou write on the card?;
mettez au pluriel ... put ... into the plural

6 (*supposer*): **mettons que ...** let's suppose ou say that ...

7 y mettre du sien to pull one's weight

se mettre *vi* **1** (*se placer*): **vous pouvez vous mettre là** you can sit (ou stand) there; **où ça se met?** where does it go?; **se mettre au lit** to get into bed; **se mettre au piano** to sit down at the piano; **se mettre de l'encre sur les doigts** to get ink on one's fingers

2 (*s'habiller*): **se mettre en maillot de bain** to get into ou put on a swimsuit; **n'avoir rien à se mettre** to have nothing to wear

3: **se mettre à** to begin, start; **se mettre à faire** to begin doing ou to do; **se mettre au piano** to start learning the piano; **se mettre au régime** to go on a diet; **se mettre au travail/à l'étude** to get down to work/one's studies

meuble [mœbl] *nm* piece of furniture;
des ~s furniture; **meublé** *nm* furnished flatlet (BRIT) ou room; **meubler** *vt* to furnish

meuf [mœf] *nf* (*fam*) woman

meugler [møgle] *vi* to low, moo

meule [møl] *nf* (*de foin, blé*) stack; (*de fromage*) round; (*à broyer*) millstone

meunier [mønje] *nm* miller

meurs *etc* [mœʀ] *vb voir* **mourir**

meurtre [mœʀtʀ] *nm* murder;
meurtrier, -ière *adj* (*arme etc*) deadly; (*fureur, instincts*) murderous ▷ *nm/f* murderer(-eress)

meurtrir [mœʀtʀiʀ] *vt* to bruise; (*fig*) to wound

meus *etc* [mœ] *vb voir* **mouvoir**

meute [møt] *nf* pack

mexicain, e [mɛksikɛ̃, ɛn] *adj* Mexican ▷ *nm/f*: **M~, e** Mexican

Mexico [mɛksiko] *n* Mexico City

Mexique [mɛksik] *nm*: **le ~** Mexico

mi [mi] nm (Mus) E; (en chantant la gamme) mi ▷ préfixe: **mi...** half(-):

mid-: **à la mi-janvier** in mid-January; **à mi-jambes/corps** (up ou down) to the knees/waist; **à mi-hauteur** halfway up

miauler [mjole] vi to mew

miche [miʃ] nf round ou cob loaf

mi-chemin [miʃmɛ̃]: **à ~** adv halfway, midway

mi-clos, e [miklo, kloz] adj half-closed

micro [mikʀo] nm mike, microphone; (Inform) micro

microbe [mikʀɔb] nm germ, microbe

micro...: **micro-onde** nf: **four à micro-ondes** microwave oven; **micro-ordinateur** nm microcomputer; **microscope** nm microscope; **microscopique** adj microscopic

midi [midi] nm midday, noon; (moment du déjeuner) lunchtime; (sud) south: **à ~** at 12 (o'clock) ou midday ou noon; **le M~** the South (of France), the Midi

mie [mi] nf crumb (of the loaf)

miel [mjɛl] nm honey; **mielleux, -euse** adj (personne) unctuous, syrupy

mien, ne [mjɛ̃, mjɛn] pron: **le(la) ~(ne), les ~(ne)s** mine; **les ~s** my family

miette [mjɛt] nf (de pain, gâteau) crumb; (fig: de la conversation etc) scrap; **en ~s** in pieces ou bits

---

MOT-CLÉ

mieux [mjø] adv 1 (d'une meilleure façon): **mieux (que)** better (than); **elle travaille/mange mieux** she works/ eats better; **aimer mieux** to prefer; **elle va mieux** she is better; **de mieux en mieux** better and better

2 (de la meilleure façon) best; **ce que je connais le mieux** what I know best; **les livres les mieux faits** the best-made books

▷ adj 1 (plus à l'aise, en meilleure forme) better; **se sentir mieux** to feel better

2 (plus satisfaisant) better; **c'est mieux ainsi** it's better like this; **c'est le mieux**

des deux it's the better of the two; **le(la) mieux, les mieux** the best; **demandez-lui, c'est le mieux** ask him, it's the best thing

3 (plus joli) better-looking; **il est mieux que son frère** (plus beau) he's better-looking than his brother; (plus gentil) he's nicer than his brother; **il est mieux sans moustache** he looks better without a moustache

4: **au mieux** at best; **au mieux avec** on the best of terms with; **pour le mieux** for the best

▷ nm 1 (progrès) improvement

2: **de mon/ton mieux** as best I/you can (ou could); **faire de son mieux** to do one's best

---

mignon, ne [miɲɔ̃, ɔn] adj sweet, cute

migraine [migʀɛn] nf headache; (Méd) migraine

mijoter [miʒɔte] vt to simmer; (préparer avec soin) to cook lovingly; (fam: tramer) to plot, cook up ▷ vi to simmer

milieu, x [miljø] nm (centre) middle; (Bio, Géo) environment; (entourage social) milieu; (provenance) background; (pègre): **le ~** the underworld; **au ~ de** in the middle of; **au beau ou au ~ (de)** right in the middle (of); **un juste ~** a happy medium

militaire [militɛʀ] adj military, army cpd ▷ nm serviceman

militant, e [militɑ̃, ɑ̃t] adj, nm/f militant

militer [milite] vi to be a militant

mille [mil] num a ou one thousand ▷ nm (mesure): **~ (marin)** nautical mile; **mettre dans le ~** (fig) to be bang on target; **millefeuille** nm cream ou vanilla slice; **millénaire** nm millennium ▷ adj thousand-year-old; (fig) ancient; **mille-pattes** nm inv centipede

millet [mijɛ] nm millet

milliard [miljaʀ] nm milliard, thousand million (BRIT), billion (US); **milliardaire** nm/f multimillionaire

(BRIT), billionaire (US)
millier [milje] nm thousand; **un ~ (de)** a thousand or so, about a thousand; **par ~s** in (their) thousands, by the thousand
milligramme [miligram] nm milligramme
millimètre [milimɛtʀ] nm millimetre
million [miljɔ̃] nm million; **deux ~s de** two million; **millionnaire** nm/f millionaire
mime [mim] nm/f (acteur) mime(r) ⊳ nm (art) mime, miming; **mimer** vt to mime; (singer) to mimic, take off
minable [minabl] adj (décrépit) shabby(-looking); (médiocre) pathetic
mince [mɛ̃s] adj thin; (personne, taille) slim, slender; (fig: profit, connaissances) slight, small, weak ⊳ excl: ~ **alors!** drat it!, darn it! (US); **minceur** nf thinness; (d'une personne) slimness, slenderness; **mincir** vi to get slimmer
mine [min] nf (physionomie) expression, look; (allure) exterior, appearance; (de crayon) lead; (gisement, explosif, fig: source) mine; **avoir bonne ~** (personne) to look well; (ironique) to look an utter idiot; **avoir mauvaise ~** to look unwell ou poorly; **faire ~ de faire** to make a pretence of doing; **~ de rien** although you wouldn't think so
miner [mine] vt (saper) to undermine, erode; (Mil) to mine
minerai [minʀɛ] nm ore
minéral, e, -aux [mineʀal, o] adj, nm mineral
minéralogique [mineʀalɔʒik] adj: **plaque ~** number (BRIT) ou license (US) plate; **numéro ~** registration (BRIT) ou license (US) number
minet, te [minɛ, ɛt] nm/f (chat) pussycat; (péj) young trendy
mineur, e [minœʀ] adj minor ⊳ nm/f (Jur) minor, person under age ⊳ nm (travailleur) miner
miniature [minjatyʀ] adj, nf miniature
minibus [minibys] nm minibus

minier, -ière [minje, jɛʀ] adj mining
mini-jupe [miniʒyp] nf mini-skirt
minime [minim] adj minor, minimal
minimessage [minimesaʒ] nm text message
minimiser [minimize] vt to minimize; (fig) to play down
minimum [minimɔm] adj, nm minimum; **au ~** (au moins) at the very least
ministère [ministɛʀ] nm (aussi Rel) ministry; (cabinet) government
ministre [ministʀ] nm (aussi Rel) minister; **ministre d'État** senior minister ou secretary
Minitel® [minitɛl] nm videotext terminal and service

◦ **MINITEL®**

◦ Minitel® is a public information
◦ system provided by France-Télécom
◦ to telephone subscribers since
◦ the early 80s. Among the services
◦ available are a computerized
◦ telephone directory and information
◦ on travel timetables, stock-market
◦ news and situations vacant.
◦ Subscribers pay for their time on
◦ screen as part of their phone bill.
◦ Although this information is now
◦ also available on the Internet, the
◦ special Minitel® screens, terminals
◦ and keyboards are still very much a
◦ part of French daily life.

minoritaire [minɔʀitɛʀ] adj minority
minorité [minɔʀite] nf minority; **être en ~** to be in the ou a minority
minuit [minɥi] nm midnight
minuscule [minyskyl] adj minute, tiny ⊳ nf: (lettre) ~ small letter
minute [minyt] nf minute; **à la ~** (just) this instant; (faire) there and then; **minuter** vt to time; **minuterie** nf time switch
minutieux, -euse [minysjø, jøz] adj (personne) meticulous; (travail)

minutely detailed

mirabelle [mirabɛl] *nf* (cherry) plum

miracle [mirakl] *nm* miracle

mirage [miraʒ] *nm* mirage

mire [mir] *nf*: **point de ~** (*fig*) focal point

miroir [mirwar] *nm* mirror

miroiter [mirwate] *vi* to sparkle, shimmer; **faire ~ qch à qn** to paint sth in glowing colours for sb, dangle sth in front of sb's eyes

mis, e [mi, miz] *pp de* **mettre** ▷ *adj*: **bien ~** well-dressed

mise [miz] *nf* (*argent*: *au jeu*) stake; (*tenue*) clothing, attire; **être de ~** to be acceptable *ou* in season; **mise à jour** updating; **mise au point** (*fig*) clarification; **mise de fonds** capital outlay; **mise en plis** set; **mise en scène** production

miser [mize] *vt* (*enjeu*) to stake, bet; **~ sur** (*cheval, numéro*) to bet on; (*fig*) to bank *ou* count on

misérable [mizerabl] *adj* (*lamentable, malheureux*) pitiful, wretched; (*pauvre*) poverty-stricken; (*insignifiant, mesquin*) miserable ▷ *nm/f* wretch

misère [mizer] *nf* (*extreme*) poverty, destitution; **misères** *nfpl* (*malheurs*) woes, miseries; (*ennuis*) little troubles; **salaire de ~** starvation wage

missile [misil] *nm* missile

mission [misjɔ̃] *nf* mission; **partir en ~** (*Admin, Pol*) to go on an assignment; **missionnaire** *nm/f* missionary

mité, e [mite] *adj* moth-eaten

mi-temps [mitɑ̃] *nf inv* (*Sport*: *période*) half; (*pause*) half-time; **à ~** part-time

miteux, -euse [mitø, øz] *adj* (*lieu*) seedy

mitigé, e [mitiʒe] *adj*: **sentiments ~s** mixed feelings

mitoyen, ne [mitwajɛ̃, ɛn] *adj* (*mur*) common, party *cpd*; **maisons ~nes** semi-detached houses; (*plus de deux*) terraced (BRIT) *ou* row (US) houses

mitrailler [mitraje] *vt* to machine-gun; (*fig*) to pelt, bombard;

(: *photographier*) to take shot after shot of; **mitraillette** *nf* submachine gun; **mitrailleuse** *nf* machine gun

mi-voix [mivwa]: **à ~** *adv* in a low *ou* hushed voice

mixage [miksaʒ] *nm* (*Cinéma*) (sound) mixing

mixer [miksœr] *nm* (food) mixer

mixte [mikst] *adj* (*gén*) mixed; (*Scol*) mixed, coeducational; **cuisinière ~** combined gas and electric cooker (BRIT) *ou* stove (US)

mixture [mikstyr] *nf* mixture; (*fig*) concoction

Mlle (*pl* **~s**) *abr* = **Mademoiselle**

MM *abr* = **Messieurs**

Mme (*pl* **~s**) *abr* = **Madame**

mobile [mɔbil] *adj* mobile; (*pièce de machine*) moving ▷ *nm* (*motif*) motive; (*œuvre d'art*) mobile; (**téléphone**) **~** mobile (phone)

mobilier, -ière [mɔbilje, jɛr] *nm* furniture

mobiliser [mɔbilize] *vt* to mobilize

mocassin [mɔkasɛ̃] *nm* moccasin

moche [mɔʃ] (*fam*) *adj* (*laid*) ugly; (*mauvais*) rotten

modalité [mɔdalite] *nf* form, mode

mode [mɔd] *nf* fashion ▷ *nm* (*manière*) form, mode; (*Ling*) mood; (*Mus, Inform*) mode; **à la ~** fashionable, in fashion; **mode d'emploi** directions *pl* (for use); **mode de paiement** method of payment; **mode de vie** lifestyle

modèle [mɔdɛl] *adj, nm* model; (*qui pose: de peintre*) sitter; **modèle déposé** registered design; **modèle réduit** small-scale model; **modeler** *vt* to model

modem [mɔdɛm] *nm* modem

modéré, e [mɔdere] *adj, nm/f* moderate

modérer [mɔdere] *vt* to moderate; **se modérer** *vi* to restrain o.s.

moderne [mɔdɛrn] *adj* modern ▷ *nm* (*style*) modern style; (*meubles*) modern furniture; **moderniser** *vt* to modernize

modeste [mɔdɛst] *adj* modest;

modestie nf modesty

modifier [mɔdifje] vt to modify, alter; **se modifier** vi to alter

modique [mɔdik] adj modest

module [mɔdyl] nm module

moelle [mwal] nf marrow

moelleux, -euse [mwalø, øz] adj soft; (gâteau) light and moist

mœurs [mœʀ] nfpl (conduite) morals; (manières) manners; (pratiques sociales, mode de vie) habits

moi [mwa] pron me; (emphatique) ~, **je ...** for my part, I ..., I myself ...; **c'est qui l'ai fait** it was me who did it; **apporte-le-~** bring it to me; **à ~mine** (dans un jeu) my turn; **moi-même** pron myself; (emphatique) I myself

moindre [mwɛ̃dʀ] adj lesser; lower; **le(la)~, les ~s** the least, the slightest; **merci — c'est à ~ des choses!** thank you — it's a pleasure!

moine [mwan] nm monk, friar

moineau, X [mwano] nm sparrow

🔵 **MOT-CLÉ**

moins [mwɛ̃] adv **1** (comparatif): **moins (que)** less (than); **moins grand que** less tall than, not as tall as; **il a 3 ans de moins que moi** he's 3 years younger than me; **moins je travaille, mieux je me porte** the less I work, the better I feel

2 (superlatif): **le moins** (the) least; **c'est ce que j'aime le moins** it's what I like (the) least; **le(la) moins doué(e)** the least gifted; **au moins, du moins** at least; **pour le moins** at the very least

3: **moins de** (quantité) less (than); (nombre) fewer (than); **moins de sable/d'eau** less sand/water; **moins de livres/gens** fewer books/people; **moins de 2 ans** less than 2 years; **moins de midi** not yet midday

4: **de moins, en moins**: **100 euros/3 jours de moins** 100 euros/3 days less; **3 livres en moins** 3 books fewer, 3 books too few; **de l'argent en moins**

less money; **le soleil en moins** but for the sun, minus the sun; **de moins en moins** less and less

5: **à moins de, à moins que** unless; **à moins de faire** unless we do (ou he does etc); **à moins que tu ne fasses** unless you do; **à moins d'un accident** barring any accident

▷ prép: **4 moins 2** 4 minus 2; **il est moins 5** it's 5 to; **il fait moins 5** it's 5 (degrees) below freezing, it's minus 5

mois [mwa] nm month

moisi [mwazi] nm mould, mildew; **odeur de ~** musty smell; **moisir** vi to go mouldy; **moisissure** nf mould no pl

moisson [mwasɔ̃] nf harvest; **moissonner** vt to harvest, reap; **moissonneuse** nf (machine) harvester

moite [mwat] adj sweaty, sticky

moitié [mwatje] nf half; **la ~ half; la ~ de** half (of); **la ~ du temps** half the time; **à la ~ de** halfway through; **à ~** (avant le verbe) half; (avant l'adjectif) half-; **à ~ prix** (at) half-price

molaire [mɔlɛʀ] nf molar

molester [mɔlɛste] vt to manhandle, maul (about)

molle [mɔl] adj voir **mou; mollement** adv (péj: travailler) sluggishly; (protester) feebly

mollet [mɔlɛ] nm calf ▷ adj m: **œuf ~** soft-boiled egg

molletonné, e [mɔltɔne] adj fleece-lined

mollir [mɔliʀ] vi (fléchir) to relent; (substance) to go soft

mollusque [mɔlysk] nm mollusc

môme [mom] (fam) nm/f (enfant) brat

moment [mɔmɑ̃] nm moment; **ce n'est pas le ~** this is not the (right) time; **au même ~** at the same time; (instant) at the same moment; **pour un bon ~** for a good while; **pour le ~** for the moment, for the time being; **au ~ de** at the time of; **au ~ où** just as; **à tout ~** (peut arriver etc) at any moment ou time; (constamment) constantly, continually;

en ce ~ at the moment; at present; **sur le** ~ at the time now; **par** ~**s** now and then, at times; **d'un** ~ **à l'autre** any time (now); **du** ~ **où** ou **que** seeing that, since; **momentané, e** adj temporary, momentary; **momentanément** adv (court instant) for a short while

momie [mɔmi] nf mummy

mon, ma [mɔ̃, ma] (pl **mes**) adj my

Monaco [mɔnako] nf Monaco

monarchie [mɔnaʀʃi] nf monarchy

monastère [mɔnastɛʀ] nm monastery

mondain, e [mɔ̃dɛ̃, ɛn] adj (vie) society cpd

monde [mɔ̃d] nm world; (haute société): **le** ~ (high) society; **il y a du** ~ (beaucoup de gens) there are a lot of people; (quelques personnes) there are some people; **beaucoup/peu de** ~ many/few people; **mettre au** ~ to bring into the world; **pas le moins du** ~ not in the least; **mondial, e, -aux** adj (population) world cpd; (influence) world-wide; **mondialement** adv throughout the world; **mondialisation** nf globalization

monégasque [mɔnegask] adj Monegasque, of ou from Monaco ▷ nm/f: **M**~ Monegasque, person from ou inhabitant of Monaco

monétaire [mɔnetɛʀ] adj monetary

moniteur, -trice [mɔnitœʀ, tʀis] nm/f (Sport) instructor(-tress); (de colonie de vacances) supervisor ▷ nm (écran) monitor

monnaie [mɔnɛ] nf (Econ, gén: moyen d'échange) currency; (petites pièces): **avoir de la** ~ to have (some) change; **une pièce de** ~ a coin; **faire de la** ~ to get (some) change; **avoir/faire la** ~ **de 20 euros** to have change of/get change for 20 euros; **rendre à qn la** ~ (**sur 20 euros**) to give sb the change (out of ou from 20 euros); **gardez la** ~ keep the change; **désolé, je n'ai pas de** ~ sorry, I don't have any change; **avez-vous de la** ~? do you have any change

monologue [mɔnɔlɔg] nm monologue, soliloquy; **monologuer** vi to soliloquize

monopole [mɔnɔpɔl] nm monopoly

monotone [mɔnɔtɔn] adj monotonous

Monsieur [məsjø] (pl **Messieurs**) titre Mr ▷ nm (homme quelconque): **un/le monsieur** a/the gentleman; ~, ... (en tête de lettre) Dear Sir, ...; voir aussi **Madame**

monstre [mɔ̃stʀ] nm monster ▷ adj (fam: colossal) monstrous; **un travail** ~ a fantastic amount of work; **monstrueux, -euse** adj monstrous

mont [mɔ̃] nm: **par** ~**s et par vaux** up hill and down dale; **le Mont Blanc** Mont Blanc

montage [mɔ̃taʒ] nm (assemblage: d'appareil) assembly; (Photo) photomontage; (Cinéma) editing

montagnard, e [mɔ̃taɲaʀ, aʀd] adj mountain cpd ▷ nm/f mountain-dweller

montagne [mɔ̃taɲ] nf (cime) mountain; (région): **la** ~ the mountains pl; **montagnes russes** big dipper sg, switchback sg; **montagneux, -euse** adj mountainous; (basse montagne) hilly

montant, e [mɔ̃tɑ̃, ɑ̃t] adj rising; **pull à col** ~ high-necked jumper ▷ nm (somme, total) (sum) total, (total) amount; (de fenêtre) upright; (de lit) post

monte-charge [mɔ̃tʃaʀʒ] nm inv goods lift, hoist

montée [mɔ̃te] nf (des prix, hostilités) rise; (escalade) climb; (côte) hill; **au milieu de la** ~ halfway up

monter [mɔ̃te] vt (escalier, côte) to go (ou come) up; (valise, paquet) to take (ou bring) up; (étagère) to put up; (tente, échafaudage) to put up; (machine) to assemble; (Cinéma) to edit; (Théâtre) to put on, stage; (société etc) to set up ▷ vi to go (ou come) up; (prix, niveau, température) to go up, rise; (passager) to get on; ~ **à cheval** (faire du cheval) to ride (a horse); ~ **sur** to climb up onto; ~

sur ou **à un arbre/une échelle** to climb (up) a tree/ladder; **se monter à** (*frais etc*) to add up to, come to

montgolfière [mɔ̃gɔlfjɛʀ] *nf* hot-air balloon

montre [mɔ̃tʀ] *nf* watch; **contre la –** (*Sport*) against the clock

Montréal [mɔ̃ʀeal] *n* Montreal

montrer [mɔ̃tʀe] *vt* to show; **~ qch à qn** to show sb sth; **pouvez-vous me ~ où c'est?** can you show me where it is?

monture [mɔ̃tyʀ] *nf* (*cheval*) mount; (*de lunettes*) frame; (*d'une bague*) setting

monument [mɔnymã] *nm* monument; **monument aux morts** war memorial

moquer [mɔke]: **se moquer de** *vt* to make fun of, laugh at; (*fam: se désintéresser de*) not to care about; (*tromper*): **se ~ de qn** to take sb for a ride

moquette [mɔkɛt] *nf* fitted carpet

moqueur, -euse [mɔkœʀ, øz] *adj* mocking

moral, e, -aux [mɔʀal, o] *adj* moral ▷ *nm* morale; **avoir le – (fam)** to be in good spirits; **avoir le – à zéro** (*fam*) to be really down; **morale** *nf* (*mœurs*) morals *pl*; (*valeurs*) moral standards *pl*, morality; (*d'une fable etc*) moral; **faire la morale à** to lecture, preach at; **moralité** *nf* morality; (*de fable*) moral

morceau, x [mɔʀso] *nm* piece, bit; (*d'une œuvre*) passage, extract; (*Mus*) piece; (*Culin: de viande*) cut; (*de sucre*) lump; **mettre en ~x** to pull to pieces ou bits; **manger un ~** to have a bite (to eat)

morceler [mɔʀsəle] *vt* to break up, divide up

mordant, e [mɔʀdɑ̃, ɑ̃t] *adj* (*ton, remarque*) scathing, cutting; (*ironie, froid*) biting ▷ *nm* (*style*) bite, punch

mordiller [mɔʀdije] *vt* to nibble at, chew at

mordre [mɔʀdʀ] *vt* to bite ▷ *vi* (*poisson*) to bite; **~ sur** (*fig*) to go over into, overlap into; **~ à l'hameçon** to bite, rise to the bait

mordu, e [mɔʀdy] (*fam*) *nm/f* enthusiast; **un ~ de jazz** a jazz fanatic

morfondre [mɔʀfɔ̃dʀ]: **se morfondre** *vi* to mope

morgue [mɔʀg] *nf* (*arrogance*) haughtiness; (*lieu: de la police*) morgue; (: *à l'hôpital*) mortuary

morne [mɔʀn] *adj* dismal, dreary

morose [mɔʀoz] *adj* sullen, morose

mors [mɔʀ] *nm* bit

morse [mɔʀs] *nm* (*Zool*) walrus; (*Tél*) Morse (code)

morsure [mɔʀsyʀ] *nf* bite

mort¹ [mɔʀ] *nf* death

mort², e [mɔʀ, mɔʀt] *pp de* **mourir** ▷ *adj* dead ▷ *nm/f* (*défunt*) dead man ou woman; (*victime*): **il y a eu plusieurs ~s** several people were killed, there were several killed; **~ de peur/fatigue** frightened to death/dead tired

mortalité [mɔʀtalite] *nf* mortality, death rate

mortel, le [mɔʀtɛl] *adj* (*poison etc*) deadly, lethal; (*accident, blessure*) fatal; (*silence, ennemi*) deadly; (*péché*) mortal; (*fam: ennuyeux*) deadly boring

mort-né, e [mɔʀne] *adj* (*enfant*) stillborn

mortuaire [mɔʀtɥɛʀ] *adj*: **avis ~** death announcement

morue [mɔʀy] *nf* (*Zool*) cod *inv*

mosaïque [mɔzaik] *nf* mosaic

Moscou [mɔsku] *n* Moscow

mosquée [mɔske] *nf* mosque

mot [mo] *nm* word; (*message*) line, note; **~ à ~** word for word; **mot de passe** password; **mots croisés** crossword (puzzle) *sg*

motard [mɔtaʀ] *nm* biker; (*policier*) motorcycle cop

motel [mɔtɛl] *nm* motel

moteur, -trice [mɔtœʀ, tʀis] *adj* (*Anat, Physiol*) motor; (*Tech*) driving; (*Auto*): **à 4 roues motrices** 4-wheel drive ▷ *nm* engine, motor; **à ~** power-driven, motor *cpd*; **moteur de recherche** search engine

motif [mɔtif] *nm* (*cause*) motive;

(décoratif) design, pattern, motif; **sans ~** groundless

motivation [mɔtivasjɔ̃] nf motivation

motiver [mɔtive] vt to motivate; (justifier) to justify, account for

moto [moto] nf (motor)bike; **motocycliste** nm/f motorcyclist

motorisé, e [mɔtɔrize] adj (personne) having transport ou a car

motrice [mɔtris] adj voir **moteur**

motte [mɔt] nf: **~ de terre** lump of earth, clod (of earth); **motte de beurre** lump of butter

mou (mol), molle [mu, mɔl] adj soft; (personne) lethargic; (protestations) weak ▷ nm: **avoir du mou** to be slack

mouche [muʃ] nf fly

moucher [muʃe]: **se moucher** vi to blow one's nose

moucheron [muʃrɔ̃] nm midge

mouchoir [muʃwar] nm handkerchief, hanky; **mouchoir en papier** tissue, paper hanky

moudre [mudr] vt to grind

moue [mu] nf pout; **faire la ~** to pout; (fig) to pull a face

mouette [mwet] nf (sea)gull

moufle [mufl] nf (gant) mitt(en)

mouillé, e [muje] adj wet

mouiller [muje] vt (humecter) to wet, moisten; (tremper): **~ qn/qch** to make sb/sth wet ▷ vi (Navig) to lie ou be at anchor; **se mouiller** to get wet; (fam: prendre des risques) to commit o.s.

moulant, e [mulɑ̃, ɑ̃t] adj figure-hugging

moule [mul] nf mussel ▷ nm (Culin) mould; **moule à gâteaux** nm cake tin (BRIT) ou pan (US)

mouler [mule] vt (suj: vêtement) to hug, fit closely round

moulin [mulɛ̃] nm mill; **moulin à café** coffee mill; **moulin à eau** watermill; **moulin à légumes** (vegetable) shredder; **moulin à paroles** (fig) chatterbox; **moulin à poivre** pepper mill; **moulin à vent** windmill

moulinet [mulinɛ] nm (de canne à

pêche) reel; (mouvement): **faire des ~s avec qch** to whirl sth around

moulinette® [mulinɛt] nf (vegetable) shredder

moulu, e [muly] pp de **moudre**

mourant, e [murɑ̃, ɑ̃t] adj dying

mourir [murir] vi to die; (civilisation) to die out; **~ de froid/faim** to die of exposure/hunger; **~ de faim/d'ennui** (fig) to be starving/be bored to death; **~ d'envie de faire** to be dying to do

mousse [mus] nf (Bot) moss; (de savon) lather; (écume: sur eau, bière) froth, foam; (Culin) mousse ▷ nm (Navig) ship's boy; **mousse à raser** shaving foam

mousseline [muslin] nf muslin; **pommes ~** mashed potatoes

mousser [muse] vi (bière, détergent) to foam; (savon) to lather; **mousseux, -euse** adj frothy ▷ nm: **(vin) mousseux** sparkling wine

mousson [musɔ̃] nf monsoon

moustache [mustaʃ] nf moustache; **moustaches** nfpl (du chat) whiskers pl; **moustachu, e** adj with a moustache

moustiquaire [mustikɛr] nf mosquito net

moustique [mustik] nm mosquito

moutarde [mutard] nf mustard

mouton [mutɔ̃] nm sheep inv; (peau) sheepskin; (Culin) mutton

mouvement [muvmɑ̃] nm movement; (fig: impulsion) gesture; **avoir un bon ~** to make a nice gesture; **en ~** in motion; on the move; **mouvementé, e** adj (vie, poursuite) eventful; (réunion) turbulent

mouvoir [muvwar]: **se mouvoir** vi to move

moyen, ne [mwajɛ̃, jɛn] adj average; (tailles, prix) medium; (de grandeur moyenne) medium-sized ▷ nm (façon) means sg, way; **moyens** nmpl (capacités) means; **très ~** (résultats) pretty poor; **je n'en ai pas les ~s** I can't afford it; **au ~ de** by means of; **par tous les ~s** by every possible means, every possible way; **par ses propres ~s** all by oneself; **moyen âge** Middle Ages pl; **moyen de transport** means of transport

moyennant [mwajɛnɑ̃] prép (somme) for; (service, conditions) in return for; (travail, effort) with

moyenne [mwajɛn] nf average; (Math) mean; (Scol) pass mark; **en ~ on** (an) average; **moyenne d'âge** average age

Moyen-Orient [mwajɛnɔʀjɑ̃] nm: **le ~** the Middle East

moyeu, x [mwajø] nm hub

MST sigle f (= maladie sexuellement transmissible) = STD

mû, mue [my] pp de **mouvoir**

muer [mɥe] vi (oiseau, mammifère) to moult; (serpent) to slough; (jeune garçon): **il mue** his voice is breaking

muet, te [mɥɛ, mɥɛt] adj dumb; (fig): **~ d'admiration** etc speechless with admiration etc; (Cinéma) silent ▷ nm/f mute

mufle [myfl] nm muzzle; (fam: goujat) boor

mugir [myʒiʀ] vi (taureau) to bellow; (vache) to low; (fig) to howl

muguet [mygɛ] nm lily of the valley

mule [myl] nf (Zool) (she-)mule

mulet [mylɛ] nm (Zool) (he-)mule

multinationale [myltinasjɔnal] nf multinational

multiple [myltipl] adj multiple; numerous; (varié) many, manifold; **multiplication** nf multiplication; **multiplier** vt to multiply; **se multiplier** vi to multiply

municipal, e, -aux [mynisipal, o] adj municipal; (élections, stade) municipal; (conseil) town cpd; **piscine/bibliothèque ~e** public swimming pool/library; **municipalité** (ville) municipality; (conseil) town council

munir [myniʀ] vt: **~ qch de** to equip sth with; **se ~ de** to arm o.s. with

munitions [mynisjɔ̃] nfpl ammunition sg

mur [myʀ] nm wall; **mur du son** sound barrier

mûr, e [myʀ] adj ripe; (personne) mature

muraille [myʀaj] nf (high) wall

mural, e, -aux [myʀal, o] adj wall cpd; (art) mural

mûre [myʀ] nf blackberry

muret [myʀɛ] nm low wall

mûrir [myʀiʀ] vi (fruit, blé) to ripen; (abcès) to come to a head; (fig: idée, personne) to mature ▷ vt (projet) to nurture; (personne) to (make) mature

murmure [myʀmyʀ] nm murmur; **murmurer** vi to murmur

muscade [myskad] nf (aussi: **noix (de) ~**) nutmeg

muscat [myska] nm (raisins) muscat grape; (vin) muscatel (wine)

muscle [myskl] nm muscle; **musclé, e** adj muscular; (fig) strong-arm

museau, x [myzo] nm muzzle; (Culin) brawn

musée [myze] nm museum; (de peinture) art gallery

museler [myz(ə)le] vt to muzzle; **muselière** nf muzzle

musette [myzɛt] nf (sac) lunchbag

musical, e, -aux [myzikal, o] adj musical

music-hall [myzikol] nm (salle) variety theatre; (genre) variety

musicien, ne [myzisjɛ̃, jɛn] adj musical ▷ nm/f musician

musique [myzik] nf music

◾ FÊTE DE LA MUSIQUE

- The **Fête de la Musique** is a music
- festival which takes place every year
- on 21 June. Throughout France, local
- musicians perform free of charge in
- parks, streets and squares.

musulman, e [myzylmɑ̃, an] adj, nm/f Moslem, Muslim

mutation [mytasjɔ̃] nf (Admin) transfer

muter [myte] vt to transfer, move

mutilé, e [mytile] nm/f disabled

person (through loss of limbs)

mutiler [mytile] vt to mutilate, maim

mutin, e [mytɛ̃, in] adj (air, ton) mischievous, impish ▷ nm/f (Mil, Navig) mutineer; **mutinerie** nf mutiny

mutisme [mytism] nm silence

mutuel, le [mytɥɛl] adj mutual; **mutuelle** nf voluntary insurance premiums for back-up health cover

myope [mjɔp] adj short-sighted

myosotis [mjɔzɔtis] nm forget-me-not

myrtille [miʁtij] nf bilberry

mystère [mistɛʁ] nm mystery; **mystérieux, -euse** adj mysterious

mystifier [mistifje] vt to fool

mythe [mit] nm myth

mythologie [mitɔlɔʒi] nf mythology

n

n' [n] adv voir **ne**

nacre [nakʁ] nf mother of pearl

nage [naʒ] nf swimming; (manière) style of swimming, stroke; **traverser/ s'éloigner à la ~** to swim across/away; **en ~** bathed in sweat; **nageoire** nf fin; **nager** vi to swim; **nageur, -euse** nm/f swimmer

naïf, -ïve [naif, naiv] adj naïve

nain, e [nɛ̃, nɛn] nm/f dwarf

naissance [nɛsɑ̃s] nf birth; **donner ~ à** to give birth to; (fig) to give rise to; **lieu de ~** place of birth

naître [nɛtʁ] vi to be born; (fig): **~ de** to arise from, be born out of; **il est né en 1960** he was born in 1960; **faire ~** (fig) to give rise to, arouse

naïveté [naivte] nf naïvety

nana [nana] (fam) nf (fille) chick, bird (BRIT)

nappe [nap] nf tablecloth; (de pétrole, gaz) layer; **napperon** nm table-mat

naquit etc [naki] vb voir **naître**

narguer [naʁge] vt to taunt

narine [naʀin] nf nostril

natal, e [natal] adj native; **natalité** nf birth rate

natation [natasjɔ̃] nf swimming

natif, -ive [natif, iv] adj native

nation [nasjɔ̃] nf nation; **national, e, -aux** adj national; **nationale** nf: **(route) nationale** ≈ A road (BRIT), ≈ state highway (US); **nationaliser** vt to nationalize; **nationalisme** nm nationalism; **nationalité** nf nationality

natte [nat] nf (cheveux) plait; (tapis) mat

naturaliser [natyralize] vt to naturalize

nature [natyʀ] nf nature ▷ adj, adv (Culin) plain, without seasoning or sweetening; (café, thé) black, without sugar; (yaourt) natural; **payer en ~** to pay in kind; **nature morte** still life; **naturel, le** adj (gén, aussi enfant) natural ▷ nm (absence d'affectation) naturalness; (caractère) disposition, nature; **naturellement** adv naturally; (bien sûr) of course

naufrage [nofʀaʒ] nm (ship)wreck; **faire ~** to be shipwrecked

nausée [noze] nf nausea; **avoir la ~** to feel sick

nautique [notik] adj nautical, water cpd; **sports ~s** water sports

naval, e [naval] adj naval; (industrie) shipbuilding

navet [navɛ] nm turnip; (péj: film) rubbishy film

navette [navɛt] nf shuttle; **faire la ~ (entre)** to go to and fro ou shuttle (between)

navigateur [navigatœʀ] nm (Navig) seafarer; (Inform) browser

navigation [navigasjɔ̃] nf navigation, sailing

naviguer [navige] vi to navigate, sail; **~ sur Internet** to browse the Internet

navire [naviʀ] nm ship

navrer [navʀe] vt to upset, distress; **je suis navré** I'm so sorry

ne, n' [n(ə)] adv voir **pas**; **plus**; **jamais** etc; (sans valeur négative: non traduit): **c'est plus loin que je ne le croyais** it's further than I thought

né, e [ne] pp (voir naître): **né en 1960** born in 1960; **née Scott** née Scott

néanmoins [neãmwɛ̃] adv nevertheless

néant [neã] nm nothingness; **réduire à ~** to bring to nought; (espoir) to dash

nécessaire [neseseʀ] adj necessary ▷ nm necessary; (sac) kit; **je vais faire le ~** I'll see to it; **nécessaire de couture** sewing kit; **nécessaire de toilette** toilet bag; **nécessité** nf necessity; **nécessiter** vt to require

nectar [nɛktaʀ] nm nectar

néerlandais, e [neɛʀlɑ̃dɛ, ɛz] adj Dutch

nef [nɛf] nf (d'église) nave

néfaste [nefast] adj (nuisible) harmful; (funeste) ill-fated

négatif, -ive [negatif, iv] adj negative ▷ nm (Photo) negative

négligé, e [negliʒe] adj (en désordre) slovenly ▷ nm (tenue) negligee

négligeable [negliʒabl] adj negligible

négligent, e [negliʒã, ãt] adj careless, negligent

négliger [negliʒe] vt (tenue) to be careless about; (avis, précautions) to disregard; (épouse, jardin) to neglect; **~ de faire** to fail to do, not bother to do

négociant, e [negɔsjã, jãt] nm/f merchant

négociation [negɔsjasjɔ̃] nf negotiation

négocier [negɔsje] vi, vt to negotiate

nègre [nɛgʀ] nm (péj) (écrivain) ghost (writer)

neige [nɛʒ] nf snow; **neiger** vi to snow

nénuphar [nenyfaʀ] nm water-lily

néon [neɔ̃] nm neon

néo-zélandais, e [neozelɑ̃dɛ, ɛz] adj New Zealand cpd ▷ nm/f: **Néo-Zélandais, e** New Zealander

Népal [nepal] nm: **le ~** Nepal

nerf [nɛʀ] nm nerve; **être sur les ~s**

to be all keyed up; **nerveux, -euse**
adj nervous; (irritable) touchy, nervy;
(voiture) nippy, responsive; **nervosité**
nf excitability, tenseness; (irritabilité
passagère) irritability, nervness

n'est-ce pas? [nɛspɑ] adv isn't it?,
won't you? etc, selon le verbe qui précède

Net [nɛt] nm (Internet): **le ~** the Net

net, nette [nɛt] adj (sans équivoque,
distinct) clear; (évident: amélioration,
différence) marked, distinct; (Comm: prix, salaire) net
▷ adv (refuser) flatly ▷ nm: **mettre au ~**
to copy out; **s'arrêter ~** to stop dead;
nettement adv clearly, distinctly;
(incontestablement) decidedly; **netteté**
nf clearness

nettoyage [netwajaʒ] nm cleaning;
nettoyage à sec dry cleaning

nettoyer [netwaje] vt to clean

neuf¹ [nœf] num nine

neuf², neuve [nœf, nœv] adj new;
remettre à ~ to do up (as good as new),
refurbish; **quoi de ~?** what's new?

neutre [nøtr] adj neutral; (Ling) neuter

neuve [nœv] adj voir **neuf²**

neuvième [nœvjɛm] num ninth

neveu, x [n(ə)vø] nm nephew

New York [njujɔrk] n New York

nez [ne] nm nose; **~ à ~ avec** face to face
with; **avoir du ~** to have flair

ni [ni] conj: **ni ... ni** neither ... nor; **je
n'aime ni les lentilles ni les épinards**
I like neither lentils nor spinach; **il n'a
dit ni oui ni non** he didn't say either yes
or no; **elles ne sont venues ni l'une
ni l'autre** neither of them came; **il n'a
rien vu ni entendu** he didn't see or
hear anything

niche [niʃ] nf (du chien) kennel; (de mur)
recess, niche; **nicher** vi to nest

nid [ni] nm nest; **nid de poule** pothole

nièce [njɛs] nf niece

nier [nje] vt to deny

Nil [nil] nm: **le ~** the Nile

n'importe [nɛ̃pɔrt] adv: **n'importe
qui/quoi/où** anybody/anything/
anywhere; **n'importe quand** any time;

n'importe quel/quelle any; **n'importe
lequel/laquelle** any (one); **n'importe
comment** carelessly

niveau, x [nivo] nm level; (des élèves,
études) standard; **niveau de vie**
standard of living

niveler [niv(ə)le] vt to level

noble [nɔbl] adj noble; **noblesse** nf
nobility; (d'une action etc) nobleness

noce [nɔs] nf wedding; (gens) wedding
party (ou guests pl); **faire la ~** (fam)
to go on a binge; **noces d'argent/d'or/de
diamant** silver/golden/diamond
wedding (anniversary)

nocif, -ive [nɔsif, iv] adj harmful

nocturne [nɔktyrn] adj nocturnal ▷ nf
late-night opening

Noël [nɔɛl] nm Christmas

nœud [nø] nm knot; (ruban) bow; **nœud
papillon** bow tie

noir, e [nwar] adj black; (obscur, sombre)
dark ▷ nm/f black man/woman ▷ nm:
dans le ~ in the dark; **travail au ~**
moonlighting; **travailler au ~** to work
on the side; **noircir** vt, vi to blacken;
noire nf (Mus) crotchet (BRIT), quarter
note (US)

noisette [nwazɛt] nf hazelnut

noix [nwa] nf walnut; (Culin): **une ~ de
beurre** a knob of butter; **à la ~** (fam)
worthless; **noix de cajou** cashew nut;
noix de coco coconut; **noix muscade**
nutmeg

nom [nɔ̃] nm name; (Ling) noun; **nom
de famille** surname; **nom de jeune
fille** maiden name

nomade [nɔmad] nm/f nomad

nombre [nɔ̃br] nm number; **venir en
~** to come in large numbers; **depuis ~
d'années** for many years; **au ~ de
mes amis** among my friends;
nombreux, -euse adj many,
numerous; (avec nom sg: foule etc)
large; **peu nombreux** few; **de
nombreux cas** many cases

nombril [nɔ̃bri(l)] nm navel

nommer [nɔme] vt to name; (élire) to
appoint, nominate; **se nommer: il se**

nomme Pascal his name's Pascal, he's called Pascal

non [nɔ̃] adv (réponse) no; (avec sans, seulement) not; **~ (pas) que** not that; **moi ~ plus** neither do I, I don't either; **c'est bon ~** (exprimant le doute) it's good, isn't it?; **je pense que ~** I don't think so

non alcoolisé, e [nɔ̃alkɔlize] adj non alcoholic

nonchalant, e [nɔ̃ʃalɑ̃, ɑ̃t] adj nonchalant

non-fumeur, -euse [nɔ̃fymœʀ, øz] nm/f non-smoker

non-sens [nɔ̃sɑ̃s] nm absurdity

nord [nɔʀ] nm North ▷ adj northern; north; **au ~** (situation) in the north; (direction) to the north; **au ~ de** (to the north of; **nord-africain, e** adj North-African ▷ nm/f: **Nord-Africain, e** North African; **nord-est** nm North-East; **nord-ouest** nm North-West

normal, e, -aux [nɔʀmal, o] adj normal; **c'est tout à fait ~** it's perfectly natural; **vous trouvez ça ~?** does it seem right to you?; **normale** nf: **la normale** the norm, the average; **normalement** adv (en général) normally

normand, e [nɔʀmɑ̃, ɑ̃d] adj of Normandy ▷ nm/f: **N~, e** (de Normandie) Norman

Normandie [nɔʀmɑ̃di] nf Normandy

norme [nɔʀm] nf norm, (Tech) standard

Norvège [nɔʀvɛʒ] nf Norway; **norvégien, ne** adj Norwegian ▷ nm/f: **Norvégien, ne** Norwegian ▷ nm (Ling) Norwegian

nos [no] adj voir **notre**

nostalgie [nɔstalʒi] nf nostalgia; **nostalgique** adj nostalgic

notable [nɔtabl] adj (fait) notable, noteworthy; (marqué) noticeable, marked ▷ nm prominent citizen

notaire [nɔtɛʀ] nm solicitor

notamment [nɔtamɑ̃] adv in particular, among others

note [nɔt] nf (écrite, Mus) note; (Scol) mark (BRIT), grade; (facture) bill; **note de service** memorandum

noter [nɔte] vt (écrire) to write down; (remarquer) to note, notice; (devoir) to mark, grade

notice [nɔtis] nf summary, short article; (brochure) leaflet, instruction book

notifier [nɔtifje] vt: **~ qch à qn** to notify sb of sth, notify sth to sb

notion [nosjɔ̃] nf notion, idea

notoire [nɔtwaʀ] adj widely known; (en mal) notorious

notre [nɔtʀ] (pl **nos**) adj our

nôtre [notʀ] pron: **le ~, la ~, les ~s** ▷ adj ours; **les ~s** ours; (alliés etc) our own people; **soyez des ~s** join us

nouer [nwe] vt to tie, knot; (fig: alliance etc) to strike up

noueux, -euse [nwø, øz] adj gnarled

nourrice [nuʀis] nf (gardienne) child-minder

nourrir [nuʀiʀ] vt to feed; (fig: espoir) to harbour, nurse; **nourrissant, e** adj nourishing, nutritious; **nourrisson** nm (unweaned) infant; **nourriture** nf food

nous [nu] pron (sujet) we; (objet) us; **nous-mêmes** pron ourselves

nouveau (nouvel), -elle, x [nuvo, nuvɛl] adj new ▷ nm: **y a-t-il du nouveau?** is there anything new on this? ▷ nm/f new pupil (ou employee); **de nouveau, à nouveau** again; **nouveau venu, nouvelle venue** newcomer; **nouveaux mariés** newly-weds; **nouveau-né, e** nm/f newborn baby; **nouveauté** nf novelty; (objet) new thing ou article

nouvel [nuvɛl] adj voir **nouveau**; **Nouvel An** New Year

nouvelle [nuvɛl] adj voir **nouveau** ▷ nf (piece of) news sg; (Littérature) short story; **les ~s** (Presse, TV) the news; **je suis sans ~s de lui** I haven't heard from him; **Nouvelle-Calédonie** nf New Caledonia; **Nouvelle-Zélande** nf New Zealand

novembre [nɔvɑ̃br] *nm* November

noyade [nwajad] *nf* drowning *no pl*

noyau, x [nwajo] *nm* (*de fruit*) stone;
(*Bio, Physique*) nucleus; (*fig: centre*) core

noyer [nwaje] *nm* walnut (tree); (*bois*)
walnut ▷ *vt* to drown; (*moteur*) to flood;
se noyer *vi* to be drowned; drown;
(*suicide*) to drown o.s.

nu, e [ny] *adj* naked; (*membres*) naked,
bare; (*pieds, mains, chambre, fil électrique*)
bare ▷ *nm* (*Art*) nude; **tout nu** stark
naked; **se mettre nu** to strip

nuage [nɥaʒ] *nm* cloud; **nuageux,
-euse** *adj* cloudy

nuance [nɥɑ̃s] *nf* (*de couleur, sens*)
shade; **il y a une ~ (entre)** there's a
slight difference (between); **nuancer**
vt (*opinion*) to bring some reservations
ou qualifications to

nucléaire [nykleɛr] *adj* nuclear ▷ *nm*:
le ~ nuclear energy

nudiste [nydist] *nm/f* nudist

nuée [nɥe] *nf*: **une ~ de** a cloud *ou* host
ou swarm of

nuire [nɥir] *vi* to be harmful; **~ à** to
harm, do damage to; **nuisible** *adj*
harmful; **animal nuisible** pest

nuit [nɥi] *nf* night; **il fait ~** it's dark;
cette ~ (*hier*) last night; (*aujourd'hui*)
tonight; **de ~** (*vol, service*) night *cpd*;
nuit blanche sleepless night

nul, nulle [nyl] *adj* (*aucun*) no; (*minime*)
nil, non-existent; (*non valable*) null; (*péj*):
être ~ (en) to be useless *ou* hopeless
(at) ▷ *pron* none, no one; **match ou
résultat ~** draw; **~le part** nowhere;
nullement *adv* by no means

numérique [nymerik] *adj* numerical;
(*affichage, son, télévision*) digital

numéro [nymero] *nm* number;
(*spectacle*) act, turn; (*Presse*) issue,
number; **numéro de téléphone**
(tele)phone number; **numéro vert**
≈ freefone® number (*BRIT*), ≈ toll-free
number (*US*); **numéroter** *vt* to number

nuque [nyk] *nf* nape of the neck

nu-tête [nytɛt] *adj inv, adv* bareheaded

nutritif, -ive [nytritif, iv] *adj* (*besoins,
valeur*) nutritional; (*nourrissant*)
nutritious

nylon [nilɔ̃] *nm* nylon

O

oasis [ɔazis] *nf* oasis
obéir [ɔbeir] *vi* to obey; **~ à** to obey;
  obéissance *nf* obedience;
  obéissant, e *adj* obedient
obèse [ɔbɛz] *adj* obese; **obésité** *nf*
  obesity
objecter [ɔbʒɛkte] *vt*: **~ que** to object
  that; **objecteur** *nm*: **objecteur de
  conscience** conscientious objector
objectif, -ive [ɔbʒɛktif, iv] *adj*
  objective ▷ *nm* objective; (*Photo*) lens
  sg, objective
objection [ɔbʒɛksjɔ̃] *nf* objection
objectivité [ɔbʒɛktivite] *nf* objectivity
objet [ɔbʒɛ] *nm* object; (*d'une discussion,
  recherche*) subject; **être** *ou* **faire l'~
  de** (*discussion*) to be the subject of;
  (*soins*) to be given *ou* shown; **sans ~**
  purposeless; (*craintes*) groundless;
  (bureau des) ~s trouvés lost property
  sg (BRIT), lost-and-found *sg* (US); **objet
  d'art** objet d'art; **objets de valeur**
  valuables; **objets personnels** personal
  items

obligation [ɔbligasjɔ̃] *nf* obligation;
  (*Comm*) bond, debenture; **obligatoire**
  adj compulsory, obligatory;
  obligatoirement *adv* necessarily;
  (*fam: sans aucun doute*) inevitably
obliger [ɔbliʒe] *vt* (*contraindre*): **~ qn à
  faire** to force *ou* oblige sb to do; **je suis
  bien obligé (de le faire)** I have to (do it)
oblique [ɔblik] *adj* oblique; **en ~**
  diagonally
oblitérer [ɔblitere] *vt* (*timbre-poste*)
  to cancel
obnubiler [ɔbnybile] *vt* to obsess
obscène [ɔpsɛn] *adj* obscene
obscur, e [ɔpskyr] *adj* dark; (*méconnu*)
  obscure; **obscurcir** *vt* to darken; (*fig*)
  to obscure; **s'obscurcir** *vi* to grow
  dark; **obscurité** *nf* darkness; **dans
  l'obscurité** in the dark, in darkness
obsédé, e [ɔpsede] *nm/f*: **un ~ de jazz** a
  jazz fanatic; **obsédé sexuel** sex maniac
obséder [ɔpsede] *vt* to obsess, haunt
obsèques [ɔpsɛk] *nfpl* funeral *sg*
observateur, -trice [ɔpsɛrvatœr,
  tris] *adj* observant, perceptive ▷ *nm/f*
  observer
observation [ɔpsɛrvasjɔ̃] *nf*
  observation; (*d'un règlement etc*)
  observance; (*reproche*) reproof; **être en
  ~** (*Méd*) to be under observation
observatoire [ɔpsɛrvatwar] *nm*
  observatory
observer [ɔpsɛrve] *vt* (*regarder*) to
  observe, watch; (*scientifiquement; aussi
  règlement etc*) to observe; (*surveiller*) to
  watch; (*remarquer*) to observe, notice;
  faire ~ qch à qn (*dire*) to point out
  sth to sb
obsession [ɔpsesjɔ̃] *nf* obsession
obstacle [ɔpstakl] *nm* obstacle;
  (*Équitation*) jump, hurdle; **faire ~ à**
  (*lumière*) to block out; (*projet*) to hinder, put obstacles in
  the path of
obstiné, e [ɔpstine] *adj* obstinate
obstiner [ɔpstine] : **s'obstiner** *vi* to
  insist, dig one's heels in; **s'~ à faire** to
  persist (obstinately) in doing
obstruer [ɔpstrye] *vt* to block,

obstruct

obtenir [ɔptǝniʀ] vt to obtain, get; (résultat) to achieve, obtain; **~ de pouvoir faire** to obtain permission to do

obturateur [ɔptyʀatœʀ] nm (Photo) shutter

obus [ɔby] nm shell

occasion [ɔkazjɔ̃] nf (aubaine, possibilité) opportunity; (circonstance) occasion; (Comm: article non neuf) secondhand buy; (acquisition avantageuse) bargain; **à plusieurs ~s** on several occasions; **à l'~** sometimes, on occasions; **d'~** secondhand; **occasionnel, le** adj (non régulier) occasional

occasionner [ɔkazjɔne] vt to cause

occident [ɔksidɑ̃] nm: **l'O~** the West; **occidental, e, ~aux** adj western; (Pol) Western ▷ nm/f Westerner

occupation [ɔkypasjɔ̃] nf occupation

occupé, e [ɔkype] adj (personne) busy; (place, sièges) taken; (toilettes) engaged; (Mil, Pol) occupied; **la ligne est ~e** the line's engaged (BRIT) ou busy (US)

occuper [ɔkype] vt to occupy; (poste) to hold; **s'occuper de** (être responsable de) to be in charge of; (se charger de: affaire) to take charge of, deal with; (: clients etc) to attend to; **s'~ (à qch)** to occupy o.s. ou keep o.s. busy (with sth)

occurrence [ɔkyʀɑ̃s] nf: **en l'~** in this case

océan [ɔseɑ̃] nm ocean

octet [ɔktɛ] nm byte

octobre [ɔktɔbʀ] nm October

oculiste [ɔkylist] nm/f eye specialist

odeur [ɔdœʀ] nf smell

odieux, -euse [ɔdjø, jøz] adj hateful

odorant, e [ɔdɔʀɑ̃, ɑ̃t] adj sweet-smelling, fragrant

odorat [ɔdɔʀa] nm (sense of) smell

œil [œj] (pl yeux) nm: **avoir un ~ au beurre noir** ou **poché** to have a black eye; **à l'~** (fam) for free; **à l'~ nu** with the naked eye; **ouvrir l'~** (fig) to keep one's eyes open ou an eye out; **fermer**

les yeux (sur) (fig) to turn a blind eye (to); **les yeux fermés** (aussi fig) with one's eyes shut

œillères [œjɛʀ] nfpl blinkers (BRIT), blinders (US)

œillet [œjɛ] nm (Bot) carnation

œuf [œf, pl œ] nm egg; **œuf à la coque** boiled egg; **œuf au plat** fried egg; **œuf dur** hard-boiled egg; **œuf de Pâques** Easter egg; **œufs brouillés** scrambled eggs

œuvre [œvʀ] nf (tâche) task, undertaking; (livre, tableau etc) work; (ensemble de la production artistique) works pl ▷ nm (Constr): **le gros ~** the shell; **mettre en ~** (moyens) to make use of; **œuvre de bienfaisance** charity; **œuvre d'art** work of art

offense [ɔfɑ̃s] nf insult; **offenser** vt to offend, hurt; **s'offenser de qch** to take offence (BRIT) ou offense (US) at sth

offert, e [ɔfɛʀ, ɛʀt] pp de **offrir**

office [ɔfis] nm (agence) bureau, agency; (Rel) service ▷ nm ou nf (pièce) pantry; **faire ~ de** to act as; **d'~** automatically; **office du tourisme** tourist bureau

officiel, le [ɔfisjɛl] adj, nm/f official

officier [ɔfisje] nm officer

officieux, -euse [ɔfisjø, jøz] adj unofficial

offrande [ɔfʀɑ̃d] nf offering

offre [ɔfʀ] nf offer; (aux enchères) bid; (Admin: soumission) tender; (Écon): **l'~ et la demande** supply and demand; **"~s d'emploi"** "situations vacant"; offre d'emploi job advertised; **offre publique d'achat** takeover bid

offrir [ɔfʀiʀ] vt: **~ (à qn)** to offer (to sb); (faire cadeau de) to give (to sb); **s'offrir** vt (vacances, voiture) to treat o.s. to; **~ (à qn) de faire qch** to offer to do sth (for sb); **~ à boire à qn** (chez soi) to offer sb a drink; **je vous offre un verre** I'll buy you a drink

OGM sigle m (= organisme génétiquement modifié) GMO

oie [wa] nf (Zool) goose

oignon [ɔɲɔ̃] nm onion; (de tulipe)

etc) bulb

oiseau, x [wazo] nm bird; **oiseau de proie** bird of prey

oisif, -ive [wazif, iv] adj idle

oléoduc [ɔleɔdyk] nm (oil) pipeline

olive [ɔliv] nf (Bot) olive; **olivier** nm olive (tree)

OLP sigle f (= Organisation de libération de la Palestine) PLO

olympique [ɔlɛ̃pik] adj Olympic

ombragé, e [ɔ̃braʒe] adj shaded, shady

ombre [ɔ̃bR] nf (espace non ensoleillé) shade; (ombre portée, tache) shadow; **à l'~** in the shade; **dans l'~** (fig) in the dark; **ombre à paupières** eyeshadow

omelette [ɔmlɛt] nf omelette; **omelette norvégienne** baked Alaska

omettre [ɔmɛtR] vt to omit, leave out

omoplate [ɔmɔplat] nf shoulder blade

MOT-CLÉ

on [ɔ̃] pron **1** (indéterminé) you, one; **on peut le faire ainsi** you ou one can do it like this, it can be done like this
2 (quelqu'un): **on les a attaqués** they were attacked; **on vous demande au téléphone** there's a phone call for you, you're wanted on the phone
3 (nous): **on va y aller demain** we're going tomorrow
4 (les gens) we: **autrefois, on croyait ...** they used to believe ...
5: on ne peut plus adv: **on ne peut plus stupide** as stupid as can be

oncle [ɔ̃kl] nm uncle

onctueux, -euse [ɔ̃ktɥø, øz] adj creamy, smooth

onde [ɔ̃d] nf wave; **~s courtes/moyennes** short/medium wave sg; **grandes ~s** long wave sg

ondée [ɔ̃de] nf shower

on-dit [ɔ̃di] nm inv rumour

onduler [ɔ̃dyle] vi to undulate; (cheveux) to wave

onéreux, -euse [ɔnerø, øz] adj costly

ongle [ɔ̃gl] nm nail

ont [ɔ̃] vb voir **avoir**

ONU sigle f (= Organisation des Nations Unies) UN

onze [ɔ̃z] num eleven; **onzième** num eleventh

OPA sigle f = **offre publique d'achat**

opaque [ɔpak] adj opaque

opéra [ɔpera] nm opera; (édifice) opera house

opérateur, -trice [ɔperatœr, tris] nm/f operator; **opérateur (de prise de vues)** cameraman

opération [ɔperasjɔ̃] nf operation; (Comm) dealing

opératoire [ɔperatwar] adj (choc etc) post-operative

opérer [ɔpere] vt (personne) to operate on; (faire, exécuter) to carry out, make ▷ vi (remède: faire effet) to act, work; (Méd) to operate; **s'opérer** vi (avoir lieu) to occur, take place; **se faire ~** to have an operation

opérette [ɔperɛt] nf operetta, light opera

opinion [ɔpinjɔ̃] nf opinion; **l'opinion (publique)** public opinion

opportun, e [ɔpɔrtœ̃, yn] adj timely, opportune; **opportuniste** nm/f opportunist

opposant, e [ɔpozɑ̃, ɑ̃t] nm/f opponent

opposé, e [ɔpoze] adj (direction) opposite; (faction) opposing; (opinions, intérêts) conflicting; (contre): **~ à** opposed to, against ▷ nm: **l'~** the other ou opposite side (ou direction); (contraire) the opposite; **à l'~** (fig) on the other hand; **à l'~ de** (fig) contrary to, unlike

opposer [ɔpoze] vt (personnes, équipes) to oppose; (couleurs) to contrast; **s'opposer** vi (équipes) to confront each other; (opinions) to conflict; (couleurs, styles) to contrast; **s'~ à** (interdire) to oppose; **~ qch à** (comme obstacle, défense) to set sth against; (comme objection) to put sth forward against

opposition [ɔpozisjɔ̃] nf opposition;
par ~ à as opposed to; **entrer en ~ avec**
to come into conflict with; **faire ~ à un
chèque** to stop a cheque

oppressant, e [ɔpresɑ̃, ɑ̃t] adj
oppressive

oppresser [ɔprese] vt to oppress;
oppression nf oppression

opprimer [ɔprime] vt to oppress

opter [ɔpte] vi: **~ pour** to opt for

opticien, ne [ɔptisjɛ̃, jɛn] nm/f
optician

optimisme [ɔptimism] nm optimism;
optimiste nm/f optimist ▷ adj
optimistic

option [ɔpsjɔ̃] nf option; **matière à ~**
(Scol) optional subject

optique [ɔptik] adj (nerf) optic;
(verres) optical ▷ nf (fig: manière de voir)
perspective

or [ɔʀ] nm gold ▷ conj now, but; **en or**
(objet) gold cpd; **une affaire en or** a
real bargain; **il croyait gagner et il a
perdu** he was sure he would win and
yet he lost

orage [ɔʀaʒ] nm (thunder)storm;
orageux, -euse adj stormy

oral, e, -aux [ɔʀal, o] adj, nm oral; **par
voie -e** (Méd) orally

orange [ɔʀɑ̃ʒ] nf orange ▷ adj inv
orange; **orangé, e** adj orangey,
orange-coloured; **orangeade** nf
orangeade; **oranger** nm orange tree

orateur [ɔʀatœʀ] nm speaker

orbite [ɔʀbit] nf (Anat) (eye-)socket;
(Physique) orbit

Orcades [ɔʀkad] nfpl: **les ~** the
Orkneys, the Orkney Islands

orchestre [ɔʀkɛstʀ] nm orchestra;
(de jazz) band; (places) stalls pl (BRIT),
orchestra (US)

orchidée [ɔʀkide] nf orchid

ordinaire [ɔʀdinɛʀ] adj ordinary;
(qualité) standard; (péj: commun)
common ▷ nm ordinary; (menus)
everyday fare ▷ nf (essence) ≈ two-star
(petrol) (BRIT), ≈ regular gas (US); **d'~**
usually, normally; **comme à l'~** as usual

ordinateur [ɔʀdinatœʀ] nm
computer; **ordinateur individuel
ou personnel** personal computer;
ordinateur portable laptop
(computer)

ordonnance [ɔʀdɔnɑ̃s] nf (Méd)
prescription; (Mil) orderly, batman
(BRIT); **pouvez-vous me faire une ~?**
can you write me a prescription?

ordonné, e [ɔʀdɔne] adj tidy, orderly

ordonner [ɔʀdɔne] vt (agencer) to
organize, arrange; (donner un ordre):
~ à qn de faire to order sb to do; (Rel)
to ordain; (Méd) to prescribe

ordre [ɔʀdʀ] nm order; (propreté et
soin) orderliness, tidiness; (nature)
d'~ pratique of a practical nature;
ordres nmpl (Rel) holy orders; **mettre
en ~** to tidy (up), put in order; **par
~ alphabétique/d'importance**
in alphabetical order/in order of
importance; **à l'~ de qn** payable to
sb; **être aux ~s de qn/sous les ~s de
qn** to be at sb's disposal, under sb's
command; **jusqu'à nouvel ~** until
further notice; **de premier ~** first-rate;
ordre du jour (d'une réunion) agenda;
à l'ordre du jour (fig) topical; **ordre
public** law and order

ordure [ɔʀdyʀ] nf filth no pl; **ordures**
nfpl (balayures, déchets) rubbish
sg, refuse sg; **ordures ménagères**
household refuse

oreille [ɔʀɛj] nf ear; **avoir de l'~** to have
a good ear (for music)

oreiller [ɔʀeje] nm pillow

oreillons [ɔʀejɔ̃] nmpl mumps sg

ores [ɔʀ]: **d'~ et déjà** adv already

orfèvrerie [ɔʀfɛvʀəʀi] nf goldsmith's
(ou silversmith's) trade; (ouvrage) gold
(ou silver) plate

organe [ɔʀgan] nm organ; (porte-parole)
representative, mouthpiece

organigramme [ɔʀganigʀam] nm
(tableau hiérarchique) organization
chart; (schéma) flow chart

organique [ɔʀganik] adj organic

organisateur, -trice [ɔʀganizatœʀ,

tris] *nm/f* organizer
organisation [ɔʀganizasjɔ̃] *nf*
organization; **Organisation des
Nations Unies** United Nations
(Organization)
organiser [ɔʀganize] *vt* to organize;
(mettre sur pied: service etc) to set up;
s'organiser to get organized
organisme [ɔʀganism] *nm (Bio)*
organism; *(corps, Admin)* body
organiste [ɔʀganist] *nm/f* organist
orgasme [ɔʀgasm] *nm* orgasm, climax
orge [ɔʀʒ] *nf* barley
orgue [ɔʀg] *nm* organ
orgueil [ɔʀgœj] *nm* pride; **orgueilleux,
-euse** *adj* proud
oriental, e, -aux [ɔʀjɑ̃tal, -o] *adj
(langue, produit)* oriental; *(frontière)*
eastern
orientation [ɔʀjɑ̃tasjɔ̃] *nf (de
recherches)* orientation; *(d'une maison
etc)* aspect; *(d'un journal)* leanings *pl*;
avoir le sens de l' ~ to have a (good)
sense of direction; **orientation
professionnelle** careers advisory
service
orienté, e [ɔʀjɑ̃te] *adj (fig: article,
journal)* slanted; **bien/mal ~**
(appartement) well/badly positioned; **~
au sud** facing south, with a southern
aspect
orienter [ɔʀjɑ̃te] *vt (tourner: antenne)*
to direct, turn; *(personne, recherches)*
to direct; *(fig: élève)* to orientate;
s'orienter *(se repérer)* to find one's
bearings; **s' ~ vers** *(fig)* to turn towards
origan [ɔʀigɑ̃] *nm* oregano
originaire [ɔʀiʒinɛʀ] *adj*: **être ~ de** to
be a native of
original, e, -aux [ɔʀiʒinal, o] *adj*
original; *(bizarre)* eccentric ▷ *nm/f*
eccentric ▷ *nm (document etc, Art)*
original
origine [ɔʀiʒin] *nf* origin; **origines** *nfpl
(d'une personne)* origins; **d' ~** *(pays)* of
origin; **d' ~ suédoise** of Swedish origin;
(pneus etc) original; **à l' ~** originally;
originel, le *adj* original

orme [ɔʀm] *nm* elm
ornement [ɔʀnəmɑ̃] *nm* ornament
orner [ɔʀne] *vt* to decorate, adorn
ornière [ɔʀnjɛʀ] *nf* rut
orphelin, e [ɔʀfəlɛ̃, in] *adj* orphan(ed)
▷ *nm/f* orphan; **orphelin de
mère/de père** motherless/fatherless;
orphelinat *nm* orphanage
orteil [ɔʀtɛj] *nm* toe; **gros ~** big toe
orthographe [ɔʀtɔgʀaf] *nf* spelling
ortie [ɔʀti] *nf* (stinging) nettle
os [ɔs] *nm* bone; **os à moelle**
marrowbone
osciller [ɔsile] *vi (au vent etc)* to rock;
(fig): **~ entre** to waver *ou* fluctuate
between
osé, e [oze] *adj* daring, bold
oseille [ozɛj] *nf* sorrel
oser [oze] *vi, vt* to dare; **~ faire** to dare
(to) do
osier [ozje] *nm* willow; **d' ~, en ~**
wicker(work)
osseux, -euse [ɔsø, øz] *adj* bony;
(tissu, maladie, greffe) bone *cpd*
otage [ɔtaʒ] *nm* hostage; **prendre qn
comme ~** to take sb hostage
OTAN *sigle f (= Organisation du traité de
l'Atlantique Nord)* NATO
otarie [ɔtaʀi] *nf* sea-lion
ôter [ote] *vt* to remove; *(soustraire)*
to take away; **~ qch à qn** to take sth
(away) from sb; **~ qch de** to remove
sth from
otite [ɔtit] *nf* ear infection
ou [u] *conj* or; **ou ... ou** either ... or; **ou
bien** or (else)

 MOT-CLÉ

où [u] *pron relatif* **1** *(position, situation)*
where, that *(souvent omis)*; **la chambre
où il était** the room (that) he was in,
the room where he was; **la ville où
je l'ai rencontré** the town where I
met him; **la pièce d'où il est sorti** the
room he came out of; **le village d'où
je viens** the village I come from; **les
villes par où il est passé** the towns he

went through

2 (temps, état) that (souvent omis); **le jour où il est parti** the day (that) he left; **au prix où c'est** at the price it is ⊳ adv **1** (interrogation) where; **où est-il/va-t-il?** where is he/is he going?; **par où?** which way?; **d'où vient que ...?** how come ...?

2 (position) where; **je sais où il est** I know where he is; **où que l'on aille** wherever you go

ouate ['wat] nf cotton wool (BRIT), cotton (US)

oubli [ubli] nm (acte): **l'~ de** forgetting; (trou de mémoire) lapse of memory; (négligence) omission, oversight; **tomber dans l'~** to sink into oblivion

oublier [ublije] vt to forget; (laisser quelque part: chapeau etc) to leave behind; (ne pas voir: erreurs etc) to miss; **j'ai oublié ma clé/mon passeport** I've forgotten my key/passport

ouest [wɛst] nm west ⊳ adj inv west; (région) western; **à l'~** in the west; (direction) (to the) west, westwards; **à l'~ de** (to the) west of

ouf ['uf] excl phew!

oui ['wi] adv yes

ouï-dire ['widiʀ]: **par ~** adv by hearsay

ouïe [wi] nf hearing; **ouïes** nfpl (de poisson) gills

ouragan [uʀaɡɑ̃] nm hurricane

ourlet [uʀlɛ] nm hem

ours [uʀs] nm bear; **ours blanc/brun** polar/brown bear; **ours (en peluche)** teddy (bear)

oursin [uʀsɛ̃] nm sea urchin

ourson [uʀsɔ̃] nm (bear-)cub

ouste [ust] excl hop it!

outil [uti] nm tool; **outiller** vt to equip

outrage [utʀaʒ] nm insult; **outrage à la pudeur** indecent conduct no pl

outrance [utʀɑ̃s]: **à ~** adv excessively, to excess

outre [utʀ] prép besides ⊳ adv: **passer ~ à** to disregard, take no notice of; **en ~** besides, moreover; **~ mesure** to excess;

(manger, boire) immoderately; **outre-Atlantique** adv across the Atlantic; **outre-mer** adv overseas

ouvert, e [uvɛʀ, ɛʀt] pp de **ouvrir** ⊳ adj open; (robinet, gaz etc) on; **ouvertement** adv openly; **ouverture** nf opening; (Mus) overture; **heures d'ouverture** (Comm) opening hours; **ouverture d'esprit** open-mindedness

ouvrable [uvʀabl] adj: **jour ~** working day, weekday

ouvrage [uvʀaʒ] nm (tâche, de tricot etc) work no pl; (texte, livre) work

ouvre-boîte(s) [uvʀəbwat] nm inv tin (BRIT) ou can opener

ouvre-bouteille(s) [uvʀəbutɛj] nm inv bottle-opener

ouvreuse [uvʀøz] nf usherette

ouvrier, -ière [uvʀije, ijɛʀ] nm/f worker ⊳ adj working-class; (conflit) industrial; (mouvement) labour cpd; **classe ouvrière** working class

ouvrir [uvʀiʀ] vt (gén) to open; (brèche, passage, Méd: abcès) to open up; (commencer l'exploitation de, créer) to open (up); (eau, électricité, chauffage, robinet) to turn on ⊳ vi to open; to open up; **s'ouvrir** vi to open; **s'~ à qn** to open one's heart to sb; **est-ce ouvert au public?** is it open to the public?; **quand est-ce que le musée est ouvert?** when is the museum open?; **à quelle heure ouvrez-vous?** what time do you open?; **~ l'appétit à qn** to whet sb's appetite

ovaire [ovɛʀ] nm ovary

ovale [ɔval] adj oval

OVNI [ɔvni] sigle m (= objet volant non identifié) UFO

oxyder [ɔkside]: **s'oxyder** vi to become oxidized

oxygène [ɔksiʒɛn] nm oxygen

oxygéné, e [ɔksiʒene] adj: **eau ~e** hydrogen peroxide

ozone [ozon] nf ozone; **la couche d'~** the ozone layer

P

brown/wholemeal (BRIT) ou wholewheat (US) bread; **pain d'épice** = gingerbread; **pain de mie** sandwich loaf; **pain grillé** toast

pair, e [pɛʀ] adj (nombre) even ▷ nm peer; **aller de ~** to go hand in hand ou together; **jeune fille au ~** au pair; **paire** nf pair

paisible [pezibl] adj peaceful, quiet

paix [pɛ] nf peace; **faire/avoir la ~** to make/have peace; **fiche-lui la ~!** (fam) leave him alone!

Pakistan [pakistɑ̃] nm: **le ~** Pakistan

palais [palɛ] nm palace; (Anat) palate

pâle [pal] adj pale; **bleu ~** pale blue

Palestine [palɛstin] nf: **la ~** Palestine

palette [palɛt] nf (de peintre) palette; (produits) range

pâleur [palœʀ] nf paleness

palier [palje] nm (d'escalier) landing; (fig) level, plateau; **par ~s** in stages

pâlir [paliʀ] vi to turn ou go pale; (couleur) to fade

pallier [palje] vt to offset, make up for

palme [palm] nf (de plongeur) flipper; **palmé, e** adj (pattes) webbed

palmier [palmje] nm palm tree; (gâteau) heart-shaped biscuit made of flaky pastry

pâlot, te [palo, ɔt] adj pale, peaky

palourde [paluʀd] nf clam

palper [palpe] vt to feel, finger

palpitant, e [palpitɑ̃, ɑ̃t] adj thrilling

palpiter [palpite] vi (cœur, pouls) to beat; (: plus fort) to pound, throb

paludisme [palydism] nm malaria

pamphlet [pɑ̃flɛ] nm lampoon, satirical tract

pamplemousse [pɑ̃pləmus] nm grapefruit

pan [pɑ̃] nm section, piece ▷ excl bang!

panache [panaʃ] nm plume; panache

panaché, e [panaʃe] adj: **glace ~e** mixed-flavour ice cream ▷ nm (bière) shandy

pancarte [pɑ̃kaʀt] nf sign, notice

pancréas [pɑ̃kʀeas] nm pancreas

---

pacifique [pasifik] adj peaceful ▷ nm: **le P~, l'océan P~** the Pacific (Ocean)

pack [pak] nm pack

pacotille [pakotij] nf cheap junk

PACS sigle m (= pacte civil de solidarité) contract of civil partnership; **pacser: se pacser** vi to sign a contract of civil partnership

pacte [pakt] nm pact, treaty

pagaille [pagaj] nf mess, shambles sg

page [paʒ] nf page ▷ nm page (boy); **à la ~** (fig) up-to-date; **page d'accueil** (Inform) home page; **page Web** (Inform) web page

paiement [pemɑ̃] nm payment

païen, ne [pajɛ̃, pajɛn] adj, nm/f pagan, heathen

paillasson [pajasɔ̃] nm doormat

paille [paj] nf straw

pain [pɛ̃] nm (substance) bread; (unité) loaf (of bread); (morceau): **~ de savon** etc bar of soap etc; **pain au chocolat** chocolate-filled pastry; **pain aux raisins** currant bun; **pain bis/complet**

pané, e [pane] adj fried in breadcrumbs

panier [panje] nm basket; **mettre au ~** to chuck away; **panier à provisions** shopping basket; **panier-repas** nm packed lunch

panique [panik] nf, adj panic; **paniquer** vi to panic

panne [pan] nf breakdown; **être/ tomber en ~** to have broken down/ break down; **être en ~ d'essence** ou **sèche** to have run out of petrol (BRIT) ou gas (US); **ma voiture est en ~** my car has broken down; **panne d'électricité** ou **de courant** power cut ou failure

panneau, x [pano] nm (écriteau) sign, notice; **panneau d'affichage** notice board; **panneau de signalisation** roadsign; **panneau indicateur** signpost

panoplie [panɔpli] nf (jouet) outfit; (fig) array

panorama [panɔʀama] nm panorama

panse [pɑ̃s] nf paunch

pansement [pɑ̃smɑ̃] nm dressing, bandage; **pansement adhésif** sticking plaster

pantacourt [pɑ̃takuʀ] nm three-quarter length trousers pl

pantalon [pɑ̃talɔ̃] nm trousers pl, pair of trousers; **pantalon de ski** ski pants pl

panthère [pɑ̃tɛʀ] nf panther

pantin [pɑ̃tɛ̃] nm puppet

pantoufle [pɑ̃tufl] nf slipper

paon [pɑ̃] nm peacock

papa [papa] nm dad(dy)

pape [pap] nm pope

paperasse [papʀas] nf (péj) bumf no pl, papers pl; **paperasserie** [-ʀi] nf paperwork no pl; (tracasserie) red tape no pl

papeterie [papɛtʀi] nf (magasin) stationer's (shop)

papi nm (fam) granddad

papier [papje] nm paper; (article) article; **papiers** nmpl (aussi: **~s d'identité**) (identity) papers; **papier à lettres** writing paper, notepaper;

papier (d')aluminium aluminium (BRIT) ou aluminum (US) foil, tinfoil; **papier calque** tracing paper; **papier de verre** sandpaper; **papier hygiénique** ou **de toilette** toilet paper; **papier journal** newspaper; **papier peint** wallpaper

papillon [papijɔ̃] nm butterfly; (fam: contravention) (parking) ticket; **papillon de nuit** moth

papillote [papijɔt] nf: **en ~** cooked in tinfoil

papoter [papɔte] vi to chatter

paquebot [pak(ə)bo] nm liner

pâquerette [pakʀɛt] nf daisy

Pâques [pak] nm, nfpl Easter

> **PÂQUES**
>
> In France, Easter eggs are said to be brought by the Easter bells or **cloches de Pâques** which fly from Rome and drop them in people's gardens.

paquet [pakɛ] nm packet; (colis) parcel; (fig: tas): **~ de** pile ou heap of; **un ~ de cigarettes, s'il vous plaît** a packet of cigarettes, please; **paquet-cadeau** nm: **pouvez-vous me faire un paquet-cadeau, s'il vous plaît?** can you gift-wrap it for me, please?

par [paʀ] prép by; **finir** etc **~** to end etc with; **~ amour** out of love; **passer ~ Lyon/la côte** to go via ou through Lyons/along the coast; **~ la fenêtre** (jeter, regarder) out of the window; **3 ~ jour/personne** 3 a ou per day/person; **2 ~ 2** in twos; **~ ici** this way; (dans le coin) round here; **~-ci, ~-là** here and there; **~ temps de pluie** in wet weather

parabolique [paʀabɔlik] adj: **antenne ~** parabolic ou dish aerial

parachute [paʀaʃyt] nm parachute; **parachutiste** nm/f parachutist; (Mil) paratrooper

parade [paʀad] nf (spectacle, défilé) parade; (Escrime, Boxe) parry

paradis [paradi] nm heaven, paradise

paradoxe [paradɔks] nm paradox

paraffine [parafin] nf paraffin

parages [paraʒ] nmpl: **dans les ~ (de)** in the area ou vicinity (of)

paragraphe [paragraf] nm paragraph

paraître [paʀɛtʀ] vb +attrib to seem, look, appear ▷ vi to appear; (être visible) to show; (Presse, Édition) to be published, come out, appear ▷ vb impers: **il paraît que** it seems ou appears that, they say that

parallèle [paralɛl] adj parallel; (non officiel) unofficial ▷ adj (comparaison): **faire un ~ entre** to draw a parallel between ▷ nf parallel (line)

paralyser [paralize] vt to paralyse

paramédical, e, -aux [paramedikal, o] adj: **personnel ~** paramedics pl, paramedical workers pl

paraphrase [parafraz] nf paraphrase

parapluie [paraplɥi] nm umbrella

parasite [parazit] nm parasite; **parasites** nmpl (Tél) interference sg

parasol [parasɔl] nm parasol, sunshade

paratonnerre [paratɔnɛʀ] nm lightning conductor

parc [park] nm (public) park, gardens pl; (de château etc) grounds pl; (d'enfant) playpen; **parc à thème** theme park; **parc d'attractions** amusement park; **parc de stationnement** car park

parcelle [parsɛl] nf fragment, scrap; (de terrain) plot, parcel

parce que [parsk(ə)] conj because

parchemin [parʃəmɛ̃] nm parchment

parc(o)mètre [park(o)mɛtʀ] nm parking meter

parcourir [parkurir] vt (trajet, distance) to cover; (article, livre) to skim ou glance through; (lieu) to go all over, travel up and down; (suj: frisson) to run through

parcours [parkur] nm (trajet) journey; (itinéraire) route

par-dessous [pard(ə)su] prép, adv under(neath)

pardessus [pardəsy] nm overcoat

par-dessus [pard(ə)sy] prép over (the top of) ▷ adv over (the top): **~ le marché** on top of all that; **~ tout** above all; **en avoir ~ la tête** to have had enough

par-devant [pard(ə)vã] adv (passer) round the front

pardon [pardɔ̃] nm forgiveness no pl ▷ excl sorry!; (pour interpeller etc) excuse me!; **demander ~ à qn (de)** to apologize to sb (for); **je vous demande ~** I'm sorry; (pour interpeller) excuse me; **pardonner** vt to forgive; **pardonner qch à qn** to forgive sb for sth

pare...: **pare-brise** nm inv windscreen (BRIT), windshield (US); **pare-chocs** nm inv bumper; **pare-feu** nm inv (de foyer) fireguard; (Inform) firewall

pareil, le [parɛj] adj (identique) the same, alike; (similaire) similar; (tel): **un courage/livre ~** such courage/a book, courage/a book like this; **de ~s livres** such books; **faire ~** to do the same (thing); **~ à** the same as; (similaire) similar to; **sans ~** unparalleled, unequalled

parent, e [parã, ãt] nm/f: **un(e) ~(e)** a relative ou relation; **parents** nmpl (père et mère) parents; **parenté** nf (lien) relationship

parenthèse [parãtɛz] nf (ponctuation) bracket, parenthesis; (digression) parenthesis, digression; **entre ~s** in brackets; (fig) incidentally

paresse [parɛs] nf laziness; **paresseux, -euse** adj lazy

parfait, e [parfɛ, ɛt] adj perfect ▷ nm (Ling) perfect (tense); **parfaitement** adv perfectly ▷ excl (most) certainly

parfois [parfwa] adv sometimes

parfum [parfɛ̃] nm (produit) perfume, scent; (odeur: de fleur) scent, fragrance; (goût) flavour; **quels ~s avez-vous?** what flavours do you have?; **parfumé, e** adj (fleur, fruit) fragrant; (femme) perfumed; **parfumé au café** coffee-flavoured; **parfumer** vt (suj: odeur, bouquet) to perfume; (crème, gâteau) to flavour; **parfums** nf (produits) perfumes pl; (boutique) perfume shop

pari [paʀi] nm bet; **parier** vt to bet

Paris [paʀi] n Paris; **parisien, ne** adj Parisian; (Géo, admin) Paris cpd ▷ nm/f: **Parisien, ne** Parisian

parité [paʀite] nf (Pol): **~ hommes-femmes** balanced representation of men and women

parjure [paʀʒyʀ] nm perjury

parking [paʀkiŋ] nm (lieu) car park

⚠ Attention à ne pas traduire *parking* par le mot anglais *parking*.

parlant, e [paʀlɑ̃, ɑ̃t] adj (regard) eloquent; (Cinéma) talking

parlement [paʀləmɑ̃] nm parliament; **parlementaire** adj parliamentary ▷ nm/f member of parliament

parler [paʀle] vi to speak, talk; (avouer) to talk; **~ (à qn) de** to talk (to sb) (about); **le/en français** to speak French/in French; **~ affaires** to talk business; **sans ~ de** (fig) not to mention, to say nothing of; **tu parles!** (fam: bien sûr) you bet!; **parlez-vous français?** do you speak French?; **je ne parle pas anglais** I don't speak English; **est-ce que je peux ~ à …?** can I speak to …?

parloir [paʀlwaʀ] nm (de prison, d'hôpital) visiting room

parmi [paʀmi] prép among(st)

paroi [paʀwa] nf wall; (cloison) partition

paroisse [paʀwas] nf parish

parole [paʀɔl] nf (faculté): **la ~** speech; (mot, promesse) word; **paroles** nfpl (Mus) words, lyrics; **tenir ~** to keep one's word; **prendre la ~** to speak; **demander la ~** to ask for permission to speak; **je te crois sur ~** I'll take your word for it

parquet [paʀkɛ] nm (parquet) floor; (Jur): **le ~** the Public Prosecutor's department

parrain [paʀɛ̃] nm godfather;

parrainer vt (suj: entreprise) to sponsor

pars [paʀ] vb voir **partir**

parsemer [paʀsəme] vt (suj: feuilles, papiers) to be scattered over; **~ qch de** to scatter sth with

part [paʀ] nf (qui revient à qn) share; (fraction, portion) part; **à ~** adv (séparément) separately; (de côté) aside ▷ prép apart from, except for; **prendre ~ à** (débat etc) to take part in; (soucis, douleur de qn) to share in; **faire ~ de qch à qn** to announce sth to sb, inform sb of sth; **pour ma ~** as for me, as far as I'm concerned; **à ~ entière** full; **de la ~ de** (au nom de) on behalf of; (donné par) from; **de toute(s) ~(s)** from all sides ou quarters; **de ~ et d'autre** on both sides, on either side; **d'une ~ … d'autre ~** on the one hand … on the other hand; **d'autre ~** (de plus) moreover; **faire la ~ des choses** to make allowances

partage [paʀtaʒ] nm (fractionnement) dividing up; (répartition) sharing (out) no pl, share-out

partager [paʀtaʒe] vt to share; (distribuer, répartir) to share (out); (morceler, diviser) to divide (up); **se partager** vt (héritage etc) to share between themselves (ou ourselves)

partenaire [paʀtənɛʀ] nm/f partner

parterre [paʀtɛʀ] nm (de fleurs) (flower) bed; (Théâtre) stalls pl

parti [paʀti] nm (Pol) party; (décision) course of action; (personne à marier) match; **tirer ~ de** to take advantage of, turn to good account; **prendre ~ (pour/contre)** to take a stand (for/against); **parti pris** bias

partial, e, -aux [paʀsjal, jo] adj biased, partial

participant, e [paʀtisipɑ̃, ɑ̃t] nm/f participant; (à un concours) entrant

participation [paʀtisipasjɔ̃] nf participation; (financière) contribution

participer [paʀtisipe]: **~ à** vt (course, réunion) to take part in; (frais etc) to contribute to; (chagrin, succès de qn) to share (in)

particularité [paʀtikylaʀite] *nf* (distinctive) characteristic

particulier, -ière [paʀtikylje, jɛʀ] *adj* (*spécifique*) particular; (*spécial*) special, particular; (*personnel, privé*) private; (*étrange*) peculiar, odd ▷ *nm* (*individu*: Admin) private individual; **~ à** peculiar to; **en ~** (*surtout*) in particular, particularly; (*en privé*) in private; **particulièrement** *adv* particularly

partie [paʀti] *nf* (*gén*) part; (*Jur etc*: *protagonistes*) party; (*de cartes, tennis etc*) game; **une ~ de pêche** a fishing party *ou* trip; **en ~** partly, in part; **faire ~ de** (*suj: chose*) to be part of; **prendre qn à ~** to take sb to task; **en grande ~** largely, in the main; **partie civile** (*Jur*) party claiming damages in a criminal case

partiel, le [paʀsjɛl] *adj* partial ▷ *nm* (*Scol*) class exam

partir [paʀtiʀ] *vi* (*gén*) to go; (*quitter*) to go, leave; (*tache*) to go, come out; **~ de** (*lieu: quitter*) to leave; (*: commencer à*) to start from; **~ pour/à** (*lieu, pays etc*) to leave for/go off to; **à ~ de** from; **le train/le bus part à quelle heure?** what time does the train/bus leave?

partisan, e [paʀtizã, an] *nm/f* partisan ▷ *adj*: **être ~ de qch/de faire** to be in favour of sth/doing

partition [paʀtisjɔ̃] *nf* (*Mus*) score

partout [paʀtu] *adv* everywhere; **~ où il allait** everywhere *ou* wherever he went

paru [paʀy] *pp de* **paraître**

parution [paʀysjɔ̃] *nf* publication

parvenir [paʀvəniʀ]: **~ à** *vt* (*atteindre*) to reach; (*réussir*): **~ à faire** to manage to do, succeed in doing; **faire ~ qch à qn** to have sth sent to sb

pas¹ [pɑ] *nm* (*enjambée, Danse*) step; (*allure, mesure*) pace; (*bruit*) (foot)step; (*trace*) footprint; **~ à ~** step by step; **au ~** at walking pace; **marcher à grands ~** to stride along; **à ~ de loup** stealthily; **faire les cent ~** to pace up and down; **faire le premier ~** to make the first move; **sur le ~ de la porte** on the doorstep

MOT-CLÉ

pas² [pɑ] *adv* 1 (*en corrélation avec* ne, non etc) not; **il ne pleure pas** (*habituellement*) he does not *ou* doesn't cry; (*maintenant*) he's not *ou* isn't crying; **il n'a pas pleuré/ne pleurera pas** he did not *ou* didn't/will not *ou* won't cry; **ils n'ont pas de voiture/d'enfants** they don't have *ou* haven't got a car/any children; **il m'a dit de ne pas le faire** he told me not to do it; **non pas que** … not that …

2 (*employé sans ne etc*): **pas moi** not me, I don't (*ou* can't *etc*); **elle travaille, (mais) lui pas** *ou* **pas lui** she works but he doesn't *ou* does not; **une pomme pas mûre** an unripe apple; **pas du tout** not at all; **pas de sucre, merci** no sugar, thanks; **ceci est à vous *ou* pas?** is this yours or not?, is this yours or isn't it?

3: **pas mal** (*joli: personne, maison*) not bad; **pas mal fait** not badly done *ou* made; **comment ça va? — pas mal** how are things? — not bad; **pas mal de** quite a lot of

passage [pɑsaʒ] *nm* (*fait de passer*) voir **passer**; (*lieu, prix de la traversée, extrait*) passage; (*chemin*) way; **de ~** (*touristes*) passing through; **passage à niveau** level crossing; **passage clouté** pedestrian crossing; **passage interdit** no entry; **passage souterrain** subway (*BRIT*), underpass

passager, -ère [pɑsaʒe, ɛʀ] *adj* passing ▷ *nm/f* passenger

passant, e [pɑsã, ãt] *adj* (*rue, endroit*) busy ▷ *nm/f* passer-by; **en ~** in passing

passe [pɑs] *nf* (*Sport, Navig*) pass; **être en ~ de faire** to be on the way to doing; **être dans une mauvaise ~** to be going through a rough patch

passé, e [pɑse] *adj* (*révolu*) past; (*dernier: semaine etc*) last; (*couleur*) faded ▷ *prép* after ▷ *nm* past; (*Ling*) past (tense); **~ de mode** out of fashion; **passé composé** perfect (tense); **passé simple** past historic (tense)

passe-partout [pɑspaʀtu] *nm inv* master ou skeleton key ▷ *adj inv* all-purpose

passeport [pɑspɔʀ] *nm* passport

passer [pɑse] *vi* (*aller*) to go; (*voiture, piétons: défiler*) to pass (by), go by; (*facteur, laitier etc*) to come, call; (*pour rendre visite*) to call ou drop in; (*film, émission*) to be on; (*temps, jours*) to pass, go by; (*couleur*) to fade; (*mode*) to die out; (*douleur*) to pass, go away; (*Scol*): **~ dans la classe supérieure** to go up to the next class ▷ *vt* (*frontière, rivière etc*) to cross; (*douane*) to go through; (*examen*) to sit, take; (*visite médicale etc*) to have; (*journée, temps*) to spend; (*enfiler: vêtement*) to slip on; (*film, pièce*) to show, put on; (*disque*) to play, put on; (*commande*) to place; (*marché, accord*) to agree on; **se passer** *vi* (*avoir lieu: scène, action*) to take place; (*se dérouler: entretien etc*) to go; (*s'écouler: semaine etc*) to pass, go by; (*arriver*) **que s'est-il passé?** what happened?; **~ qch à qn** (*sel etc*) to pass sth to sb; (*prêter*) to lend sth to sb; (*lettre, message*) to pass sth on to sb; (*tolérer*) to let sb get away with sth; **~ par** to go through; **~ avant qch/qn** (*fig*) to come before sth/sb; **un coup de fil à qn** (*fam*) to give sb a ring; **laisser ~ qch** (*air, lumière, personne*) to let through; (*occasion*) to let slip, miss; (*erreur*) to overlook; **~ à la radio/télévision** to be on the radio/on television; **~ à table** to sit down to eat; **~ au salon** to go into the sitting-room; **~ son tour** to miss one's turn; **~ la seconde** (*Auto*) to change into second; **~ le balai/ l'aspirateur** to sweep up/hoover; **je vous passe M. Dupont** (*je vous mets en communication avec lui*) I'm putting you through to Mr Dupont; (*je lui passe l'appareil*) here is Mr Dupont, I'll hand you over to Mr Dupont; **se ~ de** to go ou

do without

passerelle [pɑsʀɛl] *nf* footbridge; (*de navire, avion*) gangway

passe-temps [pɑstɑ̃] *nm inv* pastime

passif, -ive [pɑsif, iv] *adj* passive

passion [pɑsjɔ̃] *nf* passion; **passionnant, e** *adj* fascinating; **passionné, e** *adj* (*personne*) passionate; (*récit*) impassioned; **être passionné de** to have a passion for; **passionner** *vt* (*personne*) to fascinate, grip

passoire [pɑswaʀ] *nf* sieve; (*à légumes*) colander; (*à thé*) strainer

pastèque [pastɛk] *nf* watermelon

pasteur [pastœʀ] *nm* (*protestant*) minister, pastor

pastille [pastij] *nf* (*à sucer*) lozenge, pastille

patate [patat] *nf* (*fam: pomme de terre*) spud; **patate douce** sweet potato

patauger [patoʒe] *vi* to splash about

pâte [pɑt] *nf* (*à tarte*) pastry; (*à pain*) dough; (*à frire*) batter; **pâtes** *nfpl* (*macaroni etc*) pasta *sg*; **pâte à modeler** modelling clay, Plasticine® (*BRIT*); **pâte brisée** shortcrust pastry; **pâte d'amandes** almond paste, marzipan; **pâte de fruits** crystallized fruit *no pl*; **pâte feuilletée** puff ou flaky pastry

pâté [pɑte] *nm* (*charcuterie*) pâté; (*tache*) ink blot; **pâté de maisons** block (of houses); **pâté (de sable)** sandpie; **pâté en croûte** pork pie

pâtée [pɑte] *nf* mash, feed

patente [patɑ̃t] *nf* (*Comm*) trading licence

paternel, le [patɛʀnɛl] *adj* (*amour, soins*) fatherly; (*ligne, autorité*) paternal

pâteux, -euse [pɑtø, øz] *adj* pasty; (*langue*) coated

pathétique [patetik] *adj* moving

patience [pasjɑ̃s] *nf* patience

patient, e [pasjɑ̃, ɑ̃t] *adj, nm/f* patient; **patienter** *vi* to wait

patin [patɛ̃] *nm* skate; (*sport*) skate; **patins (à glace)** (ice) skates; **patins à roulettes** roller skates

patinage [patinaʒ] *nm* skating

patiner [patine] vi to skate; (roue,
voiture) to spin; **se patiner** vi (meuble,
cuir) to acquire a sheen; **patineur,
-euse** nm/f skater; **patinoire** nf
skating rink, (ice) rink

pâtir [pɑtiʀ]: **~ de** vt to suffer because
of

pâtisserie [pɑtisʀi] nf (boutique) cake
shop; (gâteau) cake, pastry; (à la maison)
pastry- ou cake-making, baking;
pâtissier, -ière nm/f pastrycook

patois [patwa] nm dialect, patois

patrie [patʀi] nf homeland

patrimoine [patʀimwan] nm (culture)
heritage

○ **JOURNÉES DU PATRIMOINE**

● Once a year, important public
  buildings are open to the public for
  a weekend. During these **Journées
  du Patrimoine**, there are guided
  visits and talks based on a particular
  theme.

patriotique [patʀijɔtik] adj patriotic

patron, ne [patʀɔ̃, ɔn] nm/f boss; (Rel)
patron saint ▷ nm (Couture) pattern;
patronat nm employers pl; **patronner**
vt to sponsor, support

patrouille [patʀuj] nf patrol

patte [pat] nf (jambe) leg; (pied: de chien,
chat) paw; (: d'oiseau) foot

pâturage [pɑtyʀaʒ] nm pasture

paume [pom] nf palm

paumé, e [pome] (fam) nm/f drop-out

paupière [popjɛʀ] nf eyelid

pause [poz] nf (arrêt) break; (en parlant,
Mus) pause

pauvre [povʀ] adj poor; **les pauvres**
nmpl the poor; **pauvreté** nf (état)
poverty

pavé, e [pave] adj (cour) (chaussée)
cobbled ▷ nm (bloc) paving
stone; cobblestone

pavillon [pavijɔ̃] nm (de banlieue)
small (detached) house; pavilion;
(drapeau) flag

payant, e [pejɑ̃, ɑ̃t] adj (spectateurs
etc) paying; (fig: entreprise) profitable;
(effort) which pays off; **c'est ~** you have
to pay, there is a charge

paye [pɛj] nf pay, wages pl

payer [peje] vt (créancier, employé, loyer)
to pay; (achat, réparations, fig: faute)
to pay for ▷ vi to pay; (métier) to be
well-paid; (tactique etc) to pay off; **il me
l'a fait ~ 10 euros** he charged me 10
euros for it; **~ qch à qn** to buy sth for sb,
buy sb sth; **se ~ la tête de qn** (fam) to
take the mickey out of sb; **est-ce que je
peux ~ par carte de crédit?** can I pay
by credit card?

pays [pei] nm country; (région) region;
du ~ local

paysage [peizaʒ] nm landscape

paysan, ne [peizɑ̃, an] nm/f farmer;
(péj) peasant ▷ adj (agricole) farming;
(rural) country

Pays-Bas [peiba] nmpl: **les ~** the
Netherlands

PC nm (Inform) PC

PDA sigle m (= personal digital assistant)
PDA

PDG sigle m = **président directeur
général**

péage [peaʒ] nm toll; (endroit) tollgate

peau, x [po] nf skin; **gants de ~** fine
leather gloves; **être bien/mal dans sa
~** to be at ease/ill-at-ease; **peau
de chamois** (chiffon) chamois leather,
shammy

pêche [pɛʃ] nf (fruit) peach; (sport,
activité) fishing; (poissons pêchés) catch;
pêche à la ligne (en rivière) angling

péché [peʃe] nm sin

pécher [peʃe] vi (Rel) to sin

pêcher [peʃe] nm peach tree ▷ vi to go
fishing ▷ vt (attraper) to catch; (être
pêcheur ou) to fish for

pécheur, -eresse [peʃœʀ, peʃʀɛs]
nm/f sinner

pêcheur [peʃœʀ] nm fisherman; (à la
ligne) angler

pédagogie [pedagɔʒi] nf educational
methods pl, pedagogy; **pédagogique**

adj educational

pédale [pedal] *nf* pedal

pédalo [pedalo] *nm* pedal-boat

pédant, e [pedã, ãt] *(péj) adj* pedantic

pédestre [pedɛstʀ] *adj*: **randonnée ~** ramble; **sentier ~** pedestrian footpath

pédiatre [pedjatʀ] *nm/f* paediatrician, child specialist

pédicure [pedikyʀ] *nm/f* chiropodist

pègre [pɛgʀ] *nf* underworld

peigne [pɛɲ] *nm* comb; **peigner** *vt* to comb (the hair of); **se peigner** *vi* to comb one's hair; **peignoir** *nm* dressing gown; **peignoir de bain** bathrobe

peindre [pɛ̃dʀ] *vt* to paint; *(fig)* to portray, depict

peine [pɛn] *nf (affliction)* sorrow, sadness *no pl; (mal, effort)* trouble *no pl*, effort; *(difficulté)* difficulty; *(Jur)* sentence; **avoir de la ~** to be sad; **faire de la ~ à qn** to distress ou upset sb; **prendre la ~ de faire** to go to the trouble of doing; **se donner de la ~** to make an effort; **ce n'est pas la ~ de faire** there's no point in doing, it's not worth doing; **à ~** scarcely, barely; **à ~ ... que** hardly ... than, no sooner ... than; **peine capitale** capital punishment; **peine de mort** death sentence *ou* penalty; **peiner** *vi (personne)* to work hard; *(moteur, voiture)* to labour ▷ *vt* to grieve, sadden

peintre [pɛ̃tʀ] *nm* painter; **peintre en bâtiment** painter (and decorator)

peinture [pɛ̃tyʀ] *nf* painting; *(matière)* paint; *(surfaces peintes: aussi:* **~s)** paintwork; **"~ fraîche"** "wet paint"

péjoratif, -ive [peʒɔʀatif, iv] *adj* pejorative, derogatory

Pékin [pekɛ̃] *n* Beijing

pêle-mêle [pɛlmɛl] *adv* higgledy-piggledy

peler [pəle] *vt, vi* to peel

pèlerin [pɛlʀɛ̃] *nm* pilgrim

pèlerinage [pɛlʀinaʒ] *nm* pilgrimage

pelle [pɛl] *nf* shovel; *(d'enfant, de terrassier)* spade

pellicule [pelikyl] *nf* film; **pellicules**

nfpl *(Méd)* dandruff *sg;* **je voudrais une ~ de 36 poses** I'd like a 36-exposure film

pelote [p(ə)lɔt] *nf (de fil, laine)* ball; **pelote basque** pelota

peloton [p(ə)lɔtɔ̃] *nm* group, squad; *(Cyclisme)* pack

pelotonner [p(ə)lɔtɔne]: **se pelotonner** *vi* to curl (o.s.) up

pelouse [p(ə)luz] *nf* lawn

peluche [p(ə)lyʃ] *nf*: **(animal en) ~** fluffy animal, soft toy; **chien/lapin en ~** fluffy dog/rabbit

pelure [p(ə)lyʀ] *nf* peeling, peel *no pl*

pénal, e, -aux [penal, o] *adj* penal; **pénalité** *nf* penalty

penchant [pɑ̃ʃɑ̃] *nm (tendance)* tendency, propensity; *(faible) liking*, fondness

pencher [pɑ̃ʃe] *vi* to tilt, lean over ▷ *vt* to tilt; **se pencher** *vi* to lean over; *(se baisser)* to bend down; **se ~ sur** *(fig: problème)* to look into; **~ pour** to be inclined to favour

pendant [pɑ̃dɑ̃] *prép (au cours de)* during; *(indique la durée) for*; **~ que** while

pendentif [pɑ̃dɑ̃tif] *nm* pendant

penderie [pɑ̃dʀi] *nf* wardrobe

pendre [pɑ̃dʀ] *vt, vi* to hang; **se ~** *(se suicider)* to hang o.s.; **~ qch à** *(mur)* to hang sth (up) on; *(plafond)* to hang sth (up) from

pendule [pɑ̃dyl] *nf* clock ▷ *nm* pendulum

pénétrer [penetʀe] *vi, vt* to penetrate; **~ dans** to enter

pénible [penibl] *adj (travail)* hard; *(sujet)* painful; *(personne)* tiresome; **péniblement** *adv* with difficulty

péniche [peniʃ] *nf* barge

pénicilline [penisilin] *nf* penicillin

péninsule [penɛ̃syl] *nf* peninsula

pénis [penis] *nm* penis

pénitence [penitɑ̃s] *nf (peine)* penance; *(repentir)* penitence; **pénitencier** *nm* penitentiary

pénombre [penɔ̃bʀ] *nf (faible clarté)* half-light; *(obscurité)* darkness

pensée [pɑ̃se] *nf* thought; *(démarche,*

doctrine) thinking *no pl*; (*fleur*) pansy; **en ~** in one's mind

penser [pɑ̃se] *vi, vt* to think; **~ à** (*ami, vacances*) to think of *ou* about; (*réfléchir à: problème, offre*) to think about *ou* over; (*prévoir*) to think of; **faire ~ à** to remind one of; **~ faire qch** to be thinking of doing sth, intend to do sth; **pensif, -ive** *adj* pensive, thoughtful

pension [pɑ̃sjɔ̃] *nf* (*allocation*) pension; (*prix du logement*) board and lodgings, bed and board; (*école*) boarding school; **pension alimentaire** (*de divorcée*) maintenance allowance, alimony; **pension complète** full board; **pension de famille** boarding house, guesthouse; **pensionnaire** *nm/f* (Scol) boarder; **pensionnat** *nm* boarding school

pente [pɑ̃t] *nf* slope; **en ~** sloping

Pentecôte [pɑ̃tkot] *nf*: **la ~** Whitsun (BRIT), Pentecost

pénurie [penyri] *nf* shortage

pépé [pepe] (*fam*) *nm* grandad

pépin [pepɛ̃] *nm* (Bot: *graine*) pip; (*ennui*) snag, hitch

pépinière [pepinjɛr] *nf* nursery

perçant, e [pɛrsɑ̃, ɑ̃t] *adj* (*cri*) piercing, shrill; (*regard*) piercing

percepteur, -trice [pɛrsɛptœr, tris] *nm/f* tax collector

perception [pɛrsɛpsjɔ̃] *nf* perception; (*bureau*) tax office

percer [pɛrse] *vt* to pierce; (*ouverture etc*) to make; (*mystère, énigme*) to penetrate ▷ *vi* to break through; **perceuse** *nf* drill

percevoir [pɛrsəvwar] *vt* (*distinguer*) to perceive, detect; (*taxe, impôt*) to collect; (*revenu, indemnité*) to receive

perche [pɛrʃ] *nf* (*bâton*) pole

percher [pɛrʃe] *vt, vi* to perch; **se percher** *vi* to perch; **perchoir** *nm* perch

perçois *etc* [pɛrswa] *vb voir* **percevoir**

perçu, e [pɛrsy] *pp de* **percevoir**

percussion [pɛrkysjɔ̃] *nf* percussion

percuter [pɛrkyte] *vt* to strike; (*suj:*

véhicule) to crash into

perdant, e [pɛrdɑ̃, ɑ̃t] *nm/f* loser

perdre [pɛrdr] *vt* to lose; (*gaspiller: temps, argent*) to waste; (*personne: moralement etc*) to ruin ▷ *vi* to lose; (*sur une vente etc*) to lose out; **se perdre** *vi* (*s'égarer*) to get lost, lose one's way; (*denrées*) to go to waste; **j'ai perdu mon portefeuille/passeport** I've lost my wallet/passport; **je me suis perdu** (*et je le suis encore*) I'm lost; (*et je ne le suis plus*) I got lost

perdrix [pɛrdri] *nf* partridge

perdu, e [pɛrdy] *pp de* **perdre** ▷ *adj* (*isolé*) out-of-the-way; (Comm: *emballage*) non-returnable; (*malade*): **il est ~** there's no hope left for him; **à vos moments ~s** in your spare time

père [pɛr] *nm* father; **père de famille** father; **le père Noël** Father Christmas

perfection [pɛrfɛksjɔ̃] *nf* perfection; **à la ~** to perfection; **perfectionné, e** *adj* sophisticated; **perfectionner** *vt* to improve, perfect; **se perfectionner en anglais** to improve one's English

perforer [pɛrfɔre] *vt* (*poinçonner*) to punch

performant, e [pɛrfɔrmɑ̃, ɑ̃t] *adj*: **très ~** high-performance *cpd*

perfusion [pɛrfyzjɔ̃] *nf*: **faire une ~ à qn** to put sb on a drip

péril [peril] *nm* peril

périmé, e [perime] *adj* (Admin) out-of-date, expired

périmètre [perimɛtr] *nm* perimeter

période [perjɔd] *nf* period; **périodique** *adj* periodic ▷ *nm* periodical; **garniture** *ou* **serviette périodique** sanitary towel (BRIT) *ou* napkin (US)

périphérique [periferik] *adj* (*quartiers*) outlying ▷ *nm* (Auto): **boulevard ~** ring road (BRIT), beltway (US)

périr [perir] *vi* to die, perish

périssable [perisabl] *adj* perishable

perle [pɛrl] *nf* pearl; (*de plastique, métal, sueur*) bead

permanence [pɛrmanɑ̃s] *nf*

permanence; (local) (duty) office; **assurer une ~** (service public, bureaux) to operate ou maintain a basic service; **être de ~** to be on call ou duty; **en ~** continuously

permanent, e [pɛrmanɑ̃, ɑ̃t] adj permanent; (spectacle) continuous; **permanente** nf perm

perméable [pɛrmeabl] adj permeable; **~ à** (fig) receptive ou open to

permettre [pɛrmɛtr] vt to allow, permit; **~ à qn de faire/qch** to allow sb to do/sth; **se ~ de faire** to take the liberty of doing

permis [pɛrmi] nm permit, licence; **permis de conduire** driving licence (BRIT), driver's license (US); **permis de construire** planning permission (BRIT), building permit (US); **permis de séjour** residence permit; **permis de travail** work permit

permission [pɛrmisjɔ̃] nf permission; (Mil) leave; **avoir la ~ de faire** to have permission to do; **en ~** on leave

Pérou [peru] nm Peru

perpétuel, le [pɛrpetɥɛl] adj perpetual; **perpétuité** nf: **à perpétuité** for life; **être condamné à perpétuité** to receive a life sentence

perplexe [pɛrplɛks] adj perplexed, puzzled

perquisitionner [pɛrkizisjɔne] vi to carry out a search

perron [pɛrɔ̃] nm steps pl (leading to entrance)

perroquet [pɛrɔkɛ] nm parrot

perruche [pɛryʃ] nf budgerigar (BRIT), budgie (BRIT), parakeet (US)

perruque [pɛryk] nf wig

persécuter [pɛrsekyte] vt to persecute

persévérer [pɛrsevere] vi to persevere

persil [pɛrsi] nm parsley

Persique [pɛrsik] adj: **le golfe ~** the (Persian) Gulf

persistant, e [pɛrsistɑ̃, ɑ̃t] adj persistent

persister [pɛrsiste] vi to persist; **~ à faire qch** to persist in doing sth

personnage [pɛrsɔnaʒ] nm (individu) character, individual; (célébrité) important person; (de roman, film) character; (Peinture) figure

personnalité [pɛrsɔnalite] nf personality; (personnage) prominent figure

personne [pɛrsɔn] nf person ⊳ pron nobody, no one; (avec négation en anglais) anybody, anyone; **personne âgée** elderly person; **personnel, le** adj personal; (égoïste) selfish ⊳ nm staff, personnel; **personnellement** adv personally

perspective [pɛrspɛktiv] nf (Art) perspective; (vue) view; (point de vue) viewpoint, angle; (chose envisagée) prospect; **en ~** in prospect

perspicace [pɛrspikas] adj clear-sighted, gifted with (ou showing) insight; **perspicacité** nf clear-sightedness

persuader [pɛrsɥade] vt: **~ qn (de faire)** to persuade sb (to do); **persuasif, -ive** adj persuasive

perte [pɛrt] nf loss; (de temps) waste; (fig: morale) ruin; **à ~ de vue** as far as the eye can (ou could) see; **pertes blanches** (vaginal) discharge sg

pertinent, e [pɛrtinɑ̃, ɑ̃t] adj apt, relevant

perturbation [pɛrtyrbasjɔ̃] nf: **perturbation (atmosphérique)** atmospheric disturbance

perturber [pɛrtyrbe] vt to disrupt; (Psych) to perturb, disturb

pervers, e [pɛrvɛr, ɛrs] adj perverted

pervertir [pɛrvɛrtir] vt to pervert

pesant, e [pəzɑ̃, ɑ̃t] adj heavy; (fig: présence) burdensome

pèse-personne [pɛzpɛrsɔn] nm (bathroom) scales pl

peser [pəze] vt to weigh ⊳ vi to weigh; (fig: avoir de l'importance) to carry weight; **~ lourd** to be heavy

pessimiste [pesimist] adj pessimistic

▷ nm/f pessimist

peste [pɛst] nf plague

pétale [petal] nm petal

pétanque [petɑ̃k] nf type of bowls

○ **PÉTANQUE**

Pétanque is a version of the game of 'boules', played on a variety of hard surfaces. Standing with their feet together, players throw steel bowls at a wooden jack. **Pétanque** originated in the South of France and is still very much associated with that area.

pétard [petaʀ] nm banger (BRIT), firecracker

péter [pete] vi (fam: casser) to bust; (fam!) to fart (!)

pétillant, e [petijɑ̃, ɑ̃t] adj (eau etc) sparkling

pétiller [petije] vi (feu) to crackle; (champagne) to bubble; (yeux) to sparkle

petit, e [p(ə)ti, it] adj small; (avec nuance affective) little; (voyage) short, little; (bruit etc) faint, slight ▷ nm/f (petit enfant) little boy/girl, child; **petits** nmpl (d'un animal) young no pl; **faire des ~s** to have kittens (ou puppies etc); **la classe des ~s** the infant class; **les tout-~s** the little ones, the tiny tots (fam); **~ à ~** bit by bit, gradually; **petit(e) ami(e)** boyfriend/girlfriend; **petit déjeuner** breakfast; **le petit déjeuner est à quelle heure?** what time is breakfast?; **petit four** petit four; **petit pain** (bread) roll; **les petites annonces** the small ads; **petits pois** (garden) peas; **petite-fille** nf granddaughter; **petit-fils** nm grandson

pétition [petisjɔ̃] nf petition

petits-enfants [pətizɑ̃fɑ̃] nmpl grandchildren

pétrin [petʀɛ̃] nm (fig): **dans le ~** (fam) in a jam ou fix

pétrir [petʀiʀ] vt to knead

pétrole [petʀɔl] nm oil; (pour lampe, réchaud etc) paraffin (oil); **pétrolier, -ière** nm oil tanker

‖ Attention à ne pas traduire **pétrole** par le mot anglais **petrol**.

○ **MOT-CLÉ**

peu [pø] adv 1 (modifiant verbe, adjectif, adverbe): **il boit peu** he doesn't drink (very) much; **il est peu bavard** he's not very talkative; **peu avant/après** shortly before/afterwards

2 (modifiant nom): **peu de: peu de gens/d'arbres** few ou not (very) many people/trees; **il a peu d'espoir** he hasn't (got) much hope, he has little hope; **pour peu de temps** for (only) a short while

3: **peu à peu** little by little; **à peu près** just about, more or less; **à peu près 10 kg/10 euros** approximately 10 kg/10 euros

▷ nm 1: **le peu de gens qui** the few people who; **le peu de sable qui** what little sand, the little sand which

2: **un peu** a little; **un petit peu** a little bit; **un peu d'espoir** a little hope; **elle est un peu bavarde** she's quite ou rather talkative; **un peu plus de** slightly more than; **un peu moins de** slightly less than; (avec pluriel) slightly fewer than

▷ pron: **peu le savent** few know (it); **de peu** (only) just

peuple [pœpl] nm people; **peupler** vt (pays, région) to populate; (étang) to stock; (suj: hommes, poissons) to inhabit

peuplier [pøplije] nm poplar (tree)

peur [pœʀ] nf fear; **avoir ~ (de/de faire/que)** to be frightened ou afraid (of/of doing/that); **faire ~ à** to frighten; **de ~ de/que** for fear of/that; **peureux, -euse** adj fearful, timorous

peut [pø] vb voir **pouvoir**

peut-être [pøtɛtʀ] adv perhaps, maybe; **~ que** perhaps, maybe; **~ bien qu'il fera/est** he may well do/be

phare [faʀ] nm (en mer) lighthouse; (de véhicule) headlight

pharmacie [faʀmasi] nf (magasin) chemist's (BRIT), pharmacy, (de salle de bain) medicine cabinet; **pharmacien, ne** nm/f pharmacist, chemist (BRIT)

phénomène [fenɔmɛn] nm phenomenon

philosophe [filɔzɔf] nm/f philosopher ▷ adj philosophical

philosophie [filɔzɔfi] nf philosophy

phobie [fɔbi] nf phobia

phoque [fɔk] nm seal

phosphorescent, e [fɔsfɔʀesɑ̃, ɑ̃t] adj luminous

photo [fɔto] nf photo(graph); **prendre en ~** to take a photo of; **pourriez-vous nous prendre en ~, s'il vous plaît?** would you take a picture of us, please?; **faire de la ~** to take photos; **photo d'identité** passport photograph

photocopie nf photocopy

photocopier vt to photocopy

photocopieur nm photocopier

photographe nm/f photographer

photographie nf (technique) photography; (cliché) photograph

photographier vt to photograph

phrase [fʀaz] nf sentence

physicien, ne [fizisjɛ̃, jɛn] nm/f physicist

physique [fizik] adj physical ▷ nm physique ▷ nf physics sg; **au ~** physically; **physiquement** adv physically

pianiste [pjanist] nm/f pianist

piano [pjano] nm piano; **pianoter** vi to tinkle away (at the piano)

pic [pik] nm (instrument) pick(axe); (montagne) peak; (Zool) woodpecker; **à ~** vertically; (fig: tomber, arriver) just at the right time

pichet [piʃɛ] nm jug

picorer [pikɔʀe] vt to peck

pie [pi] nf magpie

pièce [pjɛs] nf (d'un logement) room; (Théâtre) play; (de machine) part; (de monnaie) coin; (document) document; (fragment, de collection) piece; **dix euros ~** ten euros each; **vendre à la ~** to sell separately; **travailler à la ~** to do piecework; **un maillot une ~** a one-piece swimsuit; **un deux-~s cuisine** a two-room(ed) flat (BRIT) ou apartment (US) with kitchen; **pièce à conviction** exhibit; **pièce d'eau** ornamental lake ou pond; **pièce de rechange** spare (part); **pièce d'identité: avez-vous une pièce d'identité?** have you got any (means of) identification?; **pièce jointe** (Comput) attachment; **pièce montée** tiered cake; **pièces détachées** spares, (spare) parts; **pièces justificatives** supporting documents

pied [pje] nm foot; (de table) leg; (de lampe) base; **~s nus** ou **nus-~** barefoot; **à ~** on foot; **au ~ de la lettre** literally; **avoir ~** to be able to touch the bottom, not to be out of one's depth; **avoir le ~ marin** to be a good sailor; **sur ~** (debout, rétabli) up and about; **mettre sur ~** (entreprise) to set up; **c'est le ~** (fam) it's brilliant; **mettre les ~s dans le plat** (fam) to put one's foot in it; **il se débrouille comme un ~** (fam) he's completely useless; **pied-noir** nm Algerian-born Frenchman

piège [pjɛʒ] nm trap; **prendre au ~** to trap; **piéger** vt (avec une bombe) to booby-trap; **lettre/voiture piégée** letter-/car-bomb

piercing [pjɛʀsiŋ] nm body piercing

pierre [pjɛʀ] nf stone; **pierre tombale** tombstone; **pierreries** nfpl gems, precious stones

piétiner [pjetine] vi (trépigner) to stamp (one's foot); (fig) to be at a standstill ▷ vt to trample on

piéton, ne [pjetɔ̃, ɔn] nm/f pedestrian; **piétonnier, -ière** adj: **rue** ou **zone piétonnière** pedestrian precinct

pieu, x [pjø] nm post; (pointu) stake

pieuvre [pjœvʀ] nf octopus

pieux, -euse [pjø, pjøz] adj pious

pigeon [piʒɔ̃] nm pigeon

piger[piʒe] (fam) vi, vt to understand

pigiste[piʒist] nm/f freelance(r)

pignon[piɲɔ̃] nm (de mur) gable

pile[pil] nf (tas) pile; (Élec) battery
▷ adv (fam: s'arrêter etc) dead: **à deux
heures ~** at two on the dot; **jouer à ~
ou face** to toss up (for it); **~ ou face?**
heads or tails?

piler[pile] vt to crush, pound

pilier[pilje] nm pillar

piller[pije] vt to pillage, plunder, loot

pilote[pilɔt] nm pilot; (de véhicule) driver
▷ adj nm pilot cpd: **pilote de course** racing
driver; **pilote de ligne** airline pilot;
piloter vt (avion) to pilot, fly; (voiture)
to drive

pilule[pilyl] nf pill; **prendre la ~** to be
on the pill

piment[pimɑ̃] nm (aussi: **~ rouge**)
chilli; (fig) spice, piquancy; **~ doux**
pepper, capsicum; **pimenté, e** adj
(plat) hot, spicy

pin[pɛ̃] nm pine

pinard[pinaʀ] (fam) nm (cheap) wine,
plonk (BRIT)

pince[pɛ̃s] nf (outil) pliers pl; (de homard,
crabe) pincer, claw; (Couture: pli) dart;
pince à épiler tweezers pl; **pince à
linge** clothes peg (BRIT) ou pin (US)

pincé, e[pɛ̃se] adj (air) stiff

pinceau, x[pɛ̃so] nm (paint)brush

pincer[pɛ̃se] vt to pinch; (fam) to nab

pinède[pinɛd] nf pinewood, pine forest

pingouin[pɛ̃gwɛ̃] nm penguin

ping-pong®[piŋpɔ̃g] nm table tennis

pinson[pɛ̃sɔ̃] nm chaffinch

pintade[pɛ̃tad] nf guinea-fowl

pion[pjɔ̃] nm (Échecs) pawn; (Dames)
piece; (Scol) supervisor

pionnier[pjɔnje] nm pioneer

pipe[pip] nf pipe; **fumer la ~** to smoke
a pipe

piquant, e[pikɑ̃, ɑ̃t] adj (barbe, rosier
etc) prickly; (saveur, sauce) hot, pungent;
(détail) titillating; (froid) biting ▷ nm
(épine) thorn, prickle; (fig) spiciness,
spice

pique[pik] nf pike; (fig) cutting remark
▷ nm (Cartes) spades pl

pique-nique[piknik] nm picnic;
pique-niquer vi to have a picnic

piquer[pike] vt (suj: guêpe, fumée, orties)
to sting; (: moustique) to bite; (: barbe)
to prick; (: froid) to bite; (Méd) to give a jab
to; (: chien, chat) to put to sleep; (intérêt)
to arouse; (fam: voler) to pinch ▷ vi
(avion) to go into a dive

piqûre[pikyʀ] nf (d'épingle) prick;
(d'ortie) sting; (de moustique) bite; (Méd)
injection, shot (US); **faire une ~ à qn** to
give sb an injection

pirate[piʀat] nm, adj pirate; **pirate de
l'air** hijacker

pire[piʀ] adj, (comparatif) worse; (superlatif): **le(la)
~ ...** the worst ... ▷ nm: **le ~ (de)** the
worst (of); **au ~** at (the very) worst

pis[pi] nm (de vache) udder ▷ adj, adv
worse; **de mal en ~** from bad to worse

piscine[pisin] nf (swimming) pool;
piscine couverte indoor (swimming)
pool

pissenlit[pisɑ̃li] nm dandelion

pistache[pistaʃ] nf pistachio (nut)

piste[pist] nf (d'un animal, sentier) track,
trail; (indice) lead; (de stade) track; (de
cirque) ring; (de danse) floor; (de patinage)
rink; (de ski) run; (Aviat) runway; **piste
cyclable** cycle track

pistolet[pistɔlɛ] nm (arme) pistol,
gun; (à peinture) spray gun; **pistolet-
mitrailleur** nm submachine gun

piston[pistɔ̃] nm (Tech) piston; **avoir
du ~** (fam) to have friends in the right
places; **pistonner** vt (candidat) to pull
strings for

piteux, -euse[pitø, øz] adj pitiful,
sorry (avant le nom); **en ~ état** in a
sorry state

pitié[pitje] nf pity; **il me fait ~** I feel
sorry for him; **avoir ~ de** (compassion)
to pity, feel sorry for; (merci) to have pity
ou mercy on

pitoyable[pitwajabl] adj pitiful

pittoresque[pitɔʀɛsk] adj

picturesque
PJ sigle f (= police judiciaire) ≈ CID (BRIT)
≈ FBI (US)
placard [plakaʀ] nm (armoire)
cupboard; (affiche) poster, notice
place [plas] nf (emplacement, classement)
place; (de ville, village) square; (espace
libre) room, space; (de parking) space;
(siège: de train, cinéma, voiture) seat;
(emploi) job; **en ~** (mettre) in its place;
sur ~ on the spot; **faire ~ à** to give way
to; **ça prend de la ~** it takes up a lot
of room ou space; **à la ~ de** in place of,
instead of; **à votre ~ ...** if I were you ...;
je voudrais réserver deux ~s I'd like to
book two seats; **la ~ est prise?** is this
seat taken?; **se mettre à la ~ de qn** to
put o.s. in sb's shoes
placé, e [plase] adj: **haut ~** (fig) high-
ranking; **être bien/mal ~** (spectateur)
to have a good/a poor seat; (concurrent)
to be in a good/bad position; **il est
bien ~ pour le savoir** he is in a position
to know
placement [plasmɑ̃] nm (Finance)
investment; **agence** ou **bureau de ~**
employment agency
placer [plase] vt to place; (convive,
spectateur) to seat; (argent) to place,
invest; **se ~ au premier rang** to go and
stand (ou sit) in the first row
plafond [plafɔ̃] nm ceiling
plage [plaʒ] nf beach; **plage arrière**
(Auto) parcel ou back shelf
plaider [plede] vi (avocat) to plead
▷ vt to plead; **~ pour** (fig) to speak
for; **plaidoyer** nm (Jur) speech for the
defence; (fig) plea
plaie [ple] nf wound
plaignant, e [plɛɲɑ̃, ɑ̃t] nm/f plaintiff
plaindre [plɛ̃dʀ] vt to pity, feel sorry
for; **se plaindre** vi (gémir) to moan;
(protester): **se ~ (à qn) (de)** to complain
(to sb) (about); (souffrir): **se ~ de** to
complain of
plaine [plɛn] nf plain
plain-pied [plɛ̃pje] adv: **de ~ (avec)** on
the same level (as)

plainte [plɛ̃t] nf (gémissement) moan,
groan; (doléance) complaint; **porter ~** to
lodge a complaint
plaire [plɛʀ] vi to be a success, be
successful; **ça plaît beaucoup aux
jeunes** it's very popular with young
people; **~ à: cela me plaît** I like it; **se ~
quelque part** to like being somewhere
ou like something somewhere; **s'il vous
plaît** please
plaisance [plɛzɑ̃s] nf (aussi:
navigation de ~) (pleasure) sailing,
yachting
plaisant, e [plɛzɑ̃, ɑ̃t] adj pleasant;
(histoire, anecdote) amusing
plaisanter [plɛzɑ̃te] vi to joke;
plaisanterie nf joke
plaisir [plɛziʀ] nm pleasure; **faire ~
à qn** (délibérément) to be nice to sb,
please sb; **ça me fait ~** I like (doing) it;
j'espère que ça te fera ~ I hope you'll
like it; **pour le ~** for pleasure
plaît [ple] vb voir **plaire**
plan, e [plɑ̃, an] adj flat ▷ nm plan;
(fig) level, plane; (Cinéma) shot; **au
premier/second ~** in the foreground/
middle distance; **à l'arrière ~** in the
background; **plan d'eau** lake
planche [plɑ̃ʃ] nf (pièce de bois) plank,
(wooden) board; (illustration) plate;
planche à repasser ironing board;
planche (à roulettes) skateboard;
planche (à voile) (sport) windsurfing
plancher [plɑ̃ʃe] nm floor; floorboards
pl ▷ vi (fam) to work hard
planer [plane] vi to glide; (fam: rêveur)
to have one's head in the clouds; **~ sur**
(fig: danger) to hang over
planète [planɛt] nf planet
planeur [planœʀ] nm glider
planifier [planifje] vt to plan
planning [planiŋ] nm programme,
schedule; **planning familial** family
planning
plant [plɑ̃] nm seedling, young plant
plante [plɑ̃t] nf plant; **la plante du
pied** the sole (of the foot); **plante verte**
ou **d'appartement** house plant

planter [plɑ̃te] vt (plante) to plant; (enfoncer) to hammer ou drive in; (tente) to put up, pitch; (fam: personne) to dump; **se planter** (fam: se tromper) to get it wrong

plaque [plak] nf plate; (de verglas, d'eczéma) patch; (avec inscription) plaque; **plaque chauffante** hotplate; **plaque de chocolat** bar of chocolate; **plaque tournante** (fig) centre

plaqué, e [plake] adj: **~ or/argent** gold-/silver-plated

plaquer [plake] vt (Rugby) to bring down; (fam: laisser tomber) to drop

plaquette [plaket] nf (de chocolat) bar; (beurre) pack(et); **plaquette de frein** brake pad

plastique [plastik] adj, nm plastic; **plastiquer** vt to blow up (with a plastic bomb)

plat, e [pla, -at] adj flat; (cheveux) straight; (style) flat, dull ▷ nm (récipient, Culin) dish; (d'un repas) course; **à ~ ventre** face down; **à ~** (pneu, batterie) flat; (fam: personne) dead beat; **plat cuisiné** pre-cooked meal; **plat de résistance** main course; **plat du jour** dish of the day

platane [platan] nm plane tree

plateau, x [plato] nm (support) tray; (Géo) plateau; (Cinéma) set; **plateau à fromages** cheese board

plate-bande [platbɑ̃d] nf flower bed

plate-forme [platfɔʀm] nf platform; **plate-forme de forage/pétrolière** drilling/oil rig

platine [platin] nm platinum ▷ nf (d'un tourne-disque) turntable; **platine laser** compact disc ou CD player

plâtre [plɑtʀ] nm (matériau) plaster; (statue) plaster statue; (Méd) (plaster) cast; **avoir un bras dans le ~** to have an arm in plaster

plein, e [plɛ̃, plɛn] adj full ▷ nm: **faire le ~ (d'essence)** to fill up (with petrol); **à ~es mains** (ramasser) in handfuls; **à ~ temps** full-time; **en ~ air** in the open air; **en ~ soleil** in direct sunlight; **en ~e**

nuit/rue in the middle of the night/street; **en ~ jour** in broad daylight; **le ~, s'il vous plaît** fill it up, please

pleurer [plœʀe] vi to cry; (yeux) to water ▷ vt to mourn (for); **~ sur** to lament (over), to bemoan

pleurnicher [plœʀniʃe] vi to snivel, whine

pleurs [plœʀ] nmpl: **en ~** in tears

pleut [plø] vb voir **pleuvoir**

pleuvoir [pløvwaʀ] vb impers to rain ▷ vi (coups) to rain down; (critiques, invitations) to shower down; **il pleut** it's raining; **il pleut des cordes** it's pouring (down), it's raining cats and dogs

pli [pli] nm fold; (de jupe) pleat; (de pantalon) crease

pliant, e [plijɑ̃, plijɑ̃t] adj folding

plier [plije] vt to fold; (pour ranger) to fold up; (genou, bras) to bend ▷ vi to bend; (fig) to yield; **se ~ à** to submit to

plisser [plise] vt (jupe) to put pleats in; (yeux) to screw up; (front) to crease

plomb [plɔ̃] nm (métal) lead; (d'une cartouche) (lead) shot; (Pêche) sinker; (Élec) fuse; **sans ~** (essence etc) unleaded

plomberie [plɔ̃bʀi] nf plumbing

plombier [plɔ̃bje] nm plumber

plonge [plɔ̃ʒ] nf washing-up

plongeant, e [plɔ̃ʒɑ̃, ɑ̃t] adj (vue) from above; (décolleté) plunging

plongée [plɔ̃ʒe] nf (Sport) diving no pl; (sans scaphandre) skin diving; **~ sous-marine** diving

plongeoir [plɔ̃ʒwaʀ] nm diving board

plongeon [plɔ̃ʒɔ̃] nm dive

plonger [plɔ̃ʒe] vi to dive ▷ vt: **~ qch dans** to plunge sth into; **se ~ dans** (études, lecture) to bury ou immerse o.s. in; **plonger** von **dive**

plu [ply] pp de **plaire**; de **pleuvoir**

pluie [plɥi] nf rain

plume [plym] nf feather; (pour écrire) (pen) nib; (fig) pen

plupart [plypaʀ]: **la ~** pron the majority, most (of them); **la ~ des** most, the majority of; **la ~ du temps/d'entre nous** most of the time/of us;

pour la ~ for the most part, mostly

pluriel [plyʀjɛl] nm plural

plus¹ [ply] vb voir **plaire**

○ MOT-CLÉ

plus¹ [ply] adv 1 (forme négative): **ne ... plus** no more, no longer; **je n'ai plus d'argent** I've got no more money ou no money left; **il ne travaille plus** he's no longer working, he doesn't work any more

2 [ply, plyz + voyelle] (comparatif) more, ...+er; (superlatif): **le plus** the most, the ...+est; **plus grand/intelligent (que)** bigger/more intelligent (than); **le plus grand/intelligent** the biggest/most intelligent; **tout au plus** at the very most

3 [plys, plyz + voyelle] (davantage) more; **il travaille plus (que)** he works more (than); **plus il travaille, plus il est heureux** the more he works, the happier he is; **plus de 10 personnes/3 heures** more than ou over 10 people/3 hours; **3 heures de plus que** 3 hours more than; **de plus** what's more, moreover; **il a 3 ans de plus que moi** he's 3 years older than me; **3 kilos en plus** 3 kilos more; **en plus de** in addition to; **de plus en plus** more and more; **plus ou moins** more or less; **ni plus ni moins** no more, no less
▷ prép [plys]: **4 plus 2** 4 plus 2

plusieurs [plyzjœʀ] dét, pron several; **ils sont ~** there are several of them

plus-value [plyvaly] nf (bénéfice) surplus

plutôt [plyto] adv rather; **je préfère ~ celui-ci** I'd rather have this one; **~ que (de) faire** rather than ou instead of doing

pluvieux, -euse [plyvjø, jøz] adj rainy, wet

PME sigle f (= petite(s) et moyenne(s) entreprise(s)) small business(es)

PMU sigle m (= Pari mutuel urbain) system

of betting on horses; (café) betting agency

PNB sigle m (= produit national brut) GNP

pneu [pnø] nm tyre (BRIT), tire (US); **j'ai un ~ crevé** I've got a flat tyre

pneumonie [pnømɔni] nf pneumonia

poche [pɔʃ] nf pocket; (sous les yeux) bag, pouch; **argent de ~** pocket money

pochette [pɔʃɛt] nf (d'aiguilles etc) case; (mouchoir) breast pocket handkerchief; (sac à main) clutch bag; **pochette de disque** record sleeve

poêle [pwal] nm stove ▷ nf: **~ (à frire)** frying pan

poème [pɔɛm] nm poem

poésie [pɔezi] nf (poème) poem; (art): **la ~** poetry

poète [pɔɛt] nm poet

poids [pwa] nm weight; (Sport) shot; **vendre au ~** to sell by weight; **perdre/prendre du ~** to lose/put on weight; **poids lourd** (camion) lorry (BRIT), truck (US)

poignant, e [pwaɲɑ̃, ɑ̃t] adj poignant

poignard [pwaɲaʀ] nm dagger; **poignarder** vt to stab, knife

poigne [pwaɲ] nf grip; **avoir de la ~** (fig) to rule with a firm hand

poignée [pwaɲe] nf (de sel etc, fig) handful; (de couvercle, porte) handle; **poignée de main** handshake

poignet [pwaɲɛ] nm (Anat) wrist; (de chemise) cuff

poil [pwal] nm (Anat) hair; (de pinceau, brosse) bristle; (de tapis) strand; (pelage) coat; **à ~** (fam) starkers; **au ~** (fam) hunky-dory; **poilu, e** adj hairy

poinçonner [pwɛ̃sɔne] vt (bijou) to hallmark; (billet) to punch

poing [pwɛ̃] nm fist; **coup de ~** punch

point [pwɛ̃] nm (endroit) spot; (marque, signe) dot; (: de ponctuation) full stop, period (US); (Couture, Tricot) stitch ▷ adv = **pas¹**; **faire le ~** (fig) to take stock (of the situation); **sur le ~ de faire** (just) about to do; **à tel que** so much so that; **mettre au ~** (procédé) to develop; (affaire) to settle; **à ~** (Culin: viande) medium; **à ~ (nommé)**

just at the right time; **deux ~s** colon; **point de côté** stitch (pain); **point d'exclamation/d'interrogation** exclamation/question mark; **point de repère** landmark; (dans le temps) point of reference; **point de vente** retail outlet; **point de vue** viewpoint; (fig: opinion) point of view; **point faible** weak spot; **point final** full stop, period (us); **point mort: au point mort** (Auto) in neutral; **points de suspension** suspension points

pointe [pwɛ̃t] nf point; (clou) tack; (fig): **une ~ de** a hint of; **être à la ~ de** (fig) to be in the forefront of; **sur la ~ des pieds** on tiptoe; **en ~** pointed, tapered; **de ~** (technique etc) leading; **heures de ~** peak hours

pointer [pwɛte] vt (diriger: canon, doigt): **~ sur qch** to point at sth ▷ vi (employé) to clock in

pointillé [pwɛtije] nm (trait) dotted line

pointilleux, -euse [pwɛtijø, øz] adj particular, pernickety

pointu, e [pwɛty] adj pointed; (voix) shrill; (analyse) precise

pointure [pwɛtyʀ] nf size

point-virgule [pwɛ̃viʀgyl] nm semi-colon

poire [pwaʀ] nf pear; (fam: péj) mug

poireau, x [pwaʀo] nm leek

poirier [pwaʀje] nm pear tree

pois [pwa] nm (Bot) pea; (sur une étoffe) dot, spot; **~ chiche** chickpea; **à ~** (cravate etc) spotted, polka-dot cpd

poison [pwazɔ̃] nm poison

poisseux, -euse [pwasø, øz] adj sticky

poisson [pwasɔ̃] nm fish gén inv; (Astrol): **P~s** Pisces; **~ d'avril** April fool; (blague) April Fool's Day trick; see note; **poisson rouge** goldfish; **poissonnerie** nf fish-shop; **poissonnier, -ière** nm/f fishmonger (BRIT), fish merchant (us)

● The traditional April Fools' Day prank in France involves attaching a cut-

out paper fish, known as a 'poisson d'avril', to the back of one's victim, without being caught.

poitrine [pwatʀin] nf chest; (seins) bust, bosom; (Culin) breast

poivre [pwavʀ] nm pepper

poivron [pwavʀɔ̃] nm pepper, capsicum

polaire [pɔlɛʀ] adj polar

pôle [pol] nm (Géo, Élec) pole; **le ~ Nord/Sud** the North/South Pole

poli, e [pɔli] adj polite; (lisse) smooth

police [pɔlis] nf police; **police judiciaire** ≈ Criminal Investigation Department (BRIT), ≈ Federal Bureau of Investigation (us); **police secours** ≈ emergency services (BRIT), ≈ paramedics nf pl (us); **policier, -ière** adj police cpd ▷ nm policeman; (aussi: **roman policier**) detective novel

polir [pɔliʀ] vt to polish

politesse [pɔlitɛs] nf politeness

politicien, ne [pɔlitisjɛ̃, jɛn] (péj) nm/f politician

politique [pɔlitik] adj political ▷ nf politics sg; (mesures, méthode) policies pl

politiquement [pɔlitikmɑ̃] adv politically; **~ correct** politically correct

pollen [pɔlɛn] nm pollen

polluant, e [pɔlɥɑ̃, ɑ̃t] adj polluting ▷ nm (produit): ~ pollutant; **non-** non-polluting

polluer [pɔlɥe] vt to pollute; **pollution** nf pollution

polo [pɔlo] nm (chemise) polo shirt

Pologne [pɔlɔɲ] nf: **la ~** Poland; **polonais, e** adj Polish ▷ nm/f: **Polonais, e** Pole ▷ nm (Ling) Polish

poltron, ne [pɔltʀɔ̃, ɔn] adj cowardly

polycopier [pɔlikɔpje] vt to duplicate

Polynésie [pɔlinezi] nf: **la ~** Polynesia; **la ~ française** French Polynesia

polyvalent, e [pɔlivalɑ̃, ɑ̃t] adj (rôle) varied; (salle) multi-purpose

pommade [pɔmad] nf ointment, cream

pomme [pɔm] nf apple; **tomber**

dans les ~s (fam) to pass out; **pomme d'Adam** Adam's apple; **pomme de pin** pine ou fir cone; **pomme de terre** potato

pommette [pɔmɛt] nf cheekbone

pommier [pɔmje] nm apple tree

pompe [pɔ̃p] nf pump; (faste) pomp (and ceremony); **pompe (à essence)** petrol pump; **pompes funèbres** funeral parlour sg, undertaker's sg; **pomper** vt to pump; (aspirer) to pump up; (absorber) to soak up

pompeux, -euse [pɔ̃pø, øz] adj pompous

pompier [pɔ̃pje] nm fireman

pompiste [pɔ̃pist] nm/f petrol (BRIT) ou gas (US) pump attendant

poncer [pɔ̃se] vt to sand (down)

ponctuation [pɔ̃ktɥasjɔ̃] nf punctuation

ponctuel, le [pɔ̃ktɥɛl] adj punctual

pondéré, e [pɔ̃deʀe] adj level-headed, composed

pondre [pɔ̃dʀ] vt to lay

poney [pɔnɛ] nm pony

pont [pɔ̃] nm bridge; (Navig) deck; **faire le ~** to take the extra day off; see note; **pont suspendu** suspension bridge; **pont-levis** nm drawbridge

○ PONT
○
○ The expression 'faire le pont' refers
○ to the practice of taking a Monday
○ or Friday off to make a long weekend
○ if a public holiday falls on a Tuesday
○ or Thursday. The French commonly
○ take an extra day of work to give
○ four consecutive days' holiday at
○ 'l'Ascension', 'le 14 juillet' and 'le
○ 15 août'.

pop [pɔp] adj inv pop

populaire [pɔpylɛʀ] adj popular; (manifestation) mass cpd; (milieux, quartier) working-class; (expression) vernacular

popularité [pɔpylaʀite] nf popularity

population [pɔpylasjɔ̃] nf population

populeux, -euse [pɔpylø, øz] adj densely populated

porc [pɔʀ] nm pig; (Culin) pork

porcelaine [pɔʀsəlɛn] nf porcelain, china; piece of china(ware)

porc-épic [pɔʀkepik] nm porcupine

porche [pɔʀʃ] nm porch

porcherie [pɔʀʃəʀi] nf pigsty

pore [pɔʀ] nm pore

porno [pɔʀno] adj porno ▷ nm porn

port [pɔʀ] nm harbour, port; (ville) port; (de l'uniforme etc) wearing; (pour lettre) postage; (pour colis, aussi: posture) carriage; **port d'arme** (Jur) carrying of a firearm; **port payé** postage paid

portable [pɔʀtabl] adj (portatif) portable; (téléphone) mobile ▷ nm (Comput) laptop (computer); (téléphone) mobile (phone)

portail [pɔʀtaj] nm gate

portant, e [pɔʀtɑ̃, ɑ̃t] adj: **bien/mal ~** in good/poor health

portatif, -ive [pɔʀtatif, iv] adj portable

porte [pɔʀt] nf door; (de ville, jardin) gate; **mettre à la ~** to throw out; **porte-avions** nm inv aircraft carrier; **porte-bagages** nm inv luggage rack; **porte-bonheur** nm inv lucky charm; **porte-clefs** nm inv key ring; **porte-documents** nm inv attaché ou document case

porté, e [pɔʀte] adj: **être ~ à faire** to be inclined to do; **être ~ sur qch** to be keen on sth; **portée** nf (d'une arme) range; (fig: effet) impact, import; (: capacité) scope, capability; (de chatte etc) litter; (Mus) stave, staff; **à/hors de portée (de)** within/out of reach (of); **à portée de (la) main** within (arm's) reach; **à la portée de qn** (fig) at sb's level, within sb's capabilities

porte...: **portefeuille** nm wallet; **portemanteau, x** nm (cintre) coat hanger; (au mur) coat rack; **porte-monnaie** nm inv purse; **porte-parole** nm inv spokesman

porter [pɔʀte] vt to carry; (sur soi: vêtement, barbe, bague) to wear; (fig: responsabilité etc) to bear, carry; (inscription, nom, fruits) to bear; (coup) to deal; (attention) to turn; (apporter): **~ qch à qn** to take sth to sb ▷ vi (voix) to carry; (coup, argument) to hit home; **se porter** vi (se sentir): **se ~ bien/mal** to be well/unwell; **~ sur** (recherches) to be concerned with; **se faire ~ malade** to report sick

porteur, -euse [pɔʀtœʀ, øz] nm/f (de bagages) porter; (de chèque) bearer

porte-voix [pɔʀtavwa] nm inv megaphone

portier [pɔʀtje] nm doorman

portière [pɔʀtjɛʀ] nf door

portion [pɔʀsjɔ̃] nf (part) portion, share; (partie) portion, section

porto [pɔʀto] nm port (wine)

portrait [pɔʀtʀɛ] nm (peinture) portrait; (photo) photograph; **portrait-robot** nm Identikit ® ou photo-fit® picture

portuaire [pɔʀtɥɛʀ] adj port cpd, harbour cpd

portugais, e [pɔʀtɥgɛ, ɛz] adj Portuguese ▷ nm/f: **P~, e** Portuguese ▷ nm (Ling) Portuguese

Portugal [pɔʀtɥgal] nm: **le ~** Portugal

pose [poz] nf (de moquette) laying; (attitude, d'un modèle) pose; (Photo) exposure

posé, e [poze] adj serious

poser [poze] vt to put; (installer: moquette, carrelage) to lay; (rideaux, papier peint) to hang; (question) to ask; (principe, conditions) to lay ou set down; (difficulté) to pose; (formuler: problème) to formulate ▷ vi (modèle) to pose; **se poser** vi (oiseau, avion) to land; (question) to arise; **~ qch (sur)** (déposer) to put sth down (on); **~ qch sur/quelque part** (placer) to put sth on/somewhere; **~ sa candidature à un poste** to apply for a post

positif, -ive [pozitif, iv] adj positive

position [pozisjɔ̃] nf position; **prendre**

~ (fig) to take a stand

posologie [pozɔlɔʒi] nf dosage

posséder [posede] vt to own, possess; (qualité, talent) to have, possess; (sexuellement) to possess; **possession** nf ownership no pl, possession; **prendre possession de qch** to take possession of sth

possibilité [posibilite] nf possibility; **possibilités** nfpl (potentiel) potential sg

possible [posibl] adj possible; (projet, entreprise) feasible ▷ nm: **faire son ~** to do all one can, do one's utmost; **le plus/moins de livres ~** as many/few books as possible; **le plus vite ~** as quickly as possible; **aussitôt/dès que ~** as soon as possible

postal, e, -aux [pɔstal, o] adj postal

poste¹ [pɔst] nf (service) post, postal service; (administration, bureau) post office; **mettre à la ~** to post; **poste restante** poste restante (BRIT), general delivery (US)

poste² [pɔst] nm (fonction, Mil) post; (Tél) extension; (de radio etc) set; **poste (de police)** police station; **poste de secours** first-aid post; **poste d'essence** filling station; **poste d'incendie** fire point; **poste de pilotage** cockpit, flight deck

poster [pɔste] vt (lettre): **où est-ce que je peux ~ ces cartes postales?** where can I post these cards?

postérieur, e [pɔsteʀjœʀ] adj (date) later; (partie) back ▷ nm (fam) behind

postuler [pɔstyle] vi: **à ou pour un emploi** to apply for a job

pot [po] nm (en verre) jar; (en terre) pot; (en plastique, carton) carton; (en métal) tin; (fam: chance) luck; **avoir du ~** (fam) to be lucky; **boire ou prendre un ~** (fam) to have a drink; **petit ~ (pour bébé)** (jar of) baby food; **~ catalytique** catalytic converter; **pot d'échappement** exhaust pipe

potable [pɔtabl] adj: **eau (non) ~** (non-)drinking water

potage [pɔtaʒ] nm soup; **potager,**

-ère adj: **(jardin) potager** kitchen ou vegetable garden

pot-au-feu [pɔtofø] nm inv (beef) stew

pot-de-vin [podvɛ̃] nm bribe

pote [pɔt] (fam) nm pal

poteau, x [pɔto] nm post; **poteau indicateur** signpost

potelé, e [pɔt(ə)le] adj plump, chubby

potentiel, le [pɔtɑ̃sjɛl] adj, nm potential

poterie [pɔtri] nf pottery; (objet) piece of pottery

potier, -ière [pɔtje, jɛʀ] nm/f potter

potiron [pɔtiʀɔ̃] nm pumpkin

pou, x [pu] nm louse

poubelle [pubɛl] nf (dust)bin

pouce [pus] nm thumb

poudre [pudʀ] nf powder; (fard) (face) powder; (explosif) gunpowder; **en ~**: **café en ~** instant coffee; **lait en ~** dried ou powdered milk; **poudreuse** nf powder snow; **poudrier** nm (powder) compact

pouffer [pufe] vi: **~ (de rire)** to burst out laughing

poulailler [pulaje] nm henhouse

poulain [pulɛ̃] nm foal; (fig) protégé

poule [pul] nf hen; (Culin) (boiling) fowl; **poule mouillée** coward

poulet [pulɛ] nm chicken; (fam) cop

poulie [puli] nf pulley

pouls [pu] nm pulse; **prendre le ~ de qn** to feel sb's pulse

poumon [pumɔ̃] nm lung

poupée [pupe] nf doll

pour [puʀ] prép for ▷ nm: **le ~ et le contre** the pros and cons; **~ faire** (so as) to do, in order to do; **~ avoir fait** for having done; **~ que** so that, in order that; **~ fermé (cause de) travaux** closed for refurbishment ou alterations; **c'est ~ ça que ...** that's why ...; **~ quoi faire?** what for?; **~ 20 euros d'essence** 20 euros' worth of petrol; **~ cent** per cent; **~ ce qui est de** as for

pourboire [puʀbwaʀ] nm tip; **combien de ~ est-ce qu'il faut laisser?** how much should I tip?

pourcentage [puʀsɑ̃taʒ] nm percentage

pourchasser [puʀʃase] vt to pursue

pourparlers [puʀpaʀle] nmpl talks, negotiations

pourpre [puʀpʀ] adj crimson

pourquoi [puʀkwa] adv, conj why ▷ nm inv: **le ~ (de)** the reason (for)

pourrai etc [puʀe] vb voir **pouvoir**

pourri, e [puʀi] adj rotten

pourrir [puʀiʀ] vi to rot; (fruit) to go rotten ou bad ▷ vt to rot; (fig) to spoil thoroughly; **pourriture** nf rot

poursuite [puʀsɥit] nf pursuit, chase; **poursuites** nfpl (Jur) legal proceedings

poursuivre [puʀsɥivʀ] vt to pursue, chase (after); (obséder) to haunt; (Jur) to bring proceedings against, prosecute; (: au civil) to sue; (but) to strive towards; (continuer: études etc) to carry on with, continue; **se poursuivre** vi to go on, continue

pourtant [puʀtɑ̃] adv yet; **c'est ~ facile** (and) yet it's easy

pourtour [puʀtuʀ] nm perimeter

pourvoir [puʀvwaʀ] vt: **~ qch/qn de** to equip sth/sb with ▷ vi: **~ à** to provide for; **pourvu, e** adj: **pourvu de** equipped with; **pourvu que** (si) provided that, so long as; (espérons que) let's hope (that)

pousse [pus] nf growth; (bourgeon) shoot

poussée [puse] nf thrust; (d'acné) eruption; (fig: prix) upsurge

pousser [puse] vt to push; (émettre: cri, soupir) to give; (stimuler: élève) to urge on; (poursuivre: études etc) to carry on (further) ▷ vi to push; (croître) to grow; **se pousser** vi to move over; **~ qn à** (inciter) to urge ou press sb to; (acculer) to drive sb to; **faire ~ (plante)** to grow

poussette [pusɛt] nf push chair (BRIT), stroller (US)

poussière [pusjɛʀ] nf dust; **poussiéreux, -euse** adj dusty

poussin [pusɛ̃] nm chick
poutre [putʀ] nf beam

 MOT-CLÉ

pouvoir [puvwaʀ] nm power; (Pol: dirigeants): **le pouvoir** those in power; **les pouvoirs publics** the authorities; **pouvoir d'achat** purchasing power
▷ vb semi-aux **1** (être en état de) can, be able to; **je ne peux pas le réparer** I can't ou I am not able to repair it; **déçu de ne pas pouvoir le faire** disappointed not to be able to do it **2** (avoir la permission) can, may, be allowed to; **vous pouvez aller au cinéma** you can ou may go to the pictures **3** (probabilité, hypothèse) may, might, could; **il a pu avoir un accident** he may ou might ou could have had an accident; **il aurait pu le dire!** he might ou could have said (so!)
▷ vb impers may, might, could; **il peut arriver que** it may ou might ou could happen that; **il pourrait pleuvoir** it might rain
▷ vt can, be able to; **j'ai fait tout ce que j'ai pu** I did all I could; **je n'en peux plus** (épuisé) I'm exhausted; (à bout) I can't take any more
▷ vi: **se pouvoir: il se peut que** it may ou might be that; **cela se pourrait** that's quite possible

prairie [pʀeʀi] nf meadow
praline [pʀalin] nf sugared almond
praticable [pʀatikabl] adj passable, practicable
pratiquant, e [pʀatikɑ̃, ɑ̃t] nm/f (regular) churchgoer
pratique [pʀatik] nf practice ▷ adj practical; **pratiquement** adv (pour ainsi dire) practically, virtually; **pratiquer** vt to practise; (l'équitation, la pêche) to go in for; (le golf, football) to play; (intervention, opération) to carry out
pré [pʀe] nm meadow

préalable [pʀealabl] adj preliminary; **au ~** beforehand
préambule [pʀeɑ̃byl] nm preamble; (fig) prelude; **sans ~** straight away
préau [pʀeo] nm (Scol) covered playground
préavis [pʀeavi] nm notice
précaution [pʀekosjɔ̃] nf precaution; **avec ~** cautiously; **par ~** as a precaution
précédemment [pʀesedamɑ̃] adv before, previously
précédent, e [pʀesedɑ̃, ɑ̃t] adj previous ▷ nm precedent; **sans ~** unprecedented; **le jour ~** the day before, the previous day
précéder [pʀesede] vt to precede
précher [pʀeʃe] vt to preach
précieux, -euse [pʀesjø, jøz] adj precious; (aide, conseil) invaluable
précipice [pʀesipis] nm drop, chasm
précipitamment [pʀesipitamɑ̃] adv hurriedly, hastily
précipitation [pʀesipitasjɔ̃] nf (hâte) haste
précipité, e [pʀesipite] adj hurried, hasty
précipiter [pʀesipite] vt (hâter: départ) to hasten; (faire tomber): ~ **qn/qch du haut de** to throw ou hurl sb/sth off ou from; **se précipiter** vi to speed up; **se ~ sur/vers** to rush at/towards
précis, e [pʀesi, iz] adj (mesures) accurate, precise; **à 4 heures ~es** at 4 o'clock sharp; **précisément** adv precisely; **préciser** vt (expliquer) to be more specific about, clarify; (spécifier) to state, specify; **se préciser** vi to become clear(er); **précision** nf precision; (détail) point ou detail; **demander des précisions** to ask for further explanation
précoce [pʀekɔs] adj early; (enfant) precocious
préconçu, e [pʀekɔ̃sy] adj preconceived
préconiser [pʀekɔnize] vt to advocate
prédécesseur [pʀedesesœʀ] nm predecessor

predecessor

prédilection [pʀedilɛksjɔ̃] nf: **avoir une ~ pour** to be partial to

prédire [pʀediʀ] vt to predict

prédominer [pʀedɔmine] vi to predominate

préface [pʀefas] nf preface

préfecture [pʀefɛktyʀ] nf prefecture; **préfecture de police** police headquarters pl

préférable [pʀefeʀabl] adj preferable

préféré, e [pʀefeʀe] adj, nm/f favourite

préférence [pʀefeʀɑ̃s] nf preference; **de ~** preferably

préférer [pʀefeʀe] vt: **~ qn/qch (à)** to prefer sb/sth (to), like sb/sth better (than); **~ faire** to prefer to do; **je préférerais du thé** I would rather have tea, I'd prefer tea

préfet [pʀefɛ] nm prefect

préhistorique [pʀeistɔʀik] adj prehistoric

préjudice [pʀeʒydis] nm (matériel) loss; (moral) harm no pl; **porter ~ à** to harm, be detrimental to; **au ~ de** at the expense of

préjugé [pʀeʒyʒe] nm prejudice; **avoir un ~ contre** to be prejudiced ou biased against

prélasser [pʀelɑse]: **se prélasser** vi to lounge

prélèvement [pʀelɛvmɑ̃] nm (montant) deduction; **faire un ~ de sang** to take a blood sample

prélever [pʀel(ə)ve] vt (échantillon) to take; **~ (sur)** (montant) to deduct (from); (argent: sur son compte) to withdraw (from)

prématuré, e [pʀematyʀe] adj premature ▷ nm premature baby

premier, -ière [pʀəmje, jɛʀ] adj first; (rang) front; (fig: objectif) basic; **le ~ venu** the first person to come along; **de ~ ordre** first-rate; **Premier ministre** Prime Minister; **première** nf (Scol) year 12 (BRIT), eleventh grade (US); (Aviat, Rail etc) first class; **premièrement** adv firstly

prémonition [pʀemɔnisjɔ̃] nf premonition

prenant, e [pʀənɑ̃, ɑ̃t] adj absorbing, engrossing

prénatal, e [pʀenatal] adj (Méd) antenatal

prendre [pʀɑ̃dʀ] vt to take; (repas) to have; (se procurer) to get; (malfaiteur, poisson) to catch; (passager) to pick up; (personnel) to take on; (traiter: personne) to handle; (voix, ton) to put on; (ôter): **~ qch à** to take sth from; (coincer): **se ~ les doigts dans** to get one's fingers caught in ▷ vi (liquide, ciment) to set; (greffe, vaccin) to take; (feu: foyer) to go; (se diriger): **à gauche** to turn (to the) left; **~ froid** to catch cold; **se ~ pour** to think one is; **s'en ~ à** to attack; **se ~ d'amitié pour** to befriend; **s'y ~** (procéder) to set about it

preneur [pʀənœʀ] nm: **être/trouver ~** to be willing to buy/find a buyer

prénom [pʀenɔ̃] nm first ou Christian name

préoccupation [pʀeɔkypasjɔ̃] nf (souci) concern; (idée fixe) preoccupation

préoccuper [pʀeɔkype] vt (inquiéter) to worry; (absorber) to preoccupy; **se ~ de** to be concerned with

préparatifs [pʀepaʀatif] nmpl preparations

préparation [pʀepaʀasjɔ̃] nf preparation

préparer [pʀepaʀe] vt to prepare; (café, thé) to make; (examen) to prepare for; (voyage, entreprise) to plan; **se préparer** vi (orage, tragédie) to brew, be in the air; **~ qch à qn** (surprise etc) to have sth in store for sb; **se ~ (à qch/faire)** to prepare (o.s.) ou get ready (for sth/to do)

prépondérant, e [pʀepɔ̃deʀɑ̃, ɑ̃t] adj major, dominating

préposé, e [pʀepoze] nm/f employee; (facteur) postman

préposition [pʀepozisjɔ̃] nf preposition

près [pʀɛ] adv near, close; **~ de** near (to), close to; (environ) nearly, almost; **de ~** closely; **à 5 kg ~** to within about 5 kg; **il n'est pas à 10 minutes ~** he can spare 10 minutes; **est-ce qu'il y a une banque ~ d'ici?** is there a bank nearby?

présage [pʀezaʒ] nm omen

presbyte [pʀɛsbit] adj long-sighted

presbytère [pʀɛsbitɛʀ] nm presbytery

prescription [pʀɛskʀipsjɔ̃] nf prescription

prescrire [pʀɛskʀiʀ] vt to prescribe

présence [pʀezɑ̃s] nf presence; (au bureau, à l'école) attendance

présent, e [pʀezɑ̃, ɑ̃t] adj, nm present; **à ~ (que)** now (that)

présentation [pʀezɑ̃tasjɔ̃] nf presentation; (de nouveau venu) introduction; (allure) appearance; **faire les ~s** to do the introductions

présenter [pʀezɑ̃te] vt to present; (excuses, condoléances) to offer; (invité, conférencier): **~ qn (à)** to introduce sb (to) ▷ vi: **~ bien** to have a pleasing appearance; **se présenter** (occasion) to arise; **se ~ à** (examen) to sit; (élection) to stand for, run for; **je vous présente Nadine** this is Nadine, could I introduce you to Nadine?

préservatif [pʀezɛʀvatif] nm condom, sheath

préserver [pʀezɛʀve] vt: **~ de** (protéger) to protect from

président [pʀezidɑ̃] nm (Pol) president; (d'une assemblée, Comm) chairman; **président directeur général** chairman and managing director; **présidentielles** nfpl presidential elections

présider [pʀezide] vt to preside over; (dîner) to be the guest of honour at

presque [pʀɛsk] adv almost, nearly; **~ personne** hardly anyone; **~ rien** hardly anything; **~ pas** hardly (at all); **~ pas (de)** hardly any

presqu'île [pʀɛskil] nf peninsula

pressant, e [pʀesɑ̃, ɑ̃t] adj urgent

presse [pʀɛs] nf press; (affluence):

heures de ~ busy times

pressé, e [pʀese] adj in a hurry; (travail) urgent; **orange ~e** freshly-squeezed orange juice

pressentiment [pʀesɑ̃timɑ̃] nm foreboding, premonition

pressentir [pʀesɑ̃tiʀ] vt to sense

presse-papiers [pʀɛspapje] nm inv paperweight

presser [pʀese] vt (fruit, éponge) to squeeze; (bouton) to press; (allure) to speed up; (inciter): **~ qn de faire** to urge ou press sb to do ▷ vi to be urgent; **se presser** vi (se hâter) to hurry (up); **se ~ contre qn** to squeeze up against sb; **le temps presse** there's not much time; **rien ne presse** there's no hurry

pressing [pʀesiŋ] nm (magasin) dry-cleaner's

pression [pʀesjɔ̃] nf pressure; (bouton) press stud; (fam: bière) draught beer; **faire ~ sur** to put pressure on; **sous ~** pressurized, under pressure; (fig) under pressure; **pression artérielle** blood pressure

prestataire [pʀɛstatɛʀ] nm/f supplier

prestation [pʀɛstasjɔ̃] nf (allocation) benefit; (d'une entreprise) service provided; (d'un artiste) performance

prestidigitateur, -trice [pʀɛstidiʒitatœʀ, tʀis] nm/f conjurer

prestige [pʀɛstiʒ] nm prestige; **prestigieux, -euse** adj prestigious

présumer [pʀezyme] vt: **~ que** to presume ou assume that

prêt, e [pʀɛ, pʀɛt] adj ready ▷ nm (somme) loan; **quand est-ce que mes photos seront ~es?** when will my photos be ready?; **prêt-à-porter** nm ready-to-wear ou off-the-peg (BRIT) clothes pl

prétendre [pʀetɑ̃dʀ] vt (affirmer): **~ que** to claim that; (avoir l'intention de): **~ faire qch** to mean ou intend to do sth; **prétendu, e** adj (supposé) so-called

Attention à ne pas traduire **prétendre** par to pretend.

prétentieux, -euse [pʀetɑ̃sjø, jøz]

adj pretentious

prétention [pʀetɑ̃sjɔ̃] *nf* claim; (*vanité*) pretentiousness

prêter [pʀete] *vt* (*livres, argent*): **~ qch (à)** to lend sth (to); (*supposer*): **~ à qn** (*caractère, propos*) to attribute to sb; **pouvez-vous me ~ de l'argent?** can you lend me some money?

prétexte [pʀetɛkst] *nm* pretext, excuse; **sous aucun ~** on no account; **prétexter** *vt* to give as a pretext *ou* an excuse

prêtre [pʀɛtʀ] *nm* priest

preuve [pʀœv] *nf* proof; (*indice*) proof, evidence *no pl*; **faire ~ de** to show; **faire ses ~s** to prove o.s. (*ou itself*)

prévaloir [pʀevalwaʀ] *vi* to prevail

prévenant, e [pʀev(ə)nɑ̃, ɑ̃t] *adj* thoughtful, kind

prévenir [pʀev(ə)niʀ] *vt* (*éviter*: catastrophe etc) to avoid, prevent; (*anticiper*: désirs, besoins) to anticipate; **~ qn (de)** (*avertir*) to warn sb (about); (*informer*) to tell *ou* inform sb (about)

préventif, -ive [pʀevɑ̃tif, iv] *adj* preventive

prévention [pʀevɑ̃sjɔ̃] *nf* prevention; **prévention routière** road safety

prévenu, e [pʀev(ə)ny] *nm/f* (*Jur*) defendant, accused

prévision [pʀevizjɔ̃] *nf*: **~s** predictions; (*Écon*) forecast *sg*; **en ~ de** in anticipation of; **prévisions météorologiques** weather forecast *sg*

prévoir [pʀevwaʀ] *vt* (*anticiper*) to foresee; (*s'attendre à*) to expect, reckon on; (*organiser*: voyage etc) to plan; (*envisager*) to allow; **comme prévu** as planned; **prévoyant, e** *adj* gifted with (*ou showing*) foresight; **prévu, e** *pp de* **prévoir**

prier [pʀije] *vi* to pray ▷ *vt* (*Dieu*) to pray to; (*implorer*) to beg; (*demander*): **~ qn de faire** to ask sb to do; **se faire ~** to need coaxing *ou* persuading; **je vous en prie** (*allez-y*) please do; (*de rien*) don't mention it; **prière** *nf* prayer; **"prière de ..."** "please ..."

primaire [pʀimɛʀ] *adj* primary ▷ *nm* (*Scol*) primary education

prime [pʀim] *nf* (*bonus*) bonus; (*subvention*) premium; (*Comm*: cadeau) free gift; (*Assurances, Bourse*) premium ▷ *adj*: **de ~ abord** at first glance; **primer** *vt* (*récompenser*) to award a prize to ▷ *vi* to dominate; to be most important

primevère [pʀimvɛʀ] *nf* primrose

primitif, -ive [pʀimitif, iv] *adj* primitive; (*originel*) original

prince [pʀɛ̃s] *nm* prince; **princesse** *nf* princess

principal, e, -aux [pʀɛ̃sipal, o] *adj* principal, main ▷ *nm* (*Scol*) principal, head(master); (*essentiel*) main thing

principe [pʀɛ̃sip] *nm* principle; **par ~** on principle; **en ~** (*habituellement*) as a rule; (*théoriquement*) in principle

printemps [pʀɛ̃tɑ̃] *nm* spring

priorité [pʀijɔʀite] *nf* priority; (*Auto*) right of way; **priorité à droite** right of way to vehicles coming from the right

pris, e [pʀi, pʀiz] *pp de* **prendre** ▷ *adj* (*place*) taken; (*mains*) full; (*personne*) busy; **avoir le nez/la gorge ~(e)** to have a stuffy nose/a hoarse throat; **être ~ de panique** to be panic-stricken

prise [pʀiz] *nf* (*d'une ville*) capture; (*Pêche, Chasse*) catch; (*point d'appui ou pour empoigner*) hold; (*Élec*: fiche) plug; (: *femelle*) socket; **être aux ~s avec** to be grappling with; **prise de courant** power point; **prise de sang** blood test; **prise multiple** adaptor

priser [pʀize] *vt* (*estimer*) to prize, value

prison [pʀizɔ̃] *nf* prison; **aller/être en ~** to go to/be in prison *ou* jail; **prisonnier, -ière** *nm/f* prisoner ▷ *adj* captive

privé, e [pʀive] *adj* private; (*en punition*): **tu es ~ de télé!** no TV for you! ▷ *nm* (*Comm*) private sector; **en ~** in private

priver [pʀive] *vt*: **~ qn de** to deprive sb of; **se priver de** to go *ou* do without

privilège [pʀivilɛʒ] *nm* privilege

prix [pʀi] *nm* price; (*récompense, Scol*) prize; **hors de ~** exorbitantly priced;

à aucun ~ not at any price; **à tout ~** at all costs

probable [pʀɔbabl] adj likely, probable; **probablement** adv probably

problème [pʀɔblɛm] nm problem

procédé [pʀɔsede] nm (méthode) process; (comportement) behaviour no pl

procéder [pʀɔsede] vi to proceed; (moralement) to behave; **~ à** to carry out

procès [pʀɔsɛ] nm trial; (poursuites) proceedings pl; **être en ~ avec** to be involved in a lawsuit with

processus [pʀɔsesys] nm process

procès-verbal, -aux [pʀɔsɛvɛʀbal, o] nm (de réunion) minutes pl; (aussi: **P.-V.**) parking ticket

prochain, e [pʀɔʃɛ̃, ɛn] adj next; (proche: départ, arrivée) impending; **mon ~** fellow man; **la ~e fois/semaine ~e** next time/week; **prochainement** adv soon, shortly

proche [pʀɔʃ] adj nearby; (dans le temps) imminent; (parent, ami) close; **proches** nmpl (parents) close relatives; **être ~ (de)** to be near, be close (to)

proclamer [pʀɔklame] vt to proclaim

procuration [pʀɔkyʀasjɔ̃] nf proxy

procurer [pʀɔkyʀe] vt: **~ qch à qn** (fournir) to obtain sth for sb; (causer: plaisir etc) to bring sb sth; **se procurer** vt to get; **procureur** nm public prosecutor

prodige [pʀɔdiʒ] nm marvel, wonder; (personne) prodigy; **prodiguer** vt (soins, attentions) **prodiguer qch à qn** to give sb sth

producteur, -trice [pʀɔdyktœʀ, tʀis] nm/f producer

productif, -ive [pʀɔdyktif, iv] adj productive

production [pʀɔdyksjɔ̃] nf production; (rendement) output

productivité [pʀɔdyktivite] nf productivity

produire [pʀɔdɥiʀ] vt to produce; **se produire** vi (événement) to happen, occur; (acteur) to perform, appear

produit [pʀɔdɥi] nm product;

produit chimique chemical; **produits agricoles** farm produce sg; **produits de beauté** beauty products, cosmetics; **produits d'entretien** cleaning products

prof [pʀɔf] (fam) nm teacher

proférer [pʀɔfeʀe] vt to utter

professer [pʀɔfese] vt to profess

professeur, e [pʀɔfesœʀ] nm/f teacher; (de faculté) (university) lecturer; (titulaire d'une chaire) professor

profession [pʀɔfesjɔ̃] nf occupation; **~ libérale** (liberal) profession; **sans ~** unemployed; **professionnel, le** adj, nm/f professional

profil [pʀɔfil] nm profile; **de ~** in profile

profit [pʀɔfi] nm (avantage) benefit, advantage; (Comm, Finance) profit; **au ~ de** in aid of; **tirer ~ de** to profit from; **profitable** adj (utile) beneficial; (lucratif) profitable; **profiter** vi: **profiter de** (situation, occasion) to take advantage of; (vacances, jeunesse etc) to make the most of

profond, e [pʀɔfɔ̃, ɔ̃d] adj deep; (sentiment, intérêt) profound; **profondément** adv deeply; **il dort profondément** he is sound asleep; **profondeur** nf depth; **l'eau à quelle profondeur?** how deep is the water?

programme [pʀɔgʀam] nm programme; (Scol) syllabus, curriculum; (Inform) program; **programmer** vt (émission) to schedule; (Inform) to program; **programmeur, -euse** nm/f programmer

progrès [pʀɔgʀɛ] nm progress no pl; **faire des ~** to make progress; **progresser** vi to progress; **progressif, -ive** adj progressive

proie [pʀwa] nf prey no pl

projecteur [pʀɔʒɛktœʀ] nm (pour film) projector; (de théâtre, cirque) spotlight

projectile [pʀɔʒɛktil] nm missile

projection [pʀɔʒɛksjɔ̃] nf projection; (séance) showing

projet [pʀɔʒɛ] nm plan; (ébauche) draft; **projet de loi** bill; **projeter** vt (envisager) to plan; (film, photos) to project; (ombre, lueur) to throw, cast; (jeter) to throw up (ou off ou out)

prolétaire [prɔletɛr] adj, nmf proletarian

prolongement [prɔlɔ̃ʒmɑ̃] nm extension; **dans le ~s** the running on from

prolonger [prɔlɔ̃ʒe] vt (débat, séjour) to prolong; (délai, billet, rue) to extend; **se prolonger** vi to go on

promenade [prɔm(ə)nad] nf walk (ou drive ou ride); **faire une ~** to go for a walk; **une ~ en voiture/à vélo** a drive/(bicycle) ride

promener [prɔm(ə)ne] vt (chien) to take out for a walk; (doigts, regard): **~ qch sur** to run sth over; **se promener** vi to go for (ou be out for) a walk

promesse [prɔmɛs] nf promise

promettre [prɔmɛtr] vt to promise ▷ vi to be ou look promising; **à qn de faire** to promise sb that one will do

promiscuité [prɔmiskɥite] nf (chambre) lack of privacy

promontoire [prɔmɔ̃twar] nm headland

promoteur, -trice [prɔmɔtœr, tris] nm/f: **promoteur (immobilier)** property developer (BRIT), real estate promoter (us)

promotion [prɔmɔsjɔ̃] nf promotion; **en ~** on special offer

promouvoir [prɔmuvwar] vt to promote

prompt, e [prɔ̃(pt), prɔ̃(p)t] adj swift, rapid

prôner [prone] vt (préconiser) to advocate

pronom [prɔnɔ̃] nm pronoun

prononcer [prɔnɔ̃se] vt (dire) to utter; (discours) to deliver; **se prononcer** vi to be pronounced; **comment est-ce que ça se prononce?** how do you pronounce ou say it?; **se ~ (sur)** (se décider) to reach a decision (on ou about), give a verdict (on); **prononciation** nf pronunciation

pronostic [prɔnɔstik] nm (Méd) prognosis; (fig: aussi: **~s**) forecast

propagande [prɔpagɑ̃d] nf propaganda

propager [prɔpaʒe] vt to spread; **se propager** vi to spread

prophète [prɔfɛt] nm prophet

prophétie [prɔfesi] nf prophecy

propice [prɔpis] adj favourable

proportion [prɔpɔrsjɔ̃] nf proportion; **toute(s) ~(s) gardée(s)** making due allowance(s)

propos [prɔpo] nm (intention) intention, aim; (sujet): **à quel ~?** what about? ▷ nmpl (paroles) talk no pl, remarks; **à ~ de** regarding; **à tout ~** for the slightest reason ou; **à ~** by the way; (opportunément) at the right moment

proposer [prɔpoze] vt to propose; **~ qch (à qn)** (suggérer) to suggest sth (to sb), propose sth (to sb); (offrir) to offer sth (to sb); **se ~ (pour faire)** to offer one's services (to do); **proposition** (suggestion) nf proposal, suggestion; (Ling) clause

propre [prɔpr] adj clean; (net) neat, tidy; (possessif) own; (sens) literal; (particulier): **~ à** peculiar to; (approprié): **~ à** suitable for ▷ nm: **recopier au ~** to make a fair copy of; **proprement** adv (avec propreté) cleanly; **le village proprement dit** the village itself; **à proprement parler** strictly speaking; **propreté** nf cleanliness

propriétaire [prɔprijetɛr] nm/f owner; (pour le locataire) landlord(-lady)

propriété [prɔprijete] nf property; (droit) ownership

propulser [prɔpylse] vt to propel

prose [proz] nf (style) prose

prospecter [prɔspɛkte] vt to prospect; (Comm) to canvass

prospectus [prɔspɛktys] nm leaflet

prospère [prɔspɛr] adj prosperous; **prospérer** vi to prosper

prosterner [prɔstɛrne]: **se prosterner** vi to bow low, prostrate o.s.

prostituée [pʀɔstitɥe] nf prostitute

prostitution [pʀɔstitysjɔ̃] nf
prostitution

protecteur, -trice [pʀɔtɛktœʀ, tʀis]
adj protective; (air, ton: péj) patronizing
▷ nm/f protector

protection [pʀɔtɛksjɔ̃] nf protection;
(d'un personnage influent: aide) patronage

protéger [pʀɔteʒe] vt to protect; **se ~
de/contre** to protect o.s. from

protège-slip [pʀɔtɛʒslip] nm panty
liner

protéine [pʀɔtein] nf protein

protestant, e [pʀɔtɛstɑ̃, ɑ̃t] adj, nm/f
Protestant

protestation [pʀɔtɛstasjɔ̃] nf (plainte)
protest

protester [pʀɔtɛste] vi: **~ (contre)** to
protest (against ou about); **~ de** (son
innocence) to protest

prothèse [pʀɔtɛz] nf: **prothèse
dentaire** denture

protocole [pʀɔtɔkɔl] nm (fig) etiquette

proue [pʀu] nf bow(s pl), prow

prouesse [pʀuɛs] nf feat

prouver [pʀuve] vt to prove

provenance [pʀɔv(ə)nɑ̃s] nf origin;
avion en ~ de plane (arriving) from

provenir [pʀɔv(ə)niʀ]: **~ de** vt to
come from

proverbe [pʀɔvɛʀb] nm proverb

province [pʀɔvɛ̃s] nf province

proviseur [pʀɔvizœʀ] nm
≈ head(teacher) (BRIT), ≈ principal (US)

provision [pʀɔviziɔ̃] nf (réserve)
stock, supply; **provisions** nfpl (vivres)
provisions, food no pl

provisoire [pʀɔvizwaʀ] adj
temporary; **provisoirement** adv
temporarily

provocant, e [pʀɔvɔkɑ̃, ɑ̃t] adj
provocative

provoquer [pʀɔvɔke] vt (défier) to
provoke; (causer) to cause, bring about;
(inciter): **~ qn à** to incite sb to

proxénète [pʀɔksenɛt] nm procurer

proximité [pʀɔksimite] nf nearness,

closeness; (dans le temps) imminence,
closeness; **à ~** near ou close by; **à ~ de**
near (to), close to

prudemment [pʀydamɑ̃] adv
carefully; wisely, sensibly

prudence [pʀydɑ̃s] nf carefulness;
avec ~ carefully; **par ~** as a precaution

prudent, e [pʀydɑ̃, ɑ̃t] adj (pas
téméraire) careful; (: en général) safety-
conscious; (sage, conseillé) wise,
sensible; **c'est plus ~** it's wiser

prune [pʀyn] nf plum

pruneau, x [pʀyno] nm prune

prunier [pʀynje] nm plum tree

PS sigle m = **parti socialiste**

pseudonyme [psødɔnim] nm (gén)
fictitious name; (d'écrivain) pseudonym,
pen name

psychanalyse [psikanaliz] nf
psychoanalysis

psychiatre [psikjatʀ] nm/f
psychiatrist; **psychiatrique** adj
psychiatric

psychique [psiʃik] adj psychological

psychologie [psikɔlɔʒi] nf
psychology; **psychologique** adj
psychological; **psychologue** nm/f
psychologist

pu [py] pp de **pouvoir**

puanteur [pɥɑ̃tœʀ] nf stink, stench

pub [pyb] nf (fam: annonce) ad, advert;
(pratique) advertising

public, -ique [pyblik] adj public;
(école, instruction) state cpd ▷ nm public;
(assistance) audience; **en ~** in public

publicitaire [pyblisitɛʀ] adj
advertising cpd; (film) publicity cpd

publicité [pyblisite] nf (méthode,
profession) advertising; (annonce)
advertisement; (révélations) publicity

publier [pyblije] vt to publish

publipostage [pyblipɔstaʒ] nm
mailing m

publique [pyblik] adj voir **public**

puce [pys] nf flea; (Inform) chip; **carte
à ~** smart card; **(marché aux) ~s** flea
market sg

pudeur [pydœʀ] nf modesty; **pudique**

adj (chaste) modest; (discret) discreet

puer [pɥe] (péj) *vi* to stink

puéricultrice [pɥerikyltris] *nf* p(a)ediatric nurse

puéril, e [pɥeril] *adj* childish

puis [pɥi] *vb voir* **pouvoir** ▷ *adv* then

puiser [pɥize] *vt*: ~ (dans) to draw (from)

puisque [pɥisk] *conj* since

puissance [pɥisɑ̃s] *nf* power; en ~ *adj* potential

puissant, e [pɥisɑ̃, ɑ̃t] *adj* powerful

puits [pɥi] *nm* well

pull(-over) [pyl(ɔvɛr)] *nm* sweater

pulluler [pylyle] *vi* to swarm

pulpe [pylp] *nf* pulp

pulvériser [pylverize] *vt* to pulverize; (liquide) to spray

punaise [pynɛz] *nf* (Zool) bug; (clou) drawing pin (BRIT), thumbtack (US)

punch [pɔ̃ʃ] *nm* (boisson) punch

punir [pynir] *vt* to punish; **punition** *nf* punishment

pupille [pypij] *nf* (Anat) pupil ▷ *nm/f* (enfant) ward

pupitre [pypitr] *nm* (Scol) desk

pur, e [pyr] *adj* pure; (vin) undiluted; (whisky) neat; en ~ perte to no avail; c'est de la folie ~e it's sheer madness

purée [pyre] *nf*: ~ (de pommes de terre) mashed potatoes *pl*; purée de marrons chestnut purée

purement [pyrmɑ̃] *adv* purely

purgatoire [pyrgatwar] *nm* purgatory

purger [pyrʒe] *vt* (Méd, Pol) to purge; (Jur: peine) to serve

pur-sang [pyrsɑ̃] *nm inv* thoroughbred

pus [py] *nm* pus

putain [pytɛ̃] (fam!) *nf* whore(!)

puzzle [pœzl] *nm* jigsaw (puzzle)

P.-V. [peve] *sigle m* = **procès-verbal**

pyjama [piʒama] *nm* pyjamas *pl* (BRIT), pajamas *pl* (US)

pyramide [piramid] *nf* pyramid

Pyrénées [pirene] *nfpl*: les ~ the Pyrenees

q

QI *sigle m* (= quotient intellectuel) IQ

quadragénaire [k(w)adraʒener] *nm/f* man/woman in his/her forties

quadruple [k(w)adrypl] *nm*: le ~ de four times as much as

quai [ke] *nm* (de port) quay; (de gare) platform; être à ~ (navire) to be alongside; de quel ~ part le train pour Paris? which platform does the Paris train go from?

qualification [kalifikasjɔ̃] *nf* (aptitude) qualification

qualifier [kalifje] *vt* to qualify; se **qualifier** *vi* to qualify; ~ qch/qn de to describe sth/sb as

qualité [kalite] *nf* quality

quand [kɑ̃] *conj, adv* when; ~ je serai riche when I'm rich; ~ même all the same; ~ même, il exagère! really, he overdoes it!; ~ bien même even though

quant [kɑ̃]: ~ à *prép* (pour ce qui est de) as for, as to; (au sujet de) regarding

quantité [kɑ̃tite] *nf* quantity, amount; (grand nombre): une *ou* des ~(s) de a

great deal of

quarantaine [kaʁɑ̃tɛn] nf (Méd) quarantine; **avoir la ~ (âge)** to be around forty; **une ~ (de)** forty or so, about forty

quarante [kaʁɑ̃t] num forty

quart [kaʁ] nm (fraction) quarter; (surveillance) watch; **un ~ de vin** a quarter litre of wine; **le ~ de** a quarter of; **quart d'heure** quarter of an hour; **quarts de finale** quarter finals pl

quartier [kaʁtje] nm (de ville) district, area; (de boeuf) quarter; (de fruit) piece; **cinéma de ~** local cinema; **avoir ~ libre** (fig) to be free; **quartier général** headquarters pl

quartz [kwaʁts] nm quartz

quasi [kazi] adv almost, nearly; **quasiment** adv almost, nearly; **quasiment jamais** hardly ever

quatorze [katɔʁz] num fourteen

quatorzième [katɔʁzjɛm] num fourteenth

quatre [katʁ] num four; **à ~ pattes** on all fours; **se mettre en ~ pour qn** to go out of one's way for sb; **~ à ~** (monter, descendre) four at a time; **quatre-vingt-dix** num ninety; **quatre-vingts** num eighty; **quatrième** num fourth ▷ nf (Scol) year 9 (BRIT), eighth grade (US)

quatuor [kwatɥɔʁ] nm quartet(te)

 MOT-CLÉ

que [kə] conj 1 (introduisant complétive) that; **il sait que tu es là** he knows (that) you're here; **je veux que tu acceptes** I want you to accept; **il a dit que oui** he said he would (ou it was so)
2 (reprise d'autres conjonctions): **quand il rentrera et qu'il aura mangé** when he gets back and (when) he has eaten; **si vous y allez et que vous ...** if you go there and if you ...
3 (en tête de phrase: hypothèse, souhait etc): **qu'il le veuille ou non** whether he likes it or not; **qu'il fasse ce qu'il voudra!** let him do as he pleases!

4 (après comparatif) than, as; voir aussi **plus**; **aussi**; **autant** etc
5 (seulement): **ne ... que** only; **il ne boit que de l'eau** he only drinks water
6 (temps): **il y a 4 ans qu'il est parti** it is 4 years since he left, he left 4 years ago
▷ adv (exclamation): **qu'il ou qu'est-ce qu'il est bête/court vite!** he's so silly!/he runs so fast!; **que de livres!** what a lot of books!
▷ pron 1 (relatif: personne) whom; (: chose) that, which; **l'homme que je vois** the man (whom) I see; **le livre que tu vois** the book (that ou which) you see; **un jour que j'étais ...** a day when I was ...
2 (interrogatif) what; **que fais-tu?, qu'est-ce que tu fais?** what are you doing?; **qu'est-ce que c'est?** what is it?, what's that?; **que faire?** what can one do?

Québec [kebɛk] n: **le ~** Quebec; **québecois, e** adj Quebec ▷ nm/f: **Québécois, e** Quebecker ▷ nm (Ling) Quebec French

 MOT-CLÉ

quel, quelle [kɛl] adj 1 (interrogatif: personne) who; (: chose) what; **quel est cet homme?** who is this man?; **quel est ce livre?** what is this book?; **quel livre/homme?** what book/man?; (parmi un certain choix) which book/man?; **quels acteurs préférez-vous?** which actors do you prefer?; **dans quels pays êtes-vous allé?** which ou what countries did you go to?
2 (exclamatif): **quelle surprise!** what a surprise!
3: **quel que soit le coupable** whoever is guilty; **quel que soit votre avis** whatever your opinion

quelconque [kɛlkɔ̃k] adj (indéfini): **un ami/prétexte ~** some friend/pretext or other; (*médiocre: repas*) indifferent, poor; (*laid: personne*) plain-looking

○ **MOT-CLÉ**

quelque [kɛlk] *adj* **1** (*au singulier*) some; (*au pluriel*) a few, some; (*tournure interrogative*) any; **quelque espoir** some hope; **il a quelques amis** he has a few *ou* some friends; **a-t-il quelques amis?** does he have any friends?; **les quelques livres qui** the few books which; **20 kg et quelque(s)** a bit over 20 kg
2: **quelque ... que**: **quelque livre qu'il choisisse** whatever (*ou* whichever) book he chooses
3: **quelque chose** something; (*tournure interrogative*) anything; **quelque chose d'autre** something else; anything else; **quelque part** somewhere; anywhere; **en quelque sorte** as it were
▷ *adv* **1** (*environ*): **quelque 100 mètres** some 100 metres
2: **quelque peu** rather, somewhat

quelquefois [kɛlkəfwa] *adv* sometimes

quelques-uns, -unes [kɛlkəzœ̃ yn] *pron* a few, some

quelqu'un [kɛlkœ̃] *pron* someone, somebody; (+ *tournure interrogative*) anyone, anybody; **quelqu'un d'autre** someone *ou* somebody else; (+ *tournure interrogative*) anybody else

qu'en dira-t-on [kɑ̃diratɔ̃] *nm inv*: **le qu'en dira-t-on** gossip, what people say

querelle [kəʀɛl] *nf* quarrel; **quereller**: **se quereller** *vi* to quarrel

qu'est-ce que [kɛskə] *vb + conj voir* **que**

qu'est-ce qui [kɛski] *vb + conj voir* **qui**

question [kɛstjɔ̃] *nf* question; (*fig*) matter, issue; **il a été ~ de** we (*ou* they) spoke about; **de quoi est-il ~?** what is it about?; **il n'en est pas ~** there's no question of it; **en ~** in question; **hors de ~** out of the question; **remettre**

en ~ to question; **questionnaire** *nm* questionnaire; **questionner** *vt* to question

quête [kɛt] *nf* collection; (*recherche*) quest, search; **faire la ~** (*à l'église*) to take the collection; (*artiste*) to pass the hat round

quetsche [kwɛtʃ] *nf* kind of dark-red plum

queue [kø] *nf* tail; (*fig: du classement*) bottom; (*: de poêle*) handle; (*: de fruit, feuille*) stalk; (*: de train, colonne, file*) rear; **faire la ~** to queue (up) (*BRIT*), line up (*US*); **queue de cheval** ponytail; **queue de poisson** (*Auto*): **faire une queue de poisson à qn** to cut in front of sb

○ **MOT-CLÉ**

qui [ki] *pron* **1** (*interrogatif: personne*) who; (*: chose*): **qu'est-ce qui est sur la table?** what is on the table?; **qui est-ce qui?** who?; **qui est-ce que?** who?; **à qui est ce sac?** whose bag is this?; **à qui parlais-tu?** who were you talking to?, to whom were you talking?; **chez qui allez-vous?** whose house are you going to?
2 (*relatif: personne*) who; (+ *prép*) whom; **l'ami de qui je vous ai parlé** the friend I told you about; **la dame chez qui je suis allé** the lady whose house I went to
3 (*sans antécédent*): **amenez qui vous voulez** bring who you like; **qui que ce soit** whoever it may be

quiconque [kikɔ̃k] *pron* (*celui qui*) whoever, anyone who; (*n'importe qui*) anyone, anybody

quille [kij] *nf*: (*jeu de*) **~s** skittles *sg* (*BRIT*), bowling (*US*)

quincaillerie [kɛ̃kajʀi] *nf* (*ustensiles*) hardware; (*magasin*) hardware shop

quinquagénaire [kɛ̃kaʒenɛʀ] *nm/f* man/woman in his/her fifties

quinquennat [kɛ̃kena] *nm* five year term of office (of French President)

quinte [kɛ̃t] *nf*: **~ (de toux)** coughing fit

quintuple [kɛ̃typl] *nm*: **le ~ de** five times as much as

quinzaine [kɛ̃zɛn] *nf*: **une ~ (de)** about fifteen, fifteen or so; **une ~ (de jours)** a fortnight (BRIT), two weeks

quinze [kɛ̃z] *num* fifteen; **dans ~ jours** in a fortnight('s time), in two weeks('time)

quinzième [kɛ̃zjɛm] *num* fifteenth

quiproquo [kipʀɔko] *nm* misunderstanding

quittance [kitɑ̃s] *nf (reçu)* receipt

quitte [kit] *adj*: **être ~ envers qn** to be no longer in sb's debt; *(fig)* to be quits with sb; **~ à faire** even if it means doing

quitter [kite] *vt* to leave; *(vêtement)* to take off; **se quitter** *vi (couples, interlocuteurs)* to part; **ne quittez pas** *(au téléphone)* hold the line

qui-vive [kiviv] *nm*: **être sur le ~** to be on the alert

○ **MOT-CLÉ**

quoi [kwa] *pron interrog* 1 what; **quoi de neuf?** what's new?; **quoi?** *(qu'est-ce que tu dis?)* what?

2 *(avec prép)*: **à quoi tu penses?** what are you thinking about?; **de quoi parlez-vous?** what are you talking about?; **à quoi bon?** what's the use?
▷ *pron rel*: **as-tu de quoi écrire?** do you have anything to write with?; **il n'y a pas de quoi** (please) don't mention it; **il n'y a pas de quoi rire** there's nothing to laugh about
▷ *pron (locutions)*: **quoi qu'il arrive** whatever happens; **quoi qu'il en soit** be that as it may; **quoi que ce soit** anything at all
▷ *excl* what!

quoique [kwak] *conj* (al)though

quotidien, ne [kɔtidjɛ̃, jɛn] *adj* daily; *(banal)* everyday ▷ *nm (journal)* daily (paper); **quotidiennement** *adv* daily

---

r

r. *abr* = **route; rue**

rab [ʀab] *(fam) nm (nourriture)* extra; **est-ce qu'il y a du ~?** are there any seconds?

rabâcher [ʀabɑʃe] *vt* to keep on repeating

rabais [ʀabɛ] *nm* reduction, discount; **rabaisser** *vt (dénigrer)* to belittle; *(rabattre: prix)* to reduce

Rabat [ʀaba(t)] *n* Rabat

rabattre [ʀabatʀ] *vt (couvercle, siège)* to pull down; *(déduire)* to reduce; **se rabattre** *vi (se refermer: couvercle)* to fall shut; *(véhicule, coureur)* to cut in; **se ~ sur** to fall back on

rabbin [ʀabɛ̃] *nm* rabbi

rabougri, e [ʀabugʀi] *adj* stunted

raccommoder [ʀakɔmɔde] *vt* to mend, repair

raccompagner [ʀakɔ̃paɲe] *vt* to take ou see back

raccord [ʀakɔʀ] *nm* link; *(retouche)* touch up; **raccorder** *vt* to join (up), link up; *(suj: pont etc)* to connect, link

raccourci [ʀakuʀsi] nm short cut

raccourcir [ʀakuʀsiʀ] vt to shorten
▷ vi (jours) to grow shorter, draw in

raccrocher [ʀakʀɔʃe] vt (tableau) to
hang back up; (récepteur) to put down
▷ vi (Tél) to hang up, ring off

race [ʀas] nf race; (d'animaux, fig) breed;
de ~ purebred, pedigree

rachat [ʀaʃa] nm buying, buying back

racheter [ʀaʃ(ə)te] vt (article perdu) to
buy another; (après avoir vendu) to buy
back; (d'occasion) to buy; (Comm: part,
firme) to buy up; (davantage): **~ du lait/3
œufs** to buy more milk/another 3 eggs
ou 3 more eggs; **se racheter** vi (fig) to
make amends

racial, e, -aux [ʀasjal, jo] adj racial

racine [ʀasin] nf root; **racine carrée/
cubique** square/cube root

racisme [ʀasism] nm racism

raciste [ʀasist] adj, nm/f racist

racket [ʀaket] nm racketeering no pl

raclée [ʀɑkle] (fam) nf hiding,
thrashing

racler [ʀɑkle] vt (surface) to scrape; **se
la gorge** to clear one's throat

racontars [ʀakɔ̃taʀ] nmpl story, lie

raconter [ʀakɔ̃te] vt: **~ (à qn)** (décrire)
to relate (to sb), tell (sb) about; (dire de
mauvaise foi) to tell (sb); **~ une histoire**
to tell a story

radar [ʀadaʀ] nm radar

rade [ʀad] nf (natural) harbour; **rester
en ~** (fig) to be left stranded

radeau, x [ʀado] nm raft

radiateur [ʀadjatœʀ] nm radiator,
heater; (Auto) radiator; **radiateur
électrique** electric heater ou fire

radiation [ʀadjasjɔ̃] nf (Physique)
radiation

radical, e, -aux [ʀadikal, o] adj
radical

radieux, -euse [ʀadjø, jøz] adj radiant

radin, e [ʀadɛ̃, in] (fam) adj stingy

radio [ʀadjo] nf radio; (Méd) X-ray
▷ nm radio operator; **à la ~** on the
radio; **radioactif, -ive** adj radioactive;

radiocassette nm cassette radio,
radio cassette player; **radiographie** nf
radiography; (photo) X-ray photograph;
radiophonique adj radio cpd; **radio-
réveil** (pl **radios-réveils**) nm radio
alarm clock

radis [ʀadi] nm radish

radoter [ʀadɔte] vi to ramble on

radoucir [ʀadusiʀ]: **se radoucir** vi
(temps) to become milder; (se calmer)
to calm down

rafale [ʀafal] nf (vent) gust (of wind);
(tir) burst of gunfire

raffermir [ʀafɛʀmiʀ] vt to firm up

raffiner [ʀafine] vt to refine; **raffinerie**
nf refinery

raffoler [ʀafɔle]: **~ de** vt to be very
keen on

rafle [ʀafl] nf (de police) raid; **rafler** (fam)
vt to swipe, nick

rafraîchir [ʀafʀeʃiʀ] vt (atmosphère,
température) to cool (down); (aussi:
mettre à ~) to chill; (fig: rénover) to
brighten up; **se rafraîchir** vi (temps)
to grow cooler; (en se lavant) to
freshen up; (en buvant) to refresh o.s.;
rafraîchissant, e adj refreshing;
rafraîchissement nm (boisson) cool
drink; **rafraîchissements** nmpl
(boissons, fruits etc) refreshments

rage [ʀaʒ] nf (Méd): **la ~** rabies; (fureur)
rage, fury; **faire ~** to rage; **rage de
dents** (raging) toothache

ragot [ʀago] (fam) nm malicious
gossip no pl

ragoût [ʀagu] nm stew

raide [ʀed] adj stiff; (câble) taut, tight;
(escarpé) steep; (droit: cheveux) straight;
(fam: sans argent) flat broke; (osé)
daring, bold ▷ adv (en pente) steeply;
~ mort stone dead; **raideur** nf (rigidité)
stiffness; **avec raideur** (répondre) stiffly,
abruptly; **raidir** vt (muscles) to stiffen;
se raidir vi (tissu) to stiffen; (personne)
to tense up; (: se préparer moralement) to
brace o.s.; (fig: position) to harden

raie [ʀɛ] nf (Zool) skate; ray; (rayure)
stripe; (des cheveux) parting

raifort [ʀɛfɔʀ] nm horseradish

rail [ʀaj] nm rail; (chemins de fer) railways pl; **par ~** by rail

railler [ʀaje] vt to scoff at, jeer at

rainure [ʀɛnyʀ] nf groove

raisin [ʀɛzɛ̃] nm (aussi: **~s**) grapes pl; **raisins secs** raisins

raison [ʀɛzɔ̃] nf reason; **avoir ~** to be right; **donner ~ à qn** to agree with sb; (événement) to prove sb right; **perdre la ~** to become insane; **se faire une ~** to learn to live with it; **~ de plus** all the more reason; **à plus forte ~** all the more so; **en ~ de** because of; **à ~ de** at the rate of; **sans ~** for no reason; **raison sociale** corporate name; **raisonnable** adj reasonable, sensible

raisonnement [ʀɛzɔnmɑ̃] nm (façon de réfléchir) reasoning; (argumentation) argument

raisonner [ʀɛzɔne] vi (penser) to reason; (argumenter, discuter) to argue ▷ vt (personne) to reason with

rajeunir [ʀaʒœniʀ] vt (suj: coiffure, robe): **~ qn** to make sb look younger; (fig: personnel) to inject new blood into ▷ vi to become (ou look) younger

rajouter [ʀaʒute] vt to add

rajuster [ʀaʒyste] vt (vêtement) to straighten, tidy; (salaires) to adjust

ralenti [ʀalɑ̃ti] nm: **au ~** (fig) at a slower pace; **tourner au ~** (Auto) to tick over, idle

ralentir [ʀalɑ̃tiʀ] vt to slow down

râler [ʀɑle] vi to groan; (fam) to grouse, moan (and groan)

rallier [ʀalje] vt (rejoindre) to rejoin; (gagner à sa cause) to win over

rallonge [ʀalɔ̃ʒ] nf (de table) (extra) leaf

rallonger [ʀalɔ̃ʒe] vt to lengthen

rallye [ʀali] nm rally; (Pol) march

ramassage [ʀamasaʒ] nm: **ramassage scolaire** school bus service

ramasser [ʀamase] vt (objet tombé ou par terre, fam) to pick up; (recueillir: copies, ordures) to collect; (récolter) to gather; **ramassis** (péj) nm (de voyous) bunch; (d'objets) jumble

rambarde [ʀɑ̃baʀd] nf guardrail

rame [ʀam] nf (aviron) oar; (de métro) train; (de papier) ream

rameau, x [ʀamo] nm (small) branch; **les Rameaux** (Rel) Palm Sunday sg

ramener [ʀam(ə)ne] vt to bring back; (reconduire) to take back; **~ qch à** (réduire à) to reduce sth to

ramer [ʀame] vi to row

ramollir [ʀamɔliʀ] vt to soften; **se ramollir** vi to go soft

rampe [ʀɑ̃p] nf (d'escalier) banister(s pl); (dans un garage) ramp; (Théâtre): **la ~** the footlights pl; **rampe de lancement** launching pad

ramper [ʀɑ̃pe] vi to crawl

rancard [ʀɑ̃kaʀ] (fam) nm (rendez-vous) date

rancart [ʀɑ̃kaʀ] nm: **mettre au ~** (fam) to scrap

rance [ʀɑ̃s] adj rancid

rancœur [ʀɑ̃kœʀ] nf rancour

rançon [ʀɑ̃sɔ̃] nf ransom

rancune [ʀɑ̃kyn] nf grudge, rancour; **garder ~ à qn (de qch)** to bear sb a grudge (for sth); **sans ~!** no hard feelings!; **rancunier, -ière** adj vindictive, spiteful

randonnée [ʀɑ̃dɔne] nf (pédestre) walk, ramble; (: en montagne) hike, hiking no pl; **la ~** (activité) hiking, walking; **une ~ à cheval** a pony trek

rang [ʀɑ̃] nm (rangée) row; (grade, classement) rank; **rangs** nmpl (Mil) ranks; **se mettre en ~s** to get into ou form rows; **au premier ~** in the first row; (fig) ranking first

rangé, e [ʀɑ̃ʒe] adj (vie) well-ordered; (personne) steady

rangée [ʀɑ̃ʒe] nf row

ranger [ʀɑ̃ʒe] vt (mettre de l'ordre dans) to tidy up; (classer, grouper) to order, arrange; (mettre à sa place) to put away; (fig: classer): **~ qn/qch parmi** to rank sb/sth among; **se ranger** vi (véhicule, conducteur) to pull over ou in; (piéton) to step aside; (s'assagir) to settle down; **se ~ à** (avis) to come round to

ranimer [ʀanime] vt (personne) to bring round; (douleur, souvenir) to revive; (feu) to rekindle

rapace [ʀapas] nm bird of prey

râpe [ʀɑp] nf (Culin) grater; **râper** vt (Culin) to grate

rapide [ʀapid] adj fast; (prompt: coup d'œil, mouvement) quick ▷ nm express (train); (de cours d'eau) rapid; **rapidement** adv fast; quickly

rapiécer [ʀapjese] vt to patch

rappel [ʀapɛl] nm (Théâtre) curtain call; (Méd: vaccination) booster; (deuxième avis) reminder; **rappeler** vt to call back; (ambassadeur, Mil) to recall; (faire se souvenir): **rappeler qch à qn** to remind sb of sth; **se rappeler** vt (se souvenir de) to remember, recall; **pouvez-vous rappeler plus tard?** can you call back later?

rapport [ʀapɔʀ] nm (lien, analogie) connection; (compte rendu) report; (profit) yield, return; (entre personnes, pays) relations; **avoir ~ à** to have something to do with; **être/se mettre en ~ avec qn** to be/get in touch with sb; **par ~ à** in relation to; **rapports (sexuels)** (sexual) intercourse sg; **rapport qualité-prix** value (for money)

rapporter [ʀapɔʀte] vt (rendre, ramener) to bring back; (bénéfice) to yield, bring in; (mentionner, répéter) to report ▷ vi (investissement) to give a good return ou yield; (activité) to be very profitable; **se ~ à** to relate to

rapprochement [ʀapʀɔʃmã] nm (de nations) reconciliation; (rapport) parallel

rapprocher [ʀapʀoʃe] vt (deux objets) to bring closer together; (fig: ennemis, partis etc) to bring together; (comparer) to establish a parallel between; (chaise d'une table): **~ qch (de)** to bring sth closer (to); **se rapprocher** vi to draw closer ou nearer; **se ~ de** to come closer to; (présenter une analogie avec:) to be close to

raquette [ʀakɛt] nf (de tennis) racket; (de ping-pong) bat

rare [ʀaʀ] adj rare; **se faire ~** to become scarce; **rarement** adv rarely, seldom

ras, e [ʀɑ, ʀɑz] adj (poil, herbe) short; (tête) close-cropped ▷ adv short; **en ~e campagne** in open country; **à ~ bords** to the brim; **en avoir ~ le bol** to be fed up

raser [ʀɑze] vt (barbe, cheveux) to shave off; (menton, personne) to shave; (fam: ennuyer) to bore; (démolir) to raze (to the ground); (frôler) to graze, skim; **se raser** vi to shave; (fam) to be bored (to tears); **rasoir** nm razor

rassasier [ʀasazje] vt: **être rassasié** to have eaten one's fill

rassemblement [ʀasãbləmã] nm (groupe) gathering; (Pol) union

rassembler [ʀasãble] vt (réunir) to assemble, gather; (documents, notes) to gather together, collect; **se rassembler** vi to gather

rassurer [ʀasyʀe] vt to reassure; **se rassurer** vi to reassure o.s.; **rassure-toi** don't worry

rat [ʀa] nm rat

rate [ʀat] nf spleen

raté, e [ʀate] adj (tentative) unsuccessful, failed ▷ nm/f (fam: personne) failure

râteau, x [ʀɑto] nm rake

rater [ʀate] vi (affaire, projet etc) to go wrong, fail ▷ vt (fam: cible, train, occasion) to miss; (plat) to spoil; (fam: examen) to fail; **nous avons raté notre train** we missed our train

ration [ʀasjɔ̃] nf ration

RATP sigle f (= Régie autonome des transports parisiens) Paris transport authority

rattacher [ʀataʃe] vt (animal, cheveux) to tie up again; (fig: relier): **~ qch à** to link sth with

rattraper [ʀatʀape] vt (fugitif) to recapture; (empêcher de tomber) to catch (hold of); (atteindre, rejoindre) to catch up with; (réparer: erreur) to make up for; **se rattraper** vi to make up for it; **se ~**

(à) (se raccrocher) to stop o.s. falling (by catching hold of)

rature [RatyR] nf deletion, erasure

rauque [Rok] adj (voix) hoarse

ravages [Ravaʒ] nmpl: **faire des ~** to wreak havoc

ravi, e [Ravi] adj: **être ~ de/que** to be delighted with/that

ravin [Ravɛ̃] nm gully, ravine

ravir [RaviR] vt (enchanter) to delight; **à ~** adv beautifully

raviser [Ravize]: **se raviser** vi to change one's mind

ravissant, e [Ravisɑ̃, ɑ̃t] adj delightful

ravisseur, -euse [RavisœR, øz] nm/f abductor, kidnapper

ravitailler [Ravitaje] vt (en vivres, munitions) to provide with fresh supplies; (avion) to refuel: **se ~ (en)** to get fresh supplies of

raviver [Ravive] vt (feu, douleur) to revive; (couleurs) to brighten up

rayé, e [Reje] adj (à rayures) striped

rayer [Reje] vt (érafler) to scratch; (barrer) to cross out; (d'une liste) to cross off

rayon [Rejɔ̃] nm (de soleil etc) ray; (Géom) radius; (de roue) spoke; (étagère) shelf; (de grand magasin) department; **dans un ~ de** within a radius of; **rayon de soleil** sunbeam; **rayons X** X-rays

rayonnement [Rejɔnmɑ̃] nm (fig: d'une culture) influence

rayonner [Rejɔne] vi (fig) to shine forth; (personne: de joie, de beauté) to be radiant; (touriste) to go touring (from one base)

rayure [RejyR] nf (motif) stripe; (éraflure) scratch; **à ~s** striped

raz-de-marée [Radmare] nm inv tidal wave

ré [Re] nm (Mus) D; (en chantant la gamme) re

réaction [Reaksjɔ̃] nf reaction

réadapter [Readapte]: **se réadapter (à)** vi to readjust (to)

réagir [Reaʒir] vi to react

réalisateur, -trice [RealizatœR, tRis]

nm/f (TV, Cinéma) director

réalisation [Realizasjɔ̃] nf realization; (cinéma) production; **en cours de ~** under way

réaliser [Realize] vt (projet, opération) to carry out, realize; (rêve, souhait) to realize, fulfil; (exploit) to achieve; (film) to produce; (se rendre compte de) to realize; **se réaliser** vi to be realized

réaliste [Realist] adj realistic

réalité [Realite] nf reality; **en ~** in (actual) fact; **dans la ~** in reality

réanimation [Reanimasjɔ̃] nf resuscitation; **service de ~** intensive care unit

rébarbatif, -ive [RebaRbatif, iv] adj forbidding

rebattu, e [R(ə)baty] adj hackneyed

rebelle [Rəbɛl] nm/f rebel ▷ adj (troupes) rebel; (enfant) rebellious; (mèche etc) unruly

rebeller [R(ə)bele]: **se rebeller** vi to rebel

rebondir [R(ə)bɔ̃diR] vi (ballon: au sol) to bounce; (: contre un mur) to rebound; (fig) to get moving again

rebord [R(ə)bɔR] nm edge; **le ~ de la fenêtre** windowsill

rebours [R(ə)buR]: **à ~** adv the wrong way

rebrousser [R(ə)bruse] vt: **~ chemin** to turn back

rebuter [Rəbyte] vt to put off

récalcitrant, e [Rekalsitrɑ̃, ɑ̃t] adj refractory

récapituler [Rekapityle] vt to recapitulate, sum up

receler [R(ə)səle] vt (produit d'un vol) to receive; (fig) to conceal; **receleur, -euse** nm/f receiver

récemment [Resamɑ̃] adv recently

recensement [R(ə)sɑ̃smɑ̃] nm (population) census

recenser [R(ə)sɑ̃se] vt (population) to take a census of; (inventorier) to list

récent, e [Resɑ̃, ɑ̃t] adj recent

récépissé [Resepise] nm receipt

récepteur [ReseptœR] nm receiver

réception [ʀesɛpsjɔ̃] nf receiving no pl; (accueil) welcome; (bureau) reception desk; (réunion mondaine) reception, party; **réceptionniste** nm/f receptionist

recette [ʀ(ə)sɛt] nf recipe; (Comm) takings pl; **recettes** nfpl (Comm: rentrées) receipts; **faire ~** (spectacle, exposition) to be a winner

recevoir [ʀ(ə)səvwaʀ] vt to receive; (client, patient) to see; **être reçu (à un examen)** to pass

rechange [ʀ(ə)ʃɑ̃ʒ]: **de ~** adj (pièces, roue) spare; (fig: solution) alternative; **des vêtements de ~** a change of clothes

recharge [ʀ(ə)ʃaʀʒ] nf refill; **rechargeable** adj (stylo etc) refillable; **recharger** vt (stylo) to refill; (batterie) to recharge

réchaud [ʀeʃo] nm (portable) stove

réchauffer [ʀeʃofe] vt (plat) to reheat; (mains, personne) to warm; **se réchauffer** vi (température) to get warmer; (personne) to warm o.s. (up)

rêche [ʀɛʃ] adj rough

recherche [ʀ(ə)ʃɛʀʃ] nf (action) search; (raffinement) studied elegance; (scientifique etc): **la ~** research; **recherches** nfpl (de la police) investigations; (scientifiques) research sg; **la ~ de** the search for sth; **être à la ~ de qch** to be looking for sth

recherché, e [ʀ(ə)ʃɛʀʃe] adj (rare, demandé) much sought-after; (raffiné: style) mannered; (: tenue) elegant

rechercher [ʀ(ə)ʃɛʀʃe] vt (objet égaré, personne) to look for; (causes, nouveau procédé) to try to find; (bonheur, compliments) to seek

rechute [ʀ(ə)ʃyt] nf (Méd) relapse

récidiver [ʀesidive] vi to commit a subsequent offence; (fig) to do it again

récif [ʀesif] nm reef

récipient [ʀesipjɑ̃] nm container

réciproque [ʀesipʀɔk] adj reciprocal

récit [ʀesi] nm story; **récital** nm recital; **réciter** vt to recite

réclamation [ʀeklamasjɔ̃] nf complaint; **(service des) ~s** complaints department

réclame [ʀeklam] nf ad, advert(isement); **en ~** on special offer; **réclamer** vt to ask for; (revendiquer) to claim, demand ▷ vi to complain

réclusion [ʀeklyzjɔ̃] nf imprisonment

recoin [ʀəkwɛ̃] nm nook, corner

reçois etc [ʀəswa] vb voir **recevoir**

récolte [ʀekɔlt] nf harvesting, gathering; (produits) harvest, crop; **récolter** vt to harvest, gather (in); (fig) to collect

recommandé [ʀ(ə)kɔmɑ̃de] nm (Postes): **en ~** by registered mail

recommander [ʀ(ə)kɔmɑ̃de] vt to recommend; (Postes) to register

recommencer [ʀ(ə)kɔmɑ̃se] vt (reprendre: lutte, séance) to resume, start again; (refaire: travail, explications) to start afresh, start (over) again ▷ vi to start again; (récidiver) to do it again

récompense [ʀekɔ̃pɑ̃s] nf reward; (prix) award; **récompenser** vt: **récompenser qn (de ou pour)** to reward sb (for)

réconcilier [ʀekɔ̃silje] vt to reconcile; **se réconcilier (avec)** to make up (with)

reconduire [ʀ(ə)kɔ̃dɥiʀ] vt (raccompagner) to take ou see back; (renouveler) to renew

réconfort [ʀekɔ̃fɔʀ] nm comfort; **réconforter** vt (consoler) to comfort

reconnaissance [ʀ(ə)kɔnɛsɑ̃s] nf (gratitude) gratitude, gratefulness; (action de reconnaître) recognition; (Mil) reconnaissance, recce; **reconnaissant, e** adj grateful; **je vous serais reconnaissant de bien vouloir ...** I would be most grateful if you would (kindly) ...

reconnaître [ʀ(ə)kɔnɛtʀ] vt to recognize; (Mil: lieu) to reconnoitre; (Jur: enfant, torts) to acknowledge; **~ que** to admit ou acknowledge that; **~ qn/qch à** (l'identifier grâce à) to recognize sb/sth by; **reconnu, e** adj (indiscuté, connu) recognized

reconstituer [R(ə)kɔ̃stitɥe] vt (événement, accident) to reconstruct; (fresque, vase brisé) to piece together, reconstitute

reconstruire [R(ə)kɔ̃stRɥiR] vt to rebuild

reconvertir [R(ə)kɔ̃vɛRtiR] **se reconvertir dans** vr (un métier, une branche) to go into

record [R(ə)kɔR] nm, adj record

recoupement [R(ə)kupmɑ̃] nm: **par ~** by cross-checking

recouper [R(ə)kupe]: **se recouper** vi (témoignages) to tie up; match up

recourbé [R(ə)kuRbe]: **se recourber** vi to curve (up), bend (up)

recourir [R(ə)kuRiR]: **~ à** vt (ami, agence) to turn ou appeal to; (force, ruse, emprunt) to resort to

recours [R(ə)kuR] nm: **avoir ~ à = recourir à; en dernier ~** as a last resort

recouvrer [R(ə)kuvRe] vt (vue, santé etc) to recover, regain

recouvrir [R(ə)kuvRiR] vt (couvrir à nouveau) to re-cover; (couvrir entièrement, aussi fig) to cover

récréation [RekReasjɔ̃] nf (Scol) break

recroqueviller [R(ə)kRɔk(ə)vije]: **se recroqueviller** vi (personne) to huddle up

recrudescence [R(ə)kRydesɑ̃s] nf fresh outbreak

recruter [R(ə)kRyte] vt to recruit

rectangle [Rɛktɑ̃gl] nm rectangle; **rectangulaire** adj rectangular

rectificatif [Rɛktifikatif] nm correction

rectifier [Rɛktifje] vt (calcul, adresse, paroles) to correct; (erreur) to rectify

rectiligne [Rɛktiliɲ] adj straight

recto [Rɛkto] nm front (of a page); **~ verso** on both sides (of paper)

reçu, e [R(ə)sy] pp de **recevoir** ▷ adj (candidat) successful; (admis, consacré) accepted ▷ nm (Comm) receipt; **je peux**

avoir un ~, s'il vous plaît? can I have a receipt, please?

recueil [Rəkœj] nm collection;
recueillir vt to collect; (voix, suffrages) to win; (accueillir: réfugiés, chat) to take in; **se recueillir** vi to gather one's thoughts, meditate

recul [R(ə)kyl] nm (éloignement) distance; (déclin) decline; **être en ~** to be on the decline; **avec du ~** with hindsight; **prendre du ~** to stand back; **reculé, e** adj remote; **reculer** vi to move back, back away; (Auto) to reverse, back up; (fig) to be on the decline ▷ vt to move back; (véhicule) to reverse, back up; (date, décision) to postpone; **reculer devant** (danger, difficulté) to shrink from; **reculons: à reculons** adv backwards

récupérer [RekypeRe] vt to recover, get back; (heures de travail) to make up; (déchets) to salvage ▷ vi to recover

récurer [RekyRe] vt to scour; **poudre à ~** scouring powder

reçut [Rəsy] vb voir **recevoir**

recycler [R(ə)sikle] vt (Tech) to recycle; **se recycler** vi to retrain

rédacteur, -trice [RedaktœR, tRis] nm/f (journaliste) writer; subeditor; (d'ouvrage de référence) editor, compiler

rédaction [Redaksjɔ̃] nf writing; (rédacteurs) editorial staff; (Scol: devoir) essay, composition

redescendre [R(ə)desɑ̃dR] vi to go back down ▷ vt (pente etc) to go down

rédiger [Rediʒe] vt to write; (contrat) to draw up

redire [R(ə)diR] vt to repeat; **trouver à ~ à** to find fault with

redoubler [R(ə)duble] vi (tempête, violence) to intensify; (Scol) to repeat a year; **~ de patience/prudence** to be doubly patient/careful

redoutable [R(ə)dutabl] adj formidable, fearsome

redouter [R(ə)dute] vt to dread

redressement [R(ə)dRɛsmɑ̃]

(économique) recovery

redresser [R(ə)dʀese] vt (relever) to set upright; (pièce tordue) to straighten out; (situation, économie) to put right; **se redresser** vi (personne) to sit (ou stand) up (straight); (économie) to recover

réduction [Redyksjɔ̃] nf reduction; **y a-t-il une ~ pour les étudiants?** is there a reduction for students?

réduire [Redɥiʀ] vt to reduce; (prix, dépenses) to cut, reduce; **réduit** nm (pièce) tiny room

rééducation [Reedykasjɔ̃] nf (d'un membre) re-education; (de délinquants, d'un blessé) rehabilitation

réel, le [Reel] adj real; **réellement** adv really

réexpédier [ʀeekspedje] vt (à l'envoyeur) to return, send back; (au destinataire) to send on, forward

refaire [R(ə)fɛʀ] vt (faire de nouveau; sport) to take up again; (réparer, restaurer) to do up

réfectoire [Refɛktwaʀ] nm refectory

référence [Refeʀɑ̃s] nf reference; **références** nfpl (recommandations) reference sg

référer [Refeʀe]: **se référer à** vt to refer to

refermer [R(ə)fɛʀme] vt to close ou shut again; **se refermer** vi (porte) to close ou shut (again)

refiler [R(ə)file] vi (fam) to palm off

réfléchi, e [Refleʃi] adj (caractère) thoughtful; (action) well-thought-out; (Ling) reflexive; **c'est tout ~** my mind's made up

réfléchir [RefleʃiR] vt to reflect ▷ vi to think; **~ à** to think about

reflet [R(ə)flɛ] nm reflection; (sur l'eau etc) sheen no pl, glint; **refléter** vt to reflect; **se refléter** vi to be reflected

réflexe [Reflɛks] nm, adj reflex

réflexion [Refleksjɔ̃] nf (de la lumière etc) reflection; (fait de penser) thought; (remarque) remark; **~ faite, à la ~** on reflection

réflexologie [Reflɛksɔlɔʒi] nf

reflexology

réforme [Refɔʀm] nf reform; (Rel): **la R~** the Reformation; **réformer** vt to reform; (Mil) to declare unfit for service

refouler [R(ə)fule] vt (envahisseurs) to drive back; (larmes) to force back; (désir, colère) to repress

refrain [R(ə)frɛ̃] nm refrain, chorus

refréner, réfréner [RafRene, RefRene] vt to curb, check

réfrigérateur [RefRiʒeʀatœʀ] nm refrigerator, fridge

refroidir [R(ə)fRwadiʀ] vt to cool; (fig: personne) to put off ▷ vi to cool (down); **se refroidir** vi (temps) to get cooler ou colder; (fig: ardeur) to cool (off); **refroidissement** nm (grippe etc) chill

refuge [R(ə)fyʒ] nm refuge; **réfugié, e** adj, nm/f refugee; **réfugier**: **se réfugier** vi to take refuge

refus [R(ə)fy] nm refusal; **ce n'est pas de ~** I won't say no, it's welcome; **refuser** vt to refuse; (Scol: candidat) to fail; **refuser qch à qn** to refuse sb sth; **refuser du monde** to have to turn people away; **se refuser à faire** to refuse to do

regagner [R(ə)gaɲe] vt (faveur) to win back; (lieu) to get back to

régal [Regal] nm treat; **régaler**: **se régaler** vi to have a delicious meal; (fig) to enjoy o.s.

regard [R(ə)gaʀ] nm (coup d'œil) look, glance; (expression) look (in one's eye); **au ~ de** (loi, morale) from the point of view of; **en ~ de** in comparison with

regardant, e [R(ə)gaʀdɑ̃, ɑ̃t] adj (économe) tight-fisted; **peu ~ (sur)** very free (about)

regarder [R(ə)gaʀde] vt to look at; (film, télévision, match) to watch; (concerner) to concern ▷ vi to look; **ne pas ~ à la dépense** to spare no expense; **~ qn/qch comme** to regard sb/sth as

régie [Reʒi] nf (Comm, Industrie) state-owned company; (Théâtre, Cinéma) production; (Radio, TV) control room

régime [ʀeʒim] nm (Pol) régime; (Méd) diet; (Admin: carcéral, fiscal etc) system; (de bananes, dattes) bunch; **se mettre au/suivre un ~** to go on/be on a diet

régiment [ʀeʒimɑ̃] nm regiment

région [ʀeʒjɔ̃] nf region; **régional, e, -aux** adj regional

régir [ʀeʒiʀ] vt to govern

régisseur [ʀeʒisœʀ] nm (d'un domaine) steward; (Cinéma, TV) assistant director; (Théâtre) stage manager

registre [ʀaʒistʀ] nm register

réglage [ʀeglaʒ] nm adjustment

règle [ʀɛgl] nf (instrument) ruler; (loi) rule; **règles** nfpl (menstruation) period sg; **en ~** (papiers d'identité) in order; **en ~ générale** as a (general) rule

réglé, e [ʀegle] adj (vie) well-ordered; (arrangé) settled

règlement [ʀɛglamɑ̃] nm (paiement) settlement; (arrêté) regulation; (règles, statuts) regulations pl, rules pl; **réglementaire** adj conforming to the regulations; (tenue) regulation cpd; **réglementation** nf (règles) regulations pl; **réglementer** vt to regulate

régler [ʀegle] vt (conflit, facture) to settle; (personne) to settle up with; (mécanisme, machine) to regulate, adjust; (thermostat etc) to set, adjust

réglisse [ʀeglis] nf liquorice

règne [ʀɛɲ] nm (d'un roi etc, fig) reign; **le ~ végétal/animal** the vegetable/animal kingdom; **régner** vi (roi) to rule, reign; (fig) to reign

regorger [ʀ(ə)gɔʀʒe] vi: **~ de** to overflow with, be bursting with

regret [ʀ(ə)gʀɛ] nm regret; **à ~** with regret; **sans ~** with no regrets; **regrettable** adj regrettable; **regretter** vt to regret; (personne) to miss; **je regrette mais ...** I'm sorry but ...

regrouper [ʀ(ə)gʀupe] vt (grouper) to group together; (contenir) to include, comprise; **se regrouper** vi to gather (together)

régulier, -ière [ʀegylje, jɛʀ] adj (gén)

regular; (vitesse, qualité) steady; (égal: couche, ligne) even; (Transports: ligne, service) scheduled, regular; (légal) lawful, in order; (honnête) straight, on the level; **régulièrement** adv regularly; (uniformément) evenly

rehausser [ʀaose] vt (relever) to heighten, raise; (fig: souligner) to set off, enhance

rein [ʀɛ̃] nm kidney; **reins** nmpl (dos) back sg

reine [ʀɛn] nf queen

reine-claude [ʀɛnklod] nf greengage

réinscriptible [ʀeɛ̃skʀiptibl] adj (CD, DVD) rewritable

réinsertion [ʀeɛ̃sɛʀsjɔ̃] nf (de délinquant) reintegration, rehabilitation

réintégrer [ʀeɛ̃tegʀe] vt (lieu) to return to; (fonctionnaire) to reinstate

rejaillir [ʀ(ə)ʒajiʀ] vi to splash up; **~ sur** (fig: scandale) to rebound on; (: gloire) to be reflected on

rejet [ʀaʒɛ] nm rejection; **rejeter** vt (relancer) to throw back; (écarter) to reject; (déverser) to throw out, discharge; (vomir) to bring ou throw up; **rejeter la responsabilité de qch sur qn** to lay the responsibility for sth at sb's door

rejoindre [ʀ(ə)ʒwɛdʀ] vt (famille, régiment) to rejoin, return to; (lieu) to get (back) to; (suj: route etc) to meet, join; (rattraper) to catch up (with); **se rejoindre** vi to meet; **je te rejoins à la gare** I'll see ou meet you at the station

réjouir [ʀeʒwiʀ] vt to delight; **se ~ (de qch/de faire)** to be delighted (about sth/to do); **réjouissances** nfpl (fête) festivities

relâche [ʀəlɑʃ] nm ou nf: **sans ~** without respite ou a break; **relâché, e** adj loose, lax; **relâcher** vt (libérer) to release; (desserrer) to loosen; **se relâcher** vi (discipline) to become slack ou lax; (élève) to slacken off

relais [ʀ(ə)lɛ] nm (Sport): **(course de) ~** relay (race); **prendre le ~ (de)** to take over (from); **relais routier** ≈ transport café (BRIT), ≈ truck stop (US)

relancer [R(ə)lɑ̃se] vt (balle) to throw back; (moteur) to restart; (fig) to boost, revive; (harceler): ~ **qn** to pester sb

relatif, -ive [R(ə)latif, iv] adj relative

relation [R(ə)lasjɔ̃] nf (rapport) relation(ship); (connaissance) acquaintance; **relations** nfpl (rapports) relations; (connaissances) connections; **être/entrer en ~(s) avec** to get/be in contact with

relaxer [Rəlakse]: **se relaxer** vi to relax

relayer [R(ə)leje] vt (collaborateur, coureur etc) to relieve; **se relayer** vi (dans une activité) to take it in turns

reléguer [R(ə)lege] vt to relegate

relevé, e [Rəl(ə)ve] adj (manches) rolled-up; (sauce) highly-seasoned ▷ nm (de compteur) reading; **relevé bancaire ou de compte** bank statement

relève [Rələv] nf (personne) relief; **prendre la ~** to take over

relever [Rəl(ə)ve] vt (meuble) to stand up again; (personne tombée) to help up; (vitre, niveau de vie) to raise; (inf) to turn up; (style) to elevate; (plat, sauce) to season; (sentinelle, équipe) to relieve; (fautes) to pick out; (défi) to accept, take up; (noter: adresse etc) to take down, note; (: plan) to sketch; (compteur) to read; (ramasser: cahiers) to collect, take in; **se relever** vi (se remettre debout) to get up; ~ **de** (maladie) to be recovering from; (être du ressort de) to be a matter for; (fig) to pertain to; ~ **qn de** (fonctions) to relieve sb of; ~ **la tête** to look up

relief [Rəljɛf] nm relief; **mettre en ~** (fig) to bring out, highlight

relier [Rəlje] vt to link up with; (livre) to bind; ~ **qch à** to link sth to

religieux, -euse [R(ə)liʒjø, jøz] adj religious ▷ nm monk

religion [R(ə)liʒjɔ̃] nf religion

relire [R(ə)liR] vt (à nouveau) to reread, read again; (vérifier) to read over

reluire [R(ə)lɥiR] vi to gleam

remanier [R(ə)manje] vt to reshape,

recast; (Pol) to reshuffle

remarquable [R(ə)maRkabl] adj remarkable

remarque [R(ə)maRk] nf remark; (écrite) note

remarquer [R(ə)maRke] vt (voir) to notice; **se remarquer** vi to be noticeable; **faire ~ (à qn) que** to point out (to sb) that; **faire ~ qch (à qn)** to point sth out (to sb); **remarquez, ...** mind you ...; **se faire ~** to draw attention to o.s.

rembourrer [Rɑ̃bure] vt to stuff

remboursement [Rɑ̃bursəmɑ̃] nm (de dette, d'emprunt) repayment; (de frais) refund; **rembourser** vt to pay back, repay; (frais, billet etc) to refund; **se faire rembourser** to get a refund

remède [R(ə)mɛd] nm (médicament) medicine; (traitement, fig) remedy, cure

remémorer [R(ə)memɔRe]: **se remémorer** vt to recall, recollect

remerciements [RəmɛRsimɑ̃] nmpl thanks; **(avec) tous mes ~** (with) grateful ou many thanks

remercier [R(ə)mɛRsje] vt to thank; (congédier) to dismiss; ~ **qn de/d'avoir fait** to thank sb for/for having done

remettre [R(ə)mɛtR] vt (replacer) to put back; (vêtement) to put back on; (ajouter) to add; (ajourner): ~ **qch (à)** to postpone sth (until); **se remettre** vi: **se ~ (de)** to recover (from); ~ **qch à qn** (donner: lettre, clé etc) to hand over sth to sb; (: prix, décoration) to present sb with sth; **se ~ à faire qch** to start doing sth again; **s'en ~ à** to leave it (up) to

remise [R(ə)miz] nf (rabais) discount; (local) shed; **remise de peine** reduction of sentence; **remise des prix** prize-giving; **remise en cause ou question** calling into question, challenging; **remise en jeu** (Football) throw-in

remontant [R(ə)mɔ̃tɑ̃] nm tonic, pick-me-up

remonte-pente [R(ə)mɔ̃tpɑ̃t] nm ski-lift

remonter [R(ə)mɔ̃te] vi to go back

up; (prix, température) to go up again
▷ vt (pente) to go up; (fleuve) to sail (ou swim etc) up; (manches, pantalon) to roll up; (col) to turn up; (niveau, limite) to raise; (fig: personne) to buck up; (qch de démonté) to put back together, reassemble; (montre) to wind up; **~ le moral à qn** to raise sb's spirits; **~ à** (dater de) to date ou go back to

remords [R(ə)mɔR] nm remorse no pl; **avoir des ~** to feel remorse

remorque [R(ə)mɔRk] nf trailer; **remorquer** vt to tow; **remorqueur** nm tug(boat)

remous [Rəmu] nm (d'un navire) (back)wash no pl; (de rivière) swirl, eddy ▷ nmpl (fig) stir sg

remparts [RãpaR] nmpl walls, ramparts

remplaçant, e [Rãplasã, ãt] nm/f replacement, stand-in; (Scol) supply teacher

remplacement [Rãplasmã] nm replacement; **faire des ~s** (professeur) to do supply teaching; (secrétaire) to do temping

remplacer [Rãplase] vt to replace; **~ qch/qn par** to replace sth/sb with

rempli, e [Rãpli] adj (emploi du temps) full, busy; **~ de** full of, filled with

remplir [RãpliR] vt to fill (up); (questionnaire) to fill out ou up; (obligations, fonction, condition) to fulfil; **se remplir** vi to fill up

remporter [RãpɔRte] vt (marchandise) to take away; (fig) to win, achieve

remuant, e [Rəmɥã, ãt] adj restless

remue-ménage [R(ə)mymenaʒ] nm inv commotion

remuer [Rəmɥe] vt to move; (café, sauce) to stir ▷ vi to move; **se remuer** vi to move; (fam: s'activer) to get a move on

rémunérer [Remyneʀe] vt to remunerate

renard [R(ə)naR] nm fox

renchérir [RãʃeRiR] vi (fig): **~ (sur)** (en paroles) to add something (to)

rencontre [RãkɔtR] nf meeting; (imprévue) encounter; **aller à la ~ de qn**

to go and meet sb; **rencontrer** vt to meet; (mot, expression) to come across; (difficultés) to meet with; **se rencontrer** vi to meet

rendement [Rãdmã] nm (d'un travailleur, d'une machine) output; (d'un champ) yield

rendez-vous [Rãdevu] nm appointment; (d'amoureux) date; (lieu) meeting place; **donner ~ à qn** to arrange to meet sb; **avoir/prendre ~ (avec)** to have/make an appointment (with); **j'ai ~ avec ...** I have an appointment with ...; **je voudrais prendre ~** I'd like to make an appointment

rendre [RãdR] vt (restituer) to give back, return; (invitation) to return, repay; (vomir) to bring up; (exprimer, traduire) to render; (faire devenir): **~ qn célèbre/qch possible** to make sb famous/sth possible; **se rendre** vi (capituler) to surrender, give o.s. up; (aller): **se ~ quelque part** to go somewhere; **~ la monnaie à qn** to give sb his change; **se ~ compte de qch** to realize sth

rênes [Rɛn] nfpl reins

renfermé, e [RãfɛRme] adj (fig) withdrawn ▷ nm: **sentir le ~** to smell stuffy

renfermer [RãfɛRme] vt to contain

renforcer [RãfɔRse] vt to reinforce; **renfort: renforts** nmpl reinforcements; **à grand renfort de** with a great deal of

renfrogné, e [RãfRɔɲe] adj sullen

renier [Rənje] vt (personne) to disown, repudiate; (foi) to renounce

renifler [R(ə)nifle] vi, vt to sniff

renne [Rɛn] nm reindeer inv

renom [Rənɔ̃] nm reputation; (célébrité) renown; **renommé, e** adj celebrated, renowned; **renommée** nf fame

renoncer [R(ə)nɔ̃se]: **~ à** vt to give up; **~ à faire** to give up the idea of doing

renouer [Rənwe] vt: **~ avec** (habitude) to take up again

renouveler [R(ə)nuv(ə)le] vt to

renew; (exploit, méfait) to repeat; **se renouveler** vi (incident) to recur, happen again; **renouvellement** nm (remplacement) renewal

rénover [ʀenɔve] vt (immeuble) to renovate, do up; (quartier) to redevelop

renseignement [ʀɑ̃sɛɲmɑ̃] nm information no pl, piece of information; **(guichet des) ~s** information office; **(service des) ~s** (Tél) directory enquiries (BRIT), information (US)

renseigner [ʀɑ̃seɲe] vt: **~ qn (sur)** to give information to sb (about); **se renseigner** vi to ask for information, make inquiries

rentabilité [ʀɑ̃tabilite] nf profitability

rentable [ʀɑ̃tabl] adj profitable

rente [ʀɑ̃t] nf private income; (pension) pension

rentrée [ʀɑ̃tʀe] nf: **~ (d'argent)** cash no pl coming in; **la ~ (des classes)** the start of the new school year

rentrer [ʀɑ̃tʀe] vi (revenir chez soi) to go (ou come) (back) home; (entrer de nouveau) to go (ou come) back in; (entrer) to go (ou come) in; (air, clou: pénétrer) to go in; (revenu) to come in ▶ vt to bring in; (véhicule) to put away; (chemise dans pantalon etc) to tuck in; (griffes) to draw in; **~ le ventre** to pull in one's stomach; **~ dans** (heurter) to crash into; **~ dans l'ordre** to be back to normal; **~ dans ses frais** to recover one's expenses; **je rentre mardi** I'm going ou coming home on Tuesday

renverse [ʀɑ̃vɛʀs]: **à la ~** adv backwards

renverser [ʀɑ̃vɛʀse] vt (faire tomber: chaise, verre) to knock over, overturn; (liquide, contenu) to spill, upset; (piéton) to knock down; (retourner) to turn upside down; (: ordre des mots etc) to reverse; (fig: gouvernement etc) to overthrow; (fam: stupéfier) to bowl over; **se renverser** vi (verre, vase) to fall over; (contenu) to spill

renvoi [ʀɑ̃vwa] nm (d'employé) dismissal; (d'élève) expulsion; (référence)

cross-reference; (éructation) belch; **renvoyer** vt to send back; (congédier) to dismiss; (élève: définitivement) to expel; (lumière) to reflect; (ajourner): **renvoyer qch (à)** to put sth off ou postpone sth (until)

repaire [ʀ(ə)pɛʀ] nm den

répandre [ʀepɑ̃dʀ] vt (renverser) to spill; (étaler, diffuser) to spread; (odeur) to give off; **se répandre** vi to spill; (se propager) to spread; **répandu, e** adj (opinion, usage) widespread

réparation [ʀepaʀasjɔ̃] nf repair

réparer [ʀepaʀe] vt to repair; (fig: offense) to make up for, atone for; (: oubli, erreur) to put right; **où est-ce que je peux le faire ~?** where can I get it fixed?

repartie [ʀepaʀti] nf retort; **avoir de la ~** to be quick at repartee

repartir [ʀ(ə)paʀtiʀ] vi to leave again; (voyageur) to set off again; (fig) to get going again; **~ à zéro** to start from scratch (again)

répartir [ʀepaʀtiʀ] vt (pour attribuer) to share out; (pour disperser, disposer) to divide up; (poids) to distribute; **se répartir** vt (travail, rôles) to share out between themselves; **répartition** nf (des richesses etc) distribution

repas [ʀ(ə)pɑ] nm meal

repassage [ʀ(ə)pɑsaʒ] nm ironing

repasser [ʀ(ə)pɑse] vi to come (ou go) back ▶ vt (vêtement, tissu) to iron; (examen) to retake, resit; (film) to show again; (leçon: revoir) to go over (again)

repentir [ʀɑ̃pɑ̃tiʀ] nm repentance; **se repentir** vi to repent; **se ~ d'avoir fait qch** (regretter) to regret having done sth

répercussions [ʀepɛʀkysjɔ̃] nfpl (fig) repercussions

répercuter [ʀepɛʀkyte]: **se répercuter** vi (bruit) to reverberate; (fig): **se ~ sur** to have repercussions on

repère [ʀ(ə)pɛʀ] nm mark; (monument, événement) landmark

repérer [ʀ(ə)peʀe] vt (fam: erreur, personne) to spot; (: endroit) to locate; **se**

repérer vi to find one's way about

répertoire [ʀepɛʀtwaʀ] nm (liste) (alphabetical) list; (carnet) index notebook; (Inform) folder, directory; (d'un artiste) repertoire

répéter [ʀepete] vt to repeat: (préparer: leçon) to learn, go over; (Théâtre) to rehearse; **se répéter** vi (redire) to repeat o.s.; (se reproduire) to be repeated, recur; **pouvez-vous ~, s'il vous plaît?** can you repeat that, please?

répétition [ʀepetisjɔ̃] nf repetition; (Théâtre) rehearsal; **~ générale** (final) dress rehearsal

répit [ʀepi] nm respite; **sans ~** without letting up

replier [ʀ(ə)plije] vt (rabattre) to fold down ou over; **se replier** vi (troupes, armée) to withdraw, fall back; (sur soi-même) to withdraw into o.s.

réplique [ʀeplik] nf (repartie, fig) reply; (Théâtre) line; (copie) replica; **répliquer** vi to reply; (riposter) to retaliate

répondeur [ʀepɔ̃dœʀ] nm: **~ (automatique)** (Tél) answering machine

répondre [ʀepɔ̃dʀ] vi to answer, reply; (freins) to respond; **~ à** to reply to, answer; (affection, salut) to return; (provocation) to respond to; (correspondre à: besoin) to answer; (: conditions) to meet; (: description) to match; (avec impertinence) **~ à qn** to answer sb back; **~ de** to answer for

réponse [ʀepɔ̃s] nf answer, reply; **en ~ à** in reply to

reportage [ʀ(ə)pɔʀtaʒ] nm report

reporter¹ [ʀapɔʀtɛʀ] nm reporter

reporter² [ʀapɔʀte] vt (ajourner): **~ qch (à)** to postpone sth (until); (transférer): **~ qch sur** to transfer sth to; **se reporter à** (époque) to think back to; (document) to refer to

repos [ʀ(ə)po] nm rest; (tranquillité) peace (and quiet); (Mil): **~!** stand at easel; **ce n'est pas de tout ~!** it's no picnic!

reposant, e [ʀ(ə)pozã, ãt] adj restful

reposer [ʀ(ə)poze] vt (verre, livre) to put down; (délasser) to rest ▷ vi: **laisser ~** (pâte) to leave to stand; **se reposer** vi to rest; **se ~ sur qn** to rely on sb; **~ sur** (fig) to rest on

repoussant, e [ʀ(ə)pusã, ãt] adj repulsive

repousser [ʀ(ə)puse] vi to grow again ▷ vt to repel, repulse; (offre) to turn down, reject; (personne) to push back; (différer) to put back

reprendre [ʀ(ə)pʀãdʀ] vt (objet prêté, donné) to take back; (prisonnier, ville) to recapture; (firme, entreprise) to take over; (le travail) to resume; (emprunt: argument, idée) to take up, use; (refaire: article etc) to go over again; (vêtement) to alter; (réprimander) to tell off; (corriger) to correct; (chercher): **je viendrai te ~ à 4 h** I'll come and fetch you at 4; **se reservir de: ~ du pain/un œuf** to take (eat) more bread/another egg ▷ vi (classes, pluie) to start (up) again; (activités, travaux, combats) to resume, start (up) again; (affaires) to pick up; (dire): **reprit-il** he went on; **~ des forces** to recover one's strength; **~ courage** to take new heart; **~ la route** to resume one's journey, set off again; **~ haleine** ou **son souffle** to get one's breath back

représentant, e [ʀ(ə)pʀezãtã, ãt] nm/f representative

représentation [ʀ(ə)pʀezãtasjɔ̃] nf (symbole, image) representation; (spectacle) performance

représenter [ʀ(ə)pʀezãte] vt to represent; (donner: pièce, opéra) to perform; **se représenter** vt (se figurer) to imagine

répression [ʀepʀesjɔ̃] nf repression

réprimer [ʀepʀime] vt (émotions) to suppress; (peuple etc) to repress

repris [ʀ(ə)pʀi] nm: **~ de justice** ex-prisoner, ex-convict

reprise [ʀ(ə)pʀiz] nf (recommencement) resumption; (économique) recovery; (TV) repeat; (Comm) trade-in, part exchange; (raccommodage) mend; **à plusieurs ~s** on several occasions

repriser [R(ə)pRize] vt (chaussette, lainage) to darn; (tissu) to mend

reproche [R(ə)pRɔʃ] nm (remontrance) reproach; **faire des ~s à qn** to reproach sb; **sans ~(s)** beyond reproach; **reprocher** vt: **reprocher qch à qn** to reproach ou blame sb for sth; **reprocher qch à** (critiquer) to have sth against

reproduction [R(ə)pRɔdyksjɔ̃] nf reproduction

reproduire [R(ə)pRɔdɥiR] vt to reproduce; **se reproduire** vi (Bio) to reproduce; (recommencer) to recur, re-occur

reptile [Rɛptil] nm reptile

république [Repyblik] nf republic

répugnant, e [Repyɲɑ̃, ɑ̃t] adj disgusting

répugner [Repyɲe]: **~ à** vt : **~ à qn** to repel ou disgust sb; **~ à faire** to be loath ou reluctant to do

réputation [Repytasjɔ̃] nf reputation; **réputé, e** adj renowned

requérir [RəkeRiR] vt (nécessiter) to require, call for

requête [Rəkɛt] nf request

requin [Rəkɛ̃] nm shark

requis, e [Rəki, iz] adj required

RER sigle m (= réseau express régional) Greater Paris high-speed train service

rescapé, e [Rɛskape] nm/f survivor

rescousse [Rɛskus] nf: **aller à la ~ de qn** to go to sb's aid ou rescue

réseau, x [Rezo] nm network

réservation [RezɛRvasjɔ̃] nf booking, reservation; **j'ai confirmé ma ~ par fax/e-mail** I confirmed my booking by fax/e-mail

réserve [RezɛRv] nf (retenue) reserve; (entrepôt) storeroom; (restriction, d'Indiens) reservation; (de pêche, chasse) preserve; **de ~** (provisions etc) in reserve

réservé, e adj reserved; **chasse/pêche ~e** private hunting/fishing

réserver [RezɛRve] vt to reserve; (chambre, billet etc) to book, reserve; (fig: destiner) to have in store; (garder): **~ qch pour/à** to keep ou save sth for: **je voudrais ~ une chambre pour deux personnes** I'd like to book a double room; **j'ai réservé une table au nom de ... I** booked a table in the name of ...

réservoir [RezɛRvwaR] nm tank

résidence [Rezidɑ̃s] nf residence; **résidence secondaire** second home; **résidence universitaire** hall of residence (BRIT), dormitory (US); **résidentiel, le** adj residential; **résider** vi: **résider à/dans/en** to reside in; **résider dans** (fig) to lie in

résidu [Rezidy] nm residue no pl

résigner [Reziɲe]: **se résigner** vi: se **~ (à qch/à faire)** to resign o.s. (to sth/to doing)

résilier [Rezilje] vt to terminate

résistance [Rezistɑ̃s] nf resistance; (de réchaud, bouilloire: fil) element

résistant, e [Rezistɑ̃, ɑ̃t] adj (personne) robust, tough; (matériau) strong, hard-wearing

résister [Reziste] vi to resist; **~ à** (assaut, tentation) to resist; (supporter: gel etc) to withstand; (désobéir à) to stand up to; **~ à** (assaut, tentation) to resist;

résolu, e [Rezɔly] pp de **résoudre** ▷ adj: **être~ à qch/faire** to be set upon sth/doing

résolution [Rezɔlysjɔ̃] nf (fermeté, décision) resolution; (d'un problème) solution

résolve etc [Rezɔlv] vb voir **résoudre**

résonner [Rezɔne] vi (cloche, pas) to reverberate, resound; (salle) to be resonant

résorber [RezɔRbe]: **se résorber** vi (fig: chômage) to be reduced; (: déficit) to be absorbed

résoudre [RezudR] vt to solve; **se ~ à faire** to bring o.s. to do

respect [Rɛspɛ] nm respect; **tenir en ~** to keep at bay; **présenter ses ~s à qn** to pay one's respects to sb; **respecter** vt to respect; **respectueux, -euse** adj respectful

respiration [ʀɛspiʀasjɔ̃] *nf*
breathing *no pl*

respirer [ʀɛspiʀe] *vi* to breathe; (*fig: se détendre*) to get one's breath; (*: se rassurer*) to breathe again ▷ *vt* to breathe (in), inhale; (*manifester: santé, calme etc*) to exude

resplendir [ʀɛsplɑ̃diʀ] *vi* to shine; (*fig*): **~ (de)** to be radiant (with)

responsabilité [ʀɛspɔ̃sabilite] *nf* responsibility; (*légale*) liability

responsable [ʀɛspɔ̃sabl] *adj* responsible ▷ *nm/f* (*coupable*) person responsible; (*personne compétente*) person in charge; (*de parti, syndicat*) official; **~ de** responsible for

ressaisir [ʀ(ə)seziʀ]: **se ressaisir** *vi* to regain one's self-control

ressasser [ʀ(ə)sase] *vt* to keep going over

ressemblance [ʀ(ə)sɑ̃blɑ̃s] *nf* resemblance, similarity, likeness

ressemblant, e [ʀ(ə)sɑ̃blɑ̃, ɑ̃t] *adj* (*portrait*) lifelike, true to life

ressembler [ʀ(ə)sɑ̃ble]: **~ à** *vt* to be like, resemble; (*visuellement*) to look like; **se ressembler** *vi* to be (*ou* look) alike

ressentiment [ʀ(ə)sɑ̃timɑ̃] *nm* resentment

ressentir [ʀ(ə)sɑ̃tiʀ] *vt* to feel; **se ~ de** to feel (*ou* show) the effects of

resserrer [ʀ(ə)seʀe] *vt* (*nœud, boulon*) to tighten (up); (*fig: liens*) to strengthen

resservir [ʀ(ə)seʀviʀ] *vi* to do ou serve again; **~ qn (d'un plat)** to give sb a second helping (of a dish); **se ~ de** (*plat*) to take a second helping of; (*outil etc*) to use again

ressort [ʀəsɔʀ] *nm* (*pièce*) spring; (*énergie*) spirit; (*recours*): **en dernier ~** as a last resort; (*compétence*): **être du ~ de** to fall within the competence of

ressortir [ʀəsɔʀtiʀ] *vi* to go (*ou* come) out (*again*); (*contraster*) to stand out; **~ de** to emerge from; **faire ~** (*fig: souligner*) to bring out

ressortissant, e [ʀ(ə)sɔʀtisɑ̃, ɑ̃t] *nm/f* national

ressources [ʀ(ə)suʀs] *nfpl* (*moyens*) resources

ressusciter [ʀesysite] *vt* (*fig*) to revive, bring back ▷ *vi* to rise (from the dead)

restant, e [ʀɛstɑ̃, ɑ̃t] *adj* remaining ▷ *nm*: **le ~ (de)** the remainder (of); **un ~ de** (*de trop*) some left-over

restaurant [ʀɛstɔʀɑ̃] *nm* restaurant; **pouvez-vous m'indiquer un bon ~?** can you recommend a good restaurant?

restauration [ʀɛstɔʀasjɔ̃] *nf* restoration; (*hôtellerie*) catering; **restauration rapide** fast food

restaurer [ʀɛstɔʀe] *vt* to restore; **se restaurer** *vi* to have something to eat

reste [ʀɛst] *nm* (*restant*): **le ~ (de)** the rest (of); (*de trop*): **un ~ (de)** some left-over; **restes** *nmpl* (*nourriture*) leftovers; (*d'une cité etc, dépouille mortelle*) remains; **du ~, au ~** besides, moreover

rester [ʀɛste] *vi* to stay, remain; (*subsister*) to remain, be left; (*durer*) to last, live on ▷ *vb impers*: **il reste du pain/2 œufs** there's some bread/there are 2 eggs left (over); **restons-en là** let's leave it at that; **il me reste assez de temps** I have enough time left; **il ne me reste plus qu'à ...** I've just got to ...

restituer [ʀɛstitɥe] *vt* (*objet, somme*): **~ qch (à qn)** to return sth (to sb)

restreindre [ʀɛstʀɛ̃dʀ] *vt* to restrict, limit

restriction [ʀɛstʀiksjɔ̃] *nf* restriction

résultat [ʀezylta] *nm* result; **résultats** *nmpl* (*d'examen, d'élection*) results *pl*

résulter [ʀezylte]: **~ de** *vt* to result from, be the result of

résumé [ʀezyme] *nm* summary, résumé; **en ~** in brief; (*pour conclure*) to sum up

résumer [ʀezyme] *vt* (*texte*) to summarize; (*récapituler*) to sum up
  Attention à ne pas traduire **résumer** par *to resume*.

résurrection [ʀezyʀɛksjɔ̃] *nf*

resurrection

rétablir [Retablir] vt to restore, re-establish; **se rétablir** vi (guérir) to recover; (silence, calme) to return, restoring; (guérison) recovery

retaper [R(ə)tape] (fam) vt (maison, voiture etc) to do up; (revigorer) to buck up

retard [R(ə)taR] nm (d'une personne attendue) lateness no pl; (sur l'horaire, un programme) delay; (fig: scolaire, mental etc) backwardness; **en ~ (de 2 heures)** (2 hours) late; **avoir du ~** to be late; (sur un programme) to be behind (schedule); **prendre du ~** (train, avion) to be delayed; **sans ~** without delay; **désolé d'être en ~** sorry I'm late; **le vol a deux heures de ~** the flight is two hours late

retardataire [R(ə)taRdatɛR] nmf latecomer

retardement [R(ə)taRdəmã]: **à ~** adj delayed action cpd; **bombe à ~** time bomb

retarder [R(ə)taRde] vt to delay; (montre) to put back ▷ vi (montre) to be slow; **~ qn (d'une heure)** (sur un horaire) to delay sb (an hour); (départ, date) to put sth back (by 2 days)

retenir [Rət(ə)niR] vt (garder, retarder) to keep, detain; (maintenir: objet qui glisse, fig: colère, larmes) to hold back; (se rappeler) to retain; (réserver) to reserve; (accepter: proposition etc) to accept; (fig: empêcher d'agir): **~ qn (de faire)** to hold sb back (from doing); **se ~** (se cramponner): **se ~ à** to hold onto; (se contenir): **se ~ de faire** to restrain o.s. from doing: **~ son souffle** to hold one's breath

retentir [R(ə)tãtiR] vi to ring out; **retentissant, e** adj resounding

retenue [Rət(ə)ny] nf (prélèvement) deduction; (Scol) detention; (modération) (self-)restraint

réticence [Retisãs] nf reluctance no pl, hesitation

hesitant, reluctant

rétine [Retin] nf retina

retiré, e [R(ə)tiRe] adj (vie) secluded; (lieu) remote

retirer [R(ə)tiRe] vt (vêtement, lunettes) to take off, remove; (argent, plainte) to withdraw; (reprendre: bagages, billets) to collect, pick up; (extraire): **~ qch de** to take sth out of, remove sth from

retomber [R(ə)tɔ̃be] vi (à nouveau) to fall again; (atterrir: après un saut etc) to land; (échoir): **~ sur qn** to fall on sb

rétorquer [RetɔRke] vt: **~ (à qn) que** to retort (to sb) that

retouche [R(ə)tuʃ] nf (sur vêtement, photographie) alteration; **retoucher** vt (texte, vêtement) to alter

retour [R(ə)tuR] nm return; **au ~** (en route) on the way back; **à mon retour** when I get/got back; **être de ~ (de)** to be back (from); **par ~ du courrier** by return of post; **quand serons-nous de ~?** when do we get back?

retourner [R(ə)tuRne] vt (dans l'autre sens: matelas, crêpe etc) to turn (over); (:sac, vêtement) to turn inside out; (fam: bouleverser) to shake; (renvoyer, restituer): **~ qch à qn** to return sth to sb ▷ vi (aller, revenir): **~ quelque part/à** to go back ou return somewhere/to; **se retourner** vi to turn over; (tourner la tête) to turn round; **se ~ contre** (fig) to turn against

retrait [R(ə)tRɛ] nm (d'argent) withdrawal; **en ~** set back; **retrait du permis (de conduire)** disqualification from driving (BRIT), revocation of driver's license (US)

retraite [R(ə)tRɛt] nf (d'un employé) retirement; (revenu) pension; (d'une armée, Rel) retreat; **prendre sa ~** to retire; **retraite anticipée** early retirement; **retraité, e** adj retired ▷ nm/f pensioner

retrancher [R(ə)tRãʃe] vt (nombre, somme): **~ qch de** to take ou deduct sth from; **se ~ derrière/dans** to take refuge behind/in

rétrécir [retresir] vt (vêtement) to take in ▸ vi to shrink; **se rétrécir** (route, vallée) to narrow

rétro [retro] adj inv rétro; **la mode -** the nostalgia vogue

rétroprojecteur [retroprojεktœr] nm overhead projector

rétrospective [retrospεktiv] nf (Art) retrospective; (Cinéma) season, retrospective. **rétrospectivement** adv in retrospect

retroussé [r(ə)truse] vt to roll up

retrouvailles [r(ə)truvaj] nfpl reunion sg

retrouver [r(ə)truve] vt (fugitif, objet perdu) to find; (calme, santé) to regain; (revoir) to see again; (rejoindre) to meet (again), join; **se retrouver** vi to meet; (s'orienter) to find one's way; **se - quelque part** to make sense of sth, somewhere; **s'y -** (y voir clair) to break even; **je ne retrouve plus mon portefeuille** I can't find my wallet

retroviseur [retrovizœr] nm (rear-view) mirror

réunion [reynjɔ̃] nf (séance) meeting

réunir [reynir] vt (rassembler) to gather together; (inviter: amis, famille) to have round, have in (cumuler: qualités etc) to combine, have in (rapprocher: ennemis) to bring together (again), reunite; (rattacher: parties) to join (together); **se réunir** vi (se rencontrer) to meet (together)

réussi, e [reysi] adj successful

réussir [reysir] vi to succeed, be successful; (à un examen) to pass ▸ vt to make a success of; **- à faire** to succeed in doing; **- à qn** (études) to be beneficial to sb; **réussite** [reysit] nf success; (Cartes) patience

revaloir [r(ə)valwar] vt: **je vous revaudrai cela** I'll repay you some day; (en mal) I'll pay you back for this

revanche [r(ə)vɑ̃ʃ] nf revenge; (Sport) revenge match; **en -** on the other hand

rêve [rεv] nm dream; **de -** dream; cpd: **faire un -** to have a dream

réveil [revεj] nm waking up no pl; (fig) awakening; (pendule) alarm (clock); **au -** on waking; (fig) to awaken, revive; **se réveiller** [reveje] vt (personne) to wake up; (fig) to awaken. se réveiller vi **me réveiller à 7 heures, s'il vous plaît** could have an alarm call at

réveillon [revεjɔ̃] nm Christmas Eve; (de la Saint-Sylvestre) New Year's Eve; **réveillonner** vi to celebrate Christmas Eve (ou New Year's Eve)

révélateur, -trice [revelatœr, tris] adj **- (de qch)** revealing (sth)

révéler [revele] vt to reveal; **se révéler** vi to be revealed, reveal itself ▸ vb +attrib: **se - difficile/aisé** to prove difficult/easy

revenant, e [r(ə)vənɑ̃, ɑ̃t] nm/f ghost

revendeur, -euse [r(ə)vɑ̃dœr, øz] nm/f (détaillant) retailer; (de drogue) (drug-)dealer

revendication [r(ə)vɑ̃dikasjɔ̃] nf claim, demand

revendiquer [r(ə)vɑ̃dike] vt to claim, demand; (responsabilité) to claim

revendre [r(ə)vɑ̃dr] vt (occasion) to resell; (détailler) to sell ▸ **- (en abondance)** to spare

revenir [rəv(ə)nir] vi to come back; (coûter) **- cher/à 100 euros (à qn)** to cost (sb) a lot/100 euros; **- à** (reprendre: études, projet) to return to, go back to; (équivaloir à) to amount to; **- à qn** (part, honneur) to go to, be sb's; (souvenir, nom) to come back to sb; **- sur** (question, sujet) to go back over; (engagement) to go back on; **- à soi** to come round; **n'en pas - : je n'en reviens pas** I can't get over it; **- sur ses pas** to retrace one's steps; **cela revient à dire que/au même** it amounts to saying that/the same thing; **faire -** (Culin) to brown

revenu [rəv(ə)ny] nm income; **revenus** nmpl income sg

rêver [reve] vi, vt to dream; **- de/à** to dream of

réverbère [ʀeveʀbɛʀ] nm street lamp ou light; **réverbérer** vt to reflect

revers [ʀ(ə)vɛʀ] nm (de feuille, main) back; (d'étoffe) wrong side; (de pièce, médaille) back, reverse; (Tennis, Ping-Pong) backhand; (de veste) lapel; (fig: échec) setback

revêtement [ʀ(ə)vɛtmã] nm (de sols) flooring; (de chaussée) surface

revêtir [ʀ(ə)vetiʀ] vt (habit) to don, put on; (prendre: importance, apparence) to take on; **~ qch de** to cover sth with

rêveur, -euse [ʀɛvœʀ, øz] adj dreamy ▷ nm/f dreamer

revient [ʀəvjɛ̃] vb voir **revenir**

revigorer [ʀ(ə)vigɔʀe] vt (air frais) to invigorate, brace up; (repas, boisson) to revive, buck up

revirement [ʀ(ə)viʀmã] nm change of mind; (d'une situation) reversal

réviser [ʀevize] vt to revise; (machine) to overhaul, service

révision [ʀevizjɔ̃] nf revision; (de voiture) servicing no pl

revivre [ʀ(ə)vivʀ] vi (reprendre des forces) to come alive again ▷ vt (épreuve, moment) to relive

revoir [ʀəvwaʀ] vt to see again; (réviser) to revise ▷ nm: **au ~** goodbye

révoltant, e [ʀevɔltã, ãt] adj revolting, appalling

révolte [ʀevɔlt] nf rebellion, revolt

révolter [ʀevɔlte] vt to revolt; **se révolter (contre)** to rebel (against)

révolu, e [ʀevɔly] adj past; (Admin): **âgé de 18 ans ~s** over 18 years of age

révolution [ʀevɔlysjɔ̃] nf revolution; **révolutionnaire** adj, nm/f revolutionary

revolver [ʀevɔlvɛʀ] nm gun; (à barillet) revolver

révoquer [ʀevɔke] vt (fonctionnaire) to dismiss; (arrêt, contrat) to revoke

revue [ʀ(ə)vy] nf review; (périodique) review, magazine; (de music-hall) variety show; **passer en ~** (mentalement) to go through

rez-de-chaussée [ʀed(ə)ʃose] nm inv ground floor

RF sigle f = **République française**

Rhin [ʀɛ̃] nm Rhine.

rhinocéros [ʀinɔseʀɔs] nm rhinoceros

Rhône [ʀon] nm Rhone

rhubarbe [ʀybaʀb] nf rhubarb

rhum [ʀɔm] nm rum

rhumatisme [ʀymatism] nm rheumatism no pl

rhume [ʀym] nm cold; **rhume de cerveau** head cold; **le rhume des foins** hay fever

ricaner [ʀikane] vi (avec méchanceté) to snigger; (bêtement) to giggle

riche [ʀiʃ] adj rich; (personne, pays) rich, wealthy; **~ en** rich in; **richesse** nf wealth; (fig: de sol, musée etc) richness; **richesses** nfpl (ressources, argent) wealth sg; (fig: trésors) treasures

ricochet [ʀikɔʃɛ] nm: **faire des ~s** to skip stones

ride [ʀid] nf wrinkle

rideau, X [ʀido] nm curtain; **rideau de fer** (boutique) metal shutter(s)

rider [ʀide] vt to wrinkle; **se rider** vi to become wrinkled

ridicule [ʀidikyl] adj ridiculous ▷ nm: **le ~** ridicule; **ridiculiser** vt to ridicule; **se ridiculiser** vi to make a fool of o.s.

 MOT-CLÉ

rien [ʀjɛ̃] pron 1: **(ne) ... rien** nothing, tournure négative + anything; **qu'est-ce que vous avez? — rien** what have you got? — nothing; **il n'a rien dit/fait** he said/did nothing; he hasn't said/done anything; **n'avoir peur de rien** not to be afraid ou frightened of nothing, not to be afraid ou frightened of anything; **il n'a rien** (n'est pas blessé) he's all right; **ça ne fait rien** it doesn't matter; **de rien!** not at all!

2: **rien de: rien d'intéressant** nothing interesting; **rien d'autre** nothing else; **rien du tout** nothing at all

3: **rien que** just, only; nothing but; **rien que pour lui faire plaisir** only ou just to please him; **rien que la vérité** nothing but the truth; **rien que cela** that alone ▷ *nm*: **un petit rien** (*cadeau*) a little something; **des riens** trivia *pl*; **un rien de** a hint of; **en un rien de temps** in no time at all

rieur, -euse [R(i)jœR, R(i)jøz] *adj* cheerful

rigide [Riʒid] *adj* stiff; (*fig*) rigid; strict

rigoler [Rigɔle] *vi* (*fam: rire*) to laugh; (*s'amuser*) to have (some) fun; (*plaisanter*) to be joking *ou* kidding; **rigolo, -ote** (*fam*) *adj* funny ▷ *nm/f* comic; (*péj*) fraud, phoney

rigoureusement [RiguRøzmɑ̃] *adv* (*vrai*) absolutely; (*interdit*) strictly

rigoureux, -euse [RiguRø, øz] *adj* rigorous; (*hiver*) hard, harsh

rigueur [RigœR] *nf* rigour; **"tenue de soirée de -"** "formal dress only"; **à la -** at a pinch; **tenir - à qn de qch** to hold sth against sb

rillettes [Rijɛt] *nfpl* potted meat (*made from pork or goose*)

rime [Rim] *nf* rhyme

rinçage [Rɛ̃saʒ] *nm* rinsing (out); (*opération*) rinse

rincer [Rɛ̃se] *vt* to rinse; (*récipient*) to rinse out

ringard, e [Rɛ̃gaR, aRd] (*fam*) *adj* old-fashioned

riposter [Ripɔste] *vi* to retaliate ▷ *vt*: **- que** to retort that

rire [RiR] *vi* to laugh; (*se divertir*) to have fun ▷ *nm* laugh; **le -** laughter; **- de** to laugh at; **pour -** (*pas sérieusement*) for a joke *ou* a laugh

risible [Rizibl] *adj* laughable

risque [Risk] *nm* risk; **- danger**; **à ses -s et périls** at his own risk; **risqué, e** *adj* risky; (*plaisanterie*) risqué, daring; **risquer** *vt* to risk; (*allusion, question*) to venture, hazard; **il ne risque pas de recommencer** there's no chance of him doing that again; **se risquer à faire** (*tenter*) to venture *ou* dare to do

rissoler [Risɔle] *vi, vt*: **(faire) -** to brown

ristourne [RistuRn] *nf* discount

rite [Rit] *nm* rite; (*fig*) ritual

rivage [Rivaʒ] *nm* shore

rival, e, -aux [Rival, o] *adj, nm/f* rival; **rivaliser** *vi*: **rivaliser avec** (*personne*) to rival, vie with; **rivalité** *nf* rivalry

rive [Riv] *nf* shore; (*de fleuve*) bank; **riverain, e**, *nm/f* riverside (*ou* lakeside) resident; (*d'une route*) local resident

rivière [RivjɛR] *nf* river

riz [Ri] *nm* rice; **rizière** *nf* paddy-field, ricefield

RMI *sigle m* (= *revenu minimum d'insertion*) ≈ income support (BRIT), ≈ welfare (US)

RN *sigle f* = **route nationale**

robe [Rɔb] *nf* dress; (*de juge*) robe; (*pelage*) coat; **robe de chambre** dressing gown; **robe de mariée** wedding dress; **robe de soirée** evening dress

robinet [Rɔbinɛ] *nm* tap (BRIT), faucet (US)

robot [Rɔbo] *nm* robot; **robot de cuisine** food processor

robuste [Rɔbyst] *adj* robust, sturdy; **robustesse** *nf* robustness, sturdiness

roc [Rɔk] *nm* rock

rocade [Rɔkad] *nf* bypass

rocaille [Rɔkaj] *nf* loose stones *pl*; (*jardin*) rockery, rock garden

roche [Rɔʃ] *nf* rock

rocher [Rɔʃe] *nm* rock

rocheux, -euse [Rɔʃø, øz] *adj* rocky

rodage [Rɔdaʒ] *nm*: **en -** running in

rôder [Rode] *vi* to roam about; (*de façon suspecte*) to lurk (about *ou* around); **rôdeur, -euse** *nm/f* prowler

rogne [Rɔɲ] (*fam*) *nf*: **être en -** to be in a temper

rogner [Rɔɲe] *vt* to clip; **- sur** (*fig*) to cut down *ou* back on

rognons [Rɔɲɔ̃] *nmpl* (*Culin*) kidneys

roi [Rwa] *nm* king; **la fête des Rois, les**

Rois Twelfth Night

rôle [ʁol] nm role, part

rollers [ʁɔlœʀ] nmpl Rollerblades®

romain, e [ʁɔmɛ̃, ɛn] adj Roman ▷ nm/f: **R~, e** Roman

roman, e [ʁɔmɑ̃, an] adj (Archit) Romanesque ▷ nm novel; **(roman) policier** detective story

romancer [ʁɔmɑ̃se] vt (agrémenter) to romanticize; **romancier, -ière** nm/f novelist; **romanesque** adj (amours, aventures) storybook cpd; (sentimental: personne) romantic

roman-feuilleton [ʁɔmɑ̃fœjtɔ̃] nm serialized novel

romanichel, le [ʁɔmaniʃɛl] (péj) nm/f gipsy

romantique [ʁɔmɑ̃tik] adj romantic

romarin [ʁɔmaʁɛ̃] nm rosemary

Rome [ʁɔm] n Rome

rompre [ʁɔ̃pʀ] vt to break; (entretien, fiançailles) to break off ▷ vi (fiancés) to break it off; **se rompre** vi to break; **rompu, e** adj (fourbu) exhausted

ronces [ʁɔ̃s] nfpl brambles

ronchonner [ʁɔ̃ʃɔne] (fam) vi to grouse, grouch

rond, e [ʁɔ̃, ʁɔ̃d] adj round; (joues, mollets) well-rounded; (fam: ivre) tight ▷ nm (cercle) ring; (fam: sou): **je n'ai plus un ~** I haven't a penny left; **en ~** (s'asseoir, danser) in a ring; **ronde** nf (gén: de surveillance) rounds pl, patrol; (danse) round (dance); (Mus) semibreve (BRIT), whole note (US); **à la ronde** (alentour): **à 10 km à la ronde** for 10 km round; **rondelet, le** adj plump

rondelle [ʁɔ̃dɛl] nf (tranche) slice, round; (Tech) washer

rond-point [ʁɔ̃pwɛ̃] nm roundabout

ronflement [ʁɔ̃fləmɑ̃] nm snore, snoring

ronfler [ʁɔ̃fle] vi to snore; (moteur, poêle) to hum

ronger [ʁɔ̃ʒe] vt to gnaw (at); (suj: vers, rouille) to eat into; **se ~ les ongles** to bite one's nails; **se ~ les sangs** to worry o.s. sick; **rongeur** nm rodent

ronronner [ʁɔ̃ʀɔne] vi to purr

rosbif [ʁɔsbif] nm: **du ~** roasting beef; (cuit) roast beef

rose [ʁoz] nf rose ▷ adj pink; **rose bonbon** adj inv candy pink

rosé, e [ʁoze] adj pinkish; **(vin) ~** rosé

roseau, x [ʁozo] nm reed

rosée [ʁoze] nf dew

rosier [ʁozje] nm rosebush, rose tree

rossignol [ʁɔsiɲɔl] nm (Zool) nightingale

rotation [ʁɔtasjɔ̃] nf rotation

roter [ʁɔte] (fam) vi to burp, belch

rôti [ʁoti] nm: **du ~** roasting meat; (cuit) roast meat; **un ~ de bœuf/porc** a joint of beef/pork

rotin [ʁɔtɛ̃] nm rattan (cane); **fauteuil en ~** cane (arm)chair

rôtir [ʁotiʁ] vi, vt (aussi: **faire ~**) to roast; **rôtisserie** nf (restaurant) steakhouse; (traiteur) roast meat shop; **rôtissoire** nf (roasting) spit

rotule [ʁɔtyl] nf kneecap

rouage [ʁwaʒ] nm cog(wheel), gearwheel; **les ~s de l'État** the wheels of State

roue [ʀu] nf wheel; **roue de secours** spare wheel

rouer [ʀwe] vt: **~ qn de coups** to give sb a thrashing

rouge [ʀuʒ] adj, nm/f red ▷ nm red; **(vin) ~** red wine; **sur la liste ~** ex-directory (BRIT), unlisted (US); **passer au ~** (signal) to go red; (automobiliste) to go through a red light; **rouge à joue** blusher; **rouge (à lèvres)** lipstick; **rouge-gorge** nm robin (redbreast)

rougeole [ʀuʒɔl] nf measles sg

rougeoyer [ʀuʒwaje] vi to glow red

rouget [ʀuʒɛ] nm mullet

rougeur [ʀuʒœʀ] nf redness; (Méd: tache) red blotch

rougir [ʀuʒiʀ] vi to turn red; (de honte, timidité) to blush, flush; (de plaisir, colère) to flush

rouille [ʀuj] nf rust; **rouillé, e** adj rusty; **rouiller** vt to rust ▷ vi to rust, go rusty

roulant, e [ʀulɑ̃, ɑ̃t] adj (meuble) on

wheels; (tapis etc) moving; **escalier ~** escalator

rouleau, x [Rulo] nm roll; (à mise en plis, à peinture, vague) roller; **rouleau à pâtisserie** rolling pin

roulement [Rulmã] nm (rotation) rotation; (bruit) rumbling no pl, rumble; **travailler par ~** to work on a rota (BRIT) ou rotation (US) basis; **roulement (à billes)** ball bearings pl; **roulement de tambour** drum roll

rouler [Rule] vt to roll; (papier, tapis) to roll up; (Culin: pâte) to roll out; (fam: duper) to do, con ▷ vi (bille, boule) to roll; (voiture, train) to go, run; (automobiliste) to drive; (bateau) to roll; **se ~ dans** (boue) to roll in; (couverture) to roll o.s. (up) in

roulette [Rulεt] nf (de table, fauteuil) castor; (de dentiste) drill; (jeu) roulette; **à ~s** on castors; **ça a marché comme sur des ~s** (fam) it went off very smoothly

roulis [Ruli] nm roll(ing)

roulotte [Rulɔt] nf caravan

roumain, e [Rumɛ̃, εn] adj Rumanian ▷ nm/f; **R~, e** Rumanian

Roumanie [Rumani] nf Rumania

rouquin, e [Rukɛ̃, in] (péj) nm/f redhead

rouspéter [Ruspete] (fam) vi to moan

rousse [Rus] adj voir **roux**

roussir [RusiR] vt to scorch ▷ vi (Culin): **faire ~** to brown

route [Rut] nf road; (fig: chemin) way; (itinéraire, parcours) route; (fig: voie) road, path; **il y a 3 h de ~** it's a 3-hour ride ou journey; **en ~** on the way; **en ~!** let's go!; **mettre en ~** to start up; **se mettre en ~** to set off; **quelle ~ dois-je prendre pour aller à ...?** which road do I take for ...?; **route nationale** = A road (BRIT), = state highway (US); **routier, -ière** adj road cpd ▷ nm (camionneur) (long-distance) lorry (BRIT) ou truck (US) driver; (restaurant) = transport café (BRIT), = truck stop (US)

routine [Rutin] nf routine; **routinier, -ière** (péj) adj (activité) humdrum;

(personne) addicted to routine

rouvrir [RuvRiR] vt, vi to reopen, open again; **se rouvrir** vi to reopen, open again

roux, rousse [Ru, Rus] adj red; (personne) red-haired ▷ nm/f redhead

royal, e, -aux [Rwajal, o] adj royal; (cadeau etc) fit for a king

royaume [Rwajom] nm kingdom; (fig) realm; **le Royaume-Uni** the United Kingdom

royauté [Rwajote] nf (régime) monarchy

ruban [Rybã] nm ribbon; **ruban adhésif** adhesive tape

rubéole [Rybeɔl] nf German measles sg, rubella

rubis [Rybi] nm ruby

rubrique [RybRik] nf (titre, catégorie) heading; (Presse: article) column

ruche [Ryʃ] nf hive

rude [Ryd] adj (au toucher) rough; (métier, tâche) hard, tough; (climat) severe, harsh; (bourru) harsh, rough; (fruste: manières) rugged, tough; (fam: fameux) jolly good; **rudement** (fam) adv (très) terribly

rudimentaire [RydimãtεR] adj rudimentary, basic

rudiments [Rydimã] nmpl: **avoir des ~ d'anglais** to have a smattering of English

rue [Ry] nf street

ruée [Rɥe] nf rush

ruelle [Rɥεl] nf alley(-way)

ruer [Rɥe] vi (cheval) to kick out; **se ruer vi: se ~ sur** to pounce on; **se ~ vers/dans/hors de** to rush towards/into/out of

rugby [Rygbi] nm rugby (football)

rugir [RyʒiR] vi to roar

rugueux, -euse [Rygø, øz] adj rough

ruine [Rɥin] nf ruin; **ruiner** vt to ruin; **ruineux, -euse** adj ruinous

ruisseau, x [Rɥiso] nm stream, brook

ruisseler [Rɥis(ə)le] vi to stream

rumeur [RymœR] nf (nouvelle) rumour; (bruit confus) rumbling

ruminer [ʀymine] *vt (herbe)* to ruminate; *(fig)* to ruminate on *ou* over, chew over

rupture [ʀyptyʀ] *nf (séparation, désunion)* break-up, split; *(de négociations etc)* breakdown; *(de contrat)* breach; *(dans continuité)* break

rural, e, -aux [ʀyʀal, o] *adj* rural, country *cpd*

ruse [ʀyz] *nf:* **la ~** cunning, craftiness; *(pour tromper)* trickery; **une ~** a trick, a ruse; **rusé, e** *adj* cunning, crafty

russe [ʀys] *adj* Russian ▷ *nm/f:* **R~** Russian ▷ *nm (Ling)* Russian

Russie [ʀysi] *nf:* **la ~** Russia

rustine® [ʀystin] *nf* rubber repair patch *(for bicycle tyre)*

rustique [ʀystik] *adj* rustic

rythme [ʀitm] *nm* rhythm; *(vitesse)* rate; *(: de la vie)* pace, tempo; **rythmé, e** *adj* rhythmic(al)

S

s' [s] *pron voir* **se**

sa [sa] *adj voir* **son¹**

sable [sabl] *nm* sand

sablé [sable] *nm* shortbread biscuit

sabler [sable] *vt (contre le verglas)* to grit; **~ le champagne** to drink champagne

sabot [sabo] *nm* clog; *(de cheval)* hoof; **sabot de frein** brake shoe

saboter [sabote] *vt* to sabotage; *(bâcler)* to make a mess of, botch

sac [sak] *nm* bag; *(à charbon etc)* sack; **mettre à ~** to sack; **sac à dos** rucksack; **sac à main** handbag; **sac de couchage** sleeping bag; **sac de voyage** travelling bag

saccadé, e [sakade] *adj* jerky; *(respiration)* spasmodic

saccager [sakaʒe] *vt (piller)* to sack; *(dévaster)* to create havoc in

saccharine [sakaʀin] *nf* saccharin

sachet [saʃɛ] *nm (small)* bag; *(de sucre, café)* sachet; **du potage en ~** packet soup; **sachet de thé** tea bag

sacoche [sakɔʃ] nf (gén) bag; (de bicyclette) saddlebag

sacré, e [sakʀe] adj sacred; (fam: satané) blasted; (: fameux): **un ~ toupet** a heck of a cheek

sacrement [sakʀəmɑ̃] nm sacrament

sacrifice [sakʀifis] nm sacrifice; **sacrifier** vt to sacrifice

sacristie [sakʀisti] nf (catholique) sacristy; (protestante) vestry

sadique [sadik] adj sadistic

safran [safʀɑ̃] nm saffron

sage [saʒ] adj wise; (enfant) good

sage-femme [saʒfam] nf midwife

sagesse [saʒɛs] nf wisdom

Sagittaire [saʒitɛʀ] nm: **le ~** Sagittarius

Sahara [saaʀa] nm: **le ~** the Sahara (desert)

saignant, e [sɛɲɑ̃, ɑ̃t] adj (viande) rare

saigner [seɲe] vi to bleed ▷ vt to bleed; (animal) to kill (by bleeding); **~ du nez** to have a nosebleed

saillir [sajiʀ] vi to project, stick out; (veine, muscle) to bulge

sain, e [sɛ̃, sɛn] adj healthy; **~ et sauf** safe and sound, unharmed; **~ d'esprit** sound in mind, sane

saindoux [sɛ̃du] nm lard

saint, e [sɛ̃, sɛ̃t] adj holy ▷ nm/f saint; **le Saint Esprit** the Holy Spirit ou Ghost; **la Sainte Vierge** the Blessed Virgin; **la Saint-Sylvestre** New Year's Eve; **sainteté** nf holiness

sais etc [sɛ] vb voir **savoir**

saisie [sezi] nf seizure; **saisie (de données)** (data) capture

saisir [seziʀ] vt to take hold of, grab; (fig: occasion) to seize; (comprendre) to grasp; (entendre) to get, catch; (données) to capture; (Culin) to fry quickly; (Jur: biens, publication) to seize; **saisissant, e** adj startling, striking

saison [sɛzɔ̃] nf season; **haute/basse/morte** high/low/slack season; **saisonnier, -ière** adj seasonal

salade [salad] nf (Bot) lettuce etc; (Culin) (green) salad; (fam: confusion) tangle, muddle; **salade composée** mixed salad; **salade de fruits** fruit salad; **saladier** nm (salad) bowl

salaire [salɛʀ] nm (annuel, mensuel) salary; (hebdomadaire, journalier) pay, wages pl; **salaire minimum interprofessionnel de croissance** index-linked guaranteed minimum wage

salarié, e [salaʀje] nm/f salaried employee; wage-earner

salaud [salo] (fam!) nm sod (!), bastard (!)

sale [sal] adj dirty, filthy; (fam: mauvais) nasty

salé, e [sale] adj (mer, goût) salty; (Culin: amandes, beurre etc) salted; (: gâteaux) savoury; (fam: grivois) spicy; (: facture) steep

saler [sale] vt to salt

saleté [salte] nf (état) dirtiness; (crasse) dirt, filth; (tache etc) dirt no pl; (fam: méchanceté) dirty trick; (: camelote) rubbish no pl; (: obscénité) filthy thing (to say)

salière [saljɛʀ] nf saltcellar

salir [saliʀ] vt to (make) dirty; (fig: quelqu'un) to soil the reputation of; **se salir** vi to get dirty; **salissant, e** (tissu) which shows the dirt; (travail) dirty, messy

salle [sal] nf room; (d'hôpital) ward; (de restaurant) dining room; (d'un cinéma) auditorium; (: public) audience; **salle à manger** dining room; **salle d'attente** waiting room; **salle de bain(s)** bathroom; **salle de classe** classroom; **salle de concert** concert hall; **salle d'eau** shower-room; **salle d'embarquement** (à l'aéroport) departure lounge; **salle de jeux** (pour enfants) playroom; **salle de séjour** living room; **salle des ventes** saleroom

salon [salɔ̃] nm lounge, sitting room; (mobilier) lounge suite; (exposition) exhibition, show; **salon de coiffure** hairdressing salon; **salon de thé** tearoom

salope [salɔp] (fam!) nf bitch (!)

saloperie [salɔpʀi] (fam!) nf (action) dirty trick; (chose sans valeur) rubbish no pl

salopette [salɔpɛt] nf (de dungarees pl; (d'ouvrier) overall(s)

salsifis [salsifi] nm salsify

salubre [salybʀ] adj healthy, salubrious

saluer [salɥe] vt (pour dire bonjour, fig) to greet; (pour dire au revoir) to take one's leave; (Mil) to salute

salut [saly] nm (geste) wave; (parole) greeting; (Mil: salut: (sauvegarde) safety; (Rel) salvation ▷ excl (fam: bonjour) hi (there); (: au revoir) see you, bye

salutations [salytasjɔ̃] nfpl greetings; **Veuillez agréer, Monsieur, mes ~ distinguées** yours faithfully

samedi [samdi] nm Saturday

SAMU [samy] sigle m (= service d'assistance médicale d'urgence) ≈ ambulance (service) (BRIT), ≈ paramedics pl (US)

sanction [sɑ̃ksjɔ̃] nf sanction; **sanctionner** vt (loi, usage) to sanction; (punir) to punish

sandale [sɑ̃dal] nf sandal

sandwich [sɑ̃dwi(t)ʃ] nm sandwich; **je voudrais un ~ au jambon/fromage** I'd like a ham/cheese sandwich

sang [sɑ̃] nm blood; **en ~** covered in blood; **se faire du mauvais ~** to fret, get in a state; **sang-froid** nm calm, sangfroid; **de sang-froid** in cold blood; **sanglant, e** adj bloody

sangle [sɑ̃gl] nf strap

sanglier [sɑ̃glije] nm (wild) boar

sanglot [sɑ̃glo] nm sob; **sangloter** vi to sob

sangsue [sɑ̃sy] nf leech

sanguin, e [sɑ̃gɛ̃, in] adj blood cpd

sanitaire [sanitɛʀ] adj health cpd; **sanitaires** nmpl (lieu) bathroom sg

sans [sɑ̃] prép without; **un pull ~ manches** a sleeveless jumper; **~ faute** without fail; **~ arrêt** without a break; **~ ça** (fam) otherwise; **~ qu'il s'en aperçoive** without him

ou his noticing; **sans-abri** nmpl homeless; **sans-emploi** nm/f inv unemployed person; **les sans-emploi** the unemployed; **sans-gêne** adj inv inconsiderate

santé [sɑ̃te] nf health; **en bonne ~** in good health; **boire à la ~ de qn** to drink (to) sb's health; **à ta/votre ~!** cheers!

saoudien, ne [saudjɛ̃, jɛn] adj Saudi Arabian ▷ nm/f: **S~, ne** Saudi Arabian

saoul, e [su, sul] adj = **soûl**

saper [sape] vt to undermine

sapeur-pompier [sapœʀpɔ̃pje] nm fireman

saphir [safiʀ] nm sapphire

sapin [sapɛ̃] nm fir (tree); (bois) fir; **sapin de Noël** Christmas tree

sarcastique [saʀkastik] adj sarcastic

Sardaigne [saʀdɛɲ] nf: **la ~** Sardinia

sardine [saʀdin] nf sardine

SARL sigle f (= société à responsabilité limitée) ≈ plc (BRIT), ≈ Inc. (US)

sarrasin [saʀazɛ̃] nm buckwheat

satané, e [satane] (fam) adj confounded

satellite [satelit] nm satellite

satin [satɛ̃] nm satin

satire [satiʀ] nf satire; **satirique** adj satirical

satisfaction [satisfaksjɔ̃] nf satisfaction

satisfaire [satisfɛʀ] vt to satisfy; **~ à** (conditions) to meet; **satisfaisant, e** adj (acceptable) satisfactory; **satisfait, e** adj satisfied; **satisfait de** happy ou satisfied with

saturer [satyʀe] vt to saturate

sauce [sos] nf sauce; (avec un rôti) gravy; **sauce tomate** tomato sauce; **saucière** nf sauceboat

saucisse [sosis] nf sausage

saucisson [sosisɔ̃] nm (slicing) sausage

sauf, sauve [sof, sov] adj unharmed, unhurt; (fig: honneur) intact, saved ▷ prép except; **laisser la vie sauve à qn** to spare sb's life; **~ si** (à moins que) unless; **~ erreur** if I'm not mistaken;

~ avis contraire unless you hear to the contrary

sauge [soʒ] nf sage

saugrenu, e [sogrəny] adj preposterous

saule [sol] nm willow (tree)

saumon [somɔ̃] nm salmon inv

saupoudrer [sopudre] vt: **~ qch de** to sprinkle sth with

saur [sɔr] adj m: **hareng ~** smoked herring, kipper

saut [so] nm jump; (discipline sportive) jumping; **faire un ~ chez qn** to pop over to sb's (place); **saut à l'élastique** bungee jumping; **saut à la perche** pole vaulting; **saut en hauteur/longueur** high/long jump; **saut périlleux** somersault

sauter [sote] vi to jump, leap; (exploser) to blow up, explode; (: fusibles) to blow; (se détacher) to pop out ou off ▷ vt to jump (over), leap (over); (fig: omettre) to skip, miss (out); **faire ~** to blow up; (Culin) to sauté; **~ à la corde** to skip; **~ au cou de qn** to fly into sb's arms; **~ sur une occasion** to jump at an opportunity; **~ aux yeux** to be (quite) obvious

sauterelle [sotrɛl] nf grasshopper

sautiller [sotije] vi (oiseau) to hop; (enfant) to skip

sauvage [sovaʒ] adj (gén) wild; (peuplade) savage; (farouche: personne) unsociable; (barbare) wild, savage; (non officiel) unauthorized, unofficial; **faire du camping ~** to camp in the wild ▷ nm/f savage; (timide) unsociable type

sauve [sov] adj f voir **sauf**

sauvegarde [sovgard] nf safeguard; (Inform) backup; **sauvegarder** vt to safeguard; (Inform: enregistrer) to save; (: copier) to back up

sauve-qui-peut [sovkipø] excl run for your life!

sauver [sove] vt to save; (porter secours à) to rescue; (récupérer) to salvage, rescue; **se sauver** vi (s'enfuir) to run away; (fam: partir) to be off; **sauvetage**

nm rescue; **sauveteur** nm rescuer; **sauvette**: **à la sauvette** adv (se marier etc) hastily, hurriedly; **sauveur** nm saviour (BRIT), savior (US)

savant, e [savɑ̃, ɑ̃t] adj scholarly, learned ▷ nm scientist

saveur [savœr] nf flavour; (fig) savour

savoir [savwar] vt to know; (être capable de): **il sait nager** he can swim ▷ nm knowledge; **se savoir** vi (être connu) to be known: **je ne sais pas** I don't know; **je ne sais pas parler français** I don't speak French; **savez-vous où je peux ...?** do you know where I can ...?; **je n'en sais rien** I (really) don't know; **à ~** that is, namely; **faire ~ qch à qn** to let sb know sth; **pas que je sache** not as far as I know

savon [savɔ̃] nm (produit) soap; (morceau) bar of soap; (fam): **passer un ~ à qn** to give sb a good dressing-down; **savonner** vt to soap; **savonnette** nf bar of soap

savourer [savure] vt to savour; **savoureux, -euse** adj tasty; (fig: anecdote) spicy, juicy

saxo(phone) [sakso(fɔn)] nm sax(ophone)

scabreux, -euse [skabrø, øz] adj risky; (indécent) improper, shocking

scandale [skɑ̃dal] nm scandal; **faire un ~** (scène) to make a scene; (Jur) to create a disturbance; **faire ~** to scandalize people; **scandaleux, -euse** adj scandalous, outrageous

scandinave [skɑ̃dinav] adj Scandinavian ▷ nm/f: **S~** Scandinavian

Scandinavie [skɑ̃dinavi] nf Scandinavia

scarabée [skarabe] nm beetle

scarlatine [skarlatin] nf scarlet fever

scarole [skarɔl] nf endive

sceau, x [so] nm seal

sceller [sele] vt to seal

scénario [senarjo] nm scenario

scène [sɛn] nf (gén) scene; (estrade, de théâtre) stage; **entrer en ~** to come on stage; **mettre en ~** (Théâtre) to stage;

(*Cinéma*) to direct; **faire une ~ (à qn)** to make a scene (with sb); **scène de ménage** domestic scene

sceptique [sɛptik] *adj* sceptical

schéma [ʃema] *nm* (*diagramme*) diagram, sketch; **schématique** *adj* diagrammatic(al), schematic; (*fig*) oversimplified

sciatique [sjatik] *nf* sciatica

scie [si] *nf* saw

sciemment [sjamɑ̃] *adv* knowingly

science [sjɑ̃s] *nf* (*savoir*) knowledge; **sciences humaines/ sociales** social sciences; **sciences naturelles** (*Scol*) natural science *sg*, biology *sg*; **sciences po** political science *ou* studies *pl*; **science-fiction** *nf* science fiction; **scientifique** *adj* scientific ▷ *nm/f* scientist; (*étudiant*) science student

scier [sje] *vt* to saw; (*retrancher*) to saw off; **scierie** *nf* sawmill

scintiller [sɛ̃tije] *vi* to sparkle; (*étoile*) to twinkle

sciure [sjyʀ] *nf*: **~ (de bois)** sawdust

sclérose [skleʀoz] *nf*: **sclérose en plaques** multiple sclerosis

scolaire [skɔlɛʀ] *adj* school *cpd*; **scolariser** *vt* to provide with schooling/schools; **scolarité** *nf* schooling

scooter [skutœʀ] *nm* (motor) scooter

score [skɔʀ] *nm* score

scorpion [skɔʀpjɔ̃] *nm* (*signe*): **le S~** Scorpio

scotch [skɔtʃ] *nm* (*whisky*) scotch, whisky; **S~®** (*adhésif*) Sellotape® (*BRIT*), Scotch® tape (*US*)

scout, e [skut] *adj, nm* scout

script [skʀipt] *nm* (*écriture*) printing; (*Cinéma*) (shooting) script

scrupule [skʀypyl] *nm* scruple

scruter [skʀyte] *vt* to scrutinize; (*l'obscurité*) to peer into

scrutin [skʀytɛ̃] *nm* (*vote*) ballot; (*ensemble des opérations*) poll

sculpter [skylte] *vt* to sculpt; (*bois*) to carve; **sculpteur** *nm* sculptor;

sculpture *nf* sculpture

SDF *sigle m*: **sans domicile fixe** homeless person; **les ~** the homeless

○ **MOT-CLÉ**

se [sə], **s'** *pron* 1 (*emploi réfléchi*) oneself; (: *masc*) himself; (: *fém*) herself; (: *sujet non humain*) itself; (: *pl*) themselves; **se savonner** to soap o.s.

2 (*réciproque*) one another, each other; **ils s'aiment** they love one another *ou* each other

3 (*passif*): **cela se répare facilement** it is easily repaired

4 (*possessif*): **se casser la jambe/se laver les mains** to break one's leg/ wash one's hands

séance [seɑ̃s] *nf* (*d'assemblée*) meeting, session; (*de tribunal*) sitting, session; (*musicale, Cinéma, Théâtre*) performance

seau [so] *nm* bucket, pail

sec, sèche [sɛk, sɛʃ] *adj* dry; (*raisins, figues*) dried; (*cœur: insensible*) hard, cold ▷ *nm*: **tenir au ~** to keep in a dry place ▷ *adv*: **je le bois ~** I drink it straight *ou* neat; **à ~** (*puits*) dried up

sécateur [sekatœʀ] *nm* secateurs *pl* (*BRIT*), shears *pl*

sèche [sɛʃ] *adj f voir* **sec**; **sèche- cheveux** *nm inv* hair-drier; **sèche- linge** *nm inv* tumble dryer; **sèchement** *adv* (*répondre*) drily

sécher [seʃe] *vt* to dry; (*dessécher: peau, blé*) to dry (out); (: *étang*) to dry up; (*fam: cours*) to skip ▷ *vi* to dry; to dry out; to dry up; (*fam: candidat*) to be stumped; **se sécher** (*après le bain*) to dry o.s.; **sécheresse** *nf* dryness; (*absence de pluie*) drought; **séchoir** *nm* drier

second, e¹ [s(ə)gɔ̃, ɔ̃d] *adj* second ▷ *nm* (*assistant*) second in command; (*Navig*) first mate ▷ *nf* (*Scol*) year 11 (*BRIT*), tenth grade (*US*); (*Aviat, Rail etc*) second class; **voyager en ~** to travel second-class; **secondaire** *adj* secondary; **seconde²** *nf* second; **seconder** *vt* to assist

secouer [s(ǝ)kwe] vt to shake; (passagers) to rock; (traumatiser) to shake (up)

secourir [s(ǝ)kuʀiʀ] vt (venir en aide à) to assist, aid; **secourisme** nm first aid; **secouriste** nf/f first-aid worker

secours [s(ǝ)kuʀ] nm help, aid, assistance ▷ nmpl aid sg; **au ~!** help!; **appeler au ~** to shout or call for help; **porter ~ à qn** to give sb assistance, help sb; **les premiers ~** first aid sg

▪ **ÉQUIPES DE SECOURS**

▪ Emergency phone numbers can
▪ be dialled free from public phones.
▪ For the police ('la police') dial 17; for
▪ medical services (le SAMU) dial
▪ 15; for the fire brigade ('les sapeurs
▪ pompiers'), dial 18.

secousse [s(ǝ)kus] nf jolt, bump; (électrique) shock; (fig: psychologique) jolt, shock

secret, -ète [sǝkʀɛ, ɛt] adj secret; (fig: renfermé) reticent, reserved ▷ nm secret; (discrétion absolue): **le ~** secrecy; **en ~** in secret, secretly; **secret professionel** professional secrecy

secrétaire [s(ǝ)kʀetɛʀ] nm/f secretary ▷ nm (meuble) writing desk; **secrétaire de direction** private or personal secretary; **secrétaire d'État** junior minister; **secrétariat** nm (profession) secretarial work; (bureau) office; (: d'organisation internationale) secretariat

secteur [sɛktœʀ] nm sector; (zone) area; (Élec): **branché sur ~** plugged into the mains (supply)

section [sɛksjɔ̃] nf (de parcours d'autobus) fare stage; (Mil: unité) platoon; **sectionner** vt to sever

sécu [seky] abr f = **sécurité sociale**

sécurité [sekyʀite] nf (absence de danger) safety; (absence de troubles) security; **système de ~** security system; **être en ~** to be safe; **la sécurité routière** road safety; **la sécurité sociale** ≈ (the) Social Security (BRIT), ≈ Welfare (US)

sédentaire [sedɑ̃tɛʀ] adj sedentary

séduction [sedyksjɔ̃] nf seduction; (charme, attrait) appeal, charm

séduire [seduiʀ] vt to charm; (femme: abuser de) to seduce; **séduisant, e** adj (femme) seductive; (homme, offre) very attractive

ségrégation [segʀegasjɔ̃] nf segregation

seigle [sɛgl] nm rye

seigneur [sɛɲœʀ] nm lord

sein [sɛ̃] nm breast; (entrailles) womb; **au ~ de** (équipe, institution) within

séisme [seism] nm earthquake

seize [sɛz] num sixteen; **seizième** num sixteenth

séjour [seʒuʀ] nm stay; (pièce) living room; **séjourner** vi to stay

sel [sɛl] nm salt; (fig: piquant) spice

sélection [selɛksjɔ̃] nf selection; **sélectionner** vt to select

self-service [sɛlfsɛʀvis] adj, nm self-service

selle [sɛl] nf saddle; **selles** nfpl (Méd) stools; **seller** vt to saddle

selon [s(ǝ)lɔ̃] prép according to; (en se conformant à) in accordance with; **~ que** according to whether; **~ moi** as I see it

semaine [s(ǝ)mɛn] nf week; **en ~** during the week, on weekdays

semblable [sɑ̃blabl] adj similar; (de ce genre): **de ~s mésaventures** such mishaps ▷ nm fellow creature ou man; **~ à** similar to, like

semblant [sɑ̃blɑ̃] nm: **un ~ de ...** a semblance of ...; **faire ~ (de faire)** to pretend (to do)

sembler [sɑ̃ble] vb +attrib to seem ▷ vb impers: **il semble (bien) que/inutile de** it (really) seems or appears that/ useless to; **il me semble que** it seems to me that; **comme bon lui semble** as he sees fit

semelle [s(ǝ)mɛl] nf sole; (intérieure) insole, inner sole

semer [s(ə)me] vt to sow; (fig: éparpiller) to scatter; (: confusion) to spread; (fam: poursuivants) to lose, shake off; **semé de** (difficultés) riddled with

semestre [s(ə)mɛstʀ] nm half-year; (Scol) semester

séminaire [seminɛʀ] nm seminar

semi-remorque [səmiʀəmɔʀk] nm articulated lorry (BRIT), semi(trailer) (US)

semoule [s(ə)mul] nf semolina

sénat [sena] nm senate; **sénateur** nm senator

Sénégal [senegal] nm: **le ~** Senegal

sens [sɑ̃s] nm (Physiol.) sense; (signification) meaning, sense; (direction) direction; **à mon ~** to my mind; **dans le ~ des aiguilles d'une montre** clockwise; **dans le ~ contraire des aiguilles d'une montre** anticlockwise; **dans le mauvais ~** (aller) the wrong way, in the wrong direction; **le bon ~** common sense; **sens dessus dessous** upside down; **sens interdit/unique** one-way street

sensation [sɑ̃sɑsjɔ̃] nf sensation; **à ~** (péj) sensational; **faire ~** to cause ou create a sensation; **sensationnel, le** adj (fam) fantastic, terrific

sensé, e [sɑ̃se] adj sensible

sensibiliser [sɑ̃sibilize] vt: **~ qn à** to make sb sensitive to

sensibilité [sɑ̃sibilite] nf sensitivity

sensible [sɑ̃sibl] adj sensitive; (aux sens) perceptible; (appréciable: différence, progrès) appreciable, noticeable; **~ à** sensitive to; **sensiblement** adv (à peu près): **ils sont sensiblement du même âge** they are approximately the same age; **sensiblerie** nf sentimentality

⚠ Attention à ne pas traduire **sensible** par le mot anglais **sensible**.

sensuel, le [sɑ̃sɥɛl] adj (personne) sensual; (musique) sensuous

sentence [sɑ̃tɑ̃s] nf (jugement) sentence

sentier [sɑ̃tje] nm path

sentiment [sɑ̃timɑ̃] nm feeling; **recevez mes ~s respectueux**

(personne nommée) yours sincerely; (personne non nommée) yours faithfully; **sentimental, e, -aux** adj sentimental; (vie, aventure) love cpd

sentinelle [sɑ̃tinɛl] nf sentry

sentir [sɑ̃tiʀ] vt (par l'odorat) to smell; (par le goût) to taste; (au toucher, fig) to feel; (répandre une odeur de) to smell of; (: ressemblance) to smell like ▷ vi to smell; **~ mauvais** to smell bad; **se ~ bien** to feel good; **se ~ mal** (être indisposé) to feel unwell ou ill; **se ~ le courage/la force de faire** to feel brave/strong enough to do; **il ne peut pas le ~** (fam) he can't stand him; **je ne me sens pas bien** I don't feel well

séparation [sepaʀɑsjɔ̃] nf separation; (cloison) division, partition

séparé, e [sepaʀe] adj (distinct) separate; (époux) separated; **séparément** adv separately

séparer [sepaʀe] vt to separate; (désunir) to drive apart; (détacher): **~ qch de** to pull sth (off) from; (dissocier): **~ de** (époux) to separate from; (employé, objet personnel) to part with

sept [sɛt] num seven; **septante** (BELGIQUE, SUISSE) adj inv seventy

septembre [sɛptɑ̃bʀ] nm September

septicémie [sɛptisemi] nf blood poisoning, septicaemia

septième [sɛtjɛm] num seventh

séquelles [sekel] nfpl after-effects; (fig) aftermath sg

serbe [sɛʀb(ə)] adj Serbian

Serbie [sɛʀbi] nf: **la ~** Serbia

serein, e [səʀɛ̃, ɛn] adj serene

sergent [sɛʀʒɑ̃] nm sergeant

série [seʀi] nf series inv; (de clés, casseroles, outils) set; (catégorie: Sport) rank; **en ~** in quick succession; (Comm) mass cpd; **de ~** (voiture) standard; **hors ~** (Comm) custom-built; **série noire** (crime) thriller

sérieusement [seʀjøzmɑ̃] adv seriously

sérieux, -euse [serjø, jøz] adj serious; (élève, employé) reliable, responsible; (client, maison) reliable, dependable ▷ nm seriousness; (d'une entreprise etc) reliability; **garder son ~** to keep a straight face; **prendre qch/qn au ~** to take sth/sb seriously

serin [s(ə)rɛ̃] nm canary

seringue [s(ə)rɛ̃g] nf syringe

serment [sɛrmɑ̃] nm (juré) oath; (promesse) pledge, vow

sermon [sɛrmɔ̃] nm sermon

séropositif, -ive [seropozitif, iv] adj (Méd) HIV positive

serpent [sɛrpɑ̃] nm snake; **serpenter** vi to wind

serpillière [sɛrpijɛr] nf floorcloth

serre [sɛr] nf (Agr) greenhouse; **serres** nfpl (griffes) claws, talons

serré, e [sere] adj (habits) tight; (fig: lutte, match) tight, close-fought; (passagers etc) (tightly) packed; (réseau) dense; **avoir le cœur ~** to have a heavy heart

serrer [sere] vt (tenir) to grip ou hold tight; (comprimer, coincer) to squeeze; (poings, mâchoires) to clench; (suj: vêtement) to be too tight for; (ceinture, nœud, vis) to tighten ▷ vi: **~ à droite** to keep ou get over to the right

serrure [seryr] nf lock; **serrurier** nm locksmith

sert etc [sɛr] vb voir **servir**

servante [sɛrvɑ̃t] nf (maid) servant

serveur, -euse [sɛrvœr, øz] nm/f waiter (waitress)

serviable [sɛrvjabl] adj obliging, willing to help

service [sɛrvis] nm service; (assortiment de vaisselle) set, service; (bureau: de la vente etc) department, section; (travail) duty; **premier ~** (série de repas) first sitting; **être de ~** to be on duty; **faire le ~** to serve; **rendre un ~ à qn** to do sb a favour; (objet: s'avérer utile) to come in useful ou handy for sb; **mettre en ~** to put into service ou operation; **~ compris/non compris**

service included/not included; **hors ~** out of order; **service après vente** after sales service; **service d'ordre** police (ou stewards) in charge of maintaining order; **service militaire** military service; see note; **services secrets** secret service sg

● **SERVICE MILITAIRE**
●
● Until 1997, French men over the age
● of 18 who were passed as fit, and
● who were not in full-time higher
● education, were required to do
● ten months "service militaire".
● Conscientious objectors were
● required to do two years' community
● service.
● Since 1997, military service has been
● suspended in France. However, all
● sixteen-year-olds, both male and
● female, are required to register for
● a compulsory one-day training
● course, the "JAPD" ("journée d'appel
● de préparation à la défense"), which
● covers basic information on the
● principles and organization of
● defence in France, and also advises
● on career opportunities in the
● military and in the voluntary sector.
● Young people must attend the
● training day before their eighteenth
● birthday.

serviette [sɛrvjɛt] nf (de table) (table) napkin, serviette; (de toilette) towel; (porte-documents) briefcase; **serviette hygiénique** sanitary towel

servir [sɛrvir] vt to serve; (au restaurant) to wait on; (au magasin) to serve, attend to ▷ vi (Tennis) to serve; (Cartes) to deal ▷ vt servir vi (servir d'un plat) to help o.s.; **vous êtes servi?** are you being served?; **~ à qn** (diplôme, livre) to be of use to sb; **~ à qch/faire** (outil etc) to be used for sth/doing; **ça ne sert à rien** it's no use; **~ (à qn) de** to serve as (for sb); **se ~ de** (plat) to help o.s. to, *(voiture, outil, relations)* to use; **sers-toi!** help yourself!

serviteur [sɛʀvitœʀ] *nm* servant

ses [se] *adj voir* **son'**

seuil [sœj] *nm* doorstep; *(fig)* threshold

seul, e [sœl] *adj (unique)*: **un ~ livre** only one book, a single book ▷ *adv (vivre)* alone, on one's own ▷ *nm, nf*: **il en reste un(e) ~(e)** there's only one left; **le ~ livre** the only book; **parler tout ~** to talk to oneself; **faire qch (tout)** ~ to do sth (all) on one's own *ou* (all) by oneself; **à lui (tout)** ~ single-handed, on his own; **se sentir** ~ to feel lonely; **seulement** *adv* only; **non seulement ... mais aussi** *ou* **encore** not only ... but also

sève [sɛv] *nf* sap

sévère [sevɛʀ] *adj* severe

sexe [sɛks] *nm* sex; *(organes génitaux)* genitals, sex organs; **sexuel, le** *adj* sexual

shampooing [ʃɑ̃pwɛ̃] *nm* shampoo

Shetland [ʃɛtlɑ̃d] *n*: **les Îles ~** the Shetland Islands, Shetland

short [ʃɔʀt] *nm* (pair of) shorts *pl*

⭕ **MOT-CLÉ**

si [si] *adv* **1** *(oui)* yes; **"Paul n'est pas venu" — "si!"** "Paul hasn't come" — "yes, he has!"; **je vous assure que si** I assure you he did *ou* she is *etc*
2 *(tellement)* so; **si gentil/rapidement** so kind/fast; **(tant et)** **si bien que** so much so that; **si rapide qu'il soit** however fast he may be
▷ *conj* **1** *if*; **si tu veux** if you want; **je me demande si** I wonder if *ou* whether; **si seulement** if only
▷ *nm* (Mus) B; *(en chantant la gamme)* ti

Sicile [sisil] *nf*: **la ~** Sicily

SIDA [sida] *sigle m* (= *syndrome immuno-déficitaire acquis*) AIDS *sg*

sidéré, e [sideʀe] *adj* staggered

sidérurgie [sideʀyʀʒi] *nf* steel industry

siècle [sjɛkl] *nm* century

siège [sjɛʒ] *nm* seat; *(d'entreprise)* head office; *(d'organisation)* headquarters *pl*; *(Mil)* siege; **siège social** registered office; **siéger** *vi* to sit

sien, ne [sjɛ̃, sjɛn] *pron*: **le(la) ~(ne), les ~(ne)s** *(homme)* his; *(femme)* hers; *(chose, animal)* its

sieste [sjɛst] *nf* (afternoon) snooze *ou* nap; **faire la** ~ to have a snooze *ou* nap

sifflement [sifləmɑ̃] *nm*: **un** ~ a whistle

siffler [sifle] *vi (gén)* to whistle; *(en respirant)* to wheeze; *(serpent, vapeur)* to hiss ▷ *vt (chanson)* to whistle; *(chien etc)* to whistle for; *(fille)* to whistle at; *(pièce, orateur)* to hiss, boo; *(fin de match, départ)* to blow one's whistle for; *(fam: verre)* to guzzle

sifflet [siflɛ] *nm* whistle; **coup de** ~ whistle

siffloter [siflɔte] *vi, vt* to whistle

sigle [sigl] *nm* acronym

signal, -aux [siɲal, o] *nm* signal; *(indice, écriteau)* sign; **donner le ~ de** to give the signal for sth; **signal d'alarme** alarm signal; **signalement** *nm* description, particulars *pl*

signaler [siɲale] *vt* to indicate; *(personne: faire un signe)* to signal; *(perte)* to report; *(faire remarquer)*: ~ **qch à qn/(à qn) que** to point out sth to sb/(to sb) that; **je voudrais** ~ **un vol** I'd like to report a theft

signature [siɲatyʀ] *nf* signature; *(action)* signing

signe [siɲ] *nm* sign; *(Typo)* mark; **faire un ~ de la main** to give a sign with one's hand; **faire** ~ **à qn** *(fig: contacter)* to get in touch with sb; **faire** ~ **à qn d'entrer** to motion (to) sb to come in; **signer** *vt* to sign; **se signer** *vi* to cross o.s.; **où dois-je signer?** where do I sign?

significatif, -ive [siɲifikatif, iv] *adj* significant

signification [siɲifikasjɔ̃] *nf* meaning

signifier [siɲifje] *vt (vouloir dire)* to mean; *(faire connaître)*: ~ **qch (à qn)**

make sth known (to sb)

silence [silɑ̃s] nm silence; (Mus) rest;
garder le ~ to keep silent, say nothing;
silencieux, -euse adj quiet, silent
▷ nm silencer

silhouette [silwɛt] nf outline,
silhouette; (allure) figure

sillage [sijaʒ] nm wake

sillon [sijɔ̃] nm furrow; (de disque)
groove; **sillonner** vt to criss-cross

simagrées [simagʁe] nfpl fuss sg

similaire [similɛʁ] adj similar;
similicuir nm imitation leather;
similitude nf similarity

simple [sɛ̃pl] adj simple; (non multiple)
single ▷ nm: **~ messieurs/dames**
men's/ladies' singles sg ▷ **~
d'esprit** simpleton

simplicité [sɛ̃plisite] nf simplicity; **en
toute ~** quite simply

simplifier [sɛ̃plifje] vt to simplify

simuler [simyle] vt to sham, simulate

simultané, e [simyltane] adj
simultaneous

sincère [sɛ̃sɛʁ] adj sincere;
sincèrement adv sincerely; (pour parler
franchement) honestly, really; **sincérité**
nf sincerity

Singapour [sɛ̃gapuʁ] nm Singapore

singe [sɛ̃ʒ] nm monkey; (de grande taille)
ape; **singer** vt to ape, mimic; **singeries**
nfpl antics

singulariser [sɛ̃gylaʁize]: **se
singulariser** vi to call attention to o.s.

singularité [sɛ̃gylaʁite] nf peculiarity

singulier, -ière [sɛ̃gylje, jɛʁ] adj
remarkable, singular ▷ nm singular

sinistre [sinistʁ] adj sinister ▷ nm
(incendie) blaze; (catastrophe) disaster;
(Assurances) damage (giving rise to a
claim); **sinistré, e** adj disaster-stricken
▷ nm/f disaster victim

sinon [sinɔ̃] conj (autrement, sans quoi)
otherwise, or else; (sauf) except, other
than; (si ce n'est) if not

sinueux, -euse [sinɥø, øz] adj
winding

sinus [sinys] nm (Anat) sinus; (Géom)

sine; sinusite nf sinusitis

sirène [siʁɛn] nf siren; **sirène d'alarme**
fire alarm; (en temps de guerre) air-raid
siren

sirop [siʁo] nm (à diluer: de fruit etc)
syrup; (pharmaceutique) syrup, mixture;
~ pour la toux cough mixture

siroter [siʁɔte] vt to sip

sismique [sismik] adj seismic

site [sit] nm (paysage, environnement)
setting; (d'une ville etc: emplacement)
site; **site** (pittoresque) beauty spot;
sites touristiques places of interest;
site Web (Inform) website

sitôt [sito] adv: **~ parti** as soon as he etc
had left; **~ que** as soon as; **pas de ~** not
for a long time

situation [sitɥasjɔ̃] nf situation; (d'un
édifice, d'une ville) position, location;
situation de famille marital status

situé, e [sitɥe] adj situated

situer [sitɥe] vt to site, situate; (en
pensée) to set, place; **se situer** vi to be
situated

six [sis] num six; **sixième** num sixth ▷ B
(Scol) nf year 7 (BRIT), sixth grade (US)

skaï® [skaj] nm Leatherette®

ski [ski] nm (objet) ski; (sport) skiing;
faire du ~ to ski; **ski de fond** cross-
country skiing; **ski nautique** water-
skiing; **ski de piste** downhill skiing; **ski
de randonnée** cross-country skiing;
skier vi to ski; **skieur, -euse** nm/f skier

slip [slip] nm (sous-vêtement) pants pl,
briefs pl; (de bain: d'homme) trunks pl; (:
du bikini) (bikini) briefs pl

slogan [slɔgɑ̃] nm slogan

Slovaquie [slɔvaki] nf: **la ~** Slovakia

SMIC [smik] sigle m = **salaire minimum
interprofessionnel de croissance**

smoking [smɔkiŋ] nm dinner ou
evening suit

SMS sigle m (= short message service)
(service) SMS; (message) text message

SNCF sigle f (= Société nationale des
chemins de fer français) French railways

snob [snɔb] adj snobbish ▷ nm/f snob;
snobisme nm snobbery, snobbishness

sobre [sɔbʀ] *adj* (*personne*) temperate, abstemious; (*élégance, style*) sober

sobriquet [sɔbʀikɛ] *nm* nickname

social, e, -aux [sɔsjal, jo] *adj* social

socialisme [sɔsjalism] *nm* socialism; **socialiste** *nm/f* socialist

société [sɔsjete] *nf* society; (*sportive*) club; (*Comm*) company; **la ~ de consommation** the consumer society; **société anonyme** ≈ limited (BRIT) ou incorporated (US) company

sociologie [sɔsjɔlɔʒi] *nf* sociology

socle [sɔkl] *nm* (*de colonne, statue*) plinth, pedestal; (*de lampe*) base

socquette [sɔkɛt] *nf* ankle sock

sœur [sœʀ] *nf* sister; (*religieuse*) nun, sister

soi [swa] *pron* oneself; **en ~ (intrinsèquement)** in itself; **cela va de ~** that *ou* it goes without saying; **soi-disant** *adj inv* so-called ⊳ *adv* supposedly

soie [swa] *nf* silk; **soierie** *nf* (*tissu*) silk

soif [swaf] *nf* thirst; **avoir ~** to be thirsty; **donner ~ à qn** to make sb thirsty

soigné, e [swaɲe] *adj* (*tenue*) well-groomed, neat; (*travail*) careful, meticulous

soigner [swaɲe] *vt* (*malade, maladie*: suj: *docteur*) to treat; (suj: *infirmière, mère*) to nurse, look after; (*travail, détails*) to take care over; (*jardin, invités*) to look after; **soigneux, -euse** *adj* (*propre*) tidy, neat; (*appliqué*) painstaking, careful

soi-même [swamɛm] *pron* oneself

soin [swɛ̃] *nm* (*application*) care; (*propreté, ordre*) tidiness, neatness; **soins** *nmpl* (*à un malade, blessé*) treatment *sg*, medical attention *sg*; (*hygiène*) care *sg*; **prendre ~ de** to take care of, look after; **prendre ~ de faire** to take care to do; **les premiers ~s** first aid *sg*

soir [swaʀ] *nm* evening; **ce ~** this evening, tonight; **à ce ~!** see you this evening (*ou* tonight)!; **sept/dix heures du ~** seven in the evening/ten at

night; **demain ~** tomorrow evening, tomorrow night; **soirée** *nf* evening; (*réception*) party

soit[1] [swa] *vb* voir **être** ⊳ *conj* (à savoir) namely; (*ou*): **~ ... ~** either ... or; **~ que ... ~ que** *ou* **ou que** whether ... or whether

soit[2] [swat] *adv* so be it, very well

soixantaine [swasɑ̃tɛn] *nf*: **une ~ (de)** sixty *ou* so, about sixty; **avoir la ~ (âge)** to be around sixty

soixante [swasɑ̃t] *num* sixty; **soixante-dix** *num* seventy

soja [sɔʒa] *nm* soya; (*graines*) soya beans *pl*; **germes de ~** beansprouts

sol [sɔl] *nm* ground; (*de logement*) floor; (*Agr*) soil; (*Mus*) G; (: *en chantant la gamme*) so(h)

solaire [sɔlɛʀ] *adj* (*énergie etc*) solar; (*crème etc*) sun *cpd*

soldat [sɔlda] *nm* soldier

solde [sɔld] *nf* pay ⊳ *nm* (*Comm*) balance; **soldes** *nm ou f pl* (*articles*) sale goods; (*vente*) sales; **en ~** at sale price; **solder** *vt* (*marchandise*) to sell at sale price, sell off

sole [sɔl] *nf* sole *inv* (*fish*)

soleil [sɔlɛj] *nm* sun; (*lumière*) sun(light); (*temps ensoleillé*) sun(shine); **il fait du ~** it's sunny; **au ~** in the sun

solennel, le [sɔlanɛl] *adj* solemn

solfège [sɔlfɛʒ] *nm* musical theory

solidaire [sɔlidɛʀ] *adj*: **être ~s** to show solidarity, stand *ou* stick together; **être ~ de** (*collègues*) to stand by; **solidarité** *nf* solidarity; **par solidarité (avec)** in sympathy (with)

solide [sɔlid] *adj* solid; (*mur, maison, meuble*) solid, sturdy; (*connaissances, argument*) sound; (*personne, estomac*) robust, sturdy ⊳ *nm* solid

soliste [sɔlist] *nm/f* soloist

solitaire [sɔlitɛʀ] *adj* (*sans compagnie*) solitary, lonely; (*lieu*) lonely ⊳ *nm/f* (*ermite*) recluse; (*fig*: *ours*) loner

solitude [sɔlityd] *nf* loneliness; (*tranquillité*) solitude

solliciter [sɔlisite] *vt* (*personne*) to appeal to; (*emploi, faveur*) to seek

sollicitude [sɔlisityd] nf concern

soluble [sɔlybl] adj soluble

solution [sɔlysjɔ̃] nf solution; **solution de facilité** easy way out

solvable [sɔlvabl] adj solvent

sombre [sɔ̃bʀ] adj dark; (fig) gloomy; **sombrer** vi (bateau) to sink; **sombrer dans** (misère, désespoir) to sink into

sommaire [sɔmɛʀ] adj (simple) basic; (expéditif) summary ▷ nm summary

somme [sɔm] nf (Math) sum; (quantité) amount; (argent) sum, amount ▷ nm: **faire un ~** to have a (short) nap; **en ~** in all; **~ toute** all in all

sommeil [sɔmɛj] nm sleep; **avoir ~** to be sleepy; **~ toute** all in all

sommet [sɔme] nm top; (d'une montagne) summit, top; (fig: de la perfection, gloire) height

sommier [sɔmje] nm (bed) base

somnambule [sɔmnɑ̃byl] nm/f sleepwalker

somnifère [sɔmnifɛʀ] nm sleeping drug no pl (ou pill)

somnoler [sɔmnɔle] vi to doze

somptueux, -euse [sɔ̃ptɥø, øz] adj sumptuous

son¹, sa [sɔ̃, sa] (pl **ses**) adj (antécédent humain: mâle) his; (: femelle) her; (: valeur indéfinie) one's, his/her; (antécédent non humain) its

son² [sɔ̃] nm sound; (de blé) bran

sondage [sɔ̃daʒ] nm: **sondage (d'opinion)** (opinion) poll

sonde [sɔ̃d] nf (Navig) lead ou sounding line; (Méd) probe; (Tech: de forage) borer, driller

sonder [sɔ̃de] vt (Navig) to sound; (Tech) to bore, drill; (fig: personne) to sound out; **~ le terrain** (fig) to test the ground

songe [sɔ̃ʒ] nm dream; **songer** vi: **songer à** (penser à) to think over; (envisager) to consider, think of; **songer que** to think that; **songeur, -euse** adj pensive

sonnant, e [sɔnɑ̃, ɑ̃t] adj: **à 8 heures ~es** on the stroke of 8

sonné, e [sɔne] adj (fam) cracked; **il est**

midi – it's gone twelve

sonner [sɔne] vi to ring ▷ vt (cloche) to ring; (glas, tocsin) to sound; (portier, infirmière) to ring for; **~ faux** (instrument) to sound out of tune; (rire) to ring false

sonnerie [sɔnʀi] nf (son) ringing; (sonnette) bell; (de portable) ringtone; **sonnerie d'alarme** alarm bell

sonnette [sɔnɛt] nf bell; **sonnette d'alarme** alarm bell

sonore [sɔnɔʀ] adj (voix) sonorous, ringing; (salle) resonant; (film, signal) sound cpd; **sonorisation** nf (équipement: de salle de conférences) public address system, P.A. system; (: de discothèque) sound system; **sonorité** nf (de piano, violon) tone; (d'une salle) acoustics pl

sophistiqué, e [sɔfistike] adj sophisticated

sorbet [sɔʀbe] nm water ice, sorbet

sorcier [sɔʀsje] nm sorcerer

sordide [sɔʀdid] adj (lieu) squalid; (action) sordid

sort [sɔʀ] nm (destinée) fate; (condition) lot; (magique) curse, spell; **tirer au ~** to draw lots

sorte [sɔʀt] nf sort, kind; **de la ~** in that way; **de (telle) ~ que** so that; **en quelque ~** in a way; **faire en ~ que** to see to it that; **quelle ~ de ...?** what kind of ...?

sortie [sɔʀti] nf (issue) way out, exit; (remarque drôle) sally; (promenade) outing; (le soir: au restaurant etc) night out; (Comm: d'un disque) release; (: d'un livre) publication; (: d'un modèle) launching; **où est la ~?** where's the exit?; **sortie de bain** (vêtement) bathrobe

sortilège [sɔʀtilɛʒ] nm (magic) spell

sortir [sɔʀtiʀ] vi (gén) to come out; (partir, se promener, aller au spectacle) to go out; (numéro gagnant) to come up ▷ vt (gén) to take out; (produit, modèle) to bring out; (fam: dire) to come out with; **~ avec qn** to be going out with sb; **s'en ~** (malade) to pull through;

(d'une difficulté etc) to get through; **~ de** (endroit) to go (ou come) out of, leave; (provenir de) to come from; (compétence) to be outside

sosie [sɔzi] nm double

sot, sotte [so, sɔt] adj silly, foolish ▷ nm/f fool; **sottise** nf (caractère) silliness, foolishness; (action) silly ou foolish thing

sou [su] nm: **près de ses ~s** tight-fisted; **sans le ~** penniless

soubresaut [subrəso] nm start; (cahot) jolt

souche [suʃ] nf (d'arbre) stump; (de carnet) counterfoil (BRIT), stub

souci [susi] nm (inquiétude) worry; (préoccupation) concern; (Bot) marigold; **se faire du ~** to worry; **soucier**: **se soucier de** vt to care about; **soucieux, -euse** adj concerned, worried

soucoupe [sukup] nf saucer; **soucoupe volante** flying saucer

soudain, e [sudɛ̃, ɛn] adj (douleur, mort) sudden ▷ adv suddenly, all of a sudden

Soudan [sudɑ̃] nm: **le ~** Sudan

soude [sud] nf soda

souder [sude] vt (avec fil à souder) to solder; (par soudure autogène) to weld; (fig) to bind together

soudure [sudyr] nf soldering; welding; (joint) soldered joint; weld

souffle [sufl] nm (en expirant) breath; (en soufflant) puff, blow; (respiration) breathing; (d'explosion, de ventilateur) blast; (du vent) blowing; **être à bout de ~** to be out of breath; **un ~ d'air** a breath of air

soufflé, e [sufle] adj (fam: stupéfié) staggered ▷ nm (Culin) soufflé

souffler [sufle] vi (gén) to blow; (haleter) to puff (and blow) ▷ vt (feu, bougie) to blow out; (chasser: poussière etc) to blow away; (Tech: verre) to blow; (dire): **~ qch à qn** to whisper sth to sb

souffrance [sufrɑ̃s] nf suffering; **en ~** (affaire) pending

souffrant, e [sufrɑ̃, ɑ̃t] adj unwell

souffre-douleur [sufrǝduloer] nm inv

butt, underdog

souffrir [sufrir] vi to suffer, be in pain ▷ vt to suffer, endure; (supporter) to bear, stand; **~ de** (maladie, froid) to suffer from; **elle ne peut pas le ~** she can't stand ou bear him

soufre [sufr] nm sulphur

souhait [swɛ] nm wish; **tous nos ~s pour la nouvelle année** (our) best wishes for the New Year; **à vos ~s!** bless you!; **souhaitable** adj desirable

souhaiter [swete] vt to wish for; **~ la bonne année à qn** to wish sb a happy New Year; **~ que** to hope that

soûl, e [su, sul] adj drunk ▷ nm: **tout son ~** to one's heart's content

soulagement [sulaʒmɑ̃] nm relief

soulager [sulaʒe] vt to relieve

soûler [sule] vt: **~ qn** to get sb drunk; (suj: boisson) to make sb drunk; (fig) to make sb's head spin ou reel; **se soûler** vi to get drunk

soulever [sul(ə)ve] vt to lift; (poussière) to send up; (enthousiasme) to arouse; (question, débat) to raise; **se soulever** vi (peuple) to rise up; (personne couchée) to lift o.s. up

soulier [sulje] nm shoe

souligner [suliɲe] vt to underline; (fig) to emphasize, stress

soumettre [sumɛtr] vt (pays) to subject, subjugate; (rebelle) to put down, subdue; **~ qch à qn** (projet etc) to submit sth to sb; **se soumettre (à)** to submit (to)

soumis, e [sumi, iz] adj submissive; **soumission** nf submission

soupçon [supsɔ̃] nm suspicion; (petite quantité): **un ~ de** a hint ou touch of; **soupçonner** vt to suspect; **soupçonneux, -euse** adj suspicious

soupe [sup] nf soup

souper [supe] vi to have supper ▷ nm supper

soupeser [supǝze] vt to weigh in one's hand(s); (fig) to weigh up

soupière [supjɛr] nf (soup) tureen

soupir [supir] nm sigh; **pousser un**

~ de soulagement to heave a sigh of relief

soupirer [supiʀe] vi to sigh

souple [supl] adj supple; (fig: règlement, caractère) flexible; (: démarche, taille) lithe, supple; **souplesse** nf suppleness; (de caractère) flexibility

source [suʀs] nf (point d'eau) spring; (d'un cours d'eau, fig) source; **de bonne ~** on good authority

sourcil [suʀsi] nm (eye)brow;

sourciller vi: **sans sourciller** without turning a hair ou batting an eyelid

sourd, e [suʀ, suʀd] adj (son) muffled; (douleur) dull ▷ nm/f deaf person; **faire la ~e oreille** to turn a deaf ear; **sourdine** (Mus) mute; **en sourdine** softly, quietly; **sourd-muet, sourde-muette** adj deaf-and-dumb ▷ nm/f deaf-mute

souriant, e [suʀjɑ̃, jɑ̃t] adj cheerful

sourire [suʀiʀ] nm smile ▷ vi to smile; **~ à qn** to smile at sb; (fig: plaire à) to appeal to sb; (suj: chance) to smile on sb; **garder le ~** to keep smiling

souris [suʀi] nf mouse

sournois, e [suʀnwa, waz] adj deceitful, underhand

sous [su] prép under; **~ la pluie** in the rain; **~ terre** underground; **~ peu** shortly, before long; **sous-bois** nm inv undergrowth

souscrire [suskʀiʀ]: **~ à** vt to subscribe to

sous...: **sous-directeur, -trice** nm/f assistant manager (-manageress); **sous-entendre** vt to imply, infer; **sous-entendu, e** adj implied ▷ nm innuendo, insinuation; **sous-estimer** vt to underestimate; **sous-jacent, e** adj underlying; **sous-louer** vt to sublet; **sous-marin, e** adj (flore, faune) submarine; (pêche) underwater ▷ nm submarine; **sous-pull** nm thin poloneck jersey; **soussigné, e** adj: **je soussigné** I the undersigned; **sous-sol** nm basement; **sous-titre** nm subtitle

soustraction [sustʀaksjɔ̃] nf subtraction

soustraire [sustʀɛʀ] vt to subtract, take away; (dérober): **~ qch à qn** to remove sth from sb; **se soustraire à** (autorité etc) to elude, escape from

sous...: **sous-traitant** nm sub-contractor; **sous-traiter** vt to sub-contract; **sous-vêtements** nmpl underwear sg

soutane [sutan] nf cassock, soutane

soute [sut] nf hold

soutenir [sut(ə)niʀ] vt to support; (assaut, choc) to stand up to, withstand; (intérêt, effort) to keep up; (assurer): **~ que** to maintain that; **soutenu, e** adj (efforts) sustained, unflagging; (style) elevated

souterrain, e [suteʀɛ̃, ɛn] adj underground ▷ nm underground passage

soutien [sutjɛ̃] nm support; **soutien-gorge** nm bra

soutirer [sutiʀe] vt: **~ qch à qn** to squeeze ou get sth out of sb

souvenir [suv(ə)niʀ] nm (réminiscence) memory; (objet) souvenir ▷ vb: **se ~ de** to remember; **se ~ que** to remember that; **en ~ de** in memory ou remembrance of; **avec mes affectueux/meilleurs ~s, ...** with love from, .../regards, ...

souvent [suvɑ̃] adv often; **peu ~** seldom, infrequently

souverain, e [suv(ə)ʀɛ̃, ɛn] nm/f sovereign, monarch

soyeux, -euse [swajø, øz] adj silky

spacieux, -euse [spasjø, jøz] adj spacious, roomy

spaghettis [spageti] nmpl spaghetti sg

sparadrap [spaʀadʀa] nm sticking plaster (BRIT), Bandaid® (US)

spatial, e, -aux [spasjal, jo] adj (Aviat) space cpd

speaker, ine [spikœʀ, kʀin] nm/f announcer

spécial, e, -aux [spesjal, jo] adj special; (bizarre) peculiar; **spécialement** adv especially, particularly; (tout exprès) specially; **spécialiser: se spécialiser** vi to specialize; **spécialiste** nm/f specialist; **spécialité** nf speciality; (branche) special field

spécifier [spesifje] vt to specify, state

spécimen [spesimɛn] nm specimen

spectacle [spɛktakl] nm (scène) sight; (représentation) show; (industrie) show business; **spectaculaire** adj spectacular

spectateur, -trice [spɛktatœʀ, tʀis] nm/f (Cinéma etc) member of the audience; (Sport) spectator; (d'un événement) onlooker, witness

spéculer [spekyle] vi to speculate

spéléologie [speleɔlɔʒi] nf potholing

sperme [spɛʀm] nm semen, sperm

sphère [sfɛʀ] nf sphere

spirale [spiʀal] nf spiral

spirituel, le [spiʀitɥɛl] adj spiritual; (fin, piquant) witty

splendide [splɑ̃did] adj splendid

spontané, e [spɔ̃tane] adj spontaneous; **spontanéité** nf spontaneity

sport [spɔʀ] nm sport ▷ adj inv (vêtement) casual; **faire du ~** to do sport; **sports d'hiver** winter sports; **sportif, -ive** adj (journal, association, épreuve) sports cpd; (allure, démarche) athletic; (attitude, esprit) sporting

spot [spɔt] nm (lampe) spot (light); (annonce) **spot** (publicitaire) commercial (break)

square [skwaʀ] nm public garden(s)

squelette [skəlɛt] nm skeleton; **squelettique** adj scrawny

SRAS [sʀas] sigle m (= syndrome respiratoire aigu sévère) SARS

Sri Lanka [sʀilɑ̃ka] nm: **le ~** Sri Lanka

stabiliser [stabilize] vt to stabilize

stable [stabl] adj stable, steady

stade [stad] nm (Sport) stadium; (phase, niveau) stage

stage [staʒ] nm (cours) training course; **~ de formation (professionnelle)** vocational (training) course; **~ de**

perfectionnement advanced training course; **stagiaire** nm/f, adj trainee Attention à ne pas traduire stage par le mot anglais stage.

stagner [stagne] vi to stagnate

stand [stɑ̃d] nm (d'exposition) stand; (de foire) stall; **stand de tir** (à la foire, Sport) shooting range

standard [stɑ̃daʀ] adj inv standard ▷ nm switchboard; **standardiste** nm/f switchboard operator

standing [stɑ̃diŋ] nm standing; **de grand ~** luxury

starter [staʀtɛʀ] nm (Auto) choke

station [stasjɔ̃] nf station; (de bus) stop; (de villégiature) resort; **station de ski** ski resort; **station de taxis** taxi rank (BRIT) ou stand (US); **stationnement** nm parking; **stationner** vi to park; **station-service** nf service station

statistique [statistik] nf (science) statistics sg; (rapport, étude) statistic ▷ adj statistical

statue [staty] nf statue

statu quo [statykwo] nm status quo

statut [staty] nm status; **statuts** nmpl (Jur, Admin) statutes; **statutaire** adj statutory

Sté abr = **société**

steak [stɛk] nm steak; **~ haché** hamburger

sténo(graphie) [steno(gʀafi)] nf shorthand

stérile [steʀil] adj sterile

stérilet [steʀilɛ] nm coil, loop

stériliser [steʀilize] vt to sterilize

stimulant [stimylɑ̃] nm (fig) stimulus, incentive; (physique) stimulant

stimuler [stimyle] vt to stimulate

stipuler [stipyle] vt to stipulate

stock [stɔk] nm stock; **stocker** vt to stock

stop [stɔp] nm (Auto: écriteau) stop sign; (: feu arrière) brake-light; **faire du ~** (fam) to hitch(hike); **stopper** vt, vi to stop, halt

store [stɔʀ] nm blind; (de magasin)

shade, awning

strabisme [strabism] nm squinting

strapontin [strapɔ̃tɛ̃] nm jump ou foldaway seat

stratégie [strateʒi] nf strategy; **stratégique** adj strategic

stress [stres] nm stress; **stressant, e** adj stressful; **stresser** vt: **stresser qn** to make sb (feel) tense

strict, e [strikt] adj strict; (tenue, décor) severe, plain; **le ~ nécessaire/ minimum** the bare essentials/ minimum

strident, e [stridɑ̃, ɑ̃t] adj shrill, strident

strophe [strɔf] nf verse, stanza

structure [stryktyr] nf structure; **~s d'accueil** reception facilities

studieux, -euse [stydjø, jøz] adj studious

studio [stydjo] nm (logement) (one-roomed) flatlet (BRIT) ou apartment (US); (d'artiste, TV etc) studio

stupéfait, e [stypefɛ, ɛt] adj astonished

stupéfiant, e [stypefjɑ̃, jɑ̃t] adj (étonnant) stunning, astounding ▷ nm (Méd) drug, narcotic

stupéfier [stypefje] vt (étonner) to stun, astonish

stupeur [stypœr] nf astonishment

stupide [stypid] adj stupid; **stupidité** nf stupidity; (parole, acte) stupid thing (to do ou say)

style [stil] nm style

stylé, e [stile] adj well-trained

styliste [stilist] nm/f designer

stylo [stilo] nm: **~ (à encre)** (fountain) pen; **stylo (à) bille** ball-point pen

su, e [sy] pp de **savoir** ▷ nm: **au su de** with the knowledge of

suave [sɥav] adj sweet

subalterne [sybaltern] adj (employé, officier) junior; (rôle) subordinate, subsidiary ▷ nm/f subordinate

subconscient [sybkɔ̃sjɑ̃] nm subconscious

subir [sybir] vt (affront, dégâts) to suffer;

(opération, châtiment) to undergo

subit, e [sybi, it] adj sudden; **subitement** adv suddenly, all of a sudden

subjectif, -ive [sybʒektif, iv] adj subjective

subjonctif [sybʒɔ̃ktif] nm subjunctive

subjuguer [sybʒyge] vt to captivate

submerger [sybmɛrʒe] vt to submerge; (fig) to overwhelm

subordonné, e [sybɔrdɔne] adj, nm/f subordinate

subrepticement [sybrɛptismɑ̃] adv surreptitiously

subside [sybzid] nm grant

subsidiaire [sybzidjɛr] adj: **question ~** deciding question

subsister [sybziste] vi (rester) to remain, subsist; (survivre) to live on

substance [sypstɑ̃s] nf substance

substituer [sypstitɥe] vt: **~ qn/qch à** to substitute sb/sth for; **se ~ à qn** (évincer) to substitute o.s. for sb

substitut [sypstity] nm (succédané) substitute

subterfuge [sypterfyʒ] nm subterfuge

subtil, e [syptil] adj subtle

subvenir [sybvənir]: **~ à** vt to meet

subvention [sybvɑ̃sjɔ̃] nf subsidy, grant; **subventionner** vt to subsidize

suc [syk] nm (Bot) sap; (de viande, fruit) juice

succéder [syksede]: **~ à** vt to succeed; **se succéder** vi (accidents, années) to follow one another

succès [syksɛ] nm success; **avoir du ~** to be a success, be successful; **à ~** successful; **succès de librairie** bestseller

successeur [syksesœr] nm successor

successif, -ive [syksesif, iv] adj successive

succession [syksesjɔ̃] nf (série, Pol) succession; (Jur: patrimoine) estate, inheritance

succomber [sykɔ̃be] vi to die, succumb; (fig): **~ à** to succumb to

succulent, e [sykylɑ̃, ɑ̃t] adj (repas,

mets) delicious

succursale [sykyʀsal] *nf* branch

sucer [syse] *vt* to suck; **sucette** *nf* (*bonbon*) lollipop; (*de bébé*) dummy (BRIT), pacifier (US)

sucre [sykʀ] *nm* (*substance*) sugar; (*morceau*) lump of sugar, sugar lump *ou* cube; **sucre d'orge** barley sugar; **sucre en morceaux/cristallisé/en poudre** lump/granulated/caster sugar; **sucre glace** icing sugar (BRIT), confectioner's sugar (US); **sucré, e** *adj* (*produit alimentaire*) sweetened; (*au goût*) sweet; **sucrer** *vt* (*thé, café*) to sweeten, put sugar in; **sucreries** *nfpl* (*bonbons*) sweets, sweet things; **sucrier** *nm* (*récipient*) sugar bowl

sud [syd] *nm*: **le ~** the south ▷ *adj inv* south; (*côte*) south, southern; **au ~** (*situation*) in the south; (*direction*) to the south; **au ~ de** (to the) south of; **sud-africain, e** *adj* South African ▷ *nm/f*: **Sud-Africain, e** *adj* South African; **sud-américain, e** *adj* South American ▷ *nm/f*: **Sud-Américain, e** *adj* South American; **sud-est** *nm, adj inv* south-east; **sud-ouest** *nm, adj inv* south-west

Suède [sɥɛd] *nf*: **la ~** Sweden; **suédois, e** *adj* Swedish ▷ *nm/f*: **Suédois, e** Swede ▷ *nm* (Ling) Swedish

suer [sɥe] *vi* to sweat; (*suinter*) to ooze; **sueur** *nf* sweat; **en sueur** sweating, in a sweat; **donner des sueurs froides à qn** to put sb in(to) a cold sweat

suffire [syfiʀ] *vi* (*être assez*): **~ (à qn/pour qch/pour faire)** to be enough *ou* sufficient (for sb/for sth/to do); **il suffit d'une négligence ...** it only takes one act of carelessness ...; **il suffit qu'on oublie pour que ...** one only needs to forget for ...; **ça suffit!** that's enough!

suffisamment [syfizamɑ̃] *adv* sufficiently, enough; **~ de** sufficient, enough

suffisant, e [syfizɑ̃, ɑ̃t] *adj* sufficient; (*résultats*) satisfactory; (*vaniteux*) self-important, bumptious

suffixe [syfiks] *nm* suffix

suffoquer [syfɔke] *vt* to choke, suffocate; (*stupéfier*) to astound ▷ *vi* to choke, suffocate

suffrage [syfʀaʒ] *nm* (Pol: *voix*) vote

suggérer [sygʒeʀe] *vt* to suggest; **suggestion** *nf* suggestion

suicide [sɥisid] *nm* suicide; **suicider: se suicider** *vi* to commit suicide

suie [sɥi] *nf* soot

suisse [sɥis] *adj* Swiss ▷ *nm*: **S~** Swiss *pl inv* ▷ *nf*: **la S~** Switzerland; **la S~ romande/allemande** French-speaking/German-speaking Switzerland

suite [sɥit] *nf* (*continuation: d'énumération etc*) rest, remainder; (: de *feuilleton*) continuation; (: *film etc sur le même thème*) sequel; (*série*) series, succession; (*conséquence*) result; (*ordre, liaison logique*) coherence; (*appartement, Mus*) suite; (*escorte*) retinue, suite; **suites** *nfpl* (*d'une maladie etc*) effects; **prendre la ~ de** (*directeur etc*) to succeed, take over from; **donner ~ à** (*requête, projet*) to follow up; **faire ~ à** to follow; (*faisant*) **~ à votre lettre du ...** further to your letter of the ...; **de ~** (*d'affilée*) in succession; (*immédiatement*) at once; **par la ~** afterwards, subsequently; **à la ~** one after the other; **à la ~ de** (*derrière*) behind; (*en conséquence de*) following

suivant, e [sɥivɑ̃, ɑ̃t] *adj* next, following ▷ *prép* (*selon*) according to; **au ~!** next!

suivi, e [sɥivi] *adj* (*effort, qualité*) consistent; (*cohérent*) even; **très/peu ~** (*cours*) well-/poorly-attended

suivre [sɥivʀ] *vt* (*gén*) to follow; (Scol: *cours*) to attend; (*comprendre*) to keep up with; (Comm: *article*) to continue to stock ▷ *vi* to follow; (*élève: assimiler*) to keep up; **se suivre** *vi* (*accidents etc*) to follow one after the other; **faire ~** (*lettre*) to forward; **"à ~"** to be continued"

sujet, te [syʒɛ, ɛt] *adj*: **être ~ à** (*vertige etc*) to be liable *ou* subject to ▷ *nm/f*

(d'un souverain) subject ▷ nm subject;
au ~ de about; **sujet de conversation**
topic ou subject of conversation;
sujet d'examen (Scol) examination
question

super [sypɛʀ] (fam) adj inv terrific,
great, fantastic, super

superbe [sypɛʀb] adj magnificent,
superb

superficie [sypɛʀfisi] nf (surface) area

superficiel, le [sypɛʀfisjɛl] adj
superficial

superflu, e [sypɛʀfly] adj superfluous

supérieur, e [sypeʀjœʀ] adj (lèvre,
étages, classes) upper; (plus élevé:
température, niveau, enseignement): **~ (à)**
higher (than); (meilleur: qualité, produit):
~ (à) superior (to); (excellent, hautain)
superior ▷ nm, nf superior; **supériorité**
nf superiority

supermarché [sypɛʀmaʀʃe] nm
supermarket

superposer [sypɛʀpoze] vt (faire
chevaucher) to superimpose; **lits
superposés** bunk beds

superpuissance [sypɛʀpɥisɑ̃s] nf
super-power

superstitieux, -euse [sypɛʀstisjø,
jøz] adj superstitious

superviser [sypɛʀvize] vt to
supervise

supplanter [syplɑ̃te] vt to supplant

suppléant, e [sypleɑ̃, -ɑ̃t] adj
(professeur) supply cpd; (juge,
fonctionnaire) deputy cpd ▷ nm/f
(professeur) supply teacher

suppléer [syplee] vt (ajouter: mot
manquant etc) to supply, provide;
(compenser: lacune) to fill in; **~ à** to
make up for

supplément [syplemɑ̃] nm
supplement; (de frites etc) extra portion;
un ~ de travail extra ou additional
work; **payer un ~** to pay an additional
charge; **le vin est en ~** wine is extra;
supplémentaire adj additional,
further; (train, bus) relief cpd, extra

supplications [syplikasjɔ̃] nfpl pleas,

entreaties

supplice [syplis] nm torture no pl

supplier [syplije] vt to implore,
beseech

support [sypɔʀ] nm support;
(publicitaire) medium; (audio-visuel) aid

supportable [sypɔʀtabl] adj (douleur)
bearable

supporter¹ [sypɔʀtɛʀ] nm supporter,
fan

supporter² [sypɔʀte] vt (conséquences,
épreuve) to bear, endure; (défauts,
personne) to put up with; (suj: chose:
chaleur etc) to withstand; (: personne:
chaleur, vin) to be able to take

 Attention à ne pas traduire
supporter par **to support**.

supposer [sypoze] vt to suppose;
(impliquer) to presuppose; **à ~ que**
supposing (that)

suppositoire [sypozitwaʀ] nm
suppository

suppression [sypʀesjɔ̃] nf (voir
supprimer) cancellation; removal;
deletion

supprimer [sypʀime] vt (congés,
service d'autobus etc) to cancel; (emplois,
privilèges, témoin gênant) to do away
with; (cloison, cause, anxiété) to remove;
(clause, mot) to delete

suprême [sypʀɛm] adj supreme

⊙ MOT-CLÉ

sur [syʀ] prép 1 (position) on; (par-dessus)
over; (au-dessus) above; **pose-le sur
la table** put it on the table; **je n'ai
pas d'argent sur moi** I haven't any
money on me
2 (direction) towards; **en allant sur
Paris** going towards Paris; **sur votre
droite** on ou to your right
3 (à propos de) on, about; **un livre/une
conférence sur Balzac** a book/lecture
on ou about Balzac
4 (proportion) out of; **un sur 10** one in
10; (Scol) one out of 10
5 (mesures) by; **4 m sur 2** 4 m by 2

6 (*succession*): **avoir accident sur accident** to have one accident after the other

sûr, e [syʀ] *adj* sure, certain; (*digne de confiance*) reliable; (*sans danger*) safe; (*diagnostic, goût*) reliable; **le plus - de** the safest thing is to: **sûr de soi** self-assured, self-confident

surcharge [syʀʃaʀʒ] *nf* (*de passagers, marchandises*) excess load; **surcharger** *vt* to overload

surcroît [syʀkʀwa] *nm:* **un - de** additional *+nom*; **par** *ou* **de -** moreover; **en -** in addition

surdité [syʀdite] *nf* deafness

sûrement [syʀmɑ̃] *adv* (*certainement*) certainly; (*sans risques*) safely

surenchère [syʀɑ̃ʃɛʀ] *nf* (*aux enchères*) higher bid; **surenchérir** *vi* to bid higher; (*fig*) to try and outbid each other

surestimer [syʀɛstime] *vt* to overestimate

sûreté [syʀte] *nf* (*sécurité*) safety; (*exactitude: de renseignements etc*) reliability; (*d'un geste*) steadiness; **mettre en -** to put in a safe place; **pour plus de -** as an extra precaution, to be on the safe side

surf [sœʀf] *nm* surfing

surface [syʀfas] *nf* surface; (*superficie*) surface area; **une grande -** a supermarket; **faire -** to surface; **en -** near the surface; (*fig*) superficially

surfait, e [syʀfɛ, ɛt] *adj* overrated

surfer [syʀfe] *vi:* **- sur Internet** to surf *ou* browse the Internet

surgelé, e [syʀʒəle] *adj* (deep-)frozen ▷ *nm:* **les -s** (deep-)frozen food

surgir [syʀʒiʀ] *vi* to appear suddenly; (*fig: problème, conflit*) to arise

sur...: **surhumain, e** *adj* superhuman; **sur-le-champ** *adv* immediately; **le surlendemain (soir)** two days later (in the evening); **le surlendemain de** two days after; **surmenage** *nm* overwork(ing);

surmener: se surmener *vi* to overwork

surmonter [syʀmɔ̃te] *vt* (*vaincre*) to overcome; (*être au-dessus de*) to top

surnaturel, le [syʀnatyʀɛl] *adj, nm* supernatural

surnom [syʀnɔ̃] *nm* nickname

surnombre [syʀnɔ̃bʀ] *nm:* **être en -** to be too many (*ou* one too many)

surpeuplé, e [syʀpœple] *adj* overpopulated

surplace [syʀplas] *nm:* **faire du -** to mark time

surplomber [syʀplɔ̃be] *vt, vi* to overhang

surplus [syʀply] *nm* (*Comm*) surplus; (*reste*): **- de bois** wood left over

surprenant, e [syʀpʀənɑ̃, ɑ̃t] *adj* amazing

surprendre [syʀpʀɑ̃dʀ] *vt* (*étonner*) to surprise; (*tomber sur: intrus etc*) to catch; (*entendre*) to overhear

surpris, e [syʀpʀi, iz] *adj:* **- (de/que)** surprised (at/that); **surprise** *nf* surprise; **faire une surprise à qn** to give sb a surprise; **surprise-partie** *nf* party

sursaut [syʀso] *nm* start, jump; (*de énergie, indignation*) sudden fit *ou* burst of; **en -** with a start; **sursauter** *vi* to (give a) start, jump

sursis [syʀsi] *nm* (*Jur: gén*) suspended sentence; (*fig*) reprieve

surtout [syʀtu] *adv* (*avant tout, d'abord*) above all; (*spécialement, particulièrement*) especially; **-, ne dites rien!** whatever you do don't say anything!; **- pas!** certainly *ou* definitely not!; **- que ...** especially as ...

surveillance [syʀvejɑ̃s] *nf* watch; (*Police, Mil*) surveillance; **sous - médicale** under medical supervision

surveillant, e [syʀvejɑ̃, ɑ̃t] *nm/f* (*de prison*) warder; (*Scol*) monitor

surveiller [syʀveje] *vt* (*enfant, élèves, bagages*) to watch, keep an eye on; (*prisonnier, suspect*) to keep (a) watch on; (*territoire, bâtiment*) to (keep) watch over; (*travaux, cuisson*) to supervise; (*Scol: examen*) to invigilate; **~ son langage/sa ligne** to watch one's language/figure

survenir [syʀvəniʀ] *vi* (*incident, retards*) to occur, arise; (*événement*) to take place

survêtement [syʀvɛtmɑ̃] *nm* tracksuit

survie [syʀvi] *nf* survival; **survivant, e** *nm/f* survivor; **survivre** *vi* to survive; **survivre à** (*accident etc*) to survive

survoler [syʀvɔle] *vt* to fly over; (*fig: livre*) to skim through

survolté, e [syʀvɔlte] *adj* (*fig*) worked up

sus [sy(s)]: **en ~ de** *prép* in addition to, over and above; **en ~** in addition

susceptible [syseptibl] *adj* touchy, sensitive; **~ de faire** (*hypothèse*) liable to do

susciter [sysite] *vt* (*admiration*) to arouse; (*ennuis*): **~ (à qn)** to create (for sb)

suspect, e [syspɛ(kt), ɛkt] *adj* suspicious; (*témoignage, opinions*) suspect ▷ *nm/f* suspect; **suspecter** *vt* to suspect; (*honnêteté de qn*) to question, have one's suspicions about

suspendre [syspɑ̃dʀ] *vt* (*accrocher: vêtement*): **~ qch (à)** to hang sth up (on); (*interrompre, démettre*) to suspend

suspendu, e [syspɑ̃dy] *adj* (*accroché*): **~ à** hanging on (ou from); (*perché*): **au-dessus de** suspended over

suspens [syspɑ̃]: **en ~** *adv* (*affaire*) in abeyance; **tenir en ~** to keep in suspense

suspense [syspɛns, syspɑ̃s] *nm* suspense

suspension [syspɑ̃sjɔ̃] *nf* suspension; (*lustre*) light fitting ou fitment

suture [sytyʀ] *nf* (*Méd*): **point de ~** stitch

svelte [svɛlt] *adj* slender, svelte

SVP *abr* (= *s'il vous plaît*) please

sweat [swɛt] *nm* (*fam*) sweatshirt

sweat-shirt [switʃœʀt] (*pl* **~s**) *nm* sweatshirt

syllabe [si(l)lab] *nf* syllable

symbole [sɛ̃bɔl] *nm* symbol; **symbolique** *adj* symbolic(al); (*geste, offrande*) token *cpd*; **symboliser** *vt* to symbolize

symétrique [simetʀik] *adj* symmetrical

sympa [sɛ̃pa] (*fam*) *adj inv* nice; **sois ~, prête-le moi** be a pal and lend it to me

sympathie [sɛ̃pati] *nf* (*inclination*) liking; (*affinité*) friendship; (*condoléances*) sympathy; **j'ai beaucoup de ~ pour lui** I like him a lot; **sympathique** *adj* nice, friendly

⚠ Attention à ne pas traduire *sympathique* par *sympathetic*.

sympathisant, e [sɛ̃patizɑ̃, ɑ̃t] *nm/f* sympathizer

sympathiser [sɛ̃patize] *vi* (*voisins etc: s'entendre*) to get on (BRIT) ou along (US) (well)

symphonie [sɛ̃fɔni] *nf* symphony

symptôme [sɛ̃ptom] *nm* symptom

synagogue [sinagɔg] *nf* synagogue

syncope [sɛ̃kɔp] *nf* (*Méd*) blackout; **tomber en ~** to faint, pass out

syndic [sɛ̃dik] *nm* (*d'immeuble*) managing agent

syndical, e, -aux [sɛ̃dikal, o] *adj* (trade) union *cpd*; **syndicaliste** *nm/f* trade unionist

syndicat [sɛ̃dika] *nm* (*d'ouvriers, employés*) (trade) union; **syndicat d'initiative** tourist office; **syndiqué, e** *adj* belonging to a (trade) union; **syndiquer**: **se syndiquer** *vi* to form a trade union; (*adhérer*) to join a trade union

synonyme [sinɔnim] *adj* synonymous ▷ *nm* synonym; **~ de** synonymous with

syntaxe [sɛ̃taks] *nf* syntax

synthèse [sɛ̃tɛz] *nf* synthesis

synthétique [sɛ̃tetik] *adj* synthetic

Syrie [siʀi] *nf*: **la ~** Syria

systématique [sistematik] *adj* systematic

système [sistɛm] *nm* system; **le ~ D** resourcefulness

t

t' [t] pron voir **te**

ta [ta] adj voir **ton'**

tabac [taba] nm tobacco; (magasin) tobacconist's (shop)

tabagisme [tabagism] nm: **tabagisme passif** passive smoking

table [tabl] nf table; **à ~!** dinner etc is ready!; **se mettre à ~** to sit down to eat; **mettre la ~** to lay the table; **une ~ pour 4, s'il vous plaît** a table for 4, please; **table à repasser** ironing board; **table de cuisson** hob; **table de nuit** ou **de chevet** bedside table; **table des matières** (table of) contents pl; **table d'orientation** viewpoint indicator; **table roulante** trolley (BRIT), tea wagon (US)

tableau, x [tablo] nm (peinture) painting; (reproduction, fig) picture; (panneau) board; (schéma) table, chart; **tableau d'affichage** notice board; **tableau de bord** dashboard; (Aviat) instrument panel; **tableau noir** blackboard

tablette [tablɛt] nf (planche) shelf; **tablette de chocolat** bar of chocolate

tablier [tablije] nm apron

tabou [tabu] nm taboo

tabouret [taburɛ] nm stool

tac [tak] nm: **il m'a répondu du ~ au ~** he answered me right back

tache [taʃ] nf (saleté) stain, mark; (Art, de couleur, lumière) spot; **tache de rousseur** freckle

tâche [taʃ] nf task

tacher [taʃe] vt to stain, mark

tâcher [taʃe] vi: **~ de faire** to try ou endeavour to do

tacheté, e [taʃte] adj spotted

tact [takt] nm tact; **avoir du ~** to be tactful

tactique [taktik] adj tactical ▷ nf (technique) tactics sg; (plan) tactic

taie [tɛ] nf: **~ (d'oreiller)** pillowslip, pillowcase

taille [taj] nf cutting; (d'arbre etc) pruning; (milieu du corps) waist; (hauteur) height; (grandeur) size; **de ~ à faire** capable of doing; **de ~** sizeable; **taille-crayon(s)** nm pencil sharpener

tailler [taje] vt (pierre, diamant) to cut; (arbre, plante) to prune; (vêtement) to cut out; (crayon) to sharpen

tailleur [tajœʀ] nm (couturier) tailor; (vêtement) suit; **en ~** (assis) cross-legged

taillis [taji] nm copse

taire [tɛʀ] vt: **faire ~ qn** to make sb be quiet; **se taire** vi to be silent ou quiet; **taisez-vous!** be quiet!

Taiwan [tajwan] nf Taiwan

talc [talk] nm talc, talcum powder

talent [talɑ̃] nm talent

talkie-walkie [tokiwoki] nm walkie-talkie

talon [talɔ̃] nm heel; (de chèque, billet) stub, counterfoil; **talons plats/ aiguilles** flat/stiletto heels

talus [taly] nm embankment

tambour [tɑ̃buʀ] nm (Mus, aussi Tech) drum; (musicien) drummer; (porte) revolving door(s pl); **tambourin** nm tambourine

Tamise [tamiz] *nf*: **la ~** the Thames

tamisé, e [tamize] *adj* (*lumière*) subdued, soft

tampon [tɑ̃pɔ̃] *nm* (*de coton, d'ouate*) wad, pad; (*amortisseur*) buffer; (*bouchon*) plug, stopper; (*cachet, timbre*) stamp; (**mémoire**) ~ (*Inform*) buffer; **tampon (hygiénique)** tampon; **tamponner** *vt* (*timbres*) to stamp; (*heurter*) to crash *ou* ram into; **tamponneuse** *adj f*: **autos tamponneuses** dodgems

tandem [tɑ̃dɛm] *nm* tandem

tandis [tɑ̃di]: **~ que** *conj* while

tanguer [tɑ̃ɡe] *vi* to pitch (and toss)

tanière [tanjɛʀ] *nf* lair, den

tannière [tanjɛʀ] *nf* lair, den

tant [tɑ̃] *adv* so much; **~** (*de*) (*sable, eau*) so much; (*gens, livres*) so many; **~ que** as long as; (*autant que*) as much as; **~ mieux** that's great; (*avec une certaine réserve*) so much the better; **~ pis** too bad; (*conciliant*) never mind; **~ bien que mal** as well as can be expected

tante [tɑ̃t] *nf* aunt

tantôt [tɑ̃to] *adv* (*parfois*): **~ ... now ...** now; (*cet après-midi*) this afternoon

taon [tɑ̃] *nm* horsefly

tapage [tapaʒ] *nm* uproar, din

tapageur, -euse [tapaʒœʀ, øz] *adj* noisy; (*voyant*) loud, flashy

tape [tap] *nf* slap

tape-à-l'œil [tapalœj] *adj inv* flashy, showy

taper [tape] *vt* (*porte*) to bang, slam; (*enfant*) to slap; (*dactylographier*) to type (out); (*fam: emprunter*): **~ qn de 10 euros** to touch sb for 10 euros ▷ *vi* (*soleil*) to beat down; **se taper** *vt* (*repas*) to put away; (*fam: corvée*) to get landed with; **~ sur qn** to thump sb; (*fig*) to run sb down; **~ sur un clou** to hit a nail; **~ sur la table** to bang on the table; **~ à** (*porte etc*) to knock on; **~ dans** (*se servir*) to dig into; **~ des mains/pieds** to clap one's hands/stamp one's feet; **~ (à la machine)** to type

tapi, e [tapi] *adj* (*blotti*) crouching; (*caché*) hidden away

tapis [tapi] *nm* carpet; (*petit*) rug; **tapis de sol** (*de tente*) groundsheet;

tapis de souris (*Inform*) mouse mat; **tapis roulant** (*pour piétons*) moving walkway; (*pour bagages*) carousel

tapisser [tapise] *vt* (*avec du papier peint*) to paper; (*recouvrir*): **~ qch (de)** to cover sth (with); **tapisserie** *nf* (*tenture, broderie*) tapestry; (*papier peint*) wallpaper; **tapissier-décorateur** *nm* interior decorator

tapoter [tapɔte] *vt* (*joue, main*) to pat; (*objet*) to tap

taquiner [takine] *vt* to tease

tard [taʀ] *adv* late; **plus ~** later (on); **au plus ~** at the latest; **sur le ~** late in life; **il est trop ~** it's too late

tarder [taʀde] *vi* (*chose*) to be a long time coming; (*personne*): **~ à faire** to delay doing; **il me tarde d'être** I am longing to be; **sans (plus) ~** without (further) delay

tardif, -ive [taʀdif, iv] *adj* late

tarif [taʀif] *nm*: **~ des consommations** price list; **~s postaux/douaniers** postal/customs rates; **~ des taxis** taxi fares; **~ plein/réduit** (*train*) full/reduced price; (*téléphone*) peak/off-peak rate

tarir [taʀiʀ] *vi* to dry up, run dry

tarte [taʀt] *nf* tart; **~ aux fraises** strawberry tart; **~ Tatin** ≈ apple upside-down tart

tartine [taʀtin] *nf* slice of bread; **tartine de miel** slice of bread and honey; **tartiner** *vt* to spread; **fromage à tartiner** cheese spread

tartre [taʀtʀ] *nm* (*des dents*) tartar; (*de bouilloire*) fur, scale

tas [tɑ] *nm* heap, pile; (*fig*): **un ~ de** heaps *ou* lots of; **en ~** in a heap *ou* pile; **formé sur le ~** trained on the job

tasse [tɑs] *nf* cup; **tasse à café** coffee cup

tassé, e [tɑse] *adj*: **bien ~** (*café etc*) strong

tasser [tɑse] *vt* (*terre, neige*) to pack down; (*entasser*): **~ qch dans** to cram sth into; **se tasser** *vi* (*se serrer*) to squeeze up; (*s'affaisser*) to settle; (*fig*) to settle down

tâter [tate] vt to feel; (fig) to try out; **se tâter** (hésiter) to be in two minds; **~ de** (prison etc) to have a taste of

tatillon, ne [tatijɔ̃, ɔn] adj pernickety

tâtonnement [tatɔnmɑ̃] nm: **par ~s** (fig) by trial and error

tâtonner [tatɔne] vi to grope one's way along

tâtons [tatɔ̃]: **à ~** adv: chercher/ avancer **à ~** to grope around for/grope one's way forward

tatouage [tatwaʒ] nm tattoo

tatouer [tatwe] vt to tattoo

taudis [todi] nm hovel, slum

taule [tol] (fam) nf nick (fam), prison

taupe [top] nf mole

taureau, x [tɔʀo] nm bull; (signe): **le T~** Taurus

taux [to] nm rate; (d'alcool) level; **taux d'intérêt** interest rate

taxe [taks] nf tax; (douanière) duty; **toutes ~s comprises** inclusive of tax; **la boutique hors ~s** the duty-free shop; **taxe à la valeur ajoutée** value-added tax; **taxe de séjour** tourist tax

taxer [takse] vt (personne) to tax; (produit) to put a tax on, tax

taxi [taksi] nm taxi; (chauffeur: fam) taxi driver; **pouvez-vous m'appeler un ~, s'il vous plaît?** can you call me a taxi, please?

Tchécoslovaquie [tʃekɔslɔvaki] nf Czechoslovakia; **tchèque** adj Czech ▷ nm/f: **Tchèque** Czech ▷ nm (Ling) Czech; **la République tchèque** the Czech Republic

Tchétchénie [tʃetʃeni] nf: **la ~** Chechnya

te, t' [tə] pron you; (réfléchi) yourself

technicien, ne [tɛknisjɛ̃, jɛn] nm/f technician

technico-commercial, e, -aux [tɛknikɔkɔmɛʀsjal, jo] adj: **agent ~** sales technician

technique [tɛknik] adj technical ▷ nf technique; **techniquement** adv technically

techno [tɛkno] nf (Mus) techno (music)

technologie [tɛknɔlɔʒi] nf technology; **technologique** adj technological

teck [tɛk] nm teak

tee-shirt [tiʃœʀt] nm T-shirt, tee-shirt

teindre [tɛ̃dʀ] vt to dye; **se ~ les cheveux** to dye one's hair; **teint, e** adj dyed ▷ nm (du visage) complexion; (momentané) colour ▷ nf shade; **grand teint** colourfast

teinté, e [tɛ̃te] adj: **~ de** (fig) tinged with

teinter [tɛ̃te] vt (verre, papier) to tint; (bois) to stain

teinture [tɛ̃tyʀ] nf dye; **teinture d'iode** tincture of iodine; **teinturerie** nf dry cleaner's; **teinturier** nm dry cleaner

tel, telle [tɛl] adj (pareil) such; (comme): **~ un/des ~** like a/like ...; (indéfini) such-and-such a; (intensif): **un ~/de ~s ...** such (a)/such ...; **rien de ~** nothing like it; **~ que** like, such as; **~ quel** as it is ou stands (ou was etc); **venez ~ jour** come on such-and-such a day

télé [tele] (fam) nf TV; **à la ~** on TV ou telly

télé...: télécabine nf (benne) cable car; **télécarte** nf phonecard; **téléchargeable** adj downloadable; **téléchargement** nm (action) downloading; (fichier) download; **télécharger** vt to download; **télécommande** nf remote control; **télécopieur** nm fax machine; **télédistribution** nf cable TV; **télégramme** nm telegram; **télégraphier** vt to telegraph, cable; **téléguider** vt to radio-control; **télématique** nf telematics sg; **téléobjectif** nm telephoto lens sg; **télépathie** nf telepathy; **téléphérique** nm cable car

téléphone [telefɔn] nm telephone; **avoir le ~** to be on the (tele)phone; **au ~** on the phone; **téléphoner** vi to make a phone call; **téléphoner à** to phone, call up; **est-ce que je peux téléphoner d'ici?** can I make a call from here?; **téléphonique** adj (tele)phone cpd

télé... téléréalité nf reality TV

télescope [teleskɔp] nm telescope

télescoper [teleskɔpe] vt to smash up; **se télescoper** (véhicules) to concertina

télé... téléscripteur nm teleprinter; **télésiège** nm chairlift; **téléski** nm ski-tow; **téléspectateur, -trice** nm/f (television) viewer; **télétravail** nm telecommuting; **télévente** nf telesales; **téléviseur** nm television set; **télévision** nf television; **à la télévision** on television; **télévision numérique** digital TV; **télévision par câble/satellite** cable/satellite television

télex [teleks] nm telex

telle [tɛl] adj voir **tel**; **tellement** adv (tant) so much; (si) so; **tellement de** (sable, eau) so much; (gens, livres) so many; **il s'est endormi tellement il était fatigué** he was so tired (that) he fell asleep; **pas tellement** not (all) that much; not (all) that +adjectif

témeraire [temerɛr] adj reckless, rash

témoignage [temwaɲaʒ] nm (Jur: déclaration) testimony no pl, evidence no pl; (rapport, récit) account; (fig: d'affection etc: cadeau) token, mark; (: geste) expression

témoigner [temwaɲe] vt (intérêt, gratitude) to show ▷ vi (Jur) to testify, give evidence; **~ de** to bear witness to; to testify to

témoin [temwɛ̃] nm witness ▷ adj: **appartement ~** show flat (BRIT); **être ~ de** to witness; **témoin oculaire** eyewitness

tempe [tɑ̃p] nf temple

tempérament [tɑ̃peramɑ̃] nm temperament, disposition; **à ~ (=vente)** on deferred (payment) terms; (achat) by instalments, hire purchase cpd

température [tɑ̃peratyr] nf temperature; **avoir ou faire de la ~** to be running ou have a temperature

tempête [tɑ̃pɛt] nf storm; **tempête de sable/neige** sand/snowstorm

temple [tɑ̃pl] nm temple; (protestant) church

temporaire [tɑ̃pɔrɛr] adj temporary

temps [tɑ̃] nm (atmosphérique) weather; (durée) time; (époque) time, times pl; (Ling) tense; (Mus) beat; (Tech) stroke; **un ~ de chien** (fam) rotten weather; **quel ~ fait-il?** what's the weather like?; **il fait beau/mauvais ~** the weather is fine/bad; **avoir le ~/tout son ~** to have time/plenty of time; **en ~ de paix/ guerre** in peacetime/wartime; **en ~ utile ou voulu** in due time ou course; **ces derniers ~** lately; **dans quelque ~** in a (little) while; **de ~ en ~, de ~ à autre** from time to time; **à ~ (partir, arriver)** in time; **à ~ complet, à plein ~** full-time; **à ~ partiel, à mi-~** part-time; **dans le ~** at one time; **temps d'arrêt** pause, halt; **temps libre** free ou spare time; **temps mort** (Comm) slack period

tenable [t(ə)nabl] adj bearable

tenace [tənas] adj tenacious

tenant, e [tənɑ̃, ɑ̃t] nm/f (Sport): **~ du titre** title-holder

tendance [tɑ̃dɑ̃s] nf tendency; (opinions) leanings pl, sympathies pl; (évolution) trend; **avoir ~ à** to have a tendency to, tend to

tendeur [tɑ̃dœr] nm (attache) elastic strap

tendre [tɑ̃dr] adj tender; (bois, roche, couleur) soft ▷ vt (élastique, peau) to stretch; (corde) to tighten; (muscle) to tense; (fig: piège) to set, lay; (donner): **~ qch à qn** to hold sth out to sb; (offrir) to offer sth to sb; **se tendre** vi (corde) to tighten; (relations) to become strained; **~ à qch/à faire** to tend towards sth/to do; **~ l'oreille** to prick up one's ears; **~ la main/le bras** to hold out one's hand/ stretch out one's arm; **tendrement** adv tenderly; **tendresse** nf tenderness

tendu, e [tɑ̃dy] pp de **tendre** ▷ adj (corde) tight; (muscles) tense; (relations) strained

ténèbres [tenɛbʀ] nfpl darkness sg

teneur [tənœʀ] nf content; (d'une lettre) terms pl, content

tenir [t(ə)niʀ] vt to hold; (magasin, hôtel) to run; (promesse) to keep ▷ vi to hold; (neige, gel) to last; **se tenir** vi (avoir lieu) to be held, take place; (être: personne) to stand; **~ à** (personne, objet) to be attached to; (réputation) to care about; **~ à faire** to be determined to do; **~ de** (ressembler à) to take after; **ça ne tient qu'à lui** it is entirely up to him; **~ qn pour** to regard sb as; **~ qch de qn** (histoire) to have heard ou learnt sth from sb; (qualité, défaut) to have inherited ou got sth from sb; **~ dans** to fit into; **~ compte de qch** to take sth into account; **~ les comptes** to keep the books; **~ bon** to stand fast; **le coup** to hold out; **~ au chaud** (café, plat) to keep hot; **un manteau qui tient chaud** a warm coat; **tiens/tenez, voilà le stylo** there's the pen!; **tiens, voilà Alain!** look, here's Alain!; **tiens?** (surprise) really?; **se ~ droit** to stand (ou sit) up straight; **bien se ~** to behave well; **se ~ à qch** to hold on to sth; **s'en ~ à qch** to confine o.s. to sth

tennis [tenis] nm tennis; (court) tennis court ▷ nm ou f pl (aussi: **chaussures de ~**) tennis ou gym shoes; **tennis de table** table tennis; **tennisman** nm tennis player

tension [tɑ̃sjɔ̃] nf tension; (Méd) blood pressure; **avoir de la ~** to have high blood pressure

tentation [tɑ̃tasjɔ̃] nf temptation

tentative [tɑ̃tativ] nf attempt

tente [tɑ̃t] nf tent

tenter [tɑ̃te] vt (éprouver, attirer) to tempt; (essayer): **~ qch/de faire** to attempt ou try sth to do; **~ sa chance** to try one's luck

tenture [tɑ̃tyʀ] nf hanging

tenu, e [t(ə)ny] pp de **tenir** ▷ adj (maison, comptes): **bien ~** well-kept; (obligé): **~ de faire** obliged to do ▷ nf (vêtements) clothes pl; (comportement)

(good) manners pl, good behaviour; (d'une maison) upkeep; **en petite ~e** scantily dressed ou clad

ter [tɛʀ] adj: **16** = **16b** ou **a**

terme [tɛʀm] nm term; (fin) end; **à court/long ~** adj short-/long-term ▷ adv in the short/long term; **avant ~** (Méd) prematurely; **mettre un ~ à** to put an end ou a stop to; **en bons ~s** on good terms

terminaison [tɛʀminɛzɔ̃] nf (Ling) ending

terminal, -aux [tɛʀminal, o] nm terminal; terminale nf (Scol) = year 13 (BRIT), = twelfth grade (US)

terminer [tɛʀmine] vt to finish; **se terminer** vi to end; **quand est-ce que le spectacle se termine?** when does the show finish?

terne [tɛʀn] adj dull

ternir [tɛʀniʀ] vt to dull; (fig) to sully, tarnish; **se ternir** vi to become dull

terrain [teʀɛ̃] nm (sol, fig) ground; (Comm: étendue de terre) land no pl; (parcelle) plot (of land); (à bâtir) site; **sur le ~** (fig) on the field; **terrain d'aviation** airfield; **terrain de camping** campsite; **terrain de football/rugby** football/rugby pitch (BRIT) ou field (US); **terrain de golf** golf course; **terrain de jeu** games field; (pour les petits) playground; **terrain de sport** sports ground; **terrain vague** waste ground no pl

terrasse [teʀas] nf terrace; **à la ~** (café) outside; **terrasser** vt (adversaire) to floor; (suj: maladie etc) to strike down

terre [tɛʀ] nf (gén, aussi Élec) earth; (substance) soil, earth; (opposé à mer) land no pl; (contrée) land; **terres** nfpl (terrains) lands, land sg; **en ~** (pipe, poterie) clay cpd; **à ~** ou **par ~** (mettre, être, s'asseoir) on the ground; (jeter, tomber) to the ground, down; **terre à terre** adj inv (considération, personne) down-to-earth; **terre cuite** terracotta; **la terre ferme** dry land; **terre glaise** clay

terreau [teʀo] nm compost

terre-plein [tɛʀplɛ̃] *nm* platform; (*sur chaussée*) central reservation

terrestre [tɛʀɛstʀ] *adj* (*surface*), of the earth; (*Bot, Zool, Mil*) land *cpd*; (*Rel*) earthly

terreur [tɛʀœʀ] *nf* terror *no pl*

terrible [tɛʀibl] *adj* terrible, dreadful; (*fam*) terrific; **pas ~** nothing special

terrien, ne [tɛʀjɛ̃, jɛn] *adj*: **propriétaire ~** landowner ▷ *nm/f* (*non martien etc*) earthling

terrier [tɛʀje] *nm* burrow, hole; (*chien*) terrier

terrifier [tɛʀifje] *vt* to terrify

terrine [tɛʀin] *nf* (*récipient*) terrine; (*Culin*) pâté

territoire [tɛʀitwaʀ] *nm* territory

terroriser [tɛʀɔʀize] *vt* to terrorize

terrorisme [tɛʀɔʀism] *nm* terrorism; **terroriste** *nm/f* terrorist

tertiaire [tɛʀsjɛʀ] *adj* tertiary ▷ *nm* (*Écon*) service industries *pl*

tes [te] *adj voir* **ton'**

test [tɛst] *nm* test

testament [tɛstamɑ̃] *nm* (*Jur*) will; (*Rel*) Testament; (*fig*) legacy

tester [tɛste] *vt* to test

testicule [tɛstikyl] *nm* testicle

tétanos [tetanos] *nm* tetanus

têtard [tɛtaʀ] *nm* tadpole

tête [tɛt] *nf* head; (*cheveux*) hair *no pl*; (*visage*) face; **de ~** (*comme adj: wagon etc*) front *cpd*; (*comme adv: calculer*) in one's head, mentally; **perdre la ~** (*fig: s'affoler*) to lose one's head; (*: devenir fou*) to go off one's head; **tenir ~ à qn** to stand up to sb; **la ~ en bas** with one's head down; **la ~ la première** (*tomber*) headfirst; **faire une ~** (*Football*) to head the ball; **faire la ~** (*fig*) to sulk; **en ~** at the front; (*Sport*) in the lead; **à la ~ de** at the head of; **à ~ reposée** in a more leisurely moment; **n'en faire qu'à sa ~** to do as one pleases; **en avoir par-dessus la ~** to be fed up; **en ~ à ~** in private, alone together; **de la ~ aux pieds** from head to toe; **tête de lecture** (*playback*) head; **tête de liste** (*Pol*) chief candidate; **tête**

de mort skull and crossbones; **tête de série** (*Tennis*) seeded player, seed; **tête de Turc** (*fig*) whipping boy (*BRIT*), butt; **tête-à-queue** *nm inv*: **faire un tête-à-queue** to spin round

téter [tete] *vt*: **~ (sa mère)** to suck at one's mother's breast, feed

tétine [tetin] *nf* teat; (*sucette*) dummy (*BRIT*), pacifier (*US*)

têtu, e [tɛty] *adj* stubborn, pigheaded

texte [tɛkst] *nm* text; (*morceau choisi*) passage

textile [tɛkstil] *adj* textile *cpd* ▷ *nm* textile; **le ~** the textile industry

Texto® [tɛksto] *nm* text message

texture [tɛkstyʀ] *nf* texture

TGV *sigle m* (= *train à grande vitesse*) high-speed train

thaïlandais, e [tajlɑ̃dɛ, ɛz] *adj* Thai ▷ *nm/f*: **T~, e** Thai

Thaïlande [tajlɑ̃d] *nf* Thailand

thé [te] *nm* tea; **~ au citron** lemon tea; **~ au lait** tea with milk; **prendre le ~** to have tea; **faire le ~** to make the tea

théâtral, e, -aux [teatʀal, o] *adj* theatrical

théâtre [teatʀ] *nm* theatre; (*péj: simulation*) playacting; (*fig: lieu*): **le ~ de** the scene of; **faire du ~** to act

théière [tejɛʀ] *nf* teapot

thème [tɛm] *nm* theme; (*Scol: traduction*) prose (composition)

théologie [teolɔʒi] *nf* theology

théorie [teoʀi] *nf* theory; **théorique** *adj* theoretical

thérapie [teʀapi] *nf* therapy

thermal, e, -aux [tɛʀmal, o] *adj*: **station ~e** spa; **cure ~e** water cure

thermomètre [tɛʀmɔmɛtʀ] *nm* thermometer

thermos® [tɛʀmos] *nm ou nf*: **(bouteille) thermos** vacuum *ou* Thermos® flask

thermostat [tɛʀmɔsta] *nm* thermostat

thèse [tɛz] *nf* thesis

thon [tɔ̃] *nm* tuna (fish)

thym [tɛ̃] *nm* thyme

Tibet [tibɛ] nm: **le ~** Tibet

tibia [tibja] nm shinbone, tibia; *(partie antérieure de la jambe)* shin

TIC sigle fpl *(= technologies de l'information et de la communication)* ICT sg

tic [tik] nm tic, *(nervous)* twitch; *(de langage etc)* mannerism

ticket [tikɛ] nm ticket; **ticket de caisse** receipt; **je peux avoir un ticket de caisse, s'il vous plaît?** can I have a receipt, please?

tiède [tjɛd] adj lukewarm; *(vent, air)* mild, warm; **tiédir** vi to cool; *(se réchauffer)* to grow warmer

tien, ne [tjɛ̃, tjɛn] pron: **le ~ (la) ~(ne), les ~(ne)s** yours; **à la ~ne!** cheers!

tiens [tjɛ̃] vb, excl voir **tenir**

tiercé [tjɛrse] nm system of forecast betting giving first 3 horses

tiers, tierce [tjɛr, tjɛrs] adj third ▷ nm *(Jur)* third party; *(fraction)* third; **le tiers monde** the Third World

tige [tiʒ] nf stem; *(baguette)* rod

tignasse [tiɲas] *(péj)* nf mop of hair

tigre [tigr] nm tiger; **tigré, e** adj *(rayé)* striped; *(tacheté)* spotted; *(chat)* tabby; **tigresse** nf tigress

tilleul [tijœl] nm lime (tree), linden (tree); *(boisson)* lime(-blossom) tea

timbre [tɛ̃br] nm *(tampon)* stamp; *(aussi:* **~-poste)** (postage) stamp; *(Mus: de voix, instrument)* timbre, tone

timbré, e [tɛ̃bre] *(fam)* adj cracked

timide [timid] adj *(timoré)* timid; **timidement** adv shyly; timidly; **timidité** nf shyness; timidity

tintamarre [tɛ̃tamar] nm din, uproar

tinter [tɛ̃te] vi to ring, chime; *(argent, clefs)* to jingle

tique [tik] nf *(parasite)* tick

tir [tir] nm *(sport)* shooting; *(fait ou manière de tirer)* firing no pl; *(rafale)* fire; *(stand)* shooting gallery; **tir à l'arc** archery

tirage [tiraʒ] nm *(action)* printing; *(Photo)* print; *(de journal)* circulation; *(de livre: nombre d'exemplaires)* (print) run; *(: édition)* edition; *(de loterie)* draw; **par ~**

au sort by drawing lots

tire [tir] nf: **vol à la ~** pickpocketing

tiré, e [tire] adj *(traits)* drawn; **~ par les cheveux** far-fetched

tire-bouchon [tirbuʃɔ̃] nm corkscrew

tirelire [tirlir] nf moneybox

tirer [tire] vt *(gén)* to pull; *(trait, rideau, carte, conclusion, chèque)* to draw; *(langue)* to stick out; *(en faisant feu: balle, coup)* to fire; *(: animal)* to shoot; *(journal, livre, photo)* to print; *(Football: corner etc)* to take ▷ vi *(faire feu)* to fire; *(Football)* to shoot; **se tirer** vi *(fam)* to push off; **s'en ~** *(éviter le pire)* to get off; *(survivre)* to pull through; *(se débrouiller)* to manage; **~ qch de** *(extraire)* to take ou pull sth out of; **~ qn de** *(embarras etc)* to help ou get sb out of; **~ sur** *(corde)* to pull on ou at; *(faire feu sur)* to shoot ou fire at; *(pipe)* to draw on; *(approcher de: couleur)* to verge ou border on; **~ à l'arc/la carabine** to shoot with a bow and arrow/with a rifle; **~ à sa fin** to be drawing to a close; **~ qch au clair** to clear sth up; **~ au sort** to draw lots; **~ parti de** to take advantage of; **~ profit de** to profit from; **~ les cartes** to read ou tell the cards

tiret [tirɛ] nm dash

tireur [tirœr] nm gunman; **tireur d'élite** marksman

tiroir [tirwar] nm drawer; **tiroir-caisse** nm till

tisane [tizan] nf herb tea

tisser [tise] vt to weave

tissu [tisy] nm fabric, material, cloth no pl; *(Anat, Bio)* tissue; **tissu-éponge** nm (terry) towelling no pl

titre [titr] nm *(gén)* title; *(de journal)* headline; *(diplôme)* qualification; *(Comm)* security; **en ~** *(champion)* official; **à juste ~** rightly; **à quel ~?** on what grounds? **à aucun ~** on no account; **au même ~ (que)** in the same way (as); **à ~ d'information** for (your) information; **à ~ gracieux** free of charge; **à ~ d'essai** on a trial basis; **à ~ privé** in a private capacity;

titre de propriété title deed; **titre de transport** ticket

tituber [titybe] vi to stagger (along)

titulaire [titylɛʀ] adj (Admin) with tenure ▷ nm/f (de permis) holder; **être ~ de** (diplôme, permis) to hold

toast [tost] nm slice ou piece of toast; (de bienvenue) (welcoming) toast; **porter un ~ à qn** to propose ou drink a toast to sb

toboggan [tɔbɔgã] nm slide; (Auto) flyover

toc [tɔk] excl: **~, ~** knock knock ▷ nm: **en ~** fake

tocsin [tɔksɛ̃] nm alarm (bell)

tohu-bohu [tɔyboy] nm hubbub

toi [twa] pron you

toile [twal] nf (tableau) canvas; **de ou en ~** (pantalon) cotton; (sac) canvas; **la T~** (Internet) the Web; **toile cirée** oilcloth; **toile d'araignée** cobweb; **toile de fond** (fig) backdrop

toilette [twalɛt] nf (habits) outfit; **toilettes** nfpl (w.-c.) toilet sg; **faire sa ~** to have a wash, get washed; **articles de ~** toiletries; **où sont les ~s?** where's the toilet?

toi-même [twamɛm] pron yourself

toit [twa] nm roof; **toit ouvrant** sunroof

toiture [twatyʀ] nf roof

Tokyo [tɔkjo] n Tokyo

tôle [tol] nf (plaque) steel ou iron sheet; **tôle ondulée** corrugated iron

tolérable [tɔleʀabl] adj tolerable

tolérant, e [tɔleʀã, ãt] adj tolerant

tolérer [tɔleʀe] vt to tolerate; (Admin: hors taxe etc) to allow

tollé [tɔ(l)le] nm outcry

tomate [tɔmat] nf tomato; **~s farcies** stuffed tomatoes

tombe [tɔ̃b] nf (sépulture) grave; (avec monument) tomb

tombeau, x [tɔ̃bo] nm tomb

tombée [tɔ̃be] nf: **à la ~ de la nuit** at nightfall

tomber [tɔ̃be] vi to fall; (fièvre, vent) to drop; **laisser ~** (objet) to drop;

(personne) to let down; (activité) to give up; **laisse ~!** forget it!; **faire ~** to knock over; **~ sur** (rencontrer) to bump into; **~ de fatigue/sommeil** to drop from exhaustion/be falling asleep on one's feet; **ça tombe bien** that's come at the right time; **il est bien tombé** he's been lucky; **à l'eau** (projet) to fall through; **~ en panne** to break down

tombola [tɔ̃bɔla] nf raffle

tome [tom] nm volume

ton¹, ta [tɔ̃, ta] (pl **tes**) adj your

ton² [tɔ̃] nm (gén) tone; (couleur) shade, tone; **de bon ~** in good taste

tonalité [tɔnalite] nf (au téléphone) dialling tone

tondeuse [tɔ̃døz] nf (à gazon) (lawn)mower; (du coiffeur) clippers pl; (pour les moutons) shears pl

tondre [tɔ̃dʀ] vt (pelouse, herbe) to mow; (haie) to cut, clip; (mouton, toison) to shear; (cheveux) to crop

tongs [tɔ̃g] nfpl flip-flops

tonifier [tɔnifje] vt (peau, organisme) to tone up

tonique [tɔnik] adj fortifying ▷ nm tonic

tonne [tɔn] nf metric ton, tonne

tonneau, x [tɔno] nm (à vin, cidre) barrel; **faire des ~x** (voiture, avion) to roll over

tonnelle [tɔnɛl] nf bower, arbour

tonner [tɔne] vi to thunder; **il tonne** it is thundering, there's some thunder

tonnerre [tɔnɛʀ] nm thunder

tonus [tɔnys] nm energy

top [tɔp] nm: **au 3ème ~** at the 3rd stroke ▷ adj: **~ secret** top secret

topinambour [tɔpinãbuʀ] nm Jerusalem artichoke

torche [tɔʀʃ] nf torch

torchon [tɔʀʃɔ̃] nm cloth; (à vaisselle) tea towel ou cloth

tordre [tɔʀdʀ] vt (chiffon) to wring; (barre, fig: visage) to twist; **se tordre** vi: **se ~ le poignet/la cheville** to twist one's wrist/ankle; **se ~ de douleur/rire** to be doubled up with pain/laughter;

tordu, e [tɔʀdy] adj bent; (fig) crazy

tornade [tɔʀnad] nf tornado

torrent [tɔʀɑ̃] nm mountain stream

torsade [tɔʀsad] nf: **un pull à ~s** a cable sweater

torse [tɔʀs] nm chest; (Anat, Sculpture) torso; **~ nu** stripped to the waist

tort [tɔʀ] nm (défaut) fault; **torts** nmpl (Jur) fault sg; **avoir ~** to be wrong; **être dans son ~** to be in the wrong; **donner ~ à qn** to lay the blame on sb; **causer du ~ à qn** to harm sb; **à ~** wrongly; **à ~ et à travers** wildly

torticolis [tɔʀtikɔli] nm stiff neck

tortiller [tɔʀtije] vt to twist; (moustache) to twirl; **se tortiller** vi to wriggle; (en dansant) to wiggle

tortionnaire [tɔʀsjɔnɛʀ] nm torturer

tortue [tɔʀty] nf tortoise; (d'eau douce) terrapin; (d'eau de mer) turtle

tortueux, -euse [tɔʀtɥø, øz] adj (rue) twisting; (fig) tortuous

torture [tɔʀtyʀ] nf torture; **torturer** vt to torture; (fig) to torment

tôt [to] adv early; **~ ou tard** sooner or later; **si ~** so early; (déjà) so soon; **plus ~** earlier; **au plus ~** at the earliest

total, e, -aux [tɔtal, o] adj, nm total; **au ~** in total; (fig) on the whole; **faire le ~** to work out the total; **totalement** adv totally; **totaliser** vt to total; **totalitaire** adj totalitarian; **totalité** nf: **la totalité de** all (of); (the whole +sg; **en totalité** entirely

toubib [tubib] (fam) nm doctor

touchant, e [tuʃɑ̃, ɑ̃t] adj touching

touche [tuʃ] nf (de piano, de machine à écrire) key; (de téléphone) button; (Peinture etc) stroke, touch; (fig: de nostalgie) touch; (Football: aussi: **remise en ~**) throw-in; (aussi: **ligne de ~**) touch-line; **touche dièse** nf (de téléphone, clavier) hash key

toucher [tuʃe] nm touch ▷ vt to touch; (palper) to feel; (atteindre: d'un coup de feu etc) to hit; (concerner) to concern, affect; (contacter) to reach, contact; (recevoir: récompense) to receive, get; (: salaire) to

draw, get; (: chèque) to cash; **se toucher** (être en contact) to touch; **au ~** to the touch; **~ à** to touch; (concerner) to have to do with, concern; **je vais lui en ~ un mot** I'll have a word with him about it; **~ au but** (fig) to near one's goal; **~ à sa fin** to be drawing to a close

touffe [tuf] nf tuft

touffu, e [tufy] adj thick, dense

toujours [tuʒuʀ] adv always; (encore) still; (constamment) forever; **~ plus** more and more; **pour ~** forever; **~ est-il que** the fact remains that; **essaie ~** (you can) try anyway

toupie [tupi] nf (spinning) top

tour [tuʀ] nf tower; (immeuble) high-rise block (BRIT) ou building (US); (Échecs) castle, rook; **tour de contrôle** nf control tower; **la tour Eiffel** the Eiffel Tower

tour [tuʀ] nm (excursion) trip; (à pied) stroll, walk; (en voiture) run, ride; (Sport: aussi: **~ de piste**) lap; (d'être servi ou de jouer etc) turn; (de roue etc) revolution; (Pol: aussi: **~ de scrutin**) ballot; (ruse, de prestidigitation) trick; (de potier) wheel; (à bois, métaux) lathe; (circonférence): **de 3 m de ~** 3 m round, with a circumference ou girth of 3 m; **faire le ~ de** to go round; (à pied) to walk round; **c'est au ~ de Renée** it's Renée's turn; **à ~ de rôle, à ~ in turn; tour de chant** nm song recital; **tour de force** tour de force; **tour de garde** nm spell of duty; **tour d'horizon** nm (fig) general survey; **tour de taille/tête** nm waist/head measurement; **un 33 tours** an LP; **un 45 tours** a single

tourbe [tuʀb] nf peat

tourbillon [tuʀbijɔ̃] nm whirlwind; (d'eau) whirlpool; (fig) whirl, swirl; **tourbillonner** vi to whirl (round)

tourelle [tuʀɛl] nf turret

tourisme [tuʀism] nm tourism; **agence de ~** tourist agency; **faire du ~** to go touring; (en ville) to go sightseeing; **touriste** nm/f tourist; **touristique** adj tourist cpd; (région) touristic

tourment [tuʀmɑ̃] nm torment;
tourmenter vt to torment; **se
tourmenter** to fret, worry o.s.

tournage [tuʀnaʒ] nm (Cinéma)
shooting

tournant [tuʀnɑ̃] nm (de route) bend;
(fig) turning point

tournée [tuʀne] nf (du facteur etc)
round; (d'artiste, politicien) tour; (au café)
round (of drinks)

tourner [tuʀne] vt to turn; (sauce,
mélange) to stir; (Cinéma: faire les prises
de vues) to shoot; (: produire) to make
▷ vi to turn; (moteur) to run; (taximètre)
to tick away; (lait etc) to turn (sour); **se
tourner** vi to turn round; **tournez à
gauche/droite au prochain carrefour**
turn left/right at the next junction;
mal ~ to go wrong; **~ autour de** to go
round; (péj) to hang round; **~ à/en** to
turn into; **~ qn en ridicule** to ridicule
sb; **~ le dos à** (mouvement) to turn one's
back on; (position) to have one's back
to; **~ de l'œil** to pass out; **se ~ vers** to
turn towards; (fig) to turn to; **se ~ les
pouces** to twiddle one's thumbs

tournesol [tuʀnəsɔl] nm sunflower

tournevis [tuʀnəvis] nm screwdriver

tournoi [tuʀnwa] nm tournament

tournure [tuʀnyʀ] nf (Ling) turn of
phrase; (évolution): **la ~ de qch** the way
sth is developing; **tournure d'esprit**
turn ou cast of mind

tourte [tuʀt] nf pie

tourterelle [tuʀtəʀɛl] nf turtledove

tous [tu] adj, pron voir **tout**

Toussaint [tusɛ̃] nf: **la ~** All Saints' Day

○ **TOUSSAINT**

La Toussaint, 1 November, or All
Saints' Day, is a public holiday in
France. People traditionally visit the
graves of friends and relatives to lay
chrysanthemums on them.

tousser [tuse] vi to cough

○ **MOT-CLÉ**

tout, e [tu, tut] (mpl **tous**, fpl **toutes**)
adj 1 (avec article singulier) all; **tout le
lait** all the milk; **toute la nuit** all night,
the whole night; **tout le livre** the whole
book; **tout un pain** a whole loaf; **tout
le temps** all the time; the whole time;
tout le monde everybody; **c'est tout
le contraire** it's quite the opposite
2 (avec article pluriel) all; every; **tous les
livres** all the books; **toutes les nuits**
every night; **toutes les fois** every time;
toutes les trois/deux semaines every
third/other ou second week, every
three/two weeks; **tous les deux** both
ou each of us (ou them ou you); **toutes
les trois** all three of us (ou them ou you)
3 (sans article): **à tout âge** at any age;
pour toute nourriture, il avait ... his
only food was ...
▷ pron everything, all; **il a tout fait**
he's done everything; **je les vois tous**
I can see them all ou all of them; **nous y
sommes tous allés** all of us went, we
all went; **c'est tout** that's all; **en tout** in
all; **tout ce qu'il sait** all he knows
▷ nm whole; **le tout** all of it (ou them);
le tout est de ... the main thing is to ...;
pas du tout not at all
▷ adv 1 (très, complètement) very; **tout
près** very near; **le tout premier** the
very first; **tout seul** all alone; **le livre
tout entier** the whole book; **tout en
haut** right at the top; **tout droit**
straight ahead
2: **tout en** while; **tout en travaillant**
while working, as he etc works ou worked
3: **tout d'abord** first of all; **tout à coup**
suddenly; **tout à fait** absolutely; **tout
à l'heure** a short while ago; (futur) in a
short while, shortly; **à tout à l'heure!**
see you later!; **tout de même** all the
same; **tout de suite** immediately,
straight away; **tout simplement**
quite simply

toutefois [tutfwa] adv however

toutes [tut] adj, pron voir **tout**

tout-terrain [tutɛʀɛ̃] adj: **vélo ~** mountain bike; **véhicule ~** four-wheel drive

toux [tu] nf cough

toxicomane [tɔksikɔman] nm/f drug addict

toxique [tɔksik] adj toxic

trac [tʀak] nm (au théâtre, en public) stage fright; (aux examens) nerves pl; **avoir le ~** (au théâtre, en public) to have stage fright; (aux examens) to be feeling nervous

tracasser [tʀakase] vt to worry, bother; **se tracasser** to worry

trace [tʀas] nf (empreintes) tracks pl; (marques, aussi fig) mark; (quantité infime, indice, vestige) trace; **traces de pas** footprints

tracer [tʀase] vt to draw; (piste) to open up

tract [tʀakt] nm tract, pamphlet

tracteur [tʀaktœʀ] nm tractor

traction [tʀaksjɔ̃] nf: **~ avant/arrière** front-wheel/rear-wheel drive

tradition [tʀadisjɔ̃] nf tradition; **traditionnel, le** adj traditional

traducteur, -trice [tʀadyktœʀ, tʀis] nm/f translator

traduction [tʀadyksjɔ̃] nf translation

traduire [tʀaduiʀ] vt to translate; (exprimer) to convey; **~ qn en justice** to bring sb before the courts; **pouvez-vous me ~ ceci?** can you translate this for me?

trafic [tʀafik] nm traffic; **trafic d'armes** arms dealing; **trafiquant, e** nm/f trafficker; (d'armes) dealer; **trafiquer** (péj) vt (vin) to doctor; (moteur, document) to tamper with

tragédie [tʀaʒedi] nf tragedy; **tragique** adj tragic

trahir [tʀaiʀ] vt to betray; **trahison** nf betrayal; (Jur) treason

train [tʀɛ̃] nm (Rail) train; (allure) pace; **être en ~ de faire qch** to be doing sth; **c'est bien le ~ pour …?** is this the train for …?; **train d'atterrissage** undercarriage; **train de vie** lifestyle; **train électrique** (jouet) (electric) train set

traîne [tʀɛn] nf (de robe) train; **être à la ~** to lag behind

traîneau, x [tʀɛno] nm sleigh, sledge

traîner [tʀene] vt (remorque) to pull; (enfant, chien) to drag ou trail along ▷ vi (robe, manteau) to trail; (être en désordre) to lie around; (aller lentement) to dawdle (along); (vagabonder, agir lentement) to hang about; (durer) to drag on; **se traîner** vi: **se ~ par terre** to crawl (on the ground); **~ les pieds** to drag one's feet

train-train [tʀɛ̃tʀɛ̃] nm humdrum routine

traire [tʀɛʀ] vt to milk

trait [tʀɛ] nm (ligne) line; (de dessin) stroke; (caractéristique) feature, trait; **traits** nmpl (du visage) features; **d'un ~** (boire) in one gulp; **de ~** (animal) draught; **avoir ~ à** to concern; **trait d'union** hyphen

traitant, e [tʀɛtɑ̃, ɑ̃t] adj (shampooing) medicated; **votre médecin ~** your usual ou family doctor

traite [tʀɛt] nf (Comm) draft; (Agr) milking; **d'une ~** without stopping

traité [tʀete] nm treaty

traitement [tʀetmɑ̃] nm treatment; (salaire) salary; **traitement de données** data processing; **traitement de texte** word processing; (logiciel) word processing package

traiter [tʀete] vt to treat; (qualifier): **~ qn d'idiot** to call sb a fool ▷ vi to deal; **~ de** to deal with

traiteur [tʀetœʀ] nm caterer

traître, -esse [tʀɛtʀ, tʀɛtʀɛs] adj (dangereux) treacherous ▷ nm traitor

trajectoire [tʀaʒɛktwaʀ] nf path

trajet [tʀaʒɛ] nm (parcours, voyage) journey; (itinéraire) route; (distance à parcourir) distance; **il y a une heure de ~** the journey takes one hour

trampoline [tʀɑ̃pɔlin] nm trampoline

tramway [tʀamwɛ] nm tram(way);

(voiture) tram(car) (BRIT), streetcar (US)

tranchant, e [tʀɑ̃ʃɑ̃, ɑ̃t] adj sharp; (fig) peremptory ▷ nm (d'un couteau) cutting edge; (de la main) edge; **à double ~** double-edged

tranche [tʀɑ̃ʃ] nf (morceau) slice; (arête) edge; **~ d'âge/de salaires** age/wage bracket

tranché, e [tʀɑ̃ʃe] adj (couleurs) distinct; (opinions) clear-cut

trancher [tʀɑ̃ʃe] vt to cut, sever ▷ vi to take a decision; **~ avec** to contrast sharply with

tranquille [tʀɑ̃kil] adj quiet; (rassuré) easy in one's mind, with one's mind at rest; **se tenir ~** (enfant) to be quiet; **laisse-moi/laisse-ça ~** leave me/it alone; **avoir la conscience ~** to have a clear conscience; **tranquillisant** nm tranquillizer; **tranquillité** nf peace (and quiet); (d'esprit) peace of mind

transférer [tʀɑ̃sfeʀe] vt to transfer; **transfert** nm transfer

transformation [tʀɑ̃sfɔʀmasjɔ̃] nf change, alteration; (radicale) transformation; (Rugby) conversion; **transformations** nfpl (travaux) alterations

transformer [tʀɑ̃sfɔʀme] vt to change; (radicalement) to transform; (vêtement) to alter; (matière première, appartement, Rugby) to convert; **(se) ~ en** to turn into

transfusion [tʀɑ̃sfyzjɔ̃] nf: **~ sanguine** blood transfusion

transgénique [tʀɑ̃sʒenik] adj transgenic

transgresser [tʀɑ̃sgʀese] vt to contravene

transi, e [tʀɑ̃zi] adj numb (with cold), chilled to the bone

transiger [tʀɑ̃ziʒe] vi to compromise

transit [tʀɑ̃zit] nm transit; **transiter** vi to pass in transit

transition [tʀɑ̃zisjɔ̃] nf transition; **transitoire** adj transitional

transmettre [tʀɑ̃smɛtʀ] vt (passer): **~ qch à qn** to pass sth on to sb;

(Tech, Tél, Méd) to transmit; (TV, Radio: retransmettre) to broadcast; **transmission** nf transmission

transparent, e [tʀɑ̃spaʀɑ̃, ɑ̃t] adj transparent

transpercer [tʀɑ̃spɛʀse] vt (froid, pluie) to go through, pierce; (balle) to go through

transpiration [tʀɑ̃spiʀasjɔ̃] nf perspiration

transpirer [tʀɑ̃spiʀe] vi to perspire

transplanter [tʀɑ̃splɑ̃te] vt (Méd, Bot) to transplant

transport [tʀɑ̃spɔʀ] nm transport; **transports en commun** public transport sg; **transporter** vt to carry, move; (Comm) to transport, convey; **transporteur** nm haulage contractor (BRIT), trucker (US)

transvaser [tʀɑ̃svaze] vt to decant

transversal, e, -aux [tʀɑ̃svɛʀsal, o] adj (rue) which runs across; **coupe ~e** cross section

trapèze [tʀapɛz] nm (au cirque) trapeze

trappe [tʀap] nf trap door

trapu, e [tʀapy] adj squat, stocky

traquenard [tʀaknaʀ] nm trap

traquer [tʀake] vt to track down; (harceler) to hound

traumatiser [tʀomatize] vt to traumatize

travail, -aux [tʀavaj] nm (gén) work; (tâche, métier) work no pl, job; (Écon, Méd) labour; **être sans ~** (employé) to be unemployed; voir aussi **travaux**; **travail (au) noir** moonlighting

travailler [tʀavaje] vi to work; (bois) to warp ▷ vt (bois, métal) to work; (objet d'art, discipline) to work on; **cela le travaille** it is on his mind; **travailleur, -euse** adj hard-working ▷ nm/f worker; **travailleur social** social worker; **travailliste** adj ≈ Labour cpd

travaux [tʀavo] nmpl de réparation, agricoles etc) work sg; (sur route) roadworks pl; (de construction) building) work; **travaux des champs** farmwork sg; **travaux dirigés** (Scol) tutorial sg; **travaux forcés** hard labour no pl; **travaux manuels** (Scol) handicrafts; **travaux ménagers** housework no pl; **travaux pratiques** (Scol) practical work; (en laboratoire) lab work

travers [TRAVER] nm fault, failing; **en ~ (de)** across; **au ~ (de)/à ~** through; **de ~** (nez, bouche) crooked; (chapeau) askew; **comprendre de ~** to misunderstand; **regarder de ~** (fig) to look askance at

traverse [TRAVERS] nf (de voie ferrée) sleeper; **chemin de ~** shortcut

traversée [TRAVERSE] nf crossing; **combien de temps dure la ~?** how long does the crossing take?

traverser [TRAVERSE] vt (gén) to cross; (ville, tunnel, aussi: percer, fig) to go through; (suj: ligne, trait) to run across

traversin [TRAVERSẼ] nm bolster

travesti [TRAVESTI] nm transvestite

trébucher [TREbyfe] vi: **~ (sur)** to stumble (over), trip (against)

trèfle [TREfl] nm (Bot) clover; (Cartes: couleur) clubs pl; (: carte) club; **à quatre feuilles** four-leaf clover

treize [TREZ] num thirteen; **treizième** num thirteenth

tréma [TREMA] nm diaeresis

tremblement [TRĀblǝmā] nm: **tremblement de terre** earthquake

trembler [TRĀble] vi to tremble, shake; **~ de** (froid, fièvre) to shiver ou tremble with; (peur) to shake ou tremble with; **pour qn** to fear for sb

trémousser [TREmuse]: **se trémousser** vi to jig about, wriggle about

trempé, e [TRĀpe] adj soaking (wet), drenched; (Tech) tempered

tremper [TRĀpe] vt to soak, drench; (aussi: **faire ~, mettre à ~**) to soak; (plonger): **~ qch dans** to dip sth in(to) ▷ vi to soak; (fig): **~ dans** to be involved ou have a hand in; **se tremper** vi to have a quick dip

tremplin [TRĀplẽ] nm springboard; (Ski) ski-jump

trentaine [TRĀten] nf: **une ~ (de)** thirty or so, about thirty; **avoir la ~** (âge) to be around thirty

trente [TRĀt] num thirty; **être sur son ~ et un** to be wearing one's Sunday best; **trentième** num thirtieth

trépidant, e [TRepidā, āt] adj (fig: rythme) pulsating; (: vie) hectic

trépigner [TREpine] vi to stamp (one's feet)

très [TRE] adv very; much +pp, highly +pp

trésor [TREzɔR] nm treasure; **Trésor (public)** public revenue; **trésorerie** (gestion) accounts pl; (bureaux) accounts department; **difficultés de trésorerie** cash problems, shortage of cash funds; **trésorier, -ière** nm/f treasurer

tressaillir [TResajiR] vi to shiver, shudder

tressauter [TResote] vi to start, jump

tresse [TRES] nf braid, plait; **tresser** vt (cheveux) to braid, plait; (fil, jonc) to plait; (corbeille) to weave; (corde) to twist

tréteau, x [TReto] nm trestle

treuil [TRœj] nm winch

trêve [TREv] nf (Mil, Pol) truce; (fig) respite; **~ de ...** enough of this ...

tri [TRi] nm: **faire le ~ (de)** to sort out; **le (bureau de) ~** (Postes) the sorting office

triangle [TRijāgl] nm triangle; **triangulaire** adj triangular

tribord [TRibɔR] nm: **à ~** to starboard, on the starboard side

tribu [TRiby] nf tribe

tribunal, -aux [TRibynal, o] nm (Jur) court; (Mil) tribunal

tribune [TRibyn] nf (estrade) platform, rostrum; (débat) forum; (d'église, de tribunal) gallery; (de stade) stand

tribut [TRiby] nm tribute

tributaire [TRibyteR] adj: **être ~ de** to be dependent on

tricher [TRife] vi to cheat; **tricheur, -euse** nm/f cheat(er)

tricolore [TRikɔlɔR] adj three-coloured; (français) red, white and blue

tricot [tʀiko] *nm (technique, ouvrage)* knitting *no pl*; *(vêtement)* jersey, sweater; **~ de peau** vest; **tricoter** *vt* to knit

tricycle [tʀisikl] *nm* tricycle

trier [tʀije] *vt* to sort out; *(Postes, fruits)* to sort

trimestre [tʀimɛstʀ] *nm (Scol)* term; *(Comm)* quarter; **trimestriel, le** *adj* quarterly; *(Scol)* end-of-term

trinquer [tʀɛke] *vi* to clink glasses

triomphe [tʀijɔf] *nm* triumph; **triompher** *vi* to triumph, win; **triompher de** to triumph over, overcome

tripes [tʀip] *nfpl (Culin)* tripe *sg*

triple [tʀipl] *adj* triple ▷ *nm*: **le ~ (de)** *(comparaison)* three times as much (as); **en ~ exemplaire** in triplicate; **tripler** *vi, vt* to triple, treble

triplés, -ées [tʀiple] *nm/fpl* triplets

tripoter [tʀipɔte] *vt* to fiddle with

triste [tʀist] *adj* sad; *(couleur, temps, journée)* dreary; *(péj)*: **~ personnage/ affaire** sorry individual/affair; **tristesse** *nf* sadness

trivial, e, -aux [tʀivjal, jo] *adj* coarse, crude; *(commun)* mundane

troc [tʀɔk] *nm* barter

trognon [tʀɔɲɔ] *nm (de fruit)* core; *(de légume)* stalk

trois [tʀwa] *num* three; **troisième** *num* third ▷ *nf (Scol)* year 10 *(BRIT)*, ninth grade *(us)*; **le troisième âge** *(période de vie)* one's retirement years; *(personnes âgées)* senior citizens *pl*

trombe [tʀɔb] *nf*: **des ~s d'eau** a downpour; **en ~** like a whirlwind

trombone [tʀɔbɔn] *nm (Mus)* trombone; *(de bureau)* paper clip

trompe [tʀɔp] *nf (d'éléphant)* trunk; *(Mus)* trumpet, horn

tromper [tʀɔpe] *vt* to deceive; *(vigilance, poursuivants)* to elude; **se tromper** *vi* to make a mistake, be mistaken; **se ~ de voiture/jour** to take the wrong car/get the day wrong; **se ~ de 3 cm/20 euros** to be out by 3 cm/20

euros; **je me suis trompé de route** I took the wrong road

trompette [tʀɔpɛt] *nf* trumpet; **en ~** *(nez)* turned-up

trompeur, -euse [tʀɔpœʀ, øz] *adj* deceptive

tronc [tʀɔ] *nm (Bot, Anat)* trunk; *(d'église)* collection box

tronçon [tʀɔsɔ] *nm* section; **tronçonner** *vt* to saw up; **tronçonneuse** *nf* chainsaw

trône [tʀon] *nm* throne

trop [tʀo] *adv (+vb)* too much; *(+adjectif, adverbe)* too; **~ (nombreux)** too many; **peu (nombreux)** too few; **~ (souvent)** too often; **~ (longtemps)** (for) too long; **~ de** *(nombre)* too many; *(quantité)* too much; **de ~, en ~**: **des livres en ~** a few books too many; **du lait en ~** too much milk; **3 livres/3 euros de ~** 3 books too many/3 euros too much; **ça coûte ~ cher** it's too expensive

tropical, e, -aux [tʀɔpikal, o] *adj* tropical

tropique [tʀɔpik] *nm* tropic

trop-plein [tʀoplɛ] *nm (tuyau)* overflow ou outlet pipe; *(liquide)* overflow

troquer [tʀɔke] *vt*: **~ qch contre** to barter ou trade sth for; *(fig)* to swap sth for

trot [tʀo] *nm* trot; **trotter** *vi* to trot

trottinette [tʀɔtinɛt] *nf (child's)* scooter

trottoir [tʀɔtwaʀ] *nm* pavement *(BRIT)*, sidewalk *(us)*; **faire le ~** *(péj)* to walk the streets; **trottoir roulant** moving walkway, travellator

trou [tʀu] *nm* hole; *(Comm)* gap; *(Comm)* deficit; **trou d'air** air pocket; **trou de mémoire** blank, lapse of memory

troublant, e [tʀublɑ, ɑt] *adj* disturbing

trouble [tʀubl] *adj (liquide)* cloudy; *(image, photo)* blurred; *(affaire)* shady, murky ▷ *adv*: **voir ~** to have blurred vision ▷ *nm* agitation; **troubles** *nmpl* *(Pol)* disturbances, troubles, unrest *pl*;

(*Méd*) trouble sg, disorders; **trouble-fête** nm spoilsport

troubler[tʀuble] vt to disturb; (*liquide*) to make cloudy; (*intriguer*) to bother; **se troubler** vi (*personne*) to become flustered ou confused

trouer[tʀue] vt to make a hole (ou holes) in

trouille[tʀuj] (*fam*) nf: **avoir la ~** to be scared to death

troupe[tʀup] nf troop; **troupe (de théâtre)** (theatrical) company

troupeau, x[tʀupo] nm (*de moutons*) flock; (*de vaches*) herd

trousse[tʀus] nf case, kit; (*d'écolier*) pencil case; **aux ~s de** (*fig*) on the heels ou tail of; **trousse à outils** toolkit; **trousse de toilette** toilet bag

trousseau, x[tʀuso] nm (*de mariée*) trousseau; **trousseau de clefs** bunch of keys

trouvaille[tʀuvaj] nf find

trouver[tʀuve] vt to find; (*rendre visite*): **aller/venir ~ qn** to go/come and see sb; **se trouver** vi (*être*) to be; **je trouve que** I find ou think that; **~ à boire/critiquer** to find something to drink/criticize; **se ~ mal** to pass out

truand[tʀyɑ̃] nm gangster; **truander** vt: **se faire truander** to be swindled

truc[tʀyk] nm (*astuce*) way, trick; (*de cinéma, prestidigitateur*) trick, effect; (*chose*) thing, thingumajig; **avoir le ~** to have the knack; **c'est pas mon ~** (*fam*) it's not really my thing

truffe[tʀyf] nf truffle; (*nez*) nose

truffé, e[tʀyfe] adj (*Culin*) garnished with truffles; **~ de** (*fig: citations*) peppered with; (: *fautes*) riddled with; (: *pièges*) bristling with

truie[tʀɥi] nf sow

truite[tʀɥit] nf trout inv

truquage[tʀyka3] nm special effects pl

truquer[tʀyke] vt (*élections, serrure, dés*) to fix

TSVP sigle (= *tournez svp*) PTO

TTC sigle (= *toutes taxes comprises*) inclusive of tax

tu¹[ty] pron you; **dire tu à qn** to use the "tu" form to sb

tu², e[ty] pp de **taire**

tuba[tyba] nm (*Mus*) tuba; (*Sport*) snorkel

tube[tyb] nm tube; (*chanson*) hit

tuberculose[tybɛʀkyloz] nf tuberculosis

tuer[tɥe] vt to kill; **se tuer** vi to be killed; (*suicide*) to kill o.s.; **~ au travail** (*fig*) to work o.s. to death; **tuerie** nf slaughter no pl

tue-tête[tytɛt]: **à ~** adv at the top of one's voice

tueur[tɥœʀ] nm killer; **tueur à gages** hired killer

tuile[tɥil] nf tile; (*fam*) spot of bad luck, blow

tulipe[tylip] nf tulip

tuméfié, e[tymefje] adj puffed-up, swollen

tumeur[tymœʀ] nf growth, tumour

tumulte[tymylt] nm commotion; **tumultueux, -euse** adj stormy, turbulent

tunique[tynik] nf tunic

Tunis[tynis] n Tunis

Tunisie[tynizi] nf: **la ~** Tunisia; **tunisien, ne** adj Tunisian ▷ nm/f: **Tunisien, ne** Tunisian

tunnel[tynɛl] nm tunnel; **le ~ sous la Manche** the Channel Tunnel

turbulent, e[tyʀbylɑ̃, ɑ̃t] adj boisterous, unruly

turc, turque[tyʀk] adj Turkish ▷ nm/f: **T~, Turque** Turk/Turkish woman ▷ nm (*Ling*) Turkish

turf[tyʀf] nm racing; **turfiste** nm/f racegoer

Turquie[tyʀki] nf: **la ~** Turkey

turquoise[tyʀkwaz] nf turquoise ▷ adj inv turquoise

tutelle[tytɛl] nf (*Jur*) guardianship; (*Pol*) trusteeship; **sous la ~ de** (*fig*) under the supervision of

tuteur[tytœʀ] nm (*Jur*) guardian; (*de plante*) stake, support

tutoyer[tytwaje] vt: **~ qn** to address

sb as "tu"

tuyau, x [tɥijo] *nm* pipe; *(flexible)* tube; *(fam)* tip; **tuyau d'arrosage** hosepipe; **tuyau d'échappement** exhaust pipe; **tuyauterie** *nf* piping *no pl*

TVA *sigle f* (= *taxe à la valeur ajoutée*) VAT

tympan [tɛ̃pɑ̃] *nm* (*Anat*) eardrum

type [tip] *nm* type; *(fam)* chap, guy ▷ *adj* typical, classic

typé, e [tipe] *adj* ethnic

typique [tipik] *adj* typical

tyran [tirɑ̃] *nm* tyrant; **tyrannique** *adj* tyrannical

tzigane [dzigan] *adj* gipsy, tzigane

ulcère [ylsɛʀ] *nm* ulcer

ultérieur, e [ylteʀjœʀ] *adj* later, subsequent; **remis à une date ~e** postponed to a later date; **ultérieurement** *adv* later, subsequently

ultime [yltim] *adj* final

 MOT-CLÉ

un, une [œ̃, yn] *art indéf* a; (*devant voyelle*) an; **un garçon/vieillard** a boy/an old man; **une fille** a girl ▷ *pron* one; **l'un des meilleurs** one of the best; **l'un ..., l'autre** (the) one ..., the other; **les uns ..., les autres** some ..., others; **l'un et l'autre** both (of them); **l'un ou l'autre** either (of them); **l'un l'autre** each other; **les uns les autres** one another; **pas un seul** not a single one; **un par un** one by one ▷ *num* one; **un pamplemousse seulement** one grapefruit only, just

one grapefruit
▷ *nf*: **la une** (*Presse*) the front page

unanime [ynanim] *adj* unanimous;
unanimité *nf*: **à l'unanimité**
unanimously

uni, e [yni] *adj* (*ton, tissu*) plain; (*surface*)
smooth, even; (*famille*) close(-knit);
(*pays*) united

unifier [ynifje] *vt* to unite, unify

uniforme [yniform] *adj* uniform;
(*surface, ton*) even ▷ *nm* uniform;
uniformiser *vt* (*systèmes*) to
standardize

union [ynjɔ̃] *nf* union; **union de
consommateurs** consumers'
association; **union libre: vivre en
union libre** (*en concubinage*) to cohabit;
Union européenne European Union;
Union soviétique Soviet Union

unique [ynik] *adj* (*seul*) only;
(*exceptionnel*) unique; (*le même*): **un
prix/système** ~ a single price/system;
fils/fille ~ only son/daughter,
only child; **sens** ~ one-way street;
uniquement *adv* only, solely; (*juste*)
only, merely

unir [ynir] *vt* (*nations*) to unite; (*en
mariage*) to unite, join together;
s'unir *vi* to unite; (*en mariage*) to be joined
together

unitaire [yniter] *adj*: **prix** ~ unit price

unité [ynite] *nf* unit; (*harmonie,
cohésion*) unity

univers [yniver] *nm* universe;
universel, le *adj* universal

universitaire [yniversiter] *adj*
university *cpd*; (*diplôme, études*)
academic, university *cpd* ▷ *nm/f*
academic

université [yniversite] *nf* university

urbain, e [yrbɛ̃, ɛn] *adj* urban, city
cpd, town *cpd*; **urbanisme** *nm* town
planning

urgence [yrʒɑ̃s] *nf* urgency; (*Méd etc*)
emergency; **d'**~ *adj* emergency *cpd*
▷ *adv* as a matter of urgency; (**service
des**) ~**s** casualty

urgent, e [yrʒɑ̃, ɑ̃t] *adj* urgent

urine [yrin] *nf* urine; **urinoir** *nm*
(public) urinal

urne [yrn] *nf* (*électorale*) ballot box;
(*vase*) urn

urticaire [yrtiker] *nf* nettle rash

us [ys] *nmpl*: **us et coutumes** (habits
and) customs

usage [yzaʒ] *nm* (*emploi, utilisation*) use;
(*coutume*) custom; **à l'**~ with use; **à l'**~
de (*pour*) for (use of); **en** ~ in use; **hors
d'**~ out of service; **à** ~ **interne** (*Méd*) to
be taken (internally); **à** ~ **externe** (*Méd*)
for external use only; **usagé, e** *adj* (*usé*)
worn; **usager, -ère** *nm/f* user

usé, e [yze] *adj* worn; (*banal: argument
etc*) hackneyed

user [yze] *vt* (*outil*) to wear down;
(*vêtement*) to wear out; (*matière*) to wear
away; (*consommer: charbon etc*) to use;
s'user *vi* (*tissu, vêtement*) to wear out;
~ **de** (*moyen, procédé*) to use, employ;
(*droit*) to exercise

usine [yzin] *nf* factory

usité, e [yzite] *adj* common

ustensile [ystɑ̃sil] *nm* implement;
ustensile de cuisine kitchen utensil

usuel, le [yzɥɛl] *adj* everyday, common

usure [yzyr] *nf* wear

utérus [yterys] *nm* uterus, womb

utile [ytil] *adj* useful

utilisation [ytilizasjɔ̃] *nf* use

utiliser [ytilize] *vt* to use

utilitaire [ytiliter] *adj* utilitarian

utilité [ytilite] *nf* usefulness *no pl*; **de
peu d'**~ of little use or help

utopie [ytɔpi] *nf* utopia

V

va [va] *vb voir* **aller**

vacance [vakɑ̃s] *nf* (*Admin*) vacancy;
vacances *nfpl* holiday(s pl (BRIT)),
vacation *sg* (US); **les grandes ~s** the
summer holidays; **prendre des/ses ~s**
to take a holiday/one's holiday(s); **aller
en ~s** to go on holiday; **je suis ici en ~s**
I'm here on holiday; **vacancier, -ière**
nm/f holiday-maker

vacant, e [vakɑ̃, ɑ̃t] *adj* vacant

vacarme [vakaʀm] *nm* (*bruit*) racket

vaccin [vaksɛ̃] *nm* vaccine; (*opération*)
vaccination; **vaccination** *nf*
vaccination; **vacciner** *vt* to vaccinate;
être vacciné contre qch (*fam*) to be
cured of sth

vache [vaʃ] *nf* (*Zool*) cow; (*cuir*) cowhide
▷ *adj* (*fam*) rotten, mean; **vachement**
(*fam*) *adv* (*très*) really; (*pleuvoir, travailler*)
a hell of a lot; **vacherie** *nf* (*action*) dirty
trick; (*remarque*) nasty remark

vaciller [vasije] *vi* to sway, wobble;
(*bougie, lumière*) to flicker; (*fig*) to be
failing, falter

va-et-vient [vaevjɛ̃] *nm inv* (*de
personnes, véhicules*) comings and
goings pl, to-ings and fro-ings pl

vagabond [vagabɔ̃] *nm* (*rôdeur*)
tramp, vagrant; (*voyageur*) wanderer;
vagabonder *vi* to roam, wander

vagin [vaʒɛ̃] *nm* vagina

vague [vag] *nf* wave ▷ *adj* vague;
(*regard*) faraway; (*manteau, robe*)
loose(-fitting); (*quelconque*) **un ~
bureau/cousin** some office/cousin
or other; **vague de fond** ground swell;
vague de froid cold spell

vaillant, e [vajɑ̃, ɑ̃t] *adj* (*courageux*)
gallant; (*robuste*) hale and hearty

vain, e [vɛ̃, vɛn] *adj* vain; **en ~** in vain

vaincre [vɛ̃kʀ] *vt* to defeat; (*fig*) to
conquer, overcome; **vaincu, e** *nm/f*
defeated party; **vainqueur** *nm* victor;
(*Sport*) winner

vaisseau, x [veso] *nm* (*Anat*) vessel;
(*Navig*) ship, vessel; **vaisseau spatial**
spaceship

vaisselier [vesəlje] *nm* dresser

vaisselle [vesɛl] *nf* (*service*) crockery;
(*plats et à laver*) (dirty) dishes pl; **faire
la ~** to do the washing-up (BRIT) ou
the dishes

valable [valabl] *adj* valid; (*acceptable*)
decent, worthwhile

valet [valɛ] *nm* manservant; (*Cartes*)
jack

valeur [valœʀ] *nf* (*gén*) value; (*mérite*)
worth, merit; (*Comm: titre*) security;
valeurs *nfpl* (*morales*) values; **mettre
en ~** (*détail*) to highlight; (*objet décoratif*)
to show off to advantage; **avoir de
la ~** to be valuable; **sans ~** worthless;
prendre de la ~ to go up ou gain in
value

valide [valid] *adj* (*en bonne santé*) fit;
(*valable*) valid; **valider** *vt* to validate

valise [valiz] *nf* (*suit*)case; **faire ses ~s**
to pack one's bags

vallée [vale] *nf* valley

vallon [valɔ̃] *nm* small valley

valoir [valwaʀ] *vi* (*être valable*) to
hold, apply ▷ *vt* (*prix, valeur, effort*)

to be worth; (causer): ~ **qch à qn** to earn sb sth; **se valoir** vi to be of equal merit; (péj) to be two of a kind; **faire** ~ (droits, prérogatives) to assert; **se faire** ~ to make the most of o.s.; **à ~ sur** to be deducted from; **vaille que vaille** somehow or other; **cela ne me vaut rien** this climate doesn't suit me; **le coup** ou **la peine** to be worth the trouble ou worth it; ~ **mieux: il vaut mieux se taire** it's better to say nothing; **ça ne vaut rien** it's worthless; **que vaut ce candidat?** how good is this applicant?

valse [vals] nf waltz
vandalisme [vɑ̃dalism] nm vandalism
vanille [vanij] nf vanilla
vanité [vanite] nf vanity; **vaniteux, -euse** adj vain, conceited
vanne [van] nf gate; (fig) joke
vannerie [vanʀi] nf basketwork
vantard, e [vɑ̃taʀ, aʀd] adj boastful
vanter [vɑ̃te] vt to speak highly of, praise; **se vanter** to boast, brag; **se ~ de** to pride o.s. on; (péj) to boast of
vapeur [vapœʀ] nf steam; (émanation) vapour, fumes pl; **vapeurs** nfpl (bouffées) vapours; **à ~** steam-powered, steam cpd; **cuit à la ~** steamed; **vaporeux, -euse** adj (flou) hazy, misty; (léger) filmy; **vaporisateur** nm spray; **vaporiser** vt (parfum etc) to spray
varappe [vaʀap] nf rock climbing
vareuse [vaʀøz] nf (blouson) pea jacket; (d'uniforme) tunic
variable [vaʀjabl] adj variable; (temps, humeur) changeable; (divers: résultats) varied, various
varice [vaʀis] nf varicose vein
varicelle [vaʀisɛl] nf chickenpox
varié, e [vaʀje] adj varied; (divers) various; **hors d'œuvre ~s** selection of hors d'œuvres
varier [vaʀje] vi (temps, humeur) to change ▷ vt to vary; **variété** nf variety; **variétés** nfpl: **spectacle/émission de variétés** variety show

variole [vaʀjɔl] nf smallpox
Varsovie [vaʀsɔvi] n Warsaw
vas [va] vb voir **aller**; ~-**y!** [vazi] go on!
vase [vaz] nm vase ▷ nf silt, mud; **vaseux, -euse** adj silty, muddy; (fig: confus) woolly, hazy; (: fatigué) woozy
vasistas [vazistas] nm fanlight
vaste [vast] adj vast, immense
vautour [votuʀ] nm vulture
vautrer [votʀe] vb: **se ~ dans/sur** to wallow in/sprawl on
va-vite [vavit]: **à la ~** adv in a rush ou hurry
VDQS sigle (= vin délimité de qualité supérieure) label guaranteeing the quality of wine
veau, x [vo] nm (Zool) calf; (Culin) veal; (peau) calfskin
vécu, e [veky] pp de **vivre**
vedette [vadɛt] nf (artiste etc) star; (canot) motor boat; (police) launch
végétal, e, -aux [veʒetal, o] adj vegetable ▷ nm vegetable, plant; **végétalien, ne** adj, nm/f vegan
végétarien, ne [veʒetaʀjɛ̃, jɛn] adj, nm/f vegetarian; **avez-vous des plats ~s?** do you have any vegetarian dishes?
végétation [veʒetasjɔ̃] nf vegetation; **végétations** nfpl (Méd) adenoids
véhicule [veikyl] nm vehicle; **véhicule utilitaire** commercial vehicle
veille [vɛj] nf (état) wakefulness; (jour): **la ~ (de)** the day before; **la ~ au soir** the previous evening; **à la ~ de** on the eve of; **la ~ de Noël** Christmas Eve; **la ~ du jour de l'An** New Year's Eve
veillée [veje] nf (soirée) evening; (réunion) evening gathering; **veillée (funèbre)** wake
veiller [veje] vi to stay up ▷ vt (malade, mort) to watch over, sit up with; ~ **à** to attend to, see to; ~ **à ce que** to make sure that; ~ **sur** to watch over; **veilleur** nm: **veilleur de nuit** night watchman; **veilleuse** nf (lampe) night light; (Auto) sidelight; (flamme) pilot light
veinard, e [venaʀ, aʀd] nm/f lucky devil

veine [vɛn] nf (Anat, du bois etc) vein; (filon) vein, seam; (fam: chance): **avoir de la ~** to be lucky

véliplanchiste [veliplɑ̃ʃist] nm/f windsurfer

vélo [velo] nm bike, cycle; **faire du ~** to go cycling; **vélomoteur** nm moped

velours [v(ə)luʀ] nm velvet; **velours côtelé** corduroy; **velouté, e** adj velvety ▷ nm: **velouté de tomates** cream of tomato soup

velu, e [valy] adj hairy

vendange [vɑ̃dɑ̃ʒ] nf (aussi: **~s**) grape harvest; **vendanger** vi to harvest the grapes

vendeur, -euse [vɑ̃dœʀ, øz] nm/f shop assistant ▷ nm (Jur) vendor, seller

vendre [vɑ̃dʀ] vt to sell; **~ qch à qn** to sell sb sth; **"à ~"** for sale"

vendredi [vɑ̃dʀədi] nm Friday; **vendredi saint** Good Friday

vénéneux, -euse [venenø, øz] adj poisonous

vénérien, ne [veneʀjɛ̃, jɛn] adj venereal

vengeance [vɑ̃ʒɑ̃s] nf vengeance no pl, revenge no pl

venger [vɑ̃ʒe] vt to avenge; **se venger** vi to avenge o.s.; **se ~ de qch** to avenge o.s. for sth, take one's revenge for sth; **se ~ de qn** to take revenge on sb; **se ~ sur** to take revenge on

venimeux, -euse [vanimø, øz] adj poisonous, venomous; (fig: haineux) venomous, vicious

venin [vanɛ̃] nm venom, poison

venir [v(ə)niʀ] vi to come; **~ de** to come from; **~ de faire: je viens d'y aller/de le voir** I've just been there/seen him; **s'il vient à pleuvoir** if it should rain; **j'en viens à croire que** I have come to believe that; **où veux-tu en ~?** what are you getting at?; **faire ~** (docteur, plombier) to call (out)

vent [vɑ̃] nm wind; **il y a du ~** it's windy; **c'est du ~** it's all hot air; **dans le ~** (fam) trendy

vente [vɑ̃t] nf sale; **la ~** (activité) selling;

(secteur) sales pl; **mettre en ~** (produit) to put on sale; (maison, objet personnel) to put up for sale; **vente aux enchères** auction sale; **vente de charité** jumble sale

venteux, -euse [vɑ̃tø, øz] adj windy

ventilateur [vɑ̃tilatœʀ] nm fan

ventiler [vɑ̃tile] vt to ventilate

ventouse [vɑ̃tuz] nf (de caoutchouc) suction pad

ventre [vɑ̃tʀ] nm (Anat) stomach; (légèrement péj) belly; (utérus) womb; **avoir mal au ~** to have stomach ache (BRIT) ou a stomach ache (US)

venu, e [v(ə)ny] pp de **venir** ▷ adj: **bien ~** timely; **mal** out of place; **être mal ~ à** ou **de faire** to have no grounds for doing, be in no position to

ver [vɛʀ] nm worm; (des fruits etc) maggot; (du bois) woodworm no pl; voir aussi **vers**; **ver à soie** silkworm; **ver de terre** earthworm; **ver luisant** glow-worm; **ver solitaire** tapeworm

verbe [vɛʀb] nm verb

verdâtre [vɛʀdɑtʀ] adj greenish

verdict [vɛʀdik(t)] nm verdict

verdir [vɛʀdiʀ] vi, vt to turn green; **verdure** nf greenery

véreux, -euse [veʀø, øz] adj worm-eaten; (malhonnête) shady, corrupt

verge [vɛʀʒ] nf (Anat) penis

verger [vɛʀʒe] nm orchard

verglacé, e [vɛʀglase] adj icy, iced-over

verglas [vɛʀgla] nm (black) ice

véridique [veʀidik] adj truthful

vérification [veʀifikɑsjɔ̃] nf (action) checking no pl; (contrôle) check

vérifier [veʀifje] vt to check; (corroborer) to confirm, bear out

véritable [veʀitabl] adj real (amour) true; **un ~ désastre** an absolute disaster

vérité [veʀite] nf truth; **en ~** really, actually

verlan [vɛʀlɑ̃] nm (fam) (back) slang

vermeil, le [vɛʀmɛj] adj ruby red

vermine [vɛʀmin] nf vermin pl

vermoulu, e [vɛʀmuly] *adj* worm-eaten

verni, e [vɛʀni] *adj* (fam) lucky; **cuir ~** patent leather

vernir [vɛʀniʀ] *vt* (bois, tableau, ongles) to varnish; (poterie) to glaze; **vernis** *nm* (enduit) varnish; glaze; (fig) veneer; **vernis à ongles** nail polish ou varnish; **vernissage** *nm* (d'une exposition) preview

vérole [veʀɔl] *nf* (variole) smallpox

verre [vɛʀ] *nm* glass; (de lunettes) lens *sg*; **boire** ou **prendre un ~** to have a drink; **verres de contact** contact lenses; **verrière** (paroi vitrée) glass wall; (toit vitré) glass roof

verrou [veʀu] *nm* (targette) bolt; **mettre qn sous les ~s** to put sb behind bars; **verrouillage** *nm* locking; **verrouillage centralisé** central locking; **verrouiller** *vt* (porte) to bolt; (ordinateur) to lock

verrue [veʀy] *nf* wart

vers [vɛʀ] *nm* line ▷ *nmpl* (poésie) verse *sg* ▷ *prép* (en direction de) toward(s); (près de) around (about); (temporel) about, around

versant [vɛʀsɑ̃] *nm* slopes *pl*, side

versatile [vɛʀsatil] *adj* fickle, changeable

verse [vɛʀs]: **à ~** *adv*: **il pleut à ~** it's pouring (with rain)

Verseau [vɛʀso] *nm*: **le ~** Aquarius

versement [vɛʀsəmɑ̃] *nm* payment; **en 3 ~s** in 3 instalments

verser [vɛʀse] *vt* (liquide, grains) to pour; (larmes, sang) to shed; (argent) to pay; **~ qch sur un compte** to pay sth into an account

version [vɛʀsjɔ̃] *nf* version; (Scol) translation (into the mother tongue); **film en ~ originale** film in the original language

verso [vɛʀso] *nm* back; **voir au ~** see over(leaf)

vert, e [vɛʀ, vɛʀt] *adj* green; (vin) young; (vigoureux) sprightly ▷ *nm* green; **les V~s** (Pol) the Greens

vertèbre [vɛʀtɛbʀ] *nf* vertebra

vertement [vɛʀtəmɑ̃] *adv* (réprimander) sharply

vertical, e, -aux [vɛʀtikal, o] *adj* vertical; **verticale** *nf* vertical; **à la verticale** vertically; **verticalement** *adv* vertically

vertige [vɛʀtiʒ] *nm* (peur du vide) vertigo; (étourdissement) dizzy spell; (fig) fever; **vertigineux, -euse** *adj* breathtaking

vertu [vɛʀty] *nf* virtue; **en ~ de** in accordance with; **vertueux, -euse** *adj* virtuous

verve [vɛʀv] *nf* witty eloquence; **être en ~** to be in brilliant form

verveine [vɛʀvɛn] *nf* (Bot) verbena, vervain; (infusion) verbena tea

vésicule [vezikyl] *nf* vesicle; **vésicule biliaire** gall-bladder

vessie [vesi] *nf* bladder

veste [vɛst] *nf* jacket; **veste droite/croisée** single/double-breasted jacket

vestiaire [vɛstjɛʀ] *nm* (au théâtre etc) cloakroom; (de stade etc) changing-room (BRIT), locker-room (US)

vestibule [vɛstibyl] *nm* hall

vestige [vɛstiʒ] *nm* relic; (fig) trace; **vestiges** *nmpl* (de ville) remains

vestimentaire [vɛstimɑ̃tɛʀ] *adj* (détail) of dress; (élégance) sartorial; **dépenses ~s** clothing expenditure

veston [vɛstɔ̃] *nm* jacket

vêtement [vɛtmɑ̃] *nm* garment, item of clothing; **vêtements** *nmpl* clothes

vétérinaire [veteʀinɛʀ] *nm/f* vet, veterinary surgeon

vêtir [vetiʀ] *vt* to clothe, dress

vêtu, e [vety] *pp de* **vêtir** ▷ *adj*: **~ de** dressed in, wearing

vétuste [vetyst] *adj* ancient, timeworn

veuf, veuve [vœf, vœv] *adj* widowed ▷ *nm* widower

veuve [vœv] *nf* widow

vexant, e [vɛksɑ̃, ɑ̃t] *adj* (contrariant) annoying; (blessant) hurtful

vexation [vɛksasjɔ̃] *nf* humiliation

vexer [vɛkse] vt: **~ qn** to hurt sb's feelings; **se vexer** vi to be offended

viable [vjabl] adj viable; (économie, industrie etc) sustainable

viande [vjɑ̃d] nf meat; **je ne mange pas de ~** I don't eat meat

vibrer [vibʀe] vi to vibrate; (son, voix) to be stirred; (fig) to be stirred; **faire ~** (cause to) vibrate; (fig) to stir, thrill

vice [vis] nm vice; (défaut) fault ▷ préfixe: **~ ...** vice-; **vice de forme** legal flaw ou irregularity

vicié, e [visje] adj (air) polluted, tainted; (Jur) invalidated

vicieux, -euse [visjø, jøz] adj (pervers) lecherous; (rétif) unruly ▷ nm/f lecher

vicinal, e, -aux [visinal, o] adj: **chemin ~** by-road, byway

victime [viktim] nf victim; (d'accident) casualty

victoire [viktwaʀ] nf victory

victuailles [viktwaj] nfpl provisions

vidange [vidɑ̃ʒ] nf (d'un fossé, réservoir) emptying; (Auto) oil change; (de lavabo: bonde) waste outlet; **vidanges** nfpl (matières) sewage sg; **vidanger** vt to empty

vide [vid] adj empty ▷ nm (Physique) vacuum; (espace) (empty) space, gap; (futilité, néant) void; **avoir peur du ~** to be afraid of heights; **emballé sous ~** vacuum packed; **à ~** (sans occupants) empty; (sans charge) unladen

vidéo [video] nf video ▷ adj: **cassette ~** video cassette; **jeu ~** video game; **vidéoclip** nm music video; **vidéoconférence** nf videoconference

vide-ordures [vidɔʀdyʀ] nm inv (rubbish) chute

vider [vide] vt to empty; (Culin: volaille, poisson) to gut, clean out; **se vider** vi to empty; **~ les lieux** to quit ou vacate the premises; **videur** nm (de boîte de nuit) bouncer, doorman

vie [vi] nf life; **être en ~** to be alive; **sans ~** lifeless; **à ~** for life; **que faites-vous dans la ~?** what do you do?

vieil [vjɛj] adj m voir **vieux**; **vieillard**

nm old man; **vieille** adj, nf voir **vieux**; **vieilleries** nfpl old things; **vieillesse** nf old age; **vieillir** vi (prendre de l'âge) to grow old; (population, vin) to age; (doctrine, auteur) to become dated ▷ vt to age; **vieillissement** nm growing old; ageing

Vienne [vjɛn] nf Vienna

viens [vjɛ̃] vb voir **venir**

vierge [vjɛʀʒ] adj virgin; (page) clean, blank ▷ nf virgin; (signe): **la V~** Virgo

Vietnam, Viêt-Nam [vjɛtnam] nm Vietnam; **vietnamien, ne** adj Vietnamese ▷ nm/f: **Vietnamien, ne** Vietnamese

vieux, vieil, vieille [vjø, vjɛj] adj old ▷ nm/f old man (woman); **les vieux** nmpl old people; **un petit ~** a little old man; **mon ~/ma vieille** (fam) old man/girl; **prendre un coup de ~** to put years on; **vieux garçon** bachelor; **vieux jeu** adj inv old-fashioned

vif, vive [vif, viv] adj (animé) lively; (alerte, brusque, aigu) sharp; (lumière, couleur) bright; (air) crisp; (vent, émotion) keen; (fort: regret, déception) great, deep; (vivant): **brûlé ~** burnt alive; **de vive voix** personally, orally; **avoir l'esprit ~** to be quick-witted; **piquer qn au ~** to cut to the quick; **à ~** (plaie) open; **avoir les nerfs à ~** to be on edge

vigne [viɲ] nf (plante) vine; (plantation) vineyard; **vigneron** nm wine grower

vignette [viɲɛt] nf (Admin) ≈ (road) tax disc (BRIT), ≈ license plate sticker (US); (de médicament) price label (used for reimbursement)

vignoble [viɲɔbl] nm (plantation) vineyard; (vignes d'une région) vineyards pl

vigoureux, -euse [viguʀø, øz] adj vigorous, robust

vigueur [vigœʀ] nf vigour; **entrer en ~** to come into force; **en ~** current

vilain, e [vilɛ̃, ɛn] adj (laid) ugly; (affaire, blessure) nasty; (pas sage: enfant) naughty; **vilain mot** naughty ou bad word

villa [vila] nf (detached) house; **~ en multipropriété** time-share villa

village [vilaʒ] nm village; **villageois, e** adj village cpd ▷ nm/f villager

ville [vil] nf town; (*importante*) city; (*administration*): **la ~** (the) town council, the local authority; **ville d'eaux** spa; **ville nouvelle** new town

vin [vɛ̃] nm wine; **avoir le ~ gai** to get happy after a few drinks; **vin d'honneur** reception (*with wine and snacks*); **vin de pays** local wine; **vin ordinaire** ou **de table** table wine

vinaigre [vinɛgʀ] nm vinegar; **vinaigrette** nf vinaigrette, French dressing

vindicatif, -ive [vɛ̃dikatif, iv] adj vindictive

vingt [vɛ̃] num twenty; **~-quatre heures sur ~-quatre** twenty-four hours a day, round the clock; **vingtaine** nf: **une vingtaine (de)** about twenty, twenty or so; **vingtième** num twentieth

vinicole [vinikɔl] adj wine cpd, wine-growing

vinyle [vinil] nm vinyl

viol [vjɔl] nm (*d'une femme*) rape; (*d'un lieu sacré*) violation

violacé, e [vjɔlase] adj purplish, mauvish

violemment [vjɔlamɑ̃] adv violently

violence [vjɔlɑ̃s] nf violence

violent, e [vjɔlɑ̃, ɑ̃t] adj violent; (*remède*) drastic

violer [vjɔle] vt (*femme*) to rape; (*sépulture, loi, traité*) to violate

violet, te [vjɔle, ɛt] adj, nm purple, mauve; **violette** nf (*fleur*) violet

violon [vjɔlɔ̃] nm violin; (*fam: prison*) lock-up; **violon d'Ingres** hobby; **violoncelle** nm cello; **violoniste** nm/f violinist

vipère [vipɛʀ] nf viper, adder

virage [viʀaʒ] nm (*d'un véhicule*) turn; (*d'une route, piste*) bend

virée [viʀe] nf trip; (*à pied*) walk; (*longue*) walking tour; (*dans les cafés*) tour

virement [viʀmɑ̃] nm (Comm) transfer

virer [viʀe] vt (Comm): **~ qch (sur)** to transfer qch (into); (*fam: expulser*): **~ qn** to kick sb out ▷ vi to turn; (*Chimie*) to change colour; **~ au bleu/rouge** to turn blue/red; **~ de bord** to tack

virevolter [viʀvɔlte] vi to twirl around

virgule [viʀgyl] nf comma; (Math) point

viril, e [viʀil] adj (*propre à l'homme*) masculine; (*énergique, courageux*) manly, virile

virtuel, le [viʀtɥɛl] adj potential; (*théorique*) virtual

virtuose [viʀtɥoz] nm/f (Mus) virtuoso; (*gén*) master

virus [viʀys] nm virus

vis [vi] vb voir **voir**; **vivre**

vis² [vis] nf screw

visa [viza] nm (*sceau*) stamp; (*validation de passeport*) visa

visage [vizaʒ] nm face

vis-à-vis [vizavi] prép: **~ de qn** to(wards) sb; **en ~** facing each other

visées [vize] nfpl (*intentions*) designs

viser [vize] vi to aim ▷ vt to aim at; (*concerner*) to be aimed ou directed at; (*apposer un visa sur*) to stamp, visa; **~ à qch/faire** to aim at sth/at doing ou to do

visibilité [vizibilite] nf visibility

visible [vizibl] adj visible; (*disponible*): **est-il ~?** can he see me?, will he see visitors?

visière [vizjɛʀ] nf (*de casquette*) peak; (*qui s'attache*) eyeshade

vision [vizjɔ̃] nf vision; (*sens*) (eye)sight, vision; (*fait de voir*): **la ~ de** the sight of; **visionneuse** nf viewer

visiophone [vizjɔfɔn] nm videophone

visite [vizit] nf visit; **~ médicale** medical examination; **~ accompagnée** ou **guidée** guided tour; **la ~ guidée commence à quelle heure?** what time does the guided tour start?; **faire une ~ à qn** to call on sb, pay sb a visit; **rendre ~ à qn** to visit sb, pay sb a visit; **être en ~ (chez qn)** to be visiting (sb); **avoir**

de la ~ to have visitors; **heures de ~** (hôpital, prison) visiting hours

visiter [vizite] vt to visit; **visiteur, -euse** nm/f visitor

vison [vizɔ̃] nm mink

visser [vise] vt: **~ qch** (fixer, serrer) to screw sth on

visuel, le [vizɥɛl] adj visual

vital, e, -aux [vital, o] adj vital

vitamine [vitamin] nf vitamin

vite [vit] adv (rapidement) quickly, fast; (sans délai) quickly; (sous peu) soon; **~!** quick!; **faire ~** to be quick; **le temps passe ~** time flies

vitesse [vitɛs] nf speed; (Auto: dispositif) gear; **prendre de la ~** to pick up ou gather speed; **à toute ~** at full ou top speed; **en ~** (rapidement) quickly; (en hâte) in a hurry

LIMITE DE VITESSE

- The speed limit in France is 50 km/h
  in built-up areas, 90 km/h on main
  roads, and 130 km/h on motorways
  (110 km/h when it is raining).

viticulteur [vitikyltœr] nm wine grower

vitrage [vitraʒ] nm: **double ~** double glazing

vitrail, -aux [vitraj, o] nm stained-glass window

vitre [vitr] nf (window) pane; (de portière, voiture) window; **vitré, e** adj glass cpd

vitrine [vitrin] nf (shop) window; (petite armoire) display cabinet; **en ~** in the window

vivable [vivabl] adj (personne) livable-with; (maison) fit to live in

vivace [vivas] adj (arbre, plante) hardy; (fig) indestructible, inveterate

vivacité [vivasite] nf liveliness, vivacity

vivant, e [vivã, ãt] adj (qui vit) living, alive; (animé) lively; (preuve, exemple) living ▷ nm: **du ~ de qn** in sb's lifetime;

les ~s the living

vive [viv] adj voir **vif** ▷ vb voir **vivre** ▷ excl: **~ le roi!** long live the king!; **vivement** adv deeply ▷ excl: **vivement les vacances!** roll on the holidays!

vivier [vivje] nm (étang) fish tank; (réservoir) fishpond

vivifiant, e [vivifjã, jãt] adj invigorating

vivoter [vivote] vi to scrape a living, get by; (fig: affaire etc) to struggle along

vivre [vivr] vi, vt to live; (période) to live through; **vivres** nmpl provisions, food supplies; **~ de** to live on; **il vit encore** he is still alive; **se laisser ~** to take life as it comes; **ne plus ~** (être anxieux) to live on one's nerves; **il a vécu** (eu une vie aventureuse) he has seen life; **être facile à ~** to be easy to get on with; **faire ~ qn** (pourvoir à sa subsistance) to provide (a living) for sb

vlan [vlã] excl wham!, bang!

VO [veo] nf: **film en VO** film in the original version; **en VO sous-titrée** in the original version with subtitles

vocabulaire [vɔkabylɛr] nm vocabulary

vocation [vɔkasjɔ̃] nf vocation, calling

vœu, x [vø] nm wish; (promesse) vow; **faire ~ de** to take a vow of; **tous nos ~x de bonne année, meilleurs ~x** best wishes for the New Year

vogue [vɔg] nf fashion, vogue; **en ~** in fashion, in vogue

voici [vwasi] prép (pour introduire, désigner) here is +sg, here are +pl; **et ~ que ...** and now it (ou he) ...; voir aussi **voilà**

voie [vwa] nf way; (Rail) track, line; (Auto) lane; **être en bonne ~** to be going well; **mettre qn sur la ~** to put sb on the right track; **pays en ~ de développement** developing country; **être en ~ d'achèvement/de rénovation** to be nearing completion/in the process of renovation; **par ~ buccale ou orale** orally; **route à ~**

unique single-track road; **route à 2/3 ~s** 2-/3-lane road; **voie de garage** (Rail) siding; **voie express** expressway; **voie ferrée** track; railway line (BRIT), railroad (US); **la voie lactée** the Milky Way; **la voie publique** the public highway

voilà [vwala] *prép* (*en désignant*) there is *+sg*, there are *+pl*; **les ~ ou voici** here ou there they are; **en ~ ou voici un** here's one, there's one; **voici mon frère et ma sœur** this is my brother and that's my sister; **~ ou voici deux ans** two years ago; **~ ou voici deux ans que** it's two years since; **et ~!** there we are!; **~ tout** that's all; **en ~ ou voici** (*en offrant etc*) there ou here you are; **tiens! ~ Paul** look! there's Paul

voile [vwal] *nm* veil (*tissu léger*) net ▷ *nf* sail; (*sport*) sailing; **voiler** *vt* to veil; (*fausser: roue*) to buckle; (: *bois*) to warp; **se voiler** *vi* (*lune, regard*) to mist over; (*voix*) to become husky; (*roue, disque*) to buckle; (*planche*) to warp; **voilier** *nm* sailing ship; (*de plaisance*) sailing boat; **voilure** *nf* (*de voilier*) sails *pl*

voir [vwaʀ] *vi, vt* to see; **se voir** *vi* (*être visible*) to show; (*se fréquenter*) to see each other; (*se produire*) to happen; **cela se voit** (*c'est visible*) that's obvious, it shows; **faire ~ qch à qn** to show sb sth; **en faire ~ à qn** (*fig*) to give sb a hard time; **ne pas pouvoir ~ qn** not to be able to stand sb; **voyons!** let's see now; (*indignation etc*) come on!; **ça n'a rien à ~ avec lui** that has nothing to do with him

voire [vwaʀ] *adv* even

voisin, e [vwazɛ̃, in] *adj* (*proche*) neighbouring; (*contigu*) next; (*ressemblant*) connected ▷ *nm/f* neighbour; **voisinage** *nm* (*proximité*) proximity; (*environs*) vicinity; (*quartier, voisins*) neighbourhood

voiture [vwatyʀ] *nf* car; (*wagon*) coach, carriage; **voiture de course** racing car; **voiture de sport** sports car

voix [vwa] *nf* voice; (*Pol*) vote; **à haute ~** aloud; **à ~ basse** in a low voice; **à 2/4 ~** (*Mus*) in 2/4 parts; **avoir ~ au chapitre** to have a say in the matter

vol [vɔl] *nm* (*d'oiseau, d'avion*) flight; (*larcin*) theft; **~ régulier** scheduled flight; **à ~ d'oiseau** as the crow flies; **au ~: attraper qch au ~** to catch sth as it flies past; **en ~** in flight; **je voudrais signaler un ~** I'd like to report a theft; **vol à main armée** armed robbery; **vol libre** hang-gliding

volage [vɔlaʒ] *adj* fickle

volaille [vɔlaj] *nf* (*oiseaux*) poultry *pl*; (*viande*) poultry *no pl*; (*oiseau*) fowl

volant, e [vɔlɑ̃, ɑ̃t] *adj voir* **feuille** *etc* ▷ *nm* (*d'automobile*) (steering) wheel; (*de commande*) wheel; (*objet lancé*) shuttlecock; (*bande de tissu*) flounce

volcan [vɔlkɑ̃] *nm* volcano

volée [vɔle] *nf* (*Tennis*) volley; **à la ~: rattraper à la ~** to catch in mid-air; **à toute ~** (*sonner les cloches*) vigorously; (*lancer un projectile*) with full force

voler [vɔle] *vi* (*avion, oiseau, fig*) to fly; (*voleur*) to steal ▷ *vt* (*objet*) to steal; (*personne*) to rob; **~ qch à qn** to steal sth from sb; **on m'a volé mon portefeuille** my wallet (BRIT) ou billfold (US) has been stolen; **il ne l'a pas volé!** he asked for it!

volet [vɔlɛ] *nm* (*de fenêtre*) shutter; (*de feuillet, document*) section

voleur, -euse [vɔlœʀ, øz] *nm/f* thief ▷ *adj* thieving; **"au ~!"** "stop thief!"

volontaire [vɔlɔ̃tɛʀ] *adj* (*acte, enrôlement, prisonnier*) voluntary; (*oubli*) intentional; (*caractère, personne*) decided self-willed ▷ *nm/f* volunteer

volonté [vɔlɔ̃te] *nf* (*faculté de vouloir*) will; (*énergie, fermeté*) will(power); (*souhait, désir*) wish; **à ~** as much as one likes; **bonne ~** goodwill, willingness; **mauvaise ~** lack of goodwill, unwillingness

volontiers [vɔlɔ̃tje] *adv* (*avec plaisir*) willingly, gladly; (*habituellement, souvent*) readily, willingly; **voulez-vous boire quelque chose? — ~!** I would you

like something to drink? — yes, please!
volt [vɔlt] nm volt
volte-face [vɔltəfas] nf inv: **faire ~** to
turn round
voltige [vɔltiʒ] nf (Équitation) trick
riding; (au cirque) acrobatics sg;
voltiger vi to flutter (about)
volubile [vɔlybil] adj voluble
volume [vɔlym] nm volume; (Géom:
solide) solid; **volumineux, -euse** adj
voluminous, bulky
volupté [vɔlypte] nf sensual delight
ou pleasure
vomi [vɔmi] nm vomit; **vomir** vi to
vomit, be sick ▷ vt to vomit, bring up;
(fig) belch out, spew out; (exécrer) to
loathe, abhor
vorace [vɔʀas] adj voracious
vos [vo] adj voir **votre**
vote [vɔt] nm vote; **vote par
correspondance/procuration** postal/
proxy vote; **voter** vi to vote ▷ vt (projet
de loi) to vote for; (loi, réforme) to pass
votre [vɔtʀ] (pl **vos**) adj your
vôtre [votʀ] pron: **le ~, la ~, les ~s** yours;
les ~s (fig) your family ou folks; **à la ~**
(toast) your (good) health!
vouer [vwe] vt: **~ sa vie à** (étude, cause
etc) to devote one's life to; **~ une
amitié éternelle à qn** to undying
friendship to sb

⭕ **MOT-CLÉ**

vouloir [vulwaʀ] nm: **le bon vouloir de
qn** sb's goodwill; sb's pleasure
▷ vt 1 (exiger, désirer) to want; **vouloir
faire/que qn fasse** to want to do/sb
to do; **voulez-vous du thé?** would you
like ou do you want some tea?; **que
me veut-il?** what does he want with
me?; **sans le vouloir** (involontairement)
without meaning to, unintentionally;
je voudrais ceci/faire I would ou I'd
like this/to do; **le hasard a voulu
que ...** as fate would have it ...; **la
tradition veut que ...** it is a tradition
that ...

2 (consentir): **je veux bien** (bonne
volonté) I'll be happy to; (concession) fair
enough, that's fine; **je peux le faire, si
vous voulez** I can do it if you like; **oui,
si on veut** (en quelque sorte) yes, if you
like; **veuillez attendre** please wait;
veuillez agréer ... (formule épistolaire:
personne nommée) yours sincerely;
(personne non nommée) yours faithfully
3: **en vouloir à qn** to bear sb a grudge;
s'en vouloir (de) to be annoyed with
o.s. (for); **il en veut à mon argent** he's
after my money
4: **vouloir de: l'entreprise ne veut
plus de lui** the firm doesn't want him
any more; **elle ne veut pas de son aide**
she doesn't want his help
5: **vouloir dire** to mean

voulu, e [vuly] adj (requis) required,
requisite; (délibéré) deliberate,
intentional; voir aussi **vouloir**
vous [vu] pron you; (objet indirect)
(to) you; (réfléchi: sg) yourself; (: pl)
yourselves; (réciproque) each other
▷ nm: **employer le ~** to use
the "vous" form; **~-même** yourself;
~-mêmes yourselves
vouvoyer [vuvwaje] vt: **~ qn** to
address sb as "vous"
voyage [vwajaʒ] nm journey, trip; (fait
de voyager): **le ~** travel(ling); **partir/être
en ~** to go off/be away on a journey
ou trip; **faire bon ~** to have a good
journey; **votre ~ s'est bien passé?** how
was your journey?; **voyage d'affaires/
d'agrément** business/pleasure trip;
voyage de noces honeymoon; **nous
sommes en voyage de noces** we're
on honeymoon; **voyage organisé**
package tour
voyager [vwajaʒe] vi to travel;
voyageur, -euse nm/f traveller;
(passager) passenger; **voyageur de
commerce** sales representative,
commercial traveller
voyant, e [vwajɑ̃, ɑ̃t] adj (couleur) loud,
gaudy ▷ nm (signal) (warning) light

voyelle [vwajɛl] nf vowel

voyou [vwaju] nm hooligan

vrac [vʀak]: **en ~** adv (au détail) loose; (en gros) in bulk; (en désordre) in a jumble

vrai, e [vʀɛ] adj (véridique: récit, faits) true; (non factice, authentique) real; **à ~ dire** to tell the truth; **vraiment** adv really; **vraisemblable** adj likely; (excuse) convincing; **vraisemblablement** adj probably; **vraisemblance** nf likelihood; (romanesque) verisimilitude

vrombir [vʀɔ̃biʀ] vi to hum

VRP sigle m (= voyageur, représentant, placier) sales rep (fam)

VTT sigle m (= vélo tout-terrain) mountain bike

vu, e [vy] pp de **voir** ▷ adj: **bien/mal vu** (fig: personne) popular/unpopular; (: chose) approved/disapproved of ▷ prép (en raison de) in view of; **vu que** in view of the fact that

vue [vy] nf (fait de voir): **la ~** the sight of; (sens, faculté) (eye)sight; (panorama, image, photo) view; **vues** nfpl (idées) views; (dessein) designs; **hors de ~** out of sight; **avoir en ~** to have in mind; **tirer à ~** to shoot on sight; **à ~ d'œil** visibly; **à première ~** at first sight; **de ~** by sight; **perdre de ~** to lose sight of; **en ~ (visible)** in sight; (célèbre) in the public eye; **en ~ de faire** with a view to doing; **perdre la ~** to lose one's (eye)sight; **avoir ~ sur** to have a view of; **vue d'ensemble** overall view

vulgaire [vylgɛʀ] adj (grossier) vulgar, coarse; (ordinaire) commonplace, mundane; (péj: quelconque): **de ~s touristes** common tourists; (Bot, Zool: non latin) common; **vulgariser** vt to popularize

vulnérable [vylneʀabl] adj vulnerable

W

wagon [vagɔ̃] nm (de voyageurs) carriage; (de marchandises) truck, wagon; **wagon-lit** nm sleeper, sleeping car; **wagon-restaurant** nm restaurant ou dining car

wallon, ne [walɔ̃, ɔn] adj Walloon ▷ nm (Ling) Walloon ▷ nm/f: **W~, ne** Walloon

watt [wat] nm watt

w-c sigle mpl (= water-closet(s)) toilet

Web [wɛb] nm inv: **le ~** the (World Wide) Web; **webmaster** [-mastœʀ], **webmestre** [-mɛstʀ] nm/f webmaster

week-end [wikɛnd] nm weekend

western [wɛstɛʀn] nm western

whisky [wiski] (pl **whiskies**) nm whisky

xénophobe [gzenɔfɔb] *adj*
xenophobic ▷ *nm/f* xenophobe
xérès [gzeʀɛs] *nm* sherry
xylophone [gzilɔfɔn] *nm* xylophone

y [i] *adv* (*à cet endroit*) there; (*dessus*) on
it (*ou* them); (*dedans*) in it (*ou* them)
▷ *pron* (*about ou* on *ou* of) it (*d'après le
verbe employé*); **j'y pense** I'm thinking
about it; **ça y est!** that's it!; *voir aussi*
aller; **avoir**
yacht [jɔt] *nm* yacht
yaourt [jauʀt] *nm* yoghourt; **~ nature/**
aux fruits plain/fruit yogurt
yeux [jø] *nmpl de* œil
yoga [jɔga] *nm* yoga
yoghourt [jɔguʀt] *nm* =**yaourt**
yougoslave [jugɔslav] (*Histoire*) *adj*
Yugoslav(ian) ▷ *nm/f:* **Y~** Yugoslav
Yougoslavie [jugɔslavi] *nf* (*Histoire*)
Yugoslavia; **l'ex-~** the former
Yugoslavia

Z

≈ restricted parking area; **zone industrielle** industrial estate

zoo [zo(o)] *nm* zoo

zoologie [zɔɔlɔʒi] *nf* zoology; **zoologique** *adj* zoological

zut [zyt] *excl* dash (it)! (*BRIT*), nuts! (*US*)

zapper [zape] *vi* to zap

zapping [zapiŋ] *nm*: **faire du ~** to flick through the channels

zèbre [zɛbR(ə)] *nm* (*Zool*) zebra; **zébré, e** *adj* striped, streaked

zèle [zɛl] *nm* zeal; **faire du ~** (*péj*) to be over-zealous; **zélé, e** *adj* zealous

zéro [zero] *nm* zero, nought (*BRIT*); **au-dessous de ~** below zero (Centigrade) ou freezing; **partir de ~** to start from scratch; **trois (buts) à ~** 3 (goals to) nil

zeste [zɛst] *nm* peel, zest

zézayer [zezeje] *vi* to have a lisp

zigzag [zigzag] *nm* zigzag; **zigzaguer** *vi* to zigzag

Zimbabwe [zimbabwe] *nm*: **le ~** Zimbabwe

zinc [zɛ̃g] *nm* (*Chimie*) zinc

zipper [zipe] *vt* (*Inform*) to zip

zizi [zizi] *nm* (*langage enfantin*) willy

zodiaque [zɔdjak] *nm* zodiac

zona [zona] *nm* shingles *sg*

zone [zon] *nf* zone, area; (*fam: quartiers pauvres*): **la ~** the slums; **zone bleue**

A [eɪ] n (Mus) la m

KEYWORD

a [eɪ, ə] (before vowel or silent h **an**) indef art **1** un(e); **a book** un livre; **an apple** une pomme; **she's a doctor** elle est médecin

2 (instead of the number "one") un(e); **a year ago** il y a un an; **a hundred/ thousand** etc **pounds** cent/mille etc livres

3 (in expressing ratios, prices etc): **3 a day/week** 3 par jour/semaine; **10 km an hour** 10 km à l'heure; **£5 a person** 5£ par personne; **30p a kilo** 30p le kilo

A2 n (BRIT: Scol) deuxième partie de l'examen équivalent au baccalauréat

A.A. n abbr (BRIT: = Automobile Association) ≈ ACF m; (= Alcoholics Anonymous) AA

A.A.A. n abbr (= American Automobile Association) ≈ ACF m

aback [ə'bæk] adv: **to be taken ~** être décontenancé(e)

abandon [ə'bændən] vt abandonner

abattoir ['æbətwɑ:'] n (BRIT) abattoir m

abbey ['æbɪ] n abbaye f

abbreviation [əbri:vɪ'eɪʃən] n abréviation f

abdomen ['æbdəmən] n abdomen m

abduct [æb'dʌkt] vt enlever

abide [ə'baɪd] vt souffrir, supporter; **I can't ~ it/him** je ne le supporte pas; **abide by** vt fus observer, respecter

ability [ə'bɪlɪtɪ] n compétence f; capacité f; (skill) talent m

able ['eɪbl] adj compétent(e); **to be ~ to do sth** pouvoir faire qch, être capable de faire qch

abnormal [æb'nɔ:məl] adj anormal(e)

aboard [ə'bɔ:d] adv à bord ▷ prep à bord de; (train) dans

abolish [ə'bɔlɪʃ] vt abolir

abolition [æbə'lɪʃən] n abolition f

abort [ə'bɔ:t] vt (Med) faire avorter; (Comput, fig) faire avorter; **abortion** [ə'bɔ:ʃən] n avortement m; **to have an abortion** se faire avorter

KEYWORD

about [ə'baut] adv **1** (approximately) environ, à peu près; **about a hundred/ thousand** etc environ cent/mille etc, une centaine (de)/un millier (de) etc; **it takes about 10 hours** ça prend environ or à peu près 10 heures; **at about 2 o'clock** vers 2 heures; **I've just about finished** j'ai presque fini

2 (referring to place) çà et là, de-ci de-là; **to run about** courir çà et là; **to walk about** se promener, aller et venir; **they left all their things lying about** ils ont laissé traîner toutes leurs affaires

3: **to be about to do sth** être sur le point de faire qch

▷ prep **1** (relating to) au sujet de, à propos de; **a book about London** un livre sur Londres; **what is it about?** de quoi s'agit-il?; **we talked about it** nous en avons parlé; **what** or **how about doing this?** et si nous faisions ceci? **2** (*referring to place*) dans; **to walk about the town** se promener dans la ville

above [ə'bʌv] *adv* au-dessus ▷ *prep* au-dessus de; (*more than*) plus de; **mentioned** ~ mentionné ci-dessus; ~ **all** par-dessus tout, surtout

abroad [ə'brɔːd] *adv* à l'étranger

abrupt [ə'brʌpt] *adj* (*steep, blunt*) abrupt(e); (*sudden, gruff*) brusque

abscess ['æbsɪs] *n* abcès *m*

absence ['æbsəns] *n* absence *f*

absent ['æbsənt] *adj* absent(e); **absent-minded** *adj* distrait(e)

absolute ['æbsəluːt] *adj* absolu(e); **absolutely** [æbsə'luːtlɪ] *adv* absolument

absorb [əb'zɔːb] *vt* absorber; **to be ~ed in a book** être plongé(e) dans un livre; **absorbent cotton** *n* (*us*) coton *m* hydrophile; **absorbing** *adj* absorbant(e); (*book, film etc*) captivant(e)

abstain [əb'steɪn] *vi*: **to ~ (from)** s'abstenir (de)

abstract ['æbstrækt] *adj* abstrait(e)

absurd [əb'səːd] *adj* absurde

abundance [ə'bʌndəns] *n* abondance *f*

abundant [ə'bʌndənt] *adj* abondant(e)

abuse *n* [ə'bjuːs] (*insults*) insultes *fpl*, injures *fpl*; (*ill-treatment*) mauvais traitements *mpl*; (*of power etc*) abus *m* ▷ *vt* [ə'bjuːz] (*insult*) insulter; (*ill-treat*) malmener; (*power etc*) abuser de; **abusive** *adj* grossier(-ière), injurieux(-euse)

abysmal [ə'bɪzməl] *adj* exécrable; (*ignorance etc*) sans bornes

academic [ækə'dɛmɪk] *adj* universitaire; (*person: scholarly*) intellectuel(-le); (*pej: issue*) oiseux(-euse), purement théorique ▷ *n* universitaire *m/f*; **academic year** *n*

(*University*) année *f* universitaire; (*Scol*) année scolaire

academy [ə'kædəmɪ] *n* (*learned body*) académie *f*; (*school*) collège *m*; ~ **of music** conservatoire *m*

accelerate [æk'sɛləreɪt] *vt, vi* accélérer; **acceleration** [ækselə'reɪʃən] *n* accélération *f*; **accelerator** *n* (*BRIT*) accélérateur *m*

accent ['æksɛnt] *n* accent *m*

accept [ək'sɛpt] *vt* accepter; **acceptable** *adj* acceptable; **acceptance** *n* acceptation *f*

access ['æksɛs] *n* accès *m*; **to have ~ to** (*information, library etc*) avoir accès à, pouvoir utiliser or consulter; (*person*) avoir accès auprès de; **accessible** [æk'sɛsəbl] *adj* accessible

accessory [æk'sɛsərɪ] *n* accessoire *m*; ~ **to** (*Law*) accessoire à

accident ['æksɪdənt] *n* accident *m*; (*chance*) hasard *m*; **I've had an ~** j'ai eu un accident; **by** ~ (*by chance*) par hasard; (*not deliberately*) accidentellement; **accidental** [æksɪ'dɛntl] *adj* accidentel(le); **accidentally** [æksɪ'dɛntəlɪ] *adv* accidentellement; **Accident and Emergency Department** *n* (*BRIT*) service *m* des urgences; **accident insurance** *n* assurance *f* accident

acclaim [ə'kleɪm] *vt* acclamer ▷ *n* acclamations *fpl*

accommodate [ə'kɔmədeɪt] *vt* loger, recevoir; (*oblige, help*) obliger; (*car etc*) contenir

accommodation (*us* **accommodations**) [əkɔmə'deɪʃən(z)] *n(pl)* logement *m*

accompaniment [ə'kʌmpənɪmənt] *n* accompagnement *m*

accompany [ə'kʌmpənɪ] *vt* accompagner

accomplice [ə'kʌmplɪs] *n* complice *m/f*

accomplish [ə'kʌmplɪʃ] *vt* accomplir; **accomplishment** *n* (*skill: gen pl*) talent *m*; (*completion*) accomplissement *m*;

(*achievement*) réussite *f*

accord [əˈkɔːd] *n* accord *m* ▷ *vt* accorder; **of his own ~** de son plein gré; **accordance with**: **in accordance with** conformément à; **according**: **according to** *prep* selon; **accordingly** *adv* (*appropriately*) en conséquence; (*as a result*) par conséquent

account [əˈkaunt] *n* (*Comm*) compte *m*; (*report*) compte rendu, récit *m*; **accounts** *npl* (*Comm*: *records*) comptabilité *f*, comptes; **of no ~** sans importance; **on ~** en acompte; **to buy sth on ~** acheter qch à crédit; **on no ~** en aucun cas; **on ~ of** à cause de; **to take into ~**, **take ~ of** tenir compte de; **account for** *vt fus* (*explain*) expliquer, rendre compte de; (*represent*) représenter; **accountable** *adj*: **accountable (to)** responsable (devant); **accountant** *n* comptable *m/f*; **account number** *n* numéro *m* de compte

accumulate [əˈkjuːmjuleit] *vt* accumuler, amasser ▷ *vi* s'accumuler, s'amasser

accuracy [ˈækjurəsɪ] *n* exactitude *f*, précision *f*

accurate [ˈækjurɪt] *adj* exact(e), précis(e); (*device*) précis; **accurately** *adv* avec précision

accusation [ækjuˈzeɪʃən] *n* accusation *f*

accuse [əˈkjuːz] *vt* ~ **sb** (**of sth**) accuser qn (de qch); **accused** *n* (*Law*) accusé(e)

accustomed [əˈkʌstəmd] *adj*: **~ to** habitué(e) à ou accoutumé(e) à

ace [eɪs] *n* as *m*

ache [eɪk] *n* mal *m*, douleur *f* ▷ *vi* (*be sore*) faire mal, être douloureux(-euse); **my head ~s** j'ai mal à la tête

achieve [əˈtʃiːv] *vt* (*aim*) atteindre; (*victory, success*) remporter, obtenir; **achievement** *n* exploit *m*, réussite *f*; (*of aims*) réalisation *f*

acid [ˈæsɪd] *adj*, *n* acide (*m*)

acknowledge [əkˈnɔlɪdʒ] *vt* (*also*: ~

receipt of) accuser réception de; (*fact*) reconnaître; **acknowledgement** *n* (*of letter*) accusé *m* de réception

acne [ˈæknɪ] *n* acné *m*

acorn [ˈeɪkɔːn] *n* gland *m*

acoustic [əˈkuːstɪk] *adj* acoustique

acquaintance [əˈkweɪntəns] *n* connaissance *f*

acquire [əˈkwaɪər] *vt* acquérir; **acquisition** [ækwɪˈzɪʃən] *n* acquisition *f*

acquit [əˈkwɪt] *vt* acquitter; **to ~ o.s. well** s'en tirer très honorablement

acre [ˈeɪkər] *n* acre *f* (= 4047 *m²*)

acronym [ˈækrənɪm] *n* acronyme *m*

across [əˈkrɔs] *prep* (*on the other side of*) de l'autre côté de; (*crosswise*) en travers de ▷ *adv* de l'autre côté; en travers; **to run/swim ~** traverser en courant/à la nage; **~ from** en face de

acrylic [əˈkrɪlɪk] *adj*, *n* acrylique (*m*)

act [ækt] *n* acte *m*, action *f*; (*Theat: part of play*) acte; (: *of performer*) numéro *m*; (*Law*) loi *f* ▷ *vi* agir; (*Theat*) jouer; (*pretend*) jouer la comédie ▷ *vt* (*role*) jouer, tenir; **to catch sb in the ~** prendre qn sur le fait or en flagrant délit; **to ~ as** servir de; **act up** (*inf*) ▷ *vi* (*person*) se conduire mal; (*knee, back, injury*) jouer des tours; (*machine*) être capricieux(-ieuse); **acting** *adj* suppléant(e), par intérim ▷ *n* (*activity*): **to do some acting** faire du théâtre (*or* du cinéma)

action [ˈækʃən] *n* action *f*; (*Mil*) combat(s) *m* (pl); (*Law*) procès *m*, action en justice; **out of ~** hors de combat; (*machine etc*) hors d'usage; **to take ~** agir, prendre des mesures; **action replay** *n* (BRIT TV) ralenti *m*

activate [ˈæktɪveɪt] *vt* (*mechanism*) actionner, faire fonctionner

active [ˈæktɪv] *adj* actif(-ive); (*volcano*) en activité; **actively** *adv* activement; (*discourage*) vivement

activist [ˈæktɪvɪst] *n* activiste *m/f*

activity [ækˈtɪvɪtɪ] *n* activité *f*; **activity holiday** *n* vacances actives

actor ['æktə^r] n acteur m
actress ['æktrɪs] n actrice f
actual ['æktjuəl] adj réel(le), véritable; (emphatic use) lui-même (elle-même)
⚠ Be careful not to translate **actual** by the French word **actuel**.
actually ['æktjuəlɪ] adv réellement, véritablement; (in fact) en fait
⚠ Be careful not to translate **actually** by the French word **actuellement**.
acupuncture ['ækjupʌŋktʃə^r] n acuponcture f
acute [ə'kju:t] adj aigu(ë); (mind, observer) pénétrant(e)
A.D. adv abbr (= Anno Domini) ap. J.-C.
ad [æd] n abbr = **advertisement**
adamant ['ædəmənt] adj inflexible
adapt [ə'dæpt] vt adapter ▷ vi: **to ~ (to)** s'adapter (à); **adapter, adaptor** m (Elec) adaptateur m; (for several plugs) prise f multiple
add [æd] vt ajouter; (figures: also: **~ up**) additionner ▷ vi (fig): **it doesn't ~ up** cela ne rime à rien; **add up to** vt fus (Math) s'élever à; (fig: mean) signifier
addict ['ædɪkt] n toxicomane m/f; (fig) fanatique m/f; **addicted** [ə'dɪktɪd] adj: **to be addicted to** (drink, drugs) être adonné(e) à; (fig: football etc) être un(e) fanatique de; **addiction** [ə'dɪkʃən] n (Med) dépendance f; **addictive** [ə'dɪktɪv] adj qui crée une dépendance
addition [ə'dɪʃən] n (adding up) addition f; (thing added) ajout m; **in ~** de plus, de surcroît; **in ~ to** en plus de; **additional** adj supplémentaire
additive ['ædɪtɪv] n additif m
address [ə'drɛs] n adresse f; (talk) discours m, allocution f ▷ vt adresser; (speak to) s'adresser à; **my ~ is ...** mon adresse, c'est ...; **address book** n carnet m d'adresses
adequate ['ædɪkwɪt] adj (enough) suffisant(e); (satisfactory) satisfaisant(e)
adhere [əd'hɪə^r] vi: **to ~ to** adhérer à; (fig: rule, decision) se tenir à
adhesive [əd'hi:zɪv] n adhésif m;

adhesive tape n (BRIT) ruban m adhésif; (US Med) sparadrap m
adjacent [ə'dʒeɪsənt] adj adjacent(e), contigu(ë); **~ to** adjacent à
adjective ['ædʒɛktɪv] n adjectif m
adjoining [ə'dʒɔɪnɪŋ] adj voisin(e), adjacent(e), attenant(e)
adjourn [ə'dʒə:n] vt ajourner ▷ vi suspendre la séance; lever la séance; clore la session
adjust [ə'dʒʌst] vt (machine) ajuster, régler; (prices, wages) rajuster ▷ vi: **to ~ (to)** s'adapter (à); **adjustable** adj réglable; **adjustment** n (of machine) ajustage m, réglage m; (of prices, wages) rajustement m; (of person) adaptation f
administer [əd'mɪnɪstə^r] vt administrer; **administration** [ədmɪnɪs'treɪʃən] n (management) administration f; (government) gouvernement m; **administrative** [əd'mɪnɪstrətɪv] adj administratif(-ive)
administrator [əd'mɪnɪstreɪtə^r] n administrateur(-trice)
admiral ['ædmərəl] n amiral m
admiration [ædmə'reɪʃən] n admiration f
admire [əd'maɪə^r] vt admirer; **admirer** n (fan) admirateur(-trice)
admission [əd'mɪʃən] n admission f; (to exhibition, night club etc) entrée f; (confession) aveu m
admit [əd'mɪt] vt laisser entrer; (agree) reconnaître, admettre; (crime) reconnaître avoir commis; **"children not ~ted"** "entrée interdite aux enfants"; **admit to** vt fus reconnaître, avouer; **admittance** n admission f, (droit m d')entrée f; **admittedly** adv il faut en convenir
adolescent [ædəu'lɛsnt] adj, n adolescent(e)
adopt [ə'dɔpt] vt adopter; **adopted** adj adoptif(-ive), adopté(e); **adoption** [ə'dɔpʃən] n adoption f
adore [ə'dɔ:^r] vt adorer
adorn [ə'dɔ:n] vt orner

Adriatic (Sea) [eɪdrɪˈætɪk-] n, adj: **the Adriatic (Sea)** la mer Adriatique, l'Adriatique f

adrift [əˈdrɪft] adv à la dérive

adult [ˈædʌlt] n adulte m/f ▷ adj (grown-up) adulte; (for adults) pour adultes; **adult education** n éducation f des adultes

adultery [əˈdʌltərɪ] n adultère m

advance [ədˈvɑːns] n avance f ▷ vt avancer ▷ vi s'avancer; **in ~** en avance, d'avance; **to make ~s to sb** (gen) faire des propositions à qn; (amorously) faire des avances à qn; **~ booking** location f; **~ notice, ~ warning** préavis m; (verbal) avertissement m; **do I need to book in ~?** est-ce qu'il faut réserver à l'avance?; **advanced** adj avancé(e); (Scol: studies) supérieur(e)

advantage [ədˈvɑːntɪdʒ] n (also Tennis) avantage m; **to take ~ of** (person) exploiter; (opportunity) profiter de

advent [ˈædvənt] n avènement m, venue f; **A~** (Rel) avent m

adventure [ədˈvɛntʃər] n aventure f; **adventurous** [ədˈvɛntʃərəs] adj aventureux(-euse)

adverb [ˈædvɜːb] n adverbe m

adversary [ˈædvəsərɪ] n adversaire m/f

adverse [ˈædvɜːs] adj adverse; (effect) négatif(-ive); (weather, publicity) mauvais(e); (wind) contraire

advert [ˈædvɜːt] n abbr (BRIT) = **advertisement**

advertise [ˈædvətaɪz] vi faire de la publicité ou de la réclame; (in classified ads etc) mettre une annonce ▷ vt faire de la publicité ou de la réclame pour; (in classified ads etc) mettre une annonce pour vendre; **~ for** (staff) recruter par (voie d')annonce; **advertisement** [ədˈvɜːtɪsmənt] n (Comm) publicité f, réclame f; (in classified ads etc) annonce f; **advertiser** n annonceur m; **advertising** n publicité f

advice [ədˈvaɪs] n conseils mpl; (notification) avis m; **a piece of ~** un conseil; **to take legal ~** consulter un avocat

advisable [ədˈvaɪzəbl] adj recommandable, indiqué(e)

advise [ədˈvaɪz] vt conseiller; **to ~ sb of sth** aviser or informer qn de qch; **to ~ against sth/doing sth** déconseiller qch/conseiller de ne pas faire qch; **adviser, advisor** n conseiller(-ère); **advisory** adj consultatif(-ive)

advocate n [ˈædvəkɪt] (lawyer) avocat (plaidant); (upholder) défenseur m, avocat(e) ▷ vt [ˈædvəkeɪt] recommander, prôner; **to be an ~ of** être partisan(e) de

Aegean [iːˈdʒiːən] n, adj: **the ~ (Sea)** la mer Égée, l'Égée f

aerial [ˈɛərɪəl] n antenne f ▷ adj aérien(ne)

aerobics [ɛəˈrəubɪks] n aérobic m

aeroplane [ˈɛərəpleɪn] n (BRIT) avion m

aerosol [ˈɛərəsɒl] n aérosol m

affair [əˈfɛər] n affaire f; (also: **love ~**) liaison f; aventure f

affect [əˈfɛkt] vt affecter; (subj: disease) atteindre; **affected** adj affecté(e)

affection [əˈfɛkʃən] n affection f; **affectionate** adj affectueux(-euse)

afflict [əˈflɪkt] vt affliger

affluent [ˈæfluənt] adj (person, family, surroundings) aisé(e), riche; **the ~ society** la société d'abondance

afford [əˈfɔːd] vt (behaviour) se permettre; (provide) fournir, procurer; **can we ~ a car?** avons-nous de quoi acheter ou les moyens d'acheter une voiture?; **affordable** adj abordable

Afghanistan [æfˈɡænɪstæn] n Afghanistan m

afraid [əˈfreɪd] adj effrayé(e); **to be ~ of or to** avoir peur de; **I am ~ that** je crains que + sub; **I'm ~ so/not** oui/non, malheureusement

Africa [ˈæfrɪkə] n Afrique f; **African** adj africain(e) ▷ n africain(e); **African-American** adj afro-américain(e) ▷ n Afro-Américain(e)

after [ˈɑːftər] prep, adv après ▷ conj

après jour; **it's quarter ~ two** (us) il est deux heures et quart; **~ having done/~ he left** après avoir fait/après son départ; **to name sb ~ sb** donner à qn le nom de qn; **to ask ~ sb** demander des nouvelles de qn; **what/who are you ~?** que/qui cherchez-vous? **~ you!** après vous!; **~ all** après tout; **after-effects** npl (of disaster, radiation, drink etc) répercussions fpl; (of illness) séquelles fpl, suites fpl; **aftermath** n conséquences fpl; **afternoon** n après-midi m or f; **after-shave (lotion)** n lotion f après-rasage; **after-sun (lotion/cream)** n après-soleil m inv; **afterwards** (us **afterward**) adv après

again [ə'gen] adv de nouveau, encore (une fois); **to do sth ~** refaire qch; **~ and ~** à plusieurs reprises

against [ə'genst] prep contre; (compared to) par rapport à

age [eɪdʒ] n âge m ▷ vt, vi vieillir; **he is 20 years of ~** il a 20 ans; **to come of ~** atteindre sa majorité; **it's been ~s since I saw you** ça fait une éternité que je ne t'ai pas vu; **~d** 10 âgé(e) de 10 ans; **age group** n tranche f d'âge; **age limit** n limite f d'âge

agency ['eɪdʒənsɪ] n agence f

agenda [ə'dʒɛndə] n ordre du jour
Be careful not to translate agenda by the French word agenda.

agent ['eɪdʒənt] n agent m; (firm) concessionnaire m

aggravate ['ægrəveɪt] vt (situation) aggraver; (annoy) exaspérer, agacer

aggression [ə'grɛʃən] n agression f

aggressive [ə'grɛsɪv] adj agressif(-ive)

agile ['ædʒaɪl] adj agile

agitated ['ædʒɪteɪtɪd] adj inquiet(-ète)

AGM n abbr (= annual general meeting) AG f

ago [ə'gəu] adv: **2 days ~** il y a 2 jours; **not long ~** il n'y a pas longtemps; **how long ~?** il y a combien de temps (de cela)?

agony ['ægənɪ] n (pain) douleur f atroce; (distress) angoisse f; **to be in ~**

souffrir le martyre

agree [ə'gri:] vt (price) convenir de ▷ vi: **to ~ with** (person) être d'accord avec; (statements etc) concorder avec; (Ling) s'accorder avec; **to ~ to do** accepter de or consentir à faire; **to ~ to sth** consentir à qch; **to ~ that** (admit) convenir or reconnaître que; **garlic doesn't ~ with me** je ne supporte pas l'ail; **agreeable** adj (pleasant) agréable; (willing) consentant(e), d'accord; **agreed** adj (time, place) convenu(e); **agreement** n accord m; **in agreement** d'accord

agricultural [ægrɪ'kʌltʃərəl] adj agricole

agriculture ['ægrɪkʌltʃər] n agriculture f

ahead [ə'hɛd] adv en avant; devant; **go right or straight ~** (direction) allez tout droit; **go ~!** (permission) allez-y!; **~ of** devant; (fig: schedule etc) en avance sur; **~ of time** en avance

aid [eɪd] n aide f; (device) appareil m ▷ vt aider; **in ~ of** en faveur de

aide [eɪd] n (person) assistant(e)

AIDS [eɪdz] n abbr (= acquired immune (or immuno-)deficiency syndrome) SIDA m

ailing ['eɪlɪŋ] adj (person) souffreteux(euse); (economy) malade

ailment ['eɪlmənt] n affection f

aim [eɪm] vt: **to ~ sth (at)** (gun, camera) braquer or pointer qch (sur); (missile) lancer qch (à or contre or en direction de); (remark, blow) destiner or adresser qch (à); **to ~** (also: **to take ~**) viser ▷ n but m; (skill): **his ~ is bad** il vise mal; **to ~ at** viser; (fig) viser à; **to ~ to do** avoir l'intention de faire

ain't [eɪnt] (inf) = **am not**; **aren't**; **isn't**

air [ɛə] n air m ▷ vt aérer; (idea, grievance, views) mettre sur le tapis ▷ cpd (currents, attack etc) aérien(ne); **to throw sth into the ~** (ball etc) jeter qch en l'air; **by ~** par avion; **to be on the ~** (Radio, TV: programme) être diffusé(e); (: station) émettre; **airbag** n airbag m; **airbed** n (BRIT) matelas

m pneumatique; **airborne** *adj* (plane)
en vol; **as soon as the plane was
airborne** dès que l'avion eut décollé;
air-conditioned *adj* climatisé(e), à
air conditionné; **air conditioning** n
climatisation f; **aircraft** n inv avion m;
airfield n terrain m d'aviation; **Air
Force** n Armée f de l'air; **air hostess**
n (BRIT) hôtesse f de l'air; **airing
cupboard** n (BRIT) placard qui contient
la chaudière et dans lequel on met le linge
à sécher; **airlift** n pont aérien; **airline** n
ligne aérienne, compagnie aérienne;
airliner n avion m de ligne; **airmail**
n: **by airmail** par avion; **airplane** n
(US) avion m; **airport** n aéroport m;
air raid n attaque aérienne; **airsick**
adj: **to be airsick** avoir le mal de l'air;
airspace n espace m aérien; **airstrip** n
terrain m d'atterrissage; **air terminal**
n aérogare f; **airtight** *adj* hermétique;
air-traffic controller n aiguilleur m
du ciel; **airy** *adj* bien aéré(e); (manners)
dégagé(e)

aisle [aɪl] n (of church: central) allée f
centrale; (: side) nef f latérale, bas-côté
m; (in theatre, supermarket) allée; (on
plane) couloir; **aisle seat** n place f
côté couloir

ajar [əˈdʒɑːʳ] *adj* entrouvert(e)

à la carte [ælæˈkɑːt] *adv* à la carte

alarm [əˈlɑːm] n alarme f ▷ vt alarmer;
alarm call n coup m de fil pour
réveiller; **could I have an alarm call at
7 am, please?** pouvez-vous me réveiller
à 7 heures, s'il vous plaît?; **alarm
clock** n réveille-matin m inv, réveil m;
alarmed *adj* (frightened) alarmé(e);
(protected by an alarm) protégé(e) par
un système d'alarme; **alarming** *adj*
alarmant(e)

Albania [ælˈbeɪnɪə] n Albanie f

albeit [ɔːlˈbiːɪt] conj bien que + sub,
encore que + sub

album [ˈælbəm] n album m

alcohol [ˈælkəhɒl] n alcool m;
alcohol-free *adj* sans alcool; **alcoholic**
[ælkəˈhɒlɪk] *adj*, n alcoolique (m/f)

alcove [ˈælkəuv] n alcôve f

ale [eɪl] n bière f

alert [əˈlɜːt] *adj* alerte, vif (vive);
(watchful) vigilant(e) ▷ n alerte f ▷ vt
alerter; **on the ~** sur le qui-vive; (Mil) en
état d'alerte

algebra [ˈældʒɪbrə] n algèbre m

Algeria [ælˈdʒɪərɪə] n Algérie f

Algerian [ælˈdʒɪərɪən] *adj* algérien(ne)
▷ n Algérien(ne)

Algiers [ælˈdʒɪəz] n Alger m

alias [ˈeɪlɪæs] *adv* alias ▷ n faux nom,
nom d'emprunt

alibi [ˈælɪbaɪ] n alibi m

alien [ˈeɪlɪən] n (from abroad)
étranger(-ère); (from outer space)
extraterrestre ▷ *adj*: **~ (to)**
étranger(-ère) (à); **alienate** vt aliéner;
(subj: person) s'aliéner

alight [əˈlaɪt] *adj* en feu ▷ vi mettre
pied à terre; (passenger) descendre;
(bird) se poser

align [əˈlaɪn] vt aligner

alike [əˈlaɪk] *adj* semblable, pareil(le)
▷ *adv* de même; **to look ~** se ressembler

alive [əˈlaɪv] *adj* vivant(e), (active)
plein(e) de vie

⊙ **KEYWORD**

all [ɔːl] *adj* (singular) tout(e); (plural)
tous (toutes); **all day** toute la journée;
all night toute la nuit; **all men** tous
les hommes; **all five** tous les cinq; **all
the books** tous les livres; **all his life**
toute sa vie

▷ *pron* **1** tout; **I ate it all, I ate all of it**
j'ai tout mangé; **all of us went** nous
y sommes tous allés; **all of the boys
went** tous les garçons y sont allés;
is that all? c'est tout?; (in shop) ce
sera tout?

2 (in phrases): **above all** surtout;
after all après tout; **at
all: not at all** (in answer to question) pas
du tout; (in answer to thanks) je vous en
prie!; **I'm not at all tired** je ne suis pas
du tout fatigué(e); **anything at all will**

do n'importe quoi fera l'affaire; **all in all** tout bien considéré, en fin de compte ▷ adv: **all alone** tout(e) seul(e); **it's not as hard as all that** ce n'est pas si difficile que ça; **all the more/the better** d'autant plus/mieux; **all but** presque, pratiquement; **the score is 2 all** le score est de 2 partout

Allah ['ælə] n Allah m

allegation [ælɪ'geɪʃən] n allégation f

alleged [ə'lɛdʒd] adj prétendu(e); **allegedly** adv à ce que l'on prétend, paraît-il

allegiance [ə'liːdʒəns] n fidélité f, obéissance f

allergic [ə'lɜːdʒɪk] adj: **~ to** allergique à; **I'm ~ to penicillin** je suis allergique à la pénicilline

allergy ['ælədʒɪ] n allergie f

alleviate [ə'liːvɪeɪt] vt soulager, adoucir

alley ['ælɪ] n ruelle f

alliance [ə'laɪəns] n alliance f

allied ['ælaɪd] adj allié(e)

alligator ['ælɪgeɪtə'] n alligator m

all-in [ɔːlɪn] adj, adv (BRIT: charge) tout compris

allocate ['æləkeɪt] vt (share out) répartir, distribuer; **to ~ sth to** (duties) assigner or attribuer qch à; (sum, time) allouer qch à

allot [ə'lɒt] vt (share out) répartir, distribuer; **to ~ sth to** (time) allouer qch à; (duties) assigner qch à

all-out ['ɔːlaʊt] adj (effort etc) total(e)

allow [ə'laʊ] vt (practice, behaviour) permettre, autoriser; (sum to spend etc) accorder, allouer; (sum time estimated) compter, prévoir; (claim, goal) admettre; (concede): **to ~ that** convenir que; **to ~ sb to do** permettre à qn de faire, autoriser qn à faire; **he is ~ed to ...** on lui permet de ...; **allow for** vt fus tenir compte de; **allowance** n (money received) allocation f; (: from parent etc) subside m; (: for expenses) indemnité f; (us: pocket money) argent m

de poche; (Tax) somme f déductible du revenu imposable, abattement m; **to make allowances for** (person) essayer de comprendre; (thing) tenir compte de

all right adv (feel, work) bien; (as answer) d'accord

ally n ['ælaɪ] allié m ▷ vt [ə'laɪ]: **to ~ o.s. with** s'allier avec

almighty [ɔːl'maɪtɪ] adj tout(e)-puissant(e); (tremendous) énorme

almond ['ɑːmənd] n amande f

almost ['ɔːlməʊst] adv presque

alone [ə'ləʊn] adj, adv seul(e); **to leave sb ~** laisser qn tranquille; **to leave sth ~** ne pas toucher à qch; **let ~ ...** sans parler de ...; encore moins ...

along [ə'lɒŋ] prep le long de ▷ adv: **is he coming ~ with us?** vient-il avec nous?; **he was hopping/limping ~** il venait or avançait en sautillant/boitant; **~ with** avec, en plus de; (person) en compagnie de; **all ~** (all the time) depuis le début; **alongside** prep (along) le long de; (beside) à côté de ▷ adv bord à bord; côte à côte

aloof [ə'luːf] adj distant(e) ▷ adv: **to stand ~** se tenir à l'écart or à distance

aloud [ə'laʊd] adv à haute voix

alphabet ['ælfəbɛt] n alphabet m

Alps [ælps] npl: **the ~** les Alpes fpl

already [ɔːl'rɛdɪ] adv déjà

alright ['ɔːl'raɪt] adv (BRIT) = **all right**

also ['ɔːlsəʊ] adv aussi

altar ['ɔltə'] n autel m

alter ['ɔltə'] vt, vi changer; **alteration** [ɔltə'reɪʃən] n changement m, modification f; **alterations** npl (Sewing) retouches fpl; (Archit) modifications fpl

alternate adj [ɔl'tɜːnɪt] alterné(e), alternant(e), alternatif(-ive); (us = **alternative**) ▷ vi ['ɔltəːneɪt] alterner; **to ~ with** alterner avec; **on ~ days** un jour sur deux, tous les deux jours

alternative [ɔl'tɜːnətɪv] adj (solution, plan) autre, de remplacement; (lifestyle) parallèle ▷ n (choice) alternative f; (other possibility) autre possibilité f;

~ **medicine** médecine alternative, médecine douce; **alternatively** adv: **alternatively one could ...** une autre ou l'autre solution serait de ...

although [ɔːlˈðəu] conj bien que + sub

altitude [ˈæltɪtjuːd] n altitude f

altogether [ɔːltəˈgɛðə^r] adv entièrement, tout à fait; (on the whole) tout compte fait; (in all) en tout

aluminium [æljuˈmɪnɪəm] (BRIT **aluminum**) [əˈluːmɪnəm] (US) n aluminium m

always [ˈɔːlweɪz] adv toujours

Alzheimer's (disease) [ˈæltshaɪməz-] n maladie f d'Alzheimer

am [æm] vb see **be**

a.m. adv abbr (= ante meridiem) du matin

amalgamate [əˈmælgəmeɪt] vt, vi fusionner

amass [əˈmæs] vt amasser

amateur [ˈæmətə^r] n amateur m

amaze [əˈmeɪz] vt stupéfier; **to be ~d (at)** être stupéfait(e) (de); **amazed** adj stupéfait(e); **amazement** n surprise f, étonnement m; **amazing** adj étonnant(e), incroyable; (bargain, offer) exceptionnel(le)

Amazon [ˈæməzən] n (Geo) Amazone f

ambassador [æmˈbæsədə^r] n ambassadeur m

amber [ˈæmbə^r] n ambre m; **at ~** (BRIT Aut) à l'orange

ambiguous [æmˈbɪgjuəs] adj ambigu(ë)

ambition [æmˈbɪʃən] n ambition f; **ambitious** [æmˈbɪʃəs] adj ambitieux(-euse)

ambulance [ˈæmbjuləns] n ambulance f; **call an ~!** appelez une ambulance!

ambush [ˈæmbuʃ] n embuscade f ▷ vt tendre une embuscade à

amen [ɑːˈmɛn] excl amen

amend [əˈmɛnd] vt (law) amender; (text) corriger; **to make ~s** réparer ses torts, faire amende honorable; **amendment** n (to law) amendement m; (to text) correction f

amenities [əˈmiːnɪtɪz] npl aménagements mpl, équipements mpl

America [əˈmɛrɪkə] n Amérique f; **American** adj américain(e) ▷ n Américain(e); **American football** n (BRIT) football m américain

amicable [ˈæmɪkəbl] adj amical(e); (Law) à l'amiable

amid(st) [əˈmɪd(st)] prep parmi, au milieu de

ammunition [æmjuˈnɪʃən] n munitions fpl

amnesty [ˈæmnɪstɪ] n amnistie f

among(st) [əˈmʌŋ(st)] prep parmi, entre

amount [əˈmaunt] n (sum of money) somme f; (total) montant m; (quantity) quantité f; nombre m ▷ vi: **to ~ to** (total) s'élever à; (be same as) équivaloir à, revenir à

amp(ère) [ˈæmp(ɛə^r)] n ampère m

ample [ˈæmpl] adj ample, spacieux(-euse); (enough): **this is ~** c'est largement suffisant; **to have ~ time/room** avoir bien assez de temps/place

amplifier [ˈæmplɪfaɪə^r] n amplificateur m

amputate [ˈæmpjuteɪt] vt amputer

Amtrak [ˈæmtræk] (US) n société mixte de transports ferroviaires interurbains pour voyageurs

amuse [əˈmjuːz] vt amuser; **amusement** n amusement m; (pastime) distraction f; **amusement arcade** n salle f de jeu; **amusement park** n parc m d'attractions

amusing [əˈmjuːzɪŋ] adj amusant(e), divertissant(e)

an [æn, ən, n] indef art see **a**

anaemia [əˈniːmɪə] (US **anemia**) n anémie f

anaemic [əˈniːmɪk] (US **anemic**) adj anémique

anaesthetic [ænɪsˈθɛtɪk] (US **anesthetic**) n anesthésique m

analog(ue) [ˈænəlɔg] adj (watch, computer) analogique

analogy [əˈnælədʒɪ] n analogie f

analyse ['ænəlaɪz] (us **analyze**) vt analyser; **analysis** (pl **analyses**) [ə'næləsis, -si:z] n analyse f; **analyst** ['ænəlɪst] n (political analyst etc) analyste m/f; (us) psychanalyste m/f

analyze ['ænəlaɪz] vt (us) = **analyse**

anarchy ['ænəkɪ] n anarchie f

anatomy [ə'nætəmɪ] n anatomie f

ancestor ['ænsɪstə*] n ancêtre m, aïeul m

anchor ['æŋkə*] n ancre f ▷ vi (also: **to drop ~**) jeter l'ancre, mouiller ▷ vt mettre à l'ancre; (fig): **to ~ sth to** fixer qch à

anchovy ['æntʃəvɪ] n anchois m

ancient ['eɪnʃənt] adj ancien(ne), antique; (person) d'un âge vénérable; (car) antédiluvien(ne)

and [ænd] conj et; **~ so on** et ainsi de suite; **try ~ come** tâchez de venir; **come ~ sit here** venez vous asseoir ici; **he talked ~ talked** il a parlé pendant des heures; **better ~ better** de mieux en mieux; **more ~ more** de plus en plus

Andorra [æn'dɔ:rə] n (principauté d')Andorre f

anemia etc [ə'ni:mɪə] (us) = **anaemia** etc

anesthetic [ænɪs'θetɪk] (us) = **anaesthetic**

angel ['eɪndʒəl] n ange m

anger ['æŋgə*] n colère f

angina [æn'dʒaɪnə] n angine f de poitrine

angle ['æŋgl] n angle m; **from the ~ of** leur point de vue

angler ['æŋglə*] n pêcheur(-euse) à la ligne

Anglican ['æŋglɪkən] adj, n anglican(e)

angling ['æŋglɪŋ] n pêche f à la ligne

angrily ['æŋgrɪlɪ] adv avec colère

angry ['æŋgrɪ] adj en colère, furieux(-euse); (wound) enflammé(e); **to be ~ with sb/at sth** être furieux contre qn/au sujet de qch; **to get ~** se fâcher, se mettre en colère

anguish ['æŋgwɪʃ] n angoisse f

animal ['ænɪməl] n animal m ▷ adj animal(e)

animated ['ænɪmeɪtɪd] adj animé(e)

animation [ænɪ'meɪʃən] n (of person) entrain m; (of street, Cine) animation f

aniseed ['ænɪsi:d] n anis m

ankle ['æŋkl] n cheville f

annex ['æneks] n (BRIT: also: **-e**) annexe f ▷ vt [ə'neks] annexer

anniversary [ænɪ'və:sərɪ] n anniversaire m

announce [ə'naʊns] vt annoncer; (birth, death) faire part de; **announcement** n annonce f; (for births etc: in newspaper) avis m de faire-part; (: letter, card) faire-part m; **announcer** n (Radio, TV: between programmes) speaker(ine); (: in a programme) présentateur(-trice)

annoy [ə'nɔɪ] vt agacer, ennuyer, contrarier; **don't get ~ed!** ne vous fâchez pas!; **annoying** adj agaçant(e), contrariant(e)

annual ['ænjuəl] adj annuel(le) ▷ n (Bot) plante annuelle; (book) album m; **annually** adv annuellement

annum ['ænəm] n see **per**

anonymous [ə'nɒnɪməs] adj anonyme

anorak ['ænəræk] n anorak m

anorexia [ænə'reksɪə] n (also: **~ nervosa**) anorexie f

anorexic [ænə'reksɪk] adj, n anorexique (m/f)

another [ə'nʌðə*] adj: **~ book** (one more) un autre livre, encore un livre, un livre de plus; (a different one) un autre livre ▷ pron un(e) autre, encore un(e), un(e) de plus; see also **one**

answer ['ɑ:nsə*] n réponse f; (to problem) solution f ▷ vi répondre ▷ vt (reply to) répondre à; (problem) résoudre; (prayer) exaucer; **in ~ to your letter** suite à or en réponse à votre lettre; **to ~ the phone** répondre (au téléphone); **to ~ the bell** or **the door** aller or venir ouvrir (la porte); **answer back** vi répondre, répliquer; **answerphone** n (esp BRIT) répondeur m (téléphonique)

ant [ænt] n fourmi f

Antarctic [ænt'ɑːktɪk] n: **the ~** l'Antarctique m

antelope [ˈæntɪləʊp] n antilope f

antenatal [ˈæntɪˈneɪtl] adj prénatal(e)

antenna (pl **-e**) [ænˈtenə, -niː] n antenne f

anthem [ˈænθəm] n: **national ~** hymne national

anthology [ænˈθɒlədʒɪ] n anthologie f

anthrax [ˈænθræks] n anthrax m

anthropology [ænθrəˈpɒlədʒɪ] n anthropologie f

anti [ˈæntɪ] prefix anti-: **antibiotic** [ˈæntɪbaɪˈɒtɪk] n antibiotique m; **antibody** [ˈæntɪbɒdɪ] n anticorps m

anticipate [ænˈtɪsɪpeɪt] vt s'attendre à, prévoir; (wishes, request) aller au devant de, devancer; **anticipation** [æntɪsɪˈpeɪʃən] n attente f

anticlimax [æntɪˈklaɪmæks] n déception f

anticlockwise [æntɪˈklɒkwaɪz] (BRIT) adv dans le sens inverse des aiguilles d'une montre

antics [ˈæntɪks] npl singeries fpl

anti: antidote [ˈæntɪdəʊt] n antidote m, contrepoison m; **antifreeze** [ˈæntɪfriːz] n antigel m; **anti-globalization** [æntɪgləʊbəlaɪˈzeɪʃən] n antimondialisation f; **antihistamine** [æntɪˈhɪstəmiːn] n antihistaminique m; **antiperspirant** [æntɪˈpəːspɪrənt] n déodorant m

antique [ænˈtiːk] n (ornament) objet m d'art ancien; (furniture) meuble ancien ▷ adj ancien(ne); **antique shop** n magasin m d'antiquités

antiseptic [æntɪˈseptɪk] adj, n antiseptique (m)

antisocial [æntɪˈsəʊʃəl] adj (unfriendly) peu liant(e), insociable; (against society) antisocial(e)

antlers [ˈæntləz] npl bois mpl, ramure f

anxiety [æŋˈzaɪətɪ] n anxiété f; (keenness): **~ to do** grand désir or impatience f de faire

anxious [ˈæŋkʃəs] adj (très) inquiet(-ète); (always worried)

anxieux(-euse); (worrying) angoissant(e); (keen): **~ to do/that** qui tient beaucoup à faire/à ce que + sub; impatient(e) de faire/que + sub

○ **KEYWORD**

any [ˈenɪ] adj **1** (in questions etc: singular) du, de l', de la; (: plural) des; **do you have any butter/children/ink?** avez-vous du beurre/des enfants/de l'encre?

2 (with negative) de, d'; **I don't have any money/books** je n'ai pas d'argent/de livres

3 (no matter which) n'importe quel(le); (each and every) tout(e), chaque; **choose any book you like** vous pouvez choisir n'importe quel livre; **any teacher you ask will tell you** n'importe quel professeur vous le dira

4 (in phrases): **in any case** de toute façon; **any day now** d'un jour à l'autre; **at any moment** à tout moment, d'un instant à l'autre; **at any time** en tout cas; **any time** n'importe quand; **he might come (at) any time** il pourrait venir n'importe quand; **come (at) any time** venez quand vous voulez

▷ pron **1** (in questions etc) en; **have you got any?** est-ce que vous en avez?; **can any of you sing?** est-ce que parmi vous il y en a qui savent chanter?

2 (with negative) en; **I don't have any (of them)** je n'en ai pas, je n'en ai aucun

3 (no matter which one(s)) n'importe lequel or laquelle; (anybody) n'importe qui; **take any of those books you like** vous pouvez prendre n'importe lequel de ces livres

▷ adv **1** (in questions etc): **do you want any more soup/sandwiches?** voulez-vous encore de la soupe/des sandwichs?; **are you feeling any better?** est-ce que vous vous sentez mieux?

2 (with negative): **I can't hear him any more** je ne l'entends plus; **don't wait any longer** n'attendez pas plus longtemps; **anybody** pron n'importe qui; (in interrogative sentences) quelqu'un; (in negative sentences): **I don't see anybody** je ne vois personne; **if anybody should phone ...** si quelqu'un téléphone ...; **anyhow** adv quoi qu'il en soit; (haphazardly) n'importe comment; **do it anyhow you like** faites-le comme vous voulez; **she leaves things just anyhow** elle laisse tout traîner; **I shall go anyhow** j'irai de toute façon; **anyone** pron = **anybody**; **anything** pron (no matter what) n'importe quoi; (in questions) quelque chose; (with negative) ne ... rien; **can you see anything?** tu vois quelque chose?; **if anything happens to me ...** s'il m'arrive quoi que ce soit ...; **you can say anything you like** vous pouvez dire ce que vous voulez; **anything will do** n'importe quoi fera l'affaire; **he'll eat anything** il mange de tout; **anytime** adv (at any moment) à un moment à l'autre; (whenever) n'importe quand; **anyway** adv de toute façon; **anyway, I couldn't come even if I wanted to** de toute façon, je ne pouvais pas venir même si je le voulais; **I shall go anyway** j'irai quand même; **why are you phoning, anyway?** au fait, pourquoi tu me téléphones?; **anywhere** adv n'importe où; (in interrogative sentences) quelque part; (in negative sentences): **I can't see him anywhere** je ne le vois nulle part; **can you see him anywhere?** tu le vois quelque part?; **put the books down anywhere** pose les livres n'importe où; **anywhere in the world** (no matter where) n'importe où dans le monde

apart [ə'pɑːt] adv (to one side) à part; de côté; à l'écart; (separately) séparément; **to take/pull ~** démonter; **10 miles/10 years long way ~** à 10 miles/très éloignés l'un de l'autre; **~ from** prep à part, excepté

apartment [ə'pɑːtmənt] n (US)

appartement m, logement m; (room) chambre f; **apartment building** n (US) immeuble m; maison divisée en appartements

apathy ['æpəθɪ] n apathie f, indifférence f

ape [eɪp] n (grand) singe ▷ vt singer

aperitif [ə'perɪtɪf] n apéritif m

aperture ['æpətʃjuə'] n orifice m, ouverture f; (Phot) ouverture (du diaphragme)

APEX ['eɪpeks] n abbr (Aviat: = advance purchase excursion) APEX m

apologize [ə'pɒlədʒaɪz] vi: **to ~ (for sth to sb)** s'excuser (de qch auprès de qn), présenter des excuses (à qn pour qch)

apology [ə'pɒlədʒɪ] n excuses fpl

apostrophe [ə'pɒstrəfɪ] n apostrophe f

appal [ə'pɔːl] (us **appall**) vt consterner, atterrer, horrifier; **appalling** adj épouvantable; (stupidity) consternant(e)

apparatus [æpə'reɪtəs] n appareil m, dispositif m; (in gymnasium) agrès mpl

apparent [ə'pærənt] adj apparent(e); **apparently** adv apparemment

appeal [ə'piːl] vi (Law) faire ou interjeter appel ▷ n (Law) appel m; (request) prière f; (charm) attrait m, charme m; **to ~ for** demander (instamment); implorer; **to ~ to** (beg) faire appel à; (be attractive) plaire à; **it doesn't ~ to me** cela ne m'attire pas; **appealing** adj (attractive) attrayant(e)

appear [ə'pɪə'] vi apparaître, se montrer; (Law) comparaître; (publication) paraître, sortir, être publié(e); (seem) paraître, sembler; **it would ~ that** il semble que; **to ~ in Hamlet** jouer dans Hamlet; **to ~ on TV** passer à la télé; **appearance** n apparition f; parution f; (look, aspect) apparence f, aspect m

appendices [ə'pendɪsiːz] npl of **appendix**

appendicitis [əpendɪ'saɪtɪs] n appendicite f

appendix (pl **appendices**) [ə'pendɪks,

-si:z] *n* appendice *m*

appetite ['æpitait] *n* appétit *m*

appetizer ['æpitaizə*r*] *n* (food) amuse-gueule *m*; (drink) apéritif *m*

applaud [ə'plɔ:d] *vt, vi* applaudir

applause [ə'plɔ:z] *n* applaudissements *mpl*

apple ['æpl] *n* pomme *f*; **apple pie** *n* tarte *f* aux pommes

appliance [ə'plaiəns] *n* appareil *m*

applicable [ə'plikəbl] *adj* applicable; **to be ~ to** (relevant) valoir pour

applicant ['æplikənt] *n*: **~ (for)** candidat(e) (à)

application [æpli'keiʃən] *n* application *f*; (for a job, a grant etc) demande *f*, candidature *f*; **application form** *n* formulaire *m* de demande

apply [ə'plai] *vt*: **to ~ to** (paint, ointment) appliquer (sur); (law, etc) appliquer à ▷ *vi*: **to ~ to** (ask) s'adresser à; (be suitable for, relevant to) s'appliquer à; **to ~ (for)** (permit, grant) faire une demande (en vue d'obtenir); (job) poser sa candidature (pour), faire une demande d'emploi (concernant); **to ~ o.s. to** s'appliquer à

appoint [ə'pɔint] *vt* (to post) nommer, engager; (date, place) fixer, désigner; **appointment** *n* (to post) nomination *f*; (job) poste *m*; (arrangement to meet) rendez-vous *m*; **to have an appointment** avoir un rendez-vous; **to make an appointment (with)** prendre rendez-vous (avec); **I'd like to make an appointment** je voudrais prendre rendez-vous

appraisal [ə'preizl] *n* évaluation *f*

appreciate [ə'pri:ʃieit] *vt* (like) apprécier, faire cas de; (be grateful for) être reconnaissant(e) de; (be aware of) comprendre, se rendre compte de ▷ *vi* (Finance) prendre de la valeur; **appreciation** [əpri:ʃi'eiʃən] *n* appréciation *f*; (gratitude) reconnaissance *f*; (Finance) hausse *f*, valorisation *f*

apprehension [æpri'hɛnʃən] *n*

appréhension *f*, inquiétude *f*

apprehensive [æpri'hɛnsiv] *adj* inquiet(-ète), appréhensif(-ive)

apprentice [ə'prɛntis] *n* apprenti *m*

approach [ə'prəutʃ] *vi* approcher ▷ *vt* (come near) approcher de; (ask, apply to) s'adresser à; (subject, passer-by) aborder ▷ *n* approche *f*; accès *m*, abord *m*; démarche (intellectuelle)

appropriate [adj ə'prəupriit] (tool etc) qui convient, approprié(e); (moment, remark) opportun(e) ▷ *vt* [ə'prəuprieit] (take) s'approprier

approval [ə'pru:vəl] *n* approbation *f*; **on ~** (Comm) à l'examen

approve [ə'pru:v] *vt* approuver; **approve of** *vt fus* (thing) approuver; (person): **they don't ~ of her** ils n'ont pas bonne opinion d'elle

approximate [ə'prɔksimit] *adj* approximatif(-ive); **approximately** *adv* approximativement

Apr. *abbr* = **April**

apricot ['eiprikɔt] *n* abricot *m*

April ['eiprəl] *n* avril *m*; **April Fools' Day** *n* le premier avril

▶ **APRIL FOOLS' DAY**

April Fools' Day est le 1er avril, à l'occasion duquel on fait des farces de toutes sortes. Les victimes de ces farces sont les "April fools". Traditionnellement, on n'est censé faire des farces que jusqu'à midi.

apron ['eiprən] *n* tablier *m*

apt [æpt] *adj* (suitable) approprié(e); (likely): **~ to do** susceptible de faire, ayant tendance à faire

aquarium [ə'kwɛəriəm] *n* aquarium *m*

Aquarius [ə'kwɛəriəs] *n* le Verseau

Arab ['ærəb] *n* Arabe *m/f* ▷ *adj* arabe

Arabia [ə'reibiə] *n* Arabie *f*; **Arabian** *adj* arabe; **Arabic** ['ærəbik] *adj, n* arabe (*m*)

arbitrary ['a:bitrəri] *adj* arbitraire

arbitration [a:bi'treiʃən] *n*

arbitrage *m*

arc [ɑːk] *n* arc *m*

arcade [ɑːˈkeɪd] *n* arcade *f*; (*passage with shops*) passage *m*, galerie *f*; (*with games*) salle *f* de jeu

arch [ɑːtʃ] *n* arche *f*; (*of foot*) cambrure *f*, voûte *f* plantaire ▷ *vt* arquer, cambrer

archaeology [ɑːkɪˈɒlədʒɪ] (*us* **archeology**) *n* archéologie *f*

archbishop [ɑːtʃˈbɪʃəp] *n* archevêque *m*

archeology [ɑːkɪˈɒlədʒɪ] (*us*) = **archaeology**

architect [ˈɑːkɪtɛkt] *n* architecte *m*; **architectural** [ɑːkɪˈtɛktʃərəl] *adj* architectural(e); **architecture** *n* architecture *f*

archive [ˈɑːkaɪv] *n* (*often pl*) archives *fpl*

Arctic [ˈɑːktɪk] *adj* arctique ▷ *n*: **the ~** l'Arctique *m*

are [ɑː] *vb* see **be**

area [ˈɛərɪə] *n* (*Geom*) superficie *f*; (*zone*) région *f*; (: *smaller*) secteur *m*; (*in room*) coin *m*; (*knowledge, research*) domaine *m*; **area code** (*us*) (*Tel*) indicatif *m* de zone

arena [əˈriːnə] *n* arène *f*

aren't [ɑːnt] = **are not**

Argentina [ɑːdʒənˈtiːnə] *n* Argentine *f*; **Argentinian** [ɑːdʒənˈtɪnɪən] *adj* argentin(e) ▷ *n* Argentin(e)

arguably [ˈɑːɡjʊəblɪ] *adv*: **it is ~ ...** on peut soutenir que c'est ...

argue [ˈɑːɡjuː] *vi* (*quarrel*) se disputer; (*reason*) argumenter; **to ~ that** objecter or alléguer que, donner comme argument que

argument [ˈɑːɡjʊmənt] *n* (*quarrel*) dispute *f*, discussion *f*; (*reasons*) argument *m*

Aries [ˈɛərɪz] *n* le Bélier

arise (*pt* **arose**, *pp* **~n**) [əˈraɪz, əˈrəʊz, əˈrɪzn] *vi* survenir, se présenter

arithmetic [əˈrɪθmətɪk] *n* arithmétique *f*

arm [ɑːm] *n* bras *m* ▷ *vt* armer; **arms** *npl* (*weapons, Heraldry*) armes *fpl*; **~ in ~** bras dessus bras dessous; **armchair** *n* fauteuil *m*

armed [ɑːmd] *adj* armé(e); **armed forces** *npl*: **the armed forces** les forces armées; **armed robbery** *n* vol *m* à main armée

armour (*us* **armor**) [ˈɑːmə] *n* armure *f*; (*Mil: tanks*) blindés *mpl*

armpit [ˈɑːmpɪt] *n* aisselle *f*

armrest [ˈɑːmrɛst] *n* accoudoir *m*

army [ˈɑːmɪ] *n* armée *f*

A road (*BRIT*) = route nationale

aroma [əˈrəʊmə] *n* arôme *m*; **aromatherapy** *n* aromathérapie *f*

arose [əˈrəʊz] *pt* of **arise**

around [əˈraʊnd] *adv* (tout) autour; (*nearby*) dans les parages ▷ *prep* autour de; (*near*) près de; (*fig: about*) environ; (: *date, time*) vers; **is he ~?** est-il dans les parages?

arouse [əˈraʊz] *vt* (*sleeper*) éveiller; (*curiosity, passions*) éveiller, susciter; (*anger*) exciter

arrange [əˈreɪndʒ] *vt* arranger; **to ~ to do sth** prévoir de faire qch; **arrangement** *n* arrangement *m*; **arrangements** *npl* (*plans etc*) arrangements *mpl*, dispositions *fpl*

array [əˈreɪ] *n* (*of objects*) déploiement *m*, étalage *m*

arrears [əˈrɪəz] *npl* arriéré *m*; **to be in ~ with one's rent** devoir un arriéré de loyer

arrest [əˈrɛst] *vt* arrêter; (*sb's attention*) retenir, attirer ▷ *n* arrestation *f*; **under ~** en état d'arrestation

arrival [əˈraɪvl] *n* arrivée *f*; **new ~** nouveau venu/nouvelle venue; (*baby*) nouveau-né(e)

arrive [əˈraɪv] *vi* arriver; **arrive at** *vt fus* (*decision, solution*) parvenir à

arrogance [ˈærəɡəns] *n* arrogance *f*

arrogant [ˈærəɡənt] *adj* arrogant(e)

arrow [ˈærəʊ] *n* flèche *f*

arse [ɑːs] *n* (*BRIT infl*) cul *m* (*!*)

arson [ˈɑːsn] *n* incendie criminel

art [ɑːt] *n* art *m*; **Arts** *npl* (*Scol*) les lettres *fpl*; **art college** *n* école *f* des beaux-arts

artery [ˈɑːtərɪ] n artère f

art gallery n musée m d'art; (saleroom) galerie f de peinture

arthritis [ɑːˈθraɪtɪs] n arthrite f

artichoke [ˈɑːtɪtʃəuk] n artichaut m; **Jerusalem ~** topinambour m

article [ˈɑːtɪkl] n article m

articulate adj [ɑːˈtɪkjulɪt] (person) qui s'exprime clairement et aisément; (speech) bien articulé(e), prononcé(e) clairement ▷ vb [ɑːˈtɪkjuleɪt] ▷ vi articuler, parler distinctement ▷ vt articuler

artificial [ɑːtɪˈfɪʃəl] adj artificiel(le)

artist [ˈɑːtɪst] n artiste m/f; **artistic** [ɑːˈtɪstɪk] adj artistique

art school n = école f des beaux-arts

⭕ **KEYWORD**

as [æz] conj 1 (time: moment) comme, alors que; à mesure que; **he came in as I was leaving** il est arrivé comme je partais; **as the years went by** à mesure que les années passaient; **as from tomorrow** à partir de demain

2 (since, because) comme, puisque; **he left early as he had to be home by 10** comme il or puisqu'il devait être de retour avant 10h, il est parti de bonne heure

3 (referring to manner, way) comme; **do as you wish** faites comme vous voudrez; **as she said** comme elle disait ▷ adv 1 (in comparisons): **as big as** aussi grand que; **twice as big as** deux fois plus grand que; **as much as** autant que; **as much money/many books as** autant d'argent/de livres que; **as soon as** dès que

2 (concerning): **as for or to that** quant à cela, pour ce qui est de cela

3: **as if or though** comme si; **he looked as if he was ill** il avait l'air de malade; see also **long; such; well** ▷ prep (in the capacity of) en tant que, en qualité de; **he works as a driver** il travaille comme chauffeur; **as**

chairman of the company, he ... en tant que président de la société, il ...; **he gave me it as a present** il me l'a offert, il m'en a fait cadeau

a.s.a.p. abbr = **as soon as possible**

asbestos [æzˈbɛstəs] n asbeste m, amiante m

ascent [əˈsɛnt] n (climb) ascension f

ash [æʃ] n (dust) cendre f; (also: ~ **tree**) frêne m

ashamed [əˈʃeɪmd] adj honteux(-euse), confus(e); **to be ~ of** avoir honte de

ashore [əˈʃɔː*] adv à terre

ashtray [ˈæʃtreɪ] n cendrier m

Ash Wednesday n mercredi m des Cendres

Asia [ˈeɪʃə] n Asie f; **Asian** n (from Asia) Asiatique m/f; (BRIT: from Indian subcontinent) Indo-Pakistanais(-e) ▷ adj asiatique; indo-pakistanais(-e)

aside [əˈsaɪd] adv de côté; à l'écart ▷ n aparté m

ask [ɑːsk] vt demander; (invite) inviter; **to ~ sb sth/to do sth** demander à qn qch/de faire qch; **to ~ sb about sth** questionner qn au sujet de qch; se renseigner auprès de qn au sujet de qch; **to ~ (sb) a question** poser une question (à qn); **to ~ sb out to dinner** inviter qn au restaurant; **ask for** vt fus demander; **it's just ~ing for trouble** or **for it** ce serait chercher des ennuis

asleep [əˈsliːp] adj endormi(e); **to fall ~** s'endormir

AS level n abbr (= Advanced Subsidiary level) première partie de l'examen équivalent au baccalauréat

asparagus [əsˈpærəgəs] n asperges fpl

aspect [ˈæspɛkt] n aspect m; (direction in which a building etc faces) orientation f, exposition f

aspirations [æspəˈreɪʃənz] npl (hopes, ambition) aspirations fpl

aspire [əsˈpaɪə*] vi: **to ~ to** aspirer à

aspirin [ˈæsprɪn] n aspirine f

ass [æs] n âne m; (inf) imbécile m/f; (us)

infl) cul m (l)

assassin [əˈsæsɪn] n assassin m;
assassinate vt assassiner

assault [əˈsɔːlt] n (Mil) assaut m; (gen:
attack) agression f ▷ vt attaquer;
(sexually) violenter

assemble [əˈsɛmbl] vt assembler ▷ vi
s'assembler, se rassembler

assembly [əˈsɛmblɪ] n (meeting)
rassemblement m; (parliament)
assemblée f; (construction)
assemblage m

assert [əˈsɜːt] vt affirmer, déclarer;
(authority) faire valoir; (innocence)
protester de; **assertion** [əˈsɜːʃən] n
assertion f, affirmation f

assess [əˈsɛs] vt évaluer, estimer; (tax,
damages) établir or fixer le montant de;
(person) juger la valeur de; **assessment**
n évaluation f, estimation f; (of tax)
fixation f

asset [ˈæsɛt] n avantage m, atout m;
(person) atout; **assets** npl (Comm)
capital m; (movable) avoir(s) m(pl); actif m

assign [əˈsaɪn] vt (date) fixer, arrêter; **to
~ sth to** (task) assigner qch à; (resources)
affecter qch à; **assignment** n (task)
mission f; (homework) devoir m

assist [əˈsɪst] vt aider, assister;
assistance n aide f, assistance f;
assistant n assistant(e), adjoint(e);
(BRIT: also: **shop assistant**)
vendeur(-euse)

associate adj, n [əˈsəʊʃiɪt] associé(e)
▷ vb [əˈsəʊʃieɪt] vt associer ▷ vi: **to ~
with sb** fréquenter qn

association [əsəʊsɪˈeɪʃən] n
association f

assorted [əˈsɔːtɪd] adj assorti(e)

assortment [əˈsɔːtmənt] n
assortiment m; (of people) mélange m

assume [əˈsjuːm] vt supposer;
(responsibilities etc) assumer; (attitude,
name) prendre; adopter

assumption [əˈsʌmpʃən] n
supposition f, hypothèse f; (of power)
assomption f, prise f

assurance [əˈʃʊərəns] n assurance f

assure [əˈʃʊəʳ] vt assurer

asterisk [ˈæstərɪsk] n astérisque m

asthma [ˈæsmə] n asthme m

astonish [əˈstɒnɪʃ] vt étonner,
stupéfier; **astonished** adj étonné(e);
to be astonished at être étonné(e)
de; **astonishing** adj étonnant(e),
stupéfiant(e); **I find it astonishing
that ...** je trouve incroyable que ... + sub;
astonishment n (grand) étonnement m,
stupéfaction f

astound [əˈstaʊnd] vt stupéfier,
sidérer

astray [əˈstreɪ] adv: **to go ~** s'égarer;
(fig) quitter le droit chemin; **to lead ~**
(morally) détourner du droit chemin

astrology [əˈstrɒlədʒɪ] n astrologie f

astronaut [ˈæstrənɔːt] n
astronaute m/f

astronomer [əˈstrɒnəməʳ] n
astronome m

astronomical [æstrəˈnɒmɪkl] adj
astronomique

astronomy [əˈstrɒnəmɪ] n
astronomie f

astute [əˈstjuːt] adj astucieux(-euse),
malin(-igne)

asylum [əˈsaɪləm] n asile m; **asylum
seeker** [-siːkəʳ] n demandeur(-euse)
d'asile

KEYWORD

at [æt] prep 1 (referring to position,
direction) à; **at the top** au sommet; **at
home/school** à la maison or chez soi/à
l'école; **at the baker's** à la boulangerie,
chez le boulanger; **to look at sth**
regarder qch

2 (referring to time) **at 4 o'clock** à 4
heures; **at Christmas** à Noël; **at night**
la nuit; **at times** par moments, parfois

3 (referring to rates, speed etc) à; **at £1
a kilo** une livre le kilo; **two at a time**
deux à la fois; **at 50 km/h** à 50 km/h

4 (referring to manner): **at a stroke** d'un
seul coup; **at peace** en paix

5 (referring to activity): **to be at work** (in

the office etc) être au travail; *(working)* travailler; **to play at cowboys** jouer aux cowboys; **to be good at sth** être bon en qch

6 *(referring to cause):* **shocked/surprised/annoyed at sth** choqué par/étonné de/agacé par qch; **I went at his suggestion** j'y suis allé sur son conseil

7 *(symbol)* arobase f

ate [eɪt] *pt of* **eat**
atheist ['eɪθɪɪst] *n* athée *m/f*
Athens ['æθɪnz] *n* Athènes
athlete ['æθliːt] *n* athlète *m/f*
athletic [æθ'letɪk] *adj* athlétique; **athletics** *n* athlétisme *m*
Atlantic [ət'læntɪk] *adj* atlantique ▷ *n:* **the ~ (Ocean)** l'(océan *m*) Atlantique *m*
atlas ['ætləs] *n* atlas *m*
A.T.M. *n abbr* (= *Automated Telling Machine)* guichet *m* automatique
atmosphere ['ætməsfɪə] *n* (*air)* atmosphère *f*; *(fig: of place etc)* atmosphère, ambiance *f*
atom ['ætəm] *n* atome *m*; **atomic** [ə'tɒmɪk] *adj* atomique; **atom(ic) bomb** *n* bombe *f* atomique
A to Z® *n* (*map)* plan *m* des rues
atrocity [ə'trɒsɪtɪ] *n* atrocité *f*
attach [ə'tætʃ] *vt* (*gen)* attacher; (*document, letter)* joindre; **to be ~ed to sb/sth** (*to like)* être attaché à qn/qch; **attachment** *n* (*tool)* accessoire *m*; (*Comput)* fichier *m* joint; (*love):* **attachment (to)** affection *f* (pour), attachement *m* (à)
attack [ə'tæk] *vt* attaquer; (*task etc)* s'attaquer à ▷ *n* attaque *f*; **heart ~** crise *f* cardiaque; **attacker** *n* attaquant *m*, agresseur *m*
attain [ə'teɪn] *vt* (*also: ~ to)* parvenir à, atteindre; (*knowledge)* acquérir
attempt [ə'tempt] *n* tentative *f* ▷ *vt* essayer, tenter
attend [ə'tend] *vt* (*course)* suivre; (*meeting, talk)* assister à; (*school, church)* aller à, fréquenter; (*patient)* soigner,

s'occuper de; **attend to** *vt fus* (*needs, affairs etc)* s'occuper de; (*customer)* s'occuper de, servir; **attendance** *n* (*being present)* présence *f*; (*people present)* assistance *f*; **attendant** *n* employé(e), gardien(ne) ▷ *adj* concomitant(e), qui accompagne or s'ensuit

> Be careful not to translate **to attend** by the French word **attendre**.

attention [ə'tenʃən] *n* attention *f* ▷ *excl* (*Mil)* garde-à-vous!; **for the ~ of** (*Admin)* à l'attention de
attic ['ætɪk] *n* grenier *m*, combles *mpl*
attitude ['ætɪtjuːd] *n* attitude *f*
attorney [ə'tɜːnɪ] *n* (*us: lawyer)* avocat *m*; **Attorney General** *n* (*BRIT)* = procureur général; (*us)* = garde *m* des Sceaux, ministre *m* de la Justice
attract [ə'trækt] *vt* attirer; **attraction** [ə'trækʃən] *n* (*gen pl: pleasant things)* attraction *f*, attrait *m*; (*Physics)* attraction; (*fig: towards sb, sth)* attirance *f*; **attractive** *adj* séduisant(e), attrayant(e)
attribute *n* ['ætrɪbjuːt] attribut *m* ▷ *vt* [ə'trɪbjuːt]: **to ~ sth to** attribuer qch à
aubergine ['əubəʒiːn] *n* aubergine *f*
auburn ['ɔːbən] *adj* auburn *inv*, châtain roux *inv*
auction ['ɔːkʃən] *n* (*also: sale by ~)* vente *f* aux enchères ▷ *vt* (*also: to sell by ~)* vendre aux enchères
audible ['ɔːdɪbl] *adj* audible
audience ['ɔːdɪəns] *n* (*people)* assistance *f*, public *m*; (*on radio)* auditeurs *mpl*; (*at theatre)* spectateurs *mpl*; (*interview)* audience *f*
audit ['ɔːdɪt] *vt* vérifier
audition [ɔː'dɪʃən] *n* audition *f*
auditor ['ɔːdɪtə] *n* vérificateur *m* des comptes
auditorium [ɔːdɪ'tɔːrɪəm] *n* auditorium *m*, salle *f* de concert or de spectacle
Aug. *abbr* = **August**
August ['ɔːɡəst] *n* août *m*
aunt [ɑːnt] *n* tante *f*; **auntie, aunty** *n* diminutive of **aunt**

au pair ['əʊ'peəʳ] n (also: ~ **girl**) jeune fille f au pair

aura ['ɔːrə] n atmosphère f; (of person) aura f

austerity [ɔsˈtɛrɪtɪ] n austérité f

Australia [ɔsˈtreɪlɪə] n Australie f; **Australian** adj australien(ne) ▷ n Australien(ne)

Austria ['ɒstrɪə] n Autriche f; **Austrian** adj autrichien(ne) ▷ n Autrichien(ne)

authentic [ɔːˈθɛntɪk] adj authentique

author ['ɔːθəʳ] n auteur m

authority [ɔːˈθɒrɪtɪ] n autorité f; (permission) autorisation (formelle); **the authorities** les autorités fpl, l'administration f

authorize ['ɔːθəraɪz] vt autoriser

auto ['ɔːtəʊ] n (us) auto f, voiture f; **autobiography** [ɔːtəbaɪˈɒgrəfɪ] n autobiographie f; **autograph** ['ɔːtəgrɑːf] n autographe m ▷ vt signer, dédicacer; **automatic** [ɔːtəˈmætɪk] adj automatique ▷ n (gun) automatique m; (car) voiture f à transmission automatique; **automatically** adv automatiquement; **automobile** ['ɔːtəməbiːl] n (us) automobile f; **autonomous** [ɔːˈtɒnəməs] adj autonome; **autonomy** [ɔːˈtɒnəmɪ] n autonomie f

autumn ['ɔːtəm] n automne m

auxiliary [ɔːgˈzɪlɪərɪ] adj, n auxiliaire (m/f)

avail [əˈveɪl] vt: **to ~ o.s. of** user de; profiter de ▷ n: **to no ~** sans résultat, en vain, en pure perte

availability [əveɪləˈbɪlɪtɪ] n disponibilité f

available [əˈveɪləbl] adj disponible

avalanche ['ævəlɑːnʃ] n avalanche f

Ave. abbr = **avenue**

avenue ['ævənjuː] n avenue f; (fig) moyen m

average ['ævərɪdʒ] n moyenne f ▷ adj moyen(ne) ▷ vt (a certain figure) atteindre or faire etc en moyenne; **on ~** en moyenne

avert [əˈvɜːt] vt (danger) prévenir, écarter; (one's eyes) détourner

avid ['ævɪd] adj avide

avocado [ævəˈkɑːdəʊ] n (BRIT: also: ~ **pear**) avocat m

avoid [əˈvɔɪd] vt éviter

await [əˈweɪt] vt attendre

awake [əˈweɪk] adj éveillé(e) ▷ vb (pt **awoke**, pp **awoken**) ▷ vt éveiller ▷ vi s'éveiller; **to be ~** être réveillé(e)

award [əˈwɔːd] n (for bravery) récompense f; (prize) prix m; (Law: damages) dommages-intérêts mpl ▷ vt (prize) décerner; (Law: damages) accorder

aware [əˈweəʳ] adj: ~ **of** (conscious) conscient(e) de; (informed) au courant de; **to become ~ of/that** prendre conscience de/que; se rendre compte de/que; **awareness** n conscience f, connaissance f

away [əˈweɪ] adv (au) loin; (movement): **she went ~** elle est partie ▷ adj (not in, not here) absent(e); **far ~** (au) loin; **two kilometres ~** à (une distance de) deux kilomètres, à deux kilomètres de distance; **two hours ~ by car** à deux heures de voiture or de route; **the holiday was two weeks ~** il restait deux semaines jusqu'aux vacances; **he's ~ for a week** il est parti (pour) une semaine; **to take sth ~ from sb** prendre qch à qn; **to take sth ~ from sth** (subtract) ôter qch de qch; **to work/pedal ~** travailler/pédaler à cœur joie; **to fade ~** (colour) s'estomper; (sound) s'affaiblir

awe [ɔː] n respect mêlé de crainte, effroi mêlé d'admiration; **awesome** ['ɔːsəm] (us) adj (inf: excellent) génial(e)

awful ['ɔːfəl] adj affreux(-euse); **an ~ lot of** énormément de; **awfully** adv (very) terriblement, vraiment

awkward ['ɔːkwəd] adj (clumsy) gauche, maladroit(e); (inconvenient) peu pratique; (embarrassing) gênant

awoke [əˈwəʊk] pt of **awake**

awoken [əˈwəʊkən] pp of **awake**

axe [æks] (*US* **ax**) *n* hache *f* ▷ *vt* (*project etc*) abandonner; (*jobs*) supprimer

axle ['æksl] *n* essieu *m*

ay(e) [aɪ] *excl* (*yes*) oui

azalea [ə'zeɪlɪə] *n* azalée *f*

B [biː] *n* (*Mus*): **B** si *m*

B.A. *abbr* (*Scol*) = **Bachelor of Arts**

baby ['beɪbɪ] *n* bébé *m*; **baby carriage** *n* (*US*) voiture *f* d'enfant; **baby-sit** *vi* garder les enfants; **baby-sitter** *n* baby-sitter *m/f*; **baby wipe** *n* lingette *f* (*pour bébé*)

bachelor ['bætʃ(ə)lə^r] *n* célibataire *m*; **B~ of Arts/Science (BA/BSc)** ≈ licencié(e) ès or en lettres/sciences

back [bæk] *n* (*of person, horse*) dos *m*; (*of hand*) dos, revers *m*; (*of house*) derrière *m*; (*of car, train*) arrière *m*; (*of chair*) dossier *m*; (*of page*) verso *m*; (*of crowd*): **can the people at the ~ hear me properly?** est-ce que les gens du fond peuvent m'entendre?; (*Football*) arrière *m*; **~ to front** à l'envers ▷ *vt* (*financially*) soutenir (financièrement); (*candidate: also:* **~ up**) soutenir, appuyer; (*horse: at races*) parier or miser sur; (*car*) (faire) reculer ▷ *vi* reculer; (*car etc*) faire marche arrière ▷ *adj* (*in compounds*) de derrière, à l'arrière; **~ seat/wheel** (*Aut*)

siège m/roue f arrière inv; **~ payments/ rent** arriéré m de paiements/loyer; **~ garden/room** jardin/pièce sur l'arrière ▷ adv (not forward) en arrière; (returned): **he's ~** il est rentré, il est de retour; **he ran ~** il est revenu en courant; (restitution): **throw the ball ~** renvoie la balle; **can I have it ~?** puis-je le ravoir?, peux-tu me le rendre?; (again): **he called ~** il a rappelé; **back down** vi rabattre de ses prétentions; **back out** vi (of promise) se dédire; **back up** vt (person) soutenir; (Comput) faire une copie de sauvegarde de; **backache** n mal m au dos; **backbencher** (BRIT) n membre du parlement sans portefeuille; **backbone** n colonne vertébrale, épine dorsale; **back door** n porte f de derrière; **backfire** vi (Aut) pétarader; (plans) mal tourner; **backgammon** n trictrac m; **background** n arrière-plan m; (of events) situation f, conjoncture f; (basic knowledge) éléments mpl de base; (experience) formation f; **family background** milieu familial; **backing** n (fig) soutien m, appui m; **backlog** n: **backlog of work** travail m en retard; **backpack** n sac m à dos; **backpacker** n randonneur(-euse); **backslash** n barre oblique inversée; **backstage** adv dans les coulisses; **backstroke** n dos crawlé; **backup** adj (train, plane) supplémentaire, de réserve; (Comput) de sauvegarde ▷ n (support) appui m, soutien m; (Comput: also: **backup file**) sauvegarde f; **backward** adj (movement) en arrière; (person, country) arriéré(e), attardé(e); **backwards** adv (move, go) en arrière; (read a list) à l'envers, à rebours; (fall) à la renverse; (walk) à reculons; **backyard** n arrière-cour f
bacon ['beɪkən] n bacon m, lard m
bacteria [bæk'tɪərɪə] npl bactéries fpl
bad [bæd] adj mauvais(e); (child) vilain(e); (mistake, accident) grave; (meat, food) gâté(e), avarié(e); **his ~ leg** sa jambe malade; **to go ~** (meat, food) se gâter; (milk) tourner

bade [bæd] pt of **bid**
badge [bædʒ] n insigne m; (of policeman) plaque f; (stick-on, sew-on) badge m
badger ['bædʒə] n blaireau m
badly ['bædlɪ] adv (work, dress etc) mal; **to reflect ~ on sb** donner une mauvaise image de qn; **~ wounded** grièvement blessé; **he needs it ~** il en a absolument besoin; **~ off** adj, adv dans la gêne
bad-mannered ['bæd'mænəd] adj mal élevé(e)
badminton ['bædmɪntən] n badminton m
bad-tempered ['bæd'tempəd] adj (by nature) ayant mauvais caractère; (on one occasion) de mauvaise humeur
bag [bæg] n sac m; **~s of** (inf: lots of) des tas de; **baggage** n bagages mpl; **baggage allowance** n franchise f de bagages; **baggage reclaim** n (at airport) livraison f des bagages; **baggy** adj avachi(e), qui fait des poches; **bagpipes** npl cornemuse f
bail [beɪl] n caution f ▷ vt (prisoner: also: **grant ~ to**) mettre en liberté sous caution; (boat: also: **~ out**) écoper; **to be released on ~** être libéré(e) sous caution; **bail out** vt (prisoner) payer la caution de
bait [beɪt] n appât m ▷ vt appâter; (fig: tease) tourmenter
bake [beɪk] vt (faire) cuire au four ▷ vi (bread etc) cuire (au four); (make cakes etc) faire de la pâtisserie; **baked beans** npl haricots blancs à la sauce tomate; **baked potato** n pomme f de terre en robe des champs; **baker** n boulanger m; **bakery** n boulangerie f; **baking** n (process) cuisson f; **baking powder** n levure f (chimique)
balance ['bæləns] n équilibre m; (Comm: sum) solde m; (remainder) reste m; (scales) balance f ▷ vt mettre ou faire tenir en équilibre; (pros and cons) peser; (budget) équilibrer; (account) balancer; (compensate) compenser,

contrebalancer: **~ of trade/payments**
balance commerciale/des comptes ou
paiements; **balanced** adj (personality,
diet) équilibré(e); (report) objectif(-ive)
balance sheet n bilan m

balcony ['bælkənɪ] n balcon m; **do you
have a room with a ~?** avez-vous une
chambre avec balcon?

bald [bɔːld] adj chauve; (tyre) lisse

ball [bɔːl] n boule f; (football) ballon m;
(for tennis, golf) balle f; (dance) bal m; **to
play ~** jouer au ballon (or à la balle);
(fig) coopérer

ballerina [bælə'riːnə] n ballerine f

ballet ['bæleɪ] n ballet m; (art)
danse f (classique); **ballet dancer** n
danseur(-euse) de ballet

balloon [bə'luːn] n ballon m

ballot ['bælət] n scrutin m

ballpoint (pen) ['bɔːlpɔɪnt-] n stylo
m à bille

ballroom ['bɔːlrum] n salle f de bal

Baltic ['bɔːltɪk] n: **the ~ (Sea)** la (mer)
Baltique

bamboo [bæm'buː] n bambou m

ban [bæn] n interdiction f ▷ vt interdire

banana [bə'nɑːnə] n banane f

band [bænd] n bande f; (at a dance)
orchestre m; (Mil) musique f, fanfare f

bandage ['bændɪdʒ] n bandage m,
pansement m ▷ vt (wound, leg) mettre
un pansement or un bandage sur

Band-Aid® ['bændeɪd] n (us)
pansement adhésif

B. & B. n abbr = **bed and breakfast**

bandit ['bændɪt] n bandit m

bang [bæŋ] n détonation f; (of door)
claquement m; (blow) coup (violent)
▷ vt frapper (violemment); (door)
claquer ▷ vi détoner, claquer

Bangladesh [bæŋglə'deʃ] n
Bangladesh m

Bangladeshi [bæŋglə'deʃɪ] adj du
Bangladesh ▷ n habitant(e) du
Bangladesh

bangle ['bæŋgl] n bracelet m

bangs [bæŋz] npl (us: fringe) frange f

banish ['bænɪʃ] vt bannir

banister(s) ['bænɪstə(z)] n(pl) rampe
f (d'escalier)

banjo (pl **~es** or **~s**) ['bændʒəu] n
banjo m

bank [bæŋk] n banque f; (of river, lake)
bord m, rive f; (of earth) talus m, remblai
m ▷ vi (Aviat) virer sur l'aile; **bank on** vt
fus miser or tabler sur; **bank account**
n compte m en banque; **bank balance**
n solde m bancaire; **bank card** (BRIT)
n carte f d'identité bancaire; **bank
charges** npl (BRIT) frais mpl de banque;
banker n banquier m; **bank holiday**
n (BRIT) jour férié (où les banques
sont fermées); voir encadré; **banking**
n opérations fpl bancaires; profession
f de banquier; **bank manager** n
directeur m d'agence (bancaire);
banknote n billet m de banque

● **BANK HOLIDAY**

Le terme **bank holiday** s'applique
au Royaume-Uni aux jours fériés
pendant lesquels banques et
commerces sont fermés. Les
principaux **bank holidays** à part
Noël et Pâques se situent au mois
de mai et fin août, et contrairement
aux pays de tradition catholique, ne
coïncident pas nécessairement avec
une fête religieuse.

bankrupt ['bæŋkrʌpt] adj en faillite;
to go ~ faire faillite; **bankruptcy** n
faillite f

bank statement n relevé m de
compte

banner ['bænər] n bannière f

bannister(s) ['bænɪstə(z)] n(pl)
= **banister(s)**

banquet ['bæŋkwɪt] n banquet m,
festin m

baptism ['bæptɪzəm] n baptême m

baptize [bæp'taɪz] vt baptiser

bar [bɑːr] n (pub) bar m; (counter)
comptoir m, bar; (rod: of metal etc) barre
f; (of window etc) barreau m; (of chocolate)

tablette f, plaque f; (fig: obstacle)
obstacle m; (prohibition) mesure f
d'exclusion; (Mus) mesure f ▷ vt (road)
barrer; (person) exclure; (activity)
interdire; **~ of soap** savonnette
f; **behind ~s** (prisoner) derrière les
barreaux; **the B~** (Law) le barreau; **~
none** sans exception

barbaric [baː'bærɪk] adj barbare

barbecue ['baːbɪkjuː] n barbecue m

barbed wire ['baːbd-] n fil m de fer
barbelé

barber ['baːbəʳ] n coiffeur m (pour
hommes); **barber's (shop)** (us **barber
(shop)**) n salon m de coiffure (pour
hommes)

bar code n code m à barres, code-
barre m

bare [bɛəʳ] adj nu(e) ▷ vt mettre à nu,
dénuder; (teeth) montrer; **barefoot** adj,
adv nu-pieds, (les) pieds nus; **barely**
adv à peine

bargain ['baːgɪn] n (transaction)
marché m; (good buy) affaire f, occasion
f ▷ vi (haggle) marchander; (negotiate)
négocier, traiter; **into the ~** par-dessus
le marché; **bargain for** vt fus (inf): **he
got more than he ~ed for!** il en a eu
pour son argent!

barge [baːdʒ] n péniche f; **barge in** vi
(walk in) faire irruption; (interrupt talk)
intervenir mal à propos

bark [baːk] n (of tree) écorce f; (of dog)
aboiement m ▷ vi aboyer

barley ['baːlɪ] n orge f

barmaid ['baːmeɪd] n serveuse f (de
bar), barmaid f

barman ['baːmən] n serveur m (de bar),
barman m

barn [baːn] n grange f

barometer [bə'rɔmɪtəʳ] n baromètre m

baron ['bærən] n baron m; **baroness**
n baronne f

barracks ['bærəks] npl caserne f

barrage ['bæraːʒ] n (Mil) tir m de
barrage; (dam) barrage m; (of criticism)
feu m

barrel ['bærəl] n tonneau m; (of gun)

canon m

barren ['bærən] adj stérile

barrette [bə'ret] (us) n barrette f

barricade [bærɪ'keɪd] n barricade f

barrier ['bærɪəʳ] n barrière f

barring ['baːrɪŋ] prep sauf

barrister ['bærɪstəʳ] n (BRIT) avocat
(plaidant)

barrow ['bærəu] n (cart) charrette
f à bras

bartender ['baːtendəʳ] n (us) serveur
m (de bar), barman m

base [beɪs] n base f ▷ vt (opinion, belief):
to ~ sth on baser or fonder qch sur ▷ adj
vil(e), bas(se)

baseball ['beɪsbɔːl] n base-ball m;
baseball cap n casquette f de base-ball

Basel ['baːl] n = **Basle**

basement ['beɪsmənt] n sous-sol m

bases ['beɪsiːz] npl of **basis**

bash [bæʃ] vt (inf) frapper, cogner

basic ['beɪsɪk] adj (precautions, rules)
élémentaire; (principles, research)
fondamental(e); (vocabulary, salary) de
base; (minimal) réduit(e) au minimum,
rudimentaire; **basically** adv (in fact) en
fait; (essentially) fondamentalement;
basics npl: **the basics** l'essentiel m

basil ['bæzl] n basilic m

basin ['beɪsn] n (vessel, also Geo) cuvette
f, bassin m; (BRIT: for food) bol m; (also:
wash~) lavabo m

basis (pl **bases**) ['beɪsɪs, -siːz] n base
f; **on a part-time/trial ~** à temps
partiel/à l'essai

basket ['baːskɪt] n corbeille f; (with
handle) panier m; **basketball** n
basket-ball m

Basle ['baːl] n Bâle

Basque [bæsk] adj basque ▷ n Basque
m/f; **the ~ Country** le Pays basque

bass [beɪs] n (Mus) basse f

bastard ['baːstəd] n enfant naturel(le),
bâtard(e); (inf!) salaud m (!)

bat [bæt] n chauve-souris f; (for baseball
etc) batte f; (BRIT: for table tennis)
raquette f ▷ vt: **he didn't ~ an eyelid** il
n'a pas sourcillé or bronché

batch [bætʃ] n (of bread) fournée f; (of papers) liasse f; (of applicants, letters) paquet m

bath (pl **-s**) [bɑːθ, bɑːðz] n bain m; (bathtub) baignoire f ▷ vt baigner, donner un bain à; **to have a ~** prendre un bain; see also **baths**

bathe [beɪð] vi se baigner ▷ vt baigner; (wound etc) laver

bathing ['beɪðɪŋ] n baignade f; **bathing costume** (us **bathing suit**) n maillot m (de bain)

bath: **bathrobe** n peignoir m de bain; **bathroom** n salle f de bains; **baths** [bɑːðz] npl (BRIT: also: **swimming baths**) piscine f; **bath towel** n serviette f de bain; **bathtub** n baignoire f

baton ['bætən] n bâton m; (Mus) baguette f; (club) matraque f

batter ['bætəʳ] vt battre ▷ n pâte f à frire; **battered** adj (hat, pan) cabossé(e); **battered wife/child** épouse/enfant maltraité(e) or martyr(e)

battery ['bætərɪ] n (for torch, radio) pile f; (Aut, Mil) batterie f; **battery farming** n élevage m en batterie

battle ['bætl] n bataille f, combat m ▷ vi se battre, lutter; **battlefield** n champ m de bataille

bay [beɪ] n (of sea) baie f; (BRIT: for parking) place f de stationnement; (: for loading) aire f de chargement; **B~ of Biscay** golfe m de Gascogne; **to hold sb at ~** tenir qn à distance or en échec

bay leaf n laurier m

bazaar [bə'zɑːʳ] n (shop, market) bazar m; (sale) vente f de charité

BBC n abbr (= British Broadcasting Corporation) office de la radiodiffusion et télévision britannique

B.C. adv abbr (= before Christ) av. J.-C.

⊙ **KEYWORD**

be [biː] (pt **was, were**, pp **been**) aux vb 1 (with present participle: forming continuous tenses): **what are you doing?** que faites-vous?; **they're coming tomorrow** ils viennent demain; **I've been waiting for you for 2 hours** je t'attends depuis 2 heures

2 (with pp: forming passives): **to be killed** être tué(e); **the box had been opened** la boîte avait été ouverte; **he was nowhere to be seen** on ne le voyait nulle part

3 (in tag questions): **it was fun, wasn't it?** c'était drôle, n'est-ce pas?; **he's good-looking, isn't he?** il est beau, n'est-ce pas?; **she's back, is she?** elle est rentrée, n'est-ce pas or alors?

4 (+to +infinitive): **the house is to be sold** (necessity) la maison doit être vendue; (future) la maison va être vendue; **he's not to open it** il ne doit pas l'ouvrir

▷ vb + complement 1 (gen) être; **I'm English** je suis anglais(e); **I'm tired** je suis fatigué(e); **I'm hot/cold** j'ai chaud/froid; **he's a doctor** il est médecin; **be careful/good/quiet!** faites attention/soyez sages/taisez-vous!; **2 and 2 are 4** 2 et 2 font 4

2 (of health): **how are you?** comment allez-vous?; **I'm better now** je vais mieux maintenant; **he's very ill** il est très malade

3 (of age): **how old are you?** quel âge avez-vous?; **I'm sixteen (years old)** j'ai seize ans

4 (cost) coûter; **how much was the meal?** combien a coûté le repas?; **that'll be £5, please** ça fera 5 livres, s'il vous plaît; **this shirt is £17** cette chemise coûte 17 livres

▷ vi 1 (exist, occur etc) être, exister; **the prettiest girl that ever was** la fille la plus jolie qui ait jamais existé; **is there a God?** y a-t-il un dieu?; **be that as it may** quoi qu'il en soit; **so be it** soit

2 (referring to place) être, se trouver; **I won't be here tomorrow** je ne serai pas là demain

3 (referring to movement) aller; **where have you been?** où êtes-vous allé(s)?

▷ *impers vb* **1** (*referring to time*) être; **it's 5 o'clock** il est 5 heures; **it's the 28th of April** c'est le 28 avril
2 (*referring to distance*): **it's 10 km to the village** le village est à 10 km
3 (*referring to the weather*) faire; **it's too hot/cold** il fait trop chaud/froid; **it's windy today** il y a du vent aujourd'hui
4 (*emphatic*): **it's me/the postman** c'est moi/le facteur; **it was Maria who paid the bill** c'est Maria qui a payé la note

beach [biːtʃ] *n* plage *f* ▷ *vt* échouer
beacon ['biːkən] *n* (*lighthouse*) fanal *m*; (*marker*) balise *f*
bead [biːd] *n* perle *f*; (*of dew, sweat*) goutte *f*; **beads** *npl* (*necklace*) collier *m*
beak [biːk] *n* bec *m*
beam [biːm] *n* (*Archit*) poutre *f*; (*of light*) rayon *m* ▷ *vi* rayonner
bean [biːn] *n* haricot *m*; (*of coffee*) grain *m*; **beansprouts** *npl* pousses *fpl* or germes *mpl* de soja
bear [bɛəʳ] *n* ours *m* ▷ *vb* (*pt* **bore**, *pp* **borne**) ▷ *vt* porter; (*endure*) supporter, rapporter ▷ *vi*: **to ~ right/left** obliquer à droite/gauche, se diriger vers la droite/gauche
beard [bɪəd] *n* barbe *f*
bearer ['bɛərəʳ] *n* porteur *m*; (*of passport etc*) titulaire *m/f*
bearing ['bɛərɪŋ] *n* maintien *m*, allure *f*; (*connection*) rapport *m*; (*Tech*): (**ball**) **bearings** *npl* roulement *m* (à billes)
beast [biːst] *n* bête *f*; (*inf: person*) brute *f*
beat [biːt] *n* battement *m*; (*Mus*) temps *m*, mesure *f*; (*of policeman*) ronde *f* ▷ *vt* (*pt* **~**, *pp* **~en**) battre; **off the ~en track** hors des chemins or sentiers battus; **to ~ it** (*inf*) ficher le camp; **beat up** *vt* (*inf: person*) tabasser; **beating** *n* raclée *f*
beautiful ['bjuːtɪful] *adj* beau (belle); **beautifully** *adv* admirablement
beauty ['bjuːtɪ] *n* beauté *f*; **beauty parlour** (*us* **beauty parlor**) *n* institut *m* de beauté; **beauty salon** *n* institut *m* de beauté; **beauty spot**

n (*on skin*) grain *m* de beauté; (*BRIT Tourism*) site naturel (d'une grande beauté)
beaver ['biːvəʳ] *n* castor *m*
became [bɪ'keɪm] *pt of* **become**
because [bɪ'kɒz] *conj* parce que; **~ of** *prep* à cause de
beckon ['bɛkən] *vt* (*also*: **~ to**) faire signe (de venir) à
become [bɪ'kʌm] *vt* devenir; **to ~ fat/thin** grossir/maigrir; **to ~ angry** se mettre en colère
bed [bɛd] *n* lit *m*; (*of flowers*) parterre *m*; (*of coal, clay*) couche *f*; (*of sea, lake*) fond *m*; **to go to ~** aller se coucher; **bed and breakfast** *n* (*terms*) chambre *f* et petit déjeuner; (*place*) ≈ chambre *f* d'hôte; *voir encadré*; **bedclothes** *npl* couvertures *fpl* et draps *mpl*; **bedding** *n* literie *f*; **bed linen** *n* draps *mpl* de lit (et taies *fpl* d'oreillers); **bedroom** *n* chambre *f* (à coucher); **bedside** *n*: **at sb's bedside** au chevet de qn; **bedside lamp** *n* lampe *f* de chevet; **bedside table** *n* table *f* de chevet; **bedsit(ter)** *n* (*BRIT*) chambre meublée, studio *m*; **bedspread** *n* couvre-lit *m*, dessus-de-lit *m*; **bedtime** *n*: **it's bedtime** c'est l'heure de se coucher

● **BED AND BREAKFAST**

● Un **bed and breakfast** est une
● petite pension dans une maison
● particulière ou une ferme où l'on
● peut louer une chambre avec
● petit déjeuner compris pour un
● prix modique par rapport à ce que
● l'on paierait dans un hôtel. Ces
● établissements sont communément
● appelés "B & B", et sont signalés par
● une pancarte dans le jardin ou au-
● dessus de la porte.

bee [biː] *n* abeille *f*
beech [biːtʃ] *n* hêtre *m*
beef [biːf] *n* bœuf *m*; **roast ~** rosbif *m*; **beefburger** *n* hamburger *m*;

Beefeater n hallebardier m (de la tour de Londres)

been [bi:n] pp of **be**

beer [bɪər] n bière f; **beer garden** n (BRIT) jardin m d'un pub (où l'on peut emmener ses consommations)

beet [bi:t] n (vegetable) betterave f; (US: also: **red ~**) betterave (potagère)

beetle ['bi:tl] n scarabée m, coléoptère m

beetroot ['bi:tru:t] n (BRIT) betterave f

before [bɪ'fɔ:r] prep (of time) avant; (of space) devant ▷ conj avant que + sub; avant de ▷ adv avant; **~ going** avant de partir; **~ she goes** avant qu'elle (ne) parte; **the week ~** la semaine précédente or d'avant; **I've never seen it ~** c'est la première fois que je le vois; **beforehand** adv au préalable, à l'avance

beg [beg] vi mendier ▷ vt demander (forgiveness, mercy etc) demander; (entreat) supplier; **to ~ sb to do sth** supplier qn de faire qch; see also **pardon**

began [bɪ'gæn] pt of **begin**

beggar ['begər] n mendiant(e)

begin [bɪ'gɪn] (pt **began**, pp **begun**) vt, vi commencer; **to ~ doing** or **to do sth** commencer à faire qch; **beginner** n débutant(e); **beginning** n commencement m, début m

begun [bɪ'gʌn] pp of **begin**

behalf [bɪ'hɑ:f] n: **on ~ of, (US) in ~ of** (representing) de la part de; (for benefit of) pour le compte de; **on my/his ~** de ma/sa part

behave [bɪ'heɪv] vi se conduire, se comporter; (well: also: **~ o.s.**) se conduire bien or comme il faut; **behaviour**, (US) **behavior** n comportement m, conduite f

behind [bɪ'haɪnd] prep derrière; (time) en retard sur; (supporting) **to be ~ sb** soutenir qn ▷ adv derrière ▷ n derrière m; **~ the scenes** dans les coulisses; **to be ~ (schedule) with sth** être en retard dans qch

beige [beɪʒ] adj beige

Beijing ['beɪ'dʒɪŋ] n Pékin

being ['bi:ɪŋ] n être m; **to come into ~** prendre naissance

belated [bɪ'leɪtɪd] adj tardif(-ive)

belch [beltʃ] vi avoir un renvoi, roter ▷ vt (also: **~ out**: smoke etc) vomir, cracher

Belgian ['bɛldʒən] adj belge, de Belgique ▷ n Belge m/f

Belgium ['bɛldʒəm] n Belgique f

belief [bɪ'li:f] n (opinion) conviction f; (trust, faith) foi f

believe [bɪ'li:v] vt, vi croire, estimer; **to ~ in** (God) croire en; (ghosts, method) croire à; **believer** n (in idea, activity) partisan(e); (Rel) croyant(e)

bell [bɛl] n cloche f; (small) clochette f; (on door) sonnette f; (electric) sonnerie f

bellboy ['bɛlbɔɪ] (US **bellhop** ['bɛlhɔp]) n groom m, chasseur m

bellow ['bɛləu] vi (bull) meugler; (person) brailler

bell pepper n (esp US) poivron m

belly ['bɛlɪ] n ventre m; **belly button** (inf) n nombril m

belong [bɪ'lɔŋ] vi: **to ~ to** appartenir à; (club etc) faire partie de; **this book ~s here** ce livre va ici, la place de ce livre est ici; **belongings** npl affaires fpl, possessions fpl

beloved [bɪ'lʌvɪd] adj bien-aimé(e), chéri(e)

below [bɪ'ləu] prep sous, au-dessous de ▷ adv en dessous; en contre-bas; **see ~** voir plus bas or plus loin or ci-dessous

belt [bɛlt] n ceinture f; (Tech) courroie f ▷ vt (thrash) donner une raclée à; **beltway** n (US Aut) route f de ceinture; (: motorway) périphérique m

bemused [bɪ'mju:zd] adj médusé(e)

bench [bɛntʃ] n banc m; (in workshop) établi m; **the B~** (Law: judges) la magistrature, la Cour

bend [bɛnd] vb (pt, pp **bent**) ▷ vt courber; (leg, arm) plier ▷ vi se courber ▷ n (BRIT: in road) virage m, tournant m; (in pipe, river) coude m; **bend down** vi se baisser; **bend over** vi se pencher

beneath [bɪ'niːθ] prep sous, au-dessous de; (unworthy of) indigne de ▷ adv dessous, au-dessous, en bas

beneficial [benɪ'fɪʃəl] adj: ~ (to) salutaire (pour), bénéfique (à)

benefit ['benɪfɪt] n avantage m, profit m; (allowance of money) allocation f ▷ vt faire du bien à, profiter à ▷ vi: **he'll ~ from it** cela lui fera du bien, il y gagnera or s'en trouvera bien

Benelux ['benɪlʌks] n Bénélux m

benign [bɪ'naɪn] adj (person, smile) bienveillant(e), affable; (Med) bénin(-igne)

bent [bent] pt, pp of **bend** ▷ n inclination f, penchant m ▷ adj: **to be ~ on** être résolu(e) à

bereaved [bɪ'riːvd] n: **the ~** la famille du disparu

beret ['bereɪ] n béret m

Berlin [bəː'lɪn] n Berlin

Bermuda [bəː'mjuːdə] n Bermudes fpl

Bern [bəːn] n Berne

berry ['berɪ] n baie f

berth [bəːθ] n (bed) couchette f; (for ship) poste m d'amarrage, mouillage m ▷ vi (in harbour) venir à quai; (at anchor) mouiller

beside [bɪ'saɪd] prep à côté de; (compared with) par rapport à; **that's ~ the point** ça n'a rien à voir; **to be ~ o.s. (with anger)** être hors de soi; **besides** adv en outre, de plus ▷ prep en plus de; (except) excepté

best [best] adj meilleur(e) ▷ adv le mieux; **the ~ part of** (quantity) le plus clair de, la plus grande partie de; **at ~** au mieux; **to make the ~ of sth** s'accommoder de qch (du mieux que l'on peut); **to do one's ~** faire de son mieux; **to the ~ of my knowledge** pour autant que je sache; **to the ~ of my ability** du mieux que je pourrai; **best-before date** n date f de limite d'utilisation or de consommation; **best man** (irreg) n garçon m d'honneur; **bestseller** n best-seller m, succès m

de librairie

bet [bet] n pari m ▷ vt, vi (pt, pp ~ -ted) parier; **to ~ sb sth** parier qch à qn

betray [bɪ'treɪ] vt trahir

better ['betə*] adj meilleur(e) ▷ adv mieux ▷ vt améliorer ▷ n: **to get the ~ of** triompher de, l'emporter sur; **you had ~ do it** vous feriez mieux de le faire; **he thought ~ of it** il s'est ravisé; **to get ~** (Med) aller mieux; (improve) s'améliorer

betting ['betɪŋ] n paris mpl; **betting shop** n (BRIT) bureau m de paris

between [bɪ'twiːn] prep entre ▷ adv au milieu, dans l'intervalle

beverage ['bevərɪdʒ] n boisson f (gén sans alcool)

beware [bɪ'wɛə*] vi: **to ~ (of)** prendre garde (à); **"~ of the dog"** (attention) chien méchant"

bewildered [bɪ'wɪldəd] adj dérouté(e), ahuri(e)

beyond [bɪ'jɔnd] prep (in space, time) au-delà de; (exceeding) au-dessus de ▷ adv au-delà; **~ doubt** hors de doute; **~ repair** irréparable

bias ['baɪəs] n (prejudice) préjugé m, parti pris m; (preference) prévention f; **bias(s)ed** adj partial(e), montrant un parti pris

bib [bɪb] n bavoir m

Bible ['baɪbl] n Bible f

bicarbonate of soda [baɪˈkɑːbənɪt-] n bicarbonate m de soude

biceps ['baɪseps] n biceps m

bicycle ['baɪsɪkl] n bicyclette f; **bicycle pump** n pompe f à vélo

bid [bɪd] n offre f; (at auction) enchère f; (attempt) tentative f ▷ vb (pt ~ or **bade**, pp ~ or **~den**) ▷ vi faire une enchère or offre ▷ vt faire une enchère or offre de; **to ~ sb good day** souhaiter le bonjour à qn; **bidder** n: **the highest bidder** le plus offrant

bidet ['biːdeɪ] n bidet m

big [bɪg] adj (in height: person, building, tree) grand(e); (in bulk, amount: person, parcel, book) gros(se); **bigheaded** adj prétentieux(-euse); **big toe** n gros orteil

● **BIG APPLE**

■ Si l'on sait que "The Big Apple" désigne la ville de New York ("apple" est en réalité un terme d'argot signifiant "grande ville"), on connaît moins les surnoms donnés aux autres grandes villes américaines. Chicago est surnommée "Windy City" à cause des rafales soufflant du lac Michigan, La Nouvelle-Orléans doit son sobriquet de "Big Easy" à son style de vie décontracté, et l'industrie automobile a donné à Detroit son surnom de "Motown".

bike [baɪk] n vélo m; **bike lane** n piste f cyclable

bikini [bɪ'kiːnɪ] n bikini m

bilateral [baɪ'lætərl] adj bilatéral(e)

bilingual [baɪ'lɪŋgwəl] adj bilingue

bill [bɪl] n note f, facture f; (in restaurant) addition f, note f; (Pol) projet m de loi; (us: banknote) billet m (de banque); (notice) affiche f; (of bird) bec m; **put it on my ~** mettez-le sur mon compte; **"post no ~s"** "défense d'afficher"; **to fit** or **fill the ~** (fig) faire l'affaire; **billboard** (us) n panneau m d'affichage

billfold ['bɪlfəʊld] n (us) portefeuille m

billiards ['bɪljədz] n (jeu m de) billard m

billion ['bɪljən] n (BRIT) billion m (million de millions); (us) milliard m

bin [bɪn] n boîte f; (BRIT: also: **dust-litter ~**) poubelle f; (for coal) coffre m

bind (pt, pp **bound**) [baɪnd, baʊnd] vt attacher; (book) relier; (oblige) obliger, contraindre ▷ n (inf: nuisance) scie f

binge [bɪndʒ] n (inf): **to go on a ~** faire la bringue

bingo ['bɪŋgəʊ] n sorte de jeu de loto pratiqué dans les établissements publics

binoculars [bɪ'nɒkjʊləz] npl jumelles fpl

bio... [baɪə'] prefix: **biochemistry** n biochimie f; **biodegradable** ['baɪəʊdɪ'greɪdəbl] adj biodégradable

biography [baɪ'ɒgrəfɪ] n biographie f

biological adj biologique; **biology** [baɪ'ɒlədʒɪ] n biologie f; **biometric** [baɪə'metrɪk] adj biométrique

birch [bəːtʃ] n bouleau m

bird [bəːd] n oiseau m; (BRIT inf: girl) nana f; **bird flu** n grippe f aviaire; **bird of prey** n oiseau m de proie; **birdwatching** n ornithologie f (d'amateur)

Biro® ['baɪərəʊ] n stylo m à bille

birth [bəːθ] n naissance f; **to give ~ to** donner naissance à, mettre au monde; (subj: animal) mettre bas; **birth certificate** n acte m de naissance; **birth control** n (policy) limitation f des naissances; (method) méthode(s) contraceptive(s); **birthday** n anniversaire m ▷ cpd (cake, card etc) d'anniversaire; **birthmark** n envie f, tache f de vin; **birthplace** n lieu m de naissance

biscuit ['bɪskɪt] n (BRIT) biscuit m; (us) petit pain au lait

bishop ['bɪʃəp] n évêque m; (Chess) fou m

bistro ['biːstrəʊ] n petit restaurant m, bistrot m

bit [bɪt] pt of **bite** ▷ n morceau m; (Comput) bit m; (of tool) mèche f; (of horse) mors m; **a ~ of** un peu de; **a ~ mad/dangerous** un peu fou/risqué; **~ by ~** petit à petit

bitch [bɪtʃ] n (dog) chienne f; (inf!) salope f (!), garce f

bite [baɪt] vt, vi (pt **bit**, pp **bitten**) mordre; (insect) piquer ▷ n morsure f; (insect bite) piqûre f; (mouthful) bouchée f; **let's have a ~ (to eat)** mangeons un morceau; **to ~ one's nails** se ronger les ongles

bitten ['bɪtn] pp of **bite**

bitter ['bɪtə'] adj amer(-ère); (criticism) cinglant(e); (icy: weather, wind) glacial(e) ▷ n (BRIT: beer) bière f (à forte teneur en houblon)

bizarre [bɪ'zaː'] adj bizarre

black [blæk] *adj* noir(e) ▷ *n* (colour) noir *m*; (person): **B~** noir(e) ▷ *vt* (BRIT Industry) boycotter; **to give sb a ~ eye** pocher l'œil à qn; **to be in the ~** (in credit) avoir un compte créditeur; **~ and blue** (bruised) couvert(e) de bleus; **black out** *vi* (faint) s'évanouir; **blackberry** *n* mûre *f*; **blackbird** *n* merle *m*; **blackboard** *n* tableau noir; **black coffee** *n* café noir; **blackcurrant** *n* cassis *m*; **black ice** *n* verglas *m*; **blackmail** *n* chantage *m* ▷ *vt* faire chanter, soumettre au chantage; **black market** *n* marché noir; **blackout** *n* panne *f* d'électricité; (in wartime) black-out *m*; (TV) interruption *f* d'émission; (fainting) syncope *f*; **black pepper** *n* poivre noir; **black pudding** *n* boudin (noir); **Black Sea** *n*: **the Black Sea** la mer Noire

bladder ['blædə'] *n* vessie *f*

blade [bleɪd] *n* lame *f*; (of propeller) pale *f*; **a ~ of grass** un brin d'herbe

blame [bleɪm] *n* faute *f*, blâme *m* ▷ *vt*: **to ~ sb/sth for sth** attribuer à qn/qch la responsabilité de qch; reprocher qch à qn/qch; **I'm not to ~** ce n'est pas ma faute

bland [blænd] *adj* (taste, food) doux (douce), fade

blank [blæŋk] *adj* blanc (blanche); (look) sans expression, dénué(e) d'expression ▷ *n* espace *m* vide, blanc *m*; (cartridge) cartouche *f* à blanc; **his mind was a ~** il avait la tête vide

blanket ['blæŋkɪt] *n* couverture *f*; (of snow, cloud) couche *f*

blast [blɑ:st] *n* explosion *f*; (shock wave) souffle *m*; (of air, steam) bouffée *f* ▷ *vt* faire sauter ou exploser

blatant ['bleɪtənt] *adj* flagrant(e), criant(e)

blaze [bleɪz] *n* (fire) incendie *m*; (fig) flamboiement *m* ▷ *vi* (fire) flamber; (fig) flamboyer, resplendir ▷ *vt*: **to ~ a trail** (fig) montrer la voie; **in a ~ of publicity** à grand renfort de publicité

blazer ['bleɪzə'] *n* blazer *m*

bleach [bli:tʃ] *n* (also: **household ~**) eau *f* de Javel ▷ *vt* (linen) blanchir; **bleachers** *npl* (us Sport) gradins *mpl* (en plein soleil)

bleak [bli:k] *adj* morne, désolé(e); (weather) triste, maussade; (smile) lugubre; (prospect, future) morose

bled [bled] *pt, pp of* **bleed**

bleed (pt, pp **bled**) [bli:d, bled] *vt* saigner; (brakes, radiator) purger ▷ *vi* saigner; **my nose is ~ing** je saigne du nez

blemish ['blemɪʃ] *n* défaut *m*; (on reputation) tache *f*

blend [blend] *n* mélange *m* ▷ *vt* mélanger ▷ *vi* (colours etc: also: **~ in**) se mélanger, se fondre, s'allier; **blender** *n* (Culin) mixeur *m*

bless (pt, pp **~ed** or **blest**) [bles, blest] *vt* bénir; **~ you!** (after sneeze) à tes souhaits!; **blessing** *n* bénédiction *f*; (godsend) bienfait *m*

blew [blu:] *pt of* **blow**

blight [blaɪt] *vt* (hopes etc) anéantir, briser

blind [blaɪnd] *adj* aveugle ▷ *n* (for window) store *m* ▷ *vt* aveugler; **the blind** *npl* les aveugles *mpl*; **blind alley** *n* impasse *f*; **blindfold** *n* bandeau *m* ▷ *adj, adv* les yeux bandés ▷ *vt* bander les yeux à

blink [blɪŋk] *vi* cligner des yeux; (light) clignoter

bliss [blɪs] *n* félicité *f*, bonheur *m* sans mélange

blister ['blɪstə'] *n* (on skin) ampoule *f*, cloque *f*; (on paintwork) boursouflure *f* ▷ *vi* (paint) se boursoufler, se cloquer

blizzard ['blɪzəd] *n* blizzard *m*, tempête *f* de neige

bloated ['bləutɪd] *adj* (face) bouffi(e); (stomach, person) gonflé(e)

blob [blɒb] *n* (drop) goutte *f*; (stain, spot) tache *f*

block [blɒk] *n* bloc *m*; (in pipes) obstruction *f*; (toy) cube *m*; (of buildings) pâté *m* (de maisons) ▷ *vt* bloquer;

(fig) faire obstacle à; **the sink is ~ed** l'évier est bouché; **~ of flats** (BRIT) immeuble (locatif); **mental** ~ blocage m; **block up** vt boucher; **blockade** [blɔ'keɪd] n blocus m ▷ vt faire le blocus de; **blockage** n obstruction f; **blockbuster** n (film, book) grand succès; **block capitals** npl majuscules fpl d'imprimerie; **block letters** npl majuscules fpl

blog [blɔg] n blog m, blogue m

bloke [bləʊk] n (BRIT inf) type m

blond(e) [blɔnd] adj, n blond(e)

blood [blʌd] n sang m; **blood donor** n donneur(-euse) de sang; **blood group** n groupe sanguin; **blood poisoning** n empoisonnement m du sang; **blood pressure** n tension (artérielle); **bloodshed** n effusion f de sang, carnage m; **bloodshot** adj: **bloodshot eyes** yeux injectés de sang; **bloodstream** n sang m, système sanguin; **blood test** n analyse f de sang; **blood transfusion** n transfusion f de sang; **blood type** n groupe sanguin; **blood vessel** n vaisseau sanguin; **bloody** adj sanglant(e); (BRIT infl): **this bloody** ... ce foutu ..., ce putain de ... (!) ▷ adv: **bloody strong/good** (BRIT: infl) vachement or sacrément fort/bon

bloom [bluːm] n fleur f ▷ vi être en fleur

blossom [ˈblɔsəm] n fleur(s) f(pl) ▷ vi être en fleurs; (fig) s'épanouir

blot [blɔt] n tache f ▷ vt tacher; (ink) sécher

blouse [blauz] n (feminine garment) chemisier m, corsage m

blow [bləʊ] n coup m ▷ vb (pt **blew**, pp **~n**) ▷ vi souffler ▷ vt (instrument) jouer de; (fuse) faire sauter; **to ~ one's nose** se moucher; **blow away** vi s'envoler ▷ vt chasser, faire s'envoler; **blow out** vi (fire, flame) s'éteindre; (tyre) éclater; (fuse) sauter; **blow up** vi exploser, sauter ▷ vt faire sauter; (tyre) gonfler; (Phot) agrandir; **blow-dry** n (hairstyle) brushing m

blown [bləʊn] pp of **blow**

blue [bluː] adj bleu(e); (depressed) triste; **~ film/joke** film m/histoire f pornographique; **out of the ~** (fig) à l'improviste, sans qu'on s'y attende; **bluebell** n jacinthe f des bois; **blueberry** n myrtille f, airelle f; **blue cheese** n (fromage) bleu m; **blues** npl: **the blues** (Mus) le blues; **to have the blues** (inf: feeling) avoir le cafard; **bluetit** n mésange bleue

bluff [blʌf] vi bluffer ▷ n bluff m; **to call sb's ~** mettre qn au défi d'exécuter ses menaces

blunder [ˈblʌndəʳ] n gaffe f, bévue f ▷ vi faire une gaffe or une bévue

blunt [blʌnt] adj (knife) émoussé(e), peu tranchant(e); (pencil) mal taillé(e); (person) brusque, ne mâchant pas ses mots

blur [bləːʳ] n (shape): **to become a ~** devenir flou ▷ vt brouiller, rendre flou(e); **blurred** adj flou(e)

blush [blʌʃ] vi rougir ▷ n rougeur f; **blusher** n rouge m à joues

board [bɔːd] n (wooden) planche f; (on wall) panneau m; (for chess etc) plateau m; (cardboard) carton m; (committee) conseil m, comité m; (in firm) conseil d'administration; (Naut, Aviat): **on ~** à bord de ▷ vt (ship) monter à bord de; (train) monter dans; **full ~** (BRIT) pension complète; **half ~** (BRIT) demi-pension f; **~ and lodging** n chambre f avec pension; **to go by the ~** (hopes, principles) être abandonné(e); **board game** n jeu m de société; **boarding card** n (Aviat, Naut) carte f d'embarquement; **boarding pass** n (BRIT) = **boarding card**; **boarding school** n internat m, pensionnat m; **board room** n salle f du conseil d'administration

boast [bəʊst] vi: **to ~ (about or of)** se vanter de

boat [bəʊt] n bateau m; (small) canot m; barque f

bob [bɔb] vi (boat, cork on water: also: **~**

up and down danser, se balancer

bobby pin ['bɒbɪ-] n (US) pince f à cheveux

body ['bɒdɪ] n corps m; (of car) carrosserie f; (fig: society) organe m, organisme m; **body-building** n body-building m, culturisme m; **bodyguard** n garde m du corps; **bodywork** n carrosserie f

bog [bɒg] n tourbière f ▷ vt: **to get ~ged down (in)** (fig) s'enliser (dans)

bogus ['bəʊgəs] adj bidon inv; fantôme

boil [bɔɪl] vt (faire) bouillir ▷ n (Med) furoncle m ▷ vi bouillir; **to come to the** or (US) **a ~** bouillir; **boil down** vi (fig): **to ~ down to** se réduire ou ramener à; **boil over** vi déborder; **boiled egg** n œuf m à la coque; **boiled potatoes** n pommes fpl à l'anglaise or à l'eau; **boiler** n chaudière f; **boiling** ['bɔɪlɪŋ] adj: **I'm boiling (hot)** (inf) je crève de chaud; **boiling point** n point m d'ébullition

bold [bəʊld] adj hardi(e), audacieux(-euse); (pej) effronté(e); (outline, colour) franc (franche), tranché(e), marqué(e)

bollard ['bɒləd] n (BRIT Aut) borne lumineuse or de signalisation

bolt [bəʊlt] n verrou m; (with nut) boulon m ▷ adv: **~ upright** droit(e) comme un piquet ▷ vt (door) verrouiller; (food) engloutir ▷ vi se sauver, filer (comme une flèche); (horse) s'emballer

bomb [bɒm] n bombe f ▷ vt bombarder; **bombard** [bɒm'bɑːd] vt bombarder; **bomber** n (Aviat) bombardier m; (terrorist) poseur m de bombes; **bomb scare** n alerte f à la bombe

bond [bɒnd] n lien m; (binding promise) engagement m, obligation f; (Finance) obligation; **bonds** npl (chains) chaînes fpl; **in ~** (of goods) en entrepôt

bone [bəʊn] n os m; (of fish) arête f ▷ vt désosser, ôter les arêtes de

bonfire ['bɒnfaɪə*] n feu m (de joie); (for rubbish) feu

bonnet ['bɒnɪt] n bonnet m; (BRIT: of car) capot m

bonus ['bəʊnəs] n (money) prime f; (advantage) avantage m

boo [buː] excl hou!, peuh! ▷ vt huer

book [buk] n livre m; (of stamps, tickets etc) carnet m; (Comm): **books** npl comptes mpl, comptabilité f ▷ vt (ticket) prendre; (seat, room) réserver; (football player) prendre le nom de, donner un carton à; **I ~ed a table in the name of ...** j'ai réservé une table au nom de ...; **book in** vi (BRIT: at hotel) prendre sa chambre; **book up** vt réserver; **the hotel is ~ed up** l'hôtel est complet; **bookcase** n bibliothèque f (meuble); **booking** n (BRIT) réservation f; **I confirmed my booking by fax/e-mail** j'ai confirmé ma réservation par fax/e-mail; **booking office** n (BRIT) bureau m de location; **book-keeping** n comptabilité f; **booklet** n brochure f; **bookmaker** n bookmaker m; **bookmark** n (for book) marque-page m; (Comput) signet m; **bookseller** n libraire m/f; **bookshelf** n (single) étagère f (à livres); (bookcase) bibliothèque f; **bookshop, bookstore** n librairie f

boom [buːm] n (noise) grondement m; (in prices, population) forte augmentation; (busy period) boom m, vague f de prospérité ▷ vi gronder; prospérer

boost [buːst] n stimulant m, remontant m ▷ vt stimuler

boot [buːt] n botte f; (for hiking) chaussure f (de marche); (ankle boot) bottine f; (BRIT: of car) coffre m (à bagages); (Comput) lancer, mettre en route; **to ~** (in addition) par-dessus le marché, en plus

booth [buːð] n (at fair) baraque (foraine); (of telephone etc) cabine f; (also: **voting ~**) isoloir m

booze [buːz] (inf) n boissons fpl alcooliques, alcool m

border ['bɔːdə*] n bordure f; bord m; (of a country) frontière f; **borderline** n (fig) ligne f de démarcation

bore [bɔːˀ] pt of **bear** ▷ vt (person) ennuyer, raser; (hole) percer; (well, tunnel) creuser ▷ n (person) raseur(-euse); (boring thing) barbe f; (of gun) calibre m; **bored** adj: **to be bored** s'ennuyer; **boredom** n ennui m

boring ['bɔːrɪŋ] adj ennuyeux(-euse)

born [bɔːn] adj: **to be ~** naître; **I was ~ in 1960** je suis né en 1960

borne [bɔːn] pp of **bear**

borough ['bʌrə] n municipalité f

borrow ['bɔrəu] vt: **to ~ sth (from sb)** emprunter qch (à qn)

Bosnia(-Herzegovina)
['bɔːsnɪə(hɜːzə'gəuvɪnə)] n Bosnie-Herzégovine f; **Bosnian** ['bɔznɪən] adj bosniaque, bosnien(ne) ▷ n Bosniaque m/f, Bosnien(ne)

bosom ['buzəm] n poitrine f; (fig) sein m

boss [bɔs] n patron m ▷ vt (also: **~ about, ~ around**) mener à la baguette; **bossy** adj autoritaire

both [bəuθ] adj: les deux, l'un(e) et l'autre ▷ pron: **~ (of them)** les deux, tous (toutes) (les) deux; l'un(e) et l'autre; **~ of us went, we ~ went** nous y sommes allés tous les deux ▷ adv: **~ A and B** A et B

bother ['bɔðəˀ] vt (worry) tracasser; (needle, plague) importuner, ennuyer; (disturb) déranger ▷ vi (also: **~ o.s.**) se tracasser, se faire du souci ▷ n (trouble) ennuis mpl; **to ~ doing** prendre la peine de faire; **don't ~** ce n'est pas la peine; **it's no ~** aucun problème

bottle ['bɔtl] n bouteille f; (baby's) biberon m; (of perfume, medicine) flacon m ▷ vt mettre en bouteille(s); **bottle bank** n conteneur m de bouteilles; **bottle-opener** n ouvre-bouteille m

bottom ['bɔtəm] n (of container, sea etc) fond m; (buttocks) derrière m; (of page, list) bas m; (of mountain, tree, hill) pied m ▷ adj (shelf, step) du bas

bought [bɔːt] pt, pp of **buy**

boulder ['bəuldəˀ] n gros rocher (gén lisse, arrondi)

bounce [bauns] vi (ball) rebondir; (cheque) être refusé (étant donné sans provision) ▷ vt faire rebondir ▷ n (rebound) rebond m; **bouncer** n (inf: at dance, club) videur m

bound [baund] pt, pp of **bind** ▷ n (gen pl) limite f; (leap) bond m ▷ vi (leap) bondir ▷ vt (limit) borner ▷ adj: **to be ~ to do sth** (obliged) être obligé(e) ou avoir obligation de faire qch; **he's ~ to fail** (likely) il est sûr d'échouer, son échec est inévitable ou assuré; **~ by** (law, regulation) engagé(e) par; **~ for à** destination de; **out of ~s** dont l'accès est interdit

boundary ['baundrɪ] n frontière f

bouquet ['bukeɪ] n bouquet m

bourbon ['buəbən] n (us: also: **~ whiskey**) bourbon m

bout [baut] n période f; (of malaria etc) accès m, crise f, attaque f; (Boxing etc) combat m, match m

boutique [buː'tiːk] n boutique f

bow¹ [bəu] n (knot) nœud m; (weapon) arc m; (Mus) archet m

bow² [bau] n (with body) révérence f, inclination f (du buste ou corps); (Naut: also: **~s**) proue f ▷ vi faire une révérence, s'incliner

bowels [bauəlz] npl intestins mpl; (fig) entrailles fpl

bowl [bəul] n (for eating) bol m; (for washing) cuvette f; (ball) boule f ▷ vi (Cricket) lancer (la balle); **bowler** n (Cricket) lanceur m (de la balle); (BRIT: also: **bowler hat**) (chapeau m) melon m

bowling ['bəulɪŋ] n (game) jeu m de boules, jeu de quilles; **bowling alley** n bowling m; **bowling green** n terrain m de boules (gazonné et carré); **bowls** n (jeu m de) boules fpl

bow tie [bəu-] n nœud m papillon

box [bɔks] n boîte f; (also: **cardboard ~**) carton m; (Theat) loge f ▷ vt mettre en boîte ▷ vi boxer, faire de la boxe; **boxer** n (person) boxeur m; **boxer shorts** npl caleçon m; **boxing** ['bɔksɪŋ] n (sport) boxe f; **Boxing Day**

n (BRIT) le lendemain de Noël; voir encadré;
boxing gloves npl gants mpl de boxe;
boxing ring n ring m; **box junction** n
(BRIT Aut) zone f (de carrefour) d'accès
réglementé; **box office** n bureau m
de location

● **BOXING DAY**

Boxing Day est le lendemain de
Noël, férié en Grande-Bretagne. Ce
nom vient d'une coutume du XIXe
siècle qui consistait à donner des
cadeaux de Noël (dans des boîtes à
ses employés etc le 26 décembre.

boy [bɔɪ] n garçon m; **boy band** n boys
band m
boycott ['bɔɪkɒt] n boycottage m ▷ vt
boycotter
boyfriend ['bɔɪfrɛnd] n (petit) ami
bra [brɑː] n soutien-gorge m
brace [breɪs] n (support) attache f,
agrafe f; (BRIT: also: ~s: on teeth) appareil
m (dentaire); (tool) vilebrequin m ▷ vt
(support) consolider, soutenir; **braces**
npl (BRIT: for trousers) bretelles fpl; **to ~
o.s.** (fig) se préparer mentalement
bracelet ['breɪslɪt] n bracelet m
bracket ['brækɪt] n (Tech) tasseau m,
support m; (group) classe f, tranche f;
(also: **brace ~**) accolade f; (also: **round
~**) parenthèse f; (also: **square ~**) crochet
m ▷ vt mettre entre parenthèses; **in ~s**
entre parenthèses ou crochets
brag [bræg] vi se vanter
braid [breɪd] n (trimming) galon m; (of
hair) tresse f, natte f
brain [breɪn] n cerveau m; **brains** npl
(intellect, food) cervelle f
braise [breɪz] vt braiser
brake [breɪk] n frein m ▷ vt, vi freiner;
brake light n feu m de stop
bran [bræn] n son m
branch [brɑːntʃ] n branche f; (Comm)
succursale f; (: of bank) agence f; **branch
off** vi (road) bifurquer; **branch out** vi
diversifier ses activités

brand [brænd] n marque
(commerciale) ▷ vt (cattle) marquer (au
fer rouge); **brand name** n nom m de
marque; **brand-new** adj tout(e) neuf
(neuve), flambant neuf
brandy ['brændɪ] n cognac m
brash [bræʃ] adj effronté(e)
brass [brɑːs] n cuivre m (jaune), laiton
m; **the ~** (Mus) les cuivres; **brass band**
n fanfare f
brat [bræt] n (pej) mioche m/f, môme
m/f
brave [breɪv] adj courageux(-euse),
brave ▷ vt braver, affronter; **bravery**
n bravoure f, courage m
brawl [brɔːl] n rixe f, bagarre f
Brazil [brə'zɪl] n Brésil m; **Brazilian** adj
brésilien(ne) ▷ n Brésilien(ne)
breach [briːtʃ] vt ouvrir une brèche
dans ▷ n (gap) brèche f; (breaking): ~ of
contract rupture f de contrat; **~ of the
peace** attentat m à l'ordre public
bread [brɛd] n pain m; **breadbin**
n (BRIT) boîte f or huche f à pain;
breadbox n (US) boîte f or huche f à
pain; **breadcrumbs** npl miettes fpl de
pain; (Culin) chapelure f, panure f
breadth [brɛtθ] n largeur f
break [breɪk] (pt broke, pp broken) vt
casser, briser; (promise) rompre; (law)
violer ▷ vi se casser, se briser; (weather)
tourner; (storm) éclater; (day) se lever
▷ n (gap) brèche f; (fracture) cassure f;
(rest) interruption f, arrêt m; (: short
pause): **t : at school** récréation f; (chance)
chance f, occasion f favorable; **to ~
one's leg** etc se casser la jambe etc; **to ~
~ a record** battre un record; **to ~ the
news to sb** annoncer la nouvelle à qn;
break down vt (door etc) enfoncer;
(figures, data) décomposer, analyser ▷ vi
s'effondrer; (Med) faire une dépression
(nerveuse); (Aut) tomber en panne; **my
car has broken down** ma voiture est
en panne; **break in** vt (horse etc) dresser
▷ vi (burglar) entrer par effraction;
(interrupt) interrompre; **break into** vt
fus (house) s'introduire or pénétrer par

effraction dans; **break off** vi (speaker) s'interrompre; (branch) se rompre ▷ vt (talks, engagement) rompre; **break out** vi éclater, se déclarer; (prisoner) s'évader; **to ~ out in spots** se couvrir de boutons; **break up** vi (partnership) cesser, prendre fin; (marriage) se briser; (crowd, meeting) se séparer; (ship) se disloquer; (Scol: pupils) être en vacances; (line) couper; **the line's or you're ~ing up** ça coupe ▷ vt fracasser, casser; (fight etc) interrompre; (marriage) désunir; **breakdown** n (Aut) panne f; (in communications, marriage) rupture f; (Med: also: **nervous breakdown**) dépression (nerveuse); (of figures) ventilation f, répartition f; **breakdown truck** (us **breakdown van**) n dépanneuse f

breakfast ['brɛkfəst] n petit déjeuner m; **what time is ~?** le petit déjeuner est à quelle heure?

break: break-in n cambriolage m; **breakthrough** n percée f

breast [brɛst] n (of woman) sein m; (chest) poitrine f; (of chicken, turkey) blanc m; **breast-feed** vt, vi (irreg: like **feed**) allaiter; **breast-stroke** n brasse f

breath [brɛθ] n haleine f, souffle m; **to take a deep ~** respirer à fond; **out of ~** à bout de souffle, essoufflé(e)

Breathalyser® ['brɛθəlaɪzəʳ] (BRIT) n alcootest m

breathe [briːð] vt, vi respirer; **breathe in** vi inspirer ▷ vt aspirer; **breathe out** vt, vi expirer; **breathing** n respiration f

breath: breathless adj essoufflé(e), haletant(e); **breathtaking** adj stupéfiant(e), à vous couper le souffle; **breath test** n alcootest m

bred [brɛd] pt, pp de **breed**

breed [briːd] (pt, pp **bred**) vt élever; l'élevage de ▷ vi se reproduire ▷ n race f, variété f

breeze [briːz] n brise f

breezy ['briːzɪ] adj (day, weather) venteux(-euse); (manner) désinvolte; (person) jovial(e)

brew [bruː] vt (tea) faire infuser; (beer) brasser ▷ vi (fig) se préparer, couver; **brewery** n brasserie f (fabrique)

bribe [braɪb] n pot-de-vin m ▷ vt acheter; soudoyer; **bribery** n corruption f

bric-a-brac ['brɪkəbræk] n bric-à-brac m

brick [brɪk] n brique f; **bricklayer** n maçon m

bride [braɪd] n mariée f, épouse f; **bridegroom** n marié m, époux m; **bridesmaid** n demoiselle f d'honneur

bridge [brɪdʒ] n pont m; (Naut) passerelle f (de commandement); (of nose) arête f; (Cards, Dentistry) bridge m ▷ vt (gap) combler

bridle ['braɪdl] n bride f

brief [briːf] adj bref (brève) ▷ n (Law) dossier m, cause f; (gen) tâche f ▷ vt mettre au courant; **briefs** npl slip m; **briefcase** n serviette f, porte-documents m inv; **briefing** n instructions fpl; (Press) briefing m; **briefly** adv brièvement

brigadier [brɪgəˈdɪəʳ] n brigadier général

bright [braɪt] adj brillant(e); (room, weather) clair(e); (person: clever) intelligent(e), doué(e); (: cheerful) gai(e); (idea) génial(e); (colour) vif (vive)

brilliant ['brɪljənt] adj brillant(e); (light, sunshine) éclatant(e); (inf: great) super

brim [brɪm] n bord m

brine [braɪn] n (Culin) saumure f

bring [brɪŋ] (pt, pp **brought**) vt (thing) apporter; (person) amener; **bring about** vt provoquer, entraîner; **bring back** vt rapporter; (person) ramener; **bring down** vt (lower) abaisser; (shoot down) abattre; (government) faire s'effondrer; **bring in** vt (person) faire entrer; (object) rentrer; (Pol: legislation) introduire; (produce: income) rapporter; **bring on** vt (illness, attack) provoquer; (player, substitute) amener; **bring out** vt sortir; (meaning) faire ressortir, mettre en relief; **bring up** vt élever; (carry up) monter; (*question*) soulever; (*food: vomit*) vomir, rendre

brink [brɪŋk] *n* bord *m*

brisk [brɪsk] *adj* vif (vive); (*abrupt*) brusque; (*trade etc*) actif(-ive)

bristle ['brɪsl] *n* poil *m* ▷ *vi* se hérisser

Brit [brɪt] *n abbr* (*inf*: = British person) Britannique *m/f*

Britain ['brɪtən] *n* (*also*: **Great ~**) la Grande-Bretagne

British ['brɪtɪʃ] *adj* britannique ▷ *npl*: **the ~** les Britanniques *mpl*; **British Isles** *npl*: **the British Isles** les îles *fpl* Britanniques

Briton ['brɪtən] *n* Britannique *m/f*

Brittany ['brɪtənɪ] *n* Bretagne *f*

brittle ['brɪtl] *adj* cassant(e), fragile

B road *n* (BRIT) = route départementale

broad [brɔːd] *adj* large; (*distinction*) général(e); (*accent*) prononcé(e); **in ~ daylight** en plein jour; **broadband** *n* transmission *f* à haut débit; **broad bean** *n* fève *f*; **broadcast** *n* émission *f* ▷ *vb* (*pt, pp* **broadcast**) ▷ *vt* (*Radio*) radiodiffuser; (*TV*) téléviser ▷ *vi* émettre; **broaden** *vt* élargir; **to broaden one's mind** élargir ses horizons ▷ *vi* s'élargir; **broadly** *adv* en gros, généralement; **broad-minded** *adj* large d'esprit

broccoli ['brɔkəlɪ] *n* brocoli *m*

brochure ['brəʊʃjʊə*ʳ*] *n* prospectus *m*, dépliant *m*

broil [brɔɪl] (us) *vt* rôtir

broiler ['brɔɪlə*ʳ*] *n* (*fowl*) poulet *m* (à rôtir); (us: *grill*) gril *m*

broke [brəʊk] *pt of* **break** ▷ *adj* (*inf*) fauché(e)

broken ['brəʊkn] *pp of* **break** ▷ *adj* (*stick, leg etc*) cassé(e); (*machine: also*: ~ **down**) fichu(e); **in ~ French/English** dans un français/anglais approximatif *or* hésitant

broker ['brəʊkə*ʳ*] *n* courtier *m*

bronchitis [brɔŋ'kaɪtɪs] *n* bronchite *f*

bronze [brɔnz] *n* bronze *m*

brooch [brəʊtʃ] *n* broche *f*

brood [bruːd] *n* couvée *f* ▷ *vi* (*person*)

méditer (sombrement), ruminer

broom [brum] *n* balai *m*; (*Bot*) genêt *m*

Bros. *abbr* (*Comm*: = *brothers*) Frères

broth [brɔθ] *n* bouillon *m* de viande et de légumes

brothel ['brɔθl] *n* maison close, bordel *m*

brother ['brʌðə*ʳ*] *n* frère *m*; **brother-in-law** *n* beau-frère *m*

brought [brɔːt] *pt, pp of* **bring**

brow [brau] *n* front *m*; (*eyebrow*) sourcil *m*; (*of hill*) sommet *m*

brown [braun] *adj* brun(e), marron *inv*; (*hair*) châtain *inv*; (*tanned*) bronzé(e) ▷ *n* (*colour*) brun *m*, marron *m* ▷ *vt* brunir; (*Culin*) faire dorer, faire roussir; **brown bread** *n* pain *m* bis

Brownie ['braunɪ] *n* jeannette *f* éclaireuse (cadette)

brown rice *n* riz *m* complet

brown sugar *n* cassonade *f*

browse [brauz] *vi* (*in shop*) regarder (*sans acheter*); **to ~ through a book** feuilleter un livre; **browser** *n* (*Comput*) navigateur *m*

bruise [bruːz] *n* bleu *m*, ecchymose *f*, contusion *f* ▷ *vt* contusionner, meurtrir

brunette [bruː'nɛt] *n* (*femme*) brune

brush [brʌʃ] *n* brosse *f*; (*for painting*) pinceau *m*; (*for shaving*) blaireau *m*; (*quarrel*) accrochage *m*, prise *f* de bec ▷ *vt* brosser; (*also*: ~ **past**, ~ **against**) effleurer, frôler

Brussels ['brʌslz] *n* Bruxelles

Brussels sprout [-spraut] *n* chou *m* de Bruxelles

brutal ['bruːtl] *adj* brutal(e)

B.Sc. *n abbr* = **Bachelor of Science**

BSE *n abbr* = (*bovine spongiform encephalopathy*) ESB *f*, BSE *f*

bubble ['bʌbl] *n* bulle *f* ▷ *vi* bouillonner, faire des bulles; (*sparkle, fig*) pétiller; **bubble bath** *n* bain moussant; **bubble gum** *n* chewing-gum *m*; **bubblejet printer** ['bʌbldʒɛt-] *n* imprimante *f* à bulle d'encre

buck [bʌk] *n* mâle *m* (*d'un lapin, lièvre,*

daim etc); (US inf) dollar m ▷ vi ruer, lancer une ruade; **to pass the ~ (to sb)** se décharger de la responsabilité (sur qn)

bucket ['bʌkɪt] n seau m

buckle ['bʌkl] n boucle f ▷ vt (belt etc) boucler, attacher ▷ vi (warp) tordre, gauchir; (: wheel) se voiler

bud [bʌd] n bourgeon m; (of flower) bouton m ▷ vi bourgeonner; (flower) éclore

Buddhism ['budɪzəm] n bouddhisme m

Buddhist ['budɪst] adj bouddhiste ▷ n Bouddhiste m/f

buddy ['bʌdɪ] n (US) copain m

budge [bʌdʒ] vt faire bouger ▷ vi bouger

budgerigar ['bʌdʒərɪgɑːʳ] n perruche f

budget ['bʌdʒɪt] n budget m ▷ vi: **to ~ for sth** inscrire qch au budget

budgie ['bʌdʒɪ] n = **budgerigar**

buff [bʌf] adj (couleur) chamois ▷ n (inf: enthusiast) mordu(e)

buffalo (pl ~ or ~es) ['bʌfələu] n (BRIT) buffle m; (US) bison m

buffer ['bʌfəʳ] n tampon m; (Comput) mémoire f tampon

buffet ['bufeɪ] (food BRIT: bar) buffet m ▷ vt ['bʌfɪt] secouer, ébranler; **buffet car** n (BRIT Rail) voiture-bar f

bug [bʌg] n (bedbug etc) punaise f; (esp US: any insect) insecte m, bestiole f; (fig: germ) virus m, microbe m; (spy device) dispositif m d'écoute (électronique), micro clandestin; (Comput: of program) erreur f ▷ vt (room) poser des micros dans; (inf: annoy) embêter

buggy ['bʌgɪ] n poussette f

build [bɪld] n (of person) carrure f, charpente f ▷ vt (pt, pp **built**) construire, bâtir; **build up** vt accumuler, amasser; (business) développer; (reputation) bâtir; **builder** n entrepreneur m; **building** n (trade) construction f; (structure) bâtiment m, construction f; (: residential, offices) immeuble m; **building site** n chantier

m (de construction); **building society** n (BRIT) société f de crédit immobilier

built [bɪlt] pt, pp of **build**; **built-in** adj (cupboard) encastré(e); (device) incorporé(e); intégré(e); **built-up** adj: **built-up area** zone urbanisée

bulb [bʌlb] n (Bot) bulbe m, oignon m; (Elec) ampoule f

Bulgaria [bʌl'gɛərɪə] n Bulgarie f; **Bulgarian** adj bulgare ▷ n Bulgare m/f

bulge [bʌldʒ] n renflement m, gonflement m ▷ vi faire saillie; présenter un renflement; (pocket, file): **to be bulging with** être plein(e) à craquer de

bulimia [bə'lɪmɪə] n boulimie f

bulimic [bju:'lɪmɪk] adj, n boulimique (m/f)

bulk [bʌlk] n masse f, volume m; **in ~** (Comm) en gros, en vrac; **the ~ of** la plus grande or grosse partie de; **bulky** adj volumineux(-euse), encombrant(e)

bull [bul] n taureau m; (male elephant, whale) mâle m

bulldozer ['buldəuzəʳ] n bulldozer m

bullet ['bulɪt] n balle f (de fusil etc)

bulletin ['bulɪtɪn] n bulletin m, communiqué m; (also: **news ~**) (bulletin d'informations fpl; **bulletin board** n (Comput) messagerie f (électronique)

bullfight ['bulfaɪt] n corrida f, course f de taureaux; **bullfighter** n torero m; **bullfighting** n tauromachie f

bully ['bulɪ] n brute f, tyran m ▷ vt tyranniser, rudoyer

bum [bʌm] n (inf: backside) derrière m; (: esp US: tramp) vagabond(e), traîne-savates m/f inv; (: idler) glandeur m

bumblebee ['bʌmblbi:] n bourdon m

bump [bʌmp] n (blow) coup m, choc m; (jolt) cahot m; (on road etc, on head) bosse f ▷ vt heurter, cogner; **bump into** vt fus rentrer dans, tamponner; (inf) tomber sur; **bumper** n pare-chocs m inv ▷ adj: **bumper crop/harvest** récolte/ moisson exceptionnelle; **bumpy** adj (road) cahoteux(-euse); **it was a**

bumpy flight/ride on a été secoués
dans l'avion/la voiture

bun [bʌn] n (cake) petit gâteau; (bread)
petit pain au lait; (of hair) chignon m

bunch [bʌntʃ] n (of flowers) bouquet
m; (of keys) trousseau m; (of bananas)
régime m; (of people) groupe m;
bunches npl (in hair) couettes fpl; **~ of
grapes** grappe f de raisin

bundle [bʌndl] n paquet m ▷ vt (also:
~ up) faire un paquet de; (put): **to ~
sth/sb into** fourrer or enfourner
qch/qn dans

bungalow [bʌŋgələu] n bungalow m

bungee jumping [bʌndʒiː-dʒʌmpɪŋ]
n saut m à l'élastique

bunion [bʌnjən] n oignon m (au pied)

bunk [bʌŋk] n couchette f; **bunk beds**
npl lits superposés

bunker [bʌŋkəʳ] n (coal store) soute f
à charbon; (Mil, Golf) bunker m

bunny [bʌnɪ] n (also: **~ rabbit**) lapin m

buoy [bɔɪ] n bouée f; **buoyant** adj (ship)
flottable; (carefree) gai(e), plein(e)
d'entrain; (Comm: market, economy)
actif(-ive)

burden [bəːdn] n fardeau m, charge
f ▷ vt charger; (oppress) accabler,
surcharger

bureau (pl **-x**) [bjuərəu, -z] n (BRIT:
writing desk) bureau m, secrétaire m;
(us: chest of drawers) commode f; (office)
bureau, office m

bureaucracy [bjuəˈrɔkrəsɪ] n
bureaucratie f

bureaucrat [bjuərəkræt] n
bureaucrate m/f; **rond-de-cuir** m

bureau de change [-dəˈʃɑ̃ʒ] (pl
bureaux de change) n bureau m de
change

bureaux [bjuərəuz] npl of **bureau**

burger [bəːgəʳ] n hamburger m

burglar [bəːgləʳ] n cambrioleur m;
burglar alarm n sonnerie f d'alarme;
burglary n cambriolage m

Burgundy [bəːgəndɪ] n Bourgogne f

burial [bɛrɪəl] n enterrement m

burn [bəːn] vt, vi (pt, pp **-ed** or **~t**) brûler

▷ n brûlure f; **burn down** vt incendier,
détruire par le feu; **burn out** vt (writer
etc): **to ~ o.s. out** s'user (à force de
travailler); **burning** adj (building, forest)
en flammes; (issue, question) brûlant(e);
(ambition) dévorant(e)

Burns' Night [bəːnz-] n fête écossaise à
la mémoire du poète Robert Burns

- **BURNS NIGHT**
-
- **Burns Night** est une fête qui a lieu
- le 25 janvier, à la mémoire du poète
- écossais Robert Burns (1759 - 1796),
- à l'occasion de laquelle les Écossais
- partout dans le monde organisent
- un souper, en général arrosé de
- whisky. Le plat principal est toujours
- le haggis, servi avec de la purée de
- pommes de terre et de la purée de
- rutabagas. On apporte le haggis au
- son des cornemuses et au cours du
- repas on lit des poèmes de Burns et
- on chante des chansons.

burnt [bəːnt] pt, pp of **burn**

burp [bəːp] (inf) n rot m ▷ vi roter

burrow [bʌrəu] n terrier m ▷ vi
creuser un terrier; (rummage) fouiller

burst [bəːst] (pt, pp **burst**) vt faire éclater;
(river: banks etc) rompre ▷ vi éclater;
(tyre) crever ▷ n explosion f; (also: **~
pipe**) fuite f (due à une rupture); **a ~
of enthusiasm/energy** un accès
d'enthousiasme/d'énergie; **to ~ into
flames** s'enflammer soudainement; **to
~ out laughing** éclater de rire; **to ~ into
tears** fondre en larmes; **to ~ open** vi
s'ouvrir violemment or soudainement;
to be ~ing with (container) être plein(e)
(à craquer) de, regorger de; (fig) être
débordant(e) de; **burst into** vt fus
(room etc) faire irruption dans

bury [bɛrɪ] vt enterrer

bus (pl **-es**) [bʌs, bʌsɪz] n autobus m,
bus m; **bus conductor** n receveur(-euse)
m/f de bus

bush [buʃ] n buisson m; (scrub land)

brousse f; **to beat about the ~** tourner autour du pot

business ['bɪznɪs] n (matter, firm) affaire f; (trading) affaires fpl; (job, duty) travail m; **to be away on ~** être en déplacement d'affaires; **it's none of my ~** cela ne me regarde pas, ce ne sont pas mes affaires; **he means ~** il ne plaisante pas, il est sérieux; **business class** n (on plane) classe f affaires; **businesslike** adj sérieux(-euse), efficace; **businessman** (irreg) n homme m d'affaires; **business trip** n voyage m d'affaires; **businesswoman** (irreg) n femme f d'affaires

busker ['bʌskə^r] n (BRIT) artiste ambulant(e)

bus: bus pass n carte f de bus; **bus shelter** n abribus m; **bus station** n gare f routière; **bus-stop** n arrêt m d'autobus

bust [bʌst] n buste m; (measurement) tour m de poitrine ▷ adj (inf: broken) fichu(e), fini(e); **to go ~** faire faillite

bustling ['bʌslɪŋ] adj (town) très animé(e)

busy ['bɪzɪ] adj occupé(e); (shop, street) très fréquenté(e); (us: telephone, line) occupé ▷ vt: **to ~ o.s.** s'occuper; **busy signal** n (us) tonalité f occupé inv

🔑 **KEYWORD**

but [bʌt] conj mais; **I'd love to come, but I'm busy** j'aimerais venir mais je suis occupé; **he's not English but French** il n'est pas anglais mais français; **but that's far too expensive!** mais c'est bien trop cher!

▷ prep (apart from, except) sauf, excepté; **nothing but** rien d'autre que; **we've had nothing but trouble** nous n'avons eu que des ennuis; **no-one but him can do it** lui seul peut le faire; **who but a lunatic would do such a thing?** qui sinon un fou ferait une chose pareille?; **but for you/your help** sans toi/ton aide; **anything but that** tout sauf or

excepté ça, tout mais pas ça

▷ adv (just, only) ne ... que; **she's but a child** elle n'est qu'une enfant; **had I but known** si seulement j'avais su; **I can but try** je peux toujours essayer; **all but finished** pratiquement terminé

butcher ['butʃə^r] n boucher m ▷ vt massacrer; (cattle etc for meat) tuer; **butcher's (shop)** n boucherie f

butler ['bʌtlə^r] n maître m d'hôtel

butt [bʌt] n (cask) gros tonneau; (of gun) crosse f; (of cigarette) mégot m; (BRIT fig: target) cible f ▷ vt donner un coup de tête à

butter ['bʌtə^r] n beurre m ▷ vt beurrer; **buttercup** n bouton m d'or

butterfly ['bʌtəflaɪ] n papillon m; (Swimming: also: **~ stroke**) brasse f papillon

buttocks ['bʌtəks] npl fesses fpl

button ['bʌtn] n bouton m; (us: badge) pin m ▷ vt (also: **~ up**) boutonner ▷ vi se boutonner

buy [baɪ] (pt, pp **bought**) vt acheter ▷ n achat m; **to ~ sb sth/sth from sb** acheter qch à qn; **to ~ sb a drink** offrir un verre or à boire à qn; **can I ~ you a drink?** je vous offre un verre?; **where can I ~ some postcards?** où est-ce que je peux acheter des cartes postales?; **buy out** vt (partner) désintéresser; **buy up** vt acheter en bloc, rafler; **buyer** n acheteur(-euse) m/f

buzz [bʌz] n bourdonnement m; (inf: phone call): **to give sb a ~** passer un coup de fil à qn ▷ vi bourdonner; **buzzer** n timbre m électrique

🔑 **KEYWORD**

by [baɪ] prep 1 (referring to cause, agent) par, de; **killed by lightning** tué par la foudre; **surrounded by a fence** entouré d'une barrière; **a painting by Picasso** un tableau de Picasso

2 (referring to method, manner, means): **by bus/car** en autobus/voiture; **by train**

par le or en train; **to pay by cheque** payer par chèque; **by moonlight/candlelight** à la lueur de la lune/d'une bougie; **by saving hard, he …** à force d'économiser, il …

3 (via, through) par; **we came by Dover** nous sommes venus par Douvres

4 (close to, past) à côté de; **the house by the school** la maison à côté de l'école; **a holiday by the sea** des vacances au bord de la mer; **she went by me** elle est passée à côté de moi; **I go by the post office every day** je passe devant la poste tous les jours

5 (with time: not later than) avant; (: during): **by daylight** à la lumière du jour; **by night** la nuit, de nuit; **by 4 o'clock** avant 4 heures; **by this time tomorrow** d'ici demain à la même heure; **by the time I got here it was too late** lorsque je suis arrivé il était déjà trop tard

6 (amount) à; **by the kilo/metre** au kilo/au mètre; **paid by the hour** payé à l'heure

7 (Math: measure): **to divide/multiply by 3** diviser/multiplier par 3; **a room 3 metres by 4** une pièce de 3 mètres sur 4; **it's broader by a metre** c'est plus large d'un mètre

8 (according to) d'après, selon; **it's 3 o'clock by my watch** il est 3 heures à ma montre; **it's all right by me** je n'ai rien contre

9: **(all) by oneself** etc tout(e) seul(e) ▷ adv **1** see go; pass etc

2: **by and by** un peu plus tard, bientôt; **by and large** dans l'ensemble

bye(-bye) ['baɪ('baɪ)] excl au revoir!, salut!

by-election ['baɪɪlekʃən] n (BRIT) élection (législative) partielle

bypass ['baɪpɑːs] n rocade f; (Med) pontage m ▷ vt éviter

byte [baɪt] n (Comput) octet m

C

C [siː] n (Mus): **C** do m

cab [kæb] n taxi m; (of train, truck) cabine f

cabaret ['kæbəreɪ] n (show) spectacle m de cabaret

cabbage ['kæbɪdʒ] n chou m

cabin ['kæbɪn] n (house) cabane f, hutte f; (on ship) cabine f; (on plane) compartiment m; **cabin crew** n (Aviat) équipage m

cabinet ['kæbɪnɪt] n (Pol) cabinet m; (furniture) petit meuble à tiroirs et rayons; (also: **display ~**) vitrine f, cabine f; **cabinet minister** n ministre m (membre du cabinet)

cable ['keɪbl] n câble m ▷ vt câbler, télégraphier; **cable car** n téléphérique m; **cable television** n télévision f par câble

cactus (pl **cacti**) ['kæktəs, -taɪ] n cactus m

café ['kæfeɪ] n ≈ café(-restaurant) m (sans alcool)

cafeteria [kæfɪ'tɪərɪə] n cafétéria f

caffein(e) ['kæfi:n] *n* caféine *f*
cage [keɪdʒ] *n* cage *f*
cagoule [kə'gu:l] *n* K-way® *m*
Cairo ['kaɪərəʊ] *n* le Caire
cake [keɪk] *n* gâteau *m*; **~ of soap** savonnette *f*
calcium ['kælsɪəm] *n* calcium *m*
calculate ['kælkjuleɪt] *vt* calculer; *(estimate: chances, effect)* évaluer; **calculation** [kælkju'leɪʃən] *n* calcul *m*; **calculator** *n* calculatrice *f*
calendar ['kæləndə^r] *n* calendrier *m*
calf *(pl* **calves)** [kɑ:f, kɑ:vz] *n (of cow)* veau *m*; *(of other animals)* petit *m*; *(also:* **~skin)** veau *m*, vachette *f*; *(Anat)* mollet *m*
calibre *(us* **caliber)** ['kælɪbə^r] *n* calibre *m*
call [kɔ:l] *vt* appeler; *(meeting)* convoquer ▷ *vi* appeler; *(visit: also:* **~ in, ~ round)** passer ▷ *n (shout)* appel *m*, cri *m*; *(also:* **telephone ~)** coup *m* de téléphone; **to be on ~** être de permanence; **to be ~ed** s'appeler; **can I make a ~ from here?** est-ce que je peux téléphoner d'ici?; **call back** *vi (return)* repasser; *(Tel)* rappeler ▷ *vt (Tel)* rappeler; **can you ~ back later?** pouvez-vous rappeler plus tard?; **call for** *vt fus (demand)* demander; *(fetch)* passer prendre; **call off** *vt* annuler; **call on** *vt fus (visit)* rendre visite à, passer voir; *(request):* **to ~ on sb to do** inviter qn à faire; **call out** *vi* pousser un cri ou des cris; **call up** *vt (Mil)* appeler, mobiliser; *(Tel)* appeler; **callbox** *n (BRIT)* cabine *f* téléphonique; **call centre** *(us* **call center)** *n* centre *m* d'appels; **caller** *n (Tel)* personne *f* qui appelle; *(visitor)* visiteur *m*
callous ['kæləs] *adj* dur(e), insensible
calm [kɑ:m] *adj* calme ▷ *n* calme *m* ▷ *vt* calmer, apaiser; **calm down** *vi* se calmer ▷ *vt* calmer, apaiser; **calmly** ['kɑ:mlɪ] *adv* calmement, avec calme
Calor gas® ['kælə^r-] *n (BRIT)* butane *m*,

butagaz® *m*
calorie ['kælərɪ] *n* calorie *f*
calves [kɑ:vz] *npl of* **calf**
Cambodia [kæm'bəʊdɪə] *n* Cambodge *m*
camcorder ['kæmkɔ:də^r] *n* caméscope *m*
came [keɪm] *pt of* **come**
camel ['kæməl] *n* chameau *m*
camera ['kæmərə] *n* appareil-photo *m*; *(Cine, TV)* caméra *f*; **in ~** à huis clos, en privé; **cameraman** *n* caméraman *m*; **camera phone** *n* téléphone *m* avec appareil photo numérique intégré
camouflage ['kæməflɑ:ʒ] *n* camouflage *m* ▷ *vt* camoufler
camp [kæmp] *n* camp *m* ▷ *vi* camper ▷ *adj (man)* efféminé(e)
campaign [kæm'peɪn] *n (Mil, Pol etc)* campagne *f* ▷ *vi (also fig)* faire campagne; **campaigner** *n*; **campaigner for** partisan(e) de; **campaigner against** opposant(e) à
camp: **campbed** *n (BRIT)* lit *m* de camp; **camper** *n* campeur(-euse); *(vehicle)* camping-car *m*; **campground** *(us) n (terrain *m* de)* camping *m*; **camping** *n* camping *m*; **to go camping** faire du camping; **campsite** *n (terrain *m* de)* camping *m*
campus ['kæmpəs] *n* campus *m*
can¹ [kæn] *n (of milk, oil, water)* bidon *m*; *(tin)* boîte *f (de conserve)* ▷ *vt* mettre en conserve

KEYWORD

can² [kæn] *(negative* **cannot, can't,** *conditional and pt* **could)** *aux vb* **1** *(be able to)* pouvoir; **you can do it if you try** vous pouvez le faire si vous essayez; **I can't hear you** je ne t'entends pas
2 *(know how to)* savoir; **I can swim/ play tennis/drive** je sais nager/jouer au tennis/conduire; **can you speak French?** parlez-vous français?
3 *(may)* pouvoir; **can I use your phone?** puis-je me servir de votre téléphone?

4 (expressing disbelief, puzzlement etc):
it can't be true! ce n'est pas possible!;
what CAN he want? qu'est-ce qu'il peut
bien vouloir?

5 (expressing possibility, suggestion etc):
he could be in the library il se peut-
être dans la bibliothèque; **she could
have been delayed** il se peut qu'il ait
été retardée

Canada ['kænədə] n Canada m;
Canadian [kə'neɪdɪən] adj
canadien(ne) ▷ n Canadien(ne)
canal [kə'næl] n canal m
canary [kə'nɛərɪ] n canari m, serin m
cancel ['kænsəl] vt annuler; (train)
supprimer; (appointment)
décommander; (cross out) barrer, rayer;
(cheque) faire opposition à; **I would
like to ~ my booking** je voudrais
annuler ma réservation; **cancellation**
[kænsə'leɪʃən] n annulation f;
suppression f
Cancer ['kænsə'] n (Astrology) le Cancer
cancer ['kænsə'] n cancer m
candidate ['kændɪdeɪt] n candidat(e)
candle ['kændl] n bougie f; (in church)
cierge m; **candlestick** n (also: **candle
holder**) bougeoir m; (bigger, ornate)
chandelier m
candy ['kændɪ] n sucre candi; (us)
bonbon m; **candy bar** (us) n barref
chocolatée; **candyfloss** (BRIT) n barbe
fà papa
cane [keɪn] n cannef; (for baskets, chairs
etc) rotin m ▷ vt (BRIT Scol) administrer
des coups de bâton à
canister ['kænɪstə'] n boîtef (gén en
métal); (of gas) bombef
cannabis ['kænəbɪs] n (drug)
cannabis m
canned [kænd] adj (food) en boîte,
en conserve; (inf: music) enregistré(e);
(BRIT inf: drunk) bourré(e); (us inf: worker)
mis(e) à la porte
cannon (pl ~ or ~s) ['kænən] n (gun)
canon m
cannot ['kænɔt] = **can not**

canoe [kə'nu:] n pirogue f; (Sport)
canoë m; **canoeing** n (sport) canoë m
canon ['kænən] n (clergyman) chanoine
m; (standard) canon m
can-opener [-'əʊpnə'] n ouvre-boîte f
can't [kɑ:nt] = **can not**
canteen [kæn'ti:n] n (eating place)
cantinef; (BRIT: of cutlery) ménagèref
canter ['kæntə'] vi aller au petit galop
canvas ['kænvəs] n toilef
canvass ['kænvəs] vi (Pol): **to ~ for**
faire campagne pour ▷ vt (citizens,
opinions) sonder
canyon ['kænjən] n cañon m, gorge
(profonde)
cap [kæp] n casquette f; (for swimming)
bonnet m de bain; (of pen) capuchon m;
(of bottle) capsule f; (contraceptive:
also: **Dutch ~**) diaphragme m ▷ vt
(outdo) surpasser; (put limit on)
plafonner
capability [keɪpə'bɪlɪtɪ] n aptitude
f, capacité f
capable ['keɪpəbl] adj capable
capacity [kə'pæsɪtɪ] n (of container)
capacité f, contenance f; (ability)
aptitude f
cape [keɪp] n (garment) cape f; (Geo)
cap m
caper ['keɪpə'] n (Culin: gen pl) câpref;
(prank) farcef
capital ['kæpɪtl] n (also: **~ city**)
capitale f; (money) capital m; (also:
~ letter) majuscule f; **capitalism**
n capitalisme m; **capitalist** adj, n
capitaliste m/f; **capital punishment** n
peine capitale
Capitol ['kæpɪtl] n: **the ~** le Capitole
Capricorn ['kæprɪkɔ:n] n le Capricorne
capsize [kæp'saɪz] vt faire chavirer
▷ vi chavirer
capsule ['kæpsju:l] n capsule f
captain ['kæptɪn] n capitaine m
caption ['kæpʃən] n légende f
captivity [kæp'tɪvɪtɪ] n captivité f
capture ['kæptʃə'] vt (prisoner, animal)
capturer; (town) prendre; (attention)
capter; (Comput) saisir ▷ n capture f; (of

data) saisie f de données
car [kɑːʳ] n voiture f, auto f; (US Rail) wagon m, voiture
carafe [kəˈræf] n carafe f
caramel [ˈkærəməl] n caramel m
carat [ˈkærət] n carat m
caravan [ˈkærəvæn] n caravane f; **caravan site** (BRIT) camping m pour caravanes
carbohydrate [kɑːbəuˈhaɪdreɪt] n hydrate m de carbone; (food) féculent m
carbon [ˈkɑːbən] n carbone m; **carbon dioxide** [-daɪˈɒksaɪd] n gaz m carbonique, dioxyde m de carbone; **carbon monoxide** [-mɔˈnɒksaɪd] n oxyde m de carbone
car boot sale n voir encadré

● CAR BOOT SALE

Type de brocante très populaire, où chacun vide sa cave ou son grenier. Les articles sont présentés dans des coffres de voitures et la vente a souvent lieu sur un parking ou dans un champ. Les brocanteurs d'un jour doivent s'acquitter d'une petite contribution pour participer à la vente.

carburettor (US **carburetor**) [kɑːbjuˈretəʳ] n carburateur m
card [kɑːd] n carte f; (material) carton m; **cardboard** n carton m; **card game** n jeu m de cartes
cardigan [ˈkɑːdɪgən] n cardigan m
cardinal [ˈkɑːdɪnl] adj cardinal(e); (importance) capital(e) ▷ n cardinal m
cardphone [ˈkɑːdfəun] n téléphone m à carte (magnétique)
care [kɛəʳ] n soin m, attention f; (worry) souci m ▷ vi: **to ~ about** (feel interest for) se soucier de, s'intéresser à; (person: love) être attaché à; **in sb's ~** à la garde de qn, confié à qn; **~ of** (on letter) chez; **to take ~ (to do)** faire attention (à faire); **to take ~ of** vt s'occuper de; **I don't ~** ça m'est bien

égal, peu m'importe; **I couldn't ~ less** cela m'est complètement égal, je m'en fiche complètement; **care for** vt fus s'occuper de; (like) aimer
career [kəˈrɪəʳ] n carrière f ▷ vi (also: **~ along**) aller à toute allure
care: **carefree** adj sans souci, insouciant(e); **careful** adj soigneux(-euse); (cautious) prudent(e); **(be) careful!** (fais) attention!; **carefully** adv avec soin, soigneusement; prudemment; **caregiver** (US) n (professional) travailleur social; (unpaid) personne qui s'occupe d'un proche qui est malade; **careless** adj négligent(e); (heedless) insouciant(e); **carelessness** n manque m de soin, négligence f; insouciance f; **carer** [ˈkɛərəʳ] n (professional) travailleur social; (unpaid) personne qui s'occupe d'un proche qui est malade; **caretaker** n gardien(ne), concierge m/f
car-ferry [ˈkɑːferɪ] n (on sea) ferry(-boat) m; (on river) bac m
cargo (pl **-es**) [ˈkɑːgəu] n cargaison f, chargement m
car hire n (BRIT) location f de voitures
Caribbean [kærɪˈbiːən] adj, n: **the ~ (Sea)** la mer des Antilles or des Caraïbes
caring [ˈkɛərɪŋ] adj (person) bienveillant(e); (society, organization) humanitaire
carnation [kɑːˈneɪʃən] n œillet m
carnival [ˈkɑːnɪvl] n (public celebration) carnaval m; (US: funfair) fête foraine
carol [ˈkærəl] n: **(Christmas) ~** chant m de Noël
carousel [kærəˈsɛl] n (for luggage) carrousel m; (US) manège m
car park (BRIT) n parking m, parc m de stationnement
carpenter [ˈkɑːpɪntəʳ] n charpentier m; (joiner) menuisier m
carpet [ˈkɑːpɪt] n tapis m ▷ vt recouvrir (d'un tapis); **fitted ~** (BRIT) moquette f
car rental n (US) location f de voitures
carriage [ˈkærɪdʒ] n (BRIT Rail)

wagon *n* (*horse-drawn*) voiture *f*; (*of goods*) transport *m*; (*cost*) port *m*; **carriageway** *n* (BRIT: *part of road*) chaussée *f*; **carrier** ['kærɪə'] *n* transporteur *m*, camionneur *m*; (*company*) entreprise *f* de transport; (*Med*) porteur(-euse); **carrier bag** *n* (BRIT) sac *m* en papier *or* en plastique

carrot ['kærət] *n* carotte *f*

carry ['kærɪ] *vt* (*subj: person*) porter; (: *vehicle*) transporter; (*involve: responsibilities etc*) comporter, impliquer; (*disease*) être porteur de ▷ *vi* (*sound*) porter; **to get carried away** (*fig*) s'emballer, s'enthousiasmer; **carry on** *vi* (*continue*) continuer ▷ *vt* (*conduct: business*) diriger; (: *conversation*) entretenir; (*continue: business, conversation*) continuer; **to ~ on with sth/doing** continuer qch/à faire; **carry out** *vt* (*orders*) exécuter; (*investigation*) effectuer

cart [kɑːt] *n* charrette *f* ▷ *vt* (*inf*) transporter

carton ['kɑːtən] *n* (*box*) carton *m*; (*of yogurt*) pot *m* (en carton)

cartoon [kɑː'tuːn] *n* (*Press*) dessin *m* (humoristique); (*satirical*) caricature *f*; (*comic strip*) bande dessinée; (*Cine*) dessin animé

cartridge ['kɑːtrɪdʒ] *n* (*for gun, pen*) cartouche *f*

carve [kɑːv] *vt* (*meat: also: ~ up*) découper; (*wood, stone*) tailler, sculpter; **carving** *n* (*in wood etc*) sculpture *f*

car wash *n* station *f* de lavage (de voitures)

case [keɪs] *n* cas *m*; (*Law*) affaire *f*, procès *m*; (*box*) caisse *f*, boîte *f*; (*for glasses*) étui *m*; (BRIT: *also*: **suit~**) valise *f*; **in ~ of** en cas de; **in ~ he** au cas où il; **just in ~** à tout hasard; **in any ~** en tout cas, de toute façon

cash [kæʃ] *n* argent *m*; (*Comm*) (*argent m*) liquide *m*, argent *m* en encaissant; **to pay (in) ~** payer (en argent) comptant *or* en espèces; **~ with order/on delivery**

(*Comm*) payable *or* paiement à la commande/livraison; **I haven't got any ~** je n'ai pas de liquide; **cashback** *n* (*discount*) remise *f*; (*at supermarket etc*) retrait *m* (*à la caisse*); **cash card** *n* carte *f* de retrait; **cash desk** *n* (BRIT) caisse *f*; **cash dispenser** *n* distributeur *m* automatique de billets

cashew [kæˈʃuː] *n* (*also*: **~ nut**) noix *f* de cajou

cashier [kæˈʃɪə'] *n* caissier(-ère)

cashmere ['kæʃmɪə'] *n* cachemire *m*

cash point *n* distributeur *m* automatique de billets

cash register *n* caisse enregistreuse

casino [kəˈsiːnəu] *n* casino *m*

casket ['kɑːskɪt] *n* coffret *m*; (US: *coffin*) cercueil *m*

casserole ['kæsərəul] *n* (*pot*) cocotte *f*; (*food*) ragoût *m* (en cocotte)

cassette [kæˈsɛt] *n* cassette *f*; **cassette player** *n* lecteur *m* de cassettes

cast [kɑːst] (*vb: pt, pp* **~**) *vt* (*throw*) jeter; (*shadow: lit*) projeter; (: *fig*) jeter; (*glance*) jeter ▷ *n* (*Theat*) distribution *f*; (*also*: **plaster ~**) plâtre *m*; **to ~ sb as Hamlet** attribuer à qn le rôle de Hamlet; **to ~ one's vote** voter, exprimer son suffrage; **to ~ doubt on** jeter un doute sur; **cast off** *vi* (*Naut*) larguer les amarres; (*Knitting*) arrêter les mailles

castanets [kæstə'nɛts] *npl* castagnettes *fpl*

caster sugar ['kɑːstə-] *n* (BRIT) sucre *n* semoule

cast-iron ['kɑːstaɪən] *adj* (*lit*) de *or* en fonte; (*fig: will*) de fer; (*alibi*) en béton

castle ['kɑːsl] *n* château *m*; (*fortress*) château-fort *m*; (*Chess*) tour *f*

casual ['kæʒjul] *adj* (*by chance*) de hasard, fait(e) au hasard, fortuit(e); (*irregular: work etc*) temporaire; (*unconcerned*) désinvolte; **~ wear** vêtements *mpl* sport *inv*

casualty ['kæʒjultɪ] *n* accidenté(e), blessé(e); (*dead*) victime *f*, mort(e); (BRIT: *Med: department*) urgences *fpl*

cat [kæt] *n* chat *m*

Catalan ['kætələn] adj catalan(e)

catalogue (US **catalog**) ['kætələg] n catalogue m ▷ vt cataloguer

catalytic converter [kætə'lɪtɪkkən'vɜːtəʳ] n pot m catalytique

cataract ['kætərækt] n (also Med) cataracte f

catarrh [kə'tɑːʳ] n rhume m chronique, catarrhe f

catastrophe [kə'tæstrəfi] n catastrophe f

catch [kætʃ] (pt, pp **caught**) vt attraper; (person: by surprise) prendre, surprendre; (understand) saisir; (get entangled) accrocher ▷ vi (fire) prendre; (get entangled) s'accrocher ▷ n (fish etc) prise f; (hidden problem) attrapé f; (Tech) loquet m; cliquet m; **to ~ sb's attention** **or eye** attirer l'attention de qn; **to ~ fire** prendre feu; **to ~ sight of** apercevoir; **catch up** vi (with work) se rattraper, combler son retard ▷ vt (also: **~ up with**) rattraper; **catching** ['kætʃɪŋ] adj (Med) contagieux(-euse)

category ['kætɪgəri] n catégorie f

cater ['keɪtəʳ] vi: **to ~ for** (BRIT: needs) satisfaire, pourvoir à; (: readers, consumers) s'adresser à, pourvoir aux besoins de; (Comm: parties etc) préparer des repas pour

caterpillar ['kætəpɪləʳ] n chenille f

cathedral [kə'θiːdrəl] n cathédrale f

Catholic ['kæθəlɪk] (Rel) adj catholique ▷ n catholique m/f

Catseye® ['kæts'aɪ] n (BRIT Aut) (clou m à) catadioptre m

cattle ['kætl] npl bétail m, bestiaux mpl

catwalk ['kætwɔːk] n passerelle f; (for models) podium m (de défilé de mode)

caught [kɔːt] pt, pp of **catch**

cauliflower ['kɔlɪflauəʳ] n chou-fleur m

cause [kɔːz] n cause f ▷ vt causer

caution ['kɔːʃən] n prudence f; (warning) avertissement m ▷ vt avertir, donner un avertissement à; **cautious** adj prudent(e)

cave [keɪv] n caverne f, grotte f; **cave in** vi (roof etc) s'effondrer

caviar(e) ['kæviɑːʳ] n caviar m

cavity ['kævɪtɪ] n cavité f; (Med) carie f

cc abbr (= cubic centimetre) cm³; (on letter etc) = **carbon copy**

CCTV n abbr = **closed-circuit television**

CD n abbr (= compact disc) CD m; **CD** **burner** n graveur m de CD; **CD player** n platine f laser; **CD-ROM** ['siːdiː'rɔm] n abbr (= compact disc read-only memory) CD-ROM m inv; **CD writer** n graveur m de CD

cease [siːs] vt, vi cesser; **ceasefire** n cessez-le-feu m

cedar ['siːdəʳ] n cèdre m

ceilidh ['keɪlɪ] n bal m folklorique écossais or irlandais

ceiling ['siːlɪŋ] n (also fig) plafond m

celebrate ['sɛlɪbreɪt] vt, vi célébrer; **celebration** [sɛlɪ'breɪʃən] n célébration f

celebrity [sɪ'lɛbrɪtɪ] n célébrité f

celery ['sɛlərɪ] n céleri m (en branches)

cell [sɛl] n (gen) cellule f; (Elec) élément m (de pile)

cellar ['sɛləʳ] n cave f

cello ['tʃɛləu] n violoncelle m

Cellophane® ['sɛləfeɪn] n cellophane® f

cellphone ['sɛlfəun] n téléphone m cellulaire

Celsius ['sɛlsɪəs] adj Celsius inv

Celtic ['kɛltɪk, 'sɛltɪk] adj celte, celtique

cement [sə'mɛnt] n ciment m

cemetery ['sɛmɪtri] n cimetière m

censor ['sɛnsəʳ] n censeur m ▷ vt censurer; **censorship** n censure f

census ['sɛnsəs] n recensement m

cent [sɛnt] n (unit of dollar, euro) cent m (= un centième du dollar, de l'euro); see also **per**

centenary [sɛn'tiːnəri] (US **centennial**) [sɛn'tɛnɪəl] n centenaire m

center ['sɛntəʳ] (US) = **centre**

centi... [sɛntɪ] prefix: **centigrade** adj centigrade; **centimetre** (US

centimeter) n centimètre m;

centipede ['sɛntɪpiːd] n mille-
pattes m inv

central ['sɛntrəl] adj central(e);
Central America n Amérique centrale;
central heating n chauffage central;
central reservation n (BRIT Aut) terre-
plein central

centre (US **center**) ['sɛntəʳ] n centre m
▷ vt centrer; **centre-forward** n (Sport)
avant-centre m; **centre-half** n (Sport)
demi-centre m

century ['sɛntjurɪ] n siècle m; **in the
twentieth ~** au vingtième siècle

CEO n abbr (US) = **chief executive
officer**

ceramic [sɪ'ræmɪk] adj céramique

cereal ['siːrɪəl] n céréale f

ceremony ['sɛrɪmənɪ] n cérémonie f;
to stand on ~ faire des façons

certain ['sɜːtən] adj certain(e);
to make ~ of s'assurer de; **for ~**
certainement, sûrement; **certainly**
adv certainement; **certainty** n
certitude f

certificate [sə'tɪfɪkɪt] n certificat m

certify ['sɜːtɪfaɪ] vt certifier; (award
diploma to) conférer un diplôme etc
à; (declare insane) déclarer malade
mental(e)

cf. abbr (= compare) cf., voir

CFC n abbr (= chlorofluorocarbon) CFC m

chain [tʃeɪn] n chaîne f ▷ vt
(also: ~ up) enchaîner, attacher (avec
une chaîne); **chain-smoke** vi fumer
cigarette sur cigarette

chair [tʃɛəʳ] n chaise f; (armchair)
fauteuil m; (of university) chaire f; (of
meeting) présidence f ▷ vt (meeting)
présider; **chairlift** n télésiège m;
chairman n président m; **chairperson**
n président(e); **chairwoman** n
présidente f

chalet ['ʃæleɪ] n chalet m

chalk [tʃɔːk] n craie f; **chalkboard** (US)
n tableau noir

challenge ['tʃælɪndʒ] n défi m ▷ vt
défier; (statement, right) mettre en

question, contester; **to ~ sb to do**
mettre qn au défi de faire; **challenging**
adj (task, career) qui représente un défi
ou une gageure; (tone, look) de défi,
provocateur(-trice)

chamber ['tʃeɪmbəʳ] n chambre f; (BRIT
Law: gen pl) cabinet m; **~ of commerce**
chambre de commerce; **chambermaid**
n femme f de chambre

champagne [ʃæm'peɪn] n
champagne m

champion ['tʃæmpɪən] n (also of cause)
champion(ne); **championship** n
championnat m

chance [tʃɑːns] n (luck) hasard m;
(opportunity) occasion f, possibilité f;
(hope, likelihood) chance f; (risk) risque
m ▷ vt (risk) risquer > adj fortuit(e), de
hasard; **to take a ~** prendre un risque;
by ~ par hasard; **to ~ it** risquer le coup,
essayer

chancellor ['tʃɑːnsələʳ] n chancelier m;
Chancellor of the Exchequer
[-ɪks'tʃɛkəʳ] (BRIT) n chancelier m de
l'Échiquier

chandelier [ʃændə'lɪəʳ] n lustre m

change [tʃeɪndʒ] vt (alter, replace:
Comm: money) changer; (switch,
substitute: hands, trains, clothes,
one's name etc) changer de ▷ vi (gen)
changer; (change clothes) se changer;
(be transformed) **to ~ into** se changer
ou transformer en ▷ n changement
m; (money) monnaie f; **to ~ gear** (Aut)
changer de vitesse; **to ~ one's mind**
changer d'avis; **a ~ of clothes** des
vêtements de rechange; **for a ~** pour
changer; **do you have ~ for £10?** vous
avez la monnaie de 10 livres?; **where
can I ~ some money?** où est-ce que je
peux changer de l'argent?; **keep the
~!** gardez la monnaie!; **change over**
vi (swap) échanger; (change: drivers
etc) changer; (change sides: players etc)
changer de côté; **to ~ over from sth
to sth** passer de qch à qch; **changeable**
adj (weather) variable; **change
machine** n distributeur m de monnaie

changing room n (BRIT: in shop) salon m d'essayage; (: Sport) vestiaire m

channel ['tʃænl] n (TV) chaîne f; (waveband, groove, fig: medium) canal m; (of river, sea) chenal m ▷ vt canaliser; **the (English) C~** la Manche; **Channel Islands** npl: **the Channel Islands** les îles fpl Anglo-Normandes; **Channel Tunnel** n: **the Channel Tunnel** le tunnel sous la Manche

chant [tʃɑ:nt] n chant m; (Rel) psalmodie f ▷ vt chanter, scander

chaos ['keɪɒs] n chaos m

chaotic [keɪ'ɒtɪk] adj chaotique

chap [tʃæp] n (BRIT inf: man) type m

chapel ['tʃæpl] n chapelle f

chapped [tʃæpt] adj (skin, lips) gercé(e)

chapter ['tʃæptə'] n chapitre m

character ['kærɪktə'] n caractère m; (in novel, film) personnage m; (eccentric person) numéro m, phénomène m; **characteristic** ['kærɪktə'rɪstɪk] adj, n caractéristique (f); **characterize** ['kærɪktəraɪz] vt caractériser

charcoal ['tʃɑ:kəʊl] n charbon m de bois; (Art) charbon

charge [tʃɑ:dʒ] n (accusation) accusation f; (Law) inculpation f; (cost) prix (demandé) ▷ vt (gun, battery, Mil: enemy) charger; (customer, sum) faire payer ▷ vi foncer; **charges** npl (costs) frais mpl; (Tel): **to reverse the ~s** téléphoner en PCV; **to take ~ of** se charger de; **to be in ~ of** être responsable de, s'occuper de; **to ~ sb (with)** (Law) inculper qn (de); **charge card** n carte f de client (émise par un grand magasin); **charger** n (also: **battery charger**) chargeur m

charismatic [kærɪz'mætɪk] adj charismatique

charity ['tʃærɪtɪ] n charité f; (organization) institution f charitable or de bienfaisance, œuvre f (de charité); **charity shop** n (BRIT) boutique vendant des articles d'occasion au profit d'une organisation caritative

charm [tʃɑ:m] n charme m; (on bracelet)

breloque f ▷ vt charmer, enchanter; **charming** adj charmant(e)

chart [tʃɑ:t] n tableau m, diagramme m; graphique m; (map) carte marine ▷ vt dresser or établir la carte de; (sales, progress) établir la courbe de; **charts** npl (Mus) hit-parade m; **to be in the ~s** (record, pop group) figurer au hit-parade

charter ['tʃɑ:tə'] vt (plane) affréter ▷ n (document) charte f; **chartered accountant** n (BRIT) expert-comptable m; **charter flight** n charter m

chase [tʃeɪs] vt poursuivre, pourchasser; (also: **~ away**) chasser ▷ n poursuite f, chasse f

chat [tʃæt] vi (also: **have a ~**) bavarder, causer; (on Internet) papoter ▷ n conversation f; **chat up** vt (BRIT inf: girl) baratiner; **chat room** n (Internet) forum m de discussion; **chat show** n (BRIT) talk-show m

chatter ['tʃætə'] vi (person) bavarder, papoter ▷ n bavardage m, papotage m; **my teeth are ~ing** je claque des dents

chauffeur ['ʃəʊfə'] n chauffeur m (de maître)

chauvinist ['ʃəʊvɪnɪst] n (also: **male ~**) phallocrate m, macho m; (nationalist) chauvin(e)

cheap [tʃi:p] adj bon marché inv, pas cher (chère); (reduced: ticket) à prix réduit; (: fare) réduit(e); (joke) facile, d'un goût douteux; (poor quality) à bon marché, de qualité médiocre ▷ adv à bon marché, pour pas cher; **can you recommend a ~ hotel/restaurant, please?** pourriez-vous m'indiquer un hôtel/restaurant bon marché?; **cheap day return** n billet m d'aller et retour réduit (valable pour la journée); **cheaply** adv à bon marché, à bon compte

cheat [tʃi:t] vi tricher; (in exam) copier ▷ vt tromper, duper; (rob): **to ~ sb out of sth** escroquer qch à qn ▷ n tricheur(-euse) m/f; escroc m; **cheat on** vt fus tromper

Chechnya [tʃɪtʃ'njɑ:] n Tchétchénie f

check [tʃɛk] vt vérifier; (passport, ticket) contrôler; (halt) enrayer; (restrain) maîtriser ▷ vi (official etc) se renseigner ▷ n vérification f; contrôle m; (curb) frein m; (BRIT: bill) addition f; (US) **= cheque**; (pattern: gen) carreaux mpl; **to ~ with sb** demander à qn; **check in** vi (in hotel) remplir sa fiche (d'hôtel); (at airport) se présenter à l'enregistrement ▷ vt (luggage) (faire) enregistrer; **check off** vt (tick off) cocher; **check out** vi (in hotel) régler sa note ▷ vt (investigate: story) vérifier; **check up** vi: **to ~ up on sth** vérifier (qch); **to ~ up on sb** se renseigner sur le compte de qn; (checkbook (US) **= chequebook**; **checked** adj (pattern, cloth) à carreaux; **checkers** n (US) jeu m de dames; **check-in** n (also: **check-in desk**) (at airport) enregistrement m; **checking account** n (US) compte courant; **checklist** n liste f de contrôle; **checkmate** n échec et mat m; **checkout** n (in supermarket) caisse f; **checkpoint** n contrôle m; **checkroom** (US) n consigne f; **checkup** n (Med) examen médical, check-up m

cheddar ['tʃɛdə'] n (also: **~ cheese**) cheddar m

cheek [tʃiːk] n joue f; (impudence) toupet m, culot m; **what a ~!** quel toupet!; **cheekbone** n pommette f; **cheeky** adj effronté(e), culotté(e)

cheer [tʃɪə'] vt acclamer, applaudir; (gladden) réjouir, réconforter ▷ vi applaudir ▷ n (gen pl) acclamations fpl, applaudissements mpl; bravos mpl, hourras mpl; **~s!** à la vôtre!; **cheer up** vi se dérider, reprendre courage ▷ vt remonter le moral à or de, dérider, égayer; **cheerful** adj gai(e), joyeux(-euse)

cheerio ['tʃɪərɪ'əʊ] excl (BRIT) salut!, au revoir!

cheerleader ['tʃɪəliːdə'] n membre d'un groupe de majorettes qui chantent et dansent pour soutenir leur équipe pendant les matchs de football américain

cheese [tʃiːz] n fromage m; **cheeseburger** n cheeseburger m; **cheesecake** n tarte f au fromage

chef [ʃɛf] n chef (cuisinier)

chemical ['kɛmɪkl] adj chimique ▷ n produit m chimique

chemist ['kɛmɪst] n (BRIT: pharmacist) pharmacien(ne); (scientist) chimiste m/f; **chemistry** n chimie f; **chemist's (shop)** n (BRIT) pharmacie f

cheque (US **check**) [tʃɛk] n chèque m; **chequebook** (US **checkbook**) n chéquier m, carnet m de chèques; **cheque card** n (BRIT) carte f (d'identité) bancaire

cherry ['tʃɛrɪ] n cerise f; (also: **~ tree**) cerisier m

chess [tʃɛs] n échecs mpl

chest [tʃɛst] n poitrine f; (box) coffre m, caisse f

chestnut ['tʃɛsnʌt] n châtaigne f; (also: **~ tree**) châtaignier m

chest of drawers n commode f

chew [tʃuː] vt mâcher; **chewing gum** n chewing-gum m

chic [ʃiːk] adj chic, élégant(e)

chick [tʃɪk] n poussin m; (inf) pépée f

chicken ['tʃɪkɪn] n poulet m; (inf: coward) poule mouillée; **chicken out** vi (inf) se dégonfler; **chickenpox** n varicelle f

chickpea ['tʃɪkpiː] n pois m chiche

chief [tʃiːf] n chef m ▷ adj principal(e); **chief executive** (US **chief executive officer**) n directeur(-trice) général(e); **chiefly** adv principalement, surtout

child (pl **~ren**) [tʃaɪld, 'tʃɪldrən] n enfant m/f; **child abuse** n maltraitance f d'enfants; (sexual) abus mpl sexuels sur des enfants; **child benefit** n (BRIT) = allocations familiales; **childbirth** n accouchement m; **child-care** n (for working parents) garde f des enfants (pour les parents qui travaillent); **childhood** n enfance f; **childish** adj puéril(e), enfantin(e); **child minder** n (BRIT) garde f d'enfants; **children** ['tʃɪldrən] npl of **child**

Chile ['tʃɪlɪ] n Chili m

chill [tʃɪl] n (of water) froid m; (of air) fraîcheur f; (Med) refroidissement m, coup m de froid ▷ vt (person) faire frissonner; (Culin) mettre au frais, rafraîchir; **chill out** vi (inf: esp us) se relaxer

chil(l)i ['tʃɪlɪ] n piment m (rouge)

chilly ['tʃɪlɪ] adj froid(e), glacé(e); (sensitive to cold) frileux(-euse)

chimney ['tʃɪmnɪ] n cheminée f

chimpanzee [tʃɪmpæn'zi:] n chimpanzé m

chin [tʃɪn] n menton m

China [tʃaɪnə] n Chine f

china ['tʃaɪnə] n (material) porcelaine f; (crockery) (vaisselle f en) porcelaine f

Chinese [tʃaɪ'ni:z] adj chinois(e) ▷ n (pl inv) Chinois(e); (Ling) chinois m

chip [tʃɪp] n (gen pl: Culin: BRIT) frite f; (: US: also: **potato ~**) chip m; (of wood) copeau m; (of glass, stone) éclat m; (also: **micro~**) puce f; (in gambling) fiche f ▷ vt (cup, plate) ébrécher; **chip shop** n (BRIT) friterie f

CHIP SHOP

- Un **chip shop**, que l'on appelle également la **fish-and-chip shop**, est un magasin où l'on vend des plats à emporter. Les **chip shops** sont d'ailleurs à l'origine des "takeaways". On y achète en particulier du poisson frit et des frites, mais on y trouve également des plats traditionnels britanniques ("steak pies", saucisses, etc). Tous les plats étaient à l'origine emballés dans du papier journal. Dans certains de ces magasins, on peut s'asseoir pour consommer sur place.

chiropodist [kɪ'rɔpədɪst] n (BRIT) pédicure m/f

chisel ['tʃɪzl] n ciseau m

chives [tʃaɪvz] npl ciboulette f, civette f

chlorine ['klɔ:ri:n] n chlore m

choc-ice ['tʃɔkaɪs] n (BRIT) esquimau® m

chocolate ['tʃɔklɪt] n chocolat m

choice [tʃɔɪs] n choix m ▷ adj de choix

choir ['kwaɪə] n chœur m, chorale f

choke [tʃəuk] vi étouffer ▷ vt étrangler; étouffer; (block) boucher, obstruer ▷ n (Aut) starter m

cholesterol [kə'lɛstərɔl] n cholestérol m

choose (pt **chose**, pp **chosen**) [tʃu:z, tʃəuz, 'tʃəuzn] vt choisir; **to ~ to do** décider de faire, juger bon de faire

chop [tʃɔp] vt (wood) couper (à la hache); (Culin: also: **~ up**) couper (fin), émincer, hacher (en morceaux) ▷ n (Culin) côtelette f; **chop down** vt (tree) abattre; **chop off** vt trancher; **chopsticks** ['tʃɔpstɪks] npl baguettes fpl

chord [kɔ:d] n (Mus) accord m

chore [tʃɔ:] n travail m de routine; **household ~s** travaux mpl du ménage

chorus ['kɔ:rəs] n chœur m; (repeated part of song, also fig) refrain m

chose [tʃəuz] pt of **choose**

chosen ['tʃəuzn] pp of **choose**

Christ [kraɪst] n Christ m

christen ['krɪsn] vt baptiser; **christening** n baptême m

Christian ['krɪstɪən] adj, n chrétien(ne); **Christianity** [krɪstɪ'ænɪtɪ] n christianisme m; **Christian name** n prénom m

Christmas ['krɪsməs] n Noël m or f; **happy** or **merry ~!** joyeux Noël!; **Christmas card** n carte f de Noël; **Christmas carol** n chant m de Noël; **Christmas Day** n le jour de Noël; **Christmas Eve** n la veille de Noël, la nuit de Noël; **Christmas pudding** n (esp BRIT) Christmas pudding m; **Christmas tree** n arbre m de Noël

chrome [krəum] n chrome m

chronic ['krɔnɪk] adj chronique

chrysanthemum [krɪ'sænθəməm] n chrysanthème m

chubby ['tʃʌbɪ] adj potelé(e),

rondelet(te)

chuck [tʃʌk] vt (inf) lancer, jeter; (BRIT: also: ~ **up**: job) lâcher; **chuck out** vt (inf: person) flanquer dehors or à la porte; (: rubbish etc) jeter

chuckle ['tʃʌkl] vi glousser

chum [tʃʌm] n copain (copine)

chunk [tʃʌŋk] n gros morceau

church [tʃəːtʃ] n église f; **churchyard** n cimetière m

churn [tʃəːn] n (for butter) baratte f; (also: **milk ~**) (grand) bidon à lait

chute [ʃuːt] n goulotte f; (also: **rubbish ~**) vide-ordures m inv; (BRIT: children's slide) toboggan m

chutney ['tʃʌtnɪ] n chutney m

CIA n abbr (= Central Intelligence Agency) CIA f

CID n abbr (= Criminal Investigation Department) ≈ P.J. f

cider ['saɪdə'] n cidre m

cigar [sɪ'gɑː'] n cigare m

cigarette [sɪgə'rɛt] n cigarette f; **cigarette lighter** n briquet m

cinema ['sɪnəmə] n cinéma m

cinnamon ['sɪnəmən] n cannelle f

circle ['səːkl] n cercle m; (in cinema) balcon m ▷ vi faire ou décrire des cercles ▷ vt (surround) entourer, encercler; (move round) faire le tour de, tourner autour de

circuit ['səːkɪt] n circuit m; (lap) tour m

circular ['səːkjələ'] adj circulaire ▷ n circulaire f; (as advertisement) prospectus m

circulate ['səːkjəleɪt] vi circuler ▷ vt faire circuler; **circulation** [səːkjə'leɪʃən] n circulation f; (of newspaper) tirage m

circumstances ['səːkəmstənsɪz] npl circonstances fpl; (financial condition) moyens mpl, situation financière

circus ['səːkəs] n cirque m

cite [saɪt] vt citer

citizen ['sɪtɪzn] n (Pol) citoyen(ne); (resident): **the ~s of this town** les habitants de cette ville; **citizenship** n citoyenneté f; (BRIT: Scol) ≈ éducation

f civique

citrus fruits ['sɪtrəs-] npl agrumes mpl

city ['sɪtɪ] n (grande) ville f; **the C~** la Cité de Londres (centre des affaires); **city centre** n centre ville m; **city technology college** n (BRIT) établissement m d'enseignement technologique (situé dans un quartier défavorisé)

civic ['sɪvɪk] adj civique; (authorities) municipal(e)

civil ['sɪvɪl] adj civil(e); (polite) poli(e), civil(e); **civilian** [sɪ'vɪlɪən] adj, n civil(e)

civilization [sɪvɪlaɪ'zeɪʃən] n civilisation f

civilized ['sɪvɪlaɪzd] adj civilisé(e); (fig) où règnent les bonnes manières

civil: **civil law** n code civil; (study) droit civil m; **civil rights** npl droits mpl civiques; **civil servant** n fonctionnaire m/f; **Civil Service** n fonction publique, administration f; **civil war** n guerre civile

CJD n abbr (= Creutzfeldt-Jakob disease) MCJ f

claim [kleɪm] vt (rights etc) revendiquer; (compensation) réclamer; (assert) déclarer, prétendre ▷ vi (for insurance) faire une déclaration de sinistre ▷ n revendication f; prétention f; (right) droit m; **(insurance) ~** demande f d'indemnisation, déclaration f de sinistre; **claim form** n (gen) formulaire m de demande

clam [klæm] n palourde f

clamp [klæmp] n crampon m; (on workbench) valet m; (on car) sabot m de Denver ▷ vt attacher; (car) mettre un sabot à; **clamp down on** vt fus sévir contre, prendre des mesures draconiennes à l'égard de

clan [klæn] n clan m

clap [klæp] vi applaudir

claret ['klærət] n (vin m de) bordeaux m (rouge)

clarify ['klærɪfaɪ] vt clarifier

clarinet [klærɪ'nɛt] n clarinette f

clarity ['klærɪtɪ] n clarté f

clash [klæʃ] n (sound) choc m, fracas m; (with police) affrontement m; (fig) conflit m ▷ vi se heurter; être or entrer en conflit; (colours) jurer; (dates, events) tomber en même temps

clasp [klɑːsp] n (of necklace, bag) fermoir m ▷ vt serrer, étreindre

class [klɑːs] n (gen) classe f; (group, category) catégorie f ▷ vt classer, classifier

classic [ˈklæsɪk] adj classique ▷ n (author, work) classique m; **classical** adj classique

classification [klæsɪfɪˈkeɪʃən] n classification f

classify [ˈklæsɪfaɪ] vt classifier, classer

classmate [ˈklɑːsmeɪt] n camarade m/f de classe

classroom [ˈklɑːsrum] n (salle f de) classe f; **classroom assistant** n assistant(-e) d'éducation

classy [ˈklɑːsɪ] (inf) adj classe (inf)

clatter [ˈklætə] n cliquetis m ▷ vi cliqueter

clause [klɔːz] n clause f; (Ling) proposition f

claustrophobic [klɔːstrəˈfəubɪk] adj (person) claustrophobe; (place) où l'on se sent claustrophobe

claw [klɔː] n griffe f; (of bird of prey) serre f; (of lobster) pince f

clay [kleɪ] n argile f

clean [kliːn] adj propre; (clear, smooth) net(te); (record, reputation) sans tache; (joke, story) correct(e) ▷ vt nettoyer; **clean up** vt nettoyer; (fig) remettre de l'ordre dans; **cleaner** n (person) nettoyeur(-euse), femme f de ménage; (product) détachant m; **cleaner's** n (also: **dry cleaner's**) teinturier m; **cleaning** n nettoyage m

cleanser [ˈklɛnzə] n (for face) démaquillant m

clear [klɪə] adj clair(e); (glass, plastic) transparent(e); (road, way) libre, dégagé(e); (profit, majority) net(te); (conscience) tranquille; (skin) frais (fraîche); (sky) dégagé(e) ▷ vt (road)

dégager, déblayer; (table) débarrasser; (room etc: of people) faire évacuer; (cheque) compenser; (Law: suspect) innocenter; (obstacle) franchir or sauter sans heurter ▷ vi (weather) s'éclaircir; (fog) se dissiper ▷ adv: ~ of à distance de, à l'écart de; **to ~ the table** débarrasser la table, desservir; **clear away** vt (things, clothes etc) enlever, retirer; **to ~ away the dishes** débarrasser la table; **clear up** vt ranger, mettre en ordre; (mystery) éclaircir, résoudre; **clearance** n (removal) déblayage m; (permission) autorisation f; **clear-cut** adj précis(e), nettement défini(e); **clearing** n (in forest) clairière f; **clearly** adv clairement; (obviously) de toute évidence; **clearway** n (BRIT) route f à stationnement interdit

clench [klɛntʃ] vt serrer

clergy [ˈklɜːdʒɪ] n clergé m

clerk [klɑːk, US klɜːrk] n (BRIT) employé(e) de bureau; (US: salesman/woman) vendeur(-euse) m

clever [ˈklɛvə] adj (intelligent) intelligent(e); (skilful) habile, adroit(e); (device, arrangement) ingénieux(-euse), astucieux(-euse)

cliché [ˈkliːʃeɪ] n cliché m

click [klɪk] n (Comput) cliquer ▷ vt: **to ~ one's tongue** faire claquer sa langue; **to ~ one's heels** claquer des talons; **to ~ on an icon** cliquer sur une icône

client [ˈklaɪənt] n client(e)

cliff [klɪf] n falaise f

climate [ˈklaɪmɪt] n climat m; **climate change** n changement m climatique

climax [ˈklaɪmæks] n apogée m, point culminant; (sexual) orgasme m

climb [klaɪm] vi grimper, monter; (plane) prendre de l'altitude ▷ vt (stairs) monter; (mountain) escalader; (tree) grimper à ▷ n montée f, escalade f; **to ~ over a wall** passer par dessus un mur; **climb down** vi (re)descendre; (BRIT fig) rabattre de ses prétentions; **climber** n (also: **rock climber**) grimpeur(-euse), varappeur(-euse); (plant) plante grimpante; **climbing** n (also: **rock climbing**) escalade f, varappe f

clinch [klɪntʃ] vt (deal) conclure, sceller

cling (pt, pp **clung**) [klɪŋ, klʌŋ] vi: **~ (to)** se cramponner (à), s'accrocher (à); (clothes) coller (à)

Clingfilm® ['klɪŋfɪlm] n film m alimentaire

clinic ['klɪnɪk] n clinique f; centre médical

clip [klɪp] n (for hair) barrette f; (also: **paper ~**) trombone m; (TV, Cinema) clip m ▷ vt (also: **~ together**: papers) attacher; (hair, nails) couper; (hedge) tailler; **clipping** n (from newspaper) coupure f de journal

cloak [kləuk] n grande cape f ▷ vt (fig) masquer, cacher; **cloakroom** n (for coats etc) vestiaire m; (BRIT: W.C.) toilettes fpl

clock [klɔk] n (large) horloge f; (small) pendule f; **clock in** or **on** (BRIT) vi (with card) pointer (en arrivant); (start work) commencer à travailler; **clock off** or **out** (BRIT) vi (with card) pointer (en partant); (leave work) quitter le travail; **clockwise** adv dans le sens des aiguilles d'une montre; **clockwork** n rouages mpl, mécanisme m; (of clock) mouvement m (d'horlogerie) ▷ adj (toy, train) mécanique

clog [klɔg] n sabot m ▷ vt boucher, encrasser ▷ vi: **~ up** se boucher, s'encrasser

clone [kləun] n clone m ▷ vt cloner

close¹ [kləus] adj (near): **~ (to)** près (de), proche (de); (contact, link, watch) étroit(e); (examination) attentif(-ive), minutieux(-euse); (contest) très serré(e); (weather) lourd(e), étouffant(e) ▷ adv près, à proximité; **~ to** prep près de; **~ by, ~ at hand** adj, adv tout(e) près; **a ~ friend** un ami intime; **to have a ~ shave** (fig) l'échapper belle

close² [kləuz] vt fermer ▷ vi (shop etc) fermer; (lid, door etc) se fermer; (end) se terminer, se conclure ▷ n (end)

conclusion f; **what time do you ~?** à quelle heure fermez-vous?; **close down** vi fermer (définitivement); **closed** adj (shop etc) fermé(e)

closely ['kləuslɪ] adv (examine, watch) de près

closet ['klɔzɪt] n (cupboard) placard m, réduit m

close-up ['kləusʌp] n gros plan

closing time n heure f de fermeture

closure ['kləuʒə²] n fermeture f

clot [klɔt] n (of blood, milk) caillot m; (inf: person) ballot m ▷ vi (: external bleeding) se coaguler

cloth [klɔθ] n (material) tissu m, étoffe f; (BRIT: also: **tea ~**) torchon m; lavette f; (also: **table~**) nappe f

clothes [kləuðz] npl vêtements mpl, habits mpl; **clothes line** n corde f (à linge); **clothes peg** (us **clothes pin**) n pince f à linge

clothing ['kləuðɪŋ] n = **clothes**

cloud [klaud] n nuage m; **cloud over** vi se couvrir; (fig) s'assombrir; **cloudy** adj nuageux(-euse), couvert(e); (liquid) trouble

clove [kləuv] n clou m de girofle; **a ~ of garlic** une gousse d'ail

clown [klaun] n clown m ▷ vi (also: **~ about, ~ around**) faire le clown

club [klʌb] n (society) club m; (weapon) massue f, matraque f; (also: **golf ~**) club m ▷ vt matraquer ▷ vi: **to ~ together** s'associer; **clubs** npl (Cards) trèfle m; **club class** n (Aviat) classe f club

clue [klu:] n indice m; (in crosswords) définition f; **I haven't a ~** je n'en ai pas la moindre idée

clump [klʌmp] n: **~ of trees** bouquet m d'arbres

clumsy ['klʌmzɪ] adj (person) gauche, maladroit(e); (object) malcommode, peu maniable

clung [klʌŋ] pt, pp of **cling**

cluster ['klʌstə²] n (petit) groupe; (of flowers) grappe f ▷ vi se rassembler

clutch [klʌtʃ] n (Aut) embrayage m; (grasp): **~es** étreinte f, prise f ▷ vt (grasp) agripper; (hold tightly) serrer fort; (hold on to) se cramponner à

cm abbr (= centimetre) cm

Co. abbr = **company, county**

c/o abbr (= care of) c/o, aux bons soins de

coach [kəutʃ] n (bus) autocar m; (horse-drawn) diligence f; (of train) voiture f, wagon m; (Sport: trainer) entraîneur(-euse); (school: tutor) répétiteur(-trice) ▷ vt (Sport) entraîner; (student) donner des leçons particulières à; **coach station** (BRIT) n gare routière; **coach trip** n excursion f en car

coal [kəul] n charbon m

coalition [kəuə'lɪʃən] n coalition f

coarse [kɔːs] adj grossier(-ère), rude; (vulgar) vulgaire

coast [kəust] n côte f ▷ vi (car, cycle) descendre en roue libre; **coastal** adj côtier(-ère); **coastguard** n garde-côte m; **coastline** n côte f, littoral m

coat [kəut] n manteau m; (of animal) pelage m, poil m; (of paint) couche f ▷ vt couvrir, enduire; **coat hanger** n cintre m; **coating** n couche f, enduit m

coax [kəuks] vt persuader par des cajoleries

cob [kɒb] n see **corn**

cobbled [ˈkɒbld] adj pavé(e)

cobweb [ˈkɒbwɛb] n toile f d'araignée

cocaine [kəˈkeɪn] n cocaïne f

cock [kɒk] n (rooster) coq m; (male bird) mâle m ▷ vt (gun) armer; **cockerel** n jeune coq m

cockney [ˈkɒknɪ] n cockney m/f (habitant des quartiers populaires de l'East End de Londres); = faubourien(ne)

cockpit [ˈkɒkpɪt] n (in aircraft) poste m de pilotage, cockpit m

cockroach [ˈkɒkrəutʃ] n cafard m, cancrelat m

cocktail [ˈkɒkteɪl] n cocktail m

cocoa [ˈkəukəu] n cacao m

coconut [ˈkəukənʌt] n noix f de coco

C.O.D. abbr = **cash on delivery**

cod [kɒd] n morue f fraîche, cabillaud m

code [kəud] n code m; (Tel: area code)

indicatif m

coeducational [ˈkəuɛdjuˈkeɪʃənl] adj mixte

coffee [ˈkɒfɪ] n café m; **coffee bar** (BRIT) n café m; **coffee bean** n grain m de café; **coffee break** n pause-café f; **coffee maker** n cafetière f; **coffeepot** n cafetière f; **coffee shop** n café m; **coffee table** n (petite) table basse

coffin [ˈkɒfɪn] n cercueil m

cog [kɒg] n (wheel) roue dentée; (tooth) dent f (d'engrenage)

cognac [ˈkɒnjæk] n cognac m

coherent [kəuˈhɪərənt] adj cohérent(e)

coil [kɔɪl] n rouleau m, bobine f; (contraceptive) stérilet m ▷ vt enrouler

coin [kɔɪn] n pièce f (de monnaie) ▷ vt (word) inventer

coincide [kəunˈsaɪd] vi coïncider; **coincidence** [kəuˈɪnsɪdəns] n coïncidence f

Coke® [kəuk] n coca m

coke [kəuk] n (coal) coke m

colander [ˈkɒləndə] n passoire f (à légumes)

cold [kəuld] adj froid(e) ▷ n froid m; (Med) rhume m; **it's** ~ il fait froid; **to be** ~ (person) avoir froid; **to catch a** ~ s'enrhumer, attraper un rhume; **in** ~ **blood** de sang-froid; **cold cuts** (US) npl viandes froides; **cold sore** n bouton m de fièvre

coleslaw [ˈkəulslɔː] n sorte de salade de chou cru

colic [ˈkɒlɪk] n colique(s) f(pl)

collaborate [kəˈlæbəreɪt] vi collaborer

collapse [kəˈlæps] vi s'effondrer, s'écrouler; (Med) avoir un malaise ▷ n effondrement m, écroulement m; (of government) chute f

collar [ˈkɒlə] n (of coat, shirt) col m; (for dog) collier m; **collarbone** n clavicule f

colleague [ˈkɒliːg] n collègue m/f

collect [kəˈlɛkt] vt rassembler; (pick up) ramasser; (as a hobby) collectionner; (BRIT: call for) (passer) prendre; (mail) faire la levée de; (money owed) encaisser; (*donations, subscriptions*) recueillir ▷ vi (*people*) se rassembler; (*dust, dirt*) s'amasser; **to call ~** (*Tel*) téléphoner en PCV; **collection** [kə'lekʃən] n collection f; (*of mail*) levée f; (*for money*) collecte f, quête f; **collective** [kə'lektɪv] adj collectif (-ive); **collector** n collectionneur m

college ['kɔlɪdʒ] n collège m; (*of technology, agriculture etc*) institut m

collide [kə'laɪd] vi **to ~ (with)** entrer en collision (avec)

collision [kə'lɪʒən] n collision f, heurt m

cologne [kə'ləun] n (*also:* **eau de ~**) eau f de cologne

colon ['kəulən] n (*sign*) deux-points mpl; (*Med*) côlon m

colonel ['kɜːnl] n colonel m

colonial [kə'ləunɪəl] adj colonial(e)

colony ['kɔlənɪ] n colonie f

colour etc (us *color*) ['kʌlə'] n couleur f ▷ vt colorier; (*dye*) teindre; (*paint*) peindre; (*with crayons*) colorier; (*news*) fausser, exagérer ▷ vi (*blush*) rougir; **I'd like a different ~** je le voudrais dans une autre coloris; **colour in** vt colorier; **colour-blind** adj daltonien(ne); **coloured** adj coloré(e); (*photo*) en couleur; **colour film** n (*for camera*) pellicule f(en) couleur; **colourful** adj coloré(e), vif (vive); (*personality*) pittoresque, haut(e) en couleurs; **colouring** n colorant m; (*complexion*) teint m; **colour television** n télévision f(en) couleur

column ['kɔləm] n colonne f; (*fashion column, sports column etc*) rubrique f

coma ['kəumə] n coma m

comb [kəum] n peigne m ▷ vt (*hair*) peigner; (*area*) ratisser, passer au peigne fin

combat ['kɔmbæt] n combat m ▷ vt combattre, lutter contre

combination [kɔmbɪ'neɪʃən] n (*gen*) combinaison f

combine vb [kəm'baɪn] ▷ vt combiner ▷ vi s'associer; (*Chem*) se combiner ▷ n

[kɔmbaɪn] (*Econ*) trust m; **to ~ sth with sth** (*one quality with another*) joindre au allier qch à qch

come (pt **came**, pp ~) [kʌm, keɪm] vi 1 (*movement towards*) venir; **to ~ running** arriver en courant; **he's ~ here to work** il est venu ici pour travailler; **~ with me** suivez-moi

2 (*arrive*) arriver; **to ~ home** rentrer (chez soi ou à la maison); **we've just ~ from Paris** nous arrivons de Paris

3 (*reach*): **to ~ to** (*decision etc*) parvenir à, arriver à; **the bill came to £40** la note s'est élevée à 40 livres

4 (*occur*): **an idea came to me** il m'est venu une idée

5 (*be, become*): **to ~ loose/undone** se défaire/desserrer; **I've ~ to like him** j'ai fini par bien l'aimer; **come across** vt fus rencontrer par hasard, tomber sur; **come along** vi (BRIT: *pupil, work*) faire des progrès, avancer; **come back** vi revenir; **come down** vi descendre; (*prices*) baisser; (*buildings*) s'écrouler; (*: be demolished*) être démoli(e); **come from** vt fus (*source*) venir de; (*place*) venir de, être originaire de; **come in** vi entrer; (*train*) arriver; (*fashion*) entrer en vogue; (*on deal etc*) participer; **come off** vi (*button*) se détacher; (*attempt*) réussir; **come on** vi (*lights, electricity*) s'allumer; (*central heating*) se mettre en marche; (*pupil, work, project*) faire des progrès, avancer; **~ on!** viens!; allons!, allez!; **come out** vi (*sun*) se montrer; (*book*) paraître; (*stain*) s'enlever; (*strike*) cesser le travail, se mettre en grève; **come round** vi (*after faint, operation*) revenir à soi, reprendre connaissance; **come to** vi revenir à soi; (*problem*) se poser; (*event*) survenir; (*in conversation*) être soulevé; **come up with** vt fus (*money*) fournir; **he came up with an idea** il a eu une idée, il a proposé quelque chose

comeback ['kʌmbæk] n (*Theat etc*) rentrée f

comedian [kəˈmiːdɪən] n (comic) comique m; (Theat) comédien m

comedy [ˈkɒmɪdɪ] n comédie f; (humour) comique m

comet [ˈkɒmɪt] n comète f

comfort [ˈkʌmfət] n confort m, bien-être m; (solace) consolation f, réconfort m ▷ vt consoler, réconforter; **comfortable** adj confortable; (person) à l'aise; (financially) aisé(e); (patient) dont l'état est stationnaire; **comfort station** n (us) toilettes fpl

comic [ˈkɒmɪk] adj (also: **~al**) comique ▷ n (person) comique m; (BRIT: magazine: for children) magazine m de bandes dessinées or de BD; (: for adults) illustré m; **comic book** (us) n (for children) magazine m de bandes dessinées or de BD; (for adults) illustré m; **comic strip** n bande dessinée

comma [ˈkɒmə] n virgule f

command [kəˈmɑːnd] n ordre m, commandement m; (Mil: authority) commandement m; (mastery) maîtrise f ▷ vt (troops) commander; **to ~ sb to do** donner l'ordre or commander à qn de faire; **commander** n (Mil) commandant m

commemorate [kəˈmɛməreɪt] vt commémorer

commence [kəˈmɛns] vt, vi commencer; **commencement** (us) n (University) remise f des diplômes

commend [kəˈmɛnd] vt louer; (recommend) recommander

comment [ˈkɒmɛnt] n commentaire m ▷ vi: **to ~ on** faire des remarques sur; **"no ~"** "je n'ai rien à déclarer"; **commentary** [ˈkɒməntərɪ] n commentaire m; (Sport) reportage m (en direct); **commentator** [ˈkɒməntɪtə²] n commentateur m; (Sport) reporter m

commerce [ˈkɒmɜːs] n commerce m

commercial [kəˈmɜːʃəl] adj commercial(e) ▷ n (Radio, TV) annonce f publicitaire, spot m (publicitaire); **commercial break** n (Radio, TV) spot m (publicitaire)

commission [kəˈmɪʃən] n (committee, fee) commission f ▷ vt (work of art) commander, charger un artiste de l'exécution de; **out of ~** (machine) hors service; **commissioner** n (Police) préfet m (de police)

commit [kəˈmɪt] vt (act) commettre; (resources) consacrer; (to sb's care) confier (à); **to ~ o.s. (to do)** s'engager (à faire); **to ~ suicide** se suicider; **commitment** n engagement m; (obligation) responsabilité(s) (fpl)

committee [kəˈmɪtɪ] n comité m; commission f

commodity [kəˈmɒdɪtɪ] n produit m, marchandise f, article m

common [ˈkɒmən] adj (gen) commun(e); (usual) courant(e) ▷ n terrain communal; **commonly** adv communément, généralement; couramment; **commonplace** adj banal(e), ordinaire; **Commons** npl (BRIT Pol): **the (House of) Commons** la chambre des Communes; **common sense** n bon sens; **Commonwealth** n: **the Commonwealth** le Commonwealth

communal [ˈkɒmjuːnl] adj (life) communautaire; (for common use) commun(e)

commune n [ˈkɒmjuːn] (group) communauté f ▷ vi [kəˈmjuːn]: **to ~ with** (nature) communier avec

communicate [kəˈmjuːnɪkeɪt] vt communiquer, transmettre ▷ vi: **to ~ (with)** communiquer (avec)

communication [kəmjuːnɪˈkeɪʃən] n communication f

communion [kəˈmjuːnɪən] n (also: **Holy C~**) communion f

communism [ˈkɒmjunɪzəm] n communisme m; **communist** adj, n communiste m/f

community [kəˈmjuːnɪtɪ] n communauté f; **community centre** (us **community center**) n foyer socio-éducatif, centre m de loisirs;

community service n ~ travail m
d'intérêt général, TIG m

commute [kə'mju:t] vi faire le trajet
journalier (de son domicile à un lieu
de travail assez éloigné) ▷ vt (Law)
commuer; **commuter** n banlieusard(e)
(qui fait un trajet journalier pour se rendre
à son travail)

compact adj [kəm'pækt] compact(e)
▷ n ['kɒmpækt] (also: **powder ~**)
poudrier m; **compact disc** n disque
compact; **compact disc player** n
lecteur m de disques compacts

companion [kəm'pænjən] n
compagnon (compagne)

company ['kʌmpənɪ] n compagnie
f; **to keep sb ~** tenir compagnie
à qn; **company car** n voiture f de
fonction; **company director** n
administrateur(-trice)

comparable ['kɒmpərəbl] adj
comparable

comparative [kəm'pærətɪv] adj
(study) comparatif(-ive); (relative)
relatif(-ive); **comparatively** adv
(relatively) relativement

compare [kəm'pɛə'] vt: **to ~ sth/sb
with** or **to** comparer qch/qn avec or
à ▷ vi: **to ~ (with)** se comparer (à);
être comparable (à); **comparison**
[kəm'pærɪsn] n comparaison f

compartment [kəm'pɑːtmənt]
n (also Rail) compartiment m; **a
non-smoking ~** un compartiment
non-fumeurs

compass ['kʌmpəs] n boussole f;
compasses npl (Math) compas m

compassion [kəm'pæʃən] n
compassion f, humanité f

compatible [kəm'pætɪbl] adj
compatible

compel [kəm'pɛl] vt contraindre,
obliger; **compelling** adj (fig: argument)
irrésistible

compensate ['kɒmpənseɪt] vt
indemniser, dédommager ▷ vi: **to
~ for** compenser; **compensation**
[kɒmpən'seɪʃən] n compensation

f; (money) dédommagement m,
indemnité f

compete [kəm'piːt] vi (take part)
concourir; (vie): **to ~ (with)** rivaliser
(avec), faire concurrence (à)

competent ['kɒmpɪtənt] adj
compétent(e), capable

competition [kɒmpɪ'tɪʃən] n (contest)
compétition f, concours m; (Econ)
concurrence f

competitive [kəm'pɛtɪtɪv] adj
(Econ) concurrentiel(le); (sports) de
compétition; (person) qui a l'esprit
de compétition

competitor [kəm'pɛtɪtə'] n
concurrent(e)

complacent [kəm'pleɪsnt] adj (trop)
content(e) de soi

complain [kəm'pleɪn] vi: **to ~ (about)**
se plaindre (de); (in shop etc) réclamer
(au sujet de); **complaint** n plainte f; (in
shop etc) réclamation f; (Med) affection f

complement ['kɒmplɪmənt] n
complément m; (esp of ship's crew
etc) effectif complet ▷ vt (enhance)
compléter; **complementary**
[kɒmplɪ'mɛntərɪ] adj complémentaire

complete [kəm'pliːt] adj
complet(-ète); (finished) achevé(e)
▷ vt achever, parachever; (set,
group) compléter; (a form) remplir;
completely adv complètement;
completion [kəm'pliːʃən] n
achèvement m; (of contract) exécution f

complex ['kɒmplɛks] adj complexe ▷ n
(Psych, buildings etc) complexe m

complexion [kəm'plɛkʃən] n (of face)
teint m

compliance [kəm'plaɪəns] n
(submission) docilité f; (agreement): **~
with** le fait de se conformer à; **in ~ with**
en conformité avec, conformément à

complicate ['kɒmplɪkeɪt] vt
compliquer; **complicated** adj
compliqué(e); **complication**
[kɒmplɪ'keɪʃən] n complication f

compliment n ['kɒmplɪmənt]
compliment m ▷ vt ['kɒmplɪmɛnt]

complimenter; **complimentary** [kɒmplɪˈmɛntərɪ] *adj* flatteur(-euse); (*free*) à titre gracieux

comply [kəmˈplaɪ] *vi*: **to ~ with** se soumettre à, se conformer à

component [kəmˈpəʊnənt] *adj* composant(e), constituant(e) ⊳ *n* composant *m*, élément *m*

compose [kəmˈpəʊz] *vt* (*form*): **to be ~d of** se composer de; **to ~ o.s.** se calmer, se maîtriser; **composer** *n* (*Mus*) compositeur *m*; **composition** [kɒmpəˈzɪʃən] *n* composition *f*

composure [kəmˈpəʊʒəʳ] *n* calme *m*, maîtrise *f* de soi

compound [ˈkɒmpaʊnd] *n* (*Chem*, *Ling*) composé *m*; (*enclosure*) enclos *m*, enceinte *f* ⊳ *adj* composé(e); (*fracture*) compliqué(e)

comprehension [kɒmprɪˈhɛnʃən] *n* compréhension *f*

comprehensive [kɒmprɪˈhɛnsɪv] *adj* (très) complet(-ète); **~ policy** (*Insurance*) assurance *f* tous risques; **comprehensive (school)** *n* (BRIT) école secondaire non sélective avec libre circulation d'une section à l'autre, ≈ CES *m*

> Be careful not to translate **comprehensive** by the French word **compréhensif**.

compress *vt* [kəmˈprɛs] comprimer; (*text, information*) condenser ⊳ *n* [ˈkɒmprɛs] (*Med*) compresse *f*

comprise [kəmˈpraɪz] *vt* (*also*: **be ~d of**) comprendre; (*constitute*) constituer, représenter

compromise [ˈkɒmprəmaɪz] *n* compromis *m* ⊳ *vt* compromettre ⊳ *vi* transiger, accepter un compromis

compulsive [kəmˈpʌlsɪv] *adj* (*Psych*) compulsif(-ive); (*book, film etc*) captivant(e)

compulsory [kəmˈpʌlsərɪ] *adj* obligatoire

computer [kəmˈpjuːtəʳ] *n* ordinateur *m*; **computer game** *n* jeu *m* vidéo; **computer-generated** *adj* de synthèse; **computerize** *vt* (*data*)

traiter par ordinateur; (*system, office*) informatiser; **computer programmer** *n* programmeur(-euse) *m/f*; **computer programming** *n* programmation *f*; **computer science** *n* informatique *f*; **computer studies** *npl* informatique *f*; **computing** [kəmˈpjuːtɪŋ] *n* informatique *f*

con [kɒn] *vt* duper; (*cheat*) escroquer ⊳ *n* escroquerie *f*

conceal [kənˈsiːl] *vt* cacher, dissimuler

concede [kənˈsiːd] *vt* concéder ⊳ *vi* céder

conceited [kənˈsiːtɪd] *adj* vaniteux(-euse), suffisant(e)

conceive [kənˈsiːv] *vt*, *vi* concevoir

concentrate [ˈkɒnsəntreɪt] *vi* se concentrer ⊳ *vt* concentrer

concentration [kɒnsənˈtreɪʃən] *n* concentration *f*

concept [ˈkɒnsɛpt] *n* concept *m*

concern [kənˈsəːn] *n* affaire *f*; (*Comm*) entreprise *f*, firme *f*; (*anxiety*) inquiétude *f*, souci *m* ⊳ *vt* (*worry*) inquiéter; (*involve*) concerner; (*relate to*) se rapporter à; **to be ~ed (about)** s'inquiéter (de), être inquiet(-ète) (au sujet de); **concerning** *prep* en ce qui concerne, à propos de

concert [ˈkɒnsət] *n* concert *m*; **concert hall** *n* salle *f* de concert

concerto [kənˈtʃəːtəʊ] *n* concerto *m*

concession [kənˈsɛʃən] *n* (*compromise*) concession *f*; (*reduced price*) réduction *f*; **tax ~** dégrèvement fiscal; **"~s"** tarif réduit

concise [kənˈsaɪs] *adj* concis(e)

conclude [kənˈkluːd] *vt* conclure; **conclusion** [kənˈkluːʒən] *n* conclusion *f*

concrete [ˈkɒŋkriːt] *n* béton *m* ⊳ *adj* concret(-ète); (*Constr*) en béton

concussion [kənˈkʌʃən] *n* (*Med*) commotion (cérébrale)

condemn [kənˈdɛm] *vt* condamner

condensation [kɒndɛnˈseɪʃən] *n* condensation *f*

condense [kənˈdɛns] *vi* se condenser

▷ vt condenser

condition [kən'dɪʃən] n condition f; (disease) maladie f ▷ vt déterminer, conditionner; **on ~ that** à condition que + sub, à condition de; **conditional** [kən'dɪʃənl] adj conditionnel(le); **conditioner** n (for hair) baume démêlant; (for fabrics) assouplissant m

condo ['kɒndəʊ] n (us inf) = **condominium**

condom ['kɒndəm] n préservatif m

condominium [kɒndə'mɪnɪəm] n (us: building) immeuble m (en copropriété); (: rooms) appartement m (dans un immeuble en copropriété)

condone [kən'dəʊn] vt fermer les yeux sur, approuver (tacitement)

conduct n ['kɒndʌkt] conduite f ▷ vt [kən'dʌkt] conduire; (manage) mener, diriger; (Mus) diriger; **to ~ o.s.** se conduire, se comporter; **conducted tour** (BRIT) n voyage organisé; (of building) visite guidée; **conductor** n (of orchestra) chef m d'orchestre; (on bus) receveur m; (us: on train) chef m de train; (Elec) conducteur m

cone [kəʊn] n cône m; (for ice-cream) cornet m; (Bot) pomme f de pin, cône

confectioner [kən'fekʃənr] n (sweets) confiseur(-euse); **confectionery** n confiserie f

confer [kən'fəːr] vt: **to ~ sth on** conférer qch à ▷ vi conférer, s'entretenir

conference ['kɒnfərns] n conférence f

confess [kən'fes] vt confesser, avouer ▷ vi (admit sth) avouer; (Rel) se confesser; **confession** [kən'feʃən] n confession f

confide [kən'faɪd] vi: **to ~ in** s'ouvrir à, se confier à

confidence ['kɒnfɪdns] n confiance f; (also: **self-~**) assurance f, confiance en soi; (secret) confidence f; **in ~** (speak, write) en confidence, confidentiellement; **confident** adj (self-assured) sûr(e) de soi; (sure) sûr; **confidential** [kɒnfɪ'denʃəl] adj confidentiel(le)

confine [kən'faɪn] vt limiter, borner,

(shut up) confiner, enfermer; **confined** adj (space) restreint(e), réduit(e)

confirm [kən'fəːm] vt (report, Rel) confirmer; (appointment) ratifier; **confirmation** [kɒnfə'meɪʃən] n confirmation f; ratification f

confiscate ['kɒnfɪskeɪt] vt confisquer

conflict n ['kɒnflɪkt] conflit m, lutte f ▷ vi [kən'flɪkt] (opinions) s'opposer, se heurter

conform [kən'fɔːm] vi: **to ~ (to)** se conformer à

confront [kən'frʌnt] vt (two people) confronter; (enemy, danger) affronter, faire face à; (problem) faire face à; **confrontation** [kɒnfrən'teɪʃən] n confrontation f

confuse [kən'fjuːz] vt (person) troubler; (situation) embrouiller; (one thing with another) confondre; **confused** adj (person) dérouté(e), désorienté(e); (situation) embrouillé(e); **confusing** adj peu clair(e), déroutant(e); **confusion** [kən'fjuːʒən] n confusion f

congestion [kən'dʒestʃən] n (Med) congestion f; (fig: traffic) encombrement m

congratulate [kən'grætjuleɪt] vt: **to ~ sb (on)** féliciter qn (de); **congratulations** [kəngrætju'leɪʃənz] npl: **congratulations (on)** félicitations fpl (pour) ▷ excl: **congratulations!** (toutes mes) félicitations!

congregation [kɒŋgrɪ'geɪʃən] n assemblée f (des fidèles)

congress ['kɒŋgres] n congrès m; (Pol): **C~** Congrès m; **congressman** n membre m du Congrès; **congresswoman** n membre m du Congrès

conifer ['kɒnɪfər] n conifère m

conjugate ['kɒndʒugeɪt] vt conjuguer; **conjugation** [kɒndʒə'geɪʃən] n conjugaison f

conjunction [kən'dʒʌŋkʃən] n conjonction f; **in ~ with** (conjointement) avec

conjure ['kʌndʒər] vi faire des tours de

passe-passe

connect [kə'nɛkt] vt joindre, relier; (Elec) connecter; (Tel: caller) mettre en connexion; (: subscriber) brancher; (fig) établir un rapport entre, faire un rapprochement entre ▷ vi (train): **to ~ with** assurer la correspondance avec; **to be ~ed with** avoir un rapport avec; (have dealings with) avoir des rapports avec, être en relation avec; **connecting flight** n (vol m de) correspondance f; **connection** [kə'nɛkʃən] n relation f, lien m; (Elec) connexion f; (Tel) communication f; (train etc) correspondance f

conquer ['kɔŋkə*] vt conquérir; (feelings) vaincre, surmonter

conquest ['kɔŋkwɛst] n conquête f

cons [kɔnz] npl see **convenience; pro**

conscience ['kɔnʃəns] n conscience f

conscientious [kɔnʃɪ'ɛnʃəs] adj conscencieux(-euse)

conscious ['kɔnʃəs] adj conscient(e); (deliberate: insult, error) délibéré(e); **consciousness** n conscience f; (Med) connaissance f

consecutive [kən'sɛkjutɪv] adj consécutif(-ive); **on three ~ occasions** trois fois de suite

consensus [kən'sɛnsəs] n consensus m

consent [kən'sɛnt] n consentement m ▷ vi: **to ~ (to)** consentir (à)

consequence ['kɔnsɪkwəns] n suites fpl, conséquence f; (significance) importance f

consequently ['kɔnsɪkwəntlɪ] adv par conséquent, donc

conservation [kɔnsə'veɪʃən] n préservation f, protection f; (also: **nature ~**) défense f de l'environnement

conservative [kən'sə:vətɪv] adj conservateur(-trice); (cautious) prudent(e); **Conservative** adj, n (BRIT Pol) conservateur(-trice)

conservatory [kən'sə:vətrɪ] n (room) jardin m d'hiver; (Mus) conservatoire m

consider [kən'sɪdə*] vt (study)

considérer, réfléchir à; (take into account) penser à, prendre en considération; (regard, judge) considérer, estimer; **to ~ doing sth** envisager de faire qch; **considerable** adj considérable; **considerably** adv nettement; **considerate** adj prévenant(e), plein(e) d'égards; **consideration** [kənsɪdə'reɪʃən] n considération f; (reward) rétribution f, rémunération f; **considering** prep: **considering (that)** étant donné (que)

consignment [kən'saɪnmənt] n arrivage m, envoi m

consist [kən'sɪst] vi: **to ~ of** consister en, se composer de

consistency [kən'sɪstənsɪ] n (thickness) consistance f; (fig) cohérence f

consistent [kən'sɪstənt] adj logique, cohérent(e)

consolation [kɔnsə'leɪʃən] n consolation f

console¹ [kən'səul] vt consoler

console² ['kɔnsəul] n console f

consonant ['kɔnsənənt] n consonne f

conspicuous [kən'spɪkjuəs] adj voyant(e), qui attire l'attention

conspiracy [kən'spɪrəsɪ] n conspiration f, complot m

constable ['kʌnstəbl] n (BRIT) ≈ agent m de police, gendarme m; **chief ~** ≈ préfet m de police

constant ['kɔnstənt] adj constant(e); incessant(e); **constantly** adv constamment, sans cesse

constipated ['kɔnstɪpeɪtɪd] adj constipé(e); **constipation** [kɔnstɪ'peɪʃən] n constipation f

constituency [kən'stɪtjuənsɪ] n (Pol: area) circonscription électorale; (: electors) électorat m

constitute ['kɔnstɪtjuːt] vt constituer

constitution [kɔnstɪ'tjuːʃən] n constitution f

constraint [kən'streɪnt] n contrainte f

construct [kən'strʌkt] vt construire; **construction** [kən'strʌkʃən] n

construction f; **constructive** adj
constructif(-ive)

consul ['kɒnsl] n consul m; **consulate**
['kɒnsjʊlɪt] n consulat m

consult [kən'sʌlt] vt consulter;
consultant n (Med) médecin
consultant; (other specialist) consultant
m, (expert-)conseil m; **consultation**
[kɒnsəl'teɪʃən] n consultation f;
consulting room n (BRIT) cabinet m de
consultation

consume [kən'sju:m] vt consommer;
(subj: flames, hatred, desire) consumer;
consumer n consommateur(-trice)

consumption [kən'sʌmpʃən] n
consommation f

cont. abbr (= continued) suite

contact ['kɒntækt] n contact m;
(person) connaissance f, relation f ▷ vt
se mettre en contact or en rapport
avec; **contact lenses** npl verres mpl
de contact

contagious [kən'teɪdʒəs] adj
contagieux(-euse)

contain [kən'teɪn] vt contenir;
to ~ o.s. se contenir, se maîtriser;
container n récipient m; (for shipping
etc) conteneur m

contaminate [kən'tæmɪneɪt] vt
contaminer

cont'd abbr (= continued) suite

contemplate ['kɒntəmpleɪt] vt
contempler; (consider) envisager

contemporary [kən'tempərərɪ] adj
contemporain(e); (design, wallpaper)
moderne ▷ n contemporain(e)

contempt [kən'tempt] n mépris m,
dédain m; **~ of court** (Law) outrage m à
l'autorité de la justice

contend [kən'tend] vt: **to ~ that**
soutenir or prétendre que ▷ vi: **to ~
with** (compete) rivaliser avec; (struggle)
lutter avec

content [kən'tent] adj content(e),
satisfait(e) ▷ vt contenter, satisfaire
▷ n ['kɒntent] contenu m; (of fat,
moisture) teneur f; **contents** npl (of
container etc) contenu m; **(table of) ~s**

table f des matières; **contented** adj
content(e), satisfait(e)

contest n ['kɒntest] combat m, lutte f;
(competition) concours m ▷ vt [kən'test]
contester, discuter; (compete for)
disputer; (Law) attaquer; **contestant**
[kən'testənt] n concurrent(e); (in fight)
adversaire m/f

context ['kɒntekst] n contexte m

continent ['kɒntɪnənt] n continent
m; **the C~** (BRIT) l'Europe continentale;
continental [kɒntɪ'nentl] adj
continental(e); **continental breakfast**
n café or thé complet; **continental
quilt** n (BRIT) couette f

continual [kən'tɪnjuəl] adj
continuel(le); **continually** adv
continuellement, sans cesse

continue [kən'tɪnju:] vi continuer ▷ vt
continuer; (start again) reprendre

continuity [kɒntɪ'nju:ɪtɪ] n continuité
f; (TV etc) enchaînement m

continuous [kən'tɪnjuəs] adj
continu(e), permanent(e); (Ling)
progressif(-ive); **continuous
assessment** (BRIT) n contrôle
continu; **continuously** adv (repeatedly)
continuellement; (uninterruptedly) sans
interruption

contour ['kɒntuəʳ] n contour m, profil
m; (also: ~ **line**) courbe f de niveau

contraception [kɒntrə'sepʃən] n
contraception f

contraceptive [kɒntrə'septɪv]
adj contraceptif(-ive),
anticonceptionnel(le) ▷ n
contraceptif m

contract n ['kɒntrækt] contrat m ▷ vb
[kən'trækt] vi (become smaller) se
contracter, se resserrer ▷ vt contracter;
(Comm): **to ~ to do sth** s'engager (par
contrat) à faire qch; **contractor** n
entrepreneur m

contradict [kɒntrə'dɪkt] vt contredire;
contradiction [kɒntrə'dɪkʃən] n
contradiction f

contrary[1] ['kɒntrərɪ] adj contraire,
opposé(e) ▷ n contraire m; **on the ~** au

contraire; **unless you hear to the ~** sauf avis contraire

contrary² [kən'trɛərɪ] adj (perverse) contrariant(e), entêté(e)

contrast n ['kɒntrɑːst] contraste m ▷ vt [kən'trɑːst] mettre en contraste, contraster; **in ~ to** or **with** contrairement à, par opposition à

contribute [kən'trɪbjuːt] vi contribuer ▷ vt: **to ~ £10/an article to** donner 10 livres/un article à; **to ~ to** (gen) contribuer à; (newspaper) collaborer à; (discussion) prendre part à; **contribution** [kɒntrɪ'bjuːʃən] n contribution f; (BRIT: for social security) cotisation f; (to publication) article m; **contributor** n (to newspaper) collaborateur(-trice); (of money, goods) donateur(-trice)

control [kən'trəul] vt (process, machinery) commander; (temper) maîtriser; (disease) enrayer ▷ n maîtrise f; (power) autorité f; **controls** npl (of machine etc) commandes fpl; (on radio) boutons mpl de réglage; **to be in ~ of** être maître de, maîtriser; (in charge of) être responsable de; **everything is under ~** j'ai (or il a etc) la situation en main; **the car went out of ~** j'ai (or il a etc) perdu le contrôle du véhicule; **control tower** n (Aviat) tour f de contrôle

controversial [kɒntrə'vəːʃl] adj discutable, controversé(e)

controversy ['kɒntrəvəːsɪ] n controverse f, polémique f

convenience [kən'viːnɪəns] n commodité f; **at your ~** quand or comme cela vous convient; **all modern ~s, all mod cons** (BRIT) avec tout le confort moderne, tout confort

convenient [kən'viːnɪənt] adj commode

convent ['kɒnvənt] n couvent m

convention [kən'vɛnʃən] n convention f; (custom) usage m; **conventional** adj conventionnel(le)

conversation [kɒnvə'seɪʃən] n

conversation f

conversely [kɒn'vəːslɪ] adv inversement, réciproquement

conversion [kən'vəːʃən] n conversion f; (BRIT: of house) transformation f, aménagement m; (Rugby) transformation f

convert vt [kən'vəːt] (Rel, Comm) convertir; (alter) transformer; (house) aménager ▷ n ['kɒnvəːt] converti(e); **convertible** adj convertible ▷ n (voiture f) décapotable f

convey [kən'veɪ] vt transporter; (thanks) transmettre; (idea) communiquer; **conveyor belt** n convoyeur m tapis roulant

convict vt [kən'vɪkt] déclarer (or reconnaître) coupable ▷ n ['kɒnvɪkt] forçat m, convict m; **conviction** [kən'vɪkʃən] n (Law) condamnation f; (belief) conviction f

convince [kən'vɪns] vt convaincre, persuader; **convinced** adj: **convinced of/that** convaincu(e) de/que; **convincing** adj persuasif(-ive), convaincant(e)

convoy ['kɒnvɔɪ] n convoi m

cook [kuk] vt (faire) cuire ▷ vi cuire; (person) faire la cuisine ▷ n cuisinier(-ière); **cookbook** n livre m de cuisine; **cooker** n cuisinière f; **cookery** n cuisine f; **cookery book** n (BRIT) = **cookbook**; **cookie** n (US) biscuit m, petit gâteau sec; **cooking** n cuisine f

cool [kuːl] adj frais (fraîche); (not afraid) calme; (unfriendly) froid(e); (inf: trendy) cool inv (inf); (: great) super inv (inf) ▷ vt, vi rafraîchir, refroidir; **cool down** vi refroidir; (fig: person, situation) se calmer; **cool off** vi (become calmer) se calmer; (lose enthusiasm) perdre son enthousiasme

cop [kɒp] n (inf) flic m

cope [kəup] vi s'en sortir, tenir le coup; **to ~ with** (problem) faire face à

copper ['kɒpə*] n cuivre m; (BRIT: inf: policeman) flic m

copy ['kɒpɪ] n copie f; (book etc)

exemplaire *m* ▷ *vt* copier; (*imitate*) imiter; **copyright** *n* droit *m* d'auteur, copyright *m*

coral ['kɔrəl] *n* corail *m*

cord [kɔ:d] *n* corde *f*; (*fabric*) velours côtelé; (*Elec*) cordon *m* d'alimentation, fil *m* (électrique); **cords** *npl* (*trousers*) pantalon *m* de velours côtelé; **cordless** *adj* sans fil

corduroy ['kɔ:dərɔɪ] *n* velours côtelé

core [kɔ:ʳ] *n* (*of fruit*) trognon *m*, cœur *m*; (*fig: of problem etc*) cœur ▷ *vt* enlever le trognon or le cœur de

coriander [kɔrɪ'ændəʳ] *n* coriandre *f*

cork [kɔ:k] *n* (*material*) liège *m*; (*of bottle*) bouchon *m*; **corkscrew** *n* tire-bouchon *m*

corn [kɔ:n] *n* (*BRIT: wheat*) blé *m*; (*US: maize*) maïs *m*; (*on foot*) cor *m*; ~ **on the cob** (*Culin*) épi *m* de maïs au naturel

corned beef ['kɔ:nd-] *n* corned-beef *m*

corner ['kɔ:nəʳ] *n* coin *m*; (*in road*) tournant *m*, virage *m*; (*Football*) corner *m* ▷ *vt* (*trap: prey*) acculer; (*fig*) coincer; (*Comm: market*) accaparer ▷ *vi* prendre un virage; **corner shop** (*BRIT*) *n* magasin *m* du coin

cornflakes ['kɔ:nfleɪks] *npl* cornflakes *mpl*

cornflour ['kɔ:nflauəʳ] *n* (*BRIT*) farine *f* de maïs, maïzena® *f*

cornstarch ['kɔ:nstɑ:tʃ] *n* (*US*) farine *f* de maïs, maïzena® *f*

Cornwall ['kɔ:nwəl] *n* Cornouailles *f*

coronary ['kɔrənərɪ] *n*: ~ (**thrombosis**) infarctus *m* (du myocarde), thrombose *f* coronaire

coronation [kɔrə'neɪʃən] *n* couronnement *m*

coroner ['kɔrənəʳ] *n* coroner *m*, officier de police judiciaire chargé de déterminer les causes d'un décès

corporal ['kɔ:pərl] *n* caporal *m*, brigadier *m* ▷ *adj*: ~ **punishment** châtiment corporel

corporate ['kɔ:pərɪt] *adj* (*action, ownership*) en commun; (*Comm*) de la société

corporation [kɔ:pə'reɪʃən] *n* (*of town*) municipalité *f*, conseil municipal; (*Comm*) société *f*

corps [kɔ:ʳ, *pl* kɔ:z] *n* corps *m*; **the diplomatic ~** le corps diplomatique; **the press ~** la presse

corpse [kɔ:ps] *n* cadavre *m*

correct [kə'rɛkt] *adj* (*accurate*) correct(e), exact(e); (*proper*) correct, convenable ▷ *vt* corriger; **correction** [kə'rɛkʃən] *n* correction *f*

correspond [kɔrɪs'pɔnd] *vi* correspondre; **to ~ to sth** (*be equivalent to*) correspondre à qch; **correspondence** *n* correspondance *f*; **correspondent** *n* correspondant(e); **corresponding** *adj* correspondant(e)

corridor ['kɔrɪdɔ:ʳ] *n* couloir *m*, corridor *m*

corrode [kə'rəud] *vt* corroder, ronger ▷ *vi* se corroder

corrupt [kə'rʌpt] *adj* corrompu(e); (*Comput*) altéré(e) ▷ *vt* corrompre; (*Comput*) altérer; **corruption** *n* corruption *f*; (*Comput*) altération *f* (de données)

Corsica ['kɔ:sɪkə] *n* Corse *f*

cosmetic [kɔz'mɛtɪk] *n* produit de beauté, cosmétique *m* ▷ *adj*: (*fig: reforms*) symbolique, superficiel(le); **cosmetic surgery** *n* chirurgie *f* esthétique

cosmopolitan [kɔzmə'pɔlɪtn] *adj* cosmopolite

cost [kɔst] *n* coût *m* ▷ *vb* (*pt*, *pp* ~) ▷ *vi* coûter ▷ *vt* établir or calculer le prix de revient de; **costs** *npl* (*Comm*) frais *mpl*; (*Law*) dépens *mpl*; **how much does it ~?** combien ça coûte?; **to ~ sb time/effort** demander du temps/un effort à qn; **it ~ him his life/job** ça lui a coûté la vie/son emploi; **at all ~s** coûte que coûte, à tout prix

co-star ['kəustɑ:ʳ] *n* partenaire *m/f*

costly ['kɔstlɪ] *adj* coûteux(-euse)

cost of living *n* coût *m* de la vie

costume ['kɔstjuːm] *n* costume *m*; (*BRIT: also:* **swimming ~**) maillot *m*

(de bain)

cosy (US **cozy**) ['kəʊzɪ] adj (room, bed) douillet(te); **to be ~** (person) être bien (au chaud)

cot [kɒt] n (BRIT: child's) lit m d'enfant, petit lit; (US: campbed) lit de camp

cottage ['kɒtɪdʒ] n petite maison (à la campagne), cottage m; **cottage cheese** n fromage blanc (maigre)

cotton ['kɒtn] n coton m; (thread) fil m (de coton); **cotton on** vi (inf): **to ~ on (to sth)** piger (qch); **cotton bud** (BRIT) n coton-tige ® m; **cotton candy** (US) n barbe f à papa; **cotton wool** n (BRIT) ouate f, coton m hydrophile

couch [kaʊtʃ] n canapé m; divan m

cough [kɒf] vi tousser ▷ n toux f; **I've got a ~** j'ai la toux; **cough mixture**, **cough syrup** n sirop m pour la toux

could [kʊd] pt of **can**[2]; **couldn't** = **could not**

council ['kaʊnsl] n conseil m; **city or town ~** conseil municipal; **council estate** n (BRIT) (quartier m or zone f de) logements loués à/par la municipalité; **council house** n (BRIT) maison f (à loyer modéré) louée par la municipalité; **councillor** (US **councilor**) n conseiller(-ère); **council tax** n (BRIT) impôts locaux

counsel ['kaʊnsl] n conseil m; (lawyer) avocat(e) ▷ vt: **to ~ (sb to do sth)** conseiller (à qn de faire qch); **counselling** (US **counseling**) n (Psych) aide psychosociale; **counsellor** (US **counselor**) n conseiller(-ère); (US Law) avocat m

count [kaʊnt] vt, vi compter ▷ n compte m; (nobleman) comte m; **count in** vt (inf): **to ~ sb in on sth** inclure qn dans qch; **count on** vt fus compter sur; **countdown** n compte m à rebours

counter ['kaʊntəʳ] n comptoir m; (in post office, bank) guichet m; (in game) jeton m ▷ vt aller à l'encontre de, opposer ▷ adv: **to ~ to** à l'encontre de; contrairement à; **counterclockwise** (US) adv en sens inverse des aiguilles

d'une montre

counterfeit ['kaʊntəfɪt] n faux m, contrefaçon f ▷ vt contrefaire ▷ adj faux (fausse)

counterpart ['kaʊntəpɑːt] n (of person) homologue m/f

countess ['kaʊntɪs] n comtesse f

countless ['kaʊntlɪs] adj innombrable

country ['kʌntrɪ] n pays m; (native land) patrie f; (as opposed to town) campagne f; (region) région f, pays; **country and western (music)** n musique f country; **country house** n manoir m, (petit) château; **countryside** n campagne f

county ['kaʊntɪ] n comté m

coup [kuː, pl kuːz] n (achievement) beau coup; (also: **~ d'état**) coup d'État

couple ['kʌpl] n couple m; **a ~ of (two)** deux; (a few) deux ou trois

coupon ['kuːpɒn] n (voucher) bon m de réduction; (detachable form) coupon m détachable, coupon-réponse m

courage ['kʌrɪdʒ] n courage m; **courageous** [kə'reɪdʒəs] adj courageux(-euse)

courgette [kʊə'ʒet] n (BRIT) courgette f

courier ['kʊrɪəʳ] n messager m, courrier m; (for tourists) accompagnateur(-trice)

course [kɔːs] n cours m; (of ship) route f; (for golf) terrain m; (part of meal) plat m; **of ~** adv bien sûr; **(no,) of ~ not!** bien sûr que non!, évidemment que non!; **~ of treatment** (Med) traitement m

court [kɔːt] n cour f; (Law) cour, tribunal m; (Tennis) court m ▷ vt (woman) courtiser, faire la cour à; **to take to ~** actionner or poursuivre en justice

courtesy ['kəːtəsɪ] n courtoisie f, politesse f; **(by) ~ of** avec l'aimable autorisation de; **courtesy bus**, **courtesy coach** n navette gratuite

court: **court-house** n (US) palais m de justice; **courtroom** ['kɔːtruːm] n salle f de tribunal; **courtyard** ['kɔːtjɑːd] n cour f

cousin ['kʌzn] n cousin(e); **first ~** cousin(e) germain(e)

cover ['kʌvəʳ] vt couvrir; (Press: report

on) faire un reportage sur; (*feelings, mistake*) cacher; (*include*) englober; (*discuss*) traiter ▷ n (*of book, Comm*) couverture f; (*of pan*) couvercle m; (*over furniture*) housse f; (*shelter*) abri m; **covers** npl (*on bed*) couvertures f; **to take** ~ se mettre à l'abri; **under** ~ à l'abri; **under** ~ **of darkness** à la faveur de la nuit; **under separate** ~ (*Comm*) sous pli séparé; **cover up** vi: **to** ~ **up for sb** (*fig*) couvrir qn; **coverage** n (*in media*) reportage m; **cover charge** n couvert m (*supplément à payer*); **cover-up** n tentative f pour étouffer une affaire

cow [kau] n vache f ▷ vt effrayer, intimider

coward ['kauəd] n lâche m/f; **cowardly** adj lâche

cowboy ['kaubɔɪ] n cow-boy m

cozy ['kəuzɪ] adj (us) = **cosy**

crab [kræb] n crabe m

crack [kræk] n (*split*) fente f, fissure f; (*in cup, bone*) fêlure f; (*in wall*) lézarde f; (*noise*) craquement m, coup (sec); (*Drugs*) crack m ▷ vt fendre, fissurer; fêler; lézarder; (*whip*) faire claquer; (*nut*) casser; (*problem*) résoudre; (*code*) déchiffrer ▷ cpd (*athlete*) de première classe, d'élite; **crack down on** vt fus (*crime*) sévir contre, réprimer; **cracked** adj (*cup, bone*) fêlé(e); (*broken*) cassé(e); (*wall*) lézardé(e); (*surface*) craquelé(e); (*inf*) toqué(e), timbré(e); **cracker** n (*also:* **Christmas cracker**) pétard m; (*biscuit*) biscuit (salé), craquelin m

crackle ['krækl] vi crépiter, grésiller

cradle ['kreɪdl] n berceau m

craft [krɑːft] n ruse f (*artisanale*); (*cunning*) ruse f, astuce f; (*boat: pl inv*) embarcation f, barque f; (*plane: pl inv*) appareil m; **craftsman** (*irreg*) n artisan m ouvrier (*qualifié*); **craftsmanship** n métier m, habileté f

cram [kræm] vt (*fill*): **to** ~ **sth with** bourrer qch de; (*put*): **to** ~ **sth into** fourrer qch dans ▷ vi (*for exams*) bachoter

cramp [kræmp] n crampe f; **I've got** ~ **in my leg** j'ai une crampe à la jambe; **cramped** adj à l'étroit, très serré(e)

cranberry ['krænbərɪ] n canneberge f

crane [kreɪn] n grue f

crap [kræp] n (*inf: nonsense*) conneries fpl (!); (: *excrement*) merde f (!)

crash [kræʃ] n (*noise*) fracas m; (*of car, plane*) collision f; (*of business*) faillite f ▷ vt (*plane*) écraser ▷ vi (*plane*) s'écraser; (*two cars*) se percuter, s'emboutir; (*business*) s'effondrer; (*plane*) se jeter ou se fracasser contre; **crash course** n cours intensif; **crash helmet** n casque (*protecteur*)

crate [kreɪt] n cageot m; (*for bottles*) caisse f

crave [kreɪv] vt, vi: **to** ~ (**for**) avoir une envie irrésistible de

crawl [krɔːl] vi ramper; (*vehicle*) avancer au pas ▷ n (*Swimming*) crawl m

crayfish ['kreɪfɪʃ] n (*pl inv: freshwater*) écrevisse f; (*saltwater*) langoustine f

crayon ['kreɪən] n crayon m (de couleur)

craze [kreɪz] n engouement m

crazy ['kreɪzɪ] adj fou (folle); **to be** ~ **about sb/sth** (*inf*) être fou de qn/qch

creak [kriːk] vi (*hinge*) grincer; (*floor, shoes*) craquer

cream [kriːm] n crème f ▷ adj (*colour*) crème inv; **cream cheese** n fromage m à la crème, fromage blanc; **creamy** adj crémeux(-euse)

crease [kriːs] n pli m ▷ vt froisser, chiffonner ▷ vi se froisser, se chiffonner

create [kriː'eɪt] vt créer; **creation** [kriː'eɪʃən] n création f; **creative** adj créatif(-ive); **creator** n créateur(-trice)

creature ['kriːtʃə] n créature f

crèche [krɛʃ] n garderie f, crèche f

credentials [krɪ'dɛnʃlz] npl (*references*) références fpl; (*identity papers*) pièce f d'identité

credibility [krɛdɪ'bɪlɪtɪ] n crédibilité f

credible ['krɛdɪbl] adj digne de foi, crédible

credit ['krɛdɪt] n crédit m; (*recognition*)

honneur m; (Scol) unité f de valeur ▷ vt (Comm) créditer; (believe: also: **give ~ to**) ajouter foi à, croire; **credits** npl (Cine) générique m; **to be in ~** (person, bank account) être créditeur(-trice); **to ~ sb with** (fig) prêter ou attribuer à qn; **credit card** n carte f de crédit; **do you take credit cards?** acceptez-vous les cartes de crédit?

creek [kriːk] n (inlet) crique f, anse f; (us: stream) ruisseau m, petit cours d'eau

creep (pt, pp **crept**) [kriːp, krɛpt] vi ramper

cremate [krɪ'meɪt] vt incinérer

crematorium (pl **crematoria**) [krɛmə'tɔːrɪəm, -'tɔːrɪə] n four m crématoire

crept [krɛpt] pt, pp of **creep**

crescent ['krɛsnt] n croissant m; (street) rue f (en arc de cercle)

cress [krɛs] n cresson m

crest [krɛst] n crête f; (of coat of arms) timbre m

crew [kruː] n équipage m; (Cine) équipe f (de tournage); **crew-neck** n col ras

crib [krɪb] n lit m d'enfant; (for baby) berceau m ▷ vt (inf) copier

cricket ['krɪkɪt] n (insect) grillon m, cri-cri m inv; (game) cricket m; **cricketer** n joueur m de cricket

crime [kraɪm] n crime m; **criminal** ['krɪmɪnl] adj, n criminel(le)

crimson ['krɪmzn] adj cramoisi(e)

cringe [krɪndʒ] vi avoir un mouvement de recul

cripple ['krɪpl] n boiteux(-euse), infirme m/f ▷ vt (person) estropier, paralyser; (ship, plane) immobiliser; (production, exports) paralyser

crisis (pl **crises**) ['kraɪsɪs, -siːz] n crise f

crisp [krɪsp] adj croquant(e); (weather) vif (vive); (manner etc) brusque; **crisps** (BRIT) npl (pommes fpl) chips fpl; **crispy** adj croustillant(e)

criterion (pl **criteria**) [kraɪ'tɪərɪən, -'tɪərɪə] n critère m

critic ['krɪtɪk] n critique m/f; **critical** adj critique; **criticism** ['krɪtɪsɪzəm]

n critique f; **criticize** ['krɪtɪsaɪz] vt critiquer

Croat ['krəʊæt] adj, n = **Croatian**

Croatia [krəʊ'eɪʃə] n Croatie f; **Croatian** adj croate ▷ n Croate m/f; (Ling) croate m

crockery ['krɔkərɪ] n vaisselle f

crocodile ['krɔkədaɪl] n crocodile m

crocus ['krəʊkəs] n crocus m

croissant ['krwasɑ̃] n croissant m

crook [kruk] n escroc m; (of shepherd) houlette f; **crooked** ['krukɪd] adj courbé(e), tordu(e); (action) malhonnête

crop [krɔp] n (produce) culture f; (amount produced) récolte f; (riding crop) cravache f ▷ vt (hair) tondre; **crop up** vi surgir, se présenter, survenir

cross [krɔs] n croix f; (Biol) croisement m ▷ vt (street etc) traverser; (arms, legs, Biol) croiser; (cheque) barrer ▷ adj en colère, fâché(e); **cross off** ou **out** vt barrer, rayer; **cross over** vi traverser; **cross-Channel ferry** ['krɔs'tʃænl-] n ferry m qui fait la traversée de la Manche; **crosscountry (race)** n cross(-country) m; **crossing** n (sea passage) traversée f; (also: **pedestrian crossing**) passage clouté; **how long does the crossing take?** combien de temps dure la traversée?; **crossing guard** (us) n contractuel qui fait traverser la rue aux enfants; **crossroads** n carrefour m; **crosswalk** n (us) passage clouté; **crossword** n mots mpl croisés

crotch [krɔtʃ] n (of garment) entrejambe m; (Anat) entrecuisse m

crouch [krautʃ] vi s'accroupir; (hide) se tapir; (before springing) se ramasser

crouton ['kruːtɔn] n croûton m

crow [krəʊ] n (bird) corneille f; (of cock) chant m du coq, cocorico m ▷ vi (cock) chanter

crowd [kraud] n foule f ▷ vt bourrer, remplir ▷ vi affluer, s'attrouper, s'entasser; **crowded** adj bondé(e), plein(e)

crown [kraun] n couronne f; (of head)

sommet m de la tête; (of hill) sommet
m ▷ vt (also tooth) couronner; **crown
jewels** npl joyaux mpl de la Couronne
crucial ['kru:ʃl] adj crucial(e),
décisif(-ive)
crucifix ['kru:sɪfɪks] n crucifix m
crude [kru:d] adj (materials) brut(e);
non raffiné(e); (basic) rudimentaire,
sommaire; (vulgar) cru(e),
grossier(-ière); **crude (oil)** n (pétrole)
brut m
cruel ['kruəl] adj cruel(le); **cruelty** n
cruauté f
cruise [kru:z] n croisière f ▷ vi (ship)
croiser; (car) rouler; (aircraft) voler
crumb [krʌm] n miette f
crumble ['krʌmbl] vt émietter ▷ vi
(plaster etc) s'effriter; (land, earth)
s'ébouler; (building) s'écrouler, crouler;
(fig) s'effondrer
crumpet ['krʌmpɪt] n petite crêpe
(épaisse)
crumple ['krʌmpl] vt froisser, friper
crunch [krʌntʃ] vt croquer; (underfoot)
faire craquer, écraser; faire crisser ▷ n
(fig) instant m or moment m critique,
moment de vérité; **crunchy** adj
croquant(e), croustillant(e)
crush [krʌʃ] n (crowd) foule f, cohue f;
(love): **to have a ~ on sb** avoir le béguin
pour qn; (drink): **lemon ~** citron pressé
▷ vt écraser; (crumple) froisser; (grind,
break up: garlic, ice) piler; (: grapes)
presser; (hopes) anéantir
crust [krʌst] n croûte f; **crusty** adj
(bread) croustillant(e); (inf: person)
revêche, bourru(e)
crutch [krʌtʃ] n béquille f; (also: **crotch**)
entrejambe m
cry [kraɪ] vi pleurer; (shout: also: ~
out) crier ▷ n cri m; **cry out** vi (call out,
shout) pousser un cri ▷ vt crier
crystal ['krɪstl] n cristal m
cub [kʌb] n petit m (d'un animal); (also: ~
scout) louveteau m
Cuba ['kju:bə] n Cuba m
cube [kju:b] n cube m ▷ vt (Math) élever
au cube

cubicle ['kju:bɪkl] n (in hospital) box m;
(at pool) cabine f
cuckoo ['kuku:] n coucou m
cucumber ['kju:kʌmbə'] n
concombre m
cuddle ['kʌdl] vt câliner, caresser ▷ vi
se blottir l'un contre l'autre
cue [kju:] n queue f de billard; (Theat
etc) signal m
cuff [kʌf] n (BRIT: of shirt, coat etc)
poignet m, manchette f; (us: on trousers)
revers m; (blow) gifle f; **off the ~** adv à
l'improviste; **cufflinks** n boutons m de
manchette
cuisine [kwɪ'zi:n] n cuisine f
cul-de-sac ['kʌldəsæk] n cul-de-sac
m, impasse f
cull [kʌl] vt sélectionner ▷ n (of animals)
abattage sélectif
culminate ['kʌlmɪneɪt] vi: **to ~ in** finir
or se terminer par; (lead to) mener à
culprit ['kʌlprɪt] n coupable m/f
cult [kʌlt] n culte m
cultivate ['kʌltɪveɪt] vt cultiver
cultural ['kʌltʃərəl] adj culturel(le)
culture ['kʌltʃə'] n culture f
cumin ['kʌmɪn] n (spice) cumin m
cunning ['kʌnɪŋ] n ruse f, astuce f ▷ adj
rusé(e), malin(-igne); (clever: device,
idea) astucieux(-euse)
cup [kʌp] n tasse f; (prize, event) coupe f;
(of bra) bonnet m
cupboard ['kʌbəd] n placard m
cup final n (BRIT Football) finale f de
la coupe
curator [kjuə'reɪtə'] n conservateur
(d'un musée etc)
curb [kə:b] vt refréner, mettre un frein à
▷ n (fig) frein m; (us) bord m du trottoir
curdle ['kə:dl] vi (se) cailler
cure [kjuə'] vt guérir; (Culin: salt)
saler; (: smoke) fumer; (: dry) sécher ▷ n
remède m
curfew ['kə:fju:] n couvre-feu m
curiosity [kjuərɪ'ɔsɪtɪ] n curiosité f
curious ['kjuərɪəs] adj curieux(-euse);
I'm ~ about him il m'intrigue
curl [kə:l] n boucle f (de cheveux) ▷ vt,

vi boucler; *(tightly)* friser; **curl up** vi
s'enrouler; *(person)* se pelotonner;
curler n bigoudi m, rouleau m; **curly**
adj bouclé(e); *(tightly curled)* frisé(e)

currant ['kʌrnt] n raisin m de Corinthe,
raisin sec; *(fruit)* groseille f

currency ['kʌrnsɪ] n monnaie f; **to ~
gain** *(fig)* s'accréditer

current ['kʌrnt] n courant m ⊳ adj
(common) courant(e); *(tendency, price,
event)* actuel(le); **current account**
n *(BRIT)* compte courant; **current
affairs** npl *(questions fpl d')* actualité f;
currently adv actuellement

curriculum (pl **~s** or **curricula**)
[kə'rɪkjuləm, -lə] n programme m
d'études; **curriculum vitae** ['-'vi:taɪ] n
curriculum vitae (CV) m

curry ['kʌrɪ] n curry m ⊳ vt: **to ~ favour
with** chercher à gagner la faveur or à
s'attirer les bonnes grâces de; **curry
powder** n poudre f de curry

curse [kə:s] vi jurer, blasphémer ⊳ vt
maudire ⊳ n *(gen)* malédiction f;
(problem, scourge) fléau m; *(swearword)*
juron m

cursor ['kə:sə*] n *(Comput)* curseur m

curt [kə:t] adj brusque, sec (sèche)

curtain ['kə:tn] n rideau m

curve [kə:v] n courbe f; *(in the road)*
tournant m, virage m ⊳ vi se courber;
(road) faire une courbe; **curved** adj
courbe

cushion ['kuʃən] n coussin m ⊳ vt *(fall,
shock)* amortir

custard ['kʌstəd] n *(for pouring)* crème
anglaise

custody ['kʌstədɪ] n *(of child)* garde f;
(for offenders): **to take sb into ~** placer
qn en détention préventive

custom ['kʌstəm] n coutume f, usage
m; *(Comm)* clientèle f

customer ['kʌstəmə*] n client m

customized ['kʌstəmaɪzd] adj
personnalisé(e); *(car etc)* construit sur
sur commande

customs ['kʌstəmz] npl douane f;
customs officer n douanier m

cut [kʌt] vb (pt, pp **~**) ⊳ vt couper;
(meat) découper; *(reduce)* réduire ⊳ vi
couper ⊳ n *(gen)* coupure f; *(of clothes)*
coupe f; *(in salary etc)* réduction f; *(of
meat)* morceau m; **to ~ a tooth** percer
une dent; **to ~ one's finger** se couper
le doigt; **to get one's hair ~** se faire
couper les cheveux; **I've ~ myself** je me
suis coupé(e); **cut back** vt *(plants)* tailler;
(production, expenditure) réduire; **cut
down** vt *(tree)* abattre; *(reduce)* réduire;
cut off vt couper; *(fig)* isoler; **cut
out** vt *(picture etc)* découper; *(remove)*
supprimer; **cut up** vt découper;
cutback n réduction f

cute [kju:t] adj mignon(ne), adorable

cutlery ['kʌtlərɪ] n couverts mpl

cutlet ['kʌtlɪt] n côtelette f

cut-price ['kʌt'praɪs] *(us* **cut-rate**
['kʌt'reɪt])* adj au rabais, à prix réduit

cutting ['kʌtɪŋ] adj *(fig)* cinglant(e)
⊳ n *(BRIT: from newspaper)* coupure f *(de
journal)*; *(from plant)* bouture f

CV n abbr **= curriculum vitae**

cwt abbr **= hundredweight(s)**

cyberspace ['saɪbəspeɪs] n
cyberespace m

cycle ['saɪkl] n cycle m; *(bicycle)*
bicyclette f, vélo m ⊳ vi faire de la
bicyclette; **cycle hire** n location f de
vélos; **cycle lane, cycle path** n piste f
cyclable; **cycling** n cyclisme m; **cyclist**
n cycliste m/f

cyclone ['saɪkləun] n cyclone m

cylinder ['sɪlɪndə*] n cylindre m

cymbals ['sɪmblz] npl cymbales fpl

cynical ['sɪnɪkl] adj cynique

Cypriot ['sɪprɪət] adj cypriote,
chypriote ⊳ n Cypriote m/f, Chypriote
m/f

Cyprus ['saɪprəs] n Chypre f

cyst [sɪst] n kyste m; **cystitis** [sɪs'taɪtɪs]
n cystite f

czar [zɑ:*] n tsar m

Czech [tʃɛk] adj tchèque ⊳ n Tchèque
m/f; *(Ling)* tchèque m; **Czech Republic**
n: **the Czech Republic** la République
tchèque

d

D [di:] n (Mus): **D** ré m

dab [dæb] vt (eyes, wound) tamponner; (paint, cream) appliquer (par petites touches or rapidement)

dad, daddy [dæd, 'dædɪ] n papa m

daffodil ['dæfədɪl] n jonquille f

daft [dɑːft] adj (inf) idiot(e), stupide

dagger ['dægə'] n poignard m

daily ['deɪlɪ] adj quotidien(ne), journalier(-ière) ▷ adv tous les jours

dairy ['dɛərɪ] n (shop) crèmerie f, laiterie f; (on farm) laiterie f; **dairy produce** n produits laitiers

daisy ['deɪzɪ] n pâquerette f

dam [dæm] n (wall) barrage m; (water) réservoir m, lac m de retenue ▷ vt endiguer

damage ['dæmɪdʒ] n dégâts mpl, dommages mpl; (fig) tort m ▷ vt endommager, abîmer; (fig) faire du tort à; **damages** npl (Law) dommages-intérêts mpl

damn [dæm] vt condamner; (curse) maudire ▷ n (inf): **I don't give a ~** je m'en fous ▷ adj (inf: also: **~ed**): **this ~ ...** ce sacré or foutu ...; **~ (it)!** zut!

damp [dæmp] adj humide ▷ n humidité f ▷ vt (also: **~en**: cloth, rag) humecter; (: enthusiasm etc) refroidir

dance [dɑːns] n danse f; (ball) bal m ▷ vi danser; **dance floor** n piste f de danse; **dancer** n danseur(-euse); **dancing** n danse f

dandelion ['dændɪlaɪən] n pissenlit m

dandruff ['dændrəf] n pellicules fpl

D & T n abbr (BRIT: Scol) = **design and technology**

Dane [deɪn] n Danois(e)

danger ['deɪndʒə'] n danger m; **~!** (on sign) danger!; **in ~** en danger; **he was in ~ of falling** il risquait de tomber; **dangerous** adj dangereux(-euse)

dangle ['dæŋgl] vt balancer ▷ vi pendre, se balancer

Danish ['deɪnɪʃ] adj danois(e) ▷ n (Ling) danois m

dare [dɛə'] vt: **to ~ sb to do** défier qn or mettre qn au défi de faire ▷ vi: **to ~ (to) do sth** oser faire qch; **I ~ say** (I suppose) il est probable qu'il viendra; **daring** adj hardi(e), audacieux(-euse) ▷ n audace f, hardiesse f

dark [dɑːk] adj (night, room) obscur(e), sombre; (colour, complexion) foncé(e), sombre ▷ n: **in the ~** dans le noir; **to be in the ~ about** (fig) ignorer tout de; **after ~** après la tombée de la nuit; **darken** vt obscurcir, assombrir ▷ vi s'obscurcir, s'assombrir; **darkness** n obscurité f; **darkroom** n chambre noire

darling ['dɑːlɪŋ] adj, n chéri(e)

dart [dɑːt] n fléchette f; (in sewing) pince f ▷ vi: **to ~ towards** se précipiter or s'élancer vers; **dartboard** n cible f (de jeu de fléchettes); **darts** n jeu m de fléchettes

dash [dæʃ] n (sign) tiret m; (small quantity) goutte f, larme f ▷ vt (throw) jeter or lancer violemment; (hopes) anéantir ▷ vi: **to ~ towards** se précipiter or se ruer vers

dashboard ['dæʃbɔːd] n (Aut) tableau m de bord

data ['deɪtə] npl données fpl; **database** n base f de données; **data processing** n traitement m (électronique) de l'information

date [deɪt] n date f; (with sb) rendez-vous m; (fruit) datte f ▷ vt dater; (person) sortir avec; **~ of birth** date de naissance; **to ~** adv à ce jour; **out of ~** périmé(e); **up to ~** à la page, mis(e) à jour, moderne; **dated** adj démodé(e)

daughter ['dɔːtə'] n fille f; **daughter-in-law** n belle-fille f, bru f

daunting ['dɔːntɪŋ] adj décourageant(e), intimidant(e)

dawn [dɔːn] n aube f, aurore f ▷ vi (day) se lever, poindre; **it ~ed on him that ...** il lui vint à l'esprit que ...

day [deɪ] n jour m; (as duration) journée f; (period of time, age) époque f, temps m; **the ~ before** la veille, le jour précédent; **the ~ after, the following ~** le lendemain, le jour suivant; **the ~ before yesterday** avant-hier; **the ~ after tomorrow** après-demain; **by ~** de jour; **day-care centre** ['deɪkeə-] n (for elderly etc) centre m d'accueil de jour; (for children) garderie f; **daydream** vi rêver (tout éveillé); **daylight** n (lumière f du) jour m; **day return** n (BRIT) billet m d'aller-retour (valable pour la journée); **daytime** n jour m, journée f; **day-to-day** adj (routine, expenses) journalier(-ière); **day trip** n excursion f (d'une journée)

dazed [deɪzd] adj abruti(e)

dazzle ['dæzl] vt éblouir, aveugler; **dazzling** adj (light) aveuglant(e), éblouissant(e); (fig) éblouissant(e)

DC abbr (Elec) = **direct current**

dead [dɛd] adj mort(e); (numb) engourdi(e), insensible; (battery) à plat ▷ adv (completely) absolument, complètement; (exactly) juste; **he was shot ~** il a été tué d'un coup de revolver; **~ tired** éreinté(e), complètement fourbu(e); **to stop ~** s'arrêter pile ou net;

the line is ~ (Tel) la ligne est coupée; **dead end** n impasse f; **deadline** n date f or heure f limite; **deadly** adj mortel(le); (weapon) meurtrier(-ière); **Dead Sea** n: **the Dead Sea** la mer Morte

deaf [dɛf] adj sourd(e); **deafen** vt rendre sourd(e); **deafening** adj assourdissant(e)

deal [diːl] n affaire f, marché m ▷ vt (pt, pp **~t**) (blow) porter; (cards) donner, distribuer; **a great ~ of** beaucoup de; **deal with** vt fus (handle) s'occuper or se charger de; (be about: book etc) traiter de; **dealer** n (Comm) marchand m; (Cards) donneur m; **dealings** npl (in goods, shares) opérations fpl, transactions fpl; (relations) relations fpl, rapports mpl

dealt [dɛlt] pt, pp of **deal**

dean [diːn] n (Rel, BRIT Scol) doyen m; (US Scol) conseiller principal (conseillère principale) d'éducation

dear [dɪə'] adj cher (chère); (expensive) cher, coûteux(-euse) ▷ n: **my ~** mon cher (ma chère) ▷ excl: **~ me!** mon Dieu!; **D~ Sir/Madam** (in letter) Monsieur/Madame; **D~ Mr/Mrs X** Cher Monsieur X (Chère Madame X); **dearly** adv (love) tendrement; (pay) cher

death [dɛθ] n mort f; (Admin) décès m; **death penalty** n peine f de mort; **death sentence** n condamnation f à mort

debate [dɪ'beɪt] n discussion f, débat m ▷ vt discuter, débattre

debit ['dɛbɪt] n débit m ▷ vt: **to ~ a sum to sb** or **to sb's account** porter une somme au débit de qn, débiter qn d'une somme; **debit card** n carte f de paiement

debris ['dɛbriː] n débris mpl, décombres mpl

debt [dɛt] n dette f; **to be in ~** avoir des dettes, être endetté(e)

debut ['deɪbjuː] n début(s) m(pl)

Dec. abbr (= December) déc

decade ['dɛkeɪd] n décennie f, décade f

decaffeinated [dɪˈkæfɪneɪtɪd] adj décaféiné(e)

decay [dɪˈkeɪ] n (of building) délabrement m; (also: **tooth ~**) carie f (dentaire) ▷ vi (rot) se décomposer, pourrir; (: teeth) se carier

deceased [dɪˈsiːst] n: **the ~** le (la) défunt(e)

deceit [dɪˈsiːt] n tromperie f, supercherie f; **deceive** [dɪˈsiːv] vt tromper

December [dɪˈsɛmbə] n décembre m

decency [ˈdiːsənsɪ] n décence f

decent [ˈdiːsənt] adj (proper) décent(e), convenable

deception [dɪˈsɛpʃən] n tromperie f

deceptive [dɪˈsɛptɪv] adj trompeur(-euse)

decide [dɪˈsaɪd] vt (subj: person) décider; (question, argument) trancher, régler ▷ vi se décider, décider; **to ~ to do/that** décider de faire/que; **to ~ on** décider, se décider pour

decimal [ˈdɛsɪməl] adj décimal(e) ▷ n décimale f

decision [dɪˈsɪʒən] n décision f

decisive [dɪˈsaɪsɪv] adj décisif(-ive); (manner, person) décidé(e), catégorique

deck [dɛk] n (Naut) pont m; (of cards) jeu m; (record deck) platine f; (of bus): **top ~** impériale f; **deckchair** n chaise longue

declaration [dɛkləˈreɪʃən] n déclaration f

declare [dɪˈklɛə] vt déclarer

decline [dɪˈklaɪn] n (decay) déclin m; (lessening) baisse f ▷ vt refuser, décliner ▷ vi décliner; (business) baisser

decorate [ˈdɛkəreɪt] vt (adorn, give a medal to) décorer; (paint and paper) peindre et tapisser; **decoration** [dɛkəˈreɪʃən] n (medal etc, adornment) décoration f; **decorator** n peintre m en bâtiment

decrease n [ˈdiːkriːs] diminution f ▷ vt, vi [diːˈkriːs] diminuer

decree [dɪˈkriː] n (Pol, Rel) décret m; (Law) arrêt m, jugement m

dedicate [ˈdɛdɪkeɪt] vt consacrer; (book etc) dédier; **dedicated** adj (person) dévoué(e); (Comput) spécialisé(e), dédié(e); **dedicated word processor** station f de traitement de texte

dedication [dɛdɪˈkeɪʃən] n (devotion) dévouement m; (in book) dédicace f

deduce [dɪˈdjuːs] vt déduire, conclure

deduct [dɪˈdʌkt] vt: **to ~ sth (from)** déduire qch (de), retrancher qch (de); **deduction** [dɪˈdʌkʃən] n (deducting, deducing) déduction f; (from wage etc) prélèvement m, retenue f

deed [diːd] n action f, acte m; (Law) acte notarié, contrat m

deem [diːm] vt (formal) juger, estimer

deep [diːp] adj profond(e); (voice) grave ▷ adv: **spectators stood 20 ~** il y avait 20 rangs de spectateurs; **4 metres ~** de 4 mètres de profondeur; **how ~ is the water?** l'eau a quelle profondeur?; **deep-fry** vt faire frire (dans une friteuse); **deeply** adv profondément; (regret, interested) vivement

deer [dɪə] n (pl inv): **(red) ~** cerf m; **(fallow) ~** daim m; **(roe) ~** chevreuil m

default [dɪˈfɔːlt] n (Comput: also: **~ value**) valeur f par défaut; **by ~** (Law) par défaut, par contumace; (Sport) par forfait

defeat [dɪˈfiːt] n défaite f ▷ vt (team, opponents) battre

defect n [ˈdiːfɛkt] défaut m ▷ vi [dɪˈfɛkt]: **to ~ to the enemy/the West** passer à l'ennemi/l'Ouest; **defective** [dɪˈfɛktɪv] adj défectueux(-euse)

defence (us **defense**) [dɪˈfɛns] n défense f

defend [dɪˈfɛnd] vt défendre; **defendant** n défendeur(-deresse); (in criminal case) accusé(e), prévenu(e); **defender** n défenseur m

defense [dɪˈfɛns] (us) = **defence**

defensive [dɪˈfɛnsɪv] adj défensif(-ive) ▷ n: **on the ~** sur la défensive

defer [dɪˈfəː] vt (postpone) différer, ajourner

defiance [dɪˈfaɪəns] n défi m; **in ~ of** au mépris de; **defiant** [dɪˈfaɪənt] adj provocant(e), de défi; (*person*) rebelle, intraitable

deficiency [dɪ'fɪʃənsɪ] *n* (*lack*) insuffisance *f*; (: *Med*) carence *f*; (*flaw*) faiblesse *f*; **deficient** [dɪ'fɪʃənt] *adj* (*inadequate*) insuffisant(e); **to be deficient in** manquer de

deficit ['defɪsɪt] *n* déficit *m*

define [dɪ'faɪn] *vt* définir

definite ['defɪnɪt] *adj* (*fixed*) défini(e), (*bien*) déterminé(e); (*clear, obvious*) net(te), manifeste; (*certain*) sûr(e); **he was ~ about it** il a été catégorique; **definitely** *adv* sans aucun doute

definition [defɪ'nɪʃən] *n* définition *f*; (*clearness*) netteté *f*

deflate [diː'fleɪt] *vt* dégonfler

deflect [dɪ'flekt] *vt* détourner, faire dévier

defraud [dɪ'frɔːd] *vt*: **to ~ sb of sth** escroquer qch à qn

defrost [diː'frɔst] *vt* (*fridge*) dégivrer; (*frozen food*) décongeler

defuse [diː'fjuːz] *vt* désamorcer

defy [dɪ'faɪ] *vt* défier; (*efforts etc*) résister à; **it defies description** cela défie toute description

degree [dɪ'griː] *n* degré *m*; (*Scol*) diplôme *m* (*universitaire*); **a (first) ~ in maths** (*BRIT*) une licence en maths; **by ~s** (*gradually*) par degrés; **to some ~** jusqu'à un certain point, dans une certaine mesure

dehydrated [diːhaɪ'dreɪtɪd] *adj* déshydraté(e); (*milk, eggs*) en poudre

de-icer ['diː'aɪsə*r*] *n* dégivreur *m*

delay [dɪ'leɪ] *vt* (*train*) retarder; (*payment*) différer ▷ *vi* s'attarder ▷ *n* délai *m*, retard *m*; **to be ~ed** être en retard

delegate *n* ['delɪgɪt] délégué(e) ▷ ['delɪgeɪt] déléguer

delete [dɪ'liːt] *vt* rayer, supprimer; (*Comput*) effacer

deli ['delɪ] *n* épicerie fine

deliberate *adj* [dɪ'lɪbərɪt] (*intentional*) délibéré(e); (*slow*) mesuré(e) ▷ *vi* [dɪ'lɪbəreɪt] délibérer, réfléchir; **deliberately** *adv* (*on purpose*) exprès,

délibérément

delicacy ['delɪkəsɪ] *n* délicatesse *f*; (*choice food*) mets fin or délicat, friandise *f*

delicate ['delɪkɪt] *adj* délicat(e)

delicatessen [delɪkə'tesn] *n* épicerie fine

delicious [dɪ'lɪʃəs] *adj* délicieux(-euse)

delight [dɪ'laɪt] *n* (*grande*) joie, grand plaisir *m* ▷ *vt* enchanter; **she's a ~ to work with** c'est un plaisir de travailler avec elle; **to take ~ in** prendre grand plaisir à; **delighted** *adj*: **delighted (at or with sth)** ravi(e) (de qch); **to be delighted to do sth/that** être enchanté(e) or ravi(e) de faire qch/que; **delightful** *adj* (*person*) adorable; (*meal, evening*) merveilleux(-euse)

delinquent [dɪ'lɪŋkwənt] *adj*, *n* délinquant(e)

deliver [dɪ'lɪvə*r*] *vt* (*mail*) distribuer; (*goods*) livrer; (*message*) remettre; (*speech*) prononcer; (*Med*: *baby*) mettre au monde; **delivery** *n* (*of mail*) distribution *f*; (*of goods*) livraison *f*; (*of speaker*) élocution *f*; (*Med*) accouchement *m*; **to take delivery of** prendre livraison de

delusion [dɪ'luːʒən] *n* illusion *f*

de luxe [də'lʌks] *adj* de luxe

delve [delv] *vi*: **to ~ into** fouiller dans

demand [dɪ'mɑːnd] *vt* réclamer, exiger ▷ *n* exigence *f*; (*claim*) revendication *f*; (*Econ*) demande *f*; **in ~** demandé(e), recherché(e); **on ~** sur demande

> Be careful not to translate **to demand** by the French word **demander**.

demise [dɪ'maɪz] *n* décès *m*

demo ['deməu] *n abbr* (*inf*) = **demonstration** (*protest*) manif *f*; (*Comput*) démonstration *f*

democracy [dɪ'mɔkrəsɪ] *n* démocratie *f*; **democrat** ['deməkræt] *n* démocrate *m/f*; **democratic** [demə'krætɪk] *adj* démocratique

demolish [dɪˈmɒlɪʃ] vt démolir
demolition [deməˈlɪʃən] n
démolition f
demon [ˈdiːmən] n démon m
demonstrate [ˈdemənstreɪt] vt
démontrer, prouver; (show) faire
une démonstration de ▷ vi: to
~ (for/against) manifester (en
faveur de/contre); **demonstration**
[demənˈstreɪʃən] n manifestation
f; (Pol etc) manifestation f;
demonstrator n (Pol etc)
manifestant(e)
demote [dɪˈməʊt] vt rétrograder
den [den] n (of lion) tanière f; (room)
repaire m
denial [dɪˈnaɪəl] n (of accusation)
démenti m; (of rights, guilt, truth)
dénégation f
denim [ˈdenɪm] n jean m; **denims** npl
(blue-)jeans mpl
Denmark [ˈdenmɑːk] n Danemark m
denomination [dɪnɒmɪˈneɪʃən] n
(money) valeur f; (Rel) confession f
denounce [dɪˈnaʊns] vt dénoncer
dense [dens] adj dense; (inf: stupid)
obtus(e)
density [ˈdensɪtɪ] n densité f;
single-/double-~ disk (Comput)
disquette f(à) simple/double densité
dent [dent] n bosse f ▷ vt (also: **make a
~ in**) cabosser
dental [ˈdentl] adj dentaire; **dental
floss** [-flɒs] n fil m dentaire; **dental
surgery** n cabinet m de dentiste
dentist [ˈdentɪst] n dentiste m/f
dentures [ˈdentʃəz] npl dentier mpl
deny [dɪˈnaɪ] vt nier; (refuse) refuser
deodorant [diːˈəʊdərənt] n
déodorant m
depart [dɪˈpɑːt] vi partir; to ~ **from** (fig:
differ from) s'écarter de
department [dɪˈpɑːtmənt] n (Comm)
rayon m; (Scol) section f; (Pol) ministère
m, département m; **department store**
n grand magasin
departure [dɪˈpɑːtʃə] n départ m; (fig):
a new ~ une nouvelle voie; **departure**

lounge n salle f de départ
depend [dɪˈpend] vi: to ~ (up)on
dépendre de; (rely on) compter sur; **it
~s** cela dépend; **~ing on the result ...**
selon le résultat ...; **dependant** n
personne f à charge; **dependent** adj: to
be dependent (on) dépendre (de) ▷ n
= **dependant**
depict [dɪˈpɪkt] vt (in picture)
représenter; (in words) (dé)peindre,
décrire
deport [dɪˈpɔːt] vt déporter, expulser
deposit [dɪˈpɒzɪt] n (Chem, Comm, Geo)
dépôt m; (of ore, oil) gisement m; (part
payment) arrhes fpl, acompte m; (on
bottle etc) consigne f; (for hired goods
etc) cautionnement m, garantie f ▷ vt
déposer; **deposit account** n compte
m sur livret
depot [ˈdepəʊ] n dépôt m; (us: Rail)
gare f
depreciate [dɪˈpriːʃɪeɪt] vi se déprécier,
se dévaloriser
depress [dɪˈpres] vt déprimer; (press
down) appuyer sur, abaisser; (wages etc)
faire baisser; **depressed** adj (person)
déprimé(e); (area) en déclin, touché(e)
par le sous-emploi; **depressing** adj
déprimant(e); **depression** [dɪˈpreʃən]
n dépression f
deprive [dɪˈpraɪv] vt: to ~ **sb of** priver
qn de; **deprived** adj déshérité(e)
dept. abbr (= department) dépt, dép t
depth [depθ] n profondeur f; **to be in
the ~s of despair** être au plus profond
du désespoir; **to be out of one's ~**
(BRIT: swimmer) ne plus avoir pied; (fig)
être dépassé(e), nager
deputy [ˈdepjʊtɪ] n (second in command)
adjoint(e); (Pol) député m; (us: also:
~ **sheriff**) shérif adjoint ▷ adj: ~ **head**
(Scol) directeur(-trice) adjoint(e), sous-
directeur(-trice)
derail [dɪˈreɪl] vt: **to be ~ed** dérailler
derelict [ˈderɪlɪkt] adj abandonné(e),
à l'abandon
derive [dɪˈraɪv] vt: **to ~ sth from** tirer
qch de; trouver qch dans ▷ vi: **to ~ from**

provenir de, dériver de

descend [dɪ'sɛnd] vt, vi descendre; **to ~ from** descendre de, être issu(e) de; **to ~ to** s'abaisser à; **descendant** n descendant(e); **descent** n descente f; (origin) origine f

describe [dɪs'kraɪb] vt décrire; **description** [dɪs'krɪpʃən] n description f; (sort) sorte f, espèce f

desert n ['dɛzət] désert m ▷ vb [dɪ'zə:t] ▷ vt déserter, abandonner ▷ vi (Mil) déserter; **deserted** [dɪ'zə:tɪd] adj désert(e)

deserve [dɪ'zə:v] vt mériter

design [dɪ'zaɪn] n (sketch) plan m, dessin m; (layout, shape) conception f, ligne f; (pattern) dessin m, motif s) m(pl); (of dress, car) modèle m; (art) design m, stylisme m; (intention) dessein m ▷ vt dessiner; (plan) concevoir; **design and technology** n (BRIT: Scol) technologie f

designate [dɪ'zɪgneɪt] vt désigner ▷ adj ['dɛzɪgnɪt] désigné(e)

designer [dɪ'zaɪnə*] n (Archit, Art) dessinateur(-trice); (Industry) concepteur m, designer m; (Fashion) styliste m/f

desirable [dɪ'zaɪərəbl] adj (property, location, purchase) attrayant(e)

desire [dɪ'zaɪə*] n désir m ▷ vt désirer, vouloir

desk [dɛsk] n (in office) bureau m; (for pupil) pupitre m; (BRIT: in shop, restaurant) caisse f; (in hotel, at airport) réception f; **desk-top publishing** ['dɛsktɔp-] n publication assistée par ordinateur, PAO f

despair [dɪs'pɛə*] n désespoir m ▷ vi: **to ~ of** désespérer de

despatch [dɪs'pætʃ] n, vt = **dispatch**

desperate ['dɛspərɪt] adj désespéré(e); (fugitive) prêt(e) à tout; **to be ~ for sth/ to do sth** avoir désespérément besoin de qch/de faire qch; **desperately** adv désespérément; (very) terriblement, extrêmement; **desperation** [dɛspə'reɪʃən] n désespoir m; **in (sheer) desperation** en désespoir

de cause

despise [dɪs'paɪz] vt mépriser

despite [dɪs'paɪt] prep malgré, en dépit de

dessert [dɪ'zə:t] n dessert m; **dessertspoon** n cuiller f à dessert

destination [dɛstɪ'neɪʃən] n destination f

destined ['dɛstɪnd] adj: **~ for London** à destination de Londres

destiny ['dɛstɪnɪ] n destinée f, destin m

destroy [dɪs'trɔɪ] vt détruire; (injured horse) abattre; (dog) faire piquer

destruction [dɪs'trʌkʃən] n destruction f

destructive [dɪs'trʌktɪv] adj destructeur(-trice)

detach [dɪ'tætʃ] vt détacher; **detached** adj (attitude) détaché(e); **detached house** n pavillon m maison(semi) (individuelle)

detail ['di:teɪl] n détail m ▷ vt raconter en détail, énumérer; **in ~** en détail; **detailed** adj détaillé(e)

detain [dɪ'teɪn] vt retenir; (in captivity) détenir

detect [dɪ'tɛkt] vt déceler, percevoir; (Med, Police) dépister; (Mil, Radar, Tech) détecter; **detection** [dɪ'tɛkʃən] n découverte f, dépistage m; **detective** n policier m; **private detective** détective privé; **detective story** n roman policier

detention [dɪ'tɛnʃən] n détention f; (Scol) retenue f, consigne f

deter [dɪ'tə:*] vt dissuader

detergent [dɪ'tə:dʒənt] n détersif m, détergent m

deteriorate [dɪ'tɪərɪəreɪt] vi se détériorer, se dégrader

determination [dɪtə:mɪ'neɪʃən] n détermination f

determine [dɪ'tə:mɪn] vt déterminer; **to ~ to do** prendre la résolution de, se déterminer à faire; **determined** adj (person) déterminé(e), décidé(e); **determined to do** bien décidé à faire

deterrent [dɪ'tɛrənt] n effet m de dissuasion; force f de dissuasion

detest [dɪ'tɛst] vt détester, avoir horreur de

detour ['di:tuə'] n détour m; (us Aut: diversion) déviation f

detract [dɪ'trækt] vt: **to ~ from** (quality, pleasure) diminuer; (reputation) porter atteinte à

detrimental [dɛtrɪ'mɛntl] adj: **~ to** préjudiciable or nuisible à

devastating ['dɛvəsteɪtɪŋ] adj dévastateur(-trice); (news) accablant(e)

develop [dɪ'vɛləp] vt (gen) développer; (disease) commencer à souffrir de; (resources) exploiter; (land) aménager ▷ vi se développer; (situation, disease: evolve) évoluer; (facts, symptoms: appear) se manifester, se produire; **can you ~ this film?** pouvez-vous développer cette pellicule?; **developing country** n pays m en voie de développement; **development** n développement m; (of land) exploitation f; (new fact, event) rebondissement m, fait(s) nouveau(x)

device [dɪ'vaɪs] n (apparatus) appareil m, dispositif m

devil ['dɛvl] n diable m; démon m

devious ['di:vɪəs] adj (person) sournois(e), dissimulé(e)

devise [dɪ'vaɪz] vt imaginer, concevoir

devote [dɪ'vəut] vt: **to ~ sth to** consacrer qch à; **devoted** adj dévoué(e); **to be devoted to** être dévoué(e) or très attaché(e) à; (book etc) être consacré(e) à; **devotion** n dévouement m, attachement m; (Rel) dévotion f, piété f

devour [dɪ'vauə'] vt dévorer

devout [dɪ'vaut] adj pieux(-euse), dévot(e)

dew [dju:] n rosée f

diabetes [daɪə'bi:ti:z] n diabète m

diabetic [daɪə'bɛtɪk] n diabétique m/f ▷ adj (person) diabétique

diagnose [daɪəg'nəuz] vt diagnostiquer

diagnosis (pl **diagnoses**) [daɪəg'nəusɪs, -si:z] n diagnostic m

diagonal [daɪ'ægənl] adj diagonal(e) ▷ n diagonale f

diagram ['daɪəgræm] n diagramme m, schéma m

dial ['daɪəl] n cadran m ▷ vt (number) faire, composer

dialect ['daɪəlɛkt] n dialecte m

dialling code ['daɪəlɪŋ-] (us **dial code**) n indicatif m (téléphonique); **what's the ~ for Paris?** quel est l'indicatif de Paris?

dialling tone ['daɪəlɪŋ-] (us **dial tone**) n tonalité f

dialogue (us **dialog**) ['daɪəlɔg] n dialogue m

diameter [daɪ'æmɪtə'] n diamètre m

diamond ['daɪəmənd] n diamant m; (shape) losange m; **diamonds** npl (Cards) carreau m

diaper ['daɪəpə'] n (us) couche f

diarrhoea (us **diarrhea**) [daɪə'ri:ə] n diarrhée f

diary ['daɪərɪ] n (daily account) journal m; (book) agenda m

dice [daɪs] n (pl inv) dé m ▷ vt (Culin) couper en dés or en cubes

dictate [dɪk'teɪt] vt dicter; **dictation** [dɪk'teɪʃən] n dictée f

dictator [dɪk'teɪtə'] n dictateur m

dictionary ['dɪkʃənrɪ] n dictionnaire m

did [dɪd] pt of **do**

didn't [dɪdnt] = **did not**

die [daɪ] vi mourir; **to be dying for sth** avoir une envie folle de qch; **to be dying to do sth** mourir d'envie de faire qch; **die down** vi se calmer, s'apaiser; **die out** vi disparaître, s'éteindre

diesel ['di:zl] n (vehicle) diesel m; (also: ~ oil) carburant m diesel, gas-oil m

diet ['daɪət] n alimentation f; (restricted food) régime m ▷ vi (also: **be on a ~**) suivre un régime

differ ['dɪfə'] vi: **to ~ from sth** (be different) être différent(e) de qch, différer de qch; **to ~ from sb over sth** ne pas être d'accord avec qn au sujet de qch; **difference** n différence f; (quarrel) différend m, désaccord m; **different**

adj différent(e); **differentiate** [dɪfə'rɛnʃɪeɪt] *vi*: **to differentiate between** faire une différence entre; **differently** *adv* différemment

difficult ['dɪfɪkəlt] *adj* difficile; **difficulty** *n* difficulté *f*

dig [dɪɡ] *vt* (*pt, pp* **dug**) (*hole*) creuser; (*garden*) bêcher ▷ *n* (*prod*) coup *m* de coude; (*fig: remark*) coup de griffe or de patte; (*Archaeology*) fouille *f*; **to ~ one's nails into** enfoncer ses ongles dans; **dig up** *vt* déterrer

digest [daɪ'dʒɛst] *vt* digérer ▷ *n* ['daɪdʒɛst] sommaire *m*, résumé *m*; **digestion** [dɪ'dʒɛstʃən] *n* digestion *f*

digit ['dɪdʒɪt] *n* (*number*) chiffre *m* (de 0 à 9); (*finger*) doigt *m*; **digital** *adj* (*system, recording, radio*) numérique; (*watch*) à affichage numérique or digital; **digital camera** *n* appareil *m* photo numérique; **digital TV** *n* télévision *f* numérique

dignified ['dɪɡnɪfaɪd] *adj* digne

dignity ['dɪɡnɪtɪ] *n* dignité *f*

digs [dɪɡz] *npl* (*BRIT inf*) piaule *f*, chambre meublée

dilemma [daɪ'lɛmə] *n* dilemme *m*

dill [dɪl] *n* aneth *m*

dilute [daɪ'luːt] *vt* diluer

dim [dɪm] *adj* (*light, eyesight*) faible; (*memory, outline*) vague, indécis(e); (*room*) sombre; (*inf: stupid*) borné(e), obtus(e) ▷ *vt* (*light*) réduire, baisser; (*us Aut*) mettre en code, baisser

dime [daɪm] *n* (*us*) pièce *f* de 10 cents

dimension [daɪ'mɛnʃən] *n* dimension *f*

diminish [dɪ'mɪnɪʃ] *vt, vi* diminuer

din [dɪn] *n* vacarme *m*

dine [daɪn] *vi* dîner; **diner** *n* (*person*) dîneur(-euse); (*us: eating place*) petit restaurant

dinghy ['dɪŋɡɪ] *n* youyou *m*; (*inflatable*) canot *m* pneumatique; (*also:* **sailing ~**) voilier *m*, dériveur *m*

dingy ['dɪndʒɪ] *adj* miteux(-euse), minable

dining car ['daɪnɪŋ-] *n* (*BRIT*) voiture-restaurant *f*, wagon-restaurant *m*

dining room ['daɪnɪŋ-] *n* salle *f* à manger

dining table [daɪnɪŋ-] *n* table *f* de (la) salle à manger

dinner ['dɪnə'] *n* (*evening meal*) dîner *m*; (*lunch*) déjeuner *m*; (*public*) banquet *m*; **dinner jacket** *n* smoking *m*; **dinner party** *n* dîner *m*; **dinner time** *n* (*evening*) heure *f* du dîner; (*midday*) heure du déjeuner

dinosaur ['daɪnəsɔː'] *n* dinosaure *m*

dip [dɪp] *n* (*slope*) déclivité *f*; (*in sea*) baignade *f*, bain *m*; (*Culin*) sauce *f* ▷ *vt* tremper, plonger; (*BRIT Aut: lights*) mettre en code, baisser ▷ *vi* plonger

diploma [dɪ'pləʊmə] *n* diplôme *m*

diplomacy [dɪ'pləʊməsɪ] *n* diplomatie *f*

diplomat ['dɪpləmæt] *n* diplomate *m*; **diplomatic** [dɪplə'mætɪk] *adj* diplomatique

dipstick ['dɪpstɪk] *n* (*BRIT Aut*) jauge *f* de niveau d'huile

dire [daɪə'] *adj* (*poverty*) extrême; (*awful*) affreux(-euse)

direct [daɪ'rɛkt] *adj* direct(e) ▷ *vt* (*tell way*) diriger, orienter; (*letter, remark*) adresser; (*Cine, TV*) réaliser; (*Theat*) mettre en scène; (*order*) **to ~ sb to do sth** ordonner à qn de faire qch ▷ *adv* directement; **can you ~ me to ...?** pouvez-vous m'indiquer la chemin de ...?; **direct debit** *n* (*BRIT Banking*) prélèvement *m* automatique

direction [dɪ'rɛkʃən] *n* direction *f*; **directions** *npl* (*to a place*) indications *fpl*; **~s for use** mode *m* d'emploi; **sense of ~** sens *m* de l'orientation

directly [dɪ'rɛktlɪ] *adv* (*in straight line*) directement, tout droit; (*at once*) tout de suite, immédiatement

director [dɪ'rɛktə'] *n* directeur *m*; (*Theat*) metteur *m* en scène; (*Cine, TV*) réalisateur(-trice)

directory [dɪ'rɛktərɪ] *n* annuaire *m*; (*Comput*) répertoire *m*; **directory enquiries** (*us* **directory assistance**)

(Tel: service) renseignements *mpl*

dirt [dəːt] *n* saleté *f*; *(mud)* boue *f*; **dirty** *adj* sale; *(joke)* cochon(ne) ⊳ *vt* salir

disability [dɪsə'bɪlɪtɪ] *n* invalidité *f*, infirmité *f*

disabled [dɪs'eɪbld] *adj* handicapé(e); *(maimed)* mutilé(e)

disadvantage [dɪsəd'vɑːntɪdʒ] *n* désavantage *m*, inconvénient *m*

disagree [dɪsə'griː] *vi (differ)* ne pas concorder; *(be against, think otherwise)*: **to ~ (with)** ne pas être d'accord (avec); **disagreeable** *adj* désagréable; **disagreement** *n* désaccord *m*, différend *m*

disappear [dɪsə'pɪə^r] *vi* disparaître; **disappearance** *n* disparition *f*

disappoint [dɪsə'pɔɪnt] *vt* décevoir; **disappointed** *adj* déçu(e); **disappointing** *adj* décevant(e); **disappointment** *n* déception *f*

disapproval [dɪsə'pruːvəl] *n* désapprobation *f*

disapprove [dɪsə'pruːv] *vi*: **to ~ of** désapprouver

disarm [dɪs'ɑːm] *vt* désarmer; **disarmament** [dɪs'ɑːməmənt] *n* désarmement *m*

disaster [dɪ'zɑːstə^r] *n* catastrophe *f*, désastre *m*; **disastrous** *adj* désastreux(-euse)

disbelief ['dɪsbə'liːf] *n* incrédulité *f*

disc [dɪsk] *n* disque *m*; *(Comput)* = **disk**

discard [dɪs'kɑːd] *vt (old things)* se débarrasser de; *(fig)* écarter, renoncer à

discharge *vt* [dɪs'tʃɑːdʒ] *(duties)* s'acquitter de; *(waste etc)* déverser; décharger; *(patient)* renvoyer (chez lui); *(employee, soldier)* licencier ⊳ *n* ['dɪstʃɑːdʒ] *(Elec, Med)* émission *f*; *(dismissal)* renvoi *m*; licenciement *m*

discipline ['dɪsɪplɪn] *n* discipline *f* ⊳ *vt* discipliner; *(punish)* punir

disc jockey *n* disque-jockey *m* (DJ)

disclose [dɪs'kləuz] *vt* révéler, divulguer

disco ['dɪskəu] *n abbr* discothèque *f*

discoloured [dɪs'kʌləd] *(us*

discolored) *adj* décoloré(e), jauni(e)

discomfort [dɪs'kʌmfət] *n* malaise *m*, gêne *f*; *(lack of comfort)* manque *m* de confort

disconnect [dɪskə'nekt] *vt (Elec, Radio)* débrancher; *(gas, water)* couper

discontent [dɪskən'tent] *n* mécontentement *m*

discontinue [dɪskən'tɪnjuː] *vt* cesser, interrompre; **"~d"** *(Comm)* "fin de série"

discount *n* ['dɪskaunt] remise *f*, rabais *m* ⊳ *vt* [dɪs'kaunt] *(report etc)* ne pas tenir compte de

discourage [dɪs'kʌrɪdʒ] *vt* décourager

discover [dɪs'kʌvə^r] *vt* découvrir; **discovery** *n* découverte *f*

discredit [dɪs'kredɪt] *vt (idea)* mettre en doute; *(person)* discréditer

discreet [dɪ'skriːt] *adj* discret(-ète)

discrepancy [dɪ'skrepənsɪ] *n* divergence *f*, contradiction *f*

discretion [dɪ'skreʃən] *n* discrétion *f*; **at the ~ of** à la discrétion de

discriminate [dɪ'skrɪmɪneɪt] *vi*: **to ~ between** établir une distinction entre, faire la différence entre; **to ~ against** pratiquer une discrimination contre; **discrimination** [dɪskrɪmɪ'neɪʃən] *n* discrimination *f*; *(judgment)* discernement *m*

discuss [dɪ'skʌs] *vt* discuter de; *(debate)* discuter; **discussion** [dɪ'skʌʃən] *n* discussion *f*

disease [dɪ'ziːz] *n* maladie *f*

disembark [dɪsɪm'bɑːk] *vt, vi* débarquer

disgrace [dɪs'greɪs] *n* honte *f*; *(disfavour)* disgrâce *f* ⊳ *vt* déshonorer, couvrir de honte; **disgraceful** *adj* scandaleux(-euse), honteux(-euse)

disgruntled [dɪs'grʌntld] *adj* mécontent(e)

disguise [dɪs'gaɪz] *n* déguisement *m* ⊳ *vt* déguiser; **in ~** déguisé(e)

disgust [dɪs'gʌst] *n* dégoût *m*, aversion *f* ⊳ *vt* dégoûter, écœurer

disgusted [dɪs'gʌstɪd] *adj* dégoûté(e), écœuré(e)

disgusting [dɪs'gʌstɪŋ] adj
dégoûtant(e)

dish [dɪʃ] n plat m; **to do** or **wash the ~es** faire la vaisselle; **dishcloth** n (for drying) torchon m; (for washing) lavette f

dishonest [dɪs'ɒnɪst] adj malhonnête

dishtowel ['dɪʃtauəl] n (us) torchon m
(à vaisselle)

dishwasher ['dɪʃwɔʃə] n lave-vaisselle m

disillusion [dɪsɪ'luːʒən] vt désabuser,
désenchanter

disinfectant [dɪsɪn'fɛktənt] n
désinfectant m

disintegrate [dɪs'ɪntɪgreɪt] vi se
désintégrer

disk [dɪsk] n (Comput) disquette f;
single-/double-sided ~ disquette une
face/double face; **disk drive** n lecteur
m de disquette; **diskette** (Comput)
disquette f

dislike [dɪs'laɪk] n aversion f,
antipathie f ▷ vt ne pas aimer

dislocate ['dɪsləkeɪt] vt disloquer,
déboîter

disloyal [dɪs'lɔɪəl] adj déloyal(e)

dismal ['dɪzml] adj (gloomy) lugubre,
maussade; (very bad) lamentable

dismantle [dɪs'mæntl] vt démonter

dismay [dɪs'meɪ] n consternation f ▷ vt
consterner

dismiss [dɪs'mɪs] vt congédier,
renvoyer; (idea) écarter; (Law) rejeter;
dismissal n renvoi m

disobedient [dɪsə'biːdɪənt] adj
désobéissant(e), indiscipliné(e)

disobey [dɪsə'beɪ] vt désobéir à

disorder [dɪs'ɔːdə] n désordre
m; (rioting) désordres mpl; (Med)
troubles mpl

disorganized [dɪs'ɔːgənaɪzd] adj
désorganisé(e)

disown [dɪs'əun] vt renier

dispatch [dɪs'pætʃ] vt expédier,
envoyer ▷ n envoi m, expédition f; (Mil,
Press) dépêche f

dispel [dɪs'pɛl] vt dissiper, chasser

dispense [dɪs'pɛns] vt (medicine)

préparer (et vendre); **dispense with** vt
fus se passer de; **dispenser** n (device)
distributeur m

disperse [dɪs'pəːs] vt disperser ▷ vi se
disperser

display [dɪs'pleɪ] n (of goods) étalage
m; affichage m; (Comput: information)
visualisation f; (: device) visuel m; (of
feeling) manifestation f ▷ vt montrer;
(goods) mettre à l'étalage, exposer;
(results, departure times) afficher; (pej)
faire étalage de

displease [dɪs'pliːz] vt mécontenter,
contrarier

disposable [dɪs'pəuzəbl] adj (pack etc)
jetable; (income) disponible

disposal [dɪs'pəuzl] n (of rubbish)
évacuation f, destruction f; (of property
etc: by selling) vente f; (: by giving away)
cession f; **at one's ~** à sa disposition

dispose [dɪs'pəuz] vi: **to ~ of** (unwanted
goods) se débarrasser de, se défaire
de; (problem) expédier; **disposition**
[dɪspə'zɪʃən] n disposition f;
(temperament) naturel m

disproportionate [dɪsprə'pɔːʃənət]
adj disproportionné(e)

dispute [dɪs'pjuːt] n discussion f; (also:
industrial ~) conflit m ▷ vt (question)
contester; (matter) discuter

disqualify [dɪs'kwɔlɪfaɪ] vt (Sport)
disqualifier; **to ~ sb for sth/from
doing** rendre qn inapte à qch/à faire

disregard [dɪsrɪ'gɑːd] vt ne pas tenir
compte de

disrupt [dɪs'rʌpt] vt (plans, meeting,
lesson) perturber, déranger; **disruption**
[dɪs'rʌpʃən] n perturbation f,
dérangement m

dissatisfaction [dɪssætɪs'fækʃən] n
mécontentement m, insatisfaction f

dissatisfied [dɪs'sætɪsfaɪd] adj: ~
(with) insatisfait(e) (de)

dissect [dɪ'sɛkt] vt disséquer

dissent [dɪ'sɛnt] n dissentiment m,
différence f d'opinion

dissertation [dɪsə'teɪʃən] n (Scol)
mémoire m

dissolve [dɪ'zɔlv] vt dissoudre ▷ vi se
dissoudre, fondre; **to ~ in(to) tears**
fondre en larmes

distance ['dɪstns] n distance f; **in the
~** au loin

distant ['dɪstnt] adj lointain(e),
éloigné(e); (manner) distant(e), froid(e)

distil (us **distill**) [dɪs'tɪl] vt distiller;
distillery n distillerie f

distinct [dɪs'tɪŋkt] adj distinct(e);
(clear) marqué(e); **as ~ from** par
opposition à; **distinction** [dɪs'tɪŋkʃən]
n distinction f; (in exam) mention f très
bien; **distinctive** adj distinctif(-ive)

distinguish [dɪs'tɪŋgwɪʃ] vt
distinguer; **to ~ o.s.** se distinguer;
distinguished adj (eminent, refined)
distingué(e)

distort [dɪs'tɔːt] vt déformer

distract [dɪs'trækt] vt distraire,
déranger; **distracted** adj (not
concentrating) distrait(e); (worried)
affolé(e); **distraction** [dɪs'trækʃən] n
distraction f

distraught [dɪs'trɔːt] adj éperdu(e)

distress [dɪs'tres] n détresse
f ▷ vt affliger; **distressing** adj
douloureux(-euse), pénible

distribute [dɪs'trɪbjuːt] vt distribuer;
distribution [dɪstrɪ'bjuːʃən] n
distribution f; **distributor** n (gen:
Tech) distributeur m; (Comm)
concessionnaire m/f

district ['dɪstrɪkt] n (of country) région f;
(of town) quartier m; (Admin) district m;
district attorney n (us) ≈ procureur m
de la République

distrust [dɪs'trʌst] n méfiance f, doute
m ▷ vt se méfier de

disturb [dɪs'təːb] vt troubler;
(inconvenience) déranger; **disturbance**
n dérangement m; (political etc)
troubles mpl; **disturbed** adj (worried,
upset) agité(e), troublé(e); **to be
emotionally disturbed** avoir des
problèmes affectifs; **disturbing** adj
troublant(e), inquiétant(e)

ditch [dɪtʃ] n fossé m; (for irrigation)

rigole f ▷ vt (inf) abandonner; (person)
plaquer

ditto ['dɪtəu] adv idem

dive [daɪv] n plongeon m; (of submarine)
plongée f ▷ vi plonger; **to ~ into** (bag
etc) plonger la main dans; (place) se
précipiter dans; **diver** n plongeur m

diverse [daɪ'vəːs] adj divers(e)

diversion [daɪ'vəːʃən] n (BRIT Aut)
déviation f; (distraction, Mil) diversion f

diversity [daɪ'vəːsɪti] n diversité f,
variété f

divert [daɪ'vəːt] vt (BRIT: traffic) dévier;
(plane) dérouter; (train, river) détourner

divide [dɪ'vaɪd] vt diviser; (separate)
séparer ▷ vi se diviser; **divided
highway** (us) n route f à quatre voies

divine [dɪ'vaɪn] adj divin(e)

diving ['daɪvɪŋ] n plongée (sous-
marine); **diving board** n plongeoir m

division [dɪ'vɪʒən] n division f;
(separation) séparation f; (Comm)
service m

divorce [dɪ'vɔːs] n divorce m ▷ vt
divorcer d'avec; **divorced** adj
divorcé(e); **divorcee** [dɪvɔː'siː] n
divorcé(e)

D.I.Y. adj, n abbr (BRIT) = **do-it-yourself**

dizzy ['dɪzɪ] adj: **I feel ~** la tête me
tourne, j'ai la tête qui tourne

DJ n abbr = **disc jockey**

DNA n abbr (= deoxyribonucleic acid)
ADN m

 KEYWORD

do [duː] (pt **did**, pp **done**) n (inf: party etc)
soirée f, fête f
▷ vb 1 (in negative constructions) non
traduit; **I don't understand** je ne
comprends pas
2 (to form questions) non traduit; **didn't
you know?** vous ne le saviez pas?; **what
do you think?** qu'en pensez-vous?
3 (for emphasis, in polite expressions):
**people do make mistakes
sometimes** on peut toujours se
tromper; **she does seem rather late** je

trouve qu'elle est bien en retard; **do sit
down/help yourself** asseyez-vous/
servez-vous je vous en prie; **do take
care!** faites bien attention à vous!
4 (*used to avoid repeating vb*): **she swims
better than I do** elle nage mieux que
moi; **do you agree? - yes, I do/no I
don't** vous êtes d'accord? - oui/non;
she lives in Glasgow - so do I elle
habite Glasgow - moi aussi; **he didn't
like it and neither did we** il n'a pas
aimé ça, et nous non plus; **who broke
it? - I did** qui l'a cassé? - c'est moi;
he asked me to help him and I did il
m'a demandé de l'aider, et c'est ce
que j'ai fait
5 (*in question tags*): **you like him, don't
you?** vous l'aimez bien, n'est-ce pas?; **I
don't know him, do I?** je ne crois pas
le connaître
▷ **vt 1** (*gen: carry out, perform etc*) faire;
(*visit: city, museum*) visiter; **what
are you doing tonight?** qu'est-ce que
vous faites ce soir?; **what do you do?**
(*job*) que faites-vous dans la vie?; **what
can I do for you?** que puis-je faire pour
vous?; **to do the cooking/washing-
up** faire la cuisine/la vaisselle; **to do
one's teeth/hair/nails** se brosser les
dents/se coiffer/se faire les ongles
2 (*Aut etc: distance*) faire; (*: speed*) faire
du; **we've done 200 km already** nous
avons déjà fait 200 km; **the car was
doing 100** la voiture faisait du 100 (à
l'heure); **he can do 100 in that car** il
peut faire du 100 (à l'heure) dans cette
voiture-là
▷ **vi 1** (*act, behave*) faire; **do as I do**
comme moi
2 (*get on, fare*) marcher; **the firm is
doing well** l'entreprise marche bien;
he's doing well/badly at school ça
marche bien/mal pour lui à l'école);
how do you do? comment allez-vous?
(*on being introduced*) enchanté(e)!
3 (*suit*) aller; **will it do?** est-ce que ça
ça ira?
4 (*be sufficient*) suffire, aller; **will £10**

do? est-ce que 10 livres suffiront?;
that'll do ça suffit, ça ira; **that'll do!** (*in
annoyance*) ça va or suffit comme ça!; **to
make do (with)** se contenter (de)
do up *vt* (*laces, dress*) attacher; (*buttons*)
boutonner; (*zip*) fermer; (*renovate: room*)
refaire; (*: house*) remettre à neuf
do with *vt fus* (*need*): **I could do with
a drink/some help** quelque chose à
boire/un peu d'aide ne serait pas de
refus; **it could do with a wash** ça ne
lui ferait pas de mal d'être lavé; (*be
connected with*): **that has nothing to
do with you** cela ne vous concerne pas;
I won't have anything to do with it je
ne veux pas m'en mêler
do without *vi* s'en passer; **if you're
late for tea then you'll do without**
si vous êtes en retard pour le dîner il
faudra vous en passer
▷ *vt fus* se passer de; **I can do without
a car** je peux me passer de voiture

dock [dɔk] *n* dock *m*; (*wharf*) quai *m*;
(*Law*) banc *m* des accusés ▷ *vi* se mettre
à quai; (*Space*) s'arrimer; **docks** *npl*
(*Naut*) docks

doctor [ˈdɔktəʳ] *n* médecin *m*, docteur
m; (*PhD etc*) docteur *m* ▷ *vt* (*drink*) frelater;
call a ~! appelez un docteur or un
médecin!; **Doctor of Philosophy (PhD)**
n (*degree*) doctorat *m*; (*person*) titulaire
m/f d'un doctorat

document [ˈdɔkjumənt] *n*
document *m*; **documentary**
[dɔkjuˈmɛntərɪ] *adj, n*
documentaire (*m*); **documentation**
[dɔkjumənˈteɪʃən] *n* documentation *f*

dodge [dɔdʒ] *n* truc *m*; combine *f* ▷ *vt*
esquiver, éviter

dodgy [ˈdɔdʒɪ] *adj* (*inf: uncertain*)
douteux(-euse); (*: shady*) louche

does [dʌz] *vb see* **do**

doesn't [ˈdʌznt] = **does not**

dog [dɔg] *n* chien(ne) ▷ *vt* (*follow
closely*) suivre de près; (*fig: memory etc*)
poursuivre, harceler; **doggy bag**
[ˈdɔgɪ-] *n* petit sac pour emporter les restes

do-it-yourself ['du:ɪtjɔː'self] n
bricolage m

dole [dəul] n (BRIT: payment) allocation f
de chômage; **on the ~** au chômage

doll [dɒl] n poupée f

dollar ['dɒlə*] n dollar m

dolphin ['dɒlfɪn] n dauphin m

dome [dəum] n dôme m

domestic [də'mestɪk] adj (duty,
happiness) familial(e); (policy,
affairs, flight) intérieur(e); (animal)
domestique; **domestic appliance** n
appareil ménager

dominant ['dɒmɪnənt] adj
dominant(e)

dominate ['dɒmɪneɪt] vt dominer

domino ['dɒmɪnəu] (pl **-es**) n
domino m; **dominoes** n (game)
dominos mpl

donate [də'neɪt] vt faire don de,
donner; **donation** [də'neɪʃən] n
donation f, don m

done [dʌn] pp of **do**

donkey ['dɒŋkɪ] n âne m

donor ['dəunə*] n (of blood etc)
donneur(-euse); (to charity)
donateur(-trice); **donor card** n carte f
de don d'organes

don't [dəunt] = **do not**

donut ['dəunʌt] (us) n = **doughnut**

doodle ['du:dl] vi griffonner,
gribouiller

doom [du:m] n (fate) destin m ▷ vt: **to
be ~ed to failure** être voué(e) à l'échec

door [dɔː*] n porte f; (Rail, car) portière f;
doorbell n sonnette f; **door handle**
n poignée f de porte; (of car) poignée
de portière; **doorknob** n poignée f or
bouton m de porte; **doorstep** n pas
m de la porte, seuil m; **doorway** n
(embrasure f de) porte f

dope [dəup] n (inf: drug) drogue f;
(: person) andouille f ▷ vt (horse etc)
doper

dormitory ['dɔːmɪtrɪ] n (BRIT) dortoir
m; (us: hall of residence) résidence f
universitaire

DOS [dɒs] n abbr (= disk operating system)
DOS m

dosage ['dəusɪdʒ] n dose f; dosage m;
(on label) posologie f

dose [dəus] n dose f

dot [dɒt] n point m; (on material) pois m
▷ vt: **~ted with** parsemé(e) de; **on the
~** à l'heure tapante; **dotcom** [dɒt'kɒm]
n point com m, pointcom m; **dotted
line** ['dɒtɪd-] n ligne pointillée; **to sign
on the dotted line** signer à l'endroit
indiqué or sur la ligne pointillée

double ['dʌbl] adj double ▷ adv (twice):
to cost ~ (sth) coûter le double
(de qch) or deux fois plus (que qch) ▷ n
double m; (Cine) doublure f ▷ vt
doubler; (fold) plier en deux ▷ vi
doubler; **on the ~, at the ~** au pas
de course; **double back** vi (person)
revenir sur ses pas; **double bass** n
contrebasse f; **double bed** n grand
lit; **double-check** vt, vi revérifier;
double-click vi (Comput) double-
cliquer; **double-cross** vt doubler,
trahir; **doubledecker** n autobus m à
impériale; **double glazing** n (BRIT)
double vitrage m; **double room** n
chambre f pour deux; **doubles** n
(Tennis) double m; **double yellow
lines** npl (BRIT: Aut) double bande jaune
marquant l'interdiction de stationner

doubt [daut] n doute m ▷ vt douter
de; **no ~** sans doute; **to ~ that** douter
que + sub; **doubtful** adj douteux(-euse);
(person) incertain(e); **doubtless** adv
sans doute, sûrement

dough [dəu] n pâte f; **doughnut** (us
donut) n beignet m

dove [dʌv] n colombe f

Dover ['dəuvə*] n Douvres

down [daun] n (fluff) duvet m ▷ adv
en bas, vers le bas; (on the ground) par
terre ▷ prep en bas de, (along) le long
de ▷ vt (inf: drink) siffler; **to walk ~ a
hill** descendre une colline; **to run ~ the
street** descendre la rue en courant;
~ with X! à bas X!; **down-and-out** n
(tramp) clochard(e); **downfall** n chute
f; ruine f; **downhill** adv: **to go downhill**
descendre; (business) péricliter

Downing Street ['daʊnɪŋ-] n (BRIT):
10 ~ résidence du Premier ministre

● **DOWNING STREET**

> **Downing Street** est une rue de
> Westminster (à Londres) où se
> trouvent la résidence officielle
> du Premier ministre et celle du
> ministre des Finances. Le nom
> **Downing Street** est souvent utilisé
> pour désigner le gouvernement
> britannique.

down: download vt (Comput)
télécharger; **downright** adj (lie etc)
effronté(e); (refusal) catégorique
Down's syndrome [daʊnz-] n
trisomie f
down: downstairs adv (on or to
ground floor) au rez-de-chaussée; (on
or to floor below) à l'étage inférieur;
down-to-earth adj terre à terre inv;
downtown adv en ville; **down under**
adv en Australie ou Nouvelle Zélande;
downward ['daʊnwəd] adj, adv vers
le bas; **downwards** ['daʊnwədz] adv
vers le bas
doz. abbr = **dozen**
doze [daʊz] vi sommeiller
dozen ['dʌzn] n douzaine f; **a ~ books**
une douzaine de livres; **~s of** des
centaines de
Dr. abbr (= doctor) Dr; (in street names)
= **drive**
drab [dræb] adj terne, morne
draft [drɑːft] n (of letter, school
work) brouillon m; (of literary work)
ébauche f; (Comm) traite f; (us: call-up)
conscription f ▷ vt faire le brouillon de;
(Mil: send) détacher; see also **draught**
drag [dræɡ] vt traîner; (river) draguer
▷ vi traîner ▷ n (inf) casse-pieds m/f;
(women's clothing): **in ~** (en) travesti; **to
~ and drop** (Comput) glisser-poser
dragon ['dræɡən] n dragon m
dragonfly ['dræɡənflaɪ] n libellule f
drain [dreɪn] n égout m; (on resources)

saignée f ▷ vt (land, marshes) drainer,
assécher; (vegetables) égoutter;
(reservoir etc) vider ▷ vi (water) s'écouler;
drainage n (system) système m
d'égouts; (act) drainage m; **drainpipe**
n tuyau m d'écoulement
drama ['drɑːmə] n (art) théâtre m, art
m dramatique; (play) pièce f; (event)
drame m; **dramatic** [drəˈmætɪk]
adj (Theat) dramatique; (impressive)
spectaculaire
drank [dræŋk] pt of **drink**
drape [dreɪp] vt draper; **drapes** npl (us)
rideaux mpl
drastic ['dræstɪk] adj (measures)
d'urgence, énergique; (change)
radical(e)
draught (us **draft**) [drɑːft] n courant
d'air; **on ~** (beer) à la pression; **draught
beer** n bière f (à la) pression; **draughts**
n (BRIT: game) (jeu m de) dames fpl
draw [drɔː] (vb: pt **drew**, pp **drawn**) vt (tier;
(picture) dessiner; (attract) attirer; (line,
circle) tracer; (money) retirer; (wages)
toucher ▷ vi (Sport) faire match nul ▷ n
match nul; (lottery) loterie f; (: picking
of ticket) tirage m au sort; **draw out**
vi (lengthen) s'allonger ▷ vt (money)
retirer; **draw up** vi (stop) s'arrêter
▷ vt (document) établir, dresser; (plan)
formuler, dessiner; (chair) approcher;
drawback n inconvénient m,
désavantage m
drawer [drɔːˀ] n tiroir m
drawing ['drɔːɪŋ] n dessin m; **drawing
pin** n (BRIT) punaise f; **drawing room**
n salon m
drawn [drɔːn] pp of **draw**
dread [drɛd] n épouvante f, effroi m ▷ vt
redouter, appréhender; **dreadful** adj
épouvantable, affreux(-euse)
dream [driːm] n rêve m ▷ vt, vi (pt,
pp **~ed** or **~t**) rêver; **dreamer** n
rêveur(-euse)
dreamt [drɛmt] pt, pp of **dream**
dreary ['drɪərɪ] adj triste; monotone
drench [drɛntʃ] vt tremper
dress [drɛs] n robe f; (clothing)

drew | 360

habillement *m*, tenue *f* ▷ *vt* habiller; *(wound)* panser ▷ *vt*: **to get ~ed** s'habiller; **dress up** *vi* s'habiller; *(in fancy dress)* se déguiser; **dress circle** *n* (BRIT) premier balcon; **dresser** *n (furniture)* vaisselier *m*; *(: US)* coiffeuse *f*, commode *f*; **dressing** *n (Med)* pansement *m*; *(Culin)* sauce *f*, assaisonnement *m*; **dressing gown** *n* (BRIT) robe *f* de chambre; **dressing room** *n (Theat)* loge *f*; *(Sport)* vestiaire *m*; **dressing table** *n* coiffeuse *f*; **dressmaker** *n* couturière *f*

drew [dru:] *pt of* **draw**

dribble ['drɪbl] *vi (baby)* baver ▷ *vt (ball)* dribbler

dried [draɪd] *adj (fruit, beans)* sec *(sèche); (eggs, milk)* en poudre

drier ['draɪəʳ] *n* = **dryer**

drift [drɪft] *n (of current etc)* force *f*; direction *f*; *(of snow)* rafale *f*; coulée *f*; *(: on ground)* congère *f*; *(general meaning)* sens général *m* ▷ *vi (boat)* aller à la dérive, dériver; *(sand, snow)* s'amonceler, s'entasser

drill [drɪl] *n* perceuse *f*; *(bit)* foret *m*; *(of dentist)* roulette *f*, fraise *f*; *(Mil)* exercice *m* ▷ *vt* percer; *(troops)* entraîner ▷ *vi (for oil)* faire un *or* des forage(s)

drink [drɪŋk] *n* boisson *f*; *(alcoholic)* verre *m* ▷ *vt, vi (pt* **drank***, pp* **drunk)** boire; **to have a ~** boire quelque chose, boire un verre; **a ~ of water** un verre d'eau; **would you like a ~?** tu veux boire quelque chose?; **drink-driving** *n* conduite *f* en état d'ivresse; **drinker** *n* buveur(-euse); **drinking water** *n* eau *f* potable

drip [drɪp] *n (drop)* goutte *f*; *(Med: device)* goutte-à-goutte *m inv*; *(: liquid)* perfusion *f* ▷ *vi* tomber goutte à goutte; *(tap)* goutter

drive [draɪv] *n* promenade *f or* trajet *m* en voiture; *(also:* **~way)** allée *f*; *(energy)* dynamisme *m*, énergie *f*; *(push)* effort *(concerté)*; campagne *f*; *(Comput: also:* **disk ~)** lecteur *m* de disquette ▷ *vb (pt* **drove***, pp* **~n)** ▷ *vt* conduire; *(nail)*

enfoncer; *(push)* chasser, pousser; *(Tech: motor)* actionner; entraîner ▷ *vi (be at the wheel)* conduire; *(travel by car)* aller en voiture; **left-/right-hand ~** (Aut) conduite *f* à gauche/droite; **to ~ sb mad** rendre qn fou (folle); **drive out** *vt (force out)* chasser; **drive-in** *adj, n (esp US)* drive-in *m*

driven ['drɪvn] *pp of* **drive**

driver ['draɪvəʳ] *n* conducteur(-trice); *(of taxi, bus)* chauffeur *m*; **driver's license** *n* (US) permis *m* de conduire

driveway ['draɪvweɪ] *n* allée *f*

driving ['draɪvɪŋ] *n* conduite *f*; **driving instructor** *n* moniteur *m* d'auto-école; **driving lesson** *n* leçon *f* de conduite; **driving licence** *n* (BRIT) permis *m* de conduire; **driving test** *n* examen *m* du permis de conduire

drizzle ['drɪzl] *n* bruine *f*, crachin *m*

droop [dru:p] *vi (flower)* commencer à se faner; *(shoulders, head)* tomber

drop [drɔp] *n (of liquid)* goutte *f*; *(fall)* baisse *f*; *(also:* **parachute ~)** saut *m* ▷ *vt* laisser tomber; *(voice, eyes, price)* baisser; *(passenger)* déposer ▷ *vi* tomber; **drop in** *vi (inf: visit)*: **to ~ in (on)** faire un saut (chez), passer *(chez)*; **drop off** *vi (sleep)* s'assoupir ▷ *vt (passenger)* déposer; **drop out** *vi (withdraw)* se retirer; *(student etc)* abandonner, décrocher

drought [draut] *n* sécheresse *f*

drove [drəuv] *pt of* **drive**

drown [draun] *vt* noyer ▷ *vi* se noyer

drowsy ['drauzɪ] *adj* somnolent(e)

drug [drʌg] *n* médicament *m*; *(narcotic)* drogue *f* ▷ *vt* droguer; **to be on ~s** se droguer; **drug addict** *n* toxicomane *m/f*; **drug dealer** *n* revendeur(-euse) de drogue; **druggist** *n* (US) pharmacien *m*-droguiste; **drugstore** *n* (US) pharmacie-droguerie *f*, drugstore *m*

drum [drʌm] *n* tambour *m*; *(for oil, petrol)* bidon *m*; **drums** *npl (Mus)* batterie *f*; **drummer** *n (joueur m* de) tambour *m*

drunk [drʌŋk] pp of **drink** ▷ adj ivre, soûl(e) ▷ n (also: **~ard**) ivrogne m/f; **to get ~** se soûler; **drunken** adj ivre, soûl(e); (rage, stupor) ivrogne, d'ivrogne

dry [draɪ] adj sec (sèche); (day) sans pluie ▷ vt sécher; (clothes) faire sécher ▷ vi sécher; **dry off** vi, vt sécher; **dry up** vi (river, supplies) se tarir; **dry-cleaner's** n teinturerie f; **dry-cleaning** n (process) nettoyage m à sec; **dryer** n (tumble-dryer) sèche-linge m inv; (for hair) sèche-cheveux m inv

DSS n abbr (BRIT) = **Department of Social Security**

DTP n abbr (= desktop publishing) PAO f

dual [ˈdjuəl] adj double; **dual carriageway** n (BRIT) route f à quatre voies

dubious [ˈdjuːbɪəs] adj hésitant(e), incertain(e); (reputation, company) douteux(-euse)

duck [dʌk] n canard m ▷ vi se baisser vivement, baisser subitement la tête

due [djuː] adj (money, payment) dû (due); (expected) attendu(e); (fitting) qui convient ▷ adv: **~ north** droit vers le nord; **~ to** (because of) en raison de; (caused by) dû à; **the train is ~ at 8 a.m.** le train est attendu à 8 h; **she is ~ back tomorrow** elle doit rentrer demain; **he is ~ £10** on lui doit 10 livres; **to give sb his or her ~** être juste envers qn

duel [ˈdjuəl] n duel m

duet [djuːˈet] n duo m

dug [dʌg] pt, pp of **dig**

duke [djuːk] n duc m

dull [dʌl] adj (boring) ennuyeux(-euse); (not bright) morne, terne; (sound, pain) sourd(e); (weather, day) gris(e), maussade ▷ vt (pain, grief) atténuer; (mind, senses) engourdir

dumb [dʌm] adj muet(te); (stupid) bête

dummy [ˈdʌmɪ] n (tailor's dummy) mannequin m; (mock-up) factice m, maquette f; (BRIT: for baby) tétine f ▷ adj faux (fausse), factice

dump [dʌmp] n (also: **rubbish ~**) décharge (publique); (inf: place) trou m

▷ vt (put down) déposer; déverser; (get rid of) se débarrasser de; (Comput) lister

dumpling [ˈdʌmplɪŋ] n boulette f (de pâte)

dune [djuːn] n dune f

dungarees [dʌŋgəˈriːz] npl bleu(s) m(pl); (for child, woman) salopette f

dungeon [ˈdʌndʒən] n cachot m

duplex [ˈdjuːpleks] n (us: also: **~ apartment**) duplex m

duplicate [n ˈdjuːplɪkət] double m ▷ vt [ˈdjuːplɪkeɪt] faire un double de; (on machine) polycopier; **in ~** en deux exemplaires, en double

durable [ˈdjuərəbl] adj durable; (clothes, metal) résistant(e), solide

duration [djuəˈreɪʃən] n durée f

during [ˈdjuərɪŋ] prep pendant, au cours de

dusk [dʌsk] n crépuscule m

dust [dʌst] n poussière f ▷ vt (furniture) essuyer, épousseter; (cake etc): **to ~ with** saupoudrer de; **dustbin** n (BRIT) poubelle f; **duster** n chiffon m; **dustman** n (BRIT: irreg) boueux m, éboueur m; **dustpan** n pelle f à poussière; **dusty** adj poussiéreux(-euse)

Dutch [dʌtʃ] adj hollandais(e), néerlandais(e) ▷ n (Ling) hollandais m, néerlandais m ▷ adv: **to go ~** or **dutch** (inf) partager les frais; **the Dutch** npl les Hollandais, les Néerlandais; **Dutchman** (irreg) n Hollandais m; **Dutchwoman** (irreg) n Hollandaise f

duty [ˈdjuːtɪ] n devoir m; (tax) droit m, taxe f; **on ~** de service; (at night etc) de garde; **off ~** libre, pas de service or de garde; **duty-free** adj exempté(e) de douane, hors-taxe

duvet [ˈduːveɪ] n (BRIT) couette f

DVD n abbr (= digital versatile or video disc) DVD m; **DVD burner** n graveur m de DVD; **DVD player** n lecteur m de DVD; **DVD writer** n graveur m de DVD

dwarf (pl **dwarves**) [dwɔːf, dwɔːvz] n nain(e) ▷ vt écraser

dwell (pt, pp **dwelt**) [dwel, dwelt] vi

demeurer; **dwell on** vt fus s'étendre sur
dwelt [dwɛlt] pt, pp of **dwell**
dwindle ['dwɪndl] vi diminuer, décroître
dye [daɪ] n teinture f ▷ vt teindre
dying ['daɪɪŋ] adj mourant(e), agonisant(e)
dynamic [daɪ'næmɪk] adj dynamique
dynamite ['daɪnəmaɪt] n dynamite f
dyslexia [dɪs'lɛksɪə] n dyslexie f
dyslexic [dɪs'lɛksɪk] adj, n dyslexique m/f

e

E [iː] n (Mus): **E** mi m
E111 n abbr (= form E111) formulaire m E111
each [iːtʃ] adj chaque ▷ pron chacun(e);
~ **other** l'un l'autre; **they hate** ~ **other**
ils se détestent (mutuellement); **they have 2 books** ~ ils ont 2 livres chacun;
they cost £5 ~ ils coûtent 5 livres (la) pièce
eager ['iːgəʳ] adj (person, buyer) empressé(e); (keen: pupil, worker) enthousiaste; **to be** ~ **to do sth** (impatient) brûler de faire qch; (keen) désirer vivement faire qch; **to be** ~ **for** (event) désirer vivement; (vengeance, affection, information) être avide de
eagle ['iːgl] n aigle m
ear [ɪəʳ] n oreille f; (of corn) épi m;
earache n mal m aux oreilles; **eardrum** n tympan m
earl [əːl] n comte m
earlier ['əːlɪəʳ] adj (date etc) plus rapproché(e); (edition etc) plus ancien(ne), antérieur(e) ▷ adv plus tôt
early ['əːlɪ] adv tôt, de bonne heure;

(ahead of time) en avance; *(near the beginning)* au début ▷ *adj* précoce, qui se manifeste (or se fait) tôt or de bonne heure; *(Christians, settlers)* premier(-ière); *(reply)* rapide; *(death)* prématuré(e); *(work)* de jeunesse; **to have an ~ night/start** se coucher/partir tôt or de bonne heure; **in the ~ or ~ in the spring/19th century** au début or commencement du printemps/du 19ème siècle; **early retirement** *n* retraite anticipée

earmark ['ɪəmɑ:k] *vt*: **~ sth for** réserver or destiner qch à

earn [ə:n] *vt* gagner; *(Comm: yield)* rapporter; **to ~ one's living** gagner sa vie

earnest ['ə:nɪst] *adj* sérieux(-euse) ▷ *n*: **in ~** *adv* sérieusement, pour de bon

earnings ['ə:nɪŋz] *npl* salaire *m*; gains *mpl*; *(of company etc)* profits *mpl*, bénéfices *mpl*

ear: earphones *npl* écouteurs *mpl*; **earplugs** *npl* boules *fpl* Quiès®; *(to keep out water)* protège-tympans *mpl*; **earring** *n* boucle *f* d'oreille

earth [ə:θ] *n (gen, also BRIT Elec)* terre *f* ▷ *vt (BRIT Elec)* relier à la terre; **earthquake** *n* tremblement *m* de terre, séisme *m*

ease [i:z] *n* facilité *f*, aisance *f*; *(comfort)* bien-être *m* ▷ *vt (soothe: mind)* tranquilliser; *(reduce: pain, problem)* atténuer; *(: tension)* réduire; *(loosen)* relâcher, détendre; *(help: pass)*: **to ~ sth in/out** faire pénétrer/sortir qch délicatement or avec douceur, faciliter la pénétration/la sortie de qch; **at ~** à l'aise; *(Mil)* au repos

easily ['i:zɪlɪ] *adv* facilement; *(by far)* de loin

east [i:st] *n* est *m* ▷ *adj (wind)* d'est; *(side)* est *inv* ▷ *adv* à l'est, vers l'est; **the E~** l'Orient *m*; *(Pol)* les pays *mpl* de l'Est; **eastbound** *adj* en direction de l'est; *(carriageway)* est *inv*

Easter ['i:stə'] *n* Pâques *fpl*; **Easter egg** *n* œuf *m* de Pâques

eastern ['i:stən] *adj* de l'est, oriental(e)

Easter Sunday *n* le dimanche de Pâques

easy ['i:zɪ] *adj* facile; *(manner)* aisé(e) ▷ *adv*: **to take it** or **things ~** *(rest)* ne pas se fatiguer; *(not worry)* ne pas (trop) s'en faire; **easy-going** *adj* accommodant(e), facile à vivre

eat *(pt* **ate**, *pp* **~en)** [i:t, eɪt, 'i:tn] *vt*, *vi* manger; **can we have something to ~?** est-ce qu'on peut manger quelque chose?; **eat out** *vi* manger au restaurant

eavesdrop ['i:vzdrɔp] *vi*: **~ (on)** écouter de façon indiscrète

e-book ['i:buk] *n* livre *m* électronique

e-business ['i:bɪznɪs] *n (company)* entreprise *f* électronique; *(commerce)* commerce *m* électronique

EC *n abbr (= European Community)* CE *f*

eccentric [ɪk'sɛntrɪk] *adj*, *n* excentrique *m/f*

echo, echoes ['ɛkəu] *n* écho *m* ▷ *vt* répéter ▷ *vi* résonner; faire écho

eclipse [ɪ'klɪps] *n* éclipse *f*

eco-friendly [i:kəu'frɛndlɪ] *adj* non nuisible à or qui ne nuit pas à l'environnement

ecological [i:kə'lɔdʒɪkəl] *adj* écologique

ecology [ɪ'kɔlədʒɪ] *n* écologie *f*

e-commerce [i:kɔmə:s] *n* commerce *m* électronique

economic [i:kə'nɔmɪk] *adj* économique; *(profitable)* rentable; **economical** *adj* économique; *(person)* économe; **economics** *n (Scol)* économie *f* politique ▷ *npl (of project etc)* côté *m* or aspect *m* économique

economist [ɪ'kɔnəmɪst] *n* économiste *m/f*

economize [ɪ'kɔnəmaɪz] *vi* économiser, faire des économies

economy [ɪ'kɔnəmɪ] *n* économie *f*; **economy class** *n (Aviat)* classe *f* touriste; **economy class syndrome** *n* syndrome *m* de la classe économique

ecstasy ['ɛkstəsɪ] *n* extase *f*; *(Drugs)*

ecstasy *m*; **ecstatic** [eks'tætɪk] *adj* extatique, en extase

eczema ['eksɪmə] *n* eczéma *m*

edge [edʒ] *n* bord *m*; (of knife etc) tranchant *m*, fil *m* ▷ *vt* border; **on** ~ (fig) crispé(e), tendu(e)

edgy ['edʒɪ] *adj* crispé(e), tendu(e)

edible ['edɪbl] *adj* comestible; (meal) mangeable

Edinburgh ['edɪnbərə] *n* Édimbourg

● **EDINBURGH FESTIVAL**
●
● Le Festival d'Édimbourg, qui se tient
● chaque année durant trois semaines
● au mois d'août, est l'un des grands
● festivals européens. Il est réputé
● pour son programme officiel mais
● aussi pour son festival "off" (the
● Fringe) qui propose des spectacles
● aussi bien traditionnels que
● résolument d'avant-garde. Pendant
● la durée du Festival se tient par
● ailleurs, sur l'esplanade du château,
● un grand spectacle de musique
● militaire, le "Military Tattoo".

edit ['edɪt] *vt* (text, book) éditer; (report) préparer; (film) monter; (magazine) diriger; (newspaper) être le rédacteur or la rédactrice en chef de; **edition** [ɪ'dɪʃən] *n* édition *f*; **editor** *n* (of newspaper) rédacteur(-trice), rédacteur(-trice) en chef; (of sb's work) éditeur(-trice); (also: **film editor**) monteur(-euse); **political/foreign editor** rédacteur politique/au service étranger; **editorial** [edɪ'tɔːrɪəl] *adj* de la rédaction, éditorial(e) ▷ *n* éditorial *m*

educate ['edjukeɪt] *vt* (teach) instruire; (bring up) éduquer; **educated** ['edjukeɪtɪd] *adj* (person) cultivé(e)

education [edju'keɪʃən] *n* éducation *f*; (studies) études *fpl*; (teaching) enseignement *m*, instruction *f*; **educational** *adj* pédagogique; (institution) scolaire; (game, toy) éducatif(-ive)

eel [iːl] *n* anguille *f*

eerie ['ɪərɪ] *adj* inquiétant(e), spectral(e), surnaturel(le)

effect [ɪ'fekt] *n* effet *m* ▷ *vt* effectuer; **effects** *npl* (property) effets, affaires *fpl*; **to take ~** (Law) entrer en vigueur, prendre effet; (drug) agir, faire son effet; **in ~** en fait; **effective** *adj* efficace; (actual) véritable; **effectively** *adv* efficacement; (in reality) effectivement, en fait

efficiency [ɪ'fɪʃənsɪ] *n* efficacité *f*; (of machine, car) rendement *m*

efficient [ɪ'fɪʃənt] *adj* efficace; (machine, car) d'un bon rendement; **efficiently** *adv* efficacement

effort ['efət] *n* effort *m*; **effortless** *adj* sans effort, aisé(e); (achievement) facile

e.g. *adv abbr* (= exempli gratia) par exemple, p. ex.

egg [eg] *n* œuf *m*; **hard-boiled/soft-boiled ~** œuf dur/à la coque; **eggcup** *n* coquetier *m*; **egg plant** *n* (us) aubergine *f*; **eggshell** *n* coquille *f* d'œuf; **egg white** *n* blanc *m* d'œuf; **egg yolk** *n* jaune *m* d'œuf

ego ['iːgəu] *n* (self-esteem) amour-propre *m*; (Psych) moi *m*

Egypt ['iːdʒɪpt] *n* Égypte *f*; **Egyptian** [ɪ'dʒɪpʃən] *adj* égyptien(ne) ▷ *n* Égyptien(ne)

Eiffel Tower ['aɪfəl-] *n* tour *f* Eiffel

eight [eɪt] *num* huit; **eighteen** *num* dix-huit; **eighteenth** *num* dix-huitième; **eighth** *num* huitième; **eightieth** ['eɪtɪɪθ] *num* quatre-vingtième

eighty ['eɪtɪ] *num* quatre-vingt(s)

Eire ['ɛərə] *n* République *f* d'Irlande

either ['aɪðə*] *adj* l'un ou l'autre; (both, each) chaque ▷ *pron*: ~ **(of them)** l'un ou l'autre ▷ *adv* non plus ▷ *conj*: ~ **good or bad** soit bon soit mauvais; **on ~ side** de chaque côté; **I don't like ~** je n'aime ni l'un ni l'autre; **no, I don't ~** moi non plus; **which bike do you want? - ~ will do** quel vélo voulez-vous? - n'importe lequel; **answer with ~ yes or no** répondez par oui ou par non

eject [ɪ'dʒɛkt] vt (tenant etc) expulser; (object) éjecter

elaborate [ɪ'læbərɪt] adj compliqué(e), recherché(e), minutieux(-euse) ▷ vb [ɪ'læbəreɪt] ▷ vt élaborer ▷ vi entrer dans les détails

elastic [ɪ'læstɪk] adj, n élastique (m); **elastic band** (BRIT) élastique m

elbow ['ɛlbəu] n coude m

elder ['ɛldə*] adj ▷ n (tree) sureau m; **one's ~s** ses aînés; **elderly** adj âgé(e) ▷ npl: **the elderly** les personnes âgées

eldest ['ɛldɪst] adj, n: **the ~ (child)** l'aîné(e) (des enfants)

elect [ɪ'lɛkt] vt élire; (choose): **to ~ to do** choisir de faire ▷ adj: **the president ~** le président désigné; **election** [ɪ'lɛkʃən] n élection f; **electoral** adj électoral(e); **electorate** n électorat m

electric [ɪ'lɛktrɪk] adj électrique; **electrical** adj électrique; **electric blanket** n couverture chauffante; **electric fire** (BRIT) n radiateur m électrique; **electrician** [ɪlɛk'trɪʃən] n électricien m; **electricity** [ɪlɛk'trɪsɪtɪ] n électricité f; **electric shock** n choc m or décharge f électrique; **electrify** [ɪ'lɛktrɪfaɪ] vt (Rail) électrifier; (audience) électriser

electronic [ɪlɛk'trɔnɪk] adj électronique; **electronic mail** n courrier m électronique; **electronics** n électronique f

elegance ['ɛligəns] n élégance f

elegant ['ɛligənt] adj élégant(e)

element ['ɛlimənt] n (gen) élément m; (of heater, kettle etc) résistance f

elementary [ɛli'mɛntərɪ] adj élémentaire; (school, education) primaire; **elementary school** n (US) école f primaire

elephant ['ɛlɪfənt] n éléphant m

elevate ['ɛliveɪt] vt élever

elevator ['ɛliveɪtə*] n (in warehouse etc) élévateur m, monte-charge m inv; (us: lift) ascenseur m

eleven [ɪ'lɛvn] num onze; **eleventh** num onzième

eligible ['ɛlidʒəbl] adj éligible; (for membership) admissible; **an ~ young man** un beau parti; **to be ~ for sth** remplir les conditions requises pour qch

eliminate [ɪ'lɪmɪneɪt] vt éliminer

elm [ɛlm] n orme m

eloquent ['ɛləkwənt] adj éloquent(e)

else [ɛls] adv: **something ~** quelque chose d'autre, autre chose; **somewhere ~** ailleurs, autre part; **everywhere ~** partout ailleurs; **everyone ~** tous les autres; **nothing ~** rien d'autre; **where ~?** à quel autre endroit?; **little ~** pas grand-chose d'autre; **elsewhere** adv ailleurs, autre part

elusive [ɪ'luːsɪv] adj insaisissable

e-mail [ˈiːmeɪl] n abbr (= electronic mail) e-mail m, courriel m ▷ vt: **to ~ sb** envoyer un e-mail ou un courriel à qn; **e-mail address** n adresse f e-mail

embankment [ɪm'bæŋkmənt] n (of road, railway) remblai m, talus m; (of river) berge f, quai m; (dyke) digue f

embargo, embargoes [ɪm'bɑːgəu] n (Comm, Naut) embargo m; (prohibition) interdiction f

embark [ɪm'bɑːk] vi embarquer ▷ vt embarquer; **to ~ on** (journey etc) commencer, entreprendre; (fig) se lancer or s'embarquer dans

embarrass [ɪm'bærəs] vt embarrasser, gêner; **embarrassed** adj gêné(e); **embarrassing** adj gênant(e), embarrassant(e); **embarrassment** n embarras m, gêne f; (embarrassing thing, person) source f d'embarras

embassy ['ɛmbəsɪ] n ambassade f

embrace [ɪm'breɪs] vt embrasser, étreindre; (include) embrasser ▷ vi s'embrasser, s'étreindre ▷ n étreinte f

embroider [ɪm'brɔɪdə*] vt broder; **embroidery** n broderie f

embryo ['ɛmbrɪəu] n (also fig) embryon m

emerald ['ɛmərəld] n émeraude f

emerge [ɪˈməːdʒ] vi apparaître;
(from room, car) surgir; (from sleep,
imprisonment) sortir
emergency [ɪˈməːdʒənsɪ] n (crisis)
cas m d'urgence; (Med) urgence f; **in
an ~** en cas d'urgence; **state of ~** état
m d'urgence; **emergency brake** (us)
n frein m à main; **emergency exit**
n sortie f de secours; **emergency
landing** n atterrissage forcé;
emergency room n (us: Med)
urgences fpl; **emergency services** npl:
the emergency services (fire, police,
ambulance) les services mpl d'urgence
emigrate [ˈɛmɪɡreɪt] vi émigrer;
emigration [ɛmɪˈɡreɪʃən] n
émigration f
eminent [ˈɛmɪnənt] adj éminent(e)
emissions [ɪˈmɪʃənz] npl émissions fpl
emit [ɪˈmɪt] vt émettre
emotion [ɪˈməʊʃən] n sentiment m;
emotional adj (person) émotif(-ive),
très sensible; (needs) affectif(-ive);
(scene) émouvant(e); (tone, speech) qui
fait appel aux sentiments
emperor [ˈɛmpərər] n empereur m
emphasis (pl **-ases**) [ˈɛmfəsɪs, -siːz] n
accent m; **to lay** or **place ~ on sth** (fig)
mettre l'accent sur, insister sur
emphasize [ˈɛmfəsaɪz] vt (syllable,
word, point) appuyer or insister sur;
(feature) souligner, accentuer
empire [ˈɛmpaɪər] n empire m
employ [ɪmˈplɔɪ] vt employer;
employee [ɪmplɔɪˈiː] n employé(e);
employer n employeur(-euse);
employment n emploi m;
employment agency n agence f or
bureau m de placement
empower [ɪmˈpaʊər] vt: **to ~ sb to do**
autoriser or habiliter qn à faire
empress [ˈɛmprɪs] n impératrice f
emptiness [ˈɛmptɪnɪs] n vide m; (of
area) aspect m désertique
empty [ˈɛmptɪ] adj vide; (street, area)
désert(e); (threat, promise) en l'air,
vain(e) ▷ vt vider ▷ vi se vider; (liquid)
s'écouler; **empty-handed** adj les

mains vides
EMU n abbr (= European Monetary Union)
UME f
emulsion [ɪˈmʌlʃən] n émulsion f; (also:
~ paint) peinture mate
enable [ɪˈneɪbl] vt: **to ~ sb to do**
permettre à qn de faire
enamel [ɪˈnæməl] n émail m; (also: **~
paint**) (peinture f) laque f
enchanting [ɪnˈtʃɑːntɪŋ] adj
ravissant(e), enchanteur(-eresse)
encl. abbr (on letters etc: = enclosed) ci-
joint(e); (= enclosure) PJ f
enclose [ɪnˈkləʊz] vt (land) clôturer;
(space, object) entourer; (letter etc): **to
~ (with)** joindre (à); **please find ~d**
veuillez trouver ci-joint
enclosure [ɪnˈkləʊʒər] n enceinte f
encore [ɔŋˈkɔːr] excl, n bis (m)
encounter [ɪnˈkaʊntər] n rencontre f
▷ vt rencontrer
encourage [ɪnˈkʌrɪdʒ] vt encourager;
encouragement n encouragement m
encouraging [ɪnˈkʌrɪdʒɪŋ] adj
encourageant(e)
encyclop(a)edia [ɛnsaɪkləʊˈpiːdɪə] n
encyclopédie f
end [ɛnd] n fin f; (of table, street, rope
etc) bout m, extrémité f ▷ vt terminer;
(also: **bring to an ~, put an ~ to**)
mettre fin à ▷ vi se terminer, finir; **in
the ~** finalement; **on ~** (object)
debout, dressé(e); **to stand on ~** (hair)
se dresser sur la tête; **for hours on ~**
pendant des heures, des heures durant;
end up vi: **to ~ up in** (condition) finir or
se terminer par; (place) finir or aboutir à
endanger [ɪnˈdeɪndʒər] vt mettre en
danger; **an ~ed species** une espèce en
voie de disparition
endearing [ɪnˈdɪərɪŋ] adj attachant(e)
endeavour, (us) **endeavor** [ɪnˈdɛvər] n
effort m; (attempt) tentative f ▷ vt: **to ~
to do** tenter or s'efforcer de faire
ending [ˈɛndɪŋ] n dénouement m,
conclusion f; (Ling) terminaison f
endless [ˈɛndlɪs] adj sans fin,
interminable

endorse [ɪn'dɔːs] vt (cheque) endosser; (approve) appuyer, approuver, sanctionner; **endorsement** n (approval) appui m, aval m; (BRIT: on driving licence) contravention f (portée au permis de conduire)

endurance [ɪn'djuərəns] n endurance f

endure [ɪn'djuəʳ] vt (bear) supporter, endurer ▷ vi (last) durer

enemy ['ɛnəmɪ] adj, n ennemi(e)

energetic [ɛnə'dʒɛtɪk] adj énergique; (activity) très actif(-ive), qui fait se dépenser (physiquement)

energy ['ɛnədʒɪ] n énergie f

enforce [ɪn'fɔːs] vt (law) appliquer, faire respecter

engaged [ɪn'geɪdʒd] adj (BRIT: busy, in use) occupé(e); (betrothed) fiancé(e); **to get ~** se fiancer; **the line's ~** la ligne est occupée; **engaged tone** n (BRIT Tel) tonalité f occupé inv

engagement [ɪn'geɪdʒmənt] n (undertaking) obligation f, engagement m; (appointment) rendez-vous m inv; (to marry) fiançailles fpl; **engagement ring** n bague f de fiançailles

engaging [ɪn'geɪdʒɪŋ] adj engageant(e), attirant(e)

engine ['ɛndʒɪn] n (Aut) moteur m; (Rail) locomotive f

☐ Be careful not to translate **engine** by the French word **engin**.

engineer [ɛndʒɪ'nɪəʳ] n ingénieur m; (BRIT: repairer) dépanneur m; (Navy, us Rail) mécanicien m; **engineering** n engineering m, ingénierie f (of bridges, ships) génie m; (of machine) mécanique f

England ['ɪŋɡlənd] n Angleterre f

English ['ɪŋɡlɪʃ] adj anglais(e) ▷ n (Ling) anglais m; **the ~** npl les Anglais; **English Channel** n **the ~ English Channel** la Manche; **Englishman** (irreg) n Anglais m; **Englishwoman** (irreg) n Anglaise f

engrave [ɪn'ɡreɪv] vt graver

engraving [ɪn'ɡreɪvɪŋ] n gravure f

enhance [ɪn'hɑːns] vt rehausser,

mettre en valeur

enjoy [ɪn'dʒɔɪ] vt aimer, prendre plaisir à; (have benefit of: health, fortune) jouir de; (: success) connaître; **to ~ o.s.** s'amuser; **enjoyable** adj agréable; **enjoyment** n plaisir m

enlarge [ɪn'lɑːdʒ] vt accroître; (Phot) agrandir ▷ vi: **to ~ on** (subject) s'étendre sur; **enlargement** n (Phot) agrandissement m

enlist [ɪn'lɪst] vt recruter; (support) s'assurer ▷ vi s'engager

enormous [ɪ'nɔːməs] adj énorme

enough [ɪ'nʌf] adj: **~ time/books** assez or suffisamment de temps/livres ▷ adv: **big ~** assez or suffisamment grand ▷ pron: **have you got ~?** en avez-vous assez?; **~ to eat** assez à manger; **that's ~, thanks** cela suffit or c'est assez, merci; **I've had ~ of him** j'en ai assez de lui; **he has not worked ~** il n'a pas assez or suffisamment travaillé, il n'a pas travaillé assez or suffisamment; **... which, funnily** or **oddly ~ ...** qui, chose curieuse

enquire [ɪn'kwaɪəʳ] vt, vi = **inquire**

enquiry [ɪn'kwaɪərɪ] n = **inquiry**

enrage [ɪn'reɪdʒ] vt mettre en fureur or en rage, rendre furieux(-euse)

enrich [ɪn'rɪtʃ] vt enrichir

enrol (us **enroll**) [ɪn'rəul] vt inscrire ▷ vi s'inscrire; **enrolment** (us **enrollment**) n inscription f

en route [ɔn'ruːt] adv en route, en chemin

en suite ['ɔnswiːt] adj: **with ~ bathroom** avec salle de bains or attenante

ensure [ɪn'ʃuəʳ] vt assurer, garantir

entail [ɪn'teɪl] vt entraîner, nécessiter

enter [ɪn'tɜːʳ] vt (room) entrer dans, pénétrer dans; (club, army) entrer à; (competition) s'inscrire à or pour; (sb for a competition) (faire) inscrire; (write down) inscrire, noter; (Comput) entrer, introduire ▷ vi entrer

enterprise ['ɛntəpraɪz] n (company, undertaking) entreprise f; (initiative) (esprit m d'initiative f; **free ~** libre entreprise; **private ~** entreprise privée; **enterprising** adj entreprenant(e), dynamique; (scheme) audacieux(-euse)

entertain [ɛntəˈteɪn] vt amuser, distraire; (invite) recevoir (à dîner); (idea, plan) envisager; **entertainer** n artiste m/f de variétés; **entertaining** adj amusant(e), distrayant(e); **entertainment** n (amusement) distraction f, divertissement m, amusement m; (show) spectacle m

enthusiasm [ɪnˈθuːzɪæzəm] n enthousiasme m

enthusiast [ɪnˈθuːzɪæst] n enthousiaste m/f; **enthusiastic** [ɪnˈθuːzɪˈæstɪk] adj enthousiaste; **to be enthusiastic about** être enthousiasmé(e) par

entire [ɪnˈtaɪəʳ] adj (tout) entier(-ère); **entirely** adv entièrement, complètement

entitle [ɪnˈtaɪtl] vt: **to ~ sb to sth** donner droit à qch à qn; **entitled** adj (book) intitulé(e); **to be entitled to do** avoir le droit de faire

entrance n [ˈɛntrns] entrée f ⊳ vt [ɪnˈtrɑːns] enchanter, ravir; **where's the ~?** où est l'entrée?; **to gain ~ to** (university etc) être admis à; **entrance examination** n examen m d'entrée or d'admission; **entrance fee** n (to museum etc) prix m d'entrée; (to join club etc) droit m d'inscription; **entrance ramp** n (US AUT) bretelle f d'accès; **entrant** n (in race etc) participant(e), concurrent(e); (BRIT: in exam) candidat(e)

entrepreneur [ˈɔntrəprəˈnəːʳ] n entrepreneur m

entrust [ɪnˈtrʌst] vt: **to ~ sth to** confier qch à

entry [ˈɛntrɪ] n entrée f; (in register, diary) inscription f; **"no ~"** "défense d'entrer", "entrée interdite"; (AUT) "sens interdit"; **entry phone** n (BRIT) interphone m (à l'entrée d'un immeuble)

envelope [ˈɛnvələup] n enveloppe f

envious [ˈɛnvɪəs] adj envieux(-euse)

environment [ɪnˈvaɪərnmənt] n (social, moral) milieu m; (natural world): **the ~** l'environnement m; **environmental** [ɪnvaɪərnˈmɛntl] adj (of surroundings) du milieu; (issue, disaster) écologique; **environmentally** [ɪnvaɪərnˈmɛntlɪ] adv: **environmentally sound/friendly** qui ne nuit pas à l'environnement

envisage [ɪnˈvɪzɪdʒ] vt (foresee) prévoir

envoy [ˈɛnvɔɪ] n envoyé(e); (diplomat) ministre m plénipotentiaire

envy [ˈɛnvɪ] n envie f ⊳ vt envier; **to ~ sb sth** envier qch à qn

epic [ˈɛpɪk] n épopée f ⊳ adj épique

epidemic [ɛpɪˈdɛmɪk] n épidémie f

epilepsy [ˈɛpɪlɛpsɪ] n épilepsie f; **epileptic** adj, n épileptique m/f; **epileptic fit** n crise f d'épilepsie

episode [ˈɛpɪsəud] n épisode m

equal [ˈiːkwl] adj égal(e) ⊳ vt égaler; **~ to** (task) à la hauteur de; **equality** [iːˈkwɔlɪtɪ] n égalité f; **equalize** vt, vi (SPORT) égaliser; **equally** adv également; (share) en parts égales; (treat) de la même façon; (pay) autant; (just as) tout aussi

equation [ɪˈkweɪʃən] n (MATH) équation f

equator [ɪˈkweɪtəʳ] n équateur m

equip [ɪˈkwɪp] vt équiper; **to ~ sb/sth with** équiper or munir qn/qch de; **equipment** n équipement m; (electrical etc) appareillage m, installation f

equivalent [ɪˈkwɪvəlnt] adj équivalent(e) ⊳ n équivalent m; **to be ~ to** être équivalent(e) à, être équivaloir à

ER abbr (BRIT: = Elizabeth Regina) la reine Élisabeth; (US: Med: = emergency room) urgences fpl

era [ˈɪərə] n ère f, époque f

erase [ɪˈreɪz] vt effacer; **eraser** n gomme f

erect [ɪˈrɛkt] adj droit(e) ⊳ vt construire; (monument) ériger, élever; (tent etc) dresser; **erection** [ɪˈrɛkʃən] n (PHYSIOL) érection f; (of building) construction f

ERM n abbr (= Exchange Rate Mechanism) mécanisme m des taux de change

erode [ɪˈrəʊd] vt éroder; (metal) ronger

erosion [ɪˈrəʊʒən] n érosion f

erotic [ɪˈrɔtɪk] adj érotique

errand [ˈɛrnd] n course f, commission f

erratic [ɪˈrætɪk] adj irrégulier(-ière), inconstant(e)

error [ˈɛrə] n erreur f

erupt [ɪˈrʌpt] vi entrer en éruption; (fig) éclater; **eruption** [ɪˈrʌpʃən] n éruption f; (of anger, violence) explosion f

escalate [ˈɛskəleɪt] vi s'intensifier; (costs) monter en flèche

escalator [ˈɛskəleɪtə] n escalier roulant

escape [ɪˈskeɪp] n évasion f, fuite f; (of gas etc) fuite f ▷ vi s'échapper, fuir; (from jail) s'évader; (leak) s'échapper ▷ vt échapper à; **to ~ from** (person) échapper à; (place) s'échapper de; (fig) fuir; **his name ~s me** son nom m'échappe

escort vt [ɪˈskɔːt] escorter ▷ n [ˈɛskɔːt] (Mil) escorte f

especially [ɪˈspɛʃlɪ] adv (particularly) particulièrement; (above all) surtout

espionage [ˈɛspɪənɑːʒ] n espionnage m

essay [ˈeseɪ] n (Scol) dissertation f; (Literature) essai m

essence [ˈɛsns] n essence f; (Culin) extrait m

essential [ɪˈsɛnʃl] adj essentiel(le); (basic) fondamental(e); **essentials** npl éléments essentiels; **essentially** adv essentiellement

establish [ɪˈstæblɪʃ] vt établir; (business) fonder, créer; (one's power etc) asseoir, affermir; **establishment** n établissement m; (founding) création f; (institution) établissement m; **the Establishment** les pouvoirs établis, l'ordre établi

estate [ɪˈsteɪt] n (land) domaine m, propriété f; (Law) biens mpl, succession f; (BRIT: also: **housing ~**)

lotissement m; **estate agent** n (BRIT) agent immobilier; **estate car** n (BRIT) break m

estimate n [ˈɛstɪmət] estimation f; (Comm) devis m ▷ vb [ˈɛstɪmeɪt] ▷ vt estimer

etc abbr (= et cetera) etc

eternal [ɪˈtəːnl] adj éternel(le)

eternity [ɪˈtəːnɪtɪ] n éternité f

ethical [ˈɛθɪkl] adj moral(e); **ethics** [ˈɛθɪks] n éthique f ▷ npl moralité f

Ethiopia [iːθɪˈəupɪə] n Éthiopie f

ethnic [ˈɛθnɪk] adj ethnique; (clothes, food) folklorique, exotique, propre aux minorités ethniques non-occidentales; **ethnic minority** n minorité f ethnique

e-ticket [ˈiːtɪkɪt] n billet m électronique

etiquette [ˈɛtɪkɛt] n convenances fpl, étiquette f

EU n abbr (= European Union) UE f

euro [ˈjuərəu] n (currency) euro m

Europe [ˈjuərəp] n Europe f; **European** [juərəˈpiːən] adj européen(ne) ▷ n Européen(ne); **European Community** n Communauté européenne; **European Union** n Union européenne

Eurostar [ˈjuərəustɑːʳ] n Eurostar® m

evacuate [ɪˈvækjueɪt] vt évacuer

evade [ɪˈveɪd] vt échapper à; (question etc) éluder; (duties) se dérober à

evaluate [ɪˈvæljueɪt] vt évaluer

evaporate [ɪˈvæpəreɪt] vi s'évaporer; (fig: hopes, fear) s'envoler; (anger) se dissiper

eve [iːv] n: **on the ~ of** à la veille de

even [ˈiːvn] adj (level, smooth) régulier(-ière); (equal) égal(e); (number) pair(e) ▷ adv même; **~ if** même si + indic; **~ though** alors même que + cond; **~ more** encore plus; **~ faster** encore plus vite; **~ so** quand même; **not ~** pas même; **~ he was there** même lui était là; **~ on Sundays** même le dimanche; **to get ~ with sb** prendre sa revanche sur qn

evening [ˈiːvnɪŋ] n soir m; (as duration,

event) soirée *f*; **in the ~** le soir; **evening class** *n* cours *m* du soir; **evening dress** *n* (*man's*) tenue *f* de soirée, smoking *m*; (*woman's*) robe *f* de soirée

event [ɪˈvɛnt] *n* événement *m*; (*Sport*) épreuve *f*; **in the ~ of** en cas de; **eventful** *adj* mouvementé(e)

eventual [ɪˈvɛntʃuəl] *adj* final(e)

> Be careful not to translate *eventual* by the French word *éventuel*.

eventually [ɪˈvɛntʃuəlɪ] *adv* finalement

> Be careful not to translate *eventually* by the French word *éventuellement*.

ever [ˈɛvə*] *adv* jamais; (*at all times*) toujours; (*in questions*): **why ~ not?** mais enfin, pourquoi pas?; **the best ~** le meilleur qu'on ait jamais vu; **have you ~ seen it?** l'as-tu déjà vu?, as-tu eu l'occasion or t'est-il arrivé de le voir?; **~ since** (*as adv*) depuis; (*as conj*) depuis que; **~ so pretty** si joli; **evergreen** *n* arbre *m* à feuilles persistantes

KEYWORD

every [ˈɛvrɪ] *adj* **1** (*each*) chaque; **every one of them** tous (sans exception); **every shop in town was closed** tous les magasins en ville étaient fermés
2 (*all possible*) tous (toutes) les; **I gave you every assistance** j'ai fait tout mon possible pour vous aider; **I have every confidence in him** je lui fais entièrement or pleinement confiance en lui; **we wish you every success** nous vous souhaitons beaucoup de succès
3 (*showing recurrence*) tous les; **every day** tous les jours, chaque jour; **every other car** une voiture sur deux; **every other/third day** tous les deux/trois jours; **every now and then** de temps en temps; **everybody** = **everyone**; **everyday** *adj* (*expression*) courant(e), d'usage courant; (*use*) courant; (*clothes, life*) de tous les jours; (*occurrence,*

problem) quotidien(ne); **everyone** *pron* tout le monde, tous *pl*; **everything** *pron* tout; **everywhere** *adv* partout; **everywhere you go you meet ...** où qu'on aille, on rencontre ...

evict [ɪˈvɪkt] *vt* expulser

evidence [ˈɛvɪdəns] *n* (*proof*) preuve(s) *f(pl)*; (*of witness*) témoignage *m*; (*sign*): **to show ~ of** donner des signes de; **to give ~** témoigner, déposer

evident [ˈɛvɪdnt] *adj* évident(e); **evidently** *adv* de toute évidence; (*apparently*) manifestement

evil [ˈiːvl] *adj* mauvais(e) ▷ *n* mal *m*

evoke [ɪˈvəuk] *vt* évoquer

evolution [iːvəˈluːʃən] *n* évolution *f*

evolve [ɪˈvɔlv] *vt* élaborer ▷ *vi* évoluer, se transformer

ewe [juː] *n* brebis *f*

ex [ɛks] *n* (*inf*): **my ex** mon ex

ex- [ɛks] *préfix* ex-

exact [ɪɡˈzækt] *adj* exact(e) ▷ *vt*: **to ~ sth (from)** (*signature, confession*) extorquer qch (à); (*apology*) exiger qch (de); **exactly** *adv* exactement

exaggerate [ɪɡˈzædʒəreɪt] *vt, vi* exagérer; **exaggeration** [ɪɡzædʒəˈreɪʃən] *n* exagération *f*

exam [ɪɡˈzæm] *n abbr* (*Scol*) = **examination**

examination [ɪɡzæmɪˈneɪʃən] *n* (*Scol, Med*) examen *m*; **to take** or **sit an ~** (*BRIT*) passer un examen

examine [ɪɡˈzæmɪn] *vt* (*gen*) examiner; (*Scol, Law: person*) interroger; **examiner** *n* examinateur(-trice)

example [ɪɡˈzɑːmpl] *n* exemple *m*; **for ~** par exemple

exasperated [ɪɡˈzɑːspəreɪtɪd] *adj* exaspéré(e)

excavate [ˈɛkskəveɪt] *vt* (*site*) fouiller, excaver; (*object*) mettre au jour

exceed [ɪkˈsiːd] *vt* dépasser; (*one's powers*) outrepasser; **exceedingly** *adv* extrêmement

excel [ɪkˈsɛl] *vi* exceller ▷ *vt* surpasser; **to ~ o.s.** se surpasser

excellence ['eksələns] n excellence f
excellent ['eksələnt] adj excellent(e)
except [ɪk'sept] prep (also: **- for, ~ing**)
sauf, excepté, à l'exception de ▷ vt
excepter: **- if/when** sauf si/quand;
- that excepté que, si ce n'est que;
exception [ɪk'sepʃən] n exception
f; **to take exception to** s'offusquer
de; **exceptional** [ɪk'sepʃənl] adj
exceptionnel(le); **exceptionally**
[ɪk'sepʃənlɪ] adv exceptionnellement
excerpt ['eksə:pt] n extrait m
excess [ɪk'ses] n excès m; **excess
baggage** n excédent m de bagages;
excessive adj excessif(-ive)
exchange [ɪks'tʃeɪndʒ] n échange m;
(also: **telephone ~**) central m ▷ vt: **to ~
(for)** échanger (contre); **could I ~ this,
please?** est-ce que je peux échanger
ceci, s'il vous plaît?; **exchange rate** n
taux m de change
excise [ˈeksaɪz] n taxe f
excite [ɪk'saɪt] vt exciter; **excited** adj:
(tout (toute)) excité(e); **to get excited**
s'exciter; **excitement** n excitation f;
exciting adj passionnant(e)
exclaim [ɪk'skleɪm] vi s'exclamer;
exclamation [eksklə'meɪʃən] n
exclamation f; **exclamation mark**
(us **exclamation point**) n point m
d'exclamation
exclude [ɪk'sklu:d] vt exclure
excluding [ɪk'sklu:dɪŋ] prep: **~ VAT** la
TVA non comprise
exclusion [ɪk'sklu:ʒən] n exclusion f
exclusive [ɪk'sklu:sɪv] adj
exclusif(-ive); (club, district) sélect(e);
(item of news) en exclusivité; **~ of VAT**
TVA non comprise; **exclusively** adv
exclusivement
excruciating [ɪk'skru:ʃɪeɪtɪŋ]
adj (pain) atroce, déchirant(e);
(embarrassing) pénible
excursion [ɪk'skə:ʃən] n excursion f
excuse [ɪk'skju:s] excuse f ▷ vt
[ɪk'skju:z] (forgive) excuser; **to ~ sb
from** (activity) dispenser qn de; **~ me!**
excusez-moi!, pardon!; **now if you
will ~ me, ...** maintenant, si vous (le)

permettez ...
ex-directory ['eksdɪ'rektərɪ] adj (BRIT)
sur la liste rouge
execute ['eksɪkju:t] vt exécuter;
execution [eksɪ'kju:ʃən] n exécution f
executive [ɪg'zekjutɪv] n (person) cadre
m; (managing group) bureau m; (Pol)
exécutif m ▷ adj exécutif(-ive); (position,
job) de cadre
exempt [ɪg'zempt] adj: **~ from**
exempté(e) or dispensé(e) de ▷ vt: **to ~
sb from** exempter or dispenser qn de
exercise ['eksəsaɪz] n exercice m ▷ vt
exercer; (patience etc) faire preuve de;
(dog) promener ▷ vi (also: **to take ~**)
prendre de l'exercice; **exercise book**
n cahier m
exert [ɪg'zə:t] vt exercer, employer; **to
~ o.s.** se dépenser; **exertion** [ɪg'zə:ʃən]
n effort m
exhale [eks'heɪl] vt exhaler ▷ vi expirer
exhaust [ɪg'zɔ:st] n (also: **~ fumes**)
gaz mpl d'échappement; (also: **~ pipe**)
tuyau m d'échappement ▷ vt épuiser;
exhausted adj épuisé(e); **exhaustion**
[ɪg'zɔ:stʃən] n épuisement m; **nervous
exhaustion** fatigue nerveuse
exhibit [ɪg'zɪbɪt] n (Art) pièce f or objet
m exposé(e); (Law) pièce à conviction
▷ vt (Art) exposer; (courage, skill) faire
preuve de; **exhibition** [eksɪ'bɪʃən] n
exposition f
exhilarating [ɪg'zɪləreɪtɪŋ] adj
grisant(e), stimulant(e)
exile ['eksaɪl] n exil m; (person) exilé(e)
▷ vt exiler
exist [ɪg'zɪst] vi exister; **existence** n
existence f; **existing** adj actuel(le)
exit ['eksɪt] n sortie f ▷ vi (Comput,
Theat) sortir; **where's the ~?** où est la
sortie?; **exit ramp** n (us Aut) bretelle
f d'accès
exotic [ɪg'zɔtɪk] adj exotique
expand [ɪk'spænd] vt (area) agrandir;
(quantity) accroître ▷ vi (trade, etc) se
développer, s'accroître; (gas, metal)
se dilater
expansion [ɪk'spænʃən] n (territorial,

economic) expansion f; (of trade, influence etc) développement m; (of production) accroissement m; (of population) croissance f; (of gas, metal) expansion, dilatation f

expect [ɪk'spɛkt] vt (anticipate) s'attendre à, s'attendre à ce que + sub; (count on) compter sur, escompter; (require) demander, exiger; (suppose) supposer; (await: also baby) attendre ▷ vi: **to be ~ing** (pregnant woman) être enceinte; **expectation** [ɛkspɛk'teɪʃən] n (hope) attente f, espérance(s) f(pl); (belief) attente

expedition [ɛkspə'dɪʃən] n expédition f

expel [ɪk'spɛl] vt chasser, expulser; (Scol) renvoyer, exclure

expenditure [ɪk'spɛndɪtʃə'] n (act of spending) dépense f; (money spent) dépenses fpl

expense [ɪk'spɛns] n (high cost) coût m; (spending) dépense f, frais mpl; **expenses** npl frais mpl; dépenses; **at the ~ of** (fig) aux dépens de; **expense account** n (note) frais mpl

expensive [ɪk'spɛnsɪv] adj cher (chère), coûteux(-euse); **it's too ~** ça coûte trop cher

experience [ɪk'spɪərɪəns] n expérience f ▷ vt connaître; (feeling) éprouver; **experienced** adj expérimenté(e)

experiment [ɪk'spɛrɪmənt] n expérience f ▷ vi faire une expérience; **experimental** [ɪkspɛrɪ'mɛntl] adj expérimental(e)

expert [ˈɛkspəːt] adj expert(e) ▷ n expert m; **expertise** [ɛkspəː'tiːz] n (grande) compétence

expire [ɪk'spaɪə'] vi expirer; **expiry** n expiration f; **expiry date** n date f d'expiration; (on label) à utiliser avant ...

explain [ɪk'spleɪn] vt expliquer; **explanation** [ɛksplə'neɪʃən] n explication f

explicit [ɪk'splɪsɪt] adj explicite; (definite) formel(le)

explode [ɪk'spləud] vi exploser

exploit n [ˈɛksplɔɪt] exploit m ▷ vt [ɪk'splɔɪt] exploiter; **exploitation** [ɛksplɔɪ'teɪʃən] n exploitation f

explore [ɪk'splɔː'] vt explorer; (possibilities) étudier, examiner; **explorer** n explorateur(-trice)

explosion [ɪk'spləuʒən] n explosion f; **explosive** [ɪk'spləusɪv] adj explosif(-ive) ▷ n explosif m

export vt [ɛk'spɔːt] exporter ▷ n [ˈɛkspɔːt] exportation f ▷ cpd d'exportation; **exporter** n exportateur m

expose [ɪk'spəuz] vt exposer; (unmask) démasquer, dévoiler; **exposed** adj (land, house) exposé(e); **exposure** [ɪk'spəuʒə'] n exposition f; (publicity) couverture f; (Phot: speed) (temps m de) pose f; (: shot) pose; **to die of exposure** (Med) mourir de froid

express [ɪk'sprɛs] adj (definite) formel(le), exprès(-esse); (BRIT: letter etc) exprès inv ▷ n (train) rapide m ▷ vt exprimer; **expression** [ɪk'sprɛʃən] n expression f; **expressway** n (US) voie f express (à plusieurs files)

exquisite [ɛk'skwɪzɪt] adj exquis(e)

extend [ɪk'stɛnd] vt (visit, street) prolonger, remettre; (building) agrandir; (offer) présenter, offrir; (hand, arm) tendre ▷ vi (land) s'étendre; **extension** n (of visit, street) prolongation f; (building) annexe f; (telephone: in offices) poste m; (: in private house) téléphone m supplémentaire; **extension cable**, **extension lead** n (Elec) rallonge f; **extensive** adj étendu(e), vaste; (damage, alterations) considérable; (inquiries) approfondi(e)

extent [ɪk'stɛnt] n étendue f; **to some ~** dans une certaine mesure; **to the ~ of ...** au point de ...; **to what ~?** dans quelle mesure?, jusqu'à quel point?; **to such an ~ that ...** à tel point que ...

exterior [ɛk'stɪərɪə'] adj extérieur(e) ▷ n extérieur m

external [ɛk'stəːnl] adj externe

extinct [ɪkˈstɪŋkt] adj (volcano)
éteint(e); (species) disparu(e);
extinction n extinction f
extinguish [ɪkˈstɪŋgwɪʃ] vt éteindre
extra [ˈɛkstrə] adj supplémentaire,
de plus ▷ adv (in addition) en plus ▷ n
supplément m; (perk) à-côté m; (Cine,
Theat) figurant(e)
extract vt [ɪkˈstrækt] extraire; (tooth)
arracher; (money, promise) soutirer ▷ n
[ˈɛkstrækt] extrait m
extradite [ˈɛkstrədaɪt] vt extrader
extraordinary [ɪkˈstrɔːdnrɪ] adj
extraordinaire
extravagance [ɪkˈstrævəgəns]
n (excessive spending) prodigalités
fpl; (thing bought) folie f, dépense
excessive; **extravagant** adj
extravagant(e); (in spending: person)
prodigue, dépensier(-ière); (: tastes)
dispendieux(-euse)
extreme [ɪkˈstriːm] adj, n extrême (m);
extremely adv extrêmement
extremist [ɪkˈstriːmɪst] adj, n
extrémiste m/f
extrovert [ˈɛkstrəvəːt] n extraverti(e)
eye [aɪ] n œil m, (yeux) pl); (of needle)
trou m, chas m ▷ vt examiner; **to keep
an ~ on** surveiller; **eyeball** n globe
m oculaire; **eyebrow** n sourcil m;
eyedrops npl gouttes fpl pour les yeux;
eyelash n cil m; **eyelid** n paupière f;
eyeliner n eye-liner m; **eyeshadow** n
ombre f à paupières; **eyesight** n vue f;
eye witness n témoin m oculaire

f

F [ɛf] n (Mus): **F** fa m
fabric [ˈfæbrɪk] n tissu m
fabulous [ˈfæbjuləs] adj
fabuleux(-euse); (inf: super) formidable,
sensationnel(le)
face [feɪs] n visage m, figure f;
(expression) air m; (of clock) cadran m;
(of cliff) paroi f; (of mountain) face f;
(of building) façade f ▷ vt faire face à;
(facts etc) accepter; **~ down** (person)
à plat ventre; (card) face en dessous;
to lose/save ~ perdre/sauver la face;
to pull a ~ faire une grimace; **in the
~ of** (difficulties etc) face à, devant; **on
the ~ of it** à première vue; **~ to ~**
à face; **face up to** vt fus faire face à,
affronter; **face cloth** n (BRIT) gant m
de toilette; **face pack** n (BRIT) masque
m (de beauté)
facial [ˈfeɪʃl] adj facial(e) ▷ n soin
complet du visage
facilitate [fəˈsɪlɪteɪt] vt faciliter
facilities [fəˈsɪlɪtɪz] npl installations
fpl, équipement m; **credit ~** facilités

de paiement

fact [fækt] n fait m; **in ~** en fait

faction ['fækʃən] n faction f

factor ['fæktəʳ] n facteur m; (of sun cream) indice m (de protection); **I'd like a ~15 suntan lotion** je voudrais une crème solaire d'indice 15

factory ['fæktərı] n usine f, fabrique f

factual ['fæktjuəl] adj basé(e) sur les faits

faculty ['fækəltı] n faculté f; (us: teaching staff) corps enseignant

fad [fæd] n (personal) manie f; (craze) engouement m

fade [feɪd] vi se décolorer, passer; (light, sound) s'affaiblir; (flower) se faner; **fade away** vi (sound) s'affaiblir

fag [fæg] n (BRIT inf: cigarette) clope f

Fahrenheit ['fɑ:rənhaɪt] n Fahrenheit m inv

fail [feɪl] vt (exam) échouer à; (candidate) recaler; (subj: courage, memory) faire défaut à ▷ vi échouer; (eyesight, health, light: also: **be ~ing**) baisser, s'affaiblir; (brakes) lâcher; **to ~ to do sth** (neglect) négliger de or ne pas faire qch; (be unable) ne pas arriver or parvenir à faire qch; **without ~** à coup sûr; sans faute; **failing** n défaut m ▷ prep faute de; **failing that** à défaut, sinon; **failure** ['feɪljəʳ] n échec m; (person) raté(e) f; (mechanical etc) défaillance f

faint [feɪnt] adj faible; (recollection) vague; (mark) à peine visible ▷ n évanouissement m ▷ vi s'évanouir; **to feel ~** défaillir; **faintest** adj: **I haven't the faintest idea** je n'en ai pas la moindre idée; **faintly** adv faiblement; (vaguely) vaguement

fair [fɛəʳ] adj équitable, juste; (hair) blond(e); (skin, complexion) pâle, blanc (blanche); (weather) beau (belle); (good enough) assez bon(ne); (sizeable) considérable ▷ adv: **to play ~** jouer franc jeu ▷ n foire f; (BRIT: funfair) fête (foraine); **fairground** n champ m de foire; **fair-haired** adj (person) aux cheveux clairs, blond(e); **fairly** adv

(justly) équitablement; (quite) assez;

fair trade n commerce m équitable;

fairway n (Golf) fairway m

fairy ['fɛərı] n fée f; **fairy tale** n conte m de fées

faith [feɪθ] n foi f; (trust) confiance f; (sect) culte m, religion f; **faithful** adj fidèle; **faithfully** adv fidèlement; **yours faithfully** (BRIT: in letters) veuillez agréer l'expression de mes salutations les plus distinguées

fake [feɪk] n (painting etc) faux m; (person) imposteur m ▷ adj faux (fausse) ▷ vt (emotions) simuler; (painting) faire un faux de

falcon ['fɔːlkən] n faucon m

fall [fɔːl] n chute f; (decrease) baisse f; (us: autumn) automne m ▷ vi (pt **fell**, pp **~en**) tomber; (price, temperature, dollar) baisser; **falls** npl (waterfall) chute f d'eau, cascade f; **to ~ flat** vi (on one's face) tomber de tout son long; (s'étaler, (joke) tomber à plat; (plan) échouer; **fall apart** vi (object) tomber en morceaux; **fall down** vi (person) tomber; (building) s'effondrer, s'écrouler; **fall for** vt fus (trick) se laisser prendre à; (person) tomber amoureux(-euse) de; **fall off** vi tomber; (diminish) baisser, diminuer; **fall out** vi (friends etc) se brouiller; (hair, teeth) tomber; **fall over** vi tomber (par terre); **fall through** vi (plan, project) tomber à l'eau

fallen ['fɔːlən] pp of **fall**

fallout ['fɔːlaut] n retombées f (radioactives)

false [fɔːls] adj faux (fausse); **under ~ pretences** sous un faux prétexte; **false alarm** n fausse alerte; **false teeth** npl (BRIT) fausses dents, dentier m

fame [feɪm] n renommée f, renom m

familiar [fə'mɪlɪəʳ] adj familier(-ière); **to be ~ with sth** connaître qch; **familiarize** [fə'mɪlɪəraɪz] vt: **to familiarize o.s. with** se familiariser avec

family ['fæmɪlı] n famille f; **family doctor** n médecin m de famille; **family**

planning n planning familial

famine ['fæmɪn] n famine f

famous ['feɪməs] adj célèbre

fan [fæn] n (folding) éventail m; (Elec) ventilateur m; (person) fan m, admirateur(-trice); (Sport) supporter m/f ▷ vt éventer; (fire, quarrel) attiser

fanatic [fə'nætɪk] n fanatique m/f

fan belt n courroie f de ventilateur

fan club n fan-club m

fancy ['fænsɪ] n (whim) fantaisie f, envie f; (imagination) imagination f ▷ adj (luxury) de luxe; (elaborate: jewellery, packaging) fantaisie inv ▷ vt (feel like, want) avoir envie de; (imagine) imaginer; **to take a ~** se prendre d'affection pour; s'enticher de; **he fancies her** elle lui plaît; **fancy dress** n déguisement m, travesti m

fan heater n (BRIT) radiateur soufflant

fantasize ['fæntəsaɪz] vi fantasmer

fantastic [fæn'tæstɪk] adj fantastique

fantasy ['fæntəsɪ] n imagination f, fantaisie f; (unreality) fantasme m

fanzine ['fænziːn] n fanzine m

FAQ n abbr (= frequently asked question) FAQ inv, faq f inv

far [fɑː] adj (distant) lointain(e), éloigné(e) ▷ adv loin; **the ~ side/end** l'autre côté/bout; **it's not ~ (from here)** ce n'est pas loin (d'ici); **~ away, ~ off** au loin, dans le lointain; **~ better** beaucoup mieux; **~ from** loin de; **by ~** de loin, de beaucoup; **go as ~ as the bridge** allez jusqu'au pont; **as ~ as I know** pour autant que je sache; **how ~ is it to...?** combien y a-t-il jusqu'à...?; **how ~ have you got with your work?** où en êtes-vous dans votre travail?

farce [fɑːs] n farce f

fare [fɛə] n (on trains, buses) prix m du billet; (in taxi) prix de la course; (food) table f, chère f; **half ~** demi-tarif; **full ~** plein tarif

Far East n: **the ~** l'Extrême-Orient m

farewell [fɛə'wɛl] excl, n adieu m

farm [fɑːm] n ferme f ▷ vt cultiver; **farmer** n fermier(-ière); **farmhouse**

n (maison f de) ferme f; **farming** n agriculture f; (of animals) élevage m; **farmyard** n cour f de ferme

far-reaching ['fɑː'riːtʃɪŋ] adj d'une grande portée

fart [fɑːt] (infl) vi péter

farther ['fɑːðə] adv plus loin ▷ adj plus éloigné(e), plus lointain(e)

farthest ['fɑːðɪst] superlative of **far**

fascinate ['fæsɪneɪt] vt fasciner, captiver; **fascinated** adj fasciné(e)

fascinating ['fæsɪneɪtɪŋ] adj fascinant(e)

fascination [fæsɪ'neɪʃən] n fascination f

fascist ['fæʃɪst] adj, n fasciste m/f

fashion ['fæʃən] n mode f; (manner) façon f, manière f ▷ vt façonner; **in ~** à la mode; **out of ~** démodé(e); **fashionable** adj à la mode; **fashion show** n défilé m de mannequins or de mode

fast [fɑːst] adj rapide; (clock): **to be ~** avancer; (dye, colour) grand or bon teint inv ▷ adv vite, rapidement; (stuck, held) solidement ▷ n jeûne m ▷ vi jeûner; **~ asleep** profondément endormi

fasten ['fɑːsn] vt attacher, fixer; (coat) attacher, fermer ▷ vi se fermer, s'attacher

fast food n fast food m, restauration frapide

fat [fæt] adj gros(se) ▷ n graisse f; (on meat) gras m; (for cooking) matière grasse

fatal ['feɪtl] adj (mistake) fatal(e); (injury) mortel(le); **fatality** [fə'tælɪtɪ] n (road death etc) victime f, décès m; **fatally** adv fatalement; (injured) mortellement

fate [feɪt] n destin m; (of person) sort m

father ['fɑːðə] n père m; **Father Christmas** n le Père Noël; **father-in-law** n beau-père m

fatigue [fə'tiːg] n fatigue f

fattening ['fætnɪŋ] adj (food) qui fait grossir

fatty ['fætɪ] adj (food) gras(se) ▷ n (inf) gros (grosse)

faucet ['fɔːsɪt] *n* (*us*) robinet *m*
fault [fɔːlt] *n* (*defect*) défaut *m*; (*Geo*) faille *f* ▷ *vt* trouver des défauts à, prendre en défaut; **it's my ~** c'est de ma faute; **to find ~ with** trouver à redire à ou critiquer à; **at ~** fautif(-ive), coupable; **faulty** *adj* défectueux(-euse)
fauna ['fɔːnə] *n* faune *f*
favour *etc* (*us* **favor** *etc*) ['feɪvəʳ] *n* faveur *f*; (*help*) service *m* ▷ *vt* (*proposition*) être en faveur de; (*pupil etc*) favoriser; (*team, horse*) donner gagnant; **to do sb a ~** rendre un service à qn; **in ~ of** en faveur de; **to find ~ with sb** trouver grâce aux yeux de qn; **favourable** *adj* favorable; **favourite** ['feɪvrɪt] *adj, n* favori(te)
fawn [fɔːn] *n* (*deer*) faon *m* ▷ *adj* (*also*: **~-coloured**) fauve ▷ *vi*: **to ~ (up)on** flatter servilement
fax [fæks] *n* (*document*) télécopie *f*; (*machine*) télécopieur *m* ▷ *vt* envoyer par télécopie
FBI *n abbr* (*us*: = *Federal Bureau of Investigation*) FBI *m*
fear [fɪəʳ] *n* crainte *f*, peur *f* ▷ *vt* craindre; **for ~ of** de peur que + *sub* ou de + *infinitive*; **fearful** *adj* craintif(-ive); (*sight, noise*) affreux(-euse); **fearless** *adj* intrépide
feasible ['fiːzəbl] *adj* faisable, réalisable
feast [fiːst] *n* festin *m*, banquet *m*; (*Rel*: *also*: **~ day**) fête *f* ▷ *vi* festoyer
feat [fiːt] *n* exploit *m*, prouesse *f*
feather ['feðəʳ] *n* plume *f*
feature ['fiːtʃəʳ] *n* caractéristique *f*; (*article*) chronique *f*, rubrique *f* ▷ *vt* (*film*) avoir pour vedette(s) ▷ *vi* figurer (en bonne place); **features** *npl* (*of face*) traits *mpl*; **a (special) ~ on sth/sb** un reportage sur qch/qn; **feature film** *n* long métrage
Feb. *abbr* (= *February*) fév
February ['fɛbruərɪ] *n* février *m*
fed [fɛd] *pt, pp of* **feed**
federal ['fɛdərəl] *adj* fédéral(e)
federation [fɛdə'reɪʃən] *n* fédération *f*

fed up *adj*: **to be ~ (with)** en avoir marre ou plein le dos *De*
fee [fiː] *n* rémunération *f*; (*of doctor, lawyer*) honoraires *mpl*; (*of school, college etc*) frais *mpl* de scolarité; (*for examination*) droits *mpl*
feeble ['fiːbl] *adj* faible; (*attempt, excuse*) pauvre; (*joke*) piteux(-euse)
feed [fiːd] *n* (*of animal*) nourriture *f*, pâture *f*; (*on printer*) mécanisme *m* d'alimentation ▷ *vt* (*pt, pp* **fed**) (*person*) nourrir; (*BRIT: baby*): **breastfeed** allaiter; (: *with bottle*) donner le biberon à; (*horse etc*) donner à manger à; (*machine*) alimenter; (*data etc*): **to ~ sth into** enregistrer qch dans; **feedback** *n* (*Elec*) effet *m* Larsen; (*from person*) réactions *fpl*
feel [fiːl] *n* (*sensation*) sensation *f*; (*impression*) impression *f* ▷ *vt* (*pt, pp* **felt**) (*touch*) toucher; (*explore*) palper; (*cold, pain*) sentir; (*grief, anger*) ressentir, éprouver; (*think, believe*): **to ~ (that)** trouver que; **to ~ hungry/cold** avoir faim/froid; **to ~ lonely/better** se sentir seul/mieux; **I don't ~ well** je ne me sens pas bien; **it ~s soft** c'est doux au toucher; **to ~ like** (*want*) avoir envie de; **feeling** *n* (*physical*) sensation *f*; (*emotion, impression*) sentiment *m*; **to hurt sb's feelings** froisser qn
feet [fiːt] *npl of* **foot**
fell [fɛl] *pt of* **fall** ▷ *vt* (*tree*) abattre
fellow ['fɛləu] *n* type *m*; (*comrade*) compagnon *m*; (*of learned society*) membre *m* ▷ *cpd*: **their ~ prisoners/students** leurs camarades prisonniers/étudiants; **fellow citizen** *n* concitoyen *m*; **fellow countryman** *n* (*irreg*) compatriote *m*; **fellow men** *npl* semblables *mpl*; **fellowship** *n* (*society*) association *f*; (*comradeship*) amitié *f*, camaraderie *f*; (*Scol*) sorte de bourse universitaire
felony ['fɛlənɪ] *n* crime *m*, forfait *m*
felt [fɛlt] *pt, pp of* **feel** ▷ *n* feutre *m*; **felt-tip** *n* (*also*: **felt-tip pen**) stylo-feutre *m*
female ['fiːmeɪl] *n* (*Zool*) femelle *f*;

(pej: woman) bonne femme ▷ *adj (Biol)* femelle; *(sex, character)* féminin(e); *(vote etc)* des femmes

feminine ['fɛmɪnɪn] *adj* féminin(e)

feminist ['fɛmɪnɪst] *n* féministe *m/f*

fence [fɛns] *n* barrière *f* ▷ *vi* faire de l'escrime; **fencing** *n (sport)* escrime *m*

fend [fɛnd] *vi*: **to ~ for o.s.** se débrouiller *(tout seul)*; **fend off** *vt (attack etc)* parer; *(questions etc)* éluder

fender ['fɛndəʳ] *n* garde-feu *m inv*; *(on boat)* défense *f*; *(us: of car)* aile *f*

fennel ['fɛnl] *n* fenouil *m*

ferment *vi* [fə'mɛnt] fermenter ▷ *n* ['fə:mɛnt] *(fig)* agitation *f*, effervescence *f*

fern [fə:n] *n* fougère *f*

ferocious [fə'rəuʃəs] *adj* féroce

ferret ['fɛrɪt] *n* furet *m*

ferry ['fɛrɪ] *n (small)* bac *m*; *(large: also:* **~-boat)** ferry(-boat *m*) *m* ▷ *vt* transporter

fertile ['fə:taɪl] *adj* fertile; *(Biol)* fécond(e); **fertilize** ['fə:tɪlaɪz] *vt* fertiliser; *(Biol)* féconder; **fertilizer** *n* engrais *m*

festival ['fɛstɪvəl] *n (Rel)* fête *f*; *(Art, Mus)* festival *m*

festive ['fɛstɪv] *adj* de fête; **the ~ season** *(BRIT: Christmas)* la période des fêtes

fetch [fɛtʃ] *vt* aller chercher; *(BRIT: sell for)* rapporter

fête [feɪt] *n* fête *f*, kermesse *f*

fetus ['fi:təs] *n (us)* = **foetus**

feud [fju:d] *n* querelle *f*, dispute *f*

fever ['fi:vəʳ] *n* fièvre *f*; **feverish** *adj* fiévreux(-euse), fébrile

few [fju:] *adj (not many)* peu de ▷ *pron* peu; **a ~** *(as adj)* quelques; *(as pron)* quelques-uns(-unes); **quite a ~ ...** *adj* un certain nombre de ..., pas mal de ...; **in the past ~ days** ces derniers jours; **fewer** *adj* moins de; **fewest** *adj* le moins nombreux

fiancé [fɪ'ɑ̃:ŋseɪ] *n* fiancé *m*; **fiancée** *n* fiancée *f*

fiasco [fɪ'æskəu] *n* fiasco *m*

fib [fɪb] *n* bobard *m*

fibre *(us* **fiber)** ['faɪbəʳ] *n* fibre *f*; **fibreglass** *(us* **Fiberglass®)** *n* fibre *f* de verre

fickle ['fɪkl] *adj* inconstant(e), volage, capricieux(-euse)

fiction ['fɪkʃən] *n* romans *mpl*, littérature *f* romanesque; *(invention)* fiction *f*; **fictional** *adj* fictif(-ive)

fiddle ['fɪdl] *n (Mus)* violon *m*; *(cheating)* combine *f*; escroquerie *f* ▷ *vt (BRIT: accounts)* falsifier, maquiller; **fiddle with** *vt fus* tripoter

fidelity [fɪ'dɛlɪtɪ] *n* fidélité *f*

fidget ['fɪdʒɪt] *vi* se trémousser, remuer

field [fi:ld] *n* champ *m*; *(fig)* domaine *m*, champ; *(Sport: ground)* terrain *m*; **field marshal** *n* maréchal *m*

fierce [fɪəs] *adj (look, animal)* féroce, sauvage; *(wind, attack, person)* très violent(e); *(fighting, enemy)* acharné(e)

fifteen [fɪf'ti:n] *num* quinze; **fifteenth** *num* quinzième

fifth [fɪfθ] *num* cinquième

fiftieth ['fɪftɪɪθ] *num* cinquantième

fifty ['fɪftɪ] *num* cinquante; **fifty-fifty** *adv* moitié-moitié ▷ *adj*: **to have a fifty-fifty chance (of success)** avoir une chance sur deux (de réussir)

fig [fɪg] *n* figue *f*

fight [faɪt] *n (between persons)* bagarre *f*; *(argument)* dispute *f*; *(Mil)* combat *m*; *(against cancer etc)* lutte *f* ▷ *vb* (pt, pp **fought**) ▷ *vt* se battre contre; *(cancer, alcoholism, emotion)* combattre, lutter contre; *(election)* se présenter à ▷ *vi* se battre; *(argue)* se disputer; *(fig)*: **to ~ (for/against)** lutter (pour/contre); **fight back** *vi* rendre les coups; *(after illness)* reprendre le dessus ▷ *vt (tears)* réprimer; **fight off** *vt* repousser; *(disease, sleep, urge)* lutter contre; **fighting** *n* combats *mpl*; *(brawls)* bagarres *fpl*

figure ['fɪgəʳ] *n (Drawing, Geom)* figure *f*; *(number)* chiffre *m*; *(body, outline)* silhouette *f*; *(person's shape)* ligne *f*, formes *fpl*; *(person)* personnage *m*

▷ vt (us: think) supposer ▷ vi (appear)
figurer; (us: make sense) s'expliquer;
figure out vt (understand) arriver à
comprendre; (plan) calculer

file [faɪl] n (tool) lime f; (dossier)
dossier m; (folder) dossier, chemise f; (: binder)
classeur m; (Comput) fichier m; (row)
file f ▷ vt (nails, wood) limer; (papers)
classer; (Law: claim) faire enregistrer;
déposer; **filing cabinet** n classeur
m (meuble)

Filipino [fɪlɪˈpiːnəu] adj philippin(e)
▷ n (person) Philippin(e)

fill [fɪl] vt remplir; (vacancy) pourvoir à
▷ n: **to eat one's ~** manger à sa faim;
to ~ with remplir de; **fill in** vt (hole)
boucher; (form) remplir ▷ vi (Brit: details,
form) remplir; **fill out** vt (form, receipt) remplir;
fill up vt remplir
▷ vi (Aut) faire le plein

fillet [ˈfɪlɪt] n filet m; **fillet steak** n filet
m de bœuf, tournedos m

filling [ˈfɪlɪŋ] n (Culin) garniture f, farce
f; (for tooth) plombage m; **filling station**
n station-service f, station d'essence

film [fɪlm] n film m; (Phot) pellicule
f, film m; (of powder, liquid) couche
f, pellicule f ▷ vt (scene) filmer ▷ vi
tourner; **I'd like a 36-exposure ~** je
voudrais une pellicule de 36 poses; **film
star** n vedette f de cinéma

filter [ˈfɪltə*] n filtre m ▷ vt filtrer; **filter
lane** n (Brit Aut: at traffic lights) voie f
de dégagement; (: on motorway) voie
f de sortie

filth [fɪlθ] n saleté f; **filthy** adj
sale, dégoûtant(e); (language)
ordurier(-ière), grossier(-ière)

fin [fɪn] n (of fish) nageoire f; (of shark)
aileron m; (of diver) palme f

final [ˈfaɪnl] adj final(e), dernier(-ière);
(decision, answer) définitif(-ive) ▷ n
(Brit Sport) finale f; **finals** npl (Scol)
examens mpl de dernière année;
(us Sport) finale f; **finale** [fɪˈnɑːlɪ] n
finale m; **finalist** n (Sport) finaliste m/f;
finalize vt mettre au point; **finally** adv
(eventually) enfin, finalement; (lastly) en
dernier lieu

finance [faɪˈnæns] n finance
f ▷ vt financer; **finances** npl
finances fpl; **financial** [faɪˈnænʃəl]
adj financier(-ière); **financial year** n
année f budgétaire

find [faɪnd] vt (pt, pp **found**) trouver;
(lost object) retrouver ▷ n trouvaille
f, découverte f; **to ~ sb guilty** (Law)
déclarer qn coupable; **find out** vt se
renseigner sur; (truth, secret) découvrir;
(person) démasquer ▷ vi: **to ~ out
about** (make enquiries) se renseigner
sur; (by chance) apprendre; **findings**
npl (Law) conclusions fpl, verdict m; (of
report) constatations fpl

fine [faɪn] adj (weather) beau (belle);
(excellent) excellent(e); (thin, subtle, not
coarse) fin(e); (acceptable) bien inv ▷ adv
(well) très bien; (small) fin, finement
▷ n (Law) amende f; contravention f
▷ vt (Law) condamner à une amende;
donner une contravention à; **he's ~** il va
bien; **the weather is ~** il fait beau; **fine
arts** npl beaux-arts mpl

finger [ˈfɪŋgə*] n doigt m ▷ vt palper,
toucher; **index ~** index m; **fingernail**
n ongle m (de la main); **fingerprint** n
empreinte digitale; **fingertip** n bout
m du doigt

finish [ˈfɪnɪʃ] n fin f; (Sport) arrivée f;
(polish etc) finition f ▷ vt finir, terminer
▷ vi finir, se terminer; **to ~ doing sth**
finir de faire qch; **to ~ third** arriver
ou terminer troisième; **when does
the show ~?** quand est-ce que le
spectacle se termine?; **finish off** vt
finir, terminer; (kill) achever; **finish
up** vi, vt finir

Finland [ˈfɪnlənd] n Finlande f; **Finn**
n Finnois(e), Finlandais(e); **Finnish**
adj finnois(e), finlandais(e) ▷ n (Ling)
finnois m

fir [fəː*] n sapin m

fire [ˈfaɪə*] n feu m; (accidental) incendie
m; (heater) radiateur m ▷ vt (discharge):
to ~ a gun tirer un coup de feu; (fig:
interest) enflammer, animer; (inf:
dismiss) mettre à la porte, renvoyer ▷ vi

(shoot) tirer, faire feu; **~!** au feu!; **on ~** en feu; **to set ~ to sth, set sth on ~** mettre le feu à qch; **fire alarm** *n* avertisseur *m* d'incendie; **firearm** *n* arme *f* à feu; **fire brigade** *n* (*us* **fire department**) (régiment *m* de sapeurs-)pompiers *mpl*; **fire engine** *n* (*BRIT*) pompe *f* à incendie; **fire escape** *n* escalier *m* de secours; **fire exit** *n* issue *f* or sortie *f* de secours; **fire extinguisher** *n* extincteur *m*; **fireman** (*irreg*) *n* pompier *m*; **fireplace** *n* cheminée *f*; **fire station** *n* caserne *f* de pompiers; **fire truck** (*us*) *n* = **fire engine**; **firewall** *n* (*Internet*) pare-feu *m*; **firewood** *n* bois *m* de chauffage; **fireworks** *npl* (*display*) feu(x) *m*(*pl*) d'artifice

firm [fəːm] *adj* ferme ⊳ *n* compagnie *f*, firme *f*; **firmly** *adv* fermement

first [fəːst] *adj* premier(-ière) ⊳ *adv* (*before other people*) le premier, la première; (*before other things*) en premier, d'abord; (*when listing reasons etc*) en premier lieu, premièrement; (*in the beginning*) au début ⊳ *n* (*person: in race*) premier(-ière); (*BRIT Scol*) mention *f* très bien; (*Aut*) première *f*; **the ~ of January** le premier janvier; **at ~** au commencement, au début; **~ of all** tout d'abord, pour commencer; **first aid** *n* premiers secours or soins; **first-aid kit** *n* trousse *f* à pharmacie; **first-class** *adj* (*ticket etc*) de première classe; (*excellent*) excellent(e), exceptionnel(le); (*post*) en tarif prioritaire; **first-hand** *adj* de première main; **first lady** *n* (*us*) femme *f* du président; **firstly** *adv* premièrement, en premier lieu; **first name** *n* prénom *m*; **first-rate** *adj* excellent(e)

fiscal ['fɪskl] *adj* fiscal(e); **fiscal year** *n* exercice financier

fish [fɪʃ] *n* (*pl inv*) poisson *m* ⊳ *vt, vi* pêcher; **~ and chips** poisson frit et frites; **fisherman** (*irreg*) *n* pêcheur *m*; **fish fingers** *npl* (*BRIT*) bâtonnets de poisson (congelés); **fishing** *n* pêche *f*; **to go fishing** aller à la pêche;

fishing boat *n* barque *f* de pêche; **fishing line** *n* ligne *f* (de pêche); **fishmonger** *n* (*BRIT*) marchand *m* de poisson; **fishmonger's (shop)** *n* (*BRIT*) poissonnerie *f*; **fish sticks** *npl* (*us*) = **fish fingers**; **fishy** *adj* (*inf*) suspect(e), louche

fist [fɪst] *n* poing *m*

fit [fɪt] *adj* (*Med, Sport*) en (bonne) forme; (*proper*) convenable; approprié(e) ⊳ *vt* (*subj: clothes*) aller à; (*put in, attach*) installer, poser; (*equip*) équiper, garnir, munir; (*suit*) convenir à ⊳ *vi* (*clothes*) aller; (*parts*) s'adapter; (*in space, gap*) entrer, s'adapter ⊳ *n* (*Med*) accès *m*, crise *f*; (*of anger*) accès; (*of hysterics, jealousy*) crise; **~ to** (*ready to*) en état de; **~ for** (*worthy*) digne de; (*capable*) apte à; **to keep ~** se maintenir en forme; **this dress is a tight/good ~** cette robe est un peu juste/(me) va très bien; **a ~ of coughing** une quinte de toux; **by ~s and starts** par à-coups; **fit in** *vi* (*add up*) cadrer; (*integrate*) s'intégrer; (*to new situation*) s'adapter; **fitness** *n* (*Med*) forme *f* physique; **fitted** *adj* (*jacket, shirt*) ajusté(e); **fitted carpet** *n* moquette *f*; **fitted kitchen** *n* (*BRIT*) cuisine équipée; **fitted sheet** *n* drap-housse *m*; **fitting** *adj* approprié(e) ⊳ *n* (*of dress*) essayage *m*; (*of piece of equipment*) pose *f*, installation *f*; **fitting room** *n* (*in shop*) cabine *f* d'essayage; **fittings** *npl* installations *fpl*

five [faɪv] *num* cinq; **fiver** *n* (*inf: BRIT*) billet *m* de cinq livres; (*: us*) billet de cinq dollars

fix [fɪks] *vt* (*date, amount etc*) fixer; (*sort out*) arranger; (*mend*) réparer; (*make ready: meal, drink*) préparer ⊳ *n*: **to be in a ~** être dans le pétrin; **fix up** *vt* (*meeting*) arranger; **to ~ sb up with sth** faire avoir qch à qn; **fixed** *adj* (*prices etc*) fixe; **fixture** *n* installation *f* (fixe); (*Sport*) rencontre *f* (au programme)

fizzy ['fɪzɪ] *adj* pétillant(e), gazeux(-euse)

flag [flæg] *n* drapeau *m*; (*also:* **~stone**)

dalle f ▷ vi faiblir; fléchir; **flag down**
vt héler, faire signe (de s'arrêter) à;
flagpole n mât m

flair [flɛəʳ] n flair m

flak [flæk] n (Mil) tir antiaérien; (inf:
criticism) critiques fpl

flake [fleɪk] n (of rust, paint) écaille f; (of
snow, soap powder) flocon m ▷ vi (also: ~
off) s'écailler

flamboyant [flæm'bɔɪənt] adj
flamboyant(e), éclatant(e); (person)
haut(e) en couleur

flame [fleɪm] n flamme f

flamingo [flə'mɪŋgəʊ] n flamant
m (rose)

flammable ['flæməbl] adj
inflammable

flan [flæn] n (BRIT) tarte f

flank [flæŋk] n flanc m ▷ vt flanquer

flannel ['flænl] n (BRIT: also: **face ~**)
gant m de toilette; (fabric) flanelle f

flap [flæp] n (of pocket, envelope) rabat
m ▷ vt (wings) battre (de); (of) vi (sail,
flag) claquer

flare [flɛəʳ] n (signal) signal lumineux;
(Mil) fusée éclairante; (in skirt etc)
évasement m; **flares** npl (trousers)
pantalon m à pattes d'éléphant; **flare
up** vi s'embraser; (fig: person) se mettre
en colère, s'emporter; (: revolt) éclater

flash [flæʃ] n éclair m; (also: **news ~**)
flash m (d'information); (Phot) flash
m ▷ vt (switch on) allumer (brièvement);
(direct): **to ~ sth at** braquer qch sur;
(send: message) câbler; (smile) lancer
▷ vi briller; jeter des éclairs; (light
on ambulance etc) clignoter; **a ~ of
lightning** un éclair; **in a ~** en un clin
d'œil; **to ~ one's headlights** faire un
appel de phares; **he ~ed by** or **past** il
passa (devant nous) comme un éclair;
flashback n flashback m, retour m en
arrière; **flashbulb** n ampoule f de flash;
flashlight n lampe f de poche

flask [flɑːsk] n flacon m, bouteille f;
(also: **vacuum ~**) bouteille f thermos®

flat [flæt] adj plat(e); (tyre) dégonflé(e),
à plat; (beer) éventé(e); (battery) à plat;

(denial) catégorique; (Mus) bémol inv;
(: voice) faux (fausse) ▷ n (BRIT:
apartment) appartement m; (Aut)
crevaison f, pneu crevé; (Mus) bémol m;
~ out (work) sans relâche; (race) à fond;
flatten vt (also: **flatten out**) aplatir;
(crop) coucher; (house, city) raser

flatter ['flætəʳ] vt flatter; **flattering** adj
flatteur(-euse); (clothes etc) seyant(e)

flaunt [flɔːnt] vt faire étalage de

flavour etc (us **flavor** etc) ['fleɪvəʳ]
n goût m, saveur f; (of ice cream etc)
parfum m ▷ vt parfumer, aromatiser;
vanilla-~ed à l'arôme de vanille,
vanillé(e); **what ~s do you have?** quels
parfums avez-vous?; **flavouring** n
arôme m (synthétique)

flaw [flɔː] n défaut m; **flawless** adj
sans défaut

flea [fliː] n puce f; **flea market** n
marché m aux puces

flee (pt, pp **fled**) [fliː, fled] vt fuir, s'enfuir
de ▷ vi fuir, s'enfuir

fleece [fliːs] n (of sheep) toison f; (top)
(laine f) polaire f ▷ vt (inf) voler, filouter

fleet [fliːt] n flotte f; (of lorries, cars etc)
parc m; convoi m

fleeting ['fliːtɪŋ] adj fugace,
fugitif(-ive); (visit) très bref (brève)

Flemish ['flemɪʃ] adj flamand(e)
▷ n (Ling) flamand m; **the ~** npl les
Flamands

flesh [fleʃ] n chair f

flew [fluː] pt of **fly**

flex [fleks] n fil m or câble m électrique
(souple) ▷ vt (knee) fléchir; (muscles)
tendre; **flexibility** n flexibilité f;
flexible adj flexible; (person, schedule)
souple; **flexitime** (us **flextime**) n
horaire m variable or à la carte

flick [flɪk] n petit coup; (with finger)
chiquenaude f ▷ vt donner un petit
coup à; (switch) appuyer sur; **flick
through** vt fus feuilleter

flicker ['flɪkəʳ] vi (light, flame) vaciller

flies [flaɪz] npl of **fly**

flight [flaɪt] n vol m; (escape) fuite f;
(also: **~ of steps**) escalier m; **flight**

attendant n steward m, hôtesse f de l'air

flimsy ['flɪmzɪ] adj peu solide; (clothes) trop léger(-ère); (excuse) pauvre, mince

flinch [flɪntʃ] vi tressaillir; **to ~ from** se dérober à, reculer devant

fling [flɪŋ] vt (pt, pp **flung**) jeter, lancer

flint [flɪnt] n silex m; (in lighter) pierre f (à briquet)

flip [flɪp] vt (throw) donner une chiquenaude à; (switch) appuyer sur; (us: pancake) faire sauter; **to ~ sth over** retourner qch

flip-flops ['flɪpflɒps] npl (esp BRIT) tongs fpl

flipper ['flɪpə*] n (of animal) nageoire f; (for swimmer) palme f

flirt [flɜːt] vi flirter ⊳ n flirteur(-euse)

float [fləʊt] n flotteur m; (in procession) char m; (sum of money) réserve f ⊳ vi flotter

flock [flɒk] n (of sheep) troupeau m; (of birds) vol m; (of people) foule f

flood [flʌd] n inondation f; (of letters, refugees etc) flot m ⊳ vt inonder ⊳ vi (place) être inondé; (people): **to ~ into** envahir; **flooding** n inondation f; **floodlight** n projecteur m

floor [flɔː*] n sol m; (storey) étage m; (of sea, valley) fond m ⊳ vt (knock down) terrasser; (baffle) désorienter; **ground ~**, (US) **first ~** rez-de-chaussée m; **first ~**, (US) **second ~** premier étage; **what is it on?** c'est à quel étage?; **floorboard** n planche f (du plancher); **flooring** n sol m; (wooden) plancher m; (covering) revêtement m de sol; **floor show** n spectacle m de variétés

flop [flɒp] n fiasco m ⊳ vi (fail) faire fiasco; (fall) s'affaler, s'effondrer; **floppy** adj lâche, flottant(e) ⊳ n (Comput: also: **floppy disk**) disquette f

flora ['flɔːrə] n flore f

floral ['flɔːrl] adj floral(e); (dress) à fleurs

florist ['flɒrɪst] n fleuriste m/f; **florist's (shop)** n magasin m or boutique f de fleuriste

flotation [fləʊ'teɪʃən] n (of shares)

émission f; (of company) lancement m (en Bourse)

flour ['flaʊə*] n farine f

flourish ['flʌrɪʃ] vi prospérer ⊳ n (gesture) moulinet m

flow [fləʊ] n (of water, traffic etc) écoulement m; (tide, influx) flux m; (of blood, Elec) circulation f; (of river) courant m ⊳ vi couler; (traffic) s'écouler; (robes, hair) flotter

flower ['flaʊə*] n fleur f ⊳ vi fleurir; **flower bed** n parte-bande f; **flowerpot** n pot m (à fleurs)

flown [fləʊn] pp of **fly**

fl. oz. abbr = **fluid ounce**

flu [fluː] n grippe f

fluctuate ['flʌktjʊeɪt] vi varier, fluctuer

fluent ['fluːənt] adj (speech, style) coulant(e), aisé(e); **he speaks ~ French, he's ~ in French** il parle le français couramment

fluff [flʌf] n duvet m; (on jacket, carpet) peluche f; **fluffy** adj duveteux(-euse); (toy) en peluche

fluid ['fluːɪd] n fluide m; (in diet) liquide m ⊳ adj fluide; **fluid ounce** n (BRIT) = 0.028 l; 0.05 pints

fluke [fluːk] n coup m de veine

flung [flʌŋ] pt, pp of **fling**

fluorescent [fluə'rɛsnt] adj fluorescent(e)

fluoride ['fluəraɪd] n fluor m

flurry ['flʌrɪ] n (of snow) rafale f, bourrasque f; **a ~ of activity** un affairement soudain

flush [flʌʃ] n (on face) rougeur f; (fig: of youth etc) éclat m ⊳ vt nettoyer à grande eau ⊳ vi rougir ⊳ adj (level): **~ with** au ras de, de niveau avec; **to ~ the toilet** tirer la chasse (d'eau)

flute [fluːt] n flûte f

flutter ['flʌtə*] n (of panic, excitement) agitation f; (of wings) battement m ⊳ vi (bird) battre des ailes, voleter

fly [flaɪ] n (insect) mouche f; (on trousers: also: **flies**) braguette f ⊳ vb (pt **flew**, pp **flown**) ⊳ vt (plane) piloter; (passengers, *cargo*) transporter (par avion); (*distance*) parcourir ▷ vi voler; (*passengers*) aller en avion; (*escape*) s'enfuir, fuir; (*flag*) se déployer; **fly away, fly off** vi s'envoler; **fly-drive** n formule f avion plus voiture; **flying** n (*activity*) aviation f; (*action*) vol m ▷ adj: **flying visit** visite f éclair inv; **with flying colours** haut la main; **flying saucer** n soucoupe volante; **flyover** n (BRIT: *overpass*) pont routier

FM abbr (Radio: = frequency modulation) FM

foal [fəʊl] n poulain m

foam [fəʊm] n écume f; (*on beer*) mousse f; (*also:* **~ rubber**) caoutchouc m mousse ▷ vi (*liquid*) écumer; (*soapy water*) mousser

focus ['fəʊkəs] n (pl **-es**) foyer m; (*of interest*) centre m ▷ vt (*field glasses etc*) mettre au point ▷ vi: **to ~ (on)** (*with camera*) régler la mise au point (sur); (*with eyes*) fixer son regard (sur); (*concentrate*) se concentrer; **out of/in ~** (*picture*) flou(e)/net(te); (*camera*) pas au point/au point

foetus (*US* **fetus**) ['fiːtəs] n fœtus m

fog [fɒg] n brouillard m; **foggy** adj: **it's foggy** il y a du brouillard; **fog lamp** (*US* **fog light**) n (*Aut*) phare m anti-brouillard

foil [fɔɪl] vt déjouer, contrecarrer ▷ n feuille f de métal; (*kitchen foil*) papier m d'alu(minium); **to act as a ~** to (fig) servir de repoussoir or de faire-valoir à

fold [fəʊld] n (*bend, crease*) pli m; (*Agr*) parc m à moutons; (fig) bercail m ▷ vt plier; **to ~ one's arms** croiser les bras; **fold up** vi (*map etc*) se plier, se replier; (*business*) fermer boutique ▷ vt (*map etc*) plier, replier; **folder** n (*for papers*) chemise f; (*: binder*) classeur m; (*Comput*) dossier m; **folding** adj (*chair, bed*) pliant(e)

foliage ['fəʊlɪɪdʒ] n feuillage m

folk [fəʊk] npl gens mpl ▷ cpd folklorique; **folks** npl (inf: *parents*) famille f, parents mpl; **folklore**

['fəʊklɔː'] n folklore m; **folk music** n musique f folklorique; (*contemporary*) musique folk, folk m; **folk song** n chanson f folklorique; (*contemporary*) chanson folk inv

follow ['fɒləʊ] vt suivre ▷ vi suivre; (*result*) s'ensuivre; **to ~ suit** (fig) faire de même; **follow up** vt (*letter, offer*) donner suite à; (*case*) suivre; **follower** n disciple m/f, partisan(e); **following** adj suivant(e) ▷ n partisans mpl, disciples mpl; **follow-up** n suite f; (*on file, case*) suivi m

fond [fɒnd] adj (*memory, look*) tendre, affectueux(-euse); (*hopes, dreams*) un peu fou (folle); **to be ~ of** aimer beaucoup

food [fuːd] n nourriture f; **food mixer** n mixeur m; **food poisoning** n intoxication f alimentaire; **food processor** n robot m de cuisine; **food stamp** n (*US*) bon m de nourriture (pour indigents)

fool [fuːl] n idiot(e); (*Culin*) mousse f de fruits ▷ vt berner, duper; **fool about, fool around** vi (pej: *waste time*) traînailler, glandouiller; (: *behave foolishly*) faire l'idiot or l'imbécile; **foolish** adj idiot(e), stupide; (*rash*) imprudent(e); **foolproof** adj (*plan etc*) infaillible

foot (pl **feet**) [fʊt, fiːt] n pied m; (*of animal*) patte f; (*measure*) pied (= 30.48 *cm*; 12 *inches*) ▷ vt (*bill*) payer; **on ~** à pied; **footage** n (*Cine: length*) = métrage m; (*: material*) séquences fpl; **foot-and-mouth (disease)** [fʊtənd'maʊθ-] n fièvre f aphteuse; **football** n (*ball*) ballon m (de football); (*sport*: BRIT) football m; (*: US*) football américain; **footballer** n (BRIT) = **football player**; **football match** n (BRIT) match m de foot(ball); **football player** n footballeur(-euse), joueur(-euse) de football; (*US*) joueur(-euse) de football américain; **footbridge** n passerelle f; **foothills** npl contreforts mpl; **foothold** n prise f (de pied); **footing** n (fig) position f; **to lose**

one's footing perdre pied; **footnote** n note f (en bas de page); **footpath** n sentier m; **footprint** n trace f (de pied); **footstep** n pas m; **footwear** n chaussures fpl

KEYWORD

for [fɔːʳ] prep 1 (indicating destination, intention, purpose) pour; **the train for London** le train pour (or à destination de) Londres; **he left for Rome** il est parti pour Rome; **he went for the paper** il est allé chercher le journal; **is this for me?** c'est pour moi?; **it's time for lunch** c'est l'heure du déjeuner; **what's it for?** ça sert à quoi?; **what for?** (why) pourquoi?; (to what end) pour quoi faire?, à quoi bon?; **for sale** à vendre; **to pray for peace** prier pour la paix
2 (on behalf of, representing) pour; **the MP for Hove** le député de Hove; **to work for sb/sth** travailler pour qn/qch; **I'll ask him for you** je vais lui demander pour toi; **G for George** G comme Georges
3 (because of) pour; **for this reason** pour cette raison; **for fear of being criticized** de peur d'être critiqué
4 (with regard to) pour; **it's cold for July** il fait froid pour juillet; **a gift for languages** un don pour les langues
5 (in exchange for): **I sold it for £5** je l'ai vendu 5 livres; **to pay 50 pence for a ticket** payer un billet 50 pence
6 (in favour of) pour; **are you for or against us?** êtes-vous pour ou contre nous?; **I'm all for it** je suis tout à fait pour; **vote for X** votez pour X
7 (referring to distance) pendant, sur; **there are roadworks for 5 km** il y a des travaux sur or pendant 5 km; **we walked for miles** nous avons marché pendant des kilomètres
8 (referring to time) pendant; depuis; pour; **he was away for 2 years** il a été absent pendant 2 ans; **she will be away for a month** elle sera absente

(pendant) un mois; **it hasn't rained for 3 weeks** ça fait 3 semaines qu'il ne pleut pas, il ne pleut pas depuis 3 semaines; **I have known her for years** je la connais depuis des années; **can you do it for tomorrow?** est-ce que tu peux le faire pour demain?
9 (with infinitive clauses): **it is not for me to decide** ce n'est pas à moi de décider; **it would be best for you to leave** le mieux serait que vous partiez; **there is still time for you to do it** vous avez encore le temps de le faire; **for this to be possible ...** pour que cela soit possible ...
10 (in spite of): **for all that** malgré cela, néanmoins; **for all his work/efforts** malgré tout son travail/tous ses efforts; **for all his complaints, he's very fond of her** il a beau se plaindre, il l'aime beaucoup
▷ conj (since, as: rather formal) car

forbid (pt **forbad(e)**, pp **~den**) [fəˈbɪd, -ˈbæd, -ˈbɪdn] vt défendre, interdire; **to ~ sb to do** défendre or interdire à qn de faire; **forbidden** adj défendu(e)

force [fɔːs] n force f ▷ vt forcer; (push) pousser (de force); **to ~ o.s. to do** se forcer à faire; **in ~** (being used: rule, law, prices) en vigueur; (in large numbers) en force; **forced** adj forcé(e); **forceful** adj énergique

ford [fɔːd] n gué m

fore [fɔːʳ] n: **to the ~** en évidence; **forearm** n avant-bras m inv; **forecast** n prévision f, (also: **weather forecast**) prévisions fpl météorologiques, météo f ▷ vt (irreg: like **cast**) prévoir; **forecourt** n (of garage) devant m; **forefinger** n index m; **forefront** n: **in the forefront of** au premier rang or plan de; **foreground** n premier plan; **forehead** [ˈfɔrɪd] n front m

foreign [ˈfɔrɪn] adj étranger(-ère); (trade) extérieur(e); (travel) à l'étranger; **foreign currency** n devises étrangères; **foreigner** n étranger(-ère);

foreign exchange n (system) change m; (money) devises fpl; **Foreign Office** n (BRIT) ministère m des Affaires étrangères; **Foreign Secretary** n (BRIT) ministre m des Affaires étrangères

fore: **foreman** (irreg) n (in construction) contremaître m; **foremost** adj le (la) plus en vue, premier(-ière) ▷ adv: **first and foremost** avant tout, tout d'abord; **forename** n prénom m

forensic [fə'rɛnsɪk] adj: **~ medicine** médecine légale

foresee (pt **foresaw**, pp **~n**) [fɔː'siː, -'sɔː, -'siːn] vt prévoir; **foreseeable** adj prévisible

forest ['fɔrɪst] n forêt f; **forestry** n sylviculture f

forever [fə'rɛvər] adv pour toujours; (fig: endlessly) continuellement

foreword ['fɔːwəːd] n avant-propos m inv

forfeit ['fɔːfɪt] vt perdre

forgave [fə'geɪv] pt of **forgive**

forge [fɔːdʒ] n forge f ▷ vt (signature) contrefaire; (wrought iron) forger; **to ~ money** (BRIT) fabriquer de la fausse monnaie; **forger** n faussaire m; **forgery** n faux m, contrefaçon f

forget (pt **forgot**, pp **forgotten**) [fə'gɛt, -'gɔt, -'gɔtn] vt, vi oublier; **I've forgotten my key/passport** j'ai oublié ma clé/mon passeport; **forgetful** adj distrait(e), étourdi(e)

forgive (pt **forgave**, pp **~n**) [fə'gɪv, -'geɪv, -'gɪvn] vt pardonner; **to ~ sb for sth/for doing sth** pardonner qch à qn/à qn de faire qch

forgot [fə'gɔt] pt of **forget**

forgotten [fə'gɔtn] pp of **forget**

fork [fɔːk] n (for eating) fourchette f; (for gardening) fourche f; (of roads) bifurcation f ▷ vi (road) bifurquer

forlorn [fə'lɔːn] adj (deserted) abandonné(e); (hope, attempt) désespéré(e)

form [fɔːm] n forme f; (Scol) classe f; (questionnaire) formulaire m ▷ vt former; (habit) contracter; **to ~ part**

of sth faire partie de qch; **on top ~** en pleine forme

formal ['fɔːməl] adj (offer, receipt) en bonne et due forme; (person) cérémonieux(-euse); (occasion, dinner) officiel(le); (garden) à la française; (clothes) de soirée; **formality** [fɔː'mælɪtɪ] n formalité f

format ['fɔːmæt] n format m ▷ vt (Comput) formater

formation [fɔː'meɪʃən] n formation f

former ['fɔːmər] adj ancien(ne); (before n) précédent(e); **the ~ ... the latter** le premier ... le second, celui-là ... celui-ci; **formerly** adv autrefois

formidable ['fɔːmɪdəbl] adj redoutable

formula ['fɔːmjulə] n formule f

fort [fɔːt] n fort m

forthcoming [fɔːθ'kʌmɪŋ] adj qui va paraître ou avoir lieu prochainement; (character) ouvert(e), communicatif(-ive); (available) disponible

fortieth ['fɔːtɪɪθ] num quarantième

fortify ['fɔːtɪfaɪ] vt (city) fortifier; (person) remonter

fortnight ['fɔːtnaɪt] n (BRIT) quinzaine f, quinze jours mpl; **fortnightly** adj bimensuel(le) ▷ adv tous les quinze jours

fortress ['fɔːtrɪs] n forteresse f

fortunate ['fɔːtʃənɪt] adj heureux(-euse); (person) chanceux(-euse); **it is ~ that** c'est une chance que, il est heureux que; **fortunately** adv heureusement, par bonheur

fortune ['fɔːtʃən] n chance f; (wealth) fortune f; **fortune-teller** n diseuse f de bonne aventure

forty ['fɔːtɪ] num quarante

forum ['fɔːrəm] n forum m, tribune f

forward ['fɔːwəd] adj (movement, position) en avant, vers l'avant; (not shy) effronté(e); (in time) en avance ▷ adv (also: **~s**) en avant ▷ n (Sport) avant m ▷ vt (letter) faire suivre; (parcel, goods) expédier; (fig) promouvoir, favoriser; **to move ~** avancer; **forwarding address** n adresse f de réexpédition

forward slash n barre f oblique

fossil ['fɒsl] n fossile m

foster ['fɒstə'] vt (encourage) encourager, favoriser; (child) élever (sans adopter); **foster child** n enfant élevé dans une famille d'accueil

foster parent n parent qui élève un enfant sans l'adopter

fought [fɔ:t] pt, pp of **fight**

foul [faul] adj (weather, smell, food) infect(e); (language) ordurier(-ière) ▷ n (Football) faute f ▷ vt (dirty) salir, encrasser; **he's got a ~ temper** il a un caractère de chien; **foul play** n (Law) acte criminel

found [faund] pt, pp of **find** ▷ vt (establish) fonder; **foundation** [faun'deɪʃən] n (act) fondation f; (base) fondement m; (also: **foundation cream**) fond m de teint; **foundations** npl (of building) fondations fpl

founder ['faundə'] n fondateur m ▷ vi couler, sombrer

fountain ['fauntɪn] n fontaine f; **fountain pen** n stylo m (à encre)

four [fɔ:'] num quatre; **on all ~s** à quatre pattes; **four-letter word** n obscénité f, gros mot; **four-poster** n (also: **four-poster bed**) lit m à baldaquin; **fourteen** num quatorze; **fourteenth** num quatorzième; **fourth** num quatrième ▷ n (Aut: also: **fourth gear**) quatrième f; **four-wheel drive** n (Aut: car) voiture f à quatre roues motrices

fowl [faul] n volaille f

fox [fɒks] n renard m ▷ vt mystifier

foyer ['fɔɪeɪ] n (in hotel) vestibule m; (Theat) foyer m

fraction ['frækʃən] n fraction f

fracture ['fræktʃə'] n fracture f ▷ vt fracturer

fragile ['frædʒaɪl] adj fragile

fragment ['frægmənt] n fragment m

fragrance ['freɪɡrəns] n parfum m

frail [freɪl] adj fragile, délicat(e);

(person) frêle

frame [freɪm] n (of building) charpente f; (of human, animal) charpente, ossature f; (of picture) cadre m; (of door, window) encadrement m, chambranle m; (of spectacles: also: **~s**) monture f ▷ vt (picture) encadrer; **~ of mind** disposition f d'esprit; **framework** n structure f

France [frɑ:ns] n la France

franchise ['fræntʃaɪz] n (Pol) droit m de vote; (Comm) franchise f

frank [fræŋk] adj franc (franche) ▷ vt (letter) affranchir; **frankly** adv franchement

frantic ['fræntɪk] adj (hectic) frénétique; (distraught) hors de soi

fraud [frɔ:d] n supercherie f, fraude f, tromperie f; (person) imposteur m

fraught [frɔ:t] adj (tense: person) très tendu(e); (: situation) pénible; **~ with** (difficulties etc) chargé(e) de, plein(e) de

fray [freɪ] vt effilocher ▷ vi s'effilocher

freak [fri:k] n (eccentric person) phénomène m; (unusual event) hasard m extraordinaire; (pej: fanatic): **health food ~** fana m/f ou obsédé(e) de l'alimentation saine ▷ adj (storm) exceptionnel(le); (accident) exceptionnel(le)

freckle ['frɛkl] n tache f de rousseur

free [fri:] adj libre; (gratis) gratuit(e) ▷ vt (prisoner etc) libérer; (jammed object or person) dégager; **is this seat ~?** la place est libre?; **~ (of charge)** gratuitement; **freedom** n liberté f; **Freefone®** n numéro vert; **free gift** n prime f; **free kick** n (Sport) coup franc; **freelance** (journalist etc) indépendant(e), free-lance inv ▷ adv en free-lance; **freely** adv librement; (: liberally) libéralement; **Freepost®** n (BRIT) port payé; **free-range** adj (egg) de ferme; (chicken) fermier; **freeway** n (US) autoroute f; **free will** n libre arbitre m; **of one's own free will** de son plein gré

freeze [fri:z] vb (pt **froze**, pp **frozen**) ▷ vi geler ▷ vt geler; (food) congeler; (prices, salaries) bloquer, geler ▷ n gel m;

(of prices, salaries) blocage m; **freezer** n congélateur m; **freezing** adj: **freezing (cold)** *(room etc)* glacial(e); *(person, hands)* gelé(e), glacé(e) ▷ n: **3 degrees below freezing** 3 degrés au-dessous de zéro; **it's freezing** il fait un froid glacial; **freezing point** n point m de congélation

freight [freɪt] n *(goods)* fret m, cargaison f; *(money charged)* fret, prix m du transport; **freight train** n *(us)* train m de marchandises

French [frɛntʃ] adj français(e) ▷ n *(Ling)* français m; **the ~** npl les Français; **what's the ~ (word) for ...?** comment dit-on ... en français?; **French bean** n *(BRIT)* haricot vert; **French bread** n pain m français; **French dressing** n *(Culin)* vinaigrette f; **French fried potatoes** npl see **French fries**; **Frenchman** *(irreg)* n Français m; **French stick** n = baguette f; **French window** n porte-fenêtre f; **Frenchwoman** *(irreg)* n Française f

frenzy ['frɛnzɪ] n frénésie f

frequency ['friːkwənsɪ] n fréquence f

frequent adj ['friːkwənt] fréquent(e) ▷ vt [frɪ'kwɛnt] fréquenter; **frequently** ['friːkwəntlɪ] adv fréquemment

fresh [frɛʃ] adj frais (fraîche); *(new)* nouveau (nouvelle); *(cheeky)* familier(-ière), culotté(e); **freshen** vi *(wind, air)* fraîchir; **freshen up** vi faire un brin de toilette; **fresher** n *(BRIT University: inf)* bizuth m, étudiant(e) de première année; **freshly** adv nouvellement, récemment; **freshman** *(us: irreg)* n = **fresher**; **freshwater** adj *(fish)* d'eau douce

fret [frɛt] vi s'agiter, se tracasser

Fri abbr (= Friday) ven

friction ['frɪkʃən] n friction f, frottement m

Friday ['fraɪdɪ] n vendredi m

fridge [frɪdʒ] n *(BRIT)* frigo m, frigidaire® m

fried [fraɪd] adj frit(e): **- egg** œuf m sur le plat

friend [frɛnd] n ami(e); **friendly** adj amical(e); *(kind)* sympathique, gentil(le); *(place)* accueillant(e); *(Pol: country)* ami(e) ▷ n *(also: **friendly match**)* match amical; **friendship** n amitié f

fries [fraɪz] *(esp us)* npl = **French fried potatoes**

frigate ['frɪgɪt] n frégate f

fright [fraɪt] n peur f, effroi m; **to give sb a ~** faire peur à qn; **to take ~** prendre peur, s'effrayer; **frighten** vt effrayer, faire peur à; **frightened** adj: **to be frightened (of)** avoir peur (de); **frightening** adj effrayant(e); **frightful** adj affreux(-euse)

frill [frɪl] n *(of dress)* volant m; *(of shirt)* jabot m

fringe [frɪndʒ] n *(BRIT: of hair)* frange f; *(edge: of forest etc)* bordure f

Frisbee® ['frɪzbɪ] n Frisbee® m

fritter ['frɪtə'] n beignet m

frivolous ['frɪvələs] adj frivole

fro [frəu] see **to**

frock [frɔk] n robe f

frog [frɔg] n grenouille f; **frogman** *(irreg)* n homme-grenouille m

 KEYWORD

from [frɔm] prep 1 *(indicating starting place, origin etc)* de; **where do you come from?, where are you from?** d'où venez-vous?; **where has he come from?** d'où arrive-t-il?; **from London to Paris** de Londres à Paris; **to escape from sb/sth** échapper à qn/qch; **a letter/telephone call from my sister** une lettre/un appel de ma sœur; **to drink from the bottle** boire à (même) la bouteille; **tell him from me that ...** dites-lui de ma part que ...

2 *(indicating time)* (à partir) de; **from one o'clock to or until or till two** d'une heure à deux heures; **from January (on)** à partir de janvier

3 (*indicating distance*) de; **the hotel is one kilometre from the beach** l'hôtel est à un kilomètre de la plage

4 (*indicating price, number etc*) de; **prices range from £10 to £50** les prix varient entre 10 livres et 50 livres; **the interest rate was increased from 9% to 10%** le taux d'intérêt est passé de 9% à 10%

5 (*indicating difference*) de; **he can't tell red from green** il ne peut pas distinguer le rouge du vert; **to be different from sb/sth** être différent de qn/qch

6 (*because of, on the basis of*): **from what he says** ce qu'il dit; **weak from hunger** affaibli par la faim

front [frʌnt] n (*of house, dress*) devant m; (*of coach, train*) avant m; (*promenade: also:* **sea ~**) bord m de mer; (*Mil, Pol, Meteorology*) front m; (*fig: appearances*) contenance f, façade f ▷ adj de devant; (*seat, wheel*) avant inv ▷ vi: **in ~ (of)** devant; **front door** n porte f d'entrée; (*of car*) portière f avant; **frontier** ['frʌntɪəʳ] n frontière f; **front page** n première page; **front-wheel drive** n traction f avant

frost [frɒst] n gel m, gelée f; (*also:* **hoar~**) givre m; **frostbite** n gelures fpl; **frosting** n (*esp us: on cake*) glaçage m; **frosty** adj (*window*) couvert(e) de givre; (*weather, welcome*) glacial(e)

froth [frɒθ] n mousse f; écume f

frown [fraʊn] n froncement m de sourcils ▷ vi froncer les sourcils

froze [frəʊz] pt of **freeze**

frozen ['frəʊzn] pp of **freeze** ▷ adj (*food*) congelé(e); (*very cold: person; Comm: assets*) gelé(e)

fruit [fruːt] n (pl inv) fruit m; **fruit juice** n jus m de fruit; **fruit machine** n (BRIT) machine f à sous; **fruit salad** n salade f de fruits

frustrate [frʌs'treɪt] vt frustrer; **frustrated** adj frustré(e)

fry (pt, pp **fried**) [fraɪ, -d] vt (faire) frire;

small ~ le menu fretin; **frying pan** n poêle f (à frire)

ft. abbr = **foot; feet**

fudge [fʌdʒ] n (Culin) sorte de confiserie à base de sucre, de beurre et de lait

fuel [fjuəl] n (*for heating*) combustible m; (*for engine*) carburant m; **fuel tank** n (*in vehicle*) réservoir m de or à carburant

fulfil (us **fulfill**) [ful'fɪl] vt (*function, condition*) remplir; (*order*) exécuter; (*wish, desire*) satisfaire, réaliser

full [ful] adj plein(e); (*details, hotel, bus*) complet(-ète); (*busy: day*) chargé(e); (*skirt*) ample, large ▷ adv: **to know ~ well that** savoir fort bien que; **I'm ~ (up)** j'ai bien mangé; **full employment/ fare** plein emploi/tarif; **a ~ two hours** deux bonnes heures; **at ~ speed** à toute vitesse; **in ~** (*reproduce, quote, pay*) intégralement; (*write name etc*) en toutes lettres; **full-length** adj (*portrait*) en pied; (*coat*) long(ue); **full-length film** long métrage; **full moon** n pleine lune; **full-scale** adj (*model*) grandeur nature inv; (*search, retreat*) complet(-ète), total(e); **full stop** n point m; **full-time** adj, adv (*work*) à plein temps; **fully** adv entièrement, complètement; (*at least*)

fumble ['fʌmbl] vi fouiller, tâtonner; **fumble with** vt fus tripoter

fume [fjuːm] vi (*rage*) rager; **fumes** npl vapeurs fpl, émanations fpl, gaz mpl

fun [fʌn] n amusement m, divertissement m; **to have ~** s'amuser; **for ~** pour rire; **to make ~ of** se moquer de

function ['fʌŋkʃən] n fonction f; (*reception, dinner*) cérémonie f, soirée officielle ▷ vi fonctionner

fund [fʌnd] n caisse f, fonds m; (*source, store*) source f, mine f; **funds** npl (*money*) fonds mpl

fundamental [fʌndə'mɛntl] adj fondamental(e)

funeral ['fjuːnərəl] n enterrement m, obsèques fpl (*more formal occasion*); **funeral director** n entrepreneur m

des pompes funèbres; **funeral parlour** ['pɑːlə'] n (BRIT) dépôt m mortuaire
funfair ['fʌnfɛə'] n (BRIT) fête (foraine)
fungus (pl **fungi**) ['fʌŋɡəs, -ɡaɪ] n champignon m; (mould) moisissure f
funnel ['fʌnl] n entonnoir m; (of ship) cheminée f
funny ['fʌnɪ] adj amusant(e), drôle; (strange) curieux(-euse), bizarre
fur [fəː'] n fourrure f; (BRIT: in kettle etc) (dépôt m de) tartre m; **fur coat** n manteau m de fourrure
furious ['fjʊərɪəs] adj furieux(-euse); (effort) acharné(e)
furnish ['fəːnɪʃ] vt meubler; (supply) fournir; **furnishings** npl mobilier m, articles mpl d'ameublement
furniture ['fəːnɪtʃə'] n meubles mpl, mobilier m; **piece of ~** meuble m
furry ['fəːrɪ] adj (animal) à fourrure; (toy) en peluche
further ['fəːðə'] adj supplémentaire, autre; nouveau (nouvelle) ▷ adv plus loin; (more) davantage; (moreover) de plus ▷ vt faire avancer or progresser, promouvoir; **further education** n enseignement m postscolaire (recyclage, formation professionnelle); **furthermore** adv de plus, en outre
furthest ['fəːðɪst] superlative of **far**
fury ['fjʊərɪ] n fureur f
fuse (US **fuze**) [fjuːz] n fusible m; (for bomb etc) amorce f, détonateur m ▷ vt, vi (metal) fondre; (BRIT: Elec): **to ~ the lights** faire sauter les fusibles or les plombs; **fuse box** n boîte f à fusibles
fusion ['fjuːʒən] n fusion f
fuss [fʌs] n (anxiety, excitement) chichis mpl, façons fpl; (commotion) tapage m; (complaining, trouble) histoire(s) f(pl); **to make a ~** faire des façons (or des histoires); **to make a ~ of sb** dorloter qn; **fussy** adj (person) tatillon(ne), difficile, chichiteux(-euse); (dress, style) tarabiscoté(e)
future ['fjuːtʃə'] adj futur(e) ▷ n avenir m; (Ling) futur m; **futures** npl (Comm) opérations fpl à terme; **in (the) ~** à

l'avenir
fuze [fjuːz] n, vt, vi (US) = **fuse**
fuzzy ['fʌzɪ] adj (Phot) flou(e); (hair) crépu(e)

g

G [dʒiː] *n (Mus)*: **G** sol *m*

g. *abbr* (= gram) g

gadget ['gædʒɪt] *n* gadget *m*

Gaelic ['geɪlɪk] *adj, n (Ling)* gaélique (*m*)

gag [gæg] *n (on mouth)* bâillon *m; (joke)* gag *m ⊳ vt (prisoner etc)* bâillonner

gain [geɪn] *n (improvement)* gain *m; (profit)* gain, profit *m ⊳ vt* gagner ⊳ *vi (watch)* avancer; **to ~ from/by** gagner de/à; **to ~ on sb** *(catch up)* rattraper qn; **to ~ 3lbs (in weight)** prendre 3 livres; **to ~ ground** gagner du terrain

gal. *abbr* = **gallon**

gala ['gɑːlə] *n* gala *m*

galaxy ['gæləksɪ] *n* galaxie *f*

gale [geɪl] *n* coup *m* de vent

gall bladder ['gɔːl-] *n* vésicule *f* biliaire

gallery ['gælərɪ] *n (also: **art ~**)* musée *m; (: private)* galerie *f; (: in theatre)* dernier balcon

gallon ['gæln] *n* gallon *m* (BRIT = 4.543 *l*; US = 3.785 *l*)

gallop ['gæləp] *n* galop *m ⊳ vi* galoper

gallstone ['gɔːlstəun] *n* calcul *m* (biliaire)

gamble ['gæmbl] *n* pari *m*, risque calculé ⊳ *vt, vi* jouer; **to ~ on** *(fig)* miser sur; **gambler** *n* joueur *m*; **gambling** *n* jeu *m*

game [geɪm] *n* jeu *m; (event)* match *m; (of tennis, chess, cards)* partie *f; (Hunting)* gibier *m ⊳ adj (willing)*: **to be ~ (for)** être prêt(e) (à ou pour); **big ~** gros gibier; **games** *npl (Scol)* sport *m; (sport event)* jeux *mpl*; **games console** ['geɪmz-] *n* console *f* de jeux vidéo; **game show** *n* jeu télévisé

gammon ['gæmən] *n (bacon)* quartier *m* de lard fumé; *(ham)* jambon fumé *or* salé

gang [gæŋ] *n* bande *f; (of workmen)* équipe *f*

gangster ['gæŋstə*] *n* gangster *m*, bandit *m*

gap [gæp] *n* trou *m; (in time)* intervalle *m; (difference)*: **~ (between)** écart *m* (entre)

gape [geɪp] *vi (person)* être ou rester bouche bée; *(hole, shirt)* être ouvert(e)

gap year *n* année que certains étudiants prennent pour voyager ou pour travailler avant d'entrer à l'université

garage ['gærɑːʒ] *n* garage *m*; **garage sale** *n* vide-grenier *m*

garbage ['gɑːbɪdʒ] *n (US: rubbish)* ordures *fpl*, détritus *mpl; (inf: nonsense)* âneries *fpl*; **garbage can** *n (US)* poubelle *f*, boîte *f* à ordures; **garbage collector** *n (US)* éboueur *m*

garden ['gɑːdn] *n* jardin *m*; **gardens** *npl (public)* jardin public; *(private)* parc *m*; **garden centre** (BRIT) *n* pépinière *f*, jardinerie *f*; **gardener** *n* jardinier *m*; **gardening** *n* jardinage *m*

garlic ['gɑːlɪk] *n* ail *m*

garment ['gɑːmənt] *n* vêtement *m*

garnish ['gɑːnɪʃ] *(Culin) vt* garnir ⊳ *n* décoration *f*

garrison ['gærɪsn] *n* garnison *f*

gas [gæs] *n* gaz *m; (US: gasoline)* essence *f ⊳ vt* asphyxier; **I can smell ~** ça sent le gaz; **gas cooker** *n* (BRIT) cuisinière *f* à gaz; **gas cylinder** n bouteille f de gaz; **gas fire** n (BRIT) radiateur m à gaz

gasket ['gæskɪt] n (Aut) joint m de culasse

gasoline ['gæsəli:n] n (US) essence f

gasp [gɑ:sp] n halètement m; (of shock etc): **she gave a small ~ of pain** la douleur lui coupa le souffle ▷ vi haleter; (fig) avoir le souffle coupé

gas: gas pedal n (US) accélérateur m; **gas station** n (US) station-service f; **gas tank** n (US Aut) réservoir m d'essence

gate [geɪt] n (of garden) portail m; (of field, at level crossing) barrière f; (of building, town, at airport) porte f

gateau (pl **-x**) ['gætəu, -z] n gros gâteau à la crème

gatecrash ['geɪtkræʃ] vt s'introduire sans invitation dans

gateway ['geɪtweɪ] n porte f

gather ['gæðə'] vt (flowers, fruit) cueillir; (pick up) ramasser; (assemble: objects) rassembler; (: people) réunir; (: information) recueillir; (understand) comprendre; (Sewing) froncer ▷ vi (assemble) se rassembler; **to ~ speed** prendre de la vitesse; **gathering** n rassemblement m

gauge [geɪdʒ] n (instrument) jauge f ▷ vt jauger; (fig) juger de

gave [geɪv] pt of **give**

gay [geɪ] adj (homosexual) homosexuel(le); (colour) gai, vif (vive)

gaze [geɪz] n regard m fixe ▷ vi: **to ~ at** vt fixer du regard

GB abbr = **Great Britain**

GCSE n abbr (BRIT: = General Certificate of Secondary Education) examen passé à l'âge de 16 ans sanctionnant les connaissances de l'élève

gear [gɪə'] n matériel m, équipement m; (Tech) engrenage m; (Aut) vitesse f ▷ vt (fig: adapt) adapter; **top** or (US) **high/low ~** quatrième (or cinquième)/première vitesse; **in ~** en prise; **gear up** vi: **to ~ up (to do)** se préparer (à faire); **gear box** n boîte f de vitesse; **gear**

lever n levier m de vitesse; **gear shift** (US) n = **gear lever**; **gear stick** (BRIT) n = **gear lever**

geese [gi:s] npl of **goose**

gel [dʒɛl] n gelée f

gem [dʒɛm] n pierre précieuse

Gemini ['dʒɛmɪnaɪ] n les Gémeaux mpl

gender ['dʒɛndə'] n genre m; (person's sex) sexe m

gene [dʒi:n] n (Biol) gène m

general ['dʒɛnərl] n général m ▷ adj général(e); **in ~** en général; **general anaesthetic** (US **general anesthetic**) n anésthesie générale; **general election** n élection(s) législative(s); **generalize** vi généraliser; **generally** adv généralement; **general practitioner** n généraliste m/f; **general store** n épicerie f

generate ['dʒɛnəreɪt] vt engendrer; (electricity) produire

generation [dʒɛnə'reɪʃən] n génération f; (of electricity etc) production f

generator ['dʒɛnəreɪtə'] n générateur m

generosity [dʒɛnə'rɔsɪtɪ] n générosité f

generous ['dʒɛnərəs] adj généreux(-euse); (copious) copieux(-euse)

genetic [dʒɪ'nɛtɪk] adj génétique; **~ engineering** ingénierie m génétique; **~ fingerprinting** système m d'empreinte génétique; **genetically modified** adj (food etc) génétiquement modifié(e); **genetics** n génétique f

Geneva [dʒɪ'ni:və] n Genève

genitals ['dʒɛnɪtlz] npl organes génitaux

genius ['dʒi:nɪəs] n génie m

gent [dʒɛnt] n abbr (BRIT inf) = **gentleman**

gentle ['dʒɛntl] adj doux (douce); (breeze, touch) léger(-ère)

gentleman (irreg) ['dʒɛntlmən] n monsieur m; (well-bred man) gentleman m

gently ['dʒɛntlɪ] adv doucement

gents [dʒɛnts] n W.-C. mpl (pour hommes)

genuine ['dʒɛnjuɪn] adj véritable, authentique; (person, emotion) sincère; **genuinely** adv sincèrement, vraiment

geographic(al) [dʒɪə'græfɪk(l)] adj géographique

geography [dʒɪ'ɔgrəfɪ] n géographie f

geology [dʒɪ'ɔlədʒɪ] n géologie f

geometry [dʒɪ'ɔmɪtrɪ] n géométrie f

geranium [dʒɪ'reɪnɪəm] n géranium m

geriatric [dʒɛrɪ'ætrɪk] adj gériatrique
▷ n patient(e) gériatrique

germ [dʒɜːm] n (Med) microbe m

German ['dʒɜːmən] adj allemand(e)
▷ n Allemand(e) m/f; (Ling) allemand m;
German measles n rubéole f

Germany ['dʒɜːmənɪ] n Allemagne f

gesture ['dʒɛstʃə] n geste m

KEYWORD

get [gɛt] (pt, pp **got**, pp **gotten** (us)) vi
1 (become, be) devenir; **to get old/tired** devenir vieux/fatigué, vieillir/se fatiguer; **to get drunk** s'enivrer; **to get dirty** se salir; **to get married** se marier; **when do I get paid?** quand est-ce que je serai payé?; **it's getting late** il se fait tard

2 (go): **to get to/from** aller à/de; **to get home** rentrer chez soi; **how did you get here?** comment es-tu arrivé ici?

3 (begin) commencer or se mettre à; **to get to know sb** apprendre à connaître qn; **I'm getting to like him** je commence à l'apprécier; **let's get going** or **started** allons-y

4 (modal aux vb): **you've got to do it** il faut que vous le fassiez; **I've got to tell the police** je dois le dire à la police
▷ vt **1**: **to get sth done** (do) faire qch; (have done) faire faire qch; **to get sth/sb ready** préparer qch/qn; **to get one's hair cut** se faire couper les cheveux; **to get the car going** or (faire) démarrer la voiture; **to get sb to do sth**

faire faire qch à qn

2 (obtain: money, permission, results) obtenir, avoir; (buy) acheter; (find: job, flat) trouver; (fetch: person, doctor, object) aller chercher; **to get sth for sb** procurer qch à qn; **can I get you a drink?** est-ce que je peux vous servir à boire?

3 (receive: present, letter) recevoir, avoir; (acquire: reputation) avoir; (prize) obtenir; **what did you get for your birthday?** qu'est-ce que tu as eu pour ton anniversaire?; **how much did you get for the painting?** combien avez-vous vendu le tableau?

4 (catch) prendre, saisir, attraper; (hit: target etc) atteindre; **to get sb by the arm/throat** prendre or saisir or attraper qn par le bras/à la gorge; **get him!** arrête-le!; **the bullet got him in the leg** il a pris la balle dans la jambe

5 (take, move): **to get sth to sb** faire parvenir qch à qn; **do you think we'll get it through the door?** on arrivera à le faire passer par la porte?

6 (catch, take: plane, bus etc) prendre; **where do I get the train for Birmingham?** où prend-on le train pour Birmingham?

7 (understand) comprendre, saisir; (hear) entendre; **I've got it!** j'ai compris!; **I don't get your meaning** je ne vois or comprends pas ce que vous voulez dire; **I didn't get your name** je n'ai pas entendu votre nom

8 (have, possess): **to have got** avoir; **how many have you got?** vous en avez combien?

9 (illness) avoir; **I've got a cold** j'ai le rhume; **she got pneumonia and died** elle a fait une pneumonie et elle est morte

get away vi partir, s'en aller; (escape) s'échapper

get away with vt fus (punishment) en être quitte pour; (crime etc) se faire pardonner

get back vi (return) rentrer
▷ vt récupérer, recouvrer; **when do we get back?** quand serons-nous de retour?
get in vi entrer; (arrive home) rentrer; (train) arriver
get into vt fus entrer dans; (car, train etc) monter dans; (clothes) mettre, enfiler, endosser; **to get into bed/a rage** se mettre au lit/en colère
get off vi (from train etc) descendre; (depart: person, car) s'en aller
▷ vt (remove: clothes, stain) enlever
▷ vt fus (train, bus) descendre de; **where do I get off?** où est-ce que je dois descendre?
get on vi (at exam etc) se débrouiller; (agree): **to get on (with)** s'entendre (avec); **how are you getting on?** comment ça va?
▷ vt fus monter dans; (horse) monter sur
get out vi sortir; (of vehicle) descendre
▷ vt sortir
get out of vt fus sortir de; (duty etc) échapper à, se soustraire à
get over vt fus (illness) se remettre de
get through vi (Tel) avoir la communication; **to get through to sb** atteindre qn
get up vi (rise) se lever
▷ vt fus monter

getaway ['gɛtəweɪ] n fuite f
Ghana ['gɑːnə] n Ghana m
ghastly ['gɑːstlɪ] adj atroce, horrible
ghetto ['gɛtəu] n ghetto m
ghost [gəust] n fantôme m, revenant m
giant ['dʒaɪənt] n géant(e) f ▷ adj géant(e), énorme
gift [gɪft] n cadeau m; (donation, talent) don m; **gifted** adj doué(e); **gift shop** (us **gift store**) n boutique f de cadeaux; **gift token, gift voucher** n chèque-cadeau m
gig [gɪg] n (inf: concert) concert m
gigabyte ['dʒɪgəbaɪt] n gigaoctet m
gigantic [dʒaɪ'gæntɪk] adj gigantesque

giggle ['gɪgl] vi pouffer, ricaner sottement
gills [gɪlz] npl (of fish) ouïes fpl, branchies fpl
gilt [gɪlt] n dorure f ▷ adj doré(e)
gimmick ['gɪmɪk] n truc m
gin [dʒɪn] n gin m
ginger ['dʒɪndʒəʳ] n gingembre m
gipsy ['dʒɪpsɪ] n = **gypsy**
giraffe [dʒɪ'rɑːf] n girafe f
girl [gəːl] n fille f, fillette f; (young unmarried woman) jeune fille; (daughter) fille; **an English ~** une jeune Anglaise; **girl band** n girls band m; **girlfriend** n (of girl) amie f; (of boy) petite amie; **Girl Guide** n (BRIT) éclaireuse f; (Roman Catholic) guide f; **Girl Scout** n (US) = **Girl Guide**
gist [dʒɪst] n essentiel m
give [gɪv] vb (pt **gave**, pp **~n**) ▷ vt donner ▷ vi (break) céder; (stretch: fabric) se relâcher; **to ~ sb sth, ~ sth to sb** donner qch à qn; (gift) offrir qch à qn; (message) transmettre qch à qn; **to ~ sb a call/kiss** appeler/embrasser qn; **to ~ a cry/sigh** pousser un cri/un soupir; **give away** vt donner; (give free) faire cadeau de; (betray) trahir; (disclose) révéler; **give back** vt rendre; **give in** vi céder ▷ vt donner; **give out** vt (food etc) distribuer; **give up** vi renoncer ▷ vt renoncer à; **to ~ up smoking** arrêter de fumer; **to ~ o.s. up** se rendre
given ['gɪvn] pp of **give** ▷ adj (fixed: time, amount) donné(e), déterminé(e) ▷ conj: **~ the circumstances ...** étant donné les circonstances ..., vu les circonstances ...; **~ that ...** étant donné que ...
glacier ['glæsɪəʳ] n glacier m
glad [glæd] adj content(e); **gladly** ['glædlɪ] adv volontiers
glamorous ['glæmərəs] adj (person) séduisant(e); (job) prestigieux(-euse)
glamour (us **glamor**) ['glæməʳ] n éclat m, prestige m
glance [glɑːns] n coup m d'œil ▷ vi: **to ~**

at jeter un coup d'œil à
gland [glænd] n glande f
glare [glɛəʳ] n (of anger) regard furieux; (of light) lumière éblouissante; (of publicity) feux mpl ▷ vi briller d'un éclat aveuglant; **to ~ at** lancer un regard or des regards furieux à; **glaring** adj (mistake) criant(e), qui saute aux yeux
glass [glɑːs] n verre m; **glasses** npl (spectacles) lunettes fpl
glaze [gleɪz] vt (door) vitrer; (pottery) vernir ▷ n vernis m
gleam [gliːm] vi luire, briller
glen [glɛn] n vallée f
glide [glaɪd] vi glisser; (Aviat, bird) planer; **glider** n (Aviat) planeur m
glimmer [ˈɡlɪməʳ] n lueur f
glimpse [glɪmps] n vision passagère, aperçu m ▷ vt entrevoir, apercevoir
glint [glɪnt] vi étinceler
glisten [ˈglɪsn] vi briller, luire
glitter [ˈglɪtəʳ] vi scintiller, briller
global [ˈgləubl] adj (world-wide) mondial(e); (overall) global(e); **globalization** n mondialisation f; **global warming** n réchauffement m de la planète
globe [gləub] n globe m
gloom [gluːm] n obscurité f; (sadness) tristesse f, mélancolie f; **gloomy** adj (person) morose; (place, outlook) sombre
glorious [ˈglɔːrɪəs] adj glorieux(-euse); (beautiful) splendide
glory [ˈglɔːrɪ] n gloire f; splendeur f
gloss [glɔs] n (shine) brillant m, vernis m; (also: ~ **paint**) peinture brillante or laquée
glossary [ˈglɔsərɪ] n glossaire m, lexique m
glossy [ˈglɔsɪ] adj brillant(e), luisant(e) ▷ n (also: ~ **magazine**) revue f de luxe
glove [glʌv] n gant m; **glove compartment** n (Aut) boîte f à gants, vide-poches m inv
glow [gləu] vi rougeoyer; (face) rayonner; (eyes) briller
glucose [ˈgluːkəus] n glucose m
glue [gluː] n colle f ▷ vt coller

GM abbr (= genetically modified) génétiquement modifié(e)
gm abbr (= gram) g
GMO n abbr (= genetically modified organism) OGM m
GMT abbr (= Greenwich Mean Time) GMT
gnaw [nɔː] vt ronger
go [gəu] vb (pt **went**, pp **gone**) ▷ vi aller; (depart) partir, s'en aller; (work) marcher; (break) céder; (time) passer; (be sold): **to go for £10** se vendre 10 livres; (become): **to go pale/mouldy** pâlir/moisir ▷ n (pl **goes**): **to have a go (at)** essayer (de faire); **to be on the go** être en mouvement; **whose go is it?** à qui est-ce de jouer?; **he's going to do it** il va le faire, il est sur le point de le faire; **to go for a walk** aller se promener; **to go dancing/shopping** aller danser/faire les courses; **to go and see sb, go to see sb** aller voir qn; **how did it go?** comment est-ce que ça s'est passé?; **to go round the back/by the shop** passer par derrière/devant le magasin; **... to go** (US: food) ... à emporter; **go ahead** vi (take place) avoir lieu; (get going) y aller; **go away** vi partir, s'en aller; **go back** vi rentrer; revenir; (go again) retourner; **go by** vi (years, time) passer, s'écouler ▷ vt fus s'en tenir à; (believe) en croire; **go down** vi descendre; (number, price, amount) baisser; (ship) couler; (sun) se coucher ▷ vt fus descendre; **go for** vt fus (fetch) aller chercher; (like) aimer; (attack) s'en prendre à; attaquer; **go in** vi entrer; **go into** vt fus entrer dans; (investigate) étudier, examiner; (embark on) se lancer dans; **go off** vi partir, s'en aller; (food) se gâter; (milk) tourner; (bomb) sauter; (alarm clock) sonner; (alarm) se déclencher; (lights etc) s'éteindre; (event) se dérouler ▷ vt fus ne plus aimer; **the gun went off** le coup est parti; **go on** vi continuer; (happen) se passer; (lights) s'allumer ▷ vt fus: **to go on doing** continuer à faire; **go out** vi sortir; (fire, light) s'éteindre;

(*tide*) descendre; **to go out with sb** sortir avec qn; **go over** *vi, vt fus* (*check*) revoir, vérifier; **go past** *vt fus*: **to go past sth** passer devant qch; **go round** *vi* (*circulate: news, rumour*) circuler; (*revolve*) tourner; (*suffice*) suffire (pour tout le monde); (*visit*): **to go round to sb's** passer chez qn; aller chez qn; (*make a detour*): **to go round (by)** faire un détour (par); **go through** *vt fus* (*town etc*) traverser; (*search through*) fouiller; (*suffer*) subir; **go up** *vi* monter; (*price*) augmenter ▷ *vt fus* gravir; **go with** *vt fus* aller avec; **go without** *vt fus* se passer de

go-ahead ['gəʊəhɛd] *adj* dynamique, entreprenant(e) ▷ *n* feu vert

goal [gəʊl] *n* but *m*; **goalkeeper** *n* gardien *m* de but; **goal-post** *n* poteau *m* de but

goat [gəʊt] *n* chèvre *f*

gobble ['gɔbl] *vt* (*also:* **~ down, ~ up**) engloutir

god [gɔd] *n* dieu *m*; **G~** Dieu; **godchild** *n* filleul(e); **goddaughter** *n* filleule *f*; **goddess** *n* déesse *f*; **godfather** *n* parrain *m*; **godmother** *n* marraine *f*; **godson** *n* filleul *m*

goggles ['gɔglz] *npl* (*for skiing etc*) lunettes (protectrices); (*for swimming*) lunettes de piscine

going ['gəʊɪŋ] *n* (*conditions*) état *m* du terrain ▷ *adj*: **the ~ rate** le tarif (en vigueur)

gold [gəʊld] *n* or *m* ▷ *adj* en or; (*reserves*) d'or; **golden** *adj* (*made of gold*) en or; (*gold in colour*) doré(e); **goldfish** *n* poisson *m* rouge; **goldmine** *n* mine *f* d'or; **gold-plated** *adj* plaqué(e) or *inv*

golf [gɔlf] *n* golf *m*; **golf ball** *n* balle *f* de golf; (*on typewriter*) boule *f*; **golf club** *n* club *m* de golf; (*stick*) club *m*, crosse *f* de golf; **golf course** *n* terrain *m* de golf; **golfer** *n* joueur(-euse) de golf

gone [gɔn] *pp of* **go**

gong [gɔŋ] *n* gong *m*

good [gʊd] *adj* bon(ne); (*kind*) gentil(le); (*child*) sage; (*weather*) beau (belle) ▷ *n*

bien *m*; **goods** *npl* marchandise *f*, articles *mpl*; **~!** bon!, très bien!; **to be ~ at** être bon en; **to be ~ for** être bon pour; **it's no ~ complaining** cela ne sert à rien de se plaindre; **to make ~** (*deficit*) combler; (*losses*) compenser; **for ~** (*for ever*) pour de bon, une fois pour toutes; **would you be ~ enough to …?** auriez-vous la bonté or l'amabilité de …?; **is this any ~?** (*will it do?*) est-ce que ceci fera l'affaire?, est-ce que cela peut vous rendre service?; (*what's it like?*) qu'est-ce que ça vaut?; **a ~ deal (of)** beaucoup (de); **a ~ many** beaucoup de; **~ morning/afternoon!** bonjour!; **~ evening!** bonsoir!; **~ night!** bonsoir!; (*on going to bed*) bonne nuit!; **goodbye** *excl* au revoir!; **to say goodbye to sb** dire au revoir à qn; **Good Friday** *n* Vendredi saint; **good-looking** *adj* beau (belle), bien *inv*; **good-natured** *adj* (*person*) qui a un bon naturel; **goodness** *n* (*of person*) bonté *f*; **for goodness sake!** je vous en prie!; **goodness gracious!** mon Dieu!; **goods train** *n* (BRIT) train *m* de marchandises; **goodwill** *n* bonne volonté

goose (*pl* **geese**) [guːs, giːs] *n* oie *f*; **gooseberry** ['guzbəri] *n* groseille *f* à maquereau; **to play ~** (BRIT) tenir la chandelle

goose bumps, goose pimples *npl* chair *f* de poule

gorge [gɔːdʒ] *n* gorge *f* ▷ *vt*: **to ~ o.s. (on)** se gorger (de)

gorgeous ['gɔːdʒəs] *adj* splendide, superbe

gorilla [gə'rɪlə] *n* gorille *m*

gosh (*inf*) [gɔʃ] *excl* mince alors!

gospel ['gɔspl] *n* évangile *m*

gossip ['gɔsɪp] *n* (*chat*) bavardages *mpl*; (*malicious*) commérage *m*, cancans *mpl*; (*person*) commère *f* ▷ *vi* bavarder; cancaner, faire des commérages; **gossip column** *n* (*Press*) échos *mpl*

got [gɔt] *pt, pp of* **get**

gotten ['gɔtn] (US) *pp of* **get**

gourmet ['gʊəmeɪ] *n* gourmet *m*,

gastronome m/f
govern ['gʌvən] vt gouverner;
(influence) déterminer; **government**
n gouvernement m; (BRIT: ministers)
ministère m; **governor** n (of colony,
state, bank) gouverneur m; (of school,
hospital etc) administrateur(-trice);
(BRIT: of prison) directeur(-trice)
gown [gaun] n robe f; (of teacher, BRIT:
of judge) toge f
G.P. n abbr (Med) = **general practitioner**
grab [græb] vt saisir, empoigner ▷ vi: **to**
~ at essayer de saisir
grace [greis] n grâce f ▷ vt (honour)
honorer; (adorn) orner; **5 days' ~**
un répit de 5 jours; **graceful** adj
gracieux(-euse), élégant(e); **gracious**
['greiʃəs] adj bienveillant(e)
grade [greid] n (Comm: quality) qualité
f; (size) calibre m; (type) catégorie
f; (in hierarchy) grade m, échelon m;
(Scol) note f; (us: school class) classe
f; (: gradient) pente f ▷ vt classer; (by
size) calibrer; **grade crossing** n (us)
passage m à niveau; **grade school** n
(US) école f primaire
gradient ['greidiənt] n inclinaison
f, pente f
gradual ['grædjuəl] adj graduel(le),
progressif(-ive); **gradually** adv peu à
peu, graduellement
graduate n ['grædjuit] diplômé(e)
d'université; (us: of high school)
diplômé(e) de fin d'études ▷ vi
['grædjueit] obtenir un diplôme
d'université (or de fin d'études);
graduation [grædju'eiʃən] n
cérémonie f de remise des diplômes
graffiti [grə'fi:ti] npl graffiti mpl
graft [grɑ:ft] n (Agr, Med) greffe f;
(bribery) corruption f ▷ vt greffer; **hard**
~ (BRIT: inf) boulot acharné
grain [grein] n (single piece) grain m; (no
pl: cereals) céréales fpl; (us: corn) blé m
gram [græm] n gramme m
grammar ['græməʳ] n grammaire f;
grammar school n (BRIT) lycée m
gramme [græm] n = **gram**

gran (inf) [græn] n (BRIT) mamie f (inf),
mémé f (inf)
grand [grænd] adj magnifique,
splendide; (gesture etc) noble; **grandad**
(inf) n = **granddad**; **grandchild** (pl
-ren) n petit-fils m, petite-fille f;
grandchildren npl petits-enfants;
granddad n (inf) papy m (inf), papi
m (inf); **pépé** m (inf); **granddaughter**
n petite-fille f; **grandfather** n
grand-père m; **grandma** n (inf)
gran; **grandmother** n grand-
mère f; **grandpa** n (inf) = **granddad**;
grandparents npl grands-parents mpl;
grand piano n piano m à queue; **Grand**
Prix ['grɑ̃:'pri:] n (Aut) grand prix
automobile; **grandson** n petit-fils m
granite ['grænit] n granit m
granny ['græni] n (inf) = **gran**
grant [grɑ:nt] vt accorder; (a request)
accéder à; (admit) concéder ▷ n (Scol)
bourse f; (Admin) subside m, subvention
f; **to take sth for ~ed** considérer qch
comme acquis; **to take sb for ~ed**
considérer qn comme faisant partie
du décor
grape [greip] n raisin m
grapefruit ['greipfru:t] n
pamplemousse m
graph [grɑ:f] n graphique m, courbe f;
graphic ['græfik] adj graphique; (vivid)
vivant(e); **graphics** n (art) arts mpl
graphiques; (process) graphisme m
▷ npl (drawings) illustrations fpl
grasp [grɑ:sp] vt saisir ▷ n (grip) prise f;
(fig) compréhension f, connaissance f
grass [grɑ:s] n herbe f; (lawn) gazon m;
grasshopper n sauterelle f
grate [greit] n grille f de cheminée ▷ vi
grincer ▷ vt (Culin) râper
grateful ['greitful] adj
reconnaissant(e)
grater ['greitəʳ] n râpe f
gratitude ['grætitju:d] n gratitude f
grave [greiv] n tombe f ▷ adj grave,
sérieux(-euse)
gravel ['grævl] n gravier m
gravestone ['greivstəun] n pierre

tombale

graveyard ['greivjɑːd] n cimetière m

gravity ['græviti] n (Physics) gravité f; pesanteur f; (seriousness) gravité

gravy ['greivi] n jus m (de viande), sauce f (au jus de viande)

gray [grei] adj (US) = **grey**

graze [greiz] vi paître, brouter ▷ vt (touch lightly) frôler, effleurer; (scrape) écorcher ▷ n écorchure f

grease [griːs] n (fat) graisse f; (lubricant) lubrifiant m ▷ vt graisser; lubrifier; **greasy** adj gras(se), graisseux(-euse); (hands, clothes) graisseux

great [greit] adj grand(e); (heat, pain etc) très fort(e), intense; (inf) formidable; **Great Britain** n Grande-Bretagne f; **great-grandfather** n arrière-grand-père m; **great-grandmother** n arrière-grand-mère f; **greatly** adv très, grandement; (with verbs) beaucoup

Greece [griːs] n Grèce f

greed [griːd] n (also: **~iness**) avidité f; (for food) gourmandise f; **greedy** adj avide; (for food) gourmand(e)

Greek [griːk] adj grec (grecque) ▷ n Grec (Grecque); (Ling) grec m

green [griːn] adj vert(e); (inexperienced) (bien) jeune, naïf(-ive); (ecological: product etc) écologique ▷ n (colour) vert m; (on golf course) green m; (stretch of grass) pelouse f; **greens** npl (vegetables) légumes verts; **green card** n (Aut) carte verte; (US: work permit) permis m de travail; **greengage** n reine-claude f; **greengrocer** n (BRIT) marchand m de fruits et légumes; **greengrocer's (shop)** n magasin m de fruits et légumes; **greenhouse** n serre f; **greenhouse effect** n: **the greenhouse effect** l'effet m de serre

Greenland ['griːnlənd] n Groenland m

green salad n salade verte

greet [griːt] vt accueillir; **greeting** n salutation f; **Christmas/birthday greetings** souhaits mpl de Noël/de bon anniversaire; **greeting(s) card** n carte f de vœux

grew [gruː] pt of **grow**

grey (US **gray**) [grei] adj gris(e); (dismal) sombre; **grey-haired** adj aux cheveux gris; **greyhound** n lévrier m

grid [grid] n grille f; (Elec) réseau m; **gridlock** n (traffic jam) embouteillage m

grief [griːf] n chagrin m, douleur f

grievance ['griːvəns] n doléance f, grief m; (cause for complaint) grief

grieve [griːv] vi avoir du chagrin; se désoler ▷ vt faire de la peine à, affliger; **to ~ for sb** pleurer qn

grill [gril] n (on cooker) gril m; (also: **mixed ~**) grillade(s) f(pl) ▷ vt (BRIT) griller; (inf: question) cuisiner

grille [gril] n grillage m; (Aut) calandre f

grim [grim] adj sinistre, lugubre; (serious, stern) sévère

grime [graim] n crasse f

grin [grin] n large sourire m ▷ vi sourire

grind [graind] vb (pt, pp **ground**) ▷ vt écraser; (coffee, pepper etc) moudre; (US: meat) hacher ▷ n (work) corvée f

grip [grip] n (handclasp) poigne f; (control) prise f; (handle) poignée f; (holdall) sac m de voyage ▷ vt saisir, empoigner; (viewer, reader) captiver; **to come to ~s with** se colleter avec, en venir aux prises avec; **to ~ the road** (Aut) adhérer à la route; **gripping** adj prenant(e), palpitant(e)

grit [grit] n gravillon m; (courage) cran m ▷ vt (road) sabler; **to ~ one's teeth** serrer les dents

grits [grits] npl (US) gruau m de maïs

groan [grəun] n (of pain) gémissement m ▷ vi gémir

grocer ['grəusə²] n épicier m; **groceries** npl provisions fpl; **grocer's (shop)**, **grocery** n épicerie f

groin [grɔin] n aine f

groom [gruːm] n (for horses) palefrenier m; (also: **bride~**) marié m ▷ vt (horse) panser; (fig): **to ~ sb for** former qn pour

groove [gruːv] n sillon m, rainure f

grope [grəup] vi tâtonner; **to ~ for** chercher à tâtons

gross [grəʊs] *adj* grossier(-ière); (*Comm*) brut(e); **grossly** *adv* (*greatly*) très, grandement

grotesque [grə'tɛsk] *adj* grotesque

ground [graʊnd] *pt, pp of* **grind** ▷ *n* sol *m*, terre *f*; (*land*) terrain *m*, terres *fpl*; (*Sport*) terrain; (*reason: gen pl*) raison *f*; (*US: also:* **~ wire**) terre *f* ▷ *vt* (*plane*) empêcher de décoller, retenir au sol; (*US Elec*) équiper d'une prise de terre; **grounds** *npl* (*gardens etc*) parc *m*, domaine *m*; (*of coffee*) marc *m*; **on the ~, to the ~** par terre; **to gain/lose ~** gagner/perdre du terrain; **ground floor** *n* (*BRIT*) rez-de-chaussée *m*; **groundsheet** *n* (*BRIT*) tapis *m* de sol; **groundwork** *n* préparation *f*

group [gruːp] *n* groupe *m* ▷ *vt* (*also:* **~ together**) grouper ▷ *vi* (*also:* **~ together**) se grouper

grouse [graʊs] *n* (*pl inv: bird*) grouse *f* (*sorte de coq de bruyère*) ▷ *vi* (*complain*) rouspéter, râler

grovel ['grɒvl] *vi* (*fig*): **to ~ (before)** ramper (devant)

grow (*pt* **grew**, *pp* **~n**) [grəʊ, gruː, grəʊn] *vi* (*plant*) pousser, croître; (*person*) grandir; (*increase*) augmenter, se développer; (*become*) devenir: **to ~ rich/weak** s'enrichir/s'affaiblir ▷ *vt* cultiver, faire pousser; (*hair, beard*) laisser pousser; **grow on** *vt fus: that painting is ~ing on me** je finirai par aimer ce tableau; **grow up** *vi* grandir

growl [graʊl] *vi* grogner

grown [grəʊn] *pp of* **grow**; **grown-up** *n* adulte *m/f*, grande personne

growth [grəʊθ] *n* croissance *f*, développement *m*; (*what has grown*) pousse *f*, poussée *f*; (*Med*) grosseur *f*, tumeur *f*

grub [grʌb] *n* larve *f*; (*inf: food*) bouffe *f*

grubby ['grʌbɪ] *adj* crasseux(-euse)

grudge [grʌdʒ] *n* rancune *f* ▷ *vt*: **to ~ sb sth** (*in giving*) donner qch à qn à contre-cœur; (*resent*) reprocher qch à qn; **to bear sb a ~ (for)** garder rancune or en vouloir à qn (de)

gruelling (*US* **grueling**) ['grʊəlɪŋ] *adj* exténuant(e)

gruesome ['gruːsəm] *adj* horrible

grumble ['grʌmbl] *vi* rouspéter, ronchonner

grumpy ['grʌmpɪ] *adj* grincheux(-euse)

grunt [grʌnt] *vi* grogner

guarantee [gærən'tiː] *n* garantie *f* ▷ *vt* garantir

guard [gɑːd] *n* garde *f*; (*one man*) garde *m*; (*BRIT Rail*) chef *m* de train; (*safety device: on machine*) dispositif *m* de sûreté; (*also:* **fire~**) garde-feu *m inv* ▷ *vt* garder, surveiller; (*protect*): **to ~ sb/sth (against or from)** protéger qn/qch (contre); **to be on one's ~** (*fig*) être sur ses gardes; **guardian** *n* gardien(ne); (*of minor*) tuteur(-trice)

guerrilla [gə'rɪlə] *n* guérillero *m*

guess [gɛs] *vi* deviner ▷ *vt* deviner; (*estimate*) évaluer; (*US*) croire, penser ▷ *n* supposition *f*, hypothèse *f*; **to take** *or* **have a ~** essayer de deviner

guest [gɛst] *n* invité(e); (*in hotel*) client(e); **guest house** *n* pension *f*; **guest room** *n* chambre *f* d'amis

guidance ['gaɪdəns] *n* (*advice*) conseils *mpl*

guide [gaɪd] *n* (*person*) guide *m/f*; (*book*) guide *m*; (*also:* **Girl G~**) éclaireuse *f*; (*Roman Catholic*) guide *f* ▷ *vt* guider; **is there an English-speaking ~?** est-ce que l'un des guides parle anglais?; **guidebook** *n* guide *m*; **guide dog** *n* chien *m* d'aveugle; **guided tour** *n* visite guidée; **what time does the guided tour start?** la visite guidée commence à quelle heure?; **guidelines** *npl* (*advice*) instructions générales, conseils *mpl*

guild [gɪld] *n* (*History*) corporation *f*; (*sharing interests*) cercle *m*, association *f*

guilt [gɪlt] *n* culpabilité *f*; **guilty** *adj* coupable

guinea pig ['gɪnɪ-] *n* cobaye *m*

guitar [gɪ'tɑː*] *n* guitare *f*; **guitarist** *n* guitariste *m/f*

gulf [gʌlf] *n* golfe *m*; (*abyss*) gouffre *m*

gull [gʌl] *n* mouette *f*

gulp [gʌlp] vi avaler sa salive; (from emotion) avoir la gorge serrée, s'étrangler ▷ vt (also: **~ down**) avaler

gum [gʌm] n (Anat) gencive f; (glue) colle f; (also: **chewing-~**) chewing-gum m ▷ vt coller

gun [gʌn] n (small) revolver m, pistolet m; (rifle) fusil m, carabine f; (cannon) canon m; **gunfire** n fusillade f; **gunman** (irreg) n bandit armé; **gunpoint** n: **at gunpoint** sous la menace du pistolet (or fusil); **gunpowder** n poudre f à canon; **gunshot** n coup m de feu

gush [gʌʃ] vi jaillir; (fig) se répandre en effusions

gust [gʌst] n (of wind) rafale f

gut [gʌt] n intestin m, boyau m; **guts** npl (Anat) boyaux mpl; (inf: courage) cran m

gutter ['gʌtə'] n (of roof) gouttière f; (in street) caniveau m

guy [gaɪ] n (inf: man) type m; (also: **~rope**) corde f; (figure) effigie de Guy Fawkes

Guy Fawkes' Night [gaɪ'fɔːks-] n voir encadré

● **GUY FAWKES' NIGHT**
●
● **Guy Fawkes' Night**, que l'on
● appelle également "bonfire night",
● commémore l'échec du complot (le
● "Gunpowder Plot") contre James Ist
● et son parlement le 5 novembre 1605.
● L'un des conspirateurs, Guy Fawkes,
● avait été surpris dans les caves du
● parlement alors qu'il s'apprêtait à y
● mettre le feu. Chaque année pour le
● 5 novembre, les enfants préparent à
● l'avance une effigie de Guy Fawkes
● et ils demandent aux passants "un
● penny pour le guy" avec lequel ils
● pourront s'acheter des fusées de feu
● d'artifice. Beaucoup de gens font
● encore un feu dans leur jardin sur
● lequel ils brûlent le "guy".

gym [dʒɪm] n (also: **~nasium**) gymnase m; (also: **~nastics**) gym f; **gymnasium** n gymnase m; **gymnast** n gymnaste m/f; **gymnastics** n, npl gymnastique f; **gym shoes** npl chaussures fpl de gym(nastique)

gynaecologist (us **gynecologist**) [gaɪnɪ'kɔlədʒɪst] n gynécologue m/f

gypsy ['dʒɪpsɪ] n gitan(e), bohémien(ne)

h

haberdashery [hæbə'dæʃəri] n (BRIT) mercerie f

habit ['hæbɪt] n habitude f; (costume: Rel) habit m

habitat ['hæbɪtæt] n habitat m

hack [hæk] vt hacher, tailler ▷ n (pej: writer) nègre m; **hacker** n (Comput) pirate m (informatique)

had [hæd] pt, pp of **have**

haddock (pl ~ or ~s) ['hædək] n églefin m; **smoked** ~ haddock m

hadn't ['hædnt] = **had not**

haemorrhage (US **hemorrhage**) ['hemərɪdʒ] n hémorragie f

haemorrhoids (US **hemorrhoids**) ['hemərɔɪdz] npl hémorroïdes fpl

haggle ['hægl] vi marchander

Hague [heɪg] n: **The ~** La Haye

hail [heɪl] n grêle f ▷ vt (call) héler; (greet) acclamer ▷ vi grêler; **hailstone** n grêlon m

hair [hɛə] n cheveux mpl; (on body) poils mpl; (of animal) pelage m; (single hair: on head) cheveu m; (: on body, of animal) poil m; **to do one's ~** se coiffer; **hairband** n (elasticated) bandeau m; (plastic) serre-tête m; **hairbrush** n brosse f à cheveux; **haircut** n coupe f (de cheveux); **hairdo** n coiffure f; **hairdresser** n coiffeur(-euse); **hairdresser's** n salon m de coiffure, coiffeur m; **hair dryer** n sèche-cheveux m, séchoir m; **hair gel** n gel m pour cheveux; **hair spray** n laque f (pour les cheveux); **hairstyle** n coiffure f; **hairy** adj poilu(e), chevelu(e); (inf: frightening) effrayant(e)

hake (pl ~ or ~s) [heɪk] n colin m, merlu m

half [hɑːf] n (pl halves) moitié f; (of beer: also: ~ pint) demi m; (Rail, bus: also: ~ fare) demi-tarif m; (Sport: of match) mi-temps f ▷ adj demi(e) ▷ adv (à) moitié, à demi; ~ **an hour** une demi-heure; ~ **a dozen** une demi-douzaine; ~ **a pound** une demi-livre, = 250 g; **two and a** ~ deux et demi; **to cut sth in** ~ couper qch en deux; **half board** n (BRIT: in hotel) demi-pension f; **half-brother** n demi-frère m; **half day** n demi-journée f; **half fare** n demi-tarif m; **half-hearted** adj tiède, sans enthousiasme; **half-hour** n demi-heure f; **half-price** adj à moitié prix ▷ adv (also: **at half-price**) à moitié prix; **half term** n (BRIT Scol) vacances fpl (de demi-trimestre); **half-time** n mi-temps f; **halfway** adv à mi-chemin; **halfway through** sth au milieu de qch

hall [hɔːl] n (entrance way: big) hall m; (small) entrée f; (us: corridor) couloir m; (mansion) château m, manoir m

hallmark ['hɔːlmɑːk] n poinçon m; (fig) marque f

hallo [hə'ləʊ] excl = **hello**

hall of residence n (BRIT) pavillon m or résidence f universitaire

Halloween, Hallowe'en ['hæləʊ'iːn] n veille f de la Toussaint; voir encadré

HALLOWEEN

- Selon la tradition, **Halloween** est la
  nuit des fantômes et des sorcières.
  En Écosse et aux États-Unis surtout
  (et de plus en plus en Angleterre) les
  enfants, pour fêter **Halloween**, se
  déguisent ce soir-là et ils vont ainsi
  de porte en porte en demandant de
  petits cadeaux (du chocolat, une
  pomme etc).

hallucination [həlu:sɪ'neɪʃən] *n*
hallucination *f*

hallway ['hɔ:lweɪ] *n (entrance)*
vestibule *m; (corridor)* couloir *m*

halo ['heɪləu] *n (of saint etc)* auréole *f*

halt [hɔ:lt] *n* halte *f*, arrêt *m* ⊳ *vt* faire
arrêter; *(progress etc)* interrompre ⊳ *vi*
faire halte, s'arrêter

halve [hɑ:v] *vt (apple etc)* partager ou
diviser en deux; *(reduce by half)* réduire
de moitié

halves [hɑ:vz] *npl of* **half**

ham [hæm] *n* jambon *m*

hamburger ['hæmbə:gə'] *n*
hamburger *m*

hamlet ['hæmlɪt] *n* hameau *m*

hammer ['hæmə'] *n* marteau *m* ⊳ *vt
(nail)* enfoncer; *(fig)* éreinter, démolir
⊳ *vi (at door)* frapper à coups redoublés;
to ~ a point home to sb faire rentrer
qch dans la tête de qn

hammock ['hæmək] *n* hamac *m*

hamper ['hæmpə'] *vt* gêner ⊳ *n* panier
m (d'osier)

hamster ['hæmstə'] *n* hamster *m*

hamstring ['hæmstrɪŋ] *n (Anat)*
tendon *m* du jarret

hand [hænd] *n* main *f; (of clock)* aiguille
f; (handwriting) écriture *f; (at cards)* jeu
m; (worker) ouvrier(-ière) ⊳ *vt* passer,
donner; **to give sb a ~** donner un coup
de main à qn; **at ~** à portée de la main;
in ~ *(situation)* en main; *(work)* en cours;
to be on ~ *(person)* être disponible;
(emergency services) se tenir prêt(e) à
intervenir; **to ~** *(information etc)* sous

la main, à portée de la main; **on the
one ~ ..., on the other ~** d'une part ...,
d'autre part; **hand down** *vt* passer;
(tradition, heirloom) transmettre; *(us:
sentence, verdict)* prononcer; **hand in**
vt remettre; **hand out** *vt* distribuer;
hand over *vt* remettre; *(powers etc)*
transmettre; **handbag** *n* sac *m* à main;
hand baggage *n* = **hand luggage**;
handbook *n* manuel *m;* **handbrake**
n frein *m* à main; **handcuffs** *npl*
menottes *fpl;* **handful** *n* poignée *f*

handicap ['hændɪkæp] *n* handicap *m*
⊳ *vt* handicaper; **mentally/physically
~ped** handicapé(e) mentalement/
physiquement

handkerchief ['hæŋkətʃɪf] *n*
mouchoir *m*

handle ['hændl] *n (of door etc)* poignée
f; (of cup etc) anse *f; (of knife etc)* manche
m; (of saucepan) queue *f; (for winding)*
manivelle *f* ⊳ *vt* toucher, manier;
(deal with) s'occuper de; *(treat: people)*
prendre; **"~ with care"** "fragile"; **to fly
off the ~** s'énerver; **handlebar(s)** *n(pl)*
guidon *m*

hand luggage *n* bagages *mpl*
à main; **handmade** *adj* fait(e) à la
main; **handout** *n (money)* aide *f,* don
m; (leaflet) prospectus *m; (at lecture)*
polycopié *m;* **hands-free** *adj (phone)*
mains libres *inv* ⊳ *n:* also: **hands-free
kit** kit *m* mains libres *inv*

handsome ['hænsəm] *adj* beau (belle);
(profit) considérable

handwriting ['hændraɪtɪŋ] *n*
écriture *f*

handy ['hændɪ] *adj (person)* adroit(e);
(close at hand) sous la main; *(convenient)*
pratique

hang (*pt, pp* **hung**) [hæŋ, hʌŋ] *vt*
accrocher; *(criminal: pt, pp* **-ed**) pendre
⊳ *vi* pendre; *(hair, drapery)* tomber
⊳ *n:* **to get the ~ of (doing) sth** *(inf)*
attraper le coup pour faire qch; **hang
about, hang around** *vi* traîner; **hang
down** *vi* pendre; **hang on** *vi (wait)*
attendre; **hang out** *vt (washing)*

étendre (dehors) ▷ vi (inf: live) habiter, percher; (: spend time) traîner; **hang round** vi = **hang around**; **hang up** vi (Tel) raccrocher ▷ vt (coat, painting etc) accrocher, suspendre

hanger ['hæŋə*] n cintre m, portemanteau m

hang-gliding [hæŋglaɪdɪŋ] n vol m libre or sur aile delta

hangover ['hæŋəʊvə*] n (after drinking) gueule f de bois

hankie, hanky ['hæŋkɪ] n abbr = **handkerchief**

happen ['hæpən] vi arriver, se passer, se produire; **what's -ing?** que se passe-t-il?; **she -ed to be free** il s'est trouvé (or se trouvait) qu'elle était libre; **as it -s** justement

happily ['hæpɪlɪ] adv heureusement; (cheerfully) joyeusement

happiness ['hæpɪnɪs] n bonheur m

happy ['hæpɪ] adj heureux(-euse); **- with** (arrangements etc) satisfait(e) de; **to be - to do** faire volontiers; **- birthday!** bon anniversaire!

harass ['hærəs] vt accabler, tourmenter; **harassment** n tracasseries fpl

harbour (us **harbor**) ['hɑːbə*] n port m ▷ vt héberger, abriter; (hopes, suspicions) entretenir

hard [hɑːd] adj dur(e); (question, problem) difficile; (facts, evidence) concret(-ète) ▷ adv (work) dur; (think, try) sérieusement; **to look -** at regarder fixement; (thing) regarder de près; **no - feelings!** sans rancune!; **to be - of hearing** être dur(e) d'oreille; **to be - done by** être traité(e) injustement; **hardback** n livre relié; **hardboard** n Isorel® m; **hard disk** n (Comput) disque dur; **harden** vt durcir; (fig) endurcir ▷ vi (substance) durcir

hardly ['hɑːdlɪ] adv (scarcely) à peine; (harshly) durement; **- anywhere/ever** presque nulle part/jamais

hard: hardship n (difficulties) épreuves fpl; (deprivation) privations fpl; **hard**

shoulder n (BRIT Aut) accotement stabilisé; **hard-up** adj (inf) fauché(e); **hardware** n quincaillerie f; (Comput, Mil) matériel m; **hardware shop** (us **hardware store**) n quincaillerie f; **hard-working** adj travailleur(-euse), consciencieux(-euse)

hardy ['hɑːdɪ] adj robuste; (plant) résistant(e) au gel

hare [hɛə*] n lièvre m

harm [hɑːm] n mal m; (wrong) tort m ▷ vt (person) faire du mal or du tort à; (thing) endommager; **out of -'s way** à l'abri du danger, en lieu sûr; **harmful** adj nuisible; **harmless** adj inoffensif(-ive)

harmony ['hɑːmənɪ] n harmonie f

harness ['hɑːnɪs] n harnais m ▷ vt (horse) harnacher; (resources) exploiter

harp [hɑːp] n harpe f ▷ vi: **to - on about** revenir toujours sur

harsh [hɑːʃ] adj (hard) dur(e); (severe) sévère; (unpleasant: sound) discordant(e); (: light) cru(e)

harvest ['hɑːvɪst] n (of corn) moisson f; (of fruit) récolte f; (of grapes) vendange f ▷ vt moissonner; récolter; vendanger

has [hæz] vb see **have**

hasn't ['hæznt] = **has not**

hassle ['hæsl] n (inf: fuss) histoire(s) f(pl)

haste [heɪst] n hâte f, précipitation f; **hasten** ['heɪsn] vt hâter, accélérer ▷ vi se hâter, s'empresser; **hastily** adv à la hâte; (leave) précipitamment; **hasty** adj (decision, action) hâtif(-ive); (departure, escape) précipité(e)

hat [hæt] n chapeau m

hatch [hætʃ] n (Naut: also: **-way**) écoutille f; (BRIT: also: **service -**) passe-plats m inv ▷ vi éclore

hatchback ['hætʃbæk] n (Aut) modèle m avec hayon arrière

hate [heɪt] vt haïr, détester ▷ n haine f; **hatred** ['heɪtrɪd] n haine f

haul [hɔːl] vt traîner, tirer ▷ n (of fish) prise f; (of stolen goods etc) butin m

haunt [hɔːnt] vt (subj: ghost, fear)

hanter; (: *person*) fréquenter ▷ *n*
repaire *m*; **haunted** *adj* (*castle etc*)
hanté(e); (*look*) égaré(e), hagard(e)

 KEYWORD

have [hæv] (*pt, pp* **had**) *aux vb* 1 (*gen*)
avoir; être; **to have eaten/slept** avoir
mangé/dormi; **to have arrived/gone**
être arrivé(e)/parti(e); **having finished**
or **when he had finished, he left**
quand il a eu fini, il est parti; **we'd
already eaten** nous avions déjà mangé
2 (*in tag questions*): **you've done it,
haven't you?** vous l'avez fait, n'est-ce
pas?
3 (*in short answers and questions*): **no I
haven't!/yes we have!** mais non!/
mais si!; **so I have!** ah oui, oui c'est
vrai!; **I've been there before, have
you?** j'y suis déjà allé, et vous?
▷ *modal aux vb* (*be obliged*): **to have
(got) to do sth** devoir faire qch; **to
have (got) to do it** elle doit le faire, il faut qu'elle
le fasse; **you haven't to tell her** vous
n'êtes pas obligé de le lui dire; (*must not*)
ne le lui dites surtout pas; **do you have
to book?** il faut réserver?
▷ *vt* 1 (*possess*) avoir; **he has (got) blue
eyes/dark hair** il a les yeux bleus/les
cheveux bruns
2 (*referring to meals etc*): **to have
breakfast** prendre le petit déjeuner; **to
have dinner/lunch** dîner/déjeuner; **to
have a drink** prendre un verre; **to have
a cigarette** fumer une cigarette
3 (*receive*) avoir, recevoir; (*obtain*) avoir;
may I have your address? puis-je
avoir votre adresse?; **you can have it
for £5** vous pouvez l'avoir pour 5 livres;
I must have it for tomorrow il me
le faut pour demain; **to have a baby**
avoir un bébé
4 (*maintain, allow*): **I won't have it!** ça
ne se passera pas comme ça!; **we can't
have that** nous ne tolérerons pas ça
5 (*by sth else*): **to have sth done** faire

faire qch; **to have one's hair cut** se
faire couper les cheveux; **to have sb do
sth** faire faire qch à qn
6 (*experience, suffer*) avoir; **to have a
cold/flu** avoir un rhume/la grippe;
to have an operation se faire opérer;
she had her bag stolen elle s'est fait
voler son sac
7 (*+noun*): **to have a swim/walk** nager/
se promener; **to have a bath/shower**
prendre un bain/une douche; **let's
have a look** regardons; **to have a
meeting** se réunir; **to have a party**
organiser une fête; **let me have a try**
laissez-moi essayer

haven ['heɪvn] *n* port *m*; (*fig*) havre *m*
haven't ['hævnt] = **have not**
havoc ['hævək] *n* ravages *mpl*
Hawaii [hə'waɪ:] *n* (îles *fpl*) Hawaï *m*
hawk [hɔːk] *n* faucon *m*
hawthorn ['hɔːθɔːn] *n* aubépine *f*
hay [heɪ] *n* foin *m*; **hay fever** *n* rhume *m*
des foins; **haystack** *n* meule *f* de foin
hazard ['hæzəd] *n* (*risk*) danger *m*,
risque *m* ▷ *vt* risquer, hasarder;
hazardous *adj* hasardeux(-euse),
risqué(e); **hazard warning lights** *npl*
(*Aut*) feux *mpl* de détresse
haze [heɪz] *n* brume *f*
hazel ['heɪzl] *n* (*tree*) noisetier *m*
▷ *adj* (*eyes*) noisette *inv*; **hazelnut** *n*
noisette *f*
hazy ['heɪzɪ] *adj* brumeux(-euse);
(*idea*) vague
he [hiː] *pron* il; **it is he who ...** c'est lui
qui ...; **here he is** le voici
head [hɛd] *n* tête *f*; (*leader*) chef *m*; (*of
school*) directeur(-trice); (*of secondary
school*) proviseur *m* ▷ *vt* (*list*) être
en tête de; (*group, company*) être à
la tête de; **~s or tails** pile ou face; **~
first** la tête la première; **~ over heels
in love** follement or éperdument
amoureux(-euse); **to ~ the ball** faire
une tête; **head for** *vt fus* se diriger vers;
(*disaster*) aller à; **head off** *vt* (*threat,
danger*) détourner; **headache** *n* mal *m*

de tête; **to have a headache** avoir mal à la tête; **heading** n titre m; (subject title) rubrique f; **headlamp** (BRIT) n = **headlight**; **headlight** n phare m; **headline** n titre m; **head office** n siège m, bureau m central; **headphones** npl casque m (à écouteurs); **headquarters** npl (of business) bureau or siège central; (Mil) quartier général; **headroom** n (in car) hauteur f de plafond; (under bridge) hauteur limite; **headscarf** n foulard m; **headset** n = **headphones**; **headteacher** n directeur(-trice); (of secondary school) proviseur m; **head waiter** n maître m d'hôtel

heal [hiːl] vt, vi guérir

health [hɛlθ] n santé f; **health care** n services médicaux; **health centre** n (BRIT) centre m de santé; **health food** n aliment(s) naturel(s); **Health Service** n: **the Health Service** (BRIT) = la Sécurité Sociale; **healthy** adj (person) en bonne santé; (climate, food, attitude etc) sain(e)

heap [hiːp] n tas m ▷ vt (also: ~ **up**) entasser, amonceler; **she ~ed her plate with cakes** elle a chargé son assiette de gâteaux; **~s (of)** (inf: lots) des tas de

hear [hɪər] (pt, pp ~**d**) vt entendre; (news) apprendre ▷ vi entendre; **to ~ about** entendre parler de; (have news of) avoir des nouvelles de; **to ~ from sb** recevoir des nouvelles de

heard [hɜːd] pt, pp of **hear**

hearing ['hɪərɪŋ] n (sense) ouïe f; (of witnesses) audition f; (of a case) audience f; **hearing aid** n appareil m acoustique

hearse [hɜːs] n corbillard m

heart [hɑːt] n cœur m; **hearts** npl (Cards) cœur; **at ~** au fond; **by ~** (learn, know) par cœur; **to lose/take ~** perdre/prendre courage; **heart attack** n crise f cardiaque; **heartbeat** n battement m de cœur; **heartbroken** adj: **to be heartbroken** avoir beaucoup de chagrin; **heartburn** n brûlures fpl d'estomac; **heart disease** n maladie

f cardiaque

hearth [hɑːθ] n foyer m, cheminée f

heartless ['hɑːtlɪs] adj (person) sans cœur, insensible; (treatment) cruel(le)

hearty ['hɑːtɪ] adj chaleureux(-euse); (appetite) solide; (dislike) cordial(e); (meal) copieux(-euse)

heat [hiːt] n chaleur f; (Sport: also: **qualifying ~**) éliminatoire f ▷ vt chauffer; **heat up** vi (liquid) chauffer; (room) se réchauffer ▷ vt réchauffer; **heated** adj chauffé(e); (fig) passionné(e), échauffé(e), excité(e); **heater** n appareil m de chauffage; radiateur m; (in car) chauffage m; (water heater) chauffe-eau m

heather ['hɛðər] n bruyère f

heating ['hiːtɪŋ] n chauffage m

heatwave ['hiːtweɪv] n vague f de chaleur

heaven ['hɛvn] n ciel m, paradis m; (fig) paradis; **heavenly** adj céleste, divin(e)

heavily ['hɛvɪlɪ] adv lourdement; (drink, smoke) beaucoup; (sleep, sigh) profondément

heavy ['hɛvɪ] adj lourd(e); (work, rain, user, eater) gros(se); (drinker, smoker) grand(e); (schedule, week) chargé(e)

Hebrew ['hiːbruː] adj hébraïque ▷ n (Ling) hébreu m

Hebrides ['hɛbrɪdiːz] npl: **the ~** les Hébrides fpl

hectare ['hɛktɑːr] n (BRIT) hectare m

hectic ['hɛktɪk] adj (schedule) très chargé(e); (day) mouvementé(e); (lifestyle) trépidant(e)

he'd [hiːd] = **he would; he had**

hedge [hɛdʒ] n haie f ▷ vi se dérober ▷ vt: **to ~ one's bets** (fig) se couvrir

hedgehog ['hɛdʒhɒg] n hérisson m

heed [hiːd] vt (also: **take ~ of**) tenir compte de, prendre garde à

heel [hiːl] n talon m ▷ vt retalonner

hefty ['hɛftɪ] adj (person) costaud(e); (parcel) lourd(e); (piece, price) gros(se)

height [haɪt] n (of person) taille f, grandeur f; (of object) hauteur f; (of plane, mountain) altitude f; (high ground) hauteur, éminence f; (fig: of glory, fame, power) sommet m; (: of luxury, stupidity) comble m; **at the ~ of summer** au cœur de l'été; **heighten** vt hausser, surélever; (fig) augmenter

heir [ɛəʳ] n héritier m; **heiress** n héritière f

held [hɛld] pt, pp of **hold**

helicopter ['hɛlɪkɔptəʳ] n hélicoptère f

hell [hɛl] n enfer m; **oh ~!** (inf) merde!

he'll [hi:l] = **he will; he shall**

hello [hə'ləu] excl bonjour!; (to attract attention) hé!; (surprise) tiens!

helmet ['hɛlmɪt] n casque m

help [hɛlp] n aide f; (cleaner etc) femme f de ménage ▷ vt, vi aider; **~! au secours!**; **~ yourself** servez-vous; **can you ~ me?** pouvez-vous m'aider?; **can I ~ you?** (in shop) vous désirez?; **he can't ~ it** il n'y peut rien; **help out** vi aider ▷ vt: **to ~ sb out** aider qn; **helper** n aide m/f, assistant(e); **helpful** adj serviable, obligeant(e); (useful) utile; **helping** n portion f; **helpless** adj impuissant(e); (baby) sans défense; **helpline** n service m d'assistance téléphonique; (free) ≈ numéro vert

hem [hɛm] n ourlet m ▷ vt ourler

hemisphere ['hɛmɪsfɪəʳ] n hémisphère m

hemorrhage ['hɛmərɪdʒ] n (us) = **haemorrhage**

hemorrhoids ['hɛmərɔɪdz] npl (us) = **haemorrhoids**

hen [hɛn] n poule f; (female bird) femelle f

hence [hɛns] adv (therefore) d'où, de là; **2 years ~** d'ici 2 ans

hen night, hen party n soirée f entre filles (avant le mariage de l'une d'elles)

hepatitis [hɛpə'taɪtɪs] n hépatite f

her [hə:ʳ] pron (direct) la, l' + vowel or mute; (indirect) lui; (stressed, after prep) elle ▷ adj son (sa), ses pl; see also **me; my**

herb [hə:b] n herbe f; **herbal** adj à base de plantes; **herbal tea** n tisane f

herd [hə:d] n troupeau m

here [hɪəʳ] adv ici; (time) alors ▷ excl tiens!, tenez!; **~!** (present) présent!; **~ is, ~ are** voici; **~ he/she is** le (la) voici

hereditary [hɪ'rɛdɪtrɪ] adj héréditaire

heritage ['hɛrɪtɪdʒ] n héritage m, patrimoine m

hernia ['hə:nɪə] n hernie f

hero (pl **-es**) ['hɪərəu] n héros m; **heroic** [hɪ'rəuɪk] adj héroïque

heroin ['hɛrəuɪn] n héroïne f (drogue)

heroine ['hɛrəuɪn] n héroïne f (femme)

heron ['hɛrən] n héron m

herring ['hɛrɪŋ] n hareng m

hers [hə:z] pron le (la) sien(ne), les siens (siennes); see also **mine**

herself [hə:'sɛlf] pron (reflexive) se; (emphatic) elle-même; (after prep) elle; see also **oneself**

he's [hi:z] = **he is; he has**

hesitant ['hɛzɪtənt] adj hésitant(e), indécis(e)

hesitate ['hɛzɪteɪt] vi: **to ~ (about/to do)** hésiter (sur/à faire); **hesitation** [hɛzɪ'teɪʃən] n hésitation f

heterosexual ['hɛtərəu'sɛksjuəl] adj, n hétérosexuel(le)

hexagon ['hɛksəgən] n hexagone m

hey [heɪ] excl hé!

heyday ['heɪdeɪ] n: **the ~ of** l'âge m d'or de, les beaux jours de

HGV n abbr = **heavy goods vehicle**

hi [haɪ] excl salut!; (to attract attention) hé!

hibernate ['haɪbəneɪt] vi hiberner

hiccough, hiccup ['hɪkʌp] vi hoqueter ▷ n: **to have (the) ~s** avoir le hoquet

hid [hɪd] pt of **hide**

hidden ['hɪdn] pp of **hide** ▷ adj: **~ agenda** intentions non déclarées

hide [haɪd] n (skin) peau f ▷ vb (pt **hid**, pp **hidden**) vt cacher ▷ vi: **to ~ (from sb)** se cacher (de qn)

hideous ['hɪdɪəs] adj hideux(-euse), atroce

hiding ['haɪdɪŋ] n (beating) correction f, volée f de coups; **to be in ~** (concealed) se tenir caché(e)

hi-fi ['haɪfaɪ] *adj, n abbr* (= high fidelity) hi-fi *inv*

high [haɪ] *adj* haut(e); (*speed, respect, number*) grand(e); (*price*) élevé(e); (*wind*) fort(e), violent(e); (*voice*) aigu(ë) ▷ *adv* haut, en haut; **20 m** ~ haut(e) de 20 m; ~ **in the air** haut dans le ciel; **highchair** *n* (*child's*) chaise haute; **high-class** *adj* (*neighbourhood, hotel*) chic *inv*, de grand standing; **higher education** *n* études supérieures; **high heels** *npl* talons hauts, hauts talons; **high jump** *n* (*Sport*) saut *m* en hauteur; **the Highlands** ['haɪləndz] *npl* région montagneuse; **the Highlands** (*in Scotland*) les Highlands *mpl*; **highlight** *n* (*fig: of event*) point culminant ▷ *vt* (*emphasize*) faire ressortir, souligner; **highlights** *npl* (*in hair*) reflets *mpl*; **highlighter** *n* (*pen*) surligneur (lumineux); **highly** *adv* extrêmement, très; (*unlikely*) fort; (*recommended, skilled, qualified*) hautement; **to speak highly of** dire beaucoup de bien de; **highness** *n*: **His/Her Highness** son Altesse *f*; **high-rise** *n* (*also:* **high-rise block, high-rise building**) tour *f* (d'habitation); **high school** *n* (*BRIT*) lycée *m*; (*US*) établissement *m* d'enseignement supérieur; **high season** *n* (*BRIT*) haute saison; **high street** *n* (*BRIT*) grand-rue *f*; **high-tech** (*inf*) *adj* de pointe; **highway** *n* (*US*) route *f*; (*us*) route nationale; **Highway Code** *n* (*BRIT*) code *m* de la route

hijack ['haɪdʒæk] *vt* détourner (*par la force*); **hijacker** *n* auteur *m* d'un détournement d'avion, pirate *m* de l'air

hike [haɪk] *vi* faire des excursions à pied ▷ *n* excursion *f* à pied, randonnée *f*; **hiker** *n* promeneur(-euse), excursionniste *m/f*; **hiking** *n* excursions *fpl* à pied, randonnée *f*

hilarious [hɪ'lɛərɪəs] *adj* (*behaviour, event*) désopilant(e)

hill [hɪl] *n* colline *f*, (*fairly high*) montagne *f*; (*on road*) côte *f*; **hillside** *n* (flanc *m* de) coteau *m*; **hill walking** *n*

randonnée *f* de basse montagne; **hilly** *adj* vallonné(e), montagneux(-euse)

him [hɪm] *pron* (*direct*) le, l' *before vowel or h mute*; (*stressed, indirect, after prep*) lui; *see also* **me**; **himself** *pron* (*reflexive*) se; (*emphatic*) lui-même; (*after prep*) lui; *see also* **oneself**

hind [haɪnd] *adj* de derrière

hinder ['hɪndə'] *vt* gêner; (*delay*) retarder

hindsight ['haɪndsaɪt] *n*: **with (the benefit of) ~** avec du recul, rétrospectivement

Hindu ['hɪndu:] *n* Hindou(e); **Hinduism** *n* (*Rel*) hindouisme *m*

hinge [hɪndʒ] *n* charnière *f* ▷ *vi* (*fig*): **to ~ on** dépendre de

hint [hɪnt] *n* allusion *f*; (*advice*) conseil *m*; (*clue*) indication *f* ▷ *vt*: **to ~ that** insinuer que ▷ *vi*: **to ~ at** faire une allusion à

hip [hɪp] *n* hanche *f*

hippie, hippy ['hɪpɪ] *n* hippie *m/f*

hippo ['hɪpəu] (*pl* ~**s**) *n* hippopotame *m*

hippopotamus [hɪpə'pɔtəməs] (*pl* ~**es** *or* **hippopotami**) *n* hippopotame *m*

hippy ['hɪpɪ] *n* = **hippie**

hire ['haɪə'] *vt* (*BRIT: car, equipment*) louer; (*worker*) embaucher, engager ▷ *n* location *f*; **for ~** à louer; (*taxi*) libre; **I'd like to ~ a car** je voudrais louer une voiture; **hire(d) car** (*BRIT*) voiture *f* de location; **hire purchase** *n* (*BRIT*) achat *m* (*or* vente) à tempérament *or* crédit

his [hɪz] *pron* le (la) sien(ne), les (siennes) ▷ *adj* son (sa), ses *pl*; *see also* **mine**[1]; **my**

Hispanic [hɪs'pænɪk] *adj* (*in US*) hispano-américain(e) ▷ *n* Hispano-Américain(e)

hiss [hɪs] *vi* siffler

historian [hɪ'stɔ:rɪən] *n* historien(ne)

historic(al) [hɪ'stɔrɪk(l)] *adj* historique

history ['hɪstərɪ] *n* histoire *f*

hit [hɪt] *vt* (*pt, pp* ~) frapper; (*reach: target*) atteindre, toucher; (*collide with: car*) entrer en collision avec, heurter;

(fig: affect) toucher ▷ n coup m; (success) succès m; (song) tube m; (to website) visite f; (on search engine) résultat m de recherche; **to ~ it off with sb** bien s'entendre avec qn; **to ~ back** vi: **to ~ back at sb** prendre sa revanche sur qn

hitch [hɪtʃ] vt (fasten) accrocher, attacher; (also: **~ up**) remonter d'une saccade ▷ vi faire de l'autostop ▷ n (difficulty) anicroche f, contretemps m; **to ~ a lift** faire du stop; **hitch-hike** vi faire de l'autostop; **hitch-hiker** n auto-stoppeur(-euse) f; **hitch-hiking** n auto-stop m, stop m (inf)

hi-tech ['haɪ'tɛk] adj de pointe

hitman ['hɪtmæn] (irreg) n (inf) tueur m à gages

HIV n abbr (= human immunodeficiency virus) HIV m, VIH m; **~-negative/positive** séronégatif(-ive)/positif(-ive)

hive [haɪv] n ruche f

hoard [hɔːd] n (of food) provisions fpl, réserves fpl; (of money) trésor m ▷ vt amasser

hoarse [hɔːs] adj enroué(e)

hoax [həʊks] n canular m

hob [hɒb] n plaque chauffante

hobble ['hɒbl] vi boitiller

hobby ['hɒbɪ] n passe-temps favori

hobo ['həʊbəʊ] n (us) vagabond m

hockey ['hɒkɪ] n hockey m; **hockey stick** n crosse f de hockey

hog [hɒg] n porc (châtré) m ▷ vt (fig) accaparer; **to go the whole ~** aller jusqu'au bout

Hogmanay [hɒgmə'neɪ] n réveillon m du jour de l'An, Saint-Sylvestre f; voir encadré

● HOGMANAY

● La Saint-Sylvestre ou "New Year's Eve" se nomme **Hogmanay** en Écosse. En cette occasion, la famille et les amis se réunissent pour entendre sonner les douze coups de minuit et pour fêter le "first-footing", une coutume qui veut qu'on se

● rende chez ses amis et voisins en apportant quelque chose à boire (du whisky en général) et un morceau de charbon en gage de prospérité pour la nouvelle année.

hoist [hɔɪst] n palan m ▷ vt hisser

hold [həʊld] (pt, pp **held**) vt (contain) contenir; (meeting) tenir; (keep back) retenir; (believe) considérer; (possess) avoir ▷ vi (withstand pressure) tenir (bon); (be valid) valoir; (on telephone) attendre ▷ n prise f; (find) influence f; (Naut) cale f; **to catch** or **get (a) ~ of** saisir; **to get ~ of** (find) trouver; **~ the line!** (Tel) ne quittez pas!; **to ~ one's own** (fig) (bien) se défendre; **hold back** vt retenir; (secret) cacher; **hold on** vi tenir bon; (wait) attendre; **~ on!** (Tel) ne quittez pas!; **to ~ on to sth** (grasp) se cramponner à qch; (keep) conserver or garder qch; **hold out** vt offrir ▷ vi (resist): **to ~ out (against)** résister (devant), tenir bon (devant); **hold up** vt (raise) lever; (support) soutenir; (delay) retarder; (: traffic) ralentir; (rob) braquer; **holdall** n (BRIT) fourre-tout m inv; **holder** n (container) support m; (of ticket, record) détenteur(-trice) f; (of office, title, passport etc) titulaire m/f

hole [həʊl] n trou m

holiday ['hɒlədɪ] n (BRIT: vacation) vacances fpl; (day off) jour m de congé; (public) jour férié; **to be on ~** être en vacances; **I'm here on ~** je suis ici en vacances; **holiday camp** n (also: **holiday centre**) camp m de vacances; **holiday job** n (BRIT) boulot m (inf) de vacances; **holiday-maker** n (BRIT) vacancier(-ière) f; **holiday resort** n centre m de villégiature or de vacances

Holland ['hɒlənd] n Hollande f

hollow ['hɒləʊ] adj creux(-euse); (fig) faux (fausse) ▷ n creux m; (in land) dépression f (de terrain), cuvette f ▷ vt: **to ~ out** creuser, évider

holly ['hɒlɪ] n houx m

Hollywood ['hɒlɪwʊd] n Hollywood

holocaust ['hɔləkɔːst] n holocauste m
holy ['həʊlɪ] adj saint(e); (bread, water) bénit(e); (ground) sacré(e)
home [həʊm] n foyer m, maison f; (country) pays natal, patrie f; (institution) maison ▷ adj de (safe); (Econ, Pol) national(e), intérieur(e); (Sport: team) qui reçoit; (: match, win) sur leur (or notre) terrain ▷ adv chez soi, à la maison; au pays natal; (right in: nail etc) à fond; **at ~** chez soi, à la maison; **to go (or come) ~** rentrer (chez soi), rentrer à la maison (or au pays); **make yourself at ~** faites comme chez vous; **home address** n domicile permanent; **homeland** n patrie f; **homeless** adj sans foyer, sans abri; **homely** adj (plain) simple, sans prétention; (welcoming) accueillant(e); **home-made** adj fait(e) à la maison; **home match** n match m à domicile; **Home Office** n (BRIT) ministère m de l'Intérieur; **home owner** n propriétaire occupant; **home page** n (Comput) page f d'accueil; **Home Secretary** n (BRIT) ministre m de l'Intérieur; **homesick** adj **to be homesick** avoir le mal du pays; (missing one's family) s'ennuyer de sa famille; **home town** n ville natale; **homework** n devoirs mpl
homicide ['hɔmɪsaɪd] n (us) homicide m
homoeopathic (us **homeopathic**) [həʊmɪə'pæθɪk] adj (medicine) homéopathique; (doctor) homéopathe
homoeopathy (us **homeopathy**) [həʊmɪ'ɔpəθɪ] n homéopathie f
homosexual [hɔməʊ'sɛksjuəl] adj, n homosexuel(le)
honest ['ɔnɪst] adj honnête; (sincere) franc (franche); **honestly** adv honnêtement; franchement; **honesty** n honnêteté f
honey ['hʌnɪ] n miel m; **honeymoon** n lune f de miel, voyage m de noces; **we're on honeymoon** nous sommes en voyage de noces; **honeysuckle** n chèvrefeuille m

Hong Kong ['hɔŋ'kɔŋ] n Hong Kong
honorary ['ɔnərərɪ] adj honoraire; (duty, title) honorifique; **~ degree** diplôme m honoris causa
honour (us **honor**) ['ɔnə*] vt honorer ▷ n honneur m; **to graduate with ~s** obtenir sa licence avec mention; **honourable** (us **honorable**) adj honorable; **honours degree** n (Scol) ≈ licence f avec mention
hood [hʊd] n capuchon m; (of cooker) hotte f; (BRIT Aut) capote f; (us Aut) capot m; **hoodie** ['hʊdɪ] n (top) sweat m à capuche
hoof (pl **~s** or **hooves**) [huːf, huːvz] n sabot m
hook [hʊk] n crochet m; (on dress) agrafe f; (for fishing) hameçon m ▷ vt accrocher; **off the ~** (Tel) décroché
hooligan ['huːlɪɡən] n voyou m
hoop [huːp] n cerceau m
hooray [huː'reɪ] excl = **hurray**
hoot [huːt] vi (BRIT: Aut) klaxonner; (siren) mugir; (owl) hululer
Hoover® ['huːvə*] n (BRIT) aspirateur m ▷ vt: **to hoover** (room) passer l'aspirateur dans; (carpet) passer l'aspirateur sur
hooves [huːvz] npl of **hoof**
hop [hɔp] vi sauter; (on one foot) sauter à cloche-pied; (bird) sautiller
hope [həʊp] vt, vi espérer ▷ n espoir m; **I ~ so** je l'espère; **I ~ not** j'espère que non; **hopeful** adj (person) plein(e) d'espoir; (situation) prometteur(-euse), encourageant(e); **hopefully** adv (expectantly) avec espoir, avec optimisme; (one hopes) avec un peu de chance; **hopeless** adj désespéré(e); (useless) nul(le)
hops [hɔps] npl houblon m
horizon [hə'raɪzn] n horizon m; **horizontal** [hɔrɪ'zɔntl] adj horizontal(e)
hormone ['hɔːməʊn] n hormone f
horn [hɔːn] n corne f; (Mus) cor m; (Aut) klaxon m
horoscope ['hɔrəskəʊp] n

horoscope m

horrendous [hə'rɛndəs] adj horrible, affreux(-euse)

horrible ['hɔrɪbl] adj horrible, affreux(-euse)

horrid ['hɔrɪd] adj (person) détestable; (weather, place, smell) épouvantable

horrific [hɔ'rɪfɪk] adj horrible

horrifying ['hɔrɪfaɪɪŋ] adj horrifiant(e)

horror ['hɔrə*] n horreur f; **horror film** n film m d'épouvante

hors d'œuvre [ɔ:'də:vrə] n hors d'œuvre m

horse [hɔ:s] n cheval m; **horseback**: **on horseback** adj, adv à cheval; **horse chestnut** n (nut) marron m (d'Inde); (tree) marronnier m (d'Inde); **horsepower** n puissance f en chevaux; (unit) cheval-vapeur m (CV); **horse-racing** n courses fpl de chevaux; **horseradish** n raifort m; **horse riding** n (BRIT) équitation f

hose [həuz] n (also: ~pipe) tuyau m; (also: garden ~) tuyau d'arrosage; **hosepipe** n tuyau m; (in garden) tuyau d'arrosage

hospital ['hɔspɪtl] n hôpital m; **in ~** à l'hôpital; **where's the nearest ~?** où est l'hôpital le plus proche?

hospitality [hɔspɪ'tælɪtɪ] n hospitalité f

host [həust] n hôte m; (TV, Radio) présentateur(-trice), animateur(-trice); (large number): **a ~ of** une foule de; (Rel) hostie f

hostage ['hɔstɪdʒ] n otage m

hostel ['hɔstl] n foyer m; (also: youth ~) auberge f de jeunesse

hostess ['həustɪs] n hôtesse f; (BRIT: also: air ~) hôtesse de l'air; (TV, Radio) animatrice f

hostile ['hɔstaɪl] adj hostile

hostility [hɔ'stɪlɪtɪ] n hostilité f

hot [hɔt] adj très chaud(e); (as opposed to only warm) très chaud(e); (spicy) fort(e); (fig: contest) acharné(e); (topic) brûlant(e); (temper) violent(e), passionné(e); **to be ~** (person) avoir chaud; (thing) être (très)

chaud; (weather) faire chaud; **hot dog** n hot-dog m

hotel [həu'tɛl] n hôtel m

hot-water bottle [hɔt'wɔ:tə-] n bouillotte f

hound [haund] vt poursuivre avec acharnement ▷ n chien courant

hour ['auə*] n heure f; **hourly** adj toutes les heures; (rate) horaire

house n [haus] maison f; (Pol) chambre f; (Theat) salle f; auditoire m ▷ vt [hauz] (person) loger, héberger; **on the ~** (fig) aux frais de la maison; **household** n (Admin etc) ménage m; (people) famille f, maisonnée f; **householder** n propriétaire m/f; (head of house) chef m de famille; **housekeeper** n gouvernante f; **housekeeping** n (work) ménage m; **housewife** (irreg) n ménagère f, femme f au foyer; **house wine** n cuvée f maison or du patron; **housework** n (travaux mpl du) ménage m

housing ['hauzɪŋ] n logement m; **housing development** (BRIT **housing estate**) n (blocks of flats) cité f; (houses) lotissement m

hover ['hɔvə*] vi planer; **hovercraft** n aéroglisseur m, hovercraft m

how [hau] adv comment; **~ are you?** comment allez-vous?; **~ do you do?** bonjour; (on being introduced) enchanté(e); **~ long have you been here?** depuis combien de temps êtes-vous là?; **~ lovely/awful!** que or comme c'est joli/affreux!; **~ much time/many people?** combien de temps/gens?; **~ much does it cost?** ça coûte combien?; **~ old are you?** quel âge avez-vous?; **~ tall is he?** combien mesure-t-il?; **~ is school?** ça va à l'école?; **~ was the film?** comment était le film?

however [hau'ɛvə*] conj pourtant, cependant ▷ adv: **~ I do it** de quelque manière que je m'y prenne; **~ cold it is** même s'il fait très froid; **~ did you do it?** comment êtes-vous donc arrivé?

howl [haul] n hurlement m ▷ vi hurler

(wind) mugir
H.P. n abbr (BRIT) = **hire purchase**
h.p. abbr (Aut) = **horsepower**
HQ n abbr (= headquarters) QG m
hr(s) abbr (= hour(s)) h
HTML n abbr (= hypertext markup language) HTML m
hubcap [ˈhʌbkæp] n enjoliveur m
huddle [ˈhʌdl] vi: **to ~ together** se blottir les uns contre les autres
huff [hʌf] n: **in a ~** fâché(e)
hug [hʌg] vt serrer dans ses bras; (shore, kerb) serrer ▷ n: **to give sb a ~** serrer qn dans ses bras
huge [hjuːdʒ] adj énorme, immense
hull [hʌl] n (of ship) coque f
hum [hʌm] vt (tune) fredonner ▷ vi fredonner; (insect) bourdonner; (plane, tool) vrombir
human [ˈhjuːmən] adj humain(e) ▷ n (also: ~ **being**) être humain
humane [hjuːˈmeɪn] adj humain(e), humanitaire
humanitarian [hjuːmænɪˈtɛərɪən] adj humanitaire
humanity [hjuːˈmænɪtɪ] n humanité f
human rights npl droits mpl de l'homme
humble [ˈhʌmbl] adj humble, modeste
humid [ˈhjuːmɪd] adj humide; **humidity** [hjuːˈmɪdɪtɪ] n humidité f
humiliate [hjuːˈmɪlɪeɪt] vt humilier
humiliating [hjuːˈmɪlɪeɪtɪŋ] adj humiliant(e)
humiliation [hjuːmɪlɪˈeɪʃən] n humiliation f
hummus [ˈhʊməs] n houm(m)ous m
humorous [ˈhjuːmərəs] adj humoristique
humour (us **humor**) [ˈhjuːmə*] n humour m; (mood) humeur f ▷ vt (person) faire plaisir à; se prêter aux caprices de
hump [hʌmp] n bosse f
hunch [hʌntʃ] n (premonition) intuition f
hundred [ˈhʌndrəd] num cent; **~s of** des centaines de; **hundredth** [-ɪdθ]

num centième
hung [hʌŋ] pt, pp of **hang**
Hungarian [hʌŋˈgɛərɪən] adj hongrois(e) ▷ n Hongrois(e); (Ling) hongrois m
Hungary [ˈhʌŋgərɪ] n Hongrie f
hunger [ˈhʌŋgə*] n faim f ▷ vi: **to ~ for** avoir faim de, désirer ardemment
hungry [ˈhʌŋgrɪ] adj affamé(e); **to be ~** avoir faim; **~ for** (fig) avide de
hunt [hʌnt] vt (seek) chercher; (Sport) chasser ▷ vi (search): **to ~ for** chercher (partout); (Sport) chasser ▷ n (Sport) chasse f; **hunter** n chasseur m; **hunting** n chasse f
hurdle [ˈhəːdl] n (Sport) haie f; (fig) obstacle m
hurl [həːl] vt lancer (avec violence); (abuse, insults) lancer
hurrah, **hurray** [hʊˈrɑː, ˈhʌˈreɪ] excl hourra!
hurricane [ˈhʌrɪkən] n ouragan m
hurry [ˈhʌrɪ] n hâte f, précipitation f ▷ vi se presser, se dépêcher ▷ vt (person) faire presser, faire se dépêcher; (work) presser; **to be in a ~** être pressé(e); **to do sth in a ~** faire qch en vitesse; **hurry up** vi se dépêcher
hurt [həːt] (pt, pp ~) vt (cause pain to) faire mal à; (injure, fig) blesser ▷ vi faire mal ▷ adj blessé(e); **my arm ~s** j'ai mal au bras; **to ~ o.s.** se faire mal
husband [ˈhʌzbənd] n mari m
hush [hʌʃ] n calme m, silence m ▷ vt faire taire; **~!** chut!
husky [ˈhʌskɪ] adj (voice) rauque ▷ n chien esquimau or de traîneau
hut [hʌt] n hutte f; (shed) cabane f
hyacinth [ˈhaɪəsɪnθ] n jacinthe f
hydrangea [haɪˈdreɪndʒə] n hortensia m
hydrofoil [ˈhaɪdrəfɔɪl] n hydrofoil m
hydrogen [ˈhaɪdrədʒən] n hydrogène m
hygiene [ˈhaɪdʒiːn] n hygiène f; **hygienic** [haɪˈdʒiːnɪk] adj hygiénique
hymn [hɪm] n hymne m; cantique m
hype [haɪp] n (inf) matraquage m

publicitaire or **médiatique**

hypermarket ['haɪpəmɑːkɪt] (BRIT) n
hypermarché m

hyphen ['haɪfn] n trait m d'union

hypnotize ['hɪpnətaɪz] vt hypnotiser

hypocrite ['hɪpəkrɪt] n hypocrite m/f

hypocritical [hɪpə'krɪtɪkl] adj
hypocrite

hypothesis (pl **hypotheses**)
[haɪ'pɒθɪsɪs, -siːz] n hypothèse f

hysterical [hɪ'sterɪkl] adj hystérique;
(funny) hilarant(e)

hysterics [hɪ'sterɪks] npl: **to be in/
have ~** (anger, panic) avoir une crise de
nerfs; (laughter) attraper un fou rire

I [aɪ] pron je; (before vowel) j'; (stressed)
moi

ice [aɪs] n glace f; (on road) verglas m
▷ vt (cake) glacer ▷ vi (also: **~ up**)
geler; (also: **~ up**) se givrer; **iceberg**
n iceberg m; **ice cream** n glace f; **ice
cube** n glaçon m; **ice hockey** n hockey
m sur glace

Iceland ['aɪslənd] n Islande f; **Icelander**
n Islandais(e); **Icelandic** [aɪs'lændɪk]
adj islandais(e) ▷ n (Ling) islandais m

ice: **ice lolly** n (BRIT) esquimau m;
ice rink n patinoire f; **ice skating** n
patinage m (sur glace)

icing ['aɪsɪŋ] n (Culin) glaçage m; **icing
sugar** n (BRIT) sucre m glace

icon ['aɪkɒn] n icône f

ICT n abbr (BRIT: Scol: = information and
communications technology) TIC fpl

icy ['aɪsɪ] adj glacé(e); (road) verglacé(e);
(weather, temperature) glacial(e)

I'd [aɪd] = **I would**; **I had**

ID card n carte f d'identité

idea [aɪ'dɪə] n idée f

ideal [aɪˈdɪəl] n idéal m ▷ adj idéal(e)

ideally [aɪˈdɪəlɪ] adv (preferably) dans l'idéal; (perfectly): **he is ideally suited to the job** il est parfait pour ce poste

identical [aɪˈdɛntɪkl] adj identique

identification [aɪdɛntɪfɪˈkeɪʃən] n identification f; **means of ~** pièce f d'identité

identify [aɪˈdɛntɪfaɪ] vt identifier

identity [aɪˈdɛntɪtɪ] n identité f; **identity card** n carte f d'identité; **identity theft** n usurpation f d'identité

ideology [aɪdɪˈɔlədʒɪ] n idéologie f

idiom [ˈɪdɪəm] n (phrase) expression f idiomatique; (style) style m

idiot [ˈɪdɪət] n idiot(e), imbécile m/f

idle [aɪdl] adj (doing nothing) sans occupation, désœuvré(e); (lazy) oisif(-ive), paresseux(-euse); (unemployed) au chômage; (machinery) au repos; (question, pleasures) vain(e), futile ▷ vi (engine) tourner au ralenti

idol [aɪdl] n idole f

idyllic [ɪˈdɪlɪk] adj idyllique

i.e. abbr (= id est: that is) c. à d., c'est-à-dire

if [ɪf] conj si; **if necessary** si nécessaire, le cas échéant; **if so** si c'est le cas; **if not** sinon; **if only I could!** si seulement je pouvais!; see also **as**; **even**

ignite [ɪgˈnaɪt] vt mettre le feu à, enflammer ▷ vi s'enflammer

ignition [ɪgˈnɪʃən] n (Aut) allumage m; **to switch on/off the ~** mettre/couper le contact

ignorance [ˈɪgnərəns] n ignorance f

ignorant [ˈɪgnərənt] adj ignorant(e); **to be ~ of** (subject) ne rien connaître en; (events) ne pas être au courant de

ignore [ɪgˈnɔː] vt ne tenir aucun compte de; (mistake) ne pas relever; (person: pretend not to see) faire semblant de ne pas reconnaître; (: pay no attention to) ignorer

ill [ɪl] adj (sick) malade; (bad) mauvais(e) ▷ n mal m ▷ adv: **to speak/think ~ of sb** dire/penser du mal de qn; **to be taken ~** tomber malade

I'll [aɪl] = **I will; I shall**

illegal [ɪˈliːgl] adj illégal(e)

illegible [ɪˈlɛdʒɪbl] adj illisible

illegitimate [ɪlɪˈdʒɪtɪmət] adj illégitime

ill health n mauvaise santé

illiterate [ɪˈlɪtərət] adj illettré(e)

illness [ˈɪlnɪs] n maladie f

illuminate [ɪˈluːmɪneɪt] vt (room, street) éclairer; (for special effect) illuminer

illusion [ɪˈluːʒən] n illusion f

illustrate [ˈɪləstreɪt] vt illustrer

illustration [ɪləˈstreɪʃən] n illustration f

I'm [aɪm] = **I am**

image [ˈɪmɪdʒ] n image f; (public face) image de marque

imaginary [ɪˈmædʒɪnərɪ] adj imaginaire

imagination [ɪmædʒɪˈneɪʃən] n imagination f

imaginative [ɪˈmædʒɪnətɪv] adj imaginatif(-ive); (person) plein(e) d'imagination

imagine [ɪˈmædʒɪn] vt s'imaginer; (suppose) imaginer, supposer

imbalance [ɪmˈbæləns] n déséquilibre m

imitate [ˈɪmɪteɪt] vt imiter; **imitation** [ɪmɪˈteɪʃən] n imitation f

immaculate [ɪˈmækjulət] adj impeccable; (Rel) immaculé(e)

immature [ɪməˈtjuə] adj (fruit) qui n'est pas mûr(e); (person) qui manque de maturité

immediate [ɪˈmiːdɪət] adj immédiat(e); **immediately** adv (at once) immédiatement; **immediately next to** juste à côté de

immense [ɪˈmɛns] adj immense, énorme; **immensely** adv (+adj) extrêmement; (+vb) énormément

immerse [ɪˈməːs] vt immerger, plonger; **to be ~d in** (fig) être plongé dans

immigrant [ˈɪmɪgrənt] n

immigrant(e); (already established) immigré(e); **immigration** [ɪmɪˈgreɪʃən] n immigration f

imminent [ˈɪmɪnənt] adj imminent(e)

immoral [ɪˈmɒrl] adj immoral(e)

immortal [ɪˈmɔːtl] adj, n immortel(le)

immune [ɪˈmjuːn] adj: ~ (to) immunisé(e) (contre); **immune system** n système m immunitaire

immunize [ˈɪmjunaɪz] vt immuniser

impact [ˈɪmpækt] n choc m, impact m; (fig) impact

impair [ɪmˈpɛəʳ] vt détériorer, diminuer

impartial [ɪmˈpɑːʃl] adj impartial(e)

impatience [ɪmˈpeɪʃəns] n impatience f

impatient [ɪmˈpeɪʃənt] adj impatient(e); **to get** or **grow ~** s'impatienter

impeccable [ɪmˈpekəbl] adj impeccable, parfait(e)

impending [ɪmˈpendɪŋ] adj imminent(e)

imperative [ɪmˈperətɪv] adj (need) urgent(e), pressant(e); (tone) impérieux(-euse) ▷ n (Ling) impératif m

imperfect [ɪmˈpəːfɪkt] adj imparfait(e); (goods etc) défectueux(-euse) ▷ n (Ling: also: ~ **tense**) imparfait m

imperial [ɪmˈpɪərɪəl] adj impérial(e); (BRIT: measure) légal(e)

impersonal [ɪmˈpəːsənl] adj impersonnel(le)

impersonate [ɪmˈpəːsəneɪt] vt se faire passer pour; (Theat) imiter

impetus [ˈɪmpətəs] n impulsion f; (of runner) élan m

implant [ɪmˈplɑːnt] vt (Med) implanter; (fig: idea, principle) inculquer

implement n [ˈɪmplɪmənt] outil m, instrument m; (for cooking) ustensile m ▷ vt [ˈɪmplɪment] exécuter

implicate [ˈɪmplɪkeɪt] vt impliquer, compromettre

implication [ɪmplɪˈkeɪʃən] n implication f; **by ~** indirectement

implicit [ɪmˈplɪsɪt] adj implicite; (complete) absolu(e)

imply [ɪmˈplaɪ] vt (hint) suggérer, laisser entendre; (mean) indiquer, supposer

impolite [ɪmpəˈlaɪt] adj impoli(e)

import vt [ɪmˈpɔːt] importer ▷ n [ˈɪmpɔːt] (Comm) importation f; (meaning) portée f, signification f

importance [ɪmˈpɔːtns] n importance f

important [ɪmˈpɔːtnt] adj important(e); **it's not ~** c'est sans importance, ce n'est pas important

importer [ɪmˈpɔːtəʳ] n importateur(-trice)

impose [ɪmˈpəuz] vt imposer ▷ vi: **to ~ on sb** abuser de la gentillesse de qn; **imposing** adj imposant(e), impressionnant(e)

impossible [ɪmˈpɒsɪbl] adj impossible

impotent [ˈɪmpətnt] adj impuissant(e)

impoverished [ɪmˈpɒvərɪʃt] adj pauvre, appauvri(e)

impractical [ɪmˈpræktɪkl] adj pas pratique; (person) qui manque d'esprit pratique

impress [ɪmˈpres] vt impressionner, faire impression sur; (mark) imprimer, marquer; **to ~ sth on sb** faire bien comprendre qch à qn

impression [ɪmˈpreʃən] n impression f; (of stamp, seal) empreinte f; (imitation) imitation f; **to be under the ~ that** avoir l'impression que

impressive [ɪmˈpresɪv] adj impressionnant(e)

imprison [ɪmˈprɪzn] vt emprisonner, mettre en prison; **imprisonment** n emprisonnement m; (period): **to sentence sb to 10 years' imprisonment** condamner qn à 10 ans de prison

improbable [ɪmˈprɒbəbl] adj improbable; (excuse) peu plausible

improper [ɪmˈprɒpəʳ] adj (unsuitable) déplacé(e), de mauvais goût; (indecent) indécent(e); (*dishonest*) malhonnête

improve [ɪm'pruːv] vt améliorer ▷ vi s'améliorer; (*pupil etc*) faire des progrès; **improvement** n amélioration f; (*of pupil etc*) progrès m

improvise ['ɪmprəvaɪz] vt, vi improviser

impulse ['ɪmpʌls] n impulsion f; **on** ~ impulsivement, sur un coup de tête; **impulsive** [ɪm'pʌlsɪv] adj impulsif(-ive)

⊙ **KEYWORD**

in [ɪn] prep 1 (*indicating place, position*) dans; **in the house/the fridge** dans la maison/le frigo; **in the garden** dans le or au jardin; **in town** en ville; **in the country** à la campagne; **in school** à l'école; **in here/there** ici/là

2 (*with place names: of town, region, country*) **in London** à Londres; **in England** en Angleterre; **in Japan** au Japon; **in the United States** aux États-Unis

3 (*indicating time: during*) **in spring** au printemps; **in summer** en été; **in May/2005** en mai/2005; **in the afternoon** (dans) l'après-midi; **at 4 o'clock in the afternoon** à 4 heures de l'après-midi

4 (*indicating time: in the space of*) en; (: *future*) dans; **I did it in 3 hours/days** je l'ai fait en 3 heures/jours; **I'll see you in 2 weeks** or **in a 2 weeks' time** je te verrai dans 2 semaines

5 (*indicating manner etc*) à; **in a loud/soft voice** à voix haute/basse; **in pencil** au crayon; **in writing** par écrit; **in French** en français; **the boy in the blue shirt** le garçon à or avec la chemise bleue

6 (*indicating circumstances*): **in the sun** au soleil; **in the shade** à l'ombre; **in the rain** sous la pluie; **a change in policy** un changement de politique

7 (*indicating mood, state*): **in tears** en larmes; **in anger** sous le coup de la

colère; **in despair** au désespoir; **in good condition** en bon état; **to live in luxury** vivre dans le luxe

8 (*with ratios, numbers*): **1 in 10 households, 1 household in 10** 1 ménage sur 10; **20 pence in the pound** 20 pence par livre sterling; **they lined up in twos** ils se mirent en rangs (deux) par deux; **in hundreds** par centaines

9 (*referring to people, works*) chez; **the disease is common in children** c'est une maladie courante chez les enfants; **in (the works of) Dickens** chez Dickens, dans (l'œuvre de) Dickens

10 (*indicating profession etc*) dans; **to be in teaching** être dans l'enseignement

11 (*after superlative*) de; **the best pupil in the class** le meilleur élève de la classe

12 (*with present participle*): **in saying this** en disant ceci

▷ adv: **to be in** (*person: at home, work*) être là; (*train, ship, plane*) être arrivé(e); (*in fashion*) être à la mode; **to ask sb in** inviter qn à entrer; **to run/limp** etc **in** entrer en courant/boitant etc

▷ n: **the ins and outs (of)** (*of proposal, situation etc*) les tenants et aboutissants de

---

inability [ɪnə'bɪlɪtɪ] n incapacité f; **~ to pay** incapacité de payer

inaccurate [ɪn'ækjurət] adj inexact(e); (*person*) qui manque de précision

inadequate [ɪn'ædɪkwət] adj insuffisant(e), inadéquat(e)

inadvertently [ɪnəd'vəːtntlɪ] adv par mégarde

inappropriate [ɪnə'prəuprɪət] adj inopportun(e), mal à propos; (*word, expression*) impropre

inaugurate [ɪn'nɔːgjureɪt] vt inaugurer; (*president, official*) investir de ses fonctions

Inc. abbr = **incorporated**

incapable [ɪn'keɪpəbl] adj: **~ (of)** incapable (de)

incense n ['ɪnsens] encens m ▷ vt
[ɪn'sens] (anger) mettre en colère

incentive [ɪn'sentɪv] n
encouragement m, raison f de se
donner de la peine

inch [ɪntʃ] n pouce m (=25 mm; 12 in a
foot); **within an ~** of à deux doigts de;
he wouldn't give an ~ (fig) il n'a pas
voulu céder d'un pouce

incidence ['ɪnsɪdns] n (of crime, disease)
fréquence f

incident ['ɪnsɪdnt] n incident m

incidentally [ɪnsɪ'dentəlɪ] adv (by the
way) à propos

inclination [ɪnklɪ'neɪʃən] n
inclination f; (desire) envie f

incline n ['ɪnklaɪn] pente f, plan
incliné ▷ vb [ɪn'klaɪn] ▷ vt incliner ▷ vi
(surface) s'incliner; **to be ~d to do** (have
a tendency to do) avoir tendance à faire

include [ɪn'kluːd] vt inclure,
comprendre; **service is/is not ~d** le
service est compris/n'est pas compris;
including prep y compris; **inclusion**
n inclusion f; **inclusive** adj inclus(e),
compris(e); **inclusive of tax** taxes
comprises

income ['ɪnkʌm] n revenu m; (from
property etc) rentes fpl; **income
support** n (BRIT) ≈ revenu m minimum
d'insertion, RMI m; **income tax** n
impôt sur le revenu

incoming ['ɪnkʌmɪŋ] adj (passengers,
mail) à l'arrivée; (government, tenant)
nouveau (nouvelle)

incompatible [ɪnkəm'pætɪbl] adj
incompatible

incompetence [ɪn'kɒmpɪtns] n
incompétence f, incapacité f

incompetent [ɪn'kɒmpɪtnt] adj
incompétent(e), incapable

incomplete [ɪnkəm'pliːt] adj
incomplet(-ète)

inconsistent [ɪnkən'sɪstnt] adj
qui manque de constance; (work)
irrégulier(-ière); (statement) peu
cohérent(e); **~ with** en contradiction
avec

inconvenience [ɪnkən'viːnjəns] n
inconvénient m; (trouble) dérangement
m ▷ vt déranger

inconvenient [ɪnkən'viːnjənt]
adj malcommode; (time, place) mal
choisi(e), qui ne convient pas; (visitor)
importun(e)

incorporate [ɪn'kɔːpəreɪt] vt
incorporer; (contain) contenir

incorrect [ɪnkə'rekt] adj incorrect(e);
(opinion, statement) inexact(e)

increase n ['ɪnkriːs] augmentation
f ▷ vi, vt [ɪn'kriːs] augmenter;
increasingly adv de plus en plus

incredible [ɪn'kredɪbl] adj incroyable;
incredibly adv incroyablement

incur [ɪn'kɜː] vt (expenses) encourir;
(anger, risk's) s'exposer à; (debt)
contracter; (loss) subir

indecent [ɪn'diːsnt] adj indécent(e),
inconvenant(e)

indeed [ɪn'diːd] adv (confirming,
agreeing) en effet, effectivement; (for
emphasis) vraiment; (furthermore)
d'ailleurs; **yes ~!** certainement!

indefinitely [ɪn'defɪnɪtlɪ] adv (wait)
indéfiniment

independence [ɪndɪ'pendns] n
indépendance f; **Independence Day**
n (US) fête de l'Indépendance américaine;
voir encadré

○ **INDEPENDENCE DAY**
●
● L'**Independence Day** est la fête
● nationale aux États-Unis, le 4
● juillet. Il commémore l'adoption
● de la déclaration d'Indépendance,
● en 1776, écrite par Thomas Jefferson
● et proclamant la séparation des 13
● colonies américaines de la Grande-
● Bretagne.

---

independent [ɪndɪ'pendnt]
adj indépendant(e); (radio) libre;
independent school n (BRIT) école
privée

index ['ɪndeks] n (pl -es) (in book)

index m; (: in library etc) catalogue m (pl **indices**) (ratio, sign) indice m
India ['ɪndɪə] n Inde f; **Indian** adj indien(ne) ▷ n Indien(ne); (**American Indian**) Indien(ne) (d'Amérique)
indicate ['ɪndɪkeɪt] vt indiquer ▷ vi (BRIT Aut): **to - left/right** mettre son clignotant à gauche/à droite; **indication** [ɪndɪ'keɪʃən] n indication f, signe m; **indicative** [ɪn'dɪkətɪv] adj: **to be indicative of sth** être symptomatique de qch ▷ n (Ling) indicatif m; **indicator** n (sign) indicateur m; (Aut) clignotant m
indices ['ɪndɪsi:z] npl of **index**
indict [ɪn'daɪt] vt accuser; **indictment** n accusation f
indifference [ɪn'dɪfrəns] n indifférence f
indifferent [ɪn'dɪfrənt] adj indifférent(e); (poor) médiocre, quelconque
indigenous [ɪn'dɪdʒɪnəs] adj indigène
indigestion [ɪndɪ'dʒestʃən] n indigestion f, mauvaise digestion
indignant [ɪn'dɪgnənt] adj: **- (at sth/ with sb)** indigné(e) (de qch/contre qn)
indirect [ɪndɪ'rekt] adj indirect(e)
indispensable [ɪndɪ'spensəbl] adj indispensable
individual [ɪndɪ'vɪdjuəl] n individu m ▷ adj individuel(le); (characteristic) particulier(-ière), original(e); **individually** adv individuellement
Indonesia [ɪndə'ni:zɪə] n Indonésie f
indoor ['ɪndɔ:r] adj d'intérieur; (plant) d'appartement; (swimming pool) couvert(e); (sport, games) pratiqué(e) en salle; **indoors** [ɪn'dɔ:z] adv à l'intérieur
induce [ɪn'dju:s] vt (persuade) persuader; (bring about) provoquer; (labour) déclencher
indulge [ɪn'dʌldʒ] vt (whim) céder à, satisfaire; (child) gâter ▷ vi: **to - in** (luxury) s'offrir qch, se permettre qch; (fantasies etc) se livrer à qch; **indulgent** adj indulgent(e)
industrial [ɪn'dʌstrɪəl] adj

industriel(le); (injury) du travail; (dispute) ouvrier(-ière); **industrial estate** n (BRIT) zone industrielle; **industrialist** n industriel m; **industrial park** n (US) zone industrielle
industry ['ɪndəstrɪ] n industrie f; (diligence) zèle m, application f
inefficient [ɪnɪ'fɪʃənt] adj inefficace
inequality [ɪnɪ'kwɔlɪtɪ] n inégalité f
inevitable [ɪn'evɪtəbl] adj inévitable; **inevitably** adv inévitablement, fatalement
inexpensive [ɪnɪk'spensɪv] adj bon marché inv
inexperienced [ɪnɪk'spɪərɪənst] adj inexpérimenté(e)
inexplicable [ɪnɪk'splɪkəbl] adj inexplicable
infamous ['ɪnfəməs] adj infâme, abominable
infant ['ɪnfənt] n (baby) nourrisson m; (young child) petit(e) enfant
infantry ['ɪnfəntrɪ] n infanterie f
infant school n (BRIT) classes fpl préparatoires (entre 5 et 7 ans)
infect [ɪn'fekt] vt (wound) infecter; (person, blood) contaminer; **infection** [ɪn'fekʃən] n infection f; (contagion) contagion f; **infectious** [ɪn'fekʃəs] adj infectieux(-euse); (also fig) contagieux(-euse)
infer [ɪn'fə:r] vt: **to - (from)** conclure (de), déduire (de)
inferior [ɪn'fɪərɪər] adj inférieur(e); (goods) de qualité inférieure ▷ n inférieur(e); (in rank) subalterne m/f
infertile [ɪn'fə:taɪl] adj stérile
infertility [ɪnfə'tɪlɪtɪ] n infertilité f, stérilité f
infested [ɪn'festɪd] adj: **- (with)** infesté(e) (de)
infinite ['ɪnfɪnɪt] adj infini(e); (time, money) illimité(e); **infinitely** adv infiniment
infirmary [ɪn'fə:mərɪ] n hôpital m; (in school, factory) infirmerie f
inflamed [ɪn'fleɪmd] adj enflammé(e)
inflammation [ɪnflə'meɪʃən] n

inflammation f

inflatable [ɪnˈfleɪtəbl] *adj* gonflable

inflate [ɪnˈfleɪt] *vt* (tyre, balloon)
gonfler; (fig: exaggerate) grossir;
(: increase) gonfler; **inflation** [ɪnˈfleɪʃən]
n (Econ) inflation f

inflexible [ɪnˈfleksɪbl] *adj* inflexible,
rigide

inflict [ɪnˈflɪkt] *vt*: **to ~ on** infliger à

influence [ˈɪnfluəns] *n* influence f ▷ *vt*
influencer; **under the ~ of alcohol** en
état d'ébriété; **influential** [ɪnfluˈɛnʃl]
adj influent(e)

influenza [ɪnfluˈɛnzə] *n* grippe f

influx [ˈɪnflʌks] *n* afflux m

info (inf) [ˈɪnfəu] *n* (= information)
renseignements *mpl*

inform [ɪnˈfɔːm] *vt*: **to ~ sb (of)**
informer or avertir qn (de) ▷ *vi*: **to ~ on
sb** dénoncer qn, informer contre qn

informal [ɪnˈfɔːml] *adj* (person,
manner, party) simple; (visit, discussion)
dénué(e) de formalités; (announcement,
invitation) non officiel(le); (colloquial)
familier(-ère)

information [ɪnfəˈmeɪʃən] *n*
information(s) f(pl); (knowledge)
connaissances *fpl*;
a piece of ~ un renseignement;
information office *n* bureau *m*
de renseignements; **information
technology** *n* informatique f

informative [ɪnˈfɔːmətɪv] *adj*
instructif(-ive)

infra-red [ɪnfrəˈred] *adj* infrarouge

infrastructure [ˈɪnfrəstrʌktʃəʳ] *n*
infrastructure f

infrequent [ɪnˈfriːkwənt] *adj* peu
fréquent(e), rare

infuriate [ɪnˈfjuərɪeɪt] *vt* mettre en
fureur

infuriating [ɪnˈfjuərɪeɪtɪŋ] *adj*
exaspérant(e)

ingenious [ɪnˈdʒiːnjəs] *adj*
ingénieux(-euse)

ingredient [ɪnˈɡriːdɪənt] *n* ingrédient
m; (fig) élément *m*

inhabit [ɪnˈhæbɪt] *vt* habiter;

inhabitant *n* habitant(e)

inhale [ɪnˈheɪl] *vt* inhaler; (perfume)
respirer; (smoke) avaler ▷ *vi* (breathe in)
aspirer; (in smoking) avaler la fumée;
inhaler *n* inhalateur *m*

inherent [ɪnˈhɪərənt] *adj*: **~ (in or to)**
inhérent(e) (à)

inherit [ɪnˈhɛrɪt] *vt* hériter (de);
inheritance *n* héritage *m*

inhibit [ɪnˈhɪbɪt] *vt* (Psych) inhiber;
(growth) freiner; **inhibition** [ɪnhɪˈbɪʃən]
n inhibition f

initial [ɪˈnɪʃl] *adj* initial(e) ▷ *n* initiale
f ▷ *vt* parafer; **initials** *npl* initiales *fpl*;
(as signature) parafe m; **initially** *adv*
initialement, au début

initiate [ɪˈnɪʃɪeɪt] *vt* (start)
entreprendre; amorcer; (enterprise)
lancer; (person) initier; **to ~
proceedings against sb** (Law)
intenter une action à qn, engager des
poursuites contre qn

initiative [ɪˈnɪʃətɪv] *n* initiative f

inject [ɪnˈdʒekt] *vt* injecter; (person): **to
~ sb with sth** faire une piqûre de qch à
qn; **injection** [ɪnˈdʒekʃən] *n* injection
f, piqûre f

injure [ˈɪndʒəʳ] *vt* blesser; (damage:
reputation etc) compromettre; **to ~
o.s.** se blesser; **injured** *adj* (person,
leg etc) blessé(e); **injury** *n* blessure f;
(wrong) tort *m*

injustice [ɪnˈdʒʌstɪs] *n* injustice f

ink [ɪŋk] *n* encre f; **ink-jet printer**
[ˈɪŋkdʒet-] *n* imprimante f à jet d'encre

inland *adj* [ˈɪnlənd] intérieur(e) ▷ *adv*
[ɪnˈlænd] à l'intérieur, dans les terres;
Inland Revenue *n* (BRIT) fisc *m*

in-laws [ˈɪnlɔːz] *npl* beaux-parents *mpl*;
belle famille

inmate [ˈɪnmeɪt] *n* (in prison)
détenu(e); (in asylum) interné(e)

inn [ɪn] *n* auberge f

inner [ˈɪnəʳ] *adj* intérieur(e); **inner-city**
adj (schools, problems) de quartiers
déshérités

inning [ˈɪnɪŋ] *n* (US: Baseball) tour *m*
de batte; **innings** *npl* (Cricket) tour

de batte

innocence ['ɪnəsns] n innocence f

innocent ['ɪnəsnt] adj innocent(e)

innovation [ɪnəʊ'veɪʃən] n innovation f

innovative ['ɪnəʊveɪtɪv] adj novateur(-trice); (product) innovant(e)

in-patient ['ɪnpeɪʃənt] n malade hospitalisé(e)

input ['ɪnpʊt] n (contribution) contribution f; (resources) ressources fpl; (Comput) entrée f (de données); (: data) données fpl ▷ vt (Comput) introduire, entrer

inquest ['ɪnkwest] n enquête (criminelle); (coroner's) enquête judiciaire

inquire [ɪn'kwaɪə*] vi demander ▷ vt demander; **to ~ about** s'informer de, se renseigner sur; **to ~ when/where/whether** demander quand/où/si; **inquiry** n demande f de renseignements; (Law) enquête f, investigation f; **"inquiries"** "renseignements"

ins. abbr = **inches**

insane [ɪn'seɪn] adj fou (folle); (Med) aliéné(e)

insanity [ɪn'sænɪtɪ] n folie f; (Med) aliénation (mentale)

insect ['ɪnsekt] n insecte m; **insect repellent** n crème f anti-insectes

insecure [ɪnsɪ'kjʊə*] adj (person) anxieux(-euse); (job) précaire; (building etc) peu sûr(e)

insecurity [ɪnsɪ'kjʊərɪtɪ] n insécurité f

insensitive [ɪn'sensɪtɪv] adj insensible

insert vt [ɪn'sɜːt] insérer ▷ n ['ɪnsɜːt] insertion f

inside ['ɪn'saɪd] n intérieur m ▷ adj intérieur(e) ▷ adv à l'intérieur, dedans ▷ prep à l'intérieur de; (of time): **~ 10 minutes** en moins de 10 minutes; **to go ~** rentrer; **inside lane** n (Aut: in Britain) voie f de gauche; (: in US, Europe) voie f de droite; **inside out** adv à l'envers; (know) à fond; **to turn sth inside out** retourner qch

insight ['ɪnsaɪt] n perspicacité f; (glimpse, idea) aperçu m

insignificant [ɪnsɪg'nɪfɪknt] adj insignifiant(e)

insincere [ɪnsɪn'sɪə*] adj hypocrite

insist [ɪn'sɪst] vi insister; **to ~ on doing** insister pour faire; **to ~ on sth** exiger qch; **to ~ that** insister pour que + sub; (claim) maintenir or soutenir que; **insistent** adj insistant(e), pressant(e); (noise, action) ininterrompu(e)

insomnia [ɪn'sɒmnɪə] n insomnie f

inspect [ɪn'spekt] vt inspecter; (BRIT: ticket) contrôler; **inspection** [ɪn'spekʃən] n inspection f; (BRIT: of tickets) contrôle m; **inspector** n inspecteur(-trice); (BRIT: on buses, trains) contrôleur(-euse)

inspiration [ɪnspə'reɪʃən] n inspiration f; **inspire** [ɪn'spaɪə*] vt inspirer; **inspiring** adj inspirant(e)

instability [ɪnstə'bɪlɪtɪ] n instabilité f

install (us **instal**) [ɪn'stɔːl] vt installer; **installation** [ɪnstə'leɪʃən] n installation f

instalment (us **installment**) [ɪn'stɔːlmənt] n (payment) acompte m, versement partiel; (of TV serial etc) épisode m; **in ~s** (pay) à tempérament; (receive) en plusieurs fois

instance ['ɪnstəns] n exemple m; **for ~** par exemple; **in the first ~** tout d'abord, en premier lieu

instant ['ɪnstənt] n instant m ▷ adj immédiat(e), urgent(e); (coffee, food) instantané(e), en poudre; **instantly** adv immédiatement, tout de suite; **instant messaging** n messagerie f instantanée

instead [ɪn'sted] adv au lieu de cela; **~ of** au lieu de; **~ of sb** à la place de qn

instinct ['ɪnstɪŋkt] n instinct m; **instinctive** adj instinctif(-ive)

institute ['ɪnstɪtjuːt] n institut m ▷ vt instituer, établir; (inquiry) ouvrir; (proceedings) entamer

institution [ɪnstɪ'tjuːʃən] n institution f; (school) établissement

m (scolaire); (for care) établissement
(psychiatrique etc)
instruct [ɪn'strʌkt] vt: **to ~ sb in sth**
enseigner qch à qn; **to ~ sb to do**
charger qn or ordonner à qn de faire;
instruction [ɪn'strʌkʃən] n instruction
f; **instructions** npl (orders) directives
fpl; **instructions for use** mode m
d'emploi; **instructor** n professeur m;
(for skiing, driving) moniteur m
instrument ['ɪnstrumənt] n
instrument m; **instrumental**
[ɪnstru'mentl] adj (Mus)
instrumental(e); **to be instrumental
in sth/in doing sth** contribuer à qch/à
faire qch
insufficient [ɪnsə'fɪʃənt] adj
insuffisant(e)
insulate ['ɪnsjuleɪt] vt isoler; (against
sound) insonoriser; **insulation**
[ɪnsju'leɪʃən] n isolation f; (against
sound) insonorisation f
insulin ['ɪnsjulɪn] n insuline f
insult n ['ɪnsʌlt] insulte f, affront
m ▷ vt [ɪn'sʌlt] insulter, faire un
affront à; **insulting** adj insultant(e),
injurieux(-euse)
insurance [ɪn'ʃuərəns] n assurance
f; **fire/life ~** assurance-incendie/-vie;
insurance company n compagnie f
or société f d'assurances; **insurance
policy** n police f d'assurance
insure [ɪn'ʃuə] vt assurer; **to ~ (o.s.)
against** (fig) parer à
intact [ɪn'tækt] adj intact(e)
intake ['ɪnteɪk] n (Tech) admission
f; (consumption) consommation f;
(BRIT Scol): **an ~ of 200 a year** 200
admissions par an
integral ['ɪntɪgrəl] adj (whole)
intégral(e); (part) intégrant(e)
integrate ['ɪntɪgreɪt] vt intégrer ▷ vi
s'intégrer
integrity [ɪn'tegrɪtɪ] n intégrité f
intellect ['ɪntəlekt] n intelligence f;
intellectual [ɪntə'lektjuəl] adj, n
intellectuel(le)
intelligence [ɪn'telɪdʒəns] n

intelligence f; (Mil etc) informations fpl,
renseignements mpl
intelligent [ɪn'telɪdʒənt] adj
intelligent(e)
intend [ɪn'tend] vt (gift etc): **to ~ sth
for** destiner qch à; **to ~ to do** avoir
l'intention de faire
intense [ɪn'tens] adj intense; (person)
véhément(e)
intensify [ɪn'tensɪfaɪ] vt intensifier
intensity [ɪn'tensɪtɪ] n intensité f
intensive [ɪn'tensɪv] adj intensif(-ive);
intensive care n: **to be in intensive
care** être en réanimation; **intensive
care unit** n service m de réanimation
intent [ɪn'tent] n intention f ▷ adj
attentif(-ive), absorbé(e); **to all ~s and
purposes** en fait, pratiquement; **to
be ~ on doing sth** être (bien) décidé
à faire qch
intention [ɪn'tenʃən] n intention f;
intentional adj intentionnel(le),
délibéré(e)
interact [ɪntər'ækt] vi avoir une action
réciproque; (people) communiquer;
interaction [ɪntər'ækʃən] n
interaction f; **interactive** adj (Comput)
interactif, conversationnel(le)
intercept [ɪntə'sept] vt intercepter;
(person) arrêter au passage
interchange n ['ɪntətʃeɪndʒ]
(exchange) échange m; (on motorway)
échangeur m
intercourse ['ɪntəkɔːs] n: **sexual ~**
rapports sexuels
interest ['ɪntrɪst] n intérêt m; (Comm:
stake, share) participation f, intérêts
mpl ▷ vt intéresser; **interested** adj
intéressé(e); **to be interested in sth**
s'intéresser à qch; **I'm interested
in going** ça m'intéresse d'y aller;
interesting adj intéressant(e);
interest rate n taux m d'intérêt
interface ['ɪntəfeɪs] n (Comput)
interface f
interfere [ɪntə'fɪə] vi: **to ~ in** (quarrel)
s'immiscer dans; (other people's business)
se mêler de; **to ~ with** (object) tripoter,

toucher à; (plans) contrecarrer; (duty) être en conflit avec; **interference** n (gen) ingérence f; (Radio, TV) parasites mpl

interim ['ɪntərɪm] adj provisoire; (post) intérimaire ▷ n: **in the ~** dans l'intérim

interior [ɪn'tɪərɪə] n intérieur m ▷ adj intérieur(e); (minister, department) de l'intérieur; **interior design** n architecture f d'intérieur

intermediate [ɪntə'miːdɪət] adj intermédiaire; (Scol: course, level) moyen(ne)

intermission [ɪntə'mɪʃən] n pause f; (Theat, Cine) entracte m

intern vt [ɪn'tɜːn] interner ▷ n ['ɪntɜːn] (us) interne m/f

internal [ɪn'tɜːnl] adj interne; (dispute, reform etc) intérieur(e); **Internal Revenue Service** n (us) fisc m

international [ɪntə'næʃnl] adj international(e) ▷ n (BRIT Sport) international m

Internet [ɪntə'nɛt] n: **the ~** l'Internet m; **Internet café** n cybercafé m; **Internet Service Provider** n fournisseur m d'accès à Internet; **Internet user** n internaute m/f

interpret [ɪn'tɜːprɪt] vt interpréter ▷ vi servir d'interprète; **interpretation** [ɪntɜːprɪ'teɪʃən] n interprétation f; **interpreter** n interprète m/f; **could you act as an interpreter for us?** pourriez-vous nous servir d'interprète?

interrogate [ɪn'tɛrəugeɪt] vt interroger; (suspect etc) soumettre à un interrogatoire; **interrogation** [ɪntɛrəu'geɪʃən] n interrogation f; (by police) interrogatoire m

interrogative [ɪntə'rɔgətɪv] adj interrogateur(-trice) ▷ n (Ling) interrogatif m

interrupt [ɪntə'rʌpt] vt, vi interrompre; **interruption** [ɪntə'rʌpʃən] n interruption f

intersection [ɪntə'sɛkʃən] n (of roads) croisement m

interstate ['ɪntəsteɪt] (us) n

autoroute f (qui relie plusieurs états)

interval ['ɪntəvl] n intervalle m; (BRIT: Theat) entracte m; (: Sport) mi-temps f; **at ~s** par intervalles

intervene [ɪntə'viːn] vi (time) s'écouler (entre-temps); (event) survenir; (person) intervenir

interview ['ɪntəvjuː] n (Radio, TV etc) interview f; (for job) entrevue f ▷ vt interviewer; avoir une entrevue avec; **interviewer** n (Radio, TV etc) interviewer m

intimate adj ['ɪntɪmət] intime; (friendship) profond(e); (knowledge) approfondi(e) ▷ vt ['ɪntɪmeɪt] suggérer, laisser entendre; (announce) faire savoir

intimidate [ɪn'tɪmɪdeɪt] vt intimider; **intimidating** [ɪn'tɪmɪdeɪtɪŋ] adj intimidant(e)

into ['ɪntu] prep dans; **~ pieces/French** en morceaux/français

intolerant [ɪn'tɔlərnt] adj: **~ (of)** intolérant(e) (de)

intranet [ɪn'trænet] n intranet m

intransitive [ɪn'trænsɪtɪv] adj intransitif(-ive)

intricate ['ɪntrɪkət] adj complexe, compliqué(e)

intrigue [ɪn'triːg] n intrigue f ▷ vt intriguer; **intriguing** adj fascinant(e)

introduce [ɪntrə'djuːs] vt introduire; (TV show etc) présenter; **to ~ sb (to sb)** présenter qn (à qn); **to ~ sb to** (pastime, technique) initier qn à; **introduction** [ɪntrə'dʌkʃən] n introduction f; (of person) présentation f; (to new experience) initiation f; **introductory** [ɪntrə'dʌktərɪ] adj préliminaire, introductif(-ive)

intrude [ɪn'truːd] vi (person) être importun(e); **to ~ on** ou **into** (conversation etc) s'immiscer dans; **intruder** n intrus(e)

intuition [ɪntjuː'ɪʃən] n intuition f

inundate ['ɪnʌndeɪt] vt: **to ~ with** inonder de

invade [ɪn'veɪd] vt envahir

invalid n ['ɪnvəlɪd] malade m/f; (with disability) invalide m/f ▷ adj [ɪn'vælɪd] (not valid) invalide, non valide

invaluable [ɪn'væljuəbl] adj inestimable, inappréciable

invariably [ɪn'vɛərɪəblɪ] adv invariablement; **she is ~ late** elle est toujours en retard

invasion [ɪn'veɪʒən] n invasion f

invent [ɪn'vent] vt inventer; **invention** [ɪn'venʃən] n invention f; **inventor** n inventeur(-trice)

inventory ['ɪnvəntrɪ] n inventaire m

inverted commas [ɪn'vɜːtɪd-] npl (BRIT) guillemets mpl

invest [ɪn'vest] vt investir ▷ vi: **to ~ in** placer de l'argent or investir dans; (fig: acquire) s'offrir, faire l'acquisition de

investigate [ɪn'vestɪgeɪt] vt étudier, examiner; (crime) faire une enquête sur; **investigation** [ɪnvestɪ'geɪʃən] n (of crime) enquête f, investigation f

investigator [ɪn'vestɪgeɪtə'] n investigateur(-trice); **private ~** détective privé

investment [ɪn'vestmənt] n investissement m, placement m

investor [ɪn'vestə'] n épargnant(e); (shareholder) actionnaire m/f

invisible [ɪn'vɪzɪbl] adj invisible

invitation [ɪnvɪ'teɪʃən] n invitation f

invite [ɪn'vaɪt] vt inviter; (opinions etc) demander; **inviting** adj engageant(e), attrayant(e)

invoice ['ɪnvɔɪs] n facture f ▷ vt facturer

involve [ɪn'vɔlv] vt (concern) impliquer; (concern) concerner; (require) nécessiter; **to ~ sb in** (theft etc) impliquer qn dans; (activity, meeting) faire participer qn à; **involved** adj (complicated) complexe; **to be involved in** (take part) participer à; **involvement** n (personal role) rôle m; (participation) participation f; (enthusiasm) enthousiasme m

inward ['ɪnwəd] adj (movement) vers l'intérieur; (thought, feeling) profond(e), intime ▷ adv = **inwards; inwards** adv

vers l'intérieur

IQ n abbr (= intelligence quotient) Q.I. m

IRA n abbr (= Irish Republican Army) IRA f

Iran [ɪ'rɑːn] n Iran m; **Iranian** [ɪ'reɪnɪən] adj iranien(ne) ▷ n iranien(ne)

Iraq [ɪ'rɑːk] n Irak m; **Iraqi** adj irakien(ne) ▷ n Irakien(ne)

Ireland ['aɪələnd] n Irlande f

iris, irises ['aɪrɪs, -ɪz] n iris m

Irish ['aɪrɪʃ] adj irlandais(e) ▷ npl: **the ~** les Irlandais; **Irishman** (irreg) n Irlandais m; **Irishwoman** (irreg) n Irlandaise f

iron ['aɪən] n fer m; (for clothes) fer à repasser ▷ adj de or en fer ▷ vt (clothes) repasser

ironic(al) [aɪ'rɔnɪk(l)] adj ironique; **ironically** adv ironiquement

ironing ['aɪənɪŋ] n (activity) repassage m; (clothes: ironed) linge repassé; (: to be ironed) linge à repasser; **ironing board** n planche f à repasser

irony ['aɪrənɪ] n ironie f

irrational [ɪ'ræʃənl] adj irrationnel(le); (person) qui n'est pas rationnel

irregular [ɪ'regjulə'] adj irrégulier(-ière); (surface) inégal(e); (action, event) peu orthodoxe

irrelevant [ɪ'reləvənt] adj sans rapport, hors de propos

irresistible [ɪrɪ'zɪstɪbl] adj irrésistible

irresponsible [ɪrɪ'spɔnsɪbl] adj (act) irréfléchi(e); (person) qui n'a pas le sens des responsabilités

irrigation [ɪrɪ'geɪʃən] n irrigation f

irritable ['ɪrɪtəbl] adj irritable

irritate ['ɪrɪteɪt] vt irriter; **irritating** adj irritant(e); **irritation** [ɪrɪ'teɪʃən] n irritation f

IRS n abbr (US) = **Internal Revenue Service**

is [ɪz] vb see **be**

ISDN n abbr (= Integrated Services Digital Network) RNIS m

Islam ['ɪzlɑːm] n Islam m; **Islamic** [ɪz'lɑːmɪk] adj islamique

island ['aɪlənd] n île f; (also: **traffic ~**) refuge m (pour piétons); **islander** n

habitant(e) d'une île, insulaire *m/f*
isle [aɪl] *n* île *f*
isn't [ɪznt] = **is not**
isolated ['aɪsəleɪtɪd] *adj* isolé(e)
isolation [aɪsə'leɪʃən] *n* isolement *m*
ISP *n abbr* = **Internet Service Provider**
Israel ['ɪzreɪl] *n* Israël *m*; **Israeli** [ɪz'reɪlɪ] *adj* israélien(ne) ▷ *n* Israélien(ne)
issue ['ɪʃuː] *n* question *f*, problème *m*; *(of banknotes)* émission *f*; *(of newspaper)* numéro *m*; *(of book)* publication *f*, parution *f* ▷ *vt (rations, equipment)* distribuer; *(orders)* donner; *(statement)* publier, faire; *(certificate, passport)* délivrer; *(banknotes, cheques, stamps)* émettre, mettre en circulation; **at ~** en jeu, en cause; **to take ~ with sb (over sth)** exprimer son désaccord avec qn (sur qch)
IT *n abbr* = **information technology**

 KEYWORD

it [ɪt] *pron* 1 *(specific: subject)* il (elle); *(: direct object)* le (la, l'); *(: indirect object)* lui; **it's on the table** c'est or il (or elle) est sur la table; **I can't find it** je n'arrive pas à le trouver; **give it to me** donne-le-moi
2 *(after prep)*: **about/from/of it** en; **I spoke to him about it** je lui en ai parlé; **what did you learn from it?** qu'est-ce que vous en avez retiré?; **I'm proud of it** j'en suis fier; **in/to it** y; **put the book in it** mettez-y le livre; **he agreed to it** il y a consenti; **did you go to it?** *(party, concert etc)* est-ce que vous y êtes allé(s)?
3 *(impersonal)* il; ce, cela, ça; **it's raining** il pleut; **it's Friday tomorrow** demain, c'est vendredi *or* nous sommes, vendredi; **it's 6 o'clock** il est 6 heures; **how far is it? — it's 10 miles** c'est loin? — c'est à 10 miles; **who is it? — it's me** qui est-ce? — c'est moi

Italian [ɪ'tæljən] *adj* italien(ne) ▷ *n* Italien(ne); *(Ling)* italien *m*

italics [ɪ'tælɪks] *npl* italique *m*
Italy ['ɪtəlɪ] *n* Italie *f*
itch [ɪtʃ] *n* démangeaison *f* ▷ *vi (person)* éprouver des démangeaisons; *(part of body)* démanger; **I'm ~ing to do** l'envie me démange de faire; **itchy** *adj*: **my back is itchy** j'ai le dos qui me démange
it'd ['ɪtd] = **it would**; **it had**
item ['aɪtəm] *n (gen)* article *m*; *(on agenda)* question *f*, point *m*; *(also*: **news ~**) nouvelle *f*
itinerary [aɪ'tɪnərərɪ] *n* itinéraire *m*
it'll ['ɪtl] = **it will**; **it shall**
its [ɪts] *adj* son (sa), ses *pl*
it's [ɪts] = **it is**; **it has**
itself [ɪt'sɛlf] *pron (reflexive)* se; *(emphatic)* lui-même (elle-même)
ITV *n abbr (BRIT*: = *Independent Television)* chaîne de télévision commerciale
I've [aɪv] = **I have**
ivory ['aɪvərɪ] *n* ivoire *m*
ivy ['aɪvɪ] *n* lierre *m*

j

jab [dʒæb] vt: **to ~ sth into** enfoncer or planter qch dans ▷ n (Med: inf) piqûre f

jack [dʒæk] n (Aut) cric m; (Cards) valet m

jacket ['dʒækɪt] n veste f, veston m; (of book) couverture f, jaquette f; **jacket potato** n pomme f de terre en robe des champs

jackpot ['dʒækpɔt] n gros lot

Jacuzzi® [dʒə'ku:zɪ] n jacuzzi® m

jagged ['dʒægɪd] adj dentelé(e)

jail [dʒeɪl] n prison f ▷ vt emprisonner, mettre en prison; **jail sentence** n peine f de prison

jam [dʒæm] n confiture f; (also: **traffic ~**) embouteillage m ▷ vt (passage etc) encombrer, obstruer; (mechanism, drawer etc) bloquer, coincer; (Radio) brouiller ▷ vi (mechanism, sliding part) se coincer, se bloquer; (gun) s'enrayer; **to be in a ~** (inf) être dans le pétrin; **to ~ sth into** (stuff) entasser or comprimer qch dans; (thrust) enfoncer qch dans

Jamaica [dʒə'meɪkə] n Jamaïque f

jammed [dʒæmd] adj (window etc)
coincé(e)

Jan abbr (= January) janv

janitor ['dʒænɪtə'] n (caretaker) concierge m

January ['dʒænjuərɪ] n janvier m

Japan [dʒə'pæn] n Japon m; **Japanese** [dʒæpə'ni:z] adj japonais(e) ▷ n (pl inv) Japonais(e); (Ling) japonais m

jar [dʒɑ:'] n (stone, earthenware) pot m; (glass) bocal m ▷ vi (sound) produire un son grinçant or discordant; (colours etc) détonner, jurer

jargon ['dʒɑ:gən] n jargon m

javelin ['dʒævlɪn] n javelot m

jaw [dʒɔ:] n mâchoire f

jazz [dʒæz] n jazz m

jealous ['dʒeləs] adj jaloux(-ouse); **jealousy** n jalousie f

jeans [dʒi:nz] npl jean m

Jello® ['dʒeləu] (us) n gelée f

jelly ['dʒelɪ] n (dessert) gelée f; (us: jam) confiture f; **jellyfish** n méduse f

jeopardize ['dʒepədaɪz] vt mettre en danger or péril

jerk [dʒə:k] n secousse f, saccade f; (of muscle) spasme m; (inf) pauvre type m ▷ vt (shake) donner une secousse à; (pull) tirer brusquement ▷ vi (vehicles) cahoter

jersey ['dʒə:zɪ] n tricot m; (fabric) jersey m

Jesus ['dʒi:zəs] n Jésus m

jet [dʒet] n (of gas, liquid) jet m; (Aviat) avion m à réaction, jet m; **jet lag** n décalage m horaire; **jet-ski** vi faire du jet-ski or scooter des mers

jetty ['dʒetɪ] n jetée f, digue f

Jew [dʒu:] n Juif m

jewel ['dʒu:əl] n bijou m, joyau m; (in watch) rubis m; **jeweller** (us **jeweler**) n bijoutier(-ière), joaillier m; **jeweller's (shop)** (us **jewelry store**) n bijouterie f, joaillerie f; **jewellery** (us **jewelry**) n bijoux mpl

Jewish ['dʒu:ɪʃ] adj juif (juive)

jigsaw ['dʒɪgsɔ:] n (also: **~ puzzle**) puzzle m

job [dʒɔb] n (chore, task) travail m, tâche

f: (employment) emploi m, poste m, place f; **it's a good ~ that ...** c'est heureux or c'est une chance que ... + sub; **just the ~!** (c'est) juste or exactement ce qu'il faut!; **job centre** (BRIT) n = ANPE f, = Agence nationale pour l'emploi; **jobless** adj sans travail, au chômage

jockey ['dʒɔkɪ] n jockey m ▷ vi: **to ~ for position** manœuvrer pour être bien placé

jog [dʒɔg] vt secouer ▷ vi (Sport) faire du jogging; **to ~ sb's memory** rafraîchir la mémoire de qn; **jogging** n jogging m

join [dʒɔɪn] vt (put together) unir, assembler; (become member of) s'inscrire à; (meet) rejoindre, retrouver; (queue) se joindre à ▷ vi (roads, rivers) se rejoindre, se rencontrer ▷ n raccord m; **join in** vi se mettre de la partie ▷ vt fus se mêler à; **join up** vi (meet) se rejoindre; (Mil) s'engager

joiner ['dʒɔɪnər] (BRIT) n menuisier m

joint [dʒɔɪnt] n (Tech) jointure f; joint m; (Anat) articulation f, jointure f; (BRIT Culin) rôti m; (inf: place) boîte f; (of cannabis) joint ▷ adj commun(e); (committee) mixte, paritaire; (winner) ex aequo; **joint account** n compte joint; **jointly** adv ensemble, en commun

joke [dʒəuk] n plaisanterie f; (also: **practical ~**) farce f ▷ vi plaisanter; **to play a ~ on** jouer un tour à, faire une farce à; **joker** n (Cards) joker m

jolly ['dʒɔlɪ] adj gai(e), enjoué(e) (enjoyable) amusant(e), plaisant(e) ▷ adv (BRIT inf) rudement, drôlement

jolt [dʒəult] n cahot m, secousse f; (shock) choc m ▷ vt cahoter, secouer

Jordan [dʒɔːdən] n (country) Jordanie f

journal ['dʒɜːnl] n journal m; **journalism** n journalisme m; **journalist** n journaliste m/f

journey ['dʒɜːnɪ] n voyage m; (distance covered) trajet m; **the ~ takes two hours** le trajet dure deux heures; **how was your ~?** votre voyage s'est bien passé?

joy [dʒɔɪ] n joie f; **joyrider** n

voleur(-euse) de voiture (qui fait une virée dans le véhicule volé); **joy stick** n (Aviat) manche m à balai; (Comput) manche à balai, manette f (de jeu)

Jr abbr = **junior**

judge [dʒʌdʒ] n juge m ▷ vt juger; (estimate: weight, size etc) apprécier; (consider) estimer

judo ['dʒuːdəu] n judo m

jug [dʒʌg] n pot m, cruche f

juggle ['dʒʌgl] vi jongler; **juggler** n jongleur m

juice [dʒuːs] n jus m; **juicy** adj juteux(-euse)

Jul abbr (= July) juil

July [dʒuːˈlaɪ] n juillet m

jumble ['dʒʌmbl] n fouillis m ▷ vt (also: **~ up, ~ together**) mélanger, brouiller; **jumble sale** (BRIT) vente f de charité

● **JUMBLE SALE**

● Les **jumble sales** ont lieu dans les
● églises, salles des fêtes ou halls
● d'écoles, et l'on y vend des articles
● de toutes sortes, en général bon
● marché et surtout d'occasion, pour
● collecter des fonds pour une œuvre
● de charité, une école (par exemple,
● pour acheter un ordinateur), ou
● encore une église (pour réparer un
● toit etc).

jumbo ['dʒʌmbəu] adj (also: **~ jet**) (avion) gros porteur (à réaction)

jump [dʒʌmp] vi sauter, bondir; (with fear etc) sursauter; (increase) monter en flèche ▷ vt sauter, franchir ▷ n saut m, bond m; (with fear etc) sursaut m; (fence) obstacle m; **to ~ the queue** (BRIT) passer avant son tour

jumper ['dʒʌmpər] n (BRIT: pullover) pull-over m; (US: pinafore dress) robe-chasuble f

jump leads (US **jumper cables**) npl câbles npl de démarrage

Jun. abbr = **June**; **junior**

junction ['dʒʌŋkʃən] n (BRIT:

of roads) carrefour m; (of rails)
embranchement m
June [dʒuːn] n juin m
jungle ['dʒʌŋgl] n jungle f
junior ['dʒuːnɪəʳ] adj, n: **he's ~ to me
(by 2 years), he's my ~ (by 2 years)**
il est mon cadet (de 2 ans), il est plus
jeune que moi (de 2 ans); **he's ~ to me**
(seniority) il est en dessous de moi (dans
la hiérarchie), j'ai plus d'ancienneté que
lui; **junior high school** n (US) ≈ collège
m d'enseignement secondaire; see also
high school; junior school n (BRIT)
école f primaire, cours moyen
junk [dʒʌŋk] n (rubbish) camelote f;
(cheap goods) bric-à-brac m inv; **junk
food** n snacks vite prêts (sans valeur
nutritive)
junkie ['dʒʌŋkɪ] n (inf) junkie m,
drogué(e)
junk mail n prospectus mpl; (Comput)
messages mpl publicitaires
Jupiter ['dʒuːpɪtəʳ] n (planet) Jupiter f
jurisdiction [dʒuərɪs'dɪkʃən] n
juridiction f; **it falls or comes within/
outside our ~** cela est/n'est pas de
notre compétence or ressort
jury ['dʒuərɪ] n jury m
just [dʒʌst] adj juste ▷ adv: **he's ~ done
it/left** il vient de le faire/partir; **~
right/two o'clock** exactement or juste
ce qu'il faut/deux heures; **we were ~
going** nous partions; **I was ~ about to
phone** j'allais téléphoner; **~ as he was
leaving** au moment or à l'instant précis
où il partait; **~ before/enough/here**
juste avant/assez/là; **it's ~ me/a
mistake** ce n'est que moi/(rien) qu'une
erreur; **~ missed/caught** manqué/
attrapé de justesse; **~ listen to this!**
écoutez un peu ça!; **she's ~ as clever
as you** elle est tout aussi intelligente
que vous; **it's ~ as well that you ...**
heureusement que vous ...; **~ a
minute!, ~ one moment!** un instant
(s'il vous plaît)!
justice ['dʒʌstɪs] n justice f; (US: judge)
juge m de la Cour suprême

justification [dʒʌstɪfɪ'keɪʃən] n
justification f
justify ['dʒʌstɪfaɪ] vt justifier
jut [dʒʌt] vi (also: **~ out**) dépasser,
faire saillie
juvenile ['dʒuːvənaɪl] adj juvénile;
(court, books) pour enfants ▷ n
adolescent(e)

K

K, k [keɪ] *abbr* (= *one thousand*) K;
(= *kilobyte*) Ko

kangaroo [kæŋɡəˈruː] *n* kangourou *m*

karaoke [kɑːrəˈəʊkɪ] *n* karaoké *m*

karate [kəˈrɑːtɪ] *n* karaté *m*

kebab [kəˈbæb] *n* kébab *m*

keel [kiːl] *n* quille *f*; **on an even ~**
(*fig*) à flot

keen [kiːn] *adj* (*eager*) plein(e)
d'enthousiasme; (*interest, desire,
competition*) vif (vive); (*eye, intelligence*)
pénétrant(e); (*edge*) effilé(e); **to be ~ to
do** *or* **on doing sth** désirer vivement
faire qch, tenir beaucoup à faire qch;
to be ~ on sth/sb aimer beaucoup
qch/qn

keep [kiːp] (*pt, pp* **kept**) *vt* (*retain,
preserve*) garder; (*hold back*) retenir;
(*shop, accounts, promise, diary*) tenir;
(*support*) entretenir; (*chickens, bees,
pigs etc*) élever ▷ *vi* (*food*) se conserver;
(*remain: in a certain state or place*)
rester ▷ *n* (*of castle*) donjon *m*; (*food
etc*): **enough for his ~** assez pour
(*assure*) sa subsistance; **to ~ doing
sth** (*continue*) continuer à faire qch;
(*repeatedly*) ne pas arrêter de faire
qch; **to ~ sb from doing/sth from
happening** empêcher qn de faire *or* que
qn (ne) fasse/que qch (n')arrive; **to ~ sb
happy/a place tidy** faire que qn soit
content/qu'un endroit reste propre; **to
~ sth to o.s.** garder qch pour soi, tenir
qch secret; **to ~ sth from sb** cacher qch
à qn; **to ~ time** (*clock*) être à l'heure,
ne pas retarder; **for ~s** (*inf*) pour de
bon, pour toujours; **keep away** *vt*: **to
~ sth/sb away from sb** tenir qch/qn
éloigné de qn ▷ *vi*: **to ~ away (from)**
ne pas s'approcher (de); **keep back** *vt*
(*crowds, tears, money*) retenir; (*conceal:
information*): **to ~ sth back from sb**
cacher qch à qn ▷ *vi* rester en arrière;
keep off *vt* (*dog, person*) éloigner ▷ *vi*: **if
the rain ~s off** s'il ne pleut pas; **~ your
hands off!** pas touché! (*inf*); **"~ off the
grass"** "pelouse interdite"; **keep on** *vi*
continuer; **to ~ on doing** continuer à
faire; **don't ~ on about it!** arrête (de m'en
parler)!; **keep out** *vt* empêcher d'entrer
▷ *vi* (*stay out*) rester en dehors; **"~ out"**
"défense d'entrer"; **keep up** *vi* (*fig: in
comprehension*) suivre ▷ *vt* continuer,
maintenir; **to ~ up with sb** (*in work
etc*) se maintenir au même niveau
que qn; (*in race etc*) aller aussi vite que
qn; **keeper** *n* gardien(ne); **keep-fit** *n*
gymnastique *f* (d'entretien); **keeping**
n (*care*) garde *f*; **in keeping with** en
harmonie avec

kennel [ˈkɛnl] *n* niche *f*; **kennels** *npl*
(*for boarding*) chenil *m*

Kenya [ˈkɛnjə] *n* Kenya *m*

kept [kɛpt] *pt, pp of* **keep**

kerb [kəːb] *n* (*BRIT*) bordure *f* du trottoir

kerosene [ˈkɛrəsiːn] *n* kérosène *m*

ketchup [ˈkɛtʃəp] *n* ketchup *m*

kettle [ˈkɛtl] *n* bouilloire *f*

key [kiː] *n* (*gen, Mus*) clé *f*; (*of piano,
typewriter*) touche *f*; (*on map*) légende
f ▷ *adj* (*factor, role, area*) clé *inv* ▷ *vt*
(*also:* **~ in**: *text*) saisir; **can I have my**

~? je peux avoir ma clé?; **a ~ issue** un problème fondamental; **keyboard** n clavier m; **keyhole** n trou m de la serrure; **keyring** n porte-clés m

kg abbr (= kilogram) K

khaki ['kɑːkɪ] adj, n kaki m

kick [kɪk] vt donner un coup de pied à
▷ vi (horse) ruer ▷ n coup m de pied; (inf: thrill): **he does it for ~s** il le fait parce que ça l'excite, il le fait pour le plaisir; **to ~ the habit** (inf) arrêter; **kick off** vi (Sport) donner le coup d'envoi; **kick-off** n (Sport) coup m d'envoi

kid [kɪd] n (inf: child) gamin(e); (animal, leather) chevreau m ▷ vi (inf) plaisanter, blaguer

kidnap ['kɪdnæp] vt enlever, kidnapper; **kidnapping** n enlèvement m

kidney ['kɪdnɪ] n (Anat) rein m; (Culin) rognon m; **kidney bean** n haricot m rouge

kill [kɪl] vt tuer ▷ n mise f à mort; **to ~ time** tuer le temps; **killer** n tueur(-euse); (murderer) meurtrier(-ière); **killing** n meurtre m; (of group of people) tuerie f, massacre m; (inf): **to make a killing** se remplir les poches, réussir un beau coup

kiln [kɪln] n four m

kilo ['kiːləu] n kilo m; **kilobyte** n (Comput) kilo-octet m; **kilogram(me)** n kilogramme m; **kilometre** (US **kilometer**) ['kɪləmiːtə*] n kilomètre m; **kilowatt** n kilowatt m

kilt [kɪlt] n kilt m

kin [kɪn] n see **next-of-kin**

kind [kaɪnd] adj gentil(le), aimable ▷ n sorte f, espèce f; (species) genre m; **to be two of a ~** se ressembler; **in ~** (Comm) en nature; **~ of** (inf: rather) plutôt; **a ~ of** une sorte de; **what ~ of ...?** quelle sorte de ...?

kindergarten ['kɪndəgɑːtn] n jardin m d'enfants

kindly ['kaɪndlɪ] adj bienveillant(e), plein(e) de gentillesse ▷ adv avec bonté; **will you ~ ...** auriez-vous la bonté or l'obligeance de ...

kindness ['kaɪndnɪs] n (quality) bonté f, gentillesse f

king [kɪŋ] n roi m; **kingdom** n royaume m; **kingfisher** n martin-pêcheur m; **king-size(d) bed** n grand lit (de 1,95 m de large)

kiosk ['kiːɔsk] n kiosque m; (BRIT: also: **telephone ~**) cabine f (téléphonique)

kipper ['kɪpə*] n hareng fumé et salé

kiss [kɪs] n baiser m ▷ vt embrasser; **to ~ (each other)** s'embrasser; **kiss of life** n (BRIT) bouche à bouche m

kit [kɪt] n équipement m, matériel m; (set of tools etc) trousse f; (for assembly) kit m

kitchen ['kɪtʃɪn] n cuisine f

kite [kaɪt] n (toy) cerf-volant m

kitten ['kɪtn] n petit chat, chaton m

kitty ['kɪtɪ] n (money) cagnotte f

kiwi ['kiːwiː] n (also: **~ fruit**) kiwi m

km abbr (= kilometre) km

km/h abbr (= kilometres per hour) km/h

knack [næk] n: **to have the ~ of (doing)** avoir le coup (pour faire)

knee [niː] n genou m; **kneecap** n rotule f

kneel (pt, pp **knelt**) [niːl, nɛlt] vi (also: **~ down**) s'agenouiller

knelt [nɛlt] pt, pp of **kneel**

knew [njuː] pt of **know**

knickers ['nɪkəz] npl (BRIT) culotte f (de femme)

knife [naɪf] n (pl **knives**) couteau m ▷ vt poignarder, frapper d'un coup de couteau

knight [naɪt] n chevalier m; (Chess) cavalier m

knit [nɪt] vt tricoter ▷ vi tricoter; (broken bones) se ressouder; **to ~ one's brows** froncer les sourcils; **knitting** n tricot m; **knitting needle** n aiguille f à tricoter; **knitwear** n tricots mpl, lainages mpl

knives [naɪvz] npl of **knife**

knob [nɔb] n bouton m; (BRIT): **a ~ of butter** une noix de beurre

knock [nɔk] vt frapper; (bump into) heurter; (fig: col) dénigrer ▷ vi (at

door etc): **to ~ at/on** frapper à/sur ⊳ n
coup m; **knock down** vt renverser;
(price) réduire; **knock off** vi (inf: finish)
s'arrêter (de travailler) ⊳ vt (vase,
object) faire tomber; (inf: steal) piquer;
(fig: from price etc): **to ~ off £10** faire
une remise de 10 livres; **knock out**
vt assommer; (Boxing) mettre k.-o.;
(in competition) éliminer; **knock over**
vt (object) faire tomber; (pedestrian)
renverser; **knockout** n (Boxing) knockout m, K.-O. m; **knockout competition**
(BRIT) compétition f avec épreuves
éliminatoires

knot [nɒt] n (gen) nœud m ⊳ vt nouer
know [nəu] vt (pt **knew**, pp **~n**) savoir;
(person, place) connaître; **to ~ that**
savoir que; **to ~ how to do** savoir
faire; **to ~ how to swim** savoir nager; **to ~
about/of sth** (event) être au courant
de qch; (subject) connaître qch; **I don't
~** je ne sais pas; **do you ~ where I
can ...?** savez-vous où je peux ...?;
know-all (BRIT pej) je-sais-tout
m/f; **know-how** n savoir-faire m,
technique f, compétence f; **knowing**
adj (look etc) entendu(e); **knowingly**
adv (on purpose) sciemment; (smile, look)
d'un air entendu; **know-it-all** n (US)
= **know-all**

knowledge [ˈnɒlɪdʒ] n connaissance
f; (learning) connaissances f, savoir
m; **without my ~** à mon insu;
knowledgeable adj bien informé(e)
known [nəun] pp of **know** ⊳ adj (thief,
facts) notoire; (expert) célèbre
knuckle [ˈnʌkl] n articulation f (des
phalanges), jointure f
koala [kəuˈɑːlə] n (also: ~ **bear**) koala m
Koran [kɔˈrɑːn] n Coran m
Korea [kəˈrɪə] n Corée f; **Korean** adj
coréen(ne) ⊳ n Coréen(ne)
kosher [ˈkəuʃə] adj kascher inv
Kosovar, Kosovan [ˈkɒsəvɑːʳ,
ˈkɒsəvən] adj kosovar(e)
Kosovo [ˈkɒsəvəu] n Kosovo m
Kuwait [kuˈweit] n Koweït m

L, abbr (BRIT Aut: = learner) signale un
conducteur débutant
l. abbr (= litre) l
lab [læb] n abbr (= laboratory) labo m
label [ˈleibl] n étiquette f; (brand: of
record) marque f ⊳ vt étiqueter
labor etc [ˈleibəʳ] (US) = **labour**
laboratory [ləˈbɒrətəri] n laboratoire m
Labor Day n (US, CANADA) fête f du
travail (le premier lundi de septembre)

● **LABOR DAY**
●
● La fête du Travail aux États-Unis et au
● Canada est fixée au premier lundi de
● septembre. Instituée par le Congrès
● en 1894 après avoir été réclamée par
● les mouvements ouvriers pendant
● douze ans, elle a perdu une grande
● partie de son caractère politique
● pour devenir un jour férié assez
● ordinaire et l'occasion de partir pour
● un long week-end avant la rentrée
● des classes.

labor union n (US) syndicat m

Labour ['leɪbəʳ] n (BRIT Pol: also: **the ~ Party**) le parti travailliste, les travaillistes mpl

labour (US **labor**) ['leɪbəʳ] n (work) travail m; (workforce) main-d'œuvre f ▷ vi: **to ~ (at)** travailler dur (à), peiner (sur) ▷ vt: **to ~ a point** insister sur un point; **in ~** (Med) en travail; **labourer** n manœuvre m; **farm labourer** ouvrier m agricole

lace [leɪs] n dentelle f; (of shoe etc) lacet m ▷ vt (shoe: also: **~ up**) lacer

lack [læk] n manque m ▷ vt manquer de; **through** or **for ~ of** faute de, par manque de; **to be ~ing** manquer, faire défaut; **to be ~ing in** manquer de

lacquer ['lækəʳ] n laque f

lacy ['leɪsɪ] adj (of lace) en dentelle; (like lace) comme de la dentelle

lad [læd] n garçon m, gars m

ladder ['lædəʳ] n échelle f; (BRIT: in tights) maille filée ▷ vt, vi (BRIT: tights) filer

ladle ['leɪdl] n louche f

lady ['leɪdɪ] n dame f; **"ladies and gentlemen ..."** "Mesdames (et) Messieurs ..."; **young ~** jeune fille f; (married) jeune femme f; **the ladies' (room)** les toilettes fpl des dames; **ladybird** (US **ladybug**) n coccinelle f

lag [læg] n retard m ▷ vi (also: **~ behind**) rester en arrière, traîner; (fig) rester à la traîne ▷ vt (pipes) calorifuger

lager ['lɑːgəʳ] n bière blonde

lagoon [lə'guːn] n lagune f

laid [leɪd] pt, pp of **lay**; **laid back** adj (inf) relaxe, décontracté(e)

lain [leɪn] pp of **lie**

lake [leɪk] n lac m

lamb [læm] n agneau m

lame [leɪm] adj (also fig) boiteux(-euse)

lament [lə'mɛnt] n lamentation f ▷ vt pleurer, se lamenter sur

lamp [læmp] n lampe f; **lamppost** n (BRIT) réverbère m; **lampshade** n abat-jour m inv

land [lænd] n (as opposed to sea)

terre f (ferme); (country) pays m; (soil) terre; (piece of land) terrain m; (estate) terre(s), domaine(s) m(pl) ▷ vi (from ship) débarquer; (Aviat) atterrir; (fig: fall) (re)tomber ▷ vt (passengers, goods) débarquer; (obtain) décrocher; **to ~ sb with sth** (inf) coller qch à qn; **landing** n (from ship) débarquement m; (Aviat) atterrissage m; (of staircase) palier m; **landing card** n carte f de débarquement; **landlady** n propriétaire f, logeuse f; (of pub) patronne f; **landlord** n propriétaire m, logeur m; (of pub etc) patron m; **landmark** n (point m de) repère m; **to be a landmark** (fig) faire date or époque; **landowner** n propriétaire foncier or terrien; **landscape** n paysage m; **landslide** n (Geo) glissement m (de terrain); (fig: Pol) raz-de-marée (électoral)

lane [leɪn] n (in country) chemin m; (Aut: of road) voie f; (: line of traffic) file f; (in race) couloir m

language ['læŋgwɪdʒ] n langue f; (way one speaks) langage m; **what ~s do you speak?** quelles langues parlez-vous?; **bad ~** grossièretés fpl, langage grossier; **language laboratory** n laboratoire m de langues; **language school** n école f de langue

lantern ['læntn] n lanterne f

lap [læp] n (of track) tour m (de piste); (of body): **in** or **on one's ~** sur les genoux ▷ vt (also: **~ up**) laper ▷ vi (waves) clapoter

lapel [lə'pɛl] n revers m

lapse [læps] n défaillance f; (in behaviour) écart m (de conduite) ▷ vi (Law) cesser d'être en vigueur; (contract) expirer; **to ~ into bad habits** prendre de mauvaises habitudes; **~ of time** laps m de temps, intervalle m

laptop (computer) ['læptɔp-] n portable m

lard [lɑːd] n saindoux m

larder ['lɑːdəʳ] n garde-manger m inv

large [lɑːdʒ] adj grand(e); (person,

animal) gros (grosse); **at ~** (*free*) en liberté; (*generally*) en général; pour la plupart; *see also* **by**; **largely** *adv* en grande partie; (*principally*) surtout; **large-scale** *adj* (*map, drawing etc*) à grande échelle; (*fig*) important(e)

lark [lɑːk] *n* (*bird*) alouette *f*; (*joke*) blague *f*, farce *f*

laryngitis [lærɪnˈdʒaɪtɪs] *n* laryngite *f*

lasagne [ləˈzænjə] *n* lasagne *f*

laser [ˈleɪzə*ʳ*] *n* laser *m*; **laser printer** *n* imprimante *f* laser

lash [læʃ] *n* coup *m* de fouet; (*also:* **eye~**) cil *m* ▷ *vt* fouetter; (*tie*) attacher; **lash out** *vi*: **to ~ out (at or against sb/sth)** attaquer violemment (qn/qch)

lass [læs] (*BRIT*) *n* (jeune) fille *f*

last [lɑːst] *adj* dernier(-ière) ▷ *adv* en dernier; (*most recently*) la dernière fois; (*finally*) finalement ▷ *vi* durer; **~ week** la semaine dernière; **~ night** (*evening*) hier soir; (*night*) la nuit dernière; **at ~** enfin; **~ but one** avant-dernier(-ière); **lastly** *adv* en dernier lieu, pour finir; **last-minute** *adj* de dernière minute

latch [lætʃ] *n* loquet *m*; **latch onto** *vt fus* (*cling to: person, group*) s'accrocher à; (*idea*) se mettre en tête

late [leɪt] *adj* (*not on time*) en retard; (*far on in day etc*) tardif(-ive); (*edition, delivery*) dernier(-ière); (*dead*) défunt(e) ▷ *adv* tard; (*behind time, schedule*) en retard; **to be 10 minutes ~** avoir 10 minutes de retard; **sorry I'm ~** désolé d'être en retard; **it's too ~** il est trop tard; **of ~** dernièrement; **in ~ May** vers la fin (du mois) de mai, fin mai; **the ~ Mr X** M. X ; **latecomer** *n* retardataire *m/f*; **lately** *adv* récemment; **later** *adj* (*date etc*) ultérieur(e); (*version etc*) plus récent(e) ▷ *adv* plus tard; **later on** plus tard; **latest** [ˈleɪtɪst] *adj* tout(e) dernier(-ière); **at the latest** au plus tard

lather [ˈlɑːðə*ʳ*] *n* mousse *f* (de savon) ▷ *vt* savonner

Latin [ˈlætɪn] *n* latin *m* ▷ *adj* latin(e); **Latin America** *n* Amérique latine;

Latin American *adj* latino-américain(e), d'Amérique latine ▷ *n* Latino-Américain(e)

latitude [ˈlætɪtjuːd] *n* (*also fig*) latitude *f*

latter [ˈlætə*ʳ*] *adj* deuxième, dernier(-ière) ▷ *n*: **the ~** ce dernier, celui-ci

laugh [lɑːf] *n* rire *m* ▷ *vi* rire; **(to do sth) for a ~** (faire qch) pour rire; **laugh at** *fus* se moquer de; (*joke*) rire de; **laughter** *n* rire *m*; (*of several people*) rires *mpl*

launch [lɔːntʃ] *n* lancement *m*; (*also:* **motor ~**) vedette *f* ▷ *vt* (*ship, rocket, plan*) lancer; **launch into** *vt fus* se lancer dans

launder [ˈlɔːndə*ʳ*] *vt* laver; (*fig: money*) blanchir

Launderette® [lɔːnˈdrɛt] (*BRIT*) (*US* **Laundromat®** [ˈlɔːndrəmæt]) *n* laverie *f* (automatique)

laundry [ˈlɔːndrɪ] *n* (*clothes*) linge *m*; (*business*) blanchisserie *f*; (*room*) buanderie *f*; **to do the ~** faire la lessive

lava [ˈlɑːvə] *n* lave *f*

lavatory [ˈlævətərɪ] *n* toilettes *fpl*

lavender [ˈlævəndə*ʳ*] *n* lavande *f*

lavish [ˈlævɪʃ] *adj* copieux(-euse); (*person: giving freely*): **~ with** prodigue de ▷ *vt*: **to ~ sth on sb** prodiguer qch à qn; (*money*) dépenser qch sans compter pour qn

law [lɔː] *n* loi *f*; (*science*) droit *m*; **lawful** *adj* légal(e), permis(e); **lawless** *adj* (*action*) illégal(e); (*place*) sans loi

lawn [lɔːn] *n* pelouse *f*; **lawnmower** *n* tondeuse *f* à gazon

lawsuit [ˈlɔːsuːt] *n* procès *m*

lawyer [ˈlɔːjə*ʳ*] *n* (*consultant, with company*) juriste *m*; (*for sales, wills etc*) = notaire *m*; (*partner, in court*) = avocat *m*

lax [læks] *adj* relâché(e)

laxative [ˈlæksətɪv] *n* laxatif *m*

lay [leɪ] *pt of* **lie** *adj* laïque; (*not expert*) profane ▷ *vt* (*pt, pp* **laid**) poser, mettre; (*eggs*) pondre; (*trap*) tendre; (*plans*) élaborer; **to ~ the table** mettre la table;

lay down vt poser; (*rules etc*) établir; **to ~ down the law** (*fig*) faire la loi; **lay off** vt (*workers*) licencier; (*provide: meal etc*) fournir; **lay out** vt (*design*) dessiner, concevoir; (*display*) disposer; (*spend*) dépenser; **lay-by** n (BRIT) aire f de stationnement (sur le bas-côté)

layer ['leɪə'] n couche f

layman ['leɪmən] (*irreg*) n (*Rel*) laïque m; (*non-expert*) profane m

layout ['leɪaʊt] n disposition f, plan m, agencement m; (*Press*) mise f en page

lazy ['leɪzɪ] adj paresseux(-euse)

lb. abbr (*weight*) = **pound**

lead¹ [liːd] n (*front position*) tête f; (*distance, time ahead*) avance f; (*clue*) piste f; (*Elec*) fil m; (*for dog*) laisse f; (*Theat*) rôle principal ▷ vb (*pt, pp* **led**) ▷ vt (*guide*) mener, conduire; (*be leader of*) être à la tête de ▷ vi (*Sport*) mener, être en tête; **to ~ to** (*road, pipe*) mener à, conduire à; (*result in*) conduire à; aboutir à; **to be in the ~** (*Sport: in race*) mener, être en tête; (: *in match*) mener (à la marque); **to ~ sb to do sth** amener qn à faire qch; **to ~ the way** montrer le chemin; **lead up to** vt conduire à; (*in conversation*) en venir à

lead² [lɛd] n (*metal*) plomb m; (*in pencil*) mine f

leader ['liːdə'] n (*of team*) chef m; (*of party etc*) dirigeant(e), leader m; (*Sport: in league*) leader; (: *in race*) coureur m de tête; **leadership** n (*position*) direction f; **under the leadership of ...** sous la direction de ...; **qualities of leadership** qualités fpl de chef or de meneur

lead-free ['lɛdfriː] adj sans plomb

leading ['liːdɪŋ] adj de premier plan; (*main*) principal(e); (*in race*) de tête

lead singer [liːd-] n (*in pop group*) (chanteur m) vedette f

leaf (pl **leaves**) [liːf, liːvz] n feuille f; (*of table*) rallonge f; **to turn over a new ~** (*fig*) changer de conduite or d'existence; **leaf through** vt (*book*) feuilleter

leaflet ['liːflɪt] n prospectus m, brochure f; (*Pol, Rel*) tract m

league [liːg] n ligue f; (*Football*) championnat m; **to be in ~ with** avoir partie liée avec, être de mèche avec

leak [liːk] n (*out: also fig*) fuite f ▷ vi (*pipe, liquid etc*) fuir; (*shoes*) prendre l'eau; (*ship*) faire eau ▷ vt (*liquid*) répandre; (*information*) divulguer

lean [liːn] adj maigre ▷ vb (*pt, pp* **~ed** or **~t**) ▷ vt: **to ~ sth on** appuyer qch sur ▷ vi (*slope*) pencher; (*rest*): **to ~ against** s'appuyer contre; être appuyé(e) contre; **to ~ on** s'appuyer sur; **lean forward** vi se pencher en avant; **lean over** vi se pencher; **leaning** n: **leaning (towards)** penchant m (pour)

leant [lɛnt] pt, pp de **lean**

leap [liːp] n bond m, saut m ▷ vi (*pt, pp* **~ed** or **~t**) bondir, sauter

leapt [lɛpt] pt, pp de **leap**

leap year n année f bissextile

learn (*pt, pp* **~ed** or **~t**) [ləːn, -t] vt, vi apprendre; **to ~ (how) to do sth** apprendre à faire qch; **to ~ about sth** (*Scol*) étudier qch; (*hear, read*) apprendre qch; **learner** n débutant(e); (BRIT: *also*: **learner driver**) (conducteur(-trice)) débutant(e); **learning** n savoir m

learnt [ləːnt] pp de **learn**

lease [liːs] n bail m ▷ vt louer à bail

leash [liːʃ] n laisse f

least [liːst] adj: **the ~** (+ *noun*) le (la) plus petit(e), le (la) moindre; (*smallest amount of*) le moins de ▷ pron: **(the)** ~ le moins; (+ *adj*): **the** ~ le (la) moins; (*the* ~ **money** le moins d'argent; **the** ~ **expensive** le (la) moins cher (chère); **the** ~ **possible effort** le moins d'effort possible; **at** ~ au moins; (*or rather*) du moins; **you could at** ~ **have written** tu aurais au moins pu écrire; **not in the** ~ pas le moins du monde

leather ['lɛðə'] n cuir m

leave [liːv] (*vb: pt, pp* **left**) vt laisser; (*go away from*) quitter; (*forget*) oublier ▷ vi partir, s'en aller ▷ n (*time off*) congé m; (*Mil, also: consent*) permission f; **what time does the train/bus ~?** le train/le bus part à quelle heure?; **to ~ sth to sb** (money etc) laisser qch à qn; **to be left** rester; **there's some milk left over** il reste du lait; **- it to me!** laissez-moi faire!, je m'en occupe!; **on ~** en permission; **leave behind** vt (also fig) laisser; (forget) laisser, oublier; **leave out** vt oublier, omettre

leaves [liːvz] npl of **leaf**

Lebanon ['lebənən] n Liban m

lecture ['lɛktʃər] n conférence f; (Scol) cours (magistral) ▷ vi donner des cours; enseigner ▷ vt (scold) sermonner, réprimander; **to give a ~ (on)** faire une conférence (sur), faire un cours (sur); **lecture hall** n amphithéâtre m; **lecturer** n (speaker) conférencier(-ière) f; (BRIT: at university) professeur m (d'université), prof m/f de fac (inf); **lecture theatre** n = **lecture hall**

> ⚠ Be careful not to translate *lecture* by the French word *lecture*.

led [lɛd] pt, pp of **lead¹**

ledge [lɛdʒ] n (of window, on wall) rebord m; (of mountain) saillie f, corniche f

leek [liːk] n poireau m

left [lɛft] pt, pp of **leave** ▷ adj gauche ▷ adv à gauche ▷ n gauche f; **there are two ~** il en reste deux; **on the ~, to the ~** à gauche; **the L~** (Pol) la gauche; **left-hand** adj: **the left-hand side** la gauche; **left-hand drive** n (BRIT: vehicle) véhicule m avec la conduite à gauche; **left-handed** adj gaucher(-ère); (scissors etc) pour gauchers; **left-luggage locker** n (BRIT) (casier m à) consigne f automatique; **left-luggage (office)** n (BRIT) consigne f; **left-overs** npl restes mpl; **left-wing** adj (Pol) de gauche

leg [lɛg] n jambe f; (of animal) patte f; (of furniture) pied m; (Culin: of chicken) cuisse f; (of journey) étape f; **1st/2nd ~** (Sport) match m aller/retour; **~ of lamb** (Culin) gigot m d'agneau

legacy ['lɛgəsi] n (also fig) héritage m, legs m

legal ['liːgl] adj (permitted by law) légal(e); (relating to law) juridique; **legal holiday** (us) n jour férié; **legalize** vt légaliser; **legally** adv légalement

legend ['lɛdʒənd] n légende f; **legendary** ['lɛdʒəndəri] adj légendaire

leggings ['lɛgɪŋz] npl caleçon m

legible ['lɛdʒəbl] adj lisible

legislation [lɛdʒɪs'leɪʃən] n législation f

legislative ['lɛdʒɪslətɪv] adj législatif(-ive)

legitimate [lɪ'dʒɪtɪmət] adj légitime

leisure ['lɛʒər] n (free time) temps m libre, loisirs mpl; **at ~** (tout) à loisir; **at your ~** (later) à tête reposée; **leisure centre** n (BRIT) centre m de loisirs; **leisurely** adj tranquille, fait(e) sans se presser

lemon ['lɛmən] n citron m; **lemonade** n (fizzy) limonade f; **lemon tea** n thé m au citron

lend (pt, pp lent) [lɛnd, lɛnt] vt: **to ~ sth (to sb)** prêter qch (à qn); **could you ~ me some money?** pourriez-vous me prêter de l'argent?

length [lɛŋθ] n longueur f; (section of road, pipe etc) morceau m, bout m; **~ of time** durée f; **it is 2 metres in ~** cela fait 2 mètres de long; **at ~** (at last) enfin, à la fin; (lengthily) longuement; **lengthen** vt allonger, prolonger ▷ vi s'allonger; **lengthways** adv dans le sens de la longueur, en long; **lengthy** adj (très) long (longue)

lens [lɛnz] n (of spectacles) verre m; (of camera) objectif m

Lent [lɛnt] n carême m

lent [lɛnt] pt, pp of **lend**

lentil ['lɛntl] n lentille f

Leo ['liːəu] n le Lion

leopard ['lɛpəd] n léopard m

leotard ['liːətɑːd] n justaucorps m

leprosy ['lɛprəsi] n lèpre f

lesbian ['lɛzbɪən] n lesbienne f ▷ adj lesbien(ne)

less [lɛs] adj moins de ▷ pron, adv moins ▷ prep: **~ tax/10% discount** avant impôt/moins 10% de remise; **~ than**

that/you moins que cela/vous; **~ than half** moins de la moitié; **~ than ever** moins que jamais; **~ and ~** de moins en moins; **the ~ he works ...** moins il travaille ...; **lessen** vi diminuer, s'amoindrir, s'atténuer ▷ vt diminuer, réduire, atténuer; **lesser** ['lɛsə*'*] adj moindre; **to a lesser extent** or **degree** à un degré moindre

lesson ['lɛsn] n leçon f; **to teach sb a ~** (fig) donner une bonne leçon à qn

let (pt, pp **~**) [lɛt] vt laisser; (BRIT: lease) louer; **to ~ sb do sth** laisser qn faire qch; **to ~ sb know sth** faire savoir qch à qn, prévenir qn de qch; **to ~ go** lâcher prise; **to ~ go of sth, to ~ sth go** lâcher qch; **~'s go** allons-y; **~ him come** qu'il vienne; **"to ~"** (BRIT) "à louer"; **let down** vt (lower) baisser; (BRIT: tyre) dégonfler; (disappoint) décevoir; **let in** vt laisser entrer; (visitor etc) faire entrer; **let off** vt (allow to leave) laisser partir; (not punish) ne pas punir; (firework etc) faire partir; (bomb) faire exploser; **let out** vt laisser sortir; (scream) laisser échapper; (BRIT: rent out) louer

lethal ['li:θl] adj mortel(le), fatal(e); (weapon) meurtrier(-ère)

letter ['lɛtə*'*] n lettre f; **letterbox** n (BRIT) boîte f aux or à lettres

lettuce ['lɛtɪs] n laitue f, salade f

leukaemia (US **leukemia**) [lu:'ki:mɪə] n leucémie f

level ['lɛvl] adj (flat) plat(e), plan(e), uni(e); (horizontal) horizontal(e) ▷ n niveau m ▷ vt niveler, aplanir; **"A" ~s** (BRIT) ≈ baccalauréat m; **to be ~ with** être au même niveau que; **to draw ~ with** (runner, car) arriver à la hauteur de, rattraper; **on the ~** (fig: honest) régulier(-ière); **level crossing** n (BRIT) passage m à niveau

lever ['li:və*'*] n levier m; **leverage** n (influence) **leverage (on or with)** prise f (sur)

levy ['lɛvɪ] n taxe f, impôt m ▷ vt (tax) lever; (fine) infliger

liability [laɪə'bɪlətɪ] n responsabilité f;

(handicap) handicap m

liable ['laɪəbl] adj (subject): **~ to** sujet(te) à, passible de; (responsible): **~ (for)** responsable (de); (likely): **~ to do** susceptible de faire

liaise [li:'eɪz] vi: **to ~ with** assurer la liaison avec

liar ['laɪə*'*] n menteur(-euse)

libel ['laɪbl] n diffamation f; (document) écrit m diffamatoire ▷ vt diffamer

liberal ['lɪbərl] adj libéral(e); (generous): **~ with** prodigue or généreux(-euse) avec ▷ n: **L~** (Pol) libéral(e); **Liberal Democrat** n (BRIT) libéral(e)-démocrate m/f

liberate ['lɪbəreɪt] vt libérer

liberation [lɪbə'reɪʃən] n libération f

liberty ['lɪbətɪ] n liberté f; **to be at ~** (criminal) être en liberté; **at ~ to do** libre de faire; **to take the ~ of** prendre la liberté de, se permettre de

Libra ['li:brə] n la Balance

librarian [laɪ'brɛərɪən] n bibliothécaire m/f

library ['laɪbrərɪ] n bibliothèque f

Be careful not to translate **library** by the French word **librairie**.

Libya ['lɪbɪə] n Libye f

lice [laɪs] npl of **louse**

licence (US **license**) ['laɪsns] n autorisation f, permis m; (Comm) licence f; (Radio, TV) redevance f; (also: **driving ~**, US also: **driver's license**) permis m (de conduire)

license ['laɪsns] n (US) = **licence**; **licensed** adj (for alcohol) patenté(e) pour la vente des spiritueux, qui a une patente de débit de boissons; (car) muni(e) de la vignette; **license plate** n (US Aut) plaque f minéralogique; **licensing hours** (BRIT) npl heures fpl d'ouvertures (des pubs)

lick [lɪk] vt lécher; (inf: defeat) écraser, flanquer une piquette or raclée à; **to ~ one's lips** se frotter les mains

lid [lɪd] n couvercle m; (eyelid) paupière f

lie [laɪ] n mensonge m ▷ vi (pt, pp **~d**) (tell lies) mentir; (pt **lay**, pp **lain**) (rest) être étendu(e) or allongé(e) or couché(e); (object: be situated) se trouver, être; **to ~ low** (fig) se cacher, rester caché(e); **to tell ~s** mentir; **lie about, lie around** vi (things) traîner; (BRIT: person) traînasser, fainéanter; **lie down** vi se coucher, s'étendre

Liechtenstein ['lɪktənstaɪn] n Liechtenstein m

lie-in ['laɪɪn] n (BRIT): **to have a ~** faire la grasse matinée

lieutenant [lɛf'tɛnənt, us lu:'tɛnənt] n lieutenant m

life (pl **lives**) [laɪf, laɪvz] n vie f; **to come to ~** (fig) s'animer; **life assurance** n (BRIT) = **life insurance**; **lifeboat** n canot m or chaloupe f de sauvetage; **lifeguard** n surveillant m de baignade; **life insurance** n assurance-vie f; **life jacket** n gilet m or ceinture f de sauvetage; **lifelike** adj qui semble vrai(e) or vivant(e), ressemblant(e); (painting) réaliste; **life preserver** n (US) gilet m or ceinture f de sauvetage; **life sentence** n condamnation f à perpétuité; **lifestyle** n style m de vie; **lifetime** n: **in his lifetime** de son vivant

lift [lɪft] vt soulever, lever; (end) supprimer, lever ▷ vi (fog) se lever ▷ n (BRIT: elevator) ascenseur m; **to give sb a ~** (BRIT) emmener or prendre qn en voiture; **can you give me a ~ to the station?** pouvez-vous m'emmener à la gare?; **lift up** vt soulever; **lift-off** n décollage m

light [laɪt] n lumière f; (lamp) lampe f; (Aut: rear light) feu m; (: headlamp) phare m; (for cigarette etc) **have you got a ~?** avez-vous du feu? ▷ vt (pt, pp **~ed** or **lit**) (candle, cigarette, fire) allumer; (room) éclairer ▷ adj (room, colour) clair(e); (not heavy, also fig) léger(-ère); (not strenuous) peu fatigant(e); **lights** npl (traffic lights) feux mpl; **to come to ~** être dévoilé(e) or découvert(e); **in the ~ of** à la lumière de; étant donné; **light up** vi s'allumer; (face) s'éclairer; (smoke) allumer une cigarette or une pipe etc ▷ vt (illuminate)

éclairer, illuminer; **light bulb** n ampoule f; **lighten** vt (light up) éclairer; (make lighter) éclaircir; (make less heavy) alléger; **lighter** n (also: **cigarette lighter**) briquet m; **light-hearted** adj gai(e), joyeux(-euse), enjoué(e); **lighthouse** n phare m; **lighting** n éclairage m; (in theatre) éclairages; **lightly** adv légèrement; **to get off lightly** s'en tirer à bon compte

lightning ['laɪtnɪŋ] n foudre f; (flash) éclair m

lightweight ['laɪtweɪt] adj (suit) léger(-ère) ▷ n (Boxing) poids léger

like [laɪk] vt aimer (bien) ▷ prep comme ▷ adj semblable, pareil(le) ▷ n: **the ~** (pej) (d')autres du même genre or acabit; **his ~s and dislikes** ses goûts mpl or préférences fpl; **I would ~, I'd ~** je voudrais, j'aimerais; **would you ~ a coffee?** voulez-vous du café?; **to be/look ~ sb/sth** ressembler à qn/qch; **what's he ~?** comment est-il?; **what does it look ~?** de quoi est-ce que ça a l'air?; **what does it taste ~?** quel goût est-ce que ça a?; **that's just ~ him** c'est bien de lui, ça lui ressemble; **do it ~ this** fais-le comme ceci; **it's nothing ~ ...** ce n'est pas du tout comme ...; **likeable** adj sympathique, agréable

likelihood ['laɪklɪhud] n probabilité f

likely ['laɪklɪ] adj (result, outcome) probable; (excuse) plausible; **he's ~ to leave** il va sûrement partir, il risque fort de partir; **not ~!** (inf) pas de danger!

likewise ['laɪkwaɪz] adv de même, pareillement

liking ['laɪkɪŋ] n (for person) affection f; (for thing) penchant m, goût m; **to be to sb's ~** être au goût de qn, plaire à qn

lilac ['laɪlək] n lilas m

Lilo® ['laɪləu] n matelas m pneumatique

lily ['lɪlɪ] n lis m; **~ of the valley** muguet m

limb [lɪm] n membre m

limbo ['lɪmbəu] n: **to be in ~** (fig) être tombé(e) dans l'oubli

lime [laɪm] n (tree) tilleul m; (fruit) citron vert, lime f; (Geo) chaux f

limelight ['laɪmlaɪt] n: **in the ~** (fig) en vedette, au premier plan

limestone ['laɪmstəun] n pierre f à chaux; (Geo) calcaire m

limit ['lɪmɪt] n limite f ▷ vt limiter; **limited** adj limité(e), restreint(e); **to be limited to** se limiter à, ne concerner que

limousine ['lɪməziːn] n limousine f

limp [lɪmp] n: **to have a ~** boiter ▷ vi boiter ▷ adj mou (molle)

line [laɪn] n (gen) ligne f; (stroke) trait m; (wrinkle) ride f; (rope) corde f; (wire) fil m; (of poem) vers m; (row, series) rangée f; (of people) file f, queue f; (railway track) voie f; (Comm: series of goods) article(s) m(pl), ligne de produits; (work) métier m ▷ vt: **to ~ (with)** (clothes) doubler (de); (box) garnir ou tapisser (de); (subj: trees, crowd) border; **to stand in ~** (US) faire la queue; **in his ~ of business** dans sa partie, dans son rayon; **to be in ~ for sth** (fig) être en lice pour qch; **in ~ with** en accord avec, en conformité avec; **in a ~** aligné(e); **line up** vi s'aligner, se mettre en rang(s); (in queue) faire la queue ▷ vt aligner; (event) prévoir; (find) trouver; **to have sb/sth ~d up** avoir qn/qch en vue ou de prévu(e)

linear ['lɪnɪə'] adj linéaire

linen ['lɪnɪn] n linge m (de corps ou de maison); (cloth) lin m

liner ['laɪnə'] n (ship) paquebot m de ligne; (for bin) sac-poubelle m

line-up ['laɪnʌp] n (us: queue) file f; (also: **police ~**) parade f d'identification; (Sport) (composition f de l')équipe f

linger ['lɪŋɡə'] vi s'attarder, traîner; (smell, tradition) persister

lingerie ['lænʒəriː] n lingerie f

linguist ['lɪŋɡwɪst] n linguiste m/f; **to be a good ~** être doué(e) pour les langues; **linguistic** adj linguistique

lining ['laɪnɪŋ] n doublure f; (of brakes) garniture f

link [lɪŋk] n (connection) lien m, rapport

m; (Internet) lien; (of a chain) maillon m ▷ vt relier, lier, unir; **links** npl (Golf) (terrain m de) golf m; **link up** vt relier ▷ vi (people) se rejoindre; (companies etc) s'associer

lion ['laɪən] n lion m; **lioness** n lionne f

lip [lɪp] n lèvre f; (of cup etc) rebord m; **lipread** vi lire sur les lèvres; **lip salve** [-sælv] n pommade f pour les lèvres, pommade rosat; **lipstick** n rouge m à lèvres

liqueur [lɪ'kjuə'] n liqueur f

liquid ['lɪkwɪd] n liquide m ▷ adj liquide; **liquidizer** ['lɪkwɪdaɪzə'] n (BRIT Culin) mixer m

liquor ['lɪkə'] n spiritueux m, alcool m; **liquor store** (US) n magasin m de vins et spiritueux

Lisbon ['lɪzbən] n Lisbonne

lisp [lɪsp] n zézaiement m ▷ vi zézayer

list [lɪst] n liste f ▷ vt (write down) inscrire; (make list of) faire la liste de; (enumerate) énumérer

listen ['lɪsn] vi écouter; **to ~ to** écouter; **listener** n auditeur(-trice)

lit [lɪt] pt, pp of **light**

liter ['liːtə'] n (US) = **litre**

literacy ['lɪtərəsɪ] n degré m d'alphabétisation, fait m de savoir lire et écrire

literal ['lɪtərl] adj littéral(e); **literally** adv littéralement; (really) réellement

literary ['lɪtərərɪ] adj littéraire

literate ['lɪtərət] adj qui sait lire et écrire; (educated) instruit(e)

literature ['lɪtrɪtʃə'] n littérature f; (brochures etc) copie f publicitaire, prospectus mpl

litre (US **liter**) ['liːtə'] n litre m

litter ['lɪtə'] n (rubbish) détritus mpl; (dirtier) ordures fpl; (young animals) portée f; **litter bin** n (BRIT) poubelle f; **littered** adj: **littered with** (scattered) jonché(e) de

little ['lɪtl] adj (small) petit(e); (not much): ~ **milk** peu de lait ▷ adv peu; **a ~** un peu (de); **a ~ milk** un peu de lait; **a ~ bit** un peu; **as ~ as possible**

le moins possible; **~ by** petit à petit,
peu à peu; **little finger** n auriculaire
m, petit doigt

live¹ [laɪv] adj (animal) vivant(e), en
vie; (wire) sous tension; (broadcast)
(transmis(e)) en direct; (unexploded)
non explosé(e)

live² [lɪv] vi vivre; (reside) vivre, habiter;
to ~ in London habiter (à) Londres;
where do you ~? où habitez-vous?; **live
together** vivre ensemble, cohabiter;
live up to fus se montrer à la
hauteur de

livelihood ['laɪvlɪhʊd] n moyens mpl
d'existence

lively ['laɪvlɪ] adj vif (vive), plein(e)
d'entrain; (place, book) vivant(e)

liven up ['laɪvn-] vt (room etc) égayer;
(discussion, evening) animer ▷ vi
s'animer

liver ['lɪvə'] n foie m

lives [laɪvz] npl of **life**

livestock ['laɪvstɔk] n cheptel m,
bétail m

living ['lɪvɪŋ] adj vivant(e), en vie ▷ n:
to earn or **make a ~** gagner sa vie;
living room n salle f de séjour

lizard ['lɪzəd] n lézard m

load [ləud] n (weight) poids m; (thing
carried) chargement m, charge f;
(Elec, Tech) charge ▷ vt (also: **~ up**):
to ~ (with) (lorry, ship) charger (de);
(gun, camera) charger (avec); (Comput)
charger; **a ~ of, ~s of** (fig) un or des
tas de, des masses de; **to talk a ~
of rubbish** (inf) dire des bêtises;
loaded adj (dice) pipé(e); (question)
insidieux(-euse); (inf: rich) bourré(e)
de fric

loaf (pl **loaves**) [ləuf, ləuvz] n pain m,
miche f ▷ vi (also: **~ about, ~ around**)
fainéanter, traîner

loan [ləun] n prêt m ▷ vt prêter; **on ~**
prêté(e), en prêt

loathe [ləuð] vt détester, avoir en
horreur

loaves [ləuvz] npl of **loaf**

lobby ['lɔbɪ] n hall m, entrée f; (Pol)

groupe m de pression, lobby m ▷ vt
faire pression sur

lobster ['lɔbstə'] n homard m

local ['ləukl] adj local(e) ▷ n (BRIT: pub)
pub m or café m du coin; **the locals** npl
les gens du pays or du coin; **local
anaesthetic** n anesthésie locale;
local authority n collectivité locale,
municipalité f; **local government** n
administration locale or municipale;
locally ['ləukəlɪ] adv localement; dans
les environs or la région

locate [ləu'keɪt] vt (find) trouver,
repérer; (situate) situer; **to be ~d in** être
situé à or en

location [ləu'keɪʃən] n emplacement
m; **on ~** (Cine) en extérieur

⚠ Be careful not to translate *location*
by the French word *location*.

loch [lɔx] n lac m, loch m

lock [lɔk] n (of door, box) serrure f; (of
canal) écluse f; (of hair) mèche f, boucle f
▷ vt (with key) fermer à clé ▷ vi (door etc)
fermer à clé; (wheels) se bloquer; **lock
in** vt enfermer; **lock out** vt enfermer
dehors; (on purpose) mettre à la porte;
lock up vt (person) enfermer; (house)
fermer à clé ▷ vi tout fermer (à clé)

locker ['lɔkə'] n casier m; (in station)
consigne f automatique; **locker-room**
(us) n (Sport) vestiaire m

locksmith ['lɔksmɪθ] n serrurier m

locomotive [ləukə'məutɪv] n
locomotive f

locum ['ləukəm] n (Med) suppléant(e)
de médecin etc

lodge [lɔdʒ] n pavillon m (de gardien);
(also: **hunting ~**) pavillon de chasse ▷ vi
(person) **to ~ with** être logé(e) chez,
être en pension chez; (bullet) se loger
▷ vt (appeal etc) présenter; déposer; **to
~ a complaint** porter plainte; **lodger**
n locataire m/f; (with room and meals)
pensionnaire m/f

lodging ['lɔdʒɪŋ] n logement m

loft [lɔft] n grenier m; (apartment)
grenier aménagé (en appartement)
(gén dans ancien entrepôt ou fabrique)

log [lɔg] n (of wood) bûche f; (Naut) livre m or journal m de bord; (of car) = carte grise ▷ vt enregistrer; **log in, log on** vi (Comput) ouvrir une session, entrer dans le système; **log off, log out** vi (Comput) clore une session, sortir du système

logic ['lɔdʒɪk] n logique f; **logical** adj logique

logo ['ləugəu] n logo m

Loire [lwa:] n: **the (River)** ~ la Loire

lollipop ['lɔlɪpɔp] n sucette f; **lollipop man/lady** (BRIT: irreg) n contractuel qui fait traverser la rue aux enfants

lolly ['lɔlɪ] n (inf: ice) esquimau m; (: lollipop) sucette f

London ['lʌndən] n Londres; **Londoner** n Londonien(ne)

lone [ləun] adj solitaire

loneliness ['ləunlinis] n solitude f, isolement m

lonely ['ləunlɪ] adj seul(e); (childhood etc) solitaire; (place) solitaire, isolé(e)

long [lɔŋ] adj long (longue) ▷ adv longtemps ▷ vi: **to ~ for sth/to do sth** avoir très envie de qch/de faire qch, attendre qch avec impatience/ attendre avec impatience de faire qch; **how ~ is this river/course?** quelle est la longueur de ce fleuve/la durée de ce cours?; **6 metres ~** (long) de 6 mètres; **6 months ~** qui dure 6 mois, de 6 mois; **all night ~** toute la nuit; **he no ~er comes** il ne vient plus; **I can't stand it any ~er** je ne peux plus le supporter; **~ before** longtemps avant; **before ~** (+ future) avant peu, dans peu de temps; (+ past) peu de temps après; **don't be ~!** fais vite!, dépêche-toi!; **I shan't be ~** je n'en ai pas pour longtemps; **at ~ last** enfin; **so or as ~ as** à condition que + sub; **long-distance** adj (race) de fond; (call) interurbain(e); **long-haul** adj (flight) long-courrier; **longing** n désir m, envie f; (nostalgia) nostalgie f ▷ adj plein(e) d'envie or de nostalgie

longitude ['lɔŋgɪtju:d] n longitude f

long: long jump n saut m en longueur;

long-life adj (batteries etc) longue durée inv; (milk) longue conservation; **long-sighted** adj (BRIT) presbyte; (fig) prévoyant(e); **long-standing** adj de longue date; **long-term** adj à long terme

loo [lu:] n (BRIT inf) w.-c mpl, petit coin

look [luk] vi regarder; (seem) sembler, paraître, avoir l'air; (building etc): **to ~ south/on to the sea** donner sur le sud/ sur la mer ▷ n regard m; (appearance) air m, allure f, aspect m; **looks** npl (good looks) physique m, beauté f; **to ~ like** ressembler à; **to ~** + adj: regarder; **to have a ~** + regarder; **to have a ~ at sth** jeter un coup d'œil à qch; **~ (here)!** (annoyance) écoutez!; **look after** vt fus s'occuper de; (luggage etc: watch over) garder, surveiller; **look around** vi regarder autour de soi; **look at** vt fus regarder; (problem etc) examiner; **look back** vi: **to ~ back at sth/sb** se retourner pour regarder qch/qn; **to ~ back on** (time, period) évoquer, repenser à; **look down on** vt fus (fig) regarder de haut, dédaigner; **look for** vt fus chercher; **we're ~ing for a hotel/restaurant** nous cherchons un hôtel/restaurant; **look forward to** vt fus attendre avec impatience; **~ing forward to hearing from you** (in letter) dans l'attente de vous lire; **look into** vt fus (matter, possibility) examiner, étudier; **look out** vi (beware): **to ~ out (for)** prendre garde (à), faire attention (à); **~ out!** attention!; **look out for** vt fus (seek) être à la recherche de; (try to spot) guetter; **look round** vt fus (house, shop) faire le tour de ▷ vi (turn) regarder derrière soi, se retourner; **look through** vt fus (papers, book) regarder; (: briefly) parcourir; **look up** vi lever les yeux; (improve) s'améliorer ▷ vt (word) chercher; **look up to** vt fus avoir du respect pour; **lookout** n (tower etc) poste m de guet; (person) guetteur m; **to be on the lookout (for)** guetter

loom [lu:m] vi (also: ~ **up**) surgir; (event) paraître imminent(e); (threaten) menacer

loony ['lu:nɪ] adj, n (inf) timbré(e), cinglé(e) m/f

loop [lu:p] n boucle f ▷ vt: **to ~ sth round sth** passer qch autour de qch; **loophole** n (fig) porte f de sortie; échappatoire f

loose [lu:s] adj (knot, screw) desserré(e); (clothes) vague, ample, lâche; (hair) dénoué(e), épars(e); (not firmly fixed) pas solide; (morals, discipline) relâché(e); (translation) approximatif(-ive) ▷ n: **to be on the ~** être en liberté; **~ connection** (Elec) mauvais contact; **to be at a ~ end** or (us) **at ~s ends** (fig) ne pas trop savoir quoi faire; **loosely** adv sans serrer; (imprecisely) approximativement; **loosen** vt desserrer, relâcher, défaire

loot [lu:t] n butin m ▷ vt piller

lop-sided ['lɔp'saɪdɪd] adj de travers, asymétrique

lord [lɔ:d] n seigneur m; **L~ Smith** lord Smith; **the L~** (Rel) le Seigneur; **my L~** (to noble) Monsieur le comte/le baron; (to judge) Monsieur le juge; (to bishop) Monseigneur; **good L~!** mon Dieu!; **Lords** npl (Brit: Pol): **the (House of) Lords** la Chambre des Lords

lorry ['lɔrɪ] n (Brit) camion m; **lorry driver** n (Brit) camionneur m, routier m

lose (pt, pp **lost**) [lu:z, lɔst] vt perdre ▷ vi perdre; **I've lost my wallet/passport** j'ai perdu mon portefeuille/passeport; **to ~ (time)** (clock) retarder; **lose out** vi être perdant(e); **loser** n perdant(e)

loss [lɔs] n perte f; **to make a ~** enregistrer une perte; **to be at a ~** être perplexe or embarrassé(e)

lost [lɔst] pt, pp of **lose** ▷ adj perdu(e); **to get ~** vi se perdre; **I'm ~** je me suis perdu; **~ and found property** n (us) objets trouvés; **~ and found** n (us) (bureau m des) objets trouvés; **lost property** n (Brit) objets trouvés; **lost property office** or **department** (bureau m des) objets trouvés

lot [lɔt] n (at auctions, set) lot m; (destiny) sort m, destinée f; **the ~** (everything) le tout; (everyone) tous mpl, toutes fpl; **a ~** beaucoup; **a ~ of** beaucoup de; **~s of** des tas de; **to draw ~s (for sth)** tirer (qch) au sort

lotion ['ləʊʃən] n lotion f

lottery ['lɔtərɪ] n loterie f

loud [laʊd] adj bruyant(e), sonore; (voice) fort(e); (condemnation etc) vigoureux(-euse); (gaudy) voyant(e), tapageur(-euse) ▷ adv (speak etc) fort; **out ~** tout haut; **loudly** adv fort, bruyamment; **loudspeaker** n haut-parleur m

lounge [laundʒ] n salon m; (of airport) salle f; (Brit: also: **~ bar**) (salle de) café m or bar m ▷ vi (also: **~ about** or **around**) se prélasser, paresser

louse (pl lice) [laus, laɪs] n pou m

lousy ['laʊzɪ] (inf) adj (bad quality) infect(e), moche; **I feel ~** je suis mal fichu(e)

love [lʌv] n amour m ▷ vt aimer; (caringly, kindly) aimer beaucoup; **I ~ chocolate** j'adore le chocolat; **to ~ to do** aimer beaucoup or adorer faire; **"15 ~"** (Tennis) "15 à rien or zéro"; **to be/fall in ~ with** être/tomber amoureux(-euse) de; **to make ~** faire l'amour; **from Anne, ~, Anne** affectueusement, Anne; **I ~ you** je t'aime; **love affair** n liaison (amoureuse); **love life** n vie sentimentale

lovely ['lʌvlɪ] adj (pretty) ravissant(e); (friend, wife) charmant(e); (holiday, surprise) très agréable, merveilleux(-euse)

lover ['lʌvə'] n amant m; (person in love) amoureux(-euse); (amateur): **a ~ of** un(e) ami(e) de, un(e) amoureux(-euse) de

loving ['lʌvɪŋ] adj affectueux(-euse), tendre, aimant(e)

low [ləʊ] adj bas (basse); (quality) mauvais(e), inférieur(e) ▷ adv bas ▷ n (Meteorology) dépression f; **to feel ~** se sentir déprimé(e); **he's very ~** (*ill*) il est bien bas *or* très affaibli; **to turn (down) ~** *vt* baisser; **to be ~ on** (*supplies etc*) être à court de; **to reach a new** *or* **an all-time ~** tomber au niveau le plus bas; **low-alcohol** *adj* à faible teneur en alcool, peu alcoolisé(e); **low-calorie** *adj* hypocalorique

lower ['ləʊə^r] *adj* inférieur(e) ▷ *vt* baisser; (*resistance*) diminuer; **to ~ o.s. to** s'abaisser à

low-fat ['ləʊ'fæt] *adj* maigre

loyal ['lɔɪəl] *adj* loyal(e), fidèle; **loyalty** *n* loyauté *f*, fidélité *f*; **loyalty card** *n* carte *f* de fidélité

L.P. *n abbr* = **long-playing record**

L-plates ['elpleɪts] *npl* (BRIT) plaques *fpl* (obligatoires) d'apprenti conducteur

Lt *abbr* (= *lieutenant*) Lt.

Ltd *abbr* (Comm: company: = *limited*) = S.A.

luck [lʌk] *n* chance *f*; **bad ~** malchance *f*, malheur *m*; **good ~!** bonne chance!; **bad** *or* **hard ~!** pas de chance!; **luckily** *adv* heureusement, par bonheur; **lucky** *adj* (*person*) qui a de la chance; (*coincidence*) heureux(-euse); (*number etc*) qui porte bonheur

lucrative ['lu:krətɪv] *adj* lucratif(-ive), rentable, qui rapporte

ludicrous ['lu:dɪkrəs] *adj* ridicule, absurde

luggage ['lʌgɪdʒ] *n* bagages *mpl*; **our ~ hasn't arrived** nos bagages ne sont pas arrivés; **could you send someone to collect our ~?** pourriez-vous envoyer quelqu'un chercher nos bagages?; **luggage rack** *n* (*in train*) porte-bagages *m inv*; (: *on car*) galerie *f*

lukewarm ['lu:kwɔ:m] *adj* tiède

lull [lʌl] *n* accalmie *f*; (*in conversation*) pause *f* ▷ *vt*: **to ~ sb to sleep** bercer qn pour qu'il s'endorme; **to be ~ed into a false sense of security** s'endormir dans une fausse sécurité

lullaby ['lʌləbaɪ] *n* berceuse *f*

lumber ['lʌmbə^r] *n* (*wood*) bois *m* de charpente; (*junk*) bric-à-brac *m inv* ▷ *vt* (BRIT inf): **to ~ sb with sth/sb** coller *or*

refiler qch/qn à qn

luminous ['lu:mɪnəs] *adj* lumineux(-euse)

lump [lʌmp] *n* morceau *m*; (*in sauce*) grumeau *m*; (*swelling*) grosseur *f* ▷ *vt* (*also*: **~ together**) réunir, mettre en tas; **lump sum** *n* somme globale *or* forfaitaire; **lumpy** *adj* (*sauce*) qui a des grumeaux; (*bed*) défoncé(e), peu confortable

lunatic ['lu:nətɪk] *n* fou (folle), dément(e) ▷ *adj* fou (folle), dément(e)

lunch [lʌntʃ] *n* déjeuner *m* ▷ *vi* déjeuner; **lunch break, lunch hour** *n* pause *f* de midi, heure *f* du déjeuner; **lunchtime** *n*: **it's lunchtime** c'est l'heure du déjeuner

lung [lʌŋ] *n* poumon *m*

lure [luə^r] *n* (*attraction*) attrait *m*, charme *m*; (*in hunting*) appât *m*, leurre *m* ▷ *vt* attirer *or* persuader par la ruse

lurk [lə:k] *vi* se tapir, se cacher

lush [lʌʃ] *adj* luxuriant(e)

lust [lʌst] *n* (*sexual*) désir (sexuel); (*Rel*) luxure *f*; (*fig*): **~ for** soif *f* de

Luxembourg ['lʌksəmbə:g] *n* Luxembourg *m*

luxurious [lʌg'zjuərɪəs] *adj* luxueux(-euse)

luxury ['lʌkʃərɪ] *n* luxe *m* ▷ *cpd* de luxe

Lycra® ['laɪkrə] *n* Lycra® *m*

lying ['laɪɪŋ] *n* mensonge(s) *m(pl)* ▷ *adj* (*statement, account*) mensonger(-ère), faux (fausse); (*person*) menteur(-euse)

Lyons ['lɪɔ̃] *n* Lyon *m*

lyrics ['lɪrɪks] *npl* (*of song*) paroles *fpl*

m

m. abbr (= metre) m; (= million) M; (= mile) mi

M.A. n abbr (Scol) = **Master of Arts**

ma [mɑː] (inf) n maman f

mac [mæk] n (BRIT) imper(méable m) m

macaroni [mækəˈrəʊnɪ] n macaronis mpl

Macedonia [mæsɪˈdəʊnɪə] n Macédoine f; **Macedonian** [mæsɪˈdəʊnɪən] adj macédonien(ne) ▷ n Macédonien(ne); (Ling) macédonien m

machine [məˈʃiːn] n machine f ▷ vt (dress etc) coudre à la machine; (Tech) usiner; **machine gun** n mitrailleuse f; **machinery** n machinerie f, machines fpl; (fig) mécanisme(s) m(pl); **machine washable** adj (garment) lavable en machine

macho [ˈmætʃəʊ] adj macho inv

mackerel [ˈmækrl] n (pl inv) maquereau m

mackintosh [ˈmækɪntɒʃ] n (BRIT) imperméable m

mad [mæd] adj fou (folle); (foolish) insensé(e); (angry) furieux(-euse); **to be ~ (keen) about** or **on sth** (inf) être follement passionné de qch, être fou de qch

Madagascar [mædəˈgæskə] n Madagascar m

madam [ˈmædəm] n madame f

mad cow disease n maladie f des vaches folles

made [meɪd] pt, pp of **make**; **made-to-measure** adj (garment) fait(e) sur mesure; **made-up** [ˈmeɪdʌp] adj (story) inventé(e), fabriqué(e)

madly [ˈmædlɪ] adv follement; **~ in love** éperdument amoureux(-euse)

madman [ˈmædmən] (irreg) n fou m, aliéné m

madness [ˈmædnɪs] n folie f

Madrid [məˈdrɪd] n Madrid

Mafia [ˈmæfɪə] n maf(f)ia f

mag [mæg] n abbr (BRIT inf: = magazine) magazine m

magazine [mægəˈziːn] n (Press) magazine m, revue f; (Radio, TV) magazine

maggot [ˈmægət] n ver m, asticot m

magic [ˈmædʒɪk] n magie f ▷ adj magique; **magical** adj magique; (experience, evening) merveilleux(-euse); **magician** [məˈdʒɪʃən] n magicien(ne)

magistrate [ˈmædʒɪstreɪt] n magistrat m; juge m

magnet [ˈmægnɪt] n aimant m; **magnetic** [mægˈnɛtɪk] adj magnétique

magnificent [mægˈnɪfɪsnt] adj superbe, magnifique; (splendid: robe, building) somptueux(-euse), magnifique

magnify [ˈmægnɪfaɪ] vt grossir; (sound) amplifier; **magnifying glass** n loupe f

magpie [ˈmægpaɪ] n pie f

mahogany [məˈhɒgənɪ] n acajou m

maid [meɪd] n bonne f; (in hotel) femme f de chambre; **old ~** (pej) vieille fille

maiden name n nom m de jeune fille

mail [meɪl] n poste f; (letters) courrier m ▷ vt envoyer (par la poste); **by ~** par la poste; **mailbox** n (us: also mailbox) boîte f aux lettres; **mailing list** n liste f d'adresses; **mailman** (irreg) n (us) facteur m; **mail-order** n vente f par achat m par correspondance

main [meɪn] adj principal(e) ▷ n (pipe) conduite principale, canalisation f; **the ~s** (Elec) le secteur; **the ~ thing** l'essentiel m; **in the ~** dans l'ensemble; **main course** n (Culin) plat m de résistance; **mainland** n continent m; **mainly** adv principalement, surtout; **main road** n grand axe, route nationale; **mainstream** n (fig) courant principal; **main street** n rue f principale

maintain [meɪn'teɪn] vt entretenir; (continue) maintenir, préserver; (affirm) soutenir; **maintenance** [ˈmeɪntənəns] n entretien m; (Law: alimony) pension f alimentaire

maisonette [meɪzəˈnɛt] n (BRIT) appartement m en duplex

maize [meɪz] n (BRIT) maïs m

majesty [ˈmædʒɪstɪ] n majesté f; (title): **Your M~** Votre Majesté

major [ˈmeɪdʒəʳ] n (Mil) commandant m ▷ adj (important) important(e); (most important) principal(e); (Mus) majeur(e) ▷ vi (us Scol): **to ~ (in)** se spécialiser en

Majorca [məˈjɔːkə] n Majorque f

majority [məˈdʒɔrɪtɪ] n majorité f

make [meɪk] vt (pt, pp made) faire; (manufacture) faire, fabriquer; (earn) gagner; (decision) prendre; (friend) se faire; (speech) prononcer; (cause to be): **to ~ sb sad** etc rendre qn triste etc; (force): **to ~ sb do sth** obliger qn à faire qch, faire faire qch à qn; (equal): **2 and 2 ~ 4** 2 et 2 font 4 ▷ n (manufacture) fabrication f; (brand) marque f; **to ~ the bed** faire le lit; **to ~ a fool of sb** (ridicule) ridiculiser qn; (trick) avoir ou duper qn; **to ~ a profit** faire un ou des bénéfice(s); **to ~ a loss** essuyer une perte; **to ~ it** (in time etc) y arriver; (succeed) réussir;

what time do you ~ it? quelle heure avez-vous?; **I ~ it £249** d'après mes calculs ça fait 249 livres; **to be made of** être en; **to ~ do with** se contenter de; se débrouiller avec; **make off** vi filer; **make out** vt (write out: cheque) faire; (decipher) déchiffrer; (understand) comprendre; (see) distinguer; (claim, imply) prétendre, vouloir faire croire; **make up** vt (invent) inventer, imaginer; (constitute) constituer; (parcel, bed) faire ▷ vi se réconcilier; (with cosmetics) se maquiller, se farder; **to be made up of** se composer de; **make up for** vt fus compenser; (lost time) rattraper; **makeover** [ˈmeɪkəʊvəʳ] n (by beautician) soins mpl de maquillage; (change of image) changement m d'image; **maker** n fabricant m; (of film, programme) réalisateur(-trice); **makeshift** adj provisoire, improvisé(e); **make-up** n maquillage m

making [ˈmeɪkɪŋ] n (fig): **in the ~** en formation ou gestation; **to have the ~s of** (actor, athlete) avoir l'étoffe de

malaria [məˈlɛərɪə] n malaria f, paludisme m

Malaysia [məˈleɪzɪə] n Malaisie f

male [meɪl] n (Biol, Elec) mâle m ▷ adj (sex, attitude) masculin(e); (animal) mâle; (child etc) du sexe masculin

malicious [məˈlɪʃəs] adj méchant(e), malveillant(e)

> Be careful not to translate *malicious* by the French word *malicieux*.

malignant [məˈlɪgnənt] adj (Med) malin(-igne)

mall [mɔːl] n (also: **shopping ~**) centre commercial

mallet [ˈmælɪt] n maillet m

malnutrition [mælnjuːˈtrɪʃən] n malnutrition f

malpractice [mælˈpræktɪs] n faute professionnelle; négligence f

malt [mɔːlt] n ▷ cpd (whisky) pur malt

Malta ['mɔːltə] n Malte f; **Maltese** [mɔːl'tiːz] adj maltais(e) ▷ n (pl inv) Maltais(e)

mammal ['mæml] n mammifère m

mammoth ['mæməθ] n mammouth m ▷ adj géant(e), monstre

man (pl **men**) [mæn, mɛn] n homme m; (Sport) joueur m; (Chess) pièce f ▷ vt (Naut: ship) garnir d'hommes; (machine) assurer le fonctionnement de; (Mil: gun) servir; (: post) être de service à; **an old ~** un vieillard; **~ and wife** mari et femme

manage ['mænɪdʒ] vi se débrouiller; (succeed) y arriver, réussir ▷ vt (business) gérer; (team, operation) diriger; (control: ship) manier, manœuvrer; (: person) savoir s'y prendre avec; **to ~ to do** se débrouiller pour faire; (succeed) réussir à faire; **manageable** adj maniable; (task etc) faisable; (number) raisonnable; **management** n (running) administration f, direction f; (people in charge of business, firm) dirigeants mpl, cadres mpl; (: of hotel, shop, theatre) direction; **manager** n (of business) directeur m; (of institution etc) administrateur m; (of department, unit) responsable m/f, chef m; (of hotel etc) gérant m; (Sport) manager m; (of artist) impresario m; **manageress** n directrice f; (of hotel etc) gérante f; **managerial** [mænɪ'dʒɪərɪəl] adj directorial(e); (skills) de cadre, de gestion; **managing director** n directeur général

mandarin ['mændərɪn] n (also: ~ **orange**) mandarine f

mandate ['mændeɪt] n mandat m

mandatory ['mændətəri] adj obligatoire

mane [meɪn] n crinière f

maneuver [mə'nuːvə] (US) = **manoeuvre**

mangetout ['mɔnʒ'tuː] n mangetout m inv

mango (pl **~es**) ['mæŋɡəu] n mangue f

man: **manhole** n trou m d'homme; **manhood** n (age) âge m d'homme m;

(manliness) virilité f

mania ['meɪnɪə] n manie f; **maniac** ['meɪnɪæk] n maniaque m/f; (fig) fou (folle)

manic ['mænɪk] adj maniaque

manicure ['mænɪkjuə] n manucure f

manifest ['mænɪfest] vt manifester ▷ adj manifeste, évident(e)

manifesto [mænɪ'festəu] n (Pol) manifeste m

manipulate [mə'nɪpjuleɪt] vt manipuler; (system, situation) exploiter

man: **mankind** [mæn'kaɪnd] n humanité f, genre humain; **manly** adj viril(e); **man-made** adj artificiel(le); (fibre) synthétique

manner ['mænə] n manière f, façon f; (behaviour) attitude f, comportement m; **manners** npl (good) **~s** (bonnes) manières; **bad ~s** mauvaises manières; **all ~ of** toutes sortes de

manoeuvre (us **maneuver**) [mə'nuːvə] vt (move) manœuvrer; (manipulate: person) manipuler; (: situation) exploiter ▷ n manœuvre f

manpower ['mænpauə] n main-d'œuvre f

mansion ['mænʃən] n château m, manoir m

manslaughter ['mænslɔːtə] n homicide m involontaire

mantelpiece ['mæntlpiːs] n cheminée f

manual ['mænjuəl] adj manuel(le) ▷ n manuel m

manufacture [mænju'fæktʃə] vt fabriquer ▷ n fabrication f; **manufacturer** n fabricant m

manure [mə'njuə] n fumier m; (artificial) engrais m

manuscript ['mænjuskrɪpt] n manuscrit m

many ['mɛnɪ] adj beaucoup de, de nombreux(-euses) ▷ pron beaucoup, un grand nombre; **a great ~** un grand nombre (de); **~ a ...** bien des ..., plus d'un(e) ...

map [mæp] n carte f; (of town) plan

m; **can you show it to me on the ~?** pouvez-vous me l'indiquer sur la carte?; **map out** *vt* tracer; (*fig: task*) planifier

maple ['meɪpl] *n* érable *m*

Mar *abbr* = **March**

mar [mɑːʳ] *vt* gâcher, gâter

marathon ['mærəθən] *n* marathon *m*

marble ['mɑːbl] *n* marbre *m*; (*toy*) bille *f*

March [mɑːtʃ] *n* mars *m*

march [mɑːtʃ] *vi* marcher au pas; (*demonstrators*) défiler ▷ *n* marche *f*; (*demonstration*) manifestation *f*

mare [mɛəʳ] *n* jument *f*

margarine [mɑːdʒə'riːn] *n* margarine *f*

margin ['mɑːdʒɪn] *n* marge *f*; **marginal** *adj* marginal(e); **marginal seat** (*Pol*) siège disputé; **marginally** *adv* très légèrement, sensiblement

marigold ['mærɪɡəʊld] *n* souci *m*

marijuana [mærɪ'wɑːnə] *n* marijuana *f*

marina [mə'riːnə] *n* marina *f*

marinade *n* [mærɪ'neɪd] marinade *f* ▷ *vt* **marinate**

marinate ['mærɪneɪt] *vt* (faire) mariner

marine [mə'riːn] *adj* marin(e) ▷ *n* fusilier marin; (*us*) marine *m*

marital ['mærɪtl] *adj* matrimonial(e); **marital status** *n* situation *f* de famille

maritime ['mærɪtaɪm] *adj* maritime

marjoram ['mɑːdʒərəm] *n* marjolaine *f*

mark [mɑːk] *n* marque *f*; (*of skid etc*) trace *f*; (*BRIT Scol*) note *f*; (*oven temperature*): **(gas) ~ 4** thermostat *m* 4 ▷ *vt* (*also Sport: player*) marquer; (*stain*) tacher; (*BRIT Scol*) corriger, noter; **to ~ time** marquer le pas; **marked** *adj* (*obvious*) marqué(e), net(te); **marker** *n* (*sign*) jalon *m*; (*bookmark*) signet *m*

market ['mɑːkɪt] *n* marché *m* ▷ *vt* (*Comm*) commercialiser; **marketing** *n* marketing *m*; **marketplace** *n* place *f* du marché; (*Comm*) marché *m*; **market research** *n* étude *f* de marché

marmalade ['mɑːməleɪd] *n* confiture *f* d'oranges

maroon [mə'ruːn] *vt*: **to be ~ed** être

abandonné(e); (*fig*) être bloqué(e) ▷ *adj* (*colour*) bordeaux *inv*

marquee [mɑː'kiː] *n* chapiteau *m*

marriage ['mærɪdʒ] *n* mariage *m*; **marriage certificate** *n* extrait *m* d'acte de mariage

married ['mærɪd] *adj* marié(e); (*life, love*) conjugal(e)

marrow ['mærəʊ] *n* (*of bone*) moelle *f*; (*vegetable*) courge *f*

marry ['mærɪ] *vt* épouser, se marier avec; (*subj: father, priest etc*) marier ▷ *vi* (*also:* **get married**) se marier

Mars [mɑːz] *n* (*planet*) Mars *f*

Marseilles [mɑː'seɪ] *n* Marseille

marsh [mɑːʃ] *n* marais *m*, marécage *m*

marshal ['mɑːʃl] *n* maréchal *m*; (*us: fire, police*) ≈ capitaine *m*; (*for demonstration, meeting*) membre *m* du service d'ordre ▷ *vt* rassembler

martyr ['mɑːtəʳ] *n* martyr(e)

marvel ['mɑːvl] *n* merveille *f* ▷ *vi*: **to ~ (at)** s'émerveiller (de); **marvellous**, (*us*) **marvelous** *adj* merveilleux(-euse)

Marxism ['mɑːksɪzəm] *n* marxisme *m*

Marxist ['mɑːksɪst] *adj*, *n* marxiste (*m/f*)

marzipan ['mɑːzɪpæn] *n* pâte *f* d'amandes

mascara [mæs'kɑːrə] *n* mascara *m*

mascot ['mæskət] *n* mascotte *f*

masculine ['mæskjʊlɪn] *adj* masculin(e) ▷ *n* masculin *m*

mash [mæʃ] *vt* (*Culin*) faire une purée de; **mashed potato(es)** *n(pl)* purée *f* de pommes de terre

mask [mɑːsk] *n* masque *m* ▷ *vt* masquer

mason ['meɪsn] *n* (*also:* **stone~**) maçon *m*; (*also:* **free~**) franc-maçon *m*; **masonry** *n* maçonnerie *f*

mass [mæs] *n* multitude *f*, masse *f*; (*Physics*) masse; (*Rel*) messe *f* ▷ *cpd* (*communication*) de masse; (*unemployment*) massif(-ive) ▷ *vi* se masser; **masses** *npl*: **the ~es** les masses; **~es of** (*inf*) des tas de

massacre ['mæsəkəʳ] *n* massacre *m*

massage ['mæsɑːʒ] n massage m
▷ vt masser
massive ['mæsɪv] adj énorme,
massif(-ive)
mass media npl mass-media mpl
mass-produce ['mæsprə'djuːs] vt
fabriquer en série
mast [mɑːst] n mât m; (Radio, TV)
pylône m
master ['mɑːstə'] n maître m; (in
secondary school) professeur m; (in
primary school) instituteur m; (for
boys): **M- X** Monsieur X ▷ vt maîtriser;
(learn) apprendre à fond; **M- of Arts/
Science (MA/MSc)** n = titulaire m/f
d'une maîtrise (en lettres/science); **M-
of Arts/Science degree (MA/MSc)**
n = maîtrise f; **mastermind** n esprit
supérieur ▷ vt diriger, être le cerveau
de; **masterpiece** n chef-d'œuvre m
masturbate ['mæstəbeɪt] vi se
masturber
mat [mæt] n petit tapis; (also: **door-**)
paillasson m; (also: **table-**) set m de
table ▷ adj = **matt**
match [mætʃ] n allumette f; (game)
match m, partie f; (fig) égal(e) ▷ vt (also:
~ up) assortir; (go well with) aller bien
avec, s'assortir à; (equal) égaler, valoir
▷ vi être assorti(e); **to be a good -** être
bien assorti(e); **matchbox** n boîte f
d'allumettes; **matching** adj assorti(e)
mate [meɪt] n (inf) copain (copine);
(animal) partenaire m/f, mâle (femelle);
(in merchant navy) second m ▷ vi
s'accoupler
material [mə'tɪərɪəl] n (substance)
matière f, matériau m; (cloth) tissu m,
étoffe f; (information, data) données fpl
▷ adj matériel(le); (relevant: evidence)
pertinent(e); **materials** npl (equipment)
matériaux mpl
materialize [mə'tɪərɪəlaɪz] vi se
matérialiser, se réaliser
maternal [mə'tə:nl] adj maternel(le)
maternity [mə'tə:nɪtɪ] n maternité f;
maternity hospital n maternité f;
maternity leave n congé m de

maternité
math [mæθ] n (us: = mathematics)
maths fpl
mathematical [mæθə'mætɪkl] adj
mathématique
mathematician [mæθəmə'tɪʃən] n
mathématicien(ne)
mathematics [mæθə'mætɪks] n
mathématiques fpl
maths [mæθs] n abbr (BRIT:
= mathematics) maths fpl
matinée ['mætɪneɪ] n matinée f
matron ['meɪtrən] n (in hospital)
infirmière-chef f; (in school) infirmière f
matt [mæt] adj mat(e)
matter ['mætə'] n question f; (Physics)
matière f, substance f; (Med: pus) pus
m ▷ vi importer; **matters** npl (affairs,
situation) la situation; **it doesn't ~** cela
n'a pas d'importance; (I don't mind) cela
ne fait rien; **what's the ~?** qu'est-ce
qu'il y a?, qu'est-ce qui ne va pas?; **no
what** quoi qu'il arrive; **as a - of course**
tout naturellement; **as a - of fact** en
fait; **reading ~** (BRIT) de quoi lire, de
la lecture
mattress ['mætrɪs] n matelas m
mature [mə'tjuə'] adj mûr(e); (cheese)
fait(e); (wine) arrivé(e) à maturité ▷ vi
mûrir; (cheese, wine) se faire; **mature
student** n étudiant(e) plus âgé(e) que la
moyenne; **maturity** n maturité f
maul [mɔːl] vt lacérer
mauve [məuv] adj mauve
max abbr = **maximum**
maximize ['mæksɪmaɪz] vt (profits etc,
chances) maximiser
maximum ['mæksɪməm] (pl **maxima**)
adj maximum ▷ n maximum m
May [meɪ] n mai m
may [meɪ] (conditional **might**) vi
(indicating possibility): **he ~ come** il se
peut qu'il vienne; (be allowed to): **~ I
smoke?** puis-je fumer?; (wishes): **~ God
bless you!** (que) Dieu vous bénisse!;
you - as well go vous feriez aussi
bien d'y aller
maybe ['meɪbiː] adv peut-être; **~**

he'll ... peut-être qu'il ...

May Day n le Premier mai

mayhem ['meɪhɛm] n grabuge m

mayonnaise [meɪə'neɪz] n mayonnaise f

mayor [mɛəʳ] n maire m; **mayoress** n (female mayor) maire m; (wife of mayor) épouse f du maire

maze [meɪz] n labyrinthe m, dédale m

MD n abbr (Comm) = **managing director**

me [miː] pron me, m' + vowel or h mute; (stressed, after prep) moi; **it's me** c'est moi; **he heard me** il m'a entendu; **give me a book** donnez-moi un livre; **it's for me** c'est pour moi

meadow ['mɛdəu] n prairie f, pré m

meagre (us **meager**) ['miːgəʳ] adj maigre

meal [miːl] n repas m; (flour) farine f; **mealtime** n heure f du repas

mean [miːn] adj (with money) avare, radin(e); (unkind) mesquin(e), méchant(e); (shabby) misérable; (average) moyen(ne) ▷ vt (pt, pp ~t) (signify) signifier, vouloir dire; (refer to) faire allusion à, parler de; (intend): **to ~ to do** avoir l'intention de faire ▷ n moyenne f; **means** npl (way, money) moyens mpl; **by ~s of** (instrument) au moyen de; **by all ~s** je vous en prie; **to be ~t for** être destiné(e) à; **do you ~ it?** vous êtes sérieux?; **what do you ~?** que voulez-vous dire?

meaning ['miːnɪŋ] n signification f, sens m; **meaningful** adj significatif(-ive); (relationship) valable; **meaningless** adj dénué(e) de sens

meant [mɛnt] pt, pp of **mean**

meantime ['miːntaɪm] adv (also: **in the ~**) pendant ce temps

meanwhile ['miːnwaɪl] adv = **meantime**

measles ['miːzlz] n rougeole f

measure ['mɛʒəʳ] vt, vi mesurer ▷ n mesure f; (ruler) règle (graduée)

measurements ['mɛʒəmənts] npl mesures fpl; **chest/hip ~** tour m de poitrine/hanches

meat [miːt] n viande f; **I don't eat ~** je ne mange pas de viande; **cold ~s** (BRIT) viandes froides; **meatball** n boulette f de viande

Mecca ['mɛkə] n la Mecque

mechanic [mɪ'kænɪk] n mécanicien m; **can you send a ~?** pouvez-vous nous envoyer un mécanicien?; **mechanical** adj mécanique; **mechanism** ['mɛkənɪzəm] n mécanisme m

medal ['mɛdl] n médaille f; **medallist** (us **medalist**) n (Sport) médaillé(e)

meddle ['mɛdl] vi: **to ~ in** se mêler de, s'occuper de; **to ~ with** toucher à

media ['miːdɪə] npl média mpl ▷ npl of **medium**

mediaeval [mɛdɪ'iːvl] adj = **medieval**

mediate ['miːdɪeɪt] vi servir d'intermédiaire

medical ['mɛdɪkl] adj médical(e) ▷ n (also: **~ examination**) visite médicale; (private) examen médical; **medical certificate** n certificat médical

medicated ['mɛdɪkeɪtɪd] adj traitant(e), médicamenteux(-euse)

medication [mɛdɪ'keɪʃən] n (drugs etc) médication f

medicine ['mɛdsɪn] n médecine f; (drug) médicament m

medieval [mɛdɪ'iːvl] adj médiéval(e)

mediocre [miːdɪ'əukəʳ] adj médiocre

meditate ['mɛdɪteɪt] vi: **to ~ (on)** méditer (sur)

meditation [mɛdɪ'teɪʃən] n méditation f

Mediterranean [mɛdɪtə'reɪnɪən] adj méditerranéen(ne); **the ~ (Sea)** la (mer) Méditerranée

medium ['miːdɪəm] adj moyen(ne) ▷ n (pl **media**: means) moyen m; (pl **~s**: person) médium m; **the happy ~** le juste milieu; **medium-sized** adj de taille moyenne; **medium wave** n (Radio) ondes moyennes, petites ondes

meek [miːk] adj doux (douce), humble

meet (pt, pp **met**) [miːt, mɛt] vt rencontrer; (by arrangement) retrouver, rejoindre; (for the first time) faire la connaissance de; (go and fetch) **I'll ~ you at the station** j'irai te chercher à la gare; (opponent, danger, problem) faire face à; (requirements) satisfaire à, répondre à ▷ vi (friends) se rencontrer; se retrouver; (in session) se réunir; (join: lines, roads) se joindre; **nice ~ing you** ravi d'avoir fait votre connaissance; **meet up** vi: **to ~ up with sb** rencontrer qn; **meet with** vt fus (difficulty) rencontrer; **to ~ with success** être couronné(e) de succès; **meeting** n (of group of people) réunion f; (between individuals) rendez-vous m; **she's at or in a meeting** (Comm) elle est en réunion; **meeting place** n lieu m de (la) réunion; (for appointment) lieu de rendez-vous

megabyte ['mɛgəbaɪt] n (Comput) méga-octet m

megaphone ['mɛgəfəun] n porte-voix m inv

megapixel ['mɛgəpɪksl] n mégapixel m

melancholy ['mɛlənkəlɪ] n mélancolie f ▷ adj mélancolique

melody ['mɛlədɪ] n mélodie f

melon ['mɛlən] n melon m

melt [mɛlt] vi fondre ▷ vt faire fondre

member ['mɛmbə*] n membre m; **Member of Congress** (US) n membre m du Congrès, ≈ député m; **Member of Parliament (MP)** n (BRIT) député m; **Member of the European Parliament (MEP)** n Eurodéputé m; **Member of the House of Representatives (MHR)** n (US) membre m de la Chambre des représentants; **Member of the Scottish Parliament (MSP)** n (BRIT) député m au Parlement écossais; **membership** n (becoming a member) adhésion f; admission f; (the members) membres mpl, adhérents mpl; **membership card** n carte f de membre

memento [mə'mɛntəu] n souvenir m

memo ['mɛməu] n note f (de service)

memorable ['mɛmərəbl] adj mémorable

memorandum (pl **memoranda**) [mɛmə'rændəm, -də] n note f (de service)

memorial [mɪ'mɔːrɪəl] n mémorial m ▷ adj commémoratif(-ive)

memorize ['mɛmərɑɪz] vt apprendre or retenir par cœur

memory ['mɛmərɪ] n (also Comput) mémoire f; (recollection) souvenir m; **in ~ of** à la mémoire de; **memory card** n (for digital camera) carte f mémoire

men [mɛn] npl of **man**

menace ['mɛnɪs] n menace f; (inf: nuisance) peste f, plaie f ▷ vt menacer

mend [mɛnd] vt réparer; (darn) raccommoder, repriser ▷ n: **on the ~** en voie de guérison; **to ~ one's ways** s'amender

meningitis [mɛnɪn'dʒaɪtɪs] n méningite f

menopause ['mɛnəupɔːz] n ménopause f

men's room (US) n: **the men's room** les toilettes fpl pour hommes

menstruation [mɛnstru'eɪʃən] n menstruation f

menswear ['mɛnzwɛə*] n vêtements mpl d'hommes

mental ['mɛntl] adj mental(e); **mental hospital** n hôpital m psychiatrique; **mentality** [mɛn'tælɪt] n mentalité f; **mentally** adv: **to be mentally handicapped** être handicapé(e) mental(e); **the mentally ill** les malades mentaux

menthol ['mɛnθɔl] n menthol m

mention ['mɛnʃən] n mention f ▷ vt mentionner, faire mention de; **don't ~ it!** je vous en prie, il n'y a pas de quoi

menu ['mɛnjuː] n (set menu, Comput) menu m; (list of dishes) carte f; **could we see the ~?** est-ce qu'on peut voir la carte?

MEP n abbr = **Member of the European Parliament**

mercenary ['məːsɪnərɪ] adj (person) intéressé(e), mercenaire n ▷ n mercenaire m

merchandise ['mə:tʃəndaɪz] n marchandises fpl

merchant ['mə:tʃənt] n négociant m, marchand m; (BRIT) banque f d'affaires; **merchant bank** (BRIT) banque f d'affaires; **merchant navy** (US **merchant marine**) n marine marchande

merciless ['mə:sɪlɪs] adj impitoyable, sans pitié

mercury ['mə:kjurɪ] n mercure m

mercy ['mə:sɪ] n pitié f, merci f; (Rel) miséricorde f; **at the ~ of** à la merci de

mere [mɪə*] adj simple; (chance) pur(e); **a ~ two hours** seulement deux heures; **merely** adv simplement, purement

merge [mə:dʒ] vt unir; (Comput) fusionner, interclasser ▷ vi (colours, shapes, sounds) se mêler; (roads) se joindre; (Comm) fusionner; **merger** n (Comm) fusion f

meringue [mə'ræŋ] n meringue f

merit ['merɪt] n mérite m, valeur f ▷ vt mériter

mermaid ['mə:meɪd] n sirène f

merry ['merɪ] adj gai(e); **M~ Christmas!** joyeux Noël; **merry-go-round** n manège m

mesh [meʃ] n mailles fpl

mess [mes] n désordre m, fouillis m, pagaille f; (muddle: of life) gâchis m; (: of economy) pagaille f; (dirt) saleté f; (Mil) mess m, cantine f; **to be (in) a ~** être en désordre; **to be/get in a ~** (fig) être/se mettre dans le pétrin; **mess about** or **around** (inf) vi perdre son temps; **mess up** vt (dirty) salir; (spoil) gâcher; **mess with** (inf) vt fus (challenge, confront) se frotter à; (interfere with) toucher à

message ['mesɪdʒ] n message m; **can I leave a ~?** est-ce que je peux laisser un message?; **are there any ~s for me?** est-ce que j'ai des messages?

messenger ['mesɪndʒə*] n messager m

Messrs, Messrs. ['mesəz] abbr (on letters: = messieurs) MM

messy ['mesɪ] adj (dirty) sale; (untidy) en désordre

met [met] pt, pp of **meet**

metabolism [me'tæbəlɪzəm] n métabolisme m

metal ['metl] n métal m ▷ cpd en métal; **metallic** [me'tælɪk] adj métallique

metaphor ['metəfə*] n métaphore f

meteor ['mi:tɪə*] n météore m; **meteorite** ['mi:tɪəraɪt] n météorite m or f

meteorology [mi:tɪə'rɔlədʒɪ] n météorologie f

meter ['mi:tə*] n (instrument) compteur m; (also: **parking ~**) parc(o)mètre m; (US: unit) = **metre** ▷ vt (US Post) affranchir à la machine

method ['meθəd] n méthode f; **methodical** [mɪ'θɔdɪkl] adj méthodique

methylated spirit ['meθɪleɪtɪd-] (BRIT: also: **meths**) n alcool m à brûler

meticulous [me'tɪkjuləs] adj méticuleux(-euse)

metre (US **meter**) ['mi:tə*] n mètre m

metric ['metrɪk] adj métrique

metro ['metrəu] n métro m

metropolitan [metrə'pɔlɪtən] adj métropolitain(e); **the M~ Police** (BRIT) la police londonienne

Mexican ['meksɪkən] adj mexicain(e) ▷ n Mexicain(e)

Mexico ['meksɪkəu] n Mexique m

mg abbr (= milligram) mg

mice [maɪs] npl of **mouse**

micro... ['maɪkrəu] prefix: **microchip** n (Elec) puce f; **microphone** n microphone m; **microscope** n microscope m; **microwave** n (also: **microwave oven**) four m à micro-ondes

mid [mɪd] adj: **~ May** la mi-mai; **~ afternoon** le milieu de l'après-midi; **in ~ air** en plein ciel; **he's in his ~ thirties** il a dans les trente-cinq ans; **midday** n midi m

middle ['mɪdl] n milieu m; (waist) ceinture f, taille f ▷ adj du milieu; (average) moyen(ne); **in the ~ of the night** au milieu de la nuit; **middle-**

aged adj d'un certain âge; ni vieux ni jeune; **Middle Ages** npl: **the Middle Ages** le moyen âge; **middle-class** adj bourgeois(e); **middle class(es)** n(pl): **the middle class(es)** = les classes moyennes; **Middle East** n: **the Middle East** le Proche-Orient, le Moyen-Orient; **middle name** n second prénom; **middle school** n (US) école pour les enfants de 12 à 14 ans; = collège m; (BRIT) école pour les enfants de 8 à 14 ans

midge [mɪdʒ] n moucheron m

midget ['mɪdʒɪt] n nain(e) f

midnight ['mɪdnaɪt] n minuit m

midst [mɪdst] n: **in the ~ of** au milieu de

midsummer [mɪd'sʌmə'] n milieu m de l'été

midway [mɪd'weɪ] adj, adv: **~ (between)** à mi-chemin (entre); **~ through ...** au milieu de ..., en plein(e) ...

midweek [mɪd'wiːk] adv au milieu de la semaine, en pleine semaine

midwife (pl **midwives**) ['mɪdwaɪf, -vz] n sage-femme f

midwinter [mɪd'wɪntə'] n milieu de l'hiver

might [maɪt] vb see **may** ▷ n puissance f, force f; **mighty** adj puissant(e)

migraine ['miːɡreɪn] n migraine f

migrant ['maɪɡrənt] n (bird, animal) migrateur m; (person) migrant(e) f ▷ adj migrateur(-trice); (worker) saisonnier(-ière)

migrate [maɪ'ɡreɪt] vi migrer

migration [maɪ'ɡreɪʃən] n migration f

mike [maɪk] n abbr (= microphone) micro m

mild [maɪld] adj doux (douce); (reproach, infection) léger(-ère); (illness) bénin(-igne); (interest) modéré(e); (taste) peu relevé(e); **mildly** ['maɪldlɪ] adv doucement; légèrement; **to put it mildly** (inf) c'est le moins qu'on puisse dire

mile [maɪl] n mil(l)e m (= 1609 m); **mileage** n distance f en milles, = kilométrage m; **mileometer**

mileometer [maɪ'lɔmɪtə'] n compteur m kilométrique; **milestone** n borne f; (fig) jalon m

military ['mɪlɪtərɪ] adj militaire

militia [mɪ'lɪʃə] n milice f

milk [mɪlk] n lait m ▷ vt (cow) traire; (fig: person) dépouiller, plumer; (: situation) exploiter à fond; **milk chocolate** n chocolat m au lait; **milkman** (irreg) n laitier m; **milky** adj (drink) au lait; (colour) laiteux(-euse)

mill [mɪl] n moulin m; (factory) usine f, fabrique f; (spinning mill) filature f; (flour mill) minoterie f ▷ vt moudre, broyer ▷ vi (also: **~ about**) grouiller

millennium (pl **~s** or **millennia**) [mɪ'lɛnɪəm, -'lɛnɪə] n millénaire m

milli... ['mɪlɪ] prefix milli...;
milligram(me) n milligramme m;
millilitre (US **milliliter**) n millilitre m; **millimetre** (US **millimeter**) n millimètre m

million ['mɪljən] n million m; **a ~ pounds** un million de livres sterling; **millionaire** [mɪljə'nɛə'] n millionnaire m; **millionth** [-θ] num millionième

milometer [maɪ'lɔmɪtə'] n = **mileometer**

mime [maɪm] n mime m ▷ vt, vi mimer

mimic ['mɪmɪk] n imitateur(-trice) ▷ vt, vi imiter, contrefaire

min. abbr (= minute(s)) mn.; (= minimum) min.

mince [mɪns] vt hacher ▷ n (BRIT Culin) viande hachée, hachis m; **mincemeat** n hachis de fruits secs utilisés en pâtisserie; (US) viande hachée, hachis m; **mince pie** n sorte de tarte aux fruits secs

mind [maɪnd] n esprit m ▷ vt (attend to, look after) s'occuper de; (be careful) faire attention à; (object to): **I don't ~ the noise** je ne crains pas le bruit, le bruit ne me dérange pas; **it is on my ~** cela me préoccupe; **to change one's ~** changer d'avis; **to my ~** à mon avis, selon moi; **to bear sth in ~** tenir compte de qch; **to have sb/sth**

in ~ avoir qn/qch en tête; **to make
up one's ~** se décider; **do you ~ if ...?**
est-ce que cela vous gêne si ...?; **I don't
~** cela ne me dérange pas; *(don't care)*
ça m'est égal; **~ you, ...** remarquez, ...;
never ~ peu importe, ça ne fait rien;
(don't worry) ne vous en faites pas; **"~
the step"** "attention à la marche"
mindless *adj* irréfléchi(e); *(violence,
crime)* insensé(e); *(boring: job)* idiot(e)
mine² [maɪn] *pron* le (la) mien(ne), les
miens (miennes); **a friend of ~** un de
mes amis, un ami à moi; **this book is ~**
ce livre est à moi
mine² [maɪn] *n* mine *f* ▷ *vt* *(coal)*
extraire; *(ship, beach)* miner; **minefield**
n champ *m* de mines; **miner** *n*
mineur *m*
mineral [ˈmɪnərəl] *adj* minéral(e)
▷ *n* minéral *m*; **mineral water** eau
minérale
mingle [ˈmɪŋɡl] *vi*: **to ~ with** se mêler à
miniature [ˈmɪnətʃə*] *adj* (en)
miniature ▷ *n* miniature *f*
minibar [ˈmɪnɪbɑː*] *n* minibar *m*
minibus [ˈmɪnɪbʌs] *n* minibus *m*
minicab [ˈmɪnɪkæb] *n* (*BRIT*) taxi *m*
indépendant
minimal [ˈmɪnɪml] *adj* minimal(e)
minimize [ˈmɪnɪmaɪz] *vt* *(reduce)*
réduire au minimum; *(play down)*
minimiser
minimum [ˈmɪnɪməm] *n* (*pl* **minima**)
minimum *m* ▷ *adj* minimum
mining [ˈmaɪnɪŋ] *n* exploitation
minière
miniskirt [ˈmɪnɪskəːt] *n* mini-jupe *f*
minister [ˈmɪnɪstə*] *n* (*BRIT Pol*)
ministre *m*; *(Rel)* pasteur *m*
ministry [ˈmɪnɪstrɪ] *n* (*BRIT Pol*)
ministère *m*; *(Rel)*: **to go into the ~**
devenir pasteur
minor [ˈmaɪnə*] *adj* petit(e), de peu
d'importance; *(Mus, poet, problem)*
mineur(e) ▷ *n* (*Law*) mineur(e)
minority [maɪˈnɔrɪtɪ] *n* minorité *f*
mint [mɪnt] *n* *(plant)* menthe *f*; *(sweet)*
bonbon *m* à la menthe ▷ *vt* *(coins)*

battre; **the (Royal) M~**, **the (US)
M~** l'hôtel *m* de la Monnaie; **in ~
condition** à l'état de neuf
minus [ˈmaɪnəs] *n* *(also:* **~ sign**) signe *m*
moins ▷ *prep* moins; **12 ~ 6 equals 6**
moins 6 égal 6; **~ 24 °C** moins 24 °C
minute¹ *n* [ˈmɪnɪt] minute *f*; **minutes**
npl (of meeting) procès-verbal *m*,
compte rendu; **wait a ~!** (attendez)
un instant!; **at the last ~** à la dernière
minute
minute² *adj* [maɪˈnjuːt] minuscule;
(detailed) minutieux(-euse); **in ~ detail**
par le menu
miracle [ˈmɪrəkl] *n* miracle *m*
miraculous [mɪˈrækjuləs] *adj*
miraculeux(-euse)
mirage [ˈmɪrɑːʒ] *n* mirage *m*
mirror [ˈmɪrə*] *n* miroir *m*, glace *f*; *(in
car)* rétroviseur *m*
misbehave [mɪsbɪˈheɪv] *vi* mal se
conduire
misc. *abbr* = **miscellaneous**
miscarriage [ˈmɪskærɪdʒ] *n* (*Med*)
fausse couche *f*; **~ of justice** erreur *f*
judiciaire
miscellaneous [mɪsɪˈleɪnɪəs] *adj*
(items, expenses) divers(es); *(selection)*
varié(e)
mischief [ˈmɪstʃɪf] *n* *(naughtiness)*
sottises *fpl*; *(playfulness)* espièglerie
f; *(harm)* mal *m*, dommage *m*;
(maliciousness) méchanceté *f*
mischievous [ˈmɪstʃɪvəs] *adj* *(playful,
naughty)* coquin(e), espiègle
misconception [ˈmɪskənˈsepʃən] *n*
idée fausse
misconduct [mɪsˈkɒndʌkt] *n*
inconduite *f*; **professional ~** faute
professionnelle
miser [ˈmaɪzə*] *n* avare *m/f*
miserable [ˈmɪzərəbl] *adj* *(person,
expression)* malheureux(-euse);
(conditions) misérable; *(weather)*
maussade; *(offer, donation)* minable;
(failure) pitoyable
misery [ˈmɪzərɪ] *n* *(unhappiness)*
tristesse *f*; *(pain)* souffrances *fpl*;

(wretchedness) misère f

misfortune [mɪsˈfɔːtʃən] n malchance f, malheur m

misgiving [mɪsˈgɪvɪŋ] n (apprehension) craintes fpl; **to have ~s about sth** avoir des doutes quant à qch

misguided [mɪsˈgaɪdɪd] adj malavisé(e)

mishap [ˈmɪshæp] n mésaventure f

misinterpret [mɪsɪnˈtɜːprɪt] vt mal interpréter

misjudge [mɪsˈdʒʌdʒ] vt méjuger, se méprendre sur le compte de

mislay [mɪsˈleɪ] vt (irreg: like lay) égarer

mislead [mɪsˈliːd] vt (irreg: like lead) induire en erreur; **misleading** adj trompeur(-euse)

misplace [mɪsˈpleɪs] vt égarer; **to be ~d** (trust etc) être mal placé(e)

misprint [ˈmɪsprɪnt] n faute f d'impression

misrepresent [mɪsreprɪˈzent] vt présenter sous un faux jour

Miss [mɪs] n Mademoiselle

miss [mɪs] vt (fail to get, attend, see) manquer, rater; (regret the absence of): **I ~ him/it** il/cela me manque ▷ vi manquer ▷ n (shot) coup manqué; **we ~ed our train** nous avons raté notre train; **you can't ~ it** vous ne pouvez pas vous tromper; **miss out** vt (BRIT) oublier; **miss out on** vt fus (fun, party) rater, manquer; (chance, bargain) laisser passer

missile [ˈmɪsaɪl] n (Aviat) missile m; (object thrown) projectile m

missing [ˈmɪsɪŋ] adj manquant(e); (after escape, disaster) disparu(e); **to go ~** disparaître; **~ in action** (Mil) porté(e) disparu(e)

mission [ˈmɪʃən] n mission f; **on a ~ to sb** en mission auprès de qn; **missionary** n missionnaire m/f

misspell [ˈmɪsspel] vt (irreg: like spell) mal orthographier

mist [mɪst] n brume f ▷ vi (also: **~ over**, **~ up**) devenir brumeux(-euse); (BRIT: windows) s'embuer

mistake [mɪsˈteɪk] n erreur f, faute

f ▷ vt (irreg: like take) (meaning) mal comprendre; (intentions) se méprendre sur; **to ~ for** prendre pour; **by ~** par erreur, par inadvertance; **to make a ~** (in writing) faire une faute; (in calculating etc) faire une erreur; **there must be some ~** il doit y avoir une erreur, se tromper; **mistaken** pp of **mistake** ▷ adj (idea etc) erroné(e); **to be mistaken** faire erreur, se tromper

mister [ˈmɪstər] n (inf) Monsieur m; see **Mr**

mistletoe [ˈmɪsltəu] n gui m

mistook [mɪsˈtuk] pt of **mistake**

mistress [ˈmɪstrɪs] n maîtresse f; (BRIT: in primary school) institutrice f; (: in secondary school) professeur m

mistrust [mɪsˈtrʌst] vt se méfier de

misty [ˈmɪstɪ] adj brumeux(-euse); (glasses, window) embué(e)

misunderstand [mɪsʌndəˈstænd] vt, vi (irreg: like stand) mal comprendre; **misunderstanding** n méprise f, malentendu m; **there's been a misunderstanding** il y a eu un malentendu

misunderstood [mɪsʌndəˈstud] pt, pp of **misunderstand** ▷ adj (person) incompris(e)

misuse n [mɪsˈjuːs] mauvais emploi; (of power) abus m ▷ vt [mɪsˈjuːz] mal employer; abuser de

mitt(en) [ˈmɪt(n)] n moufle f; (fingerless) mitaine f

mix [mɪks] vt mélanger; (sauce, drink etc) préparer ▷ vi se mélanger; (socialize): **he doesn't ~ well** il est peu sociable ▷ n mélange m; **to ~ sth with sth** mélanger qch à qch; **cake ~** préparation f pour gâteau; **mix up** vt mélanger; (confuse) confondre; **to be ~ed up in sth** être mêlé(e) à qch ou impliqué(e) dans qch; **mixed** adj (feelings, reactions) contradictoire; (school, marriage) mixte; **mixed grill** n (BRIT) assortiment m de grillades; **mixed salad** n salade f de crudités; **mixed-up** adj (person) désorienté(e), embrouillé(e); **mixer**

n (for food) batteur *m*, mixeur *m*; (drink) boisson gazeuse (servant à couper un alcool); (person): **he is a good mixer** il est très sociable; **mixture** *n* assortiment *m*, mélange *m*; (Med) préparation *f*; **mix-up** *n*: **there was a mix-up** il y a eu confusion

ml *abbr* (= millilitre(s)) ml

mm *abbr* (= millimetre) mm

moan [məun] *n* gémissement *m* ▷ *vi* gémir; (*inf*: complain): **to ~ (about)** se plaindre (de)

moat [məut] *n* fossé *m*, douves *fpl*

mob [mɔb] *n* foule *f*; (disorderly) cohue *f* ▷ *vt* assaillir

mobile ['məubaɪl] *adj* mobile ▷ *n* (Art) mobile *m*; **mobile home** *n* caravane *f*; **mobile phone** *n* téléphone portatif

mobility [məu'bɪlɪtɪ] *n* mobilité *f*

mobilize ['məubɪlaɪz] *vt*, *vi* mobiliser

mock [mɔk] *vt* ridiculiser; (laugh at) se moquer de ▷ *adj* faux (fausse); **mocks** *npl* (BRIT: Scol) examens blancs; **mockery** *n* moquerie *f*, raillerie *f*

mod cons ['mɔd'kɔnz] *npl abbr* (BRIT) = **modern conveniences**; *see* **convenience**

mode [məud] *n* mode *m*; (of transport) moyen *m*

model ['mɔdl] *n* modèle *m*; (person: for fashion) mannequin *m*; (: for artist) modèle *m* ▷ *vt* (with clay etc) modeler ▷ *vi* travailler comme mannequin ▷ *adj* (railway: toy) modèle réduit *inv*; (child, factory) modèle; **to ~ clothes** présenter des vêtements; **to ~ o.s. on** imiter

modem ['məudem] *n* modem *m*

moderate *adj* ['mɔdərət] modéré(e); (amount, change) peu important(e) ▷ *vb* ['mɔdəreɪt] ▷ *vi* se modérer, se calmer ▷ *vt* modérer; **moderation** [mɔdə'reɪʃən] *n* modération *f*, mesure *f*; **in ~** à dose raisonnable, pris(e) or pratiqué(e) avec modération

modern ['mɔdən] *adj* moderne; **modernize** *vt* moderniser; **modern languages** *npl* langues vivantes

modest ['mɔdɪst] *adj* modeste;

modesty *n* modestie *f*

modification [mɔdɪfɪ'keɪʃən] *n* modification *f*

modify ['mɔdɪfaɪ] *vt* modifier

module ['mɔdjuːl] *n* module *m*

mohair ['məuhɛəʳ] *n* mohair *m*

Mohammed [mə'hæmɛd] *n* Mahomet *m*

moist [mɔɪst] *adj* humide, moite; **moisture** ['mɔɪstʃəʳ] *n* humidité *f*; (on glass) buée *f*; **moisturizer** ['mɔɪstʃəraɪzəʳ] *n* crème hydratante

mold *etc* [məuld] (us) = **mould** *etc*

mole [məul] *n* (animal, spy) taupe *f*; (spot) grain *m* de beauté

molecule ['mɔlɪkjuːl] *n* molécule *f*

molest [məu'lɛst] *vt* (assault sexually) attenter à la pudeur de

molten ['məultən] *adj* fondu(e); (rock) en fusion

mom [mɔm] *n* (us) = **mum**

moment ['məumənt] *n* moment *m*, instant *m*; **at the ~** en ce moment; **momentarily** ['məuməntrɪlɪ] *adv* momentanément; (us: soon) bientôt; **momentary** *adj* momentané(e), passager(-ère); **momentous** [məu'mɛntəs] *adj* important(e), capital(e)

momentum [məu'mɛntəm] *n* élan *m*, vitesse acquise; (fig) dynamique *f*; **to gather ~** prendre de la vitesse; (fig) gagner du terrain

mommy ['mɔmɪ] *n* (us: mother) maman *f*

Mon *abbr* (= Monday) l.

Monaco ['mɔnəkəu] *n* Monaco *f*

monarch ['mɔnək] *n* monarque *m*; **monarchy** *n* monarchie *f*

monastery ['mɔnəstərɪ] *n* monastère *m*

Monday ['mʌndɪ] *n* lundi *m*

monetary ['mʌnɪtərɪ] *adj* monétaire

money ['mʌnɪ] *n* argent *m*; **to make ~** (person) gagner de l'argent; (business) rapporter; **money belt** *n* ceinture-portefeuille *f*; **money order** *n* mandat *m*

mongrel ['mʌŋgrəl] n (dog) bâtard m
monitor ['mɒnɪtəʳ] n (TV, Comput) écran m, moniteur m ▷ vt contrôler; (foreign station) être à l'écoute de; (progress) suivre de près
monk [mʌŋk] n moine m
monkey ['mʌŋkɪ] n singe m
monologue ['mɒnəlɒg] n monologue m
monopoly [mə'nɒpəlɪ] n monopole m
monosodium glutamate [mɒnə'səudɪəm 'glu:təmeɪt] n glutamate m de sodium
monotonous [mə'nɒtənəs] adj monotone
monsoon [mɒn'su:n] n mousson f
monster ['mɒnstəʳ] n monstre m
month [mʌnθ] n mois m; **monthly** adj mensuel(le) ▷ adv mensuellement
Montreal [mɒntrɪ'ɔːl] n Montréal
monument ['mɒnjumənt] n monument m
mood [mu:d] n humeur f, disposition f; **to be in a good/bad ~** être de bonne/mauvaise humeur; **moody** adj (variable) d'humeur changeante, lunatique; (sullen) morose, maussade
moon [mu:n] n lune f; **moonlight** n clair m de lune
moor [muəʳ] n lande f ▷ vt (ship) amarrer ▷ vi mouiller
moose [mu:s] n (pl inv) élan m
mop [mɒp] n balai m à laver; (for dishes) lavette f à vaisselle ▷ vt éponger, essuyer; **~ of hair** tignasse f; **mop up** vt éponger
mope [məup] vi avoir le cafard, se morfondre
moped ['məuped] n cyclomoteur m
moral ['mɒrl] adj moral(e) ▷ n morale f; **morals** npl moralité f
morale [mɒ'rɑːl] n moral m
morality [mə'rælɪtɪ] n moralité f
morbid ['mɔːbɪd] adj morbide

O **KEYWORD**

more [mɔːʳ] adj 1 (greater in number etc) plus (de), davantage (de); **more people/work (than)** plus de gens/de travail (que)
2 (additional) encore (de); **do you want (some) more tea?** voulez-vous encore du thé?; **is there any more wine?** reste-t-il du vin?; **I have no** or **I don't have any more money** je n'ai plus d'argent; **it'll take a few more weeks** ça prendra encore quelques semaines ▷ pron plus, davantage; **more than 10** plus de 10; **it cost more than we expected** cela a coûté plus que prévu; **I want more** j'en veux plus or davantage; **is there any more?** est-ce qu'il en reste?; **there's no more** il n'y en a plus; **a little more** un peu plus; **many/much more** beaucoup plus, bien davantage ▷ adv plus; **more dangerous/easily (than)** plus dangereux/facilement (que); **more and more expensive** de plus en plus cher; **more or less** plus ou moins; **more than ever** plus que jamais; **once more** encore une fois, une fois de plus

moreover [mɔː'rəuvəʳ] adv de plus
morgue [mɔːg] n morgue f
morning ['mɔːnɪŋ] n matin m; (as duration) matinée f ▷ cpd matinal(e); (paper) du matin; **in the ~** le matin; **7 o'clock in the ~** 7 heures du matin; **morning sickness** n nausées matinales
Moroccan [mə'rɒkən] adj marocain(e) ▷ n Marocain(e)
Morocco [mə'rɒkəu] n Maroc m
moron ['mɔːrɒn] n idiot(e), minus m/f
morphine ['mɔːfiːn] n morphine f
morris dancing ['mɒrɪs-] n (BRIT) danses folkloriques anglaises

■ **MORRIS DANCING**

● Le **Morris dancing** est une
● danse folklorique anglaise
● traditionnellement réservée aux
● hommes. Habillés tout en blanc
● et portant des clochettes, ils

- exécutent différentes figures avec des mouchoirs et de longs bâtons.
- Cette danse est très populaire dans les fêtes de village.

Morse [mɔːs] n (also: ~ **code**) morse m
mortal ['mɔːtl] adj, n mortel(le)
mortar ['mɔːtəʳ] n mortier m
mortgage ['mɔːɡɪdʒ] n hypothèque f; (loan) prêt m (or crédit m) hypothécaire ⊳ vt hypothéquer
mortician [mɔːˈtɪʃən] n (us) entrepreneur m de pompes funèbres
mortified ['mɔːtɪfaɪd] adj mort(e) de honte
mortuary ['mɔːtjuərɪ] n morgue f
mosaic [məuˈzeɪɪk] n mosaïque f
Moscow ['mɔskəu] n Moscou
Moslem ['mɔzləm] adj, n = **Muslim**
mosque [mɔsk] n mosquée f
mosquito (pl ~**es**) [mɔsˈkiːtəu] n moustique m
moss [mɔs] n mousse f
most [məust] adj (majority of) la plupart de; (greatest amount of) le plus de ⊳ pron la plupart ⊳ adv le plus; (very) très, extrêmement; **the** ~ le plus; ~ **fish** la plupart des poissons; **the** ~ **beautiful woman in the world** la plus belle femme du monde; ~ **of** (with plural) la plupart de; (with singular) la plus grande partie de; ~ **of them** la plupart d'entre eux; ~ **of the time** la plupart du temps; **I saw** ~ (a lot but not all) j'en ai vu la plupart; (more than anyone else) c'est moi qui en ai vu le plus; **at the (very)** ~ au plus; **to make the** ~ **of** profiter au maximum de; **mostly** adv (chiefly) surtout, principalement; (usually) généralement
MOT n abbr (BRIT) = **Ministry of Transport**; **the** ~ (**test**) visite technique (annuelle) obligatoire des véhicules à moteur
motel [məuˈtel] n motel m
moth [mɔθ] n papillon m de nuit; (in clothes) mite f
mother ['mʌðəʳ] n mère f ⊳ vt (pamper, protect) dorloter; **motherhood** n maternité f; **mother-in-law** n belle-mère f; **mother-of-pearl** n nacre f; **Mother's Day** n fête f des Mères; **mother-to-be** n future maman; **mother tongue** n langue maternelle
motif [məuˈtiːf] n motif m
motion ['məuʃən] n mouvement m; (gesture) geste m; (at meeting) motion f ⊳ vt, vi: **to** ~ (**to**) **sb to do** faire signe à qn de faire; **motionless** adj immobile, sans mouvement; **motion picture** n film m
motivate ['məutɪveɪt] vt motiver
motivation [məutɪ'veɪʃən] n motivation f
motive ['məutɪv] n motif m, mobile m
motor ['məutəʳ] n moteur m; (BRIT inf: vehicle) auto f; cpd: **motorbike** n moto f; **motorboat** n bateau m à moteur; **motorcar** n (BRIT) automobile f; **motorcycle** n moto f; **motorcyclist** n motocycliste m/f; **motoring** (BRIT) n tourisme m automobile; **motorist** n automobiliste m/f; **motor racing** n (BRIT) course f automobile; **motorway** n (BRIT) autoroute f
motto (pl ~**es**) ['mɔtəu] n devise f
mould, (us) **mold** [məuld] n moule m; (mildew) moisissure f ⊳ vt mouler, modeler; (fig) façonner; **mouldy** adj moisi(e); (smell) de moisi
mound [maund] n monticule m, tertre m
mount [maunt] n (hill) mont m, montagne f; (horse) monture f; (for picture) carton m de montage ⊳ vt monter; (horse) monter; (bike) monter sur; (picture) monter sur carton ⊳ vi (inflation, tension) augmenter; **mount up** vi s'élever, monter; (bills, problems, savings) s'accumuler
mountain ['mauntɪn] n montagne f ⊳ cpd de (la) montagne; **mountain bike** n VTT m, vélo m tout terrain; **mountaineer** n alpiniste m/f; **mountaineering** n alpinisme m; **mountainous** adj montagneux(-euse)

mountain range n chaîne f de montagnes

mourn [mɔːn] vt pleurer ▷ vi: **to ~ for sb** pleurer qn; **to ~ for sth** se lamenter sur qch; **mourner** n parent(e) or ami(e) du défunt; personne f en deuil or venue rendre hommage au défunt; **mourning** n deuil m; **in mourning** en deuil

mouse (pl **mice**) [maus, maɪs] n (also Comput) souris f; **mouse mat** n (Comput) tapis m de souris

moussaka [muˈsɑːkə] n moussaka f

mousse [muːs] n mousse f

moustache (us **mustache**) [məsˈtɑːʃ] n moustache(s) f(pl)

mouth [mauθ, pl -ðz] n bouche f; (of dog, cat) gueule f; (of river) embouchure f; (of hole, cave) ouverture f; **mouthful** n bouchée f; **mouth organ** n harmonica m; **mouthpiece** n (of musical instrument) bec m, embouchure f; (spokesperson) porte-parole m inv; **mouthwash** n eau f dentifrice

move [muːv] n (movement) mouvement m; (in game) coup m; (: turn to play) tour m; (change of house) déménagement m; (change of job) changement m d'emploi ▷ vt déplacer, bouger; (emotionally) émouvoir; (Pol: resolution etc) proposer ▷ vi (gen) bouger, remuer; (traffic) circuler; (also: **~ house**) déménager; (in game) jouer; **can you ~ your car, please?** pouvez-vous déplacer votre voiture, s'il vous plaît?; **to ~ sb to do sth** pousser or inciter qn à faire qch; **to get a ~ on** se dépêcher, se remuer; **move back** vi revenir, retourner; **move in** vi (to a house) emménager; (police, soldiers) intervenir; **move off** vi s'éloigner, s'en aller; **move on** vi se remettre en route; **move out** vi (of house) déménager; **move over** vi se pousser, se déplacer; **move up** vi avancer; (employee) avoir de l'avancement; (pupil) passer dans la classe supérieure; **movement** n mouvement m

movie [ˈmuːvɪ] n film m; **movies** npl: **the ~s** le cinéma; **movie theater** (us) n cinéma m

moving [ˈmuːvɪŋ] adj en mouvement; (touching) émouvant(e)

mow (pt **-ed**, pp **-ed** or **-n**) [məu, -d, -n] vt faucher; (lawn) tondre; **mower** n (also: **lawnmower**) tondeuse f à gazon

Mozambique [məuzəmˈbiːk] n Mozambique m

MP n abbr (BRIT) = **Member of Parliament**

MP3 n mp3 m; **MP3 player** n lecteur m mp3

mpg n abbr = **miles per gallon** (30 mpg = 9,4 l. aux 100 km)

m.p.h. abbr = **miles per hour** (60 mph = 96 km/h)

Mr (us **Mr.**) [ˈmɪstər] n: **Mr X** Monsieur X, M. X

Mrs (us **Mrs.**) [ˈmɪsɪz] n: **X** Madame X, Mme X

Ms (us **Ms.**) [mɪz] n (Miss or Mrs): **Ms X** Madame X, Mme X

MSP n abbr (= Member of the Scottish Parliament) député m au Parlement écossais

Mt abbr (Geo: = mount) Mt

much [mʌtʃ] adj beaucoup de ▷ adv, n or pron beaucoup; **we don't have ~ time** nous n'avons pas beaucoup de temps; **how ~ is it?** combien est-ce que ça coûte?; **it's not ~** ce n'est pas beaucoup; **too ~** trop (de); **so ~** tant (de); **I like it very/so ~** j'aime beaucoup/tellement ça; **as ~ as** autant de; **that's ~ better** c'est beaucoup mieux

muck [mʌk] n (mud) boue f; (dirt) ordures fpl; **muck up** vt (inf: ruin) gâcher, esquinter; (: dirty) salir; (: exam, interview) se planter à; **mucky** adj (dirty) boueux(-euse), sale

mucus [ˈmjuːkəs] n mucus m

mud [mʌd] n boue f

muddle [ˈmʌdl] n (mess) pagaille f, fouillis m; (mix-up) confusion f ▷ vt (also: **~ up**) brouiller, embrouiller; **to get in a ~** (while explaining etc)

s'embrouiller
muddy ['mʌdɪ] adj boueux(-euse)
mudguard ['mʌdɡɑːd] n garde-boue m inv
muesli ['mjuːzlɪ] n muesli m
muffin ['mʌfɪn] n (roll) petit pain rond et plat; (cake) petit gâteau au chocolat ou aux fruits
muffled ['mʌfld] adj étouffé(e), voilé(e)
muffler ['mʌflə*] n (scarf) cache-nez m inv; (US Aut) silencieux m
mug [mʌɡ] n (cup) tasse f (sans soucoupe); (: for beer) chope f; (inf: face) bouille f; (: fool) poire f ▷ vt (assault) agresser; **mugger** n agresseur m; **mugging** n agression f
muggy ['mʌɡɪ] adj lourd(e), moite
mule [mjuːl] n mule f
multicoloured (US **multicolored**) ['mʌltɪkʌləd] adj multicolore
multimedia [mʌltɪ'miːdɪə] adj multimédia inv
multinational [mʌltɪ'næʃənl] n multinationale f ▷ adj multinational(e)
multiple ['mʌltɪpl] adj multiple ▷ n multiple m; **multiple choice (test)** n QCM m, questionnaire m à choix multiple; **multiple sclerosis** [-sklɪ'rəʊsɪs] n sclérose f en plaques
multiplex (cinema) ['mʌltɪpleks-] n (cinéma m) multisalles m
multiplication [mʌltɪplɪ'keɪʃən] n multiplication f
multiply ['mʌltɪplaɪ] vt multiplier ▷ vi se multiplier
multistorey ['mʌltɪ'stɔːrɪ] adj (BRIT: building) à étages, (: car park) à étages or niveaux multiples
mum [mʌm] n (BRIT) maman f ▷ adj: **to keep** ~ ne pas souffler mot
mumble ['mʌmbl] vt, vi marmotter, marmonner
mummy ['mʌmɪ] n (BRIT: mother) maman f; (embalmed) momie f
mumps [mʌmps] n oreillons mpl
munch [mʌntʃ] vt, vi mâcher
municipal [mjuː'nɪsɪpl] adj municipal(e)

mural ['mjʊərl] n peinture murale
murder ['mɜːdə*] n meurtre m, assassinat m ▷ vt assassiner; **murderer** n meurtrier m, assassin m
murky ['mɜːkɪ] adj sombre, ténébreux(-euse); (water) trouble
murmur ['mɜːmə*] n murmure m ▷ vt, vi murmurer
muscle ['mʌsl] n muscle m; (fig) force f; **muscular** ['mʌskjulə*] adj musculaire; (person, arm) musclé(e)
museum [mjuː'zɪəm] n musée m
mushroom ['mʌʃrum] n champignon m ▷ vi (fig) pousser comme un (or des) champignon(s)
music ['mjuːzɪk] n musique f; **musical** adj musical(e); (person) musicien(ne) ▷ n (show) comédie musicale; **musical instrument** n instrument m de musique; **musician** [mjuː'zɪʃən] n musicien(ne)
Muslim ['mʌzlɪm] adj, n musulman(e)
muslin ['mʌzlɪn] n mousseline f
mussel ['mʌsl] n moule f
must [mʌst] aux vb (obligation): **I ~ do it** je dois le faire, il faut que je le fasse; (probability): **he ~ be there by now** il doit y être maintenant, il y est probablement maintenant; (suggestion, invitation): **you ~ come and see me** il faut que vous veniez me voir ▷ n nécessité f, impératif m; **it's a ~** c'est indispensable; **I ~ have made a mistake** j'ai dû me tromper
mustache ['mʌstæʃ] n (US) =**moustache**
mustard ['mʌstəd] n moutarde f
mustn't ['mʌsnt] = **must not**
mute [mjuːt] adj, n muet(te)
mutilate ['mjuːtɪleɪt] vt mutiler
mutiny ['mjuːtɪnɪ] n mutinerie f ▷ vi se mutiner
mutter ['mʌtə*] vt, vi marmonner, marmotter
mutton ['mʌtn] n mouton m
mutual ['mjuːtʃuəl] adj mutuel(le), réciproque; (benefit, interest) commun(e)

muzzle ['mʌzl] n museau m; (protective device) muselière f; (of gun) gueule f
▷ vt museler

my [maɪ] adj mon (ma), mes pl; **my house/car/gloves** ma maison/ma voiture/mes gants; **I've washed my hair/cut my finger** je me suis lavé les cheveux/coupé le doigt; **is this my pen or yours?** c'est mon stylo ou c'est le vôtre?

myself [maɪ'sɛlf] pron (reflexive) me; (emphatic) moi-même; (after prep) moi; see also **oneself**

mysterious [mɪs'tɪərɪəs] adj mystérieux(-euse)

mystery ['mɪstərɪ] n mystère m

mystical ['mɪstɪkl] adj mystique

mystify ['mɪstɪfaɪ] vt (deliberately) mystifier; (puzzle) ébahir

myth [mɪθ] n mythe m; **mythology** [mɪ'θɔlədʒɪ] n mythologie f

n

n/a abbr (= not applicable) n.a.

nag [næg] vt (scold) être toujours après, reprendre sans arrêt

nail [neɪl] n (human) ongle m; (metal) clou m ▷ vt clouer; **to ~ sth to sth** clouer qch à qch; **to ~ sb down to a date/price** contraindre qn à accepter or donner une date/un prix; **nailbrush** n brosse f à ongles; **nailfile** n lime f à ongles; **nail polish** n vernis m à ongles; **nail polish remover** n dissolvant m; **nail scissors** npl ciseaux mpl à ongles; **nail varnish** n (BRIT) = **nail polish**

naïve [naɪ'iːv] adj naïf(-ïve)

naked ['neɪkɪd] adj nu(e)

name [neɪm] n nom m; (reputation) réputation f ▷ vt nommer; (identify: accomplice etc) citer; (price, date) fixer, donner; **by ~** par son nom; de nom; **in the ~ of** au nom de; **what's your ~?** comment vous appelez-vous?, quel est votre nom?; **namely** adv à savoir

nanny ['nænɪ] n bonne f d'enfants

nap [næp] n (sleep) (petit) somme

napkin ['næpkɪn] n serviette f (de table)

nappy ['næpɪ] n (BRIT) couche f

narcotics [nɑː'kɒtɪkz] npl (illegal drugs) stupéfiants mpl

narrative ['nærətɪv] n récit m ▷ adj narratif(-ive)

narrator [nə'reɪtə'] n narrateur(-trice)

narrow ['nærəu] adj étroit(e); (fig) restreint(e), limité(e) ▷ vi (road) devenir plus étroit, se rétrécir; (gap, difference) se réduire; **to have a ~ escape** l'échapper belle; **narrow down** vt restreindre; **narrowly** adv: **he narrowly missed injury/the tree** il a failli se blesser/rentrer dans l'arbre; **he only narrowly missed the target** il a manqué la cible de peu or de justesse; **narrow-minded** adj à l'esprit étroit, borné(e); (attitude) borné(e)

nasal ['neɪzl] adj nasal(e)

nasty ['nɑːstɪ] adj (person: malicious) méchant(e); (: rude) très désagréable; (smell) dégoûtant(e); (wound, situation) mauvais(e), vilain(e)

nation ['neɪʃən] n nation f

national ['næʃənl] adj national(e) ▷ n (abroad) ressortissant(e); (when home) national(e); **national anthem** n hymne national; **national dress** n costume national; **National Health Service** n (BRIT) service national de santé; ≈ Sécurité Sociale; **National Insurance** n (BRIT) ≈ Sécurité Sociale; **nationalist** adj, n nationaliste m/f; **nationality** [næʃə'nælɪtɪ] n nationalité f; **nationalize** vt nationaliser; **national park** n parc national; **National Trust** n (BRIT) ≈ Caisse f nationale des monuments historiques et des sites

NATIONAL TRUST

Le **National Trust** est un organisme indépendant, à but non lucratif, dont la mission est de protéger et de mettre en valeur les monuments et les sites britanniques en raison de leur intérêt historique ou de leur beauté naturelle.

nationwide ['neɪʃənwaɪd] adj s'étendant à l'ensemble du pays; (problem) à l'échelle du pays entier

native ['neɪtɪv] n habitant(e) du pays, autochtone m/f ▷ adj du pays, indigène; (country) natal(e); (language) maternel(le); (ability) inné(e); **Native American** n Indien(ne) d'Amérique ▷ adj amérindien(ne); **native speaker** n locuteur natif

NATO ['neɪtəu] n abbr (= North Atlantic Treaty Organization) OTAN f

natural ['nætʃrəl] adj naturel(le); **natural gas** n gaz naturel; **natural history** n histoire naturelle; **naturally** adv naturellement; **natural resources** npl ressources naturelles

nature ['neɪtʃə'] n nature f; **by ~** par tempérament, de nature; **nature reserve** n (BRIT) réserve naturelle

naughty ['nɔːtɪ] adj (child) vilain(e), pas sage

nausea ['nɔːsɪə] n nausée f

naval ['neɪvl] adj naval(e)

navel ['neɪvl] n nombril m

navigate ['nævɪgeɪt] vt (steer) diriger, piloter ▷ vi (Aut) indiquer la route à suivre; **navigation** [nævɪ'geɪʃən] n navigation f

navy ['neɪvɪ] n marine f

navy-blue ['neɪvɪ'bluː] adj bleu marine inv

Nazi ['nɑːtsɪ] n Nazi(e)

NB abbr (= nota bene) NB

near [nɪə'] adj proche ▷ adv près ▷ prep (also: **~ to**) près de ▷ vt approcher de; **in the ~ future** dans un proche avenir; **nearby** [nɪə'baɪ] adj proche ▷ adv tout près, à proximité; **nearly** adv presque; **I nearly fell** j'ai failli tomber; **it's not nearly big enough** ce n'est vraiment pas assez grand, c'est loin d'être assez grand; **near-sighted** adj myope

neat [niːt] adj (person, work) soigné(e);

(*room etc*) bien tenu(e) or rangé(e); (*solution, plan*) habile; (*spirits*) pur(e); **neatly** *adv* avec soin or ordre; (*skilfully*) habilement

necessarily ['nɛsɪsrɪlɪ] *adv* nécessairement; **not ~** pas nécessairement or forcément

necessary ['nɛsɪsrɪ] *adj* nécessaire; **if ~** si besoin est, le cas échéant

necessity [nɪ'sɛsɪtɪ] *n* nécessité *f*; chose nécessaire or essentielle

neck [nɛk] *n* cou *m*; (*of garment*) encolure *f*; (*of bottle*) goulot *m*; **~ and ~** à égalité; **necklace** ['nɛklɪs] *n* collier *m*; **necktie** ['nɛktaɪ] *n* (*esp US*) cravate *f*

nectarine ['nɛktərɪn] *n* brugnon *m*, nectarine *f*

need [niːd] *n* besoin *m* ▷ *vt* avoir besoin de; **to ~ to do** devoir faire; avoir besoin de faire; **you don't ~ to go** vous n'avez pas besoin or vous n'êtes pas obligé de partir; **a signature is ~ed** il faut une signature; **there's no ~ to do ....** il n'y a pas lieu de faire ..., il n'est pas nécessaire de faire ...

needle ['niːdl] *n* aiguille *f* ▷ *vt* (*inf*) asticoter, tourmenter

needless ['niːdlɪs] *adj* inutile; **~ to say,** ... inutile de dire que ...

needlework ['niːdlwəːk] *n* (*activity*) travaux *mpl* d'aiguille; (*object*) ouvrage *m*

needn't ['niːdnt] = **need not**

needy ['niːdɪ] *adj* nécessiteux(-euse)

negative ['nɛɡətɪv] *n* (*Phot, Elec*) négatif *m*; (*Ling*) terme *m* de négation ▷ *adj* négatif(-ive)

neglect [nɪ'ɡlɛkt] *vt* négliger; (*garden*) ne pas entretenir; (*duty*) manquer à ▷ *n* (*of person, duty, garden*) le fait de négliger; **(state of) ~** abandon *m*; **to ~ to do sth** négliger or omettre de faire qch; **to ~ one's appearance** se négliger

negotiate [nɪ'ɡəʊʃɪeɪt] *vi* négocier ▷ *vt* négocier; (*obstacle*) franchir, négocier; **to ~ with sb for sth** négocier avec qn en vue d'obtenir qch

negotiation [nɪɡəʊʃɪ'eɪʃən] *n*

négociation *f*, pourparlers *mpl*

negotiator [nɪ'ɡəʊʃɪeɪtə^r] *n* négociateur(-trice)

neighbour (*us* **neighbor** *etc*) ['neɪbə^r] *n* voisin(e); **neighbourhood** *n* (*place*) quartier *m*; (*people*) voisinage *m*; **neighbouring** *adj* voisin(e), avoisinant(e)

neither ['naɪðə^r] *adj, pron* aucun(e) (des deux), ni l'un(e) ni l'autre ▷ *conj*: **~ do I** moi non plus ▷ *adv*: **~ good nor bad** ni bon ni mauvais; **~ of them** ni l'un ni l'autre

neon ['niːɔn] *n* néon *m*

Nepal [nɪ'pɔːl] *n* Népal *m*

nephew ['nɛvjuː] *n* neveu *m*

nerve [nəːv] *n* nerf *m*; (*bravery*) sangfroid *m*, courage *m*; (*cheek*) aplomb *m*, toupet *m*; **nerves** *npl* (*nervousness*) nervosité *f*; **he gets on my ~s** il m'énerve

nervous ['nəːvəs] *adj* nerveux(-euse); (*anxious*) inquiet(-ète), plein(e) d'appréhension; (*timid*) intimidé(e); **nervous breakdown** *n* dépression nerveuse

nest [nɛst] *n* nid *m* ▷ *vi* (se) nicher, faire son nid

Net [nɛt] *n* (*Comput*): **the ~** (*Internet*) le Net

net [nɛt] *n* filet *m*; (*fabric*) tulle *f* ▷ *adj* net(te) ▷ *vt* (*fish etc*) prendre au filet; **netball** *n* netball *m*

Netherlands ['nɛðələndz] *npl*: **the ~** les Pays-Bas *mpl*

nett [nɛt] *adj* = **net**

nettle ['nɛtl] *n* ortie *f*

network ['nɛtwəːk] *n* réseau *m*

neurotic [njuə'rɔtɪk] *adj* névrosé(e)

neuter ['njuːtə^r] *adj* neutre ▷ *vt* (*cat etc*) châtrer, couper

neutral ['njuːtrəl] *adj* neutre ▷ *n* (*Aut*) point mort

never ['nɛvə^r] *adv* (ne ...) jamais; **I ~ went** je n'y suis pas allé; **I've ~ been to Spain** je ne suis jamais allé en Espagne; **~ again** plus jamais; **~ in my life** jamais de ma vie; *see also* **mind**; **never-ending**

adj interminable; **nevertheless** [nɛvəðə'lɛs] *adv* néanmoins, malgré tout

new [njuː] *adj* nouveau (nouvelle); *(brand new)* neuf (neuve); **New Age** *n* New Age *m*; **newborn** *adj* nouveau-né(e); **newcomer** ['njuːkʌmə*r*] *n* nouveau venu (nouvelle venue); **newly** *adv* nouvellement, récemment

news [njuːz] *n* nouvelle(s) *f(pl)*; *(Radio, TV)* informations *fpl*, actualités *fpl*; **a piece of ~** une nouvelle; **news agency** *n* agence *f* de presse; **newsagent** *n (BRIT)* marchand *m* de journaux; **newscaster** *(Radio, TV)* présentateur(-trice); **news dealer** *n (US)* marchand *m* de journaux; **newsletter** *n* bulletin *m*; **newspaper** *n* journal *m*; **newsreader** *n* = **newscaster**

newt [njuːt] *n* triton *m*

New Year *n* Nouvel An; **Happy ~!** Bonne Année!; **New Year's Day** *n* le jour de l'An; **New Year's Eve** *n* la Saint-Sylvestre

New York [-'jɔːk] *n* New York

New Zealand [-'ziːlənd] *n* Nouvelle-Zélande *f*; **New Zealander** *n* Néo-Zélandais(e)

next [nɛkst] *adj (in time)* prochain(e); *(seat, room)* voisin(e), d'à côté; *(meeting, bus stop)* suivant(e) ▷ *adv* la fois suivante; la prochaine fois; *(afterwards)* ensuite; **~ to** *prep* à côté de; **~ to nothing** presque rien; **~ time** *adv* la prochaine fois; **the ~ day** le lendemain, le jour suivant *or* d'après; **~ year** l'année prochaine; **~ please!** *(at doctor's etc)* au suivant!; **the week after ~** dans deux semaines; **next door** *adv* à côté ▷ *adj (neighbour)* d'à côté; **next-of-kin** *n* parent *m* le plus proche

NHS *n abbr (BRIT)* = **National Health Service**

nibble ['nɪbl] *vt* grignoter

nice [naɪs] *adj (holiday, trip, taste)* agréable; *(flat, picture)* joli(e); *(person)* gentil(le); *(distinction, point)* subtil(e);

nicely *adv* agréablement; joliment; gentiment; subtilement

niche [niːʃ] *n (Archit)* niche *f*

nick [nɪk] *n (indentation)* encoche *f*; *(wound)* entaille *f*; *(BRIT inf):* **in good ~** en bon état ▷ *vt (cut):* **to ~ o.s.** se couper; *(inf: steal)* faucher, piquer; **in the ~ of time** juste à temps

nickel ['nɪkl] *n* nickel *m*; *(US)* pièce *f* de 5 cents

nickname ['nɪkneɪm] *n* surnom *m* ▷ *vt* surnommer

nicotine ['nɪkətiːn] *n* nicotine *f*

niece [niːs] *n* nièce *f*

Nigeria [naɪ'dʒɪərɪə] *n* Nigéria *m or f*

night [naɪt] *n* nuit *f*; *(evening)* soir *m*; **at ~** la nuit; **by ~** de nuit; **last ~** *(evening)* hier soir; *(night-time)* la nuit dernière; **night club** *n* boîte *f* de nuit; **nightdress** *n* chemise *f* de nuit; **nightie** ['naɪtɪ] *n* chemise *f* de nuit; **nightlife** *n* vie *f* nocturne; **nightly** *adj (news)* de soir; *(by night)* nocturne ▷ *adv (every evening)* tous les soirs; *(every night)* toutes les nuits; **nightmare** *n* cauchemar *m*; **night school** *n* cours *mpl* du soir; **night shift** *n* équipe *f* de nuit; **night-time** *n* nuit *f*

nil [nɪl] *n (BRIT Sport)* zéro *m*

nine [naɪn] *num* neuf; **nineteen** [naɪn'tiːn] *num* dix-neuf; **nineteenth** [naɪn'tiːnθ] *num* dix-neuvième; **ninetieth** ['naɪntɪɪθ] *num* quatre-vingt-dixième; **ninety** *num* quatre-vingt-dix

ninth [naɪnθ] *num* neuvième

nip [nɪp] *vt* pincer ▷ *vi (BRIT inf):* **to ~ out/down/up** sortir/descendre/ monter en vitesse

nipple ['nɪpl] *n (Anat)* mamelon *m*, bout *m* du sein

nitrogen ['naɪtrədʒən] *n* azote *m*

 KEYWORD

no [nəu] *(pl* **noes)** *adv (opposite of "yes")* non; **are you coming? — no (I'm not)** est-ce que vous venez? — non; **would you like some more? — no thank you**

vous en voulez encore? — non merci
▷ *adj* (*not any*) (ne ...) pas de,
aucun(e); **I have no money/books** je
n'ai pas d'argent/de livres; **no smoking**
"défense de fumer"; **"no dogs"** les chiens ne sont
pas admis"
▷ *n* non *m*

nobility [nəʊˈbɪlɪtɪ] *n* noblesse *f*
noble [ˈnəʊbl] *adj* noble
nobody [ˈnəʊbədɪ] *pron* (ne ...)
personne
nod [nɔd] *vi* faire un signe de (la) tête
(*affirmatif ou amical*); (*sleep*) somnoler
▷ *vt*: **to ~ one's head** faire un signe de
(la) tête; (*in agreement*) faire signe que
oui ▷ *n* signe *m* de (la) tête; **nod off** *vi*
s'assoupir
noise [nɔɪz] *n* bruit *m*; **I can't sleep for
the ~** je n'arrive pas à dormir à cause du
bruit; **noisy** *adj* bruyant(e)
nominal [ˈnɔmɪnl] *adj* (*rent, fee*)
symbolique; (*value*) nominal(e)
nominate [ˈnɔmɪneɪt] *vt* (*propose*)
proposer; (*appoint*) nommer;
nomination [nɔmɪˈneɪʃən] *n*
nomination *f*; **nominee** [nɔmɪˈniː] *n*
candidat agréé; personne nommée
none [nʌn] *pron* aucun(e); **~ of you**
aucun d'entre vous, personne parmi
vous; **I have ~ left** je n'en ai plus; **he's
~ the worse for it** il ne s'en porte pas
plus mal
nonetheless [ˈnʌnðəˈlɛs] *adv*
néanmoins
non-fiction [nɔnˈfɪkʃən] *n* littérature *f*
non-romanesque
nonsense [ˈnɔnsəns] *n* absurdités *fpl*,
idioties *fpl*; **~!** ne dites pas d'idioties!
non: **non-smoker** *n* non-fumeur *m*;
non-smoking *adj* non-fumeur; **non-
stick** *adj* qui n'attache pas
noodles [ˈnuːdlz] *npl* nouilles *fpl*
noon [nuːn] *n* midi *m*
no-one [ˈnəʊwʌn] *pron* = **nobody**
nor [nɔːʳ] *conj* = **neither** ▷ *adv* see

neither
norm [nɔːm] *n* norme *f*
normal [ˈnɔːml] *adj* normal(e);
normally *adv* normalement
Normandy [ˈnɔːməndɪ] *n* Normandie *f*
north [nɔːθ] *n* nord *m* ▷ *adj* nord *inv*;
(*wind*) du nord ▷ *adv* au or vers le nord;
North Africa *n* Afrique *f* du Nord;
North African *adj* nord-africain(e),
d'Afrique du Nord ▷ *n* Nord-Africain(e);
North America *n* Amérique *f* du Nord;
North American *n* Nord-Américain(e)
▷ *adj* nord-américain(e), d'Amérique
du Nord; **northbound** [ˈnɔːθbaʊnd]
adj (*traffic*) en direction du nord;
(*carriageway*) nord *inv*; **north-east** *n*
nord-est *m*; **northeastern** *adj* (du)
nord-est *inv*; **northern** [ˈnɔːðən] *adj*
du nord, septentrional(e); **Northern
Ireland** *n* Irlande *f* du Nord; **North
Korea** *n* Corée *f* du Nord; **North
Pole** *n*: **the North Pole** le pôle Nord;
North Sea *n*: **the North Sea** la mer
du Nord; **north-west** *n* nord-ouest *m*;
northwestern [ˈnɔːθˈwɛstən] *adj* (du)
nord-ouest *inv*
Norway [ˈnɔːweɪ] *n* Norvège *f*;
Norwegian [nɔːˈwiːdʒən] *adj*
norvégien(ne) ▷ *n* Norvégien(ne);
(*Ling*) norvégien *m*
nose [nəʊz] *n* nez *m*; (*of dog, cat*)
museau *m*; (*fig*) flair *m*; **nose about,
nose around** *vi* fouiner or fureter
(partout); **nosebleed** *n* saignement *m*
de nez; **nosey** *adj* (*inf*) curieux(-euse)
nostalgia [nɔsˈtældʒɪə] *n* nostalgie *f*;
nostalgic [nɔsˈtældʒɪk] *adj*
nostalgique
nostril [ˈnɔstrɪl] *n* narine *f*; (*of horse*)
naseau *m*
nosy [ˈnəʊzɪ] (*inf*) *adj* = **nosey**
not [nɔt] *adv* (ne ...) pas; **he is ~ or isn't
here** il n'est pas ici; **you must ~ or
mustn't do that** tu ne dois pas faire
ça; **I hope ~** j'espère que non; **~ at
all** pas du tout; (*after thanks*) je t'en
prie; **it's too late, isn't it?** c'est trop tard,
n'est-ce pas?; **~ yet/now** pas encore/

maintenant; *see also* **only**

notable ['nəʊtəbl] *adj* notable;
notably *adv* (*particularly*) en
particulier; (*markedly*) spécialement

notch [nɒtʃ] *n* encoche *f*

note [nəʊt] *n* note *f*; (*letter*) mot *m*;
(*banknote*) billet *m* ▷ *vt* (*also*: ~ **down**)
noter; (*notice*) constater; **notebook**
n carnet *m*; (*for shorthand etc*) bloc-
notes *m*; **noted** ['nəʊtɪd] *adj* réputé(e);
notepad *n* bloc-notes *m*; **notepaper** *n*
papier *m* à lettres

nothing ['nʌθɪŋ] *n* rien *m*; **he does** ~ il
ne fait rien; ~ **new** rien de nouveau; **for**
~ (*free*) pour rien, gratuitement; (*in vain*)
pour rien; ~ **at all** rien du tout; ~ **much**
pas grand-chose

notice ['nəʊtɪs] *n* (*announcement,
warning*) avis *m* ▷ *vt* remarquer,
s'apercevoir de; **advance** ~ préavis *m*;
at short ~ dans un délai très court;
until further ~ jusqu'à nouvel ordre;
to give ~, **hand in one's** ~ (*employee*)
donner sa démission, démissionner;
to take ~ **of** prêter attention à;
to bring sth to sb's ~ porter qch à la
connaissance de qn; **noticeable** *adj*
visible

notice board *n* (BRIT) panneau *m*
d'affichage

notify ['nəʊtɪfaɪ] *vt*: **to** ~ **sb of sth**
avertir qn de qch

notion ['nəʊʃən] *n* idée *f*; (*concept*)
notion *f*; **notions** *npl* (US: haberdashery)
mercerie *f*

notorious [nəʊ'tɔːrɪəs] *adj* notoire
(*souvent en mal*)

notwithstanding [nɒtwɪθ'stændɪŋ]
adv néanmoins ▷ *prep* en dépit de

nought [nɔːt] *n* zéro *m*

noun [naʊn] *n* nom *m*

nourish ['nʌrɪʃ] *vt* nourrir;
nourishment *n* nourriture *f*

Nov. *abbr* (= *November*) nov

novel ['nɒvl] *n* roman *m* ▷ *adj* nouveau
(nouvelle), original(e); **novelist** *n*
romancier *m*; **novelty** *n* nouveauté *f*

November [nəʊ'vɛmbəʳ] *n*

novembre *m*

novice ['nɒvɪs] *n* novice *m/f*

now [naʊ] *adv* maintenant ▷ *conj*: ~
(**that**) maintenant (que); **right** ~ tout
de suite; **by** ~ à l'heure qu'il est; **just** ~:
that's the fashion just ~ c'est la mode
en ce moment or maintenant; ~ **and
then**, ~ **and again** de temps en temps;
from ~ **on** dorénavant; **nowadays**
['naʊədeɪz] *adv* de nos jours

nowhere ['nəʊwɛəʳ] *adv* (ne ...)
nulle part

nr *abbr* (BRIT) = **near**

nozzle ['nɒzl] *n* (*of hose*) jet *m*, lance *f*;
(*of vacuum cleaner*) suceur *m*

nuclear ['njuːklɪəʳ] *adj* nucléaire

nucleus (*pl* **nuclei**) ['njuːklɪəs,
'njuːklɪaɪ] *n* noyau *m*

nude [njuːd] *adj* nu(e) ▷ *n* (Art) nu *m*; **in
the** ~ (tout(e)) nu(e)

nudge [nʌdʒ] *vt* donner un (petit) coup
de coude à

nudist ['njuːdɪst] *n* nudiste *m/f*

nudity ['njuːdɪtɪ] *n* nudité *f*

nuisance ['njuːsns] *n*: **it's a** ~ c'est
(très) ennuyeux or gênant; **he's a** ~ il est
assommant or casse-pieds; **what a** ~!
quelle barbe!

numb [nʌm] *adj* engourdi(e); (*with fear*)
paralysé(e)

number ['nʌmbəʳ] *n* nombre *m*;
(*numeral*) chiffre *m*; (*of house, car,
telephone, newspaper*) numéro *m* ▷ *vt*
(*amount to*) compter; **a** ~ **of** un certain
nombre de; **they were seven in** ~ ils
étaient (au nombre de) sept; **to be** ~**ed
among** compter parmi; **number plate**
n (BRIT Aut) plaque *f* minéralogique *or*
d'immatriculation; **Number Ten** (BRIT: 10
Downing Street) résidence *f* du Premier
ministre

numerical [njuː'mɛrɪkl] *adj*
numérique

numerous ['njuːmərəs] *adj*
nombreux(-euse)

nun [nʌn] *n* religieuse *f*, sœur *f*

nurse [nɜːs] *n* infirmière *f*; (*also*: ~**maid**)
bonne *f* d'enfants ▷ *vt* (*patient, cold*)

soigner

nursery ['nɜːsərɪ] n (room) nursery f; (institution) crèche f, garderie f; (for plants) pépinière f; **nursery rhyme** n comptine f, chansonnette f pour enfants; **nursery school** n école maternelle; **nursery slope** n (BRIT Ski) piste f pour débutants

nursing ['nɜːsɪŋ] n (profession) profession f d'infirmière; (care) soins mpl; **nursing home** n clinique f; (for convalescence) maison f de convalescence or de repos; (for old people) maison de retraite

nurture ['nɜːtʃəʳ] vt élever

nut [nʌt] n (of metal) écrou m; (fruit: walnut) noix f; (: hazelnut) noisette f; (: peanut) cacahuète f (terme générique en anglais)

nutmeg ['nʌtmɛg] n (noix f) muscade f

nutrient ['njuːtrɪənt] n substance nutritive

nutrition [njuː'trɪʃən] n nutrition f, alimentation f

nutritious [njuː'trɪʃəs] adj nutritif(-ive), nourrissant(e)

nuts [nʌts] (inf) adj dingue

NVQ n abbr (BRIT) = **National Vocational Qualification**

nylon ['naɪlɔn] n nylon m ▷ adj de or en nylon

O

oak [əuk] n chêne m ▷ cpd de or en (bois de) chêne

O.A.P. n abbr (BRIT) = **old age pensioner**

oar [ɔːʳ] n aviron m, rame f

oasis (pl oases) [əu'eɪsɪs, əu'eɪsiːz] n oasis f

oath [əuθ] n serment m; (swear word) juron m; **on** (BRIT) or **under ~** sous serment; assermenté(e)

oatmeal ['əutmiːl] n flocons mpl d'avoine

oats [əuts] n avoine f

obedience [ə'biːdɪəns] n obéissance f

obedient [ə'biːdɪənt] adj obéissant(e)

obese [əu'biːs] adj obèse

obesity [əu'biːsɪtɪ] n obésité f

obey [ə'beɪ] vt obéir à; (instructions, regulations) se conformer à ▷ vi obéir

obituary [ə'bɪtjuərɪ] n nécrologie f

object n ['ɔbdʒɪkt] objet m; (purpose) but m, objet; (Ling) complément m d'objet ▷ vi [əb'dʒɛkt]: **to ~ to** (attitude) désapprouver; (proposal) protester

contre; élever une objection contre; **I ~!** je proteste!; **he ~ed that ...** il a fait valoir or a objecté que ...; **money is no ~** l'argent n'est pas un problème; **objection** [əb'dʒɛkʃən] n objection f; **if you have no objection** si vous n'y voyez pas d'inconvénient; **objective** n objectif m ⊳ adj objectif(-ive)
obligation [ɔblɪ'geɪʃən] n obligation f, devoir m; (debt) dette f (de reconnaissance)
obligatory [ə'blɪgətərɪ] adj obligatoire
oblige [ə'blaɪdʒ] vt (force): **to ~ sb to do** obliger or forcer qn à faire; (do a favour) rendre service à, obliger; **to be ~d to sb for sth** être obligé(e) à qn de qch
oblique [ə'bli:k] adj oblique; (allusion) indirect(e)
obliterate [ə'blɪtəreɪt] vt effacer
oblivious [ə'blɪvɪəs] adj: **~ of** oublieux(-euse) de
oblong ['ɔblɔŋ] adj oblong(ue) ⊳ n rectangle m
obnoxious [əb'nɔkʃəs] adj odieux(-euse); (smell) nauséabond(e)
oboe ['əubəu] n hautbois m
obscene [əb'si:n] adj obscène
obscure [əb'skjuə'] adj obscur(e) ⊳ vt obscurcir; (hide: sun) cacher
observant [əb'zə:vnt] adj observateur(-trice)
observation [ɔbzə'veɪʃən] n observation f; (by police etc) surveillance f
observatory [əb'zə:vətrɪ] n observatoire m
observe [əb'zə:v] vt observer; (remark) faire observer or remarquer; **observer** n observateur(-trice)
obsess [əb'sɛs] vt obséder; **obsession** [əb'sɛʃən] n obsession f; **obsessive** adj obsédant(e)
obsolete ['ɔbsəli:t] adj dépassé(e), périmé(e)
obstacle ['ɔbstəkl] n obstacle m
obstinate ['ɔbstɪnɪt] adj obstiné(e); (pain, cold) persistant(e)

obstruct [əb'strʌkt] vt (block) boucher, obstruer; (hinder) entraver; **obstruction** [əb'strʌkʃən] n obstruction f; (to plan, progress) obstacle m
obtain [əb'teɪn] vt obtenir
obvious ['ɔbvɪəs] adj évident(e), manifeste; **obviously** adv manifestement; (of course): **obviously!** bien sûr!; **obviously not!** évidemment pas!, bien sûr que non!
occasion [ə'keɪʒən] n occasion f; (event) événement m; **occasional** adj pris(e) (or fait(e)) de temps en temps; (worker, spending) occasionnel(le); **occasionally** adv de temps en temps, quelquefois
occult [ɔ'kʌlt] adj occulte ⊳ n: **the ~** le surnaturel
occupant ['ɔkjupənt] n occupant m
occupation [ɔkju'peɪʃən] n occupation f; (job) métier m, profession f
occupy ['ɔkjupaɪ] vt occuper; **to ~ o.s. with** or **by doing** s'occuper à faire
occur [ə'kə:'] vi se produire; (difficulty, opportunity) se présenter; (phenomenon, error) se rencontrer; **to ~ to sb** venir à l'esprit de qn; **occurrence** [ə'kʌrəns] n (existence) présence f, existence f; (event) cas m, fait m
ocean ['əuʃən] n océan m
o'clock [ə'klɔk] adv: **it is 5 o'clock** il est 5 heures
Oct. abbr (= October) oct
October [ɔk'təubə'] n octobre m
octopus ['ɔktəpəs] n pieuvre f
odd [ɔd] adj (strange) bizarre, curieux(-euse); (number) impair(e); (not of a pair) dépareillé(e); **60-~** 60 et quelques; **at ~ times** de temps en temps; **the ~ one out** l'exception f; **oddly** adv bizarrement, curieusement; **odds** npl (in betting) cote f; **it makes no odds** cela n'a pas d'importance; **odds and ends** de petites choses; **at odds** en désaccord
odometer [ɔ'dɔmɪtə'] n (us) odomètre m

odour (us **odor**) ['əudə'] n odeur f

⊙ **KEYWORD**

of [ɔv, əv] prep **1** (gen) de; **a friend of ours** un de nos amis; **a boy of 10** un garçon de 10 ans; **that was kind of you** c'était gentil de votre part
2 (expressing quantity, amount, dates etc) de; **a kilo of flour** un kilo de farine; **how much of this do you need?** combien vous en faut-il?; **there were three of them** (people) ils étaient 3; (objects) il y en avait 3; **three of us went** 3 d'entre nous y sont allé(e)s; **the 5th of July** le 5 juillet; **a quarter of 4** (us) 4 heures moins le quart
3 (from, out of) en, de; **a statue of marble** une statue de or en marbre; **made of wood** (fait) en bois

off [ɔf] adj, adv (engine) coupé(e); (light, TV) éteint(e); (tap) fermé(e); (BRIT: food) mauvais(e), avancé(e); (: milk) tourné(e); (absent) absent(e); (cancelled) annulé(e); (removed): **the lid was ~** le couvercle était retiré or n'était pas mis; (away): **to run/drive ~** partir en courant/en voiture ▷ prep de; **to be ~** (to leave) partir, s'en aller; **to be ~ sick** être absent pour cause de maladie; **a day ~** un jour de congé; **to have an ~ day** n'être pas en forme; **he had his coat ~** il avait enlevé son manteau; **10% ~** (Comm) 10% de rabais; **5 km ~ (the road)** à 5 km (de la route); **~ the coast** au large de la côte; **it's a long way ~** c'est loin (d'ici); **I'm ~ meat** je ne mange plus de viande; je n'aime plus la viande; **on the ~ ~ chance** à tout hasard; **~ and on, on and ~** de temps à autre

offence (us **offense**) [ə'fɛns] n (crime) délit m, infraction f; **to take ~ at** se vexer de, s'offenser de

offend [ə'fɛnd] vt (person) offenser, blesser; **offender** n délinquant(e); (against regulations) contrevenant(e)

offense [ə'fɛns] n (us) = **offence**

offensive [ə'fɛnsɪv] adj offensant(e), choquant(e); (smell etc) très déplaisant(e); (weapon) offensif(-ive) ▷ n (Mil) offensive f

offer ['ɔfə'] n offre f, proposition f ▷ vt offrir, proposer; **"on ~"** (Comm) "en promotion"

offhand [ɔf'hænd] adj désinvolte ▷ adv spontanément

office ['ɔfɪs] n (place) bureau m; (position) charge f, fonction f; **doctor's ~** (us) cabinet (médical); **to take ~** entrer en fonctions; **office block** (us **office building**) n immeuble m de bureaux; **office hours** npl heures fpl de bureau; (us Med) heures de consultation

officer ['ɔfɪsə'] n (Mil etc) officier m; (also: **police ~**) agent m (de police); (of organization) membre m du bureau directeur

office worker n employé(e) de bureau

official [ə'fɪʃl] adj (authorized) officiel(le) ▷ n officiel m; (civil servant) fonctionnaire m/f; (of railways, post office, town hall) employé(e)

off: off-licence n (BRIT: shop) débit m de vins et de spiritueux; **off-line** adj (Comput) (en mode) autonome; (: switched off) non connecté(e); **off-peak** adj aux heures creuses; (electricity, ticket) au tarif heures creuses; **off-putting** adj (BRIT: remark) rébarbatif(-ive); (person) rebutant(e), peu engageant(e); **off-season** adj, adv hors-saison inv

offset ['ɔfsɛt] vt (irreg: like **set**) (counteract) contrebalancer, compenser

offshore [ɔf'ʃɔ:'] adj (breeze) de terre; (island) proche du littoral; (fishing) côtier(-ière)

offside ['ɔf'saɪd] adj (Sport) hors jeu; (Aut: in Britain) de droite; (: in US, Europe) de gauche

offspring ['ɔfsprɪŋ] n progéniture f

often ['ɔfn] adv souvent; **how ~ do you go?** vous y allez tous les combien?; **every so ~** de temps en temps, de temps à autre

oh [əu] excl ô!, oh!, ah!

oil [ɔɪl] n huile f; (petroleum) pétrole m; (for central heating) mazout m ▷ vt (machine) graisser; **oil filter** n (Aut) filtre m à huile; **oil painting** n peinture f à l'huile; **oil refinery** n raffinerie f de pétrole; **oil rig** n derrick m; (at sea) plate-forme pétrolière; **oil slick** n nappe f de mazout; **oil tanker** n (ship) pétrolier m; (truck) camion-citerne m; **oil well** n puits m de pétrole; **oily** adj huileux(-euse); (food) gras(se)

ointment ['ɔɪntmənt] n onguent m

O.K., okay ['əu'keɪ] (inf) excl d'accord! ▷ vt approuver, donner son accord à ▷ adj (not bad) pas mal; **is it O.K.?, are you O.K.?** ça va?

old [əuld] adj vieux (vieille); (person) vieux, âgé(e); (former) ancien(ne), vieux; **how ~ are you?** quel âge avez-vous?; **he's 10 years ~** il a 10 ans, il est âgé de 10 ans; **~er brother/sister** frère/sœur aîné(e); **old age** n vieillesse f; **old-age pension** n (BRIT) pension f de retraite f (de la sécurité sociale); **old-age pensioner** n (BRIT) retraité(e); **old-fashioned** adj démodé(e); (person) vieux jeu inv; **old people's home** n (esp BRIT) maison f de retraite

olive ['ɔlɪv] n (fruit) olive f; (tree) olivier m ▷ adj (also: **~-green**) (vert) olive inv; **olive oil** n huile f d'olive

Olympic [əu'lɪmpɪk] adj olympique; **the ~ Games, the ~s** les Jeux mpl olympiques

omelet(te) ['ɔmlɪt] n omelette f

omen ['əumən] n présage m

ominous ['ɔmɪnəs] adj menaçant(e), inquiétant(e); (event) de mauvais augure

omit [əu'mɪt] vt omettre

KEYWORD

on [ɔn] prep 1 (indicating position) sur; **on the table** sur la table; **on the wall** sur le or au mur; **on the left** à gauche

2 (indicating means, method, condition

etc): **on foot** à pied; **on the train/plane** (be) dans le train/l'avion; (go) en train/avion; **on the telephone/radio/television** au téléphone/à la radio/à la télévision; **to be on drugs** se droguer; **on holiday** (BRIT), **on vacation** (US) en vacances

3 (referring to time): **on Friday** vendredi; **on Fridays** le vendredi; **on June 20th** le 20 juin; **a week on Friday** vendredi en huit; **on arrival** à l'arrivée; **on seeing this** en voyant ceci

4 (about, concerning) sur; **a book on Balzac/physics** un livre sur Balzac/de physique

▷ adv 1 (referring to dress): **to have one's coat on** avoir (mis) son manteau; **to put one's coat on** mettre son manteau; **what's she got on?** qu'est-ce qu'elle porte?

2 (referring to covering): **screw the lid on tightly** vissez bien le couvercle

3 (further, continuously): **to walk** etc **on** continuer à marcher etc; **from that day on** depuis ce jour

▷ adj 1 (in operation: machine) en marche; (: radio, TV, light) allumé(e); (: tap, gas) ouvert(e); (: brakes) mis(e); **is the meeting still on?** (not cancelled) est-ce que la réunion a bien lieu?; (in progress) la réunion dure-t-elle encore?; **when is this film on?** quand passe ce film?

2 (inf): **that's not on!** (not acceptable) cela ne se fait pas!; (not possible) pas question!

once [wʌns] adv une fois; (formerly) autrefois ▷ conj une fois que + sub; **~ he had left/it was done** une fois qu'il fut parti/ que ce fut terminé; **at ~** tout de suite, immédiatement; (simultaneously) à la fois; **all at ~** adv tout d'un coup; **~ a week** une fois par semaine; **~ more** encore une fois; **~ and for all** une fois pour toutes; **~ upon a time there was ...** il y avait une fois ..., il était une fois ...

oncoming [ˈɒnkʌmɪŋ] adj (traffic) venant en sens inverse

○ **KEYWORD**

one [wʌn] num un(e); **one hundred and fifty** cent cinquante; **one by one** un(e) à un or par un(e); **one day** un jour ▷ adj **1** (sole) seul(e), unique; **the one book which** l'unique or le seul livre qui; **the one man who** le seul (homme) qui **2** (same) même; **they came in the one car** ils sont venus dans la même voiture
▷ pron **1**: **this one** celui-ci (celle-ci); **that one** celui-là (celle-là); **I've already got one/a red one** j'en ai déjà un(e)/un(e) rouge; **which one do you want?** lequel voulez-vous?
2: **one another** l'un(e) l'autre; **to look at one another** se regarder
3 (impersonal) on; **one never knows** on ne sait jamais; **to cut one's finger** se couper le doigt; **one needs to eat** il faut manger

one-off [wʌnˈɒf] (BRIT inf) n exemplaire m unique

oneself [wʌnˈsɛlf] pron se; (after prep, also emphatic) soi-même; **to hurt ~** se faire mal; **to keep sth for ~** garder qch pour soi; **to talk to ~** se parler à soi-même; **by ~** tout seul

one-shot [wʌnˈʃɒt] (US) n = **one-off**; **one-sided** adj (argument, decision) unilatéral(e); **one-to-one** adj (relationship) univoque; **one-way** adj (street, traffic) à sens unique

ongoing [ˈɒngəʊɪŋ] adj en cours; (relationship) suivi(e)

onion [ˈʌnjən] n oignon m

on-line [ˈɒnlaɪn] adj (Comput) en ligne; (: switched on) connecté(e)

onlooker [ˈɒnlʊkər] n spectateur(-trice)

only [ˈəʊnlɪ] adv seulement ▷ adj seul(e), unique ▷ conj seulement, mais; **an ~ child** un enfant unique; **not ~ ... but also** non seulement ... mais aussi;

~ took one j'en ai seulement pris un, je n'en ai pris qu'un

on-screen [ɒnˈskriːn] adj à l'écran

onset [ˈɒnsɛt] n début m; (of winter, old age) approche f

onto [ˈɒntu] prep = **on to**

onward(s) [ˈɒnwəd(z)] adv (move) en avant; **from that time ~** à partir de ce moment

oops [ups] excl houp!

ooze [uːz] vi suinter

opaque [əʊˈpeɪk] adj opaque

open [ˈəʊpn] adj ouvert(e); (car) découvert(e); (road, view) dégagé(e); (meeting) public(-ique); (admiration) manifeste ▷ vt ouvrir ▷ vi (flower, eyes, door, debate) s'ouvrir; (shop, bank, museum) ouvrir; (book etc: commence) commencer, débuter; **is it ~ to public?** est-ce ouvert au public?; **what time do you ~?** à quelle heure ouvrez-vous?; **in the ~ (air)** en plein air; **open up** vt ouvrir; (blocked road) dégager ▷ vi s'ouvrir; **open-air** adj en plein air; **opening** n ouverture f; (opportunity) occasion f; (work) débouché m; (job) poste vacant; **opening hours** npl heures fpl d'ouverture; **open learning** n enseignement universitaire à la carte, notamment par correspondance; (distance learning) télé-enseignement m; **openly** adv ouvertement; **open-minded** adj à l'esprit ouvert; **open-necked** adj à col ouvert; **open-plan** adj sans cloisons; **Open University** n (BRIT) cours universitaires par correspondance

○ **OPEN UNIVERSITY**

● L'**Open University** a été fondée en
● 1969. L'enseignement comprend
● des cours (certaines plages horaires
● sont réservées à cet effet à la
● télévision et à la radio), les devoirs
● qui sont envoyés par l'étudiant à son
● directeur ou sa directrice d'études, et
● un séjour obligatoire en université
● d'été. Il faut préparer un certain

- nombre d'unités de valeur pendant une période de temps déterminée
- et obtenir la moyenne à un certain nombre d'entre elles pour recevoir le diplôme visé.

opera ['ɔpərə] n opéra m; **opera house** n opéra m; **opera singer** n chanteur(-euse) d'opéra

operate ['ɔpəreɪt] vt (machine) faire marcher, faire fonctionner ▷ vi fonctionner; **to ~ on sb (for)** (Med) opérer qn (de)

operating room n (us: Med) salle f d'opération

operating theatre n (BRIT: Med) salle f d'opération

operation [ɔpə'reɪʃən] n opération f; (of machine) fonctionnement m; **to have an ~ (for)** se faire opérer (de); **to be in ~** (machine) être en service; (system) être en vigueur; **operational** adj opérationnel(le); (ready for use) en état de marche

operative ['ɔpərətɪv] adj (measure) en vigueur ▷ n (in factory) ouvrier(-ière)

operator ['ɔpəreɪtə'] n (of machine) opérateur(-trice); (Tel) téléphoniste m/f

opinion [ə'pɪnjən] n opinion f, avis m; **in my ~** à mon avis; **opinion poll** n sondage m d'opinion

opponent [ə'pəunənt] n adversaire m/f

opportunity [ɔpə'tju:nɪtɪ] n occasion f; **to take the ~ to do** or **of doing** profiter de l'occasion pour faire

oppose [ə'pəuz] vt s'opposer à; **to be ~d to sth** être opposé(e) à qch; **as ~d to** par opposition à

opposite ['ɔpəzɪt] adj (house etc) d'en face ▷ adv en face ▷ prep en face de ▷ n opposé m, contraire m; (of word) contraire

opposition [ɔpə'zɪʃən] n opposition f

oppress [ə'prɛs] vt opprimer

opt [ɔpt] vi: **to ~ for** opter pour; **to ~ to do** choisir de faire; **opt out** vi: **to ~ out of** choisir de ne pas participer à or de

ne pas faire

optician [ɔp'tɪʃən] n opticien(ne)

optimism ['ɔptɪmɪzəm] n optimisme m

optimist ['ɔptɪmɪst] n optimiste m/f; **optimistic** [ɔptɪ'mɪstɪk] adj optimiste

optimum ['ɔptɪməm] adj optimum

option ['ɔpʃən] n choix m, option f; (Scol) matière f à option; **optional** adj facultatif(-ive)

or [ɔ:'] conj ou; (with negative): **he hasn't seen or heard anything** il n'a rien vu ni entendu; **or else** sinon; ou bien

oral ['ɔ:rəl] adj oral(e) ▷ n oral m

orange ['ɔrɪndʒ] n (fruit) orange f ▷ adj orange inv; **orange juice** n jus m d'orange; **orange squash** n orangeade f

orbit ['ɔ:bɪt] n orbite f ▷ vt graviter autour de

orchard ['ɔ:tʃəd] n verger m

orchestra ['ɔ:kɪstrə] n orchestre m; (us: seating) (fauteuils mpl d')orchestre

orchid ['ɔ:kɪd] n orchidée f

ordeal [ɔ:'di:l] n épreuve f

order ['ɔ:də'] n ordre m; (Comm) commande f; **in ~** en ordre; (of document) en règle; **out of ~** (not in correct order) en désordre; (machine) hors service; (telephone) en dérangement; **a machine in working ~** une machine en état de marche; **in ~ to do/that** pour faire/que + sub; **could I ~ now, please?** je peux commander, s'il vous plaît?; **to be on ~** être en commande; **to ~ sb to do** ordonner à qn de faire; **order form** n bon m de commande; **orderly** n (Mil) ordonnance f; (Med) garçon m de salle ▷ adj (room) en ordre; (mind) méthodique; (person) qui a de l'ordre

ordinary ['ɔ:dnrɪ] adj ordinaire, normal(e); (pej) ordinaire, quelconque; **out of the ~** exceptionnel(le)

ore [ɔ:'] n minerai m

oregano [ɔrɪ'gɑ:nəu] n origan m

organ ['ɔ:gən] n organe m; (Mus) orgue m, orgues fpl; **organic** [ɔ:'gænɪk] adj

organique; (*crops etc*) biologique,
naturel(le); **organism** *n* organisme *m*
organization [ɔːgənaɪˈzeɪʃən] *n*
organisation *f*
organize [ˈɔːgənaɪz] *vt* organiser;
organized [ˈɔːgənaɪzd] *adj* (*planned*)
organisé(e); (*efficient*) bien organisé(e);
organizer *n* organisateur(-trice)
orgasm [ˈɔːgæzəm] *n* orgasme *m*
orgy [ˈɔːdʒɪ] *n* orgie *f*
oriental [ɔːrɪˈɛntl] *adj* oriental(e)
orientation [ɔːrɪɛnˈteɪʃən] *n* (*attitudes*)
tendance *f*; (*in job*) orientation *f*; (*of
building*) orientation, exposition *f*
origin [ˈɔrɪdʒɪn] *n* origine *f*
original [əˈrɪdʒɪnl] *adj* (*first*);
(*earliest*) originel(le) ▷ *n* original *m*;
originally *adv* (*at first*) à l'origine
originate [əˈrɪdʒɪneɪt] *vi*: **to ~ from**
être originaire de; (*suggestion*) provenir
de; **to ~ in** (*custom*) prendre naissance
dans, avoir son origine dans
Orkney [ˈɔːknɪ] *n* (*also*: **the ~s, the ~
Islands**) les Orcades *fpl*
ornament [ˈɔːnəmənt] *n* ornement *m*;
(*trinket*) bibelot *m*; **ornamental**
[ɔːnəˈmɛntl] *adj* décoratif(-ive),
(*garden*) d'agrément
ornate [ɔːˈneɪt] *adj* très orné(e)
orphan [ˈɔːfn] *n* orphelin(e)
orthodox [ˈɔːθədɔks] *adj* orthodoxe
orthopaedic (*us* **orthopedic**)
[ɔːθəˈpiːdɪk] *adj* orthopédique
osteopath [ˈɔstɪəpæθ] *n* ostéopathe
m/f
ostrich [ˈɔstrɪtʃ] *n* autruche *f*
other [ˈʌðəʳ] *adj* autre ▷ *pron*: **the ~
(one)** l'autre; **~s** (*other people*) d'autres
▷ *adv*: **~ than** autrement que; à part;
the ~ day l'autre jour; **otherwise** *adv*,
conj autrement
Ottawa [ˈɔtəwə] *n* Ottawa
otter [ˈɔtəʳ] *n* loutre *f*
ouch [autʃ] *excl* aïe!
ought (*pt* ~) [ɔːt] *aux vb*: **I ~ to do it** je
devrais le faire; il faudrait que je le
fasse; **this ~ to have been corrected**
cela aurait dû être corrigé; **he ~ to win**

(*probability*) il devrait gagner
ounce [auns] *n* once *f* (28.35g; 16 in
a pound)
our [ˈauəʳ] *adj* notre, nos *pl*; *see also* **my**;
ours *pron* le (la) nôtre, les nôtres; *see
also* **mine**[1]; **ourselves** *pron pl* (*reflexive,
after preposition*) nous; (*emphatic*) nous-
mêmes; *see also* **oneself**
oust [aust] *vt* évincer
out [aut] *adv* dehors; (*published, not at
home etc*) sorti(e); (*light, fire*) éteint(e); **~
there** là-bas; **he's ~** (*absent*) il est sorti;
to be ~ in one's calculations s'être
trompé dans ses calculs; **to run/back
etc ~** sortir en courant/en reculant
etc; **~ loud** *adv* à haute voix; **~ of** *prep*
(*outside*) en dehors de; (*because of: anger
etc*) par; (*from among*): **10 ~ of 10** 10 sur
10; (*without*): **~ of petrol** sans essence,
à court d'essence; **~ of order** (*machine*)
en panne; (*Tel: line*) en dérangement;
outback *n* (*in Australia*) intérieur *m*;
outbound *adj*: **outbound (from/for)**
en partance (de/pour); **outbreak**
[ˈautbreɪk] *n* (*of violence*) éruption *f*, explosion
f; (*of disease*) de nombreux cas;
the outbreak of war south of the border
la guerre qui s'est déclarée au sud de
la frontière; **outburst** *n* explosion *f*,
accès *m*; **outcast** *n* exilé(e); (*socially*)
paria *m*; **outcome** *n* issue *f*, résultat *m*;
outcry *n* tollé (général); **outdated** *adj*
démodé(e); **outdoor** *adj* de or en plein
air; **outdoors** *adv* dehors; au grand air
outer [ˈautəʳ] *adj* extérieur(e); **outer
space** *n* espace *m* cosmique
outfit [ˈautfɪt] *n* (*clothes*) tenue *f*
out: **outgoing** *adj* (*president, tenant*)
sortant(e); (*character*) ouvert(e),
extraverti(e); **outgoings** *npl* (*BRIT*:
expenses) dépenses *fpl*; **outhouse** *n*
appentis *m*, remise *f*
outing [ˈautɪŋ] *n* sortie *f*; excursion *f*
out: **outlaw** *n* hors-la-loi *m inv* ▷ *vt*
(*person*) mettre hors la loi; (*practice*)
proscrire; **outlay** *n* dépenses *fpl*;
(*investment*) mise *f* de fonds; **outlet**
n (*for liquid etc*) issue *f*, sortie *f*; (*for

emotion) exutoire m; (*also*: **retail outlet**) point m de vente; (*us*: Elec) prise f de courant; **outline** n (*shape*) contour m; (*summary*) esquisse f, grandes lignes ▷ vt (*fig*: *theory*, *plan*) exposer à grands traits; **outlook** n perspective f; (*point of view*) attitude f; **outnumber** vt surpasser en nombre; **out-of-date** adj (*passport*, *ticket*) périmé(e); (*theory*, *idea*) dépassé(e); (*custom*) désuet(-ète); (*clothes*) démodé(e); **out-of-doors** adv = **outdoors**; **out-of-the-way** adj loin de tout; **out-of-town** adj (*shopping centre etc*) en périphérie; **outpatient** n malade m/f en consultation externe; **outpost** n avant-poste m; **output** n rendement m, production f; (*Comput*) sortie f ▷ vt (*Comput*) sortir

outrage ['autreɪdʒ] n (*anger*) indignation f; (*violent act*) atrocité f, acte m de violence; (*scandal*) scandale m ▷ vt outrager; **outrageous** [aut'reɪdʒəs] adj atroce; (*scandalous*) scandaleux(-euse)

outright adv [aut'raɪt] complètement; (*deny*, *refuse*) catégoriquement; (*ask*) carrément; (*kill*) sur le coup ▷ adj ['autraɪt] complet(-ète); catégorique

outset ['autset] n début m

outside [aut'saɪd] n extérieur m ▷ adj extérieur(e) ▷ adv (au) dehors, à l'extérieur ▷ prep hors de, à l'extérieur de; (*in front of*) devant; **at the ~** (*fig*) au plus or maximum; **outside lane** n (*Aut*: *in Britain*) voie f de droite; (*in US*, *Europe*) voie de gauche; **outside line** n (*Tel*) ligne extérieure; **outsider** n (*stranger*) étranger(-ère)

out: **outsize** adj énorme; (*clothes*) grande taille inv; **outskirts** npl faubourgs mpl; **outspoken** adj très franc (franche); **outstanding** adj remarquable, exceptionnel(le); (*unfinished*: *work*, *business*) en suspens, en souffrance; (*debt*) impayé(e); (*problem*) non réglé(e)

outward ['autwəd] adj (*sign*, *appearances*) extérieur(e); (*journey*)

(d')aller; **outwards** adv (*esp BRIT*) = **outward**

outweigh [aut'weɪ] vt l'emporter sur

oval ['əuvl] adj, n ovale m

ovary ['əuvəri] n ovaire m

oven ['ʌvn] n four m; **oven glove** n gant m de cuisine; **ovenproof** adj allant au four; **oven-ready** adj prêt(e) à cuire

over ['əuvə'] adv (par-)dessus ▷ adj (or adv) (*finished*) fini(e), terminé(e); (*too much*) en plus ▷ prep sur; par-dessus; (*above*) au-dessus de; (*on the other side of*) de l'autre côté de; (*more than*) plus de; (*during*) pendant; (*about*, *concerning*): **they fell out ~ money/her** ils se sont brouillés pour des questions d'argent/à cause d'elle; **~ here** ici; **~ there** là-bas; **all ~** (*everywhere*) partout; **~ and ~ (again)** à plusieurs reprises; **~ and above** en plus de; **to ask sb ~** inviter qn (à passer); **to fall ~** tomber; **to turn sth ~** retourner qch

overall adj [əuvər'ɔːl] (*length*) total(e); (*study*, *impression*) d'ensemble ▷ n (*BRIT*) blouse f ▷ adv [əuvər'ɔːl] dans l'ensemble, en général; **overalls** npl (*boiler suit*) bleus mpl (de travail)

overboard ['əuvəbɔːd] adv (Naut) par-dessus bord

overcame [əuvə'keɪm] pt of **overcome**

overcast ['əuvəkɑːst] adj couvert(e)

overcharge [əuvə'tʃɑːdʒ] vt: **to ~ sb for sth** faire payer qch trop cher à qn

overcoat ['əuvəkəut] n pardessus m

overcome [əuvə'kʌm] vt (*irreg*: *like* **come**) (*defeat*) triompher de; (*difficulty*) surmonter ▷ adj (*emotionally*) bouleversé(e); **~ with grief** accablé(e) de douleur

over: **overcrowded** adj bondé(e); (*city*, *country*) surpeuplé(e); **overdo** vt (*irreg*: *like* **do**) exagérer; (*overcook*) trop cuire; **to overdo it**, **to overdo things** (*work too hard*) en faire trop, se surmener; **overdone** [əuvə'dʌn] adj (*vegetables*, *steak*) trop cuit(e); **overdose** n dose excessive; **overdraft** n découvert m;

overdrawn adj (account) à découvert;
overdue adj en retard; (bill) impayé(e);
(change) qui tarde; **overestimate** vt
surestimer

overflow vi [əuvə'fləu] déborder
▷ n ['əuvəfləu] (also: ~ **pipe**) tuyau m
d'écoulement, trop-plein m

overgrown [əuvə'grəun] adj (garden)
envahi(e) par la végétation

overhaul vt [əuvə'hɔ:l] réviser ▷ n
['əuvəhɔ:l] révision f

overhead adv [əuvə'hɛd] au-dessus
▷ adj, n ['əuvəhɛd] ▷ adj aérien(ne);
(lighting) vertical(e) ▷ n (us)
= **overheads**; **overhead projector**
n rétroprojecteur m; **overheads** npl
(BRIT) frais généraux

over: overhear vt (irreg: like **hear**)
entendre (par hasard); **overheat** vi
(engine) chauffer; **overland** adj, adv par
voie de terre; **overlap** vi se chevaucher;
overleaf adv au verso; **overload** vt
surcharger; **overlook** vt (have view of)
donner sur; (miss) oublier, négliger;
(forgive) fermer les yeux sur

overnight adv [əuvə'naɪt] (happen)
durant la nuit; (fig) soudain ▷ adj
['əuvənaɪt] d'une (or de) nuit;
soudain(e); **to stay ~ (with sb)** passer
la nuit (chez qn); **overnight bag** n
nécessaire m de voyage

overpass ['əuvəpɑ:s] n (us: for cars)
pont autoroutier; (: for pedestrians)
passerelle f, pont m

overpower [əuvə'pauə'] vt vaincre;
(fig) accabler; **overpowering** adj
irrésistible; (heat, stench) suffocant(e)

over: overreact [əuvəri:'ækt] vi
réagir de façon excessive; **overrule**
vt (decision) annuler; (claim) rejeter;
(person) rejeter l'avis de; **overrun** vt
(irreg: like **run**) (Mil: country etc) occuper;
(time limit etc) dépasser ▷ vi dépasser le
temps imparti

overseas [əuvə'si:z] adv outre-mer;
(abroad) à l'étranger ▷ adj (trade)
extérieur(e); (visitor) étranger(-ère)

oversee [əuvə'si:] vt (irreg: like **see**)

surveiller

overshadow [əuvə'ʃædəu] vt (fig)
éclipser

oversight ['əuvəsaɪt] n omission f,
oubli m

oversleep [əuvə'sli:p] vi (irreg: like
sleep) se réveiller (trop) tard

overspend [əuvə'spɛnd] vi (irreg: like
spend) dépenser de trop

overt [əu'və:t] adj non dissimulé(e)

overtake [əuvə'teɪk] vt (irreg: like **take**)
dépasser; (BRIT: Aut) dépasser, doubler

over: overthrow vt (irreg: like **throw**)
(government) renverser; **overtime** n
heures fpl supplémentaires

overtook [əuvə'tuk] pt of **overtake**

over: overturn vt renverser; (decision,
plan) annuler ▷ vi se retourner;
overweight adj (person) trop gros(se);
overwhelm vt (subj: emotion) accabler,
submerger; (enemy, opponent) écraser;
overwhelming adj (victory, defeat)
écrasant(e); (desire) irrésistible

ow [au] excl aïe!

owe [əu] vt devoir; **to ~ sb sth, to ~ sth
to sb** devoir qch à qn; **how much do I ~
you?** combien est-ce que je vous dois?;
owing to prep à cause de, en raison de

owl [aul] n hibou m

own [əun] vt posséder ▷ adj propre;
a room of my ~ une chambre à moi,
ma propre chambre; **to get one's ~
back** prendre sa revanche; **on one's
~** tout(e) seul(e); **own up** vi avouer;
owner n propriétaire m/f; **ownership**
n possession f

ox (pl **oxen**) [ɔks, 'ɔksn] n bœuf m

Oxbridge ['ɔksbrɪdʒ] n (BRIT) les
universités d'Oxford et de Cambridge

oxen ['ɔksən] npl of **ox**

oxygen ['ɔksɪdʒən] n oxygène m

oyster ['ɔɪstə'] n huître f

oz. abbr = **ounce(s)**

ozone ['əuzəun] n ozone m; **ozone
friendly** adj qui n'attaque pas or qui
préserve la couche d'ozone; **ozone
layer** n couche f d'ozone

P

p abbr (BRIT) = **penny**; **pence**

P.A. n abbr = **personal assistant**; **public address system**

p.a. abbr = **per annum**

pace [peis] n pas m; (speed) allure f, vitesse f ▷ vi: **to ~ up and down** faire les cent pas; **to keep ~ with** aller à la même vitesse que; (events) se tenir au courant de; **pacemaker** n (Med) stimulateur m cardiaque; (Sport: also: **pacesetter**) meneur(-euse) de train

Pacific [pə'sɪfɪk] n: **the ~ (Ocean)** le Pacifique, l'océan m Pacifique

pacifier [ˈpæsɪfaɪəʳ] n (us: dummy) tétine f

pack [pæk] n paquet m; (of hounds) meute f; (of thieves, wolves etc) bande f; (of cards) jeu m; (us: of cigarettes) paquet m; (back pack) sac m à dos ▷ vt (goods) empaqueter, emballer; (in suitcase etc) emballer; (box) remplir; (cram) entasser ▷ vi: **to ~ (one's bags)** faire ses bagages; **pack in** (BRIT inf) ▷ vi (machine) tomber en panne ▷ vt (boyfriend) plaquer; **~ it in!** laisse tomber!; **pack off** vt: **to ~ sb off to** expédier qn à; **pack up** vi (BRIT inf: machine) tomber en panne; (: person) se tirer ▷ vt (belongings) ranger; (goods, presents) empaqueter, emballer

package [ˈpækɪdʒ] n paquet m; (also: ~ **deal**: agreement) marché global; (: purchase) forfait m; (Comput) progiciel m ▷ vt (goods) conditionner; **package holiday** n (BRIT) vacances organisées; **package tour** n voyage organisé

packaging [ˈpækɪdʒɪŋ] n (wrapping materials) emballage m

packed [pækt] adj (crowded) bondé(e); **packed lunch** n (BRIT) repas froid

packet [ˈpækɪt] n paquet m

packing [ˈpækɪŋ] n emballage m

pact [pækt] n pacte m, traité m

pad [pæd] n bloc(-notes) m m; (to prevent friction) tampon m ▷ vt rembourrer; **padded** adj (jacket) matelassé(e); (bra) rembourré(e)

paddle [ˈpædl] n (oar) pagaie f; (us: for table tennis) raquette f de ping-pong ▷ vi (with feet) barboter, faire trempette ▷ vt: **to ~ a canoe** etc pagayer; **paddling pool** n petit bassin

paddock [ˈpædək] n enclos m; (Racing) paddock m

padlock [ˈpædlɔk] n cadenas m

paedophile (us **pedophile**) [ˈpiːdəʊfaɪl] n pédophile m

page [peidʒ] n (of book) page f; (also: ~ **boy**) groom m, chasseur m; (at wedding) garçon m d'honneur ▷ vt (in hotel etc) (faire) appeler

pager [ˈpeidʒəʳ] n bip m (fam), Alphapage® m

paid [peid] pt, pp of **pay** ▷ adj (work, official) rémunéré(e); (holiday) payé(e); **to put ~ to** (BRIT) mettre fin à, mettre par terre

pain [pein] n douleur f; (inf: nuisance) plaie f; **to be in ~** souffrir, avoir mal; **to take ~s to do** se donner du mal pour faire; **painful** adj douloureux(-euse); (difficult) difficile, pénible; **painkiller**

n calmant *m*, analgésique *m*;
painstaking ['peɪnzteɪkɪŋ] *adj* (person)
soigneux(-euse); (work) soigné(e)
paint [peɪnt] *n* peinture *f* ▷ *vt* peindre;
to ~ the door blue peindre la porte en
bleu; **paintbrush** *n* pinceau *m*; **painter**
n peintre *m*; **painting** *n* peinture *f*;
(picture) tableau *m*
pair [pɛə] *n* (of shoes, gloves etc) paire
f; (of people) couple *m*; **~ of scissors**
(paire de) ciseaux *mpl*; **~ of trousers**
pantalon *m*
pajamas [pə'dʒɑːmæz] *npl* (US)
pyjama(s) *m*(*pl*)
Pakistan [pɑːkɪ'stɑːn] *n* Pakistan *m*;
Pakistani *adj* pakistanais(e) ▷ *n*
Pakistanais(e)
pal [pæl] *n* (inf) copain (copine)
palace ['pæləs] *n* palais *m*
pale [peɪl] *adj* pâle; **~ blue** *adj* bleu
pâle *inv*
Palestine ['pælɪstaɪn] *n* Palestine *f*;
Palestinian [pælɪs'tɪnɪən] *adj*
palestinien(ne) ▷ *n* Palestinien(ne)
palm [pɑːm] *n* (Anat) paume *f*; (also: **~
tree**) palmier *m* ▷ *vt*: **to ~ sth off on sb**
(inf) refiler qch à qn
pamper ['pæmpə] *vt* gâter, dorloter
pamphlet ['pæmflət] *n* brochure *f*
pan [pæn] *n* (also: **sauce~**) casserole *f*;
(also: **frying ~**) poêle *f*
pancake ['pænkeɪk] *n* crêpe *f*
panda ['pændə] *n* panda *m*
pane [peɪn] *n* carreau *m* (de fenêtre),
vitre *f*
panel ['pænl] *n* (of wood, cloth etc)
panneau *m*; (Radio, TV) panel *m*, invités
mpl; (for interview, exams) jury *m*
panhandler ['pænhændlə] *n* (US inf)
mendiant *m*
panic ['pænɪk] *n* panique *f*, affolement
m ▷ *vi* s'affoler, paniquer
panorama [pænə'rɑːmə] *n*
panorama *m*
pansy ['pænzɪ] *n* (Bot) pensée *f*
pant [pænt] *vi* haleter
panther ['pænθə] *n* panthère *f*
panties ['pæntɪz] *npl* slip *m*, culotte *f*

pantomime ['pæntəmaɪm] *n* (BRIT)
spectacle *m* de Noël; voir encadré

● **PANTOMIME**
●
● Une **pantomime** (à ne pas confondre
● avec le mot tel qu'on l'utilise en
● français), qu'on appelle également
● de façon familière "panto", est un
● genre de farce où le personnage
● principal est souvent un jeune
● garçon et où il y a toujours une
● "dame", c'est-à-dire une vieille
● femme jouée par un homme, et
● un méchant. La plupart du temps,
● l'histoire est basée sur un conte de
● fées comme Cendrillon ou Le Chat
● botté, et le public est encouragé
● à participer en prévenant le héros
● d'un danger imminent. Ce genre de
● spectacle, qui s'adresse surtout aux
● enfants, vise également un public
● d'adultes au travers des nombreuses
● plaisanteries faisant allusion à des
● faits d'actualité.

pants [pænts] *n* (BRIT: woman's) culotte
f, slip *m*; (man's) slip, caleçon *m*; (us:
trousers) pantalon *m*
pantyhose ['pæntɪhəʊz] (US) *npl*
collant *m*
paper ['peɪpə] *n* papier *m*; (also:
wall~) papier peint; (also: **news~**)
journal *m*; (academic essay) article *m*;
(exam) épreuve écrite ▷ *adj* en or de
papier ▷ *vt* tapisser (de papier peint);
papers *npl* (also: **identity ~s**) papiers
mpl (d'identité); **paperback** *n* livre
broché or non relié; (small) livre *m* de
poche; **paper bag** *n* sac *m* en papier;
paper clip *n* trombone *m*; **paper shop**
n (BRIT) marchand *m* de journaux;
paperwork *n* papiers *mpl*; (pej)
paperasserie *f*
paprika ['pæprɪkə] *n* paprika *m*
par [pɑː] *n* pair *m*; (Golf) normale *f* du
parcours; **on a ~ with** à égalité avec, au
même niveau que

paracetamol [pærə'si:təmɒl] (BRIT) n paracétamol m

parachute ['pærəʃu:t] n parachute m

parade [pə'reɪd] n défilé m ▷ vt (fig) faire étalage de ▷ vi défiler

paradise ['pærədaɪs] n paradis m

paradox ['pærədɒks] n paradoxe m

paraffin ['pærəfɪn] n (BRIT): ~ (oil) pétrole (lampant)

paragraph ['pærəgrɑ:f] n paragraphe m

parallel ['pærəlɛl] adj: ~ (with or to) parallèle (à); (fig) analogue (à) ▷ n (line) parallèle f; (fig, Geo) parallèle m

paralysed ['pærəlaɪzd] adj paralysé(e)

paralysis (pl paralyses) [pə'rælɪsɪs, -si:z] n paralysie f

paramedic [pærə'mɛdɪk] n auxiliaire m/f médical(e)

paranoid ['pærənɔɪd] adj (Psych) paranoïaque; (neurotic) paranoïde

parasite ['pærəsaɪt] n parasite m

parcel ['pɑ:sl] n paquet m, colis m ▷ vt (also: ~ up) empaqueter

pardon ['pɑ:dn] n pardon m; (Law) grâce f ▷ vt pardonner à; (Law) gracier; ~! pardon!; ~ me! (after burping etc) excusez-moi!; I beg your ~! (I'm sorry) pardon!, je suis désolé!; (I beg your) ~?, (us) ~ me? (what did you say?) pardon?

parent ['pɛərənt] n (father) père m; (mother) mère f; **parents** npl parents mpl; **parental** [pə'rɛntl] adj parental(e), des parents

Paris ['pærɪs] n Paris

parish ['pærɪʃ] n paroisse f; (BRIT: civil) ≈ commune f

Parisian [pə'rɪzɪən] adj parisien(ne), de Paris ▷ n Parisien(ne)

park [pɑ:k] n parc m, jardin public ▷ vt garer ▷ vi se garer; **can I ~ here?** est-ce que je peux me garer ici?

parking ['pɑ:kɪŋ] n stationnement m; "**no ~**" "stationnement interdit"; **parking lot** n (us) parking m, parc m de stationnement; **parking meter** n parc(o)mètre m; **parking ticket** n P.-V. m

> Be careful not to translate *parking* by the French word *parking*.

parkway ['pɑ:kweɪ] n (us) route f express (en site vert ou aménagé)

parliament ['pɑ:ləmənt] n parlement m; **parliamentary** [pɑ:lə'mɛntərɪ] adj parlementaire

Parmesan [pɑ:mɪ'zæn] n (also: ~ cheese) Parmesan m

parole [pə'rəʊl] n: on ~ en liberté conditionnelle

parrot ['pærət] n perroquet m

parsley ['pɑ:slɪ] n persil m

parsnip ['pɑ:snɪp] n panais m

parson ['pɑ:sn] n ecclésiastique m; (Church of England) pasteur m

part [pɑ:t] n partie f; (of machine) pièce f; (Theat etc) rôle m; (of serial) épisode m; (us: in hair) raie f ▷ adv = partly ▷ vt séparer ▷ vi (people) se séparer; (crowd) s'ouvrir; **to take ~ in** participer à, prendre part à; **to take sb's ~** prendre le parti de qn, prendre parti pour qn; **for my ~** en ce qui me concerne; **for the most ~** en grande partie; dans la plupart des cas; **in ~** en partie; **to take sth in good/bad ~** prendre qch du bon/mauvais côté; **part with** vt fus (person) se séparer de; (possessions) se défaire de

partial ['pɑ:ʃl] adj (incomplete) partiel(le); **to be ~ to** aimer, avoir un faible pour

participant [pɑ:'tɪsɪpənt] n (in competition, campaign) participant(e)

participate [pɑ:'tɪsɪpeɪt] vi: to ~ (in) participer (à), prendre part (à)

particle ['pɑ:tɪkl] n particule f; (of dust) grain m

particular [pə'tɪkjʊlə] adj (specific) particulier(-ière); (special) particulier, spécial(e); (fussy) difficile, exigeant(e); (careful) méticuleux(-euse); **in ~** en particulier, surtout; **particularly** adv particulièrement; (in particular) en particulier; **particulars** npl détails mpl; (information) renseignements mpl

parting ['pɑ:tɪŋ] n séparation f; (BRIT:

in hair) raie f

partition [pɑːˈtɪʃən] n (Pol) partition f,
division f; (wall) cloison f

partly [ˈpɑːtlɪ] adv en partie,
partiellement

partner [ˈpɑːtnəʳ] n (Comm)
associé(e); (Sport) partenaire m/f;
(spouse) conjoint(e); (lover) ami(e); (at
dance) cavalier(-ière); **partnership** n
association f

part of speech n (Ling) partie f du
discours

partridge [ˈpɑːtrɪdʒ] n perdrix f

part-time [ˈpɑːtˈtaɪm] adj, adv à mi-
temps, à temps partiel

party [ˈpɑːtɪ] n (Pol) parti m; (celebration)
fête f; (: formal) réception f; (: in evening)
soirée f; (group) groupe m; (Law) partie f

pass [pɑːs] vt (time, object) passer;
(place) passer devant; (friend) croiser;
(exam) être reçu(e) à, réussir; (overtake)
dépasser; (approve) approuver, accepter
▷ vi passer; (Scol) être reçu(e) or
admis(e), réussir ▷ n (permit) laissez-
passer m inv; (membership card) carte f
d'accès or d'abonnement; (in mountains)
col m; (Sport) passe f; (Scol: also: ~ **mark**):
to get a ~ être reçu(e) (sans mention);
to ~ sth to sb passer qch à qn; **could you
~ the salt/oil, please?** pouvez-vous
me passer le sel/l'huile, s'il vous plaît?;
to make a ~ at sb (inf) faire des avances
à qn; **pass away** vi mourir; **pass by** vi
passer ▷ vt (ignore) négliger; **pass on**
vt (hand on): **to ~ on (to)** transmettre
(à); **pass out** vi s'évanouir; **pass over**
vt (ignore) passer sous silence; **pass up**
vt (opportunity) laisser passer; **passable**
adj (road) praticable; (work) acceptable

Be careful not to translate **to pass
an exam** by the French expression
passer un examen.

passage [ˈpæsɪdʒ] n (also: **~way**)
couloir m; (gen, in book) passage m; (by
boat) traversée f

passenger [ˈpæsɪndʒəʳ] n
passager(-ère)

passer-by [pɑːsəˈbaɪ] n passant(e)

passing place n (Aut) aire f de
croisement

passion [ˈpæʃən] n passion f;
passionate adj passionné(e); **passion
fruit** n fruit m de la passion

passive [ˈpæsɪv] adj (also Ling)
passif(-ive)

passport [ˈpɑːspɔːt] n passeport m;
passport control n contrôle m des
passeports; **passport office** n bureau
m de délivrance des passeports

password [ˈpɑːswəːd] n mot m de
passe

past [pɑːst] prep (in front of) devant;
(further than) au delà de, plus loin que;
(later than) après ▷ adv: **to run**
~ passer en courant ▷ adj passé(e);
(president etc) ancien(ne) ▷ n passé m;
he's ~ forty il a plus de or passé quarante
ans; **ten/quarter ~ eight** huit heures
dix/un or et quart; **for the ~ few/3 days**
depuis quelques/3 jours; ces derniers/3
derniers jours

pasta [ˈpæstə] n pâtes fpl

paste [peɪst] n pâte f; (Culin: meat)
pâté m (à tartiner); (: tomato) purée
f, concentré m; (glue) colle f (de pâte)
▷ vt coller

pastel [ˈpæstl] adj pastel inv ▷ n (Art:
pencil) (crayon m) pastel m; (: drawing)
(dessin m au) pastel; (colour) ton m
pastel inv

pasteurized [ˈpæstəraɪzd] adj
pasteurisé(e)

pastime [ˈpɑːstaɪm] n passe-temps m
inv, distraction f

pastor [ˈpɑːstəʳ] n pasteur m

past participle [-ˈpɑːtɪsɪpl] n (Ling)
participe passé

pastry [ˈpeɪstrɪ] n pâte f; (cake)
pâtisserie f

pasture [ˈpɑːstʃəʳ] n pâturage m

pasty n [ˈpæstɪ] petit pâté (en croûte)

pasty [ˈpeɪstɪ] adj (complexion)
terreux(-euse)

pat [pæt] vt donner une petite tape à;
(dog) caresser

patch [pætʃ] n (of material) pièce f; (eye patch) cache m; (spot) tache f; (of land) parcelle f; (on tyre) rustine f ▷ vt (clothes) rapiécer; **a bad ~** (BRIT) une période difficile; **patchy** adj inégal(e); (incomplete) fragmentaire

pâté ['pæteɪ] n pâté m, terrine f

patent ['peɪtnt, us 'pætnt] n brevet m (d'invention) ▷ vt faire breveter ▷ adj patent(e), manifeste

paternal [pə'tɜ:nl] adj paternel(le)

paternity leave [pə'tɜ:nɪtɪ-] n congé m de paternité

path [pɑ:θ] n chemin m, sentier m; (in garden) allée f; (of missile) trajectoire f

pathetic [pə'θetɪk] adj (pitiful) pitoyable; (very bad) lamentable, minable

pathway ['pɑ:θweɪ] n chemin m, sentier m; (in garden) allée f

patience ['peɪʃns] n patience f; (BRIT: Cards) réussite f

patient ['peɪʃnt] n malade m/f; (of dentist etc) patient(e) ▷ adj patient(e)

patio ['pætɪəu] n patio m

patriotic [pætrɪ'ɒtɪk] adj patriotique; (person) patriote

patrol [pə'trəul] n patrouille f ▷ vt patrouiller dans; **patrol car** n voiture f de police

patron ['peɪtrən] n (in shop) client(e); (of charity) patron(ne); **~ of the arts** mécène m

patronizing ['pætrənaɪzɪŋ] adj condescendant(e)

pattern ['pætən] n (Sewing) patron m; (design) motif m; **patterned** adj à motifs

pause [pɔːz] n pause f, arrêt m ▷ vi faire une pause, s'arrêter

pave [peɪv] vt paver, dallar; **to ~ the way for** ouvrir la voie à

pavement ['peɪvmənt] n (BRIT) trottoir m; (us) chaussée f

pavilion [pə'vɪlɪən] n pavillon m; (Sport) stand m

paving ['peɪvɪŋ] n (material) pavé m, dalle f

paw [pɔ:] n patte f

pawn [pɔ:n] n (Chess, also fig) pion m ▷ vt mettre en gage; **pawnbroker** n prêteur m sur gages

pay [peɪ] n salaire m; (of manual worker) paie f ▷ vb (pt, pp **paid**) ▷ vt payer ▷ vi payer; (be profitable) être rentable; **can I ~ by credit card?** est-ce que je peux payer par carte de crédit?; **to ~ attention (to)** prêter attention (à); **to ~ sb a visit** rendre visite à qn; **to ~ one's respects to sb** présenter ses respects à qn; **pay back** vt rembourser; **pay for** vt fus payer; **pay in** vt verser; **pay off** vt (debts) régler, acquitter; (person) rembourser ▷ vi (scheme, decision) se révéler payant(e); **pay out** vt (money) payer, sortir de sa poche; **pay up** vt (amount) payer; **payable** adj payable; **to make a cheque payable to sb** établir un chèque à l'ordre de qn; **pay day** n jour m de paie; **pay envelope** n (us) paie f; **payment** n paiement m; (of bill) règlement m; (of deposit, cheque) versement m; **monthly payment** mensualité f; **payout** n (from insurance) dédommagement m; (in competition) prix m; **pay packet** n (BRIT) paie f; **pay phone** n cabine f téléphonique, téléphone public; **pay raise** n (us) = **pay rise**; **pay rise** n (BRIT) augmentation f (de salaire); **payroll** n registre m du personnel; **pay slip** n (BRIT) bulletin m de salaire, feuille f de paie; **pay television** n chaînes fpl payantes

PC n abbr = **personal computer**; (BRIT) = **police constable** ▷ adj abbr = **politically correct**

p.c. abbr = **per cent**

PDA n abbr (= personal digital assistant) agenda m électronique

PE n abbr (= physical education) EPS f

pea [pi:] n (petit) pois

peace [pi:s] n paix f; (calm) calme m, tranquillité f; **peaceful** adj paisible, calme

peach [pi:tʃ] n pêche f

peacock ['pi:kɔk] n paon m

peak [pi:k] n (mountain) pic m, cime f; (of cap) visière f; (fig: highest level) maximum m; (: of career, fame) apogée m; **peak hours** npl heures fpl d'affluence or de pointe

peanut ['pi:nʌt] n arachide f, cacahuète f; **peanut butter** n beurre m de cacahuète

pear [pɛəʳ] n poire f

pearl [pə:l] n perle f

peasant ['pɛznt] n paysan(ne)

peat [pi:t] n tourbe f

pebble ['pɛbl] n galet m, caillou m

peck [pɛk] vt (also: ~ **at**) donner un coup de bec à; (food) picorer ▷ n coup m de bec; (kiss) bécot m; **peckish** adj (BRIT inf): **I feel peckish** je mangerais bien quelque chose, j'ai la dent

peculiar [pɪ'kju:lɪəʳ] adj (odd) étrange, bizarre, curieux(-euse); (particular): **~ to** particulier(-ière) à

pedal ['pɛdl] n pédale f ▷ vi pédaler

pedalo ['pɛdələu] n pédalo m

pedestal ['pɛdəstl] n piédestal m

pedestrian [pɪ'dɛstrɪən] n piéton m; **pedestrian crossing** n (BRIT) passage clouté; **pedestrianized** adj: **a pedestrianized street** une rue piétonne; **pedestrian precinct** (US **pedestrian zone**) n (BRIT) zone piétonne

pedigree ['pɛdɪgri:] n ascendance f; (of animal) pedigree m ▷ cpd (animal) de race

pedophile ['pi:dəufail] (US) n = **paedophile**

pee [pi:] vi (inf) faire pipi, pisser

peek [pi:k] vi jeter un coup d'œil (furtif)

peel [pi:l] n pelure f, épluchure f; (of orange, lemon) écorce f ▷ vt peler, éplucher ▷ vi (paint etc) s'écailler; (wallpaper) se décoller; (skin) peler

peep [pi:p] n (BRIT: look) coup d'œil furtif; (sound) pépiement m ▷ vi (BRIT) jeter un coup d'œil (furtif)

peer [pɪəʳ] vi: **to ~ at** regarder attentivement, scruter ▷ n (noble) pair m; (equal) pair m, égal(e)

peg [pɛg] n (for coat etc) patère f; (BRIT: also: **clothes ~**) pince f à linge

pelican ['pɛlɪkən] n pélican m; **pelican crossing** n (BRIT Aut) feu m à commande manuelle

pelt [pɛlt] vt: **to ~ sb (with)** bombarder qn (de) ▷ vi (rain) tomber à seaux; (inf: run) courir à toutes jambes ▷ n peau f

pelvis ['pɛlvɪs] n bassin m

pen [pɛn] n (for writing) stylo m; (for sheep) parc m

penalty ['pɛnltɪ] n pénalité f; sanction f; (fine) amende f; (Sport) pénalité f; (Football) penalty m; (Rugby) pénalité f

pence [pɛns] npl of **penny**

pencil ['pɛnsl] n crayon m; **pencil in** vt noter provisoirement; **pencil case** n trousse f (d'écolier); **pencil sharpener** n taille-crayon(s) m inv

pendant ['pɛndnt] n pendentif m

pending ['pɛndɪŋ] prep en attendant ▷ adj en suspens

penetrate ['pɛnɪtreɪt] vt pénétrer dans; (enemy territory) entrer en

penfriend ['pɛnfrɛnd] n (BRIT) correspondant(e)

penguin ['pɛŋgwɪn] n pingouin m

penicillin [pɛnɪ'sɪlɪn] n pénicilline f

peninsula [pə'nɪnsjulə] n péninsule f

penis ['pi:nɪs] n pénis m, verge f

penitentiary [pɛnɪ'tɛnʃərɪ] n (US) prison f

penknife ['pɛnnaɪf] n canif m

penniless ['pɛnɪlɪs] adj sans le sou

penny (pl **pennies** or **pence**) ['pɛnɪ, 'pɛnɪz, pɛns] n (BRIT) penny m; (US) cent m

penpal ['pɛnpæl] n correspondant(e)

pension ['pɛnʃən] n (from company) retraite f; **pensioner** n (BRIT) retraité(e)

pentagon ['pɛntəgən] n: **the P~** (US Pol) le Pentagone

penthouse ['pɛnthaus] n appartement m (de luxe) en attique

penultimate [pɪ'nʌltɪmət] adj pénultième, avant-dernier(-ière)

people ['pi:pl] npl gens mpl; personnes

fpl; (inhabitants) population f; (Pol) peuple m ▷ n (nation, race) peuple m; **several ~ came** plusieurs personnes sont venues; **~ say that ...** on dit or les gens disent que ...

pepper ['pepə'] n poivre m; (vegetable) poivron m ▷ vt (Culin) poivrer; **peppermint** n (sweet) pastille f de menthe

per [pə:'] prep par; **~ hour** (miles etc) à l'heure; (fee) (de) l'heure; **~ kilo** etc le kilo etc; **~ day/person** par jour/personne; **~ annum** per an

perceive [pə'si:v] vt percevoir; (notice) remarquer, s'apercevoir de

per cent adv pour cent

percentage [pə'sɛntɪdʒ] n pourcentage m

perception [pə'sɛpʃən] n perception f; (insight) sensibilité f

perch [pə:tʃ] n (fish) perche f; (for bird) perchoir m ▷ vi (se) percher

percussion [pə'kʌʃən] n percussion f

perennial [pə'rɛnɪəl] adj (Bot) vivace f, plante pluriannuelle

perfect adj ['pə:fɪkt] adj parfait(e) ▷ n (also: **~ tense**) parfait m ▷ vt [pə'fɛkt] (technique, skill, work of art) parfaire; (method, plan) mettre au point; **perfection** [pə'fɛkʃən] n perfection f; **perfectly** ['pə:fɪktlɪ] adv parfaitement

perform [pə'fɔ:m] vt (carry out) exécuter; (concert etc) jouer, donner ▷ vi (actor, musician) jouer; **performance** n représentation f, spectacle m; (of an artist) interprétation f; (Sport: of car, engine) performance f; (of company, economy) résultats mpl; **performer** n artiste m/f

perfume ['pə:fju:m] n parfum m

perhaps [pə'hæps] adv peut-être

perimeter [pə'rɪmɪtə'] n périmètre m

period ['pɪərɪəd] n période f; (History) époque f; (Scol) cours m; (full stop) point m; (Med) règles fpl ▷ adj (costume, furniture) d'époque; **periodical** [pɪərɪ'ɔdɪkl] n périodique m; **periodically** adv périodiquement

perish ['perɪʃ] vi périr, mourir; (decay) se détériorer

perjury ['pə:dʒərɪ] n (Law: in court) faux témoignage; (breach of oath) parjure m

perk [pə:k] n (inf) avantage m, à-côté m

perm [pə:m] n (for hair) permanente f

permanent [pə:mənənt] adj permanent(e); **permanently** adv de façon permanente; (move abroad) définitivement; (open, closed) en permanence; (tired, unhappy) constamment

permission [pə'mɪʃən] n permission f, autorisation f

permit n ['pə:mɪt] permis m

perplex [pə'plɛks] vt (person) rendre perplexe

persecute ['pə:sɪkju:t] vt persécuter

persecution [pə:sɪ'kju:ʃən] n persécution f

persevere [pə:sɪ'vɪə'] vi persévérer

Persian ['pə:ʃən] adj persan(e); **the ~ Gulf** le golfe Persique

persist ['pə:sɪst] vi: **to ~ (in doing)** persister (à faire), s'obstiner (à faire); **persistent** adj persistant(e), tenace

person ['pə:sn] n personne f; **in ~** en personne; **personal** adj personnel(le); **personal assistant** n secrétaire personnel(le); **personal computer** n ordinateur individuel, PC m; **personality** [pə:sə'nælɪtɪ] n personnalité f; **personally** adv personnellement; **to take sth personally** se sentir visé(e) par qch; **personal organizer** n agenda (personnel) (style Filofax®); (electronic) agenda électronique; **personal stereo** n Walkman® m, baladeur m

personnel [pə:sə'nɛl] n personnel m

perspective [pə'spɛktɪv] n perspective f

perspiration [pə:spɪ'reɪʃən] n transpiration f

persuade [pə'sweɪd] vt: **to ~ sb to do sth** persuader qn de faire qch, amener or décider qn à faire qch

persuasion [pə'sweɪʒən] n persuasion f

persuasive [pəˈsweɪsɪv] adj
persuasif(-ive)

perverse [pəˈvɜːs] adj pervers(e);
(contrary) entêté(e), contrariant(e)

pervert n [ˈpɜːvəːt] perverti(e) ▷ vt
[pəˈvəːt] pervertir; (words) déformer

pessimism [ˈpɛsɪmɪzəm] n
pessimisme m

pessimist [ˈpɛsɪmɪst] n pessimiste
m/f; **pessimistic** [pɛsɪˈmɪstɪk] adj
pessimiste

pest [pɛst] n animal m (or insecte m)
nuisible; (fig) fléau m

pester [ˈpɛstə*] vt importuner, harceler

pesticide [ˈpɛstɪsaɪd] n pesticide m

pet [pɛt] n animal familier m ▷ cpd
(favourite) favori(te) ▷ vt (stroke)
caresser, câliner; **teacher's ~** chouchou
m du professeur; **~ hate** bête noire

petal [ˈpɛtl] n pétale m

petite [pəˈtiːt] adj menu(e)

petition [pəˈtɪʃən] n pétition f

petrified [ˈpɛtrɪfaɪd] adj (fig) mort(e)
de peur

petrol [ˈpɛtrəl] n (BRIT) essence f; **I've
run out of ~** je suis en panne d'essence
  Be careful not to translate petrol by
  the French word pétrole.

petroleum [pəˈtrəʊlɪəm] n pétrole m

petrol: petrol pump n (BRIT: in car,
at garage) pompe f à essence; **petrol
station** n (BRIT) station-service f;
petrol tank n (BRIT) réservoir m
d'essence

petticoat [ˈpɛtɪkəʊt] n jupon m

petty [ˈpɛtɪ] adj (mean) mesquin(e);
(unimportant) insignifiant(e), sans
importance

pew [pjuː] n banc m (d'église)

pewter [ˈpjuːtə*] n étain m

phantom [ˈfæntəm] n fantôme m

pharmacist [ˈfɑːməsɪst] n
pharmacien(ne)

pharmacy [ˈfɑːməsɪ] n pharmacie f

phase [feɪz] n phase f, période f; **phase
in** vt introduire progressivement;
phase out vt supprimer
progressivement

Ph.D. abbr = **Doctor of Philosophy**

pheasant [ˈfɛznt] n faisan m

phenomena [fəˈnɒmɪnə] npl of
phenomenon

phenomenal [fəˈnɒmɪnl] adj
phénoménal(e)

phenomenon (pl **phenomena**)
[fəˈnɒmɪnən, -nə] n phénomène m

Philippines [ˈfɪlɪpiːnz] npl (also:
Philippine Islands): **the ~** les
Philippines fpl

philosopher [fɪˈlɒsəfə*] n
philosophe m

philosophical [fɪləˈsɒfɪkl] adj
philosophique

philosophy [fɪˈlɒsəfɪ] n philosophie f

phlegm [flɛm] n flegme m

phobia [ˈfəʊbjə] n phobie f

phone [fəʊn] n téléphone m ▷ vt
téléphoner à ▷ vi téléphoner; **to be
on the ~** avoir le téléphone; (be calling)
être au téléphone; **phone back** vt, vi
rappeler; **phone up** vt téléphoner à ▷ vi
téléphoner; **phone book** n annuaire m;
phone box (US **phone booth**) n cabine
f téléphonique; **phone call** n coup m
de fil or de téléphone; **phonecard** n
télécarte f; **phone number** n numéro
m de téléphone

phonetics [fəˈnɛtɪks] n phonétique f

phoney [ˈfəʊnɪ] adj faux (fausse),
factice; (person) pas franc (franche)

photo [ˈfəʊtəʊ] n photo f; **photo album**
n album m de photos; **photocopier** n
copieur m; **photocopy** n photocopie f
▷ vt photocopier

photograph [ˈfəʊtəɡrɑːf] n
photographie f ▷ vt photographier;
photographer [fəˈtɒɡrəfə*] n
photographe m/f; **photography**
[fəˈtɒɡrəfɪ] n photographie f

phrase [freɪz] n expression f; (Ling)
locution f ▷ vt exprimer; **phrase
book** n recueil m d'expressions (pour
touristes)

physical [ˈfɪzɪkl] adj physique;
physical education n éducation

f physique; **physically** adv physiquement

physician [fɪ'zɪʃən] n médecin m
physicist ['fɪzɪsɪst] n physicien(ne)
physics ['fɪzɪks] n physique f
physiotherapist [fɪzɪəʊ'θerəpɪst] n kinésithérapeute m/f
physiotherapy [fɪzɪəʊ'θerəpɪ] n kinésithérapie f
physique [fɪ'ziːk] n (appearance) physique m; (health etc) constitution f
pianist ['piːənɪst] n pianiste m/f
piano [pɪ'ænəʊ] n piano m
pick [pɪk] n (tool: also: **~-axe**) pic m, pioche f ▷ vt choisir; (gather) cueillir; (remove) prendre; (lock) forcer; **take your ~** faites votre choix; **the ~ of** le (la) meilleur(e) de; **to ~ one's nose** se mettre les doigts dans le nez; **to ~ one's teeth** se curer les dents; **to ~ a quarrel with sb** chercher noise à qn; **pick on** vt fus (person) harceler; **pick out** vt choisir; (distinguish) distinguer; **pick up** vi (improve) remonter, s'améliorer ▷ vt ramasser; (collect) passer prendre; (Aut: give lift to) prendre; (learn) apprendre; (Radio) capter; **to ~ up speed** prendre de la vitesse; **to ~ o.s. up** se relever
pickle ['pɪkl] n (also: **~s:** as condiment) pickles mpl ▷ vt conserver dans du vinaigre ou dans de la saumure; **in a ~** (fig) dans le pétrin
pickpocket ['pɪkpɒkɪt] n pickpocket m
pick-up ['pɪkʌp] n (also: **~ truck**) pick-up m inv
picnic ['pɪknɪk] n pique-nique m ▷ vi pique-niquer; **picnic area** n aire f de pique-nique
picture ['pɪktʃə*] n (also TV) image f; (painting) peinture f, tableau m; (photograph) photo(graphie) f; (drawing) dessin m; (film) film m; (fig: description) description f ▷ vt (imagine) se représenter; **pictures** npl: **the ~s** (BRIT) le cinéma; **to take a ~ of sb/sth** prendre qn/qch en photo; **would you take a ~ of us, please?** pourriez-vous

nous prendre en photo, s'il vous plaît?;
picture frame n cadre m; **picture messaging** n picture messaging m, messagerie f d'images
picturesque [pɪktʃə'resk] adj pittoresque
pie [paɪ] n tourte f; (of fruit) tarte f; (of meat) pâté m en croûte
piece [piːs] n morceau m; (item): **a ~ of furniture/advice** un meuble/conseil ▷ vt: **to ~ together** rassembler; **to take to ~s** démonter
pie chart n graphique m à secteurs, camembert m
pier [pɪə*] n jetée f
pierce [pɪəs] vt percer, transpercer; **pierced** adj (ears) percé(e)
pig [pɪg] n cochon m, porc m; (pej: unkind person) mufle m; (: greedy person) goinfre m
pigeon ['pɪdʒən] n pigeon m
piggy bank ['pɪgɪ-] n tirelire f
pigsty ['pɪgstaɪ] n porcherie f
pigtail ['pɪgteɪl] n natte f, tresse f
pike [paɪk] n (fish) brochet m
pilchard ['pɪltʃəd] n pilchard m (sorte de sardine)
pile [paɪl] n (pillar, of books) pile f; (heap) tas m; (of carpet) épaisseur f; **pile up** vi (accumulate) s'entasser, s'accumuler ▷ vt (put in heap) empiler, entasser; (accumulate) accumuler; **piles** npl hémorroïdes fpl; **pile-up** n (Aut) télescopage m, collision f en série
pilgrim ['pɪlgrɪm] n pèlerin m

● **PILGRIM FATHERS**

● Les "Pères pèlerins" sont un
● groupe de puritains qui quittèrent
● l'Angleterre en 1620 pour fuir les
● persécutions religieuses. Ayant
● traversé l'Atlantique à bord du
● "Mayflower", ils fondèrent New
● Plymouth en Nouvelle-Angleterre,
● dans ce qui est aujourd'hui le
● Massachusetts. Ces Pères pèlerins
● sont considérés comme les

- fondateurs des États-Unis, et l'on
- commémore chaque année, le jour
- de "Thanksgiving", la réussite de leur
- première récolte.

pilgrimage ['pɪlgrɪmɪdʒ] *n*
pèlerinage *m*

pill [pɪl] *n* pilule *f*; **the ~** la pilule

pillar ['pɪlə'] *n* pilier *m*

pillow ['pɪləʊ] *n* oreiller *m*; **pillowcase,
pillowslip** *n* taie *f* d'oreiller

pilot ['paɪlət] *n* pilote *m* ▷ *cpd (scheme
etc)* pilote, expérimental(e) ▷ *vt* piloter;
pilot light *n* veilleuse *f*

pimple ['pɪmpl] *n* bouton *m*

PIN *n abbr (= personal identification
number)* code *m* confidentiel

pin [pɪn] *n* épingle *f*; *(Tech)* cheville *f* ▷ *vt*
épingler; **~s and needles** fourmis *fpl*; **to
~ sb down** *(fig)* coincer qn; **to ~ sth on
sb** *(fig)* mettre qch sur le dos de qn

pinafore ['pɪnəfɔː'] *n* tablier *m*

pinch [pɪntʃ] *n* pincement *m*; *(of salt
etc)* pincée *f* ▷ *vt* pincer; *(inf: steal)*
piquer, chiper ▷ *vi (shoe)* serrer; **at a ~**
à la rigueur

pine [paɪn] *n (also: ~ tree)* pin *m* ▷ *vi*: **to
~ for** aspirer à, désirer ardemment

pineapple ['paɪnæpl] *n* ananas *m*

ping [pɪŋ] *n (noise)* tintement *m*; **ping-
pong®** ['pɪŋpɔŋ] *n* ping-pong® *m*

pink [pɪŋk] *adj* rose ▷ *n (colour)* rose *m*

pinpoint ['pɪnpɔɪnt] *vt* indiquer *(avec
précision)*

pint [paɪnt] *n* pinte *f (BRIT = 0.57 l; US =
0.47 l)*; *(BRIT inf)* ≈ demi *m*, ≈ pot *m*

pioneer [paɪə'nɪə'] *n* pionnier *m*

pious ['paɪəs] *adj* pieux(-euse)

pip [pɪp] *n (seed)* pépin *m*; **pips** *npl*: **the
~s** *(BRIT: time signal on radio)* le top

pipe [paɪp] *n* tuyau *m*, conduite *f*; *(for
smoking)* pipe *f* ▷ *vt* amener par tuyau;
pipeline *n (for gas)* gazoduc *m*, pipeline
m; *(for oil)* oléoduc *m*, pipeline; **piper** *n
(flautist)* joueur(-euse) de pipeau; *(of
bagpipes)* joueur(-euse) de cornemuse

pirate ['paɪərət] *n* pirate *m* ▷ *vt (CD,
video, book)* pirater

Pisces ['paɪsiːz] *n* les Poissons *mpl*

piss [pɪs] *vi (inf!)* pisser (!); **pissed** *(inf!)*
adj (BRIT: drunk) bourré(e); *(US: angry)*
furieux(-euse)

pistol ['pɪstl] *n* pistolet *m*

piston ['pɪstən] *n* piston *m*

pit [pɪt] *n* trou *m*, fosse *f*; *(also: coal ~)*
puits *m* de mine; *(also: orchestra ~)*
fosse d'orchestre; *(US: fruit stone)* noyau
m ▷ *vt*: **to ~ o.s. or one's wits against**
se mesurer à

pitch [pɪtʃ] *n (BRIT SPORT)* terrain *m*; *(Mus)*
ton *m*; *(fig: degree)* degré *m*; *(tar)* poix
f ▷ *vt (throw)* lancer; *(tent)* dresser ▷ *vi
(fall)*: **to ~ into/off** tomber dans/de;
pitch-black *adj* noir(e) comme poix

pitfall ['pɪtfɔːl] *n* piège *m*

pith [pɪθ] *n (of orange etc)* intérieur *m* de
l'écorce

pitiful ['pɪtɪful] *adj (touching)* pitoyable;
(contemptible) lamentable

pity ['pɪtɪ] *n* pitié *f* ▷ *vt* plaindre; **what a
~!** quel dommage!

pizza ['piːtsə] *n* pizza *f*

placard ['plækɑːd] *n* affiche *f*; *(in march)*
pancarte *f*

place [pleɪs] *n* endroit *m*, lieu *m*;
(proper position, job, rank, seat) place
f; *(home)*: **at/to his ~** chez lui ▷ *vt
(position)* placer, mettre; *(identify)*
situer; reconnaître; **to take ~** avoir
lieu; **to change ~s with sb** changer
de place avec qn; **out of ~** *(not suitable)*
déplacé(e), inopportun(e); **in the first
~** d'abord, premièrement; **place mat** *n* set
m de table; *(in linen etc)* napperon *m*;
placement *n (during studies)* stage *m*

placid ['plæsɪd] *adj* placide

plague [pleɪg] *n (Med)* peste *f* ▷ *vt (fig)*
tourmenter

plaice [pleɪs] *n (pl inv)* carrelet *m*

plain [pleɪn] *adj (in one colour)* uni(e);
(clear) clair(e), évident(e); *(simple)*
simple; *(not handsome)* quelconque,
ordinaire ▷ *adv* franchement,
carrément ▷ *n* plaine *f*; **plain
chocolate** *n* chocolat *m* à croquer;
plainly *adv* clairement; *(frankly)*

carrément, sans détours

plaintiff ['pleɪntɪf] n plaignant(e)

plait [plæt] n tresse f, natte f

plan [plæn] n plan m; (scheme) projet m ▷ vt (think in advance) projeter; (prepare) organiser ▷ vi faire des projets; **to ~ to do** projeter de faire

plane [pleɪn] n (Aviat) avion m; (also: **~ tree**) platane m; (tool) rabot m; (Art, Math etc) plan m; (fig) niveau m, plan ▷ vt (with tool) raboter

planet ['plænɪt] n planète f

plank [plæŋk] n planche f

planning ['plænɪŋ] n planification f; **family ~** planning familial

plant [plɑːnt] n plante f; (machinery) matériel m; (factory) usine f ▷ vt planter; (bomb) déposer, poser; (microphone, evidence) cacher

plantation [plæn'teɪʃən] n plantation f

plaque [plæk] n plaque f

plaster ['plɑːstə²] n plâtre m; (also: **~ of Paris**) plâtre à mouler; (BRIT: also: **sticking ~**) pansement adhésif ▷ vt plâtrer; (cover): **to ~ with** couvrir de; **plaster cast** n (Med) plâtre m; (model, statue) moule m

plastic ['plæstɪk] n plastique m ▷ adj (made of plastic) en plastique; **plastic bag** n sac m en plastique; **plastic surgery** n chirurgie f esthétique

plate [pleɪt] n (dish) assiette f; (sheet of metal, on door: Phot) plaque f; (in book) gravure f; (dental) dentier m

plateau (pl **~s** or **~x**) ['plætəu, -z] n plateau m

platform ['plætfɔːm] n (at meeting) tribune f; (stage) estrade f; (Rail) quai m; (Pol) plateforme f

platinum ['plætɪnəm] n platine m

platoon [plə'tuːn] n peloton m

platter ['plætə²] n plat m

plausible ['plɔːzɪbl] adj plausible; (person) convaincant(e)

play [pleɪ] n jeu m; (Theat) pièce f de théâtre) ▷ vt (game) jouer à; (team, opponent) jouer contre; (instrument)

jouer de; (part, piece of music, note) jouer; (CD etc) passer ▷ vi jouer; **to ~ safe** ne prendre aucun risque; **play back** vt repasser, réécouter; **play up** vi (cause trouble) faire des siennes; **player** n joueur(-euse); (Mus) musicien(ne); **playful** adj enjoué(e); **playground** n cour f de récréation; (in park) aire f de jeux; **playgroup** n garderie f; **playing card** n carte f à jouer; **playing field** n terrain m de sport; **playschool** n = **playgroup**; **playtime** n (Scol) récréation f; **playwright** n dramaturge m

plc abbr (BRIT: = public limited company) ≈ SARL f

plea [pliː] n (request) appel m; (Law) défense f

plead [pliːd] vt plaider; (give as excuse) invoquer ▷ vi (Law) plaider; (beg): **to ~ with sb (for sth)** implorer qn (d'accorder qch); **to ~ guilty/not guilty** plaider coupable/non coupable

pleasant ['pleznt] adj agréable

please [pliːz] excl s'il te (or vous) plaît ▷ vt plaire à ▷ vi (think fit): **do as you ~** faites comme il vous plaira; **~ yourself!** (inf) (faites) comme vous voulez!; **pleased** adj: **pleased (with)** content(e) (de); **pleased to meet you** enchanté (de faire votre connaissance)

pleasure ['pleʒə²] n plaisir m; **"it's a ~"** "je vous en prie"

pleat [pliːt] n pli m

pledge [pledʒ] n (promise) promesse f ▷ vt promettre

plentiful ['plentɪful] adj abondant(e), copieux(-euse)

plenty ['plentɪ] n: **~ of** beaucoup de; (sufficient) (bien) assez de

pliers ['plaɪəz] npl pinces fpl

plight [plaɪt] n situation f critique

plod [plɔd] vi avancer péniblement; (fig) peiner

plonk [plɔŋk] (inf) n (BRIT: wine) pinard m, piquette f ▷ vt: **to ~ sth down** poser brusquement qch

plot [plɔt] n complot m, conspiration f;

(of story, play) intrigue f; *(of land)* lot m de terrain, lopin m ▷ vt *(mark out)* tracer point par point; *(Naut)* pointer; *(make graph of)* faire le graphique de; *(conspire)* comploter ▷ vi comploter

plough *(us* **plow)** [plau] n charrue f ▷ vt *(earth)* labourer; **to ~ money into** investir dans; **ploughman's lunch** n *(BRIT)* assiette froide avec du pain, du fromage et des pickles

plow [plau] *(us)* = **plough**

ploy [plɔɪ] n stratagème m

pluck [plʌk] vt *(fruit)* cueillir; *(musical instrument)* pincer; *(bird)* plumer; **to ~ one's eyebrows** s'épiler les sourcils; **to ~ up courage** prendre son courage à deux mains

plug [plʌg] n *(stopper)* bouchon m, bonde f; *(Elec)* prise f de courant; *(Aut: also:* **spark(ing) ~)** bougie f ▷ vt *(hole)* boucher; *(inf: advertise)* faire du battage pour, matraquer; **plug in** vt *(Elec)* brancher; **plughole** n *(BRIT)* trou m d'écoulement)

plum [plʌm] n *(fruit)* prune f

plumber ['plʌmə'] n plombier m

plumbing ['plʌmɪŋ] n *(trade)* plomberie f; *(piping)* tuyauterie f

plummet ['plʌmɪt] vi *(person, object)* plonger; *(sales, prices)* dégringoler

plump [plʌmp] adj rondelet(te), dodu(e), bien en chair; **plump for** vt fus *(inf: choose)* se décider pour

plunge [plʌndʒ] n plongeon m; *(fig)* chute f ▷ vt plonger ▷ vi *(fall)* tomber, dégringoler; *(dive)* plonger; **to take the ~** se jeter à l'eau

pluperfect [pluː'pə:fɪkt] n *(Ling)* plus-que-parfait m

plural ['pluərl] adj pluriel(le) ▷ n pluriel m

plus [plʌs] n *(also:* **~ sign)** signe m plus; *(advantage)* atout m ▷ prep plus; **ten/twenty ~** plus de dix/vingt

ply [plaɪ] n *(of wool)* fil m ▷ vt *(a trade)* exercer ▷ vi *(ship)* faire la navette; **to ~ sb with drink** donner continuellement à boire à qn; **plywood**

n contreplaqué m

P.M. n abbr *(BRIT)* = **prime minister**

p.m. adv abbr *(= post meridiem)* de l'après-midi

PMS n abbr *(= premenstrual syndrome)* syndrome prémenstruel

PMT n abbr *(= premenstrual tension)* syndrome prémenstruel

pneumatic drill [njuː'mætɪk-] n marteau-piqueur m

pneumonia [njuː'məunɪə] n pneumonie f

poach [pəutʃ] vt *(cook)* pocher; *(steal)* pêcher *(or chasser)* sans permis ▷ vi braconner; **poached** adj *(egg)* poché(e)

P.O. Box n abbr = **post office box**

pocket ['pɔkɪt] n poche f ▷ vt empocher; **to be (£5) out of ~** *(BRIT)* en être de sa poche *(pour £5 livres)*; **pocketbook** n *(us: wallet)* portefeuille m; **pocket money** n argent m de poche

pod [pɔd] n cosse f

podcast n podcast m

podiatrist [pɔ'di:ætrɪst] n *(us)* pédicure m/f

podium ['pəudɪəm] n podium m

poem ['pəuɪm] n poème m

poet ['pəuɪt] n poète m; **poetic** [pəu'ɛtɪk] adj poétique; **poetry** n poésie f

poignant ['pɔɪnjənt] adj poignant(e)

point [pɔɪnt] n point m; *(tip)* pointe f; *(in time)* moment m; *(in space)* endroit m; *(subject, idea)* point, sujet m; *(purpose)* but m; *(also:* **decimal ~**): **2 ~ 3 (2.3)** = 2 virgule 3 (2,3); *(BRIT Elec: also:* **power ~**) prise f de courant ▷ vt *(show)* indiquer; *(gun etc)*: **to ~ sth at** braquer or diriger qch sur ▷ vi: **to ~ at** montrer du doigt; **points** npl *(Rail)* aiguillage m; **to make a ~ of doing sth** ne pas manquer de faire qch; **to get/miss the ~** comprendre/ne pas comprendre; **to come to the ~** en venir au fait; **there's no ~ (in doing)** cela ne sert à rien *(de faire)*, à quoi ça sert?; **to be on the ~ of doing sth** être sur le point de faire qch; **point out** vt (mention) faire remarquer, souligner; **point-blank** adv (fig) catégoriquement; (also: **at point-blank range**) à bout portant; **pointed** adj (shape) pointu(e); (remark) plein(e) de sous-entendus; **pointer** n (needle) aiguille f; (clue) indication f; (advice) tuyau m; **pointless** adj inutile, vain(e); **point of view** n point m de vue

poison ['pɔɪzn] n poison m ▷ vt empoisonner; **poisonous** adj (snake) venimeux(-euse); (substance, plant) vénéneux(-euse); (fumes) toxique

poke [pəuk] vt (jab with finger, stick etc) piquer; (pousser du doigt; (put): **to ~ sth in(to)** fourrer or enfoncer qch dans; **poke about** vi fureter; **poke out** vi (stick out) sortir

poker ['pəukə'] n tisonnier m; (Cards) poker m

Poland ['pəuland] n Pologne f

polar ['pəulə'] adj polaire; **polar bear** n ours blanc

Pole [pəul] n Polonais(e)

pole [pəul] n (of wood) mât m, perche f; (Elec) poteau m; (Geo) pôle m; **pole bean** n (us) haricot m (à rames); **pole vault** n saut m à la perche

police [pə'li:s] npl police f ▷ vt maintenir l'ordre dans; **police car** n voiture f de police; **police constable** n (BRIT) agent m de police; **police force** n police f, forces fpl de l'ordre; **policeman** (irreg) n agent m de police, policier m; **police officer** n agent m de police; **police station** n commissariat m de police; **policewoman** (irreg) n femme-agent f

policy ['pɔlɪsɪ] n politique f; (also: **insurance ~**) police f (d'assurance)

polio ['pəulɪəu] n polio f

Polish ['pəulɪʃ] adj polonais(e) ▷ n (Ling) polonais m

polish ['pɔlɪʃ] n (for shoes) cirage m; (for floor) cire f, encaustique f; (for nails) vernis m; (shine) éclat m, poli m; (fig: refinement) raffinement m ▷ vt (put polish on: shoes, wood) cirer; (make

shiny) astiquer, faire briller; **polish off** vt (food) liquider; **polished** adj (fig) raffiné(e)

polite [pə'laɪt] adj poli(e); **politeness** n politesse f

political [pə'lɪtɪkl] adj politique; **politically** adv politiquement; **politically correct** politiquement correct(e)

politician [pɔlɪ'tɪʃən] n homme/ femme politique, politicien(ne)

politics ['pɔlɪtɪks] n politique f

poll [pəul] n scrutin m, vote m; (also: **opinion ~**) sondage m (d'opinion) ▷ vt (votes) obtenir

pollen ['pɔlən] n pollen m

polling station n (BRIT) bureau m de vote

pollute [pə'lu:t] vt polluer

pollution [pə'lu:ʃən] n pollution f

polo ['pəuləu] n polo m; **polo-neck** adj à col roulé ▷ n (sweater) pull m à col roulé; **polo shirt** n polo m

polyester [pɔlɪ'ɛstə'] n polyester m

polystyrene [pɔlɪ'staɪri:n] n polystyrène m

polythene ['pɔlɪθi:n] n (BRIT) polyéthylène m; **polythene bag** n sac m en plastique

pomegranate ['pɔmɪɡrænɪt] n grenade f

pompous ['pɔmpəs] adj pompeux(-euse)

pond [pɔnd] n étang m; (stagnant) mare f

ponder ['pɔndə'] vt considérer, peser

pony ['pəunɪ] n poney m; **ponytail** n queue f de cheval; **pony trekking** n (BRIT) randonnée f équestre or à cheval

poodle ['pu:dl] n caniche m

pool [pu:l] n (of rain) flaque f; (pond) mare f; (artificial) bassin m; (also: **swimming ~**) piscine f; (sth shared) fonds commun; (billiards) poule f ▷ vt mettre en commun; **pools** npl (football) = loto sportif

poor [puə'] adj pauvre; (mediocre) médiocre, faible, mauvais(e) ▷ npl: **the ~s** les pauvres mpl; **poorly** adv (badly) mal, médiocrement ▷ adj souffrant(e), malade

pop [pɒp] n (noise) bruit sec; (Mus) musique f pop; (inf: drink) soda m; (us inf: father) papa m ▷ vt (put) fourrer, mettre (rapidement) ▷ vi éclater; (cork) sauter; **pop in** vi entrer en passant; **pop out** vi sortir; **popcorn** n pop-corn m

pope [pəup] n pape m

poplar ['pɒplə^r] n peuplier m

popper ['pɒpə^r] n (BRIT) bouton-pression m

poppy ['pɒpɪ] n (wild) coquelicot m; (cultivated) pavot m

Popsicle® ['pɒpsɪkl] n (us) esquimau m (glace)

pop star n pop star f

popular ['pɒpjulə^r] adj populaire; (fashionable) à la mode; **popularity** [pɒpju'lærɪtɪ] n popularité f

population [pɒpju'leɪʃən] n population f

pop-up adj (Comput: menu, window) pop up inv ▷ n pop up m inv, fenêtre f pop up

porcelain ['pɔːslɪn] n porcelaine f

porch [pɔːtʃ] n porche m; (us) véranda f

pore [pɔː^r] n pore m ▷ vi: **to ~ over** s'absorber dans, être plongé(e) dans

pork [pɔːk] n porc m; **pork chop** n côte f de porc; **pork pie** n pâté m de porc en croûte

porn [pɔːn] adj (inf) porno ▷ n (inf) porno m; **pornographic** [pɔːnə'græfɪk] adj pornographique; **pornography** [pɔː'nɔgrəfɪ] n pornographie f

porridge ['pɔrɪdʒ] n porridge m

port [pɔːt] n (harbour) port m; (Naut: left side) bâbord m; (wine) porto m; (Comput) port m, accès m; **~ of call** (port d')escale f

portable ['pɔːtəbl] adj portatif(-ive)

porter ['pɔːtə^r] n (for luggage) porteur m; (doorkeeper) gardien n; portier m

portfolio [pɔːt'fəuliəu] n portefeuille m; (of artist) portfolio m

portion ['pɔːʃən] n portion f, part f

portrait ['pɔːtreɪt] n portrait m

portray [pɔː'treɪ] vt faire le portrait de; (in writing) dépeindre, représenter; (subj: actor) jouer

Portugal ['pɔːtjugl] n Portugal m

Portuguese [pɔːtju'giːz] adj portugais(e) ▷ n (pl inv) Portugais(e); (Ling) portugais m

pose [pəuz] n pose f ▷ vi poser; (pretend): **to ~ as** se faire passer pour ▷ vt poser; (problem) créer

posh [pɒʃ] adj (inf) chic inv

position [pə'zɪʃən] n position f; (job, situation) situation f ▷ vt mettre en place or en position

positive ['pɒzɪtɪv] adj positif(-ive); (certain) sûr(e), certain(e); (definite) formel(le), catégorique; **positively** adv (affirmatively, enthusiastically) de façon positive; (inf: really) carrément

possess [pə'zɛs] vt posséder; **possession** [pə'zɛʃən] n possession f; **possessions** npl (belongings) affaires fpl; **possessive** adj possessif(-ive)

possibility [pɒsɪ'bɪlɪtɪ] n possibilité f; (event) éventualité f

possible ['pɒsɪbl] adj possible; **as big as ~** aussi gros que possible; **possibly** adv (perhaps) peut-être; **I cannot possibly come** il m'est impossible de venir

post [pəust] n (BRIT: mail) poste f; (: letters, delivery) courrier m; (job, situation) poste m; (pole) poteau m ▷ vt (BRIT: send by post) poster; (: appoint): **to ~ to** affecter à; **where can I ~ these cards?** où est-ce que je peux poster ces cartes postales?; **postage** n tarifs mpl d'affranchissement; **postal** adj postal(e); **postal order** n mandat(-poste m) m; **postbox** n (BRIT) boîte f aux lettres (publique); **postcard** n carte postale; **postcode** n (BRIT) code postal

poster ['pəustə^r] n affiche f

postgraduate ['pəust'grædjuət] n = étudiant(e) de troisième cycle

postman ['pəustmən] (BRIT: irreg) n

facteur m

postmark ['pəʊstmɑːk] n cachet m (de la poste)

post-mortem [pəʊst'mɔːtəm] n autopsie f

post office n (building) poste f; (organization): **the Post Office** les postes fpl

postpone [pəs'pəʊn] vt remettre (à plus tard), reculer

posture ['pɒstʃə'] n posture f; (fig) attitude f

postwoman ['pəʊst'wʊmən] n (irreg) n factrice f

pot [pɒt] n (for cooking) marmite f; casserole f; (teapot) théière f; (for coffee) cafetière f; (for plants, jam) pot m; (inf: marijuana) herbe f ▷ vt (plant) mettre en pot; **to go to ~** (inf) aller à vau-l'eau

potato (pl **-es**) [pə'teɪtəʊ] n pomme f de terre; **potato peeler** n épluche-légumes m

potent ['pəʊtnt] adj puissant(e); (drink) fort(e), très alcoolisé(e); (man) viril

potential [pə'tenʃl] adj potentiel(le) ▷ n potentiel m

pothole ['pɒthəʊl] n (in road) nid m de poule; (BRIT: underground) gouffre m, caverne f

pot plant n plante f d'appartement

potter ['pɒtə'] n potier m ▷ vi (BRIT): to **~ around** or **about** bricoler; **pottery** n poterie f

potty ['pɒtɪ] n (child's) pot m

pouch [paʊtʃ] n (Zool) poche f; (for tobacco) blague f; (for money) bourse f

poultry ['pəʊltrɪ] n volaille f

pounce [paʊns] vi: **to ~ (on)** bondir (sur), fondre (sur)

pound [paʊnd] n livre f (weight = 453g, 16 ounces; money = 100 pence); (for dogs, cars) fourrière f ▷ vt (beat) bourrer de coups, marteler; (crush) piler, pulvériser ▷ vi (heart) battre violemment, taper; **pound sterling** n livre f sterling

pour [pɔː'] vt verser ▷ vi couler à flots; (rain) pleuvoir à verse; **to ~ sb a drink** verser or servir à boire à qn; **pour in**

vi (people) affluer, se précipiter; (news, letters) arriver en masse; **pour out** vi (people) sortir en masse ▷ vt vider; (fig) déverser; (serve: a drink) verser; **pouring** adj: **pouring rain** pluie torrentielle

pout [paʊt] vi faire la moue

poverty ['pɒvətɪ] n pauvreté f, misère f

powder ['paʊdə'] n poudre f ▷ vt poudrer; **powdered milk** n lait m en poudre

power ['paʊə'] n (strength, nation) puissance f, force f; (ability, Pol: of party, leader) pouvoir m; (of speech, thought) faculté f; (Elec) courant m; **to be in ~** être au pouvoir; **power cut** n (BRIT) coupure f de courant; **power failure** n panne f de courant; **powerful** adj puissant(e); (performance etc) très fort(e); **powerless** adj impuissant(e); **power point** n (BRIT) prise f de courant; **power station** n centrale f électrique

p.p. abbr (= per procurationem: by proxy) p.p.

PR n abbr = **public relations**

practical ['præktɪkl] adj pratique; **practical joke** n farce f; **practically** adv (almost) pratiquement

practice ['præktɪs] n pratique f; (of profession) exercice m; (at football etc) entraînement m; (business) cabinet m ▷ vt, vi (us) = **practise**; **in ~** (in reality) en pratique; **out of ~** rouillé(e)

practise (us **practice**) ['præktɪs] vt (work at: piano, backhand etc) s'exercer à, travailler; (train for: sport) s'entraîner à; (a sport, religion, method) pratiquer; (profession) exercer ▷ vi s'exercer, travailler; (train) s'entraîner; (lawyer, doctor) exercer; **practising** (us **practicing**) adj (Christian etc) pratiquant(e); (lawyer) en exercice

practitioner [præk'tɪʃənə'] n praticien(ne)

pragmatic [præg'mætɪk] adj pragmatique

prairie ['prɛərɪ] n savane f

praise [preɪz] n éloge(s) m(pl), louange(s) f(pl) ▷ vt louer, faire l'éloge de

pram [præm] n (BRIT) landau m, voiture f d'enfant

prank [præŋk] n farce f

prawn [prɔ:n] n crevette f (rose); **prawn cocktail** n cocktail m de crevettes

pray [preɪ] vi prier; **prayer** [preə^r] n prière f

preach [pri:tʃ] vi prêcher; **preacher** n prédicateur m; (us: clergyman) pasteur m

precarious [prɪ'kɛəriəs] adj précaire

precaution [prɪ'kɔ:ʃən] n précaution f

precede [prɪ'si:d] vt, vi précéder; **precedent** ['prɛsɪdənt] n précédent m; **preceding** [prɪ'si:dɪŋ] adj qui précède (or précédait)

precinct ['pri:sɪŋkt] n (us: district) circonscription f, arrondissement m; **pedestrian ~** (BRIT) zone piétonnière; **shopping ~** (BRIT) centre commercial

precious ['prɛʃəs] adj précieux(-euse)

precise [prɪ'saɪs] adj précis(e); **precisely** adv précisément

precision [prɪ'sɪʒən] n précision f

predator ['prɛdətə^r] n prédateur m, rapace m

predecessor ['pri:dɪsɛsə^r] n prédécesseur m

predicament [prɪ'dɪkəmənt] n situation f difficile

predict [prɪ'dɪkt] vt prédire; **predictable** adj prévisible; **prediction** [prɪ'dɪkʃən] n prédiction f

predominantly [prɪ'dɔmɪnəntlɪ] adv en majeure partie; (especially) surtout

preface ['prɛfəs] n préface f

prefect ['pri:fɛkt] n (BRIT: in school) élève chargé de certaines fonctions de discipline

prefer [prɪ'fə:^r] vt préférer; **preferable** ['prɛfrəbl] adj préférable; **preferably** ['prɛfrəblɪ] adv de préférence; **preference** ['prɛfrəns] n préférence f

prefix ['pri:fɪks] n préfixe m

pregnancy ['prɛgnənsɪ] n grossesse f

pregnant ['prɛgnənt] adj enceinte adj f, (animal) pleine

prehistoric ['pri:hɪs'tɔrɪk] adj

préhistorique

prejudice ['prɛdʒudɪs] n préjugé m; **prejudiced** adj (person) plein(e) de préjugés; (in a matter) partial(e)

preliminary [prɪ'lɪmɪnərɪ] adj préliminaire

prelude ['prɛlju:d] n prélude m

premature ['prɛmətʃuə] adj prématuré(e)

premier ['prɛmɪə^r] adj premier(-ière), principal(e) ▷ n (Pol: Prime Minister) premier ministre; (Pol: President) chef m de l'État

premiere ['prɛmɪɛə^r] n première f

Premier League n première division

premises ['prɛmɪsɪz] npl locaux mpl; **on the ~** sur les lieux; sur place

premium ['pri:mɪəm] n prime f; **to be at a ~** (fig: housing etc) être très demandé(e), être rarissime

premonition [prɛmə'nɪʃən] n prémonition f

preoccupied [pri:'ɔkjupaɪd] adj préoccupé(e)

prepaid [pri:'peɪd] adj payé(e) d'avance

preparation [prɛpə'reɪʃən] n préparation f; **preparations** npl (for trip, war) préparatifs mpl

preparatory school n école primaire privée; (us) lycée privé

prepare [prɪ'pɛə^r] vt préparer ▷ vi: **to ~ for** se préparer à

prepared [prɪ'pɛəd] adj: **~ for** préparé(e) à; **~ to** prêt(e) à

preposition [prɛpə'zɪʃən] n préposition f

prep school n = **preparatory school**

prerequisite [pri:'rɛkwɪzɪt] n condition f préalable

preschool [pri:'sku:l] adj préscolaire; (child) d'âge préscolaire

prescribe [prɪ'skraɪb] vt prescrire

prescription [prɪ'skrɪpʃən] n (Med) ordonnance f; (: medicine) médicament m (obtenu sur ordonnance); **could you write me a ~?** pouvez-vous me faire une ordonnance?

presence ['prɛzns] n présence f; **in**

sb's ~ en présence de qn; **~ of mind**
présence d'esprit

present ['preznt] *adj* présent(e);
(current) présent, actuel(le) ▷ *n* cadeau
m; *(actuality)* présent *m* ▷ *vt* [prɪ'zent]
présenter; *(prize, medal)* remettre;
(give): **to ~ sb with sth** offrir qch à
qn; **at ~** en ce moment; **to give sb a**
~ offrir un cadeau à qn; **presentable**
[prɪ'zentəbl] *adj* présentable;
presentation [prezn'teɪʃən] *n*
présentation *f*; *(ceremony)* remise *f* du
cadeau *(or de la médaille etc)*; **present-**
day *adj* contemporain(e); **presenter**
[prɪ'zentə*] *n* (BRIT Radio,
TV) présentateur(-trice); **presently**
adv (soon) tout à l'heure, bientôt; *(with*
verb in past) peu après; *(at present)* en ce
moment; **present participle**
[-'pɑːtɪsɪpl] *n* participe *m* présent
preservation [prezə'veɪʃən] *n*
préservation *f*, conservation *f*
preservative [prɪ'zəːvətɪv] *n* agent *m*
de conservation
preserve [prɪ'zəːv] *vt (keep safe)*
préserver, protéger; *(maintain)*
conserver, garder; *(food)* mettre en
conserve ▷ *n (for game, fish)* réserve *f*;
(often pl: jam) confiture *f*
preside [prɪ'zaɪd] *vi* présider
president ['prezɪdənt] *n* président(e);
presidential [prezɪ'denʃl] *adj*
présidentiel(le)
press [pres] *n (tool, machine, newspapers)*
presse *f*; *(for wine)* pressoir *m* ▷ *vt (push)*
appuyer sur; *(squeeze)* presser, serrer;
(clothes: iron) repasser; *(insist)*: **to ~**
sth on sb presser qn d'accepter qch; *(urge,*
entreat): **to ~ sb to do** *or* **into doing sth**
pousser qn à faire qch ▷ *vi* appuyer;
we are ~ed for time le temps nous
manque; **to ~ for sth** faire pression
pour obtenir qch; **press conference**
n conférence *f* de presse; **pressing** *adj*
urgent(e), pressant(e); **press stud** *n*
(BRIT) bouton-pression *m*; **press-up** *n*
(BRIT) traction *f*
pressure ['preʃə*] *n* pression *f*; *(stress)*

tension *f*; **to put ~ on sb (to do sth)**
faire pression sur qn (pour qu'il fasse
qch); **pressure cooker** *n* cocotte-
minute *f*; **pressure group** *n* groupe *m*
de pression
prestige [pres'tiːʒ] *n* prestige *m*
prestigious [pres'tɪdʒəs] *adj*
prestigieux(-euse)
presumably [prɪ'zjuːməblɪ] *adv*
vraisemblablement
presume [prɪ'zjuːm] *vt* présumer,
supposer
pretence (us **pretense**) [prɪ'tens] *n*
(claim) prétention *f*; **under false ~s**
sous de faux prétextes fallacieux
pretend [prɪ'tend] *vt (feign)* feindre,
simuler ▷ *vi (feign)* faire semblant
pretense [prɪ'tens] *n* (us) = **pretence**
pretentious [prɪ'tenʃəs] *adj*
prétentieux(-euse)
pretext ['priːtekst] *n* prétexte *m*
pretty ['prɪtɪ] *adj* joli(e) ▷ *adv* assez
prevail [prɪ'veɪl] *vi (win)* l'emporter,
prévaloir; *(be usual)* avoir cours;
prevailing *adj (widespread)* courant(e),
répandu(e); *(wind)* dominant(e)
prevalent ['prevələnt] *adj* répandu(e),
courant(e)
prevent [prɪ'vent] *vt*: **to ~ (from doing)**
empêcher (de faire); **prevention**
[prɪ'venʃən] *n* prévention *f*; **preventive**
adj préventif(-ive)
preview ['priːvjuː] *n (of film)* avant-
première *f*
previous ['priːvɪəs] *adj (last)*
précédent(e); *(earlier)* antérieur(e);
previously *adv* précédemment,
auparavant
prey [preɪ] *n* proie *f* ▷ *vi*: **to ~**
s'attaquer à; **it was ~ing on his mind**
ça le rongeait *or* minait
price [praɪs] *n* prix *m* ▷ *vt (goods)* fixer
le prix de; **priceless** *adj* sans prix,
inestimable; **price list** *n* tarif *m*
prick [prɪk] *n (sting)* piqûre *f* ▷ *vt*
piquer; **to ~ up one's ears** dresser *or*
tendre l'oreille
prickly ['prɪklɪ] *adj* piquant(e),

épineux(-euse); (fig: person) irritable
pride [praɪd] n fierté f; (pej) orgueil
m ▷ vt: **to ~ o.s. on** se flatter de;
s'enorgueillir de
priest [priːst] n prêtre m
primarily ['praɪmərɪlɪ] adv
principalement, essentiellement
primary ['praɪmərɪ] adj primaire;
(first in importance) premier(-ière),
primordial(e) ▷ n (us: election)
f) primaire; **primary school** (BRIT)
école f primaire
prime [praɪm] adj primordial(e),
fondamental(e); (excellent) excellent(e)
▷ vt (fig) mettre au courant ▷ n: **in the
~ of life** dans la fleur de l'âge; **Prime
Minister** n Premier ministre
primitive ['prɪmɪtɪv] adj primitif(-ive)
primrose ['prɪmrəuz] n primevère f
prince [prɪns] n prince m
princess [prɪn'sɛs] n princesse f
principal ['prɪnsɪpl] adj principal(e)
▷ n (head teacher) directeur m,
principal m; **principally** adv
principalement
principle ['prɪnsɪpl] n principe m; **in ~**
en principe, **on ~** par principe
print [prɪnt] n (mark) empreinte f;
(letters) caractères mpl; (fabric) imprimé
m; (Art) gravure f, estampe f; (Phot)
épreuve f ▷ vt imprimer; (publish)
publier; (write in capitals) écrire en
majuscules; **out of ~** épuisé(e); **print
out** vt (Comput) imprimer; **printer** n
(machine) imprimante f; (person)
imprimeur m; **printout** n (Comput)
sortie f imprimante
prior ['praɪə*] adj antérieur(e),
précédent(e); (more important)
prioritaire ▷ adv: **~ to doing** avant
de faire
priority [praɪ'ɔrɪtɪ] n priorité f; **to have
or take ~ over sth/sb** avoir la priorité
sur qch/qn
prison ['prɪzn] n prison f ▷ cpd
pénitentiaire; **prisoner** n
prisonnier(-ière); **prisoner of war** n
prisonnier(-ière) de guerre

pristine ['prɪstiːn] adj virginal(e)
privacy ['prɪvəsɪ] n intimité f, solitude f
private ['praɪvɪt] adj (not public)
privé(e); (personal) personnel(le);
(house, car, lesson) particulier(-ière);
(quiet: place) tranquille ▷ n soldat m
de deuxième classe; **"~"** (on envelope)
"personnelle"; (on door) "privé"; **in ~** en
privé; **privately** adv en privé; (within
oneself) intérieurement; **private
property** n propriété privée; **private
school** n école privée
privatize ['praɪvɪtaɪz] vt privatiser
privilege ['prɪvɪlɪdʒ] n privilège m
prize [praɪz] n prix m ▷ adj (example,
idiot) parfait(e); (bull, novel) primé(e)
▷ vt priser, faire grand cas de; **prize-
giving** n distribution f des prix;
prizewinner n gagnant(e)
pro [prəu] n (inf: Sport) professionnel(le)
▷ prep pro ...; **pros** npl: **the ~s and cons**
le pour et le contre
probability [prɔbə'bɪlɪtɪ] n probabilité
f; **in all ~** très probablement
probable ['prɔbəbl] adj probable
probably ['prɔbəblɪ] adv probablement
probation [prə'beɪʃən] n: **on ~**
(employee) à l'essai; (Law) en liberté
surveillée
probe [prəub] n (Med, Space) sonde f;
(enquiry) enquête f, investigation f ▷ vt
sonder, explorer
problem ['prɔbləm] n problème m
procedure [prə'siːdʒə*] n (Admin, Law)
procédure f; (method) marche f à suivre,
façon f de procéder
proceed [prə'siːd] vi (go forward)
avancer; (act) procéder; (continue): **to ~
(with)** continuer, poursuivre; **to ~ to
do** se mettre à faire; **proceedings** npl
(measures) mesures fpl; (Law: against
sb) poursuites fpl; (meeting) réunion
f, séance f; (records) compte rendu;
actes mpl; **proceeds** ['prəusiːdz] npl
produit m, recette f
process ['prəusɛs] n processus m;
(method) procédé m ▷ vt traiter
procession [prə'sɛʃən] n défilé m,

cortège m; **funeral ~** (on foot) cortège funèbre; (in cars) convoi m mortuaire
proclaim [prəˈkleɪm] vt déclarer, proclamer
prod [prɒd] vt pousser
produce n [ˈprɒdjuːs] (Agr) produits mpl ▷ vt [prəˈdjuːs] produire; (show) présenter; (cause) provoquer, causer; (Theat) monter, mettre en scène; (TV: programme) réaliser; (: play, film) mettre en scène; (Radio: programme) réaliser; (: play) mettre en ondes; **producer** n (Theat) metteur m en scène; (Agr, Comm, Cine) producteur m; (TV: of programme) réalisateur m; (: of play, film) metteur m en scène; (Radio: of programme) réalisateur m; (: of play) metteur m en ondes
product [ˈprɒdʌkt] n produit m; production [prəˈdʌkʃən] n production f; (Theat) mise f en scène; **productive** [prəˈdʌktɪv] adj productif(-ive); **productivity** [prɒdʌkˈtɪvɪtɪ] n productivité f
Prof. [prɒf] abbr (= professor) Prof
profession [prəˈfɛʃən] n profession f; **professional** n professionnel(le) ▷ adj professionnel(le); (work) de professionnel
professor [prəˈfɛsəʳ] n professeur m (titulaire d'une chaire); (us: teacher) professeur m
profile [ˈprəʊfaɪl] n profil m
profit [ˈprɒfɪt] n (from trading) bénéfice m; (advantage) profit m ▷ vi: **to ~ (by or from)** profiter (de); **profitable** adj lucratif(-ive), rentable
profound [prəˈfaʊnd] adj profond(e)
programme (us **program**) [ˈprəʊɡræm] n (Comput: also BRIT: **program**) programme m; (Radio, TV) émission f ▷ vt programmer; **programmer** (us **programer**) n programmeur(-euse); **programming** (us **programing**) n programmation f
progress n [ˈprəʊɡrɛs] progrès m(pl) ▷ vi [prəˈɡrɛs] progresser, avancer; **in ~** en cours; **progressive** [prəˈɡrɛsɪv] adj progressif(-ive); (person) progressiste

prohibit [prəˈhɪbɪt] vt interdire, défendre
project n [ˈprɒdʒɛkt] (plan) projet m, plan m; (venture) opération f, entreprise f; (Scol: research) étude f, dossier m ▷ vb [prəˈdʒɛkt] vt projeter ▷ vi (stick out) faire saillie, s'avancer; **projection** [prəˈdʒɛkʃən] n projection f; (overhang) saillie f; **projector** [prəˈdʒɛktəʳ] n projecteur m
prolific [prəˈlɪfɪk] adj prolifique
prolong [prəˈlɒŋ] vt prolonger
prom [prɒm] n abbr = **promenade** (us: ball) bal m d'étudiants; **the P~s** série de concerts de musique classique; voir encadré

● **PROM**

En Grande-Bretagne, un **promenade concert** ou **prom** est un concert de musique classique, ainsi appelé car, à l'origine, le public restait debout et se promenait au lieu de rester assis. De nos jours, une partie du public reste debout, mais il y a également des places assises (plus chères). Les **Proms** les plus connus sont les Proms londoniens. La dernière séance (le "Last Night of the Proms") est un grand événement médiatique où se jouent des airs traditionnels et patriotiques. Aux États-Unis et au Canada, le **prom** ou **promenade** est un bal organisé par le lycée.

promenade [prɒməˈnɑːd] n (by sea) esplanade f, promenade f
prominent [ˈprɒmɪnənt] adj (standing out) proéminent(e); (important) important(e)
promiscuous [prəˈmɪskjuəs] adj (sexually) de mœurs légères
promise [ˈprɒmɪs] n promesse f ▷ vt, vi promettre; **promising** adj prometteur(-euse)
promote [prəˈməʊt] vt promouvoir; (new product) lancer; **promotion**

[prə'məuʃən] n promotion f

prompt [prɒmpt] adj rapide ▷ n (Comput) message m (de guidage) ▷ vt (cause) entraîner, provoquer; (Theat) souffler (son rôle or ses répliques) à; **at 8 o'clock -** à 8 heures précises; **to - sb to do** inciter or pousser qn à faire; **promptly** adv rapidement, sans délai; (on time) ponctuellement

prone [prəun] adj (lying) couché(e) (face contre terre); (liable): **- to** enclin(e) à

prong [prɒŋ] n (of fork) dent f

pronoun ['prəunaun] n pronom m

pronounce [prə'nauns] vt prononcer; **how do you - it?** comment est-ce que ça se prononce?

pronunciation [prənʌnsɪ'eɪʃən] n prononciation f

proof [pruːf] n preuve f ▷ adj: **- against** à l'épreuve de

prop [prɒp] n support m, étai m; (fig) soutien m ▷ vt (also: **- up**) étayer, soutenir; **props** npl accessoires mpl

propaganda [prɒpə'gændə] n propagande f

propeller [prə'pelər] n hélice f

proper ['prɒpər] adj (suited, right) approprié(e), bon (bonne); (seemly) correct(e), convenable; (authentic) vrai(e), véritable; (referring to place): **the village -** le village proprement dit; **properly** adv correctement, convenablement; **proper noun** n nom m propre

property ['prɒpətɪ] n (possessions) biens mpl; (house etc) propriété f; (land) terres fpl, domaine m

prophecy ['prɒfɪsɪ] n prophétie f

prophet ['prɒfɪt] n prophète m

proportion [prə'pɔːʃən] n proportion f; (share) part f; partie f; **proportions** npl (size) dimensions fpl; **proportional, proportionate** adj proportionnel(le)

proposal [prə'pəuzl] n proposition f, offre f; (plan) projet m; (of marriage) demande f en mariage

propose [prə'pəuz] vt proposer, suggérer ▷ vi faire sa demande en

mariage; **to - to do** avoir l'intention de faire

proposition [prɒpə'zɪʃən] n proposition f

proprietor [prə'praɪətər] n propriétaire m/f

prose [prəuz] n prose f; (Scol: translation) thème m

prosecute ['prɒsɪkjuːt] vt poursuivre; **prosecution** [prɒsɪ'kjuːʃən] n poursuites fpl judiciaires; (accusing side: in criminal case) accusation f; (: in civil case) la partie plaignante; **prosecutor** n (lawyer) procureur m; (us: **public prosecutor**) ministère public; (us: plaintiff) plaignant(e)

prospect n ['prɒspekt] perspective f; (hope) espoir m, chances fpl ▷ vt, vi [prə'spekt] prospecter; **prospects** npl (for work etc) possibilités f d'avenir, débouchés mpl; **prospective** [prə'spektɪv] adj (possible) éventuel(le); (future) futur(e)

prospectus [prə'spektəs] n prospectus m

prosper ['prɒspər] vi prospérer; **prosperity** [prɒ'sperɪtɪ] n prospérité f; **prosperous** adj prospère

prostitute ['prɒstɪtjuːt] n prostituée f; **male -** prostitué m

protect [prə'tekt] vt protéger; **protection** [prə'tekʃən] n protection f; **protective** adj protecteur(-trice); (clothing) de protection

protein ['prəutiːn] n protéine f

protest n ['prəutest] protestation f ▷ vb [prə'test] ▷ vi: **to - against/ about** protester contre/à propos de; **to - (that)** protester que

Protestant ['prɒtɪstənt] adj, n protestant(e)

protester, protestor [prə'testər] n (in demonstration) manifestant(e)

protractor [prə'træktər] n (Geom) rapporteur m

proud [praud] adj fier(-ère); (pej) orgueilleux(-euse)

prove [pruːv] vt prouver, démontrer

▷ *vi*: **to ~ correct** *etc* s'avérer juste *etc*; **to ~ o.s.** montrer ce dont on est capable

proverb ['prɒvɜːb] *n* proverbe *m*

provide [prə'vaɪd] *vt* fournir; **to ~ sb with sth** fournir qch à qn; **provide** for *vt fus* (*person*) subvenir aux besoins de; (*future event*) prévoir; **provided** *conj*: **provided (that)** à condition que + *sub*; **providing** [prə'vaɪdɪŋ] *conj* à condition que + *sub*

province ['prɒvɪns] *n* province *f*; (*fig*) domaine *m*; **provincial** [prə'vɪnʃəl] *adj* provincial(e)

provision [prə'vɪʒən] *n* (*supplying*) fourniture *f*; approvisionnement *m*; (*stipulation*) disposition *f*; **provisions** *npl* (*food*) provisions *fpl*; **provisional** *adj* provisoire

provocative [prə'vɒkətɪv] *adj* provocateur(-trice), provocant(e)

provoke [prə'vəʊk] *vt* provoquer

prowl [praʊl] *vi* (*also*: **~ about, ~ around**) rôder

proximity [prɒk'sɪmɪtɪ] *n* proximité *f*

proxy ['prɒksɪ] *n*: **by ~** par procuration

prudent ['pruːdnt] *adj* prudent(e)

prune [pruːn] *n* pruneau *m* ▷ *vt* élaguer

pry [praɪ] *vi*: **to ~ into** fourrer son nez dans

PS *n abbr* (= *postscript*) PS *m*

pseudonym ['sjuːdənɪm] *n* pseudonyme *m*

PSHE *n abbr* (BRIT: Scol: = *personal, social and health education*) cours d'éducation personnelle, sanitaire et sociale préparant à la vie adulte

psychiatric [saɪkɪ'ætrɪk] *adj* psychiatrique

psychiatrist [saɪ'kaɪətrɪst] *n* psychiatre *m/f*

psychic ['saɪkɪk] *adj* (*also*: **~al**) (méta)psychique; (*person*) doué(e) de télépathie ou d'un sixième sens

psychoanalysis (*pl* **-ses**) [saɪkəʊə'nælɪsɪs, -siːz] *n* psychanalyse *f*

psychological [saɪkə'lɒdʒɪkl] *adj* psychologique

psychologist [saɪ'kɒlədʒɪst] *n* psychologue *m/f*

psychology [saɪ'kɒlədʒɪ] *n* psychologie *f*

psychotherapy [saɪkəʊ'θerəpɪ] *n* psychothérapie *f*

pt *abbr* = **pint(s)**; **point(s)**

PTO *abbr* (= *please turn over*) TSVP

pub [pʌb] *n abbr* (= *public house*) pub *m*

puberty ['pjuːbətɪ] *n* puberté *f*

public ['pʌblɪk] *adj* public(-ique) ▷ *n* public *m*; **in ~** en public; **to make ~** rendre public

publication [pʌblɪ'keɪʃən] *n* publication *f*

public: **public company** *n* société *f* anonyme; **public convenience** *n* (BRIT) toilettes *fpl*; **public holiday** *n* (BRIT) jour férié; **public house** *n* (BRIT) pub *m*

publicity [pʌb'lɪsɪtɪ] *n* publicité *f*

publicize ['pʌblɪsaɪz] *vt* (*make known*) faire connaître, rendre public; (*advertise*) faire de la publicité pour

public: **public limited company** *n* = société *f* anonyme (SA) (cotée en Bourse); **publicly** *adv* publiquement, en public; **public opinion** *n* opinion publique; **public relations** *n or npl* relations publiques (RP); **public school** *n* (BRIT) école privée; (US) école publique; **public transport** (US **public transportation**) *n* transports *mpl* en commun

publish ['pʌblɪʃ] *vt* publier; **publisher** *n* éditeur *m*; **publishing** *n* (*industry*) édition *f*

pub lunch *n* repas *m* de bistrot

pudding ['pʊdɪŋ] *n* (BRIT: *dessert*) dessert *m*, entremets *m*; (*sweet dish*) pudding *m*, gâteau *m*

puddle ['pʌdl] *n* flaque *f* d'eau

puff [pʌf] *n* bouffée *f* ▷ *vt*: **to ~ out**: sails, cheeks) gonfler ▷ *vi* (*pant*) haleter; **puff pastry** (US **puff paste**) *n* pâte feuilletée

pull [pʊl] *n* (*tug*): **to give sth a ~** tirer sur qch ▷ *vt* tirer; (*trigger*) presser;

(strain: muscle, tendon) se claquer ▷ vi tirer; **to ~ to pieces** mettre en morceaux; **to ~ one's punches** (also fig) ménager son adversaire; **to ~ one's weight** y mettre du sien (fig); **to ~ o.s. together** se ressaisir; **to ~ sb's leg** (fig) faire marcher qn; **pull apart** vt (break) mettre en pièces, démantibuler; **pull away** vi (vehicle: move off) partir; (draw back) s'éloigner; **pull back** vt (lever etc) tirer sur; (curtains) ouvrir ▷ vi (refrain) s'abstenir; (Mil: withdraw) se retirer; **pull down** vt baisser, abaisser; (house) démolir; **pull in** vi (car) entrer en gare; **pull off** vt enlever, ôter; (deal etc) conclure; **pull out** vi démarrer, partir; (Aut: come out of line) déboîter ▷ vt (from bag, pocket) sortir; (remove) arracher; **pull over** vi (Aut) se ranger; **pull up** vi (stop) s'arrêter ▷ vt remonter; (uproot) déraciner, arracher

pulley ['pʊlɪ] n poulie f

pullover ['pʊləʊvə*] n pull-over m, tricot m

pulp [pʌlp] n (of fruit) pulpe f; (for paper) pâte f à papier

pulpit ['pʊlpɪt] n chaire f

pulse [pʌls] n (of blood) pouls m; (of heart) battement m; **pulses** npl (Culin) légumineuses fpl

puma ['pju:mə] n puma m

pump [pʌmp] n pompe f; (shoe) escarpin m ▷ vt pomper; **pump up** vt gonfler

pumpkin ['pʌmpkɪn] n potiron m, citrouille f

pun [pʌn] n jeu m de mots, calembour m

punch [pʌntʃ] n (blow) coup m de poing; (tool) poinçon m; (drink) punch m ▷ vt (make a hole in) poinçonner, perforer; (hit): **to ~ sb/sth** donner un coup de poing à qn/sur qch; **punch-up** n (BRIT inf) bagarre f

punctual ['pʌŋktjuəl] adj ponctuel(le)

punctuation [pʌŋktju'eɪʃən] n ponctuation f

puncture ['pʌŋktʃə*] n (BRIT) crevaison f ▷ vt crever

punish ['pʌnɪʃ] vt punir; **punishment** n punition f, châtiment m

punk [pʌŋk] n (person: also: **~ rocker**) punk m/f; (music: also: **~ rock**) le punk; (us inf: hoodlum) voyou m

pup [pʌp] n chiot m

pupil ['pju:pl] n élève m/f; (of eye) pupille f

puppet ['pʌpɪt] n marionnette f, pantin m

puppy ['pʌpɪ] n chiot m, petit chien

purchase ['pə:tʃɪs] n achat m ▷ vt acheter

pure [pjʊə*] adj pur(e); **purely** adv purement

purify ['pjʊərɪfaɪ] vt purifier, épurer

purity ['pjʊərɪtɪ] n pureté f

purple ['pə:pl] adj violet(te); (face) cramoisi(e)

purpose ['pə:pəs] n intention f, but m; **on ~** exprès

purr [pə:*] vi ronronner

purse [pə:s] n (BRIT: for money) porte-monnaie m inv; (us: handbag) sac m (à main) ▷ vt serrer, pincer

pursue [pə'sju:] vt poursuivre

pursuit [pə'sju:t] n poursuite f; (occupation) occupation f, activité f

pus [pʌs] n pus m

push [pʊʃ] n poussée f ▷ vt pousser; (button) appuyer sur; (fig: product) mettre en avant, faire de la publicité pour ▷ vi pousser; **to ~ for** (better pay, conditions) réclamer; **push in** vi s'introduire de force; **push off** vi (inf) filer, ficher le camp; **push on** vi (continue) continuer; **push over** vt renverser; **push through** vi (in crowd) se frayer un chemin; **pushchair** n (BRIT) poussette f; **pusher** n (also: **drug pusher**) revendeur(-euse) (de drogue), ravitailleur(-euse) (en drogue); **push-up** n (us) traction f

pussy(-cat) ['pʊsɪ-] n (inf) minet m

put [pʊt, pt, pp] vt mettre; (place) poser, placer; (say) dire, exprimer; (a question) poser; (case, view) exposer, présenter; (estimate) estimer; **put**

aside vt mettre de côté; **put away**
vt (store) ranger; **put back** vt (replace)
remettre, replacer; (postpone) remettre;
put by vt (money) mettre de côté,
économiser; **put down** vt (parcel etc)
poser, déposer; (in writing) mettre
par écrit, inscrire; (suppress: revolt
etc) réprimer, écraser; (attribute)
attribuer; (animal) abattre; (cat, dog)
faire piquer; **put forward** vt (ideas)
avancer, proposer; **put in** vt (complaint)
soumettre; (time, effort) consacrer; **put
off** vt (postpone) remettre à plus tard,
ajourner; (discourage) dissuader; **put
on** vt (clothes, lipstick, CD) mettre; (light
etc) allumer; (play etc) monter; (weight)
prendre; (assume: accent, manner)
prendre; **put out** vt (take outside)
mettre dehors; (one's hand) tendre; (light
etc) éteindre; (person: inconvenience)
déranger, gêner; **put through** vt (Tel:
caller) mettre en communication;
(: call) passer; (plan) faire accepter;
put together vt mettre ensemble;
(assemble: furniture) monter, assembler;
(meal) préparer; **put up** vt (raise) lever,
relever, remonter; (hang) accrocher;
(build) construire, ériger; (increase)
augmenter; (accommodate) loger; **put
up with** vt fus supporter

putt [pʌt] n putt m; **putting green**
n green m

puzzle ['pʌzl] n énigme f, mystère m;
(game) jeu m, casse-tête m; (jigsaw)
puzzle m; (also: **crossword ~**) mots
croisés ▷ vt intriguer, rendre perplexe
▷ vi: **to ~ over** chercher à comprendre;
puzzled adj perplexe; **puzzling** adj
déconcertant(e), inexplicable

pyjamas [pɪ'dʒɑːməz] npl (BRIT)
pyjama m s

pylon ['paɪlən] n pylône m

pyramid ['pɪrəmɪd] n pyramide f

Pyrenees [pɪrə'niːz] npl Pyrénées fpl

q

quack [kwæk] n (of duck) coin-coin m
inv; (pej: doctor) charlatan m

quadruple [kwɔ'druːpl] vt, vi
quadrupler

quail [kweɪl] n (Zool) caille f ▷ vi: **to ~ at**
or **before** reculer devant

quaint [kweɪnt] adj bizarre; (old-
fashioned) désuet(-ète); (picturesque) au
charme vieillot, pittoresque

quake [kweɪk] vi trembler ▷ n abbr
= **earthquake**

qualification [kwɔlɪfɪ'keɪʃən]
n (often pl: degree etc) diplôme m;
(training) qualification(s) f(pl); (ability)
compétence(s) f(pl); (limitation) réserve
f, restriction f

qualified ['kwɔlɪfaɪd] adj (trained)
qualifié(e); (professionally) diplômé(e);
(fit, competent) compétent(e),
qualifié(e); (limited) conditionnel(le)

qualify ['kwɔlɪfaɪ] vt qualifier; (modify)
atténuer, nuancer ▷ vi: **to ~ (as)**
obtenir son diplôme (de); **to ~ (for)**
remplir les conditions requises (pour)

(Sport) se qualifier (pour)

quality ['kwɔlɪtɪ] n qualité f

qualm [kwɑ:m] n doute m; scrupule m

quantify ['kwɔntɪfaɪ] vt quantifier

quantity ['kwɔntɪtɪ] n quantité f

quarantine ['kwɔrnti:n] n
quarantaine f

quarrel ['kwɔrl] n querelle f, dispute f
▷ vi se disputer, se quereller

quarry ['kwɔrɪ] n (for stone) carrière f;
(animal) proie f, gibier m

quart [kwɔ:t] n ≈ litre m

quarter ['kwɔ:tə'] n quart m; (of year)
trimestre m; (district) quartier m;
(US, CANADA: 25 cents) (pièce f de) vingt-cinq
cents m ▷ vt partager en quartiers ou
en quatre; (Mil) caserner, cantonner;
quarters npl logement m; (Mil)
quartiers mpl, cantonnement m; **a ~
of an hour** un quart d'heure; **quarter
final** n quart m de finale; **quarterly** adj
trimestriel(le) ▷ adv tous les trois mois

quartet(te) [kwɔ:'tet] n quatuor m;
(jazz players) quartette m

quartz [kwɔ:ts] n quartz m

quay [ki:] n (also: ~side) quai m

queasy ['kwi:zɪ] adj: **to feel ~** avoir
mal au cœur

Quebec [kwɪ'bek] n (city) Québec;
(province) Québec m

queen [kwi:n] n (gen) reine f; (Cards
etc) dame f

queer [kwɪə'] adj étrange,
curieux(-euse); (suspicious) louche ▷ n
(inf: highly offensive) homosexuel m

quench [kwentʃ] vt: **to ~ one's thirst**
se désaltérer

query ['kwɪərɪ] n question f ▷ vt
(disagree with, dispute) mettre en doute,
questionner

quest [kwest] n recherche f, quête f

question ['kwestʃən] n question f ▷ vt
(person) interroger; (plan, idea) mettre
en question ou en doute; **beyond**
~ sans aucun doute; **out of the**
~ hors de question; **questionable** adj
discutable; **question mark** n point
m d'interrogation; **questionnaire**

[kwestʃə'neə'] n questionnaire m

queue [kju:] n (BRIT) queue f, file f ▷ vi
(also: **~ up**) faire la queue

quiche [ki:ʃ] n quiche f

quick [kwɪk] adj rapide; (mind) vif
(vive); (agile) agile, vif (vive) ▷ n: **cut
to the ~** (fig) touché(e) au vif; **be ~!**
dépêche-toi!; **quickly** adv (fast) vite,
rapidement; (immediately) tout de suite

quid [kwɪd] n (pl inv: BRIT inf) livre f

quiet ['kwaɪət] adj tranquille,
calme; (voice) bas(se); (ceremony,
colour) discret(-ète) ▷ n tranquillité
f, calme m; (silence) silence m;
quietly adv tranquillement;
(silently) silencieusement; (discreetly)
discrètement

quilt [kwɪlt] n édredon m; (continental
quilt) couette f

quirky ['kwɜ:kɪ] adj singulier(-ère)

quit [kwɪt] (pt, pp ~ or ~**ted**) vt quitter
▷ vi (give up) abandonner, renoncer;
(resign) démissionner

quite [kwaɪt] adv (rather) assez, plutôt;
(entirely) complètement, tout à fait;
~ a few of them un assez grand
nombre d'entre eux; **that's not ~ right**
ce n'est pas tout à fait juste; **~ (so!)**
exactement!

quits [kwɪts] adj: **~ (with)** quitte
(envers); **let's call it ~** restons-en là

quiver ['kwɪvə'] vi trembler, frémir

quiz [kwɪz] n (on TV) jeu-concours m
(télévisé); (in magazine etc) test m de
connaissances ▷ vt interroger

quota ['kwəʊtə] n quota m

quotation [kwəʊ'teɪʃən] n citation f;
(estimate) devis m; **quotation marks**
npl guillemets mpl

quote [kwəʊt] n citation f; (estimate)
devis m ▷ vt (sentence, author) citer;
(price) donner, soumettre ▷ vi: **to**
~ from citer; **quotes** npl (inverted
commas) guillemets mpl

r

Rabat [rə'bɑːt] n Rabat
rabbi ['ræbaɪ] n rabbin m
rabbit ['ræbɪt] n lapin m
rabies ['reɪbiːz] n rage f
RAC n abbr (BRIT: = Royal Automobile Club) ≈ ACF m
rac(c)oon [rə'kuːn] n raton m laveur
race [reɪs] n (species) race f; (competition, rush) course f ▷ vt (person) faire la course avec ▷ vi (compete) faire la course, courir; (pulse) battre très vite; **race car** n (US) = **racing car**; **racecourse** n champ m de courses; **racehorse** n cheval m de course; **racetrack** n piste f
racial ['reɪʃl] adj racial(e)
racing ['reɪsɪŋ] n courses fpl; **racing car** n (BRIT) voiture f de course; **racing driver** n (BRIT) pilote m de course
racism ['reɪsɪzəm] n racisme m; **racist** ['reɪsɪst] adj, n raciste m/f
rack [ræk] n (for guns, tools) râtelier m; (for clothes) portant m; (for bottles) casier m; (also: **luggage ~**) filet m à bagages;

(also: **roof ~**) galerie f; (also: **dish ~**) égouttoir m ▷ vt tourmenter; **to ~ one's brains** se creuser la cervelle
racket ['rækɪt] n (for tennis) raquette f; (noise) tapage m, vacarme m; (swindle) escroquerie f
racquet ['rækɪt] n raquette f
radar ['reɪdɑː'] n radar m
radiation [reɪdɪ'eɪʃən] n rayonnement m; (radioactive) radiation f
radiator ['reɪdɪeɪtə'] n radiateur m
radical ['rædɪkl] adj radical(e)
radio ['reɪdɪəu] n radio f ▷ vt (person) appeler par radio; **on the ~** à la radio; **radioactive** adj radioactif(-ive); **radio station** n station f de radio
radish ['rædɪʃ] n radis m
RAF n abbr (BRIT) = **Royal Air Force**
raffle ['ræfl] n tombola f
raft [rɑːft] n (craft: also: **life ~**) radeau m; (logs) train m de flottage
rag [ræg] n chiffon m; (pej: newspaper) feuille f, torchon m; (for charity) attractions organisées par les étudiants au profit d'œuvres de charité; **rags** npl haillons mpl
rage [reɪdʒ] n (fury) rage f, fureur f ▷ vi (person) être fou (folle) de rage; (storm) faire rage, être déchaîné(e); **it's all the ~** cela fait fureur
ragged ['rægɪd] adj (edge) inégal(e), qui accroche; (clothes) en loques; (appearance) déguenillé(e)
raid [reɪd] n (Mil) raid m; (criminal) hold-up m inv; (by police) descente f, rafle f ▷ vt faire un raid sur ou un hold-up dans ou une descente dans
rail [reɪl] n (on stair) rampe f; (on bridge, balcony) balustrade f; (of ship) bastingage m; (for train) rail m; **railcard** n (BRIT) carte f de chemin de fer; **railing(s)** n(pl) grille f; **railway** (US **railroad**) n chemin m de fer; (track) voie ferrée f; **railway line** n (BRIT) ligne f de chemin de fer; (track) voie ferrée; **railway station** n (BRIT) gare f
rain [reɪn] n pluie f ▷ vi pleuvoir; **in the ~** sous la pluie; **it's ~ing** il pleut;

rainbow n arc-en-ciel m; **raincoat** n imperméable m; **raindrop** n goutte f de pluie; **rainfall** n chute f de pluie; (measurement) hauteur f des précipitations; **rainforest** n forêt tropicale; **rainy** adj pluvieux(-euse)

raise [reɪz] n augmentation f ▷ vt (lift) lever; hausser; (increase) augmenter; (morale) remonter; (standards) améliorer; (a protest, doubt) provoquer, causer; (a question) soulever; (cattle, family) élever; (crop) faire pousser; (army, funds) rassembler; (loan) obtenir; **to ~ one's voice** élever la voix

raisin ['reɪzn] n raisin sec

rake [reɪk] n (tool) râteau m; (person) débauché m ▷ vt (garden) ratisser

rally ['rælɪ] n (Pol etc) meeting m, rassemblement m; (Aut) rallye m; (Tennis) échange m ▷ vt rassembler, rallier; (support) gagner ▷ vi (sick person) aller mieux; (Stock Exchange) reprendre

RAM [ræm] n abbr (Comput: = random access memory) mémoire vive

ram [ræm] n bélier m ▷ vt (push) enfoncer; (crash into: vehicle) emboutir; (: lamppost etc) percuter

Ramadan [ræmə'dæn] n Ramadan m

ramble ['ræmbl] n randonnée f ▷ vi (walk) se promener, faire une randonnée; (pej: also: **~ on**) discourir, pérorer; **rambler** n promeneur(-euse), randonneur(-euse); **rambling** adj (speech) décousu(e); (house) plein(e) de coins et de recoins; (Bot) grimpant(e)

ramp [ræmp] n (incline) rampe f; (Aut) dénivellation f; (in garage) pont m; **on/off~** (us Aut) bretelle f d'accès

rampage [ræm'peɪdʒ] n: **to be on the ~** se déchaîner

ran [ræn] pt of **run**

ranch [rɑːntʃ] n ranch m

random ['rændəm] adj fait(e) or établi(e) au hasard; (Comput, Math) aléatoire ▷ n: **at ~** au hasard

rang [ræŋ] pt of **ring**

range [reɪndʒ] n (of mountains) chaîne f; (of missile, voice) portée f; (of products)

choix m, gamme f; (also: **shooting ~**) champ m de tir; (also: **kitchen ~**) fourneau m (de cuisine) ▷ vt (place) mettre en rang, placer ▷ vi: **to ~ over** couvrir; **to ~ from ... to** aller de ... à

ranger ['reɪndʒər] n garde m forestier

rank [ræŋk] n rang m; (Mil) grade m; (BRIT: also: **taxi ~**) station f de taxis ▷ vi: **to ~ among** compter or se classer parmi ▷ adj (smell) nauséabond(e); **the ~ and file** (fig) la masse, la base

ransom ['rænsəm] n rançon f; **to hold sb to ~** (fig) exercer un chantage sur qn

rant [rænt] vi fulminer

rap [ræp] n (music) rap m ▷ vt (door) frapper sur or à; (table etc) taper sur

rape [reɪp] n viol m; (Bot) colza m ▷ vt violer

rapid ['ræpɪd] adj rapide; **rapidly** adv rapidement; **rapids** npl (Geo) rapides mpl

rapist ['reɪpɪst] n auteur m d'un viol

rapport [ræ'pɔːr] n entente f

rare [reər] adj rare; (Culin: steak) saignant(e); **rarely** adv rarement

rash [ræʃ] adj imprudent(e), irréfléchi(e) ▷ n (Med) rougeur f, éruption f; (of events) série f (noire)

rasher ['ræʃər] n fine tranche (de lard)

raspberry ['rɑːzbərɪ] n framboise f

rat [ræt] n rat m

rate [reɪt] n (ratio) taux m, pourcentage m; (speed) vitesse f, rythme m; (price) tarif m ▷ vt (price) évaluer, estimer; (people) classer; **rates** npl (BRIT: property tax) impôts locaux; **to ~ sb/sth as** considérer qn/qch comme

rather ['rɑːðər] adv (somewhat) assez, plutôt; (to some extent) un peu; **it's ~ expensive** c'est assez cher; (too much) c'est un peu cher; **there's ~ a lot** il y en a beaucoup; **I would** or **I'd ~ go** j'aimerais mieux or je préférerais partir; **or ~** (more accurately) ou plutôt

rating ['reɪtɪŋ] n (assessment) évaluation f; (score) classement m; (Finance) cote f; **ratings** npl (Radio) indice(s) m(pl) d'écoute; (TV) Audimat®

ratio ['reɪʃɪəʊ] n proportion f: **in the ~ of 100 to 1** dans la proportion de 100 contre 1

ration ['ræʃən] n ration f ▷ vt rationner; **rations** npl (food) vivres mpl

rational ['ræʃənl] adj raisonnable, sensé(e); (solution, reasoning) logique; (Med: person) rationnel

rat race n foire f d'empoigne

rattle ['rætl] n (of door, window) battement m; (of coins, chain) cliquetis m; (of train, engine) bruit m de ferraille; (for baby) hochet m ▷ vi cliqueter; (car, bus): **to ~ along** rouler en faisant un bruit de ferraille ▷ vt agiter (bruyamment); (inf: disconcert) décontenancer

rave [reɪv] vi (in anger) s'emporter; (with enthusiasm) s'extasier; (Med) délirer ▷ n (inf: party) rave f, soirée f techno

raven ['reɪvən] n grand corbeau

ravine [rə'vi:n] n ravin m

raw [rɔ:] adj (uncooked) cru(e); (not processed) brut(e); (sore) à vif, irrité(e); (inexperienced) inexpérimenté(e); **~ materials** matières premières

ray [reɪ] n rayon m; **~ of hope** lueur f d'espoir

razor ['reɪzə'] n rasoir m; **razor blade** n lame f de rasoir

Rd abbr = **road**

RE n abbr (BRIT) = **religious education**

re [ri:] prep concernant

reach [ri:tʃ] n portée f, atteinte f; (of river etc) étendue f ▷ vt atteindre, arriver à; (conclusion, decision) parvenir à ▷ vi s'étendre; **out of/within ~** (object) hors de/à portée; **reach out** vt tendre ▷ vi: **to ~ out (for)** allonger le bras (pour prendre)

react [ri:'ækt] vi réagir; **reaction** [ri:'ækʃən] n réaction f; **reactor** [ri:'æktə'] n réacteur m

read (pt, pp ~) [ri:d, rɛd] vi lire ▷ vt lire; (understand) comprendre, interpréter; (study) étudier; (meter) relever; (subj: instrument etc) indiquer, marquer; **read out** vt lire à haute voix; **reader** n

lecteur(-trice)

readily ['rɛdɪlɪ] adv volontiers, avec empressement; (easily) facilement

reading ['ri:dɪŋ] n lecture f; (understanding) interprétation f; (on instrument) indications fpl

ready ['rɛdɪ] adj prêt(e); (willing) prêt, disposé(e); (available) disponible ▷ n: **at the ~** (Mil) prêt à faire feu; **when will my photos be ~?** quand est-ce que mes photos seront prêtes?; **to get ~** (as vi) se préparer; (as vt) préparer; **ready-cooked** adj précuit(e); **ready-made** adj tout(e) fait(e)

real [rɪəl] adj (world, life) réel(le); (genuine) véritable; (proper) vrai(e) ▷ adv (us inf: very) vraiment; **real ale** n bière traditionnelle; **real estate** n biens fonciers ou immobiliers; **realistic** [rɪə'lɪstɪk] adj réaliste; **reality** [ri:'ælɪtɪ] n réalité f

reality TV n téléréalité f

realization [rɪəlaɪ'zeɪʃən] n (awareness) prise f de conscience; (fulfilment: also: of asset) réalisation f

realize ['rɪəlaɪz] vt (understand) se rendre compte de, prendre conscience de; (a project, Comm: asset) réaliser

really ['rɪəlɪ] adv vraiment; **~?** vraiment?, c'est vrai?

realm [rɛlm] n royaume m; (fig) domaine m

realtor ['rɪəltɔ:'] n (us) agent immobilier

reappear [ri:ə'pɪə'] vi réapparaître, reparaître

rear [rɪə'] adj de derrière, arrière inv; (Aut: wheel etc) arrière ▷ n arrière m ▷ vt (cattle, family) élever ▷ vi (also: **~ up**) (animal) se cabrer

rearrange [ri:ə'reɪndʒ] vt réarranger

rear-view mirror n (Aut) rétroviseur m; **rear-wheel drive** n (Aut) traction f arrière

reason ['ri:zn] n raison f ▷ vi: **to ~ with sb** raisonner qn, faire entendre raison à qn; **it stands to ~ that** il va sans dire que; **reasonable** adj raisonnable;

(not bad) acceptable; **reasonably** adv
(behave) raisonnablement; (fairly) assez;
reasoning n raisonnement m

reassurance [riːəˈʃuərəns] n (factual)
assurance f, garantie f; (emotional)
réconfort m

reassure [riːəˈʃuəʳ] vt rassurer

rebate [ˈriːbeɪt] n (on tax etc)
dégrèvement m

rebel n [ˈrɛbl] rebelle m/f ▷ vi [rɪˈbɛl]
se rebeller, se révolter; **rebellion**
[rɪˈbɛljən] n rébellion f, révolte f;
rebellious [rɪˈbɛljəs] adj rebelle

rebuild [riːˈbɪld] vt (irreg: like build)
reconstruire

recall [rɪˈkɔːl] rappeler; (remember)
se rappeler, se souvenir de ▷ n [rɪˈkɔːl]
rappel m; (ability to remember) mémoire f

rec'd abbr (=received)

receipt [rɪˈsiːt] n (document) reçu m;
(for parcel etc) accusé m de réception;
(act of receiving) réception f; **receipts**
npl (Comm) recettes fpl; **can I have a
~, please?** je peux avoir un reçu, s'il
vous plaît?

receive [rɪˈsiːv] vt recevoir; (guest)
recevoir, accueillir; **receiver** n (Tel)
récepteur m, combiné m; (Radio)
récepteur; (of stolen goods) receleur
m; (for bankruptcies) administrateur
m judiciaire

recent [ˈriːsnt] adj récent(e); **recently**
adv récemment

reception [rɪˈsɛpʃən] n réception
f; (welcome) accueil m, réception;
reception desk n réception f;
receptionist n réceptionniste m/f

recession [rɪˈsɛʃən] n (Econ) récession f

recharge [riːˈtʃɑːdʒ] vt (battery)
recharger

recipe [ˈrɛsɪpɪ] n recette f

recipient [rɪˈsɪpɪənt] n (of payment)
bénéficiaire m/f; (of letter) destinataire
m/f

recital [rɪˈsaɪtl] n récital m

recite [rɪˈsaɪt] vt (poem) réciter

reckless [ˈrɛkləs] adj (driver
etc) imprudent(e); (spender etc)

insouciant(e)

reckon [ˈrɛkən] vt (count) calculer,
compter; (consider) estimer;
(think): **I ~ (that) ...** je pense (que) ...,
j'estime (que) ...

reclaim [rɪˈkleɪm] vt (land: from sea)
assécher; (demand back) réclamer (le
remboursement ou la restitution de);
(waste materials) récupérer

recline [rɪˈklaɪn] vi être allongé(e) or
étendu(e)

recognition [rɛkəɡˈnɪʃən] n
reconnaissance f; **transformed
beyond ~** méconnaissable

recognize [ˈrɛkəɡnaɪz] vt: **to ~ (by/as)**
reconnaître (à/comme étant)

recollection [rɛkəˈlɛkʃən] n
souvenir m

recommend [rɛkəˈmɛnd] vt
recommander; **can you ~ a good
restaurant?** pouvez-vous me
conseiller un bon restaurant?;
recommendation [rɛkəmənˈdeɪʃən] n
recommandation f

reconcile [ˈrɛkənsaɪl] vt (two people)
réconcilier; (two facts) concilier,
accorder; **to ~ o.s. to** se résigner à

reconsider [riːkənˈsɪdəʳ] vt
reconsidérer

reconstruct [riːkənˈstrʌkt] vt
(building) reconstruire; (crime, system)
reconstituer

record n [ˈrɛkɔːd] rapport m, récit
m; (of meeting etc) procès-verbal m;
(register) registre m; (file) dossier m;
(Comput) article m; (also: **police ~**)
casier m judiciaire; (Mus: disc) disque
m; (Sport) record m ▷ adj record inv ▷ vt
[rɪˈkɔːd] (set down) noter; (Mus: song
etc) enregistrer; **public ~s** archives
fpl; **in ~ time** dans un temps record;
recorded delivery (Brit Post): **to
send sth recorded delivery** ≈ envoyer
qch en recommandé; **recorder** n
(Mus) flûte f à bec; **recording** n (Mus)
enregistrement m; **record player** n
tourne-disque m

recount [rɪˈkaunt] vt raconter

recover [rɪˈkʌvə] vt récupérer ▷ vi (from illness) se rétablir; (from shock) se remettre; **recovery** n récupération f; rétablissement m; (Econ) redressement m

recreate [riːkrɪˈeɪt] vt recréer

recreation [rɛkrɪˈeɪʃən] n (leisure) récréation f, détente f; **recreational drug** n drogue récréative; **recreational vehicle** n (us) camping-car m

recruit [rɪˈkruːt] n recrue f ▷ vt recruter; **recruitment** n recrutement m

rectangle [ˈrɛktæŋgl] n rectangle m; **rectangular** [rɛkˈtæŋgjulə] adj rectangulaire

rectify [ˈrɛktɪfaɪ] vt (error) rectifier, corriger

rector [ˈrɛktə] n (Rel) pasteur m

recur [rɪˈkəː] vi se reproduire; (idea, opportunity) se retrouver; (symptoms) réapparaître; **recurring** adj (problem) périodique, fréquent(e); (Math) périodique

recyclable [riːˈsaɪklæbl] adj recyclable

recycle [riːˈsaɪkl] vt, vi recycler

recycling [riːˈsaɪklɪŋ] n recyclage m

red [rɛd] n rouge m; (Pol: pej) rouge m/f ▷ adj rouge; (hair) roux (rousse); **in the ~** (account) à découvert; (business) en déficit; **Red Cross** n Croix-Rouge f; **redcurrant** n groseille f rouge

redeem [rɪˈdiːm] vt (debt) rembourser; (sth in pawn) dégager; (fig, also Rel) racheter

red: red-haired adj roux (rousse); **redhead** n roux (rousse), rousse f; **red-hot** adj chauffé(e) au rouge, brûlant(e); **red light** n: **to go through a red light** (Aut) brûler un feu rouge; **red-light district** n quartier mal famé

red meat n viande f rouge

reduce [rɪˈdjuːs] vt réduire; (lower) abaisser; **"~ speed now"** (Aut) "ralentir"; **to ~ sb to tears** faire pleurer qn; **reduced** adj réduit(e); **"greatly reduced prices"** "gros rabais"; **at a**

reduced price (goods) au rabais; (ticket etc) à prix réduit; **reduction** [rɪˈdʌkʃən] n réduction f; (of price) baisse f; (discount) rabais m; réduction; **is there a reduction for children/students?** y a-t-il une réduction pour les enfants/les étudiants?

redundancy [rɪˈdʌndənsɪ] n (BRIT) licenciement m, mise f au chômage

redundant [rɪˈdʌndənt] adj (BRIT: worker) licencié(e), mis(e) au chômage; (detail, object) superflu(e); **to be made ~** (worker) être licencié, être mis au chômage

reed [riːd] n (Bot) roseau m

reef [riːf] n (at sea) récif m, écueil m

reel [riːl] n bobine f; (Fishing) moulinet m; (Cine) bande f; (dance) quadrille écossais ▷ vi (sway) chanceler

ref [rɛf] n abbr (inf: = referee) arbitre m

refectory [rɪˈfɛktərɪ] n réfectoire m

refer [rɪˈfəː] vt: **to ~ sb to** (inquirer, patient) adresser qn à; (reader: to text) renvoyer qn à ▷ vi: **to ~ to** (allude to) parler de, faire allusion à; (consult) se reporter à; (apply to) s'appliquer à

referee [rɛfəˈriː] n arbitre m; (BRIT: for job application) répondant(e) ▷ vt arbitrer

reference [ˈrɛfrəns] n référence f, renvoi m; (mention) allusion f, mention f; for job application: letter) références; lettre f de recommandation; **with ~ to** en ce qui concerne; (Comm: in letter) me référant à; **reference number** n (Comm) numéro m de référence

refill vt [riːˈfɪl] remplir à nouveau; (pen, lighter etc) recharger ▷ n [ˈriːfɪl] (for pen etc) recharge f

refine [rɪˈfaɪn] vt (sugar, oil) raffiner; (taste) affiner; (idea, theory) peaufiner; **refined** adj (person, taste) raffiné(e); **refinery** n raffinerie f

reflect [rɪˈflɛkt] vt (light, image) réfléchir, refléter ▷ vi (think) réfléchir, méditer; **it ~s badly on him** cela le discrédite; **it ~s well on him** c'est son honneur; **reflection** [rɪˈflɛkʃən] *n* réflexion *f*; (image) reflet *m*; **on reflection** réflexion faite

reflex ['ri:fleks] *adj*, *n* réflexe (*m*)

reform [rɪ'fɔ:m] *n* réforme *f* ▷ *vt* réformer

refrain [rɪ'freɪn] *vi*: **to ~ from doing** s'abstenir de faire ▷ *n* refrain *m*

refresh [rɪ'freʃ] *vt* rafraîchir; (subj: food, sleep etc) redonner des forces à; **refreshing** *adj* (drink) rafraîchissant(e); (sleep) réparateur(-trice); **refreshments** *npl* rafraîchissements *mpl*

refrigerator [rɪ'frɪdʒəreɪtə'] *n* réfrigérateur *m*, frigidaire *m*

refuel [ri:'fjuəl] *vi* se ravitailler en carburant

refuge ['refju:dʒ] *n* refuge *m*; **to take in** se réfugier dans; **refugee** [refju'dʒi:] *n* réfugié(e)

refund *n* ['ri:fʌnd] remboursement *m* ▷ *vt* [rɪ'fʌnd] rembourser

refurbish [ri:'fə:bɪʃ] *vt* remettre à neuf

refusal [rɪ'fju:zəl] *n* refus *m*; **to have first - on sth** avoir droit de préemption sur qch

refuse[1] ['refju:s] *n* ordures *fpl*, détritus *mpl*

refuse[2] [rɪ'fju:z] *vt*, *vi* refuser; **to ~ to do sth** refuser de faire qch

regain [rɪ'geɪn] *vt* (lost ground) regagner; (strength) retrouver

regard [rɪ'gɑ:d] *n* respect *m*, estime *f*, considération ▷ *vt* considérer; **to give one's ~s to** faire ses amitiés à; **"with kindest ~s"** "bien amicalement"; **as ~s, with ~ to** en ce qui concerne; **regarding** *prep* en ce qui concerne; **regardless** *adv* quand même; **regardless of** sans se soucier de

regenerate [rɪ'dʒenəreɪt] *vt* régénérer ▷ *vi* se régénérer

reggae ['regeɪ] *n* reggae *m*

regiment ['redʒɪmənt] *n* régiment *m*

region ['ri:dʒən] *n* région *f*; **in the ~** (fig) aux alentours de; **regional** *adj* régional(e)

register ['redʒɪstə'] *n* registre *m*;

(also: **electoral ~**) liste électorale ▷ *vt* enregistrer, inscrire; (birth) déclarer; (vehicle) immatriculer; (letter) envoyer en recommandé; (subj: instrument) marquer ▷ *vi* s'inscrire; (at hotel) signer le registre; (make impression) être (bien) compris(e); **registered** *adj* (BRIT: letter) recommandé(e)

registered trademark *n* marque déposée

registrar ['redʒɪstrɑ:'] *n* officier *m* de l'état civil

registration [redʒɪs'treɪʃən] *n* (act) enregistrement *m*; (of student) inscription *f*; (BRIT Aut: also: **~ number**) numéro *m* d'immatriculation

registry office ['redʒɪstrɪ-] *n* (BRIT) bureau *m* de l'état civil; **to get married in a ~** se marier à la mairie

regret [rɪ'gret] *n* regret *m* ▷ *vt* regretter; **regrettable** *adj* regrettable, fâcheux(-euse)

regular ['regjulə'] *adj* régulier(-ière); (usual) habituel(le), normal(e); (soldier) de métier; (Comm: size) ordinaire ▷ *n* (client etc) habitué(e); **regularly** *adv* régulièrement

regulate ['regjuleɪt] *vt* régler; **regulation** [regju'leɪʃən] *n* (rule) règlement *m*; (adjustment) réglage *m*

rehabilitation ['ri:əbɪlɪ'teɪʃən] *n* (of offender) réhabilitation *f*; (of addict) réadaptation *f*

rehearsal [rɪ'hə:səl] *n* répétition *f*

rehearse [rɪ'hə:s] *vt* répéter

reign [reɪn] *n* règne *m* ▷ *vi* régner

reimburse [ri:ɪm'bə:s] *vt* rembourser

rein [reɪn] *n* (for horse) rêne *f*

reincarnation [ri:ɪnkɑ:'neɪʃən] *n* réincarnation *f*

reindeer ['reɪndɪə'] *n* (pl inv) renne *m*

reinforce [ri:ɪn'fɔ:s] *vt* renforcer; **reinforcements** *npl* (Mil) renfort(s) *m(pl)*

reinstate [ri:ɪn'steɪt] *vt* rétablir, réintégrer

reject *n* ['ri:dʒekt] (Comm) article *m* de rebut ▷ *vt* [rɪ'dʒekt] refuser; (idea) rejeter;**rejection** [rɪ'dʒekʃən] n rejet m, refus m

rejoice [rɪ'dʒɔɪs] vi: to ~ (at or over) se réjouir (de)

relate [rɪ'leɪt] vt (tell) raconter; (connect) établir un rapport entre ▷ vi: to ~ to (connect) se rapporter à; **to ~ to sb** (interact) entretenir des rapports avec qn; **related** adj apparenté(e); **related to** (subject) lié(e) à; **relating to** prep concernant

relation [rɪ'leɪʃən] n (person) parent(e); (link) rapport m, lien m; **relations** npl (relatives) famille f; **relationship** n rapport m, lien m; (personal ties) relations fpl, rapports m; (also: **family relationship**) lien de parenté; (affair) liaison f

relative ['relətɪv] n parent(e) ▷ adj relatif(-ive); (respective) respectif(-ive); **relatively** adv relativement

relax [rɪ'læks] vi (muscle) se relâcher; (person: unwind) se détendre ▷ vt relâcher; (mind, person) détendre; **relaxation** [riːlæk'seɪʃən] n relâchement m; (of mind) détente f; (recreation) détente, délassement m; **relaxed** adj relâché(e); détendu(e); **relaxing** adj délassant(e)

relay ['riːleɪ] n (Sport) course f de relais ▷ vt (message) retransmettre, relayer

release [rɪ'liːs] n (from prison, obligation) libération f; (of gas etc) émission f; (of film etc) sortie f; (new recording) disque m ▷ vt (prisoner) libérer; (book, film) sortir; (report, news) rendre public, publier; (gas etc) émettre, dégager; (free: from wreckage etc) dégager; (Tech: catch, spring etc) déclencher; (let go: person, animal) relâcher; (: hand, object) lâcher; (: grip, brake) desserrer

relegate ['relɪgeɪt] vt reléguer; (BRIT Sport): **to be ~d** descendre dans une division inférieure

relent [rɪ'lent] vi se laisser fléchir; **relentless** adj implacable; (non-stop) continuel(le)

relevant ['reləvənt] adj (question,

pertinent(e); (corresponding) approprié(e); (fact) significatif(-ive); (information) utile

reliable [rɪ'laɪəbl] adj (person, firm) sérieux(-euse), fiable; (method, machine) fiable; (news, information) sûr(e)

relic ['relɪk] n (Rel) relique f; (of the past) vestige m

relief [rɪ'liːf] n (from pain, anxiety) soulagement m; (help, supplies) secours m(pl); (Art, Geo) relief m

relieve [rɪ'liːv] vt (pain, patient) soulager; (fear, worry) dissiper; (bring help) secourir; (take over from: gen) relayer; (: guard) relever; **to ~ sb of sth** débarrasser qn de qch; **to ~ o.s.** (euphemism) se soulager, faire ses besoins; **relieved** adj soulagé(e)

religion [rɪ'lɪdʒən] n religion f

religious [rɪ'lɪdʒəs] adj religieux(-euse); (book) de piété; **religious education** n instruction religieuse

relish ['relɪʃ] n (Culin) condiment m; (enjoyment) délectation f ▷ vt (food etc) savourer; **to ~ doing** se délecter à faire

relocate [riːləʊ'keɪt] vt (business) transférer ▷ vi se transférer, s'installer or s'établir ailleurs

reluctance [rɪ'lʌktəns] n répugnance f

reluctant [rɪ'lʌktənt] adj peu disposé(e), qui hésite; **reluctantly** adv à contrecœur, sans enthousiasme

rely on [rɪ'laɪ-] vt fus (be dependent on) dépendre de; (trust) compter sur

remain [rɪ'meɪn] vi rester; **remainder** n reste m; (Comm) fin f de série; **remaining** adj qui reste; **remains** npl restes mpl

remand [rɪ'mɑːnd] n: **on ~** en détention préventive ▷ vt: **to be ~ed in custody** être placé(e) en détention préventive

remark [rɪ'mɑːk] n remarque f, observation f ▷ vt (faire) remarquer, dire; **remarkable** adj remarquable

remarry [riː'mærɪ] vi se remarier

remedy ['remədɪ] n: **~ (for)** remède m

(contre or à) ▷ vt remédier à

remember [rɪˈmɛmbər] vt se rappeler, se souvenir de; (send greetings): ~ **me to him** saluez-le de ma part; **Remembrance Day** [rɪˈmɛmbrəns-] n (BRIT) ≈ (le jour de) l'Armistice m, ≈ le 11 novembre

● REMEMBRANCE DAY

● **Remembrance Day** ou
● **Remembrance Sunday** est le
● dimanche le plus proche du 11
● novembre, jour où la Première
● Guerre mondiale a officiellement
● pris fin. Il rend hommage aux
● victimes des deux guerres
● mondiales. À cette occasion, on
● observe deux minutes de silence
● à 11h, heure de la signature de
● l'armistice avec l'Allemagne en
● 1918; certains membres de la
● famille royale et du gouvernement
● déposent des gerbes de coquelicots
● au cénotaphe de Whitehall, et des
● couronnes sont placées sur les
● monuments aux morts dans toute
● la Grande-Bretagne; par ailleurs,
● les gens portent des coquelicots
● artificiels fabriqués et vendus
● par des membres de la légion
● britannique blessés au combat, au
● profit des blessés de guerre et de
● leur famille.

remind [rɪˈmaɪnd] vt: **to ~ sb of sth** rappeler qch à qn; **to ~ sb to do** faire penser à qn à faire, rappeler à qn qu'il doit faire; **reminder** n (Comm: letter) rappel m; (note etc) pense-bête m; (souvenir) souvenir m

reminiscent [rɛmɪˈnɪsnt] adj: ~ **of** qui rappelle, qui fait penser à

remnant [ˈrɛmnənt] n reste m, restant m; (of cloth) coupon m

remorse [rɪˈmɔːs] n remords m

remote [rɪˈməut] adj éloigné(e), lointain(e); (person) distant(e);

(possibility) vague; **remote control** n télécommande f; **remotely** adv au loin; (slightly) très vaguement

removal [rɪˈmuːvəl] n (taking away) enlèvement m; suppression f; (BRIT: from house) déménagement m; (from office: dismissal) renvoi m; (of stain) nettoyage m; (Med) ablation f; **removal man** (irreg) (BRIT) déménageur m; **removal van** n (BRIT) camion m de déménagement

remove [rɪˈmuːv] vt enlever, retirer; (employee) renvoyer; (stain) faire partir; (abuse) supprimer; (doubt) chasser

Renaissance [rɪˈneɪsãs] n: **the ~** la Renaissance

rename [riːˈneɪm] vt rebaptiser

render [ˈrɛndər] vt rendre

rendezvous [ˈrɔndɪvuː] n rendez-vous m inv

renew [rɪˈnjuː] vt renouveler; (negotiations) reprendre; (acquaintance) renouer

renovate [ˈrɛnəveɪt] vt rénover; (work of art) restaurer

renowned [rɪˈnaund] adj renommé(e)

rent [rɛnt] pt, pp of **rend** ▷ n loyer m ▷ vt louer; **rental** n (for television, car) (prix m de) location f

reorganize [riːˈɔːɡənaɪz] vt réorganiser

rep [rɛp] n abbr (Comm) = **representative**

repair [rɪˈpɛər] n réparation f ▷ vt réparer; **in good/bad** ~ en bon/mauvais état; **where can I get this** ~? où est-ce que je peux faire réparer ceci?; **repair kit** n trousse f de réparations

repay [riːˈpeɪ] vt (irreg: like **pay**) (money, creditor) rembourser; (sb's efforts) récompenser; **repayment** n remboursement m

repeat [rɪˈpiːt] n (Radio, TV) reprise f ▷ vt répéter; (promise, attack, also Comm: order) renouveler; (Scol: a class) redoubler ▷ vi répéter; **can you ~ that, please?** pouvez-vous répéter,

s'il vous plaît?; **repeatedly** adv
souvent, à plusieurs reprises; **repeat
prescription** (BRIT): **I'd like a repeat
prescription** je voudrais renouveler
mon ordonnance
repellent [rɪˈpɛlənt] adj repoussant(e)
▷ n: **insect ~** insectifuge m
repercussions [ri:pəˈkʌʃənz] npl
répercussions fpl
repetition [rɛpɪˈtɪʃən] n répétition f
repetitive [rɪˈpɛtɪtɪv] adj (movement,
work) répétitif(-ive); (speech) plein(e)
de redites
replace [rɪˈpleɪs] vt (put back)
remettre, replacer; (take the place
of) remplacer; **replacement** n
(substitution) remplacement m; (person)
remplaçant(e)
replay [ˈriːpleɪ] n (of match) match
rejoué; (of tape, film) répétition f
replica [ˈrɛplɪkə] n réplique f, copie
exacte
reply [rɪˈplaɪ] n réponse f ▷ vi répondre
report [rɪˈpɔːt] n rapport m; (Press
etc) reportage m; (BRIT: also: **school
~**) bulletin m (scolaire); (of gun)
détonation f ▷ vt rapporter, faire un
compte rendu de; (Press etc) faire un
reportage sur; (notify: accident) signaler;
(: culprit) dénoncer ▷ vi (make a report)
faire un rapport; **I'd like to ~ a theft**
je voudrais signaler un vol; (present
o.s.): **to ~ (to sb)** se présenter (chez
qn); **report card** n (us, SCOTTISH)
bulletin m (scolaire); **reportedly** adv:
she is reportedly living in Spain elle
habiterait en Espagne; **he reportedly
told them to ...** il leur aurait dit de ...;
reporter n reporter m
represent [rɛprɪˈzɛnt] vt représenter;
(view, belief) présenter, expliquer;
(describe): **to ~ sth as** présenter or
décrire qch comme; **representation**
[rɛprɪzɛnˈteɪʃən] n représentation f;
representative n représentant(e); (us
Pol) député m ▷ adj représentatif(-ive),
caractéristique
repress [rɪˈprɛs] vt réprimer;

repression [rɪˈprɛʃən] n répression f
reprimand [ˈrɛprɪmɑːnd] n
réprimande f ▷ vt réprimander
reproduce [riːprəˈdjuːs] vt reproduire
▷ vi se reproduire; **reproduction**
[riːprəˈdʌkʃən] n reproduction f
reptile [ˈrɛptaɪl] n reptile m
republic [rɪˈpʌblɪk] n république f;
republican adj, n républicain(e)
reputable [ˈrɛpjutəbl] adj de bonne
réputation; (occupation) honorable
reputation [rɛpjuˈteɪʃən] n
réputation f
request [rɪˈkwɛst] n demande f;
(formal) requête f ▷ vt: **to ~ (of or from
sb)** demander (à qn); **request stop** n
(BRIT: for bus) arrêt facultatif
require [rɪˈkwaɪə*] vt (need: subj: person)
avoir besoin de; (: thing, situation)
nécessiter, demander; (want) exiger;
(order): **to ~ sb to do sth/sth of sb**
exiger que qn fasse qch/qch de qn;
requirement n (need) exigence f;
besoin m; (condition) condition f
(requise)
resat [riːˈsæt] pt, pp of **resit**
rescue [ˈrɛskjuː] n (from accident)
sauvetage m; (help) secours mpl ▷ vt
sauver
research [rɪˈsəːtʃ] n recherche(s) f(pl)
▷ vt faire des recherches sur
resemblance [rɪˈzɛmbləns] n
ressemblance f
resemble [rɪˈzɛmbl] vt ressembler à
resent [rɪˈzɛnt] vt être contrarié(e)
par; **resentful** adj irrité(e), plein(e)
de ressentiment; **resentment** n
ressentiment m
reservation [rɛzəˈveɪʃən] n (booking)
réservation f; **to make a ~ (in an
hotel/a restaurant/on a plane)**
réserver or retenir une chambre/une
table/une place; **reservation desk** n
(us: in hotel) réception f
reserve [rɪˈzəːv] n réserve f; (Sport)
remplaçant(e) ▷ vt (seats etc) réserver,
retenir; **reserved** adj réservé(e)
reservoir [ˈrɛzəvwɑː*] n réservoir m

reshuffle [riːˈʃʌfl] n: **Cabinet ~** (Pol) remaniement ministériel

residence [ˈrezɪdəns] n résidence f; **residence permit** n (BRIT) permis de séjour

resident [ˈrezɪdənt] n (of country) résident(e); (of area, house) habitant(e); (in hotel) pensionnaire ▷ adj résidant(e); **residential** [rezɪˈdenʃəl] adj de résidence; (area) résidentiel(le); (course) avec hébergement sur place

residue [ˈrezɪdjuː] n (Chem, Physics) résidu m

resign [rɪˈzaɪn] vt (one's post) se démettre de ▷ vi démissionner; **to ~ o.s. to** (endure) se résigner à; **resignation** [rezɪɡˈneɪʃən] n (from post) démission f; (state of mind) résignation f

resin [ˈrezɪn] n résine f

resist [rɪˈzɪst] vt résister à; **resistance** n résistance f

resit (BRIT) vt [riːˈsɪt] (pt, pp **resat**) (exam) repasser ▷ n [ˈriːsɪt] deuxième session f (d'un examen)

resolution [rezəˈluːʃən] n résolution f

resolve [rɪˈzɒlv] n résolution f ▷ vt (decide): **to ~ to do** résoudre ou décider de faire; (problem) résoudre

resort [rɪˈzɔːt] n (seaside town) station f balnéaire; (for skiing) station f de ski; (recourse) recours m ▷ vi: **to ~ to** avoir recours à; **in the last ~** en dernier ressort

resource [rɪˈsɔːs] n ressource f; **resourceful** adj ingénieux(-euse), débrouillard(e)

respect [rɪsˈpekt] n respect m ▷ vt respecter; **respectable** adj respectable; (quite good: result etc) honorable; **respectful** adj respectueux(-euse); **respective** adj respectif(-ive); **respectively** adv respectivement

respite [ˈrespaɪt] n répit m

respond [rɪsˈpɒnd] vi répondre; (react) réagir; **response** [rɪsˈpɒns] n réponse f; (reaction) réaction f

responsibility [rɪsˌpɒnsɪˈbɪlɪtɪ] n responsabilité f

responsible [rɪsˈpɒnsɪbl] adj (liable): **~ (for)** responsable (de); (person) digne de confiance; (job) qui comporte des responsabilités; **responsibly** adv avec sérieux

responsive [rɪsˈpɒnsɪv] adj (student, audience) réceptif(-ive); (brakes, steering) sensible

rest [rest] n repos m; (stop) arrêt m, pause f; (Mus) silence m; (support) support m, appui m; (remainder) reste m, restant m ▷ vi se reposer; (be supported): **to ~ on** s'appuyer sur ▷ vt (lean): **to ~ sth on/against** appuyer qch sur/contre; **the ~ of them** les autres

restaurant [ˈrestərɒn] n restaurant m; **restaurant car** n (BRIT Rail) wagon-restaurant m

restless [ˈrestlɪs] adj agité(e)

restoration [restəˈreɪʃən] n (of building) restauration f; (of stolen goods) restitution f

restore [rɪˈstɔː] vt (building) restaurer; (sth stolen) restituer; (peace, health) rétablir; (to former state) ramener à

restrain [rɪsˈtreɪn] vt (feeling) contenir; (person): **to ~ (from doing)** retenir (de faire); **restraint** n (restriction) contrainte f; (moderation) retenue f; (of style) sobriété f

restrict [rɪsˈtrɪkt] vt restreindre, limiter; **restriction** [rɪsˈtrɪkʃən] n restriction f, limitation f

rest room n (US) toilettes fpl

restructure [riːˈstrʌktʃə] vt restructurer

result [rɪˈzʌlt] n résultat m ▷ vi: **to ~ in** aboutir à, se terminer par; **as a ~ of** à la suite de

resume [rɪˈzjuːm] vt (work, journey) reprendre ▷ vi (work etc) reprendre

résumé [ˈreɪzjuːmeɪ] n (summary) résumé m; (US: curriculum vitae) curriculum vitae m inv

resuscitate [rɪˈsʌsɪteɪt] vt (Med) réanimer

retail ['ri:teɪl] adj de or au détail ▷ adv
au détail;**retailer** n détaillant(e)

retain [rɪ'teɪn] vt (keep) garder,
conserver

retaliation [rɪtælɪ'eɪʃən] n représailles
fpl, vengeance f

retarded [rɪ'tɑ:dɪd] adj retardé(e)

retire [rɪ'taɪə'] vi (give up work) prendre
sa retraite; (withdraw) se retirer, partir;
(go to bed) se coucher;**retired**
adj (person) retraité(e);**retirement**
n retraite f

retort [rɪ'tɔ:t] vi riposter

retreat [rɪ'tri:t] n retraite f ▷ vi battre
en retraite

retrieve [rɪ'tri:v] vt (sth lost) récupérer;
(situation, honour) sauver; (error, loss)
réparer; (Comput) rechercher

retrospect ['rɛtrəspɛkt] n: **in ~**
rétrospectivement, après coup;
retrospective [rɛtrə'spɛktɪv] adj
rétrospectif(-ive); (law) rétroactif(-ive)
▷ n (Art) rétrospective f

return [rɪ'tə:n] n (going or coming back)
retour m; (of sth stolen etc) restitution
f; (Finance: from land, shares) rapport
m ▷ cpd (journey, match) de retour; (BRIT:
ticket) aller et retour; (match) retour
▷ vi (person etc: come back) revenir;
(: go back) retourner ▷ vt rendre; (bring
back) rapporter; (send back) renvoyer;
(put back) remettre; (Pol: candidate)
élire; **returns** npl (Comm) recettes fpl;
(Finance) bénéfices mpl; **many happy
~s (of the day)!** bon anniversaire!; **by
~ (of post)** par retour du courrier); **in ~
(for)** en échange (de); **a ~ (ticket) for ...**
un billet aller et retour pour ...;**return
ticket** n (esp BRIT) billet m aller-retour

reunion [ri:'ju:nɪən] n réunion f

reunite [ri:ju:'naɪt] vt réunir

revamp [ri:'væmp] vt (house) retaper;
(firm) réorganiser

reveal [rɪ'vi:l] vt (make known) révéler;
(display) laisser voir;**revealing** adj
révélateur(-trice); (dress) au décolleté
généreux or suggestif

revel ['rɛvl] vi: **to ~ in sth/in doing** se

délecter de qch/à faire

revelation [rɛvə'leɪʃən] n révélation f

revenge [rɪ'vɛndʒ] n vengeance f; (in
game etc) revanche f ▷ vt venger; **to
take ~ (on)** se venger (sur)

revenue ['rɛvənju:] n revenu m

Reverend ['rɛvərənd] adj (in titles):
the ~ John Smith (Anglican) le révérend
John Smith; (Catholic) l'abbé (John)
Smith; (Protestant) le pasteur (John)
Smith

reversal [rɪ'və:sl] n (of opinion)
revirement m; (of order) renversement
m; (of direction) changement m

reverse [rɪ'və:s] n contraire m, opposé
m; (back) dos m, envers m; (of paper)
verso m; (of coin) revers m; (Aut: also:
~ gear) marche arrière ▷ adj (order,
direction) opposé(e), inverse ▷ vt (order,
position) changer, inverser; (direction,
policy) changer complètement de;
(decision) annuler; (roles) renverser
▷ vi (BRIT Aut) faire marche arrière;
reverse-charge call n (BRIT Tel)
communication f en PCV;**reversing
lights** npl (BRIT Aut) feux mpl de marche
arrière or de recul

revert [rɪ'və:t] vi: **to ~ to** revenir à,
retourner à

review [rɪ'vju:] n revue f; (of book, film)
critique f; (of situation, policy) examen
m, bilan m; (US: examination) examen
▷ vt passer en revue; faire la critique
de; examiner

revise [rɪ'vaɪz] vt réviser, modifier;
(manuscript) revoir, corriger ▷ vi (study)
réviser;**revision** [rɪ'vɪʒən] n révision f

revival [rɪ'vaɪvl] n reprise f;
(recovery) rétablissement m; (of faith)
renouveau m

revive [rɪ'vaɪv] vt (person) ranimer;
(custom) rétablir; (economy) relancer;
(hope, courage) raviver; faire renaître;
(play, fashion) reprendre ▷ vi (person)
reprendre connaissance; (: from ill
health) se rétablir; (hope etc) renaître;
(activity) reprendre

revolt [rɪ'vəʊlt] n révolte f ▷ vi se

révolter, se rebeller ▷ vt révolter, dégoûter;**revolting** adj dégoûtant(e)

revolution [rɛvə'lu:ʃən] n révolution f; (of wheel etc) tour m, révolution; **revolutionary** adj, n révolutionnaire (m/f)

revolve [rɪ'vɒlv] vi tourner

revolver [rɪ'vɒlvə*] n revolver m

reward [rɪ'wɔːd] n récompense f ▷ vt: **to ~ (for)** récompenser (de);**rewarding** adj (fig) qui (en) vaut la peine, gratifiant(e)

rewind [ri:'waɪnd] vt (irreg: like **wind**) (tape) réembobiner

rewritable [ri:'raɪtəbl] adj (CD, DVD) réinscriptible

rewrite [ri:'raɪt] (pt rewrote, pp **rewritten**) vt récrire

rheumatism ['ru:mətɪzəm] n rhumatisme m

Rhine [raɪn] n: **the (River) ~** le Rhin

rhinoceros [raɪ'nɒsərəs] n rhinocéros m

Rhône [rəʊn] n: **the (River) ~** le Rhône

rhubarb ['ru:bɑ:b] n rhubarbe f

rhyme [raɪm] n rime f; (verse) vers mpl

rhythm ['rɪðm] n rythme m

rib [rɪb] n (Anat) côte f

ribbon ['rɪbən] n ruban m; **in ~s** (torn) en lambeaux

rice [raɪs] n riz m;**rice pudding** n riz m au lait

rich [rɪtʃ] adj riche; (gift, clothes) somptueux(-euse); **to be ~** sth être riche en qch

rid [rɪd] (pt, pp ~) vt: **to ~ sb of** débarrasser qn de; **to get ~ of** se débarrasser de

riddle ['rɪdl] n (puzzle) énigme f ▷ vt: **to be ~d with** être criblé(e) de; (fig) être en proie à

ride [raɪd] n promenade f, tour m; (distance covered) trajet m ▷ vb (pt **rode**, pp **ridden**) ▷ vi (as sport) monter (à cheval), faire du cheval; (go somewhere: on horse, bicycle) aller (à cheval ou bicyclette etc); (travel: on bicycle, motor cycle, bus) rouler ▷ vt (a horse) monter;

(distance) parcourir, faire; **to ~ a horse/ bicycle** monter à cheval/à bicyclette; **to take sb for a ~** (fig) faire marcher qn; (cheat) rouler qn;**rider** n cavalier(-ière); (in race) jockey m; (on bicycle) cycliste m/f; (on motorcycle) motocycliste m/f

ridge [rɪdʒ] n (of hill) faîte m; (of roof, mountain) arête f; (on object) strie f

ridicule ['rɪdɪkju:l] n ridicule m; dérision f ▷ vt ridiculiser, tourner en dérision;**ridiculous** [rɪ'dɪkjʊləs] adj ridicule

riding ['raɪdɪŋ] n équitation f; **riding school** n manège m, école f d'équitation

rife [raɪf] adj répandu(e); **~ with** abondant(e) en

rifle ['raɪfl] n fusil m (à canon rayé) ▷ vt vider, dévaliser

rift [rɪft] n fente f, fissure f; (fig: disagreement) désaccord m

rig [rɪg] n (also: **oil ~**: on land) derrick m; (: at sea) plate-forme pétrolière f ▷ vt (election etc) truquer

right [raɪt] adj (true) juste, exact(e); (correct) bon (bonne); (suitable) approprié(e), convenable; (just) juste, équitable; (morally good) bien inv; (not left) droit(e) ▷ n (moral good) bien m; (title, claim) droit m; (not left) droite f ▷ adv (answer) correctement; (treat) bien, comme il faut; (not on the left) à droite ▷ vt redresser ▷ excl bon!; **do you have the ~ time?** avez-vous l'heure juste ou exacte?; **to be ~** (person) avoir raison; (answer) être juste ou correct(e); **by ~s** en toute justice; **on the ~** à droite; **to be in the ~** avoir raison; **~ in the middle** en plein milieu; **~ away** immédiatement;**right angle** n (Math) angle droit;**rightful** adj (heir) légitime; **right-hand** adj: **the right-hand side** la droite;**right-hand drive** n (BRIT) conduite f à droite; (vehicle) véhicule m avec la conduite à droite;**right-handed** adj (person) droitier(-ière); **rightly** adv bien, correctement; (with reason) à juste titre;**right of way** n (on path etc) droit m de passage; (Aut) priorité f; **right-wing** adj (Pol) de droite

rigid['rɪdʒɪd] adj rigide; (principle, control) strict(e)

rigorous['rɪgərəs] adj rigoureux(-euse)

rim[rɪm] n bord m; (of spectacles) monture f; (of wheel) jante f

rind[raɪnd] n (of bacon) couenne f; (of lemon etc) écorce f, zeste m; (of cheese) croûte f

ring[rɪŋ] n anneau m; (on finger) bague f; (also: **wedding ~**) alliance f; (of people, objects) cercle m; (of spies) réseau m; (of smoke etc) rond m; (arena) piste f, arène f; (for boxing) ring m; (sound of bell) sonnerie f ▷ vb (pt **rang**, pp **rung**) ▷ vi (telephone, bell) sonner; (person: by telephone) téléphoner; (ears) bourdonner; (also: **~ out**: voice, words) retentir ▷ vt (BRIT Tel: also: **~ up**) téléphoner à, appeler; **to ~ the bell** sonner; **to give sb a ~** (Tel) passer un coup de téléphone ou de fil à qn; **ring back** vt, vi (BRIT Tel) rappeler; **ring off** vi (BRIT Tel) raccrocher; **ring up** vt (BRIT) (Tel) appeler; **ringing tone** n (BRIT Tel) tonalité f d'appel; **ringleader** n (of gang) chef m, meneur m; **ring road** n (BRIT) rocade f; (motorway) périphérique m; **ringtone** n (on mobile) sonnerie f (de téléphone portable)

rink[rɪŋk] n (also: **ice ~**) patinoire f

rinse[rɪns] n rinçage m ▷ vt rincer

riot['raɪət] n émeute f, bagarres fpl ▷ vi (demonstrators) manifester avec violence; (population) se soulever, se révolter; **to run ~** se déchaîner

rip[rɪp] n déchirure f ▷ vt déchirer ▷ vi se déchirer; **rip off** vt (inf: cheat) arnaquer; **rip up** vt déchirer

ripe[raɪp] adj (fruit) mûr(e); (cheese) fait(e)

rip-off['rɪpɔf] n (inf): **it's a ~!** c'est du vol manifeste!, c'est de l'arnaque!

ripple['rɪpl] n ride f, ondulation f; (of applause, laughter) cascade f ▷ vi se rider, onduler

rise[raɪz] n (slope) côte f, pente f; (hill) élévation f; (increase: in wages: BRIT) augmentation f; (: in prices, temperature) hausse f, augmentation f; (fig: to power etc) ascension f ▷ vi (pt **rose**, pp **~n**) s'élever, monter; (prices, numbers) augmenter, monter; (waters, river) monter; (sun, wind, person: from chair, bed) se lever; (also: **~ up**: tower, building) s'élever; (: rebel) se révolter; se rebeller; (in rank) s'élever; **to give ~ to** donner lieu à; **to ~ to the occasion** se montrer à la hauteur; **risen**['rɪzn] pp of **rise**; **rising** adj (increasing: number, prices) en hausse; (tide) montant(e); (sun, moon) levant(e)

risk[rɪsk] n risque m ▷ vt risquer; **to take** ou **run the ~ of doing** courir le risque de faire; **at ~** en danger; **at one's own ~** à ses risques et périls; **risky** adj risqué(e)

rite[raɪt] n rite m; **the last ~s** les derniers sacrements

ritual['rɪtjuəl] adj rituel(le) ▷ n rituel m

rival['raɪvl] n rival(e); (in business) concurrent(e) ▷ adj rival(e); qui fait concurrence à ▷ vt (match) égaler; **rivalry** n rivalité f; (in business) concurrence f

river['rɪvə*] n rivière f; (major: also big) fleuve m ▷ cpd (port, traffic) fluvial(e); **up/down ~** en amont/aval; **riverbank** n rive f, berge f

rivet['rɪvɪt] n rivet m ▷ vt (fig) river, fixer

Riviera[rɪvɪ'ɛərə] n: **the (French) ~** la Côte d'Azur

road[rəud] n route f; (in town) rue f; (fig) chemin, voie f ▷ cpd (accident) de la route; **major/minor ~** route principale ou à priorité/voie secondaire; **which ~ do I take for ...?** quelle route dois-je prendre pour aller à...?; **roadblock** n barrage routier; **road map** n carte routière; **road rage** n comportement très agressif de certains usagers de la route; **road safety** n sécurité routière; **roadside** n bord m de la route, bas-côté m; **roadsign** n panneau m de signalisation; **road tax** n (BRIT Aut) taxe f sur les automobiles; **roadworks** npl travaux mpl (de réfection des routes)

roam [rəum] vi errer, vagabonder

roar [rɔː⁷] n rugissement m; (of crowd) hurlements mpl; (of vehicle, thunder, storm) grondement m ▷ vi rugir; hurler; gronder; **to ~ with laughter** rire à gorge déployée; **to do a ~ing trade** faire des affaires en or

roast [rəust] n rôti m ▷ vt (meat) (faire) rôtir; (coffee) griller, torréfier; **roast beef** n rôti m de bœuf, rosbif m

rob [rɔb] vt (person) voler; (bank) dévaliser; **to ~ sb of sth** voler ou dérober qch à qn; (fig: deprive) priver qn de qch; **robber** n bandit m, voleur m; **robbery** n vol m

robe [rəub] n (for ceremony etc) robe f; (also: **bath~**) peignoir m; (us: blanket) couverture f ▷ vt revêtir (d'une robe)

robin [rɔbɪn] n rouge-gorge m

robot [rəubɔt] n robot m

robust [rəuˈbʌst] adj robuste; (material, appetite) solide

rock [rɔk] n (substance) roche f, roc m; (boulder) rocher m, roche; (us: small stone) caillou m; (BRIT: sweet) = sucre m d'orge ▷ vt (swing gently: cradle) balancer; (: child) bercer; (shake) ébranler, secouer ▷ vi se balancer, être ébranlé(e) or secoué(e); **on the ~s** (drink) avec des glaçons; (marriage etc) en train de craquer; **rock and roll** n rock (and roll) m, rock'n'roll m; **rock climbing** n varappe f

rocket [rɔkɪt] n fusée f; (Mil) fusée, roquette f; (Culin) roquette f

rocking chair [rɔkɪŋ-] n fauteuil m à bascule

rocky [rɔkɪ] adj (hill) rocheux(-euse); (path) rocailleux(-euse)

rod [rɔd] n (metallic) tringle f; (Tech) tige f; (wooden) baguette f; (also: **fishing ~**) canne f à pêche

rode [rəud] pt of **ride**

rodent [rəudnt] n rongeur m

rogue [rəug] n coquin(e)

role [rəul] n rôle m; **role-model** n modèle m à émuler

roll [rəul] n rouleau m; (of banknotes) liasse f; (also: **bread ~**) petit pain; (register) liste f; (sound of drums etc) roulement m ▷ vt rouler; (also: **~ up**: string) enrouler; (also: **~ out**: pastry) étendre au rouleau, abaisser ▷ vi rouler; **roll up** vi (inf: arrive) arriver, s'amener; **roll over** vi se retourner; **roll up** vi (inf: arrive) arriver, s'amener; (carpet, cloth, map) rouler; (sleeves) retrousser; **roller** n rouleau m; (wheel) roulette f; (for road) rouleau compresseur; (for hair) bigoudi m; **roller coaster** n montagnes fpl russes; **roller skates** npl patins mpl à roulettes; **roller-skating** n patin m à roulettes; **to go roller-skating** faire du patin à roulettes; **rolling pin** n rouleau m à pâtisserie

ROM [rɔm] n abbr (Comput: = read-only memory) mémoire morte, ROM f

Roman [rəumən] adj romain(e) ▷ n Romain(e); **Roman Catholic** adj, n catholique (m/f)

romance [rəˈmæns] n (love affair) idylle f; (charm) poésie f; (novel) roman m à l'eau de rose

Romania etc [rəuˈmeɪnɪə] = **Rumania** etc

Roman numeral n chiffre romain

romantic [rəˈmæntɪk] adj romantique; (novel, attachment) sentimental(e)

Rome [rəum] n Rome f

roof [ruːf] n toit m; (of tunnel, cave) plafond m ▷ vt (also: **~ over**) couvrir (d'un toit); **the ~ of the mouth** la voûte du palais; **roof rack** n (Aut) galerie f

rook [ruk] n (bird) freux m; (Chess) tour f

room [ruːm] n (in house) pièce f; (also: **bed~**) chambre f (à coucher); (in school etc) salle f; (space) place f; **roommate** n camarade m/f de chambre; **room service** n service m des chambres (dans un hôtel); **roomy** adj spacieux(-euse) (garment) ample

rooster ['ruːstə'] n coq m

root [ruːt] n (Bot, Math) racine f; (fig: of problem) origine f, fond m ▷ vi (plant) s'enraciner

rope [rəʊp] n corde f; (Naut) cordage m ▷ vt (tie up or together) attacher; (climbers: also: ~ together) encorder; (area: also: ~ off) interdire l'accès de; (: divide off) séparer; **to know the ~s** (fig) être au courant, connaître les ficelles

rose [rəʊz] pt of **rise** ▷ n rose f; (also: **~bush**) rosier m

rosé ['rəʊzeɪ] n rosé m

rosemary ['rəʊzmərɪ] n romarin m

rosy ['rəʊzɪ] adj rose; **a ~ future** un bel avenir

rot [rɒt] n (decay) pourriture f; (fig: pej: nonsense) idioties fpl, balivernes fpl ▷ vt, vi pourrir

rota ['rəʊtə] n liste f, tableau m de service

rotate [rəʊ'teɪt] vt (revolve) faire tourner; (change round: crops) alterner; (: jobs) faire à tour de rôle ▷ vi (revolve) tourner

rotten ['rɒtn] adj (decayed) pourri(e); (dishonest) corrompu(e); (inf: bad) mauvais(e), moche; **to feel ~** (ill) être mal fichu(e)

rough [rʌf] adj (cloth, skin) rêche, rugueux(-euse); (terrain) accidenté(e); (path) rocailleux(-euse); (voice) rauque, rude; (person, manner: coarse) rude, fruste; (: violent) brutal(e); (district, weather) mauvais(e); (sea) houleux(-euse); (plan) ébauché(e); (guess) approximatif(-ive) ▷ n (Golf) rough m ▷ vt: **to ~ it** vivre à la dure; **to sleep ~** (BRIT) coucher à la dure; **roughly** adv (handle) rudement, brutalement; (speak) avec brusquerie; (make) grossièrement; (approximately) à peu près, en gros

roulette [ruː'let] n roulette f

round [raʊnd] adj rond(e) ▷ n rond m, cercle m; (BRIT: of toast) tranche f; (duty: of policeman, milkman etc)

tournée f; (: of doctor) visites fpl; (game: of cards, in competition) partie f; (Boxing) round m; (of talks) série f ▷ vt (corner) tourner ▷ prep autour de ▷ adv: **right ~, all ~** tout autour; **~ of ammunition** cartouche f; **~ of applause** applaudissements mpl; **~ of drinks** tournée f; **~ of sandwiches** (BRIT) sandwich m; **the long way ~** (par) le chemin le plus long; **all (the) year ~** toute l'année; **it's just ~ the corner** (fig) c'est tout près; **to go ~ to sb's (house)** aller chez qn; **go ~ the back** passez par derrière; **there's enough to go ~** assez pour tout le monde; **she arrived ~ (about) noon** (BRIT) elle est arrivée vers midi; **~ the clock** 24 heures sur 24; **round off** vt (speech etc) terminer; **round up** vt rassembler; (criminals) effectuer une rafle de; (prices) arrondir (au chiffre supérieur)

roundabout n (BRIT Aut) rond-point m (à sens giratoire); (at fair) manège m (de chevaux de bois) ▷ adj (route, means) détourné(e); **round trip** n (voyage m) aller et retour m; **roundup** n rassemblement m; (of criminals) rafle f

rouse [raʊz] vt (wake up) réveiller; (stir up) susciter, provoquer; (interest) éveiller; (suspicions) susciter, éveiller

route [ruːt] n itinéraire m; (of bus) parcours m; (of trade, shipping) route f

routine [ruː'tiːn] adj (work) ordinaire, courant(e); (procedure) d'usage ▷ n (habits) habitudes fpl; (pej) train-train m; (Theat) numéro m

row¹ [rəʊ] n (line) rangée f; (of people, seats, Knitting) rang m; (behind one another: of cars, people) file f ▷ vi (in boat) ramer; (as sport) faire de l'aviron ▷ vt (boat) faire aller à la rame ou à l'aviron; **in a ~** (fig) d'affilée

row² [raʊ] n (noise) vacarme m; (dispute) dispute f, querelle f; (scolding) réprimande f, savon m ▷ vi (also: **to have a ~**) se disputer, se quereller

rowboat ['rəʊbəʊt] n (US) canot m (à rames)

rowing ['rəʊɪŋ] n canotage m; (as sport) aviron m; **rowing boat** n (BRIT) canot m (à rames)

royal ['rɔɪəl] adj royal(e); **royalty** n (royal persons) (membres mpl de la) famille royale; (payment: to author) droits mpl d'auteur; (: to inventor) royalties fpl

rpm abbr (= revolutions per minute) t/mn (= tours/minute)

R.S.V.P. abbr (= répondez s'il vous plaît) RSVP

Rt. Hon. abbr (BRIT: = Right Honourable) titre donné aux députés de la Chambre des communes

rub [rʌb] n: **to give sth a ~** donner un coup de chiffon or de torchon à qch ▷ vt frotter; (person) frictionner; (hands) se frotter; **to ~ sb up** (BRIT) or **to ~ sb** (US) **the wrong way** prendre qn à rebrousse-poil; **rub in** vt (ointment) faire pénétrer; **rub off** vi partir; **rub out** vt effacer

rubber ['rʌbə*] n caoutchouc m; (BRIT: eraser) gomme f (à effacer); **rubber band** n élastique m; **rubber gloves** npl gants mpl en caoutchouc

rubbish ['rʌbɪʃ] n (from household) ordures fpl; (fig: pej) choses fpl sans valeur; camelote f; (nonsense) bêtises fpl, idioties fpl; **rubbish bin** n (BRIT) boîte f à ordures, poubelle f; **rubbish dump** n (BRIT: in town) décharge publique, dépotoir m

rubble ['rʌbl] n décombres mpl; (smaller) gravats mpl; (Constr) blocage m

ruby ['ru:bɪ] n rubis m

rucksack ['rʌksæk] n sac m à dos

rudder ['rʌdə*] n gouvernail m

rude [ru:d] adj (impolite: person) impoli(e); (: word, manners) grossier(-ière); (shocking) indécent(e), inconvenant(e)

ruffle ['rʌfl] vt (hair) ébouriffer; (clothes) chiffonner; (fig: person): **to get ~d** s'énerver

rug [rʌg] n petit tapis; (BRIT: blanket) couverture f

rugby ['rʌgbɪ] n (also: ~ **football**) rugby m

rugged ['rʌgɪd] adj (landscape) accidenté(e); (features, character) rude

ruin ['ru:ɪn] n ruine f ▷ vt (spoil: clothes) abîmer; (: event) gâcher; **ruins** npl (of building) ruine(s)

rule [ru:l] n règle f; (regulation) règlement m; (government) autorité f, gouvernement m ▷ vt (country) gouverner; (person) dominer; (decide) décider ▷ vi commander; (law): **as a ~** normalement, en règle générale; **rule out** vt exclure; **ruler** n (sovereign) souverain(e); (leader) chef m (d'État); (for measuring) règle f; **ruling** adj (party) au pouvoir; (class) dirigeant(e) ▷ n (Law) décision f

rum [rʌm] n rhum m

Rumania [ru:'meɪnɪə] n Roumanie f; **Rumanian** adj roumain(e) ▷ n Roumain(e); (Ling) roumain m

rumble ['rʌmbl] n grondement m; (of stomach, pipe) gargouillement m ▷ vi gronder; (stomach, pipe) gargouiller

rumour (US **rumor**) ['ru:mə*] n rumeur f, bruit m (qui court) ▷ vt: **it is ~ed that** le bruit court que

rump steak n romsteck m

run [rʌn] n (race) course f; (outing) tour m or promenade f (en voiture); (distance travelled) parcours m, trajet m; (series) suite f, série f; (Theat) série de représentations; (Ski) piste f; (Cricket, Baseball) point m; (in tights, stockings) maille filée, échelle f ▷ vb (pt **ran**, pp **~**) ▷ vt (business) diriger; (competition, course) organiser; (hotel, house) tenir; (race) participer à; (Comput: program) exécuter; (to pass: hand, finger): **to ~ sth over** promener or passer qch sur; (water, bath) faire couler; (Press: feature) publier ▷ vi courir; (pass: road etc) passer; (work: machine, factory) marcher; (bus, train) circuler; (continue: play) se jouer, être à l'affiche; (: contract) être valide or en vigueur; (flow: river, bath, nose) couler; (colours, washing) déteindre; (*in election*) être candidat, se présenter; **at a ~** au pas de course; **to go for a ~** aller courir ou faire un peu de course à pied; (*in car*) faire un tour ou une promenade (en voiture); **there was a ~ on** (*meat, tickets*) les gens se sont rués sur; **in the long ~** à la longue; **on the ~** en fuite; **I'll ~ you to the station** je vais vous emmener or conduire à la gare; **to ~ a risk** courir un risque; **run after** vt fus (*to catch up*) courir après; (*chase*) poursuivre; **run away** vi s'enfuir; **run down** vt (*Aut: knock over*) renverser; (*BRIT: reduce: production*) réduire progressivement; (*: factory/shop*) réduire progressivement la production/ l'activité de; (*criticize*) critiquer, dénigrer; **to be ~ down** (*tired*) être fatigué(e) or à plat; **run into** vt fus (*meet: person*) rencontrer par hasard; (*: trouble*) se heurter à; (*collide with*) heurter; **run off** vi s'enfuir ⊳ vt (*copies*) tirer; **run out** vi (*person*) sortir en courant; (*liquid*) couler; (*lease*) expirer; (*money*) être épuisé(e); **run out of** vt fus se trouver à court de; **run over** vt (*Aut*) écraser ⊳ vt fus (*revise*) revoir, reprendre; **run through** vt fus (*recap*) reprendre, revoir; (*play*) répéter; **run up** vi: **to ~ up against** (*difficulties*) se heurter à; **runaway** adj (*horse*) emballé(e); (*truck*) fou (folle); (*person*) fugitif(-ive); (*child*) fugueur(-euse)

rung [rʌŋ] pp of **ring** ⊳ n (*of ladder*) barreau m

runner [ˈrʌnəʳ] n (*in race: person*) coureur(-euse); (*: horse*) partant m; (*on sledge*) patin m; (*for drawer etc*) coulisseau m; **runner bean** n (*BRIT*) haricot m (à rames); **runner-up** n second(e)

running [ˈrʌnɪŋ] n (*in race etc*) course f; (*of business, organization*) direction f, gestion f ⊳ adj (*water*) courant(e); (*commentary*) suivi(e); **6 days** ~ 6 jours de suite; **to be in/out of the ~ for sth**

être/ne pas être sur les rangs pour qch

runny [ˈrʌnɪ] adj qui coule

run-up [ˈrʌnʌp] n (*BRIT*): **~ to sth** période f précédant qch

runway [ˈrʌnweɪ] n (*Aviat*) piste f (d'envol or d'atterrissage)

rupture [ˈrʌptʃəʳ] n (*Med*) hernie f

rural [ˈruərl] adj rural(e)

rush [rʌʃ] n (*of crowd, Comm: sudden demand*) ruée f; (*hurry*) hâte f; (*of anger, joy*) accès m; (*current*) flot m; (*Bot*) jonc m ⊳ vt (*hurry*) transporter or envoyer d'urgence ⊳ vi se précipiter; **to ~ sth off** (*do quickly*) faire qch à la hâte; **rush hour** n heures fpl de pointe or d'affluence

Russia [ˈrʌʃə] n Russie f; **Russian** adj russe ⊳ n Russe m/f; (*Ling*) russe m

rust [rʌst] n rouille f ⊳ vi rouiller

rusty [ˈrʌstɪ] adj rouillé(e)

ruthless [ˈruːθlɪs] adj sans pitié, impitoyable

RV n abbr (*us*) = **recreational vehicle**

rye [raɪ] n seigle m

S

Sabbath ['sæbəθ] n (Jewish) sabbat m; (Christian) dimanche m

sabotage ['sæbətɑːʒ] n sabotage m ▷ vt saboter

saccharin(e) ['sækərɪn] n saccharine f

sachet ['sæʃeɪ] n sachet m

sack [sæk] n (bag) sac m ▷ vt (dismiss) renvoyer, mettre à la porte; (plunder) piller, mettre à sac; **to get the ~** être renvoyé(e) or mis(e) à la porte

sacred ['seɪkrɪd] adj sacré(e)

sacrifice ['sækrɪfaɪs] n sacrifice m ▷ vt sacrifier

sad [sæd] adj (unhappy) triste; (deplorable) triste, fâcheux(-euse); (inf: pathetic: thing) triste, lamentable; (: person) minable

saddle ['sædl] n selle f ▷ vt (horse) seller; **to be ~d with sth** (inf) avoir qch sur les bras

sadistic [sə'dɪstɪk] adj sadique

sadly ['sædlɪ] adv tristement; (unfortunately) malheureusement; (seriously) fort

sadness ['sædnɪs] n tristesse f

s.a.e. n abbr (BRIT: = stamped addressed envelope) enveloppe affranchie pour la réponse

safari [sə'fɑːrɪ] n safari m

safe [seɪf] adj (out of danger) hors de danger, en sécurité; (not dangerous) sans danger; (cautious) prudent(e); (sure: bet etc) assuré(e) ▷ n coffre-fort m; **could you put this in the ~, please?** pourriez-vous mettre ceci dans le coffre-fort?; **~ and sound** sain(e) et sauf (sauve); **(just) to be on the ~ side** pour plus de sûreté, par précaution; **safely** adv (assume, say) sans risque d'erreur; (drive, arrive) sans accident; **safe sex** n rapports sexuels protégés

safety ['seɪftɪ] n sécurité f; **safety belt** n ceinture f de sécurité; **safety pin** n épingle f de sûreté or de nourrice

saffron ['sæfrən] n safran m

sag [sæg] vi s'affaisser, fléchir; (hem, breasts) pendre

sage [seɪdʒ] n (herb) sauge f; (person) sage m

Sagittarius [sædʒɪ'tɛərɪəs] n le Sagittaire

Sahara [sə'hɑːrə] n: **the ~ (Desert)** le (désert du) Sahara m

said [sɛd] pt, pp of **say**

sail [seɪl] n (on boat) voile f; (trip): **to go for a ~** faire un tour en bateau ▷ vt (boat) manœuvrer, piloter ▷ vi (travel: ship) avancer, naviguer; (set off) partir, prendre la mer; (Sport) faire de la voile; **they ~ed into Le Havre** ils sont entrés dans le port du Havre; **sailboat** n (us) bateau m à voiles, voilier m; **sailing** n (Sport) voile f; **to go sailing** faire de la voile; **sailing boat** n bateau m à voiles, voilier m; **sailor** n marin m, matelot m

saint [seɪnt] n saint(e)

sake [seɪk] n: **for the ~ of** (out of concern for) pour (l'amour de), dans l'intérêt de; (out of consideration for) par égard pour

salad ['sæləd] n salade f; **salad cream** n (BRIT) (sorte f de) mayonnaise f; **salad dressing** n vinaigrette f

salami [sə'lɑːmɪ] n salami m

salary ['sælərɪ] n salaire m, traitement m

sale [seɪl] n vente f; (at reduced prices) soldes mpl; **sales** npl (total amount sold) chiffre m de ventes; **"for -"** "à vendre"; **on -** en vente; **sales assistant** (us **sales clerk**) n vendeur(-euse)

salesman (irreg) n (in shop) vendeur m; **salesperson** (irreg) n (in shop) vendeur(-euse); **sales rep** n (Comm) représentant(e) m/f; **saleswoman** (irreg) n (in shop) vendeuse f

saline ['seɪlaɪn] adj salin(e)

saliva [sə'laɪvə] n salive f

salmon ['sæmən] n (pl inv) saumon m

salon ['sælɒn] n salon m

saloon [sə'luːn] n (us) bar m; (BRIT Aut) berline f; (ship's lounge) salon m

salt [sɔːlt] n sel m ⊳ vt saler; **saltwater** adj (fish etc) (d'eau) de mer; **salty** adj salé(e)

salute [sə'luːt] n salut m; (of guns) salve f ⊳ vt saluer

salvage ['sælvɪdʒ] n (saving) sauvetage m; (things saved) biens sauvés or récupérés ⊳ vt sauver, récupérer

Salvation Army [sæl'veɪʃən-] n Armée f du Salut

same [seɪm] adj même ⊳ pron: **the - le (la) même, les mêmes; the - book as le même livre que; at the - time** en même temps; (yet) néanmoins; **all or just the -** tout de même, quand même; **to do the -** faire de même, en faire autant; **to do the - as sb** faire comme qn; **and the - to you!** et à vous de même!; (after insult) toi-même!

sample ['sɑːmpl] n échantillon m; (Med) prélèvement m ⊳ vt (food, wine) goûter

sanction ['sæŋkʃən] n approbation f, sanction f ⊳ vt cautionner; **sanctions** npl (Pol) sanctions

sanctuary ['sæŋktjuərɪ] n (holy place) sanctuaire m; (refuge) asile m; (for wildlife) réserve f

sand [sænd] n sable m ⊳ vt (also: - **down**: wood etc) poncer

sandal ['sændl] n sandale f

sand: sandbox n (us: for children) tas m de sable; **sandcastle** n château m de sable; **sand dune** n dune f de sable; **sandpaper** n papier m de verre; **sandpit** n (BRIT: for children) tas m de sable; **sands** npl plage f (de sable); **sandstone** ['sændstəun] n grès m

sandwich ['sændwɪtʃ] n sandwich m ⊳ vt (also: - **in**) intercaler; **-ed between** pris en sandwich entre; **cheese/ham -** sandwich au fromage/jambon

sandy ['sændɪ] adj sablonneux(-euse); (colour) sable inv, blond roux inv

sane [seɪn] adj (person) sain(e) d'esprit; (outlook) sensé(e), sain(e)

sang [sæŋ] pt of **sing**

sanitary towel (us **sanitary napkin**) ['sænɪtərɪ-] n serviette f hygiénique

sanity ['sænɪtɪ] n santé mentale; (common sense) bon sens

sank [sæŋk] pt of **sink**

Santa Claus [sæntə'klɔːz] n le Père Noël

sap [sæp] n (of plants) sève f ⊳ vt (strength) saper, miner

sapphire ['sæfaɪə'] n saphir m

sarcasm ['sɑːkæzm] n sarcasme m, raillerie f

sarcastic [sɑː'kæstɪk] adj sarcastique

sardine [sɑː'diːn] n sardine f

SASE n abbr (us: = self-addressed stamped envelope) enveloppe affranchie pour la réponse

sat [sæt] pt, pp of **sit**

Sat. abbr (= Saturday) sa

satchel ['sætʃl] n cartable m

satellite ['sætəlaɪt] n satellite m; **satellite dish** n antenne f parabolique; **satellite television** n télévision f par satellite

satin ['sætɪn] n satin m ⊳ adj en or de satin, satiné(e)

satire ['sætaɪə'] n satire f

satisfaction [sætɪs'fækʃən] n satisfaction f

satisfactory [sætɪsˈfæktərɪ] adj satisfaisant(e)

satisfied [ˈsætɪsfaɪd] adj satisfait(e); **to be ~ with sth** être satisfait de qch

satisfy [ˈsætɪsfaɪ] vt satisfaire, contenter; (convince) convaincre, persuader

Saturday [ˈsætədɪ] n samedi m

sauce [sɔːs] n sauce f; **saucepan** n casserole f

saucer [ˈsɔːsəʳ] n soucoupe f

Saudi Arabia [ˈsaudɪ-] n Arabie f Saoudite

sauna [ˈsɔːnə] n sauna m

sausage [ˈsɔsɪdʒ] n saucisse f; (salami etc) saucisson m; **sausage roll** n friand m

sautéed [ˈsəuteɪd] adj sauté(e)

savage [ˈsævɪdʒ] adj (cruel, fierce) brutal(e), féroce; (primitive) primitif(-ive), sauvage ▷ n sauvage m/f ▷ vt attaquer férocement

save [seɪv] vt (person, belongings) sauver; (money) mettre de côté, économiser; (time) (faire) gagner; (keep) garder; (Comput) sauvegarder; (Sport: stop) arrêter; (avoid: trouble) éviter ▷ n (Sport) arrêt m (du ballon) ▷ prep sauf, à l'exception de

savings [ˈseɪvɪŋz] npl économies fpl; **savings account** n compte m d'épargne; **savings and loan association** (us) ≈ société f de crédit immobilier

savoury (us **savory**) [ˈseɪvərɪ] adj savoureux(-euse); (dish: not sweet) salé(e)

saw [sɔː] pt of **see** ▷ n (tool) scie f ▷ vt (pt ~ed, pp ~ed or ~n) scier; **sawdust** n sciure f

sawn [sɔːn] pp of **saw**

saxophone [ˈsæksəfəun] n saxophone m

say [seɪ] n: **to have one's ~** dire ce qu'on a à dire ▷ vt (pt, pp **said**) dire; **to have a ~** avoir voix au chapitre; **could you ~ that again?** pourriez-vous répéter ce

que vous venez de dire?; **to ~ yes/no** dire oui/non; **my watch ~s 3 o'clock** ma montre indique 3 heures, il est 3 heures à ma montre; **that is to ~** c'est-à-dire, cela va sans dire, cela va de soi; **saying** n dicton m, proverbe m

scab [skæb] n croûte f; (pej) jaune m

scaffolding [ˈskæfəldɪŋ] n échafaudage m

scald [skɔːld] n brûlure f ▷ vt ébouillanter

scale [skeɪl] n (of fish) écaille f; (Mus) gamme f; (of ruler, thermometer etc) graduation f, échelle (graduée); (of salaries, fees etc) barème m; (of map, also size, extent) échelle f ▷ vt (mountain) escalader; **scales** npl balance f; (larger) bascule f; (also: **bathroom ~s**) pèse-personne m inv; **~ of charges** tableau m des tarifs; **on a large ~** sur une grande échelle, en grand

scallion [ˈskæljən] n (us: salad onion) ciboule f

scallop [ˈskɔləp] n coquille f Saint-Jacques; (Sewing) feston m

scalp [skælp] n cuir chevelu ▷ vt scalper

scalpel [ˈskælpl] n scalpel m

scam [skæm] n (inf) arnaque f

scampi [ˈskæmpɪ] npl langoustines (frites), scampi mpl

scan [skæn] vt (examine) scruter, examiner; (glance at quickly) parcourir; (TV, Radar) balayer ▷ n (Med) scanographie f

scandal [ˈskændl] n scandale m; (gossip) ragots mpl

Scandinavia [skændɪˈneɪvɪə] n Scandinavie f; **Scandinavian** adj scandinave ▷ n Scandinave m/f

scanner [ˈskænəʳ] n (Radar, Med) scanner m, scanographe m; (Comput) scanner m, numériseur m

scapegoat [ˈskeɪpgəut] n bouc m émissaire

scar [skɑːʳ] n cicatrice f ▷ vt laisser une cicatrice ou une marque à

scarce [skɛəs] adj rare, peu

abondant(e); **to make o.s. ~** (inf) se sauver; **scarcely** adv à peine, presque pas

scare [skɛəʳ] n peur f, panique f ▷ vt effrayer, faire peur à; **to ~ sb stiff** faire une peur bleue à qn; **bomb ~** alerte f à la bombe; **scarecrow** n épouvantail m; **scared** adj: **to be scared** avoir peur

scarf (pl **scarves**) [skɑːf, skɑːvz] n (long) écharpe f; (square) foulard m

scarlet [ˈskɑːlɪt] adj écarlate

scarves [skɑːvz] npl of **scarf**

scary [ˈskɛərɪ] adj (inf) effrayant(e); (film) qui fait peur

scatter [ˈskætəʳ] vt éparpiller, répandre; (crowd) disperser ▷ vi se disperser

scenario [sɪˈnɑːrɪəu] n scénario m

scene [siːn] n (Theat, fig etc) scène f; (of crime, accident) lieu(x) m(pl), endroit m; (sight, view) spectacle m, vue f; **scenery** n (Theat) décor(s) m(pl); (landscape) paysage m; **scenic** adj offrant de beaux paysages or panoramas

scent [sɛnt] n parfum m, odeur f; (fig: track) piste f

sceptical (Us **skeptical**) [ˈskɛptɪkl] adj sceptique

schedule [ˈʃɛdjuːl, us ˈskɛdjuːl] n programme m, plan m; (of trains) horaire m; (of prices etc) barème m, tarif m ▷ vt prévoir; **on ~** à l'heure (prévue); à la date prévue; **to be ahead of/behind ~** avoir de l'avance/du retard; **scheduled flight** n vol régulier

scheme [skiːm] n plan m, projet m; (plot) complot m, combine f; (arrangement) arrangement m, classification f; (pension scheme etc) régime m ▷ vt, vi comploter, manigancer

schizophrenic [skɪtsəˈfrɛnɪk] adj schizophrène

scholar [ˈskɒləʳ] n érudit(e); (pupil) boursier(-ère); **scholarship** n érudition f; (grant) bourse f (d'études)

school [skuːl] n (gen) école f; (secondary school) collège m, lycée m; (in university)

faculté f; (us: university) université f ▷ cpd scolaire; **schoolbook** n livre m scolaire or de classe; **schoolboy** n écolier m; (at secondary school) collégien m, lycéen m; **schoolchildren** npl écoliers mpl; (at secondary school) collégiens mpl, lycéens mpl; **schoolgirl** n écolière f; (at secondary school) collégienne f, lycéenne f; **schooling** n instruction f, études fpl; **schoolteacher** n (primary) instituteur(-trice); (secondary) professeur m

science [ˈsaɪəns] n science f; **science fiction** n science-fiction f; **scientific** [saɪənˈtɪfɪk] adj scientifique; **scientist** n scientifique m/f; (eminent) savant m

sci-fi [ˈsaɪfaɪ] n abbr (inf: = science fiction) SF f

scissors [ˈsɪzəz] npl ciseaux mpl; **a pair of ~** une paire de ciseaux

scold [skəuld] vt gronder

scone [skɒn] n sorte de petit pain rond au lait

scoop [skuːp] n pelle f (à main); (for ice cream) boule f à glace; (Press) reportage exclusif or à sensation

scooter [ˈskuːtəʳ] n (motor cycle) scooter m; (toy) trottinette f

scope [skəup] n (capacity: of plan, undertaking) portée f, envergure f; (: of person) compétence f, capacités fpl; (opportunity) possibilités fpl

scorching [ˈskɔːtʃɪŋ] adj torride, brûlant(e)

score [skɔːʳ] n score m, décompte m des points; (Mus) partition f ▷ vt (goal, point) marquer; (success) remporter; (cut: leather, wood, card) entailler, inciser ▷ vi marquer des points; (Football) marquer un but; (keep score) compter les points; **on that ~** à cet égard, à ce sujet; **a ~ (of)** (twenty) vingt; **~s of** (fig) des tas de; **to ~ 6 out of 10** obtenir 6 sur 10; **score out** vt rayer, barrer, biffer; **scoreboard** n tableau m; **scorer** n (Football) auteur m du but; buteur m; (keeping score) marqueur m

scorn [skɔːn] n mépris m, dédain m

Scorpio ['skɔːpɪəu] n le Scorpion
scorpion ['skɔːpɪən] n scorpion m
Scot [skɔt] n Écossais(e)
Scotch [skɔtʃ] n whisky m, scotch m
Scotch tape® (us) n scotch® m, ruban adhésif
Scotland ['skɔtlənd] n Écosse f
Scots [skɔts] adj écossais(e); **Scotsman** (irreg) n Écossais m; **Scotswoman** (irreg) n Écossaise f; **Scottish** ['skɔtɪʃ] adj écossais(e); **Scottish Parliament** n Parlement m écossais
scout [skaut] n (Mil) éclaireur m; (also: **boy ~**) scout m; **girl ~** guide f
scowl [skaul] vi se renfrogner, avoir l'air maussade; **to ~ at** regarder de travers
scramble ['skræmbl] n (rush) bousculade f, ruée f ▷ vi grimper/descendre tant bien que mal; **to ~ for** se bousculer or se disputer pour (avoir); **to go scrambling** (Sport) faire du trial; **scrambled eggs** npl œufs brouillés
scrap [skræp] n bout m, morceau m; (fight) bagarre f; (also: **~ iron**) ferraille f ▷ vt jeter, mettre au rebut; (fig) abandonner, laisser tomber ▷ vi se bagarrer; **scraps** npl (waste) déchets mpl; **scrapbook** n album m
scrape [skreɪp] vt, vi gratter, racler ▷ n: **to get into a ~** s'attirer des ennuis; **scrape through** vi (exam etc) réussir de justesse
scrap paper n papier m brouillon
scratch [skrætʃ] n égratignure f, rayure f; (on paint) éraflure f; (from claw) coup m de griffe ▷ vt (rub) se gratter; (paint etc) érafler; (with claw, nail) griffer ▷ vi (se) gratter; **to start from ~** partir de zéro; **to be up to ~** être à la hauteur; **scratch card** n carte f à gratter
scream [skriːm] n cri perçant, hurlement m ▷ vi crier, hurler
screen [skriːn] n écran m; (in room) paravent m; (fig) écran, rideau m ▷ vt masquer, cacher; (from the wind etc) abriter, protéger; (film) projeter; (candidates etc) filtrer; **screening** n (of film) projection f; (Med) test m (or

tests) de dépistage; **screenplay** n scénario m; **screen saver** n (Comput) économiseur m d'écran
screw [skruː] n vis f ▷ vt (also: **~ in**) visser; **screw up** vt (paper etc) froisser; **to ~ up one's eyes** se plisser les yeux; **screwdriver** n tournevis m
scribble ['skrɪbl] n gribouillage m ▷ vt griffonner, gribouiller
script [skrɪpt] n (Cine etc) scénario m, texte m; (writing) écriture f script m
scroll [skrəul] n rouleau m ▷ vt (Comput) faire défiler (sur l'écran)
scrub [skrʌb] n (land) broussailles fpl ▷ vt (floor) nettoyer à la brosse; (pan) récurer; (washing) frotter
scruffy ['skrʌfɪ] adj débraillé(e)
scrum(mage) ['skrʌm(ɪdʒ)] n mêlée f
scrutiny ['skruːtɪnɪ] n examen minutieux
scuba diving ['skuːbə-] n plongée sous-marine (autonome)
sculptor ['skʌlptə'] n sculpteur m
sculpture ['skʌlptʃə'] n sculpture f
scum [skʌm] n écume f, mousse f; (pej: people) rebut m, lie f
scurry ['skʌrɪ] vi filer à toute allure; **to ~ off** détaler, se sauver
sea [siː] n mer f ▷ cpd marin(e), de (la) mer, maritime; **by** or **beside the ~** (holiday, town) au bord de la mer; **by ~** par mer, en bateau; **out to ~** au large; **(out) at ~** en mer; **to be all at ~** (fig) nager complètement; **seafood** n fruits mpl de mer; **sea front** n bord m de mer; **seagull** n mouette f
seal [siːl] n (animal) phoque m; (stamp) sceau m, cachet m ▷ vt sceller; (envelope) coller; (: with seal) cacheter; **seal off** vt (forbid entry to) interdire l'accès de
sea level n niveau m de la mer
seam [siːm] n couture f; (of coal) veine f, filon m
search [səːtʃ] n (for person, thing, Comput) recherche(s) f(pl); (of drawer, pockets) fouille f; (Law: at sb's home) perquisition f ▷ vt fouiller; (examine)

examiner minutieusement; scruter
▷ vi: **to ~ for** chercher; **in ~ of** à la
recherche de; **search engine** n
(Comput) moteur de recherche;
search party n expédition f de secours

sea: seashore n rivage m, plage f,
bord m de (la) mer; **seasick** adj: **to be
seasick** avoir le mal de mer; **seaside**
n bord m de mer; **seaside resort** n
station f balnéaire

season ['siːzn] n saison f ▷ vt
assaisonner, relever; **to be in/out of ~**
être/ne pas être de saison; **seasonal**
adj saisonnier(-ière); **seasoning** n
assaisonnement m; **season ticket** n
carte f d'abonnement

seat [siːt] n siège m; (in bus, train:
place) place f; (buttocks) postérieur m;
(of trousers) fond m ▷ vt faire asseoir,
placer; (have room for) avoir des places
assises pour, pouvoir accueillir; **I'd like
to book two ~s** je voudrais réserver
deux places; **to be ~ed** être assis; **seat
belt** n ceinture f de sécurité; **seating** n
sièges fpl, places assises

sea: sea water n eau f de mer; **seaweed**
n algues fpl

sec. abbr (= second) sec

secluded [sɪ'kluːdɪd] adj retiré(e),
à l'écart

second ['sɛkənd] num deuxième,
second(e) ▷ adv (in race etc) en seconde
position ▷ n (unit of time) seconde f;
(Aut: also: **~ gear**) seconde f; (Comm:
imperfect) article m de second choix;
(BRIT Scol) ≈ licence f avec mention f
(motion) appuyer; **seconds** npl (inf: food)
rab m (inf); **secondary** adj secondaire;
secondary school n collège m; lycée
m; **second-class** adj de deuxième classe;
(Rail) de seconde (classe); (Post) au
tarif réduit; (pej) de qualité inférieure
▷ adv (Rail) en seconde; (Post) au tarif
réduit; **secondhand** adj d'occasion;
(information) de seconde main;
secondly adv deuxièmement; **second-
rate** adj de deuxième ordre, de qualité
inférieure; **second thoughts** npl: **to**

have second thoughts changer d'avis;
on second thoughts or **thought** (us)
à la réflexion

secrecy ['siːkrəsɪ] n secret m

secret ['siːkrɪt] adj secret(-ète)
▷ n secret m; **in ~** adv en secret,
secrètement, en cachette

secretary ['sɛkrətrɪ] n secrétaire m/f;
S~ of State (for) (Brit Pol) ministre
m (de)

secretive ['siːkrətɪv] adj réservé(e);
(pej) cachottier(-ière), dissimulé(e)

secret service n services secrets

sect [sɛkt] n secte f

section ['sɛkʃən] n section f; (Comm)
rayon m; (of document) section, article
m, paragraphe m; (cut) coupe f

sector ['sɛktə] n secteur m

secular ['sɛkjulə] adj laïque

secure [sɪ'kjuə] adj (free from anxiety)
sans inquiétude, sécurisé(e); (firmly
fixed) solide, bien attaché(e) (or
fermé(e) etc); (in safe place) en lieu sûr,
en sûreté ▷ vt (fix) fixer, attacher; (get)
obtenir, se procurer

security [sɪ'kjuərɪtɪ] n sécurité f,
mesures fpl de sécurité; (for loan)
caution f, garantie f; **securities** npl
(Stock Exchange) valeurs fpl, titres mpl;
security guard n garde chargé
de la sécurité; (transporting money)
convoyeur m de fonds

sedan [sə'dæn] n (us Aut) berline f

sedate [sɪ'deɪt] adj calme; posé(e) ▷ vt
donner des sédatifs à

sedative ['sɛdɪtɪv] n calmant m,
sédatif m

seduce [sɪ'djuːs] vt séduire; **seductive**
[sɪ'dʌktɪv] adj séduisant(e);
(smile) séducteur(-trice); (fig: offer)
alléchant(e)

see [siː] vb (pt saw, pp ~n) ▷ vt (gen)
voir; (accompany): **to ~ sb to the
door** reconduire or raccompagner qn
jusqu'à la porte ▷ vi voir; **to ~ that**
(ensure) veiller à ce que + sub, faire en
sorte que + sub, s'assurer que; **~ you
soon/later/tomorrow!** à bientôt/plus

tard/demain!; **see off** vt accompagner (à la gare or à l'aéroport etc); **see out** vt (take to door) raccompagner à la porte; **see through** vt mener à bonne fin ▷ vt fus voir clair dans; **see to** vt fus s'occuper de, se charger de

seed [siːd] n graine f; (fig) germe m; (Tennis etc) tête f de série; **to go to ~** (plant) monter en graine; (fig) se laisser aller

seeing ['siːɪŋ] conj: **~ (that)** vu que, étant donné que

seek (pt, pp **sought**) [siːk, sɔːt] vt chercher, rechercher

seem [siːm] vi sembler, paraître; **there ~s to be ...** il semble qu'il y a ..., on dirait qu'il y a ...; **seemingly** adv apparemment

seen [siːn] pp of **see**

seesaw ['siːsɔː] n (jeu m de) bascule f

segment ['seɡmənt] n segment m; (of orange) quartier m

segregate ['seɡrɪɡeɪt] vt séparer, isoler

Seine [seɪn] n: **the (River) ~** la Seine

seize [siːz] vt (grasp) saisir, attraper; (take possession of) s'emparer de; (opportunity) saisir

seizure ['siːʒəʳ] n (Med) crise f, attaque f; (of power) prise f

seldom ['seldəm] adv rarement

select [sɪ'lekt] adj choisi(e), d'élite; (hotel, restaurant, club) chic inv, sélect inv ▷ vt sélectionner, choisir; **selection** n sélection f, choix m; **selective** adj sélectif(-ive); (school) à recrutement sélectif

self [self] n (pl **selves**): **the ~** le moi inv ▷ prefix auto-; **self-assured** adj sûr(e) de soi, plein(e) d'assurance; **self-catering** adj (BRIT: flat) avec cuisine, où l'on peut faire sa cuisine; (: holiday) en appartement (or chalet etc) loué; **self-centred** (US **self-centered**) adj égocentrique; **self-confidence** n confiance f en soi; **self-confident** adj sûr(e) de soi, plein(e) d'assurance; **self-conscious** adj timide, qui manque d'assurance; **self-contained**

adj (BRIT: flat) avec entrée particulière, indépendant(e); **self-control** n maîtrise f de soi; **self-defence** (US **self-defense**) n autodéfense f; (Law) légitime défense f; **self-drive** adj (BRIT): **self-drive car** voiture f de location; **self-employed** adj qui travaille à son compte; **self-esteem** n amour-propre m; **self-indulgent** adj qui ne se refuse rien; **self-interest** n intérêt personnel; **selfish** adj égoïste; **self-pity** n apitoiement m sur soi-même; **self-raising** [self'reɪzɪŋ] (US **self-rising** [self'raɪzɪŋ]) adj: **self-raising flour** farine f pour gâteaux (avec levure incorporée); **self-respect** n respect m de soi, amour-propre m; **self-service** adj, n libre-service m, self-service (m)

sell (pt, pp **sold**) [sel, səuld] vt vendre ▷ vi se vendre; **to ~ at or for 10 euros** se vendre 10 euros; **sell off** vt liquider; **sell out** vi: **to ~ out (of sth)** (use up stock) vendre tout son stock (de qch); **sell-by date** n date f limite de vente; **seller** n vendeur(-euse), marchand(e)

Sellotape® ['seləuteɪp] n (BRIT) scotch® m

selves [selvz] npl of **self**

semester [sɪ'mestəʳ] n (esp US) semestre m

semi... ['semɪ] prefix semi-, demi-; à demi, à moitié; **semicircle** n demi-cercle m; **semidetached (house)** n (BRIT) maison jumelée or jumelle; **semi-final** n demi-finale f

seminar ['semɪnɑːʳ] n séminaire m

semi-skimmed ['semɪ'skɪmd] adj demi-écrémé(e)

senate ['senɪt] n sénat m; (US): **the S~** le Sénat; **senator** n sénateur m

send (pt, pp **sent**) [send, sent] vt envoyer; **send back** vt renvoyer; **send for** vt fus (by post) se faire envoyer, commander par correspondance; **send in** vt (report, application, resignation) remettre; **send off** vt (goods) envoyer, expédier; (BRIT Sport: player) expulser or renvoyer du terrain; **send on** vt

(BRIT: letter) faire suivre; (luggage etc: in advance) (faire) expédier à l'avance; **send out** vt (invitation) envoyer (par la poste); (emit: light, heat, signal) émettre; **send up** vt (person, price) faire monter; (BRIT: parody) mettre en boîte, parodier; **sender** n expéditeur(-trice); **send-off** n: **a good send-off** des adieux chaleureux

senile ['si:naɪl] adj sénile

senior ['si:nɪə'] adj (high-ranking) de haut niveau; (of higher rank): **to be ~ to sb** être le supérieur de qn; **senior citizen** n personne du troisième âge; **senior high school** n (us) = lycée m

sensation [sɛn'seɪʃən] n sensation f; **sensational** adj qui fait sensation; (marvellous) sensationnel(le)

sense [sɛns] n sens m; (feeling) sentiment m; (meaning) signification f; (wisdom) bon sens ▷ vt sentir, pressentir; **it makes ~** c'est logique; **senseless** adj insensé(e), stupide; (unconscious) sans connaissance; **sense of humour** (us **sense of humor**) n sens m de l'humour

sensible ['sɛnsɪbl] adj sensé(e), raisonnable; (shoes etc) pratique

⬛ Be careful not to translate **sensible** by the French word **sensible**.

sensitive ['sɛnsɪtɪv] adj: **~ (to)** sensible (à)

sensual ['sɛnsjuəl] adj sensuel(le)

sensuous ['sɛnsjuəs] adj voluptueux(-euse), sensuel(le)

sent [sɛnt] pt, pp of **send**

sentence ['sɛntns] n (Ling) phrase f; (Law: judgment) condamnation f, sentence f; (: punishment) peine f ▷ vt: **to ~ sb to death/to 5 years** condamner qn à mort/à 5 ans

sentiment ['sɛntɪmənt] n sentiment m; (opinion) opinion f, avis m; **sentimental** [sɛntɪ'mɛntl] adj sentimental(e)

Sep. abbr (= September) septembre

separate adj ['sɛprɪt] séparé(e); (organization) indépendant(e); (day,

occasion, issue) différent(e) ▷ vb ['sɛpəreɪt] ▷ vt séparer; (distinguish) distinguer ▷ vi se séparer; **separately** adv séparément; **separates** npl (clothes) coordonnés mpl; **separation** [sɛpə'reɪʃən] n séparation f

September [sɛp'tɛmbə'] n septembre m

septic ['sɛptɪk] adj (wound) infecté(e); **septic tank** n fosse f septique

sequel ['si:kwl] n conséquence f; séquelles fpl; (of story) suite f

sequence ['si:kwəns] n ordre m, suite f; (in film) séquence f; (dance) numéro m

sequin ['si:kwɪn] n paillette f

Serb [sə:b] adj, n = **Serbian**

Serbia ['sə:bɪə] n Serbie f

Serbian ['sə:bɪən] adj serbe ▷ n Serbe m/f; (Ling) serbe m

sergeant ['sɑ:dʒənt] n sergent m; (Police) brigadier m

serial ['sɪərɪəl] n feuilleton m; **serial killer** n meurtrier m tuant en série; **serial number** n numéro m de série

series ['sɪərɪz] n série f; (Publishing) collection f

serious ['sɪərɪəs] adj sérieux(-euse); (accident etc) grave; **seriously** adv sérieusement; (hurt) gravement

sermon ['sə:mən] n sermon m

servant ['sə:vənt] n domestique m/f; (fig) serviteur (servante)

serve [sə:v] vt (employer etc) servir, être au service de; (purpose) servir à; (customer, food, meal) servir; (subj: train) desservir; (apprenticeship) faire, accomplir; (prison term) faire; purger ▷ vi (Tennis) servir; (be useful): **to ~ as/for/to do** servir de/à/à faire ▷ n (Tennis) service m; **it ~s him right** c'est bien fait pour lui; **server** n (Comput) serveur m

service ['sə:vɪs] n (gen) service m; (Aut) révision f; (Rel) office m ▷ vt (car etc) réviser; **services** npl (Econ: tertiary sector) (secteur m) tertiaire m, secteur des services; (BRIT: on motorway) station-service f; (Mil): **the**

S~s *npl* les forces armées; **to be of ~ to sb**, **to do sb a ~** rendre service à qn; **~ included/not included** service compris/non compris; **service area** *n* (on motorway) aire *f* de services; **service charge** *n* (BRIT) service *m*; **serviceman** (*irreg*) *n* militaire *m*; **service station** *n* station-service *f*

serviette [sɜːˈviˈɛt] *n* (BRIT) serviette *f* (de table)

session [ˈsɛʃən] *n* (sitting) séance *f*; **to be in ~** (sitting) siéger, être en session or en séance

set [sɛt] *n* série *f*, assortiment *m*; (of tools etc) jeu *m*; (Radio, TV) poste *m*; (Tennis) set *m*; (group of people) cercle *m*, milieu *m*; (Cine) plateau *m*; (Theat: stage) scène *f*; (: scenery) décor *m*; (Math) ensemble *m*; (Hairdressing) mise *f* en plis ▷ *adj* (fixed) fixe, déterminé(e); (ready) prêt(e) ▷ *vb* (*pt, pp* ~) ▷ *vt* (place) mettre, poser, placer; (fix, establish) fixer; (: record) établir; (assign: task, homework) donner; (exam) composer; (adjust) régler; (decide: rules etc) fixer, choisir ▷ *vi* (sun) se coucher; (jam, jelly, concrete) prendre; (bone) se ressouder; **to be ~ on doing** être résolu(e) à faire; **to ~ to music** mettre en musique; **to ~ on fire** mettre le feu à; **to ~ free** libérer; **to ~ sth going** déclencher qch; **to ~ sail** partir, prendre la mer; **set aside** *vt* mettre de côté; (time) garder; **set down** *vt* (subj: bus, train) déposer; **set in** *vi* (infection, bad weather) s'installer; (complications) survenir, surgir; **set off** *vi* se mettre en route, partir ▷ *vt* (bomb) faire exploser; (cause to start) déclencher; (show up well) mettre en valeur, faire valoir; **set out** *vi*: **to ~ out (from)** partir (de) ▷ *vt* (arrange) disposer; (state) présenter, exposer; **to ~ out to do** entreprendre de faire; avoir pour but or intention de faire; **set up** *vt* (organization) fonder, créer; **setback** *n* (hitch) revers *m*, contretemps *m*; **set menu** *n* menu *m*

settee [sɛˈtiː] *n* canapé *m*

setting [ˈsɛtɪŋ] *n* cadre *m*; (of jewel)

monture *f*; (position: of controls) réglage *m*

settle [ˈsɛtl] *vt* (argument, matter, account) régler; (problem) résoudre; (Med: calm) calmer ▷ *vi* (bird, dust etc) se poser; **to ~ for sth** accepter qch, se contenter de qch; **to ~ on sth** opter or se décider pour qch; **settle down** *vi* (get comfortable) s'installer; (become calmer) se calmer, se ranger; (live quietly) se fixer; **settle in** *vi* s'installer; **settle up** *vi*: **to ~ up with sb** régler (ce que l'on doit à) qn; **settlement** *n* (payment) règlement *m*; (agreement) accord *m*; (village etc) village *m*, hameau *m*

setup [ˈsɛtʌp] *n* (arrangement) manière *f* dont les choses sont organisées; (situation) situation *f*, allure *f* des choses

seven [ˈsɛvn] *num* sept; **seventeen** *num* dix-sept; **seventeenth** [sɛvnˈtiːnθ] *num* dix-septième; **seventh** *num* septième; **seventieth** [ˈsɛvntɪɪθ] *num* soixante-dixième; **seventy** *num* soixante-dix

sever [ˈsɛvəʳ] *vt* couper, trancher; (relations) rompre

several [ˈsɛvərl] *adj, pron* plusieurs *pl*; **~ of us** plusieurs d'entre nous

severe [sɪˈvɪəʳ] *adj* (stern) sévère, strict(e); (serious) grave, sérieux(-euse); (plain) sévère, austère

sew (*pt* ~ed, *pp* ~n) [səʊ, səʊd, səʊn] *vt, vi* coudre

sewage [ˈsuːɪdʒ] *n* vidange(s) *f*(pl)

sewer [ˈsuːəʳ] *n* égout *m*

sewing [ˈsəʊɪŋ] *n* couture *f*; (item(s)) ouvrage *m*; **sewing machine** *n* machine *f* à coudre

sewn [səʊn] *pp* of **sew**

sex [sɛks] *n* sexe *m*; **to have ~ with** avoir des rapports (sexuels) avec; **sexism** [ˈsɛksɪzəm] *n* sexisme *m*; **sexist** *adj* sexiste; **sexual** [ˈsɛksjʊəl] *adj* sexuel(le); **sexual intercourse** *n* rapports sexuels; **sexuality** [sɛksjʊˈælɪtɪ] *n* sexualité *f*; **sexy** *adj* sexy *inv*

shabby [ˈʃæbɪ] *adj* miteux(-euse)

(behaviour) mesquin(e), méprisable

shack [ʃæk] *n* cabane *f*, hutte *f*

shade [ʃeɪd] *n* ombre *f*; *(for lamp)* abat-jour *m inv*; *(of colour)* nuance *f*, ton *m*; *(us: window shade)* store *m*; *(small quantity)*: **a ~ of** un soupçon de ▷ *vt* abriter du soleil, ombrager; **shades** *npl* *(us: sunglasses)* lunettes *fpl* de soleil; **in the ~** à l'ombre; **a ~ smaller** un tout petit peu plus petit

shadow [ˈʃædəu] *n* ombre *f* ▷ *vt* *(follow)* filer; **shadow cabinet** *n* (BRIT Pol) *cabinet parallèle formé par le parti qui n'est pas au pouvoir*

shady [ˈʃeɪdɪ] *adj* ombragé(e); *(fig: dishonest)* louche, véreux(-euse)

shaft [ʃɑːft] *n* *(of arrow, spear)* hampe *f*; *(Aut, Tech)* arbre *m*; *(of mine)* puits *m*; *(of lift)* cage *f*; *(of light)* rayon *m*, trait *m*

shake [ʃeɪk] *vb (pt shook, pp shaken)* ▷ *vt* secouer; *(bottle, cocktail)* agiter; *(house, confidence)* ébranler ▷ *vi* trembler; **to ~ one's head** *(in refusal also or in agreement)* dire ou faire non de la tête; *(in dismay)* secouer la tête; **to ~ hands with sb** serrer la main à qn; **shake off** *vt* secouer; *(pursuer)* se débarrasser de; **shake up** *vt* secouer; **shaky** *adj* *(hand, voice)* tremblant(e); *(building)* branlant(e), peu solide

shall [ʃæl] *aux vb*: **I ~ go** j'irai; **~ I open the door?** j'ouvre la porte?; **I'll get the coffee, ~ I?** je vais chercher le café, d'accord?

shallow [ˈʃæləu] *adj* peu profond(e); *(fig)* superficiel(le), qui manque de profondeur

sham [ʃæm] *n* frime *f*

shambles [ˈʃæmblz] *n* confusion *f*, pagaïe *f*, fouillis *m*

shame [ʃeɪm] *n* honte *f* ▷ *vt* faire honte à; **it is a ~ (that/to do)** c'est dommage (que + sub/de faire); **what a ~!** quel dommage!; **shameful** *adj* honteux(-euse), scandaleux(-euse)

shameless *adj* éhonté(e), effronté(e)

shampoo [ʃæmˈpuː] *n* shampooing *m* ▷ *vt* faire un shampooing à

shandy [ˈʃændɪ] *n* bière panachée

shan't [ʃɑːnt] = **shall not**

shape [ʃeɪp] *n* forme *f* ▷ *vt* façonner, modeler; *(sb's ideas, character)* former; *(sb's life)* déterminer ▷ *vi* *(also: ~ up)* *(events)* prendre tournure; *(: person)* faire des progrès, se former; **to take ~** prendre forme ou tournure

share [ʃɛəʳ] *n* part *f*; (Comm) action *f* ▷ *vt* partager; *(have in common)* avoir en commun; **to ~ out (among** *or* **between)** partager (entre); **shareholder** *n* (BRIT) actionnaire *m/f*

shark [ʃɑːk] *n* requin *m*

sharp [ʃɑːp] *adj* *(razor, knife)* tranchant(e), bien aiguisé(e); *(point, voice)* aigu(ë); *(nose, chin)* pointu(e); *(outline, increase)* net(te); *(cold, pain)* vif (vive); *(taste)* piquant(e), âcre; (Mus) dièse; *(person: quick-witted)* vif (vive), éveillé(e); *(: unscrupulous)* malhonnête ▷ *n* (Mus) dièse *m* ▷ *adv*: **at 2 o'clock ~** à 2 heures pile ou tapantes; **sharpen** *vt* aiguiser; *(pencil)* tailler; *(fig)* aviver; **sharpener** *n* *(also:* **pencil sharpener)** taille-crayon(s) *m inv*; **sharply** *adv* *(turn, stop)* brusquement; *(stand out)* nettement; *(criticize, retort)* sèchement, vertement

shatter [ˈʃætəʳ] *vt* briser; *(fig: upset)* bouleverser; *(: ruin)* briser, ruiner ▷ *vi* voler en éclats, se briser; **shattered** *adj* *(overwhelmed, grief-stricken)* bouleversé(e); *(inf: exhausted)* éreinté(e)

shave [ʃeɪv] *vt* raser ▷ *vi* se raser ▷ *n*: **to have a ~** se raser; **shaver** *n* *(also:* **electric shaver)** rasoir *m* électrique

shaving cream *n* crème *f* à raser

shaving foam *n* mousse *f* à raser

shavings [ˈʃeɪvɪŋz] *npl* *(of wood etc)* copeaux *mpl*

shawl [ʃɔːl] *n* châle *m*

she [ʃiː] *pron* elle

sheath [ʃiːθ] *n* gaine *f*, fourreau *m*, étui *m*; *(contraceptive)* préservatif *m*

shed [ʃed] *n* remise *f*, resserre *f* ▷ *vt* *(pt, pp ~)* *(leaves, fur etc)* perdre; *(tears)* verser, répandre; *(workers)* congédier

she'd [ʃiːd] = **she had; she would**

sheep [ʃiːp] n (pl inv) mouton m;
sheepdog n chien m de berger;
sheepskin n peau f de mouton

sheer [ʃɪəʳ] adj (utter) pur(e), pur et
simple; (steep) à pic, abrupt(e); (almost
transparent) extrêmement fin(e) ▷ adv à
pic, abruptement

sheet [ʃiːt] n (on bed) drap m; (of paper)
feuille f; (of glass, metal etc) feuille,
plaque f

sheik(h) [ʃeɪk] n cheik m

shelf (pl **shelves**) [ʃɛlf, ʃɛlvz] n étagère
f, rayon m

shell [ʃɛl] n (on beach) coquillage m; (of
egg, nut etc) coquille f; (explosive) obus
m; (of building) carcasse f ▷ vt (peas)
écosser; (Mil) bombarder (d'obus)

she'll [ʃiːl] = **she will**; **she shall**

shellfish [ʃɛlfɪʃ] n (pl inv: crab etc)
crustacé m; (: scallop etc) coquillage m
▷ npl (as food) fruits mpl de mer

shelter [ʃɛltəʳ] n abri m, refuge
m ▷ vt abriter, protéger; (give lodging to)
donner asile à ▷ vi s'abriter, se mettre
à l'abri; **sheltered** adj (life) retiré(e), à
l'abri des soucis; (spot) abrité(e)

shelves [ʃɛlvz] npl of **shelf**

shelving [ʃɛlvɪŋ] n (shelves)
rayonnage(s) m(pl)

shepherd [ʃɛpəd] n berger m ▷ vt
(guide) guider, escorter; **shepherd's pie**
n ≈ hachis m Parmentier

sheriff [ʃɛrɪf] (us) n shérif m

sherry [ʃɛrɪ] n xérès m, sherry m

she's [ʃiːz] = **she is**; **she has**

Shetland [ʃɛtlənd] n (also: **the ~s, the
~ Isles** or **Islands**) les îles fpl Shetland

shield [ʃiːld] n bouclier m; (protection)
écran m de protection ▷ vt: **to ~ (from)**
protéger (de ou contre)

shift [ʃɪft] n (change) changement m;
(work period) période f de travail; (of
workers) équipe f, poste m ▷ vt déplacer,
changer de place; (remove) enlever ▷ vi
changer de place, bouger

shin [ʃɪn] n tibia m

shine [ʃaɪn] n éclat m, brillant m ▷ vb
(pt, pp **shone**) ▷ vi briller ▷ vt (torch): **to**

~ on braquer sur; (polish: pt, pp **-d**) faire
briller or reluire

shingles [ʃɪŋɡlz] n (Med) zona m

shiny [ʃaɪnɪ] adj brillant(e)

ship [ʃɪp] n bateau m; (large) navire
m ▷ vt transporter (par mer); (send)
expédier (par mer); **shipment** n
cargaison f; **shipping** n (ships)
navires mpl; (traffic) navigation f; (the
industry) industrie navale; (transport)
transport m; **shipwreck** n épave
f; (event) naufrage m ▷ vt: **to be
shipwrecked** faire naufrage; **shipyard**
n chantier naval

shirt [ʃəːt] n chemise f; (woman's)
chemisier m; **in ~ sleeves** en bras de
chemise

shit [ʃɪt] excl (inf!) merde (!)

shiver [ʃɪvəʳ] n frisson m ▷ vi frissonner

shock [ʃɔk] n choc m; (Elec) secousse
f, décharge f; (Med) commotion
f, choc ▷ vt (scandalize) choquer,
scandaliser; (upset) bouleverser;
shocking adj (outrageous) choquant(e),
scandaleux(-euse); (awful)
épouvantable

shoe [ʃuː] n chaussure f, soulier m;
(also: **horse~**) fer m à cheval ▷ vt (pt, pp
shod) (horse) ferrer; **shoelace** n lacet
m (de soulier); **shoe polish** n cirage m;
shoeshop n magasin m de chaussures

shone [ʃɔn] pt, pp of **shine**

shook [ʃuk] pt of **shake**

shoot [ʃuːt] n (on branch, seedling)
pousse f ▷ vb (pt, pp **shot**) ▷ vt (game:
hunt) chasser; (: aim at) tirer; (: kill)
abattre; (person) blesser/tuer d'un
coup de fusil (or de revolver); (execute)
fusiller; (arrow) tirer; (gun) tirer un
coup de; (Cine) tourner ▷ vi (with gun,
bow): **to ~ (at)** tirer (sur); (Football)
shooter, tirer; **shoot down** vt (plane)
abattre; **shoot up** vi (fig: prices etc)
monter en flèche; **shooting** n (shots)
coups mpl de feu; (attack) fusillade f;
(murder) homicide m (à l'aide d'une arme
à feu); (Hunting) chasse f

shop [ʃɔp] n magasin m; (workshop)

atelier m ▷ vi (also: **~ping**) faire ses courses or ses achats; **shop assistant** n (BRIT) vendeur(-euse); **shopkeeper** n marchand(e), commerçant(e); **shoplifting** n vol m à l'étalage; **shopping** n (goods) achats mpl, provisions fpl; **shopping bag** n sac m (à provisions); **shopping centre** (US **shopping center**) n centre commercial; **shopping mall** n centre commercial; **shopping trolley** n (BRIT) Caddie® m; **shop window** n vitrine f

shore [ʃɔːʳ] n (of sea, lake) rivage m, rive f ▷ vt: **to ~ (up)** étayer; **on ~** à terre

short [ʃɔːt] adj (not long) court(e); (soon finished) court, bref (brève); (person, step) petit(e); (curt) brusque, sec (sèche); (insufficient) insuffisant(e) ▷ n (also: **~ film**) court métrage; (Elec) court-circuit m; **to be ~ of sth** être à court de or manquer de qch; **in ~** bref; **en bref; ~ of doing** à moins de faire; **everything ~ of** tout sauf; **it is ~ for** c'est l'abréviation or le diminutif de; **to cut ~** (speech, visit) abréger, écourter; **to fall ~ of** ne pas être à la hauteur de; **to run ~ of** arriver à court de, venir à manquer de; **to stop ~** s'arrêter net; **to stop ~ of** ne pas aller jusqu'à; **shortage** n manque m, pénurie f; **shortbread** n sablé m; **shortcoming** n défaut m; **short(crust) pastry** (BRIT) pâte brisée; **shortcut** n raccourci m; **shorten** vt raccourcir; (text, visit) abréger; **shortfall** n déficit m; **shorthand** n (BRIT) sténo(graphie) f; **shortlist** n (BRIT: for job) liste f des candidats sélectionnés; **short-lived** adj de courte durée; **shortly** adv bientôt, sous peu; **shorts** npl: **(a pair of) shorts** un short; **short-sighted** adj (BRIT) myope; (fig) qui manque de clairvoyance; **short-sleeved** adj à manches courtes; **short story** n nouvelle f; **short-tempered** adj qui s'emporte facilement; **short-term** adj (effect) à court terme

shot [ʃɔt] pt, pp of **shoot** ▷ n coup m

(de feu); (try) coup, essai m; (injection) piqûre f; (Phot) photo f; **to be a good/poor ~** (person) tirer bien/mal; **like a ~** comme une flèche; (very readily) sans hésiter; **shotgun** n fusil m de chasse

should [ʃud] aux vb: **I ~ go now** je devrais partir maintenant; **he ~ be there now** il devrait être arrivé maintenant; **I ~ go if I were you** si j'étais vous j'irais; **I ~ like to** j'aimerais bien, volontiers

shoulder [ˈʃəʊldəʳ] n épaule f ▷ vt (fig) endosser, se charger de; **shoulder blade** n omoplate f

shouldn't [ˈʃudnt] = **should not**

shout [ʃaut] n cri m ▷ vt crier ▷ vi crier, pousser des cris

shove [ʃʌv] vt pousser; (inf: put): **to ~ sth in** fourrer or ficher qch dans ▷ n poussée f

shovel [ˈʃʌvl] n pelle f ▷ vt pelleter, enlever (or enfourner) à la pelle

show [ʃəʊ] n (of emotion) manifestation f, démonstration f; (semblance) semblant m, apparence f; (exhibition) exposition f, salon m; (Theat, TV) spectacle m; (Cine) séance f ▷ vb (pt **~ed**, pp **~n**) ▷ vt montrer; (film) passer; (courage etc) faire preuve de, manifester; (exhibit) exposer ▷ vi se voir, être visible; **can you ~ me where it is, please?** pouvez-vous me montrer où c'est?; **to be on ~** être exposé(e); **it's just for ~** c'est juste pour l'effet; **show in** vt faire entrer; **show off** vi (pej) crâner ▷ vt (display) faire valoir; (pej) faire étalage de; **show out** vt reconduire à la porte; **show up** vi (stand out) ressortir; (inf: turn up) se montrer ▷ vt (unmask) démasquer, dénoncer; (flaw) faire ressortir; **show business** n le monde du spectacle

shower [ˈʃaʊəʳ] n (for washing) douche f; (rain) averse f; (of stones etc) pluie f, grêle f; (US: party) réunion organisée pour la remise de cadeaux ▷ vi prendre une douche, se doucher ▷ vt: **to ~ sb with** (gifts etc) combler qn de; **to have**

or **take a ~** prendre une douche, se doucher; **shower cap** n bonnet m de douche; **shower gel** n gel m douche

showing ['ʃəʊɪŋ] n (of film) projection f

show jumping [-dʒʌmpɪŋ] n concours m hippique

shown [ʃəʊn] pp of **show**

show: show-off n (inf: person) crâneur(-euse), m'as-tu-vu(e); **showroom** n magasin m ou salle f d'exposition

shrank [ʃræŋk] pt of **shrink**

shred [ʃred] n (gen pl) lambeau m, petit morceau; (fig: of truth, evidence) parcelle f ▷ vt mettre en lambeaux, déchirer; (documents) détruire; (Culin: grate) râper; (: lettuce etc) couper en lanières

shrewd [ʃruːd] adj astucieux(-euse), perspicace; (business person) habile

shriek [ʃriːk] n cri perçant ou aigu, hurlement m ▷ vi, vt hurler, crier

shrimp [ʃrɪmp] n crevette grise

shrine [ʃraɪn] n (place) lieu m de pèlerinage

shrink (pt **shrank**, pp **shrunk**) [ʃrɪŋk, ʃræŋk, ʃrʌŋk] vi rétrécir; (fig) diminuer; (also: **~ away**) reculer ▷ vt (wool) (faire) rétrécir ▷ n (inf: pej) psychanalyste m/f; **to ~ from (doing) sth** reculer devant (la pensée de) faire qch

shrivel ['ʃrɪvl] (also: **~ up**) vt ratatiner, flétrir ▷ vi se ratatiner, se flétrir

shroud [ʃraʊd] n linceul m ▷ vt: **~ed in mystery** enveloppé(e) de mystère

Shrove Tuesday ['ʃrəʊv-] n (le) Mardi gras

shrub [ʃrʌb] n arbuste m

shrug [ʃrʌg] n haussement m d'épaules ▷ vt, vi: **to ~ (one's shoulders)** hausser les épaules; **shrug off** vt faire fi de

shrunk [ʃrʌŋk] pp of **shrink**

shudder ['ʃʌdə*] n frisson m, frémissement m ▷ vi frissonner, frémir

shuffle ['ʃʌfl] vt (cards) battre; **to ~ (one's feet)** traîner les pieds

shun [ʃʌn] vt éviter, fuir

shut (pt, pp **~**) [ʃʌt] vt fermer ▷ vi (se) fermer; **shut down** vt fermer

définitivement ▷ vi fermer définitivement; **shut up** vi (inf: keep quiet) se taire ▷ vt (close) fermer; (silence) faire taire; **shutter** n volet m; (Phot) obturateur m

shuttle ['ʃʌtl] n navette f; (also: **~ service**) (service m de) navette f; **shuttlecock** n volant m (de badminton)

shy [ʃaɪ] adj timide

siblings ['sɪblɪŋz] npl (formal) frères et sœurs mpl (de mêmes parents)

Sicily ['sɪsɪlɪ] n Sicile f

sick [sɪk] adj (ill) malade; (BRIT: vomiting): **to be ~** vomir; (humour) noir(e), macabre; **to feel ~** avoir envie de vomir, avoir mal au cœur; **to be ~ of** (fig) en avoir assez de; **sickening** adj (fig) écœurant(e), révoltant(e), répugnant(e); **sick leave** n congé m de maladie; **sickly** adj maladif(-ive), souffreteux(-euse); (causing nausea) écœurant(e); **sickness** n maladie f; (vomiting) vomissement(s) m(pl)

side [saɪd] n côté m; (of lake, road) bord m; (of mountain) versant m; (fig: aspect) côté, aspect m; (team: Sport) équipe f; (TV: channel) chaîne f ▷ adj (door, entrance) latéral(e) ▷ vi: **to ~ with sb** prendre le parti de qn, se ranger du côté de qn; **by the ~ of** au bord de; **side by ~** côte à côte; **to rock from ~ to ~** se balancer; **to take ~s (with)** prendre parti (pour); **sideboard** n buffet m; **sideboards** (BRIT), **sideburns** npl (whiskers) pattes fpl; **side effect** n effet m secondaire; **sidelight** n (Aut) veilleuse f; **sideline** n (Sport) (ligne f de) touche f; (fig) activité f secondaire; **side order** n garniture f; **side road** n petite route, route transversale; **side street** n rue transversale; **sidetrack** vt (fig) faire dévier de son sujet; **sidewalk** n (US) trottoir m; **sideways** adv de côté

siege [siːdʒ] n siège m

sieve [sɪv] n tamis m, passoire f ▷ vt tamiser, passer (au tamis)

sift [sɪft] vt passer au tamis ou au crible; (fig) passer au crible

sigh [saɪ] n soupir m ▷ vi soupirer, pousser un soupir

sight [saɪt] n (faculty) vue f; (spectacle) spectacle m; (on gun) mire f ▷ vt apercevoir; **in ~** visible; (fig) en vue; **out of ~** hors de vue; **sightseeing** n tourisme m; **to go sightseeing** faire du tourisme

sign [saɪn] n (gen) signe m; (with hand etc) signe, geste m; (notice) panneau m, écriteau m; (also: **road~**) panneau de signalisation ▷ vt signer; **where do I ~?** où dois-je signer?; **sign for** vt fus (item) signer le reçu pour; **sign in** vi signer le registre (en arrivant); **sign on** vi (BRIT: as unemployed) s'inscrire au chômage; (enrol) s'inscrire ▷ vt (employee) embaucher; **sign over** vt: **to ~ sth over to sb** céder qch par écrit à qn; **sign up** vi (Mil) s'engager; (for course) s'inscrire

signal ['sɪɡnl] n signal m ▷ vi (Aut) mettre son clignotant ▷ vt (person) faire signe à; (message) communiquer par signaux

signature ['sɪɡnətʃə] n signature f

significance [sɪɡ'nɪfɪkəns] n signification f; importance f

significant [sɪɡ'nɪfɪkənt] adj significatif(-ive); (important) important(e), considérable

signify ['sɪɡnɪfaɪ] vt signifier

sign language n langage m par signes

signpost ['saɪnpəust] n poteau m indicateur

Sikh [siːk] adj, n Sikh m/f

silence ['saɪləns] n silence m ▷ vt faire taire, réduire au silence

silent ['saɪlənt] adj silencieux(-euse); (film) muet(te); **to keep** or **remain ~** garder le silence, ne rien dire

silhouette [sɪluː'ɛt] n silhouette f

silicon chip ['sɪlɪkən-] n puce f électronique

silk [sɪlk] n soie f ▷ cpd de or en soie

silly ['sɪlɪ] adj stupide, sot(te), bête

silver ['sɪlvə] n argent m; (money) monnaie f (en pièces d'argent); (also: **~ware**) argenterie f ▷ adj (made of

silver) d'argent, en argent; (in colour) argenté(e); **silver-plated** adj plaqué(e) argent

similar ['sɪmɪlə] adj: **~ (to)** semblable (à); **similarity** [sɪmɪ'lærɪtɪ] n ressemblance f, similarité f; **similarly** adv de la même façon, de même

simmer ['sɪmə] vi cuire à feu doux, mijoter

simple ['sɪmpl] adj simple; **simplicity** [sɪm'plɪsɪtɪ] n simplicité f; **simplify** ['sɪmplɪfaɪ] vt simplifier; **simply** adv simplement; (without fuss) avec simplicité; (absolutely) absolument

simulate ['sɪmjuleɪt] vt simuler, feindre

simultaneous [sɪməl'teɪnɪəs] adj simultané(e); **simultaneously** adv simultanément

sin [sɪn] n péché m ▷ vi pécher

since [sɪns] adv, prep depuis ▷ conj (time) depuis que; (because) puisque, étant donné que, comme; **~ then**, **ever ~** depuis ce moment-là

sincere [sɪn'sɪə] adj sincère; **sincerely** adv sincèrement; **Yours sincerely** (at end of letter) veuillez agréer, Monsieur (or Madame) l'expression de mes sentiments distingués or les meilleurs

sing (pt **sang**, pp **sung**) [sɪŋ, sæŋ, sʌŋ] vt, vi chanter

Singapore [sɪŋɡə'pɔː] n Singapour m

singer ['sɪŋə] n chanteur(-euse)

singing ['sɪŋɪŋ] n (of person, bird) chant m

single ['sɪŋɡl] adj seul(e), unique; (unmarried) célibataire; (not double) simple ▷ n (BRIT: also: **~ ticket**) aller m (simple); (record) 45 tours m; **singles** npl (Tennis) simple m; **every ~ day** chaque jour sans exception; **single out** vt choisir; (distinguish) distinguer; **single bed** n lit m d'une personne or à une place; **single file** n: **in single file** en file indienne; **single-handed** adv tout(e) seul(e), sans (aucune) aide; **single-minded** adj résolu(e), tenace; **single parent** n parent unique (or

célibataire); single-parent family
famille monoparentale; **single room** n
chambre f à un lit or pour une personne

singular ['sɪŋɡjʊlə'] adj
singulier(-ière); (odd) singulier,
étrange; (outstanding) remarquable;
(Ling) (au) singulier, du singulier ⊳ n
(Ling) singulier m

sinister ['sɪnɪstə'] adj sinistre

sink [sɪŋk] n évier m; (washbasin)
lavabo m ⊳ vb (pt **sank**, pp **sunk**) ⊳ vt
(ship) (faire) couler, faire sombrer;
(foundations) creuser ⊳ vi couler,
sombrer; (ground:level) s'affaisser; **to ~
into sth** (chair) s'enfoncer dans qch;
sink in vi (explanation) rentrer (inf),
être compris

sinus ['saɪnəs] n (Anat) sinus m inv

sip [sɪp] n petite gorgée f ⊳ vt boire à
petites gorgées

sir [sə'] n monsieur m; **S~ John Smith** sir
John Smith; **yes ~** oui Monsieur

siren ['saɪərn] n sirène f

sirloin ['sə:lɔɪn] n (also: **~ steak**)
aloyau m

sister ['sɪstə'] n sœur f; (nun) religieuse
f; (Brit: nurse) infirmière f
en chef; **sister-in-law** n belle-sœur f

sit (pt, pp **sat**) [sɪt, sæt] vi s'asseoir; (be
sitting) être assis(e); (assembly) être en
séance, siéger; (for painter) poser ⊳ vt
(exam) passer, se présenter à; **sit back**
vi (in seat) bien s'installer, se carrer; **sit
down** vi s'asseoir; **sit on** vt fus (jury,
committee) faire partie de; **sit up** vi
s'asseoir; (straight) se redresser; (not go
to bed) rester debout, ne pas se coucher

sitcom ['sɪtkɔm] n abbr (TV: = situation
comedy) sitcom f, comédie f de situation

site [saɪt] n emplacement m, site m;
(also: **building ~**) chantier m ⊳ vt placer

sitting ['sɪtɪŋ] n (of assembly etc) séance
f; (in canteen) service m; **sitting room**
n salon m

situated ['sɪtjʊeɪtɪd] adj situé(e)

situation [sɪtjʊ'eɪʃən] n situation f;
"~s vacant/wanted" (Brit) "offres/
demandes d'emploi"

six [sɪks] num six; **sixteen** num seize;
sixteenth [sɪks'ti:nθ] num seizième;
sixth ['sɪksθ] num sixième; **sixth form**
n (Brit) = classes fpl de première et
de terminale; **sixth-form college**
n lycée n'ayant que des classes de première
et de terminale; **sixtieth** ['sɪkstiɪθ] num
soixantième; **sixty** num soixante

size [saɪz] n dimensions fpl; (of person)
taille f; (of clothing) taille f; (of shoes)
pointure f; (of problem) ampleur f; (of
glue) colle f ⊳ vt; **sizeable** adj assez grand(e);
(amount, problem, majority) assez
important(e)

sizzle ['sɪzl] vi grésiller

skate [skeɪt] n patin m; (fish: pl inv)
raie f ⊳ vi patiner; **skateboard** n
skateboard m, planche f à roulettes;
skateboarding n skateboard m;
skater n patineur(-euse); **skating**
n patinage m; **skating rink** n patinoire f

skeleton ['skelɪtn] n squelette m;
(outline) schéma m

skeptical ['skeptɪkl] (us) = **sceptical**

sketch [skɛtʃ] n (drawing) croquis
m, esquisse f; (outline plan) aperçu
m; (Theat) sketch m, saynète f ⊳ vt
esquisser, faire un croquis or une
esquisse de; (plan etc) esquisser

skewer ['skju:ə'] n brochette f

ski [ski:] n ski m ⊳ vi skier, faire du ski;
ski boot n chaussure f de ski

skid [skɪd] n dérapage m ⊳ vi déraper

ski: skier n skieur(-euse); **skiing** n ski m;
to go skiing (aller) faire du ski

skilful (us **skillful**) ['skɪlful] adj habile,
adroit(e)

ski lift n remonte-pente m inv

skill [skɪl] n (ability) habileté f,
adresse f, talent m; (requiring training)
compétences fpl; **skilled** adj habile,
adroit(e); (worker) qualifié(e)

skim [skɪm] vt (soup) écumer; (glide
over) raser, effleurer ⊳ vi: **to ~ through**
(fig) parcourir; **skimmed milk** (us **skim
milk**) n lait écrémé

skin [skɪn] n peau f ⊳ vt (fruit etc)
éplucher; (animal) écorcher; **skinhead**

n skinhead *m*; **skinny** *adj* maigre, maigrichon(ne)

skip [skɪp] *n* petit bond *or* saut *m*; (BRIT: container) benne *f* ▷ *vi* gambader, sautiller; (with rope) sauter à la corde ▷ *vt* (pass over) sauter

ski: ski pass *n* forfait-skieur(s) *m*; **ski pole** *n* bâton *m* de ski

skipper ['skɪpə'] *n* (Naut, Sport) capitaine *m*; (in race) skipper *m*

skipping rope ['skɪpɪŋ-] (US **skip rope**) *n* (BRIT) corde *f* à sauter

skirt [skə:t] *n* jupe *f* ▷ *vt* longer, contourner

skirting board ['skə:tɪŋ-] *n* (BRIT) plinthe *f*

ski slope *n* piste *f* de ski

ski suit *n* combinaison *f* de ski

skull [skʌl] *n* crâne *m*

skunk [skʌŋk] *n* mouffette *f*

sky [skaɪ] *n* ciel *m*; **skyscraper** *n* gratte-ciel *m inv*

slab [slæb] *n* (of stone) dalle *f*; (of meat, cheese) tranche épaisse

slack [slæk] *adj* (loose) lâche, desserré(e); (slow) stagnant(e); (careless) négligent(e), peu sérieux(-euse) *or* consciencieux(-euse); **slacks** *npl* pantalon *m*

slain [sleɪn] *pp of* **slay**

slam [slæm] *vt* (door) (faire) claquer; (throw) jeter violemment, flanquer; (inf: criticize) éreinter, démolir ▷ *vi* claquer

slander ['slɑ:ndə'] *n* calomnie *f*; (Law) diffamation *f*

slang [slæŋ] *n* argot *m*

slant [slɑ:nt] *n* inclinaison *f*; (fig) angle *m*, point *m* de vue

slap [slæp] *n* claque *f*, gifle *f*; (on the back) tape *f* ▷ *vt* donner une claque *or* une gifle *or* une tape à; **to ~ on** (paint) appliquer rapidement ▷ *adv* (directly) tout droit, en plein

slash [slæʃ] *vt* entailler, taillader; (fig: prices) casser

slate [sleɪt] *n* ardoise *f* ▷ *vt* (fig: criticize) éreinter, démolir

slaughter ['slɔ:tə'] *n* carnage *m*,

massacre *m*; (of animals) abattage *m* ▷ *vt* (animal) abattre; (people) massacrer; **slaughterhouse** *n* abattoir *m*

Slav [slɑ:v] *adj* slave

slave [sleɪv] *n* esclave *m/f* ▷ *vi* (also: **~ away**) trimer, travailler comme un forçat; **slavery** *n* esclavage *m*

slay (*pt* **slew**, *pp* **slain**) [sleɪ, slu:, sleɪn] *vt* (literary) tuer

sleazy ['sli:zɪ] *adj* miteux(-euse), minable

sled [sled] (US) = **sledge**

sledge [sledʒ] *n* luge *f*

sleek [sli:k] *adj* (hair, fur) brillant(e), luisant(e); (car, boat) aux lignes pures *or* élégantes

sleep [sli:p] *n* sommeil *m* ▷ *vi* (*pt, pp* **slept**) dormir; **to go to ~** s'endormir; **sleep in** *vi* (oversleep) se réveiller trop tard; (on purpose) faire la grasse matinée; **sleep together** *vi* (have sex) coucher ensemble; **sleeper** *n* (person) dormeur(-euse); (BRIT Rail: on track) traverse *f*; (: train) train-couchettes *m*; (: berth) couchette *f*; **sleeping bag** *n* sac *m* de couchage; **sleeping car** *n* wagon-lits *m*, voiture-lits *f*; **sleeping pill** *n* somnifère *m*; **sleepover** *n* nuit *f* chez un copain *or* une copine; **we're having a sleepover at Jo's** nous allons passer la nuit chez Jo; **sleepwalk** *vi* marcher en dormant; **sleepy** *adj* (fig) endormi(e)

sleet [sli:t] *n* neige fondue

sleeve [sli:v] *n* manche *f*; (of record) pochette *f*; **sleeveless** *adj* (garment) sans manches

sleigh [sleɪ] *n* traîneau *m*

slender ['slendə'] *adj* svelte, mince; (fig) faible, ténu(e)

slept [slept] *pt, pp of* **sleep**

slew [slu:] *pt of* **slay**

slice [slaɪs] *n* tranche *f*; (round) rondelle *f*; (utensil) spatule *f*; (also: **fish ~**) pelle *f* à poisson ▷ *vt* couper en tranches *or* en rondelles

slick [slɪk] *adj* (skilful) bien ficelé(e);

(salesperson) qui a du bagout ▷ n (also: **oil ~**) nappe f de pétrole, marée noire

slide [slaɪd] n (in playground) toboggan m; (Phot) diapositive f (Brit: also: **hair ~**) barrette f; (in prices) chute f, baisse f ▷ vb (pt, pp **slid**) ▷ vt (faire) glisser ▷ vi glisser; **sliding** (door) coulissant(e)

slight [slaɪt] adj (slim) mince, menu(e); (frail) frêle; (trivial) faible, insignifiant(e); (small) petit(e), léger(-ère) before n to offense(e), affront m ▷ vt (offend) blesser, offenser; **not in the ~est** pas le moins du monde, pas du tout; **slightly** adv légèrement, un peu

slim [slɪm] adj mince ▷ vi maigrir; (diet) suivre un régime amaigrissant; **slimming** n amaigrissement m ▷ adj (diet, pills) amaigrissant(e), pour maigrir; (food) qui ne fait pas grossir

slimy ['slaɪmɪ] adj visqueux(-euse), gluant(e)

sling [slɪŋ] n (Med) écharpe f; (for baby) porte-bébé m; (weapon) fronde f, lance-pierre m ▷ vt (pt, pp **slung**) lancer, jeter

slip [slɪp] n faux pas; (mistake) erreur f, bévue f; (underskirt) combinaison f; (of paper) petite feuille, fiche f ▷ vt (slide) glisser ▷ vi (slide) glisser; (move smoothly): **to ~ into/out of** se glisser ou se faufiler dans/hors de; (decline) baisser; **to ~ sth on/off** enfiler/enlever qch; **to give sb the ~** fausser compagnie à qn; **a ~ of the tongue** un lapsus; **slip up** vi faire une erreur, gaffer

slipped disc [slɪpt-] n déplacement m de vertèbre

slipper ['slɪpə'] n pantoufle f

slippery ['slɪpərɪ] adj glissant(e)

slip road n (Brit: to motorway) bretelle f d'accès

slit [slɪt] n fente f; (cut) incision f ▷ vt (pt, pp ~) fendre; couper, inciser

slog [slɒg] n (Brit: effort) gros effort; (: work) tâche fastidieuse ▷ vi travailler très dur

slogan ['sləʊgən] n slogan m

slope [sləʊp] n pente f, côte f; (side of mountain) versant m; (slant) inclinaison f ▷ vi: **to ~ down** être ou descendre en pente; **to ~ up** monter; **sloping** adj en pente, incliné(e); (handwriting) penché(e)

sloppy ['slɒpɪ] adj (work) peu soigné(e), bâclé(e); (appearance) négligé(e), débraillé(e)

slot [slɒt] n fente f ▷ vt: **to ~ sth into** encastrer ou insérer qch dans; **slot machine** n (Brit: vending machine) distributeur m (automatique, machine f à sous; (for gambling) appareil m or machine à sous

Slovakia [sləʊˈvækɪə] n Slovaquie f

Slovene [sləʊˈviːn] adj slovène ▷ n Slovène m/f; (Ling) slovène m

Slovenia [sləʊˈviːnɪə] n Slovénie f; **Slovenian** adj, n = **Slovene**

slow [sləʊ] adj lent(e); (watch): **to be ~** retarder ▷ adv lentement ▷ vt, vi ralentir; **"~"** (road sign) "ralentir"; **slow down** vi ralentir; **slowly** adv lentement; **slow motion** n: **in slow motion** au ralenti

slug [slʌg] n limace f; (bullet) balle f; **sluggish** adj (person) mou (molle), lent(e); (stream, engine, trading) lent(e)

slum [slʌm] n (house) taudis m; **slums** npl (area) quartiers mpl pauvres

slump [slʌmp] n baisse soudaine, effondrement m; (Econ) crise f ▷ vi s'effondrer, s'affaisser

slung [slʌŋ] pt, pp of **sling**

slur [slɜː'] n (smear): **~ (on)** atteinte f (à); insinuation f (contre) ▷ vt mal articuler

slush [slʌʃ] n neige fondue

sly [slaɪ] adj (person) rusé(e); (smile, expression, remark) sournois(e)

smack [smæk] n (slap) tape f; (on face) gifle f ▷ vt donner une tape à; (on face) gifler; (on bottom) donner la fessée à ▷ vi: **to ~ of** avoir des relents de, sentir

small [smɔːl] adj petit(e); **small ads** npl (Brit) petites annonces; **small change** n petite or menue monnaie

smart [smɑːt] adj élégant(e), chic

inv; (*clever*) intelligent(e); (*quick*) vif
(vive), prompt(e) ▷ *vi* faire mal, brûler;
smartcard *n* carte *f* à puce

smash [smæʃ] *n* (*also*: **~-up**) collision
f, accident *m*; (*Mus*) succès foudroyant
▷ *vt* casser, briser, fracasser; (*opponent*)
écraser; (*Sport: record*) pulvériser ▷ *vi* se
briser, se fracasser; s'écraser; **smashing**
adj (*inf*) formidable

smear [smɪə⁰] *n* (*stain*) tache *f*; (*mark*)
trace *f*; (*Med*) frottis *m* ▷ *vt* enduire;
(*make dirty*) salir; **smear test** *n* (*BRIT
Med*) frottis *m*

smell [smɛl] *n* odeur *f*; (*sense*) odorat
m ▷ *vb* (*pt, pp* **smelt** *or* **~ed**) ▷ *vt* sentir
▷ *vi* (*pej*) sentir mauvais; **smelly** *adj* qui
sent mauvais, malodorant(e)

smelt [smɛlt] *pt, pp of* **smell**

smile [smaɪl] *n* sourire *m* ▷ *vi* sourire

smirk [sməːk] *n* petit sourire suffisant
or affecté

smog [smɔg] *n* brouillard mêlé de
fumée

smoke [sməuk] *n* fumée *f* ▷ *vt, vi*
fumer; **do you mind if I ~?** ça ne vous
dérange pas que je fume?; **smoke
alarm** *n* détecteur *m* de fumée;
smoked *adj* (*bacon, glass*) fumé(e);
smoker *n* (*person*) fumeur(-euse); (*Rail*)
wagon *m* fumeurs; **smoking** *n*: **"no
smoking"** (*sign*) "défense de fumer";
smoky *adj* enfumé(e); (*taste*) fumé(e)

smooth [smuːð] *adj* lisse; (*sauce*)
onctueux(-euse); (*flavour, whisky*)
moelleux(-euse); (*movement*)
régulier(-ière), sans à-coups *or* heurts;
(*flight*) sans secousses; (*pej: person*)
doucereux(-euse), mielleux(-euse) ▷ *vt*
(*also*: **~ out**) lisser, défroisser; (*creases,
difficulties*) faire disparaître

smother [ˈsmʌðə⁰] *vt* étouffer

SMS *n abbr* (= *short message service*)
SMS *m*; **SMS message** *n* message
m SMS

smudge [smʌdʒ] *n* tache *f*, bavure *f* ▷ *vt*
salir, maculer

smug [smʌg] *adj* suffisant(e),
content(e) de soi

smuggle [ˈsmʌgl] *vt* passer en
contrebande *or* en fraude; **smuggling**
n contrebande *f*

snack [snæk] *n* casse-croûte *m inv*;
snack bar *n* snack(-bar) *m*

snag [snæg] *n* inconvénient *m*,
difficulté *f*

snail [sneɪl] *n* escargot *m*

snake [sneɪk] *n* serpent *m*

snap [snæp] *n* (*sound*) claquement
m, bruit sec; (*photograph*) photo *f*,
instantané *m* ▷ *adj* subit(e), fait(e) sans
réfléchir ▷ *vt* (*fingers*) faire claquer;
(*break*) casser net *or* avec un bruit sec ▷ *vi*
se casser net *or* avec un bruit sec; (*speak sharply*) parler
d'un ton brusque; **to ~ open/shut**
s'ouvrir/se refermer brusquement;
snap at *vt fus* (*subj: dog*) essayer de
mordre; **snap up** *vt* sauter sur, saisir;
snapshot *n* photo *f*, instantané *m*

snarl [snɑːl] *vi* gronder

snatch [snætʃ] *n* (*small amount*) ▷ *vt*
saisir (*d'un geste vif*); (*steal*) voler; **to ~
some sleep** arriver à dormir un peu

sneak [sniːk] (*us: pt* **snuck**) *vi*: **to ~
in/out** entrer/sortir furtivement ou à
la dérobée ▷ *n* (*inf: pej: informer*) faux
jeton; **to ~ up on sb** s'approcher de qn
sans faire de bruit; **sneakers** *npl* tennis
mpl, baskets *fpl*

sneer [snɪə⁰] *vi* ricaner; **to ~ at sb/sth**
se moquer de qn/qch avec mépris

sneeze [sniːz] *vi* éternuer

sniff [snɪf] *vi* renifler ▷ *vt* renifler,
flairer; (*glue, drug*) sniffer, respirer

snigger [ˈsnɪgə⁰] *vi* ricaner

snip [snɪp] *n* (*cut*) entaille *f*; (*BRIT: inf:
bargain*) (bonne) occasion *or* affaire *f*
▷ *vt* couper

sniper [ˈsnaɪpə⁰] *n* (*marksman*) tireur
embusqué

snob [snɔb] *n* snob *m/f*

snooker [ˈsnuːkə⁰] *n* sorte de jeu de
billard

snoop [snuːp] *vi*: **to ~ about** fureter

snooze [snuːz] *n* petit somme *m* ▷ *vi*
faire un petit somme

snore [snɔː⁰] *vi* ronfler ▷ *n*

ronflement m

snorkel ['snɔːkl] n (of swimmer) tuba m

snort [snɔːt] n grognement m ▷ vi grogner; (horse) renâcler

snow [snəʊ] n neige f ▷ vi neiger; **snowball** n boule f de neige; **snowdrift** n congère f; **snowman** (irreg) n bonhomme m de neige; **snowplough** (us **snowplow**) n chasse-neige m inv; **snowstorm** n tempête f de neige

snub [snʌb] vt repousser, snober ▷ n rebuffade f

snug [snʌg] adj douillet(te), confortable; (person) bien au chaud

○ **KEYWORD**

so [səʊ] adv 1 (thus, likewise) ainsi, de cette façon; **if so** si oui; **so do or have I** moi aussi; **it's 5 o'clock - so it is!** il est 5 heures - en effet! or c'est vrai!; **I hope/think so** je l'espère/le crois; **so far** jusqu'ici, jusqu'à maintenant; (in past) jusque-là

2 (in comparisons: to such a degree) si, tellement; **so big (that)** si or tellement grand (que); **she's not so clever as her brother** elle n'est pas aussi intelligente que son frère

3: **so much** adj, adv tant (de); **I've got so much work** j'ai tant de travail; **I love you so much** je vous aime tant; **so many** tant (de)

4 (phrases): **10 or so** à peu près or environ 10; **so long!** (inf: goodbye) au revoir!, à un de ces jours!; **so (what?)** (inf) (bon) et alors?, et après?

▷ conj 1 (expressing purpose): **so as to** pour faire, afin de faire; **so (that)** pour que or afin que + sub

2 (expressing result) donc, par conséquent; **so that** si bien que, de (telle) sorte que; **so that's the reason!** c'est donc (pour) ça!; **so you see, I could have gone** alors tu vois, j'aurais pu y aller

soak [səʊk] vt faire or laisser tremper;

(drench) tremper ▷ vi tremper; **soak up** vt absorber; **soaking** adj (also: **soaking wet**) trempé(e)

so-and-so ['səʊənsəʊ] n (somebody) un(e) tel(le)

soap [səʊp] n savon m; **soap opera** n feuilleton télévisé (quotidienneté réaliste ou embellie); **soap powder** n lessive f, détergent m

soar [sɔː] vi (on wing) monter (en flèche), s'élancer; (building) s'élancer

sob [sɔb] n sanglot m ▷ vi sangloter

sober ['səʊbə] adj qui n'est pas (or plus) ivre; (serious) sérieux(-euse), sensé(e); (colour, style) sobre, discret(-ète); **sober up** vi se dégriser

so-called ['səʊ'kɔːld] adj soi-disant inv

soccer ['sɔkə] n football m

sociable ['səʊʃəbl] adj sociable

social ['səʊʃl] adj (also: sociable) sociable ▷ n (petite) fête; **socialism** n socialisme m; **socialist** adj, n socialiste (m/f); **socialize** vi: **to socialize with** (meet often) fréquenter; (get to know) lier connaissance or parler avec; **social life** n vie sociale; **socially** adv socialement, en société; **social security** n aide sociale; **social services** npl services sociaux; **social work** n assistance sociale; **social worker** n assistant(e) social(e)

society [sə'saɪətɪ] n société f; (club) société, association f; (also: **high ~**) (haute) société, grand monde

sociology [səʊsɪ'ɔlədʒɪ] n sociologie f

sock [sɔk] n chaussette f

socket ['sɔkɪt] n cavité f; (Elec: also: **wall ~**) prise f de courant

soda ['səʊdə] n (Chem) soude f; (also: **~ water**) eau f de Seltz; (us: also: **~ pop**) soda m

sodium ['səʊdɪəm] n sodium m

sofa ['səʊfə] n sofa m, canapé m; **sofa bed** n canapé-lit m

soft [sɔft] adj (not rough) doux (douce); (not hard) doux, mou (molle); (not loud) doux, léger(-ère); (kind) doux, gentil(le); **soft drink** n boisson non alcoolisée;

soft drugs npl drogues douces; **soften**
['sɔfn] vt (r)amollir; (fig) adoucir ▷ vi
se ramollir; (fig) s'adoucir; **softly** adv
doucement; (touch) légèrement; (kiss)
tendrement; **software** n (Comput)
logiciel m, software m

soggy ['sɔgɪ] adj (clothes) trempé(e);
(ground) détrempé(e)

soil [sɔɪl] n (earth) sol m, terre f ▷ vt salir;
(fig) souiller

solar ['səʊləʳ] adj solaire; **solar power**
n énergie f solaire; **solar system** n
système m solaire

sold [səʊld] pt, pp of **sell**

soldier ['səʊldʒəʳ] n soldat m,
militaire m

sold out adj (Comm) épuisé(e)

sole [səʊl] n (of foot) plante f; (of shoe)
semelle f; (fish: pl inv) sole f ▷ adj
seul(e), unique; **solely** adv seulement,
uniquement

solemn ['sɔləm] adj solennel(le);
(person) sérieux(-euse), grave

solicitor [sə'lɪsɪtəʳ] n (BRIT: for wills etc)
≈ notaire m; (: in court) ≈ avocat m

solid ['sɔlɪd] adj (not liquid) solide; (not
hollow: mass) compact(e); (: metal, rock,
wood) massif(-ive) ▷ n solide m

solitary ['sɔlɪtərɪ] adj solitaire

solitude ['sɔlɪtjuːd] n solitude f

solo ['səʊləʊ] n solo m ▷ adv (fly) en
solitaire; **soloist** n soliste m/f

soluble ['sɔljʊbl] adj soluble

solution [sə'luːʃən] n solution f

solve [sɔlv] vt résoudre

solvent ['sɔlvənt] adj (Comm) solvable
▷ n (Chem) (dis)solvant m

sombre, (us **somber**) ['sɔmbəʳ] adj
sombre, morne

KEYWORD

some [sʌm] adj **1** (a certain amount
or number of): **some tea/water/ice
cream** du thé/de l'eau/de la glace;
some children/apples des enfants/
pommes; **I've got some money but
not much** j'ai de l'argent mais pas

beaucoup

2 (certain: in contrasts): **some people
say that ...** il y a des gens qui disent
que ...; **some films were excellent,
but most were mediocre** certains
films étaient excellents, mais la plupart
étaient médiocres

3 (unspecified): **some woman was
asking for you** il y avait une dame qui
vous demandait; **he was asking for
some book (or other)** il demandait un
livre quelconque; **some day** un de ces
jours; **some day next week** un jour la
semaine prochaine
▷ pron **1** (a certain number) quelques-
un(e)s, certain(e)s; **I've got some
(books etc)** j'en ai (quelques-uns); **some
(of them) have been sold** certains ont
été vendus

2 (a certain amount) un peu; **I've got
some** (money, milk) j'en ai (un peu);
would you like some? est-ce que vous
en voulez?, en voulez-vous?; **could I
have some of that cheese?** pourrais-
je avoir un peu de ce fromage?; **I've
read some of the book** j'ai lu une
partie du livre
▷ adv: **some 10 people** quelque 10
personnes, 10 personnes environ;
somebody ['sʌmbədɪ] pron
= **someone**; **somehow** adv d'une
façon ou d'une autre; (for some
reason) pour une raison ou une
autre; **someone** pron quelqu'un;
someplace adv (us) = **somewhere**;
something pron quelque chose m;
something interesting quelque
chose d'intéressant; **something to do**
quelque chose à faire; **sometime** adv
(in future) un de ces jours, un jour ou
l'autre; (in past): **sometime last month**
au cours du mois dernier; **sometimes**
adv quelquefois, parfois; **somewhat**
adv quelque peu, un peu; **somewhere**
adv quelque part; **somewhere else**
ailleurs, autre part

son [sʌn] n fils m

song [sɒŋ] n chanson f; (of bird) chant m

son-in-law ['sʌnɪnlɔː] n gendre m, beau-fils m

soon [suːn] adv bientôt; (early) tôt; **~ afterwards** peu après; see also **as**; **sooner** adv (time) plus tôt; (preference): **I would sooner do that** j'aimerais autant ou je préférerais faire ça; **sooner or later** tôt ou tard

soothe [suːð] vt calmer, apaiser

sophisticated [sə'fɪstɪkeɪtɪd] adj raffiné(e), sophistiqué(e); (machinery) hautement perfectionné(e), très complexe

sophomore ['sɒfəmɔːʳ] n (us) étudiant(e) de seconde année

soprano [sə'prɑːnəu] n (singer) soprano m/f

sorbet ['sɔːbeɪ] n sorbet m

sordid ['sɔːdɪd] adj sordide

sore [sɔːʳ] adj (painful) douloureux(-euse), sensible ▷ n plaie f

sorrow ['sɒrəu] n peine f, chagrin m

sorry ['sɒrɪ] adj désolé(e); (condition, excuse, tale) triste, déplorable; **~!** pardon!, excusez-moi!; **~?** pardon?; **to feel ~ for sb** plaindre qn

sort [sɔːt] n genre m, espèce f, sorte f; (make: of coffee, car etc) marque f ▷ vt (also: **~ out**: select which to keep) trier; (classify) classer; (tidy) ranger; **sort out** vt (problem) résoudre, régler

SOS n SOS m

so-so ['səusəu] adv comme ci comme ça

sought [sɔːt] pt, pp of **seek**

soul [səul] n âme f

sound [saund] adj (healthy) en bonne santé, sain(e); (safe, not damaged) solide, en bon état; (reliable, not superficial) sérieux(-euse), solide; (sensible) sensé(e) ▷ adv: **~ asleep** profondément endormi(e) ▷ n (noise, volume) son m; (louder) bruit m; (Geo) détroit m, bras m de mer ▷ vt (alarm) sonner ▷ vi sonner, retentir; (fig: seem) sembler (être); **to ~ like** ressembler à; **sound bite** n phrase toute faite (pour

être citée dans les médias); **soundtrack** n (of film) bande f sonore

soup [suːp] n soupe f, potage m

sour ['sauəʳ] adj aigre; **it's ~ grapes** c'est du dépit

source [sɔːs] n source f

south [sauθ] n sud m ▷ adj sud inv; (wind) du sud ▷ adv au sud, vers le sud; **South Africa** n Afrique f du Sud; **South African** adj sud-africain(e) ▷ n Sud-Africain(e); **South America** n Amérique f du Sud; **South American** adj sud-américain(e) ▷ n Sud-Américain(e); **southbound** adj en direction du sud; (carriageway) sud inv; **south-east** n sud-est m; **southeastern** [sauθ'iːstən] adj du ou au sud-est; **southern** ['sʌðən] adj (du) sud; méridional(e); **South Korea** n Corée f du Sud; **South of France n: the South of France** le Sud de la France, le Midi; **South Pole** n Pôle m Sud; **southward(s)** adv vers le sud; **south-west** n sud-ouest m; **southwestern** [sauθ'westən] adj du ou au sud-ouest

souvenir [suːvə'nɪəʳ] n souvenir m (objet)

sovereign ['sɒvrɪn] adj, n souverain(e)

sow¹ [sau] (pt **~ed**, pp **~n**) vt semer

sow² n [sau] truie f

soya ['sɔɪə] (us **soy** [sɔɪ]) n: **~ bean** graine f de soja; **~ sauce** sauce f au soja

spa [spɑː] n (town) station thermale; (us: **health ~**) établissement m de cure de rajeunissement

space [speɪs] n (gen) espace m; (room) place f; espace; (length of time) laps m de temps ▷ cpd spatial(e) ▷ vt (also: **~ out**) espacer; **spacecraft** n engin ou vaisseau spatial; **spaceship** n = **spacecraft**

spacious ['speɪʃəs] adj spacieux(-euse), grand(e)

spade [speɪd] n (tool) bêche f, pelle f; (child's toy) pelle; **spades** npl (Cards) pique m

spaghetti [spə'ɡetɪ] n spaghetti mpl

Spain [speɪn] n Espagne f

spam [spæm] n (Comput) spam m
span [spæn] n (of bird, plane) envergure f; (of arch) portée f; (in time) espace m de temps, durée f ▷ vt enjamber, franchir; (fig) couvrir, embrasser
Spaniard ['spænjəd] n Espagnol(e)
Spanish ['spænɪʃ] adj espagnol(e), d'Espagne ▷ n (Ling) espagnol m; **the Spanish** npl les Espagnols
spank [spæŋk] vt donner une fessée à
spanner ['spænə'] n (BRIT) clé f (de mécanicien)
spare [spɛə'] adj de réserve, de rechange; (surplus) de or en trop, de reste ▷ n (part) pièce f de rechange, pièce détachée ▷ vt (do without) se passer de; (afford to give) donner, accorder, passer; (not hurt) épargner; **to ~** (surplus) en surplus, de trop; **spare part** n pièce f de rechange, pièce détachée; **spare room** n chambre f d'ami; **spare time** n moments mpl de loisir; **spare tyre** (US **spare tire**) n (Aut) pneu m de rechange; **spare wheel** n (Aut) roue f de secours
spark [spɑːk] n étincelle f; **spark(ing) plug** n bougie f
sparkle ['spɑːkl] n scintillement m, étincellement m, éclat m ▷ vi étinceler, scintiller
sparkling ['spɑːklɪŋ] adj (wine) mousseux(-euse), pétillant(e); (water) pétillant(e), gazeux(-euse)
sparrow ['spærəu] n moineau m
sparse [spɑːs] adj clairsemé(e)
spasm ['spæzəm] n (Med) spasme m
spat [spæt] pt, pp of **spit**
spate [speɪt] n (fig): **~ of** avalanche f or torrent m de
spatula ['spætjulə] n spatule f
speak (pt **spoke**, pp **spoken**) [spiːk, spəuk, 'spəukn] vt (language) parler; (truth) dire ▷ vi parler; (make a speech) prendre la parole; **to ~ to sb/of or about sth** parler à qn/de qch; **I don't ~ French** je ne parle pas français; **do you ~ English?** parlez-vous anglais?; **can I ~ to ...?** est-ce que je peux parler

à ...?; **speaker** n (in public) orateur m; (also: **loudspeaker**) haut-parleur m; (for stereo etc) baffle m, enceinte f; (Pol): **the Speaker** (BRIT) le président de la Chambre des communes ou des représentants; (US) le président de la Chambre
spear [spɪə'] n lance f ▷ vt transpercer
special ['spɛʃl] adj spécial(e); **special delivery** n (Post): **by special delivery** en express; **special effects** npl (Cine) effets spéciaux; **specialist** n spécialiste m/f; **speciality** [spɛʃɪˈælɪtɪ] n (BRIT) spécialité f; **specialize** vi: **to specialize (in)** se spécialiser (dans); **specially** adv spécialement, particulièrement; **special needs** npl (BRIT) difficultés fpl d'apprentissage scolaire; **special offer** n (Comm) réclame f; **special school** n (BRIT) établissement d'enseignement spécialisé; **specialty** n (US) = **speciality**
species ['spiːʃiːz] n (pl inv) espèce f
specific [spəˈsɪfɪk] adj (not vague) précis(e), explicite; (particular) particulier(-ière); **specifically** adv explicitement, précisément; (intend, ask, design) expressément, spécialement
specify ['spɛsɪfaɪ] vt spécifier, préciser
specimen ['spɛsɪmən] n spécimen m, échantillon m; (Med: of blood) prélèvement m; (: of urine) échantillon m
speck [spɛk] n petite tache, petit point; (particle) grain m
spectacle ['spɛktəkl] n spectacle m; **spectacles** npl (BRIT) lunettes fpl; **spectacular** [spɛkˈtækjulə'] adj spectaculaire
spectator [spɛkˈteɪtə'] n spectateur(-trice)
spectrum (pl **spectra**) ['spɛktrəm, -rə] n spectre m; (fig) gamme f
speculate ['spɛkjuleɪt] vi spéculer; (try to guess): **to ~ about** s'interroger sur
sped [spɛd] pt, pp of **speed**
speech [spiːtʃ] n (faculty) parole f; (talk) discours m, allocution f; (manner of speaking) façon f de parler, langage m;

(enunciation) élocution f; **speechless** adj muet(te)

speed [spi:d] n vitesse f; *(promptness)* rapidité f ▷ vi: **to go ~** aller très vite; ▷ vb see **speed**: **exceed the speed limit** faire un excès de vitesse; **at full** ou **top ~** à toute vitesse ou allure; **speed up** *(pt, pp* **~ed up)** vi aller plus vite, accélérer ▷ vt accélérer; **speedboat** n vedette f, hors-bord m inv; **speeding** n *(Aut)* excès m de vitesse; **speed limit** n limitation f de vitesse, vitesse maximale permise; **speedometer** [spɪ'dɔmɪtə'] n compteur m (de vitesse); **speedy** adj rapide, prompt(e)

spell [spɛl] n *(also:* **magic** ~**)** sortilège m, charme m; *(period of time)* (courte) période ▷ vt *(pt, pp* **spelt** ou **~ed)** *(in writing)* écrire, orthographier; *(aloud)* épeler; *(fig)* signifier; **to cast a ~ on sb** jeter un sort à qn; **he can't ~** il fait des fautes d'orthographe; **spell out** vt *(explain):* **to ~ sth out for sb** expliquer qch clairement à qn; **spellchecker** ['spɛltʃɛkə'] n *(Comput)* correcteur m ou vérificateur m orthographique; **spelling** n orthographe f

spelt [spɛlt] pt, pp of **spell**

spend *(pt, pp* **spent)** [spɛnd, spɛnt] vt *(money)* dépenser; *(time, life)* passer; *(devote)* consacrer; **spending** n: **government spending** les dépenses publiques

spent [spɛnt] pt, pp of **spend** ▷ adj *(cartridge, bullets)* vide

sperm [spə:m] n spermatozoïde m; *(semen)* sperme m

sphere [sfɪə'] n sphère f; *(fig)* sphère, domaine m

spice [spaɪs] n épice f ▷ vt épicer

spicy ['spaɪsɪ] adj épicé(e), relevé(e); *(fig)* piquant(e)

spider ['spaɪdə'] n araignée f

spike [spaɪk] n pointe f; *(Bot)* épi m

spill *(pt, pp* **spilt** ou **~ed)** [spɪl, -t, -d] vt renverser; répandre ▷ vi se répandre; **spill over** vi déborder

spin [spɪn] n *(revolution of wheel)* tour m; *(Aviat)* (chute f en) vrille f; *(trip in car)* petit tour, balade f; *(on ball)* effet m ▷ vb *(pt, pp* **spun)** ▷ vt *(wool etc)* filer; *(wheel)* faire tourner ▷ vi *(turn)* tourner, tournoyer

spinach ['spɪnɪtʃ] n épinards mpl

spinal ['spaɪnl] adj vertébral(e), spinal(e)

spinal cord n moelle épinière

spin doctor n *(inf)* personne employée pour présenter un parti politique sous un jour favorable

spin-dryer [spɪn'draɪə'] n *(BRIT)* essoreuse f

spine [spaɪn] n colonne vertébrale; *(thorn)* épine f, piquant m

spiral ['spaɪərl] n spirale f ▷ vi *(fig: prices etc)* monter en flèche

spire ['spaɪə'] n flèche f, aiguille f

spirit ['spɪrɪt] n *(soul)* esprit m, âme f; *(ghost)* esprit, revenant m; *(mood)* esprit, état m d'esprit; *(courage)* courage m, énergie f; **spirits** npl *(drink)* spiritueux mpl, alcool m; **in good ~s** de bonne humeur

spiritual ['spɪrɪtjuəl] adj spirituel(le); *(religious)* religieux(-euse)

spit [spɪt] n *(for roasting)* broche f; *(spittle)* crachat m; *(saliva)* salive f ▷ vi *(pt, pp* **spat)** cracher; *(sound)* crépiter; *(rain)* crachiner

spite [spaɪt] n rancune f, dépit m ▷ vt contrarier, vexer; **in ~ of** en dépit de, malgré; **spiteful** adj malveillant(e), rancunier(-ière)

splash [splæʃ] n *(sound)* plouf m; *(of colour)* tache f ▷ vt éclabousser ▷ vi *(also:* **~ about)** barboter, patauger; **splash out** vi *(BRIT)* faire une folie

splendid ['splɛndɪd] adj splendide, superbe, magnifique

splinter ['splɪntə'] n *(wood)* écharde f; *(metal)* éclat m ▷ vi *(wood)* se fendre; *(glass)* se briser

split [splɪt] n fente f, déchirure f; *(fig: Pol)* scission f ▷ vb *(pt, pp* **~)** ▷ vt fendre, déchirer; *(party)* diviser; *(work, profits)* partager, répartir ▷ vi *(break)* se fendre,

se briser; (divide) se diviser; **split up** vi
(couple) se séparer, rompre; (meeting)
se disperser

spoil (pt, pp **-ed** o **-t**) [spɔɪl, -d, -t] vt
(damage) abîmer; (mar) gâcher; (child)
gâter

spoilt [spɔɪlt] pt, pp of **spoil** ▷ adj (child)
gâté(e); (ballot paper) nul(le)

spoke [spəuk] pt of **speak** ▷ n rayon m

spoken ['spəukn] pp of **speak**

spokesman ['spəuksmən] (irreg) n
porte-parole m inv

spokesperson ['spəukspɜːsn] n
porte-parole m inv

spokeswoman ['spəukswumən]
(irreg) n porte-parole m inv

sponge [spʌndʒ] n éponge f; (Culin:
also: **~ cake**) ≈ biscuit m de Savoie
▷ vt éponger; **to ~ off** o **on** vivre
aux crochets de; **sponge bag** n (BRIT)
trousse f de toilette

sponsor ['spɒnsə*] n (Radio, TV, Sport)
sponsor m; (for application) parrain m,
marraine f; (BRIT: for fund-raising event)
donateur(-trice) ▷ vt sponsoriser,
parrainer, faire un don à; **sponsorship**
n sponsoring m, parrainage m; dons mpl

spontaneous [spɒn'teɪnɪəs] adj
spontané(e)

spooky ['spuːkɪ] adj (inf) qui donne la
chair de poule

spoon [spuːn] n cuiller f; **spoonful** n
cuillerée f

sport [spɔːt] n sport m; (person) chic
type m/chic fille f ▷ vt (wear) arborer;
sport jacket n (US) = **sports jacket**;
sports car n voiture f de sport;
sports centre (BRIT) n centre sportif;
sports jacket n (BRIT) veste f de sport;
sportsman (irreg) n sportif m; **sports
utility vehicle** n véhicule m de loisirs
(de type SUV); **sportswear** n vêtements
mpl de sport; **sportswoman** (irreg) n
sportive f; **sporty** adj sportif(-ive)

spot [spɒt] n tache f; (dot: on pattern)
pois m; (pimple) bouton m; (place)
endroit m, coin m; (small amount): **a ~
of** un peu de ▷ vt (notice) apercevoir,

repérer; **on the ~** sur place, sur les lieux;
(immediately) sur le champ; **spotless** adj
immaculé(e); **spotlight** n projecteur
m; (Aut) phare m auxiliaire

spouse [spauz] n époux (épouse)

sprain [spreɪn] n entorse f, foulure
f ▷ vt: **to ~ one's ankle** se fouler ou se
tordre la cheville

sprang [spræŋ] pt of **spring**

sprawl [sprɔːl] vi s'étaler

spray [spreɪ] n jet m (en fines
gouttelettes); (from sea) embruns
mpl; (aerosol) vaporisateur m, bombe
f; (for garden) vaporisateur m; (of
flowers) petit bouquet ▷ vt vaporiser,
pulvériser; (crops) traiter

spread [spred] n (distribution)
répartition f; (Culin) pâte f à tartiner;
(inf: meal) festin m ▷ vb (pt, pp **~**)
(paste, contents) étendre, étaler; (rumour,
disease) répandre, propager; (wealth)
répartir ▷ vi s'étendre; se répandre; se
propager; (stain) s'étaler; **spread out**
vi (people) se disperser; **spreadsheet** n
(Comput) tableur m

spree [spriː] n: **to go on a ~** faire la fête

spring [sprɪŋ] n (season) printemps
m; (leap) bond m, saut m; (coiled metal)
ressort m; (of water) source f ▷ vb (pt
sprang, pp **sprung**) ▷ vi bondir, sauter;
spring up vi (problem) se présenter,
surgir; (plant, buildings) surgir de terre;
spring onion n (BRIT) ciboule f, cive f

sprinkle ['sprɪŋkl] vt: **to ~ water** etc
on, **~ with water** etc asperger d'eau
etc; **to ~ sugar** etc **on**, **~ with sugar** etc
saupoudrer de sucre etc

sprint [sprɪnt] n sprint m ▷ vi courir à
toute vitesse; (Sport) sprinter

sprung [sprʌŋ] pp of **spring**

spun [spʌn] pt, pp of **spin**

spur [spɜː*] n éperon m; (fig) aiguillon
m ▷ vt (also: **~ on**) éperonner;
aiguillonner; **on the ~ of the moment**
sous l'impulsion du moment

spurt [spɜːt] n jet m; (of blood)
jaillissement m; (of energy) regain m,
sursaut m ▷ vi jaillir, gicler

spy [spaɪ] n espion(ne) ▷ vi: **to ~ on** espionner, épier ▷ vt (see) apercevoir

sq. abbr = **square**

squabble ['skwɔbl] vi se chamailler

squad [skwɔd] n (Mil, Police) escouade f, groupe m; (Football) contingent m

squadron ['skwɔdrn] n (Mil) escadron m; (Aviat, Naut) escadrille f

squander ['skwɔndə'] vt gaspiller, dilapider

square [skwɛə'] n carré m; (in town) place f ▷ adj carré(e) ▷ vt (arrange) régler; arranger; (Math) élever au carré; (reconcile) concilier; **all ~** quitte; à égalité; **a ~ meal** un repas convenable; **2 metres ~** (de) 2 mètres sur 2; **1 ~ metre** 1 mètre carré; **square root** racine carrée

squash [skwɔʃ] n (BRIT: drink): **lemon/ orange ~** citronnade f/orangeade f; (Sport) squash m; (US: vegetable) courge f ▷ vt écraser

squat [skwɔt] adj petit(e) et épais(se), ramassé(e) ▷ vi (also: ~ **down**) s'accroupir; **squatter** n squatter m

squeak [skwi:k] vi (hinge, wheel) grincer; (mouse) pousser un petit cri

squeal [skwi:l] vi pousser un ou des cri(s) aigu(s) ou perçant(s); (brakes) grincer

squeeze [skwi:z] n pression f ▷ vt presser; (hand, arm) serrer

squid [skwɪd] n calmar m

squint [skwɪnt] vi loucher

squirm [skwə:m] vi se tortiller

squirrel ['skwɪrəl] n écureuil m

squirt [skwə:t] vi, vt jaillir, gicler ▷ vt faire gicler

Sr abbr = **senior**

Sri Lanka [srɪ'læŋkə] n Sri Lanka m

St abbr = **saint; street**

stab [stæb] n (with knife etc) coup m (de couteau etc); (of pain) lancée f; (inf: try): **to have a ~ (at doing) sth** s'essayer à (faire) qch ▷ vt poignarder

stability [stə'bɪlɪtɪ] n stabilité f

stable ['steɪbl] n écurie f ▷ adj stable

stack [stæk] n tas m, pile f ▷ vt empiler,

entasser

stadium ['steɪdɪəm] n stade m

staff [stɑ:f] n (work force) personnel m; (BRIT Scol: also: **teaching ~**) professeurs mpl, enseignants mpl, personnel enseignant ▷ vt pourvoir en personnel

stag [stæg] n cerf m

stage [steɪdʒ] n scène f; (platform) estrade f; (point) étape f, stade m; (profession): **the ~** le théâtre ▷ vt (play) monter, mettre en scène; (demonstration) organiser; **in ~s** par étapes, par degrés

> Be careful not to translate *stage* by the French word *stage*.

stagger ['stægə'] vi chanceler, tituber ▷ vt (person: amaze) stupéfier; (hours, holidays) étaler, échelonner; **staggering** adj (amazing) stupéfiant(e), renversant(e)

stagnant ['stægnənt] adj stagnant(e)

stag night, stag party n enterrement m de vie de garçon

stain [steɪn] n tache f; (colouring) colorant m ▷ vt tacher; (wood) teindre; **stained glass** (decorative) verre coloré; (in church) vitraux mpl; **stainless steel** n inox m, acier m inoxydable

staircase ['stɛəkeɪs] n = **stairway**

stairs [stɛəz] npl escalier m

stairway ['stɛəweɪ] n escalier m

stake [steɪk] n pieu m, poteau m; (Betting) enjeu m; (Comm: interest) intérêts mpl; (also: ~ **out**: area) marquer, délimiter; **to be at ~** être en jeu

stale [steɪl] adj (bread) rassis(e); (food) pas frais (fraîche); (beer) éventé(e); (smell) de renfermé; (air) confiné(e)

stalk [stɔ:k] n tige f ▷ vt traquer

stall [stɔ:l] n (BRIT: in street, market etc) éventaire m, étal m; (in stable) stalle f ▷ vt (Aut) caler; (fig: delay) retarder ▷ vi (Aut) caler; (fig) essayer de gagner du temps; **stalls** npl (BRIT: in cinema, theatre) orchestre m

stamina ['stæmɪnə] n vigueur f, endurance f

stammer ['stæmə^r] n bégaiement m
▷ vi bégayer

stamp [stæmp] n timbre m; (also:
rubber ~) tampon m; (mark, also fig)
empreinte f; (on document) cachet
m ▷ vi (also: **~ one's foot**) taper du
pied ▷ vt (letter) timbrer; (with rubber
stamp) tamponner; **stamp out** vt (fire)
piétiner; (crime) éradiquer; (opposition)
éliminer; **stamped addressed
envelope** n (BRIT) enveloppe
affranchie pour la réponse

stampede [stæm'piːd] n ruée f; (of
cattle) débandade f

stance [stæns] n position f

stand [stænd] n (position) position f;
(for taxis) station f (de taxis); (comm)
étalage m, stand m; (Sport: also: **~s**)
tribune f; (also: **music ~**) pupitre m
▷ vb (pt, pp **stood**) ▷ vi être ou se tenir
(debout); (rise) se lever, se mettre
debout; (be placed) se trouver; (remain:
offer etc) rester valable ▷ vt (place)
mettre, poser; (tolerate, withstand)
supporter; (treat, invite) offrir, payer;
to make a ~ prendre position; **to ~
for parliament** (BRIT) se présenter
aux élections (comme candidat à la
députation); **I can't ~ him** je ne peux
pas le voir; **stand back** vi (move back)
reculer, s'écarter; **stand by** vi (be ready)
se tenir prêt(e) ▷ vt fus (opinion) s'en
tenir à; (person) ne pas abandonner,
soutenir; **stand down** vi (withdraw)
se retirer; **stand for** vt fus (signify)
représenter, signifier; (tolerate)
supporter, tolérer; **stand in for** vt fus
remplacer; **stand out** vi (be prominent)
ressortir; **stand up** vi (rise) se lever,
se mettre debout; **stand up for** vt fus
défendre; **stand up to** vt fus tenir tête
à, résister à

standard ['stændəd] n (norm) norme
f, étalon m; (level) niveau m (voulu);
(criterion) critère m; (flag) étendard m
▷ adj (size) ordinaire, normal(e);
(model, feature) standard inv; (practice)
courant(e); (text) de base; **standards**

npl (morals) morale f, principes mpl;
standard of living n niveau m de vie

stand-by ticket n (Aviat) billet m
stand-by

standing ['stændɪŋ] adj debout
inv; (permanent) permanent(e) ▷ n
réputation f, rang m, standing m; **of
many years'** qui dure ou existe depuis
longtemps; **standing order** n (BRIT:
at bank) virement m automatique,
prélèvement m bancaire

stand: **standpoint** n point m de vue;
standstill n: **at a standstill** à l'arrêt;
(fig) au point mort; **to come to a
standstill** s'immobiliser, s'arrêter

stank [stæŋk] pt of **stink**

staple ['steɪpl] n (for papers) agrafe f
▷ adj (food, crop, industry etc) de base
principal(e) ▷ vt agrafer

star [stɑː^r] n étoile f; (celebrity) vedette f
▷ vt (Cine) avoir pour vedette; **stars** npl:
the ~s (Astrology) l'horoscope m

starboard ['stɑːbəd] n tribord m

starch [stɑːtʃ] n amidon m; (in food)
fécule f

stardom ['stɑːdəm] n célébrité f

stare [stɛə^r] n regard m fixe ▷ vi: **to ~ at**
regarder fixement

stark [stɑːk] adj (bleak) désolé(e),
morne ▷ adv: **~ naked** complètement
nu(e)

start [stɑːt] n commencement m,
début m; (of race) départ m; (sudden
movement) sursaut m ▷ vt (advantage)
avance f, avantage m ▷ vt commencer;
(cause: fight) déclencher; (rumour)
donner naissance à; (fashion) lancer;
(found: business, newspaper) lancer, créer;
(engine) mettre en marche ▷ vi (begin)
commencer; (begin journey) partir, se
mettre en route; (jump) sursauter;
when does the film ~? à quelle heure
est-ce que le film commence? **to ~
doing or to do sth** se mettre à faire qch;
start off vi (begin) commencer; (leave) partir;
start out vi (begin) commencer; (set
out) partir; **start up** vi commencer;
(car) démarrer ▷ vt (fight) déclencher;

(business) créer; (car) mettre en marche; **starter** n (Aut) démarreur m; (Sport: official) starter m; (BRIT Culin) entrée f; **starting point** n point m de départ

startle ['stɑ:tl] vt faire sursauter; donner un choc à; **startling** adj surprenant(e), saisissant(e)

starvation [stɑ:'veɪʃən] n faim f, famine f

starve [stɑ:v] vi mourir de faim ▷ vt laisser mourir de faim

state [steɪt] n état m; (Pol) État m ▷ vt (declare) déclarer, affirmer; (specify) indiquer, spécifier; **States** npl: **the S~s** les États-Unis; **to be in a ~** être dans tous ses états; **stately** adj noble, majestueux(-euse); **stately home** n manoir m ou château m (ouvert au public); **statement** n déclaration f; (Law) déposition f; **state school** n école publique; **statesman** (irreg) n homme m d'État

static ['stætɪk] n (Radio) parasites mpl; (also: **~ electricity**) électricité f statique ▷ adj statique

station ['steɪʃən] n gare f; (also: **police ~**) poste m ou commissariat m (de police) ▷ vt placer, poster

stationary ['steɪʃnərɪ] adj à l'arrêt, immobile

stationer's (shop) n (BRIT) papeterie f

stationery ['steɪʃnərɪ] n papier m à lettres, petit matériel de bureau

station wagon n (US) break m

statistic [stə'tɪstɪk] n statistique f; **statistics** n (science) statistique f

statue ['stætju:] n statue f

stature ['stætʃər] n stature f; (fig) envergure f

status ['steɪtəs] n position f, situation f; (prestige) prestige m; (Admin, official position) statut m; **status quo** [-'kwəʊ] n: **the status quo** le statu quo

statutory ['stætjʊtrɪ] adj statutaire, prévu(e) par un article de loi

staunch [stɔ:ntʃ] adj sûr(e), loyal(e)

stay [steɪ] n (period of time) séjour m ▷ vi rester; (reside) loger; (spend some time)

séjourner; **to ~ put** ne pas bouger; **to ~ the night** passer la nuit; **stay away** vi (from person, building) ne pas s'approcher; (from event) ne pas venir à; **stay behind** vi rester en arrière; **stay in** vi (at home) rester à la maison; **stay on** vi rester; **stay out** vi (of house) ne pas rentrer; (strikers) rester en grève; **stay up** vi (at night) ne pas se coucher

steadily ['stedɪlɪ] adv (regularly) progressivement; (firmly) fermement; (walk) d'un pas ferme; (fixedly: look) sans détourner les yeux

steady ['stedɪ] adj stable, solide, ferme; (regular) constant(e), régulier(-ière); (person) calme, pondéré(e) ▷ vt assurer, stabiliser; (nerves) calmer; **a ~ boyfriend** un petit ami

steak [steɪk] n (meat) bifteck m, steak m; (fish, pork) tranche f

steal (pt **stole**, pp **stolen**) [sti:l, stəʊl, 'stəʊln] vt, vi voler; (move) se faufiler, se déplacer furtivement; **my wallet has been stolen** m'a volé mon portefeuille

steam [sti:m] n vapeur f ▷ vt (Culin) cuire à la vapeur ▷ vi fumer; **steam up** vi (window) se couvrir de buée; **to get ~ed up about sth** (fig: inf) s'exciter à propos de qch; **steamy** adj humide; (window) embué(e); (also) torride

steel [sti:l] n acier m ▷ cpd d'acier

steep [sti:p] adj raide, escarpé(e); (price) très élevé(e), excessif(-ive) ▷ vt (food) tremper

steeple ['sti:pl] n clocher m

steer [stɪər] vt diriger; (boat) gouverner; (lead: person) guider, conduire ▷ vi tenir le gouvernail; **steering** n (Aut) conduite f; **steering wheel** n volant m

stem [stem] n (of plant) tige f; (of glass) pied m ▷ vt contenir, endiguer; (attack, spread of disease) juguler

step [step] n pas m; (stair) marche f; (action) mesure f, disposition f ▷ vi: **to ~ forward/back** faire un pas en avant/reculer; **steps** npl (BRIT) = **stepladder**; **to be in/out of**

stereo | 538

~ (with) (fig) aller dans le sens (de)/être déphasé(e) (par rapport à); **step down** vi (fig) se retirer, se désister; **step in** vi (fig) intervenir; **step up** vt (production, sales) augmenter; (campaign, efforts) intensifier; **stepbrother** n demi-frère m; **stepchild** (pl **~ren**) n beau-fils m, belle-fille f; **stepdaughter** n belle-fille f; **stepfather** n beau-père m; **stepladder** n (BRIT) escabeau m; **stepmother** n belle-mère f; **stepsister** n demi-sœur f; **stepson** n beau-fils m

stereo ['stɛrɪəʊ] n (sound) stéréo f; (hi-fi) chaîne f stéréo ▷ adj (also: **~phonic**) stéréo(phonique)

stereotype ['stɪərɪətaɪp] n stéréotype m ▷ vt stéréotyper

sterile ['stɛraɪl] adj stérile; **sterilize** ['stɛrɪlaɪz] vt stériliser

sterling ['stɜːlɪŋ] adj (silver) de bon aloi, fin(e) ▷ n (currency) livre f sterling inv

stern [stɜːn] adj sévère ▷ n (Naut) arrière m, poupe f

steroid ['stɪərɔɪd] n stéroïde m

stew [stjuː] n ragoût m ▷ vt, vi cuire à la casserole

steward [stjuːəd] n (Aviat, Naut, Rail) steward m; **stewardess** n hôtesse f

stick [stɪk] n bâton m; (for walking) canne f; (of chalk etc) morceau m ▷ vb (pt, pp **stuck**) ▷ vt (glue) coller; (thrust): **to ~ sth into** piquer or planter or enfoncer qch dans; (inf: put) mettre, fourrer; (: tolerate) supporter ▷ vi (adhere) tenir, coller; (remain) rester; (get jammed: door, lift) se bloquer; **stick out** vi dépasser, sortir; **stick up** vi dépasser, sortir; **stick up for** vt fus défendre; **sticker** n auto-collant m; **sticking plaster** n sparadrap m, pansement adhésif; **stick insect** n phasme m; **stick shift** n (US Aut) levier m de vitesses

sticky ['stɪkɪ] adj poisseux(-euse); (label) adhésif(-ive); (fig: situation) délicat(e)

stiff [stɪf] adj (gen) raide, rigide; (door, brush) dur(e); (difficult) difficile, ardu(e);

(cold) froid(e), distant(e); (strong, high) fort(e), élevé(e) ▷ adv: **to be bored/scared/frozen ~** s'ennuyer à mourir/être mort(e) de peur/froid

stifling ['staɪflɪŋ] adj (heat) suffocant(e)

stigma ['stɪɡmə] n stigmate m

stiletto [stɪ'lɛtəʊ] n (BRIT also: **~ heel**) talon m aiguille

still [stɪl] adj immobile ▷ adv (up to this time) encore, toujours; (even) encore; (nonetheless) quand même, tout de même

stimulate ['stɪmjuleɪt] vt stimuler

stimulus (pl **stimuli**) ['stɪmjuləs, 'stɪmjulaɪ] n stimulant m; (Biol, Psych) stimulus m

sting [stɪŋ] n piqûre f; (organ) dard m ▷ vt, vi (pt, pp **stung**) piquer

stink [stɪŋk] n puanteur f ▷ vi (pt **stank** pp **stunk**) puer, empester

stir [stɜː] n agitation f, sensation f ▷ vt remuer ▷ vi remuer, bouger; **stir up** vt (trouble) fomenter, provoquer; **stir-fry** vt faire sauter ▷ n: **vegetable stir-fry** légumes sautés à la poêle

stitch [stɪtʃ] n (Sewing) point m; (Knitting) maille f; (Med) point de suture; (pain) point de côté ▷ vt coudre, piquer; (Med) suturer

stock [stɒk] n réserve f, provision f; (Comm) stock m; (Agr) cheptel m, bétail m; (Culin) bouillon m; (Finance) valeurs fpl, titres mpl; (descent, origin) souche f ▷ adj (fig: reply etc) classique ▷ vt (have in stock) avoir, vendre; **in ~** en stock, en magasin; **out of ~** épuisé(e); **to take ~** (fig) faire le point; **~s and shares** valeurs (mobilières), titres; **stockbroker** ['stɒkbrəʊkə] n agent m de change; **stock cube** n (BRIT Culin) bouillon-cube m; **stock exchange** n Bourse f (des valeurs); **stockholder** ['stɒkhəʊldə] n (US) actionnaire m/f

stocking ['stɒkɪŋ] n bas m

stock market n Bourse f, marché financier

stole [stəʊl] pt of **steal** ▷ n étole f

stolen ['stəʊln] pp of **steal**

stomach ['stʌmək] n estomac m; (abdomen) ventre m ▷ vt supporter, digérer; **stomachache** n mal m à l'estomac ou au ventre

stone [stəun] n pierre f; (pebble) caillou m, galet m; (in fruit) noyau m; (Med) calcul m; (BRIT: weight) = 6.348 kg; 14 pounds ▷ cpd de or en pierre ▷ vt (person) lancer des pierres sur, lapider; (fruit) dénoyauter

stood [stud] pt, pp of **stand**

stool [stu:l] n tabouret m

stoop [stu:p] vi (also: **have a ~**) être voûté(e); (also: **~ down**: bend) se baisser, se courber

stop [stɔp] n arrêt m; (in punctuation) point m ▷ vt arrêter; (break off) interrompre; (also: **put a ~ to**) mettre fin à; (prevent) empêcher ▷ vi s'arrêter; (rain, noise etc) cesser, s'arrêter; **to ~ doing sth** cesser or arrêter de faire qch; **to ~ sb (from) doing sth** empêcher qn de faire qch; **~ it!** arrête!; **stop by** vi s'arrêter (au passage); **stop off** vi faire une courte halte; **stopover** n halte f; (Aviat) escale f; **stoppage** n (strike) arrêt m de travail; (obstruction) obstruction f

storage ['stɔ:rɪdʒ] n emmagasinage m

store [stɔ:] n (stock) provision f, réserve f; (depot) entrepôt m; (BRIT: large shop) grand magasin; (us: shop) magasin m ▷ vt emmagasiner; (information) enregistrer; **stores** npl (food) provisions f; **who knows what is in ~ for us?** qui sait ce que l'avenir nous réserve or ce qui nous attend?; **storekeeper** n (us) commerçant m

storey, (us **story**) ['stɔ:rɪ] n étage m

storm [stɔ:m] n tempête f; (thunderstorm) orage m ▷ vi (fig) fulminer ▷ vt prendre d'assaut; **stormy** adj orageux(-euse)

story ['stɔ:rɪ] n histoire f; (Press: article) article m; (us) = **storey**

stout [staut] adj (strong) solide; (fat) gros(se), corpulent(e) ▷ n bière brune

stove [stəuv] n (for cooking) fourneau m;

(: small) réchaud m; (for heating) poêle m

straight [streɪt] adj droit(e); (hair) raide; (frank) franc(he), franche); (simple) simple ▷ adv (tout) droit; (drink) sec, sans eau; **to put** or **get ~** mettre en ordre, mettre de l'ordre dans; (fig) mettre au clair; **~ away**, **~ off** (at once) tout de suite; **straighten** vt ajuster; (bed) arranger; **straighten out** vt (fig) débrouiller; **straighten up** (stand up) se redresser; **straightforward** adj simple; (frank) honnête, direct(e)

strain [streɪn] n (Tech) tension f; pression f; (physical) effort m; (mental) tension (nerveuse); (Med) entorse f; (breed: of plants) variété f; (: of animals) race f ▷ vt (fig: resources etc) mettre à rude épreuve, grever; (hurt: back etc) se faire mal à; (vegetables) égoutter; **strains** npl (Mus) accords mpl; **strained** adj (muscle) froissé(e); (laugh etc) forcé(e); (relations) tendu(e); **strainer** n passoire f

strait [streɪt] n (Geo) détroit m; **straits** npl: **to be in dire ~s** (fig) avoir de sérieux ennuis

strand [strænd] n (of thread) fil m, brin m; (of rope) toron m; (of hair) mèche f ▷ vt (boat) échouer; **stranded** adj en rade, en plan

strange [streɪndʒ] adj (not known) inconnu(e); (odd) étrange, bizarre; **strangely** adv étrangement, bizarrement; see also **enough**; **stranger** n (unknown) inconnu(e); (from somewhere else) étranger(-ère)

strangle ['stræŋgl] vt étrangler

strap [stræp] n lanière f, courroie f, sangle f; (of slip, dress) bretelle f

strategic [strə'ti:dʒɪk] adj stratégique

strategy ['strætɪdʒɪ] n stratégie f

straw [strɔ:] n paille f; **that's the last ~!** ça c'est le comble!

strawberry ['strɔ:bərɪ] n fraise f

stray [streɪ] adj (animal) perdu(e), errant(e); (scattered) isolé(e) ▷ vi s'égarer; **~ bullet** balle perdue

streak [striːk] n bande f, filet m; (in hair) raie f ▷ vt zébrer, strier

stream [striːm] n (brook) ruisseau m; (current) courant m, flot m; (of people) défilé ininterrompu, flot m ▷ vi ruisseler; to ~ in/out entrer/sortir à flots

street [striːt] n rue f; **streetcar** n (us) tramway m; **street light** n réverbère m; **street map, street plan** n plan m des rues

strength [strɛŋθ] n force f; (of girder, knot etc) solidité f; **strengthen** vt renforcer; (muscle) fortifier; (building, Econ) consolider

strenuous ['strɛnjuəs] adj vigoureux(-euse), énergique; (tiring) ardu(e), fatigant(e)

stress [strɛs] n (force, pressure) pression f; (mental strain) tension (nerveuse), stress m; (accent) accent m; (emphasis) insistance f ▷ vt insister sur, souligner; (syllable) accentuer; **stressed** adj (tense) stressé(e); (syllable) accentué(e); **stressful** adj (job) stressant(e)

stretch [strɛtʃ] n (of sand etc) étendue f ▷ vi s'étirer; (extend): to ~ to or as far as s'étendre jusqu'à ▷ vt tendre, étirer; (fig) pousser (au maximum); at a ~ d'affilée; **stretch out** vi s'étendre ▷ vt (arm etc) allonger, tendre; (to spread) étendre

stretcher ['strɛtʃər] n brancard m, civière f

strict [strikt] adj strict(e); **strictly** adv strictement

stride [straid] n grand pas, enjambée f ▷ vi (pt **strode**, pp **stridden**) marcher à grands pas

strike [straik] n grève f; (of oil etc) découverte f; (attack) raid m ▷ vt (pt, pp **struck**) n frapper; (oil etc) trouver, découvrir; (make: agreement, deal) conclure ▷ vi faire grève; (attack) attaquer; (clock) sonner; to go on or come out on ~ se mettre en grève, faire grève; to ~ a match frotter une allumette; **striker** n gréviste

m/f; (Sport) buteur m; **striking** adj frappant(e), saisissant(e); (attractive) éblouissant(e)

string [striŋ] n ficelle f, fil m; (row: of beads) rang m; (Mus) corde f ▷ vt (pt, pp **strung**) to ~ out échelonner; to ~ together enchaîner; the strings npl (Mus) les instruments mpl à cordes; to pull ~s (fig) faire jouer le piston

strip [strip] n bande f; (Sport) tenue f ▷ vt (undress) déshabiller; (paint) décaper; (fig) dégarnir, dépouiller; (also: ~ down: machine) démonter ▷ vi se déshabiller; **strip off** vt (paint etc) décaper ▷ vi (person) se déshabiller

stripe [straip] n raie f, rayure f; (Mil) galon m; **striped** adj rayé(e), à rayures

stripper ['stripər] n strip-teaseuse f

strip-search ['stripsɜːtʃ] vt: to ~ sb fouiller qn (en le faisant se déshabiller)

strive (pt **strove**, pp ~n) [straiv, strəuv, 'strivn] vi: to ~ to do/for sth s'efforcer de faire/d'obtenir qch

strode [strəud] pt of **stride**

stroke [strəuk] n coup m; (Med) attaque f; (Swimming: style) (sorte f de) nage f ▷ vt caresser; at a ~ en un (seul) coup

stroll [strəul] n petite promenade f ▷ vi flâner, se promener nonchalamment; **stroller** n (us: for child) poussette f

strong [strɒŋ] adj (gen) fort(e); (healthy) vigoureux(-euse); (heart, nerves) solide; they are 50 ~ ils sont au nombre de 50; **stronghold** n forteresse f, fort m; (fig) bastion m; **strongly** adv fortement, avec force; vigoureusement; solidement

strove [strəuv] pt of **strive**

struck [strʌk] pt, pp of **strike**

structure ['strʌktʃər] n structure f; (building) construction f

struggle ['strʌgl] n lutte f ▷ vi lutter, se battre

strung [strʌŋ] pt, pp of **string**

stub [stʌb] n (of cigarette) bout m, mégot m; (of ticket etc) talon m ▷ vt: to ~ one's toe (on sth) se heurter le doigt de pied (contre qch); **stub out** vt écraser

stubble ['stʌbl] n chaume m; (on chin) barbe f de plusieurs jours

stubborn ['stʌbən] adj têtu(e), obstiné(e), opiniâtre

stuck [stʌk] pt, pp of **stick** ▷ adj (jammed) bloqué(e), coincé(e)

stud [stʌd] n (on boots also:) clou m; (collar stud) bouton m de col; (earring) petite boucle d'oreille; (of horses: also: ~ farm) écurie f, haras m; (also: ~ horse) étalon m ▷ vt (fig): **~ded with** parsemé(e), criblé(e) de

student ['stju:dənt] n étudiant(e) ▷ adj (life) estudiantin(e), étudiant(e), d'étudiant; (residence, restaurant) universitaire; (loan, movement) étudiant; **student driver** n (US) (conducteur-trice) débutant(e); **students' union** n (BRIT: association) ≈ union f des étudiants; (: building) ≈ foyer m des étudiants

studio ['stju:dɪəʊ] n studio m, atelier m; (TV etc) studio; **studio flat** (US) **studio apartment**) n studio m

study ['stʌdɪ] n étude f; (room) bureau m ▷ vt étudier; (examine) examiner ▷ vi étudier, faire ses études

stuff [stʌf] n (gen) chose(s) f(pl), truc m; (belongings) affaires fpl, trucs; (substance) substance f ▷ vt rembourrer; (Culin) farcir; (inf: push) fourrer; **stuffing** n bourre f, rembourrage m; (Culin) farce f; **stuffy** adj (room) mal ventilé(e) or aéré(e); (ideas) vieux jeu inv

stumble ['stʌmbl] vi trébucher; **to ~ across** or **on** (fig) tomber sur

stump [stʌmp] n souche f; (of limb) moignon m ▷ vt: **to be ~ed** sécher, ne pas savoir que répondre

stun [stʌn] vt (blow) étourdir; (news) abasourdir, stupéfier

stung [stʌŋ] pt, pp of **sting**

stunk [stʌŋk] pp of **stink**

stunned [stʌnd] adj assommé(e); (fig) sidéré(e)

stunning ['stʌnɪŋ] adj (beautiful) étourdissant(e); (news etc)

stupéfiant(e)

stunt [stʌnt] n (in film) cascade f, acrobatie f; (publicity) truc m publicitaire ▷ vt retarder, arrêter

stupid ['stju:pɪd] adj stupide, bête; **stupidity** [stju:'pɪdɪtɪ] n stupidité f, bêtise f

sturdy ['stɜ:dɪ] adj (person, plant) robuste, vigoureux(-euse); (object) solide

stutter ['stʌtə*] n bégaiement m ▷ vi bégayer

style [staɪl] n style m; (distinction) allure f, cachet m, style; (design) modèle m; **stylish** adj élégant(e), chic inv; **stylist** n (hair stylist) coiffeur(-euse)

sub... [sʌb] prefix sub..., sous-; **subconscious** adj subconscient(e)

subdued [səb'dju:d] adj (light) tamisé(e); (person) qui a perdu de son entrain

subject n ['sʌbdʒɪkt] sujet m; (Scol) matière f ▷ vt [səb'dʒekt]: **to ~ sb/sth to** soumettre à; **to be ~ to** (law) être soumis(e) à; **subjective** [səb'dʒektɪv] adj subjectif(-ive); **subject matter** n (content) contenu m

subjunctive [səb'dʒʌŋktɪv] n subjonctif m

submarine [sʌbmə'ri:n] n sous-marin m

submission [səb'mɪʃən] n soumission f

submit [səb'mɪt] vt soumettre ▷ vi se soumettre

subordinate [sə'bɔ:dɪnət] adj (junior) subalterne; (Grammar) subordonné(e) ▷ n subordonné(e)

subscribe [səb'skraɪb] vi cotiser; **to ~ to** (opinion, fund) souscrire à; (newspaper) s'abonner à; être abonné(e) à

subscription [səb'skrɪpʃən] n (to magazine etc) abonnement m

subsequent ['sʌbsɪkwənt] adj ultérieur(e), suivant(e); **subsequently** adv par la suite

subside [səb'saɪd] vi (land) s'affaisser;

(flood) baisser; *(wind, feelings)* tomber

subsidiary [səb'sɪdɪərɪ] *adj*
subsidiaire; accessoire; *(BRIT Scol: subject)* complémentaire ▷ *n* filiale *f*

subsidize ['sʌbsɪdaɪz] *vt*
subventionner

subsidy ['sʌbsɪdɪ] *n* subvention *f*

substance ['sʌbstəns] *n* substance *f*

substantial [səb'stænʃl] *adj*
substantiel(le); *(fig)* important(e)

substitute ['sʌbstɪtjuːt] *n (person)*
remplaçant(e); *(thing)* succédané *m*
▷ *vt*: **to ~ sth/sb for** substituer qch/qn
à, remplacer par qch/qn; **substitution**
n substitution *f*

subtitles ['sʌbtaɪtlz] *npl (Cine)* sous-
titres *mpl*

subtle ['sʌtl] *adj* subtil(e)

subtract [səb'trækt] *vt* soustraire,
retrancher

suburb ['sʌbɜːb] *n* faubourg *m*; **the ~s** la
banlieue; **suburban** [sə'bɜːbən] *adj* de
banlieue, suburbain(e)

subway ['sʌbweɪ] *n (BRIT: underpass)*
passage souterrain; *(us: railway)*
métro *m*

succeed [sək'siːd] *vi* réussir ▷ *vt*
succéder à; **to ~ in doing** réussir à faire

success [sək'ses] *n* succès *m*; réussite *f*;
successful *adj (business)* prospère,
qui réussit; *(attempt)* couronné(e) de
succès; **to be successful (in doing)**
réussir (à faire); **successfully** *adv*
avec succès

succession [sək'seʃən] *n* succession *f*

successive [sək'sesɪv] *adj*
successif(-ive)

successor [sək'sesə'] *n* successeur *m*

succumb [sə'kʌm] *vi* succomber

such [sʌtʃ] *adj* tel (telle); *(of that kind)*:
~ a book un livre de ce genre ou pareil,
un tel livre; *(so much)*: **~ courage** un
tel courage ▷ *adv* si; **~ a long trip** un
si long voyage; **~ a lot of** tellement
or tant de; **~ as** *(like)* tel (telle) que,
comme; **as ~** *adv* en tant que tel (telle),
à proprement parler; **such-and-such**
adj tel ou tel (telle ou telle)

suck [sʌk] *vt* sucer; *(breast, bottle)* téter

Sudan [suː'dɑːn] *n* Soudan *m*

sudden ['sʌdn] *adj* soudain(e),
subit(e); **all of a ~** soudain, tout à coup;
suddenly *adv* brusquement, tout à
coup, soudain

sue [suː] *vt* poursuivre en justice,
intenter un procès à

suede [sweɪd] *n* daim *m*, cuir suédé

suffer ['sʌfə'] *vt* souffrir, subir; *(bear)*
tolérer, supporter, subir ▷ *vi* souffrir;
to ~ from *(illness)* souffrir de, avoir;
suffering *n* souffrance(s) *f(pl)*

suffice [sə'faɪs] *vi* suffire

sufficient [sə'fɪʃənt] *adj* suffisant(e)

suffocate ['sʌfəkeɪt] *vi* suffoquer,
étouffer

sugar ['ʃʊgə'] *n* sucre *m* ▷ *vt* sucrer

suggest [sə'dʒest] *vt* suggérer,
proposer; *(indicate)* sembler
indiquer; **suggestion** [sə'dʒestʃən] *n*
suggestion *f*

suicide ['suːɪsaɪd] *n* suicide *m*; **~
bombing** attentat *m* suicide; *see also*
commit; **suicide bomber** *n* kamikaze
m/f

suit [suːt] *n (man's)* costume *m*, complet
m; *(woman's)* tailleur *m*, ensemble *m*;
(Cards) couleur *f*; *(lawsuit)* procès *m*
▷ *vt (subj: clothes, hairstyle)* aller à; *(be
convenient for)* convenir à; *(adapt)*: **to
~ sth to** adapter ou approprier qch à;
well ~ed *(couple)* faits l'un pour l'autre,
très bien assortis; **suitable** *adj* qui
convient; approprié(e), adéquat(e);
suitcase *n* valise *f*

suite [swiːt] *n (of rooms, also Mus)* suite
f; *(furniture)*: **bedroom/dining room ~**
(ensemble m de) chambre *f* à coucher/
salle *f* à manger; **a three-piece ~** un
salon *(canapé et deux fauteuils)*

sulfur ['sʌlfə'] *(us)* *n* = **sulphur**

sulk [sʌlk] *vi* bouder

sulphur ['sʌlfə'] *(us* **sulfur)** *n* soufre *m*

sultana [sʌl'tɑːnə] *n (fruit)* raisin *(sec)*
de Smyrne

sum [sʌm] *n* somme *f*; *(Scol etc)* calcul *m*;
sum up *vt* résumer ▷ *vi* résumer

summarize ['sʌməraɪz] vt résumer

summary ['sʌmərɪ] n résumé m

summer ['sʌmə*] n été m ▷ cpd d'été,
estival(e); **in (the) ~** en été, pendant
l'été; **summer holidays** npl grandes
vacances; **summertime** n (season)
été m

summit ['sʌmɪt] n sommet m; (also:
~ conference) (conférence f au)
sommet m

summon ['sʌmən] vt appeler,
convoquer; **to ~ a witness** citer or
assigner un témoin

Sun. abbr (= Sunday) dim

sun [sʌn] n soleil m; **sunbathe** vi
prendre un bain de soleil; **sunbed** n lit
pliant; (with sun lamp) lit à ultra-violets;
sunblock n écran m total; **sunburn**
n coup m de soleil; **sunburned**,
sunburnt adj bronzé(e), hâlé(e);
(painfully) brûlé(e) par le soleil

Sunday ['sʌndɪ] n dimanche m

sunflower ['sʌnflauə*] n tournesol m

sung [sʌŋ] pp of **sing**

sunglasses ['sʌnglɑːsɪz] npl lunettes
fpl de soleil

sunk [sʌŋk] pp of **sink**

sun:sunlight n (lumière f du) soleil m;
sun lounger n chaise longue; **sunny**
adj ensoleillé(e); **it is sunny** il fait (du)
soleil, il y a du soleil; **sunrise** n lever m
du soleil; **sun roof** n (Aut) toit ouvrant;
sunscreen n crème f solaire; **sunset**
n coucher m de soleil; **sunshade** n (over
table) parasol m; **sunshine** n (lumière f
du) soleil m; **sunstroke** n insolation f,
coup m de soleil; **suntan** n bronzage m;
suntan lotion n lotion f or lait m
solaire; **suntan oil** n huile f solaire

super ['suːpə*] adj (inf) formidable

superb [suː'pəːb] adj superbe,
magnifique

superficial [suːpə'fɪʃəl] adj
superficiel(le)

superintendent [suːpərɪn'tendənt]
n directeur(-trice); (Police)
≈ commissaire m

superior [su'pɪərɪə*] adj supérieur(e);

(smug) condescendant(e), méprisant(e)
▷ n supérieur(e)

superlative [su'pəːlətɪv] n (Ling)
superlatif m

supermarket [suːpəmɑːkɪt] n
supermarché m

supernatural [suːpə'nætʃərəl] adj
surnaturel(le) ▷ n: **the ~** le surnaturel

superpower ['suːpəpauə*] n (Pol)
superpuissance f

superstition [suːpə'stɪʃən] n
superstition f

superstitious [suːpə'stɪʃəs] adj
superstitieux(-euse)

superstore ['suːpəstɔː*] n (Brit)
hypermarché m, grande surface

supervise ['suːpəvaɪz] vt (children
etc) surveiller; (organization, work)
diriger; **supervision** [suːpə'vɪʒən] n
surveillance f; (monitoring) contrôle m;
(management) direction f; **supervisor** n
surveillant(e); (in shop) chef m de rayon

supper ['sʌpə*] n dîner m; (late)
souper m

supple ['sʌpl] adj souple

supplement n ['sʌplɪmənt]
supplément m ▷ vt ['sʌplɪ'ment]
ajouter à, compléter

supplier [sə'plaɪə*] n fournisseur m

supply [sə'plaɪ] vt (provide) fournir;
(equip): **to ~ (with)** approvisionner
or ravitailler (en); fournir (en) ▷ n
provision f, réserve f; (supplying)
approvisionnement m; **supplies** npl
(food) vivres mpl; (Mil) subsistances fpl

support [sə'pɔːt] n (moral, financial
etc) soutien m, appui m; (Tech) support
m, soutien ▷ vt soutenir, supporter;
(financially) subvenir aux besoins
de; (uphold) être pour, être partisan
de, appuyer; (Sport: team) être pour;
supporter n (Pol etc) partisan(e);
(Sport) supporter m

suppose [sə'pəuz] vt, vi supposer;
imaginer; **to be ~d to do/be** être
censé(e) faire/être; **supposedly**
[sə'pəuzɪdlɪ] adv soi-disant;
supposing conj si, à supposer que + sub

suppress [sə'pres] vt (revolt, feeling) réprimer; (information) faire disparaître; (scandal, yawn) étouffer

supreme [su'pri:m] adj suprême

surcharge ['sə:tʃɑ:dʒ] n surcharge f

sure [ʃuəʳ] adj (gen) sûr; (definite, convinced) sûr, certain(e); ~! (of course) bien sûr!; ~ **enough** effectivement; **to make ~ of sth/that** s'assurer de qch/que, vérifier qch/que; **surely** adv sûrement; certainement

surf [sə:f] n (waves) ressac m ▷ vt: **to ~ the Net** surfer sur Internet, surfer sur le net

surface ['sə:fɪs] n surface f ▷ vt (road) poser un revêtement sur ▷ vi remonter à la surface; (fig) faire surface; **by mail** par voie de terre; (by sea) par voie maritime

surfboard ['sə:fbɔ:d] n planche f de surf

surfer ['sə:fəʳ] n (in sea) surfeur(-euse); **web** or **net ~** internaute m/f

surfing ['sə:fɪŋ] n surf m

surge [sə:dʒ] n (of emotion) vague f ▷ vi déferler

surgeon ['sə:dʒən] n chirurgien m

surgery ['sə:dʒərɪ] n chirurgie f; (BRIT: room) cabinet m (de consultation); (also: ~ **hours**) heures fpl de consultation

surname ['sə:neɪm] n nom m de famille

surpass [sə:'pɑ:s] vt surpasser, dépasser

surplus ['sə:pləs] n surplus m, excédent m ▷ adj en surplus, de trop; (Comm) excédentaire

surprise [sə'praɪz] n (gen) surprise f; (astonishment) étonnement m ▷ vt surprendre, étonner; **surprised** adj (look, smile) surpris(e), étonné(e); **to be surprised** être surpris; **surprising** adj surprenant(e), étonnant(e); **surprisingly** adv (easy, helpful) étonnamment, étrangement; (somewhat) surprisingly, he agreed curieusement, il a accepté

surrender [sə'rɛndəʳ] n reddition f,

capitulation f ▷ vi se rendre, capituler

surround [sə'raund] vt entourer; (Mil etc) encercler; **surrounding** adj environnant(e); **surroundings** npl environs mpl, alentours mpl

surveillance [sə:'veɪləns] n surveillance f

survey n ['sə:veɪ] enquête f, étude f; (in house buying etc) inspection f, (rapport m d')expertise f; (of land) levé m ▷ vt [sə:'veɪ] (situation) passer en revue; (examine carefully) inspecter; (building) expertiser; (land) faire le levé de; (look at) embrasser du regard; **surveyor** n (of building) expert m; (of land) (arpenteur m) géomètre m

survival [sə'vaɪvl] n survie f

survive [sə'vaɪv] vi survivre; (custom etc) subsister ▷ vt (accident etc) survivre à, réchapper de; (person) survivre à; **survivor** n survivant(e)

suspect adj, n ['sʌspekt] suspect(e) ▷ vt [sə'spekt] soupçonner, suspecter

suspend [sə'spend] vt suspendre; **suspended sentence** f (Law) condamnation f avec sursis; **suspenders** npl (BRIT) jarretelles fpl; (us) bretelles fpl

suspense [sə'spens] n attente f, incertitude f; (in film etc) suspense m; **to keep sb in ~** tenir qn en suspens, laisser qn dans l'incertitude

suspension [sə'spenʃən] n (gen, Aut) suspension f; (of driving licence) retrait m provisoire; **suspension bridge** n pont suspendu

suspicion [sə'spɪʃən] n soupçon(s) m(pl); **suspicious** adj (suspecting) soupçonneux(-euse), méfiant(e); (causing suspicion) suspect(e)

sustain [sə'steɪn] vt soutenir; (subj: food) nourrir, donner des forces à; (damage) subir; (injury) recevoir

SUV n abbr (esp us: = sports utility vehicle) SUV m, véhicule m de loisirs

swallow ['swɔləʊ] n (bird) hirondelle f ▷ vt avaler; (fig: story) gober

swam [swæm] *pt of* **swim**

swamp [swɒmp] *n* marais *m*, marécage *m* ▷ *vt* submerger

swan [swɒn] *n* cygne *m*

swap [swɒp] *n* échange *m*, troc *m* ▷ *vt*: **to ~ (for)** échanger (contre), troquer (contre)

swarm [swɔːm] *n* essaim *m* ▷ *vi* (*bees*) essaimer; (*people*) grouiller; **to be ~ing with** grouiller de

sway [sweɪ] *vi* se balancer, osciller ▷ *vt* (*influence*) influencer

swear [swɛəʳ] (*pt* **swore**, *pp* **sworn**) *vt*, *vi* jurer; **swear in** *vt* assermenter; **swearword** *n* gros mot, juron *m*

sweat [swɛt] *n* sueur *f*, transpiration *f* ▷ *vi* suer

sweater ['swɛtəʳ] *n* tricot *m*, pull *m*

sweatshirt ['swɛtʃəːt] *n* sweat-shirt *m*

sweaty ['swɛtɪ] *adj* en sueur, moite or mouillé(e) de sueur

Swede [swiːd] *n* Suédois(e)

swede [swiːd] *n* (BRIT) rutabaga *m*

Sweden ['swiːdn] *n* Suède *f*; **Swedish** ['swiːdɪʃ] *adj* suédois(e) ▷ *n* (Ling) suédois *m*

sweep [swiːp] *n* (*curve*) grande courbe; (*also*: **chimney ~**) ramoneur *m* ▷ *vb* (*pt, pp* **swept**) ▷ *vt* balayer; (*subj: current*) emporter

sweet [swiːt] *n* (BRIT: *pudding*) dessert *m*; (*candy*) bonbon *m* ▷ *adj* doux (douce); (*not savoury*) sucré(e); (*kind*) gentil(le); (*baby*) mignon(ne); **sweetcorn** *n* maïs doux; **sweetener** ['swiːtnəʳ] *n* (Culin) édulcorant *m*; **sweetheart** *n* amoureux(-euse); **sweetshop** *n* (BRIT) confiserie *f*

swell [swɛl] *n* (*of sea*) houle *f* ▷ *adj* (US: *inf: excellent*) chouette ▷ *vb* (*pt* **-ed**, *pp* **swollen** or **-ed**) ▷ *vt* (*increase*) grossir, augmenter ▷ *vi* (*increase*) grossir, augmenter; (*sound*) s'enfler; (Med: *also*: **~ up**) enfler; **swelling** *n* (Med) enflure *f*; (: *lump*) grosseur *f*

swept [swɛpt] *pt, pp of* **sweep**

swerve [swəːv] *vi* (*to avoid obstacle*) faire une embardée or un écart; (*off the road*) dévier

swift [swɪft] *n* (*bird*) martinet *m* ▷ *adj* rapide, prompt(e)

swim [swɪm] *n*: **to go for a ~** aller nager or se baigner ▷ *vb* (*pt* **swam**, *pp* **swum**) ▷ *vi* nager; (Sport) faire de la natation; (*fig: head, room*) tourner ▷ *vt* traverser (à la nage); **to ~ a length** nager une longueur; **swimmer** *n* nageur(-euse); **swimming** *n* nage *f*, natation *f*; **swimming costume** *n* (BRIT) maillot *m* (de bain); **swimming pool** *n* piscine *f*; **swimming trunks** *npl* maillot *m* de bain; **swimsuit** *n* maillot *m* (de bain)

swing [swɪŋ] *n* (*in playground*) balançoire *f*; (*movement*) balancement *m*, oscillations *fpl*; (*change in opinion etc*) revirement *m* ▷ *vb* (*pt, pp* **swung**) ▷ *vt* balancer, faire osciller; (*also*: **~ round**) tourner, faire virer ▷ *vi* se balancer, osciller; (*also*: **~ round**) virer, tourner; **to be in full ~** battre son plein

swipe card [swaɪp-] *n* carte *f* magnétique

swirl [swəːl] *vi* tourbillonner, tournoyer

Swiss [swɪs] *adj* suisse ▷ *n* (*pl inv*) Suisse(-esse)

switch [swɪtʃ] *n* (*for light, radio etc*) bouton *m*; (*change*) changement *m*, revirement *m* ▷ *vt* (*change*) changer; **switch off** *vt* éteindre; (*engine, machine*) arrêter; **could you ~ off the light?** pouvez-vous éteindre la lumière?; **switch on** *vt* allumer; (*engine, machine*) mettre en marche; **switchboard** *n* (Tel) standard *m*

Switzerland ['swɪtsələnd] *n* Suisse *f*

swivel ['swɪvl] *vi* (*also*: **~ round**) pivoter, tourner

swollen ['swəʊlən] *pp of* **swell**

swoop [swuːp] *n* (*by police etc*) rafle *f*, descente *f* ▷ *vi* (*bird: also*: **~ down**) descendre en piqué, piquer

swop [swɒp] *n, vt* = **swap**

sword [sɔːd] *n* épée *f*; **swordfish** *n* espadon *m*

swore [swɔːʳ] *pt of* **swear**

sworn [swɔːn] *pp of* **swear** ▷ *adj*

(*statement, evidence*) donné(e) sous
serment; (*enemy*) juré(e)
swum [swʌm] *pp of* **swim**
swung [swʌŋ] *pt, pp of* **swing**
syllable ['sɪləbl] *n* syllabe *f*
syllabus ['sɪləbəs] *n* programme *m*
symbol ['sɪmbl] *n* symbole *m*;
  symbolic(al) [sɪm'bɒlɪk(l)] *adj*
  symbolique
symmetrical [sɪ'metrɪkl] *adj*
  symétrique
symmetry ['sɪmɪtrɪ] *n* symétrie *f*
sympathetic [sɪmpə'θetɪk] *adj*
  (*showing pity*) compatissant(e);
  (*understanding*) bienveillant(e),
  compréhensif(-ive); ~ **towards** bien
  disposé(e) envers

> Be careful not to translate
> *sympathetic* by the French word
> *sympathique*.

sympathize ['sɪmpəθaɪz] *vi*: **to ~
  with sb** plaindre qn; (*in grief*) s'associer
  à la douleur de qn; **to ~ with sth**
  comprendre qch
sympathy ['sɪmpəθɪ] *n* (*pity*)
  compassion *f*
symphony ['sɪmfənɪ] *n* symphonie *f*
symptom ['sɪmptəm] *n* symptôme
  m; indice *m*
synagogue ['sɪnəgɒg] *n* synagogue *f*
syndicate ['sɪndɪkɪt] *n* syndicat *m*,
  coopérative *f*; (*Press*) agence *f* de presse
syndrome ['sɪndrəum] *n* syndrome *m*
synonym ['sɪnənɪm] *n* synonyme *m*
synthetic [sɪn'θetɪk] *adj* synthétique
Syria ['sɪrɪə] *n* Syrie *f*
syringe ['sɪrɪndʒ] *n* seringue *f*
syrup ['sɪrəp] *n* sirop *m*; (*BRIT: also:*
  golden ~) mélasse raffinée
system ['sɪstəm] *n* système *m*;
  (*Anat*) organisme *m*; **systematic**
  [sɪstə'mætɪk] *adj* systématique;
  méthodique; **systems analyst** *n*
  analyste-programmeur *m/f*

t

ta [tɑː] *excl* (*BRIT inf*) merci!
tab [tæb] *n* (*label*) étiquette *f*; (*on drinks
  can etc*) languette *f*; **to keep ~s on** (*fig*)
  surveiller
table ['teɪbl] *n* table *f* ▷ *vt* (*BRIT: motion
  etc*) présenter; **a ~ for 4, please** une
  table pour 4, s'il vous plaît; **to lay** *ou*
  set the ~ mettre le couvert *ou* la table;
  tablecloth *n* nappe *f*; **table d'hôte**
  [tɑːbl'dəut] *adj* (*meal*) à prix fixe; **table
  lamp** *n* lampe décorative *ou* de table;
  tablemat *n* (*for plate*) napperon *m*,
  set *m*; (*for hot dish*) dessous-de-plat *m
  inv*; **tablespoon** *n* cuiller *f* de service;
  (*also:* **tablespoonful**: *as measurement*)
  cuillerée *f* à soupe
tablet ['tæblɪt] *n* (*Med*) comprimé *m*; (*of
  stone*) plaque *f*
table tennis *n* ping-pong *m*, tennis
  m de table
tabloid ['tæblɔɪd] *n* (*newspaper*)
  quotidien *m* populaire
taboo [tə'buː] *adj, n* tabou (*m*)
tack [tæk] *n* (*nail*) petit clou *m*; (*fig*)

direction f ▷ vt (nail) clouer; (sew) bâtir ▷ vi (Naut) tirer un or des bord(s); **to ~ sth on to (the end of) sth** (of letter, book) rajouter qch à la fin de qch

tackle ['tækl] n matériel m, équipement m; (for lifting) appareil m de levage; (Football, Rugby) plaquage m ▷ vt (difficulty, animal, burglar) s'attaquer à; (person: challenge) s'expliquer avec; (Football, Rugby) plaquer

tacky ['tæki] adj collant(e); (paint) pas sec (sèche); (pej: poor-quality) minable; (: showing bad taste) ringard(e)

tact [tækt] n tact m; **tactful** adj plein(e) de tact

tactics ['tæktɪks] npl tactique f

tactless ['tæktlɪs] adj qui manque de tact

tadpole ['tædpəul] n têtard m

taffy ['tæfɪ] n (us) (bonbon m au) caramel m

tag [tæg] n étiquette f

tail [teɪl] n queue f; (of shirt) pan m ▷ vt (follow) suivre, filer; **tails** npl (suit) habit m; see also **head**

tailor ['teɪlər] n tailleur m (artisan)

Taiwan ['taɪ'wɑːn] n Taïwan (no article); **Taiwanese** [taɪwɑ'niːz] adj taïwanais(e) ▷ n inv Taïwanais(e)

take [teɪk] vb (pt **took**, pp **~n**) ▷ vt prendre; (gain: prize) remporter; (require: effort, courage) demander; (tolerate) accepter, supporter; (hold: passengers etc) contenir; (accompany) emmener, accompagner; (bring, carry) apporter, emporter; (exam) passer, se présenter à; **to ~ sth from** (drawer etc) prendre qch dans; (person) prendre qch à; **I ~ it that** je suppose que; **to be ~n ill** tomber malade; **it won't ~ long** ça ne prendra pas longtemps; **I was quite ~n with her/it** elle/cela m'a beaucoup plu; **take after** vt fus ressembler à; **take apart** vt démonter; **take away** vt (carry off) emporter; (remove) enlever; (subtract) soustraire; **take back** vt (return) rendre, rapporter; (one's words) retirer; **take down** vt

(building) démolir; (letter etc) prendre, écrire; **take in** vt (deceive) tromper, rouler; (understand) comprendre, saisir; (include) couvrir, inclure; (lodger) prendre; (dress, waistband) reprendre; **take off** vi (Aviat) décoller ▷ vt (remove) enlever; **take on** vt (work) accepter, se charger de; (employee) prendre, embaucher; (opponent) accepter de se battre contre; **take out** vt sortir; (remove) enlever; (invite) sortir avec; **to ~ sth out of** (out of drawer etc) prendre qch dans; **to ~ sb out to a restaurant** emmener qn au restaurant; **take over** vt (business) reprendre ▷ vi: **to ~ over from sb** prendre la relève de qn; **take up** vt (one's story) reprendre; (dress) raccourcir; (occupy: time, space) prendre, occuper; (engage in: hobby etc) se mettre à; (accept: offer, challenge) accepter; **takeaway** (BRIT) adj (food) à emporter ▷ n (shop, restaurant) = magasin m qui vend des plats à emporter; **taken** pp of **take**; **is this seat taken?** la place est prise?; **takeoff** n (Aviat) décollage m; **takeout** adj, n (us) = **takeaway**; **takeover** n (Comm) rachat m; **takings** npl (Comm) recette f

talc [tælk] n (also: **~um powder**) talc m

tale [teɪl] n (story) conte m, histoire f; (account) récit m; **to tell ~s** (fig) rapporter

talent ['tælnt] n talent m, don m; **talented** adj doué(e), plein(e) de talent

talk [tɔːk] n (a speech) causerie f, exposé m; (conversation) discussion f; (interview) entretien m; (gossip) racontars mpl (pej) ▷ vi parler; (chatter) bavarder; **talks** npl (Pol etc) entretiens mpl; **to ~ about** parler de; **to ~ sb out of/into doing** persuader qn de ne pas faire/de faire; **to ~ shop** parler métier or affaires; **talk over** vt discuter (de); **talk show** n (TV, Radio) émission-débat f

tall [tɔːl] adj (person) grand(e); (building, tree) haut(e); **to be 6 feet ~** mesurer 1 mètre 80

tambourine [tæmbə'riːn] n

tambourin m

tame [teɪm] adj apprivoisé(e); (fig: story, style) insipide

tamper ['tæmpə] vi: **to ~ with** toucher à (en cachette ou sans permission)

tampon ['tæmpɒn] n tampon m hygiénique or périodique

tan [tæn] n (also: **sun~**) bronzage m ▷ vt, vi bronzer, brunir ▷ adj (colour) marron clair inv

tandem ['tændəm] n tandem m

tangerine [tændʒə'riːn] n mandarine f

tangle ['tæŋgl] n enchevêtrement m; **to get in(to) a ~** s'emmêler

tank [tæŋk] n réservoir m; (for fish) aquarium m; (Mil) char m d'assaut, tank m

tanker ['tæŋkə] n (ship) pétrolier m, tanker m; (truck) camion-citerne m

tanned [tænd] adj bronzé(e)

tantrum ['tæntrəm] n accès m de colère

Tanzania [tænzə'niːə] n Tanzanie f

tap [tæp] n (on sink etc) robinet m; (gentle blow) petite tape f ▷ vt frapper or taper légèrement; (resources) exploiter, utiliser; (telephone) mettre sur écoute; **on ~** (fig: resources) disponible; **tap dancing** n claquettes fpl

tape [teɪp] n (for tying) ruban m; (also: **magnetic ~**) bande f (magnétique); (cassette) cassette f; (sticky) Scotch® m ▷ vt (record) enregistrer (au magnétoscope or sur cassette); (stick) coller avec du Scotch®; **tape measure** n mètre m à ruban; **tape recorder** n magnétophone m

tapestry ['tæpɪstrɪ] n tapisserie f

tar [tɑː] n goudron m

target ['tɑːgɪt] n cible f; (fig: objective) objectif m

tariff ['tærɪf] n (Comm) tarif m; (taxes) tarif douanier

tarmac ['tɑːmæk] n (BRIT: on road) macadam m; (Aviat) aire f d'envol

tarpaulin [tɑː'pɔːlɪn] n bâche goudronnée

tarragon ['tærəgən] n estragon m

tart [tɑːt] n (Culin) tarte f, (BRIT inf: pej:

prostitute) poule f ▷ adj (flavour) âpre, aigrelet(te)

tartan ['tɑːtn] n tartan m ▷ adj écossais(e)

tartar(e) sauce n sauce f tartare

task [tɑːsk] n tâche f; **to take to ~** prendre à partie

taste [teɪst] n goût m; (fig: glimpse, idea) idée f, aperçu m ▷ vt goûter ▷ vi: **to ~ of** (fish etc) avoir le or un goût de; **you can ~ the garlic (in it)** on sent bien l'ail; **to have a ~ of sth** goûter (à) qch; **can I have a ~?** je peux goûter?; **to be in good/bad or poor ~** être de bon/mauvais goût; **tasteful** adj de bon goût; **tasteless** adj (food) insipide; (remark) de mauvais goût; **tasty** adj savoureux(-euse), délicieux(-euse)

tatters ['tætəz] npl: **in ~** (also: **tattered**) en lambeaux

tattoo [tə'tuː] n tatouage m; (spectacle) parade f militaire ▷ vt tatouer

taught [tɔːt] pt, pp of **teach**

taunt [tɔːnt] n raillerie f ▷ vt railler

Taurus ['tɔːrəs] n le Taureau

taut [tɔːt] adj tendu(e)

tax [tæks] n (on goods etc) taxe f; (on income) impôts mpl, contributions fpl ▷ vt taxer; imposer; (fig: patience etc) mettre à l'épreuve; **tax disc** n (BRIT Aut) vignette f (automobile); **tax-free** adj exempt(e) d'impôts

taxi ['tæksɪ] n taxi m ▷ vi (Aviat) rouler (lentement) au sol; **can you call me a ~, please?** pouvez-vous m'appeler un taxi, s'il vous plaît?; **taxi driver** n chauffeur m de taxi; **taxi rank** (BRIT), **taxi stand** n station f de taxis

tax payer [-peɪə] n contribuable m/f

tax return n déclaration f d'impôts or de revenus

TB n abbr = **tuberculosis**

tea [tiː] n thé m; (BRIT: snack: for children) goûter m; **high ~** (BRIT) collation combinant goûter et dîner; **tea bag** n sachet m de thé; **tea break** n (BRIT) pause-thé f

teach (pt, pp **taught**) [tiːtʃ, tɔːt] vt: **to**

~ sb sth, to ~ sth to sb apprendre qch à qn; (in school etc) enseigner qch à qn ▷ vi enseigner; **teacher** n (in secondary school) professeur m; (in primary school) instituteur(-trice); **teaching** n enseignement m

tea cloth n (BRIT) torchon m; **teacup** n tasse f à thé

tea leaves npl feuilles fpl de thé

team [ti:m] n équipe f; (of animals) attelage m; **team up** vi: to ~ up (with) faire équipe (avec)

teapot ['ti:pɒt] n théière f

tear[¹] ['tɪə'] n larme f; **in ~s** en larmes

tear[²] [tɛə'] déchirure f; ▷ vb (pt **tore**, pp **torn**) ▷ vt déchirer; ▷ vi se déchirer; **tear apart** vt (also fig) déchirer; **tear down** vt (building, statue) démolir; (poster, flag) arracher; **tear off** vt (sheet of paper etc) arracher; (one's clothes) enlever à toute vitesse; **tear up** vt (sheet of paper etc) déchirer, mettre en morceaux or pièces

tearful ['tɪəful] adj larmoyant(e)

tear gas ['tɪə–] n gaz m lacrymogène

tearoom ['ti:ru:m] n salon m de thé

tease [ti:z] vt taquiner; (unkindly) tourmenter

tea: **teaspoon** n petite cuiller; (also: **teaspoonful**: as measurement) ≈ cuillerée f à café; **teatime** n l'heure f du thé; **tea towel** n (BRIT) torchon m (à vaisselle)

technical ['tɛknɪkl] adj technique

technician [tɛk'nɪʃən] n technicien(ne)

technique [tɛk'ni:k] n technique f

technology [tɛk'nɒlədʒɪ] n technologie f

teddy (bear) ['tɛdɪ–] n ours m (en peluche)

tedious ['ti:dɪəs] adj fastidieux(-euse)

tee [ti:] n (Golf) tee m

teen [ti:n] adj = **teenage** ▷ n (us) = **teenager**

teenage ['ti:neɪdʒ] adj (fashions etc) pour jeunes, pour adolescents; (child) qui est adolescent(e); **teenager** n

adolescent(e)

teens [ti:nz] npl: to be in one's ~ être adolescent(e)

teeth [ti:θ] npl of **tooth**

teetotal ['ti:'təutl] adj (person) qui ne boit jamais d'alcool

telecommunications ['tɛlɪkəmju:nɪ'keɪʃənz] n télécommunications fpl

telegram ['tɛlɪgræm] n télégramme m

telegraph pole ['tɛlɪgrɑː-f-] n poteau m télégraphique

telephone ['tɛlɪfəun] n téléphone m ▷ vt (person) téléphoner à; (message) téléphoner; **to be on the ~** (be speaking) être au téléphone; **telephone book**, **telephone directory**; **telephone booth** (BRIT), **telephone box** n cabine f téléphonique; **telephone call** n appel m téléphonique; **telephone directory** n annuaire m (du téléphone); **telephone number** n numéro m de téléphone

telesales ['tɛlɪseɪlz] npl télévente f

telescope ['tɛlɪskəup] n télescope m

televise ['tɛlɪvaɪz] vt téléviser

television ['tɛlɪvɪʒən] n télévision f; **on ~** à la télévision; **television programme** n émission f de télévision

tell (pt, pp **told**) [tɛl, təuld] vt dire; (relate: story) raconter; (distinguish): **to ~ sth from** distinguer qch de ▷ vi (talk): **to ~ of** parler de; (have effect) se faire sentir, se voir; **to ~ sb to do** dire à qn de faire qch; **to ~ the time** (know how to) savoir lire l'heure; **tell off** vt réprimander, gronder; **teller** n (in bank) caissier(-ière)

telly ['tɛlɪ] n abbr (BRIT inf: = television) télé f

temp [tɛmp] n (BRIT = temporary worker) intérimaire m/f ▷ vi travailler comme intérimaire

temper ['tɛmpə'] n (nature) caractère m; (mood) humeur f; (fit of anger) colère f ▷ vt (moderate) tempérer, adoucir; **to be in a ~** être en colère; **to lose one's ~** se mettre en colère

temperament [ˈtɛmprəmənt]
n (nature) tempérament *m*;

temperamental [tɛmprəˈmɛntl] *adj*
capricieux(-euse)

temperature [ˈtɛmprətʃəʳ]
n température *f*; **to have** or **run a ~** avoir
de la fièvre

temple [ˈtɛmpl] *n* (building) temple *m*;
(Anat) tempe *f*

temporary [ˈtɛmpərərɪ] *adj*
temporaire, provisoire; (job, worker)
temporaire

tempt [tɛmpt] *vt* tenter; **to ~ sb into
doing** induire qn à faire; **temptation** *n*
tentation *f*; **tempting** *adj* tentant(e);
(food) appétissant(e)

ten [tɛn] *num* dix

tenant [ˈtɛnənt] *n* locataire *m/f*

tend [tɛnd] *vt* s'occuper de ▷ *vi*: **to ~ to
do** avoir tendance à faire; **tendency**
[ˈtɛndənsɪ] *n* tendance *f*

tender [ˈtɛndəʳ] *adj* tendre; (delicate)
délicat(e); (sore) sensible ▷ *n* (Comm:
offer) soumission *f*; (money): **legal ~**
cours légal ▷ *vt* offrir

tendon [ˈtɛndən] *n* tendon *m*

tenner [ˈtɛnəʳ] *n* (BRIT inf) billet *m* de
dix livres

tennis [ˈtɛnɪs] *n* tennis *m*; **tennis ball**
n balle *f* de tennis; **tennis court** *n*
(court *m* de) tennis *m*; **tennis match**
n match *m* de tennis; **tennis player** *n*
joueur(-euse) de tennis; **tennis racket**
n raquette *f* de tennis

tenor [ˈtɛnəʳ] *n* (Mus) ténor *m*

tenpin bowling [ˈtɛnpɪn-] *n* (BRIT)
bowling *m* (à 10 quilles)

tense [tɛns] *adj* tendu(e) ▷ *n* (Ling)
temps *m*

tension [ˈtɛnʃən] *n* tension *f*

tent [tɛnt] *n* tente *f*

tentative [ˈtɛntətɪv] *adj* timide,
hésitant(e); (conclusion) provisoire

tenth [tɛnθ] *num* dixième

tent: **tent peg** *n* piquet *m* de tente; **tent
pole** *n* montant *m* de tente

tepid [ˈtɛpɪd] *adj* tiède

term [tə:m] *n* terme *m*; (Scol) trimestre

m ▷ *vt* appeler; **terms** *npl* (conditions)
conditions *fpl*; (Comm) tarif *m*; **in the
short/long ~** à court/long terme; **to
come to ~s with** (problem) faire face à;
to be on good ~s with bien s'entendre
avec, être en bons termes avec

terminal [ˈtə:mɪnl] *adj* (disease) dans sa
phase terminale; (patient) incurable ▷ *n*
(Elec) borne *f*; (for oil, ore etc, also Comput)
terminal *m*; (also: **air ~**) aérogare *f*;
(BRIT: also: **coach ~**) gare routière

terminate [ˈtə:mɪneɪt] *vt* mettre fin à;
(pregnancy) interrompre

termini [ˈtə:mɪnaɪ] *npl of* **terminus**

terminology [tə:mɪˈnɔlədʒɪ] *n*
terminologie *f*

terminus (*pl* **termini**) [ˈtə:mɪnəs,
ˈtə:mɪnaɪ] *n* terminus *m inv*

terrace [ˈtɛrəs] *n* terrasse *f*; (BRIT: row of
houses) rangée *f* de maisons (attenantes
les unes aux autres); **the ~s** (BRIT Sport)
les gradins *mpl*; **terraced** *adj* (garden)
en terrasses; (in a row: house, cottage etc)
attenant(e) aux maisons voisines

terrain [tɛˈreɪn] *n* terrain *m* (sol)

terrestrial [tɪˈrɛstrɪəl] *adj* terrestre

terrible [ˈtɛrɪbl] *adj* terrible, atroce;
(weather, work) affreux(-euse),
épouvantable; **terribly** *adv*
terriblement; (very badly) affreusement
mal

terrier [ˈtɛrɪəʳ] *n* terrier *m* (chien)

terrific [təˈrɪfɪk] *adj* (very
great) fantastique, incroyable,
terrible; (wonderful) formidable,
sensationnel(le)

terrified [ˈtɛrɪfaɪd] *adj* terrifié(e); **to be
~ of sth** avoir très peur de qch

terrify [ˈtɛrɪfaɪ] *vt* terrifier; **terrifying**
adj terrifiant(e)

territorial [tɛrɪˈtɔ:rɪəl] *adj*
territorial(e)

territory [ˈtɛrɪtərɪ] *n* territoire *m*

terror [ˈtɛrəʳ] *n* terreur *f*; **terrorism** *n*
terrorisme *m*; **terrorist** *n* terroriste
m/f; **terrorist attack** *n* attentat *m*
terroriste

test [tɛst] *n* (trial, check) essai *m*; (: of

courage etc) épreuve *f*; (*Med*) examen *m*; (*Chem*) analyse *f*; (*Scol*) interrogation *f* de contrôle; (*also*: **driving ~**) (examen du) permis *m* de conduire ▷ *vt* essayer; mettre à l'épreuve; examiner; analyser; faire subir une interrogation (de contrôle) à

testicle ['tɛstɪkl] *n* testicule *m*

testify ['tɛstɪfaɪ] *vi* (*Law*) témoigner, déposer; **to ~ to sth** (*Law*) attester qch

testimony ['tɛstɪmənɪ] *n* (*Law*) témoignage *m*, déposition *f*

test match *n* (*Cricket*, *Rugby*) match international; **test tube** *n* éprouvette *f*

tetanus ['tɛtənəs] *n* tétanos *m*

text [tɛkst] *n* texte *m*; (*on mobile phone*) texto *m*, SMS *m inv* ▷ *vt* (*inf*) envoyer un texto *or* SMS à; **textbook** *n* manuel *m*

textile ['tɛkstaɪl] *n* textile *m*

text message *n* texto *m*, SMS *m inv*

text messaging [-'mɛsɪdʒɪŋ] *n* messagerie textuelle

texture ['tɛkstʃə[r]] *n* texture *f*; (*of skin, paper etc*) grain *m*

Thai [taɪ] *adj* thaïlandais(e) ▷ *n* Thaïlandais(e)

Thailand ['taɪlænd] *n* Thaïlande *f*

Thames [tɛmz] *n*: **the (River) ~** la Tamise

than [ðæn, ðən] *conj* que; (*with numerals*): **more ~ 10/once** plus de 10/d'une fois; **I have more/less ~ you** j'en ai plus/moins que toi; **she has more apples ~ pears** elle a plus de pommes que de poires; **it is better to phone ~ to write** il vaut mieux téléphoner (plutôt) qu'écrire; **she is older ~ you think** elle est plus âgée que tu crois

thank [θæŋk] *vt* remercier, dire merci à; **thanks** *npl* remerciements *mpl* ▷ *excl* merci!; **~ you (very much)** merci (beaucoup); **~ God** Dieu merci; **~s to** *prep* grâce à; **thankfully** *adv* (*fortunately*) heureusement; **Thanksgiving (Day)** *n* jour *m* d'action de grâce; *voir encadré*

● **Thanksgiving (Day)** est un
● jour de congé aux États-Unis,
● le quatrième jeudi du mois de
● novembre, commémorant la bonne
● récolte que les Pèlerins venus de
● Grande-Bretagne ont eue en 1621;
● traditionnellement, c'était un jour
● où l'on remerciait Dieu et où l'on
● organisait un grand festin. Une
● fête semblable, mais qui n'a aucun
● rapport avec les Pères Pèlerins, a
● lieu au Canada le deuxième lundi
● d'octobre.

● ● **KEYWORD**

that [ðæt] *adj* (*demonstrative: pl* **those**) ce, cet + *vowel or h mute*, cette *f*; **that man/woman/book** cet homme/cette femme/ce livre; (*not this*) cet homme-là/cette femme-là/ce livre-là; **that one** celui-là (celle-là)

▷ *pron* 1 (*demonstrative: pl* **those**) ce; (*not this one*) cela, ça; (*that one*) celui (celle); **who's that?** qui est-ce?; **what's that?** qu'est-ce que c'est?; **is that you?** c'est toi?; **I prefer this to that** je préfère ceci à cela *or* ça; **that's what he said** c'est ce qu'il a dit; **will you eat all that?** est-ce que tu vas manger tout ça?; **that is (to say)** c'est-à-dire, à savoir

2 (*relative: subject*) qui; (*: object*) que; (*: after prep*) lequel (laquelle), lesquels (lesquelles) *pl*; **the book that I read** le livre que j'ai lu; **the books that are in the library** les livres qui sont dans la bibliothèque; **all that I have** tout ce que j'ai; **the box that I put it in** la boîte dans laquelle je l'ai mis; **the people that I spoke to** les gens auxquels *or* à qui j'ai parlé

3 (*relative: of time*) où; **the day that he came** le jour où il est venu

▷ *conj* que; **he thought that I was ill** il pensait que j'étais malade

▷ *adv* (*demonstrative*): **I don't like it that much** ça ne me plaît pas tant que ça; **I didn't know it was that bad** je ne savais pas que c'était si or aussi mauvais; **it's about that high** c'est à peu près de cette hauteur

thatched [θætʃt] *adj* (*roof*) de chaume; **~ cottage** chaumière *f*

thaw [θɔː] *n* dégel *m* ▷ *vi* (*ice*) fondre; (*food*) dégeler ▷ *vt* (*food*) (faire) dégeler

 KEYWORD

the [ðiː, ðə] *def art* **1** (*gen*) le, la *f*, l' + *vowel or h mute*, les *pl* (NB: à + le(s) = **au(x)**; de + le = **du**; de + les = **des**): **the boy/girl/ink** le garçon/la fille/l'encre; **the children** les enfants; **the history of the world** l'histoire du monde; **give it to the postman** donne-le au facteur; **to play the piano/flute** jouer du piano/de la flûte
2 (+ *adj to form n*) le, la *f*, l' + *vowel or h mute*, les *pl*: **the rich and the poor** les riches et les pauvres; **to attempt the impossible** tenter l'impossible
3 (*in titles*): **Elizabeth the First** Elisabeth première; **Peter the Great** Pierre le Grand
4 (*in comparisons*): **the more he works, the more he earns** plus il travaille, plus il gagne de l'argent

theatre (*us* **theater**) [ˈθɪətəʳ] *n* théâtre *m*; (*Med: also:* **operating ~**) salle *f* d'opération

theft [θɛft] *n* vol *m* (*larcin*)

their [ðɛəʳ] *adj* leur, leurs *pl*; *see also* **my**; **theirs** *pron* le (la) leur, les leurs; *see also* **mine¹**

them [ðɛm, ðəm] *pron* (*direct*) les; (*indirect*) leur; (*stressed, after prep*) eux (elles); **give me a few of ~** donnez m'en quelques uns (or quelques unes); *see also* **me**

theme [θiːm] *n* thème *m*; **theme park** *n* parc *m* à thème

themselves [ðəmˈsɛlvz] *pl pron* (*reflexive*) se; (*emphatic, after prep*) eux-mêmes (elles-mêmes); **between ~** entre eux (elles); *see also* **oneself**

then [ðɛn] *adv* (*at that time*) alors, à ce moment-là; (*next*) puis, ensuite; (*and also*) et puis ▷ *conj* (*therefore*) alors, dans ce cas ▷ *adj*: **the ~ president** le président d'alors *or* de l'époque; **by ~** (*past*) à ce moment-là; (*future*) d'ici là; **from ~ on** dès lors; **until ~** jusqu'à ce moment-là, jusque-là

theology [θɪˈɔlədʒɪ] *n* théologie *f*

theory [ˈθɪərɪ] *n* théorie *f*

therapist [ˈθɛrəpɪst] *n* thérapeute *m/f*

therapy [ˈθɛrəpɪ] *n* thérapie *f*

 KEYWORD

there [ðɛəʳ] *adv* **1**: **there is**, **there are** il y a; **there are 3 of them** (*people, things*) il y en a 3; **there is no-one here/no bread left** il n'y a personne/il n'y a plus de pain; **there has been an accident** il y a eu un accident
2 (*referring to place*) là, là-bas; **it's there** c'est là(-bas); **in/on/up/down there** là-dedans/là-dessus/là-haut/en bas; **he went there on Friday** il y est allé vendredi; **I want that book there** je veux ce livre-là; **there he is!** le voilà!
3: **there, there** (*esp to child*) allons, allons!

there: **thereabouts** *adv* (*place*) par là, près de là; (*amount*) environ, à peu près; **thereafter** *adv* par la suite; **thereby** *adv* ainsi; **therefore** *adv* donc, par conséquent

there's [ˈðɛəz] = **there is**; **there has**

thermal [ˈθəːml] *adj* thermique; **~ underwear** sous-vêtements *mpl* en Thermolactyl®

thermometer [θəˈmɔmɪtəʳ] *n* thermomètre *m*

thermostat [ˈθəːməustæt] *n* thermostat *m*

these [ðiːz] *pl pron* ceux-ci (celles-ci) ▷ *pl adj* ces; (*not those*): **~ books** ces

livres-ci

thesis (*pl* **theses**) ['θiːsɪs, 'θiːsiːz] *n* thèse *f*

they [ðeɪ] *pl pron* ils (elles); (*stressed*) eux (elles); **~ say that …** (*it is said that*) on dit que …; **they'd = they had; they would; they'll = they shall; they will; they're = they are; they've = they have**

thick [θɪk] *adj* épais(se); (*stupid*) bête, borné(e) ▷ *n*: **in the ~ of** au beau milieu de, en plein cœur de; **it's 20 cm ~** ça a 20 cm d'épaisseur; **thicken** *vi* s'épaissir ▷ *vt* (*sauce etc*) épaissir; **thickness** *n* épaisseur *f*

thief (*pl* **thieves**) [θiːf, θiːvz] *n* voleur(-euse)

thigh [θaɪ] *n* cuisse *f*

thin [θɪn] *adj* mince; (*skinny*) maigre; (*soup*) peu épais(se); (*hair, crowd*) clairsemé(e) ▷ *vt* (*also*: ~ **down**: *sauce, paint*) délayer

thing [θɪŋ] *n* chose *f*; (*object*) objet *m*; (*contraction*) truc *m*; **things** *npl* (*belongings*) affaires *fpl*; **the ~ is …** c'est que …; **the best ~ would be to** le mieux serait de; **how are ~s?** comment ça va?; **to have a ~ about** (*be obsessed by*) être obsédé(e) par; (*hate*) détester; **poor ~!** le (or la) pauvre!

think (*pt, pp* **thought**) [θɪŋk, θɔːt] *vi* penser, réfléchir ▷ *vt* penser, croire; (*imagine*) s'imaginer; **what did you ~ of them?** qu'avez-vous pensé d'eux?; **to ~ about sth/sb** penser à qch/qn; **I'll ~ about it** je vais y réfléchir; **to ~ of doing** avoir l'idée de faire; **I ~ so/not** je crois or pense que oui/non; **to ~ well of** avoir une haute opinion de; **think over** *vt* bien réfléchir à; **think up** *vt* inventer, trouver

third [θəːd] *num* troisième ▷ *n* (*fraction*) tiers *m*; (*Aut*) troisième (vitesse) *f*; (*BRIT Scol: degree*) = licence *f* avec mention passable; **thirdly** *adv* troisièmement; **third party insurance** *n* (*BRIT*) assurance *f* au tiers; **Third World** *n*: **the Third World** le Tiers-Monde

thirst [θəːst] *n* soif *f*; **thirsty** *adj* qui a soif, assoiffé(e); (*work*) qui donne soif; **to be thirsty** avoir soif

thirteen [θəː'tiːn] *num* treize

thirteenth [-'tiːnθ] *num* treizième

thirtieth ['θəːtɪɪθ] *num* trentième

thirty ['θəːtɪ] *num* trente

KEYWORD

this [ðɪs] *adj* (*demonstrative: pl* **these**) ce, cet + *vowel or h* mute, cette *f*; **this man/woman/book** cet homme/cette femme/ce livre; (*not that*) cet homme-ci/cette femme-ci/ce livre-ci; **this one** celui-ci (celle-ci)
▷ *pron* (*demonstrative: pl* **these**) ce; (*not that one*) celui-ci (celle-ci), ceci; **who's this?** qui est-ce?; **what's this?** qu'est-ce que c'est?; **I prefer this to that** je préfère ceci à cela; **this is where I live** c'est ici que j'habite; **this is what he said** voici ce qu'il a dit; **this is Mr Brown** (*in introductions*) je vous présente Mr Brown; (*in photo*) c'est Mr Brown; (*on telephone*) ici Mr Brown
▷ *adv* (*demonstrative*): **it was about this big** c'était à peu près de cette grandeur or grand comme ça; **I didn't know it was this bad** je ne savais pas que c'était si or aussi mauvais

thistle ['θɪsl] *n* chardon *m*

thorn [θɔːn] *n* épine *f*

thorough ['θʌrə] *adj* (*search*) minutieux(-euse); (*knowledge, research*) approfondi(e); (*work, person*) consciencieux(-euse); (*cleaning*) à fond; **thoroughly** *adv* (*search*) minutieusement; (*study*) en profondeur; (*clean*) à fond; (*very*) tout à fait

those [ðəuz] *pl pron* ceux-là (celles-là) ▷ *pl adj* ces; (*not these*): **~ books** ces livres-là

though [ðəu] *conj* bien que + *sub*, quoique + *sub* ▷ *adv* pourtant

thought [θɔːt] *pt, pp of* **think** ▷ *n*

pensée f; (idea) idée f; (opinion) avis m; **thoughtful** adj (deep in thought) pensif(-ive); (serious) réfléchi; (considerate) prévenant; **thoughtless** adj qui manque de considération

thousand ['θaʊzənd] num mille; **one ~** mille; **two ~** deux mille; **~s of** des milliers de; **thousandth** num millième

thrash [θræʃ] vt rouer de coups; (as punishment) donner une correction à; (inf: defeat) battre à plate(s) couture(s)

thread [θrεd] n film; (of screw) pas m; filetage m ▷ vt (needle) enfiler

threat [θrεt] n menace f; **threaten** vi (storm) menacer ▷ vt: **to threaten sb with sth/to do** menacer qn de qch/de faire; **threatening** adj menaçant(e)

three [θri:] num trois; **three-dimensional** adj à trois dimensions; **three-piece suite** n salon m (canapé et deux fauteuils); **three-quarters** mpl trois-quarts mpl; **three-quarters full** aux trois-quarts plein

threshold ['θrεʃhəʊld] n seuil m

threw [θru:] pt of **throw**

thrill [θrɪl] n (excitement) émotion f, sensation forte; (shudder) frisson m ▷ vt (audience) électriser; **thrilled** adj: **thrilled (with)** ravi(e) de; **thriller** n film m (or roman m or pièce f) à suspense; **thrilling** adj (book, play etc) saisissant(e); (news, discovery) excitant(e)

thriving ['θraɪvɪŋ] adj (business, community) prospère

throat [θrəʊt] n gorge f; **to have a sore ~** avoir mal à la gorge

throb [θrɒb] vi (heart) palpiter; (engine) vibrer; **my head is ~bing** j'ai des élancements dans la tête

throne [θrəʊn] n trône m

through [θru:] prep à travers; (time) pendant, durant; (by means of) par, par l'intermédiaire de; (owing to) à cause de ▷ adj (ticket, train, passage) direct(e) ▷ adv à travers; (from) **Monday-Friday** (us) de lundi à vendredi; **to put sb ~ to sb** (Tel) passer qn à qn; **to be**

~ (BRIT: Tel) avoir la communication; (esp us: have finished) avoir fini; **"no ~ traffic"** (us) "passage interdit"; **"no ~ road"** (BRIT) "impasse"; **throughout** prep (place) partout dans; (time) durant tout(e) le (la) ▷ adv partout

throw [θrəʊ] n jet m; (Sport) lancer m ▷ vt (Sport) lancer; (rider) désarçonner; (fig) décontenancer; **to ~ a party** donner une réception; **throw away** vt jeter; (money) gaspiller; **throw in** vt (Sport: ball) remettre en jeu; (include) ajouter; **throw off** vt se débarrasser de; **throw out** vt jeter; (reject) rejeter; (person) mettre à la porte; **throw up** vi vomir

thru [θru:] (us) = **through**

thrush [θrʌʃ] n (Zool) grive f

thrust [θrʌst] vt (pt, pp ~) pousser brusquement; (push in) enfoncer

thud [θʌd] n bruit sourd

thug [θʌg] n voyou m

thumb [θʌm] n (Anat) pouce m ▷ vt: **to ~ a lift** faire de l'auto-stop, arrêter une voiture; **thumbtack** n (us) punaise f (clou)

thump [θʌmp] n grand coup; (sound) bruit sourd ▷ vt cogner sur ▷ vi cogner, frapper

thunder ['θʌndə'] n tonnerre m ▷ vi tonner; (train etc): **to ~ past** passer dans un grondement ou un bruit de tonnerre; **thunderstorm** n orage m

Thur(s) abbr (= Thursday) jeu

Thursday ['θɜːzdɪ] n jeudi m

thus [ðʌs] adv ainsi

thwart [θwɔːt] vt contrecarrer

thyme [taɪm] n thym m

Tibet [tɪ'bεt] n Tibet m

tick [tɪk] n (sound: of clock) tic-tac m; (mark) coche f; (Zool) tique f; (BRIT inf): **in a ~** dans un instant ▷ vi faire tic-tac ▷ vt (item on list) cocher; **tick off** vt (item on list) cocher; (person) réprimander, attraper

ticket ['tɪkɪt] n billet m; (for bus, tube) ticket m; (in shop: on goods) étiquette f; (for library) carte f (also: **parking ~**)

contravention f. p.-v. m; **ticket barrier**
n (BRIT: Rail) portillon m automatique;
ticket collector n contrôleur(-euse);
ticket inspector n contrôleur(-euse);
ticket machine n billetterie f
automatique; **ticket office** n guichet
m, bureau m de vente des billets

tickle ['tɪkl] vi chatouiller ▷ vt
chatouiller; **ticklish** adj (person)
chatouilleux(-euse); (problem)
épineux(-euse)

tide [taɪd] n marée f; (fig: of events)
cours m

tidy ['taɪdɪ] adj (room) bien rangé(e);
(dress, work) net (nette), soigné(e);
(person) ordonné(e), qui a de l'ordre ▷ vt
(also: ~ up) ranger

tie [taɪ] n (string etc) cordon m; (BRIT:
also: **neck~**) cravate f; (fig: link) lien m;
(Sport: draw) égalité f de points; match
nul ▷ vt (parcel) attacher; (ribbon)
nouer ▷ vi (Sport) faire match nul; faire
à égalité de points; **to ~ sth in a bow**
faire un nœud à or avec qch; **to ~ a knot
in sth** faire un nœud à qch; **tie down**
vt (fig): **to ~ sb down to** contraindre
qn à accepter; **to feel ~d down** (by
relationship) se sentir coincé(e); **tie up**
vt (parcel) ficeler; (dog, boat) attacher;
(prisoner) ligoter; (arrangements)
conclure; **to be ~d up** (busy) être pris(e)
or occupé(e)

tier [tɪə'] n gradin m; (of cake) étage m

tiger ['taɪɡə'] n tigre m

tight [taɪt] adj (rope) tendu(e), raide;
(clothes) étroit(e), très juste; (budget,
programme, bend) serré(e); (control)
strict(e), sévère; (inf: drunk) ivre, rond(e)
▷ adv (squeeze) très fort; (shut) à bloc,
hermétiquement; **hold ~!** accrochez-
vous bien!; **tighten** vt (rope) tendre;
(screw) resserrer; (control) renforcer
▷ vi se tendre, se resserrer; **tightly** adv
(grasp) bien, très fort; **tights** npl (BRIT)
collant m

tile [taɪl] n (on roof) tuile f; (on wall or
floor) carreau m

till [tɪl] n caisse (enregistreuse) ▷ prep,

conj = **until**

tilt [tɪlt] vt pencher, incliner ▷ vi
pencher, être incliné(e)

timber ['tɪmbə'] n (material) bois m de
construction

time [taɪm] n temps m; (epoch: often
pl) époque f, temps; (by clock) heure
f; (moment) moment m; (occasion, also
Math) fois f; (Mus) mesure f ▷ vt (race)
chronométrer; (programme) minuter;
(visit) fixer; (remark etc) choisir le
moment de; **a long ~** un long moment,
longtemps; **four at a ~** à quatre à la
fois; **for the ~ being** pour le moment;
from ~ to ~ de temps en temps; **at ~s**
parfois; **in ~** (soon enough) à temps;
(after some time) avec le temps, à la
longue; (Mus) en mesure; **in a week's
~** dans une semaine; **in no ~** en un rien
de temps; **any ~** n'importe quand;
on ~ à l'heure; **5 ~s 5** 5 fois 5; **what ~
is it?** quelle heure est-il?; **what ~ is
the museum/shop open?** à quelle
heure ouvre le musée/magasin?; **to
have a good ~** bien s'amuser; **time
limit** n limite f de temps, délai m;
timely adj opportun(e); **timer** n (in
kitchen) compte-minutes m inv; (Tech)
minuteur m; **time-share** n maison
f/appartement m en multipropriété;
timetable n (Rail) (indicateur m)
horaire m; (Scol) emploi m du temps;
time zone n fuseau m horaire

timid ['tɪmɪd] adj timide; (easily scared)
peureux(-euse)

timing ['taɪmɪŋ] n (Sport)
chronométrage m; **the ~ of his
resignation** le moment choisi pour sa
démission

tin [tɪn] n étain m; (also: ~ **plate**)
fer-blanc m; (BRIT: can) boîte f (de
conserve); (for baking) moule m (à
gâteau); (for storage) boîte f; **tinfoil** n
papier m d'étain or d'aluminium

tingle ['tɪŋɡl] vi picoter; (person) avoir
des picotements

tinker ['tɪŋkə']; **tinker with** vt fus
bricoler, rafistoler

tinned [tɪnd] adj (BRIT: food) en boîte, en conserve

tin opener [-'əupnə*] n (BRIT) ouvre-boîte(s) m

tinsel ['tɪnsl] n guirlandes fpl de Noël (argentées)

tint [tɪnt] n teinte f; (for hair) shampooing colorant; **tinted** adj (hair) teinté(e); (spectacles, glass) teinté(e)

tiny ['taɪnɪ] adj minuscule

tip [tɪp] n (end) bout m; (gratuity) pourboire m; (BRIT: for rubbish) décharge f; (advice) tuyau m ▷ vt (waiter) donner un pourboire à; (tilt) incliner; (overturn: also: ~ over) renverser; (empty: also: ~ out) déverser; **how much should I ~?** combien de pourboire est-ce qu'il faut laisser?; **tip off** vt prévenir, avertir

tiptoe ['tɪptəu] n: **on ~** sur la pointe des pieds

tire ['taɪə*] n (US) = **tyre** ▷ vt fatiguer ▷ vi se fatiguer; **tired** adj fatigué(e); **to be tired of** en avoir assez de, être las (lasse) de; **tire pressure** (US) = **tyre pressure**; **tiring** adj fatigant(e)

tissue ['tɪʃu:] n tissu m; (paper handkerchief) mouchoir m en papier, kleenex® m; **tissue paper** n papier m de soie

tit [tɪt] n (bird) mésange f; **to give ~ for tat** rendre coup pour coup

title ['taɪtl] n titre m

T-junction ['ti:'dʒʌŋkʃən] n croisement m en T

TM n abbr = **trademark**

○ **KEYWORD**

to [tu:, tə] prep 1 (direction) à; (towards) vers; envers; **to go to France/Portugal/London/school** aller en France/au Portugal/à Londres/à l'école; **to go to Claude's/the doctor's** aller chez Claude/le docteur; **the road to Edinburgh** la route d'Édimbourg

2 (as far as) (jusqu')à; **to count to 10** compter jusqu'à 10; **from 40 to 50**

people de 40 à 50 personnes

3 (with expressions of time): **a quarter to 5** 5 heures moins le quart; **it's twenty to 3** il est 3 heures moins vingt

4 (for, of) de: **the key to the front door** la clé de la porte d'entrée; **a letter to his wife** une lettre (adressée) à sa femme

5 (expressing indirect object) à: **to give sth to sb** donner qch à qn; **to talk to sb** parler à qn; **to be a danger to sb** être dangereux(-euse) pour qn

6 (in relation to) à: **3 goals to 2** 3 (buts) à 2; **30 miles to the gallon** = 9.4 litres aux cent (km)

7 (purpose, result): **to come to sb's aid** venir au secours de qn, porter secours à qn; **to sentence sb to death** condamner qn à mort; **to my surprise** à ma grande surprise

▷ with vb 1 (simple infinitive): **to go/eat** aller/manger

2 (following another vb): **to want/try/start to do** vouloir/essayer de/commencer à faire

3 (with vb omitted): **I don't want to** je ne veux pas

4 (purpose, result): **I did it to help you** je l'ai fait pour vous aider

5 (equivalent to relative clause): **I have things to do** j'ai des choses à faire; **the main thing is to try** l'important est d'essayer

6 (after adjective etc): **ready to go** prêt(e) à partir; **too old/young to ...** trop vieux/jeune pour ...

▷ adv: **push/pull the door to** tirez/poussez la porte

toad [təud] n crapaud m; **toadstool** n champignon (vénéneux)

toast [təust] n (Culin) pain grillé, toast m; (drink, speech) toast m ▷ vt (Culin) faire griller; (drink to) porter un toast à; **toaster** n grille-pain m inv

tobacco [tə'bækəu] n tabac m

toboggan [tə'bɔgən] n toboggan m; (child's) luge f

today [tə'deɪ] adv, n (also fig) aujourd'hui (m)

toddler ['tɒdlə*] n enfant m/f qui commence à marcher, bambin m

toe [təu] n doigt m de pied, orteil m; (of shoe) bout m ▷ vt: **to ~ the line** (fig) obéir, se conformer; **toenail** n ongle m de l'orteil

toffee ['tɒfɪ] n caramel m

together [tə'geðə*] adv ensemble; (at same time) en même temps; **~ with** prep avec

toilet ['tɔɪlət] n (BRIT: lavatory) toilettes fpl, cabinets mpl; **to go to the ~** aller aux toilettes; **where's the ~?** où sont les toilettes?; **toilet bag** n (BRIT) nécessaire m de toilette; **toilet paper** n papier m hygiénique; **toiletries** ['tɔɪlətrɪz] npl articles mpl de toilette; **toilet roll** n rouleau m de papier hygiénique

token ['təukən] n (sign) marque f, témoignage m; (metal disc) jeton m ▷ adj (fee, strike) symbolique; **book/record-** (BRIT) chèque-livre/-disque m

Tokyo ['təukjəu] n Tokyo

told [təuld] pt, pp of **tell**

tolerant ['tɔlərnt] adj: **~ (of)** tolérant(e) (à l'égard de)

tolerate ['tɔləreɪt] vt supporter

toll [təul] n (tax, charge) péage m ▷ vi (bell) sonner; **the accident ~ on the roads** le nombre des victimes de la route; **toll call** n (US Tel) appel m (à) longue distance; **toll-free** adj (US) gratuit(e) ▷ adv gratuitement

tomato [tə'mɑːtəu] n (pl **-es**) tomate f; **tomato sauce** n sauce f tomate

tomb [tuːm] n tombe f; **tombstone** n pierre tombale

tomorrow [tə'mɔrəu] adv, n (also fig) demain (m); **the day after ~** après-demain; **a week ~** demain en huit; **~ morning** demain matin

ton [tʌn] n tonne f (BRIT: = 1016 kg; US = 907 kg; metric = 1000 kg); **~s of** (inf) des tas de

tone [təun] n ton m; (of radio, BRIT Tel) tonalité f ▷ vi (also: **~ in**) s'harmoniser;

tone down vt (colour, criticism) adoucir

tongs [tɒŋz] npl pinces fpl; (for coal) pincettes fpl; (for hair) fer m à friser

tongue [tʌŋ] n langue f; **~ in cheek** adv ironiquement

tonic ['tɒnɪk] n (Med) tonique m; (also: **~ water**) Schweppes® m

tonight [tə'naɪt] adv, n cette nuit; (this evening) ce soir

tonne [tʌn] n (BRIT: metric ton) tonne f

tonsil ['tɒnsl] n amygdale f; **tonsillitis** [tɒnsɪ'laɪtɪs] n: **to have tonsillitis** avoir une angine or une amygdalite

too [tuː] adv (excessively) trop; (also) aussi; **~ much** (as adv) trop; (as adj) trop de; **~ many** adj trop de

took [tuk] pt of **take**

tool [tuːl] n outil m; **tool box** n boîte f à outils; **tool kit** n trousse f à outils

tooth (pl **teeth**) [tuːθ, tiːθ] n (Anat, Tech) dent f; **to brush one's teeth** se laver les dents; **toothache** n mal m de dents; **to have toothache** avoir mal aux dents; **toothbrush** n brosse f à dents; **toothpaste** n (pâte f) dentifrice m; **toothpick** n cure-dent m

top [tɒp] n (of mountain, head) sommet m; (of page, ladder) haut m; (of box, cupboard, table) dessus m; (lid: of box, jar) couvercle m; (: of bottle) bouchon m; (toy) toupie f; (Dress: blouse etc) haut m; (: of pyjamas) veste f du haut; (in rank) premier(-ière); (best) meilleur(e) ▷ vt (exceed) dépasser; (be first in) être en tête de; **from ~ to bottom** de fond en comble; **on ~ of** sur; (in addition to) en plus de; **over the ~** (inf: behaviour etc) qui dépasse les limites; **top up** (US **top off**) vt (bottle) remplir; (salary) compléter; **to ~ up one's mobile (phone)** recharger son compte; **top floor** n dernier étage; **top hat** n haut-de-forme m

topic ['tɒpɪk] n sujet m, thème m; **topical** adj d'actualité

topless ['tɒplɪs] adj (bather etc) aux seins nus

topping ['tɒpɪŋ] n (Culin) couche de

crème, fromage etc qui recouvre un plat

topple ['tɒpl] vt renverser, faire tomber
▷ vi basculer; tomber

top-up ['tɒpʌp] n (for mobile phone)
recharge f, minutes fpl; **top-up card** n
(for mobile phone) recharge f

torch [tɔːtʃ] n torche f; (BRIT: electric)
lampe f de poche

tore [tɔː] pt of **tear²**

torment n ['tɔːmɛnt] tourment m
▷ vt [tɔːˈmɛnt] tourmenter; (fig: annoy)
agacer

torn [tɔːn] pp of **tear²**

tornado [tɔːˈneɪdəʊ] (pl ~es) n
tornade f

torpedo [tɔːˈpiːdəʊ] (pl ~es) n torpille f

torrent ['tɒrənt] n torrent m; **torrential**
[tɒˈrɛnʃl] adj torrentiel(le)

tortoise ['tɔːtəs] n tortue f

torture ['tɔːtʃə] n torture f ▷ vt
torturer

Tory ['tɔːrɪ] adj, n (BRIT Pol) tory m/f,
conservateur(-trice)

toss [tɒs] vt lancer, jeter; (BRIT: pancake)
faire sauter; (head) rejeter en arrière
▷ vi: **to ~ up for sth** (BRIT) jouer qch à
pile ou face; **to ~ a coin** jouer à pile ou
face; **to ~ and turn** (in bed) se tourner
et se retourner

total ['təʊtl] adj total(e) ▷ n total m ▷ vt
(add up) faire le total de, additionner;
(amount to) s'élever à

totalitarian [təʊtælɪˈtɛərɪən] adj
totalitaire

totally ['təʊtəlɪ] adv totalement

touch [tʌtʃ] n contact m, toucher m;
(sense, skill: of pianist etc) toucher ▷ vt
(gen) toucher; (tamper with) toucher à;
a ~ of (fig) un petit peu de, une touche
de; **to get in ~ with** prendre contact
avec; **to lose ~** (friends) se perdre de
vue; **touch down** vi (Aviat) atterrir;
(on sea) amerrir; **touchdown** n (Aviat)
atterrissage m; (on sea) amerrissage
m; (US Football) essai m; **touched**
adj (moved) touché(e); **touching**
adj touchant(e), attendrissant(e);
touchline n (Sport) (ligne f de) touche

f; **touch-sensitive** adj (keypad) à
effleurement; (screen) tactile

tough [tʌf] adj dur(e); (resistant)
résistant(e), solide; (meat) dur, coriace;
(firm) inflexible; (task, problem, situation)
difficile

tour ['tʊə] n voyage m; (also: **package
~**) voyage organisé; (of town, museum)
tour m, visite f; (by band) tournée f ▷ vt
visiter; **tour guide** n (person) guide m/f

tourism ['tʊərɪzm] n tourisme m

tourist ['tʊərɪst] n touriste m/f ▷ cpd
touristique; **tourist office** n syndicat
m d'initiative

tournament ['tʊənəmənt] n
tournoi m

tour operator n (BRIT) organisateur m
de voyages, tour-opérateur m

tow [təʊ] vt remorquer; (caravan,
trailer) tracter; **"on ~"**, (us) **"in ~"** (Aut)
"véhicule en remorque"; **tow away** vt
(subj: police) emmener à la fourrière;
(: breakdown service) remorquer

towards (s) [təˈwɔːd(z)] prep vers;
(of attitude) envers, à l'égard de; (of
purpose) pour

towel ['taʊəl] n serviette f (de toilette);
towelling n (fabric) tissu-éponge m

tower ['taʊə] n tour f; **tower block** n
(BRIT) tour f (d'habitation)

town [taʊn] n ville f; **to go to ~** = aller
en ville; (fig) y mettre le paquet; **town
centre** n (BRIT) centre m de la ville,
centre-ville m; **town hall** n ≈ mairie f

tow truck n (us) dépanneuse f

toxic ['tɒksɪk] adj toxique

toy [tɔɪ] n jouet m; **toy with** vt fus
jouer avec; (idea) caresser; **toyshop** n
magasin m de jouets

trace [treɪs] n trace f ▷ vt (draw) tracer,
dessiner; (follow) suivre la trace de;
(locate) retrouver

tracing paper ['treɪsɪŋ-] n papier-
calque m

track [træk] n (mark) trace f; (path:
gen) chemin m, piste f; (: of bullet etc)
trajectoire f; (: of suspect, animal) piste
f; (Rail) voie ferrée, rails mpl; (on tape,

Comput, Sport) piste; (on CD) piste f; (on record) plage f ▷ vt suivre la trace or la piste de; **to keep ~ of** suivre; **track down** vt (prey) trouver et capturer; (sth lost) finir par retrouver; **tracksuit** n survêtement m

tractor ['træktə] n tracteur m

trade [treɪd] n commerce m; (skill, job) métier m ▷ vi faire du commerce ▷ vt (exchange): **to ~ sth (for sth)** échanger qch (contre qch); **to ~ with/in** faire du commerce avec/le commerce de; **trade in** vt (old car etc) faire reprendre; **trademark** n marque f de fabrique; **trader** n commerçant(e), négociant(e); **tradesman** (irreg) n (shopkeeper) commerçant m; **trade union** n syndicat m

trading ['treɪdɪŋ] n affaires fpl, commerce m

tradition [trə'dɪʃən] n tradition f; **traditional** adj traditionnel(le)

traffic ['træfɪk] n trafic m; (cars) circulation f ▷ vi: **to ~ in** (pej: liquor, drugs) faire le trafic de; **traffic circle** n (us) rond-point m; **traffic island** n refuge m (pour piétons); **traffic jam** n embouteillage m; **traffic lights** npl feux mpl (de signalisation); **traffic warden** n contractuel(le)

tragedy ['trædʒədɪ] n tragédie f

tragic ['trædʒɪk] adj tragique

trail [treɪl] n (tracks) trace f, piste f; (path) chemin m, piste f; (of smoke etc) traînée f ▷ vt (drag) traîner, tirer; (follow) suivre ▷ vi traîner; (in game, contest) être en retard; **trailer** n (Aut) remorque f; (us) caravane f; (Cine) bande-annonce f

train [treɪn] n train m; (in underground) rame f; (of dress) traîne f; (BRIT: series): **~ of events** série f d'événements ▷ vt (apprentice, doctor etc) former; (Sport) entraîner; (dog) dresser; (memory) exercer; (point: gun etc): **to ~ sth on** braquer qch sur ▷ vi recevoir sa formation; s'entraîner; **one's ~ of thought** le fil de sa pensée; **what**

time does the **~ from Paris get in?** à quelle heure arrive le train de Paris?; **is this the ~ for ...?** c'est bien le train pour...?; **trainee** [treɪ'niː] n stagiaire m/f; (in trade) apprenti(e); **trainer** n (Sport) entraîneur(-euse); (of dogs etc) dresseur(-euse); **trainers** fpl (shoes) chaussures fpl de sport; **training** n formation f; (Sport) entraînement m; (of dog etc) dressage m; **in training** (Sport) à l'entraînement; (fit) en forme; **training course** n cours m de formation professionnelle; **training shoes** npl chaussures fpl de sport

trait [treɪt] n trait m (de caractère)

traitor ['treɪtə] n traître m

tram [træm] n (BRIT: also: **~car**) tram(way) m

tramp [træmp] n (person) vagabond(e), clochard(e); (inf: pej: woman): **to be a ~** être coureuse

trample ['træmpl] vt: **to ~ (underfoot)** piétiner

trampoline ['træmpəliːn] n trampoline m

tranquil ['træŋkwɪl] adj tranquille; **tranquillizer** (us **tranquilizer**) n (Med) tranquillisant m

transaction [træn'zækʃən] n transaction f

transatlantic ['trænzət'læntɪk] adj transatlantique

transcript ['trænskrɪpt] n transcription f (texte)

transfer n ['trænsfə'] (gen, also Sport) transfert m; (Pol: of power) passation f; (of money) virement m; (picture, design) décalcomanie f; (: stick-on) autocollant m ▷ vt [træns'fə:'] transférer; passer; virer; **to ~ the charges** (BRIT Tel) téléphoner en P.C.V.

transform [træns'fɔːm] vt transformer; **transformation** n transformation f

transfusion [træns'fjuːʒən] n transfusion f

transit ['trænzɪt] n: **in ~** en transit

transition [træn'zɪʃən] n transition f

transitive ['trænzɪtɪv] adj (Ling) transitif(-ive)

translate [trænz'leɪt] vt: **to ~ (from/into)** traduire (du/en); **can you ~ this for me?** pouvez-vous me traduire ceci?; **translation** [trænz'leɪʃən] n traduction f; (Scol: as opposed to prose) version f; **translator** n traducteur(-trice)

transmission [trænz'mɪʃən] n transmission f

transmit [trænz'mɪt] vt transmettre n; (Radio, TV) émettre; **transmitter** n émetteur n

transparent [træns'pærnt] adj transparent(e)

transplant n ['trænspla:nt] (Med) transplantation f

transport n ['trænspɔ:t] transport m ▷ vt [træns'pɔ:t] transporter; **transportation** [trænspɔ:'teɪʃən] n (moyen m de) transport m

transvestite [trænz'vestaɪt] n travesti(e)

trap [træp] n (snare, trick) piège m; (carriage) cabriolet m ▷ vt prendre au piège; (confine) coincer

trash [træʃ] n (pej: goods) camelote f; (: nonsense) sottises fpl; (us: rubbish) ordures fpl; **trash can** n (us) poubelle f

trauma ['trɔ:mə] n traumatisme m; **traumatic** [trɔ:'mætɪk] adj traumatisant(e)

travel ['trævl] n voyage(s) m(pl) ▷ vi voyager; (news, sound) se propager ▷ vt (distance) parcourir; **travel agency** n agence f de voyages; **travel agent** n agent m de voyages; **travel insurance** n assurance-voyage f; **traveller** (us **traveler**) n voyageur(-euse); **traveller's cheque** (us **traveler's check**) n chèque m de voyage; **travelling** (us **traveling**) n voyage(s) m(pl); **travel-sick** adj: **to get travel-sick** avoir le mal de la route (or de mer or de l'air); **travel sickness** n mal m de la route (or de mer or de l'air)

tray [treɪ] n (for carrying) plateau m; (on

desk) corbeille f

treacherous ['tretʃərəs] adj traître(sse); (ground, tide) dont il faut se méfier

treacle ['tri:kl] n mélasse f

tread [tred] n (step) pas m; (sound) bruit m de pas; (of tyre) chape f, bande f de roulement ▷ vi (pt **trod**, pp **trodden**) marcher; **tread on** vt fus marcher sur

treasure ['treʒə'] n trésor m ▷ vt (value) tenir beaucoup à; **treasurer** n trésorier(-ière)

treasury ['treʒərɪ] n: **the T~**, (us) **the T~ Department** = le ministère des Finances

treat [tri:t] n petit cadeau, petite surprise ▷ vt traiter; **to ~ sb to sth** offrir qch à qn; **treatment** n traitement m

treaty ['tri:tɪ] n traité m

treble ['trebl] adj triple ▷ vt, vi tripler

tree [tri:] n arbre m

trek [trek] n (long walk) randonnée f; (tiring walk) longue marche, trotte f

tremble ['trembl] vi trembler

tremendous [trɪ'mendəs] adj (enormous) énorme; (excellent) formidable, fantastique

trench [trentʃ] n tranchée f

trend [trend] n (tendency) tendance f; (of events) cours m; (fashion) mode f; **trendy** adj (idea, person) dans le vent; (clothes) dernier cri m

trespass ['trespəs] vi: **to ~ on** s'introduire sans permission dans; **"no ~ing"** "propriété privée", "défense d'entrer"

trial ['traɪəl] n (Law) procès m, jugement m; (test: of machine etc) essai m; **trials** npl (unpleasant experiences) épreuves fpl; **trial period** n période f d'essai

triangle ['traɪæŋgl] n (Math, Mus) triangle m

triangular [traɪ'æŋgjulə'] adj triangulaire

tribe [traɪb] n tribu f

tribunal [traɪ'bju:nl] n tribunal m

tribute ['trɪbju:t] n tribut m, hommage

m; **to pay ~ to** rendre hommage à

trick [trɪk] n (magic) tour m; (joke, prank) tour, farce f; (skill, knack) astuce f; (Cards) levée f ▷ vt attraper, rouler; **to play a ~ on sb** jouer un tour à qn; **that should do the ~** (fam) ça devrait faire l'affaire

trickle ['trɪkl] n (of water etc) filet m ▷ vi couler en un filet or goutte à goutte

tricky ['trɪkɪ] adj difficile, délicat(e)

tricycle ['traɪsɪkl] n tricycle m

trifle ['traɪfl] n bagatelle f; (Culin) = diplomate m ▷ adv: **a ~ long** un peu long

trigger ['trɪɡər] n (of gun) gâchette f

trim [trɪm] adj (house, garden) bien tenu(e); (figure) svelte ▷ n (haircut etc) légère coupe; (on car) garnitures fpl ▷ vt (cut) couper légèrement; (decorate): **to ~ (with)** décorer (de); (Naut: a sail) gréer

trio ['triːəu] n trio m

trip [trɪp] n voyage m; (excursion) excursion f; (stumble) faux pas ▷ vi faire un faux pas, trébucher; **trip up** vi trébucher ▷ vt faire un croc-en-jambe à

triple ['trɪpl] adj triple

triplets ['trɪplɪts] npl triplés(-ées)

tripod ['traɪpɔd] n trépied m

triumph ['traɪʌmf] n triomphe m ▷ vi: **to ~ (over)** triompher (de); **triumphant** [traɪʌmfənt] adj triomphant(e)

trivial ['trɪvɪəl] adj insignifiant(e); (commonplace) banal(e)

trod [trɔd] pt of **tread**

trodden ['trɔdn] pp of **tread**

trolley ['trɔlɪ] n chariot m

trombone [trɔm'bəun] n trombone m

troop [truːp] n bande f, groupe m; **troops** npl (Mil) troupes fpl; (: men) hommes mpl, soldats mpl

trophy ['trəufɪ] n trophée m

tropical ['trɔpɪkl] adj tropical(e)

trot [trɔt] n trot m ▷ vi trotter; **on the ~** (BRIT: fig) d'affilée

trouble ['trʌbl] n difficulté(s) f(pl), problème(s) m(pl); (worry) ennuis mpl, soucis mpl; (bother, effort) peine f; (Pol)

conflit(s) m(pl); troubles mpl; (Med): **stomach** etc ~ troubles gastriques etc ▷ vt (disturb) déranger, gêner; (worry) inquiéter ▷ vi: **to ~ to do** prendre la peine de faire; **troubles** npl (Pol etc) troubles; (personal) ennuis, soucis; **to be in ~** avoir des ennuis; (ship, climber etc) être en difficulté; **to have ~ doing sth** avoir du mal à faire qch; **it's no ~!** je vous en prie!; **the ~ is ...** le problème, c'est que ...; **what's the ~?** qu'est-ce qui ne va pas?; **troubled** adj (person) inquiet(-ète); (times, life) agité(e); **troublemaker** n élément perturbateur, fauteur m de troubles; **troublesome** adj (child) fatigant(e), difficile; (cough) gênant(e)

trough [trɔf] n (also: **drinking ~**) abreuvoir m; (also: **feeding ~**) auge f; (depression) creux m

trousers ['trauzəz] npl pantalon m; **short ~** (BRIT) culottes courtes

trout [traut] n (pl inv) truite f

trowel ['trauəl] n truelle f; (garden tool) déplantoir m

truant ['truənt] n: **to play ~** (BRIT) faire l'école buissonnière

truce [truːs] n trêve f

truck [trʌk] n camion m; (Rail) wagon m à plate-forme; **truck driver** n camionneur m

true [truː] adj vrai(e); (accurate) exact(e); (genuine) vrai, véritable; (faithful) fidèle; **to come ~** se réaliser

truly ['truːlɪ] adv vraiment, réellement; (truthfully) sans mentir; **yours ~** (in letter) je vous prie d'agréer, Monsieur (or Madame) mes, l'expression de mes sentiments respectueux

trumpet ['trʌmpɪt] n trompette f

trunk [trʌŋk] n (of tree, person) tronc m; (of elephant) trompe f; (case) malle f; (us Aut) coffre m; **trunks** npl (also: **swimming ~s**) maillot m or slip m de bain

trust [trʌst] n confiance f; (responsibility): **to place sth in sb's ~** confier la responsabilité de qch à qn; (Law) fidéicommis m ▷ vt (rely on) avoir confiance en; (entrust): **to ~ sth to sb** confier qch à qn; (hope): **to ~ (that)** espérer (que); **to take sth on ~** accepter qch les yeux fermés; **trusted** adj en qui l'on a confiance; **trustworthy** adj digne de confiance

truth [truːθ] (pl **truths**) n vérité f; **truthful** adj (person) qui dit la vérité; (answer) sincère

try [traɪ] n essai m, tentative f; (Rugby) essai f ▷ vt (attempt) essayer, tenter; (test: sth new: also: **~ out**) essayer, tester; (Law: person) juger; (strain) éprouver ▷ vi essayer; **to ~ to do** essayer de faire; (seek) chercher à faire; **try on** vt (clothes) essayer; **trying** adj pénible

T-shirt ['tiːʃəːt] n tee-shirt m

tub [tʌb] n cuve f; (for washing clothes) baquet m; (bath) baignoire f

tube [tjuːb] n tube m; (BRIT: underground) métro m; (for tyre) chambre f à air

tuberculosis [tjubəːkjuˈləʊsɪs] n tuberculose f

tube station n (BRIT) station f de métro

tuck [tʌk] vt (put) mettre; **tuck away** vt cacher, ranger; (money) mettre de côté; (building): **to be ~ed away** être caché(e); **tuck in** vt rentrer; (child) border ▷ vi (eat) manger de bon appétit; attaquer le repas; **tuck shop** n (BRIT Scol) boutique f à provisions

Tue(s) abbr (= Tuesday) ma

Tuesday ['tjuːzdɪ] n mardi m

tug [tʌg] n (ship) remorqueur m ▷ vt tirer (sur)

tuition [tjuːˈɪʃən] n (BRIT: lessons) leçons fpl; (: private) cours particuliers; (us: fees) frais mpl de scolarité

tulip ['tjuːlɪp] n tulipe f

tumble ['tʌmbl] n (fall) chute f, culbute f ▷ vi tomber, dégringoler; **to ~ to sth** (inf) réaliser qch; **tumble dryer** n (BRIT) séchoir m (à linge) à air chaud

tumbler ['tʌmblə¹] n verre (droit), gobelet m

tummy ['tʌmɪ] n (inf) ventre m

tumour (us **tumor**) ['tjuːmə¹] n tumeur f

tuna ['tjuːnə] n (pl inv: also: **~ fish**) thon m

tune [tjuːn] n (melody) air m ▷ vt (Mus) accorder; (Radio, TV, Aut) régler, mettre au point; **to be in/out of ~** (instrument) être accordé/désaccordé; (singer) chanter juste/faux; **tune in** vi (Radio, TV): **to ~ in (to)** se mettre à l'écoute (de); **tune up** vi (musician) accorder son instrument

tunic ['tjuːnɪk] n tunique f

Tunis ['tjuːnɪs] n Tunis

Tunisia [tjuːˈnɪzɪə] n Tunisie f

Tunisian [tjuːˈnɪzɪən] adj tunisien(ne) ▷ n Tunisien(ne)

tunnel ['tʌnl] n tunnel m; (in mine) galerie f ▷ vi creuser un tunnel (or une galerie)

turbulence ['təːbjuləns] n (Aviat) turbulence f

turf [təːf] n gazon m; (clod) motte f (de gazon) ▷ vt gazonner

Turk [təːk] n Turc (Turque)

Turkey ['təːkɪ] n Turquie f

turkey ['təːkɪ] n dindon m, dinde f

Turkish ['təːkɪʃ] adj turc (turque) ▷ n (Ling) turc m

turmoil ['təːmɔɪl] n trouble m, bouleversement m

turn [təːn] n tour m; (in road) tournant m; (tendency: of mind, events) tournure f; (performance) numéro m; (Med) crise f, attaque f ▷ vt tourner; (collar, steak) retourner; (change): **to ~ sth into** changer qch en; (age) atteindre ▷ vi (object, wind, milk) tourner; (person: look back): se retourner; (reverse direction) faire demi-tour; (become) devenir; **to ~ into** se changer en, se transformer en; **a good ~** un service; **it gave me quite a ~** ça m'a fait un coup; **"no left ~"** (Aut) "défense de tourner à gauche"; **~ left/right at the next junction** tournez à gauche/droite au prochain carrefour; **it's your ~** c'est (à) votre tour; **in ~** à son tour;

à tour de rôle; **to take ~s** se relayer; **turn around** vi (person) se retourner ▷ vt (object) tourner; **turn away** vi se détourner, tourner la tête ▷ vt (reject: person) renvoyer; (: business) refuser; **turn back** vi revenir, faire demi-tour; **turn down** vt (refuse) refuser, repousser; (reduce) baisser; (fold) rabattre; **turn in** vi (inf: go to bed) aller se coucher ▷ vt (fold) rentrer; **turn off** vi (from road) tourner ▷ vt (light, radio etc) éteindre; (tap) fermer; (engine) arrêter; **I can't ~ the heating off** je n'arrive pas à éteindre le chauffage; **turn on** vt (light, radio etc) allumer; (tap) ouvrir; (engine) mettre en marche; **I can't ~ the heating on** je n'arrive pas à allumer le chauffage; **turn out** vt (light, gas) éteindre; (produce) produire ▷ vi (voters, troops) se présenter; **to ~ out to be** ...: s'avérer ..., se révéler ...; **turn over** vi (person) se retourner ▷ vt (object) retourner; (page) tourner; **turn round** vi faire demi-tour; (rotate) tourner; **turn to** vt fus: **to ~ to sb** s'adresser à qn; **turn up** vi (person) arriver, se pointer (inf); (lost object) être retrouvé(e) ▷ vt (collar) remonter; (radio, heater) mettre plus fort; **turning** n (in road) tournant m; **turning point** n (fig) tournant m, moment décisif

turnip ['tə:nɪp] n navet m

turn: **turnout** n (of voters) taux m de participation; **turnover** n (Comm: amount of money) chiffre m d'affaires; (: of goods) roulement m; (: of staff) renouvellement m, changement m; **turnstile** n tourniquet m (d'entrée); **turn-up** n (BRIT: on trousers) revers m

turquoise ['tə:kwɔɪz] n (stone) turquoise f ▷ adj turquoise inv

turtle ['tə:tl] n tortue marine; **turtleneck (sweater)** n pullover m à col montant

tusk [tʌsk] n défense f (d'éléphant)

tutor ['tju:tə*] n (BRIT Scol: in college) directeur(-trice) d'études; (private

teacher) précepteur(-trice); **tutorial** [tju:'tɔ:rɪəl] n (Scol) (séance f de) travaux mpl pratiques

tuxedo [tʌk'si:dəu] n (us) smoking m

TV [ti:'vi:] n abbr (= television) télé f, TV f

tweed [twi:d] n tweed m

tweezers ['twi:zəz] npl pince f à épiler

twelfth [twelfθ] num douzième

twelve [twelv] num douze; **at ~ (o'clock)** à midi; (midnight) à minuit

twentieth ['twentɪθ] num vingtième

twenty ['twentɪ] num vingt

twice [twaɪs] adv deux fois; **~ as much** deux fois plus

twig [twɪg] n brindille f ▷ vt, vi (inf) piger

twilight ['twaɪlaɪt] n crépuscule m

twin [twɪn] adj -e jumeau(-elle) ▷ vt jumeler; **twin(-bedded) room** n chambre f à deux lits; **twin beds** npl lits mpl jumeaux

twinkle ['twɪŋkl] vi scintiller; (eyes) pétiller

twist [twɪst] n torsion f, tour m; (in wire, flex) tortillon m; (bend: in road) tournant m; (in story) coup m de théâtre ▷ vt tordre; (weave) entortiller; (roll around) enrouler; (fig) déformer ▷ vi (road, river) serpenter; **to ~ one's ankle/wrist** (Med) se tordre la cheville/le poignet

twit [twɪt] n (inf) crétin(e)

twitch [twɪtʃ] n (pull) coup sec, saccade f; (nervous) tic m ▷ vi se convulser, avoir un tic

two [tu:] num deux; **to put ~ and ~ together** (fig) faire le rapprochement

type [taɪp] n (category) genre m, espèce f; (model) modèle m; (example) type m; (Typ) type, caractère m ▷ vt (letter etc) taper (à la machine); **typewriter** n machine f à écrire

typhoid ['taɪfɔɪd] n typhoïde f

typhoon [taɪ'fu:n] n typhon m

typical ['tɪpɪkl] adj typique, caractéristique; **typically** adv (as usual) comme d'habitude; (characteristically) typiquement

typing ['taɪpɪŋ] *n* dactylo(graphie) *f*
typist ['taɪpɪst] *n* dactylo *m/f*
tyre (*us* **tire**) ['taɪə'] *n* pneu *m*; **I've got a flat ~** j'ai un pneu crevé; **tyre pressure** *n* (*BRIT*) pression *f* (de gonflage)

UFO ['juːfəu] *n abbr* (= *unidentified flying object*) ovni *m*
Uganda [juːˈgændə] *n* Ouganda *m*
ugly ['ʌglɪ] *adj* laid(e), vilain(e); (*fig*) répugnant(e)
UHT *adj abbr* = **ultra-heat treated**; **~ milk** lait *m* UHT *or* longue conservation
UK *n abbr* = **United Kingdom**
ulcer ['ʌlsə'] *n* ulcère *m*; **mouth~** aphte *f*
ultimate ['ʌltɪmət] *adj* ultime, final(e); (*authority*) suprême; **ultimately** *adv* (*at last*) en fin de compte; (*fundamentally*) finalement; (*eventually*) par la suite
ultimatum (*pl* **~s** *or* **ultimata**) [ʌltɪˈmeɪtəm, -tə] *n* ultimatum *m*
ultrasound ['ʌltrəsaund] *n* (*Med*) ultrason *m*
ultraviolet ['ʌltrəˈvaɪəlɪt] *adj* ultraviolet(te)
umbrella [ʌmˈbrɛlə] *n* parapluie *m*; (*for sun*) parasol *m*
umpire ['ʌmpaɪə'] *n* arbitre *m*; (*Tennis*) juge *m* de chaise

UN n abbr = **United Nations**

unable [ʌnˈeɪbl] adj: **to be ~ to** ne (pas) pouvoir, être dans l'impossibilité de; (not capable) être incapable de

unacceptable [ʌnəkˈsɛptəbl] adj (behaviour) inadmissible; (price, proposal) inacceptable

unanimous [juːˈnænɪməs] adj unanime

unarmed [ʌnˈɑːmd] adj (person) non armé(e); (combat) sans armes

unattended [ʌnəˈtɛndɪd] adj (car, child, luggage) sans surveillance

unattractive [ʌnəˈtræktɪv] adj peu attrayant(e); (character) peu sympathique

unavailable [ʌnəˈveɪləbl] adj (article, room, book) qui n'est pas disponible; (person) qui n'est pas libre

unavoidable [ʌnəˈvɔɪdəbl] adj inévitable

unaware [ʌnəˈwɛəʳ] adj: **to be ~ of** ignorer, ne pas savoir, être inconscient(e) de; **unawares** adv à l'improviste, au dépourvu

unbearable [ʌnˈbɛərəbl] adj insupportable

unbeatable [ʌnˈbiːtəbl] adj imbattable

unbelievable [ʌnbɪˈliːvəbl] adj incroyable

unborn [ʌnˈbɔːn] adj à naître

unbutton [ʌnˈbʌtn] vt déboutonner

uncalled-for [ʌnˈkɔːldfɔːʳ] adj déplacé(e), injustifié(e)

uncanny [ʌnˈkænɪ] adj étrange, troublant(e)

uncertain [ʌnˈsəːtn] adj incertain(e); (hesitant) hésitant(e); **uncertainty** n incertitude f, doutes mpl

unchanged [ʌnˈtʃeɪndʒd] adj inchangé(e)

uncle [ˈʌŋkl] n oncle m

unclear [ʌnˈklɪəʳ] adj qui (n'est pas) clair(e) ou évident(e); **I'm still ~ about what I'm supposed to do** je ne sais pas encore exactement ce que je dois faire

uncomfortable [ʌnˈkʌmfətəbl] adj inconfortable, peu confortable; (uneasy) mal à l'aise, gêné(e); (situation) désagréable

uncommon [ʌnˈkɔmən] adj rare, singulier(-ière), peu commun(e)

unconditional [ʌnkənˈdɪʃənl] adj sans conditions

unconscious [ʌnˈkɔnʃəs] adj sans connaissance, évanoui(e); (unaware): **~ (of)** inconscient(e) (de) ▷ n: **the ~** l'inconscient m

uncontrollable [ʌnkənˈtrəuləbl] adj (child, dog) indiscipliné(e); (temper, laughter) irrépressible

unconventional [ʌnkənˈvɛnʃənl] adj peu conventionnel(le)

uncover [ʌnˈkʌvəʳ] vt découvrir

undecided [ʌndɪˈsaɪdɪd] adj indécis(e), irrésolu(e)

undeniable [ʌndɪˈnaɪəbl] adj indéniable, incontestable

under [ˈʌndəʳ] prep sous; (less than) (de) moins de; au-dessous de; (according to) selon, en vertu de ▷ adv au-dessous; en dessous; **~ there** là-dessous; **~ the circumstances** étant donné les circonstances; **~ repair** en cours (de) réparation; **undercover** adj secret(-ète), clandestin(e); **underdone** adj (Culin) saignant(e); (: pej) pas assez cuit(e); **underestimate** vt sous-estimer, mésestimer; **undergo** vt (irreg: like **go**) subir; (treatment) suivre; **undergraduate** n étudiant(e) (qui prépare la licence); **underground** adj souterrain(e); (fig) clandestin(e) ▷ n (BRIT: railway) métro m; (Pol) clandestinité f; **undergrowth** n broussailles fpl, sous-bois m; **underline** vt souligner; **undermine** vt saper, miner; **underneath** [ʌndəˈniːθ] adv (en) dessous ▷ prep sous, au-dessous de; **underpants** npl caleçon m, slip m; **underpass** n (BRIT: for pedestrians) passage souterrain; (: for cars) passage inférieur;

underprivileged adj défavorisé(e);
underscore vt souligner; **undershirt**
n (US) tricot m de corps; **underskirt** n
(BRIT) jupon m
understand [Andə'stænd] vt, vi (irreg:
like **stand**) comprendre; **I don't ~** je
ne comprends pas; **understandable**
adj compréhensible; **understanding**
adj compréhensif(-ive) ▷ n
compréhension f; (agreement) accord m
understatement ['Andəsteıtmənt]
n: **that's an ~** c'est (bien) peu dire, le
terme est faible
understood [Andə'stud] pt, pp of
understand ▷ adj entendu(e); (implied)
sous-entendu(e)
undertake [Andə'teık] vt (irreg: like
take) (job, task) entreprendre; (duty)
se charger de; **to ~ to do sth** s'engager
à faire qch
undertaker ['Andəteıkə'] n (BRIT)
entrepreneur m des pompes funèbres,
croque-mort m
undertaking ['Andəteıkıŋ] n
entreprise f; (promise) promesse f
under: underwater adv sous l'eau
▷ adj sous-marin(e); **underway**
adj: **to be underway** (meeting,
investigation) être en cours; **underwear**
n sous-vêtements mpl; (women's
only) dessous mpl; **underwent** pt of
undergo; underworld n (of crime)
milieu m, pègre f
undesirable [Andı'zaıərəbl] adj peu
souhaitable; (person, effect) indésirable
undisputed ['Andıs'pju:tıd] adj
incontesté(e)
undo [An'du:] vt (irreg: like **do**) défaire;
undone [An'dʌn] pp of **undo** ▷ adj: **to
come ~** se défaire
undoubtedly [An'dautıdlı] adv sans
aucun doute
undress [An'drɛs] vi se déshabiller
unearth [An'ə:θ] vt déterrer; (fig)
dénicher
uneasy [An'i:zı] adj mal à l'aise,
gêné(e); (worried) inquiet(-ète); (feeling)
désagréable; (peace, truce) fragile

unemployed [Anım'plɔıd] adj sans
travail, au chômage ▷ n: **the ~** les
chômeurs mpl
unemployment [Anım'plɔımənt] n
chômage m; **unemployment benefit**
(US **unemployment compensation**) n
allocation f de chômage
unequal [An'i:kwəl] adj inégal(e)
uneven [An'i:vn] adj inégal(e); (quality,
work) irrégulier(-ière)
unexpected [Anık'spɛktıd]
adj inattendu(e), imprévu(e);
unexpectedly adv (succeed) contre
toute attente; (arrive) à l'improviste
unfair [An'fɛə'] adj: **~ (to)** injuste
(envers)
unfaithful [An'feıθful] adj infidèle
unfamiliar [Anfə'mılıə'] adj étrange,
inconnu(e); **to be ~ with sth** mal
connaître qch
unfashionable [An'fæʃnəbl] adj
(clothes) démodé(e); (place) peu chic inv
unfasten [An'fɑ:sn] vt défaire; (belt,
necklace) détacher; (open) ouvrir
unfavourable (US **unfavorable**)
[An'feıvrəbl] adj défavorable
unfinished [An'fınıʃt] adj inachevé(e)
unfit [An'fıt] adj (physically: ill) en
mauvaise santé; (: out of condition)
pas en forme; (incompetent): **~ (for)**
impropre (à); (work, service) inapte (à)
unfold [An'fəuld] vt déplier ▷ vi se
dérouler
unforgettable [Anfə'gɛtəbl] adj
inoubliable
unfortunate [An'fɔ:tʃnət] adj
malheureux(-euse); (event, remark)
malencontreux(-euse); **unfortunately**
adv malheureusement
unfriendly [An'frɛndlı] adj peu
aimable, froid(e)
unfurnished [An'fə:nıʃt] adj non
meublé(e)
unhappiness [An'hæpınıs] n tristesse
f, peine f
unhappy [An'hæpı] adj triste,
malheureux(-euse); (: unfortunate:
remark etc) malheureux(-euse); (not

pleased): ~ **with** mécontent(e) de, peu satisfait(e) de

unhealthy [ʌnˈhɛlθɪ] *adj* (gen) malsain(e); (person) maladif(-ive)

unheard-of [ʌnˈhəːdɔv] *adj* inouï(e), sans précédent

unhelpful [ʌnˈhɛlpful] *adj* (person) peu serviable; (advice) peu utile

unhurt [ʌnˈhəːt] *adj* indemne, sain(e) et sauf (sauve)

unidentified [ʌnaɪˈdɛntɪfaɪd] *adj* non identifié(e); *see also* **UFO**

uniform [ˈjuːnɪfɔːm] *n* uniforme *m* ▷ *adj* uniforme

unify [ˈjuːnɪfaɪ] *vt* unifier

unimportant [ʌnɪmˈpɔːtənt] *adj* sans importance

uninhabited [ʌnɪnˈhæbɪtɪd] *adj* inhabité(e)

unintentional [ʌnɪnˈtɛnʃənəl] *adj* involontaire

union [ˈjuːnjən] *n* union *f*; (also: **trade** ~) syndicat *m* ▷ *cpd* syndical(e), syndical(e); **Union Jack** *n* drapeau du Royaume-Uni

unique [juːˈniːk] *adj* unique

unisex [ˈjuːnɪsɛks] *adj* unisexe

unit [ˈjuːnɪt] *n* unité *f*; (section: of furniture, equipment) élément *m*, bloc *m*; (team, squad) groupe *m*, service *m*; **kitchen** ~ élément de cuisine

unite [juːˈnaɪt] *vt* unir ▷ *vi* s'unir; **united** *adj* uni(e); (country, party) unifié(e); (efforts) conjugué(e); **United Kingdom** *n* Royaume-Uni *m* (R.U.); **United Nations (Organization)** *n* (Organisation *f* des) Nations unies (ONU); **United States (of America)** *n* États-Unis *mpl*

unity [ˈjuːnɪtɪ] *n* unité *f*

universal [juːnɪˈvəːsl] *adj* universel(le)

universe [ˈjuːnɪvəːs] *n* univers *m*

university [juːnɪˈvəːsɪtɪ] *n* université *f* ▷ *cpd* (student, professor) d'université; (education, year, degree) universitaire

unjust [ʌnˈdʒʌst] *adj* injuste

unkind [ʌnˈkaɪnd] *adj* peu gentil(le), méchant(e)

unknown [ʌnˈnəun] *adj* inconnu(e)

unlawful [ʌnˈlɔːful] *adj* illégal(e)

unleaded [ʌnˈlɛdɪd] *n* (also: ~ **petrol**) essence *f* sans plomb

unleash [ʌnˈliːʃ] *vt* déchaîner, (fig) déclencher

unless [ʌnˈlɛs] *conj*: ~ **he leaves** à moins qu'il (ne) parte; ~ **otherwise stated** sauf indication contraire

unlike [ʌnˈlaɪk] *adj* dissemblable, différent(e) ▷ *prep* à la différence de, contrairement à

unlikely [ʌnˈlaɪklɪ] *adj* (result, event) improbable; (explanation) invraisemblable

unlimited [ʌnˈlɪmɪtɪd] *adj* illimité(e)

unlisted [ʌnˈlɪstɪd] *adj* (US Tel) sur la liste rouge

unload [ʌnˈləud] *vt* décharger

unlock [ʌnˈlɔk] *vt* ouvrir

unlucky [ʌnˈlʌkɪ] *adj* (person) malchanceux(-euse); (object, number) qui porte malheur; **to be** ~ (person) ne pas avoir de chance

unmarried [ʌnˈmærɪd] *adj* célibataire

unmistak(e)able [ʌnmɪsˈteɪkəbl] *adj* indubitable; qu'on ne peut pas ne pas reconnaître

unnatural [ʌnˈnætʃrəl] *adj* non naturel(le); (perversion) contre nature

unnecessary [ʌnˈnɛsəsərɪ] *adj* inutile, superflu(e)

UNO [ˈjuːnəu] *n abbr* = **United Nations Organization**

unofficial [ʌnəˈfɪʃl] *adj* (news) officieux(-euse), non officiel(le); (strike) ~ sauvage

unpack [ʌnˈpæk] *vi* défaire sa valise ▷ *vt* (suitcase) défaire; (belongings) déballer

unpaid [ʌnˈpeɪd] *adj* (bill) impayé(e); (holiday) non-payé(e), sans salaire; (work) non rétribué(e)

unpleasant [ʌnˈplɛznt] *adj* déplaisant(e), désagréable

unplug [ʌnˈplʌg] *vt* débrancher

unpopular [ʌnˈpɔpjulər] *adj* impopulaire

unprecedented [ʌn'presɪdəntɪd] *adj*
sans précédent

unpredictable [ʌnprɪ'dɪktəbl] *adj*
imprévisible

unprotected ['ʌnprə'tektɪd] *adj (sex)*
non protégé(e)

unqualified [ʌn'kwɒlɪfaɪd] *adj*
(teacher) non diplômé(e), sans titres;
(success) sans réserve, total(e); *(disaster)*
total(e)

unravel [ʌn'rævl] *vt* démêler

unreal [ʌn'rɪəl] *adj* irréel(le);
(extraordinary) incroyable

unrealistic ['ʌnrɪə'lɪstɪk] *adj (idea)*
irréaliste; *(estimate)* peu réaliste

unreasonable [ʌn'riːznəbl] *adj* qui
n'est pas raisonnable

unrelated [ʌnrɪ'leɪtɪd] *adj* sans
rapport; *(people)* sans lien de parenté

unreliable [ʌnrɪ'laɪəbl] *adj* sur qui
(or quoi) on ne peut compter,
peu fiable

unrest [ʌn'rest] *n* agitation *f*,
troubles *mpl*

unroll [ʌn'rəʊl] *vt* dérouler

unruly [ʌn'ruːlɪ] *adj* indiscipliné(e)

unsafe [ʌn'seɪf] *adj (in danger)* en
danger; *(journey, car)* dangereux(-euse)

unsatisfactory ['ʌnsætɪs'fæktərɪ] *adj*
peu satisfaisant(e)

unscrew [ʌn'skruː] *vt* dévisser

unsettled [ʌn'setld] *adj (restless)*
perturbé(e); *(unpredictable)* instable;
incertain(e); *(not finalized)* non résolu(e)

unsettling [ʌn'setlɪŋ] *adj* qui a un effet
perturbateur

unsightly [ʌn'saɪtlɪ] *adj*
disgracieux(-euse), laid(e)

unskilled [ʌn'skɪld] *adj*: ~ **worker**
manœuvre *m*

unspoilt [ʌn'spɔɪlt], **unspoiled**
['ʌn'spɔɪld] *adj (place)* non dégradé(e)

unstable [ʌn'steɪbl] *adj* instable

unsteady [ʌn'stedɪ] *adj* mal assuré(e),
chancelant(e), instable

unsuccessful [ʌnsək'sesfʊl] *adj*
(attempt) infructueux(-euse); *(writer,
proposal)* qui n'a pas de succès; **to be**

~ *(in attempting sth)* ne pas réussir, ne
pas avoir de succès; *(application)* ne pas
être retenu(e)

unsuitable [ʌn'suːtəbl] *adj* qui ne
convient pas, peu approprié(e); *(time)*
inopportun(e)

unsure [ʌn'ʃuə?] *adj* pas sûr(e); **to be ~
of o.s.** ne pas être sûr de soi, manquer
de confiance en soi

untidy [ʌn'taɪdɪ] *adj (room)* en
désordre; *(appearance, person)*
débraillé(e); *(person: in character)* sans
ordre, désordonné; *(work)* peu
soigné(e)

untie [ʌn'taɪ] *vt (knot, parcel)* défaire;
(prisoner, dog) détacher

until [ən'tɪl] *prep* jusqu'à; *(after negative)*
avant ▷ *conj* jusqu'à ce que + *sub*; *(in
past, after negative)* avant que + *sub*; ~ **he
comes** jusqu'à ce qu'il vienne, jusqu'à
son arrivée; ~ **now** jusqu'à présent,
jusqu'ici; ~ **then** jusque-là

untrue [ʌn'truː] *adj (statement)* faux
(fausse)

unused¹ [ʌn'juːzd] *adj (new)* neuf
(neuve)

unused² [ʌn'juːst] *adj*: **to be ~ to sth/
to doing sth** ne pas avoir l'habitude de
qch/de faire qch

unusual [ʌn'juːʒʊəl] *adj* insolite,
exceptionnel(le), rare; **unusually** *adv*
exceptionnellement, particulièrement

unveil [ʌn'veɪl] *vt* dévoiler

unwanted [ʌn'wɒntɪd] *adj (child,
pregnancy)* non désiré(e); *(clothes etc)*
à donner

unwell [ʌn'wel] *adj* souffrant(e); **to feel
~** ne pas se sentir bien

unwilling [ʌn'wɪlɪŋ] *adj*: **to be ~ to do**
ne pas vouloir faire

unwind [ʌn'waɪnd] *vb (irreg: like* **wind**)
▷ *vt* dérouler ▷ *vi (relax)* se détendre

unwise [ʌn'waɪz] *adj* imprudent(e),
peu judicieux(-euse)

unwittingly [ʌn'wɪtɪŋlɪ] *adv*
involontairement

unwrap [ʌn'ræp] *vt* défaire; ouvrir

unzip [ʌn'zɪp] *vt* ouvrir (la fermeture

éclair de); (Comput) dézipper

○ **KEYWORD**

up [ʌp] prep: **he went up the stairs/the hill** il a monté l'escalier/la colline; **the cat was up a tree** le chat était dans un arbre; **they live further up the street** ils habitent plus haut dans la rue; **go up that road and turn left** remontez la rue et tournez à gauche

▷ adv 1 en haut; en l'air; (upwards, higher): **up in the sky/the mountains** (là-haut) dans le ciel/les montagnes; **put it a bit higher up** mettez-le un peu plus haut; **to stand up** (get up) se lever, se mettre debout; (be standing) être debout; **up there** là-haut; **up above** au-dessus

2: **to be up** (out of bed) être levé(e); (prices) avoir augmenté ou monté; (finished): **when the year was up** à la fin de l'année

3: **up to** (as far as) jusqu'à; **up to now** jusqu'à présent

4: **to be up to** (depending on): **it's up to you** c'est à vous de décider; (equal to): **he's not up to it** (job, task etc) il n'en est pas capable; (inf: be doing): **what is he up to?** qu'est-ce qu'il peut bien faire?

▷ n: **ups and downs** hauts et bas mpl

up-and-coming [ʌpənd'kʌmɪŋ] adj plein(e) d'avenir ou de promesses
upbringing ['ʌpbrɪŋɪŋ] n éducation f
update [ʌp'deɪt] vt mettre à jour
upfront [ʌp'frʌnt] adj (open) franc (franche) ▷ adv (pay) d'avance; **to be ~ about sth** ne rien cacher de qch
upgrade [ʌp'greɪd] vt (person) promouvoir; (job) revaloriser; (property, equipment) moderniser
upheaval [ʌp'hiːvl] n bouleversement m; (in room) branle-bas m; (event) crise f
uphill [ʌp'hɪl] adj qui monte; (fig: task) difficile, pénible ▷ adv (face, look) vers le haut; (go): **to go** ~ monter en amont, vers l'amont; **to go** ~ monter
upholstery [ʌp'həʊlstərɪ] n

rembourrage m; (cover) tissu m d'ameublement; (of car) garniture f
upmarket [ʌp'mɑːkɪt] adj (product) haut de gamme inv; (area) chic inv
upon [ə'pɒn] prep sur
upper ['ʌpə] adj supérieur(e); du dessus ▷ n (of shoe) empeigne f
upper-class adj de la haute société, aristocratique; (district) élégant(e), huppé(e); (accent, attitude) caractéristique des classes supérieures
upright ['ʌpraɪt] adj droit(e); (fig) droit, honnête
uprising ['ʌpraɪzɪŋ] n soulèvement m, insurrection f
uproar ['ʌprɔː] n tumulte m, vacarme m; (protests) protestations fpl
upset [ʌp'sɛt] n dérangement m
▷ vt (irreg: like set [ʌp'sɛt]) (glass etc) renverser; (plan) déranger; (person: offend) contrarier; (: grieve) faire de la peine à; bouleverser ▷ adj [ʌp'sɛt] contrarié(e); peiné(e); **to have a stomach** ~ (BRIT) avoir une indigestion
upside down ['ʌpsaɪd-] adv à l'envers; **to turn sth** ~ (fig: place) mettre sens dessus dessous
upstairs [ʌp'stɛəz] adv en haut ▷ adj (room) du dessus, d'en haut ▷ n: **the** ~ l'étage m
up-to-date ['ʌptə'deɪt] adj moderne; (information) très récent(e)
uptown ['ʌptaʊn] (us) adv (live) dans les quartiers chics; (go) vers les quartiers chics ▷ adj des quartiers chics
upward ['ʌpwəd] adj ascendant(e); vers le haut; **upward(s)** adv vers le haut; (more than): **upward(s) of** plus de
uranium [juə'reɪnɪəm] n uranium m
Uranus [juə'reɪnəs] n Uranus f
urban ['əːbən] adj urbain(e)
urge [əːdʒ] n besoin (impératif), envie (pressante) ▷ vt (person): **to** ~ **sb to do** exhorter qn à faire, pousser qn à faire, recommander vivement à qn de faire
urgency ['əːdʒənsɪ] n urgence f; (of tone) insistance f

urgent ['ə:dʒənt] adj urgent(e); (plea, tone) pressant(e)

urinal ['juərɪnl] n (BRIT: place) urinoir m

urinate ['juərɪneɪt] vi uriner

urine ['juərɪn] n urine f

URL abbr (= uniform resource locator) URL f

US n abbr = **United States**

us [ʌs] pron nous; see also **me**

USA n abbr = **United States of America**

use n [ju:s] emploi m, utilisation f; (usefulness) utilité f ▷ vt [ju:z] se servir de, utiliser, employer; **in ~** en usage; **out of ~** hors d'usage; **to be of ~** servir, être utile; **it's no ~** ça ne sert à rien; **to have the ~ of** avoir l'usage de; **she ~d to do it** elle le faisait (autrefois), elle avait coutume de le faire; **to be ~d to** avoir l'habitude de, être habitué(e) à; **use up** vt finir, épuiser; (food) consommer; **used** [ju:zd] adj (car) d'occasion; **useful** adj utile; **useless** adj inutile; (inf: person) nul(le); **user** n utilisateur(-trice), usager m; **user-friendly** adj convivial(e), facile d'emploi

usual ['ju:ʒuəl] adj habituel(le); **as ~** comme d'habitude; **usually** adv d'habitude, d'ordinaire

utensil [ju:'tɛnsl] n ustensile m; **kitchen ~s** batterie f de cuisine

utility [ju:'tɪlɪtɪ] n utilité f; (also: **public ~**) service public

utilize ['ju:tɪlaɪz] vt utiliser; (make good use of) exploiter

utmost ['ʌtməust] adj extrême, le (la) plus grand(e) ▷ n: **to do one's ~** faire tout son possible

utter ['ʌtə*] adj total(e), complet(-ète) ▷ vt prononcer, proférer; (sounds) émettre; **utterly** adv complètement, totalement

U-turn ['ju:'tə:n] n demi-tour m; (fig) volte-face f inv

V

v. abbr = **verse** (= vide) v.; (= versus) c.; (= volt) V

vacancy ['veɪkənsɪ] n (BRIT: job) poste vacant; (room) chambre f disponible; **"no vacancies"** "complet"

vacant ['veɪkənt] adj (post) vacant(e); (seat etc) libre, disponible; (expression) distrait(e)

vacate [və'keɪt] vt quitter

vacation [və'keɪʃən] n (esp us) vacances fpl; **on ~** en vacances; **vacationer** (us **vacationist**) n vacancier(-ière)

vaccination [væksɪ'neɪʃən] n vaccination f

vaccine ['væksi:n] n vaccin m

vacuum ['vækjuːm] n vide m; **vacuum cleaner** n aspirateur m

vagina [və'dʒaɪnə] n vagin m

vague [veɪg] adj vague, imprécis(e); (blurred: photo, memory) flou(e)

vain [veɪn] adj (useless) vain(e); (conceited) vaniteux(-euse); **in ~** en vain

Valentine's Day ['væləntaɪnz-] n

Saint-Valentin f
valid ['vælɪd] adj (document) valide, valable; (excuse) valable
valley ['vælɪ] n vallée f
valuable ['væljuəbl] adj (jewel) de grande valeur; (time, help) précieux(-euse); **valuables** npl objets mpl de valeur
value ['vælju:] n valeur f ⊳ vt (fix price) évaluer, expertiser; (appreciate) apprécier; **values** npl (principles) valeurs fpl
valve [vælv] n (in machine) soupape f, (on tyre) valve f; (Med) valve, valvule f
vampire ['væmpaɪə'] n vampire m
van [væn] n (Aut) camionnette f
vandal ['vændl] n vandale m/f; **vandalism** n vandalisme m; **vandalize** vt saccager
vanilla [və'nɪlə] n vanille f
vanish ['vænɪʃ] vi disparaître
vanity ['vænɪtɪ] n vanité f
vapour (us **vapor**) ['veɪpə'] n vapeur f; (on window) buée f
variable ['vɛərɪəbl] adj variable; (mood) changeant(e)
variant ['vɛərɪənt] n variante f
variation [vɛərɪ'eɪʃən] n variation f; (in opinion) changement m
varied ['vɛərɪd] adj varié(e), divers(e)
variety [və'raɪətɪ] n (variety) variété f; (quantity) nombre m, quantité f
various ['vɛərɪəs] adj divers(es), différent(e); (several) divers, plusieurs
varnish ['vɑːnɪʃ] n vernis m ⊳ vt vernir
vary ['vɛərɪ] vt, vi varier, changer
vase [vɑːz] n vase m
Vaseline® ['væsɪliːn] n vaseline f
vast [vɑːst] adj vaste, immense; (amount, success) énorme
VAT [væt] n abbr (BRIT: = value added tax) TVA f
vault [vɔːlt] n (of roof) voûte f; (tomb) caveau m; (in bank) salle f des coffres; chambre f forte ⊳ vt (also: ~ **over**) sauter (d'un bond)
VCR n abbr = **video cassette recorder**
VDU n abbr = **visual display unit**

veal [viːl] n veau m
veer [vɪə'] vi tourner; (car, ship) virer
vegan ['viːgən] n végétalien(ne)
vegetable ['vɛdʒtəbl] n légume m ⊳ adj végétal(e)
vegetarian [vɛdʒɪ'tɛərɪən] adj, n végétarien(ne); **do you have any ~ dishes?** avez-vous des plats végétariens?
vegetation [vɛdʒɪ'teɪʃən] n végétation f
vehicle ['viːɪkl] n véhicule m
veil [veɪl] n voile m
vein [veɪn] n veine f; (on leaf) nervure f
Velcro® ['vɛlkrəu] n velcro® m
velvet ['vɛlvɪt] n velours m
vending machine ['vɛndɪŋ-] n distributeur automatique
vendor ['vɛndə'] n vendeur(-euse); **street ~** marchand ambulant
Venetian blind [vɪ'niːʃən-] n store vénitien
vengeance ['vɛndʒəns] n vengeance f; **with a ~** (fig) vraiment, pour de bon
venison ['vɛnɪsn] n venaison f
venom ['vɛnəm] n venin m
vent [vɛnt] n conduit m d'aération; (in dress, jacket) fente f ⊳ vt (fig: one's feelings) donner libre cours à
ventilation [vɛntɪ'leɪʃən] n ventilation f, aération f
venture ['vɛntʃə'] n entreprise f ⊳ vt risquer, hasarder ⊳ vi s'aventurer, se risquer; **a business ~** une entreprise commerciale
venue ['vɛnjuː] n lieu m
Venus ['viːnəs] n (planet) Vénus f
verb [vəːb] n verbe m; **verbal** adj verbal(e)
verdict ['vəːdɪkt] n verdict m
verge [vəːdʒ] n bord m; **"soft ~s"** (BRIT) "accotements non stabilisés"; **on the ~ of doing** sur le point de faire
verify ['vɛrɪfaɪ] vt vérifier
versatile ['vəːsətaɪl] adj polyvalent(e)
verse [vəːs] n vers mpl; (stanza) strophe f; (in Bible) verset m
version ['vəːʃən] n version f

versus ['vəːsəs] prep contre

vertical ['vəːtɪkl] adj vertical(e)

very ['vɛrɪ] adv très ▷ adj: **the ~
book which** le livre même que; **the ~ last** le
tout dernier; **at the ~ least** au moins; **~
much** beaucoup

vessel ['vɛsl] n (Anat, Naut) vaisseau m;
(container) récipient m; see also **blood**

vest [vɛst] n (BRIT: underwear) tricot m
de corps; (us: waistcoat) gilet m

vet [vɛt] n abbr (BRIT: = veterinary
surgeon) vétérinaire m/f; (us: = veteran)
ancien(ne) combattant(e) ▷ vt
examiner minutieusement

veteran ['vɛtərn] n vétéran m; (also:
war ~) ancien combattant

veterinary surgeon ['vɛtrɪnərɪ-]
(BRIT) (us **veterinarian** [vɛtrɪ'nɛərɪən])
n vétérinaire m/f

veto ['viːtəu] n (pl **~es**) veto m ▷ vt
opposer son veto à

via ['vaɪə] prep par, via

viable ['vaɪəbl] adj viable

vibrate [vaɪ'breɪt] vi: **to ~ (with)**
vibrer (de)

vibration [vaɪ'breɪʃən] n vibration f

vicar ['vɪkə'] n pasteur m (de l'Église
anglicane)

vice [vaɪs] n (evil) vice m; (Tech) étau m;
vice-chairman n vice-président(e)

vice versa ['vaɪsɪ'vəːsə] adv vice versa

vicinity [vɪ'sɪnɪtɪ] n environs mpl,
alentours mpl

vicious ['vɪʃəs] adj (remark) cruel(le),
méchant(e); (blow) brutal(e); (dog)
méchant(e), dangereux(-euse); **a ~
circle** un cercle vicieux

victim ['vɪktɪm] n victime f

victor ['vɪktə'] n vainqueur m

Victorian [vɪk'tɔːrɪən] adj
victorien(ne)

victorious [vɪk'tɔːrɪəs] adj
victorieux(-euse)

victory ['vɪktərɪ] n victoire f

video ['vɪdɪəu] n (video film) vidéo f;
(also: **~ cassette**) vidéocassette f; (also:
~ cassette recorder) magnétoscope
m ▷ vt (with recorder) enregistrer;

(with camera) filmer; **video camera** n
caméra f vidéo inv; **video (cassette)
recorder** n magnétoscope m; **video
game** n jeu m vidéo inv; **video shop**
n vidéoclub m; **video tape** n bande f
vidéo inv; (cassette) vidéocassette f

vie [vaɪ] vi: **to ~ with** lutter avec,
rivaliser avec

Vienna [vɪ'ɛnə] n Vienne

Vietnam, Viet Nam ['vjɛt'næm] n
Viêt-nam or Vietnam m; **Vietnamese**
[vjɛtnə'miːz] adj vietnamien(ne) ▷ n
(pl inv) Vietnamien(ne)

view [vjuː] n vue f, (opinion) avis m,
vue ▷ vt voir, regarder; (situation)
considérer; (house) visiter; **on ~** (in
museum etc) exposé(e); **in full ~ of sb**
sous les yeux de qn; **in my ~** à mon avis;
in ~ of the fact that étant donné que;
viewer n (TV) téléspectateur(-trice);
viewpoint n point m de vue

vigilant ['vɪdʒɪlənt] adj vigilant(e)

vigorous ['vɪgərəs] adj
vigoureux(-euse)

vile [vaɪl] adj (action) vil(e); (smell, food)
abominable; (temper) massacrant(e)

villa ['vɪlə] n villa f

village ['vɪlɪdʒ] n village m; **villager** n
villageois(e)

villain ['vɪlən] n (scoundrel) scélérat m;
(BRIT: criminal) bandit m; (in novel etc)
traître m

vinaigrette [vɪneɪ'grɛt] n vinaigrette f

vine [vaɪn] n vigne f

vinegar ['vɪnɪgə'] n vinaigre m

vineyard ['vɪnjɑːd] n vignoble m

vintage ['vɪntɪdʒ] n (year) année f,
millésime m ▷ cpd (car) d'époque; (wine)
de grand cru

vinyl ['vaɪnl] n vinyle m

viola [vɪ'əulə] n alto m

violate ['vaɪəleɪt] vt violer

violation [vaɪə'leɪʃən] n violation f;
in ~ of (rule, law) en infraction à, en
violation de

violence ['vaɪələns] n violence f

violent ['vaɪələnt] adj violent(e)

violet ['vaɪələt] adj (colour) violet(te)

▷ n (plant) violette f

violin [vaɪəˈlɪn] n violon m

VIP n abbr (= very important person) VIP m

virgin [ˈvɜːdʒɪn] n vierge f

Virgo [ˈvɜːgəʊ] n la Vierge

virtual [ˈvɜːtjʊəl] adj (Comput, Physics) virtuel(le); (in effect): **it's a ~ impossibility** c'est quasiment impossible; **virtually** adv (almost) pratiquement; **virtual reality** n (Comput) réalité virtuelle

virtue [ˈvɜːtjuː] n vertu f; (advantage) mérite m, avantage m; **by ~ of** en vertu or raison de

virus [ˈvaɪərəs] n (Med, Comput) virus m

visa [ˈviːzə] n visa m

vise [vaɪs] n (US Tech) = **vice**

visibility [vɪzɪˈbɪlɪtɪ] n visibilité f

visible [ˈvɪzəbl] adj visible

vision [ˈvɪʒən] n (sight) vue f, vision f; (foresight, in dream) vision

visit [ˈvɪzɪt] n visite f; (stay) séjour m ▷ vt (person: us: also: **~ with**) rendre visite à; (place) visiter; **visiting hours** npl heures fpl de visite; **visitor** n visiteur(-euse); (to one's house) invité(e); **visitor centre** (US **visitor center**) n hall m or centre m d'accueil

visual [ˈvɪzjʊəl] adj visuel(le); **visualize** vt se représenter

vital [ˈvaɪtl] adj vital(e); **of ~ importance (to sb/sth)** d'une importance capitale (pour qn/qch)

vitality [vaɪˈtælɪtɪ] n vitalité f

vitamin [ˈvɪtəmɪn] n vitamine f

vivid [ˈvɪvɪd] adj (account) frappant(e), vivant(e); (light, imagination) vif (vive)

V-neck [ˈviːnɛk] n décolleté m en V

vocabulary [vəʊˈkæbjʊlərɪ] n vocabulaire m

vocal [ˈvəʊkl] adj vocal(e); (articulate) qui n'hésite pas à s'exprimer, qui sait faire entendre ses opinions

vocational [vəʊˈkeɪʃənl] adj professionnel(le)

vodka [ˈvɔdkə] n vodka f

vogue [vəʊg] n: **to be in ~** être en vogue or à la mode

voice [vɔɪs] n voix f ▷ vt (opinion) exprimer, formuler; **voice mail** n (system) messagerie f vocale; (device) boîte f vocale

void [vɔɪd] n vide m ▷ adj (invalid) nul(le); (empty): **~ of** vide de, dépourvu(e) de

volatile [ˈvɔlətaɪl] adj volatil(e); (fig: person) versatile; (: situation) explosif(-ive)

volcano (pl **~es**) [vɔlˈkeɪnəʊ] n volcan m

volleyball [ˈvɔlɪbɔːl] n volley(-ball) m

volt [vəʊlt] n volt m; **voltage** n tension f, voltage m

volume [ˈvɔljuːm] n volume m; (of tank) capacité f

voluntarily [ˈvɔləntrɪlɪ] adv volontairement

voluntary [ˈvɔləntərɪ] adj volontaire; (unpaid) bénévole

volunteer [vɔlənˈtɪə] n volontaire m/f ▷ vt (information) donner spontanément ▷ vi (Mil) s'engager comme volontaire; **to ~ to do** se proposer pour faire

vomit [ˈvɔmɪt] n vomissure f ▷ vt, vi vomir

vote [vəʊt] n vote m, suffrage m; (votes cast) voix f, vote; (franchise) droit m de vote ▷ vt (chairman) élire; (propose): **to ~ that** proposer que + sub ▷ vi voter; **~ of thanks** discours m de remerciement; **voter** n électeur(-trice); **voting** n scrutin m, vote m

voucher [ˈvaʊtʃə] n (for meal, petrol, gift) bon m

vow [vaʊ] n vœu m, serment m ▷ vi jurer

vowel [ˈvaʊəl] n voyelle f

voyage [ˈvɔɪɪdʒ] n voyage m par mer, traversée f

vulgar [ˈvʌlgə] adj vulgaire

vulnerable [ˈvʌlnərəbl] adj vulnérable

vulture [ˈvʌltʃə] n vautour m

W

waddle ['wɔdl] vi se dandiner

wade [weɪd] vi: **to ~ through** marcher dans, patauger dans; (fig: book) venir à bout de

wafer ['weɪfə*] n (Culin) gaufrette f

waffle ['wɔfl] n (Culin) gaufre f ▷ vi parler pour ne rien dire; faire du remplissage

wag [wæg] vt agiter, remuer ▷ vi remuer

wage [weɪdʒ] n (also: **~s**) salaire m, paye f ▷ vt: **to ~ war** faire la guerre

wag(g)on ['wægən] n (horse-drawn) chariot m; (BRIT Rail) wagon m (de marchandises)

wail [weɪl] n gémissement m; (of siren) hurlement m ▷ vi gémir; (siren) hurler

waist [weɪst] n taille f, ceinture f; **waistcoat** n (BRIT) gilet m

wait [weɪt] n attente f ▷ vi attendre; **to ~ for sb/sth** attendre qn/qch; **to keep sb ~ing** faire attendre qn; **~ for me, please** attendez-moi, s'il vous plaît; **I can't ~ to ...** (fig) je meurs

d'envie de ...; **to lie in ~ for** guetter; **wait on** vt fus servir; **waiter** n garçon m (de café), serveur m; **waiting list** n liste f d'attente; **waiting room** n salle f d'attente; **waitress** ['weɪtrɪs] n serveuse f

waive [weɪv] vt renoncer à, abandonner

wake [weɪk] vb (pt **woke** or **~d**, pp **woken** or **~d**) ▷ vt (also: **~ up**) réveiller ▷ vi (also: **~ up**) se réveiller ▷ n (for dead person) veillée f mortuaire; (Naut) sillage m

Wales [weɪlz] n pays m de Galles; **the Prince of ~** le prince de Galles

walk [wɔːk] n promenade f; (short) petit tour; (gait) démarche f; (path) chemin m; (in park etc) allée f ▷ vi marcher; (for pleasure, exercise) se promener ▷ vt (distance) faire à pied; (dog) promener; **10 minutes' ~ from** à 10 minutes de marche de; **to go for a ~** faire une promenade; faire un tour; **from all ~s of life** de toutes conditions sociales; **walk out** vi (go out) sortir; (as protest) partir (en signe de protestation); (strike) se mettre en grève; **to ~ out on sb** quitter qn; **walker** n (person) marcheur(-euse); **walkie-talkie** ['wɔːkɪ'tɔːkɪ] n talkie-walkie m; **walking** n marche f à pied; **walking shoes** npl chaussures fpl de marche; **walking stick** n canne f; **Walkman®** n Walkman® m; **walkway** n promenade f, cheminement piéton

wall [wɔːl] n mur m; (of tunnel, cave) paroi f

wallet ['wɔlɪt] n portefeuille m; **I can't find my ~** je ne retrouve plus mon portefeuille

wallpaper ['wɔːlpeɪpə*] n papier peint ▷ vt tapisser

walnut ['wɔːlnʌt] n noix f; (tree, wood) noyer m

walrus (pl **~** or **~es**) ['wɔːlrəs] n morse m

waltz [wɔːlts] n valse f ▷ vi valser

wand [wɔnd] n (also: **magic ~**) baguette f (magique)

wander ['wɔndə*] vi (person) errer, aller

sans but; (thoughts) vagabonder ▷ vt
errer dans

want [wɒnt] vt vouloir; (need) avoir
besoin de ▷ n: **for ~ of** par manque de,
faute de; **to ~ to do** vouloir faire; **to ~
sb to do** vouloir qu'on fasse; **wanted**
adj (criminal) recherché(e) par la police;
"cook wanted" "on recherche un
cuisinier"

war [wɔːr] n guerre f; **to make ~ (on)**
faire la guerre (à)

ward [wɔːd] n (in hospital) salle f; (Pol)
section électorale; (Law: child: also: **~ of
court**) pupille m/f

warden ['wɔːdn] n (BRIT: of institution)
directeur(-trice); (of park, game reserve)
gardien(ne); (BRIT: also: **traffic ~**)
contractuel(le)

wardrobe ['wɔːdrəʊb] n (cupboard)
armoire f; (clothes) garde-robe f

warehouse ['wɛəhaʊs] n entrepôt m

warfare ['wɔːfɛər] n guerre f

warhead ['wɔːhɛd] n (Mil) ogive f

warm [wɔːm] adj chaud(e);
(person, thanks, welcome, applause)
chaleureux(-euse); **it's ~** il fait
chaud; **I'm ~** j'ai chaud; **warm up** vi
(person, room) se réchauffer; (athlete,
discussion) s'échauffer ▷ vt (food) (faire)
réchauffer; (water) (faire) chauffer;
(engine) faire chauffer; **warmly** adv
(dress) chaudement; (thank, welcome)
chaleureusement; **warmth** n chaleur f

warn [wɔːn] vt avertir, prévenir; **to ~
sb (not) to do** conseiller à qn de (ne
pas) faire; **warning** n avertissement
m; (notice) avis m; **warning light** n
avertisseur lumineux

warrant ['wɒrnt] n (guarantee) garantie
f; (Law: to arrest) mandat m d'arrêt;
(: to search) mandat de perquisition ▷ vt
(justify, merit) justifier

warranty ['wɒrəntɪ] n garantie f

warrior ['wɒrɪər] n guerrier(-ière)

Warsaw ['wɔːsɔː] n Varsovie

warship ['wɔːʃɪp] n navire m de guerre

wart [wɔːt] n verrue f

wartime ['wɔːtaɪm] n: **in ~** en temps

de guerre

wary ['wɛərɪ] adj prudent(e)

was [wɒz] pt of **be**

wash [wɒʃ] vt laver ▷ vi se laver; (sea): **to
~ over/against sth** inonder/baigner
qch ▷ n (clothes) lessive f; (washing
programme) lavage m; (of ship) sillage m;
to have a ~ se laver, faire sa toilette;
wash up vi (BRIT) faire la vaisselle;
(us: have a wash) se débarbouiller;
washbasin n lavabo m; **wash cloth** n
(us) gant m de toilette; **washer** n (Tech)
rondelle f, joint m; **washing** n (BRIT:
linen etc: dirty) linge m; (: clean) lessive f;
washing line n (BRIT) corde f à linge;
washing machine n machine f à laver;
washing powder n (BRIT) lessive f
(en poudre)

Washington ['wɒʃɪŋtən] n
Washington m

wash: washing-up n (BRIT) vaisselle f;
washing-up liquid n (BRIT) produit
m pour la vaisselle; **washroom** n (us)
toilettes fpl

wasn't ['wɒznt] = **was not**

wasp [wɒsp] n guêpe f

waste [weɪst] n gaspillage m; (of time)
perte f; (rubbish) déchets mpl; (also:
household ~) ordures fpl ▷ adj (land,
ground: in city) à l'abandon; (leftover):
~ material déchets ▷ vt gaspiller; (time,
opportunity) perdre; **waste ground** n
(BRIT) terrain m vague; **wastepaper
basket** n corbeille f à papier

watch [wɒtʃ] n montre f; (act of
watching) surveillance f; (guard: Mil)
sentinelle f; (Naut) homme m de quart;
(Naut: spell of duty) quart m ▷ vt (look at)
observer; (: match, programme) regarder;
(spy on, guard) surveiller; (be careful of)
faire attention à ▷ vi regarder; (keep
guard) monter la garde; **to keep ~** faire
le guet; **watch out** vi faire attention;
watchdog n chien m de garde; (fig)
gardien(ne); **watch strap** n bracelet
m de montre

water ['wɔːtər] n eau f ▷ vt (plant,
garden) arroser ▷ vi (eyes) larmoyer; **in**

British **~s** dans les eaux territoriales Britanniques; **to make sb's mouth ~** mettre l'eau à la bouche de qn; **water down** vt (milk etc) couper avec de l'eau; (fig: story) édulcorer; **watercolour** ou **watercolor** n aquarelle f; **watercress** n cresson m (de fontaine); **waterfall** n chute f d'eau; **watering can** n arrosoir m; **watermelon** n pastèque f; **waterproof** adj imperméable; **water-skiing** n ski m nautique

watt [wɔt] n watt m

wave [weɪv] n (of water) vague f; (of hand) geste m, signe m; (Radio) onde f; (in hair) ondulation f; (of enthusiasm, strikes etc) vague ▷ vi faire signe de la main; (flag) flotter au vent; (grass) ondoyer ▷ vt (handkerchief) agiter; (stick) brandir; **wavelength** n longueur f d'ondes

waver ['weɪvər] vi vaciller; (voice) trembler; (person) hésiter

wavy ['weɪvɪ] adj (hair, surface) ondulé(e); (line) onduleux(-euse)

wax [wæks] n cire f; (for skis) fart m ▷ vt cirer; (car) lustrer; (skis) farter ▷ vi (moon) croître

way [weɪ] n chemin m, voie f; (distance) distance f; (direction) chemin, direction f; (manner) manière f; (habit) habitude f, façon; **which ~?** - **this ~/that ~** par où or de quel côté? - par ici/par là; **to lose one's ~** perdre son chemin; **on the ~ (to)** en route (pour); **to be on one's ~** être en route; **to be in the ~** bloquer le passage; (fig) gêner; **it's a long ~** c'est loin d'ici; **to go out of one's ~ to do (fig)** se donner beaucoup de mal pour faire; **to be under ~** (work, project) être en cours; **in a ~** dans un sens; **by the ~** à propos; **"~ in"** (BRIT) "entrée"; **"~ out"** (BRIT) "sortie"; **the ~ back** le chemin du retour; **"give ~"** (BRIT Aut) "cédez le priorité"; **no ~! (inf)** pas question!

W.C. n abbr (BRIT: = water closet) w.-c. mpl, waters mpl

we [wi:] pl pron nous

weak [wi:k] adj faible; (health) fragile; (beam, structure) peu solide; (tea, coffee) léger(-ère); **weaken** vi faiblir ▷ vt affaiblir; **weakness** n faiblesse f; (fault) point m faible

wealth [welθ] n (money, resources) richesse(s) f(pl); (of details) profusion f; **wealthy** adj riche

weapon ['wepən] n arme f; **~s of mass destruction** armes fpl de destruction massive

wear [weər] n (use) usage m; (deterioration through use) usure f ▷ vb (pt wore, pp worn) ▷ vt (clothes) porter; (put on) mettre; (damage: through use) user ▷ vi (last) faire de l'usage; (rub etc through) s'user; **sports/baby-** vêtements mpl de sport/pour bébés; **evening ~** tenue f de soirée; **wear off** vi disparaître; **wear out** vt user; (person, strength) épuiser

weary ['wɪərɪ] adj (tired) épuisé(e); (dispirited) las(lasse), abattu(e) ▷ vi: **to ~ of** se lasser de

weasel ['wi:zl] n (Zool) belette f

weather ['weðər] n temps m ▷ vt (storm: lit, fig) essuyer; (crisis) survivre à; **under the ~** (fig: ill) mal fichu(e); **weather forecast** n prévisions fpl météorologiques, météo f; **weatherman** (irreg) n météorologue m

weave (pt wove, pp woven) [wi:v, wəʊv, 'wəʊvn] vt (cloth) tisser; (basket) tresser

web [web] n (of spider) toile f; (on duck's foot) palmure f; (fig) tissu m; (Comput): **the (World-Wide) W~** le Web; **web page** n (Comput) page f Web; **website** n (Comput) site m web

wed [wed] (pt, pp **~ded**) vt épouser ▷ vi se marier

Wed abbr (= Wednesday) me

we'd [wi:d] = we had; we would

wedding ['wedɪŋ] n mariage m; **wedding anniversary** n anniversaire m de mariage; **silver/golden wedding anniversary** noces fpl d'argent/d'or; **wedding day** n jour m du mariage; **wedding dress** n robe f de mariée;

wedding ring n alliance f
wedge [wedʒ] n (of wood etc) coin m; (under door etc) cale f; (of cake) part f ▷ vt (fix) caler; (push) enfoncer, coincer
Wednesday ['wednzdɪ] n mercredi m
wee [wiː] adj (SCOTTISH) petit(e); tout(e) petit(e)
weed [wiːd] n mauvaise herbe f ▷ vt désherber; **weedkiller** n désherbant m
week [wiːk] n semaine f; **a ~ today/on Tuesday** aujourd'hui/mardi en huit; **weekday** n jour m de semaine; (Comm) jour ouvrable; **weekend** n week-end m; **weekly** adv une fois par semaine, chaque semaine ▷ adj, n hebdomadaire m
weep [wiːp] (pt, pp **wept**) vi (person) pleurer
weigh [weɪ] vt, vi peser; **to ~ anchor** lever l'ancre; **weigh up** vt examiner
weight [weɪt] n poids m; **to put on/lose ~** grossir/maigrir; **weightlifting** n haltérophilie f
weir [wɪə*] n barrage m
weird [wɪəd] adj bizarre; (eerie) surnaturel(le)
welcome ['welkəm] adj bienvenu(e) ▷ n accueil m ▷ vt accueillir; (also: **bid ~**) souhaiter la bienvenue à; (be glad of) se réjouir de; **you're ~!** (after thanks) de rien, il n'y a pas de quoi
weld [weld] vt souder
welfare ['welfɛə*] n (wellbeing) bien-être m; (social aid) assistance sociale; **welfare state** n État-providence m
well [wel] n puits m ▷ adv bien ▷ adj: **to be ~** aller bien ▷ excl eh bien!; (relief also) bon!; (resignation) enfin!; **~ done!** bravo!; **get ~ soon!** remets-toi vite!; **to do ~** bien réussir; (business) prospérer; **as ~** (in addition) aussi, également; **as ~ as** aussi bien que or de; en plus de
we'll [wiːl] = **we will**; **we shall**
well: **well-behaved** adj sage, obéissant(e); **well-built** adj (person) bien bâti(e); **well-dressed** adj bien habillé(e), bien vêtu(e); **well-groomed** ['-'gruːmd] adj très

soigné(e)
wellies ['welɪz] (inf) npl (BRIT) = **wellingtons**
wellingtons ['welɪŋtənz] npl (also: **wellington boots**) bottes fpl en caoutchouc
well-known adj (person) bien connu(e); **well-off** adj aisé(e), assez riche; **well-paid** ['wel'peɪd] adj bien payé(e)
Welsh [welʃ] adj gallois(e) ▷ n (Ling) gallois m; **the Welsh** npl (people) les Gallois; **Welshman** (irreg) n Gallois m; **Welshwoman** (irreg) n Galloise f
went [went] pt of **go**
wept [wept] pt, pp of **weep**
were [wəː*] pt of **be**
we're [wɪə*] = **we are**
weren't [wəːnt] = **were not**
west [west] n ouest m ▷ adj (wind) d'ouest; (side) ouest inv ▷ adv à or vers l'ouest; **the W~** l'Occident m, l'Ouest; **westbound** ['westbaund] adj (traffic) en direction de l'ouest; (carriageway) ouest inv; **western** adj occidental(e), de or à l'ouest ▷ n (Cine) western m; **West Indian** adj antillais(e) ▷ n Antillais(e)
West Indies [-'ɪndɪz] npl Antilles fpl
wet [wet] adj mouillé(e); (damp) humide; (soaked: also: **~ through**) trempé(e); (rainy) pluvieux(-euse); **to get ~** se mouiller; "**~ paint**" "attention peinture fraîche"; **wetsuit** n combinaison f de plongée
we've [wiːv] = **we have**
whack [wæk] vt donner un grand coup à
whale [weɪl] n (Zool) baleine f
wharf (pl **wharves**) [wɔːf, wɔːvz] n quai m

 KEYWORD

what [wɔt] adj 1 (in questions) quel(le); **what size is he?** quelle taille fait-il?; **what colour is it?** de quelle couleur est-ce?; **what books do you need?**

quels livres vous faut-il?
2 (*in exclamations*): **what a mess!** quel désordre!; **what a fool I am!** que je suis bête!
▷ *pron* **1** (*interrogative*) que; de/à/en etc quoi; **what are you doing?** que faites-vous?, qu'est-ce que vous faites?; **what is happening?** qu'est-ce qui se passe?, que se passe-t-il?; **what are you talking about?** de quoi parlez-vous?; **what are you thinking about?** à quoi pensez-vous?; **what is it called?** comment est-ce que ça s'appelle?; **what about me?** et moi?; **what about doing ...?** et si on faisait ...?
2 (*relative: subject*) ce qui; (: *direct object*) ce que; (: *indirect object*) ce à quoi, ce dont; **I saw what you did/was on the table** j'ai vu ce que vous avez fait/ce qui était sur la table; **tell me what you remember** dites-moi ce dont vous vous souvenez; **what I want is a cup of tea** ce que je veux, c'est une tasse de thé
▷ *excl* (*disbelieving*) quoi!, comment!

whatever [wɔtˈɛvəʳ] *adj*: **take ~ book you prefer** prenez le livre que vous préférez, peu importe lequel; **~ book you take** quel que soit le livre que vous preniez ▷ *pron*: **do ~ is necessary** faites (tout) ce qui est nécessaire; **~ happens** quoi qu'il arrive; **no reason ~** *or* **whatsoever** pas la moindre raison; **nothing ~** *or* **whatsoever** rien du tout

whatsoever [wɔtsəʊˈɛvəʳ] *adj see* **whatever**

wheat [wiːt] *n* blé *m*, froment *m*

wheel [wiːl] *n* roue *f*; (*Aut: also*: **steering ~**) volant *m*; (*Naut*) gouvernail *m* ▷ *vt* (*pram etc*) pousser, rouler ▷ *vi* (*birds*) tournoyer; (*also*: **~ round: person**) se retourner, faire volte-face; **wheelbarrow** *n* brouette *f*; **wheelchair** *n* fauteuil roulant; **wheel clamp** *n* (*Aut*) sabot *m* (de Denver)

wheeze [wiːz] *vi* respirer bruyamment

🔑 **KEYWORD**

when [wɛn] *adv* quand; **when did he go?** quand est-ce qu'il est parti?
▷ *conj* **1** (*at, during, after the time that*) quand, lorsque; **she was reading when I came in** elle lisait quand *or* lorsque je suis entré
2 (*on, at which*): **on the day when I met him** le jour où je l'ai rencontré
3 (*whereas*) alors que; **I thought I was wrong when in fact I was right** j'ai cru que j'avais tort alors qu'en fait j'avais raison

whenever [wɛnˈɛvəʳ] *adv* quand donc
▷ *conj* quand; (*every time that*) chaque fois que

where [wɛəʳ] *adv, conj* où; **this is ~** c'est là que; **whereabouts** *adv* où donc ▷ *n*: **nobody knows his whereabouts** personne ne sait où il se trouve; **whereas** *conj* alors que; **whereby** *adv* (*formal*) par lequel (*or* laquelle *etc*); **wherever** *adv* où donc ▷ *conj* où que + *sub*; **sit wherever you like** asseyez-vous (là) où vous voulez

whether [ˈwɛðəʳ] *conj* si; **I don't know ~ to accept or not** je ne sais pas si je dois accepter ou non; **it's doubtful ~** il est peu probable que + *sub*; **~ you go or not** que vous y alliez ou non

🔑 **KEYWORD**

which [wɪtʃ] *adj* **1** (*interrogative: direct, indirect*) quel(le); **which picture do you want?** quel tableau voulez-vous?; **which one?** lequel (laquelle)?
2: in which case auquel cas; **we got there at 8pm, by which time the cinema was full** quand nous sommes arrivés à 20h, le cinéma était complet
▷ *pron* **1** (*interrogative*) lequel (laquelle),

lesquels (lesquelles) pl; **I don't mind
which** peu importe lequel; **which
(of these) are yours?** lesquels sont à
vous?; **tell me which you want**
dites-moi lesquels or ceux que vous
voulez

2 (relative: subject) qui; (: object) que;
sur/vers etc lequel (laquelle) (NB: à +
lequel = **auquel**; de + lequel = **duquel**);
**the apple which you ate/which is
on the table** la pomme que vous avez
mangée/qui est sur la table; **the
chair on which you are sitting** la
chaise sur laquelle vous êtes assis;
the book of which you spoke le livre
dont vous avez parlé; **he said he
knew, which is true/I was afraid
of** il a dit qu'il le savait, ce qui est
vrai/ce que je craignais; **after which**
après quoi

whichever [wɪtʃˈɛvəʳ] adj: **take ~ book
you prefer** prenez le livre que vous
préférez, peu importe lequel; **~ book
you take** quel que soit le livre que
vous preniez

while [waɪl] n moment m ▷ conj
pendant que; (as long as) tant que; (as,
whereas) alors que; (though) bien que
+ sub, quoique + sub; **for a ~** pendant
quelque temps; **in a ~** dans un
moment

whilst [waɪlst] conj = **while**

whim [wɪm] n caprice m

whine [waɪn] n gémissement m; (of
engine, siren) plainte stridente ▷ vi
gémir, geindre, pleurnicher; (dog,
engine, siren) gémir

whip [wɪp] n fouet m; (for riding)
cravache f; (Pol: person) chef m de file
(assurant la discipline dans son groupe
parlementaire) ▷ vt fouetter; (snatch)
enlever (or sortir) brusquement;
whipped cream n crème fouettée

whirl [wəːl] vi tournoyer; (dancers)
tournoyer ▷ vt faire tournoyer;
faire tourner

whisk [wɪsk] n (Culin) fouet m ▷ vt

(eggs) fouetter, battre; **to ~ sb away** or
off emmener qn rapidement

whiskers [ˈwɪskəz] npl (of animal)
moustaches fpl; (of man) favoris mpl

whisky (IRISH, US **whiskey**) [ˈwɪskɪ] n
whisky m

whisper [ˈwɪspəʳ] n chuchotement m
▷ vt, vi chuchoter

whistle [ˈwɪsl] n (sound) sifflement m;
(object) sifflet m ▷ vi siffler ▷ vt siffler,
siffloter

white [waɪt] adj blanc (blanche); (with
fear) blême ▷ n blanc m; (person) blanc
(blanche); **White House** n (us): **the
White House** la Maison-Blanche;
whitewash n (paint) lait m de chaux
▷ vt blanchir à la chaux; (fig) blanchir

whiting [ˈwaɪtɪŋ] n (pl inv: fish)
merlan m

Whitsun [ˈwɪtsn] n la Pentecôte

whittle [ˈwɪtl] vt: **to ~ away** or **~ down**
(costs) réduire, rogner

whizz [wɪz] vi aller (or passer) à toute
vitesse

who [huː] pron qui

whoever [huːˈɛvəʳ] pron: **~ finds it**
celui (celle) qui le trouve (, qui que ce
soit), quiconque le trouve; **ask ~ you
like** demandez à qui vous voulez; **~ he
marries** qui que ce soit or quelle que
soit la personne qu'il épouse; **~ told
you that?** qui a bien pu vous dire ça?,
qui donc vous a dit ça?

whole [həʊl] adj (complete)
entier(-ière), tout(e); (not broken)
intact(e), complet(-ète) ▷ n (all):
the ~ of la totalité de, tout(e) le (la);
(entire unit) tout m; **the ~ of the town**
la ville tout entière; **on the ~, as a
~** dans l'ensemble; **wholefood(s)** n(pl)
aliments complets; **wholeheartedly**
[həʊlˈhɑːtɪdlɪ] adv sans réserve;
to agree wholeheartedly être
entièrement d'accord; **wholemeal**
adj (BRIT: flour, bread) complet(-ète);
wholesale n (vente f en) gros m
▷ adj (price) de gros; (destruction)
systématique; **wholewheat**

adj = **wholemeal; wholly** adv entièrement, tout à fait

O **KEYWORD**

whom [huːm] pron **1** (interrogative) qui; **whom did you see?** qui avez-vous vu?; **to whom did you give it?** à qui l'avez-vous donné?

2 (relative) que; à/de etc qui; **the man whom I saw/to whom I spoke** l'homme que j'ai vu/à qui j'ai parlé

whore [hɔːʳ] n (inf: pej) putain f

O **KEYWORD**

whose [huːz] adj **1** (possessive: interrogative): **whose book is this?**, **whose is this book?** à qui est ce livre?; **whose pencil have you taken?** à qui est le crayon que vous avez pris?, c'est le crayon de qui de vous avez pris?; **whose daughter are you?** de qui êtes-vous la fille?

2 (possessive: relative): **the man whose son you rescued** l'homme dont or de qui vous avez sauvé le fils; **the girl whose sister you were speaking to** la fille à la sœur de qui or de laquelle vous parliez; **the woman whose car was stolen** la femme dont la voiture a été volée

▷ pron à qui; **whose is this?** à qui est ceci?; **I know whose it is** je sais à qui c'est

O **KEYWORD**

why [waɪ] adv pourquoi; **why not?** pourquoi pas?

▷ conj: **I wonder why he said that** je me demande pourquoi il a dit ça; **that's not why I'm here** ce n'est pas pour ça que je suis là; **the reason why** la raison pour laquelle

▷ excl eh bien!, tiens!; **why, it's**

you! tiens, c'est vous!; **why, that's impossible!** voyons, c'est impossible!

wicked ['wɪkɪd] adj méchant(e); (mischievous: grin, look) espiègle, malicieux(-euse); (crime) pervers(e); (inf: very good) génial(e) (inf)

wicket ['wɪkɪt] n (Cricket: stumps) guichet m; (: grass area) espace compris entre les deux guichets

wide [waɪd] adj large; (area, knowledge) vaste, très étendu(e); (choice) grand(e)
▷ adv: **to open** ~ ouvrir tout grand; **to shoot** ~ tirer à côté; **it is 3 metres** ~ cela fait 3 mètres de large; **widely** adv (different) radicalement; (spaced) sur une grande étendue; (believed) généralement; (travelled) beaucoup; **widen** vt élargir ▷ vi s'élargir; **wide open** adj grand(e) ouvert(e); **widespread** adj (belief etc) très répandu(e)

widow ['wɪdəu] n veuve f; **widower** n veuf m

width [wɪdθ] n largeur f

wield [wiːld] vt (sword) manier; (power) exercer

wife (pl **wives**) [waɪf, waɪvz] n femme f, épouse f

wig [wɪg] n perruque f

wild [waɪld] adj sauvage; (sea) déchaîné(e); (idea, life) fou (folle); (behaviour) déchaîné(e), extravagant(e); (inf: angry) hors de soi, furieux(-euse)
▷ n: **the** ~ la nature; **wilderness** ['wɪldənɪs] n désert m, région f sauvage; **wildlife** n faune f (et flore f); **wildly** adv (behave) de manière déchaînée; (applaud) frénétiquement; (hit, guess) au hasard; (happy) follement

O **KEYWORD**

will [wɪl] aux vb **1** (forming future tense): **I will finish it tomorrow** je le finirai demain; **I will have finished it by tomorrow** je l'aurai fini d'ici demain; **will you do it? – yes I will/no I won't**

ferez-vous? – oui/non

2 (in conjectures, predictions): **he will** or **he'll be there by now** il doit être arrivé à l'heure qu'il est; **that will be the postman** ça doit être le facteur

3 (in commands, requests, offers): **will you be quiet!** voulez-vous bien vous taire!; **will you help me?** est-ce que vous pouvez m'aider?; **will you have a cup of tea?** voulez-vous une tasse de thé?; **I won't put up with it!** je ne le tolérerai pas!

▷ vt (pt, pp **willed**): **to will sb to do** souhaiter ardemment que qn fasse; **he willed himself to go on** par un suprême effort de volonté, il continua ▷ n volonté f; (document) testament m; **against one's will** à contre-cœur

willing ['wɪlɪŋ] adj de bonne volonté, serviable; **he's ~ to do it** il est disposé à le faire, il veut bien le faire; **willingly** adv volontiers

willow ['wɪləʊ] n saule m

willpower ['wɪl'paʊə'] n volonté f

wilt [wɪlt] vi dépérir

win [wɪn] n (in sports etc) victoire f ▷ vb (pt, pp **won**) ▷ vt (battle, money) gagner; (prize, contract) remporter; (popularity) acquérir ▷ vi gagner; **win over**, **win round** vt convaincre

wince [wɪns] vi tressaillir

winch [wɪntʃ] n treuil m

wind¹ [wɪnd] n (also Med) vent m; (breath) souffle m ▷ vt (take breath away) couper le souffle à; **the ~(s)** (Mus) les instruments mpl à vent

wind² [waɪnd] (pt, pp **wound**) vt enrouler; (wrap) envelopper; (clock, toy) remonter ▷ vi (road, river) serpenter; **wind down** vt (car window) baisser; (fig: production, business) réduire progressivement; **wind up** vt (clock) remonter; (debate) terminer, clôturer

windfall ['wɪndfɔːl] n coup m de chance

winding ['waɪndɪŋ] adj (road) sinueux(-euse); (staircase) tournant(e)

windmill ['wɪndmɪl] n moulin m à vent

window ['wɪndəʊ] n fenêtre f; (in car, train: also: **~-pane**) vitre f; (in shop etc) vitrine f; **window box** n jardinière f; **window cleaner** n (person) laveur(-euse) de vitres; **window pane** n vitre f, carreau m; **window seat** n (in vehicle) place f côté fenêtre; **windowsill** n (inside) appui m de la fenêtre; (outside) rebord m de la fenêtre

windscreen ['wɪndskriːn] n pare-brise m inv; **windscreen wiper** n essuie-glace m inv

windshield ['wɪndʃiːld] (us) n = **windscreen**

windsurfing ['wɪndsɜːfɪŋ] n planche f à voile

windy ['wɪndɪ] adj (day) de vent, venteux(-euse); (place, weather) venteux; **it's ~** il y a du vent

wine [waɪn] n vin m; **wine bar** n bar m à vin; **wine glass** n verre m à vin; **wine list** n carte f des vins; **wine tasting** n dégustation f (de vins)

wing [wɪŋ] n aile f; **wings** npl (Theat) coulisses fpl; **wing mirror** n (BRIT) rétroviseur latéral

wink [wɪŋk] n clin m d'œil ▷ vi faire un clin d'œil; (blink) cligner des yeux

winner ['wɪnə'] n gagnant(e)

winning ['wɪnɪŋ] adj (team) gagnant(e); (goal) décisif(-ive); (charming) charmeur(-euse)

winter ['wɪntə'] n hiver m ▷ vi hiverner; **in ~** en hiver; **winter sports** npl sports mpl d'hiver; **wintertime** n hiver m

wipe [waɪp] n: **to give sth a ~** donner un coup de torchon/de chiffon/d'éponge à qch ▷ vt essuyer; (erase: tape) effacer; **to ~ one's nose** se moucher; **wipe out** vt (debt) éteindre, amortir; (memory) effacer; (destroy) anéantir; **wipe up** vt essuyer

wire ['waɪə'] n fil m (de fer); (Elec) fil électrique; (Tel) télégramme m ▷ vt (house) faire l'installation électrique de; (also: **~ up**) brancher; (person: send telegram to) télégraphier à

wiring ['waɪərɪŋ] n (Elec) installation f électrique

wisdom ['wɪzdəm] n sagesse f; (of action) prudence f; **wisdom tooth** n dent f de sagesse

wise [waɪz] adj sage, prudent(e); (remark) judicieux(-euse)

wish [wɪʃ] n (desire) désir m; (specific desire) souhait m, vœu m ▷ vt souhaiter, désirer, vouloir; **best ~es** (on birthday etc) meilleurs vœux; **with best ~es** (in letter) bien amicalement; **to ~ sb goodbye** dire au revoir à qn; **he ~ed me well** il m'a souhaité bonne chance; **to ~ to do/sb to do** désirer or vouloir faire/que qn fasse; **to ~ for** souhaiter

wistful ['wɪstful] adj mélancolique

wit [wɪt] n (also: **~s**: intelligence) intelligence f, esprit m; (presence of mind): présence f d'esprit; (wittiness) esprit; (person) homme/femme d'esprit

witch [wɪtʃ] n sorcière f

with [wɪð, wɪθ] prep 1 (in the company of) avec; (at the home of) chez; **we stayed with friends** nous avons logé chez des amis; **I'll be with you in a minute** je suis à vous dans un instant

2 (descriptive): **a room with a view** une chambre avec vue; **the man with the grey hat/blue eyes** l'homme au chapeau gris/aux yeux bleus

3 (indicating manner, means, cause): **with tears in her eyes** les larmes aux yeux; **to walk with a stick** marcher avec une canne; **red with anger** rouge de colère; **to shake with fear** trembler de peur; **to fill sth with water** remplir qch d'eau

4 (in phrases): **I'm with you** (I understand) je vous suis; **to be with it** (inf: up-to-date) être dans le vent

withdraw [wɪð'drɔː] vt (irreg: like draw) retirer ▷ vi se retirer; **withdrawal** n retrait m; (Med) état m de manque

withdrawn pp of **withdraw** ▷ adj (person) renfermé(e)

withdrew [wɪð'druː] pt of **withdraw**

wither ['wɪðə*] vi se faner

withhold [wɪð'həuld] vt (irreg: like hold) (money) retenir; (decision) remettre; (permission): **to ~ (from)** refuser (à); (information): **to ~ (from)** cacher (à)

within [wɪð'ɪn] prep à l'intérieur de ▷ adv à l'intérieur; **~ his reach** à sa portée; **~ sight of** en vue de; **~ a mile of** à moins d'un mille de; **~ the week** avant la fin de la semaine

without [wɪð'aut] prep sans; **~ a coat** sans manteau; **~ speaking** sans parler; **to go or do ~ sth** se passer de qch

withstand [wɪð'stænd] vt (irreg: like stand) résister à

witness ['wɪtnɪs] n (person) témoin m ▷ vt (event) être témoin de; (document) attester l'authenticité de; **to bear ~ to sth** témoigner de qch

witty ['wɪtɪ] adj spirituel(le), plein(e) d'esprit

wives [waɪvz] npl of **wife**

wizard ['wɪzəd] n magicien m

wk abbr = **week**

wobble ['wɔbl] vi trembler; (chair) branler

woe [wəu] n malheur m

woke [wəuk] pt of **wake**

woken ['wəukn] pp of **wake**

wolf (pl **wolves**) [wulf, wulvz] n loup m

woman (pl **women**) ['wumən, 'wɪmɪn] n femme f ▷ cpd: **~ doctor** femme f médecin; **~ teacher** professeur m femme

womb [wuːm] n (Anat) utérus m

women ['wɪmɪn] npl of **woman**

won [wʌn] pt, pp of **win**

wonder ['wʌndə*] n merveille f, miracle m; (feeling) émerveillement m ▷ vi: **to ~ whether/why** se demander si/pourquoi; **to ~ at** (surprise) s'étonner de; (admiration) s'émerveiller de; **to ~ about** songer à; **it's no ~ that** il n'est pas étonnant que + sub; **wonderful** adj merveilleux(-euse)

won't [wəʊnt] = **will not**

wood [wʊd] n (timber, forest) bois m;
wooden adj en bois; (fig: actor) raide;
(: performance) qui manque de naturel;
woodwind n: **the woodwind** (Mus) les
bois mpl; **woodwork** n menuiserie f

wool [wʊl] n laine f; **to pull the ~ over
sb's eyes** (fig) en faire accroire à qn;
woollen (us **woolen**) adj de or en laine;
woolly (us **wooly**) adj laineux(-euse);
(fig: ideas) confus(e)

word [wəːd] n mot m; (spoken) mot,
parole f; (promise) parole; (news)
nouvelles fpl ▷ vt rédiger, formuler; **in
other ~s** en d'autres termes; **to have
a ~ with sb** toucher un mot à qn; **to
break/keep one's ~** manquer à sa
parole/tenir (sa) parole; **wording** n
termes mpl, langage m; (of document)
libellé m; **word processing** n
traitement m de texte; **word processor**
n machine f de traitement de texte

wore [wɔːʳ] pt of **wear**

work [wəːk] n travail m; (Art, Literature)
œuvre f ▷ vi travailler; (mechanism)
marcher, fonctionner; (plan etc)
marcher; (medicine) agir ▷ vt (clay,
wood etc) travailler; (mine etc) exploiter;
(machine) faire marcher or fonctionner;
(miracles etc) faire; **works** n (BRIT:
factory) usine f; **how does this ~?**
comment est-ce que ça marche?; **the
TV isn't ~ing** la télévision est en
panne or ne marche pas; **to be out of
~** être au chômage or sans emploi; **to
~ loose** se défaire, se desserrer; **work
out** vi (plans etc) marcher; (Sport)
s'entraîner ▷ vt (problem) résoudre;
(plan) élaborer; **it ~s out at £100** ça fait
100 livres; **worker** n travailleur(-euse),
ouvrier(-ière); **work experience** n
stage m; **workforce** n main-d'œuvre f;
working class n classe ouvrière ▷ adj:
working-class ouvrier(-ière), de la
classe ouvrière; **working week** n
semaine f de travail; **workman** (irreg)
n ouvrier m; **work of art** n œuvre

f d'art; **workout** n (Sport) séance
f d'entraînement; **work permit** n
permis m de travail; **workplace** n lieu
m de travail; **worksheet** n (Scol) feuille
f d'exercices; **workshop** n atelier m;
work station n poste m de travail;
work surface n plan m de travail;
worktop n plan m de travail

world [wəːld] n monde m ▷ cpd
(champion) du monde; (power, war)
mondial(e); **to think the ~ of sb** (fig)
ne jurer que par qn; **World Cup** n:
the World Cup (Football) la Coupe du
monde; **world-wide** adj universel(le);
World-Wide Web n: **the World-Wide
Web** le Web

worm [wəːm] n (also: **earth~**) ver m

worn [wɔːn] pp of **wear** adj usé(e);
worn-out adj (object) complètement
usé(e); (person) épuisé(e)

worried [ˈwʌrɪd] adj inquiet(-ète); **to
be ~ about sth** être inquiet au sujet
de qch

worry [ˈwʌrɪ] n souci m ▷ vt inquiéter
▷ vi s'inquiéter, se faire du souci;
worrying adj inquiétant(e)

worse [wəːs] adj pire, plus mauvais(e)
▷ adv plus mal ▷ n pire m; **to get
~** (condition, situation) empirer,
se dégrader; **a change for the** ~
une détérioration; **worsen** vt, vi
empirer; **worse off** adj moins à l'aise
financièrement; (fig): **you'll be worse
off this way** ça ira moins bien de
cette façon

worship [ˈwəːʃɪp] n culte m ▷ vt (God)
rendre un culte à; (person) adorer

worst [wəːst] adj le (la) pire, le (la) plus
mauvais(e) ▷ adv le plus mal ▷ n pire
m; **at ~** au pis aller

worth [wəːθ] n valeur f ▷ adj: **to be ~**
valoir; **it's ~ it** cela en vaut la peine,
ça vaut la peine; **it is ~ one's while
(to do)** ça vaut le coup (inf) (de faire);
worthless adj qui ne vaut rien;
worthwhile adj (activity) qui en vaut la
peine; (cause) louable

worthy [ˈwəːðɪ] adj (person) digne;

(motive) louable; **~ of** digne de

⭕ **KEYWORD**

would [wud] *aux vb* **1** *(conditional tense)*:
if you asked him he would do it si
vous le lui demandiez, il le ferait; **if
you had asked him he would have
done it** si vous le lui aviez demandé, il
l'aurait fait
2 *(in offers, invitations, requests)*: **would
you like a biscuit?** voulez-vous un
biscuit?; **would you close the door
please?** voulez-vous fermer la porte,
s'il vous plaît?
3 *(in indirect speech)*: **I said I would do it**
j'ai dit que je le ferais
4 *(emphatic)*: **it WOULD have to
snow today!** naturellement il neige
aujourd'hui! or il fallait qu'il neige
aujourd'hui!
5 *(insistence)*: **she wouldn't do it** elle
n'a pas voulu or elle a refusé de le faire
6 *(conjecture)*: **it would have been
midnight** il devait être minuit; **it
would seem so** on dirait bien
7 *(indicating habit)*: **he would go there
on Mondays** il y allait le lundi

wouldn't ['wudnt] = **would not**
wound¹ [wu:nd] *n* blessure *f* ▷ *vt*
blesser
wound² [waund] *pt, pp of* **wind**
wove [wəuv] *pt of* **weave**
woven ['wəuvn] *pp of* **weave**
wrap [ræp] *vt (also:* ~ **up)** envelopper;
(parcel) emballer; *(wind)* enrouler;
wrapper *n (on chocolate etc)* papier *m*;
(BRIT: of book) couverture *f*; **wrapping
paper** *n (of sweet, chocolate)* papier *m*;
(of parcel) emballage *m*; **wrapping paper**
n papier *m* d'emballage; *(for gift)* papier
cadeau
wreath [ri:θ, *pl* ri:ðz] *n* couronne *f*
wreck [rɛk] *n (sea disaster)* naufrage
m; *(ship)* épave *f*; *(vehicle)* véhicule
accidenté; *(pej: person)* loque
(humaine) ▷ *vt* démolir; *(fig)* briser,

ruiner; **wreckage** *n* débris *mpl*; *(of
building)* décombres *mpl*; *(of ship)*
naufrage *m*
wren [rɛn] *n (Zool)* troglodyte *m*
wrench [rɛntʃ] *n (Tech)* clé *f* (à
écrous); *(tug)* violent mouvement de
torsion; *(fig)* déchirement *m* ▷ *vt* tirer
violemment sur, tordre; **to ~ sth from**
arracher qch *(violemment)* à or de
wrestle ['rɛsl] *vi*: **to ~ (with sb)** lutter
(avec qn); **wrestler** *n* lutteur(-euse);
wrestling *n* lutte *f*; *(also:* **all-in
wrestling**: *BRIT)* catch *m*
wretched ['rɛtʃɪd] *adj* misérable
wriggle ['rɪgl] *vi (also:* ~ **about)** se
tortiller
wring *(pt, pp* **wrung)** [rɪŋ, rʌŋ] *vt*
tordre; *(wet clothes)* essorer; *(fig)*: **to ~
sth out of** arracher qch à
wrinkle ['rɪŋkl] *n (on skin)* ride *f*; *(on
paper etc)* pli *m* ▷ *vt* rider, plisser ▷ *vi*
se plisser
wrist [rɪst] *n* poignet *m*
write *(pt* **wrote,** *pp* **written)** [raɪt, rəut,
'rɪtn] *vt, vi* écrire; *(prescription)* rédiger;
write down *vt* noter; *(put in writing)*
mettre par écrit; **write off** *vt (debt)*
passer aux profits et pertes; *(project)*
mettre une croix sur; *(smash up: car etc)*
démolir complètement; **write out**
vt écrire; *(copy)* recopier; **write-off** *n*
perte totale; **the car is a write-off** la
voiture est bonne pour la casse; **writer**
n auteur *m*, écrivain *m*
writing ['raɪtɪŋ] *n* écriture *f*; *(of author)*
œuvres *fpl*; **in ~** par écrit; **writing paper**
n papier *m* à lettres
written ['rɪtn] *pp of* **write**
wrong [rɔŋ] *adj (incorrect)* faux
(fausse); *(incorrectly chosen: number,
road etc)* mauvais(e); *(not suitable)* qui
ne convient pas; *(wicked)* mal; *(unfair)*
injuste ▷ *adv* mal ▷ *n* tort *m* ▷ *vt* faire
du tort à, léser; **you are ~ to do it** tu as
tort de le faire; **you are ~ about that,
you've got it ~** tu te trompes; **what's
~?** qu'est-ce qui ne va pas?; **what's ~
with the car?** qu'est-ce qu'elle a, la

voiture?; **to go ~** (person) se tromper; (plan) mal tourner; (machine) se détraquer; **I took a ~ turning** je me suis trompé de route; **wrongly** adv à tort; (answer, do, count) mal, incorrectement; **wrong number** n (Tel): **you have the wrong number** vous vous êtes trompé de numéro

wrote [rəut] pt of **write**

wrung [rʌŋ] pt, pp of **wring**

WWW n abbr = **World-Wide Web**; **the ~** le Web

XL abbr (= extra large) XL

Xmas ['eksməs] n abbr = **Christmas**

X-ray ['eksreɪ] n (ray) rayon m X; (photograph) radio(graphie) f ▷ vt radiographier

xylophone ['zaɪləfəun] n xylophone m

y

yacht [jɔt] *n* voilier *m*; *(motor, luxury yacht)* yacht *m*; **yachting** *n* yachting *m*, navigation *f* de plaisance

yard [jɑːd] *n (of house etc)* cour *f*; *(us: garden)* jardin *m*; *(measure)* yard *m* (= 914 *mm*; 3 *feet)*; **yard sale** *n (us)* brocante *f* (dans son propre jardin)

yarn [jɑːn] *n* fil *m*; *(tale)* longue histoire

yawn [jɔːn] *n* bâillement *m* ▷ *vi* bâiller

yd. *abbr* = **yard(s)**

yeah [jɛə] *adv (inf)* ouais

year [jɪə'] *n* an *m*, année *f*; *(Scol etc)* année; **to be 8 ~s old** avoir 8 ans; **an eight-~-old child** un enfant de huit ans; **yearly** *adj* annuel(le) ▷ *adv* annuellement; **twice yearly** deux fois par an

yearn [jəːn] *vi*: **to ~ for sth/to do** aspirer à qch/à faire

yeast [jiːst] *n* levure *f*

yell [jɛl] *n* hurlement *m*, cri *m* ▷ *vi* hurler

yellow [ˈjɛləʊ] *adj, n* jaune (*m*); **Yellow Pages®** *npl (Tel)* pages *fpl* jaunes

yes [jɛs] *adv* oui; *(answering negative question)* si ▷ *n* oui *m*; **to say ~ (to)** dire oui (à)

yesterday [ˈjɛstədɪ] *adv, n* hier (*m*); **~ morning/evening** hier matin/soir; **all day ~** toute la journée d'hier

yet [jɛt] *adv* encore; *(in questions)* déjà ▷ *conj* pourtant, néanmoins; **it is not finished** – ce n'est pas encore fini *or* toujours pas fini; **have you eaten ~?** vous avez déjà mangé?; **the best ~** le meilleur jusqu'ici *or* jusque-là; **as ~** jusqu'ici, encore

yew [juː] *n* if *m*

Yiddish [ˈjɪdɪʃ] *n* yiddish *m*

yield [jiːld] *n* production *f*, rendement *m*; *(Finance)* rapport *m* ▷ *vt* produire, rendre, rapporter; *(surrender)* céder ▷ *vi* céder; *(us Aut)* céder la priorité

yob(bo) [ˈjɔb(əʊ)] *n* (BRIT *inf*) loubar(d) *m*

yoga [ˈjəʊɡə] *n* yoga *m*

yog(h)ourt *n* = **yog(h)urt**

yog(h)urt [ˈjɔɡət] *n* yaourt *m*

yolk [jəʊk] *n* jaune *m* (d'œuf)

⭕ KEYWORD

you [juː] *pron* **1** *(subject)* tu; *(polite form)* vous; *(plural)* vous; **you are very kind** vous êtes très gentil; **you French enjoy your food** vous autres Français, vous aimez bien manger; **you and I will go** toi et moi *or* vous et moi, nous irons; **there you are!** vous voilà!
2 *(object: direct, indirect)* te, t' + *vowel*; vous; **I know you** je te *or* vous connais; **I gave it to you** je te l'ai donné, je vous l'ai donné
3 *(stressed)* toi; vous; **I told YOU to do it** c'est à toi *or* vous que j'ai dit de le faire
4 *(after prep, in comparisons)* toi; vous; **it's for you** c'est pour toi *or* vous; **she's younger than you** elle est plus jeune que toi *or* vous
5 *(impersonal: one)* on; **fresh air does you good** l'air frais fait du bien; **you**

never know on ne sait jamais; **you can't do that!** ça ne se fait pas!

you'd [juːd] = **you had; you would**

you'll [juːl] = **you will; you shall**

young [jʌŋ] *adj* jeune ▷ *npl* (*of animal*) petits *mpl*; (*people*): **the ~** les jeunes, la jeunesse; **my ~er brother** mon frère cadet; **youngster** *n* jeune *m/f*; (*child*) enfant *m/f*

your [jɔːʳ] *adj* ton (ta), tes *pl*; (*polite form, pl*) votre, vos *pl*; *see also* **my**

you're [juəʳ] = **you are**

yours [jɔːz] *pron* le (la) tien(ne), les tiens (tiennes); (*polite form, pl*) le (la) vôtre, les vôtres; **is it ~?** c'est à toi (*or* à vous)?; **a friend of ~** un(e) de tes (*or* de vos) amis; *see also* **faithfully; mine¹; sincerely**

yourself [jɔːˈsɛlf] *pron* (*reflexive*) te; (: *polite form*) vous; (*after prep*) toi; vous; (*emphatic*) toi-même; vous-même; *see also* **oneself**; **yourselves** *pl pron* vous; (*emphatic*) vous-mêmes; *see also* **oneself**

youth [juːθ] *n* jeunesse *f*; (*young man*) (*pl* **-s**) jeune homme *m*; **youth club** *n* centre *m* de jeunes; **youthful** *adj* jeune; (*enthusiasm etc*) juvénile; **youth hostel** *n* auberge *f* de jeunesse

you've [juːv] = **you have**

Yugoslav [ˈjuːɡəʊslɑːv] *adj* yougoslave ▷ *n* Yougoslave *m/f*

Yugoslavia [juːɡəʊˈslɑːvɪə] *n* (*Hist*) Yougoslavie *f*

Z

zeal [ziːl] *n* (*revolutionary etc*) ferveur *f*; (*keenness*) ardeur *f*, zèle *m*

zebra [ˈziːbrə] *n* zèbre *m*; **zebra crossing** *n* (*BRIT*) passage clouté *or* pour piétons

zero [ˈzɪərəʊ] *n* zéro *m*

zest [zɛst] *n* entrain *m*, élan *m*; (*of lemon etc*) zeste *m*

zigzag [ˈzɪɡzæɡ] *n* zigzag *m* ▷ *vi* zigzaguer, faire des zigzags

Zimbabwe [zɪmˈbɑːbwɪ] *n* Zimbabwe *m*

zinc [zɪŋk] *n* zinc *m*

zip [zɪp] *n* (*also*: **- fastener**) fermeture *f* éclair® *or* à glissière ▷ *vt* (*file*) (*also*: **- up**) fermer (avec une fermeture éclair®); **zip code** *n* (*US*) code postal; **zip file** *n* (*Comput*) fichier *m* zip *inv*; **zipper** *n* (*US*) = **zip**

zit [zɪt] (*inf*) *n* bouton *m*

zodiac [ˈzəʊdɪæk] *n* zodiaque *m*

zone [zəʊn] *n* zone *f*

zoo [zuː] *n* zoo *m*

zoology [zuːˈɒlədʒɪ] *n* zoologie *f*

zoom [zu:m] *vi:* **to ~ past** passer en
trombe; **zoom lens** *n* zoom *m*
zucchini [zu:ˈkiːnɪ] *n(pl)* (us)
courgette(s) *f(pl)*

Phrasefinder

Phrases utiles

TOPICS | THEMES

TOPICS | THEMES

Good evening!	Bonsoir!
Good night!	Bonne nuit!
Goodbye!	Au revoir!
What's your name?	Comment vous appelez-vous?
My name is ...	Je m'appelle ...
This is ...	Je vous présente ...
my wife.	ma femme.
my husband.	mon mari.
my partner.	mon compagnon/ma compagne.
Where are you from?	D'où venez-vous?
I come from ...	Je suis de ...
How are you?	Comment allez-vous?
Fine, thanks.	Bien, merci.
And you?	Et vous?
Do you speak English?	Parlez-vous anglais?
I don't understand French.	Je ne comprends pas le français.
Thanks very much!	Merci beaucoup!

Asking the Way | Demander son chemin

Where is the nearest …?	Où est le/la … le/la plus proche?
How do I get to …?	Comment est-ce qu'on va à/au/à la …?
Is it far?	Est-ce que c'est loin?
How far is it from here?	C'est à combien d'ici?
Is this the right way to …?	C'est la bonne direction pour aller à/au/à la …?
I'm lost.	Je suis perdu.
Can you show me on the map?	Pouvez-vous me le montrer sur la carte?
You have to turn round.	Vous devez faire demi-tour.
Go straight on.	Allez tout droit.
Turn left/right.	Tournez à gauche/à droite.
Take the second street on the left/right.	Prenez la deuxième rue à gauche/à droite.

Car Hire | Location de voitures

I want to hire …	Je voudrais louer …
a car.	*une voiture.*
a moped.	*une mobylette.*
a motorbike.	*une moto.*
How much is it for …?	C'est combien pour …?
one day	*une journée*
a week	*une semaine*
What is included in the price?	Qu'est-ce qui est inclus dans le prix?
I'd like a child seat for a …-year-old child.	Je voudrais un siège-auto pour un enfant de … ans.
What do I do if I have an accident/if I break down?	Que dois-je faire en cas d'accident/de panne?

Breakdowns — Pannes

My car has broken down.	Je suis en panne.
Where is the next garage?	Où est le garage le plus proche?
The exhaust	Le pot d'échappement
The gearbox	La boîte de vitesse
The windscreen	Le pare-brise
… is broken.	… est cassé(e).
The brakes	Les freins
The headlights	Les phares
The windscreen wipers	Les essuie-glace
… are not working.	… ne fonctionnent pas.
The battery is flat.	La batterie est à plat.
The car won't start.	Le moteur ne démarre pas.
The engine is overheating.	Le moteur surchauffe.
I have a flat tyre.	J'ai un pneu à plat.
Can you repair it?	Pouvez-vous le réparer?
When will the car be ready?	Quand est-ce que la voiture sera prête?

Parking — Stationnement

Can I park here?	Je peux me garer ici?
Do I need to buy a (car-parking) ticket?	Est-ce qu'il faut acheter un ticket de stationnement?
Where is the ticket machine?	Où est l'horodateur?
The ticket machine isn't working.	L'horodateur ne fonctionne pas.

Petrol Station — Station service

Where is the nearest petrol station?	Où est la station service la plus proche?
Fill it up, please.	Le plein, s'il vous plaît.

30 euros' worth of...	30 euros de ...
diesel.	*diesel.*
(unleaded) economy petrol.	*sans plomb.*
premium unleaded.	*super.*
Pump number ... please.	Pompe numéro ..., s'il vous plaît.
Please check ...	Pouvez-vous vérifier ...
the tyre pressure.	*la pression des pneus?*
the oil.	*le niveau de l'huile?*
the water.	*le niveau de l'eau?*

Accident | Accidents

Please call ...	Appelez ..., s'il vous plaît.
the police.	*la police*
an ambulance.	*une ambulance*
Here are my insurance details.	Voici les références de mon assurance.
Give me your insurance details, please.	Donnez-moi les références de votre assurance , s'il vous plaît.
Can you be a witness for me?	Pouvez-vous me servir de témoin?
You were driving too fast.	Vous conduisiez trop vite.
It wasn't your right of way.	Vous n'aviez pas la priorité.

Travelling by Car | Voyager en voiture

What's the best route to ...?	Quel est le meilleur chemin pour aller à ...?
I'd like a motorway tax sticker ...	Je voudrais une vignette de péage ...
for a week.	*pour une semaine.*
for a year.	*pour un an.*
Do you have a road map of this area?	Avez-vous une carte de la région?

Cycling · À vélo

Where is the cycle path to …?	Où est la piste cyclable pour aller à …?
Can I keep my bike here?	Est-ce que je peux laisser mon vélo ici?
My bike has been stolen.	On m'a volé mon vélo.
Where is the nearest bike repair shop?	Où se trouve le réparateur de vélos le plus proche?
The brakes	Les freins
The gears	Les vitesses
… aren't working.	… ne marchent pas.
The chain is broken.	La chaîne est cassée.
I've got a flat tyre.	J'ai une crevaison.
I need a puncture repair kit.	J'ai besoin d'un kit de réparation.

Train · En train

How much is …?	Combien coûte …?
a single	un aller simple
a return	un aller-retour
A single to …, please.	Un aller simple pour …, s'il vous plaît.
I would like to travel first/second class.	Je voudrais voyager en première/seconde classe.
Two returns to …, please.	Deux allers-retours pour …, s'il vous plaît.
Is there a reduction …?	Il y a un tarif réduit …?
for students	pour les étudiants
for pensioners	pour les seniors
for children	pour les enfants
with this pass	avec cette carte

I'd like to reserve a seat on the train to … please.	Je voudrais faire une réservation pour le train qui va à …, s'il vous plaît.
Non smoking/smoking, please.	Non-fumeurs/Fumeurs, s'il vous plaît.
I want to book a sleeper to …	Je voudrais réserver une couchette pour …
When is the next train to …?	À quelle heure part le prochain train pour …?
Is there a supplement to pay?	Est-ce qu'il faut payer un supplément?
Do I need to change?	Est-ce qu'il y a un changement?
Where do I change?	Où est-ce qu'il faut changer?
Which platform does the train for … leave trom?	De quel quai part le train pour …?
Is this the train for …?	C'est bien le train pour …?
Excuse me, that's my seat.	Excusez-moi, c'est ma place.
I have a reservation.	J'ai réservé.
Is this seat free?	La place est libre?
Please let me know when we get to …	Pourriez-vous me prévenir lorsqu'on arrivera à …?
Where is the buffet car?	Où est la voiture-bar?
Where is coach number …?	Où est la voiture numéro …?

Ferry | En ferry

Is there a ferry to …?	Est-ce qu'il y a un ferry pour …?
When is the next/first/last ferry to …?	Quand part le prochain/premier/dernier ferry pour …?
How much is it for a camper/car with … people?	Combien coûte la traversée pour un camping-car/une voiture avec … personnes?

How long does the crossing take?	Combien de temps dure la traversée?
Where is …?	Où est …?
the restaurant	*le restaurant*
the bar	*le bar*
the duty-free shop	*le magasin hors-taxe*
Where is cabin number …?	Où est la cabine numéro …?
Do you have anything for seasickness?	Avez-vous quelque chose pour le mal de mer?

Plane   En avion

Where is …?	Où est …?
the taxi rank	*la station de taxis*
the bus stop	*l'arrêt de bus*
the information office	*le bureau de renseignements*
Where do I check in for the flight to …?	Où dois-je enregistrer pour le vol pour …?
Which gate for the flight to …?	À quelle porte faut-il embarquer pour le vol pour …?
When is the latest I can check in?	Quelle est l'heure limite d'enregistrement?
When does boarding begin?	À quelle heure commence l'embarquement?
Window/aisle, please.	Fenêtre/couloir, s'il vous plaît.
I've lost my boarding pass/ my ticket.	J'ai perdu mon ticket d'embarquement/mon billet.
Where is the luggage for the flight from …?	Où sont les bagages du vol provenant de…?
My luggage hasn't arrived.	Mes bagages ne sont pas arrivés.

Local Public Transport   Transports en commun

How do I get to …?	Comment est-ce qu'on va à …?
Where is the bus station?	Où est la gare routière?

Where is the nearest …?	Où est … le/la plus proche?
bus stop	*l'arrêt de bus*
underground station	*la station de métro*
A ticket to…, please.	Un ticket pour…, s'il vous plaît.
Is there a reduction …?	Il y a un tarif réduit …?
for students	*pour les étudiants*
for pensioners	*pour les seniors*
for children	*pour les enfants*
for the unemployed	*pour les chômeurs*
with this pass	*avec cette carte*
How does the (ticket) machine work?	Comment fonctionne le distributeur de tickets?
Do you have a map of the underground?	Avez-vous un plan du métro?
Please tell me when to get off.	Pourriez-vous me prévenir quand je dois descendre?
What is the next stop?	Quel est le prochain arrêt?

Taxi | En taxi

Where can I get a taxi?	Où puis-je trouver un taxi?
Call me a taxi, please.	Pouvez-vous m'appeler un taxi, s'il vous plaît?
To the airport/station, please.	À l'aéroport/À la gare, s'il vous plaît.
To this address, please.	À cette adresse, s'il vous plaît.
I'm in a hurry.	Je suis pressé.
How much is it?	Combien est-ce?
I need a receipt.	Il me faut un reçu.
Keep the change.	Gardez la monnaie.
Stop here, please.	Arrêtez-moi ici, s'il vous plaît.

Camping | Camping

Is there a campsite here?	Est-ce qu'il y a un camping ici?
We'd like a site for ...	Nous voudrions un emplacement pour ...
a tent.	*une tente.*
a camper van.	*un camping-car.*
a caravan.	*une caravane.*
We'd like to stay one night/ ... nights.	Nous voudrions rester une nuit/... nuits.
How much is it per night?	Combien est-ce par nuit?
Where are ...?	Où sont ...?
the toilets	*les toilettes*
the showers	*les douches*
Where is ...?	Où est ...?
the shop	*le magasin*
the site office	*le bureau*
the restaurant	*le restaurant*
Can we camp here overnight?	Est-ce qu'on peut camper ici pour la nuit?
Can we park here overnight?	Est-ce qu'on peut stationner ici pour la nuit?

Self-Catering | Location de vacances

Where do we get the key for the apartment/house?	Où est-ce qu'il faut aller chercher la clé de l'appartement/la maison?
Do we have to pay extra for electricity/gas?	Est-ce que l'électricité/l'eau est à payer en plus?
How does ... work?	Comment fonctionne ...?
the washing maching	*la machine à laver*
the heating	*le chauffage*
the water heater	*le chauffe-eau*

Who do I contact if there are any problems?	Qui dois-je contacter en cas de problème?
We need ...	Il nous faut ...
a second key.	*un double de la clé.*
more sheets.	*des draps supplémentaires.*
more crockery.	*de la vaisselle en plus.*
The gas has run out.	Il n'y a plus de gaz.
There is no electricity.	Il n'y a pas d'électricité.
Do we have to clean the apartment/the house before we leave?	Est-ce qu'on doit nettoyer l'appartement/la maison avant de partir?

Hotel | Hotel

Do you have a ... for tonight?	Avez-vous une ... pour ce soir?
single room	*chambre pour une personne*
double room	*chambre pour deux personnes*
room for ... people	*chambre pour ... personnes*
Do you have a room ...?	Avez-vous une chambre ...?
with bath	*avec baignoire*
with shower	*avec douche*
I want to stay for one night/ ... nights.	Je voudrais rester une nuit/ ... nuits.
I booked a room in the name of ...	J'ai réservé une chambre au nom de ...
I'd like another room.	Je voudrais une autre chambre.
What time is breakfast?	On sert le petit déjeuner à quelle heure?
Can I have breakfast in my room?	Pouvez-vous me servir le petit déjeuner dans ma chambre?
Where is ...?	Où est ...?
the restaurant	*le restaurant*

the bar	*le bar*
the gym	*la salle de sport*
the swimming pool	*la piscine*
I'd like an alarm call for tomorrow morning at ...	Je voudrais qu'on me réveille demain matin à ...
I'd like to get these things washed/cleaned.	Pourriez-vous laver/faire nettoyer ceci?
Please bring me ...	S'il vous plaît, apportez-moi ...
The... doesn't work.	Le/la ... ne marche pas.
Room number ...	Chambre numéro ...
Are there any messages for me?	Est-ce que j'ai reçu des messages?

I'd like ...	Je voudrais ...
Do you have ...?	Avez-vous ...?
Do you have this ...?	Avez-vous ceci ...?
in another size	*dans une autre taille*
in another colour	*dans une autre couleur*
I take size ...	Je fais du ...
My feet are a size 5½.	Je fais du trente-neuf.
I'll take it.	Je le prends.
Do you have anything else?	Avez-vous autre chose?
That's too expensive.	C'est trop cher.
I'm just looking.	Je regarde juste.
Do you take credit cards?	Acceptez-vous la carte bleue?

Food shopping | Alimentation

Where is the nearest ...?	Où est ... le/la plus proche?
supermarket	*le supermarché*
baker's	*la boulangerie*
butcher's	*la boucherie*
Where is the market?	Où est le marché?
When is the market on?	Quand est-ce qu'est le marché?
a kilo/pound of ...	un kilo/demi-kilo de ...
200 grams of ...	deux cents grammes de ...
... slices of ...	... tranches de ...
a litre of ...	un litre de ...
a bottle/packet of ...	une bouteille/un paquet de ...

Post Office | Poste

Where is the nearest post office?	Où est la poste la plus proche?
When does the post office open?	La poste ouvre à quelle heure?
Where can I buy stamps?	Où peut-on acheter des timbres?

SHOPPING | ACHATS

I'd like … stamps for postcards/letters to Britain/the United States.	Je voudrais … timbres pour cartes postales/lettres pour la Grande-Bretagne/les États-Unis.
I'd like to send …	Je voudrais envoyer …
this letter.	*cette lettre.*
this parcel.	*ce colis.*
by airmail/express mail/registered mail	par avion/en courrier urgent/en recommandé
Is there any mail for me?	Est-ce que j'ai du courrier?
Where is the nearest postbox?	Où est la boîte aux lettres la plus proche?

Photos and Videos | Photographie et vidéo

A colour/black and white film, please.	Une pellicule couleur/noir et blanc, s'il vous plaît.
With twenty-four/thirty-six exposures.	De vingt-quatre/trente-six poses.
Can I have batteries for this camera, please?	Je voudrais des piles pour ce caméscope, s'il vous plaît.
The camera is sticking.	Le caméscope se bloque.
Can you develop this film, please?	Pourriez-vous développer cette pellicule, s'il vous plaît?
I'd like the photos …	Je voudrais les photos …
matt.	*en mat.*
glossy.	*en brillant.*
ten by fifteen centimetres.	*en format dix sur quinze.*
When will the photos be ready?	Quand est-ce que les photos seront prêtes?
How much do the photos cost?	Combien coûtent les photos?
Could you take a photo of us, please?	Pourriez-vous nous prendre en photo, s'il vous plaît?

Sightseeing | Visites touristiques

Where is the tourist office?	Où se trouve l'office de tourisme?
Do you have any leaflets about ...?	Avez-vous des dépliants sur ...?
Are there any sightseeing tours of the town?	Est-ce qu'il existe des visites guidées de la ville?
When is ... open?	À quelle heure ouvre ...?
the museum	*le musée*
the church	*l'église*
the castle	*le château*
How much does it cost to get in?	Combien coûte l'entrée?
Are there any reductions ...?	Il y a un tarif réduit ...?
for students	*pour les étudiants*
for children	*pour les enfants*
for pensioners	*pour les seniors*
for the unemployed	*pour les chômeurs*
Is there a guided tour in English?	Est-ce qu'il y a une visite guidée en anglais?
Can I take photos here?	Je peux prendre des photos ici?
Can I film here?	Je peux filmer ici?

Entertainment | Loisirs

What is there to do here?	Qu'est-ce qu'il y a à faire ici?
Where can we ...?	Où est-ce qu'on peut ...?
go dancing	*danser*
hear live music	*écouter de la musique live*
Where is there ...?	Où est-ce qu'il y a ...?
a nice bar	*un bon bar*
a good club	*une bonne discothèque*
What's on tonight ...?	Qu'est-ce qu'il y a ce soir ...?

LEISURE | LOISIRS

at the cinema	au cinéma
at the theatre	au théâtre
at the opera	à l'opéra
at the concert hall	à la salle de concert
Where can I buy tickets for ...?	Où est-ce que je peux acheter des places ...?
the theatre	de théâtre
the concert	de concert
the opera	d'opéra
the ballet	pour le ballet
How much is it to get in?	Combien coûte l'entrée?
I'd like a ticket/... tickets for ...	Je voudrais un billet/... billets pour ...
Are there any reductions ...?	Il y a un tarif réduit ...?
for children	pour les enfants
for pensioners	pour les seniors
for students	pour les étudiants
for the unemployed	pour les chômeurs

At the Beach | À la plage

Where is the nearest beach?	Où se trouve la plage la plus proche?
Is it safe to swim here?	Est-ce qu'on peut nager ici sans danger?
How deep is the water?	La profondeur de l'eau est de combien?
Is there a lifeguard?	Est-ce qu'il y a un maître nageur?
Where can you ...?	Où peut-on ...?
go surfing	faire du surf
go waterskiing	faire du ski nautique
go diving	faire de la plongée
go paragliding	faire du parapente

I'd like to hire ...	Je voudrais louer ...
a deckchair.	una chaise longue.
a sunshade.	un parasol.
a surfboard.	une planche de surf.
a jet-ski.	un scooter des mers.
a rowing boat.	une barque.
a pedal boat.	un pédalo.

Sport | Sport

Where can we ...?	Où peut-on ...?
play tennis/golf	jouer au tennis/golf
go swimming	aller nager
go riding	faire de l'équitation
go fishing	aller pêcher
How much is it per hour?	Combien est-ce que ça coûte de l'heure?
Where can I book a court?	Où peut-on réserver un court?
Where can I hire rackets?	Où peut-on louer des raquettes de tennis?
Where can I hire a rowing boat/a pedal boat?	Où peut-on louer une barque/ un pédalo?
Do you need a fishing permit?	Est-ce qu'il faut un permis de pêche?

Skiing | Ski

Where can I hire skiing equipment?	Où peut-on louer un équipement de ski?
I'd like to hire ...	Je voudrais louer ...
downhill skis.	des skis de piste.
cross-country skis.	des skis de fond.
ski boots.	des chaussures de ski.
ski poles.	des bâtons de ski.
Can you tighten my bindings, please?	Pourriez-vous resserrer mes fixations, s'il vous plaît?

LEISURE | LOISIRS

Where can I buy a ski pass?	Où est-ce qu'on peut acheter un forfait?
I'd like a ski pass ...	Je voudrais un forfait ...
for a day.	*pour une journée.*
for five days.	*pour cinq jours.*
for a week.	*pour une semaine.*
How much is a ski pass?	Combien coûte le forfait?
When does the first/last chair-lift leave?	À quelle heure part le premier/ dernier télésiège?
Do you have a map of the ski runs?	Avez-vous une carte des pistes?
Where are the beginners' slopes?	Où sont les pistes pour débutants?
How difficult is this slope?	Quelle est la difficulté de cette piste?
Is there a ski school?	Y a-t-il une école de ski?
What's the weather forecast for today?	Quel est le temps prévu pour aujourd'hui?
What is the snow like?	Comment est la neige?
Is there a danger of avalanches?	Est-ce qu'il y a un risque d'avalanches?

A table for ... people, please.	Une table pour ... personnes, s'il vous plaît.
The ... please.	La ..., s'il vous plaît.
menu	*carte*
wine list	*carte des vins*
What do you recommend?	Qu'est-ce que vous me conseillez?
Do you have ...?	Servez-vous ...?
any vegetarian dishes	*des plats végétariens*
children's portions	*des portions pour enfants*
Does that contain ...?	Est-ce que cela contient...?
peanuts	*des cacahuètes*
alcohol	*de l'alcool*
Can you bring (more) ... please?	Vous pourriez m'apporter (plus de) ..., s'il vous plaît?
I'll have ...	Je vais prendre ...
The bill, please.	L'addition, s'il vous plaît.
All together, please.	Sur une seule note, s'il vous plaît.
Separate bills, please.	Sur des notes séparées, s'il vous plaît.
Keep the change.	Gardez la monnaie.
This isn't what I ordered.	Ce n'est pas ce que j'ai commandé.
The bill is wrong.	Il y a une erreur dans l'addition.
The food is cold/too salty.	C'est froid/trop salé.

TELEPHONE | TELEPHONE

Where can I make a phone call?	Où est-ce que je peux téléphoner?
Where is the nearest card phone?	Où est la cabine à cartes la plus proche?
Where is the nearest coin box?	Où est le téléphone à pièces le plus proche?
I'd like a twenty-five euro phone card.	Je voudrais une carte téléphonique de vingt-cinq euros.
I'd like some coins for the phone, please.	Je voudrais de la monnaie pour téléphoner.
I'd like to make a reverse charge call.	Je voudrais téléphoner en PCV.
Hello.	Allô.
This is …	C'est …
Who's speaking, please?	Qui est à l'appareil?
Can I speak to Mr/Ms …, please?	Puis-je parler à Monsieur/Madame … s'il vous plaît?
Extension …, please.	Poste numéro …, s'il vous plaît.
I'll phone back later.	Je rappellerai plus tard.
Can you text me your answer?	Pouvez-vous me répondre par (minimessage) SMS?
Where can I charge my mobile phone?	Où est-ce que je peux recharger mon portable?
I need a new battery.	Il me faut une pile neuve.
Where can I buy a top-up card?	Où est-ce que je peux acheter une carte prépayée?
I can't get a network.	Je n'ai pas de réception.

Passport/Customs | Passeport/Douane

Here is ...	Voici ...
my passport.	*mon passeport.*
my identity card.	*ma carte d'identité.*
my driving licence.	*mon permis de conduire.*
Here are my vehicle documents.	Voici les documents de mon véhicule.
This is a present.	C'est un cadeau.
This is for my own personal use.	C'est pour mon usage personnel.

At the Bank | À la banque

Where can I change money?	Où puis-je changer de l'argent?
Is there a bank/bureau de change here?	Est-ce qu'il y a une banque/un bureau de change par ici?
When is the bank open?	La banque ouvre à quelle heure?
I'd like ... euros.	Je voudrais ... euros.
I'd like to cash these traveller's cheques.	Je voudrais encaisser ces chèques de voyage.
What's the commission?	Combien prenez-vous de commission?
Can I use my card to get cash?	Je peux me servir de ma carte pour retirer de l'argent?
Is there a cash machine here?	Il y a un distributeur par ici?
The cash machine swallowed my card.	Le distributeur m'a pris ma carte.

Repairs — Réparations

Where can I get this repaired?	Où puis-je faire réparer ceci?
Can you repair ...?	Pouvez-vous réparer ...?
these shoes	ces chaussures
this watch	cette montre
How much will the repairs cost?	Combien coûte la réparation?

Emergency Services — Urgences

Help!	Au secours!
Fire!	Au feu!
Please call ...	Pouvez-vous appeler ...
the emergency doctor.	le médecin d'urgence.
the fire brigade.	les pompiers.
the police.	la police.
I need to make an urgent phone call.	Je dois téléphoner d'urgence.
I need an interpreter.	J'ai besoin d'un interprète.
Where is the police station?	Où est le commissariat?
Where is the hospital?	Où est l'hopital?
I want to report a theft.	Je voudrais signaler un vol.
.... has been stolen.	On m'a volé ....
There's been an accident.	Il y a eu un accident.
There are ... people injured.	Il y a ... blessés.
I've been ...	On m'a ...
robbed.	volé.
attacked.	attaqué.
raped.	violé.
I'd like to phone my embassy.	Je voudrais appeler mon ambassade.

Pharmacy | Pharmacie

Where is the nearest pharmacy?	Où est la pharmacie la plus proche?
Which pharmacy provides emergency service?	Quelle est la pharmacie de garde?
I'd like something ...	Je voudrais quelque chose ...
for diarrhoea.	contre la diarrhée.
for a temperature.	contre la fièvre.
for travel sickness.	contre le mal des transports.
for a headache.	contre le mal de tête.
for a cold.	contre le rhume.
I'd like ...	Je voudrais ...
plasters.	des pansements.
a bandage.	un bandage .
some paracetamol.	du paracétamol.
I can't take ...	Je suis allergique à ...
aspirin.	l'aspirine.
penicillin.	la pénicilline.
Is it safe to give to children?	C'est sans danger pour les enfants?

At the Doctor's | Chez le médecin

I need a doctor.	J'ai besoin de voir un médecin.
Where is casualty?	Où sont les urgences?
I have a pain here.	J'ai mal ici.
I feel ...	J'ai ...
hot.	chaud.
cold.	froid.
I feel sick.	je me sens mal.
I feel dizzy.	J'ai la tête qui tourne.
I'm allergic to ...	Je suis allergique à ...

HEALTH | SANTÉ

I am ...	Je suis ...
pregnant.	*enceinte.*
diabetic.	*diabétique.*
HIV-positive.	*séropositif(-ive).*
I'm on this medication.	Je prends ces médicaments.
My blood group is ...	Mon groupe sanguin est ...

At the Hospital | À l'hôpital

Which ward is ... in?	Dans quelle salle se trouve ...?
When are visiting hours?	Quelles sont les heures de visite?
I'd like to speak to ...	Je voudrais parler à ...
a doctor.	*un médecin.*
a nurse.	*une infirmière.*
When will I be discharged?	Quand vais-je pouvoir sortir?

At the Dentist's | Chez le dentiste

I need a dentist.	J'ai besoin de voir un dentiste.
This tooth hurts.	J'ai mal à cette dent.
One of my fillings has fallen out.	J'ai perdu un de mes plombages.
I have an abscess.	J'ai un abscès.
Can you repair my dentures?	Pouvez-vous réparer mon dentier?
I need a receipt for the insurance.	J'ai besoin d'un reçu pour mon assurance.

Business Travel | Voyages d'affaires

I'd like to arrange a meeting with …	Je voudrais organiser une réunion avec …
I have an appointment with Mr/Ms …	J'ai rendez-vous avec Monsieur/Madame …
Here is my card.	Voici ma carte de visite.
I work for …	Je travaille pour …
How do I get to …?	Où se trouve …?
your office	*votre bureau*
Mr/Ms …'s office	*le bureau de Monsieur/ Madame …*
I need an interpreter.	J'ai besoin d'un interprète.
May I use …?	Je peux me servir …?
your phone	*de votre téléphone*
your computer	*de votre ordinateur*
your desk	*de votre bureau*

Disabled Travellers | Voyageurs handicappés

Is it possible to visit … with a wheelchair?	Est-ce qu'on peut visiter … en chaise roulante?
Where is the wheelchair-accessible entrance?	Où est l'entrée pour les chaises roulantes?
Is your hotel accessible to wheelchairs?	Votre hôtel est-il accessible aux chaises roulantes?
I need a room …	Je voudrais une chambre …
on the ground floor.	*au rez-de-chaussée.*
with wheelchair access.	*accessible aux chaises roulantes.*
Do you have a lift for wheelchairs?	Y a-t-il un ascenseur pour chaises roulantes?
Where is the disabled toilet?	Où sont les toilettes pour handicappés?
Can you help me get on/off please?	Pouvez-vous m'aider à monter /descendre, s'il vous plaît?

The tyre has burst.	Le pneu est crevé.
The battery is flat.	La batterie est à plat.

Travelling with children | Voyager avec des enfants

Is it OK to bring children here?	Est-ce que les enfants sont admis?
Is there a reduction for children?	Il y a un tarif réduit pour les enfants?
Do you have children's portions?	Vous servez des portions pour enfants?
Do you have ...?	Avez-vous ...?
a high chair	*une chaise pour bébé*
a cot	*un berceau*
a child's seat	*un siège pour enfant*
Where can I change the baby?	Où est-ce que je peux changer mon bébé?
Where can I breast-feed the baby?	Où est-ce que je peux allaiter mon bébé?
Can you warm this up, please?	Vous pouvez me réchauffer ceci, s'il vous plaît?
What is there for children to do?	Qu'est-ce qu'il y a à faire pour les enfants ?
Where is the nearest playground?	Où est l'aire de jeux la plus proche?
Is there a child-minding service?	Est-ce qu'il y a un service de garderie?

I'd like to make a complaint.	Je voudrais faire une réclamation.
To whom can I complain?	À qui dois-je m'adresser pour faire un réclamation?
I'd like to speak to the manager, please.	Je voudrais parler au responsable, s'il vous plaît.
The light	*La lumière*
The heating	*Le chauffage*
The shower	*La douche*
... doesn't work.	... ne marche pas.
The room is ...	La chambre est ...
dirty.	*sale.*
too small.	*trop petite.*
The room is too cold.	Il fait trop froid dans la chambre.
Can you clean the room, please?	Pourriez-vous nettoyer ma chambre, s'il vous plaît?
Can you turn down the TV/the radio, please?	Pourriez-vous baisser le son de votre télé/radio, s'il vous plaît?
The food is ...	C'est ...
cold.	*froid.*
too salty.	*trop salé.*
This isn't what I ordered.	Ce n'est pas ce que j'ai commandé.
We've been waiting for a very long time.	Ça fait longtemps que nous attendons.
The bill is wrong.	Vous vous êtes trompé dans l'addition.
I want my money back.	Je veux qu'on me rembourse.
I'd like to exchange this.	Je voudrais échanger ceci.
I'm not satisfied with this.	Je ne suis pas satisfait(e).

Contents

Preface

The number of clinically important drugs increases every year, as does the nurse's responsibility for drug therapy. No practitioner can memorize all the drug information necessary to provide safe and efficacious drug therapy. Compound the growing list of drugs with a continuing shortage of pharmacists and an anticipated shortage of nurses, and there is an ever-increasing risk of medication errors that lead to poor patient outcomes.

The *2017 Lippincott Pocket Drug Guide for Nurses* provides need-to-know information in an abbreviated format. Drugs are listed alphabetically. Monographs are concise. Each monograph provides the key information needed to ensure safe patient care:

- Drug class
- Pregnancy and Controlled Substance category
- Black box warning, if appropriate
- Indications and dosages
- Dosage adjustments that also alert you, when appropriate, to the need to consult a complete drug guide
- Most common and most critical adverse effects
- Clinically important interactions
- Key nursing and patient teaching points to ensure safe drug use.

The pocket size makes this book easy to carry into the clinical setting for a quick check before administering the drug.

Following the drug monographs, a new section on patient safety reviews the rights of medication administration, safety-oriented patient and family teaching, and other aspects of safe drug administration. Appendices cover biological agents, topical drugs, ophthalmic agents, laxatives, combination drugs, and contraceptives. To keep the book short and sweet, common abbreviations are used throughout; these are listed in the abbreviations list on pages vii–ix.

In the rush of the clinical setting, this guide will provide the critical information you need immediately. However, it is important to check complete facts and details as soon as time allows to ensure that the best outcomes are achieved for each patient.

Amy M. Karch, RN, MS

Guide to abbreviations

Abbreviations in headings

BBW	Black Box Warning
CLASS	Therapeutic/Pharmacologic Class
PREG/CONT	Pregnancy Risk Category/Controlled Substance Schedule
IND & DOSE	Indications & Dosages
ADJUST DOSE	Dosage Adjustment
ADV EFF	Adverse Effects
NC/PT	Nursing Considerations/Patient Teaching

Abbreviations in text

abd	abdominal	CBC	complete blood count
ABG	arterial blood gas	CDAD	*Clostridium difficile*–associated diarrhea
ACE	angiotensin-converting enzyme		
ACT	activated clotting time	CDC	Centers for Disease Control and Prevention
ACTH	adrenocorticotropic hormone	CK	creatine kinase
		CML	chronic myelogenous leukemia
ADH	antidiuretic hormone		
ADHD	attention-deficit hyperactivity disorder	CNS	central nervous system
		conc	concentration
adjunct	adjunctive	COPD	chronic obstructive pulmonary disease
AHA	American Heart Association		
AIDS	acquired immunodeficiency syndrome	CR	controlled-release
		CrCl	creatinine clearance
ALL	acute lymphocytic leukemia	CSF	cerebrospinal fluid
ALT	alanine transaminase	CV	cardiovascular
a.m.	morning	CVP	central venous pressure
AML	acute myelogenous leukemia	CYP450	cytochrome P-450
		D_5W	dextrose 5% in water
ANA	anti-nuclear antibodies	DIC	disseminated intravascular coagulopathy
ANC	absolute neutrophil count		
aPTT	activated partial thromboplastin time	dL	deciliter (100 mL)
		DR	delayed-release
ARB	angiotensin II receptor blocker	DVT	deep venous thrombosis
		dx	diagnosis
ASA	acetylsalicylic acid	dysfx	dysfunction
AST	aspartate transaminase	ECG	electrocardiogram
AV	atrioventricular	ED	erectile dysfunction
bid	twice a day *(bis in die)*	EEG	electroencephalogram
BP	blood pressure	ER	extended-release
BPH	benign prostatic hypertrophy	ET	endotracheal
		FDA	Food and Drug Administration
BSA	body surface area		
BUN	blood urea nitrogen	5-FU	fluorouracil
CABG	coronary artery bypass graft	5-HIAA	5-hydroxyindole acetic acid
CAD	coronary artery disease	FSH	follicle-stimulating hormone
cAMP	cyclic adenosine monophosphate	g	gram
		GABA	gamma-aminobutyric acid

GERD	gastroesophageal reflux disease	mg	milligram
GFR	glomerular filtration rate	mgt	management
GGTP	gamma-glutamyl transpeptidase	MI	myocardial infarction
		min	minute
GI	gastrointestinal	mL	milliliter
G6PD	glucose-6-phosphate dehydrogenase	mo	month
		MRSA	methicillin-resistant *Staphylococcus aureus*
GU	genitourinary		
HCG	human chorionic gonadotropin	MS	multiple sclerosis
		NA	not applicable
Hct	hematocrit	NG	nasogastric
HDL	high-density lipoprotein	ng	nanogram
HF	heart failure	NMJ	neuromuscular junction
Hg	mercury	NMS	neuroleptic malignant syndrome
Hgb	hemoglobin		
Hib	*Haemophilus influenzae* type b	NRTI	nucleoside reverse transcriptase inhibitor
HIV	human immunodeficiency virus	NSAID	nonsteroidal anti-inflammatory drug
HMG-CoA	3-hydroxy-3-methylglutaryl coenzyme A	NSS	normal saline solution
		n/v	nausea and vomiting
HPA	hypothalamic-pituitary axis	n/v/d	nausea, vomiting, and diarrhea
hr	hour		
HR	heart rate	OCD	obsessive-compulsive disorder
HSV	herpes simplex virus		
hx	history	oint	ointment
IBS	irritable bowel syndrome	OTC	over-the-counter
ICU	intensive care unit	P	pulse
IHSS	idiopathic hypertrophic subaortic stenosis	PABA	para-aminobenzoic acid
		PDA	patent ductus arteriosus
IM	intramuscular	PE	pulmonary embolus
INR	International Normalized Ratio	PEG	percutaneous endoscopic gastrostomy
IOP	intraocular pressure	periop	perioperative
IV	intravenous	PFT	pulmonary function test
kg	kilogram	PG	prostaglandin
L	liter	pH	hydrogen ion concentration
lb	pound	PID	pelvic inflammatory disease
LDL	low-density lipoprotein	PKSK9	proprotein convertase subtilism kexin type 9
LFT	liver function test		
LH	luteinizing hormone	p.m.	evening
LHRH	luteinizing hormone-releasing hormone	PMDD	premenstrual dysphoric disorder
m	meter	PMS	premenstrual syndrome
MAC	*Mycobacterium avium* complex	PO	orally, by mouth *(per os)*
		postop	postoperative
maint	maintenance	preop	preoperative
MAO	monoamine oxidase	PRN	when required *(pro re nata)*
MAOI	monoamine oxidase inhibitor	PSA	prostate-specific antigen
		pt	patient
max	maximum	PT	prothrombin time
mcg	microgram	PTCA	percutaneous transluminal coronary angioplasty

PTSD	post-traumatic stress disorder
PTT	partial thromboplastin time
PVCs	premature ventricular contractions
px	prophylaxis
q	every
qid	four times a day *(quarter in die)*
R	respiratory rate
RBC	red blood cell
RDA	recommended dietary allowance
RDS	respiratory distress syndrome
RPLS	posterior reversible leukoencephalopathy syndrome
RSV	respiratory syncytial virus
SA	sinoatrial
SBE	subacute bacterial endocarditis
sec	second
SIADH	syndrome of inappropriate antidiuretic hormone secretion
SLE	systemic lupus erythematosus
sol	solution
sp	species
SR	sustained-release
SSRI	selective serotonin reuptake inhibitor
STD	sexually transmitted disease
subcut	subcutaneous
SWSD	shift-work sleep disorder
s&sx	signs and symptoms
sx	symptoms
T_3	triiodothyronine
T_4	thyroxine (tetraiodothyronine)
TB	tuberculosis
tbsp	tablespoon
TCA	tricyclic antidepressant
temp	temperature
TIA	transient ischemic attack
tid	three times a day *(ter in die)*
TNF	tumor necrosis factor
TPA	tissue plasminogen activator
TPN	total parenteral nutrition
TSH	thyroid-stimulating hormone
tsp	teaspoon

tx	treatment
unkn	unknown
URI	upper respiratory (tract) infection
USP	United States Pharmacopeia
UTI	urinary tract infection
UV	ultraviolet
VLDL	very–low-density lipoprotein
VREF	vancomycin-resistant *Enterococcus faecium*
w/	with
WBC	white blood cell
wk	week
XR	extended-release
yr	year

abacavir (Ziagen)
CLASS Antiviral, NRTI
PREG/CONT C/NA

BBW Risk of severe to fatal hypersensitivity reactions; increased w/ HLA-B*5701 allele. Monitor for lactic acidosis, severe hepatomegaly.
IND & DOSE HIV infection (w/other antiretrovirals). *Adult:* 300 mg PO bid or 600 mg/day PO. *Child 3 mo–18 yr:* 8 mg/kg PO bid or 16 mg/day PO once daily; max, 600 mg/day.
ADJUST DOSE Mild hepatic impairment
ADV EFF Fatigue, headache, insomnia, malaise, **MI**, n/v/d, rash, **severe to fatal hepatomegaly, severe to fatal lactic acidosis, severe hypersensitivity reactions,** weakness
INTERACTIONS Alcohol, methadone, other abacavir-containing drugs
NC/PT Give w/other antiretrovirals. Suggest use of barrier contraceptives; breast-feeding not recommended. Monitor for s&sx of lactic acidosis, liver dysfx, hypersensitivity reactions.

abatacept (Orencia)
CLASS Antiarthritic, immune modulator
PREG/CONT C/NA

IND & DOSE Tx of adult rheumatoid arthritis. *Over 100 kg:* 1,000 mg/day IV. *60–100 kg:* 750 mg/day IV. *Under 60 kg:* 500 mg/day IV. After initial dose, give at 2 and 4 wk, then q 4 wk. Tx of juvenile idiopathic arthritis in child 6 yr and older. *75 kg or more:* Use adult dose; max, 1,000 mg/day. *Under 75 kg:* 10 mg/kg IV. After initial dose, give at 2 and 4 wk.
ADV EFF Headache, hypersensitivity reactions and anaphylaxis, potentially serious infection
INTERACTIONS Live vaccines; TNF antagonists (contraindicated)
NC/PT Monitor for s&sx of infection. Pretest for TB before beginning therapy. Do not give w/TNF antago-

nists. Do not give live vaccines during or for 3 mo after tx.

abciximab (ReoPro)
CLASS Antiplatelet, glycoprotein IIb/IIIa inhibitor
PREG/CONT C/NA

IND & DOSE Adjunct to percutaneous coronary intervention (PCI) to prevent acute ischemic complications in pt undergoing PCI. *Adult:* 0.25 mcg/kg by IV bolus 10–60 min before procedure, then continuous IV infusion of 0.125 mcg/kg/min for 12 hr (max, 10 mcg/min). **Unstable angina not responding to conventional therapy w/when PCI is planned within 24 hr, w/heparin and aspirin therapy.** *Adult:* 0.25 mcg/kg by IV bolus over at least 1 min, then 10 mcg/min by IV infusion for 19–24 hr, ending 1 hr after PCI.
ADV EFF Bleeding, edema, hypotension, n/v, pain, **thrombocytopenia**
INTERACTIONS Anticoagulants, antiplatelets, thrombolytics
NC/PT Provide safety measures to protect pt from bleeding and monitor for signs of bleeding. Monitor CBC. Give w/heparin and aspirin therapy. Clearly mark chart that pt is on drug.

abiraterone (Zytiga)
CLASS Antineoplastic, CYP17 inhibitor
PREG/CONT X/NA

IND & DOSE Tx of pts w/metastatic castration-resistant prostate cancer. *Adult:* 1,000 mg PO once daily w/5 mg prednisone PO bid
ADJUST DOSE Hepatic impairment
ADV EFF Adrenocortical insufficiency, arrhythmias, **cardiotoxicity,** cough, diarrhea, dyspepsia, dyspnea, edema, **hepatotoxicity,** hot flushes, hypertension, hypokalemia, nocturia, URI, UTI
INTERACTIONS CYP3A4 enzyme inducers, inhibitors; avoid use w/CYP2D6 substrates

NC/PT Must be taken on empty stomach w/no food 1 hr before or 2 hr after dosing; tab should swallow tablet whole and not cut, crush, or chew. Not for use in pregnancy/breast-feeding. Monitor closely for cardiotoxicity, hepatotoxicity, adrenal insufficiency. Corticosteroids may be needed in stressful situations.

abobotulinumtoxinA (Dysport)
CLASS Neurotoxin
PREG/CONT C/NA

BBW Drug not for tx of muscle spasticity; toxin may spread from injection area and cause s&sx of botulism (CNS alterations, trouble speaking and swallowing, loss of bladder control). Use only for approved indications.
IND & DOSE Improvement of glabellar lines. 50 units in five equal injections q 4 mo. Cervical dystonia. *Adult:* 250–1,000 units IM q 12 wk.
ADV EFF Anaphylactic reactions, dizziness, headache, local reactions, MI, spread of toxin that can lead to death
INTERACTIONS Aminoglycosides, anticholinesterases, lincosamides, magnesium sulfate, NMJ blockers, polymyxin, quinidine, succinylcholine
NC/PT Store in refrigerator. Have epinephrine available in case of anaphylactic reactions. Do not use w/ allergy to cow's milk proteins. Effects may not appear for 1–2 days; will persist for 3–4 mo. Not for use in pregnancy.

acamprosate calcium (Campral)
CLASS Antialcoholic, GABA analogue
PREG/CONT C/NA

IND & DOSE Maint of abstinence from alcohol as part of comprehensive psychosocial tx mgt program. *Adult:* 666 mg PO tid; begin as soon as abstinence achieved.
ADJUST DOSE Renal impairment
ADV EFF Diarrhea, **suicidality**
INTERACTIONS Alcohol
NC/PT Ensure pt is abstaining from alcohol and is in comprehensive tx program. Pt may take drug even if relapse occurs. Not for use in pregnancy/breast-feeding. Pt should report thoughts of suicide.

acarbose (Precose)
CLASS Alpha-glucosidase inhibitor, antidiabetic
PREG/CONT B/NA

IND & DOSE Adjunct to diet/ exercise to lower blood glucose in pts w/type 2 diabetes. *Adult:* 25 mg PO tid w/first bite of meal. Max for pt 60 kg or less, 50 mg PO tid; over 60 kg, 100 mg PO tid. **Combination tx w/sulfonylureas, metformin, or insulin to enhance glycemic control.** *Adult:* Adjust dose based on blood glucose levels in combination w/dosage of other drugs used.
ADV EFF Abd pain, flatulence, hypoglycemia, n/v/d, pneumatosis cystoides intestinalis
INTERACTIONS Antidiabetics, celery, charcoal, coriander, dandelion root, digestive enzymes, digoxin, fenugreek, garlic, ginseng, juniper berries
NC/PT Give w/food. Monitor blood glucose. Pt should follow diet and exercise program and report diarrhea w/mucus discharge, rectal bleeding, constipation.

acebutolol hydrochloride (Sectral)
CLASS Antiarrhythmic, antihypertensive, beta-adrenergic blocker
PREG/CONT B/NA

IND & DOSE Tx of hypertension. *Adult:* 400 mg/day PO. Maint dose, 200–1,200 mg/day PO (larger dose in

two divided doses). **Mgt of PVCs.**
Adult: 200 mg PO bid. Range to control PVCs, 600–1,200 mg/day PO. Discontinue gradually over 3 wk.
ADJUST DOSE Renal, hepatic impairment; elderly pts
ADV EFF Arrhythmias (bradycardia, tachycardia, heart block), **bronchospasm,** constipation, decreased exercise tolerance, ED, flatulence, gastric pain, HF, n/v
INTERACTIONS Alpha blockers, aspirin, beta blockers, bismuth subsalicylate, calcium channel blockers, clonidine, insulin, magnesium salicylate, NSAIDs, prazosin
NC/PT Monitor apical P; do not give if P is less than 45. May give w/food. Withdraw slowly over 3 wk after long-term therapy.

---

acetaminophen
(Acephen, Ofirmev, Tylenol, etc)
CLASS Analgesic, antipyretic
PREG/CONT B/NA

BBW Risk of medication error and severe hepatotoxicity; monitor for overdose through use of multiple acetaminophen-containing products; monitor liver function at higher end of dosage range.
IND & DOSE Temporary reduction of fever; temporary relief of minor aches and pains caused by common cold and influenza; headache, sore throat, toothache (pts 2 yr and older); backache, menstrual cramps, minor arthritis pain, muscle aches (pts over 12 yr). *Adult, child over 12 yr* (PO or rectal suppositories): 325–560 mg q 4–6 hr or 1,300 mg (ER) PO q 8 hr. *Adult, child 13 yr and older, 50 kg or more:* 1,000 mg IV q 6 hr or 650 mg IV q 4 hr; max, 1,000 mg/dose IV or 4,000 mg/day IV. *Child 13 yr, under 50 kg:* 15 mg/kg IV q 6 hr or 12.5 mg/kg IV q 4 hr; max, 750 mg or 75 mg/kg/day. *Child 2–12 yr:* 15 mg/kg IV q 6 hr or 12 mg/kg IV q 4 hr; max, 75 mg/kg/day. *Child:* May repeat PO or rectal doses

four to five times/day; max, five doses in 24 hr or 10 mg/kg. PO doses: 11 yr, 480 mg/dose; 9–10 yr, 400 mg/dose; 6–8 yr, 320 mg/dose; 4–5 yr, 240 mg/dose; 2–3 yr, 160 mg/dose; 12–23 mo, 120 mg/dose; 4–11 mo, 80 mg/dose; 0–3 mo, 40 mg/dose. PR doses: 6–12 yr, 325 mg q 4–6 hr; 3–6 yr, 120 mg q 4–6 hr; 12–36 mo, 80 mg q 4 hr; 3–11 mo, 80 mg q 6 hr.
ADJUST DOSE Active liver disease, severe liver impairment, severe renal disease
ADV EFF Hepatic failure, hepatotoxicity, myocardial damage, serious skin reactions
INTERACTIONS Alcohol, anticholinergics, barbiturates, charcoal, carbamazepine, hydantoins, oral anticoagulants, rifampin, sulfinpyrazone, zidovudine
NC/PT Do not exceed recommended dosage. Avoid combining (many products contain acetaminophen). Administer IV over 15 min. Not recommended for longer than 10 days. Overdose tx: acetylcysteine, possible life support. Pt should report difficulty breathing, rash.

---

acetazolamide (Diamox Sequels)
CLASS Antiepileptic, antiglaucoma, carbonic anhydrase inhibitor, diuretic
PREG/CONT C/NA

BBW Fatalities have occurred due to severe reactions; discontinue immediately if s&sx of serious reactions. Use caution if pt receiving high-dose aspirin; anorexia, tachypnea, lethargy, coma, death have occurred.
IND & DOSE Open-angle glaucoma. *Adult:* 250 mg–1 g/day PO, usually in divided doses, or 1 ER capsule bid (a.m. and p.m.). Max, 1 g/day. **Acute congestive angle-closure glaucoma.** *Adult:* 500 mg (ER) PO bid or 250 mg PO q 4 hr. **Secondary glaucoma and preoperatively.** *Adult:* 250 mg PO q 4 hr, or 250 mg PO bid, or 500 mg PO

bid (ER capsules), or 500 mg PO followed by 125–250 mg PO q 4 hr. May give IV for rapid relief of increased IOP: 500 mg IV, then 125–250 mg PO q 4 hr. **Diuresis in HF.** *Adult:* 250–375 mg PO (5 mg/kg) daily in a.m. **Drug-induced edema.** *Adult:* 250–375 mg PO once q day or for 1 or 2 days alternating w/day of rest. **Epilepsy.** *Adult:* 8–30 mg/kg/day PO in divided doses. Range, 375–1,000 mg/day. **Acute altitude sickness.** *Adult, child 12 yr and older:* 500 mg–1 g/day PO in divided doses.
ADV EFF Urinary frequency
INTERACTIONS Amphetamines, lithium, procainamide, quinidine, salicylates, TCAs
NC/PT Do not give IM. Make oral liquid by crushing tablets and suspending in sweet syrup (do not use alcohol or glycerin). Have IOP checked periodically. May cause dizziness, increased urination. Pt should report flank pain, bleeding, weight gain of more than 3 lb/day. Name confusion between *Diamox* and *Trimox* (ampicillin).

acetylcysteine (Acetadote)
CLASS Antidote, mucolytic
PREG/CONT B/NA

IND & DOSE Mucolytic adjuvant therapy for abnormal, viscid, or inspissated mucus secretions in acute and chronic bronchopulmonary disease. *Adult, child:* Nebulization w/face mask, mouthpiece, tracheostomy: 3–5 mL of 20% sol or 6–10 mL of 10% sol tid or qid. Nebulization w/tent, croupette: Up to 300 mL during a tx period. Direct or by tracheostomy: 1–2 mL of 10%–20% sol q 1–4 hr. Percutaneous intratracheal catheter: 1–2 mL of 20% sol or 2–4 mL of 10% sol q 1–4 hr. **To prevent or lessen hepatic injury that may occur after ingestion of potentially hepatotoxic dose of acetaminophen.** *Adult, child:* PO, 140 mg/kg oading dose, then 17 maint doses of

70 mg/kg q 4 hr, starting 4 hr after loading dose. IV, loading dose, 150 mg/kg in 200 mL IV over 60 min; maint dose 50 mg/kg in 500 mL IV over 4 hr followed by second maint dose of 100 mg/kg in 1,000 mL IV over 16 hr. Total IV dose, 300 mg/kg over 21 hr.
ADV EFF Anaphylactoid reactions, bronchospasm, n/v, rhinorrhea
INTERACTIONS (in sol) Amphotericin B, erythromycin, hydrogen peroxide, lactobiotate, tetracycline
NC/PT Use water to remove sol from pt's face. Monitor nebulizer for buildup of drug. Have suction equipment available. May mix 20% sol w/soft drinks to concentration of 5%. Dilute oral sol w/water if using gastric tube. Warn pt of possible disagreeable odor as nebulization begins. Pt should report difficulty breathing.

acitretin (Soriatane)
CLASS Antipsoriatic, retinoic acid
PREG/CONT X/NA

BBW Do not use in pregnancy; serious fetal harm possible. Males should not father a child during and for 3 mo after tx.
IND & DOSE Tx of severe psoriasis. *Adult:* 25–50 mg/day PO w/main meal.
ADV EFF Hepatotoxicity, hypervitaminosis A, ossification abnormalities
INTERACTIONS Methotrexate, phenytoin, retinoids, St. John's wort, tetracyclines, vitamin D
NC/PT Pt must have monthly negative pregnancy tests and agree to use two forms of contraception. Dispensed in 1-mo supply only. Must have signed pt agreement in medical record. Pt may not donate blood for 3 yr after tx. Pt should swallow tablets whole and not cut, crush, or chew them; stop drug when lesions resolve; avoid sun exposure.

aclidinium bromide
(Tudorza Pressair)
CLASS Anticholinergic, bronchodilator
PREG/CONT C/NA

IND & DOSE Long-term maint tx of bronchospasm associated w/COPD. *Adult:* 400 mcg/actuation bid.
ADJUST DOSE Over 80 yr; under 60 kg; renal, hepatic impairment
ADV EFF Dry mouth, glaucoma, headache, hypersensitivity reactions, nasopharyngitis, **paradoxical bronchospasm**, urine retention
INTERACTIONS Other anticholinergics; avoid this combination
NC/PT Ensure appropriate use of drug; use only w/provided inhaler. Not for acute bronchospasem; rescue inhaler should be provided. Monitor for hypersensitivity, more likely in pts w/severe hypersensitivity to milk proteins. Stop drug w/paradoxical bronchospasm. Not for use in breastfeeding. Monitor for glaucoma. Have pt void before each dose if urine retention occurs.

acyclovir (Zovirax)
CLASS Antiviral, purine nucleoside analogue
PREG/CONT B/NA

IND & DOSE Herpes genitalis. *Adult:* 5 mg/kg IV infused over 1 hr q 8 hr for 5 days. Herpes encephalitis. *Adult:* 10 mg/kg IV infused over 1 hr q 8 hr for 10 days. Herpes simplex (immunocompromised pts). *Adult:* 5 mg/kg IV infused over 1 hr q 8 hr for 7 days. Varicella zoster (immunocompromised pts). *Adult:* 10 mg/kg IV infused over 1 hr q 8 hr for 7 days. Initial genital herpes. *Adult:* 200 mg PO q 4 hr five times daily (1,000 mg/day) for 10 days. Long-term suppressive therapy. *Adult:* 400 mg PO bid for up to 12 mo. Recurrent therapy. *Adult:* 200 mg IV q 4 hr five times daily for 5 days. HSV infection. *Child*

under 12 yr: 10 mg/kg IV infused over 1 hr q 8 hr for 7 days. Varicella zoster. *Child under 12 yr:* 20 mg/kg IV over 1 hr q 8 hr for 7 days. Shingles, HSV encephalitis. *Child 3 mo to 12 yr:* 20 mg/kg IV over 1 hr q 8 hr for 14–21 days. Neonatal HSV. 10 mg/kg IV infused over 1 hr q 8 hr for 10 days. *2 yr or older and 40 kg or less:* 20 mg/kg/dose PO qid (80 mg/kg/day) for 5 days. *Over 12 yr, over 40 kg:* Give adult dose. Ointment. *All ages:* Apply sufficient quantity to cover all lesions six times/day (q 3 hr) for 7 days. 1.25-cm (0.5-in) ribbon of ointment covers 2.5 cm² (4 in²) surface area. Cream. *12 yr and older:* Apply enough to cover all lesions five times/day for 4 days.
ADJUST DOSE Elderly pts, renal impairment
ADV EFF Inflammation or phlebitis at injection sites, n/v/d, transient topical burning w/topical use
INTERACTIONS Nephrotoxic drugs, probenecid, zidovudine
NC/PT Ensure pt well hydrated. Wear rubber glove or finger cot when applying topically. Drug not a cure and will not prevent recurrence. Pt should avoid sexual intercourse when lesions are present; use condoms to prevent spread.

adalimumab (Humira)
CLASS Antiarthritic, TNF blocker
PREG/CONT B/NA

BBW Risk of serious infection, activation of TB; risk of lymphoma and other potentially fatal malignancies in children, adolescents.
IND & DOSE Tx of rheumatoid arthritis, psoriatic arthritis, ankylosing spondylitis. *Adult:* 40 mg subcut every other wk. Crohn's disease/ulcerative colitis. *Adult, child 40 kg or over:* Four 40-mg subcut injections in 1 day followed by 80 mg 2 wk later; 2 wk later begin 40 mg every other wk maint. *Child 17 to under 40 kg:* Two

40-mg subcut injections in 1 day; then 40 mg 2 wk later; then begin 20 mg subcut every other wk. **Plaque psoriasis.** *Adult:* 80 mg subcut, then 40 mg every other wk starting 1 wk later. **Juvenile idiopathic arthritis:** *Child 30 kg and over:* 40 mg subcut every other wk. *Child 15 to under 30 kg:* 20 mg subcut every other wk. *Child 10 to under 15 kg:* 10 mg subcut every other wk.
ADV EFF Anaphylaxis, bone marrow suppression, demyelinating diseases, headache, HF, injection-site reactions, **malignancies, serious infections**
INTERACTIONS Anakinra, immunosuppressants, live vaccines
NC/PT High risk of infection; monitor pt, protect as appropriate. Monitor CNS for s&sx of demyelinating disorders. Advise pt to avoid pregnancy. Teach proper administration/disposal of syringes. Tell pt to mark calendar for injection days.

---

adefovir dipivoxil (Hepsera)

CLASS Antiviral, reverse transcriptase inhibitor
PREG/CONT C/NA

BBW Worsening hepatitis when discontinued. HIV resistance if used in undiagnosed HIV infection (test before use). Monitor for renal and hepatic toxicity. Withdraw drug and monitor if s&sx of lactic acidosis or steatosis.
IND & DOSE **Tx of chronic hepatitis B.** *Adult, child 12 yr and older:* 10 mg/day PO.
ADJUST DOSE Renal impairment
ADV EFF Asthenia, elevated LFTs, **hepatitis exacerbation if discontinued, lactic acidosis, nephrotoxicity, severe hepatomegaly w/steatosis**
INTERACTIONS Nephrotoxic drugs; tenofovir (contraindicated)
NC/PT Test for HIV infection before starting tx. Monitor for renal/hepatic dysfx, lactic acidosis, steatosis. Advise against use in pregnancy/

breast-feeding. Drug does not cure disease; use precautions. Advise pt to not run out of drug; serious hepatitis can occur w/sudden stopping.

---

adenosine (Adenocard, Adenoscan)

CLASS Antiarrhythmic, diagnostic agent
PREG/CONT C/NA

IND & DOSE **Conversion to sinus rhythm from supraventricular tachycardia** *(Adenocard)*. *Pts over 50 kg:* 6 mg IV bolus; may repeat within 1–2 min w/12-mg IV bolus up to two times. *Pts under 50 kg:* 0.05–0.1 mg/kg rapid IV bolus; may repeat in 1–2 min. Max single dose, 0.3 mg/kg. **Diagnosis of suspected CAD, w/thallium** *(Adenoscan)*. *Adult:* 0.14 mg/kg/min IV over 6 min (total dose, 0.84 mg/kg); inject thallium at 3 min.
ADV EFF Bronchoconstriction, *facial flushing, fatal cardiac events,* heart block, hypersensitivity reactions, hypertension, hypotension, seizures, stroke
INTERACTIONS Carbamazepine, digoxin, dipyridamole, theophylline, verapamil
NC/PT Do not refrigerate; discard unused portions. Have emergency equipment on standby and continuously monitor pt. Do not use in pts w/AV block, sinus node disease, suspected bronchoconstrictic disease. Have methylxanthines on hand as antidote.

---

ado-trastuzumab (Kadcyla)

CLASS Antineoplastic, microtubular inhibitor
PREG/CONT D/NA

BBW Risk of hepatotoxicity, cardiac dysfunction, death. Can cause fetal harm. Do not substitute for trastuzumab.
IND & DOSE **Tx of HER2-positive metastatic breast cancer in pts who**

have had prior tx or have developed recurrence during or within 6 mo of tx. *Adult:* 3.6 mg/kg as IV infusion every 3 wk until disease progression or toxicity.

ADV EFF Constipation, fatigue, headache, **hemorrhage, hepatotoxicity, infusion reactions, left ventricular impairment,** musculoskeletal pain, neurotoxicity, **pulmonary toxicity,** thrombocytopenia

INTERACTIONS Strong CYP3A4 inhibitors; avoid this combination. Do not use w/5% dextrose solutions

NC/PT Ensure proper use; HER-2 testing required. Rule out pregnancy before starting tx (contraceptives advised); not for use in breast-feeding. Monitor LFTs, platelet count (before and periodically during tx), cardiac output, respiratory function. Infusion reaction may require slowing or interrupting infusion. Pt should mark calendar for infusion dates; take safety precautions w/neurotoxicity; report difficulty breathing, dark urine, yellowing of skin/ eyes, abdominal pain, swelling, dizziness, unusual bleeding.

DANGEROUS DRUG

afatinib (Gilotrif)

CLASS Antineoplastic, kinase inhibitor
PREG/CONT D/NA

IND & DOSE First-line tx of pts w/metastatic non-small-cell lung cancer whose tumors have epidermal growth factor receptor exon 19 deletions or exon 21 substitution *Adult:* 40 mg/day PO at least 1 hr before or 2 hr after meal.

ADV EFF Abd pain, bullous/exfoliative skin disorders, dehydration, diarrhea, hepatotoxicity, interstitial lung disease, keratitis, n/v/d, rash, stomatitis, weight loss

INTERACTIONS P-glycoprotein inducers/inhibitors

NC/PT Ensure proper dx. Monitor renal function/LFTs. Risk of dehydration. Pt should avoid pregnancy/

breast-feeding; perform proper mouth care; eat small, frequent meals; report rash, difficulty breathing; severe n/v; urine/stool color changes.

---

aflibercept (Eylea)

CLASS Fusion protein, ophthalmic agent
PREG/CONT C/NA

IND & DOSE Tx of pts w/neovascular (wet) age-related macular degeneration. *Adult:* 2 mg (0.05 mL) by intravitreal injection q 4 wk for first 3 mo, then 2 mg once q 8 wk. **Tx of macular edema after retinal vein occlusion.** *Adult:* 2 mg by intravitreal injection q 4 wk. **Tx of diabetic macular edema, diabetic retinopathy.** *Adult:* 2 mg by intravitreal injection q 4 wk for five injections, then once q 8 wk

ADV EFF Cataract, endophthalmitis, eye infections, eye pain, increased IOP, intraocular infection, retinal detachment, **thrombotic events,** vision changes, vitreous floaters

NC/PT Monitor pt closely during and immediately after injection. Advise pt to immediately report eye redness, sensitivity to light, sudden vision changes.

---

agalsidase beta (Fabrazyme)

CLASS Enzyme
PREG/CONT B/NA

IND & DOSE Tx of Fabry disease. *Adult:* 1 mg/kg IV q 2 wk at no more than 0.25 mg/min.

ADV EFF Anaphylaxis, potentially serious infusion reactions (chills, fever, dyspnea, n/v, flushing, headache, chest pain, tachycardia, facial edema, rash)

NC/PT Ensure appropriate supportive measures available during infusion. Premedicate w/antipyretics; immediately discontinue if infusion reaction occurs.

DANGEROUS DRUG

albiglutide (Tanzeum)
CLASS Antidiabetic, GLP-1 receptor agonist
PREG/CONT C/NA

BBW Risk of thyroid C-cell tumors, including medullary thyroid carcinoma; not for use w/hx or family hx of thyroid cancer or multiple endocrine neoplasia.

IND & DOSE Adjunct to diet/exercise to improve glycemic control in pts w/type 2 diabetes. *Adult:* 30 mg subcut in abdomen, thigh, upper arm wkly; max, 50 mg/wk subcut.

ADV EFF Hypersensitivity reactions, hypoglycemia, injection-site reactions, n/v/d, **pancreatitis**, renal impairment

INTERACTIONS Oral medications (delays gastric emptying)

NC/PT Ensure proper use; not a first-line tx. Inject into abdomen, thigh, upper arm; rotate injection sites. Monitor glucose, renal function. May be combined w/other antidiabetics. Not for use in pregnancy/breast-feeding, type 1 diabetes, ketoacidosis, preexisting GI disease. Pt should continue diet/exercise program; properly dispose of needles, syringes; report hypoglycemia episodes, severe abd pain, injection-site reactions.

albumin (human) (Albuminar, Buminate, Plasbumin)
CLASS Blood product, plasma protein
PREG/CONT C/NA

IND & DOSE Plasma volume expansion related to shock, burns, nephrosis, etc. *Adult:* 5%—500 mL by IV infusion as rapidly as possible; additional 500 mg in 15–30 min; 20% or ... maintain plasma albumin conc ...5 g/100 mL. *Child:* 0.6–1 g/kg, ... V of 20% or 25%.

ADV EFF BP changes, chills, fever, flushing, HF, n/v, rash
NC/PT Monitor BP during infusion; discontinue if hypotension occurs. Stop infusion if headache, fever, BP changes occur; treat w/antihistamine. Adjust infusion rate based on pt response.

albuterol sulfate (AccuNeb, Proventil HFA, Ventolin HFA, VoSpire ER)
CLASS Antiasthmatic, beta agonist, bronchodilator, sympathomimetic
PREG/CONT C/NA

IND & DOSE Relief, prevention of bronchospasm in COPD. *Adult:* 2–4 mg PO tid–qid or 4–8 mg ER tablets q 12 hr. *Child 6–12 yr:* 2 mg PO three to four times/day or 4 mg ER tablet PO q 12 hr. *Child 2–5 yr:* 0.1 mg/kg PO tid; max, 4 mg PO tid. Acute bronchospasm. *Adult:* 1–2 inhalations q 4–6 hr; max, 12 inhalations/day; 2.5 mg tid–qid by nebulization. *Child 2–12 yr, over 15 kg:* 2.5 mg bid–tid by nebulization; *under 15 kg:* 0.5% sol tid–qid by nebulization over 5–15 min. Exercise-induced bronchospasm. *Adult:* 2 inhalations 15–30 min before exercise.

ADJUST DOSE Elderly pts, pts sensitive to beta-adrenergic stimulation

ADV EFF Anxiety, apprehension, **bronchospasm, cardiac arrhythmias,** fear, flushing, n/v, pallor, sweating

INTERACTIONS Aminophylline, beta-adrenergics, digoxin, insulin, linezolid, QT-prolonging drugs, sympathomimetics

NC/PT Do not exceed recommended doses. Have beta blocker on standby. Pt should not cut, crush, or chew tablets. Dizziness may occur; use caution. Use inhalation for acute bronchospasm.

DANGEROUS DRUG

aldesleukin (Proleukin)

CLASS Antineoplastic, immune modulator (interleukin-2 product)
PREG/CONT C/NA

BBW Restrict use in pts w/abnormal pulmonary or cardiac tests or hx of pulmonary or cardiac disease. Risk of capillary leak syndrome, disseminated infections (antibiotic px recommended). Withhold if severe lethargy or somnolence.

IND & DOSE Tx of metastatic renal carcinoma, metastatic melanoma. *Adult:* 600,000 international units/kg IV q 8 hr over 15 min over total of 14 doses; 9 days of rest, then repeat. Max, 28 doses/course.

ADV EFF Bone marrow suppression, cardiac arrhythmias, cardiotoxicity, hepatotoxicity, hypotension, n/v/d, **nephrotoxicity, pulmonary toxicity**

INTERACTIONS Bone marrow suppressants, cardiotoxic drugs, CNS depressants, dexamethasone, hepatotoxic drugs, nephrotoxic drugs

NC/PT Obtain baseline ECG. Protect pt from infection (antibiotic px). Ensure proper mouth care. Pt should avoid pregnancy/breast-feeding; report s&sx of bleeding, infection, severe lethargy.

alectinib (Alecensa)

CLASS Antineoplastic, kinase inhibitor
PREG/CONT High risk/NA

IND & DOSE Tx of pts w/anaplastic lymphoma kinase-positive, metastatic non-small-cell lung cancer who have had crizotinib. *Adult:* 600 mg/day PO w/food.

ADV EFF Bradycardia, constipation, edema, fatigue, **hepatotoxicity**, interstitial pneumonitis, severe myalgia and CK elevation

NC/PT Ensure proper dx. Perform LFTs before and q 2 wk for first 2 mo, then periodically during use; dose adjustment may be needed. Monitor CK levels q 2 wk during first mo and w/complaints of muscle pain/weakness. Monitor lungs/HR regularly; adjust dose as needed. Not for use in pregnancy (contraceptives advised)/breast-feeding. Pt should take daily w/food; report difficulty breathing, shortness of breath, muscle pain/weakness, urine/stool color changes.

alemtuzumab (Lemtrada)

CLASS Monoclonal antibody, MS drug
PREG/CONT C/NA

BBW Risk of serious to fatal autoimmune conditions; serious to life-threatening infusion reactions. Increased risk of malignancies. Ensure proper use; monitor pt closely.

IND & DOSE Tx of relapsing, remitting MS in pts intolerant to other tx. *Adult:* 12 mg/day IV over 4 hr on 5 consecutive days, then 21 mg/day IV over 4 hr for 3 consecutive days 12 mo after first tx course.

ADV EFF Autoimmune cytopenias, cancer development, hypersensitivity reactions, infusion reaction, n/v/d, thyroid disorders, URI, urticaria

NC/PT Limit use to pts w/inadequate response to two or more other drugs. Premedicate w/corticosteroids, antivirals for herpes px. Monitor CBC monthly during and for 48 mo after last infusion. Monitor thyroid function q 3 mo until 48 mo after last infusion. Monitor pt closely during infusion; reaction can occur after infusion ends. Not for use in pregnancy/breast-feeding. Protect pt from infection; ensure standard cancer screening. Pt should take small, frequent meals; report fever, s&sx of infection, difficulty breathing.

alendronate sodium
(Binosto, Fosamax)
CLASS Bisphosphonate, calcium regulator
PREG/CONT C/NA

IND & DOSE Tx of postmenopausal osteoporosis; men w/osteoporosis. *Adult:* 10 mg/day PO or 70 mg PO once a wk. **Prevention of osteoporosis.** *Adult:* 5 mg/day PO or 35 mg PO once wkly. **Tx of Paget disease.** *Adult:* 40 mg/day PO for 6 mo; may retreat after 6-mo tx-free period. **Tx of glucocorticoid-induced osteoporosis.** *Adult:* 5 mg/day PO (10 mg/day PO for postmenopausal women not on estrogen)
ADJUST DOSE Renal impairment
ADV EFF Bone pain, esophageal erosion, femur fractures, GI irritation, headache, hypocalcemia, n/v/d, osteonecrosis of jaw
INTERACTIONS Antacids, aspirin, calcium, iron, NSAIDs, ranitidine
NC/PT Give w/full glass of water or dissolve effervescent tablet in ½ glass water, wait 5 min, stir, then have pt swallow in a.m. at least 30 min before other food or medication; have pt stay upright for 30 min and until first food of day. Monitor serum calcium level; ensure pt has adequate calcium and vitamin D intake. Consider limiting use to 3–5 yr to decrease risk of long-bone fractures. Pt should report difficulty swallowing.

alfuzosin hydrochloride (Uroxatral)
CLASS Alpha-adrenergic blocker, BPH drug
PREG/CONT B/NA

IND & DOSE Tx of s&sx of BPH. *Adult:* 10 mg/day PO after same meal each day.
ADJUST DOSE Hepatic impairment
ADV EFF Dizziness, intraoperative floppy iris syndrome, orthostatic hypotension, prolonged QT

INTERACTIONS Adrenergic blockers, antihypertensives, itraconazole, ketoconazole, nitrates, phosphodiesterase inhibitors, protease inhibitors, QT-prolonging drugs, ritonavir
NC/PT Ensure pt does not have prostate cancer. Monitor for orthostatic hypotension. Advise pt to change positions slowly, take safety precautions for dizziness. Pt should not cut, crush, or chew tablets; store tablets in dry place, protected from light.

alglucosidase alfa
(Lumizyme, Myozyme)
CLASS Enzyme, Pompe's disease drug
PREG/CONT B/NA

BBW Risk of life-threatening anaphylactic reactions; have medical support readily available. Potential for rapid disease progression. Risk of cardiorespiratory failure; monitor pts w/cardiorespiratory disorders carefully *(Myozyme)*.
IND & DOSE To increase ventilator-free survival in pts w/infantile-onset Pompe's disease *(Myozyme)*; tx of pts 8 yr and older w/Pompe's disease *(Lumizyme)*. *Adult, child:* 20 mg/kg IV infusion over 4 hr q 2 wk.
ADV EFF Anaphylaxis, **cardiopulmonary failure**, chest discomfort, dyspnea, flushing, neck pain, **rapid progression of disease**, rash, urticaria, v/d
NC/PT Have medical support readily available during administration. Begin infusion at 1 mg/kg/hr; increase by 2 mg/kg/hr to reach desired dose, carefully monitoring pt response. *Lumizyme* available only by limited access program. Monitor for disease progression.

alirocumab (Praluent)

CLASS PCSK9 inhibitor antibody

PREG/CONT Moderate risk/NA

IND & DOSE Adjunct to diet/exercise for tx of pts w/heterozygous familial hypercholesterolemeia w/ maximal tolerance to statin therapy or clinical atherosclerotic CV disease. *Adult:* 75 mg subcut once every 2 wk; max, 150 mg subcut once every 2 wk.

ADV EFF Flulike sx, **hypersensitivity reactions,** injection-site reactions, nasopharyngitis

NC/PT Monitor LDL at baseline and periodically. Monitor for severe hypersensitivity reaction; stop drug, provide supportive care. Use caution in pregnancy/breast-feeding. Ensure use of die/exercise program. Teach proper administration, not to reuse or share syringe or pen, disposal of needles/syringes. Pt should rotate injection sites w/each use, mark calendar for injection days, review information w/each prescription; report difficulty breathing, rash, injection-site pain/ inflammation.

aliskiren (Tekturna)

CLASS Antihypertensive, renin inhibitor

PREG/CONT D/NA

BBW Use during pregnancy can cause fetal injury or death.

IND & DOSE Tx of hypertension, alone or w/other antihypertensives. *Adult:* 150–300 mg/day PO.

ADJUST DOSE Severe renal impairment

ADV EFF Angioedema w/respiratory sx, cough, diarrhea, dizziness, dyspepsia, fatigue, GERD, headache, hyperkalemia, hypotension, impaired renal function, URI

INTERACTIONS ACE inhibitors, ARBs, cyclosporine, furosemide, itraconazole, NSAIDs, thiazides

NC/PT Rule out pregnancy; not for use in breast-feeding. Monitor potassium level, renal function tests. Store drug in dry place at room temp. Other drugs may also be needed to control BP. Pt should report difficulty breathing, neck swelling, dizziness.

allopurinol (Aloprim, Zyloprim)

CLASS Antigout, purine analogue

PREG/CONT C/NA

IND & DOSE Gout, hyperuricemia. *Adult:* 100–800 mg/day PO in divided doses. **Hyperuricosuria.** *Adult:* 200–300 mg/day PO. **Px of acute gout attacks.** *Adult:* 100 mg/day PO; increase by 100 mg/day at wkly intervals until uric acid is 6 mg/dL or less. **Px of uric acid nephropathy in certain malignancies.** *Adult:* 600–800 mg/day PO for 2–3 days w/high fluid intake. *Child 6–10 yr:* 300 mg/day PO. *Child under 6 yr:* 150 mg/day PO. **Recurrent calcium oxalate stones.** *Adult:* 200–300 mg/day PO. **Parenteral use.** *Adult:* 200–400 mg/ m²/day IV to max of 600 mg/day as continuous infusion at 6-, 8-, 12-hr intervals. *Child:* 200 mg/m²/day IV as continuous infusion at 6-, 8-, 12-hr intervals.

ADJUST DOSE Elderly pts, renal impairment

ADV EFF Drowsiness, headache, n/v/d, **serious to fatal skin reactions**

INTERACTIONS ACE inhibitors, amoxicillin, ampicillin, anticoagulants, cyclophosphamide, theophylline, thiazides, thiopurines

NC/PT Give after meals; encourage 2.5–3 L/day fluid intake. Check urine alkalinity. Pt should discontinue at first sign of rash; avoid OTC medications.

almotriptan malate
(Axert)

CLASS Antimigraine, serotonin selective agonist, triptan
PREG/CONT C/NA

IND & DOSE Tx of acute migraines w/or without aura. Adult, child 12–17 yr: 6.25–12.5 mg PO as single dose at first sign of migraine; may repeat in 2 hr. Max, 2 doses/24 hr.
ADJUST DOSE Hepatic, renal impairment
ADV EFF BP changes, dizziness, dry mouth, medication-overuse headache, MI, nausea, potentially fatal cerebrovascular events, pressure in chest, serotonin syndrome
INTERACTIONS Antifungals, antivirals, ergots, ketoconazole, macrolides, MAOIs, nefazodone, SSRIs
NC/PT For acute migraine, not px. Ensure pt has not used ergots within 24 hr. Not for use in pregnancy. Pt should not take more than two doses/24 hr; discontinue if s&sx of angina; monitor environment. Drug overuse headache may require detoxification. Pt should report GI problems, numbness/tingling, chest pain.

alogliptin (Nesina)
CLASS Antidiabetic, DPP-4 inhibitor
PREG/CONT B/NA

IND & DOSE Adjunct to diet/exercise to improve glycemic control in type 2 diabetes. Adult: 25 mg/day PO.
ADJUST DOSE Renal impairment
ADV EFF Headache, hepatotoxicity, hypoglycemia, nasopharyngitis, pancreatitis, potentially debilitating arthralgia, URI
NC/PT Ensure continued diet/exercise program. Not for use in type 1 diabetes. Monitor blood glucose, renal, liver, pancreatic function. May give w/other antidiabetics. Pt should continue diet/exercise program,

report severe joint pain (drug should be discontinued), uncontrolled blood glucose, all herbs/other drugs used.

alosetron (Lotronex)
CLASS 5-HT$_3$ antagonist, IBS drug
PREG/CONT B/NA

BBW Only indicated for women w/severe diarrhea-dominant IBS who have failed to respond to conventional tx. Ensure pt understands risks of use and warning signs to report. Discontinue immediately at signs of constipation, ischemic colitis.
IND & DOSE Tx of severe diarrhea-predominant IBS in women w/chronic IBS, no anatomic or biochemical abnormalities of GI tract, and who have failed to respond to conventional therapy. Adult: 0.5–1 mg PO bid.
ADJUST DOSE Elderly pts, mild to moderate hepatic impairment
ADV EFF Constipation, ischemic colitis
INTERACTIONS Cimetidine, clarithromycin, fluoroquinolones, fluvoxamine, GI motility drugs, itraconazole, ketoconazole, telithromycin, voriconazole
NC/PT Ensure pt has signed physician-pt agreement. Give w/or without food. Monitor for signs of constipation. Not for use in pregnancy. Regular follow-up required. Pt should report constipation.

alpha$_1$-proteinase inhibitor (Aralast NP, Prolastin-C, Zemaira)
CLASS Blood product
PREG/CONT C/NA

IND & DOSE Chronic replacement tx for pts w/congenital alpha$_1$-antitrypsin deficiency; tx of pts w/early evidence of panacinar emphysema. Adult: 60 mg/kg IV once wkly (Aralast NP, Prolastin). Chronic augmen-

tation and maint therapy of pts w/alpha$_1$-proteinase inhibitor deficiency w/emphysema. *Adult:* 0.08 mL/kg/min IV over 15 min once a wk *(Zemaira)*.
ADV EFF Dizziness, fever, flulike sx, light-headedness
NC/PT Warn pt that this is blood product and can carry risk of blood-borne diseases. Discontinue if s&sx of hypersensitivity. Pt should report fever, chills, joint pain.

---

alprazolam (Xanax)
CLASS Anxiolytic, benzodiazepine
PREG/CONT D/C-IV

IND & DOSE Mgt of anxiety disorders; short-term relief of anxiety sx; anxiety associated w/depression. *Adult:* 0.25–0.5 mg PO tid; adjust to max 4 mg/day in divided doses. **Panic disorder.** *Adult:* 0.5 mg PO tid; increase at 3- to 4-day intervals to 1–10 mg/day or 0.5–1 mg/day ER tablets. Range, 3–6 mg/day.
ADJUST DOSE Elderly pts, advanced hepatic disease, debilitation
ADV EFF Anger, apathy, confusion, constipation, crying, **CV collapse**, diarrhea, disorientation, drowsiness (initially), drug dependence (withdrawal syndrome when drug is discontinued), dry mouth, fatigue, hostility, lethargy, light-headedness, mild paradoxical excitatory reactions during first 2 wk of tx, restlessness, sedation
INTERACTIONS Alcohol, carbamazepine, cimetidine, digoxin, disulfiram, grapefruit juice, hormonal contraceptives, isoniazid, kava, ketoconazole, levodopa, omeprazole, valerian root, valproic acid
NC/PT Taper gradually when discontinuing. Pt should not cut, crush, or chew ER tablet; avoid alcohol, grapefruit juice; take safety measures w/CNS effects. Name confusion w/*Xanax* (alprazolam), *Celexa* (citalopram), and *Cerebyx*

(fosphenytoin), and between alprazolam and lorazepam.

---

alprostadil (Caverject, Muse, Prostin VR Pediatric)
CLASS Prostaglandin
PREG/CONT Unkn/NA

BBW Apnea occurs in 10%–12% of neonates treated w/alprostadil, particularly those weighing under 2 kg. Monitor respiratory status continuously; have ventilatory assistance readily available. Move neonate often during first hr of infusion.
IND & DOSE Tx of ED. *Adult:* Intracavernous injection, 0.2–60 mcg using 0.5-in, 27–30 gauge needle; may repeat up to three times/wk. Urogenital system, 125–250 mcg; max, 2 systems/24 hr. **Palliative tx to temporarily maintain patency of ductus arteriosus.** *Child:* 0.025–0.05 mcg/kg/min IV infusion; max, 0.4 mcg/kg/min if needed.
ADV EFF Apnea, bradycardia, **cardiac arrest**, flushing, hypotension, respiratory distress, tachycardia; w/intracavernous injection: **penile fibrosis**
NC/PT Constantly monitor arterial pressure and blood gases w/IV use. Use extreme caution. Teach pt injection technique, proper disposal of needles/syringes. Name confusion w/*Prostin VR Pediatric* (alprostadil), *Prostin F$_2$* (dinoprost—available outside US), *Prostin E$_2$* (dinoprostone), and *Prostin 15M* (carboprost in Europe).

---

alteplase recombinant (Activase, Cathflo Activase)
CLASS Thrombolytic enzyme, TPA
PREG/CONT C/NA

IND & DOSE Acute MI. *Adult over 67 kg:* 100 mg as 15-mg IV bolus followed by 50 mg infused over 30 min;

then 35 mg over next 60 min. *Adult 67 kg or less:* 15-mg IV bolus followed by 0.75 mg/kg infused over 30 min (max, 50 mg); then 0.5 mg/kg over next 60 min (max, 35 mg). For 3-hr infusion, 60 mg in first hr (6–10 mg as bolus); 20 mg over second hr; 20 mg over third hr. Pts under 65 kg should receive 1.25 mg/kg over 3 hr. **Pulmonary embolism.** *Adult:* 100 mg IV infusion over 2 hr, followed immediately by heparin therapy when PTT or thrombin time returns to twice normal or less. **Acute ischemic stroke.** *Adult:* 0.9 mg/kg (max, 90 mg total dose) infused over 60 min w/10% given as IV bolus over first min. **Restoration of central venous access devices.** *Adult:* 2 mg *(Cathflo Activase)* in 2 mL sterile water for injection; may repeat after 2 hr.
ADV EFF Bleeding, cardiac arrhythmias, intracranial hemorrhage, n/v, urticaria
INTERACTIONS Anticoagulants, aspirin, dipyridamole
NC/PT Discontinue heparin and alteplase if serious bleeding occurs. Monitor coagulation studies; apply pressure or pressure dressings as needed to control bleeding. Type and cross-match blood. Initiate tx within first 6 hr of MI, within 3 hr of stroke.

DANGEROUS DRUG

altretamine (Hexalen)
CLASS Antineoplastic
PREG/CONT D/NA

BBW Must be used under supervision of oncologist. Monitor blood counts regularly; monitor neurologic exams regularly for neurotoxicity.
IND & DOSE **Palliative tx of pts w/persistent or recurrent ovarian cancer following first-line therapy w/cisplatin and/or alkylating agent–based combination.** *Adult:* 260 mg/m^2/day PO for 14 or 21 consecutive days of 28-day cycle w/meals or at bedtime.
ADV EFF Bone marrow depression, neurotoxicity, n/v/d

INTERACTIONS Antidepressants, cimetidine, MAOIs, pyridoxine
NC/PT Not for use in pregnancy/ breast-feeding. Monitor blood counts regularly. Perform neurologic exam before and regularly during tx. Give antiemetic if n/v severe.

---

aluminum hydroxide gel (generic)
CLASS Antacid
PREG/CONT Unkn/NA

IND & DOSE **Hyperacidity, symptomatic relief of upset stomach associated w/hyperacidity.** *Adult:* Tablets/ capsules, 500–1,500 mg three to six times/day PO between meals and at bedtime. Liquid, 5–10 mL between meals and at bedtime. *Child:* 5–15 mL PO q 3–6 hr or 1–3 hr after meals and at bedtime. **Px of GI bleeding in critically ill infants.** 2–5 mL/dose PO q 1–2 hr.
ADV EFF Constipation, **intestinal obstruction**
INTERACTIONS Benzodiazepines, corticosteroids, diflunisal, digoxin, fluoroquinolones, iron, isoniazid, oral drugs, penicillamine, phenothiazines, ranitidine, tetracyclines
NC/PT Do not give oral drugs within 1–2 hr of this drug. Monitor serum phosphorus levels w/long-term therapy. Advise pt to chew tables thoroughly and follow w/water. Constipation may occur.

---

alvimopan (Entereg)
CLASS Peripheral mu-opioid receptor antagonist
PREG/CONT B/NA

BBW For short-term use in hospitalized pts only; risk of MI.
IND & DOSE **To accelerate time to upper and lower GI recovery after partial large or small bowel resection surgery w/primary anastomosis.** *Adult:* 12 mg 30 min–5 hr before surgery, then 12 mg PO bid for up to 7 days. Max, 15 doses.

ADJUST DOSE Renal, hepatic impairment
ADV EFF Anemia, back pain, constipation, dyspepsia, flatulence, hypokalemia, **MI**, urine retention
NC/PT Not for use w/severe hepatic or renal dysfx. For short-term, in-hospital use only. Recent use of opioids may lead to increased adverse effects.

amantadine (generic)
CLASS Antiparkinsonian, antiviral
PREG/CONT C/NA

IND & DOSE **Influenza A virus px or tx.** *Adult:* 200 mg/day PO or 100 mg PO bid for 10 days. *Child 9–12 yr:* 100 mg PO bid. *Child 1–9 yr:* 4.4–8.8 mg/kg/day PO in one or two divided doses; max, 150 mg/day. **Parkinsonism tx.** *Adult:* 100 mg PO bid (up to 400 mg/day). **Drug-induced extrapyramidal reactions.** *Adult:* 100 mg PO bid, up to 300 mg/day in divided doses.
ADJUST DOSE Elderly pts, seizure disorders, renal disease
ADV EFF Dizziness, insomnia, n/d
INTERACTIONS Anticholinergics, hydrochlorothiazide, QT-prolonging drugs, triamterene
NC/PT Do not discontinue abruptly w/Parkinson's disease. Dispense smallest amount possible. Safety precautions if dizziness occurs.

ambrisentan (Letairis)
CLASS Antihypertensive, endothelin receptor antagonist
PREG/CONT X/NA

BBW Rule out pregnancy before starting tx; may cause fetal harm. Pt should use two forms of contraception.
IND & DOSE **Tx of pulmonary arterial hypertension to improve exercise ability and delay clinical worsening.** *Adult:* 5–10 mg/day PO.

ADV EFF Abd pain, anemia, constipation, edema, fluid retention, flushing, **hepatic impairment**, nasal congestion, nasopharyngitis, sinusitis, reduced sperm count
INTERACTIONS Cyclosporine
NC/PT Available only through restricted access program. Not for use in pregnancy/breast-feeding; negative pregnancy test, use of two forms of contraception required. Pt should not cut, crush, or chew tablets; report swelling, difficulty breathing.

amifostine (Ethyol)
CLASS Cytoprotective
PREG/CONT C/NA

IND & DOSE **To reduce cumulative renal toxicity associated w/cisplatin therapy in pts w/advanced ovarian cancer; to reduce incidence of moderate to severe xerostomia in pts w/ postoperative radiation for head and neck cancer.** *Adult:* 910 mg/m² IV daily over 15 min before chemotherapy, over 3 min before radiation therapy.
ADJUST DOSE Elderly pts, CV disease
ADV EFF Cutaneous reactions, dizziness, hypocalcemia, hypotension, n/v
INTERACTIONS Cyclosporine
NC/PT Premedicate w/antiemetic, dexamethasone. Monitor BP carefully during tx. Discontinue at s&sx of cutaneous reaction.

amikacin sulfate (generic)
CLASS Aminoglycoside
PREG/CONT D/NA

BBW Monitor for nephrotoxicity, ototoxicity w/baseline and periodic renal function and neurologic examinations. Risk of serious toxicity, including neuromuscular blockade and respiratory paralysis.
IND & DOSE **Short-term tx of serious infections caused by susceptible strains of *Pseudomonas* sp,**

Escherichia coli, indole-positive and indole-negative *Proteus* sp, *Providencia* sp, *Klebsiella* sp, *Enterobacter* sp, *Serratia* sp, *Acinetobacter* sp, suspected gram-negative infections before susceptibility is known; initial tx of staphylococcal infection if penicillin contraindicated. *Adult, child:* 15 mg/kg/day IM or IV in two to three equal doses at equal intervals, not to exceed 1.5 g/day, for 7–10 days. **UTIs.** *Adult, child:* 250 mg IM or IV bid.

ADJUST DOSE Elderly pts, renal failure

ADV EFF Anorexia, **nephrotoxicity,** n/v/d, ototoxicity, pain at injection site, superinfections

INTERACTIONS Hetastarch in IV sol, NMJ blockers, ototoxic drugs, penicillin

NC/PT Culture before tx. Monitor renal function, length of tx. Ensure pt well hydrated. Give IM dose by deep injection. Pt should report loss of hearing. Name confusion between amikacin and anakinra.

amiloride hydrochloride (Midamor)
CLASS Potassium-sparing diuretic
PREG/CONT B/NA

BBW Monitor pt for hyperkalemia.
IND & DOSE Adjunctive tx for edema of HF or hypertension; to prevent hypokalemia in pts at risk.
Adult: Add 5 mg/day PO to usual anti-hypertensive dose; may increase dose to 10–20 mg/day w/careful electrolyte monitoring.
ADV EFF Anorexia, ED, n/v/d, weakness
INTERACTIONS ACE inhibitors, digoxin, potassium supplements, spironolactone, triamterene
NC/PT Give early in day w/food. Monitor weight, edema, serum electrolytes. Advise pt to take early in day (so increased urination will not disturb sleep) and avoid foods high in potassium.

amino acids (Aminosyn, FreAmine, HepatAmine, ProcalAmine, etc)
CLASS Calorie agent, protein substrate
PREG/CONT C/NA

IND & DOSE To provide nutrition to pts in negative nitrogen balance and unable to maintain in other ways.
Adult: 1–1.5 g/kg/day amino acid injection IV into peripheral vein; 250–500 mL/day amino acid injection IV mixed w/appropriate dextrose, vitamins, and electrolytes as part of TPN sol. Must be individualized. **Hepatic encephalopathy.** *Adult:* 80–120 g amino acid/day; 500 mL *HepatAmine* w/500 mL 50% dextrose and electrolyte sol IV over 8–12 hr/day. **Child w/renal failure.** 0.5–1 g/kg/day amino acid IV mixed w/dextrose as appropriate. **Amino acids replacement.** *Adult, child 16 yr and older:* 1.5 g/kg/day IV. *Child 13–15 yr:* 1.7 g/kg/day IV. *Child 4–12 yr:* 2 g/kg/day IV. *Child 1–3 yr:* 2–2.5 g/kg/day IV.
ADV EFF Dizziness, headache, infection, n/v, pain at infusion site, **pulmonary edema**
INTERACTIONS Tetracyclines
NC/PT Use strict aseptic technique in preparation, administration. Individualize dose based on lab values. Replace all IV apparatus daily. Infuse slowly; monitor closely.

aminocaproic acid (Amicar)
CLASS Systemic hemostatic
PREG/CONT C/NA

IND & DOSE Tx of excessive bleeding due to systemic hyperfibrinolysis/urinary fibrinolysis. *Adult:* Initially, 5 g PO or IV followed by 1–1.25 g every hr to produce and sustain plasma levels of 0.13 mg/mL; do not give more than 30 g/day. **Acute bleeding.** *Adult:* 4–5 g IV in 250 mL diluent during first hr of infusion; then

continuous infusion of 1 g/hr in 50 mL diluent. Continue for 8 hr or until bleeding stops. **Px of recurrence of subarachnoid hemorrhage.** *Adult:* 36 g/day PO or IV in six divided doses.
ADV EFF Abd cramps, dizziness, headache, malaise, n/v/d, **pulmonary embolism**, tinnitus
INTERACTIONS Estrogen, hormonal contraceptives
NC/PT Pt on oral therapy may need up to 10 tablets first hr and around-the-clock dosing. Orient, support pt if CNS effects occur. Monitor for s&sx of clotting.

aminolevulinic acid hydrochloride (Levulan Kerastick)
CLASS Photosensitizer
PREG/CONT C/NA

IND & DOSE Tx of nonkeratotic actinic keratosis of face and scalp w/light therapy. *Adult:* 20% sol applied directly to lesions, followed by light therapy within next 14–18 hr; once q 8 wk if needed.
ADV EFF Local crusting, local erosion, itching, photosensitivity, scaling
NC/PT Clean and dry area; break ampule and apply directly to lesions. Light therapy must be done in 14–18 hr. May repeat in 8 wk.

aminophylline (generic)
CLASS Bronchodilator, xanthine
PREG/CONT C/NA

IND & DOSE Symptomatic relief or prevention of bronchial asthma, reversible bronchospasm associated w/chronic bronchitis and emphysema; adjunct to inhaled beta$_2$-selective adrenergic agonists and systemic corticosteroids for tx of acute exacerbations of s&sx and reversible airflow obstruction associated w/asthma. *Adult:* Initially, 300 mg PO in divided doses q 6–8 hr; after 3 days increase to 400 mg/day

PO in divided doses q 6–8 hr; after 3 more days, if tolerated, 600 mg/day PO in divided doses q 6–8 hr; adjust dose based on peak theophylline levels. *Child:* Adjust dose based on response. *Child 1–15 yr:* Initially, 12–14 mg/kg/day PO in divided doses q 4–6 hr (max, 300 mg/day); after 3 days, 16 mg/kg/day PO in divided doses q 4–6 hr (max, 400 mg/day); after 3 more days, 20 mg/kg/day PO in divided doses q 4–6 hr (max, 600 mg/day). **IV infusion rate for rapid tx.** Loading dose, 5.7 mg/kg over 30 min. Then, *adult over 60 yr:* 0.3 mg/kg/hr (max, 400 mg theophylline/day); *healthy nonsmoking adult:* 0.4 mg/kg/hr (max, 900 mg theophylline/day); *adult w/cardiac decompensation, cor pulmonale, hepatic impairment, sepsis w/multiorgan failure, shock:* 0.2 mg/kg/hr (max, 400 mg theophylline/day, 17 mg/hr); *adolescent (nonsmoking) 12–16 yr:* 0.5 mg/kg/hr (max, 900 mg theophylline/day); *adolescent smokers/child 9–12 yr:* 0.7 mg/kg/hr; *child 1–9 yr:* 0.8 mg/kg/hr; *infants 6–52 wk:* mg/kg/hr = 0.008 × age in wks + 0.21; *neonates over 24 days:* 1.5 mg/kg q 12 hr; *neonates 24 days or younger:* 1 mg/kg q 12 hr.
ADV EFF Related to serum theophylline levels: Anorexia, **brain damage, circulatory failure,** dizziness, irritability, n/v/d, **respiratory arrest, seizures,** tachycardia
INTERACTIONS Acyclovir, allopurinol, beta blockers, cimetidine, clindamycin, diltiazem, disulfiram, enoxacin, erythromycin, fluoroquinolones, fluvoxamine, hormonal contraceptives, nicotine, NMJ blockers, pentoxifylline, phenytoin, sympathomimetics, tetracyclines, thiabendazole, ticlopidine, verapamil, zileuton
NC/PT Maintain adequate hydration. Monitor serum theophylline levels carefully. Use in pregnancy only if clearly needed. Pt should avoid excessive intake of caffeinated beverages, report changes in smoking habits (smoking affects drug's effectiveness).

DANGEROUS DRUG

amiodarone hydrochloride
(Cordarone, Pacerone)

CLASS Adrenergic blocker, antiarrhythmic
PREG/CONT D/NA

BBW Reserve use for life-threatening arrhythmias; serious toxicity, including arrhythmias, pulmonary toxicity, possible.

IND & DOSE Tx of life-threatening recurrent ventricular arrhythmias.
Adult: Loading dose, 800–1,600 mg/day PO in divided doses for 1–3 wk; reduce dose to 600–800 mg/day PO in divided doses for 1 mo; if rhythm stable, reduce dose to 400 mg/day PO in one to two divided doses for maint dose. Or, 1,000 mg IV over 24 hr: 150 mg IV loading dose over 10 min, followed by 360 mg IV over 6 hr at 1 mg/min, then 540 mg IV at 0.5 mg/min over next 18 hr. After first 24 hr, maint infusion of 0.5 mg/min (720 mg/24 hr) or less IV can be cautiously continued for 2–3 wk. Switch to PO form as soon as possible. Convert to PO dose based on duration of IV therapy: Less than 1 wk, initial PO dose is 800–1,600 mg; 1–3 wk, initial PO dose is 600–800 mg; more than 3 wk, initial PO dose is 400 mg.

ADV EFF Anorexia, ataxia, **cardiac arrest, cardiac arrhythmias,** constipation, corneal microdeposits, fatigue, **hepatotoxicity,** hyperthyroidism, hypothyroidism, n/v, photosensitivity, **pulmonary toxicity**

INTERACTIONS Azole antifungals, beta blockers, calcium channel blockers, digoxin, ethotoin, fluoroquinolones, grapefruit juice, macrolide antibiotics, phenytoin, quinidine, ranolazine, simvastatin, thioridazine, trazodone, vardenafil, warfarin, ziprasidone

NC/PT Monitor cardiac rhythm continually and pulmonary function w/ periodic chest X-ray. Regular blood tests and serum-level checks needed.

Obtain baseline ophthalmic exam, then periodically. Not for use in pregnancy. Pt should avoid grapefruit juice, report vision or breathing changes.

amitriptyline hydrochloride (generic)

CLASS Antidepressant, TCA
PREG/CONT D/NA

BBW Increased risk of suicidality in children, adolescents, young adults; monitor carefully.

IND & DOSE Relief of sx of depression (endogenous). *Adult, hospitalized pts:* Initially, 100 mg/day PO in divided doses; gradually increase to 200–300 mg/day as needed. *Outpt:* Initially, 75 mg/day PO in divided doses; may increase to 150 mg/day. Maint dose, 40–100 mg/day (may give as single bedtime dose). *Child 12 yr and older:* 10 mg PO tid, then 20 mg at bedtime. **Chronic pain.** *Adult:* 75–150 mg/day PO.

ADJUST DOSE Elderly pts

ADV EFF Anticholinergic effects, confusion, constipation, disturbed concentration, dry mouth, **MI,** orthostatic hypotension, photosensitivity, sedation, **stroke**

INTERACTIONS Anticholinergics, barbiturates, cimetidine, clonidine, disulfiram, ephedrine, epinephrine, fluoxetine, furazolidone, hormonal contraceptives, levodopa, MAOIs, methylphenidate, nicotine, norepinephrine, phenothiazines, QT-prolonging drugs, thyroid medication

NC/PT Restrict drug access in depressed or suicidal pts; give major portion at bedtime. Pt should be aware of sedative effects and avoid driving, etc; not mix w/other sleep-inducing drugs, avoid prolonged exposure to sun or sunlamps, report thoughts of suicide.

amlodipine besylate
(Norvasc)
CLASS Antianginal, antihypertensive, calcium channel blocker
PREG/CONT C/NA

IND & DOSE Tx of chronic stable angina, Prinzmetal's angina; to reduce angina risk and need for revascularization procedures in pts w/CAD without HF; tx of essential hypertension. *Adult:* Initially, 5 mg/day PO; may gradually increase dose over 7–14 days to max 10 mg/day PO. **Tx of hypertension.** *Child 6–17 yr:* 2.5–5 mg/day PO.
ADJUST DOSE Elderly pts, hepatic impairment
ADV EFF Angina, dizziness, fatigue, flushing, headache, hypotension, lethargy, light-headedness, MI, nausea, peripheral edema
INTERACTIONS Anticholinergics, barbiturates, cimetidine, clonidine, disulfiram, ephedrine, epinephrine, fluoxetine, furazolidone, hormonal contraceptives, levodopa, MAOIs, methylphenidate, nicotine, norepinephrine, phenothiazines, QT-prolonging drugs, simvastatin, thyroid medication
NC/PT Monitor closely when adjusting dose; monitor BP w/hx of nitrate use. Monitor cardiac rhythm during initiation and periodically during tx. Not for use in breast-feeding. Name confusion between *Norvasc* (amlodipine) and *Navane* (thiothixene).

ammonium chloride
(generic)
CLASS Electrolyte, urine acidifier
PREG/CONT C/NA

IND & DOSE Tx of hypochloremic states and metabolic alkalosis; urine acidification. *Adult:* Dosage determined by pt's condition and tolerance. Monitor dosage rate and amount by repeated serum bicarbonate determinations. IV infusion should not exceed conc of 1%–2% of ammonium chloride
ADV EFF Ammonia toxicity, hepatic impairment, pain at injection site
INTERACTIONS Amphetamine, chlorpropamide, dextroamphetamine, ephedrine, flecainide, methadone, methamphetamine, mexiletine, pseudoephedrine
NC/PT Give IV slowly. Monitor for possible fluid overload, acidosis; have sodium bicarbonate or sodium lactate available in case of overdose.

amoxapine (generic)
CLASS Anxiolytic, TCA
PREG/CONT C/NA

BBW Increased risk of suicidality in children, adolescents, young adults; monitor carefully.
IND & DOSE Relief of sx of depression; tx of depression w/anxiety or agitation. *Adult:* Initially, 50 mg PO bid–tid; gradually increase to 100 mg PO bid–tid by end of first wk if tolerated; increase above 300 mg/day only if dosage ineffective for at least 2 wk. Usual effective dose, 200–300 mg/day.
ADJUST DOSE Elderly pts
ADV EFF Anticholinergic effects, confusion, constipation, disturbed concentration, dry mouth, MI, orthostatic hypotension, photosensitivity, sedation, stroke
INTERACTIONS Anticholinergics, barbiturates, cimetidine, clonidine, disulfiram, ephedrine, epinephrine, fluoxetine, furazolidone, hormonal contraceptives, levodopa, MAOIs, methylphenidate, nicotine, norepinephrine, phenothiazines, QT-prolonging drugs, thyroid medication
NC/PT Restrict drug access in depressed or suicidal pts; give major portion at bedtime. Pt should be aware of sedative effects and avoid driving, etc, should not mix w/other sleep-inducing drugs, should avoid

prolonged exposure to sun or sunlamps, report thoughts of suicide.

amoxicillin trihydrate
(Amoxil, Moxatag)
CLASS Antibiotic, penicillin-type
PREG/CONT B/NA

IND & DOSE Tx of tonsillitis and pharyngitis caused by *Streptococcus pyogenes* (ER tablet); infections due to susceptible strains of *Haemophilus influenzae, Escherichia coli, Proteus mirabilis, Neisseria gonorrhoeae, Streptococcus pneumoniae, Enterococcus faecalis,* streptococci, non–penicillinase-producing staphylococci, *Helicobacter pylori* infection in combination w/other agents; postexposure px against *Bacillus anthracis.* *Adult, child over 40 kg:* URIs, GU, skin and soft-tissue infections, 250 mg PO q 8 hr or 500 mg PO q 12 hr; severe infection, 500 mg PO q 8 hr or 875 mg PO q 12 hr; postexposure anthrax px, 500 mg PO tid to complete 60-day course after 14–21 days of a fluoroquinolone or doxycycline tx; lower respiratory infection, 500 mg PO q 8 hr or 875 mg PO bid; uncomplicated gonococcal infections, 3 g amoxicillin PO as single dose; *C. trachomatis* in pregnancy, 500 mg PO tid for 7 days or 875 mg PO bid; tonsillitis/pharyngitis, 775 mg PO for 10 days w/food (ER tablet); *H. pylori* infection, 1 g PO bid w/clarithromycin 500 mg PO bid and lansoprazole 30 mg PO bid for 14 days. *Child 3 mo and older, under 40 kg:* URIs, GU infections, skin and soft-tissue infections, 20 mg/kg/day PO in divided doses q 8 hr or 25 mg/kg/day PO in divided doses q 12 hr; severe infection, 40 mg/kg/day PO in divided doses q 8 hr or 45 mg/kg/day PO in divided doses q 12 hr; postexposure anthrax px, 80 mg/kg/day PO divided in three doses to complete 60-day course after 14–21 days of fluoroquinolone or doxycycline tx. *Child 3 mo and older:* Mild to moderate URIs, GU infections, skin infections, 20 mg/kg PO daily in divided doses q 8 hr or 25 mg/kg PO in divided doses q 12 hr; acute otitis media, 80–90 mg/kg/day PO for 10 days (severe cases) or 5–7 days (moderate cases); gonorrhea in prepubertal children, 50 mg/kg PO w/25 mg/kg probenecid PO as single dose; lower respiratory infections/severe URI, GU, and skin infections, 40 mg/kg PO daily in divided doses q 8 hr or 45 mg/kg PO daily in divided doses q 12 hr. *Child up to 12 wk:* 30 mg/kg PO daily in divided doses q 12 hr.
ADJUST DOSE Renal impairment
ADV EFF Abd pain, anaphylaxis, fever, gastritis, glossitis, n/v/d, sore mouth, superinfections, wheezing
INTERACTIONS Chloramphenicol, hormonal contraceptives, probenecid, tetracyclines
NC/PT Culture before tx. Monitor for superinfections; n/v/d may occur. Pt should not cut, crush, or chew ER tablets; should continue until at least 2 days after s&sx resolve; complete full course.

amphetamine (Adzenys XR-ODT)
CLASS CNS stimulant
PREG/CONT C/C-II

BBW High risk of abuse and dependence; monitor pt closely.
IND & DOSE Tx of ADHD in pts 6 yr and older. *Adult:* 12.5 mg/day PO in a.m. *Children 6–17 yr:* 6.3 mg/day PO in a.m.; max: 18.8 mg/day for child 6–12 yr, 12.5 mg/day for child 13–17 yr.
ADV EFF Abd pain, agitation, anorexia, growth suppression, hypertension, nervousness, n/v/d, peripheral vascular disease, psychiatric adverse reactions, **sudden death,** tachycardia, weight loss
INTERACTIONS Acidifying, alkalinizing agents
NC/PT Ensure proper dx, baseline ECG. Monitor BP, P regularly. Monitor growth/weight in child. Evaluate for

bipolar disorder before use. Arrange for periodic breaks to evaluate need for drug. Pt must allow tablet to dissolve in saliva on the tongue, then swallow; take once daily in a.m.; secure drug (a controlled substance). Pt should report numbness/tingling, chest pain, significant weight loss, abnormal thoughts, palpitations.

DANGEROUS DRUG

amphotericin B; amphotericin B cholesteryl sulfate; amphotericin B liposome (Abelcet, AmBisome, Amphotec)

CLASS Antifungal
PREG/CONT B/NA

BBW Reserve systemic use for progressive or potentially fatal infections. Not for use in noninvasive disease; toxicity can be severe.
IND & DOSE Tx of potentially fatal, progressive fungal infections not responsive to other tx. *Adult, child:* 5 mg/kg/day IV as single infusion at 2.5 mg/kg/hr *(Abelcet).* **Aspergillosis.** *Adult, child:* Initially, 3–4 mg/kg/day IV; Infuse at 1 mg/kg/hr *(Amphotec).* Or, 3 mg/kg/day IV over more than 2 hr *(AmBisome).* **Presumed fungal infection in febrile neutropenic pts.** *Adult, child:* 3 mg/kg/day IV *(AmBisome).* **Cryptococcal meningitis in HIV pts.** *Adult, child:* 6 mg/kg/day IV *(AmBisome).* **Leishmaniasis.** *Adult, child:* 3 mg/kg/day IV, days 1–5, 14, and 21 for immunocompetent pts; 4 mg/kg/day IV, days 1–5, 10, 17, 24, 31, and 38 for immunocompromised pts *(AmBisome).*
ADV EFF Cramping, dyspepsia, electrolyte disturbances, n/v/d, pain at injection site, **renal toxicity**
INTERACTIONS Antineoplastics, corticosteroids, cyclosporine, digitalis, nephrotoxic drugs, thiazide diuretics, zidovudine
NC/PT Dose varies among brand names; check carefully. Culture

before tx. Monitor injection sites, electrolytes, kidney function. Use antihistamines, aspirin, antiemetics, meperidine to improve comfort, drug tolerance.

---

ampicillin (generic)

CLASS Antibiotic, penicillin
PREG/CONT B/NA

IND & DOSE Tx of bacterial infections caused by susceptible strains; tx of GU infections: *Adult:* 500 mg IM, IV, PO q 6 hr. **Tx of respiratory tract infections.** *Adult:* 250 mg IM, IV, PO q 6 hr. **Tx of digestive system infections.** *Adult:* 500 mg PO q 6 hr for 48–72 hr after pt asymptomatic or eradication evident. **Tx of STDs in pts allergic to tetracycline.** *Adult:* 3.5 g ampicillin PO w/1 g probenecid. **Prevention of bacterial endocarditis for dental, oral, or upper respiratory procedures in pts at high risk.** *Adult:* 2 g ampicillin IM or IV within 30 min of procedure. Child: 50 mg/kg ampicillin IM or IV within 30 min of procedure. Six hr later, 25 mg/kg ampicillin IM or IV or 25 mg/kg amoxicillin PO. **Tx of respiratory and soft-tissue infections.** *Adult, child 40 kg or more:* 250–500 mg IV or IM q 6 hr. *Under 40 kg:* 25–50 mg/kg/day IM or IV in equally divided doses at 6- to 8-hr intervals. *20 kg to 40 kg:* 250 mg PO q 6 hr. *Under 20 kg:* 50 mg/kg/day PO in equally divided doses q 6–8 hr. **Tx of GI and GU infections, including women w/N. gonorrhoeae.** *Adult, child over 40 kg:* 500 mg IM or IV q 6 hr. *40 kg or less:* 50 mg/kg/day IM or IV in equally divided doses q 6–8 hr. *20 kg to 40 kg:* 500 mg PO q 6 hr. *Under 20 kg:* 100 mg/kg/day PO in equally divided doses q 6–8 hr. **Tx of bacterial meningitis.** *Adult, child:* 150–200 mg/kg/day by continuous IV drip, then IM injections in equally divided doses q 3–4 hr. **Tx of septicemia.** *Adult, child:* 150–200 mg/kg/day IV for at least 3 days, then IM q 3–4 hr.

ADJUST DOSE Renal impairment
ADV EFF Abd pain, **anaphylaxis**, fever, gastritis, glossitis, n/v/d, sore mouth, superinfections, wheezing
INTERACTIONS Atenolol, chloramphenicol, hormonal contraceptives, probenecid, tetracyclines
NC/PT Culture before tx. Give on empty stomach. Do not give IM injections in same site. Check IV site for thrombosis. Monitor for superinfections. Pt should use second form of contraception while on drug. May experience n/v/d.

anagrelide (Agrylin)
CLASS Antiplatelet
PREG/CONT C/NA

IND & DOSE Tx of essential thrombocythemia secondary to myeloproliferative disorders to reduce elevated platelet count and risk of thrombosis; to improve associated s&sx, including thrombohemorrhagic events. *Adult:* Initially, 0.5 mg PO qid or 1 mg PO bid; do not increase by more than 0.5 mg/day each wk. Max, 10 mg/day or 2.5 mg as single dose. *Child:* Initially, 0.5 mg/day PO; do not increase by more than 0.5 mg/day each wk. Max, 10 mg/day or 2.5 mg in single dose.
ADJUST DOSE Moderate hepatic impairment
ADV EFF Abd pain, asthenia, **bleeding, complete heart block**, headache, HF, MI, n/v/d, palpitations, **pancreatitis, prolonged QT**, thrombocytopenia
INTERACTIONS Aspirin, drugs that affect bleeding, grapefruit juice, NSAIDs
NC/PT Pretreatment ECG. Obtain platelet count q 2 days for first wk, then wkly. Provide safety measures. Monitor for bleeding; mark chart for alert in invasive procedures. Not for use in pregnancy. Pt should not drink grapefruit juice; should take on empty stomach. Name confusion between *Agrylin* and *Aggrastat* (tirofiban).

anakinra (Kineret)
CLASS Antiarthritic, interleukin-1 receptor antagonist
PREG/CONT B/NA

IND & DOSE To reduce s&sx and slow progression of moderately to severely active rheumatoid arthritis in pts who have failed on one or more disease-modifying antirheumatic drugs. *Adult 18 yr and older:* 100 mg/day subcut at about same time each day. Tx of neonatal-onset multisystem inflammatory disease. *Child:* 1–2 mg/kg/day subcut to max 8 mg/kg/day.
ADJUST DOSE Renal impairment, elderly pts
ADV EFF Hypersensitivity reactions, infections, injection-site reactions, sinusitis, URI
INTERACTIONS Etanercept; immunizations; TNF blockers (increased risk of serious infection; combination not recommended)
NC/PT Store refrigerated, protected from light. Monitor neutrophil counts regularly. Not for use in pregnancy. Rotate inject sites. Other antiarthritics may also be needed. Pt should dispose of syringes, needles appropriately. Name confusion between anakinra and amikacin.

DANGEROUS DRUG

anastrozole (Arimidex)
CLASS Antiestrogen, antineoplastic, aromatase inhibitor
PREG/CONT X/NA

IND & DOSE Tx of advanced breast cancer in postmenopausal women w/disease progression following tamoxifen tx; first-line tx of postmenopausal women w/hormone receptor–positive or hormone receptor–unkn locally advanced or metastatic breast cancer; adjuvant tx of postmenopausal women w/hormone receptor–positive early breast cancer. *Adult:* 1 mg/day PO.

ADV EFF Asthenia, back pain, bone pain, CV events, decreased bone density, fractures, hot flashes, insomnia, n/v, pharyngitis
INTERACTIONS Estrogens, tamoxifen
NC/PT Monitor lipid levels periodically, bone density. Use analgesics for pain. Not for use in pregnancy.

anidulafungin (Eraxis)
CLASS Antifungal, echinocandin
PREG/CONT C/NA

IND & DOSE Tx of candidemia and other *Candida* infections. *Adult:* 200 mg by IV infusion on day 1, then 100 mg/day by IV infusion; generally for minimum of 14 days. **Tx of esophageal candidiasis.** *Adult:* 100 mg by IV infusion on day 1, then 50 mg/day by IV infusion for minimum of 14 days.
ADV EFF Liver toxicity, n/v/d
NC/PT Culture before tx. Monitor LFTs. Not for use in pregnancy/breastfeeding. Maintain fluid, food intake.

antihemophilic factor
(Advate, Hemofil M, Humate-P, ReFacto, Wilate, Xyntha)
CLASS Antihemophilic
PREG/CONT C/NA

IND & DOSE Tx of hemophilia A; short-term px (*ReFacto*) to reduce frequency of spontaneous bleeding; surgical or invasive procedures in pts w/von Willebrand disease in whom desmopressin is ineffective or contraindicated. *Adult, child:* Dose depends on weight, severity of deficiency, severity of bleeding; monitor factor VIII levels to establish dose needed. Follow tx carefully w/factor VIII level assays. Formulas used as dosage guide:

$$\text{(\% of normal)} = \frac{\text{AHF/IU given} \times 2}{\text{weight in kg}}$$

Expected Factor VIII increase

AHF/IU required = weight (kg)
× desired factor VIII increase
(% of normal) × 0.5

ADV EFF AIDS (from repeated use of blood products), **bronchospasm, hemolysis, hepatitis,** stinging at infusion site, tachycardia
NC/PT Monitor factor VIII levels regularly. Monitor pulse. Reduce infusion rate w/significant tachycardia. Pt should wear or carry medical alert information.

antihemophilic factor
(Factor VIII) (recombinant) (Nuwiq)
CLASS Clotting factor
PREG/CONT Unkn /NA

IND & DOSE Tx/control of bleeding episodes, periop bleeding mgt in pts w/hemophilia A. *Adult, child:* International units (IU) – body wt in kg × desired factor VIII rise (IU/dL) × 0.5 (IU/kg/IU/dL) IV. **Px to reduce bleeding episodes in hemophilia A.** *Adult, child 12–17 yr:* 30–40 international units/kg IV every other day. *Child 2–11 yr:* 30–50 international units/kg every other day or three times/wk.
ADV EFF Back pain, dry mouth, headache, **hypersensitivity reactions,** factor VIII antibody production, injection-site reaction, vertigo
NC/PT Ensure dx; not for tx of von Willebrand disease. For acute use, refer to guidelines for usual dosage; use formula to determine actual dose. Use caution in pregnancy/breast-feeding. For px, teach proper storage/administration/reconstitution, disposal of needles/syringes; recommend med-alert identification. Pt should report difficulty breathing, chest pain, numbness/tingling, continued bleeding.

antihemophilic factor (recombinant) Fc fusion protein (Eloctate)
CLASS Antihemophilic
PREG/CONT C/NA

IND & DOSE Tx of congenital hemophilia A (for bleeding episodes, periop use). *Adult, child:* Given IV:

$$\text{(\% of normal)} = \frac{\text{AHF/IU given} \times 2}{\text{weight in kg}}$$

AHF/IU required = weight (kg) × desired factor VIII increase (% of normal) × 0.5

Routine px of bleeding in congenital hemophilia A. 50 international units/kg IV q 4 days; based on response, range 25–65 international units/kg q 3–5 days.
ADV EFF Anaphylaxis, arthralgia, myalgia
NC/PT Monitor factor VIII levels regularly. Monitor pulse. Reduce infusion rate w/significant tachycardia. Pt should wear or carry medical alert information; use caution in pregnancy.

antihemophilic factor (recombinant) porcine sequence (Obizur)
CLASS Antihemophilic
PREG/CONT C/NA

IND & DOSE Tx of bleeding episodes in adults w/acquired hemophilia A. *Adult:* 200 units/kg IV; titrate based on response and factor VIII recovery.
ADV EFF Anaphylaxis, inhibitory antibody production
NC/PT Monitor factor VIII levels and pt closely during infusion. Pt should wear or carry medical alert information; use caution in pregnancy.

antithrombin, recombinant (ATryn)
CLASS Coagulation inhibitor
PREG/CONT C/NA

IND & DOSE Prevention of periop and peripartum thromboembolic events in pts w/hereditary antithrombin deficiency. *Adult:* Individualize dose based on antithrombin level; loading dose over 15 min IV followed by maint dose to keep antithrombin activity levels 80%–120% of normal. Surgical pts, use formula 100 − baseline antithrombin activity ÷ 2.3 × body wt; maint, divide by 10.2. Pregnant women, 100 − baseline antithrombin activity ÷ 1.3 × body wt; maint, divide by 5.4.
ADV EFF Hemorrhage, infusion-site reactions
INTERACTIONS Heparin, low-molecular-weight heparin
NC/PT Not for use w/allergy to goats or goat products. Follow clotting studies closely.

antithrombin III (Thrombate III)
CLASS Coagulation inhibitor
PREG/CONT C/NA

IND & DOSE Tx of pts w/hereditary antithrombin III deficiency in connection w/surgical or obstetrical procedures or when suffering from thromboembolism; replacement tx in congenital antithrombin III deficiency. *Adult:* Dosage units = desired antithrombin level (%) − baseline antithrombin level (%) × body wt (kg) ÷ 1.4 q 2–8 days IV.
ADV EFF Hemorrhage, infusion-site reactions
INTERACTIONS Heparin, low-molecular-weight heparin
NC/PT Frequent blood tests required. Dosage varies widely. Monitor for bleeding. Human blood product; slight risk of blood-transmitted diseases.

DANGEROUS DRUG

apixaban (Eliquis)
CLASS Anticoagulant, direct thrombin inhibitor
PREG/CONT B/NA

BBW Premature discontinuation increases risk of thrombotic events; consider coverage w/another anticoagulant if discontinued for reasons other than pathological bleeding. Risk of epidural, spinal hematomas if used in pts w/spinal puncture of anesthesia.
IND & DOSE Reduction of stroke, embolism in pts w/nonvalvular atrial fibrillation. *Adult:* 5 mg PO bid; reduce to 2.5 mg PO bid if age over 80 yr, weight over 60 kg, serum creatinine over 1.5 mg.dL. **Px of DVT after hip/knee replacement.** *Adult:* 2.5 mg PO bid. **Tx of DVT, PE.** *Adult:* 10 mg PO bid for 7 days, then 5 mg PO bid. **Reduction of risk of recurrent DVT, PE.** *Adult:* 2.5 mg PO bid.
ADJUST DOSE Elderly pts, severe renal impairment
ADV EFF Bleeding, rebound thrombotic events w/discontinuation, severe hypersensitivity reactions
INTERACTIONS Carbamazepine, clarithromycin, itraconazole, ketoconazole, other drugs that increase bleeding, phenytoin, rifampin, ritonavir, St. John's wort
NC/PT Not for use w/artificial heart valves. Monitor for bleeding; do not stop suddenly. Pt should avoid pregnancy/breast-feeding, OTC drugs that affect bleeding; ensure that drug is not stopped suddenly; take safety precautions to avoid injury; report increased bleeding, chest pain, headache, dizziness.

apomorphine (Apokyn)
CLASS Antiparkinsonian, dopamine agonist
PREG/CONT C/NA

IND & DOSE Intermittent tx of hypomobility "off" episodes caused by advanced Parkinson's disease. *Adult:* 2 mg subcut; increase slowly to max of 6 mg. Give 300 mg trimethobenzamide PO tid for 3 days before starting to completion of 2 mo of tx.
ADV EFF Chest pain, compulsive behaviors, dizziness, dyskinesia, edema, fibrotic complications, flushing, hallucinations, hepatic impairment, hypotension, loss of impulse control, melanoma, n/v, renal impairment, rhinorrhea, sedation, somnolence, sweating, yawning
INTERACTIONS Antihypertensives, dopamine antagonists, 5-HT$_3$ antagonists (granisetron, ondansetron, etc), QT-prolonging drugs, vasodilators
NC/PT Give subcut injection in stomach, upper arm, or leg; rotate sites. Protect pt when CNS effects occur. Teach proper drug administration/disposal of needles/syringes; many CNS effects possible; safety precautions w/CNS changes, hypotension.

apremilast (Otezla)
CLASS Antiarthritic, phosphodiesterase-4 inhibitor
PREG/CONT C/NA

IND & DOSE Tx of adults w/active psoriatic arthritis. *Adult:* 30 mg PO bid. Titrate as follows: Day 1, 10 mg PO in a.m.; day 2, 10 mg PO in a.m. and p.m.; day 3, 10 mg PO in a.m. and 20 mg PO in p.m.; day 4, 20 mg PO in a.m. and p.m.; day 5, 20 mg in a.m. and 30 mg PO in p.m.; day 6, 30 mg PO bid.
ADJUST DOSE Renal disease
ADV EFF Depression, headache, n/v/d, weight loss

INTERACTIONS Carbamazepine, phenobarbital, phenytoin, rifampin
NC/PT Titrate dose to effective level to decrease GI effects. Give small, frequent meals. Monitor weight loss; stop drug if significant. Watch for depression, possible suicidality. Pt should take daily as directed, report severe GI upset, significant weight loss, thoughts of suicide, increasing depression.

---

aprepitant (Emend), fosaprepitant (Emend for Injection)

CLASS Antiemetic, substance P and neurokinin 1 receptor antagonist
PREG/CONT B/NA

IND & DOSE W/other antiemetics for prevention of acute and delayed n/v associated w/initial and repeat courses of moderately or highly emetogenic cancer chemotherapy. *Adult:* Aprepitant, 125 mg PO 1 hr before chemotherapy (day 1) and 80 mg PO once daily in a.m. on days 2 and 3 w/dexamethasone, ondansetron; or parenteral administration, fosaprepitant, 115 mg IV 30 min before chemotherapy on day 1 of antiemetic regimen; infuse over 15 min. *Child 12 yr and older or under 12 yr weighing at least 30 kg:* 115 mg IV 30 min before chemotherapy infused over 15 min on day 1 of antiemetic regimen; 125 mg/day PO days 2 and 3. **Postop n/v.** *Adult:* 40 mg PO within 3 hr before anesthesia induction.
ADV EFF Alopecia, anorexia, constipation, diarrhea, dizziness, fatigue
INTERACTIONS Docetaxel, etoposide, hormonal contraceptives, ifosfamide, imatinib, irinotecan, paclitaxel, pimozide, vinblastine, vincristine, vinorelbine, warfarin
NC/PT Give first dose w/dexamethasone 1 hr before start of chemotherapy; give additional doses of dexamethasone and ondansetron as indicated as part of antiemetic

regimen. Give within 3 hr before anesthesia induction if used to prevent postop n/v. Provide safety precautions, analgesics as needed. Not for use in pregnancy/breast-feeding. Pt should use caution if dizziness, drowsiness occur.

---

arformoterol tartrate (Brovana)

CLASS Bronchodilator, long-acting beta agonist
PREG/CONT R/NA

BBW Increased risk of asthma-related death; alert pt accordingly. Contraindicated in asthma without use of long-term control medication.
IND & DOSE Long-term maint tx of bronchoconstriction in pts w/COPD. *Adult:* 15 mcg bid (a.m. and p.m.) by nebulization. Max, 30 mcg total daily dose.
ADV EFF Asthma-related deaths, paradoxical bronchospasm
INTERACTIONS Beta-adrenergic blockers, diuretics, MAOIs, QT-prolonging drugs, TCAs
NC/PT Not for use in acute bronchospasm. Ensure pt continues other drugs to manage COPD, especially long-term control drugs. Not for use in pregnancy/breast-feeding. Teach proper use of nebulizer. Pt should have periodic evaluation of respiratory status.

DANGEROUS DRUG

argatroban (Argatroban)

CLASS Anticoagulant
PREG/CONT B/NA

IND & DOSE Px or tx of thrombosis in pts w/heparin-induced thrombocytopenia, including pts at risk undergoing percutaneous coronary intervention (PCI). *Adult:* 2 mcg/kg/min IV; PCI, bolus of 350 mcg/kg IV over 3–5 min, then 25 mcg/kg/min IV.
ADV EFF Bleeding, cardiac arrest, chest pain, dyspnea, fever, headache, hypotension, n/v/d

INTERACTIONS Heparin, thrombolytics, warfarin
NC/PT Not for use in pregnancy/breast-feeding. Monitor for s&sx of bleeding.

aripiprazole (Abilify, Abilify Discmelt, Abilify Maintena, Aristada)

CLASS Atypical antipsychotic, dopamine/serotonin agonist and antagonist
PREG/CONT C/NA

BBW Elderly pts w/dementia-related psychosis have increased risk of death if given atypical antipsychotics; not approved for this use. Risk of suicidal ideation increases w/antidepressant use, especially in children, adolescents, young adults; monitor accordingly.
IND & DOSE Oral sol may be substituted on mg-to-mg basis up to 25 mg of tablet. Pts taking 30-mg tablets should receive 25 mg if switched to sol. **Tx of schizophrenia.** *Adult:* 10–15 mg/day PO. Increase dose q 2 wk to max of 30 mg/day. Or 441 mg IM in deltoid muscle q 4 wk or 662–882 mg IM in gluteal muscle q 4–6 wk. *Child 13–17 yr:* Initially, 2 mg/day PO. Adjust to 5 mg/day after 2 days, then to target dose of 10 mg/day; max, 30 mg/day. **Tx of bipolar disorder.** *Adult:* 15 mg/day PO as one dose; maint, 15–30 mg/day PO. *Child 10–17 yr:* Initially, 2 mg/day PO; titrate to 5 mg/day after 2 days, then to 10 mg/day after another 2 days. Target dose, 10 mg/day; max, 30 mg/day. **Tx of major depressive disorder.** *Adult:* Initially, 2–5 mg/day PO; maint, 2–15 mg/day as adjunct therapy. **Tx of agitation.** *Adult:* 5.25–15 mg IM; usual dose, 9.75 mg IM. May give cumulative doses of up to 30 mg/day PO. **Irritability associated w/autistic disorder.** *Child 6–17 yr:* 2 mg/day PO; titrate to maint dose of 5–15 mg/day.
ADV EFF Akathisia, bone marrow suppression, cognitive/motor impairment, dyslipidemia, hyperglycemia,

NMS, orthostatic hypotension, **seizures** (potentially life-threatening), suicidality, weight gain
INTERACTIONS Alcohol, carbamazepine, CNS depressants, CYP2D6 inhibitors (fluoxetine, paroxetine, quinidine), CYP3A4 inhibitors (ketoconazole), lorazepam
NC/PT Dispense least amount possible to suicidal pts. Ensure pt well hydrated. Switch to oral sol w/difficulty swallowing. Adjust ER injection dose based on current oral use; see manufacturer's guideline. Not for use in pregnancy/breast-feeding. Monitor weight; assess for hyperglycemia. May react w/many medications; monitor drug regimen. Take safety precautions for cognitive/motor impairment. Confusion between aripiprazole and proton pump inhibitors; use extreme caution.

armodafinil (Nuvigil)

CLASS CNS stimulant, narcoleptic
PREG/CONT C/C-IV

IND & DOSE To improve wakefulness in pts w/excessive sleepiness associated w/obstructive sleep apnea/hypopnea syndrome; narcolepsy. *Adult:* 150–250 mg/day PO as single dose in a.m. **Shift work sleep disorder.** *Adult:* 150 mg/day PO taken 1 hr before start of work shift.
ADJUST DOSE Elderly pts, severe hepatic impairment
ADV EFF Angioedema, **anaphylaxis,** dizziness, headache, insomnia, nausea, psychiatric sx, **Stevens-Johnson syndrome**
INTERACTIONS Cyclosporine, ethinyl estradiol, hormonal contraceptives, midazolam, omeprazole, phenytoin, TCAs, triazolam, warfarin
NC/PT Rule out underlying medical conditions; not intended for tx of obstruction. Should be part of comprehensive program for sleep. Provide safety measures if CNS effects occur. Stop drug if psychiatric sx

occur. Not for use in pregnancy/breast-feeding. Pt should use barrier contraceptives, avoid alcohol.

DANGEROUS DRUG

arsenic trioxide
(Trisenox)
CLASS Antineoplastic
PREG/CONT D/NA

BBW Extremely toxic and carcinogenic; monitor blood counts, electrolytes. Prolonged QT, arrhythmias; monitor ECG.
IND & DOSE Induction and remission of acute promyelocytic leukemia in pts refractory to retinoid or anthracycline chemotherapy w/t(15:17) translocation or PML/RAR-alpha gene expression. *Adult:* Induction, 0.15 mg/kg/day IV until bone marrow remission; max, 60 doses. Consolidation, 0.15 mg/kg/day IV starting 3–6 wk after induction.
ADJUST DOSE Severe hepatic impairment
ADV EFF Abd pain, APL differentiation syndrome, cancer, complete heart block, cough, dizziness, dyspnea, edema, fatigue, headache, hyperleukocytosis, leukocytosis, n/v/d, prolonged QT
INTERACTIONS Cyclosporine, ethinyl estradiol, hormonal contraceptives, midazolam, omeprazole, phenytoin, TCAs, triazolam, warfarin
NC/PT Monitor CBC, ECG, electrolytes closely. Provide comfort measures for GI effects, safety measures for CNS effects. Not for use in pregnancy/breast-feeding.

---

asenapine (Saphris)
CLASS Atypical antipsychotic, dopamine/serotonin antagonist
PREG/CONT C/NA

BBW Elderly pts w/dementia-related psychosis have increased risk of death if given atypical antipsychotics; not approved for this use. Risk of sui-

cidal ideation increases w/antidepressant use, especially in children, adolescents, young adults; monitor accordingly.
IND & DOSE Tx of schizophrenia. *Adult:* 5–10 mg sublingually bid. **Acute tx of manic or mixed episodes associated w/bipolar I disorder; adjunctive therapy w/lithium or valproate for acute tx of manic or mixed episodes associated w/bipolar I disorder.** *Adult:* 5–10 mg sublingually bid; may decrease to 5 mg/day if needed. **Tx of manic or mixed episodes w/bipolar I disorder.** *Child 10–17 yr:* 2.5–10 mg sublingually bid.
ADJUST DOSE Severe hepatic impairment
ADV EFF Akathisia, bone marrow suppression, dizziness, dyslipidemia, extrapyramidal sx, hyperglycemia, NMS, orthostatic hypotension, prolonged QT, somnolence, suicidality, weight gain
INTERACTIONS Alcohol, antihypertensives, CNS depressants, fluvoxamine, QT-prolonging drugs
NC/PT Monitor ECG periodically. Provide safety measures for CNS effects. Monitor weight gain and blood glucose. Pt should not swallow tablet; should place under tongue (where it will dissolve within sec) and not eat or drink for 10 min. Not for use in pregnancy/breast-feeding. Pt should change positions slowly, take safety measures w/CNS effects, report thoughts of suicide.

---

asfotase alfa (Strensiq)
CLASS Alkaline phosphatase
PREG/CONT Low risk/NA

IND & DOSE Tx of perinatal, juvenile-onset hypophosphatasia. *Adult, child:* 2 mg/kg subcut three times/wk or 1 mg/kg subcut six times/wk; max, 3 mg/kg three times/wk.
ADV EFF Ectopic calcifications (eye, kidneys), hypersensitivity reactions, lipodystrophy

NC/PT Ensure proper dx. Monitor phosphate level. Rotate injection sites; do not give in inflamed, swollen areas. Teach caregiver proper administration/disposal of needles/ syringes.

DANGEROUS DRUG

asparaginase Erwinia chrysanthemi (Erwinaze)

CLASS Antineoplastic
PREG/CONT C/NA

IND & DOSE Tx of pts w/ALL who have developed sensitivity to asparaginase or pegaspargase. *Adult, child:* 25,000/m² international units IM for each scheduled dose of pegaspargase or asparaginase; limit volume to 2 mL/injection.
ADV EFF Anaphylaxis, arthralgia, coagulation disorders, hyperglycemia, n/v, pancreatitis, rash, seizures, thrombotic events, urticaria
NC/PT Monitor for severe reaction, hyperglycemia, pancreatitis, coagulation disorders. Not for use in pregnancy. Prepare calendar to keep track of appointments. Pt should have regular blood tests.

---

aspirin (Bayer, Bufferin, Heartline, Norwich, St. Joseph's, etc)

CLASS Analgesic, antiplatelet, antipyretic, salicylate
PREG/CONT D/NA

IND & DOSE Tx of mild to moderate pain, fever. *Adult:* 325–1,000 mg PO q 4–6 hr; max, 4,000 mg/day. SR tablets, 1,300 mg PO, then 650–1,300 mg q 8 hr; max, 3,900 mg/day. Suppositories, 1 rectally q 4 hr. *Child:* 10–15 mg/kg/dose PO q 4 hr; up to 60–80 mg/kg/day. Do not give to pts w/chickenpox or flu sx. **Arthritis.** *Adult:* Up to 3 g/day PO in divided doses. *Child:* 90–130 mg/kg/24 h PO in divided doses at 6- to 8-hr

intervals. Maintain serum level of 150–300 mcg/mL. **Ischemic stroke, TIA.** *Adult:* 50–325 mg/day PO. **Angina, recurrent MI prevention.** *Adult:* 75–325 mg/day PO. **Suspected MI.** *Adult:* 160–325 mg PO as soon as possible; continue daily for 30 days. **CABG.** *Adult:* 325 mg PO 6 hr after procedure, then daily for 1 yr. **Acute rheumatic fever.** *Adult:* 5–8 g/day PO; modify to maintain serum salicylate level of 15–30 mg/dL. *Child:* Initially, 100 mg/kg/day PO, then decrease to 75 mg/kg/day for 4–6 wk. Therapeutic serum salicylate level, 150–300 mcg/mL. **Kawasaki disease.** *Child:* 80–100 mg/kg/day PO divided q 6 hr; after fever resolves, 1–5 mg/kg/day once daily.
ADV EFF Acute aspirin toxicity, bleeding, dizziness, difficulty hearing, dyspepsia, epigastric discomfort, nausea, occult blood loss, tinnitus
INTERACTIONS Alcohol, alkalinizers, antacids, anticoagulants, corticosteroids, furosemide, nitroglycerin, NSAIDs, urine acidifiers
NC/PT Do not use in children w/ chickenpox or flu sx. Monitor dose for use in children. Give w/full glass of water. Pt should not cut, crush, or chew SR preparations; check OTC products for aspirin content to avoid overdose; report ringing in ears, bloody stools.

---

atazanavir sulfate (Reyataz)

CLASS Antiretroviral, protease inhibitor
PREG/CONT B/NA

IND & DOSE W/other antiretrovirals for tx of HIV-1 infection. *Adult:* Therapy-naïve, 300 mg/day PO w/100 mg ritonavir PO once daily; if unable to tolerate ritonavir, can give 400 mg PO once daily; therapy-experienced, 300 mg/day PO w/100 mg ritonavir PO taken w/food. *Child 3 mo and at least 10 kg–under 18 yr:* Therapy-naïve, base dose on weight, 150–300 mg/day

atazanavir PO w/80–100 mg ritonavir daily PO; therapy-experienced, base dose on weight, 200–300 mg/day atazanavir PO w/100 mg ritonavir PO. Must be taken w/food.
ADJUST DOSE Hepatic, renal impairment
ADV EFF Cardiac conduction problems, headache, liver enzyme elevation, nausea, phenylketonuria (w/oral powder in pts w/phenylketonuria), rash, **severe hepatomegaly w/ steatosis** (sometimes fatal).
INTERACTIONS Antacids, bosentan, indinavir, irinotecan, lovastatin, proton pump inhibitors, rifampin, sildenafil, simvastatin, St. John's wort, warfarin. Contraindicated w/ ergot derivatives, midazolam, pimozide, triazolam
NC/PT Ensure HIV testing has been done. Monitor LFTs. Ensure pt takes drug w/other antiretrovirals. Withdraw drug at s&sx of lactic acidosis. Not for use in pregnancy/breast-feeding. Does not cure disease. Oral powder only for children between 10 and 25 kg. Must be taken with ritonavir and food. Pt should avoid St. John's wort, report use to all health care providers.

atenolol (Tenormin)

CLASS Antianginal, antihypertensive, beta₁-adrenergic blocker

PREG/CONT D/NA

BBW Do not discontinue drug abruptly during long-term therapy; taper drug gradually over 2 wk w/ monitoring; risk of MI, arrhythmias.
IND & DOSE *Hypertension. Adult:* 50 mg PO once/day; after 1–2 wk, may increase to 100 mg/day. *Angina pectoris. Adult:* Initially, 50 mg/day PO; up to 200 mg/day may be needed. *Acute MI. Adult:* 100 mg/day PO or 50 mg PO bid for 6–9 days or until discharge.
ADJUST DOSE Elderly pts, renal impairment

ADV EFF Bradycardia, **bronchospasm**, cardiac arrhythmias, ED, exercise tolerance decrease, flatulence, gastric pain, **laryngospasm**, n/v/d
INTERACTIONS Ampicillin, anticholinergics, aspirin, bismuth subsalicylate, calcium salts, clonidine, hormonal contraceptives, insulin, lidocaine, prazosin, quinidine, verapamil
NC/PT Do not stop suddenly; taper over 2 wk. Pt should take safety precautions w/CNS effects, report difficulty breathing.

atomoxetine hydrochloride (Strattera)

CLASS Selective norepinephrine reuptake inhibitor

PREG/CONT C/NA

BBW Increased risk of suicidality in children, adolescents. Monitor closely; alert caregivers of risk.
IND & DOSE *Tx of ADHD as part of total tx program. Adult, child over 70 kg:* 40 mg/day PO; increase after minimum of 3 days to target total daily dose of 80 mg PO. Max, 100 mg/day. *Child 6 yr and older, 70 kg or less:* 0.5 mg/kg/day PO; increase after minimum of 3 days to target total daily dose of about 1.2 mg/kg/day PO. Max, 1.4 mg/kg or 100 mg/day, whichever is less.
ADJUST DOSE Hepatic impairment
ADV EFF Aggressive behavior/hostility, constipation, cough, dry mouth, insomnia, n/v, priapism, **sudden cardiac death, suicidality**
INTERACTIONS CYP3A4 substrates, fluoxetine, MAOIs (do not give within 14 days of atomoxetine), paroxetine, quinidine
NC/PT Ensure proper dx of ADHD; part of comprehensive tx program. Rule out cardiac abnormalities; baseline ECG suggested. Monitor growth. Provide drug vacation periodically. Give before 6 p.m. to allow sleep. Not for use in pregnancy. Pt should avoid

OTC drugs, herbs that may be stimulants.

atorvastatin calcium
(Lipitor)

CLASS Antihyperlipidemic, HMG-CoA inhibitor
PREG/CONT X/NA

IND & DOSE Adjunct to diet to lower total cholesterol, serum triglycerides, LDL and increase HDL in pts w/primary hypercholesterolemia, mixed dyslipidemia, familial hypercholesterolemia, elevated serum triglycerides; to prevent MI, CV disease in pts w/many risk factors; to reduce risk of MI and CV events in pts w/hx of CAD. *Adult:* 10–20 mg PO once daily without regard to meals; maint, 10–80 mg/day PO. *Child 10–17 yr:* 10 mg PO daily; max, 20 mg/day.
ADV EFF Abd pain, constipation, cramps, flatulence, headache, **liver failure, rhabdomyolysis w/renal failure, stroke**
INTERACTIONS Antifungals, cimetidine, clarithromycin, cyclosporine, digoxin, diltiazem, erythromycin, fibric acid derivatives, grapefruit juice, hormonal contraceptives, nefazodone, niacin, protease inhibitors, tacrolimus
NC/PT Obtain baseline and periodic LFTs. Withhold drug in acute or serious conditions. Give in p.m. Ensure pt is using diet/exercise program. Not for use in pregnancy. Pt should report muscle pain. Name confusion between written orders for *Lipitor* (atorvastatin) and *Zyrtec* (cetirizine).

atovaquone (Mepron)

CLASS Antiprotozoal
PREG/CONT C/NA

IND & DOSE Prevention and acute oral tx of mild to moderate *Pneumocystis jiroveci* pneumonia in pts intolerant of trimethoprim-sulfamethoxazole. *Adult, child 13–16 yr:* Prevention of *P. jiroveci* pneumonia, 1,500 mg PO daily w/meal. Tx of *P. jiroveci* pneumonia, 750 mg PO bid w/food for 21 days.
ADJUST DOSE Elderly pts
ADV EFF Dizziness, fever, headache, insomnia, n/v/d
INTERACTIONS Rifampin
NC/PT Give w/meals. Ensure drug is taken for 21 days for tx. Pt should report severe GI reactions.

atropine sulfate
(AtroPen, Isopoto Atropine)

CLASS Anticholinergic, antidote, belladonna
PREG/CONT C/NA

IND & DOSE Antisialagogue, tx of parkinsonism, bradycardia, pylorospasm, urinary bladder relaxation, uterine relaxation. *Adult:* 0.4–0.6 mg PO, IM, IV, subcut. *Child:* Base dose on weight, 0.1–0.4 mg PO, IM, IV, subcut. **Bradyarrhythmia.** *Adult:* 0.4–1 mg (max, 2 mg) IV q 1–2 hr as needed. *Child:* 0.01–0.03 mg/kg IV. **Antidote for cholinergic drug overdose, organophosphorus insecticides; initial tx for nerve agent poisoning.** *Adult:* 2–3 mg parenterally; repeat until signs of atropine intoxication appear. Use of auto-injector recommended. **Ophthalmic sol for eye refraction.** *Adult:* 1–2 drops into eye 1 hr before refracting. **Ophthalmic sol for uveitis.** *Adult:* 1–2 drops into eye tid.
ADJUST DOSE Elderly pts
ADV EFF Altered taste perception, bradycardia, decreased sweating, dry mouth, n/v, palpitations, **paralytic ileus**, predisposition to heat prostration, urinary hesitancy, urine retention
INTERACTIONS Anticholinergics, antihistamines, haloperidol, MAOIs, phenothiazines, TCAs
NC/PT Ensure adequate hydration. Provide temp control. Monitor heart rate. Pt should empty bladder before taking if urine retention occurs. Sugarless lozenges may help dry mouth.

auranofin (Ridaura)

CLASS Antirheumatic, gold salt
PREG/CONT C/NA

BBW Discontinue at first sign of toxicity. Severe bone marrow depression, renal toxicity, diarrhea possible.
IND & DOSE Mgt of pts w/active classic rheumatoid arthritis who have insufficient response to NSAIDs. Adult: 3 mg PO bid or 6 mg/day PO; after 6 mo may increase to 3 mg PO tid. Max, 9 mg/day.
ADV EFF Angioedema, bone marrow suppression, diarrhea, eye changes, GI bleeding, gingivitis, interstitial pneumonitis, peripheral neuropathy, photosensitivity, rash, renal failure, stomatitis
NC/PT Monitor blood counts; renal, lung function. Corticosteroids may help w/mild reactions. Pt should avoid ultraviolet light, use sunscreen or protective clothes.

avanafil (Stendra)

CLASS ED drug,
phosphodiesterase-5 inhibitor
PREG/CONT C/NA

IND & DOSE Tx of ED. Adult: 100 mg PO 15 min before sexual activity; range, 50–200 mg no more than once/day.
ADJUST DOSE Severe renal, hepatic impairment
ADV EFF Back pain, dyspepsia, flushing, headache, MI, nasal congestion, nasopharyngitis, nonarteritic ischemic optic neuropathy, sudden hearing loss
INTERACTIONS Alcohol, alpha blockers, amprenavir, antihypertensives, aprepitant, diltiazem, fluconazole, fosamprenavir, grapefruit juice, guanylate cyclase inhibitors, itraconazole, ketoconazole, nitrates, ritonavir, verapamil
NC/PT Ensure proper dx. Does not prevent STDs; does not work in absence of sexual stimulation. Pt should not use w/nitrates, antihypertensives, grapefruit juice, alcohol; report sudden loss of vision or hearing, erection lasting over 4 hr.

axitinib (Inlyta)

CLASS Antineoplastic, kinase inhibitor
PREG/CONT D/NA

IND & DOSE Tx of advanced renal cell cancer after failure of one prior systemic therapy. Adult: 5 mg PO bid 12 hr apart w/full glass of water.
ADJUST DOSE Hepatic impairment
ADV EFF Anorexia, asthenia, cardiac failure, constipation, diarrhea, dysphonia, fatigue, hand-foot syndrome, GI perforation/fistula, hemorrhage, hepatic injury, hypertension, hypertensive crisis, hypothyroidism, proteinuria, RPLS, thrombotic events, vomiting, weight loss
INTERACTIONS Strong CYP3A4/5 inhibitors or inducers (carbamazepine, dexamethasone, ketoconazole, phenobarbital, phenytoin, rifabutin, rifampin, rifapentine, St. John's wort); avoid these combinations
NC/PT Monitor closely for adverse reactions; have supportive measures readily available. Stop at least 24 hr before scheduled surgery. Not for use in pregnancy. Pt should take w/full glass of water, report s&sx of bleeding, severe headache, severe GI effects, urine/stool changes, swelling, difficulty breathing.

azacitidine (Vidaza)

CLASS Antineoplastic,
nucleoside metabolic inhibitor
PREG/CONT D/NA

IND & DOSE Tx of myelodysplastic syndrome, including refractory anemias and chronic myelomonocytic leukemia. Adult: 75 mg/m²/day subcut for 7 days q 4 wk; may increase to 100 mg/m²/day after two cycles if no response. Pt should have at least four cycles.

ADJUST DOSE Hepatic impairment
ADV EFF Bone marrow suppression, fever, **hepatic impairment**, injection-site reactions, n/v/d, pneumonia, **renal impairment**
NC/PT Not for use in pregnancy. Men on drug should not father a child. Monitor CBC, LFTs, renal function. Premedicate w/antiemetic.

azathioprine (Azasan, Imuran)

CLASS Immunosuppressant
PREG/CONT D/NA

BBW Monitor blood counts regularly; severe hematologic effects may require stopping drug. Increases risk of neoplasia; alert pt accordingly.
IND & DOSE Px of rejection w/ **renal homotransplantation.** *Adult:* 3–5 mg/kg/day PO or IV as single dose on day of transplant; maint, 1–3 mg/kg/day PO. **Tx of classic rheumatoid arthritis not responsive to other therapy.** *Adult:* 1 mg/kg PO as single dose or bid. May increase at 6–8 wk and thereafter by steps at 4-wk intervals; max, 2.5 mg/kg/day.
ADJUST DOSE Elderly pts, renal impairment
ADV EFF Carcinogenesis, hepatotoxicity, leukopenia, macrocytic anemia, n/v, **serious infection,** thrombocytopenia
INTERACTIONS Allopurinol, NMJ blockers
NC/PT Switch to oral form as soon as possible; monitor blood counts carefully. Give w/food if GI upset a problem. Protect from infection.

azilsartan medoxomil (Edarbi)

CLASS Antihypertensive, ARB
PREG/CONT D/NA

BBW Rule out pregnancy before starting tx. Suggest use of barrier contraceptives during tx; fetal injury and death have been reported.

IND & DOSE Tx of hypertension, alone or w/other antihypertensives. *Adult:* 80 mg/day PO. For pts on high-dose diuretics or who are volume-depleted, consider starting dose of 40 mg/day; titrate if tolerated.
ADV EFF Diarrhea, hyperkalemia, renal impairment
INTERACTIONS ARBs, lithium, NSAIDs, renin blockers
NC/PT Rule out pregnancy; suggest use of barrier contraceptives. Monitor in situations that could lead to lower BP. Mark chart if pt is going to surgery; possible volume problems after surgery. Not for use in breast-feeding.

azithromycin (AzaSite, Zithromax, Zmax)

CLASS Macrolide antibiotic
PREG/CONT B/NA

IND & DOSE Tx of mild to moderate acute bacterial exacerbations of COPD, pneumonia, pharyngitis/tonsillitis (as second-line), uncomplicated skin and skin-structure infections. *Adult:* 500 mg PO as single dose on first day, then 250 mg PO daily on days 2–5 for total dose of 1.5 g or 500 mg/day PO for 3 days. **Tx of nongonococcal urethritis, genital ulcer disease, cervicitis due to *Chlamydia trachomatis.* ** *Adult:* Single 1-g PO dose. **Tx of gonococcal urethritis/ cervicitis, mild to moderate acute bacterial sinusitis, community-acquired pneumonia.** *Adult:* Single 2-g PO dose. *Child 6 mo and older:* 10 mg/kg/day PO for 3 days. **Disseminated MAC infections.** *Adult:* Prevention, 1,200 mg PO once wkly. Tx, 600 mg/day PO w/ethambutol. **Tx of acute sinusitis.** *Adult:* 500 mg/day PO for 3 days or single 2-g dose of *Zmax.* Tx of community-acquired pneumonia. *Adult, child 16 yr and older:* 500 mg IV daily for at least 2 days, then 500 mg PO for 7–10 days. *Child 6 mo–15 yr:* 10 mg/kg PO as single dose on first day, then 5 mg/kg PO on days 2–5, or 60 mg/kg *Zmax* as single

dose. **Tx of mild community-acquired pneumonia.** *Adult:* 500 mg PO on day 1, then 250 mg PO for 4 days. **Tx of PID.** *Adult:* 500 mg IV daily for 1–2 days, then 250 mg PO for 7 days. **Tx of otitis media.** *Child 6 mo and older:* 10 mg/kg PO as single dose, then 5 mg/kg PO on days 2–5, or 30 mg/kg PO as single dose, or 10 mg/kg/day PO for 3 days. **Tx of pharyngitis/tonsillitis.** *Child 12 yr and older:* 12 mg/kg/day PO on days 1–5; max, 500 mg/day. **Tx of bacterial conjunctivitis.** *Adult, child:* 1 drop to affected eye bid for 2 days; then 1 drop/day for 5 days.
ADV EFF Abd pain, angioedema, diarrhea, prolonged QT, superinfections
INTERACTIONS Aluminum- and magnesium-containing antacids, QT-prolonging drugs, theophylline, warfarin
NC/PT Culture before tx. Give on empty stomach 1 hr before or 2 hr after meals. Prepare sol by adding 60 mL water to bottle and shaking well; pt should drink all at once. May experience superinfections.

---

aztreonam (Azactam, Cayston)
CLASS Monobactam antibiotic
PREG/CONT B/NA

IND & DOSE **Tx of UTIs.** *Adult:* 500 mg–1 g IV or IM q 8–12 hr. **Tx of moderately severe systemic infection.** *Adult:* 1–2 g IV or IM q 8–12 hr. *Child 9 mo and older:* 30 mg/kg IV or IM q 8 hr. **Tx of severe systemic infection.** *Adult:* 2 g IV or IM q 6–8 hr. *Child 9 mo and older:* 30 mg/kg IV or IM q 8 hr. **Tx of cystic fibrosis pts w/ *Pseudomonas aeruginosa* infections.** *Adult, child 7 yr and older:* 75 mg inhalation using *Altera Nebulizer System* tid for 28 days; space doses at least 4 hr apart. Then 28 days off.
ADJUST DOSE Renal impairment
ADV EFF Anaphylaxis, injection-site reactions, n/v/d, pruritus, rash
NC/PT Culture before tx. Discontinue, provide supportive tx if anaphy-

laxis occurs. Monitor for injection-site reactions. Use inhaled form only w/ provided nebulizer system.

---

bacitracin (Baci-IM)
CLASS Antibiotic
PREG/CONT C/NA

BBW Monitor renal function tests daily w/IM tx; risk of serious renal toxicity.
IND & DOSE **Pneumonia, empyema caused by susceptible strains of staphylococci in infants.** *Over 2.5 kg:* 1,000 units/kg/day IM in two to three divided doses. *Under 2.5 kg:* 900 units/kg/day IM in two to three divided doses. **Px of minor skin abrasions; tx of superficial skin infections.** *Adult, child:* Apply topical ointment to affected area one to three times/day; cover w/sterile bandage if needed. Do not use longer than 1 wk. **Superficial infections of conjunctiva or cornea.** *Adult, child:* Dose varies by product; see package insert.
ADV EFF Contact dermatitis (topical), **nephrotoxicity**, pain at injection site, superinfections
INTERACTIONS Aminoglycosides, NMJs
NC/PT Culture before tx. Reconstituted IM sol stable for 1 wk. Ensure adequate hydration. Monitor renal function closely (IM).

---

baclofen (Gablofen, Lioresal)
CLASS Centrally acting skeletal muscle relaxant
PREG/CONT C/NA

BBW Taper gradually to prevent rebound spasticity, hallucinations, possible psychosis, rhabdomyolysis, other serious effects; abrupt discontinuation can cause serious reactions.
IND & DOSE **Alleviation of s&sx of spasticity from MS or spinal cord injuries (intrathecal).** *Adult:* Testing usually done w/50 mcg/mL injected

into intrathecal space over 1 min. Pt is observed for 4–8 hr, then 75 mcg/1.5 mL is given; pt is observed for 4–8 hr; final screening bolus of 100 mcg/2 mL is given 24 hr later if response still inadequate. Maint for spasticity of cerebral origin, 22–1,400 mcg/day; maint for spasticity of spinal cord origin, 12–2,003 mcg/day. **Spinal cord injuries, other spinal cord diseases** (oral). *Adult:* 5 mg PO tid for 3 days; 10 mg PO tid for 3 days; 15 mg PO tid for 3 days; 20 mg PO tid for 3 days. Thereafter, additional increases may be needed. Max, 80 mg/day.
ADJUST DOSE Elderly pts, renal impairment
ADV EFF Confusion, dizziness, drowsiness, fatigue, headache, hypotension, insomnia, urinary frequency, weakness
INTERACTIONS CNS depressants
NC/PT Use caution if spasticity needed to stay upright. Monitor implantable intrathecal delivery site, system. Do not inject directly into pump catheter access port, risk of life-threatening infection. Taper slowly if discontinuing. Not for use in pregnancy. Pt should avoid OTC sleeping drugs and alcohol.

balsalazide disodium
(Colazal, Giazo)
CLASS Anti-inflammatory
PREG/CONT B/NA

IND & DOSE Tx of mildly to moderately active ulcerative colitis. *Adult:* Three 750-mg capsules PO tid (total daily dose, 6.75 g) for up to 12 wk. Or, three 1.1-g tablets PO bid (total daily dose 6.6 g) for up to 8 wk. *Child 5–17 yr:* Three 750-mg capsules PO tid (6.75 g/day) for 8 wk, or one 750-mg capsule PO tid (2.25 g/day) for up to 8 wk.
ADV EFF Abd pain, cramps, depression, fatigue, flatulence, flulike sx, n/v/d, renal impairment

NC/PT Serious effects; use extreme caution. Not for use in pts w/salicylate hypersensitivity. Maintain hydration. Observe for worsening of ulcerative colitis. Pt should take w/meals, continue all restrictions and tx used for ulcerative colitis. Drug is high in sodium; monitor sodium intake. Name confusion between *Colazal* (balsalazide) and *Clozaril* (clozapine).

basiliximab (Simulect)
CLASS Immunosuppressant
PREG/CONT B/NA

BBW Only physicians experienced in immunosuppressive therapy and mgt of organ transplant pts should prescribe. Pts should be managed in facilities equipped and staffed w/adequate laboratory and supportive medical resources.
IND & DOSE Px of acute rejection in renal transplant pts, w/other immunosuppressants. *Adult:* Two doses of 20 mg IV—first dose 2 hr before transplant, second dose on day 4 posttransplant.
ADV EFF Abd pain, cramps, hypersensitivity reactions, hypertension, infections, n/v/d, pain
NC/PT Not for use in pregnancy/breastfeeding. Monitor for hypersensitivity reactions; protect pt from infections.

BCG intravesical
(TheraCys, Tice BCG)
CLASS Antineoplastic
PREG/CONT C/NA

BBW Use precautions when handling. Contains live mycobacteria; infections can occur.
IND & DOSE Intravesical use in tx and px of carcinoma in situ of urinary bladder; px of primary or recurrent stage Ta and T1 papillary tumors after transurethral resection. *Adult:* 1 ampule in 50 mL diluent

instilled via catheter into bladder by gravity.

ADV EFF Bone marrow suppression, chills, cystitis, dysuria, hematuria, infections, malaise, n/v, urinary urgency, UTI

INTERACTIONS Antibiotics, isoniazid

NC/PT Monitor for infection, local reactions. Pt should avoid fluids 4 hr before tx; empty bladder before instillation; lie down for first hr (turning side to side), then upright for 1 hr; try to retain fluid in bladder for 2 hr; empty bladder trying not to splash liquid; and increase fluid intake over next few hours.

beclomethasone dipropionate (QNASL, QVAR), beclomethasone dipropionate monohydrate (Beconase AQ)

CLASS Corticosteroid
PREG/CONT C/NA

IND & DOSE Maintenance, control, prophylactic tx of asthma. *Adult, child 12 yr and older:* 40–160 mcg by inhalation bid; max, 320 mcg/bid. Titrate to response: "Low" dose: 80–240 mcg/day; "medium" dose: 240–480 mcg/day; "high" dose: Over 480 mcg/day. *Child 5–11 yr:* 40 mcg bid; max, 80 mcg bid. Relief of s&sx of seasonal or perennial and nonallergic rhinitis; prevention of recurrence of nasal polyps after surgical removal. *Adult, child 12 yr and older:* 1–2 inhalations (42–84 mcg) in each nostril bid (total, 168–336 mcg/day). *Child 6–12 yr:* 1 inhalation in each nostril bid (total, 168 mcg).

ADV EFF Cushing's syndrome, epistaxis, headache, local irritation, nausea rebound congestion

NC/PT Taper oral steroids slowly in switching to inhaled forms. If using nasal spray, use nose decongestant to facilitate penetration of drug. If using other inhalants, use several min

before using this drug. If using respiratory inhalant, allow at least 1 min between puffs; pt should rinse mouth after each inhalation.

bedaquiline (Sirturo)

CLASS Antimycobacterial, antituberculotic
PREG/CONT B/NA

BBW Increased risk of death; reserve for pts resistant to other effective therapy. Prolonged QT, risk of serious to fatal arrhythmias. Monitor ECG; avoid other QT-prolonging drugs.

IND & DOSE Tx of adults w/multidrug-resistant pulmonary TB, w/other antituberculotics when effective TB program cannot be provided. *Adult:* 400 mg PO for 2 wk; then 200 mg PO three times/wk for 22 wk, w/other antituberculotics.

ADJUST DOSE Hepatic impairment, severe renal impairment

ADV EFF Arthralgia, headache, hepatic impairment, nausea, prolonged QT

INTERACTIONS Ketoconazole, lopinavir, QT-prolonging drugs, rifampin, ritonavir

NC/PT Obtain baseline ECG; monitor periodically. Monitor LFTs. Ensure proper use of drug and use w/other antituberculotics; must give using directly observed therapy. Not for use in breast-feeding. Pt should mark calendar for tx days; swallow capsule whole and not cut, crush, or chew it; ensure also taking other drugs for TB; avoid alcohol; report urine/stool color changes, abnormal heartbeat.

belatacept (Nulojix)

CLASS T-cell costimulation blocker
PREG/CONT C/NA

BBW Increased risk of posttransplant lymphoproliferative disorder involving CNS, more likely without immunity to Epstein-Barr virus.

Increased risk of cancers and serious infections.

IND & DOSE Px of organ rejection in pts w/renal transplants, w/other immunosuppressants. *Adult:* days 1 and 5, 10 mg/kg IV over 30 min; repeat end of wk 2, 4, 8, 12. Maint starting at wk 16 and q 4 wk thereafter, 5 mg/kg IV over 30 min. Must be given with basiliximab, mycophenolate, and corticosteroids.

ADV EFF Anemia, constipation, cough, edema, graft dysfxn, headache, hyperkalemia, hypokalemia, **infections** (potentially fatal), **malignancies, posttransplant lymphoproliferative disorder, progressive multifocal leukoencephalopathy,** UTI

INTERACTIONS Live vaccines
NC/PT Not for use in liver transplants. Not for use in pregnancy/breast-feeding. Use only provided silicone-free syringe to prepare drug. Ensure use of concomitant drugs. Monitor blood counts, s&sx of infection, orientation, mood. Protect from infection. Encourage cancer screening exams.

belimumab (Benlysta)
CLASS B-cell activating factor inhibitor
PREG/CONT C/NA

IND & DOSE Tx of pts w/active, antibody-positive SLE, w/standard therapy. *Adult:* 10 mg/kg IV over 1 hr at 2-wk intervals for first three doses, then at 4-wk intervals.
ADV EFF Bronchitis, **death, depression/suicidality, hypersensitivity reactions, malignancies,** migraine, n/v/d, pain, pharyngitis, **progressive multifocal leukoencephalopathy, serious to fatal infections**
INTERACTIONS Live vaccines
NC/PT Not for use in pregnancy/breast-feeding. Premedicate w/antihistamines, corticosteroids. Do not use w/acute infection; monitor for

infections. Encourage cancer screening. Protect pt w/suicidal thoughts.

belinostat (Beleodaq)
CLASS Antineoplastic, histone deacetylase inhibitor
PREG/CONT D/NA

IND & DOSE Tx of relapsed/refractory peripheral T-cell lymphoma. *Adult:* 1,000 mg/m^2/day IV over 30 min on days 1–5 of 21-day cycle; repeat until disease progression or unacceptable toxicity.
ADV EFF Bone marrow suppression, fatigue, fever, **hepatotoxicity,** n/v/d, **serious to fatal infection, tumor lysis syndrome**
NC/PT Rule out pregnancy. Monitor bone marrow, LFTs, tumor lysis syndrome; modify dose, support pt as needed. Not for use in pregnancy (contraceptives advised). Protect from infection; encourage cancer screening. Advise small, frequent meals; rest periods. Pt should report urine/stool color changes, unusual bleeding, severe n/v/d.

benazepril hydrochloride (Lotensin)
CLASS ACE inhibitor, antihypertensive
PREG/CONT D/NA

BBW Rule out pregnancy; fetal abnormalities and death have occurred if used during second or third trimester. Encourage contraceptive measures.
IND & DOSE Tx of hypertension, alone or as part of combination therapy. *Adult:* 10 mg PO daily. Maint, 20–40 mg/day PO; max, 80 mg/day. *Child 6 yr and older:* 0.1–0.6 mg/kg/day; max, 40 mg/day.
ADJUST DOSE Renal impairment
ADV EFF Cough, hepatotoxicity, hyperkalemia, renal toxicity, **Stevens-Johnson syndrome**

INTERACTIONS Allopurinol, ARBs, capsaicin, indomethacin, lithium, NSAIDs, potassium-sparing diuretics, renin inhibitors
NC/PT Use caution before surgery; mark chart. Protect pt w/decreased fluid volume. Not for use in pregnancy. Cough may occur. Pt should change position slowly if dizzy, light-headed.

DANGEROUS DRUG

bendamustine hydrochloride (Bendeka, Treanda)
CLASS Alkylating agent, antineoplastic
PREG/CONT D/NA

IND & DOSE Chronic lymphocytic leukemia. *Adult:* 100 mg/m² IV over 30 min (*Treanda*), 10 min (*Bendeka*) on days 1 and 2 of 28-day cycle for up to six cycles. **Indolent non–B cell Hodgkin lymphoma.** *Adult:* 120 mg/m² IV over 60 min (*Treanda*), 10 min (*Bendeka*) on days 1 and 2 of 21-day cycle for up to eight cycles.
ADJUST DOSE Hepatic, renal impairment
ADV EFF Extravasation injury, Fatigue, fever, infections, infusion reaction, **malignancies, myelosuppression,** n/v/d, **rash to toxic skin reactions, tumor lysis syndrome**
INTERACTIONS Ciprofloxacin, fluvoxamine, nicotine, omeprazole
NC/PT Monitor blood counts closely; dosage adjustment may be needed. Protect pt from infection, bleeding. Monitor pt closely during infusion; note infusion times for specific drug being used. Premedicate w/ antihistamines, antipyretics, corticosteroids. Assess skin regularly. Not for use in pregnancy/breast-feeding. Pt may feel very tired; should plan activities accordingly.

---

benzonatate (Tessalon, Zonatuss)
CLASS Antitussive
PREG/CONT C/NA

IND & DOSE Symptomatic relief of nonproductive cough. *Adult, child 10 yr and older:* 100–200 mg PO tid; max, 600 mg/day.
ADV EFF Constipation, dizziness, headache, nausea, rash, sedation
NC/PT Pt should not cut, crush, or chew capsules; must swallow capsule whole. Use caution if CNS effects occur.

---

benztropine mesylate (Cogentin)
CLASS Anticholinergic, antiparkinsonian
PREG/CONT C/NA

IND & DOSE Adjunct to tx of parkinsonism. *Adult:* Initially, 0.5–1 mg PO at bedtime; total daily dose, 0.5–6 mg at bedtime or in two to four divided doses; may give IM or IV at same dose. **Control of drug-induced extrapyramidal disorders.** *Adult:* 1–2 mg IM (preferred) or IV to control condition, then 1–4 mg PO daily or bid to prevent recurrences. **Extrapyramidal disorders occurring early in neuroleptic tx.** *Adult:* 2 mg PO bid to tid. Withdraw drug after 1 or 2 wk to determine continued need.
ADJUST DOSE Elderly pts
ADV EFF Blurred vision, constipation, decreased sweating, dry mouth, urinary hesitancy, urine retention
INTERACTIONS Alcohol, anticholinergics, haloperidol, phenothiazines, TCAs
NC/PT Pt should discontinue if dry mouth makes swallowing or speaking difficulty, use caution in hot weather when decreased sweating could lead to heat prostration, avoid alcohol and OTC drugs that could cause serious CNS effects, empty bladder before each dose if urine retention a problem; use caution if CNS effects occur.

beractant (natural lung surfactant) (Survanta)
CLASS Lung surfactant
PREG/CONT Unkn/NA

IND & DOSE Px for infants at risk for RDS. Give first dose of 100 mg phospholipids/kg birth weight (4 mL/kg) intratracheally soon after birth, preferably within 15 min. After determining needed dose, inject ¼ of dose into endotracheal (ET) tube over 2–3 sec; may repeat no sooner than 6 hr after dose. Rescue tx of premature infants w/RDS. Give 100 mg phospholipids/kg birth weight (4 mL/kg) intratracheally. Give first dose as soon as possible within 8 hr of birth after RDS diagnosis is made and pt is on ventilator; may repeat after 6 hr from previous dose.
ADV EFF Bradycardia, hypotension, intraventricular hemorrhage, nonpulmonary infections, patent ductus arteriosus, sepsis
NC/PT Monitor ECG and O_2 saturation continuously during and for at least 30 min after administration. Ensure ET tube is correctly placed. Suction immediately before dosing; do not suction for 1 hr after dosing.

betamethasone (generic), betamethasone dipropionate (Diprolene AF, Maxivate), betamethasone sodium phosphate and acetate (Celestone Soluspan), betamethasone valerate (Beta-Val, Luxiq)
CLASS Corticosteroid
PREG/CONT C/NA

IND & DOSE Tx of primary or secondary adrenocortical insufficiency; hypercalcemia w/cancer; short-term mgt of inflammatory and allergic disorders; thrombocytopenia purpura; ulcerative colitis; MS exacerbations; trichinosis w/neurological or cardiac involvement.
Adult: Oral (betamethasone), initially, 0.6–7.2 mg/day. IM (betamethasone sodium phosphate, betamethasone sodium phosphate and acetate), initially, 0.5–9 mg/day. Intrabursal, intra-articular, intradermal, intralesional (betamethasone sodium phosphate and acetate), 1.5–12 mg intra-articular (depending on joint size), 0.2 mL/cm³ intradermally (max, 1 mL/wk); 0.25–1 mL at 3- to 7-day intervals for foot disorders. Topical dermatologic cream, ointment (betamethasone dipropionate), apply sparingly to affected area daily or bid.
ADV EFF Aggravation of infection, headache, immunosuppression, increased appetite, local stinging and burning, masking of infection, vertigo, weight gain
INTERACTIONS Live vaccines
NC/PT Give oral dose at 9 a.m. Taper dosage when discontinuing. Pt should avoid overusing joints after injection; be cautious w/occlusive dressings; do not stop drug suddenly; wear medical alert tag; apply sparingly if using topically; avoid exposure to infection; monitor blood glucose w/long-term use.

betaxolol hydrochloride valerate (Betoptic S)
CLASS Antiglaucoma drug, antihypertensive, beta-selective blocker
PREG/CONT C/NA

IND & DOSE Hypertension, used alone or w/other antihypertensives. *Adult:* 10 mg PO daily, alone or added to diuretic therapy. Tx of ocular hypertension and open-angle glaucoma alone or w/other antiglaucoma drugs. *Adult:* 1 or 2 drops ophthalmic sol bid to affected eye(s).
ADJUST DOSE Elderly pts, severe renal impairment, dialysis pts

ADV EFF Allergic reactions, bradycardia, cardiac arrhythmias, decreased exercise tolerance, dizziness, HF, n/v/d, ocular itching/tearing (ophthalmic)
INTERACTIONS Anticholinergics, aspirin, hormonal contraceptives, insulin, prazosin, salicylates, verapamil
NC/PT Do not discontinue abruptly; taper over 2 wk. Protect eyes or joints from injury after dosing. Give eyedrops as instructed to avoid systemic absorption.

bethanechol chloride
(Urecholine)
CLASS Cholinergic, parasympathomimetic
PREG/CONT C/NA

IND & DOSE Acute postop and postpartum nonobstructive urine retention; neurogenic atony of urinary bladder w/retention. *Adult:* 10–50 mg PO three/four times a day.
ADV EFF Abd discomfort, **cardiac arrest,** flushing, n/v/d, sweating
INTERACTIONS Cholinergics, ganglionic blockers
NC/PT Give on empty stomach 1 hr before or 2 hr after meals. Keep atropine on hand for severe response. Safety precautions if CNS effects occur.

DANGEROUS DRUG

bevacizumab (Avastin)
CLASS Antineoplastic, monoclonal antibody
PREG/CONT C/NA

BBW GI perforation, wound healing impairment, severe to fatal hemorrhage possible; monitor pt closely.
IND & DOSE Tx of metastatic cancer of colon/rectum, w/5-FU. *Adult:* 5–10 mg/kg IV q 14 days with progression; first infusion over 90 min, second over 60 min, then over 30 min. Tx of metastatic, unresectable or locally advanced nonsquamous, non-

small-cell lung cancer. *Adult:* 15 mg/kg IV q 3 wk. Tx of glioblastoma. *Adult:* 10 mg/kg IV q 2 wk. Tx of metastatic renal cell carcinoma. *Adult:* 10 mg/kg IV q 2 wk w/interferon alfa. Tx of resistant, metastatic or recurrent cervical cancer. *Adult:* 15 mg/kg IV q 3 wk w/other drugs. Tx of platinum-resistant epithelial ovarian, fallopian tube, or primary peritoneal cancer. *Adult:* 10 mg/kg IV q 2 wk w/doxorubicin or wkly topotecan, or 15 mg/kg q 3 wk w/topotecan q 3 wk.
ADV EFF Arterial thrombotic events, back pain, epistaxis, exfoliative dermatitis, headache, hypertension, infusion reactions, non-GI fistula formation, proteinuria, ovarian failure, rectal hemorrhage, RPLS, rhinitis
NC/PT Do not initiate within 28 days of major surgery and until surgical wound is completely healed. Do not give as IV push or bolus. Monitor BP, wounds (for healing issues), during infusion (for infusion reactions). Not for use in pregnancy (risk of embryofetal toxicity)/breast-feeding. Pt should report rectal bleeding, high fever, changes in neurologic function.

DANGEROUS DRUG

bexarotene (Targretin)
CLASS Antineoplastic
PREG/CONT X/NA

BBW Not for use in pregnancy; fetal harm can occur.
IND & DOSE Cutaneous manifestations of cutaneous T-cell lymphoma in pts refractory to other tx. *Adult:* 300 mg/m²/day PO; may adjust to 200 mg/m²/day PO, then 100 mg/m²/day PO.
ADV EFF Abd pain, asthenia, dry skin, headache, **hepatic impairment,** hyperlipidemia, hypothyroidism, lipid abnormalities, nausea, **pancreatitis,** photosensitivity, rash
INTERACTIONS Atorvastatin, carboplatin, gemfibrozil, paclitaxel, tamoxifen

NC/PT Rule out pregnancy before start of tx; ensure pt is using contraceptives. Monitor LFTs, amylase, lipids, thyroid function. Protect pt from exposure to sunlight. Pt should swallow capsules whole, not cut, crush, or chew them. Not for use in breast-feeding.

---

bicalutamide (Casodex)

CLASS Antiandrogen
PREG/CONT X/NA

IND & DOSE Tx of stage D2 metastatic carcinoma of prostrate, w/LHRH.
Adult: 50 mg/day PO a.m. or p.m.
ADJUST DOSE Hepatic, renal impairment
ADV EFF Anemia, asthenia, constipation, diarrhea, dyspnea, edema, gynecomastia, hematuria, hot flashes, nausea, nocturia, pain, **severe hepatic injury to fatal hepatic failure**
INTERACTIONS Midazolam, warfarin
NC/PT Used w/LHRH only. Monitor LFTs regularly, PSA levels, glucose levels. Not for use in pregnancy. Pt should report trouble breathing, blood in urine, yellowing of eyes or skin.

---

bismuth subsalicylate (Kaopectate, Pepto-Bismol, Pink Bismuth)

CLASS Antidiarrheal
PREG/CONT C (1st, 2nd trimesters); D (3rd trimester)/ NA

IND & DOSE To control diarrhea, gas, upset stomach, indigestion, heartburn, nausea; to reduce number of bowel movements and help firm stool. *Adult, child 12 yr and older:* 2 tablets or 30 mL (524 mg) PO; repeat q 30 min–1 hr as needed (max, eight doses/24 hr). *Child 9–11 yr:* 1 tablet or 15 mL PO. *Child 6–8 yr:* 2/3 tablet or 10 mL PO. *Child 3–5 yr:*

1/3 tablet or 5 mL PO. **Tx of traveler's diarrhea.** *Adult, child 12 yr and older:* 1 oz (524 mg) PO q 30 min for total of eight doses.
ADV EFF Darkening of stool
INTERACTIONS Antidiabetics, aspirin, methotrexate, sulfinpyrazone, tetracyclines, valproic acid
NC/PT Shake liquid well. Have pt chew tablets (not swallow whole). Pt should not take w/drugs containing aspirin. Pt should report ringing in ears; stools may be dark.

---

bisoprolol fumarate (Zebeta)

CLASS Antihypertensive, beta-selective adrenergic blocker
PREG/CONT C/NA

IND & DOSE Mgt of hypertension, alone or w/other antihypertensives.
Adult: 5 mg PO daily, alone or added to diuretic therapy; 2.5 mg may be appropriate. Max, 20 mg PO daily.
ADJUST DOSE Renal, hepatic impairment
ADV EFF Bradycardia, **broncho-spasm**, cardiac arrhythmias, constipation, decreased exercise tolerance, ED, fatigue, flatulence, headache, n/v/d
INTERACTIONS Anticholinergics, hormonal contraceptives, insulin, NSAIDs, prazosin, salicylates
NC/PT Do not discontinue abruptly; taper over 2 wk. Controversial need to stop before surgery. If diabetic pt, monitor glucose levels regularly. Pt should avoid OTC drugs. Name confusion between *Zebeta* (bisoprolol) and *DiaBeta* (glyburide).

---

bivalirudin (Angiomax)

CLASS Anticoagulant, thrombin inhibitor
PREG/CONT B/NA

IND & DOSE Pts w/unstable angina undergoing PTCA. *Adult:* 0.75 mg/kg IV, then 1.75 mg/kg/hr during procedure. **Tx or px of heparin-induced thrombocytopenia in pts undergoing PTCA.** *Adult:* 0.75 mg/kg IV, then 1.75 mg/kg/hr during procedure; may continue for up to 4 hr, then 0.2 mg/kg/hr for up to 20 hr if needed.

ADJUST DOSE Renal impairment
ADV EFF Bleeding, fever, headache, hypotension, thrombocytopenia
INTERACTIONS Heparin, thrombolytics, warfarin
NC/PT Used w/aspirin therapy. Monitor for bleeding; could indicate need to discontinue.

> ### DANGEROUS DRUG

bleomycin sulfate (BLM)
CLASS Antibiotic, antineoplastic
PREG/CONT D/NA

> **BBW** Monitor pulmonary function regularly and chest X-ray wkly or bi-wkly for onset of pulmonary toxicity. Be alert for rare, severe idiosyncratic reaction, including fever, chills, hypertension, in lymphoma pts.

IND & DOSE Palliative tx of squamous cell carcinoma, lymphomas, testicular carcinoma, alone or w/ other drugs. *Adult:* 0.25–0.5 unit/kg IV, IM, or subcut once or twice wkly. **Tx of malignant pleural effusion.** *Adult:* 60 units dissolved in 50–100 mL NSS via thoracotomy tube.

ADJUST DOSE Renal impairment
ADV EFF Chills, dyspnea, fever, hair loss, hyperpigmentation, idiosyncratic reactions to **anaphylaxis,** pneumonitis, **pulmonary fibrosis,** stomatitis, striae, vesiculation, vomiting
INTERACTIONS Digoxin, oxygen, phenytoin
NC/PT Label reconstituted sol and use within 24 hr. Monitor LFTs, renal function tests, pulmonary function regularly; consult physician immediately if s&sx of toxicity. Not for use in pregnancy. Pt should mark calendar for injection dates, cover head w/temp extremes (hair loss possible).

blinatumomab (Blincyto)
CLASS Antineoplastic, monoclonal antibody
PREG/CONT C/NA

> **BBW** Life-threatening cytokine release syndrome and neurologic toxicities possible. Monitor closely; interrupt or stop as recommended.

IND & DOSE Tx of Philadelphia chromosome–negative relapsed or refractory B-cell precursor ALL. *Adult at least 45 kg:* Cycle 1, 9 mcg/day as continuous IV on days 1–7 and 28 mcg/day on days 8–28; subsequent cycles, 28 mcg/day on days 1–28.

ADV EFF CNS toxicity, constipation, **cytokine release syndrome,** edema, fever, infections, nausea, hypokalemia, rash
NC/PT Hospitalize for first 9 days of cycle 1, first 2 days of cycle 2. Follow reconstitution directions carefully. Premedicate w/dexamethasone 20 mg IV 1 hr before first dose or if interrupting for 4 or more hr. Administer using infusion pump to ensure constant flow rate. Monitor for infection. Not for use in pregnancy/breast-feeding. Pt should take safety precautions w/CNS effects; mark calendar for tx days; report difficulty breathing, dizziness, edema, rash.

> ### DANGEROUS DRUG

bortezomib (Velcade)
CLASS Antineoplastic, proteasome inhibitor
PREG/CONT D/NA

IND & DOSE Tx of multiple myeloma; tx of mantle cell lymphoma in pts who have received at least one other therapy. *Adult:* 1.3 mg/m² as 3–5 sec IV bolus or subcut for nine 6-day cycles (days 1, 4, 8, 11, then 10 days of rest, then days 22, 25, 29, 32; may repeat tx for multiple myeloma if 6 mo since failed tx.

ADJUST DOSE Hepatic impairment

ADV EFF Anemia, anorexia, asthenia, constipation, HF, hypotension, leukopenia, neutropenia, n/v/d, **peripheral neuropathies, pulmonary infiltrates,** thrombocytopenia, tumor lysis syndrome
INTERACTIONS Ketoconazole, omeprazole, ritonavir, St. John's wort
NC/PT Monitor for neurologic changes. Monitor CBC. Try to maintain hydration if GI effects are severe. Not for use in pregnancy/breast-feeding. Diabetic pts, pts w/CV disease require close monitoring. Pt should use care when driving or operating machinery until drug's effects are known.

---

bosentan (Tracleer)
CLASS Endothelin receptor antagonist, pulmonary antihypertensive
PREG/CONT X/NA

BBW Rule out pregnancy before starting tx; ensure pt is using two forms of contraception during tx and for 1 mo after tx ends. Verify pregnancy status monthly. Obtain baseline then monthly liver enzyme levels. Dose reduction or drug withdrawal indicated if liver enzymes elevated; liver failure possible. Available only through restricted access program.
IND & DOSE Tx of pulmonary arterial hypertension in pts w/WHO class II–IV sx. *Adult, child over 12 yr:* 62.5 mg PO bid for 4 wk. Then, for pts 40 kg or more, maint dose is 125 mg PO bid. For pts under 40 kg but over 12 yr, maint dose is 62.5 mg PO bid.
ADJUST DOSE Hepatic impairment
ADV EFF Decreased hemoglobin/hematocrit, decreased sperm count, edema, flushing, headache, hypotension, **liver injury,** nasopharyngitis
INTERACTIONS Atazanavir, cyclosporine A, glyburide, hormonal contraceptives, ritonavir (serious toxicity), statins
NC/PT Available only through restricted access program. Obtain

baseline Hgb, at 1 and 3 mo, then q 3 mo. Monitor LFTs. Do not use w/ cyclosporine or glyburide. Taper if discontinuing. Not for use in pregnancy (barrier contraceptives advised)/breast-feeding. Pt should keep chart of activity tolerance to monitor drug's effects.

---

bosutinib (Bosulif)
CLASS Antineoplastic, kinase inhibitor
PREG/CONT D/NA

IND & DOSE Tx of accelerated blast phase Philadelphia chromosome–positive CML w/resistance or intolerance to other tx. *Adult:* 500 mg/day PO, up to 600 mg/day if complete hematologic response does not occur by wk 12 and no serious adverse effects. Adjust dose based on toxicity.
ADJUST DOSE Hepatic impairment
ADV EFF Abd pain, anemia, edema, fatigue, fever, **fluid retention, GI toxicity, hepatotoxicity, myelosuppression,** n/v/d, rash, renal toxicity
INTERACTIONS CYP3A inhibitors/inducers (carbamazepine, dexamethasone, ketoconazole, phenobarbital, phenytoin, rifabutin, rifampin, rifapentine, St. John's wort), P-glycoprotein inhibitors; avoid these combinations. Proton pump inhibitors
NC/PT Monitor closely for bone marrow suppression, GI toxicity; monitor renal function. Not for use in pregnancy. Pt should take once a day, report s&sx of bleeding, severe GI effects, urine/stool changes, swelling.

---

brentuximab (Adcetris)
CLASS Monoclonal antibody
PREG/CONT D/NA

BBW Risk of potentially fatal progressive multifocal leukoencephalopathy (PML).
IND & DOSE Tx of Hodgkin lymphoma after failure of autologous

stem-cell transplant or if high risk for relapse or progression; tx of systemic anaplastic large-cell lymphoma. *Adult:* 1.8 mg/kg IV over 30 min q 3 wk for max of 16 cycles. **ADV EFF Anaphylactic reactions,** chills, cough, dyspnea, fever, **hematologic toxicities,** hepatotoxicity, infections, infusion reactions, nausea, neutropenia, **peripheral neuropathy, PML, pulmonary toxicity, Stevens-Johnson syndrome, tumor lysis syndrome**
INTERACTIONS Bleomycin, ketoconazole, rifampin
NC/PT Monitor pt during infusion. Monitor neutrophil count, LFTs, pulmonary function; dose adjustment may be needed. Protect pt w/peripheral neuropathies. Not for use in pregnancy/breast-feeding. Pt should report mood or behavior changes, changes in vision or walking, weakness, rash, infections.

---

brexpiprazole (Rexulti)
CLASS Atypical antipsychotic, dopamine/serotonin agonist/antagonist
PREG/CONT High risk/NA

BBW Elderly pts w/dementia-related psychosis have increased risk of death if given atypical antipsychotics; not approved for this use. Risk of suicidal ideation increases w/antidepressant use, especially in child, adolescents, young adults; monitor accordingly. Not approved for use in child.
IND & DOSE Tx of schizophrenia. *Adult:* 1 mg/day PO; max, 4 mg/day. Adjunct tx for major depressive disorder. *Adult:* 0.5–1 mg/day PO; max, 3 mg/day.
ADV EFF Akathisia, bone marrow suppression, cognitive/motor impairment, dyslipidemia, hyperglycemia, **NMS,** orthostatic hypotension, **seizures** (potentially life-threatening), suicidality, syncope, tardive dyskinesia, weight gain

INTERACTIONS Alcohol, carbamazepine, CNS depressants, CYP2D6 inhibitors (fluoxetine, paroxetine, quinidine), CYP3A4 inhibitors (ketoconazole), lorazepam
NC/PT Dispense least amount possible to suicidal pts. Not for use in pregnancy (risk of abnormal muscle movements, withdrawal)/breast-feeding. Monitor weight; assess for hyperglycemia. May react w/many drugs; monitor regimen. Take safety precautions for cognitive/motor impairment; use cautiously if low BP possible; ensure hydration. Pt should report suicidal thoughts, signs of infection, abnormal muscle movements. Confusion between brexpiprazole and proton pump inhibitors; use extreme caution.

---

brivaracetam (Briviact)
CLASS Antiepileptic
PREG/CONT High risk/NA

IND & DOSE Adjunct tx of partial-onset seizures in pts 16 and over. *Adult:* 50 mg PO or IV bid; range, 25–100 mg bid.
ADJUST DOSE Hepatic impairment
ADV EFF Bronchospasm, dizziness, fatigue, n/v, **psychiatric reactions,** sedation, somnolence. **suicidality**
INTERACTIONS Carbamazepine, levetiracetam, phenytoin, rifampin
NC/PT Use same dose for PO, IV; switch to PO as soon as feasible. Sol form is available. Must taper drug when discontinuing. Not for use in pregnancy/breast-feeding. Monitor for behavioral changes/suicidality. Pt should swallow tablets whole and not cut, crush, or chew them; take safety precautions for sedation, cognitive/motor impairment; report difficulty breathing, changes in thoughts/behavior, excessive fatigue.

bromocriptine mesylate (Cycloset, Parlodel)

CLASS Antidiabetic, antiparkinsonian, dopamine receptor agonist
PREG/CONT B/NA

IND & DOSE Tx of postencephalitic or idiopathic Parkinson's disease. *Adult, child 15 yr and older:* 11.25 mg PO bid. Assess q 2 wk, and adjust dose; max, 100 mg/day. **Tx of hyperprolactinemia.** *Adult, child 15 yr and older:* 1.25–2.5 mg PO daily; range, 2.5–15 mg/day. **Tx of acromegaly.** *Adult, child 15 yr and older:* 1.25–2.5 mg PO for 3 days at bedtime; add 1.25–2.5 mg as tolerated q 3–7 days until optimal response. Range, 20–30 mg/day. **Tx of type 2 diabetes.** *Adult:* 0.8 mg/day PO in a.m. within 2 hr of waking; increase by 1 tablet/ wk to max 6 tablets (4.8 mg) daily (*Cycloset* only).
ADV EFF Abd cramps, constipation, dyspnea, fatigue, n/v/d, orthostatic hypotension
INTERACTIONS Erythromycin, phenothiazines, sympathomimetics
NC/PT Ensure proper diagnosis before starting tx. Taper dose if used in parkinsonism. Not for use in pregnancy/breast-feeding. Pt should take drug for diabetes once a day in a.m., use safety precautions if dizziness, orthostatic hypotension occur.

brompheniramine maleate (BroveX, J-Tan, Lo-Hist 12, Respa-AR)

CLASS Antihistamine
PREG/CONT C/NA

IND & DOSE Relief of sx of seasonal rhinitis, common cold; tx of nonallergic pruritic sx. *Adult, child 12 yr and older:* Products vary. ER tablets, 6–12 mg PO q 12 hr. Chewable tablets, 12–24 mg PO q 12 hr (max, 48 mg/day). ER capsules,

12–24 mg/day PO. Oral suspension (*BroveX*), 5–10 mL (12–24 mg) PO q 12 hr (max, 48 mg/day). Oral liquid, 10 mL (4 mg) PO four times/day. Oral suspension 5 mL PO q 12 hr (max, two doses/day). *Child 6–12 yr:* ER tablets, 6 mg PO q 12 hr. Chewable tablets, 6–12 mg PO q 12 hr (max, 24 mg/day). ER capsules, 12 mg/day PO. Oral liquid, 5 mL (2 mg) PO four times/day. Oral suspension (*BroveX*), 5 mL (12 mg) PO q 12 hr (max, 24 mg/day). Oral suspension, 2.5 mL PO q 12 hr (max, 5 mL/day). *Child 2–6 yr:* Chewable tablets, 6 mg PO q 12 hr (max, 12 mg/day). Oral liquid, 2.5 mL (1 mg) PO 4 times/day. Oral suspension (*BroveX*), 2.5 mL (6 mg) PO q 12 hr up (max, 12 mg/day). Oral suspension 1.25 mL PO q 12 hr (max, 2.5 mL/day). *Child 12 mo–2 yr:* Oral suspension, 1.25 mL (3 mg) PO q 12 hr (max, 2.5 mL [6 mg]/day). Oral liquid, titrate dose based on 0.5 mg/kg/day PO in equally divided doses four times/day.
ADJUST DOSE Elderly pts
ADV EFF Anaphylactic shock, disturbed coordination, dizziness, drowsiness, faintness, thickening bronchial secretions
INTERACTIONS Alcohol, anticholinergics, CNS depressants
NC/PT Double-check dosages; products vary widely. Pt should not cut, crush, or chew ER tablets; should avoid alcohol, take safety precautions if CNS effects occur.

budesonide (Entocort EC, Pulmicort Flexhaler, Pulmicort Respules, Rhinocort)

CLASS Corticosteroid
PREG/CONT B (inhalation); C (oral)/NA

IND & DOSE Nasal spray mgt of sx of allergic rhinitis. *Adult, child 6 yr and older:* 64 mcg/day as 1 spray (32 mcg) in each nostril once daily. Max for pts over 12 yr, 256 mcg/day as 4 sprays per nostril once daily. Max

for pts 6 to under 12 yr, 128 mcg/day (given as 2 sprays per nostril once daily). **Maint tx of asthma as prophylactic therapy.** *Adult, child 12 yr and older:* 360 mcg by inhalation bid; max, 720 mcg/day. "Low" dose, 180–600 mcg/day; "medium" dose, 600–1,200 mcg/day; "high" dose, more than 1,200 mcg/day. *Child 5–11 yr:* 180 mcg by inhalation bid; max, 360 mcg bid. "Low" dose, 180–400 mcg/day; "medium" dose, 400–800 mcg/day; "high" dose, over 800 mcg/day. *Child 0–11 yr:* 0.5–1 mg by inhalation once daily or in two divided doses using jet nebulizer. Max, 1 mg/day. "Low" dose, 0.25–0.5 mg/day (0–4 yr), 0.5 mg/day (5–11 yr); "medium" dose, 0.5–1 mg/day (0–4 yr), 1 mg/day (5–11 yr); "high" dose, over 1 mg/day (0–4 yr), 2 mg/day (5–11 yr). **Tx, maint of clinical remission for up to 3 mo of mild to moderate active Crohn's disease involving ileum/ascending colon.** *Adult:* 9 mg/day PO in a.m. for up to 8 wk. May retreat recurrent episodes for 8-wk periods. Maint, 6 mg/day PO for up to 3 mo, then taper until cessation complete.
ADJUST DOSE Hepatic impairment
ADV EFF Back pain, cough, dizziness, fatigue, headache, lethargy, nasal irritation, pharyngitis
INTERACTIONS Erythromycin, grapefruit juice, indinavir, itraconazole, ketoconazole, ritonavir, saquinavir
NC/PT Taper systemic steroids when switching to inhaled form. Ensure proper administration technique for nasal spray, inhalation. Monitor for potential hypercorticism. Pt should not cut, crush, or chew PO tablets.

bumetanide (generic)
CLASS Loop diuretic
PREG/CONT C/NA

BBW Monitor electrolytes, hydration, hepatic function w/long-term tx; water and electrolyte depletion possible.

IND & DOSE Tx of edema associated w/HF, renal and hepatic diseases. *Adult:* Oral, 0.5–2 mg/day PO; may repeat at 4- to 5-hr intervals. Max, 10 mg/day. Intermittent therapy, 3–4 days on, then 1–2 off. Parenteral, 0.5–1 mg IV/IM over 1–2 min; may repeat in 2–3 hr; max, 10 mg/day.
ADJUST DOSE Elderly pts, renal impairment
ADV EFF Anorexia, asterixis, drowsiness, headache, hypokalemia, nocturia, n/v/d, orthostatic hypotension, pain at injection site, polyuria
INTERACTIONS Aminoglycosides, cardiac glycosides, cisplatin, NSAIDs, probenecid
NC/PT Switch to PO as soon as possible. Monitor electrolytes. Give early in day to avoid disrupting sleep. Pt should eat potassium-rich diet, check weight daily (report loss/gain of over 3 lb/day).

DANGEROUS DRUG

buprenorphine hydrochloride (Buprenex, Butrans Transdermal)
CLASS Opioid agonist-antagonist analgesic
PREG/CONT C/C-III

BBW Risk of addiction, abuse, misuse; life-threatening respiratory depression; accidental exposure to children; neonatal opioid withdrawal syndrome. Secure drug, limit access. Not for use in pregnancy.
IND & DOSE Relief of moderate to severe pain (parenteral). *Adult:* 0.3 mg IM or by slow (over 2 min) IV injection. May repeat once, 30–60 min after first dose; repeat q 6 hr. *Child 2–12 yr:* 2–6 mcg/kg body weight IM or slow IV injection q 4–6 hr. **Tx of opioid dependence** (oral). *Adult:* 8 mg on day 1, 16 mg on day 2 and subsequent induction days (can be 3–4 days). Maint, 12–16 mg/day sublingually (*Suboxone*). **Mgt of moderate to severe chronic pain in pts needing continuous, around-the-clock opioid**

analgesic for extended period
(transdermal). *Adult:* Initially,
5 mcg/hr, intended to be worn for
7 days; max, 20 mcg/hr.
ADJUST DOSE Elderly, debilitated
pts
ADV EFF Dizziness, headache,
hypotension, hypoventilation, miosis,
n/v, sedation, sweating, vertigo
INTERACTIONS Barbiturates, benzodiazepines, general anesthetics,
opioid analgesics, phenothiazines,
sedatives
NC/PT Have opioid antagonists,
facilities for assisted respiration on
hand. Taper as part of comprehensive
tx plan. Not for use in pregnancy/
breast-feeding. Pt should place translingual tablet under tongue until dissolved, then swallow; apply
transdermal patch to clean, dry area,
leave for 7 days. Remove old patch
before applying new one. Do not
repeat use of site for 3 wk. Safety precautions if CNS effects occur.

DANGEROUS DRUG

**buPROPion
hydrobromide (Aplenzin),
buPROPion
hydrochloride (Wellbutrin,
Zyban)**
CLASS Antidepressant,
smoking deterrent
PREG/CONT C/NA

BBW Monitor response and behavior; suicide risk in depressed pts,
children, adolescents, young adults.
Serious mental health events possible, including changes in behavior,
depression, and hostility. Aplenzin not
indicated for smoking cessation; risk
of serious neuropsychiatric events,
including suicide, when used for this
purpose.
IND & DOSE Tx of major depressive disorder. *Adult:* 300 mg PO as
100 mg tid; max, 450 mg/day. SR,
150 mg PO bid. ER, 150 mg/day PO.
Aplenzin, 174–348 mg/day PO; max,
522 mg/day. **Smoking cessation.**

Adult: 150 mg (Zyban) PO daily for
3 days; increase to 300 mg/day in two
divided doses at least 8 hr apart. Treat
for 7–12 wk. **Tx of seasonal affective
disorder.** *Adult:* 150 mg (Wellbutrin
XL) PO daily in a.m.; max, 300 mg/day.
Begin in autumn; taper off (150 mg/day
for 2 wk before discontinuation) in
early spring. Aplenzin, 174–348 mg/day
PO; continue through winter season.
ADJUST DOSE Renal, hepatic
impairment
ADV EFF Agitation, constipation,
depression, dry mouth, headache,
migraine, **suicidality**, tachycardia,
tremor, weight loss
INTERACTIONS Alcohol, amantadine, cyclophosphamide, levodopa,
MAOIs, paroxetine, sertraline
NC/PT Check labels carefully; dose
varies between Wellbutrin forms.
Avoid use w/hx of seizure disorder.
Monitor hepatic, renal function.
Smoking cessation: Pt should quit
smoking within 2 wk of tx. May be
used w/transdermal nicotine. Pt
should avoid alcohol, take safety precautions if CNS effects occur, report
thoughts of suicide.

---

busPIRone (generic)
CLASS Anxiolytic
PREG/CONT B/NA

IND & DOSE Mgt of anxiety disorders; short-term relief of sx of anxiety.** *Adult:* 15 mg/day PO; may
increase slowly to optimum therapeutic effect. Max, 60 mg/day.
ADV EFF Abd distress, dizziness,
dry mouth, headache, insomnia,
light-headedness, n/v/d
INTERACTIONS Alcohol, CNS
depressants, erythromycin, fluoxetine, grapefruit juice, haloperidol,
itraconazole, MAOIs
NC/PT Suggest sugarless lozenges
for dry mouth, analgesic for headache. Pt should avoid OTC sleeping
drugs, alcohol, grapefruit juice, take
safety measures if CNS effects occur.

DANGEROUS DRUG

busulfan (Busulfex, Myleran)

CLASS Alkylating agent, antineoplastic

PREG/CONT D/NA

BBW Arrange for blood tests to evaluate bone marrow function before tx, wkly during, and for at least 3 wk after tx ends. Severe bone marrow suppression possible. Hematopoietic progenitor cell transplantation required to prevent potentially fatal complications of prolonged myelosuppression.

IND & DOSE Palliative tx of chronic myelogenous leukemia; bone marrow transplantation (oral). *Adult:* Remission induction, 4–8 mg or 60 mcg/kg PO. Maint, resume tx w/ induction dosage when WBC count reaches 50,000/mm³; if remission shorter than 3 mo, maint of 1–3 mg PO daily advised to control hematologic status. *Child:* May give 60–120 mcg/kg/day PO, or 1.8–4.6 mg/m²/day PO for remission induction. **W/cyclophosphamide as conditioning regimen before allogenic hematopoietic progenitor cell transplant for CML** (parenteral). *Adult:* 0.8 mg/kg IV of ideal body weight or actual body weight, whichever is lower, as 2-hr infusion q 6 hr for 4 consecutive days; total of 16 doses.

ADJUST DOSE Hepatic impairment

ADV EFF Amenorrhea, anemia, hyperpigmentation, leukopenia, menopausal sx, n/v/d, ovarian suppression, pancytopenia, pulmonary dysplasia, seizures, Stevens-Johnson syndrome

NC/PT Arrange for respiratory function test before and periodically during tx; monitor CBC. Reduce dose w/ bone marrow depression. Ensure pt is hydrated. Give IV through central venous catheter. Premedicate for IV tx w/phenytoin, antiemetics. Not for use in pregnancy (barrier contraceptives advised)/breast-feeding. Pt should drink 10–12 glasses of fluid each day, report difficulty breathing, severe skin reactions.

DANGEROUS DRUG

butorphanol tartrate (generic)

CLASS Opioid agonist-antagonist analgesic

PREG/CONT C (pregnancy); D (labor & delivery)/C-IV

IND & DOSE Relief of moderate to severe pain; preop or preanesthetic medication; to supplement balanced anesthesia. *Adult:* 2 mg IM q 3–4 hr or 1 mg IV q 3–4 hr; range, 0.5–2 mg IV q 3–4 hr. *During labor:* 1–2 mg IV/IM at full term during early labor; repeat q 4 hr. **Relief of moderate to severe pain** (nasal spray). 1 mg (1 spray/nostril); repeat in 60–90 min if adequate relief not achieved; may repeat two-dose sequence q 3–4 hr.

ADJUST DOSE Elderly pts; hepatic, renal impairment

INTERACTIONS Barbiturate anesthetics

ADV EFF Nausea, sedation, slow shallow respirations

NC/PT Ensure ready access to respiratory assist devices when giving IV/IM. Protect from falls; sedation, visual disturbances possible. Pt should not drive or perform other tasks requiring alertness.

C1-inhibitor (human) (Cinryze)

CLASS Blood product, esterase inhibitor

PREG/CONT C/NA

IND & DOSE Px against angioedema attacks in adults, adolescents w/hereditary angioedema. *Adult, adolescent:* 1,000 units IV at 1 mL/min over 10 min q 3–4 days.

ADV EFF Blood-related infections, headache, hypersensitivity reactions, n/v, rash, thrombotic events

NC/PT Have epinephrine available in case of severe hypersensitivity reactions. Slight risk of blood-related diseases. Not for use in pregnancy/breast-feeding. Pt should report difficulty breathing, hives, chest tightness.

C1-inhibitor (recombinant) (Ruconest)
CLASS Blood product, esterase inhibitor
PREG/CONT C/NA

IND & DOSE Tx of acute angioedema attacks in adults, adolescents w/hereditary angioedema. *Adult, adolescent 84 kg:* 50 international units/kg IV over 5 min. *84 kg and over:* 4,200 international units IV over 5 min. No more than two doses/24 hr.
ADV EFF Headache, **hypersensitivity reactions,** n/d, **serious thrombotic events**
NC/PT Have epinephrine available in case of severe hypersensitivity reactions. Use in pregnancy/breast-feeding only if clearly needed. Teach pt/significant other how to prepare, administer drug at onset of attack, proper disposal of needles/syringes. Pt should report difficulty breathing, chest tightness.

cabazitaxel (Jevtana)
CLASS Antineoplastic, microtubular inhibitor
PREG/CONT D/NA

BBW Severe hypersensitivity reactions possible; prepare to support pt. Severe neutropenia, deaths have occurred; monitor blood counts closely. Not for use w/hx of severe reactions to cabazitaxel or polysorbate 80.
IND & DOSE W/oral prednisone for tx of pts w/hormone-refractory metastatic prostate cancer previously treated w/docetaxel. *Adult:* 25 mg/m^2 IV over 1 hr q 3 wk.
ADJUST DOSE Elderly pts, hepatic impairment
ADV EFF Abd pain, alopecia, anorexia, arthralgia, asthenia, **bone marrow suppression,** constipation, cough, dysgeusia, dyspnea, fever, **hepatic impairment, hypersensitivity reactions,** n/v/d, **neutropenia, renal failure**
INTERACTIONS Strong CYP3A inhibitors, inducers
NC/PT Premedicate w/antihistamine, corticosteroid, and H$_2$ antagonist; antiemetic if needed. Always give w/oral prednisone. Drug requires two dilutions before administration. Monitor blood count; dose adjustment needed based on neutrophil count; do not administer if neutrophil count <1,500/mm^3. Monitor LFTs, renal function. Ensure hydration; tx w/antidiarrheals may be needed. Not for use in pregnancy/breast-feeding. Pt should mark calendar w/dates for tx, try to maintain food and liquid intake, report difficulty breathing, rash.

cabozantinib (Cometriq)
CLASS Antineoplastic, kinase inhibitor
PREG/CONT D/NA

BBW Risk of GI perforation, fistulas; monitor pt. Severe to fatal hemorrhage has occurred; monitor for s&sx of bleeding.
IND & DOSE Tx of progressive, metastatic medullary thyroid cancer. *Adult:* 140 mg/day PO.
ADJUST DOSE Hepatic impairment
ADV EFF Abd pain, anorexia, constipation, fatigue, hair color change, **hypertension,** nausea, **osteonecrosis of jaw, palmar-plantar erythrodysesthesia syndrome, proteinuria, RPLS, thromboembolic events,** weight loss, **wound complications**

INTERACTIONS Strong CYP3A4 inducers/inhibitors, grapefruit juice; avoid these combinations
NC/PT Monitor for s&sx of bleeding, GI perforation, drug interactions. Not for use in pregnancy/breast-feeding. Pt should take as directed on empty stomach, at least 2 hr before or after food; swallow capsule whole and not cut, crush, or chew it; avoid grapefruit juice; report s&sx of bleeding (bruising, coughing up blood, tarry stools, bleeding that won't stop); acute stomach pain; choking, difficulty swallowing; swelling or pain in mouth or jaw; chest pain, acute leg pain, difficulty breathing.

caffeine (Caffedrine, Enerjets, NoDoz, Vivarin), caffeine citrate (Cafcit)
CLASS Analeptic, CNS stimulant, xanthine
PREG/CONT C/NA

IND & DOSE Aid in staying awake; adjunct to analgesic preparations. *Adult:* 100–200 mg PO q 3–4 hr as needed. **Tx of respiratory depression associated w/overdose of CNS depressants.** *Adult:* 500 mg–1 g caffeine and sodium benzoate (250–500 mg caffeine) IM; max, 2.5 g/day. May give IV in severe emergency. **Short-term tx of apnea of prematurity in infants between 28 and 33 wk gestation.** *Premature infants:* 20 mg/kg IV over 30 min followed 24 hours later by 5 mg/kg/day IV over 10 min or PO as maint *(Cafcit).*
ADV EFF Diuresis, excitement, insomnia, restlessness, tachycardia, withdrawal syndrome (headache, anxiety, muscle tension)
INTERACTIONS Cimetidine, ciprofloxacin, clozapine, disulfiram, ephedra, guarana, hormonal contraceptives, iron, ma huang, mexiletine, theophylline
NC/PT should avoid foods high in caffeine; not stop abruptly because withdrawal sx possible; avoid

dangerous activities if CNS effects occur. Ensure parental support w/premature infant use.

calcitonin, salmon (Miacalcin)
CLASS Calcium regulator, hormone
PREG/CONT C/NA

IND & DOSE Tx of Paget's disease. *Adult:* 100 units/day IM or subcut. **Tx of postmenopausal osteoporosis when other tx not suitable.** *Adult:* 100 units/day IM or subcut. **Tx of hypercalcemia.** *Adult:* 4 units/kg q 12 hr IM or subcut. If response unsatisfactory after 1–2 days, increase to 8 units/kg q 12 hr; if response still unsatisfactory after 2 more days, increase to 8 units/kg q 6 hr.
ADV EFF Flushing of face or hands, hypocalcemia, **hypersensitivity reactions,** local inflammatory reactions at injection site, **malignancy,** n/v, rash, urinary frequency
INTERACTIONS Lithium
NC/PT Before use, give skin test to pt w/hx of allergies; give w/calcium carbonate (1.5 g/day) and vitamin D (400 units/day). Monitor for hypocalcemia. Monitor serum alkaline phosphatase and urinary hydroxyproline excretion before and during first 3 mo of therapy, then q 3–6 mo. Inject doses of more than 2 mL IM, not subcut. Teach pt proper technique and proper disposal of needles/syringes. Pt should report difficulty breathing, facial edema, chest discomfort.

calcium salts: calcium acetate (Eliphos, PhosLo), **calcium carbonate** (Caltrate, Chooz, Tums), **calcium chloride**, **calcium citrate** (Cal-Cee, Cal-Citrate), **calcium glubionate** (Calcionate, Calciquid), **calcium gluconate** (generic), **calcium lactate** (Cal-Lac)
CLASS Antacid, electrolyte
PREG/CONT C/NA

IND & DOSE RDA (carbonate or lactate). *Adult over 50 yr:* 1,200 mg/day PO. *Adult 19–50 yr:* 1,000 mg/day PO. *Child 14–18 yr:* 1,300 mg/day PO. *Child 9–13 yr:* 1,300 mg/day PO. *Child 4–8 yr:* 800 mg/day PO. *Child 1–3 yr:* 500 mg/day PO. *Child 7–12 mo:* 270 mg/day PO. *Child 0–6 mo:* 210 mg/day PO. *Pregnancy/breast-feeding, 19–50 yr:* 1,000 mg/day PO. *Pregnancy/breast-feeding, 14–18 yr:* 1,300 mg/day PO. **Dietary supplement** (carbonate or lactate). *Adult:* 500 mg–2 g PO bid–qid. **Antacid.** *Adult:* 0.5–2 g PO calcium carbonate as needed. **Tx of hypocalcemic disorders.** *Adult:* 500 mg–1 g calcium chloride IV at intervals of 1–3 days. *Child:* 2.7–5 mg/kg or 0.027–0.05 mL/kg calcium chloride IV q 4–6 hr, or 200–500 mg/day IV (2–5 mL of 10% sol); for infants, no more than 200 mg IV (2 mL of 10% sol) in divided doses (calcium gluconate). **Tx of magnesium intoxication.** *Adult:* 500 mg calcium chloride IV promptly. **Tx of hyperphosphatemia.** *Adult:* 2,001–2,668 mg PO w/each meal (calcium acetate). **Cardiac resuscitation.** *Adult:* 500 mg–1 g IV or 200–800 mg calcium chloride into ventricular cavity.
ADV EFF Anorexia, bradycardia, constipation, hypercalcemia, hypotension, irritation at injection site,

n/v, peripheral vasodilation, rebound hyperacidity, tingling
INTERACTIONS Fluoroquinolones, quinidine, salicylates, tetracyclines, thyroid hormone, verapamil
NC/PT Do not give oral drugs within 1–2 hr of antacid. Avoid extravasation of IV fluid; tissue necrosis possible. Monitor serum phosphate levels periodically. Monitor cardiac response closely w/parenteral tx. Pt should take drug between meals and at bedtime; chew antacid tablets thoroughly before swallowing and follow w/glass of water; not take w/other oral drugs; space at least 1–2 hr after antacid.

calfactant (natural lung surfactant) (Infasurf)
CLASS Lung surfactant
PREG/CONT Unkn/NA

IND & DOSE Prophylactic tx of infants at risk for developing RDS; rescue tx of premature infants up to 72 hr of age who have developed RDS. Instill 3 mL/kg of birth weight in two doses of 1.5 mL/kg each intratracheally. Repeat doses of 3 mL/kg (to total of three doses) given 12 hr apart.
ADV EFF Bradycardia, hyperbilirubinemia, hypotension, intraventricular hemorrhage, nonpulmonary infections, patent ductus arteriosus, sepsis
NC/PT Monitor ECG and O_2 saturation continuously during and for at least 30 min after administration. Ensure ET tube correctly placed; suction immediately before dosing. Do not suction for 1 hr after dosing. Maintain appropriate interventions for critically ill infant.

canagliflozin (Invokana)
CLASS Antidiabetic, sodium-glucose cotransporter 2 inhibitor
PREG/CONT C/NA

IND & DOSE W/diet/exercise to improve glycemic control in type

2 diabetes. *Adult:* 100 mg/day w/first meal of day; max, 300 mg/day.
ADJUST DOSE Severe hepatic/renal impairment
ADV EFF Bone fracture, dehydration, diabetic ketoacidosis, genital yeast infections, hypoglycemia, hypotension, hyperkalemia, hyperlipidemia, polyuria, UTI
INTERACTIONS Celery, coriander, dandelion root, digoxin, fenugreek, garlic, ginger, juniper berries, phenobarbital, phenytoin, rifampin
NC/PT Not for use w/type 1 diabetes, pregnancy/breast-feeding. Monitor blood glucose, HbA1c, BP periodically; also monitor for UTI, genital infections. Pt should continue diet/exercise program, other antidiabetics as ordered; take safety measures w/dehydration; report sx of UTI, genital infections.

canakinumab (Ilaris)
CLASS Interleukin blocker
PREG/CONT C/NA

IND & DOSE Tx of cryopyrin-associated periodic syndromes, including familial cold autoinflammatory syndrome and Muckle-Wells syndrome. *Adult, child 4 yr and older:* Over 40 kg, 150 mg subcut; 15 kg to under 40 kg, 2 mg/kg subcut; 15–40 kg w/inadequate response, 3 mg/kg subcut. Injections given q 8 wk. **Tx of juvenile rheumatoid arthritis.** *Adult, child 2 yr and older:* 4 mg/kg subcut q 4 wk.
ADV EFF Diarrhea, flulike sx, headache, nasopharyngitis, nausea, **serious infections**
INTERACTIONS Immunosuppressants, live vaccines
NC/PT Use extreme caution in pts w/infections; monitor for infections. Not for use in pregnancy/breast-feeding. Pt should report s&sx of infection.

candesartan cilexetil (Atacand)
CLASS Antihypertensive, ARB
PREG/CONT D/NA

BBW Rule out pregnancy before starting tx. Suggest barrier birth control; fetal injury and deaths have occurred. If pregnancy detected, discontinue as soon as possible.
IND & DOSE Tx of hypertension. *Adult:* 16 mg PO daily; range, 8–32 mg/day. *Child 6–under 17 yr:* Over 50 kg, 8–16 mg/day PO; range, 4–32 mg/day PO; under 50 kg, 4–8 mg/day PO; range, 4–16 mg/day PO. *Child 1–under 6 yr:* 0.20 mg/kg/day oral suspension; range, 0.05–0.4 mg/kg/day. **Tx of HF.** *Adult:* 4 mg/day PO; may be doubled at 2-wk intervals. Target dose, 32 mg/day PO as single dose.
ADJUST DOSE Volume depletion
ADV EFF Abd pain, diarrhea, dizziness, headache, hyperkalemia, hypotension, renal impairment, URI sx
INTERACTIONS ARBs, lithium, NSAIDs, renin inhibitors
NC/PT If BP not controlled, can add other antihypertensives. Use caution if pt goes to surgery; volume depletion possible. Not for use in pregnancy (barrier contraception advised)/breast-feeding. Pt should use care in situations that could lead to fluid volume loss; monitor fluid intake.

cangrelor (Kengreal)
CLASS Platelet inhibitor
PREG/CONT Unkn/NA

IND & DOSE Adjunct to percutaneous coronary intervention to reduce risk of periprocedural MI, repeat revascularization, stent thrombosis in pts who have not received platelet inhibitors. *Adult:* 30 mcg/kg as IV bolus before procedure; then 4 mcg/kg/min IV infusion for at least 2 hr or for duration of procedure (whichever longer).

ADV EFF Bleeding, hypersensitivity reactions

INTERACTIONS Clopidogrel, prasugrel; do not coadminister

NC/PT Monitor pt for bleeding. Administer by dedicated IV line. Switch to oral ticagrelor, prasugrel, or clopidogrel after infusion ends to maintain platelet inhibition. Use caution in pregnancy/breast-feeding. Pt should report difficulty breathing, chest pain.

DANGEROUS DRUG

capecitabine (Xeloda)
CLASS Antimetabolite, antineoplastic
PREG/CONT D/NA

BBW Increased risk of excessive bleeding, even death, if combined w/ warfarin; avoid this combination. If combination must be used, monitor INR and PT levels closely; adjust anticoagulant dose as needed.

IND & DOSE Tx of metastatic breast and colorectal cancer; adjuvant postop Dukes C colon cancer. *Adult:* 2,500 mg/m²/day PO in two divided doses 12 hr apart within 30 min after meal for 2 wk, followed by 1 wk rest. Given as 3-wk cycles for eight cycles (24 wk); adjuvant tx for total of 6 mo. If used w/docetaxel, 1,250 PO bid a.m. and p.m. within 30 min after meal for 2 wk, combined w/docetaxel 75 mg/m² IV over 1 hr q 3 wk.

ADJUST DOSE Elderly pts; renal impairment (contraindicated with severe renal impairment)

ADV EFF Anorexia, **cardiomyopathy, coagulopathy,** constipation, dehydration, dermatitis, hand-and-foot syndrome, hyperbilirubinemia, leukopenia, **mucocutaneous toxicity, myelosuppression, MI,** n/v/d, **renal impairment, Stevens-Johnson syndrome,** stomatitis

INTERACTIONS Antacids, docetaxel, leucovorin (risk of severe toxicity, death), phenytoin, warfarin

NC/PT Obtain baseline and periodic renal function tests, CBC; monitor for s&sx of toxicity. Monitor nutritional status, fluid intake. Give frequent mouth care; correct dehydration. Not for use in pregnancy (barrier contraceptives advised)/breast-feeding. Pt should mark calendar for tx days; avoid exposure to infection; report s&sx of infection, rash, chest pain, severe diarrhea.

---

capreomycin (Capastat Sulfate)
CLASS Antibiotic, antituberculotic
PREG/CONT C/NA

BBW Arrange for audiometric testing and assessment of vestibular function, renal function tests, and serum potassium before and regularly during tx; severe risk of renal failure, auditory damage. Drug's safety not established in children or pregnant women.

IND & DOSE Tx of pulmonary TB not responsive to first-line antituberculotics, as part of combination therapy. *Adult:* 1 g daily (max, 20 mg/kg/day) IM or IV for 60–120 days, followed by 1 g IM two to three times/wk for 12–24 mo.

ADJUST DOSE Elderly pts, renal impairment

ADV EFF Nephrotoxicity, ototoxicity

INTERACTIONS Nephrotoxic drugs, NMJ blockers

NC/PT Culture and sensitivity before tx. Use w/other antituberculotics. Give by deep IM injection. Obtain audiometric testing regularly. Monitor renal function, potassium levels regularly.

---

captopril (generic)
CLASS ACE inhibitor, antihypertensive
PREG/CONT D/NA

BBW Rule out pregnancy; fetal abnormalities and death have occurred if used during second or third trimester. Encourage use of contraceptive measures.

IND & DOSE Tx of hypertension, alone or as part of combination therapy. *Adult:* 25 mg PO bid or tid. Range, 25–150 mg bid–tid; max, 450 mg/day. **Tx of heart failure.** *Adult:* 6.25–12.5 mg PO tid. Maint, 50–100 mg PO tid; max, 450 mg/day. **Left ventricular dysfx after MI.** *Adult:* 6.25 mg PO tid, then 12.5 mg PO tid; increase slowly to 50 mg PO tid starting as early as 3 days post-MI. **Tx of diabetic nephropathy.** *Adult:* Reduce dosage; suggested dose, 25 mg PO tid.

ADJUST DOSE Elderly pts, renal impairment

ADV EFF Agranulocytosis, aphthous ulcers, cough, dysgeusia, **HF**, **MI**, pancytopenia, proteinuria, rash, tachycardia

INTERACTIONS Allopurinol, indomethacin, lithium, probenecid

NC/PT Use caution before surgery; mark chart. Give 1 hr before meals. Protect pt in situations of decreased fluid volume. Not for use in pregnancy. Cough may occur. Pt should change position slowly if dizzy, lightheaded; avoid OTC preparations; consult prescriber before stopping drug.

---

carbamazepine
(Carbatrol, Equetro, Tegretol)
CLASS Antiepileptic
PREG/CONT D/NA

BBW Risk of aplastic anemia and agranulocytosis; obtain CBC, including platelet/reticulocyte counts, and serum iron determination before starting tx; repeat wkly for first 3 mo and monthly thereafter for at least 2–3 yr. Discontinue if evidence of marrow suppression. Increased risk of suicidality; monitor accordingly. Risk of serious to fatal dermatologic reactions, including Stevens-Johnson syndrome, in pts w/HLA-B*1502

allele with *Tegretol*. Pts at risk should be screened for this allele.

IND & DOSE Refractory seizure disorders. *Adult:* 200 mg PO bid on first day. Increase gradually by up to 200 mg/day in divided doses q 6–8 hr, or 100 mg PO qid suspension; range, 800–1,200 mg/day. *Child 6–12 yr:* 100 mg PO bid on first day. Increase gradually by adding 100 mg/day at 6- to 8-hr intervals until best response achieved; max, 1,000 mg/day. *Child under 6 yr:* Optimal daily dose, less than 35 mg/kg/day PO. **Tx of trigeminal neuralgia.** *Adult:* 100 mg PO bid on first day. May increase by up to 200 mg/day, using 100-mg increments q 12 hr as needed. Range, 200–1,200 mg/day; max, 1,200 mg/day. **Tx of bipolar I disorder.** *Adult:* 400 mg/day PO in divided doses; max, 1, 600 mg/day (*Equetro* only).

ADJUST DOSE Elderly pts

ADV EFF Bone marrow suppression, CV complications, dizziness, drowsiness, **hepatic cellular necrosis w/total loss of liver tissue, hepatitis, HF**, n/v, **Stevens-Johnson syndrome**, unsteadiness

INTERACTIONS Barbiturates, charcoal, cimetidine, danazol, doxycycline, erythromycin, isoniazid, lithium, MAOIs, NMJ blockers, phenytoin, primidone, valproic acid, verapamil, warfarin

NC/PT Use only for indicated uses. Taper dose if withdrawing; abrupt removal can precipitate seizures. Obtain baseline and frequent LFTs, monitor CBC; dose adjustment made accordingly. Evaluate for therapeutic serum levels (usually 4–12 mcg/mL). Not for use in pregnancy (barrier contraceptives advisable). Pt should swallow ER tablets whole; wear medical alert tag; avoid CNS depressants (alcohol). May open *Equetro* capsule and sprinkle over food.

carbinoxamine maleate (Karbinal ER)

CLASS Antihistamine
PREG/CONT C/NA

IND & DOSE Tx of seasonal/perennial allergic rhinitis; vasomotor rhinitis; allergic conjunctivitis; allergic skin reactions; dermatographism; anaphylactic reactions; allergic reactions to blood, blood products. *Adult, child 12 yr and older:* 6–16 mg PO q 12 hr. *Child 6–11 yr:* 6–12 mg PO q 12 hr. *Child 2–3 yr:* 3–4 mg PO q 12 hr.
ADV EFF Dizziness, drowsiness, dry mouth, epigastric distress, rash, thickened secretions, urine retention
INTERACTIONS CNS depressants, MAOIs; avoid this combination
NC/PT Ensure pt can tolerate anticholinergic effects; suggest increased fluids, humidifier. Pt should measure drug using mL measure provided; take safety measures w/CNS effects; use humidifier, increase fluid intake; report difficulty breathing, fainting.

DANGEROUS DRUG

carboplatin (generic)

CLASS Alkylating agent, antineoplastic
PREG/CONT D/NA

BBW Evaluate bone marrow function before and periodically during tx; do not give next dose if marked bone marrow depression. Consult physician for dosage. Ensure epinephrine, corticosteroids, antihistamines readily available in case of anaphylactic reactions, which may occur within min of administration.
IND & DOSE Initial, palliative tx of pts w/advanced ovarian cancer. *Adult:* As single agent, 360 mg/m2 IV over at least 15 min on day 1 q 4 wk; adjust dose based on blood counts.

ADJUST DOSE Elderly pts, renal impairment
ADV EFF Abd pain, alopecia, asthenia, **anaphylactic reactions, bone marrow suppression, bronchospasm, cancer,** constipation, electrolyte abnormalities, n/v/d, peripheral neuropathies, renal impairment
INTERACTIONS Aluminum (in sol)
NC/PT Antiemetic may be needed. Obtain CBC regularly; dose adjustment may be needed. Ensure emergency equipment available in case of anaphylactic reaction. Not for use in pregnancy. Hair loss, GI effects possible.

---

carboprost tromethamine (Hemabate)

CLASS Abortifacient, prostaglandin
PREG/CONT C/NA

IND & DOSE Termination of pregnancy 13–20 wk from first day of last menstrual period; evacuation of uterus in missed abortion or intrauterine fetal death. *Adult:* 250 mcg (1 mL) IM; give 250 mcg IM at 1.5- to 3.5-hr intervals. Max, 12 mg total dose. Tx of postpartum hemorrhage. *Adult:* 250 mcg IM as one dose; may use multiple doses at 15- to 90-min intervals. Max, 2 mg (eight doses).
ADV EFF Diarrhea, flushing, hypotension, nausea, **perforated uterus, uterine rupture**
NC/PT Pretreat w/antiemetics and antidiarrheals. Give by deep IM injection. Ensure abortion complete; monitor for infection. Ensure adequate hydration. Several IM injections may be needed.

---

carfilzomib (Kyprolis)

CLASS Antineoplastic, proteasome inhibitor
PREG/CONT D/NA

IND & DOSE Tx of relapsed multiple myeloma in pts w/disease progression after at least two prior therapies; as monotherapy or in combination with lenalidomide and dexamethasone. *Adult:* Cycle 1: 20 mg/m²/day IV over 10 min on two consecutive days each wk for three wk (days 1, 2, 8, 9, 15, 16) followed by 12-day rest period. Cycle 2 and beyond: Increase to 27 mg/m²/day IV over 10 min, following same dosing-days schedule.

ADV EFF Anemia, dyspnea, fatigue, fever, **heart failure/ischemia, hepatotoxicity, infusion reactions, liver failure,** n/v/d, **pulmonary complications, pulmonary hypertension,** renal failure, **RPLS,** thrombocytopenia, **tumor lysis syndrome, venous thrombosis**

NC/PT Premedicate w/dexamethasone; hydrate before and after tx. Monitor for potentially severe adverse reactions; arrange for supportive measures, dosage adjustment. Not for use in pregnancy. Pt should mark calendar for tx days; report difficulty breathing, swelling, urine/stool color changes, chest pain.

carglumic acid (Carbaglu)
CLASS Carbamoyl phosphate synthetase I activator
PREG/CONT C/NA

IND & DOSE Adjunctive/maint tx of acute hyperammonemia due to hepatic *N*-acetylglutamate synthase deficiency. *Adult, child:* 100–250 mg/kg/day PO in divided doses; may be made into sol and given through NG tube.

ADV EFF Abd pain, anemia, fever, headache, infections, nasopharyngitis, n/v/d

NC/PT Monitor ammonia levels during tx; dose adjustment may be needed. Restrict protein intake until ammonia level regulated. Not for use in pregnancy/breast-feeding. Store in refrigerator until opened, then room temp. Date bottle; discard after 1 mo.

cariprazine (Vraylar)
CLASS Atypical antipsychotic, dopamine/serotonin agonist and antagonist
PREG/CONT High risk/NA

BBW Elderly pts w/dementia-related psychosis have increased risk of death if given atypical antipsychotics; not approved for this use. Risk of suicidal ideation increases w/antidepressant use, especially in children, adolescents, young adults; monitor accordingly; not approved for use in children.

IND & DOSE Tx of schizophrenia. *Adult:* 1.5–6 mg/day PO. Tx of manic or mixed episodes of bipolar I disorder. *Adult:* 1.5–3 mg/day PO.

ADV EFF Akathisia, bone marrow suppression, cognitive/motor impairment, dyslipidemia, hyperglycemia, **NMS,** orthostatic hypotension, **seizures** (potentially life-threatening), suicidality, syncope, tardive dyskinesia; weight gain

INTERACTIONS Alcohol, carbamazepine, CNS depressants, CYP2D6 inhibitors (fluoxetine, paroxetine, quinidine), CYP3A4 inhibitors (ketoconazole), lorazepam

NC/PT Dispense least amount possible to suicidal pts. Not for use in pregnancy (risk of abnormal muscle movements, withdrawal)/breast-feeding. Monitor weight; assess for hyperglycemia. May react w/many drugs; monitor regimen. Take safety precautions for cognitive/motor impairment; use cautiously if low BP possible; ensure hydration. Pt should report thoughts of suicide, signs of infection, abnormal muscle movements.

carisoprodol (Soma)
CLASS Centrally acting skeletal muscle relaxant
PREG/CONT C/NA

IND & DOSE Relief of discomfort associated w/acute, painful

musculoskeletal conditions, as adjunct. Adult, child over 16 yr: 250–350 mg PO tid–qid. Pt should take last dose at bedtime for max of 2–3 wk.
ADJUST DOSE Hepatic, renal impairment
ADV EFF Allergic/idiosyncratic reaction, agitation, **anaphylactoid shock,** ataxia, dizziness, drowsiness, irritability, tremor, vertigo
NC/PT Monitor for idiosyncratic reaction, most likely w/first doses. Provide safety measures w/CNS effects. May become habit-forming; use caution. Pt should avoid other CNS depressants.

DANGEROUS DRUG

carmustine (BCNU) (BiCNU, Gliadel)
CLASS Alkylating agent, antineoplastic
PREG/CONT D/NA

BBW Do not give more often than q 6 wk because of delayed bone marrow toxicity. Evaluate hematopoietic function before, wkly during, and for at least 6 wk after tx to monitor for bone marrow suppression. Monitor for pulmonary toxicity and delayed toxicity, which can occur yrs after therapy; death possible. Cumulative doses of 1,400 mg/m² increase risk.
IND & DOSE Palliative tx alone or w/other agents (injection) for brain tumors, Hodgkin lymphoma, non-Hodgkin lymphoma, multiple myeloma. Adult, child: 150–200 mg/m² IV q 6 wk as single dose or in divided daily injections (75–100 mg/m² on 2 successive days); adjust dose based on CBC. Adjunct to surgery for tx of recurrent glioblastoma as implantable wafer (w/prednisone); tx of newly diagnosed high-grade malignant glioma (wafer). Adult, child: Wafers implanted in resection cavity as part of surgical procedure; up to 8 wafers at a time.
ADV EFF Bone marrow suppression (may be delayed 4–6 wk), **cancer,**

hepatotoxicity, local burning at injection site, **pulmonary fibrosis,** pulmonary infiltrates, **renal failure,** stomatitis
INTERACTIONS Cimetidine, digoxin, mitomycin, phenytoin
NC/PT Monitor CBC before and wkly during tx. Do not give full dose within 2–3 wk of radiation or other chemotherapy. Monitor pulmonary function; toxicity can be delayed. Monitor LFTs, renal function, injection site for local reaction. Premedicate w/antiemetic. Not for use in pregnancy. Pt should try to maintain fluid intake, nutrition.

---

carvedilol (Coreg)
CLASS Alpha and beta blocker, antihypertensive
PREG/CONT C/NA

IND & DOSE Mgt of hypertension, alone or w/other drugs. Adult: 6.25 mg PO bid; maintain for 7–14 days, then increase to 12.5 mg PO bid. Max, 50 mg/day. **Tx of mild to severe HF.** Adult: 3.125 mg PO bid for 2 wk, then may increase to 6.25 mg PO bid. Max, 25 mg/day if under 85 kg, 50 mg/ if over 85 kg. **Tx of left ventricular dysfx after MI.** Adult: 6.25 mg PO bid; increase after 3–10 days to 25 mg PO bid. **Converting to once-daily CR capsules.** 3.125 mg bid, give 10 mg CR; 6.25 mg bid, give 20 mg CR; 12.5 mg bid, give 40 mg CR; 25 mg bid, give 80 mg CR.
ADJUST DOSE Hepatic impairment
ADV EFF Bradycardia, bronchospasm, constipation, diabetes, diarrhea, dizziness, fatigue, flatulence, gastric pain, **hepatic injury, HF,** hypotension, rhinitis, tinnitus, vertigo
INTERACTIONS Amiodarone, antidiabetics, clonidine, cyclosporine, digoxin, diltiazem, hypotensives, rifampin, verapamil
NC/PT Do not discontinue abruptly; taper when discontinuing (risk of CAD exacerbation). Use caution if surgery planned. Use care in conversion to CR capsules. Monitor for orthostatic

hypotension. Monitor LFTs. Provide safety measures. Pt should not cut, crush, or chew CR capsules; take w/ food; change position slowly if lowered BP occurs; if diabetic, should use caution and monitor glucose level carefully.

caspofungin acetate (Cancidas)

CLASS Antifungal, echinocandin
PREG/CONT C/NA

IND & DOSE Tx of invasive aspergillosis; tx of esophageal candidiasis; tx of candidemia and other *Candida* infections; empirical tx when fungal infection suspected in neutropenic pts. *Adult:* Loading dose, 70 mg IV, then 50 mg/day IV infusion at least 14 days. *Child 3 mo–17 yr:* Loading dose, 70 mg/m² IV, then 50 mg/m² IV daily for 14 days.
ADJUST DOSE Hepatic impairment, concurrent rifampin or inducers of drug clearance
ADV EFF Decreased serum potassium, diarrhea, fever, **hepatic damage**, hypersensitivity reactions, hypotension, increased liver enzymes
INTERACTIONS Cyclosporine, rifampin
NC/PT Monitor for IV complications. Monitor potassium levels; monitor LFTs before and during tx. Not for use in pregnancy/breast-feeding. Pt should report difficulty breathing, swelling, rash.

cefadroxil (generic)

CLASS Cephalosporin
PREG/CONT B/NA

IND & DOSE Tx of pharyngitis/ tonsillitis caused by **susceptible bacteria strains.** *Adult:* 1 g/day PO in single dose or two divided doses for 10 days. *Child:* 30 mg/kg/day PO in single or two divided doses; continue for 10 days. Tx of UTIs caused by **susceptible bacteria strains.** *Adult:* 1–2 g/day PO in single dose or two divided doses for uncomplicated lower UTIs. For all other UTIs, 2 g/day in two divided doses. *Child:* 30 mg/kg/day PO in divided doses q 12 hr. **Tx of skin, skin-structure infections caused by susceptible bacteria strains.** *Adult:* 1 g/day PO in single dose or two divided doses. *Child:* 30 mg/kg/day PO in divided doses.
ADJUST DOSE Elderly pts, renal impairment
ADV EFF Abd pain, **anaphylaxis,** anorexia, **bone marrow depression, colitis,** flatulence, n/v/d, rash, super-infections
INTERACTIONS Aminoglycosides, bacteriostatic agents, probenecid
NC/PT Culture before tx. Give w/ meals to decrease GI discomfort; give oral vancomycin for serious colitis. Refrigerate suspension. Pt should not cut, crush, or chew ER tablets; complete full course of therapy; report diarrhea w/blood or mucus.

cefdinir (generic)

CLASS Cephalosporin
PREG/CONT B/NA

IND & DOSE Tx of community-acquired pneumonia, uncomplicated skin, skin-structure infections. *Adult, adolescent:* 300 mg PO q 12 hr for 10 days. **Tx of acute exacerbation of chronic bronchitis, acute maxillary sinusitis, pharyngitis, tonsillitis.** *Adult, adolescent:* 300 mg PO q 12 hr for 10 days or 600 mg PO q 24 hr for 10 days. **Tx of otitis media, acute maxillary sinusitis, pharyngitis, tonsillitis.** *Child 6 mo–12 yr:* 7 mg/kg PO q 12 hr or 14 mg/kg PO q 24 hr for 10 days; max, 600 mg/day. **Tx of skin, skin-structure infections.** *Child 6 mo–12 yr:* 7 mg/kg PO q 12 hr for 10 days.
ADJUST DOSE Renal impairment
ADV EFF Abd pain, **anaphylaxis,** anorexia, **colitis,** flatulence, n/v/d, rash, superinfections

INTERACTIONS Aminoglycosides, antacids, oral anticoagulants
NC/PT Culture before tx. Give w/ meals to decrease GI discomfort; give oral vancomycin for serious colitis. Arrange for tx of superinfections. Store suspension at room temp; discard after 10 days. Pt should complete full course of therapy; report diarrhea w/blood or mucus.

cefditoren pivoxil
(Spectracef)
CLASS Cephalosporin
PREG/CONT B/NA

IND & DOSE Tx of uncomplicated skin/skin-structure infections, pharyngitis, tonsillitis caused by susceptible bacteria. Adult, child over 12 yr: 200 mg PO bid for 10 days. Tx of acute exacerbation of chronic bronchitis, community-acquired pneumonia caused by susceptible bacteria strains. Adult, child over 12 yr: 400 mg PO bid for 10 days (chronic bronchitis) or 14 days (pneumonia).
ADJUST DOSE Renal impairment
ADV EFF Abd pain, anaphylaxis, anorexia, colitis, flatulence, hepatotoxicity, n/v/d, rash, superinfections
INTERACTIONS Antacids, oral anticoagulants
NC/PT Culture before tx. Do not give longer than 10 days; risk of carnitine deficiency. Give w/meals to decrease GI discomfort; give oral vancomycin for serious colitis. Provide tx for superinfections. Not for pts w/allergy to milk proteins. Pt should not take w/antacids; should complete full course of therapy; report diarrhea w/blood or mucus.

cefepime hydrochloride (generic)
CLASS Cephalosporin
PREG/CONT B/NA

IND & DOSE Tx of mild to moderate UTI. Adult: 0.5–1 g IM or IV q 12 hr for 7–10 days. Tx of severe UTI. Adult: 2 g IV q 12 hr for 10 days. Tx of moderate to severe pneumonia. Adult: 1–2 g IV q 12 hr for 10 days. Tx of moderate to severe skin infections. Adult: 2 g IV q 12 hr for 10 days. Empiric therapy for febrile neutropenic pts. Adult: 2 g IV q 8 hr for 7 days. Tx of complicated intra-abdominal infections. Adult: 2 g IV q 12 hr for 7–10 days. Children over 2 mo, under 40 kg: 50 mg/kg/day IV or IM q 12 hr for 7–10 days depending on infection severity. If treating febrile neutropenia, give q 8 hr (max, 2 g/day).
ADJUST DOSE Elderly pts, renal impairment
ADV EFF Abd pain, anaphylaxis, anorexia, colitis, disulfiram reaction w/alcohol, flatulence, hepatotoxicity, n/v/d, phlebitis, rash, superinfections
INTERACTIONS Alcohol, aminoglycosides, oral anticoagulants
NC/PT Culture before tx. Administer IV over 30 min. Have vitamin K available if hypoprothrombinemia occurs. Pt should avoid alcohol during and for 3 days after tx; report diarrhea w/ blood or mucus, difficulty breathing, rash.

cefotaxime sodium
(Claforan)
CLASS Cephalosporin
PREG/CONT B/NA

IND & DOSE Tx of lower respiratory tract, skin, intra-abdominal, CNS, bone and joint infections; UTIs; peritonitis caused by susceptible bacteria. Adult: 2–8 g/day IM or IV in equally divided doses q 6–8 hr; max, 12 g/day. Child 1 mo–12 yr under 50 kg: 50–180 mg/kg/day IV or IM in four to six divided doses. Child 1–4 wk: 50 mg/kg IV q 8 hr. Child 0–1 wk: 50 mg/kg IV q 12 hr. Tx of gonorrhea. Adult: 0.5–1 g IM in single injection. Disseminated infection. Adult: 1–2 g IV q 8 hr. Periop px. Adult: 1 g IV or IM 30–90 min before surgery. Cesarean section. Adult: 1 g

IV after cord is clamped, then 1 g IV or IM at 6 and 12 hr.
ADJUST DOSE Elderly pts, renal impairment
ADV EFF Abd pain, **anaphylaxis**, anorexia, **bone marrow depression**, **colitis**, disulfiram reaction w/alcohol, flatulence, **hepatotoxicity**, n/v/d, phlebitis, rash, superinfections
INTERACTIONS Alcohol, aminoglycosides, oral anticoagulants
NC/PT Culture before tx. Ensure no hx of hypersensitivity to penicillin or other cephalosporins; have ephinephrine and emergency equipment on standby in pts with hx of type 1 allergic reactions. Give IV slowly. Pt should avoid alcohol during and for 3 days after tx; report diarrhea w/blood or mucus, difficulty breathing.

cefoxitin sodium (generic)
CLASS Cephalosporin
PREG/CONT B/NA

IND & DOSE Tx of lower respiratory tract, skin, intra-abdominal, CNS, bone and joint infections; UTIs, peritonitis caused by susceptible bacteria. *Adult:* 2–8 g/day IM or IV in equally divided doses q 6–8 hr. *Child 3 mo and older:* 80–160 mg/kg/day IM or IV in divided doses q 4–6 hr. Max, 12 g/day. **Tx of gonorrhea.** *Adult:* 2 g IM w/1 g oral probenecid. **Uncomplicated lower respiratory tract infections, UTIs, skin infections.** *Adult:* 1 g q 6–8 hr IV. **Moderate to severe infections.** *Adult:* 1 g q 4 hr IV to 2 g q 6–8 hr IV. **Severe infections.** *Adult:* 2 g q 4 hr IV or 3 g q 6–8 hr IV. **Periop px.** *Adult:* 2 g IV or IM 30–60 min before initial incision, q 6 hr for 24 hr after surgery. **Cesarean section.** *Adult:* 2 g IV as soon as cord clamped, then 2 g IM or IV at 4 and 8 hr, then q 6 hr for up to 24 hr. **Transurethral prostatectomy.** *Adult:* 1 g before surgery, then 1 g q 8 hr for up to 5 days.
ADJUST DOSE Elderly pts, renal impairment

ADV EFF Abd pain, **anaphylaxis**, anorexia, **bone marrow depression**, **colitis**, disulfiram reaction w/alcohol, flatulence, **hepatotoxicity**, n/v/d, phlebitis, rash, superinfections
INTERACTIONS Alcohol, aminoglycosides, oral anticoagulants
NC/PT Culture before tx. Give IV slowly. Have vitamin K available for hypoprothrombinemia. Pt should avoid alcohol during and for 3 days after tx; report diarrhea w/blood or mucus.

cefpodoxime proxetil (generic)
CLASS Cephalosporin
PREG/CONT B/NA

IND & DOSE Tx of upper and lower respiratory tract infections, skin and skin-structure infections, UTIs, otitis media caused by susceptible strains; STD caused by *Neisseria gonorrhoeae. Adult:* 100–400 mg PO q 12 hr depending on infection severity for 5–14 days. *Child:* 5 mg/kg/dose PO q 12 hr; max, 100–200 mg/dose for 10 days. **Tx of acute otitis media.** *Child:* 10 mg/kg/day PO divided q 12 hr; max, 400 mg/day for 5 days.
ADJUST DOSE Elderly pts, renal impairment
ADV EFF Abd pain, **anaphylaxis**, anorexia, **bone marrow depression**, **colitis**, flatulence, **hepatotoxicity**, n/v/d, phlebitis, rash, superinfections
INTERACTIONS Aminoglycosides, oral anticoagulants
NC/PT Culture before tx. Refrigerate suspension. Give oral vancomycin for serious colitis. Pt should take w/food; complete full course of therapy; report diarrhea w/blood or mucus.

cefprozil (generic)
CLASS Cephalosporin
PREG/CONT B/NA

IND & DOSE Tx of upper and lower respiratory tract infections, skin

and skin-structure infections, otitis media, acute sinusitis caused by susceptible strains. *Adult:* 250–500 mg PO q 12–24 hr for 10 days. **Tx of acute otitis media, sinusitis.** *Child 6 mo–12 yr:* 7.5–15 mg/kg PO q 12 hr for 10 days. **Tx of pharyngitis, tonsillitis.** *Child 2–12 yr:* 7.5 mg/kg PO q 12 hr for 10 days. **Tx of skin and skin-structure infections.** *Child 2–12 yr:* 20 mg/kg PO once daily for 10 days.
ADJUST DOSE Elderly pts, renal impairment
ADV EFF Abd pain, anaphylaxis, anorexia, bone marrow depression, colitis, flatulence, hepatotoxicity, n/v/d, phlebitis, rash, superinfections
INTERACTIONS Aminoglycosides, oral anticoagulants
NC/PT Culture before tx. Refrigerate suspension. Give oral vancomycin for serious colitis. Pt should take w/food; complete full course of therapy; report diarrhea w/blood or mucus.

ceftaroline fosamil (Teflaro)
CLASS Cephalosporin
PREG/CONT B/NA

IND & DOSE Tx of skin, skin-structure infections; community-acquired pneumonia caused by susceptible strains. *Adult:* 600 mg by IV infusion over 1 hr q 12 hr for 5–14 days (skin, skin-structure infections) or 5–7 days (community-acquired pneumonia).
ADJUST DOSE Renal impairment
ADV EFF CDAD, dizziness, hemolytic anemia, hypersensitivity reactions, injection-site reactions, rash, renal failure
NC/PT Culture before tx. Small, frequent meals may help GI effects. Monitor injection site, CBC. Not for use in pregnancy/breast-feeding. Pt should report severe diarrhea.

ceftazidime (Fortaz, Tazicef)
CLASS Cephalosporin
PREG/CONT B/NA

IND & DOSE Tx of lower respiratory, skin and skin-structure, intra-abdominal, CNS, bone and joint infections; UTIs, septicemia caused by susceptible strains, gynecologic infections caused by *Escherichia coli.* *Adult:* Usual dose, 1 g (range, 250 mg–2 g) q 8–12 hr IM or IV; max, 6 g/day. *Child 1 mo–12 yr:* 30 mg/kg IV q 12 hr. *Child 0–4 wk:* 30 mg/kg IV q 12 hr. **Tx of UTIs caused by susceptible bacteria strains.** *Adult:* 250–500 mg IV or IM q 8–12 hr. **Tx of pneumonia, skin and skin-structure infections caused by susceptible bacteria strains.** *Adult:* 500 mg–1 g IV or IM q 8 hr. **Tx of bone and joint infections caused by susceptible bacteria strains.** *Adult:* 2 g IV q 12 hr. Tx of gynecologic, intra-abdominal, life-threatening infections; meningitis. *Adult:* 2 g IV q 8 hr.
ADJUST DOSE Elderly pts, renal impairment
ADV EFF Abd pain, anaphylaxis, anorexia, bone marrow depression, CDAD, colitis, disulfiram-like reaction w/alcohol, flatulence, injection-site reactions, n/v/d, pain, phlebitis, superinfections
INTERACTIONS Aminoglycosides, alcohol, oral anticoagulants
NC/PT Culture before tx. Do not mix in sol w/aminoglycosides. Have vitamin K available if hypoprothrombinemia occurs. Pt should avoid alcohol during and for 3 days after tx; report diarrhea w/blood or mucus.

ceftibuten (Cedax)
CLASS Cephalosporin
PREG/CONT B/NA

IND & DOSE Tx of acute bacterial exacerbations of chronic bronchitis, acute bacterial otitis media,

pharyngitis, tonsillitis caused by susceptible strains. *Adult:* 400 mg PO daily for 10 days. *Child:* 9 mg/kg/day PO for 10 days; max, 400 mg/day.
ADJUST DOSE Renal impairment
ADV EFF Abd pain, **anaphylaxis,** anorexia, **bone marrow depression, colitis,** disulfiram-like reactions w/ alcohol, flatulence, **hepatotoxicity,** n/v/d, pain, superinfections
INTERACTIONS Aminoglycosides, alcohol, oral anticoagulants
NC/PT Culture before tx. Give w/ meals. Refrigerate suspension; discard after 14 days. Arrange tx for superinfections. Pt should avoid alcohol during and for 3 days after tx; complete full course of therapy; report diarrhea w/blood or mucus.

ceftriaxone sodium
(Rocephin)
CLASS Cephalosporin
PREG/CONT B/NA

IND & DOSE Tx of lower respiratory tract, intra-abdominal, skin and skin-structure, bone and joint infections; acute bacterial otitis media, UTIs, septicemia caused by susceptible strains. *Adult:* 1–2 g/day IM or IV as one dose or in equal divided doses bid; max, 4 g/day. *Child:* 50–75 mg/kg/day IV or IM in divided doses q 12 hr; max, 2 g/day. Tx of gonorrhea and PID caused by *Neisseria gonorrhoeae. Adult:* Single 250-mg IM dose. Tx of meningitis. *Adult:* 1–2 g/day IM or IV as one dose or in equal divided doses bid for 14–14 days; max, 4 g/day. Loading dose of 100 mg/kg may be used. Periop px. *Adult:* 1 g IV 30–120 min before surgery.
ADV EFF Abd pain, **anaphylaxis,** anorexia, **bone marrow depression, colitis,** disulfiram-like reactions w/ alcohol, flatulence, **hepatotoxicity,** n/v/d, pain, superinfections
INTERACTIONS Aminoglycosides, alcohol, oral anticoagulants
NC/PT Culture before tx. Give w/ meals. Protect drug from light. Have

vitamin K available if hypoprothrombinemia occurs. Do not mix w/other antimicrobials. Arrange tx for superinfections. Pt should avoid alcohol during and for 3 days after tx; complete full course of therapy; report diarrhea w/blood or mucus.

cefuroxime axetil
(Ceftin), **cefuroxime sodium** (Zinacef)
CLASS Cephalosporin
PREG/CONT B/NA

IND & DOSE Tx of upper respiratory tract, skin and skin-structure infections; acute bacterial otitis media, uncomplicated gonorrhea, bacterial sinusitis, UTIs, early Lyme disease caused by susceptible strains. *Adult, child 12 yr and older:* 250 mg PO bid. For severe infections, may increase to 500 mg PO bid. Treat for up to 10 days. Or 750 mg–1.5 g IM or IV q 8 hr, depending on infection severity, for 5–10 days. *Child over 3 mo:* 50–100 mg/kg/day IM or IV in divided doses q 6–8 hr. Tx of acute otitis media. *Child 3 mo–12 yr:* 250 mg PO bid for 10 days. Tx of pharyngitis/tonsillitis. *Child 3 mo–12 yr:* 125 mg PO q 12 hr for 10 days. Tx of acute sinusitis. *Child 3 mo–12 yr:* 250 mg PO bid for 10 days. Tx of impetigo. *Child 3 mo–12 yr:* 30 mg/kg/day (max, 1 g/day) in two divided doses for 10 days. Uncomplicated gonorrhea. *Adult:* 1.5 g IM (at two different sites) w/1 g oral probenecid. Periop px. *Adult:* 1.5 g IV 30–60 min before initial incision, then 750 mg IV or IM q 8 hr for 24 hr after surgery. Tx of bacterial meningitis. *Child:* 200–240 mg/kg/day IV in divided doses q 6–8 hr.
ADJUST DOSE Elderly pts, impaired renal function
ADV EFF Abd pain, **anaphylaxis,** anorexia, **bone marrow depression,** CDAD, **colitis,** disulfiram-like reactions w/alcohol, flatulence, **hepatotoxicity,** n/v/d, pain, superinfections

INTERACTIONS Aminoglycosides, alcohol, oral anticoagulants
NC/PT Culture before tx. Give w/ meals. Have vitamin K available for hypoprothrombinemia. Do not mix w/ other antimicrobials. Arrange for tx of superinfections. Use oral suspension for children who cannot swallow tablets. Pt should avoid alcohol during and for 3 days after tx; complete full course of therapy; report diarrhea w/ blood or mucus.

---

celecoxib (Celebrex)
CLASS Cox-2 specific inhibitor, NSAID
PREG/CONT C (1st, 2nd trimesters); D (3rd trimester)/NA

BBW Increased risk of CV events, GI bleeding; monitor accordingly.
IND & DOSE Tx of acute pain, dysmenorrhea; mgt of rheumatoid arthritis. *Adult:* 100 mg PO bid; may increase to 200 mg/day PO bid as needed. **Tx of osteoarthritis.** *Adult:* 200 mg/day PO. **Tx of ankylosing spondylitis.** *Adult:* 200 mg/day PO; after 6 wk, may try 400 mg/day for 6 wk. **Tx of juvenile rheumatoid arthritis.** *Child 2 yr and older:* Over 25 kg, 100 mg capsule PO bid. Ten kg to 25 kg or less, 50 mg capsule PO bid.
ADJUST DOSE Hepatic, renal impairment
ADV EFF Agranulocytosis, anaphylactoid reactions, dizziness, dyspepsia, headache, insomnia, MI, rash, somnolence, stroke
INTERACTIONS Alcohol, lithium, nicotine, warfarin
NC/PT Give w/food if GI upset occurs. Use comfort measures to help relieve pain, safety measures if CNS effects occur. Name confusion w/*Celebrex* (celecoxib), *Celexa* (citalopram), *Xanax* (alprazolam), and *Cerebyx* (fosphenytoin); use caution.

---

cephalexin (Keflex)
CLASS Cephalosporin
PREG/CONT B/NA

IND & DOSE Tx of respiratory tract infections, acute bacterial otitis media, bone infections, UTIs caused by susceptible strains. *Adult:* 1–4 g/day in divided doses; usual dose, 250 mg PO q 6 hr. *Child:* 25–50 mg/kg/day PO in divided doses. **Tx of skin, skin-structure infections, uncomplicated cystitis, streptococcal pharyngitis.** *Adult:* 500 mg PO q 12 hr. May need larger doses in severe cases; max, 4 g/day. *Child:* Divide usual daily dose; give q 12 hr. **Tx of otitis media.** *Child:* 75–100 mg/kg/day PO in four divided doses.
ADV EFF Abd pain, anaphylaxis, anorexia, bone marrow depression, colitis, disulfiram-like reactions w/ alcohol, flatulence, hepatotoxicity, n/v/d, pain, superinfections
INTERACTIONS Aminoglycosides, alcohol, oral anticoagulants
NC/PT Culture before tx. Give w/ meal. Pt should avoid alcohol during and for 3 days after tx; report diarrhea w/blood or mucus.

---

certinib (Zykadia)
CLASS Antineoplastic, kinase inhibitor
PREG/CONT D/NA

IND & DOSE Tx of anaplastic lymphoma kinase-positive metastatic non-small-cell lung cancer w/ progression after crizotinib. *Adult:* 750 mg/day PO on empty stomach.
ADV EFF Bradycardia, constipation, GI toxicity, hepatotoxicity, hyperglycemia, n/v/d, pancreatitis, prolonged QT, serious to fatal pneumonitis
INTERACTIONS CYP3A inducers/inhibitors, grapefruit juice, QT-prolonging drugs
NC/PT Ensure pt has been tested for appropriate sensitivity. Monitor LFTs, pulmonary function, glucose

(in diabetics). Pt should avoid pregnancy (contraceptives advised)/breast-feeding, grapefruit juice; take on empty stomach; report difficulty breathing, urine/stool color changes, severe diarrhea.

certolizumab (Cimzia)
CLASS Immune modulator, TNF blocker
PREG/CONT C/NA

BBW Risk of serious infections, cancer, CNS demyelinating disorders. Prescreen for TB and hepatitis B; monitor pt carefully.
IND & DOSE To reduce s&sx of Crohn's disease; tx of moderately to severely active rheumatoid arthritis. *Adult:* 400 mg subcut repeated at 2 wk and 4 wk; maint, 400 mg q wk (Crohn's), 200 mg q 4 wk (arthritis).
ADV EFF Anaphylaxis, lupuslike syndrome, malignancies, serious to fatal infections, rash, URIs, UTIs
INTERACTIONS Abatacept, anakinra, live vaccines, natalizumab, rituximab
NC/PT Monitor carefully for s&sx of allergic reaction, infection. Not for use in pregnancy. Pt should report s&sx of infection.

cetirizine hydrochloride (Zyrtec)
CLASS Antihistamine
PREG/CONT B/NA

IND & DOSE Mgt of seasonal and perennial allergic rhinitis; tx of chronic, idiopathic urticaria. *Adult, child 6 yr and older:* 10 mg/day PO or 5 mg PO bid; max, 10 mg. *Child 6–11 yr:* 5 or 10 mg PO daily. *Child 2–6 yr:* 2.5 mg PO once daily; max, 5 mg/day.
ADJUST DOSE Elderly pts; renal, hepatic impairment
ADV EFF Bronchospasm, sedation, somnolence
NC/PT Provide syrup or chewable tablets for children. Pt should main-

tain intake of fluids, use humidifier if secretions thicken; take safety precautions if sedation occurs. Name confusion between *Zyrtec* (cetirizine) and *Zyprexa* (olanzapine) and between *Zyrtec* (cetirizine) and *Zantac* (ranitidine); use caution.

cetrorelix acetate (Cetrotide)
CLASS Fertility drug
PREG/CONT X/NA

IND & DOSE Inhibition of premature LH surges in women undergoing controlled ovarian stimulation. *Adult:* 3 mg subcut. If HCG not given within 4 days, continue 0.25 mg/kg/day subcut until HCG is given.
ADV EFF Headache, hypersensitivity reactions, injection-site reactions, nausea, ovarian overstimulation
NC/PT Part of comprehensive fertility program; many follow-up tests will be needed. Pt should learn proper administration/disposal of needles/syringes.

DANGEROUS DRUG

cetuximab (Erbitux)
CLASS Antineoplastic, monoclonal antibody
PREG/CONT C/NA

BBW Serious to fatal infusion reactions, cardiac arrest, and sudden death have occurred. Closely monitor serum electrolytes during and after tx.
IND & DOSE Tx of advanced colorectal cancer; *K-Ras* wild-type, EGFR-expressing colorectal cancer; advanced squamous cell carcinoma of head and neck w/radiation or as monotherapy after failure of platinum therapy. *Adult:* 400 mg/m² IV loading dose over 120 min, then 250 mg/m² IV over 60 min wkly.
ADV EFF Cardiac arrest, dermatologic toxicity, diarrhea, headache, hypomagnesemia, increased tumor progression, increased death with

Ras-mutant mCRC, infections, **infusion reactions, pulmonary toxicity,** rash, pruritus
NC/PT Premedicate w/H₁ antagonist IV 30–60 min before first dose. Base future doses on clinical response. Do not infuse faster than 10 mg/min. Have emergency equipment on hand. Monitor electrolytes; assess lungs and skin for s&sx of toxicity. Males and females should use contraception during and for 6 mo after tx; females should not breast-feed during or for 2 mo after tx. Pt should report s&sx of infection, difficulty breathing, rash.

cevimeline hydrochloride (Evoxac)
CLASS Parasympathomimetic
PREG/CONT C/NA

IND & DOSE Tx of dry mouth in pts w/Sjögren's syndrome. *Adult:* 30 mg PO tid w/food.
ADV EFF Cardiac arrhythmias, bronchial narrowing, dehydration, dyspepsia, excessive sweating, headache, n/v/d, URIs, visual blurring
INTERACTIONS Beta-adrenergic antagonists
NC/PT Give w/meals. Monitor for dehydration. Pt should take safety precautions if visual changes occur.

charcoal, activated
(Actidose-Aqua, Liqui-Char)
CLASS Antidote
PREG/CONT C/NA

IND & DOSE Emergency tx in poisoning by most drugs and chemicals. *Adult:* 50–60 g or 1 g/kg PO, or approximately 8–10 times by volume amount of poison ingested, as oral suspension. Give as soon as possible after poisoning. W/gastric dialysis, 20–40 g PO q 6 hr for 1–2 days for severe poisonings; for optimum effect, give within 30 min of poisoning. *Child 1–12 yr:* Over 32 kg, 50–60 g PO; 16–32 kg, 25–30 g PO;

under 16 kg and under 1 yr, not recommended.
ADV EFF Black stools, constipation, diarrhea, vomiting
INTERACTIONS Laxatives, milk products, oral medications
NC/PT For use w/conscious pts only. Take steps to prevent aspiration; have life-support equipment readily available. Pt should drink 6–8 glasses of liquid/day to avoid constipation. Name confusion between *Actidose* (charcoal) and *Actos* (pioglitazone); use caution.

chenodiol (Chenodal)
CLASS Gallstone solubilizer
PREG/CONT X/NA

BBW Highly toxic to liver. Reserve use for select pts where benefit clearly outweighs risk.
IND & DOSE Tx of selected pts w/ radiolucent gallstones when surgery not an option. *Adult:* 250 mg PO bid for 2 wk, then 13–16 mg/kg/day in 2 divided doses a.m. and p.m. for up to 6–9 mo.
ADV EFF Colon cancer, diarrhea, **hepatotoxicity,** neutropenia
INTERACTIONS Clofibrate, warfarin
NC/PT Ensure correct selection of pt. Monitor LFTs carefully. Not for use in pregnancy (barrier contraceptives advised). Long-term therapy requires frequent tests. Diarrhea will occur.

DANGEROUS DRUG
chlorambucil (Leukeran)
CLASS Antineoplastic, nitrogen mustard
PREG/CONT D/NA

BBW Arrange for blood tests to evaluate hematopoietic function before and wkly during tx. Severe bone marrow suppression possible. Drug is carcinogenic; monitor pt regularly. Rule out pregnancy before starting tx. Encourage use of barrier contraceptives; drug is teratogenic. May cause infertility.

IND & DOSE Palliative tx of chronic lymphocytic leukemia (CLL); malignant lymphoma, including lymphosarcoma; giant follicular lymphoma; Hodgkin lymphoma. *Adult:* Initial dose and short-course therapy, 0.1–0.2 mg/kg PO for 3–6 wk; may give single daily dose. CLL alternative regimen, 0.4 mg/kg PO q 2 wk, increasing by 0.1 mg/kg w/each dose until therapeutic or toxic effect occurs. Maint, 0.03–0.1 mg/kg/day PO; max, 0.1 mg/kg/day.

ADV EFF Acute leukemia, alopecia, bone marrow depression

NC/PT Monitor CBC regularly. Rule out pregnancy. Do not give full dose within 4 wk of radiation or other chemotherapy. Divide dose w/severe n/v; maintain hydration. Sterility can occur. Name confusion w/*Leukeran* (chlorambucil), *Myleran* (busulfan), *Alkeran* (melphalan), and leucovorin; use caution.

chloramphenicol sodium succinate
(generic)
CLASS Antibiotic
PREG/CONT C/NA

BBW Severe, sometimes fatal blood dyscrasias (in adults) and severe, sometimes fatal gray syndrome (in newborns, premature infants) possible. Restrict use to situations in which no other antibiotic effective. Monitor serum levels at least wkly to minimize toxicity risk (therapeutic conc: peak, 10–20 mcg/mL; trough, 5–10 mcg/mL).

IND & DOSE Severe infections caused by susceptible strains. *Adult:* 50 mg/kg/day IV in divided doses q 6 hr up to 100 mg/kg/day in severe cases. Severe infections and cystic fibrosis regimen. *Child:* 50–100 mg/kg/day IV in divided doses q 6 hr. Neonates, children w/immature metabolic processes, 25 mg/kg/day IV; individualize doses at 6-hr intervals.

ADJUST DOSE Elderly pts; hepatic, renal impairment

ADV EFF Anaphylaxis, bone marrow depression, gray baby syndrome, n/v/d, superinfections

INTERACTIONS Bone marrow suppressants, glipizide, glyburide, phenytoins, tolazamide, tolbutamide, vitamin B_{12}, warfarin

NC/PT Culture before tx. Do not give IM. Monitor serum levels. Monitor CBC carefully. Change to another antibiotic as soon as possible.

chlordiazepoxide
(Librium)
CLASS Anxiolytic, benzodiazepine
PREG/CONT D/C-IV

IND & DOSE Mgt of anxiety disorders. *Adult:* 5 or 10 mg PO, up to 20 or 25 mg, tid–qid. *Child over 6 yr:* Initially, 5 mg PO bid–qid; may increase to 10 mg bid–tid. Preop apprehension. *Adult:* 5–10 mg PO tid–qid on days preceding surgery. Alcohol withdrawal. *Adult:* 50–100 mg PO, then repeated doses as needed (max, 300 mg/day).

ADJUST DOSE Elderly pts, debilitating disease

ADV EFF Apathy, confusion, constipation, **CV collapse**, depression, diarrhea, disorientation, drowsiness, drug dependence w/withdrawal, fatigue, incontinence, lethargy, lightheadedness, restlessness, urine retention

INTERACTIONS Alcohol, aminophylline, cimetidine, disulfiram, dyphylline, hormonal contraceptives, smoking, theophylline

NC/PT Monitor LFTs, renal function, CBC periodically during long-term therapy. Taper gradually after long-term use. Not for use in pregnancy (barrier contraceptives advised). Pt should take safety precautions w/ CNS effects.

chloroquine phosphate (Aralen Phosphate)

CLASS Amebicide, 4-aminoquinoline, antimalarial
PREG/CONT C/NA

IND & DOSE Tx of extraintestinal amebiasis. *Adult:* 1 g (600 mg base)/day PO for 2 days, then 500 mg (300 mg base)/day for 2–3 wk. **Px and tx of acute malaria attacks caused by susceptible strains.** *Adult:* Suppression, 300 mg base PO once a wk on same day for 2 wk before exposure, continuing until 8 wk after exposure; acute attack, 600 mg base PO initially, then 300 mg 6–8 hr, 24 hr, and 48 hr after initial dose for total dose of 1.5 g in 3 days. *Child:* Suppression, 5 mg base/kg PO once a wk on same day for 2 wk before exposure, continuing until 8 wk after exposure; acute attack, 10 mg base/kg PO initially; then 5 mg base/kg 6 hr later; then third dose 18 hr later; then last dose 24 hr after third dose. Max, 10 mg base/kg/day or 300 mg base/day.
ADV EFF N/v/d, permanent retinal changes, visual distortion
INTERACTIONS Cimetidine
NC/PT Double-check child doses; child very susceptible to overdose. Give w/food if GI effects occur. Arrange for ophthalmologic exam before and during long-term tx. Pt should take safety measures if vision changes.

chlorothiazide (Diuril), chlorothiazide sodium (generic)

CLASS Thiazide diuretic
PREG/CONT C/NA

IND & DOSE Adjunctive tx for edema; tx of hypertension. *Adult:* 0.5–2 g daily PO or IV. *Child:* Generally, 10–20 mg/kg/day PO in single dose or two divided doses. *Child 2–12 yr:* 375 mg–1 g PO in two divided doses. *Child 6 mo–2 yr:* 125–375 mg PO in two divided doses. *Child under 6 mo:* Up to 30 mg/kg/day PO in two doses.
ADV EFF Agranulocytosis, anorexia, aplastic anemia, constipation, ED, n/v/d, nocturia, polyuria, vertigo
INTERACTIONS Alcohol, antidiabetics, cholestyramine, corticosteroids, diazoxide, digoxin, lithium, opioids
NC/PT Do not give IM or subcut. Monitor and record weight daily. Pt should take w/food if GI upset occurs, take early in day so sleep will not be disturbed. Increased urination will occur; pt should plan day accordingly.

chlorpheniramine maleate (Aller-Chlor, Allergy, Chlor-Trimeton Allergy)

CLASS Antihistamine
PREG/CONT C/NA

IND & DOSE Symptomatic relief of s&sx associated w/perennial and seasonal allergic rhinitis; vasomotor rhinitis; common cold; allergic conjunctivitis. *Adult, child over 12 yr:* 4 mg PO q 4–6 hr; max, 24 mg in 24 hr (tablets, syrup). ER tablets, 16 mg w/liquid PO q 24 hr. SR tablets, 8–12 mg PO at bedtime or q 8–12 hr during day. ER capsules, 12 mg/day PO; max, 24 mg/day. Caplets, 8–12 mg/day PO q 12 hr. *Child 6–12 yr:* 2 mg q 4–6 hr PO; max, 12 mg in 24 hr (tablets, syrup).
ADJUST DOSE Elderly pts
ADV EFF Anaphylactic shock, aplastic anemia, bronchial secretion thickening, disturbed coordination, dizziness, drowsiness, epigastric distress, sedation
INTERACTIONS Alcohol, CNS depressants
NC/PT Periodic CBC w/long-term tx. Pt should take w/food; not cut, crush, or chew SR/ER forms; avoid alcohol; take safety precautions w/CNS effects.

chlorproMAZINE hydrochloride (generic)
CLASS Antiemetic, antipsychotic, anxiolytic, dopamine blocker, phenothiazine
PREG/CONT C/NA

BBW Risk of death in elderly pts w/ dementia-related psychoses; not approved for this use.

IND & DOSE Tx of excessive anxiety, agitation. *Adult:* 25 mg IM; may repeat in 1 hr w/25–50 mg IM. Increase gradually in inpts, up to 400 mg q 4–6 hr. Switch to oral dose as soon as possible, 10 mg PO tid–qid; increase to 25 mg PO bid–tid. 25–50 mg PO tid for outpts; up to 2,000 mg/day PO for inpatients. *Child 6 mo–12 yr:* 0.5 mg/kg PO q 4–6 hr; 1 mg/kg rectally q 6–8 hr; 0.55 mg/kg IM q 6–8 hr; max, 40 mg/day (up to 5 yr) or 75 mg/day (5–12 yr). *Child, inpts:* 50–100 mg/day PO; max, 40 mg/day IM (up to 5 yr), 75 mg/day IM (5–12 yr). **Preop, postop anxiety.** *Adult:* Preop, 25–50 mg PO 2–3 hr before surgery or 12.5–25 mg IM 1–2 hr before surgery; intraop, 12.5 mg IM repeated in 30 min or 2 mg IV repeated q 2 min (up to 25 mg total) to control vomiting (if no hypotension occurs); postop, 10–25 mg PO q 4–6 hr or 12.5–25 mg IM repeated in 1 hr (if no hypotension occurs). *Child 6 mo–12 yr:* Preop, 0.55 mg/kg PO 2–3 hr before surgery or 0.55 mg/kg IM 1–2 hr before surgery; intraop, 0.25 mg/kg IM or 1 mg (diluted) IV, repeated at 2-min intervals up to total IM dose; postop, 0.55 mg/kg PO q 4–6 hr or 0.55 mg/kg IM, repeated in 1 hr (if no hypotension occurs). **Tx of acute intermittent porphyria.** *Adult:* 25–50 mg PO or 25 mg IM tid–qid until pt can take oral tx. **Adjunct tx of tetanus.** *Adult:* 25–50 mg IM tid–qid, usually w/barbiturates, or 25–50 mg IV diluted and infused at 1 mg/min. *Child:* 0.55 mg/kg IM q 6–8 hr or 0.5 mg/min IV; max, 40 mg/day (up to 23 kg), 75 mg/day (23–45 kg).

Antiemetic. *Adult:* 10–25 mg PO q 4–6 hr, or 50–100 mg rectally q 6–8 hr, or 25 mg IM. If no hypotension, give 25–50 mg q 3–4 hr. Switch to oral dose when vomiting ends. *Child:* 0.55 mg/kg PO q 4–6 hr, or 0.55 mg/kg IM q 6–8 hr. Max IM dose, 40 mg/day (up to 5 yr), 75 mg/day (5–12 yr). **Tx of intractable hiccups.** *Adult:* 25–50 mg PO tid–qid. If sx persist for 2–3 days, give 25–50 mg IM; if inadequate response, give 25–50 mg IV in 500–1,000 mL saline.
ADJUST DOSE Elderly pts

ADV EFF Anaphylactoid reactions, aplastic anemia, blurred vision, bronchospasm, cardiac arrest, cardiomegaly, drowsiness, dry mouth, extrapyramidal syndromes, HF, hypotension, laryngospasm, n/v/d, NMS, orthostatic hypotension, photophobia, pulmonary edema, urine retention, urticaria, vertigo
INTERACTIONS Alcohol, anticholinergics, barbiturate anesthetics, beta blockers, epinephrine, meperidine, norepinephrine

NC/PT Do not give by subcut injection; give slowly by deep IM injection into upper outer quadrant of buttock. If giving drug via continuous infusion for intractable hiccups, keep pt flat in bed; avoid skin contact w/parenteral drug sol; monitor renal function, CBC; withdraw slowly after high-dose use. Aspiration risk w/loss of cough reflex. Pt should avoid alcohol, take safety measures if CNS effects occur, protect from sun exposure. Name confusion between chlorpromazine, chlorpropamide, and clomipramine.

chlorproPAMIDE (generic)
CLASS Antidiabetic, sulfonylurea
PREG/CONT C/NA

IND & DOSE Tx of type 2 diabetes w/diet and exercise. *Adult:* 100–250 mg/day PO; max, 750 mg/day.
ADJUST DOSE Elderly pts

ADV EFF Anorexia, **CV events,** disulfiram reaction w/alcohol, dizziness, headache, hypoglycemia, n/v
INTERACTIONS Alcohol, beta blockers, MAOIs, miconazole, NSAIDs, salicylates, warfarin
NC/PT Monitor serum glucose; switch to insulin therapy in times of high stress. Not for use in pregnancy. Pt should take w/food; continue diet and exercise program, avoid alcohol.

---

chlorzoxazone (Parafon Forte DSC, Remular-S)
CLASS Centrally acting skeletal muscle relaxant
PREG/CONT C/NA

IND & DOSE Relief of discomfort associated w/acute, painful musculoskeletal conditions as adjunct to rest, physical therapy, other measures. *Adult:* 250 mg PO tid–qid; may need 500 mg PO tid–qid. Max, 750 mg tid–qid.
ADV EFF Anaphylaxis, dizziness, drowsiness, GI disturbances, **hepatic impairment,** light-headedness, orange to red urine
INTERACTIONS Alcohol, CNS depressants
NC/PT Use other measures to help pain. Pt should avoid alcohol and sleep-inducing drugs, take safety measures if CNS effects occur.

---

cholestyramine (Prevalite)
CLASS Bile acid sequestrant, antihyperlipidemic
PREG/CONT C/NA

IND & DOSE Adjunct to reduce elevated serum cholesterol in pts w/ primary hypercholesterolemia; pruritus associated w/partial biliary obstruction. *Adult:* 4 g PO once to twice a day; w/constipation, start w/4 g once a day; maint, 8–16 g/day divided into two doses. Max, 6 packets or scoopfuls (24 g/day). *Child:*

240 mg/kg/day PO in two to three divided doses; max, 8 g/day.
ADV EFF Constipation to fecal impaction, hemorrhoid exacerbation, increased bleeding tendencies
INTERACTIONS Corticosteroids, digitalis, diuretics, fat-soluble vitamins, thiazide preparations, thyroid medication, warfarin
NC/PT Mix packet contents w/water, milk, fruit juice, noncarbonated beverages, soup, applesauce, pineapple; do not give in dry form. Monitor for constipation, which could be severe. Pt should take w/meals, take other oral drugs 1 hr before or 4–6 hr after this drug.

---

cholic acid (Cholbam)
CLASS Bile acid
PREG/CONT Unkn/NA

IND & DOSE Tx of bile acid synthesis disorders; adjunct tx of peroxisomal disorders. *Adult, child:* 10–15 mg/kg/day PO; w/concomitant familial hypertriglyceridemia, use 11–17 mg/kg/day PO.
ADV EFF Abd pain, **hepatotoxicity,** intestinal polyps, malaise, n/v/d, peripheral neuropathies, reflux esophagitis, skin lesions, UTI
INTERACTIONS Aluminum-containing antacids, bile acid resins, bile salt efflux inhibitors, cyclosporine
NC/PT Monitor LFTs before, q mo for 3 mo; then at 3, 6, 9 mo; then q 6 mo for 3 yr; then annually. Give w/ food. Pt should not cut, crush, or chew capsule (capsule may be opened and sprinkled on drink/food); should allow 4–6 hr between aluminum-based antacids/bile acid resins and this drug; take safety precaution w/CNS effects; eat small meals for GI problems; enroll in pregnancy registry if pregnancy occurs.

choline magnesium trisalicylate (Tricosal)
CLASS NSAID, salicylate
PREG/CONT C/NA

IND & DOSE Tx of osteoarthritis, rheumatoid arthritis. *Adult:* 1.5–2.5 g/day PO; max, 4.5 g/day in divided doses. **Tx of pain/fever.** *Adult:* 2–3 g/day PO in divided doses. *Child:* 217.5–652.5 mg PO q 4 hr as needed.
ADV EFF Anaphylactoid reactions, dizziness, drowsiness, GI bleeding, headache, heartburn, indigestion, n/v, sweating
INTERACTIONS ACE inhibitors, antidiabetics, carbonic anhydrase inhibitors, corticosteroids, insulin, meglitinide, methotrexate, valproic acid
NC/PT Pt should take w/full glass of water and not lie down for 30 min after taking; take w/food if GI effects are severe; use safety precautions if CNS effects occur.

chorionic gonadotropin (Pregnyl)
CLASS Hormone
PREG/CONT X/NA

BBW Drug has no known effect on fat metabolism and is not for tx of obesity.
IND & DOSE Tx of prepubertal cryptorchidism not due to anatomic obstruction. *Adult, child over 4 yr:* 4,000 USP units IM three times/wk for 3 wk; then 5,000 USP units IM every second day for four injections; then 15 injections of 500–1,000 USP units over 6 wk; then 500 USP units three times/wk for 4–6 wk. If unsuccessful, start another course 1 mo later, giving 1,000 USP units/injection. Tx of hypogonadotropic hypogonadism in males. *Adult, child over 4 yr:* 500–1,000 USP units IM three times/wk for 3 wk; then same dose twice/wk for 3 wk; then 1,000–2,000 USP units IM three times/wk; then 4,000 USP units

three times/wk for 6–9 mo. Reduce dose to 2,000 USP units three times/wk for additional 3 mo. **Induction of ovulation and pregnancy.** *Adult:* 5,000–10,000 units IM 1 day after last menotropins dose.
ADV EFF Gynecomastia, headache, irritability, ovarian cancer, ovarian hyperstimulation, pain at injection site
NC/PT Must give IM. Prepare calendar of tx schedule. Discontinue if s&sx of ovarian overstimulation. Provide comfort measures for headache, pain at injection site.

chorionic gonadotropin alfa (Ovidrel)
CLASS Fertility drug
PREG/CONT X/NA

IND & DOSE Ovulation induction in infertile women. *Adult:* 250 mcg subcut 1 day after 1 day after last FSH dose.
ADV EFF Abd pain, injection-site pain, multiple births, n/v, ovarian enlargement, ovarian hyperstimulation; pulmonary, vascular thromboembolic events
NC/PT Part of comprehensive fertility program. Inject into abdomen. Risk of multiple births. Pt should report difficulty breathing, sudden abd or leg pain.

cidofovir (generic)
CLASS Antiviral
PREG/CONT C/NA

BBW Risk of severe renal impairment; monitor renal function closely. Risk of neutropenia; monitor CBC closely. Cancer, impaired fertility, tetragenic effects reported.
IND & DOSE Tx of CMV retinitis in AIDS pts. *Adult:* 5 mg/kg IV over 1 hr for 2 wk, then 5 mg/kg IV q 2 wk.
ADV EFF Decreased IOP, dyspnea, fever, infection, n/v, neutropenia, pneumonia, proteinuria, **renal failure**

NC/PT Use only for stated indication; not for other diseases. Give w/ PO probenecid (2 g before each dose, then 1 g at 2 and 8 hr after each dose). Monitor renal function, CBC. Protect pt from infection. Not for use in pregnancy/breast-feeding. Mark calendar for tx days.

cilostazol (Pletal)
CLASS Antiplatelet, phosphodiesterase III inhibitor
PREG/CONT C/NA

BBW Do not give to pts w/HF; decreased survival reported.
IND & DOSE To reduce s&sx of intermittent claudication, allowing increased walking distance. *Adult:* 100 mg PO bid at least 30 min before or 2 hr after breakfast and dinner; may not reduce response for 2–12 wk.
ADJUST DOSE Administration with CYP3A4, CYP2C19 inhibitors
ADV EFF Bleeding, diarrhea, dizziness, dyspepsia, flatulence, headache, **HF**, nausea, rhinitis
INTERACTIONS Azole antifungals, diltiazem, grapefruit juice, high-fat meal, macrolide antibiotics, omeprazole, smoking
NC/PT Not for use in pregnancy (barrier contraceptives advised). Pt should take on empty stomach 30 min before or 2 hr after breakfast and dinner, take safety precautions to prevent injury, avoid grapefruit juice, continue tx for up to 12 wk to see results.

cimetidine (Tagamet HB)
CLASS Histamine₂ antagonist
PREG/CONT B/NA

IND & DOSE Tx of heartburn, acid indigestion. *Adult:* 200 mg PO as s&sx occur; max, 400 mg/24 hr for max of 2 wk. Tx of active duodenal ulcer. *Adult:* 800 mg PO at bedtime or 300 mg PO qid w/meals and at bedtime or 400 mg PO bid; continue for 4–6 wk. Intractable ulcers, 300 mg

IM or IV q 6–8 hr. Maint, 400 mg PO at bedtime. Tx of active benign gastric ulcer. *Adult:* 300 mg PO qid w/ meals and at bedtime or 800 mg at bedtime for 8 wk. Tx of pathologic hypersecretory syndrome. *Adult:* 300 mg PO w/meals and at bedtime or 300 mg IV or IM q 6 hr. Individualize doses as needed; max, 2,400 mg/day. Tx of erosive GERD. *Adult:* 1,600 mg PO in divided doses bid–qid for 12 wk. Prevention of upper GI bleeding. *Adult:* 50 mg/hr continuous IV infusion for up to 7 days.
ADJUST DOSE Elderly pts, renal impairment
ADV EFF Cardiac arrhythmias, confusion, diarrhea, dizziness, hallucinations, ED
INTERACTIONS Alcohol, alkylating agents, benzodiazepines, beta-adrenergic blockers, carbamazepine, chloroquine, lidocaine, nifedipine, pentoxifylline, phenytoin, procainamide, quinidine, smoking, theophylline, TCAs
NC/PT Give w/meals and at bedtime. Give IM undiluted into large muscle group. Pt should report smoking so dose can be regulated, take safety precautions w/CNS effects.

cinacalcet hydrochloride (Sensipar)
CLASS Calcimimetic, calcium-lowering drug
PREG/CONT C/NA

IND & DOSE Tx of hypercalcemia associated w/parathyroid carcinoma or severe hypercalcemia in pts w/primary parathyroidism. *Adult:* Initially, 30 mg PO bid to maintain calcium levels within normal range; adjust dose q 2–4 wk in sequential doses of 60 mg bid, then 90 mg bid to max 90 mg tid–qid. Tx of secondary hyperparathyroidism. *Adult:* 30 mg/day PO. Monitor serum calcium and phosphorus levels within 1 wk; may increase dose 30 mg q 2–4 wk to max 180 mg/day. Target intact parathyroid hormone levels, 150–300 pg/mL.

ADV EFF Dizziness, hallucinations, **hepatic impairment**, hypocalcemia, myalgia, n/v, **seizures**

INTERACTIONS Amitriptyline, erythromycin, flecainide, ketoconazole, itraconazole, TCAs, thioridazine, vinblastine

NC/PT Monitor serum calcium levels before and regularly during tx. If pt on dialysis, also give vitamin D and phosphate binders. Give w/food. Not for use in breast-feeding. Pt should not cut, crush, or chew tablets, should take safety measures if CNS effects occur.

---

ciprofloxacin (Ciloxan, Cipro)
CLASS Antibacterial, fluoroquinolone
PREG/CONT C/NA

BBW Risk of tendinitis and tendon rupture; risk higher in pts over 60 yr, those on steroids, and those w/renal, heart, or lung transplant. Avoid use in pts w/hx of myasthenia gravis; drug may exacerbate weakness.

IND & DOSE Tx of uncomplicated UTIs. *Adult:* 250 mg PO q 12 hr for 3 days or 500 mg (ER tablets) PO daily for 3 days. Tx of mild to moderate UTIs. *Adult:* 250 mg PO q 12 hr for 7–14 days or 200 mg IV q 12 hr for 7–14 days. Tx of complicated UTIs. *Adult:* 500 mg PO q 12 hr for 7–14 days or 400 mg IV q 12 hr or 1,000 mg (ER tablets) PO daily q 7–14 days. Tx of chronic bacterial prostatitis. *Adult:* 500 mg PO q 12 hr for 28 days or 400 mg IV q 12 hr for 28 days. Tx of infectious diarrhea. *Adult:* 500 mg PO q 12 hr for 5–7 days. Anthrax postexposure. *Adult:* 500 mg PO q 12 hr for 60 days or 400 mg IV q 12 hr for 60 days. *Child:* 15 mg/kg/dose PO q 12 hr for 60 days or 10 mg/kg dose IV q 12 hr for 60 days; max, 500 mg/dose PO or 400 mg/dose IV. Tx of respiratory infections. *Adult:* 500–

750 mg PO q 12 hr or 400 mg IV q 8–12 hr for 7–14 days. Tx of acute sinusitis. *Adult:* 500 mg PO q 12 hr or 400 mg IV q 12 hr for 10 days. Tx of acute uncomplicated pyelonephritis. *Adult:* 1,000 mg (ER tablets) PO daily q 7–14 days. Tx of bone, joint, skin infections. 500–750 mg PO q 12 hr or 400 mg IV q 8–12 hr for 4–6 wk. Tx of nosocomial pneumonia. *Adult:* 400 mg IV q 8 hr for 10–14 days. Tx of plaque. *Adults:* 400 mg IV q 8–12 hr for 14 days. *Child:* 10 mg/kg IV (max, 400 mg/dose) q 8–12 hr for 10–21 days. Tx of ophthalmic infections caused by susceptible organisms not responsive to other tx. *Adult:* 1 or 2 drops q 2 hr in affected eye(s) while awake for 2 days or q 4 hr for 5 days; or ½-inch ribbon ointment into conjunctival sac tid on first 2 days, then ½-inch ribbon bid for next 5 days. Tx of acute otitis externa. *Adult:* 4 drops in infected ear tid–qid, or 1 single-use container (0.25 mL) in infected ear bid for 7 days.

ADJUST DOSE Renal impairment
ADV EFF CDAD, headache, **hepatotoxicity**, n/v/d, peripheral neuropathy, rash, **tendinitis, tendon rupture**
INTERACTIONS Antacids, antidiabetic agents, didanosine, foscarnet, methotrexate, phenytoin, St. John's wort, sucralfate, theophylline, warfarin
NC/PT Avoid use in pts w/hx of myasthenia gravis; may exacerbate weakness. Use cautiously w/children; increased incidence of joint/tissue injury. Culture before tx. Give antacids at least 2 hr apart from dosing. Ensure hydration. Pt should not cut, crush, or chew ER form; report diarrhea, urine/stool color changes, sudden muscle pain.

DANGEROUS DRUG

cisplatin (CDDP) (generic)
CLASS Alkylating agent, antineoplastic, platinum agent
PREG/CONT D/NA

BBW Arrange for audiometric testing before starting tx and before subsequent doses. Do not give if audiometric acuity outside normal limits. Monitor renal function; severe toxicity related to dose possible. Have epinephrine, corticosteroids available for anaphylaxis-like reactions. Use caution to avoid inadvertent overdose. Avoid name confusion with carboplatin.

IND & DOSE Tx of metastatic testicular tumors. *Adult:* Remission induction: Cisplatin, 20 mg/m[2]/day IV for 5 consecutive days (days 1–5) q 3 wk for three courses; bleomycin, 30 units IV wkly (day 2 of each wk) for 12 consecutive doses; vinblastine, 0.15–0.2 mg/kg IV twice wkly (days 1 and 2) q 3 wk for four courses. Maint: Vinblastine, 0.3 mg/kg IV q 4 wk for 2 yr. **Tx of metastatic ovarian tumors.** *Adult:* 75–100 mg/m[2] IV once q 4 wk. For combination therapy, give sequentially: Cisplatin, 75–100 mg/m[2] IV once q 3–4 wk; cyclophosphamide, 600 mg/m[2] IV once q 3–4 wk. Single dose: 100 mg/m[2] IV once q 4 wk. **Tx of advanced bladder cancer.** *Adult:* 50–70 mg/m[2] IV once q 3–4 wk; in heavily pretreated (radiotherapy or chemotherapy) pts, give initial dose of 50 mg/m[2] repeated q 4 wk. Do not give repeated courses until serum creatinine under 1.5 mg/dL, BUN under 25 mg/dL, or platelets over 100,000/mm[3] or WBCs over 4,000/mm[3]. Do not give subsequent doses until audiometry indicates hearing within normal range.

ADJUST DOSE Renal impairment
ADV EFF Anaphylaxis-like reactions, anorexia, **bone marrow suppression, nephrotoxicity,** n/v/d, ototoxicity
INTERACTIONS Aminoglycosides, bumetanide, ethacrynic acid, furosemide, phenytoins
NC/PT Monitor renal function before and regularly during tx. Monitor hearing. Maintain hydration. Use antiemetics if needed. Monitor electrolytes regularly. Do not use needles containing aluminum. Use gloves when preparing IV. Not for use in

pregnancy. Pt should report changes in hearing, difficulty breathing, unusual bleeding. Name confusion w/ carboplatin; use extreme caution.

---

citalopram hydrobromide (Celexa)
CLASS Antidepressant, SSRI
PREG/CONT C/NA

BBW Increased risk of suicidality in children, adolescents, young adults; monitor suicidality.
IND & DOSE Tx of depression. *Adult:* 20 mg/day PO as single daily dose. May increase to 40 mg/day; max, 40 mg/day.
ADJUST DOSE Elderly pts; renal, hepatic impairment
ADV EFF Dizziness, dry mouth, ejaculatory disorders, insomnia, nausea, **prolonged QT interval,** somnolence, **suicidality,** tremor
INTERACTIONS Azole antifungals, beta blockers, citalopram, erythromycin, linezolid, macrolide antibiotics, MAOIs, pimozide, QT-prolonging drugs, St. John's wort, TCAs, warfarin
NC/PT Avoid doses over 40 mg; increased risk of prolonged QT interval. Limit drug to suicidal pts; monitor for suicidality. May take several wk to see effects. Not for use in pregnancy/breast-feeding. Pt should avoid St. John's wort, report thoughts of suicide. Name confusion w/ *Celexa* (citalopram), *Celebrex* (celecoxib), *Xanax* (alprazolam), and *Cerebyx* (fosphenytoin).

DANGEROUS DRUG

cladribine (generic)
CLASS Antimetabolite, antineoplastic, purine analogue
PREG/CONT D/NA

BBW Monitor complete hematologic profile, LFTs, renal function tests before and frequently during tx. Consult physician at first sign of toxicity;

consider delaying dose or discontinuing if neurotoxicity or renal toxicity occurs.

IND & DOSE Tx of active hairy cell leukemia. *Adult:* Single course of 0.09–0.1 mg/kg/day by continuous IV infusion for 7 days.

ADV EFF Abnormal breath sounds, anorexia, arthralgia, **bone marrow suppression,** chills, cough, fatigue, fever, headache, **hepatotoxicity,** injection-site reactions, **nephrotoxicity, neurotoxicity,** n/v/d

NC/PT Use gloves when handling drug. Must be given by continuous infusion for 7 days. Monitor renal function, LFTs, CBC before and regularly during tx. Not for use in pregnancy; pt should use contraception during and for several wk after tx ends. Pt should report numbness/tingling, pain at injection site.

clarithromycin (Biaxin)
CLASS Macrolide antibiotic
PREG/CONT C/NA

IND & DOSE Tx of pharyngitis, tonsillitis; pneumonia; skin, skin-structure infections; lower respiratory infections caused by susceptible strains. *Adult:* 250 mg PO q 12 hr for 7–14 days. *Child:* 15 mg/kg/day PO divided q 12 hr for 10 days. Tx of acute maxillary sinusitis, acute otitis media, lower respiratory infections caused by susceptible strains. *Adult:* 500 mg PO q 12 hr for 14 days or 1,000 mg (ER tablets) PO q 24 hr. Tx of mycobacterial infections. *Adult:* 500 mg PO bid. *Child:* 7.5 mg/kg PO bid; max, 500 mg PO bid. Tx of duodenal ulcers. *Adult:* 500 mg PO tid plus omeprazole 40 mg PO q a.m. for 14 days, then omeprazole 20 mg PO q a.m. for 14 days. Tx of community-acquired pneumonia. *Adult:* 250 mg PO q 12 hr for 7–14 days or 1,000 mg (ER tablets) PO q 24 hr for 7 days.

ADJUST DOSE Elderly pts, renal impairment

ADV EFF Abd pain, CDAD, diarrhea, prolonged QT, superinfections

INTERACTIONS Antidiabetics, carbamazepine, colchicine, grapefruit juice, lovastatin, phenytoin, theophylline

NC/PT Culture before tx. Arrange for tx of superinfections. Do not refrigerate suspension. Not for use in pregnancy/breast-feeding. Pt should take w/food if GI upset occurs; avoid grapefruit juice; not cut, crush, or chew ER tablets; report persistent diarrhea.

clemastine fumarate (Dayhist-1, Tavist Allergy)
CLASS Antihistamine
PREG/CONT B/NA

IND & DOSE Symptomatic relief of s&sx of allergic rhinitis. *Adult:* 1.34 mg PO bid. Max, 8.04 mg/day (syrup), 2.68 mg/day (tablets). *Child 6–12 yr:* (syrup only) 0.67 mg PO bid; max, 4.02 mg/day. Tx of mild, uncomplicated urticaria and angioedema. *Adult:* 2.68 mg PO daily–tid; max, 8.04 mg/day. *Child 6–12 yr:* (syrup only) 1.34 mg PO bid; max, 4.02 mg/day.

ADJUST DOSE Elderly pts

ADV EFF Anaphylactic shock, bronchial secretion thickening, disturbed coordination, dizziness, drowsiness, epigastric distress, sedation

INTERACTIONS Alcohol, CNS depressants, MAOIs

NC/PT Use syrup if pt cannot swallow tablets. Give w/food if GI upset occurs. Pt should drink plenty of fluids, use humidifier, avoid alcohol, report difficulty breathing/irregular heartbeat.

clevidipine butyrate (Cleviprex)
CLASS Antihypertensive, calcium channel blocker
PREG/CONT C/NA

IND & DOSE To reduce BP when oral therapy not possible or desirable. *Adult:* 1–2 mg/hr IV infusion;

titrate quickly by doubling dose q 90 sec to achieve desired BP; maint, 4–6 mg/hr; max, 21 mg/hr/24 hr.
ADV EFF Headache, **HF,** n/v
NC/PT Continuously monitor BP, ECG during administration. Taper beta blockers before use. Handle drug w/ strict aseptic technique. Use within 4 hr of puncturing stopper. Rebound hypertension possible within 8 hr of stopping drug; switch to oral antihypertensive as soon as possible.

clindamycin hydrochloride (Cleocin), clindamycin palmitate hydrochloride (generic), clindamycin phosphate (Cleocin T, Clindagel)
CLASS Lincosamide antibiotic
PREG/CONT B/NA

BBW Serious to fatal colitis, including CDAD, possibly up to several wk after tx ends. Reserve use; monitor pt closely.
IND & DOSE Serious infections caused by susceptible bacteria strains. Reserve use for penicillin-allergic pts or when penicillin inappropriate. *Adult:* 150–300 mg PO q 6 hr (up to 300–450 mg PO q 6 hr in more severe infections) or 600–2,700 mg/day IV or IM in two to four equal doses (up to 4.8 g/day IV or IM for life-threatening situations). *Child:* Clindamycin hydrochloride, 8–16 mg/kg/day PO (serious infections) or 16–20 mg/kg/day PO (more serious infections in three or four equal doses). *Child under 10 kg:* 37.5 mg/kg PO tid as min dose. *Child over 1 mo:* 20–40 mg/kg/day IV or IM in three or four equal doses or 350–450 mg/m²/day. *Neonates:* 15–20 mg/kg/day IV or IM in three or four equal doses. **Tx of bacterial vaginosis.** *Adult:* 1 applicator (100 mg clindamycin phosphate) intravaginally, preferably at bedtime for 7 consecutive days in pregnant women and 3 or 7 days in nonpregnant women. **Tx of acne**

vulgaris. *Adult:* Apply thin film to affected area bid.
ADJUST DOSE Renal impairment
ADV EFF Abd pain, **agranulocytosis, anaphylactic reactions,** anorexia, **cardiac arrest,** CDAD, contact dermatitis, esophagitis, n/v/d, pain following injection, **pseudomembranous colitis,** rash
INTERACTIONS Aluminum salts, kaolin, NMJ blockers
NC/PT Culture before tx. Give orally w/full glass of water or food. Do not give IM injection of more than 600 mg; inject deeply into muscle. Monitor LFTs, renal function. Pt should avoid eye contact w/topical sol, give intravaginally at bedtime, report severe or watery diarrhea, diarrhea w/blood or mucus.

clobazam (Onfi)
CLASS Benzodiazepine, antiepileptic
PREG/CONT C/C-IV

IND & DOSE Adjunct tx of seizures associated w/Lennox-Gastaut syndrome. *Adult, child 2 yr and older:* Over 30 kg, initially 5 mg PO bid; increase to 10 mg PO bid starting on day 7; increase to 20 mg PO bid starting on day 14. 30 kg or less, initially 5 mg/day PO; increase to 5 mg PO bid starting on day 7; increase to 10 mg PO bid starting on day 14.
ADJUST DOSE Elderly pts, mild to moderate hepatic impairment, poor CYP2C19 metabolizers
ADV EFF Aggression, ataxia, constipation, drooling, dysarthria, fatigue, fever, insomnia, sedation, somnolence, **suicidality**
INTERACTIONS Alcohol, fluconazole, fluvoxamine, hormonal contraceptives, omeprazole, ticlopidine
NC/PT Taper drug after long-term use; dispense least amount feasible. Administer whole or crush and mix in applesauce. Not for use in pregnancy/breast-feeding. Dizziness, sleepiness possible. Pt should take bid, swallow

whole or crush and take in apple-sauce, avoid alcohol, report thoughts of suicide, increase in seizure activity.

clofarabine (Clolar)
CLASS Antimetabolite, antineoplastic
PREG/CONT D/NA

IND & DOSE Tx of pts w/ALL who relapsed after at least two other regimens. *Child 1–21 yr:* 52 mg/m² IV over 2 hr daily for 5 consecutive days of 28-day cycle; repeat q 2–6 wk.
ADV EFF Anxiety, **bone marrow suppression, capillary leak syndrome,** fatigue, flushing, headache, **hemorrhage, hepatotoxicity, hyperuricemia, infections,** mucosal inflammation, n/v/d, pruritus, rash, **renal toxicity, skin reactions, tumor lysis syndrome**
NC/PT Premedicate w/antiemetic. Monitor LFTs, renal function, CBC regularly; dose adjustment may be needed. Protect pt from infection, injury. Not for use in pregnancy/breast-feeding. Pt should report bleeding, urine/stool color changes, signs of infection, rash.

clomiPHENE citrate (Clomid)
CLASS Fertility drug, hormone
PREG/CONT X/NA

IND & DOSE Tx of ovulatory failure in pts w/normal liver function, normal endogenous estrogen level. *Adult:* 50 mg/day PO for 5 days started anytime there has been no recent uterine bleeding. If no ovulation occurs, 100 mg/day PO for 5 days as early as 30 days after first. May repeat if no response.
ADV EFF Abd discomfort/distention, bloating, breast tenderness, flushing, multiple births, n/v, ovarian enlargement, ovarian overstimulation, visual disturbances

NC/PT Perform pelvic exam, obtain urine estrogen and estriol levels before tx. Discontinue if s&sx of ovarian overstimulation. Prepare calendar of tx days. Risk of multiple births. Failure after three courses indicates tx not effective and will be discontinued. Name confusion between *Serophene* (clomiphene) and *Sarafem* (fluoxetine).

clomiPRAMINE hydrochloride (Anafranil)
CLASS Anxiolytic, TCA
PREG/CONT C/NA

BBW Increased risk of suicidality in children, adolescents, young adults; monitor pt carefully.
IND & DOSE Tx of obsessions, compulsions in pts w/OCD. *Adult:* Initially, 25 mg PO daily. Increase as tolerated to approximately 100 mg during first 2 wk; max, 250 mg/day. Maint, adjust dose to maintain lowest effective dose; effectiveness after 10 wk not documented. *Child:* Initially, 25 mg PO daily. Increase as tolerated during first 2 wk; max, 3 mg/kg or 100 mg, whichever smaller. Maint, adjust dose to maintain lowest effective dosage; effectiveness after 10 wk not documented.
ADV EFF **Agranulocytosis,** anticholinergic effects, confusion, constipation, disturbed concentration, dry mouth, **MI,** nasal congestion, orthostatic hypotension, photosensitivity, sedation, **seizures,** serotonin syndrome, **stroke**
INTERACTIONS Anticholinergics, barbiturates, cimetidine, clonidine, disulfiram, ephedrine, epinephrine, fluoxetine, furazolidone, hormonal contraceptives, levodopa, MAOIs, methylphenidate, nicotine, norepinephrine, phenothiazines, QT-prolonging drugs, St. John's wort, thyroid medication
NC/PT Restrict drug access in depressed, suicidal pts. Give major

portion at bedtime. Obtain periodic CBC w/long-term therapy. Pt should not mix w/other sleep-inducing drugs; avoid driving, etc, until drug's effects known; avoid St. John's wort, prolonged exposure to sun and sun-lamps; report thoughts of suicide. Name confusion between clomip-ramine and chlorpromazine.

clonazepam (Klonopin)
CLASS Antiepileptic, benzodiazepine
PREG/CONT D/C-IV

IND & DOSE Tx of Lennox-Gastaut syndrome (petit mal variant); akinetic and myoclonic seizures. *Adult:* 1.5 mg/day PO divided into three doses; increase in increments of 0.5–1 mg PO q 3 days until seizures adequately controlled. Max, 20 mg/day. *Child at least 10 yr or 30 kg:* 0.01–0.03 mg/kg/day PO. Max, 0.05 mg/kg/day PO in two or three doses; maint, 0.1–0.2 mg/kg. Tx of panic disorder w/or without agoraphobia. *Adult:* Initially, 0.25 mg PO bid; gradually increase to target dose of 1 mg/day.
ADV EFF **Agranulocytosis**, apathy, confusion, constipation, **CV collapse**, depression, diarrhea, disorientation, drowsiness, drug dependence w/withdrawal, fatigue, incontinence, lethargy, light-headedness, restless-ness, **suicidality**, urine retention
INTERACTIONS Alcohol, amino-phylline, cimetidine, digoxin, disulfiram, dyphylline, hormonal contraceptives, omeprazole, theophylline
NC/PT Monitor suicidal and addiction-prone pts closely. Monitor LFTs. Monitor for therapeutic level (20–80 ng/mL). Taper gradually after long-term tx. Pt should avoid alcohol, wear or carry medical alert notice, take safety precautions if CNS effects occur. Name confusion between *Klonopin* (clonazepam) and clonidine.

clonidine hydrochloride (Catapres, Duraclon, Kapvay)
CLASS Antihypertensive, central analgesic, sympatholytic
PREG/CONT C/NA

BBW Epidural route not recom-mended for obstetric, postpartum, or periop pain because of risk of hemo-dynamic instability.
IND & DOSE Tx of hypertension. *Adult:* 0.1 mg bid PO. For maint, increase in increments of 0.1 or 0.2 mg to reach desired response; common range, 0.2–0.6 mg/day or 0.1-mg transdermal system (releases 0.1 mg/24 hr). If, after 1–2 wk desired BP reduction not achieved, add another 0.1-mg system or use larger system. More than two 0.3-mg systems does not improve efficacy. **Pain mgt.** *Adult:* 30 mcg/hr by epidural infusion. Tx of **ADHD.** *Child 6–17 yr:* 0.1 mg PO at bedtime; titrate at 0.1 mg/wk to total of 0.2 mg, w/0.1 mg in a.m. and 0.1 mg in p.m., then 0.1 mg in a.m. and 0.2 mg in p.m. Maint, 0.2 mg in a.m. and 0.2 mg in p.m. (*Kapvay* only).
ADV EFF Cardiac conduction abnor-malities, constipation, dizziness, drowsiness, dry mouth, hypotension, local reactions to transdermal sys-tem, sedation, somnolence
INTERACTIONS Alcohol, antihy-pertensives, drugs affecting cardiac conduction, CNS depressants, pro-pranolol, TCAs
NC/PT Taper when withdrawing to avoid rebound effects. *Kapvay* not interchangeable w/other form; must be remove old patch before applying new to clean, dry skin; rotate skin sites. Remove transdermal patch before defibrillation and MRI. Pt should swallow tablet whole and not cut, crush or chew; avoid alcohol; take safety precautions w/CNS effects. Name confusion between clonidine and *Klonopin* (clonazepam).

clopidogrel bisulfate (Plavix)

CLASS ADP receptor antagonist, antiplatelet
PREG/CONT B/NA

BBW Slow metabolizers may experience less effects, as drug is activated in liver by CYP2C19. Genotype testing for poor metabolizers suggested before tx.

IND & DOSE Tx of pts at risk for ischemic events (recent MI, stroke, established peripheral arterial disease). *Adult:* 75 mg/day PO. **Tx of acute coronary syndrome.** *Adult:* 300 mg PO loading dose, then 75 mg/day PO w/aspirin, at dose from 75–325 mg once daily.
ADV EFF Bleeding risk, dizziness, GI bleed, headache, rash
INTERACTIONS NSAIDs, warfarin
NC/PT Genotype testing before tx. Monitor for bleeding. May give w/ meals. Pt should report unusual bleeding.

clorazepate dipotassium bisulfate (Tranxene)

CLASS Antiepileptic, anxiolytic, benzodiazepine
PREG/CONT D/C-IV

IND & DOSE Mgt of anxiety disorders. *Adult:* 30 mg/day PO in divided doses tid. **Adjunct to antiepileptics.** *Adult:* Max initial dose, 7.5 mg PO tid. Increase dose by no more than 7.5 mg q wk; max, 90 mg/day. *Child 9–12 yr:* Max initial dose, 7.5 mg PO bid. Increase dose by no more than 7.5 mg q wk; max, 60 mg/day. **Acute alcohol withdrawal.** *Adult:* Day 1, 30 mg PO initially, then 30–60 mg PO in divided doses. Day 2, 45–90 mg PO in divided doses. Day 3, 22.5–45 mg PO in divided doses. Day 4, 15–30 mg PO in divided doses. Thereafter, gradually reduce dose to 7.5–15 mg/day PO; stop as soon as condition stable.

ADJUST DOSE Elderly pts, debilitating disease
ADV EFF Agranulocytosis, apathy, CV collapse, constipation, depression, diarrhea, disorientation, dizziness, drowsiness, dry mouth, lethargy, light-headedness, mild paradoxical excitatory reactions during first 2 wk
INTERACTIONS Alcohol, cimetidine, CNS depressants, digoxin, disulfiram, hormonal contraceptives, kava, omeprazole, theophylline
NC/PT Taper gradually after longterm use. Monitor for suicidality. Encourage use of medical alert tag. Not for use in pregnancy. Pt should avoid alcohol, take safety precautions for CNS effects. Name confusion between clorazepate and clofibrate; use caution.

clotrimazole (Cruex, Desenex, Gyne-Lotrimin, Lotrimin)

CLASS Antifungal
PREG/CONT B (topical/vaginal); C (oral)/NA

IND & DOSE Tx of oropharyngeal candidiasis; prevention of oropharyngeal candidiasis in immunocompromised pts receiving radiation, chemotherapy, steroid therapy (troche). *Adult, child 2 yr and older:* Dissolve slowly in mouth five times daily for 14 days. For prevention, tid for duration of chemotherapy, radiation. **Local tx of vulvovaginal candidiasis (moniliasis).** *Adult, child 12 yr and older:* 100-mg suppository intravaginally at bedtime for 7 consecutive nights, or 200-mg suppository for 3 consecutive nights, or 1 applicator (5 g/day) vaginal cream, preferably at bedtime for 3–7 consecutive days. **Topical tx of susceptible fungal infections.** *Adult, child 2 yr and older:* Gently massage into affected area and surrounding skin bid in a.m. and p.m. for 14 days. Treat for 2–4 wk.

ADV EFF Abd cramps, abnormal LFTs, local reaction to topical forms, n/v, urinary frequency
NC/PT Culture before tx. Dissolve troche in mouth. Insert vaginal suppository or cream high into vagina using applicator; apply even during menstrual period. Apply topically to clean, dry area. Pt should take full course of tx. Name confusion between clotrimazole and co-trimoxazole; use caution.

clozapine (Clozaril, FazaClo)
CLASS Antipsychotic, dopaminergic blocker
PREG/CONT B/NA

BBW Use only when pt unresponsive to conventional antipsychotics. Risk of serious CV and respiratory effects, including myocarditis. Risk of severe neutropenia; monitor WBC count wkly during and for 4 wk after tx; dosage must be adjusted based on WBC count. Potentially fatal agranulocytosis has occurred. Elderly pts w/ dementia-related psychosis are at increased risk for death; drug not approved for these pts. Monitor for seizures; risk increases in pts w/hx of seizures and as dose increases. Available only through restricted access program.
IND & DOSE Mgt of severely ill schizophrenics unresponsive to standard antipsychotics; to reduce risk of recurrent suicidal behavior in pts w/schizophrenia. *Adult:* 12.5 mg PO daily or bid. Continue to 25 mg PO daily or bid, then gradually increase w/daily increments of 25–50 mg/day, if tolerated, to 300–450 mg/day by end of second wk; max, 900 mg/day. Maintain at lowest effective dose. Withdraw slowly over 2–4 wk when discontinuing.
ADV EFF Agranulocytosis, cognitive changes, constipation, dizziness, drowsiness, dry mouth, fever, headache, hypotension, **myocarditis**

(potentially fatal), n/v, NMS, PE, sedation, **seizures**, syncope
INTERACTIONS Anticholinergics, caffeine, cimetidine, CYP450 inducers/inhibitors, ethotoin, phenytoin
NC/PT Obtain through limited access program. Monitor WBC closely; ensure adequate neutrophil count before starting drug. Monitor temp; report fever. Monitor for seizures. Monitor cardiac status. Ensure hydration in elderly pts. Not for use in pregnancy. Pt should empty bladder before taking, use sugarless lozenges for dry mouth, obtain wkly blood tests, take safety precautions w/CNS effects, report s&sx of infection. Name confusion between *Clozaril* (clozapine) and *Colazal* (balsalazide); dangerous effects possible.

coagulation factor VIIa (recombinant) (NovoSeven RT)
CLASS Antihemophilic
PREG/CONT C/NA

BBW Serious thrombotic events associated w/off-label use. Use only for approved indication.
IND & DOSE Tx of bleeding episodes, in hemophilia A or B pts w/ inhibitors to factor VIII or IX. *Adult:* 90 mcg/kg as IV bolus q 2 hr until bleeding controlled. Continue dosing at 3- to 6-hr intervals after hemostasis in severe bleeds.
ADV EFF Arthralgia, edema, fever, headache, **hemorrhage, hypersensitivity reactions**, hypertension, hypotension, injection-site reactions, n/v, rash, **thromboembolic events**
INTERACTIONS Do not mix in sol w/other drugs
NC/PT Use only for approved indication. Monitor for hypersensitivity reactions, thrombotic events; alert pt to warning signs of each.

coagulation factor IX, recombinant (Rixubis)

CLASS Antihemophilic factor
PREG/CONT C/NA

IND & DOSE Control/px of bleeding, periop mgt w/hemophilia B. *Adult:* International units (IU) needed = body weight (kg) × desired factor IX increase (% of normal) × reciprocal of observed recovery (IU/kg per IU/dL). *Routine px of hemophilia B. Adult:* 40–60 international units/kg IV twice wkly. *Child:* 60–80 international units/kg IV twice wkly.

ADV EFF Hypersensitivity reactions, nephrotic syndrome, neutralizing antibody development, thrombotic events

NC/PT Ensure proper dx. Do not use w/DIC; fibrinolysis; known hypersensitivity to hamster proteins; pregnancy/breast-feeding. Pt should take safety measures to prevent injury, blood loss; report difficulty breathing, rash, chest pain, increased bleeding.

coagulation factor X (human) (Coagadex)

CLASS Clotting factor
PREG/CONT Unkn/NA

IND & DOSE Tx, control of bleeding episodes, w/factor X deficiency. *Adult, child 12 and over:* 25 international units/kg IV repeated q 24 hr until bleeding stops. *Mgt of periop bleeding w/mild hereditary factor X deficiency. Adult, child 12 and over:* Raise factor X levels to 70–90 international units/dL: required dose = body wt in kg × desired factor X rise in international units/dL × 0.5 infused IV. Postop: repeat dose as necessary to maintain factor X level at minimum 50 international units/dL.

ADV EFF Back pain, factor X antibody production, fatigue, hypersensitivity reactions, injection-site reaction

NC/PT Drug is a blood product; explain disease risk to pt. Reconstitute w/Sterile Water for Injection, resulting in 100 international units/mL. Use caution in pregnancy/breast-feeding. Pt should report difficulty breathing, chest pain, pain at injection site.

cobimetinib (Cotellic)

CLASS Antineoplastic, kinase inhibitor
PREG/CONT High risk/NA

IND & DOSE Tx of unresectable or metastatic melanoma w/BRAF V600E or V600K mutation, w/vemurafenib. *Adult:* 60 mg/day PO for first 21 days of 28-day cycle until progression.

ADV EFF Cardiomyopathy, fever, hemorrhage, hepatotoxicity, n/v/d, new malignancies, retinopathy/retinal vein occlusion, rhabdomyolysis, severe photosensitivity
INTERACTIONS Strong CYP3A inducers/inhibitors; avoid combination

NC/PT Ensure proper dx. Perform LFTs before and periodically during use. Monitor liver function, vision. Evaluate skin for skin cancers every 2 mo. Not for use in pregnancy (contraceptive use advised)/breast-feeding during and for 2 wk after tx. Pt should avoid sun exposure, wear protective clothing; report difficulty breathing, swelling, shortness of breath, bleeding, skin/vision changes, muscle pain, urine/stool color changes.

DANGEROUS DRUG

codeine sulfate (generic)

CLASS Antitussive, opioid agonist analgesic
PREG/CONT C (pregnancy); D (labor)/C-II

BBW Death related to ultrarapid metabolism of codeine to morphine in children after tonsillectomy/adenoidectomy (T&A).

IND & DOSE Relief of mild to moderate pain. *Adult:* 15–60 mg PO, IM, IV, or subcut q 4–6 hr; max, 360 mg/24 hr. *Child 1 yr and older:* 0.5 mg/kg or 15 mg/m² IM or subcut q 4 hr. **Suppression of coughing induced by chemical or mechanical irritation.** *Adult:* 10–20 mg PO q 4–6 hr; max, 120 mg/24 hr. *Child 6–12 yr:* 5–10 mg PO q 4–6 hr; max, 60 mg/24 hr. *Child 2–6 yr:* 2.5–5 mg PO q 4–6 hr; max, 12–18 mg/day.

ADJUST DOSE Elderly pts, impaired adults

ADV EFF Cardiac arrest, clamminess, confusion, constipation, dizziness, floating feeling, lethargy, light-headedness, n/v, sedation, **shock**

INTERACTIONS Anticholinergics, barbiturate anesthetics, CNS depressants

NC/PT Do not give IV in children. Do not use to manage postop pain in children w/T&A. Ensure opioid antagonist available during parenteral administration. Ensure perfusion of subcut area before injecting. Monitor bowel function; use of laxatives advised. Use in pregnancy only if benefit clearly outweighs risk to fetus. Breast-feeding women should receive drug 4–6 hr before next feeding and should monitor baby closely for signs of sedation or difficulty breathing. Pt should take safety precautions for CNS effects. Name confusion between codeine and *Cardene* (nicardipine); use caution.

---

colchicine (Colcrys)

CLASS Antigout drug
PREG/CONT C/NA

IND & DOSE Tx of acute gout flares. *Adult:* 1.2 mg PO at first sign of gout flare, then 0.6 mg 1 hr later; max, 1.8 mg over 1-hr period. **Px of gout flares.** *Adult, child 16 yr and older:* 0.6 mg PO once or twice daily; max, 1.2 mg/day.

Tx of familial Mediterranean fever. *Adult:* 1.2–2.4 mg/day PO in one or two divided doses; increase or decrease in 0.3-mg increments as needed. *Child over 12 yr:* Use adult dosage. *Child 6–12 yr:* 0.9–1.8 mg/day PO. *Child 4–6 yr:* 0.3–1.8 mg/day PO.

ADJUST DOSE Hepatic, renal impairment

ADV EFF Abd pain, **bone marrow suppression,** n/v/d, rash, **rhabdomyolysis**

INTERACTIONS Amprenavir, aprepitant, atazanavir, atorvastatin, clarithromycin, cyclosporine, digoxin, diltiazem, erythromycin, fibrates, fluconazole, fluvastatin, fosamprenavir, gemfibrozil, grapefruit juice, indinavir, itraconazole, ketoconazole, nefazodone, nelfinavir, ranolazine, pravastatin, ritonavir, saquinavir, simvastatin, telithromycin, verapamil

NC/PT Obtain baseline and periodic CBC, LFTs, renal function tests. Check complete drug list; many drug interactions require dose adjustments. Monitor for pain relief. Fatal overdoses have occurred; keep out of reach of children. Pt should avoid grapefruit juice, report to all providers all drugs and herbs taken (many potentially serious drug interactions possible), ensure protection from infection and injury, obtain periodic medical exams.

---

coleselvelam hydrochloride (WelChol)

CLASS Antihyperlipidemic, bile acid sequestrant
PREG/CONT B/NA

IND & DOSE Monotherapy for tx of hyperlipidemia. *Adult:* 3 tablets PO bid w/meals or 6 tablets/day PO w/ meal; max, 7 tablets/day. **To lower lipid levels, w/HMG-CoA inhibitor.** *Adult:* 3 tablets PO bid w/meals or 6 tablets PO once a day w/meal; max, 6 tablets/day. **To improve glycemic control in type 2 diabetes.** *Adult:* 6 tablets/day PO or 3 tablets PO bid.

Tx of familial hypercholesterolemia.
Child 10–17 yr: 1.8 g PO bid or 3.7 g/day
PO oral suspension.
ADV EFF Constipation to fecal
impaction, flatulence, increased
bleeding tendencies
INTERACTIONS Fat-soluble vitamins, oral drugs, verapamil
NC/PT Used w/diet/exercise program. Give other oral drugs 1 hr
before or 4–6 hr after drug. Monitor
blood lipids. Mix oral suspension in
4–8 oz water; do not use dry. Suspension contains phenylalanine; use
caution w/phenylketonuria. Establish
bowel program for constipation. Pt
should report unusual bleeding,
severe constipation.

colestipol hydrochloride (Colestid)
CLASS Antihyperlipidemic, bile
acid sequestrant
PREG/CONT C/NA

IND & DOSE Adjunctive tx for pri-
mary hypercholesterolemia. *Adult:*
5–30 g/day PO suspension once a
day or in divided doses bid–qid. Start
w/5 g PO daily or bid; increase in 5-g/
day increments at 1- to 2-mo intervals. For tablets, 2–16 g/day PO in
one to two divided doses; initially, 2 g
once or twice daily, increasing in 2-g
increments at 1- to 2-mo intervals.
ADV EFF Constipation to fecal
impaction, flatulence, headache,
increased bleeding tendencies
INTERACTIONS Digoxin, fat-soluble
vitamins, oral drugs, thiazide diuretics
NC/PT Used w/diet/exercise program. Give other oral drugs 1 hr
before or 4–6 hr after drug. Give
before meals. Monitor blood lipids.
Mix in liquids, soups, cereal, carbon-
ated beverages; do not give dry (inhalation and esophageal distress
possible). Contains phenylalanine;
use caution w/phenylketonuria.
Establish bowel program for constipation. Pt should swallow tablets
whole and not cut, crush, or chew

them; report unusual bleeding, severe
constipation; use analgesic for headache.

collagenase clostridium histolyticum (Xiaflex)
CLASS Proteinase enzyme
PREG/CONT B/NA

BBW Risk of corporal rupture (penile
fracture) or other serious penile injury
when used in tx of Peyronie's disease.
Available for this use only through
restricted access program.
IND & DOSE Tx of pts w/Dupuytren's
contraction w/palpable cord. *Adult:*
0.58 mg injected into palpable cord;
may repeat up to three times/cord at
4-wk intervals. **Tx of pts w/Peyronie's
disease w/penile curvature defor-
mity of 30 degrees or more.** *Adult:*
2 injections into the collagen-
containing structure followed by
penile remodeling; may repeat max
of eight times.
ADV EFF Corporal rupture, hypersensitivity reactions, injection-site
reactions, pain, **severe allergic reactions, severe penile hematoma, tendon rupture,** swelling in involved hand
INTERACTIONS Anticoagulants,
aspirin
NC/PT Be prepared for possible
severe allergic reaction. Risk of
bleeding if pt on anticoagulants. Tendon rupture, damage to nerves and
tissue of hand possible. Monitor
penile injection site closely for
adverse reactions.

corticotropin (ACTH) (H.P. Acthar Gel)
CLASS Anterior pituitary
hormone, diagnostic agent
PREG/CONT C/NA

IND & DOSE Tx of allergic states,
glucocorticoid-sensitive disorders,
nonsuppurative thyroiditis, tubercu-
lous meningitis, trichinosis w/CNS

and cardiac involvement; rheumatic disorders; palliative mgt of leukemias, lymphomas. *Adult:* 40–80 units IM or subcut q 24–72 hr. **Tx of acute exacerbations of MS.** *Adult:* 80–120 units/day IM for 2–3 wk.
ADV EFF Acne, amenorrhea, **ana-phylactoid reactions,** depression, ecchymoses, euphoria, fluid and electrolyte disturbances, fragile skin, hypertension, immunosuppression, impaired wound healing, infections, muscle weakness, petechiae
INTERACTIONS Anticholinesterases, antidiabetics, barbiturates, live vaccines
NC/PT Verify adrenal responsiveness before tx. Give only IM or subcut. Taper dose when discontinuing after long-term use. Give rapidly acting corticosteroid in times of stress. Pt should avoid exposure to infections, monitor blood glucose levels periodically, avoid immunizations.

---

cosyntropin (Cortrosyn)
CLASS Diagnostic agent
PREG/CONT C/NA

IND & DOSE **Diagnostic tests of adrenal function.** *Adult:* 0.25–0.75 mg IV or IM or as IV infusion at 0.04 mg/hr.
ADV EFF Anaphylactoid reactions, bradycardia, edema, hypertension, rash, **seizures,** tachycardia
INTERACTIONS Diuretics
NC/PT Plasma cortisol levels usually peak within 45–60 min of injection. Normally, expect doubling of baseline levels. Pt should report difficulty breathing.

---

crizotinib (Xalkori)
CLASS Antineoplastic, kinase inhibitor
PREG/CONT D/NA

IND & DOSE **Tx of locally advanced or metastatic non–small-cell lung cancer that is anaplastic lymphoma** kinase–positive as detected by **Vysis ALK Break Apart FISH Probe Kit.** *Adult:* 250 mg PO bid without regard to food. Reduce to 200 mg PO bid based on pt safety.
ADJUST DOSE Renal impairment
ADV EFF Bradycardia, constipation, **hepatotoxicity, prolonged QT, serious to fatal pneumonitis,** vision changes including blurry vision, light sensitivity, floaters, flashes of light
INTERACTIONS CYP3A inducers/inhibitors, QT-prolonging drugs
NC/PT Ensure pt has been tested for appropriate sensitivity. Monitor LFTs, pulmonary function. Institute bowel program as needed; advise safety precautions w/vision changes. Pt should avoid pregnancy (contraceptives advised)/breast-feeding; driving, operating machinery w/vision changes. Pt should report difficulty breathing, urine/stool color changes.

---

crofelemer (Fulyzaq)
CLASS Antidiarrheal, calcium channel stimulator
PREG/CONT C/NA

IND & DOSE **Relief of noninfectious diarrhea in adults w/HIV/AIDS on antiretroviral therapy.** *Adult:* 125 mg PO bid.
ADV EFF Bronchitis, cough, flatulence, possible URI
NC/PT Ensure cause of diarrhea is not infectious and pt also taking antiretroviral. Not for use in pregnancy/breast-feeding. Monitor diarrhea. Pt should take as directed; swallow capsule whole and not cut, crush, or chew it; report cough, increased diarrhea.

---

cromolyn sodium (Crolom)
CLASS Antiallergy drug
PREG/CONT C/NA

IND & DOSE **Prevention, tx of allergic rhinitis.** *Adult, child 2 yr and older:* 1 spray in each nostril

3–6 times/day as needed. **Tx of allergic eye disorders.** *Adult:* 1 or 2 drops in each eye 4–6 times/day as needed.
ADV EFF Allergic reaction, burning or stinging, shortness of breath, wheezing
NC/PT Eyedrops not for use w/soft contact lenses. May take several days to 2 wk for noticeable effects; pt should continue use. If pregnant or breast-feeding, consult provider.

cyanocobalamin, intranasal (Nascobal)
CLASS Synthetic vitamin
PREG/CONT C/NA

IND & DOSE Maint of pts in hematologic remission after IM vitamin B₁₂ tx for pernicious anemia, inadequate secretion of intrinsic factor, dietary deficiency, malabsorption, competition by intestinal bacteria or parasites, inadequate utilization of vitamin B₁₂; maint of effective therapeutic vitamin B₁₂ levels in pts w/ HIV infection, AIDS, MS, Crohn's disease. *Adult:* 1 spray (500 mcg) in one nostril once/wk
ADV EFF Headache, nasal congestion, rhinitis
INTERACTIONS Alcohol, antibiotics, colchicine, methotrexate, para-aminosalicylic acid
NC/PT Confirm diagnosis before tx. Monitor serum vitamin B₁₂ levels before, at 1 mo, then q 3–6 mo during tx. Do not give w/nasal congestion, rhinitis, URI. Pt should take drug 1 hr before or after ingesting hot foods or liquids, which can cause nasal congestion.

cyclobenzaprine hydrochloride (Amrix)
CLASS Centrally acting skeletal muscle relaxant
PREG/CONT B/NA

IND & DOSE Relief of discomfort associated w/acute, painful musculoskeletal conditions, as adjunct to rest, physical therapy. *Adult:* 5 mg PO tid, up to 10 mg PO tid. Do not use for longer than 2–3 wk. For ER capsules, 15 mg once/day PO.
ADJUST DOSE Elderly pts, hepatic impairment
ADV EFF Dizziness, drowsiness, dry mouth, **MI**
INTERACTIONS Alcohol, barbiturates, CNS depressants, MAOIs, TCAs, tramadol
NC/PT Give analgesics for headache. Monitor elderly pts closely. Pt should take safety precautions for CNS effects, avoid alcohol.

DANGEROUS DRUG

cyclophosphamide (generic)
CLASS Alkylating agent, antineoplastic, nitrogen mustard
PREG/CONT D/NA

IND & DOSE Tx of malignant lymphoma, multiple myeloma, leukemias, mycosis fungoides, neuroblastoma, adenocarcinoma of ovary, retinoblastoma, carcinoma of breast; used concurrently or sequentially w/other antineoplastics. *Adult:* Induction, 40–50 mg/kg IV in divided doses over 2–5 days or 1–5 mg/kg/day PO for 2–5 days. Or, 1–5 mg/kg/day PO, 10–15 mg/kg IV q 7–10 days, or 3–5 mg/kg IV twice wkly. **Tx of minimal change nephrotic syndrome.** *Child:* 2.5–3 mg/kg PO for 60–90 days.
ADJUST DOSE Renal, hepatic impairment
ADV EFF Alopecia, anorexia, **bone marrow suppression,** hematuria to potentially fatal hemorrhagic cystitis, interstitial pulmonary fibrosis, n/v/d, stomatitis
INTERACTIONS Allopurinol, anticoagulants, chloramphenicol, digoxin, doxorubicin, grapefruit juice, succinylcholine
NC/PT Monitor CBC; dose adjustment may be needed. Do not give full dose within 4 wk of radiation or

chemotherapy. Ensure pt well hydrated. Pts should use contraceptive measures; can cause fetal abnormalities. Pt should take oral drug on empty stomach, wear protective gloves when handling drug, not drink grapefruit juice, cover head at temp extremes (hair loss may occur).

cycloSERINE (Seromycin Pulvules)
CLASS Antibiotic, antituberculotic
PREG/CONT C/NA

IND & DOSE Tx of active pulmonary, extrapulmonary (including renal) TB not responsive to first-line antituberculotics, w/other antituberculotics; UTIs caused by susceptible bacteria. *Adult:* 250 mg PO bid at 12-hr intervals for first 2 wk. Max, 1 g/day; maint, 500 mg–1 g/day PO in divided doses.
ADV EFF Confusion, drowsiness, headache, **HF**, somnolence, tremor, vertigo
INTERACTIONS Alcohol, high-fat meals
NC/PT Culture before tx. Use only when other drugs have failed. Use w/ other anti-TB agents. Pt should avoid alcohol, take safety precautions for CNS effects, should not take w/high-fat meal or discontinue drug without consulting prescriber. Name confusion w/cycloserine, cyclosporine, and cyclophosphamide; use caution.

cycloSPORINE (Gengraf, Neoral, Sandimmune)
CLASS Immunosuppressant
PREG/CONT C/NA

BBW Monitor pts for infections, malignancies; risks increase. Monitor LFTs, renal function before and during tx; marked decreases in function may require dose adjustment or discontinuation. Monitor BP. Heart transplant pts may concomitant antihypertensive tx. Should be used only by physicians trained in tx w/ immunosuppressants.
IND & DOSE Px and tx of organ rejection in w/kidney, liver, heart transplants. *Adult:* 15 mg/kg/day PO (Sandimmune) initially given 4–12 hr before transplantation; continue dose postop for 1–2 wk, then taper by 5% per wk to maint level of 5–10 mg/kg/day. Or by IV infusion (Sandimmune) at 1/3 oral dose (ie, 5–6 mg/kg/day 4–12 hr before transplantation as slow infusion over 2–6 hr); continue this daily dose postop. Switch to oral drug as soon as possible. Tx of rheumatoid arthritis. *Adult:* 2.5 mg/kg/day (Gengraf, Neoral) PO in divided doses bid; may increase up to 4 mg/kg/day. If no benefit after 16 wk, discontinue. Tx of recalcitrant plaque psoriasis. *Adult:* 2.5 mg/kg/day (Gengraf, Neoral) PO divided bid for 4 wk, then may increase up to 4 mg/kg/day. If response unsatisfactory after 6 wk at 4 mg/kg/day, discontinue.
ADV EFF Acne, diarrhea, gum hyperplasia, hirsutism, hyperkalemia, hypertension, hypomagnesemia, renal impairment, tremors
INTERACTIONS Amiodarone, androgens, azole antifungals, carbamazepine, colchicine, diltiazem, foscarnet, grapefruit juice, high-fat meal, HMG-CoA reductase inhibitors, hormonal contraceptives, hydantoins, macrolides, metoclopramide, nephrotoxic agents, nicardipine, orlistat, phenobarbital, rifampin, St. John's wort, SSRIs
NC/PT Mix oral sol w/milk, chocolate milk, orange juice at room temp; do not allow to stand before drinking. Do not refrigerate. Use parenteral route only if pt cannot take oral form. Monitor LFTs, renal function, CBC, BP carefully; toxicity possible. Not for use in pregnancy (barrier contraceptives advised). Pt should avoid grapefruit juice, St. John's wort, exposure to infection; should not take w/high-fat meal or discontinue without

consulting prescriber. Interacts w/ many drugs; pt should inform all caregivers he is taking drug. Some confusion w/cyclosporine, cycloserine, and cyclophosphamide; use caution.

cyproheptadine hydrochloride (generic)
CLASS Antihistamine
PREG/CONT B/NA

IND & DOSE Relief of s&sx associated w/perennial, seasonal allergic rhinitis; other allergic reactions; tx of cold urticaria. *Adult:* 4 mg PO tid. Maint, 4–20 mg/day in three divided doses; max, 0.5 mg/kg/day. *Child 7–14 yr:* 4 mg PO bid–tid. Max, 16 mg/day. *Child 2–6 yr:* 2 mg PO bid. Max, 12 mg/day.
ADJUST DOSE Elderly pts
ADV EFF Agranulocytosis, anaphylactic shock, bronchial secretion thickening, dizziness, drowsiness, epigastric distress, disturbed coordination, **pancytopenia**
INTERACTIONS Alcohol, anticholinergics, CNS depressants, fluoxetine, metyrapone, MAOIs
NC/PT Use syrup if pt cannot swallow tablets. Give w/food. Monitor response.

DANGEROUS DRUG
cytarabine (cytosine arabinoside) (DepoCyt, Tarabine PFS)
CLASS Antimetabolite, antineoplastic
PREG/CONT D/NA

BBW Chemical arachnoiditis (n/v, headache, fever) can be fatal if untreated; concurrently treat w/dexamethasone.
IND & DOSE AML, ALL induction, maint of remission. *Adult:* For induction, 100 mg/m2/day by continuous IV infusion (days 1–7) or 100 mg/m2 IV q 12 hr (days 1–7); same dose for maint. Longer rest period may be

needed. *Child:* Dose based on body weight and surface area. **Tx of meningeal leukemia.** *Adult:* 5–75 mg/m2 IV once daily for 4 days or once q 4 days. Most common dose, 30 mg/m2 q 4 days until CSF normal, then one more tx. **Tx of lymphomatous meningitis.** *Adult:* 50 mg liposomal cytarabine intrathecal q 14 days for two doses, then q 14 days for three doses. Repeat q 28 days for four doses.
ADV EFF Alopecia, anorexia, **bone marrow depression**, fever, n/v/d, neurotoxicity, rash, stomatitis, thrombophlebitis
INTERACTIONS Digoxin
NC/PT Monitor CBC; dose adjustment based on bone marrow response. Monitor neurologic function; reduce dose as needed. Premedicate w/antiemetics. Do not come in contact w/liposomal forms. Provide mouth care, comfort measures. Not for use in pregnancy. Pt should take safety measures w/CNS effects, avoid exposure to infection, cover head at temp extremes (hair loss possible).

dabigatran etexilate mesylate hydrochloride (Pradaxa)
CLASS Anticoagulant, direct thrombin inhibitor
PREG/CONT C/NA

BBW Increased risk of thrombotic events when discontinuing. Consider adding another anticoagulant if stopping drug for any reason other than pathological bleeding. Spinal/epidural hematoma in pts w/spinal puncture/ anesthesia.
IND & DOSE To reduce risk of stroke, systemic embolism in pts w/nonvalvular atrial fibrillation. *Adult:* 150 mg PO bid. Converting from warfarin: Stop warfarin and begin dabigatran when INR is under 2. Converting from parenteral anticoagulant: Start dabigatran 0–2 hr before next dose of parenteral drug

would have been given, or at discontinuation of continuous infusion of parenteral anticoagulant. If starting on parenteral anticoagulant, wait 12 hr (if CrCl 30 mL/min or more) or 24 hr (if CrCl under 30 mL/min) after last dose of dabigatran before starting parenteral drug. **Tx of DVT and PE in pts treated w/parenteral anticoagulant for 5 to 10 days.** *Adult:* 150 mg PO bid after 5 to 10 days of parenteral anticoagulation. **Px of recurrent DVT and PE in previously treated pts.** *Adult:* 150 mg PO bid after previous tx.
ADJUST DOSE Renal impairment Px o DVT, PE in pts undergoing hip replacement surgery. *Adult:* 110 mg PO bid
ADV EFF Bleeding, dyspepsia, **gastric hemorrhage,** gastritis, gastritislike s&sx, **rebound increased risk of thrombotic events w/abrupt withdrawal, serious hypersensitivity reactions**
INTERACTIONS Aspirin, NSAIDs, platelet inhibitors, rifampin, warfarin
NC/PT Contraindicated in pts w/ artificial heart valves. Increased risk of bleeding; use caution. Consider using another anticoagulant if stopping drug. Reverse effects w/idarucizumab (*Praxbind*) for life-threatening bleeds, emergency surgery. Not for use in pregnancy/breast-feeding. Pt should take at about same time each day; swallow capsule whole and not cut, crush, or chew it; not double-up doses; not stop drug suddenly; ensure prescription does not run out (risk of thrombotic events); protect drug from moisture; keep in original container or blister pack; mark container and use within 4 mo; alert all health care providers he is taking drug; report chest pain, difficulty breathing, unusual bleeding, swelling, rash.

dabrafenib (Tafinlar)
CLASS Antineoplastic, kinase inhibitor
PREG/CONT D/NA

IND & DOSE Tx of unresectable or metastatic melanoma w/BRAF V600E or V600K mutations alone or w/trametinib. *Adult:* 150 mg PO bid at least 1 hr before or 2 hr after meal; if combination being used, add trametinib 2 mg/day PO.
ADV EFF Alopecia, arthralgia, **cardiomyopathy, cutaneous malignancies, DVT,** fever, headache, **hemolytic anemia, hemorrhage,** hyperglycemia, hyperkeratosis, ocular toxicity, palmar-plantar erythrodysesthesia, **tumor promotion of wild-type BRAF melanoma,** uveitis/iritis
INTERACTIONS CYP3A4/CYP2C8 inhibitors/inducers
NC/PT Ensure proper dx and appropriate BRAF mutation. Not for use in wild-type BRAF melanoma. Assess for other malignancies; monitor temp, CBC, blood glucose; have pt schedule eye exams. Pt should avoid pregnancy/breast-feeding; use analgesics for headache; monitor skin; report vision changes, rash or skin lesions, fever.

DANGEROUS DRUG
dacarbazine hydrochloride (DTIC-Dome)
CLASS Alkylating agent, antineoplastic
PREG/CONT C/NA

BBW Arrange for lab tests (LFTs; WBC, RBC, platelet count) before and frequently during tx; serious bone marrow suppression, hepatotoxicity possible. Carcinogenic in animals; monitor accordingly.
IND & DOSE Tx of metastatic malignant melanoma. *Adult, child:* 2–4.5 mg/kg/day IV for 10 days,

repeated at 4-wk intervals, or 250 mg/m^2/day IV for 5 days, repeated q 3 wk. **Second line tx of Hodgkin disease.** *Adult, child:* 150 mg/m^2/day IV for 5 days w/other drugs, repeated q 4 wk, or 375 mg/m^2 IV on day 1 w/ other drugs, repeated q 15 days.
ADV EFF Anaphylaxis, anorexia, **bone marrow suppression, hepatic necrosis,** local tissue damage w/ extravasation, n/v/d, photosensitivity
NC/PT Monitor CBC, LFTs carefully; may limit dose. Give IV only; monitor site carefully. Extravasation can cause serious local damage; apply hot packs if this occurs. Restrict fluids and food for 4–6 hr before tx; may use antiemetics. Prepare calendar of tx days. Pt should avoid exposure to infection, sun.

---

daclatasvir (Daklinza)
CLASS Antiviral, hepatitis C virus inhibitor
PREG/CONT Unkn/NA

IND & DOSE Tx of hepatitis C, genotype 3, w/sofosbuvir. *Adult:* 60 mg/ day PO for 12 wk.
ADJUST DOSE Concurrent use of CYP3A inducers/inhibitors
ADV EFF Bradycardia, fatigue, headache, n/d
INTERACTIONS Amiodarone, carbamazepine, phenytoin, rifampin, St John's wort, strong CYP3A inducers; contraindicated
NC/PT Give w/sofosbuvir. Monitor cardiac function in pt w/cardiac comorbidities. Carefully review drug regimen; many potentially serious interactions possible. Monitor lungs/ HR regularly; adjust dose as needed. Use caution in pregnancy/breast-feeding. Pt should take daily for 12 wk w/sofosbuvir; avoid St. John's wort; report all drugs being taken, dizziness, chest pain, severe fatigue.

> **DANGEROUS DRUG**

dactinomycin (Cosmegen)
CLASS Antibiotic, antineoplastic
PREG/CONT D/NA

BBW Use strict handling procedures; extremely toxic to skin and eyes. If extravasation, burning, stinging occur at injection site, stop infusion immediately; apply cold compresses to area, and restart in another vein. Local infiltration w/injectable corticosteroid and flushing w/saline may lessen reaction.
IND & DOSE Tx of Wilms' tumor, rhabdomyosarcoma, Ewing's sarcoma, in combination therapy; testicular cancer (metastatic nonseminomatous). *Adult:* 1,000 mcg/m^2 IV on day 1 of combination regimen or daily for 5 days; max, 15 mcg/kg/day or 400–600 mcg/m^2 IV for 5 days. *Child:* 15 mcg/kg/day IV for 5 days; max, 15 mcg/kg/day or 400–600 mcg/m^2/day IV for 5 days. **Tx of gestational trophoblastic neoplasia.** *Adult:* 12 mcg/kg/day IV for 5 days when used as monotherapy; 500 mcg IV on days 1 and 2 in combination therapy. **Palliative tx or adjunct to tumor resection via isolation-perfusion technique for solid malignancies.** *Adult:* 50 mcg/kg for lower extremity or pelvis; 35 mcg/kg for upper extremity.
ADV EFF Agranulocytosis, alopecia, anemia, **aplastic anemia, bone marrow suppression,** cheilitis, dysphagia, esophagitis, fatigue, fever, **hepatotoxicity,** lethargy, myalgia, skin eruptions, stomatitis, tissue necrosis w/extravasation
NC/PT Use strict handling procedures; toxic to skin and eyes. Monitor CBC, LFTs carefully; may limit dose. Give IV only. Monitor site carefully; extravasation can cause serious local damage. Monitor for adverse effects, which may worsen 1–2 wk after tx. Prepare calendar of tx days. Pt should cover head at temp extremes (hair loss possible). Name confusion between dactinomycin and daptomycin; use caution.

dalbavancin (Dalvance)
CLASS Lipoglycopeptide antibiotic
PREG/CONT C/NA

IND & DOSE Tx of acute skin/skin-structure infections caused by susceptible strains of gram-positive bacteria. *Adult:* 1,000 units IV over 30 min, then 500 mg IV over 30 min 1 wk later.
ADJUST DOSE Renal impairment
ADV EFF CDAD, headache, **hypersensitivity reactions**, LFT changes, n/v/d, skin reactions
NC/PT Perform culture before tx. Ensure appropriate use of drug. Monitor pt during infusion; reactions possible. Not for use in pregnancy/breast-feeding. Pt should mark calendar for return date for second infusion; report difficulty breathing, severe diarrhea, diarrhea w/blood or mucus, rash.

dalfampridine (Ampyra)
CLASS Potassium channel blocker, MS drug
PREG/CONT C/NA

IND & DOSE To improve walking in pts w/MS. *Adult:* 10 mg PO bid, 12 hr apart.
ADJUST DOSE Renal impairment, seizure disorder
ADV EFF Anaphylaxis, asthenia, back pain, balance disorder, constipation, dizziness, dyspepsia, headache, insomnia, MS relapse, nasopharyngitis, nausea, paresthesia, pharyngolaryngeal pain, **seizures**, UTIs
NC/PT Do not use w/hx of seizure disorders, renal impairment. Not for use in pregnancy/breast-feeding. Pt should swallow tablet whole and not cut, crush, or chew it; use safety precautions w/CNS effects; report difficulty breathing, facial swelling.

dalteparin sodium (Fragmin)
CLASS Anticoagulant, low-molecular-weight heparin
PREG/CONT C/NA

BBW Carefully monitor pts w/spinal epidural anesthesia for neurologic impairment. Risk of spinal hematoma and paralysis; provide urgent tx as necessary.
IND & DOSE Tx of unstable angina. *Adult:* 120 international units/kg subcut q 12 hr w/aspirin therapy for 5–8 days; max, 10,000 international units q 12 hr. **DVT px, abd surgery.** *Adult:* 2,500 international units subcut 1–2 hr before surgery, repeated once daily for 5–8 days after surgery. High-risk pts, 5,000 international units subcut starting evening before surgery, then daily for 5–10 days. **DVT px w/hip replacement surgery.** *Adult:* 5,000 international units subcut evening before surgery *or* 2,500 international units within 2 hr before surgery *or* 2,500 international units 4–8 hr after surgery. Then, 5,000 international units subcut each day for 5–10 days or up to 14 days *or* 2,500 international units subcut 4–8 hr after surgery, then 5,000 international units subcut once daily. **Px for DVT in pts w/restricted mobility.** *Adult:* 5,000 international units/day subcut. **Extended tx of venous thromboembolism.** *Adult:* Mo 1, 200 international units/kg/day subcut; max, 18,000 international units/day. Mo 2–6, 150 international units/kg/day subcut; max, 18,000 international units/day.
ADJUST DOSE Thrombocytopenia, renal impairment
ADV EFF Bruising, chills, fever, **hemorrhage**, injection-site reaction
INTERACTIONS Antiplatelet drugs, chamomile, clopidogrel, garlic, ginger, ginkgo, ginseng, heparin, high-dose vitamin E, oral anticoagulants, salicylates, ticlopidine

NC/PT Do not give IM. Give subcut, alternating left and right abd wall. Cannot be interchanged w/other heparin product. Check dosing; timing varies per indication. Do not mix w/ other injection or infusion. Have protamine sulfate on hand as antidote. Teach proper handling/disposal of needles/syringes. Pt should avoid injury, report excessive bleeding.

dantrolene sodium
(Dantrium, Ryanodex)
CLASS Direct acting skeletal muscle relaxant
PREG/CONT C/NA

BBW Monitor LFTs periodically. Arrange to discontinue at first sign of abnormality; early detection of liver abnormalities may permit reversion to normal function. Hepatotoxicity possible.
IND & DOSE Control of clinical spasticity resulting from upper motor neuron disorders. *Adult:* 25 mg PO daily. Increase to 25 mg PO tid for 7 days; then increase to 50 mg PO tid and to 100 mg PO tid if needed. *Child over 5 yr:* 0.5 mg/kg PO once daily for 7 days, then 0.5 mg/kg PO tid for 7 days, then 1 mg/kg PO tid for 7 days, then 2 mg/kg PO tid if needed. Max, 100 mg PO qid. **Preop px of malignant hyperthermia.** *Adult, child:* 4–8 mg/kg/day PO in three to four divided doses for 1–2 days before surgery; give last dose about 3–4 hr before scheduled surgery. Or, for adult, child over 5 yr, 2.5 mg/kg IV 1¼ hr before surgery infused over 1 hr. **Postcrisis follow-up.** 4–8 mg/kg PO in four divided doses for 1–3 days to prevent recurrence. **Tx of malignant hyperthermia.** *Adult, child over 5 yr:* Discontinue all anesthetics as soon as problem recognized. Give dantrolene by continuous rapid IV push beginning at minimum of 1 mg/kg and continuing until sx subside or maximum cumulative dose of 10 mg/kg reached.

ADV EFF Aplastic anemia, diarrhea, dizziness, drowsiness, fatigue, **hepatitis, HF,** malaise, weakness
INTERACTIONS Alcohol, verapamil
NC/PT Monitor baseline and periodic LFTs. Monitor IV site to prevent extravasation. Use all appropriate support and tx for malignant hyperthermia, including mannitol. Establish tx goal w/oral drug; stop occasionally to assess spasticity. Discontinue if diarrhea is severe. Pt should take safety precautions, avoid alcohol.

dapagliflozin (Farxiga)
CLASS Antidiabetic, sodium-glucose cotransporter 2 inhibitor
PREG/CONT C/NA

IND & DOSE Adjunct to diet/exercise to improve glycemic control in type 2 diabetes. *Adult:* 5 mg/day PO in a.m.; max, 10 mg/day.
ADJUST DOSE Severe renal impairment
ADV EFF Bladder cancer, dehydration, genital mycotic infections, hypoglycemia, hyponatremia, hypotension, increased LDLs, ketoacidosis, **renal impairment,** UTI
INTERACTIONS Celery, coriander, dandelion root, digoxin, fenugreek, garlic, ginger, juniper berries, phenobarbital, phenytoin, rifampin
NC/PT Not for use w/type 1 diabetes, diabetic ketoacidosis. Monitor blood glucose, HbA$_{1c}$, BP periodically. Not for use in pregnancy/breast-feeding. Pt should continue diet/exercise program, other antidiabetics as ordered; take safety measures w/ dehydration; monitor for UTI, genital infections.

dapsone (generic)
CLASS Leprostatic
PREG/CONT C/NA

IND & DOSE Tx of leprosy. *Adult, child:* 50–100 mg/day PO. Adults may need up to 300 mg/day; max in

children, 100 mg/day PO. **Tx of dermatitis herpetiformis.** *Adult:* 50–300 mg/day PO. Smaller doses in children; max, 100 mg/day.
ADV EFF Blurred vision, headache, hepatic impairment, insomnia, n/v/d, photosensitivity, ringing in ears, **severe allergic reactions,** tinnitus
INTERACTIONS Probenecid, rifampin, trimethoprim
NC/PT Obtain baseline, periodic LFTs. Not for use in pregnancy/breast-feeding. Pt should complete full course of therapy, avoid sun exposure, take safety precautions w/vision changes.

daptomycin (Cubicin)
CLASS Cyclic-lipopeptide antibiotic
PREG/CONT B/NA

IND & DOSE Tx of complicated skin, skin-structure infections caused by susceptible strains of gram-positive bacteria. *Adult:* 4 mg/kg IV over 30 min or as IV injection over 2 min in normal saline injection q 24 hr for 7–14 days. **Tx of *Staphylococcus aureus* bacteremia.** *Adult:* 6 mg/kg IV over 30 min or as IV injection over 2 min for 2–6 wk or longer.
ADJUST DOSE Renal impairment
ADV EFF Anaphylaxis, CNS and musculoskeletal system effects in children under 12 mo, CDAD, constipation, dizziness, dyspnea, eosinophilic pneumonia, injection-site reactions, insomnia, myopathy, n/v/d, peripheral neuropathy, **pseudomembranous colitis,** superinfections
INTERACTIONS HMG-CoA inhibitors, oral anticoagulants, tobramycin
NC/PT Culture before tx. Ensure proper use. Do not use in children under 12 mo. Monitor CK for myopathy. Discontinue and give support for pseudomembranous colitis. Discontinue if s&sx of eosinophilic pneumonia. Treat superinfections. Pt should report persistent diarrhea, chest pain, difficulty breathing, numbness/tingling. Name confusion between dactinomycin and daptomycin; use caution.

daratumumab (Darzalex)
CLASS Antineoplastic, monoclonal antibody
PREG/CONT Unkn/NA

IND & DOSE Tx of multiple myeloma in pts who have had at least three prior lines of therapy. *Adult:* 16 mg/kg IV weekly in wk 1–8, q 2 wk in wk 9–24, and q 4 wk thereafter until progression.
ADV EFF Back pain, cough, fatigue, fever, infusion reactions, URI
NC/PT Ensure proper dx. Premedicate w/corticosteroids/antipyretics/antihistamines. Dilute and administer at initially 50 mL/hr; max, 200 mL/hr. Give corticosteroids on days 1 and 2 post infusion. Monitor for infusion reactions; stop if life-threatening reactions occur. Use caution in pregnancy/breast-feeding. Pt should mark calendar for tx days, report difficulty breathing, rash, fever.

darbepoetin alfa (Aranesp)
CLASS Erythropoiesis-stimulating hormone
PREG/CONT C/NA

BBW Increased risk of death and serious CV events if Hgb target exceeds 11 g/dL. Use lowest level of drugs needed to increase Hgb to lowest level needed to avoid transfusion. Risk of DVT is higher in pts receiving erythropoietin-stimulating agents preop to decrease need for transfusion; note darbepoetin not approved for this use. Increased risk of death or tumor progression when drug used in cancer pts w/Hgb target range exceeding 11 g/dL; monitor Hgb closely in these pts.
IND & DOSE Tx of anemia associated w/chronic renal failure, including during dialysis. *Adult:* 0.45 mcg/kg IV

or subcut once/wk. Target Hgb level, 11 g/dL. **Tx of chemotherapy-induced anemia in pts w/nonmyeloid malignancies.** 2.25 mcg/kg subcut once/wk; adjust to maintain acceptable Hgb level. Or 500 mcg by subcut injection once q 3 wk; adjust to maintain Hgb level no higher than 11 g/dL.

ADJUST DOSE Chronic renal failure
ADV EFF Abd pain, arthralgia, asthenia, cough, **development of anti-erythropoietin antibodies w/subsequent pure red cell aplasia and extreme anemia,** diarrhea, dizziness, dyspnea, edema, fatigue, headache, hypotension, hypertension, **MI,** myalgias, n/v/d, **rapid cancer growth, seizure, stroke,** thromboembolism, URI
NC/PT Ensure correct diagnosis; not substitute for emergency transfusion. Monitor Hgb levels closely; max, 11 g/dL. Monitor preop pt for increased risk of DVTs. Do not give in sol w/other drugs. Evaluate iron stores before and periodically during tx. Frequent blood tests will be needed. Teach pt proper administration/disposal of needle/syringes. Pt should take safety precautions for CNS effects, mark calendar for injection dates.

darifenacin hydrobromide (Enablex)
CLASS Urinary antispasmodic, muscarinic receptor antagonist
PREG/CONT C/NA

IND & DOSE Tx of overactive bladder. *Adult:* 7.5 mg/day PO w/liquid and swallowed whole. May increase to 15 mg/day PO as early as wk 2.
ADJUST DOSE Gastric retention, hepatic impairment, somnolence, urine retention
INTERACTIONS Anticholinergics, clarithromycin, flecainide, itraconazole, ketoconazole, nefazodone, nelfinavir, ritonavir, thioridazine, TCAs
NC/PT Ensure correct diagnosis; rule out underlying medical issues. Moni-

tor IOP. Not for use in pregnancy/breast-feeding. Pt should swallow tablet whole and not cut, crush, or chew it; use sugarless lozenges for dry mouth; use safety precautions w/somnolence.

darunavir (Prezista)
CLASS Antiviral/protease inhibitor
PREG/CONT C/NA

IND & DOSE Tx of pts w/HIV infection that has progressed following standard tx. *Adult:* 600 mg PO bid w/ritonavir 100 mg PO bid w/food (tx-experienced) 800 mg PO bid w/ritonavir 100 mg PO bid (tx-naïve). *Child 3–under 18 yr, 10 kg or more:* Base dose on weight and surface area (see manufacturer's guidelines).
ADJUST DOSE Hepatic impairment
ADV EFF Abd pain, diabetes, headache, **hepatitis,** hyperglycemia, **increased bleeding w/hemophilia,** n/v/d, rash to **Stevens-Johnson syndrome,** redistribution of body fat
INTERACTIONS Alfuzosin, cisapride, dihydroergotamine, ergotamine, lovastatin, methylergonovine, pimozide, oral midazolam, rifampin, St. John's wort, sildenafil, simvastatin, triazolam
NC/PT Contraindicated for use w/many other drugs; check complete drug list before tx. Monitor LFTs regularly; not for use w/severe hepatic impairment. Not for use in children under 3; fatalities have occurred. Monitor blood glucose. Not for use in pregnancy/breast-feeding. Pt should report rash, urine/stool color changes.

DANGEROUS DRUG

dasatinib (Sprycel)
CLASS Antineoplastic, kinase inhibitor
PREG/CONT D/NA

IND & DOSE Tx of adults w/all stages of CML; newly diagnosed or

resistant Philadelphia chromosome-positive ALL. *Adult:* Chronic CML, 100 mg/day PO. ALL/other phases of CML, 140 mg/day PO.
ADV EFF Bone marrow suppression, cardiac dysfunction, diarrhea, dyspnea, fatigue, fluid retention, hemorrhage, **HF**, nausea, **pulmonary artery hypertension, prolonged QT,** rash to severe dermatologic reactions
INTERACTIONS Antacids; CYP3A4 inducers/inhibitors; grapefruit juice, proton pump inhibitors
NC/PT Obtain baseline and periodic ECG. Monitor CBC closely; dose adjustment may be needed. Not for use in pregnancy/breast-feeding. Men should not father a child during tx. Pt should swallow tablet whole and not cut, crush, or chew it; avoid grapefruit juice; avoid exposure to infection, injury; report severe swelling, bleeding, chest pain, difficulty breathing.

DANGEROUS DRUG

DAUNOrubicin citrate (DaunoXome)
CLASS Antineoplastic
PREG/CONT D/NA

BBW Cardiotoxicity possible; monitor ECG, enzymes (dose adjustment may be needed). Serious bone marrow depression possible; monitor CBC (dose adjustment may be needed).
IND & DOSE Tx of advanced HIV-associated Kaposi's sarcoma. *Adult:* 400 mg/m² IV over 1hr q 2 wk.
ADJUST DOSE Renal, hepatic impairment
ADV EFF Abd pain, anorexia, **bone marrow suppression, cancer, cardiotoxicity,** fatigue, fever, headache, **hepatotoxicity,** n/v/d
INTERACTIONS Cyclophosphamide, hepatotoxic drugs, myelosuppressants
NC/PT Obtain baseline and periodic ECG, enzymes. Monitor CBC closely; dose adjustment may be needed. Encourage cancer screening. Monitor injection site; extravasation can

cause serious damage. Not for use in pregnancy/breast-feeding.

DANGEROUS DRUG

decitabine (Dacogen)
CLASS Antineoplastic antibiotic, nucleoside metabolic inhibitor
PREG/CONT D/NA

IND & DOSE Tx of pts w/myelodysplastic syndromes. *Adult:* 15 mg/m² IV over 3 hr q 8 hr for 3 days; repeat q 6 wk *or* 20 mg/m² IV over 1 hr daily for 5 days, repeated every 4 wk
ADJUST DOSE Renal, hepatic impairment
ADV EFF Anemia, constipation, cough, diarrhea, fatigue, hyperglycemia, nausea, neutropenia, petechiae, pyrexia, thrombocytopenia
NC/PT Monitor CBC closely; dose adjustment may be needed. Premedicate w/antiemetic. Not for use in pregnancy (contraceptive use during and for 1 mo after tx)/breast-feeding. Men should not father a child during and for 2 mo after tx. Pt should avoid exposure to infection, injury.

---

deferasirox (Exjade, Jadenu)
CLASS Chelate
PREG/CONT C/NA

BBW May cause potentially fatal renal/hepatic reactions, gastric hemorrhage; monitor closely.
IND & DOSE Tx of chronic iron overload from blood transfusions. *Adult, child 2 yr and older:* 20 mg/kg/day PO; max, 30 mg/kg/day. Adjust dose based on serum ferritin levels. Tx of iron overload related to thalassemia. *Adult, child 10 yr and older:* 10 mg/kg/day PO. Adjust dose based on serum ferritin levels.
ADJUST DOSE Moderate hepatic impairment, renal impairment
ADV EFF Abd pain, **bone marrow suppression, GI hemorrhage, hepatic/renal impairment,** n/v/d,

rash to **Stevens-Johnson syndrome**; vision/hearing changes

INTERACTIONS Aluminum-containing drugs, bisphosphonates, iron chelating agents

NC/PT Monitor LFTs, renal function before, wkly for 2 wk, then monthly during tx. Dose adjusted based on serum ferritin levels. Pt should not chew or swallow tablets whole but should disperse in water or apple or orange juice; resuspend any residue and swallow liquid. Pt should take on empty stomach at least 30 min before food, take safety precautions for CNS effects, report unusual bleeding, rash, urine/stool color changes.

deferoxamine mesylate (Desferal)
CLASS Chelate
PREG/CONT C/NA

IND & DOSE Tx of chronic iron overload. *Adult, child 2 yr and older:* 0.5–1 g IM qid; 2 g IV w/each unit of blood, or 2,040 mg/kg/day as continuous subcut infusion over 8–24 hr. IM preferred. **Tx of acute iron toxicity.** *Adult, child:* 1 g IM or IV, then 0.5 g q 4 hr for two doses, then q 4–12 hr based on pt response. Max for child, 6 g/day.

ADV EFF Abd pain, hearing/vision changes, infections, injection-site reactions, n/v/d, **respiratory distress syndrome**, rash, discolored urine

NC/PT Not for use in primary hemochromatosis. Monitor hearing, vision, lung function. Use caution in pregnancy/breast-feeding. Urine may be discolored. Pt should take safety measures for CNS effects.

degarelix (Firmagon)
CLASS Antineoplastic
PREG/CONT X/NA

IND & DOSE Tx of advanced prostate cancer. *Adult:* 240 mg subcut as two 120-mg injections, then maint of 80 mg subcut q 28 days.

ADV EFF Hot flashes, **hypersensitivity reactions**, injection-site reaction, loss of libido, **prolonged QT**, weight gain

INTERACTIONS QT-prolonging drugs

NC/PT Obtain baseline and periodic ECG. Monitor injection sites for reaction. Alert pt that flushing, hot flashes, changes in libido possible. Pt should report rash, difficulty breathing, facial swelling.

delavirdine mesylate (Rescriptor)
CLASS Antiviral, nonnucleoside reverse transcriptase inhibitor
PREG/CONT C/NA

BBW Give concurrently w/appropriate antiretrovirals; not for monotherapy.
IND & DOSE Tx of HIV-1 infection w/other appropriate antiretrovirals. *Adult, child over 16 yr:* 400 mg PO tid w/appropriate antiretrovirals.
ADV EFF Diarrhea, flulike sx, headache, nausea, rash
INTERACTIONS Antacids, antiarrhythmics, benzodiazepines, calcium channel blockers, clarithromycin, dapsone, ergot derivatives, indinavir, quinidine, rifabutin, saquinavir, St. John's wort, warfarin
NC/PT Must give w/other antiretrovirals. Monitor T cells, LFTs. Monitor for opportunistic infections. Disperse 100-mg tablets in water before giving; let stand. Stir to form uniform dispersion. Have pt drink, rinse glass, and drink the rinse. Pt should use appropriate precautions (drug not a cure); consult all health care providers (drug interacts w/many drugs); avoid St. John's wort.

demeclocycline hydrochloride (generic)

CLASS Tetracycline
PREG/CONT D/NA

IND & DOSE Tx of infections caused by susceptible bacteria strains; when penicillin contraindicated. *Adult:* General guidelines, 150 mg PO qid or 300 mg PO bid. *Child 8 yr and older:* 3–6 mg/lb/day (6.6–13.2 mg/kg/day) PO in two to four divided doses. **Tx of gonococcal infections.** *Adult:* 600 mg PO, then 300 mg q 12 hr for 4 days to total 3 g. **Tx of streptococcal infections.** *Adult:* 150 mg PO qid for 10 days.

ADV EFF Anemia; anorexia; discoloration, inadequate calcification of fetal primary teeth if used in pregnancy; discoloration, inadequate calcification of permanent teeth if used during dental development; **eosinophilia;** glossitis; **hemolytic thrombocytopenia; leukocytosis; leukopenia; liver failure; neutropenia;** n/v/d; phototoxic reaction; rash

INTERACTIONS Antacids, dairy products, digoxin, hormonal contraceptives, iron, magnesium, penicillin

NC/PT Not for use in pregnancy (use of barrier contraceptives advised)/breast-feeding. Pt should take on empty stomach w/full glass of water, not take w/iron or dairy products, avoid sun exposure.

denileukin diftitox (Ontak)

CLASS Biological protein
PREG/CONT D/NA

BBW Severe hypersensitivity reactions possible; have life support equipment on hand. Capillary leak syndrome possible; pt may lose visual acuity, color vision.

IND & DOSE Tx of cutaneous T-cell lymphoma in pts who express CD25 component of IL-2 receptor. *Adult:* 9 or 18 mcg/kg/day IV over 30–60 min for 5 consecutive days q 21 days for eight cycles

ADV EFF Capillary leak syndrome, cough, diarrhea, dyspnea, fatigue, headache, **infusion reaction,** n/v, peripheral edema, pruritus, pyrexia, rigors, vision changes

NC/PT Premedicate w/antihistamine and acetaminophen. Have emergency equipment available for hypersensitivity reactions. Warn pt of potential vision loss. Use caution in pregnancy; not for use in breast-feeding. Pt should report sudden weight gain, rash, difficulty breathing, vision changes.

denosumab (Prolia, Xgeva)

CLASS RANK ligand inhibitor
PREG/CONT D (Xgeva), X (Prolia)/NA

IND & DOSE Tx of postmenopausal osteoporosis in women at high risk for fracture; tx of bone loss in breast cancer pts receiving aromatase inhibitors; tx of bone loss in prostate cancer pts receiving androgen deprivation therapy. *Adult:* 60 mg by subcut injection in upper arm, thigh, or abdomen q 6 mo (*Prolia* only). **Px of skeletal-related events in pts w/bone metastases from solid tumors.** *Adult:* 120 mg by subcut injection q 4 wk (*Xgeva* only). **Tx of unresectable giant cell tumor of the bone** (*Xgeva*). *Adult, adolescent:* 120 mg subcut q 4 wk w/additional 120 mg subcut on days 8, 15 of first month, w/calcium, vitamin D. **Tx of hypercalcemia of malignancy refractory to bisphosphonates** (*Xgeva*). *Adult:* 120 mg subcut q 4 wk w/added 120-mg doses on days 8 and 15 of first mo.

ADJUST DOSE Renal impairment
ADV EFF Atypical femur fractures, back pain, **cancer, constipation,** cystitis, hypercholesterolemia, hypocalcemia, **infection (serious to life-threatening),** osteonecrosis of jaw, **serious skin infections**

NC/PT Obtain baseline serum calcium levels; repeat regularly. Give subcut into abdomen, upper thigh, or upper arm; rotate injection sites. Not for use in pregnancy/breast-feeding. Pt should take 1,000 mg/day calcium and 400 units/day vitamin D; have regular cancer screening; avoid exposure to infection; report signs of infection, rash, jaw pain; get regular dental care to prevent jaw problems.

---

deoxycholic acid (Kybella)
CLASS Cytolytic agent
PREG/CONT Moderate risk/NA

IND & DOSE To improve appearance of moderate to severe convexity in fullness associated with submental fat "double chin" in adults. *Adult:* 0.2 mL injected 1 cm apart at all sites in mandibular tx area; up to 50 injections/session, up to six sessions at intervals no less than 1 mo apart.
ADV EFF Dysphagia, local edema/swelling, local redness/pain, mandibular nerve injury, numbness, submental bruising
NC/PT Follow prescribed injection technique to avoid injury. Avoid injection if infection in tx area. Use caution in pregnancy/breast-feeding. Pt should mark calendar for possible tx days, report difficulty swallowing, continued pain/swelling/bruising at injection site.

---

desipramine hydrochloride (Norpramin)
CLASS Antidepressant, TCA
PREG/CONT C/NA

BBW Risk of suicidality in children, adolescents, young adults. Monitor pt; inform caregivers.
IND & DOSE Relief of depression sx. *Adult:* 100–200 mg/day PO as single dose or in divided doses; max, 300 mg/day.

ADJUST DOSE Adolescents, elderly pts
ADV EFF Agranulocytosis, anticholinergic effects, confusion, constipation, disturbed concentration, dry mouth, MI, nasal congestion, orthostatic hypotension, photosensitivity, sedation, serotonin syndrome, stroke, urine retention, withdrawal sx after prolonged use
INTERACTIONS Anticholinergics, cimetidine, clonidine, fluoxetine, MAOIs, oral anticoagulants, quinolones, sympathomimetics
NC/PT Give major portion of dose at bedtime. Monitor elderly pts for increased adverse effects. Screen for bipolar disorder. Obtain CBC if fever, signs of infection occur. Pt should avoid alcohol, sun exposure; use sugarless lozenges for dry mouth; take safety precautions w/CNS effects; report difficulty urinating, fever, thoughts of suicide.

DANGEROUS DRUG

desirudin (Iprivask)
CLASS Anticoagulant, thrombin inhibitor
PREG/CONT C/NA

BBW Risk of epidural, spinal hematoma w/resultant long-term or permanent paralysis. Weigh risks before using epidural or spinal anesthesia, spinal puncture.
IND & DOSE PX of DVT in pts undergoing elective hip replacement. *Adult:* 15 mg subcut q 12 hr given up to 5–15 min before surgery after induction of anesthesia.
ADJUST DOSE Renal impairment
ADV EFF Hemorrhage, injection-site reactions
INTERACTIONS Drugs/herbs that prolong bleeding
NC/PT Give by deep subcut injection; alternate sites. Monitor blood clotting tests w/treatment. Protect pt from injury. Pt should report difficulty breathing, numbness/tingling, unusual bleeding.

desloratadine (Clarinex, Clarinex Reditabs)

CLASS Antihistamine
PREG/CONT C/NA

IND & DOSE Relief of nasal and nonnasal sx of seasonal allergic rhinitis in pts 2 yr and older; tx of chronic idiopathic urticaria and perennial allergies caused by indoor and outdoor allergens in pts 6 mo and older. *Adult, child 12 yr and older:* 5 mg/day PO or 2 tsp (5 mg/10 mL) syrup/day PO. *Child 6–11 yr:* 1 tsp syrup (2.5 mg/5 mL)/day PO, or 2.5-mg rapidly disintegrating tablet/day PO. *Child 12 mo–5 yr:* ½ tsp syrup/day (1.25 mg/2.5 mL) PO. *Child 6–11 mo:* 2 mL syrup/day (1 mg) PO.

ADJUST DOSE Renal, hepatic impairment

ADV EFF Dry mouth/throat, dizziness, hypersensitivity reactions

NC/PT Do not use *Clarinex Reditabs* w/phenylketonuria. Pt should use humidifier if dryness a problem, suck sugarless lozenges for dry mouth, take safety precautions if dizzy.

desmopressin acetate (DDAVP, Stimate)

CLASS Hormone
PREG/CONT B/NA

IND & DOSE Tx of neurogenic diabetes insipidus. *Adult:* 0.1–0.4 mL/day intranasally as single dose or divided into two to three doses, or 0.5–1 mL/day subcut or IV divided into two doses, or 0.05 mg PO bid; adjust according to water turnover pattern (DDAVP only). *Child 3 mo–12 yr:* 0.05–0.3 mL/day intranasally as single dose or divided into two doses, or 0.05 mg PO daily; adjust according to water turnover pattern (DDAVP only). **Tx of hemophilia A, von Willebrand disease (type I).** *Adult:* 0.3 mcg/kg diluted in 50 mL sterile physiologic saline; infuse IV slowly over 15–30 min 30 min preop;

intranasal, 1 spray/nostril 2 hr preop for total dose of 300 mcg. *Child 11 mo and older:* 1 spray/nostril (150 mcg); total dose, 300 mcg. Less than 50 kg, 150 mcg as single spray.

ADV EFF Local redness, swelling, burning at injection site; **water intoxication**

INTERACTIONS Carbamazepine, chlorpropamide, SSRIs, TCAs

NC/PT Refrigerate some sol, injection (check label; some no longer need refrigeration). Use rhinal tube to deposit deep into nasal cavity; use air-filled syringe or blow into tube. Monitor nasal passages. Monitor water balance closely. Monitor for hyponatremia. Monitor pts w/CV disorders. Individualize dose to establish diurnal water turnover patterns to allow sleep.

desvenlafaxine succinate (Pristiq)

CLASS Antidepressant, serotonin-norepinephrine reuptake inhibitor
PREG/CONT C/NA

BBW High risk of suicidality in children, adolescents, young adults; monitor for suicidal ideation, especially when beginning tx or changing dose. Not approved for children.

IND & DOSE Tx of major depressive disorders. *Adult:* 50 mg/day PO w/or without food; reduce dose gradually when stopping.

ADJUST DOSE Hepatic/renal impairment

ADV EFF Activation of mania, angle-closure glaucoma, bleeding, constipation, decreased appetite, dizziness, dry mouth, **eosinophilic pneumonia,** fatigue, glaucoma, headache, hyperhidrosis, **hypertension, interstitial lung disease,** n/v/d, **seizures, serotonin syndrome, suicidal ideation**

INTERACTIONS Alcohol, aspirin, CNS depressants, MAOIs, NSAIDs, SSRIs, St. John's wort, venlafaxine, warfarin

NC/PT Limit access in suicidal pts. Do not give within 14 days of MAOIs. Taper gradually when stopping. Monitor IOP periodically. Not for use in pregnancy/breast-feeding. May take several wks to see effects. Tablet matrix may appear in stool. Pt should swallow tablet whole and not cut, crush, or chew it; report thoughts of suicide, abnormal bleeding, difficulty breathing.

dexamethasone (generic), dexamethasone sodium phosphate (generic)
CLASS Glucocorticoid, hormone
PREG/CONT C/NA

IND & DOSE Short-term tx of various inflammatory, allergic disorders. *Adult:* 0.75–9 mg/day PO, or 0.5–9 mg/day IM or IV. *Child:* Base dose on formulas for child dosing using age, body weight. *Tx of cerebral edema. Adult:* 10 mg IV, then 4 mg IM q 6 hr until cerebral edema sx subside. Change to oral form, 1–3 mg tid, as soon as possible; taper over 5–7 days. *Tx of unresponsive shock. Child:* 1–6 mg/kg as single IV injection (as much as 20 mg initially); repeated injections q 2–6 hr have been used). *Intra-articular or soft-tissue administration for tx of arthritis, psoriatic plaques. Adult:* 0.2–6 mg (depending on joint or soft-tissue injection site). *Control of bronchial asthma requiring corticosteroids. Adult:* 3 inhalations tid–qid; max, 12 inhalations/day. *Child:* 2 inhalations tid–qid; max, 8 inhalations/day. *Relief of seasonal or perennial rhinitis sx. Adult:* 2 sprays (168 mcg) in each nostril bid–tid; max, 12 sprays (1,008 mcg)/day. *Child:* 1 or 2 sprays (84–168 mcg) into each nostril bid, depending on age; max, 8 sprays (672 mcg)/day. *Tx of inflammation of eyelid, conjunctiva, cornea, globe. Adult, child:* Instill 1 or 2 drops into conjunctival sac q hr during day and q 2 hr during night; taper as 1 drop q 4 hr, then 1 drop tid–qid. For ointment, apply thin coating in lower conjunctival sac tid–qid; reduce dose to bid, then once daily. *Relief of inflammatory and pruritic manifestations of dermatoses. Adult, child:* Apply sparingly to affected area bid–qid.
ADV EFF Acne, amenorrhea, depression, euphoria, fluid/electrolyte disturbances, headache, HPA suppression, hyperglycemia, hypertension, immunosuppression, impaired wound healing, infection, insomnia, irregular menses, local irritation, muscle weakness, secondary adrenal suppression, **seizures,** vertigo
INTERACTIONS Corticotropin, live vaccines, phenobarbital, phenytoin, rifampin, salicylates
NC/PT Give daily doses before 9 a.m. to mimic normal peak corticosteroid blood levels. Taper dose w/ high doses or long-term use. Monitor serum glucose. Protect pt from exposure to infection; do not give to pt w/ active infection. Not for use in breast-feeding. Apply topical drug sparingly to intact skin. Pt should not overuse joints after intra-articular injection.

dexchlorpheniramine maleate (generic)
CLASS Antihistamine
PREG/CONT B/NA

IND & DOSE Relief of sx associated w/perennial, seasonal allergic rhinitis; vasomotor rhinitis; allergic conjunctivitis; mild, uncomplicated urticaria, angioedema; amelioration of allergic reactions to blood or plasma; dermatographism; adjunct tx in anaphylactic reactions. *Adult, child over than 12 yr:* 4–6 mg PO at bedtime or q 8–10 hr during day. *Child 6–12 yr:* 4 mg PO once daily at bedtime.
ADJUST DOSE Elderly pts
ADV EFF Agranulocytosis, **anaphylactic shock,** disturbed coordination, dizziness, drowsiness, epigastric

distress, **pancytopenia**, sedation, thickening of bronchial secretions, **thrombocytopenia**
INTERACTIONS Alcohol, CNS depressants
NC/PT Adjust dose to lowest possible to manage sx. Available in oral syrup only. Pt should avoid alcohol; take safety precautions for CNS effects.

---

dexlansoprazole
(Dexilant)
CLASS Antisecretory, proton pump inhibitor
PREG/CONT B/NA

IND & DOSE Healing, maint of healing of erosive esophagitis. *Adult:* 60 mg/day PO for up to 8 wk, then 30 mg/day PO. **Tx of heartburn, GERD.** *Adult:* 30 mg/day PO for up to 4 wk.
ADJUST DOSE Hepatic impairment
ADV EFF Acute interstitial nephritis, gastric cancer, hypomagnesemia, n/v/d, possible increase in CDAD, possible loss of bone density and fracture, vitamin B_{12} deficiency
INTERACTIONS Ampicillin, atazanavir, digoxin, iron salts, ketoconazole, methotrexate, tacrolimus, warfarin
NC/PT Not for use in breast-feeding. May be opened, contents sprinkled over 1 tbsp applesauce, and swallowed immediately. Pt should swallow capsule whole and not cut, crush, or chew it; report severe diarrhea.

---

dexmedetomidine hydrochloride (Precedex)
CLASS Sedative/hypnotic
PREG/CONT C/NA

IND & DOSE ICU sedation of mechanically ventilated pts. *Adult:* 1 mcg/kg IV over 10 min, then 0.2–0.7 mcg/kg/hr using IV infusion pump. **Sedation of nonintubated pts before**

and/or during surgery or procedures. *Adult:* 1 mcg/kg IV over 10 min, then maint dose 0.6 mcg/kg/hr; range 0.2–1 mcg/kg/hr.
ADJUST DOSE Elderly pts, hepatic impairment
ADV EFF Agitation, bradycardia, dry mouth, hypotension, **respiratory failure**
INTERACTIONS Anesthetics, CNS depressants, opioids
NC/PT Not for use in pregnancy/breast-feeding. Monitor pt continuously during tx. Do not use for longer than 24 hr.

---

dexmethylphenidate hydrochloride (Focalin, Focalin XR)
CLASS CNS stimulant
PREG/CONT C/C-II

BBW Use caution w/hx of substance dependence or alcoholism. Dependence, severe depression, psychotic reactions possible w/withdrawal.
IND & DOSE Tx of ADHD as part of total tx program. *Adult, child 6 yr and older:* 2.5 mg PO bid; may increase as needed in 2.5- to 5-mg increments to max 10 mg PO bid. ER capsules: Initially 5 mg/day PO for children; increase in 5-mg increments to 30 mg/day. Start adults at 10 mg/day PO; increase in 10-mg increments to 20 mg/day. *Already on methylphenidate:* Start at one-half methylphenidate dose w/max of 10 mg PO bid.
ADV EFF Abd pain, anorexia, dizziness, insomnia, nausea, nervousness, tachycardia
INTERACTIONS Alcohol, antihypertensives, dopamine, epinephrine, MAOIs, phenobarbital, phenytoin, primidone, SSRIs, TCAs, warfarin
NC/PT Ensure proper diagnosis before use; interrupt periodically to reevaluate. Do not give within 14 days of MAOIs. Monitor growth in children. Controlled substance; secure storage. May sprinkle contents on applesauce; pt should take immediately. Pt should

swallow ER capsules whole and not cut, crush, or chew them; take as part of comprehensive tx program; take early in day to avoid interrupting sleep; avoid alcohol and OTC products; report chest pain, insomnia.

dexpanthenol
(Panthoderm)

CLASS Emollient
PREG/CONT C/NA

IND & DOSE Topical tx of mild eczema, dermatosis, bee stings, diaper rash, chafing. *Adult, child:* Apply once or twice daily to affected areas.
ADV EFF Local irritation
NC/PT Promote hydration; remove old skin. Pt should avoid contact w/ eyes; report application-site reaction.

dexrazoxane (Totect)

CLASS Lyophilizate
PREG/CONT D/NA

IND & DOSE Tx of extravasation of IV anthracycline chemotherapy. *Adult:* Days 1, 2: 1,000 mg/m² IV; max, 2,000 mg IV. Day 3: 500 mg/m² IV; max, 1,000 mg infused over 2 hr.
ADJUST DOSE Renal impairment
ADV EFF Bone marrow suppression, injection-site pain, n/v/d, pyrexia
NC/PT Available in emergency kit. Monitor bone marrow. Not for use in pregnancy/breast-feeding. Use pain-relief measures for extravasation site.

dextran, low-molecular-weight
(Dextran 40, 10% LMD, Rheomacrodex)

CLASS Plasma volume expander
PREG/CONT C/NA

IND & DOSE Adjunct tx of shock or impending shock when blood or blood products are not available. *Adult, child:* Total dose of 20 mL/kg IV

in first 24 hr; max, 10 mL/kg beyond 24 hr. Discontinue after 5 days. **Hemodilurent in extracorporeal circulation.** *Adult:* 10–20 mL/kg added to perfusion circuit; max, 20 mL/kg. **Px for DVT, PE in pts undergoing procedures w/high risk of thromboembolic events.** *Adult:* 500–1,000 mL IV on day of surgery. Continue at 500 mL/day IV for additional 2–3 days. Thereafter, may give 500 mL q second to third day for up to 2 wk.
ADV EFF Hypotension, hypervolemia, injection-site reactions
NC/PT Give IV only. Use clear sols only. Monitor for hypervolemia. Monitor urine output. Pt should report difficulty breathing.

dextroamphetamine sulfate (Dexedrine)

CLASS Amphetamine, CNS stimulant
PREG/CONT C/C-II

BBW High abuse potential. Avoid prolonged use; prescribe sparingly. Misuse may cause sudden death or serious CV events. Increased risk w/ heart problems or structural heart anomalies.
IND & DOSE Tx of narcolepsy. *Adult, child over 12 yr:* 10 mg/day PO in divided doses. Increase in 10-mg/day increments at wkly intervals; range, 5–60 mg/day PO in divided doses. *Child 6–12 yr:* 5 mg/day PO. Increase in 5-mg increments at wkly intervals until optimal response obtained. **Adjunct tx for ADHD w/hyperactivity.** *Adult:* 5 mg PO once or twice daily; max, 40 mg/day. *Child 6 yr and older:* 5 mg PO daily–bid. Increase in 5-mg/day increments at wkly intervals; max, 40 mg/day. *Child 3–5 yr:* 2.5 mg/day PO. Increase in 2.5-mg/day increments at wkly intervals.
ADV EFF Diarrhea, dizziness, dry mouth, hypertension, insomnia, overstimulation, palpitations, restlessness, tachycardia, unpleasant taste

INTERACTIONS Acetazolamide, antihypertensives, furazolidone, MAOIs, sodium bicarbonate, urinary acidifiers

NC/PT Baseline ECG recommended. Ensure proper diagnosis. Do not give within 14 days of MAOIs. Incorporate into comprehensive social and behavioral tx plan. Controlled substance; store securely. Give early in day. Provide periodic drug breaks. Monitor BP, growth in children. Not for use in pregnancy. Pt/caregiver should report manic or aggressive behavior, numbness in fingers or toes, chest pain, shortness of breath.

dextromethorphan hydrobromide (Creo-Terpin, Delsym, DexAlone, Hold DM, etc)
CLASS Nonopioid antitussive
PREG/CONT C/NA

IND & DOSE Control of nonproductive cough. *Adult, child 12 yr and older:* Gelcaps, 30 mg PO q 6–8 hr; max, 120 mg/day. Lozenges, 5–15 mg PO q 1–4 hr; max, 120 mg/day. Liquid, syrup, strips, 10–20 mg PO q 4 hr or 30 mg q 6–8 hr; max, 120 mg/day. ER suspension, 60 mg PO q 12 hr; max, 120 mg/day. *Child 6–11 yr:* Lozenges, 5–10 mg PO q 1–4 hr; max, 60 mg/day. Liquid, syrup, strips, 15 mg PO q 6–8 hr; max, 60 mg/day. Freezer pops, 2 pops q 6–8 hr. *Child 2–6 yr:* Liquid, syrup, 7.5 mg PO q 6–8 hr; max, 30 mg/day. Freezer pops, 1 pop q 6–8 hr.

ADV EFF Respiratory depression (w/overdose)
INTERACTIONS MAOIs
NC/PT Ensure proper use and advisability of suppressing cough. Do not use within 14 days of MAOIs. Pt should avoid OTC products w/same ingredients, report persistent cough w/fever.

diazepam (Diastat, Diastat AcuDial, Valium)
CLASS Antiepileptic, anxiolytic, benzodiazepine
PREG/CONT D/C-IV

IND & DOSE Tx of anxiety disorders, skeletal muscle spasm, seizure disorders. *Adult:* 2–10 mg PO bid–qid, or 0.2 mg/kg rectally. Treat no more than one episode q 5 days. May give second dose in 4–12 hr. *Child 6–11 yr:* 0.3 mg/kg rectally. *Child 2–5 yr:* 0.5 mg/kg rectally.
ADJUST DOSE Elderly pts, debilitating diseases
ADV EFF Apathy, bradycardia, confusion, constipation, **CV collapse**, depression, diarrhea, disorientation, fatigue, incontinence, lethargy, libido changes, light-headedness, paradoxical excitement, tachycardia, urine retention
INTERACTIONS Alcohol, cimetidine, disulfiram, hormonal contraceptives, omeprazole, ranitidine, theophylline
NC/PT Taper dose after long-term use. Suggest medical alert ID. Not for use in pregnancy (barrier contraceptives advised). Pt should take safety precautions w/CNS effects.

diazoxide (Proglycem)
CLASS Glucose-elevating drug
PREG/CONT C/NA

IND & DOSE Mgt of hypoglycemia due to hyperinsulinism in infants and children and to inoperable pancreatic islet cell malignancies. *Adult, child:* 3–8 mg/kg/day PO in two to three divided doses q 8–12 hr. *Infant, newborn:* 8–15 mg/kg/day PO in two to three doses q 8–12 hr.
ADJUST DOSE Renal impairment
ADV EFF Anxiety, hirsutism, hyperglycemia, hypotension, **HF**, n/v, pulmonary hypertension in newborns, **thrombocytopenia**

INTERACTIONS Chlorpropamide, glipizide, glyburide, hydantoins, tolazamide, tolbutamide, thiazides
NC/PT Check serum glucose, daily weight to monitor fluid retention. Protect suspension from light; have insulin on hand if hyperglycemia occurs. Excessive hair growth will end when drug stopped. Pt should report weight gain of more than 3 lb/day.

---

diclofenac (Zorvolex),
diclofenac epolamine
(Flector, Voltaren),
diclofenac potassium
(Cambia, Cataflam, Zipsor),
diclofenac sodium
(Solaraze)
CLASS Analgesic
PREG/CONT C (1st, 2nd trimesters); D (3rd trimester)/NA

BBW Possible increased risk of CV events, GI bleed, renal insufficiency; monitor accordingly.
IND & DOSE Tx of pain, including dysmenorrhea. *Adult:* 50 mg PO tid or 1 transdermal patch *(Flector)* applied to most painful area bid. Tx of osteoarthritis. *Adult:* 100–150 mg/day PO in divided doses *(Voltaren),* or 50 mg bid–tid PO *(Cataflam).* For upper extremities, apply 2 g gel to affected area qid; for lower extremities, apply 4 g gel to affected area qid *(Voltaren).* Tx of rheumatoid arthritis. *Adult:* 150–200 mg/day PO in divided doses *(Voltaren),* or 50 mg bid–tid PO *(Cataflam).* Tx of ankylosing spondylitis. *Adult:* 100–125 mg/day PO. Give as 25 mg qid, w/extra 25-mg dose at bedtime *(Voltaren),* or 25 mg qid PO w/additional 25 mg at bedtime if needed *(Cataflam).* Tx of acute migraine. *Adult:* 1 PO packet mixed in 30 to 60 mL water PO as single dose at onset of headache *(Cambia).* Tx of mild to moderate pain. *Adult:* 25 mg liquid-filled capsule PO qid *(Zipsor;* not interchangeable w/other forms of diclofenac). Tx of actinic keratosis. *Adult:*

Cover lesion w/topical gel, smooth into skin; do not cover w/dressings or cosmetics *(Solaraze).* Relief of postop inflammation from cataract extraction. *Adult:* 1 drop to affected eye qid starting 24 hr after surgery for 2 wk. Tx of osteoarthritis pain. *Adult:* 35 mg PO tid *(Zorvolex).* Tx of mild to moderate acute pain. *Adult:* 18–35 mg PO tid *(Zorvolex).*
ADV EFF Anaphylactoid reactions to fatal anaphylactic shock, constipation, diarrhea, dizziness, **CV events,** dyspepsia, GI pain, headache, nausea
INTERACTIONS Anticoagulants, lithium
NC/PT Be aware forms are not interchangeable. Give w/meals if GI upset occurs. Add packets for oral suspension to 30–60 mL water. Remove old transdermal patch before applying new one to intact, dry skin. Institute emergency procedures if overdose occurs. Pt should swallow tablets whole and not cut, crush, or chew them; avoid sun if using topical gel; take safety precautions for CNS effects.

---

dicyclomine
hydrochloride (Bentyl)
CLASS Anticholinergic, antispasmodic, parasympatholytic
PREG/CONT B/NA

IND & DOSE Tx of functional bowel or IBS. *Adult:* 160 mg/day PO divided into four equal doses or 40–80 mg/day IM in four divided doses for no longer than 1–2 days; do not give IV.
ADJUST DOSE Elderly pts
ADV EFF Altered taste perception, blurred vision, decreased sweating, dry mouth, dysphagia, irritation at injection site, n/v/d, urinary hesitancy, urine retention
INTERACTIONS Amantadine, antacids, anticholinergics, antipsychotics, atenolol, digoxin, TCAs

NC/PT IM use is only temporary; switch to oral form as soon as possible. Ensure hydration, temp control. Pt should avoid hot environments, empty bladder before taking if urine retention occurs, perform mouth care for dry mouth.

didanosine (ddl, dideoxyinosine) (Videx, Videx EC)
CLASS Antiviral
PREG/CONT B/NA

BBW Monitor for pancreatitis (abd pain, elevated enzymes, n/v). Stop drug; resume only if pancreatitis ruled out. Monitor pts w/hepatic impairment; decrease may be needed if toxicity occurs. Fatal liver toxicity w/lactic acidosis possible. Noncirrhotic portal hypertension, sometimes fatal, has occurred.
IND & DOSE Tx of pts w/HIV infection w/other antiretrovirals. *Adult, child:* DR capsules: 60 kg or more, 400 mg/day PO; 25–60 kg, 250 mg/day PO; 20–25 kg, 200 mg/day PO. Oral sol: 60 kg or more, 200 mg PO bid or 400 mg/day PO; under 60 kg, 125 mg PO bid or 250 mg/day PO. *Child over 8 mo:* Pediatric powder, 120 mg/m² PO bid. *Child 2 wk–8 mo:* 100 mg/m² PO bid.
ADJUST DOSE Renal, hepatic impairment
ADV EFF Abd pain, headache, hemopoietic depression, **hepatotoxicity, lactic acidosis,** n/v, **pancreatitis**
INTERACTIONS Antifungals, allopurinol, fluoroquinolones, ganciclovir, methadone, tetracyclines
NC/PT Monitor CBC, pancreatic enzymes, LFTs. Give on empty stomach 1 hr before or 2 hr after meals. Pediatric sol can be made by pharmacists; refrigerate. Pt should not cut, crush, or chew ER forms; report abd pain, urine/stool color changes.

diflunisal (generic)
CLASS Analgesic, anti-inflammatory, antipyretic, NSAIDs
PREG/CONT C/NA

BBW Possible increased risk of CV events, GI bleeding; monitor accordingly. Do not use to treat periop pain after CABG surgery.
IND & DOSE Tx of mild to moderate pain. *Adult, child over 12 yr:* 1,000 mg PO initially, then 500 mg q 8–12 hr PO. Tx of osteoarthritis, rheumatoid arthritis. *Adult, child over 12 yr:* 500–1,000 mg/day PO in two divided doses; maint, no more than 1,500 mg/day.
ADV EFF Anaphylactoid reactions to anaphylactic shock, CV event, diarrhea, dizziness, dyspepsia, GI pain, headache, insomnia, nausea, rash
INTERACTIONS Acetaminophen, antacids, aspirin
NC/PT Give w/food if GI upset. Pt should swallow tablets whole and not cut, crush, or chew them; take safety precautions for CNS effects; report unusual bleeding.

digoxin (Lanoxin)
CLASS Cardiac glycoside
PREG/CONT C/NA

IND & DOSE Tx of HF, atrial fibrillation. *Adult:* Loading dose, 0.25 mg/day IV or PO for pts over 70 yr w/good renal function; 0.125 mg/day PO or IV for pts over 70 yr or w/impaired renal function; 0.0625 mg/day PO or IV w/marked renal impairment. Maint, 0.125–0.5 mg/day PO in two divided doses. *Child:* Premature, 20 mcg/kg PO or 15–25 mcg/kg IV; neonate, 30 mcg/kg PO or 20–30 mcg/kg IV; 1–24 mo, 40–50 mcg/kg PO or 30–50 mcg/kg IV; 2–10 yr, 30–40 mcg/kg PO or 25–35 mcg/kg IV; over 10 yr, 10–15 mcg/kg PO or 8–12 mcg/kg IV as loading dose. Maint, 25%–35% of loading dose in divided doses; range, 0.125–0.5 mg/day PO.

ADJUST DOSE Elderly pts, impaired renal function

ADV EFF Arrhythmias, GI upset, headache, weakness, yellow vision

INTERACTIONS Amiodarone, bleomycin, charcoal, cholestyramine, colestipol, cyclophosphamide, cyclosporine, dobutamine in sol, erythromycin, ginseng, hawthorn, licorice, loop diuretics, metoclopramide, methotrexate, oral aminoglycosides, penicillamine, psyllium, quinidine, St. John's wort, tetracyclines, thiazide diuretics, thyroid hormone, verapamil

NC/PT Monitor apical pulse; withhold if under 60 in adults, under 90 in children. Check dose carefully. Do not give IM. Give on empty stomach. Monitor for therapeutic drug levels: 0.5–2 ng/mL. Pt should learn to take pulse, weigh self daily, consult prescriber before taking OTC drugs or herbs, avoid St. John's wort, report slow or irregular pulse, yellow vision.

digoxin immune fab (DigiFab)
CLASS Antidote
PREG/CONT C/NA

IND & DOSE Tx of potentially life-threatening digoxin toxicity (serum digoxin over 10 ng/mL, serum potassium over 5 mEq/L in setting of digoxin toxicity). *Adult, child:* Dose determined by serum digoxin level or estimate of amount of digoxin ingested. If no estimate possible and serum digoxin level unavailable, use 800 mg IV (20 vials). See manufacturer's details; dose varies by digoxin level.

ADV EFF Anaphylaxis, HF, low cardiac output, hypokalemia

NC/PT Ensure no sheep allergies. Monitor serum digoxin before tx. Have life-support equipment on hand. Do not redigitalize until drug has cleared (several days to a wk). Serum digoxin levels unreliable for up to

3 days after administration. Pt should report difficulty breathing.

dihydroergotamine mesylate (D.H.E. 45, Migranal)
CLASS Antimigraine, ergot
PREG/CONT X/NA

BBW Serious to life-threatening ischemia if taken w/potent CYP3A4 inhibitors, including protease inhibitors, macrolide antibiotics; concurrent use contraindicated.

IND & DOSE Tx of migraine w/or without aura; acute tx of cluster headaches. *Adult:* 1 mg IM, IV, or subcut at first sign of headache; may repeat at 1-hr intervals. Max, 3 mg, or 1 intranasal spray (0.5 mg) in each nostril followed in 15 min by another spray in each nostril (max, 3 mg).

ADV EFF CV events, nausea, numbness, rhinitis, tingling

INTERACTIONS CYP3A4 inhibitors, peripheral vasoconstrictors, sumatriptan

NC/PT Not for use in pregnancy/breast-feeding. May give antiemetic if nausea severe. Monitor BP; look for signs of vasospasm. Pt should prime pump four times before use (nasal spray), report numbness/tingling, chest pain.

diltiazem hydrochloride (Cardizem, Cardizem LA, Cartia XT, Diltzac, Taztia XT, Tiazac)
CLASS Antianginal, antihypertensive, calcium channel blocker
PREG/CONT C/NA

IND & DOSE Tx of angina pectoris. *Adult:* Initially, 30 mg PO qid before meals and at bedtime; gradually increase at 1- to 2-day intervals to 180–360 mg PO in three to four divided doses. Or, 120–360 mg/day (ER, SR forms) PO, depending on brand. Tx of

essential hypertension. *Adult:* 180–240 mg PO daily *(Cardizem CD, Cartia XT).* 120–540 mg PO daily *(Cardizem LA).* 180–240 mg PO daily. 120–240 mg PO daily *(Tiazac, Taztia XT).* **Tx of supraventricular tachycardia, atrial fibrillation, atrial flutter.** *Adult:* Direct IV bolus, 0.25 mg/kg over 2 min; second bolus of 0.35 mg/kg over 2 min after 15 min if response inadequate. Or, 5–10 mg/hr by continuous IV infusion w/increases up to 15 mg/hr; may continue for up to 24 hr. **ADV EFF** Asthenia, **asystole,** bradycardia, dizziness, edema, flushing, light-headedness, nausea **INTERACTIONS** Beta blockers, cyclosporine, grapefruit juice **NC/PT** Monitor closely while establishing dose. Pt should swallow ER/SR tablets whole and not cut, crush, or chew them; avoid grapefruit juice; report irregular heart beat, swelling.

dimenhyDRINATE
(Dimetabs, Dramanate, Dymenate)
CLASS Anticholinergic, antihistamine, anti–motion sickness drug
PREG/CONT B/NA

IND & DOSE Px, tx of n/v or vertigo of motion sickness. *Adult:* 50–100 mg PO q 4–6 hr; for px, pt should take first dose 30 min before exposure to motion. Max, 400 mg/24 hr. Or, 50 mg IM as needed, or 50 mg in 10 mL sodium chloride injection IV over 2 min. *Child 6–12 yr:* 25–50 mg PO q 6–8 hr; max, 150 mg/day.
ADJUST DOSE Elderly pts
ADV EFF Anaphylaxis, confusion, dizziness, drowsiness, headache, heaviness/weakness of hands, lassitude, nervousness, restlessness, vertigo
INTERACTIONS Alcohol, CNS depressants
NC/PT Have epinephrine on hand during IV use. Pt should use 30 min before motion sickness–inducing

event, avoid alcohol, take safety precautions w/CNS effects.

dimercaprol (BAL in Oil)
CLASS Antidote, chelate
PREG/CONT C/NA

IND & DOSE Tx of arsenic, gold poisoning. *Adult, child:* 25 mg/kg deep IM four times/day for 2 days, two times/day on third day, then once daily for 10 days. **Tx of mercury poisoning.** *Adult, child:* 5 mg/kg IM, then 2.5 mg/kg once daily or bid for 10 days. **Tx of lead poisoning w/edetate calcium.** *Adult, child:* 4 mg/kg IM for first dose, then at 4-hr intervals w/edetate calcium for 2–7 days.
ADJUST DOSE Hepatic impairment
ADV EFF Abd pain, burning sensation in lips/mouth, constricted feeling in throat/chest, headache, nausea, sweating
INTERACTIONS Alcohol, CNS depressants
NC/PT Use extreme caution w/peanut allergy. Use deep IM injection. Pt should report constricted feeling in throat/chest, difficulty breathing.

dimethyl fumarate
(Tecfidera)
CLASS MS drug, nicotinic receptor agonist
PREG/CONT C/NA

IND & DOSE Tx of relapsing MS. *Adult:* 120 mg PO bid for 7 days; then 240 mg PO bid.
ADV EFF Abd pain, **anaphylaxis, angioedema,** dizziness, dyspepsia, flushing, lymphopenia, n/v/d, progressive multifocal leukoencephalopathy, rash
NC/PT Obtain baseline and periodic CBC, LFTs; withhold w/serious infection. Use caution in pregnancy/breast-feeding. Pt should swallow capsule whole and not cut, crush, or chew it (may open and sprinkle on food); avoid infections; dress in

layers if flushing occurs; report continued n/v/d, severe rash, worsening of MS sx.

dinoprostone (Cervidil, Prepidil, Prostin E2)
CLASS Abortifacient, prostaglandin
PREG/CONT C/NA

IND & DOSE Termination of pregnancy 12–20 wk from first day of last menstrual period; evacuation of uterus in mgt of missed abortion. *Adult:* 1 suppository (20 mg) high into vagina; keep pt supine for 10 min after insertion. May give additional suppositories at 3- to 5-hr intervals, based on uterine response and tolerance, for up to 2 days. **Initiation of cervical ripening before labor induction.** *Adult:* 0.5 mg gel via provided cervical catheter w/pt in dorsal position and cervix visualized using speculum. May repeat dose if no response in 6 hr. Wait 6–12 hr before beginning oxytocin IV to initiate labor. For insert: Place 1 insert transversely in posterior fornix of vagina. Keep pt supine for 2 hr (1 insert delivers 0.3 mg/hr over 12 hr). Remove, using retrieval system, at onset of active labor or 12 hr after insertion.
ADV EFF Dizziness, headache, hypotension, n/v/d, **perforated uterus**
NC/PT Store suppositories in freezer; bring to room temp before insertion. Keep pt supine after vaginal insertion. Ensure abortion complete. Give antiemetics, antidiarrheals if needed. Monitor for uterine tone, bleeding. Give support, encouragement for procedure/progressing labor. Name confusion among *Prostin VR Pediatric* (alprostadil), *Prostin FZ* (dinoprost), *Prostin E2* (dinoprostone), *Prostin 15* (carboprost in Europe); use extreme caution.

dinutuximab (Unituxin)
CLASS Antineoplastic, monoclonal antibody
PREG/CONT D/NA

BBW Risk of life-threatening infusion reactions; prehydrate, premedicate. Interrupt severe reaction and stop if anaphylaxis occurs. Risk of severe neuropathic pain: Give IV opioid before, during, and for 2 hr after infusion; stop w/severe unresponsive pain, severe sensory neuropathy, or moderate to severe motor neuropathy.
IND & DOSE As part of combination therapy in tx of child w/high-risk neuroblastoma w/at least partial response to prior first-line regimens. *Child:* 17.5 mg/m²/day IV over 10–20 hr for 4 consecutive days for 5 cycles: days 4, 5, 6, 7 for cycles 1, 3, and 5 (24-day cycles); days 8, 9, 10, and 11 for cycles 2 and 4 (32-day cycles).
ADV EFF Bone marrow suppression, capillary leak syndrome, fever, hemolytic uremic syndrome, infusion reactions, hypokalemia, hypotension, infection, n/v/d, neuropathies
NC/PT Prehydrate w/0.9% Sodium Chloride Injection 10 mL/kg over 1 hr before starting infusion. Premedicate with IV morphine before and continuously during infusion; continue for 2 hr after infusion. Give antihistamine IV over 10–15 min starting 20 min before infusion and q 4–6 hr during infusion, and acetaminophen 10–15 mg/kg PO starting 20 min before and q 4–6 hr during infusion. Give ibuprofen 5–10 mg/kg PO q 4–6 hr for fever, pain control. Not for use in pregnancy/breast-feeding. Alert pt/caregiver of risks, adverse effects to anticipate. Pt should take safety precautions w/CNS effects; report s&sx of infection, difficulty breathing, swelling, dizziness, severe pain, vision changes.

diphenhydrAMINE hydrochloride (Benadryl, Diphen AF, Diphenhist)

CLASS Antihistamine, anti-motion sickness, antiparkinsonian, sedative
PREG/CONT B/NA

IND & DOSE Relief of sx of various allergic reactions, motion sickness. *Adult:* 25–50 mg PO q 4–6 hr; max, 300 mg/24 hr. Or, 10–50 mg IV or deep IM or up to 100 mg if needed; max, 400 mg/day. *Child 6–12 yr:* 12.5–25 mg PO tid–qid, or 5 mg/kg/day PO, or 150 mg/m²/day PO; max, 150 mg/day. Or, 5 mg/kg/day or 150 mg/m²/day IV or deep IM injection. Max, 300 mg/day divided into four doses. **Nighttime sleep aid.** *Adult:* 50 mg PO at bedtime. **Cough suppression.** *Adult:* 25 mg PO q 4 hr; max, 150 mg/day (syrup). *Child 6–12 yr:* 12.5 mg PO q 4 hr. Max, 75 mg/24 hr (syrup).
ADJUST DOSE Elderly pts
ADV EFF Agranulocytosis, anaphylactic shock, bronchial secretion thickening, disturbed coordination, dizziness, drowsiness, epigastric distress, **hemolytic anemia, hypoplastic anemia, leukopenia, pancytopenia, thrombocytopenia**
INTERACTIONS Alcohol, CNS depressants, MAOIs
NC/PT Monitor response; use smallest dose possible. Use syrup if swallowing tablets difficult. Pt should avoid alcohol, take safety precautions w/CNS effects.

dipyridamole (Persantine)

CLASS Antianginal, antiplatelet, diagnostic agent
PREG/CONT B/NA

IND & DOSE Px of thromboembolism in pts w/artificial heart valves, w/warfarin. *Adult:* 75–100 mg PO qid. **Diagnostic aid to assess CAD in** pts unable to exercise. *Adult:* 0.142 mg/kg/min IV over 4 min.
ADV EFF Abd distress, dizziness, headache
INTERACTIONS Adenosine
NC/PT Monitor continually w/IV use. Give oral drug at least 1 hr before meals. Pt should take safety precautions for light-headedness.

disopyramide phosphate (Norpace, Norpace CR)

CLASS Antiarrhythmic
PREG/CONT C/NA

BBW Monitor for possible refractory arrhythmias that can be life-threatening; reserve use for life-threatening arrhythmias.
IND & DOSE Tx of life-threatening ventricular arrhythmias. *Adult, child:* 400–800 mg/day PO in divided doses q 6 hr, or q 12 hr if using CR forms. **Rapid control of ventricular arrhythmias.** *Adult:* 300 mg (immediate-release) PO. If no response within 6 hr, 200 mg PO q 6 hr; may increase to 250–300 mg q 6 hr if no response in 48 hr. For pts w/cardiomyopathy, no loading dose; 100 mg (immediate-release) PO q 6–8 hr.
ADJUST DOSE Renal, hepatic failure
ADV EFF Blurred vision, constipation, dry nose/eye/throat, **HF**, itching, malaise, muscle aches and pains, urinary hesitancy, urine retention
INTERACTIONS Antiarrhythmics, erythromycin, phenytoin, quinidine
NC/PT Monitor ECG carefully. Make pediatric suspension (1–10 mg/mL) by adding contents of immediate-release capsule to cherry syrup, if desired. Store in amber glass bottle; refrigerate up to 1 mo. Evaluate pt for safe, effective serum levels (2–8 mcg/mL). Pt should swallow CR forms whole and not cut, crush, or chew them; not stop taking without consulting prescriber; maintain hydration, empty bladder before taking.

disulfiram (Antabuse)

CLASS Antialcoholic, enzyme inhibitor

PREG/CONT C/NA

BBW Never give to intoxicated pt with or without pt's knowledge. Do not give until pt has abstained from alcohol for at least 12 hr.

IND & DOSE Aid in mgt of selected chronic alcoholics who want to remain in state of enforced sobriety. *Adult:* 500 mg/day PO in single dose for 1–2 wk. If sedative effect occurs, give at bedtime or decrease dose. Maint, 125–500 mg/day PO; max, 500 mg/day.

ADV EFF Dizziness, fatigue, headache, metal- or garlic-like aftertaste, skin eruptions; if taken w/alcohol, **arrhythmias, CV collapse, death, HF, MI**

INTERACTIONS Alcohol, caffeine, chlordiazepoxide, diazepam, metronidazole, oral anticoagulants, theophyllines

NC/PT Do not give until pt has abstained from alcohol for at least 12 hr. Monitor LFTs, CBC before and q 6 mo of tx. May crush tablets and mix w/ liquid beverages. Institute supportive measures if pt drinks alcohol during tx. Pt should abstain from all forms of alcohol (serious to fatal reactions possible if combined), wear/carry medical ID, take safety precautions for CNS effects.

DANGEROUS DRUG

DOBUTamine hydrochloride (generic)

CLASS Beta₁-selective adrenergic agonist, sympathomimetic

PREG/CONT B/NA

IND & DOSE Short-term tx of cardiac decompensation. *Adult:* Usual rate, 2–20 mcg/kg/min IV to increase cardiac output; rarely, rates up to 40 mcg/kg/min.

Child: 0.5–1 mcg/kg/min as continuous IV infusion. Maint, 2–20 mcg/kg/min.

ADV EFF Headache, hypertension, nausea, PVCs, tachycardia

INTERACTIONS Methyldopa, TCAs

NC/PT Monitor urine flow, cardiac output, pulmonary wedge pressure, ECG, BP closely during infusion; adjust dose, rate accordingly. Arrange to digitalize pt w/atrial fibrillation w/ rapid ventricular rate before giving dobutamine (dobutamine facilitates AV conduction). Name confusion between dobutamine and dopamine; use caution.

DANGEROUS DRUG

docetaxel (Docefrez, Taxotere)

CLASS Antineoplastic

PREG/CONT D/NA

BBW Do not give unless blood counts are within acceptable range (neutrophils over 1,500 cells/m²). Do not give w/hepatic impairment; increased risk of toxicity and death. Monitor LFTs carefully. Monitor for hypersensitivity reactions, possibly severe. Do not give w/hx of hypersensitivity. Monitor carefully for fluid retention; treat accordingly.

IND & DOSE Tx of breast cancer. *Adult:* 60–100 mg/m² IV infused over 1 hr q 3 wk. Tx of non-small-cell lung cancer. *Adult:* 75 mg/m² IV over 1 hr q 3 wk. First-line tx of non-small-cell lung cancer. *Adult:* 75 mg/m² over 1 hr, then 75 mg/m² cisplatin IV over 30–60 min q 3 wk. Tx of androgen-independent metastatic prostate cancer. *Adult:* 75 mg/m² IV q 3 wk as 1-hr infusion w/5 mg prednisone PO bid constantly throughout tx. Reduce dose to 60 mg/m² if febrile neutropenia, severe or cumulative cutaneous reactions, moderate neurosensory s&sx, or neutrophil count under 500/mm³ occurs for longer than 1 wk. Stop tx if reactions continue w/reduced dose. Tx of operable node-positive breast cancer. *Adult:*

75 mg/m² IV 1 hr after doxorubicin 50 mg/m² and cyclophosphamide 500 mg/m² q 3 wk for 6 courses. **Induction for squamous cell cancer of head and neck before radiotherapy.** *Adult:* 75 mg/m² as 1-hr IV infusion, then cisplatin 75 mg/m² IV over 1 hr on day 1, then 5-FU 750 mg/m²/day IV for 5 days. Repeat q 3 wk for four cycles before radiotherapy starts. **Induction for squamous cell cancer of head and neck before chemoradiotherapy.** *Adult:* 75 mg/m² as 1-hr IV infusion, then cisplatin 100 mg/m² as 30-min–3-hr infusion, then 5-FU 1,000 mg/m²/day as continuous infusion on days 1–4. Give q 3 wk for three cycles before chemoradiotherapy starts. **Tx of advanced gastric adenocarcinoma.** *Adult:* 75 mg/m² IV as 1-hr infusion, then cisplatin 75 mg/m² IV as 1–3-hr infusion (both on day 1), then 5-FU 750 mg/m²/day IV as 24-hr infusion for 5 days. Repeat cycle q 3 wk.
ADJUST DOSE Hepatic impairment
ADV EFF Acute myeloid leukemia, alopecia, arthralgia, asthenia, **bone marrow suppression, CNS impairment, cystoid macular edema, fluid retention,** hypersensitivity reactions, infection, myalgia, n/v/d, pain, **skin toxicity,** stomatitis
INTERACTIONS Cyclosporine, erythromycin, immunosuppressants, ketoconazole
NC/PT Handle drug carefully. Premedicate w/oral corticosteroids to reduce fluid retention. Monitor CBC before each dose; adjust dose as needed. Monitor LFTs; do not give w/ hepatic impairment. Monitor for fluid retention; treat accordingly. Protect from infection. Give antiemetics if needed. High alcohol level in *Taxotere* may impair pt. Pt should cover head at temp extremes (hair loss possible), mark calendar for tx days, take safety precautions for CNS effects. Name confusion between *Taxotere* (docetaxel) and *Taxol* (paclitaxel); use extreme caution.

dofetilide (Tikosyn)
CLASS Antiarrhythmic
PREG/CONT C/NA

BBW Monitor ECG before and periodically during administration. Monitor pt continually for at least 3 days. May adjust dose based on maint of sinus rhythm. Risk of induced arrhythmias.

IND & DOSE Conversion of atrial fibrillation (AF) or flutter to normal sinus rhythm; maint of sinus rhythm after conversion from AF. *Adult:* Dose based on ECG response and CrCl. CrCl over 60 mL/min, 500 mcg PO bid; CrCl 40–60 mL/min, 250 mcg PO bid; CrCl 20–under 40 mL/min, 125 mcg PO bid; CrCl under 20 mL/min, use contraindicated.
ADJUST DOSE Renal impairment
ADV EFF Fatigue, dizziness, headache, **ventricular arrhythmias**
INTERACTIONS Antihistamines, cimetidine, ketoconazole, phenothiazines, TCAs, trimethoprim, verapamil; contraindicated w/amiodarone, disopyramide, procainamide, quinidine, sotalol
NC/PT Determine time of arrhythmia onset. Monitor ECG before and periodically during tx. Have pt in facility for continual monitoring and cardiac resuscitation for 3 days when beginning or reinitiating tx. Monitor serum creatinine before and q 3 mo during tx. Do not attempt cardioversion within 24 hr of starting tx. Pt should take bid at about same time each day, keep follow-up appointments, take safety precautions w/ CNS effects.

dolasetron mesylate (Anzemet)
CLASS Antiemetic, serotonin receptor blocker
PREG/CONT B/NA

IND & DOSE Px, tx of n/v associated w/emetogenic chemotherapy (oral only). *Adult:* 100 mg PO within 1 hr before chemotherapy. *Child 2–16 yr:* 1.8 mg/kg PO tablets or injection diluted in apple or apple-grape juice within 1 hr before chemotherapy. **Px, tx of postop n/v.** *Adult:* 100 mg PO within 2 hr before surgery, or 12.5 mg IV about 15 min before stopping anesthesia for px, or 12.5 mg IV as soon as needed for tx. *Child 2–16 yr:* 1.2 mg/kg PO tablets or injection diluted in apple or apple-grape juice within 2 hr before surgery, or 0.35 mg/kg IV about 15 min before stopping anesthesia for px, or 0.35 mg/kg IV as soon as needed for tx. Max, 12.5 mg/dose.

ADV EFF Fatigue, diarrhea, dizziness, headache, prolonged QT, serotonin syndrome, tachycardia

INTERACTIONS Anthracycline, QT-prolonging drugs, rifampin

NC/PT Do not use IV for chemotherapy-induced n/v. Monitor ECG before and regularly during tx. Pt should perform proper mouth care, use sugarless lozenges, use analgesics for headache, take safety precautions w/CNS effects.

---

dolutegravir (Tivicay)
CLASS Antiviral, integrase inhibitor
PREG/CONT B/NA

IND & DOSE Tx of HIV-1 infection in combination w/other antiretrovirals. *Adult, child 12 yr and older weighing at least 40 kg:* Treatment-naïve: 50 mg/day PO; treatment-naïve or experienced w/efavirenz, fosamprenavir/ritonavir, tipranavir/ritonavir, rifampin, or suspected resistance: 50 mg PO bid.

ADV EFF Abd pain, diarrhea, fat redistribution, headache, hepatotoxicity in pts w/hepatitis B or C, **hypersensitivity reactions,** insomnia, nausea

INTERACTIONS Antacids, buffered drugs, calcium supplements, efavirenz, fosamprenavir/ritonavir, iron supplements, laxatives, rifampin, sucralfate, tipranavir/ritonavir

NC/PT Screen for hepatitis B or C before tx. Must be given w/other antiretrovirals; give cation-containing drugs at least 2 hr before or 6 hr after dolutegravir. Pt should continue other HIV tx; space antacids apart from dosing; avoid pregnancy/breast-feeding; take precautions to avoid spread; not run out of prescription; report sx of infection, difficulty breathing, urine/stool color changes, rash.

---

donepezil hydrochloride (Aricept, Aricept ODT)
CLASS Alzheimer drug, anticholinesterase inhibitor
PREG/CONT C/NA

IND & DOSE Tx of Alzheimer-type dementia, including severe dementia. *Adult:* 5 mg/day PO at bedtime; may increase to 10 mg daily after 4–6 wk; 10 mg PO daily for severe disease. For severe disease, may use 23 mg/day after 10 mg/day for at least 3 mo.

ADV EFF Abd pain, anorexia, bradycardia, dyspepsia, fatigue, GI bleed, **hepatotoxicity,** insomnia, muscle cramps, n/v/d, rash

INTERACTIONS Anticholinergics, cholinesterase inhibitors, NMJ blockers, NSAIDs, theophylline

NC/PT Monitor hepatic function. Give at bedtime. Pt should place disintegrating tablet on tongue, allow to dissolve, then drink water; take safety precautions; report severe n/v/d. Name confusion between *Aricept* (donepezil) and *Aciphex* (rabeprazole); use caution.

DANGEROUS DRUG
DOPamine hydrochloride (generic)
CLASS Dopaminergic, sympathomimetic
PREG/CONT C/NA

BBW To prevent sloughing/necrosis after extravasation, infiltrate area w/10–15 mL saline containing 5–10 mg phentolamine as soon as possible after extravasation.

IND & DOSE Correction of hemodynamic imbalance, low cardiac output, hypotension. *Adult:* Pts likely to respond to modest increments of cardiac contractility and renal perfusion, 2–5 mcg/kg/min IV initially. More seriously ill pts, 5 mcg/kg/min IV initially. Increase in increments of 5–10 mcg/kg/min to rate of 20–50 mcg/kg/min.

ADV EFF Angina, dyspnea, ectopic beats, hypotension, n/v, palpitations, tachycardia

INTERACTIONS MAOIs, methyldopa, phenytoin, TCAs; do not mix in IV sol w/other drugs

NC/PT Use extreme caution in calculating doses. Base dosing on pt response. Give in large vein; avoid extravasation. Monitor urine output, cardiac output, BP during infusion. Name confusion between dopamine and dobutamine; use caution.

doripenem (Doribax)
CLASS Carbapenem antibiotic
PREG/CONT B/NA

IND & DOSE Tx of complicated intra-abdominal infections, UTIs caused by susceptible bacteria strains. *Adult:* 500 mg IV over 1 hr q 8 hr for 5–14 days (intra-abdominal infection) or 10 days (UTI, pyelonephritis).

ADJUST DOSE Renal impairment
ADV EFF Diarrhea including CDAD, headache, **hypersensitivity reactions,** increased risk of death in ventilator-associated bacterial pneumonia, nausea, phlebitis, rash, **seizures**
INTERACTIONS Probenecid, valproic acid
NC/PT Culture, sensitivity before tx. Monitor injection site for phlebitis. Not for use in pregnancy (barrier contraceptives advised)/breast-feeding. Monitor for CDAD. Provide supportive tx for up to 2 mo after tx ends. Pt

should report difficulty breathing, severe diarrhea.

dornase alfa (Pulmozyme)
CLASS Cystic fibrosis drug
PREG/CONT B/NA

IND & DOSE Mgt of cystic fibrosis to improve pulmonary function, w/ other drugs. *Adult, child:* 2.5 mg inhaled through recommended nebulizer; bid use beneficial to some.

ADV EFF Chest pain, laryngitis, pharyngitis, rash, rhinitis
NC/PT Assess respiratory function regularly. Store in refrigerator; not stable after 24 hr at room temp. Do not mix in nebulizer w/other drugs; review proper use of nebulizer. Pt should continue other drugs for cystic fibrosis.

doxapram hydrochloride (Dopram)
CLASS Analeptic, respiratory stimulant
PREG/CONT B/NA

IND & DOSE Stimulation of respiration in pts w/drug-induced postanesthesia respiratory depression. *Adult:* Single injection of 0.5–1 mg/kg IV; max, 1.5 mg/kg as total single injection or 2 mg/kg when given as multiple injections at 5-min intervals. **Tx of COPD associated acute hypercapnia.** *Adult:* Mix 400 mg in 180 mL IV infusion; start infusion at 1–2 mg/min (0.5–1 mL/min); no longer than 2 hr. Max, 3 mg/min. **Mgt of drug-induced CNS depression.** 1–2 mg/kg IV; repeat in 5 min. Repeat q 1–2 hr until pt awakens. Or, priming dose of 1–2 mg/kg IV; if no response, infuse 250 mg in 250 mL dextrose or saline sol at rate of 1–3 mg/min; discontinue after 2 hr if pt awakens; repeat in 30 min–2 hr if relapse occurs. Max, 3 g/day.

ADV EFF Bronchospasm, cough, hypertension, increased reflexes, **seizures**

INTERACTIONS Aminophylline, enflurane, halothane, MAOIs, muscle relaxants, sympathomimetics, theophylline

NC/PT Give IV only. Monitor for extravasation. Continuously monitor pt until fully awake. Discontinue if sudden hypotension, deterioration occur.

---

doxazosin mesylate
(Cardura, Cardura XL)
CLASS Antihypertensive, alpha-adrenergic blocker
PREG/CONT C/NA

IND & DOSE Tx of mild to moderate hypertension. *Adult:* 1 mg PO daily; maint, 2, 4, 8, or 16 mg PO daily. May increase q 2 wk. Do not use ER tablets. Tx of BPH. *Adult:* 1 mg PO daily; maint, 2, 4, 8 mg daily. Or, ER tablets, 4 mg PO once daily at breakfast. Max, 8 mg/day PO.
ADV EFF Diarrhea, dizziness, dyspepsia, edema, fatigue, headache, lethargy, nausea, orthostatic hypotension, palpitations, priapism, sexual dysfx, tachycardia
INTERACTIONS Alcohol, antihypertensives, nitrates, sildenafil
NC/PT Monitor pt carefully w/first dose; chance of orthostatic hypotension, dizziness, syncope greatest w/ first dose. Monitor for edema, BPH s&sx. Pt should swallow ER tablets whole and not cut, crush, or chew them, take safety precautions.

---

doxepin hydrochloride
(Silenor, Zonalon)
CLASS Antidepressant, TCA
PREG/CONT C/NA

BBW Increased risk of suicidality in children, adolescents, young adults; monitor carefully.
IND & DOSE Tx of mild to moderate anxiety, depression. *Adult:* 25 mg PO tid. Individualize dose; range, 75–150 mg/day. Tx of more severe anxiety, depression. *Adult:* 50 mg PO tid; max, 300 mg/day. Tx of mild sx or emotional sx accompanying organic disease. *Adult:* 25–50 mg PO. Tx of pruritus. *Adult:* Apply cream four times/day at least 3–4 hr apart for 8 days. Do not cover dressing. Tx of insomnia w/difficulty in sleep maintenance (*Silenor*). *Adult:* 3–6 mg PO 30 min before bed.
ADV EFF Anticholinergic effects, confusion, constipation, disturbed concentration, dry mouth, **MI**, orthostatic hypotension, photosensitivity, sedation, **stroke**, urine retention, withdrawal sx w/prolonged use
INTERACTIONS Alcohol, anticholinergics, barbiturates, cimetidine, clonidine, disulfiram, ephedrine, epinephrine, fluoxetine, furazolidone, hormonal contraceptives, levodopa, MAOIs, methylphenidate, nicotine, norepinephrine, phenothiazines, QT-prolonging drugs, thyroid medication
NC/PT Restrict drug access in depressed, suicidal pts. Give major portion at bedtime. Dilute oral concentrate w/approximately 120 mL water, milk, fruit juice just before administration. Pt should be aware of sedative effects (avoid driving, etc); not mix w/other sleep-inducing drugs, alcohol; avoid prolonged exposure to sun, sunlamps; report thoughts of suicide. Name confusion between *Sinequan* and saquinavir; use caution.

---

doxercalciferol
(Hectorol)
CLASS Vitamin D analogue
PREG/CONT B/NA

IND & DOSE To reduce parathyroid hormone in mgt of secondary hyperparathyroidism in pts undergoing chronic renal dialysis; secondary hyperparathyroidism in pts w/stage 3, 4 chronic kidney disease without dialysis. *Adult:* 10 mcg PO three times/wk at dialysis; max, 20 mcg

three times/wk. Without dialysis, 1 mcg/day PO; max, 3.5 mcg/day.
ADV EFF Dizziness, dyspnea, edema, headache, malaise, n/v
INTERACTIONS Cholestyramine, magnesium-containing antacids, mineral oil, phenothiazines, QT-prolonging drugs, thyroid medication
NC/PT Monitor for vitamin D toxicity. Give w/non-aluminum-containing phosphate binders. Monitor vitamin D levels predialysis.

DANGEROUS DRUG

DOXOrubicin hydrochloride (Doxil)

CLASS Antineoplastic
PREG/CONT D/NA

BBW Accidental substitution of liposomal form for conventional form has caused serious adverse reactions; check carefully before giving. Monitor for extravasation, burning, stinging. If these occur, discontinue; restart in another vein. For local subcut extravasation, local infiltration w/corticosteroid may be ordered. Flood area w/ normal saline; apply cold compress. If ulceration, arrange consult w/plastic surgeon. Monitor pt's response often at start of tx: serum uric acid, cardiac output (listen for S_3). CBC changes may require dose decrease; consult physician. Risk of HF, myelosuppression, liver damage. Record doses given to monitor total dosage; toxic effects often dose-related, as total dose approaches 550 mg/m².
IND & DOSE To produce regression in ALL, AML; Wilms' tumor; neuroblastoma; soft-tissue, bone sarcoma; breast, ovarian carcinoma; transitional cell bladder carcinoma; thyroid carcinoma; Hodgkin, non-Hodgkin lymphoma; bronchogenic carcinoma. *Adult:* 60–75 mg/m² as single IV injection given at 21-day intervals. Alternate schedule: 30 mg/m² IV on each of 3 successive days, repeated q 4 wk. **Tx of AIDS-related Kaposi sarcoma (liposomal form).**

Adult: 20 mg/m² IV q 3 wk starting w/ initial rate of 1 mg/min. **Tx of ovarian cancer that has progressed or recurred after platinum-based chemotherapy.** *Adult:* 50 mg/m² IV at 1 mg/min; if no adverse effects, complete infusion in 1 hr. Repeat q 4 wk.
ADJUST DOSE Elevated bilirubin
ADV EFF Anaphylaxis, **cardiotoxicity,** complete but reversible alopecia, hand-foot syndrome, hypersensitivity reactions, mucositis, myelosuppression, n/v, red urine
INTERACTIONS Digoxin
NC/PT Do not give IM or subcut. Monitor for extravasation. Ensure hydration. Not for use in pregnancy. Pt should report difficulty breathing, chest pain. Name confusion between conventional doxorubicin and liposomal doxorubicin; use caution.

---

doxycycline (Atridox, Doryx, Doxy 100, Oracea, Vibramycin)

CLASS Tetracycline
PREG/CONT D/NA

IND & DOSE Tx of infections caused by susceptible bacteria strains; tx of infections when penicillin contraindicated. *Adult, child over 8 yr, over 45 kg:* 200 mg IV in one or two infusions (each over 1–4 hr) on first tx day, then 100–200 mg/day IV, depending on infection severity. Or, 200 mg PO on day 1, then 100 mg/day PO. *Child over 8 yr, under 45 kg:* 4.4 mg/kg IV in one or two infusions, then 2.2–4.4 mg/kg/day IV in one or two infusions. Or, 4.4 mg/kg PO in two divided doses on first tx day, then 2.2–4.4 mg/kg/day on subsequent days. **Tx of rosacea.** *Adult:* 40 mg/day PO in a.m. on empty stomach w/full glass of water for up to 9 mo. **Tx of primary or secondary syphilis.** *Adult, child over 8 yr, over 45 kg:* 100 mg PO bid for 14 days. **Tx of acute gonococcal infection.** *Adult, child over 8 yr, over 45 kg:* 100 mg PO, then 100 mg at bedtime, then 100 mg

bid for 3 days. Or, 300 mg PO, then 300 mg in 1 hr. **Px of traveler's diarrhea.** *Adult, child over 8 yr, over 45 kg:* 100 mg/day PO. **Px of malaria.** *Adult, child over 8 yr, over 45 kg:* 100 mg PO daily. *Child over 8 yr, under 45 kg:* 2 mg/kg/day PO; max, 100 mg/day. **Px of anthrax.** *Adult, child over 8 yr, over 45 kg:* 100 mg PO bid for 60 days. *Child over 8 yr, under 45 kg:* 2.2 mg/kg PO bid for 60 days. **CDC recommendations for STDs.** *Adult, child over 8 yr, over 45 kg:* 100 mg PO bid for 7–28 days depending on disease. **Periodontal disease.** *Adult, child over 8 yr, over 45 kg:* 20 mg PO bid, after scaling, root planing. **Tx of Lyme disease.** *Child over 8 yr, less than 45 kg:* 2.2 mg/kg PO bid for 60 days or 100 mg PO bid for 14–21 days.
ADJUST DOSE Elderly pts, renal impairment
ADV EFF Anorexia, **bone marrow suppression, CDAD,** discoloring of teeth/inadequate bone calcification (of fetus when used during pregnancy, of child when used if under 8 yr), **exfoliative dermatitis,** glossitis, **hepatic failure,** hypertension, n/v/d, **phototoxic reactions,** rash, superinfections
INTERACTIONS Alkali, antacids, barbiturates, carbamazepine, dairy foods, digoxin, iron, penicillins, phenytoins
NC/PT Culture before tx. Give w/ food if GI upset severe. Not for use in pregnancy/breast-feeding. Pt should complete full course of therapy, avoid sun exposure, report severe diarrhea, urine/stool color changes.

---

dronabinol (delta-9-tetrahydrocannabinol, delta-9-THC) (Marinol)
CLASS Antiemetic, appetite suppressant
PREG/CONT C/C-III

IND & DOSE Tx of n/v associated w/ cancer chemotherapy. *Adult, child:* 5 mg/m² PO 1–3 hr before chemotherapy administration. Repeat q 2–4 hr after chemotherapy, for total of four to six doses/day. If 5 mg/m² ineffective and no significant side effects, increase by 2.5-mg/m² increments to max, 15 mg/m²/dose. **Tx of anorexia associated w/weight loss in pts w/ AIDS.** *Adult, child:* 2.5 mg PO bid before lunch and dinner. May reduce to 2.5 mg/day as single evening or bedtime dose; max, 10 mg PO bid (max not recommended for children).
ADV EFF Dependence w/use over 30 days, depression, dry mouth, dizziness, drowsiness, hallucinations, headache, heightened awareness, impaired coordination, irritability, sluggishness, unsteadiness, visual disturbances
INTERACTIONS Alcohol, anticholinergics, antihistamines, CNS depressants, dofetilide, ritonavir, TCAs
NC/PT Store capsules in refrigerator. Supervise pt during first use to evaluate CNS effects. Discontinue if psychotic reactions; warn pt about CNS effects. Pt should avoid marijuana (drug contains same active ingredient), take safety precautions for CNS effects, avoid alcohol and OTC sleeping aids.

---

dronedarone (Multaq)
CLASS Antiarrhythmic
PREG/CONT X/NA

BBW Contraindicated in pts w/ symptomatic HF, recent hospitalization for HF; doubles risk of death. Contraindicated in pts w/atrial fibrillation (AF) who cannot be cardioverted; doubles risk of death, stroke.
IND & DOSE To reduce risk of CV hospitalization in pts w/paroxysmal or persistent AF or atrial flutter w/ recent episode of either and associated CV risk factors who are in sinus rhythm or will be cardioverted. *Adult:* 400 mg PO bid w/a.m. and p.m. meal.
ADV EFF Asthenia, **HF,** hypokalemia, n/v/d, prolonged QT, rash, renal impairment, **serious hepatotoxicity, serious pulmonary toxicity, stroke**

INTERACTIONS Antiarrhythmics, beta blockers, calcium channel blockers, CYP3A inhibitors/inducers, digoxin, grapefruit juice, sirolimus, statins, St. John's wort, tacrolimus, warfarin
NC/PT Obtain baseline, periodic ECG. Do not use in pt w/permanent AF or serious HF. Monitor LFTs, pulmonary function, serum potassium during tx. Not for use in pregnancy/breast-feeding. Pt should avoid grapefruit juice, St. John's wort; keep complete list of all drugs and report use to all health care providers; comply w/frequent ECG monitoring; not make up missed doses; report difficulty breathing, rapid weight gain, extreme fatigue.

---

droperidol (generic)
CLASS General anesthetic
PREG/CONT C/NA

BBW May prolong QT; reserve use for pts unresponsive to other tx. Monitor pt carefully.
IND & DOSE To reduce n/v associated w/surgical procedures. *Adult:* 2.5 mg IM or IV. May use additional 1.2 mg w/caution. *Child 2–12 yr:* 0.1 mg/kg IM or IV.
ADJUST DOSE Renal, hepatic impairment
ADV EFF Chills, drowsiness, hallucinations, hypotension, **prolonged QT w/potentially fatal arrhythmias**, tachycardia
INTERACTIONS CNS depressants, opioids, QT-prolonging drugs
NC/PT Reserve use. Monitor ECG continually during tx and recovery. Pt should take safety precautions for CNS effects.

---

droxidopa (Northera)
CLASS Norepinephrine precursor
PREG/CONT C/NA

BBW Risk of supine hypertension. Raise head of bed to lessen effects; lower dose or discontinue drug if supine hypertension cannot be managed.
IND & DOSE Tx of orthostatic hypotension in adults w/neurogenic orthostatic hypotension caused by autonomic failure. *Adult:* 100 mg PO tid; titrate in 100-mg-tid segments to max 600 mg PO tid. Effectiveness beyond 2 wk is unkn.
ADJUST DOSE Renal impairment
ADV EFF Confusion, dizziness, **exacerbation of ischemic heart disease**, fatigue, fever, headache, hypertension, nausea, **supine hypertension**
INTERACTIONS Carbidopa, levodopa
NC/PT Monitor BP carefully; raise head of bed to decrease supine hypertension. Administer last dose at least 3 hr before bedtime. Pt should avoid breast-feeding; take safety precautions w/CNS changes; report drugs used for tx of Parkinson's disease, severe headache, chest pain, palpitations.

---

dulaglutide (Trulicity)
CLASS Antidiabetic, glucagonlike peptide-1 agonist
PREG/CONT C/NA

BBW Increased risk of thyroid C-cell cancer, medullary thyroid cancers. Contraindicated w/history of thyroid cancer or multiple endocrine neoplasia syndrome type 2.
IND & DOSE Adjunct to diet/exercise to improve glycemic control in pts w/type 2 diabetes. *Adult:* 0.75 mg subcut once/wk. May increase to 1.5 mg subcut once/wk if needed and tolerated.
ADV EFF Abd pain, hypoglycemia, hypersensitivity reactions, microvascular events, n/v/d, **pancreatitis**, renal impairment, **thyroid C-cell tumors**
INTERACTIONS Oral medications (slow GI emptying; may impact absorption)

NC/PT Ensure safe use of drug; screen for thyroid cancers. Teach proper subcut administration/disposal of needles/syringes. Not for use in pregnancy/breast-feeding. Monitor for hypoglycemia, dehydration. Pt should continue diet/exercise program; report serious diarrhea, difficulty breathing, lack of glycemic control.

duloxetine hydrochloride (Cymbalta)

CLASS Antidepressant, serotonin/norepinephrine reuptake inhibitor
PREG/CONT C/NA

BBW Monitor for increased depression (agitation, irritability, increased suicidality), especially at start of tx and dose change. Most likely in children, adolescents, young adults. Provide appropriate interventions, protection. Drug not approved for children.
IND & DOSE Tx of major depressive disorder. *Adult:* 20 mg PO bid; max, 120 mg/day. Allow at least 14 days if switching from MAOI, 5 days if switching to MAOI. Tx of generalized anxiety disorder. *Adult:* 60 mg/day PO; max, 120 mg/day. Tx of diabetic neuropathic pain. *Adult:* 60 mg/day PO as single dose. Tx of fibromyalgia; chronic musculoskeletal pain. *Adult:* 30 mg/day PO for 1 wk; then increase to 60 mg/day.
ADV EFF Constipation, diarrhea, dizziness, dry mouth, fatigue, **hepatotoxicity**, orthostatic hypotension, serotonin syndrome, sweating, urinary hesitancy
INTERACTIONS Alcohol, aspirin, flecainide, fluvoxamine, linezolid, lithium, MAOIs, NSAIDs, phenothiazines, propafenone, quinidine, SSRIs, St. John's wort, tramadol, TCAs, triptans, warfarin
NC/PT Not for use in pregnancy/breast-feeding. Taper when discontinuing. Pt should swallow capsules whole and not cut, crush, or chew them; avoid alcohol, St. John's wort; report thoughts of suicide; take safety precautions w/dizziness.

dutasteride (Avodart)

CLASS Androgen hormone inhibitor, BPH drug
PREG/CONT X/NA

IND & DOSE Tx of symptomatic BPH in men w/an enlarged prostate gland. *Adult:* 0.5 mg/day PO. W/tamsulosin, 0.5 mg/day PO w/tamsulosin 0.4. mg/day PO.
ADV EFF Decreased libido, enlarged breasts, GI upset
INTERACTIONS Cimetidine, ciprofloxacin, diltiazem, ketoconazole, ritonavir, saw palmetto, verapamil
NC/PT Assess to ensure BPH dx. Monitor prostate periodically. Pt should not father child and will not be able to donate blood during and for 6 mo after tx. Pregnant women should not handle capsule. Pt should swallow capsule whole and not cut, crush, or chew it; avoid saw palmetto.

dyphylline (Lufyllin, Lufyllin-400)

CLASS Bronchodilator, xanthine
PREG/CONT C/NA

IND & DOSE Symptomatic relief or px of bronchial asthma, reversible bronchospasm associated w/chronic bronchitis, emphysema. *Adult:* Up to 15 mg/kg PO q 6 hr.
ADJUST DOSE Elderly, impaired pts
ADV EFF Headache, insomnia, n/v/d, **seizures**
INTERACTIONS Benzodiazepines, beta blockers, caffeine, halothane, mexiletine, NMJs, probenecid
NC/PT Give around the clock. Pt should avoid excessive intake of caffeine-containing beverages, take w/food if GI effects severe.

ecallantide (Kalbitor)
CLASS Plasma kallikrein inhibitor
PREG/CONT C/NA

BBW Risk of severe anaphylaxis; have medical support on hand.
IND & DOSE Tx of acute attacks of hereditary angioedema. *Adult, child 12 yr and older:* 30 mg subcut as three 10-mg injections; may repeat once in 24 hr.
ADV EFF Anaphylaxis, fever, headache, injection-site reactions, nasopharyngitis, n/v/d
NC/PT Give only when able to provide medical support for anaphylaxis; not for self-administration. Not for use in pregnancy/breast-feeding. Pt should report difficulty breathing.

eculizumab (Soliris)
CLASS Complement inhibitor, monoclonal antibody
PREG/CONT C/NA

BBW Pt must have received meningococcal vaccine at least 2 wk before tx. Drug increases risk of infection; serious to fatal meningococcal infections have occurred. Monitor closely for early signs of meningitis.
IND & DOSE Tx of pts w/paroxysmal nocturnal hemoglobinuria to reduce hemolysis. *Adult:* 600 mg IV over 35 min q 7 days for first 4 wk, then 900 mg IV as fifth dose 7 days later, then 900 mg IV q 14 days. *Child under 18 yr:* Base dose on body weight; see manufacturer's recommendations. Tx of pts w/atypical hemolytic uremic syndrome to inhibit complement-mediated thrombotic microangiopathy. *Adult:* 900 mg IV over 35 min for first 4 wk, then 1,200 mg IV for fifth dose 1 wk later, then 1,200 mg IV q 2 wk.
ADV EFF Back pain, headache, hemolysis, hypertension, **meningococcal infections**, nasopharyngitis, n/v/d, UTI

NC/PT Monitor for s&sx of meningococcal infection. Stopping drug can cause serious hemolysis. Must monitor pt for 8 wk after stopping; inform pt of risk for meningococcal infections. Not for use in pregnancy/breast-feeding. Pt should wear medical alert tag; report s&sx of infection.

edetate calcium disodium (Calcium Disodium Versenate)
CLASS Antidote
PREG/CONT B/NA

BBW Reserve use for serious conditions requiring aggressive therapy; serious toxicity possible.
IND & DOSE Tx of acute/chronic lead poisoning, lead encephalopathy. *Adult, child:* For blood levels 20–70 mcg/dL, 1,000 mg/m²/day IV or IM for 5 days. Interrupt tx for 2–4 days; follow w/another 5 days of tx if indicated. For blood levels higher than 70 mcg/dL, combine w/dimercaprol.
ADV EFF Electrolyte imbalance, headache, n/v/d, orthostatic hypotension
INTERACTIONS Zinc insulin
NC/PT Give IM or IV. Avoid excess fluids w/encephalopathy. Establish urine flow by IV infusion before tx. Monitor BUN, electrolytes. Keep pt supine for short period after tx to prevent orthostatic hypotension. Pt should prepare calendar of tx days.

DANGEROUS DRUG

edoxaban (Savaysa)
CLASS Anticoagulant, direct thrombin inhibitor
PREG/CONT C/NA

BBW Premature discontinuation increases risk of thrombotic events; consider coverage w/another anticoagulant if discontinued for reasons other than pathological bleeding. Risk of epidural/spinal hematomas if used in pts w/spinal puncture of anesthesia. Reduced efficacy w/renal impairment.

IND & DOSE Reduction of stroke, embolism in pts w/nonvalvular atrial fibrillation; tx of DVT, PE. *Adult:* 60 mg/day PO. Not recommended in hepatic impairment.

ADV EFF Bleeding, rebound thrombotic events w/discontinuation, severe hypersensitivity reactions

INTERACTIONS Carbamazepine, clarithromycin, itraconazole, ketoconazole, other drugs that increase bleeding, phenytoin, rifampin, ritonavir, St. John's wort

NC/PT Not for use w/artificial heart valves. Monitor for bleeding. Pt should avoid pregnancy/breast-feeding, OTC drugs that affect bleeding; not stop drug suddenly; take safety precautions to avoid injury; report increased bleeding, chest pain, headache, dizziness.

edrophonium chloride (Enlon)

CLASS Anticholinesterase, antidote, diagnostic agent, muscle stimulant
PREG/CONT C/NA

IND & DOSE Differential dx, adjunct in evaluating myasthenia gravis tx. *Adult:* Inject 10 mg IM. May retest w/2 mg IM after 30 min to rule out false-negative results. Or, 10 mg drawn into tuberculin syringe w/IV needle. Inject 2 mg IV in 15–30 sec; leave needle in vein. If no reaction after 45 sec, inject remaining 8 mg. May repeat test after 30 min. *Child over 34 kg:* 2 mg IV or 5 mg IM. *Child 34 kg or less:* 1 mg IV or 2 mg IM. *Infants:* 0.5 mg IV. **Evaluation of myasthenia gravis tx.** *Adult:* 1–2 mg IV 1 hr after oral intake of edrophonium. Response determines effectiveness of tx. **Edrophonium test in crisis.** *Adult:* Secure controlled respiration immediately if pt apneic, then give test. If pt in cholinergic crisis, giving edrophonium will increase oropha-

ryngeal secretions and further weaken respiratory muscles. If crisis myasthenic, giving edrophonium will improve respiration, and pt can be treated w/longer-acting IV anticholinesterases. To give test, draw up no more than 2 mg into syringe. Give 1 mg IV initially. Carefully observe cardiac response. If after 1 min dose does not further impair pt, inject remaining 1 mg. If after 2-mg dose no clear improvement in respiration, discontinue all anticholinesterases; control ventilation by tracheostomy, assisted respiration. **Antidote for NMJ blockers.** *Adult:* 10 mg IV slowly over 30–45 sec so that onset of cholinergic reaction can be detected; repeat when necessary. Max, 40 mg.

ADV EFF Abd cramps; **anaphylaxis;** bradycardia; **cardiac arrest;** cardiac arrhythmias; dysphagia; increased lacrimation, pharyngeal/tracheobronchial secretions; salivation; miosis; urinary frequency/incontinence

INTERACTIONS Corticosteroids, succinylcholine

NC/PT Give slowly IV; have atropine sulfate on hand as antidote and antagonist to severe reaction. Testing can frighten pt; offer support, explain procedure.

efavirenz (Sustiva)

CLASS Antiviral, nonnucleoside reverse transcriptase inhibitor
PREG/CONT D/NA

IND & DOSE Tx of HIV/AIDS w/other antiretrovirals. *Adult:* 600 mg/day PO w/protease inhibitor or other nucleoside reverse transcriptase inhibitor. In combination w/voriconazole 400 mg PO q 12 hr: 300 mg/day efavirenz PO. *Child 3 mo and older:* 40 kg or more, 600 mg/day PO; 32.5–under 40 kg, 400 mg/day PO; 25–under 32.5 kg, 350 mg/day PO; 20–under 25 kg, 300 mg/day PO; 15–under 20 kg, 250 mg/day PO; 10–under 15 kg, 200 m/day P; 5–under 10 kg,

150 mg/day PO; 3.5–under 5 kg, 100 mg/day PO.

ADJUST DOSE Hepatic impairment
ADV EFF Asthenia, body fat redistribution, CNS sx, dizziness, drowsiness, headache, hepatotoxicity, hyperlipidemia, n/v/d, rash to **Stevens-Johnson syndrome**
INTERACTIONS Alcohol, cisapride, ergot derivatives, hepatotoxic drugs, indinavir, methadone, midazolam, pimozide, rifabutin, rifampin, ritonavir, saquinavir, St. John's wort, triazolam, voriconazole
NC/PT Blood test needed q 2 wk. Ensure drug part of combination therapy. Monitor all drugs taken; many interactions possible. Give at bedtime for first 2–4 wk to minimize CNS effects. Monitor LFTs, lipids. Not for use in pregnancy/breast-feeding. Not a cure; pt should use precautions. Pt should swallow forms whole and not cut, crush, or chew them; avoid alcohol; report all drugs/herbs taken (including St. John's wort) to health care provider; seek regular medical care; report rash, urine/stool color changes.

---

efinaconazole (Jublia)
CLASS Azole antifungal
PREG/CONT C/NA

IND & DOSE Topical tx of toenail onychomycosis. *Adult:* Apply to toenail once daily using flow-through brush applicator for 48 wk.
ADV EFF Application-site dermatitis/vesicles/pain, ingrown toenails
NC/PT For external use only. Pt should completely cover entire toenail, toenail folds, toenail bed, undersurface of toenail plate; apply to clean, dry nails; avoid nail polish; avoid using near heat or open flame (drug is flammable); report s&sx of infection.

---

eletriptan hydrobromide (Relpax)
CLASS Antimigraine, triptan
PREG/CONT C/NA

IND & DOSE Tx of acute migraine w/or without aura. *Adult:* 20–40 mg PO. If headache improves, then returns, may give second dose after at least 2 hr. Max, 80 mg/day.
ADV EFF Hypertension, hypertonia, hypoesthesia, **MI**, pharyngitis, **serotonin syndrome**, sweating, vertigo
INTERACTIONS Clarithromycin, ergots, itraconazole, ketoconazole, nefazodone, nelfinavir, ritonavir, SSRIs, other triptans
NC/PT Tx only; not for migraine px. No more than two doses in 24 hr. Closely monitor BP w/known CAD; stop if s&sx of angina, peripheral vascular obstruction. Not for use in pregnancy. Pt should take safety precautions for CNS effects, maintain usual measures for migraine relief.

---

eliglustat (Cerdelga)
CLASS Glucosylceramide synthase inhibitor
PREG/CONT C/NA

IND & DOSE Long-term tx of pts w/Gaucher disease type 1 who are extensive, intermediate, or poor CYP2D6 metabolizers. *Adult:* 84 mg PO bid in extensive/intermediate metabolizers, 85 mg/day PO in poor metabolizers.
ADJUST DOSE Renal/hepatic impairment
ADV EFF Arrhythmias, back pain, fatigue, headache, n/v/d, pain, prolonged QT
INTERACTIONS CYP2D6 inhibitors/inducers, grapefruit juice, QT-prolonging drugs
NC/PT Monitor for cardiac disease before tx, then periodically. Test metabolizer status per FDA-cleared test. Check drug regimens; many interactions possible. Not for use in

pregnancy/breast-feeding. Pt should swallow capsule whole and not cut, crush, or chew it; avoid grapefruit juice; report chest pain, palpitations, severe GI s&sx.

elosulfase alfa (Vimizim)
CLASS Enzyme
PREG/CONT C/NA

BBW Risk of life-threatening anaphylaxis, hypersensitivity reaction. Monitor pt closely; be prepared to deal w/anaphylaxis. Pts w/acute respiratory illness at risk for life-threatening pulmonary complications; delay use w/respiratory illness.
IND & DOSE Tx of mucopolysaccharidosis type IVA (Morquio A syndrome). *Adult, child 5 yr and over:* 2 mg/kg IV infused over 3.5–4.5 hr once a wk.
ADV EFF Abd pain, chills, fatigue, fever, **headache, hypersensitivity reaction,** respiratory complications, vomiting
NC/PT Pretreat w/antihistamines, antipyretic 30–60 min before infusion. Slow or stop infusion if sx of hypersensitivity reaction. Use cautiously in pregnancy/breast-feeding. Pt should report difficulty breathing, cough, rash, chest pain.

elotuzumab (Empliciti)
CLASS Immunostimulatory antibody
PREG/CONT Unkn/NA

IND & DOSE Tx of multiple myeloma in pts who have received one to three prior therapies. *Adult:* 10 mg/kg IV q wk for two cycles, then every 2 wk until progression, given w/lenalidomide, dexamethasone.
ADV EFF Constipation, cough, diarrhea, fatigue, fever, **hepatotoxicity,** infections, **infusion reactions, malignancy**
NC/PT Ensure dx. Give w/lenalidomide, dexamethasone. Premedicate

w/dexamethasone, diphenhydramine, ranitidine, acetaminophen. Monitor for infusion reactions; interrupt infusion or discontinue if severe. Monitor liver function. Assess for infection, other malignancies. Pt should avoid pregnancy/breast-feeding (other drugs have high risk); report difficulty breathing, rash, fever, flulike sx, urine/stool color changes.

eltrombopag (Promacta)
CLASS Thrombopoietin receptor agonist
PREG/CONT C/NA

BBW Risk of severe to fatal hepatotoxicity w/interferon, ribavirin. Monitor LFTs closely; adjust dose or discontinue as needed.
IND & DOSE Tx of chronic immune idiopathic thrombocytopenic purpura in pts unresponsive to usual tx. *Adult, child 6 yr and over:* 50–75 mg/day PO. Start Eastern Asian pts at 25 mg/day. *Child 1–5 yr:* 25 mg/day PO. Tx of hepatitis C–associated thrombocytopenia. *Adult:* 25 mg/day PO; max, 100 mg/day. Tx of severe aplastic anemia after no response to immunosuppressants. *Adult:* 50 mg/day PO; max, 150 mg
ADJUST DOSE Moderate hepatic failure, pts of East Asian ancestry
ADV EFF Back pain, **bone marrow fibrosis,** cataracts, headache, **hepatotoxicity,** n/v/d, pharyngitis, **thrombotic events,** URI, UTI
INTERACTIONS Antacids, dairy products, oral anticoagulants, statins
NC/PT Do not give within 4 hr of antacids, dairy products. Monitor CBC, LFTs regularly for safety, dose adjustment. Target platelets at 50 × 10⁹/L or more. Not for use w/blood cancers; worsening possible. Monitor for cataracts, vision changes. Not for use in pregnancy/breast-feeding. Pt should take on empty stomach, 1 hr before or 2 hr after meals; report chest pain, bleeding, yellowing of eyes, skin.

eluxadoline (Viberzi)
CLASS Antidiarrheal, mu-opiod receptor agonist
PREG/CONT Low risk/NA

IND & DOSE Tx of IBS w/diarrhea.
Adult: 75–100 mg PO bid.
ADJUST DOSE Hepatic impairment
ADV EFF Abd pain, acute biliary pain, constipation, n/v, pancreatitis
NC/PT Ensure proper use; not for use w/biliary obstruction, alcoholism, hx of pancreatitis, sever hepatic impairment, severe constipation, GI obstruction. Stop if severe constipation for over 4 days occurs. Monitor pancreatic and liver enzymes. Pt should report constipation, severe abd pain.

empagliflozin (Jardiance)
CLASS Antidiabetic, sodium-glucose cotransporter 2 inhibitor
PREG/CONT C/NA

IND & DOSE Adjunct to diet/exercise to improve glycemic control in pts w/type 2 diabetes.
Adult: 10 mg/day PO in a.m.; max, 25 mg/day.
ADJUST DOSE Severe renal impairment
ADV EFF Dehydration, diabetic ketoacidosis, genital mycotic infections, hypoglycemia, hyponatremia, hypotension, increased LDLs, **renal impairment**, UTI
INTERACTIONS Celery, coriander, dandelion root, digoxin, fenugreek, garlic, ginger, juniper berries, phenobarbital, phenytoin, rifampin
NC/PT Not for use w/type 1 diabetes or ketoacidosis. Monitor blood glucose, HbA$_{1c}$, BP periodically. Not for use in pregnancy/breast-feeding. Pt should continue diet/exercise program, other antidiabetics as ordered; take safety measures w/dehydration; monitor for UTI, genital infections.

emtricitabine (Emtriva)
CLASS Antiviral, nucleoside reverse transcriptase inhibitor
PREG/CONT B/NA

BBW Use caution w/current/suspected hepatitis B; serious disease resurgence possible. Withdraw drug, monitor pt w/sx of lactic acidosis or hepatotoxicity, including hepatomegaly, steatosis.
IND & DOSE Tx of HIV-1 infection w/other antiretrovirals. *Adult:* 200 mg/day PO or 240 mg (24 mL) oral sol/day PO. *Child 3 mo–17 yr:* 6 mg/kg/day PO to max 240 mg (24 mL) oral sol. For child over 33 kg able to swallow capsule, one 200-mg capsule/day PO. *Child under 3 mo:* 3 mg/kg/day oral sol PO.
ADJUST DOSE Renal impairment
ADV EFF Abd pain, asthenia, cough, dizziness, headache, immune reconstitution syndrome, insomnia, **lactic acidosis**, n/v/d, rash, redistribution of body fat, rhinitis, **severe hepatomegaly w/steatosis**
INTERACTIONS Atripla, lamivudine, Truvada; contraindicated
NC/PT HIV antibody testing before tx. Monitor LFTs, renal function regularly. Ensure use w/other antiretrovirals. Not for use in pregnancy/breast-feeding. Not a cure; pt should use precautions. Pt should try to maintain nutrition, hydration (GI effects will occur); report difficulty breathing, unusual muscle pain, dizziness, unusual heartbeat.

enalapril maleate (Epaned, Vasotec), enalaprilat (generic)
CLASS ACE inhibitor, antihypertensive
PREG/CONT D/NA

BBW Possible serious fetal injury or death if used in second, third trimesters; advise contraceptive use.

IND & DOSE Tx of hypertension.
Adult: Initially, 5 mg/day PO; range,
10–40 mg/day. Discontinue diuretics
for 2–3 days before tx; if not possible,
start w/2.5 mg/day PO or 1.25 mg IV
q 6 hr; monitor pt response. If on diuretics, 0.625 mg IV over 5 min; repeat in 1 hr if needed, then 1.25 mg IV
q 6 hr. *Child 2 mo–16 yr:* 0.08 mg/kg
PO once daily; max, 5 mg. **Tx of HF.**
Adult: 2.5 mg/day PO or bid w/diuret-
ics, digitalis; max, 40 mg/day. **Tx of
asymptomatic left ventricular dysfx.**
Adult: 2.5 mg PO bid; target dose,
20 mg/day in two divided doses.
ADJUST DOSE Elderly pts, renal
impairment, HF
ADV EFF Anaphylaxis, angioedema,
cough; decreased Hct, Hgb; diarrhea;
dizziness; fatigue; hyperkalemia, **renal
failure**
INTERACTIONS ARBs, ACE inhibitors, indomethacin, lithium, NSAIDs,
renin inhibitors, rifampin
NC/PT Adjust dose if pt also on diuretic. Peak effect may not occur for
4 hr. Monitor BP before giving second
dose; monitor closely in situations
that might lead to BP drop. Monitor
potassium, renal function. Mark chart
if surgery required; pt may need fluid
support. Not for use in pregnancy
(contraceptives advised). Pt should
take safety precautions w/CNS
effects.

---

enfuvirtide (Fuzeon)
CLASS Anti-HIV drug, fusion
inhibitor
PREG/CONT B/NA

IND & DOSE Tx of HIV-1 infection
in tx-experienced pts w/evidence of
HIV-1 replication despite ongoing
tx, w/other antiretrovirals. *Adult:*
90 mg bid by subcut injection into upper arm, anterior thigh, or abdomen.
Child 6–16 yr: 2 mg/kg bid by subcut
injection; max, 90 mg/dose into upper arm, anterior thigh, or abdomen.

ADV EFF Dizziness, hypersensitivity
reactions, injection-site reactions,
n/v/d, **pneumonia**
NC/PT Ensure pt also on other antiretrovirals; rotate injection sites
(upper arm, anterior thigh, abdomen).
Reconstitute only w/sol provided. Refrigerate reconstituted sol; use within
24 hr. Not for use in pregnancy/
breast-feeding. Not a cure; pt should
use precautions. Teach pt proper
administration/disposal of needles/
syringes. Pt should report difficulty
breathing, unusual breathing.

DANGEROUS DRUG

enoxaparin (Lovenox)
CLASS Low-molecular-weight
heparin
PREG/CONT B/NA

BBW Increased risk of spinal hematoma, neurologic damage if used
w/spinal/epidural anesthesia. If must
be used, monitor pt closely.
IND & DOSE Px of DVT after hip,
knee replacement surgery. *Adult:*
30 mg subcut bid, w/initial dose
12–24 hr after surgery. Continue for
7–10 days; then may give 40 mg daily
subcut for up to 3 wk. **Px of DVT after
abd surgery.** *Adult:* 40 mg/day subcut begun within 2 hr before surgery,
continued for 7–10 days. **Px of DVT in
high-risk pts.** 40 mg/day subcut for
6–11 days; has been used up to
14 days. **Px of ischemic complications of unstable angina and non-
Q-wave MI.** *Adult:* 1 mg/kg subcut
q 12 hr for 2–8 days. **Tx of DVT.** *Adult:*
1 mg/kg subcut q 12 hr (for outpts);
1.5 mg/kg subcut or 1 mg/kg
subcut q 12 hr (for inpts). **Tx of MI.**
Adult: 75 yr and older, 0.75 mg/kg
subcut q 12 hr (max, 75 mg for first
two doses only). Under 75 yr, 30-mg
IV bolus plus 1 mg/kg subcut followed by 1 mg/kg subcut q 12 hr
w/aspirin (max, 100 mg for first two
doses only).
ADJUST DOSE Renal impairment

ADV EFF Bruising, chills, fever, **hemorrhage**, injection-site reactions, thrombocytopenia

INTERACTIONS Aspirin, cephalosporins, chamomile, garlic, ginger, ginkgo, ginseng, high-dose vitamin E, NSAIDs, penicillins, oral anticoagulants, salicylates

NC/PT Give as soon as possible after hip surgery, within 12 hr of knee surgery, and within 2 hr preop for abd surgery. Use deep subcut injection, not IM; alternate sites. Do not mix w/ other injections or sols. Store at room temp. Have protamine sulfate on hand as antidote. Check for s&sx of bleeding; protect pt from injury. Teach pt proper administration/disposal of needles/syringes.

---

entacapone (Comtan)

CLASS Antiparkinsonian
PREG/CONT C/NA

IND & DOSE Adjunct w/levodopa/carbidopa in tx of s&sx of idiopathic Parkinson's disease in pts experiencing "wearing off" of drug effects. *Adult:* 200 mg PO concomitantly w/levodopa/carbidopa; max, eight times/day.

ADV EFF Confusion, disorientation, dizziness, dry mouth, dyskinesia, falling asleep during activities of daily living, **fever, hallucinations,** hyperkinesia, hypotension, loss of impulse control, n/v, orthostatic hypotension, renal impairment, **rhabdomyolysis,** somnolence

INTERACTIONS Ampicillin, apomorphine, chloramphenicol, cholestyramine, dobutamine, dopamine, epinephrine, erythromycin, isoetharine, isoproterenol, MAOIs, methyldopa, norepinephrine, rifampin

NC/PT Give only w/levodopa/carbidopa; do not give within 14 days of MAOIs. Not for use in pregnancy (contraceptives used)/breast-feeding. Pt should use sugarless lozenges for dry mouth, take safety precautions w/CNS effects.

---

entecavir (Baraclude)

CLASS Antiviral, nucleoside analogue
PREG/CONT C/NA

BBW Withdraw drug, monitor pt if s&sx of lactic acidosis or hepatotoxicity, including hepatomegaly and steatosis. Do not use in pts w/HIV unless pt receiving highly active antiretroviral tx, because of high risk of HIV resistance. Offer HIV testing to all pts before starting entecavir. Severe, acute hepatitis B exacerbations have occurred in pts who discontinue antihepatitis B tx. Monitor pts for several mo after drug cessation; restarting antihepatitis tx may be warranted.

IND & DOSE Tx of chronic hepatitis B infection in pts w/evidence of active viral replication and active disease. *Adult, child 16 yr and older w/no previous nucleoside tx:* 0.5 mg/day PO on empty stomach at least 2 hr after meal or 2 hr before next meal. *Adult, child 16 yr and older w/hx of viremia also receiving lamivudine w/known resistance mutations:* 1 mg/day PO on empty stomach at least 2 hr after meal or 2 hr before next meal. *Child 2 yr and older at least 10 kg:* Dosage based on weight.

ADJUST DOSE Hepatic/renal impairment

ADV EFF Acute exacerbation of hepatitis B when discontinuing, **dizziness, fatigue, headache, lactic acidosis,** nausea, **severe hepatomegaly**

INTERACTIONS Nephrotoxic drugs

NC/PT Assess renal function regularly. Give on empty stomach at least 2 hr after meal or 2 hr before next meal. Not a cure; pt should take precautions. Not for use in pregnancy/breast-feeding. Pt should not run out of or stop drug suddenly (severe hepatitis possible), should take safety precautions w/dizziness, report unusual muscle pain.

enzalutamide (Xtandi)

CLASS Androgen receptor inhibitor, antineoplastic
PREG/CONT X/NA

IND & DOSE Tx of metastatic castration-resistant prostate cancer in pts previously on docetaxel. *Adult:* 160 mg/day PO once daily.
ADV EFF Arthralgia, asthenia, anxiety, back pain, diarrhea, dizziness, edema, flushing, headache, hematuria, hypertension, paresthesia, **RPLS, seizures,** weakness
INTERACTIONS Midazolam, omeprazole, pioglitazone, warfarin; avoid concurrent use. Gemfibrozil
NC/PT Monitor for CNS reactions; provide safety precautions. Not for use in pregnancy. Pt should swallow capsule whole and not cut, crush, or chew it; use caution w/CNS effects; report falls, severe headache, problems thinking clearly.

DANGEROUS DRUG

ephedrine sulfate (generic)

CLASS Bronchodilator, sympathomimetic, vasopressor
PREG/CONT C/NA

IND & DOSE Tx of hypotensive episodes, allergic disorders. *Adult:* 25–50 mg IM (fast absorption) or subcut (slower absorption), or 5–25 mg IV slowly; may repeat in 5–10 min. *Child:* 0.5 mg/kg or 16.7 mg/m² IM or subcut q 4–6 hr. Tx of acute asthma, allergic disorders. *Adult:* 12.5–25 mg PO q 4 hr.
ADJUST DOSE Elderly pts
ADV EFF Anxiety, **CV collapse w/ hypotension,** dizziness, dysuria, fear, **hypertension resulting in intracranial hemorrhage,** pallor, **palpitations, precordial pain in pts w/ischemic heart disease,** restlessness, **tachycardia,** tenseness
INTERACTIONS Caffeine, ephedra, guarana, ma huang, MAOIs,

methyldopa, TCAs, urinary acidifiers/alkalinizers
NC/PT Protect sol from light. Give only if sol clear; discard unused portion. Monitor CV status, urine output. Avoid prolonged systemic use. Pt should avoid OTC products w/similar action, take safety precautions w/CNS effects.

DANGEROUS DRUG

epinephrine bitartrate, epinephrine hydrochloride (Adrenaclick, AsthmaNefrin, EpiPen)

CLASS Antiasthmatic, cardiac stimulant, sympathomimetic, vasopressor
PREG/CONT C/NA

IND & DOSE Tx in cardiac arrest. *Adult:* 0.5–1 mg (5–10 mL of 1:10,000 sol) IV during resuscitation, 0.5 mg q 5 min. Intracardiac injection into left ventricular chamber, 0.3–0.5 mg (3–5 mL of 1:10,000 sol). Hypersensitivity, bronchospasm. *Adult:* 0.1–0.25 mg (1–2.5 mL of 1:10,000 sol) injected slowly IV or 0.2–1 mL of 1:1,000 sol subcut or IM, or 0.1–0.3 mL (0.5–1.5 mg) of 1:200 sol subcut. *Child:* 1:1,000 sol, 0.01 mg/kg or 0.3 mL/m² (0.01 mg/kg or 0.3 mg/m²) subcut. Repeat q 4 hr if needed; max, 0.5 mL (0.5 mg) in single dose. For neonates, 0.01 mg/kg subcut; for infants, 0.05 mg/kg subcut as initial dose. Repeat q 20–30 min as needed. *Child 30 kg or less:* 1:10,000 sol, 0.15 mg or 0.01 mg/kg by autoinjector. Temporary relief from acute attacks of bronchial asthma, COPD. *Adult, child 4 yr and older:* 1 inhalation, wait 1 min, then may use once more. Do not repeat for at least 3 hr. Or, place not more than 10 drops into nebulizer reservoir, place nebulizer nozzle into partially opened mouth, have pt inhale deeply while bulb is squeezed one to three times (not more than q 3 hr).
ADJUST DOSE Elderly pts

ADV EFF Anxiety, **CV collapse w/ hypotension**, dizziness, dysuria, fear, **hypertension resulting in intracranial hemorrhage**, pallor, **palpitations, precordial pain in pts w/ischemic heart disease**, restlessness, **tachycardia**, tenseness

INTERACTIONS Beta blockers, chlorpromazine, ephedra, guarana, ma huang, methyldopa, propranolol, TCAs

NC/PT Use extreme caution when calculating doses; small margin of safety. Protect sol from light, heat. Rotate subcut injection sites. Have alpha-adrenergic blocker on hand for hypertensive crises/pulmonary edema, beta blocker on hand for cardiac arrhythmias. Do not exceed recommended dose of inhalants. Pt should take safety precautions w/CNS effects.

DANGEROUS DRUG

epirubicin hydrochloride (Ellence)
CLASS Antineoplastic antibiotic
PREG/CONT D/NA

BBW Cardiotoxicity possible; monitor ECG closely. Severe tissue necrosis w/extravasation. Secondary acute myelogenous leukemia possible. Reduce dose in hepatic impairment. Monitor for severe bone marrow suppression.

IND & DOSE Adjunct tx in pts w/ evidence of axillary node tumor involvement after resection of primary breast cancer. *Adult:* 100–120 mg/m² IV in repeated 3- to 4-wk cycles, all on day 1; given w/cyclophosphamide and 5-FU.

ADJUST DOSE Elderly pts; hepatic, severe renal impairment

ADV EFF Alopecia, **bone marrow suppression, HF**, infection, **leukemia**, local injection-site toxicity/rash, n/v/d, **renal toxicity, thromboembolic events**

INTERACTIONS Cardiotoxic drugs, cimetidine, live vaccines

NC/PT Monitor baseline and periodic ECG to evaluate for toxicity.

Premedicate w/antiemetic. Monitor injection site carefully. Monitor CBC regularly; dose adjustment may be needed. Not for use in pregnancy/ breast-feeding. Pt should mark calendar of tx dates.

---

eplerenone (Inspra)
CLASS Aldosterone receptor blocker, antihypertensive
PREG/CONT B/NA

IND & DOSE Tx of hypertension. *Adult:* 50 mg/day PO as single dose; may increase to 50 mg PO bid after minimum 4-wk trial period. Max, 100 mg/day. **Tx of HF post-MI.** *Adult:* Initially, 25 mg/day PO; titrate to 50 mg/day over 4 wk. If serum potassium lower than 5, increase dose; if 5–5.4, no adjustment needed; if 5.5–5.9, decrease dose; if 6 or higher, withhold dose.

ADJUST DOSE Hyperkalemia, renal impairment

ADV EFF Dizziness, gynecomastia, headache, **hyperkalemia, MI**

INTERACTIONS ACE inhibitors, amiloride, ARBs, NSAIDs, spironolactone, triamterene; serious reactions w/erythromycin, fluconazole, itraconazole, ketoconazole, lithium, renin inhibitors, saquinavir, verapamil

NC/PT Monitor potassium, renal function; suggest limiting potassium-rich foods. Not for use in pregnancy/ breast-feeding. Pt should avoid OTC drugs that might interact; weigh self daily, report changes of 3 lb or more/ day.

---

epoetin alfa (EPO, erythropoietin) (Epogen, Procrit)
CLASS Recombinant human erythropoietin
PREG/CONT C/NA

BBW Increased risk of death, serious CV events if Hgb target is over 11 g/dL. Use lowest levels of drug needed to increase Hgb to lowest level needed to avoid transfusion. Incidence of DVT higher in pts receiving erythropoietin-stimulating agents preop to reduce need for transfusion; consider antithrombotic px if used for this purpose. Pts w/cancer at risk for more rapid tumor progression, shortened survival, death when Hgb target is over 11 g/dL. Increased risk of death in cancer pts not receiving radiation or chemotherapy.

IND & DOSE Tx of anemia of chronic renal failure. *Adult:* 50–100 units/kg three times/wk IV for dialysis pts, IV or subcut for nondialysis pts. Maint, 75–100 units/kg three times/wk. If on dialysis, median dose is 75 units/kg three times/wk. Target Hgb range, 10–11 g/dL. *Child 1 mo–16 yr:* 50 units/kg IV or subcut three times/wk.

Tx of anemia in HIV-infected pts on AZT therapy. *Adult:* For pts receiving AZT dose of 4,200 mg/wk or less w/serum erythropoietin levels of 500 milliunits/mL or less, 100 units/kg IV or subcut three times/wk for 8 wk.

Tx of anemia in cancer pts on chemotherapy (*Procrit* only). *Adult:* 150 units/kg subcut three times/wk or 40,000 units subcut wkly. After 8 wk, can increase to 300 units/kg or 60,000 units subcut wkly. *Child 1 mo–16 yr:* 600 units/kg per wk IV; max, 60,000 units/dose in child 5 yr and older. To reduce allogenic blood transfusions in surgery. *Adult:* 300 units/kg/day subcut for 10 days before surgery, on day of surgery, and 4 days after surgery. Or, 600 units/kg/day subcut 21, 14, and 7 days before surgery and on day of surgery. Tx of anemia of prematurity. *Child:* 25–100 units/kg/dose IV three times/wk.

ADV EFF Arthralgia, asthenia, chest pain, **development of anti-erythropoietin antibodies**, dizziness, edema, fatigue, headache, hypertension, n/v/d, **seizures, stroke, thrombotic events, tumor progression/ shortened survival (w/cancers)**

NC/PT Confirm nature of anemia. Do not give in sol w/other drugs. Monitor access lines for clotting. Monitor Hgb (target range, 10–11 g/dL; max, 11 g/dL). Evaluate iron stores before and periodically during tx; supplemental iron may be needed. Monitor for sudden loss of response and severe anemia w/low reticulocyte count; withhold drug and check for anti-erythropoietin antibodies. Must give subcut three times/wk. Pt should keep blood test appointments to monitor response to drug, report difficulty breathing, chest pain, severe headache.

---

epoprostenol sodium
(Flolan, Veletri)
CLASS Prostaglandin
PREG/CONT B/NA

IND & DOSE Tx of primary pulmonary hypertension in pts unresponsive to standard tx. *Adult:* 2 ng/kg/min IV w/increases of 1–2 ng/kg at at least 15-min intervals as tolerated through infusion pump using central line; 20–40 ng/kg/min common range after 6 mo.

ADV EFF Anxiety, agitation, bleeding, chest pain, flushing, headache, hypotension, muscle aches, n/v/d, pain, pulmonary edema; **rebound pulmonary hypertension** (w/sudden stopping)

INTERACTIONS Antihypertensives, diuretics, vasodilators

NC/PT Must deliver through continuous infusion pump. Use caution in pregnancy/breast-feeding. Teach pt, significant other maint and use of pump. Do not stop suddenly; taper if discontinuing. Pt should use analgesics for headache, muscle aches; report chest pain, s&sx of infection.

eprosartan mesylate (Teveten)
CLASS Antihypertensive, ARB
PREG/CONT D/NA

BBW Rule out pregnancy before starting tx. Suggest barrier birth control; fetal injury, deaths have occurred. If pregnancy detected, discontinue as soon as possible.
IND & DOSE Tx of hypertension. *Adult:* 600 mg PO daily. In divided doses bid w/target dose of 400–800 mg/day.
ADJUST DOSE Renal impairment
ADV EFF Abd pain, diarrhea, dizziness, headache, hyperkalemia, hypotension, URI sx
INTERACTIONS ACE inhibitors, ARBs, lithium, NSAIDs, potassium-elevating drugs, renin inhibitors
NC/PT If BP not controlled, may add other antihypertensives, such as diuretics, calcium channel blocker. Monitor fluid intake, BP, potassium. Use caution if pt goes to surgery; volume depletion possible. Not for use in pregnancy (barrier contraception advised)/breast-feeding. Pt should use care in situations that could lead to volume depletion.

---

eptifibatide (Integrilin)
CLASS Antiplatelet, glycoprotein IIb/IIIa receptor agonist
PREG/CONT B/NA

IND & DOSE Tx of acute coronary syndrome. *Adult:* 180 mcg/kg IV (max, 22.6 mg) over 1–2 min as soon as possible after dx, then 2 mcg/kg/min (max, 15 mg/hr) by continuous IV infusion for up to 72 hr. If pt is to undergo percutaneous coronary intervention (PCI), continue for 18–24 hr after procedure, up to 96 hr of tx. Px of ischemia w/PCI. 180 mcg/kg IV as bolus immediately before PCI, then 2 mcg/kg/min by continuous IV infu-

sion for 18–24 hr. May give second bolus of 180 mcg/kg 10 min.
ADJUST DOSE Renal impairment
ADV EFF Bleeding, dizziness, headache, hypotension, rash
INTERACTIONS Anticoagulants, clopidogrel, dipyridamole, NSAIDs, thrombolytics, ticlopidine
NC/PT Used w/aspirin, heparin. Arrange for baseline and periodic CBC, PT, aPTT, active clotting time; maintain aPTT of 50–70 sec and active clotting time of 300–350 sec. Avoid invasive procedures. Ensure compression of sites. Pt should use analgesics for headache; take safety precautions for dizziness; report unusual bleeding.

---

ergotamine tartrate (Ergomar)
CLASS Antimigraine, ergot
PREG/CONT X/NA

IND & DOSE Px, tx of vascular headaches. *Adult:* 2 mg under tongue at first sign of headache. May repeat at 30-min intervals; max, 6 mg/day or 10 mg/wk.
ADV EFF Cyanosis, gangrene, headache, hypertension, ischemia, itching, n/v, pulmonary fibrosis, tachycardia
INTERACTIONS Beta blockers, epinephrine, macrolide antibiotics, nicotine, protease inhibitors, sympathomimetics
NC/PT Not for use in pregnancy/breast-feeding. Pt should take at first sign of headache; not take more than 3 tablets in 24 hr; report difficulty breathing, numbness/tingling, chest pain.

---

eribulin mesylate (Halaven)
CLASS Antineoplastic, microtubular inhibitor
PREG/CONT D/NA

IND & DOSE Tx of metastatic breast cancer in pts previously

treated w/at least two chemotherapeutic regimens; tx of unresectable or metastatic liposarcoma in pts who have received an anthracycline-containing regimen. *Adult:* 1.4 mg/m² IV over 2–5 min on days 1 and 8 of 21-day cycle.
ADJUST DOSE Hepatic, renal impairment
ADV EFF Alopecia, asthenia, **bone marrow suppression,** constipation, nausea, **prolonged QT, peripheral neuropathy**
INTERACTIONS Dextrose-containing solutions, QT-prolonging drugs
NC/PT Obtain baseline ECG; monitor QT interval. Monitor for bone marrow suppression (adjust dose accordingly), peripheral neuropathy (dose adjustment may be needed). Not for use in pregnancy/breast-feeding. Protect from infection. Hair loss possible. Pt should cover head at extremes of temp; report fever, chills, cough, burning on urination.

---

erlotinib (Tarceva)
CLASS Antineoplastic, kinase inhibitor
PREG/CONT D/NA

IND & DOSE Tx of locally advanced or metastatic non-small-cell lung cancer as first-line tx or after failure of other chemotherapy. *Adult:* 150 mg/day PO on empty stomach. Tx of locally advanced, unresectable or metastatic pancreatic cancer, w/gemcitabine. *Adult:* 100 mg/day PO w/IV gemcitabine.
ADJUST DOSE Hepatic, renal impairment; lung dysfx
ADV EFF Abd pain, anorexia, **bleeding, corneal ulcerations,** cough, dyspnea, **exfoliative skin disorders,** fatigue, **GI perforation, hepatic failure, hemolytic anemia, interstitial pulmonary disease, MI,** n/v/d, rash, **renal failure**
INTERACTIONS Antacids, cigarette smoking, CYP3A4 inducers/inhibitors, midazolam
NC/PT Monitor LFTs, renal function regularly. Monitor pulmonary status. Assess cornea before and periodically during tx. Provide skin care, including sunscreen, alcohol-free emollient cream. Not for use in pregnancy/breast-feeding. Pt should report severe diarrhea, difficulty breathing, worsening rash, vision changes.

---

ertapenem (Invanz)
CLASS Carbapenem antibiotic
PREG/CONT B/NA

IND & DOSE Tx of community-acquired pneumonia; skin, skin-structure infections, including diabetic foot infections; complicated GU, intra-abdominal, acute pelvic infections caused by susceptible bacteria strains; px of surgical-site infection after colorectal surgery. *Adult, child 13 yr and older:* 1 g IM or IV each day. Length of tx varies w/infection: intra-abdominal, 5–14 days; urinary tract, 10–14 days; skin, skin-structure, 7–14 days; community-acquired pneumonia, 10–14 days; acute pelvic, 3–10 days. *Child 3 mo–12 yr:* 15 mg/kg IV or IM bid for 3–14 days; max, 1 g/day.
ADJUST DOSE Renal impairment
ADV EFF **Anaphylaxis,** CDAD, headache, hypersensitivity reaction, local pain/phlebitis at injection site; n/v/d, **pseudomembranous colitis, seizures,** superinfections
NC/PT Culture before tx. Give by deep IM injection; have emergency equipment on hand for hypersensitivity reactions. Monitor injection site for reaction. Treat superinfections. Pt should report severe or bloody diarrhea, pain at injection site.

erythromycin salts
(Eryc, Eryped, Ery-Tab, Erythrocin)

CLASS Macrolide antibiotic
PREG/CONT B/NA

IND & DOSE Tx of infections caused by susceptible bacteria. *Adult:* General guidelines, 15–20 mg/kg/day by continuous IV infusion or up to 4 g/day in divided doses q 6 hr; or 250 mg (400 mg ethylsuccinate) PO q 6 hr or 500 mg PO q 12 hr or 333 mg PO q 8 hr, up to 4 g/day, depending on infection severity. *Child:* General guidelines, 30–50 mg/kg/day PO in divided doses. Specific dose determined by infection severity. age, weight. Tx of streptococcal infections. *Adult:* 250 mg PO q 6 hr or 500 mg PO q 12 hr (for group A beta-hemolytic streptococcal infections, continue tx for at least 10 days). Tx of Legionnaires' disease. *Adult:* 1–4 g/day PO or IV in divided doses for 10–21 days. Tx of dysenteric amebiasis. *Adult:* 250 mg PO q 6 hr or 333 mg PO q 8 hr for 10–14 days. *Child:* 30–50 mg/kg/day PO in divided doses for 10–14 days. Tx of acute PID *(Neisseria gonorrhoeae). Adult:* 500 mg IV q 6 hr for 3 days, then 250 mg PO q 6 hr or 333 mg PO q 8 hr or 500 mg PO q 12 hr for 7 days. Tx of chlamydial infections. *Adult:* Urogenital infections during pregnancy, 500 mg PO qid or 666 mg PO q 8 hr for at least 7 days; ½ this dose q 8 hr for at least 14 days if intolerant to first regimen. Urethritis in males, 800 mg ethylsuccinate PO tid for 7 days. *Child:* 50 mg/kg/day PO in divided doses, for at least 2 (conjunctivitis of newborn) or 3 (pneumonia of infancy) wk. Tx of primary syphilis. *Adult:* 30–40 g PO in divided doses over 10–15 days. CDC recommendations for STDs. *Adult:* 500 mg PO qid for 7–30 days, depending on infection. Tx of pertussis. *Child:* 40–50 mg/kg/day PO in divided doses for 14 days. Tx of superficial ocular infections caused by susceptible strains. *Adult, child:* ½-inch ribbon instilled into conjunctival sac of affected eye two to six times/day, depending on infection severity. Tx of acne (dermatologic sol). *Adult, child:* Apply to affected areas a.m. and p.m. Tx of skin infections caused by susceptible bacteria. *Adult, child:* Apply flexible hydroactive dressings and granules; keep in place for 1–7 days.

ADV EFF Abd pain, **anaphylaxis,** anorexia, local irritation w/topical use; n/v/d, **pseudomembranous colitis,** superinfections

INTERACTIONS Calcium channel blockers, carbamazepine, corticosteroids, cyclosporine, digoxin, disopyramide, ergots, grapefruit juice, midazolam, oral anticoagulants, proton pump inhibitors, quinidine, statins, theophylline

NC/PT Culture before tx. Give oral drug on empty stomach round the clock for best results. Monitor LFTs w/long-term use. Apply topical form to clean, dry area. Pt should avoid grapefruit juice, report severe or bloody diarrhea.

escitalopram oxalate
(Lexapro)

CLASS Antidepressant, SSRI
PREG/CONT C/NA

BBW Monitor for suicidality, especially when starting tx or altering dose. Increased risk in children, adolescents, young adults. Not approved for use in pt under 12 yr.

IND & DOSE Tx of major depressive disorder. *Adult:* 10 mg/day PO as single dose; may increase to 20 mg/day after minimum of 1-wk trial period. Maint, 10–20 mg/day PO. *Child 12–17 yr:* 10 mg/day PO as single dose; max, 20 mg/day. Tx of generalized anxiety disorder. *Adult:* 10 mg/day PO; may increase to 20 mg/day after 1 wk if needed.

ADJUST DOSE Elderly pts, hepatic impairment

ADV EFF Activation of mania/hypomania, anaphylaxis, angioedema, angle-closure glaucoma, dizziness, ejaculatory problems, nausea, **seizures, serotonin syndrome,** somnolence, suicidality

INTERACTIONS Alcohol, carbamazepine, citalopram, lithium, MAOIs, SSRIs, St. John's wort

NC/PT Limit supply in suicidal pts. Do not use within 14 days of MAOIs. Taper after long-term use. Not for use in pregnancy/breast-feeding. Use safety precautions. May need 4 wk to see effects. Pt should not stop drug suddenly but should taper dose; avoid alcohol, St. John's wort; report thoughts of suicide. Name confusion between escitalopram and citalopram and *Lexapro* (escitalopram) and *Loxitane* (loxapine); use caution.

---

eslicarbazepine acetate (Aptiom)

CLASS Antiepileptic, sodium channel blocker
PREG/CONT C/NA

IND & DOSE Tx of partial-onset seizures, as monotherapy or w/other antiepileptics. *Adult:* 400 mg/day PO; after 1 wk, increase to 800 mg/day PO may increase by 400-600 mg/d weekly to max of 1600 mg/day.

ADJUST DOSE Renal impairment
ADV EFF Anaphylaxis, dizziness, double vision, drowsiness, fatigue, headache, hyponatremia, **liver damage,** n/v, suicidality

INTERACTIONS Carbamazepine, hormonal contraceptives, phenobarbital, phenytoin, primidone

NC/PT Ensure proper dx. Taper dose when stopping to minimize seizure risk. Monitor LFTs, serum electrolytes; ensure safety precautions w/CNS effects. Pt should avoid pregnancy/breast-feeding; take safety precautions w/CNS effects; report thoughts of suicide, difficulty breathing, urine/stool color changes.

---

esmolol hydrochloride (Brevibloc)

CLASS Antiarrhythmic, beta-selective adrenergic blocker
PREG/CONT C/NA

IND & DOSE Tx of supraventricular tachycardia; noncompensatory tachycardia; intraop, postop tachycardia and hypertension. *Adult:* Initial loading dose, 500 mcg/kg/min IV for 1 min, then maint of 50 mcg/kg/min for 4 min. If response inadequate after 5 min, repeat loading dose and follow w/maint infusion of 100 mcg/kg/min. Repeat titration as needed, increasing rate of maint dose in 50-mcg/kg/min increments. As desired heart rate or safe endpoint is approached, omit loading infusion and decrease incremental dose in maint infusion to 25 mcg/kg/min (or less), or increase interval between titration steps from 5 to 10 min. Usual range, 50–200 mcg/kg/min. Up to 24-hr infusions have been used; up to 48 hr may be well tolerated. Individualize dose based on pt response; max, 300 mcg/kg/min.

ADV EFF Hypoglycemia, hypotension, injection-site inflammation, light-headedness, midscapular pain, rigors, weakness

INTERACTIONS Anticholinergics, antihypertensives, calcium channel blockers, digoxin, ibuprofen, indomethacin, piroxicam, sympathomimetics

NC/PT Do not give undiluted. Do not mix in sol w/sodium bicarbonate, diazepam, furosemide, thiopental. Not for long-term use. Closely monitor BP, ECG. Pt should report difficulty breathing, chest pain.

esomeprazole magnesium (Nexium)

CLASS Antisecretory, proton pump inhibitor
PREG/CONT B/NA

IND & DOSE Healing of erosive esophagitis. *Adult:* 20–40 mg PO daily for 4–8 wk. Maint, 20 mg PO daily. *Child 1–11 yr:* 20 kg or more, 10–20 mg/day PO for up to 8 wk; under 20 kg, 10 mg/day PO for up to 8 wk. **Tx of symptomatic GERD.** *Adult:* 20 mg PO daily for 4 wk. Can use additional 4-wk course. *Child 12–17 yr:* 20–40 mg/day PO for up to 8 wk. *Child 1–11 yr:* 10 mg/day PO for up to 8 wk. **Tx of duodenal ulcer.** *Adult:* 40 mg/day PO for 10 days w/1,000 mg PO bid amoxicillin and 500 mg PO bid clarithromycin. **Reduction of risk of gastric ulcers w/NSAID use.** *Adult:* 20–40 mg PO daily for 6 mo. **Short-term tx of GERD when oral therapy not possible.** *Adult, child 1 mo–17 yr:* 20–40 mg IV by injection over at least 3 min or IV infusion over 10–30 min.
ADJUST DOSE Severe hepatic impairment
ADV EFF Abd pain, acute interstitial nephritis, atrophic gastritis, **bone loss w/long-term use, CDAD,** dizziness, headache, hypomagnesemia, n/v/d, pneumonia, sinusitis, URI, vitamin B$_{12}$ deficiency
INTERACTIONS Atazanavir, benzodiazepines, cilostazol, clopidogrel, digoxin, iron salts, ketoconazole, rifampin, St. John's wort, tacrolimus
NC/PT Reevaluate use after 8 wk. Give at least 1 hr before meals; may give through NG tube. Monitor LFTs periodically. Limit IV use to max 10 days. Pt should swallow capsules whole and not cut, crush, or chew them; take safety precautions w/CNS effects; report diarrhea, difficulty breathing. Name confusion between esomeprazole and omeprazole, *Nexium* (esomeprazole) and *Nexavar* (sorafenib); use caution.

estazolam (generic)

CLASS Benzodiazepine, sedative-hypnotic
PREG/CONT X/C-IV

IND & DOSE Tx of insomnia, recurring insomnia, acute or chronic medical conditions requiring restful sleep. *Adult:* 1 mg PO before bedtime; may need up to 2 mg.
ADJUST DOSE Elderly pts, debilitating disease
ADV EFF Anaphylaxis, angioedema, apathy, bradycardia, constipation, **CV collapse,** depression, diarrhea, disorientation, drowsiness, drug dependence w/withdrawal syndrome, dyspepsia, lethargy, lightheadedness, tachycardia, urine retention
INTERACTIONS Alcohol, aminophylline, barbiturates, opioids, phenothiazines, rifampin, TCAs, theophylline
NC/PT Monitor LFTs, renal function. Taper after long-term use. Pt should avoid alcohol, use only as needed (can be habit-forming), take safety precautions w/CNS effects.

estradiol, estradiol acetate, estradiol cypionate, estradiol hemihydrate, estradiol valerate (Delestrogen, Estrace, Estring, Evamist, Femring, Vagifem)

CLASS Estrogen
PREG/CONT X/NA

BBW Arrange for pretreatment and periodic (at least annual) hx and physical; should include BP, breasts, abdomen, pelvic organs, Pap test. May increase risk of endometrial cancer. Do not use to prevent CV events, dementia; may increase risks, including thrombophlebitis, PE, stroke, MI. Caution pt of risks of estrogen use. Stress need for pregnancy prevention during tx, frequent medical follow-up, periodic rests from tx.

IND & DOSE Relief of moderate to severe vasomotor sx, atrophic vaginitis, kraurosis vulvae associated w/menopause. *Adult:* 1–2 mg/day PO. Adjust dose to control sx. For gel, 0.25 g 0.1% gel applied to right or left upper thigh on alternating days; may increase to 0.5 or 1 g/day to control sx. For topical spray *(Evamist),* 1 spray once daily to forearm; may increase to 2–3 sprays daily. Cyclic therapy (3 wk on/1 wk off) recommended, especially in women w/no hysterectomy. 1–5 mg estradiol cypionate in oil IM q 3–4 wk. 10–20 mg estradiol valerate in oil IM q 4 wk. 0.014- to 0.05-mg system applied to skin wkly or twice wkly. If oral estrogens have been used, start transdermal system 1 wk after withdrawal of oral form. Given on cyclic schedule (3 wk on/1 wk off). Attempt to taper or discontinue q 3–6 mo. Vaginal cream: 2–4 g intravaginally daily for 1–2 wk, then reduce to ½ dose for similar period followed by maint of 1 g one to three times/wk thereafter. Discontinue or taper at 3- to 6-mo intervals. Vaginal ring: Insert one ring high into vagina. Replace q 90 days. Vaginal tablet: 1 tablet inserted vaginally daily for 2 wk, then twice wkly. Emulsion: Apply lotion to legs, thighs, or calves once daily. Apply gel to one arm once daily. **Tx of female hypogonadism, female castration, primary ovarian failure.** *Adult:* 1–2 mg/day PO. Adjust to control sx. Cyclic therapy (3 wk on/1 wk off) recommended. 1.5–2 mg estradiol cypionate in oil IM at monthly intervals. 10–20 mg estradiol valerate in oil IM q 4 wk. 0.05-mg system applied to skin twice wkly as above. **Tx of prostate cancer** (inoperable). *Adult:* 1–2 mg PO tid; give long-term. 30 mg or more estradiol valerate in oil IM q 1–2 wk. **Tx of breast cancer** (inoperable, progressing). *Adult:* 10 mg tid PO for at least 3 mo. **Prevention of postpartum breast engorgement.** *Adult:* 10–25 mg estradiol valerate in oil IM as single injection at end of first stage of labor. **Px of**

osteoporosis. *Adult:* 0.5 mg/day PO cyclically (23 days on, 5 days rest) starting as soon after menopause as possible.
ADV EFF Acute pancreatitis, abd cramps, bloating, **cancer,** chloasma, **cholestatic jaundice, colitis,** dysmenorrhea, edema, **hepatic adenoma,** menstrual flow changes, n/v/d, pain at injection site, photosensitivity, premenstrual syndrome, **thrombotic events**
INTERACTIONS Barbiturates, carbamazepine, corticosteroids, phenytoins, rifampin
NC/PT Give cyclically for short-term use. Give w/progestin for women w/intact uterus. Review proper administration for each drug type. Potentially serious adverse effects. Not for use in pregnancy/breast-feeding. Pt should get regular pelvic exams, avoid sun exposure, report pain in calves/chest, lumps in breast, vision or speech changes.

**estrogens, conjugated
(Cenestin, Enjuvia, Premarin)**
CLASS Estrogen
PREG/CONT X/NA

BBW Arrange for pretreatment and periodic (at least annual) hx and physical; should include BP, breasts, abdomen, pelvic organs, Pap test. May increase risk of endometrial cancer. Do not use to prevent CV events, dementia; may increase risks, including thrombophlebitis, PE, stroke, MI. Caution pt of risks of estrogen use. Stress need for pregnancy prevention during tx, frequent medical follow-up, periodic rests from tx.
IND & DOSE Relief of moderate to severe vasomotor sx associated w/menopause. *Adult:* 0.3–0.625 mg/day PO. **Tx of atrophic vaginitis, kraurosis vulvae associated w/menopause.** *Adult:* 0.5–2 g vaginal cream daily intravaginally or topically, depending on severity. Taper or discontinue at

3- to 6-mo intervals. Or, 0.3 mg/day PO continually. **Tx of female hypogonadism.** *Adult:* 0.3–0.625 mg/day PO for 3 wk, then 1 wk rest. **Tx of female castration, primary ovarian failure.** *Adult:* 1.25 mg/day PO. **Tx of prostate cancer** (inoperable). *Adult:* 1.25–2.5 mg PO tid. **Tx of osteoporosis.** *Adult:* 0.3 mg/day PO continuously or cyclically (25 days on/5 days off). **Breast cancer** (inoperable, progressing). *Adult:* 10 mg PO tid for at least 3 mo. **Abnormal uterine bleeding due to hormonal imbalance.** 25 mg IV or IM. Repeat in 6–12 hr as needed. More rapid response w/IV route. **ADV EFF** Acute pancreatitis, abd cramps, **anaphylaxis**, bloating, **cancer**, chloasma, **cholestatic jaundice, colitis**, dysmenorrhea, edema, gallbladder disease, headache, **hepatic adenoma**, hereditary angioedema exacerbations, menstrual flow changes, n/v/d, pain at injection site, photosensitivity, premenstrual syndrome, **thrombotic events**
INTERACTIONS Barbiturates, carbamazepine, corticosteroids, phenytoins, rifampin
NC/PT Give cyclically for short-term use. Give w/progestin for women w/intact uterus. Do not give w/undiagnosed genital bleeding. Review proper administration for each drug type. Potentially serious adverse effects. Not for use in pregnancy/breast-feeding. Pt should get regular pelvic exams, avoid sun exposure, report pain in calves/chest, lumps in breast, vision or speech changes.

---

estrogens, esterified (Menest)
CLASS Estrogen
PREG/CONT X/NA

BBW Arrange for pretreatment and periodic (at least annual) hx and physical; should include BP, breasts, abdomen, pelvic organs, Pap test. May increase risk of endometrial cancer. Do not use to prevent CV events or dementia; may increase risks, including thrombophlebitis, PE, stroke, MI. Caution pt of risks of estrogen use. Stress need for pregnancy prevention during tx, frequent medical follow-up, periodic rests from drug tx. Give cyclically for short-term only when treating postmenopausal conditions because of endometrial neoplasm risk. Taper to lowest effective dose; provide drug-free wk each mo.
IND & DOSE Relief of moderate to severe vasomotor sx, atrophic vaginitis, kraurosis vulvae associated w/menopause. *Adult:* 0.3–1.25 mg/day PO given cyclically (3 wk on/1 wk off). Use lowest possible dose. **Tx of female hypogonadism.** *Adult:* 2.5–7.5 mg/day PO in divided doses for 20 days on/10 days off. **Female castration, primary ovarian failure.** *Adult:* 1.25 mg/day PO given cyclically. **Prostate cancer (inoperable).** *Adult:* 1.25–2.5 mg PO tid. **Inoperable, progressing breast cancer.** *Adult:* 10 mg PO tid for at least 3 mo.
ADV EFF Acute pancreatitis, abd cramps, bloating, **cancer**, chloasma, **cholestatic jaundice, colitis**, dysmenorrhea, edema, headache, **hepatic adenoma**, menstrual flow changes, n/v/d, pain at injection site, photosensitivity, premenstrual syndrome, **thrombotic events**
INTERACTIONS Barbiturates, carbamazepine, corticosteroids, phenytoins, rifampin
NC/PT Give cyclically for short-term use. Give w/progestin for women w/intact uterus. Review proper administration for each drug type. Potentially serious adverse effects. Not for use in pregnancy/breast-feeding. Pt should get regular pelvic exams, avoid sun exposure, report pain in calves/chest, lumps in breast, vision or speech changes.

estropipate (generic)
CLASS Estrogen
PREG/CONT X/NA

BBW Arrange for pretreatment and periodic (at least annual) hx and physical; should include BP, breasts, abdomen, pelvic organs, Pap test. May increase risk of endometrial cancer. Do not use to prevent CV events or dementia; may increase risks, including thrombophlebitis, PE, stroke, MI. Caution pt of risks of estrogen use. Stress need for pregnancy prevention during tx, frequent medical follow-up, periodic rests from drug tx. Give cyclically for short term only when treating postmenopausal conditions because of endometrial neoplasm risk. Taper to lowest effective dose; provide drug-free wk each mo.
IND & DOSE Relief of moderate to severe vasomotor sx, atrophic vaginitis, kraurosis vulvae associated w/menopause. *Adult:* 0.75–6 mg/day PO given cyclically (3 wk on/1 wk off). Use lowest possible dose. **Tx of female hypogonadism, female castration, primary ovarian failure.** *Adult:* 1.5–9 mg/day PO for first 3 wk, then rest period of 8–10 days. Repeat if no bleeding at end of rest period. **Px of osteoporosis.** *Adult:* 0.75 mg/day PO for 25 days of 31-day cycle/mo.
ADV EFF Acute pancreatitis, abd cramps, bloating, **cancer,** chloasma, **cholestatic jaundice, colitis,** dysmenorrhea, edema, headache, **hepatic adenoma,** menstrual flow changes, n/v/d, pain at injection site, photosensitivity, premenstrual syndrome, **thromboembolic events**
INTERACTIONS Barbiturates, carbamazepine, corticosteroids, phenytoins, rifampin
NC/PT Give cyclically for short-term use. Give w/progestin for women w/ intact uterus. Review proper administration for each drug type. Potentially serious adverse effects. Not for use in pregnancy/breast-feeding. Pt should get regular pelvic exams, avoid sun exposure, report pain in calves/chest, lumps in breast, vision or speech changes.

eszopiclone (Lunesta)
CLASS Nonbenzodiazepine hypnotic, sedative-hypnotic
PREG/CONT C/C-IV

IND & DOSE Tx of insomnia. *Adult:* 1 mg PO immediately before bedtime, w/7–8 hr remaining before planned awakening. May increase to 3 mg PO. Use lowest effective dose.
ADJUST DOSE CYP3A4 inhibitor use, elderly or debilitated pts, severe hepatic impairment
ADV EFF Abnormal thinking, **anaphylaxis, angioedema,** depression, dizziness, headache, impaired alertness/motor coordination, nervousness, somnolence, **suicidality**
INTERACTIONS Alcohol, clarithromycin, itraconazole, ketoconazole, nefazodone, nelfinavir, rifampin, ritonavir
NC/PT Not for use in pregnancy/breast-feeding. Pt should swallow tablet whole and not cut, crush, or chew it; take only if in bed and able to stay in bed for up to 8 hr; avoid alcohol; not take w/high-fat meal; avoid sudden withdrawal; use safety precautions w/CNS effects; report thoughts of suicide, difficulty breathing, swelling of face or neck.

etanercept (Enbrel)
CLASS Antiarthritic, disease-modifying antirheumatic drug
PREG/CONT B/NA

BBW Monitor for infection s&sx; discontinue if infection occurs. Risk of serious infections (including TB), death. Increased risk of lymphoma, other cancers in children taking for juvenile rheumatoid arthritis, Crohn's disease, other inflammatory conditions; monitor accordingly.

IND & DOSE To reduce s&sx of ankylosing spondylitis, rheumatoid arthritis, psoriatic arthritis, juvenile idiopathic arthritis. *Adult:* 50 mg/wk subcut. *Child 2–17 yr:* 0.8 mg/kg/wk subcut; max, 50 mg/wk. **To reduce s&sx of plaque psoriasis.** *Adult:* 50 mg/dose subcut twice wkly 3 or 4 days apart for 3 mo; maint, 50 mg/wk subcut.
ADV EFF Anaphylaxis, bone marrow suppression, **demyelinating disorders (MS, myelitis, optic neuritis)**, cancers, increased risk of serious infections, dizziness, headache, HF, injection-site irritation, URIs
INTERACTIONS Immunosuppressants, vaccines
NC/PT Obtain baseline and periodic CBC, neurologic function tests. Monitor pt w/hx of hepatitis B infection; reactivation possible. Rotate injection sites (abdomen, thigh, upper arm). Monitor for infection. Do regular cancer screening. Teach proper administration/disposal of needles/syringes. Pt should avoid exposure to infection, maintain other tx for rheumatoid disorder (drug not a cure); report s&sx of infection, difficulty breathing.

---

ethacrynic acid (Edecrin)
CLASS Loop diuretic
PREG/CONT B/NA

IND & DOSE To reduce edema associated w/systemic diseases. *Adult:* 50–200 mg/day PO; may give IV as 50 mg slowly to max, 100 mg. *Child:* 25 mg/day PO; adjust in 25-mg/day increments if needed.
ADV EFF Abd pain, **agranulocytosis**, dehydration, dysphagia, fatigue, headache, hepatic impairment, hypokalemia, n/v/d, vertigo, weakness
INTERACTIONS Diuretics
NC/PT Switch to oral form as soon as possible. Give w/food if GI upset. Monitor potassium; supplement as needed. Not for use in breast-feeding. Pt should weigh self daily; report changes of 3 lb/day or more.

---

ethambutol hydrochloride (Myambutol)
CLASS Antituberculotic
PREG/CONT C/NA

IND & DOSE Tx of pulmonary TB w/at least one other antituberculotic. *Adult, child 13 yr and older:* 15 mg/kg/day PO as single oral dose. Continue until bacteriologic conversion permanent and max clinical improvement has occurred. Retreatment: 25 mg/kg/day as single oral dose. After 60 days, reduce to 15 mg/kg/day as single dose.
ADV EFF Anorexia, fever, headache, malaise, n/v/d, optic neuritis, **toxic epidermal necrolysis, thrombocytopenia**
INTERACTIONS Aluminum salts
NC/PT Ensure use w/other antituberculotics. Give w/food. Monitor CBC, LFTs, renal function, ophthalmic exam. Pt should not stop suddenly; have regular medical checkups; report changes in vision, color perception; take safety precautions w/CNS effects.

---

ethionamide (Trecator)
CLASS Antituberculotic
PREG/CONT C/NA

IND & DOSE Tx of pulmonary TB unresponsive to first-line tx, w/at least one other antituberculotic. *Adult:* 15–20 mg/kg/day PO to max 1 g/day. *Child:* 10–20 mg/kg/day PO in two or three divided doses after meals (max, 1 g/day), or 15 mg/kg/24 hr as single dose.
ADV EFF Alopecia, asthenia, depression, drowsiness, **hepatitis**, metallic taste, n/v/d, orthostatic hypotension, peripheral neuritis
NC/PT Ensure use w/other antituberculotics. Concomitant use of pyridoxine recommended to prevent or minimize s&sx of peripheral neuritis. Give w/food. Monitor LFTs before tx

and q 2–4 wk during tx. Not for use in pregnancy. Pt should not stop suddenly, have regular medical checkups, take safety precautions w/CNS effects.

ethosuximide (Zarontin)
CLASS Antiepileptic, succinimide
PREG/CONT C/NA

IND & DOSE Control of absence (petit mal) seizures. *Adult, child 6 yr and older:* 500 mg/day PO. Increase by small increments to maint level; increase by 250 mg q 4–7 days until control achieved. *Child 3–6 yr:* 250 mg/day PO. Increase in small increments until optimal 20 mg/kg/day in one dose or two divided doses.
ADV EFF Abd pain, **agranulocytosis, aplastic anemia,** ataxia, blurred vision, constipation, cramps, dizziness, drowsiness, **eosinophilia, generalized tonic-clonic seizures, granulocytopenia,** irritability, leukopenia, monocytosis, nervousness, n/v/d, **pancytopenia, Stevens-Johnson syndrome**
INTERACTIONS Alcohol, CNS depressants, primidone
NC/PT Reduce dose, discontinue, or substitute other antiepileptic gradually. Taper when discontinuing. Monitor CBC. Stop drug at signs of rash. Evaluate for therapeutic serum level (40–100 mcg/mL). Not for use in pregnancy (contraceptives advised). Pt should avoid alcohol, wear medical ID, avoid exposure to infection, take safety precautions w/CNS effects.

ethotoin (Peganone)
CLASS Antiepileptic, hydantoin
PREG/CONT D/NA

IND & DOSE Control of tonic-clonic, complex partial (psychomotor) seizures. *Adult:* 1 g/day PO in four to six divided doses; increase gradually over several days. Usual maint dose, 2–3 g/day PO in four to six divided

doses. *Child 1 yr and older:* 750 mg/day PO in four to six divided doses; maint range, 500 mg/day to 1 g/day PO in four to six divided doses.
ADV EFF Abd pain, **agranulocytosis, aplastic anemia,** ataxia, blurred vision, confusion, constipation, cramps, dizziness, drowsiness, **eosinophilia, epidermal necrolysis,** fatigue, **granulocytopenia,** gum dysplasia, **hepatotoxicity,** irritability, **leukopenia, lymphoma, monocytosis,** nervousness, n/v/d, nystagmus, **pancytopenia, pulmonary fibrosis, Stevens-Johnson syndrome**
INTERACTIONS Acetaminophen, amiodarone, antineoplastics, carbamazepine, chloramphenicol, cimetidine, corticosteroids, cyclosporine, diazoxide, disopyramide, disulfiram, doxycycline, estrogens, fluconazole, folic acid, hormonal contraceptives, isoniazid, levodopa, methadone, metyrapone, mexiletine, phenacemide, phenylbutazone, primidone, rifampin, sulfonamides, theophyllines, trimethoprim, valproic acid
NC/PT May use w/other antiepileptics. Reduce dosage, discontinue, or substitute other antiepileptic gradually. Taper when discontinuing. Monitor CBC. Stop drug at signs of rash. Monitor LFTs. Give w/food to enhance absorption. Evaluate for therapeutic serum levels (15–50 mcg/mL). Not for use in pregnancy (contraceptives advised). Evaluate lymph node enlargement during tx. Frequent medical follow-up needed. Pt should avoid alcohol, wear medical ID, avoid exposure to infection, take safety precautions w/CNS effects, use good dental care to limit gum hyperplasia.

etidronate disodium (Didronel)
CLASS Bisphosphonate, calcium regulator
PREG/CONT C/NA

IND & DOSE Tx of Paget's disease. *Adult:* 5–10 mg/kg/day PO for up to

6 mo; or 11–20 mg/kg/day PO for up to 3 mo. If retreatment needed, wait at least 90 days between tx regimens. **Tx of heterotopic ossification.** *Adult:* 20 mg/kg/day PO for 2 wk, then 10 mg/kg/day PO for 10 wk (after spinal cord injury); 20 mg/kg/day PO for 1 mo preop (if total hip replacement), then 20 mg/kg/day PO for 3 mo postop.

ADJUST DOSE Renal impairment
ADV EFF Bone pain, headache, n/v/d
INTERACTIONS Antacids, aspirin, food
NC/PT For Paget's disease, ensure 3 mo rest periods between tx. Monitor serum calcium level. Pt should take w/full glass of water 2 hr before meals, take calcium and vitamin D as needed, report muscle twitching.

etodolac (generic)
CLASS Analgesic, NSAID
PREG/CONT C/NA

BBW Increased risk of CV events, GI bleeding; monitor accordingly.
IND & DOSE **Mgt of s&sx of osteoarthritis, rheumatoid arthritis.** *Adult:* 600–1,000 mg/day PO in divided doses. Maint range, 600–1,200 mg/day in divided doses; max, 1,200 mg/day (20 mg/kg for pts under 60 kg). ER, 400–1,000 mg/day PO; max, 1,200 mg/day. **Mgt of s&sx of juvenile rheumatoid arthritis** (ER tablets). *Child 6–16 yr:* Over 60 kg, 1,000 mg/day PO as 500 mg PO bid; 46–60 kg, 800 mg PO as 400 mg PO bid; 31–45 kg, 600 mg/day PO; 20–30 kg, 400 mg/day PO. **Analgesia, acute pain.** *Adult:* 200–400 mg PO q 6–8 hr; max, 1,200 mg/day.
ADV EFF Anaphylactoid reactions, bleeding, blurred vision, constipation, **CV events**, diarrhea, dizziness, dyspepsia, GI pain, **hepatic failure, renal impairment**
INTERACTIONS Anticoagulants, antihypertensives, antiplatelets
NC/PT Pt should take w/meals, use safety precautions w/CNS effects.

etoposide (VP-16)
(Etophos)
CLASS Antineoplastic, mitotic inhibitor
PREG/CONT D/NA

BBW Obtain platelet count, Hgb, Hct, WBC count w/differential before tx and each dose. If severe response, discontinue; consult physician. Severe myelosuppression possible. Monitor for severe hypersensitivity reaction; arrange supportive care.
IND & DOSE **Tx of testicular cancer.** *Adult:* 50–100 mg/m²/day IV on days 1 to 5, or 100 mg/m²/day IV on days 1, 3, 5 q 3–4 wk w/other chemotherapeutics. **Tx of small-cell lung cancer.** *Adult:* 35 mg/m²/day IV for 4 days to 50 mg/m²/day for 5 days; repeat q 3–4 wk after recovery from toxicity or switch to oral form (two times IV dose rounded to nearest 50 mg).
ADJUST DOSE Renal impairment
ADV EFF Alopecia, **anaphylactoid reactions**, anorexia, fatigue, hypotension, **myelotoxicity**, n/v/d, somnolence
INTERACTIONS Anticoagulants, antihypertensives, antiplatelets
NC/PT Avoid skin contact; use rubber gloves. If contact occurs, immediately wash w/soap, water. Do not give IM, subcut. Monitor BP during infusion. Give antiemetic if nausea severe. Not for use in pregnancy (contraceptives advised). Pt should cover head at temp extremes (hair loss possible), mark calendar of tx days, avoid exposure to infection, have blood tests regularly.

etravirine (Intelence)
CLASS Antiviral, nonnucleoside reverse transcriptase inhibitor
PREG/CONT B/NA

IND & DOSE **Tx of HIV-1 infection in tx-experienced pts w/evidence of**

viral replication and HIV-1 strains resistant to nonnucleoside reverse transcriptase inhibitors and other antiretrovirals, w/other drugs. *Adult:* 200 mg PO bid after meal. *Child 6–under 18 yr:* 30 kg or more, 200 mg PO bid; 25 to under 30 kg, 150 mg PO bid; 20 to under 25 mg, 125 mg PO bid; 16–under 20 kg, 100 mg PO bid.

ADV EFF Altered fat distribution, diarrhea, fatigue, headache, **severe hypersensitivity reactions**

INTERACTIONS Antiarrhythmics, atazanavir, azole, carbamazepine, clarithromycin, clopidogrel, delavirdine, fosamprenavir, indinavir, maraviroc, nelfinavir, nevirapine, phenobarbital, phenytoin, rifabutin, rifampin, rifapentine, ritonavir, St. John's wort, tipranavir, warfarin

NC/PT Always give w/other antivirals. Stop at first sign of severe skin reaction. Pt should swallow tablets whole and not cut, crush, or chew them. If pt cannot swallow, put tablets in glass of water, stir; when water is milky, have pt drink whole glass, rinse several times, and drink rinse each time to get full dose. Not for use in breast-feeding. Pt should not use w/St. John's wort, take precautions to prevent transmission (drug not a cure), have blood tests regularly.

---

everolimus (Afinitor, Zortress)
CLASS Antineoplastic, kinase inhibitor
PREG/CONT D/NA

BBW *Zortress* only: Risk of serious infections, cancer development; risk of venous thrombosis, kidney loss; risk of nephrotoxicity w/cyclosporine. Increased mortality if used w/heart transplant; not approved for this use.
IND & DOSE Tx of advanced renal carcinoma after failure w/sunitinib, sorafenib; tx of subependymal giant-cell astrocytoma in pts not candidates for surgery. *Adult:* 5–10 mg/day

PO w/food. Tx of pts 1 yr and older w/tuberous sclerosis complex (TSC) who have developed brain tumor. *Adult, child:* 4.5 mg/m² PO once/day w/food. Tx of postmenopausal advanced hormone receptor-positive, HER2-negative breast cancer; advanced neuroendocrine pancreatic tumors; advanced renal cell carcinoma; renal angiomyolipoma w/TSC. *Adult:* 10 mg/day PO at same time each day. Px of organ rejection in adult at low to moderate risk receiving kidney transplant (*Zortress*). *Adult:* 0.75 mg PO bid w/cyclosporine starting as soon as possible after transplant.
ADJUST DOSE Hepatic impairment
ADV EFF Angioedema, elevated blood glucose, lipids, serum creatinine; oral ulcerations, **pneumonitis**, **serious to fatal infections**, stomatitis
INTERACTIONS Live vaccines, strong CYP3A4 inducers (increase everolimus dose to 20 mg/day), CYP3A4 inhibitors
NC/PT Give w/food. Provide oral care. Monitor respiratory status; protect from infections. Not for use in pregnancy (contraceptives advised)/breast-feeding. Mouth care may be needed. Pt should swallow tablet whole and not cut, crush, or chew it; report difficulty breathing, fever.

---

evolocumab (Repatha)
CLASS PCSK9 inhibitor antibody
PREG/CONT Moderate risk/NA

IND & DOSE Adjunct to diet/exercise for tx of heterozygous familial hypercholesterolemia in pts w/maximum tolerated statin or other lipid-lowering therapy or clinical atherosclerotic CV disease. *Adult:* 140 mg subcut once q 2 wk; or 420 mg subcut (three 140-mg injections given in 30 min) subcut once/mo.
ADV EFF Back pain, flulike sx, hypersensitivity reactions, injection-site reactions, nasopharyngitis

NC/PT Monitor LDL at baseline and periodically. Monitor for severe hypersensitivity reaction; stop drug, provide supportive care. Ensure use of diet/exercise program. Use caution in pregnancy/breast-feeding. Teach proper administration/disposal of needles/syringes, not to reuse or share syringe or pen. Pt should rotate injection sites w/each use, mark calendar for injection days, review information w/each prescription, report difficulty breathing, rash, injection-site pain/inflammation.

exemestane (Aromasin)
CLASS Antineoplastic
PREG/CONT X/NA

IND & DOSE Tx of advanced breast cancer in postmenopausal women whose disease has progressed after tamoxifen; adjunct tx of postmenopausal women w/estrogen receptor–positive early breast cancer who have received 2–3 yr of tamoxifen; switch to exemestane to finish 5-yr course. *Adult:* 25 mg/day PO w/meal.
ADV EFF Anxiety, decreased bone marrow density, depression, GI upset, headache, hot flashes, nausea, sweating
INTERACTIONS CYP3A4 inducers/inhibitors, estrogens, St. John's wort
NC/PT Monitor LFTs, renal function. Give supportive therapy for adverse effects. Not for use in pregnancy/breast-feeding. Pt should not use St. John's wort.

exenatide (Bydureon, Byetta)
CLASS Antidiabetic, incretin mimetic drug
PREG/CONT C/NA

BBW ER form increases risk of thyroid C-cell tumors; contraindicated w/personal/family hx of medullary thyroid cancer and in pts w/multiple endocrine neoplasia syndrome.

IND & DOSE Adjunct to diet/exercise for tx of type 2 diabetes; as add-on tx w/metformin to improve glycemic control in type 2 diabetes. Not a first-line therapy. *Adult:* 5–10 mcg by subcut injection bid at any time within 60 min before a.m. and p.m. meals or two meals any time of day, approximately 6 hr apart. ER form, 2 mg by subcut injection once q 7 days.
ADJUST DOSE Renal impairment
ADV EFF Anaphylaxis, angioedema, dizziness, hypoglycemia, injection-site reaction, hemorrhagic or necrotizing pancreatitis, n/v/d, renal impairment, thyroid C cell tumors
INTERACTIONS Alcohol, antibiotics, oral contraceptives, warfarin
NC/PT Not for use in type 1 diabetes, ketoacidosis. Maintain diet/exercise, other drugs used to tx diabetes. Monitor serum glucose. Monitor for pancreatitis. Rotate injection sites (thigh, abdomen, upper arm). Give within 1 hr of meal; if pt not going to eat, do not give. Use caution in pregnancy/breast-feeding. Review hypoglycemia s&sx.

ezetimibe (Zetia)
CLASS Cholesterol-absorption inhibitor, cholesterol-lowering drug
PREG/CONT C/NA

IND & DOSE Adjunct to diet, exercise to lower cholesterol. *Adult, child over 10 yr:* 10 mg/day PO without regard to food. May give at same time as HMG-CoA reductase inhibitor, fenofibrate. If combined w/bile acid sequestrant, give at least 2 hr before or 4 hr after bile acid sequestrant.
ADV EFF Abd pain, diarrhea, dizziness, headache, URI
INTERACTIONS Cholestyramine, cyclosporine, fenofibrate, gemfibrozil
NC/PT Ensure use of diet, exercise program. Monitor serum lipid profile. Not for use in pregnancy/breast-feeding. Frequent blood tests needed. Pt should use safety precautions

w/CNS effects, continue other lipid-lowering drugs if prescribed.

ezogabine (Potiga)
CLASS Antiepileptic, neuronal potassium channel opener
PREG/CONT C/NA

BBW Risk of suicidal ideation/suicidality; monitor accordingly. Risk of retinal abnormalities, vision loss. Obtain baseline and periodic ophthalmologic exams; if eye changes occur, stop drug unless no other tx possible.
IND & DOSE Adjunct to tx of partial seizures when other measures have failed. *Adult:* 100 mg PO tid for 1 wk; maint, 200–400 mg PO tid, w/other antiepileptics.
ADV EFF Abnormal coordination, aphasia, asthenia, blurred vision, confused state, dizziness, fatigue, prolonged QT, retinal abnormalities, skin discoloration, somnolence, tremor, urine retention, suicidal ideation, vertigo, vision loss
INTERACTIONS Alcohol, carbamazepine, digoxin, phenytoin
NC/PT Obtain baseline ECG; review QT interval periodically. Ensure baseline and periodic vision exam by ophthalmologist; discontinue w/pigmentary or vision changes. Taper slowly when withdrawing. Not for use in pregnancy/breast-feeding. Pt should empty bladder before taking, continue other tx for seizures as prescribed, avoid alcohol, use safety precautions for CNS effects, report thoughts of suicide, have medical ID tag.

factor IX concentrates (AlphaNine SD, Bebulin VH, BeneFIX, Mononine)
CLASS Antihemophilic
PREG/CONT C/NA

IND & DOSE Control of bleeding w/factor IX deficiency (hemophilia B, Christmas disease). *Adult:* Base dose on factor IX levels. Guidelines:

BeneFIX, 1.3 units/kg × body weight (kg) × desired increase (% of normal) IV daily to bid for up to 7 days; *Bebulin VH,* body weight (kg) × desired increase (% of normal) × 1.2 units/kg IV daily to bid for up to 7 days. *Others:* 1 international unit/kg × body weight (kg) × desired increase (% of normal) IV daily to bid. **Px of factor IX deficiency.** *Adult, child:* 20–30 units/kg IV once or twice/wk; increase if surgery planned.
ADV EFF AIDS, Creutzfeldt-Jakob disease, headache, infusion reaction, nausea, thrombotic events
NC/PT Must give IV; infuse slowly. Monitor for infusion reaction; slow infusion. Regular blood tests of clotting factors needed. Review s&sx of thrombotic events. Pt should wear medical alert ID.

factor XIII concentrate (human) (Corifact)
CLASS Clotting factor
PREG/CONT C/NA

IND & DOSE Routine px of congenital factor XIII deficiency. *Adult, child:* 40 units/kg IV over not less than 4 mL/min, then base dose on pt response. Repeat q 28 days, maintaining trough activity level of 5%–20%.
ADV EFF Anaphylaxis, arthralgia, blood-transferred diseases, chills, factor XIII antibody formation, fever, headache, hepatic impairment, thrombotic events
NC/PT Alert pt to risk of blood-related disease. Teach pt s&sx of thrombotic events, allergic reaction, immune reaction (break-through bleeding). Advise use of medical alert ID.

famciclovir sodium (Famvir)
CLASS Antiviral
PREG/CONT B/NA

IND & DOSE Mgt of herpes labialis. *Adult:* 1,500 mg PO as single dose. **Tx of genital herpes, first episode in immunocompetent pts.** *Adult:* 1,000 mg PO bid for 1 day. **Suppression of recurrent genital herpes in immunocompetent pts.** *Adult:* 250 mg PO bid for up to 1 yr. **Tx of herpes zoster.** *Adult:* 500 mg PO q 8 hr for 7 days. **Tx of recurrent orolabial or genital herpes simplex infection in HIV-infected pts.** *Adult:* 500 mg PO bid for 7 days.

ADJUST DOSE Renal impairment
ADV EFF Cancer, diarrhea, fever, **granulocytopenia**, headache, nausea, rash, renal impairment, **thrombocytopenia**
INTERACTIONS Cimetidine, digoxin, probenecid
NC/PT Not for use in breast-feeding. Pt should continue precautions to prevent transmission (drug not a cure), avoid exposure to infection, take analgesics for headache, report bleeding.

---

famotidine (Pepcid)
CLASS Histamine-2 receptor antagonist
PREG/CONT B/NA

IND & DOSE Acute tx of active duodenal ulcer. *Adult:* 40 mg PO or IV at bedtime, or 20 mg PO or IV bid; discontinue after 6–8 wk. *Child 1–12 yr:* 0.5 mg/kg/day PO at bedtime or divided into two doses (up to 40 mg/day), or 0.25 mg/kg IV q 12 hr (up to 40 mg/day) if unable to take orally. **Maint tx of duodenal ulcer.** *Adult:* 20 mg PO at bedtime. **Benign gastric ulcer.** *Adult:* 40 mg PO daily at bedtime. **Tx of hypersecretory syndrome.** *Adult:* Initially, 20 mg PO q 6 hr. Taper; up to 160 mg PO q 6 hr has been used. Or, 20 mg IV q 12 hr in pts unable to take orally. *Children 1–12 yr:* 0.25 mg/kg IV q 12 hr (up to 40 mg/day) if unable to take orally. **Tx of GERD.** *Adult:* 20 mg PO bid for up to 6 wk. For GERD w/esophagitis, 20–40 mg PO bid for up to 12 wk. *Child 1–12 yr:* 1 mg/kg/day PO divided into two doses (up to

40 mg bid). *Child 3 mo–1 yr:* 0.5 mg/kg PO bid for up to 8 wk. *Under 3 mo:* 0.5 mg/kg/dose oral suspension once daily for up to 8 wk. **Px, relief of heartburn, acid indigestion.** *Adult:* 10–20 mg PO for relief; 10–20 mg PO 15–60 min before eating for prevention. Max, 20 mg/24 hr.
ADJUST DOSE Renal impairment
ADV EFF Arrhythmias, constipation, diarrhea, headache
NC/PT Reserve IV use for pts unable to take orally; switch to oral as soon as possible. Give at bedtime. May use concurrent antacid to relieve pain. Pt should place rapidly disintegrating tablet on tongue; swallow w/or without water.

---

fat emulsion, intravenous (Intralipid)
CLASS Caloric drug, nutritional drug
PREG/CONT C/NA

BBW Give to preterm infants only if benefit clearly outweighs risk; deaths have occurred.
IND & DOSE Parenteral nutrition. *Adult:* Should not constitute more than 60% of total calorie intake. *10%:* Infuse IV at 1 mL/min for first 15–30 min; may increase to 2 mL/min. Infuse only 500 mL first day; increase following day. Max, 2.5 g/kg/day. *20%:* Infuse at 0.5 mL/min for first 15–30 min. Infuse only 250 mL *Intralipid* first day; increase following day. Max, 3 g/kg/day. *30%:* Infuse at 1 mL/min (0.1 g fat/min) for first 15–30 min; max, 2.5 g/kg/day. *Child:* Should not constitute more than 60% of total calorie intake. *10%:* Initial IV infusion rate, 0.1 mL/min for first 10–15 min. *20%:* Initial infusion rate, 0.05 mL/min for first 10–15 min. If no untoward reactions, increase rate to 1 g/kg in 4 hr; max, 3 g/kg/day. *30%:* Initial infusion rate, 0.1 mL/min (0.01 g fat/min) for first 10–15 min; max, 3 g/kg/day. **Tx of essential fatty acid**

deficiency. Supply 8%–10% of caloric intake by IV fat emulsion.
ADV EFF Headache, **leukopenia**, nausea, **sepsis**, **thrombocytopenia**, thrombophlebitis
NC/PT Supplied in single-dose containers. Do not store partially used bottles or resterilize for later use. Do not use w/filters. Do not use bottle in which there appears to be separation from emulsion. Monitor closely for fluid, fat overload. Monitor lipid profile, nitrogen balance closely; monitor for thrombotic events, sepsis. Pt should report pain at injection site.

---

febuxostat (Uloric)
CLASS Antigout drug, xanthine oxidase inhibitor
PREG/CONT C/NA

IND & DOSE Long-term mgt of hyperuricemia in pts w/gout. *Adult:* 40 mg/day PO; if serum uric acid level not under 6 mg/dL in 2 wk, may increase to 80 mg/day PO.
ADJUST DOSE Hepatic, renal impairment
ADV EFF Gout flares, **MI**, nausea, **stroke**
INTERACTIONS Azathioprine, mercaptopurine theophyllines (use contraindicated)
NC/PT Obtain baseline, periodic uric acid levels. May use w/antacids, other drugs to control gout. Store at room temp, protected from light. Use caution in pregnancy/breast-feeding. Pt should report chest pain, numbness, tingling.

---

felodipine (Plendil)
CLASS Antihypertensive, calcium channel blocker
PREG/CONT C/NA

IND & DOSE Tx of essential hypertension. *Adult:* 5 mg/day PO; range, 2.5–10 mg/day PO.
ADJUST DOSE Elderly pts, hepatic impairment

ADV EFF Dizziness, fatigue, flushing, headache, lethargy, light-headedness, nausea, peripheral edema
INTERACTIONS Antifungals, barbiturates, carbamazepine, cimetidine, grapefruit juice, hydantoins, ranitidine
NC/PT Monitor cardiac rhythm, BP carefully during dose adjustment. Pt should swallow tablet whole and not cut, crush, or chew it; avoid grapefruit juice; report swelling in hands, feet.

---

fenofibrate (Antara, Fenoglide, Lipofen, Lofibra, TriCor, Triglide, Trilipix)
CLASS Antihyperlipidemic
PREG/CONT C/NA

IND & DOSE Adjunct to diet/exercise for tx of hypertriglyceridemia. *Adult:* 48–145 mg (TriCor) PO, or 67–200 mg (Lofibra) PO w/meal, or 50–160 mg/day (Triglide) PO daily, or 43–130 mg/day (Antara), or 50–150 mg/day (Lipofen), or 40–120 mg/day (Fenoglide), or 45–135 mg/day PO (Trilipix). Adjunct to diet/exercise for tx of primary hypercholesterolemia, mixed dyslipidemia. *Adult:* 145 mg/day PO (TriCor), or 200 mg/day (Lofibra) PO w/meal, or 160 mg/day (Triglide), or 130 mg/day PO (Antara), or 150 mg/day (Lipofen), or 120 mg/day PO (Fenoglide), or 135 mg/day PO (Trilipix).
ADJUST DOSE Elderly pts, renal impairment
ADV EFF Decreased libido, ED, flulike sx, myalgia, nausea, **pancreatitis**, rash
INTERACTIONS Anticoagulants, bile acid sequestrants, immunosuppressants, nephrotoxic drugs, statins
NC/PT Obtain baseline, periodic lipid profile, LFTs, CBC w/long-term therapy. Differentiate between brand names; doses vary. Balance timing of administration if used w/other lipid-lowering drugs. Use caution in pregnancy; not for use in breast-feeding. Pt should swallow DR capsules whole and not cut, crush, or chew them;

continue exercise, diet programs; report muscle weakness, aches.

fenoprofen calcium (Nalfon)
CLASS Analgesic, NSAID
PREG/CONT B (1st, 2nd trimesters); D (3rd trimester)/NA

BBW Increased risk of CV events, GI bleeding; monitor accordingly.
IND & DOSE Tx of rheumatoid arthritis, osteoarthritis. *Adult:* 400–600 mg PO tid or qid. May take 2–3 wk before improvement seen.
Tx of mild to moderate pain. *Adult:* 200 mg PO q 4–6 hr as needed.
ADJUST DOSE Renal impairment
ADV EFF Agranulocytosis, anaphylactoid reactions to fatal anaphylactic shock, aplastic anemia, dizziness, dyspepsia, eosinophilia, GI pain, granulocytopenia, headache, impaired vision, insomnia, leukopenia, nausea, neutropenia, pancytopenia, rash, somnolence, thrombocytopenia
INTERACTIONS ACE inhibitors, anticoagulants, antiplatelets, aspirin, phenobarbital
NC/PT Not for use in pregnancy (contraceptives advised). Pt should take w/meals, use safety precautions w/CNS effects, report bleeding, tarry stools, vision changes.

DANGEROUS DRUG

fentanyl (Abstral, Actiq, Duragesic, Fentora, Lazanda, SUBSYS)
CLASS Opioid agonist analgesic
PREG/CONT C/C-II

BBW Ensure appropriate use because drug potentially dangerous; respiratory depression, death possible. Have opioid antagonist, facilities for assisted or controlled respiration on hand during parenteral administration. Use caution when switching between forms; doses vary. Transdermal, nasal forms not for use in opioid–nontolerant pts. Not for acute or postop pain. Do not substitute for other fentanyl product. Keep out of children's reach; can be fatal. Potentiation of effects possible when given w/macrolide antibiotics, ketoconazole, itraconazole, protease inhibitors; potentially fatal respiratory depression possible.
IND & DOSE Analgesic adjunct for anesthesia. *Adult:* Premedication, 50–100 mcg IM 30–60 min before surgery. Adjunct to general anesthesia, initially, 2–20 mcg/kg; maint, 2–50 mcg IV or IM. 25–100 mcg IV or IM when vital sign changes indicate surgical stress, lightening of analgesia. W/oxygen for anesthesia, total high dose, 50–100 mcg/kg IV. Adjunct to regional anesthesia, 50–100 mcg IM or slowly IV over 1–2 min. *Child 2–12 yr:* 2–3 mcg/kg IV as vital signs indicate. Control of postop pain, tachypnea, emergence delirium. *Adult:* 50–100 mcg IM; repeat in 1–2 hr if needed. Mgt of chronic pain in pts requiring continuous opioid analgesia over extended period. *Adult:* 25 mcg/hr transdermal system; may need replacement in 72 hr if pain has not subsided. Do not use torn, damaged systems; serious overdose possible. *Children 2–12 yr:* 25 mcg/hr transdermal system; pts should be opioid-tolerant and receiving at least 60 mg oral morphine equivalents/day.
Tx of breakthrough pain in cancer pts treated w/and tolerant to opioids. *Adult:* Place unit (*Actiq*) in mouth between cheek, lower gum. Start w/200 mcg; may start redosing 15 min after previous lozenge completed. No more than two lozenges/breakthrough pain episode. For buccal tablets, initially 100-mcg tablet between cheek, gum for 14–25 min; may repeat in 30 min. For buccal soluble film, remove film, place inside cheek; will dissolve within 5–30 min. For sublingual tablets (*Astral*), initially 100 mcg sublingually; wait at least 2 hr between doses. For nasal spray, 100 mcg as single spray in one nostril.

Max, 800 mcg as single spray in one nostril or single spray in each nostril/episode. Wait at least 2 hr before treating new episode. No more than four doses in 24 hr.
ADV EFF Apnea, **cardiac arrest**, clamminess, confusion, constipation, dizziness, floating feeling, headache, lethargy, light-headedness, local irritation, n/v, **respiratory depression**, sedation, **shock**, sweating, vertigo
INTERACTIONS Alcohol, barbiturates, CNS depressants, grapefruit juice, itraconazole, ketoconazole, macrolide antibiotics, MAOIs, protease inhibitors
NC/PT Adjust dose as needed, tolerated for pain relief. Apply transdermal system to nonirritated, nonirradiated skin on flat surface of upper torso. Clip, do not shave, hair. May need 12 hr for full effect. Do not use torn, damaged transdermal systems; serious overdose possible. Give to breast-feeding women 4–6 hr before next scheduled feeding. Buccal soluble film, nasal spray only available through restricted access program. Titrate carefully w/COPD. Pt should avoid grapefruit juice, remove old transdermal patch before applying new one, take safety precautions w/CNS effects, report difficulty breathing. Name confusion between fentanyl and sufentanil; use extreme caution.

ferrous salts (ferrous aspartate, ferrous fumarate, ferrous gluconate, ferrous sulfate, ferrous sulfate exsiccated) (Femiron, Feosol, Fer-In-Sol, Ferro-Sequels, Slow Release Iron)
CLASS Iron preparation
PREG/CONT A/NA

BBW Warn pt to keep out of reach of children; leading cause of fatal poisoning in child under 6 yr.

IND & DOSE Dietary iron supplement. *Adult:* Men, 8–11 mg/day PO; women, 8–18 mg/day PO. Pregnant, breast-feeding women, 9–27 mg/day PO. *Child:* 7–11 mg/day PO. **Px, tx of iron deficiency anemia.** *Adult:* 150–300 mg/day (6 mg/kg/day) PO for approximately 6–10 mo. *Child:* 3–6 mg/kg/day PO.
ADV EFF Anorexia; **coma, death w/overdose**; constipation; GI upset; n/v
INTERACTIONS Antacids, chloramphenicol, cimetidine, ciprofloxacin, coffee, eggs, levodopa, levothyroxine, milk, ofloxacin, tea, tetracycline
NC/PT Establish correct diagnosis. Regularly monitor Hct, Hgb. Use straw for liquid forms (may stain teeth). Give w/food if GI upset severe. Stool may be green to black; tx may take several mo. Laxative may be needed. Pt should avoid eggs, milk, coffee, tea; keep out of reach of children (serious to fatal toxicity possible).

ferumoxytol (Feraheme)
CLASS Iron preparation
PREG/CONT C/NA

BBW Risk of serious hypersensitivity/anaphylactic reactions; monitor pt closely during and for 30 min after infusion. Administer only when emergency support is available.
IND & DOSE Tx of iron deficiency anemia in pts w/chronic renal failure. *Adult:* 510 mg IV then 510 mg IV in 3–8 days. Infuse in 50–200 mL 0.9% NSS or 5% dextrose injection over at least 15 min.
ADV EFF Constipation, diarrhea, dizziness, **hypersensitivity reactions, hypotension, iron overload,** nausea, peripheral edema
NC/PT Alters MRI results for up to 3 mo after use; will not alter CT scans or X-rays. Do not give if iron overload. Monitor for hypersensitivity reaction up to 30 min after infusion; have life support available; risk of anaphylaxis greatest w/hx of multiple drug allergies. Monitor BP during and for 30 min

after administration. Use caution in pregnancy; not for use in breastfeeding. Pt should take safety precautions w/CNS effects, report difficulty breathing, itching, swelling.

fesoterodine fumarate (Toviaz)
CLASS Antimuscarinic
PREG/CONT C/NA

IND & DOSE Tx of overactive bladder. *Adult:* 4 mg/day PO; may increase to max 8 mg/day.
ADJUST DOSE Renal impairment; hepatic impairment (not recommended)
ADV EFF Blurred vision, constipation, decreased sweating, dry eyes, dry mouth, increased IOP, urine retention
INTERACTIONS Alcohol, anticholinergics, clarithromycin, itraconazole, ketoconazole
NC/PT Monitor IOP before, periodically during tx. Pt should swallow tablet whole and not cut, crush, or chew it; empty bladder before dose; use sugarless lozenges, mouth care for dry mouth; take safety precautions for vision changes; stay hydrated in heat conditions (decreased ability to sweat); avoid alcohol.

fexofenadine hydrochloride (Allegra)
CLASS Antihistamine
PREG/CONT C/NA

IND & DOSE Symptomatic relief of sx associated w/seasonal allergic rhinitis. *Adult, child 12 yr and older:* 60 mg PO bid or 180 mg PO once daily; or 10 mL suspension PO bid. *Child 6–12 yr:* 30 mg orally disintegrating tablet (ODT) PO bid, or 5 mL suspension PO bid. *Child 2–12 yr:* 5 mL suspension PO bid. Chronic idiopathic urticaria. *Adult, child 12 yr and older:* 60 mg PO bid or 180 mg PO once daily. *Child 6–12 yr:* 30 mg ODT PO bid,

or 5 mL suspension PO bid. *Child 2–12 yr:* 5 mL suspension PO bid.
ADJUST DOSE Elderly pts, renal impairment
ADV EFF Drowsiness, fatigue, nausea
INTERACTIONS Antacids, erythromycin, itraconazole ketoconazole
NC/PT Arrange for humidifier if nasal dryness, thickened secretions a problem; encourage hydration. Pt should use in a.m. before exposure to allergens, take safety precautions w/CNS effects.

fibrinogen concentrate, human (RiaSTAP)
CLASS Coagulation factor
PREG/CONT C/NA

IND & DOSE Tx of acute bleeding episodes in pts w/congenital fibrinogen deficiency. *Adult, child:* 70 mg/kg by slow IV injection not over 5 mL/min; adjust dose to target fibrinogen level of 100 mg/dL.
ADJUST DOSE Elderly pts, renal impairment
ADV EFF Anaphylactic reactions, arterial thrombosis, blood-transmitted diseases, chills, DVT, fever, MI, n/v, PE, rash
NC/PT Made from human blood; risk of blood-transmitted diseases. Risk of thromboembolic events, severe hypersensitivity reactions. Pt should report chest/leg pain, chest tightness, difficulty breathing, continued fever.

fidaxomicin (Dificid)
CLASS Macrolide antibiotic
PREG/CONT B/NA

IND & DOSE Tx of CDAD. *Adult:* 200 mg PO bid for 10 days.
ADV EFF Abd pain, dyspepsia, gastric hemorrhage, n/v
NC/PT Culture stool before tx. Not for systemic infections; specific to

C. difficile diarrhea. Pt should complete full course of tx, report severe vomiting, bloody diarrhea.

filgrastim (Neupogen)
CLASS Colony-stimulating factor
PREG/CONT C/NA

IND & DOSE To decrease incidence of infection in pts w/nonmyeloid malignancies receiving myelosuppressive anticancer drugs; to reduce time to neutrophil recovery, duration of fever after induction and consolidation chemotherapy tx of acute myeloid leukemia. *Adult:* 5 mcg/kg/day subcut or IV as single daily injection. May increase in increments of 5 mcg/kg for each chemotherapy cycle; range, 4–8 mcg/kg/day. To reduce duration of neutropenia after bone marrow transplant. *Adult:* 10 mcg/kg/day IV or continuous subcut infusion. Tx of severe chronic neutropenia. *Adult:* 6 mcg/kg subcut bid (congenital neutropenia); 5 mcg/kg/day subcut as single injection (idiopathic, cyclic neutropenia). To mobilize hematopoietic progenitor cells into blood for leukapheresis collection. *Adult:* 10 mcg/kg/day subcut at least 4 days before first leukapheresis; continue to last leukapheresis. To reduce incidence, duration of severe neutropenia in pts w/congenital, cyclic, or idiopathic neutropenia. *Adult:* 6 mcg/kg subcut bid (congenital), or 5 mcg/kg subcut (cyclic, idiopathic). To increase survival in pts exposed to myelosuppressive doses of radiation therapy. *Adult:* 10 mcg/kg/day subcut
ADV EFF Acute respiratory distress syndrome, alopecia, anaphylaxis, bone pain, fatal sickle cell crisis, fatal splenic rupture, glomerulonephritis, n/v/d
NC/PT Obtain CBC, platelet count before and twice wkly during tx. Do not give within 24 hr of chemotherapy. Give daily for up to 2 wk or neutrophils

are 10,000/mm³. Store in refrigerator. Do not shake vial; do not reuse vial, needles, syringes. Not for use in pregnancy/breast-feeding. Teach pt proper administration/disposal of needles/syringes. Pt should avoid exposure to infection; cover head at temp changes (hair loss possible); report difficulty breathing, severe abd or left shoulder pain.

finafloxacin (Xtoro)
CLASS Antibiotic, quinolone
PREG/CONT C/NA

IND & DOSE Tx of acute otitis externa (swimmer's ear). *Adult, child over 1 yr:* 4 drops in affected ear(s) bid for 7 days. If using otowick, initial dose is 8 drops, then 4 drops bid for 7 days.
ADV EFF Allergic reaction, superinfection
NC/PT Warm bottle in hands before use; ensure full course of therapy. Pt/caregiver should report rash, worsening of condition.

finasteride (Propecia, Proscar)
CLASS Androgen hormone inhibitor
PREG/CONT X/NA

IND & DOSE Tx of symptomatic BPH. *Adult:* 5 mg daily PO w/or without meal; may take 6–12 mo for response (*Proscar*). Px of male-pattern baldness. *Adult:* 1 mg/day PO for 3 mo or more before benefit seen (*Propecia*).
ADV EFF Decreased libido, ED, gynecomastia
INTERACTIONS Saw palmetto
NC/PT Confirm dx of BPH. Protect from light. Pregnant women should not touch tablet. Pt may not donate blood and should not father a child during or for 6 mo after tx. Pt should monitor urine flow for improvement; may experience loss of libido.

fingolimod (Gilenya)

CLASS MS drug
PREG/CONT C/NA

IND & DOSE Tx of relapsing forms of MS. *Adult:* 0.5 mg/day PO.
ADV EFF Back pain, bradycardia, cough, decreased lung capacity, depression, diarrhea, dyspnea, headache, increased liver enzymes, infections, macular edema, **progressive multifocal leukoencephalopathy, RPLS**
INTERACTIONS Ketoconazole, live vaccines
NC/PT Use caution w/hypertension or hx of CAD. Obtain baseline, periodic ophthalmic evaluation because of macular edema risk. Monitor for bradycardia for at least 6 hr after first dose. Obtain spirometry studies if dyspnea occurs. Not for use in pregnancy (contraceptives advised during and for 2 mo after tx)/breast-feeding. Pt should avoid exposure to infection, take safety precautions w/CNS effects, report difficulty breathing, chest pain, s&sx of infection.

flavoxate hydrochloride (generic)

CLASS Parasympathetic blocker, urinary antispasmodic
PREG/CONT B/NA

IND & DOSE Symptomatic relief of dysuria, urgency, nocturia, suprapubic pain, frequency/incontinence due to cystitis, prostatitis, urethritis, urethrocystitis, urethrotrigonitis. *Adult, child 12 yr and older:* 100–200 mg PO tid or qid. Reduce dose when sx improve. Use max 1,200 mg/day in severe urinary urgency after pelvic radiotherapy.
ADV EFF Blurred vision, drowsiness, dry mouth, **eosinophilia**, headache, **leukopenia**, nervousness, n/v, vertigo
INTERACTIONS Anticholinergics, cholinergics

NC/PT Treat for underlying problem leading to s&sx. Obtain eye exam before, during tx. Pt should use sugarless lozenges for dry mouth; empty bladder before dose; report blurred vision.

flecainide acetate (generic)

CLASS Antiarrhythmic
PREG/CONT C/NA

BBW Increased risk of nonfatal cardiac arrest, death in pts w/recent MI, chronic atrial fibrillation. Monitor cardiac rhythm carefully; risk of potentially fatal proarrhythmias.
IND & DOSE Px, tx of life-threatening ventricular arrhythmias. *Adult:* 100 mg PO q 12 hr. Increase in 50-mg increments bid q fourth day until efficacy achieved; max, 400 mg/day. Px of paroxysmal atrial fibrillation/flutter associated w/sx and paroxysmal supraventricular tachycardias. *Adult:* 50 mg PO q 12 hr; may increase in 50-mg increments bid q 4 days until efficacy achieved; max, 300 mg/day. Transfer to flecainide. Allow at least 2–4 plasma half-lives to elapse after other antiarrhythmics discontinued before starting flecainide.
ADJUST DOSE Elderly pts; renal, hepatic impairment
ADV EFF Abd pain, **arrhythmias**, chest pain, constipation, dizziness, drowsiness, dyspnea, fatigue, headache, **leukopenia**, n/v, visual changes
INTERACTIONS Amiodarone, cimetidine, disopyramide (avoid marked drop in cardiac output), propranolol
NC/PT Check serum potassium before starting tx; evaluate for therapeutic serum levels (0.2–1 mcg/mL). Monitor response closely; have life support equipment on hand. Pt should take q 12 hr (arrange timing to avoid interrupting sleep), use safety precautions w/CNS effects, report chest pain, palpitations.

flibanserin (Addyi)

CLASS Serotonin/dopamine agonist/antagonist
PREG/CONT Unkn/NA

BBW Risk of severe hypotension if combined w/alcohol; pt must abstain. Contraindicated with w/CYP3A4 inhibitors or heptic impairment. Available only through Restricted Access Program.

IND & DOSE Tx of premenopausal women w/acquired, generalized hypoactive sexual desire disorder. *Adult:* 100 mg/day PO at bedtime; stop after 8 wk if no improvement.

ADJUST DOSE Hepatic impairment

ADV EFF Dizziness, dry mouth, fatigue, hypotension, insomnia, nausea, sedation, somnolence

INTERACTIONS Alcohol, CYP3A4 inducers/inhibitors, CYP2C19 inhibitors, digoxin, oral contraceptives

NC/PT Ensure appropriate use; not for postmenopausal women; does not enhance sexual performance. Not for use in pregnancy/breast-feeding. Give at bedtime to decrease hypotension risks. May react w/many drugs; monitor regimen. Pt should not combine w/alcohol; should take at bedtime; avoid tasks that require alertness for at least 6 hr after each dose; take safety precautions for CNS changes; use cautiously if low BP possible; monitor response and report after 8 wk; report fainting, continued sedation.

floxuridine (generic)

CLASS Antimetabolite, antineoplastic
PREG/CONT D/NA

IND & DOSE Palliative mgt of GI adenocarcinoma metastatic to liver. *Adult:* 0.1–0.6 mg/kg/day via intra-arterial infusion.

ADV EFF Bone marrow suppression, infections, gastric ulceration, glossitis, **hepatic impairment**, n/v/d, **renal impairment**, stomatitis

INTERACTIONS Immunosuppressants, live vaccines

NC/PT Obtain baseline, periodic CBC. Check for mouth ulcerations, dental infections; mouth care essential. Protect from exposure to infections. Not for use in pregnancy/breast-feeding. Pt should report severe GI pain, bloody diarrhea.

fluconazole (Diflucan)

CLASS Antifungal
PREG/CONT D/NA

IND & DOSE Tx of oropharyngeal candidiasis. *Adult:* 200 mg PO or IV on first day, then 100 mg/day for at least 2 wk. *Child:* 6 mg/kg PO or IV on first day, then 3 mg/kg once daily for at least 2 wk. Tx of esophageal candidiasis. *Adult:* 200 mg PO or IV on first day, then 100 mg/day, up to 400 mg/day for minimum of 3 wk, at least 2 wk after resolution. *Child:* 6 mg/kg PO or IV on first day, then 3 mg/kg/day for 3 wk, at least 2 wk after resolution. Tx of vaginal candidiasis. *Adult:* 150 mg PO as single dose. Tx of systemic candidiasis. *Adult:* 400 mg PO or IV daily. *Child:* 6–12 mg/kg/day PO or IV. Tx of candidal UTI/peritonitis. *Adult:* 50–200 mg/day PO. Tx of cryptococcal meningitis. *Adult:* 400 mg PO or IV on first day, then 200 mg/day up to 400 mg/day for 10–12 wk after cultures of CSF become negative. *Child:* 12 mg/kg PO or IV on first day, then 6 mg/kg/day for 10–12 wk after cultures of CSF become negative. Suppression of cryptococcal meningitis in AIDS pts. *Adult:* 200 mg PO or IV daily. *Child:* 6 mg/kg PO or IV daily. Px of candidiasis in bone marrow transplants. *Adult:* 400 mg PO daily for several days before onset of neutropenia and for 7 days after neutrophil count above 1,000/mm³.

ADJUST DOSE Hepatic/renal impairment

ADV EFF Abd pain, **anaphylaxis, exfoliative skin disorders,** headache, **hepatotoxicity,** n/v/d, prolonged QT, **renal toxicity**
INTERACTIONS Benzodiazepines, cimetidine, cyclosporine, oral hypoglycemics, phenytoin, pinozide, quinidine, QT-prolonging drugs, rifampin, warfarin anticoagulants, zidovudine
NC/PT Culture before tx. For IV, oral use only. Monitor renal, hepatic function wkly. Frequent medical follow-up needed. Pt should take hygiene measures to prevent infection spread; use analgesics for headache; report rash, difficulty breathing, urine/stool color changes.

---

flucytosine (Ancobon)
CLASS Antifungal
PREG/CONT C/NA

BBW Monitor serum flucytosine levels in pts w/renal impairment (levels over 100 mcg/mL associated w/toxicity).
IND & DOSE Tx of serious infections caused by susceptible *Candida, Cryptococcus* strains. *Adult:* 50–150 mg/kg/day PO at 6-hr intervals.
ADJUST DOSE Renal impairment
ADV EFF Anemia, **cardiac arrest,** confusion, dizziness, **leukopenia,** n/v/d, **rash, respiratory arrest, thrombocytopenia**
NC/PT Give capsules few at a time over 15-min to decrease GI upset, diarrhea. Monitor LFTs, renal/hematologic function periodically during tx. Pt should take safety precautions w/CNS effects; report fever, difficulty breathing.

---

fludarabine phosphate (generic)
CLASS Antimetabolite, antineoplastic
PREG/CONT D/NA

BBW Stop tx if s&sx of toxicity (CNS complaints, stomatitis, esophago-pharyngitis, rapidly falling WBC count, intractable vomiting, diarrhea, GI ulceration/bleeding, thrombocytopenia, hemorrhage, hemolytic anemia); serious to life-threatening infections possible. Consult physician.
IND & DOSE Chronic lymphocytic leukemia (CLL); unresponsive B-cell CLL. *Adult:* 40 mg/m² PO or 25 mg/m² IV over 30 min for 5 consecutive days. Begin each 5-day course q 28 days.
ADJUST DOSE Renal impairment
ADV EFF Anorexia, **autoimmune hemolytic anemia,** bone marrow toxicity, chills, **CNS toxicity (including blindness, coma, death),** cough, dyspnea, edema, fatigue, fever, headache, infection, n/v/d, pneumonia, pruritus, **pulmonary toxicity,** stomatitis, **tumor lysis syndrome,** visual disturbances, weakness
INTERACTIONS Pentostatin
NC/PT Obtain CBC before tx, each dose. Monitor pulmonary function regularly. Not for use in pregnancy (contraceptives advised). Pt should not crush tablets; avoid contact w/skin, mucous membranes; mark calendar of tx days; take safety precautions for CNS effects; avoid exposure to infections; report bruising, excess bleeding, black stools, difficulty breathing.

---

fludrocortisone acetate (generic)
CLASS Corticosteroid
PREG/CONT C/NA

IND & DOSE Partial replacement tx in adrenocortical insufficiency. *Adult:* 0.05–0.1 mg/day PO. Tx of salt-losing adrenogenital syndrome. *Adult:* 0.1–0.2 mg/day PO.
ADJUST DOSE Elderly pts; hepatic, renal impairment
ADV EFF Anxiety, cardiac enlargement, depression, edema, HF, hypertension, hypokalemic acidosis, infection, weakness

INTERACTIONS Amphotericin B, anabolic steroids, antidiabetics, aspirin, barbiturates, digitalis, diuretics, hormonal contraceptives, phenytoin, rifampin, warfarin

NC/PT Monitor BP, serum electrolytes, blood glucose before, periodically during tx. Protect from infection. Frequent medical follow-up, blood tests needed. Use caution in pregnancy/breast-feeding. Pt should wear medical ID, report all drugs used to health care provider (many drug interactions possible).

flumazenil (generic)
CLASS Antidote, benzodiazepine receptor antagonist
PREG/CONT C/NA

BBW Possible increased risk of seizures, especially in pts on long-term benzodiazepine tx and pts w/serious cyclic antidepressant overdose; take appropriate precautions.

IND & DOSE Reversal of conscious sedation or in general anesthesia. *Adult:* 0.2 mg (2 mL) IV over 15 sec, wait 45 sec; if ineffectual, repeat at 60-sec intervals. Max cumulative dose, 1 mg (10 mL). *Children over 1 yr:* 0.01 mg/kg (up to 0.2 mg) IV over 15 sec; wait 45 sec. Repeat at 60-sec intervals. Max cumulative dose, 0.05 mg/kg or 1 mg, whichever lowest. Mgt of suspected benzodiazepine overdose. *Adult:* 0.2 mg IV over 30 sec; repeat w/0.3 mg IV q 30 sec. May give further doses of 0.5 mg over 30 sec at 1-min intervals. Max cumulative dose, 3 mg.

ADV EFF Amnesia, dizziness, increased sweating, n/v, pain at injection site, **seizures**, vertigo

INTERACTIONS Alcohol, CNS depressants, food

NC/PT IV use only, into running IV in large vein. Have emergency equipment on hand; continually monitor response. Provide safety measures for CNS effects for at least 18–24 hr after use. Give pt written information

(amnesia may be prolonged). Pt should avoid alcohol for 18–24 hr after administration.

flunisolide (Aerospan HFA)
CLASS Corticosteroid
PREG/CONT C/NA

IND & DOSE Intranasal relief/mgt of nasal sx of seasonal, perennial allergic rhinitis. *Adult:* 2 sprays (50 mcg) in each nostril bid; may increase to 2 sprays in each nostril tid (total dose, 300 mcg/day). Max, 400 mcg/day. *Child 6–14 yr:* 1 spray in each nostril tid or 2 sprays in each nostril bid (total dose, 150–200 mcg/day). Max, 200 mcg/day. Inhalation maint tx of asthma. *Adult:* 2 inhalations by mouth bid. Max, 640 mcg/day. *Child 12 yr and older:* Adult dosage. *Child 6–11 yr:* 1 inhalation bid. Max, 160 mcg bid.

ADV EFF Epistaxis, fungal infection, headache, nasal irritation, rebound congestion

NC/PT May use decongestant drops to facilitate penetration if needed. Not for acute asthma attack. Pt should not stop suddenly, rinse mouth after each use of inhaler.

fluorouracil (Carac, Efudex, Fluoroplex)
CLASS Antimetabolite, antineoplastic
PREG/CONT D/NA

BBW Stop tx at s&sx of toxicity (stomatitis, esophagopharyngitis, rapidly falling WBC count, intractable vomiting, diarrhea, GI ulceration/bleeding, thrombocytopenia, hemorrhage); serious to life-threatening reactions have occurred. Consult physician.

IND & DOSE Palliative mgt of carcinoma of colon, rectum, breast, stomach, pancreas in selected pts considered incurable by surgery or other means. *Adult:* 12 mg/kg/day IV for 4 successive days, infused slowly over 24 hr; max, 800 mg/day. If no toxicity, 6 mg/kg IV on days 6, 8, 10, 12, w/no drug tx on days 5, 7, 9, 11. Stop tx at end of day 12. If no toxicity, repeat q 30 days. If toxicity, 10–15 mg/kg/wk IV as single dose after s&sx of toxicity subside; max, 1 g/wk. Adjust dose based on response; tx may be prolonged (12–60 mo). **Tx of actinic or solar keratoses.** *Adult:* Apply bid to cover lesions. 0.5% and 1% used on head, neck, chest; 2% and 5% used on hands. Continue until inflammatory response reaches erosion, necrosis, and ulceration stage, then stop. Usual tx course, 2–4 wk. Complete healing may not occur for 1–2 mo after tx stops. **Tx of superficial basal cell carcinoma.** *Adult:* 5% strength bid in amount sufficient to cover lesions, for at least 3–6 wk. Tx may be needed for 10–12 wk.

ADJUST DOSE Poor risk, undernourished pts

ADV EFF Alopecia, anorexia, cramps, dermatitis, duodenal ulcer, duodenitis, enteritis, gastritis, glossitis, lethargy, **leukopenia**, local irritation w/topical use, malaise, n/v/d, photosensitivity, rash, stomatitis, **thrombocytopenia**

NC/PT Obtain CBC before and regularly during tx. Ensure dx of topical lesions. Thoroughly wash hands after applying topical form; avoid occlusive dressings w/topical form. Stop tx at s&sx of toxicity. Frequent medical follow-up needed. Pt should mark calendar for tx days; cover head at temp extremes (hair loss possible); avoid exposure to sun, infections; report black tarry stools, unusual bleeding or bruising.

---

fluoxetine hydrochloride (Prozac, Sarafem)

CLASS Antidepressant, SSRI
PREG/CONT C/NA

BBW Establish suicide precautions for severely depressed pts. Limit quantity dispensed; high risk of suicidality in children, adolescents, young adults.

IND & DOSE Tx of depression. *Adult:* 20 mg/day PO in a.m.; max, 80 mg/day. Once stabilized, may switch to 90-mg DR capsules PO weekly. *Child 8–18 yr:* 10 mg/day PO; may increase to 20 mg/day after 1 wk or after several wk for low-weight children. **Tx of depressive episodes of bipolar I disorder.** *Adult:* 20 mg/day PO w/5 mg olanzapine. **Tx of tx-resistant depression.** *Adult:* 20–50 mg/day PO w/5–20 mg olanzapine. **Tx of OCD.** *Adult:* 20 mg/day PO; range, 20–60 mg/day PO. May need up to 5 wk for effectiveness. Max, 80 mg/day. *Adolescent, higher-weight child:* 10 mg/day PO; range, 20–60 mg/day PO. *Adolescent, lower-weight child:* 10 mg/day PO; range, 20–30 mg/day. **Tx of bulimia.** *Adult:* 60 mg/day in a.m. **Tx of panic disorder.** *Adult:* 10 mg/day PO for first wk; max, 60 mg/day. **Tx of PMDD** (Sarafem). *Adult:* 20 mg/day PO. Or 20 mg/day PO starting 14 days before anticipated beginning of menses, continuing through first full day of menses; then no drug until 14 days before next menses. Max, 80 mg/day.

ADJUST DOSE Elderly pts, hepatic impairment

ADV EFF **Angle-closure glaucoma,** anorexia, anxiety, asthenia, constipation, dizziness, drowsiness, dry mouth, dyspepsia, fever, headache, insomnia, light-headedness, nervousness, n/v/d, painful menstruation, pharyngitis, pruritus, rash, **seizures**, serotonin syndrome, sexual dysfx, sweating, URI, urinary frequency, weight changes

INTERACTIONS Alcohol, benzodiazepines, ED drugs, linezolid, lithium, MAOIs, opioids, pimozide, serotonergic drugs, St. John's wort, TCAs, thioridazine

NC/PT Do not use within 14 days of MAOIs, within 5 wk of thioridazine. Do not combine w/pimozide. Give in a.m. Full antidepressant effect may not occur for up to 4–6 wk. Taper when stopping. Not for use in pregnancy. Pt should avoid alcohol, St. John's wort; take safety precautions w/CNS effects; report thoughts of suicide. Name confusion between *Sarafem* (fluoxetine) and *Serophene* (clomiphene); use caution.

flurazepam hydrochloride (generic)

CLASS Benzodiazepine, sedative-hypnotic
PREG/CONT X/C-IV

IND & DOSE *Tx of insomnia. Adult:* 15–30 mg PO at bedtime.
ADJUST DOSE Elderly pts, debilitating disease
ADV EFF Anaphylaxis, **angioedema,** apathy, bradycardia, confusion, constipation, **CV collapse,** depression, diarrhea, disorientation, drowsiness, drug dependence w/withdrawal, fatigue, gynecomastia, lethargy, light-headedness, restlessness, tachycardia, urine retention
INTERACTIONS Alcohol, aminophylline, barbiturates, cimetidine, disulfiram, hormonal contraceptives, opioids, phenothiazines, rifampin, SSRIs, theophylline, TCAs
NC/PT Monitor LFTs, renal function. Taper gradually after long-term use. Not for use in pregnancy (barrier contraceptives advised). Pt should take safety precautions w/CNS effects, report worsening depression, difficulty breathing, edema.

flurbiprofen (Ansaid, Ocufen)

CLASS Analgesic, NSAID
PREG/CONT B (oral); C (ophthalmic)/NA

BBW Increased risk of CV events, GI bleeding; monitor accordingly. Contraindicated for tx of periop CABG pain.

IND & DOSE *Acute or long-term tx of s&sx of rheumatoid arthritis, osteoarthritis; relief of moderate to mild pain. Adult:* 200–300 mg PO in divided doses bid, tid, or qid. Max, 100 mg/dose. *Inhibition of intraop miosis. Adult:* 1 drop ophthalmic sol approximately q 30 min, starting 2 hr before surgery (total, 4 drops).
ADV EFF Agranulocytosis, aplastic anemia, bleeding, bone marrow depression, bronchospasm, dizziness, dyspepsia, **eosinophilia, fatal anaphylactic shock,** fatigue, **gastric ulcer,** GI pain, **granulocytopenia,** headache, insomnia, **leukopenia,** nausea, **neutropenia, pancytopenia, renal impairment,** somnolence, **thrombocytopenia,** transient local stinging/burning w/ophthalmic sol
NC/PT Give w/food if GI upset severe. Not for use in pregnancy (barrier contraceptives advised). Pt should take safety precautions w/CNS effects; report fever, rash, black stools, swelling in ankles/fingers.

DANGEROUS DRUG

flutamide (generic)

CLASS Antiandrogen, antineoplastic
PREG/CONT D/NA

BBW Arrange for periodic monitoring of LFTs during long-term tx; severe hepatotoxicity possible.
IND & DOSE *Tx of locally advanced, metastatic prostatic carcinoma. Adult:* 250 mg PO tid. Begin tx at same time as initiation of LH-RH analogue.
ADV EFF Anemia, dizziness, drowsiness, ED, GI disturbances, gynecomastia, **hepatic necrosis, hepatitis,** hot flashes, leukopenia, loss of libido, n/v/d, photosensitivity, rash
NC/PT Give w/other drugs used for medical castration. Monitor LFTs regularly. Periodic blood tests will be needed. Pt should take safety precautions w/CNS effects, avoid exposure to sunlight.

fluvastatin sodium
(Lescol)

CLASS Antihyperlipidemic, statin

PREG/CONT X/NA

IND & DOSE Adjunct to diet/exercise to lower cholesterol, LDL; to slow progression of CAD, reduce risk of need for revascularization w/CAD. *Adult:* 40 mg/day PO. Maint, 20–80 mg/day PO; give 80 mg/day as two 40-mg doses, or use 80-mg ER form. Tx of heterozygous familial hypercholesterolemia. *Child 9–16 yr:* 20 mg/day PO. Adjust q 6 wk to max 40 mg bid or 80 mg ER form PO once/day.

ADV EFF Abd pain, blurred vision, cataracts, constipation, cramps, flatulence, headache, **rhabdomyolysis**

INTERACTIONS Azole antifungals, cyclosporine, erythromycin, gemfibrozil, grapefruit juice, niacin, other statins, phenytoin, warfarin

NC/PT Give in evening. Periodic ophthalmic exams will be needed. Not for use in pregnancy (barrier contraceptives advised). Pt should swallow ER form whole and not cut, crush, or chew it; continue diet/exercise program; avoid grapefruit juice; report muscle pain w/fever, changes in vision.

fluvoxamine maleate
(Luvox)

CLASS Antidepressant, SSRI

PREG/CONT C/NA

BBW Establish suicide precautions for severely depressed pts. Limit quantity dispensed. Increased risk of suicidal ideation, behavior in children, adolescents, young adults.

IND & DOSE Tx of OCD, social anxiety disorders. *Adult:* 50 mg PO at bedtime; range, 100–300 mg/day. Or, 100–300 mg/day CR capsules PO. *Child 8–17 yr:* 25 mg PO at bedtime. Divide doses over 50 mg/day; give larger dose at bedtime. Max for child up to 11 yr, 200 mg/day.

ADJUST DOSE Elderly pts, hepatic impairment

ADV EFF Anorexia, anxiety, asthenia, constipation, dizziness, drowsiness, dry mouth, dyspepsia, fever, headache, insomnia, light-headedness, nervousness, n/v/d, painful menstruation, pharyngitis, pruritus, rash, **seizures**, sexual dysfx, serotonin syndrome, sweating, URI, urinary frequency, weight changes

INTERACTIONS Alprazolam, beta blockers, carbamazepine, cigarette smoking, clozapine, diltiazem, MAOIs, methadone, quetiapine, serotonergic drugs, statins, St. John's wort, TCAs, theophylline, triazolam, warfarin

NC/PT Give in evening. Monitor for serotonin syndrome. Taper when stopping. Pt should swallow CR capsule whole and not cut, crush, or chew it; take safety precautions w/CNS effects; report thoughts of suicide.

folic acid (generic)

CLASS Folic acid, vitamin supplement

PREG/CONT A/NA

IND & DOSE Tx of megaloblastic anemias due to sprue, nutritional deficiency, pregnancy; anemias of infancy, childhood. *Adult:* 1 mg/day PO, IM, IV, subcut; maint, 0.4 mg/day. In pregnancy/breast-feeding, 0.8 mg/day PO. *Child (maint):* Over 4 yr, 0.4 mg/day, up to 0.3 mg/day PO; infants, 0.1 mg/day.

ADV EFF Pain, discomfort at injection site

INTERACTIONS Aminosalicylic acid, phenytoin, sulfasalazine

NC/PT Ensure correct anemia dx. Give orally if possible. Monitor for hypersensitivity reactions. Pt should report pain at injection site, difficulty breathing.

follitropin alfa (Gonal-F)

CLASS Fertility drug
PREG/CONT X/NA

IND & DOSE Induction of ovulation. *Adult:* 75 international units/day subcut. Increase by 37.5 international units/day after 14 days; may increase again after 7 days. Do not use for longer than 35 days. **Stimulation of multiple follicles for in vitro fertilization.** *Adult:* 150 international units/day subcut on days 2, 3 of cycle; continue for 10 days. Adjust based on response. Max, 450 international units subut; then 5,000–10,000 international units HCG. **Promotion of spermatogenesis.** *Adult:* 150–300 international units subcut two to three times/wk w/HCG. May use for up to 18 mo.
ADV EFF Multiple births, nausea, ovarian cyst, **ovarian hyperstimulation, pulmonary/vascular complications,** URI
NC/PT Ensure uterine health. Monitor regularly; monitor for thrombotic events. Alert pt to risk of multiple births. Teach proper administration/ disposal of needles/syringes.

follitropin beta (Follistim AQ)

CLASS Fertility drug
PREG/CONT X/NA

IND & DOSE Induction of ovulation. *Adult:* 75 international units/day subcut. Increase by 37.5 international units/day after 14 days; may increase again after 7 days. Do not use for longer than 35 days. **Stimulation of multiple follicles for in vitro fertilization.** *Adult:* 150–225 international units/day subcut or IM for at least 4 days; adjust based on response. Follow w/HCG.
ADV EFF Multiple births, nausea, ovarian cyst, **ovarian hyperstimulation, pulmonary/vascular complications,** URI

NC/PT Ensure uterine health. Give subcut in navel or abdomen. Give regularly; monitor for thrombotic events. Alert pt to risk of multiple births. Teach proper administration/ disposal of needles/syringes.

fomepizole (Antizol)

CLASS Antidote
PREG/CONT C/NA

IND & DOSE Antidote for anti-freeze, methanol poisoning. *Adult:* 15 mg/kg loading dose IV, then 10 mg/kg IV q 12 hr for 12 doses by slow IV infusion over 30 min.
ADV EFF Acidosis, bradycardia, dizziness, electrolyte disturbances, headache, hypotension, injection-site reaction, lymphangitis, **multiorgan failure,** nausea, nystagmus, phlebitis, **seizures, shock**
INTERACTIONS Alcohol
NC/PT Monitor ECG, electrolytes, renal function, LFTs, BP. Monitor IV injection site. May be used w/hemodialysis if needed to clear toxins. Give q 4 hr during dialysis. Pt should take safety precautions w/CNS effects.

DANGEROUS DRUG

fondaparinux (Arixtra)

CLASS Antithrombotic,
low-molecular-weight heparin
PREG/CONT C/NA

BBW Carefully monitor pts receiving spinal/epidural anesthesia; risk of spinal hematoma, neurologic damage.
IND & DOSE Px of venous thrombotic events in pts undergoing surgery for hip fracture, hip or knee replacement; in pts undergoing abd surgery; extended px of DVT that may lead to PE after hip surgery. *Adult:* 2.5 mg/day subcut starting 6–8 hr after surgical closure and continuing for 5–9 days. May add 24 days after initial course for pts undergoing hip fracture surgery. **Tx of DVT, acute PE, w/warfarin.** *Adult:* Over 100 kg,

10 mg/day subcut for 5–9 days; begin warfarin within 72 hr. 50–100 kg, 7.5 mg/day subcut for 5–9 days. Under 50 kg, 5 mg/day subcut for 5–9 days.
ADJUST DOSE Elderly pts, renal impairment
ADV EFF Anemia, **anaphylaxis,** bruising, fever, **hemorrhage,** hepatic impairment, local reaction at injection site, nausea
INTERACTIONS Cephalosporins, garlic, ginkgo, NSAIDs, oral anticoagulants, penicillins, platelet inhibitors, salicylates, vitamin E
NC/PT Give drug 6–8 hr after surgical closure. Give by deep subcut injections; do not give IM. Store at room temp. Do not mix w/other sols or massage injection site. Rotate injection sites. Provide safety measures to prevent bleeding. Teach proper technique for injection, disposal of needles/syringes. Needle guard contains dry natural rubber; may cause allergic reactions w/latex sensibility. Pt should avoid NSAIDs, report bleeding, black tarry stools, severe headache.

---

formoterol fumarate (Foradil Aerolizer, Perforomist)
CLASS Antiasthmatic, beta agonist
PREG/CONT C/NA

BBW Long-acting beta agonists may increase risk of asthma-related deaths; use only if clearly warranted. Use in asthma without concomitant inhaled corticosteroid contraindicated.
IND & DOSE Maintenance tx of COPD. *Adult:* Oral inhalation of contents of 1 capsule (12 mcg) using *Aerolizer* inhaler q 12 hr; max, 24 mcg daily. Or, one 20-mcg/2 mL vial by oral inhalation using jet nebulizer connected to air compressor bid (a.m. and p.m.); max, 40 mcg/day.
Prevention of exercise-induced bronchospasm. *Adult, child 12 yr and older:* Oral inhalation of contents of 1 capsule (12 mcg) using *Aerolizer* inhaler 15 min before exercise. **Maintenance tx of asthma.** *Adult, child 5 yr and older:* Oral inhalation of contents of 1 capsule (12 mcg) using *Aerolizer* inhaler q 12 hr; max, 1 capsule q 12 hr.
ADV EFF Headache, nervousness, prolonged QT, throat/mouth irritation, tremors, viral infections
INTERACTIONS Beta blockers, QT-prolonging drugs
NC/PT Teach proper use of inhaler, nebulizer; periodically monitor use. Provide safety precautions for tremors, analgesics for headache. Ensure continued use of other drugs for COPD, bronchospasm. Pt should use 15 min before activity if used for exercise-induced asthma. Name confusion between *Foradil* (formoterol) and *Toradol* (ketorolac); use extreme caution.

---

fosamprenavir (Lexiva)
CLASS Antiviral, protease inhibitor
PREG/CONT C/NA

IND & DOSE Tx of HIV infection w/other antiretrovirals. *Adult:* 1,400 mg PO bid. W/ritonavir: 1,400 mg PO bid plus ritonavir 100 mg/day PO, or 1,400 mg/day PO plus ritonavir 200 mg/day PO, or 700 mg PO bid w/ritonavir 100 mg PO bid. In protease-experienced pts: 700 mg PO bid w/ritonavir 100 mg PO bid. *Child 2–5 yr (tx-naïve):* 30 mg/kg oral suspension PO bid; max, 1,400 mg. *Child 6 yr and older (tx-naïve):* 30 mg/kg oral suspension PO bid; max, 1,400 mg bid. Or, 18 mg/kg oral suspension PO w/ritonavir 3 mg/kg PO bid; max, 700 mg fosamprenavir plus 100 mg ritonavir bid. *Child 6 yr and older (tx-experienced):* 18 mg/kg oral suspension w/3 mg/kg ritonavir PO bid; max, 700 mg fosamprenavir w/100 mg ritonavir bid.
ADJUST DOSE Hepatic impairment

ADV EFF Depression, headache, hyperglycemia, **MI**, n/v/d, redistribution of body fat, **Stevens-Johnson syndrome**

INTERACTIONS Dihydroergotamine, ergotamine, flecainide, lovastatin, methylergonovine, midazolam, pimozide, piroxicam, propafenone, rifabutin, simvastatin, triazolam—do not use w/any of preceding drugs. Amiodarone, amitriptyline, amlodipine, carbamazepine, cyclosporine, delavirdine, diltiazem, efavirenz, felodipine, hormonal contraceptives, imipramine, isradipine, itraconazole, ketoconazole, lidocaine, lopinavir/ritonavir, nevirapine, nicardipine, nifedipine, nimodipine, nisoldipine, phenobarbital, phenytoin, quinidine, rifampin, saquinavir, sildenafil, St. John's wort, tacrolimus, vardenafil, verapamil

NC/PT Carefully check other drugs being used; interacts w/many drugs; potentially serious interactions possible. Give w/other antiretrovirals. Monitor LFTs, blood glucose. Monitor for rash. Not for use in pregnancy (barrier contraceptives advised). Pt should monitor glucose carefully if diabetic; avoid St. John's wort; tell all health care providers about all drugs, herbs being taken; report rash, chest pain.

fosfomycin tromethamine (Monurol)
CLASS Antibacterial, urinary tract anti-infective
PREG/CONT B/NA

IND & DOSE Tx of uncomplicated UTIs in women caused by susceptible strains. *Adult, child 12 yr and older:* 1 packet dissolved in water PO as single dose.
ADV EFF Dizziness, headache, nausea, rash
INTERACTIONS Metoclopramide
NC/PT Culture before tx. Do not give dry. Mix in 90–120 mL water (not hot); stir to dissolve. Pt should con-

tact prescriber if no improvement, take safety precautions if dizziness occurs.

fosinopril sodium (generic)
CLASS ACE inhibitor, antihypertensive
PREG/CONT D/NA

BBW Pt should avoid pregnancy (suggest contraceptive); fetal damage possible if used in second, third trimesters. Switch to different drug if pregnancy occurs.
IND & DOSE Tx of hypertension. *Adult:* 10 mg/day PO. Range, 20–40 mg/day PO; max, 80 mg. **Adjunct tx of HF.** *Adult:* 10 mg/day PO; observe for 2 hr for hypotension. For pt w/moderate to severe renal failure, 5 mg/day PO; max, 40 mg/day.
ADV EFF Angioedema, cough, hyperkalemia, nausea, orthostatic hypotension, rash
INTERACTIONS ACE inhibitors, antacids, ARBs, indomethacin, lithium, NSAIDs, potassium-sparing diuretics, renin inhibitors
NC/PT Alert surgeon about use; post-stop fluid replacement may be needed. Not for use in pregnancy (barrier contraceptives advised). Pt should use care in situations that might lead to BP drop, change positions slowly if light-headedness occurs. Name confusion between fosinopril and lisinopril; use caution.

fosphenytoin sodium (Cerebyx)
CLASS Antiepileptic, hydantoin
PREG/CONT D/NA

BBW Pt should avoid pregnancy; fetal damage possible. Suggest use of contraceptive. Risk of serious CV toxicity w/rapid infusion; monitor CV status continuously during infusion.
IND & DOSE Short-term control of status epilepticus. *Adult:* Loading

dose, 15–20 mg PE/kg at 100–150 mg PE/min IV. **Px, tx of seizures during or after neurosurgery.** *Adult:* Loading dose, 10–20 mg PE/kg IM or IV; maint, 4–6 mg PE/kg/day. **Substitution for oral phenytoin therapy.** *Adult:* Substitute IM or IV at same total daily dose as phenytoin; for short-term use only.

ADJUST DOSE Hepatic, renal impairment

ADV EFF Ataxia, CV toxicity, dizziness, drowsiness, hypotension, nausea, pruritus, twitching

INTERACTIONS Acetaminophen, amiodarone, antineoplastics, carbamazepine, chloramphenicol, cimetidine, corticosteroids, cyclosporine, diazoxide, disopyramide, disulfiram, doxycycline, estrogens, fluconazole, folic acid, hormonal contraceptives, isoniazid, levodopa, methadone, metyrapone, mexiletine, phenacemide, phenylbutazone, primidone, rifampin, sulfonamides, theophyllines, trimethoprim, valproic acid

NC/PT Give IV slowly to prevent severe hypotension. Monitor infusion site carefully; sols are very alkaline, irritating. For short-term use (up to 5 days); switch to oral phenytoin as soon as possible. Not for use in pregnancy (contraceptives advised). Pt should take safety precautions w/ CNS effects. Name confusion w/ *Cerebyx* (fosphenytoin), *Celebrex* (celecoxib), *Celexa* (citalopram), or *Xanax* (alprazolam); use caution.

frovatriptan succinate (Frova)
CLASS Antimigraine, triptan
PREG/CONT C/NA

IND & DOSE Tx of acute migraine w/or without aura. *Adult:* 2.5 mg PO as single dose at first sign of migraine; may repeat after 2 hr. Max, 3 doses/24 hr.

ADV EFF Cerebrovascular events, dizziness, headache, **MI,** n/v, tingling, **ventricular arrhythmias**

INTERACTIONS Ergots, SSRIs

NC/PT Ensure proper dx of migraine. For tx, not px. Ensure no ergots taken within 24 hr. Ensure 2 hr between doses, no more than three doses/day. Monitor BP. Not for use in pregnancy. Pt should take safety precautions w/CNS effects, report chest pain/pressure.

> **DANGEROUS DRUG**

fulvestrant (Faslodex)
CLASS Antineoplastic, estrogen receptor antagonist
PREG/CONT D/NA

IND & DOSE Tx of hormone receptor–positive breast cancer in postmenopausal women w/disease progression after antiestrogen tx. *Adult:* 500 mg IM on days 1, 15, 29, then monthly as two concomitant 5-mL injections, one in each buttock.

ADJUST DOSE Hepatic impairment

ADV EFF Abd pain, anemia, arthritis, asthenia, back pain, bone pain, dizziness, dyspnea, hot flashes, increased cough/sweating, n/v/d, pelvic pain

INTERACTIONS Oral anticoagulants

NC/PT Rule out pregnancy; suggest contraceptives. Handle cautiously. Give by slow IM injection over 1–2 min. Hot flashes possible. Teach proper administration/disposal of needles/syringes. Pt should mark calendar of tx days, take safety precautions w/CNS effects.

furosemide (Lasix)
CLASS Loop diuretic
PREG/CONT C/NA

BBW Profound diuresis w/water, electrolyte depletion possible; careful medical supervision needed.

IND & DOSE Edema associated w/ systemic disease. *Adult:* 20–80 mg/day PO as single dose; max, 600 mg/day. Or, 20–40 mg IM or IV (slow IV injection over 1–2 min); max, 4 mg/min. *Child:*

2 mg/kg/day PO; max, 6 mg/kg/day (1 mg/kg/day in preterm infants). **Tx of acute pulmonary edema.** *Adult:* 40 mg IV over 1–2 min. May increase to 80 mg IV over 1–2 min if response unsatisfactory after 1 hr. *Child:* 1 mg/kg IV or IM. May increase by 1 mg/kg in 2 hr until desired effect achieved. Max, 6 mg/kg. **Tx of hypertension.** *Adult:* 40 mg bid PO.
ADJUST DOSE Renal impairment
ADV EFF Anemia, anorexia, dizziness, hyperglycemia, hypokalemia, leukopenia, muscle cramps, n/v, orthostatic hypotension, paresthesia, photosensitivity, pruritus, thrombocytopenia, urticaria, xanthopsia
INTERACTIONS Aminoglycosides, charcoal, cisplatin, digitalis, ibuprofen, indomethacin, NSAIDs, oral antidiabetics, phenytoin
NC/PT Give early in day so diuresis will not affect sleep. Do not expose to light. Record weight daily. Arrange for potassium replacement or potassium-rich diet. Pt should avoid sun exposure, report loss or gain of more than 3 lb/day, take safety precautions w/ CNS effects. Name confusion between furosemide and torsemide; use caution.

---

gabapentin (Neurontin, Gralise, Horizant)
CLASS Antiepileptic
PREG/CONT C/NA

IND & DOSE Adjunct tx of partial seizures. *Adult:* 300 mg PO tid. Maint, 900–1,800 mg/day PO tid in divided doses; max of 2,400–3,600 mg/day has been used. Max interval between doses, 12 hr. *Child 3–12 yr:* 10–15 mg/kg/day PO in three divided doses. Range, 25–35 mg/kg/day in three divided doses (child 5 yr and older) and up to 40 mg/kg/day in three divided doses (child 3–4 yr). **Tx of postherpetic neuralgia.** *Adult:* 300 mg PO; 300 mg PO bid on day 2; 300 mg PO tid on day 3. Or, 1,800 mg/day PO w/evening meal (*Gralise*). **Tx of mod-**

erate to severe restless legs syndrome. *Adult:* 600–800 mg/day PO w/food around 5 p.m.; max, 2,400 mg/day (*Horizant*).
ADJUST DOSE Elderly pts, renal impairment
ADV EFF Anaphylaxis, angioedema. ataxia, dizziness, insomnia, multiorgan hypersensitivity, neuropsychiatric reactions in children, **seizures**, somnolence, suicidal ideation, tremor, weight gain
INTERACTIONS Antacids
NC/PT *Gralise* not interchangeable w/other forms of gabapentin. Do not cut, crush, or allow pt to chew ER forms. Taper ER forms after longterm use. Monitor for anaphylaxis, angioedema; stop immediately. Pt may be at increased risk for suicidality; monitor. Not for use in pregnancy; use caution in breast-feeding. Suggest medical ID. Pt should take safety precautions for CNS effects; report rash, difficulty breathing, swelling.

---

gadobutrol (Gadavist)
CLASS Contrast agent
PREG/CONT C/NA

BBW Risk of nephrogenic systemic fibrosis, more common w/higher-than-normal dosing or repeated dosing; monitor total dose. Screen for kidney injury before use.
IND & DOSE Detection, visualization of areas w/disrupted blood-brain barrier and/or abnormal CNS vascularity; to assess malignant breast disease. *Adult, child (including neonates):* Dosage based on body weight: 0.1 mL/kg, given as IV bolus at 2 mL/sec; flush line w/NSS after injection.
ADV EFF Dysgeusia, feeling hot, headache, hypersensitivity reaction, injection-site reaction, nausea, **nephrogenic systemic fibrosis**
NC/PT Evaluate GFR before starting tx. Monitor total dose exposure; monitor for nephrogenic systemic fibrosis. Not for use in pregnancy. Pt

should report all exposure to contrast agents, itching, swelling or tightening, red or dark patches on skin, joint stiffness, muscle weakness, bone pain.

galantamine hydrobromide (Razadyne)

CLASS Alzheimer drug, cholinesterase inhibitor
PREG/CONT B/NA

IND & DOSE Tx of mild to moderate dementia of Alzheimer type. *Adult:* 4 mg PO bid; after 4 wk, increase to 8 mg PO bid; after 4 more wk, increase to 12 mg PO bid. Range, 16–32 mg/day in two divided doses. ER capsules, 8 mg/day PO; titrate to 16–24 mg/day PO.

ADJUST DOSE Hepatic, renal impairment
ADV EFF Abd pain, anorexia, bladder outflow obstruction, bradycardia, diarrhea, dizziness, dyspepsia, n/v/d, insomnia, **serious skin reactions**, weight loss
INTERACTIONS Anticholinergics, bethanechol, cimetidine, erythromycin, ketoconazole, paroxetine, potent CYP2D6/CYP3A4 inhibitors, succinylcholine
NC/PT Does not cure disease; may slow degeneration. Establish baseline functional profile. Mix sol w/water, fruit juice, or soda. Do not cut, crush, or allow pt to chew ER form; have pt swallow whole. Antiemetics may be helpful for GI upset. Pt should take safety measures for CNS effects; report rash, inability to empty bladder. Because of name confusion, manufacturer has changed name from *Reminyl* to *Razadyne*.

galsulfase (Naglazyme)

CLASS Enzyme
PREG/CONT B/NA

IND & DOSE Tx of pts w/mucopolysaccharidosis VI to improve walking

and stair climbing capacity. *Adult:* 1 mg/kg/wk by IV infusion, diluted and infused over 4 hr.
ADJUST DOSE Hepatic, renal impairment
ADV EFF Abd pain, **anaphylaxis and allergic reactions, cardiorespiratory failure**, chills, dyspnea, fever, headache, **immune reactions, infusion reactions**, n/v, pruritus, rash, urticaria
NC/PT Establish baseline activity. Pretreat w/antihistamines and antipyretics; consider adding corticosteroids. Monitor continually during infusion; consider lowering dose or discontinuing w/severe reactions. Clinical surveillance program available if used in pregnancy/breastfeeding.

ganciclovir sodium (Cytovene, Zirgan)

CLASS Antiviral
PREG/CONT C/NA

BBW Obtain CBC before tx, q 2 days during daily dosing, and at least wkly thereafter. Consult physician and arrange for reduced dose if WBC or platelet count falls. IV therapy is *only* for tx of CMV retinitis in immunocompromised pts and for px of CMV disease in transplant pts at risk for CMV.
IND & DOSE Tx of CMV retinitis. *Adult:* 5 mg/kg IV at constant rate over 1 hr q 12 hr for 14–21 days; maint, 5 mg/kg by IV infusion over 1 hr once daily 7 days/wk *or* 6 mg/kg once daily 5 days/wk. *Child 2 yr and older:* Ophthalmic gel, 1 drop in affected eye(s) five times daily (approximately q 3 hr while awake) until ulcer heals. Maint, 1 drop three times daily for 7 days. **Prevention of CMV disease in transplant recipients:** *Adult:* 5 mg/kg IV over 1 hr q 12 hr for 7–14 days; then 5 mg/kg/day IV once daily for 7 days/wk, *or* 6 mg/kg/day once daily for 5 days/wk. Prophylactic oral dose is 1,000 mg tid.
ADJUST DOSE Renal impairment

ADV EFF Anemia, **bone marrow suppression, cancer,** fever, granulocytopenia, hepatic changes, inflammation at injection site, pain, rash, thrombocytopenia
INTERACTIONS Bone marrow suppressants, imipenem-cilastatin, probenecid, zidovudine
NC/PT Avoid contact w/sol; proper disposal necessary. Do not give IM or subcut. Monitor CBC before and periodically during tx. Not for use in pregnancy (contraceptives for men, women advised). Frequent blood tests needed. Pt should have cancer screening, report rash, difficulty breathing.

ganirelix acetate
(generic)
CLASS Fertility drug
PREG/CONT X/NA

IND & DOSE Inhibition of premature LH surges in women in fertility programs. *Adult:* 250 mcg/day subcut starting on day 2 or 3 of cycle.
ADV EFF Abd pain, headache, injection-site reaction, n/v, **ovarian hyperstimulation,** vaginal bleeding
NC/PT Drug part of comprehensive fertility program. Show pt proper administration/disposal of needles/syringes. Pt should report swelling, shortness of breath, severe n/v, low urine output.

DANGEROUS DRUG
gemcitabine hydrochloride (Gemzar)
CLASS Antimetabolite, antineoplastic
PREG/CONT D/NA

IND & DOSE Tx of pancreatic cancer. *Adult:* 1,000 mg/m² IV over 30 min once wkly for up to 7 wk. Subsequent cycles of once wkly for 3 out of 4 consecutive wk can be given after 1-wk rest from tx. **First-line tx of inoperable, locally advanced or metastatic**

non-small-cell lung cancer, w/ cisplatin. *Adult:* 1,000 mg/m² IV over 30 min, days 1, 8, and 15 of each 28-day cycle, w/100 mg/m² cisplatin on day 1 after gemcitabine infusion, *or* 1,250 mg/m² IV over 30 min, days 1 and 8 of each 21-day cycle, w/ 100 mg/m² cisplatin on day 1 after gemcitabine infusion. **First-line therapy for metastatic breast cancer after failure of other adjuvant chemotherapy, w/paclitaxel.** *Adult:* 1,250 mg/m² IV over 30 min, days 1 and 8 of each 21-day cycle, w/ 175 mg/m² paclitaxel IV as 3-hr infusion before gemcitabine on day 1 of cycle. **Tx of advanced ovarian cancer that has relapsed at least 6 mo after completion of platinum-based therapy.** *Adult:* 1,000 mg/m² IV over 30 min, days 1 and 8 of each 21-day cycle. Carboplatin given on day 1 after gemcitabine.
ADV EFF Alopecia, **bone marrow depression,** capillary leak syndrome, edema, fever, flulike sx, hemolytic-uremic syndrome, hepatotoxicity, **interstitial pneumonitis,** n/v, pain, rash, RPLS
NC/PT Monitor CBC, renal function, LFTs carefully; dose adjustment may be needed. Infuse over 30 min; longer infusions cause increased half-life/greater toxicity. Premedicate for n/v. Not for use in pregnancy/breast-feeding. Pt should avoid exposure to infection; protect head in temp extremes (hair loss possible); report edema, difficulty breathing, urine/stool changes.

gemfibrozil (Lopid)
CLASS Antihyperlipidemic
PREG/CONT C/NA

IND & DOSE Adjunct to diet/exercise for tx of hypertriglyceridemia in pts w/very high triglycerides; reduction of CAD in pts unresponsive to traditional therapies. *Adult:* 1,200 mg/day PO in two divided doses 30 min before morning and evening meals.

ADJUST DOSE Hepatic, renal impairment
ADV EFF Abd pain, blurred vision, cataract development, dizziness, dyspepsia, eczema, epigastric pain, **eosinophilia**, fatigue, gallstone development, headache, **hepatotoxicity, leukopenia**, n/v/d, **rhabdomyolysis**
INTERACTIONS Anticoagulants, repaglinide, statins, sulfonylureas
NC/PT Use only if strongly indicated and lipid studies show definite response; hepatic tumorigenicity occurs in lab animals. Pt should take w/meals; continue diet/exercise program; take safety precautions w/CNS effects; report muscle pain w/fever, upper abd pain, urine/stool color changes.

gemifloxacin mesylate
(Factive)
CLASS Fluoroquinolone antibiotic
PREG/CONT C/NA

BBW Risk of tendinitis and tendon rupture. Risk increases in pts over 60 yr, w/concurrent corticosteroid use, and w/kidney, heart, or lung transplant; monitor these pts accordingly. Risk of exacerbation of muscle weakness and potential crisis in pts w/myasthenia gravis; contraindicated for use in pts w/hx of myasthenia gravis.
IND & DOSE Tx of acute bacterial exacerbations of chronic bronchitis caused by susceptible strains. *Adult:* 320 mg/day PO for 5 days. **Tx of community-acquired pneumonia caused by susceptible strains.** *Adult:* 320 mg/day PO for 5 days; 7 days for resistant strains.
ADJUST DOSE Renal impairment
ADV EFF Abd pain, blurred vision, CDAD, dizziness, n/v/d, peripheral neuropathies, photosensitivity, **prolonged QT, rash to Stevens-Johnson syndrome, ulcerative colitis**
INTERACTIONS Aluminum- or potassium-containing antacids, amiodarone, antidepressants, antipsychotics, calcium, didanosine, erythromycin, iron, procainamide, quinidine, QT-prolonging drugs, sotalol, sucralfate, sulfonylureas
NC/PT Culture before tx. Not for use in breast-feeding. Pt should take 3 hr before or 2 hr after taking antacids; swallow tablet whole and not cut, crush, or chew; drink plenty of fluids; avoid sun exposure; report acute pain or tenderness in muscle or tendon, bloody diarrhea, palpitations, fainting, numbness/tingling, rash.

gentamicin sulfate
(Gentak)
CLASS Fluoroquinolone antibiotic
PREG/CONT D (systemic); C (ophthalmic)/NA

BBW Monitor hearing w/long-term tx; ototoxicity possible. Monitor renal function, CBC, serum drug levels during long-term tx; carefully monitor pt if combined w/other neurotoxic or nephrotoxic drugs.
IND & DOSE Tx of community-acquired pneumonia caused by susceptible strains. *Adult:* 3 mg/kg/day IM or IV in three equal doses q 8 hr. Up to 5 mg/kg/day in three to four equal doses in severe infections, usually for 7–10 days. For IV use, may infuse loading dose of 1–2 mg/kg over 30–60 min. *Child:* 2–2.5 mg/kg IM or IV q 8 hr. *Infants, neonates:* 2.5 mg/kg IM or IV q 8 hr. *Preterm, full-term neonates 1 wk or younger:* 2.5 mg/kg IM or IV q 12 hr. *Preterm neonates under 32 wk gestational age:* 2.5 mg/kg IM or IV q 18 hr or 3 mg/kg q 24 hr. **Tx of PID.** *Adult:* 2 mg/kg IV, then 1.5 mg/kg IV tid plus clindamycin 600 mg IV qid. Continue for at least 4 days and at least 48 hr after pt improves, then continue clindamycin 450 mg PO qid for 10–14 days total tx. **Tx of superficial ocular infections due to susceptible microorganism strains.** *Adult, child:* 1–2 drops in affected eye(s) q 4 hr; up to 2 drops hrly in severe

infections or apply about ½" ointment to affected eye bid–tid. **Infection px in minor skin abrasions, tx of superficial skin infections.** *Adult, child:* Apply tid–qid. May cover w/sterile bandage.

ADJUST DOSE Elderly pts, renal failure

ADV EFF Anorexia, **apnea,** arachnoiditis at IM injection sites, **bone marrow suppression,** dizziness, local irritation, n/v/d, **nephrotoxicity, neuromuscular blockade,** ototoxicity, pain, purpura, rash, **seizures,** superinfections, tinnitus

INTERACTIONS Aminoglycosides, anesthetics, beta-lactam–type antibiotics, carbenicillin, cephalosporins, citrate-anticoagulated blood, diuretics (potent), enflurane, methoxyflurane, nondepolarizing NMJ blockers, penicillins, succinylcholine, ticarcillin, vancomycin

NC/PT Culture before tx. Give by deep IM injection if possible. Avoid long-term use. Monitor serum levels. Max peak levels, 12 mcg/mL (6–8 mcg/mL usually adequate for most infections); max trough levels, 2 mcg/mL. Monitor CBC, renal function, hearing. Teach proper administration of ophthalmic and topical preparations. Pt should take safety precautions w/CNS effects; avoid exposure to infection; report severe headache, loss of hearing, difficult breathing.

glatiramer acetate (Copaxone)
CLASS MS drug
PREG/CONT B/NA

IND & DOSE To reduce frequency of relapses in pts w/relapsing-remitting MS, including pts who have experienced a first clinical episode and have MRI features consistent w/MS. *Adult:* 20 mg/day subcut *or* 40 mg/day subcut three times/wk.

ADV EFF Anxiety, asthenia, back pain, chest pain, infections, injection-site reactions (including lipoatrophy, skin necrosis), nausea, post-injection reaction, rash

NC/PT Rotate injection sites; do not use same site within a wk. Teach proper administration/disposal of needles/syringes. Use caution w/breast-feeding. Monitor for infections. Pt should report severe injection-site reactions, chest pain w/sweating, trouble breathing.

DANGEROUS DRUG

glimepiride (Amaryl)
CLASS Antidiabetic, sulfonylurea
PREG/CONT C/NA

IND & DOSE Adjunct to diet to lower blood glucose in pts w/type 2 diabetes mellitus. *Adult:* 1–2 mg PO once daily w/breakfast or first meal of day. Range, 1–4 mg PO once daily; max, 8 mg/day. **W/metformin or insulin to better control glucose as adjunct to diet/exercise in pts w/type 2 diabetes mellitus.** *Adult:* 8 mg PO daily w/first meal of day w/low-dose insulin or metformin.

ADJUST DOSE Adrenal or pituitary insufficiency; debilitated, elderly, malnourished pts; hepatic, renal impairment

ADV EFF Allergic skin reactions, anorexia, **CV mortality,** diarrhea, epigastric distress, **eosinophilia, hypoglycemia**

INTERACTIONS Alcohol, androgens, anticoagulants, azole antifungals, beta blockers, calcium channel blockers, celery, cholestyramine, chloramphenicol, clofibrate, coriander, corticosteroids, dandelion root, diazoxide, estrogens, fenugreek, fluconazole, garlic, gemfibrozil, ginseng, histamine-2 blockers, hormonal contraceptives, hydantoins, isoniazid, juniper berries, magnesium salts, MAOIs, methyldopa, nicotinic acid, phenothiazines, probenecid, rifampin, salicylates, sulfinpyrazone, sulfonamides, sympathomimetics, TCAs,

thiazides, thyroid drugs, urinary acidifiers/alkalinizers
NC/PT Monitor blood glucose. Transfer to insulin temporarily in times of stress. Ensure diet/exercise program. Arrange for complete diabetic teaching program. Not for use in pregnancy. Pt should avoid alcohol.

glipiZIDE (Glucotrol)
CLASS Antidiabetic, sulfonylurea
PREG/CONT C/NA

IND & DOSE Adjunct to diet, exercise to lower blood glucose in pts w/type 2 diabetes mellitus. *Adult:* 5 mg PO before breakfast. Adjust dose in increments of 2.5–5 mg as determined by blood glucose response; max, 15 mg/dose. ER tablets, 5 mg/day PO; may increase to 10 mg/day after 3 mo.
ADJUST DOSE Elderly pts
ADV EFF Allergic skin reactions, anorexia, bone marrow suppression, CV mortality, diarrhea, epigastric distress, eosinophilia, hypoglycemia
INTERACTIONS Alcohol, beta blockers, chloramphenicol, clofibrate, coriander, dandelion root, diazoxide, fenugreek, garlic, gemfibrozil, ginseng, juniper berries, phenothiazines, rifampin, salicylates, sulfonamides
NC/PT Monitor blood glucose. Transfer to insulin temporarily in times of stress. Give 30 min before breakfast. Ensure diet/exercise program. Arrange for complete diabetic teaching program. Not for use in pregnancy. Pt should swallow ER tablets whole and not cut, crush, or chew them; avoid alcohol.

glucagon (GlucaGen, Glucagon Emergency Kit)
CLASS Diagnostic agent, glucose-elevating drug
PREG/CONT B/NA

IND & DOSE Tx of hypoglycemia. *Adult, child over 20 kg:* 0.5–1 mg IV,

IM, or subcut; severe hypoglycemia, 1 mL IV, IM, or subcut. Use IV if possible. *Child under 20 kg:* 0.5 mg IM, IV, or subcut, or dose equivalent to 20–30 mcg/kg. **Diagnostic aid in radiologic examination of stomach, duodenum, small bowel, colon.** *Adult, child over 20 kg:* Usual dose, 0.25–2 mg IV or 1–2 mg IM.
ADV EFF Hypokalemia, hypotension, n/v, respiratory distress
INTERACTIONS Oral anticoagulants
NC/PT Arouse pt as soon as possible. Provide supplemental carbohydrates. Evaluate insulin dose in pts w/insulin overdose. Teach pt and significant other proper administration/disposal of needles/syringes.

glucarpidase (Voraxaze)
CLASS Carboxypeptidase enzyme
PREG/CONT C/NA

IND & DOSE Tx of pts w/toxic plasma methotrexate concentrations w/delayed methotrexate clearance due to impaired renal function. *Adult, child:* 50 units/kg as single IV injection.
ADV EFF Flushing, headache, hypotension, n/v, paresthesia, serious allergic reactions
INTERACTIONS Folate, folate antimetabolites, leucovorin
NC/PT Continue hydration, alkalinization of urine. Do not administer within 2 hr of leucovorin. Monitor closely for allergic reaction during and directly after injection. Tell pt blood levels will be monitored repeatedly during tx. Pt should report fever, chills, rash, difficulty breathing, numbness/tingling, headache.

DANGEROUS DRUG

glyBURIDE
(DiaBeta, Glynase)
CLASS Antidiabetic, sulfonylurea
PREG/CONT B (Glynase); C (DiaBeta)/NA

IND & DOSE Adjunct to diet, exercise to lower blood glucose in pts w/type 2 diabetes mellitus. *Adult:* 2.5–5 mg PO w/breakfast *(DiaBeta)*; 1.5–3 mg/day PO *(Glynase)*; maint, 1.25–20 mg/day PO.
ADJUST DOSE Debilitated, elderly, malnourished pts
ADV EFF Allergic skin reactions, anorexia, blurred vision, **bone marrow suppression, CV mortality,** diarrhea, epigastric distress, **hypoglycemia**
INTERACTIONS Alcohol, beta blockers, bosentan, chloramphenicol, clofibrate, coriander, dandelion root, diazoxide, fenugreek, garlic, gemfibrozil, ginseng, juniper berries, phenothiazines, rifampin, salicylates, sulfonamides
NC/PT Note dosage difference between two forms; use w/care. Monitor blood glucose. Transfer to insulin temporarily in times of stress. Give before breakfast. Ensure diet/exercise program. Arrange for complete diabetic teaching program. Not for use in pregnancy. Pt should avoid alcohol. Name confusion between *DiaBeta* (glyburide) and *Zebeta* (bisoprolol); use caution.

glycerol phenylbutyrate (Ravicti)
CLASS Nitrogen-binding agent
PREG/CONT C/NA

IND & DOSE Long-term mgt of urea cycle disorders not managed by diet/amino acid supplementation. *Adult, child 2 yr and older:* 4.5–11.2 mL/m²/day PO divided into three equal doses, rounded to nearest 0.5 mL, w/food; max, 17.5 mL/day.
ADJUST DOSE Hepatic impairment

ADV EFF Diarrhea, flatulence, headache, **neurotoxicity**
INTERACTIONS Corticosteroids, haloperidol, probenecid, valproic acid
NC/PT Must give w/protein-restricted diet; monitor ammonia levels; adjust dose as needed. Not for use in pregnancy/breast-feeding. Pt should take w/food, report disorientation, confusion, impaired memory.

glycopyrrolate (Cuvposa, Robinul, Seebri Neohaler)
CLASS Anticholinergic, antispasmodic, bronchodilator, parasympatholytic
PREG/CONT B/NA

IND & DOSE Adjunct tx for peptic ulcer. *Adult:* 1 mg PO tid or 2 mg PO bid-tid. Maint, 1 mg bid; max, 8 mg/day. Tx of chronic, severe drooling caused by neurologic disorders. *Child: 3–16 yr:* 0.02 mg/kg PO tid; titrate in 0.02-mg increments q 5–7 days. Max, 0.1 mg/kg PO tid; do not exceed 1.5–3 mg/dose. Tx of peptic ulcer. *Adult:* 0.1–0.2 mg IM or IV tid-qid. Preanesthetic medication. *Adult:* 0.004 mg/kg IM 30–60 min before anesthesia. *Child 2 yr–under 12 yr:* 0.004 mg/kg IM 30 min–1 hr before anesthesia. *Child 1 mo–2 yr:* Up to 0.009 mg/kg IM may be needed. Intraop to decrease vagal traction reflexes. *Adult:* 0.1 mg IV; repeat as needed at 2- to 3-min intervals. *Child over 1 mo:* 0.004 mg/kg IV, not to exceed 0.1 mg in single dose. May repeat at 2- to 3-min intervals. Reversal of neuromuscular blockade. *Adult, child over 1 mo:* W/neostigmine, pyridostigmine, 0.2 mg IV for each 1 mg neostigmine or 5 mg pyridostigmine; give IV simultaneously. Long-term maint tx of airflow obstruction in COPD. *Adult:* 15.6 mcg (one oral inhalation) bid w/*Neohaler* device.
ADV EFF Altered taste perception, blurred vision, decreased sweating, dry mouth, dysphagia, irritation at injection site, n/v, **paradoxical**

bronchospasm w/oral inhalation, photosensitivity, urinary hesitancy, urine retention
INTERACTIONS Amantadine, anticholinergics, digitalis, haloperidol, phenothiazines
NC/PT Check dose carefully. Ensure adequate hydration. Oral inhalation is not for use in deteriorating COPD, acute bronchospasm. Teach proper use of *Neohaler* device for oral inhalation. Pt should empty bladder before each dose, avoid hot environments (may be subject to heat stroke) and sun exposure, suck sugarless lozenges, perform mouth care for dry mouth. Pt should not chew capsule if using *Seebri Neohaler* (only for use in *Neohaler* device); should report sudden shortness of breath, vision problems, difficult/painful urination.

golimumab (Simponi)
CLASS Monoclonal antibody, TNF inhibitor
PREG/CONT B/NA

BBW Serious infections possible, including TB, sepsis, invasive fungal infections. Discontinue if infection or sepsis develops. Perform TB test before tx. If TB present, start TB tx and monitor pt carefully throughout tx. Increased risk of lymphoma and other cancers in children and adolescents; monitor accordingly.
IND & DOSE Tx of active rheumatoid arthritis, active psoriatic arthritis, ankylosing spondylitis. *Adult:* 50 mg/mo subcut or 2 mg/kg IV over 30 min wk 0, 4, then q 8 wk. Tx of moderate to severe ulcerative colitis. *Adult:* 200 mg subcut wk 0, then 100 mg subcut wk 2, then 100 mg subcut q 4 wk
ADV EFF Dizziness, HF, increased risk of demyelinating disorders, infections, injection-site reactions, **invasive fungal infections, malignancies,** nasopharyngitis
INTERACTIONS Abatacept, anakinra, adalimumab, certolizumab,

etanercept, infliximab, live vaccines, rituximab
NC/PT TB test before tx. Store in refrigerator; bring to room temp before use. Rotate injection sites. For IV, use inline filter; do not infuse w/other drugs. Monitor for CNS changes, infection. Not for use in breast-feeding. Teach proper administration/disposal of needles/syringes. Pt should avoid live vaccines; take safety precautions for dizziness; have regular medical follow-up; report fever, numbness/tingling, worsening of arthritis, s&sx of infection, difficulty breathing.

DANGEROUS DRUG

goserelin acetate (Zoladex)
CLASS Antineoplastic, hormone
PREG/CONT X; D (w/breast cancer)/NA

IND & DOSE Palliative tx of advanced prostate or breast cancer. *Adult:* 3.6 mg q 28 days subcut (long-term use). Mgt of endometriosis. *Adult:* 3.6 mg subcut q 28 days for 6 mo. Endometrial thinning before ablation. *Adult:* One to two 3.6-mg subcut depots 4 wk apart; surgery should be done 4 wk after first dose (within 2–4 wk after second depot if two are used). Tx of stage B$_2$–C prostate cancer, w/flutamide. *Adult:* Start tx 8 wk before start of radiation therapy and continue during radiation therapy; 3.6-mg depot 8 wk before radiation, then one 10.8-mg depot 28 days later. Or, four injections of 3.6-mg depot at 28-day intervals, two depots preceding and two during radiotherapy.
ADV EFF Cancer, decreased erections, dizziness, dysmenorrhea, edema, gynecomastia, hot flashes, injection-site infections, lower urinary tract sx, prolonged QT, sexual dysfunction, vaginitis
NC/PT Implant in upper abdomen q 28 days or q 3 mo (q 6 mo for endometriosis). Mark calendar for

injection dates. Not for use in pregnancy (contraceptives advised)/breast-feeding. Pt should report pain at injection site, discuss sexual dysfx w/health care provider.

granisetron hydrochloride
(Granisol, Sancuso)

CLASS Antiemetic, 5-HT₃ receptor antagonist
PREG/CONT B/NA

IND & DOSE Px of chemotherapy-induced n/v. Adult, child over 2 yr: 10 mcg/kg IV over 5 min starting within 30 min of chemotherapy, only on days of chemotherapy, or 2 mg/day PO 1 hr before chemo, or 1 mg PO bid, given up to 1 hr before chemo, w/next dose 12 hr later. Or, for adults, apply 1 patch to clean, dry skin on upper, outer arm 24–48 hr before chemotherapy. Keep patch in place minimum of 24 hr after completion of chemotherapy, then remove; may be left in place for up to 7 days. Px of radiation-induced n/v. Adult, child over 2 yr: 2 mg/day PO 1 hr before radiation
ADV EFF Asthenia, chills, decreased appetite, fever, headache, serotonin syndrome
NC/PT Use only as directed. Apply transdermal patch to clean, dry skin; leave in place for up to 7 days. Pt should perform mouth care, use sugarless lozenges to help relieve nausea, report severe headache.

grass pollen allergy extract (Oralair)

CLASS Allergen extract
PREG/CONT C/NA

BBW Risk of severe life-threatening allergic reactions; not for use in uncontrolled asthma. Observe pt for 30 min after initial dose; have emergency equipment available. Prescribe epinephrine autoinjector and train pt in use.
IND & DOSE Tx of grass pollen-induced allergic rhinitis w/or without conjunctivitis confirmed by skin test in pts 10–65 yr. Adult 18–65 yr: 300 IR (index of reactivity) sublingually during grass season. Child 10–17 yr: 100 IR sublingually on day 1, 100 IR sublingually bid on day 2, 300 IR sublingually on day 3 onward.
ADV EFF Cough, ear pruritus, eosinophilic esophagitis, mouth edema, oropharyngeal pain/pruritus, throat/tongue pruritus
NC/PT Ensure skin test confirms dx. Not for use w/uncontrolled asthma, hx of severe reactions, eosionophilic esophagitis. Begin 4 mo before expected grass season; continue through season. Monitor for at least 30 min after first dose. Stop tx for oral wounds, inflammation; allow to heal completely before restarting. Pt should report difficulty breathing/swallowing.

guaifenesin (Altarussin, Diabetic Tussin, Mucinex, Siltussin)

CLASS Expectorant
PREG/CONT C/NA

IND & DOSE Symptomatic relief of respiratory conditions characterized by dry, nonproductive cough; mucus in respiratory tract. Adult, child over 12 yr: 200–400 mg PO q 4 hr; max, 2.4 g/day. Or 1–2 tablets PO (600-mg ER tablets) q 12 hr; max, 2.4 g/day. Child 6–12 yr: 100–200 mg PO q 4 hr; max, 1.2 g/day or 600 mg (ER) PO q 12 hr. Child 2–6 yr: 50–100 mg PO q 4 hr; max, 600 mg/day.
ADV EFF Dizziness, headache, n/v
NC/PT Pt should swallow ER tablet whole and not cut, crush, or chew it, use for no longer than 1 wk, consult prescriber if cough persists, take safety precautions for dizziness. Name confusion between Mucinex (guaifenesin) and Mucomyst (acetylcysteine); use caution.

guanfacine hydrochloride
(Intuniv, Tenex)

CLASS Antihypertensive, sympatholytic
PREG/CONT B/NA

IND & DOSE Mgt of hypertension. Adult, child over 12 yr: 1 mg/day PO at bedtime. Tx of ADHD. Adult, child 6 yr and older: 1 mg/day PO; titrate at increments of 1 mg/wk to range of 1–7 mg/day (0.05–0.12 mg/kg) (Intuniv).

ADJUST DOSE Elderly pts; hepatic, renal impairment
ADV EFF Constipation, dizziness, dry mouth, ED, sedation, weakness
NC/PT Taper when stopping; decrease by no more than 1 mg q 3–7 days. Pt should swallow ER form whole and not cut, crush, or chew it, take immediate-release form at bedtime, continue tx program for ADHD, take safety precautions for CNS effects, use sugarless lozenges for dry mouth.

haloperidol, haloperidol decanoate, haloperidol lactate
(Haldol)

CLASS Antipsychotic, dopaminergic blocker
PREG/CONT C/NA

BBW Increased risk of death in elderly pts w/dementia-related psychosis; drug not approved for this use.
IND & DOSE Tx of psychiatric disorders, Tourette syndrome. Adult: 0.5–2 mg PO bid–tid w/moderate sx; 3–5 mg PO bid–tid for more resistant pts. Or IM dose 10–15 times daily oral dose in elderly pts stabilized on 10 mg/day as needed; 20 times daily oral dose in pts stabilized on high doses and tolerant to oral haloperidol. Max, 3 mL/injection site; repeat at 4-wk intervals. Prompt control of acutely agitated pts w/severe sx. Adult: 2–5 mg (up to 10–30 mg) q 60 min or q 4–8 h IM as necessary. Tx of psychiatric disorders. Child 3–12 yr or 15–40 kg: 0.5 mg/day (25–50 mcg/kg/day) PO; may increase in increments of 0.5 mg q 5–7 days as needed in general, then 0.05–0.15 mg/day PO bid-tid. Nonpsychotic and Tourette syndromes, behavioral disorders, hyperactivity. Child 3–12 yr or 15–40 kg: 0.05–0.075 mg/day PO bid-tid.

ADJUST DOSE Elderly pts
ADV EFF Akathisia, anemia, aplastic anemia, autonomic disturbances, bronchospasm, cardiac arrest, dry mouth, dystonia, eosinophilia, hemolytic anemia, hyperthermia, hypoglycemia, laryngospasm, leukocytosis, leukopenia, NMS, photosensitivity, pseudoparkinsonism, refractory arrhythmias, seizures, sudden death related to asphyxia, tardive dyskinesia, thrombocytopenic or nonthrombocytopenic purpura
INTERACTIONS Anticholinergics, carbamazepine, ginkgo, lithium
NC/PT Do not use IM in children. Do not give IV. Gradually withdraw after maint tx. Monitor for renal toxicity. Urine may be pink to brown. Pt should take safety precautions for CNS effects, avoid sun exposure, maintain fluid intake, use sugarless lozenges for dry mouth, report difficulty breathing.

DANGEROUS DRUG

heparin sodium (generic)

CLASS Anticoagulant
PREG/CONT C/NA

IND & DOSE Px, tx of venous thrombotic events. Adult: IV loading dose, 5,000 units; then 10,000–20,000 units subcut followed by 8,000–10,000 units subcut q 8 hr or 15,000–20,000 units q 12 hr. Or initial dose, 10,000 units IV, then 5,000–10,000 units IV q 4–6 hr. Or loading dose, 5,000 units IV, then 20,000–40,000 units/day by IV infusion.

Child: IV bolus of 50 units/kg, then 100 units/kg IV q 4 hr or 20,000 units/m²/24 hr by continuous IV infusion. **Px of postop thromboembolism.** *Adult:* 5,000 units by deep subcut injection 2 hr before surgery and q 8–12 hr thereafter for 7 days or until pt fully ambulatory. **Surgery of heart and blood vessels for pts undergoing total body perfusion.** *Adult:* Not less than 150 units/kg IV. IV often-used guideline: 300 units/kg for procedures less than 60 min, 400 units/kg for longer procedures. Add 400–600 units to 100 mL whole blood. **Clot prevention in blood samples.** *Adult:* 70–150 units/10–20 mL whole blood.
ADV EFF Bleeding, bruising, chills, fever, **hemorrhage**, injection-site reactions, hair loss, liver enzyme changes, **white clot syndrome**
INTERACTIONS Aspirin, cephalosporins, chamomile, garlic, ginger, ginkgo, ginseng, high-dose vitamin E, NSAIDs, penicillins, oral anticoagulants, salicylates
NC/PT Adjust dose based on coagulation tests; target aPTT, 1.5–2.5 times control. Incompatible in sol w/many drugs; check before combining. Give by deep subcut injection; do not give IM. Apply pressure to all injection sites; check for signs of bleeding. Have protamine sulfate on hand as antidote. Pt should protect from injury, report bleeding gums, black or tarry stools, severe headache.

hetastarch (Hespan, Voluven)
CLASS Plasma expander
PREG/CONT C/NA

BBW Increased risk of death, need for renal replacement in critically ill pts, including sepsis pts. Not for use in these pts.
IND & DOSE Adjunct tx for plasma volume expansion in shock due to hemorrhage, burns, surgery, sepsis, trauma. *Adult:* 500–1,000 mL IV; max, 1,500 mL/day. In acute hemorrhagic

shock, rates approaching 20 mL/kg/hr IV often needed (*Hespan*); up to 50 mL/kg/day IV *Voluven* injection. **Adjunct in leukapheresis to improve harvesting, increase yield of granulocytes.** *Adult:* 250–700 mL infused at constant fixed ratio of 1:8 to 1:13 to venous whole blood. Safety of up to two procedures/wk and total of seven to ten procedures using hetastarch have been established.
ADJUST DOSE Critically ill pts, pts w/clotting disorders, renal impairment, severe liver impairment
ADV EFF Bleeding, chills, circulatory overload, coagulopathy, headache, hypersensitivity reactions, itching, mild flulike sx, submaxillary and parotid gland enlargement, n/v
INTERACTIONS Drugs affecting coagulation
NC/PT Do not use w/cardiac bypass pumps, severe liver disease, bleeding disorders. Monitor renal function; stop at first sign of renal injury. Do not mix in sol w/other drugs. Have emergency support on hand. Pt should report difficulty breathing, severe headache.

histrelin implant (Vantas)
CLASS Antineoplastic, GNRH
PREG/CONT X/NA

IND & DOSE Palliative tx of advanced prostate cancer. *Adult:* 1 implant inserted subcut and left for 12 mo. May be removed after 12 mo and new implant inserted.
ADV EFF Diabetes, fatigue, hot flashes, hyperglycemia, injection-site reactions **MI, renal impairment, spinal cord compression, stroke,** testicular atrophy
NC/PT Monitor serum glucose, renal function, injection site, CV status. Not for use in pregnancy. Pt should report chest pain, numbness/tingling, injection-site reactions.

hyaluronic acid derivatives (Euflexxa, Hyalgan, Synvisc)

CLASS Glucosamine polysaccharide
PREG/CONT C/NA

IND & DOSE Tx of pain in osteoarthritis of knee in pts unresponsive to traditional therapy. *Adult:* 2 mL/wk by intra-articular injection in knee for total of three to five injections.
ADV EFF Headache, joint swelling, pain at injection site
NC/PT Avoid strenuous exercise and prolonged weight bearing for 48 hr after injection. Headache may occur. Pt should report severe joint swelling, loss of movement.

hyaluronidase (Amphadase, Hylenex, Vitrase)

CLASS Enzyme
PREG/CONT C/NA

IND & DOSE To increase absorption of injected drugs. *Adult, child:* Add 150 units to injection sol. **Hypodermoclysis.** *Adult:* 150 units injected under skin close to clysis. *Child under 3 yr:* Limit total dose to 200 mL/clysis. *Premature infants:* Max, 25 mL/kg at rate of no more than 2 mL/min. **Adjunct to subcut urography.** *Adult:* 75 units subcut over each scapula followed by injection of contrast media at same sites.
ADV EFF Chills, dizziness, edema, hypotension, injection-site reactions, n/v
INTERACTIONS Benzodiazepines, furosemide, phenytoin
NC/PT Do not use w/dopamine or alpha-adrenergic drugs or in inflamed or infected areas. Do not apply to cornea or use for insect bites or stings; monitor injection site.

hydrALAZINE hydrochloride (generic)

CLASS Antihypertensive, vasodilator
PREG/CONT C/NA

IND & DOSE Tx of essential hypertension. *Adult:* 10 mg PO qid for first 2–4 days; increase to 25 mg PO qid for first wk. Second and subsequent wks: 50 mg PO qid. Or 20–40 mg IM or IV, repeated as necessary if unable to take orally. *Child:* 0.75 mg/kg/day PO in divided doses q 6 hr (max, 7.5 mg/kg/day PO in four divided doses, or 200 mg/day PO). Or 1.7–3.5 mg/kg IM or IV divided into four to six doses if unable to take orally. **Tx of eclampsia.** *Adult:* 5–10 mg q 20 min by IV bolus. If no response after 20 mg, try another drug.
ADV EFF Angina, anorexia, **blood dyscrasias,** dizziness, headache, n/v/d, orthostatic hypotension, palpitations, peripheral neuritis, rash, tachycardia
INTERACTIONS Adrenergic blockers
NC/PT Use parenteral drug immediately after opening ampule. Withdraw drug gradually, especially in pts who have experienced marked BP reduction. Pt should take safety precautions w/orthostatic hypotension, CNS effects; take w/food; report chest pain, numbness/tingling, fever.

hydrochlorothiazide (Microzide Capsules)

CLASS Thiazide diuretic
PREG/CONT B/NA

IND & DOSE Adjunct tx of edema from systemic disease. *Adult:* 25–100 mg PO daily until dry weight attained. Then, 25–100 mg/day PO or intermittently, up to 200 mg/day. *Child:* 1–2 mg/kg/day PO in one or two doses. Max, 100 mg/day in two doses (2–12 yr), 37.5 mg/day in two doses (6 mo–2 yr), up to 3 mg/kg/day in two doses (under 6 mo). *Tx of* **hypertension.** *Adult:* 12.5–50 mg PO; max, 50 mg/day.

ADJUST DOSE Elderly pts

ADV EFF Anorexia, dizziness, drowsiness, dry mouth, muscle cramps, n/v, nocturia, photosensitivity, polyuria, vertigo

INTERACTIONS Amphotericin B, antidiabetics, cholestyramine, colestipol, corticosteroids, lithium, loop diuretics, NMJ blockers

NC/PT Monitor BP; reduced dose of other antihypertensives may be needed. Give w/food. Mark calendar for intermittent therapy. Pt should measure weight daily, take early in day so sleep not interrupted, use safety precautions for CNS effects, avoid sun exposure, report weight changes of 3 lb/day.

DANGEROUS DRUG

hydrocodone bitartrate
(Hysingla ER, Zohydro ER)
CLASS Opioid agonist analgesic
PREG/CONT C/C-II

BBW Risks of addiction, severe to fatal respiratory depression, death w/ accidental consumption by children, life-threatening neonatal withdrawal if used in pregnancy, fatal plasma levels if combined w/alcohol. Initiating CYP3A4 inhibitors or stopping CYP3A4 inducers can cause fatal hydrocodone overdose; avoid this combination.

IND & DOSE Mgt of pain requiring continuous analgesic for prolonged period. *Adult:* Initially, 10 mg PO q 12 hr for opioid-naïve or opioid-nontolerant pts; increase as needed in 10-mg increments q 12 hr q 3–7 days.

ADJUST DOSE Elderly, impaired pts; severe renal, hepatic impairment

ADV EFF Abd pain, back pain, confusion, constipation, dizziness, dry mouth, fatigue, headache, hypotension, n/v/d, pruritus, respiratory depression

INTERACTIONS Alcohol, anticholinergics, barbiturate anesthetics, CNS depressants, CYP3A4 inducers/ inhibitors, MAOIs, other opioids, protease inhibitors

NC/PT Monitor pt carefully. Ensure appropriate use of drug; abuse-resistant forms decrease risk of addiction, abuse. Ensure opioid antagonist and emergency equipment readily available. Safety issues w/ CNS changes. Taper when discontinuing. Pt should swallow capsule whole, not cut, crush, or chew it; discontinue slowly; avoid pregnancy/breast-feeding, alcohol; take safety precautions for CNS changes; report difficulty breathing, severe constipation, pain unrelieved by drug.

---

hydrocortisone salts
(Cortaid, Pandel, Solu-Cortef)
CLASS Corticosteroid
PREG/CONT C/NA

IND & DOSE Replacement tx in adrenal cortical insufficiency, allergic states, inflammatory disorders, hematologic disorders, trichinosis, ulcerative colitis, MS. *Adult, child:* 5–200 mg/day PO based on severity and pt response, or 100–500 mg IM or IV q 2, 4, or 6 hr. **Retention enema for tx of ulcerative colitis, proctitis.** *Adult, child:* 100 mg nightly for 21 days. **Anorectal cream, suppositories to relieve discomfort of hemorrhoids, perianal itching or irritation.** *Adult, child:* 1 applicator daily or bid for 2 or 3 wk and q second day thereafter. **Dermatologic preparations to relieve inflammatory and pruritic manifestations of dermatoses.** *Adult, child:* Apply sparingly to affected area bid–qid. **Tx of acute/chronic ophthalmic inflammatory conditions.** *Adult, child:* 1–2 drops per eye one to two times/day.

ADV EFF Anaphylactoid reactions, amenorrhea, ecchymoses, fluid retention, headache, HF, hypokalemia, hypotension, immunosuppression, infection, irregular menses, local pain or irritation at application site, muscle

weakness, pancreatitis, peptic ulcer, **serious neurologic reactions w/ epidural use**, striae, vertigo
INTERACTIONS Anticoagulants, anticholinesterases, cholestyramine, estrogen, hormonal contraceptives, ketoconazole, live vaccines, phenobarbital, phenytoin, rifampin, salicylates
NC/PT Give daily before 9 a.m. to mimic normal peak diurnal corticosteroid levels and minimize HPA suppression. Rotate IM injection sites. IV, IM not for use in neonates; contains benzyl alcohol. Use minimal doses for minimal duration to minimize adverse effects. Taper doses when discontinuing high-dose or long-term tx; arrange for increased dose when pt is subject to unusual stress. W/topical use, use caution w/occlusive dressings; tight or plastic diapers over affected area can increase systemic absorption. Suggest medical ID. Pt should protect from infection; report swelling, difficulty breathing.

DANGEROUS DRUG

hydromorphone hydrochloride (Dilaudid, Dilaudid-HP, Exalgo)
CLASS Opioid agonist analgesic
PREG/CONT C; D (Labor & delivery)/C-II

BBW Monitor dose and intended use; vary w/form. Serious effects, addiction, abuse, misuse possible. Extended-release form for opioid-tolerant pts only; fatal respiratory depression possible. Extended-release form not for use w/acute or postop pain or as an as-needed drug. Pt must swallow extended-release tablets whole; broken, chewed, or crushed tablets allow rapid release of drug and could cause fatal overdose. Prolonged use in pregnancy can lead to potentially fatal neonatal opioid withdrawal syndrome. Accidental ingestion by children can be fatal; secure drug out of reach of children.

IND & DOSE Relief of moderate to severe pain; acute and chronic pain. *Adult:* 2–4 mg PO q 4–6 hr. Liquid, 2.5–10 mg PO q 3–6 hr. ER tablets, 8–64 mg/day PO. Or 1–2 mg IM or subcut q 4–6 hr as needed, or by slow IV injection over 2–3 min, or 3 mg rectally q 6–8 hr.
ADJUST DOSE Elderly or debilitated pts; hepatic, renal impairment
ADV EFF Apnea, **cardiac arrest, circulatory depression,** constipation, dizziness, flushing, light-headedness, n/v, **respiratory arrest, respiratory depression,** sedation, **shock,** sweating, visual disturbances
INTERACTIONS Alcohol, anticholinergics, antihistamines, barbiturate anesthetics, CNS depressants, MAOIs, opioid agonist/antagonists
NC/PT Ensure opioid antagonist and facilities for assisted or controlled respiration are readily available during parenteral administration. Monitor pt w/head injury carefully. Breast-feeding pt should take 4–6 hr before scheduled feeding. Refrigerate rectal suppositories. Pt should swallow ER tablet whole, and not cut, crush, or chew it; avoid alcohol, antihistamines; take laxative for constipation; use safety precautions for CNS effects; keep out of reach of children; report chest pain, difficulty breathing.

hydroxocobalamin (Cyanokit)
CLASS Antidote
PREG/CONT C/NA

IND & DOSE Tx of known or suspected cyanide poisoning. *Adult:* 5 g by IV infusion over 15 min; may give second dose over 15–120 min by IV infusion.
ADV EFF Anaphylaxis, chest tightness, dyspnea, edema, **hypertension,** injection-site reactions, nausea, photosensitivity, rash, red skin and mucous membranes (up to 2 wk), red urine (up to 5 wk)

NC/PT Support pt during acute poisoning. Run in separate IV line; do not mix w/other drugs. Monitor BP. Not for use in pregnancy/breast-feeding. Tell pt urine may be red for up to 5 wk; skin and mucous membranes may be red for 2 wk. Pt should avoid exposure to sunlight during that period, report difficulty breathing.

hydroxyprogesterone caproate (Makena)
CLASS Progestin
PREG/CONT B/NA

IND & DOSE To reduce risk of preterm birth in women w/singleton pregnancy and hx of singleton spontaneous preterm birth. *Adult:* 250 mg IM once wkly, beginning between 16 wk, 0 days' and 20 wk, 6 days' gestation. Continue wkly injections until wk 37 of gestation, or until delivery, whichever comes first.
ADV EFF Depression, fluid retention, glucose intolerance, injection-site reactions, nausea, pruritus, thromboembolic events, urticaria
NC/PT IM injection into upper outer area of buttocks once/wk. Vial stable for 5 wk at room temp; protect from light. Monitor injection sites; periodically check serum glucose. Mark calendar for injection days. Pt should report leg, chest pain.

DANGEROUS DRUG

hydroxyurea (Droxia, Hydrea)
CLASS Antineoplastic
PREG/CONT D/NA

BBW Risk of myelosuppression, infections, and malignancies; monitor pt closely.
IND & DOSE Concomitant therapy w/irradiation for primary squamous cell carcinoma of head and neck. *Adult:* 80 mg/kg PO as single daily dose q third day. Begin 7 days before irradiation; continue during and for a prolonged period after radiation therapy *(Hydrea)*. **Tx of resistant chronic myelocytic leukemia.** *Adult:* 20–30 mg/kg PO as single daily dose *(Hydrea)*. **To reduce sickle cell anemia crises** *(Droxia)*. *Adult:* 15 mg/kg/day PO as single dose; may increase by 5 mg/kg/day q 12 wk until max of 35 mg/kg/day reached. If blood levels become toxic, stop drug and resume at 2.5 mg/kg/day less than dose that resulted in toxicity when blood levels return to normal; increase q 12 wk in 2.5-mg/kg/day intervals if blood levels remain acceptable.
ADJUST DOSE Renal impairment
ADV EFF Anorexia, bone marrow depression, cancer, dizziness, headache, n/v, stomatitis
INTERACTIONS Antiviral drugs, uricosuric agents
NC/PT Handle w/extreme care; may cause cancer. Use gloves when handling capsule. Monitor CBC before and q 2 wk during tx. Capsule should not be cut, crushed, or chewed; have pt swallow whole. If pt unable to swallow capsule, may empty into glass of water; pt should swallow immediately. Not for use in pregnancy (barrier contraceptives advised). Pt should drink 10–12 glasses of fluid each day, take safety precautions for CNS effects, protect from exposure to infections, report unusual bleeding.

---

hydrOXYzine hydrochloride, hydrOXYzine pamoate (Vistaril)
CLASS Antiemetic, antihistamine, anxiolytic
PREG/CONT C/NA

IND & DOSE Symptomatic relief of anxiety. *Adult, child over 6 yr:* 50–100 mg PO qid. *Child under 6 yr:* 50 mg/day PO in divided doses. **Mgt of pruritus.** *Adult:* 25 mg PO tid–qid. **Sedation, antiemetic (preop/postop).** *Adult:* 50–100 mg PO. *Child:* 0.6 mg/kg PO.

ADV EFF Constipation, dizziness, drowsiness, dry mouth, fixed drug eruptions, hypersensitivity reactions, sedation, tremors, urine retention
INTERACTIONS Alcohol, barbiturates, CNS depressants, opioids
NC/PT Pt should use safety precautions for CNS effects; use sugarless lozenges for dry mouth; avoid alcohol; report rash, difficulty breathing.

hyoscyamine sulfate
(Levbid, Levsin/SL, Oscimin, Symax)

CLASS Anticholinergic, antispasmodic, belladonna alkaloid
PREG/CONT C/NA

IND & DOSE Adjunct tx in IBS, peptic ulcer, spastic or functional GI disorders, cystitis, neurogenic bladder or bowel disorders, parkinsonism, biliary or renal colic, rhinitis. *Adult:* 0.125–0.25 mg PO q 4 hr or as needed. Or 1–2 mL oral sol q 4 hr as needed (max, 12 mL/day). Or 1–2 oral sprays q 4 hr as needed (max, 12 sprays/day). Or ½–1 orally disintegrating tablet 3–4 times/day 30 min–1 hr before meals and at bedtime. Or 1–2 tsp elixir PO q 4 hr as needed (max, 12 tsp/day). Or 0.375–0.75 mg ER tablet PO q 12 hr; may give q 8 hr if needed (max, 4 capsules/day). Or 0.25–0.5 mg subcut, IM, or IV 2–4 times/day at 4-hr intervals as needed. *Child 12 yr and older:* 1–2 tablets PO q 4 hr as needed (max, 12 tablets in 24 hr). Or ½–1 orally disintegrating tablets PO tid–qid 30 min–1 hr before meals and at bedtime. Or 1–2 mL oral sol PO q 4 hr or as needed (max, 12 mL in 24 hr). Or 1–2 ER capsules PO q 12 hr; adjust to 1 capsule q 8 hr if needed (max, 4 capsules in 24 hr). Or 1–2 tsp elixir PO q 4 hr or as needed (max, 12 tsp in 24 hr). Or 1–2 oral sprays q 4 hr as needed. *Child 2 yr–under 12 yr:* ½–1 tablet PO q 4 hr as needed (max, 6 tablets in 24 hr). Or 0.25–1 mL oral sol PO q 4 hr or as

needed (max, 6 mL in 24 hr). Or may give elixir, dose based on weight. **To reduce secretions preanesthetic.** *Adult:* 0.005 mg/kg IV or IM 30–60 min before induction. *Child over 2 yr:* 5 mcg/kg IV 30–60 min before anesthesia. **To tx drug-induced bradycardia.** *Adult, child over 2 yr:* 0.125 mg (0.25 mL) IV. Repeat as needed. **Reversal of neuromuscular blockade.** *Adult, child over 2 yr:* 0.2 mg IV, IM, or subcut for q 1 mg neostigmine.
ADV EFF Anaphylaxis, decreased sweating, dizziness, drowsiness, dry mouth, fever, nausea, palpitations, urinary hesitancy, urticaria
INTERACTIONS Antacids, amantadine, anticholinergics, antihistamines, haloperidol, MAOIs, phenothiazines, TCAs
NC/PT Ensure adequate hydration. Pt should empty bladder before each dose, swallow whole (not cut, crush, or chew ER forms), take safety precautions for CNS effects, use sugarless lozenges for dry mouth, take 30–60 min before meals; report difficulty breathing, fainting, palpitations.

ibandronate sodium
(Boniva)

CLASS Bisphosphonate, calcium regulator
PREG/CONT C/NA

IND & DOSE Tx, px of osteoporosis in postmenopausal women. *Adult:* 150-mg tablet PO once/mo, or 3 mg IV over 15–30 sec q 3 mo.
ADJUST DOSE Renal impairment
ADV EFF Abd/back pain, anaphylaxis, atypical femur fractures, bronchitis, diarrhea, dizziness, dyspepsia, headache, hypertension, hypocalcemia, jaw osteonecrosis, myalgia, pneumonia, renal toxicity
INTERACTIONS Aluminum, iron, magnesium antacids; food, milk
NC/PT Monitor serum calcium levels. Ensure adequate intake of vitamin D/calcium. Use caution in pregnancy;

not for use in breast-feeding. Obtain periodic bone density exams. Safety for use longer than 3–5 yr not established. Pt should take in a.m. w/full glass of water at least 60 min before first beverage, food, or medication of day; stay upright for 60 min after taking to avoid potentially serious esophageal erosion; mark calendar for once/mo or q-3-mo tx; report difficulty breathing/swallowing, pain/burning in esophagus.

DANGEROUS DRUG

ibritumomab (Zevalin)
CLASS Antineoplastic, monoclonal antibody
PREG/CONT D/NA

BBW Risk of serious to fatal infusion reactions, prolonged bone marrow suppression, cutaneous/mucocutaneous reactions; monitor, support pt accordingly. Max, 32 mCi total dose.
IND & DOSE Tx of relapsed or refractory low-grade follicular transformed B-cell non-Hodgkin lymphoma; previously treated follicular non-Hodgkin lymphoma w/relapse after first-line tx. *Adult:* 250 mg/m² IV rituximab, then 5 mCi/kg as 10-min IV push. Repeat in 7–9 days.
ADV EFF Abd pain, asthenia, cough, fatigue, fever, **infusion reactions**, leukemia, nasopharyngitis, n/v/d, **prolonged bone marrow suppression, severe cutaneous/mucocutaneous reactions**
INTERACTIONS Live vaccines, platelet inhibitors
NC/PT Premedicate w/acetaminophen, diphenhydramine before each infusion. Monitor for extravasation; move to other limb if this occurs. Not for use in pregnancy (barrier contraceptives advised)/breast-feeding. Pt should avoid exposure to infection; report bleeding, fever or s&sx of infection, rash, mouth sores.

ibrutinib (Imbruvica)
CLASS Antineoplastic, kinase inhibitor
PREG/CONT D/NA

IND & DOSE Tx of mantle cell lymphoma with at least one other tx has been tried. *Adult:* 560 mg PO once daily. Tx of chronic lymphocytic leukemia (CLL) after at least one prior tx; tx of CLL w/17p depletion; tx of Waldenström's macroglobulinemia. *Adult:* 420 mg PO once a day.
ADJUST DOSE Hepatic impairment (contraindicated)
ADV EFF Abd pain, atrial fibrillation, anemia, **bone marrow suppression**, bruising, constipation, dyspnea, edema, fatigue, **hemorrhage**, infections, n/v/d, renal toxicity, **secondary malignancies**, tumor lysis syndrome, URI
INTERACTIONS CYP3A inducers/inhibitors
NC/PT Ensure proper dx. Monitor renal function; screen for secondary malignancies. Not for use in pregnancy (contraceptives advised)/breast-feeding. Pt must swallow capsule whole (not cut, crush, or chew it) w/ full glass of water. Pt should avoid exposure to infection; report urine/stool color changes, severe diarrhea, fever, bleeding, sx of infection.

ibuprofen (Advil, Caldolor, Motrin)
CLASS Analgesic, NSAID
PREG/CONT B (1st, 2nd trimesters); D (3rd trimester)/NA

BBW Increased risk of CV events, GI bleeding; monitor accordingly. Contraindicated for tx of periop pain after CABG.
IND & DOSE Tx of mild to moderate pain, fever, migraine headache, primary dysmenorrhea. *Adult, child 12 yr and older:* 400 mg PO q 4–6 hr; max, 3,200/day. Or, 400–800 mg IV over 30 min q 6 hr for pain. Or, 400 mg

IV over 30 min for fever; may follow w/400 mg IV q 4–6 hr or 100–200 mg IV q 4 hr to control fever. *Child 6 mo–11 yr:* Base dose on weight, given q 6–8 hr. 32–42 kg, 300 mg PO; 27–31 kg, 250 mg PO; 22–26 kg, 200 mg PO; 16–21 kg, 150 mg PO; 11–15 kg, 100 mg PO; 8–10 kg, 75 mg PO; 5–7 kg, 50 mg. Oral drops: 9–11 kg or 12–23 mo, 1.875 mL (75 mg) PO; 5–8 kg or 6–11 mo, 1.25 mL (50 mg) PO. **Tx of osteoarthritis, rheumatoid arthritis.** *Adult:* 1,200–3,200 mg/day PO (300 mg qid or 400, 600, 800 mg tid or qid; individualize dose). **Tx of juvenile arthritis.** *Child 6 mo–11 yr:* 30–50 mg/kg/day PO in three to four divided doses; 20 mg/kg/day for milder disease.

ADV EFF Agranulocytosis, anaphylactoid reactions to anaphylactic shock, bronchospasm, dizziness, dyspepsia, edema, eye changes, headache, **GI bleeding,** GI pain, **HF,** hepatic impairment, insomnia, nausea, pancytopenia, rash, renal injury, somnolence, Stevens-Johnson syndrome, stomatitis, thrombotic events
INTERACTIONS ACE inhibitors, anticoagulants, beta blockers, bisphosphonates, bumetanide, ethacrynic acid, furosemide, ginkgo, lithium
NC/PT Ensure hydration w/IV use. Stop if eye changes, renal or hepatic impairment. Give w/food if GI upset. Pt should avoid OTC products that may contain ibuprofen, take safety precautions for CNS effects, report ankle swelling, black tarry stool, vision changes.

DANGEROUS DRUG

ibutilide fumarate (Corvert)
CLASS Antiarrhythmic
PREG/CONT C/NA

BBW Have emergency equipment on hand during and for at least 4 hr after administration; can cause potentially life-threatening arrhythmias. Use caution when selecting pts for tx.

IND & DOSE Rapid conversion of atrial fibrillation (AF)/flutter of recent onset to sinus rhythm. *Adult:* 60 kg or more, 1 vial (1 mg) IV over 10 min; may repeat after 10 min if arrhythmia not terminated; under 60 kg, 0.1 mL/kg (0.01 mg/kg) IV over 10 min; may repeat after 10 min if arrhythmia not terminated.
ADV EFF Dizziness, headache, nausea, numbness/tingling in arms, ventricular arrhythmias
INTERACTIONS Amiodarone, antihistamines, digoxin, disopyramide, quinidine, phenothiazines, procainamide, sotalol, TCAs
NC/PT Determine time of arrhythmia onset; most effective if less than 90 days. Ensure pt anticoagulated for at least 2 wk if AF lasts more than 2 days. Have emergency equipment on hand. Provide follow-up for medical evaluation. Pt should report chest pain, difficulty breathing.

---

icatibant (Firazyr)
CLASS Bradykinin receptor antagonist
PREG/CONT C/NA

IND & DOSE Tx of acute attacks of hereditary angioedema. *Adult:* 30 mg subcut in abdomen; may repeat after at least 6 hr. Max, 3 injections/day.
ADV EFF Dizziness, drowsiness, fever, injection-site reaction, rash
INTERACTIONS ACE inhibitors
NC/PT Teach proper administration/disposal of needles/syringes. Rotate injection sites in abdomen; do not inject into scars, inflamed/infected areas. Use caution in pregnancy/breast-feeding. Pt should take safety precautions for CNS effects, go to emergency department after injecting if laryngeal attack occurs.

icosapent ethyl
(Vascepa)

CLASS Antihypertriglyceridemic, ethyl ester
PREG/CONT C/NA

IND & DOSE Adjunct to diet to reduce triglyceride levels in adults w/severe (500 mg/dL or higher) hypertriglyceridemia. *Adult:* 2 g PO bid w/food.

ADV EFF Arthralgia, bleeding, **hepatic impairment,** hypersensitivity reaction

INTERACTIONS Anticoagulants, platelet inhibitors

NC/PT Monitor LFTs carefully; use caution w/known fish/shellfish allergy. Pt should swallow capsule whole and not cut, crush, or chew it; continue diet/exercise program.

DANGEROUS DRUG

idarubicin hydrochloride
(Idamycin PFS)

CLASS Antineoplastic antibiotic
PREG/CONT D/NA

BBW Do not give IM, subcut because of severe local reaction, tissue necrosis; give IV only. Risk of myocardial toxicity; monitor accordingly. Monitor response to tx frequently at start of tx. Monitor serum uric acid level, CBC, cardiac output (listen for S3), LFTs. Changes in uric acid levels may need dose decrease; consult physician.

IND & DOSE Tx of AML w/other drugs. *Adult:* 12 mg/m²/day for 3 days by slow IV injection (10–15 min) w/ cytarabine. May give cytarabine as 100 mg/m²/day by continuous IV infusion for 7 days or as 25-mg/m² IV bolus, then 200 mg/m²/day IV for 5 days by continuous infusion. May give second course when toxicity has subsided, if needed, at 25% dose reduction.

ADJUST DOSE Hepatic, renal impairment

ADV EFF Alopecia, **anaphylaxis,** anorexia, **cancer, cardiac toxicity,** headache, **HF,** injection-site reactions, **myelosuppression, mucositis,** n/v

NC/PT Monitor injection site for extravasation. Monitor CBC, LFTs, renal function, cardiac output frequently during tx. Ensure adequate hydration. Not for use in pregnancy (barrier contraceptives advised). Pt should cover head at temp extremes (hair loss possible), get regular medical follow-up, report swelling, chest pain, difficulty breathing.

---

idarucizumab (Praxbind)

CLASS Monoclonal antibody, reversal agent
PREG/CONT Unkn/NA

IND & DOSE Reversal of anticoagulant effects of dabigatran in life-threatening or uncontrolled bleeding, need for emergency surgery or procedures. *Adult:* 5 g IV as two consecutive infusions of 2.5 g/50 mL; consecutive bolus injections of 2.5 g each could be used.

ADJUST DOSE Conduction defects

ADV EFF Constipation, delirium, fever, headache, hypokalemia, hypersensitivity reactions, pneumonia, **thromboembolism**

NC/PT Risk of serious reaction w/ hereditary fructose intolerance; monitor pt. Do not mix in solution w/ other drugs. Ensure consecutive infusions/injections. Risk of thromboembolism when pt off anticoagulant; restart anticoagulant when pt stable. Can restart dabigatran within 24 hr; other anticoagulants are not affected. Pt should report difficulty breathing, chest/leg pain, abnormal bleeding.

idelalisib (Zydelig)
CLASS Antineoplastic, kinase inhibitor
PREG/CONT D/NA

BBW Risk of severe to fatal hepatotoxicity; serious to fatal diarrhea, colitis; serious to fatal pneumonitis; GI perforation.
IND & DOSE Tx of relapsed chronic lymphocytic leukemia w/rituximab, relapsed follicular B-cell non-Hodgkin lymphoma after at least two other tx, relapsed small lymphocytic lymphoma after at least two other tx. *Adult:* 150 mg PO bid.
ADV EFF Abd pain, **anaphylaxis**, chills, **colitis**, cough, fatigue, **GI perforation, hepatotoxicity,** hyperglycemia, neutropenia, **pneumonitis, severe cutaneous reactions**
INTERACTIONS CYP3A inducers/ substrates
NC/PT Ensure dx. Monitor hepatic/ respiratory function, CBC. Watch for diarrhea, s&sx of intestinal perforation. Not for use in pregnancy (contraceptives advised)/breast-feeding. Frequent blood tests will be needed. Pt should take twice a day, report difficulty breathing, rash/skin sores, diarrhea w/blood or mucus, severe abd pain, urine/stool color changes.

idursulfase (Elaprase)
CLASS Enzyme
PREG/CONT C/NA

BBW Risk of severe to life-threatening anaphylactic reactions during infusion; have emergency equipment on hand. Monitor closely.
IND & DOSE Tx of Hunter's syndrome. *Adult, child over 5 yr:* 0.5 mg/kg IV infused over 1-8 hr.
ADV EFF Anaphylaxis, fever, hypertension, rash, respiratory impairment
NC/PT Start first infusion slowly to monitor for infusion reaction (8 mL/min for first 15 min, then increase by 8 mL/min at 15-min intervals; max,

100 mL/hr). Do not infuse w/other products in same line. Use caution in pregnancy/breast-feeding. Pt should report difficulty breathing, rash.

ifosfamide (Ifex)
CLASS Alkylating agent, antineoplastic, nitrogen mustard
PREG/CONT D/NA

BBW Arrange for blood tests to evaluate hematopoietic function before starting tx and wkly during tx; serious hemorrhagic toxicities have occurred. Provide extensive hydration consisting of at least 2 L oral or IV fluid/day to prevent bladder toxicity. Arrange to give protector, such as mesna, to prevent hemorrhagic cystitis, which can be severe. CNS toxicity can be severe to fatal. Nephrotoxicity can be severe and result in renal failure.
IND & DOSE Third-line chemotherapy of germ-cell testicular cancer w/ other drugs. *Adult:* 1.2 g/m²/day IV over at least 30 min for 5 consecutive days; repeat q 3 wk, or after recovery from hematologic toxicity. For px of bladder toxicity, give more than 2 L fluid/day IV or PO. Use mesna IV to prevent hemorrhagic cystitis.
ADJUST DOSE Elderly pts, renal impairment
ADV EFF Alopecia, **anaphylaxis**, anorexia, **cardiotoxicity,** confusion, hallucinations, immunosuppression, leukopenia, **neurotoxicity,** n/v, **potentially fatal hemorrhagic cystitis, pulmonary toxicity, secondary malignancies,** somnolence
INTERACTIONS CYP3A4 inducers/ inhibitors, grapefruit juice
NC/PT For px of bladder toxicity, give more than 2 L fluid/day IV or PO. Use mesna IV to prevent hemorrhagic cystitis. Maintain hydration (at least 10–12 glasses fluid/day). Can cause fetal harm; contraceptives advised (for men/women) during and for few wks after tx. Pt should avoid grapefruit juice, cover head at temp extremes

(hair loss possible), report painful urination, blood in urine, chest pain, difficulty breathing.

iloperidone (Fanapt)
CLASS Atypical antipsychotic
PREG/CONT C/NA

BBW Increased risk of death if used in elderly pts w/dementia-related psychosis. Do not use for these pts; not approved for this use.
IND & DOSE Acute tx of schizophrenia. *Adult:* Range, 12–24 mg/day PO; titrate based on orthostatic hypotension tolerance. Initially, 1 mg PO bid; then 2, 4, 6, 8, 10, 12 mg PO bid on days 2, 3, 4, 5, 6, 7 respectively.
ADJUST DOSE Hepatic impairment, poor CYP2D6 metabolizers
ADV EFF Bone marrow suppression, cognitive/motor impairment, dizziness, fatigue, hyperglycemia, nausea, **NMS,** orthostatic hypotension, priapism, **prolonged QT, seizures,** suicidality, weight gain
INTERACTIONS Alcohol, antihypertensives, CNS depressants, fluoxetine, itraconazole, ketoconazole, other QT-prolonging drugs, paroxetine, St. John's wort
NC/PT Obtain baseline ECG; periodically monitor QT interval. Titrate over first wk to decrease orthostatic hypotension. Monitor serum glucose. Use caution in pregnancy; not for use in breast-feeding. Pt should take safety measures for CNS effects, avoid alcohol/St. John's wort; change positions carefully, report fever, thoughts of suicide, fainting.

iloprost (Ventavis)
CLASS Vasodilator
PREG/CONT C/NA

IND & DOSE Tx of pulmonary artery hypertension in pts w/NY Heart Association Class II to IV sx. *Adult:* 2.5–5 mcg inhaled 6–9 times/day while awake; max, 45 mcg/day.

ADV EFF Back pain, **bronchospasm,** cough, dizziness, headache, **hypotension,** insomnia, light-headedness, muscle cramps, n/v, palpitations, **pulmonary hypotension,** syncope
INTERACTIONS Anticoagulants, antihypertensives, vasodilators
NC/PT Review proper use of inhaler. Use caution in pregnancy; not for use in breast-feeding. Pt should take safety measures for CNS effects, report difficulty breathing, fainting.

DANGEROUS DRUG

imatinib mesylate (Gleevec)
CLASS Antineoplastic, protein tyrosine kinase inhibitor
PREG/CONT D/NA

IND & DOSE Tx of chronic phase CML. *Adult:* 400 mg/day PO as once-a-day dose; may consider 600 mg/day. *Child over 2 yr:* 260 mg/m2 PO as one dose, or divided a.m. and p.m. Tx of accelerated phase or blast crisis CML. *Adult:* 600 mg/day PO as single dose; may consider 400 mg PO bid. Tx of newly diagnosed CML. *Child over 2 yr:* 340 mg/m2 PO; max, 600 mg/day. Tx of ALL. *Adult:* 600 mg/day PO. Tx of aggressive systemic mastocytosis (ASM), hypereosinophilic syndrome/chronic eosinophilic leukemia, myelodysplastic/myeloproliferative diseases, metastatic malignant GI stromal tumors; adjunct tx after surgical resection of Kit-positive GI stromal tumors. *Adult:* 400 mg/day PO. Tx of ASM w/eosinophilia. *Adult:* 100 mg/day PO. Tx of unresectable, recurrent, or metastatic dermatofibrosarcoma protuberans. *Adult:* 800 mg/day PO.
ADJUST DOSE Hepatic, renal impairment
ADV EFF Bone marrow suppression, fluid retention, GI perforations, headache, hemorrhage, hepatic impairment, **left ventricular dysfx,** n/v/d, **rash to Stevens-Johnson**

syndrome, **severe HF,** tumor lysis syndrome

INTERACTIONS Azithromycin, carbamazepine, clarithromycin, cyclosporine, dexamethasone, grapefruit juice, itraconazole, ketoconazole, levothyroxine, pimozide, phenobarbital, phenytoin, rifampin, simvastatin, St. John's wort, warfarin

NC/PT Monitor CBC. Not for use in pregnancy (barrier contraceptives advised). Monitor child for growth retardation. Give w/meals. May disperse in glass of water or apple juice; give immediately using 50 mL for 10-mg tablet, 200 mL for 400-mg tablet. Pt should not cut or crush tablet, should take analgesics for headache, avoid grapefruit juice/St. John's wort, report sudden fluid retention, unusual bleeding, rash, severe abd pain.

---

imipramine hydrochloride, imipramine pamoate
(Tofranil)
CLASS Antidepressant, TCA
PREG/CONT C/NA

BBW Limit drug access for depressed, potentially suicidal pts. Increased risk of suicidality, especially in children, adolescents, young adults; monitor accordingly.

IND & DOSE Tx of depression. *Adult:* Hospitalized pts, 100–150 mg/day PO in divided doses; may increase to 200 mg/day. After 2 wk, may increase to 250–300 mg/day. Outpts, 75 mg/day PO, increasing to 150 mg/day. Max, 200 mg/day; range, 50–150 mg/day. *Adolescent:* 30–40 mg/day PO. **Tx of childhood enuresis.** *Child 6 yr and older:* 25 mg/day PO 1 hr before bedtime. May increase to 75 mg/day nightly in child over 12 yr, 50 mg/day nightly in child under 12 yr. Max, 2.5 mg/kg/day.

ADJUST DOSE Elderly pts
ADV EFF Anticholinergic effects, arrhythmias, **bone marrow depression,** confusion, constipation, disturbed

concentration, dry mouth, **MI,** nervousness, orthostatic hypotension, photosensitivity, sedation, **stroke,** urine retention, withdrawal sx after prolonged use

INTERACTIONS Anticholinergics, clonidine, MAOIs, oral anticoagulants, St. John's wort, sympathomimetics

NC/PT Screen for bipolar disorder, angle-closure glaucoma. Give major portion at bedtime. Consider dose change w/adverse effects. Not for use in pregnancy/breast-feeding. Pt should avoid sun exposure, take safety measures for CNS effects, report thoughts of suicide, excessive sedation.

---

incobotulinumtoxinA
(Xeomin)
CLASS Neurotoxin
PREG/CONT C/NA

BBW Drug not for tx of muscle spasticity; toxin may spread from injection area and cause s&sx of botulism (CNS alterations, trouble speaking and swallowing, loss of bladder control). Use only for approved indications.

IND & DOSE Improvement of glabellar lines. *Adult:* Total of 20 units (0.5 mL) sol injected as divided doses of 0.1 mL into each of five sites—two in each corrugator muscle, one in procerus muscle. Repetition usually needed q 3–4 mo to maintain effect. **Cervical dystonia.** *Adult:* 120 units/tx IM as four separate injections. **Blepharospasm in previously treated pts.** *Adult:* 35 units per eye. **Upper limb spasticity.** *Adult:* Up to 400 units/tx IM as several separate injections; repeat no sooner than q 12 wk.

ADV EFF Anaphylactic reactions, dizziness, headache, local reactions, **MI, spread of toxin that can lead to death**

INTERACTIONS Aminoglycosides, anticholinesterases, lincosamides, magnesium sulfate, NMJ blockers, polymyxin, quinidine, succinylcholine

NC/PT Store in refrigerator. Have epinephrine available in case of anaphylactic reactions. Effects may not appear for 1–2 days; will persist for 3–4 mo. Not for use in pregnancy.

indacaterol (Arcapta Neohaler)
CLASS Bronchodilator, long-acting beta agonist
PREG/CONT C/NA

BBW Increased risk of asthma-related deaths; not indicated for tx of asthma.

IND & DOSE Long-term maint bronchodilator tx for pts w/COPD: *Adult:* 75 mcg/day inhaled w/*Arcapta Neohaler.*

ADV EFF Arrhythmias, asthma-related deaths, bronchospasm, cough, headache, **hypertension,** nausea, nasopharyngitis, pharyngeal pain, **seizures**

INTERACTIONS Adrenergic drugs, beta blockers, corticosteroids, diuretics, MAOIs, QT-prolonging drugs, TCAs, xanthines

NC/PT Not for asthma or acute or deteriorating situations. Do not exceed recommended dose. Should be used w/inhaled corticosteroid. Review proper use of inhaler. Pt should report worsening of condition, chest pain, severe difficulty breathing.

indapamide (generic)
CLASS Thiazide-like diuretic
PREG/CONT B/NA

IND & DOSE Tx of edema associated w/HF. *Adult:* 2.5–5 mg/day PO. Tx of **hypertension.** *Adult:* 1.25–2.5 mg/day PO. Consider adding another drug if control not achieved.

ADV EFF **Agranulocytosis,** anorexia, **aplastic anemia,** dizziness, dry mouth, hypotension, n/v, photosensitivity, vertigo

INTERACTIONS Antidiabetics, cholestyramine, colestipol, lithium, thiazide diuretics

NC/PT Give w/food if GI upset occurs. Give early in a.m. Pt should weigh self daily and record, report weight change of 3 lb/day, take safety precautions for CNS effects, use sugarless lozenges for dry mouth, avoid sun exposure.

indinavir sulfate (Crixivan)
CLASS Antiviral, protease inhibitor
PREG/CONT C/NA

IND & DOSE Tx of HIV infection w/ other drugs. *Adult, child 12 yr and older:* 800 mg PO q 8 hr. W/delavirdine, 600 mg PO q 8 hr; w/delavirdine, 400 mg PO tid; w/didanosine, give more than 1 hr apart on empty stomach; w/itraconazole, 600 mg PO q 8 hr; w/itraconazole, 200 mg PO bid; w/ketoconazole, 600 mg PO q 8 hr; w/ rifabutin, 1,000 mg PO q 8 hr (reduce rifabutin by 50%).

ADJUST DOSE Hepatic impairment

ADV EFF Dry skin, flulike sx, headache, hyperbilirubinemia, n/v/d, nephrolithiasis/urolithiasis

INTERACTIONS Ergots, midazolam, pimozide, triazolam; do not use w/ preceding drugs. Atazanavir, azole antifungals, benzodiazepines, carbamazepine, delavirdine, efavirenz, fentanyl, grapefruit juice, interleukins, nelfinavir, nevirapine, phenobarbital, phenytoin, rifabutin, rifampin, rifamycin, ritonavir, sildenafil, St. John's wort, venlafaxine

NC/PT Protect capsules from moisture; store in container provided and keep desiccant in bottle. Give drug q 8 hr around clock. Maintain hydration. Check all drugs pt taking; many interactions possible. Not a cure for disease; advise pt to use precautions to prevent spread. Pt should avoid grapefruit juice/St. John's wort; continue other HIV drugs; drink at least 1.5 L of water/day; report severe diarrhea, flank pain.

indomethacin, indomethacin sodium trihydrate (Indocin, Tivorbex)
CLASS NSAID
PREG/CONT B (1st, 2nd trimesters); D (3rd trimester)/NA

BBW Increased risk of CV events, GI bleeding; monitor accordingly. Adverse reactions dose-related; use lowest effective dose. Not for use for periop pain w/CABG surgery.
IND & DOSE Relief of s&sx of osteoarthritis, rheumatoid arthritis, ankylosing spondylitis. *Adult:* 25 mg PO bid or tid; may use total daily dose of 150–200 mg/day PO. **Tx of acute painful shoulder.** *Adult:* 75–150 mg/day PO in three or four divided doses for 7–14 days. **Tx of acute gouty arthritis.** *Adult:* 50 mg PO tid until pain tolerable; then decrease until not needed (within 3–5 days). Do not use SR form. **Closure of hemodynamically significant patent ductus arteriosus in preterm infants 500–1,750 g.** *Infant:* Three IV doses at 12- to 24-hr intervals. *2–7 days old:* 0.2 mg/kg IV for all three doses. *Under 48 hr old:* 0.2 mg/kg IV, then 0.1 mg/kg, then 0.1 mg/kg. **Tx of mild to moderate acute pain.** *Adult:* 20 mg PO tid or 40 mg PO two to three times/day (*Tivorbex*).
ADV EFF Anaphylactoid reactions to anaphylactic shock. aplastic anemia, apnea w/IV use, bleeding ulcer, bone marrow suppression, depression, dizziness, drowsiness, eye changes, headache, hepatic impairment, hypertension, insomnia, n/v, **MI, pulmonary hemorrhage w/ IV use,** rash
INTERACTIONS ACE inhibitors, adrenergic blockers, anticoagulants, ARBs, bisphosphonates, lithium, loop diuretics, platelet inhibitors, potassium-sparing diuretics

NC/PT Do not use SR form for gouty arthritic. Give w/food. Monitor eyes w/long-term therapy. Monitor LFTs, renal function. Pt should avoid OTC drugs without first checking w/ prescriber. Take safety precautions for CNS effects, report black or tarry stools, bleeding.

infliximab (Remicade)
CLASS Monoclonal antibody, TNF blocker
PREG/CONT B/NA

BBW Risk of serious to life-threatening infections, activation of TB, malignancies, including fatal hepatosplenic T-cell lymphoma. Monitor pt; reserve for approved uses.
IND & DOSE **Tx of Crohn's disease, ulcerative colitis, ankylosing spondylitis, psoriatic arthritis, plaque psoriasis.** *Adult, child:* 5 mg/kg IV at 0, 2, 6 wk; maint, 5 mg/kg IV q 8 wk (q 6 wk for ankylosing spondylitis). **Tx of rheumatoid arthritis.** *Adult:* 3 mg/kg IV at 0, 2, 6 wk; maint, 3 mg/kg IV q 8 wk w/methotrexate.
ADV EFF Abd pain, **bone marrow suppression, cancer, demyelinating diseases,** headache, **hepatitis B reactivation, hepatotoxicity, HF,** infusion reactions, **serious to fatal infections**
INTERACTIONS TNF blockers, tocilizumab, methotrexate, immunosuppressants, live vaccines
NC/PT Obtain TB test before starting tx. Monitor CBC before each dose; adjustment may be needed. Monitor LFTs. Assess for s&sx of infection. Pt should get routine cancer screening; mark calendar for tx days; report edema, chest pain, fever, signs of infection, numbness/tingling.

insoluble Prussian blue (Radiogardase)

CLASS Ferric hexacyanoferrate
PREG/CONT C/NA

IND & DOSE Tx of pts w/known or suspected internal contamination w/radioactive cesium and/or radioactive or nonradioactive thallium. *Adult:* 3 g PO tid. *Child 2–12 yr:* 1 g PO tid.

ADV EFF Constipation

NC/PT Monitor radioactivity levels. Take appropriate precautions to avoid exposure. Begin as soon as possible after exposure. Treat for constipation if indicated. Stool, oral mucus, teeth may turn blue. Excreted in urine, feces; pt should flush toilet several times, clean up spilled urine, feces.

DANGEROUS DRUG

insulin (Novolin-R), insulin inhaled (Afrezza), insulin lispro (Humalog), insulin aspart (Novolog), insulin degludec (Tresiba), insulin detemir (Levemir), insulin glargine (Basaglar, Lantus, Tuojeo), insulin glulisine (Apidra), isophane insulin (Novolin N)

CLASS Hormone
PREG/CONT B; C (aspart, degludec, glargine, glulisine)/NA

BBW Risk of acute bronchospasm w/inhaled insulin. Not for use w/asthma or COPD. Baseline spirometry in all pts before use.

IND & DOSE Tx of type 1 diabetes, severe ketoacidosis, diabetic coma; short-course tx when glucose control needed. *Adult,* child: 0.5–1 unit/kg/day subcut. Base adjustment on serum glucose levels, pt response. Can give regular and glulisine IV. For inhaled insulin: 1 inhalation at start of each meal. **Tx of type 2 diabetes when** glucose control cannot be maintained. *Adult:* 10 mg/day subcut; range, 2–100 units/day *(Lantus, Tresiba)* or 0.1–0.2 units/kg subcut or 10 units/day or bid subcut *(Levemir).*

ADV EFF Acute bronchospasm (inhaled), **anaphylaxis, angioedema,** HF, hypoglycemia, injection-site reactions, ketoacidosis, **lung cancer** (inhaled), **pulmonary function decline** (inhaled), rash, renal impairment

INTERACTIONS Alcohol, atypical antipsychotics, beta blockers, celery, coriander, corticosteroids, dandelion root, diuretics, fenugreek, garlic, ginseng, juniper berries, MAOIs, salicylates, thiazolidinediones (inhaled)

See *Insulin pharmacokinetics.*

NC/PT Spirometry evaluation before use of inhaled insulin. Double-check doses for child. Use caution when mixing two types of insulin; always draw regular insulin into syringe first. Change insulin reservoir at least q 6 days if using inhaled. If mixing w/lispro, draw lispro first. Use mixtures of regular and NPH or lente within 5–15 min of combining. Do not mix *Lantus* (glargine), *Levemir* (detemir) in sol w/other drugs, including other insulins. Usage based on onset, peak, duration; varies among insulins. Do not freeze; protect from heat. Adjust dosage based on pt response. Monitor, rotate injections sites. Ensure total diabetic teaching, including diet/exercise, hygiene measures, recognition of hypo-, hyperglycemia. Teach proper use of inhaler, proper injection, disposal of needles/syringes and to never reuse or share pens/needles. Pt should avoid alcohol; if using herbs, check w/prescriber for insulin dose adjustment; wear medical ID; always eat when using insulin; report uncontrolled serum glucose.

INSULIN PHARMACOKINETICS

Type	Onset	Peak	Duration
Regular	30–60 min	2–3 hr	6–12 hr
NPH	1–1.5 hr	4–12 hr	24 hr
Inhaled	<15 min	50 min	2–3 hr
Lispro	<15 min	30–90 min	2–5 hr
Aspart	10–20 min	1–3 hr	3–5 hr
Degludec	1 hr	None	24 hr
Detemir	Slow	3–6 hr	6–23 hr
Glargine	60 min	None	24 hr
Glulisine	2–5 min	30–90 min	1–2 hr
Combination insulins	30–60 min, then 1–2 hr	2–4 hr, then 6–12 hr	6–8 hr, then 18–24 hr

---

DANGEROUS DRUG

interferon alfa-2b
(Intron-A)
CLASS Antineoplastic
PREG/CONT C/NA

BBW Risk of serious to life-threatening reactions. Monitor for severe reactions (including hypersensitivity reactions), neuropsychiatric, autoimmune, ischemic, infectious disorders. Notify physician immediately if these occur; dose reduction/discontinuation may be needed.
IND & DOSE Tx of hairy cell leukemia. *Adult:* 2 million international units/m² subcut or IM three times/wk for up to 6 mo. **Tx of condylomata acuminata.** *Adult:* 1 million international units/lesion intralesionally three times/wk for 3 wk; can treat up to five lesions at one time. May repeat in 12–16 wk. **Tx of chronic hepatitis C.** *Adult:* 3 million international units subcut or IM three times/wk for 18–24 mo. **Tx of AIDS-related Kaposi sarcoma.** *Adult:* 30 million international units/m² subcut or IM three times/wk. **Tx of chronic hepatitis B.** *Adult:* 30–35 million international units/wk subcut or IM either as 5 million international units daily or 10 million international units three times/wk for 16 wk. *Child:*

3 million international units/m² subcut three times/wk for first wk, then 6 million international units/m² subcut three times/wk for total of 16–24 wk (max, 10 million international units three times/wk). **Tx of follicular lymphoma.** *Adult:* 5 million international units subcut three times/wk for 18 mo w/other chemotherapy. **Tx of malignant melanoma.** *Adult:* 20 million international units/m² IV over 20 min on 5 consecutive days/wk for 4 wk; maint, 10 million international units/m² IV three times/wk for 48 wk.
ADV EFF Anorexia, **bone marrow suppression,** confusion, dizziness, flulike sx, n/v, rash
NC/PT Obtain baseline, periodic CBC, LFTs. Do not give IV. Pt should mark calendar of tx days, get blood tests regularly, take safety precautions for CNS effects, report bleeding, signs of infection.

---

interferon beta-1a
(Avonex, Rebif)
CLASS Immunomodulator, MS drug
PREG/CONT C/NA

IND & DOSE Tx of relapsing forms of MS to slow accumulation of physical disability, decrease frequency of clinical exacerbations. *Adult:* 30 mcg IM once/wk *(Avonex).* Or, 22–44 mcg subcut three times per wk *(Rebif);* start w/8.8 mcg three times/wk; titrate up over 5 wk to full dose of 22–44 mcg.

ADV EFF Anaphylaxis, anorexia, bone marrow suppression, confusion, depression, dizziness, flulike sx, hepatotoxicity, nausea, photosensitivity, seizures, suicidality
NC/PT Obtain baseline, periodic CBC, LFTs. Rotate injection sites. Teach proper administration/disposal of needles/syringes. Maintain hydration. Pt should mark calendar of tx days; avoid exposure to infections, sun; report infection, unusual bleeding, thoughts of suicide, difficulty breathing.

interferon beta-1b
(Betaseron, Extavia)
CLASS Immunomodulator, MS drug
PREG/CONT C/NA

IND & DOSE Tx of relapsing forms of MS to slow accumulation of physical disability, decrease frequency of clinical exacerbations. *Adult:* 0.25 mg subcut q other day (target); discontinue if disease unremitting for more than 6 mo. Initially, 0.0625 mg subcut q other day, wks 1–2; then 0.125 mg subcut q other day, wks 3–4; then 0.1875 mg subcut q other day, wks 5–6; target 0.25 mg subcut q other day by wk 7.

ADV EFF Anaphylaxis, anorexia, bone marrow suppression, confusion, depression, dizziness, flulike sx, hepatotoxicity, nausea, photosensitivity
NC/PT Obtain baseline, periodic CBC, LFTs. Rotate injection sites. Not for use in pregnancy (barrier contraceptives advised). Maintain hydration. Teach proper administration/disposal of needles/syringes. Pt should mark calendar of tx day; avoid exposure to infection, sun; report

infection, unusual bleeding, thoughts of suicide, difficulty breathing.

interferon gamma-1b
(Actimmune)
CLASS Immunomodulator
PREG/CONT C/NA

IND & DOSE To reduce frequency/severity of serious infections associated w/chronic granulomatous disease; to delay time to disease progression in pts w/severe, malignant osteopetrosis. *Adult:* 50 mcg/m² (1 million international units/m²) subcut three times/wk in pts w/body surface area (BSA) over 0.5 m²; 1.5 mcg/kg/dose in pts w/BSA of 0.5 m² or less subcut three times/wk. For severe reactions, withhold or reduce dose by 50%.

ADV EFF Anorexia, confusion, depression, dizziness, flulike sx, nausea, suicidality
NC/PT Obtain baseline, periodic CBC, LFTs. Store in refrigerator. Give at night if flulike sx a problem. Rotate injection sites. Teach proper administration/disposal of needles/syringes. Not for use in pregnancy (barrier contraceptives advised). Maintain hydration. Pt should mark calendar of tx day; avoid exposure to infection, sun; report unusual bleeding, thoughts of suicide.

iodine thyroid products (Iosat, Lugol's Solution, Pima, SSKI, Strong Iodine Solution, ThyroSafe, ThyroShield)
CLASS Thyroid suppressant
PREG/CONT D/NA

IND & DOSE Tx of hyperthyroidism in preparation for surgery; thyrotoxic crisis: *Adult, child over 1 yr:* RDA, 150 mcg/day PO. Tx, 0.3 mL PO tid *(Strong Iodine Solution, Lugol's Solution);* range, 0.1–0.9 mL/day PO.

Thyroid blocking in radiation emergency. *Adult, child over 12 yr, 68 kg or more:* 130 mg PO q 24 hr *(Iosat, ThyroSafe, ThyroShield).* Child *3–18 yr, under 68 kg:* 65 mg/day PO. Child *1 mo–3 yr:* 32.5 mg/day PO. Child *birth–1 mo:* 16.25 mg/day PO.
ADV EFF Iodism, rash, swelling of salivary glands
INTERACTIONS Lithium
NC/PT Dilute strong iodine sol w/ fruit juice/water to improve taste. Crush tablets for small child. Discontinue if iodine toxicity.

---

iodoquinol (Yodoxin)
CLASS Amebicide
PREG/CONT C/NA

IND & DOSE Tx of acute, chronic intestinal amebiasis. *Adult:* 650 mg PO tid after meals for 20 days. *Child:* 10–13.3 mg/kg/day PO in three divided doses for 20 days; max, 650 mg/dose (do not exceed 1.95 g in 24 hr for 20 days).
ADV EFF Blurred vision, n/v/d, rash
INTERACTIONS Lithium
NC/PT Give after meals. Maintain nutrition. Pt should report severe GI upset, unusual fatigue.

---

ipilimumab (Yervoy)
CLASS Cytotoxic T-cell antigen 4–blocking antibody
PREG/CONT C/NA

BBW Severe to fatal immune-mediated reactions involving many organs possible; may occur during tx or wks to mos after tx ends. Permanently stop drug, treat w/high-dose systemic corticosteroids if s&sx of immune reactions appear.
IND & DOSE Tx of unresectable or metastatic melanoma. *Adult:* 3 mg/kg IV over 90 min q 3 wk; total, four doses.
ADV EFF Colitis, diarrhea, **endocrinopathies,** fatigue, **hepatitis,** pruritus, rash
NC/PT Establish baseline LFTs, thyroid/endocrine/GI function, skin

condition; assess regularly for changes. Not for use in pregnancy/breast-feeding. Pt should mark calendar for tx days, report severe diarrhea, increased thirst, unusual fatigue.

---

ipratropium bromide (Atrovent, Atrovent HFA)
CLASS Anticholinergic, bronchodilator
PREG/CONT B/NA

IND & DOSE Maint tx of bronchospasm associated w/COPD (sol, aerosol), chronic bronchitis, emphysema. *Adult, child 12 yr and older:* 500 mcg tid–qid via nebulizer, w/ doses 6–8 hr apart. Symptomatic relief of rhinorrhea associated w/ common cold. *Adult, child 12 yr and older:* 2 sprays 0.06%/nostril tid–qid. Child *5–11 yr:* 2 sprays 0.06%/nostril tid. Symptomatic relief of rhinitis. *Adult, child 6 yr and older:* 2 sprays 0.03%/nostril bid–tid. Relief of rhinorrhea in seasonal allergic rhinitis. *Adult, child over 5 yr:* 2 sprays 0.06%/nostril qid for 3 wk.
ADV EFF Cough, dizziness, dry mouth, headache, nervousness, nausea, urine retention
NC/PT Do not use w/peanut, soy allergies. Protect sol from light. May mix in nebulizer w/albuterol for up to 1 hr. Review proper use of nebulizer. Ensure hydration. Pt should empty bladder before using, take safety precautions for CNS effects, report vision changes, rash.

---

irbesartan (Avapro)
CLASS Antihypertensive, ARB
PREG/CONT D/NA

BBW Rule out pregnancy before beginning tx. Suggest barrier contraceptives during tx; fetal injury, deaths have occurred.
IND & DOSE Tx of hypertension. *Adult, child 13–16 yr:* 150 mg/day PO;

max, 300 mg/day. *Child 6–12 y:* 75 mg/day PO; max, 150 mg/day. **To slow progression of nephropathy in pts w/hypertension, type 2 diabetes.** *Adult:* 300 mg/day PO.

ADJUST DOSE Volume or salt depletion

ADV EFF Abd pain, **angioedema,** cough, dizziness, fatigue, headache, n/v/d, URI

INTERACTIONS ACE inhibitors, ARBs, CYP2C9-metabolized drugs, renin blockers

NC/PT Use caution w/surgery; volume expansion may be needed. Monitor closely when decreased BP secondary to fluid volume loss possible. Give w/meals. Not for use in pregnancy (barrier contraceptives advised)/breast-feeding. Pt should take safety precautions for CNS effects; report fever, chills.

irinotecan hydrochloride
(Camptosar, Onivyde)
CLASS Antineoplastic, DNA topoisomerase inhibitor
PREG/CONT D/NA

BBW Obtain CBC before each infusion. Do not give when baseline neutrophil count under 1,500/mm^2. Severe bone marrow depression possible; consult physician for dose reduction or withholding if bone marrow depression evident. Monitor for diarrhea; assess hydration. Arrange to reduce dose if 4–6 stools/day; omit dose if 7–9 stools/day. If 10 or more stools/day, consult physician. May prevent or ameliorate early diarrhea w/atropine 0.25–1 mg IV or subcut. Treat late diarrhea lasting more than 24 hr w/loperamide; late diarrhea can be severe to life-threatening.

IND & DOSE First-line tx w/5-FU and leucovorin for tx pts w/metastatic colon, rectal carcinomas. *Adult:* 125 mg/m^2 IV over 90 min days 1, 8, 15, 22 w/leucovorin 20 mg/m^2 IV bolus days 1, 8, 15, 22 and 5-FU

500 mg/m^2 IV days 1, 8, 15, 22. Restart cycle on day 43. Or, 180 mg/m^2 IV over 90 min days 1, 15, 29 w/leucovorin 200 mg/m^2 IV over 2 hr days 1, 2, 15, 16, 29, 30 and 5-FU 400 mg/m^2 as IV bolus days 1, 2, 15, 16, 29, 30 followed by 5-FU 600 mg/m^2 IV infusion over 22 hr on days 1, 2, 15, 16, 29, 30. Restart cycle on day 43. **Tx of pts w/metastatic colon, rectal cancer whose disease has recurred or progressed after 5-FU therapy.** *Adult:* 125 mg/m^2 IV over 90 min once wkly for 4 wk, then 2-wk rest; repeat 6-wk regimen, or 350 mg/m^2 IV over 90 min once q 3 wk. **W/5-FU and leucovorin for tx of pts w/metastatic adenocarcinoma of pancreas after gemcitabine therapy.** 70 mg/m^2 IV over 90 min q 2 wk (*Onivyde*); 50 mg/m^2 IV q 2 wk (*Onivyde*) for pts homozygous w/UGT1A1*28.

ADV EFF Alopecia, anorexia, **bone marrow suppression,** dizziness, dyspnea, fatigue, hypersensitivity reactions, interstitial pneumonitis, mucositis, n/v/d

INTERACTIONS CYP3A4 inducers/inhibitors, diuretics, ketoconazole, other antineoplastics, St. John's wort

NC/PT Check drug regimen; many interactions possible. Monitor CBC; dose adjustment based on bone marrow response. Premedicate w/corticosteroid and antiemetic 30 min before IV *Onivyde*. Monitor IV site for extravasation. Not for use in pregnancy (barrier contraceptives advised). Pt should mark calendar for tx days, cover head at temp extremes (hair loss possible), avoid exposure to infections, report pain at injection site, signs of infection, severe/bloody diarrhea.

iron dextran **(Dexferrum, INFeD)**
CLASS Iron preparation
PREG/CONT C/NA

BBW Monitor for hypersensitivity reactions; test dose highly recommended. Have epinephrine on hand for severe hypersensitivity reaction.

IND & DOSE Tx of iron deficiency anemia only when PO route not possible. *Adult, child:* 0.5 mL IM or IV test dose before tx; base dose on hematologic response w/frequent Hgb determinations. Over 25 kg: Dose (mL) = [0.0442 (desired Hgb – observed Hgb) × LBW] + (0.26 × LBW), where Hgb = Hgb in g/dL and LBW = lean body weight, IV or IM. *Child over 4 mo, 5–15 kg:* Dose (mL) = 0.0442 (desired Hgb – observed Hgb) × W + (0.26 × W), where W = actual weight in kg, IV or IM. **Iron replacement for blood loss.** *Adult, child:* Replacement iron (in mg) = blood loss (in mL) × Hct.

ADV EFF Anaphylaxis, arthritic reactivation, **cardiac arrest,** discoloration/pain at injection site, local phlebitis, lymphadenopathy, n/v

INTERACTIONS Chloramphenicol

NC/PT Ensure actual iron deficiency. Perform test dose at least 5 min before tx. Inject IM only into upper outer quadrant of buttocks using Z-track technique. Monitor serum ferritin. Pt should avoid oral iron or vitamins w/ iron added, report pain at injection site, difficulty breathing.

iron sucrose (Venofer)
CLASS Iron preparation
PREG/CONT B/NA

IND & DOSE Tx of iron deficiency anemia in chronic kidney disease. *Adult:* On dialysis, 100 mg IV injection over 2–5 min or 100 mg diluted IV infusion over at least 15 min. Not on dialysis, 200 mg IV injection over 2–5 min. Peritoneal dialysis, 300 mg over 1.5 hr on two occasions 14 days apart, then single infusion of 400 mg over 2.5 hr.

ADV EFF Anaphylaxis, arthralgia, chest pain, dizziness, headache, **hypotension,** injection-site reactions, **iron overload,** muscle cramps, n/v/d

NC/PT Ensure actual iron deficiency. Pt should avoid oral iron or vitamins w/iron added, take safety precautions for CNS effects, report pain at injection site, difficulty breathing.

isavuconazonium (Cresemba)
CLASS Antifungal, azole
PREG/CONT C/NA

IND & DOSE Tx of invasive aspergillosis, invasive mucormycosis. *Adult:* Loading dose, 372 mg PO or IV q 8 hr for six doses; maintenance, 372 mg/day PO or IV starting 12–24 hr after last loading dose.

ADV EFF Back pain, constipation, cough, dyspnea, edema, **hepatotoxicity,** hypokalemia, **infusion reactions, serious hypersensitivity reactions**

INTERACTIONS CYP3A4 inhibitors/ inducers (contraindicated), digoxin, immune suppressants

NC/PT Culture before tx. Review drug regimen; many interactions possible. Loading dose for 48 hours; then maintenance. Monitor LFTs. Administer IV through online filter. Monitor for infusion reactions; stop drug if these occur. Not for use in pregnancy/breast-feeding. Pt should mark calendar for dose changes; report difficulty breathing, rash, urine/ stool color changes.

isocarboxazid (Marplan)
CLASS MAOI
PREG/CONT C/NA

BBW Increased risk of suicidality in children, adolescents, young adults; monitor accordingly.

IND & DOSE Tx of depression (not a first choice). *Adult:* Up to 40 mg/day PO.

ADJUST DOSE Hepatic, severe renal impairment

ADV EFF Constipation, **CV events,** drowsiness, dry mouth

INTERACTIONS Anesthetics, antihypertensives, buspirone, caffeine, CNS depressants, dextromethorphan, meperidine, SSRIs, sympathomimetics, TCAs, tyramine-containing foods
NC/PT Do not use w/known cerebrovascular disorders, pheochromocytoma. Check complete drug list before giving; many interactions. Pt should avoid foods high in tyramine, use sugarless lozenges for dry mouth, report thoughts of suicide.

isoniazid (generic)
CLASS Antituberculotic
PREG/CONT C/NA

BBW Risk of serious to fatal hepatitis; monitor liver enzymes monthly.
IND & DOSE Tx of active TB. *Adult:* 5 mg/kg/day (max, 300 mg) PO or IM in single dose w/other effective drugs. Or, 15 mg/kg (max, 900 mg) PO two or three times/wk. *Child:* 10–15 mg/kg/day (max, 300 mg) PO or IM in single dose w/other effective drugs. Or, 20–40 mg/kg (max, 900 mg/day) two or three times/wk. Px for TB. *Adult:* 300 mg/day PO in single dose. *Child:* 10 mg/kg/day (max, 300 mg) PO in single dose.
ADV EFF Epigastric distress, fever, gynecomastia, hepatitis, injection-site reactions, peripheral neuropathy, thrombocytopenia
INTERACTIONS Acetaminophen, alcohol, carbamazepine, enflurane, phenytoin, rifampin, tyramine-containing foods
NC/PT Concomitant administration of 10–50 mg/day pyridoxine recommended for pts who are malnourished or predisposed to neuropathy (alcoholics, diabetics). Pt should take on empty stomach; avoid alcohol, foods high in tyramine; get regular medical checkups; take safety precautions to avoid injury (loss of sensation possible).

isoproterenol hydrochloride (Isuprel)
CLASS Antiasthmatic, beta agonist, bronchodilator, vasopressor
PREG/CONT C/NA

IND & DOSE Mgt of bronchospasm during anesthesia. *Adult:* 0.01–0.02 mg (0.5–1 mL diluted sol) by IV bolus; repeat when needed. *Child 7–19 yr:* 0.05–0.17 mcg/kg/min by IV bolus. Max, 1.3–2.7 mcg/kg/min. Vasopressor as adjunct tx of shock. *Adult:* 0.5–5 mcg/ min; infuse IV at adjusted rate based on hr, CVP, systemic BP, urine flow. Tx of cardiac standstill, arrhythmias. *Adult:* 0.02–0.06 mg IV injection using diluted sol. Or, 5 mcg/min IV infusion using diluted sol.
ADJUST DOSE Elderly pts
ADV EFF Anxiety, apprehension, bronchospasm, cardiac arrhythmias, cough, dizziness, fear, pallor, palpitations, pulmonary edema, respiratory difficulties, sweating
INTERACTIONS Antiarrhythmics, ergots, halogenated hydrocarbon anesthetics, oxytocics, TCAs
NC/PT Protect from light. Give smallest dose for minimum period. Have beta blocker on hand to reverse effects. Pt should report chest pain, tremor.

isosorbide dinitrate (Dilatrate SR, Isochron, Isordil Titradose) isosorbide mononitrate (Monoket)
CLASS Antianginal, nitrate
PREG/CONT C; B (Monoket)/NA

IND & DOSE Tx of angina (dinitrate). *Adult:* 2.5–5 mg sublingual or 5- to 20-mg oral tablets; maint, 10–40 mg PO q 6 hr (oral tablets/capsules). SR or ER: Initially, 40 mg, then 40–80 mg PO q 8–12 hr. Px of angina (mononitrate). *Adult:* 20 mg PO bid 7 hr apart. ER tablets: 30–60 mg/day PO; may increase to 120 mg/day.

Acute px of angina (dinitrate). *Adult:* 2.5–5 mg sublingual q 2–3 hr. Give 15 min before activity that may cause angina.

ADV EFF Apprehension, collapse, dizziness, headache, hypotension, orthostatic hypotension, rebound hypertension, restlessness, tachycardia, weakness

INTERACTIONS Ergots

NC/PT Reduce dose gradually when stopping. Headache possible. Pt should place sublingual form under tongue or in buccal pouch, try not to swallow; take orally on empty stomach; take safety precautions for CNS effects; orthostatic hypotension; report blurred vision, severe headache, more frequent anginal attacks. Name confusion Isordil (isosorbide) and Plendil (felodipine); use caution.

---

isotretinoin (Amnesteem, Claravis, Sotret)
CLASS Acne product, retinoid
PREG/CONT X/NA

BBW Ensure pt reads, signs consent form; place form in pt's permanent record. Rule out pregnancy before tx; test for pregnancy within 2 wk of starting tx. Advise use of two forms of contraception starting 1 mo before tx until 1 mo after tx ends. Pharmacists must register pts in iPLEDGE program before dispensing drug. Pt may obtain no more than 30-day supply.

IND & DOSE Tx of severe recalcitrant nodular acne unresponsive to conventional tx. *Adult, child 12 yr and older:* 0.5–1 mg/kg/day PO; range, 0.5–2 mg/kg/day divided into two doses for 15–20 wk. Max daily dose, 2 mg/kg. If second course needed, allow rest period of at least 8 wk between courses.

ADV EFF Abd pain, bronchospasm, cheilitis, conjunctivitis, dizziness, dry nose/skin, epistaxis, eye irritation, fatigue, headache, hematuria, insomnia, lethargy, lipid changes, n/v, papilledema, skin irritation, suicidality, visual changes

INTERACTIONS Corticosteroids, phenytoin, tetracycline, vitamin A

NC/PT Ensure pt has read, signed consent form. Rule out pregnancy; ensure pt using contraception. Allow 8 wk between tx cycles. Only 1 mo prescription can be given. Pt may be unable to wear contact lenses. Give w/food to improve absorption. Pt should swallow capsules whole and not cut, crush, or chew them; avoid donating blood; avoid vitamin supplements; take safety precautions for CNS effects; report visual changes, thoughts of suicide.

---

isradipine (generic)
CLASS Antihypertensive, calcium channel blocker
PREG/CONT C/NA

IND & DOSE Mgt of hypertension. *Adult:* 2.5 mg PO bid; max, 20 mg/day. CR, 5–10 mg/day PO.

ADJUST DOSE Elderly pts; hepatic, renal impairment

ADV EFF Dizziness, edema, headache, hypotension, nausea

INTERACTIONS Antifungals, atracurium, beta blockers, calcium, carbamazepine, digoxin, fentanyl, H_2 antagonists, pancuronium, prazosin, quinidine, rifampin, tubocurarine, vecuronium

NC/PT Monitor BP; other antihypertensives may be added as needed. Monitor BP, cardiac rhythm closely when determining dose. Pt should swallow CR tablet whole and not cut, crush, or chew it; take safety precautions for CNS effects; treat for headache; report swelling, palpitations.

itraconazole (Sporanox)

CLASS Antifungal
PREG/CONT C/NA

BBW Risk of severe HF; do not give if evidence of cardiac dysfunction, HF. Potential for serious CV events (including ventricular tachycardia, death) w/lovastatin, simvastatin, triazolam, midazolam, pimozide, dofetilide, quinidine due to significant CYP450 inhibition; avoid these combinations.
IND & DOSE Tx of empiric febrile neutropenia. *Adult:* 200 mg PO bid until clinically significant neutropenia resolves. **Tx of candidiasis.** *Adult:* 200 mg/day PO (oral sol only) for 1–2 wk (oropharyngeal); 100 mg/day PO for at least 3 wk (esophageal); 200 mg/day PO in AIDS/neutropenic pts. **Tx of blastomycosis, chronic histoplasmosis.** *Adult:* 200 mg/day PO or at least 3 mo; max, 400 mg/day. **Tx of systemic mycoses.** *Adult:* 100–200 mg/day PO for 3–6 mo. **Tx of dermatophytoses.** *Adult:* 100–200 mg/day PO to bid for 7–28 days. **Tx of fingernail onychomycosis.** *Adult:* 200 mg bid PO for 1 wk, then 3-wk rest period; repeat. **Tx of toenail onychomycosis.** *Adult:* 200 mg/day PO for 12 wk. **Tx of aspergillosis.** *Adult:* 200–400 mg/day PO.
ADJUST DOSE Renal impairment
ADV EFF Abd pain, edema, headache, **HF, hepatotoxicity,** n/v/d, rash
INTERACTIONS Antacids, benzodiazepines, buspirone, carbamazepine, colas, cyclosporine, digoxin, grapefruit juice, histamine₂ antagonists, isoniazid, lovastatin, macrolide antibiotics, nevirapine, oral hypoglycemics, phenobarbital, phenytoin, protease inhibitors, proton pump inhibitors, rifampin, warfarin anticoagulants
NC/PT Culture before tx. Monitor LFTs; stop if s&sx of active liver disease. Check all drugs being used; many interactions possible. Not for use in pregnancy (contraceptives advised). Give capsules w/food. For oral sol, give 100–200 mg (10–20 mL), have pt rinse and hold, then swallow sol daily for 1–3 wk. Pt should avoid grapefruit juice, colas; report difficulty breathing, urine/stool color changes.

ivabradine (Corlanor)

CLASS Cyclic nucleotide-gated channel blocker, HF drug
PREG/CONT High risk/NA

IND & DOSE Reduction of hospitalization for worsening HF. *Adult:* 5 mg PO bid. Adjust based on HR; max, 7.5 mg PO bid.
ADJUST DOSE Conduction defects
ADV EFF Atrial fibrillation, **bradycardia,** dizziness, hypertension, luminous phenomena, syncope
INTERACTIONS CYP3A4 inducers/inhibitors, grapefruit juice, negative chronotropes, St. John's wort
NC/PT Do not use w/pacemaker set at 60 or higher, second-degree AV block, hypotension, severe hepatic impairment. Monitor HR, BP regularly. Not for use in pregnancy (contraceptives advised)/breast-feeding. Pt should take bid with meals; learn to take P; use caution in situations where light-intensity changes may occur; avoid grapefruit juice, St. John's wort; report rapid P, chest pain, difficulty breathing, dizziness.

ivacaftor (Kalydeco)

CLASS Cystic fibrosis transmembrane conductance regulator potentiator
PREG/CONT B/NA

IND & DOSE Tx of cystic fibrosis in pts 6 yr and older w/any of 9 mutations in CFTR gene. *Adult, child 6 yr and older:* 150 mg PO q 12 hr w/fat-containing food.
ADJUST DOSE Moderate to severe hepatic impairment

ADV EFF Abd pain, congestion, dizziness, headache, **hepatic impairment**, nasopharyngitis, n/v, rash, URI **INTERACTIONS** Grapefruit juice, moderate to strong CYP3A inhibitors, St. John's wort
NC/PT Monitor LFTs before and q 3 mo during first yr, then yearly. Give w/fat-containing food; use safety precautions if dizziness occurs. Give w/fat-containing food; use safety precautions if dizziness occurs. Pt should take q 12 hr w/fat-containing food; use caution w/dizziness; avoid grapefruit juice, St. John's wort; report yellowing of eyes or skin, urine/stool color changes.

ivermectin (Stromectol)
CLASS Anthelmintic
PREG/CONT C/NA

IND & DOSE Tx of intestinal strongyloidiasis. *Adult:* 200 mcg/kg PO as single dose. **Tx of onchocerciasis.** *Adult:* 150 mcg/kg PO as single dose; may repeat in 3–12 mo.
ADV EFF Abd pain, dizziness, nausea, rash
NC/PT Culture before tx. Not for use in breast-feeding. Pt should take on empty stomach w/water; will need repeat stool cultures; may need repeat tx.

ixabepilone (Ixempra)
CLASS Antineoplastic, microtubule inhibitor
PREG/CONT D/NA

BBW Risk of severe liver failure, severe bone marrow suppression, neurotoxicities, cardiotoxicities; select pt carefully, monitor closely.
IND & DOSE Tx of metastatic or locally advanced breast cancer in pts who have failed on anthra cycline, taxane. *Adult:* 40 mg/m² IV over 3 hr q 3 wk; may combine w/ capecitabine.
ADV EFF Alopecia, anorexia, asthenia, **bone marrow suppression**, fatigue, n/v/d, **peripheral neuropathy,**

severe hypersensitivity reactions, stomatitis
INTERACTIONS CYP3A4 inducers/ inhibitors
NC/PT Follow CBC, LFTs closely. Premedicate w/corticosteroids. Not for use in pregnancy (barrier contraceptives advised). Pt should mark calendar for tx days; cover head at temp extremes (hair loss possible); avoid exposure to infections; perform mouth care (for stomatitis); take safety precautions (for neuropathies); report chest pain, palpitations, difficulty breathing, numbness/ tingling.

ixazomib (Ninlaro)
CLASS Antineoplastic, proteasome inhibitor
PREG/CONT High risk/NA

IND & DOSE Tx of multiple myeloma in pts who have received at least one prior therapy. *Adult:* 4 mg/day PO on days 1, 8, 15 of a 28-day cycle given w/lenalidomide, dexamethasone.
ADJUST DOSE Hepatic, renal impairment
ADV EFF Back pain, constipation, diarrhea, edema, **hepatotoxicity**, n/v/d, peripheral neuropathy, rash, **thrombocytopenia**
INTERACTIONS Strong CYP3A inducers; do not combine.
NC/PT Ensure dx. Give w/lenalidomide, dexamethasone. Monitor liver function, platelets at least monthly. Assess for severe GI effects, peripheral neuropathy, dose adjustment may be needed. Pt should avoid pregnancy (contraceptives advised)/ breast-feeding. Pt should report easy bruising, numbness/tingling/burning, severe GI effects, urine/stool color changes.

DANGEROUS DRUG

ketamine (Ketalar)

CLASS Nonbarbiturate anesthetic
PREG/CONT B/C-III

BBW Emergence reaction (confusion, hallucinations, delirium) possible; lessened w/smallest effective dose and use of tactile, verbal, or visual stimuli. Severe cases require small dose of short-acting barbiturate.

IND & DOSE Induction of anesthesia. *Adult:* 1–4.5 mg/kg IV slowly or 1–2 mg/kg IV at 0.5 mg/kg/min, or 6.5–13 mg/kg IM (10 mg/kg IM produces 12–25 min anesthesia). **Induction of anesthesia in cardiac surgery.** *Adult:* 0.5–1.5 mg/kg IV at 20 mg q 10 sec. **Maintenance of general anesthesia.** *Adult:* Repeat dose in increments of ½ to full induction dose.

ADV EFF Anorexia, confusion, diplopia, dreamlike state, emergence reaction, hallucinations, hypertension, nausea, pain at injection site, vomiting

INTERACTIONS Halothane, NMJ blockers, other sedative/hypnotics, thyroid hormones

NC/PT Administered by anesthesia specialist. Ensure oxygen, oximetry, cardiac monitoring; have emergency equipment nearby. Warn pt about sedative effect: Pt should avoid driving after receiving drug, tasks requiring mental alertness/coordination, making important decisions. Pt should report difficulty breathing, pain at injection site, changes in thinking.

---

ketoconazole (Extina, Nizoral A-D, Xolegel)

CLASS Antifungal
PREG/CONT C/NA

BBW Risk of serious to fatal hepatotoxicity; monitor closely.

IND & DOSE Tx of susceptible, systemic fungal infections; recalcitrant dermatophytosis. *Adult:* 200 mg PO daily; for severe infections, 400 mg/day PO for 1 wk–6 mo. *Child over 2 yr:* 3.3–6.6 mg/kg/day PO as single dose. **To reduce scaling due to dandruff.** *Adult, child:* Moisten hair, scalp thoroughly w/water; apply sufficient shampoo to produce lather; leave on for 5 min. Shampoo twice/wk for 4 wk with at least 3 days between shampooing. **Topical tx of tinea pedis, corporis, cruris; cutaneous candidiasis.** *Adult, child over 12 yr:* Apply thin film of gel, foam, cream once daily to affected area for 2 wk; do not wash area for 3 hr after applying. Wait 20 min before applying makeup, sunscreen. May need 6 wk of tx. **Tx of seborrheic dermatitis.** *Adult, child over 12 yr:* Apply foam bid for 4 wk.

ADV EFF Anaphylaxis, dizziness, **hepatotoxicity,** local stinging on application, n/v, pruritus

INTERACTIONS Antacids, corticosteroids, cyclosporine, histamine₂ blockers, proton pump inhibitors, rifampin, tacrolimus, warfarin

NC/PT Culture before tx. Have epinephrine on hand for anaphylaxis. Monitor LFTs closely. Review proper administration. Pt may need long-term tx. Pt should use proper hygiene to prevent infection spread, avoid drugs that alter stomach acid level (if needed, pt should take ketoconazole at least 2 hr after these drugs), take safety precautions for CNS effects, report urine/stool changes, unusual bleeding.

---

ketoprofen (generic)

CLASS NSAID
PREG/CONT C (1st, 2nd trimesters); D (3rd trimester)/NA

BBW Increased risk of CV events, GI bleeding; monitor accordingly. Contraindicated for tx of perioperative pain after CABG surgery; serious adverse effects have occurred.

IND & DOSE Relief of pain from rheumatoid arthritis, osteoarthritis. *Adult:* 75 mg PO tid or 50 mg PO qid.

Maint, 150–300 mg PO in three or four divided doses; max, 300 mg/day. ER form, 200 mg/day PO; or max, 200 mg/day ER. **Tx of mild to moderate pain, primary dysmenorrhea:** *Adult:* 25–50 mg PO q 6–8 hr as needed.

ADJUST DOSE Elderly pts; hepatic, renal impairment

ADV EFF Anaphylaxis, dizziness, dyspepsia, edema, gastric/duodenal ulcer, GI pain, headache, insomnia, nausea, renal impairment

INTERACTIONS Aminoglycosides, aspirin, cyclosporine, diuretics, warfarin

NC/PT Monitor renal function. Give w/food. Not for use in pregnancy. Pt should avoid OTC products that might contain NSAIDs, report swelling, difficulty breathing, black tarry stools.

---

ketorolac tromethamine
(Acular LS, Acuvail, Sprix)
CLASS Antipyretic, NSAID
PREG/CONT C (1st, 2nd trimesters); D (3rd trimester)/NA

BBW Increased risk of CV events, GI bleeding, renal failure; monitor accordingly. Do not use during labor/delivery or in breast-feeding; serious adverse effects in fetus/baby possible. May increase risk of bleeding; do not use w/high risk of bleeding or as px before surgery. Increased risk of severe hypersensitivity with known hypersensitivity to aspirin, NSAIDs.
IND & DOSE Short-term pain mgt (up to 5 days). *Adult:* 60 mg IM or 30 mg IV as single dose, or 30 mg IM or IV q 6 hr to max 120 mg/day. Or, 1 spray in one nostril q 6–8 hr; max, 63 mg/day (over 65 yr); 1 spray (15.75 mg) in each nostril q 6–8 hr; max, 126 mg/day (under 65 yr). *Transfer to oral:* 20 mg PO as first dose for pts who received 60 mg IM or 30 mg IV as single dose or 30-mg multiple dose, then 10 mg PO q 4–6 hr; max, 40 mg/24 hr. *Child 2–16 yr:*

1 mg/kg IM to max 30 mg, or 0.5 mg/kg IV to max 15 mg as single dose. **Relief of itching of allergic conjunctivitis.** *Adult:* 1 drop in affected eye(s) qid. **Relief of cataract postop pain, inflammation.** *Adult:* Dose varies by product; check manufacturer info.

ADJUST DOSE Elderly pts, renal impairment, weight under 50 kg

ADV EFF Anaphylaxis, dizziness, dyspepsia, edema, fluid retention, gastric/duodenal ulcer, GI pain, headache, insomnia, nausea, renal impairment, Stevens-Johnson syndrome

INTERACTIONS Aminoglycosides, aspirin, cyclosporine, diuretics, NSAIDs, warfarin

NC/PT Protect vials from light. Monitor renal function. Give to maintain serum levels, control pain. Not for use in pregnancy. Do not use ophthalmic drops w/contact lenses. Pt should take w/food, use safety precautions for CNS effects, avoid OTC products that might contain NSAIDs, report swelling, difficulty breathing, black tarry stools.

DANGEROUS DRUG

labetalol hydrochloride
(Trandate)
CLASS Antihypertensive, sympathetic blocker
PREG/CONT C/NA

IND & DOSE Tx of hypertension. *Adult:* 100 mg PO bid; maint, 200–400 mg bid PO; up to 2,400 mg/day has been used. **Tx of severe hypertension.** *Adult:* 20 mg (0.25 mg/kg) IV injection slowly over 2 min; can give additional doses of 40 or 80 mg at 10-min intervals until desired BP achieved or 300-mg dose has been injected. Transfer to oral therapy as soon as possible.
ADJUST DOSE Elderly pts
ADV EFF Bronchospasm, constipation, cough, dizziness, dyspnea, ED, flatulence, gastric pain, HF, n/v/d, stroke, vertigo

INTERACTIONS Calcium channel blockers, enflurane, isoflurane, nitroglycerin
NC/PT Taper after long-term tx. Keep pt supine during infusion. Pt should not stop taking suddenly, take w/meals, use safety precautions for CNS effects, report difficulty breathing, swelling, chest pain.

lacosamide (Vimpat)
CLASS Antiepileptic
PREG/CONT C/NA

BBW Increased risk of suicidal ideation in children, adolescents, young adults; monitor accordingly.
IND & DOSE Monotherapy or adjunct tx for partial-onset seizures. *Adult, child 17 yr and older:* 50 mg PO bid; range, 200–400 mg/day PO. IV dosing is same as oral, injected over 15–60 min; for short-term use if oral not possible.
ADJUST DOSE Hepatic, renal impairment
ADV EFF Ataxia, prolonged PR interval, diplopia, dizziness, headache, hypersensitivity, n/v, seizure, syncope
INTERACTIONS Other PR-prolonging drugs
NC/PT Taper after long-term tx. Not for use in pregnancy (barrier contraceptives advised)/breast-feeding. Pt should not stop taking suddenly, taper to minimize seizures, take safety precautions for CNS effects, report thoughts of suicide, personality changes.

lactulose (Constilac, Constulose, Enulose)
CLASS Ammonia-reducing drug, laxative
PREG/CONT B/NA

IND & DOSE Tx of portal-systemic encephalopathy. 30–45 mL (20–30 g) PO tid or qid. Adjust q 1–2 days to produce two or three soft stools/day.

May use 30–45 mL/hr PO if needed. Or, 300 mL (20 g) lactulose mixed w/700 mL water or physiologic saline as retention enema retained for 30–60 min; may repeat q 4–6 hr. *Child:* 2.5–10 mL/day PO in divided dose for small child or 40–90 mL/day for older child suggested. Goal: Two or three soft stools daily. Laxative. *Adult:* 15–30 mL/day (10–20 g) PO; up to 60 mL/day has been used.
ADV EFF Belching, distention, intestinal cramping, transient flatulence
NC/PT Give laxative syrup orally w/ fruit juice, water, milk to increase palatability. Monitor serum ammonia levels. Monitor for electrolyte imbalance w/long-term tx. Pt should not use other laxatives, not use as laxative for longer than 1 wk unless prescribed, have ready access to bathroom facilities, report diarrhea.

lamivudine (Epivir, Epivir-HBV)
CLASS Antiviral, reverse transcriptase inhibitor
PREG/CONT C/NA

BBW Monitor hematologic indices, LFTs q 2 wk during tx; severe hepatomegaly w/steatosis, lactic acidosis possible. Counsel, periodically test pts receiving *Epivir-HBV*; severe, acute hepatitis B virus (HBV) exacerbations have occurred in pts w/both HIV and HBV infection who stop taking lamivudine.
IND & DOSE Tx of chronic hepatitis B. *Adult:* 100 mg PO daily. *Child 2–17 yr:* 3 mg/kg PO daily; max, 100 mg daily. Tx of HIV, w/other drugs. *Adult, child 16 yr and older:* 150 mg PO bid or 300 mg/day PO as single dose, or 150 mg PO bid. *Child 3 mo–16 yr:* 4 mg/kg PO bid; max, 300 mg/day. *Over 30 kg:* 150 mg PO bid. *Over 21 kg but under 30 kg:* 75 mg PO in a.m. and 150 mg PO in p.m. *14–21 kg:* 75 mg PO bid.
ADJUST DOSE Renal impairment

ADV EFF Agranulocytosis, asthenia, diarrhea, GI pain, headache, **hepatomegaly w/lactic acidosis,** nasal s&sx, nausea, **pancreatitis, steatosis**
INTERACTIONS Trimethoprim-sulfamethoxazole, zalcitabine
NC/PT Give w/other antiretrovirals for HIV. Risk of emergence of lamivudine-resistant hepatitis B; monitor. Monitor for s&sx of pancreatitis; stop immediately if evident. Monitor for opportunistic infections. Not for use in pregnancy. Pt should use protection to prevent transmission (drug not a cure), get frequent blood tests, report severe headache, severe n/v.

lamotrigine (Lamictal)
CLASS Antiepileptic
PREG/CONT C/NA

BBW Risk of serious, life-threatening rash, including Stevens-Johnson syndrome; monitor accordingly. Stop immediately if rash appears; have appropriate life support on hand.
IND & DOSE Tx of partial-onset seizures, primary generalized tonic-clonic seizures, Lennox-Gastaut syndrome. *Adult taking enzyme-inducing antiepileptics (ie, carbamazepine, phenobarbital, phenytoin) but not valproic acid:* 50 mg PO daily for 2 wk, then 100 mg PO daily in two divided doses for 2 wk. May then increase by 100 mg/day q wk to maint of 300–500 mg/day PO in two divided doses. ER form: wk 1–2, 50 mg/day PO; wk 3–4, 100 mg/day PO; wk 5, 200 mg/day PO; wk 6, 300 mg/day PO; wk 7, 400 mg/day PO. Range, 400–600 mg/day. *Adult, child over 12 yr taking enzyme-inducing antiepileptics and valproic acid:* 25 mg PO q other day for 2 wk, then 25 mg PO daily for 2 wk. Then may increase by 25–50 mg q 1–2 wk to maint 100–400 mg/day PO in two divided doses. *Child 2–12 yr taking non-enzyme-inducing antiepileptics and valproic acid:* 0.15 mg/kg/day PO in one to two divided doses for 2 wk. Then

0.3 mg/kg/day PO in one to two divided doses, rounded down to nearest 5 mg for 2 wk. Maint, 1–5 mg/kg/day in one to two divided doses to max of 200 mg/day. *Child 2–12 yr taking single enzyme-inducing antiepileptic without valproic acid:* 0.6 mg/kg/day PO in two divided doses for 2 wk, then 1.2 mg/kg/day PO in two divided doses for 2 wk. Maint, 5–15 mg/kg/day in two divided doses to max 400 mg/day. **Tx of bipolar I disorder.** *Adult taking valproic acid:* 25 mg PO q other day for 2 wk, then 25 mg PO once daily for 2 wk. After 4 wk, may double dose at wkly intervals to target 100 mg/day. *Adult taking enzyme-inducing antiepileptics but not valproic acid:* 50 mg/day PO for 2 wk; then 100 mg PO daily in two divided doses for 2 wk. After 4 wk, may increase dose in 100-mg increments at wkly intervals to target maint of 400 mg/day PO in two divided doses. *Adult taking neither enzyme-inducing antiepileptics nor valproic acid:* 25 mg/day PO for 2 wk, then 50 mg PO daily for 2 wk. After 4 wk, may double dose at wkly intervals to maint of 200 mg/day.
ADV EFF Aseptic meningitis, ataxia, **blood dyscrasias,** dizziness, **hepatotoxicity, multiorgan hypersensitivity reactions,** nausea, **rash, Stevens-Johnson syndrome, toxic epidermal necrosis w/multiorgan failure, suicidality**
INTERACTIONS Carbamazepine, phenobarbital, phenytoin, primidone, valproic acid
NC/PT Monitor LFTs, renal function closely. Monitor for aseptic meningitis. Monitor for rash; stop if rash evident. Taper slowly over 2 wk when stopping. Ensure pt swallows ER tablets whole and does not cut, crush, or chew them. Pt should wear medical ID, take safety precautions for CNS effects, report rash, urine/stool changes. Name confusion between Lamictal (lamotrigine) and Lamisil (terbinafine); use caution.

lanreotide acetate
(Somatuline Depot)
CLASS Growth hormone (GH) inhibitor
PREG/CONT C/NA

IND & DOSE Long-term tx of acromegaly in pts unresponsive to other tx. *Adult:* 60–120 mg subcut q 4 wk for 3 mo. **Tx of unresectable, differentiated, advanced gastroenteropancreatic neuroendocrine tumors.** *Adult:* 120 mg IM q4 wk.
ADJUST DOSE Hepatic, renal impairment
ADV EFF Abd pain, cholelithiasis, diarrhea, flatulence, hyperglycemia, hypoglycemia, injection-site reactions, sinus bradycardia, thyroid dysfx
INTERACTIONS Antidiabetics, beta blockers, cyclosporine, insulin
NC/PT Drug injected into buttocks, alternating left and right; monitor for injection-site reactions. Monitor GH, insulin growth factor-1. Monitor serum glucose, thyroid function; intervene as indicated. Monitor for bradycardia. Not for use in breastfeeding. Pt should mark calendar of tx days; keep frequent follow-up appointments; report upper gastric pain, injection-site reactions.

lansoprazole (Prevacid, Prevacid 24 hr)
CLASS Proton pump inhibitor
PREG/CONT B/NA

IND & DOSE Tx of active duodenal ulcer. *Adult:* 15 mg PO daily for 4 wk; maint, 15 mg/day PO. **Tx of gastric ulcer.** *Adult:* 30 mg/day PO for up to 8 wk. **To reduce risk of gastric ulcer w/NSAIDs.** *Adult:* 15 mg/day PO for up to 12 wk. **Tx of duodenal ulcers associated w/Helicobacter pylori.** *Adult:* 30 mg lansoprazole, 500 mg clarithromycin, 1 g amoxicillin, all PO bid for 10–14 days; or 30 mg lansoprazole, 1 g amoxicillin PO tid for 14 days. **GERD.** *Adult, child 12–17 yr:* 15 mg/day PO for up to 8 wk. *Child 1–11 yr:* Over 30 kg, 30 mg/day PO for up to 12 wk. 30 kg or less, 15 mg/day PO for up to 12 wk. **Tx of erosive esophagitis, poorly responsive GERD.** *Adult, child 12–17 yr:* 30 mg/day PO daily for up to 8 wk. Additional 8-wk course may be helpful for pts not healed after 8-wk tx. Maint, 15 mg/day PO. **Tx of pathological hypersecretory conditions.** *Adult:* 60 mg/day PO; up to 90 mg bid have been used. **Short-term tx of erosive esophagitis (all grades).** *Adult:* 30 mg/day IV over 30 min for up to 7 days; switch to oral form as soon as possible for total of 8 wk. **Tx of heartburn.** *Adult:* 1 capsule *Prevacid 24 hr* PO w/full glass of water in a.m. before eating for 14 days; may repeat 14-day course q 4 mo.
ADJUST DOSE Hepatic impairment
ADV EFF Abd pain, bone loss, CDAD, dizziness, headache, hypomagnesemia, n/v/d, pneumonia, rash, URI
INTERACTIONS Ketoconazole, sucralfate, theophylline
NC/PT Give w/meals. May open capsule, sprinkle on applesauce, *Ensure,* yogurt, cottage cheese, strained pears. For NG tube, place 15- or 30-mg tablet in syringe, draw up 4 or 10 mL water; shake gently for quick dispersal. After dispersal, inject through NG tube to stomach within 15 min. If using capsules w/NG tube, mix granules from capsule w/40 mL apple juice, inject through tube, then flush tube w/more apple juice. For orally disintegrating tablet, place on tongue, follow w/water after it dissolves. For IV, switch to oral form as soon as feasible. Arrange for further evaluation if no symptom improvement. Pt should swallow capsule whole and not cut, crush, or chew it; take safety precautions for CNS effects; report severe diarrhea.

lanthanum carbonate (Fosrenol)

CLASS Phosphate binder
PREG/CONT C/NA

IND & DOSE To reduce serum phosphate level in pts w/end-stage renal disease. *Adult:* 1,500–3,000 mg/day PO w/meals; base dose on serum phosphate level.
ADJUST DOSE Hepatic impairment
ADV EFF Abd pain, allergic skin reactions, dyspepsia, **GI obstruction,** n/v/d, tooth injury
INTERACTIONS Antacids, levothyroxine, quinolone antibiotics
NC/PT Monitor serum phosphate level (target, 6 mg/dL or lower). Pt should chew or crush tablets, not swallow whole; take w/meals; separate from other oral drugs by 2 hr; report severe abd pain, constipation.

lapatinib (Tykerb)

CLASS Antineoplastic, kinase inhibitor
PREG/CONT D/NA

BBW Severe to fatal hepatotoxicity has occurred; monitor LFTs closely.
IND & DOSE Tx of advanced/ metastatic breast cancer w/tumors that overexpress HER2 in women who have received other tx. *Adult:* 1,250 mg/day PO on days 1–21 w/ capecitabine 2,000 mg/m²/day PO on days 1–14, given 12 hr apart. Repeat 21-day cycle. Tx of HER2-positive metastatic breast cancer. *Adult:* 1,500 mg/day PO w/letrozole 2.5 mg/day PO.
ADJUST DOSE Cardiotoxicities, concomitant CYP3A4 inducers/ inhibitors, hepatic impairment
ADV EFF Anaphylaxis, decreased left ventricular function, diarrhea, fatigue, **hepatotoxicity,** interstitial pneumonitis, n/v, prolonged QT, serious to fatal cutaneous reactions

INTERACTIONS Antacids, carbamazepine, digoxin, grapefruit juice, ketoconazole, midazolam, paclitaxel, QT-prolonging drugs, St. John's wort
NC/PT Monitor LFTs before and regularly during tx. Monitor cardiac/ respiratory function; evaluate lungs for pneumonia. Not for use in pregnancy (contraceptives advised). Pt should take 1 hr before or after meals; avoid grapefruit juice, St. John's wort, antacids; report difficulty breathing, swelling, dizziness, rash, urine/stool color changes.

laronidase (Aldurazyme)

CLASS Enzyme
PREG/CONT C/NA

BBW Life-threatening anaphylaxis has occurred; have medical support on hand.
IND & DOSE Tx of pts w/Hurler, Hurler-Scheie forms of mucopolysaccharidosis 1; Scheie forms w/ moderate to severe sx. *Adult, child 6 yr and older:* 0.58 mg/kg IV infused over 3–4 hr once/wk.
ADV EFF Anaphylaxis, fever, hyperreflexia, hypertension, injection-site reactions, paresthesia, tachycardia, UTI
NC/PT Pretreat w/antipyretics, antihistamines; monitor continually during infusion. Have emergency equipment on hand. Should mark calendar of tx days; report injection-site pain/ swelling, difficulty breathing.

leflunomide (Arava)

CLASS Antiarthritic, pyrimidine synthesis inhibitor
PREG/CONT X/NA

BBW Advise women of childbearing age of risks of pregnancy; provide counseling for appropriate contraceptive use during tx. If pt decides to become pregnant, withdrawal program to rid body of leflunomide recommended. May use cholestyramine to

rapidly decrease serum level if unplanned pregnancy occurs. Risk of severe liver injury; monitor LFTs before, periodically during tx. Not recommended w/preexisting liver disease or liver enzymes over 2 × ULN. Use caution w/other drugs that cause liver injury; start cholestyramine washout if ALT increases to 3 × ULN.
IND & DOSE Tx of active rheumatoid arthritis (RA); to relieve s&sx, improve functioning. *Adult:* Loading dose, 100 mg/day PO for 3 days; maint, 20 mg/day PO. May reduce to 10 mg/day PO.
ADJUST DOSE Hepatic impairment
ADV EFF Alopecia, drowsiness, diarrhea, erythematous rashes, headache, **hepatotoxicity**
INTERACTIONS Charcoal, cholestyramine, hepatotoxic drugs, rifampin
NC/PT Monitor LFTs. If ALT rise between two and three times ULN, monitor closely if continued tx desired. If ALT three times or more ULN, cholestyramine may decrease absorption; consider stopping. Not for use in pregnancy (barrier contraceptives advised). Pt should continue other RA tx, get regular medical follow-up, cover head at temp extremes (hair loss possible), take safety precautions for CNS effects.

lenalidomide (Revlimid)
CLASS Antianemic, immunomodulator
PREG/CONT X/NA

BBW Thalidomide derivative associated w/birth defects; rule out pregnancy before tx. Available under limited access program. Can cause significant bone marrow suppression. Increased risk of DVT, PE.
IND & DOSE Tx of multiple myeloma, w/dexamethasone. *Adult:* 25 mg/day PO days 1–21 of repeated 28-day cycle. Tx of transfusion-dependent anemia due to low- or intermediate-risk myelodysplastic syndromes.

Adult: 10 mg/day PO. Tx of mantle cell lymphoma in pts who progress after two prior therapies. *Adult:* 25 mg/day PO on days 1–21 of repeated 28-day cycle.
ADJUST DOSE Renal impairment
ADV EFF Anemia, back pain, **bone marrow suppression, cancer**, constipation, diarrhea, dizziness, dyspnea, edema, fatigue, fever, **hepatotoxicity**, nausea, rash, **serious to fatal cardiac events, serious to fatal skin reactions**, thrombocytopenia, tumor lysis syndrome, URI
INTERACTIONS Digoxin, erythropoietin-stimulating tx, estrogens
NC/PT Monitor CBC; adjust dose as needed. Rule out pregnancy; ensure contraceptive use. Not for use in breast-feeding. Pt should take safety precautions for CNS effects; avoid exposure to infection; get cancer screening; report s&sx of infection, unusual bleeding, muscle pain, difficulty breathing, chest pain, rash.

lenvatinib (Lenvima)
CLASS Antineoplastic, kinase inhibitor
PREG/CONT May cause fetal harm/NA

IND & DOSE Tx of locally recurrent or metastatic, progressive, radioactive iodine-refractory differentiated thyroid cancer. *Adult:* 24 mg/day PO.
ADJUST DOSE Hepatic/renal impairment
ADV EFF GI perforation, HF, hemorrhage, **hepatotoxicity**, hypertension, hypocalcemia, n/v/d, proteinuria, prolonged QT, **renal impairment, reversible posterior leukoencephalopathy**, stomatitis, thrombotic events
NC/PT Control BP before start of tx. Monitor hepatic/renal function. Watch for s&sx of intestinal perforation. Not for use in pregnancy (contraceptives advised)/breast-feeding. Pt should take once a day; report severe abd

pain, unusual bleeding, chest pain, calf pain, urine/stool color changes.

lesinurad (Zurampic)
CLASS URAT1 (uric acid transporter 1) inhibitor
PREG/CONT Unkn/NA

BBW Risk of acute renal failure, more common when used without a xanthine oxidase inhibitor.
IND & DOSE In combination w/a xanthine oxidase inhibitor for tx of hyperuricemia associated w/gout in pts who have not reached target serum uric acid level w/xanthine oxidase inhibitor alone. *Adult:* 200 mg/day PO in a.m. w/food and water; must be taken with a xanthine oxidase inhibitor.
ADJUST DOSE Hepatic, renal impairment
ADV EFF CV events, flulike sx, GERD, headache, **renal impairment**
INTERACTIONS Moderate CP4502C9 inhibitors, CYP3A substrates
NC/PT Monitor renal function before and during tx. Ensure concurrent use of xanthine oxidase inhibitor. Use caution in breast-feeding. Pt should maintain good hydration (at least 2 L/day); take once a day in a.m. w/food; report chest pain, difficulty breathing, severe headache.

letrozole (Femara)
CLASS Antiestrogen, antineoplastic, aromatase inhibitor
PREG/CONT D/NA

IND & DOSE Tx of advanced breast cancer in postmenopausal women progressing after antiestrogen tx; adjuvant tx of early receptor-positive breast cancer; extended adjuvant tx of breast cancer in postmenopausal women who have had 5 yr of tamoxifen; tx of postmenopausal women w/hormone receptor–positive or unkn advanced breast cancer. *Adult:* 2.5 mg/day PO; continue until tumor progression evident.
ADJUST DOSE Hepatic impairment
ADV EFF Decreased bone density, dizziness, fatigue, GI upset, headache, hot flashes, nausea, somnolence, **thromboembolic events**
NC/PT Not for use in pregnancy (contraceptives advised). Give comfort measures for adverse effects. Pt should take safety precautions for CNS effects; report, chest pain, leg pain, urine/stool color changes.

leucovorin calcium (generic)
CLASS Folic acid derivative
PREG/CONT C/NA

IND & DOSE Leucovorin rescue, after high-dose methotrexate. *Adult:* Start within 24 hr of methotrexate dose; 10 mg/m² PO q 6 hr for 10 doses or until methotrexate level less than 0.05 micromolar. If serum creatinine is 100% greater than pretreatment level 24 hr after methotrexate dose, or based on methotrexate levels, increase leucovorin to 150 mg IV q 3 hr until serum methotrexate less than 1.0 micromolar; then 15 mg IV q 3 hr until methotrexate is under 0.05 micromolar. **Tx of megaloblastic anemia.** *Adult:* 1 mg/day IM; max, 1 mg/day. **Palliative tx of metastatic colon cancer.** *Adult:* 200 mg/m² by slow IV injection over 3 min, then 5-FU 370 mg/m² IV. Or, 20 mg/m² IV, then 5-FU 425 mg/m² IV. Repeat daily for 5 days; may repeat at 4-wk intervals.
ADV EFF Hypersensitivity reactions, pain/discomfort at injection site
INTERACTIONS 5-FU
NC/PT Give orally if possible. Monitor for hypersensitivity reactions; have emergency support on hand. Do not use intrathecally. Pt should report rash, difficulty breathing. Name confusion between *Leukeran* (chlorambucil) and leucovorin; use care.

leuprolide acetate
(Eligard, Lupron)
CLASS GnRH analogue
PREG/CONT X/NA

IND & DOSE Palliative tx of advanced prostate cancer. *Adult:* 1 mg/day subcut, or depot 7.5 mg IM monthly (q 28–33 days), or 22.5 mg depot IM or subcut q 3 mo (84 days), or 30 mg depot IM or subcut q 4 mo, or 45 mg depot subcut q 6 mo (*Eligard*). **Tx of endometriosis.** *Adult:* 3.75 mg as single monthly IM injection, or 11.25 mg IM q 3 mo. Continue for 6 mo (*Lupron*). **Tx of uterine leiomyomata.** *Adult:* 3.75 mg as single monthly injection for 3 mo, or 11.25 mg IM once; give w/concomitant iron tx (*Lupron*). **Tx of central precocious puberty.** *Child:* 50 mcg/kg/day subcut; may increase by 10-mcg/kg/day increments. Or, 0.3 mg/kg IM depot q 4 wk. Round to nearest depot size; minimum, 7.5 mg (*Lupron*).
ADV EFF Anorexia, constipation, dizziness, headache, hematuria, hot flashes, hyperglycemia, injection-site reactions, **MI**, n/v, peripheral edema, prolonged QT, sweating, tumor flare
NC/PT Give only w/syringe provided. Give depot injections deep into muscle. Obtain periodic tests of testosterone, PSA. Not for use in pregnancy (contraceptives advised). Stop if precocious puberty before 11 yr (girls), 12 yr (boys). Teach proper administration/disposal of needles/syringes. Pt should take safety precautions for CNS effects; report injection-site reaction, chest pain, hyperglycemia.

levalbuterol hydrochloride (Xopenex), levalbuterol tartrate (Xopenex HFA)
CLASS Antiasthmatic, beta agonist, bronchodilator
PREG/CONT C/NA

IND & DOSE Tx, px of bronchospasm. *Adult, child 12 yr and older (Xopenex):* 0.63 mg tid, q 6–8 h by nebulization; may increase up to 1.25 mg tid by nebulization. *Child 6–11 yr (Xopenex):* 0.31 mg tid by nebulization; max, 0.63 mg tid. *Adult, child 4 yr and older (Xopenex HFA):* 2 inhalations (90 mcg) repeated q 4–6 h; some pts may respond to 1 inhalation (45 mcg) q 4 hr.
ADV EFF Anxiety, apprehension, BP changes, **bronchospasm**, CNS stimulation, CV events, fear, headache, hypokalemia, nausea
INTERACTIONS Aminophylline, beta blockers, MAOIs, sympathomimetics, theophylline
NC/PT Keep unopened drug in foil pouch until ready to use; protect from heat, light. Once foil pouch open, use vial within 2 wk, protected from heat, light. Once vial is removed from pouch, use immediately. If not used, protect from light, use within 1 wk. Discard vial if sol not colorless. Teach proper use of inhaler/nebulizer. Overuse may be fatal; explain dosing regimen. Pt should take safety precautions for CNS effects; report chest pain, difficulty breathing, worsening of condition, more frequent need for drug.

levetiracetam (Keppra)
CLASS Antiepileptic
PREG/CONT C/NA

IND & DOSE Tx of partial-onset seizures. *Adult, child over 16 yr:* 500 mg PO or IV bid; max, 3,000 mg/day. ER tablets: 1,000 mg/day PO; max, 3,000 mg/day. *Child 4–16 yr:* 10 mg/kg PO bid (500–1,000 mg/day); may increase q 2 wk in 20-mg/kg increments to 30 mg/kg bid (1,500–3,000 mg/day). Daily dose of oral sol: total dose (mL/day) = daily dose (mg/kg/day) × pt weight (kg) ÷ 100 mg/mL PO. **Tx of generalized tonic-clonic seizures.** *Adult, child over 16 yr:* 500 mg PO bid; increase by 1,000 mg/day q 2 wk to recommended 3,000 mg/day. *Child 6–15 yr:* 10 mg/kg PO bid; increase

q 2 wk by 20-mg/kg increments to recommended 60 mg/kg/day given as 30 mg/kg bid. **Tx of myoclonic seizures.** *Adult, child 12 yr and older:* 500 mg PO bid; slowly increase to recommended max, 3,000 mg/day.
ADJUST DOSE Renal impairment
ADV EFF Behavioral abnormalities, dizziness, dyspepsia, fatigue, headache, psychiatric reactions, **seizures w/withdrawal,** somnolence, **suicidality,** vertigo, vision changes
NC/PT Taper when stopping to minimize withdrawal seizures. Give w/ food. Not for use in pregnancy (barrier contraceptives advised). Pt should swallow ER tablet whole and not cut, crush, or chew it; take safety precautions for CNS effects; wear medical ID; report severe headache, thoughts of suicide. Name confusion between *Keppra* (levetiracetam) and *Kaletra* (lopinavir/ritonavir); use caution.

levocetirizine dihydrochloride (Xyzal)
CLASS Antihistamine
PREG/CONT B/NA

IND & DOSE Symptom relief of seasonal, perennial allergic rhinitis in pts 6 mo and older; tx of uncomplicated skin effects in chronic idiopathic urticaria in pts 2 yr and older. *Adult, child 12 yr and older:* 5 mg/day PO in evening. *Child 6–11 yr:* 2.5 mg/day PO in evening. *Child 6 mo–5 yr:* 1.25 mg/day (½ tsp oral sol) PO once daily in evening.
ADJUST DOSE Renal impairment
ADV EFF Dry mouth, fatigue, mental alertness changes, nasopharyngitis, somnolence
INTERACTIONS Alcohol, CNS depressants
NC/PT Encourage humidifiers, adequate fluid intake to help prevent severe dryness of mucous membranes; skin care for urticaria. Pt should take in evening, use safety precautions for CNS effects, avoid alcohol.

levodopa (generic)
CLASS Antiparkinsonian
PREG/CONT C/NA

IND & DOSE Tx of parkinsonism. *Adult:* 1 g/day PO in two or more doses w/food; increase gradually in increments not exceeding 0.75 g/day q 3–7 days as tolerated. Max, 8 g/day. Only available in combination products.
ADV EFF Abd pain, adventitious movements, anorexia, ataxia, dizziness, drowsiness, dry mouth, n/v, numbness, **suicidality,** weakness
INTERACTIONS Benzodiazepines, MAOIs, phenytoin, pyridoxine, TCAs
NC/PT Ensure 14 days free of MAOIs before use. Give w/meals. Decreased dose needed if tx interrupted. Observe for suicidal tendencies. Limit vitamin B₆ intake; check multivitamin use. Pt should take safety precautions for CNS effects, use sugarless lozenges for dry mouth, report uncontrollable movements, difficulty urinating. Only available in combination products.

levofloxacin (Levaquin)
CLASS Fluoroquinolone antibiotic
PREG/CONT C/NA

BBW Risk of tendinitis, tendon rupture. Risk increased in pts over 60 yr, w/concurrent corticosteroids use, and w/kidney, heart, lung transplant. Risk of exacerbation of myasthenia gravis w/serious muscle weakness; do not use w/hx of myasthenia gravis.
IND & DOSE Tx of community-acquired pneumonia. *Adults:* 500 mg/day PO or IV for 7–14 days. **Tx of sinusitis.** *Adult:* 500 mg/day PO or IV for 10–14 days, or 750 mg/day PO or IV for 5 days. **Tx of chronic bronchitis.** *Adult:* 500 mg/day PO or IV for 7 days. **Tx of skin infection.** *Adult:* 500–750 mg/day PO or IV for 7–14 days. **Tx of UTIs, pyelonephritis.** *Adults:* 250 mg daily PO or IV for 3–10 days; complicated, 750 mg/day PO or IV for 5 days.

Tx of nosocomial pneumonia. *Adult:* 750 mg/day PO or IV for 7–14 days. **Tx of chronic prostatitis.** *Adult:* 500 mg/day PO for 28 days, or 500 mg/day by slow IV infusion over 60 min for 28 days. **Postexposure anthrax.** *Adult:* 500 mg/day PO or IV for 60 days. *Child 6 mo or older over 50 kg:* 500 mg/day for 60 days. *Child 6 mo or older under 50 kg:* 8 mg/kg q 12 hr PO for 60 days. Max, 250 mg/dose. **Tx, px of plague due to** *Yersinia pestis.* *Adult, child over 50 kg:* 500 mg/day PO for 10–14 days. *Child 6 mo and older but less than 50 kg:* 8 mg/kg PO q 12 hr for 10–14 days; max, 250 mg.
ADJUST DOSE Renal impairment
ADV EFF Diarrhea, dizziness, headache, **hepatic impairment,** insomnia, muscle/joint tenderness, neuropathy, photosensitivity, **prolonged QT,** rash, renal impairment, **tendon rupture**
INTERACTIONS Antacids, iron salts, magnesium, NSAIDs, QT-prolonging drugs, St. John's wort, sucralfate, zinc
NC/PT Culture before starting tx. Ensure hydration. Stop if hypersensitivity reaction. Separate from antacids by at least 2 hr. Pt should avoid sun exposure, avoid St. John's wort, take safety precautions for CNS effects, report muscle/tendon pain, weakness, numbness/tingling, urine/stool color changes.

levoleucovorin (Fusilev)
CLASS Folate analogue
PREG/CONT C/NA

IND & DOSE Rescue after high-dose methotrexate; to diminish toxicity from impaired methotrexate elimination. *Adult:* 7.5 mg IV q 6 hr for 10 doses, starting 24 hr after start of methotrexate infusion. **Palliative tx of advanced metastatic colorectal cancer, w/5-FU.** *Adult:* 100 mg/m² by IV injection over at least 3 min, then 5-FU 370 mg/m² by IV injection. Or, or 10 mg/m² by IV injection, then 5-FU 425 mg/m² by IV injection.

ADV EFF N/v/d, stomatitis
INTERACTIONS 5-FU, phenobarbital, phenytoin, primidone, trimethoprim-sulfamethoxazole
NC/PT Inject slowly IV, no faster than 160 mg/min because of high calcium content. Give antiemetics if needed, mouth care for stomatitis. Pt should report pain at injection site, severe n/v/d.

levomilnacipran (Fetzima)
CLASS Antidepressant, serotonin/norepinephrine reuptake inhibitor
PREG/CONT C/NA

BBW Increased risk of suicidality in children, adolescents, young adults; monitor closely.
IND & DOSE Tx of major depressive disorder. *Adult:* 20 mg/day PO for 2 days; then 40 mg/day PO. May increase in increments of 40 mg/day every 2 days as needed. Max, 120 mg/day.
ADJUST DOSE Severe renal impairment
ADV EFF Activation of mania, angle-closure glaucoma, bradycardia, constipation, discontinuation syndrome, ED, hyponatremia, hypertension, n/v, palpitations, serotonin syndrome, sweating, urinary retention
INTERACTIONS Azole antifungals, buspirone, clarithromycin, diuretics, fentanyl, linezolid, lithium, methylene blue (IV), NSAIDs, St. John's wort, tramadol, tryptophan
NC/PT Monitor for hypomania, BP periodically, IOP in pts w/glaucoma, serotonin syndrome, discontinuation syndrome. Not for use in pregnancy/breast-feeding. Pt should swallow capsule whole, not cut, crush, or chew it. Pt should avoid St. John's wort; empty bladder before taking drug; take safety precautions for CNS effects; report thoughts of suicide, hallucinations, continued rapid heart rate.

DANGEROUS DRUG

levorphanol tartrate (generic)

CLASS Opioid agonist analgesic
PREG/CONT C/C-II

IND & DOSE *Relief of moderate to severe pain.* **Adult:** 2 mg PO q 3–6 hr; range, 8–16 mg/day.
ADJUST DOSE Elderly pts, impaired adults
ADV EFF Bronchospasm, cardiac **arrest**, constipation, dizziness, drowsiness, **laryngospasm**, light-headedness, n/v, **respiratory arrest, shock**, sweating
INTERACTIONS Alcohol, antihistamines, barbiturate anesthetics, CNS depressants
NC/PT Monitor closely w/first dose. Pt should take safety precautions for CNS effects, use laxative for constipation, take 4–6 hr before next feeding if breast-feeding, report difficulty breathing.

---

levothyroxine sodium (Levothroid, Levoxyl, Synthroid)

CLASS Thyroid hormone
PREG/CONT A/NA

BBW Do not use for weight loss; possible serious adverse effects w/ large doses.
IND & DOSE *Replacement tx in hypothyroidism.* **Adult:** 12.5–25 mcg PO, w/increasing increments of 25 mcg PO q 2–4 wk; maint, up to 200 mcg/day. Can substitute IV or IM injection for oral form when oral route not possible. Usual IV dose is 50% of oral dose. Start at 25 mcg/day or less in pts w/ long-standing hypothyroidism, known cardiac disease. Usual replacement, 1.7 mcg/kg/day. *Tx of myxedema coma without severe heart disease.* **Adult:** Initially, 200–500 mcg IV. May give additional 100–300 mcg or more second day if needed. *Thyroid suppression tx.* **Adult:**
2.6 mcg/kg/day PO for 7–10 days. *TSH suppression in thyroid cancer, nodules, thyroid goiters.* Individualize dose based on specific disease and pt; larger amounts than used for normal suppression. *Tx of congenital hypothyroidism.* **Child:** Over 12 yr, 2–3 mcg/kg/day PO; 6–12 yr, 4–5 mcg/kg/day PO; 1–5 yr, 5–6 mcg/kg/day PO; 6–12 mo, 6–8 mcg/kg/day PO; 3–6 mo, 8–10 mcg/kg/day PO; 0–3 mo, 10–15 mcg/kg/day PO.
ADJUST DOSE Elderly pts
ADV EFF Cardiac arrest, esophageal atresia, n/v/d, tremors
INTERACTIONS Aluminum- and magnesium-containing antacids, cholestyramine, colestipol, digoxin, iron, sucralfate, theophylline, warfarin
NC/PT Monitor thyroid function. Do not add IV form to other IV fluids. Replaces normal hormone; adverse effects should not occur. Pt should swallow whole w/full glass of water, wear medical ID, report chest pain, unusual sweating.

DANGEROUS DRUG

lidocaine hydrochloride (Numby Stuff, Otocaine, Xylocaine)

CLASS Antiarrhythmic, local anesthetic
PREG/CONT B/NA

IND & DOSE *Tx of ventricular arrhythmias.* **Adult:** Use 10% sol for IM injection: 300 mg in deltoid or thigh muscle; may repeat in 60–90 min. Switch to IV or oral form as soon as possible. Or, 1–4 mg/min (20–50 mcg/kg/min) IV; decrease as soon as cardiac rhythm stabilizes. **Child:** Safety/efficacy not established. AHA recommends bolus of 0.5–1 mg/kg IV, then 30 mcg/kg/min w/caution. *Local anesthetic.* **Adult, child:** Conc, diluent should be appropriate to particular local anesthetic use: 5% sol w/glucose for spinal anesthesia, 1.5% sol w/dextrose for low spinal or saddle block anesthesia. Dose varies

w/area to be anesthetized and reason for anesthesia; use lowest dose needed to achieve results. **Topical analgesia.** *Adult, child:* Up to 3 transdermal patches to area of pain for up to 12 hr within 24-hr period, or apply cream, ointment, gel, sol, oral patch, spray as directed 1–3 times/day.
ADJUST DOSE Elderly, debilitated pts; HF; hepatic, renal impairment
ADV EFF Anaphylactoid reactions, back pain, **cardiac arrest,** cardiac arrhythmias, dizziness, drowsiness, fatigue, headache, hypotension, light-headedness, **respiratory arrest, seizures,** urine retention
INTERACTIONS Beta blockers, cimetidine, succinylcholine
NC/PT Have life support equipment on hand; continually monitor pt response. Check conc carefully; varies by product. Monitor for safe, effective serum conc (antiarrhythmic: 1–5 mcg/mL); conc of 6 or more mcg/mL usually toxic. Pt should take safety precautions for CNS effects, local anesthesia; report difficulty speaking/breathing, numbness, pain at injection site.

linaclotide (Linzess)
CLASS Guanylate cyclase-C agonist, IBS drug
PREG/CONT C/NA

BBW Contraindicated in child up to 6 yr; avoid use in child 6–17 yr; caused deaths due to dehydration in juvenile mice.
IND & DOSE Tx of IBS w/constipation. *Adult:* 290 mcg/day PO. Tx of chronic idiopathic constipation. *Adult:* 145 mcg/day PO.
ADV EFF Abd pain, diarrhea, distention, flatulence, **severe diarrhea**
NC/PT Ensure constipation is main complaint; ensure no GI obstruction. Give on empty stomach at least 30 min before first meal of day. Have pt swallow capsule whole and not cut, crush, or chew it. Contraindicated in pts under 6 yr. Pt should swallow capsule whole and not cut, crush, or chew it; take on empty stomach; store in original container protected from moisture; not give to child under 17 yr; report severe diarrhea, severe abd pain, dehydration.

linagliptin (Tradjenta)
CLASS Antidiabetic, DPP-4 inhibitor
PREG/CONT B/NA

IND & DOSE Adjunct to diet/exercise to improve glycemic control in pts w/type 2 diabetes; tx of type 2 diabetes in pts w/severe renal impairment w/insulin; add on tx to insulin, diet/exercise to improve glycemic control in pts w/type 2 diabetes. *Adult:* 5 mg PO once/day.
ADV EFF Hypoglycemia, nasopharyngitis, **pancreatitis, severe debilitating arthralgia**
INTERACTIONS Celery, coriander, dandelion root, fenugreek, garlic, ginger, juniper berries, potent CYP3A inhibitors
NC/PT Monitor blood glucose, HbA$_{1c}$ before, periodically during tx. Not for use in type 1 diabetes or ketoacidosis. Ensure pt continues diet/exercise, other drugs for diabetes control. Use caution in pregnancy/breast-feeding. Arrange for thorough diabetic teaching program. Consider stopping drug w/reports of severe joint pain. Report OTC/herbal use that could alter blood glucose, s&sx of infection, uncontrolled glucose level, joint pain.

lincomycin hydrochloride (Lincocin)
CLASS Lincosamide antibiotic
PREG/CONT C/NA

BBW Risk of CDAD, pseudomembranous colitis; monitor closely.
IND & DOSE Tx of serious infections caused by susceptible bacteria strains. *Adult:* 600 mg IM q 12–24 hr, or 600 mg–1 g IV q 8–12 hr. *Child:*

10 mg/kg IM q 12–24 hr, or 10–20 mg/kg/day IV in divided doses.
ADJUST DOSE Renal impairment
ADV EFF Abd pain, **agranulocytosis, anaphylactic reactions,** anorexia, **cardiac arrest,** CDAD, contact dermatitis, esophagitis, n/v/d, pain after injection, **pseudomembranous colitis,** rash
INTERACTIONS Aluminum salts, kaolin, NMJ blockers
NC/PT Culture before tx. Do not give IM injection of more than 600 mg; inject deeply into muscle. Monitor LFTs, renal function. Pt should report severe, watery diarrhea.

linezolid (Zyvox)
CLASS Oxazolidinone antibiotic
PREG/CONT C/NA

IND & DOSE Tx of VREF, MRSA, pneumonia, complicated skin/skin-structure infections, including diabetic foot ulcers without osteomyelitis. *Adult, child 12 yr and older:* 600 mg IV or PO q 12 hr for 10–28 days. *Child 11 yr and under:* 10 mg/kg IV or PO q 8 hr for 10–14 days. **Tx of uncomplicated skin/skin-structure infections.** *Adult, child 12 yr and older:* 400 mg PO q 12 hr for 10–14 days. *Child 5–11 yr:* 10 mg/kg PO q 12 hr for 10–14 days.
ADV EFF Bone marrow suppression, CDAD, diarrhea, dizziness, hyperglycemia, insomnia, nausea, peripheral/optic neuropathy, **pseudomembranous colitis,** rash, serotonin syndrome
INTERACTIONS Aspirin, dipyridamole, MAOIs, NSAIDs, pseudoephedrine, SSRIs, St. John's wort, sympathomimetics, tyramine-containing foods
NC/PT Culture before tx. Ensure no MAOIs within 2 wk. Do not mix IV solution w/other solutions. Monitor platelets, CBC wkly; BP w/long-term use. Pt should complete full course; avoid foods high in tyramine; report all OTC and herbal use; report severe GI problems, bloody diarrhea. Name confusion between Zyvox (linezolid) and Zovirax (acyclovir); use caution.

liothyronine (Cytomel, Triostat)
CLASS Thyroid hormone
PREG/CONT A/NA

BBW Do not use for weight loss; serious adverse effects w/large doses possible.
IND & DOSE **Replacement tx in hypothyroidism.** *Adult:* 25 mcg PO; maint, 25–75 mcg/day. **Tx of myxedema.** 5 mcg/day PO; maint, 50–100 mcg/day. **Tx of myxedema coma, precoma.** *Adult:* 25–50 mcg IV q 4–12 hr; do not give IM or subcut. Start at 10–20 mcg IV w/heart disease. Max, 100 mcg/24 hr. **Tx of simple goiter.** *Adult:* 5 mcg/day PO; maint, 75 mcg/day. **Thyroid suppression tx.** *Adult:* 75–100 mcg/day PO for 7 days. Repeat I[131] uptake test; unaffected w/hyperthyroidism, decreased by 50% w/euthyroidism. **Tx of congenital hypothyroidism.** *Child:* Birth, 5 mcg/day PO. Usual maint, 20 mcg/day up to 1 yr; 50 mcg/day PO for 1–3 yr, adult dose over 3 yr.
ADJUST DOSE Elderly pts
ADV EFF **Cardiac arrest,** esophageal atresia, hyperthyroidism, n/v/d, tremors
INTERACTIONS Antacids containing aluminum or magnesium, cholestyramine, colestipol, digoxin, iron, sucralfate, theophylline, warfarin
NC/PT Monitor thyroid function. Do not add IV form to other IV fluids. Replaces normal hormone; adverse effects should not occur. Pt should swallow whole w/full glass of water, wear medical ID, report chest pain, unusual sweating.

liotrix (Thyrolar)
CLASS Thyroid hormone
PREG/CONT A/NA

BBW Do not use for weight loss; serious adverse effects w/large doses possible.

IND & DOSE Replacement tx in hypothyroidism. *Adult:* 30 mg/day PO; maint, 60–120 mg/day PO (thyroid equivalent). **Mgt of goiter, thyroid cancer.** Use larger doses than needed for replacement surgery. **Dx of thyroid function.** 1.56 mcg/kg/day PO for 7–10 days. **Tx of congenital hypothyroidism.** *Child:* Over 12 yr, 90 mg/day PO; 6–12 yr, 60–90 mg/day PO; 1–5 yr, 45–60 mg/day PO; 6–12 mo, 30–45 mg/day PO; 0–6 mo, 15–30 mg/day PO.

ADV EFF Cardiac arrest, esophageal atresia, hyperthyroidism, n/v/d, tremors

INTERACTIONS Antacids containing aluminum or magnesium, cholestyramine, colestipol, digoxin, iron, sucralfate, theophylline, warfarin

NC/PT Monitor thyroid function. Replaces normal hormone; adverse effects should not occur. Pt should swallow whole w/full glass of water, wear medical ID, report chest pain, unusual sweating.

DANGEROUS DRUG

liraglutide (Saxenda, Victoza)
CLASS Antidiabetic, glucagon-like peptide receptor agonist
PREG/CONT C/NA

BBW Causes thyroid medullary cancer in rodents. Not for use w/ personal, family hx of thyroid medullary cancer, multiple endocrine neoplasia syndrome type 2; monitor closely.

IND & DOSE Adjunct to diet/exercise to improve glycemic control in type 2 diabetes (*Victoza*). *Adults:* 0.6 mg/day by subcut injection; max, 1.8 mg/day. **Adjunct to diet/exercise for chronic weight mgt in adults w/ BMI of 30 kg/m² or greater (obese) or 27 kg/m² or greater (overweight) w/at least one weight-related co-morbidity** (*Saxenda*). *Adult:* Initially, 0.6 mg/wk subcut; increase gradually to 3 mg/wk.

ADV EFF Dizziness, gallbladder disease, headache, hypersensitivity reactions, **hypoglycemia**, n/v/d, **pancreatitis**, **papillary thyroid carcinoma, renal impairment, suicidality**

INTERACTIONS Antidiabetic secretagogues, celery, coriander, dandelion root, drugs that would be affected by delayed GI emptying, garlic, ginseng, fenugreek, juniper berries

NC/PT Not for tx of type 1 diabetes, ketoacidosis; not for first line tx. Monitor blood glucose, HbA₁c before, periodically during tx. Ensure pt continues diet/exercise, other drugs for diabetes. Provide complete diabetic teaching program. Teach proper administration/disposal of needles/syringes; should inject once/day subcut in abdomen, thigh, or upper arm. Use caution in pregnancy; not for use in breast-feeding. Pt should report OTC/herb use, difficulty swallowing, lump in throat, severe abd pain radiating to back, thoughts of suicide.

---

lisdexamfetamine dimesylate (Vyvanse)
CLASS Amphetamine, CNS stimulant
PREG/CONT C/C-II

BBW High risk of abuse; could lead to drug dependence. Amphetamine misuse has caused serious CV events, sudden death. Assess risk of abuse before to use; monitor continually.

IND & DOSE Tx of ADHD as part of integrated tx plan. *Adult, child 6 yr and older:* 30 mg PO in a.m.; may increase at wkly intervals in increments of 10–20 mg/day. Max, 70 mg/day. **Tx of moderate to severe binge eating disorder.** *Adult, child 6 and older:* 30 mg PO q.a.m.; titrate at rate of 20 mg/wk. Range, 50–70 mg/day; max, 70 mg/day.

ADJUST DOSE Renal impairment

ADV EFF Abd pain, **cardiac events,** decreased appetite, dizziness, dry mouth, fever, headache, insomnia, irritability, n/v/d, peripheral vascular disease, psychiatric adverse reactions, **sudden death,** tachycardia, weight loss
INTERACTIONS Chlorpromazine, haloperidol, MAOIs, meperidine, methenamine, norepinephrine, sympathomimetics, TCAs, urine acidifiers/alkalinizers
NC/PT Ensure proper dx. Baseline ECG before tx. Not indicated for weight loss. Part of comprehensive tx plan. Monitor growth in child. If pt cannot swallow whole, empty contents into glass of water, have pt drink right away. Stop periodically to validate use. Pt should avoid MAOI use within 14 days, take in a.m. to prevent insomnia, store in dry place, secure drug (controlled substance), report vision changes, manic sx, marked weight loss, chest pain.

lisinopril (Prinivil, Zestril)
CLASS ACE inhibitor, antihypertensive
PREG/CONT D/NA

BBW Contraceptives advised. If pregnancy occurs, stop drug as soon as possible; fetal injury/death possible.
IND & DOSE Tx of hypertension. *Adults:* 10 mg/day PO; range, 20–40 mg/day. If also taking diuretic, start at 5 mg/day; monitor BP. *Child 6 yr and older:* 0.07 mg/kg/day PO; max, 5 mg/day. **Adjunct tx of HF.** *Adults:* 5 mg/day PO w/diuretics, digitalis. Effective range, 5–20 mg/day (Prinivil), 5–40 mg/day (Zestril). **To improve survival post-MI.** *Adults:* Start within 24 hr of MI; 5 mg PO, then 5 mg PO in 24 hr; 10 mg PO after 48 hr; then 10 mg/day PO for 6 wk.
ADJUST DOSE Elderly pts, renal impairment
ADV EFF Airway obstruction, angioedema, anaphylactoid reactions, cough, dizziness, fatigue, gastric

irritation, headache, **hepatic failure,** hyperkalemia, hypertension, insomnia, **MI,** n/v/d, orthostatic hypotension, **pancytopenia, renal impairment**
INTERACTIONS ACE inhibitors, ARBs, capsaicin, diuretics, lithium, NSAIDs, renin inhibitors
NC/PT Mark chart if surgery scheduled; fluid replacement may be needed postop. Monitor BP; use care in situations that may lead to decreased BP. Maintain hydration, potassium. Not for use in pregnancy (contraceptives advised). Pt should take safety precautions for CNS effects, report swelling, difficulty breathing, chest pain. Name confusion between lisinopril and fosinopril; use caution.

lithium carbonate, lithium citrate (Lithobid)
CLASS Antimanic drug
PREG/CONT D/NA

BBW Monitor clinical status closely, especially during initial tx stages. Monitor for therapeutic serum level (0.6–1.2 mEq/L); toxicity closely related to serum level.
IND & DOSE Tx of manic episodes of bipolar disorder. *Adults:* 600 mg PO tid or 900 mg SR form PO bid to produce effective serum level between 1 and 1.5 mEq/L. Maint, 300 mg PO tid–qid to produce serum level of 0.6–1.2 mEq/L. Determine serum level at least q 2 mo in samples drawn immediately before dose (at least 8–12 hr after previous dose).
ADJUST DOSE Elderly pts, renal impairment
ADV EFF Related to serum levels: **Death,** lethargy, muscle weakness, **pulmonary complications,** slurred speech, tremor progressing to **CV collapse.** Other: Dizziness, drowsiness, GI upset, thirst, tremor
INTERACTIONS ACE inhibitors, antacids, ARBs, carbamazepine, dandelion root, diuretics, haloperidol, indomethacin, iodide salts, juniper,

NSAIDs, SSRIs, tromethamine, urinary alkalinizers

NC/PT Monitor serum level regularly; therapeutic range, 0.6–1.2 mEq/L. Maintain salt, fluid intake. Not for use in pregnancy (contraceptives advised). Teach toxicity warning signs. Pt should take w/food, milk; take safety precautions for CNS effects; report diarrhea, unsteady walking, slurred speech, difficulty breathing.

DANGEROUS DRUG

lomitapide (Juxtapid)
CLASS Antitriglyceride
PREG/CONT X/NA

BBW Increased transaminase elevations; monitor LFTs closely. Stop drug at s&sx of hepatotoxicity; risk of hepatic steatosis, cirrhosis.

IND & DOSE Adjunct to low-fat diet, other lipid-lowering tx to reduce LDL, total cholesterol, apolipoprotein B, non-HDL cholesterol in pts w/homozygous familial hypercholesterolemia. *Adult:* Initially 5 mg/day PO; increase after 2 wk to 10 mg/day PO, then at 4-wk intervals to 20, 40, and 60 mg/day PO.

ADJUST DOSE Hepatic/renal impairment

ADV EFF Abd pain, dyspepsia, **hepatotoxicity,** n/v/d

INTERACTIONS Bile acid sequestrants, lovastatin, simvastatin, strong or moderate CYP3A4 inhibitors, warfarin

NC/PT Available only through restricted access program. Ensure negative pregnancy test before tx and continued use of low-fat diet other lipid-lowering agents. Ensure appropriate dx. Monitor LFTs regularly. Consider supplemental vitamin E, and fatty acids, tx for severe GI effects. Not for use in pregnancy (barrier contraceptives advised)/breast-feeding. Pt should take as prescribed (dosage will be slowly increased); take w/ water (not food) in evening; swallow capsule whole and not cut, crush, or

chew it; continue low-fat diet, other lipid-lowering drugs; take vitamin E, fatty acids if prescribed; report severe GI complaints, urine/stool color changes, extreme fatigue.

DANGEROUS DRUG

lomustine (generic)
CLASS Alkylating agent, antineoplastic
PREG/CONT D/NA

BBW Arrange for blood tests to evaluate hematopoietic function before tx, then wkly for at least 6 wk; severe bone marrow suppression possible. Delayed suppression at or beyond 6 wk also possible.

IND & DOSE Tx of primary/metastatic brain tumors, secondary tx of Hodgkin disease in pts who relapse after primary tx w/other drugs. *Adult, child:* 130 mg/m² PO as single dose q 6 wk. Must make adjustments w/bone marrow suppression: Initially, reduce to 100 mg/m² PO q 6 wk; do not give repeat dose until platelets over 100,000/mm² and leukocytes over 4,000/mm².

ADV EFF Alopecia, ataxia, **bone marrow suppression,** n/v, **pulmonary fibrosis,** renal toxicity

NC/PT Monitor CBC, respiratory function. Do not give full dose within 2–3 wk of radiation therapy. Not for use in pregnancy (barrier contraceptives advised). Antiemetics may be ordered. Pt should avoid exposure to infection, report unusual bleeding, difficulty breathing, s&sx of infection.

loperamide hydrochloride (Imodium, Pepto Bismol)
CLASS Antidiarrheal
PREG/CONT B/NA

IND & DOSE Tx of acute/chronic diarrhea, traveler's diarrhea. *Adult:* 4 mg PO, then 2 mg after each unformed stool; max, 16 mg/day.

Child: 8–12 yr (over 30 kg): 2 mg PO tid; 6–8 yr (20–30 kg): 2 mg PO bid; 2–5 yr (13–20 kg): 1 mg PO tid. For traveler's diarrhea, 6–11 yr (22–43 kg): 2 mg PO after loose stool, then 1 mg w/each subsequent stool; max, 4 mg/day PO (6–8 yr) or 6 mg/day PO (9–11 yr) for 2 days.

ADV EFF Abd pain, constipation, distention, dry mouth, nausea, **pulmonary infiltrates, toxic megacolon**

NC/PT Stools may be hard. Pt should take drug after each stool; stop if no response in 48 hr; drink clear fluids to prevent dehydration; report fever, continued diarrhea, abd pain/distention, severe constipation.

---

lopinavir (lopinavir/ ritonavir) (Kaletra)
CLASS Antiviral, protease inhibitor
PREG/CONT C/NA

IND & DOSE *Note:* Doses for child under 12 yr based on weight. See manufacturer's details for specific doses. **Tx of HIV infection w/other antiretrovirals in tx-naïve pts.** *Adult, child 12 yr and older, over 40 kg:* 800 mg lopinavir, 200 mg ritonavir (four tablets or 10 mL)/day PO. *Children 14 days–12 yr:* over 40 kg, adult dose; 15–under 40 kg, 10 mg/kg PO bid; 7–under 15 kg, 12 mg/kg PO bid. *Child 14 days–12 yr using oral solution:* over 40 kg, adult dose; over 35–40 kg, 4.75 mL PO bid; over 30–35 kg, 4 mL PO bid; over 25–30 kg, 3.5 mL PO bid; over 20–25 kg, 2.75 mL PO bid; 15–20 kg, 2.25 mL PO bid; over 10–15 kg, 1.75 mL PO bid; 7–10 kg, 1.2 mL PO bid. **Tx of HIV infection w/other antiretrovirals in tx-experienced pts.** *Adult, child 12 yr and older, over 40 kg:* 400 mg lopinavir, 100 mg ritonavir (two tablets or 5 mL) PO. **Tx of HIV infection w/efavirenz, nevirapine, fosamprenavir without ritonavir, or nelfinavir.** *Adult, child 12 yr and older, over 40 kg:* 600 mg lopinavir, 150 mg ritonavir (three tablets) PO

bid for tx-experienced pts. No adjustment needed for tx-naïve pts. *Child 14 days–12 yr:* 7–15 kg, 13 mg/kg bid; 15–40 kg, 11 mg/kg PO bid; over 45 kg, adult dose. **Tx of HIV infection using oral sol w/efavirenz, nevirapine, amprenavir, or nelfinavir.** *Adult, child 12 yr and older, over 40 kg:* Adjust dose to 533 mg lopinavir, 133 mg ritonavir (6.5 mL) bid PO w/food. *Child 14 days–12 yr:* over 45 kg, adult dose; over 40–45 kg, 5.75 mL PO bid; over 35–40 kg, 5 mL PO bid; over 30–35 kg, 4.5 mL PO bid; over 25–30 kg, 4 mL PO bid; over 25–30 kg, 3.25 mL PO bid; over 20–25 kg, 2.5 mL PO bid; 15–20 kg, 2.5 mL PO bid; over 10–15 kg, 2 mL PO bid; 7–10 kg, 1.5 mL PO bid.

ADV EFF Abd pain, anorexia, asthenia, **hepatotoxicity**, hyperglycemia, lipid abnormalities, n/v/d, **pancreatitis**, paresthesia, prolonged PR/QT, rash

INTERACTIONS Hormonal contraceptives, sildenafil, St. John's wort, tadalafil, vardenafil. Fatal reactions possible; do not give w/amiodarone, bepridil, bupropion, clozapine, encainide, flecainide, meperidine, piroxicam, propafenone, quinidine, rifabutin. Extreme sedation/respiratory depression possible; do not give w/ alprazolam, clonazepam, diazepam, estazolam, flurazepam, midazolam, triazolam, zolpidem

NC/PT Obtain baseline lipid profile. Monitor LFTs, glucose. Monitor drug regimen; risk of many potentially serious drug interactions. Store sol in refrigerator; protect from light, heat. Do not use in preterm infants. Give didanosine 1 hr before or 2 hr after lopinavir sol. May make hormonal contraceptives ineffective (barrier contraceptives advised). Pt should swallow tablet whole and not cut, crush, or chew it; use precautions to prevent spread (drug not a cure); avoid other prescription drugs, OTC/ herbs until checking w/prescriber; avoid St. John's wort; report severe abd pain, numbness/tingling; urine/stool color changes. Name confusion between Kaletra (lopinavir/ritonavir) and Keppra (levetiracetam).

loratadine (Alavert, Claritin)
CLASS Antihistamine
PREG/CONT B/NA

IND & DOSE Symptomatic relief of allergic rhinitis; tx of rhinitis, urticaria. *Adult, child 6 yr and over:* 10 mg/day PO. *Child 2–5 yr:* 5 mg PO daily (syrup, chewable tablets).
ADJUST DOSE Elderly pts; hepatic, renal impairment
ADV EFF Bronchospasm, dizziness, headache, increased appetite, nervousness, thickened bronchial secretions, weight gain
INTERACTIONS Alcohol, CNS depressants
NC/PT Pt should place orally disintegrating tablet on tongue, swallow after it dissolves; avoid alcohol; use humidifier for dry mucous membranes; take safety precautions for CNS effects; report difficulty breathing.

lorazepam (Ativan)
CLASS Anxiolytic, benzodiazepine, sedative-hypnotic
PREG/CONT D/C-IV

IND & DOSE Mgt of anxiety disorders; short-term relief of anxiety sx. *Adults:* 2–6 mg/day PO; range, 1–10 mg/day in divided doses w/largest dose at bedtime. **Insomnia due to transient stress.** *Adult:* 2–4 mg PO at bedtime. **Preanesthetic sedation, anxiolytic.** *Adult:* 0.05 mg/kg IM; max, 4 mg at least 2 hr before procedure. Or, 2 mg total IV or 0.044 mg/kg, whichever smaller; may give doses as high as 0.05 mg/kg to total of 4 mg 15–20 min before procedure. **Tx of status epilepticus.** *Adult:* 4 mg slowly IV at 2 mg/min. May give another 4 mg IV after 10–15 min if needed.

ADJUST DOSE Hepatic, renal impairment
ADV EFF Apathy, confusion, depression, disorientation, drowsiness, dry mouth, **CV collapse**, gynecomastia, hostility, light-headedness, nausea, restlessness
INTERACTIONS Alcohol, CNS depressants, kava, probenecid, theophyllines
NC/PT Do not give intra-arterially. Give IM injection deep into muscle. Protect soln from light. May mix oral sol w/water, juice, soda, applesauce, pudding. Taper gradually after long-term tx. Pt should take safety precautions for CNS effects; report vision changes, chest pain, fainting. Name confusion between lorazepam and alprazolam; use caution.

lorcaserin hydrochloride (Belviq)
CLASS Serotonin receptor agonist, weight-loss drug
PREG/CONT X/NA

IND & DOSE Adjunct to diet/exercise for long-term weight management in adults w/initial body mass index of 30 kg/m^2 or more or 27 kg/m^2 or more w/at least one weight-related condition. *Adult:* 10 mg PO bid.
ADV EFF Back pain, cognitive changes, constipation, dizziness, dry mouth, fatigue, headache, hypoglycemia, **NMS, pulmonary hypertension, suicidality, valvular heart disease**
INTERACTIONS Bupropion, dextromethorphan, linezolid, lithium, MAOIs, selected serotonin norepinephrine reuptake inhibitors, SSRIs, St. John's wort, TCAs, tramadol, tryptophan; avoid these combinations
NC/PT Ensure appropriate use of drug; if 5% of body weight is not lost within 12 wk, stop drug. Be aware of risk of cognitive changes, suicidality; monitor for s&sx of valvular heart disease, NMS. Not for use in pregnancy/breast-feeding. Pt should take drug

bid, and not change dosage; continue diet/exercise program; avoid combining w/other weight-loss drugs; avoid St. John's wort; use safety precautions w/dizziness, sugarless candy for dry mouth; watch for slowed thinking, sleepiness; report thoughts of suicide, changes in heart rate, mental status.

losartan potassium (Cozaar)
CLASS Antihypertensive, ARB
PREG/CONT D/NA

BBW Rule out pregnancy before starting tx. Suggest barrier contraceptives during tx; fetal injury/death have occurred.
IND & DOSE Tx of hypertension. *Adult:* 50 mg/day PO; range, 25–100 mg/day PO once or bid. *Child 6 yr and over:* 0.7 mg/kg/day PO; max, 50 mg/day. **Tx of diabetic nephropathy.** *Adult:* 50 mg/day PO; may increase to 100 mg/day based on BP response. **Tx of hypertension w/left ventricular hypertrophy.** *Adult:* 50–100 mg/day PO w/12.5–25 mg/day hydrochlorothiazide.
ADV EFF Abd pain, cough, diarrhea, dizziness, drowsiness, hyperkalemia, nausea, URI
INTERACTIONS ACE inhibitors, ARBs, fluconazole, indomethacin, ketoconazole, phenobarbital, renin inhibitors, rifamycin
NC/PT If surgery needed, alert surgeon to drug use; volume replacement may be needed. Monitor potassium w/long-term use. Not for use in pregnancy (barrier contraceptives advised)/breast-feeding. Pt should use caution in situations that could lead to fluid loss, maintain hydration, take safety precautions for CNS effects.

lovastatin (Altoprev)
CLASS Antihyperlipidemic, statin
PREG/CONT X/NA

IND & DOSE Tx of familial hypercholesterolemia, type II hyperlipidemia (ER only); to slow progression of atherosclerosis in pts w/CAD; tx of primary hypercholesterolemia. *Adult:* 20 mg/day PO in evening w/ meals. Maint, 10–80 mg/day PO; max, 80 mg/day. For ER tablets, 10–60 mg/day PO single dose in evening. **As adjunct to diet to reduce total cholesterol, LDLs, apolipoprotein B in heterozygous familial hypercholesterolemia.** *Adolescent boy, postmenarchal girl, 10–17 yr:* 10–40 mg/day PO; may increase to max 40 mg/day.
ADJUST DOSE Renal impairment
ADV EFF Abd pain, cataracts, cramps, constipation, flatulence, headache, hepatic impairment, nausea, **rhabdomyolysis**
INTERACTIONS Amiodarone, azole antifungals, cyclosporine, erythromycin, gemfibrozil, grapefruit juice, itraconazole, ketoconazole, other statins, verapamil
NC/PT Monitor LFTs. Stop drug if myopathy occurs. Not for use in pregnancy (barrier contraceptives advised). Pt should not cut, crush, or chew ER tablets; take in evening for best effects; continue diet/exercise program; get periodic eye exams; report muscle pain w/fever, unusual bleeding.

loxapine hydrochloride, loxapine succinate (Adasuve)
CLASS Antipsychotic, dopaminergic blocker
PREG/CONT C/NA

BBW Increased risk of mortality when antipsychotics used in elderly pts w/dementia-related psychosis.

Avoid this use; not approved for this use. Increased risk of potentially fatal bronchospasm w/inhaled form; available only through limited release program; monitor pt closely.

IND & DOSE Tx of schizophrenia.
Adult: 10 mg PO bid; max, 50 mg/day. Increase fairly rapidly over first 7–10 days until sx controlled; range, 60–100 mg/day PO. Dosage over 250 mg/day PO not recommended. For maint: range, 20–60 mg/day PO.
Acute tx of agitation associated w/ schizophrenia, bipolar disorder.
Adult: 10 mg/24 hr by oral inhalation using inhaler.

ADJUST DOSE Elderly pts
ADV EFF Bone marrow suppression, bronchospasm, drowsiness, dry mouth, extrapyramidal sx, gynecomastia, laryngospasm, photosensitivity, rash, refractory arrhythmias
INTERACTIONS CNS drugs, drugs that affect airway disease (inhaled form)
NC/PT Ensure hydration of elderly pts. Monitor CBC; stop if suppressed. Screen pulmonary hx and examine pt before using inhaled form; inhaled form available only through restricted access program. Pt should take safety precautions for CNS effects, avoid sun exposure, report unusual bleeding, infections, palpitations. Name confusion w/*Loxitane* (loxapine), *Lexapro* (escitalopram), *Soriatane* (acitretin); use caution.

lurasidone hydrochloride (Latuda)
CLASS Atypical antipsychotic
PREG/CONT B/NA

BBW Increased risk of mortality when antipsychotics used in elderly pts w/dementia-related psychosis. Avoid this use; not approved for this use. Increased risk of suicidality in child, adolescent, young adult; monitor accordingly.

IND & DOSE Tx of schizophrenia.
Adult: 40 mg/day PO w/food; may titrate to max 80 mg/day PO.
ADJUST DOSE Hepatic, renal impairment
ADV EFF Akathisia, dystonia, hyperglycemia, **NMS**, n/v/d, parkinsonism, **suicidality**, weight gain
INTERACTIONS Alcohol, grapefruit juice, strong CYP3A4 inducers/ inhibitors
NC/PT Dispense least amount possible to suicidal pts. Not for use in breast-feeding. Pt should take safety measures for CNS effects, monitor serum glucose/weight gain, avoid alcohol, report increased thirst/ appetite, thoughts of suicide.

macitentan (Opsumit)
CLASS Endothelin receptor blocker, pulmonary hypertension drug
PREG/CONT X/NA

BBW Known teratogen; life-threatening birth defects possible. Available by limited access program for women. Monthly pregnancy tests required.

IND & DOSE Tx of pulmonary artery hypertension. *Adult:* 10 mg/day PO.
ADV EFF Anemia, bronchitis, decreased Hgb, headache, **hepatotoxicity**, nasopharyngitis, **pulmonary edema**, reduced sperm count, UTI
INTERACTIONS Ketoconazole, rifampin, ritonavir; these combinations
NC/PT Ensure proper dx, negative monthly pregnancy test for women. Monitor LFTs, Hgb, respiratory status. Female pt should avoid pregnancy (contraceptives required)/breast-feeding; males should be aware of reduced sperm count. Pt should monitor activity tolerance; report difficulty breathing, urine/stool color changes, extreme fatigue.

magnesium salts, magnesia, magnesium citrate, magnesium hydroxide (Milk of Magnesia), magnesium oxide (Mag-Ox)

CLASS Antacid, laxative
PREG/CONT C; A (antacids); B (laxative)/NA

IND & DOSE Laxative. *Adult:* 300 mL (citrate) PO w/full glass of water, or 15–60 mL (hydroxide) PO w/liquid. *Child 12 and older:* 30–60 mL (400 mg/5 mL) (hydroxide) PO w/ water or 15–30 mL/day (800 mg/5 mL) PO once daily at bedtime, or eight 311-mg tablets PO once daily at bedtime or in divided doses. *Child 6–11 yr:* 15–30 mL (400 mg/5 mL) (hydroxide) PO once daily at bedtime, or 7.5–15 mL/day (800 mg/5 mL) PO once daily at bedtime, or four 311-mg tablets PO once daily at bedtime. *Child 2–5 yr:* 5–15 mL (400 mg/5 mL) (hydroxide) PO once daily at bedtime, or two 311-mg tablets PO once daily at bedtime. **Antacid.** *Adult:* 5–15 mL (hydroxide) liquid or 622–1,244-mg tablets PO qid (adult, pt over 12 yr). **Supplemental magnesium replacement.** *Adult:* Magnesium oxide capsules, 140 mg PO tid–qid. Tablets, 400–800 mg/day PO.
ADV EFF Dizziness, hypermagnesemia, n/v/d, perianal irritation
INTERACTIONS Fluoroquinolones, ketoconazole, nitrofurantoin, penicillamine, tetracyclines
NC/PT Pt should avoid other oral drugs within 1–2 hr of antacids, take between meals and at bedtime, chew antacid tablet thoroughly, avoid long-term laxative use, avoid laxatives if abd pain, n/v occur, maintain hydration, report rectal bleeding, weakness.

magnesium sulfate (generic)

CLASS Antiepileptic, electrolyte, laxative
PREG/CONT D; B (laxative)/NA

IND & DOSE Control of hypertension w/acute nephritis. *Child:* 100 mg/kg (0.8 mEq/kg or 0.2 mL/kg of 50% sol) IM q 4–6 hr as needed. Or, 20–40 mg/kg (0.16–0.32 mEq/kg or 0.1–0.2 mL/kg of 20% sol) IM. Or, for severe sx, 100–200 mg/kg of 1%–3% sol IV over 1 hr w/half of dose given in first 15–20 min (seizure control). **Laxative.** *Adult:* 10–30 g/day PO. *Child 6–11 yr:* 5–10 g/day PO. *Child 2–5 yr:* 2.5–5 g/day PO; 5–15 mL/day PO. **Tx of arrhythmias.** *Adult:* 3–4 g IV over several min; then 3–20 mg/min continuous infusion for 5–48 hr. **Tx of eclampsia, severe preeclampsia.** *Adult:* 10–14 g IV. May infuse 4–5 g in 250 mL 5% dextrose injection or normal saline while giving IM doses up to 10 g (5 g or 10 mL of undiluted 50% sol in each buttock). Or, may give initial 4 g IV by diluting 50% sol to 10% or 20%; may inject diluted fluid (40 mL of 10% or 20 mL of 20% sol) IV over 3–4 min. Then inject 4–5 g (8–10 mL of 50% sol) IM into alternate buttocks q 4 hr as needed depending on patellar reflex, respiratory function. Or, after initial IV dose, may give 1–2 g/hr by constant IV infusion. Continue until paroxysms stop. To control seizures, optimal serum magnesium level is 6 mg/100 mL; max, 30–40 g/24 hr. **Correction of hypomagnesemia.** *Adult:* 1 g IM or IV q 6 hr for four doses (32.5 mEq/24 hr); up to 246 mg/kg IM within 4 hr or 5 g (40 mEq)/1,000 mL D₅W or normal saline IV infused over 3 hr for severe cases. **Parenteral nutrition.** *Adult:* 8–24 mEq/day IV.
ADJUST DOSE Renal impairment
ADV EFF Dizziness, excessive bowel activity, fainting, magnesium intoxication, perianal irritation, weakness

INTERACTIONS Alcohol, aminoglycosides, amphotericin B, cisplatin, cyclosporine, digoxin, diuretics, NMJ blockers

NC/PT Monitor serum magnesium level during parenteral tx; normal limits, 1.5–3 mEq/L. Fetal harm can occur if used beyond 5 days; use shortest time possible for preterm tx. Save IV use in eclampsia for life-threatening situations. Monitor knee-jerk reflex before repeated parenteral administration. If knee-jerk reflex suppressed, do not give. Use as temporary relief of constipation; stop if diarrhea occurs.

mannitol (Osmitrol)
CLASS Diagnostic agent, osmotic diuretic, urinary irrigant
PREG/CONT B/NA

IND & DOSE Px of oliguria in renal failure. *Adult:* 50–100 g IV as 5%–25% sol. **Tx of oliguria in renal failure.** *Adult:* 50–100 g IV as 15%–25% sol. **To reduce intracranial pressure, cerebral edema.** *Adult:* 1.5–2 g/kg IV as 15%–25% sol over 30–60 min. Reduced pressure should be evident in 15 min. **Reduction of IOP.** *Adult:* 1.5–2 g/kg IV infusion as 25%, 20%, or 15% sol over 30 min. If used preop, give 60–90 min before surgery for max effect. **Adjunct tx to promote diuresis in intoxication.** *Adult:* Max 200 g IV mannitol w/other fluids, electrolytes. **To measure GFR.** *Adult:* Dilute 100 mL of 20% sol w/180 mL sodium chloride injection. Infuse this 280 mL of 7.2% sol IV at 20 mL/min. Collect urine w/catheter for specified time to measure mannitol excreted in mg/min. Draw blood at start and end of time for mannitol measurement in mg/mL plasma. **Test dose of mannitol in pts w/inadequate renal function.** *Adult:* 0.2 g/kg IV (about 50 mL of 25% sol, 75 mL of 20% sol) in 3–5 min to produce urine flow of 30–50 mL/hr. If urine flow not increased, repeat dose. If no response to second dose, reevaluate situation.

ADV EFF Anorexia, diuresis, dizziness, dry mouth, n/v, **seizures**, thirst
NC/PT Do not give electrolyte-free mannitol w/blood. If blood must be given, add at least 20 mEq sodium chloride to each liter mannitol sol; use filter. Monitor serum electrolytes periodically. Pt should use sugarless lozenges for dry mouth, take safety precautions for CNS effects.

maprotiline hydrochloride (generic)
CLASS TCA
PREG/CONT B/NA

BBW Increased risk of suicidal thinking, behavior in children, adolescents, young adults; monitor accordingly.
IND & DOSE Tx of mild to moderate depression. *Adult:* 75 mg/day PO in outpts; after 1 wk may increase gradually in 25-mg increments. Usual dose, 150 mg/day. **Tx of severe depression.** *Adult:* 100–150 mg/day PO in inpts; may gradually increase to 225 mg/day. **Maint tx of depression.** *Adult:* Use lowest effective dose, usually 75–150 mg/day PO.
ADJUST DOSE Elderly pts
ADV EFF Confusion, constipation, disturbed conc, dry mouth, gynecomastia, **MI**, orthostatic hypotension, peripheral neuropathy, photosensitivity, rash, restlessness, sedation, **stroke**, urine retention
INTERACTIONS Alcohol, anticholinergics, phenothiazines, sympathomimetics, thyroid medication
NC/PT Limit access to depressed/potentially suicidal pts. Expect clinical response in 3 wk. Give at bedtime if orthostatic hypotension occurs. Not for use in pregnancy (barrier contraceptives advised). Pt should avoid alcohol, sun exposure; report numbness/tingling, chest pain, thoughts of suicide.

maraviroc (Selzentry)
CLASS Antiviral, CCR5 coreceptor antagonist
PREG/CONT B/NA

BBW Risk of severe hepatotoxicity, possibly preceded by systemic allergic reaction (rash, eosinophilia, elevated IgE level). Immediately evaluate, support pt w/s&sx of hepatitis, allergic reaction.
IND & DOSE Combination antiretroviral tx of pts infected only w/ detectable CCR5-tropic HIV-1. *Adult, child over 16 yr:* W/strong CYP3A inhibitors, protease inhibitors (except tipranavir/ritonavir), delavirdine, 150 mg PO bid. W/tipranavir/ritonavir, nevirapine, enfuvirtide, nucleoside reverse transcriptase inhibitors, other drugs that are not strong CYP3A inhibitors, 300 mg PO bid. W/efavirenz, rifampin, carbamazepine, phenobarbital, phenytoin, 600 mg PO bid.
ADJUST DOSE Renal impairment
ADV EFF Abd pain, cough, CV events, dizziness, fever, headache, hepatotoxicity, musculoskeletal sx, rash to potentially fatal Stevens-Johnson syndrome
INTERACTIONS CYP3A inducers/inhibitors, St. John's wort
NC/PT Give w/other antiretrovirals. Monitor LFTs, CD4. Use caution in pregnancy; not for use in breast-feeding. Pt should swallow tablet whole and not cut, crush, or chew it; take precautions to prevent spread (drug not a cure); avoid St. John's wort; take safety precautions for CNS effects; report chest pain, rash, urine/stool color changes.

mecasermin (Increlex)
CLASS Insulin-like growth factor-1
PREG/CONT C/NA

IND & DOSE Long-term tx of growth failure in child w/severe primary insulin growth factor-1 deficiency or w/growth hormone gene deletion who has developed neutralizing antibodies to growth hormone. *Child 2 yr and over:* Initially, 0.04–0.08 mg/kg (40–80 mcg/kg) bid by subcut injection shortly before meal or snack; may be increased by 0.04 mg/kg/dose to max of 0.12 mg/kg bid.
ADV EFF Hypersensitivity reactions, hypoglycemia, intracranial hypertension, progression of scoliosis, slipped capital femoral epiphysis, tonsillar hypertrophy
NC/PT Not a substitute for growth hormone. Monitor blood glucose, tonsils. Ensure given just before meal or snack. Pt should avoid pregnancy/breast-feeding; learn proper administration/disposal of needles/syringes; report difficulty breathing/swallowing, sudden limb or hip/knee pain, injection-site pain, rash.

DANGEROUS DRUG

mechlorethamine hydrochloride (Mustargen, Valchlor)
CLASS Alkylating agent, antineoplastic, nitrogen mustard
PREG/CONT D/NA

BBW Handle drug w/caution; use chemo-safe nonpermeable gloves. Drug highly toxic and a vesicant. Avoid inhaling dust, vapors; avoid contact w/skin, mucous membranes (especially eyes). If eye contact, immediately irrigate w/copious amount of ophthalmic irrigating sol, get ophthalmologic consultation. If skin contact, irrigate w/copious amount of water for 15 min, then apply 2% sodium thiosulfate. Monitor injection site for extravasation. Painful inflammation/induration, skin sloughing possible. If leakage, promptly infiltrate w/sterile isotonic sodium thiosulfate (1/6M), apply ice compress for 6–12 hr. Notify physician.
IND & DOSE Palliative tx of bronchogenic carcinoma, Hodgkin

disease, **lymphosarcoma, CML, chronic lymphocytic leukemia, mycosis fungoides, polycythemia vera.** *Adult:* Total 0.4 mg/kg IV for each course as single dose or in two to four divided doses of 0.1–0.2 mg/kg/day. Give at night if sedation needed for side effects. Interval between courses usually 3–6 wk. **Palliative tx of effusion secondary to metastatic carcinoma.** *Adult:* Dose, preparation for intracavity use vary greatly; usual dose, 0.2–0.4 mg/kg. **Tx of stage 1A, 1B mycosis fungoides–type T-cell lymphoma after direct skin tx.** *Adult:* Apply thin film to affected areas of skin; avoid eyes and mucous membranes.
ADV EFF Anorexia, **bone marrow suppression,** dizziness, drowsiness, impaired fertility, n/v/d, thrombophlebitis, weakness
INTERACTIONS Adalimumab, denosumab, infliximab, leflunomide, natalizumab, pimecrolimus, roflumilast
NC/PT Avoid skin contact w/powder for injection. Premedicate w/antiemetics, sedatives. Monitor CBC closely, injection site for extravasation. Maintain hydration. Not for use in pregnancy (contraceptives advised). Pt should take safety precautions for CNS changes; avoid smoking, open flames when using topical gel until gel dries (very flammable); dispose of tube appropriately; report burning at IV site, fever.

meclizine hydrochloride
(Bonine, Dramamine)
CLASS Anticholinergic, antiemetic, antihistamine, anti–motion sickness
PREG/CONT B/NA

IND & DOSE Px, tx of motion sickness. *Adult, child over 12 yr:* 25–50 mg/day PO 1 hr before travel. **Tx of vertigo.** *Adult, child over 12 yr:* 25–100 mg/day PO.
ADJUST DOSE Elderly pts

ADV EFF Anorexia, confusion, drowsiness, dry mouth, nausea, **respiratory depression to death,** urinary difficulty/frequency
INTERACTIONS Alcohol, CNS depressants
NC/PT For anti–motion sickness, works best if used before motion. Pt should avoid alcohol, take safety precautions for CNS depression, use sugarless lozenges for dry mouth, report difficulty breathing.

DANGEROUS DRUG

medroxyPROGESTERone acetate (Depo-Provera, depo-subQ provera 104, Provera)
CLASS Antineoplastic, contraceptive, hormone, progestin
PREG/CONT X/NA

BBW Before tx, rule out pregnancy; caution pt to avoid pregnancy and have frequent medical follow-up. Alert pt using contraceptive injections that drug does not protect from HIV, other STDs, and to take precautions. *Depo-Provera* use may result in significant bone density loss; drug should not be used for longer than 2 yr unless no other contraception form is adequate.
IND & DOSE Contraception. *Adult:* 150 mg IM q 3 mo. For *depo-subQ provera:* 104 mg subcut into thigh or abdomen q 12–14 wk. **Tx of secondary amenorrhea.** *Adult:* 5–10 mg/day PO for 5–10 days. **Tx of abnormal uterine bleeding.** *Adult:* 5–10 mg/day PO for 5–10 days, starting on 16th or 21st day of menstrual cycle. **Tx of endometrial, renal carcinoma.** *Adult:* 400–1,000 mg/wk IM. **To reduce endometrial hyperplasia.** *Adult:* 5–10 mg/day PO for 12–14 consecutive days/mo. Start on 1st or 16th day of cycle. **Mgt of endometriosis-associated pain.** *Adult:* 104 mg subcut *(depo-subQ Provera)* into anterior thigh or abdomen q 12–14 wk for no longer than 2 yr.

ADV EFF Amenorrhea, anaphylaxis, bone loss, breakthrough bleeding, **breast cancer, ectopic pregnancy,** edema, fluid retention, hepatic impairment, menstrual flow changes, rash, **thromboembolic events,** vision changes, weight changes
INTERACTIONS CYP3A4 inducers, HIV protease and nonnucleoside reverse transcriptase inhibitors, St. John's wort
NC/PT Arrange for pretreatment, periodic (at least annual) complete hx, physical. Monitor bone density. Not for use in pregnancy. Pt should know drug does not protect against STDs, HIV; protection is still required. Use second form of contraception with antibiotics, CYP3A4 inducers. Pt should mark calendar for tx days, report sudden vision loss, swelling, severe headache, chest pain, urine/stool color changes, severe abd pain.

mefenamic acid
(Ponstel)
CLASS NSAID
PREG/CONT C/NA

BBW Increased risk of CV events, GI bleeding; monitor accordingly. Do not use for periop pain in CABG surgery.
IND & DOSE Tx of acute pain.
Adult, child over 14 yr: 500 mg PO, then 250 mg q hr as needed for up to 1 wk. **Tx of primary dysmenorrhea.** *Adult, child over 14 yr:* 500 mg PO, then 250 mg q 6 hr q 6 hr w/bleeding onset. Can initiate at start of menses, then for 2–3 days.
ADJUST DOSE Elderly pts, renal impairment (not recommended)
ADV EFF Anaphylactoid reactions to anaphylactic shock, bone marrow suppression, constipation, diarrhea, dizziness, dyspepsia, edema, GI pain, headache, hypertension, nausea, rash, **renal impairment**
INTERACTIONS ASA, anticoagulants, methotrexate, NSAIDs
NC/PT Pt should take w/food, use safety precautions for CNS effects,

stop drug and report rash, diarrhea, black tarry stools, difficulty breathing, edema.

DANGEROUS DRUG
(AS ANTINEOPLASTIC)

megestrol acetate
(Megace)
CLASS Antineoplastic, hormone, progestin
PREG/CONT X (suspension); D (tablets)/NA

BBW Caution pt not to use if pregnant; fetal risks. Advise barrier contraceptives. Risk of thromboembolic events, stop drug at sx of thrombosis.
IND & DOSE Palliative tx of breast cancer. *Adult:* 160 mg/day PO (40 mg qid). **Palliative tx of endometrial cancer.** *Adult:* 40–320 mg/day PO. **Tx of cachexia w/HIV.** *Adult:* 800 mg/day PO; range, 400–800 mg/day (suspension only) or 625 mg/day PO (ES suspension).
ADV EFF Amenorrhea, breakthrough bleeding, dizziness, edema, fluid retention, menstrual flow changes, photosensitivity, rash, somnolence, **thromboembolic events,** vision changes, weight changes
NC/PT Stop if thromboembolic events. Store suspension in cool place; shake well before use. Not for use in pregnancy (barrier contraceptives advised). Pt should avoid sun exposure; take safety precautions for CNS effects; report chest/leg pain, swelling, numbness/tingling, severe headache.

meloxicam
(Mobic, Vivlodex)
CLASS NSAID
PREG/CONT C (1st, 2nd trimesters); D (3rd trimester)/NA

BBW Increased risk of CV events, GI bleeding; monitor accordingly. Do not use for periop pain in CABG surgery.

IND & DOSE Relief of s&sx of osteoarthritis, rheumatoid arthritis. *Adult:* 7.5 mg/day PO. Max, 15 mg/day. **Management of osteoarthritis pain.** *Adult:* 5 mg/day PO; max, 10 mg/day (*Vivlodex*). **Relief of s&sx of pauciarticular/polyarticular course juvenile rheumatoid arthritis.** *Child 2 yr and older:* 0.125 mg/kg/day PO; max, 7.5 mg (oral suspension).
ADV EFF Anaphylactic shock, bone marrow suppression, diarrhea, dizziness, dyspepsia, edema, GI pain, headache, hepatic impairment, hypertension, insomnia, nausea, rash, renal injury, serious skin events including Stevens-Johnson syndrome
INTERACTIONS ACE inhibitors, aspirin, anticoagulants, diuretics, lithium, methotrexate, oral corticosteroids, other NSAIDs, warfarin
NC/PT *Vivlodex* is not interchangeable w/other formulations. Pt should take w/food, use safety precautions for CNS effects, report difficulty breathing, swelling, black tarry stools, rash.

DANGEROUS DRUG

melphalan (Alkeran)
CLASS Alkylating agent, antineoplastic, nitrogen mustard
PREG/CONT D/NA

BBW Arrange for blood tests to evaluate hematopoietic function before and wkly during tx; severe bone marrow suppression possible. Caution pt to avoid pregnancy during tx; drug considered mutagenic.
IND & DOSE Tx of multiple myeloma. *Adult:* 6 mg/day PO. After 2–3 wk, stop for up to 4 wk, monitor blood counts. When counts rising, start maint of 2 mg/day PO. Or, 16 mg/m² as single IV infusion over 15–20 min at 2-wk intervals for four doses, then at 4-wk intervals. **Tx of epithelial ovarian carcinoma.** *Adult:* 0.2 mg/kg/day PO for 5 days as single course. Repeat courses q 4–5 wk.
ADJUST DOSE Renal impairment

ADV EFF Alopecia, amenorrhea, anaphylaxis, bone marrow suppression, cancer, n/v, pulmonary fibrosis, rash
NC/PT Refrigerate tablets in glass bottle. Monitor CBC regularly; dose adjustment may be needed. Maintain hydration. Give antiemetics for severe nausea. Not for use in pregnancy (barrier contraceptives advised). Pt should cover head at temp extremes (hair loss possible), avoid exposure to infection, report bleeding, signs of infection, difficulty breathing.

---

memantine hydrochloride (Namenda)
CLASS Alzheimer drug; *N*-methyl-*D*-aspartate receptor antagonist
PREG/CONT B/NA

IND & DOSE Tx of moderate to severe Alzheimer-type dementia. *Adult:* 5 mg/day PO. Increase at wkly intervals to 5 mg/day PO (10 mg/day), 15 mg/day PO (5-mg and 10-mg doses) w/at least 1 wk between increases. Target, 20 mg/day (10 mg bid). ER form: 7 mg/day PO; may increase by 7 mg/day after at least 1 wk. Maint, 28 mg/day.
ADJUST DOSE Renal impairment
ADV EFF Confusion, constipation, cough, dizziness, fatigue, headache
INTERACTIONS Amantadine, carbonic anhydrase inhibitors, dextromethorphan, ketamine, sodium bicarbonate, urine alkalinizers
NC/PT Obtain baseline functional profile. Not a cure; medical follow-up needed. Pt should swallow ER tablet whole and not cut, crush, or chew it; take safety precaution for CNS effects; report lack of improvement, swelling, respiratory problems.

menotropins (Menopur, Repronex)

CLASS Fertility drug, hormone
PREG/CONT X/NA

IND & DOSE To induce ovulation in anovulatory women w/HCG. *Adult:* 225 units IM; then 75–150 units/day subcut to max 450 units/day for no longer than 12 days (*Repronex*) or 20 days (*Menopur*). Or, pts who have received GnRH agonists or pituitary suppression: 150 international units/day subcut or IM (*Repronex*) for first 5 days; max, 450 international units/day. Use no longer than 12 days.
ADV EFF Congenital malformations, dizziness, ectopic pregnancy, febrile reactions, multiple births, ovarian enlargement, ovarian neoplasms, **ovarian overstimulation, ovarian torsion, thromboembolic events**
NC/PT Must follow w/HCG when clinical evidence shows sufficient follicular maturation based on urine excretion of estrogens. Dissolve contents of 1–6 vials in 1–2 mL sterile saline; give immediately. Monitor for ovarian overstimulation; admit pt to hosp for tx. Risk of multiple births. Teach proper administration/disposal of needles/syringes. Pt should mark calendar of tx days; report severe abd pain, fever, chest pain.

---

meperidine hydrochloride (Demerol)

CLASS Opioid agonist analgesic
PREG/CONT B; D (long-term use)/C-II

IND & DOSE Relief of moderate to severe acute pain. *Adult:* 50–150 mg IM, subcut, or PO q 3–4 hr as needed. May give diluted sol by slow IV injection. IM route preferred for repeated injections. *Child:* 1.1–1.75 mg/kg IM, subcut, or PO up to adult dose q 3–4 hr as needed. **Preop medication.** *Adult:* 50–100 mg IM or subcut 30–90 min

before anesthesia. *Child:* 1.1–2.2 mg/kg IM or subcut, up to adult dose, 30–90 min before anesthesia. **Anesthesia support.** *Adult:* Dilute to 10 mg/mL; give repeated doses by slow IV injection. Or, dilute to 1 mg/mL; infuse continuously. **Obstetric analgesia.** *Adult:* When contractions regular, 50–100 mg IM or subcut; repeat q 1–3 hr.
ADJUST DOSE Elderly, debilitated pts; hepatic, renal impairment
ADV EFF Apnea, cardiac arrest, **circulatory depression**, constipation, dizziness, light-headedness, n/v, **respiratory arrest/depression, shock**, sweating
INTERACTIONS Alcohol, barbiturate anesthetics, CNS depressants, MAOIs, phenothiazines. Incompatible w/sols of barbiturates, aminophylline, heparin, iodide, morphine sulfate, methicillin, phenytoin, sodium bicarbonate, sulfadiazine, sulfisoxazole
NC/PT Contraindicated in preterm infants. May give diluted sol by slow IV injection. IM route preferred for repeated injections. Have opioid antagonist, facilities for assisted or controlled respiration on hand during parenteral administration. Pt should take safety precautions for CNS effects; use laxative if constipated; take drug 4–6 hr before next feeding if breast-feeding; report difficulty breathing, chest pain.

---

mepolizumab (Nucala)

CLASS Antiasthmatic, interleukin antagonist monoclonal antibody
PREG/CONT Unkn/NA

IND & DOSE Adjunct maint tx of pts 12 yr and older w/severe asthma w/ eosinophilic phenotype. *Adult, child 12 yr and older:* 100 mg subcut once q 4 wk.
ADV EFF Back pain, fatigue, headache, **hypersensitivity reaction**, injection-site reaction, opportunistic infections

NC/PT Not for use in acute broncho-spasm, status asthmaticus. Discontinue systemic/inhaled corticosteroids gradually w/initiation of therapy. Monitor for opportunistic infections, herpes zoster, helminth infections. Pt should learn proper administration of subcut injections, proper disposal of needles/syringes; rotate injection sites. Pt should enroll in Pregnancy Registry (risks unkn); continue other therapies for asthma as indicated; report difficulty breathing, swelling, rash, signs of infection.

meprobamate (generic)
CLASS Anxiolytic
PREG/CONT D/C-IV

IND & DOSE Mgt of anxiety disorders. *Adult:* 1,200–1,600 mg/day PO in three or four divided doses. Max, 2,400 mg/day. *Child 6–12 yr:* 100–200 mg PO bid–tid.
ADJUST DOSE Elderly pts
ADV EFF Ataxia, **bone marrow suppression,** dependence w/withdrawal reactions, dizziness, drowsiness, headache, impaired vision, **hypotensive crisis,** n/v/d, rash, **suicidality,** vertigo
INTERACTIONS Alcohol, CNS depressants, barbiturates, opioids
NC/PT Dispense least amount possible to depressed/addiction-prone pts. Withdraw gradually over 2 wk after long-term use. Not for use in pregnancy (barrier contraceptives advised). Pt should avoid alcohol, take safety precautions for CNS effects, report thoughts of suicide.

DANGEROUS DRUG
mercaptopurine (Purixan)
CLASS Antimetabolite, antineoplastic
PREG/CONT D/NA

BBW Reserve for pts w/established dx of acute lymphatic leukemia; serious adverse effects possible.

IND & DOSE Tx of acute leukemia (lymphocytic, lymphoblastic) as part of combination therapy. *Adult, child:* Induction, 1.5–2.5 mg/kg/day PO (50–75 mg/m²).
ADJUST DOSE Renal impairment
ADV EFF Bone marrow depression, **hepatosplenic T-cell lymphoma, hepatotoxicity,** hyperuricemia, immunosuppression, n/v, stomatitis
INTERACTIONS Allopurinol, TNF blockers, warfarin
NC/PT Monitor CBC, LFTs regularly; dose adjustment may be needed. Oral suspension available. Not for use in pregnancy (barrier contraceptives advised)/breast-feeding. Maintain hydration. Pt should get regular checkups, report night sweats, fever, abd pain, weight loss.

meropenem (Merrem IV)
CLASS Carbapenem antibiotic
PREG/CONT B/NA

IND & DOSE Tx of meningitis, intra-abd infections caused by susceptible strains. *Adult:* 1 g IV q 8 hr. *Child 3 mo and older:* For meningitis: Over 50 kg, 2 g IV q 8 hr; under 50 kg, 40 mg/kg IV q 8 hr. For intra-abd infections: Over 50 kg, 1 g IV q 8 hr; under 50 kg, 20 mg/kg IV q 8 hr. *Child over 32 wk:* 20 mg/kg IV q 8 hr if gestational age (GA) and postnatal age (PNA) under 2 wk; 30 mg/kg IV q 8 hr if GA and PNA over 2 wk. *Child under 33 wk:* 20 mg/kg IV q 12 hr if GA and PNA less than 2 wk; q 8 hr if GA and PNA 2 wk and over. Tx of skin-structure infections caused by susceptible strains. *Adult:* 500 mg IV q 8 hr. *Child 3 mo and older:* Over 50 kg, 500 mg IV q 8 hr; under 50 kg, 10 mg/kg IV q 8 hr.
ADJUST DOSE Renal impairment
ADV EFF Abd pain, anorexia, CDAD, flatulence, headache, **hypersensitivity reactions,** n/v/d, phlebitis, **pseudomembranous colitis,** rash, superinfections

INTERACTIONS Probenecid, valproic acid
NC/PT Culture before tx. Do not mix in sol w/other drugs. Stop if s&sx of colitis. Pt should report severe or bloody diarrhea, pain at injection site, difficulty breathing.

mesalamine (Apriso, Asacol, Lialda, Pentasa, Rowasa)
CLASS Anti-inflammatory
PREG/CONT B/NA

IND & DOSE Tx of active mild to moderate ulcerative colitis. *Adult:* 2–4 1.2-g tablets PO once daily w/ food for total 2.4–4.8 g (*Lialda*). Or, 1.5 g/day PO (4 capsules) in a.m. for up to 6 mo (*Apriso*). Or, 1 g PO qid for total daily dose of 4 g for up to 8 wk (*Pentasa*). Or, 1.6 g/day PO in divided doses (*Asacol*). Or, 800 mg PO tid for 6 wk (*Asacol HD*). *Child 5 yr and older:* 54–90 kg: 27–44 mg/kg/day; max, 2.4 g/day (*Asacol*). 33–under 54 kg: 37–61 mg/kg/day; max, 2 g/day. *17–under 33 kg:* 36–71 mg/kg/day PO; max, 1.2 g/day. **Maint of remission of mild to moderate ulcerative colitis.** *Adult:* 1.6 g/day PO in two to four divided doses. **Tx of active, distal, mild to moderate ulcerative colitis/proctitis, proctosigmoiditis.** *Adult:* 60-mL units in 1 rectal instillation (4 g) once/day, preferably at bedtime, retained for approximately 8 hr for 3–6 wk. Effects may occur within 3–21 days. Usual course, 3–6 wk.
ADJUST DOSE Renal impairment
ADV EFF Abd pain, cramps, fatigue, fever, flatulence, flulike sx, gas, headache, hypersensitivity reactions, **liver failure**, malaise, renal impairment
INTERACTIONS Azathioprine, 6-mercaptopurine, nephrotoxic drugs, NSAIDs
NC/PT Products vary; use caution to differentiate doses. Monitor CBC, renal/hepatic function. Teach proper retention enema administration. Pt should swallow tablet whole and not

cut, crush, or chew it; report severe abd pain, difficulty breathing. Name confusion w/mesalamine, methenamine, memantine; use caution.

mesna (Mesnex)
CLASS Cytoprotective
PREG/CONT B/NA

IND & DOSE Px to reduce incidence of ifosfamide-induced hemorrhagic cystitis. *Adult:* 20% ifosfamide dose IV at time of ifosfamide infusion and at 4 and 8 hr after; timing must be exact.
ADV EFF Abd pain, alopecia, **anaphylaxis**, anemia, anorexia, constipation, fatigue, fever, n/v, **rash to Stevens-Johnson syndrome**, thrombocytopenia
NC/PT Not indicated to reduce risk of hematuria due to pathologic conditions. Contains benzyl alcohol; contraindicated in neonates, premature and low-birth-weight infants. Helps prevent chemotherapy complications; timing critical to balance chemotherapy effects. May give antiemetics. Monitor skin; stop if rash occurs. Pt should report severe abd pain, difficulty breathing, rash.

metaproterenol sulfate (generic)
CLASS Antiasthmatic, beta$_2$-selective agonist, bronchodilator
PREG/CONT C/NA

IND & DOSE Px, tx of bronchial asthma, reversible bronchospasm. *Adult, child 12 yr and older:* 20 mg PO tid to qid. Or 2 to 3 inhalations; max, 12 inhalations/day. *Child over 9–under 12 yr, over 27 kg:* 20 mg PO tid to qid. *Child 6–9 yr, under 27 kg:* 10 mg PO tid to qid.
ADJUST DOSE Elderly pts
ADV EFF Anxiety, apprehension, CNS stimulation, fear, flushing, heartburn, n/v, pallor, sweating, tachycardia

NC/PT Switch to syrup if swallowing difficult. Protect tablets from moisture. Do not exceed recommended dose. Allow 3–4 hr between inhalations; review use of inhaler. Pt should take safety precautions for CNS effects, report chest pain, difficulty breathing.

---

metaxalone (Skelaxin)
CLASS Skeletal muscle relaxant (centrally acting)
PREG/CONT C/NA

IND & DOSE Adjunct for relief of discomfort associated w/acute, painful musculoskeletal disorders. *Adult, child 12 yr and older:* 800 mg PO tid to qid.
ADV EFF Dizziness, drowsiness, hemolytic anemia, leukopenia, light-headedness, nausea
INTERACTIONS Alcohol, CNS depressants
NC/PT Arrange for other tx for muscle spasm relief. Pt should take safety precautions for CNS effects, avoid alcohol, report rash, yellowing of skin/eyes.

DANGEROUS DRUG

metformin hydrochloride (Fortamet, Glucophage, Glumetza, Riomet)
CLASS Antidiabetic
PREG/CONT B/NA

BBW Risk of severe lactic acidosis. Monitor pt; treat if suspicion of lactic acidosis.
IND & DOSE Adjunct to diet to lower blood glucose in type 2 diabetes, alone or w/sulfonylurea. *Adult:* 500 mg PO bid or 850 mg PO once daily; max, 2,550 mg/day in divided doses. ER tablet: 1,000 mg/day PO w/evening meal; max, 2,000 mg/day (2,500 mg *Fortamet*). *Child 10–16 yr:* 500 mg bid w/meals. Max, 2,000 mg/day in divided doses. ER form not recommended for child.

ADJUST DOSE Elderly pts, renal impairment
ADV EFF Allergic skin reactions, anorexia, gastric discomfort, heartburn, hypoglycemia, **lactic acidosis,** n/v/d, vitamin B_{12} deficiency
INTERACTIONS Alcohol, amiloride, celery, cimetidine, coriander, dandelion root, digoxin, fenugreek, furosemide, garlic, ginseng, iodinated contrast media, juniper berries, nifedipine, sulfonylureas, vancomycin
NC/PT Monitor serum glucose frequently to determine drug effectiveness, dose. Arrange for transfer to insulin during high-stress periods. Not for use in pregnancy. Pt should swallow ER tablet whole and not cut, crush, or chew it; take at night if GI problems; avoid alcohol; continue diet/exercise program; report all herbs used (so dose adjustment can be made), hypoglycemic episodes, urine/stool color changes, difficulty breathing.

DANGEROUS DRUG

methadone hydrochloride (Dolophine, Methadose)
CLASS Opioid agonist analgesic
PREG/CONT C/C-II

BBW Use for opioid addiction should be part of approved program; deaths have occurred during start of tx for opioid dependence. Carefully determine all drugs pt taking; respiratory depression and death have occurred. Have emergency services on standby. Monitor for prolonged QT, especially at higher doses. Neonatal withdrawal syndrome if used in pregnancy.
IND & DOSE Relief of severe pain, requiring around-the-clock tx, unresponsive to nonopioid analgesics. *Adult:* 2.5–10 mg IM, subcut, or PO q 8–12 hr as needed. Detoxification, temporary maint tx of opioid addiction. *Adult:* 20–30 mg PO or parenteral; PO preferred. Increase to suppress withdrawal s&sx; 40 mg/day in single or divided doses is usual stabilizing

dose. Continue stabilizing doses for 2–3 days, then gradually decrease q 1 or 2 days. Provide sufficient amount to keep withdrawal sx tolerable. Max, 21 days' tx; do not repeat earlier than 4 wk after completion of previous course. For maint tx: For heavy heroin users up until hospital admission, initially 20 mg PO 4–8 hr after heroin stopped or 40 mg PO in single dose; may give additional 10-mg doses if needed to suppress withdrawal syndrome. Adjust dose to max 120 mg/day PO.

ADJUST DOSE Elderly pts, impaired adults

ADV EFF Apnea, cardiac arrest, circulatory depression, constipation, dizziness, light-headedness, hypotension, n/v, prolonged QT, respiratory arrest, respiratory depression, shock, sweating

INTERACTIONS Barbiturate anesthetics, CNS depressants, CYP3A4 inducers/inhibitors, HIV antiretrovirals, hydantoins, protease inhibitors, QT-prolonging drugs, rifampin, urine acidifiers

NC/PT Have opioid antagonist, equipment for assisted or controlled respiration on hand during parenteral administration. Do not stop suddenly in physically dependent pt. Not for use in pregnancy (barrier contraceptives advised). Not for use w/impaired consciousness or coma w/head injury. Pt should take drug 4–6 hr before next feeding if breast-feeding, avoid alcohol, take safety precautions for CNS effects, report difficulty breathing, severe n/v.

---

methazolamide (generic)
CLASS Carbonic anhydrase inhibitor, glaucoma drug
PREG/CONT C/NA

IND & DOSE Tx of ocular conditions where lowering IOP is beneficial. *Adult:* 50–100 mg PO bid-tid.

ADJUST DOSE Hepatic, renal impairment

ADV EFF Anorexia, bone marrow suppression, dizziness, drowsiness, fatigue, GI disturbances, kidney stones, photosensitivity, Stevens-Johnson syndrome, taste alteration, tingling, tinnitus

INTERACTIONS Aspirin, corticosteroids

NC/PT Monitor IOP regularly. Pt should take safety precautions for CNS effects; avoid exposure sun, infection; report fever, rash.

---

methenamine (generic), methenamine hippurate (Hiprex, Urex)
CLASS Antibacterial, urinary tract anti-infective
PREG/CONT C/NA

IND & DOSE To suppress, eliminate bacteriuria associated w/UTIs. *Adult:* 1 g methenamine PO qid after meals and at bedtime, or 1 g hippurate PO bid. *Child 6–12 yr:* 500 mg methenamine PO qid, or 0.5–1 g hippurate PO bid. *Child under 6 yr:* 50 mg/kg/day PO methenamine divided into three doses.

ADV EFF Bladder irritation, dysuria, hepatotoxicity (hippurate), nausea, rash

NC/PT Culture before tx. Maintain hydration. Monitor LFTs w/hippurate form. Use additional measures for UTIs. Pt should take w/food, report rash, urine/stool color changes. Name confusion between methimazole and mesalamine; use caution.

---

methimazole (Tapazole)
CLASS Antithyroid drug
PREG/CONT D/NA

IND & DOSE Tx of hyperthyroidism; palliation in certain thyroid cancers. *Adult:* 15–60 mg/day PO in three equal doses q 8 hr. Maint, 5–15 mg/day PO. *Child:* 0.4 mg/kg/day PO, then maint of approximately ½ initial dose. Or, initially, 0.5–0.7 mg/kg/day or

15–20 mg/m²/day PO in three divided doses, then maint of ⅓–⅔ initial dose, starting when pt becomes euthyroid. Max, 30 mg/24 hr.

ADV EFF Bone marrow suppression, dizziness, neuritis, paresthesia, rash, vertigo, weakness

INTERACTIONS Cardiac glycosides, metoprolol, oral anticoagulants, propranolol, theophylline

NC/PT Monitor CBC, thyroid function. Tx will be long-term. Not for use in pregnancy (barrier contraceptives advised)/breast-feeding. Pt should take safety precautions for CNS effects, report unusual bleeding/bruising, signs of infection.

---

methocarbamol
(Robaxin)

CLASS Skeletal muscle relaxant
PREG/CONT C/NA

IND & DOSE Relief of discomfort associated w/acute, painful musculoskeletal conditions. *Adult:* 1.5 g PO qid. For first 48–72 hr, 6 g/day or up to 8 g/day recommended. Maint, 1 g PO qid, or 750 mg q 4 hr, or 1.5 g tid for total 4–4.5 g/day. Or, 1 g IM or IV; may need 2–3 g in severe cases. Do not use 3 g/day for more than 3 days. **Control of neuromuscular manifestations of tetanus.** *Adult:* Up to 24 g/day IV or 1 g IM or IV; may need 2–3 g for no longer than 3 days. *Child:* 15 mg/kg IV repeated q 6 hr as needed.

ADV EFF Bradycardia, discolored urine, dizziness, drowsiness, headache, nausea, urticaria

NC/PT Have pt remain recumbent during and for at least 15 min after IV injection. For IM, do not inject more than 5 mL into each gluteal region; repeat at 8-hr intervals. Switch from parenteral to oral route as soon as possible. Not for use in pregnancy. Urine may darken to green, brown, black on standing. Pt should take safety precautions for CNS effects, avoid alcohol.

---

methotrexate (Otrexup, Rasuvo, Rheumatrex, Trexall)

CLASS Antimetabolite, antineoplastic, antipsoriatic, antirheumatic
PREG/CONT X/NA

BBW Arrange for CBC, urinalysis, LFTs/renal function tests, chest X-ray before, during, and for several wk after tx; severe toxicity possible. Rule out pregnancy before starting tx; counsel pt on severe risks of fetal abnormalities. Reserve use for life-threatening neoplastic diseases, severe psoriasis/rheumatoid arthritis unresponsive to other tx. Monitor LFTs carefully w/long-term use; serious hepatotoxicity possible. High risk of serious opportunistic infections, interstitial pneumonitis, serious to fatal skin reactions, intestinal perforation; monitor closely during tx. Use cautiously w/malignant lymphomas, rapidly growing tumors; worsening of malignancy possible.

IND & DOSE Tx of choriocarcinoma, other trophoblastic diseases. *Adult:* 15–30 mg PO or IM daily for 5-day course. Repeat course three to five times w/rest periods of 1 wk or longer between courses until toxic sx subside. **Tx of leukemia.** *Adult:* Induction: 3.3 mg/m² methotrexate PO or IM w/60 mg/m² prednisone daily for 4–6 wk. Maint, 30 mg/m² methotrexate PO or IM twice wkly or 2.5 mg/kg IV q 14 days. **Tx of meningeal leukemia.** *Adult:* Give methotrexate intrathecally as px in lymphocytic leukemia. 12 mg/m² (max, 15 mg) intrathecally at intervals of 2–5 days; repeat until CSF cell count normal, then give one additional dose. *Child:* 3 yr or older, 12 mg intrathecally q 2–5 days. 2–3 yr, 10 mg intrathecally q 2–5 days. 1–2 yr, 8 mg intrathecally q 2–5 days. Under 1 yr, 6 mg intrathecally q 2–5 days. **Tx of lymphomas.** *Adult:* Burkitt tumor (stages I, II), 10–25 mg/day PO for

4–8 days. Stage III, use w/other neoplastic drugs. All usually require several courses of tx w/7- to 10-day rest periods between doses. **Tx of mycosis fungoides.** *Adult:* 2.5–10 mg/day PO for wks or mos, or 50 mg IM once wkly, or 25 mg IM twice wkly. Can also give IV w/combination chemotherapy regimens in advanced disease. **Tx of osteosarcoma.** *Adult:* 12 g/m² or up to 15 g/m² IV to give peak serum conc of 1,000 micromol. Must use as part of cytotoxic regimen w/leucovorin rescue. **Tx of severe psoriasis.** *Adult:* 10–25 mg/wk PO, IM, subcut, or IV as single wkly dose; max, 30 mg/wk. Or, 2.5 mg PO at 12-hr intervals for three doses each wk. **Tx of severe rheumatoid arthritis.** *Adult:* Single doses of 7.5 mg/wk PO or subcut (*Rasuvo*) or divided dose of 2.5 mg PO at 12-hr intervals for three doses as a course once wkly. Max, 20 mg/wk. **Tx of polyarticular course juvenile rheumatoid arthritis.** *Child 2–16 yr:* 10 mg/m² PO wkly; max, 20 mg/m²/wk.
ADV EFF Alopecia, **anaphylaxis**, blurred vision, chills, dizziness, fatigue, fertility alterations, fever, **interstitial pneumonitis**, n/v/d, rash, **renal failure, serious to fatal skin reactions, severe bone marrow depression, sudden death,** ulcerative stomatitis
INTERACTIONS Alcohol, digoxin, NSAIDs (serious to fatal reactions), phenytoin, probenecid, salicylates, sulfonamides, theophylline
NC/PT Monitor CBC, LFTs, renal/pulmonary function regularly. Have leucovorin or levoleucovorin on hand as antidote for methotrexate overdose or when large doses used. Not for use in pregnancy (men, women should use contraceptives during, for 3 mo after tx). Give antiemetic for n/v. Autoinjector for adults/juveniles using home injections. Pt should avoid alcohol, NSAIDs; cover head at temp extremes (hair loss possible); perform frequent mouth care; take safety precautions for CNS effects; report urine changes, abd pain, black tarry

stools, unusual bleeding, difficulty breathing, rash, s&sx of infection.

methoxsalen (8-MOP, Oxsoralen, Uvadex)
CLASS Psoralen
PREG/CONT C/NA

BBW Reserve use for severe/disabling disorders unresponsive to traditional tx; risk of eye/skin damage, melanoma. Brand names not interchangeable; use extreme caution.
IND & DOSE Tx of disabling psoriasis; repigmentation of vitiliginous skin; cutaneous T-cell lymphoma. *Adult:* Dose varies by weight. Must time tx w/UV exposure; see manufacturer's details.
ADV EFF Depression, dizziness, headache, itching, leg cramps, **melanoma, ocular/skin damage,** swelling
INTERACTIONS Anthralin, coal tar/coal tar derivatives, fluoroquinolones, griseofulvin, methylene blue, nalidixic acid, phenothiazines, sulfonamides, tetracyclines, thiazides/certain organic staining dyes
NC/PT Do not use w/actinic degeneration; basal cell carcinomas; radiation; arsenic tx; hepatic, cardiac disease. Alert pt to adverse effects, including ocular damage, melanoma. Must time tx w/UV light exposure. Pt must mark calendar for tx days, take safety precautions if dizzy, report vision changes.

methscopolamine bromide (Pamine)
CLASS Anticholinergic, antispasmodic
PREG/CONT C/NA

IND & DOSE Adjunct tx of peptic ulcer. *Adult:* 2.5 mg PO 30 min before meals, 2.5–5 mg PO at bedtime.
ADV EFF Altered taste perception, blurred vision, decreased sweating, dry mouth, dysphagia, n/v, urinary hesitancy, urine retention

INTERACTIONS Anticholinergics, antipsychotics, haloperidol, TCAs
NC/PT Pt should maintain adequate hydration, empty bladder before each dose, avoid hot environments, use sugarless lozenges for dry mouth, take safety precautions w/vision changes, report difficulty swallowing, palpitations.

methsuximide (Celontin)
CLASS Antiepileptic, succinimide
PREG/CONT C/NA

IND & DOSE Control of absence seizures. *Adult:* 300 mg/day PO for first wk; titrate to max 1.2 g/day.
ADV EFF Aggression, ataxia, **blood dyscrasias,** blurred vision, dizziness, drowsiness, headache, nervousness **hepatotoxicity,** n/v/d, **SLE, Stevens-Johnson syndrome, suicidality**
INTERACTIONS Other antiepileptics
NC/PT Monitor CBC, LFTs w/long-term tx. Not for use in pregnancy (barrier contraceptives advised). Pt should take safety precaution for CNS effects, report rash, urine/stool color changes, thoughts of suicide.

methyldopa, methyldopate hydrochloride (generic)
CLASS Antihypertensive, sympatholytic
PREG/CONT B (oral); C (IV)/NA

IND & DOSE Tx of hypertension. *Adult:* 250 mg PO bid–tid in first 48 hr; maint, 500 mg–2 g/day PO in two to four doses. If given w/other antihypertensives, limit initial dose to 500 mg/day in divided doses. *Child:* 10 mg/kg/day PO in two to four doses. Max, 65 mg/kg/day PO or 3 g/day PO, whichever less. **Tx of hypertensive crisis.** *Adult:* 250–500 mg IV q 6 hr as needed; max, 1 g q 6 hr. Switch to oral tx as soon as control attained. *Child:* 20–40 mg/kg/day IV in divided

doses q 6 hr. Max, 65 mg/kg or 3 g/day, whichever less.
ADJUST DOSE Elderly pts, renal impairment
ADV EFF Asthenia, bradycardia, constipation, decreased mental acuity, distention, headache, **hemolytic anemia, hepatotoxicity, HF, myocarditis,** n/v, rash, sedation, weakness
INTERACTIONS General anesthetics, levodopa, lithium, sympathomimetics
NC/PT Give IV slowly over 30–60 min; monitor injection site. Monitor CBC, LFTs periodically. Monitor BP carefully when stopping; hypertension usually returns within 48 hr. Pt should take safety precautions for CNS effects, report urine/stool color changes, rash, unusual tiredness.

methylene blue (generic)
CLASS Antidote, diagnostic agent, urinary tract anti-infective
PREG/CONT C/NA

IND & DOSE Tx of cyanide poisoning, drug-induced methemoglobinemia; GU antiseptic for cystitis, urethritis. *Adult, child:* 65–130 mg PO tid w/full glass of water. Or, 1–2 mg/kg IV or 25–50 mg/m² IV injected over several min. May repeat after 1 hr.
ADV EFF Blue-green stool, confusion, discolored urine, dizziness, n/v
INTERACTIONS SSRIs
NC/PT Give IV slowly over several min; do not give subcut or intrathecally. Contact w/skin will dye skin blue; may remove stain w/hypochlorite sol. Use other measures to decrease UTI incidence. Urine/stool may turn blue-green. Pt should take safety measures for CNS effects, report severe n/v.

methylergonovine maleate (generic)
CLASS Ergot derivative, oxytocic
PREG/CONT C/NA

IND & DOSE Routine mgt after delivery of placenta; tx of postpartum atony, hemorrhage; subinvolution of uterus; uterine stimulation during second stage of labor after delivery of anterior shoulder. *Adult:* 0.2 mg IM or IV slowly over at least 60 sec, after delivery of placenta/anterior shoulder, or during puerperium. May repeat q 2–4 hr, then 0.2 mg PO three or four times/day in puerperium for up to 1 wk.

ADV EFF Dizziness, headache, hypertension, nausea
INTERACTIONS CYP3A4 inhibitors, ergot alkaloids, vasoconstrictors
NC/PT Reserve IV for emergency; monitor BP/bleeding postpartum; use for no longer than 1 wk. Pt should report increased vaginal bleeding, numb/cold extremities.

methylnaltrexone bromide (Relistor)
CLASS Opioid receptor antagonist, laxative
PREG/CONT B/NA

IND & DOSE Tx of opioid-induced constipation in pts in palliative care in whom other laxatives do not work and in pts w/chronic noncancer pain. *Adult:* 62–114 kg, 12 mg subcut q other day; 38–under 62 kg, 8 mg subcut q other day. If weight not in above range, 0.15 mg/kg subcut q other day.

ADJUST DOSE Renal impairment
ADV EFF Abd pain, diarrhea, dizziness, flatulence, **GI perforation**, hyperhidrosis, nausea
NC/PT Teach proper administration/disposal of needles/syringes. Use caution in pregnancy/breast-feeding. Pt should take safety precautions w/ dizziness, report acute abd pain, severe diarrhea.

methylphenidate hydrochloride (Aptensio XR, Concerta, Daytrana, Metadate, Methylin, Quillichew ER, Quillivant XR, Ritalin)
CLASS CNS stimulant
PREG/CONT C/C-II

BBW Potential for abuse; use caution w/emotionally unstable pts, pts w/hx of drug dependence or alcoholism.
IND & DOSE Tx of narcolepsy *(Ritalin, Ritalin SR, Metadate SR, Methylin);* tx of attention-deficit disorders, hyperkinetic syndrome, minimal brain dysfunction in child, adult w/behavioral syndrome. *Adult:* Range, 10–60 mg/day PO. ER: 18 mg/day PO in a.m. May increase by 18 mg/day at 1-wk intervals; max, 54 mg/day *(Concerta).* Aptensio XR: 10 mg/day PO; titrate to max 60 mg/day. Or, 10- to 20-mg/day increments to max 60 mg/day *(Metadate CD, Ritalin LA).* *Child 13–17 yr:* 18 mg/day PO in a.m. Titrate to max 72 mg/day PO; do not exceed 2 mg/kg/day. Or, 10–30 mg/day transdermal patch; apply 2 hr before effect needed, remove after 9 hr. *Child 6–12 yr:* 5 mg PO before breakfast, lunch w/gradual increases of 5–10 mg wkly; max, 60 mg/day. ER: Use adult dose up to max 54 mg/day or 60 mg/day *(Aptensio XR, Qullichew ER, Quillivant XR)* PO. Or, 10–30 mg/day transdermal patch; apply 2 hr before effect needed, remove after 9 hr.
ADV EFF Abd pain, angina, anorexia, cardiac arrhythmias, changes in P/BP, chemical leukoderma, contact sensitization w/transdermal patch, growth changes, insomnia, nausea, nervousness, rash, visual disturbances
INTERACTIONS Alcohol, MAOIs, oral anticoagulants, phenytoin, SSRIs, TCAs
NC/PT Ensure proper dx; rule out underlying cardiac problems. Baseline ECG recommended. Stop tx periodically to evaluate sx. Used as part of overall tx

program. Monitor growth in children. Alert pts that *Quillichew ER* contains phenylalanine; risk in phenylketonurics. Monitor BP frequently when starting tx. Pt should swallow ER tablet whole and not cut, crush, or chew it; take before 6 p.m. to avoid sleep disturbances; apply patch to clean, dry area of hip (remove old patch before applying new one); avoid heating pads on patch; shake bottle vigorously before each use (suspension); keep in secure place; report chest pain, nervousness, insomnia. Controlled substance; secure drug.

methyLPREDNISolone (Medrol),
methyLPREDNISolone acetate (Depo-Medrol),
methyLPREDNISolone sodium succinate (Solu-Medrol)

CLASS Corticosteroid, hormone
PREG/CONT C/NA

IND & DOSE Short-term mgt of inflammatory/allergic disorders, thrombocytopenic purpura, erythroblastopenia, ulcerative colitis, acute exacerbations of MS, trichinosis w/neurologic/cardiac involvement; px of n/v w/chemotherapy. *Adult:* 4–48 mg/day PO. Alternate-day tx: twice usual dose q other a.m. Or, 10–40 mg IV over several min. Or, high-dose tx: 30 mg/kg IV infused over 10–30 min; repeat q 4–6 hr but not longer than 72 hr. *Child:* Minimum dose, 0.5 mg/kg/day PO; base dose on actual response. **Maint tx of rheumatoid arthritis.** *Adult:* 40–120 mg/wk IM. **Adrenogenital syndrome.** *Adult:* 40 mg IM q 2 wk. **Dermatologic lesions.** *Adult:* 40–120 mg/wk IM for 1–4 wk. **Asthma, allergic rhinitis.** *Adult:* 80–120 mg IM. **Intralesional.** *Adult:* 20–60 mg. **Intra-articular.** *Adult:* dose depends on site of injection: 4–10 mg (small joints); 10–40 mg (medium); 20–80 mg (large).

ADV EFF Aggravation of infections, amenorrhea, **anaphylactic reactions,** edema, fluid retention, headache, hyperglycemia, hypotension, immunosuppression, impaired healing, increased appetite, **shock,** vertigo
INTERACTIONS Azole antifungals, edrophonium, erythromycin, live vaccines, neostigmine, phenytoin, pyridostigmine, rifampin, salicylates, troleandomycin
NC/PT Individualize dose based on severity, response. Give daily dose before 9 a.m. to minimize adrenal suppression. For maint, reduce initial dose in small increments at intervals until lowest satisfactory clinical dose reached. If long-term tx needed, consider alternate-day tx w/short-acting corticosteroid. After long-term tx, withdraw slowly to prevent adrenal insufficiency. Monitor serum glucose. Pt should avoid exposure to infections, report signs of infection, black tarry stools.

metoclopramide (Reglan)

CLASS Antiemetic, dopaminergic, GI stimulant
PREG/CONT B/NA

BBW Long-term tx associated w/ permanent tardive dyskinesia; risk increases w/pts over 60 yr, especially women. Use smallest dose possible. Max, 3 mo of tx.
IND & DOSE Relief of sx of gastroparesis. *Adult:* 10 mg PO 30 min before each meal and at bedtime for 2–8 wk; severe, 10 mg IM or IV for up to 10 days until sx subside. **Tx of symptomatic gastroesophageal reflux.** *Adult:* 10–15 mg PO up to four times/day 30 min before meals and at bedtime for max 12 wk. **Px of postop n/v.** *Adult:* 10–20 mg IM at end of surgery. **Px of chemotherapy-induced vomiting.** *Adult:* IV infusion over at least 15 min. First dose 30 min before chemotherapy; repeat q 2 hr for two doses, then q 3 hr for three

doses. For highly emetogenic drugs (cisplatin, dacarbazine), initial two doses, 1–2 mg/kg. If extrapyramidal sx, give 50 mg diphenhydramine IM. **Facilitation of small-bowel intubation, gastric emptying.** *Adult:* 10 mg (2 mL) by direct IV injection over 1–2 min. *Child 6–14 yr:* 2.5–5 mg by direct IV injection over 1–2 min. *Child under 6 yr:* 0.1 mg/kg by direct IV injection over 1–2 min.
ADV EFF Diarrhea, drowsiness, extrapyramidal reactions, fatigue, lassitude, nausea, restlessness
INTERACTIONS Alcohol, CNS depressants, cyclosporine, digoxin, succinylcholine
NC/PT Monitor BP w/IV use. Give diphenhydramine for extrapyramidal reactions. Pt should take safety precautions for CNS effects, avoid alcohol, report involuntary movements, severe diarrhea.

metolazone (Zaroxolyn)
CLASS Thiazide diuretic
PREG/CONT B/NA

BBW Do not interchange *Zaroxolyn* w/other formulations; not therapeutically equivalent.
IND & DOSE Tx of hypertension. *Adult:* 2.5–5 mg/day PO. Tx of edema from systemic disease. *Adult:* 5–20 mg/day PO.
ADV EFF Anorexia, bone marrow depression, dizziness, dry mouth, nocturia, n/v/d, orthostatic hypotension, photophobia, polyuria, vertigo
INTERACTIONS Antidiabetics, cholestyramine, colestipol, diazoxide, dofetilide, lithium
NC/PT Withdraw drug 2–3 days before elective surgery; for emergency surgery, reduce preanesthetic/anesthetic dose. Pt should take early in day to avoid sleep interruption; avoid sun exposure; weigh self daily, report changes of 3 lb or more/day; report unusual bleeding.

DANGEROUS DRUG
metoprolol, metoprolol succinate, metoprolol tartrate (Lopressor)
CLASS Antihypertensive, selective beta blocker
PREG/CONT C/NA

BBW Do not stop abruptly after long-term tx (hypersensitivity to catecholamines possible, causing angina exacerbation, MI, ventricular arrhythmias). Taper gradually over 2 wk w/ monitoring. Pts w/bronchospastic diseases should not, in general, receive beta blockers. Use w/caution only in pts unresponsive to or intolerant of other antihypertensives.
IND & DOSE Tx of hypertension. *Adult:* 100 mg/day PO; maint, 100–450 mg/day. Or, 25–100 mg/day ER tablet PO; max, 400 mg/day. Tx of angina pectoris. *Adult:* 100 mg/day PO in two divided doses; range, 100–400 mg/day. Or, 100 mg/day ER tablet PO. Early tx of MI. *Adult:* 3 IV boluses of 5 mg each at 2-min intervals, then 50 mg PO 15 min after last IV dose and q 6 hr for 48 hr. Then maint of 100 mg PO bid. Late tx of MI. *Adult:* 100 mg PO bid as soon as possible after infarct, continuing for at least 3 mo–3 yr. Tx of HF. *Adult:* 12.5–25 mg/day ER tablet PO for 2 wk; max, 200 mg/day.
ADV EFF ANA development, bronchospasm, cardiac arrhythmias, constipation, decreased exercise tolerance/libido, dizziness, ED, flatulence, gastric pain, HF, laryngospasm, n/v/d, paresthesia
INTERACTIONS Barbiturates, cimetidine, clonidine, epinephrine, hydralazine, lidocaine, methimazole, NSAIDs, prazosin, propylthiouracil, rifampin, verapamil
NC/PT Monitor cardiac function w/ IV use. Pt should swallow ER tablet whole and not cut, crush, or chew it; take safety precautions for CNS effects; report difficulty breathing, swelling.

metreleptin (Myalept)
CLASS Leptin analogue
PREG/CONT C/NA

BBW Risk of development of anti-metreleptin antibodies, w/loss of drug efficacy and worsening metabolic issues, severe infections; test for antibodies in pts w/severe infection or loss of efficacy. Risk of T-cell lymphoma; assess risk in pts w/ hematologic abnormalities and/or acquired generalized lipodystrophy. Available only through restricted access program.

IND & DOSE Adjunct to diet as replacement tx in leptin deficiency in pts w/congenital or acquired lipodystrophy. *Adult, child 40 kg or less:* 0.06 mg/kg/day subcut; max, 0.13 mg/kg. *Males over 40 kg:* 2.5 mg/day subcut; max 10 mg/day. *Females over 40 kg:* 5 mg/day subcut; max 10 mg/day.

ADV EFF Abd pain, autoimmune disorder progression, **benzyl alcohol toxicity**, headache, hypersensitivity reactions, hypoglycemia, **T-cell lymphoma**, weight loss

NC/PT Ensure proper use of drug; only use for approved indication. Monitor for infections; test for antibody development. Dilute w/Bacteriostatic Water for Injection or Sterile Water for Injection; avoid benzyl alcohol when using drug in neonates, infants. Pt should learn proper reconstitution, subcut administration, proper disposal of syringes; avoid pregnancy/breast-feeding; report difficulty breathing, dizziness, fever, sx of infection.

metronidazole (Flagyl, MetroCream, MetroGel)
CLASS Amebicide, antibiotic, antiprotozoal
PREG/CONT B/NA

BBW Avoid use unless needed; possibly carcinogenic.

IND & DOSE Tx of amebiasis. *Adult:* 750 mg PO tid for 5–10 days. *Child:* 35–50 mg/kg/day PO in three divided doses for 10 days. **Tx of antibiotic-associated pseudomembranous colitis.** *Adult:* 1–2 g/day PO in three to four divided doses for 7–10 days. **Tx of gardnerella vaginalis.** *Adult:* 500 mg PO bid for 7 days. **Tx of giardiasis.** *Adult:* 250 mg PO tid for 7 days. **Tx of trichomoniasis.** *Adult:* 2 g PO in 1 day (1-day tx) or 250 mg PO tid for 7 days. **Tx of bacterial vaginosis.** Nonpregnant women, 750 mg/day PO daily for 7 days, or 1 applicator intravaginally one to two times/day for 5 days. Pregnant women, 750 mg/day PO for 7 days; avoid in first trimester. **Tx of anaerobic bacterial infection.** *Adult:* 15 mg/kg IV infused over 1 hr, then 7.5 mg/kg IV infused over 1 hr q 6 hr for 7–10 days; max, 4 g/day. **Preop, intraop, postop px for pts undergoing colorectal surgery.** *Adult:* 15 mg/kg infused IV over 30–60 min, completed about 1 hr before surgery; then 7.5 mg/kg infused over 30–60 min at 6- to 12-hr intervals after initial dose during day of surgery only. **Tx of inflammatory papules, pustules, erythema of rosacea.** *Adult:* 15 mg/kg, rub in thin film bid (a.m. and p.m.) to entire affected areas after washing; for 9 wk.

ADV EFF Anorexia, ataxia, darkened urine, dizziness, dry mouth, headache, injection-site reactions, n/v/d, superinfections, unpleasant metallic taste

INTERACTIONS Alcohol, barbiturates, disulfiram, oral anticoagulants

NC/PT Urine may darken. Pt should take full course; take orally w/food; avoid alcohol or alcohol-containing preparations during and for 24–72 after tx (severe reactions possible); use sugarless lozenges for dry mouth/metallic taste; report severe GI problems, fever.

metyrosine (Demser)
CLASS Enzyme inhibitor.
PREG/CONT C/NA

IND & DOSE Mgt of pheochromocytoma. *Adult, child over 12 yr:* 250–500 mg PO qid. **Preop preparation for pheochromocytoma surgery.** *Adult, child over 12 yr:* 2–3 g/day PO for 5–7 days; max, 4 g/day.
ADV EFF Anxiety, diarrhea, dysuria, extrapyramidal effects, gynecomastia, hypotension, insomnia, sedation
INTERACTIONS Alcohol, CNS depressants, haloperidol, phenothiazines
NC/PT Maintain hydration. Antidiarrheals may be needed. Give supportive care throughout surgery. Monitor for hypotension. Pt should avoid alcohol.

DANGEROUS DRUG

mexiletine hydrochloride (generic)
CLASS Antiarrhythmic
PREG/CONT C/NA

BBW Reserve for life-threatening arrhythmias; possible serious proarrhythmic effects.
IND & DOSE Tx of documented life-threatening ventricular arrhythmias. *Adult:* 200 mg PO q 8 hr. Increase in 50- to 100-mg increments q 2–3 days until desired antiarrhythmic effect. Max, 1,200 mg/day PO. Rapid control, 400 mg loading dose, then 200 mg PO q 8 hr. Transferring from other antiarrhythmics: Lidocaine, stop lidocaine w/first mexiletine dose; leave IV line open until adequate arrhythmia suppression ensured. Quinidine sulfate, initially 200 mg PO 6–12 hr after last quinidine dose. Disopyramide, 200 mg PO 6–12 hr after last disopyramide dose.
ADV EFF Cardiac arrhythmias, chest pain, coordination difficulties, dizziness, dyspnea, headache, heartburn, light-headedness, n/v, rash, tremors, visual disturbances
INTERACTIONS Hydantoins, propafenone, rifampin, theophylline
NC/PT Monitor for safe, effective serum level (0.5–2 mcg/mL); monitor cardiac rhythm frequently. Pt should not stop without consulting prescriber, take safety precautions for CNS effects, report chest pain, excessive tremors, lack of coordination.

DANGEROUS DRUG

micafungin sodium (Mycamine)
CLASS Antifungal, echinocandin
PREG/CONT C/NA

IND & DOSE Tx of esophageal candidiasis. *Adult:* 150 mg/day by IV infusion over 1 hr for 10–30 days. *Child over 30 kg:* 2.5 mg/kg/day IV; max, 150 mg/day. *Child 30 kg or less:* 3 mg/kg/day IV. **Px of candidal infections in pts undergoing hematopoietic stem-cell transplantation.** *Adult:* 50 mg/day by IV infusion over 1 hr for about 19 days. *Child:* 1 mg/kg/day IV; max, 50 mg/day. **Tx of systemic candidal infections,** *Candida* **peritonitis, abscesses.** *Adult:* 100 mg/day by IV infusion over 1 hr for 10–47 days based on infection. *Child:* 2 mg/kg/day IV.
ADV EFF Headache, **hemolytic anemia, hepatotoxicity,** nausea, phlebitis, **renal toxicity, serious hypersensitivity reaction**
INTERACTIONS Itraconazole, nifedipine, sirolimus
NC/PT Obtain baseline, periodic CBC, LFTs, renal function tests. Monitor injection site for phlebitis. Not for use in pregnancy (contraceptives advised)/breast-feeding. Pt should get periodic blood tests, report difficulty breathing, urine/stool color changes, pain at IV site.

DANGEROUS DRUG

miconazole nitrate
(Fungoid Tincture, Lotrimin AF, Monistat)
CLASS Antifungal
PREG/CONT B/NA

IND & DOSE Local tx of vulvovaginal candidiasis (moniliasis). *Adult:* 1 suppository intravaginally once daily at bedtime for 3 days *(Monistat)*. Or, 1 applicator cream or 1 suppository intravaginally daily at bedtime for 7 days *(Monistat 7)*. Repeat course if needed. Alternatively, one 1,200-mg vaginal suppository at bedtime for 1 dose. **Topical tx of susceptible fungal infections.** *Adult, child over 2 yr:* Cream/lotion, cover affected areas a.m. and p.m. Powder, spray or sprinkle powder liberally over affected area a.m. and p.m.

ADV EFF Local irritation/burning, nausea, rash

NC/PT Culture before tx. Monitor response. Pt should take full tx course; insert vaginal suppositories high into vagina; practice good hygiene to prevent spread, reinfection; report rash, pelvic pain.

DANGEROUS DRUG

midazolam hydrochloride (generic)
CLASS Benzodiazepine, CNS depressant
PREG/CONT D/C-IV

BBW Only personnel trained in general anesthesia should give. Have equipment for maintaining airway, resuscitation on hand; respiratory depression/arrest possible. Give IV w/ continuous monitoring of respiratory, CV function. Individualize dose; use lower dose in elderly/debilitated pts. Adjust according to other premedication use.

IND & DOSE Preop sedation, anxiety, amnesia. *Adult:* Over 60 yr or debilitated, 20–50 mcg/kg IM 1 hr

before surgery; usual dose, 1–3 mg. Under 60 yr, 70–80 mcg/kg IM 1 hr before surgery; usual dose, 5 mg. *Child 6 mo–16 yr:* 0.1–0.15 mg/kg IM; max, 10 mg/dose. **Conscious sedation for short procedures.** *Adult:* Over 60 yr, 1–1.5 mg IV initially. Maint, 25% initial dose; total dose, 3.5 mg. Under 60 yr, 1–2.5 mg IV initially. Maint, 25% of initial dose; total dose, 5 mg. *Child over 12 yr:* 1–2.5 mg IV; maint, 25% of initial dose. **Conscious sedation for short procedures before anesthesia.** *Child 6–12 yr:* Initially, 25–50 mcg/kg IV. May give up to 400 mcg/kg; max, 10 mg/dose. *6 mo–5 yr:* 50–100 mcg/kg IV; max, 6 mg total dose. **Induction of anesthesia.** *Adult:* Over 55 yr, 150–300 mcg/kg IV as initial dose. Under 55 yr, 300–350 mcg/kg IV (total 600 mcg/kg). Debilitated adult, 200–250 mcg/kg IV as initial dose. **Sedation in critical care areas.** *Adult:* 10–50 mcg/kg (0.5–4 mg usual dose) as loading dose. May repeat q 10–15 min; continuous infusion of 20–100 mcg/kg/hr to sustain effect. **Sedation in critical care areas for intubated child.** *Neonates over 32 wks' gestation:* 60 mcg/kg/hr IV. *Neonates under 32 wks' gestation:* 30 mcg/kg/hr IV.

ADV EFF Amnesia, bradycardia, confusion, disorientation, drowsiness, sedation, incontinence, injection-site reactions, n/v/d, rash, **respiratory depression**, slurred speech

INTERACTIONS Alcohol, antihistamines, carbamazepine, CNS depressants, grapefruit juice, opioids, phenobarbital, phenytoin, protease inhibitors, rifabutin, rifampin

NC/PT Do not give intra-arterially; may cause arteriospasm, gangrene. Keep resuscitative facilities on hand; have flumazenil available as antidote if overdose. Monitor P, BP, R during administration. Monitor level of consciousness for 2–6 hr after use. Do not let pt drive after use. Provide written information (amnesia likely). Pt should take safety precautions for

CNS effects, avoid alcohol, grapefruit juice before receiving drug; report visual/hearing disturbances, persistent drowsiness.

midodrine (generic)

CLASS Antihypotensive, alpha agonist
PREG/CONT C/NA

BBW Use only w/firm dx of orthostatic hypotension that interferes w/ daily activities; systolic pressure increase can cause serious problems.
IND & DOSE Tx of severe orthostatic hypotension. *Adult:* 10 mg tid while upright.
ADJUST DOSE Renal impairment
ADV EFF Bradycardia, dizziness, increased IOP, paresthesia, pruritus, supine hypertension, syncope, urine retention
INTERACTIONS Corticosteroids, digoxin, sympathomimetics, vasoconstrictors
NC/PT Monitor BP, orthostatic BP carefully. Monitor IOP w/long term use. Pt should take safety precautions for CNS effects, empty bladder before taking, avoid OTC cold/allergy remedies, report headache, fainting, numbness/tingling.

mifepristone (Korlym, Mifeprex)

CLASS Abortifacient
PREG/CONT X/NA

BBW Serious, fatal infection possible after abortion; monitor for sustained fever, prolonged heavy bleeding, severe abd pain. Urge pt to seek emergency medical help if these occur. Rule out pregnancy before tx and if tx stopped for 14 days or longer (*w/Korlym*).
IND & DOSE Pregnancy termination through 49 days gestational age. *Adult:* Day 1, 600 mg (3 tablets) PO as single dose. Day 3, if termination not confirmed, 400 mcg PO

(2 tablets) misoprostol *(Cytotec).* Day 14, evaluate for termination; if unsuccessful, surgical intervention suggested. **To control hyperglycemia secondary to hypercortisolism in adults w/Cushing's syndrome and type 2 diabetes or glucose intolerance who have failed other tx and are not candidates for surgery.** *Adult:* 300 mg/day PO w/meal; max, 1,200 mg/day (*Korlym*).
ADV EFF Abd pain, dizziness, headache, n/v/d, **potentially serious to fatal infection,** heavy uterine bleeding
NC/PT Alert pt that menses usually begins within 5 days of tx and lasts for 1–2 wk; arrange to follow drug within 48 hr w/prostaglandin *(Cytotec)* as appropriate. Ensure abortion complete or that other measures are used to complete abortion if drug effects insufficient. Give analgesic, antiemetic as needed for comfort. Ensure pt follow-up; serious to fatal infections possible. Pt treated for hyperglycemia should take w/meals; continue other tx for Cushing's syndrome. Not for use in pregnancy w/ this indication (contraceptives advised). Pt should swallow tablet whole, and not cut, crush, or chew it; immediately report sustained fever, severe abd pain, prolonged heavy bleeding, dizziness on arising, persistent malaise. Name confusion between mifepristone and misoprostol, *Mifeprex* and *Mirapex* (pramipexole); use caution.

DANGEROUS DRUG

miglitol (Glyset)

CLASS Alpha-glucosidase inhibitor, antidiabetic
PREG/CONT B/NA

IND & DOSE Adjunct to diet/ exercise to lower blood glucose in type 2 diabetes as monotherapy or w/sulfonylurea. *Adult:* 25 mg PO tid at first bite of each meal. After 4–8 wk, start maint: 50 mg PO tid at first bite of each meal. Max, 100 mg PO tid. If

combined w/sulfonylurea, monitor blood glucose; adjust doses accordingly.
ADV EFF Abd pain, anorexia, flatulence, hypoglycemia, n/v/d
INTERACTIONS Celery, charcoal, coriander, dandelion root, digestive enzymes, fenugreek, garlic, ginseng, juniper berries, propranolol, ranitidine
NC/PT Ensure thorough diabetic teaching, diet/exercise program. Pt should take w/first bite of each meal, monitor blood glucose, report severe abd pain.

---

miglustat (Zavesca)
CLASS Enzyme inhibitor
PREG/CONT X/NA

IND & DOSE Tx of mild to moderate type 1 Gaucher disease. *Adult:* 100 mg PO tid.
ADJUST DOSE Elderly pts, renal impairment
ADV EFF Diarrhea, GI complaints, male infertility, peripheral neuropathy, reduced platelet count, tremor, weight loss
NC/PT Not for use in pregnancy/breast-feeding; men should use barrier contraceptives during tx. Pt should use antidiarrheals for severe diarrhea, report unusual bleeding, increasing tremors.

---

milnacipran (Savella)
CLASS Selective serotonin and norepinephrine reuptake inhibitor
PREG/CONT C/NA

BBW Increased risk of suicidality; monitor accordingly. Not approved for use in children.
IND & DOSE Mgt of fibromyalgia. *Adult:* 12.5 mg/day PO; increase over 1 wk to target 50 mg PO bid.
ADJUST DOSE Elderly pts, renal impairment

ADV EFF Angle-closure glaucoma, bleeding, constipation, dizziness, dry mouth, headache, hypertension, insomnia, nausea, **NMS,** palpitations, **seizures, serotonin syndrome, suicidality**
INTERACTIONS Alcohol, clonidine, digoxin, epinephrine, MAOIs, norepinephrine, tramadol, triptans
NC/PT Not for use in breast-feeding. Taper when stopping to avoid withdrawal reactions. Pt should avoid alcohol, take safety precautions for CNS effects, report bleeding, rapid heart rate, thoughts of suicide.

> **DANGEROUS DRUG**

milrinone lactate (generic)
CLASS Inotropic
PREG/CONT C/NA

IND & DOSE Short-term mgt of pts w/acute decompensated HF. *Adult:* 50 mcg/kg IV bolus over 10 min. Maint infusion, 0.375–0.75 mcg/kg/min IV. Max, 1.13 mg/kg/day.
ADJUST DOSE Renal impairment
ADV EFF Headache, hypotension, **death,** ventricular arrhythmias
INTERACTIONS Furosemide in sol
NC/PT Do not mix in sol w/other drugs. Monitor rhythm, BP, P, I & O, electrolytes carefully. Pt should report pain at injection site, chest pain.

---

miltefosine (Impavido)
CLASS Antileishmanial drug
PREG/CONT D/NA

BBW May cause fetal harm; not for use in pregnancy. Negative pregnancy test required before use; contraceptives advised. Pt should not become pregnant during and for 5 mo after tx.
IND & DOSE Tx of visceral, cutaneous, mucosal leishmaniasis caused by susceptible strains. *Adult, child 12 yr and older:* 45 kg or more: 50 mg PO tid for 28 days; 30–44 kg: 50 mg PO bid for 28 days.

ADV EFF Abd pain, dizziness, hepatotoxicity, n/v/d, rash, renal toxicity, somnolence, **Stevens-Johnson syndrome**
NC/PT Culture to ensure proper use. Not for use in pregnancy (negative pregnancy test required, barrier contraceptives advised)/breast-feeding. Monitor for dehydration, fluid loss w/GI effects. Pt should avoid pregnancy during and for 5 mo after tx; use safety precautions for CNS effects; report severe diarrhea, dehydration, rash.

---

minocycline hydrochloride (Arestin, Dynacin, Minocin)
CLASS Tetracycline
PREG/CONT D/NA

IND & DOSE Infections caused by susceptible bacteria. *Adult:* Initially, 200 mg PO or IV, then 100 mg q 12 hr PO or IV. Or, 100–200 mg PO initially, then 50 mg PO qid. *Adult (ER):* 91–136 kg, 135 mg/day PO; 60–90 kg, 90 mg/day PO; 45–59 kg, 45 mg/day PO. *Child over 8 yr:* 4 mg/kg PO, then 2 mg/kg q 12 hr. **Tx of syphilis.** *Adult:* 100 mg PO q 12 hr for 10–15 days. **Tx of urethral, endocervical, rectal infections.** *Adult:* 100 mg PO q 12 hr for 7 days. **Tx of gonococcal urethritis in men.** *Adult:* 100 mg PO bid for 5 days. **Tx of gonorrhea.** *Adult:* 200 mg PO, then 100 mg q 12 hr for 4 days. Obtain post-tx cultures within 2–3 days. **Tx of meningococcal carrier state.** *Adult:* 100 mg PO q 12 hr for 5 days. **Tx of periodontitis.** *Adult:* Unit dose cartridge discharged in subgingival area. **Tx of moderate to severe acne vulgaris.** *Adult, child 12 yr and older:* 1 mg/kg PO for up to 12 wk (ER form).
ADJUST DOSE Elderly pts, renal impairment
ADV EFF Anorexia; **bone marrow depression;** discoloring/inadequate calcification of primary teeth of fetus if used by pregnant women, of permanent teeth if used during dental

development; glossitis; **liver failure;** n/v/d; phototoxic reactions; rash; superinfections
INTERACTIONS Alkali, antacids, dairy products, food, digoxin, hormonal contraceptives, iron, penicillin
NC/PT Culture before tx; ensure proper use. Give w/food for GI upset. Use IV only if oral not possible; switch to oral as soon as feasible. Additional form of contraception advised; hormonal contraceptives may be ineffective. Pt should avoid sun exposure, report rash, urine/stool color changes, watery diarrhea.

---

minoxidil (Rogaine)
CLASS Antihypertensive, vasodilator
PREG/CONT C/NA

BBW Arrange for echocardiographic evaluation of possible pericardial effusion if using oral drug; more vigorous diuretic therapy, dialysis, other tx (including minoxidil withdrawal) may be needed. Increased risk of exacerbation of angina, malignant hypertension. When first administering, hospitalize pt, monitor closely; use w/beta blocker and/or diuretic to decrease risk.
IND & DOSE Tx of severe hypertension. *Adult, child 12 yr and older:* 5 mg/day PO as single dose. Range, usually 10–40 mg/day PO; max, 100 mg/day. Concomitant therapy w/diuretics: Add hydrochlorothiazide 50 mg PO bid, or chlorthalidone 50–100 mg/day PO, or furosemide 40 mg PO bid. Concomitant therapy w/beta-adrenergic blockers, other sympatholytics: Add propranolol 80–160 mg/day PO; other beta blockers (dose equivalent to above); methyldopa 250–750 mg PO bid (start methyldopa at least 24 hr before minoxidil); clonidine 0.1–0.2 mg PO bid. *Child under 12 yr:* General guidelines: 0.2 mg/kg/day PO as single dose. Range, 0.25–1 mg/kg/day; max, 50 mg/day. **Topical tx of alopecia**

areata, male-pattern alopecia.
Adult: 1 mL to total affected scalp areas bid. Total daily max, 2 mL. May need 4 mo of tx to see results; balding returns if untreated 3–4 mo.
ADJUST DOSE Elderly pts, renal impairment
ADV EFF Bronchitis, dry scalp, eczema, edema, fatigue, headache, hypertrichosis, local irritation, pruritus, **Stevens-Johnson syndrome**, tachycardia, URI
NC/PT Monitor pt closely. Withdraw slowly. Do not apply other topical drugs to topically treated area. Enhanced/darkening of body, facial hair possible w/topical use. Twice-daily use will be needed to maintain hair growth; baldness will return if drug stopped. Pt should take P, report increase over 20 beats above normal; report weight gain of more than 3 lb in one day; wash hands thoroughly after applying topical form; avoid applying more than prescribed; not apply to inflamed or broken skin; report rash, difficulty breathing (w/oral drug).

---

mipomersen sodium (Kynamro)
CLASS Lipid-lowering drug, oligonucleotide inhibitor
PREG/CONT B/NA

BBW May cause transaminase increases, hepatotoxicity, hepatic steatosis; available only through restricted access program.
IND & DOSE Adjunct to other lipid-lowering drugs, diet to reduce LDL, total cholesterol, non-HDL cholesterol in pts w/familial hypercholesterolemia. *Adult:* 200 mg/wk subcut.
ADJUST DOSE Hepatic impairment
ADV EFF Arthralgia, chills, fatigue, flulike sx, injection-site reactions, **hepatotoxicity**, malaise, myalgia
NC/PT Available only through limited access program. Ensure dx before use; not for tx of other hypercholesterolemias. Monitor LFTs before and frequently during therapy. Rotate

injection sites; ensure continued diet/exercise, other drugs to lower lipids. Not for use in pregnancy (contraceptives advised)/breast-feeding. Pt should learn proper injection technique, disposal of syringes; rotate injection sites; refrigerate drug, protect from light; report urine/stool color changes; extreme fatigue.

---

mirabegron (Myrbetriq)
CLASS Beta-adrenergic agonist
PREG/CONT C/NA

IND & DOSE Tx of overactive bladder. *Adult:* 25 mg/day PO; max, 50 mg/day.
ADJUST DOSE Hepatic, renal impairment
ADV EFF Angioedema, dizziness, headache, hypertension, nasopharyngitis, UTI
INTERACTIONS Anticholinergics, desipramine, digoxin, flecainamide, metoprolol, propafenone
NC/PT Ensure dx; rule out obstruction, infection. Monitor BP; check for urine retention. Not for use in breast-feeding. Pt should swallow tablet whole and not cut, crush, or chew it; take w/full glass of water; use safety precautions w/dizziness; report swelling of face, urinary tract sx, fever, persistent headache.

---

mirtazapine (Remeron)
CLASS Antidepressant
PREG/CONT C/NA

BBW Ensure depressed/potentially suicidal pts have access only to limited quantities. Increased risk of suicidality in children, adolescents, young adults. Observe for clinical worsening of depressive disorders, suicidality, unusual changes in behavior, especially when starting tx or changing dose.
IND & DOSE Tx of major depressive disorder. *Adult:* 15 mg/day PO as single dose in evening. May

increase up to 45 mg/day as needed. Change dose only at intervals of more than 1–2 wk. Continue tx for up to 6 mo for acute episodes.

ADJUST DOSE Elderly pts; hepatic, renal impairment

ADV EFF Agranulocytosis, confusion, constipation, dry mouth, disturbed concentration, dizziness, dysphagia, gynecomastia, **heart block**, increased appetite, **MI**, neutropenia, photosensitivity, **stroke**, urine retention, weight gain

INTERACTIONS Alcohol, CNS depressants, MAOIs

NC/PT Do not give within 14 days of MAOIs; serious reactions possible. CBC needed if fever, signs of infection. Pt should take safety precautions for CNS effects; avoid alcohol, sun exposure; use sugarless lozenges for dry mouth; report signs of infection, chest pain, thoughts of suicide.

misoprostol (Cytotec)
CLASS Prostaglandin
PREG/CONT X/NA

BBW Arrange for serum pregnancy test for women of childbearing age. Women must have negative test within 2 wk of starting tx; drug possible abortifacient.

IND & DOSE Px of NSAID (including aspirin)-induced gastric ulcers in pts at high risk for gastric ulcer complications. *Adult:* 100–200 mcg PO four times/day w/food.

ADJUST DOSE Elderly pts, renal impairment

ADV EFF Abd pain, dysmenorrhea, flatulence, miscarriage, n/v/d

NC/PT Explain high risk of miscarriage if used in pregnancy (contraceptives advised). Pt should take drug w/ NSAID, not share drug w/others, report severe diarrhea, pregnancy. Name confusion between misoprostol and mifepristone; use caution.

mitomycin (generic)
CLASS Antineoplastic antibiotic
PREG/CONT D/NA

BBW Monitor CBC, renal/pulmonary function tests frequently at start of tx; risk of bone marrow suppression, hemolytic uremic syndrome w/renal failure. Adverse effects may require decreased dose or drug stoppage; consult physician.

IND & DOSE Palliative tx of disseminated adenocarcinoma of stomach, pancreas. *Adult:* 20 mg/m² IV as single dose q 6 to 8 wk; adjust according to hematologic profile.

ADV EFF Acute respiratory distress syndrome, alopecia, anorexia, bone marrow toxicity, confusion, drowsiness, fatigue, hemolytic uremic syndrome, injection-site reactions, n/v/d, pulmonary toxicity

NC/PT Do not give IM, subcut. Monitor CBC regularly, injection site for extravasation. Not for use in pregnancy (barrier contraceptives advised). Pt should mark calendar for tx days, cover head at temp extremes (hair loss possible), take safety precautions for CNS effects, report difficulty breathing, unusual bleeding.

mitotane (Lysodren)
CLASS Antineoplastic
PREG/CONT C/NA

BBW Stop temporarily during stress; adrenal hormone replacement may be needed.

IND & DOSE Tx of inoperable adrenocortical carcinoma. *Adult:* 2–6 g/day PO in divided doses; gradually increase to target 9–10 g/day.

ADV EFF Anorexia, dizziness, lethargy, n/v, orthostatic hypotension, rash, somnolence, visual disturbances

INTERACTIONS Warfarin

NC/PT Give antiemetics if needed. Pt should take safety precautions for CNS effects, hypotension.

DANGEROUS DRUG

mitoxantrone hydrochloride (generic)

CLASS Antineoplastic, MS drug
PREG/CONT D/NA

BBW Monitor CBC and LFTs carefully before and frequently during tx; dose adjustment possible if myelosuppression severe. Monitor IV site for extravasation; if extravasation occurs, stop and immediately restart at another site. Evaluate left ventricular ejection fraction (LVEF) before each dose when treating MS. Evaluate yearly after tx ends to detect late cardiac toxic effects; decreased LVEF, frank HF possible. Monitor BP, P, cardiac output regularly during tx; start supportive care for HF at first sign of failure.

IND & DOSE Tx of acute nonlymphocytic leukemia as part of comb tx. *Adult:* 12 mg/m²/day IV on days 1–3, w/100 mg/m² cytarabine for 7 days as continuous infusion on days 1–7. Consolidation tx: Mitoxantrone 12 mg/m² IV on days 1, 2, w/cytarabine 100 mg/m² as continuous 24-hr infusion on days 1–5. First course given 6 wk after induction tx if needed. Second course generally given 4 wk after first course. Tx of pain in advanced prostate cancer. *Adult:* 12–14 mg/m² as short IV infusion q 21 days. Tx of MS. *Adult:* 12 mg/m² IV over 5–15 min q 3 mo; max cumulative lifetime dose, 140 mg/m².

ADV EFF Alopecia, **bone marrow depression,** cough, fever, headache, **HF,** hyperuricemia, n/v/d

NC/PT Handle drug w/great care; gloves, gowns, goggles recommended. If drug contacts skin, wash immediately w/warm water. Clean spills w/ calcium hypochlorite sol. Monitor CBC, uric acid level, LFTs. Not for use in pregnancy (barrier contraceptives advised). Urine, whites of eyes may appear blue; should pass w/time. Pt should avoid exposure to infection, mark calendar for tx days, cover head at temp extremes (hair loss possible), report swelling, signs of infection, unusual bleeding.

modafinil (Provigil)

CLASS CNS stimulant, narcolepsy drug
PREG/CONT C/C-IV

IND & DOSE Tx of narcolepsy; improvement in wakefulness in pts w/ obstructive sleep apnea/hypopnea syndrome. *Adult:* 200 mg/day PO. Max, 400 mg/day. Tx of shift-work sleep disorder. *Adult:* 200 mg/day PO 1 hr before start of shift.

ADJUST DOSE Elderly pts, hepatic impairment

ADV EFF Anaphylaxis, angioedema, anorexia, anxiety, dry mouth, headache, insomnia, nervousness, persistent sleepiness, psychiatric sx, Stevens-Johnson syndrome

INTERACTIONS Cyclosporine, diazepam, hormonal contraceptives, omeprazole, phenytoin, TCAs, triazolam, warfarin

NC/PT Ensure accurate dx. Distribute least feasible amount of drug at any time to decrease risk of overdose. Monitor LFTs. Monitor pt w/CV disease closely. Consider stopping drug if psychiatric sx occur. Not for use in pregnancy (barrier contraceptives advised); pt using hormonal contraceptives should use second method (drug affects hormonal contraceptives). Pt should take safety precautions for CNS effects, report rash, difficulty breathing, persistent sleeping.

moexipril (Univasc)

CLASS ACE inhibitor, antihypertensive
PREG/CONT D/NA

BBW Do not give during pregnancy; serious fetal injury or death possible.
IND & DOSE Tx of hypertension.
Adult: 7.5 mg/day PO 1 hr before

meal; maint, 7.5–30 mg/day PO 1 hr before meals. If pt receiving diuretic, stop diuretic for 2 or 3 days before starting moexepril. If diuretic cannot be stopped, start w/3.75 mg; monitor for symptomatic hypotension.
ADJUST DOSE Elderly pts, renal impairment
ADV EFF Aphthous ulcers, cough, diarrhea, dizziness, dysgeusia, flulike sx, flushing, gastric irritation, hyperkalemia, **MI, pancytopenia,** peptic ulcers, proteinuria, pruritus, rash
INTERACTIONS ACE inhibitors, ARBs, diuretics, lithium, potassium supplements, renin inhibitors
NC/PT Alert surgeon if surgery required; volume support may be needed. Monitor for BP fall w/drop in fluid volume; potassium w/long-term use. Not for use in pregnancy (barrier contraceptives advised). Pt should perform mouth care for mouth ulcers, take safety precautions for CNS effects, report chest pain, signs of infection.

montelukast sodium
(Singulair)
CLASS Antiasthmatic, leukotriene receptor antagonist
PREG/CONT B/NA

IND & DOSE Px, long-term tx of asthma in pts 12 mo and older; relief of seasonal allergic rhinitis sx in pts 2 yr and older; relief of perennial allergic rhinitis sx in pts 6 mo and older; px of exercise-induced bronchoconstriction in pts 6 yr and older. *Adult, child 15 yr and older:* 10 mg/day PO in p.m. For exercise-induced bronchoconstriction, dose taken 2 hr before exercise, not repeated for at least 24 hr. *Child 6–14 yr:* 5 mg/day chewable tablet PO in p.m. *Child 2–5 yr:* 4 mg/day chewable tablet PO in p.m. *Child 6–23 mo:* 1 packet (4 mg)/day PO. For asthma only, 4 mg granules/day PO in p.m.
ADV EFF Abd pain, behavior/mood changes, dizziness, fatigue, head-

ache, nausea, systemic eosinophilia, URI
INTERACTIONS Phenobarbital
NC/PT Chewable tablets contain phenylalanine; alert pts w/phenylketonuria. Give in p.m. continually for best results. Not for acute asthma attacks. Pt should have rescue medication for acute asthma, take safety precautions for CNS effects, report increased incidence of acute attacks, changes in behavior/mood.

DANGEROUS DRUG

morphine sulfate
(Duramorph, Infumorph, Kadian, MS Contin, Roxanol)
CLASS Opioid agonist analgesic
PREG/CONT C/C-II

BBW Caution pt not to chew, crush CR, ER, SR forms; ensure appropriate use of forms. Do not substitute *Infumorph for Duramorph*; conc differs significantly, serious overdose possible. Ensure pt observed for at least 24 hr in fully equipped, staffed environment if given by epidural, intrathecal route; risk of serious adverse effects. Liposome preparation for lumbar epidural injection only; do not give liposome intrathecally, IV, IM.
IND & DOSE Relief of moderate to severe pain; analgesic adjunct during anesthesia; preop medication. *Adult:* 5–30 mg PO q 4 hr. CR, ER, SR: 30 mg q 8–12 hr PO or as directed by physician. *Kadian,* 20–100 mg/day PO. *MS Contin,* 200 mg PO q 12 hr. **Relief of intractable pain.** *Adult:* 5 mg injected in lumbar region provides relief for up to 24 hr; max, 10 mg/24 hr. For continuous infusion, initial dose of 2–4 mg/24 hr recommended. Or, intrathecally, w/dosage 1/10 epidural dosage; single injection of 0.2–1 mg may provide satisfactory relief for up to 24 hr. Do not inject more than 2 mL of 5 mg/10-mL ampule or more than 1 mL of 10 mg/10-mL ampule. Use only in lumbar area. Repeated intrathecal

injections not recommended. *Tx of pain after major surgery. Adult:* 10–15 mg liposome injection by lumbar epidural injection using catheter or needle before major surgery or after clamping umbilical cord during cesarean birth.

ADJUST DOSE Elderly pts, impaired adults

ADV EFF Apnea, bronchospasm, **cardiac arrest, circulatory depression,** dizziness, drowsiness, hypotension, impaired mental capacity, injection-site irritation, **laryngospasm,** light-headedness, n/v, **respiratory arrest/depression,** sedation, **shock,** sweating

INTERACTIONS Alcohol, barbiturate anesthetics, CNS depressants, MAOIs

NC/PT Have opioid antagonist, facilities for assisted or controlled respiration on hand during IV administration. Pt should lie down during IV use. Use caution when injecting IM, subcut into chilled areas and in pts w/ hypotension, shock; impaired perfusion may delay absorption. Excessive amount may be absorbed w/repeated doses when circulation restored. Pt should swallow CR, ER, SR forms whole and not cut, crush, or chew them; store in secure place; take safety precautions for CNS effects, report difficulty breathing.

---

moxifloxacin hydrochloride (Avelox, Moxeza, Vigamox)
CLASS Fluoroquinolone
PREG/CONT C/NA

BBW Increased risk of tendonitis, tendon rupture, especially in pts over 60 yr, pts taking corticosteroids, pts w/kidney, heart, lung transplant. Risk of exacerbated weakness in pts w/ myasthenia gravis; avoid use w/hx of myasthenia gravis.

IND & DOSE Tx of bacterial infections in adults caused by susceptible strains. *Pneumonia:* 400 mg/day PO,

IV for 7–14 days. *Sinusitis:* 400 mg/day PO, IV for 10 days. *Acute exacerbation of chronic bronchitis:* 400 mg/day PO, IV for 5 days. *Uncomplicated skin, skin-structure infections:* 400 mg/day PO for 7 days. *Complicated skin, skin-structure infections:* 400 mg/day PO, IV for 7–21 days. *Complicated intra-abd infections:* 400 mg PO, IV for 5–14 days.

ADV EFF Bone marrow suppression, cough, dizziness, drowsiness, headache, insomnia, n/v/d, photosensitivity, **prolonged QT,** rash, vision changes

INTERACTIONS Risk of prolonged QT w/amiodarone, phenothiazines, procainamide, quinidine, sotalol; do not combine. Antacids, didanosine, NSAIDs, sucralfate

NC/PT Culture before tx. Pt should take oral drug 4 hr before or 8 hr after antacids; stop if severe diarrhea, rash; take safety precautions for CNS effects; avoid sun exposure; report rash, unusual bleeding, severe GI problems.

---

mycophenolate mofetil (CellCept), mycophenolate sodium (Myfortic)
CLASS Immunosuppressant
PREG/CONT D/NA

BBW Risk of serious to life-threatening infection. Protect from exposure to infections; maintain sterile technique for invasive procedures. Monitor for possible lymphoma development related to drug action. Risk of pregnancy loss/congenital abnormalities; contraceptives strongly advised.

IND & DOSE Px of organ rejection in allogeneic transplants. *Renal. Adult:* 1 g bid PO, IV (over at least 2 hr) as soon as possible after transplant. Or, 720 mg PO bid on empty stomach (*Myfortic*). *Child:* 600 mg/m² oral suspension PO bid; max daily dose, 2 g/10 mL. Or, 400 mg/m² PO bid; max, 720 mg bid (*Myfortic*). *Cardiac.*

Adult: 1.5 g PO bid, or IV (over at least 2 hr). *Hepatic. Adult:* I g IV bid over at least 2 hr, or 1.5 g PO bid.
ADJUST DOSE Elderly pts; hepatic, renal impairment; cardiac dysfx
ADV EFF Anorexia, **bone marrow suppression,** constipation, headache, **hepatotoxicity,** hypertension, infection, insomnia, n/v/d, photosensitivity, **renal impairment**
INTERACTIONS Antacids, cholestyramine, cyclosporine, hormonal contraceptives, phenytoin, sevelamer, theophylline; avoid live vaccines
NC/PT Intended for use w/ corticosteroids, cyclosporine. Do not mix w/other drugs in infusion. Monitor LFTs, renal function regularly. Do not confuse two brand names; not interchangeable. Not for use in pregnancy (barrier contraceptives advised). Pt should swallow DR form whole and not cut, crush, or chew it; avoid exposure to sun; infection; get cancer screening; report signs of infection, unusual bleeding.

nabilone (Cesamet)
CLASS Antiemetic, cannabinoid
PREG/CONT C/C-II

IND & DOSE Tx of n/v associated w/chemotherapy in pts unresponsive to conventional antiemetics. *Adult:* 1–2 mg PO bid. Give initial dose 1–3 hr before chemotherapy. Max, 6 mg/day PO divided tid. May give daily during each chemotherapy cycle and for 48 hr after last dose in cycle, if needed. Risk of altered mental state; supervise pt closely.
ADV EFF Ataxia, concentration difficulties, drowsiness, dry mouth, euphoria, orthostatic hypotension, vertigo
INTERACTIONS Alcohol, amitriptyline, amoxapine, amphetamines, anticholinergics, antihistamines, atropine, barbiturates, benzodiazepines, buspirone, CNS depressants, cocaine, desipramine, lithium, muscle relaxants, opioids, scopolamine, sympathomimetics, TCAs
NC/PT Risk of altered mental state; supervise pt closely; stop w/sx of psychotic reaction. Use caution in pregnancy/breast-feeding. Warn pt possible altered mental state may persist for 2–3 days after use. Pt should take safety measures for CNS effects, avoid alcohol, report all drugs used (interactions possible), chest pain, psychotic episodes.

nabumetone (generic)
CLASS NSAID
PREG/CONT C (1st, 2nd trimesters); D (3rd trimester)/NA

BBW Increased risk of CV events, GI bleeding; more common in elderly. Not for use for periop pain after CABG surgery.
IND & DOSE Tx of s&sx of rheumatoid arthritis, osteoarthritis. *Adult:* 1,000 mg PO as single dose w/or without food; 1,500–2,000 mg/day has been used.
ADJUST DOSE Renal impairment
ADV EFF Anaphylactic shock, **bone marrow suppression, bronchospasm,** dizziness, dyspepsia, GI pain, headache, insomnia, n/v/d, rash, **renal impairment**
INTERACTIONS Aspirin, warfarin
NC/PT Pt should take w/food, take safety precautions for CNS effects, report swelling, signs of infection, difficulty breathing.

nadolol (Corgard)
CLASS Antianginal, antihypertensive, beta blocker
PREG/CONT C/NA

IND & DOSE Tx of hypertension; mgt of angina. *Adult:* 40 mg/day PO; gradually increase in 40- to 80-mg increments. Maint, 40–80 mg/day.
ADJUST DOSE Elderly pts, renal failure
ADV EFF Cardiac arrhythmias, constipation, decreased exercise

tolerance/libido, diarrhea, dizziness, ED, flatulence, gastric pain, HF, **laryngospasm,** n/v/d, **pulmonary edema, stroke**
INTERACTIONS Alpha-adrenergic blockers, clonidine, dihydroergotamine, epinephrine, ergotamine, lidocaine, NSAIDs, theophylline, verapamil
NC/PT To discontinue, reduce gradually over 1–2 wk. Alert surgeon if surgery required; volume replacement may be needed. Pt should take safety precautions for CNS effects, report difficulty breathing, numbness, confusion.

nafarelin acetate
(Synarel)
CLASS GnRH
PREG/CONT X/NA

IND & DOSE Tx of endometriosis. *Adult:* 400 mcg/day: One spray (200 mcg) into one nostril in a.m., 1 spray into other nostril in p.m. Start tx between days 2, 4 of menstrual cycle. May give 800-mcg dose as 1 spray into each nostril in a.m. (total of 2 sprays) and again in p.m. for pts w/persistent regular menstruation after 2 mo of tx. Tx for 6 mo recommended. Retreatment not recommended. **Tx of central precocious puberty.** *Child:* 1,600 mcg/day: Two sprays (400 mcg) in each nostril in a.m., 2 sprays in each nostril in p.m.; may increase to 1,800 mcg/day. If 1,800 mcg needed, give 3 sprays into alternating nostrils three times/day. Continue until resumption of puberty desired.
ADV EFF Acne, androgenic effects, dizziness, headache, hot flashes, hypoestrogenic effects, nasal irritation, rash, vaginal bleeding
NC/PT Rule out pregnancy before tx. Store upright, protected from light. Begin endometriosis tx during menstrual period, between days 2, 4. Advise barrier contraceptives. Low estrogen effects, masculinizing effects possible (some may not be

reversible). If nasal decongestant used, use at least 2 hr before dose. Pt should not interrupt tx; report nasal irritation, unusual bleeding.

DANGEROUS DRUG

nalbuphine hydrochloride (generic)
CLASS Opioid agonist-antagonist analgesic
PREG/CONT B; D (long-term use, high doses)/NA

IND & DOSE Relief of moderate to severe pain. *Adult, 70 kg:* 10 mg IM, IV, subcut q 3–6 hr as needed. **Supplement to anesthesia.** *Adult:* Induction, 0.3–3 mg/kg IV over 10–15 min; maint, 0.25–0.5 mg/kg IV.
ADJUST DOSE Hepatic, renal impairment
ADV EFF Bradycardia, dizziness, drowsiness, dry mouth, headache, hypotension, n/v, **respiratory depression,** sweating, vertigo
INTERACTIONS Barbiturate anesthetics
NC/PT Taper when stopping after prolonged use to avoid withdrawal sx. Have opioid antagonist, facilities for assisted or controlled respiration on hand for respiratory depression. Pt should take safety precautions for CNS effects, report difficulty breathing.

naloxegol (Movantik)
CLASS Laxative, opioid antagonist
PREG/CONT C/CII

IND & DOSE Tx of opioid-induced constipation in adults w/chronic noncancer pain. *Adult:* 25 mg PO 1 hr before or 2 hr after first meal of day.
ADJUST DOSE CYP3A4 inhibitor/inducer use, hepatic/renal impairment
ADV EFF Abd pain, flatulence, **GI perforation,** n/v/d, opioid withdrawal
INTERACTIONS CYP3A4 inducers/inhibitors

NC/PT Effective in pts using opioids for at least 4 wk. Stop other laxative tx before naloxegol; may restart if constipation remains after 3 days. Monitor for possible opioid withdrawal; stop if opioids are withdrawn. Monitor for possible GI obstruction. Not for use in pregnancy/breast-feeding. Pt should swallow tablet whole; not cut, crush, or chew it; take on empty stomach; avoid grapefruit/grapefruit juice; report worsening or severe abd pain, difficulty breathing.

naloxone hydrochloride (Evzio, Narcan Nasal Spray)
CLASS Opioid antagonist
PREG/CONT B/NA

IND & DOSE Emergency tx of known or suspected opioid overdose. *Adult, child:* 0.4 mg IM or subcut, or 4 mg intranasally sprayed into one nostril. May repeat q 2–3 min until emergency care available.
ADV EFF Hypertension, hypotension, n/v, **pulmonary edema,** sweating, tachycardia, tremors, **ventricular fibrillation**
NC/PT Monitor continually after use. Maintain open airway; provide life support as needed. Not a substitute for emergency care. Teach household members of pts w/potential opioid addiction, first responders stocked w/autoinjector how to identify overdose s&sx, proper use of autoinjector (may be used through clothes, etc), proper disposal of autoinjector, proper use of nasal spray; need to get immediate emergency medical care.

naltrexone hydrochloride (ReVia, Vivitrol)
CLASS Opioid antagonist
PREG/CONT C/NA

IND & DOSE Naloxone challenge. *Adult:* Draw 2 mL (0.8 mg) into syringe; inject 0.5 mL (0.2 mg) IV. Leave needle in vein; observe for 30 sec. If no withdrawal s&sx, inject remaining 1.5 mL (0.6 mg); observe for 20 min for withdrawal s&sx. Or, 2 mL (0.8 mg) naloxone subcut; observe for withdrawal s&sx for 20 min. If withdrawal s&sx occur or if any doubt pt opioid free, do not administer naltrexone. **Adjunct to tx of alcohol/opioid dependence.** *Adult:* 50 mg/day PO. Or, 380 mg IM q 4 wk into upper outer quadrant of gluteal muscle *(Vivitrol);* alternate buttock w/each dose. **Px of relapse to opioid dependence after opioid detoxification.** *Adult:* 25 mg PO. Observe for 1 hr. If no s&sx, complete dose w/25 mg; maint, 50 mg/24 hr PO. Can use flexible dosing schedule w/100 mg q other day or 150 mg q third day.
ADV EFF Abd pain, anxiety, chills, delayed ejaculation, joint/muscle pain, headache, **hepatocellular injury,** increased thirst, insomnia, n/v, nervousness
INTERACTIONS Opioid-containing products
NC/PT Do not use until pt opioid free for 7–10 days; check urine opioid levels. Do not give until pt has passed naloxone challenge. Ensure active participation in comprehensive tx program. Large opioid doses may overcome blocking effect but could cause serious injury, death. Pt should wear medical ID, take safety precautions for CNS effects, report unusual bleeding, urine/stool color changes.

naproxen (Naprelan, Naprosyn), naproxen sodium (Aleve, Anaprox)
CLASS Analgesic, NSAID
PREG/CONT C/NA

BBW Increased risk of CV events, GI bleeding; monitor accordingly. Contraindicated for periop pain after CABG surgery; serious complications possible.

IND & DOSE Tx of rheumatoid arthritis, osteoarthritis, ankylosing spondylitis. *Adult:* 375–500 mg DR tablet PO bid; or 750–1,000 mg/day CR tablet PO; or 275–550 mg naproxen sodium PO bid (may increase to 1.65 g/day for limited time); or 250–500 mg naproxen PO bid; or 250 mg (10 mL), 375 mg (15 mL), 500 mg (20 mL) naproxen suspension PO bid. **Tx of acute gout.** *Adult:* 1,000–1,500 mg/day CR tablet PO; or 825 mg naproxen sodium PO then 275 mg q 8 hr until attack subsides; or 750 mg naproxen PO then 250 mg q 8 hr until attack subsides. **Tx of mild to moderate pain.** *Adult:* 1,000 mg/day CR tablet PO; or 550 mg naproxen sodium PO then 275 mg q 6–8 hr; or 500 mg naproxen PO then 500 mg q 12 hr; or 250 mg naproxen PO q 6–8 hr; or OTC products 200 mg PO q 8–12 hr w/full glass of liquid while sx persist (max, 600 mg/24 hr). **Tx of juvenile arthritis.** *Child:* 10 mg/kg/day naproxen PO in two divided doses.
ADJUST DOSE Elderly pts
ADV EFF Anaphylactoid reactions to anaphylactic shock, bone marrow suppression, bronchospasm, dizziness, dyspepsia, GI pain, headache, insomnia, nausea, somnolence
INTERACTIONS Antihypertensives, lithium
NC/PT Pt should not cut, crush, or chew DR, CR forms; take w/food for GI upset; take safety precautions for CNS effects; report difficulty breathing, swelling, black tarry stools.

---

naratriptan (Amerge)
CLASS Antimigraine, triptan
PREG/CONT C/NA

IND & DOSE Tx of acute migraine attacks. *Adult:* 1 or 2.5 mg PO; may repeat in 4 hr if needed. Max, 5 mg/24 hr.
ADJUST DOSE Hepatic, renal impairment

ADV EFF Chest pain, **CV events,** dizziness, drowsiness, headache, neck/throat/jaw discomfort
INTERACTIONS Ergots, hormonal contraceptives, SSRIs
NC/PT For acute attack only; not for px. Monitor BP w/known CAD. Not for use in pregnancy (barrier contraceptives advised). Pt should take safety measures for CNS effects, continue usual migraine measures, report chest pain, visual changes, severe pain.

---

natalizumab (Tysabri)
CLASS Monoclonal antibody, MS drug
PREG/CONT C/NA

BBW Increased risk of possibly fatal progressive multifocal leukoencephalopathy (PML). Monitor closely for PML; stop drug immediately if signs occur. Drug available only to prescribers and pts in TOUCH prescribing program; pts must understand risks, need for close monitoring. Risk increases w/number of infusions. Risk of immune reconstitution inflammatory syndrome in pts who developed PML and stopped drug.
IND & DOSE Tx of relapsing MS; tx of Crohn's disease in pts unresponsive to other tx. *Adult:* 300 mg by IV infusion over 1 hr q 4 wk.
ADV EFF Abd pain, **anaphylactic reactions,** arthralgia, depression, diarrhea, dizziness, **encephalitis, fatigue,** gastroenteritis, **hepatotoxicity,** hypersensitivity reactions, infections, increased WBCs, lower respiratory tract infections, **meningitis, PML**
INTERACTIONS Corticosteroids, TNF blockers
NC/PT Withhold drug at s&sx of PML. Ensure pt not immunesuppressed or taking immunosuppressants. Refrigerate vials, protect from light; give within 8 hr of preparation. Monitor continually during and for 1 hr after infusion. Not for use in pregnancy (barrier contraceptives

advised)/breast-feeding. Pt should mark calendar of tx days; avoid exposure to infection; report signs of infection, changes in eyesight/thinking, severe headache, urine/stool color changes.

DANGEROUS DRUG

nateglinide (Starlix)
CLASS Antidiabetic, meglitinide
PREG/CONT C/NA

IND & DOSE Adjunct to diet/exercise to lower blood glucose in type 2 diabetes, alone or w/metformin, a thiazolidinedione. *Adult:* 120 mg PO tid 1–30 min before meals; may try 60 mg PO tid if pt near HbA$_{1c}$ goal.
ADV EFF Dizziness, headache, hypoglycemia, nausea, URI
INTERACTIONS Beta blockers, MAOIs, NSAIDs, salicylates
NC/PT Monitor serum glucose, HbA$_{1c}$ frequently to determine effectiveness of drug, dose being used. Arrange for thorough diabetic teaching program; ensure diet/exercise protocols. Pt should take safety precaution for dizziness, report unusual bleeding, severe abd pain.

---

nebivolol (Bystolic)
CLASS Antihypertensive, beta blocker
PREG/CONT C/NA

IND & DOSE Tx of hypertension. *Adult:* 5 mg/day PO; may increase at 2-wk intervals to max 40 mg/day PO
ADJUST DOSE Hepatic, renal impairment
ADV EFF Bradycardia, chest pain, dizziness, dyspnea, headache, hypotension
INTERACTIONS Antiarrhythmics, beta blockers, catecholamine-depleting drugs, clonidine, CYP2D6 inducers/inhibitors, digoxin, diltiazem, verapamil
NC/PT Do not stop abruptly after long-term tx; taper gradually over

2 wk while monitoring pt. Use caution in pregnancy; not for use in breast-feeding. Pt should take safety precautions for CNS effects, report difficulty breathing, fainting.

---

necitumumab (Portrazza)
CLASS Antineoplastic, epidermal growth factor antagonist
PREG/CONT High risk/NA

BBW Increased risk of cardiopulmonary arrest, sudden death; closely monitor magnesium, potassium, calcium, w/aggressive replacement if needed. Risk of hypomagnesemia; monitor electrolytes before each dose and at least 8 wk after tx ends.
IND & DOSE First-line tx of metastatic squamous non-small-cell lung cancer w/gemcitabine and cisplatin. *Adult:* 800 mg IV over 60 min on days 1, 8 of each 3-wk cycle.
ADV EFF Cardiopulmonary arrest, dermatologic reactions, hypomagnesemia, infusion reactions, thromboembolic events
NC/PT Not for use in nonsquamous non-small-cell lung cancer; ensure dx. Monitor electrolytes before, closely during, and for 8 wk after tx ends; aggressive replacement may be needed. Not for use in pregnancy (contraceptives advised)/breast-feeding. Patient should mark calendar for tx days, avoid sunlight, wear protective clothing, report difficulty breathing, fever, chills, chest pain, muscle pain.

---

nefazodone (generic)
CLASS Antidepressant
PREG/CONT C/NA

BBW Increased risk of suicidality in children, adolescents, young adults; monitor accordingly. Risk of severe to fatal liver failure; do not use if s&sx of hepatic impairment. Monitor closely; stop at first sign of liver failure.

IND & DOSE Tx of depression.
Adult: 200 mg/day PO in divided doses; range, 300–600 mg/day.
ADJUST DOSE Elderly pts, hepatic impairment
ADV EFF Abnormal vision, agitation, asthenia, confusion, constipation, dizziness, dry mouth, **hepatic failure**, insomnia, light-headedness, mania, nausea, orthostatic hypotension, priapism, **seizures, suicidality**
INTERACTIONS MAOIs, triazolam. Contraindicated w/astemizole, carbamazepine, cisapride, pimozide, terfenadine
NC/PT Monitor LFTs before, regularly during tx. Ensure no MAOI use within 14 days. Use caution in pregnancy/breast-feeding. Pt should avoid antihistamines, take safety precautions for CNS effects, report all drugs being used, urine/stool color changes, thoughts of suicide.

DANGEROUS DRUG

nelarabine (Arranon)
CLASS Antimitotic, antineoplastic
PREG/CONT D/NA

BBW Monitor for neurologic toxicity including neuropathies, demyelinating disorders. Stop if neurotoxicity; effects may not be reversible.
IND & DOSE Tx of T-cell acute lymphoblastic leukemia, T-cell lymphoblastic lymphoma. *Adult:* 1,500 mg/m^2 IV over 2 hr on days 1, 3, 5; repeat q 21 days. *Child:* 650 mg/m^2/day IV over 1 hr for 5 consecutive days; repeat q 21 days.
ADJUST DOSE Hepatic, renal impairment
ADV EFF Bone marrow suppression, constipation, cough, dizziness, fatigue, fever, **neurotoxicity,** n/v/d, somnolence
INTERACTIONS Live vaccines, pentostatin
NC/PT Monitor neuro function before, regularly during tx; stop if sign of neurotoxicity. Not for use in pregnancy (barrier contraceptives advised). Pt should avoid exposure to infection, take safety precautions for CNS effects, report numbness/tingling, unusual bleeding, signs of infection.

---

nelfinavir mesylate (Viracept)
CLASS Antiviral, protease inhibitor
PREG/CONT B/NA

IND & DOSE Tx of HIV infection w/ other drugs. *Adult, child over 13 yr:* 750 mg PO tid, or 1,250 mg PO bid. Max, 2,500 mg/day. *Child 2–13 yr:* 45–55 mg/kg PO bid, or 25–35 mg/kg PO tid.
ADV EFF Anorexia, anxiety, bleeding, diarrhea, dizziness, fat redistribution, GI pain, hyperglycemia, immune reconstitution syndrome, nausea, rash, **seizures,** sexual dysfx
INTERACTIONS Carbamazepine, dexamethasone, grapefruit juice, hormonal contraceptives, phenobarbital, phenytoin, rifabutin, St. John's wort. Avoid use w/amiodarone, ergot derivatives, lovastatin, midazolam, pimozide, rifampin, quinidine, simvastatin, triazolam; serious reactions can occur
NC/PT Given w/other antivirals. Interferes w/hormonal contraceptives (barrier contraceptives advised). Not for use in breast-feeding. Pt should take w/light meal, snack; avoid grapefruit juice, St. John's wort; take safety precautions for CNS effects; use precautions to avoid infections, prevent transmission (drug not a cure). Name confusion between *Viracept* (nelfinavir) and *Viramune* (nevirapine); use caution.

---

neomycin sulfate (Neo-fradin)
CLASS Aminoglycoside
PREG/CONT D/NA

IND & DOSE Preop suppression of GI bacteria for colorectal surgery.

Adult: See manufacturer's recommendations for complex 3-day regimen that includes oral erythromycin, bisacodyl, magnesium sulfate, enemas, dietary restrictions. **Adjunct tx in hepatic coma to reduce ammonia-forming bacteria in GI tract.** *Adult:* 12 g/day PO in divided doses for 5–6 days as adjunct to protein-free diet, supportive tx. *Child:* 50–100 mg/kg/day PO in divided doses for 5–6 days as adjunct to protein-free diet, supportive tx.
ADJUST DOSE Elderly pts, renal failure
ADV EFF Anorexia, leukemoid reaction, n/v, ototoxicity, pain, rash, superinfection
INTERACTIONS Beta-lactam antibiotics, citrate-anticoagulated blood, carbenicillin, cephalosporins, digoxin, diuretics, NMJ blockers, other aminoglycosides, penicillins, succinylcholine, ticarcillin
NC/PT Ensure hydration. Pt should report hearing changes, dizziness, s&sx of infection.

---

neostigmine bromide (generic), neostigmine methylsulfate (Bloxiverz, Prostigmin)

CLASS Antidote, parasympathomimetic, urinary tract drug
PREG/CONT C/NA

IND & DOSE **Px of postop distention, urine retention.** *Adult:* 0.25 mg methylsulfate subcut, IM as soon as possible postop. Repeat q 4–6 hr for 2–3 days. **Tx of postop distention.** *Adult:* 1 mL 1:2,000 sol (0.5 mg) methylsulfate subcut, IM. **Tx of urine retention.** *Adult:* 1 mL 1:2,000 sol (0.5 mg) methylsulfate subcut, IM. After bladder emptied, continue 0.5-mg injections q 3 hr for at least five injections. **Symptomatic control of myasthenia gravis.** *Adult:* 1 mL 1:2,000 sol (0.5 mg) subcut, IM. Use w/atropine to counteract adverse

muscarinic effects. Or, 15–375 mg/day tablets PO; average dose, 150 mg/day. *Child:* 0.01–0.04 mg/kg per dose IM, IV, subcut q 2–3 hr as needed. Or, 2 mg/kg/day tablets PO q 3–4 hr as needed. **Antidote for NMJ blockers.** *Adult, child:* 0.6–1.2 mg atropine IV several min before slow neostigmine bromide IV injection of 0.03–0.07 mg/kg. Repeat as needed. Max, 0.07 mg/kg or total of 5 mg.
ADV EFF Abd cramps, bradycardia, **bronchospasm, cardiac arrest,** cardiac arrhythmias, dizziness, drowsiness, dysphagia, increased peristalsis, increased pharyngeal/tracheobronchial secretions, increased salivation/lacrimation, **laryngospasm,** miosis, nausea, urinary frequency/incontinence, vomiting
INTERACTIONS Aminoglycosides, corticosteroids, succinylcholine
NC/PT Have atropine sulfate on hand as antidote and antagonist in case of cholinergic crisis, hypersensitivity reaction. Stop drug, consult physician for excessive salivation, emesis, frequent urination, diarrhea. Give IV slowly. Pt should take safety precautions for CNS effects, report excessive sweating/salivation, difficulty breathing, muscle weakness.

---

nesiritide (Natrecor)

CLASS Human B-type natriuretic peptide, vasodilator
PREG/CONT C/NA

IND & DOSE **Tx of acutely decompensated HF.** *Adult:* 2 mcg/kg IV bolus, then 0.01 mcg/kg/min IV infusion for no longer than 48 hr.
ADV EFF Azotemia, headache, hypotension, tachycardia
INTERACTIONS ACE inhibitors
NC/PT Replace reconstituted drug q 24 hr. Monitor continuously during administration. Monitor renal function regularly. Maintain hydration.

nevirapine (Viramune)
CLASS Antiviral, nonnucleoside reverse transcriptase inhibitor
PREG/CONT B/NA

BBW Monitor LFTs, renal function before, during tx. Stop if s&sx of hepatic impairment; severe to life-threatening hepatotoxicity possible (greatest risk at 6–18 wk of tx). Monitor closely. Do not give if severe rash occurs, especially w/fever, blisters, lesions, swelling, general malaise; stop if rash recurs on rechallenge. Severe to life-threatening reactions possible; risk greatest at 6–18 wk of tx. Monitoring during first 18 wk essential.
IND & DOSE Tx of HIV-1 infection w/other drugs. Adult: 200 mg/day PO for 14 days; if no rash, then 200 mg PO bid. Or, 400 mg/day PO ER tablet. Max, 400 mg/day. Child 15 days and over: 150 mg/m² PO once daily for 14 days, then 150 mg/m² PO bid.
ADV EFF Fat redistribution, headache, **hepatic impairment including hepatitis, hepatic necrosis**, n/v/d, rash, **Stevens-Johnson syndrome, toxic epidermal necrolysis**
INTERACTIONS Clarithromycin, hormonal contraceptives, itraconazole, ketoconazole, protease inhibitors, rifampin, St. John's wort
NC/PT Give w/nucleoside analogues. Do not switch to ER form until pt stabilized on immediate-release form (14 days). Shake suspension gently before use; rinse oral dosing cup and have pt drink rinse. Not for use in pregnancy (barrier contraceptives advised). Pt should swallow ER tablet whole and not cut, crush, or chew it; be aware drug not a cure, continue preventive measures, other drugs for HIV; report rash, urine/stool color changes. Name confusion between *Viramune* (nevirapine) and *Viracept* (nelfinavir); use caution.

niacin (Niacor, Niaspan)
CLASS Antihyperlipidemic, vitamin
PREG/CONT C/NA

IND & DOSE Tx of dyslipidemias. Adult, child over 16 yr: 100 mg PO tid, increased to 1,000 mg PO tid (immediate-release form); 500 mg/day PO at bedtime for 4 wk, then 1,000 mg/day PO at bedtime for another 4 wk (ER form); titrate to pt response, tolerance. Max, 2,000 mg/day; 1,000–2,000 mg/day PO (SR form). Child under 16 yr: 100–250 mg/day PO in three divided doses w/meals; may increase at 2- to 3-wk intervals to max 10 mg/kg/day (immediate-release form). Tx of CAD, post MI. Adult: 500 mg/day PO at bedtime, titrated at 4-wk intervals to max 1,000–2,000 mg/day. Tx of pellagra. Adult, child: 50–100 mg/day PO to max 500 mg/day.
ADV EFF Flushing, GI upset, glucose intolerance, hyperuricemia, n/v/d, rash
INTERACTIONS Anticoagulants, antihypertensives, bile acid sequestrants, statins, vasoactive drugs
NC/PT Do not substitute ER form for immediate-release form at equivalent doses; severe hepatotoxicity possible. ASA 325 mg 30 min before dose may help flushing. Pt should take at bedtime, avoid hot foods/beverages, alcohol around dose time to decrease flushing; maintain diet/exercise program; report rash, unusual bleeding/bruising.

niCARdipine hydrochloride (Cardene)
CLASS Antianginal, antihypertensive, calcium channel blocker
PREG/CONT C/NA

IND & DOSE Tx of chronic, stable angina. Adult: Immediate-release only, 20 mg PO tid; range, 20–40 mg PO tid. Tx of hypertension. Adult:

Immediate-release, 20 mg PO tid; range, 20–40 mg tid. SR, 30 mg PO bid; range, 30–60 mg bid. Or, 5 mg/hr IV. Increase by 2.5 mg/hr IV q 15 min to max 15 mg/hr. For rapid reduction, begin infusion at 5 mg/hr; switch to oral form as soon as possible.

ADJUST DOSE Hepatic, renal impairment

ADV EFF Asthenia, bradycardia, dizziness, flushing, headache, heart block, light-headedness, nausea

INTERACTIONS Cimetidine, cyclosporine, nicardipine, nitrates

NC/PT Monitor closely when titrating to therapeutic dose. Pt should have small, frequent meals for GI complaints; take safety precautions for CNS effects; report irregular heartbeat, shortness of breath.

---

nicotine (Nicoderm CQ, Nicotrol)
CLASS Smoking deterrent
PREG/CONT D/NA

IND & DOSE Temporary aid to give up cigarette smoking. *Adult:* Apply transdermal system, 5–21 mg, q 24 hr. *Nicoderm CQ:* 21 mg for first 6 wk; 14 mg/day for next 2 wk; 7 mg/day for next 2 wk. *Nicotrol:* 15 mg/day for first 6 wk; 10 mg/day for next 2 wk; 5 mg/day for last 2 wk. Or nasal spray, 1 spray in each nostril as needed, one to two doses/hr; max, five doses/hr, 40 doses/day. Or nasal inhaler, 1 spray in each nostril, one to two doses/hr. Max, 5 doses/hr, 40 doses/day; use for no longer than 6 mo. Treat for 12 wk, then wean over next 6–12 wk.

ADV EFF Cough, dizziness, GI upset, headache, insomnia, light-headedness, local reaction to patch

INTERACTIONS Adrenergic agonists, adrenergic blockers, caffeine, furosemide, imipramine, pentazocine, theophylline

NC/PT Ensure pt has stopped smoking, is using behavioral modification program. Protect dermal system from heat. Apply to nonhairy, clean, dry skin. Remove old system before applying new one; rotate sites. Wrap old system in foil pouch, fold over, dispose of immediately. If nasal spray contacts skin, flush immediately. Dispose of bottle w/cap on. Pt should take safety precautions for CNS effects, report burning/swelling at dermal system site, chest pain.

---

nicotine polacrilex (Nicorette, Nicotine Gum)
CLASS Smoking deterrent
PREG/CONT C/NA

IND & DOSE Temporary aid to give up cigarette smoking. *Adult:* Chewing gum—under 25 cigarettes/day, 2 mg; over 25 cigarettes/day, 4 mg. Have pt chew one piece when urge to smoke occurs; 10 pieces daily often needed during first month. Max, 24 pieces/day no longer than 4 mo. Lozenge—2 mg if first cigarette over 30 min after waking; 4 mg if first cigarette within 30 min of waking. Wk 1–6, 1 lozenge q 1–2 hr; wk 7–9, 1 lozenge q 2–4 hr; wk 10–12, 1 lozenge q 4–8 hr. Max, 5 lozenges in 6 hr or 20/day.

ADV EFF Dizziness, GI upset, headache, hiccups, light-headedness, mouth/throat soreness, n/v

INTERACTIONS Adrenergic agonists, adrenergic blockers, caffeine, furosemide, imipramine, pentazocine, theophylline

NC/PT For gum, have pt chew each piece slowly until it tingles, then place between cheek and gum. When tingle gone, have pt chew again, repeat process. Gum usually lasts for about 30 min to promote even, slow, buccal absorption of nicotine. For lozenge, have pt place in mouth, let dissolve over 20–30 min. Pt should avoid eating, drinking anything but water for 15 min before use. Taper use at 3 mo. Pt should not smoke (behavioral tx program advised), take safety precautions for CNS effects, report hearing/vision changes, chest pain.

NIFEdipine (Procardia)
CLASS Antianginal, antihypertensive, calcium channel blocker
PREG/CONT C/NA

IND & DOSE Tx of angina. Adult: 10 mg PO tid; range, 10–20 mg tid. Max, 180 mg/day. Tx of hypertension. Adult: 30–60 mg/day ER tablet PO; max, 90–120 mg/day.
ADV EFF Angina, asthenia, AV block, constipation, cough, dizziness, fatigue, flushing, headache, hypotension, light-headedness, mood changes, nasal congestion, nervousness, n/v, peripheral edema, tremor, weakness
INTERACTIONS Beta blockers, cimetidine, CYP3A inhibitors/inducers, digoxin, grapefruit juice
NC/PT Monitor closely while adjusting dose. Pt should swallow ER tablet whole and not cut, crush, or chew it; avoid grapefruit juice; take safety precautions for CNS effects; report irregular heartbeat, swelling of hands/feet.

nilotinib (Tasigna)
CLASS Antineoplastic, kinase inhibitor
PREG/CONT D/NA

BBW Risk of prolonged QT, sudden death. Increased risk w/hypokalemia, hypomagnesemia, known prolonged QT; avoid these combinations.
IND & DOSE Tx of Philadelphia chromosome–positive CML. Adult: 300–400 mg PO bid 12 hr apart on empty stomach.
ADJUST DOSE Hepatic impairment
ADV EFF Abd pain, anorexia, bone marrow suppression, constipation, fatigue, headache, hepatic dysfx, nasopharyngitis, n/v/d, pain, pancreatitis, prolonged QT, rash, sudden death, tumor lysis syndrome
INTERACTIONS Proton pump inhibitors, QT-prolonging drugs, strong CYP3A4 inducers/inhibitors, St. John's wort
NC/PT Obtain baseline, periodic ECG, QT measurement, LFTs, lipase levels. Not for use in pregnancy (barrier contraceptives advised)/breast-feeding, long-term tx. Pt should avoid exposure to infection; report all drugs/herbs being used, urine/stool color changes, signs of infection, unusual bleeding.

nimodipine (Nymalize)
CLASS Calcium channel blocker
PREG/CONT C/NA

BBW Do not give parenterally; serious to fatal reactions have occurred.
IND & DOSE To improve neurologic outcomes after subarachnoid hemorrhage from ruptured aneurysm. Adult: 60 mg PO q 4 hr for 21 days.
ADJUST DOSE Hepatic impairment
ADV EFF Bradycardia, hypotension, diarrhea
INTERACTIONS Antihypertensives, CYP3A4 inducers/inhibitors
NC/PT If pt unable to swallow capsule, may extract drug from capsule using syringe, give through NG or PEG tube, then flush w/normal saline. Do not give parenterally. Monitor carefully; provide life support as needed.

nintedanib (Ofev)
CLASS Kinase inhibitor
PREG/CONT D/NA

IND & DOSE Tx of idiopathic pulmonary fibrosis. Adult: 150 mg PO bid 12 hr apart w/food.
ADJUST DOSE Hepatic/renal impairment
ADV EFF Bleeding, GI perforation, hepatotoxicity, n/v/d, renal toxicity, thrombotic events
INTERACTIONS CYP3A4 inhibitors, P-gp inhibitors, smoking
NC/PT Assess lung function, LFTs before, regularly during tx. Not for use in pregnancy/breast-feeding.

Monitor hydration; consider anti-emetics, antidiarrheals if needed. Pt should report severe dehydration, vomiting, bleeding, chest pain.

nisoldipine (Sular)

CLASS Antihypertensive, calcium channel blocker
PREG/CONT C/NA

IND & DOSE Tx of hypertension. *Adult:* 17 mg/day PO; increase in wkly increments of 8.5 mg/wk until BP controlled; range, 17–34 mg/day PO. Max, 34 mg/day.
ADJUST DOSE Elderly pts, hepatic impairment
ADV EFF Angina, asthenia, dizziness, edema, fatigue, headache, high-fat meals, light-headedness, MI, nausea
INTERACTIONS Cimetidine, cyclosporine, grapefruit juice, quinidine
NC/PT Monitor closely when titrating to therapeutic dose. Pt should swallow tablet whole and not cut, crush, or chew it; take w/meals; avoid grapefruit juice, high-fat meals; report chest pain, shortness of breath.

nitazoxanide (Alinia)

CLASS Antiprotozoal
PREG/CONT B/NA

IND & DOSE Tx of diarrhea caused by Giardia lamblia. *Adult, child 12 yr and older:* 500 mg PO q 12 hr w/food, or 25 mL (500 mg) suspension PO q 12 hr w/food. *Child 4–11 yr:* 10 mL (200 mg) suspension PO q 12 hr w/food. *Child 1–3 yr:* 5 mL (100 mg) suspension PO q 12 hr w/food. Tx of diarrhea caused by Cryptosporidium parvum. *Child 4–11 yr:* 10 mL (200 mg) PO q 12 hr w/food. *Child 1–3 yr:* 5 mL (100 mg) suspension PO q 12 hr w/food.
ADV EFF Abd pain, diarrhea, headache, vomiting
NC/PT Culture before tx. Ensure hydration. Pt should take w/food, report continued diarrhea, vomiting.

nitrofurantoin (Macrobid, Macrodantin)

CLASS Antibacterial, urinary tract anti-infective
PREG/CONT B/NA

IND & DOSE Tx of UTIs. *Adult:* 50–100 mg PO qid for 10–14 days, or 100 mg PO bid for 7 days (Macrobid). Max, 400 mg/day. *Child over 1 mo:* 5–7 mg/kg/day in four divided doses PO. Long-term suppression of UTIs. *Adult:* 50–100 mg PO at bedtime. *Child:* 1 mg/kg/day PO in one or two doses.
ADV EFF Abd pain, bone marrow suppression, dizziness, drowsiness, hepatotoxicity, n/v/d, pulmonary hypersensitivity, rash, Stevens-Johnson syndrome, superinfections
NC/PT Culture before tx. Monitor CBC, LFTs regularly. Monitor pulmonary function. Urine may be brown or yellow-green. Pt should take w/food or milk, complete full course, take safety precautions for CNS effects, report difficulty breathing.

nitroglycerin (Minitran, Nitro-Dur, Nitrolingual Pumpspray, Nitromist, Nitrostat, Rectiv)

CLASS Antianginal, nitrate
PREG/CONT C/NA

IND & DOSE Tx of acute anginal attack. *Adult:* 1 sublingual tablet under tongue or in buccal pouch at first sign of anginal attack, let dissolve; repeat q 5 min until relief obtained. No more than 3 tablets/15 min. Or, for translingual spray: Spray preparation delivers 0.4 mg/metered dose. At onset of attack, one to two metered doses sprayed into oral mucosa; no more than three doses/15 min. Px of angina attacks. *Adult:* Sublingual, 1 tablet 5–10 min before activities that might precipitate attack. Buccal, 1 tablet between lip, gum; allow to dissolve over 3–5 min. Tablet should not be chewed/swallowed. Initial dose, 1 mg q 5 hr while awake; maint, 2 mg tid. SR tablet, 2.5–9 mg q 12 hr; max, 26 mg qid. Topical, ½ inch q 8 hr. Increase by ½ inch to achieve desired results. Usual dose, 1–2 inches q 8 hr; max 4–5 inches q 4 hr has been used. 1 inch ½ 15 mg nitroglycerin. Transdermal, one patch applied each day. Translingual spray, one to two metered doses sprayed into oral mucosa 5–10 min before activity that might precipitate attack. **Tx of moderate to severe pain associated w/anal fissure.** *Adult:* 1 inch ointment intraanally q 12 hr for 3 wk *(Rectiv).* **Tx of periop hypertension, HF associated w/MI, angina unresponsive to nitrates, beta blockers.** *Adult:* 5 mcg/min IV through infusion pump. Increase by 5-mcg/min increments q 3–5 min as needed. If no response at 20 mcg/min, increase increments to 10–20 mcg/min.

ADV EFF Abd pain, angina, apprehension, faintness, headache, **hypotension,** local reaction to topical use, n/v, rash

INTERACTIONS Ergots, heparin, sildenafil, tadalafil, vardenafil

NC/PT Review proper administration of each form. Sublingual should "fizzle" under tongue; replace q 6 mo. Withdraw gradually after long-term use. Pt may relieve headache by lying down. Pt should not cut, crush, or chew SR tablet; apply topical to clean, dry, hair-free area (remove old patch before applying new one); take safety precautions for CNS effects; report unrelieved chest pain, severe headache.

---

nitroprusside sodium
(Nitropress)

CLASS Antihypertensive, vasodilator

PREG/CONT C/NA

BBW Monitor BP closely. Do not let BP drop too rapidly; do not lower systolic BP below 60 mm Hg. Monitor blood acid-base balance (metabolic acidosis early sign of cyanide toxicity; serum thiocyanate level daily during prolonged tx, especially w/renal impairment.

IND & DOSE Tx of hypertensive crises; controlled hypotension during anesthesia; tx of acute HF. *Adult, child:* Not on antihypertensive: Average dose, 3 mcg/kg/min IV; range, 0.3–10 mcg/kg/min. At this rate, diastolic BP usually lowered by 30%–40% below pretreatment diastolic level. Use smaller doses in pts on antihypertensive. Max infusion rate, 10 mcg/kg/min. If this rate does not reduce BP within 10 min, stop drug.

ADJUST DOSE Elderly pts, renal impairment

ADV EFF Abd pain, apprehension, **cyanide toxicity,** diaphoresis, faintness, headache, **hypotension,** muscle twitching, n/v, restlessness

NC/PT Do not mix in sol w/other drugs. Monitor BP, IV frequently. Have amyl nitrate inhalation, materials to make 3% sodium nitrite sol, sodium thiosulfate on hand for nitroprusside overdose and depletion of body stores of sulfur, leading to cyanide toxicity. Pt should report chest pain, pain at injection site.

---

nivolumab (Opdivo)

CLASS Antineoplastic, human programmed death receptor-1 blocking antibody

PREG/CONT D/NA

IND & DOSE Tx of unresectable or metastatic melanoma w/progression after ipilimumab and BRAF inhibitor if BRAF V600 mutation–positive; advanced, metastatic non-small-cell lung cancer w/ progression after platinum-based chemotherapy; advanced renal cell carcinoma after antiangiogenic therapy. *Adult:* 3 mg/kg IV over 60 min q 2 wk.

ADV EFF Immune-mediated reactions (pneumonitis, colitis, hepatitis, thyroiditis), rash
NC/PT Give corticosteroids based on immune reaction severity; withhold drug if reaction is severe. Not for use in pregnancy (contraceptives advised)/breast-feeding. Pt should mark calendar w/return dates for infusion; report difficulty breathing, severe diarrhea, urine/stool color changes.

nizatidine (Axid)
CLASS Histamine-2 antagonist
PREG/CONT B/NA

IND & DOSE Short-term tx of active duodenal ulcer, benign gastric ulcer. *Adult:* 300 mg PO daily at bedtime. Maint tx of healed duodenal ulcer; tx of GERD. *Adult:* 150 mg PO daily at bedtime. Px of heartburn, acid indigestion. *Adult:* 75 mg PO w/water 30–60 min before problematic food, beverages.
ADJUST DOSE Elderly pts; hepatic, renal impairment
ADV EFF Bone marrow suppression, cardiac arrest, cardiac arrhythmias, confusion, diarrhea, dizziness, ED, gynecomastia, hallucinations, headache, hepatic dysfx, somnolence
INTERACTIONS Aspirin
NC/PT Monitor LFTs, renal function, CBC w/long-term use. Switch to oral sol if swallowing difficult. Pt should take drug at bedtime; avoid OTC drugs that may contain same ingredients; have regular medical follow-up; report unusual bleeding, dark tarry stools.

DANGEROUS DRUG

norepinephrine bitartrate (Levophed)
CLASS Cardiac stimulant, sympathomimetic, vasopressor
PREG/CONT C/NA

BBW Have phentolamine on standby for extravasation (5–10 mg phentol-

amine in 10–15 mL saline to infiltrate affected area).
IND & DOSE To restore BP in controlling certain acute hypotensive states; adjunct in cardiac arrest. *Adult:* Add 4 mL sol (1 mg/mL) to 1,000 mL 5% dextrose sol for conc of 4 mcg base/mL. Give 8–12 mcg base/min IV. Adjust gradually to maintain desired BP (usually 80–100 mm Hg systolic). Average maint, 2–4 mcg base/min.
ADV EFF Bradycardia, headache, hypertension
INTERACTIONS Methyldopa, phenothiazines, reserpine, TCAs
NC/PT Give whole blood, plasma separately, if indicated. Give IV infusions into large vein, preferably antecubital fossa, to prevent extravasation. Monitor BP q 2 min from start of infusion until desired BP achieved, then monitor q 5 min if infusion continued. Do not give pink, brown sols. Monitor for extravasation.

norethindrone acetate (Aygestin)
CLASS Progestin
PREG/CONT X/NA

IND & DOSE Tx of amenorrhea; abnormal uterine bleeding. *Adult:* 2.5–10 mg PO for 5–10 days during second half of theoretical menstrual cycle. Tx of endometriosis. *Adult:* 5 mg/day PO for 2 wk; increase in increments of 2.5 mg/day q 2 wk to max 15 mg/day.
ADV EFF Acne, amenorrhea, breakthrough bleeding/spotting, dizziness, edema, insomnia, menstrual changes, PE, photosensitivity, rash, thromboembolic disorders, vision changes/blindness, weight increase
NC/PT Stop if sudden vision loss, s&sx of thromboembolic event. Pt should mark calendar of tx days; avoid sun exposure, take safety precautions for CNS effects, report calf swelling/pain, chest pain, vision changes, difficulty breathing.

norgestrel (generic)

CLASS Hormonal contraceptive, progestin

PREG/CONT X/NA

IND & DOSE To prevent pregnancy.
1 tablet PO daily, starting on first day of menstruation, at same time each day, q day of year. For one missed dose, 1 tablet as soon as pt remembers, then next tablet at usual time. For two consecutive missed doses, pt takes one of missed tablets, discards other, takes daily tablet at usual time. For three consecutive missed doses, pt should discontinue immediately, use additional form of birth control until menses, or pregnancy ruled out. Found in combination contraceptive products.

ADV EFF Breakthrough bleeding/spotting, breast tenderness, **cerebral hemorrhage**, corneal curvature changes, edema, menstrual changes, migraine, **MI, PE**, thrombophlebitis

INTERACTIONS Barbiturates, carbamazepine, griseofulvin, hydantoins, penicillins, rifampin, St. John's wort, tetracyclines

NC/PT Arrange for pretreatment, periodic complete physical, Pap test. Start no earlier than 4 wk postpartum. Stop if s&sx of thrombotic event, sudden vision loss. Not for use in pregnancy. Review all drugs pt taking; additional contraceptive measure may be needed. Pt should avoid sun exposure, St. John's wort; take safety precautions for CNS effects; report calf swelling/pain, vision loss, difficulty breathing.

nortriptyline hydrochloride (Pamelor)

CLASS TCA

PREG/CONT D/NA

BBW Limit access in depressed, potentially suicidal pts. Risk of suicidality in children, adolescents, young adults; monitor accordingly.

IND & DOSE Tx of depression.
Adult: 25 PO mg tid–qid. Max,

150 mg/day. *Child 12 yr and over:* 30–50 mg/day PO in divided doses.

ADJUST DOSE Elderly pts

ADV EFF Atropine-like effects, **bone marrow depression**, constipation, disturbed concentration, dry mouth, glossitis, gynecomastia, hyperglycemia, orthostatic hypotension, photosensitivity, **seizures, stroke**, urine retention

INTERACTIONS Alcohol, cimetidine, clonidine, fluoxetine, MAOIs, sympathomimetics

NC/PT Monitor CBC. Pt should take at bedtime if drowsiness an issue; avoid sun exposure, alcohol; take safety precautions for CNS effects; use sugarless lozenges for dry mouth; report thoughts of suicide, unusual bleeding, numbness/tingling.

nystatin (generic)

CLASS Antifungal

PREG/CONT C/NA

IND & DOSE Local tx of vaginal candidiasis (moniliasis). *Adult:* 1 tablet (100,000 units) or 1 applicator cream (100,000 units) vaginally daily–bid for 2 wk. Tx of cutaneous/mucocutaneous mycotic infections caused by *Candida albicans*, other *Candida* sp. *Adult:* Apply to affected area two to three times daily until healing complete. For fungal foot infection, dust powder on feet, in shoes/socks. Tx of oropharyngeal candidiasis. *Adult, child over 1 yr:* 500,000–1,000,000 units PO tid for at least 48 hr after clinical cure, or 400,000–600,000 units suspension four times/day for 14 days and for at least 48 hr after sx subside.

ADV EFF GI distress, local reactions at application site, rash

NC/PT Culture before tx. Pt should complete full course of tx; hold suspension in mouth as long as possible (can be made into popsicle for longer retention); clean affected area before topical application; use appropriate hygiene to prevent reinfection; report worsening of condition.

obinutuzumab (Gazyva)

CLASS Antineoplastic, monoclonal antibody
PREG/CONT C/NA

BBW Risk of reactivation of hepatitis B, fulminant hepatitis, progressive multifocal leukoencephalopathy (PML), death. Monitor closely.
IND & DOSE Tx of previously untreated chronic lymphocytic leukemia, w/chlorambucil. *Adult:* 6-day cycle: 100 mg IV on day 1, cycle 1; 900 mg IV on day 2, cycle 1; 1,000 mg IV on day 8 and 15, cycle 1; 1,000 mg IV on day 1 of cycles 2–6.
ADV EFF Cough, bone marrow suppression, fever, **hepatotoxicity**, infusion reactions, n/v/d, PML, thrombocytopenia, tumor lysis syndrome
NC/PT Premedicate with glucocorticoids, acetaminophen, antihistamine. For pt with large tumor load, premedicate w/antihyperuricemics; ensure adequate hydration. Dilute and administer as IV infusion, not IV push or bolus. Do not give live vaccines before or during tx. Monitor LFTs; stop drug w/sx of hepatotoxicity. Monitor CBC; watch for progressive multifocal leukoencephalopathy, infection, bleeding; hemorrhage may require blood products. Pt should avoid pregnancy during and for 12 mo after tx; avoid breast-feeding; take safety measures for drug reaction; report urine/stool color changes, severe n/v/d, fever, dizziness, CNS changes, unusual bleeding.

octreotide acetate (Sandostatin)

CLASS Antidiarrheal, hormone
PREG/CONT B/NA

IND & DOSE Symptomatic tx of carcinoid tumors. *Adult:* First 2 wk: 100–600 mcg/day subcut in two to four divided doses; mean daily dose, 300 mcg. Tx of watery diarrhea of VIPomas. *Adult:* 200–300 mcg

subcut in two to four divided doses during first 2 wk to control sx. Depot injection, 20 mg IM q 4 wk. *Child:* 1–10 mcg/kg/day subcut. Range, 150–750 mcg subcut. Tx of acromegaly. *Adult:* 50 mcg tid subcut, adjusted up to 100–500 mcg tid. Withdraw for 4 wk once yrly. Depot injection: 20 mg IM intragluteally q 4 wk.
ADV EFF Abd pain, asthenia, anxiety, bradycardia, cholelithiasis, dizziness, fatigue, flushing, injection-site pain, hyperglycemia, hypoglycemia, lightheadedness, n/v/d
NC/PT Give subcut; rotate sites. Give depot injections deep IM; avoid deltoid region. Arrange to withdraw for 4 wk (8 wk for depot injection) once yrly for acromegaly. Monitor blood glucose, gallbladder ultrasound. Pt should take safety precautions for CNS effects, report severe abd pain, severe pain at injection site. Name confusion between *Sandostatin* (octreotide) and *Sandimmune* (cyclosporine); use caution.

ofatumumab (Arzerra)

CLASS Antineoplastic, cytotoxic
PREG/CONT C/NA

BBW Risk of hepatitis B reactivation, fulminant hepatitis, progressive multifocal leukoencephalopathy, death. Monitor closely.
IND & DOSE Tx of chronic lymphocytic leukemia (CLL) refractory to standard tx, w/chlorambucil. *Adult:* 300 mg IV, then 1,000 mg/wk IV on day 8, followed by 1,000 mg IV on day 1 of subsequent 28-day cycles. Minimum of 3 cycles, max of 12 cycles. Tx of CLL refractory to fludarabine, alemtuzumab. *Adult:* 300 mg IV, followed in 1 wk by 2,000 mg/wk IV in seven doses, followed in 4 wk by 2,000 mg IV q 4 wk for four doses.
ADV EFF Anemia, ataxia, bone marrow suppression, bronchitis, cough, diarrhea, dizziness, dyspnea, fatigue, fever, **hepatitis B reactivation**, infusion reactions, intestinal obstruction,

nausea, **progressive multifocal leukoencephalopathy**, tumor lysis syndrome, URI, vision problems
INTERACTIONS Live vaccines
NC/PT Premedicate w/acetaminophen, IV antihistamine, IV corticosteroids. Monitor CBC regularly. Not for use in pregnancy (contraceptives advised). Pt should avoid exposure to infection, take safety precautions for CNS effects, report difficulty breathing, unusual bleeding, s&sx of infection, difficulty breathing.

---

ofloxacin (Floxin Otic, Ocuflox)
CLASS Fluoroquinolone
PREG/CONT C/NA

BBW Increased risk of tendinitis, tendon rupture. Risk higher in pts over 60 yr, women, pts w/kidney/heart/lung transplant. Risk of exacerbated muscle weakness, sometimes severe, w/myasthenia gravis; do not give w/hx of myasthenia gravis.
IND & DOSE Tx of infections caused by susceptible bacteria strains. Uncomplicated UTIs: *Adult:* 200 mg q 12 hr PO for 3–7 days. Complicated UTIs: *Adult:* 200 mg PO bid for 10 days. **Bacterial exacerbations of COPD, community-acquired pneumonia, mild to moderate skin infections.** *Adult:* 400 mg PO q 12 hr for 10 days. **Prostatitis.** *Adult:* 300 mg PO q 12 hr for 6 wk. **Acute, uncomplicated gonorrhea.** *Adult:* 400 mg PO as single dose. **Cervicitis, urethritis.** *Adult:* 300 mg PO q 12 hr for 7 days. **Ocular infections.** *Adult:* 1–2 drops/eye as indicated. **Otic infections.** *Adult, child over 13 yr:* 10 drops/day in affected ear for 7 days. *Child 6 mo–13 yr:* 5 drops/day in affected ear for 7 days. *Child 1–12 yr w/tympanostomy tubes:* 5 drops in affected ear for 10 days. **Swimmer's ear.** *Adult:* 10 drops/day (1.5 mg) in affected ear for 7 days. *Child 12 yr and older:* 10 drops in affected ear bid for 10 days. *Child 6 mo–under 12 yr:*

5 drops in affected ear bid for 10 day. **Chronic suppurative otitis media.** *Adult, child:* 10 drops in affected ear bid for 14 days.
ADJUST DOSE Elderly pts, renal impairment
ADV EFF Bone marrow suppression, dizziness, drowsiness, headache, **hepatic impairment**, insomnia, n/v/d, photosensitivity, prolonged QT, tendinitis, tendon rupture
INTERACTIONS Antacids, iron salts, QT-prolonging drugs, St. John's wort, sucralfate, zinc
NC/PT Culture before tx. Teach proper administration of eye/eardrops. Pt should take oral drug 1 hr before or 2 hr after meals on empty stomach; avoid antacids within 2 hr of ofloxacin; drink plenty of fluids; avoid sun exposure; take safety precautions for CNS effects; report tendon pain, severe GI upset, unusual bleeding.

---

olanzapine (Zyprexa)
CLASS Antipsychotic, dopaminergic blocker
PREG/CONT C/NA

BBW Increased risk of death when used in elderly pts w/dementia-related psychosis; drug not approved for this use. Risk of severe sedation, including coma/delirium, after each injection of *Zyprexa Relprevv.* Monitor pt for at least 3 hr after injection, w/ ready access to emergency services. Because of risk, drug available only through *Zyprexa Relprevv* Patient Care Program.
IND & DOSE Tx of schizophrenia. *Adult:* 5–10 mg/day PO. Increase to 10 mg/day PO within several days; max, 20 mg/day. Or long-acting injection (*Zyprexa Relprevv*): 150, 210, or 300 mg IM q 2 wk, or 300 or 405 mg IM q 4 wk. *Child 13–17 yr:* 2.5–5 mg/day PO; target, 10 mg/day. **Tx of bipolar mania.** *Adult:* 10–15 mg/day PO. Max, 20 mg/day; maint, 5–20 mg/day PO. *Child 13–17 yr:* 2.5–5 mg/day PO; target, 10 mg/day. **Tx of agitation**

associated w/schizophrenia, mania.
Adult: 10 mg IM; range, 5–10 mg.
May repeat in 2 hr if needed; max,
30 mg/24 hr. **Tx-resistant depression.** *Adult:* 5 mg/day PO w/fluoxetine
20 mg/day PO; range, 5–12.5 mg/day
olanzapine w/20–50 mg/day PO
fluoxetine
ADJUST DOSE Elderly/debilitated pts
ADV EFF Constipation, diabetes mellitus, dizziness, dyslipidemia, fever,
gynecomastia, headache, hyperglycemia, hyperprolactinemia, **NMS**, orthostatic hypotension, somnolence,
weight gain
INTERACTIONS Alcohol, anticholinergics, antihypertensives, benzodiazepines, carbamazepine, CNS drugs,
dopamine agonists, fluoxetine, fluvoxamine, levodopa, omeprazole,
rifampin, smoking
NC/PT Dispense 1 wk at a time. Use
care to distinguish short-term from
long-term IM form. Monitor serum
glucose, lipids; watch for metabolic
changes, weight gain, hyperglycemia.
Not for use in pregnancy. Alert pt of
risk of gynecomastia. Pt should peel
back (not push through) foil on blister
pack of disintegrating tablet, remove
w/dry hands; avoid alcohol; report all
drugs being used (many interactions
possible); take safety precautions for
CNS effects, orthostatic hypotension;
report fever, flulike sx. Name confusion between *Zyprexa* (olanzapine) and
Zyrtec (cetirizine); use caution.

---

olmesartan medoxomil
(Benicar)
CLASS Antihypertensive, ARB
PREG/CONT D/NA

BBW Rule out pregnancy before tx;
suggest barrier contraceptives. Fetal
injury, death has occurred.
IND & DOSE Tx of hypertension.
Adult, child 6–16 yr, 35 kg or more:
20 mg/day PO; may titrate to
40 mg/day after 2 wk. *Child 6–16 yr,
20–under 35 kg:* 10 mg/day PO; max,
20 mg/day PO.

ADV EFF Abd/back pain, **angioedema**, bronchitis, cough, dizziness,
drowsiness, flulike sx, headache,
n/v/d, URI
INTERACTIONS ACE inhibitors,
ARBs, colesevelam, lithium, NSAIDs,
renin inhibitors
NC/PT Alert surgeon if surgery
scheduled; fluid volume expansion
may be needed. Not for use in pregnancy (barrier contraceptives advised)/breast-feeding. Pt should use
caution in situations that may lead to
BP drop (excessive hypotension possible); take safety precautions for
CNS effects; report swelling.

---

olodaterol (Striverdi
Respimat)
CLASS Long-acting beta-2
adrenergic agonist
PREG/CONT C/NA

BBW Increased risk of asthma-related deaths; not indicated for use
in asthma.
IND & DOSE Long-term maint bronchodilator for COPD. *Adult:* 2 inhalations once daily at same time each day.
ADV EFF Abd pain, arrhythmias,
arthralgia, bronchitis, **bronchospasm**,
cough, diarrhea, dizziness, hypertension, hypokalemia, tachycardia, URI,
UTI
INTERACTIONS Adrenergics, beta
blockers, MAOIs, steroids, xanthines
NC/PT Not for use in asthma; not
for acute attacks. Teach proper use of
inhaler. Pt should report difficulty
breathing, worsening of sx, palpitations, chest pain.

---

olsalazine sodium
(Dipentum)
CLASS Anti-inflammatory
PREG/CONT C/NA

IND & DOSE Maint of remission of
ulcerative colitis in pts resistant to
sulfasalazine. *Adult:* 1 g/day PO in
divided doses w/meals.

ADJUST DOSE Renal impairment
ADV EFF Abd pain, diarrhea, headache, itching, rash
INTERACTIONS Heparin, 6-mercaptopurine, thioguanine, varicella vaccine, warfarin
NC/PT Not for use in breast-feeding. Pt should always take w/food, report severe diarrhea.

omacetaxine mepesuccinate (Synribo)
CLASS Antineoplastic, protein synthesis inhibitor
PREG/CONT D/NA

IND & DOSE Tx of adult w/ accelerated CML w/resistance or intolerance to two or more kinase inhibitors. *Adult:* 1.25 mg/m² subcut bid for 14 consecutive days of 28-day cycle, then 1.25 mg/m² subcut bid for 7 consecutive days of 28-day cycle.
ADV EFF Bleeding, fatigue, fever, hair loss, hyperglycemia, injection-site reactions, n/v/d, severe myelosuppression
NC/PT Monitor bone marrow function frequently; dosage adjustment may be needed. Monitor blood glucose. Not for use in pregnancy/breast-feeding. Pt should avoid exposure to infections; be aware fatigue, bleeding, hair loss possible; report unusual bleeding, fever, s&sx of infection, rash.

omalizumab (Xolair)
CLASS Antiasthmatic, monoclonal antibody
PREG/CONT B/NA

BBW Anaphylaxis w/bronchospasm, hypotension, syncope, urticaria, edema possible. Monitor closely after each dose; have emergency equipment on hand.
IND & DOSE To decrease asthma exacerbation in pts w/moderate to severe asthma, positive skin test to perennial airborne allergens. *Adult, child over 12 yr:* 150–375 mg subcut

q 2–4 wk. Tx of chronic idiopathic urticaria in pts who remain symptomatic w/antihistamines. *Adult, child 12 and over:* 150–300 mg subcut q 4 wk.
ADV EFF Acute asthma sx, anaphylaxis, cancer, eosinophilic conditions, fever, injection-site reactions, pain, rash
NC/PT Base dose on weight, pretreatment immunoglobulin E level for asthma. Monitor after each injection for anaphylaxis. Not for use in breast-feeding. Pt should have appropriate cancer screening, report difficulty breathing, tongue swelling, rash, chest tightness, fever.

omega-3-acid ethyl esters (Lovaza)
CLASS Lipid-lowering drug, omega-3 fatty acid
PREG/CONT C/NA

IND & DOSE Adjunct to diet to reduce very high (over 500 mg/dL) triglycerides. *Adult:* 4 g/day PO as single dose (4 capsules) or divided into two doses (2 capsules PO bid).
ADV EFF Back pain, eructation, dyspepsia, flulike sx, infection, taste changes
INTERACTIONS Anticoagulants
NC/PT Monitor serum triglycerides. Ensure use of diet/exercise program. Use caution w/hx of fish, shellfish sensitivity. Not for use in pregnancy/breast-feeding. Make confusion between *Omacor* (former brand name of omega-3-acid ethyl esters) and *Amicar* (aminocaproic acid). Although *Omacor* has been changed to *Lovaza*, confusion possible; use caution.

omega-3-carboxylic acids (Epanova)
CLASS Lipid-lowering drug, omega-3 fatty acid
PREG/CONT C/NA

IND & DOSE Adjunct to diet to reduce very high (over 500 mg/dL)

triglycerides. *Adult:* 2–4 g/day PO as single dose.
ADV EFF Abd pain, eructation, dyspepsia, n/v/d
INTERACTIONS Drugs affecting coagulation
NC/PT Ensure proper use of drug. Monitor serum triglycerides. Ensure use of diet/exercise program. Use caution w/hx of fish, shellfish sensitivity. Not for use in pregnancy/breast-feeding.

omeprazole (Prilosec, Zegerid)

CLASS Proton pump inhibitor
PREG/CONT C/NA

IND & DOSE Tx of active duodenal ulcer. *Adult:* 20 mg/day PO for 2–8 wk. **Tx of active gastric ulcer.** *Adult:* 40 mg/day PO for 4–8 wk. **Tx of severe erosive esophagitis, poorly responsive GERD.** *Adult:* 20 mg/day PO for 4–8 wk. **Tx of pathologic hypersecretory conditions.** *Adult:* 60 mg/day PO. Up to 120 mg tid has been used. **Tx of frequent heartburn.** *Adult:* 20 mg/day (*Prilosec OTC* tablet) PO in a.m. before eating for 14 days. May repeat 14-day course q 4 mo. **Upper GI bleeding in critically ill pts.** *Adult:* 40 mg PO then 40 mg PO in 6–8 hr on day 1, then 40 mg/day for up to 14 days (*Zegerid*). **GERD, other acid-related disorders.** *Adult, child 1 yr and over:* 20 kg or more, 20 mg daily PO; 10–under 20 kg, 10 mg daily PO; 5–10 kg, 5 mg daily PO.
ADV EFF Abd pain, acute interstitial nephritis, bone fractures, CDAD, dizziness, headache, n/v/d, pneumonia, rash, URI, vitamin B_{12} deficiency
INTERACTIONS Atazanavir, benzodiazepines, cilostazol, clopidogrel, methotrexate, nelfinavir, phenytoin, saquinavir, sucralfate, tacrolimus, warfarin
NC/PT If sx persist after 8 wk, reevaluate. Pt should take w/meals; swallow capsule whole and not cut, crush, or chew it; if cannot swallow, open capsules, sprinkle contents on applesauce, swallow immediately; take safety precautions for CNS effects; report severe diarrhea, fever.

onabotulinumtoxinA (Botox, Botox Cosmetic)

CLASS Neurotoxin
PREG/CONT C/NA

BBW Drug not for tx of muscle spasticity; toxin may spread from injection area and cause s&sx of botulism (CNS alterations, difficulty speaking and swallowing, loss of bladder control). Use only for approved indications.
IND & DOSE Improvement of glabellar lines. *Adult:* Total of 20 units (0.5 mL) sol injected as divided doses of 0.1 mL in each of five sites—two in each corrugator muscle, one in procerus muscle; repetition usually needed q 3–4 mo to maintain effect. **Cervical dystonia.** *Adult:* 236 units (range, 198–300 units) divided among affected muscles and injected into each muscle in pts w/known tolerance. In pts without prior use, 100 units or less, then adjust dose based on pt response. **Primary axillary hyperhidrosis.** *Adult:* 50 units/axilla injected intradermally 0.1–0.2 mL in multiple sites (10–15), about 1–2 cm apart. Repeat as needed. **Blepharospasm associated w/dystonia.** *Adult:* 1.25–2.5 units injected into medial and lateral pretarsal orbicularis oculi of lower and upper lids. Repeat about q 3 mo. **Strabismus associated w/dystonia.** *Adult:* 1.25–50 units injected in any one muscle. **Upper limb spasticity.** *Adult:* Base dose on muscles affected and severity of activity; electromyographic guidance recommended. Use no more than 50 units per site. **Tx of chronic migraine.** *Adult:* 155 units IM as 0.1 mL (5 units) at each site; divide into seven head/neck muscle areas. **Tx of urinary incontinence in pts w/neurologic conditions.** *Adult:* 200 units as 1-mL injection across 30 sites into detrusor muscle.

ADV EFF Anaphylactic reactions, dizziness, headache, local reactions, **MI, spread of toxin that can lead to death**

INTERACTIONS Aminoglycosides, anticholinesterases, lincosamides, magnesium sulfate, NMJ blockers, polymyxin, quinidine, succinylcholine
NC/PT Store in refrigerator. Have epinephrine available in case of anaphylactic reactions. Effects may not appear for 1–2 days; will persist for 3–4 mo. Not for use in pregnancy.

ondansetron hydrochloride (Zofran, Zuplenz)
CLASS Antiemetic
PREG/CONT B/NA

IND & DOSE Px of chemotherapy-induced n/v. *Adult:* Three 0.15-mg/kg doses IV: First dose over 15 min starting 30 min before chemotherapy; subsequent doses at 4 and 8 hr. Or, single 32-mg dose infused over 15 min starting 30 min before chemotherapy. Or, 8 mg PO 30 min before chemotherapy, then 8 mg PO 8 hr later; give 8 mg PO q 12 hr for 1–2 days after chemotherapy. For highly emetogenic chemotherapy, 24 mg PO 30 min before chemotherapy. *Child 6 mo–18 yr:* Three 0.15-mg/kg doses IV over 15 min starting 30 min before chemotherapy, then 4 and 8 hr later. *Child 4–11 yr:* 4 mg PO 30 min before chemotherapy, 4 mg PO at 4 and 8 hr, then 4 mg PO tid for 1–2 days after chemotherapy. Px of n/v associated w/radiotherapy. *Adult:* 8 mg PO tid. For total-body radiotherapy, give 1–2 hr before radiation each day. For single high-dose radiotherapy to abdomen, give 1–2 hr before radiotherapy, then q 8 hr for 1–2 days after therapy. For daily fractionated radiotherapy to abdomen, give 1–2 hr before tx, then q 8 hr for each day tx given. Px of postop n/v. *Adult:* 4 mg undiluted IV, preferably over 2–5 min, or as single IM dose immediately before anesthesia

induction. Or, 16 mg PO 1 hr before anesthesia. *Child 1 mo–12 yr:* Single dose of 4 mg IV over 2–5 min if over 40 kg, 0.1 mg/kg IV over 2–5 min if under 40 kg.
ADJUST DOSE Hepatic impairment
ADV EFF Abd pain, diarrhea, dizziness, drowsiness, headache, myalgia, pain at injection site, **prolong QT, serotonin syndrome,** weakness
INTERACTIONS QT-prolonging drugs
NC/PT Obtain baseline ECG for QT interval. Ensure timing to correspond w/ surgery, chemotherapy. For *Zofran* orally disintegrating tablet, pt should peel foil back over (do not push through) one blister, immediately place on tongue, swallow w/saliva. For *Zuplenz,* pt should use dry hands, fold pouch along dotted line, carefully tear pouch along edge, remove film, place on tongue, swallow after it dissolves, then wash hands. Pt should take safety precautions for CNS effects; report pain at injection site, palpitations.

opium preparations (Opium Tincture, Deodorized; Paregoric)
CLASS Antidiarrheal, opioid agonist
PREG/CONT C/C-III (*Paregoric*); C/C-II (*Opium Tincture, Deodorized*)

IND & DOSE Tx of diarrhea. *Adult:* 5–10 mL *Paregoric* PO daily–qid (5 mL equivalent to 2 mg morphine), or 0.6 mL *Opium Tincture* qid. Max, 6 mL/day. *Child:* 0.25–0.5 mL/kg *Paregoric* PO daily–qid.
ADJUST DOSE Elderly pts, impaired adults
ADV EFF Bronchospasm, **cardiac arrest,** constipation, dizziness, drowsiness, flushing, **laryngospasm,** light-headedness, n/v, **respiratory arrest,** sedation, **shock,** sweating, ureteral spasm, vision changes
INTERACTIONS Barbiturate general anesthetics

NC/PT *Opium Tincture, Deodorized*, contains 25 times more morphine than *Paregoric*; do not confuse dosage (severe toxicity possible). Do not use in preterm infants. It should take 4–6 hr before next feeding if breastfeeding; not take leftover medication; take safety precautions for CNS effects; use laxative if constipated; report difficulty breathing. Name confusion between *Paregoric* (camphorated tincture of opium) and *Opium Tincture, Deodorized*; use caution.

oprelvekin (Neumega)
CLASS Interleukin
PREG/CONT C/NA

BBW Severe allergic reactions, including anaphylaxis, possible; monitor w/each dose.
IND & DOSE Px of severe thrombocytopenia; to reduce need for platelet transfusions after myelosuppressive chemotherapy in pts w/nonmyeloid malignancies. *Adult:* 50 mcg/kg/day subcut starting day 1 after chemotherapy for 14–21 days.
ADJUST DOSE Renal impairment
ADV EFF Anemia, **anaphylaxis, capillary leak syndrome,** cardiac arrhythmias, dyspnea, edema, fluid retention, papilledema
NC/PT Obtain baseline, periodical CBC. Monitor for anaphylaxis; stop immediately if it occurs. Not for use in pregnancy/breast-feeding. Teach proper administration/disposal of needles/syringes. Pt should mark calendar of injection days, report difficulty breathing, weight gain, fluid retention, vision changes.

oritavancin (Orbactiv)
CLASS Lipoglycopeptide antibiotic
PREG/CONT C/NA

IND & DOSE Tx of adults w/acute bacterial skin and skin-structure infections caused by susceptible strains of gram-positive bacteria. *Adult:* 1,200 mg IV over 3 hr as single dose.
ADV EFF CDAD, **hypersensitivity reactions,** infusion reactions, n/v/d, limb/subcutaneous abscesses, osteomyelitis
INTERACTIONS Warfarin
NC/PT Culture to ensure proper use. Monitor for infusion reactions; slow infusion. Check for skin abscesses; treat appropriately. Use w/caution in pregnancy/breast-feeding. Pt should report difficulty breathing, diarrhea with blood/mucus, skin sores.

orlistat (Alli, Xenical)
CLASS Lipase inhibitor, weight loss drug
PREG/CONT X/NA

BBW Severe allergic reactions, including anaphylaxis, possible; monitor w/each dose.
IND & DOSE Tx of obesity as part of weight loss program; reduction of risk of weight gain after prior weight loss. *Adult:* 120 mg PO tid w/each fat-containing meal. OTC, 60 mg PO w/each fat-containing meal; max, 3 capsules/day. *Child 12 yr and over:* 120 mg PO tid w/fat-containing meals. OTC not for use in children.
ADV EFF Dry mouth, flatulence, incontinence, loose stools, **severe hepatic injury,** vitamin deficiency
INTERACTIONS Amiodarone, antiepileptics, cyclosporine, fat-soluble vitamins, levothyroxine, oral anticoagulants
NC/PT Increased risk of severe hepatic injury; monitor LFTs before, periodically during tx. Ensure diet, exercise program. Not for use in pregnancy (contraceptives advised). Pt should use sugarless lozenges for dry mouth, use fat-soluble vitamins (take separately from orlistat doses), report right upper quadrant pain, urine/stool color changes.

orphenadrine citrate
(Banflex, Flexon)

CLASS Skeletal muscle relaxant
PREG/CONT C/NA

IND & DOSE Relief of discomfort associated w/acute, painful musculoskeletal conditions. *Adult:* 60 mg IV, IM. May repeat q 12 hr. Inject IV over 5 min. Or, 100 mg PO q.a.m. and p.m.
ADJUST DOSE Elderly pts
ADV EFF Confusion, constipation, decreased sweating, dizziness, dry mouth, flushing, gastric irritation, headache, n/v, tachycardia, urinary hesitancy, urine retention
INTERACTIONS Alcohol, anticholinergics, haloperidol, phenothiazines
NC/PT Ensure pt supine during IV injection and for at least 15 min after; assist from supine position after tx. Pt should swallow SR tablet whole and not cut, crush, or chew it; empty bladder before each dose; use caution in hot weather (sweating reduced); avoid alcohol; take safety precautions for CNS effects; use sugarless lozenges for dry mouth; report difficulty swallowing, severe GI upset.

oseltamivir phosphate
(Tamiflu)

CLASS Antiviral, neuraminidase inhibitor
PREG/CONT C/NA

IND & DOSE Tx of uncomplicated illness due to influenza virus (A or B). *Adult, child 13 yr and older:* 75 mg PO bid for 5 days, starting within 2 days of sx onset. *Child 1–12 yr:* 30–75 mg suspension PO bid for 5 days based on weight. *Child 2 wk–under 1 yr:* 3 mg/kg PO bid for 5 days. Px of influenza A and B infection. *Adult, child 13 yr and older:* 75 mg/day PO for at least 10 days; begin within 2 days of exposure. *Child 1–12 yr:* Over 40 kg, 75 mg/day PO; 23–40 kg, 60 mg/day PO; 15–23 kg, 45 mg/day PO; 15 kg

or less, 30 mg/day PO. Continue for 10 days.
ADJUST DOSE Renal impairment
ADV EFF Abnormal behavior, anorexia, confusion, dizziness, headache, n/v, rhinitis, **Stevens-Johnson syndrome**
NC/PT Give within 2 days of exposure or sx onset. Do not use intranasal flu vaccine until 48 hr after stopping oseltamivir; do not give oseltamivir until 2 wk after live nasal flu vaccine. Pt should complete full course; refrigerate sol, shake well before each use; take safety precautions w/dizziness, CNS changes; report severe GI problems, rash.

osimertinib (Tagrisso)

CLASS Antineoplastic, kinase inhibitor
PREG/CONT High risk/NA

IND & DOSE Tx of metastatic epidermal growth factor receptor T790M mutation–positive non-small-cell lung cancer. *Adult:* 800 mg/day PO.
ADV EFF Cardiomyopathy, diarrhea, dry skin, **interstitial pneumonitis**, QT prolongation
INTERACTIONS Strong CYP3A inducers/inhibitors; avoid combination
NC/PT Ensure proper dx. Perform left ventricular function tests before use and then q 3 mo. Monitor lung function. Not for use in pregnancy (contraceptives advised during and for 6 wk after tx)/breast-feeding during and for 2 wk after tx; males should use contraceptives for 4 mo after tx. Pt should place dose in 2 oz water, stir until dissolved, drink right away, then add 4–8 oz water to container and drink (tablet will not completely dissolve); pt should not crush or heat tablet. Pt should report difficulty breathing, swelling, shortness of breath, palpitations, dizziness.

ospemifene (Osphena)

CLASS Estrogen modulator
PREG/CONT X/NA

BBW Increased risk of endometrial cancer in women w/uterus and unopposed estrogens; addition of progestin strongly advised. Increased risk of stroke, DVT; monitor accordingly.
IND & DOSE Tx of moderate to severe dyspareunia (painful intercourse) related to vulvar/vaginal atrophy due to menopause. *Adult:* 60 mg once/day with food.
ADV EFF DVT, hot flashes, hyperhidrosis, muscle spasms, **PE**, vaginal discharge
INTERACTIONS Estrogen, fluconazole, other estrogen modulators, rifampin
NC/PT Rule out pregnancy (contraceptives advised). Not for use in breast-feeding. Combine w/progestin in women w/intact uterus; ensure annual pelvic/breast exam, mammogram. Monitor for DVT, PE, other thrombotic events. Reevaluate need for drug q 3–6 mo. Pt should take once/day, schedule annual complete exam and mammogram, report vision/speech changes, difficulty breathing, vaginal bleeding, chest pain, severe leg pain.

oxacillin sodium (generic)

CLASS Penicillinase-resistant penicillin
PREG/CONT B/NA

BBW Increased risk of infection by multiple drug-resistant strains; weigh benefit/risk before use.
IND & DOSE Infections due to penicillinase-producing staphylococci; to initiate tx when staphylococcal infection suspected. *Adult, child 40 kg or more:* 250–500 mg IV q 4–6 hr; up to 1 g q 4–6 hr in severe infections. Max, 6 g/day. *Child under 40 kg:* 50–100 mg/kg/day IV in equally

divided doses q 4–6 hr. *Neonates 2 kg or more:* 25–50 mg/kg IV q 8 hr. *Neonates under 2 kg:* 25–50 mg/kg IV q 12 hr.
ADV EFF Anaphylaxis, bone marrow suppression, fever, gastritis, nephritis, n/v/d, pain, phlebitis, rash, **seizures**, sore mouth, superinfections, wheezing
INTERACTIONS Aminoglycosides, tetracyclines
NC/PT Culture before tx. Do not mix in same IV sol as other antibiotics. Be prepared for serious hypersensitivity reactions. Treat superinfections. Pt should avoid exposure to infection, use mouth care for sore mouth, report rash, difficulty breathing, signs of infection.

DANGEROUS DRUG

oxaliplatin (Eloxatin)

CLASS Antineoplastic
PREG/CONT D/NA

BBW Risk of serious to fatal anaphylactic reactions.
IND & DOSE In combination w/5-FU/leucovorin as adjunct tx of stage III colon cancer in pts w/ complete resection of primary tumor; tx of advanced colorectal cancer. *Adult:* 85 mg/m² IV infusion in 250–500 mL D₅W w/leucovorin 200 mg/m² in D₅W both over 2 hr followed by 5-FU 400 mg/m² IV bolus over 2–4 min, followed by 5-FU 600 mg/m² IV infusion in 500 mL D₅W as 22-hr continuous infusion on day 1. Then leucovorin 200 mg/m² IV infusion over 2 hr followed by 5-FU 400 mg/m² bolus over 2–4 min, followed by 5-FU 600 mg/m² IV infusion in 500 mL D₅W as 22-hr continuous infusion on day 2. Repeat cycle q 2 wk.
ADJUST DOSE Severe renal impairment
ADV EFF Abd pain, anaphylaxis, anorexia, constipation, cough, dyspnea, fatigue, hyperglycemia, hypokalemia, injection-site reactions, neuropathy, n/v/d, paresthesia,

pulmonary fibrosis, rhabdomyolysis, RPLS, severe neutropenia
INTERACTIONS Nephrotoxic drugs
NC/PT Premedicate w/antiemetics, dexamethasone. Dose adjustment may be needed based on adverse effects. Monitor for potentially dangerous anaphylactic reactions. Monitor respiratory/neurologic function. Not for use in pregnancy/breast-feeding. Pt should take safety precautions for CNS effects, report severe headache, vision changes, difficulty breathing, numbness/tingling.

oxandrolone (Oxandrin)
CLASS Anabolic steroid
PREG/CONT X/C-III

BBW Monitor LFTs, serum electrolytes periodically. Consult physician for corrective measures; risk of peliosis hepatitis, liver cell tumors. Measure cholesterol periodically in pts at high risk for CAD; lipids may increase.
IND & DOSE Relief of bone pain w/ osteoporosis; adjunct tx to promote weight gain after weight loss due to extensive trauma; to offset protein catabolism associated w/prolonged corticosteroid use; HIV wasting syndrome; HIV-associated muscle weakness. *Adult:* 2.5 mg PO bid–qid; max, 20 mg. May need 2–4 wk to evaluate response. *Child:* Total daily dose, 0.1 mg/kg or less, or 0.045 mg/lb or less PO; may repeat intermittently.
ADV EFF Abd fullness, acne, anorexia, blood lipid changes, burning of tongue, excitation, gynecomastia, **hepatitis**, hirsutism in females, **intra-abdominal hemorrhage, liver cell tumors, liver failure**, virilization of prepubertal males
NC/PT May need 2–4 wk to evaluate response. Monitor effect on child w/ long-bone X-rays q 3–6 mo; stop drug well before bone age reaches norm for pt's chronologic age. Monitor LFTs, serum electrolytes, blood lipids. Not for use in pregnancy (barrier contraceptives advised). Pt

should take w/food, report urine/stool color changes, abd pain, severe n/v.

oxaprozin (Daypro), oxaprozin potassium (Daypro Alta)
CLASS NSAID
PREG/CONT C/NA

BBW Increased risk of CV events, GI bleeding; monitor accordingly. Contraindicated for periop pain associated w/CABG surgery.
IND & DOSE Tx of osteoarthritis. *Adult:* 1,200 mg/day PO. Use initial 600 mg/low body weight or milder disease. Tx of rheumatoid arthritis. *Adult:* 1,200 mg/day PO. Tx of juvenile rheumatoid arthritis. *Child 6–16 yr:* 600–1,200 mg/day PO based on body weight.
ADJUST DOSE Renal impairment
ADV EFF Anaphylactoid reactions to anaphylactic shock, constipation, dizziness, dyspepsia, n/v/d, platelet inhibition, rash
NC/PT Pt should take w/food; take safety precautions w/dizziness; report unusual bleeding, difficulty breathing, black tarry stools.

oxazepam (generic)
CLASS Anxiolytic, benzodiazepine
PREG/CONT D/C-IV

IND & DOSE Mgt of anxiety disorders, alcohol withdrawal. *Adult, child over 12 yr:* 10–15 mg PO or up to 30 mg PO tid–qid, depending on severity of anxiety sx. Higher range recommended in alcoholics.
ADJUST DOSE Elderly, debilitated pts
ADV EFF Apathy, bradycardia, constipation, **CV collapse**, depression, diarrhea, disorientation, dizziness, drowsiness, dry mouth, fatigue, fever, hiccups, lethargy, light-headedness
INTERACTIONS Alcohol, CNS depressants, theophylline

NC/PT Taper gradually after long-term tx, especially in pts w/epilepsy. Pt should take safety precautions for CNS effects, report vision changes, fainting, rash.

oxcarbazepine (Oxtellar XR, Trileptal)
CLASS Antiepileptic
PREG/CONT C/NA

BBW Monitor serum sodium before and periodically during tx; serious hyponatremia can occur. Teach pt to report sx (nausea, headache, malaise, lethargy, confusion).
IND & DOSE Tx of partial seizures. *Adult:* 300 mg PO bid; may increase to total 1,200 mg PO bid if clinically needed as adjunct tx. Converting to monotherapy: 300 mg PO bid started while reducing dose of other antiepileptics; reduce other drugs over 3–6 wk while increasing oxcarbazepine over 2–4 wk to max 2,400 mg/day. Starting as monotherapy: 300 mg PO bid; increase by 300 mg/day q third day until desired dose of 1,200 mg/day reached. Or 600 mg/day PO ER form; increase at wkly intervals of 600 mg/day to target 2,400 mg/day. **Adjunct tx of partial seizures.** *Child 4–16 yr:* 8–10 mg/kg/day PO in two equally divided doses; max, 600 mg/day. *Child 2–4 yr over 20 kg:* 8–10 mg/kg/day PO; max, 600 mg/day. *Child 2–4 yr under 20 kg:* 16–20 mg/kg/day PO; max, 600 mg/day. **Monotherapy for partial seizures in epileptic child.** *Child 4–16 yr:* 8–10 mg/kg/day PO in two divided doses. If pt taking another antiepileptic, slowly withdraw that drug over 3–6 wk. Then, increase oxcarbazepine in 10-mg/kg/day increments at wkly intervals to desired level. If pt not taking another antiepileptic, increase dose by 5 mg/kg/day q third day.
ADJUST DOSE Elderly pts, renal impairment
ADV EFF Bradycardia, **broncho-spasm,** confusion, disturbed coordi-nation, dizziness, drowsiness, hyper-tension, hyponatremia, hypotension, impaired fertility, n/v, **pulmonary edema, suicidality,** unsteadiness
INTERACTIONS Alcohol, carbama-zepine, felodipine, hormonal contra-ceptives, phenobarbital, phenytoin, valproic acid, verapamil
NC/PT Monitor for hyponatremia. Taper slowly if stopping or switching to other antiepileptic. Not for use in pregnancy (barrier contraceptives advised). Pt should swallow ER tab-lets whole, not cut, crush, or chew them; take safety precautions for CNS effects; avoid alcohol; wear medical ID; report unusual bleeding, difficulty breathing, thoughts of suicide, headache, confusion, lethargy.

oxybutynin chloride (Ditropan XL, Gelnique, Oxytrol)
CLASS Anticholinergic, urinary antispasmodic
PREG/CONT B/NA

IND & DOSE Relief of bladder in-stability sx; tx of overactive bladder (ER form). *Adult:* 5 mg PO bid or tid; max, 5 mg qid. ER tablets, 5 mg PO daily; max, 30 mg/day. Transdermal patch, 1 patch applied to dry, intact skin on abdomen, hip, or buttock q 3–4 days (twice wkly). (OTC form available for women 18 yr and older.) Topical gel, 1 mL applied to thigh, abdomen, or upper arm q 24 hr. *Child over 6 yr:* 5 mg ER tablets PO daily; max, 20 mg/day. *Child over 5 yr:* 5 mg PO bid; max, 5 mg tid.
ADJUST DOSE Elderly pts
ADV EFF Blurred vision, CNS ef-fects, decreased sweating, dizziness, drowsiness, dry mouth, esophagitis, tachycardia, urinary hesitancy
INTERACTIONS Amantadine, haloperidol, nitrofurantoin, phenothi-azines
NC/PT Arrange for cystometry, other diagnostic tests before, during tx. Monitor vision periodically. Periodic

bladder exams needed. Pt should swallow ER tablet whole and not cut, crush, or chew it; apply gel to high, abdomen, or upper arm (rotate sites); apply patch to dry, intact skin on abdomen, hip, or buttock (remove old patch before applying new one); take safety precautions for CNS effects; report vision changes vision, vomiting.

DANGEROUS DRUG

oxycodone hydrochloride
(OxyContin, Roxicodone)
CLASS Opioid agonist analgesic
PREG/CONT B/C-II

BBW *Roxicodone Intensol* highly concentrated preparation; use extreme care. Drug has abuse potential; monitor accordingly. Concurrent use of CYP3A4 inhibitors may result in increased drug effects, potentially fatal respiratory depression. Accidental ingestion by child can be fatal. Prolonged use in pregnancy can result in neonatal opioid withdrawal.

IND & DOSE Relief of moderate to moderately severe pain. *Adult:* Tablets, 5–15 mg PO q 4–6 hr; opioid-naïve, 10–30 mg PO q 4 hr. Capsules, 5 mg PO q 6 hr. Tablets in aversion technology, 5–15 mg PO q 4 hr as needed. Oral sol, 10–30 mg PO q 4 hr as needed. **Mgt of moderate to severe pain when continuous, around-the-clock analgesic needed for extended period.** *Adult:* CR tablets, 10 mg PO q 12 hr for pts taking nonopioid analgesics and requiring around-the-clock tx for extended period. Adjust q 1–2 days as needed by increasing by 25% to 50%. *Child 11 yr and over:* Child must have been receiving opioids for at least 5 days w/ minimum 20 mg/day; dosage based on this previous use and conversion to CR oxycontin.
ADJUST DOSE Elderly pts, hepatic impairment, impaired adults
ADV EFF Bronchospasm, cardiac arrest, constipation, dizziness,

drowsiness, flushing, **laryngospasm**, light-headedness, n/v, **respiratory arrest**, sedation, **shock**, sweating, ureteral spasm, vision changes
INTERACTIONS Barbiturate general anesthetics, opioids, protease inhibitors; avoid these combinations
NC/PT CR form not for opioid-naïve child. Use pediatric formulas to determine child dose for immediate-release form. Have opioid antagonist, facilities for assisted, controlled respiration on hand. Pt should swallow CR form whole and not cut, crush, or chew it; take 4–6 hr before next feeding if breast-feeding; take safety precautions for CNS effects; use laxative for constipation; report difficulty breathing, fainting.

---

oxymetazoline (Afrin, Dristan, Neo-Synephrine 12 Hour Extra Moisturizing, Vicks Sinex 12-Hour)
CLASS Nasal decongestant
PREG/CONT C/NA

BBW Monitor BP carefully; pts w/ hypertension may experience increased hypertension related to vasoconstriction. If nasal decongestant needed, pseudoephedrine is drug of choice.
IND & DOSE Symptomatic relief of nasal, nasopharyngeal mucosal congestion. *Adult, child over 6 yr:* 2–3 sprays of 0.05% sol in each nostril bid a.m. and p.m. or q 10–12 hr for up to 3 days.
ADV EFF Anxiety, arrhythmias, **CV collapse**, dizziness, drowsiness, dysuria, fear, headache, hypertension, light-headedness, nausea, painful urination, rebound congestion, restlessness, tenseness
INTERACTIONS MAOIs, methyldopa, TCAs, urine acidifiers/alkalinizers
NC/PT Systemic adverse effects less common because drug not generally absorbed systemically. Review proper administration. Rebound congestion possible. Pt should avoid

prolonged use (over 3 days), smoky rooms; drink plenty of fluids; use humidifier; take safety precautions for CNS effects; report excessive nervousness.

oxymetholone
(Anadrol-50)
CLASS Anabolic steroid
PREG/CONT X/C-III

BBW Monitor LFTs, serum electrolytes during tx. Consult physician for corrective measures; risk of peliosis hepatis, liver cell tumors. Measure cholesterol in pts at high risk for CAD; lipids may increase.
IND & DOSE Tx of anemias, including congenital aplastic, hypoplastic. *Adult, child:* 1–5 mg/kg/day PO. Give for minimum trial of 3–6 mo.
ADV EFF Abd fullness, acne, anorexia, blood lipid changes, burning of tongue, confusion, excitation, gynecomastia, **intra-abdominal hemorrhage, hepatitis,** hirsutism in females, hyperglycemia, insomnia, **liver cell tumors, liver failure,** virilization of prepubertal males
INTERACTIONS Oral anticoagulants, oral antidiabetics
NC/PT Use w/extreme caution; risk of serious disruption of growth/development; weigh benefits, risks. Monitor LFTs, lipids, bone age in children. Not for use in pregnancy (barrier contraceptives advised). Pt should take w/food; monitor glucose closely if diabetic; take safety precautions for CNS effects; report severe nausea, urine/stool color changes.

DANGEROUS DRUG

oxymorphone hydrochloride (Opana)
CLASS Opioid agonist analgesic
PREG/CONT C/C-II

BBW Ensure pt swallows ER form whole; cutting, crushing, chewing could cause rapid release and fatal

overdose. ER form has abuse potential; monitor accordingly. ER form indicated only for around-the-clock use over extended period. Do not give PRN. Pt must not consume alcohol in any form while taking oxycodone; risk of serious serum drug level increase, potentially fatal overdose.
IND & DOSE Relief of moderate to moderately severe acute pain. *Adult:* 10–20 mg PO q 4–6 hr. Relief of moderate to moderately severe pain in pts needing around-the-clock tx. *Adult:* 5 mg ER tablet PO q 12 hr; may increase in 5- to 10-mg increments q 3–7 days. Preop medication; anesthesia support; obstetric analgesia; relief of anxiety in pts w/pulmonary edema associated w/left ventricular dysfx. *Adult:* 0.5 mg IV or 1–1.5 mg IM, subcut q 4–6 hr as needed. For analgesia during labor, 0.5–1 mg IM.
ADJUST DOSE Elderly pts, impaired adults, renal impairment
ADV EFF Cardiac arrest, bronchospasm, constipation, dizziness, dry mouth, euphoria, flushing, hypertension, hypotension, **laryngospasm,** light-headedness, n/v, **respiratory arrest,** sedation, **shock,** sweating, urine retention
INTERACTIONS Alcohol, barbiturate anesthetics, CNS depressants
NC/PT Have opioid antagonist, facilities for assisted, controlled respiration on hand during parenteral administration. Pt should swallow ER tablet whole and not cut, crush, or chew it; take 4–6 hr before next feeding if breast-feeding; avoid alcohol; use laxative for constipation; take safety precautions for CNS effects; report difficulty breathing.

DANGEROUS DRUG

oxytocin (Pitocin)
CLASS Hormone, oxytocic
PREG/CONT X/NA

BBW Reserve for medical use, not elective induction.

IND & DOSE Induction, stimulation of labor. *Adult:* 0.5–2 milliunits/min (0.0005–0.002 units/min) by IV infusion through infusion pump. Increase in increments of no more than 1–2 milliunits/min at 30- to 60-min intervals until contraction pattern similar to normal labor established. Rates exceeding 9–10 milliunits/min rarely needed. **Control of postpartum uterine bleeding.** *Adult:* Add 10–40 units to 1,000 mL nonhydrating diluent, infuse IV at rate to control uterine atony. Or, 10 units IM after delivery of placenta. **Tx of incomplete, inevitable abortion.** *Adult:* 10 units oxytocin w/500 mL physiologic saline sol or 5% dextrose in physiologic saline IV infused at 10–20 milliunits (20–40 drops)/min. Max, 30 units in 12 hr.
ADV EFF Afibrinogenemia, anaphylactic reaction, cardiac arrhythmias, fetal bradycardia, **maternal death,** neonatal jaundice, n/v, **severe water intoxication**
NC/PT Ensure fetal position/size, absence of complications. Continuously observe pt receiving IV oxytocin for induction, stimulation of labor; fetal monitoring preferred. Regulate rate to establish uterine contractions. Stop at first sign of hypersensitivity reactions, fetal distress. Pt should report difficulty breathing.

DANGEROUS DRUG

paclitaxel (Abraxane)
CLASS Antimitotic, antineoplastic
PREG/CONT D/NA

BBW Do not give unless blood counts within acceptable range. Premedicate w/one of following to prevent severe hypersensitivity reactions: Oral dexamethasone 20 mg 12 hr and 6 hr before paclitaxel, 10 mg if AIDS-related Kaposi sarcoma; diphenhydramine 50 mg IV 30–60 min before paclitaxel; cimetidine 300 mg IV or ranitidine 50 mg IV 30–60 min before paclitaxel. Do not substitute

Abraxane for other paclitaxel formulations.
IND & DOSE Tx of metastatic breast cancer after failure of combination tx. *Adult:* 260 mg/m² IV over 3 hr q 3 wk. **Tx of non-small-cell-lung cancer.** *Adult:* 100 mg/m² IV over 30 min on days 1, 8, 15 of 21-day cycle, w/carboplatin on day 1 immediately after infusion. **Tx of metastatic adenocarcinoma of pancreas w/ gemcitabine.** *Adult:* 125 mg/m² IV over 30–40 min on days 1, 8, 15 of each 28-day cycle, w/gemcitabine on days 1, 8, 15.
ADJUST/PT Hepatic impairment
ADV EFF Alopecia, arthralgia, **bone marrow depression, hypersensitivity reactions, infection,** myalgia, n/v, peripheral neuropathies, **pneumonitis,** sepsis
INTERACTIONS Cisplatin, cyclosporine, dexamethasone, diazepam, etoposide, ketoconazole, quinidine, teniposide, testosterone, verapamil, vincristine
NC/PT Monitor CBC carefully; dose based on response. Premedicate to decrease risk of hypersensitivity reactions. Not for use in pregnancy (barrier contraceptives advised). Pt should avoid exposure to infections; mark calendar of tx days; take safety precautions for CNS effects; cover head at temp extremes (hair loss possible); report signs of infection, difficulty breathing.

---

palbociclib (Ibrance)
CLASS Antineoplastic, kinase inhibitor
PREG/CONT D/NA

IND & DOSE Tx of postmenopausal estrogen receptor–positive, HER2-negative advanced breast cancer w/ letrozole. *Adult:* 125 mg/day PO w/ food for 21 days; then 7 rest days.
ADV EFF Alopecia, anemia, **bone marrow suppression,** infections, n/v/d, peripheral neuropathy

INTERACTIONS CYP3A inducers/inhibitors, grapefruit juice
NC/PT Ensure dx. Give w/letrozole. Monitor CBC; dosage adjustment may be needed. Not for use in pregnancy (contraceptives advised)/breast-feeding. Pt should take w/food; mark calendar w/tx days; swallow capsule whole and not cut, crush, or chew it; avoid grapefruit juice; cover head at temp extremes (hair loss possible); report unusual bleeding, numbness/tingling, s&sx of infection.

palifermin (Kepivance)
CLASS Keratinocyte growth factor
PREG/CONT C/NA

IND & DOSE To decrease incidence, duration of severe oral mucositis in pts w/hematologic malignancies receiving myelotoxic chemotherapy requiring hematopoietic stem-cell support. *Adult:* 60 mcg/kg/day by IV bolus for 3 consecutive days before and 3 consecutive days after chemotherapy regimen.
ADV EFF Edema, erythema, pruritus, rash, taste alterations, tongue swelling
INTERACTIONS Heparin, myelotoxic chemotherapy
NC/PT Risk of tumor growth stimulation; monitor accordingly. Not for use in breast-feeding. Provide nutrition support w/taste changes, skin care for rash. Pt should report pain at infusion site, severe rash.

paliperidone (Invega, Invega Trinza)
CLASS Atypical antipsychotic, benzisoxazole
PREG/CONT C/NA

BBW Avoid use in elderly pts w/dementia-related psychosis; increased risk of CV death. Drug not approved for this use.

IND & DOSE Tx of schizophrenia, schizoaffective disorder. *Adult:* 6 mg/day PO in a.m.; max, 12 mg/day PO. **Tx of schizophrenia.** *Adult:* 234 mg IM, then 156 mg IM in 1 wk, both in deltoid; 117 mg IM 1 wk later in gluteal or deltoid. Maint, 39–234 mg/mo IM. Once regulated on monthly injections, can switch to ER injection of 78–234 mg IM q 3 mo (*Invega Trinza*). *Child 12–17 yr:* 51 kg or more, 3 mg/day PO; range, 3–12 mg/day. Under 56 kg, 3 mg/day PO; range, 3–6 mg/day.
ADJUST DOSE Renal impairment
ADV EFF Akathisia, bone marrow suppression, cognitive/motor impairment, dizziness, dry mouth, dystonia, extrapyramidal disorders, hyperglycemia, impaired thinking, increased mortality in geriatric pts w/dementia-related psychosis, NMS, orthostatic hypotension, prolonged QT, seizures, suicidality, tachycardia, weight gain
INTERACTIONS Alcohol, antihypertensives, CNS depressants, divalproex, dopamine agonist, levodopa, QT-prolonging drugs
NC/PT For ER injection, deltoid injection: under 90 kg, use 1-inch, 22G needle; over 90 kg, use 1½-inch, 22G needle; for gluteal injection, use 1½-inch, 22G needle. Shake syringe vigorously for at least 15 sec; administer within 5 min. Monitor for hyperglycemia, weight gain. Tablet matrix may appear in stool. Not for use in pregnancy/breast-feeding. Pt should swallow tablet whole and not cut, crush, or chew it; avoid alcohol; take safety precautions for CNS effects; report fever, thoughts of suicide.

palivizumab (Synagis)
CLASS Antiviral, monoclonal antibody
PREG/CONT C/NA

IND & DOSE Px of serious lower respiratory tract disease caused by RSV in children at high risk for RSV disease. *Child:* 15 mg/kg IM as single injection monthly during RSV season; give first dose before start of RSV season.

ADV EFF Chills, fever, malaise, pharyngitis, **severe anaphylactoid reaction**

INTERACTIONS Immunosuppressants

NC/PT Give preferably in anterolateral aspect of thigh; do not use gluteal muscle. For cardiopulmonary bypass pts, give as soon as possible following procedure, even if under 1 mo since previous dose. Monitor for anaphylaxis, infection. Caregivers should protect from infection, report fever, difficulty breathing.

palonosetron hydrochloride (Aloxi)
CLASS Antiemetic, selective serotonin receptor antagonist
PREG/CONT B/NA

IND & DOSE Px of acute/delayed n/v associated w/chemotherapy. *Adult:* 0.25 mg IV as single dose over 30 sec 30 min before start of chemotherapy. *Child 1 mo–under 17 yr:* 20 mcg/kg IV as single dose over 18 min 30 min before start of chemotherapy. Px of postop n/v. *Adult:* 0.075 mg IV as single dose over 10 sec immediately before anesthesia induction.

ADV EFF Arrhythmias, constipation, drowsiness, flulike sx, headache, **hypersensitivity reaction, serotonin syndrome,** somnolence

NC/PT Coordinate dose timing. Pt should take safety precautions, analgesic for headache; report severe constipation, fever, difficulty breathing.

pamidronate disodium (Aredia)
CLASS Bisphosphonate, calcium regulator
PREG/CONT D/NA

IND & DOSE Tx of hypercalcemia. *Adult:* 60–90 mg IV over 2–24 hr as single dose; max, 90 mg/dose. **Tx of Paget disease.** *Adult:* 30 mg/day IV as 4-hr infusion on 3 consecutive days for total dose of 90 mg; max, 90 mg/dose. **Tx of osteolytic bone lesions.** *Adult:* 90 mg IV as 2-hr infusion q 3–4 wk. For bone lesions caused by multiple myeloma, monthly 4-hr infusion; max, 90 mg/dose.

ADJUST DOSE Renal impairment

ADV EFF Bone pain, diarrhea, headache, hypocalcemia, nausea, **osteonecrosis of jaw**

NC/PT Have calcium on hand for hypocalcemic tetany. Monitor serum calcium regularly. Dental exam needed before tx for cancer pts at risk for osteonecrosis of jaw. Not recommended for use beyond 3–5 yr. Maintain hydration, nutrition. Pt should not take foods high in calcium; calcium supplements within 2 hr of dose; report muscle twitching, severe diarrhea.

pancrelipase (Creon, Pancreaze, Pertyze, Ultresa, Viokace)
CLASS Digestive enzyme
PREG/CONT C/NA

IND & DOSE Replacement tx in pts w/deficient exocrine pancreatic secretions. *Adult:* 4,000–20,000 units (usually 1–3 capsules/tablets) PO w/ each meal, snacks; may increase to 8 capsules/tablets in severe cases. *Viokace:* 500 units/kg/meal PO to max 2,500 units/kg/meal. Pts w/ pancreatectomy or obstruction, 72,000 units lipase meal PO while consuming 100 g/day fat (*Creon*). *Child 4 yr and older:* 500 units lipase/ kg/meal PO to max 2,500 units/kg/ meal. *Child 1–under 4 yr:* 1,000 units/kg/meal PO to max 2,500 units/ kg/meal or 10,000 units/kg/day. *Child up to 1 yr:* 3,000 units lipase PO/120 mL formula or breast-feeding session; 2,000–4,000 units/feeding PO (*Ultresa*).

ADV EFF Abd cramps, diarrhea, hyperuricemia, nausea

NC/PT Do not mix capsules directly into infant formula, breast milk; follow dose w/formula, breast milk. *Creon* and *Viokace* are not interchangeable. Pt should not crush or chew enteric-coated capsules; may open *Ultresa* capsules and sprinkle contents in food. Pt should report difficulty breathing, joint pain.

DANGEROUS DRUG

panitumumab (Vectibix)
CLASS Antineoplastic, monoclonal antibody
PREG/CONT C/NA

BBW Monitor for possibly severe to life-threatening dermatologic toxicity.
IND & DOSE Tx of epidermal growth factor receptor–expressing metastatic colorectal carcinoma of wild-type KRAS (exon 2). *Adult:* 6 mg/kg IV over 60 min q 14 days; give doses larger than 1,000 mg over 90 min.
ADV EFF Abd pain, constipation, **dermatologic toxicity,** diarrhea, **electrolyte depletion,** fatigue, hypomagnesemia, **infusion reactions,** ocular toxicity, **pulmonary fibrosis,** tumor progression
NC/PT Ensure appropriate use. Monitor electrolytes, respiratory function; watch for ocular keratitis. Monitor constantly during infusion; stop if infusion reaction. Men, women should use barrier contraceptives during and for 6 mo after tx; not for use in breast-feeding. Pt should report difficulty breathing, pain at injection site, fever, rash, vision changes.

---

panobinostat (Farydak)
CLASS Antineoplastic, histone deacetylase inhibitor
PREG/CONT D/NA

BBW Risk of severe diarrhea. Ensure antidiarrheal tx; interrupt/stop drug if not controlled. Serious to fatal cardiac events, arrhythmias possible; monitor ECG, electrolytes before and periodically during tx.
IND & DOSE Tx of melanoma after at least 2 prior tx, w/bortezomib and dexamethasone. *Adult:* 20 mg PO every other day for three doses/wk on days 1, 3, 5, 8, 10, 12 of wk 1 and 2 of each 21-day cycle for eight cycles.
ADJUST DOSE Hepatic impairment
ADV EFF Bleeding events, fatigue, fever, **diarrhea, hepatotoxicity,** n/v/d, peripheral edema
INTERACTIONS Antiarrhythmics, QT-prolonging drugs, strong CYP3A4 inducers/inhibitors
NC/PT Ensure proper dx; use w/ bortezomib, dexamethasone. Baseline ECG, electrolytes; monitor periodically. Monitor LFTs. Monitor for diarrhea. May use antidiarrheals; stop if severe. Ensure nutrition, hydration; small meals for GI problems. Not for use in pregnancy (contraceptives advised)/ breast-feeding. Pt should report diarrhea, bleeding, swelling.

---

pantoprazole (Protonix)
CLASS Proton pump inhibitor
PREG/CONT B/NA

IND & DOSE Tx of GERD; maint tx of erosive esophagitis; tx of pathological hypersecretory disorders. *Adult:* 40 mg/day PO for 8 wk or less for maint healing of erosive esophagitis. May repeat 8-wk course if no healing. Give continually for hypersecretory disorders: 40 mg/day IV bid up to 240 mg/day (2-yr duration) or 40 mg/day IV for 7–10 days. For severe hypersecretory syndromes, 80 mg q 12 hr (up to 240 mg/day) PO, IV (6-day duration). **Tx of GERD.** *Child 5 yr and over:* 40 kg and over: 40 mg/day PO for up to 8 wk. 15–under 40 kg: 20 mg/day PO for up to 8 wk.
ADJUST DOSE Hepatic impairment
ADV EFF Abd pain, bone loss, CDAD, dizziness, headache, hypocalcemia, hypomagnesemia, insomnia, interstitial nephritis, n/v/d, pneumonia, URI

NC/PT Further evaluation needed after 4 wk of tx for GERD. Switch from IV to oral as soon as possible. Consider zinc replacement w/IV use in pts prone to zinc deficiency. Pt should swallow tablet whole and not cut, crush, or chew it; take safety measures for dizziness; report severe diarrhea, headache, fever.

parathyroid hormone (Natpara)
CLASS Hormone
PREG/CONT High risk/NA

BBW Increased risk of osteosarcoma; do not use in pts wknown risk of osteosarcoma. Available only through restricted program.
IND & DOSE Adjunct to calcium, vitamin D to control hypocalcemia in hypoparathyroidism. *Adult:* 50 mcg/day subcut into thigh. Monitor calcium level q 3–7 days; adjust dose to maintain serum calcium level above 7.5 mg/dL.
ADV EFF Arthralgia, headache, **hypercalcemia**, n/v/d, **osteosarcoma**, paresthesia, **severe hypocalcemia**
INTERACTIONS Digoxin
NC/PT Screen pt for risk of osteosarcoma. Confirm adequate vitamin D level, serum calcium level above 7.5 mg/dL before starting. Monitor serum levels; adjust vitamin D/calcium dosages based on pt response and presentation. Not for use in pregnancy (contraceptives advised)/breast-feeding. Pt should report difficulty breathing, chest pain.

paricalcitol (Zemplar)
CLASS Vitamin
PREG/CONT C/NA

IND & DOSE Px, tx of secondary hyperparathyroidism associated w/chronic renal failure. *Adult:* 0.04–0.1 mcg/kg injected during dialysis, no more often than q other day. Pts not on dialysis: 1–2 mcg/day PO, or

2–4 mcg PO three times/wk based on parathyroid level.
ADV EFF Arthralgia, chills, dry mouth, fever, flulike sx, **GI hemorrhage**, n/v
INTERACTIONS Aluminum-containing antacids, ketoconazole
NC/PT Arrange for calcium supplements; restrict phosphorus intake. Not for use in breast-feeding. Pt should avoid vitamin D; report changes in thinking, appetite/weight loss, increased thirst.

paroxetine hydrochloride (Paxil), paroxetine mesylate (Brisdelle, Pexeva)
CLASS Antidepressant, SSRI
PREG/CONT D/NA

BBW Risk of increased suicidality in children, adolescents, young adults; monitor accordingly.
IND & DOSE Tx of depression. *Adult:* 20 mg/day PO; range, 20–50 mg/day. Or, 25–62.5 mg/day CR form. Tx of OCD. *Adult:* 20 mg/day PO. May increase in 10-mg/day increments; max, 60 mg/day. Tx of panic disorder. *Adult:* 10 mg/day PO; range, 10–60 mg/day. Or 12.5–75 mg/day CR tablet; max, 75 mg/day. Tx of social anxiety disorder. *Adult:* 20 mg/day PO in a.m. Or, 12.5 mg/day PO CR form; max, 60 mg/day or 37.5 mg/day CR form. Tx of generalized anxiety disorder. *Adult:* 20 mg/day PO; range, 20–50 mg/day. Tx of PMDD. *Adult:* 12.5 mg/day PO in a.m.; range, 12.5–25 mg/day. May give daily or just during luteal phase of cycle. Tx of PTSD. *Adult:* 20 mg/day PO as single dose; range, 20–50 mg/day. Tx of vasomotor sx of menopause (hot flashes). *Adult:* 7.5 mg/day PO at bedtime (*Brisdelle*).
ADJUST DOSE Elderly pts; hepatic, renal impairment
ADV EFF Anxiety, asthenia, bone fractures, constipation, diarrhea, dizziness, dry mouth, ejaculatory

disorders, glaucoma, headache, hyponatremia, insomnia, nervousness, serotonin syndrome, somnolence, **suicidality**

INTERACTIONS Digoxin, fosamprenavir, MAOIs, phenobarbital, phenytoin, pimozide, procyclidine, ritonavir, serotonergics, St. John's wort, tamoxifen, thioridazine, tryptophan, warfarin

NC/PT Do not give within 14 days of MAOIs or give w/pimozide, thioridazine. Not for use in pregnancy/breastfeeding. Pt should take in evening; swallow CR tablet whole and not cut, crush, or chew it; shake suspension before use; take safety precautions for CNS effects; avoid St. John's wort; report blurred vision, thoughts of suicide.

pasireotide (Signifor, Signifor LAR)
CLASS Somatostatin analog
PREG/CONT C/NA

IND & DOSE Tx of Cushing's disease when pituitary surgery is not an option. Adult: 0.6–0.9 mg subcut bid; titrate based on response. Or, 40 mg IM q 28 days (LAR).
ADJUST DOSE Hepatic impairment
ADV EFF Bradycardia, cholelithiasis, diabetes, headache, hyperglycemia, hypocortisolism, **prolonged QT**
INTERACTIONS Bromocriptine, cyclosporine, QT-prolonging drugs
NC/PT Baseline and periodic fasting blood glucose, HbA$_{1c}$, LFTs, ECG, gallbladder ultrasound. Diabetic teaching, intervention may be needed. Use w/caution in pregnancy; not for use in breast-feeding. Teach proper subcut or IM administration/disposal of needles/syringes. Pt should mark calendar for IM injection dates; report abd pain, excessive thirst, fatigue, urine/stool color changes.

patiromer (Veltassa)
CLASS Potassium binder
PREG/CONT Low risk/NA

BBW Binds to many oral drugs; could decrease their effectiveness. Give oral drugs at least 6 hr before or after patiromer.
IND & DOSE Tx of hyperkalemia. Adult: 8.4 g/day PO; may increase at 1-wk intervals by 8.4 g/day to reach target potassium level.
ADV EFF Abd discomfort, constipation, flatulence, hypomagesemia, n/d
NC/PT Give other oral drugs at least 6 hr before or after patiromer. Mix drug with full glass of water, stir well; have pt drink immediately. Do not heat drug or add to heated liquids. Check potassium level before and periodically during tx. Pt should report severe constipation, diarrhea.

pazopanib (Votrient)
CLASS Antineoplastic, kinase inhibitor
PREG/CONT D/NA

BBW Risk of severe to fatal hepatotoxicity. Monitor LFTs regularly; adjust dose accordingly.
IND & DOSE Tx of advanced renal cell carcinoma; tx of soft-tissue sarcoma progressed after prior tx. Adult: 800 mg/day PO without food.
ADJUST DOSE Hepatic impairment
ADV EFF Anorexia, **arterial thrombotic events**, GI perforation, hair color changes, **hemorrhagic events**, **hepatotoxicity**, hypertension, hypothyroidism, **impaired wound healing**, interstitial pneumonitis, n/v, **prolonged QT**, proteinuria, RPLS, **serious infections**
INTERACTIONS CYP3A4 inducers/inhibitors, simvastatin
NC/PT Not for use in pregnancy. Hair may lose pigmentation. Provide nutrition support for n/v. Stop drug w/interstitial pneumonitis, RPLS. Pt should take on empty stomach at

least 1 hr before, 2 hr after meal; report all drugs/OTC/herbs used (many drug interactions possible); urine/stool color changes, yellowing of skin/eyes, severe abd pain, difficulty breathing, chest pain, fever.

pegaptanib (Macugen)

CLASS Monoclonal antibody
PREG/CONT B/NA

IND & DOSE Tx of neovascular (wet) age-related macular degeneration. *Adult:* 0.3 mg q 6 wk by intravitreal injection into affected eye.
ADV EFF Anaphylaxis; endophthalmitis; eye discharge, pain, infection; increased IOP; retinal detachment; traumatic cataract; vision changes; vitreous floaters
NC/PT Monitor IOP. Pt should mark calendar of tx days, report eye redness, sensitivity to light, sudden vision change.

DANGEROUS DRUG
---

pegaspargase (Oncaspar)

CLASS Antineoplastic
PREG/CONT C/NA

IND & DOSE Tx of ALL. *Adult:* 2,500 international units/m^2 IM, IV no more often than q 14 days.
ADV EFF Anaphylaxis, bone marrow depression, coagulopathy, glucose intolerance, hepatotoxicity, pancreatitis, renal toxicity
NC/PT IM route preferred; reserve IV for extreme situations. Monitor LFTs, renal function, amylase. Not for use in breast-feeding. Pt should report excessive thirst, severe headache, acute shortness of breath, difficulty breathing.

pegfilgrastim (Neulasta)

CLASS Colony stimulating factor
PREG/CONT C/NA

IND & DOSE To decrease incidence of infection in pts w/nonmyeloid malignancies receiving myelosuppressive anticancer drugs. *Adult, child over 45 kg:* 6 mg subcut as single dose once per chemotherapy course. Do not give within 14 days before and 24 hr after cytotoxic chemotherapy. *Child under 45 kg:* Base dosage on wt. To increase survival in pts exposed to myelosuppressive doses of radiation. *Adult, child over 45 kg:* Two doses of 6 mg each subut 1 wk apart; give first dose as soon after exposure as possible. *Child under 45 kg:* Base dosage on wt.
ADV EFF Acute respiratory distress syndrome, alopecia, anorexia, arthralgia, bone marrow suppression, bone pain, dizziness, dyspepsia, edema, fatal sickle cell crisis, fatigue, fever, generalized weakness, glomerulonephritis, mucositis, n/v/d, splenic rupture, stomatitis
INTERACTIONS Lithium
NC/PT Monitor CBC. Protect from light. Do not shake syringe. Sol should be free of particulate matter, not discolored. Pt should cover head at temp extremes (hair loss possible), avoid exposure to infection, report signs of infection, difficulty breathing, pain at injection site. Name confusion between *Neulasta* (pegfilgrastim) and *Neumega* (oprelvekin); use caution.

peginterferon alfa-2a (Pegasys)

CLASS Interferon
PREG/CONT C/NA

BBW May cause, aggravate life-threatening to fatal neuropsychiatric, autoimmune, ischemic, infectious disorders. Monitor closely; stop w/ persistent s&sx. Risk of serious fetal defects when used w/ribavirin; men, women should avoid pregnancy.

IND & DOSE Tx of hepatitis C in pts w/compensated liver disease as part of combo regimen. *Adult:* 180 mcg subcut wkly for 48 wk w/ other antivirals. *Child 5 and over:* 180 mcg/1.73 m² × BSA subcut per wk w/ribavirin. *Tx of adult w/chronic hepatitis B w/compensated liver disease, evidence of viral replication/liver inflammation. Adult:* 180 mcg subcut wkly for 48 wk w/other antivirals.

ADJUST DOSE Hepatic, renal impairment

ADV EFF Asthenia, **bone marrow suppression, colitis**, fatigue, fever, growth impairment, headache, **hemolytic anemia, hepatic impairment**, infections, myalgia, **neuropsychiatric events, pancreatitis, peripheral neuropathy, pulmonary events, Stevens-Johnson syndrome, suicidality**

INTERACTIONS Azathioprine, didanosine, methadone, nucleoside analogues, theophylline, zidovudine

NC/PT Monitor closely; adverse effects may require stopping. Evaluate use in pregnancy based on other antivirals used. Store in refrigerator. Teach proper administration/disposal of needles/syringes. Pt should avoid exposure to infection, report severe abd pain, bloody diarrhea, s&sx of infection, thoughts of suicide, difficulty breathing, rash.

---

peginterferon alfa-2b
(Pegintron, Sylatron)
CLASS Antineoplastic, interferon
PREG/CONT C/NA

BBW May cause, aggravate life-threatening to fatal neuropsychiatric, autoimmune, ischemic, infectious disorders. Monitor closely; stop w/ persistent s&sx. Risk of serious fetal defects when used w/ribavirin; men, women should avoid pregnancy.

IND & DOSE Tx of chronic hepatitis C in pts w/compensated liver disease. *Adult:* 1.5 mcg/kg/wk subcut w/800–1,400 mg/day PO ribavirin. *Child:* 60 mcg/m²/wk subcut w/ 15 mg/kg/day PO ribavirin in two divided doses.

ADJUST DOSE Hepatic/renal impairment

ADV EFF Asthenia, **bone marrow suppression, colitis**, fatigue, fever, headache, **hemolytic anemia, hepatic impairment, infections**, injection-site reactions, **ischemic cerebral events**, myalgia, **neuropsychiatric events, pancreatitis, pulmonary events, suicidality**

INTERACTIONS Azathioprine, didanosine, methadone, nucleoside analogues, theophylline, zidovudine

NC/PT Monitor closely; adverse effects may require stopping. Not for use in pregnancy; men, women should use two forms of contraception during, for 6 mo after tx. Store in refrigerator. Teach proper administration/disposal of needles/syringes; mark calendar w/tx days. Pt should avoid exposure to infection, report severe abd pain, bloody diarrhea, s&sx of infection, suicidal thoughts, difficulty breathing, chest pain.

---

pegloticase (Krystexxa)
CLASS PEGylated uric-acid specific enzyme
PREG/CONT C/NA

BBW Severe anaphylaxis, infusion reactions have occurred; premedicate, closely monitor. Monitor serum uric acid level.

IND & DOSE Tx of chronic gout in pts refractory to conventional tx. *Adult:* 8 mg by IV infusion over no less than 120 min q 2 wk.

ADJUST DOSE Renal impairment
ADV EFF **Anaphylaxis**, chest pain, constipation, ecchymosis, gout flares, **HF**, infusion reactions, nasopharyngitis, vomiting

NC/PT Monitor serum uric acid level. Premedicate w/antihistamines, corticosteroids. Contraindicated w/G6PD deficiencies. Alert pt gout flares may occur up to 3 mo after starting tx. Not for use in breast-feeding. Pt should report difficulty breathing, edema.

pegvisomant (Somavert)
CLASS Human growth hormone analogue
PREG/CONT C/NA

IND & DOSE Tx of acromegaly in pts w/inadequate response to surgery, radiation. *Adult:* 40 mg subcut as loading dose, then 10 mg/day subcut.
ADV EFF Diarrhea, dizziness, edema, **hepatic impairment**, infection, injection-site reactions, nausea, pain, peripheral edema, sinusitis
INTERACTIONS Opioids
NC/PT Local reactions to injection common; rotate sites regularly. Monitor for infection. Monitor LFTs. Teach proper administration/disposal of needles/syringes. Not for use in breast-feeding.

pembrolizumab (Keytruda)
CLASS Antineoplastic, human programmed death receptor-1 blocking antibody
PREG/CONT D/NA

IND & DOSE Tx of unresectable or metastatic melanoma w/progression after ipilimumab w/BRAF V600 mutation; tx of non-small-cell lung cancer w/PD-L1 expression w/progression after platinum therapy. *Adult:* 2 mg/kg IV over 30 min q 3 wk.
ADV EFF Cough, fatigue, infusion reactions, n/v/d, **potentially serious immune-mediated reactions**, rash
NC/PT Ensure dx. Monitor immune-mediated reactions (LFTs, renal/thyroid function); give corticosteroids

based on severity; stop if severe. Not for use in pregnancy/breast-feeding. Frequent follow-up needed. Pt should mark calendar w/tx days, report s&sx of infection, difficulty breathing.

DANGEROUS DRUG
pemetrexed (Alimta)
CLASS Antifolate antineoplastic
PREG/CONT D/NA

IND & DOSE Tx of unresectable malignant mesothelioma; tx of locally advanced, metastatic non-small-cell lung cancer. *Adult:* 500 mg/m^2 IV infused over 10 min on day 1, then 75 mg/m^2 cisplatin (tx of mesothelioma only) IV over 2 hr; repeat cycle q 21 days.
ADJUST DOSE Renal, hepatic impairment
ADV EFF Anorexia, **bone marrow suppression**, constipation, fatigue, n/v/d, **renal impairment**, stomatitis
INTERACTIONS Nephrotoxic drugs, NSAIDs
NC/PT Pretreat w/corticosteroids, oral folic acid, IM vitamin B$_{12}$. Monitor CBC; dosage adjustment based on response. Not for use in pregnancy (barrier contraceptives advised)/breast-feeding. Pt should avoid NSAIDs, exposure to infection; report unusual bleeding, severe GI sx.

penicillamine (Cuprimine, Depen)
CLASS Antirheumatic, chelate
PREG/CONT D/NA

BBW Because of severe toxicity, including bone marrow suppression, renal damage, reserve use for serious cases; monitor closely.
IND & DOSE Tx of severe, active rheumatoid arthritis, Wilson disease, cystinuria when other measures fail. *Adult:* 125–250 mg/day PO; max, 1 g/day.
ADV EFF Agitation, anxiety, **bone marrow suppression**, fever,

myasthenia gravis, paresthesia, rash, **renal toxicity,** tinnitus
INTERACTIONS Gold salts, nephrotoxic drugs
NC/PT Monitor CBC, renal function twice/wk. Assess neurologic functioning; stop if increasing weakness. Not for use in pregnancy (barrier contraceptives advised)/breast-feeding. Pt should avoid exposure to infection, report signs of infection, muscle weakness, edema.

penicillin G benzathine
(Bicillin L-A, Permapen)
CLASS Penicillin antibiotic
PREG/CONT B/NA

BBW Not for IV use. Do not inject or mix w/other IV sols. Inadvertent IV administration has caused cardiorespiratory arrest, death.
IND & DOSE Tx of streptococcal infections. *Adult:* 1.2 million units IM. *Older child:* 900,000 units IM. *Child under 27 kg:* 300,000–600,000 units IM. **Tx of early syphilis.** *Adult:* 2.4 million units IM. **Tx of syphilis lasting longer than 1 yr.** *Adult:* 7.2 million units as 2.4 million units IM wkly for 3 wk. **Tx of yaws, bejel, pinta, erysipelas.** *Adult:* 1.2 million units IM as single dose. **Tx of congenital syphilis.** *Child 2–12 yr:* Adjust dose based on adult schedule. *Child under 2 yr:* 50,000 units/kg body weight IM. **Px of rheumatic fever, chorea.** *Adult:* 1.2 million units IM q mo; or 600,000 units q 2 wk.
ADV EFF Anaphylaxis, bone marrow suppression, gastritis, glossitis, n/v/d, pain, phlebitis, rash, superinfections
INTERACTIONS Amikacin, gentamicin, neomycin, tetracyclines, tobramycin
NC/PT Culture before tx. Use IM only: upper outer quadrant of buttock (adults), midlateral aspect of thigh (infants, small children). Pt should report difficulty breathing, rash, pain at injection site.

penicillin G potassium, penicillin G sodium
(Pfizerpen)
CLASS Penicillin antibiotic
PREG/CONT B/NA

IND & DOSE Tx of meningococcal meningitis. *Adult:* 1–2 million units q 2 hr IM, or 20–30 million units/day by continuous IV infusion. *Child:* 200,000–300,000 units/kg/day IV q 6 hr. *Infants under 7 days:* 50,000 units/kg/day IV in divided doses q 12 hr. **Tx of actinomycosis.** *Adult:* 1–6 million units/day IM in divided doses q 4–6 hr for 6 wk, or IV for cervicofacial cases. Or, 10–20 million units/day IV for thoracic, abd diseases. **Tx of clostridial infections.** *Adult:* 20 million units/day in divided doses q 4–6 hr IM or IV w/antitoxin. **Tx of fusospirochetal infections (Vincent disease).** *Adult:* 5–10 million units/day IM or IV in divided doses q 4–6 hr. **Tx of rat-bite fever.** *Adult:* 12–20 million units/day IM or IV in divided doses q 4–6 hr for 3–4 wk. **Tx of Listeria infections.** *Adult:* 15–20 million units/day IM or IV in divided doses q 4–6 hr for 2 or 4 wk (meningitis, endocarditis, respectively). **Tx of Pasteurella infections.** *Adult:* 4–6 million units/day IM or IV in divided doses q 4–6 hr for 2 wk. **Tx of erysipeloid endocarditis.** *Adult:* 12–20 million units/day IM or IV in divided doses q 4–6 hr for 4–6 wk. **Tx of diphtheria (adjunct tx w/ antitoxin to prevent carrier state).** *Adult:* 2–3 million units/day IM or IV in divided doses q 4–6 hr for 10–12 days. **Tx of anthrax.** *Adult:* Minimum 5 million units/day IM or IV in divided doses. **Tx of streptococcal infections.** *Adult:* 5–24 million units/day IM or IV in divided doses q 4–6 hr. *Child:* 150,000 units/kg/day IM or IV q 4–6 hr. *Child under 7 days:* 75,000 units/kg/day IV in divided doses q 8 hr. **Tx of syphilis.** *Adult:* 18–24 million units/day IV q 4–6 hr for 10–14 days, then benzathine penicillin G 2.4 million units IM wkly for 3 wk. **Tx of gonorrhea.**

10 million units/day IV q 4–6 hr until improvement. **Tx of group B strepto-cocci.** *Child:* 100,000 units/kg/day IV.
ADV EFF Anaphylaxis, bone mar-row suppression, gastritis, glossitis, n/v/d, pain, phlebitis, rash, superin-fections
INTERACTIONS Amikacin, genta-micin, neomycin, tetracyclines, tobramycin
NC/PT Culture before tx. Smallest volume possible for IM use. Have emergency equipment on hand w/IV infusion. Monitor serum electrolytes w/penicillin potassium. Pt should report difficulty breathing, rash, unusual bleeding, signs of infection.

penicillin G procaine (Wycillin)
CLASS Penicillin antibiotic
PREG/CONT B/NA

IND & DOSE Tx of moderately se-vere infections caused by sensitive strains of streptococci, pneumococci, staphylococci. *Adult:* 600,000–1 million units/day IM for minimum 10 days. **Tx of bacterial endocarditis (group A streptococci).** *Adult:* 600,000–1 million units/day IM. **Tx of fusospirochetal infections, rat-bite fever, erysipeloid, anthrax.** *Adult:* 600,000–1 million units/day IM. **Tx of diphtheria.** *Adult:* 300,000–600,000 units/day IM w/antitoxin. **Tx of diph-theria carrier state.** *Adult:* 300,000 units/day IM for 10 days. **Tx of syphi-lis.** *Adult, child over 12 yr:* 600,000 units/day IM for 8 days, 10–15 days for late-stage syphilis. **Tx of neuro-syphilis.** *Adult:* 2.4 million units/day IM w/500 mg probenecid PO qid for 10–14 days, then 2.4 million units benzathine penicillin G IM after com-pletion of tx regimen. **Tx of congeni-tal syphilis.** *Child under 32 kg:* 50,000 units/kg/day IM for 10 days. **Tx of group A streptococcal, staphy-lococcal pneumonia.** *Child under 27 kg:* 300,000 units/day IM.

ADV EFF Anaphylaxis, bone mar-row suppression, gastritis, glossitis, n/v/d, pain, phlebitis, rash, superin-fections
INTERACTIONS Amikacin, genta-micin, neomycin, tetracyclines, tobramycin
NC/PT Culture before tx. IM route only in upper outer quadrant of but-tock; midlateral aspect of thigh may be preferred for infants, small chil-dren. Pt should report difficulty breathing, rash, unusual bleeding, signs of infection.

penicillin V (Penicillin-VK)
CLASS Penicillin antibiotic
PREG/CONT B/NA

IND & DOSE Tx of fusospirochetal infections, staphylococcal infec-tions of skin, soft tissues. *Adult, child over 12 yr:* 250–500 mg PO q 6–8 hr. **Tx of streptococcal infections.** *Adult, child over 12 yr:* 125–250 mg PO q 6–8 hr for 10 days. **Tx of pneumo-coccal infections.** *Adult, child over 12 yr:* 250–500 mg PO q 6 hr until afebrile for 48 hr. **Px of rheumatic fever/chorea recurrence.** *Adult, child over 12 yr:* 25–250 mg PO bid. **Tx of Lyme disease.** *Adult, child over 12 yr:* 500 mg PO tid for 10–20 days. **Tx of mild, uncomplicated cutaneous anthrax.** *Adult, child over 12 yr:* 200–500 mg PO qid. *Child 2–12 yr:* 25–50 mg/kg/day PO in two or four divided doses. **Px of anthrax px.** *Adult, child over 9 yr:* 7.5 mg/kg PO qid. *Child under 9 yr:* 50 mg/kg/day PO in four divided doses. **Px of Strep-tococcus pneumoniae septicemia in sickle cell anemia.** *Child 6–9 yr:* 250 mg PO bid. *Child 3 mo–5 yr:* 125 mg PO bid.
ADV EFF Anaphylaxis, bone mar-row suppression, gastritis, glossitis, n/v/d, pain, phlebitis, rash, superin-fections
INTERACTIONS Tetracyclines
NC/PT Culture before tx. Stable for max 14 days. Pt should take w/water,

not w/milk, fruit juices, soft drinks; refrigerate suspension; report difficulty breathing, rash, unusual bleeding, signs of infection.

pentamidine isethionate (NebuPent, Pentam)

CLASS Antiprotozoal
PREG/CONT C/NA

IND & DOSE Tx of *Pneumocystis jiroveci* pneumonia. *Adult, child:* 4 mg/kg/day for 14–21 days by deep IM injection or IV infusion over 60–120 min. **Px of *P. jiroveci* pneumonia.** *Adult, child:* 300 mg once q 4 wk through *Respirgard II* nebulizer.
ADV EFF Acute renal failure, anorexia, cough, dizziness, fatigue, fever, hypotension, **laryngospasm**, metallic taste (inhalation), **severe hypotension**, pain at injection site, rash, **Stevens-Johnson syndrome**
NC/PT Culture before tx. Drug a biohazard; use safe handling procedures. Monitor CBC, LFTs, renal function. Have pt in supine position for parenteral administration. Pt should take safety precautions w/hypotension, CNS effects; learn proper use, care of *Respirgard II;* report difficulty breathing, rash.

pentazocine (Talwin)

CLASS Opioid agonist-antagonist
PREG/CONT C/C-IV

BBW Pentazocine/naloxone for oral use only; can be lethal if injected.
IND & DOSE Relief of moderate to severe pain; preanesthetic (parenteral). *Adult, child over 12 yr:* 50 mg PO q 3–4 hr; max, 600 mg/24 hr. Or, 30 mg IM, subcut or IV. May repeat q 3–4 hr; max, 360 mg/24 hr. *Women in labor:* 30 mg IM as single dose. Or, 20 mg IV two to three times at 2- to 3-hr intervals.

ADJUST DOSE Elderly pts, impaired adults
ADV EFF Bronchospasm, cardiac arrest, constipation, dizziness, euphoria, hypotension, light-headedness, **laryngospasm**, n/v, pain at injection site, sedation, **shock**, sweating, urine retention
INTERACTIONS Alcohol, barbiturate anesthetics, CNS depressants, methadone, opioids
NC/PT Doses over 30 mg IV or 60 mg IM, subcut not recommended. Oral form especially abused in combination w/tripelennamine ("Ts and Blues"); serious, fatal consequences. Have opioid antagonist, equipment for assisted, controlled respiration on hand during parenteral administration. Withdraw gradually after 4–5 days. Pt should avoid alcohol, OTC products; use laxative for constipation, take safety precautions for CNS effects; report difficulty breathing.

pentobarbital (Nembutal Sodium)

CLASS Antiepileptic, barbiturate, sedative-hypnotic
PREG/CONT D/C-II

BBW Do not administer intra-arterially; may produce arteriospasm, thrombosis, gangrene.
IND & DOSE Sedative-hypnotic, preanesthetic, emergency antiseizure. *Adult:* Give by slow IV injection (max, 50 mg/min); 100 mg in 70-kg adult. Wait at least 1 min for full effect. Base dose on response. May give additional small increments to max 200–500 mg. Minimize dose in seizure states to avoid compounding possible depression after seizures. Or, 150–200 mg IM. *Child:* Reduce initial adult dose based on age, weight, condition. Or, 25–80 mg or 2–6 mg/kg IM; max, 100 mg.
ADJUST DOSE Elderly pts, debilitated adults

ADV EFF Agitation, apnea, ataxia, bradycardia, **bronchospasm**, CNS depression, **circulatory collapse**, confusion, dizziness, hallucinations, hyperkinesia, hypotension, hyperventilation, insomnia, **laryngospasm**, pain/necrosis at injection site, somnolence, **Stevens-Johnson syndrome**, syncope, **withdrawal syndrome**
INTERACTIONS Alcohol, beta-adrenergic blockers, CNS depressants, corticosteroids, doxycycline, estrogens, hormonal contraceptives, metronidazole, oral anticoagulants, phenylbutazones, quinidine, theophylline
NC/PT Use caution in children; may produce irritability, aggression, inappropriate tearfulness. Give slowly IV or by deep IM injection. Monitor continuously during IV use; monitor injection site for irritation. Taper gradually w/long-term use. Pt should take safety precautions for CNS effects; report difficulty breathing, rash.

pentosan polysulfate sodium (Elmiron)
CLASS Bladder protectant
PREG/CONT B/NA

IND & DOSE Relief of bladder pain associated w/interstitial cystitis. *Adult:* 100 mg PO tid on empty stomach.
ADV EFF Abd pain, alopecia, bleeding, diarrhea, dizziness, dyspepsia, liver function changes, nausea
INTERACTIONS Anticoagulants, aspirin, NSAIDs
NC/PT Use caution w/hepatic insufficiency. Drug a heparin; use caution if surgery needed. Pt should cover head at temp extremes (hair loss possible), report unusual bleeding, urine/stool color changes.

---

pentostatin (Nipent)
CLASS Antineoplastic antibiotic
PREG/CONT D/NA

BBW Associated w/fatal pulmonary toxicity, bone marrow depression.
IND & DOSE Tx of alpha interferon–refractory hairy cell leukemia, chronic lymphocytic leukemia, cutaneous/peripheral T-cell lymphoma. *Adult:* 4 mg/m² IV q other wk.
ADJUST DOSE Renal impairment
ADV EFF Abd pain, anorexia, **bone marrow suppression**, chills, cough, dizziness, dyspepsia, n/v, **pulmonary toxicity**, rash
INTERACTIONS Allopurinol, cyclophosphamide, fludarabine, vidarabine
NC/PT Toxic drug; use special precautions in handling. Monitor CBC regularly; monitor pulmonary function. Not for use in pregnancy/breast-feeding. Pt should mark calendar of tx days, avoid exposure to infection, report difficulty breathing, signs of infection.

pentoxifylline (generic)
CLASS Hemorrheologic, xanthine
PREG/CONT C/NA

IND & DOSE Tx of intermittent claudication. *Adult:* 400 mg PO tid w/meals for at least 8 wk.
ADJUST DOSE Renal impairment
ADV EFF Angina, anxiety, dizziness, dyspepsia, headache, nausea, rash
INTERACTIONS Anticoagulants, theophylline
NC/PT Pt should take w/meals; swallow tablet whole and not cut, crush, or chew it; take safety precautions for CNS effects; report chest pain.

peramivir (Rapivab)
CLASS Antiviral, neuraminidase inhibitor
PREG/CONT C/NA

IND & DOSE Tx of acute uncomplicated influenza in pts w/sx for no more than 2 days. *Adult:* 600 mg IV as single dose over 15 min.
ADJUST DOSE Renal impairment
ADV EFF Diarrhea, neuropsychiatric events, **serious skin reactions to Stevens-Johnson syndrome**
INTERACTIONS Live flu vaccine (avoid use 2 wk before or 48 hr after infusion)
NC/PT Confirm dx, timing of sx. Use w/caution in pregnancy/breast-feeding. Pt should take safety precaution for CNS effects, report rash, abnormal behavior.

perampanel (Fycompa)
CLASS Antiepileptic, glutamate receptor antagonist
PREG/CONT C/NA

BBW Risk of serious to life-threatening psychiatric, behavioral reactions. Monitor pt closely, especially when starting drug or changing dose; reduce dose or stop drug if these reactions occur.
IND & DOSE Adjunct tx of partial-onset seizures; tx of primary, generalized tonic-clonic seizures. *Adult, child 12 yr and older:* 2 mg/day PO at bedtime; 4 mg/day PO at bedtime if also on enzyme-inducing antiepileptics; max, 12 mg/day PO (partial-onset seizures), 8 mg/day PO (tonic-clonic seizures).
ADJUST DOSE Elderly pts; mild to moderate hepatic impairment. Severe hepatic/renal impairment, dialysis (not recommended)
ADV EFF Ataxia, balance disorders, falls, fatigue, gait disturbances, irritability, nausea, **serious psychiatric/ behavioral reactions**, somnolence, **suicidality**, weight gain
INTERACTIONS Alcohol, carbamazepine, CNS depressants, hormonal contraceptives, oxcarbazepine, phenytoin, rifampin, St. John's wort
NC/PT Monitor closely when starting tx or changing dose; taper gradually after long-term use. Not for use in pregnancy/breast-feeding. Protect from falls; advise pt to avoid driving, operating dangerous machinery. Pt should take once a day at bedtime; not stop drug suddenly; avoid alcohol, St. John's wort; use caution to avoid falls, injury; be aware behavior changes, suicidal thoughts possible; report severe dizziness, trouble walking, suicidal thoughts, behavior changes.

perindopril erbumine (Aceon)
CLASS ACE inhibitor, antihypertensive
PREG/CONT D/NA

BBW Serious fetal injury possible; advise barrier contraceptives.
IND & DOSE Tx of hypertension. *Adult:* 4 mg/day PO; max, 16 mg/day. Tx of pts w/stable CAD to reduce risk of CV mortality, nonfatal MI. *Adult:* 4 mg/day PO for 2 wk; maint, 8 mg/day PO.
ADJUST DOSE Elderly pts, renal impairment
ADV EFF Airway obstruction, angioedema, bone marrow suppression, diarrhea, dizziness, fatigue, gastric irritation, headache, hyperkalemia, insomnia, nausea, orthostatic hypotension, somnolence
INTERACTIONS ACE inhibitors, ARBs, gold, indomethacin, lithium, NSAIDs, potassium-sparing diuretics, potassium supplements, renin inhibitors
NC/PT Have epinephrine on hand for angioedema of face, neck. Alert surgeons; volume replacement may be needed if surgery required. Use caution in conditions w/possible BP drop (diarrhea, sweating, vomiting,

dehydration). Not for use in pregnancy (barrier contraceptives advised). Pt should avoid potassium supplements, OTC drugs that might increase BP; take safety precautions for CNS effects; report difficulty breathing, signs of infection, swelling of face, neck.

pertuzumab (Perjeta)
CLASS Antineoplastic, HER2/NEU receptor antagonist
PREG/CONT D/NA

BBW Risk of embryo-fetal and/or birth defects; not for use in pregnancy.
IND & DOSE Adjunct tx of pts w/ HER2-positive metastatic breast cancer who have not received prior HER2 therapy or tx for metastatic disease, w/trastuzumab and docetaxel. *Adult:* 840 mg IV over 60 min, then 420 mg IV over 30–60 min q 3 wk, w/ trastuzumab and docetaxel.
ADV EFF Alopecia, fatigue, **infusion reaction,** left ventricular (LV) dysfunction, neutropenia, n/v, peripheral neuropathy, rash
NC/PT Perform HER2 testing before use; ensure concurrent use of trastuzumab, docetaxel. Infuse first dose over 60 min, subsequent doses over 30–60 min; do not give as bolus. Not for use in pregnancy (contraceptives advised during and for 6 mo after tx)/breast-feeding. Monitor for infusion reactions, LV dysfunction. Pt should mark calendar for injection days; be aware hair loss possible; report difficulty breathing, numbness/tingling, fever, s&sx of infection.

phenazopyridine hydrochloride
(Azo-Standard, Baridium, Pyridium)
CLASS Urinary analgesic
PREG/CONT B/NA

IND & DOSE Symptomatic relief of s&sx of lower urinary tract irritation.

Adult, child over 12 yr: 100–200 mg PO tid after meals for max 2 days. *Child 6–12 yr:* 12 mg/kg/day divided into three doses PO for max 2 days.
ADJUST DOSE Elderly pts, renal impairment
ADV EFF GI disturbances, headache, rash, yellowish orange urine
NC/PT May permanently stain contact lenses. Stop if skin, sclera become yellow; may indicate drug accumulation. Urine may be yellowish orange; will stain fabric. Pt should take after meals and not take longer than 2 days, report unusual bleeding, fever.

phenelzine sulfate (Nardil)
CLASS Antidepressant, MAOI
PREG/CONT C/NA

BBW Increased risk of suicidality in children, adolescents, young adults; monitor accordingly.
IND & DOSE Tx of depression in pts unresponsive to other tx. *Adult:* 15 mg PO tid. Rapidly increase to at least 60 mg/day. After max benefit achieved, reduce dose slowly over several wk. Maint, 15 mg/day or q other day PO.
ADJUST DOSE Elderly pts
ADV EFF Abd pain, anorexia, blurred vision, confusion, constipation, dizziness, drowsiness, dry mouth, headache, hyperreflexia, **hypertensive crisis,** hypomania, hypotension, insomnia, jitteriness, **liver toxicity,** n/v/d, orthostatic hypotension, serotonin syndrome, suicidal thoughts, twitching, vertigo
INTERACTIONS Alcohol, amphetamines, antidiabetics, beta blockers, dextromethorphan, meperidine, SSRIs, sympathomimetics, TCAs, thiazides, tyramine-containing foods
NC/PT Have phentolamine/other alpha-adrenergic blocker on hand for hypertensive crisis. Monitor LFTs, BP regularly. Pt should avoid diet high in tyramine-containing foods during, for 2 wk after tx; avoid alcohol, OTC

appetite suppressants; take safety precautions for CNS effects; change position slowly if orthostatic hypotension; report rash, urine/stool color changes, thoughts of suicide.

DANGEROUS DRUG

phenobarbital (Solfoton), phenobarbital sodium (generic)

CLASS Antiepileptic, barbiturate, sedative-hypnotic
PREG/CONT D/C-IV

BBW Increased risk of suicidality in children, adolescents, young adults; monitor accordingly.
IND & DOSE *Sedation.* *Adult:* 30–120 mg/day PO in two to three divided doses; max, 400 mg/24 hr. Or, 30–120 mg/day IM in two to three divided doses. *Child:* 6 mg/kg/day PO in divided doses. **Preop sedation.** *Adult:* 100–200 mg IM 60–90 min before surgery. *Child:* 1–3 mg/kg IM or IV 60–90 min before surgery. **Hypnotic.** *Adult:* 100–320 mg PO at bedtime, or 100–320 mg IM or IV. **Antiepileptic.** *Adult:* 60–300 mg/day PO. *Child:* 3–6 mg/kg/day PO. Or, 4–6 mg/kg/day IM or IV for 7–10 days to blood level of 10–15 mcg/mL. Or, 10–15 mg/kg/day IV or IM. **Tx of acute seizures.** *Adult:* 200–320 mg IM or IV repeated in 6 hr if needed. **Tx of status epilepticus.** *Child:* 15–20 mg/kg IV over 10–15 min.
ADJUST DOSE Elderly pts, debilitated adults; hepatic, renal impairment
ADV EFF Agitation, apnea, ataxia, bradycardia, **bronchospasm**, CNS depression, **circulatory collapse**, confusion, dizziness, hallucinations, hypotension, hypoventilation, hyperkinesia, insomnia, **laryngospasm**, pain/necrosis at injection site, somnolence, **Stevens-Johnson syndrome**, syncope, **withdrawal syndrome**
INTERACTIONS Alcohol, beta-adrenergic blockers, CNS depressants, corticosteroids, doxycycline, felodipine, fenoprofen, estrogens, hormonal contraceptives, metronidazole, oral anticoagulants, phenylbutazones, quinidine, theophylline, valproic acid
NC/PT Use caution in children; may produce irritability, aggression, inappropriate tearfulness. Do not give intra-arterially; arteriospasm, thrombosis, gangrene possible. Give slowly IV or by deep IM injection. Monitor continuously during IV use; monitor injection site for irritation. Taper gradually w/long-term use. Not for use in pregnancy (contraceptives advised). Pt should take safety precautions for CNS effects; not take longer than 2 wk for insomnia; wear medical ID for seizure disorder; report difficulty breathing, rash, thoughts of suicide.

DANGEROUS DRUG

phentolamine mesylate (OraVerse)

CLASS Alpha blocker, diagnostic agent
PREG/CONT C/NA

IND & DOSE *Px, control of hypertensive episodes in pheochromocytoma.* *Adult:* For preop reduction of elevated BP, 5 mg IV or IM 1–2 hr before surgery; repeat if necessary. Give 5 mg IV during surgery as indicated to control paroxysms of hypertension, other epinephrine toxicity effects. *Child:* 1 mg IV or IM 1–2 hr before surgery; repeat if necessary. Give 1 mg IV during surgery as indicated for epinephrine toxicity. **Px of tissue necrosis, sloughing after IV dopamine extravasation.** *Adult:* Infiltrate 10–15 mL normal saline injection containing 5–10 mg phentolamine. *Child:* Infiltrate 0.1–0.2 mg/kg to max 10 mg. **Px of tissue necrosis, sloughing after IV norepinephrine extravasation.** *Adult:* 10 mg phentolamine added to each liter IV fluids containing norepinephrine. **Dx of pheochromocytoma.** *Adult:* Use only to confirm evidence after risks carefully considered. Usual dose, 5 mg IM or IV. **Reversal**

of soft-tissue anesthesia. *Adult:* 0.2–0.8 mg based on amount of local anesthetic given, injected into anesthetized area. *Child 6 yr and older, over 30 kg:* Adult dose or max 0.4 mg. *Child 6 yr and older, 15–30 kg:* Max, 0.2 mg.

ADV EFF Acute, prolonged hypotension; arrhythmias; dizziness; **MI;** nausea; weakness

INTERACTIONS Ephedrine, epinephrine

NC/PT Give *OraVerse* after dental procedure, using same location as local anesthetic. Monitor P, BP closely. Pt should take safety precautions for CNS effects, hypotension; report palpitations, chest pain.

DANGEROUS DRUG

phenylephrine hydrochloride
(Neo-Synephrine, PediaCare Children's Decongestant, Sudafed PE, Vicks Sinex Ultra Fine Mist)
CLASS Alpha agonist, nasal decongestant, ophthalmic mydriatic, sympathomimetic
PREG/CONT C/NA

BBW Protect parenteral sol from light. Do not give unless sol is clear; discard unused sol.

IND & DOSE **Tx of mild to moderate hypotension.** *Adult:* 1–10 mg subcut, IM; max initial dose, 5 mg. Or, 0.1 or 0.5 mg IV; max initial dose, 0.5 mg. Do not repeat more often than q 10–15 min; 0.5 mg IV should raise BP for 15 min. **Tx of severe hypotension, shock.** *Adult:* For continuous infusion, add 10 mg to 500 mL dextrose or normal saline injection. Start at 100–180 mcg/min then drop factor of 20 drops/mL [100–180 drops/min]). When BP stabilized, maint, 40–60 mcg/min. **Spinal anesthesia.** *Adult:* 2–3 subcut or IM 3–4 min before spinal anesthetic injection. **Hypotensive emergencies during**

anesthesia. *Adult:* 0.2 mg IV; max, 0.5 mg/dose. *Child:* 0.5–1 mg/11.3 kg subcut, IM. **Prolongation of spinal anesthesia.** *Adult:* Adding 2–5 mg to anesthetic sol increases motor block duration by as much as 50%. **Vasoconstrictor for regional anesthesia.** *Adult:* 1:20,000 conc (add 1 mg phenylephrine to q 20 mL local anesthetic sol). **Tx of paroxysmal supraventricular tachycardia.** *Adult:* Rapid IV injection (within 20–30 sec) recommended. Max initial dose, 0.5 mg. Subsequent doses should not exceed preceding dose by more than 0.1–0.2 mg; should never exceed 1 mg. Use only after other tx failed. **Tx of nasal congestion.** *Adult:* 2–3 sprays, drops of 0.25% or 0.5% sol in each nostril q 3–4 hr. In severe cases, may need 0.5% or 1% sol. Or, 10 mg PO bid–qid. Or, 1–2 tablets PO q 4 hr. Or, 1 strip q 4 hr; max, 6 strips/24 hr. Place 1 strip on tongue; let dissolve. Or, 10 mL liquid q 6 hr. *Child 6 yr and older:* 2–3 sprays 0.25% sol in each nostril no more than q 4 hr. Or, 1 tablet PO q 4 hr. *Child 2–5 yr:* 2–3 drops 0.125% sol in each nostril q 4 hr PRN. Or, 1 dropperful (5 mL [2.5 mg]) 0.25% oral drops q 4 hr; max, 6 mL (15 mg)/day. **Vasoconstriction, pupil dilation.** *Adult:* 1 drop 2.5% or 10% sol on upper limbus. May repeat in 1 hr. **Tx of uveitis to prevent posterior synechiae.** *Adult:* 1 drop 2.5% or 10% sol on surface of cornea w/ atropine. Max, three times. **Tx of wide-angle glaucoma.** *Adult:* 1 drop 2.5% or 10% sol on upper surface of cornea repeated as necessary, w/ miotics. **Intraocular surgery.** *Adult:* 2.5% or 10% sol in eye 30–60 min before procedure. **Refraction.** *Adult:* 1 drop of cyclopegic then, in 5 min, 1 drop phenylephrine 2.5% sol and, in 10 min, another drop of cyclopegic. **Ophthalmoscopic exam.** *Adult:* 1 drop 2.5% sol in each eye. Mydriasis produced in 15–30 min, lasting 4–6 hr. **Tx of minor eye irritation.** *Adult:* 1–2 drops 0.12% sol in eye bid–qid as needed.

ADJUST DOSE Elderly pts
ADV EFF Anorexia, anxiety, blurred vision, **cardiac arrhythmias**, decreased urine output, dizziness, drowsiness, dysuria, fear, headache, light-headedness, local stinging w/ophthalmic sol, nausea, pallor, rebound congestion w/nasal sol, urine retention
INTERACTIONS Halogenated anesthetics, MAOIs, methyldopa, oxytocics, sympathomimetics, TCAs
NC/PT Have alpha-adrenergic blocker on hand. If extravasation, infiltrate area w/phentolamine (5–10 mg in 10–15 mL saline) using fine hypodermic needle; usually effective if area infiltrated within 12 hr of extravasation. Five mg IM should raise BP for 1–2 hr; 0.5 mg IV, for 15 min. Do not give within 14 days of MAOIs. Monitor closely during administration. Teach proper administration of nasal sol, eyedrops. Pt should not use longer than prescribed; take safety precautions for CNS effects; report chest pain, palpitations, vision changes.

---

phenytoin (Dilantin, Phenytek)
CLASS Antiarrhythmic, antiepileptic, hydantoin
PREG/CONT D/NA

BBW Give IV slowly to prevent severe hypotension, venous irritation; small margin of safety between full therapeutic, toxic doses. Continually monitor cardiac rhythm; check BP frequently, regularly during infusion. Suggest use of fosphenytoin sodium if IV route needed.
IND & DOSE Tx of status epilepticus. *Adult:* 10–15 mg/kg by slow IV. Maint, 100 mg PO IV q 6–8 hr; max infusion rate, 50 mg/min. *Child:* Dose based on children's formulas; may also calculate infants', children's doses based on 10–15 mg/kg IV in divided doses of 5–10 mg/kg. For neonates, 15–20 mg/kg IV in divided doses of 5–10 mg/kg recommended.

Px of seizures during neurosurgery. *Adult:* 100–200 mg IM q 4 hr during surgery, postop; not preferred route. Tx of tonic-clonic, psychomotor seizures. *Adult:* Loading dose in hospitalized pts: 1 g phenytoin capsules (phenytoin sodium, prompt) divided into three doses (400 mg, 300 mg, 300 mg) and given PO q 2 hr. When control established, may consider once-a-day dosing w/300 mg PO. W/ no previous tx: Initially, 100 mg PO tid; maint, 300–400 mg/day. *Child not previously treated:* 5 mg/kg/day PO in two to three equally divided doses. Max, 300 mg/day; maint, 4–8 mg/kg. Child over 6 yr may need minimum adult dose (300 mg/day).
Initial tx in pt previously stabilized on oral dose. *Adult:* Increase dose by 50% over oral dose. When returning to oral dose, decrease dose by 50% of original oral dose for 1 wk to prevent excessive plasma level.
ADJUST DOSE Elderly pts, hepatic impairment
ADV EFF Aplastic anemia, ataxia, dizziness, drowsiness, dysarthria, **frank malignant lymphoma, bullous/exfoliative/purpuric dermatitis, CV collapse,** gum hyperplasia, **hematopoietic complications,** insomnia, irritation, **liver damage, lupus erythematosus,** mental confusion, nausea, nystagmus, **Stevens-Johnson syndrome**
INTERACTIONS Acetaminophen, alcohol, allopurinol, amiodarone, antineoplastics, atracurium, benzodiazepines, carbamazepine, cardiac glycosides, chloramphenicol, cimetidine, corticosteroids, cyclosporine, diazoxide, disopyramide, disulfiram, doxycycline, estrogens, fluconazole, folic acid, furosemide, haloperidol, hormonal contraceptives, isoniazid, levodopa, loxapine, methadone, metronidazole, metyrapone, mexiletine, miconazole, nitrofurantoin, omeprazole, pancuronium, phenacemide, phenothiazide, phenylbutazone, primidone, pyridoxine, quinidine, rifampin, sucralfate, sulfonamides,

sulfonylureas, theophylline, trimethoprim, valproic acid, vecuronium
NC/PT Monitor for serum level (10–20 mcg/mL). Enteral tube feedings may delay absorption. Provide 2-hr window between *Dilantin* doses, tube feedings. Reduce dose, stop phenytoin, or substitute other antiepileptic gradually; stopping abruptly may precipitate status epilepticus. Stop if rash, depressed blood count, enlarged lymph node, hypersensitivity reaction, signs of liver damage, Peyronie disease (induration of corpora cavernosa of penis); start another antiepileptic promptly. Have lymph node enlargement during tx evaluated carefully. Lymphadenopathy that simulates Hodgkin lymphoma has occurred; lymph node hyperplasia may progress to lymphoma. Not for use in pregnancy (contraceptives advised). Pt should have regular dental care; take safety precautions for CNS effects; wear medical ID; report rash, unusual bleeding, urine/stool color changes, thoughts of suicide.

pilocarpine hydrochloride (Salagen)
CLASS Parasympathomimetic
PREG/CONT C/NA

IND & DOSE Tx of sx of xerostomia from salivary gland dysfx caused by radiation for head/neck cancer. *Adult:* 5–10 mg PO tid. **Tx of dry mouth in Sjögren syndrome.** *Adult:* 5 mg PO qid.
ADJUST DOSE Severe hepatic impairment
ADV EFF Bronchospasm, headache, hypertension, hypotension, n/v/d, renal colic, sweating, tearing, visual changes
INTERACTIONS Anticholinergics, beta blockers
NC/PT Maintain hydration. Not for use in breast-feeding. Pt should take safety precautions w/vision changes, report dehydration, difficulty breathing.

pimozide (Orap)
CLASS Antipsychotic, diphenylbutylpiperidine
PREG/CONT C/NA

IND & DOSE To suppress severely compromising motor, phonic tics in Tourette syndrome. *Adult:* 1–2 mg/day PO; max, 10 mg/day.
ADJUST DOSE Severe hepatic impairment
ADV EFF Akathisia, asthenia, dry mouth, extrapyramidal effects, fever, headache, increased salivation, motor restlessness, **NMS, prolonged QT,** sedation, somnolence, tardive dyskinesia, weight gain
INTERACTIONS Amphetamines, antifungals, citalopram, escitalopram, grapefruit juice, methylphenidate, nefazodone, pemoline, protease inhibitors, QT-prolonging drugs, sertraline, strong CYP2D6 inhibitors
NC/PT Ensure correct dx. Obtain baseline, periodic ECG. Not for use in breast-feeding. Check pt's drugs closely; numerous drug interactions w/contraindications. Pt should take safety precautions for CNS effects, avoid grapefruit juice.

pindolol (generic)
CLASS Antihypertensive, beta blocker
PREG/CONT B/NA

IND & DOSE Tx of hypertension. *Adult:* 5 mg PO bid; max, 60 mg/day. Usual maint, 5 mg PO tid.
ADV EFF Arrhythmias, **bronchospasm,** constipation, decreased exercise tolerance/libido, fatigue, flatulence, gastric pain, altered serum glucose changes, **HF, laryngospasm,** n/v/d
INTERACTIONS Clonidine, epinephrine, ergots, ibuprofen, indomethacin, insulin, lidocaine, naproxen, piroxicam, prazosin, sulindac, theophyllines, thioridazine, verapamil
NC/PT When stopping, taper gradually over 2 wk w/monitoring. Pt

should take safety precautions for CNS effects, report difficulty breathing, swelling. Name confusion between pindolol and *Plendil* (felodipine); use caution.

pioglitazone (Actos)
CLASS Antidiabetic, thiazolidinedione
PREG/CONT C/NA

BBW Thiazolidinediones cause or worsen HF in some pts; pioglitazone not recommended for pts w/symptomatic HF (contraindicated in NYHA Class III, IV HF). After starting or increasing, watch carefully for HF s&sx. If they occur, manage HF according to current standards of care. Pioglitazone may be reduced or stopped. Increased risk of bladder cancer when used for longer than 1 yr; monitor accordingly.
IND & DOSE Adjunct to diet/exercise to improve glucose control in type 2 diabetes as monotherapy or w/insulin, sulfonylurea, metformin. *Adult:* 15–30 mg/day PO; max, 45 mg daily PO.
ADJUST DOSE Hepatic impairment
ADV EFF Aggravated diabetes, **bladder cancer,** fatigue, fractures, headache, **hepatic injury,** HF, **hyperglycemia, hypoglycemia,** infections, macular edema, myalgia, pain
INTERACTIONS Celery, coriander, dandelion root, fenugreek, garlic, gemfibrozil, ginseng, hormonal contraceptives, juniper berries, rifampin
NC/PT Not for use in type 1 diabetes, ketoacidosis. Interferes w/hormonal contraceptives; suggest alternative birth control method or consider higher contraceptive dose. Increased risk of bladder cancer when used for longer than 1 yr; monitor accordingly. Monitor blood glucose regularly; ensure complete diabetic teaching, support. Pt should take without regard to meals; report infections, difficulty breathing, uncontrolled glucose level. Name confusion between *Actos*

(pioglitazone) and *Actonel* (risedronate); use caution.

pirfenidone (Esbriet)
CLASS Pyridone
PREG/CONT C/NA

BBW Risk of severe hepatotoxicity, bleeding, GI perforation; monitor pt closely.
IND & DOSE Tx of idiopathic pulmonary fibrosis. *Adult:* 801 mg PO tid w/food; titrate over 2 wk to full dose.
ADJUST DOSE Hepatic/renal impairment
ADV EFF Abd pain, **bleeding, GI perforation/toxicity,** GERD, **hepatotoxicity,** insomnia, n/v/d, photosensitivity, sinusitis, rash, URI, weight loss
INTERACTIONS Ciprofloxacin, fluvoxamine, smoking
NC/PT Monitor LFTs, renal function. Taper over 2 wk to reach therapeutic dose. Use w/caution in pregnancy; not for use in breast-feeding. Pt should avoid sun exposure; use sunscreen/protective clothing; avoid smoking; report severe n/v/d, urine/stool color changes.

piroxicam (Feldene)
CLASS NSAID
PREG/CONT C/NA

BBW Increased risk of CV events, GI bleeding; monitor accordingly. Contraindicated for periop pain after CABG surgery.
IND & DOSE Relief of s&sx of acute/chronic rheumatoid arthritis, osteoarthritis. *Adult:* 20 mg/day PO.
ADJUST DOSE Elderly pts
ADV EFF Anaphylactoid reactions to anaphylactic shock, bone marrow suppression, bronchospasm, constipation, dizziness, dyspepsia, edema, fatigue, GI pain, headache, hypertension, insomnia, nausea, rash, somnolence

INTERACTIONS Beta blockers, cholestyramine, lithium, oral anticoagulants
NC/PT Pt should take w/food or milk; use safety precautions for CNS effects; report swelling, difficulty breathing, rash.

pitavastatin (Livalo)

CLASS Antihyperlipidemic, statin
PREG/CONT X/NA

IND & DOSE To reduce elevated total cholesterol, LDLs, apolipoprotein B, triglycerides, increase HDL in primary hyperlipidemia, mixed dyslipidemia. *Adult:* 2 mg/day PO; max, 4 mg/day.
ADJUST DOSE Renal impairment (pts on dialysis)
ADV EFF Back pain, constipation, diarrhea, flulike sx, headache, liver toxicity, myalgias, rhabdomyolysis
INTERACTIONS Alcohol, cyclosporine, erythromycin, fibrates, lopinavir/ritonavir, niacin, rifampin
NC/PT Monitor LFTs regularly. Ensure diet/exercise program. Not for use in pregnancy (barrier contraceptives advised)/breast-feeding. Pt should get regular blood tests, avoid alcohol, report severe muscle pain w/fever, weakness, urine/stool color changes.

plasma protein fraction (Plasmanate, Plasma-Plex, Protenate)

CLASS Blood product, plasma protein
PREG/CONT C/NA

IND & DOSE Tx of hypovolemic shock. *Adult:* Initially, 250–500 mL IV. Max, 10 mL/min; do not exceed 5–8 mL/min as plasma volume nears normal. **Tx of hypoproteinemia.** *Adult:* 1,000–1,500 mL IV daily; max, 5–8 mL/min. Adjust rate based on pt response.

ADV EFF Chills, fever, HF, hypotension, n/v, pulmonary edema after rapid infusion, rash
INTERACTIONS Alcohol, cyclosporine, erythromycin, fibrates, lopinavir/ritonavir, niacin, rifampin
NC/PT Infusion only provides symptomatic relief of hypoproteinemia; consider need for whole blood based on pt's clinical condition. Give IV without regard to blood type. Monitor closely during infusion. Pt should report headache, difficulty breathing.

plerixafor (Mozobil)

CLASS Hematopoietic stem-cell mobilizer
PREG/CONT D/NA

IND & DOSE To mobilize hematopoietic stem cells to peripheral blood for collection, subsequent autologous transplantation in pts w/non-Hodgkin lymphoma/multiple myeloma, w/granulocyte-colony stimulating factor (G-CSF). *Adult:* 0.24 mg/kg subcut for up to 4 consecutive days; start after pt has received G-CSF once daily for 4 days. Give approximately 11 hours before apheresis.
ADJUST DOSE Renal impairment
ADV EFF Anaphylactic shock, dizziness, headache, injection-site reactions, n/v/d, orthostatic hypotension, rash, splenic rupture, tumor cell mobilization
NC/PT Do not use in leukemia; may mobilize leukemic cells. Not for use in pregnancy (barrier contraceptives advised)/breast-feeding. Pt should report rash, injection-site reactions, difficulty breathing.

polidocanol (Asclera)

CLASS Sclerosing agent
PREG/CONT C/NA

IND & DOSE Tx of uncomplicated spider, reticular veins in lower extremities. *Adult:* 0.1–0.3 mL as IV injection at varicose vein site; max volume/session, 10 mL.

ADV EFF Anaphylaxis, injection-site reactions

NC/PT Do not inject intra-arterially. Have emergency equipment on hand. Advise compression stockings, support hose on treated legs continuously for 2 to 3 days, then for 2 to 3 wk during the day; walk for 15–20 min immediately after procedure and daily for next few days.

---

poly-L-lactic acid
(Sculptra)
CLASS Polymer
PREG/CONT Unkn/NA

IND & DOSE To restore, correct sx of lipoatrophy in pts w/HIV syndrome. Adult: 0.1–0.2 mL injected intradermally at each injection site. May need up to 20 injections/cheek; retreat periodically.

ADV EFF Injection-site reactions

NC/PT Do not use if signs of skin infection. Apply ice packs to area immediately after injection and for first 24 hr. Massage injection sites daily. Monitor pt on anticoagulants for increased bleeding.

DANGEROUS DRUG

polymyxin B sulfate
(generic)
CLASS Antibiotic
PREG/CONT C/NA

BBW Monitor renal function carefully; nephrotoxicity possible. Avoid concurrent use of other nephrotoxics. Neurotoxicity can cause respiratory paralysis; monitor accordingly. IV, intrathecal administration for hospitalized pts only.

IND & DOSE Tx of acute infections caused by susceptible bacteria strains when less toxic drugs contraindicated. Adult, child over 2 yr: 15,000–25,000 units/kg/day IV q 12 hr; max, 25,000 units/kg/day.

Infants: 40,000 units/kg/day IV, IM.
Tx of meningeal infections caused by Pseudomonas aeruginosa. Adult, child over 2 yr: 50,000 units/day intrathecally for 3–4 days; then 50,000 units q other day for at least 2 wk after CSF cultures negative, glucose content normal. Infants: 20,000 units/day intrathecally for 3–4 days or 25,000 units q other day. Continue w/25,000 units once q other day for at least 2 wk after CSF cultures negative, glucose content normal.

ADJUST DOSE Renal impairment

ADV EFF Apnea, nephrotoxicity, neurotoxicity, pain at injection site, rash, superinfections, thrombophlebitis

INTERACTIONS Aminoglycosides, nephrotoxic drugs, NMJ blockers

NC/PT Culture before tx. Monitor renal function regularly. IM route may cause severe pain. Treat superinfections. Pt should take safety precautions for CNS effects, report swelling, difficulty breathing, vision changes.

---

pomalidomide (Pomalyst)
CLASS Antineoplastic, thalidomide analogue
PREG/CONT X/NA

BBW Known human teratogen. Can cause severe, life-threatening birth defects; not for use in pregnancy. Risk of DVT, PE in pts treated for multiple myeloma.

IND & DOSE Tx of multiple myeloma in pts who have had disease progression after at least two other therapies. Adult: 4 mg/day PO on days 1–21 of repeated 28-day cycle until progression occurs.

ADJUST DOSE Severe hepatic, renal impairment

ADV EFF Anemia, asthenia, back pain, confusion, constipation, diarrhea, dizziness, **DVT,** dyspnea, fatigue, **hepatotoxicity,** hypersensitivity reactions, nausea, neuropathy, **neutropenia, PE,** tumor lysis syndrome, URI

INTERACTIONS CYP1A2 inhibitors

NC/PT Available only through restricted access program. Rule out pregnancy before starting drug. Ensure monthly negative pregnancy test; recommend highly effective contraceptive measures for men, women. Not for use in breast-feeding. Monitor for DVT, PE. Obtain baseline, periodic CBC. Pt should take drug once/day at about same time each day; mark calendar w/tx days; swallow capsule whole w/water and not cut, crush, or chew it; obtain monthly pregnancy test; avoid donating blood during and for 1 mo after tx; take safety precautions for CNS effects; report extreme fatigue, difficulty breathing, calf pain.

DANGEROUS DRUG

ponatinib (Iclusig)
CLASS Antineoplastic, kinase inhibitor
PREG/CONT D/NA

BBW Risk of vascular occlusion, HF, hepatotoxicity, any of which can lead to death.
IND & DOSE Tx of T3151-positive CML or T3151-positive ALL. *Adult:* 45 mg/day w/food; adjust based on toxicity.
ADJUST DOSE Severe hepatic impairment
ADV EFF Abd pain, arrhythmias, arthralgia, compromised wound healing, constipation, fever, fluid retention, **HF, hepatotoxicity,** hypertension, myelosuppression, neuropathies, n/v, pancreatitis, **vascular occlusions,** vision changes
INTERACTIONS CYP3A inhibitors
NC/PT Ensure proper dx. Monitor LFTs, lipase, cardiac function, CBC, BP. Ensure comprehensive eye exam, adequate hydration; correct uric acid level. Pt should avoid pregnancy (serious fetal harm possible)/breast-feeding; report fever, extreme fatigue, urine/stool color changes, headache, vision changes.

---

poractant alfa (Curosurf)
CLASS Lung surfactant
PREG/CONT Unkn/NA

IND & DOSE Rescue tx of infants w/RDS. *Infants:* Entire contents of vial (2.5 mL/kg birth weight) intratracheally, ½ of dose into each bronchi. Give first dose as soon as possible after RDS dx and when pt on ventilator. May need up to two subsequent doses of 1.25 mL/kg birth weight at 12-hr intervals. Max total dose, 5 mL/kg (sum of initial, two repeat doses).
ADV EFF Bradycardia, flushing, hyperbilirubinemia, hypotension, infections, **intraventricular hemorrhage, patent ductus arteriosus, pneumothorax,** sepsis
NC/PT Ensure ET tube in correct position, w/bilateral chest movement, lung sounds. Store in refrigerator; protect from light. Enter vial once only. Instill slowly; inject ¼ of dose over 2–3 sec. Do not suction infant for 1 hr after completion of full dose; do not flush catheter. Maintain appropriate interventions for critically ill infant.

DANGEROUS DRUG

porfimer sodium (Photofrin)
CLASS Antineoplastic
PREG/CONT C/NA

IND & DOSE Photodynamic tx for palliation of pts w/completely/partially obstructing esophageal/transitional cancer who cannot be treated w/laser alone; transitional cell carcinoma in situ of urinary bladder; endobronchial non-small-cell lung cancer; high-grade dysplasia of Barrett esophagus. *Adult:* 2 mg/kg as slow IV injection over 3–5 min; laser tx must follow in 40–50 hr and again in 96–120 hr.
ADV EFF Abd pain, anemia, **bleeding,** chest pain, constipation, dyspnea, **GI perforation,** n/v,

photosensitivity, **pleural effusion, respiratory toxicity**
NC/PT Monitor for pleural effusion, respiratory complications. Avoid contact w/drug. Protect pt from light exposure for 30 days after tx; photosensitivity may last up to 90 days. Pt should report difficulty breathing/swallowing, unusual bleeding.

DANGEROUS DRUG

posaconazole (Noxafil)

CLASS Antifunga, azole
PREG/CONT C/NA

IND & DOSE Px of invasive *Aspergillus, Candida* infections in immunosuppressed pts. *Adult, child 13 yr and older:* 200 mg (5 mL) PO tid oral suspension; 300 mg PO bid DR tablet on day 1, then once a day. Or 300 mg IV bid on day 1, then 300 mg/day IV on day 1 (then bid oral susp). **Tx of oropharyngeal candidiasis.** *Adult, child 13 yr and older:* 100 mg (2.5 mL) PO bid on day 1; then 100 mg/day PO for 13 days (oral suspension). For refractory infection, 400 mg (10 mL) PO bid; duration based on pt response.
ADJUST DOSE Hepatic impairment, severe renal impairment
ADV EFF Abd pain, anemia, constipation, cough, dizziness, dyspnea, epistaxis, fatigue, fever, headache, **hepatotoxicity,** insomnia, n/v/d, **prolonged QT,** rash
INTERACTIONS Calcium channel blockers, cimetidine, cyclosporine, digoxin, ergots, fosamprenavir, metoclopramide, midazolam, phenytoin, quinidine, rifabutin, sirolimus, statins, tacrolimus, vincristine, vinblastine
NC/PT Culture before tx. Obtain baseline ECG; monitor LFTs. Check formulation, dose, and frequency; oral forms are not directly substitutable. Monitor drug regimen; many interactions possible. Shake bottle well before use. Give w/full meal or nutritional supplement. Maintain hydration, nutrition. Not for use in pregnancy/breast-feeding. Pt should take safety

precautions for CNS effects; report fever, urine/stool color changes.

DANGEROUS DRUG

potassium acetate, potassium chloride (K-Lyte Cl), potassium gluconate (Klor-Con, K-Tab)

CLASS Electrolyte
PREG/CONT C/NA

IND & DOSE Px of potassium deficiency. *Adult:* 16–24 mEq/day PO. **Tx of potassium deficiency.** 40–100 mEq/day PO or IV. *Child:* 2–3 mEq/kg/day or 40 mEq/m²/day PO or IV; 2–6 mEq/kg/hr PO or IV for newborns.
ADJUST DOSE Elderly pts, renal impairment
ADV EFF Abd pain, hyperkalemia, n/v/d, tissue sloughing, venospasm
INTERACTIONS Potassium-sparing diuretics, salt substitutes using potassium
NC/PT Obtain baseline, periodic serial serum potassium level. Dilute in dextrose sol to 40–80 mEq/L; do not give undiluted. Monitor for cardiac arrhythmias during IV infusion. Monitor injection site carefully. Wax tablet matrix may appear in stool. Pt should swallow tablet whole and not cut, crush, or chew it; take w/food or after meals; avoid salt substitutes, report tingling in hands/feet, black tarry stools, pain at IV injection site.

---

pralatrexate (Folotyn)

CLASS Antineoplastic, folate analogue metabolic inhibitor
PREG/CONT X/NA

IND & DOSE Tx of relapsed, refractory peripheral T-cell lymphoma. *Adult:* 30 mg/m²/wk as IV push over 3–5 min for 6 wk in 7-wk cycle.
ADJUST DOSE Elderly pts, renal impairment

ADV EFF Bone marrow suppression, dehydration, dyspnea, fatigue, mucositis, n/v/d, night sweats, pain, rash, **serious to fatal dermatologic reactions**, tumor lysis syndrome
NC/PT Monitor CBC, skin. Pt should also receive vitamin B$_{12}$ (1 mg IM q 8–10 wk) and folic acid (1–1.25 mg/day PO). Maintain hydration. Not for use in pregnancy (contraceptives advised)/breast-feeding. Provide skin care. Pt should avoid exposure to infection, report signs of infection, unusual bleeding, rash.

pralidoxime chloride
(Protopam Chloride)
CLASS Antidote
PREG/CONT C/NA

IND & DOSE Antidote in poisoning due to organophosphate pesticides, chemicals w/anticholinesterase activity. *Adult:* Atropine 2–4 mg IV. If cyanotic, 2–4 mg atropine IM while improving ventilation; repeat q 5–10 min until signs of atropine toxicity appear. Maintain atropinization for at least 48 hr. Give pralidoxime concomitantly: Initially, 1–2 g pralidoxime IV, preferably as 15–30 min infusion in 100 mL saline. After 1 hr, give second dose of 1–2 g IV if muscle weakness not relieved. Give additional doses cautiously q 10–12 hr. If IV route not feasible or pulmonary edema present, give IM or subcut. *Child 16 yr and under:* Loading dose, 20–50 mg/kg (max, 2,000 mg/dose) IV over 15–30 min, then continuous infusion of 10–20 mg/kg/hr. Or, 20–50 mg/kg (max, 2,000 mg/dose) IV over 15–30 min. Give second dose of 20–50 mg/kg in 1 hr if muscle weakness not relieved. May repeat dosing q 10–12 hr as needed. Or, for pt 40 kg and over, 1,800 mg IM/course of tx; under 40 kg, 15 mg/kg IM q 15 min if needed, to total of three doses (45 mg/kg). **Adjunct to atropine in poisoning by nerve agents w/anticholinesterase activity.** *Adult:* Give atropine, pralidoxime as soon as possible after exposure. Use autoinjectors, giving atropine first. Repeat both atropine, pralidoxime after 15 min. If after additional 15 min, repeat injections. If sx persist after third set of injections, seek medical help. **Tx of anticholinesterase overdose of myasthenia gravis drugs.** *Adult:* 1–2 g IV, then increments of 250 mg q 5 min.
ADV EFF Blurred vision, diplopia, dizziness, drowsiness, headache, pain at injection site, transient LFT increases
NC/PT For acute organophosphate poisoning, remove secretions, maintain patent airway, provide artificial ventilation as needed; then begin tx. After skin exposure to organophosphate poisoning, remove clothing, thoroughly wash hair/skin w/sodium bicarbonate or alcohol as soon as possible. Give by slow IV infusion. Have IV sodium thiopental or diazepam on hand if seizures occur. Pt should report pain at injection site, vision changes.

pramipexole dihydrochloride
(Mirapex)
CLASS Antiparkinsonian, dopamine receptor agonist
PREG/CONT C/NA

BBW Use extreme caution in pts w/ hx of hypotension, hallucinations, confusion, dyskinesias.
IND & DOSE Tx of sx of Parkinson disease. *Adult:* 0.125 mg tid for 1 wk; wk 2, 0.25 mg PO tid; wk 3, 0.5 mg PO tid; wk 4, 0.75 mg PO tid; wk 5, 1 mg PO tid; wk 6, 1.25 mg PO tid; wk 7, 1.5 mg PO tid. Once levels established, may use ER tablets for once-a-day dosing. **Tx of restless legs syndrome (*Mirapex*).** *Adult:* 0.125 mg/day PO 2–3 hr before bedtime. May increase q 4–7 days if needed, to 0.25 mg/day; max, 0.5 mg/day.
ADJUST DOSE Renal impairment

ADV EFF Asthenia, confusion, constipation, dizziness, dyskinesia, extrapyramidal sx, fever, hallucinations, headache, impulsive behaviors, insomnia, orthostatic hypotension, psychotic-like behavior, retinal changes, somnolence

INTERACTIONS Cimetidine, diltiazem, dopamine antagonists, levodopa, quinidine, quinine, ranitidine, triamterene, verapamil

NC/PT Give w/extreme caution to pts w/hx of hypotension, hallucinations, confusion, dyskinesia. Taper gradually over at least 1 wk when stopping. Not for use in pregnancy (barrier contraceptives advised). Pt should swallow ER tablet whole and not cut, crush, or chew it; take safety precautions for CNS effects; report behavior changes, hallucinations, swelling, vision changes.

DANGEROUS DRUG

pramlintide acetate
(Symlin)
CLASS Amylinomimetic,
antidiabetic
PREG/CONT C/NA

BBW Severe hypoglycemia associated w/combined use of insulin, pramlintide; usually seen within 3 hr of pramlintide injection. Monitor accordingly.

IND & DOSE Adjunct tx in pts w/ type 1, 2 diabetes who use mealtime insulin and have failed to achieve desired glucose control. *Adult w/ type 1 diabetes:* 15 mcg subcut before major meals; titrate at 15-mcg increments to maint of 30 or 60 mcg as tolerated. *Adult w/type 2 diabetes:* 60–120 mcg subcut immediately before major meals.

ADV EFF Cough, dizziness, **hypoglycemia**, injection-site reactions, n/v

INTERACTIONS Anticholinergics, oral drugs

NC/PT Doses of oral drugs, insulins will need reduction, usually by 50%

based on pt response. Drug affects gastric emptying; if rapid effect needed, give oral medication 1 hr before or 2 hr after pramlintide. Inject subcut more than 2 inches away from insulin injection site. Rotate sites. Do not mix in syringe w/insulin. Use caution in pregnancy/breast-feeding. Store unopened vial in refrigerator; may store opened vial at room temp. Teach proper administration/disposal of needles/syringes. Pt should not take if not going to eat or share pen w/ other pts; avoid alcohol; continue diet/exercise, other diabetes tx; monitor blood glucose level; report hypoglycemic reactions, injection-site pain/swelling.

DANGEROUS DRUG

prasugrel (Effient)
CLASS Platelet inhibitor
PREG/CONT B/NA

BBW Risk of serious to fatal bleeding; do not use w/active bleeding or hx of TIA, stroke. Risk increased w/ age over 75 yr, weight under 60 kg, bleeding tendency, warfarin/NSAID use. Do not use in likely candidates for CABG surgery; if pts taking drug need CABG, stop prasugrel at least 7 days before surgery. Suspect bleeding in pt who becomes hypotensive and has undergone invasive procedure. If possible, control bleeding without stopping prasugrel; stopping prematurely increases risk of thrombotic episodes.

IND & DOSE To reduce risk of thrombotic CV events (including stent thrombosis) in pts w/acute coronary syndrome who are to be managed w/percutaneous coronary intervention. *Adult:* 60 mg PO as single dose, then 10 mg/day PO without regard to food. Use 5 mg/day in pt weighing under 60 kg. Pt should also receive aspirin (75–325 mg/day).

ADV EFF Bleeding, fatigue, fever, headache, hyperlipidemia, **hypersensitivity reactions**, hypertension,

pain, rash, **risk of thrombotic episodes if stopped prematurely, thrombotic thrombocytopenic purpura**
INTERACTIONS NSAIDs
NC/PT Ensure pt also receives aspirin. Limit invasive procedures; monitor for bleeding. Stop drug 7 days before planned surgery. Protect from injury. Not for use in pregnancy (barrier contraceptives advised)/ breast-feeding. Do not stop prematurely; risk of rebound thrombotic events. Pt should wear medical ID; inform all health care providers about pramlintide use, increased risk of bleeding; report excessive bleeding, fever, purple skin patches; pink/ brown urine, black or bloody stools, difficulty breathing.

pravastatin sodium
(Pravachol)
CLASS Antihyperlipidemic, statin
PREG/CONT X/NA

IND & DOSE Adjunct to diet in tx of elevated total cholesterol, LDL cholesterol; px of MI in pts at risk for first MI; to slow progression of CAD in pts w/clinically evident CAD; to reduce risk of stroke, MI. *Adult:* 40 mg/day PO at bedtime. Max, 80 mg/day. *Adult on immunosuppressants:* 10 mg/day PO; max, 20 mg/day. **Tx of heterozygous familial hypercholesterolemia as adjunct to diet/ exercise:** *Child 14–18 yr:* 40 mg/day PO. *Child 8–13 yr:* 20 mg/day PO.
ADJUST DOSE Elderly pts; hepatic, renal impairment
ADV EFF Abd pain, blurred vision, cataracts, constipation, cramps, dizziness, flatulence, LFT elevations, n/v, **rhabdomyolysis**
INTERACTIONS Bile acid sequestrants, cyclosporine, digoxin, erythromycin, gemfibrozil, itraconazole, niacin, warfarin
NC/PT Ensure diet/exercise program for CAD. Not for use in pregnancy

(barrier contraceptives advised)/ breast-feeding. Pt should take at bedtime, have periodic eye exams, report severe GI upset, urine/stool color changes, muscle pain.

praziquantel (Biltricide)
CLASS Anthelmintic
PREG/CONT B/NA

IND & DOSE Tx of *Schistosoma* infections, liver fluke infections. *Adult, child over 4 yr:* Three doses of 20–25 mg/kg PO as one-day tx, w/ 4–6 hr between doses.
ADV EFF Abd pain, dizziness, fever, malaise, nausea, urticaria
INTERACTIONS Chloroquine, CP450 inducers, grapefruit juice
NC/PT Give w/food; GI upset common. Pt should swallow tablet whole and not cut, crush, or chew it; avoid grapefruit juice.

prazosin hydrochloride
(Minipress)
CLASS Alpha blocker, antihypertensive
PREG/CONT C/NA

IND & DOSE Tx of hypertension. *Adult:* 1 mg PO bid–tid. Increase to total 20 mg/day in divided doses; range, 6–15 mg/day. If using w/other antihypertensives, reduce dose to 1–2 mg PO tid, titrate to control BP.
ADV EFF Abd pain, dizziness, drowsiness, dry mouth, headache, hypotension, lack of energy, nausea, paresthesia, weakness
INTERACTIONS Avanafil, beta blockers, sildenafil, tadalafil, vardenafil, verapamil
NC/PT First dose may cause syncope w/sudden loss of consciousness; limit first dose to 1 mg PO, give at bedtime. Pt should take safety precautions for CNS effects, use sugarless lozenges for dry mouth, report fainting.

prednisoLONE, prednisoLONE acetate, prednisoLONE sodium phosphate (Orapred, Pred Forte, Pred Mild, Prelone)

CLASS Anti-inflammatory, corticosteroid

PREG/CONT C/NA

IND & DOSE Mgt of inflammatory disorders; tx of hypercalcemia of cancer. *Adult:* 5–60 mg/day PO based on condition, response. *Child:* 0.14–2 mg/kg/day PO in three to four divided doses. **Mgt of acute MS exacerbations.** *Adult:* 200 mg/day PO for 1 wk, then 80 mg q other day for 1 mo (sodium phosphate). **Mgt of nephrotic syndrome.** *Child:* 60 mg/m²/day PO in three divided doses for 4 wk (sodium phosphate). Then single doses for 4 wk. Or, 40 mg/m²/day PO. **Mgt of inflammation of eyelid, conjunctiva, cornea, globe.** *Adult, child:* 2 drops qid. For *Pred Mild/Forte,* sodium phosphate, 1–2 drops q hr during day, q 2 hr at night. W/favorable results, 1 drop q 4 hr, then 1 drop three to four times/day to control sx.

ADV EFF Aggravation of infections, amenorrhea, **anaphylactic reactions**, edema, fluid retention, headache, hyperglycemia, hypotension, immunosuppression, impaired healing, increased appetite, **shock**, vertigo

INTERACTIONS Barbiturates, cyclosporine, estrogens, hormonal contraceptives, ketoconazole, neostigmine, phenytoin, pyridostigmine, rifampin, salicylates

NC/PT Individualize dose, depending on severity, response. Give daily dose before 9 a.m. to minimize adrenal suppression. For maint, reduce initial dose in small increments at intervals until lowest satisfactory dose reached. If long-term tx needed, consider alternate-day tx w/short-acting corticosteroid. After long-term tx, withdraw slowly to prevent adrenal insufficiency. Monitor serum glucose level. Pt should avoid exposure to infection, bright light (eyes may be sensitive); learn proper eyedrop technique; report signs of infection, black tarry stools, difficulty breathing.

predniSONE (Prednisone Intensol, Rayos)

CLASS Corticosteroid

PREG/CONT C/NA

IND & DOSE Mgt of inflammatory disorders; tx of hypercalcemia of cancer; replacement tx w/adrenal insufficiency. *Adult:* 5–60 mg/day PO titrated based on response. *Child:* 0.05–2 mg/kg/day PO or 4–5 mg/m²/day PO in equal divided doses q 12 hr. **Mgt of acute MS exacerbations.** *Adult:* 200 mg/day PO for 1 wk, then 80 mg PO q other day for 1 mo.

ADV EFF Aggravation of infections, amenorrhea, **anaphylactic reactions**, edema, fluid retention, headache, hyperglycemia, hypotension, immunosuppression, impaired healing, increased appetite, **shock**, vertigo

INTERACTIONS Barbiturates, cyclosporine, estrogens, hormonal contraceptives, ketoconazole, neostigmine, phenytoin, pyridostigmine, rifampin, salicylates

NC/PT Individualize dose, depending on severity, response. Give daily dose before 9 a.m. to minimize adrenal suppression. For maint, reduce initial dose in small increments at intervals until lowest satisfactory dose reached. If long-term tx needed, consider alternate-day tx w/short-acting corticosteroid. After long-term tx, withdraw slowly to prevent adrenal insufficiency. Monitor serum glucose level. Pt should avoid exposure to infections, report signs of infection, worsening of condition.

pregabalin (Lyrica)

CLASS Analgesic, antiepileptic, calcium channel modulator
PREG/CONT C/C-V

BBW Increased risk of suicidal ideation; monitor accordingly.

IND & DOSE **Mgt of neuropathic pain.** *Adult:* 100 mg PO bid. Max, 300 mg/day. **Mgt of postherpetic neuralgia.** *Adult:* 75–150 mg PO bid or 50–100 mg PO tid; max, 600 mg/day. **Adjunct tx for partial-onset seizures.** 150–600 mg/day PO divided into two to three doses. **Mgt of fibromyalgia.** *Adult:* 75–150 mg PO bid. Max, 450 mg/day. **Mgt of neuropathic pain associated w/spinal cord injuries.** *Adult:* 75 mg PO bid. Increase to 150 mg PO bid within 1 wk; may increase to 300 mg PO bid if insufficient relief.
ADJUST DOSE Renal impairment
ADV EFF Angioedema, confusion, constipation, dizziness, dry mouth, infection, neuropathy, peripheral edema, somnolence, **thrombocytopenia**, weight gain
INTERACTIONS Alcohol, CNS depressants, pioglitazone, rosiglitazone
NC/PT Taper when stopping. Not for use in pregnancy (barrier contraceptives advised)/breast-feeding. Men should not father child during tx. Pt should take safety measures for CNS effects, avoid alcohol, report vision changes, weight gain, increased bleeding, thoughts of suicide.

primidone (Mysoline)

CLASS Antiepileptic
PREG/CONT D/NA

BBW Increased risk of suicidal ideation; monitor accordingly.
IND & DOSE **Control of tonic-clonic, psychomotor, focal epileptic seizures.** *Adult w/no previous tx:* Days 1–3, 100–125 mg PO at bedtime; days 4–6, 100–125 mg PO bid; days 7–9, 100–125 mg PO tid; day 10, maint, 250 mg tid. Max, 500 mg qid (2 g/day).

Adult on other epileptics: 100–125 mg PO at bedtime. When primidone alone desired, do not complete transition in under 2 wk. *Child under 8 yr:* Days 1–3, 50 mg PO at bedtime; days 4–6, 50 mg PO bid; days 7–9, 100 mg PO bid; day 10, maint, 125–250 mg tid or 10–25 mg/kg/day in divided doses.
ADV EFF Anorexia, ataxia, fatigue, hyperirritability, megaloblastic anemia, nausea, rash
INTERACTIONS Acetazolamide, alcohol, carbamazepine, isoniazid, nicotinamide, phenytoins, succinimides
NC/PT Taper when stopping; evaluate for therapeutic serum level (5–12 mcg/mL). Monitor CBC, folic acid for megaloblastic anemia. Not for use in pregnancy (barrier contraceptives advised). Pt should take safety measures for CNS effects, wear medical ID, avoid alcohol, report rash, fever, thoughts of suicide.

probenecid (Probalan)

CLASS Antigout, uricosuric
PREG/CONT B/NA

IND & DOSE **Tx of hyperuricemia associated w/gout, gouty arthritis.** *Adult:* 0.25 g PO bid for 1 wk, then 0.5 g PO at bedtime; max, 2–3 g/day. **Adjuvant to tx w/penicillins, cephalosporins.** *Adult:* 2 g/day PO in divided doses. *Child 2–14 yr:* Initially, 25 mg/kg PO, then 40 mg/kg PO in four divided doses. **Tx of gonorrhea.** *Adult:* Single 1-g dose PO 30 min before penicillin. *Child under 45 kg:* 23 mg/kg PO in one single dose 30 min before penicillin.
ADJUST DOSE Elderly pts, renal impairment
ADV EFF Anaphylaxis, anemia, anorexia, dizziness, n/v, rash, urinary frequency
INTERACTIONS Acyclovir, allopurinol, benzodiazepines, clofibrate, dapsone, dyphylline, methotrexate, NSAIDs, rifampin, sulfonamides, thiopental, zidovudine

NC/PT Check urine alkalinity; urates crystallize in acidic urine. Sodium bicarbonate, potassium citrate may be ordered to alkalinize urine. Pt should take w/meals, antacids; drink 2.5–3 L fluid/day; take safety precautions w/ dizziness; report dark urine, painful urination, difficulty breathing.

DANGEROUS DRUG

procarbazine hydrochloride (Matulane)
CLASS Antineoplastic
PREG/CONT D/NA

IND & DOSE Part of MOPP regimen for tx of stage III, IV Hodgkin lymphoma. *Adult:* 2–4 mg/kg/day PO for first wk, then 4–6 mg/kg/day PO. Maint, 1–2 mg/kg/day PO.
ADJUST DOSE Elderly pts, renal impairment
ADV EFF Bone marrow suppression, confusion, diarrhea, fever, hallucinations, **hepatotoxicity, hypertensive crisis, pneumonitis**
INTERACTIONS Alcohol, anticholinergics, antihistamines, MAOIs, oral anticoagulants, TCAs
NC/PT Monitor CBC, LFTs; do not give within 14 days of MAOIs. Not for use in pregnancy (barrier contraceptives advised)/breast-feeding. Pt should follow prescription carefully; avoid exposure to infection, injury; report severe headache, unusual bleeding, s&sx of infection, difficulty breathing.

---

prochlorperazine (Compro), prochlorperazine edisylate, prochlorperazine maleate (Procomp)
CLASS Antiemetic, antipsychotic, dopaminergic blocker, phenothiazine
PREG/CONT C/NA

BBW Increased risk of death if used to treat dementia-related psychosis

in elderly pts; not approved for this use.
IND & DOSE Mgt of manifestations of psychotic disorders. *Adult:* 5–10 mg PO tid or qid. Range, 50–75 mg/day for mild/moderate disturbances, 100–150 mg/day PO for more severe disturbances. For immediate control of severely disturbed adults, 10–20 mg IM repeated q 2–4 hr (q hour for resistant cases). *Child 2–12 yr:* 2.5 mg PO or rectally bid–tid; max, 25 mg/day (6–12 yr), 20 mg/day (2–5 yr). *Child under 12 yr:* 0.132 mg/kg by deep IM injection. Switch to oral as soon as possible (usually after one dose). **Tx of emesis.** *Adult:* 5–10 mg PO tid–qid; or 15 mg SR on arising; or 25 mg rectally bid; or 5–10 mg IM initially, then q 3–4 hr (max, 40 mg/day). *Child over 2 yr:* 18.2–38.6 kg, 2.5 mg PO or rectally tid or 5 mg bid; max, 15 mg/day. 13.6–17.7 kg, 2.5 mg PO or rectally bid–tid; max, 10 mg/day. 9.1–13.2 kg, 2.5 mg PO or rectally daily–bid; max, 7.5 mg/day. *Child 2 yr and older, at least 9 kg:* 0.132 mg/kg IM (usually one dose). **Mgt of n/v related to surgery.** *Adult:* 5–10 mg IM 1–2 hr before anesthesia or periop and postop (may repeat once in 30 min); or 5–10 mg IV 15 min before anesthesia or periop and postop (may repeat once); or 20 mg/L isotonic sol added to IV infusion 15–30 min before anesthesia. **Tx of nonpsychotic anxiety.** *Adult:* 5 mg PO tid or qid; max, 20 mg/day for no more than 12 wk.
ADV EFF Akathisia, **aplastic anemia**, blurred vision, **bone marrow suppression**, bronchospasm, dizziness, drowsiness, dystonia, **HF, laryngospasm, NMS**, photosensitivity, pink to red-brown urine, pseudoparkinsonism, rash, **refractory arrhythmias**, tardive dyskinesia
INTERACTIONS Alcohol, anticholinergics, barbiturate anesthetics
NC/PT Monitor CBC, renal function; elderly pts may be more susceptible to adverse reactions. Maintain hydration. Avoid skin contact w/oral sol. Give IM injection deep into upper

outer quadrant of buttock. Urine may be pink to red-brown. Pt should avoid sun exposure; take safety precautions for CNS effects; report unusual bleeding, swelling, fever, difficulty breathing.

progesterone (Crinone, Endometrin, Prometrium)
CLASS Hormone, progestin
PREG/CONT B (oral), X (injection)/NA

BBW Do not use for px of CV disease. Not effective for tx of CV disease. Increased risk of dementia; weigh risks. Increased risk of invasive breast cancer; monitor pts closely.
IND & DOSE Tx of primary amenorrhea. *Adult:* 5–10 mg/day IM for 6–8 consecutive days. Or, 400 mg PO in p.m. for 10 days. **Tx of secondary amenorrhea.** *Adult:* 4%–8% gel, 45–90 mg q other day; max, six doses. **Mgt of uterine bleeding.** *Adult:* 5–10 mg/day IM for six doses. If estrogen given, begin progesterone after 2 wk of estrogen tx. **Tx of endometrial hyperplasia.** *Adult:* 200 mg/day PO in p.m. for 12 days/28-day cycle w/daily conjugated estrogen. **Tx of infertility.** *Adult:* 90 mg vaginally daily in women needing progesterone supplementation; 90 mg vaginally bid for replacement. Continue for 10–12 wk into pregnancy if it occurs. **Support for embryo implantation.** *Adult:* 100 mg vaginally two to three times daily starting at oocyte retrieval, continuing for up to 10 wk.
ADV EFF Abd cramps, amenorrhea; breakthrough bleeding, spotting; breast tenderness; cervical erosion; change in menstrual flow; weight; constipation; dizziness; headache; **PE**; photosensitivity; rash; somnolence; **thromboembolic/thrombotic disease**
INTERACTIONS Grapefruit juice
NC/PT Obtain baseline, periodic (at least annual) hx, physical exam.

Insert intrauterine system during or immediately after menstrual period. Give IM by deep injection. Stop at first sign of thromboembolic problems. Not for use in pregnancy (contact prescriber if pregnancy occurs). Pt should perform monthly breast self-exams; avoid grapefruit juice, sun exposure; stop if sudden vision loss, difficulty breathing, leg pain/swelling.

DANGEROUS DRUG

promethazine hydrochloride (Phenadoz, Promethegan)
CLASS Antiemetic, antihistamine, anti–motion sickness drug, dopaminergic blocker, phenothiazine, sedative-hypnotic
PREG/CONT C/NA

BBW Do not give to child under 2 yr; risk of fatal respiratory depression. Use lowest effective dose, caution in child 2 yr and older. Give IM injection deep into muscle. Do not give subcut; tissue necrosis possible. Do not give intra-arterially; arteriospasm, limb gangrene possible. If IV route used, limit drug conc, rate of administration; ensure patent IV line.
IND & DOSE Relief of allergy s&sx. *Adult:* 25 mg PO, rectally, preferably at bedtime. If needed, 12.5 mg before meals and at bedtime. Or, 25 mg IM or IV for serious reactions. May repeat within 2 hr if needed. *Child over 2 yr:* 25 mg PO at bedtime or 6.25–12.5 mg tid. **Tx, px of motion sickness.** *Adult:* 25 mg PO bid 30–60 min before travel; repeat in 8–12 hr if needed. Then, 25 mg on rising and before evening meal. *Child over 2 yr:* 12.5–25 mg PO, rectally bid. **Tx, px of n/v.** *Adult:* 25 mg PO; repeat doses of 12.5–25 mg as needed q 4–6 hr. Give rectally or parenterally if PO not tolerated. Or, 12.5–25 mg IM or IV; max, q 4–6 hr. *Child over 2 yr:* 0.5 mg/lb body weight IM q 4–6 hr as needed.
Sedation, postop sedation, adjunctive

use w/analgesics. **Adult:** 25–50 mg PO, IM or IV. **Child over 2 yr:** 12.5–25 mg PO rectally at bedtime. For post-op sedation, 12.5–25 mg PO, IV or IM, rectally. **Preop use. Adult:** 50 mg PO night before surgery. **Child over 2 yr:** 0.5 mg/lb body weight PO. **Obstetric sedation. Adult:** 50 mg IM or IV in early stages. When labor established, 25–75 mg w/reduced opioid dose. May repeat once or twice at 4-hr intervals. Max within 24 hr, 100 mg.

ADV EFF Agranulocytosis, confusion, dizziness, drowsiness, dysuria, epigastric distress, excitation, hypotension, **pancytopenia,** photosensitivity, poor coordination, thickened bronchial secretions, urinary frequency

INTERACTIONS Alcohol, anticholinergics, methohexital, phenobarbital anesthetic, thiopental

NC/PT Do not give subcut, deep IM. Maintain hydration. Pt should take safety precautions for CNS effects, avoid sun exposure, report unusual bleeding, rash, dark urine.

DANGEROUS DRUG

propafenone hydrochloride (Rythmol)

CLASS Antiarrhythmic
PREG/CONT C/NA

BBW Arrange for periodic ECG to monitor effects on cardiac conduction; risk of serious proarrhythmias. Monitor pt response carefully, especially at start of tx; increase dosage at minimum of 3- to 4-day intervals.

IND & DOSE Tx of documented life-threatening ventricular arrhythmias; tx of paroxysmal supraventricular tachycardia w/disabling s&sx in pts w/out structural heart disease. **Adult:** 150 mg PO q 8 hr (450 mg/day). May increase at minimum of 3- to 4-day intervals to 225 mg PO q 8 hr (675 mg/day) to max 300 mg PO q 8 hr (900 mg/day). To prolong time to recurrence of symptomatic atrial fibrillation in pts w/structural heart disease. **Adult:** 225 mg ER

tablet PO q 12 hr; titrate at 5-day intervals to max 425 mg q 12 hr.

ADJUST DOSE Elderly pts; hepatic, renal impairment

ADV EFF Agranulocytosis, arrhythmias, blurred vision, constipation, dizziness, headache, **cardiac arrest, coma,** fatigue, headache, **HF,** n/v, unusual taste

INTERACTIONS Beta blockers, cimetidine, cyclosporine, digoxin, quinidine, ritonavir, SSRIs, theophylline, warfarin

NC/PT Monitor ECG periodically. Not for use in pregnancy. Pt should swallow ER tablet whole and not cut, crush, or chew it; take around the clock; use safety precautions for CNS effects; report difficulty breathing, fainting, palpitations.

---

propantheline bromide (generic)

CLASS Anticholinergic, antispasmodic, parasympatholytic
PREG/CONT C/NA

IND & DOSE Adjunct tx in peptic ulcer. **Adult:** 7.5–15 mg PO 30 min before meals and at bedtime. **Child:** 1.5 mg/kg/day PO in divided doses tid to qid.

ADJUST DOSE Elderly pts; hepatic, renal impairment

ADV EFF Blurred vision, decreased sweating, drowsiness, dry mouth, headache, n/v, urine retention

INTERACTIONS Antacids, anticholinergics, digoxin, phenothiazines

NC/PT Risk of heat prostration; maintain hydration. Pt should swallow ER tablet whole and not cut, crush, or chew it; take 30 min before meals and at bedtime; empty bladder before each dose; use sugarless lozenges for dry mouth; take safety precautions for CNS effects; report rash, eye pain.

DANGEROUS DRUG

propofol disodium
(Diprivan)
CLASS Sedative/hypnotic
PREG/CONT B/NA

IND & DOSE Induction of general anesthesia. *Adult:* 2–2.5 mg/kg IV at 40 mg/10 sec. *Children 3–16 yr:* 2.5–3.5 mg/kg IV over 20–30 sec. **Induction of general anesthesia in neurosurgery.** *Adult:* 1–2 mg/kg IV at 20 mg/10 sec. **Induction of general anesthesia in cardiac surgery.** *Adult:* 0.5–1.5 mg/kg IV at 20 mg/10 sec. **Maintenance of general anesthesia.** *Adult:* 100–200 mcg/kg/min IV or 25–50 mg intermittent IV bolus, based on pt response. *Children 3–16 yr:* 125–150 mcg/kg/min IV, based on pt response. **Monitored anesthesia care.** *Adult:* 25–75 mcg/kg/min IV, based on pt response. **ICU sedation of intubated pts.** *Adult:* 5–50 mcg/kg/min IV as continuous infusion.
ADJUST DOSE Elderly, debilitated pts
ADV EFF Anxiety, **apnea**, chills, confusion, dry mouth, **hypoxemia**, injection-site reactions, **loss of responsiveness, MI, respiratory depression**
INTERACTIONS Benzodiazepines, opioid analgesics
NC/PT Monitor continuously. Perform frequent BP checks, oximetry; give oxygen; have emergency equipment on standby; ensure pt safety for CNS effects; taper after prolonged ICU use. Pt should be aware of sedation effects (do not drive; avoid important decisions, tasks requiring alertness); report difficulty breathing, chest pain, pain at injection site.

DANGEROUS DRUG

propranolol hydrochloride
(Hemangeol, Inderal, InnoPran XL)
CLASS Antianginal, antiarrhythmic, antihypertensive, beta blocker
PREG/CONT C/NA

BBW Do not stop abruptly after long-term tx (hypersensitivity to catecholamines possible, causing angina exacerbation, MI, ventricular arrhythmias). Taper gradually over 2 wk w/monitoring.
IND & DOSE Tx of hypertension. *Adult:* 40 mg PO regular propranolol bid, or 80 mg (SR, ER) PO daily initially; range, 120–240 mg/day bid or tid or 120–160 mg (SR, ER) daily (max, 640 mg/day). **Tx of angina.** *Adult:* 80–320 mg/day PO divided bid, tid, or qid, or 80 mg (SR, ER) daily initially; usual dose, 160 mg/day (max, 320 mg/day). **Mgt of IHSS.** *Adult:* 20–40 mg PO tid or qid, or 80–160 mg (SR, ER) daily. **Post-MI.** *Adult:* 180–240 mg/day PO divided tid. After 1 mo, may titrate to 180–240 mg/day PO tid or qid (max, 240 mg/day). **Mgt of pheochromocytoma s&sx.** *Adult:* Preop, 60 mg/day PO for 3 days in divided doses; inoperable tumor, 30 mg/day in divided doses. **Px of migraine.** *Adult:* 80 mg/day PO (SR, ER) once or in divided doses; range, 160–240 mg/day. **Mgt of essential tremor.** *Adult:* 40 mg PO bid; maint, 120 mg/day (max, 320 mg/day). **Tx of arrhythmias.** *Adult:* 10–30 mg PO tid or qid, or 1–3 mg IV w/careful monitoring; max, 1 mg/min. May give second dose in 2 min, then do not repeat for 4 hr. **Tx of proliferating infantile hemangioma requiring systemic therapy.** *Child 5 wk–5 mo:* 0.6 mg/kg PO bid for 1 wk, then 1.1 mg/kg PO bid. After 2 wk, increase to maint 1.7 mg/kg PO bid; give doses at least 9 hr apart (*Hemangeol* sol only).

ADV EFF Arrhythmias, **broncho-spasm,** constipation, decreased exercise tolerance/libido, fatigue, flatulence, gastric pain, serum glucose changes, **HF, laryngospasm,** n/v/d, **stroke**
INTERACTIONS Barbiturates, clonidine, epinephrine, ergots, ibuprofen, indomethacin, insulin, lidocaine, methimazole, naproxen, phenothiazines, piroxicam, prazosin, propylthiouracil, sulindac, theophyllines, thioridazine, verapamil
NC/PT Provide continuous cardiac, regular BP monitoring w/IV form. Change to oral form as soon as possible. Do not use sol for hemangioma in premature infants, infants under 2 kg. Taper when stopping. Pt should take w/food, take safety precautions for CNS effects, report difficulty breathing, swelling, numbness/tingling.

---

propylthiouracil (PTU) (generic)
CLASS Antithyroid drug
PREG/CONT D/NA

BBW Associated w/severe, possibly fatal, liver injury. Monitor carefully for liver adverse effects, especially during first 6 mo of tx. Do not use in child unless allergic to or intolerant of other tx; risk of liver toxicity higher in children. Drug of choice when antithyroid tx needed during or just before first trimester (fetal abnormalities are associated w/methimazole).
IND & DOSE Tx of hyperthyroidism. *Adult:* 300 mg/day PO in divided doses q 8 hr, up to 400–900 mg/day in severe cases. Range, 100–150 mg/day in divided doses q 8 hr. *Child 6 and older intolerant to other tx:* 50 mg/day PO in divided doses q 8 hr. (Not drug of choice in children.)
ADV EFF Agranulocytosis, drowsiness, epigastric distress, fever, neuritis, n/v, paresthesia, rash, **severe liver injury,** vertigo

INTERACTIONS Cardiac glycosides, metoprolol, oral anticoagulants, propranolol, theophylline
NC/PT Monitor TSH, T$_3$/T$_4$. Prolonged tx will be needed. Alert surgeon that drug may increase risk of bleeding. Pt should take around the clock, use safety precautions for CNS effects, report signs of infection, urine/stool color changes.

---

protamine sulfate (generic)
CLASS Heparin antagonist
PREG/CONT C/NA

BBW Keep emergency equipment on hand in case of anaphylactic reaction.
IND & DOSE Tx of heparin, low-molecular-weight heparin overdose. *Adult, child:* 1 mg IV neutralizes not less than 100 heparin units.
ADV EFF Anaphylaxis, hypotension, n/v, rash
NC/PT Monitor coagulation studies to adjust dose; screen for heparin rebound and response. Pt should report difficulty breathing, dizziness.

---

protein C concentrate (Ceprotin)
CLASS Anticoagulant, blood product
PREG/CONT C/NA

IND & DOSE Replacement tx for pts w/severe congenital protein C deficiency. *Adult, child:* 100–120 international units/kg by IV injection. Then 60–80 international units/kg q 6 hr for three more doses. Maint, 45–60 international units/kg IV q 6–12 hr.
ADV EFF Anaphylactoid reaction, bleeding, hemothorax, hypotension, light-headedness, pruritus, rash
NC/PT Risk of disease transmission w/blood products. Protect from light. Monitor for bleeding. Pt should report difficulty breathing, hives, rash, unusual bleeding.

prothrombin complex concentrate (Kcentra)
CLASS Vitamin K anticoagulant reversal agent
PREG/CONT C/NA

BBW Risk of thromboembolic complications. Monitor closely; consider need to resume anticoagulant therapy when risks outweigh benefits.
IND & DOSE Urgent reversal of acquired coagulation factor deficiency from warfarin overactivity w/major bleeding. *Adult:* INR of 2 to less than 4, 25 units/kg IV; max, 2,500 units. INR of 4–6, 35 units/kg IV; max, 3,500 units. INR greater than 6, 50 units/kg IV; max, 5,000 units.
ADV EFF Arthralgia, blood-related infections, DVT, headache, hypotension, n/v, **serious hypersensitivity reactions, stroke**
NC/PT Monitor INR during and after tx. Monitor for hypersensitivity reactions, sx of thrombotic events. Pt should know risks of receiving blood products. Risks in pregnancy/breast-feeding unkn. Pt should report difficulty breathing, chest pain, acute leg pain, numbness/tingling, vision or speech changes, abnormal swelling.

protriptyline hydrochloride (Vivactil)
CLASS TCA
PREG/CONT C/NA

BBW Limit drug access in depressed, potentially suicidal pts. Increased risk of suicidality in children, adolescents, young adults; monitor accordingly.
IND & DOSE Relief of sx of depression. *Adult:* 15–40 mg/day PO in three to four divided doses; max, 60 mg/day.
ADJUST DOSE Elderly pts
ADV EFF Anticholinergic effects, bone marrow suppression, constipation, dry mouth, extrapyramidal effects, **MI,** orthostatic hypotension, photosensitivity, rash, **stroke**
INTERACTIONS Alcohol, cimetidine, clonidine, fluoxetine, MAOIs, ranitidine, sympathomimetics, tramadol
NC/PT Do not stop suddenly. Monitor CBC periodically. Not for use in pregnancy (contraceptives advised). Pt should avoid sun exposure, take safety precautions for CNS effects, use sugarless lozenges for dry mouth, report thoughts of suicide, excessive sedation.

pseudoephedrine hydrochloride, pseudoephedrine sulfate (Sudafed, Unifed)
CLASS Nasal decongestant, sympathomimetic
PREG/CONT C/NA

BBW Administer cautiously to pts w/ CV disease, diabetes, hyperthyroidism, glaucoma, hypertension, over 65 yr; increased sensitivity to sympathetic amines possible in these pts.
IND & DOSE Relief of nasal congestion. *Adult, child over 12 yr:* 60 mg PO q 4–6 hr (ER, 120 mg PO q 12 hr; CR, 240 mg/day PO); max, 240 mg/24 hr. *Child 6–12 yr:* 30 mg PO q 4–6 hr; max, 120 mg/24 hr. *Child 2–5 yr:* 15 mg PO (syrup) q 4–6 hr; max, 60 mg/24 hr.
ADJUST DOSE Elderly pts
ADV EFF Arrhythmias, anxiety, dizziness, drowsiness, fear, headache, hypertension, n/v, pallor, restlessness, **seizures,** tenseness, tremors
INTERACTIONS MAOIs, methyldopa, urine acidifiers/alkalinizers
NC/PT Avoid prolonged use. Underlying medical problems may be causing congestion. Pt should swallow ER tablet whole and not cut, crush, or chew it; take safety precautions for CNS effects; report sweating, sleeplessness, chest pain.

pyrantel pamoate
(Pin-Rid, Pin-X, Reese's Pinworm)
CLASS Anthelmintic
PREG/CONT C/NA

IND & DOSE Tx of enterobiasis, ascariasis. *Adult, child over 2 yr:* 11 mg/kg (5 mg/lb) PO as single oral dose. Max total dose, 1 g.
ADJUST DOSE Hepatic impairment
ADV EFF Abd cramps, anorexia, dizziness, drowsiness, headache, n/v/d
INTERACTIONS Piperazine, theophylline
NC/PT Culture before tx. Pt should shake suspension well; take w/fruit juice, milk; use strict hand washing, hygiene measures; launder undergarments, bed linens, nightclothes daily; disinfect toilet facilities daily, bathroom floors periodically; take safety precautions for CNS effects; report severe headache.

pyrazinamide (generic)
CLASS Antituberculotic
PREG/CONT C/NA

IND & DOSE Tx of active, drug-resistant TB. *Adult, child:* 15–30 mg/kg/day PO; max, 2 g/day. Always use w/up to four other antituberculotics; give for first 2 mo of 6-mo tx program.
ADV EFF Bone marrow suppression, gouty arthritis, **hepatotoxicity**, n/v, photosensitivity, rash
INTERACTIONS Piperazine, theophylline
NC/PT Give only w/other antituberculotics. Monitor LFTs during tx. Pt should have regular medical follow-up, report unusual bleeding, urine/stool color changes, severe joint pain.

pyridostigmine bromide (Mestinon, Regonol)
CLASS Antimyasthenic, cholinesterase inhibitor
PREG/CONT C/NA

IND & DOSE Control of myasthenia gravis sx. *Adult:* 600 mg PO over 24 hr; range, 60–1,500 mg. Or, 180–540 mg (ER) PO daily, bid. As supplement to oral dose preop, postop, during labor/myasthenic crisis, etc: Give 1/30 oral dose IM or very slow IV. May give 1 hr before second stage of labor completed. *Child:* 7 mg/kg/day PO divided into five or six doses (over 30 days); 5 mg/kg/day PO divided into five or six doses (29 days or younger). **Neonates w/myasthenic mothers who have difficulty swallowing, sucking, breathing.** 0.05–0.15 mg/kg IM. Change to syrup as soon as possible. **Military w/threat of sarin nerve gas exposure.** *Adult:* 30 mg PO q 8 hr starting several hr before exposure; stop if exposure occurs. **Antidote for NMJ blocker.** Atropine sulfate 0.6–1.2 mg IV immediately before slow IV injection of pyridostigmine 0.1–0.25 mg/kg; 10–20 mg pyridostigmine usually suffices. Full recovery usually within 15 min; may take 30 min.
ADV EFF Abd cramps, **anaphylaxis**, bradycardia, **bronchospasm**, cardiac arrhythmias, dysphagia, increased respiratory secretions/lacrimation/salivation, **laryngospasm**, urinary frequency/incontinence
INTERACTIONS Corticosteroids, succinylcholine
NC/PT Have atropine on hand as antidote. Give IV slowly. Pt should swallow ER tablet whole and not cut, crush, or chew it; report difficulty breathing, excessive sweating.

quetiapine fumarate
(Seroquel)
CLASS Antipsychotic
PREG/CONT C/NA

BBW Do not use in elderly pts w/ dementia-related psychosis; increased risk of CV mortality, including stroke, MI. Increased risk of suicidality in children, adolescents, young adults; monitor accordingly. Not approved for use in children.

IND & DOSE Tx of schizophrenia.
Adult: 25 mg PO bid. Increase in increments of 25–50 mg bid–tid on days 2, 3. Range by day 4, 300–400 mg/day in two to three divided doses; max, 800 mg/day. Once stabilized, switch to ER, 300 mg/day PO in p.m.; range, 400–800 mg/day. *Child 13–17 yr:* Divided dose bid. Total dose: day 1, 50 mg PO; day 2, 100 mg; day 3, 200 mg; day 4, 300 mg; day 5, 400 mg. Range, 400–800 mg/day. **Tx of manic episodes of bipolar 1 disorder.** *Adult:* 100 mg/day PO divided bid on day 1; increase to 400 mg/day PO in bid divided doses by day 4, using 100-mg/day increments. Range, 400–800 mg/day in divided doses. ER: 300 mg/day PO on day 1; 600 mg on day 2; may adjust to 800 mg on day 3 if needed. *Child 10–17 yr:* 50 mg PO day 1, 100 mg on day 2, 200 mg on day 3, 300 mg on day 4, 400 mg on day 5. Max, 600 mg/day. **Tx of depressive episodes of bipolar 1 disorder.** *Adult:* 50 mg (ER) PO on day 1, then 100 mg at bedtime on day 2; increase to desired dose of 300 mg/day by day 4. **Tx of major depressive disorder.** *Adult:* 50 mg (ER) PO at bedtime; on day 3, increase to 150 mg in evening. Range, 150–300 mg/day.
ADJUST DOSE Elderly, debilitated pts; hepatic impairment
ADV EFF Dizziness, drowsiness, dry mouth, headache, hyperglycemia, **NMS**, orthostatic hypotension, **prolonged QT**, sweating
INTERACTIONS Alcohol, anticholinergics, antihypertensives, carbamazepine, CNS depressants, dopamine antagonists, glucocorticoids, levodopa, lorazepam, phenobarbital, phenytoin, QT-prolonging drugs, rifampin, thioridazine
NC/PT Monitor for hyperglycemia. Ensure hydration in elderly pts. Not for use in pregnancy (barrier contraceptives advised). Pt should swallow ER tablet whole and not cut, crush, or chew it; avoid alcohol; take safety precautions for CNS effects; report fever, unusual bleeding, rash, suicidal thoughts.

quinapril hydrochloride (Accupril)
CLASS ACE inhibitor, antihypertensive
PREG/CONT D/NA

BBW Should not be used during pregnancy; can cause fetal injury or death. Advise barrier contraceptives.
IND & DOSE Tx of hypertension.
Adult: 10 or 20 mg/day PO; maint, 20–80 mg/day PO. **Adjunct tx of HF.** *Adult:* 5 mg PO bid; range, 10–20 mg PO bid.
ADJUST DOSE Elderly pts, renal impairment
ADV EFF Angioedema, cough, dizziness, headache, hyperkalemia, orthostatic hypotension, LFT changes, rash
INTERACTIONS ACE inhibitors, ARBs, lithium, potassium-sparing diuretics, renin inhibitors, tetracycline
NC/PT Alert surgeon to drug use; volume replacement may be needed after surgery. Maintain hydration. Not for use in pregnancy (contraceptives advised)/breast-feeding. Pt should use care in situations that may lead to BP drop; take safety precautions w/ dizziness, hypotension; report fever, difficulty breathing, swelling of lips/tongue, leg cramps.

DANGEROUS DRUG

quinine gluconate, quinidine sulfate
(generic)

CLASS Antiarrhythmic
PREG/CONT C/NA

IND & DOSE Tx of atrial arrhythmias; paroxysmal, chronic ventricular tachycardia. *Adult:* 400–600 mg (sulfate) PO q 2–3 hr until paroxysm terminated. *Child:* 30 mg/kg/24 h PO in five equally divided doses. **Conversion of atrial fibrillation (AF).** *Adult:* 648 mg (gluconate) PO q 8 hr; may increase after three to four doses if needed. Or, 324 mg (gluconate) PO q 8 hr for 2 days, then 648 mg PO q 8 hr for 2 days. Or, 5–10 mg/kg (gluconate) IV. For ER, 300 mg (sulfate) PO q 8–12 hr; may increase cautiously if serum level in therapeutic range. For immediate-release, 400 mg (sulfate) PO q 6 hr; may increase after four to five doses if no conversion. **To reduce relapse into AF.** *Adult:* 324 mg (gluconate) PO q 8–12 hr. For ER, 300 mg (sulfate) PO q 8–12 hr. For immediate-release, 200 mg (sulfate) PO q 6 hr. **Tx of *Plasmodium falciparum* malaria.** *Adult:* 24 mg/kg gluconate IV in 250 mL normal saline infused over 4 hr; then 12 mg/kg IV infused over 4 hr q 8 hr for 7 days. Or, 10 mg/kg gluconate in 5 mL/kg IV as loading dose; then maint IV infusion of 0.02 mg/kg/min. May switch to same oral dose of sulfate q 8 hr for 72 hr or until parasitemia decreased to 1% or less.

ADJUST DOSE Hepatic, renal impairment
ADV EFF Bone marrow suppression, **cardiac arrhythmias,** cinchonism, diarrhea, headache, **hepatic impairment,** light-headedness, nausea, rash, vision changes
INTERACTIONS Amiodarone, cimetidine, digoxin, grapefruit juice, hydantoins, NMJ blockers, oral anticoagulants, phenobarbital, rifampin, sodium bicarbonate, succinylcholine, sucralfate, TCAs, verapamil

NC/PT Give test dose of 200 mg PO or 200 mg IV for idiosyncratic reaction. Ensure pts w/atrial flutter, fibrillation digitalized before starting quinidine. Monitor for safe, effective serum level (2–6 mcg/mL). Pt should swallow ER tablet whole and not cut, crush, or chew it; wear medical ID; take safety precautions for CNS effects; report vision disturbances, unusual bleeding, signs of infection.

quinine sulfate
(Qualaquin)

CLASS Antimalarial, cinchonan
PREG/CONT C/NA

BBW Not for tx, px of nocturnal leg cramps; serious to life-threatening hematologic reactions possible. Chronic renal impairment has been reported. No evidence for therapeutic effectiveness for nocturnal leg cramps.
IND & DOSE Tx of uncomplicated *Plasmodium falciparum* malaria. *Adult:* 648 mg (two capsules) PO q 8 hr for 7 days.
ADJUST DOSE Renal impairment
ADV EFF Abd pain, **anaphylaxis,** blindness, blurred vision, cardiac arrhythmias, deafness, dizziness, headache, hearing impairment, hypoglycemia, n/v/d, **prolonged QT,** sweating, tinnitus, **thrombocytopenia including idiopathic thrombocytopenic purpura,** vertigo
INTERACTIONS CYP3A4 inducers/ inhibitors, digoxin, NMJ blockers, QT-prolonging drugs, rifampin
NC/PT Monitor LFTs, renal function, blood glucose, CBC. Use caution in pregnancy/breast-feeding. Pt should take safety precautions for CNS effects, report unusual bleeding, vision changes, difficulty breathing, palpitations, fainting.

rabeprazole sodium
(AcipHex)

CLASS Proton pump inhibitor
PREG/CONT C/NA

IND & DOSE Tx of GERD. *Adult, child 12 yr and older:* 20 mg/day PO for 4–8 wk; maint, 20 mg/day PO. *Child 1–11 yr:* 15 kg or more, 10 mg/day PO; under 15 kg, 5 mg/day PO for up to 12 wk. **Healing of duodenal ulcer.** *Adult:* 20 mg PO daily for up to 4 wk. **Tx of pathological hypersecretory conditions.** *Adult:* 60 mg PO daily– bid. **Helicobacter pylori eradication.** *Adult:* 20 mg PO bid w/amoxicillin 1,000 mg PO bid and clarithromycin 500 mg PO bid w/meals for 7 days.
ADJUST DOSE Hepatic impairment
ADV EFF Acute interstitial nephritis, asthenia, bone loss, CDAD, diarrhea, dizziness, dry mouth, headache, hypomagnesemia, n/v, pneumonia, URI sx, vitamin B_{12} deficiency
INTERACTIONS Atazanavir, azole antifungals, cyclosporine, digoxin, methotrexate, warfarin
NC/PT Pt should swallow tablet whole and not cut, crush, or chew it; maintain other tx for condition; take safety precautions for CNS effects; limit use in pregnancy; maintain nutrition; report worsening of condition, severe diarrhea.

radium Ra 223 dichloride (Xofigo)

CLASS Antineoplastic, radioactive particle–emitting agent
PREG/CONT X/NA

IND & DOSE Tx of castration-resistant prostate cancer w/ symptomatic bone metastases and no known visceral metastatic disease. *Adult:* 50 kBq (1.35 microcurie)/kg by slow IV injection (over 1 min) at 4-wk intervals for six injections.
ADV EFF Bone marrow suppression, n/v/d, peripheral edema

NC/PT Ensure proper dx, proper handling of drug. Monitor CBC; provide supportive measures. Use universal precautions w/body fluids. Pt should use gloves when handling body fluids; flush toilet several times; avoid pregnancy (men should use barrier contraceptives during and for 6 mo after use); report extreme fatigue, bleeding, severe vomiting, diarrhea.

ragweed pollen allergy extract (Ragwitek)

CLASS Allergen extract
PREG/CONT C/NA

BBW Risk of severe life-threatening allergic reactions. Not for use in uncontrolled asthma, pts who may be unresponsive to epinephrine or inhaled bronchodilators. Observe pt for 30 min after initial dose; have emergency equipment on hand.
IND & DOSE Immunotherapy for tx of ragweed pollen–induced allergic rhinitis w/or without conjunctivitis confirmed by skin test. *Adult 18–65 yr:* 1 tablet/day sublingually starting 12 wk before and continuing throughout season.
ADV EFF Cough, ear pruritus, mouth edema, oropharyngeal pain/pruritus, throat/tongue pruritus
NC/PT Ensure skin testing confirms allergy. Not for use w/uncontrolled asthma, hx of severe reactions/ eosinophilic esophagitis. Begin 12 wk before expected ragweed season; continue throughout season. Tell pt to place tablet under tongue, allow it to stay until completely dissolved, and not to swallow for 1 min. Monitor pt for at least 30 min after first dose; have emergency equipment on hand. Stop tx in case of oral wounds or inflammation; allow to heal completely before restarting. Pt should report and stop tx w/oral inflammation or wounds, report difficulty breathing/ swallowing.

raloxifene hydrochloride (Evista)

CLASS Selective estrogen receptor modulator
PREG/CONT X/NA

BBW Increased risk of DVT, PE; monitor accordingly. Increased risk of stroke, CV events in women w/ documented CAD; weigh benefits/risks before use in these women.
IND & DOSE Px, tx of osteoporosis in postmenopausal women; to reduce risk of invasive breast cancer in postmenopausal women w/osteoporosis and high risk of invasive breast cancer. *Adult:* 60 mg/day PO.
ADV EFF Depression, dizziness, edema, flulike sx, hot flashes, lightheadedness, rash, vaginal bleeding, **venous thromboembolism**
INTERACTIONS Cholestyramine, oral anticoagulants
NC/PT Obtain periodic CBC. Provide comfort measures for effects. Not for use in pregnancy (contraceptives advised). Pt should take safety precautions for CNS effects, report difficulty breathing, numbness/tingling, pain/swelling in legs.

raltegravir (Isentress)

CLASS Antiretroviral, integrase inhibitor
PREG/CONT C/NA

IND & DOSE Tx of HIV-1 infection, w/other antiretrovirals. *Adult, child 12 yr and older:* 400 mg PO bid w/ other antivirals; without regard to food. If given w/rifampin, 800 mg PO bid without regard to food. *Child 6–under 12 yr:* 25 kg or more, 400 mg PO bid or up to 300 mg PO bid chewable tablet; under 25 kg, chewable tablets weight-based to max 300 mg PO bid. *Child 2–under 6 yr:* 40 kg or more, 300 mg PO bid; 28–under 40 kg, 200 mg PO bid; 20–under 28 kg, 150 mg PO bid; 14–under 20 kg, 100 mg PO bid; 10–under 14 kg, 75 mg PO bid;

under 10 kg, not recommended. *Child 4 wk–under 2 yr:* 14–under 20 kg, 5 mL (100 mg) PO bid; 11–under 14 kg, 4 mL (80 mg) PO bid; 8–under 11 kg, 3 mL (60 mg) PO bid; 6–under 8 kg, 2 mL (40 mg) PO bid; 4–under 6 kg, 1.5 mL (30 mg) PO bid; 3–less than 4 kg, 1 mL (20 mg) PO bid.
ADV EFF Diarrhea, dizziness, headache, fatigue, fever, insomnia, n/v, **rhabdomyolysis, serious to life-threatening skin reactions, including Stevens-Johnson syndrome**
INTERACTIONS Rifampin, St. John's wort
NC/PT Ensure pt taking other antivirals. Not for use in pregnancy/breast-feeding. Calculate weight-based use of chewable tablets for child. Phenylalanine in chewable tablets; alert pts w/phenylketonuria. Pt should not let prescription run out or stop temporarily (virus could become resistant to antivirals); take precautions to avoid spread (drug not a cure); avoid St. John's wort; report s&sx of infection, unexplained muscle pain/weakness, rash.

ramelteon (Rozerem)

CLASS Melatonin receptor agonist, sedative-hypnotic
PREG/CONT C/NA

IND & DOSE Tx of insomnia. *Adult:* 8 mg PO within 30 min of bedtime.
ADJUST DOSE Hepatic impairment
ADV EFF Amenorrhea, **anaphylaxis, angioedema,** decreased testosterone, depression, diarrhea, galactorrhea, headache, insomnia, **suicidality**
INTERACTIONS Clarithromycin, fluconazole, fluvoxamine, itraconazole, ketoconazole, nefazodone, nelfinavir, ritonavir
NC/PT Not for use in pregnancy/breast-feeding. Pt should take 30 min before bed, avoid activities after taking, plan on 8 or more hr sleep, report difficulty breathing, swelling, thoughts of suicide.

ramipril (Altace)
CLASS ACE inhibitor, antihypertensive
PREG/CONT D/NA

BBW Not for use in pregnancy; risk of fetal harm. Advise contraceptives.
IND & DOSE Tx of hypertension. *Adult:* 2.5 mg PO daily; range, 2.5–20 mg/day. **Tx of HF first few days post MI in stable pts.** *Adult:* 2.5 mg PO bid; if hypotensive, may use 1.25 mg PO bid; target dose, 5 mg PO bid. **To decrease risk of MI, stroke, death from CV disease in stable pts.** *Adult 55 yr and older:* 2.5 mg/day PO for 1 wk, then 5 mg/day PO for 3 wk; maint, 10 mg PO daily.
ADJUST DOSE Elderly pts, renal impairment
ADV EFF Agranulocytosis, angioedema, aphthous ulcers, bone marrow suppression, cough, dizziness, dysgeusia, gastric irritation, HF, hyperkalemia, light-headedness, proteinuria, rash, Stevens-Johnson syndrome, tachycardia
INTERACTIONS ACE inhibitors, ARBs, capsaicin, diuretics, lithium, NSAIDs
NC/PT Monitor renal function, BP, potassium. Stop diuretics 2–3 days before tx. Not for use in pregnancy (barrier contraceptives advised). Alert surgeon of ramipril use; volume replacement may be needed postop. Stable for 24 hr at room temp, 48 hr if refrigerated. Pt should open capsules, sprinkle contents over small amount of applesauce or mix in applesauce/water; take safety precautions for CNS effects; use caution in situations that could lead to fluid loss, decreased BP; maintain hydration; report unusual bleeding, swelling, rash.

ramucirumab (Cyramza)
CLASS Antineoplastic, endothelial growth factor receptor antagonist
PREG/CONT C/NA

BBW Risk of serious to fatal hemorrhagic events; stop if bleeding occurs.
IND & DOSE Tx of advanced gastric or gastroesophageal junction adenocarcinoma as monotherapy or w/ paclitaxel, after other tx. *Adult:* 8 mg/kg IV push or bolus q 2 wk as single agent or w/paclitaxel. **Tx of non-small-cell lung cancer, w/ docetaxel.** *Adult:* 10 mg/kg IV on day 1 of 21-day cycle, before docetaxel infusion. **Tx of colorectal cancer, w/ leucovorin, 5-FU, irinotecan.** *Adult:* 8 mg/kg IV every 2 wk before administration of the other drugs.
ADV EFF Bleeding events, fatigue, diarrhea, GI perforation, hypertension, impaired wound healing, infusion reactions, nephrotic syndrome, RPLS, thromboembolic events, thyroid dysfunction
NC/PT Monitor for infusion reactions, bleeding, clinical deterioration, hypertension, thrombotic events, renal impairment; monitor LFTs. Not for use in pregnancy (contraceptives advised)/breast-feeding. Mark calendar w/tx days. Pt should report bleeding, severe GI pain, chest pain, difficulty breathing.

ranibizumab (Lucentis)
CLASS Monoclonal antibody, ophthalmic agent
PREG/CONT C/NA

IND & DOSE Tx of neovascular (wet) age-related macular degeneration; macular edema after retinal vein occlusion. 0.5 mg (0.05 mL) by intravitreal injection q 1–3 mo. **Tx of diabetic macular edema, diabetic retinopathy w/diabetic macular edema.** *Adult:* 0.3 mg by intravitreal injection once/mo.

ADV EFF Conjunctival hemorrhage, eye pain, hypersensitivity reactions, increased IOP, intraocular inflammation, ocular infection, retinal detachment, vision changes, vitreous floaters
NC/PT Monitor carefully for detached retina, increased IOP. Pt should be anesthetized before injection, receive antibiotic. Pt should report increased light sensitivity, vision changes, painful eye.

ranitidine hydrochloride (Zantac)
CLASS Gastric acid secretion inhibitor, histamine-2 antagonist
PREG/CONT B/NA

IND & DOSE Tx of active duodenal ulcer. Adult: 150 mg PO bid for 4–8 wk, or 300 mg PO once daily at bedtime, or 50 mg IM or IV q 6–8 hr or by intermittent IV infusion, diluted to 100 mL and infused over 15–20 min. Max, 400 mg/day; maint, 150 mg PO at bedtime. Child 1 mo–16 yr: 2–4 mg/kg PO bid for tx; once daily for maint. Max, 3,000 mg/day (tx), 1,500 mg/day (maint). Or, 2–4 mg/kg/day IV or IM q 6–8 hr; max, 50 mg q 6–8 hr. Tx of active gastric ulcer. Adult: 150 mg PO bid, or 50 mg IM or IV q 6–8 hr. Tx of pathologic hypersecretory syndrome, GERD maint, esophagitis, benign gastric ulcer. Adult: 150 mg PO bid, max, 6 g/day. Tx of heartburn, acid indigestion. Adult: 75 mg PO as needed.
ADJUST DOSE Elderly pts, renal impairment
ADV EFF Abd pain, bradycardia, bone marrow suppression, constipation, headache, n/v/d, pain at injection site, rash
INTERACTIONS Warfarin
NC/PT Give IM undiluted into large muscle; give oral drug w/meals and at bedtime. May continue antacids for pain relief. Pt should report unusual bleeding, signs of infection. Name confusion w/Zantac (ranitidine), Zyrtec (cetirizine), Xanax (alprazolam); use caution.

ranolazine (Ranexa)
CLASS Antianginal, piperazineacetamide
PREG/CONT C/NA

IND & DOSE Tx of chronic angina. Adult: 500 mg PO bid; max, 1,000 mg bid.
ADJUST DOSE Hepatic impairment (not recommended)
ADV EFF Constipation, dizziness, headache, nausea, prolonged QT, renal failure
INTERACTIONS Antipsychotics, digoxin, diltiazem, grapefruit juice, HIV protease inhibitors, ketoconazole, macrolide antibiotics, QT-prolonging drugs, rifampin, TCAs, verapamil
NC/PT Obtain baseline ECG, LFTs, renal function; monitor periodically. Continue other antianginals. Not for use in pregnancy (contraception advised)/breast-feeding. Pt should swallow tablet whole and not cut, crush, or chew it; take safety measures w/dizziness; avoid grapefruit juice; use laxative for severe constipation; report fainting, palpitations.

rasagiline (Azilect)
CLASS Antiparkinsonian, MAO type B inhibitor
PREG/CONT C/NA

IND & DOSE Tx of s&sx of all stages of idiopathic Parkinson disease. Adult: 1 mg/day PO as monotherapy; 0.5–1 mg/day PO w/levodopa.
ADJUST DOSE CYP1A2 inhibitors, hepatic impairment
ADV EFF Arthralgia, dizziness, dyspepsia, dry mouth, hallucinations, headache, hypotension, impulse control issues, melanoma, serotonin syndrome, vertigo
INTERACTIONS Cyclobenzaprine, CYP1A2 inhibitors (ciprofloxacin), dextromethorphan, MAOIs, meperidine, methadone, mirtazapine, SSRIs, St. John's wort, sympathomimetic

amines, TCAs, tramadol, tyramine-rich food
NC/PT Obtain baseline LFTs, skin evaluation. Continue other Parkinson drugs. Use caution in pregnancy/breast-feeding. Pt should avoid sun exposure, tyramine-rich foods, St. John's wort; take safety measures for CNS effects; tell all health care providers about prescribed/OTC drugs, herbs being used (drug reacts w/many other drugs); report skin changes, worsening of condition.

---

rasburicase (Elitek)
CLASS Enzyme
PREG/CONT C/NA

BBW Risk of anaphylaxis, hemolysis (in pts w/G6PD deficiency; screen before tx), methemoglobinemia, uric acid measurement alterations.
IND & DOSE Mgt of plasma uric acid level in pts w/leukemia, lymphoma, solid tumor malignancies receiving anticancer tx expected to result in tumor lysis. Adult: 0.2 mg/kg IV as single daily infusion over 30 min for 5 days. Chemotherapy should start 4–24 hr after first dose.
ADV EFF Abd pain, anaphylaxis, anxiety, constipation, fever, headache, hemolysis, methemoglobinemia, n/v/d
NC/PT Screen for G6PD deficiency. Monitor closely during infusion; stop immediately if hypersensitivity reactions. Monitor CBC. Blood drawn to monitor uric acid level to be collected in prechilled, heparinized vials and kept in ice-water bath; analysis must be done within 4 hr. Give analgesics for headache. Pt should report difficulty breathing, chest pain, rash.

---

raxibacumab (generic)
CLASS Monoclonal antibody
PREG/CONT B/NA

IND & DOSE Tx, px of inhalational anthrax, w/antibacterial drugs. Adult, child over 50 kg: 40 mg/kg IV

over 2 hr, 15 min. Child over 15 kg–50 kg: 60 mg/kg IV over 2 hr, 15 min. Child 15 kg and less: 80 mg/kg IV over 2 hr, 15 min.
ADV EFF Extremity pain, infusion reaction, pruritus, rash, somnolence
NC/PT TEACH Premedicate w/diphenhydramine. Ensure use of antibacterials. Monitor for infusion reaction; slow, interrupt infusion as needed. Pt should report itching, difficulty breathing, rash.

---

regorafenib (Stivarga)
CLASS Antineoplastic, kinase inhibitor
PREG/CONT D/NA

BBW Severe to fatal hepatotoxicity reported; monitor LFTs before, during tx.
IND & DOSE Tx of metastatic colorectal cancer in pts previously treated w/other agents; tx of advanced, unresectable GI stomal tumors. Adult: 160 mg/day PO for first 21 days of 28-day cycle. Give w/low-fat meal.
ADV EFF Anorexia, cardiac ischemia/infarction, dermatologic toxicity, diarrhea, dysphonia, GI perforation/fistula, hepatotoxicity, hypertension, mucositis, RPLS, weight loss, wound-healing complications
INTERACTIONS Grapefruit juice, St. John's wort, strong CYP3A4 inducers/inhibitors; avoid these combinations
NC/PT Monitor LFTs; arrange to decrease dose or stop drug if hepatotoxicity occurs. Monitor for skin reactions, bleeding, problems w/wound healing. Not for use in pregnancy/breast-feeding. Stop drug at least 24 hr before scheduled surgery. Pt should take daily w/low-fat meal, report chest pain, severe GI pain, bleeding, urine/stool color changes.

DANGEROUS DRUG

repaglinide (Prandin)

CLASS Antidiabetic, meglitinide
PREG/CONT C/NA

IND & DOSE Adjunct to diet/
exercise to lower blood glucose in
pts w/type 2 diabetes, as monotherapy or w/other antidiabetics. *Adult:*
0.5–4 mg PO tid or qid 15–30 min
(usually within 15 min) before meals;
max, 16 mg/day.
ADJUST DOSE Hepatic, renal
impairment
ADV EFF Diarrhea, headache,
hypoglycemia, nausea, URI
INTERACTIONS Celery, coriander,
dandelion root, fenugreek, garlic,
gemfibrozil, ginseng, itraconazole,
juniper berries
NC/PT Review complete diabetic
teaching program. Pt should always
take before meals (if meal is skipped
or added, dose should be skipped or
added appropriately), monitor serum
glucose, continue exercise/diet program, report fever, unusual bleeding/
bruising, frequent hypoglycemia.

ribavirin (Copegus, Rebetol, Ribasphere, Virazole)

CLASS Antiviral
PREG/CONT X/NA

BBW Inhaled form not for use in
adults; testicular lesions, birth defects
possible. Monotherapy not effective
for tx of chronic hepatitis C; do not
use alone for this indication. High risk
of hemolytic anemia, which could
lead to MI; do not use in significant,
unstable CV disease. Monitor respiratory status frequently; pulmonary
deterioration, death have occurred
during, shortly after tx w/inhaled
form. Risk of significant fetal defects;
caution women to avoid pregnancy
during tx (barrier contraceptives
advised). Male partners of pregnant
women should not take drug.

IND & DOSE Tx of hospitalized
infants, children w/severe RSV
infection of lower respiratory tract.
Child: Dilute aerosol powder to
20 mg/mL, deliver for 12–18 hr/day
for at least 3 but not more than 7 days.
Tx of chronic hepatitis C. *Adult over
75 kg:* Three 200-mg capsules PO in
a.m., three 200-mg capsules PO in
p.m. w/*Intron A* 3 million international
units subcut three times/wk, or w/
pegintron 180 mcg/wk subcut for
24–48 wk. *Adult 75 kg or less:* Two
200-mg capsules PO in a.m., three
200-mg capsules PO in p.m. w/*Intron
A* 3 million international units subcut
three times/wk, or w/pegintron
180 mcg/wk subcut for 24–48 wk.
Child 3 yr and older: 15 mg/kg/day PO
in divided doses a.m. and p.m. Child
25–62 kg may use oral sol. Give w/
Intron A 3 million international units/m²
subcut three times/wk.
ADJUST DOSE Anemia, renal
impairment
ADV EFF Anemia, apnea, **cardiac
arrest**, depression, deteriorating
respiratory function, growth impairment in children, **hemolytic anemia**,
nervousness, rash, **suicidality**
INTERACTIONS Antacids, nucleoside reverse transcriptase inhibitors
NC/PT Monitor CBC regularly. Review use/care of inhaler. Ensure pt on
oral tx also taking other antivirals; not
for monotherapy. Not for use in pregnancy (barrier contraceptives advised).
Pt should report thoughts of suicide,
chest pain, difficulty breathing.

rifabutin (Mycobutin)

CLASS Antibiotic
PREG/CONT B/NA

IND & DOSE Px of disseminated
Mycobacterium avium complex in
pts w/advanced HIV infection. *Adult:*
300 mg/day PO. *Child:* 5 mg/kg/day PO.
ADV EFF Abd pain, anorexia, CDAD,
headache, nausea, neutropenia, rash,
red to orange urine

INTERACTIONS Clarithromycin, delavirdine, indinavir, nelfinavir, oral contraceptives, ritonavir, saquinavir
NC/PT Negative TB test needed before starting tx. Not for use in pregnancy (barrier contraceptives advised)/breast-feeding. Urine, body fluids may turn red to orange, staining fabric, contact lenses. Pt should report diarrhea, difficulty breathing.

rifampin (Rifadin)
CLASS Antibiotic, antitubercular
PREG/CONT C/NA

IND & DOSE Tx of pulmonary TB. *Adult:* 10 mg/kg/day PO or IV; max, 600 mg/day in single dose (w/other antituberculotics). *Child:* 10–20 mg/kg/day PO or IV; max, 600 mg/day. **Tx of *Neisseria meningitidis* carriers to eliminate meningococci from nasopharynx.** *Adult:* 600 mg/day PO or IV for 4 consecutive days or 600 mg q 12 hr for 2 days. *Child over 1 mo:* 10 mg/kg PO or IV q 12 hr for 2 days; max, 600 mg/dose. *Child under 1 mo:* 5 mg/kg PO or IV q 12 hr for 2 days.
ADJUST DOSE Renal impairment
ADV EFF Acute renal failure, **bone marrow suppression**, discolored body fluids, dizziness, drowsiness, epigastric distress, fatigue, flulike sx, headache, heartburn, rash
INTERACTIONS Antiarrhythmics, benzodiazepine, buspirone, corticosteroids, cyclosporine, digoxin, doxycycline, fluoroquinolones, hormonal contraceptives, isoniazid, itraconazole, ketoconazole, methadone, metoprolol, nifedipine, oral anticoagulants, oral sulfonylureas, phenytoin, propranolol, quinidine, theophyllines, verapamil, zolpidem
NC/PT Monitor renal function, CBC, LFTs periodically. Ensure cultures and appropriate use of drug. Body fluids will turn reddish orange. Pt should take once/day on empty stomach 1 hr before or 2 hr after meals, take safety precautions for CNS effects, not wear

soft contact lenses (may become permanently stained), report signs of infection, swelling, unusual bleeding/bruising.

rifapentine (Priftin)
CLASS Antibiotic, antitubercular
PREG/CONT C/NA

IND & DOSE Tx of active pulmonary TB. *Adult, child 12 and over:* 600 mg PO twice wkly w/interval of at least 72 hr between doses. Continue for 2 mo, then 600 mg wkly PO for 4 mo w/other antituberculotics. **Tx of latent TB w/isoniazid.** *Adult, child 12 and over:* 15 mg/kg PO for 12 wk w/ isoniazid; max, 900 mg/dose. *Child 2–11 yr:* over 50 kg, 900 mg/wk PO; 32.1–50 kg, 750 mg/wk PO; 25.1–32 kg, 600 mg/wk PO; 14.1–25 kg, 450 mg/wk PO; 10–14 kg, 300 mg/wk PO.
ADJUST DOSE Elderly pts
ADV EFF Diarrhea, dizziness, headache, hematuria, **hepatotoxicity**, hyperuricemia, **hypersensitivity reactions**, proteinuria, pyuria, reddish body fluids
INTERACTIONS Antiarrhythmics, benzodiazepine, buspirone, corticosteroids, cyclosporine, digoxin, doxycycline, fluoroquinolones, hormonal contraceptives, isoniazid, itraconazole, ketoconazole, methadone, metoprolol, nifedipine, oral anticoagulants, oral sulfonylureas, phenytoin, propranolol, protease inhibitors, quinidine, theophyllines, verapamil, zolpidem
NC/PT Monitor LFTs. Always give w/other antituberculotics. Body fluids will turn reddish orange. Not for use in pregnancy (barrier contraceptives advised). Pt should mark calendar for tx days; take w/food (may crush tablets and add to semisolid food); not wear contact lenses (may become permanently stained); take safety precautions for CNS effects; report s&sx of infection, swelling, unusual bleeding/bruising, difficulty breathing.

rifaximin (Xifaxan)
CLASS Antibiotic, antidiarrheal
PREG/CONT C/NA

IND & DOSE Tx of traveler's diarrhea. *Adult, child 12 yr and older:* 200 mg PO tid for 3 days. **To reduce recurrence of hepatic encephalopathy in pts w/advanced liver disease.** *Adult:* 550 mg PO bid. **Tx of IBS w/ diarrhea.** *Adult:* 550 mg PO tid for 14 days; may retreat up to two times w/recurrence.
ADJUST DOSE Hepatic impairment
ADV EFF CDAD, dizziness, fever, flatulence, headache, **hepatotoxicity,** nausea, **pseudomembranous colitis,** rash
NC/PT Monitor LFTs w/long-term use. Do not use w/diarrhea complicated by fever, blood in stool. Not for use in pregnancy/breast-feeding. Pt should swallow tablet whole and not cut, crush, or chew it; stop if diarrhea does not resolve or worsens in 48 hr; take safety precautions w/dizziness; report bloody diarrhea, fever.

rilonacept (Arcalyst)
CLASS Anti-inflammatory, interleukin blocker
PREG/CONT C/NA

IND & DOSE Tx of cryopyrin-associated periodic syndromes, including familial cold autoinflammatory syndrome, **Muckle-Wells syndrome.** *Adult:* Loading dose, 320 mg as two 160-mg (2-mL) subcut injections at different sites; then once-wkly subcut injections of 160 mg (2 mL). *Child 12–17 yr:* Loading dose, 4.4 mg/kg subcut; max, 320 mg. May give in divided doses if needed. Then once-wkly injections of 2.2 mg/kg; max, 160 mg.
ADV EFF Injection-site reactions, lipid changes, **serious infections,** URI
INTERACTIONS Live vaccines, TNF blockers

NC/PT Stop if infection occurs. Use caution in pregnancy/breast-feeding. Teach proper administration/disposal of needles/syringes. Pt should rotate injection sites, report injection-site reactions, signs of infection.

rilpivirine (Edurant)
CLASS Antiviral, nonnucleoside reverse transcriptase inhibitor (NNRTI)
PREG/CONT B/NA

IND & DOSE Tx of HIV-1 infection in tx-naïve pts w/HIV-1 RNA of 100,000 copies/mL or less. *Adult, child over 12 yr:* 25 mg/day PO w/ food, or 50 mg/day PO w/food if taken w/rifabutin.
ADV EFF Body fat redistribution, depression, headache, hypersensitivity reactions, immune reconstitution syndrome, insomnia, **prolonged QT,** rash, severe depressive disorder, **suicidality**
INTERACTIONS Antacids, CYP3A4 inducers/inhibitors, drugs that decrease stomach acid, other NNRTIs, QT-prolonging drugs, St. John's wort
NC/PT Monitor viral load, response carefully. Ensure pt taking other antivirals. Not for use in pregnancy/breast-feeding. Body fat may redistribute to back, breasts, middle of body. Check pt drug list carefully; drug interacts w/many drugs. Pt should report all drugs, herbs, OTC products used to health care provider; take once/day w/meal; take precautions to prevent spread (drug not a cure); continue to take other antivirals; report signs of infection, depression, thoughts of suicide.

riluzole (Rilutek)
CLASS Amyotrophic lateral sclerosis (ALS) drug
PREG/CONT C/NA

IND & DOSE Tx of ALS. *Adult:* 50 mg PO q 12 hr.

ADV EFF Abd pain, asthenia, anorexia, circumoral paresthesia, diarrhea, dizziness, **interstitial pneumonitis**, **liver injury**, neutropenia, somnolence, vertigo
INTERACTIONS Allopurinol, methyldopa, sulfasalazine, warfarin
NC/PT Monitor CBC, lung function, LFTs carefully. Protect from light. Use caution in pregnancy/breast-feeding. Slows disease progress; not a cure. Pt should take on empty stomach, use safety precautions w/dizziness, report signs of infection, difficulty breathing.

---

rimabotulinumtoxinB
(Myobloc)
CLASS Neurotoxin
PREG/CONT C/NA

BBW Drug not for tx of muscle spasticity; toxin may spread from injection area and cause s&sx of botulism (CNS alterations, trouble speaking and swallowing, loss of bladder control). Use only for approved indications.
IND & DOSE Tx of cervical dystonia to reduce severity of abnormal head position and neck pain. *Adult:* 2,500–5,000 units IM injected locally into affected muscles.
ADV EFF Anaphylactic reactions, dry mouth, dyspepsia, dysphagia, **spread of toxin that can lead to death**
INTERACTIONS Aminoglycosides, anticholinesterases, lincosamides, magnesium sulfate, NMJ blockers, polymyxin, quinidine, succinylcholine
NC/PT Store in refrigerator. Have epinephrine on hand in case of anaphylactic reactions. Do not inject in area of skin infection. Effects may not appear for 1–2 days; will persist for 3–4 mo. Not for use in pregnancy/breast-feeding. Pt should report difficulty swallowing, breathing.

---

rimantadine hydrochloride
(Flumadine)
CLASS Antiviral
PREG/CONT C/NA

IND & DOSE Px of illness caused by influenza A virus. *Adult, child over 10 yr:* 100 mg/day PO bid. *Child 1–9 yr:* 5 mg/kg/day PO; max, 150 mg/dose. **Tx of illness caused by influenza A virus.** *Adult, child over 10 yr:* 100 mg/day PO bid as soon after exposure as possible, continuing for 7 days.
ADJUST DOSE Nursing home pts; hepatic, renal impairment
ADV EFF Ataxia, dizziness, dyspnea, HF, insomnia, light-headedness, mood changes, nausea
INTERACTIONS Acetaminophen, aspirin, cimetidine, intranasal influenza vaccine
NC/PT Pt should take full course of drug, take safety precautions for CNS effects, report swelling, severe mood changes.

---

riociguat (Adempas)
CLASS Cyclase stimulator, pulmonary hypertension drug
PREG/CONT X/NA

BBW Known teratogen. Serious to fatal birth defects; monthly negative pregnancy test required. Available by limited access program for women.
IND & DOSE Tx of thromboembolic pulmonary hypertension, idiopathic pulmonary hypertension. *Adult:* 1.5–2.5 mg PO tid.
ADJUST DOSE Severe renal, hepatic impairment (not recommended); smokers
ADJUST DOSE Anemia, bleeding, constipation, dizziness, dyspepsia, headache, hypotension, n/v/d, **pulmonary edema**
INTERACTIONS Antacids; CYP inhibitors; nitrates; P-glycoprotein, phosphodiesterase inhibitors

NC/PT Smokers may need higher doses. Monitor BP, respiratory status. Ensure negative pregnancy test. Not for use w/ED drugs, nitrates. Pt should avoid alcohol (during and for 1 mo after use)/breast-feeding; monitor activity tolerance, respiratory sx; take safety precautions for CNS effects; report worsening of sx, bleeding, severe n/v, difficulty breathing.

risedronate sodium (Actonel, Atelvia)
CLASS Bisphosphonate
PREG/CONT C/NA

IND & DOSE Tx, px of postmenopausal osteoporosis. *Adult:* 5 mg/day PO taken in upright position w/6–8 oz water at least 30 min before or after other beverage, food; may switch to 35-mg tablet PO once/wk, or 75 mg PO on 2 consecutive days each mo (total, 2 tablets/mo), or one 150-mg tablet PO per mo. **Tx, px of glucocorticoid osteoporosis.** *Adult:* 5 mg/day PO. **Tx of Paget disease.** *Adult:* 30 mg/day PO for 2 mo taken in upright position w/6–8 oz water at least 30 min before or after other beverage, food; may retreat after at least 2-mo posttreatment period if indicated. **To increase bone mass in men w/ osteoporosis.** *Adult:* 35 mg/day PO once/wk.

ADJUST DOSE Renal impairment
ADV EFF Anorexia, arthralgia, atypical femur fractures, diarrhea, dizziness, dyspepsia, **esophageal rupture,** headache, increased bone/muscle/joint pain, **osteonecrosis of jaw**
INTERACTIONS Aluminum, aspirin, calcium, magnesium
NC/PT Monitor serum calcium level. May increase risk of osteonecrosis of jaw; pts having invasive dental procedures should discuss risk. Not for use w/esophageal abnormalities, hypocalcemia. Not for use for longer than 3–5 yr. Give w/full glass of plain (not mineral) water at least 30 min before or after other beverage, food, medication. Have pt remain in upright position for at least 30 min to decrease GI effects. Pt should swallow DR tablet whole and not cut, crush, or chew it; mark calendar if taking wkly; take supplemental calcium, vitamin D; report muscle twitching, difficulty swallowing, edema.

risperidone (Risperdal)
CLASS Antipsychotic, benzisoxazole
PREG/CONT C/NA

BBW Not for use in elderly pts w/ dementia; increased risk of CV mortality. Not approved for this use.
IND & DOSE Tx of schizophrenia. *Adult:* 1 mg PO bid or 2 mg PO once daily; target, 3 mg PO bid by third day. Range, 4–8 mg/day or 25 mg IM q 2 wk. Max, 50 mg IM q 2 wk. Delaying relapse time in long-term tx: 2–8 mg/day PO. *Child 13–17 yr:* 0.5 mg/day PO; target, 3 mg/day. **Tx of bipolar I disorder.** *Adult:* 25–50 mg IM q 2 wk. **Tx of bipolar mania.** *Adult:* 2–3 mg/day PO; range, 1–6 mg/day. *Child 10–17 yr:* 0.5 mg/day PO; target, 2.5 mg/day. **Irritability associated w/autistic disorder.** *Child 5–17 yr:* 0.5 mg/day PO (20 kg or more), 0.25 mg/day PO (under 20 kg). After at least 4 days, may increase to 1 mg/day (20 kg or more), 0.5 mg/day (under 20 kg). Maintain dose for at least 14 days; then may increase in increments of 0.5 mg/day (20 kg or more), 0.25 mg/day (under 20 kg) at 2-wk intervals.
ADJUST DOSE Elderly pts; hepatic, renal impairment
ADV EFF Agitation, **arrhythmias,** anxiety, aggression, bone marrow depression, cognitive/motor impairment, constipation, CV events, diabetes, dizziness, drowsiness, headache, hyperglycemia, hyperprolactinemia, insomnia, n/v, **NMS,** orthostatic hypotension, photosensitivity, **seizures,** tardive dyskinesia

INTERACTIONS Alcohol, carbamazepine, clonidine, levodopa
NC/PT If restarting tx, follow initial dose guidelines, using extreme care due to increased risk of severe adverse effects w/reexposure. Stop other antipsychotics before starting risperidone. Not for use in pregnancy. Pt should open blister units of orally disintegrating tablets individually (not push tablet through foil); use dry hands to remove tablet, immediately place on tongue but do not chew; mix oral sol in 3–4 oz water, coffee, orange juice, low-fat milk (not cola, tea); take safety precautions for CNS effects; avoid sun exposure; report s&sx of infection, palpitations, increased thirst/urination, chest pain. Name confusion between *Risperdal* (risperidone) and *Requip* (ropinirole); use caution.

---

ritonavir (Norvir)
CLASS Antiviral, protease inhibitor
PREG/CONT B/NA

BBW Potentially large increase in serum conc, risk of serious arrhythmias, seizures, fatal reactions w/ alfuzosin, amiodarone, astemizole, bepridil, bupropion, clozapine, ergotamine, flecainide, meperidine, pimozide, piroxicam, propafenone, quinidine, rifabutin, terfenadine, voriconazole. Potentially large increase in serum conc of these sedatives/ hypnotics: Alprazolam, clonazepam, diazepam, estazolam, flurazepam, midazolam, triazolam, zolpidem; extreme sedation, respiratory depression possible. Do not give ritonavir w/any drugs listed above.
IND & DOSE Tx of HIV infection, w/other antiretrovirals. *Adult:* 600 mg PO bid w/food. *Child:* 250 mg/m² PO bid. Increase by 50 mg/m² bid at 2- to 3-day intervals to max 400 mg/m² PO bid. Max, 600 mg bid.
ADV EFF Abd pain, anorexia, anxiety, asthenia, body fat redistribution,

dizziness, dysuria, **hypersensitivity reactions,** n/v/d, pancreatitis, peripheral/circumoral paresthesia, prolonged PR
INTERACTIONS Grapefruit juice, QT-prolonging drugs, St. John's wort. See also *Black Box Warning* above.
NC/PT Carefully screen drug hx for potentially serious drug-drug interactions. Ensure use of other antivirals. Monitor LFTs, amylase, ECG. Pt should store capsules/oral sol in refrigerator; take w/food; avoid grapefruit juice, St. John's wort; use precautions to avoid spread (drug not a cure); report severe diarrhea, changes in drugs being taken, s&sx of infection, difficulty breathing. Name confusion between *Retrovir* (zidovudine) and ritonavir; use caution.

DANGEROUS DRUG

rituximab (Rituxan)
CLASS Antineoplastic, monoclonal antibody
PREG/CONT C/NA

BBW Fatal infusion reactions, severe cutaneous reactions, tumor lysis syndrome possible. Risk of reactivation of hepatitis B at drug initiation; screen for hepatitis B before use.
IND & DOSE Tx of lymphoma. *Adult:* 375 mg/m² IV once wkly for four or eight doses. **To reduce s&sx of rheumatoid arthritis.** *Adult:* Two 1,000-mg IV infusions separated by 2 wk, w/methotrexate. Tx of chronic lymphocytic leukemia. *Adult:* 375 mg/m² IV day before fludarabine/ cyclophosphamide; then 500 mg/m² on day 1 of cycles 2–6 (q 28 days). Tx of Wegener granulomatosis, microscopic polyangiitis. *Adult:* 375 mg/m² IV once wkly for 4 wk, w/ glucocorticoids.
ADV EFF Bowel obstruction, bronchitis, cardiac arrhythmias, infusion reactions, **infections, hepatitis B reactivation, progressive multifocal leukoencephalopathy, tumor lysis syndrome,** URI

INTERACTIONS Live vaccines
NC/PT Premedicate w/acetaminophen, diphenhydramine to decrease fever, chills associated w/infusion. Protect from infection exposure. Monitor for hepatitis B reactivation; stop if viral hepatitis occurs. Use caution in pregnancy/breast-feeding. Pt should mark calendar of tx days, report severe abd pain, headache, signs of infection, urine/stool color changes.

---

rivaroxaban (Xarelto)
CLASS Anticoagulant, factor Xa inhibitor
PREG/CONT C/NA

BBW Risk of epidural, spinal hematomas w/related neurologic impairment, possible paralysis if used in pts receiving neuraxial anesthesia or undergoing spinal puncture. Carefully consider benefits/risks of neuraxial intervention in pts who are or will be anticoagulated. If rivaroxaban used, monitor frequently for neurologic impairment; be prepared for rapid tx if necessary. Stopping drug increases risk of thromboembolic events; if stopped for any reason other than pathological bleeding, start another anticoagulant.
IND & DOSE Px of DVT, which may lead to PE in pts undergoing knee/hip replacement. *Adult:* 10 mg/day PO. Start within 6–10 hr of surgery; continue for 12 days after knee replacement, 35 days after hip replacement, continuously for atrial fibrillation (AF). **To reduce risk of stroke in pts w/nonvalvular AF; to reduce risk of recurrent DVT, PE.** *Adult:* 20 mg/day PO w/evening meal. **Tx of DVT, which may lead to PE in pts w/knee/hip replacement surgery.** *Adult:* Initially, 15 mg bid w/food for 21 days, then 20 mg PO for long-term tx.
ADJUST DOSE Renal, hepatic impairment
ADV EFF Bleeding, dysuria, elevated liver enzymes, **hemorrhage,** rash

INTERACTIONS Anticoagulants, aspirin, carbamazepine, clarithromycin, clopidogrel, erythromycin, ketoconazole, NSAIDs, phenytoin, platelet inhibitors, rifampin, ritonavir, St. John's wort, warfarin
NC/PT Not for use w/prosthetic heart valves. Monitor for bleeding. Do not stop abruptly (increased risk of stroke); taper when stopping, consider use of another anticoagulant. Not for use in pregnancy (contraceptives advised)/breast-feeding. Pt should report all prescribed/OTC drugs, herbs being taken; take precautions to prevent injury; ensure no lapse in taking drug; report stool color changes, unusual bleeding, dizziness, chest pain.

---

rivastigmine tartrate (Exelon)
CLASS Alzheimer disease drug, cholinesterase inhibitor
PREG/CONT B/NA

IND & DOSE Tx of Alzheimer disease. *Adult:* 1.5 mg PO bid w/food. Range, 6–12 mg/day; max, 12 mg/day. Transdermal patch: One 4.6-mg/24 hr patch once/day; after 4 or more wk, may increase to one 9.5-mg/24 hr patch. **Tx of Parkinson dementia.** *Adult:* Initially, 1.5 mg PO bid; titrate to effective range (3–12 mg/day PO bid in divided doses). Transdermal patch: one 4.6-mg/24 hr patch once/day; after 4 or more wk, may increase to one 9.5-mg/24 hr patch.
ADV EFF Abd pain, allergic dermatitis w/topical, anorexia, ataxia, bradycardia, confusion, fatigue, insomnia, n/v/d
INTERACTIONS Anticholinergics, beta blockers, metoclopramide, NSAIDs, other cholinesterase inhibitors, theophylline
NC/PT Establish baseline function before tx. Pt should take w/food; mix sol w/water, fruit juice, soda to improve compliance; apply patch to clean, dry skin (remove old patch before applying

new one), rotate sites; take safety precautions for CNS effects; report severe GI effects, changes in neurologic function, rash.

rizatriptan (Maxalt)

CLASS Antimigraine, serotonin selective agonist
PREG/CONT C/NA

IND & DOSE Tx of acute migraine attacks. *Adult:* 5 or 10 mg PO at onset of headache; may repeat in 2 hr if needed. Max, 30 mg/day.
ADJUST DOSE Hepatic, renal impairment
ADV EFF Chest pain, dizziness, jaw pain, paresthesia, serotonin syndrome, somnolence, throat pressure, vertigo, weakness
INTERACTIONS Ergots, MAOIs, propranolol
NC/PT Do not give within 14 days of MAOIs. For acute attack only, not px. Monitor BP in pts w/known CAD. Not for use in pregnancy. Pt should place orally disintegrating tablet on tongue, then swallow; take safety measures for CNS effects; continue normal migraine relief measures; report chest pain, numbness/tingling.

roflumilast (Daliresp)

CLASS Phosphodiesterase-4 inhibitor
PREG/CONT C/NA

IND & DOSE To reduce exacerbation risk in severe COPD. *Adult:* 500 mcg/day PO.
ADJUST DOSE Hepatic impairment
ADV EFF Bronchospasm, depression, diarrhea, dizziness, headache, insomnia, **suicidality**, weight loss
INTERACTIONS Carbamazepine, cimetidine, erythromycin, ethinyl estradiol, fluvoxamine, ketoconazole, phenobarbital, phenytoin, rifampin
NC/PT Not for acute bronchospasm. Monitor weight; if significant weight loss, stop drug. Not for use in pregnancy

(contraceptives advised)/breastfeeding. Pt should continue other COPD tx; report all drugs being taken, weight loss, thoughts of suicide, difficulty breathing.

rolapitant (Varubi)

CLASS Antiemetic, substance P/neurokinin 1 antagonist
PREG/CONT Low risk/NA

IND & DOSE Combination px of delayed n/v associated w/emetogenic chemotherapy. *Adult:* 180 mg PO 1–2 hr before start of chemotherapy, w/dexamethasone and 5-HT$_3$ receptor antagonist.
ADV EFF Anorexia, dizziness, hiccups, neutropenia
INTERACTIONS Pimozide, thioridazine (avoid use); CYP2D6 substrates, CYP3A4 inducers, digoxin, irinotecan, methotrexate, topotecan
NC/PT Premedicate w/dexamethasone and any 5-HT$_3$ receptor antagonist. Monitor drug regimen; many interactions possible. Monitor for infection. Pt should take safety precautions w/dizziness, avoid infection, report fever, syncope.

romidepsin (Istodax)

CLASS Antineoplastic, histone deacetylase inhibitor
PREG/CONT D/NA

IND & DOSE Tx of pts w/cutaneous, peripheral T-cell lymphoma who have received at least one prior systemic tx. *Adult:* 14 mg/m^2 IV over 4 hr on days 1, 8, 15 of 28-day cycle. Repeat q 28 days.
ADJUST DOSE Hepatic, severe renal impairment
ADV EFF Anemia, anorexia, **bone marrow suppression**, fatigue, **infections**, n/v/d, **prolonged QT, tumor lysis syndrome**
INTERACTIONS CYP3A4 inducers/inhibitors. QT-prolonging drugs, warfarin

NC/PT Monitor CBC, LFTs, renal function. Obtain baseline, periodic ECG. Not for use in pregnancy (contraceptives advised)/breast-feeding. Pt should mark calendar of tx days, avoid exposure to infection, report signs of infection, unusual bleeding/bruising.

romiplostim (Nplate)
CLASS Thrombopoietin receptor agonist
PREG/CONT C/NA

IND & DOSE Tx of thrombocytopenia in pts w/chronic immune thrombocytopenic purpura. *Adult:* 1 mcg/kg/wk subcut; adjust in increments of 1 mcg/kg to achieve platelet count of 50×10^9. Max, 10 mcg/kg/wk.
ADJUST DOSE Hepatic, severe renal impairment
ADV EFF Abd pain, arthralgia, dizziness, dyspepsia, headache, insomnia, myalgia, pain, paresthesia, **progression to acute myelogenous leukemia, severe thrombocytopenia, thrombotic events**
NC/PT Pt must be enrolled in *Nplate* NEXUS program; drug must be given by health care provider enrolled in program who will do blood test for platelet count before injection. Monitor platelet count; dosage adjustment may be needed. Not for use in pregnancy/breast-feeding. Not for home administration. Pt should take safety precautions w/dizziness, report difficulty breathing, numbness/tingling, leg pain.

ropinirole hydrochloride (Requip)
CLASS Antiparkinsonian, dopamine receptor agonist
PREG/CONT C/NA

IND & DOSE Tx of idiopathic Parkinson disease. *Adult:* 0.25 mg PO tid (1st wk); 0.5 mg PO tid (2nd wk); 0.75 mg PO tid (3rd wk); 1 mg PO tid (4th wk). May increase by 1.5 mg/day at 1-wk intervals to 9 mg/day, then by up to 3 mg/day at 1-wk intervals to max 24 mg/day. ER tablets: 2 mg/day PO. After 1–2 wk, may increase by 2 mg/day. Titrate w/wkly increases of 2 mg/day to max 24 mg/day. If used w/levodopa, decrease levodopa gradually; average reduction, 31% w/immediate-release ropinirole, 34% w/ER form. Tx of restless legs syndrome. *Adult:* 0.25 mg PO 1–3 hr before bed. After 2 days, increase to 0.5 mg PO; after 1 wk, to 1 mg/day PO. Wk 3, increase to 1.5 mg/day; wk 4, 2 mg/day; wk 5, 2.5 mg/day; wk 6, 3 mg/day; wk 7, 4 mg/day PO.
ADJUST DOSE Elderly pts
ADV EFF Constipation, dizziness, hallucinations, hyperkinesia, hypokinesia, insomnia, nausea, orthostatic hypotension, psychotic behavior, somnolence, sudden onset of sleep, syncope, vision changes
INTERACTIONS Alcohol, ciprofloxacin, estrogens, levodopa, warfarin
NC/PT Withdraw gradually over 1 wk if stopping. Monitor orthostatic BP. Pt should swallow ER tablet whole and not cut, crush, or chew it; take w/food; use safety precautions for CNS effects; change position slowly; report black tarry stools, hallucinations, falling asleep during daily activities. Name confusion between *Requip* (ropinirole) and *Risperdal* (risperidone); use caution.

rosiglitazone (Avandia)
CLASS Antidiabetic, thiazolidinedione
PREG/CONT C/NA

BBW Increased risk of HF, MI. Do not use in pts w/known heart disease, symptomatic HF; monitor accordingly.
IND & DOSE As adjunct to diet/exercise to improve glycemic control in pts w/type 2 diabetes. *Adult:* 4 mg PO daily; max, 8 mg/day.

ADJUST DOSE Hepatic impairment
ADV EFF Anemia, bone fractures, **CV events**, fluid retention, headache, **HF**, hypoglycemia, macular edema, **MI**, UTI, weight gain
INTERACTIONS CYP2C8 inducers/inhibitors, insulin
NC/PT Not for use w/established HF. Not for use in pregnancy/breastfeeding. Monitor weight; check for s&sx of HF. Ensure full diabetic teaching. Pt should continue diet/exercise program; report weight gain of 3 or more lb/day, chest pain, swelling.

---

rosuvastatin calcium
(Crestor)
CLASS Antihyperlipidemic, statin
PREG/CONT X/NA

IND & DOSE Tx of hypercholesterolemia, mixed dyslipidemia, primary dysbetalipoproteinemia, hypertriglyceridemia; primary px of CAD; atherosclerosis. *Adult:* 5–40 mg/day PO; 10 mg/day PO if combined w/other lipid-lowering drugs; 5 mg/day PO if combined w/cyclosporine. **Tx of heterozygous familial hypercholesterolemia.** *Child 10–17 yr:* 5–20 mg/day PO. *Child 8–under 10 yr (girls must be at least 1 yr postmenarchal):* 5–10 mg/day PO. **Tx of homozygous familial hypercholesterolemia.** *Adult:* 20 mg/day PO.
ADJUST DOSE Asian pts, renal impairment
ADV EFF Diarrhea, dizziness, flulike sx, headache, **liver failure**, myopathy, nausea, pharyngitis, **rhabdomyolysis**, rhinitis
INTERACTIONS Antacids, cyclosporine, gemfibrozil, lopinavir/ritonavir, warfarin
NC/PT Risk of increased adverse effects in Asian pts; initial tx w/5 mg/day PO and adjust based on lipid levels, adverse effects. Obtain baseline lipid profile. Not for use in pregnancy (barrier contraceptives advised)/breast-feeding. Pt should

take at bedtime; have regular blood tests; continue diet/exercise program; take antacids at least 2 hr after rosuvastatin; report muscle pain w/fever, unusual bleeding/bruising.

---

rotigotine (Neupro)
CLASS Antiparkinsonian, dopamine agonist
PREG/CONT C/NA

IND & DOSE Tx of s&sx of Parkinson's disease. *Adult:* 2 mg/24 hr transdermal patch; range, 2–8 mg/24 hr patch. **Tx of moderate to severe restless legs syndrome.** *Adult:* 1 mg/24 hr transdermal patch; max, 3 mg/24 hr transdermal patch.
ADV EFF Anorexia, application-site reactions, dizziness, dyskinesia, edema, hallucinations, headache, hyperpyrexia, hypotension, insomnia, **melanoma**, n/v, orthostatic hypotension, **severe allergic reaction**
INTERACTIONS Antipsychotics, dopamine antagonists, metoclopramide
NC/PT Apply to clean, dry skin; press firmly for 30 sec. Rotate application sites; remove old patch before applying new one. Taper after long-term use. Remove patch before MRI. Not for use in pregnancy. Pt should not open patch until ready to apply; remove old patch before applying new one; rotate application sites; not stop use suddenly; take safety precautions for CNS effects; report application-site reactions, skin reactions, difficulty breathing, fever, changes in behavior, dizziness.

---

rufinamide (Banzel)
CLASS Antiepileptic, sodium channel blocker
PREG/CONT C/NA

IND & DOSE Adjunct tx of seizures associated w/Lennox-Gastaut syndrome. *Adult:* 400–800 mg/day PO in two equally divided doses; target,

3,200 mg/day PO in two equally divided doses. *Child 1 yr and older:* 10 mg/kg/day PO in two equally divided doses; target, 45 mg/kg/day or 3,200 mg/day.
ADJUST DOSE Hepatic, renal impairment
ADV EFF Ataxia, coordination disturbances, dizziness, fatigue, headache, nausea, **seizures, severe hypersensitivity reactions,** somnolence, **suicidality**
INTERACTIONS CYP450 inducers, hormonal contraceptives, valproate
NC/PT Withdraw gradually; do not stop abruptly. Stable for 90 days. Not for use in pregnancy (hormonal contraceptives may be ineffective; second contraceptive form advised)/breast-feeding. Pt should take w/food; swallow tablet whole and not cut, crush, or chew it; store suspension upright, measure using medical measuring device; take safety precautions for CNS effects; report difficulty breathing, rash, thoughts of suicide, mood changes.

ruxolitinib (Jakafi)
CLASS Kinase inhibitor
PREG/CONT C/NA

IND & DOSE Tx of intermediate, high-risk myelofibrosis. *Adult:* 5–20 mg PO bid. Dosage based on platelet count. **Tx of polycythemia vera after inadequate response to hydroxyurea.** *Adult:* 10 mg PO bid.
ADJUST DOSE Hepatic/renal impairment
ADV EFF Anemia, **bone marrow suppression,** bruising, dizziness, headache, **serious infections,** skin cancer, thrombocytopenia
INTERACTIONS CYP450 inhibitors, fluconazole
NC/PT Monitor CBC every 2–4 wk. Stop drug after 6 mo if no spleen reduction or sx improvement. Not for use in breast-feeding. Monitor for infection. Pt should take safety

precautions w/dizziness; report signs of infection, unusual bleeding.

sacrosidase (Sucraid)
CLASS Enzyme
PREG/CONT C/NA

IND & DOSE Oral replacement of genetically determined sucrase deficiency. *Adult, child over 15 kg:* 2 mL PO or 44 drops/meal or snack PO. *Adult, child 15 kg or less:* 1 mL or 22 drops/meal or snack PO.
ADV EFF Abd pain, constipation, dehydration, headache
NC/PT Do not use in known allergy to yeast. Must dilute w/60–120 mL water, milk, infant formula before giving. Do not dilute, consume w/fruit juice. Refrigerate before opening; discard 4 wk after opening. Give cold or at room temp. Pt should report difficulty breathing, swelling of tongue/face.

saliva substitute (Entertainer's Secret, Moi-Stir, MouthKote, Salivart)
CLASS Saliva substitute
PREG/CONT Unkn/NA

IND & DOSE Mgt of dry mouth, throat in xerostomia, hyposalivation. *Adult:* Spray for ½ second or apply to oral mucosa.
ADV EFF Excessive electrolyte absorption
NC/PT Monitor pt while eating; swallowing may be impaired and additional tx needed. Pt should swish around in mouth after application, report difficulty swallowing, headache, leg cramps.

salmeterol xinafoate (Serevent Diskus)
CLASS Antiasthmatic, beta selective agonist
PREG/CONT C/NA

BBW Ensure drug not used for acute asthma or w/worsening/deteriorating asthma; risk of death. Increased risk of asthma-related hospitalization when used in children, adolescents. When long-acting sympathomimetic, inhaled corticosteroid needed, fixed-dose combination strongly recommended. Do not use for asthma unless combined w/long-term asthma-control medication; risk of death. Use only as additional tx in pts not controlled by other medications.

IND & DOSE Maint tx for asthma, bronchospasm. *Adult, child 4 yr and over:* 1 inhalation (50 mcg) bid at 12-hr intervals. **Px of exercise-induced asthma.** *Adult, child 4 yr and older:* 1 inhalation 30 min or more before exertion. **Long-term maint of bronchospasm w/COPD.** *Adult:* 1 inhalation (50 mcg) bid at 12-hr intervals.

ADV EFF Asthma-related deaths (risk higher in black pts), **bronchospasm,** headache, pain, palpitations, tachycardia, tremors

INTERACTIONS Beta blockers, diuretics, MAOIs, protease inhibitors, TCAs

NC/PT Arrange for periodic evaluation of respiratory condition. Not for tx of acute asthma attack. Review proper use of *Diskus.* Pt should never take drug alone for tx of asthma; take safety precautions w/tremors; report irregular heartbeat, difficulty breathing, worsening of asthma.

salsalate (Amigesic, Disalcid)
CLASS Analgesic, NSAID, salicylate
PREG/CONT C/NA

BBW Increased risk of GI bleeding, CV events; monitor accordingly.
IND & DOSE Relief of pain, sx of inflammatory conditions. *Adult:* 3,000 mg/day PO in divided doses.
ADV EFF Acute salicylate toxicity, anaphylactoid reactions to anaphylactic shock, bone marrow suppression, bronchospasm, constipation, **CV collapse,** dizziness, dyspepsia, GI

pain, insomnia, **renal/respiratory failure**
INTERACTIONS Alcohol, antacids, carbonic anhydrase inhibitors, corticosteroids, insulin, probenecid, spironolactone, sulfonylureas, urine alkalinizers, valproic acid
NC/PT Pt should take w/full glass of water; w/food if GI upset. Continue other measures for relief of pain, inflammation; report ringing in ears, rapid, difficult breathing.

sapropterin dihydrochloride (Kuvan)
CLASS Coenzyme factor, phenylalanine reducer
PREG/CONT C/NA

IND & DOSE W/diet to reduce blood phenylalanine level in hyperphenylalinemia caused by tetrahydrobiopterin-responsive phenylketonuria. *Pt 4 yr and older:* 10 mg/kg/day PO. May adjust to 5–20 mg/kg/day based on blood phenylalanine level.
ADV EFF Abd pain, headache, n/v/d, pharyngolaryngeal pain
NC/PT Do not use w/levodopa, ED drugs, drugs that inhibit folate metabolism. Must use w/phenylalanine dietary restrictions. Protect from moisture; do not use if outdated. Dissolve tablets in water, apple juice; have pt drink within 15 min. Monitor phenylalanine level; adjust dose as needed. Pt should report severe headache, anorexia, fever.

saquinavir mesylate (Invirase)
CLASS Antiviral, protease inhibitor
PREG/CONT B/NA

BBW Capsules, tablets not interchangeable; use tablets only when combined w/ritonavir. If saquinavir only protease inhibitor in regimen, use capsules.
IND & DOSE Tx of HIV infection, w/ritonavir and other antivirals.

Adult, child over 16 yr: 1,000 mg PO bid w/ritonavir 100 mg bid given together within 2 hr after meal. Or, w/ lopinavir 400 mg/ritonavir 100 mg PO bid (tablets). Or, 1,000 mg PO bid w/ lopinavir 400 mg/ritonavir 100 mg PO bid (capsules).

ADJUST DOSE Hepatic impairment

ADV EFF Anaphylaxis, asthenia, diabetes mellitus, diarrhea, dizziness, dyslipidemia, dyspepsia, fat redistribution, GI pain, headache, nausea, **prolonged QT**

INTERACTIONS Antiarrhythmics, carbamazepine, clarithromycin, delavirdine, dexamethasone, ergots, grapefruit juice, indinavir, ketoconazole, midazolam, nelfinavir, nevirapine, phenobarbital, phenytoin, QT-prolonging drugs, rifabutin, rifampin, ritonavir, sildenafil, statins, triazolam, St. John's wort

NC/PT Store at room temp; use by expiration date. Carefully evaluate drug hx; many potentially **DANGEROUS DRUG** interactions. Give within 2 hr after full meal, always w/ritonavir and other antivirals. Monitor for opportunistic infections. Pt should take precautions to prevent spread (drug not a cure), avoid grapefruit juice, St. John's wort; take safety precautions w/dizziness, report severe headache, urine/stool color changes. Name confusion between saquinavir and *Sinequan;* use caution.

---

sargramostim (Leukine)
CLASS Colony-stimulating factor
PREG/CONT C/NA

IND & DOSE Myeloid reconstitution after autologous, allogenic bone marrow transplantation. *Adult:* 250 mcg/m²/day for 21 days in 2-hr IV infusion starting 2–4 hr after autologous bone marrow infusion and not less than 24 hr after last dose of chemotherapy, radiation. Do not give until post-marrow infusion ANC less than 500 cells/mm³. Continue until ANC greater than 1,500 cells/mm³ for 3 consecutive days. **Bone marrow transplantation failure, engraftment delay.** *Adult:* 250 mcg/m²/day for 14 days as 2-hr IV infusion; may repeat after 7 days off tx if no engraftment. If still no engraftment, may give third dose of 500 mcg/m²/day for 14 days after another 7 days off tx. **Neutrophil recovery after chemotherapy in AML.** *Adult:* 250 mcg/m²/day IV over 4 hr starting about day 11 or 4 days after chemotherapy induction. **Mobilization of peripheral blood progenitor cells (PBPCs).** *Adult:* 250 mcg/m²/day IV over 24 hr or subcut once daily; continue throughout harvesting. **Post-PBPC transplant.** *Adult:* 250 mcg/m²/day IV over 24 hr or subcut once daily starting immediately after PBPC infusion; continue until ANC greater than 1,500 cells/mm³ for 3 consecutive days.

ADV EFF Alopecia, bone pain, diarrhea, fever, **hemorrhage,** n/v/d

INTERACTIONS Corticosteroids, lithium

NC/PT Give no less than 24 hr after cytotoxic chemotherapy and within 2–4 hr of bone marrow infusion. Store in refrigerator; do not freeze/ shake. Not for use in pregnancy (barrier contraceptives advised). Use powder within 6 hr of mixing. If using powder, use each vial for one dose; do not reenter vial. Discard unused drug. Infuse over 2 hr. Do not use in-line membrane filter or mix w/other drugs or in other diluent. Monitor CBC. Pt should cover head at temp extremes (hair loss possible); avoid exposure to infection; report fever, s&sx of infection, difficulty breathing, bleeding.

DANGEROUS DRUG

saxagliptin (Onglyza)
CLASS Antidiabetic, DPP-4 inhibitor
PREG/CONT B/NA

IND & DOSE As adjunct to diet/ exercise to improve glycemic control

in type 2 diabetics. *Adult:* 2.5–5 mg/day PO without regard to meals.
ADJUST DOSE Renal impairment
ADV EFF Headache, hypoglycemia, hypersensitivity reactions, **pancreatitis,** peripheral edema, serious to debilitating arthralgia, URI, UTI
INTERACTIONS Atazanavir, celery, clarithromycin, coriander, dandelion root, fenugreek, garlic, ginseng, indinavir, itraconazole, juniper berries, ketoconazole, nefazodone, nelfinavir, ritonavir, saquinavir, telithromycin
NC/PT Not for use in type 1 diabetes, ketoacidosis. Reduce dose if given w/strong CYP3A4/5 inhibitors. Monitor blood glucose, HbA$_{1c}$, renal function before, periodically during tx. Ensure thorough diabetic teaching program. Pt may be switched to insulin during times of stress. Pt should continue diet/exercise program, other prescribed diabetes drugs; report all other prescribed/OTC drugs, herbs being taken (dose adjustment may be needed); report uncontrolled glucose levels, severe headache, sx of infection, joint pain, rash, difficulty breathing.

scopolamine hydrobromide
(Transderm-Scop)
CLASS Anticholinergic, antiemetic, anti–motion sickness drug, antiparkinsonian, belladonna alkaloid, parasympatholytic
PREG/CONT C/NA

IND & DOSE Tx of motion sickness. *Adult:* Apply 1 transdermal system to postauricular skin at least 4 hr before antiemetic effect needed or in evening before scheduled surgery; leave scopolamine 1 mg over 3 days. May replace system q 3 days. **Obstetric amnesia, preoperative sedation.** *Adult:* 0.32–0.65 mg subcut or IM. May give IV after dilution in sterile water for injection. May repeat up to qid. *Child:* General guidelines, 0.006 mg/kg subcut, IM or IV; max,

0.3 mg. *3 yr–6 yr:* 0.2–0.3 mg IM or IV. *6 mo–3 yr:* 0.1–0.15 mg IM or IV.
Sedation, tranquilization. *Adult:* 0.6 mg subcut or IM tid–qid. **Antiemetic.** *Adult:* 0.6–1 mg subcut. *Child:* 0.006 mg/kg subcut. **Refraction.** *Adult:* Instill 1–2 drops into eye(s) 1 hr before refracting. **Uveitis.** *Adult:* Instill 1–2 drops into eye(s) up to qid.
ADJUST DOSE Elderly pts
ADV EFF **Anaphylaxis,** blurred vision, constipation, decreased sweating, dizziness, drowsiness, dry mouth, nasal congestion, photophobia, pupil dilation, urinary hesitancy, urine retention
INTERACTIONS Alcohol, antidepressants, antihistamines, haloperidol, phenothiazines
NC/PT Ensure adequate hydration. Provide temp control to prevent hyperpyrexia. W/transdermal system, have pt wash hands thoroughly after handling patch, dispose of patch properly to avoid contact w/children/pets, remove old patch before applying new one, do not cut patch. Pt should empty bladder before each dose; avoid alcohol, hot environments; use laxative for constipation; take safety precautions for CNS effects; report severe dry mouth, difficulty breathing.

sebelipase (Kanuma)
CLASS Hydrolytic lysosomal cholesteryl ester
PREG/CONT Mild risk/NA

IND & DOSE Tx of lysosomal acid lipase deficiency. *Adult:* 1 mg/kg IV over at least 2 hr once every other wk. *Child 6 mo or less with rapidly progressive deficiency:* 1–3 mg/kg IV once a wk.
ADV EFF Anemia, asthenia, constipation, cough, fever, headache, **hypersensitivity reactions,** nasopharyngitis, n/v/d, rash
NC/PT Increased risk of hypersensitivity reaction w/known egg or

egg-product allergies. Monitor for hypersensitivity reactions, slow infusion, consider pretreatment w/ antipyretics, antihistamines. Pt should report difficulty breathing, chest pain, rash.

DANGEROUS DRUG

secobarbital sodium
(Seconal Sodium)
CLASS Antiepileptic, barbiturate, sedative-hypnotic
PREG/CONT D/C-II

IND & DOSE Intermittent use as sedative-hypnotic. *Adult:* 100 mg PO at bedtime for up to 2 wk. **Preop sedation.** *Adult:* 200–300 mg PO 1–2 hr before surgery. *Child:* 2–6 mg/kg PO 1–2 hr before surgery; max, 100 mg/dose.
ADJUST DOSE Elderly, debilitated pts; hepatic, renal impairment
ADV EFF Anaphylaxis, angioedema, agitation, anxiety, apnea, ataxia, bradycardia, confusion, constipation, dizziness, epigastric pain, hallucinations, hyperkinesia, hypotension, hyperventilation, insomnia, laryngospasm, n/v/d, psychiatric disturbances, respiratory depression, sleep disorders, somnolence, **Stevens-Johnson syndrome,** syncope
INTERACTIONS Alcohol, anticoagulants, antihistamines, corticosteroids, doxycycline, estrogens, hormonal contraceptives, hypnotics, metoprolol, metronidazole, oxyphenbutazone, phenylbutazone, propranolol, quinidine, sedatives, theophylline, verapamil
NC/PT Monitor blood levels, watch for anaphylaxis, angioedema w/above interacting drugs. Not for use in pregnancy (barrier contraceptives advised)/breast-feeding. Barbiturates may produce irritability, excitability, inappropriate tearfulness, aggression in children; stay w/children who receive preop sedation. Taper gradually after repeated use. Pt should avoid alcohol,

take safety precautions, report difficulty breathing, swelling, rash.

---

secretin (ChiRhoStim)
CLASS Diagnostic agent
PREG/CONT C/NA

IND & DOSE To stimulate pancreatic secretions to aid in dx of pancreatic exocrine dysfx, gastric secretions to aid in dx of gastrinoma. *Adult:* 0.2–0.4 mcg/kg IV over 1 min.
ADV EFF Abd pain, allergic reactions, flushing, n/v
INTERACTIONS Anticholinergics
NC/PT Monitor carefully during infusion for allergic reaction; have emergency equipment on hand. Do not use w/acute pancreatitis. Pt should report severe abd pain, difficulty breathing.

---

secukinumab (Cosentyx)
CLASS Interleukin antagonist
PREG/CONT Moderate risk/NA

IND & DOSE Tx of moderate to severe plaque psoriasis in pts who are candidates for systemic therapy or phototherapy; tx of active psoriatic arthritis; tx of active ankylosing spondylitis. *Adult:* 300 mg subcut at wk 0, 1, 2, 3, and 4 followed by 300 mg subcut q 4 wk; 150 mg subcut may be acceptable in some pts.
ADV EFF Cold sx, Crohn's disease exacerbation, diarrhea, hypersensitivity reactions, **infections,** TB activation, URI
INTERACTIONS Live vaccines
NC/PT Test for TB before tx. Monitor pts w/Crohn's disease. Use caution in pregnancy/breast-feeding. Do not inject within 2 inches of navel. Pt should refrigerate drug and learn proper use/disposal of *Sensoready Pen,* subcut administration, rotation of injection sites; report difficulty breathing, swelling, chest tightness, rash, fainting, sx of infection.

selegiline hydrochloride (Eldepryl, Emsam, Zelapar)

CLASS Antidepressant, antiparkinsonian, MAO type B inhibitor
PREG/CONT C/NA

BBW Increased risk of suicidality in children, adolescents, young adults; monitor accordingly. *Emsam* is contraindicated in children under 12 yr; risk of hypertensive crisis.
IND & DOSE Mgt of pts w/Parkinson disease whose response to levodopa/carbidopa has decreased. *Adult:* 10 mg/day PO in divided doses of 5 mg each at breakfast, lunch. After 2–3 days, attempt to reduce levodopa/carbidopa dose; reductions of 10%–30% typical. For orally disintegrating tablet, 1.25 mg/day PO in a.m. before breakfast. May increase after 6 wk to 2.5 mg/day; max, 10 mg/day. **Tx of major depressive disorder.** *Adult, child over 12 yr (Emsam)* daily to dry, intact skin on upper torso, upper thigh, or outer surface of upper arm. Start w/6-mg/24 hr system; increase to max 12 mg/24 hr if needed, tolerated.
ADJUST DOSE Elderly pts
ADV EFF Abd pain, asthma, confusion, dizziness, dyskinesia, falling asleep during daily activities, fever, hallucinations, headache, hypertension, loss of impulse control, lightheadedness, local reactions to dermal patch, melanoma risk, n/v, **serotonin syndrome,** vivid dreams
INTERACTIONS Carbamazepine, fluoxetine, meperidine, methadone, opioid analgesics, oxcarbazepine, TCAs, tramadol, tyramine-rich foods
NC/PT Pt should place oral tablet on top of tongue, avoid food, beverage for 5 min; apply dermal patch to dry, intact skin on upper torso, upper thigh, or outer upper arm, replace q 24 hr (remove old patch before applying new one); continue other par-

kinsonians; take safety precautions for CNS effects; report all drugs being used (dose adjustments may be needed); report confusion, fainting, thoughts of suicide.

selexipag (Uptravi)

CLASS Prostacyclin receptor agonist
PREG/CONT Low risk/NA

IND & DOSE Tx of pulmonary arterial hypertension. *Adult:* Initially, 200 mcg PO bid; increase at wkly intervals to 1,600 mcg PO bid.
ADJUST DOSE Hepatic impairment
ADV EFF Extremity/jaw pain, flushing, headache, n/v/d, **pulmonary edema**
INTERACTIONS Strong CYP2C8 inhibitors; avoid combination
NC/PT Ensure proper dx. Not for use w/severe hepatic impairment or breast-feeding. Adjust dose based on pt response. Pt should monitor activity level and breathing, report difficulty breathing, severe n/v/d.

sertraline hydrochloride (Zoloft)

CLASS Antidepressant, SSRI
PREG/CONT C/NA

BBW Increased risk of suicidality in children, adolescents, young adults; monitor accordingly.
IND & DOSE Tx of major depressive disorder, OCD. *Adult:* 50 mg PO once daily, a.m. or p.m.; may increase to max 200 mg/day. *Child 13–17 yr:* For OCD, 50 mg/day PO; max, 200 mg/day. *Child 6–12 yr:* For OCD, 25 mg/day PO; max, 200 mg/day. **Tx of panic disorder, PTSD.** *Adult:* 25–50 mg/day PO, up to max 200 mg/day. **Tx of PMDD.** *Adult:* 50 mg/day PO daily or just during luteal phase of menstrual cycle. Range, 50–150 mg/day. **Tx of social anxiety disorder.** *Adult:* 25 mg/day PO; range, 50–200 mg/day.
ADJUST DOSE Hepatic, renal impairment

ADV EFF Anxiety, diarrhea, dizziness, drowsiness, dry mouth, fatigue, headache, insomnia, nausea, nervousness, painful menstruation, rhinitis, **suicidality,** vision changes
INTERACTIONS Cimetidine, MAOIs, pimozide, St. John's wort
NC/PT Do not give within 14 days of MAOIs. Dilute oral concentrate in 4 oz water, ginger ale, lemon-lime soda, lemonade, orange juice only; give immediately after diluting. Not for use in pregnancy (barrier contraceptives advised). May take up to 4–6 wk to see depression improvement. Pt should take safety precautions for CNS effects, avoid St. John's wort, report difficulty breathing, thoughts of suicide.

sevelamer hydrochloride (Renagel)
CLASS Calcium-phosphate binder
PREG/CONT C/NA

IND & DOSE To reduce serum phosphorus level in hemodialysis pts w/ end-stage renal disease. *Adult:* 1–4 tablets PO w/each meal based on serum phosphorus level; may increase by one tablet/meal to achieve desired serum phosphorus level.
ADV EFF Bowel obstruction/perforation, cough, diarrhea, dyspepsia, fecal impaction, headache, hypotension, thrombosis, vomiting
NC/PT Do not use w/hypophosphatemia or bowel obstruction. Pt should take other oral drugs at least 1 hr before or 3 hr after sevelamer; have blood tests regularly to monitor phosphorus level, report chest pain, difficulty breathing, severe abd pain.

sildenafil citrate (Revatio, Viagra)
CLASS ED drug, phosphodiesterase-5 inhibitor
PREG/CONT B/NA

IND & DOSE Tx of ED. *Adult:* 50 mg PO 1 hr before anticipated sexual activity; range, 25–100 mg PO. May take 30 min–4 hr before sexual activity. Limit use to once/day *(Viagra).* **Tx of pulmonary arterial hypertension.** *Adult:* 20 mg PO tid at least 4–6 hr apart without regard to food *(Revatio),* or 2.5–10 mg by IV bolus tid *(Revatio).*
ADJUST DOSE Elderly pts; hepatic, renal impairment
ADV EFF Dyspepsia, flushing, headache, hearing/vision loss, hypotension, insomnia, priapism, rhinitis
INTERACTIONS Alcohol, alpha adrenergic blockers, amlodipine, cimetidine, erythromycin, grapefruit juice, itraconazole, ketoconazole, nitrates, protease inhibitors, ritonavir, saquinavir
NC/PT Ensure proper dx before tx. *Revatio* contraindicated in children 1–17 yr; deaths have been reported. Reserve IV use for pts unable to take orally. *Viagra* ineffective in absence of sexual stimulation. Pt should take appropriate measures to prevent STDs; report difficult urination, sudden hearing/vision loss, erection lasting longer than 4 hr.

silodosin (Rapaflo)
CLASS Alpha blocker, BPH drug
PREG/CONT B/NA

IND & DOSE Tx of s&sx of BPH. *Adult:* 8 mg/day PO w/meal.
ADJUST DOSE Hepatic, renal impairment
ADV EFF Abnormal/retrograde ejaculation, dizziness, headache, liver impairment, orthostatic hypotension, rash
INTERACTIONS Clarithromycin, cyclosporine, ED drugs, itraconazole, ketoconazole, other alpha blockers, nitrates, ritonavir
NC/PT Rule out prostate cancer before tx. Pt undergoing cataract surgery at risk for intraop floppy iris syndrome; alert surgeon about drug use. Pt should take safety precautions w/dizziness, orthostatic hypotension; use caution when combined w/nitrates,

ED drugs, antihypertensives; report urine/stool color changes, worsening of sx.

siltuximab (Sylvant)

CLASS Interleukin-6 antagonist
PREG/CONT C/NA

IND & DOSE Tx of multicentric Castleman's disease in pts HIV-negative and herpesvirus-negative. *Adult:* 11 mg/kg IV over 1 hr q 3 wk.
ADV EFF GI perforation, infection, infusion reaction, rash, **severe hypersensitivity reactions,** URI
INTERACTIONS Live vaccines
NC/PT Ensure proper dx. Do not give to pt w/infections. Monitor for infection during tx; provide tx. Do not give drug until infection resolves. Have emergency equipment on hand during infusion. Not for use in pregnancy (contraceptives advised)/breast-feeding. Pt should report s&sx of infection, difficulty breathing, severe abd pain.

simeprevir (Olysio)

CLASS Hepatitis C drug, protease inhibitor
PREG/CONT High risk/NA

IND & DOSE Tx of chronic hepatitis C genotype 1 or 4, w/other antiretrovirals. *Adult:* 150 mg/day PO w/food; combined w/peginterferon alfa and ribavirin for 12 wk, then peginterferon alfa and ribavirin for 24–36 wk. May combine w/sofosbuvir in genotype 1 for 12- to 24-wk course.
ADJUST DOSE Hepatic impairment (contraindicated)
ADV EFF Bradycardia, liver failure, nausea, photosensitivity, rash
INTERACTIONS CYP3A inducers/inhibitor
NC/PT Ensure concurrent use of peginterferon alfa and ribavirin or sofosbuvir; not for monotherapy. Monitor HR. Negative pregnancy test required monthly; pt should avoid

pregnancy or fathering a child (two forms of contraception advised). Not for use in breast-feeding. Pt should swallow capsule whole, not cut, crush, or chew it; avoid sun exposure; use precautions to avoid spread of disease; report rash, itching, severe nausea, urine/stool color changes.

simethicone (Flatulex, Gas-X, Phazyme)

CLASS Antiflatulent
PREG/CONT C/NA

IND & DOSE Relief of sx of excess gas in digestive tract. *Adult:* 40–360 mg PO as needed after meals, at bedtime; max, 500 mg/day. *Child 2–12 yr, over 11 kg:* 40 mg PO as needed after meals, at bedtime. *Child under 2 yr:* 20 mg PO as needed after meals, at bedtime; max, 240 mg/day.
ADV EFF Constipation, diarrhea, flatulence
NC/PT Pt should shake drops thoroughly before each use; add drops to 30 mL cool water, infant formula, other liquid to ease administration to infants; let strips dissolve on tongue; chew chewable tablets thoroughly before swallowing; report extreme abd pain, vomiting.

simvastatin (Zocor)

CLASS Antihyperlipidemic, statin
PREG/CONT X/NA

IND & DOSE Tx of hyperlipidemia; px of coronary events. *Adult:* 10–20 mg PO, up to 40 mg, daily in evening. Range, 5–40 mg/day; max, 40 mg/day. **Tx of familial hypercholesterolemia.** *Adult:* 40 mg/day PO in evening. *Child 10–17 yr:* 10 mg/day PO in evening; range, 10–40 mg/day. **Combination tx of CAD.** *Adult:* Do not use w/other statins. If used w/fibrates, niacin, max of 10 mg/day. Give regular dose if used w/bile acid sequestrants; give sequestrants at

least 4 hr before simvastatin. If used w/cyclosporine, start w/5 mg/day; max, 10 mg/day. If used w/amiodarone, verapamil, max of 10 mg/day. If used w/diltiazem, max of 40 mg/day. Do not progress to 80 mg/day; increased risk of rhabdomyolysis.
ADJUST DOSE Renal impairment; hepatic impairment (contraindicated)
ADV EFF Abd pain, **acute renal failure,** cramps, flatulence, headache, **liver failure,** n/v/d, **rhabdomyolysis/ myopathy**
INTERACTIONS Strong CYP3A4 inhibitors, cyclosporine, danazol, gemfibrozil; contraindicated w/ these drugs. Amiodarone, amlodipine, digoxin, diltiazem, dronedarone, fibrates, grapefruit juice, hepatotoxic drugs, lomitapide, niacin, ranolazine, verapamil, warfarin
NC/PT Not for use w/strong CYP3A4 inhibitors, gemfibrozil, cyclosporine, danazol. Monitor LFTs. Ensure pt has tried cholesterol-lowering diet for 3–6 mo before starting tx. Avoid 80-mg dose because of increased risk of muscle injury, rhabdomyolysis; if pt already stable on 80 mg, monitor closely. Not for use in pregnancy (barrier contraceptives advised)/breast-feeding. Pt should continue diet, take in p.m., have blood tests regularly, avoid grapefruit juice, report urine/stool color changes, muscle pain/soreness.

---

sipuleucel-T (Provenge)
CLASS Cellular immunotherapy
PREG/CONT C/NA

IND & DOSE Tx of asymptomatic, minimally symptomatic metastatic castrate-resistant prostate cancer. *Adult:* 50 million autologous CD54+ cells activated w/PAP-GM-CSF suspended in 250 mL lactated Ringer's injection IV.
ADV EFF Acute infusion reactions, back pain, chills, fatigue, fever, headache, joint ache, nausea

INTERACTIONS Immunosuppressants
NC/PT Autologous use only. Leukapheresis will be done 3 days before infusion. Ensure pt eating. Premedicate w/oral acetaminophen and antihistamine. Risk of acute infusion reactions; closely monitor pt during infusion. Universal precautions required. Pt should report difficulty breathing, signs of infection.

---

sirolimus (Rapamune)
CLASS Immunosuppressant
PREG/CONT C/NA

BBW Risk of increased susceptibility to infection; graft loss, hepatic artery thrombosis w/liver transplant; bronchial anastomotic dehiscence in lung transplants.
IND & DOSE Px for organ rejection in renal transplant. *Adult, child 13 yr and older:* 40 kg or more: Loading dose of 6 mg PO as soon after transplant as possible, then 2 mg/day PO. Under 40 kg: Loading dose of 3 mg/m^2, then 1 mg/m^2/day PO. Tx of pts w/ lymphangioleiomyomatosis. *Adult:* 2 mg/day PO; titrate to achieve trough concentrations of 5–15 ng/mL.
ADJUST DOSE Hepatic impairment
ADV EFF Abd pain, **anaphylaxis,** anemia, **angioedema,** arthralgia, delayed wound healing, edema, fever, headache, hypertension, **interstitial lung disease,** lipid profile changes, pain, pneumonitis, skin cancer, thrombocytopenia
INTERACTIONS CYP3A4 inducers/ inhibitors, grapefruit juice, live vaccines
NC/PT Always use w/adrenal corticosteroids, cyclosporine. Monitor pulmonary function, LFTs, renal function. Not for use in pregnancy (contraceptives advised)/breast-feeding. Pt should avoid grapefruit juice, sun exposure; report difficulty breathing, swelling.

DANGEROUS DRUG

sitagliptin phosphate
(Januvia)

CLASS Antidiabetic, DPP-4 inhibitor
PREG/CONT B/NA

IND & DOSE As adjunct to diet/exercise to improve glycemic control in type 2 diabetics. *Adult:* 100 mg/day PO.
ADJUST DOSE Renal impairment
ADV EFF Headache, hypersensitivity reactions, hypoglycemia, pancreatitis, renal failure, severe to disabling arthralgia, Stevens-Johnson syndrome, URI, UTI
INTERACTIONS Atazanavir, celery, clarithromycin, coriander, dandelion root, fenugreek, garlic, ginseng, indinavir, itraconazole, juniper berries, ketoconazole, nefazodone, nelfinavir, ritonavir, saquinavir, telithromycin
NC/PT Not for use in type 1 diabetics, ketoacidosis. Monitor blood glucose, HbA1c, renal function, pancreatic enzymes before, periodically during tx. Ensure thorough diabetic teaching program. Pt may be switched to insulin during times of stress. Pt should continue diet/exercise program, other prescribed diabetes drugs; report all other prescribed/OTC drugs, herbs being take, difficulty breathing, rash, joint pain.

sodium bicarbonate
(Neut)

CLASS Antacid, electrolyte; systemic, urine alkalizer
PREG/CONT C/NA

IND & DOSE Urine alkalinization. *Adult:* 3,900 mg PO, then 1,300–2,600 mg PO q 4 hr. *Child:* 84–840 mg/kg/day PO. **Antacid.** *Adult:* 300 mg–2 g PO daily-qid usually 1–3 hr after meals, at bedtime. **Adjunct to advanced CV life support during CPR.** *Adult:* Inject IV either 300–500 mL of 5% sol or 200–300 mEq of

7.5% or 8.4% sol as rapidly as possible. Base further doses on subsequent blood gas values. Or, 1 mEq/kg dose, then repeat 0.5 mEq/kg q 10 min. *Child 2 yr and older:* 1 to 2 mEq/kg (1 mL/kg 8.4% sol) by slow IV. *Child under 2 yr:* 4.2% sol; max, 8 mEq/kg/day IV. **Severe metabolic acidosis.** *Adult, child:* Dose depends on blood carbon dioxide content, pH, pt's clinical condition. Usually, 90–180 mEq/L IV during first hr, then adjust PRN. **Less urgent metabolic acidosis.** *Adult, adolescent:* 5 mEq/kg as 4–8 hr IV infusion.
ADJUST DOSE Elderly pts, renal impairment
ADV EFF Local irritation, tissue necrosis at injection site, systemic alkalosis
INTERACTIONS Amphetamines, anorexiants, doxycycline, ephedrine, flecainide, lithium, methotrexate, quinidine, pseudoephedrine, salicylates, sulfonylureas, sympathomimetics, tetracyclines
NC/PT Monitor ABGs. Calculate base deficit when giving parenteral sodium bicarbonate. Adjust dose based on response. Give slowly. Do not attempt complete correction within first 24 hr; increased risk of systemic alkalosis. Monitor cardiac rhythm, potassium level. Pt should chew tablets thoroughly before swallowing, follow w/full glass of water; avoid oral drug within 1–2 hr of other oral drugs; report pain at injection site, headache, tremors.

sodium ferric gluconate complex
(Ferrlecit)

CLASS Iron product
PREG/CONT B/NA

IND & DOSE Tx of iron deficiency in pts undergoing long-term hemodialysis who are on erythropoietin. *Adult:* Test dose: 2 mL diluted in 50 mL normal saline injection IV over 60 min. *Adult:* 10 mL diluted in 100 mL normal saline injection IV over 60 min. *Child 6 yr and over:* 0.12 kg/kg diluted in 25 mL normal saline by IV infusion over 1 hr for each dialysis session. **ADV EFF** Cramps, dizziness, dyspnea, flushing, hypotension, **hypersensitivity reactions,** injection-site reactions, **iron overload,** n/v/d, pain **NC/PT** Monitor iron level, BP. Most pts will normally need eight doses given at sequential dialysis sessions, then periodic use based on hematocrit. Do not mix w/other drugs in sol. Have emergency equipment on hand for hypersensitivity reactions. Use caution in pregnancy/breast-feeding. Pt should take safety precautions for CNS effects, report difficulty breathing, pain at injection site.

sodium fluoride
(Fluoritab, Flura, Karigel, Pharmaflur, Stop)
CLASS Mineral
PREG/CONT C/NA

IND & DOSE Px of dental caries. *Adult:* 10 mL rinse once daily or wkly; swish around teeth, spit out. Or, apply thin ribbon to toothbrush or mouth tray for 1 min; brush, rinse, spit out. *Child:* Fluoride in drinking water over 0.6 ppm: No tx. Fluoride in drinking water 0.3–0.6 ppm: 6–16 yr, 0.5 mg/day PO; 3–6 yr, 0.25 mg/day PO. Fluoride in drinking water under 0.3 ppm: 6–16 yr, 1 mg/day PO; 3–6 yr, 0.5 mg/day PO; 6 mo–3 yr, 0.25 mg/day. *Child 6–12 yr:* 10 mL/day rinse; have pt swish around teeth for 1 min, spit out. Or, 4–6 drops gel on applicator. Have pt put applicator over teeth, bite down for 6 min, spit out excess gel.
ADV EFF Eczema, gastric distress, headache, rash, teeth staining, weakness
INTERACTIONS Dairy products
NC/PT Do not give within 1 hr of milk, dairy products. Pt may chew tablets, swallow whole, or add to drinking water, juice. Pt should brush, floss teeth before using rinse, then

spit out fluid (should not swallow fluid, cream, gel, rinse); have regular dental exams; report increased salivation, diarrhea, seizures, teeth mottling.

sodium oxybate (Xyrem)
CLASS Anticataplectic, CNS depressant
PREG/CONT B/C-III

BBW Counsel pt that drug, also called GHB, is known for abuse. Pt will be asked to view educational program, agree to safety measures to ensure only pt has drug access, and agree to return for follow-up at least q 3 mo. Severe respiratory depression, coma, death possible. Available only through restricted access program.
IND & DOSE Tx of excessive daytime sleepiness, cataplexy in pts w/ narcolepsy. *Adult:* 4.5 g/day PO divided into two equal doses of 2.25 g. Give at bedtime and again 2½–4 hr later. May increase no more often than q 1–2 wk to max 9 g/day in increments of 1.5 g/day (0.75 g/dose). Range, 6–9 g daily.
ADJUST DOSE Hepatic impairment
ADV EFF CNS depression, confusion, dizziness, dyspepsia, flulike sx, headache, n/v/d, pharyngitis, **respiratory depression, sleep walking,** somnolence, suicidality, URI
INTERACTIONS Alcohol, CNS depressants
NC/PT Dilute each dose w/60 mL water in child-resistant dosing cup. Give first dose of day when pt still in bed; should stay in bed after taking. Give second dose 2½–4 hr later, w/pt sitting up in bed. After second dose, pt should lie in bed. Not for use in pregnancy (contraceptives advised). Monitor elderly pts for impaired motor/cognitive function. Pt should take safety precautions for CNS effects; avoid eating for at least 2 hr before bed; keep drug secure; avoid alcohol, CNS depressants; report difficulty breathing, confusion, suicidal thoughts.

sodium phenylacetate/ sodium benzoate (Ammonul)

CLASS Ammonia reducer, urea substitute
PREG/CONT C/NA

IND & DOSE Adjunct tx in hyperammonemia, encephalopathy in pts w/enzyme deficiencies associated w/urea cycle. *Adult, child:* Over 20 kg, 55 mL/m². 0–20 kg, 2.5 mL/kg; Give IV through central line w/arginine.
ADJUST DOSE Hepatic, renal impairment
ADV EFF Hyperglycemia, hyperventilation, hypokalemia, mental impairment, **injection-site reaction/ necrosis,** metabolic acidosis, **neurotoxicity, seizures**
NC/PT Monitor plasma ammonia level. Not for use in pregnancy; use caution in breast-feeding. Ammonia level will be monitored; when normalized, dietary protein intake can be increased. Pt should report pain at injection site, numbness/tingling, rapid respirations.

sodium polystyrene sulfonate (Kalexate, Kayexalate, Kionex)

CLASS Potassium-removing resin
PREG/CONT C/NA

IND & DOSE Tx of hyperkalemia. *Adult:* 15–60 g/day PO best given as 15 g daily–qid. May give powder as suspension w/water, syrup (20–100 mL). May introduce into stomach via NG tube. Or, 30–50 g by enema q 6 hr, retained for 30–60 min or as long as possible. *Child:* Give lower doses, using exchange ratio of 1 mEq potassium/g resin as basis for calculation.
ADV EFF Anorexia, constipation, gastric irritation, hypokalemia, n/v
INTERACTIONS Antacids

NC/PT Give resin through plastic stomach tube, or mixed w/diet appropriate for renal failure. Give powder form in oral suspension w/ syrup base to increase palatability. Give enema after cleansing enema; help pt retain for at least 30 min. Monitor serum electrolytes; correct imbalances. If severe constipation, stop drug until function returns; do not use sorbitol, magnesium-containing laxatives. Pt should report confusion, constipation, irregular heartbeat.

sofosbuvir (Sovaldi)

CLASS Hepatitis C drug, nucleoside analog inhibitor
PREG/CONT C/NA

IND & DOSE Tx of hepatitis C, w/peginterferon alfa and ribavirin (genotype 1 or 4) or w/ribavirin (genotypes 2 and 3). *Adult:* 400 mg/ day PO w/peginterferon and ribavirin for 12 wk (genotype 1 or 4); w/ribavirin for 12 wk (genotype 2) or 24 wk (genotype 3).
ADJUST DOSE Hepatitis C virus/ HIV coinfection, pts w/hepatocellular carcinoma awaiting liver transplant
ADV EFF Anemia, bradycardia, fatigue, headache, insomnia, nausea
INTERACTIONS Amiodarone, rifampin, St. John's wort
NC/PT Ensure proper dx. Monthly negative pregnancy test required (use of barrier contraceptives advised for men and women during and for 6 mo after use). Drug is not a cure. Pt should eat small meals for nausea; take analgesic for headache; avoid St. John's wort; consult health care provider before stopping drug; take precautions to avoid spread of disease; report severe headache, urine/ stool color changes.

solifenacin succinate (VESIcare)

CLASS Muscarinic receptor antagonist, urinary antispasmodic
PREG/CONT C/NA

IND & DOSE Tx of overactive bladder. *Adult:* 5–10 mg/day PO swallowed whole w/water.

ADJUST DOSE Moderate to severe hepatic impairment, severe renal impairment

ADV EFF Constipation, dizziness, dry eyes, dry mouth, **prolonged QT**, tachycardia, urine retention

INTERACTIONS CYP3A4 inhibitors, ketoconazole, potassium chloride, QT-prolonging drugs

NC/PT Arrange tx for underlying cause. Not for use in breast-feeding. Pt should empty bladder before each dose if urine retention an issue; swallow tablet whole and not cut, crush, or chew it; use sugarless lozenges for dry mouth, laxatives for constipation; take safety precautions w/dizziness; report inability to void, fever, blurred vision.

somatropin (Genotropin, Humatrope, Norditropin Flexpro, Nutropin, Omnitrope, Saizen, Serostim, Zomactin, Zorbtive)

CLASS Hormone
PREG/CONT C; B (Genotropin, Omnitrope, Saizen, Serostim, Zorbtive)/NA

IND & DOSE (Adult) Tx of GH deficiency, replacement of endogenous GH in adults w/GHD w/multiple hormone deficiencies *(Genotropin, Humatrope, HumatroPen, Norditropin, Nutropin, Nutropin AQ, Omnitrope, Saizen)*. *Genotropin, Omnitrope,* 0.04–0.08 mg/kg/wk subcut divided into seven daily injections. *Humatrope,*

HumatroPen, 0.006–0.0125 mg/kg/day subcut. *Nutropin, Nutropin AQ,* usual, 0.006 mg/kg/day subcut; max, 0.0125 mg/kg/day (over 35 yr), 0.025 mg/kg/day (under 35 yr). *Norditropin,* 0.004–0.016 mg/kg/day subcut. *Saizen,* up to 0.005 mg/kg/day subcut; may increase up to 0.01 mg/kg/day after 4 wk. **Tx of AIDS-wasting or cachexia.** *Serostim,* over 55 kg: 6 mg/day subcut; 45–55 kg: 5 mg/day subcut; 35–45 kg: 4 mg/day subcut; under 35 kg: 0.1 mg/kg/day subcut. **Tx of short bowel syndrome in pts receiving specialized nutritional support** *(Zorbtive).* 0.1 mg/kg/day subcut for 4 wk; max, 8 mg/day.

IND & DOSE (Child) Tx of growth failure related to renal dysfx. 0.35 mg/kg/wk subcut divided into daily doses *(Nutropin, Nutropin AQ).* **Tx of girls w/Turner syndrome.** 0.33 mg/kg/wk divided into six to seven subcut injections *(Genotropin).* Or, up to 0.375 mg/kg/wk subcut divided into equal doses six to seven times/wk *(Humatrope, HumatroPen).* Or, up to 0.067 mg/kg/day subcut *(Norditropin).* Or, up to 0.375 mg/kg/wk subcut divided into equal doses *(Nutropin, Nutropin AQ).* **Long-term tx of growth failure due to Prader-Willi syndrome.** 0.24 mg/kg/wk subcut divided into daily doses *(Genotropin).* **Small for gestational age.** 0.48 mg/kg/wk subcut *(Genotropin).* **Tx of short stature, growth failure in short stature homeobox (SHOX)-containing gene deficiency.** 0.35 mg/kg/wk subcut *(Humatrope, HumatroPen).* **Tx of short stature in Noonan syndrome.** Up to 0.066 mg/kg/day subcut *(Norditropin).* **Long-term tx of idiopathic short stature when epiphyses not closed and diagnostic evaluation excludes other causes treatable by other means.** 0.47 mg/kg/wk subcut divided into six to seven doses *(Genotropin).* Or, 0.18–0.3 mg/kg/wk subcut or IM given in divided doses 3 time/wk *(Humatrope, HumatroPen).* Or, 0.3 mg/kg/wk subcut in divided

daily doses *(Nutropin, Nutropin AQ)*. **Long-term tx of growth failure due to lack of adequate endogenous GH secretion.** 0.18–0.3 mg/kg/wk subcut divided into doses six to seven 7 times/wk *(Humatrope, HumatroPen).* Or, 0.3 mg/kg/wk subcut in divided daily doses *(Nutropin, Nutropin AQ).* Or, 0.16–0.24 mg/kg/wk subcut divided into daily doses *(Genotropin).* Or, 0.16–0.24 mg/kg/wk subcut divided into daily doses *(Omnitrope).* Or, 0.06 mg/kg subcut, IM three times/wk *(Saizen)*. Or, 0.024–0.034 mg/kg subcut, six to seven days/wk *(Norditropin).* Or, up to 0.1 mg/kg subcut three times/wk *(Zomactin).* **Tx of short stature w/no catch-up growth by 2–4 yr.** 0.35 mg/kg/wk subcut injection divided into equal daily doses *(Humatrope, HumatroPen),* 0.024–0.034 mg/kg subcut six to seven times/wk *(Norditropin).*
ADV EFF Development of GH antibodies, headache, hypothyroidism, insulin resistance, **leukemia, neoplasms,** pain, pain at injection site
INTERACTIONS CYP450 inducers/inhibitors
NC/PT Arrange tests for glucose tolerance, thyroid function, growth hormone antibodies; tx as indicated. Ensure cancer screening during tx. Rotate injection sites. Teach proper administration/disposal of needles/syringes. Pt should have frequent blood tests; report increased thirst/voiding, fatigue, cold intolerance.

---

sonidegib (Odomzo)
CLASS Antineoplastic, hedgehog pathway inhibitor
PREG/CONT High risk/NA

BBW Can cause embryo-fetal death, birth defects. Advise contraceptives for women. Advise males of risk through semen and need for condom use during and for at least 8 mo after tx ends.
IND & DOSE Tx of locally advanced basal cell carcinoma recurring after surgery or radiation or if pt not candidate for surgery/radiation. *Adult:* 200 mg/day PO at least 1 hr before or 2 hr after meal.
ADV EFF Abd pain, alopecia, anorexia, fatigue, headache, myalgia, n/v/d, rash, skeletal pain, weight loss
INTERACTIONS CYP3A inducers/inhibitors
NC/PT Rule out pregnancy before use (contraceptives advised). Men should use condoms during and for 8 mo after tx. Not for use in breastfeeding. Pt cannot donate blood during and for 20 mo after last dose. Pt should take on empty stomach 1 hr before or 2 hr after meals; try small, frequent meals; report severe musculoskeletal pain, weight loss.

DANGEROUS DRUG

sorafenib tosylate (Nexavar)
CLASS Antineoplastic, kinase inhibitor
PREG/CONT D/NA

IND & DOSE Tx of advanced renal cell, hepatocellular carcinoma, differentiated thyroid carcinoma refractory to other tx. *Adult:* 400 mg PO bid on empty stomach.
ADV EFF Alopecia, fatigue, **GI perforation, hand-foot syndrome, hemorrhage, hepatitis,** hypertension, **MI,** n/v/d, **prolonged QT,** skin reactions, weight loss, wound-healing complications
INTERACTIONS CYP3A4 inducers, grapefruit juice
NC/PT Obtain baseline, periodic ECG; monitor BP regularly. Not for use in pregnancy (contraceptives advised). Pt should take on empty stomach, avoid grapefruit juice, cover head at temp extremes (hair loss possible), report headache, rash, nonhealing wounds, bleeding.

sotalol hydrochloride
(Betapace, Betapace AF, Sorine)

CLASS Antiarrhythmic, beta blocker

PREG/CONT B/NA

BBW Do not give for ventricular arrhythmias unless pt unresponsive to other antiarrhythmics and has life-threatening ventricular arrhythmia. Monitor response carefully; proarrhythmic effect can be pronounced. Do not initiate tx if baseline QT interval over 450 msec. If QT interval increases to 500 msec or more during tx, reduce dose, extend infusion time, or stop drug.

IND & DOSE *Tx of life-threatening ventricular arrhythmias (Betapace); maint of sinus rhythm after atrial fibrillation (AF) conversion (Betapace AF).* **Adult:** 80 mg PO bid. Adjust gradually, q 3 days, until appropriate response; may need 240–320 mg/day PO *(Betapace);* up to 120 mg bid PO *(Betapace AF).* Or, 75 mg IV over 5 hr bid; may increase in increments of 75 mg/day q 3 days. Range, 225–300 mg once or twice a day for ventricular arrhythmias; 112.5 mg once or twice a day IV for AF if oral not possible. Converting between oral, IV doses: 80 mg oral–75 mg IV; 120 mg oral–112.5 mg IV; 160 mg oral–150 mg IV. *Child over 2 yr w/normal renal function:* 30 mg/m² tid PO. Max, 60 mg/m² tid.

ADJUST DOSE Elderly pts, renal impairment

ADV EFF Bronchospasm, cardiac arrhythmias, constipation, decreased exercise tolerance/libido, ED, flatulence, gastric pain, **HF, laryngospasm,** n/v/d, **pulmonary edema, stroke**

INTERACTIONS Antacids, aspirin, bismuth subsalicylate, clonidine, hormonal contraceptives, insulin, magnesium salicylate, NSAIDs, prazosin, QT-prolonging drugs, sulfinpyrazone

NC/PT Monitor QT interval. Switch from IV to oral as soon as possible. Do not stop abruptly; withdraw gradually. Pt should take on empty stomach, take safety precautions w/dizziness, report difficulty breathing, confusion, edema, chest pain.

spironolactone
(Aldactone)

CLASS Aldosterone antagonist, potassium-sparing diuretic

PREG/CONT C; D (gestational hypertension)/NA

BBW Drug a tumorigen, w/chronic toxicity in rats; avoid unnecessary use.

IND & DOSE *Dx of hyperaldosteronism.* **Adult:** Long test, 400 mg/day PO for 3–4 wk; correction of hypokalemia, hypertension presumptive evidence of primary hyperaldosteronism. Short test, 400 mg/day PO for 4 days. If serum potassium increases but decreases when drug stopped, presumptive dx can be made. *Tx of edema.* **Adult:** 100 mg/day PO; range, 25–200 mg/day. **Tx of hypertension.** *Adult:* 50–100 mg/day PO for at least 2 wk. **Tx of hypokalemia.** *Adult:* 25–100 mg/day PO. *Tx of hyperaldosteronism.* **Adult:** 100–400 mg/day PO in preparation for surgery. **Tx of severe HF.** *Adult:* 25–50 mg/day PO if potassium 5 mEq/L or less, creatinine 2.5 mg/dL or less.

ADV EFF Cramping, diarrhea, dizziness, drowsiness, gynecomastia, headache, hirsutism, **hyperkalemia,** voice deepening

INTERACTIONS ACE inhibitors, anticoagulants, antihypertensives, ganglionic blockers, licorice, potassium-rich diet, salicylates

NC/PT Monitor electrolytes periodically. Pt should avoid potassium-rich foods, excessive licorice intake; take safety precautions w/dizziness; weigh self daily, report change of 3 lb or more/day; report swelling, muscle cramps/weakness.

stavudine (d4T) (Zerit)

CLASS Antiviral, nucleoside reverse transcriptase inhibitor
PREG/CONT C/NA

BBW Monitor closely for pancreatitis during tx; fatal, nonfatal pancreatitis has occurred. Monitor LFTs; lactic acidosis, severe hepatomegaly possible.

IND & DOSE Tx of HIV-1 infection w/other antivirals. *Adult, child over 13 days:* 60 kg or more, 40 mg PO q 12 hr; 30–less than 60 kg, 30 mg PO q 12 hr; under 30 kg, 1 mg/kg/dose PO q 12 hr. *Child birth–13 days:* 0.5 mg/kg/dose PO q 12 hr.

ADJUST DOSE Renal impairment
ADV EFF Agranulocytopenia, asthenia, dizziness, fever, GI pain, headache, **hepatomegaly w/steatosis, lactic acidosis,** n/v/d, **pancreatitis,** paresthesia
INTERACTIONS Didanosine, doxorubicin, ribavirin, zidovudine
NC/PT Monitor LFTs, pancreatic function, neurologic status before, q 2 wk during tx. Always give w/other antivirals. Not for use in pregnancy (barrier contraceptives advised). Pt should take precautions to prevent spread (drug not a cure), avoid infections, take safety precautions for CNS effects, report numbness/tingling, severe headache, difficulty breathing.

streptomycin sulfate (generic)

CLASS Antibiotic
PREG/CONT D/NA

BBW Risk of severe neurotoxic, nephrotoxic reactions; monitor closely. Do not use w/other neurotoxic, nephrotoxic drugs.

IND & DOSE Tx of subacute bacterial endocarditis, resistant TB. *Adult:* 15 mg/kg/day IM, or 25–30 mg/kg IM two or three times/wk. *Child:* 20–40 mg/kg/day IM or 25–30 mg/kg/IM two or three times/wk. Tx of tularemia. *Adult:* 1–2 g/day IM for 7–14 days. Tx of plaque. *Adult:* 2 g/day IM in two divided doses for at least 10 days.

ADJUST DOSE Renal impairment
ADV EFF Dizziness, hearing loss, injection-site reactions, **renal toxicity, respiratory paralysis,** ringing in ears
INTERACTIONS Diuretics
NC/PT Monitor renal function, hearing/balance. Monitor injection sites. Teach appropriate administration/disposal of needles/syringes. Ensure pt w/TB is also receiving other drugs. Not for use in pregnancy (barrier contraceptives advised)/breast-feeding. Pt should take safety precautions for CNS effects, report difficulty breathing, dizziness, edema, hearing changes.

streptozocin (Zanosar)

CLASS Alkylating drug, antineoplastic
PREG/CONT D/NA

BBW Monitor for renal, liver toxicity. Special drug handling required.
IND & DOSE Tx of metastatic islet cell carcinoma of pancreas. *Adult:* 500 mg/m² IV for 5 consecutive days q 6 wk; or 1,000 mg/m² IV once/wk for 2 wk, then increase to 1,500 mg/m² IV each wk.

ADJUST DOSE Renal impairment
ADV EFF Bone marrow suppression, dizziness, drowsiness, glucose intolerance, n/v/d, **severe to fatal renal toxicity**
INTERACTIONS Doxorubicin
NC/PT Monitor LFTs, renal function closely. Handle drug as biohazard. Monitor CBC to determine dose. Give antiemetics for n/v. Not for use in pregnancy/breast-feeding. Pt should avoid exposure to infection, maintain nutrition, report unusual bleeding/bruising, increased thirst, swelling.

succimer (Chemet)
CLASS Antidote, chelate
PREG/CONT C/NA

IND & DOSE Tx of lead poisoning in child w/blood level over 45 mcg/dL. *Child:* 10 mg/kg or 350 mg/m² PO q 8 hr for 5 days; reduce to 10 mg/kg or 350 mg/m² PO q 12 hr for 2 wk (tx runs for 19 days).
ADV EFF Back pain, dizziness, drowsiness, flank pain, headache, n/v, rash, urination difficulties
INTERACTIONS EDTA
NC/PT Monitor serum lead level, transaminase levels before, q 2 wk during tx. Continue tx for full 19 days. Have pt swallow capsule whole; if unable to swallow capsule, open and sprinkle contents on soft food or give by spoon followed by fruit drink. Pt should maintain hydration, report difficulty breathing, tremors.

sucralfate (Carafate)
CLASS Antiulcer drug
PREG/CONT B/NA

IND & DOSE Tx, maint of duodenal, esophageal ulcers. *Adult:* 1 g PO qid on empty stomach for 4–8 wk; maint, 1 g PO bid.
ADV EFF Constipation, dizziness, dry mouth, gastric discomfort, rash, vertigo
INTERACTIONS Antacids, ciprofloxacin, digoxin, ketoconazole, levothyroxine, norfloxacin, penicillamine, phenytoin, quinidine, tetracycline, theophylline, warfarin
NC/PT Pt should take on empty stomach, 1 hr before or 2 hr after meals, and at bedtime; avoid antacids within 30 min of sucralfate; take safety precautions for CNS effects; use laxative for constipation; report severe gastric pain.

---

sufentanil citrate
(Sufenta)
CLASS Opioid agonist analgesic
PREG/CONT C/C-II

IND & DOSE Adjunct to general anesthesia. *Adult:* Initially, 1–2 mcg/kg IV. Maint, 10–25 mcg; max, 1 mcg/kg/hr of expected surgical time. Anesthesia. *Adult:* Initially, 8–30 mcg/kg IV; supplement w/doses of 0.5–10 mcg/kg IV. Max, 30 mcg/kg for procedure. Give w/oxygen, skeletal muscle relaxant. *Child 2–12 yr:* Initially, 10–25 mcg/kg IV; supplement w/ doses of 25–50 mcg IV. Give w/ oxygen, skeletal muscle relaxant. **Epidural analgesia.** *Adult:* 10–15 mcg via epidural administration w/10 mL bupivacaine 0.125%. May repeat twice at 1-hr or longer intervals (total, three doses).
ADV EFF Arrhythmias, bradycardia, bronchospasm, cardiac arrest, clamminess, confusion, constipation, dizziness, dry mouth, headache, floating feeling, laryngospasm, lethargy, light-headedness, n/v, sedation, shock, tachycardia, urinary hesitancy, urine retention, vertigo
INTERACTIONS Barbiturates beta blockers, calcium channel blockers, general anesthetics, grapefruit juice, hypnotics, opiate agonists, sedatives
NC/PT Protect vials from light. Provide opioid antagonist. Have equipment for assisted, controlled respiration on hand during parenteral administration. Give to breast-feeding women 4–6 hr before next feeding. Pt should avoid grapefruit juice, take safety precautions for CNS effects, report difficulty breathing, palpitations. Name confusion between sufentanil and fentanyl; use extreme caution.

sugammadex (Bridion)

CLASS Modified gamma
cyclodextrin, reversal agent
PREG/CONT Low risk/NA

IND & DOSE Reversal of neuromuscular blockade induced by
rocuronium/vecuronium in adults
undergoing surgery. *Adult:* For ro-
curonium/vecuronium: 4 mg/kg IV as
a single bolus, based on twitch response; 2 mg/kg if response is faster.
Rocuronium only: 16 mg/kg IV as a
single bolus if there is need to reverse
blockade within 3 min after single
dose of rocuronium.
ADJUST DOSE Severe renal
impairment
ADV EFF Bradycardia, extremity
pain, headache, hypotension, n/v/d,
pain
INTERACTIONS Hormonal contraceptives, toremifene
NC/PT Monitor cardiac/respiratory
function. Pt should be on ventilator
support. Use of anticholinergic for
bradycardia is recommended. Twitch
response should determine success
and dosing. Pt should use second
method of contraception (hormonal
contraceptives may be ineffective)
and continue for 7 days post drug
administration.

sulfADIAZINE (generic)

CLASS Sulfonamide antibiotic
PREG/CONT C; D (labor &
delivery)/NA

IND & DOSE Tx of acute infections
caused by susceptible bacteria
strains. *Adult:* 2–4 g PO, then 2–
4 g/day PO in three to six divided doses.
Child over 2 mo: 75 mg/kg PO, then
150 mg/kg/day PO in four to six
divided doses; max 6 g/day Tx of
toxoplasmosis. *Adult:* 1–1.5 g PO
w/pyrimethamine for 3–4 wk. *Child
over 2 mo:* 100–200 mg/kg/day PO
w/pyrimethamine for 3–4 wk. Suppressive, maint tx in HIV pts. *Adult:*
0.5–1 g PO q 6 hr w/oral pyrimethamine, leucovorin. *Infant, child:* 85–
120 mg/kg/day PO in two to four
divided doses w/oral pyrimethamine,
leucovorin. *Adolescent:* 0.5–1 g PO q
6 hr w/oral pyrimethamine, leucovorin.
Px of recurrent attacks of rheumatic
fever. *Adult:* Over 30 kg, 1 g/day PO.
Under 30 kg, 0.5 g/day PO.
ADV EFF Abd pain, crystalluria,
headache, hematuria, **hepatocellular
necrosis**, n/v, photosensitivity, rash,
Stevens-Johnson syndrome
INTERACTIONS Acetohexamide,
chlorpropamide, cyclosporine, glyburide, glipizide, oral anticoagulants,
phenytoin, tolbutamide, tolazamide
NC/PT Culture before tx. Pt should
take on empty stomach 1 hr before or
2 hr after meals w/full glass of water;
drink 8 glasses of water/day; avoid
sun exposure; take safety precautions
for CNS effects; report bloody urine,
ringing in ears, difficulty breathing.
Name confusion between sulfadiazine
and *Silvadene* (silver sulfadiazine);
use caution.

sulfasalazine (Azulfidine)

CLASS Anti-inflammatory,
antirheumatic, sulfonamide
PREG/CONT B/NA

IND & DOSE Tx of ulcerative colitis;
to prolong time between acute attacks. *Adult:* 3–4 g/day PO in evenly
divided doses. Maint, 2 g/day PO in
evenly spaced doses (500 mg qid);
max, 4 g/day. *Child 6 yr and over:*
40–60 mg/kg/24 hr PO in three to six
divided doses. Maint, 30 mg/kg/24 hr
PO in four equally divided doses;
max, 2 g/day.
ADV EFF Abd pain, agranulocytosis,
aplastic anemia, crystalluria, headache, hematuria, **hepatocellular
necrosis**, n/v, paresthesia, photosensitivity, Stevens-Johnson syndrome,
thrombocytopenia
INTERACTIONS Digoxin, folate
NC/PT Pt should take w/meals;
swallow DR tablet whole and not cut,

crush, or chew it; drink 8 glasses of water/day; avoid sun exposure; take safety precautions for CNS effects; report difficulty breathing, bloody urine, rash.

sulindac (Clinoril)
CLASS NSAID
PREG/CONT B (1st, 2nd trimesters); D (3rd trimester)/NA

BBW Increased risk of CV events, GI bleeding; monitor accordingly. Contraindicated for periop pain in CABG surgery.
IND & DOSE Tx of pain of rheumatoid arthritis, osteoarthritis, ankylosing spondylitis. *Adult:* 150 mg PO bid. **Tx of acute painful shoulder, acute gouty arthritis.** *Adult:* 200 mg PO bid for 7–14 days (acute painful shoulder), 7 days (acute gouty arthritis).
ADJUST DOSE Hepatic, renal impairment
ADV EFF Anaphylactoid reactions to fatal anaphylactic shock, bone marrow suppression, constipation, dizziness, drowsiness, dyspepsia, edema, fatigue, GI pain, headache, insomnia, **HF,** n/v, vision disturbances
INTERACTIONS Beta blockers, diuretics, lithium
NC/PT Pt should take w/food, milk if GI upset, take safety precautions for CNS effects, report swelling, difficulty breathing, black tarry stools.

sumatriptan succinate (Alsuma, Imitrex, Onzetra Xsail, Zecuity)
CLASS Antimigraine drug, triptan
PREG/CONT C/NA

IND & DOSE Tx of acute migraine attacks. *Adult:* 25, 50, or 100 mg PO; may repeat in 2 hr or more. Max, 200 mg/day. Or, 6 mg subcut; may repeat in 1 hr. Max, 12 mg/24 hr. Or, 5, 10, or 20 mg into one nostril, or

10 mg divided into two doses (5 mg each), one in each nostril, repeated q 2 hr; max, 40 mg/24 hr. Or, 22 mg nasal powder via nosepiece in each nostril (each side delivers 11 mg [*Onzetra Xsail*]); max, 44 mg/day. Battery-powered transdermal patch delivers 6.5 mg over 4 hr. **Tx of cluster headaches.** *Adult:* 6 mg subcut; may repeat in 1 hr. Max, 12 mg/24 hr.
ADJUST DOSE Hepatic impairment
ADV EFF Altered BP, arrhythmias, burning/tingling sensation, chest pain/pressure, dizziness, feeling of tightness, GI ischemic reactions, headache, injection-site reactions, **MI, serotonin syndrome, shock**
INTERACTIONS Ergots, MAOIs, St. John's wort
NC/PT For tx, not px, of acute migraines. May repeat dose in 2 hr if needed. Teach proper administration of each form; use of Xsail powdered nasal delivery device; disposal of needles/syringes for subcut use. Not for use in pregnancy (barrier contraceptives advised). Pt should continue migraine comfort measures, take safety precautions for CNS effects, avoid St. John's wort, report chest pain, swelling, numbness/tingling.

DANGEROUS DRUG

sunitinib (Sutent)
CLASS Antineoplastic, kinase inhibitor
PREG/CONT D/NA

BBW Risk of serious to fatal hepatotoxicity; monitor LFTs closely.
IND & DOSE Tx of GI stromal tumor, advanced renal cell carcinoma. *Adult:* 50 mg/day PO for 4 wk, then 2 wk of rest. Repeat cycle. **Tx of progressive neuroendocrine cancerous pancreatic tumors.** 37.5 mg/day PO continuously.
ADJUST DOSE Hepatic impairment
ADV EFF Abd pain, arthralgia, asthenia, anorexia, **cardiotoxicity,** constipation, cough, **dermatologic toxicity to Stevens-Johnson syndrome,**

dyspnea, edema, fatigue, fever, **hemorrhage, hepatotoxicity,** hypoglycemia, **hypertension,** mucositis, n/v/d, **prolonged QT,** proteinuria, skin color changes, **thyroid dysfx,** thrombotic microangiopathy

INTERACTIONS CYP3A4 inducers/inhibitors; grapefruit juice

NC/PT Obtain baseline, periodic ECG, BP. Monitor LFTs, renal function. Not for use in pregnancy (barrier contraceptives advised)/breast-feeding. Pt should mark calendar for tx days, take safety precaution for CNS effects, report unusual bleeding, palpitations, urine/stool color changes, rash, chest pain.

---

suvorexant (Belsomra)
CLASS Insomnia drug, orexin receptor antagonist
PREG/CONT C/NA

IND & DOSE Tx of insomnia w/ difficulty w/sleep onset or maint.
Adult: 10 mg PO within 30 min of going to bed w/at least 7 hr til planned awakening; may increase to 20 mg/day.

ADJUST DOSE Hepatic impairment
ADV EFF Daytime somnolence, depression, respiratory impairment, sleep driving, sleep paralysis
INTERACTIONS CYP3A4 inducers/inhibitors; digoxin
NC/PT Ensure timing of dose; allow 7 hr for sleep. Not for use in pregnancy; use w/caution in breast-feeding. Pt should use safety precautions w/ daytime somnolence, sleep driving, CNS effects; report cognitive impairment, difficulty breathing.

---

tacrolimus (Prograf, Protopic)
CLASS Immunosuppressant
PREG/CONT C/NA

BBW High risk of infection, lymphoma. Protect from infection; monitor closely. ER form not recommended for liver transplants; risk of death in female liver transplant pts.

IND & DOSE Px of rejection after kidney transplant. *Adult:* 0.2 mg/kg/day PO divided q 12 hr, or 0.03–0.05 mg/kg/day as continuous IV infusion. Or, 0.1 mg/kg/day PO ER capsule preop, 0.2 mg/kg/day PO ER capsule postop; if using basiliximab, 0.15 mg/kg/day PO ER capsule. Px of rejection after liver transplant. *Adult:* 0.10–0.15 mg/kg/day PO divided q 12 hr; give initial dose no sooner than 6 hr after transplant. Or, 0.03–0.05 mg/kg/day as continuous IV infusion. *Child:* 0.15–0.20 mg/kg/day PO, or 0.03–0.05 mg/kg/day IV infusion. Px of rejection after heart transplant. *Adult:* 0.075 mg/kg/day PO or IV in two divided doses q 12 hr; give first dose no sooner than 6 hr after transplant. Tx of atopic dermatitis. *Adult:* Apply thin layer 0.03% or 0.1% ointment to affected area bid; rub in gently, completely. *Child 2–15 yr:* Apply thin layer 0.03% ointment bid.
ADJUST DOSE Hepatic, renal impairment
ADV EFF Abd pain, **anaphylaxis,** constipation, diarrhea, fever, **GI perforation,** headache, **hepatotoxicity,** hyperglycemia, **infections, RPLS, prolonged QT,** renal impairment
INTERACTIONS Calcium channel blockers, carbamazepine, cimetidine, clarithromycin, cyclosporine (contraindicated), erythromycin, grapefruit juice, live vaccines, metoclopramide, nicardipine, phenobarbital, phenytoin, QT-prolonging drugs, rifampicin, sirolimus (contraindicated), statins, St. John's wort
NC/PT Check drug regimen; many interactions possible. Ensure concurrent use of corticosteroids in liver transplants; use w/mycophenolate or azathioprine in heart/kidney transplants. Monitor LFTs, serum tacrolimus. Use IV route only if PO not possible; switch to PO as soon as possible. Not for use in pregnancy. Pt should avoid sun exposure (topical form); infection; avoid grapefruit juice,

St. John's wort, live vaccines; report unusual bleeding, signs of infection, all drugs being taken, severe GI pain

tadalafil (Adcirca, Cialis)
CLASS Impotence drug, phosphodiesterase-5 inhibitor
PREG/CONT B/NA

IND & DOSE Tx of ED, BPH w/ED (*Cialis*). *Adult:* 10 mg PO before anticipated sexual activity; range, 5–20 mg PO. Limit use to once/day. Or, 2.5–5 mg/day PO without regard to timing of sexual activity. **Tx of pulmonary arterial hypertension** (*Adcirca*). 40 mg/day PO.
ADJUST DOSE Hepatic, renal impairment; tx w/CYP3A4 inhibitors
ADV EFF Diarrhea, dizziness, dyspepsia, dry mouth, flulike sx, flushing, headache, **MI, priapism, Stevens-Johnson syndrome,** vision loss
INTERACTIONS Alcohol, alpha blockers, erythromycin, grapefruit juice, indinavir, itraconazole, ketoconazole, nitrates, rifampin, ritonavir; riociguat (contraindicated)
NC/PT Ensure proper dx. For pulmonary hypertension, pt should monitor activity and limitations. For ED, does not protect against STDs, will not work in absence of sexual stimulation. Pt should not use w/nitrates, antihypertensives, grapefruit juice, alcohol; report vision changes, loss of vision, erection lasting more than 4 hr, sudden hearing loss.

talc, USP (Sterile Talc Powder)
CLASS Sclerosing drug
PREG/CONT B/NA

IND & DOSE To decrease recurrence of malignant pleural effusion. *Adult:* 5 g in 50–100 mL sodium chloride injection injected into chest tube after pleural fluid drained; clamp chest tube, have pt change positions

for 2 hr; unclamp chest tube, continue external suction.
ADV EFF Acute pneumonitis, dyspnea, hypotension, localized bleeding, **MI, RDS,** tachycardia
NC/PT Ensure proper chest tube placement, pt positioning, draining. Pt should report difficulty breathing, chest pain.

taliglucerase alfa (Elelyso)
CLASS Enzyme
PREG/CONT B/NA

IND & DOSE Long-term enzyme replacement tx for adult, child w/ type I Gaucher disease. *Adult, child 4 yr and over:* 60 units/kg IV q other wk as 60- to 120-min infusion. If switching from imiglucerase, start at unit/kg dose used in last imiglucerase dose.
ADV EFF Anaphylaxis, arthralgia, back pain, headache, influenza, **infusion reaction,** pain, pharyngitis, throat infection, URI
NC/PT Give IV only. Monitor for infusion reactions; decrease infusion rate, consider use of antipyretics, antihistamines. Pt should mark calendar for infusion dates; report difficulty breathing, fever, chest/back pain, rash.

talimogene laherparepvec (Imlygic)
CLASS Oncolytic viral therapy
PREG/CONT High risk/NA

IND & DOSE Local tx of unresectable cutaneous, subcut, nodal lesions in melanoma recurrent after surgery. *Adult:* Initially, up to 4 mL at concentration of 10^6 plaque-forming units (pfu)/mL injected into lesions; subsequent doses up to 4 mL at concentration of 10^8 pfu/mL.
ADV EFF Chills, fatigue, fever, flulike sx, herpetic infections, injection-site reaction, plasmacytoma at injection site

NC/PT Accidental drug exposure may lead to herpetic infection; should not be prepared or handled by immunocompromised or pregnant providers. Providers and pt contacts should avoid exposure to dressings or bodily fluids of pt receiving drug. Provide proper treatment to pt who develops herpetic infections. Monitor injection site; treat appropriately if infection, delayed healing occurs. Monitor pt for plasmacytoma at injection site. Not for use in pregnancy (contraceptives advised)/breast-feeding. Pt should keep injection sites covered; wear gloves when changing dressings; avoid touching or scratching injection sites; caution pregnant or immunocompromised contacts to avoid dressings, bodily fluids, injection sites; report pain, signs of infection at injection site, continued fever.

DANGEROUS DRUG

tamoxifen citrate
(Soltamox)

CLASS Antiestrogen, antineoplastic
PREG/CONT D/NA

BBW Alert women w/ductal carcinoma in situ (DCIS) and those at high risk for breast cancer of risks of serious to potentially fatal drug effects, including stroke, embolic events, uterine malignancies; discuss benefits/risks.

IND & DOSE Tx of metastatic breast cancer. *Adult:* 20–40 mg/day PO for 5 yr. Give doses of more than 20 mg/day in divided doses, a.m. and p.m. **To reduce breast cancer incidence in high-risk women; tx of DCIS.** *Adult:* 20 mg/day PO for 5 yr.
ADV EFF Corneal changes, depression, dizziness, **DVT**, edema, hot flashes, n/v, **PE**, rash, **stroke**, vaginal bleeding
INTERACTIONS Bromocriptine, cytotoxic agents, grapefruit juice, oral anticoagulants

NC/PT Monitor CBC periodically. Not for use in pregnancy (barrier contraceptives advised). Pt should have regular gynecologic exams, take safety precautions for CNS effects, report leg pain/swelling, chest pain, difficulty breathing.

---

tamsulosin hydrochloride (Flomax)

CLASS Alpha-adrenergic blocker, BPH drug
PREG/CONT B/NA

IND & DOSE Tx of s&sx of BPH. *Adult:* 0.4–0.8 mg PO daily 30 min after same meal each day.
ADV EFF Abnormal ejaculation, dizziness, headache, insomnia, intraop floppy iris syndrome, orthostatic hypotension, priapism, somnolence
INTERACTIONS Alpha-adrenergic antagonists, avanafil, cimetidine, saw palmetto, sildenafil, tadalafil, vardenafil
NC/PT Ensure accurate dx. Alert surgeon; increased risk of intraop floppy iris syndrome w/cataract/glaucoma surgery. Monitor for prostate cancer. Pt should swallow capsule whole and not cut, crush, or chew it; change position slowly to avoid dizziness; not take w/ED drugs; take safety precautions for CNS effects; avoid saw palmetto; report fainting, worsening of sx, prolonged erection. Name confusion between *Flomax* (tamsulosin) and *Fosamax* (alendronate); use caution.

---

tapentadol (Nucynta, Nucynta ER)

CLASS Norepinephrine reuptake inhibitor, opioid receptor analgesic
PREG/CONT C/C-II

BBW Risk of abuse; limit use w/hx of addiction. Risk of fatal respiratory depression, highest at start and w/ dose changes; monitor accordingly.

Accidental ingestion of ER form can cause fatal overdose in child; secure drug. Risk of fatally high tapentadol level w/alcohol; pt should avoid alcohol, all medications containing alcohol.

IND & DOSE Relief of moderate to severe pain. *Adult:* 50–100 mg PO q 4–6 hr. Mgt of moderate to severe chronic pain when round-the-clock opioid use needed (ER form). *Adult:* 100–250 mg PO bid. Reduce initial dose to 50 mg in analgesic-naive pt; max, 500 mg/day. Relief of pain of diabetic peripheral neuropathy (*Nucynta ER*). *Adult:* 50 mg PO bid.

ADJUST DOSE Elderly, debilitated pts; hepatic impairment

ADV EFF Dizziness, drowsiness, headache, n/v, respiratory depression, **serotonin syndrome, seizures,** withdrawal sx

INTERACTIONS Alcohol, CNS depressants, general anesthetics, hypnotics, MAOIs, opioids, phenothiazines, sedatives, St. John's wort, SSRIs, TCAs, triptans

NC/PT Assess pain before, periodically during tx. Withdraw gradually. Do not give within 14 days of MAOIs. Pt should avoid alcohol, St. John's wort; if breast-feeding, take at least 3–4 hr before next feeding; take safety precautions for CNS effects; report difficulty breathing, rash.

---

tasimelteon (Hetlioz)
CLASS Melatonin receptor agonist
PREG/CONT C/NA

IND & DOSE Tx of non-24 hr-sleep-wake disorder in totally blind pts. *Adult:* 20 mg before bedtime at same time each night.

ADJUST DOSE Severe hepatic impairment, smokers

ADV EFF Elevated alanine aminotransferase, headache, nightmares, somnolence, URI, UTI

INTERACTIONS Fluvoxamine, ketoconazole, rifampin

NC/PT Monitor LFTs. Pt should swallow capsule whole, not cut, crush, or chew it; avoid pregnancy/breast-feeding; limit activities after taking drug; take safety measures w/somnolence; report changes in behavior, severe somnolence.

---

tbo-filgrastim (Granix)
CLASS Leukocyte growth factor
PREG/CONT C/NA

IND & DOSE To reduce duration of severe neutropenia w/nonmyeloid malignancies in pts receiving myelosuppressive anticancer drugs. *Adult:* 5 mcg/kg/day subcut, first dose no earlier than 24 hr after myelosuppressive chemotherapy. Continue until neutrophil count has recovered to normal range.

ADV EFF Acute respiratory distress syndrome, allergic reactions, bone pain, capillary leak syndrome, sickle cell crisis, splenic rupture

NC/PT Monitor CBC, respiratory function. Do not give within 24 hr before scheduled chemotherapy. Stop if sickle cell crisis suspected. Use w/caution in pregnancy/breast-feeding. Teach proper subcut injection technique, proper disposal of needles/syringes. Pt should report difficulty breathing, edema, rash.

---

tedizolid (Sivextro)
CLASS Antibacterial, oxazolidinone
PREG/CONT C/NA

IND & DOSE Tx of acute skin, skin-structure infections caused by susceptible bacteria. *Adult:* 200 mg/day PO, or IV infused over 1 hr for 6 days.

ADV EFF CDAD, dizziness, headache, n/v/d

NC/PT Perform culture/sensitivity to ensure proper use. Safety for use in neutropenia not known; consider other tx in pts w/neutropenia. Use w/caution in pregnancy/breast-feeding.

Pt should complete full course; use safety precautions w/dizziness; report diarrhea w/blood or mucus.

teduglutide (Gattex)
CLASS Glucagon-like peptide-2
PREG/CONT B/NA

IND & DOSE Tx of adults w/short bowel syndrome who are dependent on parenteral support. *Adult:* 0.05 mg/kg subcut.
ADJUST DOSE Renal impairment
ADV EFF Abd pain/distention, **biliary and pancreatic disease, fluid overload,** headache, **intestinal obstruction, neoplastic growth,** n/v
INTERACTIONS Oral drugs
NC/PT Subcut use only. Single-use vial; discard within 3 hr of reconstitution. Ensure complete colonoscopy, polyp removal before tx and at least q 5 yr. Rotate injection sites. Monitor for fluid overload; support as needed. Oral drugs may not be absorbed; monitor pt, consider need for oral drug dosage adjustment. Monitor pancreatic function. Pt should learn preparation of subcut injection, disposal of needles/syringes; rotate injection sites; schedule periodic blood tests; report severe abd pain, chest pain, swelling in extremities, severe epigastric pain, difficulty swallowing.

telavancin (Vibativ)
CLASS Antibiotic, lipoglycopeptide
PREG/CONT C/NA

BBW Fetal risk; women of childbearing age should have serum pregnancy test before start of tx. Avoid use in pregnancy; advise contraceptive use. Nephrotoxicity possible, not for use in severe renal impairment; balance risk in moderate impairment. Monitor renal function in all pts.
IND & DOSE Tx of complicated skin, skin-structure infections caused by susceptible strains of gram-positive organisms. Tx of hospital-acquired and ventilator-assisted pneumonia caused by *Staphylococcus aureus* when other tx not suitable. *Adult:* 10 mg/kg IV infused over 60 min once q 24 hr for 7–14 days.
ADJUST DOSE Renal impairment
ADV EFF Bleeding, CDAD, dizziness, foamy urine, **nephrotoxicity,** n/v, **prolonged QT, red man syndrome** (w/rapid infusion), taste disturbance
INTERACTIONS Heparin, nephrotoxic drugs, QT-prolonging drugs
NC/PT Culture before tx. Infuse over at least 60 min. Monitor clotting time, renal function periodically. Not for use in pregnancy (contraceptives advised)/breast-feeding. Negative pregnancy test needed before tx. Urine may become foamy. Pt should take safety precautions for CNS effects, report fever, unusual bleeding, irregular heartbeat.

telbivudine (Tyzeka)
CLASS Antiviral, nucleoside
PREG/CONT B/NA

BBW Monitor for myopathy, severe lactic acidosis w/hepatic failure w/ steatosis, hepatitis B exacerbation w/drug discontinuation.
IND & DOSE Tx of chronic hepatitis B. *Adult, child over 16 yr:* 600 mg/day PO w/ or without food.
ADJUST DOSE Renal impairment
ADV EFF Abd pain, arthralgia, back pain, cough, diarrhea, dyspepsia, headache, **hepatitis B exacerbation, hepatomegaly w/steatosis,** insomnia, **myopathy, nephrotoxicity, peripheral neuropathy**
INTERACTIONS Nephrotoxic drugs, peginterferon alfa-2a
NC/PT Monitor LFTs, renal function. Not for use in pregnancy (contraceptives advised)/breast-feeding. Pt should take safety precautions for CNS effects, report unusual bleeding, urine/stool color changes, numbness/ tingling.

telithromycin (Ketek)
CLASS Ketolide antibiotic
PREG/CONT C/NA

BBW Contraindicated w/myasthenia gravis; life-threatening respiratory failure possible.
IND & DOSE Tx of mild to moderately severe community-acquired pneumonia caused by susceptible strains. *Adult:* 800 mg/day PO for 7–10 days.
ADJUST DOSE Renal impairment
ADV EFF **Anaphylaxis**, CDAD, diarrhea, dizziness, headache, **hepatic impairment**, n/v, **prolonged QT, pseudomembranous colitis**, superinfections, visual disturbances
INTERACTIONS Serious reactions w/atorvastatin, lovastatin, midazolam, pimozide, simvastatin; avoid these combinations. Also, carbamazepine, digoxin, metoprolol, phenobarbital, phenytoin, rifampin, theophylline
NC/PT Culture before tx. Monitor LFTs. Treat superinfections. Pt should swallow tablet whole and not cut, crush, or chew it; take safety precautions w/dizziness; avoid quickly looking between distant and nearby objects (if visual difficulties); report bloody diarrhea, difficulty breathing, unusual bleeding.

telmisartan (Micardis)
CLASS Antihypertensive, ARB
PREG/CONT D/NA

BBW Rule out pregnancy before tx. Suggest barrier contraceptives during tx; fetal injury, deaths have occurred.
IND & DOSE Tx of hypertension. *Adult:* 40 mg/day PO. Range, 20–80 mg/day; max, 80 mg/day. **To reduce CV risk in high-risk pts unable to take ACE inhibitors.** *Adult:* 80 mg/day PO.
ADJUST DOSE Hepatic/renal impairment
ADV EFF Dermatitis, dizziness, flatulence, gastritis, headache,

hyperkalemia, hypotension, lightheadedness, palpitations, rash
INTERACTIONS ACE inhibitors, ARBs, digoxin, potassium-sparing diuretics, renin inhibitors
NC/PT Monitor renal function, LFTs, potassium level. Monitor BP carefully. Alert surgeon; volume replacement may be needed postop. Not for use in pregnancy (contraceptives advised)/breast-feeding. Pt should take safety precautions for CNS effects, report fever, severe dizziness.

temazepam (Restoril)
CLASS Benzodiazepine, sedative-hypnotic
PREG/CONT X/C-IV

BBW Taper dosage gradually after long-term use; risk of refractory seizures.
IND & DOSE Short-term tx of insomnia. *Adult:* 15–30 mg PO before bedtime for 7–10 days; 7.5 mg may be sufficient for some pts.
ADJUST DOSE Elderly, debilitated pts
ADV EFF **Anaphylaxis, angioedema,** bradycardia, confusion, constipation, **CV collapse,** diarrhea, drowsiness, drug dependence, fatigue, hiccups, nervousness, tachycardia, urticaria
INTERACTIONS Alcohol, aminophylline, CNS depressants, dyphylline, theophylline
NC/PT Not for use in pregnancy (contraceptives advised). Pt should take for no longer than 7–10 days, avoid alcohol, take safety precautions for CNS effects, report difficulty breathing, face/eye swelling, continued sleep disorders.

DANGEROUS DRUG

temozolomide (Temodar)
CLASS Alkylating agent, antineoplastic
PREG/CONT D/NA

IND & DOSE Tx of refractory astrocytoma. *Adult:* 150 mg/m²/day PO or

IV for 5 consecutive days for 28-day tx cycle. **Tx of glioblastoma multiforme. Adult:** 75 mg/m²/day PO or IV for 42 days w/focal radiation therapy; then six cycles: cycle 1, 150 mg/m²/day PO, IV for 5 days then 23 days rest; cycles 2–6, 200 mg/m²/day PO or IV for 5 days then 23 days rest.
ADJUST DOSE Elderly pts; hepatic, renal impairment
ADV EFF Alopecia, amnesia, **bone marrow suppression, cancer,** constipation, dizziness, headache, **hepatotoxicity,** insomnia, n/v/d, **PJP,** rash, **seizures**
INTERACTIONS Valproic acid
NC/PT Monitor LFTs. Monitor CBC before each dose; adjustment may be needed. Not for use in pregnancy (contraceptives advised)/breast-feeding. Pt should take safety precautions for CNS effects, avoid exposure to infection, report unusual bleeding, difficulty breathing.

DANGEROUS DRUG

temsirolimus (Torisel)
CLASS Antineoplastic, kinase inhibitor
PREG/CONT D/NA

IND & DOSE Tx of advanced renal cell carcinoma. Adult: 25 mg/wk IV infused over 30–60 min; give 30 min after giving prophylactic diphenhydramine 25–50 mg IV.
ADJUST DOSE Elderly pts; hepatic impairment
ADV EFF Abd pain, alopecia, body aches, **bowel perforation,** confusion, constipation, drowsiness, **hepatic impairment,** hyperglycemia, **hypersensitivity/infusion reactions, infections, interstitial pneumonitis, nephrotoxicity,** n/v/d, painful urination, rash, wound-healing problems
INTERACTIONS CYP3A4 inducers/inhibitors, grapefruit juice, live vaccines, St. John's wort
NC/PT Monitor LFTs, renal/respiratory function. Premedicate to decrease infusion reaction risk. Not for use in

pregnancy (barrier contraceptives advised)/breast-feeding. Pt should mark calendar of tx days; cover head at temp extremes (hair loss possible); take safety precautions for CNS effects; avoid St. John's wort, grapefruit juice; report difficulty breathing, severe abd pain, urine/stool color changes.

DANGEROUS DRUG

tenecteplase (TNKase)
CLASS Thrombolytic enzyme
PREG/CONT C/NA

BBW Arrange to stop concurrent heparin, tenecteplase if serious bleeding occurs.
IND & DOSE To reduce mortality associated w/acute MI. Adult: Initiate tx as soon as possible after onset of acute MI. Give as IV bolus over 5 sec. Dose based on weight (max, 50 mg/dose): 90 kg or more, 50 mg; 80–89 kg, 45 mg; 70–79 kg, 40 mg; 60–69 kg, 35 mg; under 60 kg, 30 mg.
ADJUST DOSE Elderly pts
ADV EFF Bleeding, cardiac arrhythmias, **MI,** rash, urticaria
INTERACTIONS Aminocaproic acid, anticoagulants, aspirin, clopidogrel, dipyridamole, heparin, ticlopidine
NC/PT Can only give IV under close supervision. Do not add other drugs to infusion sol. Stop current heparin tx. Apply pressure to all dressings. Avoid invasive procedures. Monitor coagulation studies; watch for signs of bleeding. Pt should report blood in urine, bleeding, chest pain, difficulty breathing.

---

tenofovir disoproxil fumarate (Viread)
CLASS Antiviral, nucleoside reverse transcriptase inhibitor
PREG/CONT B/NA

BBW Risk of lactic acidosis, severe hepatotoxicity; monitor hepatic function closely. Severe hepatitis B exacerbation has occurred when

anti–hepatitis B tx stopped; monitor for several mo if drug discontinued.
IND & DOSE Tx of HIV-1 infection, w/other antivirals. *Adult, child 12 yr and older, 35 kg or more:* 300 mg/day PO. *Child 2–11 yr:* 8 mg/kg/day PO. Tx of chronic hepatitis B. *Adult, child 12 yr and older, 35 kg or more:* 300 mg/day PO.
ADJUST DOSE Renal impairment
ADV EFF Asthenia, body fat redistribution, headache, **lactic acidosis, n/v/d, severe hepatomegaly w/ steatosis**
INTERACTIONS Atazanavir, didanosine, lopinavir, ritonavir
NC/PT Always give w/other antivirals. Monitor LFTs, renal function regularly; stop at first sign of lactic acidosis. Not for use in pregnancy/breast-feeding. Body fat may redistribute to back, middle, chest. Pt should take precautions to avoid disease spread (drug not a cure), avoid exposure to infections, report urine/stool color changes, rapid respirations.

terazosin hydrochloride (Hytrin)
CLASS Alpha blocker, antihypertensive, BPH drug
PREG/CONT C/NA

BBW Give first dose just before bed to lessen likelihood of first-dose syncope due to orthostatic hypotension.
IND & DOSE Tx of hypertension. *Adult:* 1 mg PO at bedtime. Slowly increase to achieve desired BP response. Usual range, 1–5 mg PO daily. Tx of BPH. *Adult:* 1 mg PO at bedtime. Increase to 2, 5, or 10 mg PO daily. May need 10 mg/day for 4–6 wk to assess benefit.
ADV EFF Allergic anaphylaxis, blurred vision, dizziness, drowsiness, dyspnea, headache, nasal congestion, n/v, orthostatic hypotension, palpitations, priapism, sinusitis
INTERACTIONS ED drugs, nitrates, other antihypertensives

NC/PT If not taken for several days, restart w/initial dose. Always start first dose at bedtime to lessen likelihood of syncope; have pt lie down if syncope occurs. Pt should take safety precautions for CNS effects, use caution w/ED drugs, report fainting, dizziness.

terbinafine hydrochloride (Lamisil)
CLASS Allylamine, antifungal
PREG/CONT B/NA

BBW Monitor regularly for s&sx of hepatic impairment; liver failure possible.
IND & DOSE Tx of onychomycosis of fingernail, toenail. *Adult:* 250 mg/day PO for 6 wk (fingernail), 12 wk (toenail). Tx of tinea capitis. *Adult:* 250 mg/day PO for 6 wk. *Child 4 yr and over:* Over 35 kg, 250 mg/day PO for 6 wk; 25–35 kg, 187.5 mg/day PO for 6 wk; under 25 kg, 125 mg/day PO for 6 wk. Tx of athlete's foot. *Adult, child:* Apply topically between toes bid for 1 wk. Tx of ring worm, jock itch. *Adult, child:* Apply topically once daily for 1 wk.
ADV EFF Abd pain, dyspepsia, headache, **hepatic failure,** nausea, pruritus, rash
INTERACTIONS Cimetidine, cyclosporine, dextromethorphan, rifampin
NC/PT Culture before tx. Monitor LFTs regularly. Not for use in pregnancy/breast-feeding. Pt should sprinkle oral granules on spoonful of nonacidic food such as mashed potatoes, swallow entire spoonful without chewing; take analgesics for headache; report urine/stool color changes, unusual bleeding, rash. Name confusion w/*Lamisil* (terbinafine), *Lamictal* (lamotrigine), *Lamisil AF* (tolnaftate), *Lamisil AT* (terbinafine); use caution.

terbutaline sulfate
(generic)

CLASS Antiasthmatic, beta selective agonist, bronchodilator, sympathomimetic
PREG/CONT B/NA

BBW Do not use injectable form in pregnant women for px, prolonged tx (beyond 48–72 hr) of preterm labor in hospital or outpt setting; risk of serious maternal heart problems, death.
IND & DOSE Px, tx of bronchial asthma, reversible bronchospasm. *Adult, child over 15 yr:* 2.5–5 mg PO tid at 6-hr intervals during waking hours; max, 15 mg/day. Or, 0.25 mg subcut into lateral deltoid one. If no significant improvement in 15–30 min, give another 0.25-mg dose. Max, 0.5 mg/4 hr. *Child 12–15 yr:* 2.5 mg PO tid; max, 7.5 mg/24 hr.
ADJUST DOSE Elderly pts
ADV EFF Anxiety, apprehension, **bronchospasm**, cardiac arrhythmias, cough, fear, nausea, palpitations, **pulmonary edema, respiratory difficulties**, restlessness, sweating
INTERACTIONS Diuretics, halogenated hydrocarbons, MAOIs, sympathomimetics, TCAs, theophylline
NC/PT Due to similar packaging, terbutaline injection confused w/ *Methergine* injection (methylergonovine maleate); use extreme caution. Have beta blocker on hand for arrhythmias, respiratory distress. Pt should take safety precautions for CNS effects, report chest pain, difficulty breathing, irregular heartbeat, failure to respond to usual dose.

teriflunomide (Aubagio)

CLASS MS drug, pyrimidine synthesis inhibitor
PREG/CONT X/NA

BBW Risk of severe hepatotoxicity; monitor LFTs before tx and at least monthly for 6 mo. Risk of major birth defects. Contraindicated in pregnancy; contraceptives required.
IND & DOSE Tx of relapsing MS. *Adult:* 7 or 14 mg/day PO.
ADJUST DOSE Severe hepatic impairment
ADV EFF Alopecia, **BP changes,** hyperkalemia, influenza, **neutropenia,** n/v, paresthesia, **peripheral neuropathy, renal failure, severe skin reactions**
INTERACTIONS Alosetron, cholestyramine, duloxetine, hormonal contraceptives, paclitaxel, pioglitazone, repaglinide, rosiglitazone, theophylline, tizanidine, warfarin
NC/PT Do not begin tx if acute infection; monitor for signs of infection, changes in potassium levels, BP changes, peripheral neuropathy, skin reactions. Monitor LFTs before, during tx. Not for use in pregnancy (contraceptives required)/breast-feeding; advise pt of risk of fetal harm. Pt should take once daily; avoid exposure to infection; report urine/stool color changes, extreme fatigue, fever, infection, skin reactions, muscle cramping, numbness/tingling.

teriparatide (Forteo)

CLASS Calcium regulator, parathyroid hormone
PREG/CONT C/NA

BBW Increased risk of osteosarcoma in rats; do not use in pts w/increased risk of osteosarcoma (Paget disease, unexplained alkaline phosphatase elevations, open epiphyses, prior external beam, implant radiation involving skeleton). Not recommended for bone disease other than osteoporosis.
IND & DOSE Tx of postmenopausal women w/osteoporosis, glucocorticoid-related osteoporosis, hypogonadal osteoporosis in men. *Adult:* 20 mcg/day subcut in thigh or abd wall for no more than 2 yr.

ADV EFF Arthralgia, hypercalcemia, nausea, orthostatic hypotension, pain, urolithiasis

INTERACTIONS Digoxin

NC/PT Do not use in pts at risk for osteosarcoma; use for no more than 2 yr. Monitor serum calcium. Not for use in pregnancy/breast-feeding. Teach proper administration/disposal of needles, delivery device. Pt should rotate injection sites, have blood tests to monitor calcium level, change positions slowly after injection, report constipation, muscle weakness.

tesamorelin (Egrifta)
CLASS GHRF analogue
PREG/CONT X/NA

IND & DOSE To reduce excess abd fat in HIV-infected pts w/lipodystrophy related to antiviral use. *Adult:* 2 mg/day subcut into abd skin.

ADV EFF Acute illness, arthralgia, **cancer**, edema, fluid retention, glucose intolerance, hypersensitivity reactions, injection-site reactions, **neoplasms**

INTERACTIONS Anticonvulsants, corticosteroids, cyclosporine, estrogen, progesterone, testosterone

NC/PT Monitor blood glucose. Arrange for cancer screening. Teach proper administration/disposal of needles/syringes. Not for use in pregnancy/breast-feeding. Pt should rotate injection sites, report signs of infection, injection-site reaction, increased thirst.

testosterone
(Androderm, AndroGel, Aveed, Axiron, Delatestryl, Fortesta, Natesto, Striant, Testim, Testopel)
CLASS Androgen, hormone
PREG/CONT X/C-III

BBW Risk of toxic effects (enlarged genitalia, greater-than-normal bone age) in children exposed to pt using

transdermal form (AndroGel, Testim). Pt should wash hands after applying, cover treated area w/clothing to reduce exposure. Risk of serious pulmonary oil microembolism, anaphylaxis (Aveed); observe pt for 30 min and be prepared for supportive tx. Risk of thrombotic events; monitor accordingly.

IND & DOSE Replacement tx in hypogonadism. *Adult:* 50–400 mg (cypionate, enanthate) IM q 2–4 wk; or 750 mg (Aveed) IM, then 750 mg 4 wk later, then q 10 wk; or 150–450 mg (enanthate pellets) implanted subcut q 3–6 mo. Or, initially 4-mg/day system (patch) applied to nonscrotal skin; then 2 mg/day system (Androderm). Or, 50 mg/day AndroGel, Testim (preferably in a.m.) applied to clean, dry, intact skin of shoulders, upper arms, or abdomen. Or, 4 actuations (40 mg) Fortesta applied to inner thighs in a.m. Or, 1 pump actuation (30 mg) Axiron to each axilla once/day. Or, 4 actuations (50 mg) AndroGel 1.62% once daily in a.m. to shoulders or upper arms. Or, 1 buccal system (30 mg) (Striant) to gum region bid (a.m. and p.m.). Rotate sites; usual position is above incisor on either side of mouth. Or 11 mg (Natesto) intranasally tid (2 pumps, one in each nostril). Tx of males w/delayed puberty. *Adult:* 50–200 mg enanthate IM q 2–4 wk for 4–6 mo. or 150 mg pellets subcut q 3–6 mo. Tx of carcinoma of breast, metastatic mammary cancer. *Adult:* 200–400 mg IM enanthate q 2–4 wk.

ADV EFF Androgenic effects, chills, dizziness, fatigue, fluid retention, headache, **hepatocellular carcinoma**, hypoestrogenic effects, leukopenia, nasal reactions (Natesto), polycythemia, rash, **thrombotic events**

INTERACTIONS Anticoagulants, corticosteroids, grapefruit juice, insulin, metronidazole

NC/PT Obtain testosterone level before use; efficacy in age-related low testosterone has not been established. Monitor blood glucose, serum calcium, serum electrolytes, lipids, LFTs. Review proper administration of each delivery form; sprays not interchangeable. Women using drug should avoid pregnancy. Pt should mark calendar of tx days; remove old transdermal patch before applying new one; cover topical gel application sites if in contact w/children; avoid grapefruit juice; report swelling, urine/stool color changes, unusual bleeding/bruising, chest pain, difficult breathing.

tetrabenazine (Xenazine)
CLASS Anti-chorea drug, monoamine depletor
PREG/CONT C/NA

BBW Increased risk of depression, suicidality; monitor accordingly.
IND & DOSE Tx of chorea associated w/Huntington disease. *Adult:* 12.5 mg/day PO in a.m. After 1 wk, increase to 12.5 mg PO bid; max, 100 mg/day in divided doses.
ADV EFF Akathisia, anxiety, confusion, depression, fatigue, insomnia, nausea, Parkinson-like sx, **prolonged QT**, sedation, URI
INTERACTIONS Alcohol, antiarrhythmics, antipsychotics, dopamine agonists, fluoxetine, MAOIs, paroxetine, quinidine
NC/PT Obtain accurate depression evaluation before use. Obtain baseline of chorea sx. Do not give within 14 days of MAOIs. Not for use in pregnancy (contraceptives advised)/breast-feeding. Pt should take safety measures for CNS effects, avoid alcohol; report tremors, behavior changes, depression, thoughts of suicide.

tetracycline hydrochloride (generic)
CLASS Antibiotic
PREG/CONT D/NA

IND & DOSE Tx of infections caused by susceptible bacteria.
Adult: 1–2 g/day PO in two to four equal doses; max, 500 mg PO qid. *Child over 8 yr:* 25–50 mg/kg/day PO in four equal doses. **Tx of brucellosis.** *Adult:* 500 mg PO qid for 3 wk w/1 g streptomycin IM bid first wk and daily second wk. **Tx of syphilis.** *Adult:* 30–40 g PO in divided doses over 10–15 days (*Sumycin*); 500 mg PO qid for 15–30 days (all others). **Tx of uncomplicated gonorrhea.** *Adult:* 500 mg PO q 6 hr for 7 days. **Tx of gonococcal urethritis.** *Adult:* 500 mg PO q 4–6 hr for 4–6 days. **Tx of uncomplicated urethral, endocervical, rectal infections w/Chlamydia trachomatis.** *Adult:* 500 mg PO qid for at least 7 days. **Tx of severe acne.** *Adult:* 1 g/day PO in divided doses; then 125–500 mg/day.
ADV EFF Anaphylaxis; **bone marrow suppression**; discoloring, inadequate calcification of primary teeth of fetus if used by pregnant women, of permanent teeth if used during dental development; **hepatic impairment**; phototoxic reactions; superinfections
INTERACTIONS Aluminum, bismuth, calcium salts; charcoal; dairy products; food; hormonal contraceptives; iron, magnesium salts; penicillins; urinary alkalinizers; zinc salts
NC/PT Culture before tx. Arrange tx of superinfections. Not for use in pregnancy (hormonal contraceptives may be ineffective; barrier contraceptives advised). Pt should take on empty stomach 1 hr before or 2 hr after meals; do not use outdated drugs; report rash, urine/stool color changes.

tetrahydrozoline hydrochloride (Murine Plus, Opticlear, Tyzine, Visine)
CLASS Alpha agonist; decongestant; ophthalmic vasoconstrictor, mydriatic
PREG/CONT C/NA

IND & DOSE Relief of nasal, nasopharyngeal mucosal congestion.

Adult, child 6 yr and older: 2–4 drops 0.1% sol in each nostril three to four times/day; or 3–4 sprays in each nostril q 4 hr as needed. Not more often than q 3 hr. *Child 2–6 yr:* 2–3 drops 0.05% sol in each nostril q 4–6 hr as needed Not more often than q 3 hr.
Temporary relief of eye redness, burning, irritation. *Adult:* 1–2 drops into eye(s) up to qid.

ADV EFF Anxiety, **CV collapse w/ hypotension,** dizziness, drowsiness, headache, light-headedness, pallor, rebound congestion, restlessness, tenseness

INTERACTIONS Methyldopa, MAOIs, reserpine, TCAs, urine acidifiers/alkalinizers

NC/PT Monitor BP in pt w/CAD. Review proper administration. Rebound congestion may occur when drug stopped. Pt should remove contact lenses before using drops, drink plenty of fluids, use humidifier for at least 72 hr, take safety precautions for CNS effects, report blurred vision, fainting.

---

thalidomide (Thalomid)
CLASS Immunomodulator
PREG/CONT X/NA

BBW Associated w/severe birth defects. Women must have pregnancy test, signed consent to use birth control to avoid pregnancy during tx (STEPS program). Significant risk of venous thromboembolic events when used in multiple myeloma; monitor accordingly.

IND & DOSE Tx of erythema nodosum leprosum. *Adult* 100–300 mg/day PO at bedtime for at least 2 wk. Up to 400 mg/day for severe lesions. Taper in decrements of 50 mg q 2–4 wk.
Tx of newly diagnosed multiple myeloma. *Adult:* 200 mg/day PO w/ dexamethasone.

ADV EFF Agitation, anorexia, anxiety, bradycardia, dizziness, dry skin, dyspnea, headache, nausea, **neutropenia,** orthostatic hypotension, **MI,**

peripheral neuropathy, rash, somnolence, **Stevens-Johnson syndrome,** tumor lysis syndrome

INTERACTIONS Alcohol, CNS depressants, dexamethasone, hormonal contraceptives

NC/PT Rule out pregnancy; ensure pt has read, agreed to contraceptive use. Monitor BP, WBC count. Not for use in breast-feeding. Pt should take safety precautions for CNS effects, avoid exposure to infection, report chest pain, dizziness, rash, signs of infection.

---

theophylline (Elixophyllin, Theo-24, Theochron)
CLASS Bronchodilator, xanthine
PREG/CONT C/NA

IND & DOSE Sx relief or px of bronchial asthma, reversible bronchospasm. *Note:* For dosages for specific populations, see manufacturer's details. *Adult, child over 45 kg:* 300–600 mg/day PO, or 0.4 mg/kg IV. *Child under 45 kg:* Total dose in mg = [(0.2 × age in wk) + 5] × body wt in kg PO/day in four equal doses. Or, 0.7–0.8 mg/kg/hr IV (1–1.5 mg/kg/12 hr IV for neonate).

ADV EFF Anorexia, **death,** dizziness, headache, insomnia, irritability, **life-threatening ventricular arrhythmias,** n/v, restlessness, **seizures**

INTERACTIONS Barbiturates, benzodiazepines, beta blockers, charcoal, cigarette smoking, cimetidine, ciprofloxacin, erythromycin, halothane, hormonal contraceptives, NMJ blockers, norfloxacin, ofloxacin, phenytoin, rifampin, ranitidine, St. John's wort, ticlopidine, thioamides, thyroid hormones

NC/PT Maintain serum level in therapeutic range (5–15 mcg/mL); adverse effects related to serum level. Do not add in sol w/other drugs. Not for use in pregnancy (barrier contraceptives advised). Pt should take ER form on empty stomach 1 hr before or 2 hr after meals, do not cut, crush or chew it; limit caffeine intake; avoid St. John's wort; report smoking changes (dose adjustment needed); take safety precautions for CNS effects; report irregular heartbeat, severe GI pain.

DANGEROUS DRUG

thioguanine (Tabloid)
CLASS Antimetabolite, antineoplastic
PREG/CONT D/NA

IND & DOSE Remission induction, consolidation, maint tx of acute nonlymphocytic leukemias. *Adult, child 3 yr and over:* 2 mg/kg/day PO for 4 wk. If no clinical improvement, no toxic effects, increase to 3 mg/kg/day PO.
ADV EFF Anorexia, **bone marrow suppression, hepatotoxicity,** hyperuricemia, n/v, stomatitis, weakness
NC/PT Monitor CBC (dose adjustment may be needed), LFTs. Not for use in pregnancy (contraceptives advised). Pt should drink 8–10 glasses of fluid/day; avoid exposure to infection; have regular blood tests; perform mouth care for mouth sores; report signs of infection, urine/stool color changes, swelling.

DANGEROUS DRUG

thiotepa (generic)
CLASS Alkylating agent, antineoplastic
PREG/CONT D/NA

IND & DOSE Tx of adenocarcinoma of breast, ovary. *Adult:* 0.3–0.4 mg/kg IV at 1- to 4-wk intervals. Or, diluted in sterile water to conc of 10 mg/mL, then 0.6–0.8 mg/kg injected directly into tumor after local anesthetic injected through same needle. Maint, 0.6–0.8 mg/kg IV q 1–4 wk. Or, 0.6–0.8 mg/kg intracavity q 1–4 wk through same tube used to remove fluid from bladder. **Superficial papillary carcinoma of urinary bladder.**

Adult: Dehydrate pt for 8–12 hr before tx. Instill 30–60 mg in 60 mL normal saline injection into bladder by catheter. Have pt retain for 2 hr. If pt unable to retain 60 mL, give in 30 mL. Repeat once/wk for 4 wk. **Control of intracavity effusions secondary to neoplasms of various serosal cavities.** *Adult:* 0.6–0.8 mg/kg infused directly into cavity using same tubing used to remove fluid from cavity.
ADV EFF Amenorrhea, **bone marrow suppression,** dizziness, fever, headache, n/v, skin reactions
NC/PT Monitor CBC; dose adjustment may be needed. IV sol should be clear w/out solutes. Not for use in pregnancy. Pt should mark calendar of tx days, avoid exposure to infections, take safety precautions w/dizziness, report unusual bleeding, signs of infection, rash.

---

thiothixene (Navane)
CLASS Antipsychotic, dopaminergic blocker, thioxanthene
PREG/CONT C/NA

BBW Increased risk of death if antipsychotics used to treat elderly pts w/dementia-related psychosis; not approved for this use.
IND & DOSE Mgt of schizophrenia. *Adult, child over 12 yr:* 2 mg PO tid (mild conditions), 5 mg bid (more severe conditions). Range, 20–30 mg/day; max, 60 mg/day.
ADJUST DOSE Elderly, debilitated pts
ADV EFF Aplastic anemia, autonomic disturbances, blurred vision, **bronchospasm,** drowsiness, dry mouth, extrapyramidal effects, gynecomastia, **HF, laryngospasm, nonthrombocytopenic purpura, pancytopenia,** photophobia, pink to red-brown urine, **refractory arrhythmias**
INTERACTIONS Alcohol, antihypertensives, carbamazepine

NC/PT Monitor renal function, CBC. Urine will turn pink to red-brown. Pt should avoid sun exposure, take safety precautions for CNS effects, maintain fluid intake, report signs of infection, unusual bleeding, difficulty breathing. Name confusion between *Navane* (thiothixene) and *Norvasc* (amlodipine); use caution.

thyroid, desiccated (Armour Thyroid, Nature-Throid, Thyroid USP, Westhroid)
CLASS Thyroid hormone
PREG/CONT A/NA

BBW Do not use to treat obesity. Large doses in euthyroid pts may produce serious to life-threatening s&sx of toxicity.
IND & DOSE Tx of hypothyroidism. *Adult:* 30 mg/day PO, increased by 15 mg/day q 2–3 wk. Usual maint, 60–120 mg/day PO daily. *Child:* Over 12 yr, 90 mg/day PO; 6–12 yr, 60–90 mg/day PO; 1–5 yr, 45–60 mg/day PO; 6–12 mo, 30–45 mg/day PO; 0–6 mo, 7.5–30 mg/day PO.
ADJUST DOSE Elderly pts, long-standing heart disease
ADV EFF Cardiac arrest, hyperthyroidism, n/v/d, skin reactions
INTERACTIONS Antacids, cholestyramine, digoxin, theophylline, warfarin
NC/PT Monitor thyroid function to establish dose, then at least yearly. Pt should wear medical ID, report headache, palpitations, heat/cold intolerance.

tiagabine hydrochloride (Gabitril)
CLASS Antiepileptic
PREG/CONT C/NA

BBW Increased risk of suicidal ideation; monitor accordingly.
IND & DOSE Adjunctive tx in partial seizures. *Adult:* 4 mg/day PO for 1 wk; may increase by 4–8 mg/wk until desired response. Usual maint,

32–56 mg daily; max, 56 mg/day in two to four divided doses. *Child 12–18 yr:* 4 mg/day PO for 1 wk; may increase to 8 mg/day in two divided doses for 1 wk, then by 4–8 mg/wk. Max, 32 mg/day in two to four divided doses.
ADV EFF Asthenia, dizziness, GI upset, incontinence, eye changes, **potentially serious rash**, somnolence
INTERACTIONS Alcohol, carbamazepine, CNS depressants, phenobarbital, phenytoin, primidone, valproate
NC/PT Taper when stopping. Not for use in pregnancy (contraceptives advised). Pt should not stop suddenly; take w/food; avoid alcohol, sleeping pills; wear medical ID; take safety precautions w/dizziness, vision changes; report rash, thoughts of suicide, vision changes.

ticagrelor (Brilinta)
CLASS Antiplatelet
PREG/CONT C/NA

BBW Significant to fatal bleeding possible; do not use w/active bleeding, CABG planned within 5 days, surgery. Maint aspirin doses above 100 mg reduce effectiveness; maintain aspirin dose at 75–100 mg/day.
IND & DOSE To reduce rate of thrombotic CV events in pts w/acute coronary syndrome or hx of MI. *Adult:* Loading dose, 180 mg PO; then 90 mg PO bid w/325 mg PO aspirin as loading dose, then aspirin dose of 75–100 mg/day PO for first year after event, then 60 mg/day PO maintenance.
ADV EFF Bleeding, dyspnea, hepatotoxicity
INTERACTIONS Potent CYP3A4 inducers (carbamazepine, dexamethasone, phenobarbital, phenytoin, rifampin), potent CYP3A4 inhibitors (atazanavir, clarithromycin, indinavir, itraconazole, ketoconazole, nefazodone, nelfinavir, ritonavir, saquinavir, telithromycin, voriconazole); avoid these combinations. Digoxin, drugs affecting coagulation, lovastatin, simvastatin

NC/PT Continually monitor for s&sx of bleeding. Not for use w/hx of intracranial bleeding. Ensure concurrent use of 75–100 mg aspirin; do not stop drug except for pathological bleeding. Increased risk of CV events; if drug must be stopped, start another anticoagulant. Assess pt w/dyspnea for potential underlying cause. Not for use in pregnancy (barrier contraceptive advised)/breast-feeding. Pt should take drug exactly as prescribed w/prescribed dose of aspirin; not increase doses; not stop drug suddenly; report other drugs or herbs being used (many reactions possible; bleeding time may be prolonged), excessive bleeding, difficulty breathing, chest pain, numbness/tingling, urine/stool color changes.

ticlopidine hydrochloride (generic)
CLASS Antiplatelet
PREG/CONT B/NA

BBW Monitor WBC count before, frequently while starting tx; if neutropenia present, stop drug immediately.
IND & DOSE To reduce thrombotic stroke risk in pts who have experienced stroke precursors; px of stent thrombosis in coronary arteries. *Adult:* 250 mg PO bid w/food.
ADV EFF Abd pain, **bleeding**, dizziness, **neutropenia**, n/v/d, pain, rash
INTERACTIONS Antacids, aspirin, cimetidine, digoxin, NSAIDs, theophylline
NC/PT Mark chart to alert all health care providers of use. Monitor WBC; watch for signs of bleeding. Pt should take w/meals, report unusual bleeding/bruising, signs of infection.

tigecycline (Tygacil)
CLASS Glycylcycline antibiotic
PREG/CONT D/NA

BBW All-cause mortality higher in pts using tigecycline; reserve use for when no other tx is suitable.

IND & DOSE Tx of complicated skin, skin-structure infections; community-acquired pneumonia; intra-abdominal infections caused by susceptible bacteria strains. *Adult:* 100 mg IV, then 50 mg IV q 12 hr for 5–14 days; infuse over 30–60 min.
ADJUST DOSE Severe hepatic impairment
ADV EFF Anaphylaxis, cough, **death**, dizziness, dyspnea, headache, **hepatic dysfunction**, n/v/d, **pancreatitis**, photosensitivity, **pseudomembranous colitis**, superinfections
INTERACTIONS Oral contraceptives, warfarin
NC/PT Culture before tx. Limit use to serious tx. Monitor LFTs, pancreatic function. Not for use in pregnancy/breast-feeding. Pt should avoid sun exposure, report bloody diarrhea, difficulty breathing, rash, pain at injection site.

timolol maleate (Betimol, Istalol, Timoptic)
CLASS Antiglaucoma, antihypertensive, beta blocker
PREG/CONT C/NA

BBW Do not stop abruptly after long-term tx (hypersensitivity to catecholamines possible, causing angina exacerbation, MI, ventricular arrhythmias). Taper gradually over 2 wk w/monitoring.
IND & DOSE Tx of hypertension. *Adult:* 10 mg bid PO; max, 60 mg/day in two divided doses. Usual range, 20–40 mg/day in two divided doses. **Px of reinfarction in MI.** 10 mg PO bid within 1–4 wk of infarction. **Px of migraine.** *Adult:* 10 mg PO bid; during maint, may give 20 mg/day as single dose. **To reduce IOP in chronic open-angle glaucoma.** 1 drop 0.25% sol bid into affected eye(s); adjust based on response to 1 drop 0.5% sol bid or 1 drop 0.25% sol daily. Or, 1 drop in affected eye(s) each morning *(Istalol).*

ADV EFF Arrhythmias, **broncho-spasm,** constipation, decreased exercise tolerance, dizziness, ED, flat-ulence, gastric pain, **HF,** hyperglyce-mia, **laryngospasm,** n/v/d, ocular irritation w/eyedrops, **PE, stroke**
INTERACTIONS Antacids, aspirin, calcium, indomethacin
NC/PT Alert surgeon if surgery required. Do not stop abruptly; must be tapered. Teach proper eyedrop administration. Pt should take safety precautions w/dizziness, report diffi-culty breathing, swelling, numbness/tingling.

Timothy grass pollen allergen extract (Grastek)
CLASS Allergen extract
PREG/CONT C/NA

BBW Risk of severe, life-threatening allergic reactions. Not for use in un-controlled asthma. Observe pt for 30 min after first dose; have emergency equipment on hand. Prescribe autoin-jectable epinephrine; teach use.
IND & DOSE Immunotherapy for tx of timothy grass pollen–induced allergic rhinitis w/or without con-junctivitis confirmed by skin test in pts 5–65 yr. Adult, child 5 yr and over: 1 tablet/day sublingually starting 12 wk before and continuing throughout season.
ADV EFF Cough, ear pruritus, mouth edema, oropharyngeal pain/pruritus, throat/tongue pruritus
NC/PT Ensure skin testing confirms allergy. Not for use in uncontrolled asthma, hx of severe reactions, eosionophilic esophagitis. Begin 12 wk before expected grass season and continue throughout season. First dose should be given under medical supervision; observe pt for at least 30 min and have emergency equip-ment on hand. Place tablet under tongue, allow to stay until completely dissolved; pt should not swallow for 1 min. Stop tx if oral wounds/

inflammation; allow to heal completely before restarting. Pt should report difficulty breathing/swallowing.

tinidazole (Tindamax)
CLASS Antiprotozoal
PREG/CONT C/NA

BBW Avoid use unless clearly needed; carcinogenic in lab animals.
IND & DOSE Tx of trichomoniasis, giardiasis. Adult: Single dose of 2 g PO w/food. Child over 3 yr: For giardi-asis, single dose of 50 mg/kg PO (up to 2 g) w/food. Tx of amebiasis. Adult: 2 g/day PO for 3 days w/food. Child over 3 yr: 50 mg/kg/day PO (up to 2 g/day) for 3 days w/food. For giardiasis, Tx of amebic liver ab-scess. Adult: 2 g/day PO for 3–5 days w/food. Child over 3 yr: 50 mg/kg/day PO (up to 2 g/day) for 3–5 days w/food.
ADV EFF Anorexia, dizziness, drowsiness, metallic taste, neutro-penia, **seizures,** superinfections, **severe hypersensi-tivity reactions,** superinfections, weakness
INTERACTIONS Alcohol, cholestyr-amine, cimetidine, cyclosporine, di-sulfiram, 5-FU, ketoconazole, lithium, oral anticoagulants, oxytetracycline, phenytoin, tacrolimus
NC/PT Give w/food. Ensure proper hygiene, tx of superinfections. Urine may become very dark. Pt should take safety precautions w/dizziness; avoid alcohol during, for 3 days after tx; report vaginal itching, white patches in mouth, difficulty breathing, rash.

tiopronin (Thiola)
CLASS Thiol compound
PREG/CONT C/NA

IND & DOSE Px of cystine kidney stone formation in severe homozy-gous cystinuria. Adult: 800 mg/day PO; increase to 1,000 mg/day in di-vided doses on empty stomach. Child 9 yr and over: 15 mg/kg/day PO on empty stomach; adjust based on urine cystine level.

ADV EFF Hepatotoxicity, nephrotoxicity, n/v/d, rash, skin/taste changes

NC/PT Monitor cystine at 1 mo, then q 3 mo. Monitor LFTs, renal function. Not for use in breast-feeding. Pt should drink fluids liberally (to 3 L/day), report urine/stool color changes, rash.

---

tiotropium bromide
(Spiriva)

CLASS Anticholinergic, bronchodilator

PREG/CONT C/NA

IND & DOSE Long-term once-daily maint tx of bronchospasm associated w/COPD. *Adult:* 2 inhalations/day of contents of one capsule using *HandiHaler* device.

ADV EFF Abd pain, blurred vision, constipation, dry mouth, epistaxis, glaucoma, rash, urine retention

INTERACTIONS Anticholinergics

NC/PT Evaluate for glaucoma; stop drug if increased IOP. Not for use in acute attacks. Review proper use of *HandiHaler* device. Pt should empty bladder before each dose, use sugarless lozenges for dry mouth, report eye pain, vision changes.

---

tipranavir (Aptivus)

CLASS Antiviral, protease inhibitor

PREG/CONT C/NA

BBW Increased risk of hepatotoxicity in pts w/hepatitis; assess liver function before, periodically during tx. Giving w/ritonavir has caused nonfatal, fatal intracranial hemorrhage; monitor carefully.

IND & DOSE Tx of HIV infection, w/other antiretrovirals. *Adult:* 500 mg/day PO w/ritonavir 200 mg, w/food. *Child 2–18 yr:* 14 mg/kg w/ritonavir 6 mg/kg PO bid (375 mg/m² w/ritonavir 150 mg/m² PO bid). Max,

500 mg bid w/ritonavir 200 mg bid, w/food.

ADV EFF Abd pain, cough, depression, fever, flulike sx, headache, **hepatomegaly and steatosis,** n/v/d, **potentially fatal liver impairment**

INTERACTIONS Amprenavir, atorvastatin, calcium channel blockers, cyclosporine, desipramine, didanosine, disulfiram, hormonal contraceptives, itraconazole, ketoconazole, lopinavir, meperidine, methadone, metronidazole, oral antidiabetics, saquinavir, sildenafil, sirolimus, SSRIs, St. John's wort, tacrolimus, tadalafil, vardenafil, voriconazole, warfarin. Contraindicated w/amiodarone, dihydroergotamine, ergotamine, flecainide, lovastatin, methylergonovine, midazolam, pimozide, propafenone, quinidine, rifampin, simvastatin, triazolam

NC/PT Ensure pt also taking ritonavir. Review drug hx before tx; multiple interactions possible. Serious complications possible. Monitor LFTs. Not for use in pregnancy/breast-feeding. Pt should take w/food; swallow capsule whole and not cut, crush, or chew it; store capsules in refrigerator (do not refrigerate sol); not use after expiration date; use precautions to prevent spread (drug not a cure); avoid exposure to infection, St. John's wort; report general malaise, urine/stool color changes, yellowing of skin/eyes.

---

tirofiban hydrochloride
(Aggrastat)

CLASS Antiplatelet

PREG/CONT B/NA

IND & DOSE Tx of acute coronary syndromes, w/heparin; px of cardiac ischemic complications in percutaneous coronary intervention. *Adult:* Initially, 25 mcg/kg IV within 5 min, then 0.15 mcg/kg/min IV for up to 18 hr.

ADJUST DOSE Renal impairment

ADV EFF Bleeding, bradycardia, dizziness, flushing, hypotension, syncope

INTERACTIONS Antiplatelets, aspirin, chamomile, don quai, feverfew, garlic, ginger, ginkgo, ginseng, grape seed extract, green leaf tea, heparin, horse chestnut seed, NSAIDs, turmeric, warfarin
NC/PT Obtain baseline, periodic CBC, PT, aPTT, active clotting time. Maintain aPTT between 50 and 70 sec, and active clotting time between 300 and 350 sec. Avoid noncompressible IV access sites to prevent excessive, uncontrollable bleeding. Pt should report light-headedness, palpitations, pain at injection site. Name confusion between *Aggrastat* (tirofiban) and argatroban; use caution.

---

tizanidine (Zanaflex)

CLASS Alpha agonist, antispasmodic
PREG/CONT C/NA

IND & DOSE Acute, intermittent mgt of increased muscle tone associated w/spasticity. *Adult:* Initially, 2 mg PO; can repeat at 6- to 8-hr intervals, up to three doses/24 hr. Increase by 2–4 mg/dose q 1–4 days; max, 36 mg/day.
ADJUST DOSE Hepatic, renal impairment
ADV EFF Asthenia, constipation, dizziness, drowsiness, dry mouth, hepatic injury, hypotension, sedation
INTERACTIONS Alcohol, baclofen, CNS depressants, hormonal contraceptives, other alpha$_2$-adrenergic agonists, QT-prolonging drugs
NC/PT Stop slowly to decrease risk of withdrawal, rebound CV effects. Continue all supportive measures for neurologically damaged pt. Not for use in pregnancy (hormonal contraceptives may be ineffective; barrier contraceptives advised). Pt should take around the clock for best results; use sugarless lozenges for dry mouth; avoid alcohol; take safety precautions for CNS effects; report vision changes, difficulty swallowing, fainting.

---

tobramycin sulfate
(Bethkis, TOBI, Tobrex Ophthalmic)

CLASS Aminoglycoside antibiotic
PREG/CONT D (injection, inhalation); B (ophthalmic)/NA

BBW Injection may cause serious ototoxicity, nephrotoxicity, neurotoxicity. Monitor closely for changes in renal, CNS function.
IND & DOSE Tx of serious infections caused by susceptible bacteria strains. *Adult:* 3 mg/kg/day IM or IV in three equal doses q 8 hr; max, 5 mg/kg/day. *Child over 1 wk:* 6–7.5 mg/kg/day IM or IV in three to four equally divided doses. *Premature infants, neonates 1 wk or younger:* Up to 4 mg/kg/day IM or IV in two equal doses q 12 hr. Mgt of cystic fibrosis pts w/*Pseudomonas aeruginosa.* *Adult, child 6 yr and older:* 300 mg bid by nebulizer inhaled over 10–15 min. Give in 28-day cycles: 28 days on, 28 days rest. Tx of superficial ocular infections due to susceptible organism strains. *Adult, child 6 yr and older:* 1–2 drops into conjunctival sac of affected eye(s) q 4 hr, 2 drops/hr in severe infections. Or, ½ inch ribbon bid–tid.
ADJUST DOSE Elderly pts, renal impairment
ADV EFF Anorexia, leukemoid reaction, palpitations, ototoxicity, **nephrotoxicity,** numbness/tingling, n/v/d, purpura, rash, superinfections, vestibular paralysis
INTERACTIONS Aminoglycosides, beta-lactam antibiotics, cephalosporins, NMJ blockers, penicillin, succinylcholine
NC/PT Culture before tx. Monitor renal function. Limit tx duration to 7–14 days to decrease toxic reactions. Do not mix in sol w/other drugs. Review proper administration of eyedrops, nebulizer. Pt should mark calendar of tx days; store in refrigerator.

protected from light; drink 8–10 glasses of fluid/day; take safety precautions for CNS effects; report hearing changes, dizziness, pain at injection site.

tocilizumab (Actemra)
CLASS Antirheumatic, interleukin-6 receptor inhibitor
PREG/CONT C/NA

BBW Serious to life-threatening infections possible, including TB and bacterial, invasive fungal, viral, opportunistic infections. Perform TB test before tx. Interrupt tx if serious infection occurs; monitor for TB s&sx during tx.
IND & DOSE Tx of moderately to severely active rheumatoid arthritis. *Adult:* 4 mg/kg by IV infusion over 1 hr, then increase to 8 mg/kg based on clinical response; may repeat once q 4 wk; max, 800 mg/infusion. Tx of active systemic juvenile arthritis/Still disease (systemic idiopathic juvenile arthritis). *Child 2 yr and over:* 30 kg or more, 8 mg/kg IV q 2 wk; under 30 kg, 12 mg/kg IV q 2 wk.
ADV EFF Anaphylaxis, dizziness, GI perforation, hypertension, increased liver enzymes, nasopharyngitis, potentially serious infections, URI
INTERACTIONS Anti-CD20 monoclonal antibodies, cyclosporine, interleukin receptor antagonists, live vaccines, omeprazole, statins, TNF antagonists, warfarin
NC/PT Do not mix in sol w/other drugs. Monitor CBC, LFTs, lipids carefully; dosage adjustment may be needed. Not for use in pregnancy/breast-feeding. Pt should continue other drugs for arthritis; avoid live vaccines, exposure to infection; report signs of infection, difficulty breathing, easy bruising/bleeding.

tofacitinib (Xeljanz)
CLASS Antirheumatic, kinase inhibitor
PREG/CONT C/NA

BBW Risk of serious to fatal infections, including TB; test for TB before tx; do not give w/active infections. Risk of lymphoma, other malignancies. Epstein-Barr virus–associated post-transplant lymphoproliferative disorder when used in renal transplant.
IND & DOSE Tx of adults w/moderately to severely active rheumatoid arthritis intolerant to other therapies. *Adult:* 5 mg PO bid.
ADJUST DOSE Hepatic, renal impairment
ADV EFF Diarrhea, GI perforation, headache, lymphoma, malignancies, serious to fatal infections, URI
INTERACTIONS Fluconazole, ketoconazole, rifampin, live vaccines
NC/PT Screen for TB, active infection before tx; monitor for signs of infection. Monitor for lymphoma, other malignancies. May combine w/other antirheumatics. Not for use in pregnancy. Pt should take as directed bid; avoid exposure to infections; avoid vaccines; report severe GI pain, fever, signs of infection.

TOLAZamide (generic)
CLASS Antidiabetic, sulfonylurea
PREG/CONT C/NA

BBW Increased risk of CV mortality; monitor accordingly.
IND & DOSE Adjunct to diet/exercise to control blood glucose in pts w/type 2 diabetes; w/insulin to control blood glucose in select pts w/type 1 diabetes. *Adult:* 100–250 mg/day PO; max, 1 g/day.
ADJUST DOSE Elderly pts
ADV EFF Bone marrow suppression, dizziness, fatigue, heartburn, hypoglycemia, rash, vertigo

INTERACTIONS Beta-adrenergic blockers, calcium channel blockers, chloramphenicol, corticosteroids, coumarins, estrogens, isoniazid, MAOIs, miconazole, nicotinic acid, oral contraceptives, phenothiazines, phenytoin, probenecid, salicylates, sulfonamides, sympathomimetics, thyroid products
NC/PT Review complete diabetic teaching program. Pt should take in a.m. w/breakfast (do not take if not eating that day); continue diet/exercise program; avoid exposure to infection; report uncontrolled blood glucose, dizziness.

TOLBUTamide (generic)

CLASS Antidiabetic, sulfonylurea
PREG/CONT C/NA

BBW Increased risk of CV mortality; monitor accordingly.
IND & DOSE Adjunct to diet/exercise to control blood glucose in pts w/type 2 diabetes; w/insulin to control blood glucose in select pts w/type1 diabetes. *Adult:* 1–2 g/day PO in a.m. before breakfast. Maint, 0.25–3 g/day PO; max, 3 g/day.
ADJUST DOSE Elderly pts
ADV EFF Bone marrow suppression, dizziness, fatigue, heartburn, hypoglycemia, rash, vertigo
INTERACTIONS Beta-adrenergic blockers, calcium channel blockers, chloramphenicol, corticosteroids, coumarins, estrogens, isoniazid, MAOIs, miconazole, nicotinic acid, oral contraceptives, phenothiazines, phenytoin, probenecid, salicylates, sulfonamides, sympathomimetics, thyroid products
NC/PT Review complete diabetic teaching program. Pt may be switched to insulin during high stress. Pt should take in a.m. w/breakfast (do not take if not eating that day); continue diet/exercise program; avoid exposure to infection; report uncontrolled blood glucose, dizziness.

tolcapone (Tasmar)

CLASS Antiparkinsonian, COMT inhibitor
PREG/CONT C/NA

BBW Risk of potentially fatal acute fulminant liver failure. Monitor LFTs before, q 2 wk during tx; discontinue if signs of liver damage. Use for pts no longer responding to other therapies.
IND & DOSE Adjunct w/levodopa/carbidopa in tx of s&sx of idiopathic Parkinson disease. *Adult:* 100 mg PO tid; max, 600 mg.
ADJUST DOSE Hepatic, renal impairment
ADV EFF Confusion; constipation; disorientation; dry mouth; falling asleep during daily activities; **fulminant, possibly fatal liver failure;** hallucinations; hypotension; lightheadedness; n/v, rash, **renal toxicity,** somnolence, weakness
INTERACTIONS MAOIs
NC/PT Monitor LFTs before, q 2 wk during tx. Always give w/levodopa/carbidopa. Do not give within 14 days of MAOIs. Taper dose w 2 wk when stopping. Not for use in pregnancy/breast-feeding. Pt should take w/meals, use sugarless lozenges for dry mouth, take safety precautions for CNS effects, use laxative for constipation, report urine/stool color changes, fever.

tolmetin sodium (generic)

CLASS NSAID
PREG/CONT C (1st, 2nd trimesters); D (3rd trimester)/NA

BBW Increased risk of CV events, GI bleeding; monitor accordingly. Not for use for periop pain in CABG surgery.
IND & DOSE Tx of acute flares; long-term mgt of rheumatoid arthritis **(RA)**, osteoarthritis. *Adult:* 400 mg PO tid (1,200 mg/day) preferably including dose on arising and at

bedtime. Maint, 600–1,800 mg/day in three to four divided doses for RA, 600–1,600 mg/day in three to four divided doses for osteoarthritis. **Tx of juvenile RA.** *Child 2 yr and older:* 20 mg/kg/day PO in three to four divided doses. Usual dose, 15–30 mg/kg/day; max, 30 mg/kg/day.
ADV EFF Anaphylactoid reactions to fatal anaphylactic shock, **bone marrow suppression,** bronchospasm, diarrhea, dizziness, dyspepsia, dysuria, GI pain, headache, hypertension, insomnia, rash, somnolence, vision problems
NC/PT Pt should take w/milk if GI upset a problem, have periodic eye exams, take safety precautions for CNS effects, report signs of infection, difficulty breathing, unusual bleeding.

tolterodine tartrate (Detrol)
CLASS Antimuscarinic
PREG/CONT C/NA

IND & DOSE Tx of overactive bladder. *Adult:* 1–2 mg PO bid. ER form, 2–4 mg/day PO.
ADJUST DOSE Hepatic, renal impairment
ADV EFF Blurred vision, constipation, dizziness, dry mouth, dyspepsia, n/v, vision changes, weight gain
INTERACTIONS CYP2D6, CYP3A4 inhibitors
NC/PT Pt should swallow capsule whole and not cut, crush, or chew it; use sugarless lozenges for dry mouth; take laxative for constipation, safety precautions for CNS effects; report rash, difficulty breathing, palpitations.

tolvaptan (Samsca)
CLASS Selective vasopressin receptor antagonist
PREG/CONT C/NA

BBW Initiate tx in hospital setting, w/close supervision of sodium,

volume. Not for use when rapid correction of hyponatremia needed.
IND & DOSE Tx of clinically significant hypervolemic, euvolemic hyponatremia. *Adult:* 15 mg/day PO; may increase after at least 24 hr to max 60 mg/day.
ADV EFF Asthenia, constipation, dehydration, dry mouth, **hepatic injury,** hyperglycemia, polyuria, **serious liver toxicity,** thirst
INTERACTIONS CYP3A inducers/inhibitors
NC/PT Do not use w/hypertonic saline sol. Monitor serum electrolytes. Not for use in emergency situation, pregnancy/breast-feeding. Pt should report severe constipation, increasing thirst, fainting.

topiramate (Topamax, Topiragen)
CLASS Antiepileptic, antimigraine
PREG/CONT D/NA

BBW Increased risk of suicidality; monitor accordingly. Reduce dose, stop, or substitute other antiepileptic gradually; stopping abruptly may precipitate status epilepticus.
IND & DOSE Px of migraines: *Adult, child 17 yr and older:* 25 mg PO in p.m. for 1 wk; wk 2, 25 mg PO bid a.m. and p.m.; wk 3, 25 mg PO in a.m., 50 mg PO in p.m.; wk 4, 50 mg PO a.m. and p.m. **Tx of seizure disorders.** *Adult, child 17 yr and older:* 200–400 m/day PO in two divided doses. *Child 10 yr and older:* 25 mg PO bid, titrating to maint dose of 200 mg PO bid over 6 wk: wk 1, 25 mg bid; wk 2, 50 mg bid; wk 3, 75 mg bid; wk 4, 100 mg bid; wk 5, 150 mg bid; wk 6, 200 mg bid. Or ER form, 25 mg PO at bedtime, range 1–3 mg/kg for first wk; titrate at 1- to 2-wk intervals by 1- to 3-mg/kg increments to 5–9 mg/kg/day PO. *Child 2–16 yr:* 5–9 mg/kg/day PO in two divided doses. Start tx at nightly dose of 25 mg (or less, based on 1–3 mg/kg/day) for

first wk. May titrate up by increments of 1–3 mg/kg/day (in two divided doses) at 1- to 2-wk intervals.
ADJUST DOSE Hepatic, renal impairment
ADV EFF Ataxia, cognitive dysfunction, dizziness, dysmenorrhea, dyspepsia, fatigue, metabolic acidosis, myopia, nausea, nystagmus, paresthesia, renal stones, somnolence, **suicidality,** URI, visual field defects
INTERACTIONS Alcohol, carbamazepine, carbonic anhydrase inhibitors, CNS depressants, hormonal contraceptives, phenytoin, valproic acid
NC/PT Taper if stopping. Not for use in pregnancy (may make hormonal contraceptives ineffective; barrier contraceptives advised). Pt should not cut, crush, or chew tablets (bitter taste); may swallow sprinkle capsule whole or sprinkle contents on soft food, swallow immediately; should avoid alcohol; take safety precautions for CNS effects; report vision changes, flank pain, thoughts of suicide. Name confusion between *Topamax* and *Toprol-XL* (metoprolol); use caution.

DANGEROUS DRUG

topotecan hydrochloride (Hycamtin)
CLASS Antineoplastic
PREG/CONT D/NA

BBW Monitor bone marrow carefully; do not give dose until bone marrow responsive.
IND & DOSE Tx of metastatic ovarian cancer, small-cell lung cancer. *Adult:* 1.5 mg/m^2/day IV over 30 min for 5 days, starting on day 1 of 21-day course. Minimum four courses recommended. **Tx of persistent cervical cancer.** *Adult:* 0.75 mg/m^2/day by IV infusion over 30 min on days 1, 2, 3 followed by cisplatin on day 1. Repeat q 21 days.
ADJUST DOSE Hepatic, renal impairment

ADV EFF Alopecia, **bone marrow suppression,** constipation, fever, infections, **interstitial pneumonitis,** n/v/d, pain
INTERACTIONS Cytotoxic drugs
NC/PT Monitor CBC; dose adjustment may be needed. Not for use in pregnancy (barrier contraceptives advised)/breast-feeding. Pt should mark calendar of tx days, cover head at temp extremes (hair loss possible), avoid exposure to infection, take analgesics for pain, report difficulty breathing, unusual bleeding, signs of infection.

DANGEROUS DRUG

toremifene citrate (Fareston)
CLASS Antineoplastic, estrogen receptor modulator
PREG/CONT D/NA

BBW Risk of prolonged QT. Obtain baseline, periodic ECG; avoid concurrent use of other QT-prolonging drugs.
IND & DOSE Tx of advanced breast cancer in postmenopausal women. *Adult:* 60 mg PO daily; continue until disease progression.
ADV EFF Depression, dizziness, headache, hot flashes, n/v, **prolonged QT,** rash, vaginal discharge
INTERACTIONS Oral anticoagulants, other drugs that decrease calcium excretion, QT-prolonging drugs
NC/PT Obtain baseline ECG; monitor periodically during tx. Not for use in pregnancy (barrier contraceptives advised). Pt should take safety precautions w/dizziness; report palpitations, vision changes.

---

torsemide (Demadex)
CLASS Loop diuretic, sulfonamide
PREG/CONT B/NA

IND & DOSE Tx of edema associated w/HF. *Adult:* 10–20 mg/day PO or IV;

max, 200 mg/day. **Tx of edema associated w/chronic renal failure.** *Adult:* 20 mg/day PO or IV; max, 200 mg/day. **Tx of edema associated w/ hepatic failure.** *Adult:* 5–10 mg/day PO or IV; max, 40 mg/day. **Tx of hypertension.** *Adult:* 5 mg/day PO.
ADV EFF Anorexia, asterixis, dizziness, drowsiness, headache, hypokalemia, nocturia, n/v/d, orthostatic hypotension, ototoxicity, pain, phlebitis at injection site, polyuria
INTERACTIONS Aminoglycoside antibiotics, cisplatin, digoxin, ethacrynic acid, NSAIDs
NC/PT Monitor serum electrolytes. Pt should take early in day to prevent sleep disruption; weigh self daily, report changes of more than 3 lb/day; take safety precautions for CNS effects; report swelling, hearing loss, muscle cramps/weakness.

DANGEROUS DRUG

tositumomab and iodine I-131 tositumomab (Bexxar)
CLASS Antineoplastic, monoclonal antibody
PREG/CONT X/NA

BBW Risk of severe, prolonged cytopenia. Hypersensitivity reactions, including anaphylaxis, have occurred.
IND & DOSE Tx of CD20-positive, follicular non-Hodgkin lymphoma. *Adult:* 450 mg tositumomab IV in 50 mL normal saline over 60 min, 5 mCi I-131 w/35 mg tositumomab in 30 mL normal saline IV over 20 min; then repeat as therapeutic step, adjusting I-131 based on pt response.
ADV EFF Anorexia, asthenia, **cancer development**, fever, headache, hypothyroidism, n/v/d, **severe cytopenia**
NC/PT Radioactive; use special handling precautions. Rule out pregnancy; not for use in pregnancy (two types of contraceptives advised)/breast-feeding. Monitor CBC, renal function. Discuss limiting exposure to family; will take about 12 days to clear

body. Pt should report signs of infection, unusual bleeding.

---

trabectedin (Yondelis)
CLASS Alkylating agent, antineoplastic
PREG/CONT Can cause fetal harm/NA

IND & DOSE Tx of pts w/ unresectable metastatic liposarcoma/leiomyosarcoma after anthracycline tx. *Adult:* 1.5 mg/m² IV over 24 hr through central line q 3 wk.
ADV EFF Bone marrow suppression, **cardiomyopathy**, constipation, dyspnea, fatigue, **hepatotoxicity**, n/v/d, **neutropenic sepsis**, peripheral edema, **rhabdomyolysis**
INTERACTIONS Strong CYP3A inducers/inhibitors; avoid combination
NC/PT Monitor CBC, LFTs, creatinine levels carefully; dose based on response. Premedicate w/ dexamethasone 30 min before each infusion. Not for use in pregnancy (barrier contraceptives advised)/breast-feeding. Pt should avoid exposure to infections; mark calendar of tx days; report signs of infection, difficulty breathing, muscle pain, peripheral edema.

DANGEROUS DRUG

tramadol hydrochloride (ConZip, Ultram)
CLASS Opioid analgesic
PREG/CONT C/NA

IND & DOSE Relief of moderate to moderately severe pain. *Adult:* 50–100 mg PO q 4–6 hr; max, 400 mg/day. For chronic pain, 25 mg/day PO in a.m.; titrate in 25-mg increments q 3 days to 100 mg/day. Then, increase in 50-mg increments q 3 days to 200 mg/day. After titration, 50–100 mg q 4–6 hr PO; max, 400 mg/day. Or, 100-mg PO ER tablet once daily, titrated by 100-mg

increments q 5 days; max, 300 mg/day. For orally disintegrating tablets, max, 200 mg/day PO.
ADJUST DOSE Elderly pts; hepatic, renal impairment
ADV EFF Anaphylactoid reactions, constipation, dizziness, headache, hypotension, n/v, sedation, **seizures, suicidality,** sweating, vertigo
INTERACTIONS Alcohol, carbamazepine, CNS depressants, MAOIs, SSRIs
NC/PT Control environment; use other measures to relieve pain. Limit use w/hx of addiction. Pt should swallow ER tablet whole and not cut, crush, or chew it; dissolve orally disintegrating tablets in mouth, then swallow w/water; take safety precautions for CNS effects; report thoughts of suicide.

trametinib (Mekinist)
CLASS Antineoplastic, kinase inhibitor
PREG/CONT D/NA

IND & DOSE Tx of unresectable or metastatic melanoma w/BRAF **V600E** or **V600K** mutations. *Adult:* 2 mg/day PO 1 hr before or 2 hr after meal; may combine w/dabrafenib 150 mg PO bid.
ADJUST DOSE Severe renal/hepatic impairment
ADV EFF Cardiomyopathy, diarrhea, hyperglycemia, **interstitial lung disease,** lymphedema, **malignancies,** ocular toxicities, **retinal pigment epithelial detachment, retinal vein occlusion, serious skin toxicity**
NC/PT Ensure regular ophthalmic exams. Evaluate left ventricular ejection fraction before and every 2 mo during tx. Evaluate lung function; stop drug if sx of interstitial pneumonitis. Watch for rash, skin toxicity; stop drug if grade 2–4 rash does not improve w/3-wk interruption. Pt should take drug 1 hr before or 2 hr after meal; avoid pregnancy/breast-feeding; know frequent testing and

follow-up will be needed; be aware drug could impair fertility; report difficulty breathing, extreme fatigue, swelling of extremities, rash, vision changes.

trandolapril (Mavik)
CLASS ACE inhibitor, antihypertensive
PREG/CONT D/NA

BBW Rule out pregnancy before tx; advise use of barrier contraceptives. Fetal injury, death has occurred when used in second, third trimester.
IND & DOSE Tx of hypertension. *Adult:* African-American pts: 2 mg/day PO. All other pts: 1 mg/day PO. Maint, 2–4 mg/day; max, 8 mg/day. Tx of HF post-MI. *Adult:* 1 mg/day PO; may start 3–5 days after MI. Adjust to target 4 mg/day.
ADJUST DOSE Angioedema, diarrhea, dizziness, headache, **hepatic failure, hypersensitivity reactions, MI,** renal impairment, tachycardia
INTERACTIONS Diuretics, lithium, potassium supplements
NC/PT Monitor LFTs. If pt on diuretic, stop diuretic 2–3 days before starting trandolapril; resume diuretic only if BP not controlled. If diuretic cannot be stopped, start at 0.5 mg PO daily; adjust upward as needed. Alert surgeon; volume replacement may be needed postop. Not for use in pregnancy (barrier contraceptives advised). Pt should use care in situations that could lead to BP drop; take safety precautions for CNS effects; report difficulty breathing, swelling of lips/face, chest pain.

tranexamic acid (Lysteda)
CLASS Antifibrinolytic
PREG/CONT B/NA

IND & DOSE Tx of cyclic heavy **menstrual bleeding.** *Adult:* 1,300 mg PO tid for max 5 days during monthly menstruation.

ADJUST DOSE Hepatic, renal impairment
ADV EFF Abd pain, **anaphylactic shock, anaphylactoid reactions,** arthralgia, back pain, fatigue, headache, n/v/d, **thromboembolic events,** visual disturbances
INTERACTIONS Hormonal contraceptives, TPAs
NC/PT Obtain baseline, periodic evaluation of bleeding. Not for use in pregnancy (hormonal contraceptives may increase thromboembolic event risk; barrier contraceptives advised). Pt should report difficulty breathing, leg pain/swelling, severe headache, vision changes.

---

tranylcypromine sulfate (Parnate)
CLASS Antidepressant, MAOI
PREG/CONT C/NA

BBW Limit amount available to suicidal pts. Possible increased risk of suicidality in children, adolescents, young adults; monitor accordingly.
IND & DOSE Tx of major depressive disorder. *Adult:* 30 mg/day PO in divided doses. If no improvement within 2–3 wk, increase in 10-mg/day increments q 1–3 wk. Max, 60 mg/day.
ADJUST DOSE Elderly pts
ADV EFF Abd pain, anorexia, blurred vision, confusion, constipation, dizziness, drowsiness, dry mouth, headache, hyperreflexia, **hypertensive crises,** hypomania, hypotension, insomnia, jitteriness, **liver toxicity,** n/v/d, orthostatic hypotension, photosensitivity, suicidal thoughts, twitching, vertigo
INTERACTIONS Alcohol, amphetamines, antidiabetics, beta blockers, bupropion, buspirone, general anesthetics, meperidine, SSRIs, sympathomimetics, TCAs, thiazides, tyramine-containing foods
NC/PT Have phentolamine, another alpha-adrenergic blocker on hand for hypertensive crisis. Do not use within 14 days of other MAOIs, within 10 days

of buspirone, bupropion. Monitor LFTs, BP regularly. Pt should avoid diet high in tyramine-containing foods during, for 2 wk after tx; avoid alcohol, OTC appetite suppressants; take safety precautions for CNS effects; change position slowly w/orthostatic hypotension; report rash, urine/stool color changes, thoughts of suicide.

DANGEROUS DRUG

trastuzumab (Herceptin)
CLASS Antineoplastic, monoclonal antibody (anti-HER2)
PREG/CONT D/NA

BBW Monitor pt during infusion; provide comfort measures, analgesics as appropriate for infusion reaction. Monitor cardiac status, especially if pt receiving chemotherapy; do not give w/anthracycline chemotherapy. Have emergency equipment on hand for cardiotoxicity; cardiomyopathy possible. Monitor for possibly severe pulmonary toxicity, especially within 24 hours of infusion. Stop if s&sx of respiratory involvement. Embryotoxic; ensure pt is not pregnancy before tx (advise use of contraceptive measures).
IND & DOSE Tx of metastatic HER2 overexpressing breast cancer. *Adult:* 4 mg/kg IV once by IV infusion over 90 min. Maint, 2 mg/kg IV wk IV over at least 30 min as tolerated; max, 500 mg/dose. Adjunct tx of HER2-overexpressing breast cancer. *Adult:* After completion of doxorubicin, cyclophosphamide tx, give wkly for 52 wk. Initially, 4 mg/kg by IV infusion over 90 min; maint, 2 mg/kg/wk by IV infusion over 30 min. Or, initially, 8 mg/kg by IV infusion over 90 min; then 6 mg/kg by IV infusion over 30–90 min q 3 wk. During first 12 wk, give w/paclitaxel. Tx of HER2-overexpressing metastatic gastric or gastroesophageal junction adenocancer. *Adult:* 8 mg/kg IV over

90 min; then 6 mg/kg IV over 30–90 min q 3 wk until disease progression.

ADV EFF Abd pain, anemia, cardiomyopathy, chills, diarrhea, fever, headache, infections, injection-site reactions, leukopenia, **neutropenia,** paresthesia, **pulmonary toxicity, serious cardiotoxicity**

NC/PT Ensure HER2 testing before therapy. Do not mix w/other drug sols or add other drugs to IV line. Monitor cardiac status; have emergency equipment on hand. Monitor respiratory status, CBC. Pt should mark calendar of tx days; avoid exposure to infection; avoid pregnancy (contraceptive measures advised); report chest pain, difficulty breathing, pain at injection site.

---

trazodone hydrochloride (generic)
CLASS Antidepressant
PREG/CONT C/NA

BBW Increased risk of suicidality; limit quantities in depressed, suicidal pts.

IND & DOSE Tx of depression.
Adult: 150 mg/day PO in divided doses; max, 400 mg/day PO in divided doses. For severe depression, max, 600 mg/day PO.

ADJUST DOSE Elderly pts

ADV EFF Angle-closure glaucoma, blurred vision, constipation, dizziness, **NMS,** orthostatic hypotension, sedation, withdrawal syndrome

INTERACTIONS Alcohol, aspirin, CNS depressants, CYP3A4 inducers/inhibitors, digoxin, MAOIs, NSAIDs, phenytoin, SSRIs, St. John's wort

NC/PT Do not give within 14 days of MAOIs. Taper when stopping; do not stop abruptly. Use caution in pregnancy/breast-feeding. Pt should take safety precautions for CNS effects, report fever, severe constipation, thoughts of suicide.

---

treprostinil sodium (Remodulin, Tyvaso)
CLASS Endothelin receptor antagonist, vasodilator
PREG/CONT B/NA

IND & DOSE Tx of pulmonary arterial hypertension. *Adult:* 1.25 ng/kg/min subcly by infusion. Increase rate in increments of no more than 1.25 ng/kg/min wkly for first 4 wk, then by 2.5 ng/kg/min wkly. Max, 40 ng/kg/min or 3 breaths (18 mcg), using *Tyvaso* Inhalation System, per tx session; 4 sessions/day, approximately 4 hr apart during waking hours. Increase by additional 3 breaths/session at 1- to 2-wk intervals if needed, tolerated. Maint, 9 breaths (54 mcg)/session.

ADJUST DOSE Hepatic impairment
ADV EFF Edema, headache, infusion-site reaction, jaw pain, n/d, rash
INTERACTIONS Anticoagulants, antihypertensives, antiplatelets, diuretics, vasodilators

NC/PT See manufacturer's instructions if switching from epoprostenol (Flolan). Obtain baseline pulmonary status, exercise tolerance. Not for use in pregnancy (barrier contraceptives advised). Taper slowly when stopping. Evaluate subcut infusion site wkly; give analgesics for headache. Teach proper care, use of continuous subcut infusion; if using inhalation, review proper use. Pt should continue usual tx procedures, report swelling, injection site pain/swelling, worsening condition.

DANGEROUS DRUG

tretinoin (Atralin, Avita, Renova, Retin-A, Tretin-X)
CLASS Antineoplastic, retinoid
PREG/CONT D/NA

BBW Rule out pregnancy before tx; arrange for pregnancy test within 2 wk of starting tx. Advise use of two forms of contraception during tx, for

1 mo after tx ends. Should only be used under supervision of experienced practitioner or in institution experienced w/its use. Risk of rapid leukocytosis (40% of pts); notify physician immediately if this occurs. Stop drug, notify physician if LFTs over 5 × ULN, pulmonary infiltrates appear, or pt has difficulty breathing; serious side effects possible. Monitor for retinoic acid–APL syndrome (fever, dyspnea, acute respiratory distress, weight gain, pulmonary infiltrates, pleural/pericardial effusion, multiorgan failure); endotracheal intubation, mechanical ventilation may be needed.

IND & DOSE To induce remission in acute promyelocytic leukemia (APL). *Adult, child 1 yr and over:* 45 mg/m²/day PO in two evenly divided doses until complete remission; stop tx 30 days after complete remission obtained or after 90 days, whichever first. **Topical tx of acne vulgaris; mitigation of wrinkles; mottled hyperpigmentation.** *Adult, child 1 yr and over:* Apply once/day before bedtime. Cover entire affected area lightly, avoiding mucous membranes.

ADV EFF Cardiac arrest, dry skin, earache, fever, GI bleeding, headache, lipid changes, **MI,** n/v, **pseudotumor cerebri, rapid/evolving leukocytosis,** rash, sweating, visual disturbances

INTERACTIONS Hydroxyurea, keratolytic agents, ketoconazole, tetracyclines

NC/PT Monitor LFTs, lipids, vision. Not for use in pregnancy (two forms of contraceptives, during and for 1 mo after tx, advised). Pt cannot donate blood during tx. Pt should not cut, crush oral capsule; have frequent blood tests; avoid products containing vitamin D; take safety precautions for CNS effects; use sugarless lozenges w/dry mouth; report severe/bloody diarrhea, difficulty breathing, thoughts of suicide.

triamcinolone acetonide (Kenalog), **triamcinolone hexacetonide** (Aristospan)
CLASS Corticosteroid
PREG/CONT C/NA

IND & DOSE Hypercalcemia of cancer; mgt of various inflammatory disorders; tx of idiopathic thrombocytopenic purpura. *Adult:* Individualize dose, depending on condition severity, pt response. Give daily dose before 9 a.m. to minimize adrenal suppression. If long-term tx needed, consider alternate-day tx. After long-term tx, withdraw slowly to avoid adrenal insufficiency. Range, 2.5–100 mg/day IM. *Child:* Individualize dose based on response, not formulae; monitor growth. **Maint, tx of bronchial asthma.** *Adult, child 6–12 yr:* 200 mcg inhalant released w/each actuation delivers about 100 mcg. Two inhalations tid–qid; max, 16 inhalations/day. **Tx of seasonal, perennial allergic rhinitis.** *Adult:* 2 sprays (220 mcg total dose) in each nostril daily; max, 4 sprays/day. *Child 6–12 yr:* 1 spray in each nostril once/day (100–110 mcg dose); max, 2 sprays/nostril/day. **Intra-articular relief of inflammatory conditions.** *Adult, child:* Acetonide, 2.5–15 mg intra-articular. Hexacetonide, 2–20 mg intra-articular; up to 0.5 mg/square inch of affected area intralesional. **Relief of inflammatory, pruritic s&sx of dermatoses.** *Adult, child:* Apply sparingly to affected area bid–qid. **Tx of oral lesions.** *Adult:* Press small dab (1/4 inch) to each lesion until thin film develops, two to three times/day after meals.

ADV EFF Headache, increased appetite, immunosuppression, impaired wound healing, infections, menstrual changes, osteoporosis, sodium/fluid retention, vertigo, weight gain

INTERACTIONS Barbiturates, edrophonium, neostigmine, oral antidiabetics, phenytoin, pyridostigmine, rifampin, salicylates
NC/PT Not for acute asthmatic attack. Give in a.m. to mimic normal levels. Taper when stopping after long-term tx. Do not use occlusive dressings w/topical form. Review proper administration. Pt should avoid exposure to infection, joint overuse after intra-articular injection; keep topical forms away from eyes; report swelling, signs of infection, worsening of condition.

---

triamterene (Dyrenium)
CLASS Potassium-sparing diuretic
PREG/CONT C/NA

BBW Risk of hyperkalemia (possibly fatal), more likely w/diabetics, elderly/severely ill pts; monitor potassium carefully.

IND & DOSE Tx of edema associated w/systemic conditions. *Adult:* 100 mg PO bid; max, 300 mg/day. Tx of hypertension. *Adult:* 25 mg/day PO; usual dose, 50–100 mg/day.
ADV EFF Abd pain, anorexia, dizziness, drowsiness, dry mouth, hyperkalemia, n/v/d, rash, renal stones
INTERACTIONS Amantadine, lithium, potassium supplements
NC/PT Pt should take in a.m. to decrease sleep interruption, w/food if GI upset; weigh self regularly, report change of 3 lb/day; take safety precautions for CNS effects; avoid foods high in potassium; report swelling, difficulty breathing, flank pain, muscle cramps, tremors.

---

triazolam (Halcion)
CLASS Benzodiazepine, sedative-hypnotic
PREG/CONT X/C-IV

IND & DOSE Tx of insomnia. *Adult:* 0.125–0.25 mg PO before retiring.

May increase to max 0.5 mg. Limit use to 7–10 days.
ADJUST DOSE Elderly, debilitated pts
ADV EFF Anaphylaxis, angioedema, bradycardia, confusion, constipation, CV collapse, diarrhea, drowsiness, drug dependence, fatigue, hiccups, nervousness, tachycardia, urticaria
INTERACTIONS Alcohol, aminophylline, cimetidine, CNS depressants, disulfiram, dyphylline, grapefruit juice, hormonal contraceptives, itraconazole, ketoconazole, omeprazole, theophylline
NC/PT Taper gradually after long-term use. Monitor renal function, CBC periodically. Not for use in pregnancy (barrier contraceptives advised). Pt should avoid grapefruit juice, alcohol; take safety precautions for CNS effects; report difficulty breathing, swelling of face/eyes, continued sleep disorders.

---

trientine hydrochloride (Syprine)
CLASS Chelate
PREG/CONT C/NA

IND & DOSE Tx of pts w/Wilson disease intolerant of penicillamine. *Adult:* 750–1,250 mg/day PO in divided doses; max, 2 g/day. *Child:* 500–750 mg/day PO; max, 1,500 mg/day.
ADV EFF Abd pain, anorexia, epigastric pain, hypersensitivity reactions, iron deficiency, muscle spasm, myasthenia gravis, rash, rhabdomyolysis, SLE, weakness
NC/PT Pt should take on empty stomach 1 hr before, 2 hr after meals; swallow capsule whole and not cut, crush, or chew it; monitor temp nightly for first mo of tx; space iron supplement at least 2 hr apart from trientine; report fever, muscle weakness/pain, difficulty breathing.

trihexyphenidyl hydrochloride (generic)

CLASS Antiparkinsonian (anticholinergic type)
PREG/CONT C/NA

BBW Stop or decrease dosage if dry mouth interferes w/swallowing, speaking.

IND & DOSE Adjunct in tx of parkinsonism. *Adult:* 1 mg PO first day. Increase by 2-mg increments at 3- to 5-day intervals until total of 6–10 mg/day. Postencephalitic pts may need 12–15 mg/day PO. W/levodopa: Adjust based on response; usual, 3–6 mg/day PO. Tx of drug-induced extrapyramidal sx. *Adult:* 1 mg PO. May need to temporarily reduce tranquilizer dose to expedite control of extrapyramidal sx. Usual dose, 5–15 mg/day.
ADJUST DOSE Elderly pts
ADV EFF Blurred vision, confusion, constipation, decreased sweating, delusions, disorientation, dizziness, drowsiness, dry mouth, flushing, light-headedness, urine retention
INTERACTIONS Haloperidol, phenothiazines
NC/PT Pt should empty bladder before each dose; use caution in hot weather (decreased sweating can lead to heat stroke); use sugarless lozenges for dry mouth; take safety precautions for CNS effects; report eye pain, rash, rapid heartbeat, difficulty swallowing/speaking.

trimethobenzamide hydrochloride (Tigan)

CLASS Antiemetic (anticholinergic)
PREG/CONT C/NA

IND & DOSE Control of postop n/v, nausea associated w/gastroenteritis. *Adult:* 300 mg PO tid–qid, or 200 mg IM tid–qid.
ADJUST DOSE Elderly pts

ADV EFF Blurred vision, dizziness, drowsiness, headache, hypotension, pain/swelling at injection site
NC/PT Ensure adequate hydration. Pt should avoid alcohol (sedation possible), take safety precautions for CNS effects, report unusual bleeding, visual disturbances, pain at injection site.

trimethoprim (Primsol)

CLASS Antibiotic
PREG/CONT C/NA

IND & DOSE Uncomplicated UTIs caused by susceptible bacteria strains. *Adult, child 12 yr and older:* 100 mg PO q 12 hr or 200 mg PO q 24 hr for 10–14 days. Tx of otitis media. *Child under 12 yr:* 10 mg/kg/day PO in divided doses q 12 hr for 10 days.
ADJUST DOSE Elderly pts, renal impairment
ADV EFF Bone marrow suppression, epigastric distress, exfoliative dermatitis, hepatic impairment, pruritus, rash
INTERACTIONS Phenytoin
NC/PT Culture before tx. Protect drug from light. Monitor CBC. Pt should take full course, avoid exposure to infection, report unusual bleeding, signs of infection, rash.

trimipramine maleate (Surmontil)

CLASS TCA
PREG/CONT C/NA

BBW Limit access in depressed, potentially suicidal pts. Monitor for suicidal ideation, especially when beginning tx, changing doses. High risk of suicidality in children, adolescents, young adults.
IND & DOSE Relief of sx of depression. *Adult:* Inpts, 100 mg PO in divided doses. Gradually increase to 200 mg/day as needed; max, 250–300 mg/day. Outpts, 75 mg/day PO in divided doses. May increase to

150 mg/day; max, 200 mg/day. *Child 12 yr and older:* 50 mg/day PO w/ gradual increases up to 100 mg/day.
ADJUST DOSE Elderly pts
ADV EFF Anticholinergic effects, **bone marrow suppression,** constipation, dry mouth, extrapyramidal effects, **MI,** orthostatic hypotension, photosensitivity, rash, **stroke**
INTERACTIONS Alcohol, cimetidine, clarithromycin, clonidine, fluoroquinolones, fluoxetine, MAOIs, ranitidine, sympathomimetics, tramadol
NC/PT Monitor CBC periodically. Not for use in pregnancy (contraceptives advised). Pt should not stop suddenly; avoid sun exposure, alcohol; take safety precautions for CNS effects; use sugarless lozenges for dry mouth; report thoughts of suicide, excessive sedation.

DANGEROUS DRUG

triptorelin pamoate (Trelstar)
CLASS Antineoplastic, LHRH analogue
PREG/CONT X/NA

IND & DOSE Palliative tx of advanced prostate cancer. *Adult:* 3.75-mg depot injection IM once monthly into buttock, or 11.25-mg injection IM q 12 wk into buttock, or 22.5 mg IM q 24 wk into buttock.
ADV EFF Anaphylaxis, angioedema, bone pain, decreased erection, headache, **HF,** hot flashes, injection-site pain, insomnia, **prolonged QT,** sexual dysfx, urinary tract sx
INTERACTIONS Antipsychotics, metoclopramide, QT-prolonging drugs
NC/PT Monitor testosterone, PSA before, periodically during tx. Not for use in pregnancy. Pt should mark calendar for injection days; use comfort measures for hot flashes, pain; report swelling, difficulty breathing, signs of infection at injection sites.

trospium chloride (generic)
CLASS Antimuscarinic, antispasmodic
PREG/CONT C/NA

IND & DOSE Tx of s&sx of overactive bladder. *Adult under 75 yr:* 20 mg PO bid on empty stomach, at least 1 hr before meals. Or, 60 mg ER tablet PO once/day. *Adult over 75 yr:* Monitor pt response; adjust down to 20 mg/day.
ADJUST DOSE Renal impairment
ADV EFF Constipation, decreased sweating, dizziness, drowsiness, dry mouth, fatigue, headache, urine retention
INTERACTIONS Digoxin, metformin, morphine, other anticholinergics, procainamide, pancuronium, tenofovir, vancomycin
NC/PT Pt should empty bladder before each dose; take on empty stomach 1 hr before, 2 hr after food; not cut, crush, or chew ER tablet; use sugarless lozenges, mouth care for dry mouth; maintain hydration; use caution in hot environments (decreased sweating could lead to heat stroke); take safety precautions for CNS effects; report inability to urinate, fever.

umeclidinium (Incruse Ellipta)
CLASS Anticholinergic, bronchodilator
PREG/CONT Unkn/NA

IND & DOSE Long-term maint tx of airflow obstruction in COPD. *Adult:* 62.5 mcg (one oral inhalation)/day.
ADV EFF Allergic reactions, cough, narrow-angle glaucoma, **paradoxical bronchospasm,** URI, urinary retention
INTERACTIONS Other anticholinergics; avoid combination
NC/PT Not for use in deteriorating COPD, acute bronchospasm. Not for

use in pts w/hypersensitivity to milk proteins. Monitor closely w/known glaucoma, BPH, urinary retention. Teach proper use of inhaler device. Pt should report sudden shortness of breath, vision problems, difficult/painful urination.

uriden (Xuriden)
CLASS Pyrimidine analog
PREG/CONT Unkn/NA

IND & DOSE Tx of hereditary orotic aciduria. *Adult, child:* 60 mg/kg/day PO; may increase to 120 mg/kg/day if needed. Max, 8 g/day.
ADV EFF None reported
NC/PT Mix granules in applesauce, pudding, yogurt, milk, or baby formula; discard any granules left in basket. Administer as soon as mixed; pt should not chew granules. Tell pt blood tests will be taken regularly to monitor drug's effects.

uridine triacetate (Vistogard)
CLASS Pyrimidine analog
PREG/CONT Unkn/NA

IND & DOSE Emergency tx of 5-FU or capecitabine overdose or severe toxicity. *Adult:* 10 g PO q 6 hr for 20 doses. *Child:* 6.2 g/m² PO q 6 hr for 20 doses; max, 10 g/dose.
ADV EFF N/v/d
NC/PT Mix packet w/3–4 oz soft food (applesauce, pudding, yogurt); give within 30 min. Do not allow pt to chew granules. Follow w/at least 4 oz water. If pt vomits within 2 hr, give complete dose again; give next dose at regular time. If a dose is missed, give as soon as possible and give next dose at regular time. May give via NG or gastrostomy tube. Tablet will not completely dissolve; do not crush or heat tablet. Pt should report vomiting, severe diarrhea.

urofollitropin (Bravelle)
CLASS Fertility drug
PREG/CONT X/NA

IND & DOSE Stimulation of ovulation. *Adults who have received gonadotropin-releasing hormone agonist, antagonist suppression:* 150 units/day subcut or IM for first 5 days. Subsequent dosing should not exceed 75–150 units/adjustment. Max, 450 units/day. Tx beyond 12 days not recommended. If pt response appropriate, give HCG 5,000–10,000 units 1 day after last *Bravelle* dose. Stimulation of follicle development. *Adult:* 225 units/day subcut or IM for 5 days, then adjust dose q 2 days, not exceeding 75- to 150-unit increments; max, 450 units/day.
ADV EFF Congenital malformations, ectopic pregnancy, multiple births, nausea, ovarian cyst, **ovarian hyperstimulation,** ovarian neoplasms, ovarian torsion, **pulmonary/vascular complications,** URI
NC/PT Ensure uterine health. Alert pt to risk of multiple births. Monitor regularly; monitor for thrombotic events. Teach proper administration/disposal of needles/syringes. Pt should report abd/chest pain.

ursodiol (Actigall, URSO 250)
CLASS Gallstone-solubilizing drug
PREG/CONT B/NA

IND & DOSE Gallstone solubilization. *Adult:* 8–10 mg/kg/day PO in two to three divided doses. Px of gallstones w/rapid weight loss. *Adult:* 300 mg PO bid or 8–10 mg/kg/day PO in two to three divided doses. Tx of biliary cirrhosis. *Adult:* 13–15 mg/kg/day PO in two to four divided doses w/food.
ADV EFF Abd pain, cramps, diarrhea, epigastric distress, fatigue, headache, rash

INTERACTIONS Antacids, bile-acid sequestrants
NC/PT Drug not a cure; gallstones may recur. Schedule periodic oral cholecystograms or ultrasonograms to evaluate effectiveness at 6-mo intervals until resolution, then every 3 mo to monitor stone formation. Monitor LFTs periodically. Pt should avoid antacids, report yellowing of skin/eyes, gallstone attacks, bleeding.

---

ustekinumab (Stelara)
CLASS Monoclonal antibody
PREG/CONT B/NA

IND & DOSE Tx of mild to moderate plaque psoriasis. *Adult:* Over 100 kg, 90 mg subcut, then 90 mg in 4 wk, then q 12 wk. 100 kg or less, 45 mg subcut, then 45 mg in 4 wk, then q 12 wk. **Tx of psoriatic arthritis.** *Adult:* Initially, 45 mg subcut, then 45 mg subcut 4 wk later, then 45 mg subcut q 12 wk. **Adult w/coexisting plaque psoriasis:** 90 mg subcut, then 90 mg subcut 4 wk later, then 90 mg subcut q 12 wk.
ADV EFF Fatigue, headache, **hypersensitivity reactions, malignancies, RPLS, serious infections,** URI
INTERACTIONS Immunosuppressants, live vaccines, phototherapy
NC/PT Use caution in pregnancy/breast-feeding. Ensure appropriate cancer screening. Pt should mark calendar of injection days, avoid live vaccines, report signs of infection, worsening of condition, difficulty breathing.

---

valacyclovir hydrochloride (Valtrex)
CLASS Antiviral
PREG/CONT B/NA

IND & DOSE Tx of herpes zoster. *Adult:* 1 g PO tid for 7 days; most effective if started within 48 hr of sx onset (rash). **Tx of genital herpes.** *Adult:* 1 g PO bid for 7–10 days for initial episode. **Episodic tx of recurrent genital herpes.** *Adult:* 500 mg PO bid for 3 days, or 1 g/day for 5 days. **To suppress recurrent episodes of genital herpes.** *Adult:* 1 g/day PO; pts w/hx of less than nine episodes in 1 yr may respond to 500 mg PO daily. **To suppress recurrent episodes of genital herpes in pts w/HIV.** 500 mg PO bid for 5–10 days. **To reduce risk of herpes zoster transmission.** *Adult:* 500 mg PO for source partner. For HIV-positive pts, 500 mg PO bid. **Tx of cold sores.** *Adult, child 12 yr and over:* 2 g PO bid for 1 day, 12 hr apart. **Tx of chickenpox.** *Child 2–18 yr:* 20 mg/kg PO tid for 5 days; max, 1 g tid.
ADJUST DOSE Renal impairment
ADV EFF Abd pain, **acute renal failure,** dizziness, headache, n/v/d, rash
INTERACTIONS Cimetidine, probenecid
NC/PT Begin tx within 48–72 hr of onset of shingles sx or within 24 hr of onset of chickenpox rash. Pt should take full course of tx; avoid contact w/lesions; avoid intercourse when lesions present; take analgesics for headache; report severe diarrhea, worsening of condition. Name confusion between *Valtrex* (valacyclovir) and *Valcyte* (valganciclovir); use caution.

---

valganciclovir hydrochloride (Valcyte)
CLASS Antiviral
PREG/CONT C/NA

BBW Arrange for CBC before tx, at least wkly thereafter. Arrange for reduced dose if WBC, platelet counts fall. Toxicity includes granulocytopenia, anemia, thrombocytopenia. Advise pt drug has caused cancer, fetal damage in animals and that risk possible in humans.
IND & DOSE Tx of cytomegalovirus (CMV) infection. *Adult:* 900 mg PO bid for 21 days; maint, 900 mg/day PO. **Px of CMV infection in high-risk**

kidney, pancreas-kidney, heart transplant. *Adult:* 900 mg/day PO initiated within 10 days of transplant, continued for 100 days after transplant. **Px of CMV infection in high-risk kidney, heart transplant.** *Child 4 mo–16 yr:* Dose in mg = 7 × BSA × CrCl PO for 100 days (heart transplant), 200 days (kidney transplant). Max, 900 mg/day. May use oral sol, tablets.

ADJUST DOSE Renal impairment
ADV EFF Anemia, **bone marrow suppression**, confusion, dizziness, drowsiness, fertility impairment, fever, headache, insomnia, n/v/d, **renal failure**, tremor
INTERACTIONS Cytotoxic drugs, didanosine, mycophenolate, probenecid, zidovudine
NC/PT Cannot be substituted for ganciclovir capsules on one-to-one basis. Monitor CBC. Precautions needed for disposal of nucleoside analogues; consult pharmacy for proper disposal of unused tablets. Not for use in pregnancy; men, women should use barrier contraceptives during, for 90 days after tx. Adults should use tablets, not solution. Avoid handling broken tablets. Pt should not cut, crush, or chew tablets; drink 2–3 L water/day; have frequent blood tests, eye exams to evaluate progress; take safety precautions w/CNS effects; avoid exposure to infection; dispose of drug appropriately; report bruising/bleeding, signs of infection. Name confusion between *Valcyte* (valganciclovir) and *Valtrex* (valacyclovir): use caution.

---

valproic acid, sodium valproate (Depakene, Depacon), **divalproex sodium** (Depakote, Divalproex)
CLASS Antiepileptic
PREG/CONT D, X (migraine prophylaxis)/NA

BBW Increased risk of suicidal ideation, suicidality; monitor accordingly.

Arrange for frequent LFTs; stop drug immediately w/suspected, apparent significant hepatic impairment. Continue LFTs to determine if hepatic impairment progresses despite discontinuation. Arrange counseling for women of childbearing age who wish to become pregnant; drug may be teratogenic. Not recommended for women of childbearing age; risk of neural tube defects, lower cognitive test scores in children when drug taken during pregnancy compared to other anticonvulsants. Stop drug at any sign of pancreatitis; life-threatening pancreatitis has occurred.

IND & DOSE Tx of simple, complex absence seizures. *Adult:* 10–15 mg/kg/day PO, increasing at 1-wk intervals by 5–10 mg/kg/day until seizures controlled or side effects preclude further increases; max, 60 mg/kg/day PO. If total dose exceeds 250 mg/day, give in divided doses. *Child 10 yr and older:* 10–15 mg/kg/day PO. **Tx of acute mania, bipolar disorder.** *Adult:* 25 mg/kg/day PO. Increase rapidly to achieve lowest therapeutic dose. Max, 60 mg/kg/day (*Divalproex ER* only). **Tx of bipolar mania:** *Adult:* 750 mg/day PO in divided doses; max, 60 mg/kg/day (*Divalproex DR* only). **Px of migraine.** *Adult:* 250 mg PO bid; up to 1,000 mg/day has been used (*Divalproex DR*); 500 mg/day ER tablet.
ADV EFF Bleeding, **bone marrow suppression**, depression, dizziness, **hepatic failure**, indigestion, **life-threatening pancreatitis**, n/v/d, rash
INTERACTIONS Alcohol, carbamazepine, charcoal, cimetidine, chlorpromazine, CNS depressants, diazepam, erythromycin, ethosuximide, felbamate, lamotrigine, phenobarbital, phenytoin, primidone, rifampin, salicylates, zidovudine
NC/PT Taper when stopping. Monitor CBC, LFTs, therapeutic serum level (usually 50–100 mcg/mL). Check drug regimen; many serious interactions possible, including DRESS (drug reaction with eosinophilia and

systemic sx)/multiorgan hypersensitivity. Not for use in pregnancy (barrier contraceptives advised). May open *Depakote Sprinkle* tablets and sprinkle on applesauce, pudding. Pt should swallow tablet/capsule whole and not chew it; avoid alcohol, OTC sleeping pills; have frequent blood tests; wear medical ID; take safety precautions for CNS effects; avoid injury, exposure to infection; report bleeding, stool color changes, thoughts of suicide. Confusion between DR *Depakote and Depakote ER*. Dosage very different, serious adverse effects possible; use extreme caution.

valsartan (Diovan)
CLASS Antihypertensive, ARB
PREG/CONT D/NA

BBW Rule out pregnancy before starting tx. Suggest barrier contraceptives during tx; fetal injury, deaths have occurred.
IND & DOSE Tx of hypertension. *Adult:* 80 mg/day PO; range, 80–320 mg/day. *Child 6–16 yr:* 1.3 mg/kg/day PO (max, 40 mg). Target, 1.3–2.7 mg/kg/day PO (40–160 mg/day). **Tx of HF.** *Adult:* 40 mg PO bid; titrate to 80 mg and 160 mg bid, to highest dose tolerated by pt. Max, 320 mg/day. **Tx of post-MI left ventricular dysfx.** *Adult:* Start as early as 12 hr post-MI; 20 mg PO bid. May increase after 7 days to 40 mg PO bid. Titrate to 160 mg PO bid if tolerated.
ADJUST DOSE Hepatic, renal impairment
ADV EFF Abd pain, cough, dizziness, headache, hyperkalemia, hypotension, n/v/d, URI
INTERACTIONS ACE inhibitors, ARBs, lithium, NSAIDs, potassium-sparing diuretics, renin inhibitors
NC/PT Alert surgeon; volume replacement may be needed postop. Do not stop abruptly. Not for use in pregnancy (barrier contraceptives advised)/breast-feeding. Pt should take safety precautions for CNS effects,

use caution in situations that can lead to BP drop; report chills, pregnancy.

vancomycin hydrochloride (Vancocin)
CLASS Antibiotic
PREG/CONT C; B (pulvules)/NA

BBW Pt at risk for development of multiple drug-resistant organisms; ensure appropriate use.
IND & DOSE Tx of severe to life-threatening infections caused by susceptible bacteria strains and unresponsive to other antibiotics. *Adult:* 500 mg–2 g/day PO in three to four divided doses for 7–10 days. Or, 500 mg IV q 6 hr or 1 g IV q 12 hr. *Child:* 40 mg/kg/day PO in three to four divided doses for 7–10 days. Or, 10 mg/kg/dose IV q 6 hr. Max, 2 g/day. *Premature, full-term neonate:* Use w/ caution because of incompletely developed renal function. Initially, 15 mg/kg IV, then 10 mg/kg q 12 hr in first wk of life, then q 8 hr up to age 1 mo. **Tx of pseudomembranous colitis due to *Clostridium difficile*.** *Adult:* 500 mg–2 g/day PO in three to four divided doses for 7–10 days, or 125 mg PO tid–qid. *Child:* 40 mg/kg/day PO in four divided doses for 7–10 days. Max, 2 g/day.
ADJUST DOSE Elderly pts, renal failure
ADV EFF Fever, hypotension, nausea, **nephrotoxicity**, ototoxicity, paresthesia, "red man syndrome," superinfections, rash
INTERACTIONS Aminoglycosides, amphotericin B, atracurium, bacitracin, cisplatin, pancuronium, vecuronium
NC/PT Culture before tx. Monitor for red man syndrome during IV infusion. Monitor renal function. Monitor for safe serum level (conc of 60–80 mcg/mL toxic). Pt should take full course; perform hygiene measures to avoid possible infections of mouth, vagina; report ringing in ears, hearing loss, swelling.

vardenafil hydrochloride
(Levitra, Staxyn)
CLASS ED drug,
phosphodiesterase type 5
inhibitor
PREG/CONT B/NA

IND & DOSE Tx of ED. *Adult:* 5–10 mg
PO 1 hr before anticipated sexual
activity; range, 5–20 mg PO. Limit
use to once/day. *Staxyn* (oral disintegrating tablet) is not interchangeable
w/ *Viagra* tablet.
ADJUST DOSE Elderly pts, hepatic
impairment
ADV EFF Abnormal ejaculation,
angina, dyspnea, flushing, GERD,
headache, hearing loss, hypotension,
priapism, rhinitis, vision changes/
loss
INTERACTIONS Erythromycin,
indinavir, itraconazole, ketoconazole
nitrates, ritonavir (limit dose of these
drugs to 2.5 mg/24 hr [72 hr w/
ritonavir]); alpha blockers
NC/PT Ensure dx. Drug not effective
without sexual stimulation. Does not
protect against STDs. For oral disintegrating tablet: Place on tongue, allow
to disintegrate; do not take w/water.
Pt should avoid nitrates, alpha blocker
antihypertensives; stop drug, immediately report loss of vision/hearing;
report difficult urination, erection
lasting more than 4 hr, fainting.

varenicline tartrate
(Chantix)
CLASS Nicotine receptor
antagonist, smoking deterrent
PREG/CONT C/NA

BBW Risk of serious mental health
events, including changes in behavior,
depressed mood, hostility, suicidal
thoughts; monitor accordingly. Higher
risk of MI, stroke, death compared w/
placebo; use w/caution.

IND & DOSE Aid to smoking cessation tx. *Adult:* Pt should pick date to
stop smoking, begin tx 1 wk before
that date. Or, pt can begin drug, quit
smoking between days 8 and 35 of tx.
Days 1–3, 0.5 mg/day PO; days 4–7,
0.5 mg PO bid; day 8 to total of 12 wk,
1 mg PO bid.
ADJUST DOSE Severe renal
impairment
ADV EFF Abd pain, abnormal
dreams, constipation, fatigue,
flatulence, headache, insomnia, **MI**,
nausea, neuropsychiatric events,
rhinorrhea, **stroke**, **suicidality**
INTERACTIONS Cimetidine,
nicotine transdermal systems
NC/PT Ensure comprehensive tx
program. Not for use in pregnancy/
breast-feeding. Tx should last 12 wk;
pt who successfully quits smoking in
that time may benefit from another
12 wk to increase likelihood of long-
term abstinence. Use caution w/
known CAD. Pt should take after
eating w/full glass of water; follow
dosing protocol closely; if relapse
occurs, discuss w/prescribe; report
failure to quit smoking, behavioral
changes, thoughts of suicide, chest
pain.

vedolizumab (Entyvio)
CLASS Immunomodulator,
integrin receptor antagonist
PREG/CONT B/NA

IND & DOSE Tx of ulcerative colitis,
Crohn's disease w/loss of response
to TNF blockers, corticosteroids.
Adult: 300 mg IV over 30 min at 0, 2,
and 6 wk, then q 8 wk.
ADV EFF Arthralgia, cough, **hypersensitivity reactions, infections,**
pain, **RPLS**, URI
NC/PT Ensure proper dx, up-to-date
immunizations before use. Stop if no
evidence of benefit within 14 wk. Use
w/caution in pregnancy/breast-feeding. Pt should mark calendar for tx
days; report s&sx of infection, fever,
difficulty breathing, rash.

velaglucerase (VPRIV)
CLASS Lysosomal enzyme
PREG/CONT B/NA

IND & DOSE Long-term replacement tx for type 1 Gaucher disease.
Adult, child: 60 units/kg as 60-min IV infusion q other wk.
ADV EFF Abd pain, back pain, dizziness, headache, **hypersensitivity/infusion reactions**, joint pain, nausea, URI
NC/PT May use antihistamines, corticosteroids to alleviate infusion reactions. Consider slowing infusion or stopping tx if infusion reactions. Pt should mark calendar for infusion days; report difficulty breathing, pain at injection site.

vemurafenib (Zelboraf)
CLASS Antineoplastic, kinase inhibitor
PREG/CONT B/NA

IND & DOSE Tx of pts w/unresectable, metastatic melanoma w/BRAF V600E mutation as detected by approved BRAF test. *Adult:* 960 mg PO bid approximately 12 hr apart.
ADV EFF Alopecia, arthralgia, **cutaneous squamous cell carcinoma**, fatigue, **hepatotoxicity**, nausea, **new malignant melanomas**, photosensitivity, pruritus, **prolonged QT, radiation sensitization, serious hypersensitivity reactions, serious ophthalmologic toxicity**, skin papilloma, **Stevens-Johnson syndrome**
INTERACTIONS CYP substrates, QT-prolonging drugs, warfarin
NC/PT BRAF confirmation test required before use to ensure appropriate drug selection. Obtain baseline ECG; periodically monitor QT interval. Monitor skin, eye reactions. Not for use in pregnancy/breast-feeding. Pt should cover head at temp extremes (hair loss possible), avoid sun exposure, report rash, difficulty breathing, urine/stool color changes, vision changes.

venlafaxine hydrochloride (Effexor XR)
CLASS Antidepressant, anxiolytic
PREG/CONT C/NA

BBW Monitor pts for suicidal ideation, especially when starting tx, changing dose; high risk in children, adolescents, young adults.
IND & DOSE Tx of major depressive disorder. *Adult:* 75 mg/day PO in two to three divided doses (or once/day, ER capsule). Increase at intervals of no less than 4 days up to 225 mg/day to achieve desired effect; max, 375 mg/day in three divided doses. **Tx of generalized anxiety disorder.** *Adult:* 75–225 mg/day ER form PO. **Tx of panic disorder.** *Adult:* 37.5 mg/day PO for 7 days, then 75 mg/day for 7 days, then 75 mg/day wkly. Max, 225 mg/day (ER only). **Tx of social anxiety.** *Adult:* 75 mg/day PO; max, 75 mg/day.
ADJUST DOSE Hepatic/renal impairment
ADV EFF Abnormal ejaculation, angle-closure glaucoma, asthenia, anorexia, constipation, dizziness, dry mouth, headache, hypertension, insomnia, nausea, nervousness, serotonin syndrome, somnolence, sweating, **suicidality**
INTERACTIONS Alcohol, MAOIs, serotonergic drugs, St. John's wort, trazodone
NC/PT To transfer to, from MAOI: Allow at least 14 days to elapse from stopping MAOI to starting venlafaxine; allow at least 7 days to elapse from stopping venlafaxine to starting MAOI. Not for use in pregnancy. Pt should swallow ER capsule whole and not cut, crush, or chew it; take w/ food; avoid alcohol, St. John's wort; take safety precautions for CNS effects; use sugarless lozenges w/dry mouth; report rash, thoughts of suicide.

DANGEROUS DRUG

verapamil hydrochloride
(Calan, Verelan)

CLASS Antianginal, antihypertensive, calcium channel blocker

PREG/CONT C/NA

BBW Monitor pt carefully during drug titration; dosage may be increased more rapidly w/hospitalized, monitored pts.

IND & DOSE Tx of angina. *Adult:* 80–120 mg PO tid. Maint, 240–480 mg/day. **Tx of arrhythmias.** *Adult:* 240–480 mg/day PO in divided doses. Or, 120–240 mg/day PO in a.m. ER capsules; max, 480 mg/day. Or, 120–180 mg/day PO in a.m. ER or SR tablets. Or, 5–10 mg IV over 2 min; may repeat dose if initial response inadequate. In digitalized pts, 240–320 mg/day PO. *Child 1–15 yr:* 0.1–0.3 mg/kg IV over 2 min; max, 5 mg. Repeat dose 30 min after initial dose if response inadequate. Max for repeat dose, 10 mg. *Child 1 yr and younger:* 0.1–0.2 mg/kg IV over 2 min. **Tx of hypertension.** *Adult:* 40–80 mg PO tid.

ADJUST DOSE Elderly pts, renal impairment

ADV EFF Cardiac arrhythmias, constipation, dizziness, edema, headache, HF, hypotension, nausea

INTERACTIONS Antihypertensives, beta blockers, calcium, carbamazepine, digoxin, flecainide, grapefruit juice, prazosin, quinidine, rifampin, statins, verapamil

NC/PT When pt stabilized, may switch to ER capsules (max, 480 mg/day), ER tablets (max, 240 mg q 12 hr), SR forms (max, 480 mg in a.m.). Protect IV sol from light. Monitor BP, cardiac rhythm closely. Pt should swallow ER, SR forms whole and not cut, crush, or chew them; take safety precautions w/ dizziness; avoid grapefruit juice; report swelling, difficulty breathing.

verteporfin (Visudyne)
CLASS Ophthalmic drug

PREG/CONT C/NA

IND & DOSE Tx of age-related macular degeneration, pathologic myopia, ocular histoplasmosis. *Adult:* 6 mg/m² diluted in D_5W to total 30 mL IV into free-flowing IV over 10 min at 3 mL/min using inline filter, syringe pump.

ADJUST DOSE Hepatic impairment

ADV EFF Dizziness, headache, injection-site reactions, malaise, photosensitivity, pruritus, rash, visual disturbances

NC/PT Laser light tx should begin within 15 min of starting IV; may repeat in 3 mo if needed. Not for use in breast-feeding. Protect pt from exposure to bright light for at least 5 days after tx. Pt should report vision changes, eye pain, injection-site pain/swelling.

vigabatrin (Sabril)
CLASS Antiepileptic, GABAase inhibitor

PREG/CONT C/NA

BBW Available only through restricted distribution program. Causes progressive, permanent, bilateral vision loss. Monitor vision; stopping drug may not stop vision loss. Increased risk of suicidality; monitor accordingly.

IND & DOSE Adjunct tx of refractory complex seizures. *Adult:* 500 mg PO bid; increase slowly to max 1,500 mg PO bid. *Child 10–16 yr:* 250 mg PO bid. Increase slowly to max 1,000 mg PO bid. **Tx of infantile spasms.** *Child:* 50 mg/kg/day PO in two divided doses; max, 150 mg/kg/day in two divided doses.

ADJUST DOSE Renal impairment

ADV EFF Abnormal coordination, anemia, arthralgia, confusion, edema, fatigue, nystagmus, **permanent**

vision loss, somnolence, suicidality, tremor, weight gain

NC/PT Available only through limited access. Abnormal MRI signal changes have been reported in infants w/infantile spasms. Taper gradually to avoid withdrawal seizures. Monitor vision; permanent vision loss possible. For refractory complex seizures, give w/other antiepileptics; for infantile spasms, use as monotherapy. Not for use in pregnancy/breast-feeding. Pt should take precautions for CNS effects, report changes in vision, thoughts of suicide, extreme fatigue, weight gain.

vilazodone hydrochloride (Viibryd)
CLASS SSRI
PREG/CONT C/NA

BBW High risk of suicidality in children, adolescents, young adults. Establish suicide precautions for severely depressed pts, limit quantity of drug dispensed. Vilazodone not approved for use in children.

IND & DOSE Tx of major depressive disorder. Adult: 10 mg/day PO for 7 days, then 20 mg/day PO for 7 days; maint, 40 mg/day PO.

ADV EFF Angle-closure glaucoma, bleeding, dizziness, dry mouth, insomnia, n/v/d, NMS, paresthesia, seizures, serotonin syndrome, suicidality

INTERACTIONS Alcohol, aspirin, diltiazem, ketoconazole, MAOIs, NSAIDs, serotonergic drugs, St. John's wort, warfarin

NC/PT Therapeutic effects may not occur for 4 wk. Taper when stopping. Not for use in pregnancy/breast-feeding. Pt should take w/food in a.m.; avoid alcohol, NSAIDs, St. John's wort; take safety precautions for CNS effects; report seizures, thoughts of suicide.

DANGEROUS DRUG

vinBLAStine sulfate (generic)
CLASS Antineoplastic, mitotic inhibitor
PREG/CONT D/NA

BBW Do not give IM, subcut due to severe local reaction, tissue necrosis. Fatal if given intrathecally; use extreme caution. Watch for irritation, infiltration; extravasation causes tissue damage, necrosis. If it occurs, stop injection immediately; give remainder of dose in another vein. Arrange for hyaluronidase injection into local area, after which apply moderate heat to disperse drug, minimize pain.

IND & DOSE Palliative tx of lymphocytic/histiocytic lymphoma, generalized Hodgkin lymphoma (stages III, IV), mycosis fungoides, advanced testicular carcinoma, Kaposi sarcoma, Letterer-Siwe disease; tx of choriocarcinoma, breast cancer, Hodgkin lymphoma, advanced testicular germinal-cell cancers. Adult: Initially, 3.7 mg/m² as single IV dose, followed at wkly intervals by increasing doses at 1.8-mg/m² increments; use these increments until max 18.5 mg/m² reached. When WBC count 3,000/mm³, use dose one increment smaller for wkly maint. Do not give another dose until WBC count is 4,000/mm³ even if 7 days have passed. Child: 2.5 mg/m² as single IV dose, followed at wkly intervals by increasing doses at 1.25-mg/m² increments. Max, 12.5 mg/m² dose.

ADJUST DOSE Hepatic impairment

ADV EFF Alopecia, anorexia, bone marrow suppression, cellulitis at injection site, headache, n/v/d, paresthesia, weakness

INTERACTIONS Erythromycin, grapefruit juice, phenytoins

NC/PT Do not give IM, subcut. Monitor CBC closely. Give antiemetic for severe n/v. Not for use in pregnancy. Pt should mark calendar of tx days; take safety precautions for CNS effects; cover head at temp extremes (hair loss possible); avoid exposure to infection, injury; avoid grapefruit juice; report pain at injection site, signs of infection, bleeding. Name confusion between vinblastine and vincristine; use caution.

DANGEROUS DRUG

vinCRIStine sulfate
(Marqibo)

CLASS Antineoplastic, mitotic inhibitor

PREG/CONT D/NA

BBW Do not give IM, subcut due to severe local reaction, tissue necrosis. Fatal if given intrathecally; use extreme caution. Watch for irritation, infiltration; extravasation causes tissue damage, necrosis. If it occurs, stop injection immediately; give remainder of dose in another vein. Arrange for hyaluronidase injection into local area, after which apply moderate heat to disperse drug, minimize pain.
IND & DOSE Tx of acute leukemia, Hodgkin lymphoma, non-Hodgkin lymphoma, rhabdomyosarcoma, neuroblastoma, Wilms tumor. *Adult:* 1.4 mg/m² IV at wkly intervals. *Child over 10 kg or BSA over 1 m²:* 1–2 mg/m²/wk IV. Max, 2 mg/dose. *Child under 10 kg or BSA under 1 m²:* 0.05 mg/kg/wk IV. Tx of adults w/ Philadelphia chromosome–negative acute ALL who have relapsed after other tx. *Adult:* 2.25 mg/m² IV over 1 hr q 7 days *(Marqibo).*
ADJUST DOSE Elderly pts, hepatic impairment
ADV EFF Alopecia, ataxia, constipation, cranial nerve manifestations, **death,** neuritic pain, paresthesia, photosensitivity, renal impairment, weight loss
INTERACTIONS Digoxin, grapefruit juice, L-asparaginase
NC/PT Do not give IM, subcut. Monitor renal function. Not for use in pregnancy. Pt should use laxative for constipation, take safety precautions

---

for CNS effects, cover head at temp extremes (hair loss possible), avoid sun exposure, report pain at injection site, swelling, severe constipation. Name confusion between vinblastine and vincristine; use caution.

DANGEROUS DRUG

vinorelbine tartrate
(Navelbine)

CLASS Antineoplastic, mitotic inhibitor

PREG/CONT D/NA

BBW Do not give IM, subcut due to severe local reaction, tissue necrosis. Fatal if given intrathecally; use extreme caution. Watch for irritation, infiltration; extravasation can cause tissue damage, necrosis. If it occurs, stop injection immediately; arrange for hyaluronidase injection into local area, after which apply moderate heat to disperse drug, minimize pain. Check CBC before each dose; severe granulocytosis possible. Adjust, delay dose as appropriate.
IND & DOSE First-line tx of pts w/ unresectable advanced non-small-cell lung cancer, as monotherapy or w/cisplatin. *Adult:* 30 mg/m² IV as single IV injection as monotherapy; 25–30 mg/m²/wk as single IV injection w/cisplatin.
ADJUST DOSE Hepatic impairment
ADV EFF Alopecia, anorexia, constipation to bowel obstruction, headache, hepatic impairment, neurologic toxicity, **severe bone marrow suppression,** paresthesia, **pulmonary toxicity,** vesiculation of GI tract
INTERACTIONS CYP3A4 inhibitors
NC/PT Check CBC before each dose; adjustment may be needed. Give antiemetic if needed. Institute bowel program; monitor for severe constipation. Monitor pulmonary function. Not for use in pregnancy (contraceptives advised). Pt should make calendar of tx days; cover head at temp extremes (hair loss possible); take safety precautions for CNS effects; avoid

exposure to infection, injury; report pain at injection site, unusual bleeding, s&sx of infection, severe constipation, difficulty breathing.

vismodegib (Erivedge)
CLASS Antineoplastic, hedgehog pathway inhibitor
PREG/CONT D/NA

BBW Risk of embryo-fetal death, severe birth defects; men, women advised to use barrier contraceptives.
IND & DOSE Tx of pts w/metastatic or locally advanced basal cell carcinoma not candidates for surgery or radiation. *Adult:* 150 mg/day PO.
ADV EFF Alopecia, anorexia, arthralgia, constipation, fatigue, muscle spasms, n/v/d
NC/PT Rule out pregnancy before tx; advise men, women to use barrier contraceptives (due to risk of fetal toxicity). Not for use in breast-feeding. Pt should take as directed; not donate blood during and for 7 mo after tx; do not donate semen during and for 3 mo after tx; cover head at temp extremes (hair loss possible); report weight loss, severe GI complaints.

von Willebrand factor (recombinant) (Vonvendi)
CLASS Clotting factor
PREG/CONT Moderate risk/NA

IND & DOSE Tx and control of bleeding episodes in von Willebrand disease. *Adult:* 40–80 international units/kg q 8–24 hr based on severity/location of bleeding.
ADV EFF Hypersensitivity reactions, thrombotic events, von Willebrand antibody production, rash
NC/PT Not for use w/known allergy to mannitol, trehalose, sodium chloride, histidine, Tris, calcium chloride, polysorbate 80, hamster/mouse proteins. For each bleeding episode, administer w/approved factor VIII if factor VIII levels are below 40% or

unkn. Use within 3 hr of reconstitution. Use caution in pregnancy/breast-feeding. Teach proper administration, reconstitution, disposal of needles/syringes; recommend medical identification. Pt should report difficulty breathing, chest pain, numbness/tingling, continued bleeding.

vorapaxar (Zontivity)
CLASS Antiplatelet, protease-activated receptor-1 antagonist
PREG/CONT B/NA

BBW Do not use w/hx of stroke, TIA, intracranial hemorrhage, active pathological bleeding. Increased risk of serious to fatal bleeding.
IND & DOSE To reduce thrombotic CV events w/MI, peripheral arterial disease. *Adult:* 2.08 mg (1 tablet)/day PO, w/aspirin and/or clopidogrel.
ADV EFF Bleeding events
INTERACTIONS Drugs affecting coagulation, strong CYP3A4 inducers/inhibitors
NC/PT Give daily, w/aspirin and/or clopidogrel. Use w/caution in pregnancy; not for use in breast-feeding. Pt should alert surgeon/dentist about use; contact prescriber before stopping; report unusual bleeding.

voriconazole (Vfend)
CLASS Triazole antifungal
PREG/CONT D/NA

IND & DOSE Tx of invasive aspergillosis, serious infections caused by susceptible fungi strains; candidemia in nonneutropenic pts w/ disseminated skin infections and abd, kidney, bladder wall, and wound infections. *Adult:* Loading dose, 6 mg/kg IV q 12 hr for two doses, then 3–4 mg/kg IV q 12 hr or 200 mg PO q 12 hr. Switch to PO as soon as possible. 40 kg or more, 200 mg PO q 12 hr; may increase to 300 mg PO q 12 hr if needed. Under 40 kg, 100 mg PO q 12 hr; may

increase to 150 mg PO q 12 hr if needed. **Tx of esophageal candidiasis.** *Adult:* 200–300 mg PO q 12 hr (100–150 mg PO q 12 hr if under 40 kg) for 14 days or for at least 7 days after sx resolution.
ADV EFF Anaphylactic reaction, BP changes, dizziness, headache, **hepatotoxicity,** n/v/d, photosensitivity, **prolonged QT,** rash, **Stevens-Johnson syndrome,** visual disturbances
INTERACTIONS Benzodiazepines, calcium channel blockers, cyclosporine, omeprazole, oral anticoagulants, phenytoin, protease inhibitors, statins, St. John's wort, sulfonylureas, tacrolimus, vinblastine, vincristine, warfarin. Do not use w/carbamazepine, ergot alkaloids, mephobarbital, phenobarbital, pimozide, quinidine, rifabutin, rifampin, sirolimus
NC/PT Obtain baseline ECG, LFTs before, periodically during tx. Review drug list carefully; many interactions possible. Not for use in pregnancy (contraceptives advised). Pt should take oral drug on empty stomach 1 hr before or 2 hr after meals; avoid sun exposure, St. John's wort; report drug list changes, urine/stool color changes, rash, difficulty breathing.

DANGEROUS DRUG

vorinostat (Zolinza)
CLASS Antineoplastic, histone deacetylase inhibitor
PREG/CONT D/NA

BBW Monitor for bleeding, excessive n/v, thromboembolic events.
IND & DOSE Tx of cutaneous manifestations in cutaneous T-cell lymphoma. *Adult:* 400 mg/day PO w/ food; continue until disease progression or unacceptable toxicity.
ADJUST DOSE Hepatic impairment
ADV EFF Anorexia, diarrhea, dizziness, **GI bleeding,** hyperglycemia, n/v/d, **thromboembolic events**
INTERACTIONS Warfarin

NC/PT Monitor CBC, electrolytes, serum blood glucose. Give antiemetics if needed. Encourage fluid intake of 2 L/day to prevent dehydration. Not for use in pregnancy (barrier contraceptives advised)/breast-feeding. Pt should take safety precaution w/ dizziness, use caution in hot environments, maintain hydration, report bloody diarrhea, numbness/tingling, chest pain, difficulty breathing.

---

vortioxetine (Brintellix)
CLASS Antidepressant, SSRI
PREG/CONT C/NA

BBW Increased risk of suicidality in children, adolescents, young adults, severely depressed pts. Limit quantity; monitor pt.
IND & DOSE Tx of major depressive disorder. *Adult:* 10 mg/day PO. Increase to 20 mg/day PO as tolerated.
ADV EFF Abnormal dreams, activation of mania, angle-closure glaucoma, constipation, dizziness, dry mouth, hyponatremia, n/v/d, pruritus, **serotonin syndrome, suicidality**
INTERACTIONS Antihypertensives, aprepitant, aspirin, bupropion, carbamazepine, fluoxetine, linezolid, MAOIs, methylene blue (IV), NSAIDs, opioids, paroxetine, phenytoin, quinidine, rifampin, serotonergic drugs, SSRIs, St. John's wort
NC/PT Review drug regimen; many interactions possible. Monitor for hyponatremia, activation of mania. Taper when discontinuing. Pt should take in a.m.; not stop suddenly; avoid pregnancy/breast-feeding, St. John's wort; take safety precautions for CNS effects; eat small, frequent meals for GI upset; report rash, mania, severe n/v, thoughts of suicide.

DANGEROUS DRUG

warfarin sodium
(Coumadin, Jantoven)
CLASS Coumarin derivative, oral anticoagulant
PREG/CONT X/NA

BBW Evaluate pt regularly for signs of blood loss (petechiae, bleeding gums, bruises, dark stools, dark urine). Maintain INR of 2–3, 3–4.5 w/mechanical prosthetic valves or recurrent systemic emboli; risk of serious to fatal bleeding.
IND & DOSE Tx, px of PE, venous thrombosis; tx of thromboembolic complications of atrial fibrillation; px of systemic embolization after acute MI. *Adult:* 2–5 mg/day PO or IV. Adjust according to PT response. Maint, 2–10 mg/day PO based on INR.
ADJUST DOSE Elderly pts
ADV EFF Alopecia, dermatitis, **hemorrhage**, n/v/d, priapism, red-orange urine
INTERACTIONS Acetaminophen, alcohol, allopurinol, amiodarone, androgens, angelica, azole antifungals, barbiturates, carbamazepine, cat's claw, cefazolin, cefotetan, cefoxitin, ceftriaxone, chamomile, chloramphenicol, cholestyramine, chondroitin, cimetidine, clofibrate, co-trimoxazole, danazol, disulfiram, erythromycin, famotidine, feverfew, fish oil, fluvastatin, garlic, ginkgo, glucagon, goldenseal, grape seed extract, green leaf tea, griseofulvin, horse chestnut seed, lovastatin, meclofenamate, mefenamic acid, methimazole, metronidazole, nalidixic acid, nizatidine, NSAIDs, phenytoin, propylthiouracil, psyllium, quinidine, quinine, quinolones, ranitidine, rifampin, simvastatin, sulfinpyrazone, thyroid drugs, turmeric, vitamins E, K
NC/PT Genetic testing can help determine reasonable dose. Decreased clearance w/CYP2C9*2, CYP2C9*3 variant alleles. Monitor blood clotting; target, INR of 2–3. IV use reserved for situations in which oral warfarin not feasible. Have vitamin K and/or prothrombin complex concentrate on hand for overdose. Check pt's drug regimen closely; many interactions possible. Carefully add, remove drugs from regimen; dose adjustment may be needed. Not for use in pregnancy (contraceptives advised); use caution in breast-feeding. Urine may turn red-orange. Pt should not start, stop any drug, herb without consulting health care provider (dose adjustments may be needed); have regular blood tests; avoid injury; report bleeding/bruising.

zafirlukast (Accolate)
CLASS Antiasthmatic, leukotriene receptor antagonist
PREG/CONT B/NA

IND & DOSE Px, long-term tx of bronchial asthma. *Adult, child 12 yr and over:* 20 mg PO bid on empty stomach 1 hr before or 2 hr after meals. *Child 5–11 yr:* 10 mg PO bid on empty stomach.
ADV EFF Headache, Churg-Strauss syndrome, dizziness, n/v/d
INTERACTIONS Calcium channel blockers, corticosteroids, cyclosporine, erythromycin, theophylline, warfarin
NC/PT Not for acute asthma attack. Pt should take on empty stomach q day, consult health care provider before using OTC products, take safety precautions w/dizziness, report severe headache, fever, increased acute asthma attacks.

zaleplon (Sonata)
CLASS Sedative-hypnotic (nonbenzodiazepine)
PREG/CONT C/C-IV

IND & DOSE Short-term tx of insomnia. *Adult:* 10 mg PO at bedtime. Pt must remain in bed for 4 hr after taking. Max, 20 mg/day.
ADJUST DOSE Elderly, debilitated pts; hepatic impairment

ADV EFF Anaphylaxis, angioedema, depression, dizziness, drowsiness, headache, short-term memory impairment, sleep disorders
INTERACTIONS Alcohol, CNS depressants, cimetidine, CYP3A4 inhibitors, rifampin
NC/PT Rule out medical causes for insomnia; institute sleep hygiene protocol. Pt will feel drug's effects for 4 hr; after 4 hr, pt may safely become active again. Pt should take dose immediately before bedtime; avoid alcohol, OTC sleeping aids; take safety precautions for CNS effects; report difficulty breathing, swelling, sleep-related behaviors.

zanamivir (Relenza)
CLASS Antiviral, neuraminidase inhibitor
PREG/CONT C/NA

IND & DOSE Tx of uncomplicated acute illness due to influenza virus. *Adult, child 7 yr and over:* 2 inhalations (one 5-mg blister/inhalation administered w/*Diskhaler*, for total 10 mg) bid at 12-hr intervals for 5 days. Should start within 2 days of onset of flu sx; give two doses on first tx day, at least 2 hr apart; separate subsequent doses by 12 hr. **Px of influenza.** *Adult, child 5 yr and over:* Two inhalations (10 mg) day for 28 days w/community outbreak, 10 days for household exposure.
ADV EFF Anorexia, bronchospasm, cough, diarrhea, dizziness, headache, nausea, **serious respiratory effects**
NC/PT Caution COPD, asthma pts of bronchospasm risk; pt should have fast-acting bronchodilator on hand. Review proper use of *Diskhaler* delivery system. Pt should take full course; if using bronchodilator, use before this drug; take safety precautions w/dizziness; report worsening of sx.

ziconotide (Prialt)
CLASS Analgesic, N-type calcium channel blocker
PREG/CONT C/NA

BBW Severe neuropsychiatric reactions, neurologic impairment; monitor pt closely. Do not use w/hx of psychosis.
IND & DOSE Mgt of severe chronic pain in pts who need intrathecal tx. *Adult:* 2.4 mcg/day by continuous intrathecal pump; may titrate to max 19.2 mcg/day (0.8 mcg/hr).
ADV EFF Confusion, dizziness, meningitis, nausea, **neurologic impairment**, nystagmus, **psychotic behavior**
NC/PT Teach pt proper care of pump, injection site. Not for use in pregnancy/breast-feeding. Pt should take safety precautions for CNS effects; report changes in mood/behavior, muscle pain/weakness, rash.

zidovudine (Retrovir)
CLASS Antiviral, nucleoside reverse transcriptase inhibitor
PREG/CONT C/NA

BBW Monitor hematologic indices q 2 wk; hematologic toxicity has occurred. Monitor LFTs; lactic acidosis w/severe hepatomegaly w/steatosis possible. Increased risk of symptomatic myopathy; monitor accordingly.
IND & DOSE Tx of HIV, w/other antiretrovirals. *Adult, child over 12 yr:* 600 mg/day PO in divided doses as either 200 mg tid or 300 mg bid. Monitor hematologic indices q 2 wk. If significant anemia (Hgb under 7.5 g/dL, reduction over 25%) or granulocyte reduction over 50% below baseline occurs, dose interruption necessary until evidence of bone marrow recovery. Or, 1 mg/kg five to six times/day IV infused over 1 hr. *Child 6 wk–12 yr:* 30 kg and over, 600 mg/day PO in two to three divided

doses. 9 to under 30 kg, 18 mg/kg/day PO in two to three divided doses. 4 to under 9 kg, 24 mg/kg/day PO in two to three divided doses. *Infant born to HIV-infected mother:* 2 mg/kg PO q 6 hr starting within 12 hr of birth to 6 wk of age, or 1.5 mg/kg IV over 30 min q 6 hr until able to take oral form. **Px of maternal-fetal transmission.** *Adult:* 100 mg PO five times/day until start of labor.
ADV EFF Agranulocytosis, anorexia, asthenia, diarrhea, flulike sx, GI pain, headache, **hepatic decompensation, hypersensitivity reactions,** nausea, rash
INTERACTIONS Acyclovir, bone marrow suppressants, cyclosporine, cytotoxic drugs, ganciclovir, interferon alfa, methadone, nephrotoxic drugs, phenytoin, probenecid, St. John's wort
NC/PT Do not infuse IV w/blood product. Pt should take drug around the clock; take precautions to prevent transmission (drug not a cure); avoid exposure to infection, St. John's wort; take w/other antivirals; report signs of infection, rash, difficulty breathing, severe headache. Name confusion between *Retrovir* (zidovudine) and ritonavir; use caution.

---

zileuton (Zyflo)
CLASS Antiasthmatic leukotriene synthesis inhibitor
PREG/CONT C/NA

IND & DOSE **Px, long-term tx of asthma.** *Adult, child 12 yr and over:* CR tablets, 1,200 mg (2 tablets) PO bid within 1 hr after a.m., p.m. meals for total daily dose of 2,400 mg. Tablets, 600 mg PO qid for total daily dose of 2,400 mg.
ADJUST DOSE Hepatic impairment
ADV EFF Diarrhea, dizziness, headache, **liver enzyme elevations,** neuropsychiatric events, pain, rash
INTERACTIONS Propranolol, theophylline, warfarin
NC/PT Not for acute asthma attack. Monitor LFTs, mood, behavior. Pt

should take daily; take CR tablets on empty stomach 1 hr before or 2 hr after meals; swallow tablet whole and not cut, crush, or chew it; take safety precaution for CNS effects; report acute asthma attacks, urine/stool color changes, rash.

---

ziprasidone (Geodon)
CLASS Atypical antipsychotic, benzisoxazole
PREG/CONT C/NA

BBW Increased risk of death if used in elderly pts w/dementia-related psychosis. Do not use in these pts; not approved for this use.
IND & DOSE **Tx of schizophrenia.** *Adult:* Initially, 20 mg PO bid w/food; range, 20–100 mg PO bid. **Rapid control of agitated behavior.** *Adult:* 10–20 mg IM; may repeat 10-mg doses q 2 hr; may repeat 20-mg doses in 4 hr. Max, 40 mg/day. **Tx of bipolar mania.** *Adult:* 40 mg PO bid w/food. May increase to 60–80 mg PO bid w/food.
ADV EFF Arrhythmias, bone marrow suppression, cognitive/motor impairment, constipation, drowsiness, dyslipidemia, dyspepsia, fever, headache, hyperglycemia, hypotension, **NMS, prolonged QT,** seizures, **severe cutaneous reactions including Stevens-Johnson syndrome and DRESS (drug reaction with eosinophilia and systemic sx),** somnolence, **suicidality,** tardive dyskinesia, weight gain
INTERACTIONS Antihypertensives, QT-prolonging drugs, St. John's wort
NC/PT Obtain baseline, periodic ECG; monitor serum glucose, weight. Use caution w/renal or hepatic impairment. Not for use in pregnancy (contraceptives advised); not recommended in breast-feeding. Pt should take safety precautions w/CNS effects, avoid St. John's wort, report palpitations, sx return.

ziv-aflibercept (Zaltrap)

CLASS Antineoplastic, ligand binding factor
PREG/CONT C/NA

BBW Risk of hemorrhage; do not administer w/active bleeding. Risk of GI perforation, compromised wound healing. Stop at least 4 wk before elective surgery; do not start until all surgical wounds healed.
IND & DOSE Tx of metastatic colorectal cancer resistant to oxaliplatin, w/5-FU, leucovorin, irinotecan. *Adult:* 4 mg/kg IV over 1 hr q 2 wk.
ADV EFF Abd pain, anorexia, dehydration, diarrhea, dysphonia, epistaxis, fatigue, headache, hepatic impairment, **hypertension, neutropenia, proteinuria, RPLS, thrombotic events**
NC/PT Not for use w/active bleeding; do not use within 4 wk of surgery. Monitor urine protein, BP, nutrition/hydration status; watch for s&sx of CV events. Not for use in pregnancy (barrier contraceptives advised for men, women during and for 3 mo after tx)/breast-feeding. Pt should mark calendar for infusion dates; avoid exposure to infection; report chest pain, fever, s&sx of infection, difficulty breathing, numbness/tingling, severe diarrhea.

zoledronic acid (Reclast, Zometa)

CLASS Bisphosphonate, calcium regulator
PREG/CONT D/NA

IND & DOSE Tx of hypercalcemia of malignancy; bone metastases w/ multiple myeloma. *Adult:* 4 mg IV as single-dose infusion of not less than 15 min for hypercalcemia of malignancy w/albumin-corrected serum calcium of 12 mg/dL or more. May retreat w/4 mg IV if needed. Minimum of 7 days should elapse between doses w/careful monitoring of serum creatinine. Pts w/solid tumors should receive 4 mg IV q 3–4 wk to treat bone metastasis *(Zometa).* Tx of Paget disease, postmenopausal osteoporosis, osteoporosis in men; px of new clinical fractures in pts w/ low-trauma hip fractures; tx, px of glucocorticoid-induced osteoporosis; px of osteoporosis in postmenopausal women. *Adult:* 5 mg IV infused via vented infusion line over at least 15 min. May consider retreatment as needed once q 2 yr for osteoporosis *(Reclast).*
ADJUST DOSE Renal impairment
ADV EFF Constipation; coughing; decreased phosphate, magnesium, potassium, calcium levels; dyspnea; femur fractures; fever; hypotension; infections; insomnia; **nephrotoxicity; osteonecrosis of jaw;** pain
INTERACTIONS Aminoglycosides, loop diuretics, nephrotoxic drugs
NC/PT Do not confuse *Reclast, Zometa;* dosage varies. Pt should have dental exam before tx; mark calendar of infusion dates; drink plenty of fluids; take supplemental vitamin D, calcium; avoid exposure to infection; report difficulty breathing, swelling, jaw pain.

zolmitriptan (Zomig)

CLASS Antimigraine drug, triptan
PREG/CONT C/NA

IND & DOSE Tx of acute migraine attacks. *Adult:* 2.5 mg PO at onset of headache or w/beginning of aura; may repeat if headache persists after 2 hr. Max, 10 mg/24 hr. Or, 1 spray in nostril at onset of headache or beginning of aura; may repeat in 2 hr if needed. Max, 10 mg/24 hr (2 sprays).
ADJUST DOSE Hepatic impairment
ADV EFF BP changes, burning/pressure sensation, chest pain, dizziness, drowsiness, numbness, **prolonged QT,** vertigo, weakness

INTERACTIONS Cimetidine, ergots, hormonal contraceptives, MAOIs, QT-prolonging drugs, sibutramine
NC/PT For acute attack, not for px. Not for use in pregnancy (may make hormonal contraceptives ineffective; barrier contraceptives advised). Pt should use right after removing from blister pack; not break, crush, or chew tablet; place orally disintegrating tablet on tongue, let dissolve; use one spray only if using nasal spray (may repeat after 2 hours if needed); take safety precautions for CNS effects; report chest pain, swelling, palpitations.

zolpidem tartrate (Ambien, Edluar, Intermezzo, Zolpimist)
CLASS Sedative-hypnotic
PREG/CONT C/C-IV

BBW Risk of suicidality; limit amount dispensed to depressed or suicidal pt.
IND & DOSE Short-term tx of insomnia. *Adult:* 10 mg PO at bedtime; max, 10 mg/day. ER tablets, 12.5 mg/day PO. Oral spray, two to three sprays in mouth, over tongue at bedtime. **Short-term tx of insomnia w/middle-of-night awakening when pt has at least 4 hr of bedtime left** *(Intermezzo). Adult:* 1.75 mg (women) or 3.5 mg (men) sublingually; limit to 1.75 mg if also on CNS depressants.
ADJUST DOSE Elderly pts
ADV EFF Anaphylaxis, angioedema, dizziness, drowsiness, hangover, headache, severe injuries related to CNS effects, sleep disorders, **suicidality,** suppression of REM sleep, vision disorders
INTERACTIONS Chlorpromazine, CNS depressants, imipramine, ketoconazole, rifampin
NC/PT Limit amount of drug given to depressed pts. Withdraw gradually after long-term use. Review proper administration of various forms. Not for use in pregnancy. Pt should take

safety precautions for CNS effects; report difficulty breathing, swelling, thoughts of suicide.

zonisamide (Zonegran)
CLASS Antiepileptic
PREG/CONT C/NA

BBW Increased risk of suicidal ideation, suicidality; monitor accordingly.
IND & DOSE Adjuvant tx for partial seizures. *Adult, child 16 and over:* 100 mg PO daily as single dose, not divided; may divide subsequent doses. May increase by 100 mg/day q 2 wk to achieve control. Max, 600 mg/day.
ADJUST DOSE Renal impairment
ADV EFF Anorexia, ataxia, decrease in mental functioning, dizziness, dry mouth, metabolic acidosis, nausea, renal calculi, **suicidality,** unusual taste
INTERACTIONS Carbamazepine, phenobarbital, phenytoin, primidone
NC/PT Withdraw gradually after long-term use. Pt should drink plenty of fluids, take safety precautions w/ CNS effects, wear medical ID, report flank pain, urine/stool color changes, thoughts of suicide.

Patient Safety and Medication Administration

The seven rights of medication administration

In the clinical setting, the monumental task of ensuring medication safety can be managed by consistently using the seven rights of drug administration: right drug, right route, right dose, right time, right patient, right response, and right documentation.

Right patient: Check the patient's identification even if you think you know who the patient is.

- Review the patient's diagnosis, and verify that the drug matches the diagnosis.
- Make sure all allergies have been checked before giving a drug.
- Ask patients specifically about OTC drugs, vitamin and mineral supplements, herbal remedies, and routine drugs that they may not think to mention.
- Review the patient's drug regimen to prevent potential interactions between the drug you are about to give and drugs the patient already takes.

Right drug: Always review a drug order before administering the drug.

- Do not assume that a computer system is always right. Always double-check.
- Make sure the drug name is correct. Ask for a brand name and a generic name; the chance of reading the name incorrectly is greatly reduced if both generic and brand names are used.
- Avoid taking verbal or telephone orders whenever possible. If you must, have a second person listen in to verify and clarify the order.
- Consider whether the drug makes sense for the patient's diagnosis.

Right route: Review the available forms of a drug to make sure the drug can be given according to the order.

- Check the routes available and the appropriateness of the route.
- Make sure the patient is able to take the drug by the route indicated.
- Do not use abbreviations for routes.

Right dose: Make sure the dose about to be delivered is the dose the prescriber ordered.

- There should always be a 0 to the left of a decimal point, and there should never be a 0 to the right of a decimal point. If you see an ordered dose that starts w/a decimal point, question it. And if a dose seems much too big, question that.
- Double-check drug calculations, even if a computer did the calculations.
- Check the measuring devices used for liquid drugs. Advise patients not to use kitchen teaspoons or tablespoons to measure drug doses.
- Do not cut tablets in half to get the correct dose without checking the warnings that come w/the drug.

Right time

- Ensure the timely delivery of the patient's drugs by scheduling dosing w/other drugs, meals, or other consistent events to maintain the serum level.
- Teach patients the importance of timing critical drugs. As needed, make detailed medication schedules and prepare pill boxes.

Right response

Monitor the patient's response to the drug administered to make sure that the response is what is anticipated.

Right documentation: Document according to facility policy.

- Include the drug name, dose, route, and time of administration.
- Note special circumstances, such as the patient having difficulty swallowing or the site of the injection.
- Include the patient's response to the drug and any special nursing interventions that were used.
- Remember, "if it isn't written, it didn't happen." Accurate documentation provides continuity of care and helps prevent medication errors.

The bottom line in avoiding medication errors is simple: "If in doubt, check it out." A strange abbreviation, a drug or dosage that is new to you, and a confusing name are all examples that signal a need for follow-up. Look up the drug in your drug guide or call the prescriber or the pharmacy to double-check. Never give a drug until you have satisfied yourself that it is the right drug, given by the right route, at the right dose, at the right time, and to the right patient.

Keeping patients safe

Patient and family teaching

In today's world, the patient is usually left to manage on his/her own. The most important safety check after all is said and done is the patient. Only the patient actually knows what health care providers he or she is seeing; what prescription drugs, OTC drugs, and herbal remedies are actually being used; and how they are being used. Today's patient needs to be educated about all drugs being taken and empowered to speak up and protect himself or herself against medication errors.

Medication errors present a constant risk, particularly for patients who take multiple drugs prescribed by multiple health care providers. Educating the patient is key to preventing errors.

Patient teaching to prevent medication errors

When being prescribed medications, patients should learn these key points to reduce the risk of medication errors.

- **Keep a list:** Keep a written list of all the drugs you take, including over-the-counter drugs, herbal products, and other supplements; carry this list w/you and show it to all your health care providers, including dentists and emergency personnel. If traveling in a different country, the brand name you are using may be used for a very different drug; it is important to know the generic name as well as the brand name. Refer to your list for safety.
- **Know your drugs:** Make sure you know why you take each of your drugs.
- **Follow the directions:** Carefully read the label of each of your drugs, and follow the directions for taking it safely. Do not stop taking a drug without first consulting the prescriber. Make a calendar if you take drugs on alternating days. Using a weekly pillbox may also help to keep things straight.
- **Store carefully:** Always store drugs in a dry place safely out of the reach of children and pets and away from humidity and heat (the bathroom is a bad storage area). Make sure to keep all drugs in their original, labeled containers.
- **Speak up:** You, the patient, are the most important member of your health care team. *Never be afraid to ask questions* about your health or your treatments.

Special populations

Keeping children safe

Children present unique challenges related to medication errors. Advise the child's caregiver to take these steps to prevent medication errors:

- Keep a list of all medications you are giving your child, including prescription, over-the-counter, and herbal medications. Share this list w/any health care provider who cares for your child.
- Never use adult medications to treat a child.
- Read all labels before giving your child a drug. Check the ingredients and dosage to avoid overdose.
- Measure liquid medications using appropriate measuring devices.
- Call your health care provider immediately if your child seems to get worse or seems to be having trouble w/a drug.
- When in doubt, do not hesitate to ask questions. You are your child's best advocate.

Protecting elderly patients

The elderly population is the most rapidly growing group in our country. Frequently, these patients have chronic diseases, are on multiple drugs, and have increasing health problems that can be a challenge to following a drug regimen. They are also more likely to suffer adverse reactions to drugs and drug combinations.

- Advise them to keep a medication list w/them to share w/all health care providers and to post a list somewhere in their home for easy access by emergency personnel.
- Prepare drug boxes for the week, draw up injectables (if stable) for the week, and provide daily reminders to take their medications.
- Be an advocate for elderly patients by asking questions, supplying information to providers, and helping elderly patients stay on top of their drug regimen and monitor their response.

Protecting women of childbearing age

As a general rule, it is best to avoid taking any drugs while pregnant.

- Advise women who may be pregnant to avoid Pregnancy Category X drugs (statins, hormones) that could cause serious harm to the fetus.
- Advise pregnant women to avoid all over-the-counter drugs and herbal therapies until they have checked w/the obstetrician for safety.
- Advise pregnant women to question all prescribed drugs and to check carefully to make sure that the drugs are safe for the fetus.
- Advise breast-feeding women to question the safety of prescribed drugs, over-the-counter drugs, or herbal therapies to make sure that the drugs or therapies will not adversely affect the baby.
- Encourage pregnant women to ask questions. Supply information and be an advocate for the fetus or newborn child.

Avoiding dangerous abbreviations

Although abbreviations can save time, they also raise the risk of misinterpretation, which can lead to potentially disastrous consequences, especially when dealing w/drug administration. To help reduce the risk of being misunderstood, always take the time to write legibly and to spell out anything that could be misread. This caution extends to how you write numbers as well as drug names and other drug-related instructions. The Joint Commission is enforcing a growing list of abbreviations that should not be used in medical records to help alleviate this problem. It is important to be familiar w/the abbreviations used in your clinical area and to avoid the use of any other abbreviations.

Common dangerous abbreviations

Try to avoid these common—and dangerous—abbreviations.

Abbreviation	Intended use	Potential misreading	Preferred use
BT	bedtime	May be read as "bid" or twice daily	Spell out "bedtime."
cc	cubic centimeters	May be read as "u" or units	Use "milliliters," abbreviated as "mL" or "ml."
D/C	discharge or discontinue	May lead to premature discontinuation of drug therapy or premature discharge	Spell out "discharge" or "discontinue."
hs	at bedtime	May be read as "half-strength"	Spell out "at bedtime."
HS	half-strength	May be read as "at bedtime"	Spell out "half-strength."
IJ	injection	May be read as "IV"	Spell out "injection."
IN	intranasal	May be read as "IM" or "IV"	Spell out "intranasal" or use "NAS."
IU	international unit	May be read as "IV" or "10"	Spell out "international unit."
µg	microgram	May be read as "mg"	Use "mcg."
o.d. or O.D.	once daily	May be read as "right eye"	Spell out "once daily."
per os	by mouth	May be read as "left eye"	Use "PO" or spell out "orally."

Abbreviation	Intended use	Potential misreading	Preferred use
q.d. or QD	daily	May be read as "qid"	Spell out "daily."
q1d	once daily	May be read as "qid"	Spell out "once daily."
qhs	every bedtime	May be read as "qhr" (every hour)	Spell out "nightly" or "at bedtime."
qn	every night	May be read as "qh" (every hour)	Spell out "nightly" or "at bedtime."
q.o.d. or QOD	every other day	May be read as "q.d." (daily) or "q.i.d." (four times daily)	Spell out "every other day."
SC, SQ	subcutaneous	May be read as "SL" (sublingual) or "5 every"	Spell out "subcutaneous" or use "subcut."
U or u	unit	May be read as "0" (100 instead of 10U)	Spell out "unit."
×7d	for 7 days	May be read as "for seven doses"	Spell out "for 7 days."
°	hour	May be read as a zero	Spell out "hour" or use "hr."

Reporting medication errors

Due to increases in the number of drugs available, the aging population, and more people taking many drugs, the possibilities for medication errors seem to be increasing. Institutions have adopted policies for reporting errors, but it is also important to submit information about errors to national programs. These national programs, coordinated by the US Pharmacopeia (USP), help to gather and disseminate information about errors, to prevent their recurrence at other sites and by other providers.

Witnessing an error

If you witness or participate in an actual or potential medication error, it is important to report that error to the national clearinghouse to ultimately help other professionals avoid similar errors. The USP maintains one central reporting center, from which it disseminates information to the FDA, drug manufacturers, and the Institute for Safe Medication Practices (ISMP). You can report an actual or potential error by calling 1-800-23-ERROR, the USP Medication Errors Reporting Program. Their office will send you a mailer to fill out and return to them. Or, you can log on to www.usp.org to report an error online or to print out the form to mail or fax back to the USP. You may request to remain anonymous. If you are not sure about what you want to report, you may report errors to the USP through the ISMP website at www.ismp.org, which also offers a discussion forum on medication errors.

What kind of errors should be reported?

Errors (or potential errors) to report include administration of the wrong drug or the wrong strength or dose of a drug, incorrect routes of administration, miscalculations, misuse of medical equipment, mistakes in prescribing or transcribing (misunderstanding of verbal orders), and errors resulting from sound-alike or look-alike names. In your report, you will be asked to include the following:

1. A description of the error or preventable adverse drug reaction. What went wrong?
2. Was this an actual medication accident or are you expressing concern about a potential error or writing about an error that was discovered before it reached the patient?
3. Patient outcome. Did the patient suffer any adverse effects?
4. Type of practice site where the event occurred
5. Generic and brand names of all products involved
6. Dosage form, concentration or strength, and so forth
7. If the error was based on a communication problem, is a sample of the order available? Are package label samples or pictures available if requested?
8. Your recommendations for error prevention.

The ISMP publishes case studies and publicizes warnings and alerts based on clinician reports of medication errors. Their efforts have helped to increase recognition of the many types of errors, such as those involving sound-alike names, look-alike names and packaging, instructions on equipment and delivery devices, and others.

Guidelines for safe disposal of medications

The White House Office of National Drug Control Policy, the Department of Health and Human Services, and the Environmental Protection Agency have established guidelines for the proper disposal of unused, unneeded, or expired medications to promote consumer safety, block access to them by potential abusers, and protect the water supply and the environment from possible contamination.

Medical disposal guidelines

Disposing in trash

- Take unused, unneeded, or expired medications out of their original containers.
- Mix the medication w/an undesirable substance, such as coffee grounds or used kitty litter, and place it in an impermeable, nondescript container, such as an empty can or a sealable storage bag. These steps help keep the medication from being diverted for illicit use or being accidentally ingested by children or animals.
- Place the closed container in your household trash. This is not the ideal way to dispose of a medication. Returning it to a drug take-back site is preferable, but if one is not available, follow these instructions.

Disposing in toilet

- Flush prescription drugs down the toilet **only** if the accompanying patient information specifically instructs you to do so.

Disposing at a hospital or government-sponsored site

- Return unused, unneeded, or expired prescription drugs to a pharmaceutical take-back location that offers safe disposal. Check w/your local hospital, health department, police department, or local government for a site near you.

Appendices

Alternative and complementary therapies

Many pts are now using herbs and alternative therapies. Some of these products may contain ingredients that interact with prescribed drugs. Pt hx of alternative therapy use may explain unexpected reactions to some drugs. In the chart below, drugs that the substance interacts with are in **bold**.

Substance	Reported uses, possible risks
acidophilus (probiotics)	*Oral:* px, tx of uncomplicated diarrhea; restoration of intestinal flora. RISK: **warfarin.**
alfalfa	*Topical:* healing ointment, relief of arthritis pain. *Oral:* tx of arthritis, hot flashes; strength giving; to reduce cholesterol level. RISK: **warfarin, chlorpromazine, antidiabetics, hormonal contraceptives, hormone replacement.**
allspice	*Topical:* anesthetic for teeth, gums; soothes sore joints, muscles. *Oral:* tx of indigestion, flatulence, diarrhea, fatigue. RISK: **iron.**
aloe leaves	*Topical:* tx of burns, healing of wounds. *Oral:* tx of chronic constipation. RISK: hypokalemia; spontaneous abortion if used in third trimester.
androstenedione	*Oral, spray:* anabolic steroid to increase muscle mass/strength. RISK: CV disease, certain cancers.
angelica	*Oral:* "cure all" for gynecologic problems, headaches, backaches, appetite loss, GI spasms; increases circulation in periphery. RISK: **anticoagulants.**
anise	*Oral:* relief of dry cough, tx of flatulence, bloating. RISK: **iron.**
apple	*Oral:* blood glucose control, constipation, cancer, heart problems. RISK: **antidiabetics, fexofenadine.**
arnica	*Topical:* relief of pain from muscle, soft-tissue injury. *Oral:* immune system stimulant; very toxic to children. RISK: **antihypertensives, anticoagulants, antiplatelet drugs.**

Substance	Reported uses, possible risks
ashwagandha	*Oral:* to improve mental, physical functioning; general tonic; to protect cells during cancer chemotherapy, radiation therapy. RISK: **anticoagulants; thyroid replacement.**
astragalus	*Oral:* to increase stamina, energy; to improve immune function, resistance to disease; tx of URI, common cold. RISK: **antihypertensives.**
barberry	*Oral:* antidiarrheal, antipyretic, cough suppressant. RISK: **antihypertensives, antiarrhythmics;** spontaneous abortion if taken during pregnancy.
basil	*Oral:* analgesic, anti-inflammatory, hypoglycemic. RISK: **antidiabetics.**
bayberry	*Topical:* to promote wound healing. *Oral:* stimulant, emetic, antidiarrheal. RISK: **antihypertensives.**
bee pollen	*Oral:* to treat allergies, asthma, ED, prostatitis; suggested use to decrease cholesterol levels, premenstrual syndrome. RISK: **antidiabetics;** bee allergy.
betel palm	*Oral:* mild stimulant, digestive aid. RISK: **MAOIs; beta blockers, digoxin, antiglaucoma drugs.**
bilberry	*Oral:* tx of diabetes, diabetic retinopathy, CV problems, cataracts, night blindness; lowers cholesterol, triglycerides. RISK: **anticoagulants, alcohol.**
birch bark	*Topical:* tx of infected wounds, cuts; very toxic to children. *Oral:* as tea for relief of stomachache.
blackberry	*Oral:* generalized healing; tx of diabetes. RISK: **antidiabetics.**
black cohosh root	*Oral:* tx of PMS, menopausal disorders, rheumatoid arthritis. Contains estrogen-like components. RISK: **hormone replacement, hormonal contraceptives, sedatives, antihypertensives, anesthetics, immunosuppressants.**
bromelain	*Oral:* tx of inflammation, sports injuries, URI, PMS; adjunct in cancer treatment. RISK: **n/v/d, menstrual disorders.**
burdock	*Oral:* tx of diabetes; atropine-like adverse effects; uterine stimulant. RISK: **antidiabetics.**

Substance	Reported uses, possible risks
capsicum	*Topical*: external analgesic. *Oral*: tx of bowel disorders, chronic laryngitis, peripheral vascular disease. RISK: **warfarin, aspirin, ACE inhibitors, MAOIs, sedatives.**
catnip leaves	*Oral*: tx of bronchitis, diarrhea.
cat's claw	*Oral*: tx of allergies, arthritis; adjunct in tx of cancers, AIDS. Discourage use by transplant recipients, during pregnancy, breast-feeding. RISK: **oral anticoagulants, antihypertensives.**
cayenne pepper	*Topical*: tx of burns, wounds; relief of toothache.
celery	*Oral*: lowers blood glucose, acts as diuretic; may cause potassium depletion. RISK: **antidiabetics.**
chamomile	*Topical*: tx of wounds, ulcers, conjunctivitis. *Oral*: tx of migraines, gastric cramps; relief of anxiety, inflammatory diseases. Contains coumarin; closely monitor pts taking anticoagulants. RISK: **antidepressants**; ragweed allergies.
chaste-tree berry	*Oral*: tx of PMS, menopausal problems; to stimulate lactation. Progesterone-like effects. RISK: **hormone replacement, hormonal contraceptives.**
chicken soup	*Oral*: breaks up respiratory secretions; bronchodilator; relieves anxiety.
chicory	*Oral*: tx of digestive tract problems, gout; stimulates bile secretions.
Chinese angelica (dong quai)	*Oral*: general tonic; tx of anemias, PMS, menopausal sx, antihypertensive, laxative. Use caution w/flu, hemorrhagic diseases. RISK: **antihypertensives, vasodilators, anticoagulants, hormone replacement.**
chondroitin	*Oral*: tx of osteoarthritis, related disorders (usually w/ glucosamine). RISK: **anticoagulants.**
chong cao fungi	*Oral*: antioxidant; promotes stamina, sexual function.
Coleus forskohlii	*Oral*: tx of asthma, hypertension, eczema. RISK: **antihypertensives, antihistamines**; peptic ulcer.
comfrey	*Topical*: tx of wounds, cuts, ulcers. *Oral*: gargle for tonsillitis. RISK: **eucalyptus**; monitor LFTs.

Substance	Reported uses, possible risks
coriander	*Oral:* weight loss, lowers blood glucose. RISK: **antidiabetics.**
creatine monohydrate	*Oral:* to enhance athletic performance. RISK: **insulin, caffeine.**
dandelion root	*Oral:* tx of liver, kidney problems; decreases lactation (after delivery, w/weaning); lowers blood glucose. RISK: **antidiabetics, antihypertensives, quinolone antibiotics.**
DHEA	*Oral:* slows aging, improves vigor ("Fountain of Youth"); androgenic side effects. RISK: **alprazolam, calcium channel blockers, antidiabetics.**
di huang	*Oral:* tx of diabetes mellitus. RISK: **antidiabetics.**
dried root bark of *Lycium chinense* Miller	*Oral:* lowers cholesterol, blood glucose. RISK: **antidiabetics.**
echinacea (cone flower)	*Oral:* tx of colds, flu; stimulates immune system, attacks viruses; causes immunosuppression if used long-term. May be hepatotoxic; discourage use for longer than 12 wk. Discourage use by patients w/SLE, TB, AIDS. RISK: **hepatotoxic drugs, immunosuppressants, antifungals.**
elder bark and flowers	*Topical:* gargle for tonsillitis/pharyngitis. *Oral:* tx of fever, chills.
ephedra	*Oral:* increases energy, relieves fatigue. RISK: **serious complications, including death; increased risk of hypertension, stroke, MI; interacts w/many drugs; banned by FDA.**
ergot	*Oral:* tx of migraine headaches, menstrual problems, hemorrhage. RISK: **antihypertensives.**
eucalyptus	*Topical:* tx of wounds. *Oral:* decreases respiratory secretions; suppresses cough. Very toxic in children. RISK: **comfrey.**
evening primrose	*Oral:* tx of PMS, menopause, rheumatoid arthritis, diabetic neuropathy. Discourage use by pts w/epilepsy, schizophrenia. RISK: **phenothiazines, antidepressants.**

Substance	Reported uses, possible risks
false unicorn root	*Oral:* tx of menstrual, uterine problems. Not for use in pregnancy, breast-feeding.
fennel	*Oral:* tx of colic, gout, flatulence; enhances lactation. RISK: **ciprofloxacin.**
fenugreek	*Oral:* lowers cholesterol level; reduces blood glucose; aids in healing. RISK: **antidiabetics, anticoagulants.**
feverfew	*Oral:* tx of arthritis, fever, migraine. Not for use if surgery planned. RISK: **anticoagulants.**
fish oil	*Oral:* tx of coronary diseases, arthritis, colitis, depression, aggression, attention deficit disorder.
garlic	*Oral:* tx of colds; diuretic; px of CAD; intestinal antiseptic; lowers blood glucose; anticoagulant effects; decreases BP; anemia. RISK: **antidiabetics.**
ginger	*Oral:* tx of nausea, motion sickness, postop nausea (may increase risk of miscarriage). RISK: **anticoagulants.**
ginkgo	*Oral:* vascular dilation; increases blood flow to brain, improving cognitive function; tx of Alzheimer disease; antioxidant. Can inhibit blood clotting. Seizures reported w/high doses. RISK: **anticoagulants, aspirin, NSAIDs, phenytoin, carbamazepine, phenobarbital, TCAs, MAOIs, antidiabetics.**
ginseng	*Oral:* aphrodisiac, mood elevator, tonic; antihypertensive; decreases cholesterol levels; lowers blood glucose; adjunct in cancer chemotherapy, radiation therapy. May cause irritability if used w/caffeine. Inhibits clotting. RISK: **anticoagulants, aspirin, NSAIDs, phenelzine, MAOIs, estrogens, corticosteroids, digoxin, antidiabetics.**
glucosamine	*Oral:* tx of osteoarthritis, joint diseases; usually w/ chondroitin. RISK: diabetic pts.
goldenrod leaves	*Oral:* tx of renal disease, rheumatism, sore throat, eczema. RISK: **diuretics.**

Substance	Reported uses, possible risks
goldenseal	*Oral:* lowers blood glucose, aids healing; tx of bronchitis, colds, flulike sx, cystitis. May cause false-negative results in pts using drugs such as marijuana, cocaine. Large amounts may cause paralysis; overdose can cause death. RISK: **anticoagulants, antihypertensives, acid blockers, barbiturates, sedatives.**
gotu kola	*Topical:* chronic venous insufficiency. RISK: **antidiabetics, cholesterol-lowering drugs, sedatives.**
grape seed extract	*Oral:* tx of allergies, asthma; improves circulation; decreases platelet aggregation. RISK: **anticoagulants.**
green tea leaf	*Oral:* antioxidant; to prevent cancer, CV disease; to increase cognitive function (caffeine effects). RISK: **anticoagulants, milk.**
guarana	*Oral:* decreases appetite; promotes weight loss; increases BP, risk of CV events.
guayusa	*Oral:* lowers blood glucose; promotes weight loss. RISK: **antihypertensives, iron, lithium.**
hawthorn	*Oral:* tx of angina, arrhythmias, BP problems; decreases cholesterol. RISK: **digoxin, ACE inhibitors, CNS depressants.**
hop	*Oral:* sedative; aids healing; alters blood glucose. RISK: **CNS depressants, antipsychotics.**
horehound	*Oral:* expectorant; tx of respiratory problems, GI disorders. RISK: **antidiabetics, antihypertensives.**
horse chestnut seed	*Oral:* tx of varicose veins, hemorrhoids, venous insufficiency. RISK: **anticoagulants.**
hyssop	*Topical:* tx of cold sores, genital herpes, burns, wounds. *Oral:* tx of coughs, colds, indigestion, flatulence. Toxic in children, pets. RISK: pregnancy, pts w/seizures.
jambul	*Oral:* tx of diarrhea, dysentery; lowers blood glucose. RISK: **CNS depressants, Java plum.**
Java plum	*Oral:* tx of diabetes mellitus. RISK: **antidiabetics.**
jojoba	*Topical:* promotion of hair growth; relief of skin problems. Toxic if ingested.

Substance	Reported uses, possible risks
juniper berries	*Oral:* increases appetite, aids digestion; diuretic; urinary tract disinfectant; lowers blood glucose. RISK: **antidiabetics;** pregnancy.
kava	*Oral:* tx of nervous anxiety, stress, restlessness; tranquilizer. Warn against use w/alprazolam; may cause coma. Advise against use w/Parkinson disease, hx of stroke. Risk of serious hepatotoxicity. RISK: **St. John's wort, anxiolytics, alcohol.**
kudzu	*Oral:* reduces alcohol craving (undergoing research for use w/alcoholics). RISK: **anticoagulants, aspirin, antidiabetics, CV drugs.**
lavender	*Topical:* astringent for minor cuts, burns. Oil potentially poisonous. *Oral:* tx of insomnia, restlessness. RISK: **CNS depressants.**
ledum tincture	*Topical:* tx of insect bites, puncture wounds; dissolves some blood clots, bruises.
licorice	*Oral:* px of thirst; soothes coughs; treats "incurable" chronic fatigue syndrome; tx of duodenal ulcer. Acts like aldosterone. Blocks spironolactone effects. Can lead to digoxin toxicity because of aldosterone-lowering effects; advise extreme caution. RISK: **thyroid drugs, antihypertensives, hormonal contraceptives;** renal/liver disease, hypertension, CAD, pregnancy, breast-feeding.
ma huang	*Oral:* tx of colds, nasal congestion, asthma. Contains ephedrine. RISK: **antihypertensives, antidiabetics, MAOIs, digoxin.**
mandrake root	*Oral:* tx of fertility problems.
marigold leaves and flowers	*Oral:* relief of muscle tension; increases wound healing. RISK: pregnancy, breast-feeding.
melatonin	*Oral:* relief of jet lag; tx of insomnia. RISK: **antihypertensives, benzodiazepines, beta blockers, methamphetamine.**
milk thistle	*Oral:* tx of hepatitis, cirrhosis, fatty liver caused by alcohol/drug use. RISK: **drugs using CP450, CYP3A4, CYP2C9 systems.**
milk vetch	*Oral:* improves resistance to disease; adjunct in cancer chemotherapy, radiation therapy.

Substance	Reported uses, possible risks
mistletoe leaves	*Oral:* promotes weight loss; relief of s&sx of diabetes. RISK: **antihypertensives, CNS depressants, immunosuppressants.**
Momordica charantia (Karela)	*Oral:* blocks intestinal absorption of glucose; lowers blood glucose; weight loss. RISK: **antidiabetics.**
nettle	*Topical:* stimulation of hair growth, tx of bleeding. *Oral:* tx of rheumatism, allergic rhinitis; antispasmodic; expectorant. RISK: **diuretics;** pregnancy, breast-feeding.
nightshade leaves and roots	*Oral:* stimulates circulatory system; tx of eye disorders.
octacosanol	*Oral:* tx of parkinsonism, enhancement of athletic performance. RISK: **carbidopa-levodopa;** pregnancy, breast-feeding.
parsley seeds and leaves	*Oral:* tx of jaundice, asthma, menstrual difficulties, urinary infections, conjunctivitis. RISK: **SSRIs, lithium, opioids, antihypertensives.**
passionflower vine	*Oral:* sedative-hypnotic. RISK: **CNS depressants, MAOIs, alcohol, anticoagulants.**
peppermint leaves	*Topical:* rubbed on forehead to relieve tension headaches. *Oral:* tx of nervousness, insomnia, dizziness, cramps, coughs.
psyllium	*Oral:* tx of constipation; lowers cholesterol. Can cause severe gas, stomach pain. May interfere w/nutrient absorption. RISK: **warfarin, digoxin, lithium, oral drugs, laxatives.**
raspberry	*Oral:* healing of minor wounds; control, tx of diabetes, GI disorders, upper respiratory disorders. RISK: **antidiabetics; alcohol.**
red clover	*Oral:* estrogen replacement in menopause; suppresses whooping cough; asthma. RISK: **anticoagulants, antiplatelets;** pregnancy.
red yeast rice	*Oral:* lowers cholesterol. RISK: **cyclosporine, fibric acid, niacin, lovastatin, grapefruit juice.**
rose hips	*Oral:* laxative; to boost immune system, prevent illness. RISK: **estrogens, iron, warfarin.**

Substance	Reported uses, possible risks
rosemary	*Topical:* relief of rheumatism, sprains, wounds, bruises, eczema. *Oral:* gastric stimulation; relief of flatulence, colic; stimulation of bile release. RISK: **alcohol.**
rue extract	*Topical:* relief of pain associated w/sprains, groin pulls, whiplash. RISK: **antihypertensives, digoxin, warfarin.**
saffron	*Oral:* tx of menstrual problems; abortifacient.
sage	*Oral:* lowers BP, blood glucose. RISK: **antidiabetics, anticonvulsants, alcohol.**
SAM-e (adomet)	*Oral:* promotion of general well-being, health. May cause frequent GI complaints, headache. RISK: **antidepressants.**
sarsaparilla	*Oral:* tx of skin disorders, rheumatism. RISK: **anticonvulsants.**
sassafras	*Topical:* tx of local pain, skin eruptions. *Oral:* enhancement of athletic performance, "cure" for syphilis. **Oil may be toxic to fetus, children, adults when ingested. Interacts w/many drugs.**
saw palmetto	*Oral:* tx of BPH. RISK: **estrogen-replacement, hormonal contraceptives, iron, finasteride, testosterone replacement.**
schisandra	*Oral:* health tonic, liver protectant; adjunct in cancer chemotherapy, radiation therapy. RISK: **drugs metabolized in liver;** pregnancy (causes uterine stimulation).
squaw vine	*Oral:* diuretic, tonic; aid in labor, delivery; tx of menstrual problems. RISK: **digoxin, alcohol.**
St. John's wort	*Topical:* tx of puncture wounds, insect bites, crushed fingers/toes. *Oral:* tx of depression, PMS symptoms; antiviral. Discourage tyramine-containing foods; hypertensive crisis possible. Thrombocytopenia has occurred. Can increase light sensitivity; advise against taking w/drugs causing photosensitivity. Severe photosensitivity possible in light-skinned people. RISK: **SSRIs, MAOIs, kava, digoxin, theophylline, AIDS antivirals, sympathomimetics, antineoplastics, hormonal contraceptives, serotogenic drugs.**

Substance	Reported uses, possible risks
sweet violet flowers	*Oral:* tx of respiratory disorders; emetic. RISK: **laxatives.**
tarragon	*Oral:* weight loss; prevents cancer; lowers blood glucose. RISK: **antidiabetics.**
tea tree oil	*Topical:* antifungal, antibacterial; tx of burns, insect bites, irritated skin, acne; mouthwash.
thyme	*Topical:* liniment, gargle; tx of wounds. *Oral:* antidiarrheal; relief of bronchitis, laryngitis. May increase light sensitivity; warn against using w/photosensitivity-causing drugs. RISK: **MAOIs, SSRIs.**
turmeric	*Oral:* antioxidant, anti-inflammatory; tx of arthritis. May cause GI distress. Warn against use w/known biliary obstruction. RISK: **oral anticoagulants, NSAIDs, immunosuppressants.**
valerian	*Oral:* sedative-hypnotic; reduces anxiety, relaxes muscles. Can cause severe liver damage. RISK: **barbiturates, alcohol, CNS depressants, benzodiazepines, antihistamines.**
went rice	*Oral:* cholesterol-, triglyceride-lowering effects. Warn against use in pregnancy, liver disease, alcoholism, acute infection.
white willow bark	*Oral:* tx of fevers. RISK: **anticoagulants, NSAIDs, diuretics.**
xuan shen	*Oral:* lowers blood glucose; slows heart rate; tx of HF. RISK: **antidiabetics.**
yohimbe	*Oral:* tx of ED. Can affect BP; CNS stimulant. Has cardiac effects. Manic episodes have occurred in psychiatric pts. RISK: **SSRIs, tyramine-containing foods, TCAs.**

Topical drugs

Topical drugs are intended for surface use, not ingestion or injection. They may be very toxic if absorbed into the system, but they serve several purposes when used topically.

PREG/CONT C

ADV EFF Burning, dermatitis, local irritation (common), stinging, toxic effects if absorbed systemically

NC/PT Apply sparingly to affected area as directed. Do not use w/open wounds, broken skin. Avoid contact w/eyes. Pt should report local irritation, allergic reaction, worsening of condition.

Acne, rosacea, melasma products

adapalene (Differin): Not for use under 12 yr. Avoid use on sunburned skin, w/other products, sun exposure. Apply thin film to affected area after washing q night at bedtime. Available as cream, gel; 0.1%, 0.3% conc.

adapalene/benzyl peroxide (Epiduo): For pt 9 yr and older. Avoid use on sunburned skin, w/ other products, sun exposure. Apply thin film once a day to affected area on face and/or trunk after washing. Available as gel; 0.1%, 2.5% conc.

alitretinoin (Panretin): Tx of lesions of Kaposi sarcoma (1% gel). Apply as needed bid to cover lesions. Photosensitivity common. Inflammation, peeling, redness possible. Pregnancy Category D.

azelaic acid (Azelex, Finacea): Wash, dry skin. Massage thin layer into affected area bid. Wash hands thoroughly after applying. Improvement usually within 4 wk. Initial irritation usual; passes w/time.

brimonidine (Mirvaso): Tx of persistent facial erythema of rosacea in adult. Apply pea-size amount to forehead, chin, cheeks daily. Risk of vascular insufficiency. Wash hands immediately after application; do not ingest.

clindamycin (Clindesse, Evoclin): Tx of bacterial vaginitis (2% vaginal cream): One applicatorful (100 mg) vaginally at any time of day. Tx of acne vulgaris (1% foam): Apply once daily to affected areas that have been washed, are fully dry.

clindamycin/benzoyl peroxide (Acanya, BenzaClin): Tx of acne. Apply gel to affected areas bid. Wash area, pat dry before applying.

clindamycin/tretinoin (Veltin, Ziana): Tx of acne. Rub pea-size amount over entire face once daily at bedtime. Not for use in colitis. Avoid sun exposure.

dapsone (Aczone Gel): Tx of acne. Apply thin layer to affected areas bid. Methemoglobinemia has been reported. Closely follow Hgb, reticulocyte count in pts w/G6PD deficiencies.

fluocinolone acetonide/ hydroquinone/tretinoin (Tri-Luma): Tx of melasma. Do not use in pregnancy. Apply to depigmented area of melasma once each

407

p.m. at least 30 min before bedtime after washing, patting dry; avoid occlusive dressings. Use sunscreen, protective clothing if outside (skin dryness, peeling possible).

ingenol mebutate (Picato): Tx of acne. Apply 0.015% gel once daily to face/scalp for 5 days. Apply 0.05% gel once daily to trunk/extremities for 2 days. Avoid periocular area, lips, mouth. Risk of hypersensitivity, ophthalmic reactions.

ivermectin (Soolantra): Tx of rosacea. Apply 1% cream to affected areas daily. Not for oral, ophthalmic, intravaginal use.

metronidazole (MetroCream, MetroGel, MetroLotion, Noritate): Tx of rosacea. Apply cream to affected area bid.

sodium sulfacetamide (Klaron): Apply thin film to affected area bid. Wash affected area w/mild soap, water; pat dry. Avoid use in denuded, abraded areas.

tazarotene (Fabior, Tazorac): Tx of psoriasis. Avoid use in pregnancy. Apply thin film once daily in p.m. Do not use w/irritants, products w/high alcohol content. Drying causes photosensitivity.

tretinoin 0.025% cream (Avita): Tx of acne. Apply thin layer once daily. Discomfort, peeling, redness possible first 2–4 wk. Worsened acne possible in first few wk.

tretinoin 0.05% cream (Renova): To remove fine wrinkles. Apply thin coat in p.m.

tretinoin gel (Retin-A* Micro): Tx of acne. Apply to cover once daily after washing. Inflammation exacerbation possible initially. Therapeutic effects usually seen in first 2 wk.

Analgesics

capsaicin (Axsain, Capsin, Capzasin, Icy Hot PM, No Pain-HP, Pain Doctor, Zostrix, Zostrix-HP): Local pain relief for osteoarthritis, rheumatoid arthritis, neuralgias. Apply no more than tid–qid. Do not bandage tightly. Consult physician if condition worsens or persists after 14–28 days. **Qutenza:** Apply patch to relieve postherpetic neuralgia pain.

Antibiotics

ciprofloxacin (Otiprio): Tx of child w/bilateral otitis media w/effusion undergoing tympanostomy tube placement: 6 mg (0.1 mL) into each affected ear after middle ear suctioning. Risk of bacterial overgrowth.

ciprofloxacin/dexamethasone (Ciprodex), ciprofloxacin/hydrocortisone (Cipro-HC Otic Drops): Apply to ears of child w/acute otitis media and tympanostomy tubes; apply to outer ear canal for acute otitis externa. Use bid for 7 days.

mupirocin (Bactroban, Centany): Tx of impetigo caused by susceptible strains. Apply small amt to affected area tid; may cover w/gauze dressing. Risk of superinfection.

mupirocin calcium (Bactroban Nasal): To eradicate nasal colonization of MRSA. Apply ½ of oint from single-use tubes between nostrils bid for 5 days. Risk of CDAD.

retapamulin (Altabax): Tx of impetigo in pts 9 mo and older. Apply thin layer to affected area bid for 5 days.

Anti-diaper-rash drug

miconazole/zinc oxide/petrolatum (Vusion): Culture for *Candida* before tx. Apply gently for 7 days; change diapers frequently, wash gently.

Antifungals

butenafine hydrochloride (Mentax): Tx of athlete's foot; tinea corporis, cruris; ringworm. Apply once/day for 4 wk.

ciclopirox (Loprox, Penlac Nail Lacquer): Tx of onychomycosis of fingernails, toenails in immunosuppressed pts. Apply directly to nails.

clotrimazole (Cruex, Desenex, Lotrimin, Mycelex): Clean area; gently massage in up to bid for max 4 wk.

econazole (generic): Apply daily or bid for 2–4 wk. Clean area before applying. Change socks at least once/day for athlete's foot.

gentian violet (generic): Apply locally up to bid. Do not apply to active lesions. Will stain skin, clothing.

ketoconazole (Extina, Nizoral, Xolegel): Tx of seborrheic dermatitis. Available as cream, foam, gel, shampoo. Use as shampoo daily.

luliconazole (Luzu): Tx of tinea cruris, tinea corporis. Apply to affected area once a day for 1 wk, 2 wk for interdigital tinea pedis.

naftifine hydrochloride (Naftin): Tx of tinea cruris, tinea pedis, tinea corporis. Gently massage in bid for no more than 4 wk. Avoid occlusive dressings. Wash hands thoroughly after applying.

oxiconazole (Oxistat): Tx of tinea cruris, tinea pedis, tinea corporis. Apply q day to bid for max 1 mo.

sertaconazole (Ertaczo): Tx of interdigital tinea pedis. Apply between toes, to surrounding tissue bid for 4 wk.

terbinafine (Lamisil): Tx of onychomycosis of fingernails/ toenails. Apply bid for 1–4 wk. Avoid occlusive dressings. Stop if local irritation.

tolnaftate (Absorbine, Tinactin): Tx of athlete's foot. Apply small amount bid for 2–3 wk; 4–6 wk if skin very thick. Clean, dry area before use. Change socks qid.

Antihistamine

azelastine hydrochloride (Astelin): 2 sprays/nostril bid. Do not use w/ alcohol, OTC antihistamines; dizziness, sedation possible.

Antipsoriatics

anthralin (Balnetar, Dritho-Cream HP, Fototar, Zithranol): Apply daily; use protective dressings. Avoid contact w/eyes. May stain fabric, skin, hair, fingernails.

calcipotriene (Dovonex): Apply thin layer q day or bid. Monitor calcium w/extended use.

calcipotriene/betamethasone (Taclonex, Taclonex Scalp): Apply q day for 4 wk. Max, 100 g/wk. Avoid occlusive dressings. Limit to 30% of body area.

Antiseborrheic

selenium sulfide (Selsun Blue): Massage 5–10 mL into scalp, leave on 2–3 min, rinse; repeat. May damage jewelry.

Antiseptics

benzalkonium chloride (Benza, Mycocide NS): Mix in sol. Spray preop area; store instruments in sol (add antirust tablets). Rinse detergents, soaps from skin before use.

chlorhexidine gluconate (BactoShield, Dyna-Hex, Exidine, Hibistat): For surgical scrub, preop skin prep, wound cleansing. Scrub, leave on for 15 sec (3 min for surgical scrub), rinse.

iodine (generic): Wash area w/sol. Highly toxic. Avoid occlusive dressings. Stains skin, clothing.

povidone iodine (ACU-Dyne, Betadine, Betagen, Iodex, Minidyne, Operand, Polydine): Less irritating than iodine. May bandage area. May inactivate HIV.

sodium hypochlorite (Dakin's solution): Apply as antiseptic. Chemical burns possible.

Antivirals

acyclovir (Zovirax): Apply 0.5-inch ribbon, rub in gently six times/day for 7 days.

acyclovir/hydrocortisone (Xerese): Tx of cold sores in pts 6 yr and older. Apply five times/day for 5 days.

docosanol (Abreva): Tx of oral, facial herpes simplex cold sores. Apply five times/day for 10 days. Do not overuse.

imiquimod (Aldara): Tx of external genital, perianal warts: Apply thin layer three times/wk at bedtime for up to 16 wk; remove w/soap, water after 6–10 hr. Tx of nonhyperkeratotic actinic keratosis on face, scalp in immunosuppressed pts: Apply before bed for 16 wk. Tx of superficial basal cell carcinoma in immunosuppressed pts: 10–40 mg applied to lesion five times/wk at bedtime for 6 wk.

imiquimod (Zyclara): Tx of nonhyperkeratotic or nonhypertrophic actinic keratoses on face, balding scalp: Apply daily at bedtime for 2 wk, then 2 wk of no tx. May repeat. Tx of genital,

perianal warts in pts 12 yr and older: Apply daily.

kunecatechins (sinecatechins) (Veregen): External tx of genital, perianal warts in pts 18 yr and older. Apply to each wart tid for 16 wk. Do not cover tx area.

penciclovir (Denavir): Tx of cold sores on lips, face. Apply thin layer q 2 hr while awake for 4 days.

Burn tx

mafenide (Sulfamylon): Apply to clean, dry, debrided wound q day or bid. Cover at all times w/drug. Monitor for infection, acidosis. Pretreat for pain.

silver sulfadiazine (Silvadene, SSD Cream, Thermazene): Apply q day to bid using 1/16-inch thickness. Dressings not necessary. Monitor for fungal infection.

Corticosteroids for inflammatory disorders

alclometasone dipropionate (generic): 0.05% oint, cream

beclomethasone (Beconase AQ, Qnasl): Nasal spray for rhinitis

betamethasone dipropionate: 0.05% oint, cream, gel, lotion, aerosol

betamethasone dipropionate augmented (Diprolene, Diprolene AF): 0.05% oint, cream, lotion

betamethasone valerate (Beta-Val, Luxiq): 0.1% oint, cream, lotion; 0.12% foam

ciclesonide (Alvesco, Omnaris, Zetonna): 80 or 160 mcg/actuation as nasal spray or for inhalation

clobetasol propionate (Clobex, Cormax, Olux, Temovate): 0.05% spray, oint, cream, foam, gel

clocortolone pivalate (Cloderm): 0.1% cream

desonide (DesOwen, Verdeso): 0.05% oint, lotion, cream, foam

desoximetasone (Topicort): 0.25% oint, cream

dexamethasone (generic): 0.05% cream, gel

diflorasone diacetate (generic): 0.1% cream

fluocinolone acetate (Synalar): 0.05% oint, cream; 0.01% sol

fluocinonide (Fluonex, Lidex, Vanos): 0.025% cream, oint; 0.01% cream; 0.05% oint, cream, gel, sol; 0.1% cream

fluticasone fumarate (Veramyst): 35 mcg/spray nasal spray

fluticasone propionate (Cutivate): 0.005% oint

halcinonide (Halog): 0.1% oint, cream

halobetasol propionate (Ultravate): 0.05% oint, cream

hydrocortisone (Bactine Hydrocortisone, Cort-Dome, Dermolate, Dermtex HC, Cortizone-10, Hycort, Hytone, Tegrin-HC): 0.25%, 0.5%, 1%, 2%, 2.5% cream, lotion, oint, sol

hydrocortisone acetate (Anusol-HCL, Cortaid, Cortaid w/Aloe, Gynecort, Lanacort-5): 0.5%, 1% cream, oint

hydrocortisone buteprate (generic): 0.1% cream

hydrocortisone butyrate (Locoid): 0.1% oint, cream

hydrocortisone valerate (generic): 0.2% oint, cream

mometasone furoate (Asmanex Twisthaler, Elocon, Nasonex): 220 mcg/actuation powder for oral inhalation; 0.1% oint, cream, lotion; 0.2% nasal spray

prednicarbate (Dermatop): 0.1% cream

triamcinolone acetonide (Triderm): 0.1% cream, lotion; 0.025% lotion

Emollients

dexpanthenol (Panthoderm): To relieve itching, aids in healing skin irritation; q day to bid.

urea (Aquacare; Gordon's Urea 40%; Nutraplus; Ureacin 10, 20): Rub in bid–qid.

vitamins A, D (generic): To relieve minor burns, chafing, skin irritation; bid–qid for up to 7 days.

Estrogen

estradiol hemihydrate (Vagifem): Tx of atrophic vaginitis. One tablet/day vaginally for 2 wk, then 1 tablet two times/wk. Taper over 3–6 mo.

Growth factor

becaplermin (Regranex): Adjunct tx of diabetic foot ulcers. Must have adequate blood supply. Risk of cancer w/long-term use.

Hair removal product

eflornithine (Vaniqa): For women only. Apply to unwanted facial hair bid for 24 wk; do not wash treated area for 4 hr.

Hemostatics

absorbable gelatin (Gelfoam):
Add 3–4 mL sterile saline to contents of jar; smear or press to cut surface. Assess for infection; do not use if area infected.

absorbable fibrin sealant (TachoSil): For CV surgery when usual techniques to control bleeding ineffective. Apply yellow side of patches directly to bleeding area. Do not use intravascularly or w/known hypersensitivity to human blood products, horse protein.

human fibrin sealant (Artiss, Evicel, Tisseel): Adjunct to decrease bleeding in vascular, liver surgery; to adhere autologous skin grafts for burns. Spray or drip onto tissue in short bursts to produce thin layer; may use second layer.

human fibrin sealant (Raplixa): Adjunct to decrease bleeding in small blood vessels in standard surgical techniques. Spray directly on site. Monitor for infection.

microfibrillar collagen (Hemopad): Apply dry directly to bleeding source. Monitor for infection. Remove any excess material once bleeding stopped.

thrombin (Thrombinar, Thrombostat): 100–1,000 units/mL. Prepare in sterile distilled water or isotonic saline. Mix freely w/blood on surface of injury; watch for allergic reactions.

thrombin, recombinant (Recothrom): Apply directly to bleeding site w/absorbable gelatin sponge; reserve for minor bleeds. Not for use w/hamster, snake protein allergies.

Immunomodulator

pimecrolimus (Elidel): Tx of mild to moderate atopic dermatitis in nonimmunosuppressed pts over 2 yr. Apply bid.

Keratolytics

podofilox (Condylox): Apply to dry skin q 12 hr for 3 days.

podophyllum resin (Podocon-25, Podofin): Use minimum possible for wart removal; very toxic.

Local anesthetic

lidocaine/tetracaine (Synera): Dermal analgesia for superficial venous access, dermatologic procedures. One patch to intact skin 20–30 min before procedure.

Lotions, solutions

Burow's solution aluminum acetate (Domeboro Powder): Astringent wet dressing for inflammatory conditions, insect bites, athlete's foot, bruises. Dissolve packet, tablet in pint of water; apply q 15–30 min for 4–8 hr.

calamine lotion (generic): To relieve topical itching. Apply tid–qid.

hamamelis water (A-E-R, Witch Hazel): To relieve itching of vaginal infection, hemorrhoids; postepisiotomy, post hemorrhoidectomy care. Apply locally six times/day.

Nasal corticosteroid

fluticasone propionate (Flonase, Flovent Diskus, Flovent HFA): Px of asthma in pts over 4 yr. Two sprays/nostril/day or 88–220 mcg bid using inhalation device, nasal inhalation.

Pediculicides, scabicides

benzyl alcohol (generic): Tx of head lice in pts 6 mo and older. Apply 5% lotion to scalp, hair near scalp.

crotamiton (Eurax): Massage into skin of entire body; repeat in 24 hr. Bathe 48 hr after use. Change bed linens, clothing; wash in hot water, dry clean.

ivermectin (Sklice): Tx of head lice in pts 6 mo and older. Apply 0.5% lotion once to head for 10 min; no need for nit picking.

lindane (generic): Apply thin layer to entire body, leave on 8–12 hr, then wash thoroughly. For shampoo, 2 oz into dry hair, leave on 4 min, then rinse. Reapply in 7 days if needed.

malathion (Ovide Lotion): Apply to dry hair, leave on 8–12 hr, rinse. Repeat in 7–9 days. Contains flammable alcohol.

permethrin (Acticin, Elimite, Nix): Thoroughly massage into skin, wash off after 8–14 hr. For shampoo, work into freshly washed, towel-dried hair, leave on 10 min, then rinse.

spinosad (Natroba): Tx of head lice in pts 4 yr and older. Apply to dry scalp, leave on 10 min, rinse. May repeat q 7 days.

Ophthalmic drugs

Ophthalmic drugs are intended for direct administration into the conjunctiva of the eye.

IND & DOSE Tx of glaucoma; to aid in dx of eye problems; tx of local ophthalmic infection, inflammation; to relieve s&sx of allergic reactions. *Adult, child:* 1–2 drops to each eye bid–qid, or 0.25–0.5 inch oint to each eye.

PREG/CONT C/NA

ADV EFF Blurred vision (prolonged w/oint), burning, local irritation, stinging, tearing; headache

NC/PT Sol, drops: Wash hands thoroughly before giving; do not touch dropper to eye or other surface; have pt tilt head back or lie down and stare upward. Gently grasp lower eyelid; pull eyelid away from eyeball. Instill drop(s) into pouch formed by eyelid; release lid slowly. Have pt close eye, look downward. Apply gentle pressure to inside corner of eye for 3–5 min to retard drainage. Pt should not rub eyes, rinse eyedropper; avoid eyedrops that have changed color; separate administration by 5 min if more than one type of eyedrop used.

Oint: Wash hands thoroughly before giving; hold tube between hands for several min to warm; discard first cm of oint when opening tube for first time. Have pt tilt head back or lie down and stare upward. Gently pull out lower lid to form pouch; place 0.25–0.5 inch oint inside lower lid. Have pt close eyes for 1–2 min, roll eyeball in all directions. Remove excess oint from around eye. Separate administration by 10 min if using more than one kind of oint. Transient stinging, burning, blurred vision possible; pt should take appropriate safety measures. Sun sensitivity w/mydriatic agents (pupils will dilate); pt may need sunglasses. Pt should report severe eye discomfort, palpitations, nausea, headache.

alcaftadine (Lastacaft): Px of itching associated w/allergic conjunctivitis. 1 drop in each eye daily. Remove contacts. Not for tx of contact lens irritation.

apraclonidine (Iopidine): To control, prevent postop IOP elevation after argon-laser surgery; short-term adjunct tx in pts on max tolerated tx who need additional IOP reduction. Monitor for possible vasovagal attack. Do not give to pts w/clonidine allergy.

azelastine hydrochloride (Optivar): Tx of ocular itching associated w/allergic conjunctivitis in pts 3 yr and older. Antihistamine, mast cell stabilizer. 1 drop bid. Rapid onset, 8-hr duration.

azithromycin (Azasite): Tx of bacterial conjunctivitis in pts 1 yr and older. 1 drop bid 8–12 hr apart for 2 days, then once/day for 5 days.

bepotastine besilate (Bepreve): Tx of ocular itching from allergic rhinitis in pts 2 yr and older. Apply bid.

besifloxacin (Besivance): Tx of pink eye: 1 drop tid for 7 days (*Besivance*).

bimatoprost (Latisse, Lumigan): Tx of open-angle glaucoma, ocular hypertension: 1 drop daily in p.m. Tx of hypertrichosis of eyelashes: 1 drop each p.m.; iris darkening possible (*Latisse*).

brimonidine tartrate (Alphagan P): Tx of open-angle glaucoma, ocular hypertension. 1 drop tid. May stain contacts. Do not use w/MAOIs.

brimonidine/timolol (Combigan): Tx of increased IOP. 1 drop q 12 hr. Do not wear contacts.

brinzolamide (Azopt): To decrease IOP in open-angle glaucoma. 1 drop tid; give 10 min apart from other drops.

bromfenac (generic): Tx of postop inflammation, pain after cataract extraction. 1 drop bid starting 24 hr after surgery and for 2 wk; once/day w/*Bromday*.

carbachol (Miostat): Tx of glaucoma, miosis during surgery. 1–2 drops tid for glaucoma, one dose before surgery.

carteolol (generic): Tx of elevated IOP in open-angle glaucoma. 1 drop bid; monitor IOP closely.

ciprofloxacin (Ciloxan): Tx of ocular infections, conjunctivitis: Apply ¼-inch ribbon to eye sac tid for 2 days, then bid for 5 days, or 1–2 drops q 2 hr while awake for 2 days, then q 4 hr for 5 days.

cyclopentolate (Cyclogyl, Pare-myd): Diagnostic procedures. Pts w/ dark irises may need higher doses. Compress lacrimal sac for 2–3 min after giving.

cyclosporine emulsion (Restasis): To increase tear production. 1 drop in each eye bid approximately 12 hr apart. Remove contacts before use.

dexamethasone intravitreal (Ozurdex): Tx of macular edema after branch retinal artery, central retinal vein occlusion; tx of nonin-fectious uveitis of posterior segment of eye. Intravitreal injection. Monitor for infection, retinal detachment.

diclofenac sodium (Voltaren): Tx of photophobia in pts undergoing incisional refractive surgery; tx of postop ocular inflammation. 1 drop qid starting 24 hr after surgery and for 2 wk, or 1–2 drops within 1 hr of corneal surgery, then 1–2 drops 15 min after surgery, then qid for max 3 days.

difluprednate (Durezol): Tx of postop ocular pain, inflammation: 1 drop qid starting 24 after surgery and for 2 wk.

dorzolamide (Trusopt): Tx of in-creased IOP, open-angle glaucoma. 1 drop tid.

dorzolamide/timolol (Cosopt): To reduce IOP. 1 drop bid. Monitor for HF if absorbed systemically.

emedastine (Emadine): To relieve s&sx of allergic conjunctivitis in pts 3 yr and older. 1 drop q day to qid. Do not wear contacts. May cause headache, blurred vision.

epinastine hydrochloride (Elestat): Px of allergic conjunctivitis itching. 1 drop bid for entire time of exposure. Remove contacts.

fluocinolone acetonide (Retisert): Tx of chronic noninfectious uveitis of posterior segment of eye. 1 surgically implanted insert replaced after 30 mo if needed.

fluorometholone (Flarex, FML): Tx of inflammatory eye conditions. Stop if swelling; monitor IOP after 10 days.

ganciclovir (Zirgan): Tx of acute herpetic keratitis. 1 drop five times/day until ulcer heals, then 1 drop tid for 7 days.

gatifloxacin (Zymar, Zymaxid): Tx of conjunctivitis caused by susceptible strains. 1 drop q 2 hr while awake up to eight times/day on days 1 and 2; then 1 drop q 4 hr while awake up to four times/day for 5 days. Pt should not wear contact lenses; may cause blurred vision.

homatropine (Homatropine HBr, Isopto-Homatropine): Refraction; tx of inflammatory conditions, preop and postop when mydriasis needed. 5–10 min needed for refraction; dark irises may need bigger doses.

ketorolac (Acuvail): Tx of pain, inflammation after cataract surgery. 1 drop bid.

ketotifen (Alaway, Zaditor): Temporary relief of itching due to allergic conjunctivitis in pts 3 yr and older. 1 drop q 8–12 hr; remove contacts for 10 min.

latanoprost (Xalatan): Tx of open-angle glaucoma, ocular hypertension. Remove contacts before and for 15 min after drops. Allow 5 min between this and other drops.

levobunolol (AKBeta, Betagon Liquifilm): Tx of bacterial conjunctivitis caused by susceptible strains. 1–2 drops q 2 hr while awake on days 1, 2; then q 4 hr while awake on days 3–7.

levofloxacin (generic): Tx of conjunctivitis caused by susceptible strains. 1 or 2 drops q 2 hr while awake up to eight times/day on days 1 and 2; then 1 drop q 4 hr while awake up to four times/day for 3–7 days.

lodoxamide tromethamine (Alomide): Tx of vernal conjunctivitis, keratitis in pts over 2 yr. Do not wear contacts. Stop if stinging, burning persists.

loteprednol etabonate (Alrex, Lotemax): Tx of postop inflammation, ocular disease. 1–2 drops qid. Discard after 14 days. Prolonged use can cause eye nerve damage.

loteprednol etabonate/ tobramycin (Zylet): Tx of ocular conditions w/risk of bacterial ocular infection. 1–2 drops q 4–6 hr for 24–48 hr.

metipranolol (OptiPranolol): Tx of chronic open-angle glaucoma, ocular hypertension. Vision changes possible; may need to use w/other drugs.

mitomycin-C (Mitosol): Adjunct to ab externo glaucoma surgery. Apply fully saturated sponges to tx area for 2 min. Topical only; biohazard disposal.

moxifloxacin (Moxeza, Vigamox): Tx of bacterial conjunctivitis caused by susceptible strains. *Moxeza* (pts 4 mo and older), 1 drop bid for 7 days. *Vigamox* (pts 1 yr and older), 1 drop tid for 7 days. Do not wear contacts. Can cause blurred vision.

natamycin (Natacyn): Tx of fungal blepharitis, conjunctivitis, keratitis. 1–2 drops/day for 7 days.

nedocromil sodium (Alocril): Tx of allergic conjunctivitis itching. 1–2 drops bid through entire allergy season.

olopatadine hydrochloride (Pataday, Patanol, Pazeo): Tx of allergic conjunctivitis itching in pts 3 yr and older. 1–2 drops q 6–8 hr. Not for use w/contacts. Headache common.

phenylephrine/ketorolac (Omidria): Px of intraop miosis; pain reduction w/cataract surgery. 4 mL in 500 mL ophthalmic irrigating solution, used as needed during surgery.

pilocarpine (Adsorbocarpine, Piloptic, Pilostat): Tx of chronic, acute glaucoma; mydriasis caused by drugs. 1–2 drops up to six times/day.

rimexolone (Vexol): Tx of anterior uveitis; postop. Corticosteroid. Monitor for systemic absorption.

sulfacetamide (Bleph-10): Tx of ocular infections. 1–2 drops q 2–3 hr; gradually taper over 7–10 days.

tafluprost (Zioptan): Tx of elevated IOP in open-angle glaucoma/ocular hypertension. 1 drop in p.m.; permanent changes in eyelashes, iris color.

timolol maleate (Timoptic, Timoptic XE): Tx of increased IOP. 1 drop/day in a.m.

travoprost (Travatan Z): Tx of open-angle glaucoma, ocular hypertension. 1 drop each p.m.; iris darkening, eyelash growth common.

trifluridine (Viroptic): Tx of keratoconjunctivitis, recurrent epithelial keratitis due to herpes simplex 1, 2. Max, 9 drops/day in affected eye(s) no longer than 21 days.

tropicamide (Mydriacyl, Tropicacyl, Tropicamide): Refraction. 1–2 drops, repeat in 5 min. May repeat again in 30 min if needed.

Laxatives

Laxative use has been replaced by proper diet and exercise in many clinical situations. Most laxatives are available as OTC preparations and are often abused by people who become dependent on them for GI movement.

IND & DOSE Short-term relief of constipation; to prevent straining; to evacuate bowel for diagnostic procedures; to remove ingested poisons from lower GI tract; as adjunct in anthelmintic tx.

PREG/CONT C/NA

ADV EFF Abd cramps, cathartic dependence, dizziness, excessive bowel activity, perianal irritation, weakness

NC/PT Use as temporary measure. Swallow tablets whole. Do not take within 1 hr of other drugs. Report sweating, flushing, muscle cramps, excessive thirst.

bisacodyl (Bisa-Lax, Correctol, Dulcolax): Stimulant. 5–15 mg PO; 2.5 g in water via enema. Onset, 6–12 hr; rapid. Tartrazine in *Dulcolax* tablets. May discolor urine. Not for child under 6 yr.

cascara: Stimulant. 325 mg–6 g PO. Onset, 6–10 hr. Use caution if pt taking prescription drugs. May discolor urine. Not for children younger than 18 yr.

castor oil: Stimulant. 15–60 mL PO. Onset, 2–6 hr. May be very vigorous; may cause abd cramping.

docusate (Colace, Ex-Lax Stool Softener, Genasoft, Phillips' Liqui-Gels, Silace): Detergent, softener. 50–300 mg PO. Onset, 12–72 hr. Gentle; beneficial w/painful anorectal conditions, dry or hard feces.

glycerin (Fleet Babylax, Fleet Liquid Glycerin Suppository, Sani-Supp): Hyperosmolar agent. Rectal suppository; 4 mL liquid by rectum (child rectal liquid). Onset, 15–60 min. Insert suppository high into rectum, retain 15 min. Insert liquid dispenser. Apply gentle, steady pressure until all liquid gone; then remove.

lactulose (Constulose): Hyperosmolar agent. 15–30 mL PO. Onset, 24–48 hr. Also used for tx of portal system encephalopathy. More palatable if mixed w/fruit juice, milk, water.

lubiprostone (Amitiza): Chloride channel activator. 24 mcg PO bid w/food, water. Onset, 1–2 hr. Also used for tx of women w/IBS w/constipation. Contains sorbitol; may cause nausea, diarrhea.

magnesium citrate (Citrate of Magnesia): Saline. 1 glassful PO. Onset, 0.5–3 hr. For child dose, reduce by half.

magnesium (Milk of Magnesia, MOM, Phillip's MOM): Saline. 30–60 mL PO at bedtime; 15–30 mL of conc PO. Onset, 0.5–3 hr. Take w/liquids. Flavored forms available.

magnesium sulfate (Epsom Salts): Saline. 5–10 mL PO. Onset, 0.5–3 hr. Take mixed w/full glass of water.

Child dose, reduce to 2.5–5 mL PO in ½ glass water.

mineral oil (Kondremul): Emollient. 5–45 mL PO. Onset, 6–8 hr. May decrease absorption of fat-soluble vitamins. Child 6 yr and older, reduce dose to 5–15 mL.

polycarbophil (Equalactin, Fiber-Con, Konsyl Fiber): Bulk. 1–2 tablets PO up to qid. Onset, 12–72 hr. Good w/IBS, diverticulitis. Swallow w/full glass of water to prevent sticking in esophagus, choking.

polyethylene glycol (MiraLax): Bulk. 17 g PO in 8 oz water daily for up to 2 wk. Onset, 48–72 hr. Do not use w/bowel obstruction. Diarrhea common.

polyethylene glycolelectrolyte solution (CoLyte, GoLytely): Bulk. 4 L oral sol PO before exam. Onset, 1 hr. Used as bowel evacuant before exam. Do not use w/GI obstruction, megacolon.

polyethylene glycol, sodium sulfate, sodium chloride, potassium chloride, sodium ascorbate, ascorbic acid (MoviPrep): Osmotic. 1 L PO, then 16 oz fluid p.m. before colonoscopy. Or, 2 L PO, then 32 oz fluid p.m. before colonoscopy. Onset, 1 hr. Maintain hydration. Monitor pt w/hx of seizures.

psyllium (Fiberall, Hydrocil Instant, Konsyl, Metamucil): Bulk. 1 tsp or packet in water, juice 1–3 times/day PO. Onset, 12–72 hr. Swallow w/full glass of water to prevent esophageal sticking, choking.

senna (Agoral, Black Draught, Fletcher's Castoria, Senna-Gen, Senokot): Stimulant. 1–8 tablets/day PO at bedtime; suppository/syrup, 10–30 mL PO. Onset, 6–10 hr. May cause abd cramps, discomfort.

sodium picosulfate, magnesium oxide, anhydrous citric acid (Prepopik): Bowel cleansing before colonoscopy. Reconstitute w/cold water, swallow immediately, follow w/clear liquids; repeat. Risk of fluid/electrolyte abnormalities.

Combination products by therapeutic class

ALZHEIMER'S DISEASE DRUG

▶ memantine and donepezil
Namzaric

ER capsules: 14 mg memantine, 10 mg donepezil; 28 mg memantine, 10 mg donepezil.
Usual adult dose: 1 capsule/day PO in p.m. Pt should not cut, crush, or chew capsule; can be opened and sprinkled on applesauce.

AMPHETAMINE

▶ dextroamphetamine and amphetamine
CONTROLLED SUBSTANCE C-II
Adderall, Adderall XR

Tablets: 1.25 mg (5-mg tablet), 2.5 mg (10-mg tablet), 5 mg (20-mg tablet), 7.5 mg (30-mg tablet) each of dextroamphetamine sulfate and saccharate, amphetamine aspartate, and sulfate.
ER capsules: 1.25 mg (5-mg capsule), 1.875 (7.5-mg tablet), 2.5 mg (10-mg capsule), 3.125 (12.5-mg capsule), 3.75 mg (15-mg capsule), 5 mg (20-mg capsule), 6.25 mg (25-mg capsule), 7.5 mg (30-mg capsule) of each component.
Usual adult, child dose: 5–60 mg/day PO in divided doses to control sx of narcolepsy, ADHD. ER capsules: 10–30 mg/day. **BBW** High risk of abuse; use caution.

ANALGESICS

▶ acetaminophen and codeine
CONTROLLED SUBSTANCE C-III
Tylenol with Codeine

Elixir: 12 mg codeine, 120 mg acetaminophen/5 mL.
Tablets: No. 2: 15 mg codeine, 300 mg acetaminophen. No. 3: 30 mg codeine, 300 mg acetaminophen. No. 4: 60 mg codeine, 300 mg acetaminophen.
Usual adult dose: 1 or 2 tablets PO q 4–6 hr as needed, or 15 mL 4–6 hr.

▶ aspirin and codeine
CONTROLLED SUBSTANCE C-III
Empirin with Codeine

Tablets: No. 3: 30 mg codeine, 325 mg aspirin. No. 4: 60 mg codeine, 325 mg aspirin.
Usual adult dose: 1 or 2 tablets PO q 4–6 hr as needed.

▶ codeine, aspirin, caffeine, and butalbital
CONTROLLED SUBSTANCE C-III
Fiorinal with Codeine

Capsules: 30 mg codeine, 325 mg aspirin, 40 mg caffeine, 50 mg butabarbital.
Usual adult dose: 1 or 2 capsules PO q 4 hr as needed for pain, up to 6/day. **BBW** Risk of death in children after tonsil/adenoid removal

who are rapid metabolizers: not approved for this use.

▶ diclofenac sodium and misoprostol
PREGNANCY CATEGORY X
Arthrotec

Tablets: '50': 50 mg diclofenac, 200 mcg misoprostol. '75': 75 mg diclofenac, 200 mcg misoprostol.
Usual adult dose: *Osteoarthritis:* Arthrotec 50, PO tid. Arthrotec 50 or 75, PO bid. *Rheumatoid arthritis:* Arthrotec 50, PO tid or qid; Arthrotec 50 or 75, PO bid. **BBW** Misoprostol is abortifacient. Not for use in pregnancy; negative pregnancy test required.

▶ famotidine and ibuprofen
Duexis

Tablets: 26.6 mg famotidine, 800 mg ibuprofen.
Usual adult dose: 1 tablet PO daily for arthritis pain.

▶ hydrocodone bitartrate and acetaminophen
CONTROLLED SUBSTANCE C-II
Norco

Elixir: 2.5 mg hydrocodone, 167 mg acetaminophen/5 mL.
Tablets: 2.5 mg hydrocodone, 500 mg acetaminophen; 5 mg hydrocodone, 500 mg acetaminophen; 5, 7.5, 10 mg hydrocodone, 400 mg acetaminophen; 7.5 mg hydrocodone, 500 mg acetaminophen; 7.5 mg hydrocodone, 650 mg acetaminophen; 10 mg hydrocodone, 650 mg acetaminophen.
Norco tablets: 5 mg hydrocodone, 325 mg acetaminophen; 7.5 mg hydrocodone, 325 mg acetaminophen; 10 mg hydrocodone, 325 mg acetaminophen.
Usual adult dose: Check brand-name products to determine specific

dose combinations available. One or two tablets, capsules PO q 4–6 hr, up to 8/day. **BBW** Risk of potentially severe hepatotoxicity.

▶ hydrocodone and ibuprofen
CONTROLLED SUBSTANCE C-II
Reprexain, Vicoprofen

Tablets: 2.5 mg hydrocodone, 200 mg ibuprofen; 7.5 mg hydrocodone, 200 mg ibuprofen; 10 mg hydrocodone, 200 mg ibuprofen.
Usual adult dose: 1 tablet PO q 4–6 hr as needed.

▶ methylsalicylate and menthol
Salonpas

Dermal patch: 10% methylsalicylate, 3% menthol.
Usual adult dose: Apply 1 patch to clean, dry affected area; leave on for 8–12 hr. Remove patch, apply another as needed. To relieve pain from sprains, bruises, strains, backache.

▶ morphine and naltrexone
CONTROLLED SUBSTANCE C-II
Embeda

ER capsules: 20 mg morphine, 0.8 mg naltrexone; 30 mg morphine, 1.2 mg naltrexone; 50 mg morphine, 2 mg naltrexone; 60 mg morphine, 2.4 mg naltrexone; 80 mg morphine, 3.2 mg naltrexone; 100 mg morphine, 4 mg naltrexone.
Usual adult dose: 1 or 2 tablets PO daily when continuous, around-the-clock analgesic needed long-term. May open capsules, sprinkle over applesauce. Pt should not cut, crush, or chew capsule. **BBW** Risk of addiction, abuse, misuse; interacts w/alcohol.

▶ naproxen and esomeprazole
Vimovo

DR tablets: 375 mg naproxen, 20 mg esomeprazole; 500 mg naproxen, 20 mg esomeprazole.
Usual adult dose: 1 tablet PO bid. Not recommended in moderate to severe renal insufficiency; severe hepatic insufficiency; reduce w/mild to moderate hepatic insufficiency. **BBW** Risk of GI adverse events, CV events. Not for periop pain w/CABG.

▶ oxycodone and acetaminophen
CONTROLLED SUBSTANCE C-II
Percocet, Roxicet, Xartemis XR

Tablets: 2.25, 4.5, 5 mg oxycodone, 325 mg acetaminophen.
ER tablets: 7.5 mg oxycodone, 325 mg acetaminophen.
Usual adult dose: 1 or 2 tablets PO q 4–6 hr as needed; 2 tablets q 12 hr for ER form. **BBW** Risk of addiction, serious respiratory depression, fatal outcomes in child, hepatotoxicity; neonatal withdrawal if used in pregnancy. Use caution.

▶ oxycodone and aspirin
CONTROLLED SUBSTANCE C-II
Percodan, Roxiprin

Tablets: 4.5 mg oxycodone, 325 mg aspirin.
Usual adult dose: 1 or 2 tablets PO q 6 hr as needed.

▶ oxycodone and ibuprofen
CONTROLLED SUBSTANCE C-II
generic

Tablets: 5 mg oxycodone, 400 mg ibuprofen.

Usual adult dose: 1 tablet PO q 6 hr as needed for moderate to severe pain. Max, 4 tablets/24 hr for no more than 7 days.

▶ pentazocine and acetaminophen
CONTROLLED SUBSTANCE C-IV
generic

Tablets: 25 mg pentazocine, 650 mg acetaminophen.
Usual adult dose: 1 tablet PO q 4 hr; max, 6 tablets/day.

▶ tramadol hydrochloride and acetaminophen
Ultracet

Tablets: 37.5 mg tramadol, 325 mg acetaminophen.
Usual adult dose: 2 tablets PO q 4–6 hr as needed; max, 8 tablets/day. Reduce in elderly/renally impaired pts. **BBW** Risk of hepatotoxicity; do not exceed 4,000 mg acetaminophen/day.

ANTIACNE DRUGS

▶ ethinyl estradiol and norethindrone
Estrostep Fe

Tablets: 1 mg norethindrone, 20 mcg ethinyl estradiol; 1 mg norethindrone, 30 mcg ethinyl estradiol; 1 mg norethindrone, 35 mcg ethinyl estradiol.
Usual adult dose: 1 tablet PO each day (21 tablets have active ingredients; 7 are inert).

▶ norgestimate and ethinyl estradiol
Ortho Tri-Cyclen

Tablets: 0.18 mg norgestimate, 35 mcg ethinyl estradiol (7 tablets);

0.215 mg norgestimate, 35 mcg ethinyl estradiol (7 tablets); 0.25 mg norgestimate, 35 mcg ethinyl estradiol (7 tablets).
Usual adult dose: For women over 15 yr, 1 tablet/day PO. Birth control agent used cyclically (21 tablets have active ingredients, 7 are inert). Approved for acne only if contraception is desired. **BBW** Contraindicated in women over 35 yr who smoke; increased risk of CV events.

ANTIBACTERIALS

▶ amoxicillin and clavulanic acid
Augmentin, Augmentin ES-600, Augmentin XR

Tablets: '250': 250 mg amoxicillin, 125 mg clavulanic acid; '500': 500 mg amoxicillin, 125 mg clavulanic acid; '875': 875 mg amoxicillin, 125 mg clavulanic acid.
Powder for oral suspension: '125': 125 mg amoxicillin, 31.25 mg clavulanic acid; '250': 250 mg amoxicillin, 62.5 mg clavulanic acid; '400': 400 mg amoxicillin, 57 mg clavulanic acid.
Sol (Augmentin ES-600): 600 mg amoxicillin, 42.9 mg clavulanic acid/5 mL.
Chewable tablets: '125': 125 mg amoxicillin, 31.25 mg clavulanic acid; '200': 200 mg amoxicillin, 28.5 mg clavulanic acid; '400': 400 mg amoxicillin, 57 mg clavulanic acid.
XR tablets: 1,000 mg amoxicillin, 62.5 mg clavulanic acid.
Usual adult dose: 1 250-mg tablet or one 500-mg tablet PO q 8 hr. For severe infections, 875-mg tablet PO q 12 hr. W/difficulty swallowing, substitute 125-mg/5 mL or 250-mg/5 mL for 500-mg tablet, or 200-mg/5 mL or 400-mg/5 mL for 875-mg tablet.
Usual child dose: Under 40 kg, 20–40 mg amoxicillin/kg/day PO in divided doses q 8 hr (dose based on amoxicillin content) or q 12 hr;

90 mg/kg/day PO oral sol divided q 12 hr (Augmentin ES-600).

▶ ceftazidime and avibactam
Avycaz

Powder for injection: 2 g ceftazidime, 0.5 g avibactam.
Usual adult dose: 2.5 g IV q 8 hr over 2 hr for 5–14 days depending on infection. Tx of complicated UTI/intra-abd infections.

▶ ceftolozane and tazobactam
Zerbaxa

Powder for injection: 1 g ceftolozane, 0.5 g tazobactam; reconstitute w/0.9% Sodium Chloride.
Usual adult dose: 1.5 g (1 g ceftolozane, 0.5 g tazobactam) IV q 8 hr over 1 hr. Tx of complicated UTI/intra-abd infections. Decrease dose in renal impairment; CDAD common.

▶ co-trimoxazole (TMP-SMZ)
Bactrim, Bactrim DS, Septra, Septra DS, Sulfatrim Pediatric

Tablets: 80 mg trimethoprim (TMP), 400 mg sulfamethoxazole (SMZ); 160 mg TMP, 800 mg SMZ.
Oral suspension: 40 mg TMP, 200 mg SMZ/5 mL.
Usual adult dose: UTIs, shigellosis, acute otitis media: 160 mg TMP/800 mg SMZ PO q 12 hr. Up to 14 days (UTI) or 5 days (shigellosis). Acute exacerbations of chronic bronchitis: 160 mg TMP/800 mg SMZ PO q 12 hr for 14 days. Pneumocystis jiroveci pneumonitis: 20 mg/kg TMP/100 mg/kg SMZ q 24 hr PO in divided doses q 6 hr for 14 days. Traveler's diarrhea: 160 mg TMP/800 mg SMZ PO q 12 hr for 5 days.

Usual child dose: *UTIs, shigellosis, acute otitis media:* 8 mg/kg/day TMP/40 mg/kg/day SMZ PO in two divided doses q 12 hr. For 10–14 days (UTIs, acute otitis media), 5 days (shigellosis). *Pneumocystis jiroveci pneumonitis:* 20 mg/kg TMP/100 mg/kg SMZ q 24 hr PO in divided doses q 6 hr for 14 days.

► erythromycin and sulfisoxazole
generic

Granules for oral suspension: Erythromycin ethylsuccinate (equivalent of 200 mg erythromycin activity) and 600 mg sulfisoxazole/5 mL when reconstituted according to manufacturer's directions.
Usual child dose: *Otitis media:* 50 mg/kg/day erythromycin and 150 mg/kg/day sulfisoxazole PO in divided doses qid for 10 days. Give without regard to meals. Refrigerate after reconstitution; use within 14 days.

► imipenem and cilastatin
Primaxin

Powder for injection (IV): 250 mg imipenem, 250 mg cilastatin; 500 mg imipenem, 500 mg cilastatin.
Powder for injection (IM): 500 mg imipenem, 500 mg cilastatin. Follow manufacturer's instructions for re-constituting, diluting drug. Give each 250- to 500-mg dose by IV infusion over 20–30 min; infuse each 1-g dose over 40–60 min. Give 500–750 mg IM q 12 hr. Max, 1,500 mg/day.
Usual adult dose: Dose recommendations based on imipenem. Initially based on type, severity of infection; later on illness severity, degree of susceptibility of pathogens, and age, weight, CrCl. For adults w/normal renal function, 250 mg–1 g IV q 6–8 hr. Max, 50 mg/kg/day or 4 g/day,

whichever less. Adjust in renal impairment.

► piperacillin sodium and tazobactam sodium
Zosyn

Powder for injection: 2 g piperacillin, 0.25 g tazobactam; 3 g piperacillin, 0.375 g tazobactam; 4 g piperacillin, 0.5 g tazobactam.
Usual adult dose: 12 g/1.5 g IV as 3.375 g q 6 hr over 30 min. Recommended for appendicitis; peritonitis; postpartum endometritis; PID; community-acquired pneumonia; nosocomial pneumonia if agent responsive in sensitivity testing. Adjust in renal impairment.

► quinupristin and dalfopristin
Synercid

Streptogramin antibiotics available only in combination.
Sol for IV use: 500-mg/10-mL vial (150 mg quinupristin, 350 mg dalfopristin).
Dose in pts over 16 yr: *Complicated skin infections due to* Staphylococcus. aureus, *Streptococcus pyogenes:* 7.5 mg/kg IV q 12 hr for 7 days. *Tx of life-threatening, susceptible infections associated w/VREF:* 7.5 mg/kg IV q 8 hr. Dangerous when used w/QT-prolonging drugs.

► sulbactam and ampicillin
Unasyn

Powder for injection: 1.5-g vial (1 g ampicillin, 0.5 g sulbactam); 3-g vial (2 g ampicillin, 1 g sulbactam).
Usual adult dose: 0.5–1 g sulbactam w/1–2 g ampicillin IM or IV q 6–8 hr.
Usual child dose: 40 kg or more, adult dosage; max, 4 g/day. Under

40 kg, 300 mg/kg/day IV in divided doses q 6 hr.

ANTI–CORONARY ARTERY DISEASE DRUG

▶ amlodipine besylate and atorvastatin calcium
Caduet

Tablets: 2.5 mg amlodipine w/10, 20, 40 mg atorvastatin; 5 mg amlodipine w/10, 20, 40, 80 mg atorvastatin; 10 mg amlodipine w/10, 20, 40, 80 mg atorvastatin.
Usual adult dose: 1 tablet PO daily in p.m. Adjust using individual products, then switch to appropriate combination product.

ANTIDEPRESSANTS

▶ chlordiazepoxide and amitriptyline
CONTROLLED SUBSTANCE C-IV
generic

Tablets: 5 mg chlordiazepoxide, 12.5 mg amitriptyline; 10 mg chlordiazepoxide, 25 mg amitriptyline.
Usual adult dose: 10 mg chlordiazepoxide w/25 mg amitriptyline PO tid–qid up to six times/day. For pts intolerant of higher doses, 5 mg chlordiazepoxide w/12.5 mg amitriptyline PO tid–qid.

▶ olanzapine and fluoxetine
Symbyax

Capsules: 6 mg olanzapine, 25 mg fluoxetine; 6 mg olanzapine, 50 mg fluoxetine; 12 mg olanzapine, 25 mg fluoxetine; 12 mg olanzapine, 50 mg fluoxetine.
Usual adult dose: 1 capsule PO daily in p.m. **BBW** Risk of suicidality; increased mortality in elderly pts w/ dementia-related psychoses (not

approved for that use). Monitor pt closely.

▶ perphenazine and amitriptyline
generic

Tablets: 2 mg perphenazine, 10 mg amitriptyline; 2 mg perphenazine, 25 mg amitriptyline; 4 mg perphenazine, 10 mg amitriptyline; 4 mg perphenazine, 25 mg amitriptyline; 4 mg perphenazine, 50 mg amitriptyline.
Usual adult dose: 2–4 mg perphenazine w/10–50 mg amitriptyline PO tid–qid.

ANTIDIABETICS

▶ alogliptin and metformin
Kazano

Tablets: 12.5 mg alogliptin, 500 mg metformin; 12.5 mg alogliptin, 1,000 mg metformin.
Usual adult dose: Base on pt response, PO bid w/food; max, 25 mg alogliptin, 2,000 mg metformin/day. **BBW** Risk of lactic acidosis; monitor pt closely and stop drug, hospitalize pt.

▶ alogliptin and pioglitazone
Oseni

Tablets: 12.5 mg alogliptin, 15 mg pioglitazone; 12.5 mg alogliptin, 30 mg pioglitazone; 12.5 mg alogliptin, 45 mg pioglitazone; 25 mg alogliptin, 15 mg pioglitazone; 25 mg alogliptin, 30 mg pioglitazone; 25 mg alogliptin, 45 mg pioglitazone.
Usual adult dose: Base on pt response, PO once daily. Max, 25 mg alogliptin, 45 mg pioglitazone. Limit w/HF, renal impairment. **BBW** Risk of HF; not for use w/known HF. Monitor pt closely.

▶ canagliflozin and metformin
Invokamet

Tablets: 50 mg canagliflozin, 500 mg metformin; 50 mg canagliflozin, 1,000 mg metformin; 150 mg canagliflozin, 500 mg metformin; 150 mg canagliflozin, 1,000 mg metformin.
Usual adult dose: Base on pt response. PO bid w/meals. Max, 300 mg canagliglozin, 3,000 mg metform/day. Reduce dose w/renal impairment. **BBW** Risk of lactic acidosis; monitor pt closely and stop drug, hospitalize pt.

▶ dapagliflozin and metformin
Xigduo XR

Tablets: 5 mg dapagliflozin, 500 mg metformin; 5 mg dapagliflozin, 1,000 mg metformin; 10 mg dapagliflozin, 500 mg metformin; 10 mg dapagliflozin, 1,000 mg metformin.
Usual adult dose: Base on pt response. PO once daily in a.m. w/food. Max, 10 mg dapagliflozin, 2,000 mg metform/day. Not for use w/severe renal impairment. **BBW** Risk of lactic acidosis; monitor pt closely and stop drug, hospitalize pt.

▶ empagliflozin and linagliptin
Glyxambi

Tablets: 10 mg empagliflozin, 5 mg linagliptin; 25 mg empagliflozin, 5 mg linagliptin.
Usual adult dose: 10 mg empagliflozin/5 mg linagliptin/day in a.m.; may increase if needed. Not for use w/severe renal impairment. Monitor pt for lactic acidosis, urosepsis, severe to disabling arthralgia.

▶ empagliflozin and metformin
Synjardy

Tablets: 5 mg empagliflozin, 500 mg metformin; 5 mg empaglifloxin, 1 g metformin; 12.5 mg empagliflozin, 500 mg metformin; 12.5 mg empagliflozin, 1 g metformin.
Usual adult dose: 5 mg empagliflozin, 500 mg metformin; may increase if needed. Not for use w/ severe renal impairment. Monitor for lactic acidosis, urosepsis, severe to disabling arthralgia.

▶ glyburide and metformin
Glucovance

Tablets: 1.25 mg glyburide, 250 mg metformin; 2.5 mg glyburide, 500 mg metformin; 5 mg glyburide, 500 mg metformin.
Usual adult dose: 1 tablet/day PO w/meal, usually in a.m. **BBW** Risk of lactic acidosis; monitor pt closely and stop drug, hospitalize pt.

▶ linagliptin and metformin
Jentadueto

Tablets: 2.5 mg linagliptin, 500 mg metformin; 2.5 mg linagliptin, 850 mg metformin; 2.5 mg lingagliptin, 1,000 mg metformin.
Usual adult dose: Base on current use of each drug, PO bid w/meals. Monitor pt for severe to disabling arthralgia. **BBW** Risk of lactic acidosis; monitor pt closely and stop drug, hospitalize pt.

▶ pioglitazone and glimepiride
Duetact

Tablets: 30 mg pioglitazone w/2 or 4 mg glimepiride.

Usual adult dose: 1 tablet/day PO w/first meal of day. **BBW** Risk of HF; not for use w/known HF. Monitor pt closely.

▶ pioglitazone and metformin
ActoPlus Met, ActoPlus Met XR

Tablets: 15 mg pioglitazone, 500 mg metformin; 15 mg pioglitazone, 850 mg metformin.
ER tablets: 15 mg pioglitazone, 1,000 mg metformin; 30 mg pioglitazone, 1,000 mg metformin.
Usual adult dose: 1 tablet PO once/day or bid w/meals; ER tablets, once/day. **BBW** Risk of lactic acidosis; monitor pt closely and stop drug, hospitalize pt. Risk of HF; not for use w/known HF. Monitor pt closely.

▶ repaglinide and metformin
PrandiMet

Tablets: 1 mg repaglinide, 500 mg metformin; 2 mg repaglinide, 500 mg metformin.
Usual adult dose: 1 tablet PO once/day or in divided doses. **BBW** Risk of lactic acidosis; monitor pt closely and stop drug, hospitalize pt.

▶ rosiglitazone and glimepiride
Avandaryl

Tablets: 4 mg rosiglitazone, 1 mg glimepiride; 4 mg rosiglitazone, 2 mg glimepiride; 4 mg rosiglitazone, 4 mg glimepiride; 8 mg rosiglitazone, 2 mg glimepiride; 8 mg rosiglitazone, 4 mg glimepiride.
Usual adult dose: 4 mg rosiglitazone w/1 or 2 mg glimepiride PO once/day w/first meal of day. **BBW** Risk of HF; not for use w/known HF. Monitor pt closely.

▶ rosiglitazone and metformin
Avandamet

Tablets: 1 mg rosiglitazone, 500 mg metformin; 2 mg rosiglitazone, 500 mg metformin; 2 mg rosiglitazone, 1 g metformin; 4 mg rosiglitazone, 500 mg metformin; 4 mg rosiglitazone, 1 g metformin.
Usual adult dose: 4 mg rosiglitazone w/500 mg metformin PO once/day or in divided doses. **BBW** Risk of lactic acidosis; monitor pt closely and stop drug, hospitalize pt. Risk of HF; not for use w/known HF. Monitor pt closely.

▶ saxagliptin and metformin
Kombiglyze XR

Tablets: 5 mg saxagliptin, 500 mg metformin; 5 mg saxagliptin, 1,000 mg metformin; 2.5 mg saxagliptin, 1,000 mg metformin.
Usual adult dose: 1 tablet PO daily. Do not cut, crush, or allow pt to chew tablets. **BBW** Risk of lactic acidosis; monitor pt closely and stop drug, hospitalize pt.

▶ sitagliptin and metformin
Janumet, Janumet XR

Tablets: 50 mg sitagliptin, 500 or 1,000 mg metformin.
ER tablets: 50 mg sitagliptin, 500 mg or 1 g metformin; 100 mg sitagliptin, 1 g metformin.
Usual adult dose: 1 tablet PO bid w/meals; max, 100 mg sitagliptin, 2,000 mg metformin/day. Risk of severe to disabling arthralgia. **BBW** Risk of lactic acidosis; monitor pt closely and stop drug, hospitalize pt.

ANTIDIARRHEAL

▶ diphenoxylate hydrochloride and atropine sulfate
CONTROLLED SUBSTANCE C-V
Lomotil, Lonox

Tablets: 2.5 mg diphenoxylate hydrochloride, 0.025 mg atropine sulfate.
Liquid: 2.5 mg diphenoxylate hydrochloride, 0.025 mg atropine sulfate/5 mL.
Usual adult dose: 5 mg PO qid.
Usual child dose (use only liquid in child 2–12 yr): 0.3–0.4 mg/kg PO daily in four divided doses.

ANTIHYPERTENSIVES

▶ aliskiren and amlodipine
Tekamlo

Tablets: 150 mg aliskiren, 5 mg amlodipine; 150 mg aliskiren, 10 mg amlodipine; 300 mg aliskiren, 5 mg amlodipine; 300 mg aliskiren, 10 mg amlodipine.
Usual adult dose: 1 tablet/day PO; may give w/other antihypertensives.
BBW Risk of birth defects/fetal death; avoid use in pregnancy.

▶ aliskiren and hydrochlorothiazide
Tekturna HCT

Tablets: 150 mg aliskiren, 12.5 mg hydrochlorothiazide; 150 mg aliskiren, 25 mg hydrochlorothiazide; 300 mg aliskiren, 12.5 mg hydrochlorothiazide; 300 mg aliskiren, 25 mg hydrochlorothiazide.
Usual adult dose: 1 tablet/day PO.
BBW Risk of birth defects/fetal death; avoid use in pregnancy.

▶ amlodipine and benazepril
Lotrel

Capsules: 2.5 mg amlodipine, 10 mg benazepril; 5 mg amlodipine, 10 mg benazepril; 5 mg amlodipine, 20 mg benazepril; 5 mg amlodipine, 40 mg benazepril; 10 mg amlodipine, 20 mg benazepril; 10 mg amlodipine, 40 mg benazepril.
Usual adult dose: 1 tablet/day PO in a.m. **BBW** Risk of birth defects/fetal death; avoid use in pregnancy.

▶ amlodipine and olmesartan
Azor

Tablets: 5 mg amlodipine, 20 mg olmesartan; 10 mg amlodipine, 20 mg olmesartan; 5 mg amlodipine, 40 mg olmesartan; 10 mg amlodipine, 40 mg olmesartan.
Usual adult dose: 1 tablet/day PO.
BBW Risk of birth defects/fetal death; avoid use in pregnancy.

▶ amlodipine and perindopril
Prestalia

Capsules: 2.5 mg amlodipine, 3.5 mg perindopril; 5 mg amlodipine, 7 mg perindopril; 10 mg amlodipine, 14 mg perindopril.
Usual adult dose: Initially, 2.5 mg amlodipine/3.5 mg perindopril PO each day; adjust based on pt response.
BBW Risk of birth defects/fetal death; avoid use in pregnancy.

▶ amlodipine and valsartan
Exforge

Tablets: 5 mg amlodipine, 160 mg valsartan; 5 mg amlodipine, 320 mg valsartan; 10 mg amlodipine, 160 mg

valsartan; 10 mg amlodipine, 320 mg valsartan.
Usual adult dose: 1 tablet/day PO.
BBW Risk of birth defects/fetal death; avoid use in pregnancy.

▶ amlodipine, valsartan, and hydrochlorothiazide
Exforge HCT

Tablets: 5 mg amlodipine, 160 mg valsartan, 12.5 mg hydrochlorothiazide; 10 mg amlodipine, 160 mg valsartan, 12.5 mg hydrochlorothiazide; 5 mg amlodipine, 160 mg valsartan, 25 mg hydrochlorothiazide; 10 mg amlodipine, 320 mg valsartan, 25 mg hydrochlorothiazide.
Usual adult dose: 1 tablet/day PO.
BBW Risk of birth defects/fetal death; avoid use in pregnancy.

▶ atenolol and chlorthalidone
Tenoretic

Tablets: 50 mg atenolol, 25 mg chlorthalidone; 100 mg atenolol, 25 mg chlorthalidone.
Usual adult dose: 1 tablet/day PO in a.m.

▶ azilsartan and chlorthalidone
Edarbyclor

Tablets: 40 mg azilsartan, 12.5 mg chlorthalidone; 40 mg azilsartan, 25 mg chlorthalidone.
Usual adult dose: 1 tablet/day PO. Not for use in pregnancy, renal failure. Monitor potassium level.
BBW Risk of birth defects/fetal death; avoid use in pregnancy.

▶ bisoprolol and hydrochlorothiazide
Ziac

Tablets: 2.5 mg bisoprolol, 6.25 mg hydrochlorothiazide; 5 mg bisoprolol, 6.25 mg hydrochlorothiazide; 10 mg bisoprolol, 6.25 mg hydrochlorothiazide.
Usual adult dose: 1 tablet/day PO in a.m. Initially, 2.5/6.25-mg tablet/day PO. May need 2–3 wk for optimal antihypertensive effect.

▶ candesartan and hydrochlorothiazide
Atacand HCT

Tablets: 16 mg candesartan, 12.5 mg hydrochlorothiazide; 32 mg candesartan, 12.5 mg hydrochlorothiazide.
Usual adult dose: 1 tablet/day PO in a.m. **BBW** Risk of birth defects/fetal death; avoid use in pregnancy.

▶ chlorthalidone and clonidine
Clorpres

Tablets: 15 mg chlorthalidone, 0.1 mg clonidine hydrochloride; 15 mg chlorthalidone, 0.2 mg clonidine hydrochloride; 15 mg chlorthalidone, 0.3 mg clonidine hydrochloride.
Usual adult dose: 1 or 2 tablets/day PO in a.m.; may give once/day or bid.

▶ enalapril and hydrochlorothiazide
Vaseretic

Tablets: 5 mg enalapril maleate, 12.5 mg hydrochlorothiazide; 10 mg enalapril maleate, 25 mg hydrochlorothiazide.
Usual adult dose: 1 or 2 tablets/day PO in a.m. **BBW** Risk of birth defects/fetal death; avoid use in pregnancy.

► **fosinopril and hydrochlorothiazide**
generic

Tablets: 10 mg fosinopril, 12.5 mg hydrochlorothiazide; 20 mg fosinopril, 12.5 mg hydrochlorothiazide.
Usual adult dose: 1 tablet/day PO in a.m. **BBW** Risk of birth defects/fetal death; avoid use in pregnancy.

► **hydrochlorothiazide and benazepril**
Lotensin HCT

Tablets: 6.25 mg hydrochlorothiazide, 5 mg benazepril; 12.5 mg hydrochlorothiazide, 10 mg benazepril; 12.5 mg hydrochlorothiazide, 20 mg benazepril; 25 mg hydrochlorothiazide, 20 mg benazepril.
Usual adult dose: 1 tablet/day PO in a.m. **BBW** Risk of birth defects/fetal death; avoid use in pregnancy.

► **hydrochlorothiazide and captopril**
generic

Tablets: 15 mg hydrochlorothiazide, 25 mg captopril; 15 mg hydrochlorothiazide, 50 mg captopril; 25 mg hydrochlorothiazide, 25 mg captopril; 25 mg hydrochlorothiazide, 50 mg captopril.
Usual adult dose: 1 or 2 tablets/day PO 1 hr before or 2 hr after meals. **BBW** Risk of birth defects/fetal death; avoid use in pregnancy.

► **hydrochlorothiazide and propranolol**
generic

Tablets: 25 mg hydrochlorothiazide, 40 mg propranolol; 25 mg hydrochlorothiazide, 80 mg propranolol.
Usual adult dose: 1 or 2 tablets PO bid.

► **irbesartan and hydrochlorothiazide**
Avalide

Tablets: 150 mg irbesartan, 12.5 mg hydrochlorothiazide; 300 mg irbesartan, 12.5 mg hydrochlorothiazide; 300 mg irbesartan, 25 mg hydrochlorothiazide.
Usual adult dose: 1 or 2 tablets/day PO. **BBW** Risk of birth defects/fetal death; avoid use in pregnancy.

► **lisinopril and hydrochlorothiazide**
(Prinzide, Zestoretic)

Tablets: 10 mg lisinopril, 12.5 mg hydrochlorothiazide; 20 mg lisinopril, 12.5 mg hydrochlorothiazide; 20 mg lisinopril, 25 mg hydrochlorothiazide.
Usual adult dose: 1 tablet/day PO in a.m. **BBW** Risk of birth defects/fetal death; avoid use in pregnancy.

► **losartan and hydrochlorothiazide**
Hyzaar

Tablets: 50 mg losartan, 12.5 mg hydrochlorothiazide; 100 mg losartan, 12.5 mg hydrochlorothiazide; 100 mg losartan, 25 mg hydrochlorothiazide.
Usual adult dose: 1 tablet/day PO in a.m. Also used to reduce stroke incidence in hypertensive pts w/left ventricular hypertrophy (not effective for this use in black pts). **BBW** Risk of birth defects/fetal death; avoid use in pregnancy.

► **metoprolol and hydrochlorothiazide**
Dutoprol, Lopressor HCT

Tablets: 50 mg metoprolol, 25 mg hydrochlorothiazide; 100 mg metoprolol, 25 mg hydrochlorothiazide;

100 mg metoprolol, 50 mg hydrochlorothiazide.
ER tablets: 25 mg metoprolol, 12.5 mg hydrochlorothiazide; 50 mg metoprolol, 12.5 mg hydrochlorothiazide, 100 mg metoprolol, 12.5 mg hydrochlorothiazice.
Usual adult dose: 1 tablet/day PO. Pt should not cut, crush, or chew ER form (*Dutoprol*). **BBW** Risk of cardiac ischemia, angina, MI w/sudden cessation; taper drug. Alert pt to not stop drug.

► **moexipril and hydrochlorothiazide**
Uniretic

Tablets: 7.5 mg moexipril, 12.5 mg hydrochlorothiazide; 15 mg moexipril, 25 mg hydrochlorothiazide.
Usual adult dose: 1 or 2 tablets/day PO 1 hr before or 2 hr after meal.
BBW Risk of birth defects/fetal death; avoid use in pregnancy.

► **nadolol and bendroflumethiazide**
Corzide

Tablets: 40 mg nadolol, 5 mg bendroflumethiazide; 80 mg nadolol, 5 mg bendroflumethiazide.
Usual adult dose: 1 tablet/day PO in a.m.

► **olmesartan, amlodipine, and hydrochlorothiazide**
Tribenzor

Tablets: 40 mg olmesartan, 10 mg amlodipine, 25 mg hydrochlorothiazide.
Usual adult dose: 1 tablet/day PO.
BBW Risk of birth defects/fetal death; avoid use in pregnancy.

► **olmesartan medoxomil and hydrochlorothiazide**
Benicar HCT

Tablets: 20 mg olmesartan, 12.5 mg hydrochlorothiazide; 40 mg olmesartan, 12.5 mg hydrochlorothiazide; 40 mg olmesartan, 25 mg hydrochlorothiazide.
Usual adult dose: 1 tablet/day PO in a.m. **BBW** Risk of birth defects/fetal death; avoid use in pregnancy.

► **quinapril and hydrochlorothiazide**
Accuretic

Tablets: 10 mg quinapril, 12.5 mg hydrochlorothiazide; 20 mg quinapril, 12.5 mg hydrochlorothiazide.
Usual adult dose: 1 tablet/day PO in a.m. **BBW** Risk of birth defects/fetal death; avoid use in pregnancy.

► **telmisartan and amlodipine**
Twynsta

Tablets: 40 mg telmisartan, 5 mg amlodipine; 40 mg telmisartan, 10 mg amlodipine; 80 mg telmisartan, 5 mg amlodipine; 80 mg telmisartan, 10 mg amlodipine.
Usual adult dose: 1 tablet/day PO.
BBW Risk of birth defects/fetal death; avoid use in pregnancy.

► **telmisartan and hydrochlorothiazide**
Micardis HCT

Tablets: 40 mg telmisartan, 12.5 mg hydrochlorothiazide; 80 mg telmisartan, 12.5 mg hydrochlorothiazide; 80 mg telmisartan, 25 mg hydrochlorothiazide.
Usual adult dose: 1 tablet/day PO; max, 160 mg telmisartan and 25 mg hydrochlorothiazide/day. **BBW** Risk

of birth defects/fetal death; avoid use in pregnancy.

▶ trandolapril and verapamil
Tarka

Tablets: 1 mg trandolapril, 240 mg verapamil; 2 mg trandolapril, 180 mg verapamil; 2 mg trandolapril, 240 mg verapamil; 4 mg trandolapril, 240 mg verapamil.
Usual adult dose: 1 tablet/day PO w/food. Pt should not cut, crush, or chew tablet. **BBW** Risk of birth defects/fetal death; avoid use in pregnancy.

▶ valsartan and hydrochlorothiazide
Diovan HCT

Tablets: 80 mg valsartan, 12.5 mg hydrochlorothiazide; 160 mg valsartan, 12.5 mg hydrochlorothiazide; 160 mg valsartan, 25 mg hydrochlorothiazide; 320 mg valsartan, 12.5 mg hydrochlorothiazide; 320 mg valsartan, 25 mg hydrochlorothiazide.
Usual adult dose: 1 tablet/day PO. **BBW** Risk of birth defects/fetal death; avoid use in pregnancy.

ANTIMIGRAINE DRUGS

▶ ergotamine and caffeine
Cafergot, Migergot

Tablets: 1 mg ergotamine tartrate, 100 mg caffeine.
Suppositories: 2 mg ergotamine tartrate, 100 mg caffeine.
Usual adult dose: 2 tablets PO at first sign of attack, then 1 tablet q 30 min, if needed. Max, 6/attack, 10/wk. Or, 1 suppository at first sign of attack, then second dose after 1 hr, if needed. Max, 2/attack, 5/wk. Do not use w/ritonavir, nelfinavir,

indinavir, erythromycin, clarithromycin, troleandomycin; serious vasospasm possible.

▶ sumatriptan and naproxen sodium
Treximet

Tablets: 85 mg sumatriptan, 500 mg naproxen.
Usual adult dose: 1 tablet PO at onset of acute migraine.

ANTINAUSEA DRUGS

▶ doxylamine and pyridoxine
Diclegis

DR tablets: 10 mg doxylamine, 10 mg pyridoxine.
Usual adult dose: 1 tablet PO at bedtime; max 4 tablets/day. Tx of n/v in pregnancy in pts not responding to other tx.

▶ netupitant and palonosetron
Akynzeo

Capsules: 300 mg netupitant, 0.5 mg palonosetron.
Usual adult dose: 1 capsule 1 hr before start of emetogenic chemotherapy. Avoid use w/severe renal/hepatic impairment.

ANTIPARKINSONIANS

▶ levodopa and carbidopa
Sinemet, Sinemet CR

Tablets: 100 mg levodopa, 10 mg carbidopa; 100 mg levodopa, 25 mg carbidopa; 250 mg levodopa, 25 mg carbidopa.
Orally disintegrating tablets: 100 mg levodopa, 10 mg carbidopa;

100 mg levodopa, 25 mg carbidopa; 250 mg levodopa, 25 mg carbidopa. **CR tablets:** 100 mg levodopa, 25 mg carbidopa; 200 mg levodopa, 50 mg carbidopa.
Usual adult dose: Start w/lowest dose; titrate based on response, tolerance.

▶ **levodopa and carbidopa**
Rytary

ER capsules: 23.75 mg carbidopa, 95 mg levodopa; 36.25 mg carbidopa, 145 mg levodopa; 48.75 mg carbidopa, 195 mg levodopa; 61.25 mg carbidopa, 245 mg levodopa.
Usual adult dose: Start w/lowest dose PO tid; increase based on pt response. Max, 612.5 mg carbidopa/2,450 mg levodopa/day. Tx of Parkinson's disease, postencephalitic parkinsonism, post–carbon monoxide or manganese toxicity parkinsonism.

▶ **levodopa and carbidopa**
Duopa

Enteral suspension: 4.63 mg carbidopa and 20 mg levodopa/mL.
Usual adult dose: 2,000 mg levodopa (1 cassette)/day over 16 hr; administer into jejunum through percutaneous endoscopic gastrostomy w/jejeunal tube using protable infusion pump. Tx of motor fluctuations in advanced Parkinson's disease.

▶ **levodopa, carbidopa, and entacapone**
Stalevo 50, Stalevo 75, Stalevo 100, Stalevo 125, Stalevo 150, Stalevo 200

Tablets: 50 mg levodopa, 12.5 mg carbidopa, 200 mg entacapone; 75 mg levodopa, 18.75 mg carbidopa, 200 mg entacapone; 100 mg levodopa, 25 mg carbidopa, 200 mg entacapone;

125 mg levodopa, 31.25 mg carbidopa, 200 mg entacapone; 150 mg levodopa, 37.5 mg carbidopa, 200 mg entacapone; 200 mg levodopa, 50 mg carbidopa, 200 mg entacapone.
Usual adult dose: 1 tablet PO q 3–8 hr.

ANTIPLATELET

▶ **aspirin and dipyridamole**
Aggrenox

Capsules: 25 mg aspirin, 200 mg dipyridamole.
Usual adult dose: 1 capsule PO bid to decrease risk of stroke in pts w/ known cerebrovascular disease. Not interchangeable w/individual components of aspirin and dipyridamole tablets. Pt should not chew capsule.

ANTIULCER DRUG

▶ **lansoprazole, amoxicillin, and clarithromycin**
Prevpac

Daily administration pack: Two 30-mg lansoprazole capsules, four 500-mg amoxicillin capsules, two 500-mg clarithromycin tablets.
Usual adult dose: Divide pack equally to take PO bid, a.m. and p.m., for 10–14 days.

ANTIVIRALS

▶ **abacavir and lamivudine**
Epzicom

Tablets: 600 mg abacavir w/300 mg lamivudine.
Usual adult dose, child weighing at least 25 kg: 1 tablet PO daily w/ other antiretrovirals for tx of HIV infection. **BBW** Risk of severe

hypersensitivity reactions, lactic acidosis, severe hepatomegaly, hepatitis B exacerbation. Monitor pt accordingly.

▶ abacavir, zidovudine, and lamivudine
Trizivir

Tablets: 300 mg abacavir, 300 mg zidovudine, 150 mg lamivudine.
Usual adult dose, child weighing at least 40 kg: 1 tablet PO bid for tx of HIV infection. Carefully monitor for hypersensitivity reactions; potential increased risk of MI. **BBW** Risk of severe hypersensitivity reactions, bone marrow suppression, myopathy, lactic acidosis, severe hepatomegaly, hepatitis B exacerbation. Monitor pt accordingly.

▶ atazanavir and cobicistat
Evotaz

Tablets: 300 mg atazanavir, 150 mg cobicistat.
Usual adult dose: 1 tablet/day PO w/food, other antiretrovirals for tx of HIV infection. Not recommended w/ evere hepatic/renal impairment. Many potentially serious drug interactions.

▶ darunavir and cobicistat
Prezcobix

Tablets: 800 mg darunavir, 150 mg cobicistat.
Usual adult dose: 1 tablet/day PO w/food for tx of HIV infection.

▶ dolutegravir, abacavir, and lamivudine
Triumeq

Tablets: 50 mg dolutegravir, 600 mg abacavir, 300 mg lamivudine.

Usual adult dose: 1 tablet/day.
Many potentially serious drug interactions. **BBW** Risk of severe hypersensitivity reactions, lactic acidosis, hepatotoxicity, hepatitis B exacerbation.

▶ efavirenz, emtricitabine, and tenofovir
Atripla

Tablets: 600 mg efavirenz, 200 mg emtricitabine, 300 mg tenofovir.
Usual adult dose, child 12 and over weighing at least 40 kg: 1 tablet PO at bedtime on empty stomach for tx of HIV infection. Not recommended w/moderate or severe renal impairment. Risk of rash, fetal harm, body fat redistribution. **BBW** Risk of lactic acidosis, severe hepatomegaly, post-tx hepatitis B exacerbation.

▶ elbasvir and grazopravir
Zepatier

Tablets: 50 mg elbasvir w/100 mg grazopravir.
Usual adult dose: 1 tablet/day PO with or without ribavirin for 12–16 wk. Tx of chronic hepatitis C genotypes 1 and 4. Monitor liver function.

▶ elvitegravir, cobicistat, emtricitabine, and tenofovir alafenamide
Genvoya

Tablets: 150 mg elvitegravir, 150 mg cobicistat, 200 mg emtricitabine, 10 mg tenofovir alafenamide.
Usual adult dose: 1 tablet/day PO w/food. Redistribution of body fat. Many potentially dangerous drug interactions. **BBW** Risk of lactic acidosis, severe hepatomegaly, post-tx hepatitis B exacerbation.

▶ **elvitegravir, cobicistat, emtricitabine, and tenofovir disoproxil fumarate**
Stribild

Tablets: 150 mg elvitegravir, 150 mg cobicistat, 200 mg emtricitabine, 300 mg tenofovir.
Usual adult dose: 1 tablet PO/day for pts never treated for HIV. Many potentially serious drug interactions. **BBW** Risk of lactic acidosis, severe hepatomegaly, post-tx hepatitis B exacerbation.

▶ **emtricitabine, rilpivirine, and tenofovir**
Complera

Tablets: 200 mg emtricitabine, 25 mg rilpivirine, 300 mg tenofovir.
Usual adult dose: 1 tablet/day PO for tx of HIV infection in tx-naïve pts. Many potentially serious drug interactions, severe rash, risk of drug reaction w/eosinophilia and systemic symptoms. **BBW** Risk of lactic acidosis, severe hepatomegaly, post-tx hepatitis B exacerbation.

▶ **emtricitabine and tenofovir disoproxil fumarate**
Truvada

Tablets: 200 mg emtricitabine w/300 mg tenofovir.
Usual adult dose, child 12 yr and older weighing at least 35 kg: 1 tablet PO daily w/other antiretrovirals for tx of HIV infection. Redistribution of body fat. Many potential drug interactions. **BBW** Risk of lactic acidosis, severe hepatomegaly, post-tx hepatitis B exacerbation, drug resistance.

▶ **lamivudine and zidovudine**
Combivir

Tablets: 150 mg lamivudine, 300 mg zidovudine.
Usual adult dose, child weighing at least 30 kg: 1 tablet PO bid for tx of HIV infection. Not recommended for adult, child under 50 kg. **BBW** Risk of lactic acidosis, severe hepatomegaly, bone marrow suppression, myopathy, post-tx hepatitis B exacerbation.

▶ **ledipasvir and sofosbuvir**
Harvoni

Tablets: 90 mg ledipasvir, 400 mg sofosbuvir.
Usual adult dose: *Genotype 1:* 1 tablet/day PO w/food for 12 wk (tx-naïve) or 24 wk (tx-experienced). *Genotype 4, 5, 6:* 1 tablet/day PO w/food for 12 wk. Tx of hepatitis C.

▶ **ombitasvir, paritaprevir, and ritonavir**
Technivie

Tablets: 12.5 mg ombitasvir, 75 mg paritaprevir, 50 mg ritonavir.
Usual adult dose: 2 tablets PO once daily in a.m. for 12 wk. Tx of genotype 4 chronic hepatitis C. Many potential serious drug interactions. Not for use w/moderate hepatic impairment.

▶ **ombitasvir, paritaprevir, ritonavir, and dasabuvir**
Viekira Pak

Tablets: 12.5 mg ombitasvir, 75 mg paritaprevir, 50 mg ritonavir; packaged w/250 mg dasabuvir.
Usual adult dose: 2 ombitasvir/ paritaprevir/ritonavir tablets PO once daily in a.m. and 1 dasabuvir

tablet PO bid (a.m. and p.m.) w/food. Tx of hepatitis C. Hepatic failure possible. Many potentially serious drug interactions.

BPH DRUG

▶ dutasteride and tamsulosin
Jalyn

Capsules: 0.5 mg dutasteride, 0.4 mg tamsulosin.
Usual adult dose: 1 capsule/day PO.

DIURETICS

▶ amiloride and hydrochlorothiazide
generic

Tablets: 5 mg amiloride, 50 mg hydrochlorothiazide.
Usual adult dose: 1 or 2 tablets/day PO w/meals.

▶ hydrochlorothiazide and triamterene
Dyazide

Capsules: 25 mg hydrochlorothiazide, 37.5 mg triamterene.
Usual adult dose: 1 or 2 capsules PO once/day or bid after meals.

▶ hydrochlorothiazide and triamterene
Maxzide, Maxzide-25

Tablets: 25 mg hydrochlorothiazide, 37.5 mg triamterene; 50 mg hydrochlorothiazide, 75 mg triamterene.
Usual adult dose: 1 or 2 tablets/day PO.

▶ spironolactone and hydrochlorothiazide
Aldactazide

Tablets: 25 mg spironolactone, 25 mg hydrochlorothiazide; 50 mg spironolactone, 50 mg hydrochlorothiazide.
Usual adult dose: 1–8 tablets/day PO (25/25). 1–4 tablets/day PO (50/50).

HF DRUG

▶ isosorbide dinitrate and hydralazine hydrochloride
BiDil

Tablets: 20 mg isosorbide dinitrate, 37.5 mg hydralazine.
Usual adult dose: 1 tablet PO tid; may increase to 2 tablets tid. For adjunct tx in self-identified black pts to improve functional survival. Not for use with ED drugs.

LIPID-LOWERING DRUGS

▶ ezetimibe and simvastatin
Vytorin

Tablets: 10 mg ezetimibe, 10 mg simvastatin; 10 mg ezetimibe, 20 mg simvastatin; 10 mg ezetimibe, 40 mg simvastatin; 10 mg ezetimibe, 80 mg simvastatin.
Usual adult dose: 1 tablet/day PO in p.m. w/cholesterol-lowering diet/exercise. Must give at least 2 hr before or 4 hr after bile sequestrant (if used).

▶ niacin and lovastatin
Advicor

Tablets: 500 mg niacin, 20 mg lovastatin; 750 mg niacin, 20 mg

lovastatin; 1,000 mg niacin, 20 mg lovastatin.
Usual adult dose: 1 tablet/day PO in p.m.

▶ simvastatin and niacin
Simcor

Tablets: 20 mg simvastatin, 500 mg niacin; 20 mg simvastatin, 750 mg niacin; 20 mg simvastatin, 1,000 mg niacin.
Usual adult dose: 1 tablet/day PO. Max, 2,000 mg niacin w/40 mg simvastatin/day.

MENOPAUSE DRUGS

▶ conjugated estrogen and bazedoxifene
Duavee

Tablets: 0.45 mg conjugated estrogen, 20 mg bazedoxifene.
Usual adult dose: 1 tablet/day PO.
BBW Risk of endometrial cancer, stroke, DVT, probable dementia. Not for use to decrease CAD.

▶ drospirenone and estradiol
Angeliq

Tablets: 0.5 mg drospirenone, 1 mg estradiol.
Usual adult dose: 1 tablet/day PO. Monitor potassium level closely.
BBW Risk of endometrial cancer, stroke, DVT, probable dementia.

▶ drospirenone and ethinyl estradiol
YAZ

Tablets: 3 mg drospirenone, 0.02 mg ethinyl estradiol.
Usual adult dose: 1 tablet/day PO. Monitor potassium level closely.

BBW Risk of serious CV events in female smokers 35 yr and over.

▶ estradiol and norethindrone (transdermal)
CombiPatch

Patch: 0.05 mg/day estradiol, 0.14 mg/day norethindrone; 0.05 mg/day estradiol, 0.25 mg/day norethindrone.
Usual adult dose: Change patch twice/wk. **BBW** Risk of endometrial cancer, stroke, DVT, probable dementia.

▶ estradiol and norethindrone (oral)
Activella

Tablets: 0.5 mg estradiol, 0.1 mg norethindrone; 1 mg estradiol, 0.5 mg norethindrone.
Usual adult dose: 1 tablet/day PO.
BBW Risk of endometrial cancer, stroke, DVT, probable dementia.

▶ estrogens, conjugated, and medroxyprogesterone
Prempro

Tablets: 0.3 mg conjugated estrogen, 1.5 mg medroxyprogesterone; 0.45 mg conjugated estrogen, 1.5 mg medroxyprogesterone; 0.625 mg conjugated estrogen, 2.5 mg medroxyprogesterone; 0.625 mg conjugated estrogen, 5 mg medroxyprogesterone.
Usual adult dose: 1 tablet/day PO. Use in women w/intact uterus.
BBW Risk of endometrial cancer, stroke, DVT, probable dementia.

▶ **ethinyl estradiol and norethindrone acetate**
Femhrt

Tablets: 2.5 mcg ethinyl estradiol, 0.5 mg norethindrone acetate; 5 mcg ethinyl estradiol, 1 mg norethindrone acetate.
Usual adult dose: 1 tablet/day PO. Use in women w/intact uterus.
BBW Risk of endometrial cancer, stroke, DVT, probable dementia.

ONCOLOGY DRUG

▶ **trifluridine and tipiracil**
Lonsurf

Tablets: 15 mg trifluridine, 6.14 mg tipiracil; 20 mg trifluridine, 8.19 mg tipiracil.
Usual adult dose: 35 mg/m^2/dose PO bid on days 1–5, 8–12 of 28-day cycle within 1 hr of completing a.m. and p.m. meals. Tx of metastatic colorectal cancer after previous tx. Risk of severe bone marrow suppression, fetal toxicity.

OPIOID AGONISTS

▶ **buprenorphine and naloxone**
CONTROLLED SUBSTANCE C-III
Suboxone

Sublingual tablets: 2 mg buprenorphine, 0.5 mg naloxone; 8 mg buprenorphine, 2 mg naloxone.
Usual adult dose: 12–16 mg/day by sublingual film after induction w/ sublingual buprenorphine for tx of opioid dependence.

▶ **buprenorphine and naloxone**
CONTROLLED SUBSTANCE C-III
Zubsolv

Sublingual tablets: 1.4 mg buprenorphine, 0.36 mg naloxone; 5.7 mg buprenorphine, 1.4 mg naloxone.
Usual adult dose: 1 tablet/day sublingually.

PSYCHIATRIC DRUG

▶ **dextromethorphan and quinidine**
Nuedexta

Capsules: 20 mg dextromethorphan, 10 mg quinidine.
Usual adult dose: 1 capsule/day PO for 7 days; maint, 1 capsule PO q 12 hr. For tx of pseudobulbar affect associated w/neurologic conditions.

RESPIRATORY DRUGS

▶ **azelastine and fluticasone**
Dymista

Nasal spray: 137 mcg azelastine, 50 mcg fluticasone.
Usual dose in pts 6 yr and older: 1 spray in each nostril bid for relief of sx of seasonal allergic rhinitis.

▶ **budesonide and formoterol fumarate**
Symbicort 80/4.5, Symbicort 160/4.5

Inhalation: 80 mcg budesonide, 4.5 mcg formoterol fumarate; 160 mcg budesonide, 4.5 mcg formoterol fumarate.
Usual dose in pts 12 yr and older: Two inhalations bid, a.m. and p.m.

For long-term maint of asthma, not for acute attacks.

▶ fluticasone and salmeterol
Advair Diskus, Advair HFA

Inhalation: 100 mcg fluticasone, 50 mcg salmeterol; 250 mcg fluticasone, 50 mcg salmeterol; 500 mcg fluticasone, 50 mcg salmeterol.
Usual dose in pts 12 yr and older: 1 inhalation bid to manage asthma.
Usual dose in child 4–11 yr: 1 inhalation (100 mcg fluticasone, 50 mcg salmeterol) bid, a.m. and p.m. about 12 hr apart. **BBW** Risk of asthma-related deaths.

▶ fluticasone and vilanterol
Breo Ellipta

Powder for inhalation: 100 mcg fluticasone, 25 mcg vilanterol.
Usual adult dose: One oral inhalation daily. **BBW** Long-acting beta agonists are associated w/asthma-related deaths; not for use in asthma or tx of acute bronchospasm.

▶ hydrocodone and chlorpheniramine
Vituz

Oral sol: 5 mg hydrocodone, 4 mg chlorpheniramine/5-mL sol.
Usual adult dose: 5 mL PO q 4–6 hr; max, four doses/day.

▶ hydrocodone and pseudoephedrine
Rezira

Oral sol: 5 mg hydrocodone, 60 mg pseudoephedrine/5-mL sol.
Usual adult dose: 5 mL PO q 4–6 hr as needed; max, four doses in 24 hr.

▶ hydrocodone and pseudoephedrine and chlorpheniramine
Zutripro

Oral sol: 5 mg hydrocodone, 60 mg pseudoephedrine, 4 mg chlorpheniramine in 5-mL sol.
Usual adult dose: 5 mL PO q 4–6 hr as needed; max, four doses in 24 hr.

▶ indacaterol and glycopyrrolate
Utibron Neohaler

Powder for inhalation: 27.5 mcg indacaterol, 15.6 mcg glycopyrrolate
Usual adult dose: Oral inhalation using *Neohaler* device, 1 capsule bid. Pt should not swallow capsules.
BBW Long-acting beta agonists are associated w/asthma-related deaths; not for use in asthma or tx of acute bronchospasm.

▶ ipratropium and albuterol
Combivent Respimat

Metered-dose inhaler: 18 mcg ipratropium bromide, 90 mcg albuterol.
Usual adult dose: 2 inhalations four times/day. Not for use during acute attack. Use caution w/known sensitivity to atropine, soy beans, soya lecithin, peanuts.

▶ loratadine and pseudoephedrine
Claritin-D

ER tablets: 5 mg loratadine, 120 mg pseudoephedrine.
Usual adult dose: 1 tablet PO q 12 hr.

► **loratadine and pseudoephedrine**
Claritin-D 24 Hour

ER tablets: 10 mg loratadine, 240 mg pseudoephedrine.
Usual adult dose: 1 tablet/day PO.

► **mometasone and formoterol**
Dulera 100/5, Dulera 200/5

Metered aerosol inhaler: 100 mcg mometasone, 5 mcg formoterol; 200 mcg mometasone, 5 mcg formoterol.
Usual adult dose: For maint tx of asthma, 2 inhalations bid, a.m. and p.m. Rinse mouth after use. Not for children.

► **olodaterol and tiotropium**
Stiolto Respimat

Metered oral inhaler: 2.5 mcg olodaterol, 2.5 mcg tiotropium.
Usual adult dose: For long-term maint of COPD, 2 inhalations once a day at same time each day. Not for child. **BBW** Risk of asthma-related deaths w/long-acting beta agonists; must be combined with inhaled corticosteroid. Not for use in asthma or acute deterioriation of COPD.

► **umeclidinium and vilanterol**
Anoro Ellipta

Inhalation powder: 62.5 mcg umeclidinium, 25 mcg vilanterol.
Usual adult dose: One oral inhalation/day for maint of COPD. **BBW** Long-acting beta agonists associated w/ asthma-related deaths, not for use in asthma or acute bronchospasm.

TENSION HEADACHE DRUG

► **butalbital, acetaminophen, and caffeine**
generic

Capsules: 50 mg butalbital, 500 mg acetaminophen, 40 mg caffeine.
Usual adult dose: 1 capsule, 1 tablet, or sol PO q 4 hr as needed; max, 6/day. May be habit-forming; pt should avoid driving, dangerous tasks.

WEIGHT-LOSS DRUGS

► **naltrexone and bupropion**
Contrave

ER tablets: 8 mg naltrexone, 90 mg bupropion.
Usual adult dose: Wk 1, 1 tablet PO in a.m.; wk 2, 1 tablet PO in a.m. and 1 tablet PO in p.m.; wk 3, 2 tablets PO in a.m. and 1 tablet PO in p.m.; maint, 2 tablets PO in a.m. and 2 tablets PO in p.m. **BBW** Risk of suicidal thoughts/behaviors, neuropsychiatric events.

► **phentermine and topiramate**
Qsymia

Capsules: 3.75 mg phentermine, 23 mg topiramate; 7.5 mg phentermine, 46 mg topiramate; 11.25 mg phentermine, 69 mg topiramate; 15 mg phentermine, 92 mg topiramate.
Usual adult dose: 1 capsule/day PO in a.m. w/diet/exercise. Hormonal contraceptives may be ineffective; cardiac issues, suicidality.

Hormonal contraceptives

IND & DOSE Take 1 tablet PO daily for 21 days, starting within 5 days of first day of menstrual bleeding (day 1 of cycle is first day of menstrual bleeding). Take inert tablets or no tablets for next 7 days. Then start new course of 21 days. Sunday start: Take first tablet on first Sunday after menstruation begins.

NC/PT Suggested measures for missed doses: One tablet missed: Take tablet as soon as possible, or take 2 tablets next day. Two consecutive tablets missed: Take 2 tablets daily for next 2 days, then resume regular schedule. Three consecutive tablets missed: If Sunday starter, take 1 pill q day until Sunday; then discard pack and start new pack on that day. If day 1 starter, discard rest of pack and start new pack that same day. Use additional birth control method until start of next menstrual period. Increased risk of thromboembolic events if combined w/smoking.

Postcoital contraception ("morning after" pills): Safe, effective for emergency contraception. Regimen starts within 72 hr of unprotected intercourse w/follow-up dose of same number of pills 12 hr after first dose. *Plan B:* 0.75 mg levonorgestrel; take second tablet 12 hr later. *Plan B One-Step, Next Choice One Door, My Way:* 1.5 mg levonorgestrel; take 1 tablet within 72 hr of unprotected sexual intercourse. Available OTC. *Ella* (ulipristal; progesterone agonist/antagonist): 30 mg tablet; take within 5 days of unprotected sexual intercourse.

ORAL CONTRACEPTIVES

Trade name	Combination
MONOPHASIC	
Altavera, Chateal, Introvale, Jolessa, Kurvelo, Levora 0.15/30, Marlissa, Portia, Quasense	30 mcg ethinyl estradiol/0.15 mg levonorgestrel
Alyacen 1/35, Cyclafem 1/35, Dasetta 1/35, Necon 1/35, Norinyl 1+35, Nortrel 1/35, Ortho-Novum 1/35, Pirmella 1/35	35 mcg ethinyl estradiol/1 mg norethindrone
Apri, Desogen, Emoquette, Ortho-Cept, Reclipsen, Solia	30 mcg ethinyl estradiol/0.15 mg desogestrel
Aviane, Falmina, Lessina, Lutera, Orsythia, Sronyx	20 mcg ethinyl estradiol/0.10 mg levonorgestrel

Trade name	Combination
Balziva, Briellyn, Femcon Fe chewable tablets, Gildagia, Ovcon-35, Philith, Vylemia, Wymzya FE, Zenchent	35 mcg ethinyl estradiol/0.4 mg norethindrone
Beyaz	3 mg drospirenone/20 mcg ethinyl estradiol/0.45 mg levomefolate; must monitor potassium levels
Brevicon, Modicon, Necon 0.5/35, Nortrel 0.5/35, Wera	35 mcg ethinyl estradiol/0.5 mg norethindrone
Cryselle, Elinest, Low-Ogestrel	30 mcg ethinyl estradiol/0.3 mg norgestrel
Estarylla, Mononessa, Ortho-Cyclen, Previfem, Sprintec	35 mcg ethinyl estradiol/0.25 mg norgestimate
Generess FE	25 mg ethinyl estradiol, 0.8 mg norethindrone
Gianvi, Loryna, Nikki, Vestura, Yaz	3 mg drospirenone/20 mcg ethinyl estradiol
Gildess 1/20, Gildess Fe 1/20, Junel Fe 1/20, Junel 21 Day 1/20, Larin 1/20, Larin FE 1/20, Loestrin 21 1/20, Loestrin 21 1/20, Loestrin 24 Fe, Lomedia 24 FE, Microgestin Fe 1/20, Minastrin 24 FE	20 mcg ethinyl estradiol/1 mg norethindrone
Gildess 1.5/20, Gildess FE 1.5/30, Junel Fe 1.5/30, Junel 21 Day 1.5/30, FE 15/30, Loestrin 21 1.5/30, Loestrin Fe 1.5/30, Microgestin Fe 1.5/30	30 mcg ethinyl estradiol/1.5 mg norethindrone acetate
Kelnor 1/35, Zovia 1/35E	35 mcg ethinyl estradiol/1 mg ethynodiol diacetate
Necon 1/50, Norinyl 1+50	50 mcg mestranol/1 mg norethindrone
Ocella, Safryal, Syeda, Yasmin 28, Zarah	3 mg drospirenone/30 mcg ethinyl estradiol; must monitor potassium level
Ogestrel 0.5/50	50 mcg ethinyl estradiol/0.5 mg norgestrel
Quasense, Seasonale, Seasonique	0.15 levonorgestrel/30 mcg ethinyl estradiol taken as 84 days active tablets, 7 days inactive

Trade name	Combination
Safyral	3 mg drospirenone/30 mcg ethinyl estradiol/45 mcg levomefolate
Zovia 1/50E	50 mcg ethinyl estradiol/1 mg ethynodiol diacetate

BIPHASIC

Amethia, Camrese, Daysee, Seasonique	**phase 1:** 84 tablets, 0.15 mg levonorgestrel/30 mcg ethinyl estradiol **phase 2:** 7 tablets, 10 mcg ethinyl estradiol
Amethia Lo	**phase 1:** 84 tablets, 0.1 mg levonorgestrel/20 mcg ethinyl estradiol **phase 2:** 7 tablets, 10 mcg ethinyl estradiol
Azurette, Kariva, Mircette, Viorele	**phase 1:** 21 tablets, 0.15 mg desogestrel/20 mcg ethinyl estradiol **phase 2:** 5 tablets, 10 mcg ethinyl estradiol
Camrese Lo, LoSeasonique	**phase 1:** 84 tablets, 0.15 mg levonorgestrel/20 mcg ethinyl estradiol **phase 2:** 7 tablets, 10 mcg ethinyl estradiol
Lo Loestrin Fe, Lo Minastrin Fe	**phase 1:** 24 tablets, 1 mg norethindrone/10 mcg ethinyl estradiol **phase 2:** 2 tablets, 10 mcg ethinyl estradiol
Necon 10/11	**phase 1:** 10 tablets, 0.5 mg norethindrone/35 mcg ethinyl estradiol **phase 2:** 11 tablets, 1 mg norethindrone/35 mcg ethinyl estradiol

TRIPHASIC

Alyacen 7/7/7, Cyclafem 7/7/7, Dasetta 7/7/7, Necon 7/7/7, Nortrel 7/7/7, Ortho-Novum 7/7/7, Pirmella 7/7/7	**phase 1:** 7 tablets, 0.5 mg norethindrone (progestin)/35 mcg ethinyl estradiol (estrogen) **phase 2:** 7 tablets, 0.75 mg norethindrone (progestin)/35 mcg ethinyl estradiol (estrogen) **phase 3:** 7 tablets, 1 mg norethindrone (progestin)/35 mcg ethinyl estradiol (estrogen)

Trade name	Combination
Aranelle, Leena, Tri-Norinyl	**phase 1:** 7 tablets, 0.5 mg norethindrone (progestin)/35 mcg ethinyl estradiol (estrogen) **phase 2:** 9 tablets, 1 mg norethindrone (progestin)/35 mcg ethinyl estradiol (estrogen) **phase 3:** 5 tablets, 0.5 mg norethindrone (progestin)/35 mcg ethinyl estradiol (estrogen)
Caziant, Cesia, Cyclessa, Velivet	**phase 1:** 7 tablets, 0.1 mg desogestrel/25 mcg ethinyl estradiol **phase 2:** 7 tablets, 0.125 mg desogestrel/25 mcg ethinyl estradiol **phase 3:** 7 tablets, 0.15 mg desogestrel/25 mcg ethinyl estradiol
Enpresse, Levonest, Myzilra, Trivora	**phase 1:** 6 tablets, 0.5 mg levonorgestrel (progestin)/30 mcg ethinyl estradiol (estrogen) **phase 2:** 5 tablets, 0.075 mg levonorgestrel (progestin)/40 mcg ethinyl estradiol (estrogen) **phase 3:** 10 tablets, 0.125 mg levonorgestrel (progestin)/30 mcg ethinyl estradiol (estrogen)
Estrostep Fe, Tilia Fe, Tri-Legest Fe	**phase 1:** 5 tablets, 1 mg norethindrone/20 mcg ethinyl estradiol; w/75 mg ferrous fumarate **phase 2:** 7 tablets, 1 mg norethindrone/30 mcg ethinyl estradiol; w/75 mg ferrous fumarate **phase 3:** 9 tablets, 1 mg norethindrone/35 mcg ethinyl estradiol; w/75 mg ferrous fumarate
Ortho Tri-Cyclen, Tri-Estarylla, Tri-Linyah, TriNessa, Tri-Previfem, Tri-Sprintec	**phase 1:** 7 tablets, 0.18 mg norgestimate/35 mcg ethinyl estradiol **phase 2:** 7 tablets, 0.215 mg norgestimate/35 mcg ethinyl estradiol **phase 3:** 7 tablets, 0.25 mg norgestimate/35 mcg ethinyl estradiol
Ortho Tri-Cyclen Lo	**phase 1:** 7 tablets, 0.18 mg norgestimate/25 mcg ethinyl estradiol **phase 2:** 7 tablets, 0.215 mg norgestimate/25 mcg ethinyl estradiol **phase 3:** 7 tablets, 0.25 mg norgestimate/25 mcg ethinyl estradiol

Trade name	Combination
Tri-Legest	**phase 1:** 5 tablets, 1 mg norethindrone/ 20 mcg ethinyl estradiol **phase 2:** 7 tablets, 1 mg norethindrone/ 30 mcg ethinyl estradiol **phase 3:** 9 tablets, 1 mg norethindrone/ 35 mcg ethinyl estradiol

4-Phasic

Natazia	**phase 1:** 2 tablets, 3 mg estradiol valerate **phase 2:** 5 tablets, 2 mg estradiol valerate/2 mg dienogest **phase 3:** 17 tablets, 2 mg estradiol valerate/3 mg dienogest **phase 4:** 2 tablets, 1 mg estradiol valerate
Quartette	**phase 1:** 42 tablets, 0.15 mg levonorgestrel, 0.02 mg ethinyl estradiol **phase 2:** 21 tablets, 0.15 mg levonorgestrel, 0.025 mg ethinyl estradiol **phase 3:** 21 tablets, 0.15 mg levonorgestrel, 0.03 mg ethinyl estradiol **phase 4:** 7 tablets, 0.01 mg ethinyl estradiol

Progestin Only

Camila, Errin, Heather, Jencycla, Jolivette, Nor-Be, Nor-QD, Ortho Micronor	0.35 mg norethindrone

Implantable System

Trade name	Combination
Implanon, Nexplanon	68 mg etonogestrel implanted subdermally in inner aspect of nondominant upper arm. Left in place for no longer than 3 yr, then must be removed. May then insert new implants.

Injectable Contraceptives

Trade name	Combination
Depo-Provera	150, 400 mcg/mL medroxyprogesterone. Give 1-mL injection deep IM; repeat every 3 mo. **BBW** Risk of significant bone loss.

Trade name	Combination
depo-sub Q provera 104	104 mg medroxyprogesterone. Give 0.65 mL subcut into anterior thigh, abdomen. **BBW** Risk of significant bone loss.

INTRAUTERINE SYSTEM

Trade name	Combination
Liletta	52 mg levonorgestrel inserted into uterus for up to 3 yr.
Mirena	52 mg levonorgestrel inserted into uterus for up to 5 yr. (Also approved to treat heavy menstrual bleeding in women using intrauterine system for contraception.) Releases 20 mcg/day.
Skyla	13.5 mg levonorgestrel inserted into uterus for up to 3 yr.

TRANSDERMAL SYSTEM

Trade name	Combination
Ortho Evra, Xulane	**BBW** Higher risk of thromboembolic events, death if combined w/smoking. 6 mg norelgestromin/0.75 ethinyl estradiol in patch form; releases 150 mcg norelgestromin/20 mcg ethinyl estradiol each 24 hr for 1 wk. Patch applied on same day of wk for 3 consecutive wk, followed by patch-free wk.

VAGINAL RING

Trade name	Combination
NuvaRing	0.12 mg etonogestrel (progestin)/0.015 mg ethinyl estradiol (estrogen)/day. Insert into vagina on or before 5th day of menstrual period; remove after 3 wk. Insert new ring after 1-wk rest.

Commonly used biologicals

IND & DOSE Vaccines provide inactivated or attenuated antigens to stimulate production of antibodies; provides active immunity. Immune globulin provides acute, passive immunity by providing preformed antibodies to specific antigen; not long-term protection.

ADV EFF Anorexia, drowsiness, injection-area edema (w/redness, swelling, induration, pain that may persist for few days), fretfulness, generalized aches/pains, hypersensitivity reactions, malaise, transient fever, vomiting

NC/PT Pregnancy Category C. Use caution in pregnancy; safety not established. Defer administration of routine immunizing or booster doses if acute infection present. Usually not indicated for pts on immunosuppressants or w/cancer, active infections. Have epinephrine 1:1,000 on hand during injection for hypersensitivity reactions. Provide comfort measures for discomforts of injection. Give pt written record of immunization, booster reminder if needed.

▶ diphtheria and tetanus toxoids, adsorbed
Decavac, Tenivac

Adult, child: Three 0.5-mL IM injections, first two at least 4 wk apart and third 6 mo later. Routine booster at 11–12 yr, then q 10 yr (*Decavac*). *Adult, child 7 yr and over:* Three 0.5-mL injections IM at 8-wk intervals, booster 6–8 mo later. Routine booster at 11–12 yr, then q 10 yr (*Tenivac*).

▶ diphtheria and tetanus toxoids and acellular pertussis vaccine adsorbed (DtaP/Tdap)
Adacel, Boostrix, Daptacel, Infanrix, Tripedia

Primary immunization: 3 IM doses of 0.5 mL at 4- to 8-wk intervals. Start doses by 6–8 wk of age; finish by 7th birthday. Use same vaccine for all three doses. *Fourth dose:* 0.5 mL IM at 15–20 mo at least 6 mo after previous dose. *Fifth dose:* 0.5 mL IM at

4–6 yr or preferably before entry into school (*Infanrix, Daptacel, Tripedia*). If fourth dose given after 4-yr birthday, may omit preschool dose. *Booster injections:* 11–64 yr (*Adacel*), 0.5 mL IM. 10 yr and older (*Boostrix*), 0.5 mL IM. Allow at least 5 yr between last of series and booster dose.

▶ diphtheria and tetanus toxoids and acellular pertussis adsorbed, hepatitis B (recombinant), and inactivated poliovirus vaccine combined (DTaP-HePB-IPV)
Pediarix

Infants w/hepatitis B surface antigen (HBsAG)–negative mothers: Three 0.5-mL doses IM at 6- to 8-wk intervals (preferably 8) stating at 2 mo. *Children previously vaccinated w/one dose of hepatitis B vaccine:* Should receive three-dose series. *Children previously vaccinated w/one or more doses of Infanrix or IPV:* May use Pediarix to complete series.

► **diphtheria and tetanus toxoids and acellular pertussis adsorbed and inactivated poliovirus vaccine (DTaP-IIPV)**
Kinrix

Fifth dose in diphtheria, tetanus, acellular pertussis series and fourth dose in inactivated poliovirus series in children 4–6 yr whose previous immunizations have been w/ *Infanrix* or *Pediarix* for first three doses and *Infanrix* for fourth dose. One IM injection of 0.5 mL.

► **diphtheria and tetanus toxoids and acellular pertussis adsorbed, inactivated poliovirus vaccine, and *Haemophilus* b conjugate (tetanus toxoid conjugate) vaccine (DTaP-IPV/Hib)**
Pentacel

Four-dose series of IM injections of 0.5 mL at 2, 4, and 6 mo, followed by booster at 18 mo. Give between 6 wk and 4 yr.

► ***Haemophilus* b conjugate vaccine**
ActHIB, Hiberix, Liquid PedvaxHIB

Active immunization of infants, children against *H. influenzae* b for primary immunization, routine recall; 2–71 mo *(PedvaxHIB)*, 2–18 mo *(ActHIB w/DPT)*, or 15–18 mo *(ActHIB, Hiberix w/Tripedia)*.
ActHIB: Reconstitute w/DTP, *Tripedia*, or saline. 2–6 mo, 3 IM injections of 0.5 mL at 2, 4, and 6 mo; 0.5 mL at 15–18 mo and DPT alone at 4–6 yr. 7–11 mo, 2 IM injections of 0.5 mL at 8-wk intervals;

booster dose at 15–18 mo. 12–14 mo, 0.5 mL IM w/a booster 2 mo later. 15–18 mo, 0.5 mL IM, booster of *Tripedia* at 4–6 yr.
Hiberix: 15 mo–4 yr, booster dose of 0.5 mL IM as single dose. Booster dose at 15 mo or older but not less than 2 mo from last dose. Unvaccinated children 15–71 mo, 0.5 mL IM.
PedvaxHIB: 2–14 mo, 2 IM injections of 0.5 mL at 2 mo and 2 mo later; 0.5 mL booster at 12 mo (if two doses complete before 12 mo, not less than 2 mo after last dose). 15 mo or older, 0.5 mL IM single injection.

► ***Haemophilus* b conjugate vaccine w/hepatitis B surface antigen (recombinant)**
Comvax

Infants w/hepatitis B surface antigen (HBsAg)–negative mothers: Three 0.5-mL IM doses at 2, 4, and 12–15 mo. Children previously vaccinated w/one or more doses of hepatitis B vaccine or Haemophilus b vaccine: 0.5-mL IM doses at 2, 4, and 12–15 mo. Give only to children of HBsAg-negative mothers.

► **hepatitis A vaccine, inactivated**
Havrix, Vaqta

Adult: *Havrix,* 1,440 ELISA units (1 mL) IM; same dose booster in 6–12 mo. *Vaqta,* 50 units (1 mL) IM; same dose booster in 6–18 mo.
Child 12 mo–18 yr: *Vaqta,* 25 units/0.5 mL IM, w/repeat dose in 6–18 mo. *Havrix,* 720 ELISA units (0.5 mL) IM; repeat dose in 6–12 mo.

► hepatitis A inactivated and hepatitis B recombinant vaccine
Twinrix

Three doses (1 mL by IM injection) on 0-, 1-, and 6-month schedule. *Accelerated dosage:* Four doses (1 mL by IM injection) on days 0, 7, 21, 30, followed by booster dose at 12 mo. Safety in pts under 18 yr not established.

► hepatitis B immune globulin (HBIG)
HepaGam B, HyperHEP B S/D, Nabi-HB

Perinatal exposure: 0.5 mL IM within 12 hr of birth; repeat dose at 1 mo and 6 mo after initial dose. *Percutaneous exposure:* 0.06 mL/kg IM immediately (within 7 days); repeat 28–30 days after exposure. Usual adult dose, 3–5 mL. *Pts at high risk for infection:* 0.06 mL/kg IM at same time (but at different site) as hepatitis B vaccine is given. *HepaGam B after liver transplant:* 20,000 international units IV at 2 mL/min. Give first dose w/liver transplant, then daily on days 1–7, q 2 wk from day 14 through 12 wk, and monthly from mo 4 onward. *Sexual exposure:* Single dose of 0.06 mL/kg IM within 14 days of last sexual contact.

► hepatitis B vaccine
Engerix-B, Recombivax HB

Adults: Initial dose, 1 mL IM, then 1 mL IM at 1 mo and 6 mo after initial dose, all types. *Child 11–19 yr:* 1 mL IM, then 1 mL IM at 1 mo and 6 mo after initial dose. *Birth–10 yr:* Initial dose, 0.5 mL IM, then 0.5 mL IM at 1 mo and 6 mo after initial dose. *Dialysis, predialysis pts:* Initial dose, 40 mcg (2 mL) IM; repeat at 1, 2, and 6 mo after initial dose *(Engerix-B).*

Or, 40 mcg (1 mL) IM; repeat at 1 and 6 mo *(Recombivax HB).* **Revaccination** (consider booster dose w/anti-HBs level under 10 milli-international units/mL 1–2 mo after third dose). *Adult, child over 10 yr:* 20 mcg. *Child under 10 yr:* 10 mcg. *Hemodialysis pts (when antibody testing indicates need):* Two 20-mcg doses.

► human papillomavirus recombinant vaccine, bivalent types 16 and 18
Cervarix

Young girls, women 10–25 yr: Three doses of 0.5 mL IM at 0, 1, and 6 mo.

► human papillomavirus recombinant vaccine, quadrivalent
Gardasil

Pts 9–26 yr: Three separate IM injections of 0.5 mL each, second dose 2 mo after initial dose, last dose 6 mo after first dose. For px of cervical cancer, precancerous genital lesions, genital warts, vaginal/vulvar/anal cancer in women; px of genital warts, anal cancer, precancerous lesions in males.

▶ **immune globulin intramuscular (IG; gamma globulin; IGIM)**
GamaSTAN S/D

▶ **immune globulin intravenous (IGIV)**
Carimune NF, Flebogamma 5%, Flebogamma 10%, Gammagard Liquid, Privigen

▶ **immune globulin subcutaneous (IGSC, SCIG)**
Gamunex-C, Hizentra

BBW Risk of renal dysfunction, renal failure, death; monitor accordingly.
Hepatitis A: 0.02 mL/kg IM for household, institutional contacts. Persons traveling to areas where hepatitis A common, 0.02 mL/kg IM if staying less than 2 mo; 0.06 mL/kg IM repeated q 5 mo for prolonged stay. *Measles (rubeola):* 0.25 mL/kg IM if exposed less than 6 days previously; immunocompromised child exposed to measles, 0.5 mL/kg to max 15 mL IM immediately. *Varicella:* 0.6–1.2 mL/kg IM promptly if zoster immune globulin unavailable. *Rubella:* 0.55 mL/kg IM to pregnant women exposed to rubella but not considering therapeutic abortion; may decrease likelihood of infection, fetal damage. *Immunoglobulin deficiency:* Initially, 1.3 mL/kg IM, followed in 3–4 wk by 0.66 mL/kg IM q 3–4 wk; some pts may need more frequent injections. *Carimune NF:* 0.4–0.8 g/kg IV by infusion q 3–4 wk. *Flebogamma:* 300–600 mg/kg IV q 3–4 wk. *Primary immune deficiency, idiopathic thrombocytopenic purpura, chronic inflammatory demyelinating polyneuropathy:* 100–200 mg/kg subcut q wk. Or initially, 1.37 × previous IGIV dose (grams)/number of wk between IGIV doses *(Gamunex-C).* Adjust based on response.

▶ **influenza type A (H5N1) virus monovalent vaccine, adjuvanted**
generic

Adult: 0.5 mL IM into deltoid muscle; then 0.5 mL IM 21 days later. Prepare by mixing one vial AS03 adjuvant w/one vial H5N1 antigen just before administration; do not mix in syringe w/other vaccines. Virus grown in chicken eggs; use caution w/chicken allergies. Use caution in pregnancy. Give pt written record.

▶ **influenza type A and B virus vaccine**
Afluria, Fluarix, FluLaval, Fluvirin, Fluzone, Fluzone High Dose, Fluzone Quadrivalent

Do not give w/sensitivity to eggs, chicken, chicken feathers, chicken dander; hypersensitivity to vaccine components; hx of Guillain-Barré syndrome. Do not give to infants, children at same time as diphtheria, tetanus toxoid, pertussis vaccine (DTP) or within 14 days after measles virus vaccine. *6–35 mo:* 0.25 mL IM; repeat in 4 wk *(Afluria, Fluzone). 3 yr and older:* 0.5 mL IM *(Afluria, Fluzone, Fluarix).* If under 9 yr and receiving vaccine for first time or received only one dose last year, give repeat dose in 4 wk. *4 yr and older:* 0.5 mL IM *(Fluvirin).* If under 9 yr and receiving vaccine for first time or received only one dose last year, give repeat dose in 4 wk. *18 yr and older:* 0.5 mL IM. Shake prefilled syringe before use *(Agriflu, Afluria, Fluarix, FluLaval, Fluzone, Fluvirin). 18–64 yr:* 0.1 mL intradermally *(Fluzone Intradermal). 65 yr and older:* 0.5 mL IM *(Fluzone High Dose).*

► **influenza type A and B virus vaccine, live, intranasal**
FluMist Quadrivalent

2–8 yr, not previously vaccinated: Two doses (0.2 mL each) intranasally as one spray (0.1 mL)/nostril at least 1 mo apart. *2–8 yr, previously vaccinated:* One dose (0.2 mL) intranasally as one spray (0.1 mL)/nostril. *9–49 yr:* One dose of one spray (0.1 mL) in each nostril/flu season. *5–8 yr not previously vaccinated w/FluMist:* Two doses (0.5 mL each) 60 days apart ± 14 days. *5–8 yr previously vaccinated w/FluMist:* One dose (0.5 mL)/flu season.

► **influenza virus vaccine, H5N1**
H5N1

Adult 18–64 yr: 1 mL IM into deltoid muscle of upper arm, then 1 mL IM 21–35 days later. Virus grown in chicken eggs; use caution in pts w/chicken allergy.

► **measles, mumps, rubella vaccine, live (MMR)**
M-M-R II

Inject 0.5 mL reconstituted vaccine subcut into outer aspect of upper arm. Dose same for all pts. Booster dose recommended on entry into elementary school. Use caution if giving to pt w/hx of sensitivity to eggs, chicken, chicken feathers. Do not give within 1 mo of immunization w/other live virus vaccines. Do not give for at least 3 mo after blood, or plasma transfusions or serum immune globulin administration.

► **measles, mumps, rubella, and varicella virus vaccine, live**
ProQuad

12 mo–12 yr: 0.5 mL subcut. Allow 1 mo between administration of vaccines containing measles antigens and administration of *ProQuad.* If second varicella vaccine needed, allow 3 mo between administration of the two doses.

► **meningococcal groups C and Y, *Haemophilus* b tetanus toxoid conjugate vaccine**
MenHibrix

Four doses, 0.5 mL IM each; first as early as 6 wk, 4th as late as 18 mo. Usual timing, 2, 4, 6, and 12–15 mo.

► **meningococcal vaccine**
Menactra, Menomune A/C/ Y/W-135, Menveo

Menactra: 9 mo–55 yr, 0.5 mL IM in deltoid region as one dose. *Menomune:* 2–55 yr, 0.5 mL IM; may give booster in 3–5 yr. *Menveo:* 2 mo–55 yr, 0.5 mL IM as one dose. Children 2–5 yr may receive second dose 2 mo after first dose.

► **meningococcal vaccine, serotype B**
Bexsero, Trumenba

Adult, child 10–25 yr: Two doses, at least 1 mo apart, 0.5 mL IM (*Bexsero*). Three doses (0.5 mL IM each) on schedule of mos 0, 2, and 6 (*Trumenba*).

▶ pneumococcal vaccine, polyvalent
Pneumovax 23

One 0.5-mL dose subcut, IM. Not recommended for children under 2 yr. Give at least 2 wk before initiation of cancer chemotherapy, other immunosuppressive therapy.

▶ pneumococcal 13-valent conjugate vaccine (diphtheria CRM197 protein)
Prevnar-13

0.5 mg IM, preferably in anterolateral aspect of thigh in infants, deltoid muscle of upper arm in older children. *6 wk–5 yr:* Four-dose series given 4–8 wk apart at 2, 4, 6 mo; then at 12–15 mo. *Catch-up schedule for children 7 mo and older:* 7–11 mo, three doses, first two doses at least 4 wk apart; third dose after first birthday. 12–23 mo, two doses at least 2 mo apart. 24 mo–5 yr, one dose (before 6th birthday). *Adults 50 yr and over:* One single dose.

▶ poliovirus vaccine, inactivated (IPV, Salk)
IPOL

Do not give w/known hypersensitivity to streptomycin, neomycin (each dose contains under 25 mcg of each). *Adults:* Not usually needed in adults in United States. Recommended if unimmunized adult is exposed, traveling to high-risk area, or household contact of children receiving IPV. Give 0.5 mL subcut: two doses at 1- to 2-mo intervals, third dose 6–12 mo later. Previously vaccinated adults at risk for exposure should receive 0.5-mL dose. *Children:* 0.5 mL subcut at 2, 4, and 6–18 mo. Booster dose needed at time of entry into elementary school.

▶ RHo (D) immune globulin
HyperRHO S/D Full Dose, RhoGAM Ultra-Filtered Plus

▶ RHo (D) immune globulin micro-dose
HyperRHO S/D minidose, MICRhoGAM Ultra-Filtered Plus

▶ RHo (D) immune globulin IV (human) (RHo D IGIV)
Rhophylac, WinRho SDF

BBW Risk of intravascular hemolysis, death when used for idiopathic thrombocytopenia purpura (ITP; *WinRho*). Monitor dipstick urinalysis at baseline, then at 2, 4, 8 hr. Ask pt to report back pain, chills, discolored urine.

Postpartum prophylaxis: 1 vial IM, IV *(WinRho SDF)* within 72 hr of delivery. *Antepartum prophylaxis:* 1 vial IM, IV *(WinRho SDF)* at 26–28 wk' gestation; 1 vial within 72 hr after Rh-incompatible delivery to prevent Rh isoimmunization during pregnancy. *After amniocentesis, miscarriage, abortion, ectopic pregnancy at or beyond 13 wk' gestation:* 1 vial IM, IV. *Transfusion accidents:* Multiply volume in mL of Rh-positive whole blood given by Hct of donor unit; divide this volume (in mL) by 15 to obtain number of vials to be given. If results of calculation are fraction, give next whole number of vials. *ITP:* 250 international units/kg IV at 2 mL/15–60 sec. *Spontaneous/ induced abortion, termination of ectopic pregnancy up to and including 12 wk' gestation (unless father Rh negative):* 1 vial microdose IM as soon as possible after pregnancy termination.

► **rotavirus vaccine, live, oral pentavalent**
Rotarix, RotaTeq

Three ready-to-use liquid pouch doses (2 mL each) PO starting at age 6–12 wk, w/subsequent doses at 4- to 10-wk intervals (do not give third dose after age 32 wk) *(RotaTeq).* Two doses of 1 mL each PO starting at age 6 wk. Allow 4 wk before second dose. Must complete Series by age 24 wk *(Rotarix).*

► **typhoid vaccine**
Typhim Vi, Vivotif Berna

Complete vaccine regimen 1–2 wk before potential exposure.
Parenteral *Over 10 yr:* 2 doses of 0.5 mL subcut at intervals of 4 wk or longer. *10 yr or younger:* Two doses of 0.25 mL subcut at intervals of 4 wk or longer.
Booster dose. Given q 3 yr in cases of continued exposure. *Over 10 yr:* 0.5 mL subcut or 0.1 mL intradermally. *6 mo–10 yr:* 0.25 mL subcut or 0.1 mL intradermally.

Parenteral *(Typhim Vi). Children 2 yr and older:* 0.5 mL IM. Booster dose q 2 yr; 0.5 mL IM.
Oral *(Vivotif Berna). Pts over 6 yr:* 1 capsule on days 1, 3, 5, 7 1 hr before meal w/cold, lukewarm water. No data on need for booster dose; 4 capsules on alternating days once q 5 yr suggested.

► **varicella virus vaccine, live**
Varivax

Adult, child 13 yr and older: 0.5 mL subcut in deltoid area, then 0.5 mL 4–8 wk later. *Child 1–12 yr:* Single 0.5-mL dose subcut.

► **zoster vaccine, live**
Zostavax

Adult 50 yr and older: 1 injection of single-dose vaccine subcut in upper arm. Vaccine should be frozen and reconstituted, using supplied diluent, immediately after removal from freezer. Give immediately after reconstituting.

OTHER BIOLOGICALS

Name	Indications	Instructions
IMMUNE GLOBULINS		
anti-thymocyte globulin *(Thymoglobulin)*	Tx of renal transplant acute rejection w/ immunosuppression	1.5 mg/kg/day for 7–14 days as 6-hr IV infusion for first dose and at least 4 hr each subsequent dose. Give through 0.22-micron filter. Store in refrigerator; use within 4 hr of reconstitution.
botulism immune globulin *(BabyBIG)*	Tx of pts under 1 yr w/infant botulism caused by toxin A or B	1 mL/kg as single IV infusion as soon as dx made.

Name	Indications	Instructions
cytomegalovirus immune globulin IV (CMV-IGIV) (CytoGam)	Px of CMV disease after renal, lung, liver, pancreas, heart transplant	15 mg/kg IV over 30 min; increase to 30 mg/kg IV for 30 min, then 60 mg/kg IV to max 150 mg/kg. Infuse at 72 hr, 2 wk, then 4, 6, 8, 12, 16 wk. Monitor for allergic reactions. Use within 6 hr of entering vial. Give through IV line w/in-line filter (15 micron).
lymphocyte, immune globulin (Atgam)	Mgt of allograft rejection in renal transplant; tx of aplastic anemia	10–30 mg/kg/day IV adult transplant; 5–25 mg/kg/day IV child transplant; 10–20 mg/kg/day IV for 8–14 days for aplastic anemia. Stable for up to 12 hr after reconstitution. Give skin test before first dose.
rabies immune globulin (HyperRab S/D, Imogam Rabies-HT)	Passive protection against rabies in nonimmunized pts w/exposure to rabies	20 international units/kg IM as single dose at same time as rabies vaccine. Infuse wound area if possible. Never give in same site as vaccine. Refrigerate vial.
vaccinia immune globulin IV (VIGIV)	Tx, modification of vaccinia infections	2 mL/kg (100 mg/kg) IV.
varicella zoster immune globulin (VZIG)	Decrease severity of chickenpox sx in high-risk pts	125 units/10 kg IV or IM given within 96 hr of exposure.

ANTITOXINS, ANTIVENINS

Name	Indications	Instructions
antivenin (Micrurus fulvius)	Neutralization of venom of U.S. coral snakes	3–5 vials by slow IV injection. Give first 1 to 2 mL over 3–5 min; observe for allergic reaction. Flush w/IV fluids after antivenin infused. May need up to 100 mL.
black widow spider species antivenin (Antivenin Latrodectus mactans)	Tx of sx of black widow spider bites	2.5 mL IM. May give IV in 10–50 mL saline over 15 min. Ensure supportive tx, muscle relaxant use.
botulism antitoxin (Botulism Antitoxin Heptavalent [HBAT])	Tx of suspected/known exposure to botulinum neurotoxin	For pts 1 yr and older, base dose on CDC protocol and exposure.

Name	Indications	Instructions
centruroides (scorpion) immune fab (*Anascorp*)	Tx of scorpion stings	Initially, 3 vials infused IV over 10 min; then 1 vial at a time at intervals of 30–60 min until clinically stable. Begin as soon as possible after sting. Severe hypersensitivity reactions, delayed serum sickness reaction possible (contains equine proteins).
crotalidae immune fab (equine) (*Anavip*)	Tx of American rattlesnake bites	10 vials IV over 60 min; may repeat in 60 min as needed. Give as soon possible after bite. Reconstitute each vial w/10 mL NSS, then further dilute in 250 mL NSS. Monitor pt for at least 18 hr; reemerging or late symptoms can be treated w/4 vial IV over 60 min. Monitor for possible allergic reactions.
crotalidae polyvalent immune fab (ovine) (*CroFab*)	Tx of rattlesnake bites	4–6 vials IV; may repeat based on response. Dilute each vial w/10 mL sterile water, then w/250 mL 0.9% NSS. Give each 250 mL over 60 min. Contains specific antibody fragments that bind to four different rattlesnake toxins. Venom removal should be done at once. Monitor carefully for hypersensitivity reaction. Most effective if given within first 6 hr after snake bite.
varicella zoster immune globulin (*VariZIG*)	Decrease severity of chickenpox; used within 4 days of exposure	1.25 mL diluted IM or 2.5 mL diluted IV over 3–5 min. Do not give w/varicella vaccine.

BACTERIAL VACCINES

Name	Indications	Instructions
BCG (*TICE BCG*)	Exposure to TB of skin test negative infants and children; tx of groups w/high rates of TB; travel to areas w/high endemic TB rates	0.2–0.3 mL percutaneously using sterile multipuncture disc. Refrigerate, protect from light. Keep vaccination site clean until reaction disappears.

Name	Indications	Instructions
VIRAL VACCINES		
Japanese encephalitis vaccine *(generic)*	Active immunization in pts over 1 yr who will reside, travel in endemic or epidemic areas	3 subcut doses of 1 mL on days 0, 7, 30. Child 1–3 yr, 3 subcut doses of 0.5 mL. Refrigerate vial. Do not remove rubber stopper. Pt should not travel within 10 days of vaccination.
Japanese encephalitis virus (JEV) vaccine, inactivated, adsorbed *(Ixiaro)*	Active immunization in pts 17 yr and older	2 doses of 0.5 mL each IM 28 days apart. Should complete series at least 1 wk before exposure to JEV. Contains protamine sulfate. Use only if clearly needed in pregnancy, breast-feeding.
rabies vaccine *(Imovax Rabies, RabAvert)*	Preexposure rabies immunization for pts in high-risk area; postexposure antirabies regimen w/rabies immunoglobulin	*Preexposure:* 1 mL IM on days 0, 7, and 21 or 28. *Postexposure:* 1 mL IM on days 0, 3, 7, 14, 28. Refrigerate. If titers low, may need booster.
yellow fever vaccine *(YF-Vax)*	Immunization of pts 9 mo and older living in or traveling to endemic areas	0.5 mL subcut. Booster dose suggested q 10 yr. Use cautiously w/allergy to chicken, egg products.

Bibliography

Aschenbrenner, D., & Venable, S. (2012). *Drug therapy in nursing* (4th ed.). Philadelphia, PA: Lippincott Williams & Wilkins.

Brunton, L., Chabner, B., & Khollman, B. (2010). *Goodman and Gilman's the pharmacological basis of therapeutics* (12th ed.). New York, NY: McGraw-Hill.

Carpenito-Moyet, L. J. (2012). *Nursing diagnosis: Application to clinical practice* (14th ed.). Philadelphia, PA: Lippincott Williams & Wilkins.

Drug evaluations subscription. (2016). Chicago, IL: American Medical Association.

Drug facts and comparisons. (2016). St. Louis, MO: Facts and Comparisons.

Drug facts update: Physicians on-line. (2016). Multimedia.

Fetrow, C. W., & Avila, J. (2003). *Professional handbook of complementary and alternative medicines* (3rd ed.). Springhouse, PA: Lippincott Williams & Wilkins.

Griffiths, M. C. (Ed.). (2012). *USAN and the USP 2012 dictionary of drug names.* Rockville, MD: United States Pharmacopeial Convention.

Handbook of adverse drug interactions. (2015). New Rochelle, NY: The Medical Letter.

ISMP medication safety alert! (2015). Huntingdon Valley, PA: Institute for Safe Medication Practices.

Karch, A. M. (2013). *Focus on nursing pharmacology* (6th ed.). Philadelphia, PA: Lippincott Williams & Wilkins.

The medical letter on drugs and therapeutics. (2016). New Rochelle, NY: Medical Letter.

PDR for nonprescriptive drugs. (2016). Oradell, NJ: Medical Economics.

PDR for ophthalmic medications. (2016). Oradell, NJ: Medical Economics.

Physicians' desk reference (69th ed.). (2016). Oradell, NJ: Medical Economics.

Smeltzer, S. C., & Bare, B. G. (2013). *Brunner and Suddarth's textbook of medical-surgical nursing* (13th ed.). Philadelphia, PA: Lippincott Williams & Wilkins.

Tatro, D. S. (Ed.). (2016). *Drug interaction facts.* St. Louis, MO: Facts and Comparisons.

Index

---

*Entries in **boldface** are drug classes.*

*Entries in **boldface** are drug classes.*

*Entries in **boldface** are drug classes.*

*Entries in **boldface** are drug classes.*

*Entries in **boldface** are drug classes.*

---

*Entries in **boldface** are drug classes.*

*Entries in **boldface** are drug classes.*

*Entries in **boldface** are drug classes.*

*Entries in **boldface** are drug classes.*

Entries in **boldface** are drug classes.

*Entries in **boldface** are drug classes.*

---

*Entries in **boldface** are drug classes.*

*Entries in **boldface** are drug classes.*

Entries in **boldface** are drug classes.

*Entries in **boldface** are drug classes.*

---

*Entries in **boldface** are drug classes.*

*Entries in **boldface** are drug classes.*

*Entries in **boldface** are drug classes.*

Entries in **boldface** *are drug classes.*

Entries in **boldface** *are drug classes.*

*Entries in **boldface** are drug classes.*

Entries in **boldface** *are drug classes.*

*Entries in **boldface** are drug classes.*

*Entries in **boldface** are drug classes.*

*Entries in **boldface** are drug classes.*

*Entries in **boldface** are drug classes.*

Entries in **boldface** are drug classes.

*Entries in **boldface** are drug classes.*

*Entries in **boldface** are drug classes.*

Entries in **boldface** *are drug classes.*

*Entries in **boldface** are drug classes.*

*Entries in **boldface** are drug classes.*

*Entries in **boldface** are drug classes.*

*Entries in **boldface** are drug classes.*

Entries in boldface are drug classes.

*Entries in **boldface** are drug classes.*

---

*Entries in **boldface** are drug classes.*

*Entries in **boldface** are drug classes.*

---

*Entries in **boldface** are drug classes.*

*Entries in **boldface** are drug classes.*

*Entries in **boldface** are drug classes.*

Entries in boldface are drug classes.

*Entries in **boldface** are drug classes.*